My Name ______________________________

Address ______________________________

____

Phone ______________________________

E-Mail ______________________________

MY GROUP

Name ______________________________
Address ______________________________
City ______________________________
State ____ Zip ______ Phone ____________
E-mail ______________________________

Name ______________________________
Address ______________________________
City ______________________________
State ____ Zip ______ Phone ____________
E-mail ______________________________

Name ______________________________
Address ______________________________
City ______________________________
State ____ Zip ______ Phone ____________
E-mail ______________________________

Name ______________________________
Address ______________________________
City ______________________________
State ____ Zip ______ Phone ____________
E-mail ______________________________

Name ______________________________
Address ______________________________
City ______________________________
State ____ Zip ______ Phone ____________
E-mail ______________________________

Name ______________________________
Address ______________________________
City ______________________________
State ____ Zip ______ Phone ____________
E-mail ______________________________

Name ______________________________
Address ______________________________
City ______________________________
State ____ Zip ______ Phone ____________
E-mail ______________________________

Name ______________________________
Address ______________________________
City ______________________________
State ____ Zip ______ Phone ____________
E-mail ______________________________

Dear Teammate,

You hold in your hands the most powerful book in the world. It is God's game plan for your life, and it is everything you need as a competitor. Spending time reading the Bible has transformed my life, and the same life-change can happen to you!

FCA's theme is **ONE**:

"I will know that you are standing together with one spirit and one purpose, fighting together for the faith, which is the Good News." –Philippians 1:27

There is power in One. One passion, one purpose, and one goal can drive an athlete, coach, or team to be their very best. There is power in One Gospel. There is power in One Truth. And there is power in our One Great God who transforms hearts and brings victory in our lives. As Christian athletes, when we stand together with one passion, one power, and one purpose, there is great impact!

It's time we really dig into God's Word and learn how to make a great impact for the Lord as Christian competitors. Study hard, stand together as One, and live for Jesus Christ!

Stand Together As One,

Shane Williamson
The Fellowship of Christian Athletes

FCA PRESS
LifeWay
Biblical Solutions for Life

ISBN: 978-1-4627-4118-2

Dewey Decimal Classification: 220.52
Subject Headings: BIBLE \ATHLETES-RELIGIOUS LIFE

CONTRIBUTORS

LifeWay Writing and Editorial Team: Trevin Wax, J.D. Green, R. David Bennett ("Warm-ups" and "Athlete Studies" writer), Chad Bonham ("Meetings" writer), Lloyd Mullens (Bible text Managing Editor), Dustin Curtis, Kathy Bence, Greg Benoit, Steve Bond, LeAnne Constantine, Marilyn Duncan, Sarah Gant, John Glynn, Katharine Harris, Sarah Hogg, George Knight, Derek Leman, Keith Madsen, Dan McArthur, Bethany McShurley, Joe Snider, and Cathy Tardif.

Fellowship of Christian Athletes: Jeff Martin, Shea Vailes, Julie Martin, and the "Training Time" writers: Sarah Roberts, Dan Britton, Julie Martin, Sarah Rennicke, Kerry O'Neill, Clay Elliott, Rebekah Trittipoe, Rex Stump, Mark Jones, Chanda Rigby, Charles Gee, Amanda Tewksbury, Kristy Makris, Donna Noonan, Roger Lipe, Adrienne Sherwood.

Design and Layout: Scott Richards of Scott Richards Design (cover), Susan Browne of B&H Publishing (front and back matter), Typesetting by TF Designs (front and back matter) and 2K/Denmark (NLT Bible text), Amy Richards (Fields of Faith ad), Advanced Online, Inc. (FCAGear ad), and Danny Burns (Getting Involved with FCA).

Printed in China
RRD

TABLE OF CONTENTS

BOOKS OF THE BIBLE

OLD TESTAMENT

NEW TESTAMENT

ABBREVIATIONS KEY:

v. –verse
f –verse following
ch. –chapter(s)
e.g. –for example
vv. –verses
ff –verses following
circa(C.)–about, around
i.e. –that is
OT –Old Testament

WHAT'S UNIQUE ABOUT THIS BIBLE?

This Bible is designed specifically for students. It's filled with discussion questions and exercises that help student athletes and coaches share every aspect of their lives in the context of God's revealed Word and the illumination and power of the Holy Spirit.

HOW CAN GROUPS USE THIS BIBLE?

There are a variety of ways to use this Bible! For starters, look at the ready-made study plans on pages 15–28. Here you'll find 330 relevant topics, grouped into 14 categories (8 Life and 6 Athlete). After choosing a topic in the first eight categories, all you have to do is decide which "Workout" to use. On pages 29–31 you will find "150 Favorite Bible Study Stories." On page 32 there are "37 Bonus Bible Studies." Altogether there are nearly 25,000 possible combinations of small-group studies to help build community in your group and develop you as a passionate Christ-follower.

LIFE TOPICS: CHOICES

CHOICES

Topic	Warm-Up	Workout	Reference
AVOIDING TROUBLE	Hold on (p. 1204)	Losing Your Head (p. 843); Follow the Light (p. 1041)	Mark 6:14-29; Ephesians 5:1-21
DANGER OF DIS-OBEDIENCE	Shielded (p. 1283)	Israelite Spy Team (p. 160); Wrath and Rejoicing (p. 1152)	Numbers 13:26-14:45; Revelation 14:1-15:8
FAMILY TENSIONS	Lifetime Guarantee (p. 1288)	Family Feuds (p. 58); Parental Expectations (p. 1042)	Genesis 21:1-21; Ephesians 6:1-4
FINDING GOD'S STRENGTH	Friendly Choice (p. 1300)	The Secret of Strength (p. 245); The Question of Marriage (p. 998)	Judges 16:21-31; 1 Corinthians 7:1-40
GOING YOUR OWN WAY	Rules: Keep, Bend or Break? (p. 1318)	Faith Under Fire (p. 243); Letters of Warning (p. 1143)	Judges 14:1-20; Revelation 2:1-3:22
GOOD & BAD INFLUENCES	When I Was Ten (p. 1287)	Healing Forgiveness (p. 837); You Will Be Assimilated! (p. 984)	Mark 2:1-12; Romans 12:1-8
LUST & SEXUAL PURITY	God's Word on Love (p. 1311)	Adultery and Murder (p. 288); Choosing the Best Way (p. 1063)	2 Samuel 11:1-27; 1 Thessalonians 4:1-12
MONEY & WEALTH	Health Fan or Health Foe? (p. 1280)	Building True Wealth (p. 882); Money Issues (p. 1076)	Luke 12:13-21; 1 Timothy 6:3-21
MOTIVES & CHOICES	Likes and Loves (p. 1284)	Detrimental Desires (p. 260); Walking by the Spirit (p. 979)	1 Samuel 8:1-22; Romans 8:1-17
RISKING EVERYTHING	Walk It Off (p. 1291)	A Beauty Contest (p. 435); The Secret to Success (p. 1049)	Esther 2:1-18; Philippians 3:1-11
SEEKING GOD'S GUIDANCE	C.O.D. (p. 1303)	Daring Escape (p. 88); One Day at a Time (p. 1111)	Exodus 2:1-25; James 4:13-17
TAKING RESPONSIBILITY	Do I Hear Fifty? (p. 1300)	A Big Fish Story (p. 760); Who's Responsible (p. 1068)	Jonah 2:1-3:10; 2 Thessalonians 3:6-15
TOUGH DECISIONS	Would You Rather? (p. 1309)	Mission Improbable (p. 214); Careful Choices (p. 999)	Joshua 5:13-6:21; 1 Corinthians 8:1-13
WHAT CONTROLS YOU?	Alarming (p. 1295)	Perilous Possessions (p. 849); The Perfect Offering (p. 977)	Mark 10:17-31; Romans 6:15-23
YOUR HEART FOCUS	In a Dilemma (p. 1292)	Where's Your Treasure? (p. 883); Changing Priorities (p. 1119)	Luke 12:22-34; 1 Peter 4:1-11

17

ARE THERE ANY STUDIES BEYOND THOSE FOUND IN THE STUDY PLANS?

Yes. You can use the index of 150 favorite Bible stories on pages 29–31 to create your own meeting. On page 32, you can choose other specific topics from the bonus Bible studies not covered in the topical charts. ***(Examples: stories about David, the miracles or parables of Jesus, and Jesus' last week)***

Topic	Workout	Reference
Rejection of Jesus	Get Out of Town	Luke 4:14-30
Communion, Eucharist	Celebrating the Lord's Supper	Luke 22:7-23
Taking Sides	Divided We Fall	1 Corinthians 1:10-17
God's Coworkers	Building with Gold	1 Corinthians 3:1-23
Christian Freedom	Handling Our Freedom	1 Corinthians 10:14–11:1
Diversity in the Body	All for One	1 Corinthians 12:12-31
Spiritual Gifts	Gifted and Talented	1 Corinthians 14:1-25
Integrity	Yes, No, Maybe	2 Corinthians 1:12–2:11
Words of Life or Death	Fragrant Letters	2 Corinthians 2:12–3:6
Handling Foolish Teaching	Tolerating Fools	2 Corinthians 11:16-33
Unity in the Body	Building Up and Hanging Out	Ephesians 4:1-16
Parents	Parental Expectations	Ephesians 6:1-4
Hope in Jesus	The Lasting Hope	Colossians 1:1-4
Walking with Christ in Victory	Victory over the Enemy	Colossians 2:6-23
Gifts from God	God's Incredible Gifts	1 Thessalonians 5:12-28
Imitators of Jesus	Worthy of God's Kingdom	2 Thessalonians 1:1-12
End Times	The Man of Lawlessness	2 Thessalonians 2:1-17

CAN WE USE THIS BIBLE TO DO A BOOK STUDY?

Absolutely! There are mini-studies your group can use to study all the New Testament books from Matthew through Revelation, as well as several Old Testament books. Simply use the mini-study questionnaires where the gray boxes appear in the Scripture text. For some of the longer books, you may want to cover more than one mini-study per meeting.

CALLING HEAVEN'S NUMBER

1. When have you called on someone in authority for help? Did you get the help you needed? Why did you need it in the first place?

ROMANS 9:30–10:21

2. What is the only way to be saved, according to Paul in 10:9-10? How does this compare with other religious teachings? With the teachings of the world around you?
3. What does it mean to "call on the name of the LORD" (10:13)?
4. What does verse 14 suggest about the importance of sharing Jesus with others? How often do you tell others about Jesus? How can you do this more often?

WHAT DO THE ICONS ON THE MINI-STUDY BOXES MEAN?

They show that the mini-study is connected to a lesson plan in a particular topical category. However, all the mini-studies should be quite relevant to any group of students.

The 14 topical categories are as follows:

LIFE TOPICS	ATHLETE TOPICS
AWARENESS	FUNDAMENTALS
RELATIONSHIPS	COMPETITION
CHOICES	TEAMWORK
STRESS	TRAINING
ISSUES	PERFORMANCE
CRISIS	GAME PLAN
BELIEFS	
DISCIPLESHIP	

YOU WILL BE ASSIMILATED!

1. When have you thought of yourself more highly than you should have? How did you discover your error?

ROMANS 12:1-8

2. What does Paul mean in verse 2 when he says, "Don't copy the behavior and customs of this world, but let God transform you into a new person by changing the way you think"?
3. How can you offer your body as "a living and holy sacrifice" (v. 1)?
4. According to this passage, what is required of you to discover God's will for your life?
5. How much are you conforming to the world's standards? Are you working to transform your mind to God's way of thinking?

WHAT'S THE PURPOSE OF THE NOTES AT THE BOTTOM OF EACH BIBLE PAGE?

These commentary notes help students understand key words and concepts of the Scripture passage covered by the mini-study questionnaires. The notes also provide background information about the overall context and practical application of the passages. ***Here's an example from Romans 11:12–12:8:***

11:25 mystery. This is something that is hidden in the mind of God, but which He is now pleased to reveal to all who are willing to seek Him.
12:1 all he has done for you. Paul has just declared God's amazing mercy (11:30-32). A Christian's motivation to obedience is gratitude for God's mercy. **bodies.** The Christian lifestyle is not a matter of mystical spirituality that transcends one's bodily nature but an everyday, practical exercise of love (6:13). The idea of "bodies" also emphasizes the metaphor of sacrifice since animal bodies were put on the altar. **living . . . holy . . . the kind he would find acceptable.** In Greek, these three phrases are attached with equal weight as requirements for "sacrifices."
12:2 Don't copy. Literally, "stop allowing yourself to be conformed." Believers are no longer helpless victims of natural and supernatural forces that shape them into a distorted pattern; they now have the ability and help to resist such powers. **transform.** The force of the verb is "continue to let yourself be transformed"—a continuous action by the Holy Spirit that goes on for a lifetime. A Christian's responsibility is to stay open to this sanctification process as the Spirit works to teach him or her to look at life from God's view of reality. **changing the way you think.** Developing a spiritual sensitivity and perception—learning to look at life on the basis of God's view of reality. Paul emphasizes the need to develop understanding of God's ways. **you will learn to know God's will for you.** Christians are called to a responsible freedom of choice and action based on the inner renewing work of the Holy Spirit.
12:3 each of you. The truth about spiritual gifts applies to every believer. **be honest in your evaluation.** The command is to know oneself accurately rather than to have too high an opinion of oneself in comparison to others.
12:5 We are many parts of one body. Paul is speaking here of believers in the church, the body of Christ. The church is like a family. Although individual members of the family are distinct and different, they belong to one another because of the common Lord whom they serve.
12:6 gifts. Those endowments given by God to every believer by grace (the words *grace* and *gifts* come from the same root word) to be used in God's service. The gifts listed here (or elsewhere in the New Testament) are not meant to be exhaustive or absolute since no gift list overlaps completely. **to prophesy.** Inspired utterances, distinguished from teaching by their immediacy and spontaneous nature, the source of which is direct revelation by God.
12:7 serving others. The special capacity for rendering practical service to the needy. **a teacher.** In contrast to the prophet (with direct revelation from God), the teacher relied on the Old Testament Scriptures and the teachings of Jesus to instruct others.
12:8 encourage. This is supporting and assisting others to live a life of obedience to God. **giving.** A person with this gift takes delight in giving away his or her possessions. **leadership ability.** Those with special ability to guide a congregation are called upon to do so with zeal. **showing kindness.** Serving those who need care with cheerfulness.

IS THERE A PARTICULAR FLOW IN THE QUESTIONS IN THE MINI-STUDIES?

Yes. The questions are arranged to move across the "Disclosure Scale" from NO RISK at the beginning of the mini-study to HIGH RISK at the end. Typically, there are warm-up, Bible discussion, and application questions to aid in interactive Bible discovery.

CAN INDIVIDUALS USE THIS BIBLE FOR DAILY DEVOTIONS?

There's a "Personal Reading Plan" in the introduction to each book of the Bible. You can check off passages as you read them. For your continued study, if you used all of the mini-studies in the gray boxes located throughout the Bible text, there would be enough for every day of the year.

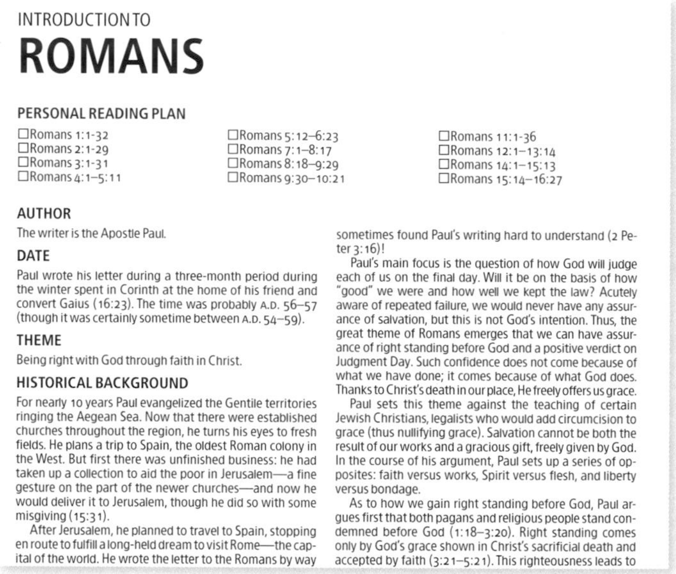

INTRODUCTION TO

ROMANS

PERSONAL READING PLAN

☐Romans 1:1-32
☐Romans 2:1-29
☐Romans 3:1-31
☐Romans 4:1–5:11
☐Romans 5:12–6:23
☐Romans 7:1–8:17
☐Romans 8:18–9:29
☐Romans 9:30–10:21
☐Romans 11:1-36
☐Romans 12:1–13:14
☐Romans 14:1–15:13
☐Romans 15:14–16:27

AUTHOR

The writer is the Apostle Paul.

DATE

Paul wrote his letter during a three-month period during the winter spent in Corinth at the home of his friend and convert Gaius (16:23). The time was probably A.D. 56–57 (though it was certainly sometime between A.D. 54–59).

THEME

Being right with God through faith in Christ.

HISTORICAL BACKGROUND

For nearly 10 years Paul evangelized the Gentile territories ringing the Aegean Sea. Now that there were established churches throughout the region, he turns his eyes to fresh fields. He plans a trip to Spain, the oldest Roman colony in the West. But first there was unfinished business: he had taken up a collection to aid the poor in Jerusalem—a fine gesture on the part of the newer churches—and now he would deliver it to Jerusalem, though he did so with some misgiving (15:31).

After Jerusalem, he planned to travel to Spain, stopping en route to fulfill a long-held dream to visit Rome—the capital of the world. He wrote the letter to the Romans by way sometimes found Paul's writing hard to understand (2 Peter 3:16)!

Paul's main focus is the question of how God will judge each of us on the final day. Will it be on the basis of how "good" we were and how well we kept the law? Acutely aware of repeated failure, we would never have any assurance of salvation, but this is not God's intention. Thus, the great theme of Romans emerges that we can have assurance of right standing before God and a positive verdict on Judgment Day. Such confidence does not come because of what we have done; it comes because of what God does. Thanks to Christ's death in our place, He freely offers us grace.

Paul sets this theme against the teaching of certain Jewish Christians, legalists who would add circumcision to grace (thus nullifying grace). Salvation cannot be both the result of our works and a gracious gift, freely given by God. In the course of his argument, Paul sets up a series of opposites: faith versus works, Spirit versus flesh, and liberty versus bondage.

As to how we gain right standing before God, Paul argues first that both pagans and religious people stand condemned before God (1:18–3:20). Right standing comes only by God's grace shown in Christ's sacrificial death and accepted by faith (3:21–5:21). This righteousness leads to

WHAT OTHER INFORMATION IS FOUND IN THE INTRODUCTION TO EACH BOOK OF THE BIBLE?

After the "Personal Reading Plan," you'll find helpful summaries about the author, date, theme, and characteristics of each book. For the books that contain mini-study questionnaires, there are charts at the bottom of the introduction page, which list those mini-studies. The passages that are used for the topical study plans (pages 15-28) are shown first, followed by the passages that are not specifically linked to a study plan.

HOW CAN OUR GROUP USE THE WARM-UP SECTION?

(PAGES 1267-1317)

The "Warm-ups" section has numerous exercises designed to kick off meetings. They contain both fun and serious affirmation exercises, which can be used to close a meeting or special event. All of these "Warm-ups" are integrated into the study plans on pages 15–28.

WARM-UPS

WIN. LOSE. TIE.

Few things in life seem to be neutral. Most of the time people either like or dislike things. And (it seems) most people prefer winning to losing.

Find a partner. Read through the following list of situations. As you read each situation, decide if it represents a win, lose, or tie for you. Indicate your choice by circling the corresponding letter: "W" for win, "L" for lose, or "T" for tie. After you've marked a choice for each situation, share your responses. Note similarities and differences. Do you and your partner define winning and losing the same way?

W L T I've got plans with friends for this weekend.
W L T I barely passed a test that I didn't study for.
W L T It looks like I have multiple chances to take the SAT and ACT.
W L T My parent travels a lot on business.
W L T I scored highest in my class on a test.
W L T According to the results of my physical, I'm perfectly healthy.
W L T Our family may adopt.
W L T There's going to be a substitute in class all week.
W L T It looks like I'm on track to get into the college of my choice.
W L T I had to sit out a game.

FLAVOR OF THE MONTH

Get in groups of around four and share your favorite ice cream flavors and combinations. Whether it's a single, double, or triple scoop, places like Baskets of Robins and Bob and Terry's can make your wildest frozen fantasy a reality. If you've got the funds, they've got the flavors.

Choose up to three of your favorite flavors — from plain vanilla to banana-rama-extravaganza. You can write them on each scoop, if you like.

Compare your favorites with other members of your group.

Now think of three words that distinctively describe you. Whether you write them down or not, share and compare your responses.

DESIGN A MEETING

ONE

PHILIPPIANS 1:27

LIFE TOPICS

ATHLETE TOPICS

BIBLE STORY STUDIES

FOUR STEPS TO **DESIGN A GREAT MEETING**

WELCOME

Begin the meeting with a greeting and announcements.

WARM-UP

Choose a targeted activity that allows people to interact with each other. Warm-up activities can be found in the "Life Topics" section (pp. 15–22) under "Warm-Up," and key questions to be used for warm-ups are featured in the "Athlete Topics" section (pp. 23–28) under "Warm-Up/Workout."

WORKOUT

Choose from one of the Bible studies listed throughout all sections located in the front and back of the Bible. This will be the spiritual growth component of the meeting.

WRAP-UP

End the meeting with any closing comments, then pray as a group.

Check out more resources for athletes and coaches at http://fcaresources.com.

LIFE TOPICS: AWARENESS

AWARENESS

Topic	Warm-Up	Workout	Reference
BEING THANKFUL & CONTENT	What's in a Name? (p. 1312)	An Attitude of Gratitude (p. 889); Carefree Contentment (p. 1050)	Luke 17:11-19; Philippians 4:10-20
CONFIDENCE & POWER	Maybe. Maybe Not (p. 1291)	Real Fire Power (p. 934); Confidence in Eternity (p. 1131)	Acts 2:1-24,36-41; 1 John 5:1-15
CONNECTING WITH GOD	Location, Location, Location (p. 1299)	In Dad's House (p. 865); Picked for the Team (p. 1037)	Luke 2:41-52; Ephesians 1:3-14
GLORIFYING GOD	Major Impact (p. 1279)	It's Alive! (p. 907); Made for God (p. 1116)	John 4:1-26; 1 Peter 2:4-12
GOD'S LEADING & PURPOSES	Mapping Me (p. 1273)	Strange but True (p. 89); Conflicting Spirits (p. 994)	Exodus 3:1-22; 1 Corinthians 2:6-16
LOVE IN ACTION	Right & Wrong (p. 1296)	A Loving Church (p. 935); God Is My Dad (p. 1129)	Acts 2:42-47; 1 John 2:28-3:10
SALVATION NOW & FOREVER	Advanced Placement (p. 1278)	Out on a Limb (p. 891); Heaven's Marriage Feast (p. 1155)	Luke 19:1-10; Revelation 18:1-19:10
STANDING STRONG	What's Your P.R.Q.? (p. 1317)	Taking a Stand (p. 851); The World's Garbage (p. 995)	Mark 11:12-19; 1 Corinthians 4:1-21
SUCCESS IN LIFE	Live It Up (p. 1276)	Overwhelmed by Temptation (p. 315); The Ultimate Reward (p. 1093)	1 Kings 10:23-11:13; Hebrews 4:1-13
THE MAIN THINGS	Ten Grand (p. 1317)	Guilty as Charged (p. 874); Doubtful Issues (p. 987)	Luke 7:36-50; Romans 14:1-15:13
USING OUR BLESSINGS	With Gratitude (p. 1292)	Blessings to Remember (p. 212); Using What You Have (p. 1019)	Joshua 3:14-4:24; 2 Corinthians 8:1-15
WALKING WITH GOD	Your Life's Work (p. 1288)	God's Perpetual Presence (p. 527); Walking in the Light (p. 914)	Psalm 139; John 8:12-20
WEAKNESSES & STRENGTHS	Best in Show (p. 1304)	A Really Bad Hair Day (p. 244); A Work in Progress (p. 1046)	Judges 16:1-22; Philippians 1:1-11
WHAT'S INSIDE	Living Will (p. 1297)	Seeing the Heart and Soul (p. 267); Been Misjudged Lately? (p. 1109)	1 Samuel 16:1-13; James 2:1-13
YOUR HEART CONDITION	I Got It! (p. 1313)	Heart Checkup (p. 93); Help for the Heart (p. 1092)	Exodus 6:28-7:24; Hebrews 3:1-19

Topic	Warm-Up	Workout	Reference
ACCEPTANCE	Facts and Fiction (p. 1275)	Accepting One Another (p. 945); Playing Judge (p. 972)	Acts 10:1-23; Romans 2:1-16
ANGER, HATRED, OR LOVE	Think About It (p. 1295)	Murder One (p. 47); The Test of Faith (p. 1128)	Genesis 4:1-16; 1 John 2:7-14
CARING & HELPING	Stress Points (p. 1304)	What I Have Is Yours! (p. 936); Love, Not Slavery (p. 1033)	Acts 3:1-16; Galatians 5:1-15
CAUTION IN TRUSTING	I'm Not Competitive... Am I? (p. 1283)	In the Pits (p. 74); Favorable Friendship (p. 1111)	Genesis 37:12-36; James 4:1-12
CHOOSING FRIENDS	Who's Your Buddy? (p. 1293)	Really? That Guy? (p. 943); Picking Your Friends (p. 1135)	Acts 9:1-19; 3 John 1-14
DATING & MARRIAGE	Lifetime Guarantee (p. 1288)	Love at First Sight (p. 66); Marriage Matters (p. 1042)	Genesis 29:1-14; Ephesians 5:22-33
FORGIVENESS	Walk It Off (p. 1291)	The Wasteful Son (p. 887); Faithful Friendships (p. 1089)	Luke 15:11-32; Philemon 1-25
GETIING ALONG	Check In (p. 1311)	"Hey, It's Mel" (p. 81); Take out the Trash (p. 1057)	Genesis 45:1-28; Colossians 3:1-25
HELPING THE NEEDY	Almost Overwhelmed (p. 1286)	The Good Samaritan (p. 879); Truth or Consequences (p. 1134)	Luke 10:25-37; 2 John 1-13
LOVE IN ACTION	Right & Wrong (p. 1296)	True Love (p. 1005); Just Do It (p. 1109)	1 Corinthians 13:1-13; James 1 :19-27
MERCY OR PUNISHMENT	Crisis Averted (p. 1316)	Forgive Him or Choke Him? (p. 818); Rage or Mercy? (p. 980)	Matthew 18: 21-35; Romans 9:1-29
ROMANCE & MARRIAGE	Your Life's Work (p. 1288)	Love Song (p. 566); Marriage that Works (p. 1118)	Song of Songs 1:1-27; 1 Peter 3:1-7
SELFLESS SERVICE	Hold On (p. 1294)	Wedding Woes (p 905); The Power of Love (p. 986)	John 2:1-11; Romans 13:8-14
SETIING BOUNDARIES	Besties (p. 1282)	Parting Company (p. 952); An Uneven Match (p. 1018)	Acts 15:36-41; 2 Corinthians 6:14-7:1
SHARING GOD'S LOVE	When I Was Ten (p. 1287)	Sharing Good News (p. 943); True Love (p. 1130)	Acts 8:26-40; 1 John 3:11-24

LIFE TOPICS: CHOICES

Topic	Warm-Up	Workout	Reference
AVOIDING TROUBLE	Hold on (p. 1294)	Losing Your Head (p. 843); Follow the Light (p. 1041)	Mark 6:14-29; Ephesians 5:1-21
DANGER OF DIS-OBEDIENCE	Shielded (p. 1283)	Israelite Spy Team (p. 160); Wrath and Rejoicing (p. 1152)	Numbers 13:26-14:45; Revelation 14:1-15:8
FAMILY TENSIONS	Lifetime Guarantee (p. 1288)	Family Feuds (p. 58); Parental Expectations (p. 1042)	Genesis 21:1-21; Ephesians 6:1-4
FINDING GOD'S STRENGTH	Friendly Choice (p. 1300)	The Secret of Strength (p. 245); The Question of Marriage (p. 998)	Judges 16:21-31; 1 Corinthians 7:1-40
GOING YOUR OWN WAY	Rules: Keep, Bend or Break? (p. 1318)	Faith Under Fire (p. 243); Letters of Warning (p. 1143)	Judges 14:1-20; Revelation 2:1-3:22
GOOD & BAD INFLUENCES	When I Was Ten (p. 1287)	Healing Forgiveness (p. 837); You Will Be Assimilated! (p. 984)	Mark 2:1-12; Romans 12:1-8
LUST & SEXUAL PURITY	God's Word on Love (p. 1311)	Adultery and Murder (p. 288); Choosing the Best Way (p. 1063)	2 Samuel 11:1-27; 1 Thessalonians 4:1-12
MONEY & WEALTH	Health Fan or Health Foe? (p. 1280)	Building True Wealth (p. 882); Money Issues (p. 1076)	Luke 12:13-21; 1 Timothy 6:3-21
MOTIVES & CHOICES	Likes and Loves (p. 1284)	Detrimental Desires (p. 260); Walking by the Spirit (p. 979)	1 Samuel 8:1-22; Romans 8:1-17
RISKING EVERYTHING	Walk It Off (p. 1291)	A Beauty Contest (p. 435); The Secret to Success (p. 1049)	Esther 2:1-18; Philippians 3:1-11
SEEKING GOD'S GUIDANCE	C.O.D. (p. 1303)	Daring Escape (p. 88); One Day at a Time (p. 1111)	Exodus 2:1-25; James 4:13-17
TAKING RESPONSIBILITY	Do I Hear Fifty? (p. 1300)	A Big Fish Story (p. 760); Who's Responsible (p. 1068)	Jonah 2:1-3:10; 2 Thessalonians 3:6-15
TOUGH DECISIONS	Would You Rather? (p. 1309)	Mission Improbable (p. 214); Careful Choices (p. 999)	Joshua 5:13-6:21; 1 Corinthians 8:1-13
WHAT CONTROLS YOU?	Alarming (p. 1295)	Perilous Possessions (p. 849); The Perfect Offering (p. 977)	Mark 10:17-31; Romans 6:15-23
YOUR HEART FOCUS	In a Dilemma (p. 1292)	Where's Your Treasure? (p. 883); Changing Priorities (p. 1119)	Luke 12:22-34; 1 Peter 4:1-11

LIFE TOPICS: STRESS

STRESS

Topic	Warm-Up	Workout	Reference
ASKING GOD FOR HELP	Wilderness Adventure (p. 1287)	Healing Phenomenon (p. 333); Enemy Outlook (p. 471)	2 Kings 5:1-16; Psalm 17
ATIITUDE IN TRIALS	You Decide (p. 1275)	Heavenly Food (p. 101); The Test of Faith (p. 1017)	Exodus 16:1-35; 2 Corinthians 6:3-13
BEING BOLD IN PRAYER	Bad Things Happen (p. 1307)	Walking on Water (p. 814); Draw Near and Hold On (p. 1100)	Matthew 14:22-33; Hebrews 10:19-39
BETRAYAL & SIN'S TRAP	Family Matters (p. 1271)	Betrayed by a Kiss (p. 829); Enslaved (p. 1032)	Matthew 26:47-56; Galatians 4:8-20
DIFFICULT OR SCARY TASKS	On My Last Nerve (p. 1274)	A Magical Staff (p. 90); The Power of Love (p. 1039)	Exodus 4:1-17; Ephesians 3:14-21
FINDING JOY IN TRIALS	Hold On (p. 1294)	Singing in Prison (p. 954); Don't Worry-Be Happy! (p. 1050)	Acts 16:22-40; Philippians 4:2-9
FOLLOWING GOD WHEN IT'S HARD	Case Closed (p. 1280)	Miracle Birth (p. 863); Passing the Test (p. 1025)	Luke 1:26-38; 2 Corinthians 13:1-14
INSECURITY & FEAR	Major Impact (p. 1279)	Calming the Storm (p. 841); Fear vs. Love (p. 1131)	Mark 4:35-41; 1 John 4:7-21
KNOWING GOD IS IN CONTROL	Stress Points (p. 1304)	Struck Blind (p. 335); Finding Joy in Troubles (p. 975)	2 Kings 6:8-23; Romans 5:1-11
PERSECUTION & HOPE	Alarming (p. 1295)	A Fiery Test (p. 723); The Point of Pain (p. 980)	Daniel 3:1-12,19-27; Romans 8:28-39
RECONNECTING WITH GOD	My Life in a Song (p. 1303)	Running Away (p. 759); A Ministry of Reconciliation (p. 1017)	Jonah 1:1-17; 2 Corinthians 5:11-6:2
RESENTMENT	Unbroken (p. 1315)	Hey-That's Not Fair! (p. 820); Pursuing Peace (p. 1103)	Matthew 20:1-16; Hebrews 12:14-29
SEEING GOD'S HAND	Win. Lose. Tie. (p. 1272)	Closed Doors (p. 953); Open Your Eyes! (p. 1037)	Acts 16:6-10; Ephesians 1:15-23
TRUSTING GOD & WAITING	Emergency Contacts (p. 1277)	Survival Tactics (p. 99); It's Tough to Wait (p. 1112)	Exodus 14:5-31; James 5:7-20
WORRY & ANXIETY	Living Will (p. 1297)	Don't Sweat It! (p. 803); One Necessary Thing (p. 879)	Matthew 6:25-34; Luke 10:38-42

LIFE TOPICS: ISSUES

ISSUES

INTRO

Topic	Warm-Up	Workout	Reference
CARING FOR CREATION & PEOPLE	My Life in a Song (p. 1303)	The Ultimate Garden (p. 45); Caring for All (p. 1029)	Genesis 2:4-25; Galatians 2:1-10
CULTS & ANTICHRISTS	Amity Assessment (p. 1298)	Anger Over the Gospel (p. 957); Seeking Truth (p. 1130)	Acts 19:23-41; 1 John 4:1-6
CULTS, OCCULT, & FALSE PROPHETS	Blessed (p. 1302)	False Prophets (p. 948); A Different Gospel (p. 1028)	Acts 13:1-12; Galatians 1:1-10
FOLLOWING GOD OR REBELLING	Difficult People (p. 1285)	Okay to Disobey (p. 271); Maturing in the Faith (p. 1122)	1 Samuel 20:1-42; 2 Peter 1:1-11
GIVING VS. EXTORTION	Live It Up (p. 1276)	Lying to Get in the Spotlight (p. 938); Generous Giving (p. 1020)	Acts 5:1-11; 2 Corinthians 8:16-9:5
JESUS WHO?	Under the Lights (p. 1313)	Four Soils (p. 811); Jesus Is #1 (p. 1096)	Matthew 13:1-23; Hebrews 7:1-28
ORDER & CHAOS	Emergency Contacts (p. 1277)	Operation Recovery (p. 49); Order vs. Chaos (p. 1006)	Genesis 8:1-22; 1 Corinthians 14:26-40
RADICAL OBEDIENCE	You Decide (p. 1275)	Moving Out (p. 52); Gouge Out Your Eyes (p. 801)	Genesis 12:1-9; Matthew 5:27-30
SEXUAL TEMPTATION	Car Chase (p. 1279)	Amnon's Rape of Tamar (p. 290); Run from Sex (p. 997)	2 Samuel 13:1-22; 1 Corinthians 6:12-20
RESPONDING TO FALSE TEACHERS	Jesus and Me (p. 1307)	Fire from Heaven (p. 323);	1 Kings 18:16-40; 1 Timothy 1:1-11
ROLES IN SOCIETY	Think About It (p. 1295)	Respecting Authority (p. 274); Roles of Husbands and Wives (p. 1003)	1 Samuel 24:1-22; 1 Corinthians 11:2-16
SEX STANDARDS	Hang Time (p. 1318)	"Everyone's Doing It" (p. 76); Sex and the Christian (p. 996)	Genesis 39:1-23; 1 Corinthians 5 1-13
SPEAKING OUT WITHOUT JUDGING	What's Your P.R.Q.? (p. 1317)	A Warning in the Night (p. 257); Judging Others (p. 997)	1 Samuel 3:1-14; 1 Corinthians 6:1-11
SUICIDE & DIVORCE	What's in a Name? (p. 1312)	Saul's Suicide (p. 279); Divorce . . . Life Shredder (p. 819)	1 Samuel 31 :1-13; Matthew 19:1-12
THE POOR & NEEDY	Think About It (p. 1295)	Sheep and Goats (p. 828); Lending a Helping Hand (p. 1075)	Matthew 25:31-46; 1 Timothy 5:1-6:2

LIFE TOPICS: CRISIS

Topic	Warm-Up	Workout	Reference
ACCUSATIONS & PERSECUTION	Car Chase (p. 1279)	The Den of Lions (p. 727); Misunderstood (p. 1062)	Daniel 6:1-24; 1 Thessalonians 2:1-16
CHOOSING SIDES	Almost Overwhelmed (p. 1286)	Weeping for Others (p. 892); The Last Battle (p. 1157)	Luke 19:28-44; Revelation 19:11-20:10
ENDURANCE & POWER	Potato Head Gone Wild (p. 1284)	Raising the Dead (p. 918); Facing Hardship (p. 1117)	John 11:17-44; 1 Peter 2:13-25
FACING OUR SINS	Crisis Averted (p. 1316)	Anyone Without Sin? (p. 913); Godly Grief (p. 1018)	John 8:1-11; 2 Corinthians 7:2-16
FAILURES & GRACE	Bad Things Happen (p. 1307)	Prayer Power (p. 56); Never Beyond God's Love (p. 1072)	Genesis 18:16-33; 1 Timothy 1:12-20
GOD RESCUES US	Emergency Contacts (p. 1277)	God, Our Refuge (p. 485); "Get Out of Jail Free" Card (p. 947)	Psalm 46:1-11; Acts 12:1-19
GOD'S POWER & COMFORT	On My Last Nerve (p. 1274)	Power in Weakness (p. 916); God's Comfort (p. 1013)	John 9:1-15,24-34; 2 Corinthians 1:3-11
JESUS' POWER & PROTECTION	Gauging How You Feel (p. 1308)	Tomb Raiders (p. 928); Sealed by Jesus from Wrath (p. 1146)	John 20:1-18; Revelation 6:1-7:17
OPPOSITION & VICTORY	Maybe, Maybe Not (p. 1291)	Dealing with Demons (p. 875); A Reason to Live (p. 1046)	Luke 8:26-39; Philippians 1:12-30
PERSEVERANCE & FAITH	Family Matters (p. 1271)	Miraculous Faith (p. 842); Passing the Test (p. 1108)	Mark 5:24-34; James 1:2-18
SUFFERING LIKE JESUS	Hold On (p. 1294)	A Crown of Thorns (p. 831); No Big Surprise (p. 1119)	Matthew 27:26-31; 1 Peter 4:12-19
TRAGEDY, LONELINESS & TRUSTING GOD	Stranded (p. 1308)	Losing Everything (p. 340); Never Alone (p.1083)	Job 1:6-22; 2 Timothy 4:9-18
TRUST & HOPE	Decision Time (p. 1290)	Suffering and Hoping (p. 979); Unwavering Confidence (p. 1016)	Romans 8:18-27; 2 Corinthians 4:1-18
WORRY & LACK OF FAITH	Tell-It-Like-It-Is Triage (p. 1281)	Help My Unbelief (p. 848); Stressed Out (p. 1120)	Mark 9:14-29; 1 Peter 5:1-11
WISDOM IN CRISES	C.O.D. (p. 1303)	Life and Death Crisis (p. 307); Living in the Light (p. 1127)	1 Kings 3:16-28; 1 John 1:5-2:6

BELIEFS

INTRO

Topic	Warm-Up	Workout	Reference
ACCEPTING THE INVITATION	Rooted (p. 1271)	The Best Invitation Ever (p. 885); Come! (p. 1160)	Luke 14:15-24; Revelation 22:7-21
LOOKING AHEAD	2050 (p. 1314)	You Gotta Believe (p. 929); The Old and New Covenants (p. 1015)	John 20:24-31; 2 Corinthians 3:7-18
EMBRACING GOD'S GRACE	Winning Categories (p. 1301)	An Eye-Opening Experience (p. 900); Grasping Grace (p. 1030)	Luke 24:13-35; Galatians 3:1-14
EVIL ENTERS PARADISE	Do I Hear Fifty? (p. 1300)	Sin Enters Paradise (p. 46); Evil in Disguise (p. 1022)	Genesis 3:1-24; 2 Corinthians 11:1-15
EXPERIENCING JESUS	Car Talk (p. 1299)	God with Us (p. 797); The Greatest Gift (p. 1038)	Matthew 1:18-25; Ephesians 2:1-10
FINAL DESTINATION	Along the Way (p. 1310)	Heaven and Hell (p. 888); Lake of Fire or Eternal Life? (p. 1158)	Luke 16:19-31; Revelation 20:11-21:8
FIRST ADAM & PERFECT ADAM	New Game (p. 1306)	Extreme Creation (p. 44); Bold Confessions (p. 1094)	Genesis 1:1-2:3; Hebrews 4:14-5:10
FUTURE JUDGMENT	Case Closed (p. 1280)	Baptized with Spirit and Fire (p. 799); Dragon Slayer (p. 1151)	Matthew 3:1-17; Revelation 12:1-13:18
JESUS DEFEATED DEATH	Jesus and Me (p. 1307)	He Is Risen! (p. 833); Victory Over Death (p. 1008)	Matthew 28:1-20; 1 Corinthians 15:35-58
JESUS' KEY PURPOSE	God's Word on Love (p. 1311)	Heavenly Purpose (p. 864); Justified by Jesus (p. 976)	Luke 2:1-20; Romans 5:12-21
JESUS-THE ONLY WAY	Amity Assessment (p. 1298)	A Spiritual Birth (p. 906); The Only Seed (p. 1031)	John 3:1-21; Galatians 3:15-26
JESUS VICTORIOUS	Most Likely (p. 1270)	On the Cross (p. 898); Lion and Lamb (p. 1145)	Luke 23:26-49; Revelation 4:1-5:14
PREPARING FOR JESUS' RETURN	Alarming (p. 1295)	Be Prepared (p. 826); Heaven's Gonna Be a Blast! (p. 1063)	Matthew 25:1-13; 1 Thessalonians 4:13-5:11
SACRIFICING FOR US	In a Dilemma (p. 1292)	The Suffering Servant (p. 512); Sacrificing for Us! (p. 857)	Isaiah 52:13-53:12; Mark 15:1-15
THE VALUE OF YOUR SOUL	For You (p. 1276)	Deny Yourself (p. 816); Works vs. Faith (p. 983)	Matthew 16:13-28; Romans 11:1-36

LIFE TOPICS: DISCIPLESHIP

DISCIPLESHIP

Topic	Warm-Up	Workout	Reference
AUTHORITY	Hold On (p. 1294)	Money Matters (p. 852); Freedom vs. Obedience (p. 1033)	Mark 12:13-17; Galatians 4:21-31
BEING EMPOWERED BYTHE SPIRIT	Case Closed (p. 1280)	Do You Really Love Me? (p. 922); Baptism of the Holy Spirit (p. 933)	John 14:15-27; Acts 1:1-11
CONNECTING WITH GOD	Living Will (p. 1297)	Precious Time (p. 847); Future Plans (p. 988)	Mark 9:2-13; Romans 15:14-33
GIVING FREELY	Live It Up (p. 1276)	Meaningful Giving (p. 853); Cheertul Giving (p. 1020)	Mark 12:41-44; 2 Corinthians 9:6-15
GOD'S CARE FOR US	Advanced Placement (p. 1278)	The Great Shepherd (p. 474); Eternal Family Ties (p. 839)	Psalm 23:1-6; Mark 3:20-35
LIVING BY FAITH	Win. Lose. Tie. (p. 1272)	Cast Your Nets (p. 929); Not Ashamed (p. 970)	John 21:1-14; Romans 1:8-17
LOVING GOD & SERVING HIM	Most Likely (p. 1270)	Making a Profit (p. 827); Love Is the Key (p. 1128)	Matthew 25:14-30; 1 John 2:15-27
PLEASING GOD	Divine Diffusion (p. 1314)	Health for Body and Mind (p. 533); Rest and Refreshment (p. 844)	Proverbs 3:1-8; Mark 6:30-44
SELF EXAMINATION & TURNING TO GOD	I'm Not Competitive... Am I? (p. 1293)	Busted! (p. 289); Evaluate Yourself (p. 1002)	2 Samuel 12:1-14; 1 Corinthians 11:17-34
SERVING OTHERS; GOOD WORKS	Stress Points (p. 1304)	Glamour Ministry (p. 939); Talk Is Cheap (p. 1110)	Acts 6:1-7; James 2:14-26
SHARING CHRIST	Car Talk (p. 1299)	Capable Christianity (p. 944); Serving Jesus (p. 970)	Acts 9:20-31; Romans 1:1-7
SPIRITUAL BATTLES & SIN	Like Christ (p. 1289)	Confronting Sin (p. 897); Weapons of War (p. 1021)	Luke 22:54-62; 2 Corinthians 10:1-18
TEMPTATION & SIN	Family Matters (p. 1271)	That's Tempting (p. 868); A New Way of Life (p. 976)	Luke 4:1-13; Romans 6:1-14
THE COST OF FOLLOWING JESUS	Likes and Loves (p. 1284)	Giving It All Up (p. 870); Salt of the Earth (p. 886)	Luke 5:1-11; Luke 14:25-35
TIME WITH GOD (PRAYER)	Wilderness Adventure (p. 1287)	Prayer Uplink (p. 803); Perfect Priorities (p. 837)	Matthew 6:5-18; Mark 1:29-39

Topic	Warm-Up	Workout	Reference
CHRIST-LIKE LOVE	Cut It Out (p. 1323)	2 Timothy 2:15-16; 22-26 (p. 1081)	Mark 12:13-17; Galatians 4:21-31
HEART FOR CHRIST	Got Heart? (p. 1325)	Colossians 3:23-24 (p. 1057)	John 14:15-27; Acts 1:1-11
GOD'S DISCIPLINE	Respecting the Ref (p. 1326)	Hebrews 12:11-1 3 (pp. 1102-03)	Mark 9:2-13; Romans 15:14-33
GOSPEL MESSAGE	The People I Trust (p. 1325)	Jeremiah 17:5-8 (p. 641)	Mark 12:41-44; 2 Corinthians 9:6-15
HANGING IN WHEN LIFE IS TOUGH	Lessons from Defeat (p. 1322)	Psalm 51:1-19 (p. 488)	Psalm 23:1-6; Mark 3:20-35
ISRAEL'S CHOICES	Realize Your Potential (p. 1322)	Ephesians 1:3-14 (p. 1037)	John 21:1-14; Romans 1:8-17
WALKING WITH GOD	Do It for Him (p. 1327)	Psalm 105:4 (p. 512)	Matthew 25:14-30; 1 John 2:15-27
PREPARING FOR BATTLE	Ready. Set. (p. 1321)	Joshua 2:1-24 (pp. 211-12)	Proverbs 3:1-8; Mark 6:30-44
DISCIPLINED PASSION	Self Discipline (p. 1324)	Judges 16:1-22 (p. 244-45)	2 Samuel 12:1-14; 1 Corinthians 11:17-34
ENDURANCE	Fans in the Stands (p. 1324)	Hebrews 12:1-2 (pp. 1102-03)	Acts 6:1-7; James 2:14-26
TRUST OVER WORRY	I Want It (p. 1328)	Matthew 6:25-33 (pp. 803-04)	Acts 9:20-31; Romans 1:1-7
LIFE BRINGER	Avoid the Killjoy (p. 1320)	John 10:10 (p. 917)	Luke 22:54-62; 2 Corinthians 10:1-18
GOD'S PROMISES	End in Sight (p. 1327)	Jeremiah 29:4-12 (p. 650)	Luke 4:1-13; Romans 6:1-14
HONORING OTHERS	Setting the Standard (p. 1321)	Romans 12:9-21 (p. 985)	Luke 5:1-11; Luke 14:25-35
THE RIGHTEOUS AND THE WICKED	They Never Win (p. 1328)	Acts 5:1-11 (p. 938)	Matthew 6:5-18; Mark 1:29-39

ATHLETE TOPICS: COMPETITION

COMPETITION

Topic	Warm-Up	Workout	Reference
NOW THE TRUTH	Louder than Words (p. 1334)	Psalm 119:69-70 (p. 520)	Mark 12:13-17; Galatians 4:21-31
ENTHUSIASTIC SERVICE TO GOD	Celebrate (p. 1330)	2 Samuel 6:1-5,12-15 (p. 285)	John 14:15-27; Acts 1:1-11
FACING GIANTS	NY Giants (Not Your Giants) (p. 1336)	1 Samuel 17:20-24; 31-51 (pp. 268-69)	Mark 9:2-13; Romans 15:14-33
HONEST BEFORE GOD	Keep It Clean (p. 1333)	Proverbs 12:13, 17 (p. 540)	Mark 12:41-44; 2 Corinthians 9:6-15
HARD WORK	It's How You Play (p. 1330)	Colossians 3:23-24 (p. 1057)	Psalm 23:1-6; Mark 3:20-35
DEALING WITH FEAR	How Are You Holding Up? (p. 1332)	Isaiah 41:10 (p. 602)	John 21:1-14; Romans 1:8-17
DEFENDING ATTACKS	Know Your Competition (p. 1331)	John 8:42-44 (p. 915); 1 Peter 5:8 (p. 1120)	Matthew 25:14-30; 1 John 2:15-27
PLAN ACCOMPLISHED	Strength from Failure (p. 1331)	Judges 16:21-30 (p. 245)	Proverbs 3:1-8; Mark 6:30-44
A RIGHT HEART	More than a Feeling (p. 1333)	Matthew 15:18-19 (p. 814); Proverbs 28:26 (p. 553); Jeremiah 17:9 (p. 641)	2 Samuel 12:1-14; 1 Corinthians 11:17-34
APPROACHING THE THRONE	Show Off! (p. 1335)	Luke 18:10-14 (p. 890)	Acts 6:1-7; James 2:14-26
STAY HUMBLE	The Humble Athlete (p. 1332)	Philippians 2:3-8 (p. 1047)	Acts 9:20-31; Romans 1:1-7
WRESTLING WITH GOD	Win Over Will (p. 1336)	Genesis 32:24-32 (p. 70)	Luke 22:54-62; 2 Corinthians 10:1-18
DEALING WITH OPPOSITION	Again and Again (p. 1335)	Nehemiah 4:1-23 (p. 422)	Luke 4:1-13; Romans 6:1-14
THE SOURCE OF ALL STRENGTH	Under Dog (p. 1334)	Judges 7:1-25 (pp. 236-37)	Luke 5:1-11; Luke 14:25-35
THE ULTIMATE QUALIFICATION	Fault (p. 1329)	Daniel 6:1-24 (pp. 724-25)	Matthew 6:5-18; Mark 1:29-39

Topic	Warm-Up	Workout	Reference
BEING SWAYED BY THE CROWD	For Real? (p. 1338)	Luke 24:36-45 (pp. 900-01)	Mark 12:13-17; Galatians 4:21-31
ACCOUNTABILITY	Rumors (p. 1343)	Proverbs 11:12-13; 16:28; 19:5; 21:23 (pp. 539; 543; 545; 547)	John 14:15-27; Acts 1:1-11
LOYALTY	Team of Teams (p. 1339)	Matthew 10:1-10 (p. 807)	Mark 9:2-13; Romans 15:14-33
HOW SIN AFFECTS OTHERS	Dragging the Team Down (p. 1340)	Jonah 1:1-15 (p. 759)	Mark 12:41-44; 2 Corinthians 9:6-15
HUMILITY	Pulling Together (p. 1344)	James 4:1-12 (p. 1111)	Psalm 23:1-6; Mark 3:20-35
FAITH IN ACTION	Get It and Go (p. 1341)	James 1:22 (p. 1108)	John 21:1-14; Romans 1:8-17
SPEAK THE TRUTH IN LOVE	Care Enough to Confront (p. 1338)	Ephesians 4:11-16 (p. 1040)	Matthew 25:14-30; 1 John 2:15-27
JUDGMENT	What Am I Doing? (p. 1344)	Genesis 4:1-16 (pp. 46-47)	Proverbs 3:1-8; Mark 6:30-44
WORKING TOGETHER	The Greatest (p. 1340)	Acts 15:22-41 (p. 952)	2 Samuel 12:1-14; 1 Corinthians 11:17-34
STRONGER TOGETHER	Share the Load (p. 1342)	Ecclesiastes 4:9-12 (p. 559); Galatians 6:2 (p. 1034)	Acts 6:1-7; James 2:14-26
PARTING COMPANY	Team Effort (p. 1337)	Luke 9:10-17 (p. 876)	Acts 9:20-31; Romans 1:1-7
PRAISE AND THANKFULNESS	Worth the Risk (p. 1339)	1 Samuel 20:1-17 (p. 271)	Luke 22:54-62; 2 Corinthians 10:1-18
UNITY IN CHRIST	No One Left Behind (p. 1343)	Ephesians 4:1-6 (p. 1040)	Luke 4:1-13; Romans 6:1-14
LIVE IT	Forgive and Forget (p. 1341)	Luke 15:11-32 (p. 886)	Luke 5:1-11; Luke 14:25-35
CHRISTIAN AFFECTION	Kiss Whom? (p. 1342)	1 Thessalonians 5:23-28 (p. 1065)	Matthew 6:5-18; Mark 1:29-39

ATHLETE TOPICS: TRAINING

TRAINING

Topic	Warm-Up	Workout	Reference
BEING A GOOD SERVANT OF CHRIST	Confident Approach (p. 1346)	Luke 11:1-13 (p. 880)	Mark 12:13-17; Galatians 4:21-31
BEING GENEROUS	Just Let Go (p. 1345)	Mark 10:17-30 (pp. 849-50)	John 14:15-27; Acts 1:1-11
WEAKNESS MADE STRONG	Push to the Limit (p. 1350)	Romans 7:7-28 (pp. 977-78)	Mark 9:2-13; Romans 15:14-33
LEARNING FROM GOD'S INSTRUCTION	Give It a Rest (p. 1350)	Exodus 18:13-23 (p. 103)	Mark 12:41-44; 2 Corinthians 9:6-15
UNITY IN THE BODY	Sober Living (p. 1352)	Romans 12:3 (p. 984)	Psalm 23:1-6; Mark 3:20-35
SACRIFICE	Selling Out (p. 1352)	Matthew 16:24-27 (p. 887)	John 21:1-14; Romans 1:8-17
PRIORITY GOALS	Inside Your Head (p. 1349)	1 Corinthians 2:11-16 (pp. 993-94)	Matthew 25:14-30; 1 John 2:15-27
SPIRITUAL BATTLES	Get Fired Up (p. 1347)	Ephesians 6:10-18 (p. 1043)	Proverbs 3:1-8; Mark 6:30-44
VICTORY IN CHRIST	Championship Bound (p. 1349)	Romans 8:31-39 (p. 980)	2 Samuel 12:1-14; 1 Corinthians 11:17-34
PROCRASTINATION	Don't Miss Out (p. 1351)	Matthew 25:1-13 (p. 922)	Acts 6:1-7; James 2:14-26
DOING THE RIGHT THING	Ethics In Athletics (p. 1348)	Proverbs 10:4; 12:2; 14:2; 22:29 (pp. 538; 539; 541; 548)	Acts 9:20-31; Romans 1:1-7
ACTING ON FAITH	Watch and Learn (p. 1347)	James 1:19-27 (pp. 1108-09)	Luke 22:54-62; 2 Corinthians 10:1-18
SUFFERING FOR CHRIST	Pain Threshold (p. 1346)	Romans 5:1-5 (p. 975); James 1:2-4 (p. 1108)	Luke 4:1-13; Romans 6:1-14
SCOUTING REPORT	Bold Assurance (p. 1348)	Numbers 13:26-33 (pp. 159-60)	Luke 5:1-11; Luke 14:25-35
TRUSTING GOD	Trouble-Free Training (p. 1351)	John 14:1-3 (p. 922)	Matthew 6:5-18; Mark 1:29-39

Topic	Warm-Up	Workout	Reference
CONSEQUENCES OF STUBBORNESS	Flex (p. 1357)	Exodus 7:14-24; 12:28-30 (pp. 93, 97)	Mark 12:13-17; Galatians 4:21-31
TIME TO PREPARE	Take a Time Out (p. 1356)	Proverbs 18:13 (p. 545); Ephesians 5:17 (p. 1041)	John 14:15-27; Acts 1:1-11
DELIGHT IN THE LORD	This One Desire (p. 1357)	Psalm 37:4 (p. 480)	Mark 9:2-13; Romans 15:14-33
PURITY	Personal Responsibility (p. 1355)	1 Thessalonians 4:1-8 (p. 1063)	Mark 12:41-44; 2 Corinthians 9:6-15
THE WAY TO PLAY	For God's Glory (p. 1354)	1 Corinthians 10:23–11:1 (pp. 101-02)	Psalm 23:1-6; Mark 3:20-35
INSTRUCTION IN WISDOM	You Can Do It (p. 1354)	James 3:1-12 (p. 1110)	John 21:1-14; Romans 1:8-17
LEADING BY EXAMPLE	Out in the Open (p. 1357)	Matthew 5:13-16 (p. 801)	Matthew 25:14-30; 1 John 2:15-27
STANDING UP FOR WHAT'S RIGHT	Gold Standard (p. 1359)	Daniel 3:1-10 (p. 723)	Proverbs 3:1-8; Mark 6:30-44
SINCERE FAITH	Goal Oriented (p. 1355)	Philippians 3:12-21 (p. 1049)	2 Samuel 12:1-14; 1 Corinthians 11:17-34
SPIRITUAL IMPACT	Off the Bench (p. 1356)	1 Samuel 3:1-21 (pp. 256-57)	Acts 6:1-7; James 2:14-26
STRENGTHENED BY GOD	You Know Me (p. 1357)	Psalm 139 (p. 526)	Acts 9:20-31; Romans 1:1-7
BUILDING OTHERS UP	Give It To 'Em (p. 1358)	Proverbs 11:24-25 (p. 539); Luke 6:30 (p. 872)	Luke 22:54-62; 2 Corinthians 10:1-18
ENDURANCE	No Shortcuts (p. 1358)	1 Samuel 15:1-23 (p. 265-66)	Luke 4:1-13; Romans 6:1-14
RIGHTEOUS ANGER	Cooling the Hot Head (p. 1353)	Ephesians 4:26-32 (p.1040-41)	Luke 5:1-11; Luke 14:25-35
YOUR BODY IS A SANCTUARY	Priority Player (p. 1359)	1 Corinthians 6:19-20 (p. 997)	Matthew 6:5-18; Mark 1:29-39

Topic	Warm-Up	Workout	Reference
ONWARD	Soldier on the Field (p. 1367)	2 Timothy 2:1-13 (pp. 1080-81)	Mark 12:13-17; Galatians 4:21-31
ALL ON THE LINE	Risk It (p. 1362)	Esther 4:1-17 (p. 435)	John 14:15-27; Acts 1:1-11
TURNING POINT	Wake Up Call (p. 1361)	Acts 9:1-18 (pp. 943-44); Proverbs 29:1 (p. 553)	Mark 9:2-13; Romans 15:14-33
TRUSTING GOD	Nothing Lasts Forever (p. 1364)	James 4:13-17 (p. 1112)	Mark 12:41-44; 2 Corinthians 9:6-15
SPIRITUAL POWER	Who Powers You? (p. 1365)	Zechariah 4:6-1 0 (p. 783)	Psalm 23:1-6; Mark 3:20-35
FAITH AND WORKS	Trust Time (p. 1367)	Exodus 14: 5-31 (p. 99)	John 21:1-14; Romans 1:8-17
RELYING ON THE HOLY SPIRIT	Power Play (p. 1364)	Acts 2:1-13 (p. 934)	Matthew 25:14-30; 1 John 2:15-27
WISDOM FROM GOD	Wise Guy (p. 1362)	I Kings 3:4-14 (pp. 306-07)	Proverbs 3:1-8; Mark 6:30-44
ETERNAL THINGS	Satisfaction Guaranteed (p. 1366)	Hebrews 13:5 (p. 1104)	2 Samuel 12:1-14; 1 Corinthians 11:17-34
GOD'S MIRACULOUS POWER	Game Forecast (p. 1363)	Joshua 10:6-14 (pp. 217-18)	Acts 6:1-7; James 2:14-26
GOD'S PLAN	Here's the Plan (p. 1368)	Genesis 6:13-22 (pp. 48-49)	Acts 9:20-31; Romans 1:1-7
THE LOVE OF GOD	God's Love Letter (p. 1366)	Song of Solomon 7:10 (p. 570)	Luke 22:54-62; 2 Corinthians 10:1-18
PURSUING GOOD	Draws and Drawbacks (p. 1363)	Luke 16:19-24 (p. 888)	Luke 4:1-13; Romans 6:1-14
FOLLOWING GOD'S VOICE	My Blind Spot (p. 1365)	Numbers 22:21-34 (p. 168)	Luke 5:1-11; Luke 14:25-35
THE END GOAL	Homecoming (p. 1368)	Hebrews 11:8-16 (pp. 1101-02); Hebrews 13:14 (p. 1104); John 14:2-3 (p. 922)	Matthew 6:5-18; Mark 1:29-39

OLD TESTAMENT

Beginnings of God's Creation

Founders of Israel

Israel's Slavery in Egypt

Journey to the Promised Land

Life in the Promised Land

Israel's Great Kings

Stories from the Prophets

Stories from the Exile

Stories of Love and Loss

NEW TESTAMENT

Jesus is Born and Grows

Jesus' Early Ministry

Miracles of Jesus

Experiences of Jesus

Parables of Jesus

Jesus' Last Week

The Christian Church Begins

Paul's Missionary Journeys

37 BONUS BIBLE STUDIES

The mini-studies for the following stories and topics are not part of the Study Plans on pages 13–28, but they can also be used for personal or group study.

Topic	Workout	Reference
Rejection of Jesus	Get Out of Town	Luke 4:14-30
Communion, Eucharist	Celebrating the Lord's Supper	Luke 22:7-23
Taking Sides	Divided We Fall	1 Corinthians 1:10-17
God's Coworkers	Building with Gold	1 Corinthians 3:1-23
Christian Freedom	Handling Our Freedom	1 Corinthians 10:14–11:1
Diversity in the Body	All for One	1 Corinthians 12:12-31
Spiritual Gifts	Gifted and Talented	1 Corinthians 14:1-25
Integrity	Yes, No, Maybe	2 Corinthians 1:12–2:11
Words of Life or Death	Fragrant Letters	2 Corinthians 2:12–3:6
Handling Foolish Teaching	Tolerating Fools	2 Corinthians 11:16-33
Unity in the Body	Building Up and Hanging Out	Ephesians 4:1-16
Parents	Parental Expectations	Ephesians 6:1-4
Hope in Jesus	The Lasting Hope	Colossians 1:1-4
Walking with Christ in Victory	Victory Over the Enemy	Colossians 2:6-23
Gifts from God	God's Incredible Gifts	1 Thessalonians 5:12-28
Imitators of Jesus	Worthy of God's Kingdom	2 Thessalonians 1:1-12
End Times	The Man of Lawlessness	2 Thessalonians 2:1-17
Our Worth and Value	Finding Worth	1 Timothy 2:1-15
False Teachers	The Dark Side	2 Timothy 3:1-9
The Bible	The Living Word	2 Timothy 3:10–4:8
Power for Living	Powerful Knowledge	Titus 1:1-4
Angels	The Role of Angels	Hebrews 1:1-14
Jesus the God-Man	Power of Shared Experiences	Hebrews 2:1-18
Trusting God	The Promise	Hebrews 6:13-20
Guilt and Restoration	A Guilty Plea	Hebrews 9:1-10
Jesus Is Superior	Passionate Sacrifice	Hebrews 9:11-28
Jesus and Salvation	Giving It Up	Hebrews 10:1-18
Faith	Lifestyle of the Rich in Faith	Hebrews 13:1-25
Money	Money Concerns	James 5:1-6
Prayer and Bible Study	Pay Attention	2 Peter 1:12-21
Lies and Truth	Dangerous Lies	2 Peter 2:1-22
Jesus' Second Return	Anticipation	2 Peter 3:1-18
The Risen Lord	A Strange Vision	Revelation 1:1-20
End Times Judgments	Incense and Death	Revelation 8:1–9:21
End Times	Two Witnesses Persecuted	Revelation 10:1–11:19
End Time Judgments	Plagues and Prostitutes	Revelation 16:1–17:18
Eternity in Heaven	Heavenly Citizenship	Revelation 21:9–22:6

INTRODUCTION TO THE
NEW LIVING TRANSLATION

TRANSLATION PHILOSOPHY AND METHODOLOGY

English Bible translations tend to be governed by one of two general translation theories. The first theory has been called "formal-equivalence," "literal," or "word-for-word" translation. According to this theory, the translator attempts to render each word of the original language into English and seeks to preserve the original syntax and sentence structure as much as possible in translation. The second theory has been called "dynamic-equivalence," "functional-equivalence," or "thought-for-thought" translation. The goal of this translation theory is to produce in English the closest natural equivalent of the message expressed by the original-language text, both in meaning and in style.

Both of these translation theories have their strengths. A formal-equivalence translation preserves aspects of the original text—including ancient idioms, term consistency, and original-language syntax—that are valuable for scholars and professional study. It allows a reader to trace formal elements of the original-language text through the English translation. A dynamic-equivalence translation, on the other hand, focuses on translating the message of the original-language text. It ensures that the meaning of the text is readily apparent to the contemporary reader. This allows the message to come through with immediacy, without requiring the reader to struggle with foreign idioms and awkward syntax. It also facilitates serious study of the text's message and clarity in both devotional and public reading.

The pure application of either of these translation philosophies would create translations at opposite ends of the translation spectrum. But in reality, all translations contain a mixture of these two philosophies. A purely formal-equivalence translation would be unintelligible in English, and a purely dynamic-equivalence translation would risk being unfaithful to the original. That is why translations shaped by dynamic-equivalence theory are usually quite literal when the original text is relatively clear, and the translations shaped by formal-equivalence theory are sometimes quite dynamic when the original text is obscure.

The translators of the New Living Translation set out to render the message of the original texts of Scripture into clear, contemporary English. As they did so, they kept the concerns of both formal-equivalence and dynamic-equivalence in mind. On the one hand, they translated as simply and literally as possible when that approach yielded an accurate, clear, and natural English text. Many words and phrases were rendered literally and consistently into English, preserving essential literary and rhetorical devices, ancient metaphors, and word choices that give structure to the text and provide echoes of meaning from one passage to the next.

On the other hand, the translators rendered the message more dynamically when the literal rendering was hard to understand, was misleading, or yielded archaic or foreign wording. They clarified difficult metaphors and terms to aid in the reader's understanding. The translators first struggled with the meaning of the words and phrases in the ancient context; then they rendered the message into clear, natural English. Their goal was to be both faithful to the ancient texts and eminently readable. The result is a translation that is both exegetically accurate and idiomatically powerful.

TRANSLATION PROCESS AND TEAM

To produce an accurate translation of the Bible into contemporary English, the translation team needed the skills necessary to enter into the thought patterns of the ancient authors and then to render their ideas, connotations, and effects into clear, contemporary English. To begin this process, qualified biblical scholars were needed to interpret the meaning of the original text and to check it against our base English translation. In order to guard against personal and theological biases, the scholars needed to represent a diverse group of Evangelicals who would employ the best exegetical tools. Then to work alongside the scholars, skilled English stylists were needed to shape the text into clear, contemporary English.

With these concerns in mind, the Bible Translation Committee recruited teams of scholars that represented a broad spectrum of denominations, theological perspectives, and backgrounds within the worldwide Evangelical community. Each book of the Bible was assigned to three different scholars with proven expertise in the book or group of books to be reviewed. Each of these scholars made a thorough review of a base translation and submitted suggested revisions to the appropriate Senior Translator. The Senior Translator then reviewed and summarized these suggestions and proposed a first-draft revision of the base text. This draft served as the basis for several additional phases of exegetical and stylistic committee review. Then the Bible Translation Committee jointly reviewed and approved every verse of the final translation.

Throughout the translation and editing process, the Senior Translators and their scholar teams were given a chance to review the editing done by the team of stylists. This ensured that exegetical errors would not be introduced late in the process and that the entire Bible Translation Committee was happy with the final result. By choosing a team of qualified scholars and skilled stylists and by setting up a process that allowed their interaction throughout the process, the New Living Translation has been refined to preserve the essential formal elements of the original biblical texts, while also creating a clear, understandable English text.

The New Living Translation was first published in 1996. Shortly after its initial publication, the Bible Translation Committee began a process of further committee review and translation refinement. The purpose of this continued revision was to increase the level of precision without sacrificing the text's easy-to-understand quality. This second-edition text was completed in 2004, and an additional update with minor changes was subsequently introduced in 2007 and 2013.

WRITTEN TO BE READ ALOUD

It is evident in Scripture that the biblical documents were written to be read aloud, often in public worship (see Nehemiah 8; Luke 4:16-20; 1 Timothy 4:13; Revelation 1:3). It is still the case today that more people will hear the Bible read aloud in church than are likely to read it for themselves. Therefore, a new translation must communicate with clarity and power when it is read publicly. Clarity was a primary goal for the NLT translators, not only to facilitate private reading and understanding, but also to ensure that it would be excellent for public reading and make an immediate and powerful impact on any listener.

THE TEXTS BEHIND THE NEW LIVING TRANSLATION

The Old Testament translators used the Masoretic Text of the Hebrew Bible as represented in *Biblia Hebraica Stuttgartensia* (1977), with its extensive system of textual notes; this is an update of Rudolf Kittel's *Biblia Hebraica* (Stuttgart, 1937). The translators also further compared the Dead Sea Scrolls, the Septuagint and other Greek manuscripts, the Samaritan Pentateuch, the Syriac Peshitta, the Latin Vulgate, and any other versions or manuscripts that shed light on the meaning of difficult passages.

The New Testament translators used the two standard editions of the Greek New Testament: the *Greek New Testament*, published by the United Bible Societies (UBS, fourth revised edition, 1993), and *Novum Testamentum Graece*, edited by Nestle and Aland (NA, twenty-seventh edition, 1993). These two editions, which have the same text but differ in punctuation and textual notes, represent, for the most part, the best in modern textual scholarship. However, in cases where strong textual or other scholarly evidence supported the decision, the translators sometimes chose to differ from the UBS and NA Greek texts and followed variant readings found in other ancient witnesses. Significant textual variants of this sort are always noted in the textual notes of the New Living Translation.

TRANSLATION ISSUES

The translators have made a conscious effort to provide a text that can be easily understood by the typical reader of modern English. To this end, we sought to use only vocabulary and language structures in common use today. We avoided using language likely to become quickly dated or that reflects only a narrow subdialect of English, with the goal of making the New Living Translation as broadly useful and timeless as possible.

But our concern for readability goes beyond the concerns of vocabulary and sentence structure. We are also concerned about historical and cultural barriers to understanding the Bible, and we have sought to translate terms shrouded in history and culture in ways that can be immediately understood. To this end:

- We have converted ancient weights and measures (for example, "ephah" [a unit of dry volume] or "cubit" [a unit of length]) to modern English (American) equivalents, since the ancient measures are not generally meaningful to today's readers. Then in the textual footnotes we offer the literal Hebrew, Aramaic, or Greek measures, along with modern metric equivalents.
- Instead of translating ancient currency values literally, we have expressed them in common terms that communicate the message. For example, in the Old Testament, "ten shekels of silver" becomes "ten pieces of silver" to convey the intended message. In the New Testament, we have often translated the "denarius" as "the normal daily wage" to facilitate understanding. Then a footnote offers: "Greek *a denarius*, the payment for a full day's labor." In general, we give a clear English rendering and then state the literal Hebrew, Aramaic, or Greek in a textual footnote.
- Since the names of Hebrew months are unknown to most contemporary readers, and since the Hebrew lunar calendar fluctuates from year to year in relation to the solar calendar used today, we have looked for clear ways to communicate the time of year the Hebrew months (such as Abib) refer to. When an expanded or interpretive rendering is given in the text, a textual note gives the literal rendering. Where it is possible to define a specific ancient date in terms of our modern calendar, we use modern dates in the text. A textual footnote then gives the literal Hebrew date and states the rationale for our rendering. For example, Ezra 6:15 pinpoints the date when the postexilic Temple was completed in Jerusalem: "the third day of the month Adar." This was during the sixth year of King Darius's reign (that is, 515 B.C.). We have translated that date as March 12, with a footnote giving the Hebrew and identifying the year as 515 B.C.
- Since ancient references to the time of day differ from our modern methods of denoting time, we have used renderings that are instantly understandable to the modern reader. Accordingly, we have rendered specific times of day by using approximate equivalents in terms of our common "o'clock" system. On occasion, translations such as "at dawn the next morning" or "as the sun was setting" have been used when the biblical reference is more general.
- When the meaning of a proper name (or a wordplay inherent in a proper name) is relevant to the message of the text, its meaning is often illuminated with a textual footnote. For example, in Exodus 2:10 the text reads: "The princess named him Moses, for she explained, 'I lifted him out of the water.'" The accompanying footnote reads: "*Moses* sounds like a Hebrew term that means 'to lift out.'"

  Sometimes, when the actual meaning of a name is clear, that meaning is included in parentheses within the text itself. For example, the text at Genesis 16:11 reads: "You are to name him Ishmael (*which means 'God hears'*), for the LORD has heard your cry of distress." Since the original hearers and readers would have instantly understood the meaning of the name "Ishmael," we have provided modern readers with the same information so they can experience the text in a similar way.

- Many words and phrases carry a great deal of cultural meaning that was obvious to the original readers but needs explanation in our own culture. For example, the phrase "they beat their breasts" (Luke 23:48) in ancient times meant that people were very upset, often in mourning. In our translation we chose to translate this phrase dynamically for clarity: "They went home *in deep sorrow*." Then we included a footnote with the literal Greek, which reads: "Greek *went home beating their breasts*." In other similar cases, however, we have sometimes chosen to illuminate the existing literal expression to make it immediately understandable. For example, here we might have expanded the literal phrase to read: "They went home beating their breasts *in sorrow*." If we had done this, we would not have included a textual footnote, since the literal Greek clearly appears in translation.
- Metaphorical language is sometimes difficult for contemporary readers to understand, so at times we have chosen to translate or illuminate the meaning of a metaphor. For example, the ancient poet writes, "Your neck is *like* the tower of David" (Song of Songs 4:4). We have rendered it "Your neck is *as beautiful as* the tower of David" to clarify the intended positive meaning of the simile. Another example comes in Ecclesiastes 12:3, which can be literally rendered: "Remember him . . . when the grinding women cease because they are few, and the women who look through the windows see dimly." We have rendered it: "Remember him before your teeth—your few remaining servants—stop grinding; and before your eyes—the women looking through the windows—see dimly." We clarified such metaphors only when we believed a typical reader might be confused by the literal text.
- When the content of the original language text is poetic in character, we have rendered it in English poetic form. We sought to break lines in ways that clarify and highlight the relationships between phrases of the text. Hebrew poetry often uses parallelism, a literary form where a second phrase (or in some instances a third or fourth) echoes the initial phrase in some way. In Hebrew parallelism, the subsequent parallel phrases continue, while also furthering and sharpening, the thought expressed in the initial line or phrase. Whenever possible, we sought to represent these parallel phrases in natural poetic English.
- The Greek term *hoi Ioudaioi* is literally translated "the Jews" in many English translations. In the Gospel of John, however, this term doesn't always refer to the Jewish people generally. In some contexts, it refers more particularly to the Jewish religious leaders. We have attempted to capture the meaning in these different contexts by using terms such as "the people" (with a footnote: Greek *the Jewish people*) or "the religious leaders," where appropriate.
- One challenge we faced was how to translate accurately the ancient biblical text that was originally written in a context where male-oriented terms were used to refer to humanity generally. We needed to respect the nature of the ancient context while also trying to make the translation clear to a modern audience that tends to read male-oriented language as applying only to males. Often the original text, though using masculine nouns and pronouns, clearly intends that the message be applied to both men and women. A typical example is found in the New Testament letters, where the believers are called "brothers" (*adelphoi*). Yet it is clear from the content of these letters that they were addressed to all the believers—male and female. Thus, we have usually translated this Greek word as "brothers and sisters" in order to represent the historical situation more accurately.

We have also been sensitive to passages where the text applies generally to human beings or to the human condition. In some instances we have used plural pronouns (they, them) in place of the masculine singular (he, him). For example, a traditional rendering of Proverbs 22:6 is: "Train up a child in the way he should go, and when he is old he will not turn from it." We have rendered it: "Direct your children onto the right path, and when they are older, they will not leave it." At times, we have also replaced third person pronouns with the second person to ensure clarity. A traditional rendering of Proverbs 26:27 is: "He who digs a pit will fall into it, and he who rolls a stone, it will come back on him." We have rendered it: "If you set a trap for others, you will get caught in it yourself. If you roll a boulder down on others, it will crush you instead."

We should emphasize, however, that all masculine nouns and pronouns used to represent God (for example, "Father") have been maintained without exception. All decisions of this kind have been driven by the concern to reflect accurately the intended meaning of the original texts of Scripture.

LEXICAL CONSISTENCY IN TERMINOLOGY

For the sake of clarity, we have translated certain original-language terms consistently, especially within synoptic passages and for commonly repeated rhetorical phrases, and within certain word categories such as divine names and non-theological technical terminology (e.g., liturgical, legal, cultural, zoological, and botanical terms). For theological terms, we have allowed a greater semantic range of acceptable English words or phrases for a single Hebrew or Greek word. We have avoided some theological terms that are not readily understood by many modern readers. For example, we avoided using words such as "justification" and "sanctification," which are carryovers from Latin translations. In place of these words, we have provided renderings such as "made right with God" and "made holy."

THE SPELLING OF PROPER NAMES

Many individuals in the Bible, especially the Old Testament, are known by more than one name (e.g., Uzziah/Azariah). For the sake of clarity, we have tried to use a single spelling for any one individual, footnoting the literal spelling whenever we differ from it. This is especially helpful in delineating the kings of Israel and Judah. King Joash/Jehoash of Israel has been consistently called Jehoash, while King Joash/Jehoash of Judah is called Joash. A similar distinction has been used to distinguish between Joram/Jehoram of Israel and Joram/Jehoram of Judah. All such decisions were made with the goal of clarifying the text for the reader. When the ancient biblical writers clearly had a theological purpose in their choice of a variant name (e.g., Esh-baal/Ishbosheth), the different names have been maintained with an explanatory footnote.

For the names Jacob and Israel, which are used interchangeably for both the individual patriarch and the nation, we generally render it "Israel" when it refers to the nation and "Jacob" when it refers to the individual. When our rendering of the name differs from the underlying Hebrew text, we provide a textual footnote, which includes this explanation: "The names 'Jacob' and 'Israel' are often interchanged throughout the Old Testament, referring sometimes to the individual patriarch and sometimes to the nation."

THE RENDERING OF DIVINE NAMES

All appearances of *'el*, *'elohim*, or *'eloah* have been translated "God," except where the context demands the translation "god(s)." We have generally rendered the tetragrammaton (*YHWH*) consistently as "the LORD," utilizing a form with small capitals that is common among English translations. This will distinguish it from the name *'adonai*, which we render "Lord." When *'adonai* and *YHWH* appear together, we have rendered it "Sovereign LORD." This also distinguishes *'adonai YHWH* from cases where *YHWH* appears with *'elohim*, which is rendered "LORD God." When YH (the short form of YHWH) and YHWH appear together, we have rendered it "LORD GOD." When *YHWH* appears with the term *tseba'oth*, we have rendered it "LORD of Heaven's Armies" to translate the meaning of the name. In a few cases, we have utilized the transliteration, *Yahweh*, when the personal character of the name is being invoked in contrast to another divine name or the name of some other god (for example, see Exodus 3:15; 6:2-3).

In the Gospels and Acts, the Greek word *christos* has normally been translated as "Messiah" when the context assumes a Jewish audience. When a Gentile audience can be assumed (which is consistently the case in the Epistles and Revelation), *christos* has been translated as "Christ." The Greek word *kurios* is consistently translated "Lord," except that it is translated "LORD" wherever the New Testament text explicitly quotes from the Old Testament, and the text there has it in small capitals.

TEXTUAL FOOTNOTES

The New Living Translation provides several kinds of textual footnotes, all designated in the text with an asterisk:

- When for the sake of clarity the NLT renders a difficult or potentially confusing phrase dynamically, we generally give the literal rendering in a textual footnote. This allows the reader to see the literal source of our dynamic rendering and how our translation relates to other more literal translations. These notes are prefaced with "Hebrew," "Aramaic," or "Greek," identifying the language of the underlying source text. For example, in Acts 2:42 we translated the literal "breaking of bread" (from the Greek) as "the Lord's Supper" to clarify that this verse refers to the ceremonial practice of the church rather than just an ordinary meal. Then we attached a footnote to "the Lord's Supper," which reads: "Greek *the breaking of bread*."
- Textual footnotes are also used to show alternative renderings, prefaced with the word "Or." These normally occur for passages where an aspect of the meaning is debated. On occasion, we also provide notes on words or phrases that represent a departure from long-standing tradition. These notes are prefaced with "Traditionally rendered." For example, the footnote to the translation "serious skin disease" at Leviticus 13:2 says: "Traditionally rendered *leprosy*. The Hebrew word used throughout this passage is used to describe various skin diseases."
- When our translators follow a textual variant that differs significantly from our standard Hebrew or Greek texts (listed earlier), we document that difference with a footnote. We also footnote cases when the NLT excludes a passage that is included in the Greek text known as the *Textus Receptus* (and familiar to readers through its translation in the King James Version). In such cases, we offer a translation of the excluded text in a footnote, even though it is generally recognized as a later addition to the Greek text and not part of the original Greek New Testament.
- All Old Testament passages that are quoted in the New Testament are identified by a textual footnote at the New Testament location. When the New Testament clearly quotes from the Greek translation of the Old Testament, and when it differs significantly in wording from the Hebrew text, we also place a textual footnote at the Old Testament location. This note includes a rendering of the Greek version, along with a cross-reference to the New Testament passage(s) where it is cited (for example, see notes on Psalms 8:2; 53:3; Proverbs 3:12).
- Some textual footnotes provide cultural and historical information on places, things, and people in the Bible that are probably obscure to modern readers. Such notes should aid the reader in understanding the message of the text. For example, in Acts 12:1, "King Herod" is named in this translation as "King Herod Agrippa" and is identified in a footnote as being "the nephew of Herod Antipas and a grandson of Herod the Great."
- When the meaning of a proper name (or a wordplay inherent in a proper name) is relevant to the meaning of the text, it is either illuminated with a textual footnote or included within parentheses in the text itself. For example, the footnote concerning the name "Eve" at Genesis 3:20 reads: "*Eve* sounds like a Hebrew term that means 'to give life.'" This wordplay in the Hebrew illuminates the meaning of the text, which goes on to say that Eve "would be the mother of all who live."

AS WE SUBMIT this translation for publication, we recognize that any translation of the Scriptures is subject to limitations and imperfections. Anyone who has attempted to communicate the richness of God's Word into another language will realize it is impossible to make a perfect translation. Recognizing these limitations, we sought God's guidance and wisdom throughout this project. Now we pray that he will accept our efforts and use this translation for the benefit of the church and of all people.

We pray that the New Living Translation will overcome some of the barriers of history, culture, and language that have kept people from reading and understanding God's Word. We hope that readers unfamiliar with the Bible will find the words clear and easy to understand and that readers well versed in the Scriptures will gain a fresh perspective. We pray that readers will gain insight and wisdom for living, but most of all that they will meet the God of the Bible and be forever changed by knowing him.

The Bible Translation Committee

BIBLE TRANSLATION TEAM

HOLY BIBLE, NEW LIVING TRANSLATION

PENTATEUCH
Daniel I. Block, Senior Translator
Wheaton College

GENESIS
Allen Ross, *Beeson Divinity School, Samford University*
Gordon Wenham, *Trinity College, Bristol*

EXODUS
Robert Bergen, *Hannibal-LaGrange College*
Daniel I. Block, *Wheaton College*
Eugene Carpenter, *Bethel College, Mishawaka, Indiana*

LEVITICUS
David Baker, *Ashland Theological Seminary*
Victor Hamilton, *Asbury College*
Kenneth Mathews, *Beeson Divinity School, Samford University*

NUMBERS
Dale A. Brueggemann, *Assemblies of God Division of Foreign Missions*
R. K. Harrison, *Wycliffe College*
Paul R. House, *Beeson Divinity School, Samford University*
Gerald L. Mattingly, *Johnson Bible College*

DEUTERONOMY
J. Gordon McConville, *University of Gloucester*
Eugene H. Merrill, *Dallas Theological Seminary*
John A. Thompson, *University of Melbourne*

HISTORICAL BOOKS
Barry J. Beitzel, Senior Translator
Trinity Evangelical Divinity School

JOSHUA, JUDGES
Carl E. Armerding, *Schloss Mittersill Study Centre*
Barry J. Beitzel, *Trinity Evangelical Divinity School*
Lawson Stone, *Asbury Theological Seminary*

1 & 2 SAMUEL
Robert Gordon, *Cambridge University*
V. Philips Long, *Regent College*
J. Robert Vannoy, *Biblical Theological Seminary*

1 & 2 KINGS
Bill T. Arnold, *Asbury Theological Seminary*
William H. Barnes, *North Central University*
Frederic W. Bush, *Fuller Theological Seminary*

1 & 2 CHRONICLES
Raymond B. Dillard, *Westminster Theological Seminary*
David A. Dorsey, *Evangelical School of Theology*
Terry Eves, Erskine College

RUTH, EZRA—ESTHER
William C. Williams, *Vanguard University*
H. G. M. Williamson, *Oxford University*

WISDOM BOOKS
Tremper Longman III, Senior Translator
Westmont College

JOB
August Konkel, *Providence Theological Seminary*
Tremper Longman III, *Westmont College*
Al Wolters, *Redeemer College*

PSALMS 1–75
Mark D. Futato, *Reformed Theological Seminary*
Douglas Green, *Westminster Theological Seminary*
Richard Pratt, *Reformed Theological Seminary*

PSALMS 76–150
David M. Howard Jr., *Bethel Theological Seminary*
Raymond C. Ortlund Jr., *Immanuel Church, Nashville, Tennessee*
Willem VanGemeren, *Trinity Evangelical Divinity School*

PROVERBS
Ted Hildebrandt, *Gordon College*
Richard Schultz, *Wheaton College*
Raymond C. Van Leeuwen, *Eastern College*

ECCLESIASTES, SONG OF SONGS
Daniel C. Fredericks, *Belhaven College*
David Hubbard, *Fuller Theological Seminary*
Tremper Longman III, *Westmont College*

PROPHETS
John N. Oswalt, Senior Translator
Asbury Theological Seminary

ISAIAH
John N. Oswalt, *Asbury Theological Seminary*
Gary Smith, *Union University*
John Walton, Wheaton College

JEREMIAH, LAMENTATIONS
G. Herbert Livingston, *Asbury Theological Seminary*
Elmer A. Martens, *Mennonite Brethren Biblical Seminary*

EZEKIEL
Daniel I. Block, *Wheaton College*
David H. Engelhard, *Calvin Theological Seminary*
David Thompson, *Asbury Theological Seminary*

DANIEL, HAGGAI—MALACHI
Joyce Baldwin Caine, *Trinity College, Bristol*
Douglas Gropp, *Catholic University of America*
Roy Hayden, *Oral Roberts School of Theology*
Andrew Hill, *Wheaton College*
Tremper Longman III, *Westmont College*

HOSEA—ZEPHANIAH
Joseph Coleson, *Nazarene Theological Seminary*
Roy Hayden, *Oral Roberts School of Theology*
Andrew Hill, Wheaton College
Richard Patterson, *Liberty University*

GOSPELS AND ACTS
Grant R. Osborne, Senior Translator
Trinity Evangelical Divinity School

MATTHEW
Craig Blomberg, *Denver Seminary*
Donald A. Hagner, *Fuller Theological Seminary*
David Turner, *Grand Rapids Baptist Seminary*

MARK
Robert Guelich, *Fuller Theological Seminary*
George Guthrie, *Union University*
Grant R. Osborne, *Trinity Evangelical Divinity School*

LUKE
Darrell Bock, *Dallas Theological Seminary*
Scot McKnight, *North Park University*
Robert Stein, *The Southern Baptist Theological Seminary*

JOHN
Gary M. Burge, *Wheaton College*
Philip W. Comfort, *Coastal Carolina University*
Marianne Meye Thompson, *Fuller Theological Seminary*

ACTS
D. A. Carson, *Trinity Evangelical Divinity School*
William J. Larkin, *Columbia International University*
Roger Mohrlang, *Whitworth University*

LETTERS AND REVELATION
Norman R. Ericson, Senior Translator
Wheaton College

ROMANS, GALATIANS
Gerald Borchert, *Northern Baptist Theological Seminary*
Douglas J. Moo, *Wheaton College*
Thomas R. Schreiner, *The Southern Baptist Theological Seminary*

1 & 2 CORINTHIANS
Joseph Alexanian, *Trinity International University*
Linda Belleville, *Bethel College, Mishawaka, Indiana*
Douglas A. Oss, *Central Bible College*
Robert Sloan, *Houston Baptist University*

EPHESIANS—PHILEMON
Harold W. Hoehner, *Dallas Theological Seminary*
Moises Silva, *Gordon-Conwell Theological Seminary*
Klyne Snodgrass, *North Park Theological Seminary*

HEBREWS, JAMES, 1 & 2 PETER, JUDE
Peter Davids, *St. Stephen's University*
Norman R. Ericson, *Wheaton College*
William Lane, *Seattle Pacific University*
J. Ramsey Michaels, *S. W. Missouri State University*

1—3 JOHN, REVELATION
Greg Beale, *Westminster Theological Seminary*
Robert Mounce, *Whitworth University*
M. Robert Mulholland Jr., *Asbury Theological Seminary*

SPECIAL REVIEWERS
F. F. Bruce, *University of Manchester*
Kenneth N. Taylor, *Translator,* The Living Bible

COORDINATING TEAM
Mark D. Taylor, *Director and Chief Stylist*
Ronald A. Beers, *Executive Director and Stylist*
Mark R. Norton, *Managing Editor and O.T. Coordinating Editor*
Philip W. Comfort, *N.T. Coordinating Editor*
Daniel W. Taylor, *Bethel University, Senior Stylist*
Sean A. Harrison, *Editor and Stylist*
James A. Swanson, *Lexical Reviewer*

THE OLD
TESTAMENT

INTRODUCTION TO

GENESIS

PERSONAL READING PLAN

- ☐Genesis 1:1–3:24
- ☐Genesis 4:1–5:32
- ☐Genesis 6:1–9:17
- ☐Genesis 9:18–11:32
- ☐Genesis 12:1–15:21
- ☐Genesis 16:1–18:33
- ☐Genesis 19:1–21:21
- ☐Genesis 21:22–23:20
- ☐Genesis 24:1–25:34
- ☐Genesis 26:1–27:40
- ☐Genesis 27:41–30:24
- ☐Genesis 30:25–31:55
- ☐Genesis 32:1–34:31
- ☐Genesis 35:1–36:43
- ☐Genesis 37:1–38:30
- ☐Genesis 39:1–41:40
- ☐Genesis 41:41–42:38
- ☐Genesis 43:1–44:34
- ☐Genesis 45:1–47:12
- ☐Genesis 47:13–48:22
- ☐Genesis 49:1–50:26

AUTHOR

Moses is assumed to be the author and editor of most of the first five books of the Old Testament (the Pentateuch).

DATE

It is difficult to set a firm date for the writing of the Pentateuch. Conservative estimates place it in either the 15th or 13th century B.C., depending on when the Exodus occurred.

THEME

Everything begins with God, who elects a people of His own.

HISTORICAL BACKGROUND AND CHARACTERISTICS

Archaeological findings and ancient history have much in common with certain details of the Genesis narrative. The socio-cultural environment of the patriarchal narratives (Gen. 12–50) fits well within the context of the Middle Bronze Age (ca 1950–1550 B.C.) in Palestine. This "book of Beginnings" is the origin for many of the major themes discussed in Scripture. Humanity's origin and mission, its fall and predicament, human responsibility and divine sovereignty, God's justice and mercy, His atonement for sin, the obedience of faith, the covenant of grace—all originate in Genesis. But Genesis is perhaps most often read for its vivid account of the pioneers of our faith—Abraham, Isaac, and Jacob—through whom God is known and can be trusted.

PASSAGES FOR TOPICAL GROUP STUDY

1:1–2:3	THE BEGINNING	Extreme Creation
2:4-25	CREATION and SEXUALITY	The Ultimate Garden
3:1-24	SIN	Sin Enters Paradise
4:1-16	SELFISHNESS and MURDER	Murder One
6:5–7:12	OBEDIENCE	Weather Alert
8:1-22	CREATION and ENVIRONMENT	Operation Recovery
12:1-9	CHARACTER and MIDDLE EAST	Moving Out
13:1-18	DOING WHAT'S RIGHT	The Right Choice
18:16-33	PRAYER and GOD'S GRACE	Prayer Power
19:1-29	SEXUALITY	Dangerous Values
21:1-21	RIVALRY and MIDDLE EAST	Family Feuds
22:1-19	SELF-SACRIFICE	The Supreme Sacrifice
25:19-34	HONOR and MOTIVATIONS	Honor and Privilege
29:1-14	LOVE and DATING	Love at First Sight
32:22-32	SPIRITUAL STRUGGLES	Wrestling with God
37:1-11	DREAMS and DESIRES	Dream On
37:12-36	SELF VS. OTHERS FOCUS	In the Pits
39:1-23	SEXUAL STANDARDS	"Everyone's Doing It"
41:1-40	GIVING GOD GLORY	An Awesome Performance
45:1-28	ARGUING and FORGIVENESS	"Hey, It's Me!"

THE ACCOUNT OF CREATION

1 In the beginning God created the heavens and the
earth.* 2 The earth was formless and empty, and
darkness covered the deep waters. And the Spirit of
God was hovering over the surface of the waters.

3 Then God said, "Let there be light," and there was
light. 4 And God saw that the light was good. Then
he separated the light from the darkness. 5 God
called the light "day" and the darkness "night."

And evening passed and morning came, marking the first day.

6 Then God said, "Let there be a space between the waters, to separate the waters of the heavens from the
waters of the earth." 7 And that is what happened.
God made this space to separate the waters of the
earth from the waters of the heavens. 8 God called
the space "sky."

And evening passed and morning came, marking the second day.

EXTREME CREATION

1. What did you create when you were a kid? Mud pies? A tree house? Other?

GENESIS 1:1–2:3

2. How does this account of creation compare with the theory of evolution?
3. Note the repetition of "God said . . ." What does that tell us about God's word? About the creation of the world?
4. What does it mean by "God created human beings in his own image" (v. 27)? What is God's image?
5. Compare God's blessing on creatures (v. 22) and on man (v. 28).
6. What does it mean to "subdue" the earth and "rule" the creatures (v. 28)? How does this apply to your life?

9 Then God said, "Let the waters beneath the sky flow
together into one place, so dry ground may appear." And that is what happened. 10 God called the
dry ground "land" and the waters "seas." And God
saw that it was good. 11 Then God said, "Let the land
sprout with vegetation—every sort of seed-bearing plant, and trees that grow seed-bearing fruit.
These seeds will then produce the kinds of plants
and trees from which they came." And that is what
happened. 12 The land produced vegetation—
all sorts of seed-bearing plants, and trees with
seed-bearing fruit. Their seeds produced plants
and trees of the same kind. And God saw that it
was good.

13 And evening passed and morning came, marking the third day.

14 Then God said, "Let lights appear in the sky to separate the day from the night. Let them be signs to
mark the seasons, days, and years. 15 Let these lights
in the sky shine down on the earth." And that is
what happened. 16 God made two great lights—the
larger one to govern the day, and the smaller one to
govern the night. He also made the stars. 17 God set
these lights in the sky to light the earth, 18 to govern
the day and night, and to separate the light from
the darkness. And God saw that it was good.
19 And evening passed and morning came, marking the fourth day.

20 Then God said, "Let the waters swarm with fish and
other life. Let the skies be filled with birds of every kind." 21 So God created great sea creatures and
every living thing that scurries and swarms in the
water, and every sort of bird—each producing offspring of the same kind. And God saw that it was
good. 22 Then God blessed them, saying, "Be fruitful
and multiply. Let the fish fill the seas, and let the
birds multiply on the earth."
23 And evening passed and morning came, marking the fifth day.

24 Then God said, "Let the earth produce every sort
of animal, each producing offspring of the same
kind—livestock, small animals that scurry along
the ground, and wild animals." And that is what
happened. 25 God made all sorts of wild animals,
livestock, and small animals, each able to produce
offspring of the same kind. And God saw that it was
good.
26 Then God said, "Let us make human beings* in
our image, to be like us. They will reign over the
fish in the sea, the birds in the sky, the livestock, all
the wild animals on the earth,* and the small animals that scurry along the ground."

27 So God created human beings* in his own
image.
In the image of God he created them;
male and female he created them.

28 Then God blessed them and said, "Be fruitful
and multiply. Fill the earth and govern it. Reign
over the fish in the sea, the birds in the sky, and all
the animals that scurry along the ground."
29 Then God said, "Look! I have given you every
seed-bearing plant throughout the earth and all
the fruit trees for your food. 30 And I have given every green plant as food for all the wild animals, the
birds in the sky, and the small animals that scurry

1:1 Or *In the beginning when God created the heavens and the earth, . . .* Or *When God began to create the heavens and the earth, . . .*
1:26a Or *man;* Hebrew reads *adam.* **1:26b** As in Syriac version; Hebrew reads *all the earth.* **1:27** Or *the man;* Hebrew reads *ha-adam.*

1:1 God created. This declaration means that God is, He created all things, and He brought us into being.

1:5 the first day. Either a literal day or a period of time. The phrase "evening passed and morning came" suggests a literal day.

1:26 image . . . like us. God created people to be like Him. Adam and Eve became unlike God only when they tried to be "like" Him in terms of authority (3:5).

1:27 male and female. Both men and women were created in the image of God and given the responsibility to take care of the earth.

1:28 reign. Man's "reign" over the world carries the idea of nurturing it with creativity and care.

along the ground—everything that has life." And
that is what happened.
31 Then God looked over all he had made, and he
saw that it was very good!
And evening passed and morning came, marking the sixth day.

2 So the creation of the heavens and the earth and
everything in them was completed. 2 On the sev-
enth day God had finished his work of creation, so
he rested* from all his work. 3 And God blessed the
seventh day and declared it holy, because it was the
day when he rested from all his work of creation.
4 This is the account of the creation of the heavens and
the earth.

THE MAN AND WOMAN IN EDEN

When the LORD God made the earth and the heavens,
5 neither wild plants nor grains were growing on the
earth. For the LORD God had not yet sent rain to wa-
ter the earth, and there were no people to cultivate
the soil. 6 Instead, springs* came up from the ground
and watered all the land. 7 Then the LORD God formed
the man from the dust of the ground. He breathed the
breath of life into the man's nostrils, and the man be-
came a living person.
8 Then the LORD God planted a garden in Eden in
the east, and there he placed the man he had made.
9 The LORD God made all sorts of trees grow up from
the ground—trees that were beautiful and that pro-
duced delicious fruit. In the middle of the garden he
placed the tree of life and the tree of the knowledge
of good and evil.
10 A river flowed from the land of Eden, watering the
garden and then dividing into four branches. 11 The first
branch, called the Pishon, flowed around the entire
land of Havilah, where gold is found. 12 The gold of that
land is exceptionally pure; aromatic resin and onyx
stone are also found there. 13 The second branch, called
the Gihon, flowed around the entire land of Cush. 14 The
third branch, called the Tigris, flowed east of the land of
Asshur. The fourth branch is called the Euphrates.
15 The LORD God placed the man in the Garden of
Eden to tend and watch over it. 16 But the LORD God
warned him, "You may freely eat the fruit of every tree
in the garden—17 except the tree of the knowledge of
good and evil. If you eat its fruit, you are sure to die."
18 Then the LORD God said, "It is not good for the
man to be alone. I will make a helper who is just right
for him." 19 So the LORD God formed from the ground
all the wild animals and all the birds of the sky. He
brought them to the man* to see what he would call
them, and the man chose a name for each one. 20 He
gave names to all the livestock, all the birds of the sky,
and all the wild animals. But still there was no helper
just right for him.

THE ULTIMATE GARDEN

1. What pets have you had? What were their names?

GENESIS 2:4-25

2. What was Adam's purpose in the Garden of Eden (v. 15)? How does this balance environmental responsibility ("watch over it") with the need to be productive ("tend")?
3. When Adam was lonely, God's solution was to create a woman (vv. 22-25). What does this say about modern views of homosexual "marriage"?
4. Death came to earth after Adam ate the forbidden fruit (v. 17). Evolution teaches that species evolve and adapt in order to avoid death. How does this prove that God could not have used "evolution" in creating humanity?

21 So the LORD God caused the man to fall into a deep
sleep. While the man slept, the LORD God took out one
of the man's ribs* and closed up the opening. 22 Then
the LORD God made a woman from the rib, and he
brought her to the man.
23 "At last!" the man exclaimed.

"This one is bone from my bone,
and flesh from my flesh!
She will be called 'woman,'
because she was taken from 'man.'"

24 This explains why a man leaves his father and
mother and is joined to his wife, and the two are unit-
ed into one.
25 Now the man and his wife were both naked, but
they felt no shame.

THE MAN AND WOMAN SIN

3 The serpent was the shrewdest of all the wild an-
imals the LORD God had made. One day he asked
the woman, "Did God really say you must not eat the
fruit from any of the trees in the garden?"
2 "Of course we may eat fruit from the trees in the
garden," the woman replied. 3 "It's only the fruit from
the tree in the middle of the garden that we are not
allowed to eat. God said, 'You must not eat it or even
touch it; if you do, you will die.'"
4 "You won't die!" the serpent replied to the woman.
5 "God knows that your eyes will be opened as soon
as you eat it, and you will be like God, knowing both
good and evil."
6 The woman was convinced. She saw that the tree
was beautiful and its fruit looked delicious, and she

2:2 Or *ceased;* also in 2:3. **2:6** Or *mist.* **2:19** Or *Adam,* and so throughout the chapter. **2:21** Or *took a part of the man's side.*

2:3 he rested. "Rested" is the same Hebrew word as "Sabbath." Though His energy is unlimited, God rested on the seventh day from His creative work.
2:7 formed. While God "created" the physical world, He "formed" humankind. Man is the product of His creative artistry.
2:9 tree of the knowledge of good and evil. God had told Adam and Eve not to eat of the fruit of this tree (v. 17). They knew they had a choice to obey God or not.
2:15 tend and watch over it. God gave human beings the role of tending and guarding creation through their role as stewards.
2:18 not good for the man. God created a man and then a woman to bring children into the world. He also brought man a "helper who is just right for him" to provide support and companionship.
2:20 names to all the livestock. This was Adam's first act of stewardship over the earth—naming the animals.
3:1 Did God really say you must not eat. The serpent tempted Eve to distrust God and her understanding of His word.
3:4 You won't die. Satan lied by telling Eve that God did not really mean what He had said.

wanted the wisdom it would give her. So she took
some of the fruit and ate it. Then she gave some to
her husband, who was with her, and he ate it, too. 7 At
that moment their eyes were opened, and they sud-
denly felt shame at their nakedness. So they sewed fig
leaves together to cover themselves.
8 When the cool evening breezes were blowing,
the man* and his wife heard the LORD God walking
about in the garden. So they hid from the LORD God
among the trees. 9 Then the LORD God called to the
man, "Where are you?"
10 He replied, "I heard you walking in the garden, so
I hid. I was afraid because I was naked."
11 "Who told you that you were naked?" the LORD
God asked. "Have you eaten from the tree whose fruit
I commanded you not to eat?"
12 The man replied, "It was the woman you gave me
who gave me the fruit, and I ate it."
13 Then the LORD God asked the woman, "What have
you done?"
"The serpent deceived me," she replied. "That's why
I ate it."
14 Then the LORD God said to the serpent,

"Because you have done this, you are cursed
more than all animals, domestic and wild.
You will crawl on your belly,
groveling in the dust as long as you live.
15 And I will cause hostility between you and the
woman,
and between your offspring and her offspring.
He will strike* your head,
and you will strike his heel."

16 Then he said to the woman,

"I will sharpen the pain of your pregnancy,
and in pain you will give birth.
And you will desire to control your husband,
but he will rule over you.*"

17 And to the man he said,

"Since you listened to your wife and ate from the
tree
whose fruit I commanded you not to eat,
the ground is cursed because of you.
All your life you will struggle to scratch a living
from it.
18 It will grow thorns and thistles for you,
though you will eat of its grains.
19 By the sweat of your brow
will you have food to eat
until you return to the ground
from which you were made.
For you were made from dust,
and to dust you will return."

PARADISE LOST: GOD'S JUDGMENT

20 Then the man—Adam—named his wife Eve, be-
cause she would be the mother of all who live.* 21 And
the LORD God made clothing from animal skins for
Adam and his wife.
22 Then the LORD God said, "Look, the human be-
ings* have become like us, knowing both good and
evil. What if they reach out, take fruit from the tree
of life, and eat it? Then they will live forever!" 23 So the
LORD God banished them from the Garden of Eden,
and he sent Adam out to cultivate the ground from
which he had been made. 24 After sending them out,
the LORD God stationed mighty cherubim to the east
of the Garden of Eden. And he placed a flaming sword
that flashed back and forth to guard the way to the
tree of life.

CAIN AND ABEL

4 Now Adam* had sexual relations with his wife,
Eve, and she became pregnant. When she gave
birth to Cain, she said, "With the LORD's help, I have
produced* a man!" 2 Later she gave birth to his broth-
er and named him Abel.
When they grew up, Abel became a shepherd,
while Cain cultivated the ground. 3 When it was time
for the harvest, Cain presented some of his crops as a
gift to the LORD. 4 Abel also brought a gift—the best
portions of the firstborn lambs from his flock. The
LORD accepted Abel and his gift, 5 but he did not ac-
cept Cain and his gift. This made Cain very angry, and
he looked dejected.

SIN ENTERS PARADISE

1. What is your favorite food? What "junk food" is hardest for you to resist?

GENESIS 3:1-24

2. Compare Eve's answer to the serpent (vv. 2-3) with God's command (2:16-17). What did she get wrong?
3. How did the serpent deceive Eve? How did he lure her into distrusting God?
4. How did God's questions (vv. 9,11) give Adam the opportunity to confess his sin and repent? What does this demonstrate about God's grace and forgiveness?
5. What was Adam's sin, according to God (v. 17)? To whom do you sometimes listen instead of God?

3:8 Or *Adam,* and so throughout the chapter. **3:15** Or *bruise;* also in 3:15b. **3:16** Or *And though you will have desire for your husband, / he will rule over you.* **3:20** *Eve* sounds like a Hebrew term that means "to give life." **3:22** Or *the man;* Hebrew reads *ha-adam.* **4:1a** Or *the man;* also in 4:25. **4:1b** Or *I have acquired. Cain* sounds like a Hebrew term that can mean "produce" or "acquire."

3:8 they hid. Sin had disrupted Adam and Eve's relationship with God. It is impossible to hide from God, who knows everything about us.

3:12-13 Adam refused to take responsibility for his actions by blaming Eve for his disobedience. Eve then passed the blame on to the serpent.

3:15 strike your head . . . strike his heel. This is the first prophecy of Christ's work in the Bible. In Adam's sin, Satan dealt a blow. But in Jesus' resurrection, He destroyed the work of Satan.

3:21 clothing from animal skins. This killing of an animal for clothing for Adam and Eve foreshadowed the blood sacrifices that would be required to cleanse people from sin, as well as the eventual sacrifice of Christ.

3:22 good and evil. After their fall into sin, Adam and Eve discovered evil and its deadly consequences (Rom. 5:12; 6:23).

4:5-8 Cain got mad because God disapproved of his offering. Then he killed his brother in a fit of jealous pride. Cain's concern was not for his relationship with God but for retribution and revenge because God had looked with favor on Abel's offering.

MURDER ONE

1. Where are you in the birth order of your family—oldest, youngest, middle? What's the best and worst part about your birth order?

GENESIS 4:1-16

2. Why did God accept Abel's offering but reject Cain's?
3. Cain was furious. What should his response have been (v. 7)?
4. Why did Cain murder Abel? Why did he blame Abel for his own sin?
5. What does Cain's answer to God (v. 9) reveal about his own selfishness? How was selfishness the root cause of Cain's murdering his own brother?
6. When has selfishness hurt your relationships with family and friends?

6 "Why are you so angry?" the LORD asked Cain. "Why
do you look so dejected? 7 You will be accepted if you do
what is right. But if you refuse to do what is right, then
watch out! Sin is crouching at the door, eager to control
you. But you must subdue it and be its master."
8 One day Cain suggested to his brother, "Let's go
out into the fields."* And while they were in the field,
Cain attacked his brother, Abel, and killed him.
9 Afterward the LORD asked Cain, "Where is your
brother? Where is Abel?"
"I don't know," Cain responded. "Am I my brother's
guardian?"
10 But the LORD said, "What have you done? Listen!
Your brother's blood cries out to me from the ground!
11 Now you are cursed and banished from the ground,
which has swallowed your brother's blood. 12 No lon-
ger will the ground yield good crops for you, no mat-
ter how hard you work! From now on you will be a
homeless wanderer on the earth."
13 Cain replied to the LORD, "My punishment* is too
great for me to bear! 14 You have banished me from
the land and from your presence; you have made me
a homeless wanderer. Anyone who finds me will kill
me!"
15 The LORD replied, "No, for I will give a sevenfold
punishment to anyone who kills you." Then the LORD
put a mark on Cain to warn anyone who might try to
kill him. 16 So Cain left the LORD's presence and settled
in the land of Nod,* east of Eden.

THE DESCENDANTS OF CAIN

17 Cain had sexual relations with his wife, and she be-
came pregnant and gave birth to Enoch. Then Cain
founded a city, which he named Enoch, after his son.
18 Enoch had a son named Irad. Irad became the fa-
ther of* Mehujael. Mehujael became the father of Me-
thushael. Methushael became the father of Lamech.
19 Lamech married two women. The first was
named Adah, and the second was Zillah. 20 Adah gave
birth to Jabal, who was the first of those who raise
livestock and live in tents. 21 His brother's name was
Jubal, the first of all who play the harp and flute. 22 La-
mech's other wife, Zillah, gave birth to a son named
Tubal-cain. He became an expert in forging tools of
bronze and iron. Tubal-cain had a sister named Naa-
mah. 23 One day Lamech said to his wives,

"Adah and Zillah, hear my voice;
  listen to me, you wives of Lamech.
I have killed a man who attacked me,
  a young man who wounded me.
24 If someone who kills Cain is punished seven times,
  then the one who kills me will be punished
    seventy-seven times!"

THE BIRTH OF SETH

25 Adam had sexual relations with his wife again, and
she gave birth to another son. She named him Seth,*
for she said, "God has granted me another son in place
of Abel, whom Cain killed." 26 When Seth grew up, he
had a son and named him Enosh. At that time people
first began to worship the LORD by name.

THE DESCENDANTS OF ADAM

5 This is the written account of the descendants of
Adam. When God created human beings,* he made
them to be like himself. 2 He created them male and fe-
male, and he blessed them and called them "human."

3 When Adam was 130 years old, he became the fa-
ther of a son who was just like him—in his very
image. He named his son Seth. 4 After the birth of
Seth, Adam lived another 800 years, and he had
other sons and daughters. 5 Adam lived 930 years,
and then he died.
6 When Seth was 105 years old, he became the father
of* Enosh. 7 After the birth of* Enosh, Seth lived an-
other 807 years, and he had other sons and daugh-
ters. 8 Seth lived 912 years, and then he died.
9 When Enosh was 90 years old, he became the father
of Kenan. 10 After the birth of Kenan, Enosh lived an-
other 815 years, and he had other sons and daugh-
ters. 11 Enosh lived 905 years, and then he died.
12 When Kenan was 70 years old, he became the father
of Mahalalel. 13 After the birth of Mahalalel, Kenan
lived another 840 years, and he had other sons and
daughters. 14 Kenan lived 910 years, and then he died.
15 When Mahalalel was 65 years old, he became the
father of Jared. 16 After the birth of Jared, Mahalalel
lived another 830 years, and he had other sons and

4:8 As in Samaritan Pentateuch, Greek and Syriac versions, and Latin Vulgate; Masoretic Text lacks *"Let's go out into the fields."* **4:13** Or *My sin.* **4:16** *Nod* means "wandering." **4:18** Or *the ancestor of,* and so throughout the verse. **4:25** *Seth* probably means "granted"; the name may also mean "appointed." **5:1** Or *man;* Hebrew reads *adam;* similarly in 5:2. **5:6** Or *the ancestor of;* also in 5:9, 12, 15, 18, 21, 25. **5:7** Or *the birth of this ancestor of;* also in 5:10, 13, 16, 19, 22, 26.

4:10 Your brother's blood cries out. The horror of this first murder reveals the depths of evil to which people can sink.

4:12-15 Cain was driven from his home and from the Lord's presence (vv. 14, 16). He would move from place to place as a restless wanderer. But God graciously placed on him some kind of identifiable sign that showed he was under divine protection.

4:25 another son. Seth would carry on the line that would eventually result in the world's Savior (Luke 3:37).

5:3 in his very image. Even after he sinned, Adam retained the image of God and passed it down to Seth.

daughters. 17 Mahalalel lived 895 years, and then
he died.
18 When Jared was 162 years old, he became the father
of Enoch. 19 After the birth of Enoch, Jared lived an-
other 800 years, and he had other sons and daugh-
ters. 20 Jared lived 962 years, and then he died.
21 When Enoch was 65 years old, he became the father
of Methuselah. 22 After the birth of Methuselah,
Enoch lived in close fellowship with God for anoth-
er 300 years, and he had other sons and daughters.
23 Enoch lived 365 years, 24 walking in close fellow-
ship with God. Then one day he disappeared, be-
cause God took him.
25 When Methuselah was 187 years old, he became
the father of Lamech. 26 After the birth of Lamech,
Methuselah lived another 782 years, and he had
other sons and daughters. 27 Methuselah lived
969 years, and then he died.
28 When Lamech was 182 years old, he became the fa-
ther of a son. 29 Lamech named his son Noah, for he
said, "May he bring us relief* from our work and the
painful labor of farming this ground that the LORD
has cursed." 30 After the birth of Noah, Lamech lived
another 595 years, and he had other sons and daugh-
ters. 31 Lamech lived 777 years, and then he died.
32 After Noah was 500 years old, he became the father
of Shem, Ham, and Japheth.

A WORLD GONE WRONG

6 Then the people began to multiply on the earth,
and daughters were born to them. 2 The sons of
God saw the beautiful women* and took any they
wanted as their wives. 3 Then the LORD said, "My Spir-
it will not put up with* humans for such a long time,
for they are only mortal flesh. In the future, their nor-
mal lifespan will be no more than 120 years."
4 In those days, and for some time after, giant Ne-
philites lived on the earth, for whenever the sons of
God had intercourse with women, they gave birth to
children who became the heroes and famous war-
riors of ancient times.
5 The LORD observed the extent of human wicked-
ness on the earth, and he saw that everything they
thought or imagined was consistently and totally
evil. 6 So the LORD was sorry he had ever made them
and put them on the earth. It broke his heart. 7 And
the LORD said, "I will wipe this human race I have cre-
ated from the face of the earth. Yes, and I will destroy
every living thing—all the people, the large animals,
the small animals that scurry along the ground, and
even the birds of the sky. I am sorry I ever made
them." 8 But Noah found favor with the LORD.

THE STORY OF NOAH

9 This is the account of Noah and his family. Noah was
a righteous man, the only blameless person living on
earth at the time, and he walked in close fellowship
with God. 10 Noah was the father of three sons: Shem,
Ham, and Japheth.
11 Now God saw that the earth had become corrupt
and was filled with violence. 12 God observed all this
corruption in the world, for everyone on earth was
corrupt. 13 So God said to Noah, "I have decided to de-
stroy all living creatures, for they have filled the earth
with violence. Yes, I will wipe them all out along with
the earth!

WEATHER ALERT

1. If your house was about to be washed away in a flood, what three things would you quickly grab?

GENESIS 6:5–7:12

2. What does 6:5 tell us about the human race? About our ability to find world peace?
3. Why did Noah find "favor in the eyes of the LORD" (6:8; see 6:22 and 7:5)?
4. Noah looked foolish building a huge boat. Why did he continue to build it? What happened when he finished?
5. How can obedience sometimes look foolish? What does this teach about obeying God? About obeying your coaches, teachers, parents, and other authorities?

14 "Build a large boat* from cypress wood* and wa-
terproof it with tar, inside and out. Then construct
decks and stalls throughout its interior. 15 Make the
boat 450 feet long, 75 feet wide, and 45 feet high.*
16 Leave an 18-inch opening* below the roof all the
way around the boat. Put the door on the side, and
build three decks inside the boat—lower, middle, and
upper.
17 "Look! I am about to cover the earth with a
flood that will destroy every living thing that
breathes. Everything on earth will die. 18 But I
will confirm my covenant with you. So enter the
boat—you and your wife and your sons and their
wives. 19 Bring a pair of every kind of animal—a
male and a female—into the boat with you to keep
them alive during the flood. 20 Pairs of every kind of
bird, and every kind of animal, and every kind of
small animal that scurries along the ground, will
come to you to be kept alive. 21 And be sure to take
on board enough food for your family and for all
the animals."

5:29 *Noah* sounds like a Hebrew term that can mean "relief" or "comfort." **6:2** Hebrew *daughters of men;* also in 6:4. **6:3** Greek version reads *will not remain in.* **6:14a** Traditionally rendered *an ark.* **6:14b** Or *gopher wood.* **6:15** Hebrew *300 cubits* [138 meters] *long, 50 cubits* [23 meters] *wide, and 30 cubits* [13.8 meters] *high.* **6:16** Hebrew *an opening of 1 cubit* [46 centimeters].

5:22-24 Enoch is the only person listed in Genesis who did not die. He walked with God in a special way, and God simply took him away (Heb. 11:5).

6:6 the LORD was sorry. God did not think He had made a mistake by creating man. But man's choice to turn from Him and His love grieved Him deeply.

6:8-9 only blameless person living on earth. Noah was the one person in the world at that time who followed the Lord.

6:14-16 God was concerned with the practical. Noah was to build a boat that had to last for 40 days of rain and 150 days of floating on the flood waters.

6:17 destroy every living thing. The Bible is clear in saying that all life on earth was destroyed in the flood. Only Noah, his family, and the animals in the ark survived.

6:18 confirm my covenant. God made an agreement with Noah to save his family, if Noah would build the ark and enter it by faith in God.

6:19 pair of every kind of animal. A pair of each animal—male and female—was needed to replenish the earth after the flood. In addition, Noah took seven pairs of the kinds of animals that could be eaten and used for sacrifice (7:2).

22 So Noah did everything exactly as God had commanded him.

THE FLOOD COVERS THE EARTH

7 When everything was ready, the LORD said to Noah, "Go into the boat with all your family, for among all the people of the earth, I can see that you alone are righteous. 2 Take with you seven pairs—male and female—of each animal I have approved for eating and for sacrifice,* and take one pair of each of the others. 3 Also take seven pairs of every kind of bird. There must be a male and a female in each pair to ensure that all life will survive on the earth after the flood. 4 Seven days from now I will make the rains pour down on the earth. And it will rain for forty days and forty nights, until I have wiped from the earth all the living things I have created."

5 So Noah did everything as the LORD commanded him.

6 Noah was 600 years old when the flood covered the earth. 7 He went on board the boat to escape the flood—he and his wife and his sons and their wives. 8 With them were all the various kinds of animals—those approved for eating and for sacrifice and those that were not—along with all the birds and the small animals that scurry along the ground. 9 They entered the boat in pairs, male and female, just as God had commanded Noah. 10 After seven days, the waters of the flood came and covered the earth.

11 When Noah was 600 years old, on the seventeenth day of the second month, all the underground waters erupted from the earth, and the rain fell in mighty torrents from the sky. 12 The rain continued to fall for forty days and forty nights.

13 That very day Noah had gone into the boat with his wife and his sons—Shem, Ham, and Japheth—and their wives. 14 With them in the boat were pairs of every kind of animal—domestic and wild, large and small—along with birds of every kind. 15 Two by two they came into the boat, representing every living thing that breathes. 16 A male and female of each kind entered, just as God had commanded Noah. Then the LORD closed the door behind them.

17 For forty days the floodwaters grew deeper, covering the ground and lifting the boat high above the earth. 18 As the waters rose higher and higher above the ground, the boat floated safely on the surface. 19 Finally, the water covered even the highest mountains on the earth, 20 rising more than twenty-two feet* above the highest peaks. 21 All the living things on earth died—birds, domestic animals, wild animals, small animals that scurry along the ground, and all the people. 22 Everything that breathed and lived on dry land died. 23 God wiped out every living thing on the earth—people, livestock, small animals that scurry along the ground, and the birds of the sky. All were destroyed. The only people who survived were Noah and those with him in the boat. 24 And the floodwaters covered the earth for 150 days.

THE FLOOD RECEDES

8 But God remembered Noah and all the wild animals and livestock with him in the boat. He sent a wind to blow across the earth, and the floodwaters began to recede. 2 The underground waters stopped flowing, and the torrential rains from the sky were stopped. 3 So the floodwaters gradually receded from the earth. After 150 days, 4 exactly five months from the time the flood began,* the boat came to rest on the mountains of Ararat. 5 Two and a half months later,* as the waters continued to go down, other mountain peaks became visible.

OPERATION RECOVERY

1. When you were a kid, what was something you used to do on a rainy day?

GENESIS 8:1-22

2. Water rapidly covered the entire earth and then it dried suddenly (a little over a year total). How would this water movement have affected the earth's surface? How does this compare with the modern belief that the earth was shaped over millions of years?
3. Note verses 21 and 22. What does this tell us about modern fears that the earth will someday become uninhabitable?

6 After another forty days, Noah opened the window he had made in the boat 7 and released a raven. The bird flew back and forth until the floodwaters on the earth had dried up. 8 He also released a dove to see if the water had receded and it could find dry ground. 9 But the dove could find no place to land because the water still covered the ground. So it returned to the boat, and Noah held out his hand and drew the dove back inside. 10 After waiting another seven days, Noah released the dove again. 11 This time the dove returned to him in the evening with a fresh olive leaf in its beak. Then Noah knew that the floodwaters were almost gone. 12 He waited another seven days and then released the dove again. This time it did not come back.

13 Noah was now 601 years old. On the first day of the new year, ten and a half months after the flood began,* the floodwaters had almost dried up from the earth. Noah lifted back the covering of the boat and saw that the surface of the ground was drying. 14 Two more months went by,* and at last the earth was dry!

15 Then God said to Noah, 16 "Leave the boat, all of you—you and your wife, and your sons and their wives. 17 Release all the animals—the birds, the livestock, and the small animals that scurry along

7:2 Hebrew *of each clean animal;* similarly in 7:8. **7:20** Hebrew *15 cubits* [6.9 meters]. **8:4** Hebrew *on the seventeenth day of the seventh month;* see 7:11. **8:5** Hebrew *On the first day of the tenth month;* see 7:11 and note on 8:4. **8:13** Hebrew *On the first day of the first month;* see 7:11. **8:14** Hebrew *The twenty-seventh day of the second month arrived;* see note on 8:13.

7:19-20 highest mountains. Even the highest mountains in the area, the mountains of Ararat (8:4), which are about 17,000 feet high, were covered by the waters.

8:1 God remembered Noah. With floodwaters covering all the territory under judgment, the Lord kept Noah and his family safe and prepared to return them to dry land.

8:17 multiply. As He had done at Creation (1:22), God gave His blessing to the creatures that would populate the planet.

the ground—so they can be fruitful and multiply throughout the earth."

18 So Noah, his wife, and his sons and their wives left the boat. 19 And all of the large and small animals and birds came out of the boat, pair by pair.

20 Then Noah built an altar to the LORD, and there he sacrificed as burnt offerings the animals and birds that had been approved for that purpose.* 21 And the LORD was pleased with the aroma of the sacrifice and said to himself, "I will never again curse the ground because of the human race, even though everything they think or imagine is bent toward evil from childhood. I will never again destroy all living things. 22 As long as the earth remains, there will be planting and harvest, cold and heat, summer and winter, day and night."

GOD CONFIRMS HIS COVENANT

9 Then God blessed Noah and his sons and told them, "Be fruitful and multiply. Fill the earth. 2 All the animals of the earth, all the birds of the sky, all the small animals that scurry along the ground, and all the fish in the sea will look on you with fear and terror. I have placed them in your power. 3 I have given them to you for food, just as I have given you grain and vegetables. 4 But you must never eat any meat that still has the lifeblood in it.

5 "And I will require the blood of anyone who takes another person's life. If a wild animal kills a person, it must die. And anyone who murders a fellow human must die. 6 If anyone takes a human life, that person's life will also be taken by human hands. For God made human beings* in his own image. 7 Now be fruitful and multiply, and repopulate the earth."

8 Then God told Noah and his sons, 9 "I hereby confirm my covenant with you and your descendants, 10 and with all the animals that were on the boat with you—the birds, the livestock, and all the wild animals—every living creature on earth. 11 Yes, I am confirming my covenant with you. Never again will floodwaters kill all living creatures; never again will a flood destroy the earth."

12 Then God said, "I am giving you a sign of my covenant with you and with all living creatures, for all generations to come. 13 I have placed my rainbow in the clouds. It is the sign of my covenant with you and with all the earth. 14 When I send clouds over the earth, the rainbow will appear in the clouds, 15 and I will remember my covenant with you and with all living creatures. Never again will the floodwaters destroy all life. 16 When I see the rainbow in the clouds, I will remember the eternal covenant between God and every living creature on earth." 17 Then God said to Noah, "Yes, this rainbow is the sign of the covenant I am confirming with all the creatures on earth."

NOAH'S SONS

18 The sons of Noah who came out of the boat with their father were Shem, Ham, and Japheth. (Ham is the father of Canaan.) 19 From these three sons of Noah came all the people who now populate the earth.

20 After the flood, Noah began to cultivate the ground, and he planted a vineyard. 21 One day he drank some wine he had made, and he became drunk and lay naked inside his tent. 22 Ham, the father of Canaan, saw that his father was naked and went outside and told his brothers. 23 Then Shem and Japheth took a robe, held it over their shoulders, and backed into the tent to cover their father. As they did this, they looked the other way so they would not see him naked.

24 When Noah woke up from his stupor, he learned what Ham, his youngest son, had done. 25 Then he cursed Canaan, the son of Ham:

"May Canaan be cursed!
May he be the lowest of servants to his relatives."

26 Then Noah said,

"May the LORD, the God of Shem, be blessed,
and may Canaan be his servant!
27 May God expand the territory of Japheth!
May Japheth share the prosperity of Shem,*
and may Canaan be his servant."

28 Noah lived another 350 years after the great flood. 29 He lived 950 years, and then he died.

10 This is the account of the families of Shem, Ham, and Japheth, the three sons of Noah. Many children were born to them after the great flood.

DESCENDANTS OF JAPHETH

2 The descendants of Japheth were Gomer, Magog, Madai, Javan, Tubal, Meshech, and Tiras.
3 The descendants of Gomer were Ashkenaz, Riphath, and Togarmah.
4 The descendants of Javan were Elishah, Tarshish, Kittim, and Rodanim.* 5 Their descendants became the seafaring peoples that spread out to various lands, each identified by its own language, clan, and national identity.

DESCENDANTS OF HAM

6 The descendants of Ham were Cush, Mizraim, Put, and Canaan.
7 The descendants of Cush were Seba, Havilah, Sabtah, Raamah, and Sabteca. The descendants of Raamah were Sheba and Dedan.
8 Cush was also the ancestor of Nimrod, who was the first heroic warrior on earth. 9 Since he was the greatest hunter in the world,* his name

8:20 Hebrew *every clean animal and every clean bird.* 9:6 Or *man;* Hebrew reads *ha-adam.* 9:27 Hebrew *May he live in the tents of Shem.* 10:4 As in some Hebrew manuscripts and Greek version (see also 1 Chr 1:7); most Hebrew manuscripts read *Dodanim.* 10:9 Hebrew *a great hunter before the LORD;* also in 10:9b.

8:20 burnt offerings. Noah had preserved and cared for the clean animals and birds on the ark for this purpose. He built an altar for sacrifice and worship of the Lord.

8:21 never . . . curse. God promised that He would never again destroy the earth by flood.

9:6 that person's life will also be taken. God gave humans the responsibility of carrying out justice for people who were found guilty of murder.

9:9 confirm My covenant. Noah was rewarded for his faithfulness with a personal promise from the Lord.

9:22 Ham. The reference is not simply to Ham's son, whose name was Canaan (10:6), but to the nation of Canaan, eventually settled by the Israelites.

10:1-2 Several nations in the Bible sprang from Noah's family members, including the Egyptians, Greeks, and Hebrews. Noah's oldest son, Japheth, represents many of the ancient nations in what is now known as Europe and Asia Minor. From Japheth, the Greeks became a small, but important nation.

became proverbial. People would say, "This man
is like Nimrod, the greatest hunter in the world."
[10] He built his kingdom in the land of Babylonia,*
with the cities of Babylon, Erech, Akkad, and Cal-
neh. [11] From there he expanded his territory to As-
syria,* building the cities of Nineveh, Rehoboth-ir,
Calah, [12] and Resen (the great city located between
Nineveh and Calah).
[13] Mizraim was the ancestor of the Ludites, Anamites,
Lehabites, Naphtuhites, [14] Pathrusites, Casluhites, and
the Caphtorites, from whom the Philistines came.*
[15] Canaan's oldest son was Sidon, the ancestor of the
Sidonians. Canaan was also the ancestor of the Hit-
tites,* [16] Jebusites, Amorites, Girgashites, [17] Hivites,
Arkites, Sinites, [18] Arvadites, Zemarites, and Ha-
mathites. The Canaanite clans eventually spread
out, [19] and the territory of Canaan extended from
Sidon in the north to Gerar and Gaza in the south,
and east as far as Sodom, Gomorrah, Admah, and
Zeboiim, near Lasha.
[20] These were the descendants of Ham, identified by
clan, language, territory, and national identity.

DESCENDANTS OF SHEM

[21] Sons were also born to Shem, the older brother of
Japheth.* Shem was the ancestor of all the descen-
dants of Eber.
[22] The descendants of Shem were Elam, Asshur, Ar-
phaxad, Lud, and Aram.
[23] The descendants of Aram were Uz, Hul, Gether, and
Mash.
[24] Arphaxad was the father of Shelah,* and Shelah
was the father of Eber.
[25] Eber had two sons. The first was named Peleg
(which means "division"), for during his lifetime
the people of the world were divided into different
language groups. His brother's name was Joktan.
[26] Joktan was the ancestor of Almodad, Sheleph, Haz-
armaveth, Jerah, [27] Hadoram, Uzal, Diklah, [28] Obal,
Abimael, Sheba, [29] Ophir, Havilah, and Jobab. All
these were descendants of Joktan. [30] The territory
they occupied extended from Mesha all the way to
Sephar in the eastern mountains.
[31] These were the descendants of Shem, identified by
clan, language, territory, and national identity.

CONCLUSION

[32] These are the clans that descended from Noah's
sons, arranged by nation according to their lines of
descent. All the nations of the earth descended from
these clans after the great flood.

THE TOWER OF BABEL

11 At one time all the people of the world spoke the
same language and used the same words. [2] As
the people migrated to the east, they found a plain in
the land of Babylonia* and settled there.
[3] They began saying to each other, "Let's make
bricks and harden them with fire." (In this region
bricks were used instead of stone, and tar was used
for mortar.) [4] Then they said, "Come, let's build a great
city for ourselves with a tower that reaches into the
sky. This will make us famous and keep us from being
scattered all over the world."
[5] But the LORD came down to look at the city and
the tower the people were building. [6] "Look!" he
said. "The people are united, and they all speak
the same language. After this, nothing they set out
to do will be impossible for them! [7] Come, let's go
down and confuse the people with different lan-
guages. Then they won't be able to understand
each other."
[8] In that way, the LORD scattered them all over
the world, and they stopped building the city. [9] That
is why the city was called Babel,* because that is
where the LORD confused the people with different
languages. In this way he scattered them all over the
world.

THE LINE OF DESCENT FROM SHEM TO ABRAM

[10] This is the account of Shem's family.

Two years after the great flood, when Shem was
100 years old, he became the father of* Arphaxad.
[11] After the birth of* Arphaxad, Shem lived another
500 years and had other sons and daughters.
[12] When Arphaxad was 35 years old, he became the
father of Shelah. [13] After the birth of Shelah, Ar-
phaxad lived another 403 years and had other sons
and daughters.*
[14] When Shelah was 30 years old, he became the fa-
ther of Eber. [15] After the birth of Eber, Shelah lived
another 403 years and had other sons and daugh-
ters.
[16] When Eber was 34 years old, he became the father
of Peleg. [17] After the birth of Peleg, Eber lived an-
other 430 years and had other sons and daughters.
[18] When Peleg was 30 years old, he became the father
of Reu. [19] After the birth of Reu, Peleg lived another
209 years and had other sons and daughters.
[20] When Reu was 32 years old, he became the father of
Serug. [21] After the birth of Serug, Reu lived another
207 years and had other sons and daughters.

10:10 Hebrew *Shinar.* **10:11** Or *From that land Assyria went out.* **10:14** Hebrew *Casluhites, from whom the Philistines came, and Caphtorites.* Compare Jer 47:4; Amos 9:7. **10:15** Hebrew *ancestor of Heth.* **10:21** Or *Shem, whose older brother was Japheth.* **10:24** Greek version reads *Arphaxad was the father of Cainan, Cainan was the father of Shelah.* Compare Luke 3:36. **11:2** Hebrew *Shinar.* **11:9** Or *Babylon. Babel* sounds like a Hebrew term that means "confusion." **11:10** Or *the ancestor of;* also in 11:12, 14, 16, 18, 20, 22, 24. **11:11** Or *the birth of this ancestor of;* also in 11:13, 15, 17, 19, 21, 23, 25. **11:12-13** Greek version reads [12] *When Arphaxad was 135 years old, he became the father of Cainan.* [13] *After the birth of Cainan, Arphaxad lived another 430 years and had other sons and daughters, and then he died. When Cainan was 130 years old, he became the father of Shelah. After the birth of Shelah, Cainan lived another 330 years and had other sons and daughters, and then he died.* Compare Luke 3:35-36.

10:12 great city. Nimrod was the great-great grandson of Noah and the founder of the "great city" of Nineveh, Assyria.

10:16 Jebusites . . . Girgashites. These people groups were already settled in Canaan when the Israelites arrived in Joshua's time.

10:21 Shem. Shem is referred to as the "chosen line" because the Hebrews descended from him. In the Hebrew language, the name Eber (a descendant of Shem) is the origin of the word "Hebrew."

10:25 the people . . . were divided. This refers to the results of the next event in chapter 11—the Tower of Babel. God dispersed the people all across the earth as a result of their prideful behavior.

11:1-5 It was not long until sin and pride—demonstrated in the building of the Tower of Babel—resurfaced. The tower builders attempted to reach God by making a high building that would enable the gods to come down to man. But God intervened, and the tower project was abandoned.

11:10-26 In 10 generations, the line of Shem is traced to the beginning of Abram's story.

22 When Serug was 30 years old, he became the father
of Nahor. 23 After the birth of Nahor, Serug lived
another 200 years and had other sons and daugh-
ters.
24 When Nahor was 29 years old, he became the fa-
ther of Terah. 25 After the birth of Terah, Nahor
lived another 119 years and had other sons and
daughters.
26 After Terah was 70 years old, he became the father
of Abram, Nahor, and Haran.

THE FAMILY OF TERAH

27 This is the account of Terah's family. Terah was the
father of Abram, Nahor, and Haran; and Haran was
the father of Lot. 28 But Haran died in Ur of the Chal-
deans, the land of his birth, while his father, Terah,
was still living. 29 Meanwhile, Abram and Nahor both
married. The name of Abram's wife was Sarai, and
the name of Nahor's wife was Milcah. (Milcah and
her sister Iscah were daughters of Nahor's brother
Haran.) 30 But Sarai was unable to become pregnant
and had no children.
31 One day Terah took his son Abram, his daughter-
in-law Sarai (his son Abram's wife), and his grandson
Lot (his son Haran's child) and moved away from Ur of
the Chaldeans. He was headed for the land of Canaan,
but they stopped at Haran and settled there. 32 Terah
lived for 205 years* and died while still in Haran.

THE CALL OF ABRAM

12 The LORD had said to Abram, "Leave your native
country, your relatives, and your father's family,
and go to the land that I will show you. 2 I will make
you into a great nation. I will bless you and make you
famous, and you will be a blessing to others. 3 I will
bless those who bless you and curse those who treat
you with contempt. All the families on earth will be
blessed through you."
4 So Abram departed as the LORD had instructed,
and Lot went with him. Abram was seventy-five
years old when he left Haran. 5 He took his wife, Sarai,
his nephew Lot, and all his wealth—his livestock and
all the people he had taken into his household at Ha-
ran—and headed for the land of Canaan. When they
arrived in Canaan, 6 Abram traveled through the land
as far as Shechem. There he set up camp beside the
oak of Moreh. At that time, the area was inhabited by
Canaanites.
7 Then the LORD appeared to Abram and said, "I
will give this land to your descendants.*" And Abram
built an altar there and dedicated it to the LORD, who
had appeared to him. 8 After that, Abram traveled
south and set up camp in the hill country, with Bethel
to the west and Ai to the east. There he built another
altar and dedicated it to the LORD, and he worshiped
the LORD. 9 Then Abram continued traveling south by
stages toward the Negev.

MOVING OUT

1. What is the longest trip you have taken with your family in a car? How many times did you have to stop to use the bathroom?

GENESIS 12:1-9

2. Abram was 75 years old when he moved his family far away from his homeland. Why did he do something so traumatic at that age? What does this highlight about Abram's character?
3. Abram was the father of the Jewish race, including modern Israel. What does God's promise to him (v. 3) suggest about modern tensions in the Middle East?

ABRAM AND SARAI IN EGYPT

10 At that time a severe famine struck the land of Ca-
naan, forcing Abram to go down to Egypt, where he
lived as a foreigner. 11 As he was approaching the bor-
der of Egypt, Abram said to his wife, Sarai, "Look, you
are a very beautiful woman. 12 When the Egyptians
see you, they will say, 'This is his wife. Let's kill him;
then we can have her!' 13 So please tell them you are
my sister. Then they will spare my life and treat me
well because of their interest in you."
14 And sure enough, when Abram arrived in Egypt,
everyone noticed Sarai's beauty. 15 When the palace
officials saw her, they sang her praises to Pharaoh,
their king, and Sarai was taken into his palace. 16 Then
Pharaoh gave Abram many gifts because of her—
sheep, goats, cattle, male and female donkeys, male
and female servants, and camels.
17 But the LORD sent terrible plagues upon Pharaoh
and his household because of Sarai, Abram's wife.
18 So Pharaoh summoned Abram and accused him
sharply. "What have you done to me?" he demanded.
"Why didn't you tell me she was your wife? 19 Why did
you say, 'She is my sister,' and allow me to take her as
my wife? Now then, here is your wife. Take her and
get out of here!" 20 Pharaoh ordered some of his men
to escort them, and he sent Abram out of the country,
along with his wife and all his possessions.

ABRAM AND LOT SEPARATE

13 So Abram left Egypt and traveled north into the
Negev, along with his wife and Lot and all that
they owned. 2 (Abram was very rich in livestock, silver,
and gold.) 3 From the Negev, they continued traveling
by stages toward Bethel, and they pitched their tents
between Bethel and Ai, where they had camped be-
fore. 4 This was the same place where Abram had built
the altar, and there he worshiped the LORD again.

11:32 Some ancient versions read *145 years;* compare 11:26 and 12:4. 12:7 Hebrew *seed.*

11:30 unable to become pregnant. Sarai, Abram's wife, was unable to have children. God would soon promise to make Abram the father of many nations by miraculously giving his wife a child.

12:1 Leave your native country. Abram had to leave the familiar in order to find his future. He left Ur to head to Haran and eventually settled in Canaan.

12:2-3 I will bless you. God's promise to Abram assured him of a land, a nation, and a blessing. Out of his descendants the entire Jewish nation, and, eventually, the Savior would arise.

12:10 Egypt. Abram found famine conditions when he arrived in Canaan. He continued on into Egypt, where the Nile River provided water for the crops.

12:11-19 Abram feared his wife Sarai's beauty would impede their travel among potentially male suitors, so he lied to the Egyptian pharaoh by telling him she was his sister. Pharaoh took Sarai into his harem and rewarded Abram with livestock. When his lie was exposed, Abram faced the pharaoh's anger.

13:1-11 After returning to Canaan from Egypt, Abram and Lot went their separate ways because the land would not support both their herds of livestock.

5 Lot, who was traveling with Abram, had also be-
come very wealthy with flocks of sheep and goats,
herds of cattle, and many tents. 6 But the land could
not support both Abram and Lot with all their flocks
and herds living so close together. 7 So disputes broke
out between the herdsmen of Abram and Lot. (At that
time Canaanites and Perizzites were also living in the
land.)
8 Finally Abram said to Lot, "Let's not allow this
conflict to come between us or our herdsmen. After
all, we are close relatives! 9 The whole countryside is
open to you. Take your choice of any section of the
land you want, and we will separate. If you want the
land to the left, then I'll take the land on the right.
If you prefer the land on the right, then I'll go to the
left."
10 Lot took a long look at the fertile plains of the
Jordan Valley in the direction of Zoar. The whole
area was well watered everywhere, like the garden
of the LORD or the beautiful land of Egypt. (This was
before the LORD destroyed Sodom and Gomorrah.)
11 Lot chose for himself the whole Jordan Valley to
the east of them. He went there with his flocks and
servants and parted company with his uncle Abram.
12 So Abram settled in the land of Canaan, and Lot
moved his tents to a place near Sodom and settled
among the cities of the plain. 13 But the people of this
area were extremely wicked and constantly sinned
against the LORD.
14 After Lot had gone, the LORD said to Abram, "Look
as far as you can see in every direction—north and
south, east and west. 15 I am giving all this land, as far
as you can see, to you and your descendants* as a per-
manent possession. 16 And I will give you so many de-
scendants that, like the dust of the earth, they cannot
be counted! 17 Go and walk through the land in every
direction, for I am giving it to you."

THE RIGHT CHOICE

1. Who is your favorite aunt, uncle, or cousin?

GENESIS 13:1-18

2. Why did Lot choose "the entire Jordan Valley for himself" (vv. 10-11)? What does this reveal about Lot?
3. Abram allowed Lot to have first choice of where to live. What does this show about Abram? About God's choice to make Abram father of His chosen people?
4. The first thing Abram did when he settled was to build an altar to God (v. 18). How is this an example for you today?
5. How often do you put self-interests over doing what's right during training and practice in your sport or other team activities?

18 So Abram moved his camp to Hebron and settled
near the oak grove belonging to Mamre. There he
built another altar to the LORD.

ABRAM RESCUES LOT

14 About this time war broke out in the region.
King Amraphel of Babylonia,* King Arioch of
Ellasar, King Kedorlaomer of Elam, and King Tidal
of Goiim 2 fought against King Bera of Sodom, King
Birsha of Gomorrah, King Shinab of Admah, King
Shemeber of Zeboiim, and the king of Bela (also called
Zoar).
3 This second group of kings joined forces in Sid-
dim Valley (that is, the valley of the Dead Sea*). 4 For
twelve years they had been subject to King Kedorla-
omer, but in the thirteenth year they rebelled against
him.
5 One year later Kedorlaomer and his allies arrived
and defeated the Rephaites at Ashteroth-karnaim,
the Zuzites at Ham, the Emites at Shaveh-kiriathaim,
6 and the Horites at Mount Seir, as far as El-paran at
the edge of the wilderness. 7 Then they turned back
and came to En-mishpat (now called Kadesh) and
conquered all the territory of the Amalekites, and
also the Amorites living in Hazazon-tamar.
8 Then the rebel kings of Sodom, Gomorrah, Ad-
mah, Zeboiim, and Bela (also called Zoar) prepared
for battle in the valley of the Dead Sea.* 9 They fought
against King Kedorlaomer of Elam, King Tidal of
Goiim, King Amraphel of Babylonia, and King Arioch
of Ellasar—four kings against five. 10 As it happened,
the valley of the Dead Sea was filled with tar pits.
And as the army of the kings of Sodom and Gomor-
rah fled, some fell into the tar pits, while the rest es-
caped into the mountains. 11 The victorious invaders
then plundered Sodom and Gomorrah and headed
for home, taking with them all the spoils of war and
the food supplies. 12 They also captured Lot—Abram's
nephew who lived in Sodom—and carried off every-
thing he owned.
13 But one of Lot's men escaped and reported every-
thing to Abram the Hebrew, who was living near the
oak grove belonging to Mamre the Amorite. Mamre
and his relatives, Eshcol and Aner, were Abram's al-
lies.
14 When Abram heard that his nephew Lot had been
captured, he mobilized the 318 trained men who had
been born into his household. Then he pursued Ked-
orlaomer's army until he caught up with them at Dan.
15 There he divided his men and attacked during the
night. Kedorlaomer's army fled, but Abram chased
them as far as Hobah, north of Damascus. 16 Abram
recovered all the goods that had been taken, and he
brought back his nephew Lot with his possessions
and all the women and other captives.

MELCHIZEDEK BLESSES ABRAM

17 After Abram returned from his victory over Kedor-
laomer and all his allies, the king of Sodom went out
to meet him in the valley of Shaveh (that is, the King's
Valley).

13:15 Hebrew *seed;* also in 13:16. **14:1** Hebrew *Shinar;* also in 14:9. **14:3** Hebrew *Salt Sea.* **14:8** Hebrew *Siddim Valley* (see 14:3); also in 14:10.

13:12 Lot . . . near Sodom. By living so close to the evil people of Sodom and Gomorrah, Lot soon joined with them and came under God's judgment.
13:16 dust of the earth. God promised Abram that he would become the father of many descendants—the nation of Israel.

14:12 Lot . . . who lived in Sodom. Note Lot's progression from having settled near the town (13:12) to living within its walls.

18 And Melchizedek, the king of Salem and a priest of God Most High,* brought Abram some bread and wine. 19 Melchizedek blessed Abram with this blessing:

"Blessed be Abram by God Most High,
Creator of heaven and earth.
20 And blessed be God Most High,
who has defeated your enemies for you."

Then Abram gave Melchizedek a tenth of all the goods he had recovered.

21 The king of Sodom said to Abram, "Give back my people who were captured. But you may keep for yourself all the goods you have recovered."

22 Abram replied to the king of Sodom, "I solemnly swear to the LORD, God Most High, Creator of heaven and earth, 23 that I will not take so much as a single thread or sandal thong from what belongs to you. Otherwise you might say, 'I am the one who made Abram rich.' 24 I will accept only what my young warriors have already eaten, and I request that you give a fair share of the goods to my allies—Aner, Eshcol, and Mamre."

THE LORD'S COVENANT PROMISE TO ABRAM

15 Some time later, the LORD spoke to Abram in a vision and said to him, "Do not be afraid, Abram, for I will protect you, and your reward will be great."

2 But Abram replied, "O Sovereign LORD, what good are all your blessings when I don't even have a son? Since you've given me no children, Eliezer of Damascus, a servant in my household, will inherit all my wealth. 3 You have given me no descendants of my own, so one of my servants will be my heir."

4 Then the LORD said to him, "No, your servant will not be your heir, for you will have a son of your own who will be your heir." 5 Then the LORD took Abram outside and said to him, "Look up into the sky and count the stars if you can. That's how many descendants you will have!"

6 And Abram believed the LORD, and the LORD counted him as righteous because of his faith.

7 Then the LORD told him, "I am the LORD who brought you out of Ur of the Chaldeans to give you this land as your possession."

8 But Abram replied, "O Sovereign LORD, how can I be sure that I will actually possess it?"

9 The LORD told him, "Bring me a three-year-old heifer, a three-year-old female goat, a three-year-old ram, a turtledove, and a young pigeon." 10 So Abram presented all these to him and killed them. Then he cut each animal down the middle and laid the halves side by side; he did not, however, cut the birds in half. 11 Some vultures swooped down to eat the carcasses, but Abram chased them away.

12 As the sun was going down, Abram fell into a deep sleep, and a terrifying darkness came down over him. 13 Then the LORD said to Abram, "You can be sure that your descendants will be strangers in a foreign land, where they will be oppressed as slaves for 400 years. 14 But I will punish the nation that enslaves them, and in the end they will come away with great wealth. 15 (As for you, you will die in peace and be buried at a ripe old age.) 16 After four generations your descendants will return here to this land, for the sins of the Amorites do not yet warrant their destruction."

17 After the sun went down and darkness fell, Abram saw a smoking firepot and a flaming torch pass between the halves of the carcasses. 18 So the LORD made a covenant with Abram that day and said, "I have given this land to your descendants, all the way from the border of Egypt* to the great Euphrates River— 19 the land now occupied by the Kenites, Kenizzites, Kadmonites, 20 Hittites, Perizzites, Rephaites, 21 Amorites, Canaanites, Girgashites, and Jebusites."

THE BIRTH OF ISHMAEL

16 Now Sarai, Abram's wife, had not been able to bear children for him. But she had an Egyptian servant named Hagar. 2 So Sarai said to Abram, "The LORD has prevented me from having children. Go and sleep with my servant. Perhaps I can have children through her." And Abram agreed with Sarai's proposal. 3 So Sarai, Abram's wife, took Hagar the Egyptian servant and gave her to Abram as a wife. (This happened ten years after Abram had settled in the land of Canaan.)

4 So Abram had sexual relations with Hagar, and she became pregnant. But when Hagar knew she was pregnant, she began to treat her mistress, Sarai, with contempt. 5 Then Sarai said to Abram, "This is all your fault! I put my servant into your arms, but now that she's pregnant she treats me with contempt. The LORD will show who's wrong—you or me!"

6 Abram replied, "Look, she is your servant, so deal with her as you see fit." Then Sarai treated Hagar so harshly that she finally ran away.

7 The angel of the LORD found Hagar beside a spring of water in the wilderness, along the road to Shur. 8 The angel said to her, "Hagar, Sarai's servant, where have you come from, and where are you going?"

"I'm running away from my mistress, Sarai," she replied.

9 The angel of the LORD said to her, "Return to your mistress, and submit to her authority." 10 Then he added, "I will give you more descendants than you can count."

11 And the angel also said, "You are now pregnant and will give birth to a son. You are to name him Ishmael (which means 'God hears'), for the LORD has heard your cry of distress. 12 This son of yours will be a wild man, as untamed as a wild donkey! He will raise his fist against everyone, and everyone will be

14:18 Hebrew *El-Elyon;* also in 14:19, 20, 22. **15:18** Hebrew *the river of Egypt,* referring either to an eastern branch of the Nile River or to the Brook of Egypt in the Sinai (see Num 34:5).

14:18 Melchizedek. This man was both a king and a priest in the city of Salem (Jerusalem). His appearance further exalts Abram as a recipient of God's blessing.

14:23 will not take. Abram saw no need for more earthly riches. His confidence was in God's provision.

15:1 I will protect you. Abram was reminded by God of His power and protection.

15:2 Eliezer. Since Abram had no heirs, he had made arrangements for his estate to go to one of his servants, Eliezer.

15:3-5 God promised Abram that he would have a son of his own who would become his heir. His descendants would be as numerous as the stars.

15:6 Abram believed the LORD. With this affirmation, Abram becomes the first person in the Bible to profess a faith relationship with the Lord.

15:18 made a covenant. The animal sacrifice was a picture of God's promise to Abram. Through this act, God declared Abram's ownership of the land before him.

16:1-15 God had not delivered on his promise of an heir for Abram. So Abram agreed, at Sarai's urging, to father a child by Sarai's Egyptian servant,

against him. Yes, he will live in open hostility against
all his relatives."
13 Thereafter, Hagar used another name to refer to
the LORD, who had spoken to her. She said, "You are
the God who sees me."* She also said, "Have I truly
seen the One who sees me?" 14 So that well was named
Beer-lahai-roi (which means "well of the Living One
who sees me"). It can still be found between Kadesh
and Bered.
15 So Hagar gave Abram a son, and Abram named
him Ishmael. 16 Abram was eighty-six years old when
Ishmael was born.

ABRAM IS NAMED ABRAHAM

17 When Abram was ninety-nine years old, the
LORD appeared to him and said, "I am El-Shad-
dai—'God Almighty.' Serve me faithfully and live a
blameless life. 2 I will make a covenant with you, by
which I will guarantee to give you countless descen-
dants."
3 At this, Abram fell face down on the ground. Then
God said to him, 4 "This is my covenant with you: I will
make you the father of a multitude of nations! 5 What's
more, I am changing your name. It will no longer be
Abram. Instead, you will be called Abraham,* for you
will be the father of many nations. 6 I will make you
extremely fruitful. Your descendants will become
many nations, and kings will be among them!
7 "I will confirm my covenant with you and your
descendants* after you, from generation to genera-
tion. This is the everlasting covenant: I will always be
your God and the God of your descendants after you.
8 And I will give the entire land of Canaan, where you
now live as a foreigner, to you and your descendants.
It will be their possession forever, and I will be their
God."

THE MARK OF THE COVENANT

9 Then God said to Abraham, "Your responsibility
is to obey the terms of the covenant. You and all
your descendants have this continual responsi-
bility. 10 This is the covenant that you and your de-
scendants must keep: Each male among you must
be circumcised. 11 You must cut off the flesh of your
foreskin as a sign of the covenant between me and
you. 12 From generation to generation, every male
child must be circumcised on the eighth day after
his birth. This applies not only to members of your
family but also to the servants born in your house-
hold and the foreign-born servants whom you have
purchased. 13 All must be circumcised. Your bodies
will bear the mark of my everlasting covenant.
14 Any male who fails to be circumcised will be cut
off from the covenant family for breaking the cov-
enant."

SARAI IS NAMED SARAH

15 Then God said to Abraham, "Regarding Sarai, your
wife—her name will no longer be Sarai. From now
on her name will be Sarah.* 16 And I will bless her and
give you a son from her! Yes, I will bless her richly,
and she will become the mother of many nations.
Kings of nations will be among her descendants."
17 Then Abraham bowed down to the ground, but
he laughed to himself in disbelief. "How could I be-
come a father at the age of 100?" he thought. "And
how can Sarah have a baby when she is ninety years
old?" 18 So Abraham said to God, "May Ishmael live
under your special blessing!"
19 But God replied, "No—Sarah, your wife, will give
birth to a son for you. You will name him Isaac,* and
I will confirm my covenant with him and his descen-
dants as an everlasting covenant. 20 As for Ishmael, I
will bless him also, just as you have asked. I will make
him extremely fruitful and multiply his descendants.
He will become the father of twelve princes, and I will
make him a great nation. 21 But my covenant will be
confirmed with Isaac, who will be born to you and
Sarah about this time next year." 22 When God had fin-
ished speaking, he left Abraham.
23 On that very day Abraham took his son, Ishma-
el, and every male in his household, including those
born there and those he had bought. Then he circum-
cised them, cutting off their foreskins, just as God had
told him. 24 Abraham was ninety-nine years old when
he was circumcised, 25 and Ishmael, his son, was thir-
teen. 26 Both Abraham and his son, Ishmael, were cir-
cumcised on that same day, 27 along with all the other
men and boys of the household, whether they were
born there or bought as servants. All were circum-
cised with him.

A SON IS PROMISED TO SARAH

18 The LORD appeared again to Abraham near the
oak grove belonging to Mamre. One day Abra-
ham was sitting at the entrance to his tent during
the hottest part of the day. 2 He looked up and noticed
three men standing nearby. When he saw them, he
ran to meet them and welcomed them, bowing low to
the ground.
3 "My lord," he said, "if it pleases you, stop here for
a while. 4 Rest in the shade of this tree while water is
brought to wash your feet. 5 And since you've honored
your servant with this visit, let me prepare some food
to refresh you before you continue on your journey."
"All right," they said. "Do as you have said."
6 So Abraham ran back to the tent and said to Sarah,
"Hurry! Get three large measures* of your best flour,
knead it into dough, and bake some bread." 7 Then
Abraham ran out to the herd and chose a tender calf
and gave it to his servant, who quickly prepared it.

16:13 Hebrew *El-roi.* **17:5** *Abram* means "exalted father"; *Abraham* sounds like a Hebrew term that means "father of many." **17:7** Hebrew *seed;* also in 17:7b, 8, 9, 10, 19. **17:15** *Sarai* and *Sarah* both mean "princess"; the change in spelling may reflect the difference in dialect between Ur and Canaan. **17:19** *Isaac* means "he laughs." **18:6** Hebrew *3 seahs,* about half a bushel or 22 liters.

17:1 live a blameless life. Abram had to wait patiently for God to fulfill His promise of a son and an heir. Trying to fulfill that promise in his own way (through Hagar) had resulted in disaster.

17:5 Abram . . . Abraham. God changed Abram's name to Abraham, meaning "father of nations." This was a sign of God's covenant promise.

17:8 possession forever. The land of Canaan would belong to Abraham's descendants, as long as they obeyed the Lord.

17:10-11 circumcised. God chose circumcision as the sign of His covenant with Abraham. This act was symbolic of God's rule over His people.

17:15 Sarai . . . Sarah. Both these names mean "princess," but the change was a sign of God's promise that she would be the mother of many descendants.

17:16 a son from her. Not through Hagar or any other person, but through Sarah this son would be born to Abraham.

17:17 Abraham . . . laughed. This was his reaction to the seeming impossibility of the promise. God then named this son Isaac (v. 19), which means, "he laughs."

17:21 My covenant will be confirmed with Isaac. God's covenant would be with the son born to Abraham and Sarah and not with Ishmael, Hagar's son.

8 When the food was ready, Abraham took some yo-
gurt and milk and the roasted meat, and he served it
to the men. As they ate, Abraham waited on them in
the shade of the trees.
9 "Where is Sarah, your wife?" the visitors asked.
"She's inside the tent," Abraham replied.
10 Then one of them said, "I will return to you about
this time next year, and your wife, Sarah, will have
a son!"
Sarah was listening to this conversation from the
tent. 11 Abraham and Sarah were both very old by
this time, and Sarah was long past the age of hav-
ing children. 12 So she laughed silently to herself and
said, "How could a worn-out woman like me enjoy
such pleasure, especially when my master—my hus-
band—is also so old?"
13 Then the LORD said to Abraham, "Why did Sarah
laugh? Why did she say, 'Can an old woman like me
have a baby?' 14 Is anything too hard for the LORD? I
will return about this time next year, and Sarah will
have a son."
15 Sarah was afraid, so she denied it, saying, "I didn't
laugh."
But the LORD said, "No, you did laugh."

ABRAHAM INTERCEDES FOR SODOM

16 Then the men got up from their meal and looked
out toward Sodom. As they left, Abraham went with
them to send them on their way.
17 "Should I hide my plan from Abraham?" the LORD
asked. 18 "For Abraham will certainly become a great
and mighty nation, and all the nations of the earth
will be blessed through him. 19 I have singled him
out so that he will direct his sons and their families
to keep the way of the LORD by doing what is right
and just. Then I will do for Abraham all that I have
promised."
20 So the LORD told Abraham, "I have heard a great
outcry from Sodom and Gomorrah, because their sin
is so flagrant. 21 I am going down to see if their actions
are as wicked as I have heard. If not, I want to know."
22 The other men turned and headed toward Sodom,
but the LORD remained with Abraham. 23 Abraham
approached him and said, "Will you sweep away both
the righteous and the wicked? 24 Suppose you find fif-
ty righteous people living there in the city—will you
still sweep it away and not spare it for their sakes?
25 Surely you wouldn't do such a thing, destroying the
righteous along with the wicked. Why, you would be
treating the righteous and the wicked exactly the
same! Surely you wouldn't do that! Should not the
Judge of all the earth do what is right?"
26 And the LORD replied, "If I find fifty righteous
people in Sodom, I will spare the entire city for their
sake."
27 Then Abraham spoke again. "Since I have begun,
let me speak further to my Lord, even though I am but
dust and ashes. 28 Suppose there are only forty-five
righteous people rather than fifty? Will you destroy
the whole city for lack of five?"

PRAYER POWER

1. When has persistence in asking for something paid off for you? When has it gotten you in trouble?

GENESIS 18:16-33

2. Why did God choose to tell Abraham about His plans to destroy Sodom and Gomorrah?
3. How is Abraham's intercession for Sodom an example that we should follow today?
4. God chose to "go down to see if what they have done justifies the cry that has come up to Me" (v. 21). What does this illustrate about God's patience and grace?
5. How have you experienced God's grace in your life and relationships?

And the LORD said, "I will not destroy it if I find for-
ty-five righteous people there."
29 Then Abraham pressed his request further. "Sup-
pose there are only forty?"
And the LORD replied, "I will not destroy it for the
sake of the forty."
30 "Please don't be angry, my Lord," Abraham plead-
ed. "Let me speak—suppose only thirty righteous
people are found?"
And the LORD replied, "I will not destroy it if I find
thirty."
31 Then Abraham said, "Since I have dared to speak
to the Lord, let me continue—suppose there are only
twenty?"
And the LORD replied, "Then I will not destroy it for
the sake of the twenty."
32 Finally, Abraham said, "Lord, please don't be an-
gry with me if I speak one more time. Suppose only
ten are found there?"
And the LORD replied, "Then I will not destroy it for
the sake of the ten."
33 When the LORD had finished his conversation
with Abraham, he went on his way, and Abraham
returned to his tent.

SODOM AND GOMORRAH DESTROYED

19 That evening the two angels came to the en-
trance of the city of Sodom. Lot was sitting there,
and when he saw them, he stood up to meet them.
Then he welcomed them and bowed with his face to
the ground. 2 "My lords," he said, "come to my home to
wash your feet, and be my guests for the night. You
may then get up early in the morning and be on your
way again."
"Oh no," they replied. "We'll just spend the night out
here in the city square."
3 But Lot insisted, so at last they went home with
him. Lot prepared a feast for them, complete with

18:18 nations . . . blessed through him. The entire world would be invited to join God's covenant family through Jesus Christ, one of Abraham's descendants.

18:21 I am going down. God visited the earth for the purpose of judgment. His holiness would not tolerate the sin of Sodom and Gomorrah.

18:25 Judge of all the earth. Abraham believed that the Lord knows all, sees all, and always does what is just.

18:32 one more time. Abraham's repetition demonstrated his desire to save his relatives from Sodom and Gomorrah's destruction.

18:33 his tent. Abraham went back to his campsite in Mamre (v. 1) to spend the night, then returned the next day to the spot where he had talked with the Lord.

19:1 entrance . . . of Sodom. People who sat at the city's entrance were community leaders. Lot apparently had become a member of Sodom's city council.

DANGEROUS VALUES

1. What's the closest you've come to rescuing someone or being rescued?

GENESIS 19:1-29

2. What were the sexual values of Sodom? How do they compare with modern values?
3. God told Lot, "I can do nothing until you arrive" to another town (v. 22). Why? How did Abraham's intercession help save this other town and Lot?
4. What happened to Lot's wife? How had living in Sodom affected her?
5. Is homosexuality a sin? What about sex before marriage?
6. How do you see the values of the world around you endangering your soul?

fresh bread made without yeast, and they ate. 4 But before they retired for the night, all the men of Sodom, young and old, came from all over the city and surrounded the house. 5 They shouted to Lot, "Where are the men who came to spend the night with you? Bring them out to us so we can have sex with them!"

6 So Lot stepped outside to talk to them, shutting the door behind him. 7 "Please, my brothers," he begged, "don't do such a wicked thing. 8 Look, I have two virgin daughters. Let me bring them out to you, and you can do with them as you wish. But please, leave these men alone, for they are my guests and are under my protection."

9 "Stand back!" they shouted. "This fellow came to town as an outsider, and now he's acting like our judge! We'll treat you far worse than those other men!" And they lunged toward Lot to break down the door.

10 But the two angels* reached out, pulled Lot into the house, and bolted the door. 11 Then they blinded all the men, young and old, who were at the door of the house, so they gave up trying to get inside.

12 Meanwhile, the angels questioned Lot. "Do you have any other relatives here in the city?" they asked. "Get them out of this place—your sons-in-law, sons, daughters, or anyone else. 13 For we are about to destroy this city completely. The outcry against this place is so great it has reached the LORD, and he has sent us to destroy it."

14 So Lot rushed out to tell his daughters' fiancés, "Quick, get out of the city! The LORD is about to destroy it." But the young men thought he was only joking.

15 At dawn the next morning the angels became insistent. "Hurry," they said to Lot. "Take your wife and your two daughters who are here. Get out right now, or you will be swept away in the destruction of the city!"

16 When Lot still hesitated, the angels seized his hand and the hands of his wife and two daughters and rushed them to safety outside the city, for the LORD was merciful. 17 When they were safely out of the city, one of the angels ordered, "Run for your lives! And don't look back or stop anywhere in the valley! Escape to the mountains, or you will be swept away!"

18 "Oh no, my lord!" Lot begged. 19 "You have been so gracious to me and saved my life, and you have shown such great kindness. But I cannot go to the mountains. Disaster would catch up to me there, and I would soon die. 20 See, there is a small village nearby. Please let me go there instead; don't you see how small it is? Then my life will be saved."

21 "All right," the angel said, "I will grant your request. I will not destroy the little village. 22 But hurry! Escape to it, for I can do nothing until you arrive there." (This explains why that village was known as Zoar, which means "little place.")

23 Lot reached the village just as the sun was rising over the horizon. 24 Then the LORD rained down fire and burning sulfur from the sky on Sodom and Gomorrah. 25 He utterly destroyed them, along with the other cities and villages of the plain, wiping out all the people and every bit of vegetation. 26 But Lot's wife looked back as she was following behind him, and she turned into a pillar of salt.

27 Abraham got up early that morning and hurried out to the place where he had stood in the LORD's presence. 28 He looked out across the plain toward Sodom and Gomorrah and watched as columns of smoke rose from the cities like smoke from a furnace.

29 But God had listened to Abraham's request and kept Lot safe, removing him from the disaster that engulfed the cities on the plain.

LOT AND HIS DAUGHTERS

30 Afterward Lot left Zoar because he was afraid of the people there, and he went to live in a cave in the mountains with his two daughters. 31 One day the older daughter said to her sister, "There are no men left anywhere in this entire area, so we can't get married like everyone else. And our father will soon be too old to have children. 32 Come, let's get him drunk with wine, and then we will have sex with him. That way we will preserve our family line through our father."

33 So that night they got him drunk with wine, and the older daughter went in and had intercourse with her father. He was unaware of her lying down or getting up again.

34 The next morning the older daughter said to her younger sister, "I had sex with our father last night. Let's get him drunk with wine again tonight, and you go in and have sex with him. That way we will preserve our family line through our father." 35 So that night they got him drunk with wine again, and the younger daughter went in and had intercourse with him. As before, he was unaware of her lying down or getting up again.

19:10 Hebrew *men;* also in 19:12, 16.

19:13 destroy this city. Because 10 righteous people could not be found in Sodom (18:32), the city would be destroyed.

19:14 thought he was only joking. Even though Lot told the truth to his daughters' husbands, they did not believe him.

19:16 Lot still hesitated. Perhaps Lot was having second thoughts about leaving his home, his possessions, and his sons-in-law.

19:24 fire and burning sulfur. Subterranean asphalt is located in this part of the world. It is possible that God caused an eruption that rained down black molten tar.

19:29 listened to Abraham's request. Abraham had interceded for all the righteous inhabitants of Sodom, but he was especially concerned for his nephew and his family. This is a reminder of the power of intercessory prayer (18:32).

36 As a result, both of Lot's daughters became pregnant by their own father. 37 When the older daughter gave birth to a son, she named him Moab.* He became the ancestor of the nation now known as the Moabites. 38 When the younger daughter gave birth to a son, she named him Ben-ammi.* He became the ancestor of the nation now known as the Ammonites.

ABRAHAM DECEIVES ABIMELECH

20 Abraham moved south to the Negev and lived for a while between Kadesh and Shur, and then he moved on to Gerar. While living there as a foreigner, 2 Abraham introduced his wife, Sarah, by saying, "She is my sister." So King Abimelech of Gerar sent for Sarah and had her brought to him at his palace.

3 But that night God came to Abimelech in a dream and told him, "You are a dead man, for that woman you have taken is already married!"

4 But Abimelech had not slept with her yet, so he said, "Lord, will you destroy an innocent nation? 5 Didn't Abraham tell me, 'She is my sister'? And she herself said, 'Yes, he is my brother.' I acted in complete innocence! My hands are clean."

6 In the dream God responded, "Yes, I know you are innocent. That's why I kept you from sinning against me, and why I did not let you touch her. 7 Now return the woman to her husband, and he will pray for you, for he is a prophet. Then you will live. But if you don't return her to him, you can be sure that you and all your people will die."

8 Abimelech got up early the next morning and quickly called all his servants together. When he told them what had happened, his men were terrified. 9 Then Abimelech called for Abraham. "What have you done to us?" he demanded. "What crime have I committed that deserves treatment like this, making me and my kingdom guilty of this great sin? No one should ever do what you have done! 10 Whatever possessed you to do such a thing?"

11 Abraham replied, "I thought, 'This is a godless place. They will want my wife and will kill me to get her.' 12 And she really is my sister, for we both have the same father, but different mothers. And I married her. 13 When God called me to leave my father's home and to travel from place to place, I told her, 'Do me a favor. Wherever we go, tell the people that I am your brother.'"

14 Then Abimelech took some of his sheep and goats, cattle, and male and female servants, and he presented them to Abraham. He also returned his wife, Sarah, to him. 15 Then Abimelech said, "Look over my land and choose any place where you would like to live." 16 And he said to Sarah, "Look, I am giving your 'brother' 1,000 pieces of silver* in the presence of all these witnesses. This is to compensate you for any wrong I may have done to you. This will settle any claim against me, and your reputation is cleared."

17 Then Abraham prayed to God, and God healed Abimelech, his wife, and his female servants, so they could have children. 18 For the LORD had caused all the women to be infertile because of what happened with Abraham's wife, Sarah.

THE BIRTH OF ISAAC

21 The LORD kept his word and did for Sarah exactly what he had promised. 2 She became pregnant, and she gave birth to a son for Abraham in his old age. This happened at just the time God had said it would. 3 And Abraham named their son Isaac. 4 Eight days after Isaac was born, Abraham circumcised him as God had commanded. 5 Abraham was 100 years old when Isaac was born.

6 And Sarah declared, "God has brought me laughter.* All who hear about this will laugh with me. 7 Who would have said to Abraham that Sarah would nurse a baby? Yet I have given Abraham a son in his old age!"

FAMILY FEUDS

1. Do you have any sibling rivalry in your family? With whom? Over what?

GENESIS 21:1-21

2. Modern Jews and Israelis are descended from Isaac, while modern Arabic nations are descended from Ishmael. How does this passage help explain modern Middle East tensions?
3. Both Abraham and Sarah were around 100 years old when Isaac was born. What meaning does this give to Isaac's birth? How does this hint at the birth of Jesus?
4. Abraham had to give up his son born to his slave, Hagar. Why did he do this?
5. When have you had to give up something for God?

HAGAR AND ISHMAEL ARE SENT AWAY

8 When Isaac grew up and was about to be weaned, Abraham prepared a huge feast to celebrate the occasion. 9 But Sarah saw Ishmael—the son of Abraham and her Egyptian servant Hagar—making fun of her son, Isaac.* 10 So she turned to Abraham and demanded, "Get rid of that slave woman and her son. He is not going to share the inheritance with my son, Isaac. I won't have it!"

11 This upset Abraham very much because Ishmael was his son. 12 But God told Abraham, "Do not be up-

19:37 *Moab* sounds like a Hebrew term that means "from father." **19:38** *Ben-ammi* means "son of my kinsman." **20:16** Hebrew *1,000 [shekels] of silver,* about 25 pounds or 11.4 kilograms in weight. **21:6** The name *Isaac* means "he laughs." **21:9** As in Greek version and Latin Vulgate; Hebrew lacks *of her son, Isaac.*

19:37-38 Moabites . . . Ammonites. The sons resulting from Lot's incest with his daughters were the ancestors of the Moabites and Ammonites. These tribes plagued Abraham's descendants, the Hebrews, for centuries.

20:3 dream. God used a dream to offer caution to Abimelech, king of Gerar, about keeping Sarah in his harem. The Lord was preparing the way for her to bear the child He had promised Abraham.

20:16 pieces of silver. The king felt obligated to compensate Abraham for the inconvenience he had caused by taking Sarah into his harem.

21:1 did . . . what he had promised. Finally, God's promise came true—the birth of a son to Abraham and Sarah (15:4; 17:15-19).

21:3 Isaac. The name means, "he laughs." Both Abraham and Sarah had once laughed, scoffing at the idea of fathering a son at their age (17:17; 18:12). This time, their laughter was filled with joy.

21:9-14 After Isaac was born, Sarah insisted that Ishmael and Hagar be driven away from their household.

set over the boy and your servant. Do whatever Sar-
ah tells you, for Isaac is the son through whom your
descendants will be counted. 13 But I will also make a
nation of the descendants of Hagar's son because he
is your son, too."
14 So Abraham got up early the next morning, pre-
pared food and a container of water, and strapped
them on Hagar's shoulders. Then he sent her away
with their son, and she wandered aimlessly in the
wilderness of Beersheba.
15 When the water was gone, she put the boy in the
shade of a bush. 16 Then she went and sat down by
herself about a hundred yards* away. "I don't want
to watch the boy die," she said, as she burst into tears.
17 But God heard the boy crying, and the angel of
God called to Hagar from heaven, "Hagar, what's
wrong? Do not be afraid! God has heard the boy cry-
ing as he lies there. 18 Go to him and comfort him, for I
will make a great nation from his descendants."
19 Then God opened Hagar's eyes, and she saw a
well full of water. She quickly filled her water con-
tainer and gave the boy a drink.
20 And God was with the boy as he grew up in the
wilderness. He became a skillful archer, 21 and he set-
tled in the wilderness of Paran. His mother arranged
for him to marry a woman from the land of Egypt.

ABRAHAM'S COVENANT WITH ABIMELECH

22 About this time, Abimelech came with Phicol, his
army commander, to visit Abraham. "God is obviously
with you, helping you in everything you do," Abime-
lech said. 23 "Swear to me in God's name that you will
never deceive me, my children, or any of my descen-
dants. I have been loyal to you, so now swear that you
will be loyal to me and to this country where you are
living as a foreigner."
24 Abraham replied, "Yes, I swear to it!" 25 Then
Abraham complained to Abimelech about a well that
Abimelech's servants had taken by force from Abra-
ham's servants.
26 "This is the first I've heard of it," Abimelech an-
swered. "I have no idea who is responsible. You have
never complained about this before."
27 Abraham then gave some of his sheep, goats, and
cattle to Abimelech, and they made a treaty. 28 But
Abraham also took seven additional female lambs
and set them off by themselves. 29 Abimelech asked,
"Why have you set these seven apart from the others?"
30 Abraham replied, "Please accept these seven
lambs to show your agreement that I dug this well."
31 Then he named the place Beersheba (which means
"well of the oath"), because that was where they had
sworn the oath.
32 After making their covenant at Beersheba, Abim-
elech left with Phicol, the commander of his army,
and they returned home to the land of the Philistines.
33 Then Abraham planted a tamarisk tree at Beer-
sheba, and there he worshiped the LORD, the Eternal
God.* 34 And Abraham lived as a foreigner in Philis-
tine country for a long time.

ABRAHAM'S FAITH TESTED

22 Some time later, God tested Abraham's faith.
"Abraham!" God called.
"Yes," he replied. "Here I am."
2 "Take your son, your only son—yes, Isaac, whom
you love so much—and go to the land of Moriah. Go
and sacrifice him as a burnt offering on one of the
mountains, which I will show you."
3 The next morning Abraham got up early. He sad-
dled his donkey and took two of his servants with
him, along with his son, Isaac. Then he chopped wood
for a fire for a burnt offering and set out for the place
God had told him about. 4 On the third day of their
journey, Abraham looked up and saw the place in the
distance. 5 "Stay here with the donkey," Abraham told
the servants. "The boy and I will travel a little farther.
We will worship there, and then we will come right
back."

THE SUPREME SACRIFICE

1. What thing in your life would be the hardest for you to give up?

GENESIS 22:1-19

2. Why did God ask Abraham to sacrifice his son? Why did Abraham obey?
3. How does this story illustrate the sacrifice made by God the Father and His Son, Jesus?
4. Is God calling you to make a large sacrifice for Him? What is it? How will you respond?
5. Does obedience to coaches or parents or other authorities sometimes require a big sacrifice on your part? How might God bless you when you make those sacrifices?

6 So Abraham placed the wood for the burnt offer-
ing on Isaac's shoulders, while he himself carried the
fire and the knife. As the two of them walked on to-
gether, 7 Isaac turned to Abraham and said, "Father?"
"Yes, my son?" Abraham replied.
"We have the fire and the wood," the boy said, "but
where is the sheep for the burnt offering?"
8 "God will provide a sheep for the burnt offering,
my son," Abraham answered. And they both walked
on together.
9 When they arrived at the place where God had
told him to go, Abraham built an altar and arranged
the wood on it. Then he tied his son, Isaac, and laid
him on the altar on top of the wood. 10 And Abraham

21:16 Hebrew *a bowshot.* **21:33** Hebrew *El-Olam.*

21:17 God heard. God heard Ishmael crying in the wilderness. His name means, "God hears."

21:19 God opened Hagar's eyes. God had to open Hagar's eyes so she could see the spring of water that God had provided to save them.

22:2 Isaac, whom you love. Isaac was the only son of God's promise (21:12). God knew how much Abraham loved his son, so He wanted to see if Abraham was totally committed to Him.

22:4 third day. It took three days to journey the region of Moriah. These were agonizing days for Abraham as he contemplated that God had asked him to sacrifice his son.

picked up the knife to kill his son as a sacrifice. 11 At that moment the angel of the LORD called to him from heaven, "Abraham! Abraham!"

"Yes," Abraham replied. "Here I am!"

12 "Don't lay a hand on the boy!" the angel said. "Do not hurt him in any way, for now I know that you truly fear God. You have not withheld from me even your son, your only son."

13 Then Abraham looked up and saw a ram caught by its horns in a thicket. So he took the ram and sacrificed it as a burnt offering in place of his son. 14 Abraham named the place Yahweh-Yireh (which means "the LORD will provide"). To this day, people still use that name as a proverb: "On the mountain of the LORD it will be provided."

15 Then the angel of the LORD called again to Abraham from heaven. 16 "This is what the LORD says: Because you have obeyed me and have not withheld even your son, your only son, I swear by my own name that 17 I will certainly bless you. I will multiply your descendants* beyond number, like the stars in the sky and the sand on the seashore. Your descendants will conquer the cities of their enemies. 18 And through your descendants all the nations of the earth will be blessed—all because you have obeyed me."

19 Then they returned to the servants and traveled back to Beersheba, where Abraham continued to live.

20 Soon after this, Abraham heard that Milcah, his brother Nahor's wife, had borne Nahor eight sons. 21 The oldest was named Uz, the next oldest was Buz, followed by Kemuel (the ancestor of the Arameans), 22 Kesed, Hazo, Pildash, Jidlaph, and Bethuel. 23 (Bethuel became the father of Rebekah.) In addition to these eight sons from Milcah, 24 Nahor had four other children from his concubine Reumah. Their names were Tebah, Gaham, Tahash, and Maacah.

THE BURIAL OF SARAH

23 When Sarah was 127 years old, 2 she died at Kiriath-arba (now called Hebron) in the land of Canaan. There Abraham mourned and wept for her.

3 Then, leaving her body, he said to the Hittite elders, 4 "Here I am, a stranger and a foreigner among you. Please sell me a piece of land so I can give my wife a proper burial."

5 The Hittites replied to Abraham, 6 "Listen, my lord, you are an honored prince among us. Choose the finest of our tombs and bury her there. No one here will refuse to help you in this way."

7 Then Abraham bowed low before the Hittites 8 and said, "Since you are willing to help me in this way, be so kind as to ask Ephron son of Zohar 9 to let me buy his cave at Machpelah, down at the end of his field. I will pay the full price in the presence of witnesses, so I will have a permanent burial place for my family."

10 Ephron was sitting there among the others, and he answered Abraham as the others listened, speaking publicly before all the Hittite elders of the town. 11 "No, my lord," he said to Abraham, "please listen to me. I will give you the field and the cave. Here in the presence of my people, I give it to you. Go and bury your dead."

12 Abraham again bowed low before the citizens of the land, 13 and he replied to Ephron as everyone listened. "No, listen to me. I will buy it from you. Let me pay the full price for the field so I can bury my dead there."

14 Ephron answered Abraham, 15 "My lord, please listen to me. The land is worth 400 pieces* of silver, but what is that between friends? Go ahead and bury your dead."

16 So Abraham agreed to Ephron's price and paid the amount he had suggested—400 pieces of silver, weighed according to the market standard. The Hittite elders witnessed the transaction.

17 So Abraham bought the plot of land belonging to Ephron at Machpelah, near Mamre. This included the field itself, the cave that was in it, and all the surrounding trees. 18 It was transferred to Abraham as his permanent possession in the presence of the Hittite elders at the city gate. 19 Then Abraham buried his wife, Sarah, there in Canaan, in the cave of Machpelah, near Mamre (also called Hebron). 20 So the field and the cave were transferred from the Hittites to Abraham for use as a permanent burial place.

A WIFE FOR ISAAC

24 Abraham was now a very old man, and the LORD had blessed him in every way. 2 One day Abraham said to his oldest servant, the man in charge of his household, "Take an oath by putting your hand under my thigh. 3 Swear by the LORD, the God of heaven and earth, that you will not allow my son to marry one of these local Canaanite women. 4 Go instead to my homeland, to my relatives, and find a wife there for my son Isaac."

5 The servant asked, "But what if I can't find a young woman who is willing to travel so far from home? Should I then take Isaac there to live among your relatives in the land you came from?"

6 "No!" Abraham responded. "Be careful never to take my son there. 7 For the LORD, the God of heaven, who took me from my father's house and my native land, solemnly promised to give this land to my descendants.* He will send his angel ahead of you, and he will see to it that you find a wife there for my son.

22:17 Hebrew *seed;* also in 22:17b, 18. 23:15 Hebrew *400 shekels,* about 10 pounds or 4.6 kilograms in weight; also in 23:16. 24:7 Hebrew *seed;* also in 24:60.

22:11 Abraham! Abraham! Abraham was about to carry out the sacrifice, doing what he had been told by God to do. An angel called out to stop him.

22:13 burnt offering. This is the first time in the Bible that the concept of substituting a sacrifice is mentioned. The ram took Isaac's place on the altar, just as Christ did for us.

22:16 by my own name. Oaths are made by calling upon someone to witness the oath; God swore by His own name.

23:4 foreigner among you. Abraham never owned any land in Canaan except the spot where he buried his beloved wife. But God had promised that all the surrounding territory would belong to his descendants one day.

23:9 cave at Machpelah. Although no one knows the exact location of this cave, according to tradition, it is beneath a Muslim shrine in Hebron.

23:10 the Hittite elders. This exchange between Ephron and Abraham took place before many witnesses (v. 16) at the city's main gateway, which was the traditional place where important matters were settled.

23:15 400 pieces of silver. Ephron acted as if his offer was generous, but 400 shekels was a high price for such a property.

23:17 field . . . cave . . . trees. Ephron negotiated the sale of the entire field and its contents as well as the cave of Machpelah.

23:19 buried his wife. By establishing this "family plot" in Canaan, Abraham was expressing his deep faith in God's promise to give his descendants the land.

24:4 my homeland. Abraham sent his most trusted servant back to where Abraham had come from to find a wife for his son, Isaac. Abraham did not want Isaac to intermarry with the Canaanites.

8 If she is unwilling to come back with you, then you are free from this oath of mine. But under no circumstances are you to take my son there."

9 So the servant took an oath by putting his hand under the thigh of his master, Abraham. He swore to follow Abraham's instructions. 10 Then he loaded ten of Abraham's camels with all kinds of expensive gifts from his master, and he traveled to distant Aram-naharaim. There he went to the town where Abraham's brother Nahor had settled. 11 He made the camels kneel beside a well just outside the town. It was evening, and the women were coming out to draw water.

12 "O LORD, God of my master, Abraham," he prayed. "Please give me success today, and show unfailing love to my master, Abraham. 13 See, I am standing here beside this spring, and the young women of the town are coming out to draw water. 14 This is my request. I will ask one of them, 'Please give me a drink from your jug.' If she says, 'Yes, have a drink, and I will water your camels, too!'—let her be the one you have selected as Isaac's wife. This is how I will know that you have shown unfailing love to my master."

15 Before he had finished praying, he saw a young woman named Rebekah coming out with her water jug on her shoulder. She was the daughter of Bethuel, who was the son of Abraham's brother Nahor and his wife, Milcah. 16 Rebekah was very beautiful and old enough to be married, but she was still a virgin. She went down to the spring, filled her jug, and came up again. 17 Running over to her, the servant said, "Please give me a little drink of water from your jug."

18 "Yes, my lord," she answered, "have a drink." And she quickly lowered her jug from her shoulder and gave him a drink. 19 When she had given him a drink, she said, "I'll draw water for your camels, too, until they have had enough to drink." 20 So she quickly emptied her jug into the watering trough and ran back to the well to draw water for all his camels.

21 The servant watched her in silence, wondering whether or not the LORD had given him success in his mission. 22 Then at last, when the camels had finished drinking, he took out a gold ring for her nose and two large gold bracelets* for her wrists.

23 "Whose daughter are you?" he asked. "And please tell me, would your father have any room to put us up for the night?"

24 "I am the daughter of Bethuel," she replied. "My grandparents are Nahor and Milcah. 25 Yes, we have plenty of straw and feed for the camels, and we have room for guests."

26 The man bowed low and worshiped the LORD. 27 "Praise the LORD, the God of my master, Abraham," he said. "The LORD has shown unfailing love and faithfulness to my master, for he has led me straight to my master's relatives."

28 The young woman ran home to tell her family everything that had happened. 29 Now Rebekah had a brother named Laban, who ran out to meet the man at the spring. 30 He had seen the nose-ring and the bracelets on his sister's wrists, and had heard Rebekah tell what the man had said. So he rushed out to the spring, where the man was still standing beside his camels. 31 Laban said to him, "Come and stay with us, you who are blessed by the LORD! Why are you standing here outside the town when I have a room all ready for you and a place prepared for the camels?"

32 So the man went home with Laban, and Laban unloaded the camels, gave him straw for their bedding, fed them, and provided water for the man and the camel drivers to wash their feet. 33 Then food was served. But Abraham's servant said, "I don't want to eat until I have told you why I have come."

"All right," Laban said, "tell us."

34 "I am Abraham's servant," he explained. 35 "And the LORD has greatly blessed my master; he has become a wealthy man. The LORD has given him flocks of sheep and goats, herds of cattle, a fortune in silver and gold, and many male and female servants and camels and donkeys.

36 "When Sarah, my master's wife, was very old, she gave birth to my master's son, and my master has given him everything he owns. 37 And my master made me take an oath. He said, 'Do not allow my son to marry one of these local Canaanite women. 38 Go instead to my father's house, to my relatives, and find a wife there for my son.'

39 "But I said to my master, 'What if I can't find a young woman who is willing to go back with me?' 40 He responded, 'The LORD, in whose presence I have lived, will send his angel with you and will make your mission successful. Yes, you must find a wife for my son from among my relatives, from my father's family. 41 Then you will have fulfilled your obligation. But if you go to my relatives and they refuse to let her go with you, you will be free from my oath.'

42 "So today when I came to the spring, I prayed this prayer: 'O LORD, God of my master, Abraham, please give me success on this mission. 43 See, I am standing here beside this spring. This is my request. When a young woman comes to draw water, I will say to her, "Please give me a little drink of water from your jug." 44 If she says, "Yes, have a drink, and I will draw water for your camels, too," let her be the one you have selected to be the wife of my master's son.'

45 "Before I had finished praying in my heart, I saw Rebekah coming out with her water jug on her shoulder. She went down to the spring and drew water. So I said to her, 'Please give me a drink.' 46 She quickly lowered her jug from her shoulder and said, 'Yes, have a drink, and I will water your camels, too!' So I drank, and then she watered the camels.

47 "Then I asked, 'Whose daughter are you?' She replied, 'I am the daughter of Bethuel, and my grandparents are Nahor and Milcah.' So I put the ring on her nose, and the bracelets on her wrists.

48 "Then I bowed low and worshiped the LORD. I praised the LORD, the God of my master, Abraham, because he had led me straight to my master's niece to be his son's wife. 49 So tell me—will you or won't you show unfailing love and faithfulness to my master?

24:22 Hebrew *a gold nose-ring weighing a beka* [0.2 ounces or 6 grams] *and two gold bracelets weighing 10 [shekels]* [4 ounces or 114 grams].

24:10 Aram-naharaim. An area in northern Syria between the Tigris and Euphrates Rivers, sometimes translated "Mesopotamia."

24:14 I will know. Eliezer prayed, asking God for a sign to discern the woman whom God had chosen for Isaac. Any woman might offer a drink to a weary traveler at the well, but for a woman to offer water for his camel would show a servant's spirit.

24:15 Rebekah. Isaac would be marrying within Abraham's extended family—Abraham's grandniece.

24:26 bowed low and worshiped the LORD. Abraham's servant was overwhelmed by God's gracious work in sending Rebekah.

Please tell me yes or no, and then I'll know what to
do next."
50 Then Laban and Bethuel replied, "The LORD has
obviously brought you here, so there is nothing we
can say. 51 Here is Rebekah; take her and go. Yes, let
her be the wife of your master's son, as the LORD has
directed."
52 When Abraham's servant heard their answer,
he bowed down to the ground and worshiped the
LORD. 53 Then he brought out silver and gold jewelry
and clothing and presented them to Rebekah. He also
gave expensive presents to her brother and mother.
54 Then they ate their meal, and the servant and the
men with him stayed there overnight.
But early the next morning, Abraham's servant
said, "Send me back to my master."
55 "But we want Rebekah to stay with us at least ten
days," her brother and mother said. "Then she can go."
56 But he said, "Don't delay me. The LORD has made
my mission successful; now send me back so I can re-
turn to my master."
57 "Well," they said, "we'll call Rebekah and ask her
what she thinks." 58 So they called Rebekah. "Are you
willing to go with this man?" they asked her.
And she replied, "Yes, I will go."
59 So they said good-bye to Rebekah and sent her away
with Abraham's servant and his men. The woman who
had been Rebekah's childhood nurse went along with
her. 60 They gave her this blessing as she parted:

"Our sister, may you become
the mother of many millions!
May your descendants be strong
and conquer the cities of their enemies."

61 Then Rebekah and her servant girls mounted the
camels and followed the man. So Abraham's servant
took Rebekah and went on his way.
62 Meanwhile, Isaac, whose home was in the Ne-
gev, had returned from Beer-lahai-roi. 63 One evening
as he was walking and meditating in the fields, he
looked up and saw the camels coming. 64 When Rebek-
ah looked up and saw Isaac, she quickly dismounted
from her camel. 65 "Who is that man walking through
the fields to meet us?" she asked the servant.
And he replied, "It is my master." So Rebekah cov-
ered her face with her veil. 66 Then the servant told
Isaac everything he had done.
67 And Isaac brought Rebekah into his mother
Sarah's tent, and she became his wife. He loved her
deeply, and she was a special comfort to him after the
death of his mother.

THE DEATH OF ABRAHAM

25 Abraham married another wife, whose name
was Keturah. 2 She gave birth to Zimran, Jok-
shan, Medan, Midian, Ishbak, and Shuah. 3 Jokshan
was the father of Sheba and Dedan. Dedan's descen-
dants were the Asshurites, Letushites, and Leum-
mites. 4 Midian's sons were Ephah, Epher, Hanoch,
Abida, and Eldaah. These were all descendants of
Abraham through Keturah.
5 Abraham gave everything he owned to his son
Isaac. 6 But before he died, he gave gifts to the sons of
his concubines and sent them off to a land in the east,
away from Isaac.
7 Abraham lived for 175 years, 8 and he died at a
ripe old age, having lived a long and satisfying life. He
breathed his last and joined his ancestors in death. 9 His
sons Isaac and Ishmael buried him in the cave of Mach-
pelah, near Mamre, in the field of Ephron son of Zohar
the Hittite. 10 This was the field Abraham had purchased
from the Hittites and where he had buried his wife Sar-
ah. 11 After Abraham's death, God blessed his son Isaac,
who settled near Beer-lahai-roi in the Negev.

ISHMAEL'S DESCENDANTS

12 This is the account of the family of Ishmael, the
son of Abraham through Hagar, Sarah's Egyptian
servant. 13 Here is a list, by their names and clans, of
Ishmael's descendants: The oldest was Nebaioth, fol-
lowed by Kedar, Adbeel, Mibsam, 14 Mishma, Dumah,
Massa, 15 Hadad, Tema, Jetur, Naphish, and Kedemah.
16 These twelve sons of Ishmael became the founders
of twelve tribes named after them, listed according to
the places they settled and camped. 17 Ishmael lived
for 137 years. Then he breathed his last and joined
his ancestors in death. 18 Ishmael's descendants occu-
pied the region from Havilah to Shur, which is east of
Egypt in the direction of Asshur. There they lived in
open hostility toward all their relatives.*

THE BIRTHS OF ESAU AND JACOB

19 This is the account of the family of Isaac, the son of
Abraham. 20 When Isaac was forty years old, he mar-
ried Rebekah, the daughter of Bethuel the Aramean
from Paddan-aram and the sister of Laban the Ara-
mean.
21 Isaac pleaded with the LORD on behalf of his
wife, because she was unable to have children. The
LORD answered Isaac's prayer, and Rebekah became
pregnant with twins. 22 But the two children strug-
gled with each other in her womb. So she went to ask
the LORD about it. "Why is this happening to me?" she
asked.
23 And the LORD told her, "The sons in your womb
will become two nations. From the very beginning,
the two nations will be rivals. One nation will be
stronger than the other; and your older son will serve
your younger son."
24 And when the time came to give birth, Rebekah
discovered that she did indeed have twins! 25 The first
one was very red at birth and covered with thick hair
like a fur coat. So they named him Esau.* 26 Then the

25:18 The meaning of the Hebrew is uncertain. **25:25** *Esau* sounds like a Hebrew term that means "hair."

24:53 presented them to Rebekah. The jewelry and clothing given to Rebekah and her family revealed the wealth of her new household and assured them that she would be provided for.

24:67 tent. After arriving in Canaan, Rebekah entered the "tent" symbolically by entering the family through marriage, and literally by intimacy with Isaac in one of the tents, which would be their home.

25:1 another wife. Abraham had been married to Sarah, but apparently had many concubines (25:6). Keturah may have been another concubine.

25:5 gave everything. Abraham left everything he owned to Isaac so all of God's promises would be kept within Isaac's line.

25:7-8 Abraham left Haran at age 75 (12:4) and died about 100 years later. God kept His promise to give him a long life (12:2; 15:15).

25:12-19 Ishmael's genealogy is followed by Isaac's. Ishmael's line includes many Arabic names, showing that he was the ancestor of that line of people.

25:23-25 Traditionally, the older son received the double portion of the inheritance. In this case, God's plan was to bless the younger son, Jacob, and continue the line of promise through him.

HONOR AND PRIVILEGE

1. What is the story behind your name? How did your parents come up with it? What does it mean?

GENESIS 25:19-34

2. What did the Lord mean when He said to Rebekah, "The sons in your womb will become two nations" (v. 23)?
3. What motivated Esau to sell his birthright? What were his top priorities?
4. What motivated Jacob to cheat his brother? What were his top priorities?
5. What is the "birthright" of every Christian? How do Christians sometimes "despise" their birthright as Esau did? How about you?
6. Does your attitude and behavior bring honor to your family, your school, and your team? How?

other twin was born with his hand grasping Esau's
heel. So they named him Jacob.* Isaac was sixty years
old when the twins were born.

ESAU SELLS HIS BIRTHRIGHT

27 As the boys grew up, Esau became a skillful hunter.
He was an outdoorsman, but Jacob had a quiet tem-
perament, preferring to stay at home. 28 Isaac loved
Esau because he enjoyed eating the wild game Esau
brought home, but Rebekah loved Jacob.
29 One day when Jacob was cooking some stew,
Esau arrived home from the wilderness exhausted
and hungry. 30 Esau said to Jacob, "I'm starved! Give
me some of that red stew!" (This is how Esau got his
other name, Edom, which means "red.")
31 "All right," Jacob replied, "but trade me your
rights as the firstborn son."
32 "Look, I'm dying of starvation!" said Esau. "What
good is my birthright to me now?"
33 But Jacob said, "First you must swear that your
birthright is mine." So Esau swore an oath, thereby
selling all his rights as the firstborn to his brother,
Jacob.
34 Then Jacob gave Esau some bread and lentil stew.
Esau ate the meal, then got up and left. He showed
contempt for his rights as the firstborn.

ISAAC DECEIVES ABIMELECH

26 A severe famine now struck the land, as had
happened before in Abraham's time. So Isaac
moved to Gerar, where Abimelech, king of the Philis-
tines, lived.
2 The LORD appeared to Isaac and said, "Do not go
down to Egypt, but do as I tell you. 3 Live here as a for-
eigner in this land, and I will be with you and bless
you. I hereby confirm that I will give all these lands to
you and your descendants,* just as I solemnly prom-
ised Abraham, your father. 4 I will cause your descen-
dants to become as numerous as the stars of the sky,
and I will give them all these lands. And through
your descendants all the nations of the earth will be
blessed. 5 I will do this because Abraham listened to
me and obeyed all my requirements, commands, de-
crees, and instructions." 6 So Isaac stayed in Gerar.
7 When the men who lived there asked Isaac about
his wife, Rebekah, he said, "She is my sister." He was
afraid to say, "She is my wife." He thought, "They will
kill me to get her, because she is so beautiful." 8 But some
time later, Abimelech, king of the Philistines, looked out
his window and saw Isaac caressing Rebekah.
9 Immediately, Abimelech called for Isaac and ex-
claimed, "She is obviously your wife! Why did you say,
'She is my sister'?"
"Because I was afraid someone would kill me to get
her from me," Isaac replied.
10 "How could you do this to us?" Abimelech ex-
claimed. "One of my people might easily have taken
your wife and slept with her, and you would have
made us guilty of great sin."
11 Then Abimelech issued a public proclamation:
"Anyone who touches this man or his wife will be put
to death!"

CONFLICT OVER WATER RIGHTS

12 When Isaac planted his crops that year, he harvest-
ed a hundred times more grain than he planted, for
the LORD blessed him. 13 He became a very rich man,
and his wealth continued to grow. 14 He acquired so
many flocks of sheep and goats, herds of cattle, and
servants that the Philistines became jealous of him.
15 So the Philistines filled up all of Isaac's wells with
dirt. These were the wells that had been dug by the
servants of his father, Abraham.
16 Finally, Abimelech ordered Isaac to leave the
country. "Go somewhere else," he said, "for you have
become too powerful for us."
17 So Isaac moved away to the Gerar Valley, where
he set up their tents and settled down. 18 He reopened
the wells his father had dug, which the Philistines
had filled in after Abraham's death. Isaac also re-
stored the names Abraham had given them.
19 Isaac's servants also dug in the Gerar Valley
and discovered a well of fresh water. 20 But then the
shepherds from Gerar came and claimed the spring.
"This is our water," they said, and they argued over it
with Isaac's herdsmen. So Isaac named the well Esek
(which means "argument"). 21 Isaac's men then dug
another well, but again there was a dispute over it.
So Isaac named it Sitnah (which means "hostility").
22 Abandoning that one, Isaac moved on and dug an-
other well. This time there was no dispute over it, so
Isaac named the place Rehoboth (which means "open
space"), for he said, "At last the LORD has created
enough space for us to prosper in this land."

25:26 *Jacob* sounds like the Hebrew words for "heel" and "deceiver." **26:3** Hebrew *seed;* also in 26:4, 24.

25:26 grasping Esau's heel. This is an early picture of the hostility that would develop between Jacob's descendants (the Israelites) and Esau's descendants (the Edomites).

25:31 your rights. Jacob, a schemer from the day he was born, was determined to take away Esau's rights as the firstborn son.

25:34 lentil stew. Lentils, similar to beans, were an important source of nourishment.

26:2 The LORD appeared. God's first recorded appearance to Isaac. God repeated to Isaac the covenant He had made with his father Abraham (15:4-5).

26:16 too powerful for us. The presence of God's people in the land, worshiping their unseen God who blessed them, was a threat to the inhabitants of Canaan even at this early time.

26:20 this is our water. Wells were greatly valued. Disagreements over the fresh water in a well were common.

23 From there Isaac moved to Beersheba, 24 where
the LORD appeared to him on the night of his arrival.
"I am the God of your father, Abraham," he said. "Do
not be afraid, for I am with you and will bless you. I
will multiply your descendants, and they will become
a great nation. I will do this because of my promise
to Abraham, my servant." 25 Then Isaac built an altar
there and worshiped the LORD. He set up his camp at
that place, and his servants dug another well.

ISAAC'S COVENANT WITH ABIMELECH

26 One day King Abimelech came from Gerar with his
adviser, Ahuzzath, and also Phicol, his army com-
mander. 27 "Why have you come here?" Isaac asked.
"You obviously hate me, since you kicked me off your
land."
28 They replied, "We can plainly see that the LORD
is with you. So we want to enter into a sworn trea-
ty with you. Let's make a covenant. 29 Swear that you
will not harm us, just as we have never troubled you.
We have always treated you well, and we sent you
away from us in peace. And now look how the LORD
has blessed you!"
30 So Isaac prepared a covenant feast to celebrate
the treaty, and they ate and drank together. 31 Early
the next morning, they each took a solemn oath not to
interfere with each other. Then Isaac sent them home
again, and they left him in peace.
32 That very day Isaac's servants came and told him
about a new well they had dug. "We've found wa-
ter!" they exclaimed. 33 So Isaac named the well Shi-
bah (which means "oath"). And to this day the town
that grew up there is called Beersheba (which means
"well of the oath").
34 At the age of forty, Esau married two Hittite
wives: Judith, the daughter of Beeri, and Basemath,
the daughter of Elon. 35 But Esau's wives made life
miserable for Isaac and Rebekah.

JACOB STEALS ESAU'S BLESSING

27 One day when Isaac was old and turning blind,
he called for Esau, his older son, and said, "My
son."
"Yes, Father?" Esau replied.
2 "I am an old man now," Isaac said, "and I don't
know when I may die. 3 Take your bow and a quiver
full of arrows, and go out into the open country to
hunt some wild game for me. 4 Prepare my favorite
dish, and bring it here for me to eat. Then I will pro-
nounce the blessing that belongs to you, my firstborn
son, before I die."
5 But Rebekah overheard what Isaac had said to his
son Esau. So when Esau left to hunt for the wild game,
6 she said to her son Jacob, "Listen. I overheard your
father say to Esau, 7 'Bring me some wild game and
prepare me a delicious meal. Then I will bless you in
the LORD's presence before I die.' 8 Now, my son, listen
to me. Do exactly as I tell you. 9 Go out to the flocks, and
bring me two fine young goats. I'll use them to prepare
your father's favorite dish. 10 Then take the food to your
father so he can eat it and bless you before he dies."
11 "But look," Jacob replied to Rebekah, "my brother,
Esau, is a hairy man, and my skin is smooth. 12 What if
my father touches me? He'll see that I'm trying to trick
him, and then he'll curse me instead of blessing me."
13 But his mother replied, "Then let the curse fall on
me, my son! Just do what I tell you. Go out and get the
goats for me!"
14 So Jacob went out and got the young goats for his
mother. Rebekah took them and prepared a delicious
meal, just the way Isaac liked it. 15 Then she took Es-
au's favorite clothes, which were there in the house,
and gave them to her younger son, Jacob. 16 She cov-
ered his arms and the smooth part of his neck with
the skin of the young goats. 17 Then she gave Jacob the
delicious meal, including freshly baked bread.
18 So Jacob took the food to his father. "My father?"
he said.
"Yes, my son," Isaac answered. "Who are you—
Esau or Jacob?"
19 Jacob replied, "It's Esau, your firstborn son. I've
done as you told me. Here is the wild game. Now sit
up and eat it so you can give me your blessing."
20 Isaac asked, "How did you find it so quickly, my
son?"
"The LORD your God put it in my path!" Jacob replied.
21 Then Isaac said to Jacob, "Come closer so I can
touch you and make sure that you really are Esau."
22 So Jacob went closer to his father, and Isaac touched
him. "The voice is Jacob's, but the hands are Esau's,"
Isaac said. 23 But he did not recognize Jacob, because
Jacob's hands felt hairy just like Esau's. So Isaac pre-
pared to bless Jacob. 24 "But are you really my son
Esau?" he asked.
"Yes, I am," Jacob replied.
25 Then Isaac said, "Now, my son, bring me the wild
game. Let me eat it, and then I will give you my bless-
ing." So Jacob took the food to his father, and Isaac
ate it. He also drank the wine that Jacob served him.
26 Then Isaac said to Jacob, "Please come a little closer
and kiss me, my son."
27 So Jacob went over and kissed him. And when
Isaac caught the smell of his clothes, he was finally
convinced, and he blessed his son. He said, "Ah! The
smell of my son is like the smell of the outdoors, which
the LORD has blessed!

28 "From the dew of heaven
  and the richness of the earth,
may God always give you abundant harvests of
  grain
  and bountiful new wine.
29 May many nations become your servants,
  and may they bow down to you.
May you be the master over your brothers,
  and may your mother's sons bow down to you.

26:25 built an altar. Isaac followed his father's practice of building an altar to worship God in a place where God appeared to him (12:7-8; 13:18).

26:30 covenant feast. To eat together signified friendship and peace. This bound the two parties to the oath they had sworn.

27:1-4 Isaac asked his son Esau to prepare a special meal of wild game so he could pronounce his blessing upon him.

27:5 Rebekah overheard. God had already told Rebekah that the inheritance would go to her younger son, Jacob (25:23). She eavesdropped and schemed to make sure this would happen.

27:29 over your brothers. The customary blessing included the fact that the elder son would be "lord over" his brothers. As Isaac spoke these words to his younger son, Jacob, he fulfilled what God had promised (25:23). Once spoken, these words could not be taken back.

All who curse you will be cursed,
and all who bless you will be blessed."

30 As soon as Isaac had finished blessing Jacob, and al-
most before Jacob had left his father, Esau returned from
his hunt. 31 Esau prepared a delicious meal and brought
it to his father. Then he said, "Sit up, my father, and eat
my wild game so you can give me your blessing."
32 But Isaac asked him, "Who are you?"
Esau replied, "It's your son, your firstborn son,
Esau."
33 Isaac began to tremble uncontrollably and said,
"Then who just served me wild game? I have already
eaten it, and I blessed him just before you came. And
yes, that blessing must stand!"
34 When Esau heard his father's words, he let out
a loud and bitter cry. "Oh my father, what about me?
Bless me, too!" he begged.
35 But Isaac said, "Your brother was here, and he
tricked me. He has taken away your blessing."
36 Esau exclaimed, "No wonder his name is Jacob,
for now he has cheated me twice.* First he took my
rights as the firstborn, and now he has stolen my
blessing. Oh, haven't you saved even one blessing for
me?"
37 Isaac said to Esau, "I have made Jacob your mas-
ter and have declared that all his brothers will be his
servants. I have guaranteed him an abundance of
grain and wine—what is left for me to give you, my
son?"
38 Esau pleaded, "But do you have only one bless-
ing? Oh my father, bless me, too!" Then Esau broke
down and wept.
39 Finally, his father, Isaac, said to him,

"You will live away from the richness of the earth,
and away from the dew of the heaven above.
40 You will live by your sword,
and you will serve your brother.
But when you decide to break free,
you will shake his yoke from your neck."

JACOB FLEES TO PADDAN-ARAM

41 From that time on, Esau hated Jacob because their
father had given Jacob the blessing. And Esau began
to scheme: "I will soon be mourning my father's death.
Then I will kill my brother, Jacob."
42 But Rebekah heard about Esau's plans. So she
sent for Jacob and told him, "Listen, Esau is consoling
himself by plotting to kill you. 43 So listen carefully,
my son. Get ready and flee to my brother, Laban, in
Haran. 44 Stay there with him until your brother cools
off. 45 When he calms down and forgets what you
have done to him, I will send for you to come back.
Why should I lose both of you in one day?"
46 Then Rebekah said to Isaac, "I'm sick and tired of
these local Hittite women! I would rather die than see
Jacob marry one of them."

28 So Isaac called for Jacob, blessed him, and said,
"You must not marry any of these Canaanite
women. 2 Instead, go at once to Paddan-aram, to the
house of your grandfather Bethuel, and marry one of
your uncle Laban's daughters. 3 May God Almighty*
bless you and give you many children. And may your
descendants multiply and become many nations!
4 May God pass on to you and your descendants* the
blessings he promised to Abraham. May you own this
land where you are now living as a foreigner, for God
gave this land to Abraham."
5 So Isaac sent Jacob away, and he went to Pad-
dan-aram to stay with his uncle Laban, his mother's
brother, the son of Bethuel the Aramean.
6 Esau knew that his father, Isaac, had blessed Jacob
and sent him to Paddan-aram to find a wife, and that
he had warned Jacob, "You must not marry a Canaan-
ite woman." 7 He also knew that Jacob had obeyed his
parents and gone to Paddan-aram. 8 It was now very
clear to Esau that his father did not like the local Ca-
naanite women. 9 So Esau visited his uncle Ishmael's
family and married one of Ishmael's daughters, in
addition to the wives he already had. His new wife's
name was Mahalath. She was the sister of Nebaioth
and the daughter of Ishmael, Abraham's son.

JACOB'S DREAM AT BETHEL

10 Meanwhile, Jacob left Beersheba and traveled to-
ward Haran. 11 At sundown he arrived at a good place
to set up camp and stopped there for the night. Jacob
found a stone to rest his head against and lay down
to sleep. 12 As he slept, he dreamed of a stairway that
reached from the earth up to heaven. And he saw the
angels of God going up and down the stairway.
13 At the top of the stairway stood the LORD, and
he said, "I am the LORD, the God of your grandfather
Abraham, and the God of your father, Isaac. The
ground you are lying on belongs to you. I am giving
it to you and your descendants. 14 Your descendants
will be as numerous as the dust of the earth! They will
spread out in all directions—to the west and the east,
to the north and the south. And all the families of the
earth will be blessed through you and your descen-
dants. 15 What's more, I am with you, and I will protect
you wherever you go. One day I will bring you back
to this land. I will not leave you until I have finished
giving you everything I have promised you."
16 Then Jacob awoke from his sleep and said, "Surely
the LORD is in this place, and I wasn't even aware of
it!" 17 But he was also afraid and said, "What an awe-
some place this is! It is none other than the house of
God, the very gateway to heaven!"
18 The next morning Jacob got up very early. He
took the stone he had rested his head against, and he
set it upright as a memorial pillar. Then he poured
olive oil over it. 19 He named that place Bethel (which
means "house of God"), although it was previously
called Luz.

27:36 *Jacob* sounds like the Hebrew words for "heel" and "deceiver." **28:3** Hebrew *El-Shaddai.* **28:4** Hebrew *seed;* also in 28:13, 14.

27:34 loud and bitter cry. The gravity of the loss of his father's blessing overwhelmed Esau.

27:43-45 Because of the deceit of Jacob and his mother, he was forced to flee to escape Esau's wrath. Rebekah would never see him again.

28:11 a stone to rest. Traditionally seen as a pillow, this stone may actually have been a sort of good luck charm in Jacob's thinking.

28:12-13 In Jacob's dream, God used a familiar picture from pagan religion, a stairway linking heaven and earth, to invite Jacob into a relationship with Him.

28:15 I will not leave you. It did not matter where Jacob went; the one true God would be with him.

28:18 memorial pillar. At this location, Jacob's grandfather, Abraham, had built an altar and called on the name of the Lord (12:8). Jacob took the stone that he had placed near his head and consecrated it with oil as a memorial.

20 Then Jacob made this vow: "If God will indeed be
with me and protect me on this journey, and if he will
provide me with food and clothing, 21 and if I return
safely to my father's home, then the LORD will certain-
ly be my God. 22 And this memorial pillar I have set
up will become a place for worshiping God, and I will
present to God a tenth of everything he gives me."

JACOB ARRIVES AT PADDAN-ARAM

29 Then Jacob hurried on, finally arriving in the
land of the east. 2 He saw a well in the distance.
Three flocks of sheep and goats lay in an open field
beside it, waiting to be watered. But a heavy stone
covered the mouth of the well.
3 It was the custom there to wait for all the flocks
to arrive before removing the stone and watering
the animals. Afterward the stone would be placed
back over the mouth of the well. 4 Jacob went over to
the shepherds and asked, "Where are you from, my
friends?"
"We are from Haran," they answered.
5 "Do you know a man there named Laban, the
grandson of Nahor?" he asked.
"Yes, we do," they replied.
6 "Is he doing well?" Jacob asked.
"Yes, he's well," they answered. "Look, here comes
his daughter Rachel with the flock now."
7 Jacob said, "Look, it's still broad daylight—too
early to round up the animals. Why don't you water
the sheep and goats so they can get back out to pas-
ture?"
8 "We can't water the animals until all the flocks
have arrived," they replied. "Then the shepherds
move the stone from the mouth of the well, and we
water all the sheep and goats."
9 Jacob was still talking with them when Rachel ar-
rived with her father's flock, for she was a shepherd.
10 And because Rachel was his cousin—the daughter
of Laban, his mother's brother—and because the
sheep and goats belonged to his uncle Laban, Jacob
went over to the well and moved the stone from its
mouth and watered his uncle's flock. 11 Then Jacob
kissed Rachel, and he wept aloud. 12 He explained to
Rachel that he was her cousin on her father's side—
the son of her aunt Rebekah. So Rachel quickly ran
and told her father, Laban.
13 As soon as Laban heard that his nephew Jacob
had arrived, he ran out to meet him. He embraced and
kissed him and brought him home. When Jacob had
told him his story, 14 Laban exclaimed, "You really are
my own flesh and blood!"

JACOB MARRIES LEAH AND RACHEL

After Jacob had stayed with Laban for about a month,
15 Laban said to him, "You shouldn't work for me with-
out pay just because we are relatives. Tell me how
much your wages should be."
16 Now Laban had two daughters. The older daugh-
ter was named Leah, and the younger one was Ra-

LOVE AT FIRST SIGHT

1. What do you know about how your parents met and fell in love?

GENESIS 29:1-14

2. Why was it important to Jacob to meet a woman who was his relative? What does this suggest about Christians dating non-Christians?
3. How was Jacob's kindness to Rachel costly and extraordinary? Why would that kindness earn him favor from Rachel?
4. What are you looking for in a potential husband or wife? What principles can you learn from Jacob's actions? From Rachel's actions?

chel. 17 There was no sparkle in Leah's eyes,* but Ra-
chel had a beautiful figure and a lovely face. 18 Since
Jacob was in love with Rachel, he told her father, "I'll
work for you for seven years if you'll give me Rachel,
your younger daughter, as my wife."
19 "Agreed!" Laban replied. "I'd rather give her to you
than to anyone else. Stay and work with me." 20 So Jacob
worked seven years to pay for Rachel. But his love for
her was so strong that it seemed to him but a few days.
21 Finally, the time came for him to marry her. "I
have fulfilled my agreement," Jacob said to Laban.
"Now give me my wife so I can sleep with her."
22 So Laban invited everyone in the neighborhood
and prepared a wedding feast. 23 But that night, when
it was dark, Laban took Leah to Jacob, and he slept
with her. 24 (Laban had given Leah a servant, Zilpah,
to be her maid.)
25 But when Jacob woke up in the morning—it was
Leah! "What have you done to me?" Jacob raged at La-
ban. "I worked seven years for Rachel! Why have you
tricked me?"
26 "It's not our custom here to marry off a young-
er daughter ahead of the firstborn," Laban replied.
27 "But wait until the bridal week is over; then we'll
give you Rachel, too—provided you promise to work
another seven years for me."
28 So Jacob agreed to work seven more years. A
week after Jacob had married Leah, Laban gave him
Rachel, too. 29 (Laban gave Rachel a servant, Bilhah, to
be her maid.) 30 So Jacob slept with Rachel, too, and he
loved her much more than Leah. He then stayed and
worked for Laban the additional seven years.

JACOB'S MANY CHILDREN

31 When the LORD saw that Leah was unloved, he en-
abled her to have children, but Rachel could not con-
ceive. 32 So Leah became pregnant and gave birth to a
son. She named him Reuben,* for she said, "The LORD

29:17 Or *Leah had dull eyes,* or *Leah had soft eyes.* The meaning of the Hebrew is uncertain. 29:32 *Reuben* means "Look, a son!" It also sounds like the Hebrew for "He has seen my misery."

28:22 this . . . pillar. The stone would be a reminder of Jacob's meeting with God at Bethel. He never forgot this meeting and its significance.
29:21-25 Jacob did not specify that it was Rachel, the younger daughter, whom he wanted to marry, and Laban took advantage of him. In an ironic twist, the rights of the firstborn were turned on Jacob, and he received Laban's firstborn daughter, Leah, as his wife.
29:28 Laban gave . . . Rachel. At least Jacob did not have to wait another seven years before taking Rachel as his wife. But he had to pay her bride price by working for Laban for seven more years (v. 30).
29:32 Reuben . . . misery. Leah was unloved by Jacob, so she lived a difficult life. Reuben's name reflected that.

has noticed my misery, and now my husband will love
me."
33 She soon became pregnant again and gave birth
to another son. She named him Simeon,* for she said,
"The LORD heard that I was unloved and has given me
another son."
34 Then she became pregnant a third time and gave
birth to another son. He was named Levi,* for she
said, "Surely this time my husband will feel affection
for me, since I have given him three sons!"
35 Once again Leah became pregnant and gave birth
to another son. She named him Judah,* for she said,
"Now I will praise the LORD!" And then she stopped
having children.

30 When Rachel saw that she wasn't having any
children for Jacob, she became jealous of her
sister. She pleaded with Jacob, "Give me children, or
I'll die!"
2 Then Jacob became furious with Rachel. "Am I
God?" he asked. "He's the one who has kept you from
having children!"
3 Then Rachel told him, "Take my maid, Bilhah,
and sleep with her. She will bear children for me,*
and through her I can have a family, too." 4 So Ra-
chel gave her servant, Bilhah, to Jacob as a wife,
and he slept with her. 5 Bilhah became pregnant
and presented him with a son. 6 Rachel named
him Dan,* for she said, "God has vindicated me! He
has heard my request and given me a son." 7 Then
Bilhah became pregnant again and gave Jacob a
second son. 8 Rachel named him Naphtali,* for she
said, "I have struggled hard with my sister, and I'm
winning!"
9 Meanwhile, Leah realized that she wasn't getting
pregnant anymore, so she took her servant, Zilpah,
and gave her to Jacob as a wife. 10 Soon Zilpah pre-
sented him with a son. 11 Leah named him Gad,* for
she said, "How fortunate I am!" 12 Then Zilpah gave
Jacob a second son. 13 And Leah named him Asher,*
for she said, "What joy is mine! Now the other women
will celebrate with me."
14 One day during the wheat harvest, Reuben found
some mandrakes growing in a field and brought
them to his mother, Leah. Rachel begged Leah, "Please
give me some of your son's mandrakes."
15 But Leah angrily replied, "Wasn't it enough that
you stole my husband? Now will you steal my son's
mandrakes, too?"
Rachel answered, "I will let Jacob sleep with you
tonight if you give me some of the mandrakes."
16 So that evening, as Jacob was coming home from
the fields, Leah went out to meet him. "You must come
and sleep with me tonight!" she said. "I have paid for
you with some mandrakes that my son found." So that
night he slept with Leah. 17 And God answered Leah's
prayers. She became pregnant again and gave birth
to a fifth son for Jacob. 18 She named him Issachar,*
for she said, "God has rewarded me for giving my ser-
vant to my husband as a wife." 19 Then Leah became
pregnant again and gave birth to a sixth son for Ja-
cob. 20 She named him Zebulun,* for she said, "God has
given me a good reward. Now my husband will treat
me with respect, for I have given him six sons." 21 Later
she gave birth to a daughter and named her Dinah.
22 Then God remembered Rachel's plight and an-
swered her prayers by enabling her to have children.
23 She became pregnant and gave birth to a son. "God
has removed my disgrace," she said. 24 And she named
him Joseph,* for she said, "May the LORD add yet an-
other son to my family."

JACOB'S WEALTH INCREASES

25 Soon after Rachel had given birth to Joseph, Jacob
said to Laban, "Please release me so I can go home
to my own country. 26 Let me take my wives and chil-
dren, for I have earned them by serving you, and let
me be on my way. You certainly know how hard I
have worked for you."
27 "Please listen to me," Laban replied. "I have be-
come wealthy, for* the LORD has blessed me because
of you. 28 Tell me how much I owe you. Whatever it is,
I'll pay it."
29 Jacob replied, "You know how hard I've worked
for you, and how your flocks and herds have grown
under my care. 30 You had little indeed before I came,
but your wealth has increased enormously. The LORD
has blessed you through everything I've done. But
now, what about me? When can I start providing for
my own family?"
31 "What wages do you want?" Laban asked again.
Jacob replied, "Don't give me anything. Just do this
one thing, and I'll continue to tend and watch over
your flocks. 32 Let me inspect your flocks today and
remove all the sheep and goats that are speckled or
spotted, along with all the black sheep. Give these to
me as my wages. 33 In the future, when you check on
the animals you have given me as my wages, you'll
see that I have been honest. If you find in my flock any
goats without speckles or spots, or any sheep that are
not black, you will know that I have stolen them from
you."
34 "All right," Laban replied. "It will be as you say."
35 But that very day Laban went out and removed the
male goats that were streaked and spotted, all the
female goats that were speckled and spotted or had

29:33 *Simeon* probably means "one who hears." 29:34 *Levi* sounds like a Hebrew term that means "being attached" or "feeling affection for." 29:35 *Judah* is related to the Hebrew term for "praise." 30:3 Hebrew *bear children on my knees.* 30:6 *Dan* means "he judged" or "he vindicated." 30:8 *Naphtali* means "my struggle." 30:11 *Gad* means "good fortune." 30:13 *Asher* means "happy." 30:18 *Issachar* sounds like a Hebrew term that means "reward." 30:20 *Zebulun* probably means "honor." 30:24 *Joseph* means "may he add." 30:27 Or *I have learned by divination that.*

30:1 I'll die! Despite enjoying Jacob's favor, Rachel felt that she needed to have children or her life would not be worth living.

30:2 Am I God? Jacob, the schemer and manipulator, could do nothing to bring about the blessing of children. That gift was in God's hands.

30:3-4 If a man's wife could not conceive, it was an ancient custom for him to sleep with her female servant to ensure the birth of a male heir. Jacob did not actually marry Bilhah; she was a concubine through whom Rachel presented Jacob with children.

30:22-23 Children were a sign of God's favor; a woman who could not have children was disgraced. For Rachel to finally give birth was a time of great joy.

30:26 let me be on my way. Jacob wanted to return to his homeland and his father's house, from which he had fled many years before (28:21; 31:13).

30:27 blessed me because of you. Jacob's hard work, marriage to Laban's daughters, and their many offspring had been a source of great blessing to Laban. This may also refer to the prophecy of 12:3.

30:35-39 Jacob agreed to stay on with Laban if he would let him keep some of the sheep and goats in his flock. Jacob selectively bred the livestock to increase his holdings.

white patches, and all the black sheep. He placed them in the care of his own sons, 36 who took them a three-days' journey from where Jacob was. Meanwhile, Jacob stayed and cared for the rest of Laban's flock.

37 Then Jacob took some fresh branches from poplar, almond, and plane trees and peeled off strips of bark, making white streaks on them. 38 Then he placed these peeled branches in the watering troughs where the flocks came to drink, for that was where they mated. 39 And when they mated in front of the white-streaked branches, they gave birth to young that were streaked, speckled, and spotted. 40 Jacob separated those lambs from Laban's flock. And at mating time he turned the flock to face Laban's animals that were streaked or black. This is how he built his own flock instead of increasing Laban's.

41 Whenever the stronger females were ready to mate, Jacob would place the peeled branches in the watering troughs in front of them. Then they would mate in front of the branches. 42 But he didn't do this with the weaker ones, so the weaker lambs belonged to Laban, and the stronger ones were Jacob's. 43 As a result, Jacob became very wealthy, with large flocks of sheep and goats, female and male servants, and many camels and donkeys.

JACOB FLEES FROM LABAN

31 But Jacob soon learned that Laban's sons were grumbling about him. "Jacob has robbed our father of everything!" they said. "He has gained all his wealth at our father's expense." 2 And Jacob began to notice a change in Laban's attitude toward him.

3 Then the LORD said to Jacob, "Return to the land of your father and grandfather and to your relatives there, and I will be with you."

4 So Jacob called Rachel and Leah out to the field where he was watching his flock. 5 He said to them, "I have noticed that your father's attitude toward me has changed. But the God of my father has been with me. 6 You know how hard I have worked for your father, 7 but he has cheated me, changing my wages ten times. But God has not allowed him to do me any harm. 8 For if he said, 'The speckled animals will be your wages,' the whole flock began to produce speckled young. And when he changed his mind and said, 'The striped animals will be your wages,' then the whole flock produced striped young. 9 In this way, God has taken your father's animals and given them to me.

10 "One time during the mating season, I had a dream and saw that the male goats mating with the females were streaked, speckled, and spotted. 11 Then in my dream, the angel of God said to me, 'Jacob!' And I replied, 'Yes, here I am.'

12 "The angel said, 'Look up, and you will see that only the streaked, speckled, and spotted males are mating with the females of your flock. For I have seen how Laban has treated you. 13 I am the God who appeared to you at Bethel,* the place where you anointed the pillar of stone and made your vow to me. Now get ready and leave this country and return to the land of your birth.'"

14 Rachel and Leah responded, "That's fine with us! We won't inherit any of our father's wealth anyway. 15 He has reduced our rights to those of foreign women. And after he sold us, he wasted the money you paid him for us. 16 All the wealth God has given you from our father legally belongs to us and our children. So go ahead and do whatever God has told you."

17 So Jacob put his wives and children on camels, 18 and he drove all his livestock in front of him. He packed all the belongings he had acquired in Paddan-aram and set out for the land of Canaan, where his father, Isaac, lived. 19 At the time they left, Laban was some distance away, shearing his sheep. Rachel stole her father's household idols and took them with her. 20 Jacob outwitted Laban the Aramean, for they set out secretly and never told Laban they were leaving. 21 So Jacob took all his possessions with him and crossed the Euphrates River,* heading for the hill country of Gilead.

LABAN PURSUES JACOB

22 Three days later, Laban was told that Jacob had fled. 23 So he gathered a group of his relatives and set out in hot pursuit. He caught up with Jacob seven days later in the hill country of Gilead. 24 But the previous night God had appeared to Laban the Aramean in a dream and told him, "I'm warning you—leave Jacob alone!"

25 Laban caught up with Jacob as he was camped in the hill country of Gilead, and he set up his camp not far from Jacob's. 26 "What do you mean by deceiving me like this?" Laban demanded. "How dare you drag my daughters away like prisoners of war? 27 Why did you slip away secretly? Why did you deceive me? And why didn't you say you wanted to leave? I would have given you a farewell feast, with singing and music, accompanied by tambourines and harps. 28 Why didn't you let me kiss my daughters and grandchildren and tell them good-bye? You have acted very foolishly! 29 I could destroy you, but the God of your father appeared to me last night and warned me, 'Leave Jacob alone!' 30 I can understand your feeling that you must go, and your intense longing for your father's home. But why have you stolen my gods?"

31 "I rushed away because I was afraid," Jacob answered. "I thought you would take your daughters from me by force. 32 But as for your gods, see if you can find them, and let the person who has taken them die! And if you find anything else that belongs to you, identify it before all these relatives of ours, and I will give it back!" But Jacob did not know that Rachel had stolen the household idols.

33 Laban went first into Jacob's tent to search there, then into Leah's, and then the tents of the two servant wives—but he found nothing. Finally, he went into Rachel's tent. 34 But Rachel had taken the household idols and hidden them in her camel saddle, and now she was sitting on them. When Laban had thoroughly searched her tent without finding them, 35 she said to

31:13 As in Greek version and an Aramaic Targum; Hebrew reads *the God of Bethel.* **31:21** Hebrew *the river.*

31:3 Return. After he had been away for 20 years (31:41), Jacob was told by the Lord that it was time to return to Canaan.

31:19 household idols. People kept small images of idols in their homes for protection. The gods Rachel stole from her father were objects of trust for the journey.

31:34 in her . . . saddle. These "gods" that Rachel had taken were mere trinkets.

31:35 I don't get up. Rachel used the excuse of menstruation (considered unclean) as a way of keeping her father from looking through the saddle on which she was sitting.

her father, "Please, sir, forgive me if I don't get up for
you. I'm having my monthly period." So Laban con-
tinued his search, but he could not find the household
idols.
36 Then Jacob became very angry, and he chal-
lenged Laban. "What's my crime?" he demanded.
"What have I done wrong to make you chase after me
as though I were a criminal? 37 You have rummaged
through everything I own. Now show me what you
found that belongs to you! Set it out here in front of
us, before our relatives, for all to see. Let them judge
between us!
38 "For twenty years I have been with you, caring
for your flocks. In all that time your sheep and goats
never miscarried. In all those years I never used a sin-
gle ram of yours for food. 39 If any were attacked and
killed by wild animals, I never showed you the car-
cass and asked you to reduce the count of your flock.
No, I took the loss myself! You made me pay for every
stolen animal, whether it was taken in broad daylight
or in the dark of night.
40 "I worked for you through the scorching heat of
the day and through cold and sleepless nights. 41 Yes,
for twenty years I slaved in your house! I worked for
fourteen years earning your two daughters, and then
six more years for your flock. And you changed my
wages ten times! 42 In fact, if the God of my father had
not been on my side—the God of Abraham and the
fearsome God of Isaac*—you would have sent me
away empty-handed. But God has seen your abuse
and my hard work. That is why he appeared to you
last night and rebuked you!"

JACOB'S TREATY WITH LABAN

43 Then Laban replied to Jacob, "These women are
my daughters, these children are my grandchildren,
and these flocks are my flocks—in fact, everything
you see is mine. But what can I do now about my
daughters and their children? 44 So come, let's make
a covenant, you and I, and it will be a witness to our
commitment."
45 So Jacob took a stone and set it up as a monument.
46 Then he told his family members, "Gather some
stones." So they gathered stones and piled them in a
heap. Then Jacob and Laban sat down beside the pile
of stones to eat a covenant meal. 47 To commemorate
the event, Laban called the place Jegar-sahadutha
(which means "witness pile" in Aramaic), and Jacob
called it Galeed (which means "witness pile" in He-
brew).
48 Then Laban declared, "This pile of stones will
stand as a witness to remind us of the covenant we
have made today." This explains why it was called
Galeed—"Witness Pile." 49 But it was also called Miz-
pah (which means "watchtower"), for Laban said,
"May the LORD keep watch between us to make sure
that we keep this covenant when we are out of each
other's sight. 50 If you mistreat my daughters or if
you marry other wives, God will see it even if no one
else does. He is a witness to this covenant between
us.
51 "See this pile of stones," Laban continued, "and see
this monument I have set between us. 52 They stand
between us as witnesses of our vows. I will never pass
this pile of stones to harm you, and you must never
pass these stones or this monument to harm me. 53 I
call on the God of our ancestors—the God of your
grandfather Abraham and the God of my grandfather
Nahor—to serve as a judge between us."
So Jacob took an oath before the fearsome God of
his father, Isaac,* to respect the boundary line. 54 Then
Jacob offered a sacrifice to God there on the mountain
and invited everyone to a covenant feast. After they
had eaten, they spent the night on the mountain.
55*Laban got up early the next morning, and he
kissed his grandchildren and his daughters and
blessed them. Then he left and returned home.

32 1*As Jacob started on his way again, angels of
God came to meet him. 2 When Jacob saw them,
he exclaimed, "This is God's camp!" So he named the
place Mahanaim.*

JACOB SENDS GIFTS TO ESAU

3 Then Jacob sent messengers ahead to his brother,
Esau, who was living in the region of Seir in the land
of Edom. 4 He told them, "Give this message to my mas-
ter Esau: 'Humble greetings from your servant Jacob.
Until now I have been living with Uncle Laban, 5 and
now I own cattle, donkeys, flocks of sheep and goats,
and many servants, both men and women. I have sent
these messengers to inform my lord of my coming,
hoping that you will be friendly to me.'"
6 After delivering the message, the messengers re-
turned to Jacob and reported, "We met your brother,
Esau, and he is already on his way to meet you—with
an army of 400 men!" 7 Jacob was terrified at the news.
He divided his household, along with the flocks and
herds and camels, into two groups. 8 He thought, "If
Esau meets one group and attacks it, perhaps the oth-
er group can escape."
9 Then Jacob prayed, "O God of my grandfather
Abraham, and God of my father, Isaac—O LORD, you
told me, 'Return to your own land and to your rela-
tives.' And you promised me, 'I will treat you kindly.'
10 I am not worthy of all the unfailing love and faith-
fulness you have shown to me, your servant. When I
left home and crossed the Jordan River, I owned noth-
ing except a walking stick. Now my household fills
two large camps! 11 O LORD, please rescue me from the
hand of my brother, Esau. I am afraid that he is com-
ing to attack me, along with my wives and children.
12 But you promised me, 'I will surely treat you kindly,
and I will multiply your descendants until they be-
come as numerous as the sands along the seashore—
too many to count.'"

31:42 Or *and the Fear of Isaac.* 31:53 Or *the Fear of his father, Isaac.* 31:55 Verse 31:55 is numbered 32:1 in Hebrew text. 32:1 Verses 32:1-32 are numbered 32:2-33 in Hebrew text. 32:2 *Mahanaim* means "two camps."

31:51-52 pile of stones . . . monument. Jacob and Laban made a pile of stones to symbolize their agreement.

31:54 sacrifice . . . covenant feast. Covenants (or agreements) in Old Testament days were sealed with a sacrifice and a shared meal (Ex. 24:5-8, 11).

32:2 Mahanaim. The name Jacob gave this place means "two camps." He knew he would soon meet his brother, Esau, who had wanted to kill him many years before (27:41-45).

32:6 on his way to meet you. The word that Esau was headed his way with 400 men must have been a source of anxiety to Jacob.

32:9 Jacob prayed. Jacob sought God's help. This is the first time we have seen him in a posture of prayer since he left Bethel (28:20-22).

32:12 as the sands along the seashore. God had promised Abraham, Isaac, and Jacob that they would have descendants too numerous to count (22:17; 26:4). Jacob was remembering God's promise to him as well (28:14).

WRESTLING WITH GOD

1. What is your nickname? How did you get it? Do you like it?

GENESIS 32:22-32

2. Why did Jacob wrestle with God? Why did God wrestle with Jacob?
3. God could have destroyed Jacob, but He chose to let him go. What does this show us about God?
4. Jacob sought God's blessing. How did God bless him?
5. Are you wrestling with God? About what?
6. How does Jacob's perseverance in seeking God's blessing give you an example to follow in your own life?

---

13 Jacob stayed where he was for the night. Then he selected these gifts from his possessions to present to his brother, Esau: 14 200 female goats, 20 male goats, 200 ewes, 20 rams, 15 30 female camels with their young, 40 cows, 10 bulls, 20 female donkeys, and 10 male donkeys. 16 He divided these animals into herds and assigned each to different servants. Then he told his servants, "Go ahead of me with the animals, but keep some distance between the herds."

17 He gave these instructions to the men leading the first group: "When my brother, Esau, meets you, he will ask, 'Whose servants are you? Where are you going? Who owns these animals?' 18 You must reply, 'They belong to your servant Jacob, but they are a gift for his master Esau. Look, he is coming right behind us.'"

19 Jacob gave the same instructions to the second and third herdsmen and to all who followed behind the herds: "You must say the same thing to Esau when you meet him. 20 And be sure to say, 'Look, your servant Jacob is right behind us.'"

Jacob thought, "I will try to appease him by sending gifts ahead of me. When I see him in person, perhaps he will be friendly to me." 21 So the gifts were sent on ahead, while Jacob himself spent that night in the camp.

JACOB WRESTLES WITH GOD

22 During the night Jacob got up and took his two wives, his two servant wives, and his eleven sons and crossed the Jabbok River with them. 23 After taking them to the other side, he sent over all his possessions.

24 This left Jacob all alone in the camp, and a man came and wrestled with him until the dawn began to break. 25 When the man saw that he would not win the match, he touched Jacob's hip and wrenched it out of its socket. 26 Then the man said, "Let me go, for the dawn is breaking!"

But Jacob said, "I will not let you go unless you bless me."

27 "What is your name?" the man asked.

He replied, "Jacob."

28 "Your name will no longer be Jacob," the man told him. "From now on you will be called Israel,* because you have fought with God and with men and have won."

29 "Please tell me your name," Jacob said.

"Why do you want to know my name?" the man replied. Then he blessed Jacob there.

30 Jacob named the place Peniel (which means "face of God"), for he said, "I have seen God face to face, yet my life has been spared." 31 The sun was rising as Jacob left Peniel,* and he was limping because of the injury to his hip. 32 (Even today the people of Israel don't eat the tendon near the hip socket because of what happened that night when the man strained the tendon of Jacob's hip.)

JACOB AND ESAU MAKE PEACE

33 Then Jacob looked up and saw Esau coming with his 400 men. So he divided the children among Leah, Rachel, and his two servant wives. 2 He put the servant wives and their children at the front, Leah and her children next, and Rachel and Joseph last. 3 Then Jacob went on ahead. As he approached his brother, he bowed to the ground seven times before him. 4 Then Esau ran to meet him and embraced him, threw his arms around his neck, and kissed him. And they both wept.

5 Then Esau looked at the women and children and asked, "Who are these people with you?"

"These are the children God has graciously given to me, your servant," Jacob replied. 6 Then the servant wives came forward with their children and bowed before him. 7 Next came Leah with her children, and they bowed before him. Finally, Joseph and Rachel came forward and bowed before him.

8 "And what were all the flocks and herds I met as I came?" Esau asked.

Jacob replied, "They are a gift, my lord, to ensure your friendship."

9 "My brother, I have plenty," Esau answered. "Keep what you have for yourself."

10 But Jacob insisted, "No, if I have found favor with you, please accept this gift from me. And what a relief to see your friendly smile. It is like seeing the face of God! 11 Please take this gift I have brought you, for God has been very gracious to me. I have more than enough." And because Jacob insisted, Esau finally accepted the gift.

12 "Well," Esau said, "let's be going. I will lead the way."

13 But Jacob replied, "You can see, my lord, that some of the children are very young, and the flocks and herds have their young, too. If they are driven too hard, even for one day, all the animals could die. 14 Please, my lord, go ahead of your servant. We will follow slowly, at a pace that is comfortable for the livestock and the children. I will meet you at Seir."

32:28 *Jacob* sounds like the Hebrew words for "heel" and "deceiver." *Israel* means "God fights." **32:31** Hebrew *Penuel,* a variant spelling of Peniel.

32:24-25 Jacob was known as a "heel grabber." Now he attempted to twist God's arm. But God revealed that He had the ultimate power.

32:28 Israel. Not only was Jacob given a new walk (his limp reminded him of God's power, v. 31); he was given a new name, Israel, signifying the nation that would spring from his descendants.

32:30 Peniel. The name of the place where Jacob wrestled with God means "face of God." He had been graced with God's presence and blessing.

33:3 bowed. Jacob's show of honor was to cool his brother's anger.

33:4 Esau ran to meet him. All Jacob's actions to pacify Esau were not needed. Esau threw his arms around the brother who had wronged him.

15 "All right," Esau said, "but at least let me assign
some of my men to guide and protect you."
Jacob responded, "That's not necessary. It's enough
that you've received me warmly, my lord!"
16 So Esau turned around and started back to Seir
that same day. 17 Jacob, on the other hand, traveled on
to Succoth. There he built himself a house and made
shelters for his livestock. That is why the place was
named Succoth (which means "shelters").
18 Later, having traveled all the way from Paddan-
aram, Jacob arrived safely at the town of Shechem,
in the land of Canaan. There he set up camp outside
the town. 19 Jacob bought the plot of land where he
camped from the family of Hamor, the father of She-
chem, for 100 pieces of silver.* 20 And there he built an
altar and named it El-Elohe-Israel.*

REVENGE AGAINST SHECHEM

34 One day Dinah, the daughter of Jacob and Leah,
went to visit some of the young women who
lived in the area. 2 But when the local prince, Shechem
son of Hamor the Hivite, saw Dinah, he seized her and
raped her. 3 But then he fell in love with her, and he
tried to win her affection with tender words. 4 He said
to his father, Hamor, "Get me this young girl. I want to
marry her."
5 Soon Jacob heard that Shechem had defiled his
daughter, Dinah. But since his sons were out in the
fields herding his livestock, he said nothing until they
returned. 6 Hamor, Shechem's father, came to discuss
the matter with Jacob. 7 Meanwhile, Jacob's sons had
come in from the field as soon as they heard what
had happened. They were shocked and furious that
their sister had been raped. Shechem had done a dis-
graceful thing against Jacob's family,* something that
should never be done.
8 Hamor tried to speak with Jacob and his sons. "My
son Shechem is truly in love with your daughter," he
said. "Please let him marry her. 9 In fact, let's arrange
other marriages, too. You give us your daughters for
our sons, and we will give you our daughters for your
sons. 10 And you may live among us; the land is open
to you! Settle here and trade with us. And feel free to
buy property in the area."
11 Then Shechem himself spoke to Dinah's father
and brothers. "Please be kind to me, and let me mar-
ry her," he begged. "I will give you whatever you ask.
12 No matter what dowry or gift you demand, I will
gladly pay it—just give me the girl as my wife."
13 But since Shechem had defiled their sister, Dinah,
Jacob's sons responded deceitfully to Shechem and
his father, Hamor. 14 They said to them, "We couldn't
possibly allow this, because you're not circumcised. It
would be a disgrace for our sister to marry a man like
you! 15 But here is a solution. If every man among you
will be circumcised like we are, 16 then we will give
you our daughters, and we'll take your daughters for
ourselves. We will live among you and become one
people. 17 But if you don't agree to be circumcised, we
will take her and be on our way."
18 Hamor and his son Shechem agreed to their
proposal. 19 Shechem wasted no time in acting on
this request, for he wanted Jacob's daughter des-
perately. Shechem was a highly respected member
of his family, 20 and he went with his father, Hamor,
to present this proposal to the leaders at the town
gate.
21 "These men are our friends," they said. "Let's in-
vite them to live here among us and trade freely. Look,
the land is large enough to hold them. We can take
their daughters as wives and let them marry ours.
22 But they will consider staying here and becoming
one people with us only if all of our men are circum-
cised, just as they are. 23 But if we do this, all their live-
stock and possessions will eventually be ours. Come,
let's agree to their terms and let them settle here
among us."
24 So all the men in the town council agreed with
Hamor and Shechem, and every male in the town
was circumcised. 25 But three days later, when their
wounds were still sore, two of Jacob's sons, Simeon
and Levi, who were Dinah's full brothers, took their
swords and entered the town without opposition.
Then they slaughtered every male there, 26 including
Hamor and his son Shechem. They killed them with
their swords, then took Dinah from Shechem's house
and returned to their camp.
27 Meanwhile, the rest of Jacob's sons arrived. Find-
ing the men slaughtered, they plundered the town
because their sister had been defiled there. 28 They
seized all the flocks and herds and donkeys—every-
thing they could lay their hands on, both inside the
town and outside in the fields. 29 They looted all their
wealth and plundered their houses. They also took all
their little children and wives and led them away as
captives.
30 Afterward Jacob said to Simeon and Levi, "You
have ruined me! You've made me stink among all the
people of this land—among all the Canaanites and
Perizzites. We are so few that they will join forces and
crush us. I will be ruined, and my entire household
will be wiped out!"
31 "But why should we let him treat our sister like a
prostitute?" they retorted angrily.

JACOB'S RETURN TO BETHEL

35 Then God said to Jacob, "Get ready and move
to Bethel and settle there. Build an altar there
to the God who appeared to you when you fled from
your brother, Esau."

33:19 Hebrew *100 kesitahs;* the value or weight of the kesitah is no longer known. **33:20** *El-Elohe-Israel* means "God, the God of Israel."
34:7 Hebrew *a disgraceful thing in Israel.*

34:7 shocked and furious. Dinah's brothers responded like this because their entire family had been violated by Shechem's actions.
34:9 your daughters . . . our daughters. Rather than fight with the clan of Israel, Hamor proposed a diplomatic solution—intermarriage between his clan and the Israelites.
34:12 dowry or gift. In this culture, fathers received gifts in exchange for the hands of their daughters.
34:15 every man . . . will be circumcised. The demands of Dinah's brothers seemed reasonable. To these Canaanites, circumcision was just a way to close a lucrative business deal.
34:24 every male in the town. All the men of the city were willing to undergo this painful ritual in order to get their hands on the property of the Israelites.
34:25 slaughtered every male. When Simeon and Levi slaughtered the males of Shechem, they were avenging the violation of their entire family, not just of their sister. Simeon and Levi paid for this in later years when their father Jacob cursed their descendants because of this horrible act (49:5-7).
35:1 Bethel. This had been the site of Jacob's dream and his covenant with God (28:10-22).

2 So Jacob told everyone in his household, "Get rid
of all your pagan idols, purify yourselves, and put on
clean clothing. 3 We are now going to Bethel, where
I will build an altar to the God who answered my
prayers when I was in distress. He has been with me
wherever I have gone."
4 So they gave Jacob all their pagan idols and ear-
rings, and he buried them under the great tree near
Shechem. 5 As they set out, a terror from God spread
over the people in all the towns of that area, so no one
attacked Jacob's family.
6 Eventually, Jacob and his household arrived at
Luz (also called Bethel) in Canaan. 7 Jacob built an
altar there and named the place El-bethel (which
means "God of Bethel"), because God had appeared
to him there when he was fleeing from his brother,
Esau.
8 Soon after this, Rebekah's old nurse, Deborah,
died. She was buried beneath the oak tree in the val-
ley below Bethel. Ever since, the tree has been called
Allon-bacuth (which means "oak of weeping").
9 Now that Jacob had returned from Paddan-aram,
God appeared to him again at Bethel. God blessed
him, 10 saying, "Your name is Jacob, but you will not be
called Jacob any longer. From now on your name will
be Israel."* So God renamed him Israel.
11 Then God said, "I am El-Shaddai—'God Almighty.'
Be fruitful and multiply. You will become a great na-
tion, even many nations. Kings will be among your
descendants! 12 And I will give you the land I once
gave to Abraham and Isaac. Yes, I will give it to you
and your descendants after you." 13 Then God went up
from the place where he had spoken to Jacob.
14 Jacob set up a stone pillar to mark the place
where God had spoken to him. Then he poured wine
over it as an offering to God and anointed the pillar
with olive oil. 15 And Jacob named the place Bethel
(which means "house of God"), because God had spo-
ken to him there.

THE DEATHS OF RACHEL AND ISAAC

16 Leaving Bethel, Jacob and his clan moved on to-
ward Ephrath. But Rachel went into labor while
they were still some distance away. Her labor pains
were intense. 17 After a very hard delivery, the mid-
wife finally exclaimed, "Don't be afraid—you have
another son!" 18 Rachel was about to die, but with
her last breath she named the baby Ben-oni (which
means "son of my sorrow"). The baby's father, how-
ever, called him Benjamin (which means "son of my
right hand"). 19 So Rachel died and was buried on the
way to Ephrath (that is, Bethlehem). 20 Jacob set up a
stone monument over Rachel's grave, and it can be
seen there to this day.
21 Then Jacob* traveled on and camped beyond
Migdal-eder. 22 While he was living there, Reuben had
intercourse with Bilhah, his father's concubine, and
Jacob soon heard about it.
These are the names of the twelve sons of Jacob:
23 The sons of Leah were Reuben (Jacob's oldest son),
Simeon, Levi, Judah, Issachar, and Zebulun.
24 The sons of Rachel were Joseph and Benjamin.
25 The sons of Bilhah, Rachel's servant, were Dan and
Naphtali.
26 The sons of Zilpah, Leah's servant, were Gad and
Asher.
These are the names of the sons who were born to Ja-
cob at Paddan-aram.

27 So Jacob returned to his father, Isaac, in Mam-
re, which is near Kiriath-arba (now called Hebron),
where Abraham and Isaac had both lived as foreign-
ers. 28 Isaac lived for 180 years. 29 Then he breathed his
last and died at a ripe old age, joining his ancestors in
death. And his sons, Esau and Jacob, buried him.

DESCENDANTS OF ESAU

36 This is the account of the descendants of Esau
(also known as Edom). 2 Esau married two
young women from Canaan: Adah, the daughter
of Elon the Hittite; and Oholibamah, the daughter
of Anah and granddaughter of Zibeon the Hivite.
3 He also married his cousin Basemath, who was
the daughter of Ishmael and the sister of Nebaioth.
4 Adah gave birth to a son named Eliphaz for Esau.
Basemath gave birth to a son named Reuel. 5 Ohol-
ibamah gave birth to sons named Jeush, Jalam, and
Korah. All these sons were born to Esau in the land
of Canaan.
6 Esau took his wives, his children, and his entire
household, along with his livestock and cattle—all
the wealth he had acquired in the land of Canaan—
and moved away from his brother, Jacob. 7 There was
not enough land to support them both because of all
the livestock and possessions they had acquired. 8 So
Esau (also known as Edom) settled in the hill country
of Seir.
9 This is the account of Esau's descendants, the
Edomites, who lived in the hill country of Seir.

10 These are the names of Esau's sons: Eliphaz, the son
of Esau's wife Adah; and Reuel, the son of Esau's
wife Basemath.
11 The descendants of Eliphaz were Teman, Omar,
Zepho, Gatam, and Kenaz. 12 Timna, the concubine of
Esau's son Eliphaz, gave birth to a son named Ama-
lek. These are the descendants of Esau's wife Adah.

35:10 *Jacob* sounds like the Hebrew words for "heel" and "deceiver." *Israel* means "God fights." **35:21** Hebrew *Israel;* also in 35:22a. The names "Jacob" and "Israel" are often interchanged throughout the Old Testament, referring sometimes to the individual patriarch and sometimes to the nation.

35:3 God who answered my prayers. After the terrible events at Shechem, God gave Jacob the opportunity to remember God's constant love and presence.

35:10 your name will be Israel. This new name had been promised in 32:28, and the promise was fulfilled here.

35:11-13 God proclaimed a blessing on Jacob and his descendants and confirmed His promises to them. These were the covenant promises made to Abraham and passed through Isaac to Jacob.

35:17 you have another son. At Joseph's birth, Rachel had asked for another son (30:24).

35:18 Ben-oni . . . Benjamin. Rachel's name for her son means "son of my trouble," a logical name for a son born with such difficulty. The name Benjamin means "son of my right hand."

35:19 Rachel died. Rachel died giving birth to Benjamin. Death in childbirth was not uncommon in that time (1 Sam. 4:20).

35:22 had intercourse with . . . his father's concubine. By this action, Reuben claimed the rights to his inheritance as the firstborn—specifically the right to inherit his father's concubine.

35:29 his sons . . . buried him. The two brothers put the past aside and buried their father peacefully.

36:1 Esau. Esau was called Edom (meaning "red") because of the red lentil stew he had traded for his birthright (25:30).

36:11 Eliphaz . . . Teman. The appearance of this Edomite name helps clarify some of Job's story. Eliphaz the Temanite was a friend of Job (Job 2:11).

13 The descendants of Reuel were Nahath, Zerah,
Shammah, and Mizzah. These are the descendants
of Esau's wife Basemath.
14 Esau also had sons through Oholibamah, the
daughter of Anah and granddaughter of Zibeon.
Their names were Jeush, Jalam, and Korah.

15 These are the descendants of Esau who became the
leaders of various clans:

The descendants of Esau's oldest son, Eliphaz, became
the leaders of the clans of Teman, Omar, Zepho, Ke-
naz, 16 Korah, Gatam, and Amalek. These are the
clan leaders in the land of Edom who descended
from Eliphaz. All these were descendants of Esau's
wife Adah.
17 The descendants of Esau's son Reuel became the
leaders of the clans of Nahath, Zerah, Shammah,
and Mizzah. These are the clan leaders in the land
of Edom who descended from Reuel. All these were
descendants of Esau's wife Basemath.
18 The descendants of Esau and his wife Oholibamah
became the leaders of the clans of Jeush, Jalam, and
Korah. These are the clan leaders who descend-
ed from Esau's wife Oholibamah, the daughter of
Anah.
19 These are the clans descended from Esau (also
known as Edom), identified by their clan leaders.

ORIGINAL PEOPLES OF EDOM

20 These are the names of the tribes that descended
from Seir the Horite. They lived in the land of Edom:
Lotan, Shobal, Zibeon, Anah, 21 Dishon, Ezer, and Di-
shan. These were the Horite clan leaders, the descen-
dants of Seir, who lived in the land of Edom.

22 The descendants of Lotan were Hori and Hemam.
Lotan's sister was named Timna.
23 The descendants of Shobal were Alvan, Manahath,
Ebal, Shepho, and Onam.
24 The descendants of Zibeon were Aiah and Anah.
(This is the Anah who discovered the hot springs
in the wilderness while he was grazing his father's
donkeys.)
25 The descendants of Anah were his son, Dishon, and
his daughter, Oholibamah.
26 The descendants of Dishon* were Hemdan, Eshban,
Ithran, and Keran.
27 The descendants of Ezer were Bilhan, Zaavan, and
Akan.
28 The descendants of Dishan were Uz and Aran.
29 So these were the leaders of the Horite clans: Lotan,
Shobal, Zibeon, Anah, 30 Dishon, Ezer, and Dishan. The
Horite clans are named after their clan leaders, who
lived in the land of Seir.

RULERS OF EDOM

31 These are the kings who ruled in the land of Edom
before any king ruled over the Israelites*:
32 Bela son of Beor, who ruled in Edom from his city of
Dinhabah.
33 When Bela died, Jobab son of Zerah from Bozrah
became king in his place.
34 When Jobab died, Husham from the land of the
Temanites became king in his place.
35 When Husham died, Hadad son of Bedad became
king in his place and ruled from the city of Avith.
He was the one who defeated the Midianites in the
land of Moab.
36 When Hadad died, Samlah from the city of Mas-
rekah became king in his place.
37 When Samlah died, Shaul from the city of Reho-
both-on-the-River became king in his place.
38 When Shaul died, Baal-hanan son of Acbor became
king in his place.
39 When Baal-hanan son of Acbor died, Hadad* be-
came king in his place and ruled from the city of
Pau. His wife was Mehetabel, the daughter of Ma-
tred and granddaughter of Me-zahab.

40 These are the names of the leaders of the clans
descended from Esau, who lived in the places named
for them: Timna, Alvah, Jetheth, 41 Oholibamah, Elah,
Pinon, 42 Kenaz, Teman, Mibzar, 43 Magdiel, and Iram.
These are the leaders of the clans of Edom, listed ac-
cording to their settlements in the land they occu-
pied. They all descended from Esau, the ancestor of
the Edomites.

JOSEPH'S DREAMS

37 So Jacob settled again in the land of Canaan,
where his father had lived as a foreigner.
2 This is the account of Jacob and his family. When
Joseph was seventeen years old, he often tended his
father's flocks. He worked for his half brothers, the
sons of his father's wives Bilhah and Zilpah. But Jo-
seph reported to his father some of the bad things his
brothers were doing.
3 Jacob* loved Joseph more than any of his other
children because Joseph had been born to him in his
old age. So one day Jacob had a special gift made for
Joseph—a beautiful robe.* 4 But his brothers hated
Joseph because their father loved him more than the
rest of them. They couldn't say a kind word to him.
5 One night Joseph had a dream, and when he told
his brothers about it, they hated him more than ever.
6 "Listen to this dream," he said. 7 "We were out in the
field, tying up bundles of grain. Suddenly my bundle
stood up, and your bundles all gathered around and
bowed low before mine!"
8 His brothers responded, "So you think you will be
our king, do you? Do you actually think you will reign
over us?" And they hated him all the more because of
his dreams and the way he talked about them.
9 Soon Joseph had another dream, and again he
told his brothers about it. "Listen, I have had anoth-
er dream," he said. "The sun, moon, and eleven stars
bowed low before me!"

36:26 Hebrew *Dishan,* a variant spelling of Dishon; compare 36:21, 28. **36:31** Or *before an Israelite king ruled over them.* **36:39** As in some Hebrew manuscripts, Samaritan Pentateuch, and Syriac version (see also 1 Chr 1:50); most Hebrew manuscripts read *Hadar.* **37:3a** Hebrew *Israel;* also in 37:13. See note on 35:21. **37:3b** Traditionally rendered *a coat of many colors.* The exact meaning of the Hebrew is uncertain.

36:31 These are the kings. This verse implies that the reader knows about the Israelite kingship established hundreds of years after these events. This notation was probably added many years later.

37:3 robe. This robe was not only a gift of love from Joseph's father, Jacob, but of favoritism as well.

37:8 reign over us? There is no indication that Joseph actually intended to rule over his brothers. His mistake was telling them about these dreams in the first place.

DREAM ON

1. What's the strangest dream you've ever had? Did it have some deep meaning?

GENESIS 37:1-11

2. Why did Joseph's brothers hate him? Who was at fault: Jacob? Joseph? The brothers?
3. What did Joseph's dreams mean? Why would the dreams have enraged his brothers even more?
4. Are you jealous of another person in your school or team? Why? Who is to blame for your jealousy?
5. Do you have dreams of becoming someone great one day? Are those dreams the same ones that God might have for you?

10 This time he told the dream to his father as well
as to his brothers, but his father scolded him. "What
kind of dream is that?" he asked. "Will your mother
and I and your brothers actually come and bow to
the ground before you?" 11 But while his brothers
were jealous of Joseph, his father wondered what the
dreams meant.
12 Soon after this, Joseph's brothers went to pasture
their father's flocks at Shechem. 13 When they had
been gone for some time, Jacob said to Joseph, "Your
brothers are pasturing the sheep at Shechem. Get
ready, and I will send you to them."
"I'm ready to go," Joseph replied.
14 "Go and see how your brothers and the flocks are
getting along," Jacob said. "Then come back and bring
me a report." So Jacob sent him on his way, and Joseph
traveled to Shechem from their home in the valley of
Hebron.
15 When he arrived there, a man from the area no-
ticed him wandering around the countryside. "What
are you looking for?" he asked.
16 "I'm looking for my brothers," Joseph replied. "Do
you know where they are pasturing their sheep?"
17 "Yes," the man told him. "They have moved on
from here, but I heard them say, 'Let's go on to Do-
than.'" So Joseph followed his brothers to Dothan and
found them there.

JOSEPH SOLD INTO SLAVERY

18 When Joseph's brothers saw him coming, they rec-
ognized him in the distance. As he approached, they
made plans to kill him. 19 "Here comes the dreamer!"
they said. 20 "Come on, let's kill him and throw him
into one of these cisterns. We can tell our father, 'A
wild animal has eaten him.' Then we'll see what be-
comes of his dreams!"
21 But when Reuben heard of their scheme, he came
to Joseph's rescue. "Let's not kill him," he said. 22 "Why
should we shed any blood? Let's just throw him into
this empty cistern here in the wilderness. Then he'll
die without our laying a hand on him." Reuben was
secretly planning to rescue Joseph and return him to
his father.
23 So when Joseph arrived, his brothers ripped
off the beautiful robe he was wearing. 24 Then they
grabbed him and threw him into the cistern. Now the
cistern was empty; there was no water in it. 25 Then,
just as they were sitting down to eat, they looked up
and saw a caravan of camels in the distance coming
toward them. It was a group of Ishmaelite traders
taking a load of gum, balm, and aromatic resin from
Gilead down to Egypt.
26 Judah said to his brothers, "What will we gain by
killing our brother? We'd have to cover up the crime.*
27 Instead of hurting him, let's sell him to those Ishma-
elite traders. After all, he is our brother—our own
flesh and blood!" And his brothers agreed. 28 So when
the Ishmaelites, who were Midianite traders, came
by, Joseph's brothers pulled him out of the cistern and
sold him to them for twenty pieces* of silver. And the
traders took him to Egypt.
29 Some time later, Reuben returned to get Joseph
out of the cistern. When he discovered that Joseph
was missing, he tore his clothes in grief. 30 Then he
went back to his brothers and lamented, "The boy is
gone! What will I do now?"
31 Then the brothers killed a young goat and dipped
Joseph's robe in its blood. 32 They sent the beautiful
robe to their father with this message: "Look at what
we found. Doesn't this robe belong to your son?"
33 Their father recognized it immediately. "Yes," he
said, "it is my son's robe. A wild animal must have
eaten him. Joseph has clearly been torn to pieces!"
34 Then Jacob tore his clothes and dressed him-
self in burlap. He mourned deeply for his son for a
long time. 35 His family all tried to comfort him, but
he refused to be comforted. "I will go to my grave*
mourning for my son," he would say, and then he
would weep.

IN THE PITS

1. What kind of pranks have you pulled? Did your pranks ever go too far? If so, when?

GENESIS 37:12-36

2. Why did Joseph's brothers want to kill him?
3. Why did Reuben try to save Joseph? Why did he say, "What am I going to do?" (v. 30) instead of "What are we going to do?"
4. What was Judah's motivation in not killing Joseph: Greed (v. 26)? Concern for his brother (v. 27)? Other?
5. Are you more concerned for the welfare of others or for how others can help you?

37:26 Hebrew *cover his blood.* **37:28** Hebrew *20 [shekels],* about 8 ounces or 228 grams in weight. **37:35** Hebrew *go down to Sheol.*

37:21-22 Reuben. As the oldest brother, Reuben should have been able to protect Joseph. But Joseph had lost his brothers' respect, and they showed him no mercy.

37:23 ripped off the . . . robe. This robe was a symbol to Joseph's brothers of their father's favoritism. They threw him in a cistern to die.

37:28 sold him . . . for twenty pieces of silver. The brothers received from a traveling band of merchants what was considered a fair price for Joseph, who was now a slave.

37:34 tore his clothes. Tearing one's clothes was a sign of loss. Jacob was heartbroken over the death of his favorite son.

36 Meanwhile, the Midianite traders* arrived in
Egypt, where they sold Joseph to Potiphar, an officer
of Pharaoh, the king of Egypt. Potiphar was captain
of the palace guard.

JUDAH AND TAMAR

38 About this time, Judah left home and moved to
Adullam, where he stayed with a man named
Hirah. 2 There he saw a Canaanite woman, the daugh-
ter of Shua, and he married her. When he slept with
her, 3 she became pregnant and gave birth to a son,
and he named the boy Er. 4 Then she became pregnant
again and gave birth to another son, and she named
him Onan. 5 And when she gave birth to a third son,
she named him Shelah. At the time of Shelah's birth,
they were living at Kezib.
6 In the course of time, Judah arranged for his first-
born son, Er, to marry a young woman named Tamar.
7 But Er was a wicked man in the LORD's sight, so the
LORD took his life. 8 Then Judah said to Er's brother
Onan, "Go and marry Tamar, as our law requires of
the brother of a man who has died. You must produce
an heir for your brother."
9 But Onan was not willing to have a child who
would not be his own heir. So whenever he had inter-
course with his brother's wife, he spilled the semen
on the ground. This prevented her from having a
child who would belong to his brother. 10 But the LORD
considered it evil for Onan to deny a child to his dead
brother. So the LORD took Onan's life, too.
11 Then Judah said to Tamar, his daughter-in-law,
"Go back to your parents' home and remain a wid-
ow until my son Shelah is old enough to marry you."
(But Judah didn't really intend to do this because
he was afraid Shelah would also die, like his two
brothers.) So Tamar went back to live in her father's
home.
12 Some years later Judah's wife died. After the time
of mourning was over, Judah and his friend Hirah
the Adullamite went up to Timnah to supervise the
shearing of his sheep. 13 Someone told Tamar, "Look,
your father-in-law is going up to Timnah to shear his
sheep."
14 Tamar was aware that Shelah had grown up, but
no arrangements had been made for her to come and
marry him. So she changed out of her widow's cloth-
ing and covered herself with a veil to disguise her-
self. Then she sat beside the road at the entrance to
the village of Enaim, which is on the road to Timnah.
15 Judah noticed her and thought she was a prostitute,
since she had covered her face. 16 So he stopped and
propositioned her. "Let me have sex with you," he said,
not realizing that she was his own daughter-in-law.
"How much will you pay to have sex with me?" Ta-
mar asked.
17 "I'll send you a young goat from my flock," Judah
promised.
"But what will you give me to guarantee that you
will send the goat?" she asked.
18 "What kind of guarantee do you want?" he re-
plied.
She answered, "Leave me your identification seal
and its cord and the walking stick you are carrying."
So Judah gave them to her. Then he had intercourse
with her, and she became pregnant. 19 Afterward she
went back home, took off her veil, and put on her wid-
ow's clothing as usual.
20 Later Judah asked his friend Hirah the Adul-
lamite to take the young goat to the woman and to
pick up the things he had given her as his guarantee.
But Hirah couldn't find her. 21 So he asked the men
who lived there, "Where can I find the shrine prosti-
tute who was sitting beside the road at the entrance
to Enaim?"
"We've never had a shrine prostitute here," they
replied.
22 So Hirah returned to Judah and told him, "I
couldn't find her anywhere, and the men of the
village claim they've never had a shrine prostitute
there."
23 "Then let her keep the things I gave her," Judah
said. "I sent the young goat as we agreed, but you
couldn't find her. We'd be the laughingstock of the
village if we went back again to look for her."
24 About three months later, Judah was told, "Ta-
mar, your daughter-in-law, has acted like a prostitute.
And now, because of this, she's pregnant."
"Bring her out, and let her be burned!" Judah de-
manded.
25 But as they were taking her out to kill her, she
sent this message to her father-in-law: "The man
who owns these things made me pregnant. Look
closely. Whose seal and cord and walking stick are
these?"
26 Judah recognized them immediately and said,
"She is more righteous than I am, because I didn't
arrange for her to marry my son Shelah." And Judah
never slept with Tamar again.
27 When the time came for Tamar to give birth,
it was discovered that she was carrying twins.
28 While she was in labor, one of the babies reached
out his hand. The midwife grabbed it and tied a
scarlet string around the child's wrist, announcing,
"This one came out first." 29 But then he pulled back
his hand, and out came his brother! "What!" the mid-
wife exclaimed. "How did you break out first?" So he
was named Perez.* 30 Then the baby with the scarlet
string on his wrist was born, and he was named Ze-
rah.*

37:36 Hebrew *the Medanites.* The relationship between the Midianites and Medanites is unclear; compare 37:28. See also 25:2. **38:29** *Perez* means "breaking out." **38:30** *Zerah* means "scarlet" or "brightness."

37:36 traders sold Joseph. Joseph went quickly from the nomadic life of a shepherd to the greatest civilization of his day, and from freedom to a life of bondage.

38:1 Judah left home. Joseph was forcibly removed from his family, but Judah was left to try his own way in the world. He seemed to have no sense of building up his family's position, just his own.

38:8-9 Without children, Tamar had no means of support. The purpose of this custom (called "levirate marriage") was to give her an heir who could take care of her. By short-circuiting his levirate duties, Onan was condemning Tamar to a life of hardship.

38:14 no arrangements. Tamar had decided that Judah had no intention of honoring his duty. Tamar had been deceived, so she decided to deceive Judah.

38:18 What kind of guarantee do you want? Tamar wanted proof of her act with Judah. If she became pregnant, she could claim that her child had inheritance rights.

38:24 Bring her out. Judah was ready to "cast the first stone" when he was told that Tamar had brought dishonor on his family.

38:29 Perez. Perez, one of the twin sons born of the union of Judah with Tamar, became head of the most important tribe in Judah and an ancestor of Jesus (Matt. 1:3).

JOSEPH IN POTIPHAR'S HOUSE

39 When Joseph was taken to Egypt by the Ishmaelite traders, he was purchased by Potiphar, an Egyptian officer. Potiphar was captain of the guard for Pharaoh, the king of Egypt.

2 The LORD was with Joseph, so he succeeded in everything he did as he served in the home of his Egyptian master. 3 Potiphar noticed this and realized that the LORD was with Joseph, giving him success in everything he did. 4 This pleased Potiphar, so he soon made Joseph his personal attendant. He put him in charge of his entire household and everything he owned. 5 From the day Joseph was put in charge of his master's household and property, the LORD began to bless Potiphar's household for Joseph's sake. All his household affairs ran smoothly, and his crops and livestock flourished. 6 So Potiphar gave Joseph complete administrative responsibility over everything he owned. With Joseph there, he didn't worry about a thing—except what kind of food to eat!

Joseph was a very handsome and well-built young man, 7 and Potiphar's wife soon began to look at him lustfully. "Come and sleep with me," she demanded.

8 But Joseph refused. "Look," he told her, "my master trusts me with everything in his entire household. 9 No one here has more authority than I do. He has held back nothing from me except you, because you are his wife. How could I do such a wicked thing? It would be a great sin against God."

10 She kept putting pressure on Joseph day after day, but he refused to sleep with her, and he kept out of her way as much as possible. 11 One day, however, no one else was around when he went in to do his work. 12 She came and grabbed him by his cloak, demanding, "Come on, sleep with me!" Joseph tore himself away, but he left his cloak in her hand as he ran from the house.

13 When she saw that she was holding his cloak and he had fled, 14 she called out to her servants. Soon all the men came running. "Look!" she said. "My husband has brought this Hebrew slave here to make fools of us! He came into my room to rape me, but I screamed. 15 When he heard me scream, he ran outside and got away, but he left his cloak behind with me."

16 She kept the cloak with her until her husband came home. 17 Then she told him her story. "That Hebrew slave you've brought into our house tried to come in and fool around with me," she said. 18 "But when I screamed, he ran outside, leaving his cloak with me!"

JOSEPH PUT IN PRISON

19 Potiphar was furious when he heard his wife's story about how Joseph had treated her. 20 So he took Joseph and threw him into the prison where the king's prisoners were held, and there he remained. 21 But the LORD was with Joseph in the prison and showed him his faithful love. And the LORD made Joseph a favorite with the prison warden. 22 Before long, the warden put Joseph in charge of all the other prisoners and over everything that happened in the prison. 23 The warden had no more worries, because Joseph took care of everything. The LORD was with him and caused everything he did to succeed.

"EVERYONE'S DOING IT"

1. Have you ever been accused of something you didn't do? What happened?

GENESIS 39:1-23

2. Why did Joseph refuse to have sex with Potiphar's wife?
3. According to Joseph, who are we sinning against when we have sex outside of marriage?
4. How did Joseph resist the temptation of Potiphar's wife? How can we imitate his example?
5. Joseph was tempted "day after day" (v. 10). What excuses could he have made to justify giving in?
6. What is the best way to respond when someone coaxes you into compromising your sexual standards?

JOSEPH INTERPRETS TWO DREAMS

40 Some time later, Pharaoh's chief cup-bearer and chief baker offended their royal master. 2 Pharaoh became angry with these two officials, 3 and he put them in the prison where Joseph was, in the palace of the captain of the guard. 4 They remained in prison for quite some time, and the captain of the guard assigned them to Joseph, who looked after them.

5 While they were in prison, Pharaoh's cup-bearer and baker each had a dream one night, and each dream had its own meaning. 6 When Joseph saw them the next morning, he noticed that they both looked upset. 7 "Why do you look so worried today?" he asked them.

8 And they replied, "We both had dreams last night, but no one can tell us what they mean."

"Interpreting dreams is God's business," Joseph replied. "Go ahead and tell me your dreams."

9 So the chief cup-bearer told Joseph his dream first. "In my dream," he said, "I saw a grapevine in front of me. 10 The vine had three branches that began to bud and blossom, and soon it produced clusters of ripe grapes. 11 I was holding Pharaoh's wine cup in my hand, so I took a cluster of grapes and squeezed the juice into the cup. Then I placed the cup in Pharaoh's hand."

12 "This is what the dream means," Joseph said. "The three branches represent three days. 13 Within three

39:1 Joseph was taken to Egypt. The scene shifts back to Egypt and to intrigue at the highest levels of Egyptian culture.
39:5 began to bless . . . for Joseph's sake. When God called Abram (12:2-3), he promised him that the nations of the earth would be blessed through him. Joseph's success was part of the fulfillment of that promise.
39:6 gave Joseph . . . responsibility. Joseph was a person whom people trusted. It was the way God worked through him that made him so effective.
39:7-9 Potiphar's wife lusted after Joseph. But Joseph would not hurt his master who trusted him, nor would he sin against God.
39:10,12 refused . . . tore himself away. Joseph knew how to deal with temptation. When the problem with his owner's wife reached the boiling point, he ran from her.
40:1 cup-bearer. The cupbearer presided in Pharaoh's household and acted as a taster of his food.
40:5 each had a dream. Pharaoh's dreams were the beginning of Joseph's rise to power.
40:8 interpreting dreams is God's business. Although Joseph had the gift of dream interpretation, the truth he spoke was God's truth.

days Pharaoh will lift you up and restore you to your position as his chief cup-bearer. 14 And please remember me and do me a favor when things go well for you. Mention me to Pharaoh, so he might let me out of this place. 15 For I was kidnapped from my homeland, the land of the Hebrews, and now I'm here in prison, but I did nothing to deserve it."

16 When the chief baker saw that Joseph had given the first dream such a positive interpretation, he said to Joseph, "I had a dream, too. In my dream there were three baskets of white pastries stacked on my head. 17 The top basket contained all kinds of pastries for Pharaoh, but the birds came and ate them from the basket on my head."

18 "This is what the dream means," Joseph told him. "The three baskets also represent three days. 19 Three days from now Pharaoh will lift you up and impale your body on a pole. Then birds will come and peck away at your flesh."

20 Pharaoh's birthday came three days later, and he prepared a banquet for all his officials and staff. He summoned* his chief cup-bearer and chief baker to join the other officials. 21 He then restored the chief cup-bearer to his former position, so he could again hand Pharaoh his cup. 22 But Pharaoh impaled the chief baker, just as Joseph had predicted when he interpreted his dream. 23 Pharaoh's chief cup-bearer, however, forgot all about Joseph, never giving him another thought.

PHARAOH'S DREAMS

41 Two full years later, Pharaoh dreamed that he was standing on the bank of the Nile River. 2 In his dream he saw seven fat, healthy cows come up out of the river and begin grazing in the marsh grass. 3 Then he saw seven more cows come up behind them from the Nile, but these were scrawny and thin. These cows stood beside the fat cows on the riverbank. 4 Then the scrawny, thin cows ate the seven healthy, fat cows! At this point in the dream, Pharaoh woke up.

5 But he fell asleep again and had a second dream. This time he saw seven heads of grain, plump and beautiful, growing on a single stalk. 6 Then seven more heads of grain appeared, but these were shriveled and withered by the east wind. 7 And these thin heads swallowed up the seven plump, well-formed heads! Then Pharaoh woke up again and realized it was a dream.

8 The next morning Pharaoh was very disturbed by the dreams. So he called for all the magicians and wise men of Egypt. When Pharaoh told them his dreams, not one of them could tell him what they meant.

9 Finally, the king's chief cup-bearer spoke up. "Today I have been reminded of my failure," he told Pharaoh. 10 "Some time ago, you were angry with the chief baker and me, and you imprisoned us in the palace of the captain of the guard. 11 One night the chief baker and I each had a dream, and each dream had its own meaning. 12 There was a young Hebrew man with us in the prison who was a slave of the captain of the guard. We told him our dreams, and he told us what each of our dreams meant. 13 And everything happened just as he had predicted. I was restored to my position as cup-bearer, and the chief baker was executed and impaled on a pole."

14 Pharaoh sent for Joseph at once, and he was quickly brought from the prison. After he shaved and changed his clothes, he went in and stood before Pharaoh. 15 Then Pharaoh said to Joseph, "I had a dream last night, and no one here can tell me what it means. But I have heard that when you hear about a dream you can interpret it."

16 "It is beyond my power to do this," Joseph replied. "But God can tell you what it means and set you at ease."

17 So Pharaoh told Joseph his dream. "In my dream," he said, "I was standing on the bank of the Nile River, 18 and I saw seven fat, healthy cows come up out of the river and begin grazing in the marsh grass. 19 But then I saw seven sick-looking cows, scrawny and thin, come up after them. I've never seen such sorry-looking animals in all the land of Egypt. 20 These thin, scrawny cows ate the seven fat cows. 21 But afterward you wouldn't have known it, for they were still as thin and scrawny as before! Then I woke up.

22 "In my dream I also saw seven heads of grain, full and beautiful, growing on a single stalk. 23 Then seven more heads of grain appeared, but these were blighted, shriveled, and withered by the east wind. 24 And the shriveled heads swallowed the seven healthy heads. I told these dreams to the magicians, but no one could tell me what they mean."

25 Joseph responded, "Both of Pharaoh's dreams mean the same thing. God is telling Pharaoh in advance what he is about to do. 26 The seven healthy

AN AWESOME PERFORMANCE

1. If the president of the United States suddenly summoned you to the White House, what would your first thought be?

GENESIS 41:1-40

2. Why did Pharaoh send for Joseph? How did he even hear of Joseph? What does this say about Joseph's faithfulness to God?
3. Why did Joseph say that he was not able to interpret Pharaoh's dreams (v. 16)?
4. How did Pharaoh know that Joseph had "the spirit of God" in him (v. 38)?
5. Who received glory for Joseph's interpretations: God? Joseph? Other?
6. Who receives glory when you perform well in school, athletics, or other visible activities?

40:20 Hebrew *He lifted up the head of.*

40:14 Mention me to Pharaoh. Though the chief cupbearer forgot about Joseph for two years, Joseph was eventually remembered and rescued.

41:13 just as . . . predicted. The testimony of the cupbearer to Pharaoh was that Joseph's interpretation of dreams was exactly correct. His ability was a gift from God.

41:16 God can tell you. Pharaoh sent for Joseph to interpret his dream. Joseph reminded the pharaoh that God's power, not his own, made all the difference.

cows and the seven healthy heads of grain both rep-
resent seven years of prosperity. 27 The seven thin,
scrawny cows that came up later and the seven thin
heads of grain, withered by the east wind, represent
seven years of famine.

28 "This will happen just as I have described it, for
God has revealed to Pharaoh in advance what he is
about to do. 29 The next seven years will be a period of
great prosperity throughout the land of Egypt. 30 But
afterward there will be seven years of famine so great
that all the prosperity will be forgotten in Egypt.
Famine will destroy the land. 31 This famine will be so
severe that even the memory of the good years will be
erased. 32 As for having two similar dreams, it means
that these events have been decreed by God, and he
will soon make them happen.

33 "Therefore, Pharaoh should find an intelligent
and wise man and put him in charge of the entire land
of Egypt. 34 Then Pharaoh should appoint supervisors
over the land and let them collect one-fifth of all the
crops during the seven good years. 35 Have them gath-
er all the food produced in the good years that are just
ahead and bring it to Pharaoh's storehouses. Store it
away, and guard it so there will be food in the cities.
36 That way there will be enough to eat when the sev-
en years of famine come to the land of Egypt. Other-
wise this famine will destroy the land."

JOSEPH MADE RULER OF EGYPT

37 Joseph's suggestions were well received by Pharaoh
and his officials. 38 So Pharaoh asked his officials, "Can
we find anyone else like this man so obviously filled
with the spirit of God?" 39 Then Pharaoh said to Joseph,
"Since God has revealed the meaning of the dreams to
you, clearly no one else is as intelligent or wise as you
are. 40 You will be in charge of my court, and all my
people will take orders from you. Only I, sitting on my
throne, will have a rank higher than yours."

41 Pharaoh said to Joseph, "I hereby put you in
charge of the entire land of Egypt." 42 Then Pharaoh
removed his signet ring from his hand and placed it
on Joseph's finger. He dressed him in fine linen cloth-
ing and hung a gold chain around his neck. 43 Then
he had Joseph ride in the chariot reserved for his
second-in-command. And wherever Joseph went, the
command was shouted, "Kneel down!" So Pharaoh put
Joseph in charge of all Egypt. 44 And Pharaoh said to
him, "I am Pharaoh, but no one will lift a hand or foot
in the entire land of Egypt without your approval."

45 Then Pharaoh gave Joseph a new Egyptian name,
Zaphenath-paneah.* He also gave him a wife, whose
name was Asenath. She was the daughter of Potiph-
era, the priest of On.* So Joseph took charge of the
entire land of Egypt. 46 He was thirty years old when
he began serving in the court of Pharaoh, the king of
Egypt. And when Joseph left Pharaoh's presence, he
inspected the entire land of Egypt.

47 As predicted, for seven years the land produced
bumper crops. 48 During those years, Joseph gathered
all the crops grown in Egypt and stored the grain
from the surrounding fields in the cities. 49 He piled up
huge amounts of grain like sand on the seashore. Fi-
nally, he stopped keeping records because there was
too much to measure.

50 During this time, before the first of the famine
years, two sons were born to Joseph and his wife,
Asenath, the daughter of Potiphera, the priest of On.
51 Joseph named his older son Manasseh,* for he said,
"God has made me forget all my troubles and every-
one in my father's family." 52 Joseph named his second
son Ephraim,* for he said, "God has made me fruitful
in this land of my grief."

53 At last the seven years of bumper crops through-
out the land of Egypt came to an end. 54 Then the seven
years of famine began, just as Joseph had predicted.
The famine also struck all the surrounding countries,
but throughout Egypt there was plenty of food. 55 Even-
tually, however, the famine spread throughout the
land of Egypt as well. And when the people cried out
to Pharaoh for food, he told them, "Go to Joseph, and do
whatever he tells you." 56 So with severe famine every-
where, Joseph opened up the storehouses and distrib-
uted grain to the Egyptians, for the famine was severe
throughout the land of Egypt. 57 And people from all
around came to Egypt to buy grain from Joseph be-
cause the famine was severe throughout the world.

JOSEPH'S BROTHERS GO TO EGYPT

42 When Jacob heard that grain was available
in Egypt, he said to his sons, "Why are you
standing around looking at one another? 2 I have
heard there is grain in Egypt. Go down there, and buy
enough grain to keep us alive. Otherwise we'll die."

3 So Joseph's ten older brothers went down to Egypt
to buy grain. 4 But Jacob wouldn't let Joseph's younger
brother, Benjamin, go with them, for fear some harm
might come to him. 5 So Jacob's* sons arrived in Egypt
along with others to buy food, for the famine was in
Canaan as well.

6 Since Joseph was governor of all Egypt and in
charge of selling grain to all the people, it was to
him that his brothers came. When they arrived, they
bowed before him with their faces to the ground. 7 Jo-
seph recognized his brothers instantly, but he pre-
tended to be a stranger and spoke harshly to them.
"Where are you from?" he demanded.

"From the land of Canaan," they replied. "We have
come to buy food."

8 Although Joseph recognized his brothers, they
didn't recognize him. 9 And he remembered the

41:45a *Zaphenath-paneah* probably means "God speaks and lives." **41:45b** Greek version reads *of Heliopolis;* also in 41:50. **41:51** *Manasseh* sounds like a Hebrew term that means "causing to forget." **41:52** *Ephraim* sounds like a Hebrew term that means "fruitful." **42:5** Hebrew *Israel's.* See note on 35:21.

41:27 famine. Seven years of famine in Egypt would be devastating.

41:40 Only I . . . will have a rank higher. Pharaoh gave Joseph an important leadership role in Egypt, making him his highest-ranking advisor.

41:45 name . . . wife. Joseph got a new job, new status, a new name, and a new wife—even the daughter of a priest.

41:49 stopped keeping records. Joseph's preparation for the coming crisis in Egypt was so thorough that no one could keep track of it.

41:51-52 Manasseh . . . Ephraim. Joseph gave both his sons Hebrew names. He brought his Hebrew heritage into his Egyptian world, honoring God's promise to His people.

41:57 people from all around. Egypt survived the famine, and Pharaoh's kingdom multiplied. As Egypt prospered, surrounding nations sought its help.

42:4 Benjamin. Joseph and Benjamin were Jacob's only sons by his wife Rachel. After losing Joseph, Jacob was protective of Benjamin and would not allow him to travel with his brothers to Egypt.

42:6 bowed before him. This is the first step in the fulfillment of Joseph's dream as a teenager that his brothers would bow down to him (37:5-8).

42:8 they didn't recognize him. Joseph was dressed in Egyptian clothes and spoke a foreign language, communicating through an interpreter.

dreams he'd had about them many years before. He
said to them, "You are spies! You have come to see how
vulnerable our land has become."
10 "No, my lord!" they exclaimed. "Your servants
have simply come to buy food. 11 We are all brothers—
members of the same family. We are honest men, sir!
We are not spies!"
12 "Yes, you are!" Joseph insisted. "You have come to
see how vulnerable our land has become."
13 "Sir," they said, "there are actually twelve of us.
We, your servants, are all brothers, sons of a man liv-
ing in the land of Canaan. Our youngest brother is
back there with our father right now, and one of our
brothers is no longer with us."
14 But Joseph insisted, "As I said, you are spies! 15 This
is how I will test your story. I swear by the life of Pha-
raoh that you will never leave Egypt unless your
youngest brother comes here! 16 One of you must go
and get your brother. I'll keep the rest of you here in
prison. Then we'll find out whether or not your story is
true. By the life of Pharaoh, if it turns out that you don't
have a younger brother, then I'll know you are spies."
17 So Joseph put them all in prison for three days.
18 On the third day Joseph said to them, "I am a
God-fearing man. If you do as I say, you will live. 19 If
you really are honest men, choose one of your broth-
ers to remain in prison. The rest of you may go home
with grain for your starving families. 20 But you must
bring your youngest brother back to me. This will
prove that you are telling the truth, and you will not
die." To this they agreed.
21 Speaking among themselves, they said, "Clearly
we are being punished because of what we did to Jo-
seph long ago. We saw his anguish when he pleaded
for his life, but we wouldn't listen. That's why we're
in this trouble."
22 "Didn't I tell you not to sin against the boy?" Reu-
ben asked. "But you wouldn't listen. And now we have
to answer for his blood!"
23 Of course, they didn't know that Joseph understood
them, for he had been speaking to them through an in-
terpreter. 24 Now he turned away from them and began
to weep. When he regained his composure, he spoke to
them again. Then he chose Simeon from among them
and had him tied up right before their eyes.
25 Joseph then ordered his servants to fill the men's
sacks with grain, but he also gave secret instructions
to return each brother's payment at the top of his
sack. He also gave them supplies for their journey
home. 26 So the brothers loaded their donkeys with the
grain and headed for home.
27 But when they stopped for the night and one of
them opened his sack to get grain for his donkey, he
found his money in the top of his sack. 28 "Look!" he ex-
claimed to his brothers. "My money has been returned;
it's here in my sack!" Then their hearts sank. Trembling,
they said to each other, "What has God done to us?"
29 When the brothers came to their father, Jacob, in
the land of Canaan, they told him everything that had
happened to them. 30 "The man who is governor of the
land spoke very harshly to us," they told him. "He ac-
cused us of being spies scouting the land. 31 But we
said, 'We are honest men, not spies. 32 We are twelve
brothers, sons of one father. One brother is no longer
with us, and the youngest is at home with our father
in the land of Canaan.'
33 "Then the man who is governor of the land told
us, 'This is how I will find out if you are honest men.
Leave one of your brothers here with me, and take
grain for your starving families and go on home.
34 But you must bring your youngest brother back to
me. Then I will know you are honest men and not
spies. Then I will give you back your brother, and you
may trade freely in the land.'"
35 As they emptied out their sacks, there in each
man's sack was the bag of money he had paid for the
grain! The brothers and their father were terrified
when they saw the bags of money. 36 Jacob exclaimed,
"You are robbing me of my children! Joseph is gone!
Simeon is gone! And now you want to take Benjamin,
too. Everything is going against me!"
37 Then Reuben said to his father, "You may kill my
two sons if I don't bring Benjamin back to you. I'll be
responsible for him, and I promise to bring him back."
38 But Jacob replied, "My son will not go down with
you. His brother Joseph is dead, and he is all I have
left. If anything should happen to him on your jour-
ney, you would send this grieving, white-haired man
to his grave.*"

THE BROTHERS RETURN TO EGYPT

43 But the famine continued to ravage the land
of Canaan. 2 When the grain they had brought
from Egypt was almost gone, Jacob said to his sons,
"Go back and buy us a little more food."
3 But Judah said, "The man was serious when he
warned us, 'You won't see my face again unless your
brother is with you.' 4 If you send Benjamin with us,
we will go down and buy more food. 5 But if you don't
let Benjamin go, we won't go either. Remember, the
man said, 'You won't see my face again unless your
brother is with you.'"
6 "Why were you so cruel to me?" Jacob* moaned.
"Why did you tell him you had another brother?"
7 "The man kept asking us questions about our fam-
ily," they replied. "He asked, 'Is your father still alive?
Do you have another brother?' So we answered his
questions. How could we know he would say, 'Bring
your brother down here'?"
8 Judah said to his father, "Send the boy with me, and
we will be on our way. Otherwise we will all die of star-
vation—and not only we, but you and our little ones. 9 I
personally guarantee his safety. You may hold me re-
sponsible if I don't bring him back to you. Then let me
bear the blame forever. 10 If we hadn't wasted all this
time, we could have gone and returned twice by now."
11 So their father, Jacob, finally said to them, "If it
can't be avoided, then at least do this. Pack your bags

42:38 Hebrew *to Sheol*. 43:6 Hebrew *Israel;* also in 43:11. See note on 35:21.

42:15 your youngest brother. Joseph could not have asked his brothers to do a more difficult thing than to bring Benjamin with them to Egypt.

42:21 anguish. Joseph's brothers immediately made the connection between their actions and the consequences they were facing.

42:24 He chose Simeon. It seems unusual that Joseph would have kept Simeon as a hostage, since Reuben, the oldest, had saved his life (37:21-22).

42:37 my two sons. Reuben's offer of laying down the lives of both his sons to secure Benjamin's safety brought little relief to Jacob. God had promised his family a host of descendants, yet he was losing sons one at a time.

43:9 I . . . guarantee his safety. While Reuben had offered the lives of his sons (42:37), Judah offered his own life in exchange for Benjamin.

43:11 do this. Jacob came up with a strategy of gift-giving to buy Joseph's favor.

with the best products of this land. Take them down
to the man as gifts—balm, honey, gum, aromatic res-
in, pistachio nuts, and almonds. 12 Also take double
the money that was put back in your sacks, as it was
probably someone's mistake. 13 Then take your broth-
er, and go back to the man. 14 May God Almighty* give
you mercy as you go before the man, so that he will
release Simeon and let Benjamin return. But if I must
lose my children, so be it."
15 So the men packed Jacob's gifts and double the
money and headed off with Benjamin. They finally
arrived in Egypt and presented themselves to Joseph.
16 When Joseph saw Benjamin with them, he said to
the manager of his household, "These men will eat
with me this noon. Take them inside the palace. Then
go slaughter an animal, and prepare a big feast." 17 So
the man did as Joseph told him and took them into Jo-
seph's palace.
18 The brothers were terrified when they saw that
they were being taken into Joseph's house. "It's be-
cause of the money someone put in our sacks last time
we were here," they said. "He plans to pretend that we
stole it. Then he will seize us, make us slaves, and take
our donkeys."

A FEAST AT JOSEPH'S PALACE

19 The brothers approached the manager of Joseph's
household and spoke to him at the entrance to the
palace. 20 "Sir," they said, "we came to Egypt once be-
fore to buy food. 21 But as we were returning home,
we stopped for the night and opened our sacks. Then
we discovered that each man's money—the exact
amount paid—was in the top of his sack! Here it is;
we have brought it back with us. 22 We also have addi-
tional money to buy more food. We have no idea who
put our money in our sacks."
23 "Relax. Don't be afraid," the household manag-
er told them. "Your God, the God of your father, must
have put this treasure into your sacks. I know I re-
ceived your payment." Then he released Simeon and
brought him out to them.
24 The manager then led the men into Joseph's pal-
ace. He gave them water to wash their feet and pro-
vided food for their donkeys. 25 They were told they
would be eating there, so they prepared their gifts for
Joseph's arrival at noon.
26 When Joseph came home, they gave him the gifts
they had brought him, then bowed low to the ground
before him. 27 After greeting them, he asked, "How is
your father, the old man you spoke about? Is he still
alive?"
28 "Yes," they replied. "Our father, your servant, is
alive and well." And they bowed low again.
29 Then Joseph looked at his brother Benjamin, the
son of his own mother. "Is this your youngest brother,
the one you told me about?" Joseph asked. "May God
be gracious to you, my son." 30 Then Joseph hurried
from the room because he was overcome with emo-
tion for his brother. He went into his private room,
where he broke down and wept. 31 After washing his
face, he came back out, keeping himself under control.
Then he ordered, "Bring out the food!"
32 The waiters served Joseph at his own table, and
his brothers were served at a separate table. The
Egyptians who ate with Joseph sat at their own table,
because Egyptians despise Hebrews and refuse to eat
with them. 33 Joseph told each of his brothers where
to sit, and to their amazement, he seated them ac-
cording to age, from oldest to youngest. 34 And Joseph
filled their plates with food from his own table, giving
Benjamin five times as much as he gave the others. So
they feasted and drank freely with him.

JOSEPH'S SILVER CUP

44 When his brothers were ready to leave, Joseph
gave these instructions to his palace manager:
"Fill each of their sacks with as much grain as they
can carry, and put each man's money back into his
sack. 2 Then put my personal silver cup at the top of
the youngest brother's sack, along with the money for
his grain." So the manager did as Joseph instructed
him.
3 The brothers were up at dawn and were sent on
their journey with their loaded donkeys. 4 But when
they had gone only a short distance and were bare-
ly out of the city, Joseph said to his palace manager,
"Chase after them and stop them. When you catch up
with them, ask them, 'Why have you repaid my kind-
ness with such evil? 5 Why have you stolen my mas-
ter's silver cup,* which he uses to predict the future?
What a wicked thing you have done!'"
6 When the palace manager caught up with the
men, he spoke to them as he had been instructed.
7 "What are you talking about?" the brothers re-
sponded. "We are your servants and would never do
such a thing! 8 Didn't we return the money we found
in our sacks? We brought it back all the way from the
land of Canaan. Why would we steal silver or gold
from your master's house? 9 If you find his cup with
any one of us, let that man die. And all the rest of us,
my lord, will be your slaves."
10 "That's fair," the man replied. "But only the one
who stole the cup will be my slave. The rest of you
may go free."
11 They all quickly took their sacks from the backs of
their donkeys and opened them. 12 The palace manag-
er searched the brothers' sacks, from the oldest to the
youngest. And the cup was found in Benjamin's sack!
13 When the brothers saw this, they tore their clothing
in despair. Then they loaded their donkeys again and
returned to the city.
14 Joseph was still in his palace when Judah and
his brothers arrived, and they fell to the ground be-
fore him. 15 "What have you done?" Joseph demanded.
"Don't you know that a man like me can predict the
future?"

43:14 Hebrew *El-Shaddai.* 44:5 As in Greek version; Hebrew lacks this phrase.

43:26 bowed low to the ground. Imagine the pressure Joseph's brothers were under to make sure Benjamin came back home safely.

43:29 his brother Benjamin. Benjamin was Joseph's only full brother. Thus, the bond between him and Benjamin was much stronger than that with his other brothers.

43:33-34 according to age. This unknown ruler seated the brothers in the exact order of their ages and then gave the youngest brother special treatment.

44:9 let that man die. The brothers proclaimed that whoever had stolen Joseph's silver cup would lose his life, and the rest would lose their freedom.

44:10 will be my slave. Joseph's servant proposed that the guilty party be enslaved and the others go free. This would create a great dilemma for the brothers—returning to their father without his youngest son.

44:14 fell to the ground. Joseph was testing his brothers. Were they still heartless? Would they treat Benjamin as they had treated him?

16 Judah answered, "Oh, my lord, what can we say to you? How can we explain this? How can we prove our innocence? God is punishing us for our sins. My lord, we have all returned to be your slaves—all of us, not just our brother who had your cup in his sack."

17 "No," Joseph said. "I would never do such a thing! Only the man who stole the cup will be my slave. The rest of you may go back to your father in peace."

JUDAH SPEAKS FOR HIS BROTHERS

18 Then Judah stepped forward and said, "Please, my lord, let your servant say just one word to you. Please, do not be angry with me, even though you are as powerful as Pharaoh himself.

19 "My lord, previously you asked us, your servants, 'Do you have a father or a brother?' 20 And we responded, 'Yes, my lord, we have a father who is an old man, and his youngest son is a child of his old age. His full brother is dead, and he alone is left of his mother's children, and his father loves him very much.'

21 "And you said to us, 'Bring him here so I can see him with my own eyes.' 22 But we said to you, 'My lord, the boy cannot leave his father, for his father would die.' 23 But you told us, 'Unless your youngest brother comes with you, you will never see my face again.'

24 "So we returned to your servant, our father, and told him what you had said. 25 Later, when he said, 'Go back again and buy us more food,' 26 we replied, 'We can't go unless you let our youngest brother go with us. We'll never get to see the man's face unless our youngest brother is with us.'

27 "Then my father said to us, 'As you know, my wife had two sons, 28 and one of them went away and never returned. Doubtless he was torn to pieces by some wild animal. I have never seen him since. 29 Now if you take his brother away from me, and any harm comes to him, you will send this grieving, white-haired man to his grave.*'

30 "And now, my lord, I cannot go back to my father without the boy. Our father's life is bound up in the boy's life. 31 If he sees that the boy is not with us, our father will die. We, your servants, will indeed be responsible for sending that grieving, white-haired man to his grave. 32 My lord, I guaranteed to my father that I would take care of the boy. I told him, 'If I don't bring him back to you, I will bear the blame forever.'

33 "So please, my lord, let me stay here as a slave instead of the boy, and let the boy return with his brothers. 34 For how can I return to my father if the boy is not with me? I couldn't bear to see the anguish this would cause my father!"

JOSEPH REVEALS HIS IDENTITY

45 Joseph could stand it no longer. There were many people in the room, and he said to his attendants, "Out, all of you!" So he was alone with his

"HEY, IT'S ME!"

1. Is there anyone you haven't seen in a long time that you would like to see again?

GENESIS 45:1-28

2. Why did Joseph tell his brothers, "don't be angry with yourselves for selling me to this place" (v. 5)?
3. How do you think Joseph was able to forgive his brothers for selling him as a slave? What's the lesson here for us?
4. Why did Joseph tell his brothers, as they were leaving, "Don't quarrel . . . along the way" (v. 24)?
5. Is there someone you need to forgive? Is there someone with whom you need to stop arguing?

brothers when he told them who he was. 2 Then he broke down and wept. He wept so loudly the Egyptians could hear him, and word of it quickly carried to Pharaoh's palace.

3 "I am Joseph!" he said to his brothers. "Is my father still alive?" But his brothers were speechless! They were stunned to realize that Joseph was standing there in front of them. 4 "Please, come closer," he said to them. So they came closer. And he said again, "I am Joseph, your brother, whom you sold into slavery in Egypt. 5 But don't be upset, and don't be angry with yourselves for selling me to this place. It was God who sent me here ahead of you to preserve your lives. 6 This famine that has ravaged the land for two years will last five more years, and there will be neither plowing nor harvesting. 7 God has sent me ahead of you to keep you and your families alive and to preserve many survivors.* 8 So it was God who sent me here, not you! And he is the one who made me an adviser* to Pharaoh—the manager of his entire palace and the governor of all Egypt.

9 "Now hurry back to my father and tell him, 'This is what your son Joseph says: God has made me master over all the land of Egypt. So come down to me immediately! 10 You can live in the region of Goshen, where you can be near me with all your children and grandchildren, your flocks and herds, and everything you own. 11 I will take care of you there, for there are still five years of famine ahead of us. Otherwise you, your household, and all your animals will starve.'"

12 Then Joseph added, "Look! You can see for yourselves, and so can my brother Benjamin, that I really am Joseph! 13 Go tell my father of my honored position here in Egypt. Describe for him everything you have seen, and then bring my father here quickly." 14 Weep-

44:29 Hebrew *to Sheol;* also in 44:31. 45:7 Or *and to save you with an extraordinary rescue.* The meaning of the Hebrew is uncertain.
45:8 Hebrew *a father.*

44:18 let your servant say. Judah begged Joseph for the life of Benjamin.
44:30 bound up. Judah described Jacob's relationship to Benjamin as "tied together." In begging for Benjamin's life, Judah was also begging for his father's life.
44:33 let me stay here. Then Judah offered himself in the place of his brother. There could be no doubt in Joseph's mind that this brother, who had once sold him into slavery, had changed.
45:1 could stand it no longer. Joseph had controlled himself as long as he could. He was ready to reveal himself to his brothers.
45:3 speechless. These brothers were now face-to-face with the brother they had wronged and an Egyptian official who had total power over them.
45:5 don't be upset. Joseph told his brothers that everything had worked out for the best because God had used him as part of His plan.
45:9 God has made me master over . . . Egypt. Note that Joseph does not say, "Pharaoh has made me lord of all Egypt." He gives God the glory. **immediately.** Joseph wants his brothers to hurry home to their father Jacob with the news.

ing with joy, he embraced Benjamin, and Benjamin
did the same. 15 Then Joseph kissed each of his broth-
ers and wept over them, and after that they began
talking freely with him.

PHARAOH INVITES JACOB TO EGYPT

16 The news soon reached Pharaoh's palace: "Joseph's
brothers have arrived!" Pharaoh and his officials
were all delighted to hear this.
17 Pharaoh said to Joseph, "Tell your brothers, 'This
is what you must do: Load your pack animals, and
hurry back to the land of Canaan. 18 Then get your fa-
ther and all of your families, and return here to me. I
will give you the very best land in Egypt, and you will
eat from the best that the land produces.'"
19 Then Pharaoh said to Joseph, "Tell your brothers,
'Take wagons from the land of Egypt to carry your
little children and your wives, and bring your father
here. 20 Don't worry about your personal belongings,
for the best of all the land of Egypt is yours.'"
21 So the sons of Jacob* did as they were told. Joseph
provided them with wagons, as Pharaoh had com-
manded, and he gave them supplies for the journey.
22 And he gave each of them new clothes—but to Ben-
jamin he gave five changes of clothes and 300 pieces*
of silver. 23 He also sent his father ten male donkeys
loaded with the finest products of Egypt, and ten fe-
male donkeys loaded with grain and bread and other
supplies he would need on his journey.
24 So Joseph sent his brothers off, and as they left, he
called after them, "Don't quarrel about all this along
the way!" 25 And they left Egypt and returned to their
father, Jacob, in the land of Canaan.
26 "Joseph is still alive!" they told him. "And he is
governor of all the land of Egypt!" Jacob was stunned
at the news—he couldn't believe it. 27 But when they
repeated to Jacob everything Joseph had told them,
and when he saw the wagons Joseph had sent to car-
ry him, their father's spirits revived.
28 Then Jacob exclaimed, "It must be true! My son
Joseph is alive! I must go and see him before I die."

JACOB'S JOURNEY TO EGYPT

46 So Jacob* set out for Egypt with all his posses-
sions. And when he came to Beersheba, he of-
fered sacrifices to the God of his father, Isaac. 2 During
the night God spoke to him in a vision. "Jacob! Jacob!"
he called.
"Here I am," Jacob replied.
3 "I am God,* the God of your father," the voice said. "Do
not be afraid to go down to Egypt, for there I will make
your family into a great nation. 4 I will go with you down
to Egypt, and I will bring you back again. You will die in
Egypt, but Joseph will be with you to close your eyes."
5 So Jacob left Beersheba, and his sons took him to
Egypt. They carried him and their little ones and their
wives in the wagons Pharaoh had provided for them.
6 They also took all their livestock and all the personal
belongings they had acquired in the land of Canaan.
So Jacob and his entire family went to Egypt—7 sons
and grandsons, daughters and granddaughters—all
his descendants.
8 These are the names of the descendants of Isra-
el—the sons of Jacob—who went to Egypt:

Reuben was Jacob's oldest son. 9 The sons of Reuben
were Hanoch, Pallu, Hezron, and Carmi.
10 The sons of Simeon were Jemuel, Jamin, Ohad, Jakin,
Zohar, and Shaul. (Shaul's mother was a Canaanite
woman.)
11 The sons of Levi were Gershon, Kohath, and Merari.
12 The sons of Judah were Er, Onan, Shelah, Perez, and
Zerah (though Er and Onan had died in the land of
Canaan). The sons of Perez were Hezron and Hamul.
13 The sons of Issachar were Tola, Puah,* Jashub,* and
Shimron.
14 The sons of Zebulun were Sered, Elon, and Jahleel.
15 These were the sons of Leah and Jacob who were
born in Paddan-aram, in addition to their daughter,
Dinah. The number of Jacob's descendants (male and
female) through Leah was thirty-three.

16 The sons of Gad were Zephon,* Haggi, Shuni, Ezbon,
Eri, Arodi, and Areli.
17 The sons of Asher were Imnah, Ishvah, Ishvi, and
Beriah. Their sister was Serah. Beriah's sons were
Heber and Malkiel.
18 These were the sons of Zilpah, the servant given to
Leah by her father, Laban. The number of Jacob's de-
scendants through Zilpah was sixteen.

19 The sons of Jacob's wife Rachel were Joseph and
Benjamin.
20 Joseph's sons, born in the land of Egypt, were
Manasseh and Ephraim. Their mother was
Asenath, daughter of Potiphera, the priest of On.*
21 Benjamin's sons were Bela, Beker, Ashbel, Gera,
Naaman, Ehi, Rosh, Muppim, Huppim, and Ard.
22 These were the sons of Rachel and Jacob. The num-
ber of Jacob's descendants through Rachel was four-
teen.

23 The son of Dan was Hushim.
24 The sons of Naphtali were Jahzeel, Guni, Jezer, and
Shillem.
25 These were the sons of Bilhah, the servant given to
Rachel by her father, Laban. The number of Jacob's
descendants through Bilhah was seven.

26 The total number of Jacob's direct descendants who
went with him to Egypt, not counting his sons' wives,
was sixty-six. 27 In addition, Joseph had two sons* who
were born in Egypt. So altogether, there were seven-
ty* members of Jacob's family in the land of Egypt.

45:21 Hebrew *Israel;* also in 45:28. See note on 35:21. **45:22** Hebrew *300 [shekels],* about 7.5 pounds or 3.4 kilograms in weight. **46:1** Hebrew *Israel;* also in 46:29, 30. See note on 35:21. **46:3** Hebrew *I am El.* **46:13a** As in Syriac version and Samaritan Pentateuch (see also 1 Chr 7:1); Hebrew reads *Puvah.* **46:13b** As in some Greek manuscripts and Samaritan Pentateuch (see also Num 26:24; 1 Chr 7:1); Hebrew reads *Iob.* **46:16** As in Greek version and Samaritan Pentateuch (see also Num 26:15); Hebrew reads *Ziphion.* **46:20** Greek version reads *of Heliopolis.* **46:27a** Greek version reads *nine sons,* probably including Joseph's grandsons through Ephraim and Manasseh (see 1 Chr 7:14-20). **46:27b** Greek version reads *seventy-five;* see note on Exod 1:5.

46:2 in a vision. God spoke to Jacob (Israel) in this same place where he had also spoken to Isaac, Jacob's father (26:4).
46:3 Do not be afraid to go down. God told Jacob to trust Him by traveling to Egypt. **I will make . . . into a great nation.** This echoes God's promise to Abraham passed down to Isaac and then to Jacob.
46:8 names of the descendants. These names are the 12 tribes of the Old Testament. The rest of the Bible describes God's people in terms of the sons of Jacob, or Israel, from whom they descended.
46:27 Jacob's family. From this small number grew a great nation (Ex. 1:5; 12:37).

JACOB'S FAMILY ARRIVES IN GOSHEN

28 As they neared their destination, Jacob sent Judah ahead to meet Joseph and get directions to the region of Goshen. And when they finally arrived there, 29 Joseph prepared his chariot and traveled to Goshen to meet his father, Jacob. When Joseph arrived, he embraced his father and wept, holding him for a long time. 30 Finally, Jacob said to Joseph, "Now I am ready to die, since I have seen your face again and know you are still alive."

31 And Joseph said to his brothers and to his father's entire family, "I will go to Pharaoh and tell him, 'My brothers and my father's entire family have come to me from the land of Canaan. 32 These men are shepherds, and they raise livestock. They have brought with them their flocks and herds and everything they own.'"

33 Then he said, "When Pharaoh calls for you and asks you about your occupation, 34 you must tell him, 'We, your servants, have raised livestock all our lives, as our ancestors have always done.' When you tell him this, he will let you live here in the region of Goshen, for the Egyptians despise shepherds."

JACOB BLESSES PHARAOH

47 Then Joseph went to see Pharaoh and told him, "My father and my brothers have arrived from the land of Canaan. They have come with all their flocks and herds and possessions, and they are now in the region of Goshen."

2 Joseph took five of his brothers with him and presented them to Pharaoh. 3 And Pharaoh asked the brothers, "What is your occupation?"

They replied, "We, your servants, are shepherds, just like our ancestors. 4 We have come to live here in Egypt for a while, for there is no pasture for our flocks in Canaan. The famine is very severe there. So please, we request permission to live in the region of Goshen."

5 Then Pharaoh said to Joseph, "Now that your father and brothers have joined you here, 6 choose any place in the entire land of Egypt for them to live. Give them the best land of Egypt. Let them live in the region of Goshen. And if any of them have special skills, put them in charge of my livestock, too."

7 Then Joseph brought in his father, Jacob, and presented him to Pharaoh. And Jacob blessed Pharaoh.

8 "How old are you?" Pharaoh asked him.

9 Jacob replied, "I have traveled this earth for 130 hard years. But my life has been short compared to the lives of my ancestors." 10 Then Jacob blessed Pharaoh again before leaving his court.

11 So Joseph assigned the best land of Egypt—the region of Rameses—to his father and his brothers, and he settled them there, just as Pharaoh had commanded. 12 And Joseph provided food for his father and his brothers in amounts appropriate to the number of their dependents, including the smallest children.

JOSEPH'S LEADERSHIP IN THE FAMINE

13 Meanwhile, the famine became so severe that all the food was used up, and people were starving throughout the lands of Egypt and Canaan. 14 By selling grain to the people, Joseph eventually collected all the money in Egypt and Canaan, and he put the money in Pharaoh's treasury. 15 When the people of Egypt and Canaan ran out of money, all the Egyptians came to Joseph. "Our money is gone!" they cried. "But please give us food, or we will die before your very eyes!"

16 Joseph replied, "Since your money is gone, bring me your livestock. I will give you food in exchange for your livestock." 17 So they brought their livestock to Joseph in exchange for food. In exchange for their horses, flocks of sheep and goats, herds of cattle, and donkeys, Joseph provided them with food for another year.

18 But that year ended, and the next year they came again and said, "We cannot hide the truth from you, my lord. Our money is gone, and all our livestock and cattle are yours. We have nothing left to give but our bodies and our land. 19 Why should we die before your very eyes? Buy us and our land in exchange for food; we offer our land and ourselves as slaves for Pharaoh. Just give us grain so we may live and not die, and so the land does not become empty and desolate."

20 So Joseph bought all the land of Egypt for Pharaoh. All the Egyptians sold him their fields because the famine was so severe, and soon all the land belonged to Pharaoh. 21 As for the people, he made them all slaves,* from one end of Egypt to the other. 22 The only land he did not buy was the land belonging to the priests. They received an allotment of food directly from Pharaoh, so they didn't need to sell their land.

23 Then Joseph said to the people, "Look, today I have bought you and your land for Pharaoh. I will provide you with seed so you can plant the fields. 24 Then when you harvest it, one-fifth of your crop will belong to Pharaoh. You may keep the remaining four-fifths as seed for your fields and as food for you, your households, and your little ones."

25 "You have saved our lives!" they exclaimed. "May it please you, my lord, to let us be Pharaoh's servants." 26 Joseph then issued a decree still in effect in the land of Egypt, that Pharaoh should receive one-fifth of all the crops grown on his land. Only the land belonging to the priests was not given to Pharaoh.

27 Meanwhile, the people of Israel settled in the region of Goshen in Egypt. There they acquired property, and they were fruitful, and their population grew rapidly. 28 Jacob lived for seventeen years after his arrival in Egypt, so he lived 147 years in all.

29 As the time of his death drew near, Jacob* called for his son Joseph and said to him, "Please do me this favor. Put your hand under my thigh and swear that you will treat me with unfailing love by honoring this last request: Do not bury me in Egypt. 30 When I die, please take my body out of Egypt and bury me with my ancestors."

47:21 As in Greek version and Samaritan Pentateuch; Hebrew reads *he moved them all into the towns.* 47:29 Hebrew *Israel;* also in 47:31b. See note on 35:21.

46:29 Goshen. Joseph's family settled in some of the most fertile land in Egypt.
46:34 shepherds. When Joseph's brothers told Pharaoh they were shepherds, he gave them land in the Egyptian backcountry. This helped Jacob's family maintain their identity as a distinct people.
47:16 in exchange. By the end of the famine, the people had sold all they owned to the government, including themselves as slaves.
47:27 acquired property. Amazingly, while the Egyptian population was selling their land, the Israelites were acquiring property.
47:29 Do not bury me in Egypt. Jacob's body would find its rest in the manner of Jacob's life—on a journey.

So Joseph promised, "I will do as you ask."
31 "Swear that you will do it," Jacob insisted. So Joseph gave his oath, and Jacob bowed humbly at the head of his bed.*

JACOB BLESSES MANASSEH AND EPHRAIM

48 One day not long after this, word came to Joseph, "Your father is failing rapidly." So Joseph went to visit his father, and he took with him his two sons, Manasseh and Ephraim.
2 When Joseph arrived, Jacob was told, "Your son Joseph has come to see you." So Jacob* gathered his strength and sat up in his bed.
3 Jacob said to Joseph, "God Almighty* appeared to me at Luz in the land of Canaan and blessed me.
4 He said to me, 'I will make you fruitful, and I will multiply your descendants. I will make you a multitude of nations. And I will give this land of Canaan to your descendants* after you as an everlasting possession.'
5 "Now I am claiming as my own sons these two boys of yours, Ephraim and Manasseh, who were born here in the land of Egypt before I arrived. They will be my sons, just as Reuben and Simeon are.
6 But any children born to you in the future will be your own, and they will inherit land within the territories of their brothers Ephraim and Manasseh.
7 "Long ago, as I was returning from Paddan-aram,* Rachel died in the land of Canaan. We were still on the way, some distance from Ephrath (that is, Bethlehem). So with great sorrow I buried her there beside the road to Ephrath."
8 Then Jacob looked over at the two boys. "Are these your sons?" he asked.
9 "Yes," Joseph told him, "these are the sons God has given me here in Egypt."
And Jacob said, "Bring them closer to me, so I can bless them."
10 Jacob was half blind because of his age and could hardly see. So Joseph brought the boys close to him, and Jacob kissed and embraced them.
11 Then Jacob said to Joseph, "I never thought I would see your face again, but now God has let me see your children, too!"
12 Joseph moved the boys, who were at their grandfather's knees, and he bowed with his face to the ground.
13 Then he positioned the boys in front of Jacob. With his right hand he directed Ephraim toward Jacob's left hand, and with his left hand he put Manasseh at Jacob's right hand.
14 But Jacob crossed his arms as he reached out to lay his hands on the boys' heads. He put his right hand on the head of Ephraim, though he was the younger boy, and his left hand on the head of Manasseh, though he was the firstborn.
15 Then he blessed Joseph and said,

"May the God before whom my grandfather Abraham
and my father, Isaac, walked—
the God who has been my shepherd
all my life, to this very day,
16 the Angel who has redeemed me from all harm—
may he bless these boys.
May they preserve my name
and the names of Abraham and Isaac.
And may their descendants multiply greatly
throughout the earth."

17 But Joseph was upset when he saw that his father placed his right hand on Ephraim's head. So Joseph lifted it to move it from Ephraim's head to Manasseh's head.
18 "No, my father," he said. "This one is the firstborn. Put your right hand on his head."
19 But his father refused. "I know, my son; I know," he replied. "Manasseh will also become a great people, but his younger brother will become even greater. And his descendants will become a multitude of nations."
20 So Jacob blessed the boys that day with this blessing: "The people of Israel will use your names when they give a blessing. They will say, 'May God make you as prosperous as Ephraim and Manasseh.'" In this way, Jacob put Ephraim ahead of Manasseh.
21 Then Jacob said to Joseph, "Look, I am about to die, but God will be with you and will take you back to Canaan, the land of your ancestors.
22 And beyond what I have given your brothers, I am giving you an extra portion of the land* that I took from the Amorites with my sword and bow."

JACOB'S LAST WORDS TO HIS SONS

49 Then Jacob called together all his sons and said, "Gather around me, and I will tell you what will happen to each of you in the days to come.

2 "Come and listen, you sons of Jacob;
listen to Israel, your father.

3 "Reuben, you are my firstborn, my strength,
the child of my vigorous youth.
You are first in rank and first in power.
4 But you are as unruly as a flood,
and you will be first no longer.
For you went to bed with my wife;
you defiled my marriage couch.

5 "Simeon and Levi are two of a kind;
their weapons are instruments of violence.

47:31 Greek version reads *and Israel bowed in worship as he leaned on his staff.* Compare Heb 11:21. **48:2** Hebrew *Israel;* also in 48:8, 10, 11, 13, 14, 21. See note on 35:21. **48:3** Hebrew *El-Shaddai.* **48:4** Hebrew *seed;* also in 48:19. **48:7** Hebrew *Paddan,* referring to Paddan-aram; compare Gen 35:9. **48:22** Or *an extra ridge of land.* The meaning of the Hebrew is uncertain.

47:30 bury me with my ancestors. Jacob was referring to the family burial plot—the cave of Machpelah (23:14-20)—purchased by Abraham to bury Sarah,

47:31 Jacob bowed humbly. Jacob (Israel) was finished with his funeral and burial arrangements. Now he waited for life to end.

48:5 I am claiming. When Jacob's descendants settled in Canaan, territory was apportioned not to the tribe of Joseph, but to the tribes named for his sons, Ephraim and Manasseh.

48:7 Rachel died. As Jacob passed on his blessing to Joseph's son, he reminisced about his beloved wife Rachel.

48:8 Are these you sons? Perhaps Jacob's eyesight was so dim he did not know who Joseph's sons were.

48:15 Joseph. Joseph's name is used here as head of the family. When Jacob gave his blessing to Joseph's children, he was actually blessing Joseph.

48:16 the Angel who has redeemed me. This could refer to Jacob's wrestling all night with God and then receiving a blessing and a new name (32:24-30).

49:2 listen to . . . your father. Jacob blessed his sons by describing their traits.

49:4 unruly as a flood. The tribe of Reuben came to be known for its indecision (Judg. 5:16).

49:5 instruments of violence. Jacob identified violence as the trait of Simeon and Levi. They had destroyed the Shechemites to avenge their sister's rape (34:25-29).

[6] May I never join in their meetings;
may I never be a party to their plans.
For in their anger they murdered men,
and they crippled oxen just for sport.
[7] A curse on their anger, for it is fierce;
a curse on their wrath, for it is cruel.
I will scatter them among the descendants of Jacob;
I will disperse them throughout Israel.

[8] "Judah, your brothers will praise you.
You will grasp your enemies by the neck.
All your relatives will bow before you.
[9] Judah, my son, is a young lion
that has finished eating its prey.
Like a lion he crouches and lies down;
like a lioness—who dares to rouse him?
[10] The scepter will not depart from Judah,
nor the ruler's staff from his descendants,*
until the coming of the one to whom it belongs,*
the one whom all nations will honor.
[11] He ties his foal to a grapevine,
the colt of his donkey to a choice vine.
He washes his clothes in wine,
his robes in the blood of grapes.
[12] His eyes are darker than wine,
and his teeth are whiter than milk.

[13] "Zebulun will settle by the seashore
and will be a harbor for ships;
his borders will extend to Sidon.

[14] "Issachar is a sturdy donkey,
resting between two saddlepacks.*
[15] When he sees how good the countryside is
and how pleasant the land,
he will bend his shoulder to the load
and submit himself to hard labor.

[16] "Dan will govern his people,
like any other tribe in Israel.
[17] Dan will be a snake beside the road,
a poisonous viper along the path
that bites the horse's hooves
so its rider is thrown off.
[18] I trust in you for salvation, O LORD!

[19] "Gad will be attacked by marauding bands,
but he will attack them when they retreat.

[20] "Asher will dine on rich foods
and produce food fit for kings.

[21] "Naphtali is a doe set free
that bears beautiful fawns.

[22] "Joseph is the foal of a wild donkey,
the foal of a wild donkey at a spring—
one of the wild donkeys on the ridge.*
[23] Archers attacked him savagely;
they shot at him and harassed him.
[24] But his bow remained taut,
and his arms were strengthened
by the hands of the Mighty One of Jacob,
by the Shepherd, the Rock of Israel.
[25] May the God of your father help you;
may the Almighty bless you
with the blessings of the heavens above,
and blessings of the watery depths below,
and blessings of the breasts and womb.
[26] May my fatherly blessings on you
surpass the blessings of my ancestors,*
reaching to the heights of the eternal hills.
May these blessings rest on the head of Joseph,
who is a prince among his brothers.

[27] "Benjamin is a ravenous wolf,
devouring his enemies in the morning
and dividing his plunder in the evening."

[28] These are the twelve tribes of Israel, and this is
what their father said as he told his sons good-bye. He
blessed each one with an appropriate message.

JACOB'S DEATH AND BURIAL

[29] Then Jacob instructed them, "Soon I will die and join
my ancestors. Bury me with my father and grand-
father in the cave in the field of Ephron the Hittite.
[30] This is the cave in the field of Machpelah, near
Mamre in Canaan, that Abraham bought from Eph-
ron the Hittite as a permanent burial site. [31] There
Abraham and his wife Sarah are buried. There Isaac
and his wife, Rebekah, are buried. And there I bur-
ied Leah. [32] It is the plot of land and the cave that my
grandfather Abraham bought from the Hittites."
[33] When Jacob had finished this charge to his sons,
he drew his feet into the bed, breathed his last, and
joined his ancestors in death.

50 Joseph threw himself on his father and wept
over him and kissed him. [2] Then Joseph told the
physicians who served him to embalm his father's
body; so Jacob* was embalmed. [3] The embalming
process took the usual forty days. And the Egyptians
mourned his death for seventy days.
[4] When the period of mourning was over, Joseph
approached Pharaoh's advisers and said, "Please do
me this favor and speak to Pharaoh on my behalf.
[5] Tell him that my father made me swear an oath. He
said to me, 'Listen, I am about to die. Take my body
back to the land of Canaan, and bury me in the tomb
I prepared for myself.' So please allow me to go and

49:10a Hebrew *from between his feet.* **49:10b** Or *until tribute is brought to him and the peoples obey;* traditionally rendered *until Shiloh comes.* **49:14** Or *sheepfolds,* or *hearths.* **49:22** Or *Joseph is a fruitful tree, / a fruitful tree beside a spring. / His branches reach over the wall.* The meaning of the Hebrew is uncertain. **49:26** Or *of the ancient mountains.* **50:2** Hebrew *Israel.* See note on 35:21.

49:8 will bow before me. Through Judah, King David descended. Also through Judah's line Jesus was born.
49:27 devouring his enemies. This trait of savagery is borne out in Benjamin's tribe. King Saul, a mighty warrior, was from this tribe (1 Sam. 10).
50:2 embalm. Joseph directed the Egyptian physicians to embalm Jacob. They removed the organs of the body and filled it with salts and preservatives.
50:3 forty days . . . seventy days. Forty days was the typical time for an Egyptian embalming. In the meantime, Jacob's family and Joseph's nation were grieving for Jacob. Seventy days to mourn was just two days shorter than the mourning period for an Egyptian Pharaoh—an indication of the respect of the Egyptians for Joseph.
50:5 allow me to go. Joseph faced the same journey to Canaan that his descendants would make 400 years later. When those descendants made that journey, they would carry Joseph's bones for burial in the promised land (Ex. 13:19).

bury my father. After his burial, I will return without
delay."
6 Pharaoh agreed to Joseph's request. "Go and bury
your father, as he made you promise," he said. 7 So Jo-
seph went up to bury his father. He was accompanied
by all of Pharaoh's officials, all the senior members
of Pharaoh's household, and all the senior officers
of Egypt. 8 Joseph also took his entire household and
his brothers and their households. But they left their
little children and flocks and herds in the land of Gos-
hen. 9 A great number of chariots and charioteers ac-
companied Joseph.
10 When they arrived at the threshing floor of
Atad, near the Jordan River, they held a very great
and solemn memorial service, with a seven-day pe-
riod of mourning for Joseph's father. 11 The local res-
idents, the Canaanites, watched them mourning at
the threshing floor of Atad. Then they renamed that
place (which is near the Jordan) Abel-mizraim,* for
they said, "This is a place of deep mourning for these
Egyptians."
12 So Jacob's sons did as he had commanded them.
13 They carried his body to the land of Canaan and
buried him in the cave in the field of Machpelah, near
Mamre. This is the cave that Abraham had bought as
a permanent burial site from Ephron the Hittite.

JOSEPH REASSURES HIS BROTHERS

14 After burying Jacob, Joseph returned to Egypt with
his brothers and all who had accompanied him to his
father's burial. 15 But now that their father was dead,
Joseph's brothers became fearful. "Now Joseph will
show his anger and pay us back for all the wrong we
did to him," they said.
16 So they sent this message to Joseph: "Before your
father died, he instructed us 17 to say to you: 'Please
forgive your brothers for the great wrong they did to
you—for their sin in treating you so cruelly.' So we,
the servants of the God of your father, beg you to for-
give our sin." When Joseph received the message, he
broke down and wept. 18 Then his brothers came and
threw themselves down before Joseph. "Look, we are
your slaves!" they said.
19 But Joseph replied, "Don't be afraid of me. Am I
God, that I can punish you? 20 You intended to harm
me, but God intended it all for good. He brought me to
this position so I could save the lives of many people.
21 No, don't be afraid. I will continue to take care of you
and your children." So he reassured them by speaking
kindly to them.

THE DEATH OF JOSEPH

22 So Joseph and his brothers and their families con-
tinued to live in Egypt. Joseph lived to the age of 110.
23 He lived to see three generations of descendants of
his son Ephraim, and he lived to see the birth of the
children of Manasseh's son Makir, whom he claimed
as his own.*
24 "Soon I will die," Joseph told his brothers, "but God
will surely come to help you and lead you out of this land
of Egypt. He will bring you back to the land he solemnly
promised to give to Abraham, to Isaac, and to Jacob."
25 Then Joseph made the sons of Israel swear an
oath, and he said, "When God comes to help you and
lead you back, you must take my bones with you."
26 So Joseph died at the age of 110. The Egyptians em-
balmed him, and his body was placed in a coffin in
Egypt.

50:11 *Abel-mizraim* means "mourning of the Egyptians." **50:23** Hebrew *who were born on Joseph's knees.*

50:15 pay us back. With their father gone, Joseph's brothers were afraid that he would take revenge against them.

50:20 You intended to harm me. Joseph's ability to forgive his brothers was grounded in his belief that God worked his will through human events.

50:23 he claimed as his own. Joseph lived to see great-great grandchildren. The custom was to place the babies on his knees, signifying that they belonged to him.

50:24 promised to give to Abraham, Isaac, and Jacob. The legacy of God's promise to Abraham was so strong that even on Joseph's deathbed, after relocating his family to the farmlands of Goshen, he held on to the promise of another place. Hundreds of years later that legacy began to be fulfilled in the exodus of Israel from Egypt slavery (Ex. 1:5-8).

50:25 take my bones with you. Joseph's desire was the same as his father's. He wanted to be buried in the home God had promised his family. His bones were eventually buried at Shechem (Ex. 13:19; Josh. 24:32).

INTRODUCTION TO
EXODUS

PERSONAL READING PLAN

☐Exodus 1:1–3:22
☐Exodus 4:1–6:12
☐Exodus 6:13–8:19
☐Exodus 8:20–10:20
☐Exodus 10:21–12:51
☐Exodus 13:1–14:31
☐Exodus 15:1–16:36
☐Exodus 17:1–18:27
☐Exodus 19:1–21:36
☐Exodus 22:1–23:33
☐Exodus 24:1–25:40
☐Exodus 26:1–28:14
☐Exodus 28:15–29:46
☐Exodus 30:1–31:18
☐Exodus 32:1–33:23
☐Exodus 34:1–35:29
☐Exodus 35:30–38:20
☐Exodus 38:21–40:38

AUTHOR

Moses is assumed to be the author and editor of most of the first five books of the Old Testament (the Pentateuch).

DATE

It is difficult to set a firm date for the writing of the Pentateuch. Conservative estimates place it in either the 15th or 13th century B.C., depending on when the Exodus occurred.

THEME

Deliverance from Egypt; giving the Law; building the Tabernacle.

HISTORICAL BACKGROUND

No direct evidence fixes the events of this book within a specifically dated historical context. The Bible does not provide the name of the pharaoh of the Exodus, and extra-biblical texts and archaeology are silent concerning the Israelites' sojourn in and escape from Egypt. Indirect evidence present throughout the Bible can be used to support a wide range of dates. Certain recent archaeological evidence from Palestine suggests a late 13th century date for the appearance of the Israelites in Canaan. If we accept this date, then Moses and the events of this book may date earlier in this same century, sometime between 1300 and 1250 B.C.

CHARACTERISTICS

The book of Exodus is dominated by the life and actions of Moses and arranged around two outstanding redemptive acts: the Exodus from Egypt and the establishment of the Covenant at Sinai. Moses and these events are fundamental to an understanding of God's plan for human redemption. It could be argued that much of the Bible is a dialogue that reacts to, explains, and completes the redemptive plan of God as it is revealed in this book.

PASSAGES FOR TOPICAL GROUP STUDY

2:1-25 . . . . . FAITH and GUIDANCE . . . . Daring Escape
3:1-22 . . . . . GOD and OUR PURPOSE . . . . . Strange but True
4:1-17 . . . . . INSECURITY . . . . A Magical Staff
5:1-21 . . . . . FOLLOWING GOD and POPULARITY . . Popularity Jeopardy
6:28–7:24. . . HARDENED HEARTS. . . . . Heart Checkup
14:5-31 . . . . . ENEMIES and FAITH . . . . Survival Tactics
16:1-35. . . . . COMPLAINING and HUMAN NATURE . . . Heavenly Food
19:10–20:21 GOD'S WAY . . . . The Ten Commandments
32:1-35 . . . . . PRAYER. . . . . Prayer Changes Things

PASSAGES FOR GENERAL GROUP STUDY

12:1-30 . . . . The Passover and Jesus

THE ISRAELITES IN EGYPT

1 These are the names of the sons of Israel (that is,
Jacob) who moved to Egypt with their father, each
with his family: 2 Reuben, Simeon, Levi, Judah, 3 Issa-
char, Zebulun, Benjamin, 4 Dan, Naphtali, Gad, and
Asher. 5 In all, Jacob had seventy* descendants in
Egypt, including Joseph, who was already there.
6 In time, Joseph and all of his brothers died, end-
ing that entire generation. 7 But their descendants, the
Israelites, had many children and grandchildren. In
fact, they multiplied so greatly that they became ex-
tremely powerful and filled the land.
8 Eventually, a new king came to power in Egypt
who knew nothing about Joseph or what he had
done. 9 He said to his people, "Look, the people of Isra-
el now outnumber us and are stronger than we are.
10 We must make a plan to keep them from growing
even more. If we don't, and if war breaks out, they
will join our enemies and fight against us. Then they
will escape from the country.*"
11 So the Egyptians made the Israelites their slaves.
They appointed brutal slave drivers over them, hop-
ing to wear them down with crushing labor. They
forced them to build the cities of Pithom and Rame-
ses as supply centers for the king. 12 But the more the
Egyptians oppressed them, the more the Israelites
multiplied and spread, and the more alarmed the
Egyptians became. 13 So the Egyptians worked the
people of Israel without mercy. 14 They made their
lives bitter, forcing them to mix mortar and make
bricks and do all the work in the fields. They were
ruthless in all their demands.
15 Then Pharaoh, the king of Egypt, gave this or-
der to the Hebrew midwives, Shiphrah and Puah:
16 "When you help the Hebrew women as they give
birth, watch as they deliver.* If the baby is a boy, kill
him; if it is a girl, let her live." 17 But because the mid-
wives feared God, they refused to obey the king's or-
ders. They allowed the boys to live, too.
18 So the king of Egypt called for the midwives.
"Why have you done this?" he demanded. "Why have
you allowed the boys to live?"
19 "The Hebrew women are not like the Egyptian
women," the midwives replied. "They are more vigor-
ous and have their babies so quickly that we cannot
get there in time."
20 So God was good to the midwives, and the Isra-
elites continued to multiply, growing more and more
powerful. 21 And because the midwives feared God, he
gave them families of their own.
22 Then Pharaoh gave this order to all his people:
"Throw every newborn Hebrew boy into the Nile Riv-
er. But you may let the girls live."

THE BIRTH OF MOSES

2 About this time, a man and woman from the tribe
of Levi got married. 2 The woman became preg-
nant and gave birth to a son. She saw that he was a
special baby and kept him hidden for three months.
3 But when she could no longer hide him, she got a
basket made of papyrus reeds and waterproofed it
with tar and pitch. She put the baby in the basket and
laid it among the reeds along the bank of the Nile Riv-
er. 4 The baby's sister then stood at a distance, watch-
ing to see what would happen to him.

DARING ESCAPE

1. How much do you know about your birth: Time? Place? Weight? Anything else?

EXODUS 2:1-25

2. Why did Moses' mother hide her baby among reeds on the Nile (Ex. 1:22)? What does this show about her faith in God?
3. How did God honor the faith of Moses' family?
4. Why did Moses give up life in the palace to fight for the Jews? Did he do the right thing in killing the Egyptian, or might God have had another path for him to follow?
5. Is there a choice you need God's guidance for at this time?

5 Soon Pharaoh's daughter came down to bathe in
the river, and her attendants walked along the river-
bank. When the princess saw the basket among the
reeds, she sent her maid to get it for her. 6 When the
princess opened it, she saw the baby. The little boy
was crying, and she felt sorry for him. "This must be
one of the Hebrew children," she said.
7 Then the baby's sister approached the princess.
"Should I go and find one of the Hebrew women to
nurse the baby for you?" she asked.
8 "Yes, do!" the princess replied. So the girl went and
called the baby's mother.
9 "Take this baby and nurse him for me," the prin-
cess told the baby's mother. "I will pay you for your
help." So the woman took her baby home and nursed
him.
10 Later, when the boy was older, his mother brought
him back to Pharaoh's daughter, who adopted him as
her own son. The princess named him Moses,* for she
explained, "I lifted him out of the water."

MOSES ESCAPES TO MIDIAN

11 Many years later, when Moses had grown up, he
went out to visit his own people, the Hebrews, and he
saw how hard they were forced to work. During his
visit, he saw an Egyptian beating one of his fellow He-
brews. 12 After looking in all directions to make sure
no one was watching, Moses killed the Egyptian and
hid the body in the sand.

1:5 Dead Sea Scrolls and Greek version read *seventy-five;* see notes on Gen 46:27. **1:10** Or *will take the country.* **1:16** Hebrew *look upon the two stones;* perhaps the reference is to a birthstool. **2:10** *Moses* sounds like a Hebrew term that means "to lift out."

1:1-5 sons of Israel . . . who moved to Egypt. Jacob (also called Israel, Gen. 32:28) and his sons had traveled to Egypt at the invitation of his son, Joseph, who had risen to prominence in Egypt (Gen. 46:1-7). Only 70 people had arrived in Egypt (46:27); settling in the land of Goshen, separate from the Egyptians (46:31-34). When the Israelites, left Egypt they numbered about 600,000 men plus women and children (12:37). The Israelites lived in Egypt for 430 years.

2:2 special. Moses was an exceptional baby (see Acts 7:20; Heb. 11:23). He had two older siblings—Miriam (v. 4) and Aaron (4:14; 7:7).

2:6-8 This must be one of the Hebrew children. When she unwrapped the baby, Pharaoh's daughter no doubt noticed he had been circumcised, since Israelites performed that rite on the eighth day after birth. Egyptians practiced circumcision but not on infants.

2:11 Moses had grown up. At this point, Moses is 40 years old (Acts 7:23).

13 The next day, when Moses went out to visit his
people again, he saw two Hebrew men fighting. "Why
are you beating up your friend?" Moses said to the
one who had started the fight.
14 The man replied, "Who appointed you to be our
prince and judge? Are you going to kill me as you
killed that Egyptian yesterday?"
Then Moses was afraid, thinking, "Everyone knows
what I did." 15 And sure enough, Pharaoh heard what
had happened, and he tried to kill Moses. But Moses
fled from Pharaoh and went to live in the land of Mid-
ian.
When Moses arrived in Midian, he sat down be-
side a well. 16 Now the priest of Midian had sev-
en daughters who came as usual to draw water
and fill the water troughs for their father's flocks.
17 But some other shepherds came and chased them
away. So Moses jumped up and rescued the girls
from the shepherds. Then he drew water for their
flocks.
18 When the girls returned to Reuel, their father, he
asked, "Why are you back so soon today?"
19 "An Egyptian rescued us from the shepherds,"
they answered. "And then he drew water for us and
watered our flocks."
20 "Then where is he?" their father asked. "Why did
you leave him there? Invite him to come and eat with
us."
21 Moses accepted the invitation, and he set-
tled there with him. In time, Reuel gave Moses his
daughter Zipporah to be his wife. 22 Later she gave
birth to a son, and Moses named him Gershom,* for
he explained, "I have been a foreigner in a foreign
land."
23 Years passed, and the king of Egypt died. But the
Israelites continued to groan under their burden of
slavery. They cried out for help, and their cry rose up
to God. 24 God heard their groaning, and he remem-
bered his covenant promise to Abraham, Isaac, and
Jacob. 25 He looked down on the people of Israel and
knew it was time to act.*

MOSES AND THE BURNING BUSH

3 One day Moses was tending the flock of his fa-
ther-in-law, Jethro,* the priest of Midian. He led
the flock far into the wilderness and came to Sinai,*
the mountain of God. 2 There the angel of the LORD ap-
peared to him in a blazing fire from the middle of a
bush. Moses stared in amazement. Though the bush
was engulfed in flames, it didn't burn up. 3 "This is
amazing," Moses said to himself. "Why isn't that bush
burning up? I must go see it."
4 When the LORD saw Moses coming to take a closer
look, God called to him from the middle of the bush,
"Moses! Moses!"
"Here I am!" Moses replied.
5 "Do not come any closer," the LORD warned. "Take
off your sandals, for you are standing on holy ground.
6 I am the God of your father*—the God of Abraham,
the God of Isaac, and the God of Jacob." When Moses
heard this, he covered his face because he was afraid
to look at God.
7 Then the LORD told him, "I have certainly seen the
oppression of my people in Egypt. I have heard their
cries of distress because of their harsh slave drivers.
Yes, I am aware of their suffering. 8 So I have come
down to rescue them from the power of the Egyptians
and lead them out of Egypt into their own fertile and
spacious land. It is a land flowing with milk and hon-
ey—the land where the Canaanites, Hittites, Amo-
rites, Perizzites, Hivites, and Jebusites now live. 9 Look!
The cry of the people of Israel has reached me, and
I have seen how harshly the Egyptians abuse them.
10 Now go, for I am sending you to Pharaoh. You must
lead my people Israel out of Egypt."

STRANGE BUT TRUE

1. Have you ever seen anything strange or experienced something that defied common sense? What was it?

EXODUS 3:1-22

2. Why did God appear in a burning bush? What might fire symbolize?
3. Why does God say that His name is "I Am Who I Am" (v. 14)? What does that mean? What does it tell us about God's character?
4. Why did God tell Moses to ask Pharaoh to let the Israelites go, when He knew that Pharaoh would say no? What does this illustrate about God's purpose for our lives?
5. What is God's purpose for your life?

11 But Moses protested to God, "Who am I to appear
before Pharaoh? Who am I to lead the people of Israel
out of Egypt?"
12 God answered, "I will be with you. And this is
your sign that I am the one who has sent you: When
you have brought the people out of Egypt, you will
worship God at this very mountain."
13 But Moses protested, "If I go to the people of Isra-
el and tell them, 'The God of your ancestors has sent
me to you,' they will ask me, 'What is his name?' Then
what should I tell them?"
14 God replied to Moses, "I AM WHO I AM.* Say this
to the people of Israel: I AM has sent me to you." 15 God

2:22 *Gershom* sounds like a Hebrew term that means "a foreigner there." 2:25 Or *and acknowledged his obligation to help them.* 3:1a Moses' father-in-law went by two names, Jethro and Reuel. 3:1b Hebrew *Horeb,* another name for Sinai. 3:6 Greek version reads *your fathers.* 3:14 Or I Will Be What I Will Be.

2:15 Pharaoh. Possibly Thutmose III (1479–1425 B.C.). **Midian.** A dry wilderness quite different than Moses' sumptuous home in Egypt. He would remain here for 40 years (Acts 7:29-30).

2:24 remembered his covenant. God had promised Abraham, Isaac, and Jacob, that He would give the promised land to their descendants (Gen. 15:18-21; 26:2-6; 28:13-15). Abraham had also been told, however, that his descendants would "be strangers in a land that does not belong to them; they will be enslaved and oppressed 400 years" (Gen. 15:13).

3:6 afraid to look at God. To see God's face, Israelites believed, was to die (Gen. 16:13; 32:30). Moses discovered a relationship with God that made him unafraid (19:3; 33:11), and would even call on God to "let me see Your glory" (33:18).

3:14 I AM WHO I AM. The name Israel would call Him expresses God's eternal, dependable, and faithful character. **I AM.** Jesus used this phrase to describe Himself, in effect, as God (John 8:53-58). The power behind the words "I am He," caused His captors to collapse (John 18:6).

also said to Moses, "Say this to the people of Isra-
el: Yahweh,* the God of your ancestors—the God of
Abraham, the God of Isaac, and the God of Jacob—
has sent me to you.

This is my eternal name,
my name to remember for all generations.

16 "Now go and call together all the elders of Israel.
Tell them, 'Yahweh, the God of your ancestors—the
God of Abraham, Isaac, and Jacob—has appeared
to me. He told me, "I have been watching closely, and
I see how the Egyptians are treating you. 17 I have
promised to rescue you from your oppression in
Egypt. I will lead you to a land flowing with milk and
honey—the land where the Canaanites, Hittites, Am-
orites, Perizzites, Hivites, and Jebusites now live."'
18 "The elders of Israel will accept your message.
Then you and the elders must go to the king of Egypt
and tell him, 'The LORD, the God of the Hebrews, has
met with us. So please let us take a three-day journey
into the wilderness to offer sacrifices to the LORD, our
God.'
19 "But I know that the king of Egypt will not let
you go unless a mighty hand forces him.* 20 So I will
raise my hand and strike the Egyptians, performing
all kinds of miracles among them. Then at last he will
let you go. 21 And I will cause the Egyptians to look fa-
vorably on you. They will give you gifts when you go
so you will not leave empty-handed. 22 Every Israelite
woman will ask for articles of silver and gold and fine
clothing from her Egyptian neighbors and from the
foreign women in their houses. You will dress your
sons and daughters with these, stripping the Egyp-
tians of their wealth."

SIGNS OF THE LORD'S POWER

4 But Moses protested again, "What if they won't
believe me or listen to me? What if they say, 'The
LORD never appeared to you'?"
2 Then the LORD asked him, "What is that in your
hand?"
"A shepherd's staff," Moses replied.
3 "Throw it down on the ground," the LORD told him.
So Moses threw down the staff, and it turned into a
snake! Moses jumped back.
4 Then the LORD told him, "Reach out and grab its
tail." So Moses reached out and grabbed it, and it
turned back into a shepherd's staff in his hand.
5 "Perform this sign," the LORD told him. "Then they
will believe that the LORD, the God of their ances-
tors—the God of Abraham, the God of Isaac, and the
God of Jacob—really has appeared to you."
6 Then the LORD said to Moses, "Now put your
hand inside your cloak." So Moses put his hand in-
side his cloak, and when he took it out again, his
hand was white as snow with a severe skin dis-

A MAGICAL STAFF

1. Are you afraid of snakes? What's the most interesting "snake story" you know?

EXODUS 4:1-17

2. Why did God make Moses' staff turn into a snake? Why did He have him pick it up by the tail, instead of near the head? What might the snake symbolize?
3. What did the miraculous healing of Moses' hand represent?
4. Why is Moses still hesitant to lead the people? Summarize God's answer (vv. 14-17) in your own words.
5. Has God asked you to do something that seems hard or scary? How might His words to Moses apply to you?

ease.* 7 "Now put your hand back into your cloak,"
the LORD said. So Moses put his hand back in, and
when he took it out again, it was as healthy as the
rest of his body.
8 The LORD said to Moses, "If they do not believe you
and are not convinced by the first miraculous sign,
they will be convinced by the second sign. 9 And if
they don't believe you or listen to you even after these
two signs, then take some water from the Nile River
and pour it out on the dry ground. When you do, the
water from the Nile will turn to blood on the ground."
10 But Moses pleaded with the LORD, "O Lord, I'm
not very good with words. I never have been, and I'm
not now, even though you have spoken to me. I get
tongue-tied, and my words get tangled."
11 Then the LORD asked Moses, "Who makes a per-
son's mouth? Who decides whether people speak or
do not speak, hear or do not hear, see or do not see? Is
it not I, the LORD? 12 Now go! I will be with you as you
speak, and I will instruct you in what to say."
13 But Moses again pleaded, "Lord, please! Send any-
one else."
14 Then the LORD became angry with Moses. "All
right," he said. "What about your brother, Aaron the
Levite? I know he speaks well. And look! He is on his
way to meet you now. He will be delighted to see you.
15 Talk to him, and put the words in his mouth. I will be
with both of you as you speak, and I will instruct you
both in what to do. 16 Aaron will be your spokesman to
the people. He will be your mouthpiece, and you will
stand in the place of God for him, telling him what to
say. 17 And take your shepherd's staff with you, and
use it to perform the miraculous signs I have shown
you."

3:15 *Yahweh* (also in 3:16) is a transliteration of the proper name *YHWH* that is sometimes rendered "Jehovah"; in this translation it is usually rendered "the LORD" (note the use of small capitals). 3:19 As in Greek and Latin versions; Hebrew reads *will not let you go, not by a mighty hand.* 4:6 Or *with leprosy.* The Hebrew word used here can describe various skin diseases.

3:15 Yahweh. Yahweh, translated LORD, is related to the verb "I am."
3:21 favorably. God had promised Abraham that Israel would leave Egypt "with many possessions" (Gen. 15:14). Indeed, when the Israelites departed, the Egyptians gladly gave them whatever they asked for (12:35-36). Later the Israelites gave these same treasures for use in God's tabernacle (chap. 35).
4:3 snake. Making a staff turn into a snake showed powerlessness of Pharaoh, who used a cobra to symbolize his authority.
4:10 tongue-tied . . . tangled. A speech impediment? Stephen described Moses as "powerful in his speech" (Acts 7:22).
4:14 Levite. Aaron, Moses, and Miriam were from the tribe of Levi (6:16-20). Through Aaron the Levites would serve as priests in God's tabernacle and temple (Num. 1:50-51).

MOSES RETURNS TO EGYPT

18 So Moses went back home to Jethro, his father-in-law. "Please let me return to my relatives in Egypt," Moses said. "I don't even know if they are still alive."

"Go in peace," Jethro replied.

19 Before Moses left Midian, the LORD said to him, "Return to Egypt, for all those who wanted to kill you have died."

20 So Moses took his wife and sons, put them on a donkey, and headed back to the land of Egypt. In his hand he carried the staff of God.

21 And the LORD told Moses, "When you arrive back in Egypt, go to Pharaoh and perform all the miracles I have empowered you to do. But I will harden his heart so he will refuse to let the people go. 22 Then you will tell him, 'This is what the LORD says: Israel is my firstborn son. 23 I commanded you, "Let my son go, so he can worship me." But since you have refused, I will now kill your firstborn son!'"

24 On the way to Egypt, at a place where Moses and his family had stopped for the night, the LORD confronted him and was about to kill him. 25 But Moses' wife, Zipporah, took a flint knife and circumcised her son. She touched his feet* with the foreskin and said, "Now you are a bridegroom of blood to me." 26 (When she said "a bridegroom of blood," she was referring to the circumcision.) After that, the LORD left him alone.

27 Now the LORD had said to Aaron, "Go out into the wilderness to meet Moses." So Aaron went and met Moses at the mountain of God, and he embraced him. 28 Moses then told Aaron everything the LORD had commanded him to say. And he told him about the miraculous signs the LORD had commanded him to perform.

29 Then Moses and Aaron returned to Egypt and called all the elders of Israel together. 30 Aaron told them everything the LORD had told Moses, and Moses performed the miraculous signs as they watched. 31 Then the people of Israel were convinced that the LORD had sent Moses and Aaron. When they heard that the LORD was concerned about them and had seen their misery, they bowed down and worshiped.

MOSES AND AARON SPEAK TO PHARAOH

5 After this presentation to Israel's leaders, Moses and Aaron went and spoke to Pharaoh. They told him, "This is what the LORD, the God of Israel, says: Let my people go so they may hold a festival in my honor in the wilderness."

2 "Is that so?" retorted Pharaoh. "And who is the LORD? Why should I listen to him and let Israel go? I don't know the LORD, and I will not let Israel go."

3 But Aaron and Moses persisted. "The God of the Hebrews has met with us," they declared. "So let us take a three-day journey into the wilderness so we can offer sacrifices to the LORD our God. If we don't, he will kill us with a plague or with the sword."

4 Pharaoh replied, "Moses and Aaron, why are you distracting the people from their tasks? Get back to work! 5 Look, there are many of your people in the land, and you are stopping them from their work."

MAKING BRICKS WITHOUT STRAW

6 That same day Pharaoh sent this order to the Egyptian slave drivers and the Israelite foremen: 7 "Do not supply any more straw for making bricks. Make the people get it themselves! 8 But still require them to make the same number of bricks as before. Don't reduce the quota. They are lazy. That's why they are crying out, 'Let us go and offer sacrifices to our God.' 9 Load them down with more work. Make them sweat! That will teach them to listen to lies!"

10 So the slave drivers and foremen went out and told the people: "This is what Pharaoh says: I will not provide any more straw for you. 11 Go and get it yourselves. Find it wherever you can. But you must produce just as many bricks as before!" 12 So the people scattered throughout the land of Egypt in search of stubble to use as straw.

13 Meanwhile, the Egyptian slave drivers continued to push hard. "Meet your daily quota of bricks, just as you did when we provided you with straw!" they demanded. 14 Then they whipped the Israelite foremen they had put in charge of the work crews. "Why haven't you met your quotas either yesterday or today?" they demanded.

15 So the Israelite foremen went to Pharaoh and pleaded with him. "Please don't treat your servants like this," they begged. 16 "We are given no straw, but the slave drivers still demand, 'Make bricks!' We are being beaten, but it isn't our fault! Your own people are to blame!"

17 But Pharaoh shouted, "You're just lazy! Lazy! That's why you're saying, 'Let us go and offer sacrifices to the LORD.' 18 Now get back to work! No straw will be given to you, but you must still produce the full quota of bricks."

POPULARITY JEOPARDY

1. Have you ever worked with bricks? If so, what did you build? If not, what sort of construction projects have you worked on?

EXODUS 5:1-21

2. Why did Pharaoh react to Moses' request by making life harder for the Israelites? What did this do to Moses' relationship with the Israelites?
3. In what ways might God's words to Moses at the burning bush (chap. 3) have encouraged him at this point?
4. How can obeying God sometimes make you unpopular in school or on your team? Is it more important to you to be obedient or popular, and why?

4:25 The Hebrew word for "feet" may refer here to the male sex organ.

4:21 I will harden his heart. Not until the sixth plague did God confirm Pharaoh's act of will against Him.

4:24 the Lord confronted him. Apparently God was angry because Moses had not obeyed Him in the matter of circumcising his son (Gen. 17:9-14). Moses may have withheld circumcision of his son in order to please his Midianite family.

4:25-26 Zipporah . . . circumcised her son. Moses' wife realized that God was displeased with her husband and quickly performed the young son's circumcision. **bridegroom of blood.** Zipporah was shocked and angry that God would require circumcision.

4:27 at the mountain of God. It's fitting that the brothers reunited where they would minister together later (19:1-25).

19 The Israelite foremen could see that they were in
serious trouble when they were told, "You must not
reduce the number of bricks you make each day." 20 As
they left Pharaoh's court, they confronted Moses and
Aaron, who were waiting outside for them. 21 The
foremen said to them, "May the LORD judge and pun-
ish you for making us stink before Pharaoh and his
officials. You have put a sword into their hands, an
excuse to kill us!"
22 Then Moses went back to the LORD and protest-
ed, "Why have you brought all this trouble on your
own people, Lord? Why did you send me? 23 Ever since
I came to Pharaoh as your spokesman, he has been
even more brutal to your people. And you have done
nothing to rescue them!"

PROMISES OF DELIVERANCE

6 Then the LORD told Moses, "Now you will see what
I will do to Pharaoh. When he feels the force of my
strong hand, he will let the people go. In fact, he will
force them to leave his land!"
2 And God said to Moses, "I am Yahweh—'the LORD.'*
3 I appeared to Abraham, to Isaac, and to Jacob as El-
Shaddai—'God Almighty'*—but I did not reveal my
name, Yahweh, to them. 4 And I reaffirmed my covenant
with them. Under its terms, I promised to give them the
land of Canaan, where they were living as foreigners.
5 You can be sure that I have heard the groans of the
people of Israel, who are now slaves to the Egyptians.
And I am well aware of my covenant with them.
6 "Therefore, say to the people of Israel: 'I am the
LORD. I will free you from your oppression and will
rescue you from your slavery in Egypt. I will redeem
you with a powerful arm and great acts of judgment.
7 I will claim you as my own people, and I will be your
God. Then you will know that I am the LORD your God
who has freed you from your oppression in Egypt. 8 I
will bring you into the land I swore to give to Abra-
ham, Isaac, and Jacob. I will give it to you as your very
own possession. I am the LORD!'"
9 So Moses told the people of Israel what the LORD had
said, but they refused to listen anymore. They had be-
come too discouraged by the brutality of their slavery.
10 Then the LORD said to Moses, 11 "Go back to Pha-
raoh, the king of Egypt, and tell him to let the people
of Israel leave his country."
12 "But LORD!" Moses objected. "My own people
won't listen to me anymore. How can I expect Pha-
raoh to listen? I'm such a clumsy speaker!*"
13 But the LORD spoke to Moses and Aaron and gave
them orders for the Israelites and for Pharaoh, the
king of Egypt. The LORD commanded Moses and Aar-
on to lead the people of Israel out of Egypt.

THE ANCESTORS OF MOSES AND AARON

14 These are the ancestors of some of the clans of Is-
rael:
The sons of Reuben, Israel's oldest son, were Hanoch,
Pallu, Hezron, and Carmi. Their descendants be-
came the clans of Reuben.
15 The sons of Simeon were Jemuel, Jamin, Ohad, Jakin,
Zohar, and Shaul. (Shaul's mother was a Canaanite
woman.) Their descendants became the clans of
Simeon.
16 These are the descendants of Levi, as listed in their
family records: The sons of Levi were Gershon, Ko-
hath, and Merari. (Levi lived to be 137 years old.)
17 The descendants of Gershon included Libni
and Shimei, each of whom became the ancestor of
a clan.
18 The descendants of Kohath included Amram,
Izhar, Hebron, and Uzziel. (Kohath lived to be
133 years old.)
19 The descendants of Merari included Mahli and
Mushi.

These are the clans of the Levites, as listed in their
family records.

20 Amram married his father's sister Jochebed, and
she gave birth to his sons, Aaron and Moses. (Am-
ram lived to be 137 years old.)
21 The sons of Izhar were Korah, Nepheg, and Zicri.
22 The sons of Uzziel were Mishael, Elzaphan, and Si-
thri.
23 Aaron married Elisheba, the daughter of Ammi-
nadab and sister of Nahshon, and she gave birth to
his sons, Nadab, Abihu, Eleazar, and Ithamar.
24 The sons of Korah were Assir, Elkanah, and
Abiasaph. Their descendants became the clans of
Korah.
25 Eleazar son of Aaron married one of the daughters
of Putiel, and she gave birth to his son, Phinehas.
These are the ancestors of the Levite families, listed
according to their clans.
26 The Aaron and Moses named in this list are the
same ones to whom the LORD said, "Lead the people of
Israel out of the land of Egypt like an army." 27 It was
Moses and Aaron who spoke to Pharaoh, the king of
Egypt, about leading the people of Israel out of Egypt.
28 When the LORD spoke to Moses in the land of Egypt,
29 he said to him, "I am the LORD! Tell Pharaoh, the king
of Egypt, everything I am telling you." 30 But Moses
argued with the LORD, saying, "I can't do it! I'm such a
clumsy speaker! Why should Pharaoh listen to me?"

AARON'S STAFF BECOMES A SERPENT

7 Then the LORD said to Moses, "Pay close attention to
this. I will make you seem like God to Pharaoh, and
your brother, Aaron, will be your prophet. 2 Tell Aaron
everything I command you, and Aaron must command
Pharaoh to let the people of Israel leave his country.
3 But I will make Pharaoh's heart stubborn so I can

6:2 *Yahweh* is a transliteration of the proper name *YHWH* that is sometimes rendered "Jehovah"; in this translation it is usually rendered "the LORD" (note the use of small capitals). **6:3** *El-Shaddai,* which means "God Almighty," is the name for God used in Gen 17:1; 28:3; 35:11; 43:14; 48:3.
6:12 Hebrew *I have uncircumcised lips;* also in 6:30.

5:23 you have done nothing to rescue them. Moses expected Pharaoh to let the Israelites go immediately, even though God had warned him otherwise (3:19; 4:21).

6:4-7 reaffirmed my covenant. These words fulfilled the covenant to Abraham, that God would choose his descendants to be a nation special to Him (Gen. 17:7).

6:12 won't listen to me. Moses was facing exactly what he had feared (4:1). In fact, he had made matters worse. In addition, his bumbling conversation with Pharaoh proved his other previous argument that he could not speak well (4:11). In essence, he was telling God, "I told you so." This is repeated in verses 29-30, with God's answer in 7:1-5.

6:13 Moses and Aaron. To assuage Israelite doubts concerning their authority (5:21), a partial genealogy is given to establish that Moses and Aaron both came from the tribe of Levi (4:14).

HEART CHECKUP

1. Have you ever seen a magician perform? Which tricks were you able to figure out?

EXODUS 6:28–7:24

2. What did God mean when he told Moses, "I will make you seem like God to Pharaoh, and your brother, Aaron, will be your prophet" (v. 1)?
3. How do you think the "magicians of Egypt" accomplished the same miracles as Moses? How can Satan or the world sometimes imitate God's miracles?
4. What does it mean that "Pharaoh's heart hardened" (v. 22)?
5. When have you hardened your heart toward God? Is it hard or soft right now, and why?

multiply my miraculous signs and wonders in the land of Egypt. 4 Even then Pharaoh will refuse to listen to you. So I will bring down my fist on Egypt. Then I will rescue my forces—my people, the Israelites—from the land of Egypt with great acts of judgment. 5 When I raise my powerful hand and bring out the Israelites, the Egyptians will know that I am the LORD."

6 So Moses and Aaron did just as the LORD had commanded them. 7 Moses was eighty years old, and Aaron was eighty-three when they made their demands to Pharaoh.

8 Then the LORD said to Moses and Aaron, 9 "Pharaoh will demand, 'Show me a miracle.' When he does this, say to Aaron, 'Take your staff and throw it down in front of Pharaoh, and it will become a serpent.*'"

10 So Moses and Aaron went to Pharaoh and did what the LORD had commanded them. Aaron threw down his staff before Pharaoh and his officials, and it became a serpent! 11 Then Pharaoh called in his own wise men and sorcerers, and these Egyptian magicians did the same thing with their magic. 12 They threw down their staffs, which also became serpents! But then Aaron's staff swallowed up their staffs. 13 Pharaoh's heart, however, remained hard. He still refused to listen, just as the LORD had predicted.

A PLAGUE OF BLOOD

14 Then the LORD said to Moses, "Pharaoh's heart is stubborn,* and he still refuses to let the people go. 15 So go to Pharaoh in the morning as he goes down to the river. Stand on the bank of the Nile and meet him there. Be sure to take along the staff that turned into a snake. 16 Then announce to him, 'The LORD, the God of the Hebrews, has sent me to tell you, "Let my people go, so they can worship me in the wilderness." Until now, you have refused to listen to him. 17 So this is what the LORD says: "I will show you that I am the LORD." Look! I will strike the water of the Nile with this staff in my hand, and the river will turn to blood. 18 The fish in it will die, and the river will stink. The Egyptians will not be able to drink any water from the Nile."'"

19 Then the LORD said to Moses: "Tell Aaron, 'Take your staff and raise your hand over the waters of Egypt—all its rivers, canals, ponds, and all the reservoirs. Turn all the water to blood. Everywhere in Egypt the water will turn to blood, even the water stored in wooden bowls and stone pots.'"

20 So Moses and Aaron did just as the LORD commanded them. As Pharaoh and all of his officials watched, Aaron raised his staff and struck the water of the Nile. Suddenly, the whole river turned to blood! 21 The fish in the river died, and the water became so foul that the Egyptians couldn't drink it. There was blood everywhere throughout the land of Egypt. 22 But again the magicians of Egypt used their magic, and they, too, turned water into blood. So Pharaoh's heart remained hard. He refused to listen to Moses and Aaron, just as the LORD had predicted. 23 Pharaoh returned to his palace and put the whole thing out of his mind. 24 Then all the Egyptians dug along the riverbank to find drinking water, for they couldn't drink the water from the Nile.

25 Seven days passed from the time the LORD struck the Nile.

A PLAGUE OF FROGS

8 1*Then the LORD said to Moses, "Go back to Pharaoh and announce to him, 'This is what the LORD says: Let my people go, so they can worship me. 2 If you refuse to let them go, I will send a plague of frogs across your entire land. 3 The Nile River will swarm with frogs. They will come up out of the river and into your palace, even into your bedroom and onto your bed! They will enter the houses of your officials and your people. They will even jump into your ovens and your kneading bowls. 4 Frogs will jump on you, your people, and all your officials.'"

5*Then the LORD said to Moses, "Tell Aaron, 'Raise the staff in your hand over all the rivers, canals, and ponds of Egypt, and bring up frogs over all the land.'" 6 So Aaron raised his hand over the waters of Egypt, and frogs came up and covered the whole land! 7 But the magicians

7:9 Hebrew *tannin,* which elsewhere refers to a sea monster. Greek version translates it "dragon." **7:14** Hebrew *heavy.* **8:1** Verses 8:1-4 are numbered 7:26-29 in Hebrew text. **8:5** Verses 8:5-32 are numbered 8:1-28 in Hebrew text.

7:3-4 make . . . heart stubborn. As in 4:21, Pharaoh's heart is hardened by God only after Pharaoh hardened his own heart. Pharaoh's hardening would give God the opportunity to unleash miraculous signs and wonders upon the land.

7:5 the Egyptians will know. With the first nine plagues, God used supernatural forces of nature to bring judgment, but in the tenth God would personally bring judgment upon Egypt.

7:11 wise men . . . sorcerers . . . magicians. The wise men were learned counselors. Sorcerers practiced divination, which God condemned (Lev. 19:26). Magicians were thought to possess occult knowledge. They were able to duplicate Moses' and Aaron's miracle—something God had not prepared them for. However, occult power is very real. These men used either tricks or demonic power to duplicate this and two other miracles (v. 22; 8:7). Finally, even they would have to admit to a power greater than their own (8:18-19).

7:17-20 water of the Nile. The Egyptians worshiped Hopi, the god of the Nile, who would kindly irrigate the fields when pleased. But even Hopi could not keep water, even water in wooden buckets and stone jars, from becoming blood at Moses' command.

7:24 dug around the riverbank. Fouled water would have been safer for drinking after being flushed through the riverbank. After this God allowed some time between plagues for the Egyptians to reflect.

8:2 plague of frogs. Heqt, a frog goddess who allegedly helped women deliver babies, had no luck delivering from frogs.

8:7 the magicians were able to do the same thing. Apparently, they could duplicate the problem, but not reverse it. For that, Pharaoh had to call Moses and Aaron (v. 8).

were able to do the same thing with their magic. They,
too, caused frogs to come up on the land of Egypt.
8 Then Pharaoh summoned Moses and Aaron and
begged, "Plead with the LORD to take the frogs away
from me and my people. I will let your people go, so
they can offer sacrifices to the LORD."
9 "You set the time!" Moses replied. "Tell me when
you want me to pray for you, your officials, and your
people. Then you and your houses will be rid of the
frogs. They will remain only in the Nile River."
10 "Do it tomorrow," Pharaoh said.
"All right," Moses replied, "it will be as you have
said. Then you will know that there is no one like the
LORD our God. 11 The frogs will leave you and your
houses, your officials, and your people. They will re-
main only in the Nile River."
12 So Moses and Aaron left Pharaoh's palace, and
Moses cried out to the LORD about the frogs he had
inflicted on Pharaoh. 13 And the LORD did just what
Moses had predicted. The frogs in the houses, the
courtyards, and the fields all died. 14 The Egyptians
piled them into great heaps, and a terrible stench
filled the land. 15 But when Pharaoh saw that relief
had come, he became stubborn.* He refused to listen
to Moses and Aaron, just as the LORD had predicted.

A PLAGUE OF GNATS

16 So the LORD said to Moses, "Tell Aaron, 'Raise your
staff and strike the ground. The dust will turn into
swarms of gnats throughout the land of Egypt.'" 17 So
Moses and Aaron did just as the LORD had command-
ed them. When Aaron raised his hand and struck the
ground with his staff, gnats infested the entire land,
covering the Egyptians and their animals. All the
dust in the land of Egypt turned into gnats. 18 Pha-
raoh's magicians tried to do the same thing with their
secret arts, but this time they failed. And the gnats
covered everyone, people and animals alike.
19 "This is the finger of God!" the magicians ex-
claimed to Pharaoh. But Pharaoh's heart remained
hard. He wouldn't listen to them, just as the LORD had
predicted.

A PLAGUE OF FLIES

20 Then the LORD told Moses, "Get up early in the morn-
ing and stand in Pharaoh's way as he goes down to the
river. Say to him, 'This is what the LORD says: Let my
people go, so they can worship me. 21 If you refuse, then
I will send swarms of flies on you, your officials, your
people, and all the houses. The Egyptian homes will be
filled with flies, and the ground will be covered with
them. 22 But this time I will spare the region of Gosh-
en, where my people live. No flies will be found there.
Then you will know that I am the LORD and that I am
present even in the heart of your land. 23 I will make a
clear distinction between* my people and your people.
This miraculous sign will happen tomorrow.'"
24 And the LORD did just as he had said. A thick
swarm of flies filled Pharaoh's palace and the houses
of his officials. The whole land of Egypt was thrown
into chaos by the flies.
25 Pharaoh called for Moses and Aaron. "All right!
Go ahead and offer sacrifices to your God," he said.
"But do it here in this land."
26 But Moses replied, "That wouldn't be right. The
Egyptians detest the sacrifices that we offer to the
LORD our God. Look, if we offer our sacrifices here
where the Egyptians can see us, they will stone us.
27 We must take a three-day trip into the wilderness
to offer sacrifices to the LORD our God, just as he has
commanded us."
28 "All right, go ahead," Pharaoh replied. "I will let
you go into the wilderness to offer sacrifices to the
LORD your God. But don't go too far away. Now hurry
and pray for me."
29 Moses answered, "As soon as I leave you, I will
pray to the LORD, and tomorrow the swarms of flies
will disappear from you and your officials and all
your people. But I am warning you, Pharaoh, don't lie
to us again and refuse to let the people go to sacrifice
to the LORD."
30 So Moses left Pharaoh's palace and pleaded with
the LORD to remove all the flies. 31 And the LORD did as
Moses asked and caused the swarms of flies to disap-
pear from Pharaoh, his officials, and his people. Not
a single fly remained. 32 But Pharaoh again became
stubborn and refused to let the people go.

A PLAGUE AGAINST LIVESTOCK

9 "Go back to Pharaoh," the LORD commanded
Moses. "Tell him, 'This is what the LORD, the God of
the Hebrews, says: Let my people go, so they can wor-
ship me. 2 If you continue to hold them and refuse to
let them go, 3 the hand of the LORD will strike all your
livestock—your horses, donkeys, camels, cattle, sheep,
and goats—with a deadly plague. 4 But the LORD will
again make a distinction between the livestock of the
Israelites and that of the Egyptians. Not a single one
of Israel's animals will die! 5 The LORD has already set
the time for the plague to begin. He has declared that
he will strike the land tomorrow.'"
6 And the LORD did just as he had said. The next
morning all the livestock of the Egyptians died, but
the Israelites didn't lose a single animal. 7 Pharaoh
sent his officials to investigate, and they discovered
that the Israelites had not lost a single animal! But
even so, Pharaoh's heart remained stubborn,* and he
still refused to let the people go.

A PLAGUE OF FESTERING BOILS

8 Then the LORD said to Moses and Aaron, "Take hand-
fuls of soot from a brick kiln, and have Moses toss it
into the air while Pharaoh watches. 9 The ashes will
spread like fine dust over the whole land of Egypt,
causing festering boils to break out on people and an-
imals throughout the land."
10 So they took soot from a brick kiln and went and
stood before Pharaoh. As Pharaoh watched, Moses

8:15 Hebrew *made his heart heavy;* also in 8:32. **8:23** As in Greek and Latin versions; Hebrew reads *I will set redemption between.* **9:7** Hebrew *heavy.*

8:19 finger of God. The magicians' powers stopped, and they could no longer duplicate Moses' acts as before (v. 7; 7:11, 22).

9:3 will strike all your livestock. The Egyptians worshiped a number of animal-headed gods including Apis and Mnevis (bull gods), Hathor (cow god) and Khnum (ram god). This plague revealed that their gods had no power to protect livestock.

9:8 handfuls of soot. Just as Moses had struck dust to begin the plague of gnats (8:16), here he took soot and tossed it into the air in Pharaoh's presence to make God's point about the effects of this coming plague.

threw the soot into the air, and boils broke out on
people and animals alike. 11 Even the magicians were
unable to stand before Moses, because the boils had
broken out on them and all the Egyptians. 12 But the
LORD hardened Pharaoh's heart, and just as the LORD
had predicted to Moses, Pharaoh refused to listen.

A PLAGUE OF HAIL

13 Then the LORD said to Moses, "Get up early in the
morning and stand before Pharaoh. Tell him, 'This
is what the LORD, the God of the Hebrews, says: Let
my people go, so they can worship me. 14 If you don't,
I will send more plagues on you* and your officials
and your people. Then you will know that there is
no one like me in all the earth. 15 By now I could have
lifted my hand and struck you and your people with
a plague to wipe you off the face of the earth. 16 But
I have spared you for a purpose—to show you my
power* and to spread my fame throughout the earth.
17 But you still lord it over my people and refuse to let
them go. 18 So tomorrow at this time I will send a hail-
storm more devastating than any in all the history of
Egypt. 19 Quick! Order your livestock and servants to
come in from the fields to find shelter. Any person or
animal left outside will die when the hail falls.'"

20 Some of Pharaoh's officials were afraid because
of what the LORD had said. They quickly brought their
servants and livestock in from the fields. 21 But those
who paid no attention to the word of the LORD left
theirs out in the open.

22 Then the LORD said to Moses, "Lift your hand
toward the sky so hail may fall on the people, the
livestock, and all the plants throughout the land of
Egypt."

23 So Moses lifted his staff toward the sky, and the
LORD sent thunder and hail, and lightning flashed
toward the earth. The LORD sent a tremendous hail-
storm against all the land of Egypt. 24 Never in all the
history of Egypt had there been a storm like that, with
such devastating hail and continuous lightning. 25 It
left all of Egypt in ruins. The hail struck down every-
thing in the open field—people, animals, and plants
alike. Even the trees were destroyed. 26 The only place
without hail was the region of Goshen, where the
people of Israel lived.

27 Then Pharaoh quickly summoned Moses and
Aaron. "This time I have sinned," he confessed. "The
LORD is the righteous one, and my people and I are
wrong. 28 Please beg the LORD to end this terrifying
thunder and hail. We've had enough. I will let you go;
you don't need to stay any longer."

29 "All right," Moses replied. "As soon as I leave the
city, I will lift my hands and pray to the LORD. Then
the thunder and hail will stop, and you will know that
the earth belongs to the LORD. 30 But I know that you
and your officials still do not fear the LORD God."

31 (All the flax and barley were ruined by the hail,
because the barley had formed heads and the flax
was budding. 32 But the wheat and the emmer wheat
were spared, because they had not yet sprouted from
the ground.)

33 So Moses left Pharaoh's court and went out of the
city. When he lifted his hands to the LORD, the thun-
der and hail stopped, and the downpour ceased. 34 But
when Pharaoh saw that the rain, hail, and thunder
had stopped, he and his officials sinned again, and
Pharaoh again became stubborn.* 35 Because his
heart was hard, Pharaoh refused to let the people
leave, just as the LORD had predicted through Moses.

A PLAGUE OF LOCUSTS

10 Then the LORD said to Moses, "Return to Pha-
raoh and make your demands again. I have
made him and his officials stubborn* so I can display
my miraculous signs among them. 2 I've also done it so
you can tell your children and grandchildren about
how I made a mockery of the Egyptians and about the
signs I displayed among them—and so you will know
that I am the LORD."

3 So Moses and Aaron went to Pharaoh and said,
"This is what the LORD, the God of the Hebrews, says:
How long will you refuse to submit to me? Let my peo-
ple go, so they can worship me. 4 If you refuse, watch
out! For tomorrow I will bring a swarm of locusts on
your country. 5 They will cover the land so that you
won't be able to see the ground. They will devour
what little is left of your crops after the hailstorm, in-
cluding all the trees growing in the fields. 6 They will
overrun your palaces and the homes of your officials
and all the houses in Egypt. Never in the history of
Egypt have your ancestors seen a plague like this
one!" And with that, Moses turned and left Pharaoh.

7 Pharaoh's officials now came to Pharaoh and ap-
pealed to him. "How long will you let this man hold
us hostage? Let the men go to worship the LORD their
God! Don't you realize that Egypt lies in ruins?"

8 So Moses and Aaron were brought back to Pharaoh.
"All right," he told them, "go and worship the LORD your
God. But who exactly will be going with you?"

9 Moses replied, "We will all go—young and old,
our sons and daughters, and our flocks and herds. We
must all join together in celebrating a festival to the
LORD."

10 Pharaoh retorted, "The LORD will certainly need to
be with you if I let you take your little ones! I can see
through your evil plan. 11 Never! Only the men may go
and worship the LORD, since that is what you request-
ed." And Pharaoh threw them out of the palace.

12 Then the LORD said to Moses, "Raise your hand
over the land of Egypt to bring on the locusts. Let
them cover the land and devour every plant that sur-
vived the hailstorm."

9:14 Hebrew *on your heart.* **9:16** Greek version reads *to display my power in you;* compare Rom 9:17. **9:34** Hebrew *made his heart heavy.*
10:1 Hebrew *have made his heart and his officials' hearts heavy.*

9:16 I have spared you for a purpose. God is in complete control of all nations and leaders (Ps. 2). God had given Pharaoh power in order to make His name known throughout the earth. Suitably, the Exodus miracle story spread far and wide. The people of Jericho had heard it and were frightened of the Israelites as a result (Josh. 2:8-12).

9:27 This time I have sinned. Pharaoh confessed his sinfulness, but Moses knew better (v. 30). Nevertheless, Moses stopped the plague at Pharaoh's request. Unfortunately, Pharaoh would take these words back in his stubbornness (v. 34).

10:7 Egypt lies in ruins. The devastation of their livestock and fields had already ruined the nation; a locust plague would be completely devastating. The officials perceived what Pharaoh would not, but in his pride, he would not be convinced.

10:11 Only the men may go. Pharaoh obviously feared that the Israelites were planning to escape slavery. So Pharaoh attempted to compromise by keeping the women and children behind to insure that the men would return.

13 So Moses raised his staff over Egypt, and the
LORD caused an east wind to blow over the land all
that day and through the night. When morning ar-
rived, the east wind had brought the locusts. 14 And
the locusts swarmed over the whole land of Egypt,
settling in dense swarms from one end of the coun-
try to the other. It was the worst locust plague in
Egyptian history, and there has never been another
one like it. 15 For the locusts covered the whole coun-
try and darkened the land. They devoured every
plant in the fields and all the fruit on the trees that
had survived the hailstorm. Not a single leaf was
left on the trees and plants throughout the land of
Egypt.

16 Pharaoh quickly summoned Moses and Aaron. "I
have sinned against the LORD your God and against
you," he confessed. 17 "Forgive my sin, just this once,
and plead with the LORD your God to take away this
death from me."

18 So Moses left Pharaoh's court and pleaded with
the LORD. 19 The LORD responded by shifting the wind,
and the strong west wind blew the locusts into the
Red Sea.* Not a single locust remained in all the land
of Egypt. 20 But the LORD hardened Pharaoh's heart
again, so he refused to let the people go.

A PLAGUE OF DARKNESS

21 Then the LORD said to Moses, "Lift your hand toward
heaven, and the land of Egypt will be covered with
a darkness so thick you can feel it." 22 So Moses lifted
his hand to the sky, and a deep darkness covered the
entire land of Egypt for three days. 23 During all that
time the people could not see each other, and no one
moved. But there was light as usual where the people
of Israel lived.

24 Finally, Pharaoh called for Moses. "Go and wor-
ship the LORD," he said. "But leave your flocks and
herds here. You may even take your little ones with
you."

25 "No," Moses said, "you must provide us with an-
imals for sacrifices and burnt offerings to the LORD
our God. 26 All our livestock must go with us, too; not a
hoof can be left behind. We must choose our sacrifices
for the LORD our God from among these animals. And
we won't know how we are to worship the LORD until
we get there."

27 But the LORD hardened Pharaoh's heart once
more, and he would not let them go. 28 "Get out of
here!" Pharaoh shouted at Moses. "I'm warning you.
Never come back to see me again! The day you see my
face, you will die!"

29 "Very well," Moses replied. "I will never see your
face again."

DEATH FOR EGYPT'S FIRSTBORN

11 Then the LORD said to Moses, "I will strike Pha-
raoh and the land of Egypt with one more blow.
After that, Pharaoh will let you leave this country. In
fact, he will be so eager to get rid of you that he will
force you all to leave. 2 Tell all the Israelite men and
women to ask their Egyptian neighbors for articles
of silver and gold." 3 (Now the LORD had caused the
Egyptians to look favorably on the people of Israel.
And Moses was considered a very great man in the
land of Egypt, respected by Pharaoh's officials and
the Egyptian people alike.)

4 Moses had announced to Pharaoh, "This is
what the LORD says: At midnight tonight I will pass
through the heart of Egypt. 5 All the firstborn sons
will die in every family in Egypt, from the oldest son
of Pharaoh, who sits on his throne, to the oldest son
of his lowliest servant girl who grinds the flour. Even
the firstborn of all the livestock will die. 6 Then a loud
wail will rise throughout the land of Egypt, a wail
like no one has heard before or will ever hear again.
7 But among the Israelites it will be so peaceful that
not even a dog will bark. Then you will know that
the LORD makes a distinction between the Egyptians
and the Israelites. 8 All the officials of Egypt will run
to me and fall to the ground before me. 'Please leave!'
they will beg. 'Hurry! And take all your followers
with you.' Only then will I go!" Then, burning with
anger, Moses left Pharaoh.

9 Now the LORD had told Moses earlier, "Pharaoh
will not listen to you, but then I will do even more
mighty miracles in the land of Egypt." 10 Moses and
Aaron performed these miracles in Pharaoh's pres-
ence, but the LORD hardened Pharaoh's heart, and he
wouldn't let the Israelites leave the country.

THE FIRST PASSOVER

12 While the Israelites were still in the land of
Egypt, the LORD gave the following instructions
to Moses and Aaron: 2 "From now on, this month will
be the first month of the year for you. 3 Announce to
the whole community of Israel that on the tenth day
of this month each family must choose a lamb or a
young goat for a sacrifice, one animal for each house-
hold. 4 If a family is too small to eat a whole animal, let
them share with another family in the neighborhood.
Divide the animal according to the size of each family
and how much they can eat. 5 The animal you select
must be a one-year-old male, either a sheep or a goat,
with no defects.

6 "Take special care of this chosen animal until the
evening of the fourteenth day of this first month.
Then the whole assembly of the community of Israel
must slaughter their lamb or young goat at twilight.
7 They are to take some of the blood and smear it on
the sides and top of the doorframes of the houses
where they eat the animal. 8 That same night they
must roast the meat over a fire and eat it along with
bitter salad greens and bread made without yeast.
9 Do not eat any of the meat raw or boiled in water.
The whole animal—including the head, legs, and in-
ternal organs—must be roasted over a fire. 10 Do not
leave any of it until the next morning. Burn whatever
is not eaten before morning.

10:19 Hebrew *sea of reeds.*

10:21 darkness so thick you can feel it. One of Egypt's chief gods was Ra, the sun god. The darkness ridiculed Ra, revealing his complete powerlessness to keep darkness from covering Egypt for three full days.

12:5 with no defects. The sacrificed lambs or goats had to be chosen from the best of the herd.

12:6-7 take some of the blood. The animal's blood was a visible sign that a sacrifice had taken place on behalf of each household and would be their only means of escaping the coming plague. Four days after selection, the lamb was to be killed and eaten.

12:8 bitter salad greens. Eating bitter salad greens found in Egypt would remind the Israelites of their years of bitter slavery every year when they sat down to eat the Passover meal (Num. 9:11).

THE PASSOVER

1. What's your favorite food for special meals or banquets?

EXODUS 12:1-30

2. Why did God name this "the Passover" (v. 27)?
3. Why did God command the people to put blood on the doorposts of their houses? How did this symbol distinguish them from the Egyptians when God's judgment came?
4. How does the sacrifice of the lamb in this story compare with the Lamb of God in the New Testament?
5. In what way does Jesus' blood protect His people from God's judgment? Hard or scary? How might His words to Moses apply to you?

11 "These are your instructions for eating this meal:
Be fully dressed,* wear your sandals, and carry your
walking stick in your hand. Eat the meal with urgen-
cy, for this is the LORD's Passover. 12 On that night I will
pass through the land of Egypt and strike down every
firstborn son and firstborn male animal in the land of
Egypt. I will execute judgment against all the gods of
Egypt, for I am the LORD! 13 But the blood on your door-
posts will serve as a sign, marking the houses where
you are staying. When I see the blood, I will pass over
you. This plague of death will not touch you when I
strike the land of Egypt.
14 "This is a day to remember. Each year, from gen-
eration to generation, you must celebrate it as a spe-
cial festival to the LORD. This is a law for all time. 15 For
seven days the bread you eat must be made without
yeast. On the first day of the festival, remove every
trace of yeast from your homes. Anyone who eats
bread made with yeast during the seven days of the
festival will be cut off from the community of Israel.
16 On the first day of the festival and again on the sev-
enth day, all the people must observe an official day
for holy assembly. No work of any kind may be done
on these days except in the preparation of food.
17 "Celebrate this Festival of Unleavened Bread, for
it will remind you that I brought your forces out of
the land of Egypt on this very day. This festival will
be a permanent law for you; celebrate this day from
generation to generation. 18 The bread you eat must
be made without yeast from the evening of the four-
teenth day of the first month until the evening of the
twenty-first day of that month. 19 During those seven
days, there must be no trace of yeast in your homes.
Anyone who eats anything made with yeast during
this week will be cut off from the community of Is-
rael. These regulations apply both to the foreigners
living among you and to the native-born Israelites.
20 During those days you must not eat anything made
with yeast. Wherever you live, eat only bread made
without yeast."
21 Then Moses called all the elders of Israel together
and said to them, "Go, pick out a lamb or young goat for
each of your families, and slaughter the Passover ani-
mal. 22 Drain the blood into a basin. Then take a bundle
of hyssop branches and dip it into the blood. Brush the
hyssop across the top and sides of the doorframes of
your houses. And no one may go out through the door
until morning. 23 For the LORD will pass through the
land to strike down the Egyptians. But when he sees
the blood on the top and sides of the doorframe, the
LORD will pass over your home. He will not permit his
death angel to enter your house and strike you down.
24 "Remember, these instructions are a permanent
law that you and your descendants must observe for-
ever. 25 When you enter the land the LORD has prom-
ised to give you, you will continue to observe this cer-
emony. 26 Then your children will ask, 'What does this
ceremony mean?' 27 And you will reply, 'It is the Pass-
over sacrifice to the LORD, for he passed over the hous-
es of the Israelites in Egypt. And though he struck the
Egyptians, he spared our families.'" When Moses had
finished speaking, all the people bowed down to the
ground and worshiped.
28 So the people of Israel did just as the LORD had
commanded through Moses and Aaron. 29 And that
night at midnight, the LORD struck down all the first-
born sons in the land of Egypt, from the firstborn son
of Pharaoh, who sat on his throne, to the firstborn son
of the prisoner in the dungeon. Even the firstborn of
their livestock were killed. 30 Pharaoh and all his offi-
cials and all the people of Egypt woke up during the
night, and loud wailing was heard throughout the
land of Egypt. There was not a single house where
someone had not died.

ISRAEL'S EXODUS FROM EGYPT

31 Pharaoh sent for Moses and Aaron during the night.
"Get out!" he ordered. "Leave my people—and take
the rest of the Israelites with you! Go and worship the
LORD as you have requested. 32 Take your flocks and
herds, as you said, and be gone. Go, but bless me as
you leave." 33 All the Egyptians urged the people of Is-
rael to get out of the land as quickly as possible, for
they thought, "We will all die!"
34 The Israelites took their bread dough before yeast
was added. They wrapped their kneading boards
in their cloaks and carried them on their shoulders.
35 And the people of Israel did as Moses had instruct-
ed; they asked the Egyptians for clothing and articles
of silver and gold. 36 The LORD caused the Egyptians to
look favorably on the Israelites, and they gave the Is-
raelites whatever they asked for. So they stripped the
Egyptians of their wealth!

12:11 Hebrew *Bind up your loins.*

12:11 Eat the meal with urgency. The phrase "eat and run" could have been coined for this meal. The Israelites were to be already dressed for their deliverance at hand. **the LORD's Passover.** God's messenger of death would only pass over the homes that had blood on the doorframes.

12:14 a law for all time. The Last Supper was a Passover (Matt. 26:17-19). In this sense, so is communion (1 Cor. 11:20).

12:17 Festival of Unleavened Bread. This seven-day festival, beginning with the Passover meal, commemorated Israel's deliverance from Egypt (Matt. 26:17; Acts 12:3; 20:6). Unleavened bread was made on the night when the people had no time to wait for bread to rise.

12:22 take a bundle of hyssop. Hyssop, a strongly scented flowering plant of the mint family found in Egypt and Palestine, was used to raise a sponge soaked in wine vinegar to Jesus' lips while he hung on the cross.

12:36 stripped the Egyptians. God had promised this (3:21; Gen. 15:14).

[37] That night the people of Israel left Rameses and started for Succoth. There were about 600,000 men,* plus all the women and children. [38] A rabble of non-Israelites went with them, along with great flocks and herds of livestock. [39] For bread they baked flat cakes from the dough without yeast they had brought from Egypt. It was made without yeast because the people were driven out of Egypt in such a hurry that they had no time to prepare the bread or other food.

[40] The people of Israel had lived in Egypt* for 430 years. [41] In fact, it was on the last day of the 430th year that all the LORD's forces left the land. [42] On this night the LORD kept his promise to bring his people out of the land of Egypt. So this night belongs to him, and it must be commemorated every year by all the Israelites, from generation to generation.

INSTRUCTIONS FOR THE PASSOVER

[43] Then the LORD said to Moses and Aaron, "These are the instructions for the festival of Passover. No outsiders are allowed to eat the Passover meal. [44] But any slave who has been purchased may eat it if he has been circumcised. [45] Temporary residents and hired servants may not eat it. [46] Each Passover lamb must be eaten in one house. Do not carry any of its meat outside, and do not break any of its bones. [47] The whole community of Israel must celebrate this Passover festival.

[48] "If there are foreigners living among you who want to celebrate the LORD's Passover, let all their males be circumcised. Only then may they celebrate the Passover with you like any native-born Israelite. But no uncircumcised male may ever eat the Passover meal. [49] This instruction applies to everyone, whether a native-born Israelite or a foreigner living among you."

[50] So all the people of Israel followed all the LORD's commands to Moses and Aaron. [51] On that very day the LORD brought the people of Israel out of the land of Egypt like an army.

DEDICATION OF THE FIRSTBORN

13 Then the LORD said to Moses, [2] "Dedicate to me every firstborn among the Israelites. The first offspring to be born, of both humans and animals, belongs to me."

[3] So Moses said to the people, "This is a day to remember forever—the day you left Egypt, the place of your slavery. Today the LORD has brought you out by the power of his mighty hand. (Remember, eat no food containing yeast.) [4] On this day in early spring, in the month of Abib,* you have been set free. [5] You must celebrate this event in this month each year after the LORD brings you into the land of the Canaanites, Hittites, Amorites, Hivites, and Jebusites. (He swore to your ancestors that he would give you this land—a land flowing with milk and honey.) [6] For seven days the bread you eat must be made without yeast. Then on the seventh day, celebrate a feast to the LORD. [7] Eat bread without yeast during those seven days. In fact, there must be no yeast bread or any yeast at all found within the borders of your land during this time.

[8] "On the seventh day you must explain to your children, 'I am celebrating what the LORD did for me when I left Egypt.' [9] This annual festival will be a visible sign to you, like a mark branded on your hand or your forehead. Let it remind you always to recite this teaching of the LORD: 'With a strong hand, the LORD rescued you from Egypt.'* [10] So observe the decree of this festival at the appointed time each year.

[11] "This is what you must do when the LORD fulfills the promise he swore to you and to your ancestors. When he gives you the land where the Canaanites now live, [12] you must present all firstborn sons and firstborn male animals to the LORD, for they belong to him. [13] A firstborn donkey may be bought back from the LORD by presenting a lamb or young goat in its place. But if you do not buy it back, you must break its neck. However, you must buy back every firstborn son.

[14] "And in the future, your children will ask you, 'What does all this mean?' Then you will tell them, 'With the power of his mighty hand, the LORD brought us out of Egypt, the place of our slavery. [15] Pharaoh stubbornly refused to let us go, so the LORD killed all the firstborn males throughout the land of Egypt, both people and animals. That is why I now sacrifice all the firstborn males to the LORD—except that the firstborn sons are always bought back.' [16] This ceremony will be like a mark branded on your hand or your forehead. It is a reminder that the power of the LORD's mighty hand brought us out of Egypt."

ISRAEL'S WILDERNESS DETOUR

[17] When Pharaoh finally let the people go, God did not lead them along the main road that runs through Philistine territory, even though that was the shortest route to the Promised Land. God said, "If the people are faced with a battle, they might change their minds and return to Egypt." [18] So God led them in a roundabout way through the wilderness toward the Red Sea.* Thus the Israelites left Egypt like an army ready for battle.*

[19] Moses took the bones of Joseph with him, for Joseph had made the sons of Israel swear to do this. He said, "God will certainly come to help you. When he does, you must take my bones with you from this place."

[20] The Israelites left Succoth and camped at Etham on the edge of the wilderness. [21] The LORD went ahead of them. He guided them during the day with a pillar of cloud, and he provided light at night with a pillar

12:37 Or *fighting men;* Hebrew reads *men on foot.* **12:40** Samaritan Pentateuch reads *in Canaan and Egypt;* Greek version reads *in Egypt and Canaan.* **13:4** Hebrew *On this day in the month of Abib.* This first month of the ancient Hebrew lunar calendar usually occurs within the months of March and April. **13:9** Or *Let it remind you always to keep the instructions of the Lord on the tip of your tongue, because with a strong hand, the Lord rescued you from Egypt.* **13:18a** Hebrew *sea of reeds.* **13:18b** Greek version reads *left Egypt in the fifth generation.*

12:37 about 600,000. The count for men only, the actual number was around two million.

12:41 430 years. God had foretold this number of Israel's years in Egypt to Abraham (Gen. 15:13).

12:46 any of its bones. The Passover lamb was not to have any bones broken. At the crucifixion, a similar decision was made to avoid breaking any of Jesus' bones. The Apostle John considered this action a fulfillment of God's commandment (Ps. 34:20; John 19:36).

13:9 Let it remind you. Some of the religious leaders in Jesus' day had taken this commandment literally by tying little boxes, called phylacteries with parchment inside, across their foreheads. Jesus condemned the act of enlarging the phylacteries for show (Matt. 23:5).

13:19 bones of Joseph. Joseph, a ruler in Egypt well before the Hebrews became slaves, believed that God would one day return his people to Canaan. He had requested that they take his bones with them (Gen. 50:24-25).

of fire. This allowed them to travel by day or by night.
22 And the LORD did not remove the pillar of cloud or
pillar of fire from its place in front of the people.

14 Then the LORD gave these instructions to Moses:
2 "Order the Israelites to turn back and camp by
Pi-hahiroth between Migdol and the sea. Camp there
along the shore, across from Baal-zephon. 3 Then Pha-
raoh will think, 'The Israelites are confused. They
are trapped in the wilderness!' 4 And once again I
will harden Pharaoh's heart, and he will chase after
you.* I have planned this in order to display my glory
through Pharaoh and his whole army. After this the
Egyptians will know that I am the LORD!" So the Isra-
elites camped there as they were told.

THE EGYPTIANS PURSUE ISRAEL

5 When word reached the king of Egypt that the Is-
raelites had fled, Pharaoh and his officials changed
their minds. "What have we done, letting all those
Israelite slaves get away?" they asked. 6 So Pharaoh
harnessed his chariot and called up his troops. 7 He
took with him 600 of Egypt's best chariots, along
with the rest of the chariots of Egypt, each with its
commander. 8 The LORD hardened the heart of Pha-
raoh, the king of Egypt, so he chased after the people
of Israel, who had left with fists raised in defiance.
9 The Egyptians chased after them with all the forces
in Pharaoh's army—all his horses and chariots, his
charioteers, and his troops. The Egyptians caught up
with the people of Israel as they were camped beside
the shore near Pi-hahiroth, across from Baal-zephon.
10 As Pharaoh approached, the people of Israel
looked up and panicked when they saw the Egyptians
overtaking them. They cried out to the LORD, 11 and
they said to Moses, "Why did you bring us out here to
die in the wilderness? Weren't there enough graves
for us in Egypt? What have you done to us? Why did
you make us leave Egypt? 12 Didn't we tell you this
would happen while we were still in Egypt? We said,
'Leave us alone! Let us be slaves to the Egyptians. It's
better to be a slave in Egypt than a corpse in the wil-
derness!'"
13 But Moses told the people, "Don't be afraid. Just
stand still and watch the LORD rescue you today. The
Egyptians you see today will never be seen again.
14 The LORD himself will fight for you. Just stay calm."

ESCAPE THROUGH THE RED SEA

15 Then the LORD said to Moses, "Why are you crying
out to me? Tell the people to get moving! 16 Pick up
your staff and raise your hand over the sea. Divide
the water so the Israelites can walk through the
middle of the sea on dry ground. 17 And I will harden
the hearts of the Egyptians, and they will charge in
after the Israelites. My great glory will be displayed
through Pharaoh and his troops, his chariots, and his
charioteers. 18 When my glory is displayed through

SURVIVAL TACTICS

1. Have you ever been chased? What happened?

EXODUS 14:5-31

2. What does it mean to "stand still and watch the LORD rescue you today" (v. 13)?
3. What would it be like to be told, "The LORD himself will fight for you; just stay calm" (v. 14), when your enemy is bearing down on top of you?
4. How are you doing with standing firm in the Lord?
5. In what area of your life do you need faith that the Lord will fight for you?

them, all Egypt will see my glory and know that I am
the LORD!"
19 Then the angel of God, who had been leading the
people of Israel, moved to the rear of the camp. The
pillar of cloud also moved from the front and stood
behind them. 20 The cloud settled between the Egyp-
tian and Israelite camps. As darkness fell, the cloud
turned to fire, lighting up the night. But the Egyptians
and Israelites did not approach each other all night.
21 Then Moses raised his hand over the sea, and
the LORD opened up a path through the water with a
strong east wind. The wind blew all that night, turn-
ing the seabed into dry land. 22 So the people of Israel
walked through the middle of the sea on dry ground,
with walls of water on each side!
23 Then the Egyptians—all of Pharaoh's horses,
chariots, and charioteers—chased them into the
middle of the sea. 24 But just before dawn the LORD
looked down on the Egyptian army from the pillar
of fire and cloud, and he threw their forces into total
confusion. 25 He twisted* their chariot wheels, making
their chariots difficult to drive. "Let's get out of here—
away from these Israelites!" the Egyptians shouted.
"The LORD is fighting for them against Egypt!"
26 When all the Israelites had reached the other
side, the LORD said to Moses, "Raise your hand over the
sea again. Then the waters will rush back and cover
the Egyptians and their chariots and charioteers."
27 So as the sun began to rise, Moses raised his hand
over the sea, and the water rushed back into its usu-
al place. The Egyptians tried to escape, but the LORD
swept them into the sea. 28 Then the waters returned
and covered all the chariots and charioteers—the en-
tire army of Pharaoh. Of all the Egyptians who had
chased the Israelites into the sea, not a single one sur-
vived.
29 But the people of Israel had walked through the
middle of the sea on dry ground, as the water stood up
like a wall on both sides. 30 That is how the LORD rescued
Israel from the hand of the Egyptians that day. And the

14:4 Hebrew *after them.* **14:25** As in Greek version, Samaritan Pentateuch, and Syriac version; Hebrew reads *He removed.*

14:2 turn back. Like a commander, God misled the enemy (v. 3) and planned their destruction (v. 4).

14:14 The LORD himself will fight. Both the victory and the glory belonged to God. The people were to proceed in faith.

14:20 lighting up the night. The pillar of cloud, which cloaked God's presence, stood between His people and their enemies. The fire representing God's glory, hidden in the cloud for protection, shone through at night.

14:21 the LORD opened up a path. Many differing opinions make the exact location of this sea impossible to determine. Nonetheless, God controlled nature to produce a strong east wind to divide the waters and deliver His people. The Lord had used the east wind previously to bring in the locust plague (10:13).

14:25 The LORD is fighting. Even the Egyptian soldiers realized that God was fighting for the Israelites (v. 14). They panicked and fled as God showed His power, just as God predicted (v. 4).

Israelites saw the bodies of the Egyptians washed up on the seashore. 31 When the people of Israel saw the mighty power that the LORD had unleashed against the Egyptians, they were filled with awe before him. They put their faith in the LORD and in his servant Moses.

A SONG OF DELIVERANCE

15 Then Moses and the people of Israel sang this song to the LORD:

"I will sing to the LORD,
for he has triumphed gloriously;
he has hurled both horse and rider
into the sea.
2 The LORD is my strength and my song;
he has given me victory.
This is my God, and I will praise him—
my father's God, and I will exalt him!
3 The LORD is a warrior;
Yahweh* is his name!
4 Pharaoh's chariots and army
he has hurled into the sea.
The finest of Pharaoh's officers
are drowned in the Red Sea.*
5 The deep waters gushed over them;
they sank to the bottom like a stone.

6 "Your right hand, O LORD,
is glorious in power.
Your right hand, O LORD,
smashes the enemy.
7 In the greatness of your majesty,
you overthrow those who rise against you.
You unleash your blazing fury;
it consumes them like straw.
8 At the blast of your breath,
the waters piled up!
The surging waters stood straight like a wall;
in the heart of the sea the deep waters became hard.

9 "The enemy boasted, 'I will chase them
and catch up with them.
I will plunder them
and consume them.
I will flash my sword;
my powerful hand will destroy them.'
10 But you blew with your breath,
and the sea covered them.
They sank like lead
in the mighty waters.

11 "Who is like you among the gods, O LORD—
glorious in holiness,
awesome in splendor,
performing great wonders?
12 You raised your right hand,
and the earth swallowed our enemies.
13 "With your unfailing love you lead
the people you have redeemed.
In your might, you guide them
to your sacred home.
14 The peoples hear and tremble;
anguish grips those who live in Philistia.
15 The leaders of Edom are terrified;
the nobles of Moab tremble.
All who live in Canaan melt away;
16 terror and dread fall upon them.
The power of your arm
makes them lifeless as stone
until your people pass by, O LORD,
until the people you purchased pass by.
17 You will bring them in and plant them on your own mountain—
the place, O LORD, reserved for your own dwelling,
the sanctuary, O Lord, that your hands have established.
18 The LORD will reign forever and ever!"

19 When Pharaoh's horses, chariots, and charioteers
rushed into the sea, the LORD brought the water
crashing down on them. But the people of Israel had
walked through the middle of the sea on dry ground!
20 Then Miriam the prophet, Aaron's sister, took a
tambourine and led all the women as they played
their tambourines and danced. 21 And Miriam sang
this song:

"Sing to the LORD,
for he has triumphed gloriously;
he has hurled both horse and rider
into the sea."

BITTER WATER AT MARAH

22 Then Moses led the people of Israel away from the
Red Sea, and they moved out into the desert of Shur.
They traveled in this desert for three days without
finding any water. 23 When they came to the oasis
of Marah, the water was too bitter to drink. So they
called the place Marah (which means "bitter").
24 Then the people complained and turned against
Moses. "What are we going to drink?" they demanded.
25 So Moses cried out to the LORD for help, and the LORD
showed him a piece of wood. Moses threw it into the
water, and this made the water good to drink.
It was there at Marah that the LORD set before them
the following decree as a standard to test their faith-
fulness to him. 26 He said, "If you will listen carefully
to the voice of the LORD your God and do what is right
in his sight, obeying his commands and keeping all
his decrees, then I will not make you suffer any of the
diseases I sent on the Egyptians; for I am the LORD
who heals you."
27 After leaving Marah, the Israelites traveled on
to the oasis of Elim, where they found twelve springs

15:3 *Yahweh* is a transliteration of the proper name *YHWH* that is sometimes rendered "Jehovah"; in this translation it is usually rendered "the LORD" (note the use of small capitals). 15:4 Hebrew *sea of reeds;* also in 15:22.

15:1-18 The Hebrews' despair and fear (14:12) has turned to joy and confidence in God. His name appears 10 times.

15:14-15 Philistia . . . Edom . . . Moab . . . Canaan. News of the miraculous deliverance at the Red Sea would travel along this route, as would the Israelites after they left Mount Sinai. As God predicted (9:16; 14:4), His glory among the nations increased.

15:21 Miriam. The sister of Moses and Aaron (2:4).

15:24 complained . . . against Moses. Only three days into the journey, there was already discontent. The Israelites changed quickly from being joyful and trusting (vv. 1-18) to fearful and questioning. This pattern would continue for many years.

15:25 to test their faithfulness. God did not give the Israelites water because they passed the test. He provided it, then took the opportunity (while His gift was fresh in their minds) to declare a test of their obedience.

and seventy palm trees. They camped there beside the water.

MANNA AND QUAIL FROM HEAVEN

16 Then the whole community of Israel set out from Elim and journeyed into the wilderness of Sin,* between Elim and Mount Sinai. They arrived there on the fifteenth day of the second month, one month after leaving the land of Egypt.* 2 There, too, the whole community of Israel complained about Moses and Aaron.

3 "If only the LORD had killed us back in Egypt," they moaned. "There we sat around pots filled with meat and ate all the bread we wanted. But now you have brought us into this wilderness to starve us all to death."

4 Then the LORD said to Moses, "Look, I'm going to rain down food from heaven for you. Each day the people can go out and pick up as much food as they need for that day. I will test them in this to see whether or not they will follow my instructions. 5 On the sixth day they will gather food, and when they prepare it, there will be twice as much as usual."

6 So Moses and Aaron said to all the people of Israel, "By evening you will realize it was the LORD who brought you out of the land of Egypt. 7 In the morning you will see the glory of the LORD, because he has heard your complaints, which are against him, not against us. What have we done that you should complain about us?" 8 Then Moses added, "The LORD will give you meat to eat in the evening and bread to satisfy you in the morning, for he has heard all your complaints against him. What have we done? Yes, your complaints are against the LORD, not against us."

9 Then Moses said to Aaron, "Announce this to the entire community of Israel: 'Present yourselves before the LORD, for he has heard your complaining.'" 10 And as Aaron spoke to the whole community of Israel, they looked out toward the wilderness. There they could see the awesome glory of the LORD in the cloud.

11 Then the LORD said to Moses, 12 "I have heard the Israelites' complaints. Now tell them, 'In the evening you will have meat to eat, and in the morning you will have all the bread you want. Then you will know that I am the LORD your God.'"

13 That evening vast numbers of quail flew in and covered the camp. And the next morning the area around the camp was wet with dew. 14 When the dew evaporated, a flaky substance as fine as frost blanketed the ground. 15 The Israelites were puzzled when they saw it. "What is it?" they asked each other. They had no idea what it was.

And Moses told them, "It is the food the LORD has given you to eat. 16 These are the LORD's instructions: Each household should gather as much as it needs. Pick up two quarts* for each person in your tent."

HEAVENLY FOOD

1. What is the strangest thing you have ever eaten?

EXODUS 16:1-35

2. Why did the Israelites start to complain? How accurate is their memory of life in Egypt?
3. Why was there no manna on the Sabbath day? Why did God command the people to rest on the Sabbath?
4. Notice the sins of the Israelites in this passage (vv. 2,20,27). What does this show you about human nature?
5. How are you like the Israelites in your own life? Which of God's commands are you having difficulty obeying?

17 So the people of Israel did as they were told. Some gathered a lot, some only a little. 18 But when they measured it out,* everyone had just enough. Those who gathered a lot had nothing left over, and those who gathered only a little had enough. Each family had just what it needed.

19 Then Moses told them, "Do not keep any of it until morning." 20 But some of them didn't listen and kept some of it until morning. But by then it was full of maggots and had a terrible smell. Moses was very angry with them.

21 After this the people gathered the food morning by morning, each family according to its need. And as the sun became hot, the flakes they had not picked up melted and disappeared. 22 On the sixth day, they gathered twice as much as usual—four quarts* for each person instead of two. Then all the leaders of the community came and asked Moses for an explanation. 23 He told them, "This is what the LORD commanded: Tomorrow will be a day of complete rest, a holy Sabbath day set apart for the LORD. So bake or boil as much as you want today, and set aside what is left for tomorrow."

24 So they put some aside until morning, just as Moses had commanded. And in the morning the leftover food was wholesome and good, without maggots or odor. 25 Moses said, "Eat this food today, for today is a Sabbath day dedicated to the LORD. There will be no food on the ground today. 26 You may gather the food for six days, but the seventh day is the Sabbath. There will be no food on the ground that day."

27 Some of the people went out anyway on the seventh day, but they found no food. 28 The LORD asked Moses, "How long will these people refuse to obey my commands and instructions? 29 They must realize that

16:1a The geographical name *Sin* is related to *Sinai* and should not be confused with the English word *sin*. **16:1b** The Exodus had occurred on the fifteenth day of the first month (see Num 33:3). **16:16** Hebrew *1 omer* [2.2 liters]; also in 16:32, 33. **16:18** Hebrew *measured it with an omer.* **16:22** Hebrew *2 omers* [4.4 liters].

16:4 as they need for that day. The food God provided would keep the Israelites alive. He would provide, but they would have to trust Him. The fact that they were to gather only enough for one day meant they were to trust God to provide daily.

16:13 quail flew in. The meat that the Lord had promised arrived right on schedule. Later in the journey God provided quail once again, but with less satisfying results (Num. 11:31-34).

16:14 flaky substance as fine as frost. Like the quail, this food came from God in an unexpected way. It came with the dew, appeared when the dew evaporated and melted in the sun.

16:23 a day of complete rest. This is the first occurrence of the word "Sabbath" in Scripture. However, the idea of a seventh day of rest and holiness is presented in the creation account (Gen. 2:2).

the Sabbath is the LORD's gift to you. That is why he
gives you a two-day supply on the sixth day, so there
will be enough for two days. On the Sabbath day you
must each stay in your place. Do not go out to pick up
food on the seventh day." 30 So the people did not gath-
er any food on the seventh day.
31 The Israelites called the food manna.* It was
white like coriander seed, and it tasted like honey
wafers.
32 Then Moses said, "This is what the LORD has com-
manded: Fill a two-quart container with manna to
preserve it for your descendants. Then later gener-
ations will be able to see the food I gave you in the
wilderness when I set you free from Egypt."
33 Moses said to Aaron, "Get a jar and fill it with
two quarts of manna. Then put it in a sacred place
before the LORD to preserve it for all future genera-
tions." 34 Aaron did just as the LORD had command-
ed Moses. He eventually placed it in the Ark of the
Covenant—in front of the stone tablets inscribed
with the terms of the covenant.* 35 So the people of
Israel ate manna for forty years until they arrived
at the land where they would settle. They ate man-
na until they came to the border of the land of Ca-
naan.
36 The container used to measure the manna was
an omer, which was one-tenth of an ephah; it held
about two quarts.*

WATER FROM THE ROCK

17 At the LORD's command, the whole community
of Israel left the wilderness of Sin* and moved
from place to place. Eventually they camped at
Rephidim, but there was no water there for the peo-
ple to drink. 2 So once more the people complained
against Moses. "Give us water to drink!" they de-
manded.
"Quiet!" Moses replied. "Why are you complaining
against me? And why are you testing the LORD?"
3 But tormented by thirst, they continued to argue
with Moses. "Why did you bring us out of Egypt? Are
you trying to kill us, our children, and our livestock
with thirst?"
4 Then Moses cried out to the LORD, "What should
I do with these people? They are ready to stone me!"
5 The LORD said to Moses, "Walk out in front of the
people. Take your staff, the one you used when you
struck the water of the Nile, and call some of the el-
ders of Israel to join you. 6 I will stand before you on
the rock at Mount Sinai.* Strike the rock, and water
will come gushing out. Then the people will be able
to drink." So Moses struck the rock as he was told, and
water gushed out as the elders looked on.
7 Moses named the place Massah (which means
"test") and Meribah (which means "arguing") because
the people of Israel argued with Moses and tested the
LORD by saying, "Is the LORD here with us or not?"

ISRAEL DEFEATS THE AMALEKITES

8 While the people of Israel were still at Rephidim,
the warriors of Amalek attacked them. 9 Moses com-
manded Joshua, "Choose some men to go out and fight
the army of Amalek for us. Tomorrow, I will stand at
the top of the hill, holding the staff of God in my hand."
10 So Joshua did what Moses had commanded and
fought the army of Amalek. Meanwhile, Moses, Aaron,
and Hur climbed to the top of a nearby hill. 11 As long as
Moses held up the staff in his hand, the Israelites had
the advantage. But whenever he dropped his hand, the
Amalekites gained the advantage. 12 Moses' arms soon
became so tired he could no longer hold them up. So
Aaron and Hur found a stone for him to sit on. Then
they stood on each side of Moses, holding up his hands.
So his hands held steady until sunset. 13 As a result,
Joshua overwhelmed the army of Amalek in battle.
14 After the victory, the LORD instructed Moses,
"Write this down on a scroll as a permanent reminder,
and read it aloud to Joshua: I will erase the memory
of Amalek from under heaven." 15 Moses built an altar
there and named it Yahweh-Nissi (which means "the
LORD is my banner"). 16 He said, "They have raised their
fist against the LORD's throne, so now* the LORD will
be at war with Amalek generation after generation."

JETHRO'S VISIT TO MOSES

18 Moses' father-in-law, Jethro, the priest of Mid-
ian, heard about everything God had done for
Moses and his people, the Israelites. He heard espe-
cially about how the LORD had rescued them from
Egypt.
2 Earlier, Moses had sent his wife, Zipporah, and
his two sons back to Jethro, who had taken them in.
3 (Moses' first son was named Gershom,* for Moses
had said when the boy was born, "I have been a for-
eigner in a foreign land." 4 His second son was named
Eliezer,* for Moses had said, "The God of my ancestors
was my helper; he rescued me from the sword of Pha-
raoh.") 5 Jethro, Moses' father-in-law, now came to
visit Moses in the wilderness. He brought Moses' wife
and two sons with him, and they arrived while Moses
and the people were camped near the mountain of
God. 6 Jethro had sent a message to Moses, saying, "I,
Jethro, your father-in-law, am coming to see you with
your wife and your two sons."
7 So Moses went out to meet his father-in-law. He
bowed low and kissed him. They asked about each
other's welfare and then went into Moses' tent.
8 Moses told his father-in-law everything the LORD
had done to Pharaoh and Egypt on behalf of Israel.
He also told about all the hardships they had experi-
enced along the way and how the LORD had rescued
his people from all their troubles. 9 Jethro was delight-
ed when he heard about all the good things the LORD
had done for Israel as he rescued them from the hand
of the Egyptians.

16:31 *Manna* means "What is it?" See 16:15. **16:34** Hebrew *He placed it in front of the Testimony;* see note on 25:16. **16:36** Hebrew *An omer is one-tenth of an ephah.* **17:1** The geographical name *Sin* is related to *Sinai* and should not be confused with the English word *sin.* **17:6** Hebrew *Horeb,* another name for Sinai. **17:16** Or *Hands have been lifted up to the* LORD's *throne, and now.* **18:3** *Gershom* sounds like a Hebrew term that means "a foreigner there." **18:4** *Eliezer* means "God is my helper."

16:34 placed it in the Ark. A jar of manna was placed in the ark with the 10 commandments (31:18).

17:4 Moses cried out to the LORD. Previously, the people had complained that Moses meant for them to starve (16:3). Here they grumbled that Moses meant for them to die of thirst, even though God had always met their needs (15:23-25). Since they were ready to kill him, Moses referred to them as "these people" instead of "My people."

17:7 Massah . . . Meribah. Psalm 95:7-8 and Hebrews 3:7-8, 15 refer to the events of verses 1-7. The names "Massah" (testing) and "Meribah" (arguing) carry ominous connotations and are reminders of the Israelites' lack of faith and obedience.

17:9 Joshua. Picking a man of wisdom (Deut. 34:9) with military prowess demonstrated Moses' ability to pick the right man as the conquest of Canaan 40 years later would show.

10 "Praise the LORD," Jethro said, "for he has rescued
you from the Egyptians and from Pharaoh. Yes, he
has rescued Israel from the powerful hand of Egypt!
11 I know now that the LORD is greater than all other
gods, because he rescued his people from the oppres-
sion of the proud Egyptians."
12 Then Jethro, Moses' father-in-law, brought a
burnt offering and sacrifices to God. Aaron and all
the elders of Israel came out and joined him in a sac-
rificial meal in God's presence.

JETHRO'S WISE ADVICE

13 The next day, Moses took his seat to hear the peo-
ple's disputes against each other. They waited before
him from morning till evening.
14 When Moses' father-in-law saw all that Moses
was doing for the people, he asked, "What are you
really accomplishing here? Why are you trying to do
all this alone while everyone stands around you from
morning till evening?"
15 Moses replied, "Because the people come to me to
get a ruling from God. 16 When a dispute arises, they
come to me, and I am the one who settles the case be-
tween the quarreling parties. I inform the people of
God's decrees and give them his instructions."
17 "This is not good!" Moses' father-in-law ex-
claimed. 18 "You're going to wear yourself out—and
the people, too. This job is too heavy a burden for
you to handle all by yourself. 19 Now listen to me,
and let me give you a word of advice, and may God
be with you. You should continue to be the people's
representative before God, bringing their disputes
to him. 20 Teach them God's decrees, and give them
his instructions. Show them how to conduct their
lives. 21 But select from all the people some capable,
honest men who fear God and hate bribes. Appoint
them as leaders over groups of one thousand, one
hundred, fifty, and ten. 22 They should always be
available to solve the people's common disputes,
but have them bring the major cases to you. Let
the leaders decide the smaller matters themselves.
They will help you carry the load, making the task
easier for you. 23 If you follow this advice, and if God
commands you to do so, then you will be able to
endure the pressures, and all these people will go
home in peace."
24 Moses listened to his father-in-law's advice and
followed his suggestions. 25 He chose capable men
from all over Israel and appointed them as leaders
over the people. He put them in charge of groups of
one thousand, one hundred, fifty, and ten. 26 These
men were always available to solve the people's
common disputes. They brought the major cases
to Moses, but they took care of the smaller matters
themselves.
27 Soon after this, Moses said good-bye to his father-
in-law, who returned to his own land.

THE LORD REVEALS HIMSELF AT SINAI

19 Exactly two months after the Israelites left
Egypt,* they arrived in the wilderness of Sinai.
2 After breaking camp at Rephidim, they came to the
wilderness of Sinai and set up camp there at the base
of Mount Sinai.
3 Then Moses climbed the mountain to appear be-
fore God. The LORD called to him from the mountain
and said, "Give these instructions to the family of Ja-
cob; announce it to the descendants of Israel: 4 'You
have seen what I did to the Egyptians. You know how
I carried you on eagles' wings and brought you to my-
self. 5 Now if you will obey me and keep my covenant,
you will be my own special treasure from among all
the peoples on earth; for all the earth belongs to me.
6 And you will be my kingdom of priests, my holy na-
tion.' This is the message you must give to the people
of Israel."
7 So Moses returned from the mountain and called
together the elders of the people and told them every-
thing the LORD had commanded him. 8 And all the
people responded together, "We will do everything
the LORD has commanded." So Moses brought the
people's answer back to the LORD.
9 Then the LORD said to Moses, "I will come to you
in a thick cloud, Moses, so the people themselves can
hear me when I speak with you. Then they will al-
ways trust you."
Moses told the LORD what the people had said.
10 Then the LORD told Moses, "Go down and prepare
the people for my arrival. Consecrate them today and
tomorrow, and have them wash their clothing. 11 Be
sure they are ready on the third day, for on that day
the LORD will come down on Mount Sinai as all the
people watch. 12 Mark off a boundary all around the
mountain. Warn the people, 'Be careful! Do not go up
on the mountain or even touch its boundaries. Any-
one who touches the mountain will certainly be put
to death. 13 No hand may touch the person or animal
that crosses the boundary; instead, stone them or
shoot them with arrows. They must be put to death.'
However, when the ram's horn sounds a long blast,
then the people may go up on the mountain.*"
14 So Moses went down to the people. He consecrat-
ed them for worship, and they washed their clothes.
15 He told them, "Get ready for the third day, and until
then abstain from having sexual intercourse."
16 On the morning of the third day, thunder roared
and lightning flashed, and a dense cloud came down
on the mountain. There was a long, loud blast from a
ram's horn, and all the people trembled. 17 Moses led
them out from the camp to meet with God, and they
stood at the foot of the mountain. 18 All of Mount Si-
nai was covered with smoke because the LORD had
descended on it in the form of fire. The smoke bil-
lowed into the sky like smoke from a brick kiln, and
the whole mountain shook violently. 19 As the blast of

19:1 Hebrew *In the third month after the Israelites left Egypt, on the very day*, i.e., two lunar months to the day after leaving Egypt. Compare Num 33:3. **19:13** Or *up to the mountain*.

18:11 I know now. God's victory over the Egyptians brought Him glory as He predicted (14:4). Whether Jethro was a true convert or simply a well-meaning Midianite priest is not explained. Some Samaritans had a similar response to Jesus (John 4:42).

18:16 God's decrees . . . instructions. Moses' authority by divine sanction extended to even practical matters.

19:4 eagles' wings. The strength and majesty of the eagle is used as a recurring image of God in His role as Savior to those who in him. (Isa. 40:31).

19:5 obey me and keep my covenant. God made a covenant with Israel at Mount Sinai based on obedience. This covenant was an extension of the one made with Abraham hundreds of years before. According to the covenant, Israel's obedience would result in being favored by God and given a special role in His kingdom.

19:15 sexual intercourse. This was a temporary abstinence so that they would be ritually clean, since sexual discharges made one unclean (Lev. 15:18).

THE TEN COMMANDMENTS

1. What is your coach's favorite "commandment"? What rule does he or she repeat often? Do you follow it?

EXODUS 19:10–20:21

2. What are some idols or false gods seen today? How can we avoid "bowing down" to them?
3. What does it mean to "misuse the name of the Lord your God" (20:7)?
4. What does it mean to "honor your father and mother" (20:12)?
5. What does it mean to "covet your neighbor's house" and possessions (20:17)?
6. Which commandments do you need to work on most in your home life? Your athletic life?

the ram's horn grew louder and louder, Moses spoke,
and God thundered his reply. 20 The LORD came down
on the top of Mount Sinai and called Moses to the top
of the mountain. So Moses climbed the mountain.
21 Then the LORD told Moses, "Go back down and
warn the people not to break through the boundar-
ies to see the LORD, or they will die. 22 Even the priests
who regularly come near to the LORD must purify
themselves so that the LORD does not break out and
destroy them."
23 "But LORD," Moses protested, "the people cannot
come up to Mount Sinai. You already warned us. You
told me, 'Mark off a boundary all around the moun-
tain to set it apart as holy.'"
24 But the LORD said, "Go down and bring Aaron
back up with you. In the meantime, do not let the
priests or the people break through to approach the
LORD, or he will break out and destroy them."
25 So Moses went down to the people and told them
what the LORD had said.

TEN COMMANDMENTS FOR THE COVENANT COMMUNITY

20 Then God gave the people all these instruc-
tions*:
2 "I am the LORD your God, who rescued you from the
land of Egypt, the place of your slavery.
3 "You must not have any other god but me.
4 "You must not make for yourself an idol of any kind
or an image of anything in the heavens or on the
earth or in the sea. 5 You must not bow down to
them or worship them, for I, the LORD your God, am
a jealous God who will not tolerate your affection
for any other gods. I lay the sins of the parents upon
their children; the entire family is affected—even
children in the third and fourth generations of
those who reject me. 6 But I lavish unfailing love for
a thousand generations on those* who love me and
obey my commands.
7 "You must not misuse the name of the LORD your God.
The LORD will not let you go unpunished if you mis-
use his name.
8 "Remember to observe the Sabbath day by keeping it
holy. 9 You have six days each week for your ordinary
work, 10 but the seventh day is a Sabbath day of rest
dedicated to the LORD your God. On that day no one
in your household may do any work. This includes
you, your sons and daughters, your male and female
servants, your livestock, and any foreigners living
among you. 11 For in six days the LORD made the heav-
ens, the earth, the sea, and everything in them; but
on the seventh day he rested. That is why the LORD
blessed the Sabbath day and set it apart as holy.
12 "Honor your father and mother. Then you will live a
long, full life in the land the LORD your God is giving
you.
13 "You must not murder.
14 "You must not commit adultery.
15 "You must not steal.
16 "You must not testify falsely against your neighbor.
17 "You must not covet your neighbor's house. You must
not covet your neighbor's wife, male or female ser-
vant, ox or donkey, or anything else that belongs to
your neighbor."

18 When the people heard the thunder and the loud
blast of the ram's horn, and when they saw the flashes
of lightning and the smoke billowing from the moun-
tain, they stood at a distance, trembling with fear.
19 And they said to Moses, "You speak to us, and we
will listen. But don't let God speak directly to us, or
we will die!"
20 "Don't be afraid," Moses answered them, "for God
has come in this way to test you, and so that your fear
of him will keep you from sinning!"
21 As the people stood in the distance, Moses ap-
proached the dark cloud where God was.

PROPER USE OF ALTARS

22 And the LORD said to Moses, "Say this to the people
of Israel: You saw for yourselves that I spoke to you
from heaven. 23 Remember, you must not make any
idols of silver or gold to rival me.
24 "Build for me an altar made of earth, and offer
your sacrifices to me—your burnt offerings and
peace offerings, your sheep and goats, and your cat-
tle. Build my altar wherever I cause my name to be
remembered, and I will come to you and bless you.
25 If you use stones to build my altar, use only natural,
uncut stones. Do not shape the stones with a tool, for
that would make the altar unfit for holy use. 26 And
do not approach my altar by going up steps. If you do,
someone might look up under your clothing and see
your nakedness.

20:1 Hebrew *all these words.* **20:6** Hebrew *for thousands of those.*

20:7 name of the Lord. Making an oath using the name of God and then failing to keep it (22:10, 11; Lev. 19:12) was to question His existence. God's name is holy and should never be used to suit our own needs.

20:8 Remember to observe the Sabbath day. God had rested on the seventh day of creation. He commanded that all work stop so that everyone, including servants, could participate in a day of rest and renewal.

20:12 Honor your father and your mother. After defining the proper relationship between people (vv. 2-11), the Law declares that Israelite sons and daughters are to treat their parents with adoration, respect, and obedience—exactly what He demanded of parents themselves in their relationship with Him.

FAIR TREATMENT OF SLAVES

21 "These are the regulations you must present to Israel.

2 "If you buy a Hebrew slave, he may serve for no more than six years. Set him free in the seventh year, and he will owe you nothing for his freedom. 3 If he was single when he became your slave, he shall leave single. But if he was married before he became a slave, then his wife must be freed with him.

4 "If his master gave him a wife while he was a slave and they had sons or daughters, then only the man will be free in the seventh year, but his wife and children will still belong to his master. 5 But the slave may declare, 'I love my master, my wife, and my children. I don't want to go free.' 6 If he does this, his master must present him before God.* Then his master must take him to the door or doorpost and publicly pierce his ear with an awl. After that, the slave will serve his master for life.

7 "When a man sells his daughter as a slave, she will not be freed at the end of six years as the men are. 8 If she does not satisfy her owner, he must allow her to be bought back again. But he is not allowed to sell her to foreigners, since he is the one who broke the contract with her. 9 But if the slave's owner arranges for her to marry his son, he may no longer treat her as a slave but as a daughter.

10 "If a man who has married a slave wife takes another wife for himself, he must not neglect the rights of the first wife to food, clothing, and sexual intimacy. 11 If he fails in any of these three obligations, she may leave as a free woman without making any payment.

CASES OF PERSONAL INJURY

12 "Anyone who assaults and kills another person must be put to death. 13 But if it was simply an accident permitted by God, I will appoint a place of refuge where the slayer can run for safety. 14 However, if someone deliberately kills another person, then the slayer must be dragged even from my altar and be put to death.

15 "Anyone who strikes father or mother must be put to death.

16 "Kidnappers must be put to death, whether they are caught in possession of their victims or have already sold them as slaves.

17 "Anyone who dishonors* father or mother must be put to death.

18 "Now suppose two men quarrel, and one hits the other with a stone or fist, and the injured person does not die but is confined to bed. 19 If he is later able to walk outside again, even with a crutch, the assailant will not be punished but must compensate his victim for lost wages and provide for his full recovery.

20 "If a man beats his male or female slave with a club and the slave dies as a result, the owner must be punished. 21 But if the slave recovers within a day or two, then the owner shall not be punished, since the slave is his property.

22 "Now suppose two men are fighting, and in the process they accidentally strike a pregnant woman so she gives birth prematurely.* If no further injury results, the man who struck the woman must pay the amount of compensation the woman's husband demands and the judges approve. 23 But if there is further injury, the punishment must match the injury: a life for a life, 24 an eye for an eye, a tooth for a tooth, a hand for a hand, a foot for a foot, 25 a burn for a burn, a wound for a wound, a bruise for a bruise.

26 "If a man hits his male or female slave in the eye and the eye is blinded, he must let the slave go free to compensate for the eye. 27 And if a man knocks out the tooth of his male or female slave, he must let the slave go free to compensate for the tooth.

28 "If an ox* gores a man or woman to death, the ox must be stoned, and its flesh may not be eaten. In such a case, however, the owner will not be held liable. 29 But suppose the ox had a reputation for goring, and the owner had been informed but failed to keep it under control. If the ox then kills someone, it must be stoned, and the owner must also be put to death. 30 However, the dead person's relatives may accept payment to compensate for the loss of life. The owner of the ox may redeem his life by paying whatever is demanded.

31 "The same regulation applies if the ox gores a boy or a girl. 32 But if the ox gores a slave, either male or female, the animal's owner must pay the slave's owner thirty silver coins,* and the ox must be stoned.

33 "Suppose someone digs or uncovers a pit and fails to cover it, and then an ox or a donkey falls into it. 34 The owner of the pit must pay full compensation to the owner of the animal, but then he gets to keep the dead animal.

35 "If someone's ox injures a neighbor's ox and the injured ox dies, then the two owners must sell the live ox and divide the price equally between them. They must also divide the dead animal. 36 But if the ox had a reputation for goring, yet its owner failed to keep it under control, he must pay full compensation—a live ox for the dead one—but he may keep the dead ox.

PROTECTION OF PROPERTY

22 1* "If someone steals an ox* or sheep and then kills or sells it, the thief must pay back five oxen for each ox stolen, and four sheep for each sheep stolen.

2* "If a thief is caught in the act of breaking into a house and is struck and killed in the process, the person who killed the thief is not guilty of murder. 3 But if

21:6 Or *before the judges.* **21:17** Greek version reads *Anyone who speaks disrespectfully of.* Compare Matt 15:4; Mark 7:10. **21:22** Or *so she has a miscarriage;* Hebrew reads *so her children come out.* **21:28** Or *bull,* or *cow;* also in 21:29-36. **21:32** Hebrew *30 shekels of silver,* about 12 ounces or 342 grams in weight. **22:1a** Verse 22:1 is numbered 21:37 in Hebrew text. **22:1b** Or *bull,* or *cow;* also in 22:4, 9, 10. **22:2** Verses 22:2-31 are numbered 22:1-30 in Hebrew text.

21:2 Hebrew slave. Voluntary slavery was a way to work out of debt. Servitude was never perpetual, except by the slave's own choice (v. 6). The period of seven years is still a part of modern bankruptcy law.

21:12-14 an accident . . . deliberately kills. Murder (intentional killing) was an evil act (20:13). Accidental manslaughter was terrible, but the punishment was not as severe and allowed for escape to a city of refuge (Num. 35:9-34).

21:23 injury. This fact weakens the case for rigid application of the law of retaliation; a person killing mother and child would have only one life to give up as punishment.

21:23-24 a life for a life, an eye for an eye. The punishment should fit the crime—not put out people's eyes. By contrast, in Hammurabi's law code, a person of low class who injured one of high class was to be put to death.

21:32 thirty silver coins. The price had gone up since Joseph was sold for twenty shekels 400 years earlier (Gen. 37:28). Judas' payment to betray Jesus was 30 shekels (Matt. 26:14; cf. Jer. 32:6-9) or four month's wages, still a princely sum in New Testament times. Yet, Judas assumed the price of slave compensation for Jesus was preferable to the cost of discipleship to Jesus. It wasn't the first time the Shepherd was ill-regarded (Zech. 11:12).

it happens in daylight, the one who killed the thief is
guilty of murder.
"A thief who is caught must pay in full for every-
thing he stole. If he cannot pay, he must be sold as a
slave to pay for his theft. 4 If someone steals an ox or a
donkey or a sheep and it is found in the thief's posses-
sion, then the thief must pay double the value of the
stolen animal.
5 "If an animal is grazing in a field or vineyard and
the owner lets it stray into someone else's field to
graze, then the animal's owner must pay compensa-
tion from the best of his own grain or grapes.
6 "If you are burning thornbushes and the fire gets
out of control and spreads into another person's field,
destroying the sheaves or the uncut grain or the
whole crop, the one who started the fire must pay for
the lost crop.
7 "Suppose someone leaves money or goods with a
neighbor for safekeeping, and they are stolen from
the neighbor's house. If the thief is caught, the com-
pensation is double the value of what was stolen. 8 But
if the thief is not caught, the neighbor must appear
before God,* who will determine if he stole the prop-
erty.
9 "Suppose there is a dispute between two people
who both claim to own a particular ox, donkey, sheep,
article of clothing, or any lost property. Both parties
must come before God, and the person whom God de-
clares* guilty must pay double compensation to the
other.
10 "Now suppose someone leaves a donkey, ox,
sheep, or any other animal with a neighbor for safe-
keeping, but it dies or is injured or is taken away,
and no one sees what happened. 11 The neighbor
must then take an oath in the presence of the LORD.
If the LORD confirms that the neighbor did not steal
the property, the owner must accept the verdict,
and no payment will be required. 12 But if the ani-
mal was indeed stolen, the guilty person must pay
compensation to the owner. 13 If it was torn to pieces
by a wild animal, the remains of the carcass must
be shown as evidence, and no compensation will be
required.
14 "If someone borrows an animal from a neighbor
and it is injured or dies when the owner is absent, the
person who borrowed it must pay full compensation.
15 But if the owner was present, no compensation is
required. And no compensation is required if the an-
imal was rented, for this loss is covered by the rental
fee.

SOCIAL RESPONSIBILITY

16 "If a man seduces a virgin who is not engaged to
anyone and has sex with her, he must pay the custom-
ary bride price and marry her. 17 But if her father re-
fuses to let him marry her, the man must still pay him
an amount equal to the bride price of a virgin.
18 "You must not allow a sorceress to live.
19 "Anyone who has sexual relations with an ani-
mal must certainly be put to death.
20 "Anyone who sacrifices to any god other than the
LORD must be destroyed.*
21 "You must not mistreat or oppress foreigners in
any way. Remember, you yourselves were once for-
eigners in the land of Egypt.
22 "You must not exploit a widow or an orphan. 23 If
you exploit them in any way and they cry out to me,
then I will certainly hear their cry. 24 My anger will
blaze against you, and I will kill you with the sword.
Then your wives will be widows and your children
fatherless.
25 "If you lend money to any of my people who are
in need, do not charge interest as a money lender
would. 26 If you take your neighbor's cloak as securi-
ty for a loan, you must return it before sunset. 27 This
coat may be the only blanket your neighbor has. How
can a person sleep without it? If you do not return it
and your neighbor cries out to me for help, then I will
hear, for I am merciful.
28 "You must not dishonor God or curse any of your
rulers.
29 "You must not hold anything back when you give
me offerings from your crops and your wine.
"You must give me your firstborn sons.
30 "You must also give me the firstborn of your cat-
tle, sheep, and goats. But leave the newborn animal
with its mother for seven days; then give it to me on
the eighth day.
31 "You must be my holy people. Therefore, do not
eat any animal that has been torn up and killed by
wild animals. Throw it to the dogs.

A CALL FOR JUSTICE

23 "You must not pass along false rumors. You
must not cooperate with evil people by lying on
the witness stand.
2 "You must not follow the crowd in doing wrong.
When you are called to testify in a dispute, do not be
swayed by the crowd to twist justice. 3 And do not
slant your testimony in favor of a person just because
that person is poor.
4 "If you come upon your enemy's ox or donkey that
has strayed away, take it back to its owner. 5 If you see
that the donkey of someone who hates you has col-
lapsed under its load, do not walk by. Instead, stop
and help.
6 "In a lawsuit, you must not deny justice to the poor.
7 "Be sure never to charge anyone falsely with evil.
Never sentence an innocent or blameless person to
death, for I never declare a guilty person to be inno-
cent.
8 "Take no bribes, for a bribe makes you ignore
something that you clearly see. A bribe makes even a
righteous person twist the truth.
9 "You must not oppress foreigners. You know what
it's like to be a foreigner, for you yourselves were once
foreigners in the land of Egypt.
10 "Plant and harvest your crops for six years, 11 but
let the land be renewed and lie uncultivated during
the seventh year. Then let the poor among you har-

22:8 Or *before the judges.* 22:9 Or *before the judges, and the person whom the judges declare.* 22:20 The Hebrew term used here refers to the complete consecration of things or people to the LORD, either by destroying them or by giving them as an offering.

22:3 if it happens in daylight. It was not permitted to kill a prowler during the day, since an assailant's vision indicated some level of premeditation.

22:16 bride price. In order to get a wife, a man was required to pay his future father-in-law for the privilege. In this case, the man who has violated the daughter must satisfy the father. A high price could be expected.

23:4-5 enemy's ox. A person's enemies must be treated with the same regard as friends, returning hostility with kindness. Here the enemy is a Hebrew.

vest whatever grows on its own. Leave the rest for
wild animals to eat. The same applies to your vine-
yards and olive groves.
12 “You have six days each week for your ordinary
work, but on the seventh day you must stop working.
This gives your ox and your donkey a chance to rest.
It also allows your slaves and the foreigners living
among you to be refreshed.
13 “Pay close attention to all my instructions. You
must not call on the name of any other gods. Do not
even speak their names.

THREE ANNUAL FESTIVALS

14 “Each year you must celebrate three festivals in my
honor. 15 First, celebrate the Festival of Unleavened
Bread. For seven days the bread you eat must be
made without yeast, just as I commanded you. Cele-
brate this festival annually at the appointed time in
early spring, in the month of Abib,* for that is the an-
niversary of your departure from Egypt. No one may
appear before me without an offering.
16 “Second, celebrate the Festival of Harvest,* when
you bring me the first crops of your harvest.
“Finally, celebrate the Festival of the Final Harvest*
at the end of the harvest season, when you have har-
vested all the crops from your fields. 17 At these three
times each year, every man in Israel must appear be-
fore the Sovereign, the LORD.
18 “You must not offer the blood of my sacrificial
offerings together with any baked goods containing
yeast. And do not leave the fat from the festival offer-
ings until the next morning.
19 “As you harvest your crops, bring the very best
of the first harvest to the house of the LORD your God.
“You must not cook a young goat in its mother’s
milk.

A PROMISE OF THE LORD’S PRESENCE

20 “See, I am sending an angel before you to protect
you on your journey and lead you safely to the place
I have prepared for you. 21 Pay close attention to him,
and obey his instructions. Do not rebel against him,
for he is my representative, and he will not forgive
your rebellion. 22 But if you are careful to obey him, fol-
lowing all my instructions, then I will be an enemy to
your enemies, and I will oppose those who oppose you.
23 For my angel will go before you and bring you into
the land of the Amorites, Hittites, Perizzites, Canaan-
ites, Hivites, and Jebusites, so you may live there. And I
will destroy them completely. 24 You must not worship
the gods of these nations or serve them in any way or
imitate their evil practices. Instead, you must utterly
destroy them and smash their sacred pillars.
25 “You must serve only the LORD your God. If you do,
I* will bless you with food and water, and I will pro-
tect you from illness. 26 There will be no miscarriages
or infertility in your land, and I will give you long, full
lives.
27 “I will send my terror ahead of you and create
panic among all the people whose lands you invade. I
will make all your enemies turn and run. 28 I will send
terror* ahead of you to drive out the Hivites, Canaan-
ites, and Hittites. 29 But I will not drive them out in a
single year, because the land would become desolate
and the wild animals would multiply and threaten
you. 30 I will drive them out a little at a time until your
population has increased enough to take possession
of the land. 31 And I will fix your boundaries from
the Red Sea to the Mediterranean Sea,* and from
the eastern wilderness to the Euphrates River.* I will
hand over to you the people now living in the land,
and you will drive them out ahead of you.
32 “Make no treaties with them or their gods. 33 They
must not live in your land, or they will cause you to
sin against me. If you serve their gods, you will be
caught in the trap of idolatry.”

ISRAEL ACCEPTS THE LORD’S COVENANT

24 Then the LORD instructed Moses: “Come up
here to me, and bring along Aaron, Nadab,
Abihu, and seventy of Israel’s elders. All of you must
worship from a distance. 2 Only Moses is allowed to
come near to the LORD. The others must not come near,
and none of the other people are allowed to climb up
the mountain with him.”
3 Then Moses went down to the people and repeat-
ed all the instructions and regulations the LORD had
given him. All the people answered with one voice,
“We will do everything the LORD has commanded.”
4 Then Moses carefully wrote down all the LORD’s
instructions. Early the next morning Moses got up
and built an altar at the foot of the mountain. He also
set up twelve pillars, one for each of the twelve tribes
of Israel. 5 Then he sent some of the young Israelite
men to present burnt offerings and to sacrifice bulls
as peace offerings to the LORD. 6 Moses drained half
the blood from these animals into basins. The other
half he splattered against the altar.
7 Then he took the Book of the Covenant and read
it aloud to the people. Again they all responded, “We
will do everything the LORD has commanded. We will
obey.”
8 Then Moses took the blood from the basins and
splattered it over the people, declaring, “Look, this
blood confirms the covenant the LORD has made with
you in giving you these instructions.”

23:15 Hebrew *appointed time in the month of Abib.* This first month of the ancient Hebrew lunar calendar usually occurs within the months of March and April. **23:16a** Or *Festival of Weeks.* This was later called the Festival of Pentecost (see Acts 2:1). It is celebrated today as Shavuot (or Shabuoth). **23:16b** Or *Festival of Ingathering.* This was later called the Festival of Shelters or Festival of Tabernacles (see Lev 23:33-36). It is celebrated today as Sukkot (or Succoth). **23:25** As in Greek and Latin versions; Hebrew reads *he.* **23:28** Often rendered *the hornet.* The meaning of the Hebrew is uncertain. **23:31a** Hebrew *from the sea of reeds to the sea of the Philistines.* **23:31b** Hebrew *from the wilderness to the river.*

23:15 Festival of Unleavened Bread. Passover week was celebrated from around mid-March to mid-April. It was in memory of the Israelites’ rapid escape from Egypt (12:17-20).

23:16 Festival of Harvest. Pentecost (Hebrew *Shavuot*) was celebrated seven weeks after the Feast of Unleavened Bread during the time of the wheat harvest. At this feast, the Israelites made offerings to God of the harvest’s firstfruits.

23:18 any . . . containing yeast. In His instructions for the Passover, God prohibited yeast, a symbol of sin and impurity, from even being in the home during that festival (12:14-16). Jesus refers to this symbol (Matt. 16:5-12).

23:20 place I have prepared. The words Jesus used to describe our place in heaven echoes the language here (John 14:2-4).

24:2 Only Moses. Only the mediator Moses is allowed direct access. Jesus, a greater middleman than Moses (v. 8; Heb. 3:3; 9:15), becomes the “mediator of a new covenant” with God (Heb. 12:24) and bridges the gulf between human and divine.

24:8 splattered it over the people. A symbol of covenant acceptance, it is also a reminder of the first Passover when blood above and beside the door marked an Israelite home for salvation. Christ’s blood seals the New covenant of forgiveness.

9 Then Moses, Aaron, Nadab, Abihu, and the seventy elders of Israel climbed up the mountain. 10 There they saw the God of Israel. Under his feet there seemed to be a surface of brilliant blue lapis lazuli, as clear as the sky itself. 11 And though these nobles of Israel gazed upon God, he did not destroy them. In fact, they ate a covenant meal, eating and drinking in his presence!

12 Then the LORD said to Moses, "Come up to me on the mountain. Stay there, and I will give you the tablets of stone on which I have inscribed the instructions and commands so you can teach the people." 13 So Moses and his assistant Joshua set out, and Moses climbed up the mountain of God.

14 Moses told the elders, "Stay here and wait for us until we come back. Aaron and Hur are here with you. If anyone has a dispute while I am gone, consult with them."

15 Then Moses climbed up the mountain, and the cloud covered it. 16 And the glory of the LORD settled down on Mount Sinai, and the cloud covered it for six days. On the seventh day the LORD called to Moses from inside the cloud. 17 To the Israelites at the foot of the mountain, the glory of the LORD appeared at the summit like a consuming fire. 18 Then Moses disappeared into the cloud as he climbed higher up the mountain. He remained on the mountain forty days and forty nights.

OFFERINGS FOR THE TABERNACLE

25 The LORD said to Moses, 2 "Tell the people of Israel to bring me their sacred offerings. Accept the contributions from all whose hearts are moved to offer them. 3 Here is a list of sacred offerings you may accept from them:

gold, silver, and bronze;
4 blue, purple, and scarlet thread;
fine linen and goat hair for cloth;
5 tanned ram skins and fine goatskin leather;
acacia wood;
6 olive oil for the lamps;
spices for the anointing oil and the fragrant incense;
7 onyx stones, and other gemstones to be set in the ephod and the priest's chestpiece.

8 "Have the people of Israel build me a holy sanctuary so I can live among them. 9 You must build this Tabernacle and its furnishings exactly according to the pattern I will show you.

PLANS FOR THE ARK OF THE COVENANT

10 "Have the people make an Ark of acacia wood—a sacred chest 45 inches long, 27 inches wide, and 27 inches high.* 11 Overlay it inside and outside with pure gold, and run a molding of gold all around it. 12 Cast four gold rings and attach them to its four feet, two rings on each side. 13 Make poles from acacia wood, and overlay them with gold. 14 Insert the poles into the rings at the sides of the Ark to carry it. 15 These carrying poles must stay inside the rings; never remove them. 16 When the Ark is finished, place inside it the stone tablets inscribed with the terms of the covenant,* which I will give to you.

17 "Then make the Ark's cover—the place of atonement—from pure gold. It must be 45 inches long and 27 inches wide.* 18 Then make two cherubim from hammered gold, and place them on the two ends of the atonement cover. 19 Mold the cherubim on each end of the atonement cover, making it all of one piece of gold. 20 The cherubim will face each other and look down on the atonement cover. With their wings spread above it, they will protect it. 21 Place inside the Ark the stone tablets inscribed with the terms of the covenant, which I will give to you. Then put the atonement cover on top of the Ark. 22 I will meet with you there and talk to you from above the atonement cover between the gold cherubim that hover over the Ark of the Covenant.* From there I will give you my commands for the people of Israel.

PLANS FOR THE TABLE

23 "Then make a table of acacia wood, 36 inches long, 18 inches wide, and 27 inches high.* 24 Overlay it with pure gold and run a gold molding around the edge. 25 Decorate it with a 3-inch border* all around, and run a gold molding along the border. 26 Make four gold rings for the table and attach them at the four corners next to the four legs. 27 Attach the rings near the border to hold the poles that are used to carry the table. 28 Make these poles from acacia wood, and overlay them with gold. 29 Make special containers of pure gold for the table—bowls, ladles, pitchers, and jars—to be used in pouring out liquid offerings. 30 Place the Bread of the Presence on the table to remain before me at all times.

PLANS FOR THE LAMPSTAND

31 "Make a lampstand of pure, hammered gold. Make the entire lampstand and its decorations of one piece—the base, center stem, lamp cups, buds, and petals. 32 Make it with six branches going out from the center stem, three on each side. 33 Each of the six branches will have three lamp cups shaped like almond blossoms, complete with buds and petals. 34 Craft the center stem of the lampstand with four lamp cups shaped like almond blossoms, complete with buds and petals. 35 There will also be an almond bud beneath each pair of branches where the six branches extend from the center stem. 36 The almond buds and branches must all be of one piece with the center stem, and they must be hammered from pure gold. 37 Then make the seven lamps for the lampstand, and set them so they reflect their light forward. 38 The lamp snuffers and trays must also be made of pure

25:10 Hebrew *2.5 cubits* [115 centimeters] *long, 1.5 cubits* [69 centimeters] *wide, and 1.5 cubits high.* **25:16** Hebrew *Place inside the Ark the Testimony;* similarly in 25:21. The Hebrew word for "testimony" refers to the terms of the LORD's covenant with Israel as written on stone tablets, and also to the covenant itself. **25:17** Hebrew *2.5 cubits* [115 centimeters] *long and 1.5 cubits* [69 centimeters] *wide.* **25:22** Or *Ark of the Testimony.* **25:23** Hebrew *2 cubits* [92 centimeters] *long, 1 cubit* [46 centimeters] *wide, and 1.5 cubits* [69 centimeters] *high.* **25:25** Hebrew *a border of a handbreadth* [8 centimeters].

24:11 eating and drinking. After a wedding it is traditional to celebrate. The Lord's Supper celebrates the New Covenant wedding of Christ and the church (v. 8; Matt. 26:26-29).

24:18 forty days and forty nights. The length of Noah's flood (Gen. 7:12) and Christ's fast (Matt. 4:2).

25:30 Bread of the Presence. Twelve loaves of (show)bread, one for each tribe of Israel, were kept on this table as a perpetual sacrifice and reminder that all blessings come from God.

25:37 reflect their light forward. Priests later insured that these lamps burned all night (27:20-21). The lighted lamps are the Israelites' response to the light of God's glory (29:43).

gold. 39 You will need 75 pounds* of pure gold for the lampstand and its accessories.

40 "Be sure that you make everything according to the pattern I have shown you here on the mountain.

PLANS FOR THE TABERNACLE

26 "Make the Tabernacle from ten curtains of finely woven linen. Decorate the curtains with blue, purple, and scarlet thread and with skillfully embroidered cherubim. 2 These ten curtains must all be exactly the same size—42 feet long and 6 feet wide.* 3 Join five of these curtains together to make one long curtain, then join the other five into a second long curtain. 4 Put loops of blue yarn along the edge of the last curtain in each set. 5 The fifty loops along the edge of one curtain are to match the fifty loops along the edge of the other curtain. 6 Then make fifty gold clasps and fasten the long curtains together with the clasps. In this way, the Tabernacle will be made of one continuous piece.

7 "Make eleven curtains of goat-hair cloth to serve as a tent covering for the Tabernacle. 8 These eleven curtains must all be exactly the same size—45 feet long and 6 feet wide.* 9 Join five of these curtains together to make one long curtain, and join the other six into a second long curtain. Allow 3 feet of material from the second set of curtains to hang over the front* of the sacred tent. 10 Make fifty loops for one edge of each large curtain. 11 Then make fifty bronze clasps, and fasten the loops of the long curtains with the clasps. In this way, the tent covering will be made of one continuous piece. 12 The remaining 3 feet* of this tent covering will be left to hang over the back of the Tabernacle. 13 Allow 18 inches* of remaining material to hang down over each side, so the Tabernacle is completely covered. 14 Complete the tent covering with a protective layer of tanned ram skins and a layer of fine goatskin leather.

15 "For the framework of the Tabernacle, construct frames of acacia wood. 16 Each frame must be 15 feet high and 27 inches wide,* 17 with two pegs under each frame. Make all the frames identical. 18 Make twenty of these frames to support the curtains on the south side of the Tabernacle. 19 Also make forty silver bases—two bases under each frame, with the pegs fitting securely into the bases. 20 For the north side of the Tabernacle, make another twenty frames, 21 with their forty silver bases, two bases under each frame. 22 Make six frames for the rear—the west side of the Tabernacle—23 along with two additional frames to reinforce the rear corners of the Tabernacle. 24 These corner frames will be matched at the bottom and firmly attached at the top with a single ring, forming a single corner unit. Make both of these corner units the same way. 25 So there will be eight frames at the rear of the Tabernacle, set in sixteen silver bases—two bases under each frame.

26 "Make crossbars of acacia wood to link the frames, five crossbars for the north side of the Tabernacle 27 and five for the south side. Also make five crossbars for the rear of the Tabernacle, which will face west. 28 The middle crossbar, attached halfway up the frames, will run all the way from one end of the Tabernacle to the other. 29 Overlay the frames with gold, and make gold rings to hold the crossbars. Overlay the crossbars with gold as well.

30 "Set up this Tabernacle according to the pattern you were shown on the mountain.

31 "For the inside of the Tabernacle, make a special curtain of finely woven linen. Decorate it with blue, purple, and scarlet thread and with skillfully embroidered cherubim. 32 Hang this curtain on gold hooks attached to four posts of acacia wood. Overlay the posts with gold, and set them in four silver bases. 33 Hang the inner curtain from clasps, and put the Ark of the Covenant* in the room behind it. This curtain will separate the Holy Place from the Most Holy Place.

34 "Then put the Ark's cover—the place of atonement—on top of the Ark of the Covenant inside the Most Holy Place. 35 Place the table outside the inner curtain on the north side of the Tabernacle, and place the lampstand across the room on the south side.

36 "Make another curtain for the entrance to the sacred tent. Make it of finely woven linen and embroider it with exquisite designs, using blue, purple, and scarlet thread. 37 Craft five posts from acacia wood. Overlay them with gold, and hang the curtain from them with gold hooks. Cast five bronze bases for the posts.

PLANS FOR THE ALTAR OF BURNT OFFERING

27 "Using acacia wood, construct a square altar 7½ feet wide, 7½ feet long, and 4½ feet high.* 2 Make horns for each of its four corners so that the horns and altar are all one piece. Overlay the altar with bronze. 3 Make ash buckets, shovels, basins, meat forks, and firepans, all of bronze. 4 Make a bronze grating for it, and attach four bronze rings at its four corners. 5 Install the grating halfway down the side of the altar, under the ledge. 6 For carrying the altar, make poles from acacia wood, and overlay them with bronze. 7 Insert the poles through the rings on the two sides of the altar. 8 The altar must be hollow, made from planks. Build it just as you were shown on the mountain.

PLANS FOR THE COURTYARD

9 "Then make the courtyard for the Tabernacle, enclosed with curtains made of finely woven linen. On the south side, make the curtains 150 feet long.*

25:39 Hebrew *1 talent* [34 kilograms]. **26:2** Hebrew *28 cubits* [12.9 meters] *long and 4 cubits* [1.8 meters] *wide.* **26:8** Hebrew *30 cubits* [13.8 meters] *long and 4 cubits* [1.8 meters] *wide.* **26:9** Hebrew *Double over the sixth sheet at the front.* **26:12** Hebrew *The half sheet that is left over.* **26:13** Hebrew *1 cubit* [46 centimeters]. **26:16** Hebrew *10 cubits* [4.6 meters] *high and 1.5 cubits* [69 centimeters] *wide.* **26:33** Or *Ark of the Testimony*, also in 26:34. **27:1** Hebrew *5 cubits* [2.3 meters] *wide, 5 cubits long, a square, and 3 cubits* [1.4 meters] *high.* **27:9** Hebrew *100 cubits* [46 meters]; also in 27:11.

25:40 pattern . . . shown . . . on the mountain. God had specific designs for items in the tabernacle (27:8). Stephen said that these designs were made by God as He directed Moses (Acts 7:44).

26:1 Tabernacle. The tabernacle was a rectangular tent covered by several layers. The inner layer was made of linen embroidered with images of cherubim. The three other layers were made of woven goat hair, dyed ram skins and manatee hides. All of its construction material was fit for a royal chamber.

26:31 special curtain. An embroidered curtain divided The Holy Place from the Most Holy Place. The Most Holy Place, representing God's throne room, contained only the ark. The Holy Place contained the table for the bread of the Presence, the lampstand and the altar of incense.

27:1 altar. This altar, outside the Holy Place in the courtyard, is known as the bronze altar or the altar of burnt offering.

27:9-18 courtyard. The entire tabernacle area was a rectangle with its long sides aligned east to west and surrounded by a seven and a half foot curtain. The tent containing the Holy Place and Most Holy Place was in the western half; the bronze altar, about seven and a half feet square, was in the eastern courtyard, which measured 150 by 75 feet. The entrance lay on the east end and was about thirty feet square.

10 They will be held up by twenty posts set securely in twenty bronze bases. Hang the curtains with silver hooks and rings. 11 Make the curtains the same on the north side—150 feet of curtains held up by twenty posts set securely in bronze bases. Hang the curtains with silver hooks and rings. 12 The curtains on the west end of the courtyard will be 75 feet long,* supported by ten posts set into ten bases. 13 The east end of the courtyard, the front, will also be 75 feet long. 14 The courtyard entrance will be on the east end, flanked by two curtains. The curtain on the right side will be 22½ feet long,* supported by three posts set into three bases. 15 The curtain on the left side will also be 22½ feet long, supported by three posts set into three bases.

16 "For the entrance to the courtyard, make a curtain that is 30 feet long.* Make it from finely woven linen, and decorate it with beautiful embroidery in blue, purple, and scarlet thread. Support it with four posts, each securely set in its own base. 17 All the posts around the courtyard must have silver rings and hooks and bronze bases. 18 So the entire courtyard will be 150 feet long and 75 feet wide, with curtain walls 7½ feet high,* made from finely woven linen. The bases for the posts will be made of bronze.

19 "All the articles used in the rituals of the Tabernacle, including all the tent pegs used to support the Tabernacle and the courtyard curtains, must be made of bronze.

LIGHT FOR THE TABERNACLE

20 "Command the people of Israel to bring you pure oil of pressed olives for the light, to keep the lamps burning continually. 21 The lampstand will stand in the Tabernacle, in front of the inner curtain that shields the Ark of the Covenant.* Aaron and his sons must keep the lamps burning in the LORD's presence all night. This is a permanent law for the people of Israel, and it must be observed from generation to generation.

CLOTHING FOR THE PRIESTS

28 "Call for your brother, Aaron, and his sons, Nadab, Abihu, Eleazar, and Ithamar. Set them apart from the rest of the people of Israel so they may minister to me and be my priests. 2 Make sacred garments for Aaron that are glorious and beautiful. 3 Instruct all the skilled craftsmen whom I have filled with the spirit of wisdom. Have them make garments for Aaron that will distinguish him as a priest set apart for my service. 4 These are the garments they are to make: a chestpiece, an ephod, a robe, a patterned tunic, a turban, and a sash. They are to make these sacred garments for your brother, Aaron, and his sons to wear when they serve me as priests. 5 So give them fine linen cloth, gold thread, and blue, purple, and scarlet thread.

DESIGN OF THE EPHOD

6 "The craftsmen must make the ephod of finely woven linen and skillfully embroider it with gold and with blue, purple, and scarlet thread. 7 It will consist of two pieces, front and back, joined at the shoulders with two shoulder-pieces. 8 The decorative sash will be made of the same materials: finely woven linen embroidered with gold and with blue, purple, and scarlet thread.

9 "Take two onyx stones, and engrave on them the names of the tribes of Israel. 10 Six names will be on each stone, arranged in the order of the births of the original sons of Israel. 11 Engrave these names on the two stones in the same way a jeweler engraves a seal. Then mount the stones in settings of gold filigree. 12 Fasten the two stones on the shoulder-pieces of the ephod as a reminder that Aaron represents the people of Israel. Aaron will carry these names on his shoulders as a constant reminder whenever he goes before the LORD. 13 Make the settings of gold filigree, 14 then braid two cords of pure gold and attach them to the filigree settings on the shoulders of the ephod.

DESIGN OF THE CHESTPIECE

15 "Then, with great skill and care, make a chestpiece to be worn for seeking a decision from God.* Make it to match the ephod, using finely woven linen embroidered with gold and with blue, purple, and scarlet thread. 16 Make the chestpiece of a single piece of cloth folded to form a pouch nine inches* square. 17 Mount four rows of gemstones* on it. The first row will contain a red carnelian, a pale-green peridot, and an emerald. 18 The second row will contain a turquoise, a blue lapis lazuli, and a white moonstone. 19 The third row will contain an orange jacinth, an agate, and a purple amethyst. 20 The fourth row will contain a blue-green beryl, an onyx, and a green jasper. All these stones will be set in gold filigree. 21 Each stone will represent one of the twelve sons of Israel, and the name of that tribe will be engraved on it like a seal.

22 "To attach the chestpiece to the ephod, make braided cords of pure gold thread. 23 Then make two gold rings and attach them to the top corners of the chestpiece. 24 Tie the two gold cords to the two rings on the chestpiece. 25 Tie the other ends of the cords to the gold settings on the shoulder-pieces of the ephod. 26 Then make two more gold rings and attach them to the inside edges of the chestpiece next to the ephod. 27 And make two more gold rings and attach them to the front of the ephod, below the shoulder-pieces, just above the knot where the decorative sash is fastened to the ephod. 28 Then attach the bottom rings of the chestpiece to the rings on the ephod with blue cords.

27:12 Hebrew *50 cubits* [23 meters]; also in 27:13. **27:14** Hebrew *15 cubits* [6.9 meters]; also in 27:15. **27:16** Hebrew *20 cubits* [9.2 meters]. **27:18** Hebrew *100 cubits* [46 meters] *long and 50 by 50* [23 meters] *wide and 5 cubits* [2.3 meters] *high.* **27:21** Hebrew *in the Tent of Meeting, outside the inner curtain that is in front of the Testimony.* See note on 25:16. **28:15** Hebrew *a chestpiece for decision.* **28:16** Hebrew *1 span* [23 centimeters]. **28:17** The identification of some of these gemstones is uncertain.

27:20 pure oil of pressed olives. Olive oil was a versatile resource—a staple for cooking and eating, and a fuel that produced almost no smoke. Pure oil would have comes from the initial extraction generally used for foods, while fatty lampstand oil usually came from the second and third pressings.

28:2 sacred garments. The special garments worn by priests gave them a certain status among the people and insured that those they were dressed in a manner appropriate to their proximity to the divine.

28:6 ephod. A sleeveless overgarment made of fine linen.

28:15 chestpiece . . . for seeking a decision from God. The high priest wore the fabric breastpiece or pouch whenever he entered the Holy Place (v. 29). Within the breastpiece, the Urim and Thummim were held.

This will hold the chestpiece securely to the ephod
above the decorative sash.
29 "In this way, Aaron will carry the names of the
tribes of Israel on the sacred chestpiece* over his
heart when he goes into the Holy Place. This will be
a continual reminder that he represents the people
when he comes before the LORD. 30 Insert the Urim
and Thummim into the sacred chestpiece so they will
be carried over Aaron's heart when he goes into the
LORD's presence. In this way, Aaron will always car-
ry over his heart the objects used to determine the
LORD's will for his people whenever he goes in before
the LORD.

ADDITIONAL CLOTHING FOR THE PRIESTS

31 "Make the robe that is worn with the ephod from a
single piece of blue cloth, 32 with an opening for Aar-
on's head in the middle of it. Reinforce the opening
with a woven collar* so it will not tear. 33 Make pome-
granates out of blue, purple, and scarlet yarn, and
attach them to the hem of the robe, with gold bells be-
tween them. 34 The gold bells and pomegranates are
to alternate all around the hem. 35 Aaron will wear
this robe whenever he ministers before the LORD, and
the bells will tinkle as he goes in and out of the LORD's
presence in the Holy Place. If he wears it, he will not
die.
36 "Next make a medallion of pure gold, and engrave
it like a seal with these words: HOLY TO THE LORD. 37 At-
tach the medallion with a blue cord to the front of
Aaron's turban, where it must remain. 38 Aaron must
wear it on his forehead so he may take on himself any
guilt of the people of Israel when they consecrate
their sacred offerings. He must always wear it on his
forehead so the LORD will accept the people.
39 "Weave Aaron's patterned tunic from fine linen
cloth. Fashion the turban from this linen as well. Also
make a sash, and decorate it with colorful embroi-
dery.
40 "For Aaron's sons, make tunics, sashes, and spe-
cial head coverings that are glorious and beautiful.
41 Clothe your brother, Aaron, and his sons with
these garments, and then anoint and ordain them.
Consecrate them so they can serve as my priests.
42 Also make linen undergarments for them, to be
worn next to their bodies, reaching from their hips
to their thighs. 43 These must be worn whenever Aar-
on and his sons enter the Tabernacle* or approach
the altar in the Holy Place to perform their priestly
duties. Then they will not incur guilt and die. This is
a permanent law for Aaron and all his descendants
after him.

DEDICATION OF THE PRIESTS

29 "This is the ceremony you must follow when
you consecrate Aaron and his sons to serve
me as priests: Take a young bull and two rams with
no defects. 2 Then, using choice wheat flour and no
yeast, make loaves of bread, thin cakes mixed with
olive oil, and wafers spread with oil. 3 Place them all
in a single basket, and present them at the entrance
of the Tabernacle, along with the young bull and the
two rams.
4 "Present Aaron and his sons at the entrance of
the Tabernacle,* and wash them with water. 5 Dress
Aaron in his priestly garments—the tunic, the robe
worn with the ephod, the ephod itself, and the chest-
piece. Then wrap the decorative sash of the ephod
around him. 6 Place the turban on his head, and fas-
ten the sacred medallion to the turban. 7 Then anoint
him by pouring the anointing oil over his head.
8 Next present his sons, and dress them in their tu-
nics. 9 Wrap the sashes around the waists of Aaron
and his sons, and put their special head coverings on
them. Then the right to the priesthood will be theirs
by law forever. In this way, you will ordain Aaron
and his sons.
10 "Bring the young bull to the entrance of the Tab-
ernacle, where Aaron and his sons will lay their
hands on its head. 11 Then slaughter the bull in the
LORD's presence at the entrance of the Tabernacle.
12 Put some of its blood on the horns of the altar with
your finger, and pour out the rest at the base of the
altar. 13 Take all the fat around the internal organs,
the long lobe of the liver, and the two kidneys and
the fat around them, and burn it all on the altar.
14 Then take the rest of the bull, including its hide,
meat, and dung, and burn it outside the camp as a
sin offering.
15 "Next Aaron and his sons must lay their hands on
the head of one of the rams. 16 Then slaughter the ram,
and splatter its blood against all sides of the altar.
17 Cut the ram into pieces, and wash off the internal
organs and the legs. Set them alongside the head and
the other pieces of the body, 18 then burn the entire an-
imal on the altar. This is a burnt offering to the LORD;
it is a pleasing aroma, a special gift presented to the
LORD.
19 "Now take the other ram, and have Aaron and his
sons lay their hands on its head. 20 Then slaughter it,
and apply some of its blood to the right earlobes of
Aaron and his sons. Also put it on the thumbs of their
right hands and the big toes of their right feet. Splat-
ter the rest of the blood against all sides of the altar.
21 Then take some of the blood from the altar and some
of the anointing oil, and sprinkle it on Aaron and his
sons and on their garments. In this way, they and
their garments will be set apart as holy.
22 "Since this is the ram for the ordination of Aaron
and his sons, take the fat of the ram, including the fat
of the broad tail, the fat around the internal organs,
the long lobe of the liver, and the two kidneys and the
fat around them, along with the right thigh. 23 Then
take one round loaf of bread, one thin cake mixed
with olive oil, and one wafer from the basket of bread
without yeast that was placed in the LORD's presence.

28:29 Hebrew *the chestpiece for decision;* also in 28:30. See 28:15. **28:32** The meaning of the Hebrew is uncertain. **28:43** Hebrew *Tent of Meeting.* **29:4** Hebrew *Tent of Meeting;* also in 29:10, 11, 30, 32, 42, 44.

28:30 Urim and Thummim. Urim ("lights") and Thummim ("perfections") were sacred lots cast to ascertain the "yes" or "no" will of God.

28:35 bells will tinkle. The bells on the robe acted like the bird that miners would take with them into a mine. If the bird died, the miners knew something was wrong.

29:7 anoint him. Aaron was anointed with fragrant oil to serve God as Christ would later be anointed (John 12:3).

29:10 lay their hands on its head. In order for priests to make atonement, a special sacrifice was needed. Laying on hands signified the declaration of ownership for the animal to which the sin of the priest was transferred.

29:13 fat around the internal organs. The richest part of the bull is offered to God. Its fat and organ meats are burned on the bronze altar.

29:18 a pleasing aroma. Burning meat is not a pleasant smell like grilled meat. The pleasing aroma is the obedience and cleansing, which pleases God.

24 Put all these in the hands of Aaron and his sons to be
lifted up as a special offering to the LORD. 25 Afterward
take the various breads from their hands, and burn
them on the altar along with the burnt offering. It is
a pleasing aroma to the LORD, a special gift for him.
26 Then take the breast of Aaron's ordination ram, and
lift it up in the LORD's presence as a special offering to
him. Then keep it as your own portion.
27 "Set aside the portions of the ordination ram that
belong to Aaron and his sons. This includes the breast
and the thigh that were lifted up before the LORD as a
special offering. 28 In the future, whenever the people
of Israel lift up a peace offering, a portion of it must be
set aside for Aaron and his descendants. This is their
permanent right, and it is a sacred offering from the
Israelites to the LORD.
29 "Aaron's sacred garments must be preserved for
his descendants who succeed him, and they will wear
them when they are anointed and ordained. 30 The de-
scendant who succeeds him as high priest will wear
these clothes for seven days as he ministers in the
Tabernacle and the Holy Place.
31 "Take the ram used in the ordination ceremony,
and boil its meat in a sacred place. 32 Then Aaron and
his sons will eat this meat, along with the bread in the
basket, at the Tabernacle entrance. 33 They alone may
eat the meat and bread used for their purification* in
the ordination ceremony. No one else may eat them,
for these things are set apart and holy. 34 If any of the
ordination meat or bread remains until the morning,
it must be burned. It may not be eaten, for it is holy.
35 "This is how you will ordain Aaron and his sons
to their offices, just as I have commanded you. The or-
dination ceremony will go on for seven days. 36 Each
day you must sacrifice a young bull as a sin offering
to purify them, making them right with the LORD.*
Afterward, cleanse the altar by purifying it*; make it
holy by anointing it with oil. 37 Purify the altar, and
consecrate it every day for seven days. After that, the
altar will be absolutely holy, and whatever touches it
will become holy.
38 "These are the sacrifices you are to offer regularly
on the altar. Each day, offer two lambs that are a year
old, 39 one in the morning and the other in the eve-
ning. 40 With one of them, offer two quarts of choice
flour mixed with one quart of pure oil of pressed ol-
ives; also, offer one quart of wine* as a liquid offering.
41 Offer the other lamb in the evening, along with the
same offerings of flour and wine as in the morning.
It will be a pleasing aroma, a special gift presented
to the LORD.
42 "These burnt offerings are to be made each day
from generation to generation. Offer them in the
LORD's presence at the Tabernacle entrance; there I
will meet with you and speak with you. 43 I will meet
the people of Israel there, in the place made holy by
my glorious presence. 44 Yes, I will consecrate the Tab-
ernacle and the altar, and I will consecrate Aaron
and his sons to serve me as priests. 45 Then I will live
among the people of Israel and be their God, 46 and
they will know that I am the LORD their God. I am the
one who brought them out of the land of Egypt so that
I could live among them. I am the LORD their God.

PLANS FOR THE INCENSE ALTAR

30 "Then make another altar of acacia wood for
burning incense. 2 Make it 18 inches square
and 36 inches high,* with horns at the corners carved
from the same piece of wood as the altar itself. 3 Over-
lay the top, sides, and horns of the altar with pure
gold, and run a gold molding around the entire altar.
4 Make two gold rings, and attach them on opposite
sides of the altar below the gold molding to hold the
carrying poles. 5 Make the poles of acacia wood and
overlay them with gold. 6 Place the incense altar just
outside the inner curtain that shields the Ark of the
Covenant,* in front of the Ark's cover—the place of
atonement—that covers the tablets inscribed with
the terms of the covenant.* I will meet with you there.
7 "Every morning when Aaron maintains the
lamps, he must burn fragrant incense on the altar.
8 And each evening when he lights the lamps, he must
again burn incense in the LORD's presence. This must
be done from generation to generation. 9 Do not offer
any unholy incense on this altar, or any burnt offer-
ings, grain offerings, or liquid offerings.
10 "Once a year Aaron must purify* the altar by
smearing its horns with blood from the offering made
to purify the people from their sin. This will be a reg-
ular, annual event from generation to generation, for
this is the LORD's most holy altar."

MONEY FOR THE TABERNACLE

11 Then the LORD said to Moses, 12 "Whenever you take
a census of the people of Israel, each man who is
counted must pay a ransom for himself to the LORD.
Then no plague will strike the people as you count
them. 13 Each person who is counted must give a
small piece of silver as a sacred offering to the LORD.
(This payment is half a shekel,* based on the sanctu-
ary shekel, which equals twenty gerahs.) 14 All who
have reached their twentieth birthday must give this
sacred offering to the LORD. 15 When this offering is
given to the LORD to purify your lives, making you
right with him,* the rich must not give more than
the specified amount, and the poor must not give less.
16 Receive this ransom money from the Israelites, and
use it for the care of the Tabernacle.* It will bring the
Israelites to the LORD's attention, and it will purify
your lives."

29:33 Or *their atonement.* **29:36a** Or *to make atonement.* **29:36b** Or *by making atonement for it;* similarly in 29:37. **29:40** Hebrew *1/10 [of an ephah]* [2.2 liters] *of choice flour . . . 1/4 of a hin* [1 liter] *of pure oil . . . 1/4 of a hin of wine.* **30:2** Hebrew *1 cubit* [46 centimeters] *long and 1 cubit wide, a square, and 2 cubits* [92 centimeters] *high.* **30:6a** Or *Ark of the Testimony;* also in 30:26. **30:6b** Hebrew *that covers the Testimony;* see note on 25:16. **30:10** Or *make atonement for;* also in 30:10b. **30:13** Or *0.2 ounces* [6 grams]. **30:15** Or *to make atonement for your lives;* similarly in 30:16. **30:16** Hebrew *Tent of Meeting;* also in 30:18, 20, 26, 36.

29:24 special offering. A special offering involved waving sacrifices before the Lord as a means of presenting them to Him. Sometimes the wave offering was followed by a burnt offering (vv. 24-26). A presentation offering was also made for that portion of the sacrificial meat that was reserved for the priests to eat (Lev. 7:30-31; 10:14).

29:38 regularly . . . Each day. Although the Law commanded certain special ceremonies where offerings were made (23:15-16), God also commanded a daily sacrifice of "two lambs a year old."

29:45 live among the people of Israel and be their God. God's presence with them in the tabernacle—even more tangible than the pillars of cloud and fire—fulfilled the covenant promise (19:5-6; 29:43).

30:12 take a census. The census could be used to select Israelites for particular service—such as the army (Num. 26:2), and was a form of state revenue (21:30).

PLANS FOR THE WASHBASIN

17 Then the LORD said to Moses, 18 "Make a bronze washbasin with a bronze stand. Place it between the Tabernacle and the altar, and fill it with water. 19 Aaron and his sons will wash their hands and feet there. 20 They must wash with water whenever they go into the Tabernacle to appear before the LORD and when they approach the altar to burn up their special gifts to the LORD—or they will die! 21 They must always wash their hands and feet, or they will die. This is a permanent law for Aaron and his descendants, to be observed from generation to generation."

THE ANOINTING OIL

22 Then the LORD said to Moses, 23 "Collect choice spices—12½ pounds of pure myrrh, 6¼ pounds of fragrant cinnamon, 6¼ pounds of fragrant calamus,* 24 and 12½ pounds of cassia*—as measured by the weight of the sanctuary shekel. Also get one gallon of olive oil.* 25 Like a skilled incense maker, blend these ingredients to make a holy anointing oil. 26 Use this sacred oil to anoint the Tabernacle, the Ark of the Covenant, 27 the table and all its utensils, the lampstand and all its accessories, the incense altar, 28 the altar of burnt offering and all its utensils, and the washbasin with its stand. 29 Consecrate them to make them absolutely holy. After this, whatever touches them will also become holy.

30 "Anoint Aaron and his sons also, consecrating them to serve me as priests. 31 And say to the people of Israel, 'This holy anointing oil is reserved for me from generation to generation. 32 It must never be used to anoint anyone else, and you must never make any blend like it for yourselves. It is holy, and you must treat it as holy. 33 Anyone who makes a blend like it or anoints someone other than a priest will be cut off from the community.'"

THE INCENSE

34 Then the LORD said to Moses, "Gather fragrant spices—resin droplets, mollusk shell, and galbanum—and mix these fragrant spices with pure frankincense, weighed out in equal amounts. 35 Using the usual techniques of the incense maker, blend the spices together and sprinkle them with salt to produce a pure and holy incense. 36 Grind some of the mixture into a very fine powder and put it in front of the Ark of the Covenant,* where I will meet with you in the Tabernacle. You must treat this incense as most holy. 37 Never use this formula to make this incense for yourselves. It is reserved for the LORD, and you must treat it as holy. 38 Anyone who makes incense like this for personal use will be cut off from the community."

CRAFTSMEN: BEZALEL AND OHOLIAB

31 Then the LORD said to Moses, 2 "Look, I have specifically chosen Bezalel son of Uri, grandson of Hur, of the tribe of Judah. 3 I have filled him with the Spirit of God, giving him great wisdom, ability, and expertise in all kinds of crafts. 4 He is a master craftsman, expert in working with gold, silver, and bronze. 5 He is skilled in engraving and mounting gemstones and in carving wood. He is a master at every craft!

6 "And I have personally appointed Oholiab son of Ahisamach, of the tribe of Dan, to be his assistant. Moreover, I have given special skill to all the gifted craftsmen so they can make all the things I have commanded you to make:

7 the Tabernacle;*
the Ark of the Covenant;*
the Ark's cover—the place of atonement;
all the furnishings of the Tabernacle;
8 the table and its utensils;
the pure gold lampstand with all its accessories;
the incense altar;
9 the altar of burnt offering with all its utensils;
the washbasin with its stand;
10 the beautifully stitched garments—the sacred garments for Aaron the priest, and the garments for his sons to wear as they minister as priests;
11 the anointing oil;
the fragrant incense for the Holy Place.

The craftsmen must make everything as I have commanded you."

INSTRUCTIONS FOR THE SABBATH

12 The LORD then gave these instructions to Moses: 13 "Tell the people of Israel: 'Be careful to keep my Sabbath day, for the Sabbath is a sign of the covenant between me and you from generation to generation. It is given so you may know that I am the LORD, who makes you holy. 14 You must keep the Sabbath day, for it is a holy day for you. Anyone who desecrates it must be put to death; anyone who works on that day will be cut off from the community. 15 You have six days each week for your ordinary work, but the seventh day must be a Sabbath day of complete rest, a holy day dedicated to the LORD. Anyone who works on the Sabbath must be put to death. 16 The people of Israel must keep the Sabbath day by observing it from generation to generation. This is a covenant obligation for all time. 17 It is a permanent sign of my covenant with the people of Israel. For in six days the LORD made heaven and earth, but on the seventh day he stopped working and was refreshed.'"

18 When the LORD finished speaking with Moses on Mount Sinai, he gave him the two stone tablets inscribed with the terms of the covenant,* written by the finger of God.

30:23 Hebrew *500 [shekels]* [5.7 kilograms] *of pure myrrh, 250 [shekels]* [2.9 kilograms] *of fragrant cinnamon, 250 [shekels] of fragrant calamus.* **30:24a** Hebrew *500 [shekels]* [5.7 kilograms] *of cassia.* **30:24b** Hebrew *1 hin* [3.8 liters] *of olive oil.* **30:36** Hebrew *in front of the Testimony;* see note on 25:16. **31:7a** Hebrew *the Tent of Meeting.* **31:7b** Hebrew *the Ark of the Testimony.* **31:18** Hebrew *the two tablets of the Testimony;* see note on 25:16.

30:34 fragrant spices—resin droplets, mollusk shell, and galbanum . . . pure frankincense. Except for frankincense, the same spices used in the anointing oil.

31:2 Hur. This man was with Aaron and Moses at Rephidim when the Israelites defeated the Amalekites (17:10-12).

31:3 great wisdom, ability, and expertise. God prepared Bezalel for the work of the tabernacle by giving him the skills and inspiration he needed. God chooses the right person for a job (like Moses) and then gives them the talents, experiences and inspiration needed to do it.

31:16-17 Sabbath . . . covenant obligation. The observance of the Sabbath was not only a command but also a symbolic act. Since God created the world in six days, then rested (Gen. 1:1–2:3), the observance of the Sabbath put Israel in the same pattern that God created. This pattern was a sign of the covenant relationship between them.

THE GOLD CALF

32 When the people saw how long it was taking
Moses to come back down the mountain, they
gathered around Aaron. "Come on," they said, "make
us some gods who can lead us. We don't know what
happened to this fellow Moses, who brought us here
from the land of Egypt."
2 So Aaron said, "Take the gold rings from the ears
of your wives and sons and daughters, and bring
them to me."
3 All the people took the gold rings from their ears
and brought them to Aaron. 4 Then Aaron took the
gold, melted it down, and molded it into the shape of
a calf. When the people saw it, they exclaimed, "O Is-
rael, these are the gods who brought you out of the
land of Egypt!"
5 Aaron saw how excited the people were, so he
built an altar in front of the calf. Then he announced,
"Tomorrow will be a festival to the LORD!"
6 The people got up early the next morning to sac-
rifice burnt offerings and peace offerings. After this,
they celebrated with feasting and drinking, and they
indulged in pagan revelry.
7 The LORD told Moses, "Quick! Go down the moun-
tain! Your people whom you brought from the land
of Egypt have corrupted themselves. 8 How quickly
they have turned away from the way I commanded
them to live! They have melted down gold and made
a calf, and they have bowed down and sacrificed to it.
They are saying, 'These are your gods, O Israel, who
brought you out of the land of Egypt.'"
9 Then the LORD said, "I have seen how stubborn
and rebellious these people are. 10 Now leave me alone
so my fierce anger can blaze against them, and I will
destroy them. Then I will make you, Moses, into a
great nation."
11 But Moses tried to pacify the LORD his God. "O LORD!"
he said. "Why are you so angry with your own people
whom you brought from the land of Egypt with such
great power and such a strong hand? 12 Why let the
Egyptians say, 'Their God rescued them with the evil
intention of slaughtering them in the mountains and
wiping them from the face of the earth'? Turn away
from your fierce anger. Change your mind about this
terrible disaster you have threatened against your
people! 13 Remember your servants Abraham, Isaac,
and Jacob.* You bound yourself with an oath to them,
saying, 'I will make your descendants as numerous as
the stars of heaven. And I will give them all of this
land that I have promised to your descendants, and
they will possess it forever.'"
14 So the LORD changed his mind about the terrible
disaster he had threatened to bring on his people.
15 Then Moses turned and went down the moun-
tain. He held in his hands the two stone tablets in-
scribed with the terms of the covenant.* They were
inscribed on both sides, front and back. 16 These tab-
lets were God's work; the words on them were writ-
ten by God himself.
17 When Joshua heard the boisterous noise of the
people shouting below them, he exclaimed to Moses,
"It sounds like war in the camp!"
18 But Moses replied, "No, it's not a shout of victory
nor the wailing of defeat. I hear the sound of a cele-
bration."
19 When they came near the camp, Moses saw the
calf and the dancing, and he burned with anger. He
threw the stone tablets to the ground, smashing them
at the foot of the mountain. 20 He took the calf they had
made and burned it. Then he ground it into powder,
threw it into the water, and forced the people to drink
it.
21 Finally, he turned to Aaron and demanded, "What
did these people do to you to make you bring such ter-
rible sin upon them?"
22 "Don't get so upset, my lord," Aaron replied. "You
yourself know how evil these people are. 23 They said
to me, 'Make us gods who will lead us. We don't know
what happened to this fellow Moses, who brought us
here from the land of Egypt.' 24 So I told them, 'Whoev-
er has gold jewelry, take it off.' When they brought it
to me, I simply threw it into the fire—and out came
this calf!"
25 Moses saw that Aaron had let the people get com-
pletely out of control, much to the amusement of their
enemies.* 26 So he stood at the entrance to the camp
and shouted, "All of you who are on the LORD's side,
come here and join me." And all the Levites gathered
around him.
27 Moses told them, "This is what the LORD, the God
of Israel, says: Each of you, take your swords and go

PRAYER CHANGES THINGS

1. What is the most memorable statue you've seen? Why was it so memorable?

EXODUS 32:1-35

2. Why do you think the Hebrews made a false idol right after all the miracles they had already seen? What does this teach us about human nature?
3. Why did God refer to the Israelites as "your people" to Moses (v. 7), instead of "my people"? How might this have encouraged Moses to intercede for them?
4. Why did Moses intercede by telling God that they are "your people" (v. 11)?
5. How can you apply Moses' example to your prayers for others on your team or in your circle of friends?

32:13 Hebrew *Israel.* The names "Jacob" and "Israel" are often interchanged throughout the Old Testament, referring sometimes to the individual patriarch and sometimes to the nation. **32:15** Hebrew *the two tablets of the Testimony;* see note on 25:16. **32:25** Or *out of control, and they mocked anyone who opposed them.* The meaning of the Hebrew is uncertain.

32:2 gold rings. The supreme irony is that the gold here, the result of a promise made by God (3:21-22; 12:35-36) and intended for the tabernacle (25:1-7; 35:4-9), is instead co-opted by the Israelites and made into what even Aaron considered to be a proper representation of Yahweh. Thus, they directly contradicted how God would use the gold to represent Himself in the sanctuary.

32:7 you brought from the land of Egypt. The phrase is thick with irony. It was God who brought Israel out of Egypt. Contrast this verse with 15:1-12 and 19:4.

32:11 you brought from . . . Egypt. Moses turns God's words back at Him (v. 7) by praising His deliverance of Israel.

32:14 the LORD changed his mind. It is inherent in God's character to execute justice within the context of mercy by giving everyone a second chance (see Jer. 18:7-8).

back and forth from one end of the camp to the other. Kill everyone—even your brothers, friends, and neighbors." 28 The Levites obeyed Moses' command, and about 3,000 people died that day.

29 Then Moses told the Levites, "Today you have ordained yourselves* for the service of the LORD, for you obeyed him even though it meant killing your own sons and brothers. Today you have earned a blessing."

MOSES INTERCEDES FOR ISRAEL

30 The next day Moses said to the people, "You have committed a terrible sin, but I will go back up to the LORD on the mountain. Perhaps I will be able to obtain forgiveness* for your sin."

31 So Moses returned to the LORD and said, "Oh, what a terrible sin these people have committed. They have made gods of gold for themselves. 32 But now, if you will only forgive their sin—but if not, erase my name from the record you have written!"

33 But the LORD replied to Moses, "No, I will erase the name of everyone who has sinned against me. 34 Now go, lead the people to the place I told you about. Look! My angel will lead the way before you. And when I come to call the people to account, I will certainly hold them responsible for their sins."

35 Then the LORD sent a great plague upon the people because they had worshiped the calf Aaron had made.

33 The LORD said to Moses, "Get going, you and the people you brought up from the land of Egypt. Go up to the land I swore to give to Abraham, Isaac, and Jacob. I told them, 'I will give this land to your descendants.' 2 And I will send an angel before you to drive out the Canaanites, Amorites, Hittites, Perizzites, Hivites, and Jebusites. 3 Go up to this land that flows with milk and honey. But I will not travel among you, for you are a stubborn and rebellious people. If I did, I would surely destroy you along the way."

4 When the people heard these stern words, they went into mourning and stopped wearing their jewelry and fine clothes. 5 For the LORD had told Moses to tell them, "You are a stubborn and rebellious people. If I were to travel with you for even a moment, I would destroy you. Remove your jewelry and fine clothes while I decide what to do with you." 6 So from the time they left Mount Sinai,* the Israelites wore no more jewelry or fine clothes.

7 It was Moses' practice to take the Tent of Meeting* and set it up some distance from the camp. Everyone who wanted to make a request of the LORD would go to the Tent of Meeting outside the camp.

8 Whenever Moses went out to the Tent of Meeting, all the people would get up and stand in the entrances of their own tents. They would all watch Moses until he disappeared inside. 9 As he went into the tent, the pillar of cloud would come down and hover at its entrance while the LORD spoke with Moses. 10 When the people saw the cloud standing at the entrance of the tent, they would stand and bow down in front of their own tents. 11 Inside the Tent of Meeting, the LORD would speak to Moses face to face, as one speaks to a friend. Afterward Moses would return to the camp, but the young man who assisted him, Joshua son of Nun, would remain behind in the Tent of Meeting.

MOSES SEES THE LORD'S GLORY

12 One day Moses said to the LORD, "You have been telling me, 'Take these people up to the Promised Land.' But you haven't told me whom you will send with me. You have told me, 'I know you by name, and I look favorably on you.' 13 If it is true that you look favorably on me, let me know your ways so I may understand you more fully and continue to enjoy your favor. And remember that this nation is your very own people."

14 The LORD replied, "I will personally go with you, Moses, and I will give you rest—everything will be fine for you."

15 Then Moses said, "If you don't personally go with us, don't make us leave this place. 16 How will anyone know that you look favorably on me—on me and on your people—if you don't go with us? For your presence among us sets your people and me apart from all other people on the earth."

17 The LORD replied to Moses, "I will indeed do what you have asked, for I look favorably on you, and I know you by name."

18 Moses responded, "Then show me your glorious presence."

19 The LORD replied, "I will make all my goodness pass before you, and I will call out my name, Yahweh,* before you. For I will show mercy to anyone I choose, and I will show compassion to anyone I choose. 20 But you may not look directly at my face, for no one may see me and live." 21 The LORD continued, "Look, stand near me on this rock. 22 As my glorious presence passes by, I will hide you in the crevice of the rock and cover you with my hand until I have passed by. 23 Then I will remove my hand and let you see me from behind. But my face will not be seen."

A NEW COPY OF THE COVENANT

34 Then the LORD told Moses, "Chisel out two stone tablets like the first ones. I will write on them the same words that were on the tablets you smashed. 2 Be ready in the morning to climb up Mount Sinai and present yourself to me on the top of the mountain. 3 No one else may come with you. In fact, no one is to appear anywhere on the mountain. Do not even let the flocks or herds graze near the mountain."

32:29 As in Greek and Latin versions; Hebrew reads *Today ordain yourselves.* 32:30 Or *to make atonement.* 33:6 Hebrew *Horeb,* another name for Sinai. 33:7 This "Tent of Meeting" is different from the Tabernacle described in chapters 26 and 36. 33:19 *Yahweh* is a transliteration of the proper name *YHWH* that is sometimes rendered "Jehovah"; in this translation it is usually rendered "the LORD" (note the use of small capitals).

32:24 out came this calf. Aaron's explanation sounds like a six-year-old child's excuse for bad behavior.

32:33 everyone who has sinned against me. This sin could not be atoned for because the people sinned defiantly (Num. 15:30) and not merely as faithful believers who strayed (Num. 15:22).

33:3-5 stubborn. Stubborn and unyielding. **would surely destroy you.** God had expressed similar frustration only once before—just prior to Noah's flood (Gen. 6:6-8).

33:11 as one speaks to a friend. Moses had experiensed God in a burning bush, a cloud, a still small voice, and a pillar of fire. He had met God on a mountain, in a desert and in the middle of a miraculously dry riverbed. Moses intimately knew God.

33:12 look favorably on you. Moses does not recall a contract or an agreement but the call of God that changed his life (chapters 3–4).

33:19 name. In ancient days, someone's name revealed his or her character. In proclaiming His name, God proclaimed His character.

4 So Moses chiseled out two tablets of stone like the
first ones. Early in the morning he climbed Mount Si-
nai as the LORD had commanded him, and he carried
the two stone tablets in his hands.
5 Then the LORD came down in a cloud and stood
there with him; and he called out his own name, Yah-
weh.* 6 The LORD passed in front of Moses, calling out,

"Yahweh!* The LORD!
The God of compassion and mercy!
I am slow to anger
and filled with unfailing love and faithfulness.
7 I lavish unfailing love to a thousand generations.*
I forgive iniquity, rebellion, and sin.
But I do not excuse the guilty.
I lay the sins of the parents upon their children
and grandchildren;
the entire family is affected—
even children in the third and fourth
generations."

8 Moses immediately threw himself to the ground
and worshiped. 9 And he said, "O Lord, if it is true that
I have found favor with you, then please travel with
us. Yes, this is a stubborn and rebellious people, but
please forgive our iniquity and our sins. Claim us as
your own special possession."
10 The LORD replied, "Listen, I am making a cov-
enant with you in the presence of all your people.
I will perform miracles that have never been per-
formed anywhere in all the earth or in any nation.
And all the people around you will see the power
of the LORD—the awesome power I will display for
you. 11 But listen carefully to everything I command
you today. Then I will go ahead of you and drive out
the Amorites, Canaanites, Hittites, Perizzites, Hivites,
and Jebusites.
12 "Be very careful never to make a treaty with
the people who live in the land where you are go-
ing. If you do, you will follow their evil ways and be
trapped. 13 Instead, you must break down their pagan
altars, smash their sacred pillars, and cut down their
Asherah poles. 14 You must worship no other gods, for
the LORD, whose very name is Jealous, is a God who is
jealous about his relationship with you.
15 "You must not make a treaty of any kind with the
people living in the land. They lust after their gods,
offering sacrifices to them. They will invite you to
join them in their sacrificial meals, and you will go
with them. 16 Then you will accept their daughters,
who sacrifice to other gods, as wives for your sons.
And they will seduce your sons to commit adultery
against me by worshiping other gods. 17 You must not
make any gods of molten metal for yourselves.
18 "You must celebrate the Festival of Unleavened
Bread. For seven days the bread you eat must be made
without yeast, just as I commanded you. Celebrate
this festival annually at the appointed time in early
spring, in the month of Abib,* for that is the anniver-
sary of your departure from Egypt.
19 "The firstborn of every animal belongs to me, in-
cluding the firstborn males* from your herds of cattle
and your flocks of sheep and goats. 20 A firstborn don-
key may be bought back from the LORD by presenting
a lamb or young goat in its place. But if you do not buy
it back, you must break its neck. However, you must
buy back every firstborn son.
"No one may appear before me without an offering.
21 "You have six days each week for your ordinary
work, but on the seventh day you must stop working,
even during the seasons of plowing and harvest.
22 "You must celebrate the Festival of Harvest* with
the first crop of the wheat harvest, and celebrate the
Festival of the Final Harvest* at the end of the harvest
season. 23 Three times each year every man in Israel
must appear before the Sovereign, the LORD, the God
of Israel. 24 I will drive out the other nations ahead of
you and expand your territory, so no one will covet
and conquer your land while you appear before the
LORD your God three times each year.
25 "You must not offer the blood of my sacrificial
offerings together with any baked goods containing
yeast. And none of the meat of the Passover sacrifice
may be kept over until the next morning.
26 "As you harvest your crops, bring the very best
of the first harvest to the house of the LORD your God.
"You must not cook a young goat in its mother's milk."
27 Then the LORD said to Moses, "Write down all
these instructions, for they represent the terms of the
covenant I am making with you and with Israel."
28 Moses remained there on the mountain with
the LORD forty days and forty nights. In all that time
he ate no bread and drank no water. And the LORD*
wrote the terms of the covenant—the Ten Command-
ments*—on the stone tablets.
29 When Moses came down Mount Sinai carrying
the two stone tablets inscribed with the terms of the
covenant,* he wasn't aware that his face had become
radiant because he had spoken to the LORD. 30 So when
Aaron and the people of Israel saw the radiance of
Moses' face, they were afraid to come near him.
31 But Moses called out to them and asked Aaron
and all the leaders of the community to come over,
and he talked with them. 32 Then all the people of Is-
rael approached him, and Moses gave them all the
instructions the LORD had given him on Mount Si-
nai. 33 When Moses finished speaking with them, he
covered his face with a veil. 34 But whenever he went

34:5 *Yahweh* is a transliteration of the proper name *YHWH* that is sometimes rendered "Jehovah"; in this translation it is usually rendered "the LORD" (note the use of small capitals). **34:6** See note on 34:5. **34:7** Hebrew *for thousands.* **34:18** Hebrew *appointed time in the month of Abib.* This first month of the ancient Hebrew lunar calendar usually occurs within the months of March and April. **34:19** As in Greek version; the meaning of the Hebrew word is uncertain. **34:22a** Hebrew *Festival of Weeks;* compare 23:16. This was later called the Festival of Pentecost. It is celebrated today as Shavuot (or Shabuoth). **34:22b** Or *Festival of Ingathering.* This was later called the Festival of Shelters or Festival of Tabernacles (see Lev 23:33-36). It is celebrated today as Sukkot (or Succoth). **34:28a** Hebrew *he.* **34:28b** Hebrew *the ten words.* **34:29** Hebrew *the two tablets of the Testimony;* see note on 25:16.

34:6-7 The LORD. God's snapshot explanation of Himself is cited many other times in Scripture (Num. 14:17-18; Neh. 9:17; Ps. 86:15; Joel 2:13; Jonah 4:2).
34:10 covenant. A covenant can be a simple promise or as complex as a fine-print contract. With God, though, a covenant is not like a contract where both parties are bound equally to their obligations. In ancient days, God did make promises to people, sometimes based on how they might respond. God made a covenant with Noah (Gen. 6:18), Abraham (Gen. 17:3-4), Abraham's heirs, the Hebrews (6:3-4), and others.
34:29 his face had become radiant. Moses' shining countenance disturbed those around him. The miracle of God's glory lingering on Moses' face shows how magnificent that glory is.
34:33 veil. This word for "veil" is used only here in the Old Testament. Its only other occurrence is in 2 Corinthians 3:13, which adds that Moses continued to wear the veil even after the glow began to fade.

into the Tent of Meeting to speak with the LORD, he
would remove the veil until he came out again. Then
he would give the people whatever instructions the
LORD had given him, 35 and the people of Israel would
see the radiant glow of his face. So he would put the
veil over his face until he returned to speak with the
LORD.

INSTRUCTIONS FOR THE SABBATH

35 Then Moses called together the whole com-
munity of Israel and told them, "These are the
instructions the LORD has commanded you to follow.
2 You have six days each week for your ordinary
work, but the seventh day must be a Sabbath day of
complete rest, a holy day dedicated to the LORD. Any-
one who works on that day must be put to death. 3 You
must not even light a fire in any of your homes on the
Sabbath."

OFFERINGS FOR THE TABERNACLE

4 Then Moses said to the whole community of Israel,
"This is what the LORD has commanded: 5 Take a sa-
cred offering for the LORD. Let those with generous
hearts present the following gifts to the LORD:

gold, silver, and bronze;
6 blue, purple, and scarlet thread;
fine linen and goat hair for cloth;
7 tanned ram skins and fine goatskin leather;
acacia wood;
8 olive oil for the lamps;
spices for the anointing oil and the fragrant
incense;
9 onyx stones, and other gemstones to be set in the
ephod and the priest's chestpiece.

10 "Come, all of you who are gifted craftsmen. Con-
struct everything that the LORD has commanded:

11 the Tabernacle and its sacred tent, its covering,
clasps, frames, crossbars, posts, and bases;
12 the Ark and its carrying poles;
the Ark's cover—the place of atonement;
the inner curtain to shield the Ark;
13 the table, its carrying poles, and all its utensils;
the Bread of the Presence;
14 for light, the lampstand, its accessories, the lamp
cups, and the olive oil for lighting;
15 the incense altar and its carrying poles;
the anointing oil and fragrant incense;
the curtain for the entrance of the Tabernacle;
16 the altar of burnt offering;
the bronze grating of the altar and its carrying
poles and utensils;
the washbasin with its stand;
17 the curtains for the walls of the courtyard;
the posts and their bases;
the curtain for the entrance to the courtyard;
18 the tent pegs of the Tabernacle and courtyard and
their ropes;
19 the beautifully stitched garments for the priests to
wear while ministering in the Holy Place—the
sacred garments for Aaron the priest, and the
garments for his sons to wear as they minister
as priests."

20 So the whole community of Israel left Moses
and returned to their tents. 21 All whose hearts were
stirred and whose spirits were moved came and
brought their sacred offerings to the LORD. They
brought all the materials needed for the Tabernacle,*
for the performance of its rituals, and for the sacred
garments. 22 Both men and women came, all whose
hearts were willing. They brought to the LORD their
offerings of gold—brooches, earrings, rings from
their fingers, and necklaces. They presented gold ob-
jects of every kind as a special offering to the LORD.
23 All those who owned the following items willingly
brought them: blue, purple, and scarlet thread; fine
linen and goat hair for cloth; and tanned ram skins
and fine goatskin leather. 24 And all who had silver
and bronze objects gave them as a sacred offering to
the LORD. And those who had acacia wood brought it
for use in the project.
25 All the women who were skilled in sewing and
spinning prepared blue, purple, and scarlet thread,
and fine linen cloth. 26 All the women who were will-
ing used their skills to spin the goat hair into yarn.
27 The leaders brought onyx stones and the special
gemstones to be set in the ephod and the priest's
chestpiece. 28 They also brought spices and olive oil
for the light, the anointing oil, and the fragrant in-
cense. 29 So the people of Israel—every man and
woman who was eager to help in the work the LORD
had given them through Moses—brought their gifts
and gave them freely to the LORD.
30 Then Moses told the people of Israel, "The LORD
has specifically chosen Bezalel son of Uri, grandson
of Hur, of the tribe of Judah. 31 The LORD has filled Bez-
alel with the Spirit of God, giving him great wisdom,
ability, and expertise in all kinds of crafts. 32 He is a
master craftsman, expert in working with gold, silver,
and bronze. 33 He is skilled in engraving and mount-
ing gemstones and in carving wood. He is a master at
every craft. 34 And the LORD has given both him and
Oholiab son of Ahisamach, of the tribe of Dan, the
ability to teach their skills to others. 35 The LORD has
given them special skills as engravers, designers, em-
broiderers in blue, purple, and scarlet thread on fine
linen cloth, and weavers. They excel as craftsmen and
as designers.

36 "The LORD has gifted Bezalel, Oholiab, and the
other skilled craftsmen with wisdom and abil-
ity to perform any task involved in building the sanc-
tuary. Let them construct and furnish the Tabernacle,
just as the LORD has commanded."
2 So Moses summoned Bezalel and Oholiab and
all the others who were specially gifted by the LORD
and were eager to get to work. 3 Moses gave them the
materials donated by the people of Israel as sacred
offerings for the completion of the sanctuary. But the

35:21 Hebrew *Tent of Meeting.*

35:2 a Sabbath of complete rest, holy day. The Sabbath was serious business to God. It was an extremely important custom directly related to God's resting from creation. By Jesus' time, some had made the Sabbath into a legalistic set of rules, a development the Lord corrected (Matt. 12:1-14).

35:30 Hur. Hur, Bezalel's grandfather, is mentioned elsewhere (17:10; 24:14; 31:2; 38:32; 1 Chron. 2:19-20), perhaps as a point of exclamation to underscore Bezalel's importance to the building of the tabernacle.

people continued to bring additional gifts each morn-
ing. 4 Finally the craftsmen who were working on the
sanctuary left their work. 5 They went to Moses and
reported, "The people have given more than enough
materials to complete the job the LORD has command-
ed us to do!"
6 So Moses gave the command, and this message
was sent throughout the camp: "Men and women,
don't prepare any more gifts for the sanctuary. We
have enough!" So the people stopped bringing their
sacred offerings. 7 Their contributions were more
than enough to complete the whole project.

BUILDING THE TABERNACLE

8 The skilled craftsmen made ten curtains of finely wo-
ven linen for the Tabernacle. Then Bezalel* decorated
the curtains with blue, purple, and scarlet thread and
with skillfully embroidered cherubim. 9 All ten cur-
tains were exactly the same size—42 feet long and
6 feet wide.* 10 Five of these curtains were joined to-
gether to make one long curtain, and the other five
were joined to make a second long curtain. 11 He made
fifty loops of blue yarn and put them along the edge of
the last curtain in each set. 12 The fifty loops along the
edge of one curtain matched the fifty loops along the
edge of the other curtain. 13 Then he made fifty gold
clasps and fastened the long curtains together with
the clasps. In this way, the Tabernacle was made of
one continuous piece.
14 He made eleven curtains of goat-hair cloth to
serve as a tent covering for the Tabernacle. 15 These
eleven curtains were all exactly the same size—
45 feet long and 6 feet wide.* 16 Bezalel joined five of
these curtains together to make one long curtain, and
the other six were joined to make a second long cur-
tain. 17 He made fifty loops for the edge of each large
curtain. 18 He also made fifty bronze clasps to fasten
the long curtains together. In this way, the tent cover-
ing was made of one continuous piece. 19 He complet-
ed the tent covering with a layer of tanned ram skins
and a layer of fine goatskin leather.
20 For the framework of the Tabernacle, Bezalel
constructed frames of acacia wood. 21 Each frame was
15 feet high and 27 inches wide,* 22 with two pegs un-
der each frame. All the frames were identical. 23 He
made twenty of these frames to support the curtains
on the south side of the Tabernacle. 24 He also made
forty silver bases—two bases under each frame,
with the pegs fitting securely into the bases. 25 For
the north side of the Tabernacle, he made another
twenty frames, 26 with their forty silver bases, two
bases under each frame. 27 He made six frames for
the rear—the west side of the Tabernacle—28 along
with two additional frames to reinforce the rear cor-
ners of the Tabernacle. 29 These corner frames were
matched at the bottom and firmly attached at the
top with a single ring, forming a single corner unit.
Both of these corner units were made the same way.
30 So there were eight frames at the rear of the Taber-
nacle, set in sixteen silver bases—two bases under
each frame.
31 Then he made crossbars of acacia wood to link
the frames, five crossbars for the north side of the
Tabernacle 32 and five for the south side. He also made
five crossbars for the rear of the Tabernacle, which
faced west. 33 He made the middle crossbar to attach
halfway up the frames; it ran all the way from one
end of the Tabernacle to the other. 34 He overlaid the
frames with gold and made gold rings to hold the
crossbars. Then he overlaid the crossbars with gold
as well.
35 For the inside of the Tabernacle, Bezalel made a
special curtain of finely woven linen. He decorated it
with blue, purple, and scarlet thread and with skill-
fully embroidered cherubim. 36 For the curtain, he
made four posts of acacia wood and four gold hooks.
He overlaid the posts with gold and set them in four
silver bases.
37 Then he made another curtain for the entrance
to the sacred tent. He made it of finely woven linen
and embroidered it with exquisite designs using blue,
purple, and scarlet thread. 38 This curtain was hung
on gold hooks attached to five posts. The posts with
their decorated tops and hooks were overlaid with
gold, and the five bases were cast from bronze.

BUILDING THE ARK OF THE COVENANT

37 Next Bezalel made the Ark of acacia wood—a
sacred chest 45 inches long, 27 inches wide,
and 27 inches high.* 2 He overlaid it inside and out-
side with pure gold, and he ran a molding of gold all
around it. 3 He cast four gold rings and attached them
to its four feet, two rings on each side. 4 Then he made
poles from acacia wood and overlaid them with gold.
5 He inserted the poles into the rings at the sides of the
Ark to carry it.
6 Then he made the Ark's cover—the place of
atonement—from pure gold. It was 45 inches long
and 27 inches wide.* 7 He made two cherubim from
hammered gold and placed them on the two ends
of the atonement cover. 8 He molded the cherubim
on each end of the atonement cover, making it all of
one piece of gold. 9 The cherubim faced each other
and looked down on the atonement cover. With their
wings spread above it, they protected it.

36:8 Hebrew *he;* also in 36:16, 20, 35. See 37:1. **36:9** Hebrew *28 cubits* [12.9 meters] *long and 4 cubits* [1.8 meters] *wide.* **36:15** Hebrew *30 cubits* [13.8 meters] *long and 4 cubits* [1.8 meters] *wide.* **36:21** Hebrew *10 cubits* [4.6 meters] *high and 1.5 cubits* [69 centimeters] *wide.* **37:1** Hebrew *2.5 cubits* [115 centimeters] *long, 1.5 cubits* [69 centimeters] *wide, and 1.5 cubits high.* **37:6** Hebrew *2.5 cubits* [115 centimeters] *long and 1.5 cubits* [69 centimeters] *wide.*

36:8-39:31 Repetition was an ancient form that placed special emphasis on the topics discussed, and the description in the following chapters of the fulfillment of the instructions given to Moses regarding the tabernacle (25:1–31:18) heightens not only the importance of the specific items being referred to but the absolute significance of the tabernacle itself as the dwelling place of God's Presence. The people obeyed God to the letter.

36:8-38 Here the tabernacle precedes the ark in proper order of construction, but the instructions for its building (26:1-37) followed the ark's instructions (25:10-22) to emphasize the central importance of the ark; upon which resided God's spiritual presence on earth. The later filling of the Most Holy Place with God's glory (40:34) mirrors the descent of the Holy Spirit on Christ (Luke 3:22) and the subsequent descent of the Spirit on Christ's church (Acts 2:2).

37:1 the Ark. The ark of the covenant (or ark of the testimony) was located in the Most Holy Place of the tabernacle. The ark was covered by the atonement seat. The Lord had told Moses "I will appear in the cloud over the atonement seat" (Lev. 16:2). Though the high priest could only appear there once a year on the day of atonement, Moses met there regularly with God to receive instructions for the Israelites (25:22). The ark was also a holy time capsule that held precious reminders of the Hebrews' journey from Egypt, such as the two tablets of the Law (40:20), Aaron's rod (Num 17:1-11), and the golden jar of manna (16:33-34). Later the ark would prove to be a visible token of God's presence in Israelite military campaigns (Josh. 6:6) and at other times just a superstitious token (1 Sam. 4).

BUILDING THE TABLE

10 Then Bezalel* made the table of acacia wood,
36 inches long, 18 inches wide, and 27 inches high.*
11 He overlaid it with pure gold and ran a gold mold-
ing around the edge. 12 He decorated it with a 3-inch
border* all around, and he ran a gold molding along
the border. 13 Then he cast four gold rings for the
table and attached them at the four corners next
to the four legs. 14 The rings were attached near the
border to hold the poles that were used to carry the
table. 15 He made these poles from acacia wood and
overlaid them with gold. 16 Then he made special
containers of pure gold for the table—bowls, ladles,
jars, and pitchers—to be used in pouring out liquid
offerings.

BUILDING THE LAMPSTAND

17 Then Bezalel made the lampstand of pure, ham-
mered gold. He made the entire lampstand and its
decorations of one piece—the base, center stem,
lamp cups, buds, and petals. 18 The lampstand had six
branches going out from the center stem, three on
each side. 19 Each of the six branches had three lamp
cups shaped like almond blossoms, complete with
buds and petals. 20 The center stem of the lampstand
was crafted with four lamp cups shaped like almond
blossoms, complete with buds and petals. 21 There was
an almond bud beneath each pair of branches where
the six branches extended from the center stem, all
made of one piece. 22 The almond buds and branches
were all of one piece with the center stem, and they
were hammered from pure gold.

23 He also made seven lamps for the lampstand,
lamp snuffers, and trays, all of pure gold. 24 The entire
lampstand, along with its accessories, was made from
75 pounds* of pure gold.

BUILDING THE INCENSE ALTAR

25 Then Bezalel made the incense altar of acacia wood.
It was 18 inches square and 36 inches high,* with
horns at the corners carved from the same piece of
wood as the altar itself. 26 He overlaid the top, sides,
and horns of the altar with pure gold, and he ran a
gold molding around the entire altar. 27 He made two
gold rings and attached them on opposite sides of the
altar below the gold molding to hold the carrying
poles. 28 He made the poles of acacia wood and over-
laid them with gold.

29 Then he made the sacred anointing oil and the
fragrant incense, using the techniques of a skilled in-
cense maker.

BUILDING THE ALTAR OF BURNT OFFERING

38 Next Bezalel* used acacia wood to construct
the square altar of burnt offering. It was
7½ feet wide, 7½ feet long, and 4½ feet high.* 2 He
made horns for each of its four corners so that the
horns and altar were all one piece. He overlaid the
altar with bronze. 3 Then he made all the altar uten-
sils of bronze—the ash buckets, shovels, basins, meat
forks, and firepans. 4 Next he made a bronze grating
and installed it halfway down the side of the altar,
under the ledge. 5 He cast four rings and attached
them to the corners of the bronze grating to hold the
carrying poles. 6 He made the poles from acacia wood
and overlaid them with bronze. 7 He inserted the poles
through the rings on the sides of the altar. The altar
was hollow and was made from planks.

BUILDING THE WASHBASIN

8 Bezalel made the bronze washbasin and its bronze
stand from bronze mirrors donated by the women
who served at the entrance of the Tabernacle.*

BUILDING THE COURTYARD

9 Then Bezalel made the courtyard, which was en-
closed with curtains made of finely woven linen. On
the south side the curtains were 150 feet long.* 10 They
were held up by twenty posts set securely in twenty
bronze bases. He hung the curtains with silver hooks
and rings. 11 He made a similar set of curtains for the
north side—150 feet of curtains held up by twen-
ty posts set securely in bronze bases. He hung the
curtains with silver hooks and rings. 12 The curtains
on the west end of the courtyard were 75 feet long,*
hung with silver hooks and rings and supported by
ten posts set into ten bases. 13 The east end, the front,
was also 75 feet long.

14 The courtyard entrance was on the east end,
flanked by two curtains. The curtain on the right side
was 22½ feet long* and was supported by three posts
set into three bases. 15 The curtain on the left side was
also 22½ feet long and was supported by three posts
set into three bases. 16 All the curtains used in the
courtyard were made of finely woven linen. 17 Each
post had a bronze base, and all the hooks and rings
were silver. The tops of the posts of the courtyard
were overlaid with silver, and the rings to hold up the
curtains were made of silver.

18 He made the curtain for the entrance to the
courtyard of finely woven linen, and he decorated
it with beautiful embroidery in blue, purple, and
scarlet thread. It was 30 feet long, and its height was
7½ feet,* just like the curtains of the courtyard walls.
19 It was supported by four posts, each set securely in
its own bronze base. The tops of the posts were over-
laid with silver, and the hooks and rings were also
made of silver.

20 All the tent pegs used in the Tabernacle and
courtyard were made of bronze.

INVENTORY OF MATERIALS

21 This is an inventory of the materials used in build-
ing the Tabernacle of the Covenant.* The Levites com-
piled the figures, as Moses directed, and Ithamar son
of Aaron the priest served as recorder. 22 Bezalel son
of Uri, grandson of Hur, of the tribe of Judah, made
everything just as the LORD had commanded Moses.
23 He was assisted by Oholiab son of Ahisamach, of the
tribe of Dan, a craftsman expert at engraving, design-
ing, and embroidering with blue, purple, and scarlet
thread on fine linen cloth.

37:10a Hebrew *he;* also in 37:17, 25. **37:10b** Hebrew *2 cubits* [92 centimeters] *long, 1 cubit* [46 centimeters] *wide, and 1.5 cubits* [69 centimeters] *high.* **37:12** Hebrew *a border of a handbreadth* [8 centimeters]. **37:24** Hebrew *1 talent* [34 kilograms]. **37:25** Hebrew *1 cubit* [46 centimeters] *long and 1 cubit wide, a square, and 2 cubits* [92 centimeters] *high.* **38:1a** Hebrew *he;* also in 38:8, 9. **38:1b** Hebrew *5 cubits* [2.3 meters] *wide, 5 cubits long, a square, and 3 cubits* [1.4 meters] *high.* **38:8** Hebrew *Tent of Meeting;* also in 38:30. **38:9** Hebrew *100 cubits* [46 meters]; also in 38:11. **38:12** Hebrew *50 cubits* [23 meters]; also in 38:13. **38:14** Hebrew *15 cubits* [6.9 meters]; also in 38:15. **38:18** Hebrew *20 cubits* [9.2 meters] *long and 5 cubits* [2.3 meters] *high.* **38:21** Hebrew *the Tabernacle, the Tabernacle of the Testimony.*

24 The people brought special offerings of gold totaling 2,193 pounds,* as measured by the weight of the sanctuary shekel. This gold was used throughout the Tabernacle.

25 The whole community of Israel gave 7,545 pounds* of silver, as measured by the weight of the sanctuary shekel. 26 This silver came from the tax collected from each man registered in the census. (The tax is one beka, which is half a shekel,* based on the sanctuary shekel.) The tax was collected from 603,550 men who had reached their twentieth birthday. 27 The hundred bases for the frames of the sanctuary walls and for the posts supporting the inner curtain required 7,500 pounds of silver, about 75 pounds for each base.* 28 The remaining 45 pounds* of silver was used to make the hooks and rings and to overlay the tops of the posts.

29 The people also brought as special offerings 5,310 pounds* of bronze, 30 which was used for casting the bases for the posts at the entrance to the Tabernacle, and for the bronze altar with its bronze grating and all the altar utensils. 31 Bronze was also used to make the bases for the posts that supported the curtains around the courtyard, the bases for the curtain at the entrance of the courtyard, and all the tent pegs for the Tabernacle and the courtyard.

CLOTHING FOR THE PRIESTS

39 The craftsmen made beautiful sacred garments of blue, purple, and scarlet cloth—clothing for Aaron to wear while ministering in the Holy Place, just as the LORD had commanded Moses.

MAKING THE EPHOD

2 Bezalel* made the ephod of finely woven linen and embroidered it with gold and with blue, purple, and scarlet thread. 3 He made gold thread by hammering out thin sheets of gold and cutting it into fine strands. With great skill and care, he worked it into the fine linen with the blue, purple, and scarlet thread.

4 The ephod consisted of two pieces, front and back, joined at the shoulders with two shoulder-pieces. 5 The decorative sash was made of the same materials: finely woven linen embroidered with gold and with blue, purple, and scarlet thread, just as the LORD had commanded Moses. 6 They mounted the two onyx stones in settings of gold filigree. The stones were engraved with the names of the tribes of Israel, just as a seal is engraved. 7 He fastened these stones on the shoulder-pieces of the ephod as a reminder that the priest represents the people of Israel. All this was done just as the LORD had commanded Moses.

MAKING THE CHESTPIECE

8 Bezalel made the chestpiece with great skill and care. He made it to match the ephod, using finely woven linen embroidered with gold and with blue, purple, and scarlet thread. 9 He made the chestpiece of a single piece of cloth folded to form a pouch nine inches* square. 10 They mounted four rows of gemstones* on it. The first row contained a red carnelian, a pale-green peridot, and an emerald. 11 The second row contained a turquoise, a blue lapis lazuli, and a white moonstone. 12 The third row contained an orange jacinth, an agate, and a purple amethyst. 13 The fourth row contained a blue-green beryl, an onyx, and a green jasper. All these stones were set in gold filigree. 14 Each stone represented one of the twelve sons of Israel, and the name of that tribe was engraved on it like a seal.

15 To attach the chestpiece to the ephod, they made braided cords of pure gold thread. 16 They also made two settings of gold filigree and two gold rings and attached them to the top corners of the chestpiece. 17 They tied the two gold cords to the rings on the chestpiece. 18 They tied the other ends of the cords to the gold settings on the shoulder-pieces of the ephod. 19 Then they made two more gold rings and attached them to the inside edges of the chestpiece next to the ephod. 20 Then they made two more gold rings and attached them to the front of the ephod, below the shoulder-pieces, just above the knot where the decorative sash was fastened to the ephod. 21 They attached the bottom rings of the chestpiece to the rings on the ephod with blue cords. In this way, the chestpiece was held securely to the ephod above the decorative sash. All this was done just as the LORD had commanded Moses.

ADDITIONAL CLOTHING FOR THE PRIESTS

22 Bezalel made the robe that is worn with the ephod from a single piece of blue woven cloth, 23 with an opening for Aaron's head in the middle of it. The opening was reinforced with a woven collar* so it would not tear. 24 They made pomegranates of blue, purple, and scarlet yarn, and attached them to the hem of the robe. 25 They also made bells of pure gold and placed them between the pomegranates along the hem of the robe, 26 with bells and pomegranates alternating all around the hem. This robe was to be worn whenever the priest ministered before the LORD, just as the LORD had commanded Moses.

27 They made tunics for Aaron and his sons from fine linen cloth. 28 The turban and the special head coverings were made of fine linen, and the undergarments were also made of finely woven linen. 29 The sashes were made of finely woven linen and embroidered with blue, purple, and scarlet thread, just as the LORD had commanded Moses.

30 Finally, they made the sacred medallion—the badge of holiness—of pure gold. They engraved it like a seal with these words: HOLY TO THE LORD.

38:24 Hebrew *29 talents and 730 shekels* [994 kilograms]. Each shekel weighed about 0.4 ounces or 11 grams. **38:25** Hebrew *100 talents and 1,775 shekels* [3,420 kilograms]. **38:26** Or *0.2 ounces* [6 grams]. **38:27** Hebrew *100 talents* [3,400 kilograms] *of silver, 1 talent* [34 kilograms] *for each base.* **38:28** Hebrew *1,775 [shekels]* [20.2 kilograms]. **38:29** Hebrew *70 talents and 2,400 shekels* [2,407 kilograms]. **39:2** Hebrew *He;* also in 39:8, 22. **39:9** Hebrew *1 span* [23 centimeters]. **39:10** The identification of some of these gemstones is uncertain. **39:23** The meaning of the Hebrew is uncertain.

38:24-31 An enormous amount of gold, silver, and bronze went into the construction, a little more than eight and a half tons. The gold and bronze had been acquired by means of a massive contribution of freewill offerings (36:3), but the nearly four tons of silver had come directly from the collection taken on behalf of the tabernacle (vv. 25-26). Each man over 20 had been required to pay a half-shekel for the census offering (30:11-16). The number of half-shekels multiplied by the 603,550 men who took part in the census (cf. 12:37; Num. 1:46) exactly equals the weight of silver listed here.

38:25 pounds . . . shekel. Often the coins were actually weights that would be placed on scales to buy that same weight of flour or grain. A shekel was about 1/5 of an ounce, and there were 75 pounds to a talent.

31 They attached the medallion with a blue cord to
Aaron's turban, just as the LORD had commanded
Moses.

MOSES INSPECTS THE WORK

32 And so at last the Tabernacle* was finished. The
Israelites had done everything just as the LORD had
commanded Moses. 33 And they brought the entire
Tabernacle to Moses:

the sacred tent with all its furnishings, clasps,
frames, crossbars, posts, and bases;
34 the tent coverings of tanned ram skins and fine
goatskin leather;
the inner curtain to shield the Ark;
35 the Ark of the Covenant* and its carrying
poles;
the Ark's cover—the place of atonement;
36 the table and all its utensils;
the Bread of the Presence;
37 the pure gold lampstand with its symmetrical
lamp cups, all its accessories, and the olive oil
for lighting;
38 the gold altar;
the anointing oil and fragrant incense;
the curtain for the entrance of the sacred tent;
39 the bronze altar;
the bronze grating and its carrying poles and
utensils;
the washbasin with its stand;
40 the curtains for the walls of the courtyard;
the posts and their bases;
the curtain for the entrance to the courtyard;
the ropes and tent pegs;
all the furnishings to be used in worship at the
Tabernacle;
41 the beautifully stitched garments for the priests to
wear while ministering in the Holy Place—the
sacred garments for Aaron the priest, and the
garments for his sons to wear as they minister
as priests.

42 So the people of Israel followed all of the LORD's
instructions to Moses. 43 Then Moses inspected all
their work. When he found it had been done just as
the LORD had commanded him, he blessed them.

THE TABERNACLE COMPLETED

40 Then the LORD said to Moses, 2 "Set up the Tab-
ernacle* on the first day of the new year.*
3 Place the Ark of the Covenant* inside, and install
the inner curtain to enclose the Ark within the Most
Holy Place. 4 Then bring in the table, and arrange the
utensils on it. And bring in the lampstand, and set up
the lamps.
5 "Place the gold incense altar in front of the Ark of
the Covenant. Then hang the curtain at the entrance
of the Tabernacle. 6 Place the altar of burnt offering in
front of the Tabernacle entrance. 7 Set the washbasin
between the Tabernacle* and the altar, and fill it with
water. 8 Then set up the courtyard around the outside
of the tent, and hang the curtain for the courtyard
entrance.

9 "Take the anointing oil and anoint the Tabernacle
and all its furnishings to consecrate them and make
them holy. 10 Anoint the altar of burnt offering and
its utensils to consecrate them. Then the altar will
become absolutely holy. 11 Next anoint the washbasin
and its stand to consecrate them.

12 "Present Aaron and his sons at the entrance of
the Tabernacle, and wash them with water. 13 Dress
Aaron with the sacred garments and anoint him, con-
secrating him to serve me as a priest. 14 Then present
his sons and dress them in their tunics. 15 Anoint them
as you did their father, so they may also serve me as
priests. With their anointing, Aaron's descendants
are set apart for the priesthood forever, from gener-
ation to generation."

16 Moses proceeded to do everything just as the
LORD had commanded him. 17 So the Tabernacle was
set up on the first day of the first month of the second
year. 18 Moses erected the Tabernacle by setting down
its bases, inserting the frames, attaching the cross-
bars, and setting up the posts. 19 Then he spread the
coverings over the Tabernacle framework and put on
the protective layers, just as the LORD had command-
ed him.

20 He took the stone tablets inscribed with the terms
of the covenant and placed them* inside the Ark.
Then he attached the carrying poles to the Ark, and
he set the Ark's cover—the place of atonement—on
top of it. 21 Then he brought the Ark of the Covenant
into the Tabernacle and hung the inner curtain to
shield it from view, just as the LORD had commanded
him.

22 Next Moses placed the table in the Tabernacle,
along the north side of the Holy Place, just outside
the inner curtain. 23 And he arranged the Bread of the
Presence on the table before the LORD, just as the LORD
had commanded him.

24 He set the lampstand in the Tabernacle across
from the table on the south side of the Holy Place.
25 Then he lit the lamps in the LORD's presence, just
as the LORD had commanded him. 26 He also placed
the gold incense altar in the Tabernacle, in the Holy
Place in front of the inner curtain. 27 On it he burned
the fragrant incense, just as the LORD had command-
ed him.

28 He hung the curtain at the entrance of the Tab-
ernacle, 29 and he placed the altar of burnt offering

39:32 Hebrew *the Tabernacle, the Tent of Meeting;* also in 39:40. **39:35** Or *Ark of the Testimony.* **40:2a** Hebrew *the Tabernacle, the Tent of Meeting;* also in 40:6, 29. **40:2b** Hebrew *the first day of the first month.* This day of the ancient Hebrew lunar calendar occurred in March or April. **40:3** Or *Ark of the Testimony;* also in 40:5, 21. **40:7** Hebrew *Tent of Meeting;* also in 40:12, 22, 24, 26, 30, 32, 34, 35. **40:20** Hebrew *He placed the Testimony;* see note on 25:16.

39:32 as the LORD had commanded. Throughout the Bible, people fail God. But here the Israelites obey Him to the letter. Noah did the same with plans for the ark (Gen. 6:22). Moses and Aaron did it in their standoff with Pharaoh (7:10). David did it in battle (2 Sam. 5:25).

39:43 Moses inspected all the work. Moses had a difficult role to play in the lives of his people. He had to rally them as well as chastise them, confront them and mitigate their differences. Here is a rare moment when Moses gets to observe their work and offer them congratulations and blessings. **it had been done.** The same word was used for God's completed work of creation (Gen. 2:2). Likewise, Moses blessed as God had blessed (Gen. 1:22,28; 2:3). Like the earth, God had designed the tabernacle and allowed His people to participate in its creation.

40:3 to enclose the Ark. As the seat of God's glory, it was important to read the ark's user manual. Once seventy men died from looking into it (1 Sam. 6:19). Another time, the ark was improperly transported in a cart that predictably tipped—into Uzzah's unfortunate hand (2 Sam. 6:6-7).

40:16 Moses proceeded to do everything. God called Moses the earth's most humble man (Num. 12:3). He did not presume to know more than God.

near the Tabernacle entrance. On it he offered a burnt
offering and a grain offering, just as the LORD had
commanded him.
[30] Next Moses placed the washbasin between the
Tabernacle and the altar. He filled it with water so
the priests could wash themselves. [31] Moses and Aar-
on and Aaron's sons used water from it to wash their
hands and feet. [32] Whenever they approached the al-
tar and entered the Tabernacle, they washed them-
selves, just as the LORD had commanded Moses.
[33] Then he hung the curtains forming the courtyard
around the Tabernacle and the altar. And he set up
the curtain at the entrance of the courtyard. So at last
Moses finished the work.

THE LORD'S GLORY FILLS THE TABERNACLE

[34] Then the cloud covered the Tabernacle, and the glo-
ry of the LORD filled the Tabernacle. [35] Moses could no
longer enter the Tabernacle because the cloud had
settled down over it, and the glory of the LORD filled
the Tabernacle.
[36] Now whenever the cloud lifted from the Taber-
nacle, the people of Israel would set out on their jour-
ney, following it. [37] But if the cloud did not rise, they
remained where they were until it lifted. [38] The cloud
of the LORD hovered over the Tabernacle during the
day, and at night fire glowed inside the cloud so the
whole family of Israel could see it. This continued
throughout all their journeys.

40:36 whenever the cloud lifted. Just as God led them with a cloud by day and a pillar of fire by night (13:21), now the cloud settled on the tabernacle and lifted when it was time to pack up.

40:38 fire glowed inside the cloud. God's glory was the fire. The cloud covered the glory so that people could see it and live. At night, the glory showed through the cloud.

INTRODUCTION TO

LEVITICUS

PERSONAL READING PLAN

☐Leviticus 1:1–3:17	☐Leviticus 12:1–13:46	☐Leviticus 20:1-27
☐Leviticus 4:1–5:13	☐Leviticus 13:47–14:32	☐Leviticus 21:1–23:8
☐Leviticus 5:14–7:10	☐Leviticus 14:33–15:33	☐Leviticus 23:9–24:23
☐Leviticus 7:11–8:36	☐Leviticus 16:1-34	☐Leviticus 25:1-55
☐Leviticus 9:1–10:20	☐Leviticus 17:1–18:30	☐Leviticus 26:1-46
☐Leviticus 11:1-47	☐Leviticus 19:1-37	☐Leviticus 27:1-34

AUTHOR

Moses is assumed to be the author and editor of most of the first five books of the Old Testament (the Pentateuch).

DATE

It is difficult to set a firm date for the writing of the Pentateuch. Conservative estimates place it in either the 15th or 13th century B.C., depending on when the Exodus occurred.

THEME

God's reconciliation and sanctification of His people.

HISTORICAL BACKGROUND

The name of this book, from the Greek and Latin versions, comes from its emphasis on the Levitical priesthood. The ministry of the tabernacle was conducted by the sons of Aaron (Moses' brother). These newly appointed priests were assisted by many of their relatives from the tribe of Levi. The events in Leviticus take place after the Exodus from Egypt and the giving of the Law at Sinai, and they concern the formalizing of Israelite religious practice. In Exodus, instructions were given for the building of the tabernacle; here in Leviticus, regulations are given for how to worship there.

CHARACTERISTICS

After the covenant at Sinai, Israel was the earthly representation of God's kingdom and, as her King, the Lord established His administration over all of Israel's life. Her religious, communal, and personal life were so regulated to establish her as God's holy people and to instruct her in holiness. To the modern reader, Leviticus may appear hopelessly outdated with its strange economic practices and the blood of animal sacrifice, yet the questions it seeks to answer are as important for us as they were for the Israelites. How do we remain reconciled to God? What is the proper way to worship a holy God? How are we to act toward each other within the context of God's covenant? Leviticus answers these and other questions faced by the Israelites using symbols familiar to them. For us, the key to understanding Leviticus is looking beyond these strange symbols to the underlying principles describing God's way of holiness and reconciliation

PROCEDURES FOR THE BURNT OFFERING

1 The LORD called to Moses from the Tabernacle* and
said to him, 2 "Give the following instructions to the
people of Israel. When you present an animal as an
offering to the LORD, you may take it from your herd
of cattle or your flock of sheep and goats.
3 "If the animal you present as a burnt offering is
from the herd, it must be a male with no defects. Bring
it to the entrance of the Tabernacle so you* may be
accepted by the LORD. 4 Lay your hand on the animal's
head, and the LORD will accept its death in your place
to purify you, making you right with him.* 5 Then
slaughter the young bull in the LORD's presence, and
Aaron's sons, the priests, will present the animal's
blood by splattering it against all sides of the altar
that stands at the entrance to the Tabernacle. 6 Then
skin the animal and cut it into pieces. 7 The sons of
Aaron the priest will build a wood fire on the altar.
8 They will arrange the pieces of the offering, includ-
ing the head and fat, on the wood burning on the al-
tar. 9 But the internal organs and the legs must first
be washed with water. Then the priest will burn the
entire sacrifice on the altar as a burnt offering. It is a
special gift, a pleasing aroma to the LORD.
10 "If the animal you present as a burnt offering
is from the flock, it may be either a sheep or a goat,
but it must be a male with no defects. 11 Slaughter the
animal on the north side of the altar in the LORD's
presence, and Aaron's sons, the priests, will splatter
its blood against all sides of the altar. 12 Then cut the
animal in pieces, and the priests will arrange the
pieces of the offering, including the head and fat, on
the wood burning on the altar. 13 But the internal or-
gans and the legs must first be washed with water.
Then the priest will burn the entire sacrifice on the
altar as a burnt offering. It is a special gift, a pleasing
aroma to the LORD.
14 "If you present a bird as a burnt offering to the
LORD, choose either a turtledove or a young pigeon.
15 The priest will take the bird to the altar, wring off its
head, and burn it on the altar. But first he must drain
its blood against the side of the altar. 16 The priest must
also remove the crop and the feathers* and throw
them in the ashes on the east side of the altar. 17 Then,
grasping the bird by its wings, the priest will tear the
bird open, but without tearing it apart. Then he will
burn it as a burnt offering on the wood burning on
the altar. It is a special gift, a pleasing aroma to the
LORD.

PROCEDURES FOR THE GRAIN OFFERING

2 "When you present grain as an offering to the
LORD, the offering must consist of choice flour. You
are to pour olive oil on it, sprinkle it with frankin-
cense, 2 and bring it to Aaron's sons, the priests. The
priest will scoop out a handful of the flour moistened
with oil, together with all the frankincense, and burn
this representative portion on the altar. It is a special
gift, a pleasing aroma to the LORD. 3 The rest of the
grain offering will then be given to Aaron and his
sons. This offering will be considered a most holy part
of the special gifts presented to the LORD.
4 "If your offering is a grain offering baked in an
oven, it must be made of choice flour, but without any
yeast. It may be presented in the form of thin cakes
mixed with olive oil or wafers spread with olive oil.
5 If your grain offering is cooked on a griddle, it must
be made of choice flour mixed with olive oil but with-
out any yeast. 6 Break it in pieces and pour olive oil
on it; it is a grain offering. 7 If your grain offering is
prepared in a pan, it must be made of choice flour and
olive oil.
8 "No matter how a grain offering for the LORD has
been prepared, bring it to the priest, who will present
it at the altar. 9 The priest will take a representative
portion of the grain offering and burn it on the altar.
It is a special gift, a pleasing aroma to the LORD. 10 The
rest of the grain offering will then be given to Aaron
and his sons as their food. This offering will be con-
sidered a most holy part of the special gifts presented
to the LORD.
11 "Do not use yeast in preparing any of the grain
offerings you present to the LORD, because no yeast
or honey may be burned as a special gift presented to
the LORD. 12 You may add yeast and honey to an offer-
ing of the first crops of your harvest, but these must
never be offered on the altar as a pleasing aroma to
the LORD. 13 Season all your grain offerings with salt to
remind you of God's eternal covenant. Never forget to
add salt to your grain offerings.
14 "If you present a grain offering to the LORD from
the first portion of your harvest, bring fresh grain
that is coarsely ground and roasted on a fire. 15 Put
olive oil on this grain offering, and sprinkle it with
frankincense. 16 The priest will take a representative
portion of the grain moistened with oil, together with
all the frankincense, and burn it as a special gift pre-
sented to the LORD.

PROCEDURES FOR THE PEACE OFFERING

3 "If you present an animal from the herd as a peace
offering to the LORD, it may be a male or a female,
but it must have no defects. 2 Lay your hand on the
animal's head, and slaughter it at the entrance of the
Tabernacle.* Then Aaron's sons, the priests, will splat-
ter its blood against all sides of the altar. 3 The priest
must present part of this peace offering as a special
gift to the LORD. This includes all the fat around the
internal organs, 4 the two kidneys and the fat around
them near the loins, and the long lobe of the liver.
These must be removed with the kidneys, 5 and Aar-
on's sons will burn them on top of the burnt offering
on the wood burning on the altar. It is a special gift, a
pleasing aroma to the LORD.
6 "If you present an animal from the flock as a peace
offering to the LORD, it may be a male or a female, but
it must have no defects. 7 If you present a sheep as your
offering, bring it to the LORD, 8 lay your hand on its

1:1 Hebrew *Tent of Meeting;* also in 1:3, 5. **1:3** Or *it.* **1:4** Or *to make atonement for you.* **1:16** Or *the crop and its contents.* The meaning of the Hebrew is uncertain. **3:2** Hebrew *Tent of Meeting;* also in 3:8, 13.

1:3 no defects. The people were to bring the best animals from their herds as **offerings** to the Lord.

1:5 slaughter. The sin offering required that a person kill his own animal, symbolically taking an innocent life for his own sins.

2:1 grain as an offering. These offerings were of flour, oil, and incense.

2:11-13 yeast or honey . . . salt. While yeast and honey were not allowed as part of the grain offering, honey *was* a part of the firstfruits offering. Salt was always a part of the offerings.

3:1-4 peace offering. This sacrifice was motivated by a person's gratitude rather than remorse over his sin.

head, and slaughter it in front of the Tabernacle. Aar-
on's sons will then splatter the sheep's blood against
all sides of the altar. 9 The priest must present the fat
of this peace offering as a special gift to the LORD. This
includes the fat of the broad tail cut off near the back-
bone, all the fat around the internal organs, 10 the two
kidneys and the fat around them near the loins, and
the long lobe of the liver. These must be removed with
the kidneys, 11 and the priest will burn them on the
altar. It is a special gift of food presented to the LORD.
12 "If you present a goat as your offering, bring it to
the LORD, 13 lay your hand on its head, and slaughter
it in front of the Tabernacle. Aaron's sons will then
splatter the goat's blood against all sides of the al-
tar. 14 The priest must present part of this offering
as a special gift to the LORD. This includes all the fat
around the internal organs, 15 the two kidneys and the
fat around them near the loins, and the long lobe of
the liver. These must be removed with the kidneys,
16 and the priest will burn them on the altar. It is a
special gift of food, a pleasing aroma to the LORD. All
the fat belongs to the LORD.
17 "You must never eat any fat or blood. This is a
permanent law for you, and it must be observed from
generation to generation, wherever you live."

PROCEDURES FOR THE SIN OFFERING

4 Then the LORD said to Moses, 2 "Give the following
instructions to the people of Israel. This is how
you are to deal with those who sin unintentionally by
doing anything that violates one of the LORD's com-
mands.
3 "If the high priest* sins, bringing guilt upon the
entire community, he must give a sin offering for the
sin he has committed. He must present to the LORD a
young bull with no defects. 4 He must bring the bull
to the LORD at the entrance of the Tabernacle,* lay
his hand on the bull's head, and slaughter it before
the LORD. 5 The high priest will then take some of the
bull's blood into the Tabernacle, 6 dip his finger in the
blood, and sprinkle it seven times before the LORD in
front of the inner curtain of the sanctuary. 7 The priest
will then put some of the blood on the horns of the al-
tar for fragrant incense that stands in the LORD's pres-
ence inside the Tabernacle. He will pour out the rest
of the bull's blood at the base of the altar for burnt
offerings at the entrance of the Tabernacle. 8 Then the
priest must remove all the fat of the bull to be offered
as a sin offering. This includes all the fat around the
internal organs, 9 the two kidneys and the fat around
them near the loins, and the long lobe of the liver. He
must remove these along with the kidneys, 10 just as he
does with cattle offered as a peace offering, and burn
them on the altar of burnt offerings. 11 But he must
take whatever is left of the bull—its hide, meat, head,
legs, internal organs, and dung—12 and carry it away
to a place outside the camp that is ceremonially clean,
the place where the ashes are dumped. There, on the
ash heap, he will burn it on a wood fire.
13 "If the entire Israelite community sins by violat-
ing one of the LORD's commands, but the people don't
realize it, they are still guilty. 14 When they become
aware of their sin, the people must bring a young
bull as an offering for their sin and present it before
the Tabernacle. 15 The elders of the community must
then lay their hands on the bull's head and slaugh-
ter it before the LORD. 16 The high priest will then take
some of the bull's blood into the Tabernacle, 17 dip his
finger in the blood, and sprinkle it seven times before
the LORD in front of the inner curtain. 18 He will then
put some of the blood on the horns of the altar for
fragrant incense that stands in the LORD's presence
inside the Tabernacle. He will pour out the rest of
the blood at the base of the altar for burnt offerings
at the entrance of the Tabernacle. 19 Then the priest
must remove all the animal's fat and burn it on the
altar, 20 just as he does with the bull offered as a sin
offering for the high priest. Through this process, the
priest will purify the people, making them right with
the LORD,* and they will be forgiven. 21 Then the priest
must take what is left of the bull and carry it outside
the camp and burn it there, just as is done with the sin
offering for the high priest. This offering is for the sin
of the entire congregation of Israel.
22 "If one of Israel's leaders sins by violating one of
the commands of the LORD his God but doesn't real-
ize it, he is still guilty. 23 When he becomes aware of
his sin, he must bring as his offering a male goat with
no defects. 24 He must lay his hand on the goat's head
and slaughter it at the place where burnt offerings
are slaughtered before the LORD. This is an offering
for his sin. 25 Then the priest will dip his finger in the
blood of the sin offering and put it on the horns of the
altar for burnt offerings. He will pour out the rest of
the blood at the base of the altar. 26 Then he must burn
all the goat's fat on the altar, just as he does with the
peace offering. Through this process, the priest will
purify the leader from his sin, making him right with
the LORD, and he will be forgiven.
27 "If any of the common people sin by violating
one of the LORD's commands, but they don't realize
it, they are still guilty. 28 When they become aware of
their sin, they must bring as an offering for their sin
a female goat with no defects. 29 They must lay a hand
on the head of the sin offering and slaughter it at the
place where burnt offerings are slaughtered. 30 Then
the priest will dip his finger in the blood and put it on
the horns of the altar for burnt offerings. He will pour
out the rest of the blood at the base of the altar. 31 Then
he must remove all the goat's fat, just as he does with
the fat of the peace offering. He will burn the fat on
the altar, and it will be a pleasing aroma to the LORD.

4:3 Hebrew *the anointed priest;* also in 4:5, 16. **4:4** Hebrew *Tent of Meeting;* also in 4:5, 7, 14, 16, 18. **4:20** Or *will make atonement for the people;* similarly in 4:26, 31, 35.

3:17 fat or blood. God's prohibition against eating blood is universal (Gen. 9:4). The fat referred to is suet, or fat surrounding the animal's organs.
4:3 bringing guilt on the entire community. When the high priest sinned, it made Israel a sinful nation.
4:5 the bull's blood. The blood cleansed the stains of sin from the altar and kept the nation ceremonially clean.
4:12 outside the camp. Since the bull had been a substitute for the priest, the entire carcass was disposed of outside of the camp. The carcass became holy and needed to be destroyed so it would not be defiled.
4:20 making them right. Or "to atone". This means to cleanse sin so forgiveness is possible. The dead animals did not change the sinful state of humanity. But the sacrifice as an act of faith—the holy God's revulsion at sin—connected the people with God's forgiveness.
4:23 male goat. When a leader sinned, he brought a goat. Since he was in a responsible position, he had to pay a greater price for his sin.

Through this process, the priest will purify the people, making them right with the LORD, and they will be forgiven.

[32] "If the people bring a sheep as their sin offering, it must be a female with no defects. [33] They must lay a hand on the head of the sin offering and slaughter it at the place where burnt offerings are slaughtered. [34] Then the priest will dip his finger in the blood of the sin offering and put it on the horns of the altar for burnt offerings. He will pour out the rest of the blood at the base of the altar. [35] Then he must remove all the sheep's fat, just as he does with the fat of a sheep presented as a peace offering. He will burn the fat on the altar on top of the special gifts presented to the LORD. Through this process, the priest will purify the people from their sin, making them right with the LORD, and they will be forgiven.

SINS REQUIRING A SIN OFFERING

5 "If you are called to testify about something you have seen or that you know about, it is sinful to refuse to testify, and you will be punished for your sin.

[2] "Or suppose you unknowingly touch something that is ceremonially unclean, such as the carcass of an unclean animal. When you realize what you have done, you must admit your defilement and your guilt. This is true whether it is a wild animal, a domestic animal, or an animal that scurries along the ground.

[3] "Or suppose you unknowingly touch something that makes a person unclean. When you realize what you have done, you must admit your guilt.

[4] "Or suppose you make a foolish vow of any kind, whether its purpose is for good or for bad. When you realize its foolishness, you must admit your guilt.

[5] "When you become aware of your guilt in any of these ways, you must confess your sin. [6] Then you must bring to the LORD as the penalty for your sin a female from the flock, either a sheep or a goat. This is a sin offering with which the priest will purify you from your sin, making you right with the LORD.*

[7] "But if you cannot afford to bring a sheep, you may bring to the LORD two turtledoves or two young pigeons as the penalty for your sin. One of the birds will be for a sin offering, and the other for a burnt offering. [8] You must bring them to the priest, who will present the first bird as the sin offering. He will wring its neck but without severing its head from the body. [9] Then he will sprinkle some of the blood of the sin offering against the sides of the altar, and the rest of the blood will be drained out at the base of the altar. This is an offering for sin. [10] The priest will then prepare the second bird as a burnt offering, following all the procedures that have been prescribed. Through this process the priest will purify you from your sin, making you right with the LORD, and you will be forgiven.

[11] "If you cannot afford to bring two turtledoves or two young pigeons, you may bring two quarts* of choice flour for your sin offering. Since it is an offering for sin, you must not moisten it with olive oil or put any frankincense on it. [12] Take the flour to the priest, who will scoop out a handful as a representative portion. He will burn it on the altar on top of the special gifts presented to the LORD. It is an offering for sin. [13] Through this process, the priest will purify those who are guilty of any of these sins, making them right with the LORD, and they will be forgiven. The rest of the flour will belong to the priest, just as with the grain offering."

PROCEDURES FOR THE GUILT OFFERING

[14] Then the LORD said to Moses, [15] "If one of you commits a sin by unintentionally defiling the LORD's sacred property, you must bring a guilt offering to the LORD. The offering must be your own ram with no defects, or you may buy one of equal value with silver, as measured by the weight of the sanctuary shekel.* [16] You must make restitution for the sacred property you have harmed by paying for the loss, plus an additional 20 percent. When you give the payment to the priest, he will purify you with the ram sacrificed as a guilt offering, making you right with the LORD, and you will be forgiven.

[17] "Suppose you sin by violating one of the LORD's commands. Even if you are unaware of what you have done, you are guilty and will be punished for your sin. [18] For a guilt offering, you must bring to the priest your own ram with no defects, or you may buy one of equal value. Through this process the priest will purify you from your unintentional sin, making you right with the LORD, and you will be forgiven. [19] This is a guilt offering, for you have been guilty of an offense against the LORD."

SINS REQUIRING A GUILT OFFERING

6 [1]*Then the LORD said to Moses, [2] "Suppose one of you sins against your associate and is unfaithful to the LORD. Suppose you cheat in a deal involving a security deposit, or you steal or commit fraud, [3] or you find lost property and lie about it, or you lie while swearing to tell the truth, or you commit any other such sin. [4] If you have sinned in any of these ways, you are guilty. You must give back whatever you stole, or the money you took by extortion, or the security deposit, or the lost property you found, [5] or anything obtained by swearing falsely. You must make restitution by paying the full price plus an additional 20 percent to the person you have harmed. On the same day you must present a guilt offering. [6] As a guilt offering to the LORD, you must bring to the priest your own ram with no defects, or you may buy one of equal value. [7] Through this process, the priest will purify you be-

5:6 Or *will make atonement for you for your sin;* similarly in 5:10, 13, 16, 18. **5:11** Hebrew $^1/_{10}$ *of an ephah* [2.2 liters]. **5:15** Each shekel was about 0.4 ounces or 11 grams in weight. **6:1** Verses 6:1-7 are numbered 5:20-26 in Hebrew text. **6:7** Or *will make atonement for you before the* Lord.

5:5 you must confess. Just offering a sacrifice did not bring about forgiveness. God wants the heart of the sinner to repent in remorse and determine to follow God. Any genuine conversion or growth in faith requires this step.

5:7 cannot afford. A poor person was allowed to bring two turtledoves as a sacrifice instead of a more valuable cow, sheep, or goat. Jesus' family offered turtledoves at Mary's purification ceremony after Jesus was born (Luke 2:24).

5:15-17 guilt offering. When a person committed a sin that required restitution, he brought an offering and was required to replace whatever loss he had caused plus 20 percent of its worth in silver.

6:2-7 The list of offenses here proves that "unintentional" sins are not unwitting sins only, but also sins of straying and giving in to temptation. Remorse and repentance demonstrate that a sin, even fraud or theft, was not defiant (Num. 15:30).

6:6 the Lord . . . the priest. In ancient days the worshipper brought his offering to the priest and by that action brought it also to the Lord. So it is today. When we bring our money or gifts to the ministries of our churches, we bring them to God.

fore the LORD, making you right with him,* and you will be forgiven for any of these sins you have committed."

FURTHER INSTRUCTIONS FOR THE BURNT OFFERING

8*Then the LORD said to Moses, 9"Give Aaron and his sons the following instructions regarding the burnt offering. The burnt offering must be left on top of the altar until the next morning, and the fire on the altar must be kept burning all night. 10 In the morning, after the priest on duty has put on his official linen clothing and linen undergarments, he must clean out the ashes of the burnt offering and put them beside the altar. 11 Then he must take off these garments, change back into his regular clothes, and carry the ashes outside the camp to a place that is ceremonially clean. 12 Meanwhile, the fire on the altar must be kept burning; it must never go out. Each morning the priest will add fresh wood to the fire and arrange the burnt offering on it. He will then burn the fat of the peace offerings on it. 13 Remember, the fire must be kept burning on the altar at all times. It must never go out.

FURTHER INSTRUCTIONS FOR THE GRAIN OFFERING

14"These are the instructions regarding the grain offering. Aaron's sons must present this offering to the LORD in front of the altar. 15 The priest on duty will take from the grain offering a handful of the choice flour moistened with olive oil, together with all the frankincense. He will burn this representative portion on the altar as a pleasing aroma to the LORD. 16 Aaron and his sons may eat the rest of the flour, but it must be baked without yeast and eaten in a sacred place within the courtyard of the Tabernacle.* 17 Remember, it must never be prepared with yeast. I have given it to the priests as their share of the special gifts presented to me. Like the sin offering and the guilt offering, it is most holy. 18 Any of Aaron's male descendants may eat from the special gifts presented to the LORD. This is their permanent right from generation to generation. Anyone or anything that touches these offerings will become holy."

PROCEDURES FOR THE ORDINATION OFFERING

19 Then the LORD said to Moses, 20"On the day Aaron and his sons are anointed, they must present to the LORD the standard grain offering of two quarts* of choice flour, half to be offered in the morning and half to be offered in the evening. 21 It must be carefully mixed with olive oil and cooked on a griddle. Then slice* this grain offering and present it as a pleasing aroma to the LORD. 22 In each generation, the high priest* who succeeds Aaron must prepare this same offering. It belongs to the LORD and must be burned up completely. This is a permanent law. 23 All such grain offerings of a priest must be burned up entirely. None of it may be eaten."

FURTHER INSTRUCTIONS FOR THE SIN OFFERING

24 Then the LORD said to Moses, 25"Give Aaron and his sons the following instructions regarding the sin offering. The animal given as an offering for sin is a most holy offering, and it must be slaughtered in the LORD's presence at the place where the burnt offerings are slaughtered. 26 The priest who offers the sacrifice as a sin offering must eat his portion in a sacred place within the courtyard of the Tabernacle. 27 Anyone or anything that touches the sacrificial meat will become holy. If any of the sacrificial blood spatters on a person's clothing, the soiled garment must be washed in a sacred place. 28 If a clay pot is used to boil the sacrificial meat, it must then be broken. If a bronze pot is used, it must be scoured and thoroughly rinsed with water. 29 Any male from a priest's family may eat from this offering; it is most holy. 30 But the offering for sin may not be eaten if its blood was brought into the Tabernacle as an offering for purification* in the Holy Place. It must be completely burned with fire.

FURTHER INSTRUCTIONS FOR THE GUILT OFFERING

7 "These are the instructions for the guilt offering. It is most holy. 2 The animal sacrificed as a guilt offering must be slaughtered at the place where the burnt offerings are slaughtered, and its blood must be splattered against all sides of the altar. 3 The priest will then offer all its fat on the altar, including the fat of the broad tail, the fat around the internal organs, 4 the two kidneys and the fat around them near the loins, and the long lobe of the liver. These are to be removed with the kidneys, 5 and the priests will burn them on the altar as a special gift presented to the LORD. This is the guilt offering. 6 Any male from a priest's family may eat the meat. It must be eaten in a sacred place, for it is most holy.

7"The same instructions apply to both the guilt offering and the sin offering. Both belong to the priest who uses them to purify someone, making that person right with the LORD.* 8 In the case of the burnt offering, the priest may keep the hide of the sacrificed animal. 9 Any grain offering that has been baked in an oven, prepared in a pan, or cooked on a griddle belongs to the priest who presents it. 10 All other grain offerings, whether made of dry flour or flour moistened with olive oil, are to be shared equally among all the priests, the descendants of Aaron.

FURTHER INSTRUCTIONS FOR THE PEACE OFFERING

11"These are the instructions regarding the different kinds of peace offerings that may be presented to the LORD. 12 If you present your peace offering as an expression of thanksgiving, the usual animal sacrifice must be accompanied by various kinds of bread made without yeast—thin cakes mixed with olive oil, wafers spread with oil, and cakes made of choice flour mixed with olive oil. 13 This peace offering of thanksgiving must also be accompanied by loaves of bread

6:8 Verses 6:8-30 are numbered 6:1-23 in Hebrew text. **6:16** Hebrew *Tent of Meeting;* also in 6:26, 30. **6:20** Hebrew 1/10 *of an ephah* [2.2 liters]. **6:21** The meaning of this Hebrew term is uncertain. **6:22** Hebrew *the anointed priest.* **6:30** Or *an offering to make atonement.* **7:7** Or *to make atonement.*

6:9 Aaron and his sons. Only God's authorized priests could prepare and present the people's sacrificial offerings to the Lord.

6:13 It must never go out. The fire on the altar never went out. It was started by God and was maintained continually (Lev. 9:24).

6:26 a sacred place. Priests and their families could eat some of the remains of the sacrifices. This is how they were provided for. The remains of the sin offering could be eaten only at the tabernacle.

7:12-15 The peace offering combined meat and grain sacrifices.

made with yeast. 14 One of each kind of bread must be presented as a gift to the LORD. It will then belong to the priest who splatters the blood of the peace offering against the altar. 15 The meat of the peace offering of thanksgiving must be eaten on the same day it is offered. None of it may be saved for the next morning.

16 "If you bring an offering to fulfill a vow or as a voluntary offering, the meat must be eaten on the same day the sacrifice is offered, but whatever is left over may be eaten on the second day. 17 Any meat left over until the third day must be completely burned up. 18 If any of the meat from the peace offering is eaten on the third day, the person who presented it will not be accepted by the LORD. You will receive no credit for offering it. By then the meat will be contaminated; if you eat it, you will be punished for your sin.

19 "Meat that touches anything ceremonially unclean may not be eaten; it must be completely burned up. The rest of the meat may be eaten, but only by people who are ceremonially clean. 20 If you are ceremonially unclean and you eat meat from a peace offering that was presented to the LORD, you will be cut off from the community. 21 If you touch anything that is unclean (whether it is human defilement or an unclean animal or any other unclean, detestable thing) and then eat meat from a peace offering presented to the LORD, you will be cut off from the community."

THE FORBIDDEN BLOOD AND FAT

22 Then the LORD said to Moses, 23 "Give the following instructions to the people of Israel. You must never eat fat, whether from cattle, sheep, or goats. 24 The fat of an animal found dead or torn to pieces by wild animals must never be eaten, though it may be used for any other purpose. 25 Anyone who eats fat from an animal presented as a special gift to the LORD will be cut off from the community. 26 No matter where you live, you must never consume the blood of any bird or animal. 27 Anyone who consumes blood will be cut off from the community."

A PORTION FOR THE PRIESTS

28 Then the LORD said to Moses, 29 "Give the following instructions to the people of Israel. When you present a peace offering to the LORD, bring part of it as a gift to the LORD. 30 Present it to the LORD with your own hands as a special gift to the LORD. Bring the fat of the animal, together with the breast, and lift up the breast as a special offering to the LORD. 31 Then the priest will burn the fat on the altar, but the breast will belong to Aaron and his descendants. 32 Give the right thigh of your peace offering to the priest as a gift. 33 The right thigh must always be given to the priest who offers the blood and the fat of the peace offering. 34 For I have reserved the breast of the special offering and the right thigh of the sacred offering for the priests. It is the permanent right of Aaron and his descendants to share in the peace offerings brought by the people of Israel. 35 This is their rightful share. The special gifts presented to the LORD have been reserved for Aaron and his descendants from the time they were set apart to serve the LORD as priests. 36 On the day they were anointed, the LORD commanded the Israelites to give these portions to the priests as their permanent share from generation to generation."

37 These are the instructions for the burnt offering, the grain offering, the sin offering, and the guilt offering, as well as the ordination offering and the peace offering. 38 The LORD gave these instructions to Moses on Mount Sinai when he commanded the Israelites to present their offerings to the LORD in the wilderness of Sinai.

ORDINATION OF THE PRIESTS

8 Then the LORD said to Moses, 2 "Bring Aaron and his sons, along with their sacred garments, the anointing oil, the bull for the sin offering, the two rams, and the basket of bread made without yeast, 3 and call the entire community of Israel together at the entrance of the Tabernacle.*"

4 So Moses followed the LORD's instructions, and the whole community assembled at the Tabernacle entrance. 5 Moses announced to them, "This is what the LORD has commanded us to do!" 6 Then he presented Aaron and his sons and washed them with water. 7 He put the official tunic on Aaron and tied the sash around his waist. He dressed him in the robe, placed the ephod on him, and attached the ephod securely with its decorative sash. 8 Then Moses placed the chestpiece on Aaron and put the Urim and the Thummim inside it. 9 He placed the turban on Aaron's head and attached the gold medallion—the badge of holiness—to the front of the turban, just as the LORD had commanded him.

10 Then Moses took the anointing oil and anointed the Tabernacle and everything in it, making them holy. 11 He sprinkled the oil on the altar seven times, anointing it and all its utensils, as well as the washbasin and its stand, making them holy. 12 Then he poured some of the anointing oil on Aaron's head, anointing him and making him holy for his work. 13 Next Moses presented Aaron's sons. He clothed them in their tunics, tied their sashes around them, and put their special head coverings on them, just as the LORD had commanded him.

14 Then Moses presented the bull for the sin offering. Aaron and his sons laid their hands on the bull's head, 15 and Moses slaughtered it. Moses took some

8:3 Hebrew *Tent of Meeting;* also in 8:4, 31, 33, 35. **8:15** Or *by making atonement for it;* or *that offerings for purification might be made on it.*

7:15-18 none . . . may be saved. The meat became holy because it was offered on the altar. Therefore, no remains could be left, lest they be defiled.
7:16 a vow or a voluntary offering. This peace offering was to thank God for help in some difficult situation.
7:20-21 cut off from the community. This was more similar to execution than excommunication. The holiness of God was at stake.
7:30-34 lift up. The breast and thigh of the sacrificial animal were lifted up and waved back and forth before being offered to the priests. This was referred to as a wave offering and a heave offering.
8:2 anointing oil. Olive oil was used for appointing people to special offices.
8:6 washed them. Moses probably washed the priests at the bronze laver that stood at the entrance of the tent to prepare them for service as mediators between God and people.
8:7 dressed him. With pomp and ceremony, Moses and his brother Aaron were organizing the worship of God, and Aaron was being vested with leadership.
8:8 Urim and Thummim. The Urim and Thummim, two onyx stones, functioned like dice, though determining God's will was no game. God gave the priests answers through the use of these stones.
8:11 seven. This was considered the perfect number in Bible times. Dashing blood seven times was a way of saying that sins were totally cleansed.
8:12 anointed . . . making him holy. Anointing a person with oil set him apart for some special task. All Christians have received the anointing of the Holy Spirit (1 John 2:20).
8:14 Aaron and his sons. Since Aaron and his sons were being consecrated, all of them were purified with a sin offering.

of the blood, and with his finger he put it on the four horns of the altar to purify it. He poured out the rest of the blood at the base of the altar. Through this process, he made the altar holy by purifying it.* 16 Then Moses took all the fat around the internal organs, the long lobe of the liver, and the two kidneys and the fat around them, and he burned it all on the altar. 17 He took the rest of the bull, including its hide, meat, and dung, and burned it on a fire outside the camp, just as the LORD had commanded him.

18 Then Moses presented the ram for the burnt offering. Aaron and his sons laid their hands on the ram's head, 19 and Moses slaughtered it. Then Moses took the ram's blood and splattered it against all sides of the altar. 20 Then he cut the ram into pieces, and he burned the head, some of its pieces, and the fat on the altar. 21 After washing the internal organs and the legs with water, Moses burned the entire ram on the altar as a burnt offering. It was a pleasing aroma, a special gift presented to the LORD, just as the LORD had commanded him.

22 Then Moses presented the other ram, which was the ram of ordination. Aaron and his sons laid their hands on the ram's head, 23 and Moses slaughtered it. Then Moses took some of its blood and applied it to the lobe of Aaron's right ear, the thumb of his right hand, and the big toe of his right foot. 24 Next Moses presented Aaron's sons and applied some of the blood to the lobes of their right ears, the thumbs of their right hands, and the big toes of their right feet. He then splattered the rest of the blood against all sides of the altar.

25 Next Moses took the fat, including the fat of the broad tail, the fat around the internal organs, the long lobe of the liver, and the two kidneys and the fat around them, along with the right thigh. 26 On top of these he placed a thin cake of bread made without yeast, a cake of bread mixed with olive oil, and a wafer spread with olive oil. All these were taken from the basket of bread made without yeast that was placed in the LORD's presence. 27 He put all these in the hands of Aaron and his sons, and he lifted these gifts as a special offering to the LORD. 28 Moses then took all the offerings back from them and burned them on the altar on top of the burnt offering. This was the ordination offering. It was a pleasing aroma, a special gift presented to the LORD. 29 Then Moses took the breast and lifted it up as a special offering to the LORD. This was Moses' portion of the ram of ordination, just as the LORD had commanded him.

30 Next Moses took some of the anointing oil and some of the blood that was on the altar, and he sprinkled them on Aaron and his garments and on his sons and their garments. In this way, he made Aaron and his sons and their garments holy.

31 Then Moses said to Aaron and his sons, "Boil the remaining meat of the offerings at the Tabernacle entrance, and eat it there, along with the bread that is in the basket of offerings for the ordination, just as I commanded when I said, 'Aaron and his sons will eat it.' 32 Any meat or bread that is left over must then be burned up. 33 You must not leave the Tabernacle entrance for seven days, for that is when the ordination ceremony will be completed. 34 Everything we have done today was commanded by the LORD in order to purify you, making you right with him.* 35 Now stay at the entrance of the Tabernacle day and night for seven days, and do everything the LORD requires. If you fail to do this, you will die, for this is what the LORD has commanded." 36 So Aaron and his sons did everything the LORD had commanded through Moses.

THE PRIESTS BEGIN THEIR WORK

9 After the ordination ceremony, on the eighth day, Moses called together Aaron and his sons and the elders of Israel. 2 He said to Aaron, "Take a young bull for a sin offering and a ram for a burnt offering, both without defects, and present them to the LORD. 3 Then tell the Israelites, 'Take a male goat for a sin offering, and take a calf and a lamb, both a year old and without defects, for a burnt offering. 4 Also take a bull* and a ram for a peace offering and flour moistened with olive oil for a grain offering. Present all these offerings to the LORD because the LORD will appear to you today.'"

5 So the people presented all these things at the entrance of the Tabernacle,* just as Moses had commanded. Then the whole community came forward and stood before the LORD. 6 And Moses said, "This is what the LORD has commanded you to do so that the glory of the LORD may appear to you."

7 Then Moses said to Aaron, "Come to the altar and sacrifice your sin offering and your burnt offering to purify yourself and the people. Then present the offerings of the people to purify them, making them right with the LORD,* just as he has commanded."

8 So Aaron went to the altar and slaughtered the calf as a sin offering for himself. 9 His sons brought him the blood, and he dipped his finger in it and put it on the horns of the altar. He poured out the rest of the blood at the base of the altar. 10 Then he burned on the altar the fat, the kidneys, and the long lobe of the liver from the sin offering, just as the LORD had commanded Moses. 11 The meat and the hide, however, he burned outside the camp.

12 Next Aaron slaughtered the animal for the burnt offering. His sons brought him the blood, and he splattered it against all sides of the altar. 13 Then they handed him each piece of the burnt offering, including the head, and he burned them on the altar. 14 Then he washed the internal organs and the legs and burned them on the altar along with the rest of the burnt offering.

15 Next Aaron presented the offerings of the people. He slaughtered the people's goat and presented it as an offering for their sin, just as he had first done with the offering for his own sin. 16 Then he presented the burnt offering and sacrificed it in the prescribed way. 17 He also presented the grain offering, burning a handful of the flour mixture on the altar, in addition to the regular burnt offering for the morning.

8:34 Or *to make atonement for you.* **9:4** Or *cow;* also in 9:18, 19. **9:5** Hebrew *Tent of Meeting;* also in 9:23. **9:7** Or *to make atonement for them.*

9:2 Present . . . to the LORD. The first official act of the high priest was to admit his own sinfulness.

9:4 the LORD will appear. Moses' instructions—first a sin offering (repentance), then a burnt offering (dedication), and then a peace offering (open hand of fellowship)—prepared priests for God's appearance.

18 Then Aaron slaughtered the bull and the ram for the people's peace offering. His sons brought him the blood, and he splattered it against all sides of the altar. 19 Then he took the fat of the bull and the ram—the fat of the broad tail and from around the internal organs—along with the kidneys and the long lobes of the livers. 20 He placed these fat portions on top of the breasts of these animals and burned them on the altar. 21 Aaron then lifted up the breasts and right thighs as a special offering to the LORD, just as Moses had commanded.

22 After that, Aaron raised his hands toward the people and blessed them. Then, after presenting the sin offering, the burnt offering, and the peace offering, he stepped down from the altar. 23 Then Moses and Aaron went into the Tabernacle, and when they came back out, they blessed the people again, and the glory of the LORD appeared to the whole community. 24 Fire blazed forth from the LORD's presence and consumed the burnt offering and the fat on the altar. When the people saw this, they shouted with joy and fell face down on the ground.

THE SIN OF NADAB AND ABIHU

10 Aaron's sons Nadab and Abihu put coals of fire in their incense burners and sprinkled incense over them. In this way, they disobeyed the LORD by burning before him the wrong kind of fire, different than he had commanded. 2 So fire blazed forth from the LORD's presence and burned them up, and they died there before the LORD.

3 Then Moses said to Aaron, "This is what the LORD meant when he said,

'I will display my holiness
through those who come near me.
I will display my glory
before all the people.'"

And Aaron was silent.

4 Then Moses called for Mishael and Elzaphan, Aaron's cousins, the sons of Aaron's uncle Uzziel. He said to them, "Come forward and carry away the bodies of your relatives from in front of the sanctuary to a place outside the camp." 5 So they came forward and picked them up by their garments and carried them out of the camp, just as Moses had commanded.

6 Then Moses said to Aaron and his sons Eleazar and Ithamar, "Do not show grief by leaving your hair uncombed* or by tearing your clothes. If you do, you will die, and the LORD's anger will strike the whole community of Israel. However, the rest of the Israelites, your relatives, may mourn because of the LORD's fiery destruction of Nadab and Abihu. 7 But you must not leave the entrance of the Tabernacle* or you will die, for you have been anointed with the LORD's anointing oil." So they did as Moses commanded.

INSTRUCTIONS FOR PRIESTLY CONDUCT

8 Then the LORD said to Aaron, 9 "You and your descendants must never drink wine or any other alcoholic drink before going into the Tabernacle. If you do, you will die. This is a permanent law for you, and it must be observed from generation to generation. 10 You must distinguish between what is sacred and what is common, between what is ceremonially unclean and what is clean. 11 And you must teach the Israelites all the decrees that the LORD has given them through Moses."

12 Then Moses said to Aaron and his remaining sons, Eleazar and Ithamar, "Take what is left of the grain offering after a portion has been presented as a special gift to the LORD, and eat it beside the altar. Make sure it contains no yeast, for it is most holy. 13 You must eat it in a sacred place, for it has been given to you and your descendants as your portion of the special gifts presented to the LORD. These are the commands I have been given. 14 But the breast and thigh that were lifted up as a special offering may be eaten in any place that is ceremonially clean. These parts have been given to you and your descendants as your portion of the peace offerings presented by the people of Israel. 15 You must lift up the thigh and breast as a special offering to the LORD, along with the fat of the special gifts. These parts will belong to you and your descendants as your permanent right, just as the LORD has commanded."

16 Moses then asked them what had happened to the goat of the sin offering. When he discovered it had been burned up, he became very angry with Eleazar and Ithamar, Aaron's remaining sons. 17 "Why didn't you eat the sin offering in the sacred area?" he demanded. "It is a holy offering! The LORD has given it to you to remove the guilt of the community and to purify the people, making them right with the LORD.* 18 Since the animal's blood was not brought into the Holy Place, you should have eaten the meat in the sacred area as I ordered you."

19 Then Aaron answered Moses, "Today my sons presented both their sin offering and their burnt offering to the LORD. And yet this tragedy has happened to me. If I had eaten the people's sin offering on such a tragic day as this, would the LORD have been pleased?" 20 And when Moses heard this, he was satisfied.

CEREMONIALLY CLEAN AND UNCLEAN ANIMALS

11 Then the LORD said to Moses and Aaron, 2 "Give the following instructions to the people of Israel.

"Of all the land animals, these are the ones you may use for food. 3 You may eat any animal that has completely split hooves and chews the cud. 4 You may not, however, eat the following animals* that have split hooves or that chew the cud, but not both. The camel chews the cud but does not have split hooves, so it is ceremonially unclean for you. 5 The hyrax* chews the cud but does not have split hooves, so it is unclean. 6 The hare chews the cud but does not have

10:6 Or *by uncovering your heads.* **10:7** Hebrew *Tent of Meeting;* also in 10:9. **10:17** Or *to make atonement for the people before the* Lord. **11:4** The identification of some of the animals, birds, and insects in this chapter is uncertain. **11:5** Or *coney,* or *rock badger.*

9:21 lifted up. The part of the animal that the priest was to eat was first presented to the Lord, probably by waving it in the air.

9:23-24 glory of the LORD. God's glory generally appears as a fire. God lit the altar fire with His own glorious appearance.

9:24 fell face down. These people felt joy as well as fear that God appeared to them, and they expressed this by falling to the ground

10:1 wrong kind. Nadab and Abihu were killed because they offered incense contrary to God's command (Lev. 16:13).

10:10 unclean. God created a symbolic system by which certain meats were unclean, as well as skin disease, menstruation, genital discharges, and corpses.

10:19-20 he was satisfied. Moses was content with Aaron's explanation; it did not seem to be a matter of open rebellion.

split hooves, so it is unclean. [7] The pig has evenly split hooves but does not chew the cud, so it is unclean. [8] You may not eat the meat of these animals or even touch their carcasses. They are ceremonially unclean for you.

[9] "Of all the marine animals, these are ones you may use for food. You may eat anything from the water if it has both fins and scales, whether taken from salt water or from streams. [10] But you must never eat animals from the sea or from rivers that do not have both fins and scales. They are detestable to you. This applies both to little creatures that live in shallow water and to all creatures that live in deep water. [11] They will always be detestable to you. You must never eat their meat or even touch their dead bodies. [12] Any marine animal that does not have both fins and scales is detestable to you.

[13] "These are the birds that are detestable to you. You must never eat them: the griffon vulture, the bearded vulture, the black vulture, [14] the kite, falcons of all kinds, [15] ravens of all kinds, [16] the eagle owl, the short-eared owl, the seagull, hawks of all kinds, [17] the little owl, the cormorant, the great owl, [18] the barn owl, the desert owl, the Egyptian vulture, [19] the stork, herons of all kinds, the hoopoe, and the bat.

[20] "You must not eat winged insects that walk along the ground; they are detestable to you. [21] You may, however, eat winged insects that walk along the ground and have jointed legs so they can jump. [22] The insects you are permitted to eat include all kinds of locusts, bald locusts, crickets, and grasshoppers. [23] All other winged insects that walk along the ground are detestable to you.

[24] "The following creatures will make you ceremonially unclean. If any of you touch their carcasses, you will be defiled until evening. [25] If you pick up their carcasses, you must wash your clothes, and you will remain defiled until evening.

[26] "Any animal that has split hooves that are not evenly divided or that does not chew the cud is unclean for you. If you touch the carcass of such an animal, you will be defiled. [27] Of the animals that walk on all fours, those that have paws are unclean. If you touch the carcass of such an animal, you will be defiled until evening. [28] If you pick up its carcass, you must wash your clothes, and you will remain defiled until evening. These animals are unclean for you.

[29] "Of the small animals that scurry along the ground, these are unclean for you: the mole rat, the rat, large lizards of all kinds, [30] the gecko, the monitor lizard, the common lizard, the sand lizard, and the chameleon. [31] All these small animals are unclean for you. If any of you touch the dead body of such an animal, you will be defiled until evening. [32] If such an animal dies and falls on something, that object will be unclean. This is true whether the object is made of wood, cloth, leather, or burlap. Whatever its use, you must dip it in water, and it will remain defiled until evening. After that, it will be ceremonially clean and may be used again.

[33] "If such an animal falls into a clay pot, everything in the pot will be defiled, and the pot must be smashed. [34] If the water from such a container spills on any food, the food will be defiled. And any beverage in such a container will be defiled. [35] Any object on which the carcass of such an animal falls will be defiled. If it is an oven or hearth, it must be destroyed, for it is defiled, and you must treat it accordingly.

[36] "However, if the carcass of such an animal falls into a spring or a cistern, the water will still be clean. But anyone who touches the carcass will be defiled. [37] If the carcass falls on seed grain to be planted in the field, the seed will still be considered clean. [38] But if the seed is wet when the carcass falls on it, the seed will be defiled.

[39] "If an animal you are permitted to eat dies and you touch its carcass, you will be defiled until evening. [40] If you eat any of its meat or carry away its carcass, you must wash your clothes, and you will remain defiled until evening.

[41] "All small animals that scurry along the ground are detestable, and you must never eat them. [42] This includes all animals that slither along on their bellies, as well as those with four legs and those with many feet. All such animals that scurry along the ground are detestable, and you must never eat them. [43] Do not defile yourselves by touching them. You must not make yourselves ceremonially unclean because of them. [44] For I am the LORD your God. You must consecrate yourselves and be holy, because I am holy. So do not defile yourselves with any of these small animals that scurry along the ground. [45] For I, the LORD, am the one who brought you up from the land of Egypt, that I might be your God. Therefore, you must be holy because I am holy.

[46] "These are the instructions regarding land animals, birds, marine creatures, and animals that scurry along the ground. [47] By these instructions you will know what is unclean and clean, and which animals may be eaten and which may not be eaten."

PURIFICATION AFTER CHILDBIRTH

12 The LORD said to Moses, [2] "Give the following instructions to the people of Israel. If a woman becomes pregnant and gives birth to a son, she will be ceremonially unclean for seven days, just as she is unclean during her menstrual period. [3] On the eighth day the boy's foreskin must be circumcised. [4] After waiting thirty-three days, she will be purified from the bleeding of childbirth. During this time of

11:2-3 split hooves . . . chews the cud. The Israelites could eat beef because cows chewed the cud and had split hooves. Camels were out because they chewed their cud but didn't have split hooves. Horses were out on both counts. Pigs were the only animals that had the right hooves but didn't chew the cud.

11:6 hare. Rabbits do not actually chew the cud, but they appear to, because of repetitive chewing movements.

11:20-21 jointed legs so they can jump. Locusts and grasshoppers, not normally in the four food groups, were the only flying insects considered suitable for eating.

11:36 cistern. When something was discovered to be unclean, there were only two options: destroy it or purify it. Here the practical nature of the law takes over. The practical reality was that people could not destroy or purify their cisterns (holding tanks for water) because cisterns were needed for survival.

11:44 be holy. Leviticus is all about God's holiness and the holiness. He desires from His people. Imagine being a people whose dietary and social customs issued from the understanding that God and His people were to be special, set apart to His service and spiritually clean.

11:45 up from the land of Egypt. The history of the Hebrews was always with them. The fact that God miraculously delivered them from Egypt was the starting point for every national policy after that. At a point in time they had been chosen and delivered. Now each day they had to decide how to live.

12:2-5 The act of childbirth did not cause a mother to be unclean. This uncleanness was a result of the blood and other body fluids that were secreted during the birth process.

purification, she must not touch anything that is set
apart as holy. And she must not enter the sanctuary
until her time of purification is over. 5 If a woman
gives birth to a daughter, she will be ceremonially
unclean for two weeks, just as she is unclean during
her menstrual period. After waiting sixty-six days,
she will be purified from the bleeding of childbirth.
6 "When the time of purification is completed for
either a son or a daughter, the woman must bring a
one-year-old lamb for a burnt offering and a young
pigeon or turtledove for a purification offering. She
must bring her offerings to the priest at the entrance
of the Tabernacle.* 7 The priest will then present them
to the LORD to purify her.* Then she will be ceremo-
nially clean again after her bleeding at childbirth.
These are the instructions for a woman after the birth
of a son or a daughter.
8 "If a woman cannot afford to bring a lamb, she
must bring two turtledoves or two young pigeons.
One will be for the burnt offering and the other for the
purification offering. The priest will sacrifice them to
purify her, and she will be ceremonially clean."

SERIOUS SKIN DISEASES

13 The LORD said to Moses and Aaron, 2 "If anyone
has a swelling or a rash or discolored skin that
might develop into a serious skin disease,* that per-
son must be brought to Aaron the priest or to one of
his sons.* 3 The priest will examine the affected area
of the skin. If the hair in the affected area has turned
white and the problem appears to be more than skin-
deep, it is a serious skin disease, and the priest who
examines it must pronounce the person ceremonially
unclean.
4 "But if the affected area of the skin is only a white
discoloration and does not appear to be more than
skin-deep, and if the hair on the spot has not turned
white, the priest will quarantine the person for seven
days. 5 On the seventh day the priest will make an-
other examination. If he finds the affected area has
not changed and the problem has not spread on the
skin, the priest will quarantine the person for seven
more days. 6 On the seventh day the priest will make
another examination. If he finds the affected area has
faded and has not spread, the priest will pronounce
the person ceremonially clean. It was only a rash.
The person's clothing must be washed, and the per-
son will be ceremonially clean. 7 But if the rash con-
tinues to spread after the person has been examined
by the priest and has been pronounced clean, the
infected person must return to be examined again.
8 If the priest finds that the rash has spread, he must
pronounce the person ceremonially unclean, for it is
indeed a skin disease.
9 "Anyone who develops a serious skin disease must
go to the priest for an examination. 10 If the priest
finds a white swelling on the skin, and some hair on
the spot has turned white, and there is an open sore
in the affected area, 11 it is a chronic skin disease, and
the priest must pronounce the person ceremonially
unclean. In such cases the person need not be quar-
antined, for it is obvious that the skin is defiled by the
disease.
12 "Now suppose the disease has spread all over the
person's skin, covering the body from head to foot.
13 When the priest examines the infected person and
finds that the disease covers the entire body, he will
pronounce the person ceremonially clean. Since the
skin has turned completely white, the person is clean.
14 But if any open sores appear, the infected person will
be pronounced ceremonially unclean. 15 The priest
must make this pronouncement as soon as he sees an
open sore, since open sores indicate the presence of
a skin disease. 16 However, if the open sores heal and
turn white like the rest of the skin, the person must
return to the priest 17 for another examination. If the
affected areas have indeed turned white, the priest
will then pronounce the person ceremonially clean
by declaring, 'You are clean!'
18 "If anyone has a boil on the skin that has started
to heal, 19 but a white swelling or a reddish white spot
develops in its place, that person must go to the priest
to be examined. 20 If the priest examines it and finds
it to be more than skin-deep, and if the hair in the
affected area has turned white, the priest must pro-
nounce the person ceremonially unclean. The boil has
become a serious skin disease. 21 But if the priest finds
no white hair on the affected area and the problem
appears to be no more than skin-deep and has faded,
the priest must quarantine the person for seven days.
22 If during that time the affected area spreads on the
skin, the priest must pronounce the person ceremo-
nially unclean, because it is a serious disease. 23 But
if the area grows no larger and does not spread, it is
merely the scar from the boil, and the priest will pro-
nounce the person ceremonially clean.
24 "If anyone has suffered a burn on the skin and the
burned area changes color, becoming either reddish
white or shiny white, 25 the priest must examine it. If
he finds that the hair in the affected area has turned
white and the problem appears to be more than skin-
deep, a skin disease has broken out in the burn. The
priest must then pronounce the person ceremonially
unclean, for it is clearly a serious skin disease. 26 But
if the priest finds no white hair on the affected area
and the problem appears to be no more than skin-
deep and has faded, the priest must quarantine the
infected person for seven days. 27 On the seventh day
the priest must examine the person again. If the af-
fected area has spread on the skin, the priest must
pronounce that person ceremonially unclean, for it
is clearly a serious skin disease. 28 But if the affected
area has not changed or spread on the skin and has
faded, it is simply a swelling from the burn. The priest
will then pronounce the person ceremonially clean,
for it is only the scar from the burn.
29 "If anyone, either a man or woman, has a sore
on the head or chin, 30 the priest must examine it. If

12:6 Hebrew *Tent of Meeting.* **12:7** Or *to make atonement for her;* also in 12:8. **13:2a** Traditionally rendered *leprosy.* The Hebrew word used throughout this passage is used to describe various skin diseases. **13:2b** Or *one of his descendants.*

13:1-46 The skin disease referred to here is not known, but it is not the same as leprosy (Hansen's disease), which is a condition of the nerve endings. Biblical skin disease involves white, hard patches of skin. This disease made a person look like a corpse, and all uncleanness related in some way to death. This passage is almost pharmaceutical in its description of symptoms and treatments.

13:2 skin. Aaron would decide whether a person's ailment was dangerous to others. The issue was not whether a person was contagious with a disease, but the ceremonial uncleanness he could pass on to others.

he finds it is more than skin-deep and has fine yellow hair on it, the priest must pronounce the person ceremonially unclean. It is a scabby sore of the head or chin. 31 If the priest examines the scabby sore and finds that it is only skin-deep but there is no black hair on it, he must quarantine the person for seven days. 32 On the seventh day the priest must examine the sore again. If he finds that the scabby sore has not spread, and there is no yellow hair on it, and it appears to be only skin-deep, 33 the person must shave off all hair except the hair on the affected area. Then the priest must quarantine the person for another seven days. 34 On the seventh day he will examine the sore again. If it has not spread and appears to be no more than skin-deep, the priest will pronounce the person ceremonially clean. The person's clothing must be washed, and the person will be ceremonially clean. 35 But if the scabby sore begins to spread after the person is pronounced clean, 36 the priest must do another examination. If he finds that the sore has spread, the priest does not need to look for yellow hair. The infected person is ceremonially unclean. 37 But if the color of the scabby sore does not change and black hair has grown on it, it has healed. The priest will then pronounce the person ceremonially clean.

38 "If anyone, either a man or woman, has shiny white patches on the skin, 39 the priest must examine the affected area. If he finds that the shiny patches are only pale white, this is a harmless skin rash, and the person is ceremonially clean.

40 "If a man loses his hair and his head becomes bald, he is still ceremonially clean. 41 And if he loses hair on his forehead, he simply has a bald forehead; he is still clean. 42 However, if a reddish white sore appears on the bald area on top of his head or on his forehead, this is a skin disease. 43 The priest must examine him, and if he finds swelling around the reddish white sore anywhere on the man's head and it looks like a skin disease, 44 the man is indeed infected with a skin disease and is unclean. The priest must pronounce him ceremonially unclean because of the sore on his head.

45 "Those who suffer from a serious skin disease must tear their clothing and leave their hair uncombed.* They must cover their mouth and call out, 'Unclean! Unclean!' 46 As long as the serious disease lasts, they will be ceremonially unclean. They must live in isolation in their place outside the camp.

TREATMENT OF CONTAMINATED CLOTHING

47 "Now suppose mildew* contaminates some woolen or linen clothing, 48 woolen or linen fabric, the hide of an animal, or anything made of leather. 49 If the contaminated area in the clothing, the animal hide, the fabric, or the leather article has turned greenish or reddish, it is contaminated with mildew and must be shown to the priest. 50 After examining the affected spot, the priest will put the article in quarantine for seven days. 51 On the seventh day the priest must inspect it again. If the contaminated area has spread, the clothing or fabric or leather is clearly contaminated by a serious mildew and is ceremonially unclean. 52 The priest must burn the item—the clothing, the woolen or linen fabric, or piece of leather—for it has been contaminated by a serious mildew. It must be completely destroyed by fire.

53 "But if the priest examines it and finds that the contaminated area has not spread in the clothing, the fabric, or the leather, 54 the priest will order the object to be washed and then quarantined for seven more days. 55 Then the priest must examine the object again. If he finds that the contaminated area has not changed color after being washed, even if it did not spread, the object is defiled. It must be completely burned up, whether the contaminated spot* is on the inside or outside. 56 But if the priest examines it and finds that the contaminated area has faded after being washed, he must cut the spot from the clothing, the fabric, or the leather. 57 If the spot later reappears on the clothing, the fabric, or the leather article, the mildew is clearly spreading, and the contaminated object must be burned up. 58 But if the spot disappears from the clothing, the fabric, or the leather article after it has been washed, it must be washed again; then it will be ceremonially clean.

59 "These are the instructions for dealing with mildew that contaminates woolen or linen clothing or fabric or anything made of leather. This is how the priest will determine whether these items are ceremonially clean or unclean."

CLEANSING FROM SKIN DISEASES

14 And the LORD said to Moses, 2 "The following instructions are for those seeking ceremonial purification from a skin disease.* Those who have been healed must be brought to the priest, 3 who will examine them at a place outside the camp. If the priest finds that someone has been healed of a serious skin disease, 4 he will perform a purification ceremony, using two live birds that are ceremonially clean, a stick of cedar,* some scarlet yarn, and a hyssop branch. 5 The priest will order that one bird be slaughtered over a clay pot filled with fresh water. 6 He will take the live bird, the cedar stick, the scarlet yarn, and the hyssop branch, and dip them into the blood of the bird that was slaughtered over the fresh water. 7 The priest will then sprinkle the blood of the dead bird seven times on the person being purified of the skin

13:45 Or *and uncover their heads.* **13:47** Traditionally rendered *leprosy.* The Hebrew term used throughout this passage is the same term used for the various skin diseases described in 13:1-46. **13:55** The meaning of the Hebrew is uncertain. **14:2** Traditionally rendered *leprosy;* see note on 13:2a. **14:4** Or *juniper;* also in 14:6, 49, 51.

13:45-46 unclean. It was up to the infected person to guard the ceremonial purity of others by dressing appropriately and giving a verbal warning about his uncleanness

13:47 mildew. The mildew mentioned here has some similarities to the mildew of today. It was a pale fungus that grew on damp objects. Priests decided how to clean the item of mildew or whether to destroy it. Mildew was unclean because it grew on dead things.

14:4 he will perform . . . hyssop. While the use of cedar stick, scarlet yarn, and hyssop branch is not explained here, these items are associated with cleansing in other passages in the Bible (Num. 19:6; Ps. 51:7). Hyssop was an herb used for medicine and as a seasoning in food.

14:5 one bird be slaughtered. The bird might have symbolized the death that the person had escaped when he was sick.

14:6 live bird. This bird probably symbolized the new life offered in cleansing from uncleanness. The person who had looked like a corpse because of his serious illness now looks alive.

14:7, 16, 51 seven. Throughout the Bible, seven is considered the number of completion and the perfect number.

14:7 release the live bird. This is a beautiful image of recovery and new life. The recovered person, like a bird, was set free to live among his own people.

disease. When the priest has purified the person, he will release the live bird in the open field to fly away.

8 "The persons being purified must then wash their clothes, shave off all their hair, and bathe themselves in water. Then they will be ceremonially clean and may return to the camp. However, they must remain outside their tents for seven days. 9 On the seventh day they must again shave all the hair from their heads, including the hair of the beard and eyebrows. They must also wash their clothes and bathe themselves in water. Then they will be ceremonially clean.

10 "On the eighth day each person being purified must bring two male lambs and a one-year-old female lamb, all with no defects, along with a grain offering of six quarts* of choice flour moistened with olive oil, and a cup* of olive oil. 11 Then the officiating priest will present that person for purification, along with the offerings, before the LORD at the entrance of the Tabernacle.* 12 The priest will take one of the male lambs and the olive oil and present them as a guilt offering, lifting them up as a special offering before the LORD. 13 He will then slaughter the male lamb in the sacred area where sin offerings and burnt offerings are slaughtered. As with the sin offering, the guilt offering belongs to the priest. It is a most holy offering. 14 The priest will then take some of the blood of the guilt offering and apply it to the lobe of the right ear, the thumb of the right hand, and the big toe of the right foot of the person being purified.

15 "Then the priest will pour some of the olive oil into the palm of his own left hand. 16 He will dip his right finger into the oil in his palm and sprinkle some of it with his finger seven times before the LORD. 17 The priest will then apply some of the oil in his palm over the blood from the guilt offering that is on the lobe of the right ear, the thumb of the right hand, and the big toe of the right foot of the person being purified. 18 The priest will apply the oil remaining in his hand to the head of the person being purified. Through this process, the priest will purify* the person before the LORD.

19 "Then the priest must present the sin offering to purify the person who was cured of the skin disease. After that, the priest will slaughter the burnt offering 20 and offer it on the altar along with the grain offering. Through this process, the priest will purify the person who was healed, and the person will be ceremonially clean.

21 "But anyone who is too poor and cannot afford these offerings may bring one male lamb for a guilt offering, to be lifted up as a special offering for purification. The person must also bring two quarts* of choice flour moistened with olive oil for the grain offering and a cup of olive oil. 22 The offering must also include two turtledoves or two young pigeons, whichever the person can afford. One of the pair must be used for the sin offering and the other for a burnt offering. 23 On the eighth day of the purification ceremony, the person being purified must bring the offerings to the priest in the LORD's presence at the entrance of the Tabernacle. 24 The priest will take the lamb for the guilt offering, along with the olive oil, and lift them up as a special offering to the LORD. 25 Then the priest will slaughter the lamb for the guilt offering. He will take some of its blood and apply it to the lobe of the right ear, the thumb of the right hand, and the big toe of the right foot of the person being purified.

26 "The priest will also pour some of the olive oil into the palm of his own left hand. 27 He will dip his right finger into the oil in his palm and sprinkle some of it seven times before the LORD. 28 The priest will then apply some of the oil in his palm over the blood from the guilt offering that is on the lobe of the right ear, the thumb of the right hand, and the big toe of the right foot of the person being purified. 29 The priest will apply the oil remaining in his hand to the head of the person being purified. Through this process, the priest will purify the person before the LORD.

30 "Then the priest will offer the two turtledoves or the two young pigeons, whichever the person can afford. 31 One of them is for a sin offering and the other for a burnt offering, to be presented along with the grain offering. Through this process, the priest will purify the person before the LORD. 32 These are the instructions for purification for those who have recovered from a serious skin disease but who cannot afford to bring the offerings normally required for the ceremony of purification."

TREATMENT OF CONTAMINATED HOUSES

33 Then the LORD said to Moses and Aaron, 34 "When you arrive in Canaan, the land I am giving you as your own possession, I may contaminate some of the houses in your land with mildew.* 35 The owner of such a house must then go to the priest and say, 'It appears that my house has some kind of mildew.' 36 Before the priest goes in to inspect the house, he must have the house emptied so nothing inside will be pronounced ceremonially unclean. 37 Then the priest will go in and examine the mildew on the walls. If he finds greenish or reddish streaks and the contamination appears to go deeper than the wall's surface, 38 the priest will step outside the door and put the house in quarantine for seven days. 39 On the seventh day the priest must return for another inspection. If he finds that the mildew on the walls of the house has spread, 40 the priest must order that the stones from those areas be removed. The contaminated material will then be taken outside the town to an area designated as ceremonially unclean. 41 Next the inside walls of the entire house must be scraped thoroughly and the scrapings dumped in the unclean place outside the town. 42 Other stones will be brought in to replace the ones that were removed, and the walls will be replastered.

43 "But if the mildew reappears after all the stones have been replaced and the house has been scraped and replastered, 44 the priest must return and inspect the house again. If he finds that the mildew has spread, the walls are clearly contaminated with a serious mildew, and the house is defiled. 45 It must be torn down, and all its stones, timbers, and plaster

14:10a Hebrew *3/10 of an ephah* [6.6 liters]. **14:10b** Hebrew *1 log* [0.3 liters]; also in 14:21. **14:11** Hebrew *Tent of Meeting;* also in 14:23. **14:18** Or *will make atonement for;* similarly in 14:19, 20, 21, 29, 31, 53. **14:21** Hebrew *1/10 of an ephah* [2.2 liters]. **14:34** Traditionally rendered *leprosy;* see note on 13:47.

14:14-18 These rites bear a resemblance to those Moses used in consecrating Aaron and his sons to the priesthood (8:23).

14:33-53 The ceremonial cleansing from mildew was similar to cleansing from skin diseases. The ritual focused on the atonement of a person or the place where he lived. The priest would examine the dwelling to determine if it was clean or unclean.

14:45 torn down. If the mildew continued to grow, the structure must be destroyed. In a society without disinfectants, there was no other choice.

must be carried out of town to the place designated as ceremonially unclean. [46] Those who enter the house during the period of quarantine will be ceremonially unclean until evening, [47] and all who sleep or eat in the house must wash their clothing.

[48] "But if the priest returns for his inspection and finds that the mildew has not reappeared in the house after the fresh plastering, he will pronounce it clean because the mildew is clearly gone. [49] To purify the house the priest must take two birds, a stick of cedar, some scarlet yarn, and a hyssop branch. [50] He will slaughter one of the birds over a clay pot filled with fresh water. [51] He will take the cedar stick, the hyssop branch, the scarlet yarn, and the live bird, and dip them into the blood of the slaughtered bird and into the fresh water. Then he will sprinkle the house seven times. [52] When the priest has purified the house in exactly this way, [53] he will release the live bird in the open fields outside the town. Through this process, the priest will purify the house, and it will be ceremonially clean.

[54] "These are the instructions for dealing with serious skin diseases,* including scabby sores; [55] and mildew,* whether on clothing or in a house; [56] and a swelling on the skin, a rash, or discolored skin. [57] This procedure will determine whether a person or object is ceremonially clean or unclean.

"These are the instructions regarding skin diseases and mildew."

BODILY DISCHARGES

15 The LORD said to Moses and Aaron, [2] "Give the following instructions to the people of Israel.

"Any man who has a bodily discharge is ceremonially unclean. [3] This defilement is caused by his discharge, whether the discharge continues or stops. In either case the man is unclean. [4] Any bed on which the man with the discharge lies and anything on which he sits will be ceremonially unclean. [5] So if you touch the man's bed, you must wash your clothes and bathe yourself in water, and you will remain unclean until evening. [6] If you sit where the man with the discharge has sat, you must wash your clothes and bathe yourself in water, and you will remain unclean until evening. [7] If you touch the man with the discharge, you must wash your clothes and bathe yourself in water, and you will remain unclean until evening. [8] If the man spits on you, you must wash your clothes and bathe yourself in water, and you will remain unclean until evening. [9] Any saddle blanket on which the man rides will be ceremonially unclean. [10] If you touch anything that was under the man, you will be unclean until evening. You must wash your clothes and bathe yourself in water, and you will remain unclean until evening. [11] If the man touches you without first rinsing his hands, you must wash your clothes and bathe yourself in water, and you will remain unclean until evening. [12] Any clay pot the man touches must be broken, and any wooden utensil he touches must be rinsed with water.

[13] "When the man with the discharge is healed, he must count off seven days for the period of purification. Then he must wash his clothes and bathe himself in fresh water, and he will be ceremonially clean. [14] On the eighth day he must get two turtledoves or two young pigeons and come before the LORD at the entrance of the Tabernacle* and give his offerings to the priest. [15] The priest will offer one bird for a sin offering and the other for a burnt offering. Through this process, the priest will purify* the man before the LORD for his discharge.

[16] "Whenever a man has an emission of semen, he must bathe his entire body in water, and he will remain ceremonially unclean until the next evening.* [17] Any clothing or leather with semen on it must be washed in water, and it will remain unclean until evening. [18] After a man and a woman have sexual intercourse, they must each bathe in water, and they will remain unclean until the next evening.

[19] "Whenever a woman has her menstrual period, she will be ceremonially unclean for seven days. Anyone who touches her during that time will be unclean until evening. [20] Anything on which the woman lies or sits during the time of her period will be unclean. [21] If any of you touch her bed, you must wash your clothes and bathe yourself in water, and you will remain unclean until evening. [22] If you touch any object she has sat on, you must wash your clothes and bathe yourself in water, and you will remain unclean until evening. [23] This includes her bed or any other object she has sat on; you will be unclean until evening if you touch it. [24] If a man has sexual intercourse with her and her blood touches him, her menstrual impurity will be transmitted to him. He will remain unclean for seven days, and any bed on which he lies will be unclean.

[25] "If a woman has a flow of blood for many days that is unrelated to her menstrual period, or if the blood continues beyond the normal period, she is ceremonially unclean. As during her menstrual period, the woman will be unclean as long as the discharge continues. [26] Any bed she lies on and any object she sits on during that time will be unclean, just as during her normal menstrual period. [27] If any of you touch these things, you will be ceremonially unclean. You must wash your clothes and bathe yourself in water, and you will remain unclean until evening.

[28] "When the woman's bleeding stops, she must count off seven days. Then she will be ceremonially clean. [29] On the eighth day she must bring two turtledoves or two young pigeons and present them to the priest at the entrance of the Tabernacle. [30] The priest will offer one for a sin offering and the other for a burnt offering. Through this process, the priest will purify her before the LORD for the ceremonial impurity caused by her bleeding.

[31] "This is how you will guard the people of Israel from ceremonial uncleanness. Otherwise they would die, for their impurity would defile my Tabernacle that stands among them. [32] These are the instruc-

14:54 Traditionally rendered *leprosy;* see note on 13:2a. **14:55** Traditionally rendered *leprosy;* see note on 13:47. **15:14** Hebrew *Tent of Meeting;* also in 15:29. **15:15** Or *will make atonement for;* also in 15:30. **15:16** Hebrew *until evening;* also in 15:18.

15:2 discharge. Some think this discharge was related to gonorrhea or some other sexually transmitted disease.

15:16 emission. An emission of semen, whether or not it was part of the sex act, was not necessarily the result of sin. Uncleanness is not identical with sin.

15:19 menstrual period. A woman was considered untouchable during her monthly menstrual period.

15:25 if the blood continues beyond the normal period. This commandment concerns blood flow beyond or at a different time than menstruation. It required more serious purification, including an offering at the sanctuary.

15:31 among them. The people's uncleanness, as well as their sins, polluted the tabernacle and required offerings to cleanse it. God graciously provided sacrifices as a way for God and man to have fellowship together.

tions for dealing with anyone who has a bodily discharge—a man who is unclean because of an emission of semen 33 or a woman during her menstrual period. It applies to any man or woman who has a bodily discharge, and to a man who has sexual intercourse with a woman who is ceremonially unclean."

THE DAY OF ATONEMENT

16 The LORD spoke to Moses after the death of Aaron's two sons, who died after they entered the LORD's presence and burned the wrong kind of fire before him. 2 The LORD said to Moses, "Warn your brother, Aaron, not to enter the Most Holy Place behind the inner curtain whenever he chooses; if he does, he will die. For the Ark's cover—the place of atonement—is there, and I myself am present in the cloud above the atonement cover.

3 "When Aaron enters the sanctuary area, he must follow these instructions fully. He must bring a young bull for a sin offering and a ram for a burnt offering. 4 He must put on his linen tunic and the linen undergarments worn next to his body. He must tie the linen sash around his waist and put the linen turban on his head. These are sacred garments, so he must bathe himself in water before he puts them on. 5 Aaron must take from the community of Israel two male goats for a sin offering and a ram for a burnt offering.

6 "Aaron will present his own bull as a sin offering to purify himself and his family, making them right with the LORD.* 7 Then he must take the two male goats and present them to the LORD at the entrance of the Tabernacle.* 8 He is to cast sacred lots to determine which goat will be reserved as an offering to the LORD and which will carry the sins of the people to the wilderness of Azazel. 9 Aaron will then present as a sin offering the goat chosen by lot for the LORD. 10 The other goat, the scapegoat chosen by lot to be sent away, will be kept alive, standing before the LORD. When it is sent away to Azazel in the wilderness, the people will be purified and made right with the LORD.*

11 "Aaron will present his own bull as a sin offering to purify himself and his family, making them right with the LORD. After he has slaughtered the bull as a sin offering, 12 he will fill an incense burner with burning coals from the altar that stands before the LORD. Then he will take two handfuls of fragrant powdered incense and will carry the burner and the incense behind the inner curtain. 13 There in the LORD's presence he will put the incense on the burning coals so that a cloud of incense will rise over the Ark's cover—the place of atonement—that rests on the Ark of the Covenant.* If he follows these instructions, he will not die. 14 Then he must take some of the blood of the bull, dip his finger in it, and sprinkle it on the east side of the atonement cover. He must sprinkle blood seven times with his finger in front of the atonement cover.

15 "Then Aaron must slaughter the first goat as a sin offering for the people and carry its blood behind the inner curtain. There he will sprinkle the goat's blood over the atonement cover and in front of it, just as he did with the bull's blood. 16 Through this process, he will purify* the Most Holy Place, and he will do the same for the entire Tabernacle, because of the defiling sin and rebellion of the Israelites. 17 No one else is allowed inside the Tabernacle when Aaron enters it for the purification ceremony in the Most Holy Place. No one may enter until he comes out again after purifying himself, his family, and all the congregation of Israel, making them right with the LORD.

18 "Then Aaron will come out to purify the altar that stands before the LORD. He will do this by taking some of the blood from the bull and the goat and putting it on each of the horns of the altar. 19 Then he must sprinkle the blood with his finger seven times over the altar. In this way, he will cleanse it from Israel's defilement and make it holy.

20 "When Aaron has finished purifying the Most Holy Place and the Tabernacle and the altar, he must present the live goat. 21 He will lay both of his hands on the goat's head and confess over it all the wickedness, rebellion, and sins of the people of Israel. In this way, he will transfer the people's sins to the head of the goat. Then a man specially chosen for the task will drive the goat into the wilderness. 22 As the goat goes into the wilderness, it will carry all the people's sins upon itself into a desolate land.

23 "When Aaron goes back into the Tabernacle, he must take off the linen garments he was wearing when he entered the Most Holy Place, and he must leave the garments there. 24 Then he must bathe himself with water in a sacred place, put on his regular garments, and go out to sacrifice a burnt offering for himself and a burnt offering for the people. Through this process, he will purify himself and the people, making them right with the LORD. 25 He must then burn all the fat of the sin offering on the altar.

26 "The man chosen to drive the scapegoat into the wilderness of Azazel must wash his clothes and bathe himself in water. Then he may return to the camp.

27 "The bull and the goat presented as sin offerings, whose blood Aaron takes into the Most Holy Place for the purification ceremony, will be carried outside the camp. The animals' hides, internal organs, and dung are all to be burned. 28 The man who burns them must wash his clothes and bathe himself in water before returning to the camp.

29 "On the tenth day of the appointed month in early autumn,* you must deny yourselves.* Neither native-born Israelites nor foreigners living among you may do any kind of work. This is a permanent

16:6 Or *to make atonement for himself and his family;* similarly in 16:11, 17b, 24, 34. **16:7** Hebrew *Tent of Meeting;* also in 16:16, 17, 20, 23, 33. **16:10** Or *wilderness, it will make atonement for the people.* **16:13** Hebrew *that is above the Testimony.* The Hebrew word for "testimony" refers to the terms of the LORD's covenant with Israel as written on stone tablets, which were kept in the Ark, and also to the covenant itself. **16:16** Or *make atonement for;* similarly in 16:17a, 18, 20, 27, 33. **16:29a** Hebrew *On the tenth day of the seventh month.* This day in the ancient Hebrew lunar calendar occurred in September or October. **16:29b** Or *must fast;* also in 16:31.

16:2 whenever he chooses. God's presence was in the Holy Place of the tabernacle. Aaron was not to come and go there at will. Instead there was one special time when he was required to enter this special place.

16:3 enters the sanctuary area. On the Day of Atonement, Aaron was to come prepared with a burnt offering to express devotion to God and a sin offering to ask for God's forgiveness.

16:13 he will not die. On several occasions God protected His people from seeing His presence, which would have brought death. The incense smoke at the ark functioned the same way for Aaron.

16:20-22 it will carry all the people's sins. The goat carried the pollution of the people's sins outside the camp. In a similar way, Jesus took our sins away forever (Isa. 53:5-6; Heb. 13:10-12).

law for you. [30] On that day offerings of purification will be made for you,* and you will be purified in the LORD's presence from all your sins. [31] It will be a Sabbath day of complete rest for you, and you must deny yourselves. This is a permanent law for you. [32] In future generations, the purification* ceremony will be performed by the priest who has been anointed and ordained to serve as high priest in place of his ancestor Aaron. He will put on the holy linen garments [33] and purify the Most Holy Place, the Tabernacle, the altar, the priests, and the entire congregation. [34] This is a permanent law for you, to purify the people of Israel from their sins, making them right with the LORD once each year."

Moses followed all these instructions exactly as the LORD had commanded him.

PROHIBITIONS AGAINST EATING BLOOD

17 Then the LORD said to Moses, [2] "Give the following instructions to Aaron and his sons and all the people of Israel. This is what the LORD has commanded.

[3] "If any native Israelite sacrifices a bull* or a lamb or a goat anywhere inside or outside the camp [4] instead of bringing it to the entrance of the Tabernacle* to present it as an offering to the LORD, that person will be as guilty as a murderer.* Such a person has shed blood and will be cut off from the community. [5] The purpose of this rule is to stop the Israelites from sacrificing animals in the open fields. It will ensure that they bring their sacrifices to the priest at the entrance of the Tabernacle, so he can present them to the LORD as peace offerings. [6] Then the priest will be able to splatter the blood against the LORD's altar at the entrance of the Tabernacle, and he will burn the fat as a pleasing aroma to the LORD. [7] The people must no longer be unfaithful to the LORD by offering sacrifices to the goat idols.* This is a permanent law for them, to be observed from generation to generation.

[8] "Give them this command as well. If any native Israelite or foreigner living among you offers a burnt offering or a sacrifice [9] but does not bring it to the entrance of the Tabernacle to offer it to the LORD, that person will be cut off from the community.

[10] "And if any native Israelite or foreigner living among you eats or drinks blood in any form, I will turn against that person and cut him off from the community of your people, [11] for the life of the body is in its blood. I have given you the blood on the altar to purify you, making you right with the LORD.* It is the blood, given in exchange for a life, that makes purification possible. [12] That is why I have said to the people of Israel, 'You must never eat or drink blood—neither you nor the foreigners living among you.'

[13] "And if any native Israelite or foreigner living among you goes hunting and kills an animal or bird that is approved for eating, he must drain its blood and cover it with earth. [14] The life of every creature is in its blood. That is why I have said to the people of Israel, 'You must never eat or drink blood, for the life of any creature is in its blood.' So whoever consumes blood will be cut off from the community.

[15] "And if any native-born Israelites or foreigners eat the meat of an animal that died naturally or was torn up by wild animals, they must wash their clothes and bathe themselves in water. They will remain ceremonially unclean until evening, but then they will be clean. [16] But if they do not wash their clothes and bathe themselves, they will be punished for their sin."

FORBIDDEN SEXUAL PRACTICES

18 Then the LORD said to Moses, [2] "Give the following instructions to the people of Israel. I am the LORD your God. [3] So do not act like the people in Egypt, where you used to live, or like the people of Canaan, where I am taking you. You must not imitate their way of life. [4] You must obey all my regulations and be careful to obey my decrees, for I am the LORD your God. [5] If you obey my decrees and my regulations, you will find life through them. I am the LORD.

[6] "You must never have sexual relations with a close relative, for I am the LORD.

[7] "Do not violate your father by having sexual relations with your mother. She is your mother; you must not have sexual relations with her.

[8] "Do not have sexual relations with any of your father's wives, for this would violate your father.

[9] "Do not have sexual relations with your sister or half sister, whether she is your father's daughter or your mother's daughter, whether she was born into your household or someone else's.

[10] "Do not have sexual relations with your granddaughter, whether she is your son's daughter or your daughter's daughter, for this would violate yourself.

[11] "Do not have sexual relations with your stepsister, the daughter of any of your father's wives, for she is your sister.

[12] "Do not have sexual relations with your father's sister, for she is your father's close relative.

[13] "Do not have sexual relations with your mother's sister, for she is your mother's close relative.

[14] "Do not violate your uncle, your father's brother, by having sexual relations with his wife, for she is your aunt.

[15] "Do not have sexual relations with your daughter-in-law; she is your son's wife, so you must not have sexual relations with her.

[16] "Do not have sexual relations with your brother's wife, for this would violate your brother.

16:30 Or *atonement will be made for you, to purify you.* **16:32** Or *atonement.* **17:3** Or *cow.* **17:4a** Hebrew *Tent of Meeting;* also in 17:5, 6, 9. **17:4b** Hebrew *will be guilty of blood.* **17:7** Or *goat demons.* **17:11** Or *to make atonement for you.*

16:30 you will be purified. The Day of Atonement was a start-over place, a renewal of God's forgiveness.

17:1-6 The Israelites apparently were offering sacrifices to idols outside the camp, then claiming they were slaughtering animals for food. To stop this practice, God required that all animals be slaughtered at the temple.

17:11 the life . . . is in its blood. The reason for animal sacrifices is because blood is life. Death is required for cleansing, since sin carries the death penalty.

18:2 I am the LORD. This phrase states the authority by which God demanded purity from His people.

18:3 not imitate their way of life. God was calling His people not to give in to the pagan culture around them.

18:16 your brother's wife. An exception to this law was Levirate marriage, which specified that a man should marry his brother's widow so she would not be destitute.

17 "Do not have sexual relations with both a wom-
an and her daughter. And do not take* her grand-
daughter, whether her son's daughter or her daugh-
ter's daughter, and have sexual relations with her.
They are close relatives, and this would be a wicked
act.
18 "While your wife is living, do not marry her sister
and have sexual relations with her, for they would be
rivals.
19 "Do not have sexual relations with a woman
during her period of menstrual impurity.
20 "Do not defile yourself by having sexual inter-
course with your neighbor's wife.
21 "Do not permit any of your children to be offered
as a sacrifice to Molech, for you must not bring shame
on the name of your God. I am the LORD.
22 "Do not practice homosexuality, having sex with
another man as with a woman. It is a detestable sin.
23 "A man must not defile himself by having sex
with an animal. And a woman must not offer herself
to a male animal to have intercourse with it. This is a
perverse act.
24 "Do not defile yourselves in any of these ways, for
the people I am driving out before you have defiled
themselves in all these ways. 25 Because the entire
land has become defiled, I am punishing the people
who live there. I will cause the land to vomit them
out. 26 You must obey all my decrees and regulations.
You must not commit any of these detestable sins. This
applies both to native-born Israelites and to the for-
eigners living among you.
27 "All these detestable activities are practiced by
the people of the land where I am taking you, and
this is how the land has become defiled. 28 So do not
defile the land and give it a reason to vomit you out,
as it will vomit out the people who live there now.
29 Whoever commits any of these detestable sins will
be cut off from the community of Israel. 30 So obey my
instructions, and do not defile yourselves by commit-
ting any of these detestable practices that were com-
mitted by the people who lived in the land before you.
I am the LORD your God."

HOLINESS IN PERSONAL CONDUCT

19 The LORD also said to Moses, 2 "Give the follow-
ing instructions to the entire community of Is-
rael. You must be holy because I, the LORD your God,
am holy.
3 "Each of you must show great respect for your
mother and father, and you must always observe my
Sabbath days of rest. I am the LORD your God.
4 "Do not put your trust in idols or make metal
images of gods for yourselves. I am the LORD your God.
5 "When you sacrifice a peace offering to the LORD,
offer it properly so you* will be accepted by God. 6 The
sacrifice must be eaten on the same day you offer it or
on the next day. Whatever is left over until the third
day must be completely burned up. 7 If any of the sac-
rifice is eaten on the third day, it will be contaminat-
ed, and I will not accept it. 8 Anyone who eats it on the
third day will be punished for defiling what is holy to
the LORD and will be cut off from the community.
9 "When you harvest the crops of your land, do not
harvest the grain along the edges of your fields, and
do not pick up what the harvesters drop. 10 It is the
same with your grape crop—do not strip every last
bunch of grapes from the vines, and do not pick up
the grapes that fall to the ground. Leave them for the
poor and the foreigners living among you. I am the
LORD your God.
11 "Do not steal.
"Do not deceive or cheat one another.
12 "Do not bring shame on the name of your God by
using it to swear falsely. I am the LORD.
13 "Do not defraud or rob your neighbor.
"Do not make your hired workers wait until the
next day to receive their pay.
14 "Do not insult the deaf or cause the blind to stum-
ble. You must fear your God; I am the LORD.
15 "Do not twist justice in legal matters by favoring
the poor or being partial to the rich and powerful. Al-
ways judge people fairly.
16 "Do not spread slanderous gossip among your
people.*
"Do not stand idly by when your neighbor's life is
threatened. I am the LORD.
17 "Do not nurse hatred in your heart for any of your
relatives.* Confront people directly so you will not be
held guilty for their sin.
18 "Do not seek revenge or bear a grudge against a
fellow Israelite, but love your neighbor as yourself. I
am the LORD.
19 "You must obey all my decrees.
"Do not mate two different kinds of animals. Do not
plant your field with two different kinds of seed. Do
not wear clothing woven from two different kinds of
thread.
20 "If a man has sex with a slave girl whose freedom
has never been purchased but who is committed to
become another man's wife, he must pay full compen-
sation to her master. But since she is not a free woman,
neither the man nor the woman will be put to death.
21 The man, however, must bring a ram as a guilt offer-
ing and present it to the LORD at the entrance of the
Tabernacle.* 22 The priest will then purify him* before
the LORD with the ram of the guilt offering, and the
man's sin will be forgiven.
23 "When you enter the land and plant fruit trees,
leave the fruit unharvested for the first three years
and consider it forbidden.* Do not eat it. 24 In the
fourth year the entire crop must be consecrated to the
LORD as a celebration of praise. 25 Finally, in the fifth
year you may eat the fruit. If you follow this pattern,
your harvest will increase. I am the LORD your God.

18:17 Or *do not marry.* **19:5** Or *it.* **19:16** Hebrew *Do not act as a merchant toward your own people.* **19:17** Hebrew *for your brother.* **19:21** Hebrew *Tent of Meeting.* **19:22** Or *make atonement for him.* **19:23** Hebrew *consider it uncircumcised.*

18:17 a wicked act. This verse outlines boundaries of decency. Much wickedness is simply the violation of decency.

18:21 Molech. Molech was the national god of the Ammonites. Children were offered to Molech as temple prostitutes and as burnt sacrifices.

18:22 homosexuality. Later in Leviticus, acts of homosexuality are listed as punishable by death.

18:28-29 vomit. God used strong imagery to describe the reaction of the earth to the indecency described in the previous verses.

19:8 defiling. Defiling holy things is bringing them into contact with uncleanness.

19:9-10 This practice of leaving leftover grain when gathering the harvest provided for the less fortunate.

19:17 Confront people directly. Talk directly to someone who has offended you rather than gossiping about him (Matt. 18:15).

19:18 love your neighbor. This sums up all the laws on how to treat other people (Rom. 13:9).

26 "Do not eat meat that has not been drained of its blood.

"Do not practice fortune-telling or witchcraft.

27 "Do not trim off the hair on your temples or trim your beards.

28 "Do not cut your bodies for the dead, and do not mark your skin with tattoos. I am the LORD.

29 "Do not defile your daughter by making her a prostitute, or the land will be filled with prostitution and wickedness.

30 "Keep my Sabbath days of rest, and show reverence toward my sanctuary. I am the LORD.

31 "Do not defile yourselves by turning to mediums or to those who consult the spirits of the dead. I am the LORD your God.

32 "Stand up in the presence of the elderly, and show respect for the aged. Fear your God. I am the LORD.

33 "Do not take advantage of foreigners who live among you in your land. 34 Treat them like native-born Israelites, and love them as you love yourself. Remember that you were once foreigners living in the land of Egypt. I am the LORD your God.

35 "Do not use dishonest standards when measuring length, weight, or volume. 36 Your scales and weights must be accurate. Your containers for measuring dry materials or liquids must be accurate.* I am the LORD your God who brought you out of the land of Egypt.

37 "You must be careful to keep all of my decrees and regulations by putting them into practice. I am the LORD."

PUNISHMENTS FOR DISOBEDIENCE

20 The LORD said to Moses, 2 "Give the people of Israel these instructions, which apply both to native Israelites and to the foreigners living in Israel.

"If any of them offer their children as a sacrifice to Molech, they must be put to death. The people of the community must stone them to death. 3 I myself will turn against them and cut them off from the community, because they have defiled my sanctuary and brought shame on my holy name by offering their children to Molech. 4 And if the people of the community ignore those who offer their children to Molech and refuse to execute them, 5 I myself will turn against them and their families and will cut them off from the community. This will happen to all who commit spiritual prostitution by worshiping Molech.

6 "I will also turn against those who commit spiritual prostitution by putting their trust in mediums or in those who consult the spirits of the dead. I will cut them off from the community. 7 So set yourselves apart to be holy, for I am the LORD your God. 8 Keep all my decrees by putting them into practice, for I am the LORD who makes you holy.

9 "Anyone who dishonors* father or mother must be put to death. Such a person is guilty of a capital offense.

10 "If a man commits adultery with his neighbor's wife, both the man and the woman who have committed adultery must be put to death.

11 "If a man violates his father by having sex with one of his father's wives, both the man and the woman must be put to death, for they are guilty of a capital offense.

12 "If a man has sex with his daughter-in-law, both must be put to death. They have committed a perverse act and are guilty of a capital offense.

13 "If a man practices homosexuality, having sex with another man as with a woman, both men have committed a detestable act. They must both be put to death, for they are guilty of a capital offense.

14 "If a man marries both a woman and her mother, he has committed a wicked act. The man and both women must be burned to death to wipe out such wickedness from among you.

15 "If a man has sex with an animal, he must be put to death, and the animal must be killed.

16 "If a woman presents herself to a male animal to have intercourse with it, she and the animal must both be put to death. You must kill both, for they are guilty of a capital offense.

17 "If a man marries his sister, the daughter of either his father or his mother, and they have sexual relations, it is a shameful disgrace. They must be publicly cut off from the community. Since the man has violated his sister, he will be punished for his sin.

18 "If a man has sexual relations with a woman during her menstrual period, both of them must be cut off from the community, for together they have exposed the source of her blood flow.

19 "Do not have sexual relations with your aunt, whether your mother's sister or your father's sister. This would dishonor a close relative. Both parties are guilty and will be punished for their sin.

20 "If a man has sex with his uncle's wife, he has violated his uncle. Both the man and woman will be punished for their sin, and they will die childless.

21 "If a man marries his brother's wife, it is an act of impurity. He has violated his brother, and the guilty couple will remain childless.

22 "You must keep all my decrees and regulations by putting them into practice; otherwise the land to which I am bringing you as your new home will vomit you out. 23 Do not live according to the customs of the people I am driving out before you. It is because they do these shameful things that I detest them. 24 But I have promised you, 'You will possess their land because I will give it to you as your possession—a land flowing with milk and honey.' I am the LORD your God, who has set you apart from all other people.

19:36 Hebrew *Use an honest ephah* [a dry measure] *and an honest hin* [a liquid measure]. **20:9** Greek version reads *Anyone who speaks disrespectfully of.* Compare Matt 15:4; Mark 7:10.

19:26 blood. Leviticus 17:13-14 explains that the life of an animal is in its blood. This is why God commands His people not to eat blood (Gen. 9:4).

19:28 cut your bodies . . . mark your bodies with tattoos. The purpose of these commands was to keep the Hebrews separate from the surrounding pagan cultures.

19:33-34 foreigners. The generosity of God would be reflected in the people's treatment of strangers in their midst.

19:35-36 dishonest standards. The ancient world had no standardized weights and measures. Cheating was easy, but integrity was still measured by the same standard.

20:3 defiled my sanctuary. God makes it clear that to offer a child to the false god Molech was a personal affront to Him.

20:6 mediums or those who consult the spirits. To consult a medium or one who consults the spirits of the dead was to trust someone besides God to direct one's future. This was a form of idolatry.

20:7 Set yourselves apart. To keep oneself separate from sin in order to honor God.

20:8 decrees. The statutes listed here were actually capital crimes. For God, holiness is a life-or-death issue.

25 "You must therefore make a distinction between ceremonially clean and unclean animals, and between clean and unclean birds. You must not defile yourselves by eating any unclean animal or bird or creature that scurries along the ground. I have identified them as being unclean for you. 26 You must be holy because I, the LORD, am holy. I have set you apart from all other people to be my very own.

27 "Men and women among you who act as mediums or who consult the spirits of the dead must be put to death by stoning. They are guilty of a capital offense."

INSTRUCTIONS FOR THE PRIESTS

21 The LORD said to Moses, "Give the following instructions to the priests, the descendants of Aaron.

"A priest must not make himself ceremonially unclean by touching the dead body of a relative. 2 The only exceptions are his closest relatives—his mother or father, son or daughter, brother, 3 or his virgin sister who depends on him because she has no husband. 4 But a priest must not defile himself and make himself unclean for someone who is related to him only by marriage.

5 "The priests must not shave their heads or trim their beards or cut their bodies. 6 They must be set apart as holy to their God and must never bring shame on the name of God. They must be holy, for they are the ones who present the special gifts to the LORD, gifts of food for their God.

7 "Priests may not marry a woman defiled by prostitution, and they may not marry a woman who is divorced from her husband, for the priests are set apart as holy to their God. 8 You must treat them as holy because they offer up food to your God. You must consider them holy because I, the LORD, am holy, and I make you holy.

9 "If a priest's daughter defiles herself by becoming a prostitute, she also defiles her father's holiness, and she must be burned to death.

10 "The high priest has the highest rank of all the priests. The anointing oil has been poured on his head, and he has been ordained to wear the priestly garments. He must never leave his hair uncombed* or tear his clothing. 11 He must not defile himself by going near a dead body. He may not make himself ceremonially unclean even for his father or mother. 12 He must not defile the sanctuary of his God by leaving it to attend to a dead person, for he has been made holy by the anointing oil of his God. I am the LORD.

13 "The high priest may marry only a virgin. 14 He may not marry a widow, a woman who is divorced, or a woman who has defiled herself by prostitution. She must be a virgin from his own clan, 15 so that he will not dishonor his descendants among his clan, for I am the LORD who makes him holy."

16 Then the LORD said to Moses, 17 "Give the following instructions to Aaron: In all future generations, none of your descendants who has any defect will qualify to offer food to his God. 18 No one who has a defect qualifies, whether he is blind, lame, disfigured, deformed, 19 or has a broken foot or arm, 20 or is hunchbacked or dwarfed, or has a defective eye, or skin sores or scabs, or damaged testicles. 21 No descendant of Aaron who has a defect may approach the altar to present special gifts to the LORD. Since he has a defect, he may not approach the altar to offer food to his God. 22 However, he may eat from the food offered to God, including the holy offerings and the most holy offerings. 23 Yet because of his physical defect, he may not enter the room behind the inner curtain or approach the altar, for this would defile my holy places. I am the LORD who makes them holy."

24 So Moses gave these instructions to Aaron and his sons and to all the Israelites.

22 The LORD said to Moses, 2 "Tell Aaron and his sons to be very careful with the sacred gifts that the Israelites set apart for me, so they do not bring shame on my holy name. I am the LORD. 3 Give them the following instructions.

"In all future generations, if any of your descendants is ceremonially unclean when he approaches the sacred offerings that the people of Israel consecrate to the LORD, he must be cut off from my presence. I am the LORD.

4 "If any of Aaron's descendants has a skin disease* or any kind of discharge that makes him ceremonially unclean, he may not eat from the sacred offerings until he has been pronounced clean. He also becomes unclean by touching a corpse, or by having an emission of semen, 5 or by touching a small animal that is unclean, or by touching someone who is ceremonially unclean for any reason. 6 The man who is defiled in any of these ways will remain unclean until evening. He may not eat from the sacred offerings until he has bathed himself in water. 7 When the sun goes down, he will be ceremonially clean again and may eat from the sacred offerings, for this is his food. 8 He may not eat an animal that has died a natural death or has been torn apart by wild animals, for this would defile him. I am the LORD.

9 "The priests must follow my instructions carefully. Otherwise they will be punished for their sin and will die for violating my instructions. I am the LORD who makes them holy.

10 "No one outside a priest's family may eat the sacred offerings. Even guests and hired workers in a priest's home are not allowed to eat them. 11 However, if the priest buys a slave for himself, the slave may eat from the sacred offerings. And if his slaves have children, they also may share his food. 12 If a priest's daughter marries someone outside the priestly family, she may no longer eat the sacred offerings. 13 But if she becomes a widow or is divorced and has no children to support her, and she returns to live in her father's home as in her youth, she may eat her father's food again. Otherwise, no one outside a priest's family may eat the sacred offerings.

14 "Any such person who eats the sacred offerings without realizing it must pay the priest for the

21:10 Or *never uncover his head.* **22:4** Traditionally rendered *leprosy;* see note on 13:2a.

21:1 the dead body of a relative. Priests were not to touch a corpse unless it was that of an immediate family member.

21:5 must not shave their heads. Some pagan priests shaved part or all of their heads. The Nazarite vow included not cutting the hair at all.

21:8 I make you holy. God gives us two foundations in this verse: He is holy, and He makes us holy.

21:16-23 any defect. In Aaron's day, handicapped priests received their share of provisions for the priesthood, but they could not receive sacrifices and could not be high priests.

21:23 the curtain. This curtain was at the entrance of the tabernacle.

amount eaten, plus an additional 20 percent. 15 The
priests must not let the Israelites defile the sacred
offerings brought to the LORD 16 by allowing unautho-
rized people to eat them. This would bring guilt upon
them and require them to pay compensation. I am the
LORD who makes them holy."

WORTHY AND UNWORTHY OFFERINGS

17 And the LORD said to Moses, 18 "Give Aaron and his
sons and all the Israelites these instructions, which
apply both to native Israelites and to the foreigners
living among you.

"If you present a gift as a burnt offering to the
LORD, whether it is to fulfill a vow or is a voluntary
offering, 19 you* will be accepted only if your offering
is a male animal with no defects. It may be a bull, a
ram, or a male goat. 20 Do not present an animal with
defects, because the LORD will not accept it on your
behalf.

21 "If you present a peace offering to the LORD
from the herd or the flock, whether it is to fulfill a
vow or is a voluntary offering, you must offer a per-
fect animal. It may have no defect of any kind. 22 You
must not offer an animal that is blind, crippled, or
injured, or that has a wart, a skin sore, or scabs.
Such animals must never be offered on the altar as
special gifts to the LORD. 23 If a bull* or lamb has a
leg that is too long or too short, it may be offered
as a voluntary offering, but it may not be offered to
fulfill a vow. 24 If an animal has damaged testicles
or is castrated, you may not offer it to the LORD. You
must never do this in your own land, 25 and you must
not accept such an animal from foreigners and then
offer it as a sacrifice to your God. Such animals will
not be accepted on your behalf, for they are mutilat-
ed or defective."

26 And the LORD said to Moses, 27 "When a calf or
lamb or goat is born, it must be left with its mother for
seven days. From the eighth day on, it will be accept-
able as a special gift to the LORD. 28 But you must not
slaughter a mother animal and her offspring on the
same day, whether from the herd or the flock. 29 When
you bring a thanksgiving offering to the LORD, sacri-
fice it properly so you will be accepted. 30 Eat the en-
tire sacrificial animal on the day it is presented. Do
not leave any of it until the next morning. I am the
LORD.

31 "You must faithfully keep all my commands by
putting them into practice, for I am the LORD. 32 Do not
bring shame on my holy name, for I will display my
holiness among the people of Israel. I am the LORD
who makes you holy. 33 It was I who rescued you from
the land of Egypt, that I might be your God. I am the
LORD."

THE APPOINTED FESTIVALS

23 The LORD said to Moses, 2 "Give the following in-
structions to the people of Israel. These are the
LORD's appointed festivals, which you are to proclaim
as official days for holy assembly.

3 "You have six days each week for your ordinary
work, but the seventh day is a Sabbath day of com-
plete rest, an official day for holy assembly. It is the
LORD's Sabbath day, and it must be observed wherev-
er you live.

4 "In addition to the Sabbath, these are the LORD's
appointed festivals, the official days for holy assem-
bly that are to be celebrated at their proper times
each year.

PASSOVER AND THE FESTIVAL OF UNLEAVENED BREAD

5 "The LORD's Passover begins at sundown on the four-
teenth day of the first month.* 6 On the next day, the
fifteenth day of the month, you must begin celebrat-
ing the Festival of Unleavened Bread. This festival to
the LORD continues for seven days, and during that
time the bread you eat must be made without yeast.
7 On the first day of the festival, all the people must
stop their ordinary work and observe an official day
for holy assembly. 8 For seven days you must present
special gifts to the LORD. On the seventh day the peo-
ple must again stop all their ordinary work to observe
an official day for holy assembly."

CELEBRATION OF FIRST HARVEST

9 Then the LORD said to Moses, 10 "Give the following
instructions to the people of Israel. When you enter
the land I am giving you and you harvest its first
crops, bring the priest a bundle of grain from the first
cutting of your grain harvest. 11 On the day after the
Sabbath, the priest will lift it up before the LORD so it
may be accepted on your behalf. 12 On that same day
you must sacrifice a one-year-old male lamb with
no defects as a burnt offering to the LORD. 13 With it
you must present a grain offering consisting of four
quarts* of choice flour moistened with olive oil. It will
be a special gift, a pleasing aroma to the LORD. You
must also offer one quart* of wine as a liquid offering.
14 Do not eat any bread or roasted grain or fresh ker-
nels on that day until you bring this offering to your
God. This is a permanent law for you, and it must be
observed from generation to generation wherever
you live.

THE FESTIVAL OF HARVEST

15 "From the day after the Sabbath—the day you
bring the bundle of grain to be lifted up as a special
offering—count off seven full weeks. 16 Keep counting

22:19 Or *it.* **22:23** Or *cow.* **23:5** This day in the ancient Hebrew lunar calendar occurred in late March, April, or early May. **23:13a** Hebrew $^2/_{10}$ *of an ephah* [4.4 liters]; also in 23:17 **23:13b** Hebrew $^1/_4$ *of a hin* [1 liter].

22:16 who makes them holy. When God gave instructions to the worshippers, it was enough to say, "I am the LORD." Because of the role of the priests, it was equally important that they acknowledge God's holiness as well as His desire to make His people holy.

22:21 perfect. While the peace offerings (7:11-36) were not for sin or guilt, they required the same standards of holiness.

23:2 appointed festivals. The biblical feasts of the Hebrews commemorated historical events and were timed to coordinate with the three annual harvests.

23:3 Sabbath. The Sabbath was a day of remembering that God created and God rested, that He is the one true God.

23:5 Passover. This feast commemorated the night in Egypt when the firstborn of each household died unless blood had been sprinkled on the doorpost of one's house (Ex. 12).

23:6 The Festival of Unleavened Bread. This feast coincided with the barley harvest (March/April).

23:15-22 This feast, known as the Feast of Weeks, or Pentecost, celebrated the end of the wheat harvest and the giving of the Ten Commandments. Later, God gave the Holy Spirit during this feast (Acts 2).

23:16 keep counting. The feast of Pentecost occurred 50 days after the Passover observance.

until the day after the seventh Sabbath, fifty days later. Then present an offering of new grain to the LORD.
17 From wherever you live, bring two loaves of bread
to be lifted up before the LORD as a special offering.
Make these loaves from four quarts of choice flour,
and bake them with yeast. They will be an offering to
the LORD from the first of your crops. 18 Along with the
bread, present seven one-year-old male lambs with
no defects, one young bull, and two rams as burnt
offerings to the LORD. These burnt offerings, together
with the grain offerings and liquid offerings, will be a
special gift, a pleasing aroma to the LORD. 19 Then you
must offer one male goat as a sin offering and two
one-year-old male lambs as a peace offering.
20 "The priest will lift up the two lambs as a special
offering to the LORD, together with the loaves representing the first of your crops. These offerings, which
are holy to the LORD, belong to the priests. 21 That same
day will be proclaimed an official day for holy assembly, a day on which you do no ordinary work. This is a permanent law for you, and it must be observed from generation to generation wherever you live.*
22 "When you harvest the crops of your land, do not harvest the grain along the edges of your fields, and do not pick up what the harvesters drop. Leave it for the poor and the foreigners living among you. I am the LORD your God."

THE FESTIVAL OF TRUMPETS

23 The LORD said to Moses, 24 "Give the following instructions to the people of Israel. On the first day of the appointed month in early autumn,* you are to observe a day of complete rest. It will be an official day for holy assembly, a day commemorated with loud blasts of a trumpet. 25 You must do no ordinary work
on that day. Instead, you are to present special gifts to the LORD."

THE DAY OF ATONEMENT

26 Then the LORD said to Moses, 27 "Be careful to celebrate the Day of Atonement on the tenth day of that same month—nine days after the Festival of Trumpets.* You must observe it as an official day for holy assembly, a day to deny yourselves* and present special gifts to the LORD. 28 Do no work during that entire day
because it is the Day of Atonement, when offerings of purification are made for you, making you right with* the LORD your God. 29 All who do not deny themselves
that day will be cut off from God's people. 30 And I will
destroy anyone among you who does any work on
that day. 31 You must not do any work at all! This is a
permanent law for you, and it must be observed from
generation to generation wherever you live. 32 This
will be a Sabbath day of complete rest for you, and on
that day you must deny yourselves. This day of rest will begin at sundown on the ninth day of the month and extend until sundown on the tenth day."

THE FESTIVAL OF SHELTERS

33 And the LORD said to Moses, 34 "Give the following
instructions to the people of Israel. Begin celebrating the Festival of Shelters* on the fifteenth day of the appointed month—five days after the Day of Atonement.* This festival to the LORD will last for seven
days. 35 On the first day of the festival you must proclaim an official day for holy assembly, when you do
no ordinary work. 36 For seven days you must present
special gifts to the LORD. The eighth day is another holy day on which you present your special gifts to the LORD. This will be a solemn occasion, and no ordinary work may be done that day.
37 ("These are the LORD's appointed festivals. Celebrate them each year as official days for holy assembly by presenting special gifts to the LORD—burnt offerings, grain offerings, sacrifices, and liquid offerings—each on its proper day. 38 These festivals must
be observed in addition to the LORD's regular Sabbath days, and the offerings are in addition to your personal gifts, the offerings you give to fulfill your vows, and the voluntary offerings you present to the LORD.)
39 "Remember that this seven-day festival to the LORD—the Festival of Shelters—begins on the fifteenth day of the appointed month,* after you have harvested all the produce of the land. The first day and the eighth day of the festival will be days of complete rest. 40 On the first day gather branches from
magnificent trees*—palm fronds, boughs from leafy trees, and willows that grow by the streams. Then celebrate with joy before the LORD your God for seven
days. 41 You must observe this festival to the LORD for
seven days every year. This is a permanent law for you, and it must be observed in the appointed month*
from generation to generation. 42 For seven days you
must live outside in little shelters. All native-born Israelites must live in shelters. 43 This will remind each
new generation of Israelites that I made their ancestors live in shelters when I rescued them from the land of Egypt. I am the LORD your God."
44 So Moses gave the Israelites these instructions
regarding the annual festivals of the LORD.

PURE OIL AND HOLY BREAD

24 The LORD said to Moses, 2 "Command the people
of Israel to bring you pure oil of pressed olives
for the light, to keep the lamps burning continually.
3 This is the lampstand that stands in the Tabernacle, in front of the inner curtain that shields the Ark of the Covenant.* Aaron must keep the lamps burning

23:21 This celebration, called the Festival of Harvest or the Festival of Weeks, was later called the Festival of Pentecost (see Acts 2:1). It is celebrated today as Shavuot (or Shabuoth). **23:24** Hebrew *On the first day of the seventh month.* This day in the ancient Hebrew lunar calendar occurred in September or October. This festival is celebrated today as Rosh Hashanah, the Jewish new year. **23:27a** Hebrew *on the tenth day of the seventh month;* see 23:24 and the note there. This day in the ancient Hebrew lunar calendar occurred in September or October. It is celebrated today as Yom Kippur. **23:27b** Or *to fast;* similarly in 23:29, 32. **23:28** Or *when atonement is made for you before.* **23:34a** Or *Festival of Booths,* or *Festival of Tabernacles.* This was earlier called the Festival of the Final Harvest or Festival of Ingathering (see Exod 23:16b). It is celebrated today as Sukkot (or Succoth). **23:34b** Hebrew *on the fifteenth day of the seventh month;* see 23:27a and the note there. **23:39** Hebrew *on the fifteenth day of the seventh month.* **23:40** Or *gather fruit from majestic trees.* **23:41** Hebrew *the seventh month.* **24:3** Hebrew *in the Tent of Meeting, outside the inner curtain of the Testimony;* see note on 16:13.

23:24 first day of the appointed month. Today this is the traditional Jewish New Year, Rosh Hashanah. In the Bible it was a day to blow ram's horns (*shofars*) in preparation for the Day of Atonement.

23:27 Day of Atonement. This was the yearly sacrifice made by the high priest for the sins of the people.

23:34 Festival of Shelters. Also called the The Festival of Booths (or Tabernacles), this festival commemorated the nomadic journey of the people of Israel after they left Egypt and began making their way across the wilderness.

in the LORD's presence all night. This is a permanent
law for you, and it must be observed from generation
to generation. 4 Aaron and the priests must tend the
lamps on the pure gold lampstand continually in the
LORD's presence.
5 "You must bake twelve flat loaves of bread from
choice flour, using four quarts* of flour for each loaf.
6 Place the bread before the LORD on the pure gold
table, and arrange the loaves in two stacks, with six
loaves in each stack. 7 Put some pure frankincense
near each stack to serve as a representative offering,
a special gift presented to the LORD. 8 Every Sabbath
day this bread must be laid out before the LORD as a
gift from the Israelites; it is an ongoing expression
of the eternal covenant. 9 The loaves of bread will
belong to Aaron and his descendants, who must eat
them in a sacred place, for they are most holy. It is the
permanent right of the priests to claim this portion of
the special gifts presented to the LORD."

AN EXAMPLE OF JUST PUNISHMENT

10 One day a man who had an Israelite mother and an
Egyptian father came out of his tent and got into a
fight with one of the Israelite men. 11 During the fight,
this son of an Israelite woman blasphemed the Name
of the LORD* with a curse. So the man was brought
to Moses for judgment. His mother was Shelomith,
the daughter of Dibri of the tribe of Dan. 12 They kept
the man in custody until the LORD's will in the matter
should become clear to them.
13 Then the LORD said to Moses, 14 "Take the blas-
phemer outside the camp, and tell all those who
heard the curse to lay their hands on his head. Then
let the entire community stone him to death. 15 Say to
the people of Israel: Those who curse their God will
be punished for their sin. 16 Anyone who blasphemes
the Name of the LORD must be stoned to death by the
whole community of Israel. Any native-born Israelite
or foreigner among you who blasphemes the Name of
the LORD must be put to death.
17 "Anyone who takes another person's life must be
put to death.
18 "Anyone who kills another person's animal must
pay for it in full—a live animal for the animal that
was killed.
19 "Anyone who injures another person must be
dealt with according to the injury inflicted—
20 a
fracture for a fracture, an eye for an eye, a tooth for
a tooth. Whatever anyone does to injure another per-
son must be paid back in kind.
21 "Whoever kills an animal must pay for it in full,
but whoever kills another person must be put to death.
22 "This same standard applies both to native-born
Israelites and to the foreigners living among you. I
am the LORD your God."
23 After Moses gave all these instructions to the Is-
raelites, they took the blasphemer outside the camp
and stoned him to death. The Israelites did just as the
LORD had commanded Moses.

THE SABBATH YEAR

25 While Moses was on Mount Sinai, the LORD said
to him, 2 "Give the following instructions to the
people of Israel. When you have entered the land I am
giving you, the land itself must observe a Sabbath rest
before the LORD every seventh year. 3 For six years you
may plant your fields and prune your vineyards and
harvest your crops, 4 but during the seventh year the
land must have a Sabbath year of complete rest. It is
the LORD's Sabbath. Do not plant your fields or prune
your vineyards during that year. 5 And don't store
away the crops that grow on their own or gather the
grapes from your unpruned vines. The land must
have a year of complete rest. 6 But you may eat what-
ever the land produces on its own during its Sabbath.
This applies to you, your male and female servants,
your hired workers, and the temporary residents who
live with you. 7 Your livestock and the wild animals in
your land will also be allowed to eat what the land
produces.

THE YEAR OF JUBILEE

8 "In addition, you must count off seven Sabbath years,
seven sets of seven years, adding up to forty-nine
years in all. 9 Then on the Day of Atonement in the
fiftieth year,* blow the ram's horn loud and long
throughout the land. 10 Set this year apart as holy, a
time to proclaim freedom throughout the land for all
who live there. It will be a jubilee year for you, when
each of you may return to the land that belonged to
your ancestors and return to your own clan. 11 This
fiftieth year will be a jubilee for you. During that year
you must not plant your fields or store away any of
the crops that grow on their own, and don't gather
the grapes from your unpruned vines. 12 It will be a
jubilee year for you, and you must keep it holy. But
you may eat whatever the land produces on its own.
13 In the Year of Jubilee each of you may return to the
land that belonged to your ancestors.
14 "When you make an agreement with your neigh-
bor to buy or sell property, you must not take advan-
tage of each other. 15 When you buy land from your
neighbor, the price you pay must be based on the
number of years since the last jubilee. The seller must
set the price by taking into account the number of
years remaining until the next Year of Jubilee. 16 The
more years until the next jubilee, the higher the price;
the fewer years, the lower the price. After all, the per-
son selling the land is actually selling you a certain
number of harvests. 17 Show your fear of God by not
taking advantage of each other. I am the LORD your
God.
18 "If you want to live securely in the land, follow
my decrees and obey my regulations. 19 Then the land

24:5 Hebrew $^2/_{10}$ *of an ephah* [4.4 liters]. **24:11** Hebrew *the Name;* also in 24:16b. **25:9** Hebrew *on the tenth day of the seventh month, on the Day of Atonement;* see 23:27a and the note there.

24:5 loaves. In Exodus these 12 loaves are called the "bread of the Presence." Twelve loaves for the 12 tribes.

24:8-9 portion. The priests shared in this bread each week. It was part of the food provided for their support by the people.

25:4 the land must have a Sabbath year. Every seventh year the land was allowed to go uncultivated. This had the same effect as our modern system of crop rotation—to keep the land productive.

25:10 jubilee. The year of Jubilee was a time for reestablishing homelands and ownership. Land that had been sold since the last Jubilee reverted to the original owners.

25:13 return to the land. God was evening things out in terms of accumulation of wealth.

25:15 based on. If the year of Jubilee was observed regularly, land sales would work as leases. When a land deal was struck, the buyer and seller would know the number of years for which the deal was valid.

will yield large crops, and you will eat your fill and
live securely in it. 20 But you might ask, 'What will we
eat during the seventh year, since we are not allowed
to plant or harvest crops that year?' 21 Be assured that
I will send my blessing for you in the sixth year, so the
land will produce a crop large enough for three years.
22 When you plant your fields in the eighth year, you
will still be eating from the large crop of the sixth
year. In fact, you will still be eating from that large
crop when the new crop is harvested in the ninth
year.

REDEMPTION OF PROPERTY

23 "The land must never be sold on a permanent basis,
for the land belongs to me. You are only foreigners
and tenant farmers working for me.
24 "With every purchase of land you must grant the
seller the right to buy it back. 25 If one of your fellow
Israelites falls into poverty and is forced to sell some
family land, then a close relative should buy it back
for him. 26 If there is no close relative to buy the land,
but the person who sold it gets enough money to buy
it back, 27 he then has the right to redeem it from the
one who bought it. The price of the land will be dis-
counted according to the number of years until the
next Year of Jubilee. In this way the original owner
can then return to the land. 28 But if the original own-
er cannot afford to buy back the land, it will remain
with the new owner until the next Year of Jubilee. In
the jubilee year, the land must be returned to the orig-
inal owners so they can return to their family land.
29 "Anyone who sells a house inside a walled town
has the right to buy it back for a full year after its sale.
During that year, the seller retains the right to buy it
back. 30 But if it is not bought back within a year, the
sale of the house within the walled town cannot be
reversed. It will become the permanent property of
the buyer. It will not be returned to the original own-
er in the Year of Jubilee. 31 But a house in a village—a
settlement without fortified walls—will be treated
like property in the countryside. Such a house may be
bought back at any time, and it must be returned to
the original owner in the Year of Jubilee.
32 "The Levites always have the right to buy back
a house they have sold within the towns allotted
to them. 33 And any property that is sold by the Le-
vites—all houses within the Levitical towns—must
be returned in the Year of Jubilee. After all, the hous-
es in the towns reserved for the Levites are the only
property they own in all Israel. 34 The open pasture-
land around the Levitical towns may never be sold. It
is their permanent possession.

REDEMPTION OF THE POOR AND ENSLAVED

35 "If one of your fellow Israelites falls into poverty and
cannot support himself, support him as you would a
foreigner or a temporary resident and allow him to
live with you. 36 Do not charge interest or make a prof-
it at his expense. Instead, show your fear of God by
letting him live with you as your relative. 37 Remem-
ber, do not charge interest on money you lend him or
make a profit on food you sell him. 38 I am the LORD
your God, who brought you out of the land of Egypt to
give you the land of Canaan and to be your God.
39 "If one of your fellow Israelites falls into poverty
and is forced to sell himself to you, do not treat him as
a slave. 40 Treat him instead as a hired worker or as a
temporary resident who lives with you, and he will
serve you only until the Year of Jubilee. 41 At that time
he and his children will no longer be obligated to you,
and they will return to their clans and go back to the
land originally allotted to their ancestors. 42 The peo-
ple of Israel are my servants, whom I brought out of
the land of Egypt, so they must never be sold as slaves.
43 Show your fear of God by not treating them harshly.
44 "However, you may purchase male and female
slaves from among the nations around you. 45 You
may also purchase the children of temporary resi-
dents who live among you, including those who have
been born in your land. You may treat them as your
property, 46 passing them on to your children as a per-
manent inheritance. You may treat them as slaves, but
you must never treat your fellow Israelites this way.
47 "Suppose a foreigner or temporary resident be-
comes rich while living among you. If any of your
fellow Israelites fall into poverty and are forced to sell
themselves to such a foreigner or to a member of his
family, 48 they still retain the right to be bought back,
even after they have been purchased. They may be
bought back by a brother, 49 an uncle, or a cousin. In
fact, anyone from the extended family may buy them
back. They may also redeem themselves if they have
prospered. 50 They will negotiate the price of their free-
dom with the person who bought them. The price will
be based on the number of years from the time they
were sold until the next Year of Jubilee—whatever it
would cost to hire a worker for that period of time. 51 If
many years still remain until the jubilee, they will re-
pay the proper proportion of what they received when
they sold themselves. 52 If only a few years remain until
the Year of Jubilee, they will repay a small amount for
their redemption. 53 The foreigner must treat them as
workers hired on a yearly basis. You must not allow a
foreigner to treat any of your fellow Israelites harshly.
54 If any Israelites have not been bought back by the
time the Year of Jubilee arrives, they and their children
must be set free at that time. 55 For the people of Israel
belong to me. They are my servants, whom I brought
out of the land of Egypt. I am the LORD your God.

BLESSINGS FOR OBEDIENCE

26 "Do not make idols or set up carved images,
or sacred pillars, or sculptured stones in your
land so you may worship them. I am the LORD your
God. 2 You must keep my Sabbath days of rest and
show reverence for my sanctuary. I am the LORD.
3 "If you follow my decrees and are careful to obey
my commands, 4 I will send you the seasonal rains.

25:24 right to buy it back. The families who first received the allotment of the land would have the right to take possession of the land again.

25:25 should buy it back. The land represented God's promise, His inheritance. If someone had sold his land because of financial difficulty, it was a relative's responsibility to make sure the land remained in the family.

25:35-36 to live with you. It was easier at times to help a wandering foreigner than a down-and-out fellow citizen. The purpose of this passage was not to forbid interest but to remind the people that making money from another person's misfortune was improper.

25:55 are my servants. The year of Jubilee was a way for God to reclaim His people and His promise to them.

26:1 worship. It was not just the image or idol that was forbidden. It was the attitude of the heart that mattered. An idol is anything that takes the place of God in our commitment.

26:3-13 if you follow. This passage outlines the blessing that God promised His people if they obeyed Him.

The land will then yield its crops, and the trees of the
field will produce their fruit. 5 Your threshing season
will overlap with the grape harvest, and your grape
harvest will overlap with the season of planting
grain. You will eat your fill and live securely in your
own land.
6 "I will give you peace in the land, and you will be
able to sleep with no cause for fear. I will rid the land
of wild animals and keep your enemies out of your
land. 7 In fact, you will chase down your enemies and
slaughter them with your swords. 8 Five of you will
chase a hundred, and a hundred of you will chase
ten thousand! All your enemies will fall beneath your
sword.
9 "I will look favorably upon you, making you fer-
tile and multiplying your people. And I will fulfill my
covenant with you. 10 You will have such a surplus of
crops that you will need to clear out the old grain to
make room for the new harvest! 11 I will live among
you, and I will not despise you. 12 I will walk among
you; I will be your God, and you will be my people. 13 I
am the LORD your God, who brought you out of the
land of Egypt so you would no longer be their slaves.
I broke the yoke of slavery from your neck so you can
walk with your heads held high.

PUNISHMENTS FOR DISOBEDIENCE

14 "However, if you do not listen to me or obey all these
commands, 15 and if you break my covenant by reject-
ing my decrees, treating my regulations with con-
tempt, and refusing to obey my commands, 16 I will
punish you. I will bring sudden terrors upon you—
wasting diseases and burning fevers that will cause
your eyes to fail and your life to ebb away. You will
plant your crops in vain because your enemies will
eat them. 17 I will turn against you, and you will be
defeated by your enemies. Those who hate you will
rule over you, and you will run even when no one is
chasing you!
18 "And if, in spite of all this, you still disobey me,
I will punish you seven times over for your sins. 19 I
will break your proud spirit by making the skies as
unyielding as iron and the earth as hard as bronze.
20 All your work will be for nothing, for your land will
yield no crops, and your trees will bear no fruit.
21 "If even then you remain hostile toward me and
refuse to obey me, I will inflict disaster on you seven
times over for your sins. 22 I will send wild animals
that will rob you of your children and destroy your
livestock. Your numbers will dwindle, and your roads
will be deserted.
23 "And if you fail to learn the lesson and contin-
ue your hostility toward me, 24 then I myself will be
hostile toward you. I will personally strike you with
calamity seven times over for your sins. 25 I will send
armies against you to carry out the curse of the cov-
enant you have broken. When you run to your towns
for safety, I will send a plague to destroy you there,
and you will be handed over to your enemies. 26 I will
destroy your food supply, so that ten women will need
only one oven to bake bread for their families. They
will ration your food by weight, and though you have
food to eat, you will not be satisfied.
27 "If in spite of all this you still refuse to listen and
still remain hostile toward me, 28 then I will give
full vent to my hostility. I myself will punish you
seven times over for your sins. 29 Then you will eat
the flesh of your own sons and daughters. 30 I will
destroy your pagan shrines and knock down your
places of worship. I will leave your lifeless corpses
piled on top of your lifeless idols,* and I will despise
you. 31 I will make your cities desolate and destroy
your places of pagan worship. I will take no pleasure
in your offerings that should be a pleasing aroma to
me. 32 Yes, I myself will devastate your land, and your
enemies who come to occupy it will be appalled at
what they see. 33 I will scatter you among the nations
and bring out my sword against you. Your land will
become desolate, and your cities will lie in ruins.
34 Then at last the land will enjoy its neglected Sab-
bath years as it lies desolate while you are in exile in
the land of your enemies. Then the land will finally
rest and enjoy the Sabbaths it missed. 35 As long as
the land lies in ruins, it will enjoy the rest you never
allowed it to take every seventh year while you lived
in it.
36 "And for those of you who survive, I will demor-
alize you in the land of your enemies. You will live in
such fear that the sound of a leaf driven by the wind
will send you fleeing. You will run as though fleeing
from a sword, and you will fall even when no one
pursues you. 37 Though no one is chasing you, you
will stumble over each other as though fleeing from
a sword. You will have no power to stand up against
your enemies. 38 You will die among the foreign na-
tions and be devoured in the land of your enemies.
39 Those of you who survive will waste away in your
enemies' lands because of their sins and the sins of
their ancestors.
40 "But at last my people will confess their sins and
the sins of their ancestors for betraying me and being
hostile toward me. 41 When I have turned their hos-
tility back on them and brought them to the land of
their enemies, then at last their stubborn hearts will
be humbled, and they will pay for their sins. 42 Then I
will remember my covenant with Jacob and my cov-
enant with Isaac and my covenant with Abraham,
and I will remember the land. 43 For the land must be
abandoned to enjoy its years of Sabbath rest as it lies
deserted. At last the people will pay for their sins, for
they have continually rejected my regulations and
despised my decrees.
44 "But despite all this, I will not utterly reject or de-
spise them while they are in exile in the land of their
enemies. I will not cancel my covenant with them by
wiping them out, for I am the LORD their God. 45 For
their sakes I will remember my ancient covenant
with their ancestors, whom I brought out of the land
of Egypt in the sight of all the nations, that I might be
their God. I am the LORD."

26:30 The Hebrew term (literally *round things*) probably alludes to dung.

26:14-39 if you do not listen to me. God couldn't have spelled out these curses any more clearly. Yet Israel often failed to follow the Lord.

26:41 stubborn hearts. A literal translation would be *uncircumcised hearts*. Circumcision showed that the Israelites belonged to God. A person with an uncircumcised, or stubborn, heart did not give evidence that he was a part of God's people.

26:44 by wiping them out. God has been true to this promise throughout history. The Israelites have been subjected to blow after blow, yet they have never been destroyed.

46 These are the decrees, regulations, and instructions that the LORD gave through Moses on Mount Sinai as evidence of the relationship between himself and the Israelites.

REDEMPTION OF GIFTS OFFERED TO THE LORD

27 The LORD said to Moses, 2 "Give the following instructions to the people of Israel. If anyone makes a special vow to dedicate someone to the LORD by paying the value of that person, 3 here is the scale of values to be used. A man between the ages of twenty and sixty is valued at fifty shekels* of silver, as measured by the sanctuary shekel. 4 A woman of that age is valued at thirty shekels* of silver. 5 A boy between the ages of five and twenty is valued at twenty shekels of silver; a girl of that age is valued at ten shekels* of silver. 6 A boy between the ages of one month and five years is valued at five shekels of silver; a girl of that age is valued at three shekels* of silver. 7 A man older than sixty is valued at fifteen shekels of silver; a woman of that age is valued at ten shekels* of silver. 8 If you desire to make such a vow but cannot afford to pay the required amount, take the person to the priest. He will determine the amount for you to pay based on what you can afford.

9 "If your vow involves giving an animal that is acceptable as an offering to the LORD, any gift to the LORD will be considered holy. 10 You may not exchange or substitute it for another animal—neither a good animal for a bad one nor a bad animal for a good one. But if you do exchange one animal for another, then both the original animal and its substitute will be considered holy. 11 If your vow involves an unclean animal—one that is not acceptable as an offering to the LORD—then you must bring the animal to the priest. 12 He will assess its value, and his assessment will be final, whether high or low. 13 If you want to buy back the animal, you must pay the value set by the priest, plus 20 percent.

14 "If someone dedicates a house to the LORD, the priest will come to assess its value. The priest's assessment will be final, whether high or low. 15 If the person who dedicated the house wants to buy it back, he must pay the value set by the priest, plus 20 percent. Then the house will again be his.

16 "If someone dedicates to the LORD a piece of his family property, its value will be assessed according to the amount of seed required to plant it—fifty shekels of silver for a field planted with five bushels of barley seed.* 17 If the field is dedicated to the LORD in the Year of Jubilee, then the entire assessment will apply. 18 But if the field is dedicated after the Year of Jubilee, the priest will assess the land's value in proportion to the number of years left until the next Year of Jubilee. Its assessed value is reduced each year. 19 If the person who dedicated the field wants to buy it back, he must pay the value set by the priest, plus 20 percent. Then the field will again be legally his. 20 But if he does not want to buy it back, and it is sold to someone else, the field can no longer be bought back. 21 When the field is released in the Year of Jubilee, it will be holy, a field specially set apart* for the LORD. It will become the property of the priests.

22 "If someone dedicates to the LORD a field he has purchased but which is not part of his family property, 23 the priest will assess its value based on the number of years left until the next Year of Jubilee. On that day he must give the assessed value of the land as a sacred donation to the LORD. 24 In the Year of Jubilee the field must be returned to the person from whom he purchased it, the one who inherited it as family property. 25 (All the payments must be measured by the weight of the sanctuary shekel,* which equals twenty gerahs.)

26 "You may not dedicate a firstborn animal to the LORD, for the firstborn of your cattle, sheep, and goats already belong to him. 27 However, you may buy back the firstborn of a ceremonially unclean animal by paying the priest's assessment of its worth, plus 20 percent. If you do not buy it back, the priest will sell it at its assessed value.

28 "However, anything specially set apart for the LORD—whether a person, an animal, or family property—must never be sold or bought back. Anything devoted in this way has been set apart as holy, and it belongs to the LORD. 29 No person specially set apart for destruction may be bought back. Such a person must be put to death.

30 "One-tenth of the produce of the land, whether grain from the fields or fruit from the trees, belongs to the LORD and must be set apart to him as holy. 31 If you want to buy back the LORD's tenth of the grain or fruit, you must pay its value, plus 20 percent. 32 Count off every tenth animal from your herds and flocks and set them apart for the LORD as holy. 33 You may not pick and choose between good and bad animals, and you may not substitute one for another. But if you do exchange one animal for another, then both the original animal and its substitute will be considered holy and cannot be bought back."

34 These are the commands that the LORD gave through Moses on Mount Sinai for the Israelites.

27:3 Or *20 ounces* [570 grams]. **27:4** Or *12 ounces* [342 grams]. **27:5** Or *A boy . . . 8 ounces* [228 grams] *of silver; a girl . . . 4 ounces* [114 grams]. **27:6** Or *A boy . . . 2 ounces* [57 grams] *of silver; a girl . . . 1.2 ounces* [34 grams]. **27:7** Or *A man . . . 6 ounces* [171 grams] *of silver; a woman . . . 4 ounces* [114 grams]. **27:16** Hebrew *50 shekels* [20 ounces or 570 grams] *of silver for a homer* [220 liters] *of barley seed.* **27:21** The Hebrew term used here refers to the complete consecration of things or people to the LORD, either by destroying them or by giving them as an offering; also in 27:28, 29. **27:25** Each shekel was about 0.4 ounces [11 grams] in weight.

27:2 special vow. Vows were like a special offering, over and above the tithe. People made vows to God out of gratitude or to please Him and receive His favor. Parents could not give daughters to God's service, but they could give money dedicating a daughter in a vow.

27:10 substitute. The prophet Malachi cited this abuse (Mal. 1:13-14). The people were dedicating healthy, acceptable animals for sacrifice to God but then switching them for sick and blemished animals.

27:28 set apart. People devoting themselves with a vow were accountable for the outcome of their vow.

27:29 set apart for destruction. When the Israelites conquered Jericho, they were instructed to destroy people and property. But Achan disobeyed this command from God. Until he was found out, God held the nation accountable for Achan's sin (Josh. 7:1-20).

27:30 One-tenth. All crops and animals were tithed (a tenth set apart).

27:34 These are the commands. This verse functioned as a kind of sign-off, giving the source (God), the author (Moses), and the place (Mount Sinai).

INTRODUCTION TO

NUMBERS

PERSONAL READING PLAN

☐Numbers 1:1-54
☐Numbers 2:1–3:51
☐Numbers 4:1-49
☐Numbers 5:1–6:27
☐Numbers 7:1-89
☐Numbers 8:1–9:14
☐Numbers 9:15–10:36
☐Numbers 11:1–12:16
☐Numbers 13:1–14:45
☐Numbers 15:1–16:50
☐Numbers 17:1–19:22
☐Numbers 20:1–21:20
☐Numbers 21:21–22:41
☐Numbers 23:1–24:25
☐Numbers 25:1–26:65
☐Numbers 27:1–28:8
☐Numbers 28:9–29:40
☐Numbers 30:1–31:54
☐Numbers 32:1-42
☐Numbers 33:1–34:29
☐Numbers 35:1–36:13

AUTHOR

Moses is assumed to be the author and editor of most of the first five books of the Old Testament (the Pentateuch).

DATE

It is difficult to set a firm date for the writing of the Pentateuch. Conservative estimates place it in either the 15th century or 13th century B.C., depending on when the Exodus occurred.

THEME

God's faithfulness despite Israel's rebellion, resulting in 40 years of misery and mercy.

HISTORICAL BACKGROUND

The name of this book in the English Bible is derived from the census taking and the mustering of the Israelite army in preparation for invading the promised land. This is detailed in chapters 1–4 and 26. The title of the book in the Hebrew Bible, meaning "in the desert" or "in the wilderness," is actually much more descriptive. The book of Numbers relates the story of the 40 years during which Israel journeyed from Mount Sinai to the edge of Canaan. This was a time of great turmoil for Israel in which the people expressed not gratitude for deliverance from Egypt but rebellion against God. Consequently, they lived out their lives in the desert.

CHARACTERISTICS

Arranged around the Israelites' wilderness wanderings, the book chronicles God's actions in leading His people toward the land of promise. What makes these actions truly remarkable is that they establish God's faithfulness in spite of the people's rebellious nature. The central human figure is Moses. He combines his many talents with a humble spirit to act as intermediary between his God and His people. The Book of Numbers provides us with a dramatic portrait of Moses, the Israelites, and God as they struggle to turn the disaster of the wilderness wanderings into success.

PASSAGES FOR TOPICAL GROUP STUDY

12:1-15 . . . . REBELLION . . . . Rebelling Against Authority
13:26–14:10,26-45 . . LACK OF FAITH. . . . . . Israelite Spy Team

REGISTRATION OF ISRAEL'S TROOPS

1 A year after Israel's departure from Egypt, the
LORD spoke to Moses in the Tabernacle* in the wil-
derness of Sinai. On the first day of the second month*
of that year he said, 2 "From the whole community of
Israel, record the names of all the warriors by their
clans and families. List all the men 3 twenty years old
or older who are able to go to war. You and Aaron
must register the troops, 4 and you will be assisted by
one family leader from each tribe.
5 "These are the tribes and the names of the leaders
who will assist you:

	Tribe	*Leader*
	Reuben	Elizur son of Shedeur
6	Simeon	Shelumiel son of Zurishaddai
7	Judah	Nahshon son of Amminadab
8	Issachar	Nethanel son of Zuar
9	Zebulun	Eliab son of Helon
10	Ephraim son of Joseph	Elishama son of Ammihud
	Manasseh son of Joseph	Gamaliel son of Pedahzur
11	Benjamin	Abidan son of Gideoni
12	Dan	Ahiezer son of Ammishaddai
13	Asher	Pagiel son of Ocran
14	Gad	Eliasaph son of Deuel
15	Naphtali	Ahira son of Enan

16 These are the chosen leaders of the community, the
leaders of their ancestral tribes, the heads of the clans
of Israel."
17 So Moses and Aaron called together these chosen
leaders, 18 and they assembled the whole community
of Israel on that very day.* All the people were regis-
tered according to their ancestry by their clans and
families. The men of Israel who were twenty years
old or older were listed one by one, 19 just as the LORD
had commanded Moses. So Moses recorded their
names in the wilderness of Sinai.
20-21 This is the number of men twenty years old or
older who were able to go to war, as their names were
listed in the records of their clans and families*:

	Tribe	*Number*
	Reuben (Jacob's* oldest son)	46,500
22-23	Simeon	59,300
24-25	Gad	45,650
26-27	Judah	74,600
28-29	Issachar	54,400
30-31	Zebulun	57,400
32-33	Ephraim son of Joseph	40,500
34-35	Manasseh son of Joseph	32,200
36-37	Benjamin	35,400
38-39	Dan	62,700
40-41	Asher	41,500
42-43	Naphtali	53,400

44 These were the men registered by Moses and Aaron
and the twelve leaders of Israel, all listed according
to their ancestral descent. 45 They were registered
by families—all the men of Israel who were twenty
years old or older and able to go to war. 46 The total
number was 603,550.
47 But this total did not include the Levites. 48 For the
LORD had said to Moses, 49 "Do not include the tribe
of Levi in the registration; do not count them with
the rest of the Israelites. 50 Put the Levites in charge
of the Tabernacle of the Covenant,* along with all its
furnishings and equipment. They must carry the Tab-
ernacle and all its furnishings as you travel, and they
must take care of it and camp around it. 51 Whenever
it is time for the Tabernacle to move, the Levites will
take it down. And when it is time to stop, they will set
it up again. But any unauthorized person who goes too
near the Tabernacle must be put to death. 52 Each tribe
of Israel will camp in a designated area with its own
family banner. 53 But the Levites will camp around the
Tabernacle of the Covenant to protect the communi-
ty of Israel from the LORD's anger. The Levites are re-
sponsible to stand guard around the Tabernacle."
54 So the Israelites did everything just as the LORD
had commanded Moses.

ORGANIZATION FOR ISRAEL'S CAMP

2 Then the LORD gave these instructions to Moses
and Aaron: 2 "When the Israelites set up camp,
each tribe will be assigned its own area. The tribal
divisions will camp beneath their family banners on
all four sides of the Tabernacle,* but at some distance
from it.
3-4 "The divisions of Judah, Issachar, and Zebulun
are to camp toward the sunrise on the east side of the
Tabernacle, beneath their family banners. These are
the names of the tribes, their leaders, and the num-
bers of their registered troops:

	Tribe	*Leader*	*Number*
	Judah	Nahshon son of Amminadab	74,600
5-6	Issachar	Nethanel son of Zuar	54,400
7-8	Zebulun	Eliab son of Helon	57,400

9 So the total of all the troops on Judah's side of the
camp is 186,400. These three tribes are to lead the
way whenever the Israelites travel to a new campsite.

1:1a Hebrew *the Tent of Meeting.* **1:1b** This day in the ancient Hebrew lunar calendar occurred in April or May. **1:18** Hebrew *on the first day of the second month;* see 1:1. **1:20-21a** In the Hebrew text, this sentence (*This is the number of men twenty years old or older who were able to go to war, as their names were listed in the records of their clans and families*) is repeated in 1:22, 24, 26, 28, 30, 32, 34, 36, 38, 40, 42. **1:20-21b** Hebrew *Israel's.* The names "Jacob" and "Israel" are often interchanged throughout the Old Testament, referring sometimes to the individual patriarch and sometimes to the nation. **1:50** Or *Tabernacle of the Testimony;* also in 1:53. **2:2** Hebrew *the Tent of Meeting;* also in 2:17.

1:2 record the names. This is the first census mentioned in the Bible. (See also ch. 26; 2 Sam. 24:1-9; and Luke 2.)

1:3 troops. This census was to form an army, so it counted only fit males.

1:4 one family leader from each tribe. This smart move reduced competition among the tribes, and it allowed minor issues to be settled by tribal representatives.

1:5-16 Ten tribes represented sons of Jacob (Israel). The other two names were the sons of Joseph.

1:32-35 Joseph. Joseph's sons, rather than Joseph, were heads of tribes. This gave Joseph's family a double portion.

1:46 total number. Just 70 people moved to Egypt as part of Jacob's family; the total of 603,550 men was phenomenal.

1:47-50 Levi. The Levites were not counted in the military census because they were responsible for maintaining and moving the tabernacle.

1:53 Levites . . . around the Tabernacle. The Levites served in the tabernacle; naturally they would set up their tents in a protective circle around it.

2:2 distance. Tribes kept their distance out of respect for the presence of God in the tabernacle.

2:3-4 Judah. Judah was not the firstborn, yet his tribe was listed first here. Jesus was born in his family line.

[10-11]"The divisions of Reuben, Simeon, and Gad are
to camp on the south side of the Tabernacle, beneath
their family banners. These are the names of the
tribes, their leaders, and the numbers of their regis-
tered troops:

	Tribe	*Leader*	*Number*
	Reuben	Elizur son of Shedeur	46,500
12-13	Simeon	Shelumiel son of Zurishaddai	59,300
14-15	Gad	Eliasaph son of Deuel*	45,650

[16] So the total of all the troops on Reuben's side of the
camp is 151,450. These three tribes will be second in
line whenever the Israelites travel.
[17] "Then the Tabernacle, carried by the Levites,
will set out from the middle of the camp. All the
tribes are to travel in the same order that they
camp, each in position under the appropriate fam-
ily banner.
[18-19] "The divisions of Ephraim, Manasseh, and Ben-
jamin are to camp on the west side of the Tabernacle,
beneath their family banners. These are the names
of the tribes, their leaders, and the numbers of their
registered troops:

	Tribe	*Leader*	*Number*
	Ephraim	Elishama son of Ammihud	40,500
20-21	Manasseh	Gamaliel son of Pedahzur	32,200
22-23	Benjamin	Abidan son of Gideoni	35,400

[24] So the total of all the troops on Ephraim's side of the
camp is 108,100. These three tribes will be third in
line whenever the Israelites travel.
[25-26] "The divisions of Dan, Asher, and Naphtali are
to camp on the north side of the Tabernacle, beneath
their family banners. These are the names of the
tribes, their leaders, and the numbers of their regis-
tered troops:

	Tribe	*Leader*	*Number*
	Dan	Ahiezer son of Ammishaddai	62,700
27-28	Asher	Pagiel son of Ocran	41,500
29-30	Naphtali	Ahira son of Enan	53,400

[31] So the total of all the troops on Dan's side of the
camp is 157,600. These three tribes will be last,
marching under their banners whenever the Israel-
ites travel."
[32] In summary, the troops of Israel listed by their
families totaled 603,550. [33] But as the LORD had com-
manded, the Levites were not included in this regis-
tration. [34] So the people of Israel did everything as the
LORD had commanded Moses. Each clan and family
set up camp and marched under their banners exact-
ly as the LORD had instructed them.

LEVITES APPOINTED FOR SERVICE

3 This is the family line of Aaron and Moses as it was
recorded when the LORD spoke to Moses on Mount
Sinai: [2] The names of Aaron's sons were Nadab (the old-
est), Abihu, Eleazar, and Ithamar. [3] These sons of Aaron
were anointed and ordained to minister as priests. [4] But
Nadab and Abihu died in the LORD's presence in the
wilderness of Sinai when they burned before the LORD
the wrong kind of fire, different than he had command-
ed. Since they had no sons, this left only Eleazar and Ith-
amar to serve as priests with their father, Aaron.
[5] Then the LORD said to Moses, [6] "Call forward the
tribe of Levi, and present them to Aaron the priest to
serve as his assistants. [7] They will serve Aaron and
the whole community, performing their sacred duties
in and around the Tabernacle.* [8] They will also main-
tain all the furnishings of the sacred tent,* serving in
the Tabernacle on behalf of all the Israelites. [9] Assign
the Levites to Aaron and his sons. They have been
given from among all the people of Israel to serve as
their assistants. [10] Appoint Aaron and his sons to car-
ry out the duties of the priesthood. But any unautho-
rized person who goes too near the sanctuary must
be put to death."
[11] And the LORD said to Moses, [12] "Look, I have cho-
sen the Levites from among the Israelites to serve as
substitutes for all the firstborn sons of the people of
Israel. The Levites belong to me, [13] for all the firstborn
males are mine. On the day I struck down all the first-
born sons of the Egyptians, I set apart for myself all
the firstborn in Israel, both of people and of animals.
They are mine; I am the LORD."

REGISTRATION OF THE LEVITES

[14] The LORD spoke again to Moses in the wilderness of
Sinai. He said, [15] "Record the names of the members of
the tribe of Levi by their families and clans. List every
male who is one month old or older." [16] So Moses listed
them, just as the LORD had commanded.
[17] Levi had three sons, whose names were Gershon,
Kohath, and Merari.
[18] The clans descended from Gershon were named af-
ter two of his descendants, Libni and Shimei.

2:14-15 As in many Hebrew manuscripts, Samaritan Pentateuch, and Latin Vulgate (see also 1:14); most Hebrew manuscripts read *son of Reuel*.
3:7 Hebrew *around the Tent of Meeting, doing service at the Tabernacle.* **3:8** Hebrew *the Tent of Meeting;* also in 3:25.

2:10 Reuben. Jacob had predicted that Reuben's tribe would be known for indecision.
2:12-13 Simeon. Jacob had predicted that Simeon's tribe would eventually be scattered.
2:14 Gad. Jacob had predicted that Gad's tribe would have a history of being attacked.
2:18-22 Ephraim, Manasseh, Benjamin. Ephraim and Manasseh were sons of Joseph. Joseph and Benjamin were Jacob's favorite sons.
2:25 Dan. Jacob once described Dan's tribe as a serpent and a viper.
2:27 Asher. Jacob foretold wealth for Asher.
2:29 Naphtali. Jacob described Naphtali's tribe as mountain people.
2:32 603,550. This counted only the able-bodied men aged 20 and over.
2:34 everything as the LORD had commanded. Moses was God's mouthpiece for the Hebrews.
3:4 the wrong kind. See Leviticus 22:9.
3:5-10 tribe of Levi . . . Aaron. Aaron's descendants were priests. All other Levites were tabernacle workers.
3:9 Assign . . . Aaron. Aaron oversaw the tabernacle service of all Levites.
3:10 put to death. The tabernacle was the place of God's presence. No one besides Aaron and his descendants and Aaron's tribe (the Levites) was allowed to work in the tabernacle or offer sacrifices or enter the Holy Place or Most Holy Place, under penalty of death.
3:12-13 all the firstborn sons. God had spared the firstborn sons of Israel when He killed all the firstborn sons of Egypt (Ex. 12:12-13). Thus, God had a right to the firstborn sons as His own. Instead, God claimed the Levite tribe to serve before Him and lead the worship.
3:15 Record. The Levites, not counted in the census, were counted here.

19 The clans descended from Kohath were named after
four of his descendants, Amram, Izhar, Hebron, and
Uzziel.
20 The clans descended from Merari were named after
two of his descendants, Mahli and Mushi.
These were the Levite clans, listed according to their
family groups.

21 The descendants of Gershon were composed of
the clans descended from Libni and Shimei. 22 There
were 7,500 males one month old or older among these
Gershonite clans. 23 They were assigned the area to
the west of the Tabernacle for their camp. 24 The lead-
er of the Gershonite clans was Eliasaph son of Lael.
25 These two clans were responsible to care for the
Tabernacle, including the sacred tent with its layers
of coverings, the curtain at its entrance, 26 the curtains
of the courtyard that surrounded the Tabernacle and
altar, the curtain at the courtyard entrance, the ropes,
and all the equipment related to their use.
27 The descendants of Kohath were composed of the
clans descended from Amram, Izhar, Hebron, and Uz-
ziel. 28 There were 8,600* males one month old or old-
er among these Kohathite clans. They were respon-
sible for the care of the sanctuary, 29 and they were
assigned the area south of the Tabernacle for their
camp. 30 The leader of the Kohathite clans was Eliza-
phan son of Uzziel. 31 These four clans were responsi-
ble for the care of the Ark, the table, the lampstand,
the altars, the various articles used in the sanctuary,
the inner curtain, and all the equipment related to
their use. 32 Eleazar, son of Aaron the priest, was the
chief administrator over all the Levites, with special
responsibility for the oversight of the sanctuary.
33 The descendants of Merari were composed of
the clans descended from Mahli and Mushi. 34 There
were 6,200 males one month old or older among
these Merarite clans. 35 They were assigned the area
north of the Tabernacle for their camp. The leader of
the Merarite clans was Zuriel son of Abihail. 36 These
two clans were responsible for the care of the frames
supporting the Tabernacle, the crossbars, the pillars,
the bases, and all the equipment related to their use.
37 They were also responsible for the posts of the
courtyard and all their bases, pegs, and ropes.
38 The area in front of the Tabernacle, in the east to-
ward the sunrise,* was reserved for the tents of Moses
and of Aaron and his sons, who had the final respon-
sibility for the sanctuary on behalf of the people of Is-
rael. Anyone other than a priest or Levite who went
too near the sanctuary was to be put to death.
39 When Moses and Aaron counted the Levite clans
at the LORD's command, the total number was 22,000
males one month old or older.

REDEEMING THE FIRSTBORN SONS

40 Then the LORD said to Moses, "Now count all the
firstborn sons in Israel who are one month old or old-
er, and make a list of their names. 41 The Levites must
be reserved for me as substitutes for the firstborn
sons of Israel; I am the LORD. And the Levites' live-
stock must be reserved for me as substitutes for the
firstborn livestock of the whole nation of Israel."
42 So Moses counted the firstborn sons of the peo-
ple of Israel, just as the LORD had commanded. 43 The
number of firstborn sons who were one month old or
older was 22,273.
44 Then the LORD said to Moses, 45 "Take the Levites
as substitutes for the firstborn sons of the people of
Israel. And take the livestock of the Levites as substi-
tutes for the firstborn livestock of the people of Isra-
el. The Levites belong to me; I am the LORD. 46 There
are 273 more firstborn sons of Israel than there are
Levites. To redeem these extra firstborn sons, 47 col-
lect five pieces of silver* for each of them (each piece
weighing the same as the sanctuary shekel, which
equals twenty gerahs). 48 Give the silver to Aaron and
his sons as the redemption price for the extra first-
born sons."
49 So Moses collected the silver for redeeming the
firstborn sons of Israel who exceeded the number of
Levites. 50 He collected 1,365 pieces of silver* on behalf
of these firstborn sons of Israel (each piece weighing
the same as the sanctuary shekel). 51 And Moses gave
the silver for the redemption to Aaron and his sons,
just as the LORD had commanded.

DUTIES OF THE KOHATHITE CLAN

4 Then the LORD said to Moses and Aaron, 2 "Record
the names of the members of the clans and fami-
lies of the Kohathite division of the tribe of Levi. 3 List
all the men between the ages of thirty and fifty who
are eligible to serve in the Tabernacle.*
4 "The duties of the Kohathites at the Tabernacle
will relate to the most sacred objects. 5 When the
camp moves, Aaron and his sons must enter the Tab-
ernacle first to take down the inner curtain and cov-
er the Ark of the Covenant* with it. 6 Then they must
cover the inner curtain with fine goatskin leather and
spread over that a single piece of blue cloth. Finally,
they must put the carrying poles of the Ark in place.
7 "Next they must spread a blue cloth over the table
where the Bread of the Presence is displayed, and on
the cloth they will place the bowls, ladles, jars, pitch-
ers, and the special bread. 8 They must spread a scar-
let cloth over all of this, and finally a covering of fine
goatskin leather on top of the scarlet cloth. Then they
must insert the carrying poles into the table.
9 "Next they must cover the lampstand with a blue
cloth, along with its lamps, lamp snuffers, trays, and
special jars of olive oil. 10 Then they must cover the
lampstand and its accessories with fine goatskin
leather and place the bundle on a carrying frame.
11 "Next they must spread a blue cloth over the gold
incense altar and cover this cloth with fine goatskin
leather. Then they must attach the carrying poles to

3:28 Some Greek manuscripts read *8,300;* see total in 3:39. **3:38** Hebrew *toward the sunrise, in front of the Tent of Meeting.* **3:47** Hebrew *5 shekels* [2 ounces or 57 grams]. **3:50** Hebrew *1,365 [shekels] of silver* [34 pounds or 15.5 kilograms]. **4:3** Hebrew *the Tent of Meeting;* also in 4:4, 15, 23, 25, 28, 30, 31, 33, 35, 37, 39, 41, 43, 47. **4:5** Or *Ark of the Testimony.*

3:21-38 These people were to see to it that God was welcomed, honored, and obeyed among the people.
3:25-26 curtain. The tabernacle was a tent made of cloth or animal hide curtains held up by stakes.
3:28 sanctuary. The sanctuary of the tabernacle, or temple, usually meant the Holy Place, a highly restricted part of the structure.
3:31 the Ark. Misuse of the ark, even if the person intended to be helpful, meant death (see 2 Sam. 6:1-7).
3:41 firstborn. See note at 3:12-13.
4:3 between the ages of thirty and fifty. These were the prime years of service in the tabernacle. A Levite's official duties began at 30.

the altar. 12 They must take all the remaining furnishings of the sanctuary and wrap them in a blue cloth, cover them with fine goatskin leather, and place them on the carrying frame.

13 "They must remove the ashes from the altar for sacrifices and cover the altar with a purple cloth. 14 All the altar utensils—the firepans, meat forks, shovels, basins, and all the containers—must be placed on the cloth, and a covering of fine goatskin leather must be spread over them. Finally, they must put the carrying poles in place. 15 The camp will be ready to move when Aaron and his sons have finished covering the sanctuary and all the sacred articles. The Kohathites will come and carry these things to the next destination. But they must not touch the sacred objects, or they will die. So these are the things from the Tabernacle that the Kohathites must carry.

16 "Eleazar son of Aaron the priest will be responsible for the oil of the lampstand, the fragrant incense, the daily grain offering, and the anointing oil. In fact, Eleazar will be responsible for the entire Tabernacle and everything in it, including the sanctuary and its furnishings."

17 Then the LORD said to Moses and Aaron, 18 "Do not let the Kohathite clans be destroyed from among the Levites! 19 This is what you must do so they will live and not die when they approach the most sacred objects. Aaron and his sons must always go in with them and assign a specific duty or load to each person. 20 The Kohathites must never enter the sanctuary to look at the sacred objects for even a moment, or they will die."

DUTIES OF THE GERSHONITE CLAN

21 And the LORD said to Moses, 22 "Record the names of the members of the clans and families of the Gershonite division of the tribe of Levi. 23 List all the men between the ages of thirty and fifty who are eligible to serve in the Tabernacle.

24 "These Gershonite clans will be responsible for general service and carrying loads. 25 They must carry the curtains of the Tabernacle, the Tabernacle itself with its coverings, the outer covering of fine goatskin leather, and the curtain for the Tabernacle entrance. 26 They are also to carry the curtains for the courtyard walls that surround the Tabernacle and altar, the curtain across the courtyard entrance, the ropes, and all the equipment related to their use. The Gershonites are responsible for all these items. 27 Aaron and his sons will direct the Gershonites regarding all their duties, whether it involves moving the equipment or doing other work. They must assign the Gershonites responsibility for the loads they are to carry. 28 So these are the duties assigned to the Gershonite clans at the Tabernacle. They will be directly responsible to Ithamar son of Aaron the priest.

DUTIES OF THE MERARITE CLAN

29 "Now record the names of the members of the clans and families of the Merarite division of the tribe of Levi. 30 List all the men between the ages of thirty and fifty who are eligible to serve in the Tabernacle.

31 "Their only duty at the Tabernacle will be to carry loads. They will carry the frames of the Tabernacle, the crossbars, the posts, and the bases; 32 also the posts for the courtyard walls with their bases, pegs, and ropes; and all the accessories and everything else related to their use. Assign the various loads to each man by name. 33 So these are the duties of the Merarite clans at the Tabernacle. They are directly responsible to Ithamar son of Aaron the priest."

SUMMARY OF THE REGISTRATION

34 So Moses, Aaron, and the other leaders of the community listed the members of the Kohathite division by their clans and families. 35 The list included all the men between thirty and fifty years of age who were eligible for service in the Tabernacle, 36 and the total number came to 2,750. 37 So this was the total of all those from the Kohathite clans who were eligible to serve at the Tabernacle. Moses and Aaron listed them, just as the LORD had commanded through Moses.

38 The Gershonite division was also listed by its clans and families. 39 The list included all the men between thirty and fifty years of age who were eligible for service in the Tabernacle, 40 and the total number came to 2,630. 41 So this was the total of all those from the Gershonite clans who were eligible to serve at the Tabernacle. Moses and Aaron listed them, just as the LORD had commanded.

42 The Merarite division was also listed by its clans and families. 43 The list included all the men between thirty and fifty years of age who were eligible for service in the Tabernacle, 44 and the total number came to 3,200. 45 So this was the total of all those from the Merarite clans who were eligible for service. Moses and Aaron listed them, just as the LORD had commanded through Moses.

46 So Moses, Aaron, and the leaders of Israel listed all the Levites by their clans and families. 47 All the men between thirty and fifty years of age who were eligible for service in the Tabernacle and for its transportation 48 numbered 8,580. 49 When their names were recorded, as the LORD had commanded through Moses, each man was assigned his task and told what to carry.

And so the registration was completed, just as the LORD had commanded Moses.

PURITY IN ISRAEL'S CAMP

5 The LORD gave these instructions to Moses: 2 "Command the people of Israel to remove from the camp anyone who has a skin disease* or a discharge, or who has become ceremonially unclean by touching a dead person. 3 This command applies to men and women alike. Remove them so they will not defile the camp in which I live among them." 4 So the Israelites did as the LORD had commanded Moses and removed such people from the camp.

5 Then the LORD said to Moses, 6 "Give the following instructions to the people of Israel: If any of the

5:2 Traditionally rendered *leprosy.* The Hebrew word used here describes various skin diseases.

4:16 Eleazar. It was no small job for Eleazar to oversee the whole process.

4:22-33 Specific duties were clearly assigned.

4:34-59 This census focused on Levite men ages 30 to 50.

5:2 skin disease or a discharge. Strict instructions were given to the people in Leviticus 13–15 about diagnosing, treating, and dealing with conditions that God defined as "unclean." Conditions deemed unclean all related to death—loss of blood or semen, skin white like a corpse, or touching a corpse. God taught separation from sin and death.

5:5-10 These verses focus on restitution. Preceding verses address cleanliness of the body and the holiness of God. These verses approach cleanliness in terms of human relationships and holiness of heart.

people—men or women—betray the LORD by doing wrong to another person, they are guilty. 7 They must confess their sin and make full restitution for what they have done, adding an additional 20 percent and returning it to the person who was wronged. 8 But if the person who was wronged is dead, and there are no near relatives to whom restitution can be made, the payment belongs to the LORD and must be given to the priest. Those who are guilty must also bring a ram as a sacrifice, and they will be purified and made right with the LORD.* 9 All the sacred offerings that the Israelites bring to a priest will belong to him. 10 Each priest may keep all the sacred donations that he receives."

PROTECTING MARITAL FAITHFULNESS

11 And the LORD said to Moses, 12 "Give the following instructions to the people of Israel.

"Suppose a man's wife goes astray, and she is unfaithful to her husband 13 and has sex with another man, but neither her husband nor anyone else knows about it. She has defiled herself, even though there was no witness and she was not caught in the act. 14 If her husband becomes jealous and is suspicious of his wife and needs to know whether or not she has defiled herself, 15 the husband must bring his wife to the priest. He must also bring an offering of two quarts* of barley flour to be presented on her behalf. Do not mix it with olive oil or frankincense, for it is a jealousy offering—an offering to prove whether or not she is guilty.

16 "The priest will then present her to stand trial before the LORD. 17 He must take some holy water in a clay jar and pour into it dust he has taken from the Tabernacle floor. 18 When the priest has presented the woman before the LORD, he must unbind her hair and place in her hands the offering of proof—the jealousy offering to determine whether her husband's suspicions are justified. The priest will stand before her, holding the jar of bitter water that brings a curse to those who are guilty. 19 The priest will then put the woman under oath and say to her, 'If no other man has had sex with you, and you have not gone astray and defiled yourself while under your husband's authority, may you be immune from the effects of this bitter water that brings on the curse. 20 But if you have gone astray by being unfaithful to your husband, and have defiled yourself by having sex with another man—'

21 "At this point the priest must put the woman under oath by saying, 'May the people know that the LORD's curse is upon you when he makes you infertile, causing your womb to shrivel* and your abdomen to swell. 22 Now may this water that brings the curse enter your body and cause your abdomen to swell and your womb to shrivel.*' And the woman will be required to say, 'Yes, let it be so.' 23 And the priest will write these curses on a piece of leather and wash them off into the bitter water. 24 He will make the woman drink the bitter water that brings on the curse. When the water enters her body, it will cause bitter suffering if she is guilty.

25 "The priest will take the jealousy offering from the woman's hand, lift it up before the LORD, and carry it to the altar. 26 He will take a handful of the flour as a token portion and burn it on the altar, and he will require the woman to drink the water. 27 If she has defiled herself by being unfaithful to her husband, the water that brings on the curse will cause bitter suffering. Her abdomen will swell and her womb will shrink,* and her name will become a curse among her people. 28 But if she has not defiled herself and is pure, then she will be unharmed and will still be able to have children.

29 "This is the ritual law for dealing with suspicion. If a woman goes astray and defiles herself while under her husband's authority, 30 or if a man becomes jealous and is suspicious that his wife has been unfaithful, the husband must present his wife before the LORD, and the priest will apply this entire ritual law to her. 31 The husband will be innocent of any guilt in this matter, but his wife will be held accountable for her sin."

NAZIRITE LAWS

6 Then the LORD said to Moses, 2 "Give the following instructions to the people of Israel.

"If any of the people, either men or women, take the special vow of a Nazirite, setting themselves apart to the LORD in a special way, 3 they must give up wine and other alcoholic drinks. They must not use vinegar made from wine or from other alcoholic drinks, they must not drink fresh grape juice, and they must not eat grapes or raisins. 4 As long as they are bound by their Nazirite vow, they are not allowed to eat or drink anything that comes from a grapevine—not even the grape seeds or skins.

5 "They must never cut their hair throughout the time of their vow, for they are holy and set apart to the LORD. Until the time of their vow has been fulfilled, they must let their hair grow long. 6 And they must not go near a dead body during the entire period of their vow to the LORD. 7 Even if the dead person is their own father, mother, brother, or sister, they must not defile themselves, for the hair on their head is the symbol of their separation to God. 8 This requirement applies as long as they are set apart to the LORD.

9 "If someone falls dead beside them, the hair they have dedicated will be defiled. They must wait for seven days and then shave their heads. Then they

5:8 Or *bring a ram for atonement, which will make atonement for them.* **5:15** Hebrew $^{1}/_{10}$ *of an ephah* [2.2 liters]. **5:21** Hebrew *when he causes your thigh to waste away.* **5:22** Hebrew *and your thigh to waste away.* **5:27** Hebrew *and her thigh will waste away.*

5:11-31 Now this chapter turns to marital relations. The Bible often uses marriage as a metaphor for our relationship with God. It is not surprising then that marital unfaithfulness carried severe penalties.

5:14 jealous. A husband was responsible to deal with his marriage even if his concern was not fully substantiated. He was not free to wait and see or to look the other way.

5:15-28 Unlike infamous witch trials in early American history, the trial described here is not deadly in and of itself. If a woman was cursed after drinking dusty water, this was a miracle showing God's judgment.

5:21 under oath. Ultimately this oath was a curse that led to sterility, if guilty.

6:2 Nazirite. Other lifetime Nazirites in the Bible included John the Baptist (Luke 1:15), Samuel (1 Sam. 1:11), and probably the most famous, Samson (Judg. 13:1-7; 16:17). For most people, the Nazirite vow was only for a period of time.

6:6-7 dead body. Touching a corpse caused uncleanness (Lev. 15), even though it was often necessary. Priests and Nazirites were forbidden to touch a corpse at all. God taught separation from sin and death.

will be cleansed from their defilement. 10 On the
eighth day they must bring two turtledoves or two
young pigeons to the priest at the entrance of the Tab-
ernacle.* 11 The priest will offer one of the birds for a
sin offering and the other for a burnt offering. In this
way, he will purify them* from the guilt they incurred
through contact with the dead body. Then they must
reaffirm their commitment and let their hair begin to
grow again. 12 The days of their vow that were com-
pleted before their defilement no longer count. They
must rededicate themselves to the LORD as a Nazirite
for the full term of their vow, and each must bring a
one-year-old male lamb for a guilt offering.

13 "This is the ritual law for Nazirites. At the con-
clusion of their time of separation as Nazirites, they
must each go to the entrance of the Tabernacle 14 and
offer their sacrifices to the LORD: a one year-old male
lamb without defect for a burnt offering, a one-year-
old female lamb without defect for a sin offering, a
ram without defect for a peace offering, 15 a basket
of bread made without yeast—cakes of choice flour
mixed with olive oil and wafers spread with olive
oil—along with their prescribed grain offerings and
liquid offerings. 16 The priest will present these of-
ferings before the LORD: first the sin offering and the
burnt offering; 17 then the ram for a peace offering,
along with the basket of bread made without yeast.
The priest must also present the prescribed grain of-
fering and liquid offering to the LORD.

18 "Then the Nazirites will shave their heads at the
entrance of the Tabernacle. They will take the hair that
had been dedicated and place it on the fire beneath the
peace-offering sacrifice. 19 After the Nazirite's head has
been shaved, the priest will take for each of them the
boiled shoulder of the ram, and he will take from the
basket a cake and a wafer made without yeast. He will
put them all into the Nazirite's hands. 20 Then the priest
will lift them up as a special offering before the LORD.
These are holy portions for the priest, along with the
breast of the special offering and the thigh of the sa-
cred offering that are lifted up before the LORD. After
this ceremony the Nazirites may again drink wine.

21 "This is the ritual law of the Nazirites, who vow to
bring these offerings to the LORD. They may also bring
additional offerings if they can afford it. And they
must be careful to do whatever they vowed when
they set themselves apart as Nazirites."

THE PRIESTLY BLESSING

22 Then the LORD said to Moses, 23 "Tell Aaron and his
sons to bless the people of Israel with this special
blessing:

24 'May the LORD bless you
and protect you.
25 May the LORD smile on you
and be gracious to you.
26 May the LORD show you his favor
and give you his peace.'

27 Whenever Aaron and his sons bless the people of Is-
rael in my name, I myself will bless them."

OFFERINGS OF DEDICATION

7 On the day Moses set up the Tabernacle, he anoint-
ed it and set it apart as holy. He also anointed
and set apart all its furnishings and the altar with
its utensils. 2 Then the leaders of Israel—the tribal
leaders who had registered the troops—came and
brought their offerings. 3 Together they brought six
large wagons and twelve oxen. There was a wagon
for every two leaders and an ox for each leader. They
presented these to the LORD in front of the Tabernacle.

4 Then the LORD said to Moses, 5 "Receive their gifts,
and use these oxen and wagons for transporting the
Tabernacle.* Distribute them among the Levites ac-
cording to the work they have to do." 6 So Moses took
the wagons and oxen and presented them to the Le-
vites. 7 He gave two wagons and four oxen to the Ger-
shonite division for their work, 8 and he gave four
wagons and eight oxen to the Merarite division for
their work. All their work was done under the leader-
ship of Ithamar son of Aaron the priest. 9 But he gave
none of the wagons or oxen to the Kohathite division,
since they were required to carry the sacred objects
of the Tabernacle on their shoulders.

10 The leaders also presented dedication gifts for the
altar at the time it was anointed. They each placed
their gifts before the altar. 11 The LORD said to Moses,
"Let one leader bring his gift each day for the dedica-
tion of the altar."

12 On the first day Nahshon son of Amminadab, leader
of the tribe of Judah, presented his offering.

13 His offering consisted of a silver platter weigh-
ing 3¹/₄ pounds and a silver basin weighing
1³/₄ pounds* (as measured by the weight of the
sanctuary shekel). These were both filled with
grain offerings of choice flour moistened with ol-
ive oil. 14 He also brought a gold container weigh-
ing four ounces,* which was filled with incense.
15 He brought a young bull, a ram, and a one-year-
old male lamb for a burnt offering, 16 and a male
goat for a sin offering. 17 For a peace offering he
brought two bulls, five rams, five male goats, and

6:10 Hebrew *the Tent of Meeting;* also in 6:13, 18. **6:11** Or *make atonement for them.* **7:5** Hebrew *the Tent of Meeting;* also in 7:89. **7:13** Hebrew *silver platter weighing 130 [shekels]* [1.5 kilograms] *and a silver basin weighing 70 shekels* [800 grams]; also in 7:19, 25, 31, 37, 43, 49, 55, 61, 67, 73, 79, 85. **7:14** Hebrew *10 [shekels]* [114 grams]; also in 7:20, 26, 32, 38, 44, 50, 56, 62, 68, 74, 80, 86.

6:9-12 This is one of the cases where the Bible demands perfection but makes practical provision for real life. Even though the Nazirite was forbidden to be around a dead body, there are provisions for resuming his vow if his proximity to death was outside his control.

6:13-20 Only a few Nazirites-for-life are mentioned in the Bible, but many took the vow for a certain period of time. This was a special time to show dedication to God.

6:14-15 burnt . . . sin . . . peace . . . grain . . . liquid offerings. A Nazirite vow was expensive and involved almost every kind of sacrifice. Paul took a Nazirite vow and offered sacrifices as a Christian (Acts 18:18; 21:23-26).

6:24-26 May the LORD bless you. This benediction has journeyed through the history of the church. Many worship services today conclude with it. **show you his favor.** Literally "turn His face toward you." When God turns His face toward His people He gives them His presence and attention. This may be the benediction Jesus gave when He ascended (Luke 24:50).

6:25 May the LORD smile on you. This has the connotation of God's pleasure in His people. Even today we describe parents watching their children as "beaming" with pride.

6:27 bless . . . in my name. God intended for them to be His special people, blessed by Him, and through them a blessing to other nations.

7:1-89 While the people had already received many instructions about the tabernacle, this passage describes the actual dedication of the tabernacle. The people brought gifts to be used in transporting the tabernacle from Mount Sinai on the journey to the promised land.

7:12-83 As with the rest of community life, the people gave their gifts according to tribe in an orderly fashion.

five one-year-old male lambs. This was the offer-
ing brought by Nahshon son of Amminadab.

18 On the second day Nethanel son of Zuar, leader of
the tribe of Issachar, presented his offering.
19 His offering consisted of a silver platter weigh-
ing $3^1/_4$ pounds and a silver basin weighing
$1^3/_4$ pounds (as measured by the weight of the
sanctuary shekel). These were both filled with
grain offerings of choice flour moistened with
olive oil. 20 He also brought a gold container
weighing four ounces, which was filled with
incense. 21 He brought a young bull, a ram, and
a one-year-old male lamb for a burnt offering,
22 and a male goat for a sin offering. 23 For a peace
offering he brought two bulls, five rams, five male
goats, and five one-year-old male lambs. This was
the offering brought by Nethanel son of Zuar.

24 On the third day Eliab son of Helon, leader of the
tribe of Zebulun, presented his offering.
25 His offering consisted of a silver platter
weighing $3^1/_4$ pounds and a silver basin weigh-
ing $1^3/_4$ pounds (as measured by the weight of
the sanctuary shekel). These were both filled
with grain offerings of choice flour moistened
with olive oil. 26 He also brought a gold container
weighing four ounces, which was filled with
incense. 27 He brought a young bull, a ram, and
a one-year-old male lamb for a burnt offering,
28 and a male goat for a sin offering. 29 For a peace
offering he brought two bulls, five rams, five
male goats, and five one-year-old male lambs.
This was the offering brought by Eliab son of
Helon.

30 On the fourth day Elizur son of Shedeur, leader of
the tribe of Reuben, presented his offering.
31 His offering consisted of a silver platter weigh-
ing $3^1/_4$ pounds and a silver basin weighing
$1^3/_4$ pounds (as measured by the weight of the
sanctuary shekel). These were both filled with
grain offerings of choice flour moistened with
olive oil. 32 He also brought a gold container
weighing four ounces, which was filled with
incense. 33 He brought a young bull, a ram, and
a one-year-old male lamb for a burnt offering,
34 and a male goat for a sin offering. 35 For a peace
offering he brought two bulls, five rams, five male
goats, and five one-year-old male lambs. This was
the offering brought by Elizur son of Shedeur.

36 On the fifth day Shelumiel son of Zurishaddai, lead-
er of the tribe of Simeon, presented his offering.
37 His offering consisted of a silver platter
weighing $3^1/_4$ pounds and a silver basin weighing
$1^3/_4$ pounds (as measured by the weight of the
sanctuary shekel). These were both filled with
grain offerings of choice flour moistened with ol-
ive oil. 38 He also brought a gold container weigh-
ing four ounces, which was filled with incense.
39 He brought a young bull, a ram, and a one-year-
old male lamb for a burnt offering, 40 and a male
goat for a sin offering. 41 For a peace offering he
brought two bulls, five rams, five male goats, and
five one-year-old male lambs. This was the offer-
ing brought by Shelumiel son of Zurishaddai.

42 On the sixth day Eliasaph son of Deuel, leader of the
tribe of Gad, presented his offering.
43 His offering consisted of a silver platter
weighing $3^1/_4$ pounds and a silver basin weigh-
ing $1^3/_4$ pounds (as measured by the weight of
the sanctuary shekel). These were both filled
with grain offerings of choice flour moistened
with olive oil. 44 He also brought a gold container
weighing four ounces, which was filled with
incense. 45 He brought a young bull, a ram, and
a one-year-old male lamb for a burnt offering,
46 and a male goat for a sin offering. 47 For a peace
offering he brought two bulls, five rams, five male
goats, and five one-year-old male lambs. This was
the offering brought by Eliasaph son of Deuel.

48 On the seventh day Elishama son of Ammihud,
leader of the tribe of Ephraim, presented his offering.
49 His offering consisted of a silver platter
weighing $3^1/_4$ pounds and a silver basin weighing
$1^3/_4$ pounds (as measured by the weight of the
sanctuary shekel). These were both filled with
grain offerings of choice flour moistened with ol-
ive oil. 50 He also brought a gold container weigh-
ing four ounces, which was filled with incense.
51 He brought a young bull, a ram, and a one-year-
old male lamb for a burnt offering, 52 and a male
goat for a sin offering. 53 For a peace offering he
brought two bulls, five rams, five male goats, and
five one-year-old male lambs. This was the offer-
ing brought by Elishama son of Ammihud.

54 On the eighth day Gamaliel son of Pedahzur, leader
of the tribe of Manasseh, presented his offering.
55 His offering consisted of a silver platter
weighing $3^1/_4$ pounds and a silver basin weighing
$1^3/_4$ pounds (as measured by the weight of the
sanctuary shekel). These were both filled with
grain offerings of choice flour moistened with
olive oil. 56 He also brought a gold container
weighing four ounces, which was filled with
incense. 57 He brought a young bull, a ram, and
a one-year-old male lamb for a burnt offering,
58 and a male goat for a sin offering. 59 For a peace
offering he brought two bulls, five rams, five
male goats, and five one-year-old male lambs.
This was the offering brought by Gamaliel son of
Pedahzur.

60 On the ninth day Abidan son of Gideoni, leader of
the tribe of Benjamin, presented his offering.
61 His offering consisted of a silver platter
weighing $3^1/_4$ pounds and a silver basin weigh-
ing $1^3/_4$ pounds (as measured by the weight of
the sanctuary shekel). These were both filled
with grain offerings of choice flour moistened
with olive oil. 62 He also brought a gold container
weighing four ounces, which was filled with
incense. 63 He brought a young bull, a ram, and
a one-year-old male lamb for a burnt offering,
64 and a male goat for a sin offering. 65 For a peace
offering he brought two bulls, five rams, five male
goats, and five one-year-old male lambs. This was
the offering brought by Abidan son of Gideoni.

66 On the tenth day Ahiezer son of Ammishaddai,
leader of the tribe of Dan, presented his offering.

67 His offering consisted of a silver platter
weighing 3¼ pounds and a silver basin weighing
1¾ pounds (as measured by the weight of the
sanctuary shekel). These were both filled with
grain offerings of choice flour moistened with ol-
ive oil. 68 He also brought a gold container weigh-
ing four ounces, which was filled with incense.
69 He brought a young bull, a ram, and a one-year-
old male lamb for a burnt offering, 70 and a male
goat for a sin offering. 71 For a peace offering he
brought two bulls, five rams, five male goats, and
five one-year-old male lambs. This was the offer-
ing brought by Ahiezer son of Ammishaddai.

72 On the eleventh day Pagiel son of Ocran, leader of
the tribe of Asher, presented his offering.
73 His offering consisted of a silver platter
weighing 3¼ pounds and a silver basin weigh-
ing 1¾ pounds (as measured by the weight of
the sanctuary shekel). These were both filled
with grain offerings of choice flour moistened
with olive oil. 74 He also brought a gold container
weighing four ounces, which was filled with
incense. 75 He brought a young bull, a ram, and
a one-year-old male lamb for a burnt offering,
76 and a male goat for a sin offering. 77 For a peace
offering he brought two bulls, five rams, five male
goats, and five one-year-old male lambs. This was
the offering brought by Pagiel son of Ocran.

78 On the twelfth day Ahira son of Enan, leader of the
tribe of Naphtali, presented his offering.
79 His offering consisted of a silver platter weigh-
ing 3¼ pounds and a silver basin weighing
1¾ pounds (as measured by the weight of the
sanctuary shekel). These were both filled with
grain offerings of choice flour moistened with
olive oil. 80 He also brought a gold container
weighing four ounces, which was filled with
incense. 81 He brought a young bull, a ram, and
a one-year-old male lamb for a burnt offering,
82 and a male goat for a sin offering. 83 For a peace
offering he brought two bulls, five rams, five male
goats, and five one-year-old male lambs. This was
the offering brought by Ahira son of Enan.

84 So this was the dedication offering brought
by the leaders of Israel at the time the altar was
anointed: twelve silver platters, twelve silver basins,
and twelve gold incense containers. 85 Each silver
platter weighed 3¼ pounds, and each silver basin
weighed 1¾ pounds. The total weight of the silver
was 60 pounds* (as measured by the weight of the
sanctuary shekel). 86 Each of the twelve gold contain-
ers that was filled with incense weighed four ounces
(as measured by the weight of the sanctuary shek-
el). The total weight of the gold was three pounds.*
87 Twelve young bulls, twelve rams, and twelve one-
year-old male lambs were donated for the burnt of-
ferings, along with their prescribed grain offerings.
Twelve male goats were brought for the sin offerings.
88 Twenty-four bulls, sixty rams, sixty male goats, and
sixty one-year-old male lambs were donated for the
peace offerings. This was the dedication offering for
the altar after it was anointed.
89 Whenever Moses went into the Tabernacle to
speak with the LORD, he heard the voice speaking to
him from between the two cherubim above the Ark's
cover—the place of atonement—that rests on the
Ark of the Covenant.* The LORD spoke to him from
there.

PREPARING THE LAMPS

8 The LORD said to Moses, 2 "Give Aaron the follow-
ing instructions: When you set up the seven lamps
in the lampstand, place them so their light shines for-
ward in front of the lampstand." 3 So Aaron did this. He
set up the seven lamps so they reflected their light for-
ward, just as the LORD had commanded Moses. 4 The
entire lampstand, from its base to its decorative blos-
soms, was made of beaten gold. It was built according
to the exact design the LORD had shown Moses.

THE LEVITES DEDICATED

5 Then the LORD said to Moses, 6 "Now set the Levites
apart from the rest of the people of Israel and make
them ceremonially clean. 7 Do this by sprinkling them
with the water of purification, and have them shave
their entire body and wash their clothing. Then they
will be ceremonially clean. 8 Have them bring a young
bull and a grain offering of choice flour moistened
with olive oil, along with a second young bull for a
sin offering. 9 Then assemble the whole community of
Israel, and present the Levites at the entrance of the
Tabernacle.* 10 When you present the Levites before
the LORD, the people of Israel must lay their hands on
them. 11 Raising his hands, Aaron must then present
the Levites to the LORD as a special offering from the
people of Israel, thus dedicating them to the LORD's
service.
12 "Next the Levites will lay their hands on the
heads of the young bulls. Present one as a sin offering
and the other as a burnt offering to the LORD, to pu-
rify the Levites and make them right with the LORD.*
13 Then have the Levites stand in front of Aaron and
his sons, and raise your hands and present them as a
special offering to the LORD. 14 In this way, you will set
the Levites apart from the rest of the people of Isra-
el, and the Levites will belong to me. 15 After this, they
may go into the Tabernacle to do their work, because
you have purified them and presented them as a spe-
cial offering.
16 "Of all the people of Israel, the Levites are re-
served for me. I have claimed them for myself in place
of all the firstborn sons of the Israelites; I have taken
the Levites as their substitutes. 17 For all the firstborn
males among the people of Israel are mine, both of
people and of animals. I set them apart for myself
on the day I struck down all the firstborn sons of the
Egyptians. 18 Yes, I have claimed the Levites in place of
all the firstborn sons of Israel. 19 And of all the Israel-
ites, I have assigned the Levites to Aaron and his sons.

7:85 Hebrew *2,400 [shekels]* [27.6 kilograms]. **7:86** Hebrew *120 [shekels]* [1.4 kilograms]. **7:89** Or *Ark of the Testimony.* **8:9** Hebrew *the Tent of Meeting;* also in 8:15, 19, 22, 24, 26. **8:12** Or *to make atonement for the Levites.*

7:84-88 twelve. Indicates the 12 tribes of Israel.
7:89 spoke to him from there. The tabernacle intended as a visual reminder of God's presence and a place for God to communicate with His people.
8:10 lay their hands. This action was a symbol that the priests represented the Israelites before the Lord.

They will serve in the Tabernacle on behalf of the Israelites and make sacrifices to purify* the people so no plague will strike them when they approach the sanctuary."

20 So Moses, Aaron, and the whole community of Israel dedicated the Levites, carefully following all the LORD's instructions to Moses. 21 The Levites purified themselves from sin and washed their clothes, and Aaron lifted them up and presented them to the LORD as a special offering. He then offered a sacrifice to purify them and make them right with the LORD.* 22 After that the Levites went into the Tabernacle to perform their duties, assisting Aaron and his sons. So they carried out all the commands that the LORD gave Moses concerning the Levites.

23 The LORD also instructed Moses, 24 "This is the rule the Levites must follow: They must begin serving in the Tabernacle at the age of twenty-five, 25 and they must retire at the age of fifty. 26 After retirement they may assist their fellow Levites by serving as guards at the Tabernacle, but they may not officiate in the service. This is how you must assign duties to the Levites."

THE SECOND PASSOVER

9 A year after Israel's departure from Egypt, the LORD spoke to Moses in the wilderness of Sinai. In the first month* of that year he said, 2 "Tell the Israelites to celebrate the Passover at the prescribed time, 3 at twilight on the fourteenth day of the first month.* Be sure to follow all my decrees and regulations concerning this celebration."

4 So Moses told the people to celebrate the Passover 5 in the wilderness of Sinai as twilight fell on the fourteenth day of the month. And they celebrated the festival there, just as the LORD had commanded Moses. 6 But some of the men had been ceremonially defiled by touching a dead body, so they could not celebrate the Passover that day. They came to Moses and Aaron that day 7 and said, "We have become ceremonially unclean by touching a dead body. But why should we be prevented from presenting the LORD's offering at the proper time with the rest of the Israelites?"

8 Moses answered, "Wait here until I have received instructions for you from the LORD."

9 This was the LORD's reply to Moses. 10 "Give the following instructions to the people of Israel: If any of the people now or in future generations are ceremonially unclean at Passover time because of touching a dead body, or if they are on a journey and cannot be present at the ceremony, they may still celebrate the LORD's Passover. 11 They must offer the Passover sacrifice one month later, at twilight on the fourteenth day of the second month.* They must eat the Passover lamb at that time with bitter salad greens and bread made without yeast. 12 They must not leave any of the lamb until the next morning, and they must not break any of its bones. They must follow all the normal regulations concerning the Passover.

13 "But those who neglect to celebrate the Passover at the regular time, even though they are ceremonially clean and not away on a trip, will be cut off from the community of Israel. If they fail to present the LORD's offering at the proper time, they will suffer the consequences of their guilt. 14 And if foreigners living among you want to celebrate the Passover to the LORD, they must follow these same decrees and regulations. The same laws apply both to native-born Israelites and to the foreigners living among you."

THE FIERY CLOUD

15 On the day the Tabernacle was set up, the cloud covered it.* But from evening until morning the cloud over the Tabernacle looked like a pillar of fire. 16 This was the regular pattern—at night the cloud that covered the Tabernacle had the appearance of fire. 17 Whenever the cloud lifted from over the sacred tent, the people of Israel would break camp and follow it. And wherever the cloud settled, the people of Israel would set up camp. 18 In this way, they traveled and camped at the LORD's command wherever he told them to go. Then they remained in their camp as long as the cloud stayed over the Tabernacle. 19 If the cloud remained over the Tabernacle for a long time, the Israelites stayed and performed their duty to the LORD. 20 Sometimes the cloud would stay over the Tabernacle for only a few days, so the people would stay for only a few days, as the LORD commanded. Then at the LORD's command they would break camp and move on. 21 Sometimes the cloud stayed only overnight and lifted the next morning. But day or night, when the cloud lifted, the people broke camp and moved on. 22 Whether the cloud stayed above the Tabernacle for two days, a month, or a year, the people of Israel stayed in camp and did not move on. But as soon as it lifted, they broke camp and moved on. 23 So they camped or traveled at the LORD's command, and they did whatever the LORD told them through Moses.

THE SILVER TRUMPETS

10 Now the LORD said to Moses, 2 "Make two trumpets of hammered silver for calling the community to assemble and for signaling the breaking of camp. 3 When both trumpets are blown, everyone

8:19 Or *make atonement for.* **8:21** Or *then made atonement for them to purify them.* **9:1** The first month of the ancient Hebrew lunar calendar usually occurs within the months of March and April. **9:3** This day in the ancient Hebrew lunar calendar occurred in late March, April, or early May. **9:11** This day in the ancient Hebrew lunar calendar occurred in late April, May, or early June. **9:15** Hebrew *covered the Tabernacle, the Tent of the Testimony.* **10:3** Hebrew *Tent of Meeting.*

8:20 all LORD's instructions. So far so good in terms of the Hebrews' obedience. Throughout Numbers, though, we see God's people not honoring God or His commands.

8:24-25 retire. This forced retirement system insured that the Levites gave God their prime years of service.

8:26 assist. The older Levites could mentor younger men.

9:7 prevented from presenting. The Israelites considered the Passover an honor and a joy, not a burden.

9:10 they may still celebrate. God wanted holiness without compromise from His people, but on day-to-day matters, God's mercy and flexibility were evident.

9:12 break any of its bones. When Moses prepared the people for the first Passover, he instructed them to roast a lamb but not to break any of its bones (Ex. 12:43-51). The instruction was repeated here as a reminder to the people. Consider Jesus, the sacrificial Lamb of God (John 1:29), whose bones were not broken (John 19:36).

9:13 fail to present. If someone did not take part in the Passover, he was, in effect, spitting on God's provision for His people.

9:14 foreigner living among you. A non-Hebrew must not only submit to dietary rules and daily rituals but must convert and be circumcised before observing the Passover.

9:15 the cloud. The cloud had been God's signal to move camp. Now at the completion of the tabernacle, the cloud hovered over it.

9:18 at the LORD's command. The Hebrews followed a personal God who provided daily guidance.

10:3-7 trumpets are blown. Using different trumpets sounds, Moses could coordinate the movements of the people.

must gather before you at the entrance of the Tabernacle.* 4 But if only one trumpet is blown, then only the leaders—the heads of the clans of Israel—must present themselves to you.

5 "When you sound the signal to move on, the tribes camped on the east side of the Tabernacle must break camp and move forward. 6 When you sound the signal a second time, the tribes camped on the south will follow. You must sound short blasts as the signal for moving on. 7 But when you call the people to an assembly, blow the trumpets with a different signal. 8 Only the priests, Aaron's descendants, are allowed to blow the trumpets. This is a permanent law for you, to be observed from generation to generation.

9 "When you arrive in your own land and go to war against your enemies who attack you, sound the alarm with the trumpets. Then the LORD your God will remember you and rescue you from your enemies. 10 Blow the trumpets in times of gladness, too, sounding them at your annual festivals and at the beginning of each month. And blow the trumpets over your burnt offerings and peace offerings. The trumpets will remind your God of his covenant with you. I am the LORD your God."

THE ISRAELITES LEAVE SINAI

11 In the second year after Israel's departure from Egypt—on the twentieth day of the second month*—the cloud lifted from the Tabernacle of the Covenant.* 12 So the Israelites set out from the wilderness of Sinai and traveled on from place to place until the cloud stopped in the wilderness of Paran.

13 When the people set out for the first time, following the instructions the LORD had given through Moses, 14 Judah's troops led the way. They marched behind their banner, and their leader was Nahshon son of Amminadab. 15 They were joined by the troops of the tribe of Issachar, led by Nethanel son of Zuar, 16 and the troops of the tribe of Zebulun, led by Eliab son of Helon.

17 Then the Tabernacle was taken down, and the Gershonite and Merarite divisions of the Levites were next in the line of march, carrying the Tabernacle with them. 18 Reuben's troops went next, marching behind their banner. Their leader was Elizur son of Shedeur. 19 They were joined by the troops of the tribe of Simeon, led by Shelumiel son of Zurishaddai, 20 and the troops of the tribe of Gad, led by Eliasaph son of Deuel.

21 Next came the Kohathite division of the Levites, carrying the sacred objects from the Tabernacle. Before they arrived at the next camp, the Tabernacle would already be set up at its new location. 22 Ephraim's troops went next, marching behind their banner. Their leader was Elishama son of Ammihud. 23 They were joined by the troops of the tribe of Manasseh, led by Gamaliel son of Pedahzur, 24 and the troops of the tribe of Benjamin, led by Abidan son of Gideoni.

25 Dan's troops went last, marching behind their banner and serving as the rear guard for all the tribal camps. Their leader was Ahiezer son of Ammishaddai. 26 They were joined by the troops of the tribe of Asher, led by Pagiel son of Ocran, 27 and the troops of the tribe of Naphtali, led by Ahira son of Enan.

28 This was the order in which the Israelites marched, division by division.

29 One day Moses said to his brother-in-law, Hobab son of Reuel the Midianite, "We are on our way to the place the LORD promised us, for he said, 'I will give it to you.' Come with us and we will treat you well, for the LORD has promised wonderful blessings for Israel!"

30 But Hobab replied, "No, I will not go. I must return to my own land and family."

31 "Please don't leave us," Moses pleaded. "You know the places in the wilderness where we should camp. Come, be our guide. 32 If you do, we'll share with you all the blessings the LORD gives us."

33 They marched for three days after leaving the mountain of the LORD, with the Ark of the LORD's Covenant moving ahead of them to show them where to stop and rest. 34 As they moved on each day, the cloud of the LORD hovered over them. 35 And whenever the Ark set out, Moses would shout, "Arise, O LORD, and let your enemies be scattered! Let them flee before you!" 36 And when the Ark was set down, he would say, "Return, O LORD, to the countless thousands of Israel!"

THE PEOPLE COMPLAIN TO MOSES

11 Soon the people began to complain about their hardship, and the LORD heard everything they said. Then the LORD's anger blazed against them, and he sent a fire to rage among them, and he destroyed some of the people in the outskirts of the camp. 2 Then the people screamed to Moses for help, and when he prayed to the LORD, the fire stopped. 3 After that, the area was known as Taberah (which means "the place of burning"), because fire from the LORD had burned among them there.

4 Then the foreign rabble who were traveling with the Israelites began to crave the good things of Egypt. And the people of Israel also began to complain. "Oh, for some meat!" they exclaimed. 5 "We remember the fish we used to eat for free in Egypt. And we had all the cucumbers, melons, leeks, onions, and garlic we wanted. 6 But now our appetites are gone. All we ever see is this manna!"

7 The manna looked like small coriander seeds, and it was pale yellow like gum resin. 8 The people would go out and gather it from the ground. They made flour by grinding it with hand mills or pounding it in mortars. Then they boiled it in a pot and made it into flat cakes. These cakes tasted like pastries baked with olive oil. 9 The manna came down on the camp with the dew during the night.

10:11a This day in the ancient Hebrew lunar calendar occurred in late April, May, or early June. **10:11b** Or *Tabernacle of the Testimony.*

10:11 second year. It should have taken them only a few months to get from Mount Sinai to the promised land. The Book of Numbers tells why it took 40 years.
10:14 banner. A banner or flag represented a family and helped keep the people marching in organized groups.
10:29 Hobab. Moses' brother-in-law (his wife, Zipporah's, brother). **Reuel.** Another name for Jethro, Moses' father-in-law (Ex. 18).
10:31 You know. Evidently Hobab knew the desert and could help the Hebrews in their crossing. He did indeed travel with them because his descendants were listed among those in the promised land (Judg. 1:16).
11:4 foreign rabble. The phrase means "mixed company." It probably applies to non-Hebrews who came out of Egypt in the Exodus—perhaps servants or in-laws.
11:7 manna. "Manna" means "What is it?" **coriander seed.** An herb in the carrot family used for cooking and for medicine. **gum resin.** A yellow, transparent resin (like powder of hardened tree sap).

10 Moses heard all the families standing in the door-
ways of their tents whining, and the LORD became
extremely angry. Moses was also very aggravated.
11 And Moses said to the LORD, "Why are you treat-
ing me, your servant, so harshly? Have mercy on me!
What did I do to deserve the burden of all these peo-
ple? 12 Did I give birth to them? Did I bring them into
the world? Why did you tell me to carry them in my
arms like a mother carries a nursing baby? How can I
carry them to the land you swore to give their ances-
tors? 13 Where am I supposed to get meat for all these
people? They keep whining to me, saying, 'Give us
meat to eat!' 14 I can't carry all these people by myself!
The load is far too heavy! 15 If this is how you intend to
treat me, just go ahead and kill me. Do me a favor and
spare me this misery!"

MOSES CHOOSES SEVENTY LEADERS

16 Then the LORD said to Moses, "Gather before me sev-
enty men who are recognized as elders and leaders of
Israel. Bring them to the Tabernacle* to stand there
with you. 17 I will come down and talk to you there.
I will take some of the Spirit that is upon you, and I
will put the Spirit upon them also. They will bear the
burden of the people along with you, so you will not
have to carry it alone.

18 "And say to the people, 'Purify yourselves, for to-
morrow you will have meat to eat. You were whining,
and the LORD heard you when you cried, "Oh, for some
meat! We were better off in Egypt!" Now the LORD will
give you meat, and you will have to eat it. 19 And it
won't be for just a day or two, or for five or ten or even
twenty. 20 You will eat it for a whole month until you
gag and are sick of it. For you have rejected the LORD,
who is here among you, and you have whined to him,
saying, "Why did we ever leave Egypt?"'"

21 But Moses responded to the LORD, "There are
600,000 foot soldiers here with me, and yet you say, 'I
will give them meat for a whole month!' 22 Even if we
butchered all our flocks and herds, would that satisfy
them? Even if we caught all the fish in the sea, would
that be enough?"

23 Then the LORD said to Moses, "Has my arm lost
its power? Now you will see whether or not my word
comes true!"

24 So Moses went out and reported the LORD's words
to the people. He gathered the seventy elders and sta-
tioned them around the Tabernacle.* 25 And the LORD
came down in the cloud and spoke to Moses. Then he
gave the seventy elders the same Spirit that was upon
Moses. And when the Spirit rested upon them, they
prophesied. But this never happened again.

26 Two men, Eldad and Medad, had stayed behind
in the camp. They were listed among the elders, but
they had not gone out to the Tabernacle. Yet the Spirit
rested upon them as well, so they prophesied there in
the camp. 27 A young man ran and reported to Moses,
"Eldad and Medad are prophesying in the camp!"

28 Joshua son of Nun, who had been Moses' assis-
tant since his youth, protested, "Moses, my master,
make them stop!"

29 But Moses replied, "Are you jealous for my sake?
I wish that all the LORD's people were prophets and
that the LORD would put his Spirit upon them all!"
30 Then Moses returned to the camp with the elders
of Israel.

THE LORD SENDS QUAIL

31 Now the LORD sent a wind that brought quail
from the sea and let them fall all around the camp.
For miles in every direction there were quail flying
about three feet above the ground.* 32 So the people
went out and caught quail all that day and through-
out the night and all the next day, too. No one gath-
ered less than fifty bushels*! They spread the quail
all around the camp to dry. 33 But while they were
gorging themselves on the meat—while it was
still in their mouths—the anger of the LORD blazed
against the people, and he struck them with a severe
plague. 34 So that place was called Kibroth-hattaavah
(which means "graves of gluttony") because there
they buried the people who had craved meat from
Egypt. 35 From Kibroth-hattaavah the Israelites trav-
eled to Hazeroth, where they stayed for some time.

THE COMPLAINTS OF MIRIAM AND AARON

12 While they were at Hazeroth, Miriam and Aar-
on criticized Moses because he had married a
Cushite woman. 2 They said, "Has the LORD spoken
only through Moses? Hasn't he spoken through us,
too?" But the LORD heard them. 3 (Now Moses was
very humble—more humble than any other person
on earth.)

4 So immediately the LORD called to Moses, Aaron,
and Miriam and said, "Go out to the Tabernacle,* all
three of you!" So the three of them went to the Tab-
ernacle. 5 Then the LORD descended in the pillar of
cloud and stood at the entrance of the Tabernacle.*
"Aaron and Miriam!" he called, and they stepped
forward. 6 And the LORD said to them, "Now listen to
what I say:

"If there were prophets among you,
  I, the LORD, would reveal myself in visions.
  I would speak to them in dreams.
7 But not with my servant Moses.
  Of all my house, he is the one I trust.
8 I speak to him face to face,
  clearly, and not in riddles!
  He sees the LORD as he is.
So why were you not afraid
  to criticize my servant Moses?"

11:16 Hebrew *the Tent of Meeting.* **11:24** Hebrew *the tent;* also in 11:26. **11:31** Or *there were quail about 3 feet* [2 cubits or 92 centimeters] *deep on the ground.* **11:32** Hebrew *10 homers* [2.2 kiloliters]. **12:4** Hebrew *the Tent of Meeting.* **12:5** Hebrew *the tent;* also in 12:10.

11:12 Did I give birth to them? In his frustration Moses wanted to pass the buck to God, the ultimate Father of "these people."

11:16-34 God helped Moses organize administratively, much like Jethro did earlier (Ex. 18:13-27).

11:20 rejected the LORD. Moses spoke bluntly. Their sin had to do with ingratitude and a lack of faith, not just an appetite for meat.

11:21 Moses responded. Compare the disciples' response when Jesus told them to feed 5,000 people (John 6:5-9).

11:23 its power. God asked Moses, in effect, "Do you not think I am able to produce so much meat?"

12:1 Miriam and Aaron. Moses' sister and brother. **Cushite.** Cush was located in what is now southern Egypt, Sudan, and northern Ethiopia.

12:2 only through Moses. Miriam and Aaron felt insecure and displaced perhaps by the 70 new elders, Moses' new wife, or simple jealousy.

12:4 immediately. The Lord knows and deals with the sin that takes place on earth. God called a meeting to address the dispute that Moses' brother and sister had with him.

12:8 why were you not afraid. To question Moses is to question God.

REBELLING AGAINST AUTHORITY

1. What's the most embarrassing situation you've ever experienced because of something you blurted out? What happened?

NUMBERS 12:1-15

2. Why do you think Miriam and Aaron were jealous of Moses? Were they right or wrong in complaining that others were not allowed to speak on behalf of God? What did God say about it?
3. What is the lesson here about rebelling against God-given authorities?
4. How do people today rebel against authority on your team? At your school? In society? In the church?
5. Do you rebel against the authority of your parents? Your coach? Your teachers? Others? What are the consequences?

9 The LORD was very angry with them, and he departed. 10 As the cloud moved from above the Tabernacle, there stood Miriam, her skin as white as snow from leprosy.* When Aaron saw what had happened to her, 11 he cried out to Moses, "Oh, my master! Please don't punish us for this sin we have so foolishly committed. 12 Don't let her be like a stillborn baby, already decayed at birth."

13 So Moses cried out to the LORD, "O God, I beg you, please heal her!"

14 But the LORD said to Moses, "If her father had done nothing more than spit in her face, wouldn't she be defiled for seven days? So keep her outside the camp for seven days, and after that she may be accepted back."

15 So Miriam was kept outside the camp for seven days, and the people waited until she was brought back before they traveled again. 16 Then they left Hazeroth and camped in the wilderness of Paran.

TWELVE SCOUTS EXPLORE CANAAN

13 The LORD now said to Moses, 2 "Send out men to explore the land of Canaan, the land I am giving to the Israelites. Send one leader from each of the twelve ancestral tribes." 3 So Moses did as the LORD commanded him. He sent out twelve men, all tribal leaders of Israel, from their camp in the wilderness of Paran. 4 These were the tribes and the names of their leaders:

Tribe	*Leader*
Reuben	Shammua son of Zaccur
5 Simeon	Shaphat son of Hori
6 Judah	Caleb son of Jephunneh
7 Issachar	Igal son of Joseph
8 Ephraim	Hoshea son of Nun
9 Benjamin	Palti son of Raphu
10 Zebulun	Gaddiel son of Sodi
11 Manasseh son of Joseph	Gaddi son of Susi
12 Dan	Ammiel son of Gemalli
13 Asher	Sethur son of Michael
14 Naphtali	Nahbi son of Vophsi
15 Gad	Geuel son of Maki

16 These are the names of the men Moses sent out to explore the land. (Moses called Hoshea son of Nun by the name Joshua.)

17 Moses gave the men these instructions as he sent them out to explore the land: "Go north through the Negev into the hill country. 18 See what the land is like, and find out whether the people living there are strong or weak, few or many. 19 See what kind of land they live in. Is it good or bad? Do their towns have walls, or are they unprotected like open camps? 20 Is the soil fertile or poor? Are there many trees? Do your best to bring back samples of the crops you see." (It happened to be the season for harvesting the first ripe grapes.)

21 So they went up and explored the land from the wilderness of Zin as far as Rehob, near Lebo-hamath. 22 Going north, they passed through the Negev and arrived at Hebron, where Ahiman, Sheshai, and Talmai—all descendants of Anak—lived. (The ancient town of Hebron was founded seven years before the Egyptian city of Zoan.) 23 When they came to the valley of Eshcol, they cut down a branch with a single cluster of grapes so large that it took two of them to carry it on a pole between them! They also brought back samples of the pomegranates and figs. 24 That place was called the valley of Eshcol (which means "cluster"), because of the cluster of grapes the Israelite men cut there.

THE SCOUTING REPORT

25 After exploring the land for forty days, the men returned 26 to Moses, Aaron, and the whole community of Israel at Kadesh in the wilderness of Paran. They reported to the whole community what they had seen and showed them the fruit they had taken from the land. 27 This was their report to Moses: "We entered the land you sent us to explore, and it is indeed a bountiful country—a land flowing with milk and honey. Here is the kind of fruit it produces. 28 But the people living there are powerful, and their towns are large and fortified. We even saw giants there, the descendants of Anak! 29 The Amalekites live in the Negev, and the Hittites, Jebusites, and Amorites live in the hill country. The Canaanites live along the coast of the Mediterranean Sea* and along the Jordan Valley."

30 But Caleb tried to quiet the people as they stood before Moses. "Let's go at once to take the land," he said. "We can certainly conquer it!"

12:10 Or *with a skin disease.* The Hebrew word used here can describe various skin diseases. **13:29** Hebrew *the sea.*

12:10 leprosy. Miriam's disease forced her to live outside the community, without prestige or position.

12:14-15 keep her outside. God responded to Aaron and Moses' appeal, but Miriam still had to endure a time of illness and separation.

13:2 each of the twelve ancestral tribes. As with the earlier census, selecting one from each tribe gave credibility and unity to their report.

13:17-20 strong or weak, few or many. Moses told the spies to report not only on the land of Canaan itself but also on the people who lived there.

13:21 explored the land. This journey of 250 miles each way probably also involved tracing a possible line of attack.

13:23 cluster of grapes. The fact that the explorers needed a pole to carry the grapes showed the bounty of the land.

13:26-29 The spies were right to give an accurate report of both the prosperity and the dangers ahead. They sinned by not trusting God to carry Israel through difficulties.

13:30 Caleb. Only Caleb is mentioned here, but Joshua also felt they should trust God and enter the land of Canaan (see 14:6-9).

ISRAELITE SPY TEAM

1. Are you more likely to stop and ask directions if you are lost or drive around until you find your way?

NUMBERS 13:26–14:10,26-45

2. Why did 10 spies recommend running away, while Joshua and Caleb recommended going in to the land of Canaan?
3. Why did the Israelites rebel against Moses and say that Egypt was better?
4. What was the result of the people's lack of faith? What does this teach about the very real danger of disobedience?

31 But the other men who had explored the land with him disagreed. "We can't go up against them! They are stronger than we are!" 32 So they spread this bad report about the land among the Israelites: "The land we traveled through and explored will devour anyone who goes to live there. All the people we saw were huge. 33 We even saw giants* there, the descendants of Anak. Next to them we felt like grasshoppers, and that's what they thought, too!"

THE PEOPLE REBEL

14 Then the whole community began weeping aloud, and they cried all night. 2 Their voices rose in a great chorus of protest against Moses and Aaron. "If only we had died in Egypt, or even here in the wilderness!" they complained. 3 "Why is the LORD taking us to this country only to have us die in battle? Our wives and our little ones will be carried off as plunder! Wouldn't it be better for us to return to Egypt?" 4 Then they plotted among themselves, "Let's choose a new leader and go back to Egypt!"

5 Then Moses and Aaron fell face down on the ground before the whole community of Israel. 6 Two of the men who had explored the land, Joshua son of Nun and Caleb son of Jephunneh, tore their clothing. 7 They said to all the people of Israel, "The land we traveled through and explored is a wonderful land! 8 And if the LORD is pleased with us, he will bring us safely into that land and give it to us. It is a rich land flowing with milk and honey. 9 Do not rebel against the LORD, and don't be afraid of the people of the land. They are only helpless prey to us! They have no protection, but the LORD is with us! Don't be afraid of them!"

10 But the whole community began to talk about stoning Joshua and Caleb. Then the glorious presence of the LORD appeared to all the Israelites at the Tabernacle.* 11 And the LORD said to Moses, "How long will these people treat me with contempt? Will they never believe me, even after all the miraculous signs I have done among them? 12 I will disown them and destroy them with a plague. Then I will make you into a nation greater and mightier than they are!"

MOSES INTERCEDES FOR THE PEOPLE

13 But Moses objected. "What will the Egyptians think when they hear about it?" he asked the LORD. "They know full well the power you displayed in rescuing your people from Egypt. 14 Now if you destroy them, the Egyptians will send a report to the inhabitants of this land, who have already heard that you live among your people. They know, LORD, that you have appeared to your people face to face and that your pillar of cloud hovers over them. They know that you go before them in the pillar of cloud by day and the pillar of fire by night. 15 Now if you slaughter all these people with a single blow, the nations that have heard of your fame will say, 16 'The LORD was not able to bring them into the land he swore to give them, so he killed them in the wilderness.'

17 "Please, Lord, prove that your power is as great as you have claimed. For you said, 18 'The LORD is slow to anger and filled with unfailing love, forgiving every kind of sin and rebellion. But he does not excuse the guilty. He lays the sins of the parents upon their children; the entire family is affected—even children in the third and fourth generations.' 19 In keeping with your magnificent, unfailing love, please pardon the sins of this people, just as you have forgiven them ever since they left Egypt."

20 Then the LORD said, "I will pardon them as you have requested. 21 But as surely as I live, and as surely as the earth is filled with the LORD's glory, 22 not one of these people will ever enter that land. They have all seen my glorious presence and the miraculous signs I performed both in Egypt and in the wilderness, but again and again they have tested me by refusing to listen to my voice. 23 They will never even see the land I swore to give their ancestors. None of those who have treated me with contempt will ever see it. 24 But my servant Caleb has a different attitude than the others have. He has remained loyal to me, so I will bring him into the land he explored. His descendants will possess their full share of that land. 25 Now turn around, and don't go on toward the land where the Amalekites and Canaanites live. Tomorrow you must set out for the wilderness in the direction of the Red Sea.*"

THE LORD PUNISHES THE ISRAELITES

26 Then the LORD said to Moses and Aaron, 27 "How long must I put up with this wicked community and its complaints about me? Yes, I have heard the complaints the Israelites are making against me. 28 Now

13:33 Hebrew *nephilim*. **14:10** Hebrew *the Tent of Meeting*. **14:25** Hebrew *sea of reeds*.

13:32 this bad report. The spies' cynical report filled the people with doubt and dismay.

14:1-2 began weeping. The people succumbed to fear of the unknown instead of trusting in the power of God.

14:3-4 a new leader and go back. The obstacles ahead seemed too great, so the people were ready to return to Egypt.

14:9 the LORD is with us. Joshua and Caleb affirmed the truth that should have blotted out all objections: God's power would make the difference in the struggle.

14:11 miraculous signs. In spite of many powerful signs, Israel demonstrated almost no faith.

14:17-19 In keeping with your magnificent, unfailing love. Moses knew God, so he trusted God to be true to His character.

14:22 again and again. The people had been unfaithful over and over. (See Ex. 14:10-12; 15:22-24; 16:1-3, 19-20, 27-30; 17:1-4; 32:1-35; Num. 11:1-3, 4-34; 14:3.)

14:24 Caleb. Caleb worshiped the Lord wholeheartedly (Josh. 14:13-14). Only he and Joshua believed God would give the people the land (v. 9).

tell them this: 'As surely as I live, declares the LORD, I will do to you the very things I heard you say. [29] You will all drop dead in this wilderness! Because you complained against me, every one of you who is twenty years old or older and was included in the registration will die. [30] You will not enter and occupy the land I swore to give you. The only exceptions will be Caleb son of Jephunneh and Joshua son of Nun.

[31] "'You said your children would be carried off as plunder. Well, I will bring them safely into the land, and they will enjoy what you have despised. [32] But as for you, you will drop dead in this wilderness. [33] And your children will be like shepherds, wandering in the wilderness for forty years. In this way, they will pay for your faithlessness, until the last of you lies dead in the wilderness.

[34] "'Because your men explored the land for forty days, you must wander in the wilderness for forty years—a year for each day, suffering the consequences of your sins. Then you will discover what it is like to have me for an enemy.' [35] I, the LORD, have spoken! I will certainly do these things to every member of the community who has conspired against me. They will be destroyed here in this wilderness, and here they will die!"

[36] The ten men Moses had sent to explore the land—the ones who incited rebellion against the LORD with their bad report— [37] were struck dead with a plague before the LORD. [38] Of the twelve who had explored the land, only Joshua and Caleb remained alive.

[39] When Moses reported the LORD's words to all the Israelites, the people were filled with grief. [40] Then they got up early the next morning and went to the top of the range of hills. "Let's go," they said. "We realize that we have sinned, but now we are ready to enter the land the LORD has promised us."

[41] But Moses said, "Why are you now disobeying the LORD's orders to return to the wilderness? It won't work. [42] Do not go up into the land now. You will only be crushed by your enemies because the LORD is not with you. [43] When you face the Amalekites and Canaanites in battle, you will be slaughtered. The LORD will abandon you because you have abandoned the LORD."

[44] But the people defiantly pushed ahead toward the hill country, even though neither Moses nor the Ark of the LORD's Covenant left the camp. [45] Then the Amalekites and the Canaanites who lived in those hills came down and attacked them and chased them back as far as Hormah.

LAWS CONCERNING OFFERINGS

15 Then the LORD told Moses, [2] "Give the following instructions to the people of Israel.

"When you finally settle in the land I am giving you, [3] you will offer special gifts as a pleasing aroma to the LORD. These gifts may take the form of a burnt offering, a sacrifice to fulfill a vow, a voluntary offering, or an offering at any of your annual festivals, and they may be taken from your herds of cattle or your flocks of sheep and goats. [4] When you present these offerings, you must also give the LORD a grain offering of two quarts* of choice flour mixed with one quart* of olive oil. [5] For each lamb offered as a burnt offering or a special sacrifice, you must also present one quart of wine as a liquid offering.

[6] "If the sacrifice is a ram, give a grain offering of four quarts* of choice flour mixed with a third of a gallon* of olive oil, [7] and give a third of a gallon of wine as a liquid offering. This will be a pleasing aroma to the LORD.

[8] "When you present a young bull as a burnt offering or as a sacrifice to fulfill a vow or as a peace offering to the LORD, [9] you must also give a grain offering of six quarts* of choice flour mixed with two quarts* of olive oil, [10] and give two quarts of wine as a liquid offering. This will be a special gift, a pleasing aroma to the LORD.

[11] "Each sacrifice of a bull, ram, lamb, or young goat should be prepared in this way. [12] Follow these instructions with each offering you present. [13] All of you native-born Israelites must follow these instructions when you offer a special gift as a pleasing aroma to the LORD. [14] And if any foreigners visit you or live among you and want to present a special gift as a pleasing aroma to the LORD, they must follow these same procedures. [15] Native-born Israelites and foreigners are equal before the LORD and are subject to the same decrees. This is a permanent law for you, to be observed from generation to generation. [16] The same instructions and regulations will apply both to you and to the foreigners living among you."

[17] Then the LORD said to Moses, [18] "Give the following instructions to the people of Israel.

"When you arrive in the land where I am taking you, [19] and you eat the crops that grow there, you must set some aside as a sacred offering to the LORD. [20] Present a cake from the first of the flour you grind, and set it aside as a sacred offering, as you do with the first grain from the threshing floor. [21] Throughout the generations to come, you are to present a sacred offering to the LORD each year from the first of your ground flour.

[22] "But suppose you unintentionally fail to carry out all these commands that the LORD has given you through Moses. [23] And suppose your descendants in the future fail to do everything the LORD has commanded through Moses. [24] If the mistake was made unintentionally, and the community was unaware of it, the whole community must present a young bull for a burnt offering as a pleasing aroma to the LORD. It must be offered along with its prescribed grain offering and liquid offering and with one male goat for a sin offering. [25] With it the priest will purify the whole community of Israel, making them right with the LORD,* and they will be forgiven. For it was an unintentional sin, and they have corrected it with

15:4a Hebrew 1/10 *of an ephah* [2.2 liters]. **15:4b** Hebrew 1/4 *of a hin* [1 liter]; also in 15:5. **15:6a** Hebrew 2/10 *of an ephah* [4.4 liters]. **15:6b** Hebrew 1/3 *of a hin* [1.3 liters]; also in 15:7. **15:9a** Hebrew 3/10 *of an ephah* [6.6 liters]. **15:9b** Hebrew 1/2 *of a hin* [2 liters]; also in 15:10. **15:25** Or *will make atonement for the whole community of Israel.*

14:28 very things I heard you say. The people wished that they had died in the desert (v. 2), so God said, "So be it."

14:39-45 the LORD is not with you. The people tried to enter the promised land without putting their faith in God, so they were defeated.

15:1-41 Because of God's judgment, the older generation would never settle the promised land. It was time to pass down traditions to the younger crowd.

15:3-12 Most of these offerings were a review of earlier teachings from Leviticus.

15:24 unintentionally. The Bible categorizes sins as either defiant (see v. 30) or sins of straying (unintentional). People who love God may sin, but they do not do so in defiance of God.

their offerings to the LORD—the special gift and the sin offering. 26 The whole community of Israel will be forgiven, including the foreigners living among you, for all the people were involved in the sin.

27 "If one individual commits an unintentional sin, the guilty person must bring a one-year-old female goat for a sin offering. 28 The priest will sacrifice it to purify* the guilty person before the LORD, and that person will be forgiven. 29 These same instructions apply both to native-born Israelites and to the foreigners living among you.

30 "But those who brazenly violate the LORD's will, whether native-born Israelites or foreigners, have blasphemed the LORD, and they must be cut off from the community. 31 Since they have treated the LORD's word with contempt and deliberately disobeyed his command, they must be completely cut off and suffer the punishment for their guilt."

PENALTY FOR BREAKING THE SABBATH

32 One day while the people of Israel were in the wilderness, they discovered a man gathering wood on the Sabbath day. 33 The people who found him doing this took him before Moses, Aaron, and the rest of the community. 34 They held him in custody because they did not know what to do with him. 35 Then the LORD said to Moses, "The man must be put to death! The whole community must stone him outside the camp." 36 So the whole community took the man outside the camp and stoned him to death, just as the LORD had commanded Moses.

TASSELS ON CLOTHING

37 Then the LORD said to Moses, 38 "Give the following instructions to the people of Israel: Throughout the generations to come you must make tassels for the hems of your clothing and attach them with a blue cord. 39 When you see the tassels, you will remember and obey all the commands of the LORD instead of following your own desires and defiling yourselves, as you are prone to do. 40 The tassels will help you remember that you must obey all my commands and be holy to your God. 41 I am the LORD your God who brought you out of the land of Egypt that I might be your God. I am the LORD your God!"

KORAH'S REBELLION

16 One day Korah son of Izhar, a descendant of Kohath son of Levi, conspired with Dathan and Abiram, the sons of Eliab, and On son of Peleth, from the tribe of Reuben. 2 They incited a rebellion against Moses, along with 250 other leaders of the community, all prominent members of the assembly. 3 They united against Moses and Aaron and said, "You have gone too far! The whole community of Israel has been set apart by the LORD, and he is with all of us. What right do you have to act as though you are greater than the rest of the LORD's people?"

4 When Moses heard what they were saying, he fell face down on the ground. 5 Then he said to Korah and his followers, "Tomorrow morning the LORD will show us who belongs to him* and who is holy. The LORD will allow only those whom he selects to enter his own presence. 6 Korah, you and all your followers must prepare your incense burners. 7 Light fires in them tomorrow, and burn incense before the LORD. Then we will see whom the LORD chooses as his holy one. You Levites are the ones who have gone too far!"

8 Then Moses spoke again to Korah: "Now listen, you Levites! 9 Does it seem insignificant to you that the God of Israel has chosen you from among all the community of Israel to be near him so you can serve in the LORD's Tabernacle and stand before the people to minister to them? 10 Korah, he has already given this special ministry to you and your fellow Levites. Are you now demanding the priesthood as well? 11 The LORD is the one you and your followers are really revolting against! For who is Aaron that you are complaining about him?"

12 Then Moses summoned Dathan and Abiram, the sons of Eliab, but they replied, "We refuse to come before you! 13 Isn't it enough that you brought us out of Egypt, a land flowing with milk and honey, to kill us here in this wilderness, and that you now treat us like your subjects? 14 What's more, you haven't brought us into another land flowing with milk and honey. You haven't given us a new homeland with fields and vineyards. Are you trying to fool these men?* We will not come."

15 Then Moses became very angry and said to the LORD, "Do not accept their grain offerings! I have not taken so much as a donkey from them, and I have never hurt a single one of them." 16 And Moses said to Korah, "You and all your followers must come here tomorrow and present yourselves before the LORD. Aaron will also be here. 17 You and each of your 250 followers must prepare an incense burner and put incense on it, so you can all present them before the LORD. Aaron will also bring his incense burner."

18 So each of these men prepared an incense burner, lit the fire, and placed incense on it. Then they all stood at the entrance of the Tabernacle* with Moses and Aaron. 19 Meanwhile, Korah had stirred up the entire community against Moses and Aaron, and they all gathered at the Tabernacle entrance. Then the glorious presence of the LORD appeared to the whole community, 20 and the LORD said to Moses and Aaron, 21 "Get away from all these people so that I may instantly destroy them!"

22 But Moses and Aaron fell face down on the ground. "O God," they pleaded, "you are the God who gives breath to all creatures. Must you be angry with all the people when only one man sins?"

23 And the LORD said to Moses, 24 "Then tell all the people to get away from the tents of Korah, Dathan, and Abiram."

15:28 Or *to make atonement for.* **16:5** Greek version reads *God has visited and knows those who are his.* Compare 2 Tim 2:19. **16:14** Hebrew *Are you trying to put out the eyes of these men?* **16:18** Hebrew *the Tent of Meeting;* also in 16:19, 42, 43, 50.

15:30 brazenly. No sacrifice covered defiant sin until the cross.

15:41 I am. The people had wavered throughout the journey, but God was still the One who had delivered them.

16:1-7 Leaders of the tribes of Levi (the priests) and Reuben challenged Moses and Aaron's leadership but missed the key point—that God had chosen them.

16:12-13 milk and honey. Now this phrase is used to describe Egypt, the land where they had been enslaved.

16:15 not taken so much as a donkey. The complainers accused Moses of abusing his authority and misleading his people. Moses contended he had taken nothing from them, but he had delivered them.

16:22 Moses and Aaron fell face down. Once again, Moses and his brother prayed for God to spare the people.

25 So Moses got up and rushed over to the tents of Dathan and Abiram, followed by the elders of Israel. 26 "Quick!" he told the people. "Get away from the tents of these wicked men, and don't touch anything that belongs to them. If you do, you will be destroyed for their sins." 27 So all the people stood back from the tents of Korah, Dathan, and Abiram. Then Dathan and Abiram came out and stood at the entrances of their tents, together with their wives and children and little ones.

28 And Moses said, "This is how you will know that the LORD has sent me to do all these things that I have done—for I have not done them on my own. 29 If these men die a natural death, or if nothing unusual happens, then the LORD has not sent me. 30 But if the LORD does something entirely new and the ground opens its mouth and swallows them and all their belongings, and they go down alive into the grave,* then you will know that these men have shown contempt for the LORD."

31 He had hardly finished speaking the words when the ground suddenly split open beneath them. 32 The earth opened its mouth and swallowed the men, along with their households and all their followers who were standing with them, and everything they owned. 33 So they went down alive into the grave, along with all their belongings. The earth closed over them, and they all vanished from among the people of Israel. 34 All the people around them fled when they heard their screams. "The earth will swallow us, too!" they cried. 35 Then fire blazed forth from the LORD and burned up the 250 men who were offering incense.

36* And the LORD said to Moses, 37 "Tell Eleazar son of Aaron the priest to pull all the incense burners from the fire, for they are holy. Also tell him to scatter the burning coals. 38 Take the incense burners of these men who have sinned at the cost of their lives, and hammer the metal into a thin sheet to overlay the altar. Since these burners were used in the LORD's presence, they have become holy. Let them serve as a warning to the people of Israel."

39 So Eleazar the priest collected the 250 bronze incense burners that had been used by the men who died in the fire, and the bronze was hammered into a thin sheet to overlay the altar. 40 This would warn the Israelites that no unauthorized person—no one who was not a descendant of Aaron—should ever enter the LORD's presence to burn incense. If anyone did, the same thing would happen to him as happened to Korah and his followers. So the LORD's instructions to Moses were carried out.

41 But the very next morning the whole community of Israel began muttering again against Moses and Aaron, saying, "You have killed the LORD's people!" 42 As the community gathered to protest against Moses and Aaron, they turned toward the Tabernacle and saw that the cloud had covered it, and the glorious presence of the LORD appeared.

43 Moses and Aaron came and stood in front of the Tabernacle, 44 and the LORD said to Moses, 45 "Get away from all these people so that I can instantly destroy them!" But Moses and Aaron fell face down on the ground.

46 And Moses said to Aaron, "Quick, take an incense burner and place burning coals on it from the altar. Lay incense on it, and carry it out among the people to purify them and make them right with the LORD.* The LORD's anger is blazing against them—the plague has already begun."

47 Aaron did as Moses told him and ran out among the people. The plague had already begun to strike down the people, but Aaron burned the incense and purified* the people. 48 He stood between the dead and the living, and the plague stopped. 49 But 14,700 people died in that plague, in addition to those who had died in the affair involving Korah. 50 Then because the plague had stopped, Aaron returned to Moses at the entrance of the Tabernacle.

THE BUDDING OF AARON'S STAFF

17 1* Then the LORD said to Moses, 2 "Tell the people of Israel to bring you twelve wooden staffs, one from each leader of Israel's ancestral tribes, and inscribe each leader's name on his staff. 3 Inscribe Aaron's name on the staff of the tribe of Levi, for there must be one staff for the leader of each ancestral tribe. 4 Place these staffs in the Tabernacle in front of the Ark containing the tablets of the Covenant,* where I meet with you. 5 Buds will sprout on the staff belonging to the man I choose. Then I will finally put an end to the people's murmuring and complaining against you."

6 So Moses gave the instructions to the people of Israel, and each of the twelve tribal leaders, including Aaron, brought Moses a staff. 7 Moses placed the staffs in the LORD's presence in the Tabernacle of the Covenant.* 8 When he went into the Tabernacle of the Covenant the next day, he found that Aaron's staff, representing the tribe of Levi, had sprouted, budded, blossomed, and produced ripe almonds!

9 When Moses brought all the staffs out from the LORD's presence, he showed them to the people. Each man claimed his own staff. 10 And the LORD said to Moses: "Place Aaron's staff permanently before the Ark of the Covenant* to serve as a warning to rebels. This should put an end to their complaints against me and prevent any further deaths." 11 So Moses did as the LORD commanded him.

12 Then the people of Israel said to Moses, "Look, we are doomed! We are dead! We are ruined! 13 Everyone who even comes close to the Tabernacle of the LORD dies. Are we all doomed to die?"

16:30 Hebrew *into Sheol;* also in 16:33. **16:36** Verses 16:36-50 are numbered 17:1-15 in Hebrew text. **16:46** Or *to make atonement for them.* **16:47** Or *and made atonement for.* **17:1** Verses 17:1-13 are numbered 17:16-28 in Hebrew text. **17:4** Hebrew *in the Tent of Meeting before the Testimony.* The Hebrew word for "testimony" refers to the terms of the LORD's covenant with Israel as written on stone tablets, which were kept in the Ark, and also to the covenant itself. **17:7** Or *Tabernacle of the Testimony;* also in 17:8. **17:10** Hebrew *before the Testimony;* see note on 17:4.

16:30 the LORD does something. Like Elijah on Mount Carmel (1 Kings 18), Moses asked God to demonstrate that He was in charge.

16:41 the community gathered to protest against Moses. As mediator between God and Israel, Moses endured constant complaints for God's decisions.

17:1-13 This chapter tells the story of Aaron's budding staff, which confirmed the Levites' preeminent role in the priesthood.

17:3 one staff for the leader of each ancestral tribe. The demonstration had to show that the Levites' power surpassed that of any other tribal head.

17:4 in front of the Ark. The staffs were placed in front of the ark. If a staff sprouted, the tribe represented by that staff was God's choice to serve in the tabernacle.

17:8 sprouted, budded, blossomed, and produced. Aaron's staff far exceeded the demands of the test. God's choice was very clear.

DUTIES OF PRIESTS AND LEVITES

18 Then the LORD said to Aaron: "You, your sons, and your relatives from the tribe of Levi will be held responsible for any offenses related to the sanctuary. But you and your sons alone will be held responsible for violations connected with the priesthood.

2 "Bring your relatives of the tribe of Levi—your ancestral tribe—to assist you and your sons as you perform the sacred duties in front of the Tabernacle of the Covenant.* 3 But as the Levites go about all their assigned duties at the Tabernacle, they must be careful not to go near any of the sacred objects or the altar. If they do, both you and they will die. 4 The Levites must join you in fulfilling their responsibilities for the care and maintenance of the Tabernacle,* but no unauthorized person may assist you.

5 "You yourselves must perform the sacred duties inside the sanctuary and at the altar. If you follow these instructions, the LORD's anger will never again blaze against the people of Israel. 6 I myself have chosen your fellow Levites from among the Israelites to be your special assistants. They are a gift to you, dedicated to the LORD for service in the Tabernacle. 7 But you and your sons, the priests, must personally handle all the priestly rituals associated with the altar and with everything behind the inner curtain. I am giving you the priesthood as your special privilege of service. Any unauthorized person who comes too near the sanctuary will be put to death."

SUPPORT FOR THE PRIESTS AND LEVITES

8 The LORD gave these further instructions to Aaron: "I myself have put you in charge of all the holy offerings that are brought to me by the people of Israel. I have given all these consecrated offerings to you and your sons as your permanent share. 9 You are allotted the portion of the most holy offerings that is not burned on the fire. This portion of all the most holy offerings—including the grain offerings, sin offerings, and guilt offerings—will be most holy, and it belongs to you and your sons. 10 You must eat it as a most holy offering. All the males may eat of it, and you must treat it as most holy.

11 "All the sacred offerings and special offerings presented to me when the Israelites lift them up before the altar also belong to you. I have given them to you and to your sons and daughters as your permanent share. Any member of your family who is ceremonially clean may eat of these offerings.

12 "I also give you the harvest gifts brought by the people as offerings to the LORD—the best of the olive oil, new wine, and grain. 13 All the first crops of their land that the people present to the LORD belong to you. Any member of your family who is ceremonially clean may eat this food.

14 "Everything in Israel that is specially set apart for the LORD* also belongs to you.

15 "The firstborn of every mother, whether human or animal, that is offered to the LORD will be yours. But you must always redeem your firstborn sons and the firstborn of ceremonially unclean animals. 16 Redeem them when they are one month old. The redemption price is five pieces of silver* (as measured by the weight of the sanctuary shekel, which equals twenty gerahs).

17 "However, you may not redeem the firstborn of cattle, sheep, or goats. They are holy and have been set apart for the LORD. Sprinkle their blood on the altar, and burn their fat as a special gift, a pleasing aroma to the LORD. 18 The meat of these animals will be yours, just like the breast and right thigh that are presented by lifting them up as a special offering before the altar. 19 Yes, I am giving you all these holy offerings that the people of Israel bring to the LORD. They are for you and your sons and daughters, to be eaten as your permanent share. This is an eternal and unbreakable covenant* between the LORD and you, and it also applies to your descendants."

20 And the LORD said to Aaron, "You priests will receive no allotment of land or share of property among the people of Israel. I am your share and your allotment. 21 As for the tribe of Levi, your relatives, I will compensate them for their service in the Tabernacle. Instead of an allotment of land, I will give them the tithes from the entire land of Israel.

22 "From now on, no Israelites except priests or Levites may approach the Tabernacle. If they come too near, they will be judged guilty and will die. 23 Only the Levites may serve at the Tabernacle, and they will be held responsible for any offenses against it. This is a permanent law for you, to be observed from generation to generation. The Levites will receive no allotment of land among the Israelites, 24 because I have given them the Israelites' tithes, which have been presented as sacred offerings to the LORD. This will be the Levites' share. That is why I said they would receive no allotment of land among the Israelites."

25 The LORD also told Moses, 26 "Give these instructions to the Levites: When you receive from the people of Israel the tithes I have assigned as your allotment, give a tenth of the tithes you receive—a tithe of the tithe—to the LORD as a sacred offering. 27 The LORD will consider this offering to be your harvest offering, as though it were the first grain from your own threshing floor or wine from your own winepress. 28 You must present one-tenth of the tithe received from the Israelites as a sacred offering to the LORD. This is the LORD's sacred portion, and you must present it to Aaron the priest. 29 Be sure to give to the LORD the best portions of the gifts given to you.

30 "Also, give these instructions to the Levites: When you present the best part as your offering, it will be considered as though it came from your own threshing floor or winepress. 31 You Levites and your

18:2 Or *Tabernacle of the Testimony.* **18:4** Hebrew *the Tent of Meeting;* also in 18:6, 21, 22, 23, 31. **18:14** The Hebrew term used here refers to the complete consecration of things or people to the LORD, either by destroying them or by giving them as an offering. **18:16** Hebrew *5 shekels* [2 ounces or 57 grams] *of silver.* **18:19** Hebrew *a covenant of salt.*

18:1-7 God, in grace and love, made Aaron's priesthood responsible for the sanctuary and the altar, and thus for the spiritual welfare of Israel.
18:8 permanent share. Since the Levites were not given any land or property, the other 11 tribes would share the task of supporting them.
18:11 Any . . . who is ceremonially clean. Families of priests were included in the "regular share" of the offerings, provided they were ceremonially clean (see Lev. 22:4-8).
18:12 olive oil, new wine, and grain. The Law required the offering of the firstfruits and the best of everything to the Lord. The priests would receive their share from this bounty.

families may eat this food anywhere you wish, for it is your compensation for serving in the Tabernacle. 32 You will not be considered guilty for accepting the LORD's tithes if you give the best portion to the priests. But be careful not to treat the holy gifts of the people of Israel as though they were common. If you do, you will die."

THE WATER OF PURIFICATION

19 The LORD said to Moses and Aaron, 2 "Here is another legal requirement commanded by the LORD: Tell the people of Israel to bring you a red heifer, a perfect animal that has no defects and has never been yoked to a plow. 3 Give it to Eleazar the priest, and it will be taken outside the camp and slaughtered in his presence. 4 Eleazar will take some of its blood on his finger and sprinkle it seven times toward the front of the Tabernacle.* 5 As Eleazar watches, the heifer must be burned—its hide, meat, blood, and dung. 6 Eleazar the priest must then take a stick of cedar,* a hyssop branch, and some scarlet yarn and throw them into the fire where the heifer is burning.

7 "Then the priest must wash his clothes and bathe himself in water. Afterward he may return to the camp, though he will remain ceremonially unclean until evening. 8 The man who burns the animal must also wash his clothes and bathe himself in water, and he, too, will remain unclean until evening. 9 Then someone who is ceremonially clean will gather up the ashes of the heifer and deposit them in a purified place outside the camp. They will be kept there for the community of Israel to use in the water for the purification ceremony. This ceremony is performed for the removal of sin. 10 The man who gathers up the ashes of the heifer must also wash his clothes, and he will remain ceremonially unclean until evening. This is a permanent law for the people of Israel and any foreigners who live among them.

11 "All those who touch a dead human body will be ceremonially unclean for seven days. 12 They must purify themselves on the third and seventh days with the water of purification; then they will be purified. But if they do not do this on the third and seventh days, they will continue to be unclean even after the seventh day. 13 All those who touch a dead body and do not purify themselves in the proper way defile the LORD's Tabernacle, and they will be cut off from the community of Israel. Since the water of purification was not sprinkled on them, their defilement continues.

14 "This is the ritual law that applies when someone dies inside a tent: All those who enter that tent and those who were inside when the death occurred will be ceremonially unclean for seven days. 15 Any open container in the tent that was not covered with a lid is also defiled. 16 And if someone in an open field touches the corpse of someone who was killed with a sword or who died a natural death, or if someone touches a human bone or a grave, that person will be defiled for seven days.

17 "To remove the defilement, put some of the ashes from the burnt purification offering in a jar, and pour fresh water over them. 18 Then someone who is ceremonially clean must take a hyssop branch and dip it into the water. That person must sprinkle the water on the tent, on all the furnishings in the tent, and on the people who were in the tent; also on the person who touched a human bone, or touched someone who was killed or who died naturally, or touched a grave. 19 On the third and seventh days the person who is ceremonially clean must sprinkle the water on those who are defiled. Then on the seventh day the people being cleansed must wash their clothes and bathe themselves, and that evening they will be cleansed of their defilement.

20 "But those who become defiled and do not purify themselves will be cut off from the community, for they have defiled the sanctuary of the LORD. Since the water of purification has not been sprinkled on them, they remain defiled. 21 This is a permanent law for the people. Those who sprinkle the water of purification must afterward wash their clothes, and anyone who then touches the water used for purification will remain defiled until evening. 22 Anything and anyone that a defiled person touches will be ceremonially unclean until evening."

MOSES STRIKES THE ROCK

20 In the first month of the year,* the whole community of Israel arrived in the wilderness of Zin and camped at Kadesh. While they were there, Miriam died and was buried.

2 There was no water for the people to drink at that place, so they rebelled against Moses and Aaron. 3 The people blamed Moses and said, "If only we had died in the LORD's presence with our brothers! 4 Why have you brought the congregation of the LORD's people into this wilderness to die, along with all our livestock? 5 Why did you make us leave Egypt and bring us here to this terrible place? This land has no grain, no figs, no grapes, no pomegranates, and no water to drink!"

6 Moses and Aaron turned away from the people and went to the entrance of the Tabernacle,* where they fell face down on the ground. Then the glorious presence of the LORD appeared to them, 7 and the LORD said to Moses, 8 "You and Aaron must take the staff and assemble the entire community. As the people watch, speak to the rock over there, and it will pour out its water. You will provide enough water from the rock to satisfy the whole community and their livestock."

9 So Moses did as he was told. He took the staff from the place where it was kept before the LORD. 10 Then he and Aaron summoned the people to come and gather

19:4 Hebrew *the Tent of Meeting.* **19:6** Or *juniper.* **20:1** The first month of the ancient Hebrew lunar calendar usually occurs within the months of March and April. The number of years since leaving Egypt is not specified. **20:6** Hebrew *the Tent of Meeting.*

19:12 purify themselves . . . with the water. A person who touched a dead body was considered unclean and required a purification ritual.

19:13 defile the LORD's Tabernacle . . . cut off. Failure to become ceremonially clean was an affront to the Law and to the tabernacle, a serious sin.

19:14 inside a tent . . . unclean. All the causes of uncleanness relate to death (corpses, mildew, skin disease like a corpse) or loss of life (loss of blood, loss of semen).

19:18 dip it into the water . . . must sprinkle. Some of the cleansing water, made with the ashes of the red heifer, was sprinkled on everything that had some contact with the dead body.

20:2 no water for the people. Forty years earlier, God had Moses strike a rock with his staff, and water flowed out (Ex. 17:5-7). Now He gave Moses different instructions for getting water.

at the rock. "Listen, you rebels!" he shouted. "Must we
bring you water from this rock?" 11 Then Moses raised
his hand and struck the rock twice with the staff, and
water gushed out. So the entire community and their
livestock drank their fill.
12 But the LORD said to Moses and Aaron, "Because
you did not trust me enough to demonstrate my holi-
ness to the people of Israel, you will not lead them into
the land I am giving them!" 13 This place was known
as the waters of Meribah (which means "arguing")
because there the people of Israel argued with the
LORD, and there he demonstrated his holiness among
them.

EDOM REFUSES ISRAEL PASSAGE

14 While Moses was at Kadesh, he sent ambassadors to
the king of Edom with this message:

> "This is what your relatives, the people of Israel,
> say: You know all the hardships we have been
> through. 15 Our ancestors went down to Egypt, and
> we lived there a long time, and we and our ances-
> tors were brutally mistreated by the Egyptians.
> 16 But when we cried out to the LORD, he heard us
> and sent an angel who brought us out of Egypt.
> Now we are camped at Kadesh, a town on the
> border of your land. 17 Please let us travel through
> your land. We will be careful not to go through
> your fields and vineyards. We won't even drink
> water from your wells. We will stay on the king's
> road and never leave it until we have passed
> through your territory."

18 But the king of Edom said, "Stay out of my land, or
I will meet you with an army!"
19 The Israelites answered, "We will stay on the
main road. If our livestock drink your water, we will
pay for it. Just let us pass through your country. That's
all we ask."
20 But the king of Edom replied, "Stay out! You may
not pass through our land." With that he mobilized
his army and marched out against them with an im-
posing force. 21 Because Edom refused to allow Israel
to pass through their country, Israel was forced to
turn around.

THE DEATH OF AARON

22 The whole community of Israel left Kadesh and ar-
rived at Mount Hor. 23 There, on the border of the land
of Edom, the LORD said to Moses and Aaron, 24 "The
time has come for Aaron to join his ancestors in
death. He will not enter the land I am giving the peo-
ple of Israel, because the two of you rebelled against
my instructions concerning the water at Meribah.
25 Now take Aaron and his son Eleazar up Mount Hor.
26 There you will remove Aaron's priestly garments
and put them on Eleazar, his son. Aaron will die there
and join his ancestors."
27 So Moses did as the LORD commanded. The
three of them went up Mount Hor together as the
whole community watched. 28 At the summit, Moses
removed the priestly garments from Aaron and
put them on Eleazar, Aaron's son. Then Aaron died
there on top of the mountain, and Moses and Ele-
azar went back down. 29 When the people realized
that Aaron had died, all Israel mourned for him
thirty days.

VICTORY OVER THE CANAANITES

21 The Canaanite king of Arad, who lived in the
Negev, heard that the Israelites were approach-
ing on the road through Atharim. So he attacked the
Israelites and took some of them as prisoners. 2 Then
the people of Israel made this vow to the LORD: "If you
will hand these people over to us, we will completely
destroy* all their towns." 3 The LORD heard the Israel-
ites' request and gave them victory over the Canaan-
ites. The Israelites completely destroyed them and
their towns, and the place has been called Hormah*
ever since.

THE BRONZE SNAKE

4 Then the people of Israel set out from Mount Hor,
taking the road to the Red Sea* to go around the land
of Edom. But the people grew impatient with the long
journey, 5 and they began to speak against God and
Moses. "Why have you brought us out of Egypt to die
here in the wilderness?" they complained. "There is
nothing to eat here and nothing to drink. And we hate
this horrible manna!"
6 So the LORD sent poisonous snakes among the peo-
ple, and many were bitten and died. 7 Then the peo-
ple came to Moses and cried out, "We have sinned by
speaking against the LORD and against you. Pray that
the LORD will take away the snakes." So Moses prayed
for the people.
8 Then the LORD told him, "Make a replica of a poi-
sonous snake and attach it to a pole. All who are bit-
ten will live if they simply look at it!" 9 So Moses made
a snake out of bronze and attached it to a pole. Then
anyone who was bitten by a snake could look at the
bronze snake and be healed!

ISRAEL'S JOURNEY TO MOAB

10 The Israelites traveled next to Oboth and camped
there. 11 Then they went on to Iye-abarim, in the wil-
derness on the eastern border of Moab. 12 From there
they traveled to the valley of Zered Brook and set up
camp. 13 Then they moved out and camped on the far
side of the Arnon River, in the wilderness adjacent to

21:2 The Hebrew term used here refers to the complete consecration of things or people to the LORD, either by destroying them or by giving them as an offering; also in 21:3. **21:3** *Hormah* means "destruction." **21:4** Hebrew *sea of reeds.*

20:10 Must we bring you water from this rock? Moses spoke in anger and frustration and implied he had some part in the miracle of water coming from the rock.

20:11 raised his hand and struck the rock . . . staff. God's direct command to Moses was to speak to the rock, not strike it. Instead, Moses used his staff in anger.

20:12 did not trust . . . you will not lead them into the land. God's punishment was quick and severe. Israel's leaders for 40 years would not enter Canaan.

20:14-21 Please let us travel through your land. Moses tried a diplomatic approach with the Edomites, distant relatives of the Israelites.

20:20 army . . . with an imposing force. The Edomites probably feared this huge migration passing through their land.

20:25-28 Aaron and his son Eleazar . . . Mount Hor . . . put them on Eleazar The mantle of family leadership passed from father to son through Aaron's priestly garments.

21:5 nothing to eat . . . drink . . . we hate this horrible manna! Certainly the Israelites were tired of manna after 40 years. Rejecting God's provision of food, however, amounted to rejecting His provision of grace.

21:8-9 replica of a poisonous snake. The bronze snake was not an idol but a symbol of God's deliverance. The snake did not save the Israelites from the snakebite, but from its consequences.

the territory of the Amorites. The Arnon is the bound-
ary line between the Moabites and the Amorites.
14 For this reason *The Book of the Wars of the LORD*
speaks of "the town of Waheb in the area of Suphah,
and the ravines of the Arnon River, 15 and the ravines
that extend as far as the settlement of Ar on the bor-
der of Moab."
16 From there the Israelites traveled to Beer,* which
is the well where the LORD said to Moses, "Assemble
the people, and I will give them water." 17 There the
Israelites sang this song:

"Spring up, O well!
 Yes, sing its praises!
18 Sing of this well,
 which princes dug,
which great leaders hollowed out
 with their scepters and staffs."

Then the Israelites left the wilderness and proceed-
ed on through Mattanah, 19 Nahaliel, and Bamoth.
20 After that they went to the valley in Moab where
Pisgah Peak overlooks the wasteland.*

VICTORY OVER SIHON AND OG

21 The Israelites sent ambassadors to King Sihon of the
Amorites with this message:

22 "Let us travel through your land. We will be
careful not to go through your fields and vine-
yards. We won't even drink water from your wells.
We will stay on the king's road until we have
passed through your territory."

23 But King Sihon refused to let them cross his ter-
ritory. Instead, he mobilized his entire army and
attacked Israel in the wilderness, engaging them in
battle at Jahaz. 24 But the Israelites slaughtered them
with their swords and occupied their land from the
Arnon River to the Jabbok River. They went only as
far as the Ammonite border because the boundary of
the Ammonites was fortified.*
25 So Israel captured all the towns of the Amorites
and settled in them, including the city of Heshbon and
its surrounding villages. 26 Heshbon had been the cap-
ital of King Sihon of the Amorites. He had defeated a
former Moabite king and seized all his land as far as
the Arnon River. 27 Therefore, the ancient poets wrote
this about him:

"Come to Heshbon and let it be rebuilt!
 Let the city of Sihon be restored.
28 A fire flamed forth from Heshbon,
 a blaze from the city of Sihon.
It burned the city of Ar in Moab;
 it destroyed the rulers of the Arnon
 heights.
29 What sorrow awaits you, O people of Moab!
 You are finished, O worshipers of Chemosh!
Chemosh has left his sons as refugees,
 his daughters as captives of Sihon, the Amorite
 king.
30 We have utterly destroyed them,
 from Heshbon to Dibon.
We have completely wiped them out
 as far away as Nophah and Medeba.*"

31 So the people of Israel occupied the territory of
the Amorites. 32 After Moses sent men to explore the
Jazer area, they captured all the towns in the region
and drove out the Amorites who lived there. 33 Then
they turned and marched up the road to Bashan, but
King Og of Bashan and all his people attacked them
at Edrei. 34 The LORD said to Moses, "Do not be afraid
of him, for I have handed him over to you, along with
all his people and his land. Do the same to him as you
did to King Sihon of the Amorites, who ruled in Hesh-
bon." 35 And Israel killed King Og, his sons, and all his
subjects; not a single survivor remained. Then Israel
occupied their land.

BALAK SENDS FOR BALAAM

22 Then the people of Israel traveled to the plains
of Moab and camped east of the Jordan River,
across from Jericho. 2 Balak son of Zippor, the Moab-
ite king, had seen everything the Israelites did to the
Amorites. 3 And when the people of Moab saw how
many Israelites there were, they were terrified. 4 The
king of Moab said to the elders of Midian, "This mob
will devour everything in sight, like an ox devours
grass in the field!"
So Balak, king of Moab, 5 sent messengers to call
Balaam son of Beor, who was living in his native
land of Pethor* near the Euphrates River.* His mes-
sage said:

"Look, a vast horde of people has arrived from
Egypt. They cover the face of the earth and are
threatening me. 6 Please come and curse these peo-
ple for me because they are too powerful for me.
Then perhaps I will be able to conquer them and
drive them from the land. I know that blessings
fall on any people you bless, and curses fall on
people you curse."

7 Balak's messengers, who were elders of Moab and
Midian, set out with money to pay Balaam to place a
curse upon Israel.* They went to Balaam and deliv-
ered Balak's message to him. 8 "Stay here overnight,"
Balaam said. "In the morning I will tell you whatever
the LORD directs me to say." So the officials from Moab
stayed there with Balaam.
9 That night God came to Balaam and asked him,
"Who are these men visiting you?"

21:16 *Beer* means "well." **21:20** Or *overlooks Jeshimon.* **21:24** Or *because the terrain of the Ammonite frontier was rugged;* Hebrew reads *because the boundary of the Ammonites was strong.* **21:30** Or *until fire spread to Medeba.* The meaning of the Hebrew is uncertain. **22:5a** Or *who was at Pethor in the land of the Amavites.* **22:5b** Hebrew *the river.* **22:7** Hebrew *set out with the money of divination in their hand.*

21:21-26 Let us travel through your land. Again the Israelites requested permission to travel through the territory of another tribe. The Amorites resisted, and Israel won a crushing victory.
21:35 occupied their land. Israel's victory over Og and his armies gave them possession of the entire Transjordan.
22:1 camped east of the Jordan River. Israel moved into position to invade Canaan from the east, with Jericho the first target.
22:5 Balaam son of Beor. Balak felt pagan divination was his one chance to save his people.
22:8 tell you whatever the LORD directs me to say. Balaam believed in many gods, but apparently he feared Israel's God. He would not give a false prophecy for money in the name of Israel's God.

10 Balaam said to God, "Balak son of Zippor, king of Moab, has sent me this message: 11 'Look, a vast horde of people has arrived from Egypt, and they cover the face of the earth. Come and curse these people for me. Then perhaps I will be able to stand up to them and drive them from the land.'"

12 But God told Balaam, "Do not go with them. You are not to curse these people, for they have been blessed!"

13 The next morning Balaam got up and told Balak's officials, "Go on home! The LORD will not let me go with you."

14 So the Moabite officials returned to King Balak and reported, "Balaam refused to come with us." 15 Then Balak tried again. This time he sent a larger number of even more distinguished officials than those he had sent the first time. 16 They went to Balaam and delivered this message to him:

> "This is what Balak son of Zippor says: Please don't let anything stop you from coming to help me. 17 I will pay you very well and do whatever you tell me. Just come and curse these people for me!"

18 But Balaam responded to Balak's messengers, "Even if Balak were to give me his palace filled with silver and gold, I would be powerless to do anything against the will of the LORD my God. 19 But stay here one more night, and I will see if the LORD has anything else to say to me."

20 That night God came to Balaam and told him, "Since these men have come for you, get up and go with them. But do only what I tell you to do."

BALAAM AND HIS DONKEY

21 So the next morning Balaam got up, saddled his donkey, and started off with the Moabite officials. 22 But God was angry that Balaam was going, so he sent the angel of the LORD to stand in the road to block his way. As Balaam and two servants were riding along, 23 Balaam's donkey saw the angel of the LORD standing in the road with a drawn sword in his hand. The donkey bolted off the road into a field, but Balaam beat it and turned it back onto the road. 24 Then the angel of the LORD stood at a place where the road narrowed between two vineyard walls. 25 When the donkey saw the angel of the LORD, it tried to squeeze by and crushed Balaam's foot against the wall. So Balaam beat the donkey again. 26 Then the angel of the LORD moved farther down the road and stood in a place too narrow for the donkey to get by at all. 27 This time when the donkey saw the angel, it lay down under Balaam. In a fit of rage Balaam beat the animal again with his staff.

28 Then the LORD gave the donkey the ability to speak. "What have I done to you that deserves your beating me three times?" it asked Balaam.

29 "You have made me look like a fool!" Balaam shouted. "If I had a sword with me, I would kill you!"

30 "But I am the same donkey you have ridden all your life," the donkey answered. "Have I ever done anything like this before?"

"No," Balaam admitted.

31 Then the LORD opened Balaam's eyes, and he saw the angel of the LORD standing in the roadway with a drawn sword in his hand. Balaam bowed his head and fell face down on the ground before him.

32 "Why did you beat your donkey those three times?" the angel of the LORD demanded. "Look, I have come to block your way because you are stubbornly resisting me. 33 Three times the donkey saw me and shied away; otherwise, I would certainly have killed you by now and spared the donkey."

34 Then Balaam confessed to the angel of the LORD, "I have sinned. I didn't realize you were standing in the road to block my way. I will return home if you are against my going."

35 But the angel of the LORD told Balaam, "Go with these men, but say only what I tell you to say." So Balaam went on with Balak's officials. 36 When King Balak heard that Balaam was on the way, he went out to meet him at a Moabite town on the Arnon River at the farthest border of his land.

37 "Didn't I send you an urgent invitation? Why didn't you come right away?" Balak asked Balaam. "Didn't you believe me when I said I would reward you richly?"

38 Balaam replied, "Look, now I have come, but I have no power to say whatever I want. I will speak only the message that God puts in my mouth." 39 Then Balaam accompanied Balak to Kiriath-huzoth, 40 where the king sacrificed cattle and sheep. He sent portions of the meat to Balaam and the officials who were with him. 41 The next morning Balak took Balaam up to Bamoth-baal. From there he could see some of the people of Israel spread out below him.

BALAAM BLESSES ISRAEL

23 Then Balaam said to King Balak, "Build me seven altars here, and prepare seven young bulls and seven rams for me to sacrifice." 2 Balak followed his instructions, and the two of them sacrificed a young bull and a ram on each altar.

3 Then Balaam said to Balak, "Stand here by your burnt offerings, and I will go to see if the LORD will respond to me. Then I will tell you whatever he reveals to me." So Balaam went alone to the top of a bare hill, 4 and God met him there. Balaam said to him, "I have prepared seven altars and have sacrificed a young bull and a ram on each altar."

5 The LORD gave Balaam a message for King Balak. Then he said, "Go back to Balak and give him my message."

6 So Balaam returned and found the king standing beside his burnt offerings with all the officials of Moab. 7 This was the message Balaam delivered:

"Balak summoned me to come from Aram;
the king of Moab brought me from the eastern hills.

22:20 go with them. But. God allowed Balaam to go, but only to do His will.

22:31 Then the LORD opened Balaam's eyes . . . the angel of the LORD. Two miracles in three verses: First, a donkey spoke—and spoke the truth. Then, Balaam's eyes were opened and he saw the truth.

22:35 Go with these men, but say only what I tell you to say. God amended His command to include the words Balaam could speak.

23:1 seven altars . . . young bulls . . . rams. Balaam may have used seven because this number was significant to God.

23:2 two of them sacrificed. Balak didn't care about God's will; he just wanted the Israelites cursed so he could drive them out of his land (22:6).

'Come,' he said, 'curse Jacob for me!
Come and announce Israel's doom.'
8 But how can I curse those
whom God has not cursed?
How can I condemn those
whom the LORD has not condemned?
9 I see them from the cliff tops;
I watch them from the hills.
I see a people who live by themselves,
set apart from other nations.
10 Who can count Jacob's descendants, as numerous as dust?
Who can count even a fourth of Israel's people?
Let me die like the righteous;
let my life end like theirs."

11 Then King Balak demanded of Balaam, "What
have you done to me? I brought you to curse my ene-
mies. Instead, you have blessed them!"
12 But Balaam replied, "I will speak only the mes-
sage that the LORD puts in my mouth."

BALAAM'S SECOND MESSAGE

13 Then King Balak told him, "Come with me to anoth-
er place. There you will see another part of the nation
of Israel, but not all of them. Curse at least that many!"
14 So Balak took Balaam to the plateau of Zophim on
Pisgah Peak. He built seven altars there and offered a
young bull and a ram on each altar.
15 Then Balaam said to the king, "Stand here by
your burnt offerings while I go over there to meet the
LORD."
16 And the LORD met Balaam and gave him a mes-
sage. Then he said, "Go back to Balak and give him my
message."
17 So Balaam returned and found the king stand-
ing beside his burnt offerings with all the officials of
Moab. "What did the LORD say?" Balak asked eagerly.
18 This was the message Balaam delivered:

"Rise up, Balak, and listen!
Hear me, son of Zippor.
19 God is not a man, so he does not lie.
He is not human, so he does not change his mind.
Has he ever spoken and failed to act?
Has he ever promised and not carried it through?
20 Listen, I received a command to bless;
God has blessed, and I cannot reverse it!
21 No misfortune is in his plan for Jacob;
no trouble is in store for Israel.
For the LORD their God is with them;
he has been proclaimed their king.
22 God brought them out of Egypt;
for them he is as strong as a wild ox.
23 No curse can touch Jacob;
no magic has any power against Israel.
For now it will be said of Jacob,
'What wonders God has done for Israel!'
24 These people rise up like a lioness,
like a majestic lion rousing itself.
They refuse to rest
until they have feasted on prey,
drinking the blood of the slaughtered!"

25 Then Balak said to Balaam, "Fine, but if you won't
curse them, at least don't bless them!"
26 But Balaam replied to Balak, "Didn't I tell you that
I can do only what the LORD tells me?"

BALAAM'S THIRD MESSAGE

27 Then King Balak said to Balaam, "Come, I will take
you to one more place. Perhaps it will please God to let
you curse them from there."
28 So Balak took Balaam to the top of Mount Peor,
overlooking the wasteland.* 29 Balaam again told Ba-
lak, "Build me seven altars, and prepare seven young
bulls and seven rams for me to sacrifice." 30 So Balak
did as Balaam ordered and offered a young bull and
a ram on each altar.

24 By now Balaam realized that the LORD was de-
termined to bless Israel, so he did not resort to
divination as before. Instead, he turned and looked
out toward the wilderness, 2 where he saw the peo-
ple of Israel camped, tribe by tribe. Then the Spirit
of God came upon him, 3 and this is the message he
delivered:

"This is the message of Balaam son of Beor,
the message of the man whose eyes see clearly,
4 the message of one who hears the words of God,
who sees a vision from the Almighty,
who bows down with eyes wide open:
5 How beautiful are your tents, O Jacob;
how lovely are your homes, O Israel!
6 They spread before me like palm groves,*
like gardens by the riverside.
They are like tall trees planted by the LORD,
like cedars beside the waters.
7 Water will flow from their buckets;
their offspring have all they need.
Their king will be greater than Agag;
their kingdom will be exalted.
8 God brought them out of Egypt;
for them he is as strong as a wild ox.
He devours all the nations that oppose him,
breaking their bones in pieces,
shooting them with arrows.
9 Like a lion, Israel crouches and lies down;
like a lioness, who dares to arouse her?
Blessed is everyone who blesses you, O Israel,
and cursed is everyone who curses you."

10 King Balak flew into a rage against Balaam. He
angrily clapped his hands and shouted, "I called you

23:28 Or *overlooking Jeshimon.* 24:6 Or *like a majestic valley.*

23:8 how can I curse . . . How can I condemn. If Balaam did the divine will, then he could not curse those whom God did not curse. If he went against God's will, he would be powerless to curse those whom God had blessed.

23:19 God is not a man, so he does not lie. As someone who gave "prophecies" to the highest bidder, Balaam knew plenty about lies.

23:21 the LORD their God is with them; he has been proclaimed their King. The first declaration of God's kingship was spoken by a pagan.

23:24 rise up like a lioness. From the outside, Israel's campaign to capture Canaan appeared to be like that of a hunting lioness: stalking the enemy, striking suddenly with great force, and devouring everything.

24:2 the Spirit of God came upon him . . . the message. In sharp contrast with Balaam's usual "sorcery," God caused Balaam to prophesy favorably toward Israel by overcoming him by the power of the Spirit.

to curse my enemies! Instead, you have blessed them
three times. 11 Now get out of here! Go back home! I
promised to reward you richly, but the LORD has kept
you from your reward."
12 Balaam told Balak, "Don't you remember what I
told your messengers? I said, 13 'Even if Balak were to
give me his palace filled with silver and gold, I would
be powerless to do anything against the will of the
LORD.' I told you that I could say only what the LORD
says! 14 Now I am returning to my own people. But
first let me tell you what the Israelites will do to your
people in the future."

BALAAM'S FINAL MESSAGES

15 This is the message Balaam delivered:

"This is the message of Balaam son of Beor,
the message of the man whose eyes see clearly,
16 the message of one who hears the words of God,
who has knowledge from the Most High,
who sees a vision from the Almighty,
who bows down with eyes wide open:
17 I see him, but not here and now.
I perceive him, but far in the distant future.
A star will rise from Jacob;
a scepter will emerge from Israel.
It will crush the heads of Moab's people,
cracking the skulls* of the people of Sheth.
18 Edom will be taken over,
and Seir, its enemy, will be conquered,
while Israel marches on in triumph.
19 A ruler will rise in Jacob
who will destroy the survivors of Ir."

20 Then Balaam looked over toward the people of Am-
alek and delivered this message:

"Amalek was the greatest of nations,
but its destiny is destruction!"

21 Then he looked over toward the Kenites and deliv-
ered this message:

"Your home is secure;
your nest is set in the rocks.
22 But the Kenites will be destroyed
when Assyria* takes you captive."

23 Balaam concluded his messages by saying:

"Alas, who can survive
unless God has willed it?
24 Ships will come from the coasts of Cyprus*;
they will oppress Assyria and afflict Eber,
but they, too, will be utterly destroyed."

25 Then Balaam left and returned home, and Balak
also went on his way.

MOAB SEDUCES ISRAEL

25 While the Israelites were camped at Acacia
Grove,* some of the men defiled themselves by
having* sexual relations with local Moabite wom-
en. 2 These women invited them to attend sacrific-
es to their gods, so the Israelites feasted with them
and worshiped the gods of Moab. 3 In this way, Isra-
el joined in the worship of Baal of Peor, causing the
LORD's anger to blaze against his people.
4 The LORD issued the following command to Moses:
"Seize all the ringleaders and execute them before the
LORD in broad daylight, so his fierce anger will turn
away from the people of Israel."
5 So Moses ordered Israel's judges, "Each of you
must put to death the men under your authority who
have joined in worshiping Baal of Peor."
6 Just then one of the Israelite men brought a Mid-
ianite woman into his tent, right before the eyes of
Moses and all the people, as everyone was weeping
at the entrance of the Tabernacle.* 7 When Phinehas
son of Eleazar and grandson of Aaron the priest saw
this, he jumped up and left the assembly. He took a
spear 8 and rushed after the man into his tent. Phin-
ehas thrust the spear all the way through the man's
body and into the woman's stomach. So the plague
against the Israelites was stopped, 9 but not before
24,000 people had died.
10 Then the LORD said to Moses, 11 "Phinehas son of
Eleazar and grandson of Aaron the priest has turned
my anger away from the Israelites by being as zeal-
ous among them as I was. So I stopped destroying all
Israel as I had intended to do in my zealous anger.
12 Now tell him that I am making my special covenant
of peace with him. 13 In this covenant, I give him and
his descendants a permanent right to the priesthood,
for in his zeal for me, his God, he purified the people of
Israel, making them right with me.*"
14 The Israelite man killed with the Midianite wom-
an was named Zimri son of Salu, the leader of a fami-
ly from the tribe of Simeon. 15 The woman's name was
Cozbi; she was the daughter of Zur, the leader of a
Midianite clan.
16 Then the LORD said to Moses, 17 "Attack the Mid-
ianites and destroy them, 18 because they assaulted
you with deceit and tricked you into worshiping Baal

24:17 As in Samaritan Pentateuch; the meaning of the Hebrew word is uncertain. **24:22** Hebrew *Asshur;* also in 24:24. **24:24** Hebrew *Kittim.* **25:1a** Hebrew *Shittim.* **25:1b** As in Greek version; Hebrew reads *some of the men began having.* **25:6** Hebrew *the Tent of Meeting.* **25:13** Or *he made atonement for the people of Israel.*

24:11 I promised to reward . . . the LORD has kept you from your reward. Balak wanted Balaam to pronounce only curses. He refused to pay for blessings.

24:15-16 knowledge from the Most High. The fourth oracle went beyond the third's claim of "visions" to "knowledge." Balaam felt his visions had given him a special understanding of the future.

24:17 star . . . scepter. This oracle predicts the rise of David and his consolidation of power over the region. Its imagery even suggests the coming of a Messiah (Rev. 2:27-28; 22:16).

25:1-18 On the very doorstep of Canaan, Israelite men were the victims of sexual seduction (v. 2) that led to Baal worship.

25:1 Acacia Grove . . . having sexual relations. Temple prostitutes sent by Balaam (Num. 31:16) lured Israelites into sexual sin as well as pagan practices.

25:4 Seize all the ringleaders and execute them . . . in broad daylight. This punishment was severe. Execution and public display of the corpses would punish the guilty, but also humiliate their families and frighten everyone.

25:6 one of the Israelite men brought a Midianite woman. The man who did this, Zimri (v. 14), was insulting his family and defying the laws against fornication. His action also was insensitive to the many deaths already caused by the plague (24,000, according to v. 9).

25:17 Attack the Midianites. Midian had been conspiring with Balak since Israel assumed the dominant position in the Transjordan (22:1-7). The Midianite women had seduced Israelite men into Baal worship.

of Peor, and because of Cozbi, the daughter of a Midianite leader, who was killed at the time of the plague because of what happened at Peor."

THE SECOND REGISTRATION OF ISRAEL'S TROOPS

26 After the plague had ended,* the LORD said to Moses and to Eleazar son of Aaron the priest,
2 "From the whole community of Israel, record the names of all the warriors by their families. List all the men twenty years old or older who are able to go to war."
3 So there on the plains of Moab beside the Jordan River, across from Jericho, Moses and Eleazar the priest issued these instructions to the leaders of Israel:
4 "List all the men of Israel twenty years old and older, just as the LORD commanded Moses."

This is the record of all the descendants of Israel who came out of Egypt.

THE TRIBE OF REUBEN

5 These were the clans descended from the sons of Reuben, Jacob's* oldest son:

The Hanochite clan, named after their ancestor Hanoch.
The Palluite clan, named after their ancestor Pallu.
6 The Hezronite clan, named after their ancestor Hezron.
The Carmite clan, named after their ancestor Carmi.

7 These were the clans of Reuben. Their registered troops numbered 43,730.
8 Pallu was the ancestor of Eliab,
9 and Eliab was the father of Nemuel, Dathan, and Abiram. This Dathan and Abiram are the same community leaders who conspired with Korah against Moses and Aaron, rebelling against the LORD.
10 But the earth opened up its mouth and swallowed them with Korah, and fire devoured 250 of their followers. This served as a warning to the entire nation of Israel.
11 However, the sons of Korah did not die that day.

THE TRIBE OF SIMEON

12 These were the clans descended from the sons of Simeon:

The Jemuelite clan, named after their ancestor Jemuel.*
The Jaminite clan, named after their ancestor Jamin.
The Jakinite clan, named after their ancestor Jakin.
13 The Zoharite clan, named after their ancestor Zohar.*
The Shaulite clan, named after their ancestor Shaul.

14 These were the clans of Simeon. Their registered troops numbered 22,200.

THE TRIBE OF GAD

15 These were the clans descended from the sons of Gad:

The Zephonite clan, named after their ancestor Zephon.
The Haggite clan, named after their ancestor Haggi.
The Shunite clan, named after their ancestor Shuni.
16 The Oznite clan, named after their ancestor Ozni.
The Erite clan, named after their ancestor Eri.
17 The Arodite clan, named after their ancestor Arodi.*
The Arelite clan, named after their ancestor Areli.

18 These were the clans of Gad. Their registered troops numbered 40,500.

THE TRIBE OF JUDAH

19 Judah had two sons, Er and Onan, who had died in the land of Canaan.
20 These were the clans descended from Judah's surviving sons:

The Shelanite clan, named after their ancestor Shelah.
The Perezite clan, named after their ancestor Perez.
The Zerahite clan, named after their ancestor Zerah.

21 These were the subclans descended from the Perezites:

The Hezronites, named after their ancestor Hezron.
The Hamulites, named after their ancestor Hamul.

22 These were the clans of Judah. Their registered troops numbered 76,500.

THE TRIBE OF ISSACHAR

23 These were the clans descended from the sons of Issachar:

The Tolaite clan, named after their ancestor Tola.
The Puite clan, named after their ancestor Puah.*
24 The Jashubite clan, named after their ancestor Jashub.
The Shimronite clan, named after their ancestor Shimron.

25 These were the clans of Issachar. Their registered troops numbered 64,300.

THE TRIBE OF ZEBULUN

26 These were the clans descended from the sons of Zebulun:

The Seredite clan, named after their ancestor Sered.
The Elonite clan, named after their ancestor Elon.
The Jahleelite clan, named after their ancestor Jahleel.

27 These were the clans of Zebulun. Their registered troops numbered 60,500.

26:1 The initial phrase in verse 26:1 is numbered 25:19 in Hebrew text. **26:5** Hebrew *Israel's;* see note on 1:20-21b. **26:12** As in Syriac version (see also Gen 46:10; Exod 6:15); Hebrew reads *Nemuelite . . . Nemuel.* **26:13** As in parallel texts at Gen 46:10 and Exod 6:15; Hebrew reads *Zerahite . . . Zerah.* **26:17** As in Samaritan Pentateuch and Greek and Syriac versions (see also Gen 46:16); Hebrew reads *Arod.* **26:23** As in Samaritan Pentateuch, Greek and Syriac versions, and Latin Vulgate (see also 1 Chr 7:1); Hebrew reads *The Punite clan, named after its ancestor Puvah.*

26:1-51 The first census had been taken over 38 years before, and nearly all the men 20 years old or older then were now dead. The new census would give the tribal leaders an idea of how many soldiers were ready to fight.

THE TRIBE OF MANASSEH

28 Two clans were descended from Joseph through Manasseh and Ephraim.

29 These were the clans descended from Manasseh:
The Makirite clan, named after their ancestor Makir.
The Gileadite clan, named after their ancestor Gilead, Makir's son.

30 These were the subclans descended from the Gileadites:
The Iezerites, named after their ancestor Iezer.
The Helekites, named after their ancestor Helek.
31 The Asrielites, named after their ancestor Asriel.
The Shechemites, named after their ancestor Shechem.
32 The Shemidaites, named after their ancestor Shemida.
The Hepherites, named after their ancestor Hepher.
33 (One of Hepher's descendants, Zelophehad, had no sons, but his daughters' names were Mahlah, Noah, Hoglah, Milcah, and Tirzah.)

34 These were the clans of Manasseh. Their registered troops numbered 52,700.

THE TRIBE OF EPHRAIM

35 These were the clans descended from the sons of Ephraim:
The Shuthelahite clan, named after their ancestor Shuthelah.
The Bekerite clan, named after their ancestor Beker.
The Tahanite clan, named after their ancestor Tahan.

36 This was the subclan descended from the Shuthelahites:
The Eranites, named after their ancestor Eran.

37 These were the clans of Ephraim. Their registered troops numbered 32,500.

These clans of Manasseh and Ephraim were all descendants of Joseph.

THE TRIBE OF BENJAMIN

38 These were the clans descended from the sons of Benjamin:
The Belaite clan, named after their ancestor Bela.
The Ashbelite clan, named after their ancestor Ashbel.
The Ahiramite clan, named after their ancestor Ahiram.
39 The Shuphamite clan, named after their ancestor Shupham.*
The Huphamite clan, named after their ancestor Hupham.

40 These were the subclans descended from the Belaites:
The Ardites, named after their ancestor Ard.*
The Naamites, named after their ancestor Naaman.

41 These were the clans of Benjamin. Their registered troops numbered 45,600.

THE TRIBE OF DAN

42 These were the clans descended from the sons of Dan:
The Shuhamite clan, named after their ancestor Shuham.

43 These were the Shuhamite clans of Dan. Their registered troops numbered 64,400.

THE TRIBE OF ASHER

44 These were the clans descended from the sons of Asher:
The Imnite clan, named after their ancestor Imnah.
The Ishvite clan, named after their ancestor Ishvi.
The Beriite clan, named after their ancestor Beriah.

45 These were the subclans descended from the Beriites:
The Heberites, named after their ancestor Heber.
The Malkielites, named after their ancestor Malkiel.

46 Asher also had a daughter named Serah.

47 These were the clans of Asher. Their registered troops numbered 53,400.

THE TRIBE OF NAPHTALI

48 These were the clans descended from the sons of Naphtali:
The Jahzeelite clan, named after their ancestor Jahzeel.
The Gunite clan, named after their ancestor Guni.
49 The Jezerite clan, named after their ancestor Jezer.
The Shillemite clan, named after their ancestor Shillem.

50 These were the clans of Naphtali. Their registered troops numbered 45,400.

RESULTS OF THE REGISTRATION

51 In summary, the registered troops of all Israel numbered 601,730.

52 Then the LORD said to Moses, 53 "Divide the land among the tribes, and distribute the grants of land in proportion to the tribes' populations, as indicated by the number of names on the list. 54 Give the larger tribes more land and the smaller tribes less land, each group

26:39 As in some Hebrew manuscripts, Samaritan Pentateuch, Greek and Syriac versions, and Latin Vulgate; most Hebrew manuscripts read *Shephupham.* **26:40** As in Samaritan Pentateuch, some Greek manuscripts, and Latin Vulgate; Hebrew lacks *named after their ancestor Ard.*

26:51 601,730. The first census, 38 years earlier, had counted 603,550 males. Despite deaths from battles, disease, old age, and disobedience, Israel had remained strong.

26:53 indicated by the number of names. Each tribe was allotted land based on population. Locations would be determined later by lot (v. 55).

receiving a grant in proportion to the size of its popu-
lation. 55 But you must assign the land by lot, and give
land to each ancestral tribe according to the number of
names on the list. 56 Each grant of land must be assigned
by lot among the larger and smaller tribal groups."

THE TRIBE OF LEVI

57 This is the record of the Levites who were counted
according to their clans:

The Gershonite clan, named after their ancestor Gershon.
The Kohathite clan, named after their ancestor Kohath.
The Merarite clan, named after their ancestor Merari.

58 The Libnites, the Hebronites, the Mahlites, the Mu-
shites, and the Korahites were all subclans of the Le-
vites.
Now Kohath was the ancestor of Amram, 59 and
Amram's wife was named Jochebed. She also was
a descendant of Levi, born among the Levites in the
land of Egypt. Amram and Jochebed became the par-
ents of Aaron, Moses, and their sister, Miriam. 60 To
Aaron were born Nadab, Abihu, Eleazar, and Itha-
mar. 61 But Nadab and Abihu died when they burned
before the LORD the wrong kind of fire, different than
he had commanded.
62 The men from the Levite clans who were one
month old or older numbered 23,000. But the Levites
were not included in the registration of the rest of
the people of Israel because they were not given an
allotment of land when it was divided among the Is-
raelites.
63 So these are the results of the registration of the
people of Israel as conducted by Moses and Eleazar
the priest on the plains of Moab beside the Jordan
River, across from Jericho. 64 Not one person on this
list had been among those listed in the previous reg-
istration taken by Moses and Aaron in the wilderness
of Sinai. 65 For the LORD had said of them, "They will
all die in the wilderness." Not one of them survived
except Caleb son of Jephunneh and Joshua son of Nun.

THE DAUGHTERS OF ZELOPHEHAD

27 One day a petition was presented by the
daughters of Zelophehad—Mahlah, Noah,
Hoglah, Milcah, and Tirzah. Their father, Zelophe-
had, was a descendant of Hepher son of Gilead, son
of Makir, son of Manasseh, son of Joseph. 2 These
women stood before Moses, Eleazar the priest, the
tribal leaders, and the entire community at the en-
trance of the Tabernacle.* 3 "Our father died in the
wilderness," they said. "He was not among Korah's
followers, who rebelled against the LORD; he died
because of his own sin. But he had no sons. 4 Why
should the name of our father disappear from his
clan just because he had no sons? Give us property
along with the rest of our relatives."
5 So Moses brought their case before the LORD.
6 And the LORD replied to Moses, 7 "The claim of the
daughters of Zelophehad is legitimate. You must give
them a grant of land along with their father's rela-
tives. Assign them the property that would have been
given to their father.
8 "And give the following instructions to the peo-
ple of Israel: If a man dies and has no son, then give
his inheritance to his daughters. 9 And if he has no
daughter either, transfer his inheritance to his broth-
ers. 10 If he has no brothers, give his inheritance to his
father's brothers. 11 But if his father has no brothers,
give his inheritance to the nearest relative in his clan.
This is a legal requirement for the people of Israel,
just as the LORD commanded Moses."

JOSHUA CHOSEN TO LEAD ISRAEL

12 One day the LORD said to Moses, "Climb one of the
mountains east of the river,* and look out over the
land I have given the people of Israel. 13 After you
have seen it, you will die like your brother, Aaron,
14 for you both rebelled against my instructions in the
wilderness of Zin. When the people of Israel rebelled,
you failed to demonstrate my holiness to them at the
waters." (These are the waters of Meribah at Kadesh*
in the wilderness of Zin.)
15 Then Moses said to the LORD, 16 "O LORD, you are
the God who gives breath to all creatures. Please ap-
point a new man as leader for the community. 17 Give
them someone who will guide them wherever they
go and will lead them into battle, so the community of
the LORD will not be like sheep without a shepherd."
18 The LORD replied, "Take Joshua son of Nun, who
has the Spirit in him, and lay your hands on him.
19 Present him to Eleazar the priest before the whole
community, and publicly commission him to lead the
people. 20 Transfer some of your authority to him so the
whole community of Israel will obey him. 21 When di-
rection from the LORD is needed, Joshua will stand be-
fore Eleazar the priest, who will use the Urim—one of
the sacred lots cast before the LORD—to determine his
will. This is how Joshua and the rest of the community
of Israel will determine everything they should do."
22 So Moses did as the LORD commanded. He pre-
sented Joshua to Eleazar the priest and the whole
community. 23 Moses laid his hands on him and com-
missioned him to lead the people, just as the LORD had
commanded through Moses.

THE DAILY OFFERINGS

28 The LORD said to Moses, 2 "Give these instructions
to the people of Israel: The offerings you present
as special gifts are a pleasing aroma to me; they are my

27:2 Hebrew *the Tent of Meeting.* 27:12 Or *the mountains of Abarim.* 27:14 Hebrew *waters of Meribath-kadesh.*

27:1-11 Zelophehad's daughters' appeal for an inheritance was an unprecedented act of courage. God's "ruling" changed the male-dominated rules that had long governed property.

27:4-5 name of our father . . . Moses brought their case before the LORD. Israelite justice looked to its source: The Lord had written the Law, and He sat as the highest judge in its application.

27:12-23 Zelophehad's daughters got their justice, but God would not bend His justice to allow Moses to enter Canaan.

27:16 appoint a new man as leader for the community. Moses' first concern was for his people, and for a smooth leadership transition.

27:18 Take Joshua son of Nun. It was important that Joshua be made Moses' successor before Moses died. One of the original spies into Canaan (13:8, 16), Joshua had shown courage and willingness to lead (13:1–14:38). He would need all his courage and fortitude as Israel's leader.

27:20 Transfer some of your authority. Moses' authority over the nation of Israel came through God's miracles, his own fortitude, and by being the mediator between God and Israel. That role would be hard for a successor to attain, so God commanded a transition period between Moses and Joshua.

food. See to it that they are brought at the appointed times and offered according to my instructions.

3 "Say to the people: This is the special gift you must present to the LORD as your daily burnt offering. You must offer two one-year-old male lambs with no defects. 4 Sacrifice one lamb in the morning and the other in the evening. 5 With each lamb you must offer a grain offering of two quarts* of choice flour mixed with one quart* of pure oil of pressed olives. 6 This is the regular burnt offering instituted at Mount Sinai as a special gift, a pleasing aroma to the LORD. 7 Along with it you must present the proper liquid offering of one quart of alcoholic drink with each lamb, poured out in the Holy Place as an offering to the LORD. 8 Offer the second lamb in the evening with the same grain offering and liquid offering. It, too, is a special gift, a pleasing aroma to the LORD.

THE SABBATH OFFERINGS

9 "On the Sabbath day, sacrifice two one-year-old male lambs with no defects. They must be accompanied by a grain offering of four quarts* of choice flour moistened with olive oil, and a liquid offering. 10 This is the burnt offering to be presented each Sabbath day, in addition to the regular burnt offering and its accompanying liquid offering.

THE MONTHLY OFFERINGS

11 "On the first day of each month, present an extra burnt offering to the LORD of two young bulls, one ram, and seven one-year-old male lambs, all with no defects. 12 These must be accompanied by grain offerings of choice flour moistened with olive oil—six quarts* with each bull, four quarts with the ram, 13 and two quarts with each lamb. This burnt offering will be a special gift, a pleasing aroma to the LORD. 14 You must also present a liquid offering with each sacrifice: two quarts* of wine for each bull, a third of a gallon* for the ram, and one quart* for each lamb. Present this monthly burnt offering on the first day of each month throughout the year.

15 "On the first day of each month, you must also offer one male goat for a sin offering to the LORD. This is in addition to the regular burnt offering and its accompanying liquid offering.

OFFERINGS FOR THE PASSOVER

16 "On the fourteenth day of the first month,* you must celebrate the LORD's Passover. 17 On the following day—the fifteenth day of the month—a joyous, seven-day festival will begin, but no bread made with yeast may be eaten. 18 The first day of the festival will be an official day for holy assembly, and no ordinary work may be done on that day. 19 As a special gift you must present a burnt offering to the LORD—two young bulls, one ram, and seven one-year-old male lambs, all with no defects. 20 These will be accompanied by grain offerings of choice flour moistened with olive oil—six quarts with each bull, four quarts with the ram, 21 and two quarts with each of the seven lambs. 22 You must also offer a male goat as a sin offering to purify yourselves and make yourselves right with the LORD.* 23 Present these offerings in addition to your regular morning burnt offering. 24 On each of the seven days of the festival, this is how you must prepare the food offering that is presented as a special gift, a pleasing aroma to the LORD. These will be offered in addition to the regular burnt offerings and liquid offerings. 25 The seventh day of the festival will be another official day for holy assembly, and no ordinary work may be done on that day.

OFFERINGS FOR THE FESTIVAL OF HARVEST

26 "At the Festival of Harvest,* when you present the first of your new grain to the LORD, you must call an official day for holy assembly, and you may do no ordinary work on that day. 27 Present a special burnt offering on that day as a pleasing aroma to the LORD. It will consist of two young bulls, one ram, and seven one-year-old male lambs. 28 These will be accompanied by grain offerings of choice flour moistened with olive oil—six quarts with each bull, four quarts with the ram, 29 and two quarts with each of the seven lambs. 30 Also, offer one male goat to purify yourselves and make yourselves right with the LORD. 31 Prepare these special burnt offerings, along with their liquid offerings, in addition to the regular burnt offering and its accompanying grain offering. Be sure that all the animals you sacrifice have no defects.

OFFERINGS FOR THE FESTIVAL OF TRUMPETS

29 "Celebrate the Festival of Trumpets each year on the first day of the appointed month in early autumn.* You must call an official day for holy assembly, and you may do no ordinary work. 2 On that day you must present a burnt offering as a pleasing aroma to the LORD. It will consist of one young bull, one ram, and seven one-year-old male lambs, all with no defects. 3 These must be accompanied by grain offerings of choice flour moistened with olive oil—six quarts* with the bull, four quarts* with the ram, 4 and two quarts* with each of the seven lambs. 5 In addition, you must sacrifice a male goat as a sin offering to purify yourselves and make yourselves right with the LORD.* 6 These special sacrifices are in addition to your regular monthly and daily burnt offerings, and they must be given with their prescribed grain offerings and liquid offerings. These offerings are given as a special gift to the LORD, a pleasing aroma to him.

28:5a Hebrew *1/10 of an ephah* [2.2 liters]; also in 28:13, 21, 29. **28:5b** Hebrew *1/4 of a hin* [1 liter]; also in 28:7. **28:9** Hebrew *2/10 of an ephah* [4.4 liters]; also in 28:12, 20, 28. **28:12** Hebrew *3/10 of an ephah* [6.6 liters]; also in 28:20, 28. **28:14a** Hebrew *1/2 of a hin* [2 liters]. **28:14b** Hebrew *1/3 of a hin* [1.3 liters]. **28:14c** Hebrew *1/4 of a hin* [1 liter]. **28:16** This day in the ancient Hebrew lunar calendar occurred in late March, April, or early May. **28:22** Or *to make atonement for yourselves;* also in 28:30. **28:26** Hebrew *Festival of Weeks.* This was later called the Festival of Pentecost (see Acts 2:1). It is celebrated today as Shavuot (or Shabuoth). **29:1** Hebrew *the first day of the seventh month.* This day in the ancient Hebrew lunar calendar occurred in September or October. This festival is celebrated today as Rosh Hashanah, the Jewish new year. **29:3a** Hebrew *3/10 of an ephah* [6.6 liters]; also in 29:9, 14. **29:3b** Hebrew *2/10 of an ephah* [4.4 liters]; also in 29:9, 14. **29:4** Hebrew *1/10 of an ephah* [2.2 liters]; also in 29:10, 15. **29:5** Or *to make atonement for yourselves.*

28:1–29:40 During this interlude before Joshua leads them into the promised land, Israel is reminded of their proper response to their God.
28:1-8 These verses restated the Law concerning the required daily sacrifices, morning and evening. (Ex. 29:38-43.)
28:16-25 These verses restated the Law concerning the observance of Passover (Lev. 23:4-8).
28:26-31 Festival of Harvest. This festival, for the offering of firstfruits of wheat, was observed 50 days after Passover. Thus, Pentecost (meaning "50") is the Greek name.
29:1-6 official day. The Festival of Trumpets was celebrated on the first of the seventh month. Today it is called *Rosh Hashanah* and is a New Year's celebration.

OFFERINGS FOR THE DAY OF ATONEMENT

7 "Ten days later, on the tenth day of the same month,*
you must call another holy assembly. On that day, the
Day of Atonement, the people must go without food and
must do no ordinary work. 8 You must present a burnt
offering as a pleasing aroma to the LORD. It will consist
of one young bull, one ram, and seven one-year-old male
lambs, all with no defects. 9 These offerings must be ac-
companied by the prescribed grain offerings of choice
flour moistened with olive oil—six quarts of choice
flour with the bull, four quarts of choice flour with the
ram, 10 and two quarts of choice flour with each of the
seven lambs. 11 You must also sacrifice one male goat for
a sin offering. This is in addition to the sin offering of
atonement and the regular daily burnt offering with its
grain offering, and their accompanying liquid offerings.

OFFERINGS FOR THE FESTIVAL OF SHELTERS

12 "Five days later, on the fifteenth day of the same
month,* you must call another holy assembly of all
the people, and you may do no ordinary work on that
day. It is the beginning of the Festival of Shelters,* a
seven-day festival to the LORD. 13 On the first day of the
festival, you must present a burnt offering as a special
gift, a pleasing aroma to the LORD. It will consist of thir-
teen young bulls, two rams, and fourteen one-year-old
male lambs, all with no defects. 14 Each of these offer-
ings must be accompanied by a grain offering of choice
flour moistened with olive oil—six quarts for each of
the thirteen bulls, four quarts for each of the two rams,
15 and two quarts for each of the fourteen lambs. 16 You
must also sacrifice a male goat as a sin offering, in ad-
dition to the regular burnt offering with its accompa-
nying grain offering and liquid offering.
17 "On the second day of this seven-day festival,
sacrifice twelve young bulls, two rams, and fourteen
one-year-old male lambs, all with no defects. 18 Each of
these offerings of bulls, rams, and lambs must be ac-
companied by its prescribed grain offering and liquid
offering. 19 You must also sacrifice a male goat as a sin
offering, in addition to the regular burnt offering with
its accompanying grain offering and liquid offering.
20 "On the third day of the festival, sacrifice eleven
young bulls, two rams, and fourteen one-year-old
male lambs, all with no defects. 21 Each of these offer-
ings of bulls, rams, and lambs must be accompanied
by its prescribed grain offering and liquid offering.
22 You must also sacrifice a male goat as a sin offering,
in addition to the regular burnt offering with its ac-
companying grain offering and liquid offering.
23 "On the fourth day of the festival, sacrifice ten
young bulls, two rams, and fourteen one-year-old
male lambs, all with no defects. 24 Each of these offer-
ings of bulls, rams, and lambs must be accompanied
by its prescribed grain offering and liquid offering.
25 You must also sacrifice a male goat as a sin offering,
in addition to the regular burnt offering with its ac-
companying grain offering and liquid offering.
26 "On the fifth day of the festival, sacrifice nine
young bulls, two rams, and fourteen one-year-old
male lambs, all with no defects. 27 Each of these offer-
ings of bulls, rams, and lambs must be accompanied
by its prescribed grain offering and liquid offering.
28 You must also sacrifice a male goat as a sin offering,
in addition to the regular burnt offering with its ac-
companying grain offering and liquid offering.
29 "On the sixth day of the festival, sacrifice eight
young bulls, two rams, and fourteen one-year-old
male lambs, all with no defects. 30 Each of these offer-
ings of bulls, rams, and lambs must be accompanied
by its prescribed grain offering and liquid offering.
31 You must also sacrifice a male goat as a sin offering,
in addition to the regular burnt offering with its ac-
companying grain offering and liquid offering.
32 "On the seventh day of the festival, sacrifice sev-
en young bulls, two rams, and fourteen one-year-old
male lambs, all with no defects. 33 Each of these offer-
ings of bulls, rams, and lambs must be accompanied
by its prescribed grain offering and liquid offering.
34 You must also sacrifice one male goat as a sin offer-
ing, in addition to the regular burnt offering with its
accompanying grain offering and liquid offering.
35 "On the eighth day of the festival, proclaim anoth-
er holy day. You must do no ordinary work on that day.
36 You must present a burnt offering as a special gift, a
pleasing aroma to the LORD. It will consist of one young
bull, one ram, and seven one-year-old male lambs, all
with no defects. 37 Each of these offerings must be ac-
companied by its prescribed grain offering and liquid
offering. 38 You must also sacrifice one male goat as a sin
offering, in addition to the regular burnt offering with
its accompanying grain offering and liquid offering.
39 "You must present these offerings to the LORD at
your annual festivals. These are in addition to the sac-
rifices and offerings you present in connection with
vows, or as voluntary offerings, burnt offerings, grain
offerings, liquid offerings, or peace offerings."
40* So Moses gave all of these instructions to the
people of Israel as the LORD had commanded him.

LAWS CONCERNING VOWS

30 1* Then Moses summoned the leaders of the
tribes of Israel and told them, "This is what the
LORD has commanded: 2 A man who makes a vow to
the LORD or makes a pledge under oath must never
break it. He must do exactly what he said he would do.
3 "If a young woman makes a vow to the LORD or
a pledge under oath while she is still living at her
father's home, 4 and her father hears of the vow or
pledge and does not object to it, then all her vows and

29:7 Hebrew *On the tenth day of the seventh month;* see 29:1 and the note there. This day in the ancient Hebrew lunar calendar occurred in September or October. It is celebrated today as Yom Kippur. **29:12a** Hebrew *On the fifteenth day of the seventh month;* see 29:1, 7 and the notes there. This day in the ancient Hebrew lunar calendar occurred in late September, October, or early November. **29:12b** Or *Festival of Booths,* or *Festival of Tabernacles.* This was earlier called the Festival of the Final Harvest or Festival of Ingathering (see Exod 23:16b). It is celebrated today as Sukkot (or Succoth). **29:40** Verse 29:40 is numbered 30:1 in Hebrew text. **30:1** Verses 30:1-16 are numbered 30:2-17 in Hebrew text.

29:7-11 holy assembly. Observed shortly after the Festival of Trumpets, this festival turned Israel's attentions inward. The high priest entered the Most Holy Place alone to make "atonement for himself, his household, and the whole community of Israel" (Lev. 16:17).

29:12-39 a seven-day festival. The Festival of Shelters is called *Sukkot,* meaning "tabernacles" or "booths," and it recalled the time after the Exodus when the Israelites lived in small "booths" (Lev. 23:42-43). The festival also celebrated the end of the yearly harvest.

30:1-16 a man who makes a vow. Moses stressed the seriousness of a vow or oath. He pointed out three exceptions related to women.

30:3-5 still living in her father's home. An unmarried woman could be released from a vow by her father's actions. If he knew of the vow and did nothing, however, the vow was binding.

pledges will stand. 5 But if her father refuses to let her fulfill the vow or pledge on the day he hears of it, then all her vows and pledges will become invalid. The LORD will forgive her because her father would not let her fulfill them.

6 "Now suppose a young woman makes a vow or binds herself with an impulsive pledge and later marries. 7 If her husband learns of her vow or pledge and does not object on the day he hears of it, her vows and pledges will stand. 8 But if her husband refuses to accept her vow or impulsive pledge on the day he hears of it, he nullifies her commitments, and the LORD will forgive her. 9 If, however, a woman is a widow or is divorced, she must fulfill all her vows and pledges.

10 "But suppose a woman is married and living in her husband's home when she makes a vow or binds herself with a pledge. 11 If her husband hears of it and does not object to it, her vow or pledge will stand. 12 But if her husband refuses to accept it on the day he hears of it, her vow or pledge will be nullified, and the LORD will forgive her. 13 So her husband may either confirm or nullify any vows or pledges she makes to deny herself. 14 But if he does not object on the day he hears of it, then he is agreeing to all her vows and pledges. 15 If he waits more than a day and then tries to nullify a vow or pledge, he will be punished for her guilt."

16 These are the regulations the LORD gave Moses concerning relationships between a man and his wife, and between a father and a young daughter who still lives at home.

CONQUEST OF THE MIDIANITES

31 Then the LORD said to Moses, 2 "On behalf of the people of Israel, take revenge on the Midianites for leading them into idolatry. After that, you will die and join your ancestors."

3 So Moses said to the people, "Choose some men, and arm them to fight the LORD's war of revenge against Midian. 4 From each tribe of Israel, send 1,000 men into battle." 5 So they chose 1,000 men from each tribe of Israel, a total of 12,000 men armed for battle. 6 Then Moses sent them out, 1,000 men from each tribe, and Phinehas son of Eleazar the priest led them into battle. They carried along the holy objects of the sanctuary and the trumpets for sounding the charge. 7 They attacked Midian as the LORD had commanded Moses, and they killed all the men. 8 All five of the Midianite kings—Evi, Rekem, Zur, Hur, and Reba—died in the battle. They also killed Balaam son of Beor with the sword.

9 Then the Israelite army captured the Midianite women and children and seized their cattle and flocks and all their wealth as plunder. 10 They burned all the towns and villages where the Midianites had lived. 11 After they had gathered the plunder and captives, both people and animals, 12 they brought them all to Moses and Eleazar the priest, and to the whole community of Israel, which was camped on the plains of Moab beside the Jordan River, across from Jericho. 13 Moses, Eleazar the priest, and all the leaders of the community went to meet them outside the camp. 14 But Moses was furious with all the generals and captains* who had returned from the battle.

15 "Why have you let all the women live?" he demanded. 16 "These are the very ones who followed Balaam's advice and caused the people of Israel to rebel against the LORD at Mount Peor. They are the ones who caused the plague to strike the LORD's people. 17 So kill all the boys and all the women who have had intercourse with a man. 18 Only the young girls who are virgins may live; you may keep them for yourselves. 19 And all of you who have killed anyone or touched a dead body must stay outside the camp for seven days. You must purify yourselves and your captives on the third and seventh days. 20 Purify all your clothing, too, and everything made of leather, goat hair, or wood."

21 Then Eleazar the priest said to the men who were in the battle, "The LORD has given Moses this legal requirement: 22 Anything made of gold, silver, bronze, iron, tin, or lead—23 that is, all metals that do not burn—must be passed through fire in order to be made ceremonially pure. These metal objects must then be further purified with the water of purification. But everything that burns must be purified by the water alone. 24 On the seventh day you must wash your clothes and be purified. Then you may return to the camp."

DIVISION OF THE PLUNDER

25 And the LORD said to Moses, 26 "You and Eleazar the priest and the family leaders of each tribe are to make a list of all the plunder taken in the battle, including the people and animals. 27 Then divide the plunder into two parts, and give half to the men who fought the battle and half to the rest of the people. 28 From the army's portion, first give the LORD his share of the plunder—one of every 500 of the prisoners and of the cattle, donkeys, sheep, and goats. 29 Give this share of the army's half to Eleazar the priest as an offering to the LORD. 30 From the half that belongs to the people of Israel, take one of every fifty of the prisoners and of the cattle, donkeys, sheep, goats, and other animals. Give this share to the Levites, who are in charge of maintaining the LORD's Tabernacle." 31 So Moses and Eleazar the priest did as the LORD commanded Moses.

32 The plunder remaining from everything the fighting men had taken totaled 675,000 sheep and goats, 33 72,000 cattle, 34 61,000 donkeys, 35 and 32,000 virgin girls.

31:14 Hebrew *the commanders of thousands, and the commanders of hundreds;* also in 31:48, 52, 54.

30:6-8 a young woman makes a vow. A husband could nullify a vow made by his wife, even if she had made it before they were married. If he knew of the vow and did nothing, however, the vow stood.

30:10-15 a woman . . . living her husband's home. A husband had the right to nullify a vow his wife had made without his knowledge.

31:1-24 As a final official act, Moses was commanded to wage war against the Midianites.

31:7 attacked Midian as the LORD had commanded Moses. Choosing to fight against the Midianites was God's idea, and God would determine the outcome.

31:8 killed Balaam son of Beor. Balaam's deception nearly toppled the Israelites.

31:9-18 the Israelite army captured the Midianite women and children. God had commanded that all but the virgin women be annihilated. The others would jeopardize Israel's moral attitudes. Nonetheless, the Israelites let all the women and children live.

31:19-24 purify yourselves. In the process of wiping out Midian, the Israelites had contaminated themselves. When contact was made with a dead human or animal, a quarantine of sorts was required. These ceremonial laws of purification were a way of emphasizing the holiness of God.

31:26-35 make a list. In these wars of the Old Testament, a portion of the spoils was to be offered to God in recognition that He was the commander-in-chief. The rest was distributed fairly among the soldiers and the community.

36 Half of the plunder was given to the fighting men. It totaled 337,500 sheep and goats, 37 of which 675 were the LORD's share; 38 36,000 cattle, of which 72 were the LORD's share; 39 30,500 donkeys, of which 61 were the LORD's share; 40 and 16,000 virgin girls, of whom 32 were the LORD's share. 41 Moses gave all the LORD's share to Eleazar the priest, just as the LORD had directed him.

42 Half of the plunder belonged to the people of Israel, and Moses separated it from the half belonging to the fighting men. 43 It totaled 337,500 sheep and goats, 44 36,000 cattle, 45 30,500 donkeys, 46 and 16,000 virgin girls. 47 From the half-share given to the people, Moses took one of every fifty prisoners and animals and gave them to the Levites, who maintained the LORD's Tabernacle. All this was done as the LORD had commanded Moses.

48 Then all the generals and captains came to Moses 49 and said, "We, your servants, have accounted for all the men who went out to battle under our command; not one of us is missing! 50 So we are presenting the items of gold we captured as an offering to the LORD from our share of the plunder—armbands, bracelets, rings, earrings, and necklaces. This will purify our lives before the LORD and make us right with him.[A]"

51 So Moses and Eleazar the priest received the gold from all the military commanders—all kinds of jewelry and crafted objects. 52 In all, the gold that the generals and captains presented as a gift to the LORD weighed about 420 pounds.* 53 All the fighting men had taken some of the plunder for themselves. 54 So Moses and Eleazar the priest accepted the gifts from the generals and captains and brought the gold to the Tabernacle* as a reminder to the LORD that the people of Israel belong to him.

THE TRIBES EAST OF THE JORDAN

32 The tribes of Reuben and Gad owned vast numbers of livestock. So when they saw that the lands of Jazer and Gilead were ideally suited for their flocks and herds, 2 they came to Moses, Eleazar the priest, and the other leaders of the community. They said, 3 "Notice the towns of Ataroth, Dibon, Jazer, Nimrah, Heshbon, Elealeh, Sibmah,* Nebo, and Beon. 4 The LORD has conquered this whole area for the community of Israel, and it is ideally suited for all our livestock. 5 If we have found favor with you, please let us have this land as our property instead of giving us land across the Jordan River."

6 "Do you intend to stay here while your brothers go across and do all the fighting?" Moses asked the men of Gad and Reuben. 7 "Why do you want to discourage the rest of the people of Israel from going across to the land the LORD has given them? 8 Your ancestors did the same thing when I sent them from Kadesh-barnea to explore the land. 9 After they went up to the valley of Eshcol and explored the land, they discouraged the people of Israel from entering the land the LORD was giving them. 10 Then the LORD was very angry with them, and he vowed, 11 'Of all those I rescued from Egypt, no one who is twenty years old or older will ever see the land I swore to give to Abraham, Isaac, and Jacob, for they have not obeyed me wholeheartedly. 12 The only exceptions are Caleb son of Jephunneh the Kenizzite and Joshua son of Nun, for they have wholeheartedly followed the LORD.'

13 "The LORD was angry with Israel and made them wander in the wilderness for forty years until the entire generation that sinned in the LORD's sight had died. 14 But here you are, a brood of sinners, doing exactly the same thing! You are making the LORD even angrier with Israel. 15 If you turn away from him like this and he abandons them again in the wilderness, you will be responsible for destroying this entire nation!"

16 But they approached Moses and said, "We simply want to build pens for our livestock and fortified towns for our wives and children. 17 Then we will arm ourselves and lead our fellow Israelites into battle until we have brought them safely to their land. Meanwhile, our families will stay in the fortified towns we build here, so they will be safe from any attacks by the local people. 18 We will not return to our homes until all the people of Israel have received their portions of land. 19 But we do not claim any of the land on the other side of the Jordan. We would rather live here on the east side and accept this as our grant of land."

20 Then Moses said, "If you keep your word and arm yourselves for the LORD's battles, 21 and if your troops cross the Jordan and keep fighting until the LORD has driven out his enemies, 22 then you may return when the LORD has conquered the land. You will have fulfilled your duty to the LORD and to the rest of the people of Israel. And the land on the east side of the Jordan will be your property from the LORD. 23 But if you fail to keep your word, then you will have sinned against the LORD, and you may be sure that your sin will find you out. 24 Go ahead and build towns for your families and pens for your flocks, but do everything you have promised."

25 Then the men of Gad and Reuben replied, "We, your servants, will follow your instructions exactly. 26 Our children, wives, flocks, and cattle will stay here in the towns of Gilead. 27 But all who are able to bear arms will cross over to fight for the LORD, just as you have said."

28 So Moses gave orders to Eleazar the priest, Joshua son of Nun, and the leaders of the clans of Israel. 29 He said, "The men of Gad and Reuben who are armed for battle must cross the Jordan with you to fight for the LORD. If they do, give them the land of Gilead as their property when the land is conquered. 30 But if they refuse to arm themselves and cross over with you, then they must accept land with the rest of you in the land of Canaan."

31 The tribes of Gad and Reuben said again, "We are your servants, and we will do as the LORD has commanded! 32 We will cross the Jordan into Canaan fully armed to fight for the LORD, but our property will be here on this side of the Jordan."

31:50 Or *will make atonement for our lives before the* Lord. **31:52** Hebrew *16,750 shekels* [191 kilograms]. **31:54** Hebrew *the Tent of Meeting.* **32:3** As in Samaritan Pentateuch and Greek version (see also 32:38); Hebrew reads *Sebam.*

32:8 Your ancestors did the same thing. Moses was suspicious when the two tribes wanted to stay on the east side of the Jordan. It reminded him of the 10 spies who refused to conquer Canaan (chaps. 13–14).

32:17 we will arm ourselves and lead. Moses was wrong. The two tribes quickly offered to fight with their brothers beyond the Jordan. Their wives and children would remain behind to stake out the land they wanted to claim.

33 So Moses assigned land to the tribes of Gad, Reu-
ben, and half the tribe of Manasseh son of Joseph. He
gave them the territory of King Sihon of the Amorites
and the land of King Og of Bashan—the whole land
with its cities and surrounding lands.
34 The descendants of Gad built the towns of Dibon,
Ataroth, Aroer, 35 Atroth-shophan, Jazer, Jogbehah,
36 Beth-nimrah, and Beth-haran. These were all forti-
fied towns with pens for their flocks.
37 The descendants of Reuben built the towns of
Heshbon, Elealeh, Kiriathaim, 38 Nebo, Baal-meon,
and Sibmah. They changed the names of some of the
towns they conquered and rebuilt.
39 Then the descendants of Makir of the tribe of
Manasseh went to Gilead and conquered it, and they
drove out the Amorites living there. 40 So Moses gave
Gilead to the Makirites, descendants of Manasseh,
and they settled there. 41 The people of Jair, another
clan of the tribe of Manasseh, captured many of the
towns in Gilead and changed the name of that region
to the Towns of Jair.* 42 Meanwhile, a man named No-
bah captured the town of Kenath and its surround-
ing villages, and he renamed that area Nobah after
himself.

REMEMBERING ISRAEL'S JOURNEY

33 This is the route the Israelites followed as they
marched out of Egypt under the leadership of
Moses and Aaron. 2 At the LORD's direction, Moses
kept a written record of their progress. These are the
stages of their march, identified by the different plac-
es where they stopped along the way.
3 They set out from the city of Rameses in early
spring—on the fifteenth day of the first month*—
on the morning after the first Passover celebration.
The people of Israel left defiantly, in full view of all
the Egyptians. 4 Meanwhile, the Egyptians were
burying all their firstborn sons, whom the LORD had
killed the night before. The LORD had defeated the
gods of Egypt that night with great acts of judg-
ment!

5 After leaving Rameses, the Israelites set up camp at Succoth.
6 Then they left Succoth and camped at Etham on the edge of the wilderness.
7 They left Etham and turned back toward Pi-hahiroth, opposite Baal-zephon, and camped near Migdol.
8 They left Pi-hahiroth* and crossed the Red Sea* into the wilderness beyond. Then they traveled for three days into the Etham wilderness and camped at Marah.
9 They left Marah and camped at Elim, where there were twelve springs of water and seventy palm trees.
10 They left Elim and camped beside the Red Sea.*
11 They left the Red Sea and camped in the wilderness of Sin.*
12 They left the wilderness of Sin and camped at Dophkah.
13 They left Dophkah and camped at Alush.
14 They left Alush and camped at Rephidim, where there was no water for the people to drink.
15 They left Rephidim and camped in the wilderness of Sinai.
16 They left the wilderness of Sinai and camped at Kibroth-hattaavah.
17 They left Kibroth-hattaavah and camped at Hazeroth.
18 They left Hazeroth and camped at Rithmah.
19 They left Rithmah and camped at Rimmon-perez.
20 They left Rimmon-perez and camped at Libnah.
21 They left Libnah and camped at Rissah.
22 They left Rissah and camped at Kehelathah.
23 They left Kehelathah and camped at Mount Shepher.
24 They left Mount Shepher and camped at Haradah.
25 They left Haradah and camped at Makheloth.
26 They left Makheloth and camped at Tahath.
27 They left Tahath and camped at Terah.
28 They left Terah and camped at Mithcah.
29 They left Mithcah and camped at Hashmonah.
30 They left Hashmonah and camped at Moseroth.
31 They left Moseroth and camped at Bene-jaakan.
32 They left Bene-jaakan and camped at Hor-haggidgad.
33 They left Hor-haggidgad and camped at Jotbathah.
34 They left Jotbathah and camped at Abronah.
35 They left Abronah and camped at Ezion-geber.
36 They left Ezion-geber and camped at Kadesh in the wilderness of Zin.
37 They left Kadesh and camped at Mount Hor, at the
border of Edom. 38 While they were at the foot of
Mount Hor, Aaron the priest was directed by the
LORD to go up the mountain, and there he died.
This happened in midsummer, on the first day of
the fifth month* of the fortieth year after Israel's
departure from Egypt. 39 Aaron was 123 years old
when he died there on Mount Hor.
40 At that time the Canaanite king of Arad, who lived in the Negev in the land of Canaan, heard that the people of Israel were approaching his land.
41 Meanwhile, the Israelites left Mount Hor and camped at Zalmonah.
42 Then they left Zalmonah and camped at Punon.
43 They left Punon and camped at Oboth.
44 They left Oboth and camped at Iye-abarim on the border of Moab.
45 They left Iye-abarim* and camped at Dibon-gad.
46 They left Dibon-gad and camped at Almon-diblathaim.
47 They left Almon-diblathaim and camped in the mountains east of the river,* near Mount Nebo.

32:41 Hebrew *Havvoth-jair.* **33:3** This day in the ancient Hebrew lunar calendar occurred in late March, April, or early May. **33:8a** As in many Hebrew manuscripts, Samaritan Pentateuch, and Latin Vulgate (see also 33:7); most Hebrew manuscripts read *left from in front of Hahiroth.* **33:8b** Hebrew *the sea.* **33:10** Hebrew *sea of reeds;* also in 33:11. **33:11** The geographical name *Sin* is related to *Sinai* and should not be confused with the English word *sin.* **33:38** This day in the ancient Hebrew lunar calendar occurred in July or August. **33:45** As in 33:44; Hebrew reads *Iyim,* another name for Iye-abarim.

32:33 and half the tribe of Manasseh son of Joseph. After Moses agreed to the arrangement with Gad and Reuben, half of another tribe decided to join the party. They too agreed to help with the conquest of Canaan.

33:1-49 Like the route on a road atlas traced with a highlighter, we can follow the progress God's people made en route to the land of promise. The number 40 is an important biblical number. When God flooded the earth it rained for 40 days. When Jesus was tempted in the wilderness He fasted for 40 days. What is recorded here is most likely a general (rather than exhaustive) summary of the rest stops during 40 years. It was compiled to give the Israelites a sacred history of God's leading.

48 They left the mountains east of the river and camped on the plains of Moab beside the Jordan River, across from Jericho. 49 Along the Jordan River they camped from Beth-jeshimoth as far as the meadows of Acacia* on the plains of Moab.

50 While they were camped near the Jordan River on the plains of Moab opposite Jericho, the LORD said to Moses, 51 "Give the following instructions to the people of Israel: When you cross the Jordan River into the land of Canaan, 52 you must drive out all the people living there. You must destroy all their carved and molten images and demolish all their pagan shrines. 53 Take possession of the land and settle in it, because I have given it to you to occupy. 54 You must distribute the land among the clans by sacred lot and in proportion to their size. A larger portion of land will be allotted to each of the larger clans, and a smaller portion will be allotted to each of the smaller clans. The decision of the sacred lot is final. In this way, the portions of land will be divided among your ancestral tribes. 55 But if you fail to drive out the people who live in the land, those who remain will be like splinters in your eyes and thorns in your sides. They will harass you in the land where you live. 56 And I will do to you what I had planned to do to them."

BOUNDARIES OF THE LAND

34 Then the LORD said to Moses, 2 "Give these instructions to the Israelites: When you come into the land of Canaan, which I am giving you as your special possession, these will be the boundaries. 3 The southern portion of your country will extend from the wilderness of Zin, along the edge of Edom. The southern boundary will begin on the east at the Dead Sea.* 4 It will then run south past Scorpion Pass* in the direction of Zin. Its southernmost point will be Kadesh-barnea, from which it will go to Hazar-addar, and on to Azmon. 5 From Azmon the boundary will turn toward the Brook of Egypt and end at the Mediterranean Sea.*

6 "Your western boundary will be the coastline of the Mediterranean Sea.

7 "Your northern boundary will begin at the Mediterranean Sea and run east to Mount Hor, 8 then to Lebo-hamath, and on through Zedad 9 and Ziphron to Hazar-enan. This will be your northern boundary.

10 "The eastern boundary will start at Hazar-enan and run south to Shepham, 11 then down to Riblah on the east side of Ain. From there the boundary will run down along the eastern edge of the Sea of Galilee,* 12 and then along the Jordan River to the Dead Sea. These are the boundaries of your land."

13 Then Moses told the Israelites, "This territory is the homeland you are to divide among yourselves by sacred lot. The LORD has commanded that the land be divided among the nine and a half remaining tribes. 14 The families of the tribes of Reuben, Gad, and half the tribe of Manasseh have already received their grants of land 15 on the east side of the Jordan River, across from Jericho toward the sunrise."

LEADERS TO DIVIDE THE LAND

16 And the LORD said to Moses, 17 "Eleazar the priest and Joshua son of Nun are the men designated to divide the grants of land among the people. 18 Enlist one leader from each tribe to help them with the task. 19 These are the tribes and the names of the leaders:

Tribe	*Leader*
Judah	Caleb son of Jephunneh
20 Simeon	Shemuel son of Ammihud
21 Benjamin	Elidad son of Kislon
22 Dan	Bukki son of Jogli
23 Manasseh son of Joseph	Hanniel son of Ephod
24 Ephraim son of Joseph	Kemuel son of Shiphtan
25 Zebulun	Elizaphan son of Parnach
26 Issachar	Paltiel son of Azzan
27 Asher	Ahihud son of Shelomi
28 Naphtali	Pedahel son of Ammihud

29 These are the men the LORD has appointed to divide the grants of land in Canaan among the Israelites."

TOWNS FOR THE LEVITES

35 While Israel was camped beside the Jordan on the plains of Moab across from Jericho, the LORD said to Moses, 2 "Command the people of Israel to give to the Levites from their property certain towns to live in, along with the surrounding pasturelands. 3 These towns will be for the Levites to live in, and the surrounding lands will provide pasture for their cattle, flocks, and other livestock. 4 The pastureland assigned to the Levites around these towns will extend 1,500 feet* from the town walls in every direction. 5 Measure off 3,000 feet* outside the town walls in every direction—east, south, west, north—with the town at the center. This area will serve as the larger pastureland for the towns.

6 "Six of the towns you give the Levites will be cities of refuge, where a person who has accidentally killed someone can flee for safety. In addition, give them forty-two other towns. 7 In all, forty-eight towns with the surrounding pastureland will be given to the Levites. 8 These towns will come from the property of the people of Israel. The larger tribes will give more towns to

33:47 Or *the mountains of Abarim;* also in 33:48. **33:49** Hebrew *as far as Abel-shittim.* **34:3** Hebrew *Salt Sea;* also in 34:12. **34:4** Or *the ascent of Akrabbim.* **34:5** Hebrew *the sea;* also in 34:6, 7. **34:11** Hebrew *Sea of Kinnereth.* **35:4** Hebrew *1,000 cubits* [460 meters]. **35:5** Hebrew *2,000 cubits* [920 meters].

33:51 When you cross the Jordan River into the land of Canaan. When you are dealing with the promises of God, it is not a question of if but when. God would be faithful to bring His people into the promised land. Because of disobedience and unbelief, the Israelites arrived in "the Land" 40 years late. But at last the time had come.

34:3-12 The tribes did not choose their own territory. Each tribe was given a specific plot of real estate according to God's map. The boundaries listed are actually larger than the land occupied by each of the tribes.

34:13-15 already received their grants of land. Since Gad, Reuben, and half the tribe of Manasseh had opted to pitch their permanent tents east of the river, the land west of the Jordan was to be distributed among only nine and a half tribes.

34:16-29 Now that the land was to be settled, Moses quickly acted on God's instruction to put reliable leaders over the task of land allocation. Here is a great formula for getting a job done. First, determine what needs to be done. Then give clear instructions to those specifically selected to oversee each part of the project.

35:1-5 Although they were not eligible for large sections of land like the other tribes (1:47-53), God wanted the Levites to have specific locations to call home. "Levite" towns were to be scattered throughout the other tribes' lands.

35:6-15 Six of the Levite towns were designated as cities of refuge. Individuals who unintentionally caused the death of another could seek protection there from those seeking revenge. Three such cities were on the west side of the Jordan, and three were on the east.

the Levites, while the smaller tribes will give fewer.
Each tribe will give property in proportion to the size
of its land."

CITIES OF REFUGE

9 The LORD said to Moses, 10 "Give the following in-
structions to the people of Israel.
"When you cross the Jordan into the land of Ca-
naan, 11 designate cities of refuge to which people can
flee if they have killed someone accidentally. 12 These
cities will be places of protection from a dead person's
relatives who want to avenge the death. The slayer
must not be put to death before being tried by the
community. 13 Designate six cities of refuge for your-
selves, 14 three on the east side of the Jordan River and
three on the west in the land of Canaan. 15 These cities
are for the protection of Israelites, foreigners living
among you, and traveling merchants. Anyone who
accidentally kills someone may flee there for safety.
16 "But if someone strikes and kills another person
with a piece of iron, it is murder, and the murderer must
be executed. 17 Or if someone with a stone in his hand
strikes and kills another person, it is murder, and the
murderer must be put to death. 18 Or if someone strikes
and kills another person with a wooden object, it is
murder, and the murderer must be put to death. 19 The
victim's nearest relative is responsible for putting the
murderer to death. When they meet, the avenger must
put the murderer to death. 20 So if someone hates an-
other person and waits in ambush, then pushes him or
throws something at him and he dies, it is murder. 21 Or
if someone hates another person and hits him with a
fist and he dies, it is murder. In such cases, the avenger
must put the murderer to death when they meet.
22 "But suppose someone pushes another person
without having shown previous hostility, or throws
something that unintentionally hits another person,
23 or accidentally drops a huge stone on someone,
though they were not enemies, and the person dies.
24 If this should happen, the community must follow
these regulations in making a judgment between the
slayer and the avenger, the victim's nearest relative:
25 The community must protect the slayer from the
avenger and must escort the slayer back to live in the
city of refuge to which he fled. There he must remain
until the death of the high priest, who was anointed
with the sacred oil.
26 "But if the slayer ever leaves the limits of the city
of refuge, 27 and the avenger finds him outside the city
and kills him, it will not be considered murder. 28 The
slayer should have stayed inside the city of refuge until
the death of the high priest. But after the death of the
high priest, the slayer may return to his own property.
29 These are legal requirements for you to observe from
generation to generation, wherever you may live.
30 "All murderers must be put to death, but only if ev-
idence is presented by more than one witness. No one
may be put to death on the testimony of only one wit-
ness. 31 Also, you must never accept a ransom payment
for the life of someone judged guilty of murder and
subject to execution; murderers must always be put
to death. 32 And never accept a ransom payment from
someone who has fled to a city of refuge, allowing a
slayer to return to his property before the death of the
high priest. 33 This will ensure that the land where you
live will not be polluted, for murder pollutes the land.
And no sacrifice except the execution of the murderer
can purify the land from murder.* 34 You must not de-
file the land where you live, for I live there myself. I am
the LORD, who lives among the people of Israel."

WOMEN WHO INHERIT PROPERTY

36 Then the heads of the clans of Gilead—de-
scendants of Makir, son of Manasseh, son of
Joseph—came to Moses and the family leaders of
Israel with a petition. 2 They said, "Sir, the LORD in-
structed you to divide the land by sacred lot among
the people of Israel. You were told by the LORD to give
the grant of land owned by our brother Zelophehad
to his daughters. 3 But if they marry men from an-
other tribe, their grants of land will go with them to
the tribe into which they marry. In this way, the total
area of our tribal land will be reduced. 4 Then when
the Year of Jubilee comes, their portion of land will
be added to that of the new tribe, causing it to be lost
forever to our ancestral tribe."
5 So Moses gave the Israelites this command from
the LORD: "The claim of the men of the tribe of Joseph
is legitimate. 6 This is what the LORD commands con-
cerning the daughters of Zelophehad: Let them mar-
ry anyone they like, as long as it is within their own
ancestral tribe. 7 None of the territorial land may pass
from tribe to tribe, for all the land given to each tribe
must remain within the tribe to which it was first al-
lotted. 8 The daughters throughout the tribes of Israel
who are in line to inherit property must marry with-
in their tribe, so that all the Israelites will keep their
ancestral property. 9 No grant of land may pass from
one tribe to another; each tribe of Israel must keep its
allotted portion of land."
10 The daughters of Zelophehad did as the LORD
commanded Moses. 11 Mahlah, Tirzah, Hoglah, Milcah,
and Noah all married cousins on their father's side.
12 They married into the clans of Manasseh son of Jo-
seph. Thus, their inheritance of land remained within
their ancestral tribe.
13 These are the commands and regulations that
the LORD gave to the people of Israel through Moses
while they were camped on the plains of Moab beside
the Jordan River, across from Jericho.

35:33 Or *can make atonement for murder.*

35:16-21 In contrast to situations of accidental manslaughter, listed here are crimes judged to be murder.

35:22 without having shown previous hostility. Crimes that were not premeditated or did not result from anger would not be judged on the same scale as those that were. This is the basis for our laws on manslaughter.

35:24 these regulations. In order to maintain the integrity of the cities of refuge, a jury of sorts determined whether a candidate for sanctuary was truly deserving. Amnesty applied only as long as the refugee remained within the city limits.

36:1-13 This passage dealt with a specific inheritance question: a man with five daughters. Upon his death his land passed to his daughters. What would happen to the land if the daughters married outside of the tribe? After all, the land was each tribe's inheritance from God. The answer proposed was that daughters marry only within their tribe.

36:10 the daughters of Zelophehad. This act of obedience seems odd in today's world, where individual choice is valued above community. However, these women belonged to a tribe that was much larger than an extended family—more than 32,000 men over 20 years old. Also, remember that the family land was at stake.

INTRODUCTION TO

DEUTERONOMY

PERSONAL READING PLAN

☐Deuteronomy 1:1-46	☐Deuteronomy 11:1–12:32	☐Deuteronomy 23:15–25:19
☐Deuteronomy 2:1–3:20	☐Deuteronomy 13:1–14:29	☐Deuteronomy 26:1–27:26
☐Deuteronomy 3:21–4:49	☐Deuteronomy 15:1–17:7	☐Deuteronomy 28:1-68
☐Deuteronomy 5:1–6:25	☐Deuteronomy 17:8–19:21	☐Deuteronomy 29:1–31:13
☐Deuteronomy 7:1–9:6	☐Deuteronomy 20:1–22:12	☐Deuteronomy 31:14–32:52
☐Deuteronomy 9:7–10:22	☐Deuteronomy 22:13–23:14	☐Deuteronomy 33:1–34:12

AUTHOR

Moses is assumed to be the author and editor of most of the first five books of the Old Testament (the Pentateuch).

DATE

It is difficult to form a firm date for the writing of the Pentateuch. Conservative estimates place it in either the 15th or 13th century B.C., depending on when the Exodus occurred.

THEME

God's covenant and Moses' personal plea with Israel.

HISTORICAL BACKGROUND

The events of this book take place on the plains of Moab as the Israelites are poised to enter the promised land. Moses oversees the important task of transferring his leadership to Joshua. At this important juncture in Israel's history, Moses gives his final instructions to the people. Moses' speeches in Deuteronomy actually were a renewal of Israel's covenant with the Lord. Much like a sermon, Moses emphasized laws that were particularly appropriate at the time. The book of Deuteronomy ends with an account of Moses' death.

CHARACTERISTICS

Arranged around three sermons given by Moses (1:1–4:43; 4:44–26:19; 29:1–32:47), the book of Deuteronomy introduces the reader to the great theological themes of Judaism. Hence, we read of a God who acts in history for the redemption of his elect; we confront the Israelite concepts of sin, punishment and reward; and we are introduced to the essential creed of Judaism, "Listen, O Israel! The Lord is our God, the Lord alone" (6:4). Behind these themes, and binding them together, is the covenant between God and Israel. It is this covenant that provides the driving force of the message of Deuteronomy, leaving no doubt as to the responsibilities, rewards, and punishments inherent in the covenant. Deuteronomy's spiritual emphasis and its call to total commitment to the Lord inspired references to its message throughout the rest of Scripture.

PASSAGES FOR TOPICAL GROUP STUDY

10:12-22. WALKING WITH GOD . . . . Circumcised Hearts

INTRODUCTION TO MOSES' FIRST ADDRESS

1 These are the words that Moses spoke to all the people of Israel while they were in the wilderness east of the Jordan River. They were camped in the Jordan Valley* near Suph, between Paran on one side and Tophel, Laban, Hazeroth, and Di-zahab on the other.

2 Normally it takes only eleven days to travel from Mount Sinai* to Kadesh-barnea, going by way of Mount Seir. 3 But forty years after the Israelites left Egypt, on the first day of the eleventh month,* Moses addressed the people of Israel, telling them everything the LORD had commanded him to say. 4 This took place after he had defeated King Sihon of the Amorites, who ruled in Heshbon, and at Edrei had defeated King Og of Bashan, who ruled in Ashtaroth.

5 While the Israelites were in the land of Moab east of the Jordan River, Moses carefully explained the LORD's instructions as follows.

THE COMMAND TO LEAVE SINAI

6 "When we were at Mount Sinai, the LORD our God said to us, 'You have stayed at this mountain long enough. 7 It is time to break camp and move on. Go to the hill country of the Amorites and to all the neighboring regions—the Jordan Valley, the hill country, the western foothills,* the Negev, and the coastal plain. Go to the land of the Canaanites and to Lebanon, and all the way to the great Euphrates River. 8 Look, I am giving all this land to you! Go in and occupy it, for it is the land the LORD swore to give to your ancestors Abraham, Isaac, and Jacob, and to all their descendants.'"

MOSES APPOINTS LEADERS FROM EACH TRIBE

9 Moses continued, "At that time I told you, 'You are too great a burden for me to carry all by myself. 10 The LORD your God has increased your population, making you as numerous as the stars! 11 And may the LORD, the God of your ancestors, multiply you a thousand times more and bless you as he promised! 12 But you are such a heavy load to carry! How can I deal with all your problems and bickering? 13 Choose some well-respected men from each tribe who are known for their wisdom and understanding, and I will appoint them as your leaders.'

14 "Then you responded, 'Your plan is a good one.' 15 So I took the wise and respected men you had selected from your tribes and appointed them to serve as judges and officials over you. Some were responsible for a thousand people, some for a hundred, some for fifty, and some for ten.

16 "At that time I instructed the judges, 'You must hear the cases of your fellow Israelites and the foreigners living among you. Be perfectly fair in your decisions 17 and impartial in your judgments. Hear the cases of those who are poor as well as those who are rich. Don't be afraid of anyone's anger, for the decision you make is God's decision. Bring me any cases that are too difficult for you, and I will handle them.'

18 "At that time I gave you instructions about everything you were to do.

SCOUTS EXPLORE THE LAND

19 "Then, just as the LORD our God commanded us, we left Mount Sinai and traveled through the great and terrifying wilderness, as you yourselves remember, and headed toward the hill country of the Amorites. When we arrived at Kadesh-barnea, 20 I said to you, 'You have now reached the hill country of the Amorites that the LORD our God is giving us. 21 Look! He has placed the land in front of you. Go and occupy it as the LORD, the God of your ancestors, has promised you. Don't be afraid! Don't be discouraged!'

22 "But you all came to me and said, 'First, let's send out scouts to explore the land for us. They will advise us on the best route to take and which towns we should enter.'

23 "This seemed like a good idea to me, so I chose twelve scouts, one from each of your tribes. 24 They headed for the hill country and came to the valley of Eshcol and explored it. 25 They picked some of its fruit and brought it back to us. And they reported, 'The land the LORD our God has given us is indeed a good land.'

ISRAEL'S REBELLION AGAINST THE LORD

26 "But you rebelled against the command of the LORD your God and refused to go in. 27 You complained in your tents and said, 'The LORD must hate us. That's why he has brought us here from Egypt—to hand us over to the Amorites to be slaughtered. 28 Where can we go? Our brothers have demoralized us with their report. They tell us, "The people of the land are taller and more powerful than we are, and their towns are large, with walls rising high into the sky! We even saw giants there—the descendants of Anak!"'

29 "But I said to you, 'Don't be shocked or afraid of them! 30 The LORD your God is going ahead of you. He will fight for you, just as you saw him do in Egypt. 31 And you saw how the LORD your God cared for you all along the way as you traveled through the wilderness, just as a father cares for his child. Now he has brought you to this place.'

32 "But even after all he did, you refused to trust the LORD your God, 33 who goes before you looking for the best places to camp, guiding you with a pillar of fire by night and a pillar of cloud by day.

34 "When the LORD heard your complaining, he became very angry. So he solemnly swore, 35 'Not one of you from this wicked generation will live to see the good land I swore to give your ancestors, 36 except Caleb son of Jephunneh. He will see this land because he has followed the LORD completely. I will give to him and his descendants some of the very land he explored during his scouting mission.'

1:1 Hebrew *the Arabah;* also in 1:7. **1:2** Hebrew *Horeb,* another name for Sinai; also in 1:6, 19. **1:3** Hebrew *In the fortieth year, on the first day of the eleventh month.* This day in the ancient Hebrew lunar calendar occurred in January or February. **1:7** Hebrew *the Shephelah.*

1:1-5 Moses is speaking to those who were children at the Exodus or who were born in the wilderness period. The people are about to enter the land, so Moses summarizes the Law for them and calls for faithful obedience to the God who saved them.

1:2 Kadesh-barnea. Where the Israelites camped while spying out Canaan (Num. 13:26).

1:21 as the LORD . . . has promised you. God's Word is the ultimate point of reference, whether spoken (to Abraham and Moses) or written (to us).

1:26 you. Moses' audience had not rebelled, while their parents and grandparents had. Moses was referring to the nation as a group, past and present.

1:30 as you saw . . . in Egypt. The character of the Lord is consistent. God led the Israelites to escape the Egyptian army and would lead them to conquer Canaan.

[37]"And the LORD was also angry with me because of
you. He said to me, 'Moses, not even you will enter the
Promised Land! [38]Instead, your assistant, Joshua son
of Nun, will lead the people into the land. Encourage
him, for he will lead Israel as they take possession of
it. [39]I will give the land to your little ones—your in-
nocent children. You were afraid they would be cap-
tured, but they will be the ones who occupy it. [40]As
for you, turn around now and go on back through the
wilderness toward the Red Sea.*'

[41]"Then you confessed, 'We have sinned against
the LORD! We will go into the land and fight for it, as
the LORD our God has commanded us.' So your men
strapped on their weapons, thinking it would be easy
to attack the hill country.

[42]"But the LORD told me to tell you, 'Do not attack,
for I am not with you. If you go ahead on your own,
you will be crushed by your enemies.'

[43]"This is what I told you, but you would not listen.
Instead, you again rebelled against the LORD's com-
mand and arrogantly went into the hill country to
fight. [44]But the Amorites who lived there came out
against you like a swarm of bees. They chased and bat-
tered you all the way from Seir to Hormah. [45]Then you
returned and wept before the LORD, but he refused to
listen. [46]So you stayed there at Kadesh for a long time.

REMEMBERING ISRAEL'S WANDERINGS

2 "Then we turned around and headed back across
the wilderness toward the Red Sea,* just as the
LORD had instructed me, and we wandered around in
the region of Mount Seir for a long time.

[2]"Then at last the LORD said to me, [3]'You have been
wandering around in this hill country long enough;
turn to the north. [4]Give these orders to the people:
"You will pass through the country belonging to your
relatives the Edomites, the descendants of Esau, who
live in Seir. The Edomites will feel threatened, so be
careful. [5]Do not bother them, for I have given them all
the hill country around Mount Seir as their property,
and I will not give you even one square foot of their
land. [6]If you need food to eat or water to drink, pay
them for it. [7]For the LORD your God has blessed you in
everything you have done. He has watched your ev-
ery step through this great wilderness. During these
forty years, the LORD your God has been with you, and
you have lacked nothing."'

[8]"So we bypassed the territory of our relatives, the
descendants of Esau, who live in Seir. We avoided the
road through the Arabah Valley that comes up from
Elath and Ezion-geber.

"Then as we turned north along the desert route
through Moab, [9]the LORD warned us, 'Do not bother
the Moabites, the descendants of Lot, or start a war
with them. I have given them Ar as their property,
and I will not give you any of their land.'"

[10](A race of giants called the Emites had once lived
in the area of Ar. They were as strong and numerous
and tall as the Anakites, another race of giants. [11]Both
the Emites and the Anakites are also known as the
Rephaites, though the Moabites call them Emites. [12]In
earlier times the Horites had lived in Seir, but they
were driven out and displaced by the descendants
of Esau, just as Israel drove out the people of Canaan
when the LORD gave Israel their land.)

[13]Moses continued, "Then the LORD said to us, 'Get
moving. Cross the Zered Brook.' So we crossed the
brook.

[14]"Thirty-eight years passed from the time we first
left Kadesh-barnea until we finally crossed the Zered
Brook! By then, all the men old enough to fight in bat-
tle had died in the wilderness, as the LORD had vowed
would happen. [15]The LORD struck them down until
they had all been eliminated from the community.

[16]"When all the men of fighting age had died, [17]the
LORD said to me, [18]'Today you will cross the border of
Moab at Ar [19]and enter the land of the Ammonites,
the descendants of Lot. But do not bother them or
start a war with them. I have given the land of Am-
mon to them as their property, and I will not give you
any of their land.'"

[20](That area was once considered the land of the
Rephaites, who had lived there, though the Ammon-
ites call them Zamzummites. [21]They were also as strong
and numerous and tall as the Anakites. But the LORD de-
stroyed them so the Ammonites could occupy their land.
[22]He had done the same for the descendants of Esau who
lived in Seir, for he destroyed the Horites so they could
settle there in their place. The descendants of Esau live
there to this day. [23]A similar thing happened when the
Caphtorites from Crete* invaded and destroyed the Av-
vites, who had lived in villages in the area of Gaza.)

[24]Moses continued, "Then the LORD said, 'Now get
moving! Cross the Arnon Gorge. Look, I will hand over
to you Sihon the Amorite, king of Heshbon, and I will
give you his land. Attack him and begin to occupy the
land. [25]Beginning today I will make people throughout
the earth terrified because of you. When they hear re-
ports about you, they will tremble with dread and fear.'"

VICTORY OVER SIHON OF HESHBON

[26]Moses continued, "From the wilderness of Kede-
moth I sent ambassadors to King Sihon of Heshbon
with this proposal of peace:

> [27]'Let us travel through your land. We will stay on
> the main road and won't turn off into the fields on
> either side. [28]Sell us food to eat and water to drink,
> and we will pay for it. All we want is permission
> to pass through your land. [29]The descendants of
> Esau who live in Seir allowed us to go through
> their country, and so did the Moabites, who live in

1:40 Hebrew *sea of reeds*. **2:1** Hebrew *sea of reeds*. **2:23** Hebrew *from Caphtor*.

1:37 angry . . . because of you. Moses blamed the people, but his sin of striking the rock in anger disqualified him from entering the land.

1:43 This is what I told you, but you would not listen. Here is what's wrong with the human race! It was true of the wandering nation in the wilderness. It was true of the man and woman in the garden. It is true of us.

2:5,9 their land. God had given the land of Edom to Esau's descendants and the land of Moab to Lot's descendants as surely as He had promised the land of Canaan to the descendants of Jacob (see Gen. 19:30-38; Am. 9:7).

2:10 Anakites. This was the tribe of giants that scared the spies sent by Moses (1:28).

2:11 Rephaites. The Moabites might have referred to these tall people as Emites (terrors).

2:12 Horites. The Horites ruled the area of Edom before Esau settled there. Esau (later named Edom) either defeated the Horites or his tribe absorbed them.

2:23 Avvites. A remnant survived (Josh. 13:3). **Caphtorites.** Caphtor was where the Philistines originated, probably modern Crete.

2:24 Arnon. The Arnon River flowed to the east of the Dead Sea about halfway between the north and south ends.

Ar. Let us pass through until we cross the Jordan
into the land the LORD our God is giving us.'

[30] "But King Sihon of Heshbon refused to allow us to
pass through, because the LORD your God made Sihon
stubborn and defiant so he could help you defeat him,
as he has now done.
[31] "Then the LORD said to me, 'Look, I have begun to
hand King Sihon and his land over to you. Begin now
to conquer and occupy his land.'
[32] "Then King Sihon declared war on us and mo-
bilized his forces at Jahaz. [33] But the LORD our God
handed him over to us, and we crushed him, his
sons, and all his people. [34] We conquered all his
towns and completely destroyed* everyone—men,
women, and children. Not a single person was
spared. [35] We took all the livestock as plunder for
ourselves, along with anything of value from the
towns we ransacked.
[36] "The LORD our God also helped us conquer Aroer
on the edge of the Arnon Gorge, and the town in the
gorge, and the whole area as far as Gilead. No town
had walls too strong for us. [37] However, we avoided
the land of the Ammonites all along the Jabbok River
and the towns in the hill country—all the places the
LORD our God had commanded us to leave alone.

VICTORY OVER OG OF BASHAN

3 "Next we turned and headed for the land of Ba-
shan, where King Og and his entire army attacked
us at Edrei. [2] But the LORD told me, 'Do not be afraid
of him, for I have given you victory over Og and his
entire army, and I will give you all his land. Treat him
just as you treated King Sihon of the Amorites, who
ruled in Heshbon.'
[3] "So the LORD our God handed King Og and all
his people over to us, and we killed them all. Not a
single person survived. [4] We conquered all sixty of
his towns—the entire Argob region in his kingdom
of Bashan. Not a single town escaped our conquest.
[5] These towns were all fortified with high walls and
barred gates. We also took many unwalled villag-
es at the same time. [6] We completely destroyed* the
kingdom of Bashan, just as we had destroyed King
Sihon of Heshbon. We destroyed all the people in ev-
ery town we conquered—men, women, and children
alike. [7] But we kept all the livestock for ourselves and
took plunder from all the towns.
[8] "So we took the land of the two Amorite kings
east of the Jordan River—all the way from the Arnon
Gorge to Mount Hermon. [9] (Mount Hermon is called
Sirion by the Sidonians, and the Amorites call it Se-
nir.) [10] We had now conquered all the cities on the pla-
teau and all Gilead and Bashan, as far as the towns of
Salecah and Edrei, which were part of Og's kingdom
in Bashan. [11] (King Og of Bashan was the last survivor
of the giant Rephaites. His bed was made of iron and
was more than thirteen feet long and six feet wide.*
It can still be seen in the Ammonite city of Rabbah.)

LAND DIVISION EAST OF THE JORDAN

[12] "When we took possession of this land, I gave to the
tribes of Reuben and Gad the territory beyond Aroer
along the Arnon Gorge, plus half of the hill country of
Gilead with its towns. [13] Then I gave the rest of Gile-
ad and all of Bashan—Og's former kingdom—to the
half-tribe of Manasseh. (This entire Argob region of
Bashan used to be known as the land of the Rephaites.
[14] Jair, a leader from the tribe of Manasseh, conquered
the whole Argob region in Bashan, all the way to the
border of the Geshurites and Maacathites. Jair re-
named this region after himself, calling it the Towns
of Jair,* as it is still known today.) [15] I gave Gilead to
the clan of Makir. [16] But I also gave part of Gilead to
the tribes of Reuben and Gad. The area I gave them
extended from the middle of the Arnon Gorge in the
south to the Jabbok River on the Ammonite frontier.
[17] They also received the Jordan Valley, all the way
from the Sea of Galilee down to the Dead Sea,* with
the Jordan River serving as the western boundary. To
the east were the slopes of Pisgah.
[18] "At that time I gave this command to the tribes
that would live east of the Jordan: 'Although the LORD
your God has given you this land as your property,
all your fighting men must cross the Jordan ahead
of your Israelite relatives, armed and ready to assist
them. [19] Your wives, children, and numerous livestock,
however, may stay behind in the towns I have given
you. [20] When the LORD has given security to the rest of
the Israelites, as he has to you, and when they occupy
the land the LORD your God is giving them across the
Jordan River, then you may all return here to the land
I have given you.'

MOSES FORBIDDEN TO ENTER THE LAND

[21] "At that time I gave Joshua this charge: 'You have
seen for yourself everything the LORD your God has
done to these two kings. He will do the same to all the
kingdoms on the west side of the Jordan. [22] Do not be
afraid of the nations there, for the LORD your God will
fight for you.'
[23] "At that time I pleaded with the LORD and said,
[24] 'O Sovereign LORD, you have only begun to show
your greatness and the strength of your hand to me,
your servant. Is there any god in heaven or on earth
who can perform such great and mighty deeds as you
do? [25] Please let me cross the Jordan to see the wonder-
ful land on the other side, the beautiful hill country
and the Lebanon mountains.'
[26] "But the LORD was angry with me because of
you, and he would not listen to me. 'That's enough!'
he declared. 'Speak of it no more. [27] But go up to Pis-
gah Peak, and look over the land in every direction.
Take a good look, but you may not cross the Jordan

2:34 The Hebrew term used here refers to the complete consecration of things or people to the LORD, either by destroying them or by giving them as an offering. **3:6** The Hebrew term used here refers to the complete consecration of things or people to the LORD, either by destroying them or by giving them as an offering; also in 3:6b. **3:11** Hebrew *9 cubits* [4.1 meters] *long and 4 cubits* [1.8 meters] *wide.* **3:14** Hebrew *Havvoth-jair.* **3:17** Hebrew *from Kinnereth to the Sea of the Arabah, the Salt Sea.*

2:30 God made. The language of the Old Testament sometimes subordinates a person's will to God's control (Ex. 7:3; see Rom. 9:18).

2:34 Not a single person was spared. This was the way to rid the land of idolatry. God put off giving Israel the land for many centuries waiting for the Canaanites to deserve this judgment (Gen. 15:16). God always gave people the opportunity to repent (see Jonah).

3:17 Pisgah. Mount Pisgah was near Mount Nebo (34:1).

3:22 God will fight for you. The Hebrew spies compared themselves to the Canaanites (Num. 13) rather than comparing the strength of the Canaanites to the strength of God.

River. 28 Instead, commission Joshua and encourage and strengthen him, for he will lead the people across the Jordan. He will give them all the land you now see before you as their possession.' 29 So we stayed in the valley near Beth-peor.

MOSES URGES ISRAEL TO OBEY

4 "And now, Israel, listen carefully to these decrees and regulations that I am about to teach you. Obey them so that you may live, so you may enter and occupy the land that the LORD, the God of your ancestors, is giving you. 2 Do not add to or subtract from these commands I am giving you. Just obey the commands of the LORD your God that I am giving you.

3 "You saw for yourself what the LORD did to you at Baal-peor. There the LORD your God destroyed everyone who had worshiped Baal, the god of Peor. 4 But all of you who were faithful to the LORD your God are still alive today—every one of you.

5 "Look, I now teach you these decrees and regulations just as the LORD my God commanded me, so that you may obey them in the land you are about to enter and occupy. 6 Obey them completely, and you will display your wisdom and intelligence among the surrounding nations. When they hear all these decrees, they will exclaim, 'How wise and prudent are the people of this great nation!' 7 For what great nation has a god as near to them as the LORD our God is near to us whenever we call on him? 8 And what great nation has decrees and regulations as righteous and fair as this body of instructions that I am giving you today?

9 "But watch out! Be careful never to forget what you yourself have seen. Do not let these memories escape from your mind as long as you live! And be sure to pass them on to your children and grandchildren. 10 Never forget the day when you stood before the LORD your God at Mount Sinai,* where he told me, 'Summon the people before me, and I will personally instruct them. Then they will learn to fear me as long as they live, and they will teach their children to fear me also.'

11 "You came near and stood at the foot of the mountain, while flames from the mountain shot into the sky. The mountain was shrouded in black clouds and deep darkness. 12 And the LORD spoke to you from the heart of the fire. You heard the sound of his words but didn't see his form; there was only a voice. 13 He proclaimed his covenant—the Ten Commandments*—which he commanded you to keep, and which he wrote on two stone tablets. 14 It was at that time that the LORD commanded me to teach you his decrees and regulations so you would obey them in the land you are about to enter and occupy.

A WARNING AGAINST IDOLATRY

15 "But be very careful! You did not see the LORD's form on the day he spoke to you from the heart of the fire at Mount Sinai. 16 So do not corrupt yourselves by making an idol in any form—whether of a man or a woman, 17 an animal on the ground, a bird in the sky, 18 a small animal that scurries along the ground, or a fish in the deepest sea. 19 And when you look up into the sky and see the sun, moon, and stars—all the forces of heaven—don't be seduced into worshiping them. The LORD your God gave them to all the peoples of the earth. 20 Remember that the LORD rescued you from the iron-smelting furnace of Egypt in order to make you his very own people and his special possession, which is what you are today.

21 "But the LORD was angry with me because of you. He vowed that I would not cross the Jordan River into the good land the LORD your God is giving you as your special possession. 22 You will cross the Jordan to occupy the land, but I will not. Instead, I will die here on the east side of the river. 23 So be careful not to break the covenant the LORD your God has made with you. Do not make idols of any shape or form, for the LORD your God has forbidden this. 24 The LORD your God is a devouring fire; he is a jealous God.

25 "In the future, when you have children and grandchildren and have lived in the land a long time, do not corrupt yourselves by making idols of any kind. This is evil in the sight of the LORD your God and will arouse his anger.

26 "Today I call on heaven and earth as witnesses against you. If you break my covenant, you will quickly disappear from the land you are crossing the Jordan to occupy. You will live there only a short time; then you will be utterly destroyed. 27 For the LORD will scatter you among the nations, where only a few of you will survive. 28 There, in a foreign land, you will worship idols made from wood and stone—gods that neither see nor hear nor eat nor smell. 29 But from there you will search again for the LORD your God. And if you search for him with all your heart and soul, you will find him.

30 "In the distant future, when you are suffering all these things, you will finally return to the LORD your God and listen to what he tells you. 31 For the LORD your God is a merciful God; he will not abandon you or destroy you or forget the solemn covenant he made with your ancestors.

THERE IS ONLY ONE GOD

32 "Now search all of history, from the time God created people on the earth until now, and search from one end of the heavens to the other. Has anything as great as this ever been seen or heard before? 33 Has any nation ever heard the voice of God* speaking from fire—as you did—and survived? 34 Has any other god dared to take a nation for himself out of another nation by means of trials, miraculous signs, wonders, war, a strong hand, a powerful arm, and terrifying acts? Yet that is what the LORD your God did for you in Egypt, right before your eyes.

35 "He showed you these things so you would know that the LORD is God and there is no other. 36 He let you

4:10 Hebrew *Horeb,* another name for Sinai; also in 4:15. **4:13** Hebrew *the ten words.* **4:33** Or *voice of a god.*

3:28 commission . . . encourage . . . strengthen. Joshua was ordained by Moses like Elisha by Elijah (1 Kings 19:19-21) and Timothy by Paul (2 Tim. 1:5-7).
4:8 what . . . nation. Pagans never knew how to please their gods (6:25).
4:19 don't be seduced. Today we face the same enticement to worship the created world more than the Creator of the world.
4:21 LORD was angry. God commanded Moses to speak to a rock, but he struck it instead (Num. 20:5-12).
4:24 fire. God's anger is like fire (Ex. 24:7; 2 Sam. 22:9; Isa. 29:6; Heb. 12:29).
4:27 LORD will scatter you. God tells the future: Israel will disobey and be scattered to every nation, as they are still today.
4:29 you will search again for the LORD. There is a day (still future) when Israel will return to God (Rom. 11:26). Also, individual Jews today can find God if they seek Him.

hear his voice from heaven so he could instruct you. He let you see his great fire here on earth so he could speak to you from it. 37 Because he loved your ancestors, he chose to bless their descendants, and he personally brought you out of Egypt with a great display of power. 38 He drove out nations far greater than you, so he could bring you in and give you their land as your special possession, as it is today.

39 "So remember this and keep it firmly in mind: The LORD is God both in heaven and on earth, and there is no other. 40 If you obey all the decrees and commands I am giving you today, all will be well with you and your children. I am giving you these instructions so you will enjoy a long life in the land the LORD your God is giving you for all time."

EASTERN CITIES OF REFUGE

41 Then Moses set apart three cities of refuge east of the Jordan River. 42 Anyone who killed another person unintentionally, without previous hostility, could flee there to live in safety. 43 These were the cities: Bezer on the wilderness plateau for the tribe of Reuben; Ramoth in Gilead for the tribe of Gad; Golan in Bashan for the tribe of Manasseh.

INTRODUCTION TO MOSES' SECOND ADDRESS

44 This is the body of instruction that Moses presented to the Israelites. 45 These are the laws, decrees, and regulations that Moses gave to the people of Israel when they left Egypt, 46 and as they camped in the valley near Beth-peor east of the Jordan River. (This land was formerly occupied by the Amorites under King Sihon, who ruled from Heshbon. But Moses and the Israelites destroyed him and his people when they came up from Egypt. 47 Israel took possession of his land and that of King Og of Bashan—the two Amorite kings east of the Jordan. 48 So Israel conquered the entire area from Aroer at the edge of the Arnon Gorge all the way to Mount Sirion,* also called Mount Hermon. 49 And they conquered the eastern bank of the Jordan River as far south as the Dead Sea,* below the slopes of Pisgah.)

TEN COMMANDMENTS FOR THE COVENANT COMMUNITY

5 Moses called all the people of Israel together and said, "Listen carefully, Israel. Hear the decrees and regulations I am giving you today, so you may learn them and obey them!

2 "The LORD our God made a covenant with us at Mount Sinai.* 3 The LORD did not make this covenant with our ancestors, but with all of us who are alive today. 4 At the mountain the LORD spoke to you face to face from the heart of the fire. 5 I stood as an intermediary between you and the LORD, for you were afraid of the fire and did not want to approach the mountain. He spoke to me, and I passed his words on to you. This is what he said:

6 "I am the LORD your God, who rescued you from the land of Egypt, the place of your slavery.

7 "You must not have any other god but me.

8 "You must not make for yourself an idol of any kind, or an image of anything in the heavens or on the earth or in the sea. 9 You must not bow down to them or worship them, for I, the LORD your God, am a jealous God who will not tolerate your affection for any other gods. I lay the sins of the parents upon their children; the entire family is affected—even children in the third and fourth generations of those who reject me. 10 But I lavish unfailing love for a thousand generations on those* who love me and obey my commands.

11 "You must not misuse the name of the LORD your God. The LORD will not let you go unpunished if you misuse his name.

12 "Observe the Sabbath day by keeping it holy, as the LORD your God has commanded you. 13 You have six days each week for your ordinary work, 14 but the seventh day is a Sabbath day of rest dedicated to the LORD your God. On that day no one in your household may do any work. This includes you, your sons and daughters, your male and female servants, your oxen and donkeys and other livestock, and any foreigners living among you. All your male and female servants must rest as you do. 15 Remember that you were once slaves in Egypt, but the LORD your God brought you out with his strong hand and powerful arm. That is why the LORD your God has commanded you to rest on the Sabbath day.

16 "Honor your father and mother, as the LORD your God commanded you. Then you will live a long, full life in the land the LORD your God is giving you.

17 "You must not murder.

18 "You must not commit adultery.

19 "You must not steal.

20 "You must not testify falsely against your neighbor.

21 "You must not covet your neighbor's wife. You must not covet your neighbor's house or land, male or female servant, ox or donkey, or anything else that belongs to your neighbor.

22 "The LORD spoke these words to all of you assembled there at the foot of the mountain. He spoke with a loud voice from the heart of the fire, surrounded by clouds and deep darkness. This was all he said at that time, and he wrote his words on two stone tablets and gave them to me.

23 "But when you heard the voice from the heart of the darkness, while the mountain was blazing with fire, all your tribal leaders and elders came to me. 24 They said, 'Look, the LORD our God has shown us his glory and greatness, and we have heard his voice from the heart of the fire. Today we have seen that God can speak to us humans, and yet we live! 25 But now, why should we risk death again? If the LORD

4:48 As in Syriac version (see also 3:9); Hebrew reads *Mount Sion.* 4:49 Hebrew *took the Arabah on the east side of the Jordan as far as the sea of the Arabah.* 5:2 Hebrew *Horeb,* another name for Sinai. 5:10 Hebrew *for thousands of those.*

4:37 he loved. God's motivation in covenanting with Abraham is the same as in John 3:16: "God loved the world."

4:39 remember this and keep it . . . in mind. God expects us to show faith by recognizing that He is the one true God.

5:6 I am the LORD. This is the basis of the Ten Commandments. When we understand who God is, what He speaks becomes priority.

5:12 Observe the Sabbath. Observing the Sabbath is not just about rest, but also about honoring God.

5:15 Remember. Before the printing press, the history of God's presence, guidance, and holiness was passed down through customs, feasts, and stories.

5:16-21 This is summed up in the command to love our neighbor as ourselves (Rom. 13:9).

5:20 testify falsely. This applies to perjury, slander, and gossip.

our God speaks to us again, we will certainly die and be consumed by this awesome fire. 26 Can any living thing hear the voice of the living God from the heart of the fire as we did and yet survive? 27 Go yourself and listen to what the LORD our God says. Then come and tell us everything he tells you, and we will listen and obey.'

28 "The LORD heard the request you made to me. And he said, 'I have heard what the people said to you, and they are right. 29 Oh, that they would always have hearts like this, that they might fear me and obey all my commands! If they did, they and their descendants would prosper forever. 30 Go and tell them, "Return to your tents." 31 But you stand here with me so I can give you all my commands, decrees, and regulations. You must teach them to the people so they can obey them in the land I am giving them as their possession.'"

32 So Moses told the people, "You must be careful to obey all the commands of the LORD your God, following his instructions in every detail. 33 Stay on the path that the LORD your God has commanded you to follow. Then you will live long and prosperous lives in the land you are about to enter and occupy.

A CALL FOR WHOLEHEARTED COMMITMENT

6 "These are the commands, decrees, and regulations that the LORD your God commanded me to teach you. You must obey them in the land you are about to enter and occupy, 2 and you and your children and grandchildren must fear the LORD your God as long as you live. If you obey all his decrees and commands, you will enjoy a long life. 3 Listen closely, Israel, and be careful to obey. Then all will go well with you, and you will have many children in the land flowing with milk and honey, just as the LORD, the God of your ancestors, promised you.

4 "Listen, O Israel! The LORD is our God, the LORD alone.* 5 And you must love the LORD your God with all your heart, all your soul, and all your strength. 6 And you must commit yourselves wholeheartedly to these commands that I am giving you today. 7 Repeat them again and again to your children. Talk about them when you are at home and when you are on the road, when you are going to bed and when you are getting up. 8 Tie them to your hands and wear them on your forehead as reminders. 9 Write them on the doorposts of your house and on your gates.

10 "The LORD your God will soon bring you into the land he swore to give you when he made a vow to your ancestors Abraham, Isaac, and Jacob. It is a land with large, prosperous cities that you did not build. 11 The houses will be richly stocked with goods you did not produce. You will draw water from cisterns you did not dig, and you will eat from vineyards and olive trees you did not plant. When you have eaten your fill in this land, 12 be careful not to forget the LORD, who rescued you from slavery in the land of Egypt. 13 You must fear the LORD your God and serve him. When you take an oath, you must use only his name.

14 "You must not worship any of the gods of neighboring nations, 15 for the LORD your God, who lives among you, is a jealous God. His anger will flare up against you, and he will wipe you from the face of the earth. 16 You must not test the LORD your God as you did when you complained at Massah. 17 You must diligently obey the commands of the LORD your God—all the laws and decrees he has given you. 18 Do what is right and good in the LORD's sight, so all will go well with you. Then you will enter and occupy the good land that the LORD swore to give your ancestors. 19 You will drive out all the enemies living in the land, just as the LORD said you would.

20 "In the future your children will ask you, 'What is the meaning of these laws, decrees, and regulations that the LORD our God has commanded us to obey?'

21 "Then you must tell them, 'We were Pharaoh's slaves in Egypt, but the LORD brought us out of Egypt with his strong hand. 22 The LORD did miraculous signs and wonders before our eyes, dealing terrifying blows against Egypt and Pharaoh and all his people. 23 He brought us out of Egypt so he could give us this land he had sworn to give our ancestors. 24 And the LORD our God commanded us to obey all these decrees and to fear him so he can continue to bless us and preserve our lives, as he has done to this day. 25 For we will be counted as righteous when we obey all the commands the LORD our God has given us.'

THE PRIVILEGE OF HOLINESS

7 "When the LORD your God brings you into the land you are about to enter and occupy, he will clear away many nations ahead of you: the Hittites, Girgashites, Amorites, Canaanites, Perizzites, Hivites, and Jebusites. These seven nations are greater and more numerous than you. 2 When the LORD your God hands these nations over to you and you conquer them, you must completely destroy* them. Make no treaties with them and show them no mercy. 3 You must not intermarry with them. Do not let your daughters and sons marry their sons and daughters, 4 for they will lead your children away from me to worship other gods. Then the anger of the LORD will burn against you, and he will quickly destroy you. 5 This is what you must do. You must break down their pagan altars and shatter their sacred pillars. Cut down their Asherah poles and burn their idols. 6 For you are a holy people, who belong to the LORD your God. Of all the

6:4 Or *The LORD our God is one LORD;* or *The LORD our God, the LORD is one;* or *The LORD is our God, the LORD is one.* 7:2 The Hebrew term used here refers to the complete consecration of things or people to the LORD, either by destroying them or by giving them as an offering; also in 7:26.

6:2 fear the LORD . . . If you obey. The essence of fearing God is obeying Him, recognizing His authority.

6:4-9 Listen, O Israel. This passage is called the *Shema* (shuh-MAH), "listen." It is repeated daily in Jewish prayers. Jesus said this was the greatest commandment (Mark 12:29).

6:4 the LORD alone. The Hebrew is a little ambiguous. Some translations render the verse as "The Lord is one." This would mean that God is a unity, the only deity who exists, and the only one to be worshipped (leaving open the later revelation of His three-in-one nature). As this translation reads, the verse teaches that God is above all others. He alone is God.

6:5 heart . . . soul. "Heart" is the seat of emotions and thoughts. "Soul" means our whole being, including our body.

6:6 wholeheartedly. This can be done by memorizing and meditating on God's truth.

6:12 be careful not to forget. People tend to turn to God in bad times and forget Him in easy times.

7:2-5 completely destroy them. God had given the Canaanites centuries to repent (Gen. 15:16).

7:3 must not intermarry. Jews were not forbidden to marry non-Jews but were forbidden to marry Canaanites. Many intercultural marriages occurred, including Joseph to an Egyptian priestess, Moses to Zipporah, a Midianite, and Boaz to Ruth, a Moabite. The important point was that the non-Israelite followed the one true God.

people on earth, the LORD your God has chosen you to be his own special treasure.

7 "The LORD did not set his heart on you and choose you because you were more numerous than other nations, for you were the smallest of all nations! 8 Rather, it was simply that the LORD loves you, and he was keeping the oath he had sworn to your ancestors. That is why the LORD rescued you with such a strong hand from your slavery and from the oppressive hand of Pharaoh, king of Egypt. 9 Understand, therefore, that the LORD your God is indeed God. He is the faithful God who keeps his covenant for a thousand generations and lavishes his unfailing love on those who love him and obey his commands. 10 But he does not hesitate to punish and destroy those who reject him. 11 Therefore, you must obey all these commands, decrees, and regulations I am giving you today.

12 "If you listen to these regulations and faithfully obey them, the LORD your God will keep his covenant of unfailing love with you, as he promised with an oath to your ancestors. 13 He will love you and bless you, and he will give you many children. He will give fertility to your land and your animals. When you arrive in the land he swore to give your ancestors, you will have large harvests of grain, new wine, and olive oil, and great herds of cattle, sheep, and goats. 14 You will be blessed above all the nations of the earth. None of your men or women will be childless, and all your livestock will bear young. 15 And the LORD will protect you from all sickness. He will not let you suffer from the terrible diseases you knew in Egypt, but he will inflict them on all your enemies!

16 "You must destroy all the nations the LORD your God hands over to you. Show them no mercy, and do not worship their gods, or they will trap you. 17 Perhaps you will think to yourselves, 'How can we ever conquer these nations that are so much more powerful than we are?' 18 But don't be afraid of them! Just remember what the LORD your God did to Pharaoh and to all the land of Egypt. 19 Remember the great terrors the LORD your God sent against them. You saw it all with your own eyes! And remember the miraculous signs and wonders, and the strong hand and powerful arm with which he brought you out of Egypt. The LORD your God will use this same power against all the people you fear. 20 And then the LORD your God will send terror* to drive out the few survivors still hiding from you!

21 "No, do not be afraid of those nations, for the LORD your God is among you, and he is a great and awesome God. 22 The LORD your God will drive those nations out ahead of you little by little. You will not clear them away all at once, otherwise the wild animals would multiply too quickly for you. 23 But the LORD your God will hand them over to you. He will throw them into complete confusion until they are destroyed. 24 He will put their kings in your power, and you will erase their names from the face of the earth. No one will be able to stand against you, and you will destroy them all.

25 "You must burn their idols in fire, and you must not covet the silver or gold that covers them. You must not take it or it will become a trap to you, for it is detestable to the LORD your God. 26 Do not bring any detestable objects into your home, for then you will be destroyed, just like them. You must utterly detest such things, for they are set apart for destruction.

A CALL TO REMEMBER AND OBEY

8 "Be careful to obey all the commands I am giving you today. Then you will live and multiply, and you will enter and occupy the land the LORD swore to give your ancestors. 2 Remember how the LORD your God led you through the wilderness for these forty years, humbling you and testing you to prove your character, and to find out whether or not you would obey his commands. 3 Yes, he humbled you by letting you go hungry and then feeding you with manna, a food previously unknown to you and your ancestors. He did it to teach you that people do not live by bread alone; rather, we live by every word that comes from the mouth of the LORD. 4 For all these forty years your clothes didn't wear out, and your feet didn't blister or swell. 5 Think about it: Just as a parent disciplines a child, the LORD your God disciplines you for your own good.

6 "So obey the commands of the LORD your God by walking in his ways and fearing him. 7 For the LORD your God is bringing you into a good land of flowing streams and pools of water, with fountains and springs that gush out in the valleys and hills. 8 It is a land of wheat and barley; of grapevines, fig trees, and pomegranates; of olive oil and honey. 9 It is a land where food is plentiful and nothing is lacking. It is a land where iron is as common as stone, and copper is abundant in the hills. 10 When you have eaten your fill, be sure to praise the LORD your God for the good land he has given you.

11 "But that is the time to be careful! Beware that in your plenty you do not forget the LORD your God and disobey his commands, regulations, and decrees that I am giving you today. 12 For when you have become full and prosperous and have built fine homes to live in, 13 and when your flocks and herds have become very large and your silver and gold have multiplied along with everything else, be careful! 14 Do not become proud at that time and forget the LORD your God, who rescued you from slavery in the land of Egypt. 15 Do not forget that he led you through the great and terrifying wilderness with its poisonous snakes and scorpions, where it was so hot and dry. He gave you water from the rock! 16 He fed you with manna in the wilderness, a food unknown to your ancestors. He did this to humble you and test you for your own good. 17 He did all this so you would never say to yourself, 'I have achieved this wealth with my own strength and energy.' 18 Remember the LORD your God. He is the one who gives you power to be successful, in order to fulfill the covenant he confirmed to your ancestors with an oath.

7:20 Often rendered *the hornet*. The meaning of the Hebrew is uncertain.

7:7-8 The LORD . . . choose you. The great truth here is that God did not love the Hebrews because they were valuable; they were valuable because He loved them.

7:26 detestable objects. They were detestable if they represented other gods or even if the people worshipped God through them. God cannot be manipulated by an idol but can be prayed to with faith.

8:3 manna. See Exodus 16:31. Jesus quoted this verse when tempted by Satan (Matt. 4:4).

8:16 test you. The manna tested the people to see if they would trust God every day and obey Him by handling the manna as He asked them to.

19 "But I assure you of this: If you ever forget the
LORD your God and follow other gods, worshiping
and bowing down to them, you will certainly be de-
stroyed. 20 Just as the LORD has destroyed other na-
tions in your path, you also will be destroyed if you
refuse to obey the LORD your God.

VICTORY BY GOD'S GRACE

9 "Listen, O Israel! Today you are about to cross the
Jordan River to take over the land belonging to
nations much greater and more powerful than you.
They live in cities with walls that reach to the sky!
2 The people are strong and tall—descendants of the
famous Anakite giants. You've heard the saying, 'Who
can stand up to the Anakites?' 3 But recognize today
that the LORD your God is the one who will cross over
ahead of you like a devouring fire to destroy them. He
will subdue them so that you will quickly conquer
them and drive them out, just as the LORD has prom-
ised.

4 "After the LORD your God has done this for you,
don't say in your hearts, 'The LORD has given us this
land because we are such good people!' No, it is be-
cause of the wickedness of the other nations that he is
pushing them out of your way. 5 It is not because you
are so good or have such integrity that you are about
to occupy their land. The LORD your God will drive
these nations out ahead of you only because of their
wickedness, and to fulfill the oath he swore to your
ancestors Abraham, Isaac, and Jacob. 6 You must rec-
ognize that the LORD your God is not giving you this
good land because you are good, for you are not—you
are a stubborn people.

REMEMBERING THE GOLD CALF

7 "Remember and never forget how angry you made
the LORD your God out in the wilderness. From the day
you left Egypt until now, you have been constantly re-
belling against him. 8 Even at Mount Sinai* you made
the LORD so angry he was ready to destroy you. 9 This
happened when I was on the mountain receiving the
tablets of stone inscribed with the words of the cov-
enant that the LORD had made with you. I was there
for forty days and forty nights, and all that time I ate
no food and drank no water. 10 The LORD gave me the
two tablets on which God had written with his own
finger all the words he had spoken to you from the
heart of the fire when you were assembled at the
mountain.

11 "At the end of the forty days and nights, the LORD
handed me the two stone tablets inscribed with the
words of the covenant. 12 Then the LORD said to me,
'Get up! Go down immediately, for the people you
brought out of Egypt have corrupted themselves.
How quickly they have turned away from the way I
commanded them to live! They have melted gold and
made an idol for themselves!'

13 "The LORD also said to me, 'I have seen how stub-
born and rebellious these people are. 14 Leave me
alone so I may destroy them and erase their name
from under heaven. Then I will make a mighty nation
of your descendants, a nation larger and more power-
ful than they are.'

15 "So while the mountain was blazing with fire I
turned and came down, holding in my hands the two
stone tablets inscribed with the terms of the covenant.
16 There below me I could see that you had sinned
against the LORD your God. You had melted gold and
made a calf idol for yourselves. How quickly you had
turned away from the path the LORD had commanded
you to follow! 17 So I took the stone tablets and threw
them to the ground, smashing them before your eyes.

18 "Then, as before, I threw myself down before the
LORD for forty days and nights. I ate no bread and
drank no water because of the great sin you had com-
mitted by doing what the LORD hated, provoking him
to anger. 19 I feared that the furious anger of the LORD,
which turned him against you, would drive him to
destroy you. But again he listened to me. 20 The LORD
was so angry with Aaron that he wanted to destroy
him, too. But I prayed for Aaron, and the LORD spared
him. 21 I took your sin—the calf you had made—and I
melted it down in the fire and ground it into fine dust.
Then I threw the dust into the stream that flows down
the mountain.

22 "You also made the LORD angry at Taberah,*
Massah,* and Kibroth-hattaavah.* 23 And at Kadesh-
barnea the LORD sent you out with this command:
'Go up and take over the land I have given you.' But
you rebelled against the command of the LORD your
God and refused to put your trust in him or obey him.
24 Yes, you have been rebelling against the LORD as
long as I have known you.

25 "That is why I threw myself down before the
LORD for forty days and nights—for the LORD said he
would destroy you. 26 I prayed to the LORD and said,
'O Sovereign LORD, do not destroy them. They are your
own people. They are your special possession, whom
you redeemed from Egypt by your mighty power and
your strong hand. 27 Please overlook the stubbornness
and the awful sin of these people, and remember in-
stead your servants Abraham, Isaac, and Jacob. 28 If
you destroy these people, the Egyptians will say, "The
Israelites died because the LORD wasn't able to bring
them to the land he had promised to give them." Or
they might say, "He destroyed them because he hated
them; he deliberately took them into the wilderness to
slaughter them." 29 But they are your people and your
special possession, whom you brought out of Egypt
by your great strength and powerful arm.'

A NEW COPY OF THE COVENANT

10 "At that time the LORD said to me, 'Chisel out
two stone tablets like the first ones. Also make
a wooden Ark—a sacred chest to store them in. Come
up to me on the mountain, 2 and I will write on the
tablets the same words that were on the ones you
smashed. Then place the tablets in the Ark.'

9:8 Hebrew *Horeb,* another name for Sinai. 9:22a *Taberah* means "place of burning." See Num 11:1-3. 9:22b *Massah* means "place of testing." See Exod 17:1-7. 9:22c *Kibroth-hattaavah* means "graves of gluttony." See Num 11:31-34.

9:4 because of the wickedness. The Hebrews would not receive the land because of their own righteousness; their victories would be as much about God judging Canaanite sin.

9:6,13 stubborn. This means stubborn and defiant, inflexible and unwilling to follow where they were guided, like a horse that refuses to turn according to a rider's commands.

9:19 again he listened. As mediator, Moses appealed to God on behalf of His people.

9:22 Taberah. The people complained, and fire destroyed part of the camp (Num. 11:1-3). **Massah.** Moses struck the rock to get water for the discontented people (Ex. 17: 6-7). **Kibroth-hattaavah.** The people craved other foods and made themselves sick on quail (Num. 11:33-34).

[3]"So I made an Ark of acacia wood and cut two
stone tablets like the first two. Then I went up the
mountain with the tablets in my hand. [4]Once again
the LORD wrote the Ten Commandments* on the tab-
lets and gave them to me. They were the same words
the LORD had spoken to you from the heart of the
fire on the day you were assembled at the foot of the
mountain. [5]Then I turned and came down the moun-
tain and placed the tablets in the Ark of the Covenant,
which I had made, just as the LORD commanded me.
And the tablets are still there in the Ark."
[6](The people of Israel set out from the wells of the
people of Jaakan* and traveled to Moserah, where
Aaron died and was buried. His son Eleazar minis-
tered as high priest in his place. [7]Then they journeyed
to Gudgodah, and from there to Jotbathah, a land with
many brooks and streams. [8]At that time the LORD set
apart the tribe of Levi to carry the Ark of the LORD's
Covenant, and to stand before the LORD as his minis-
ters, and to pronounce blessings in his name. These
are their duties to this day. [9]That is why the Levites
have no share of property or possession of land among
the other Israelite tribes. The LORD himself is their spe-
cial possession, as the LORD your God told them.)
[10]"As for me, I stayed on the mountain in the LORD's
presence for forty days and nights, as I had done the
first time. And once again the LORD listened to my
pleas and agreed not to destroy you. [11]Then the LORD
said to me, 'Get up and resume the journey, and lead
the people to the land I swore to give to their ances-
tors, so they may take possession of it.'

A CALL TO LOVE AND OBEDIENCE

[12]"And now, Israel, what does the LORD your God re-
quire of you? He requires only that you fear the LORD
your God, and live in a way that pleases him, and love
him and serve him with all your heart and soul. [13]And
you must always obey the LORD's commands and de-
crees that I am giving you today for your own good.
[14]"Look, the highest heavens and the earth and
everything in it all belong to the LORD your God. [15]Yet
the LORD chose your ancestors as the objects of his
love. And he chose you, their descendants, above all
other nations, as is evident today. [16]Therefore, change
your hearts* and stop being stubborn.
[17]"For the LORD your God is the God of gods and Lord
of lords. He is the great God, the mighty and awesome
God, who shows no partiality and cannot be bribed.
[18]He ensures that orphans and widows receive jus-
tice. He shows love to the foreigners living among
you and gives them food and clothing. [19]So you, too,
must show love to foreigners, for you yourselves were
once foreigners in the land of Egypt. [20]You must fear
the LORD your God and worship him and cling to him.
Your oaths must be in his name alone. [21]He is alone is

CIRCUMCISED HEARTS

1. What is the hardest class you've ever taken? What were the toughest requirements, and how did you meet them?

DEUTERONOMY 10:12-22

2. What is God's basic requirement for His people (v. 12)?
3. What does it mean to "change your hearts" (v. 16)? In what ways can we be "stubborn"?
4. Who is a "foreigner" in your group or school? How could you show love to that person?
5. Do you fear God and walk in all of His ways whether at home, school, or a sports event? How can you worship Him "with all your heart and all your soul"?

your God, the only one who is worthy of your praise,
the one who has done these mighty miracles that you
have seen with your own eyes. [22]When your ances-
tors went down into Egypt, there were only seventy
of them. But now the LORD your God has made you as
numerous as the stars in the sky!

11 "You must love the LORD your God and always
obey his requirements, decrees, regulations, and
commands. [2]Keep in mind that I am not talking now
to your children, who have never experienced the dis-
cipline of the LORD your God or seen his greatness and
his strong hand and powerful arm. [3]They didn't see
the miraculous signs and wonders he performed in
Egypt against Pharaoh and all his land. [4]They didn't
see what the LORD did to the armies of Egypt and to
their horses and chariots—how he drowned them in
the Red Sea* as they were chasing you. He destroyed
them, and they have not recovered to this very day!
[5]"Your children didn't see how the LORD cared for
you in the wilderness until you arrived here. [6]They
didn't see what he did to Dathan and Abiram (the
sons of Eliab, a descendant of Reuben) when the
earth opened its mouth in the Israelite camp and
swallowed them, along with their households and
tents and every living thing that belonged to them.
[7]But you have seen the LORD perform all these mighty
deeds with your own eyes!

THE BLESSINGS OF OBEDIENCE

[8]"Therefore, be careful to obey every command I am
giving you today, so you may have strength to go in

10:4 Hebrew *the ten words.* **10:6** Or *set out from Beeroth of Bene-jaakan.* **10:16** Hebrew *circumcise the foreskin of your hearts.* **11:4** Hebrew *sea of reeds.*

10:6 Eleazar. Aaron's two older sons died when they administered their duties inappropriately (Lev. 10:1-2).
10:8 to carry. Only certain people were to carry the ark. There were rings on each side so that poles could be inserted without anyone actually touching it (Ex. 25:12-15).
10:9 Levites. The Levites were treated as a distinct class of people. They were not given any land because they received their sustenance from the sacrifices of the people. They were set apart completely to administer God's worship.
10:12 And now. Moses had reviewed the history and was ready to answer the question, "Now what?" He called for the people to be totally committed to God. He was preparing the people to receive their inheritance and live in a manner worthy of it.
10:16 change your hearts. Hebrew men were "marked" with God's ownership (Gen. 17:10-14). To change their hearts would be to mark their hearts as owned by God (Deut. 30:6, Jer. 4:4; Rom. 2:29).
11:13 heart and soul. See 6:4-5.
11:14 rains. The irrigation system in Egypt was man-made (v. 10), but in Israel God would control the rains.
11:16-17 other gods. The Canaanites believed that their gods controlled the rain.

and take over the land you are about to enter. 9 If you obey, you will enjoy a long life in the land the LORD swore to give to your ancestors and to you, their descendants—a land flowing with milk and honey! 10 For the land you are about to enter and take over is not like the land of Egypt from which you came, where you planted your seed and made irrigation ditches with your foot as in a vegetable garden. 11 Rather, the land you will soon take over is a land of hills and valleys with plenty of rain—12 a land that the LORD your God cares for. He watches over it through each season of the year!

13 "If you carefully obey the commands I am giving you today, and if you love the LORD your God and serve him with all your heart and soul, 14 then he will send the rains in their proper seasons—the early and late rains—so you can bring in your harvests of grain, new wine, and olive oil. 15 He will give you lush pastureland for your livestock, and you yourselves will have all you want to eat.

16 "But be careful. Don't let your heart be deceived so that you turn away from the LORD and serve and worship other gods. 17 If you do, the LORD's anger will burn against you. He will shut up the sky and hold back the rain, and the ground will fail to produce its harvests. Then you will quickly die in that good land the LORD is giving you.

18 "So commit yourselves wholeheartedly to these words of mine. Tie them to your hands and wear them on your forehead as reminders. 19 Teach them to your children. Talk about them when you are at home and when you are on the road, when you are going to bed and when you are getting up. 20 Write them on the doorposts of your house and on your gates, 21 so that as long as the sky remains above the earth, you and your children may flourish in the land the LORD swore to give your ancestors.

22 "Be careful to obey all these commands I am giving you. Show love to the LORD your God by walking in his ways and holding tightly to him. 23 Then the LORD will drive out all the nations ahead of you, though they are much greater and stronger than you, and you will take over their land. 24 Wherever you set foot, that land will be yours. Your frontiers will stretch from the wilderness in the south to Lebanon in the north, and from the Euphrates River in the east to the Mediterranean Sea in the west.* 25 No one will be able to stand against you, for the LORD your God will cause the people to fear and dread you, as he promised, wherever you go in the whole land.

26 "Look, today I am giving you the choice between a blessing and a curse! 27 You will be blessed if you obey the commands of the LORD your God that I am giving you today. 28 But you will be cursed if you reject the commands of the LORD your God and turn away from him and worship gods you have not known before.

29 "When the LORD your God brings you into the land and helps you take possession of it, you must pronounce the blessing at Mount Gerizim and the curse at Mount Ebal. 30 (These two mountains are west of the Jordan River in the land of the Canaanites who live in the Jordan Valley,* near the town of Gilgal, not far from the oaks of Moreh.) 31 For you are about to cross the Jordan River to take over the land the LORD your God is giving you. When you take that land and are living in it, 32 you must be careful to obey all the decrees and regulations I am giving you today.

THE LORD'S CHOSEN PLACE FOR WORSHIP

12 "These are the decrees and regulations you must be careful to obey when you live in the land that the LORD, the God of your ancestors, is giving you. You must obey them as long as you live.

2 "When you drive out the nations that live there, you must destroy all the places where they worship their gods—high on the mountains, up on the hills, and under every green tree. 3 Break down their altars and smash their sacred pillars. Burn their Asherah poles and cut down their carved idols. Completely erase the names of their gods!

4 "Do not worship the LORD your God in the way these pagan peoples worship their gods. 5 Rather, you must seek the LORD your God at the place of worship he himself will choose from among all the tribes—the place where his name will be honored. 6 There you will bring your burnt offerings, your sacrifices, your tithes, your sacred offerings, your offerings to fulfill a vow, your voluntary offerings, and your offerings of the firstborn animals of your herds and flocks. 7 There you and your families will feast in the presence of the LORD your God, and you will rejoice in all you have accomplished because the LORD your God has blessed you.

8 "Your pattern of worship will change. Today all of you are doing as you please, 9 because you have not yet arrived at the place of rest, the land the LORD your God is giving you as your special possession. 10 But you will soon cross the Jordan River and live in the land the LORD your God is giving you. When he gives you rest from all your enemies and you're living safely in the land, 11 you must bring everything I command you—your burnt offerings, your sacrifices, your tithes, your sacred offerings, and your offerings to fulfill a vow—to the designated place of worship, the place the LORD your God chooses for his name to be honored.

12 "You must celebrate there in the presence of the LORD your God with your sons and daughters and all your servants. And remember to include the

11:24 Hebrew *to the western sea*. 11:30 Hebrew *the Arabah*.

11:18-20 Talk about them. Moses expected that God's ways and instructions would be a daily topic of conversation (see 6:20).

11:22-23 Be careful to obey . . . the LORD will drive out. The people's relationship to God and their success in the land were deeply connected.

11:25 fear and dread. Rahab confirmed this (Josh. 2:8-10).

12:3 Break down . . . smash . . . Burn . . . cut down . . . erase. It was very clear that the Hebrews were to allow no idol worship in the land. (7:5-6).

12:4 Do not worship the LORD your God in this way. God forbade not only worshiping other gods, but even worshiping Him through statues and images.

12:5 where his name will be honored. This referred to the place where the tabernacle would reside. Names were more symbolic in ancient days. God's name was His presence.

12:8 all of you are doing as you please. In the wilderness and earlier, God had permitted altars to be built in many places, but once in the land, God would only have one altar.

12:9 place of rest. The writer of Hebrews encouraged his readers to continue toward God's "rest"—a life of peace and faith.

12:12 must celebrate. The church today sometimes treats worship as a solemn event. Certainly in these ancient days there was a solemnity to the sacrifices and yet great joy when God was worshiped.

Levites who live in your towns, for they will receive no allotment of land among you. 13 Be careful not to sacrifice your burnt offerings just anywhere you like. 14 You may do so only at the place the LORD will choose within one of your tribal territories. There you must offer your burnt offerings and do everything I command you.

15 "But you may butcher your animals and eat their meat in any town whenever you want. You may freely eat the animals with which the LORD your God blesses you. All of you, whether ceremonially clean or unclean, may eat that meat, just as you now eat gazelle and deer. 16 But you must not consume the blood. You must pour it out on the ground like water.

17 "But you may not eat your offerings in your hometown—neither the tithe of your grain and new wine and olive oil, nor the firstborn of your flocks and herds, nor any offering to fulfill a vow, nor your voluntary offerings, nor your sacred offerings. 18 You must eat these in the presence of the LORD your God at the place he will choose. Eat them there with your children, your servants, and the Levites who live in your towns, celebrating in the presence of the LORD your God in all you do. 19 And be very careful never to neglect the Levites as long as you live in your land.

20 "When the LORD your God expands your territory as he has promised, and you have the urge to eat meat, you may freely eat meat whenever you want. 21 It might happen that the designated place of worship—the place the LORD your God chooses for his name to be honored—is a long way from your home. If so, you may butcher any of the cattle, sheep, or goats the LORD has given you, and you may freely eat the meat in your hometown, as I have commanded you. 22 Anyone, whether ceremonially clean or unclean, may eat that meat, just as you do now with gazelle and deer. 23 But never consume the blood, for the blood is the life, and you must not consume the lifeblood with the meat. 24 Instead, pour out the blood on the ground like water. 25 Do not consume the blood, so that all may go well with you and your children after you, because you will be doing what pleases the LORD.

26 "Take your sacred gifts and your offerings given to fulfill a vow to the place the LORD chooses. 27 You must offer the meat and blood of your burnt offerings on the altar of the LORD your God. The blood of your other sacrifices must be poured out on the altar of the LORD your God, but you may eat the meat. 28 Be careful to obey all my commands, so that all will go well with you and your children after you, because you will be doing what is good and pleasing to the LORD your God.

29 "When the LORD your God goes ahead of you and destroys the nations and you drive them out and live in their land, 30 do not fall into the trap of following their customs and worshiping their gods. Do not inquire about their gods, saying, 'How do these nations worship their gods? I want to follow their example.' 31 You must not worship the LORD your God the way the other nations worship their gods, for they perform for their gods every detestable act that the LORD hates. They even burn their sons and daughters as sacrifices to their gods.

32* "So be careful to obey all the commands I give you. You must not add anything to them or subtract anything from them.

A WARNING AGAINST IDOLATRY

13 1* "Suppose there are prophets among you or those who dream dreams about the future, and they promise you signs or miracles, 2 and the predicted signs or miracles occur. If they then say, 'Come, let us worship other gods'—gods you have not known before—3 do not listen to them. The LORD your God is testing you to see if you truly love him with all your heart and soul. 4 Serve only the LORD your God and fear him alone. Obey his commands, listen to his voice, and cling to him. 5 The false prophets or visionaries who try to lead you astray must be put to death, for they encourage rebellion against the LORD your God, who redeemed you from slavery and brought you out of the land of Egypt. Since they try to lead you astray from the way the LORD your God commanded you to live, you must put them to death. In this way you will purge the evil from among you.

6 "Suppose someone secretly entices you—even your brother, your son or daughter, your beloved wife, or your closest friend—and says, 'Let us go worship other gods'—gods that neither you nor your ancestors have known. 7 They might suggest that you worship the gods of peoples who live nearby or who come from the ends of the earth. 8 But do not give in or listen. Have no pity, and do not spare or protect them. 9 You must put them to death! Strike the first blow yourself, and then all the people must join in. 10 Stone the guilty ones to death because they have tried to draw you away from the LORD your God, who rescued you from the land of Egypt, the place of slavery. 11 Then all Israel will hear about it and be afraid, and no one will act so wickedly again.

12 "When you begin living in the towns the LORD your God is giving you, you may hear 13 that scoundrels among you are leading their fellow citizens astray by saying, 'Let us go worship other gods'—gods you have not known before. 14 In such cases, you must examine the facts carefully. If you find that the report is true and such a detestable act has been committed among you, 15 you must attack that town and completely destroy* all its inhabitants, as well as all the livestock. 16 Then you must pile all the plunder in the middle of the open square and burn it. Burn the entire town as a burnt offering to the LORD your God. That town must remain a ruin forever; it may never be rebuilt. 17 Keep none of the plunder that has been set apart for destruction. Then the LORD will turn from his fierce anger and be merciful to you. He will have compassion on you and make you a large nation, just as he swore to your ancestors.

18 "The LORD your God will be merciful only if you listen to his voice and keep all his commands that I am giving you today, doing what pleases him.

12:32 Verse 12:32 is numbered 13:1 in Hebrew text. **13:1** Verses 13:1-18 are numbered 13:2-19 in Hebrew text. **13:15** The Hebrew term used here refers to the complete consecration of things or people to the LORD, either by destroying them or by giving them as an offering; similarly in 13:17.

13:3 testing. To see miracles performed in the name of another god was a test of faith for the people.

13:5 they encourage rebellion. The prophet's encouragement to worship other gods, coupled with his power to astonish the people, made him a dangerous man.

CEREMONIALLY CLEAN AND UNCLEAN ANIMALS

14 "Since you are the people of the LORD your God,
never cut yourselves or shave the hair above
your foreheads in mourning for the dead. 2 You have
been set apart as holy to the LORD your God, and he
has chosen you from all the nations of the earth to be
his own special treasure.
3 "You must not eat any detestable animals that are
ceremonially unclean. 4 These are the animals* you
may eat: the ox, the sheep, the goat, 5 the deer, the ga-
zelle, the roe deer, the wild goat, the addax, the ante-
lope, and the mountain sheep.
6 "You may eat any animal that has completely split
hooves and chews the cud, 7 but if the animal doesn't
have both, it may not be eaten. So you may not eat the
camel, the hare, or the hyrax.* They chew the cud but
do not have split hooves, so they are ceremonially
unclean for you. 8 And you may not eat the pig. It has
split hooves but does not chew the cud, so it is cere-
monially unclean for you. You may not eat the meat of
these animals or even touch their carcasses.
9 "Of all the marine animals, you may eat whatever
has both fins and scales. 10 You may not, however, eat
marine animals that do not have both fins and scales.
They are ceremonially unclean for you.
11 "You may eat any bird that is ceremonially clean.
12 These are the birds you may not eat: the griffon vul-
ture, the bearded vulture, the black vulture, 13 the kite,
the falcon, buzzards of all kinds, 14 ravens of all kinds,
15 the eagle owl, the short-eared owl, the seagull,
hawks of all kinds, 16 the little owl, the great owl, the
barn owl, 17 the desert owl, the Egyptian vulture, the
cormorant, 18 the stork, herons of all kinds, the hoopoe,
and the bat.
19 "All winged insects that walk along the ground
are ceremonially unclean for you and may not be eat-
en. 20 But you may eat any winged bird or insect that
is ceremonially clean.
21 "You must not eat anything that has died a natu-
ral death. You may give it to a foreigner living in your
town, or you may sell it to a stranger. But do not eat it
yourselves, for you are set apart as holy to the LORD
your God.
"You must not cook a young goat in its mother's
milk.

THE GIVING OF TITHES

22 "You must set aside a tithe of your crops—one-tenth
of all the crops you harvest each year. 23 Bring this
tithe to the designated place of worship—the place
the LORD your God chooses for his name to be hon-
ored—and eat it there in his presence. This applies to
your tithes of grain, new wine, olive oil, and the first-
born males of your flocks and herds. Doing this will
teach you always to fear the LORD your God.
24 "Now when the LORD your God blesses you with
a good harvest, the place of worship he chooses for
his name to be honored might be too far for you to
bring the tithe. 25 If so, you may sell the tithe portion
of your crops and herds, put the money in a pouch,
and go to the place the LORD your God has chosen.
26 When you arrive, you may use the money to buy
any kind of food you want—cattle, sheep, goats,
wine, or other alcoholic drink. Then feast there in
the presence of the LORD your God and celebrate
with your household. 27 And do not neglect the Le-
vites in your town, for they will receive no allotment
of land among you.
28 "At the end of every third year, bring the entire
tithe of that year's harvest and store it in the near-
est town. 29 Give it to the Levites, who will receive
no allotment of land among you, as well as to the
foreigners living among you, the orphans, and the
widows in your towns, so they can eat and be sat-
isfied. Then the LORD your God will bless you in all
your work.

RELEASE FOR DEBTORS

15 "At the end of every seventh year you must can-
cel the debts of everyone who owes you money.
2 This is how it must be done. Everyone must cancel
the loans they have made to their fellow Israelites.
They must not demand payment from their neighbors
or relatives, for the LORD's time of release has arrived.
3 This release from debt, however, applies only to your
fellow Israelites—not to the foreigners living among
you.
4 "There should be no poor among you, for the LORD
your God will greatly bless you in the land he is giv-
ing you as a special possession. 5 You will receive this
blessing if you are careful to obey all the commands
of the LORD your God that I am giving you today. 6 The
LORD your God will bless you as he has promised. You
will lend money to many nations but will never need
to borrow. You will rule many nations, but they will
not rule over you.
7 "But if there are any poor Israelites in your towns
when you arrive in the land the LORD your God is giv-
ing you, do not be hard-hearted or tightfisted toward
them. 8 Instead, be generous and lend them whatev-
er they need. 9 Do not be mean-spirited and refuse
someone a loan because the year for canceling debts
is close at hand. If you refuse to make the loan and
the needy person cries out to the LORD, you will be
considered guilty of sin. 10 Give generously to the poor,
not grudgingly, for the LORD your God will bless you
in everything you do. 11 There will always be some in
the land who are poor. That is why I am commanding
you to share freely with the poor and with other Isra-
elites in need.

14:4 The identification of some of the animals and birds listed in this chapter is uncertain. 14:7 Or *coney*, or *rock badger*.

14:1 cut yourselves. This was an ancient custom of idol worship (1 Kings 18:28). **shave the hair.** This was a way pagan priests marked themselves.

14:2 special treasure. God chose Israel to reveal Himself to the world. The Bible and the Messiah came from Israel (Rom. 9:4-5). God still has plans to restore and save Israel (Rom. 11:26).

14:3-21 The diet of the Hebrews set them apart from other nations. Keeping kosher was an act of faith and obedience, and a mark of God's ownership.

14:21 anything that has died a natural death. This involved the prohibition on eating blood. When the animals were prepared properly, their blood was drained.

14:22-29 one-tenth. Also called a tithe, it provided for the priests and the community. It was an act of faith on the part of the giver that God was the source of provision.

14:23 the place . . . for his name to be honored. The tabernacle and later the temple.

15:3 foreigners. Israelites had to let their crops lie fallow every seventh year, so all payments on debts were suspended. Since a foreigner would not have done this, he could continue to make payments on his debts.

15:4 no poor among you. If the people obeyed, their land would produce wealth, and there would not have been poverty.

15:11 There will always be some in the land who are poor. Jesus made this same statement (Matt. 26:11). This does not contradict v. 4, which was the ideal if people obeyed (1 John 2:1).

RELEASE FOR HEBREW SLAVES

12 "If a fellow Hebrew sells himself or herself to be
your servant* and serves you for six years, in the sev-
enth year you must set that servant free.
13 "When you release a male servant, do not send
him away empty-handed. 14 Give him a generous fare-
well gift from your flock, your threshing floor, and
your winepress. Share with him some of the boun-
ty with which the LORD your God has blessed you.
15 Remember that you were once slaves in the land of
Egypt and the LORD your God redeemed you! That is
why I am giving you this command.
16 "But suppose your servant says, 'I will not leave
you,' because he loves you and your family, and he has
done well with you. 17 In that case, take an awl and
push it through his earlobe into the door. After that,
he will be your servant for life. And do the same for
your female servants.
18 "You must not consider it a hardship when you
release your servants. Remember that for six years
they have given you services worth double the wag-
es of hired workers, and the LORD your God will bless
you in all you do.

SACRIFICING FIRSTBORN MALE ANIMALS

19 "You must set aside for the LORD your God all the
firstborn males from your flocks and herds. Do not
use the firstborn of your herds to work your fields,
and do not shear the firstborn of your flocks. 20 In-
stead, you and your family must eat these animals in
the presence of the LORD your God each year at the
place he chooses. 21 But if this firstborn animal has
any defect, such as lameness or blindness, or if any-
thing else is wrong with it, you must not sacrifice it to
the LORD your God. 22 Instead, use it for food for your
family in your hometown. Anyone, whether ceremo-
nially clean or unclean, may eat it, just as anyone may
eat a gazelle or deer. 23 But you must not consume the
blood. You must pour it out on the ground like water.

PASSOVER AND THE FESTIVAL OF UNLEAVENED BREAD

16 "In honor of the LORD your God, celebrate the
Passover each year in the early spring, in the
month of Abib,* for that was the month in which the
LORD your God brought you out of Egypt by night.
2 Your Passover sacrifice may be from either the flock
or the herd, and it must be sacrificed to the LORD your
God at the designated place of worship—the place
he chooses for his name to be honored. 3 Eat it with
bread made without yeast. For seven days the bread
you eat must be made without yeast, as when you es-
caped from Egypt in such a hurry. Eat this bread—
the bread of suffering—so that as long as you live
you will remember the day you departed from Egypt.
4 Let no yeast be found in any house throughout your
land for those seven days. And when you sacrifice the
Passover lamb on the evening of the first day, do not
let any of the meat remain until the next morning.
5 "You may not sacrifice the Passover in just any of
the towns that the LORD your God is giving you. 6 You
must offer it only at the designated place of wor-
ship—the place the LORD your God chooses for his
name to be honored. Sacrifice it there in the evening
as the sun goes down on the anniversary of your exo-
dus from Egypt. 7 Roast the lamb and eat it in the place
the LORD your God chooses. Then you may go back to
your tents the next morning. 8 For the next six days
you may not eat any bread made with yeast. On the
seventh day proclaim another holy day in honor of
the LORD your God, and no work may be done on that
day.

THE FESTIVAL OF HARVEST

9 "Count off seven weeks from when you first begin to
cut the grain at the time of harvest. 10 Then celebrate
the Festival of Harvest* to honor the LORD your God.
Bring him a voluntary offering in proportion to the
blessings you have received from him. 11 This is a time
to celebrate before the LORD your God at the desig-
nated place of worship he will choose for his name
to be honored. Celebrate with your sons and daugh-
ters, your male and female servants, the Levites from
your towns, and the foreigners, orphans, and widows
who live among you. 12 Remember that you were once
slaves in Egypt, so be careful to obey all these decrees.

THE FESTIVAL OF SHELTERS

13 "You must observe the Festival of Shelters* for seven
days at the end of the harvest season, after the grain
has been threshed and the grapes have been pressed.
14 This festival will be a happy time of celebrating
with your sons and daughters, your male and female
servants, and the Levites, foreigners, orphans, and
widows from your towns. 15 For seven days you must
celebrate this festival to honor the LORD your God at
the place he chooses, for it is he who blesses you with
bountiful harvests and gives you success in all your
work. This festival will be a time of great joy for all.
16 "Each year every man in Israel must celebrate
these three festivals: the Festival of Unleavened
Bread, the Festival of Harvest, and the Festival of Shel-
ters. On each of these occasions, all men must appear
before the LORD your God at the place he chooses, but
they must not appear before the LORD without a gift
for him. 17 All must give as they are able, according to
the blessings given to them by the LORD your God.

JUSTICE FOR THE PEOPLE

18 "Appoint judges and officials for yourselves from
each of your tribes in all the towns the LORD your God
is giving you. They must judge the people fairly. 19 You
must never twist justice or show partiality. Never ac-
cept a bribe, for bribes blind the eyes of the wise and

15:12 Or *If a Hebrew man or woman is sold to you.* **16:1** Hebrew *Observe the month of Abib, and keep the Passover unto the LORD your God.* Abib, the first month of the ancient Hebrew lunar calendar, usually occurs within the months of March and April. **16:10** Hebrew *Festival of Weeks;* also in 16:16. This was later called the Festival of Pentecost (see Acts 2:1). It is celebrated today as Shavuot (or Shabuoth). **16:13** Or *Festival of Booths,* or *Festival of Tabernacles;* also in 16:16. This was earlier called the Festival of the Final Harvest or Festival of Ingathering (see Exod 23:16b). It is celebrated today as Sukkot (or Succoth).

15:19 firstborn. The first and best always belonged to God as a reminder that everything ultimately is His.

15:21 defect. Some people offered animals that were imperfect and unusable (Mal. 1:14).

16:5 Passover. This feast commemorated the last plague in Egypt (death of the firstborn). Jesus celebrated Passover at the Last Supper.

16:9 seven weeks. This was also called the Feast of the Harvest and later Pentecost (*pent* refers to the 50 days in the seven weeks). This was being celebrated when the Holy Spirit came (Acts 2:1-4).

16:13-15 Festival of Shelters. The people camped out to commemorate the journey through the desert.

corrupt the decisions of the godly. 20 Let true justice prevail, so you may live and occupy the land that the LORD your God is giving you.

21 "You must never set up a wooden Asherah pole beside the altar you build for the LORD your God. 22 And never set up sacred pillars for worship, for the LORD your God hates them.

17 "Never sacrifice sick or defective cattle, sheep, or goats to the LORD your God, for he detests such gifts.

2 "When you begin living in the towns the LORD your God is giving you, a man or woman among you might do evil in the sight of the LORD your God and violate the covenant. 3 For instance, they might serve other gods or worship the sun, the moon, or any of the stars—the forces of heaven—which I have strictly forbidden. 4 When you hear about it, investigate the matter thoroughly. If it is true that this detestable thing has been done in Israel, 5 then the man or woman who has committed such an evil act must be taken to the gates of the town and stoned to death. 6 But never put a person to death on the testimony of only one witness. There must always be two or three witnesses. 7 The witnesses must throw the first stones, and then all the people may join in. In this way, you will purge the evil from among you.

8 "Suppose a case arises in a local court that is too hard for you to decide—for instance, whether someone is guilty of murder or only of manslaughter, or a difficult lawsuit, or a case involving different kinds of assault. Take such legal cases to the place the LORD your God will choose, 9 and present them to the Levitical priests or the judge on duty at that time. They will hear the case and declare the verdict. 10 You must carry out the verdict they announce and the sentence they prescribe at the place the LORD chooses. You must do exactly what they say. 11 After they have interpreted the law and declared their verdict, the sentence they impose must be fully executed; do not modify it in any way. 12 Anyone arrogant enough to reject the verdict of the judge or of the priest who represents the LORD your God must die. In this way you will purge the evil from Israel. 13 Then everyone else will hear about it and be afraid to act so arrogantly.

GUIDELINES FOR A KING

14 "You are about to enter the land the LORD your God is giving you. When you take it over and settle there, you may think, 'We should select a king to rule over us like the other nations around us.' 15 If this happens, be sure to select as king the man the LORD your God chooses. You must appoint a fellow Israelite; he may not be a foreigner.

16 "The king must not build up a large stable of horses for himself or send his people to Egypt to buy horses, for the LORD has told you, 'You must never return to Egypt.' 17 The king must not take many wives for himself, because they will turn his heart away from the LORD. And he must not accumulate large amounts of wealth in silver and gold for himself.

18 "When he sits on the throne as king, he must copy for himself this body of instruction on a scroll in the presence of the Levitical priests. 19 He must always keep that copy with him and read it daily as long as he lives. That way he will learn to fear the LORD his God by obeying all the terms of these instructions and decrees. 20 This regular reading will prevent him from becoming proud and acting as if he is above his fellow citizens. It will also prevent him from turning away from these commands in the smallest way. And it will ensure that he and his descendants will reign for many generations in Israel.

GIFTS FOR THE PRIESTS AND LEVITES

18 "Remember that the Levitical priests—that is, the whole of the tribe of Levi—will receive no allotment of land among the other tribes in Israel. Instead, the priests and Levites will eat from the special gifts given to the LORD, for that is their share. 2 They will have no land of their own among the Israelites. The LORD himself is their special possession, just as he promised them.

3 "These are the parts the priests may claim as their share from the cattle, sheep, and goats that the people bring as offerings: the shoulder, the cheeks, and the stomach. 4 You must also give to the priests the first share of the grain, the new wine, the olive oil, and the wool at shearing time. 5 For the LORD your God chose the tribe of Levi out of all your tribes to minister in the LORD's name forever.

6 "Suppose a Levite chooses to move from his town in Israel, wherever he is living, to the place the LORD chooses for worship. 7 He may minister there in the name of the LORD his God, just like all his fellow Levites who are serving the LORD there. 8 He may eat his share of the sacrifices and offerings, even if he also receives support from his family.

A CALL TO HOLY LIVING

9 "When you enter the land the LORD your God is giving you, be very careful not to imitate the detestable customs of the nations living there. 10 For example, never sacrifice your son or daughter as a burnt offering.* And do not let your people practice fortune-telling, or use sorcery, or interpret omens, or engage in witchcraft, 11 or cast spells, or function as mediums or psychics, or call forth the spirits of the dead. 12 Anyone who does these things is detestable to the LORD. It is because the other nations have done these detestable things that the LORD your God will drive them out ahead of you. 13 But you must be blameless before the LORD your God. 14 The nations you are about to

18:10 Or *never make your son or daughter pass through the fire.*

17:1 sick or defective. Jesus was the "lamb without defect or blemish" (1 Pet. 1:19).

17:3 sun, moon, or any of the stars. God warned the people about worshiping creation over the Creator (4:19). The Israelites began this pagan practice in Egypt and often fell back into it (2 Kings 17:16; 21:3-5).

17:7 witnesses. Perjury would be a much different experience if a lying witness had to participate in putting the accused to death.

17:14 like the other nations. God was not against a king but against them wanting one for the wrong reasons. Later, the people asked for a king who could raise an army to protect them, instead of relying on God, their ultimate King (1 Sam. 8:5).

17:16 must not build up. To assure that his people remained dependent upon God, they were instructed to not upgrade their military.

18:10 never sacrifice. People who practice these things think that God is hidden and must be found by strange devices. Paul said that God "is not far from each one of us" (Acts 17:27).

displace consult sorcerers and fortune-tellers, but the
LORD your God forbids you to do such things."

TRUE AND FALSE PROPHETS

15 Moses continued, "The LORD your God will raise up
for you a prophet like me from among your fellow Is-
raelites. You must listen to him. 16 For this is what you
yourselves requested of the LORD your God when you
were assembled at Mount Sinai.* You said, 'Don't let
us hear the voice of the LORD our God anymore or see
this blazing fire, for we will die.'
17 "Then the LORD said to me, 'What they have said is
right. 18 I will raise up a prophet like you from among
their fellow Israelites. I will put my words in his
mouth, and he will tell the people everything I com-
mand him. 19 I will personally deal with anyone who
will not listen to the messages the prophet proclaims
on my behalf. 20 But any prophet who falsely claims
to speak in my name or who speaks in the name of
another god must die.'
21 "But you may wonder, 'How will we know wheth-
er or not a prophecy is from the LORD?' 22 If the proph-
et speaks in the LORD's name but his prediction does
not happen or come true, you will know that the LORD
did not give that message. That prophet has spoken
without my authority and need not be feared.

CITIES OF REFUGE

19 "When the LORD your God destroys the nations
whose land he is giving you, you will take over
their land and settle in their towns and homes. 2 Then
you must set apart three cities of refuge in the land
the LORD your God is giving you. 3 Survey the territo-
ry,* and divide the land the LORD your God is giving
you into three districts, with one of these cities in each
district. Then anyone who has killed someone can flee
to one of the cities of refuge for safety.
4 "If someone kills another person unintentional-
ly, without previous hostility, the slayer may flee to
any of these cities to live in safety. 5 For example,
suppose someone goes into the forest with a neigh-
bor to cut wood. And suppose one of them swings
an ax to chop down a tree, and the ax head flies off
the handle, killing the other person. In such cases,
the slayer may flee to one of the cities of refuge to
live in safety.
6 "If the distance to the nearest city of refuge is too
far, an enraged avenger might be able to chase down
and kill the person who caused the death. Then the
slayer would die unfairly, since he had never shown
hostility toward the person who died. 7 That is why I
am commanding you to set aside three cities of refuge.
8 "And if the LORD your God enlarges your territory,
as he swore to your ancestors, and gives you all the
land he promised them, 9 you must designate three ad-
ditional cities of refuge. (He will give you this land if
you are careful to obey all the commands I have given
you—if you always love the LORD your God and walk
in his ways.) 10 That way you will prevent the death
of innocent people in the land the LORD your God is
giving you as your special possession. You will not be
held responsible for the death of innocent people.
11 "But suppose someone is hostile toward a neigh-
bor and deliberately ambushes and murders him and
then flees to one of the cities of refuge. 12 In that case,
the elders of the murderer's hometown must send
agents to the city of refuge to bring him back and
hand him over to the dead person's avenger to be put
to death. 13 Do not feel sorry for that murderer! Purge
from Israel the guilt of murdering innocent people;
then all will go well with you.

CONCERN FOR JUSTICE

14 "When you arrive in the land the LORD your God is
giving you as your special possession, you must never
steal anyone's land by moving the boundary markers
your ancestors set up to mark their property.
15 "You must not convict anyone of a crime on the
testimony of only one witness. The facts of the case
must be established by the testimony of two or three
witnesses.
16 "If a malicious witness comes forward and accus-
es someone of a crime, 17 then both the accuser and ac-
cused must appear before the LORD by coming to the
priests and judges in office at that time. 18 The judges
must investigate the case thoroughly. If the accuser
has brought false charges against his fellow Israel-
ite, 19 you must impose on the accuser the sentence he
intended for the other person. In this way, you will
purge such evil from among you. 20 Then the rest of
the people will hear about it and be afraid to do such
an evil thing. 21 You must show no pity for the guilty!
Your rule should be life for life, eye for eye, tooth for
tooth, hand for hand, foot for foot.

REGULATIONS CONCERNING WAR

20 "When you go out to fight your enemies and
you face horses and chariots and an army
greater than your own, do not be afraid. The LORD
your God, who brought you out of the land of Egypt,
is with you! 2 When you prepare for battle, the priest
must come forward to speak to the troops. 3 He will
say to them, 'Listen to me, all you men of Israel! Do not
be afraid as you go out to fight your enemies today! Do
not lose heart or panic or tremble before them. 4 For
the LORD your God is going with you! He will fight for
you against your enemies, and he will give you vic-
tory!'
5 "Then the officers of the army must address the
troops and say, 'Has anyone here just built a new
house but not yet dedicated it? If so, you may go home!
You might be killed in the battle, and someone else
would dedicate your house. 6 Has anyone here just
planted a vineyard but not yet eaten any of its fruit?
If so, you may go home! You might die in battle, and
someone else would eat the first fruit. 7 Has anyone
here just become engaged to a woman but not yet
married her? Well, you may go home and get married!
You might die in the battle, and someone else would
marry her.'

18:16 Hebrew *Horeb,* another name for Sinai. **19:3** Or *Keep the roads in good repair.*

18:21 How will we know. We must search the Bible to see if things people say about God are true (Acts 17:11).

19:14 boundary markers. These were like a surveyor's stake. A person might move them secretly, but God knows all secrets.

19:15 two or three witnesses. By requiring more than one witness, God protected the accused from a false claim.

19:21 life for life. This law of retaliation limited vengeance by the victim and prevented cruel and unusual punishment by the judge. Though it may seem harsh, it reveals the goodness of God in protecting His people. Jesus rebuked the misuse of this law and the lack of mercy (Matt. 5:38-42).

8 "Then the officers will also say, 'Is anyone here afraid or worried? If you are, you may go home before you frighten anyone else.' 9 When the officers have finished speaking to their troops, they will appoint the unit commanders.

10 "As you approach a town to attack it, you must first offer its people terms for peace. 11 If they accept your terms and open the gates to you, then all the people inside will serve you in forced labor. 12 But if they refuse to make peace and prepare to fight, you must attack the town. 13 When the LORD your God hands the town over to you, use your swords to kill every man in the town. 14 But you may keep for yourselves all the women, children, livestock, and other plunder. You may enjoy the plunder from your enemies that the LORD your God has given you.

15 "But these instructions apply only to distant towns, not to the towns of the nations in the land you will enter. 16 In those towns that the LORD your God is giving you as a special possession, destroy every living thing. 17 You must completely destroy* the Hittites, Amorites, Canaanites, Perizzites, Hivites, and Jebusites, just as the LORD your God has commanded you. 18 This will prevent the people of the land from teaching you to imitate their detestable customs in the worship of their gods, which would cause you to sin deeply against the LORD your God.

19 "When you are attacking a town and the war drags on, you must not cut down the trees with your axes. You may eat the fruit, but do not cut down the trees. Are the trees your enemies, that you should attack them? 20 You may only cut down trees that you know are not valuable for food. Use them to make the equipment you need to attack the enemy town until it falls.

CLEANSING FOR UNSOLVED MURDER

21 "When you are in the land the LORD your God is giving you, someone may be found murdered in a field, and you don't know who committed the murder. 2 In such a case, your elders and judges must measure the distance from the site of the crime to the nearby towns. 3 When the nearest town has been determined, that town's elders must select from the herd a heifer that has never been trained or yoked to a plow. 4 They must lead it down to a valley that has not been plowed or planted and that has a stream running through it. There in the valley they must break the heifer's neck. 5 Then the Levitical priests must step forward, for the LORD your God has chosen them to minister before him and to pronounce blessings in the LORD's name. They are to decide all legal and criminal cases.

6 "The elders of the town must wash their hands over the heifer whose neck was broken. 7 Then they must say, 'Our hands did not shed this person's blood, nor did we see it happen. 8 O LORD, forgive your people Israel whom you have redeemed. Do not charge your people with the guilt of murdering an innocent person.' Then they will be absolved of the guilt of this person's blood. 9 By following these instructions, you will do what is right in the LORD's sight and will cleanse the guilt of murder from your community.

MARRIAGE TO A CAPTIVE WOMAN

10 "Suppose you go out to war against your enemies and the LORD your God hands them over to you, and you take some of them as captives. 11 And suppose you see among the captives a beautiful woman, and you are attracted to her and want to marry her. 12 If this happens, you may take her to your home, where she must shave her head, cut her nails, 13 and change the clothes she was wearing when she was captured. She will stay in your home, but let her mourn for her father and mother for a full month. Then you may marry her, and you will be her husband and she will be your wife. 14 But if you marry her and she does not please you, you must let her go free. You may not sell her or treat her as a slave, for you have humiliated her.

RIGHTS OF THE FIRSTBORN

15 "Suppose a man has two wives, but he loves one and not the other, and both have given him sons. And suppose the firstborn son is the son of the wife he does not love. 16 When the man divides his inheritance, he may not give the larger inheritance to his younger son, the son of the wife he loves, as if he were the firstborn son. 17 He must recognize the rights of his oldest son, the son of the wife he does not love, by giving him a double portion. He is the first son of his father's virility, and the rights of the firstborn belong to him.

DEALING WITH A REBELLIOUS SON

18 "Suppose a man has a stubborn and rebellious son who will not obey his father or mother, even though they discipline him. 19 In such a case, the father and mother must take the son to the elders as they hold court at the town gate. 20 The parents must say to the elders, 'This son of ours is stubborn and rebellious and refuses to obey. He is a glutton and a drunkard.' 21 Then all the men of his town must stone him to death. In this way, you will purge this evil from among you, and all Israel will hear about it and be afraid.

VARIOUS REGULATIONS

22 "If someone has committed a crime worthy of death and is executed and hung on a tree,* 23 the body must not remain hanging from the tree overnight. You

20:17 The Hebrew term used here refers to the complete consecration of things or people to the LORD, either by destroying them or by giving them as an offering. **21:22** Or *impaled on a pole;* similarly in 21:23.

20:10-15 a town. There were two sets of rules of engagement, one for taking the promised land and another for fighting neighbors. This refers to the latter.
20:11 serve you. Noah prophesied that Canaan would serve Shem (Gen. 9:25-26).
21:6 wash their hands. By this action they claim to be innocent. Pilate intended the same message regarding Christ's death (Matt. 27:24).
21:10-11 against your enemies. These are enemies outside Canaan (20:14-16).
21:12 shave her head. This act symbolizes mourning, humiliation, and leaving an old way of life.
21:14 humiliated. The divorcing husband is to treat his foreign wife with dignity.
21:15 two wives. Though God's original intention was one man and one woman (Gen. 2:23-25), polygamy became common.
21:17 double portion. The first son is to receive a double portion—and thus control over the estate—no matter what the father prefers.
21:18 stubborn and rebellious. This type of son dishonors his parents (5:16) in evil, audacious ways over a long period.
21:19 the father and mother. While elders oversaw the entire community, parents were ultimately responsible for their children.
21:21 stone him to death. See Ex. 21:15,17. **purge this evil.** God intended to protect His people from evil (13:6; 17:7,12; 19:19; 22:21,22,24; 24:7).
21:22 on a tree. The executed person was impaled on a pole (Josh. 10:26; 1 Sam. 31:10).

must bury the body that same day, for anyone who is
hung* is cursed in the sight of God. In this way, you
will prevent the defilement of the land the LORD your
God is giving you as your special possession.

22 "If you see your neighbor's ox or sheep or goat
wandering away, don't ignore your respon-
sibility.* Take it back to its owner. 2 If its owner does
not live nearby or you don't know who the owner is,
take it to your place and keep it until the owner comes
looking for it. Then you must return it. 3 Do the same
if you find your neighbor's donkey, clothing, or any-
thing else your neighbor loses. Don't ignore your re-
sponsibility.

4 "If you see that your neighbor's donkey or ox has
collapsed on the road, do not look the other way. Go
and help your neighbor get it back on its feet!

5 "A woman must not put on men's clothing, and a
man must not wear women's clothing. Anyone who
does this is detestable in the sight of the LORD your God.

6 "If you happen to find a bird's nest in a tree or
on the ground, and there are young ones or eggs in
it with the mother sitting in the nest, do not take the
mother with the young. 7 You may take the young, but
let the mother go, so that you may prosper and enjoy
a long life.

8 "When you build a new house, you must build a
railing around the edge of its flat roof. That way you
will not be considered guilty of murder if someone
falls from the roof.

9 "You must not plant any other crop between the
rows of your vineyard. If you do, you are forbidden to
use either the grapes from the vineyard or the other
crop.

10 "You must not plow with an ox and a donkey har-
nessed together.

11 "You must not wear clothing made of wool and
linen woven together.

12 "You must put four tassels on the hem of the cloak
with which you cover yourself—on the front, back,
and sides.

REGULATIONS FOR SEXUAL PURITY

13 "Suppose a man marries a woman, but after sleeping
with her, he turns against her 14 and publicly accuses
her of shameful conduct, saying, 'When I married this
woman, I discovered she was not a virgin.' 15 Then the
woman's father and mother must bring the proof of
her virginity to the elders as they hold court at the
town gate. 16 Her father must say to them, 'I gave my
daughter to this man to be his wife, and now he has
turned against her. 17 He has accused her of shameful
conduct, saying, "I discovered that your daughter was
not a virgin." But here is the proof of my daughter's
virginity.' Then they must spread her bed sheet before
the elders. 18 The elders must then take the man and
punish him. 19 They must also fine him 100 pieces of
silver,* which he must pay to the woman's father be-
cause he publicly accused a virgin of Israel of shame-
ful conduct. The woman will then remain the man's
wife, and he may never divorce her.

20 "But suppose the man's accusations are true,
and he can show that she was not a virgin. 21 The
woman must be taken to the door of her father's
home, and there the men of the town must stone her
to death, for she has committed a disgraceful crime
in Israel by being promiscuous while living in her
parents' home. In this way, you will purge this evil
from among you.

22 "If a man is discovered committing adultery, both
he and the woman must die. In this way, you will
purge Israel of such evil.

23 "Suppose a man meets a young woman, a virgin
who is engaged to be married, and he has sexual in-
tercourse with her. If this happens within a town,
24 you must take both of them to the gates of that town
and stone them to death. The woman is guilty be-
cause she did not scream for help. The man must die
because he violated another man's wife. In this way,
you will purge this evil from among you.

25 "But if the man meets the engaged woman out in
the country, and he rapes her, then only the man must
die. 26 Do nothing to the young woman; she has com-
mitted no crime worthy of death. She is as innocent as
a murder victim. 27 Since the man raped her out in the
country, it must be assumed that she screamed, but
there was no one to rescue her.

28 "Suppose a man has intercourse with a young
woman who is a virgin but is not engaged to be mar-
ried. If they are discovered, 29 he must pay her father
fifty pieces of silver.* Then he must marry the young
woman because he violated her, and he may never di-
vorce her as long as he lives.

30* "A man must not marry his father's former wife,
for this would violate his father.

REGULATIONS CONCERNING WORSHIP

23 1* "If a man's testicles are crushed or his penis is
cut off, he may not be admitted to the assembly
of the LORD.

2 "If a person is illegitimate by birth, neither he nor
his descendants for ten generations may be admitted
to the assembly of the LORD.

3 "No Ammonite or Moabite or any of their descen-
dants for ten generations may be admitted to the as-
sembly of the LORD. 4 These nations did not welcome
you with food and water when you came out of Egypt.
Instead, they hired Balaam son of Beor from Pethor in
distant Aram-naharaim to curse you. 5 But the LORD
your God refused to listen to Balaam. He turned the
intended curse into a blessing because the LORD your
God loves you. 6 As long as you live, you must never
promote the welfare and prosperity of the Ammon-
ites or Moabites.

21:23 Greek version reads *for everyone who is hung on a tree.* Compare Gal 3:13. **22:1** Hebrew *don't hide yourself;* similarly in 22:3. **22:19** Hebrew *100 [shekels] of silver,* about 2.5 pounds or 1.1 kilograms in weight. **22:29** Hebrew *50 [shekels] of silver,* about 1.25 pounds or 570 grams in weight. **22:30** Verse 22:30 is numbered 23:1 in Hebrew text. **23:1** Verses 23:1-25 are numbered 23:2-26 in Hebrew text.

21:23 is cursed in God's sight. This was a symbol of God's righteous judgment and rejection. By taking the total judgment for the sins of the world, Christ became "a curse for us" (Gal. 3:13).

22:5 woman must not put on. This rule is related to prohibitions against abnormal sexual practices (Lev. 18:22; 20:13).

22:8 railing . . . roof. This commandment calls for reasonable safety measures on property.

22:29 fifty pieces of silver. This was the bride price.

23:1 testicles are crushed. The removal of all or part of the sexual organs was a pagan practice forbidden in Israel.

23:3 Moabite. What about David, grandson of a Moabite woman? Some say that this prohibition was only for Moabite men, others that the prohibition was only for the first 10 generations after the tabernacle was built.

7 "Do not detest the Edomites or the Egyptians, be-
cause the Edomites are your relatives and you lived
as foreigners among the Egyptians. 8 The third gen-
eration of Edomites and Egyptians may enter the as-
sembly of the LORD.

MISCELLANEOUS REGULATIONS

9 "When you go to war against your enemies, be sure
to stay away from anything that is impure.
10 "Any man who becomes ceremonially defiled
because of a nocturnal emission must leave the camp
and stay away all day. 11 Toward evening he must
bathe himself, and at sunset he may return to the
camp.
12 "You must have a designated area outside the
camp where you can go to relieve yourself. 13 Each
of you must have a spade as part of your equipment.
Whenever you relieve yourself, dig a hole with the
spade and cover the excrement. 14 The camp must be
holy, for the LORD your God moves around in your
camp to protect you and to defeat your enemies. He
must not see any shameful thing among you, or he
will turn away from you.
15 "If slaves should escape from their masters and
take refuge with you, you must not hand them over to
their masters. 16 Let them live among you in any town
they choose, and do not oppress them.
17 "No Israelite, whether man or woman, may be-
come a temple prostitute. 18 When you are bringing
an offering to fulfill a vow, you must not bring to the
house of the LORD your God any offering from the
earnings of a prostitute, whether a man* or a woman,
for both are detestable to the LORD your God.
19 "Do not charge interest on the loans you make to
a fellow Israelite, whether you loan money, or food, or
anything else. 20 You may charge interest to foreign-
ers, but you may not charge interest to Israelites, so
that the LORD your God may bless you in everything
you do in the land you are about to enter and occupy.
21 "When you make a vow to the LORD your God, be
prompt in fulfilling whatever you promised him. For
the LORD your God demands that you promptly fulfill
all your vows, or you will be guilty of sin. 22 However,
it is not a sin to refrain from making a vow. 23 But once
you have voluntarily made a vow, be careful to fulfill
your promise to the LORD your God.
24 "When you enter your neighbor's vineyard, you
may eat your fill of grapes, but you must not carry any
away in a basket. 25 And when you enter your neigh-
bor's field of grain, you may pluck the heads of grain
with your hand, but you must not harvest it with a
sickle.

24 "Suppose a man marries a woman but she does
not please him. Having discovered something
wrong with her, he writes a document of divorce,
hands it to her, and sends her away from his house.
2 When she leaves his house, she is free to marry
another man. 3 But if the second husband also turns
against her, writes a document of divorce, hands it to
her, and sends her away, or if he dies, 4 the first hus-
band may not marry her again, for she has been de-
filed. That would be detestable to the LORD. You must
not bring guilt upon the land the LORD your God is
giving you as a special possession.
5 "A newly married man must not be drafted into
the army or be given any other official responsibili-
ties. He must be free to spend one year at home, bring-
ing happiness to the wife he has married.
6 "It is wrong to take a set of millstones, or even
just the upper millstone, as security for a loan, for the
owner uses it to make a living.
7 "If anyone kidnaps a fellow Israelite and treats
him as a slave or sells him, the kidnapper must die.
In this way, you will purge the evil from among you.
8 "In all cases involving serious skin diseases,*
be careful to follow the instructions of the Levitical
priests; obey all the commands I have given them.
9 Remember what the LORD your God did to Miriam as
you were coming from Egypt.
10 "If you lend anything to your neighbor, do not
enter his house to pick up the item he is giving as se-
curity. 11 You must wait outside while he goes in and
brings it out to you. 12 If your neighbor is poor and
gives you his cloak as security for a loan, do not keep
the cloak overnight. 13 Return the cloak to its owner
by sunset so he can stay warm through the night and
bless you, and the LORD your God will count you as
righteous.
14 "Never take advantage of poor and destitute la-
borers, whether they are fellow Israelites or foreign-
ers living in your towns. 15 You must pay them their
wages each day before sunset because they are poor
and are counting on it. If you don't, they might cry
out to the LORD against you, and it would be counted
against you as sin.
16 "Parents must not be put to death for the sins of
their children, nor children for the sins of their par-
ents. Those deserving to die must be put to death for
their own crimes.
17 "True justice must be given to foreigners living
among you and to orphans, and you must never ac-
cept a widow's garment as security for her debt.
18 Always remember that you were slaves in Egypt
and that the LORD your God redeemed you from your
slavery. That is why I have given you this command.
19 "When you are harvesting your crops and forget
to bring in a bundle of grain from your field, don't
go back to get it. Leave it for the foreigners, orphans,
and widows. Then the LORD your God will bless you
in all you do. 20 When you beat the olives from your
olive trees, don't go over the boughs twice. Leave
the remaining olives for the foreigners, orphans,
and widows. 21 When you gather the grapes in your
vineyard, don't glean the vines after they are picked.
Leave the remaining grapes for the foreigners,

23:18 Hebrew *a dog.* **24:8** Traditionally rendered *leprosy.* The Hebrew word used here can describe various skin diseases.

23:17 temple prostitute. In Canaanite religion, men had sexual relations with cultic prostitutes, thinking it brought fertility and prosperity.
23:19 interest. Exodus 22:25-27 outlines God's thinking on interest. Jesus would encourage even greater generosity in Luke 6:34-35.
23:24-25 enter your neighbor's vineyard . . . heads of grain. Travelers were allowed to pick grapes or grain to eat (Mark 2:23-28), but harvesting or stockpiling was prohibited.
24:1 a document of divorce. Here divorce is allowed. Later Jesus added a condition (Matt. 5:31-32), pointing to the precedent set by creation (Matt. 19:3-9).
24:8 serious skin disease. Not leprosy but a disease that whitened and hardened the skin (Lev. 13). It was not infectious but did cause ritual uncleanness.
24:16 for their own crimes. In Ezekiel 18:4-24 the prophet addresses this issue, which may have arisen from a faulty understanding of Exodus 20:5; 34:6-7.

orphans, and widows. 22 Remember that you were slaves in the land of Egypt. That is why I am giving you this command.

25 "Suppose two people take a dispute to court, and the judges declare that one is right and the other is wrong. 2 If the person in the wrong is sentenced to be flogged, the judge must command him to lie down and be beaten in his presence with the number of lashes appropriate to the crime. 3 But never give more than forty lashes; more than forty lashes would publicly humiliate your neighbor.

4 "You must not muzzle an ox to keep it from eating as it treads out the grain.

5 "If two brothers are living together on the same property and one of them dies without a son, his widow may not be married to anyone from outside the family. Instead, her husband's brother should marry her and have intercourse with her to fulfill the duties of a brother-in-law. 6 The first son she bears to him will be considered the son of the dead brother, so that his name will not be forgotten in Israel.

7 "But if the man refuses to marry his brother's widow, she must go to the town gate and say to the elders assembled there, 'My husband's brother refuses to preserve his brother's name in Israel—he refuses to fulfill the duties of a brother-in-law by marrying me.' 8 The elders of the town will then summon him and talk with him. If he still refuses and says, 'I don't want to marry her,' 9 the widow must walk over to him in the presence of the elders, pull his sandal from his foot, and spit in his face. Then she must declare, 'This is what happens to a man who refuses to provide his brother with children.' 10 Ever afterward in Israel his family will be referred to as 'the family of the man whose sandal was pulled off'!

11 "If two Israelite men get into a fight and the wife of one tries to rescue her husband by grabbing the testicles of the other man, 12 you must cut off her hand. Show her no pity.

13 "You must use accurate scales when you weigh out merchandise, 14 and you must use full and honest measures. 15 Yes, always use honest weights and measures, so that you may enjoy a long life in the land the LORD your God is giving you. 16 All who cheat with dishonest weights and measures are detestable to the LORD your God.

17 "Never forget what the Amalekites did to you as you came from Egypt. 18 They attacked you when you were exhausted and weary, and they struck down those who were straggling behind. They had no fear of God. 19 Therefore, when the LORD your God has given you rest from all your enemies in the land he is giving you as a special possession, you must destroy the Amalekites and erase their memory from under heaven. Never forget this!

HARVEST OFFERINGS AND TITHES

26 "When you enter the land the LORD your God is giving you as a special possession and you have conquered it and settled there, 2 put some of the first produce from each crop you harvest into a basket and bring it to the designated place of worship—the place the LORD your God chooses for his name to be honored. 3 Go to the priest in charge at that time and say to him, 'With this gift I acknowledge to the LORD your God that I have entered the land he swore to our ancestors he would give us.' 4 The priest will then take the basket from your hand and set it before the altar of the LORD your God.

5 "You must then say in the presence of the LORD your God, 'My ancestor Jacob was a wandering Aramean who went to live as a foreigner in Egypt. His family arrived few in number, but in Egypt they became a large and mighty nation. 6 When the Egyptians oppressed and humiliated us by making us their slaves, 7 we cried out to the LORD, the God of our ancestors. He heard our cries and saw our hardship, toil, and oppression. 8 So the LORD brought us out of Egypt with a strong hand and powerful arm, with overwhelming terror, and with miraculous signs and wonders. 9 He brought us to this place and gave us this land flowing with milk and honey! 10 And now, O LORD, I have brought you the first portion of the harvest you have given me from the ground.' Then place the produce before the LORD your God, and bow to the ground in worship before him. 11 Afterward you may go and celebrate because of all the good things the LORD your God has given to you and your household. Remember to include the Levites and the foreigners living among you in the celebration.

12 "Every third year you must offer a special tithe of your crops. In this year of the special tithe you must give your tithes to the Levites, foreigners, orphans, and widows, so that they will have enough to eat in your towns. 13 Then you must declare in the presence of the LORD your God, 'I have taken the sacred gift from my house and have given it to the Levites, foreigners, orphans, and widows, just as you commanded me. I have not violated or forgotten any of your commands. 14 I have not eaten any of it while in mourning; I have not handled it while I was ceremonially unclean; and I have not offered any of it to the dead. I have obeyed the LORD my God and have done everything you commanded me. 15 Now look down from your holy dwelling place in heaven and bless your people Israel and the land you swore to our ancestors to give us—a land flowing with milk and honey.'

A CALL TO OBEY THE LORD'S COMMANDS

16 "Today the LORD your God has commanded you to obey all these decrees and regulations. So be careful to obey them wholeheartedly. 17 You have declared today that the LORD is your God. And you have promised to walk in his ways, and to obey his decrees, commands, and regulations, and to do everything he tells

---

25:3 forty lashes. A limit is imposed on beatings so they are not inhumane.
25:4 muzzle an ox. Muzzling prevented the animal from eating while working. Paul applies this verse to ministers (1 Cor. 9:9-10 and 1 Tim. 5:17-18). **treads out the grain.** The ox walks on the grain that is spread over a hard, flat surface.
25:5-6 These practices were instituted to provide family heirs.
25:9 pull his sandal from his foot. This signifies a loss of rights.
25:17 Amalekites. See Ex. 17:8-16; Num. 14:45.
26:2 first produce. This is a one-time offering upon entering the land, distinct from the yearly offering of firstfruits (18:4).
26:5 wandering Aramean. Jacob journeyed from southern Canaan to Haran, then returned (Gen. 27–35). He also moved to Egypt with his family (Gen. 46:3-7). Two of his wives were Aramean (Gen. 28:5; 29:16,28). **large and mighty nation.** While the Israelites lived in Egypt, they grew from 70 people to over 600,000 men, plus women and children (Ex. 1:5,7).
26:12 special tithe. See 14:22-29.
26:15 holy dwelling. God is everywhere (Isa. 66:1-2), but heaven is seen as the place from which He reigns and answers prayer.
26:17 You have declared. This wording is found in treaties and covenants.

you. 18 The LORD has declared today that you are his
people, his own special treasure, just as he promised,
and that you must obey all his commands. 19 And if
you do, he will set you high above all the other na-
tions he has made. Then you will receive praise, hon-
or, and renown. You will be a nation that is holy to the
LORD your God, just as he promised."

THE ALTAR ON MOUNT EBAL

27 Then Moses and the leaders of Israel gave
this charge to the people: "Obey all these com-
mands that I am giving you today. 2 When you cross
the Jordan River and enter the land the LORD your
God is giving you, set up some large stones and coat
them with plaster. 3 Write this whole body of in-
struction on them when you cross the river to enter
the land the LORD your God is giving you—a land
flowing with milk and honey, just as the LORD, the
God of your ancestors, promised you. 4 When you
cross the Jordan, set up these stones at Mount Ebal
and coat them with plaster, as I am commanding you
today.

5 "Then build an altar there to the LORD your God,
using natural, uncut stones. You must not shape the
stones with an iron tool. 6 Build the altar of uncut
stones, and use it to offer burnt offerings to the LORD
your God. 7 Also sacrifice peace offerings on it, and
celebrate by feasting there before the LORD your God.
8 You must clearly write all these instructions on the
stones coated with plaster."

9 Then Moses and the Levitical priests addressed all
Israel as follows: "O Israel, be quiet and listen! Today
you have become the people of the LORD your God. 10 So
you must obey the LORD your God by keeping all these
commands and decrees that I am giving you today."

CURSES FROM MOUNT EBAL

11 That same day Moses also gave this charge to the
people: 12 "When you cross the Jordan River, the tribes
of Simeon, Levi, Judah, Issachar, Joseph, and Benjamin
must stand on Mount Gerizim to proclaim a blessing
over the people. 13 And the tribes of Reuben, Gad, Ash-
er, Zebulun, Dan, and Naphtali must stand on Mount
Ebal to proclaim a curse.

14 "Then the Levites will shout to all the people of
Israel:

15 'Cursed is anyone who carves or casts an idol and
secretly sets it up. These idols, the work of crafts-
men, are detestable to the LORD.'
And all the people will reply, 'Amen.'

16 'Cursed is anyone who dishonors father or mother.'
And all the people will reply, 'Amen.'

17 'Cursed is anyone who steals property from a neigh-
bor by moving a boundary marker.'
And all the people will reply, 'Amen.'

18 'Cursed is anyone who leads a blind person astray
on the road.'
And all the people will reply, 'Amen.'

19 'Cursed is anyone who denies justice to foreigners,
orphans, or widows.'
And all the people will reply, 'Amen.'

20 'Cursed is anyone who has sexual intercourse with
one of his father's wives, for he has violated his father.'
And all the people will reply, 'Amen.'

21 'Cursed is anyone who has sexual intercourse with
an animal.'
And all the people will reply, 'Amen.'

22 'Cursed is anyone who has sexual intercourse with
his sister, whether she is the daughter of his father
or his mother.'
And all the people will reply, 'Amen.'

23 'Cursed is anyone who has sexual intercourse with
his mother-in-law.'
And all the people will reply, 'Amen.'

24 'Cursed is anyone who attacks a neighbor in se-
cret.'
And all the people will reply, 'Amen.'

25 'Cursed is anyone who accepts payment to kill an
innocent person.'
And all the people will reply, 'Amen.'

26 'Cursed is anyone who does not affirm and obey the
terms of these instructions.'
And all the people will reply, 'Amen.'

BLESSINGS FOR OBEDIENCE

28 "If you fully obey the LORD your God and care-
fully keep all his commands that I am giving
you today, the LORD your God will set you high above
all the nations of the world. 2 You will experience all
these blessings if you obey the LORD your God:

3 Your towns and your fields
will be blessed.
4 Your children and your crops
will be blessed.
The offspring of your herds and flocks
will be blessed.
5 Your fruit baskets and breadboards
will be blessed.
6 Wherever you go and whatever you do,
you will be blessed.

7 "The LORD will conquer your enemies when they
attack you. They will attack you from one direction,
but they will scatter from you in seven!

26:18 his people . . . special treasure. This same idea is captured in New Testament phrases such as "chosen race" and "people for His possession" (1 Pet. 2:9). God clearly has authority over His people—and He lovingly treasures them.
27:2 large stones. It was common to commemorate important events by setting up stones and writing messages on them for people to see and remember.
27:12-13 Gerizim . . . Ebal. These mountains were on the south and north sides of Shechem.
27:15 carves or casts an idol. This activity would break the first two commandments (5:7-10). **Amen.** The people formally declare their acceptance of the covenant.
27:19 foreigners, orphans, or widows. Such people had no resources to protect themselves.
27:26 Cursed. This comprehensive curse fell on anyone who broke any part of the Law (Jms 2:10). Since not a single human fully obeys God's Law, humanity is under a curse (Gal. 3:10).
28:1-14 The terminology of the blessings parallels the terminology of the curses in verses 15-44.
28:5 baskets . . . blessed. In other words, there will be plenty to eat.

8 "The LORD will guarantee a blessing on every-
thing you do and will fill your storehouses with
grain. The LORD your God will bless you in the land
he is giving you.
9 "If you obey the commands of the LORD your God
and walk in his ways, the LORD will establish you as
his holy people as he swore he would do. 10 Then all
the nations of the world will see that you are a peo-
ple claimed by the LORD, and they will stand in awe
of you.
11 "The LORD will give you prosperity in the land he
swore to your ancestors to give you, blessing you with
many children, numerous livestock, and abundant
crops. 12 The LORD will send rain at the proper time
from his rich treasury in the heavens and will bless
all the work you do. You will lend to many nations,
but you will never need to borrow from them. 13 If you
listen to these commands of the LORD your God that I
am giving you today, and if you carefully obey them,
the LORD will make you the head and not the tail, and
you will always be on top and never at the bottom.
14 You must not turn away from any of the commands
I am giving you today, nor follow after other gods and
worship them.

CURSES FOR DISOBEDIENCE

15 "But if you refuse to listen to the LORD your God
and do not obey all the commands and decrees I am
giving you today, all these curses will come and over-
whelm you:

16 Your towns and your fields
will be cursed.
17 Your fruit baskets and breadboards
will be cursed.
18 Your children and your crops
will be cursed.
The offspring of your herds and flocks
will be cursed.
19 Wherever you go and whatever you do,
you will be cursed.

20 "The LORD himself will send on you curses, con-
fusion, and frustration in everything you do, until at
last you are completely destroyed for doing evil and
abandoning me. 21 The LORD will afflict you with dis-
eases until none of you are left in the land you are
about to enter and occupy. 22 The LORD will strike you
with wasting diseases, fever, and inflammation, with
scorching heat and drought, and with blight and mil-
dew. These disasters will pursue you until you die.
23 The skies above will be as unyielding as bronze, and
the earth beneath will be as hard as iron. 24 The LORD
will change the rain that falls on your land into pow-
der, and dust will pour down from the sky until you
are destroyed.
25 "The LORD will cause you to be defeated by your
enemies. You will attack your enemies from one di-
rection, but you will scatter from them in seven! You
will be an object of horror to all the kingdoms of the
earth. 26 Your corpses will be food for all the scaveng-
ing birds and wild animals, and no one will be there
to chase them away.
27 "The LORD will afflict you with the boils of Egypt
and with tumors, scurvy, and the itch, from which you
cannot be cured. 28 The LORD will strike you with mad-
ness, blindness, and panic. 29 You will grope around
in broad daylight like a blind person groping in the
darkness, but you will not find your way. You will be
oppressed and robbed continually, and no one will
come to save you.
30 "You will be engaged to a woman, but another
man will sleep with her. You will build a house, but
someone else will live in it. You will plant a vineyard,
but you will never enjoy its fruit. 31 Your ox will be
butchered before your eyes, but you will not eat a sin-
gle bite of the meat. Your donkey will be taken from
you, never to be returned. Your sheep and goats will
be given to your enemies, and no one will be there to
help you. 32 You will watch as your sons and daugh-
ters are taken away as slaves. Your heart will break
for them, but you won't be able to help them. 33 A for-
eign nation you have never heard about will eat the
crops you worked so hard to grow. You will suffer un-
der constant oppression and harsh treatment. 34 You
will go mad because of all the tragedy you see around
you. 35 The LORD will cover your knees and legs with
incurable boils. In fact, you will be covered from head
to foot.
36 "The LORD will exile you and your king to a na-
tion unknown to you and your ancestors. There in
exile you will worship gods of wood and stone! 37 You
will become an object of horror, ridicule, and mock-
ery among all the nations to which the LORD sends
you.
38 "You will plant much but harvest little, for lo-
custs will eat your crops. 39 You will plant vineyards
and care for them, but you will not drink the wine
or eat the grapes, for worms will destroy the vines.
40 You will grow olive trees throughout your land, but
you will never use the olive oil, for the fruit will drop
before it ripens. 41 You will have sons and daughters,
but you will lose them, for they will be led away into
captivity. 42 Swarms of insects will destroy your trees
and crops.
43 "The foreigners living among you will become
stronger and stronger, while you become weaker and
weaker. 44 They will lend money to you, but you will
not lend to them. They will be the head, and you will
be the tail!
45 "If you refuse to listen to the LORD your God and to
obey the commands and decrees he has given you, all
these curses will pursue and overtake you until you
are destroyed. 46 These horrors will serve as a sign
and warning among you and your descendants for-
ever. 47 If you do not serve the LORD your God with joy
and enthusiasm for the abundant benefits you have
received, 48 you will serve your enemies whom the
LORD will send against you. You will be left hungry,
thirsty, naked, and lacking in everything. The LORD
will put an iron yoke on your neck, oppressing you
harshly until he has destroyed you.

28:12 his rich treasury. Heaven is pictured as a gigantic treasury of all good things that God dispenses to the blessed. **You will lend.** Israel will be so blessed by God it will have more than enough.

28:13 the head and not the tail. Israel would be preeminent, honored among the nations.

28:26 Your corpses will be food. Not being properly buried showed extreme disrespect for the deceased.

28:35 incurable boils. This plague also infested the Egyptians (Ex. 9:11).

28:47 serve . . . with joy. God expects His people to respond positively and naturally to His gracious provision.

49 "The LORD will bring a distant nation against you
from the end of the earth, and it will swoop down on
you like a vulture. It is a nation whose language you
do not understand, 50 a fierce and heartless nation
that shows no respect for the old and no pity for the
young. 51 Its armies will devour your livestock and
crops, and you will be destroyed. They will leave you
no grain, new wine, olive oil, calves, or lambs, and you
will starve to death. 52 They will attack your cities un-
til all the fortified walls in your land—the walls you
trusted to protect you—are knocked down. They will
attack all the towns in the land the LORD your God has
given you.

53 "The siege and terrible distress of the enemy's
attack will be so severe that you will eat the flesh of
your own sons and daughters, whom the LORD your
God has given you. 54 The most tenderhearted man
among you will have no compassion for his own
brother, his beloved wife, and his surviving children.
55 He will refuse to share with them the flesh he is
devouring—the flesh of one of his own children—
because he has nothing else to eat during the siege
and terrible distress that your enemy will inflict on
all your towns. 56 The most tender and delicate wom-
an among you—so delicate she would not so much as
touch the ground with her foot—will be selfish to-
ward the husband she loves and toward her own son
or daughter. 57 She will hide from them the afterbirth
and the new baby she has borne, so that she herself
can secretly eat them. She will have nothing else to
eat during the siege and terrible distress that your
enemy will inflict on all your towns.

58 "If you refuse to obey all the words of instruction
that are written in this book, and if you do not fear
the glorious and awesome name of the LORD your
God, 59 then the LORD will overwhelm you and your
children with indescribable plagues. These plagues
will be intense and without relief, making you mis-
erable and unbearably sick. 60 He will afflict you with
all the diseases of Egypt that you feared so much, and
you will have no relief. 61 The LORD will afflict you
with every sickness and plague there is, even those
not mentioned in this Book of Instruction, until you
are destroyed. 62 Though you become as numerous as
the stars in the sky, few of you will be left because you
would not listen to the LORD your God.

63 "Just as the LORD has found great pleasure in
causing you to prosper and multiply, the LORD will
find pleasure in destroying you. You will be torn
from the land you are about to enter and occupy.
64 For the LORD will scatter you among all the nations
from one end of the earth to the other. There you will
worship foreign gods that neither you nor your an-
cestors have known, gods made of wood and stone!
65 There among those nations you will find no peace
or place to rest. And the LORD will cause your heart
to tremble, your eyesight to fail, and your soul to de-
spair. 66 Your life will constantly hang in the balance.
You will live night and day in fear, unsure if you
will survive. 67 In the morning you will say, 'If only
it were night!' And in the evening you will say, 'If
only it were morning!' For you will be terrified by the
awful horrors you see around you. 68 Then the LORD
will send you back to Egypt in ships, to a destination I
promised you would never see again. There you will
offer to sell yourselves to your enemies as slaves, but
no one will buy you."

29 1* These are the terms of the covenant the LORD
commanded Moses to make with the Israelites
while they were in the land of Moab, in addition to
the covenant he had made with them at Mount Sinai.*

MOSES REVIEWS THE COVENANT

2* Moses summoned all the Israelites and said to them,
"You have seen with your own eyes everything the
LORD did in the land of Egypt to Pharaoh and to all
his servants and to his whole country—3 all the great
tests of strength, the miraculous signs, and the amaz-
ing wonders. 4 But to this day the LORD has not giv-
en you minds that understand, nor eyes that see, nor
ears that hear! 5 For forty years I led you through the
wilderness, yet your clothes and sandals did not wear
out. 6 You ate no bread and drank no wine or other
alcoholic drink, but he provided for you so you would
know that he is the LORD your God.

7 "When we came here, King Sihon of Heshbon and
King Og of Bashan came out to fight against us, but
we defeated them. 8 We took their land and gave it to
the tribes of Reuben and Gad and to the half-tribe of
Manasseh as their grant of land.

9 "Therefore, obey the terms of this covenant so that
you will prosper in everything you do. 10 All of you—
tribal leaders, elders, officers, all the men of Israel—
are standing today in the presence of the LORD your
God. 11 Your little ones and your wives are with you,
as well as the foreigners living among you who chop
your wood and carry your water. 12 You are standing
here today to enter into the covenant of the LORD your
God. The LORD is making this covenant, including the
curses. 13 By entering into the covenant today, he will
establish you as his people and confirm that he is
your God, just as he promised you and as he swore to
your ancestors Abraham, Isaac, and Jacob.

14 "But you are not the only ones with whom I am
making this covenant with its curses. 15 I am making
this covenant both with you who stand here today in
the presence of the LORD our God, and also with the
future generations who are not standing here today.

16 "You remember how we lived in the land of Egypt
and how we traveled through the lands of enemy na-
tions as we left. 17 You have seen their detestable prac-
tices and their idols* made of wood, stone, silver, and
gold. 18 I am making this covenant with you so that no
one among you—no man, woman, clan, or tribe—
will turn away from the LORD our God to worship

29:1a Verse 29:1 is numbered 28:69 in Hebrew text. 29:1b Hebrew *Horeb,* another name for Sinai. 29:2 Verses 29:2-29 are numbered 29:1-28 in Hebrew text. 29:17 The Hebrew term (literally *round things*) probably alludes to dung.

28:49 end of the earth. This is a poetic way of saying "very far away." **like a vulture.** This word picture is applied to the foreign nations of Assyria and Babylonia, who attacked swiftly and powerfully (Jer. 48:40; 49:22).

28:53 you will eat the flesh of your own sons and daughters. The curse is that parents would eat the dead bodies of their children in order to stay alive during a siege (see 2 Kings 6:24-29; Lam. 2:20; 4:10).

28:58 instruction. This could refer to Deuteronomy or all five books of Moses.

29:1 These are the terms of the covenant. This is either a conclusion to the previous chapters or a preamble to chapters 29–32.

29:2 with your own eyes. This refers to the national experience of Israel, not to literal eyewitnesses.

29:4 eyes that see . . . ears that hear. Paul describes a stubborn, hardened Israel (Rom. 11:8).

29:18 bitter and poisonous fruit. Idolatry spreads if not removed and destroyed completely.

these gods of other nations, and so that no root among you bears bitter and poisonous fruit.

[19]"Those who hear the warnings of this curse should not congratulate themselves, thinking, 'I am safe, even though I am following the desires of my own stubborn heart.' This would lead to utter ruin! [20]The LORD will never pardon such people. Instead his anger and jealousy will burn against them. All the curses written in this book will come down on them, and the LORD will erase their names from under heaven. [21]The LORD will separate them from all the tribes of Israel, to pour out on them all the curses of the covenant recorded in this Book of Instruction.

[22]"Then the generations to come, both your own descendants and the foreigners who come from distant lands, will see the devastation of the land and the diseases the LORD inflicts on it. [23]They will exclaim, 'The whole land is devastated by sulfur and salt. It is a wasteland with nothing planted and nothing growing, not even a blade of grass. It is like the cities of Sodom and Gomorrah, Admah and Zeboiim, which the LORD destroyed in his intense anger.'

[24]"And all the surrounding nations will ask, 'Why has the LORD done this to this land? Why was he so angry?'

[25]"And the answer will be, 'This happened because the people of the land abandoned the covenant that the LORD, the God of their ancestors, made with them when he brought them out of the land of Egypt. [26]Instead, they turned away to serve and worship gods they had not known before, gods that were not from the LORD. [27]That is why the LORD's anger has burned against this land, bringing down on it every curse recorded in this book. [28]In great anger and fury the LORD uprooted his people from their land and banished them to another land, where they still live today!'

[29]"The LORD our God has secrets known to no one. We are not accountable for them, but we and our children are accountable forever for all that he has revealed to us, so that we may obey all the terms of these instructions.

A CALL TO RETURN TO THE LORD

30 "In the future, when you experience all these blessings and curses I have listed for you, and when you are living among the nations to which the LORD your God has exiled you, take to heart all these instructions. [2]If at that time you and your children return to the LORD your God, and if you obey with all your heart and all your soul all the commands I have given you today, [3]then the LORD your God will restore your fortunes. He will have mercy on you and gather you back from all the nations where he has scattered you. [4]Even though you are banished to the ends of the earth,* the LORD your God will gather you from there and bring you back again. [5]The LORD your God will return you to the land that belonged to your ancestors, and you will possess that land again. Then he will make you even more prosperous and numerous than your ancestors!

[6]"The LORD your God will change your heart* and the hearts of all your descendants, so that you will love him with all your heart and soul and so you may live! [7]The LORD your God will inflict all these curses on your enemies and on those who hate and persecute you. [8]Then you will again obey the LORD and keep all his commands that I am giving you today.

[9]"The LORD your God will then make you successful in everything you do. He will give you many children and numerous livestock, and he will cause your fields to produce abundant harvests, for the LORD will again delight in being good to you as he was to your ancestors. [10]The LORD your God will delight in you if you obey his voice and keep the commands and decrees written in this Book of Instruction, and if you turn to the LORD your God with all your heart and soul.

THE CHOICE OF LIFE OR DEATH

[11]"This command I am giving you today is not too difficult for you, and it is not beyond your reach. [12]It is not kept in heaven, so distant that you must ask, 'Who will go up to heaven and bring it down so we can hear it and obey?' [13]It is not kept beyond the sea, so far away that you must ask, 'Who will cross the sea to bring it to us so we can hear it and obey?' [14]No, the message is very close at hand; it is on your lips and in your heart so that you can obey it.

[15]"Now listen! Today I am giving you a choice between life and death, between prosperity and disaster. [16]For I command you this day to love the LORD your God and to keep his commands, decrees, and regulations by walking in his ways. If you do this, you will live and multiply, and the LORD your God will bless you and the land you are about to enter and occupy.

[17]"But if your heart turns away and you refuse to listen, and if you are drawn away to serve and worship other gods, [18]then I warn you now that you will certainly be destroyed. You will not live a long, good life in the land you are crossing the Jordan to occupy.

[19]"Today I have given you the choice between life and death, between blessings and curses. Now I call on heaven and earth to witness the choice you make. Oh, that you would choose life, so that you and your descendants might live! [20]You can make this choice by loving the LORD your God, obeying him, and committing yourself firmly to him. This* is the key to your life. And if you love and obey the LORD, you will live long in the land the LORD swore to give your ancestors Abraham, Isaac, and Jacob."

30:4 Hebrew *of the heavens.* **30:6** Hebrew *circumcise your heart.* **30:20** Or *He.*

29:19 congratulate themselves. For one who merely pays lip service to God, the only blessing he will ever get is the one he gives himself.
30:1-10 God foretold that Israel would not keep the Law, yet He would not reject them but restore them physically and spiritually. The return from exile did not fulfill the promise to circumcise their hearts (v. 6), suggesting that God will yet do this in the future.
30:3 restore your fortunes. This could also be translated "bring you back from captivity."
30:6 change your heart. See 10:16; see also Rom. 2:25-29; Gal. 5:6-11; 6:15; Phil. 3:3; Col. 2:11.
30:10 Book of Instruction. See 28:58.
30:12 not kept in heaven. God's word is within everyone's grasp. All are able to hear it, comprehend it, believe it, and obey it (Rom. 10:6-10).
30:15 choice between life and death. This is the choice: obedience, which brings life and blessings; or disobedience, which brings death and curses.
30:20 committing yourself firmly. This means to bond with (Gen. 2:24) or cling to (Ruth 1:14). **This is the key.** This means a full and blessed life.

JOSHUA BECOMES ISRAEL'S LEADER

31 When Moses had finished giving these instruc-
tions* to all the people of Israel, 2 he said, "I am
now 120 years old, and I am no longer able to lead you.
The LORD has told me, 'You will not cross the Jordan
River.' 3 But the LORD your God himself will cross over
ahead of you. He will destroy the nations living there,
and you will take possession of their land. Joshua will
lead you across the river, just as the LORD promised.
4 "The LORD will destroy the nations living in the
land, just as he destroyed Sihon and Og, the kings of
the Amorites. 5 The LORD will hand over to you the
people who live there, and you must deal with them
as I have commanded you. 6 So be strong and coura-
geous! Do not be afraid and do not panic before them.
For the LORD your God will personally go ahead of
you. He will neither fail you nor abandon you."
7 Then Moses called for Joshua, and as all Israel
watched, he said to him, "Be strong and courageous!
For you will lead these people into the land that the
LORD swore to their ancestors he would give them. You
are the one who will divide it among them as their
grants of land. 8 Do not be afraid or discouraged, for
the LORD will personally go ahead of you. He will be
with you; he will neither fail you nor abandon you."

PUBLIC READING OF THE BOOK OF INSTRUCTION

9 So Moses wrote this entire body of instruction in a
book and gave it to the priests, who carried the Ark of
the LORD's Covenant, and to the elders of Israel. 10 Then
Moses gave them this command: "At the end of every
seventh year, the Year of Release, during the Festival
of Shelters, 11 you must read this Book of Instruction to
all the people of Israel when they assemble before the
LORD your God at the place he chooses. 12 Call them all
together—men, women, children, and the foreigners
living in your towns—so they may hear this Book of
Instruction and learn to fear the LORD your God and
carefully obey all the terms of these instructions. 13 Do
this so that your children who have not known these
instructions will hear them and will learn to fear the
LORD your God. Do this as long as you live in the land
you are crossing the Jordan to occupy."

ISRAEL'S DISOBEDIENCE PREDICTED

14 Then the LORD said to Moses, "The time has come for
you to die. Call Joshua and present yourselves at the Tab-
ernacle,* so that I may commission him there." So Moses
and Joshua went and presented themselves at the Tab-
ernacle. 15 And the LORD appeared to them in a pillar of
cloud that stood at the entrance to the sacred tent.
16 The LORD said to Moses, "You are about to die and
join your ancestors. After you are gone, these people
will begin to worship foreign gods, the gods of the
land where they are going. They will abandon me and
break my covenant that I have made with them. 17 Then
my anger will blaze forth against them. I will abandon
them, hiding my face from them, and they will be de-
voured. Terrible trouble will come down on them, and
on that day they will say, 'These disasters have come
down on us because God is no longer among us!' 18 At
that time I will hide my face from them on account of
all the evil they commit by worshiping other gods.
19 "So write down the words of this song, and teach
it to the people of Israel. Help them learn it, so it may
serve as a witness for me against them. 20 For I will
bring them into the land I swore to give their ances-
tors—a land flowing with milk and honey. There
they will become prosperous, eat all the food they
want, and become fat. But they will begin to worship
other gods; they will despise me and break my cov-
enant. 21 And when great disasters come down on
them, this song will stand as evidence against them,
for it will never be forgotten by their descendants. I
know the intentions of these people, even now before
they have entered the land I swore to give them."
22 So that very day Moses wrote down the words of
the song and taught it to the Israelites.
23 Then the LORD commissioned Joshua son of Nun
with these words: "Be strong and courageous, for you
must bring the people of Israel into the land I swore
to give them. I will be with you."
24 When Moses had finished writing this entire
body of instruction in a book, 25 he gave this command
to the Levites who carried the Ark of the LORD's Cov-
enant: 26 "Take this Book of Instruction and place it be-
side the Ark of the Covenant of the LORD your God, so
it may remain there as a witness against the people of
Israel. 27 For I know how rebellious and stubborn you
are. Even now, while I am still alive and am here with
you, you have rebelled against the LORD. How much
more rebellious will you be after my death!
28 "Now summon all the elders and officials of your
tribes, so that I can speak to them directly and call
heaven and earth to witness against them. 29 I know
that after my death you will become utterly corrupt
and will turn from the way I have commanded you to
follow. In the days to come, disaster will come down
on you, for you will do what is evil in the LORD's sight,
making him very angry with your actions."

THE SONG OF MOSES

30 So Moses recited this entire song publicly to the as-
sembly of Israel:

32 1 "Listen, O heavens, and I will speak!
Hear, O earth, the words that I say!
2 Let my teaching fall on you like rain;
let my speech settle like dew.
Let my words fall like rain on tender grass,
like gentle showers on young plants.
3 I will proclaim the name of the LORD;
how glorious is our God!
4 He is the Rock; his deeds are perfect.

31:1 As in Dead Sea Scrolls and Greek version; Masoretic Text reads *Moses went and spoke.* **31:14** Hebrew *Tent of Meeting;* also in 31:14b.

31:2 You will not cross the Jordan River. See Num. 20:2-13.
31:4 as he destroyed Sihon and Og. See 2:26–3:22.
31:9 wrote . . . instruction in a book and gave . . . priests. Copies of a covenant, like a contract, are kept in order to be followed.
31:12 men, women, children, and the foreigners. God's Word is for all the people, including children and non-Israelites living in the land. God intended for His Word to go out from Israel to the nations.
31:19 write down . . . teach it. Moses obeys this command in verse 22. The song itself is recorded in 31:30–32:43. The use of poetic songs, sung in public worship meetings, was a way that Israel remembered what was important and worshiped the living God.
31:24 entire body of instruction. Perhaps just Deuteronomy or the whole of Genesis through Deuteronomy.
31:26 place it beside the Ark. It was standard practice to keep a copy of a covenant in a nation's holiest place.
32:1 Listen, O heavens. See Isa. 1:2; 34:1; Mic. 1:2; 6:1-2.
32:4 the Rock. A rock symbolizes strength and stability and speaks of God's protection and power (see vv. 15, 18, 30-31).

Everything he does is just and fair.
He is a faithful God who does no wrong;
how just and upright he is!

5 "But they have acted corruptly toward him;
when they act so perversely,
are they really his children?*
They are a deceitful and twisted generation.
6 Is this the way you repay the LORD,
you foolish and senseless people?
Isn't he your Father who created you?
Has he not made you and established you?
7 Remember the days of long ago;
think about the generations past.
Ask your father, and he will inform you.
Inquire of your elders, and they will tell you.
8 When the Most High assigned lands to the nations,
when he divided up the human race,
he established the boundaries of the peoples
according to the number in his heavenly court.*

9 "For the people of Israel belong to the LORD;
Jacob is his special possession.
10 He found them in a desert land,
in an empty, howling wasteland.
He surrounded them and watched over them;
he guarded them as he would guard his own eyes.*
11 Like an eagle that rouses her chicks
and hovers over her young,
so he spread his wings to take them up
and carried them safely on his pinions.
12 The LORD alone guided them;
they followed no foreign gods.
13 He let them ride over the highlands
and feast on the crops of the fields.
He nourished them with honey from the rock
and olive oil from the stony ground.
14 He fed them yogurt from the herd
and milk from the flock,
together with the fat of lambs.
He gave them choice rams from Bashan, and goats,
together with the choicest wheat.
You drank the finest wine,
made from the juice of grapes.

15 "But Israel* soon became fat and unruly;
the people grew heavy, plump, and stuffed!
Then they abandoned the God who had made them;
they made light of the Rock of their salvation.
16 They stirred up his jealousy by worshiping foreign
gods;
they provoked his fury with detestable deeds.
17 They offered sacrifices to demons, which are not
God,
to gods they had not known before,
to new gods only recently arrived,
to gods their ancestors had never feared.
18 You neglected the Rock who had fathered you;
you forgot the God who had given you birth.

19 "The LORD saw this and drew back,
provoked to anger by his own sons and daughters.
20 He said, 'I will abandon them;
then see what becomes of them.
For they are a twisted generation,
children without integrity.
21 They have roused my jealousy by worshiping
things that are not God;
they have provoked my anger with their useless
idols.
Now I will rouse their jealousy through people
who are not even a people;
I will provoke their anger through the foolish
Gentiles.
22 For my anger blazes forth like fire
and burns to the depths of the grave.*
It devours the earth and all its crops
and ignites the foundations of the mountains.
23 I will heap disasters upon them
and shoot them down with my arrows.
24 I will weaken them with famine,
burning fever, and deadly disease.
I will send the fangs of wild beasts
and poisonous snakes that glide in the dust.
25 Outside, the sword will bring death,
and inside, terror will strike
both young men and young women,
both infants and the aged.
26 I would have annihilated them,
wiping out even the memory of them.
27 But I feared the taunt of Israel's enemy,
who might misunderstand and say,
"Our own power has triumphed!
The LORD had nothing to do with this!"'

28 "But Israel is a senseless nation;
the people are foolish, without understanding.
29 Oh, that they were wise and could understand this!
Oh, that they might know their fate!
30 How could one person chase a thousand of them,
and two people put ten thousand to flight,
unless their Rock had sold them,
unless the LORD had given them up?
31 But the rock of our enemies is not like our Rock,
as even they recognize.*
32 Their vine grows from the vine of Sodom,
from the vineyards of Gomorrah.
Their grapes are poison,
and their clusters are bitter.
33 Their wine is the venom of serpents,
the deadly poison of cobras.

34 "The LORD says, 'Am I not storing up these things,
sealing them away in my treasury?

32:5 The meaning of the Hebrew is uncertain. **32:8** As in Dead Sea Scrolls, which read *the number of the sons of God,* and Greek version, which reads *the number of the angels of God;* Masoretic Text reads *the number of the sons of Israel.* **32:10** Hebrew *as the pupil of his eye.* **32:15** Hebrew *Jeshurun,* a term of endearment for Israel. **32:22** Hebrew *of Sheol.* **32:31** The meaning of the Hebrew is uncertain. Greek version reads *our enemies are fools.*

32:6 Father. This title was used by the prophets (Isa. 9:6; 63:16; Jer. 3:4; Mal. 2:10), Jesus (John 6:27), Paul (Rom. 1:7; 1 Cor. 8:6; 15:24; Gal. 1:1; Eph. 5:20; 6:23; Phil. 2:11; Col. 1:3; 3:17), Peter (1 Pet. 1:2; 2 Pet. 1:17), and John (2 John 3).
32:8 Most High. *Elyon*, a title that speaks of God's sovereign power over all the earth.
32:15 Israel. Literally Jeshurun, which is an ironic reference to Israel as the "upright one" (Isa. 44:2).
32:17 demons. Pagan gods were actually demonic powers (Ps. 106:37).
32:21 not even a people. A nation not chosen as Israel was. Paul sees the fulfillment of this in Romans 10:19; 11:11.
32:22 depths of the grave. Or the realm of the dead.
32:34 sealing them away in my treasury. God's sovereign will for the future has been established and will surely unfold.

35 I will take revenge; I will pay them back.
In due time their feet will slip.
Their day of disaster will arrive,
and their destiny will overtake them.'

36 "Indeed, the LORD will give justice to his people,
and he will change his mind about* his servants,
when he sees their strength is gone
and no one is left, slave or free.
37 Then he will ask, 'Where are their gods,
the rocks they fled to for refuge?
38 Where now are those gods,
who ate the fat of their sacrifices
and drank the wine of their offerings?
Let those gods arise and help you!
Let them provide you with shelter!
39 Look now; I myself am he!
There is no other god but me!
I am the one who kills and gives life;
I am the one who wounds and heals;
no one can be rescued from my powerful hand!
40 Now I raise my hand to heaven
and declare, "As surely as I live,
41 when I sharpen my flashing sword
and begin to carry out justice,
I will take revenge on my enemies
and repay those who reject me.
42 I will make my arrows drunk with blood,
and my sword will devour flesh—
the blood of the slaughtered and the captives,
and the heads of the enemy leaders."'

43 "Rejoice with him, you heavens,
and let all of God's angels worship him.*
Rejoice with his people, you Gentiles,
and let all the angels be strengthened in him.*
For he will avenge the blood of his children*;
he will take revenge against his enemies.
He will repay those who hate him*
and cleanse his people's land."

44 So Moses came with Joshua* son of Nun and re-
cited all the words of this song to the people.
45 When Moses had finished reciting all these words
to the people of Israel, 46 he added: "Take to heart all the
words of warning I have given you today. Pass them
on as a command to your children so they will obey
every word of these instructions. 47 These instructions
are not empty words—they are your life! By obeying
them you will enjoy a long life in the land you will oc-
cupy when you cross the Jordan River."

MOSES' DEATH FORETOLD

48 That same day the LORD said to Moses, 49 "Go to Moab,
to the mountains east of the river,* and climb Mount
Nebo, which is across from Jericho. Look out across the
land of Canaan, the land I am giving to the people of
Israel as their own special possession. 50 Then you will
die there on the mountain. You will join your ances-
tors, just as Aaron, your brother, died on Mount Hor
and joined his ancestors. 51 For both of you betrayed
me with the Israelites at the waters of Meribah at Ka-
desh* in the wilderness of Zin. You failed to demon-
strate my holiness to the people of Israel there. 52 So
you will see the land from a distance, but you may not
enter the land I am giving to the people of Israel."

MOSES BLESSES THE PEOPLE

33 This is the blessing that Moses, the man of God,
gave to the people of Israel before his death:

2 "The LORD came from Mount Sinai
and dawned upon us* from Mount Seir;
he shone forth from Mount Paran
and came from Meribah-kadesh
with flaming fire at his right hand.*
3 Indeed, he loves his people;*
all his holy ones are in his hands.
They follow in his steps
and accept his teaching.
4 Moses gave us the LORD's instruction,
the special possession of the people of Israel.*
5 The LORD became king in Israel*—
when the leaders of the people assembled,
when the tribes of Israel gathered as one."

6 Moses said this about the tribe of Reuben:*

"Let the tribe of Reuben live and not die out,
though they are few in number."

7 Moses said this about the tribe of Judah:

"O LORD, hear the cry of Judah
and bring them together as a people.
Give them strength to defend their cause;
help them against their enemies!"

8 Moses said this about the tribe of Levi:

"O LORD, you have given your Thummim and
Urim—the sacred lots—
to your faithful servants the Levites.*

32:36 Or *will take revenge for.* **32:43a** As in Dead Sea Scrolls and Greek version; Masoretic Text lacks the first two lines. Compare Heb 1:6. **32:43b** As in Greek version; Hebrew text lacks this sentence. Compare Rom 15:10. **32:43c** As in Dead Sea Scrolls and Greek version; Masoretic Text reads *his servants.* **32:43d** As in Dead Sea Scrolls and Greek version; Masoretic Text lacks this line. **32:44** Hebrew *Hoshea,* a variant name for Joshua. **32:49** Hebrew *the mountains of Abarim.* **32:51** Hebrew *waters of Meribath-kadesh.* **33:2a** As in Greek and Syriac versions; Hebrew reads *upon them.* **33:2b** Or *came from myriads of holy ones, from the south, from his mountain slopes.* The meaning of the Hebrew is uncertain. **33:3** As in Greek version; Hebrew reads *Indeed, lover of the peoples.* **33.4** Hebrew *of Jacob.* The names "Jacob" and "Israel" are often interchanged throughout the Old Testament, referring sometimes to the individual patriarch and sometimes to the nation. **33:5** Hebrew *in Jeshurun,* a term of endearment for Israel. **33:6** Hebrew lacks *Moses said this about the tribe of Reuben.* **33:8** As in Greek version; Hebrew lacks *the Levites.*

32:35 I will take revenge. The writer of Hebrews warns against ignoring the claims of Christ (Heb. 10:30).
32:35 I will pay . . . back. God alone has the right to punish evildoers (Rom. 12:19).
32:50 join your ancestors. Moses would join his deceased family members in death (Gen. 25:8).
32:51 you betrayed me. This incident is referred to in 1:37; 3:23-26; 4:21-22; 31:2; and Numbers 20:10-13.
33:1 blessing. Moses' blessing of the tribes (verses 6-25) is similar to Jacob's blessing of his sons (Gen. 49:1-28). **man of God.** This is the first time this is used of Moses (Josh. 14:6; 1 Chron. 23:14; 2 Chron. 30:16; Ezra 3:2; Ps. 90, title).
33:5 king. God Himself was to rule Israel (Judg. 8:23).
33:8 Thummim and Urim. The sacred lots used to make decisions under the direction of God (Ex. 28:30). **your faithful servants.** The High Priest. **Massah . . . Meribah.** "Testing" and "rebellion" (Exod. 17:7; Ps. 95:8)—the place where Israel stubbornly resisted God's will.

You put them to the test at Massah
and struggled with them at the waters of
Meribah.
9 The Levites obeyed your word
and guarded your covenant.
They were more loyal to you
than to their own parents.
They ignored their relatives
and did not acknowledge their own children.
10 They teach your regulations to Jacob;
they give your instructions to Israel.
They present incense before you
and offer whole burnt offerings on the altar.
11 Bless the ministry of the Levites, O LORD,
and accept all the work of their hands.
Hit their enemies where it hurts the most;
strike down their foes so they never rise
again."

12 Moses said this about the tribe of Benjamin:

"The people of Benjamin are loved by the LORD
and live in safety beside him.
He surrounds them continuously
and preserves them from every harm."

13 Moses said this about the tribes of Joseph:

"May their land be blessed by the LORD
with the precious gift of dew from the heavens
and water from beneath the earth;
14 with the rich fruit that grows in the sun,
and the rich harvest produced each month;
15 with the finest crops of the ancient mountains,
and the abundance from the everlasting hills;
16 with the best gifts of the earth and its bounty,
and the favor of the one who appeared in the
burning bush.
May these blessings rest on Joseph's head,
crowning the brow of the prince among his
brothers.
17 Joseph has the majesty of a young bull;
he has the horns of a wild ox.
He will gore distant nations,
even to the ends of the earth.
This is my blessing for the multitudes of Ephraim
and the thousands of Manasseh."

18 Moses said this about the tribes of Zebulun and Issachar*:

"May the people of Zebulun prosper in their
travels.
May the people of Issachar prosper at home in
their tents.
19 They summon the people to the mountain
to offer proper sacrifices there.
They benefit from the riches of the sea
and the hidden treasures in the sand."

20 Moses said this about the tribe of Gad:

"Blessed is the one who enlarges Gad's territory!
Gad is poised there like a lion
to tear off an arm or a head.
21 The people of Gad took the best land for
themselves;
a leader's share was assigned to them.
When the leaders of the people were assembled,
they carried out the LORD's justice
and obeyed his regulations for Israel."

22 Moses said this about the tribe of Dan:

"Dan is a lion's cub,
leaping out from Bashan."

23 Moses said this about the tribe of Naphtali:

"O Naphtali, you are rich in favor
and full of the LORD's blessings;
may you possess the west and the south."

24 Moses said this about the tribe of Asher:

"May Asher be blessed above other sons;
may he be esteemed by his brothers;
may he bathe his feet in olive oil.
25 May the bolts of your gates be of iron and bronze;
may you be secure all your days."

26 "There is no one like the God of Israel.*
He rides across the heavens to help you,
across the skies in majestic splendor.
27 The eternal God is your refuge,
and his everlasting arms are under you.
He drives out the enemy before you;
he cries out, 'Destroy them!'
28 So Israel will live in safety,
prosperous Jacob in security,
in a land of grain and new wine,
while the heavens drop down dew.
29 How blessed you are, O Israel!
Who else is like you, a people saved by the LORD?
He is your protecting shield
and your triumphant sword!
Your enemies will cringe before you,
and you will stomp on their backs!"

THE DEATH OF MOSES

34 Then Moses went up to Mount Nebo from
the plains of Moab and climbed Pisgah Peak,
which is across from Jericho. And the LORD showed
him the whole land, from Gilead as far as Dan; 2 all the
land of Naphtali; the land of Ephraim and Manasseh;
all the land of Judah, extending to the Mediterranean
Sea*; 3 the Negev; the Jordan Valley with Jericho—the
city of palms—as far as Zoar. 4 Then the LORD said to
Moses, "This is the land I promised on oath to Abra-

33:18 Hebrew lacks *and Issachar.* **33:26** Hebrew *of Jeshurun,* a term of endearment for Israel. **34:2** Hebrew *the western sea.*

33:13 Joseph. That is, Ephraim and Manasseh. **dew . . . water from beneath.** A reference to rain and springs or wells.
33:19 riches of the sea. These tribes would enjoy success in maritime trade (Gen. 49:13).
33:21 the best land. Good land was required to maintain livestock, and livestock signified wealth.
33:24 bathe his feet in olive oil. Asher would enjoy God's rich blessing.
33:26 across the skies. This description has been found in Canaanite literature in reference to Baal. Its use here (and in Ps. 68:4) indicates that Yahweh is the true God who dwells in the heavens and is sovereign over creation.

ham, Isaac, and Jacob when I said, 'I will give it to your descendants.' I have now allowed you to see it with your own eyes, but you will not enter the land."
5 So Moses, the servant of the LORD, died there in the land of Moab, just as the LORD had said. 6 The LORD buried him* in a valley near Beth-peor in Moab, but to this day no one knows the exact place. 7 Moses was 120 years old when he died, yet his eyesight was clear, and he was as strong as ever. 8 The people of Israel mourned for Moses on the plains of Moab for thirty days, until the customary period of mourning was over.
9 Now Joshua son of Nun was full of the spirit of wisdom, for Moses had laid his hands on him. So the people of Israel obeyed him, doing just as the LORD had commanded Moses.
10 There has never been another prophet in Israel like Moses, whom the LORD knew face to face. 11 The LORD sent him to perform all the miraculous signs and wonders in the land of Egypt against Pharaoh, and all his servants, and his entire land. 12 With mighty power, Moses performed terrifying acts in the sight of all Israel.

34:6 Hebrew *He buried him;* Samaritan Pentateuch and some Greek manuscripts read *They buried him.*

34:6 no one knows the exact place. God kept Moses' burial plot a secret, no doubt to prevent it from becoming a shrine. This note was obviously added by someone later with God's inspiration.

34:8 mourned . . . thirty days. This was the traditional time period for mourning. Moses had made an inestimable impact on the nation, which now had to say goodbye to its beloved leader.

34:10 never been another prophet in Israel like Moses. Moses promised that other prophets would come who spoke for God just like him (18:15). Yet Moses stood out from other prophets by his privileged relationship with God, who spoke face to face with Moses.

34:11 Moses was the supreme example of the Old Testament servant of God. The writer of Hebrews contrasts Moses with Christ, the "servant" and the "Son," in Hebrews 3:1-6.

INTRODUCTION TO

JOSHUA

PERSONAL READING PLAN

☐ Joshua 1:1–2:24
☐ Joshua 3:1–4:24
☐ Joshua 5:1–6:27
☐ Joshua 7:1–8:35
☐ Joshua 9:1–10:43
☐ Joshua 11:1–12:24
☐ Joshua 13:1–14:15
☐ Joshua 15:1–16:10
☐ Joshua 17:1–18:28
☐ Joshua 19:1–20:9
☐ Joshua 21:1–22:34
☐ Joshua 23:1–24:33

AUTHOR

The author is not identified. The book is named for its main character, Joshua, successor to Moses.

DATE

Suggested dates for Joshua range from circa 1405 to 1250 B.C.

THEME

Obedience brings long-awaited victory in the promised land.

HISTORICAL BACKGROUND

Having led the children of Israel to the entrance of the promised land, Moses is forbidden to guide them in. His servant and aide, Joshua, is chosen by God to take the people in, lead them to victory, and divide the land among them. Joshua's training has included accompanying Moses partially up Mount Sinai, being the captain of the army, and being sent as a spy into Canaan. He was one of only two spies who believed Israel could possess the land by God's enablement. The book of Joshua opens with the Israelites camped on the east side of the Jordan River. Through Joshua, the Lord commands the people to pass through the Jordan on dry ground. After recounting the series of military victories and allotments of land for the 12 tribes, the book concludes with Joshua's charge to the people before his death.

CHARACTERISTICS

This book highlights Joshua's successful leadership of Israel and God's active involvement in history. We see this most obviously in the "book of war" (chaps. 1–11), which chronicles a series of battles with victory going to the 'strong and courageous' (a theme repeated at least eight times in God's call to Joshua). When the Israelites do what God calls them to do, they defeat the enemy. When they disobey, they are unable to win.

PASSAGES FOR TOPICAL GROUP STUDY

3:14–4:24. . IMPORTANCE OF REMEMBERING . . . . . Blessings to Remember
5:13–6:21. . OBEYING GOD and WAR . . . . Mission Improbable

THE LORD'S CHARGE TO JOSHUA

1 After the death of Moses the LORD's servant, the
LORD spoke to Joshua son of Nun, Moses' assistant.
He said, 2 "Moses my servant is dead. Therefore, the
time has come for you to lead these people, the Is-
raelites, across the Jordan River into the land I am
giving them. 3 I promise you what I promised Moses:
'Wherever you set foot, you will be on land I have
given you—4 from the Negev wilderness in the south
to the Lebanon mountains in the north, from the Eu-
phrates River in the east to the Mediterranean Sea*
in the west, including all the land of the Hittites.' 5 No
one will be able to stand against you as long as you
live. For I will be with you as I was with Moses. I will
not fail you or abandon you.
6 "Be strong and courageous, for you are the one
who will lead these people to possess all the land
I swore to their ancestors I would give them. 7 Be
strong and very courageous. Be careful to obey all
the instructions Moses gave you. Do not deviate from
them, turning either to the right or to the left. Then
you will be successful in everything you do. 8 Study
this Book of Instruction continually. Meditate on it
day and night so you will be sure to obey everything
written in it. Only then will you prosper and succeed
in all you do. 9 This is my command—be strong and
courageous! Do not be afraid or discouraged. For the
LORD your God is with you wherever you go."

JOSHUA'S CHARGE TO THE ISRAELITES

10 Joshua then commanded the officers of Israel, 11 "Go
through the camp and tell the people to get their pro-
visions ready. In three days you will cross the Jordan
River and take possession of the land the LORD your
God is giving you."
12 Then Joshua called together the tribes of Reuben,
Gad, and the half-tribe of Manasseh. He told them,
13 "Remember what Moses, the servant of the LORD,
commanded you: 'The LORD your God is giving you
a place of rest. He has given you this land.' 14 Your
wives, children, and livestock may remain here in
the land Moses assigned to you on the east side of the
Jordan River. But your strong warriors, fully armed,
must lead the other tribes across the Jordan to help
them conquer their territory. Stay with them 15 until
the LORD gives them rest, as he has given you rest,
and until they, too, possess the land the LORD your God
is giving them. Only then may you return and settle
here on the east side of the Jordan River in the land
that Moses, the servant of the LORD, assigned to you."
16 They answered Joshua, "We will do whatever you
command us, and we will go wherever you send us.
17 We will obey you just as we obeyed Moses. And may
the LORD your God be with you as he was with Moses.
18 Anyone who rebels against your orders and does
not obey your words and everything you command
will be put to death. So be strong and courageous!"

RAHAB PROTECTS THE SPIES

2 Then Joshua secretly sent out two spies from the
Israelite camp at Acacia Grove.* He instructed
them, "Scout out the land on the other side of the Jor-
dan River, especially around Jericho." So the two men
set out and came to the house of a prostitute named
Rahab and stayed there that night.
2 But someone told the king of Jericho, "Some Isra-
elites have come here tonight to spy out the land."
3 So the king of Jericho sent orders to Rahab: "Bring
out the men who have come into your house, for they
have come here to spy out the whole land."
4 Rahab had hidden the two men, but she replied,
"Yes, the men were here earlier, but I didn't know
where they were from. 5 They left the town at dusk,
as the gates were about to close. I don't know where
they went. If you hurry, you can probably catch up
with them." 6 (Actually, she had taken them up to the
roof and hidden them beneath bundles of flax she had
laid out.) 7 So the king's men went looking for the spies
along the road leading to the shallow crossings of the
Jordan River. And as soon as the king's men had left,
the gate of Jericho was shut.
8 Before the spies went to sleep that night, Rahab
went up on the roof to talk with them. 9 "I know the
LORD has given you this land," she told them. "We
are all afraid of you. Everyone in the land is living
in terror. 10 For we have heard how the LORD made a
dry path for you through the Red Sea* when you left
Egypt. And we know what you did to Sihon and Og,
the two Amorite kings east of the Jordan River, whose
people you completely destroyed.* 11 No wonder our
hearts have melted in fear! No one has the courage
to fight after hearing such things. For the LORD your
God is the supreme God of the heavens above and the
earth below.
12 "Now swear to me by the LORD that you will be
kind to me and my family since I have helped you.
Give me some guarantee that 13 when Jericho is con-
quered, you will let me live, along with my father and
mother, my brothers and sisters, and all their fami-
lies."
14 "We offer our own lives as a guarantee for your
safety," the men agreed. "If you don't betray us, we
will keep our promise and be kind to you when the
LORD gives us the land."
15 Then, since Rahab's house was built into the
town wall, she let them down by a rope through the
window. 16 "Escape to the hill country," she told them.
"Hide there for three days from the men searching for
you. Then, when they have returned, you can go on
your way."
17 Before they left, the men told her, "We will be
bound by the oath we have taken only if you follow
these instructions. 18 When we come into the land, you
must leave this scarlet rope hanging from the win-
dow through which you let us down. And all your

1:4 Hebrew *the Great Sea.* **2:1** Hebrew *Shittim.* **2:10a** Hebrew *sea of reeds.* **2:10b** The Hebrew term used here refers to the complete consecration of things or people to the LORD, either by destroying them or by giving them as an offering.

1:1 Joshua . . . Moses' assistant. Joshua had served as captain of Moses' army and was one of the spies sent into the land of Canaan (Num. 14:38).

1:5 I will not fail you. God calmed Joshua's concerns about assuming leadership by assuring him of His presence.

1:10 Joshua . . . commanded. The inauguration was over. It was time for this new leader to take charge and lead his people into the land.

2:1 came to the house of a prostitute. Prostitutes in the ancient world often operated inns. The spies were seeking lodging in a public house where information about Jericho could be gathered.

2:8-12 Rahab had heard about the wonders the Lord had performed for Israel, and she apparently believed in Him. But she wanted assurance that her family would be protected when the Israelites invaded Jericho.

2:18 scarlet rope. To identify Rahab's house, the invading Israelites would look for a dyed cord dangling from her window. This would signify that her household should be spared.

family members—your father, mother, brothers, and
all your relatives—must be here inside the house. 19 If
they go out into the street and are killed, it will not be
our fault. But if anyone lays a hand on people inside
this house, we will accept the responsibility for their
death. 20 If you betray us, however, we are not bound
by this oath in any way."
21 "I accept your terms," she replied. And she sent
them on their way, leaving the scarlet rope hanging
from the window.
22 The spies went up into the hill country and stayed
there three days. The men who were chasing them
searched everywhere along the road, but they finally
returned without success.
23 Then the two spies came down from the hill coun-
try, crossed the Jordan River, and reported to Joshua
all that had happened to them. 24 "The LORD has given
us the whole land," they said, "for all the people in the
land are terrified of us."

THE ISRAELITES CROSS THE JORDAN

3 Early the next morning Joshua and all the Is-
raelites left Acacia Grove* and arrived at the
banks of the Jordan River, where they camped before
crossing. 2 Three days later the Israelite officers went
through the camp, 3 giving these instructions to the
people: "When you see the Levitical priests carrying
the Ark of the Covenant of the LORD your God, move
out from your positions and follow them. 4 Since you
have never traveled this way before, they will guide
you. Stay about half a mile* behind them, keeping a
clear distance between you and the Ark. Make sure
you don't come any closer."
5 Then Joshua told the people, "Purify yourselves,
for tomorrow the LORD will do great wonders among
you."
6 In the morning Joshua said to the priests, "Lift up
the Ark of the Covenant and lead the people across
the river." And so they started out and went ahead of
the people.
7 The LORD told Joshua, "Today I will begin to make
you a great leader in the eyes of all the Israelites.
They will know that I am with you, just as I was with
Moses. 8 Give this command to the priests who carry
the Ark of the Covenant: 'When you reach the banks
of the Jordan River, take a few steps into the river and
stop there.'"
9 So Joshua told the Israelites, "Come and listen to
what the LORD your God says. 10 Today you will know
that the living God is among you. He will surely drive
out the Canaanites, Hittites, Hivites, Perizzites, Girga-
shites, Amorites, and Jebusites ahead of you. 11 Look,
the Ark of the Covenant, which belongs to the Lord of
the whole earth, will lead you across the Jordan Riv-
er! 12 Now choose twelve men from the tribes of Israel,
one from each tribe. 13 The priests will carry the Ark
of the LORD, the Lord of all the earth. As soon as their
feet touch the water, the flow of water will be cut off
upstream, and the river will stand up like a wall."
14 So the people left their camp to cross the Jordan,
and the priests who were carrying the Ark of the Cov-
enant went ahead of them. 15 It was the harvest sea-
son, and the Jordan was overflowing its banks. But as
soon as the feet of the priests who were carrying the
Ark touched the water at the river's edge, 16 the water
above that point began backing up a great distance
away at a town called Adam, which is near Zarethan.
And the water below that point flowed on to the Dead
Sea* until the riverbed was dry. Then all the people
crossed over near the town of Jericho.
17 Meanwhile, the priests who were carrying the
Ark of the LORD's Covenant stood on dry ground in
the middle of the riverbed as the people passed by.
They waited there until the whole nation of Israel
had crossed the Jordan on dry ground.

BLESSINGS TO REMEMBER

1. What kind of souvenir do you collect to remember special times: T-shirt? Postcards? Some other kind of keepsake?

JOSHUA 3:14–4:24

2. Why did God command the people to set up a pile of stones (4:21-24)? Why was Joshua concerned about answering the children's questions?
3. Why is it important to remember God's miracles and blessings? How can remembering His blessings in your life help you in the future?
4. What is something God has done for you that's worth commemorating?

MEMORIALS TO THE JORDAN CROSSING

4 When all the people had crossed the Jordan, the
LORD said to Joshua, 2 "Now choose twelve men,
one from each tribe. 3 Tell them, 'Take twelve stones
from the very place where the priests are standing
in the middle of the Jordan. Carry them out and pile
them up at the place where you will camp tonight.'"
4 So Joshua called together the twelve men he had
chosen—one from each of the tribes of Israel. 5 He told
them, "Go into the middle of the Jordan, in front of the
Ark of the LORD your God. Each of you must pick up
one stone and carry it out on your shoulder—twelve
stones in all, one for each of the twelve tribes of Isra-
el. 6 We will use these stones to build a memorial. In
the future your children will ask you, 'What do these
stones mean?' 7 Then you can tell them, 'They remind
us that the Jordan River stopped flowing when the
Ark of the LORD's Covenant went across.' These stones
will stand as a memorial among the people of Israel
forever."

3:1 Hebrew *Shittim*. 3:4 Hebrew *about 2,000 cubits* [920 meters]. 3:16 Hebrew *the sea of the Arabah, the Salt Sea*.

3:3 Ark of the Covenant. The people stepped into the Jordan River at the first sign of the ark's appearance. The ark of the covenant represented the Lord's presence.

3:7 I am with you. God's assuring presence was as much to encourage Joshua as it was to spur the people on to battle.

3:12 choose twelve men. These men were to gather 12 large stones from the riverbed for a monument to be built on the other side of the river (4:2-3).

3:15 Jordan was overflowing its banks. God arranged for the Israelites to cross the Jordan River during the spring flood stage. The river would have been much less intimidating without the melting snow from Mt. Hermon far to the north. But less water would have required less faith.

3:17 stood on dry ground. The priests stood in the middle of the river "on dry ground" and directed the people across.

4:6 a memorial. This monument of stones taken from the Jordan River would help the Israelites remember God's faithfulness for generations to come.

8 So the men did as Joshua had commanded them. They took twelve stones from the middle of the Jordan River, one for each tribe, just as the LORD had told Joshua. They carried them to the place where they camped for the night and constructed the memorial there.

9 Joshua also set up another pile of twelve stones in the middle of the Jordan, at the place where the priests who carried the Ark of the Covenant were standing. And they are there to this day.

10 The priests who were carrying the Ark stood in the middle of the river until all of the LORD's commands that Moses had given to Joshua were carried out. Meanwhile, the people hurried across the riverbed. 11 And when everyone was safely on the other side, the priests crossed over with the Ark of the LORD as the people watched.

12 The armed warriors from the tribes of Reuben, Gad, and the half-tribe of Manasseh led the Israelites across the Jordan, just as Moses had directed. 13 These armed men—about 40,000 strong—were ready for battle, and the LORD was with them as they crossed over to the plains of Jericho.

14 That day the LORD made Joshua a great leader in the eyes of all the Israelites, and for the rest of his life they revered him as much as they had revered Moses.

15 The LORD had said to Joshua, 16 "Command the priests carrying the Ark of the Covenant* to come up out of the riverbed." 17 So Joshua gave the command. 18 As soon as the priests carrying the Ark of the LORD's Covenant came up out of the riverbed and their feet were on high ground, the water of the Jordan returned and overflowed its banks as before.

19 The people crossed the Jordan on the tenth day of the first month.* Then they camped at Gilgal, just east of Jericho. 20 It was there at Gilgal that Joshua piled up the twelve stones taken from the Jordan River.

21 Then Joshua said to the Israelites, "In the future your children will ask, 'What do these stones mean?' 22 Then you can tell them, 'This is where the Israelites crossed the Jordan on dry ground.' 23 For the LORD your God dried up the river right before your eyes, and he kept it dry until you were all across, just as he did at the Red Sea* when he dried it up until we had all crossed over. 24 He did this so all the nations of the earth might know that the LORD's hand is powerful, and so you might fear the LORD your God forever."

5 When all the Amorite kings west of the Jordan and all the Canaanite kings who lived along the Mediterranean coast* heard how the LORD had dried up the Jordan River so the people of Israel could cross, they lost heart and were paralyzed with fear because of them.

ISRAEL REESTABLISHES COVENANT CEREMONIES

2 At that time the LORD told Joshua, "Make flint knives and circumcise this second generation of Israelites.*" 3 So Joshua made flint knives and circumcised the entire male population of Israel at Gibeath-haaraloth.*

4 Joshua had to circumcise them because all the men who were old enough to fight in battle when they left Egypt had died in the wilderness. 5 Those who left Egypt had all been circumcised, but none of those born after the Exodus, during the years in the wilderness, had been circumcised. 6 The Israelites had traveled in the wilderness for forty years until all the men who were old enough to fight in battle when they left Egypt had died. For they had disobeyed the LORD, and the LORD vowed he would not let them enter the land he had sworn to give us—a land flowing with milk and honey. 7 So Joshua circumcised their sons—those who had grown up to take their fathers' places—for they had not been circumcised on the way to the Promised Land. 8 After all the males had been circumcised, they rested in the camp until they were healed.

9 Then the LORD said to Joshua, "Today I have rolled away the shame of your slavery in Egypt." So that place has been called Gilgal* to this day.

10 While the Israelites were camped at Gilgal on the plains of Jericho, they celebrated Passover on the evening of the fourteenth day of the first month.* 11 The very next day they began to eat unleavened bread and roasted grain harvested from the land. 12 No manna appeared on the day they first ate from the crops of the land, and it was never seen again. So from that time on the Israelites ate from the crops of Canaan.

THE LORD'S COMMANDER CONFRONTS JOSHUA

13 When Joshua was near the town of Jericho, he looked up and saw a man standing in front of him with sword in hand. Joshua went up to him and demanded, "Are you friend or foe?"

14 "Neither one," he replied. "I am the commander of the LORD's army."

At this, Joshua fell with his face to the ground in reverence. "I am at your command," Joshua said. "What do you want your servant to do?"

15 The commander of the LORD's army replied, "Take off your sandals, for the place where you are standing is holy." And Joshua did as he was told.

THE FALL OF JERICHO

6 Now the gates of Jericho were tightly shut because the people were afraid of the Israelites. No one was allowed to go out or in. 2 But the LORD said to Joshua, "I have given you Jericho, its king, and all its strong warriors. 3 You and your fighting men should march around the town once a day for six

4:16 Hebrew *Ark of the Testimony.* **4:19** This day in the ancient Hebrew lunar calendar occurred in late March, April, or early May. **4:23** Hebrew *sea of reeds.* **5:1** Hebrew *along the sea.* **5:2** Or *circumcise the Israelites a second time.* **5:3** *Gibeath-haaraloth* means "hill of foreskins." **5:9** *Gilgal* sounds like the Hebrew word *galal,* meaning "to roll." **5:10** This day in the ancient Hebrew lunar calendar occurred in late March, April, or early May.

4:24 all the nations of the earth. Although the miracle of the parting of Jordan's waters was specific to the Israelites at that time, God's fame would be spread throughout the world as a result.

5:6 traveled in the wilderness for forty years. The Lord waited for an entire disobedient generation to die off before bringing His people to the promised land.

5:11-12 For the first time, the Israelites would be able to enjoy the bounty of their new land. They would no longer have to eat manna, the substance that had sustained them in the wilderness.

5:13 a man standing in front. Joshua's encounter with this man was an inspiring experience for the Israelites. A supernatural army's presence, in addition to his faithful men, also bolstered Joshua's confidence.

6:1 gates of Jericho were tightly shut. News of Israel's miraculous crossing of the Jordan River apparently preceded them and terrified the inhabitants of Jericho, although they were protected by two thick walls.

6:3 should march around the town . . . once a day. Joshua's battle checklist surely never included just marching around the walls of Jericho. But he obeyed God's orders without question.

MISSION IMPROBABLE

1. What's the biggest city you've visited?

JOSHUA 5:13–6:21

2. If you were Joshua, the military commander of Israel, how would you expect to conquer a walled city? How did God choose to do it? Why?
3. Why did God forbid the Israelites to keep any of the plunder from Jericho? Why did they have to kill everyone in the city?
4. Why did God command that a prostitute should be saved, out of all the people in Jericho (6:17)?
5. How do God's commands sometimes seem odd, harsh, or demanding? Do you strive to obey, even when His commands are difficult?

days. 4 Seven priests will walk ahead of the Ark, each
carrying a ram's horn. On the seventh day you are to
march around the town seven times, with the priests
blowing the horns. 5 When you hear the priests give
one long blast on the rams' horns, have all the people
shout as loud as they can. Then the walls of the town
will collapse, and the people can charge straight into
the town."

6 So Joshua called together the priests and said,
"Take up the Ark of the LORD's Covenant, and assign
seven priests to walk in front of it, each carrying
a ram's horn." 7 Then he gave orders to the people:
"March around the town, and the armed men will
lead the way in front of the Ark of the LORD."

8 After Joshua spoke to the people, the seven priests
with the rams' horns started marching in the pres-
ence of the LORD, blowing the horns as they marched.
And the Ark of the LORD's Covenant followed behind
them. 9 Some of the armed men marched in front of
the priests with the horns and some behind the Ark,
with the priests continually blowing the horns. 10 "Do
not shout; do not even talk," Joshua commanded. "Not
a single word from any of you until I tell you to shout.
Then shout!" 11 So the Ark of the LORD was carried
around the town once that day, and then everyone
returned to spend the night in the camp.

12 Joshua got up early the next morning, and the
priests again carried the Ark of the LORD. 13 The seven
priests with the rams' horns marched in front of the
Ark of the LORD, blowing their horns. Again the armed
men marched both in front of the priests with the horns
and behind the Ark of the LORD. All this time the priests
were blowing their horns. 14 On the second day they
again marched around the town once and returned to
the camp. They followed this pattern for six days.

15 On the seventh day the Israelites got up at dawn
and marched around the town as they had done be-
fore. But this time they went around the town sev-
en times. 16 The seventh time around, as the priests
sounded the long blast on their horns, Joshua com-
manded the people, "Shout! For the LORD has given
you the town! 17 Jericho and everything in it must be
completely destroyed* as an offering to the LORD.
Only Rahab the prostitute and the others in her house
will be spared, for she protected our spies.

18 "Do not take any of the things set apart for de-
struction, or you yourselves will be completely de-
stroyed, and you will bring trouble on the camp of
Israel. 19 Everything made from silver, gold, bronze, or
iron is sacred to the LORD and must be brought into
his treasury."

20 When the people heard the sound of the rams'
horns, they shouted as loud as they could. Sudden-
ly, the walls of Jericho collapsed, and the Israelites
charged straight into the town and captured it.
21 They completely destroyed everything in it with
their swords—men and women, young and old, cat-
tle, sheep, goats, and donkeys.

22 Meanwhile, Joshua said to the two spies, "Keep
your promise. Go to the prostitute's house and bring
her out, along with all her family."

23 The men who had been spies went in and brought
out Rahab, her father, mother, brothers, and all the
other relatives who were with her. They moved her
whole family to a safe place near the camp of Israel.

24 Then the Israelites burned the town and every-
thing in it. Only the things made from silver, gold,
bronze, or iron were kept for the treasury of the
LORD's house. 25 So Joshua spared Rahab the pros-
titute and her relatives who were with her in the
house, because she had hidden the spies Joshua sent
to Jericho. And she lives among the Israelites to this
day.

26 At that time Joshua invoked this curse:

"May the curse of the LORD fall on anyone
  who tries to rebuild the town of Jericho.
At the cost of his firstborn son,
  he will lay its foundation.
At the cost of his youngest son,
  he will set up its gates."

27 So the LORD was with Joshua, and his reputation
spread throughout the land.

AI DEFEATS THE ISRAELITES

7 But Israel violated the instructions about the
things set apart for the LORD.* A man named
Achan had stolen some of these dedicated things, so
the LORD was very angry with the Israelites. Achan
was the son of Carmi, a descendant of Zimri* son of
Zerah, of the tribe of Judah.

6:17 The Hebrew term used here refers to the complete consecration of things or people to the LORD, either by destroying them or by giving them as an offering; similarly in 6:18, 21. **7:1a** The Hebrew term used here refers to the complete consecration of things or people to the LORD, either by destroying them or by giving them as an offering; similarly in 7:11, 12, 13, 15. **7:1b** As in parallel text at 1 Chr 2:6; Hebrew reads *Zabdi.* Also in 7:17, 18.

6:4 ram's horn. Priests used these "jubilee trumpets" in religious ceremonies to announce the presence of the Lord.

6:5 shout as loud as they can. The confused inhabitants inside Jericho would be stunned by the voices of thousands of warriors.

6:17 must be completely destroyed as an offering to the LORD. Literally "set apart for destruction." For a city to be "set apart" under God's judgment meant that it was to be totally destroyed.

6:25 Rahab . . . lives among the Israelites to this day. Rahab's family was saved due to her fateful encounter with the Israelite spies when they visited Jericho.

6:26 rebuild the town. As a conquered city belonging to God, Jericho would never again be restored to its former glory.

2 Joshua sent some of his men from Jericho to spy out the town of Ai, east of Bethel, near Beth-aven. 3 When they returned, they told Joshua, "There's no need for all of us to go up there; it won't take more than two or three thousand men to attack Ai. Since there are so few of them, don't make all our people struggle to go up there."

4 So approximately 3,000 warriors were sent, but they were soundly defeated. The men of Ai 5 chased the Israelites from the town gate as far as the quarries,* and they killed about thirty-six who were retreating down the slope. The Israelites were paralyzed with fear at this turn of events, and their courage melted away.

6 Joshua and the elders of Israel tore their clothing in dismay, threw dust on their heads, and bowed face down to the ground before the Ark of the LORD until evening. 7 Then Joshua cried out, "Oh, Sovereign LORD, why did you bring us across the Jordan River if you are going to let the Amorites kill us? If only we had been content to stay on the other side! 8 Lord, what can I say now that Israel has fled from its enemies? 9 For when the Canaanites and all the other people living in the land hear about it, they will surround us and wipe our name off the face of the earth. And then what will happen to the honor of your great name?"

10 But the LORD said to Joshua, "Get up! Why are you lying on your face like this? 11 Israel has sinned and broken my covenant! They have stolen some of the things that I commanded must be set apart for me. And they have not only stolen them but have lied about it and hidden the things among their own belongings. 12 That is why the Israelites are running from their enemies in defeat. For now Israel itself has been set apart for destruction. I will not remain with you any longer unless you destroy the things among you that were set apart for destruction.

13 "Get up! Command the people to purify themselves in preparation for tomorrow. For this is what the LORD, the God of Israel, says: Hidden among you, O Israel, are things set apart for the LORD. You will never defeat your enemies until you remove these things from among you.

14 "In the morning you must present yourselves by tribes, and the LORD will point out the tribe to which the guilty man belongs. That tribe must come forward with its clans, and the LORD will point out the guilty clan. That clan will then come forward, and the LORD will point out the guilty family. Finally, each member of the guilty family must come forward one by one. 15 The one who has stolen what was set apart for destruction will himself be burned with fire, along with everything he has, for he has broken the covenant of the LORD and has done a horrible thing in Israel."

ACHAN'S SIN

16 Early the next morning Joshua brought the tribes of Israel before the LORD, and the tribe of Judah was singled out. 17 Then the clans of Judah came forward, and the clan of Zerah was singled out. Then the families of Zerah came forward, and the family of Zimri was singled out. 18 Every member of Zimri's family was brought forward person by person, and Achan was singled out.

19 Then Joshua said to Achan, "My son, give glory to the LORD, the God of Israel, by telling the truth. Make your confession and tell me what you have done. Don't hide it from me."

20 Achan replied, "It is true! I have sinned against the LORD, the God of Israel. 21 Among the plunder I saw a beautiful robe from Babylon,* 200 silver coins,* and a bar of gold weighing more than a pound.* I wanted them so much that I took them. They are hidden in the ground beneath my tent, with the silver buried deeper than the rest."

22 So Joshua sent some men to make a search. They ran to the tent and found the stolen goods hidden there, just as Achan had said, with the silver buried beneath the rest. 23 They took the things from the tent and brought them to Joshua and all the Israelites. Then they laid them on the ground in the presence of the LORD.

24 Then Joshua and all the Israelites took Achan, the silver, the robe, the bar of gold, his sons, daughters, cattle, donkeys, sheep, goats, tent, and everything he had, and they brought them to the valley of Achor. 25 Then Joshua said to Achan, "Why have you brought trouble on us? The LORD will now bring trouble on you." And all the Israelites stoned Achan and his family and burned their bodies. 26 They piled a great heap of stones over Achan, which remains to this day. That is why the place has been called the Valley of Trouble* ever since. So the LORD was no longer angry.

THE ISRAELITES DEFEAT AI

8 Then the LORD said to Joshua, "Do not be afraid or discouraged. Take all your fighting men and attack Ai, for I have given you the king of Ai, his people, his town, and his land. 2 You will destroy them as you destroyed Jericho and its king. But this time you may keep the plunder and the livestock for yourselves. Set an ambush behind the town."

3 So Joshua and all the fighting men set out to attack Ai. Joshua chose 30,000 of his best warriors and sent them out at night 4 with these orders: "Hide in ambush close behind the town and be ready for action. 5 When our main army attacks, the men of Ai will come out to fight as they did before, and we will run away from them. 6 We will let them chase us until we have drawn them away from the town. For they will say,

7:5 Or *as far as Shebarim.* **7:21a** Hebrew *Shinar.* **7:21b** Hebrew *200 shekels of silver,* about 5 pounds or 2.3 kilograms in weight. **7:21c** Hebrew *50 shekels,* about 20 ounces or 570 grams in weight. **7:26** Hebrew *valley of Achor.*

7:6 tore their clothing . . . bowed face down. After their easy victory over Jericho, Israel suffered a humiliating defeat by the defenders of the city of Ai.

7:11 some of the things . . . must be set apart. All living things in Jericho were to be destroyed and burned. Anything of value was supposed to be brought into the Lord's treasury.

7:13 You will never defeat your enemies. Israel's potential for victory was based on obedience. A perfectly obedient army of ten could defeat thousands of the enemy. But one disobedient Israelite would bring defeat by even the weakest nation.

7:21 200 silver coins . . . gold weighing more than a pound. Achan kept for himself about five pounds of silver and one pound of gold from the spoils of war taken in the battle against Jericho.

7:25 burned their bodies. Because of his disobedience of the Lord's command, Achan was stoned to death and then his body was burned. This was supposed to be the destiny of every living thing in Jericho (6:18-19,24).

7:26 the LORD was no longer angry. Once the sin was removed from their midst, the Lord again walked with the Israelites.

8:1 Joshua, "Do not be afraid." God addressed Joshua's fears about returning to a city where Israel had suffered defeat. He promised to direct them in the battle.

'The Israelites are running away from us as they did
before.' Then, while we are running from them, 7 you
will jump up from your ambush and take possession
of the town, for the LORD your God will give it to you.
8 Set the town on fire, as the LORD has commanded.
You have your orders."

9 So they left and went to the place of ambush be-
tween Bethel and the west side of Ai. But Joshua
remained among the people in the camp that night.
10 Early the next morning Joshua roused his men and
started toward Ai, accompanied by the elders of Is-
rael. 11 All the fighting men who were with Joshua
marched in front of the town and camped on the
north side of Ai, with a valley between them and the
town. 12 That night Joshua sent about 5,000 men to lie
in ambush between Bethel and Ai, on the west side
of the town. 13 So they stationed the main army north
of the town and the ambush west of the town. Joshua
himself spent that night in the valley.

14 When the king of Ai saw the Israelites across the
valley, he and all his army hurried out early in the
morning and attacked the Israelites at a place over-
looking the Jordan Valley.* But he didn't realize there
was an ambush behind the town. 15 Joshua and the
Israelite army fled toward the wilderness as though
they were badly beaten. 16 Then all the men in the
town were called out to chase after them. In this way,
they were lured away from the town. 17 There was not
a man left in Ai or Bethel* who did not chase after the
Israelites, and the town was left wide open.

18 Then the LORD said to Joshua, "Point the spear in
your hand toward Ai, for I will hand the town over
to you." Joshua did as he was commanded. 19 As soon
as Joshua gave this signal, all the men in ambush
jumped up from their position and poured into the
town. They quickly captured it and set it on fire.

20 When the men of Ai looked behind them, smoke
from the town was filling the sky, and they had no-
where to go. For the Israelites who had fled in the
direction of the wilderness now turned on their pur-
suers. 21 When Joshua and all the other Israelites saw
that the ambush had succeeded and that smoke was
rising from the town, they turned and attacked the
men of Ai. 22 Meanwhile, the Israelites who were in-
side the town came out and attacked the enemy from
the rear. So the men of Ai were caught in the middle,
with Israelite fighters on both sides. Israel attacked
them, and not a single person survived or escaped.
23 Only the king of Ai was taken alive and brought to
Joshua.

24 When the Israelite army finished chasing and
killing all the men of Ai in the open fields, they went
back and finished off everyone inside. 25 So the entire
population of Ai, including men and women, was
wiped out that day—12,000 in all. 26 For Joshua kept
holding out his spear until everyone who had lived
in Ai was completely destroyed.* 27 Only the livestock
and the treasures of the town were not destroyed, for
the Israelites kept these as plunder for themselves, as
the LORD had commanded Joshua. 28 So Joshua burned
the town of Ai,* and it became a permanent mound of
ruins, desolate to this very day.

29 Joshua impaled the king of Ai on a sharpened
pole and left him there until evening. At sunset the
Israelites took down the body, as Joshua commanded,
and threw it in front of the town gate. They piled a
great heap of stones over him that can still be seen
today.

THE LORD'S COVENANT RENEWED

30 Then Joshua built an altar to the LORD, the God of
Israel, on Mount Ebal. 31 He followed the commands
that Moses the LORD's servant had written in the Book
of Instruction: "Make me an altar from stones that are
uncut and have not been shaped with iron tools."*
Then on the altar they presented burnt offerings and
peace offerings to the LORD. 32 And as the Israelites
watched, Joshua copied onto the stones of the altar*
the instructions Moses had given them.

33 Then all the Israelites—foreigners and na-
tive-born alike—along with the elders, officers, and
judges, were divided into two groups. One group
stood in front of Mount Gerizim, the other in front of
Mount Ebal. Each group faced the other, and between
them stood the Levitical priests carrying the Ark of
the LORD's Covenant. This was all done according to
the commands that Moses, the servant of the LORD,
had previously given for blessing the people of Israel.

34 Joshua then read to them all the blessings and
curses Moses had written in the Book of Instruction.
35 Every word of every command that Moses had ever
given was read to the entire assembly of Israel, in-
cluding the women and children and the foreigners
who lived among them.

THE GIBEONITES DECEIVE ISRAEL

9 Now all the kings west of the Jordan River heard
about what had happened. These were the kings
of the Hittites, Amorites, Canaanites, Perizzites, Hi-
vites, and Jebusites, who lived in the hill country, in
the western foothills,* and along the coast of the Med-
iterranean Sea* as far north as the Lebanon moun-
tains. 2 These kings combined their armies to fight as
one against Joshua and the Israelites.

3 But when the people of Gibeon heard what Josh-
ua had done to Jericho and Ai, 4 they resorted to de-
ception to save themselves. They sent ambassadors
to Joshua, loading their donkeys with weathered
saddlebags and old, patched wineskins. 5 They put on
worn-out, patched sandals and ragged clothes. And

8:14 Hebrew *the Arabah.* **8:17** Some manuscripts lack *or Bethel.* **8:26** The Hebrew term used here refers to the complete consecration of things or people to the LORD, either by destroying them or by giving them as an offering. **8:28** *Ai* means "ruin." **8:31** Exod 20:25; Deut 27:5-6. **8:32** Hebrew *onto the stones.* **9:1a** Hebrew *the Shephelah.* **9:1b** Hebrew *the Great Sea.*

8:13 stationed the main army. Israel's strategy was to exploit Ai's over-confidence. Joshua planned to lure the fighting men away from the city and then ambush them.

8:26 everyone . . . was completely destroyed. It was important that the army of Israel become known for total victory in its initial battles for control of the land of Canaan.

8:30-31 Joshua led the people to Mount Ebal for a spiritual event. Moses had spelled out the location and details of this covenant renewal ceremony before he died on the other side of the Jordan River (Deut. 27–28).

8:33 one group . . . in front of Mount Gerizim, the other in front of Mount Ebal. The two congregations of Israel faced each other across the valley between these two mountains. The Gerizim tribes called out "Amen" when the Levites read the blessings that would accompany covenant obedience (vv. 14-26). The Ebal tribes called out "Amen" when the curses that would accompany covenant disobedience were read.

9:3-6 Not willing to risk defeat by the Israelites, the leaders of the city of Gibeon lied to Joshua and succeeded in making a deal that assured them of Israel's protection.

the bread they took with them was dry and moldy.
6 When they arrived at the camp of Israel at Gilgal,
they told Joshua and the men of Israel, "We have come
from a distant land to ask you to make a peace treaty
with us."
7 The Israelites replied to these Hivites, "How do we
know you don't live nearby? For if you do, we cannot
make a treaty with you."
8 They replied, "We are your servants."
"But who are you?" Joshua demanded. "Where do
you come from?"
9 They answered, "Your servants have come from a
very distant country. We have heard of the might of the
LORD your God and of all he did in Egypt. 10 We have also
heard what he did to the two Amorite kings east of the
Jordan River—King Sihon of Heshbon and King Og of
Bashan (who lived in Ashtaroth). 11 So our elders and all
our people instructed us, 'Take supplies for a long jour-
ney. Go meet with the people of Israel and tell them, "We
are your servants; please make a treaty with us."'
12 "This bread was hot from the ovens when we left
our homes. But now, as you can see, it is dry and moldy.
13 These wineskins were new when we filled them, but
now they are old and split open. And our clothing and
sandals are worn out from our very long journey."
14 So the Israelites examined their food, but they
did not consult the LORD. 15 Then Joshua made a peace
treaty with them and guaranteed their safety, and the
leaders of the community ratified their agreement
with a binding oath.
16 Three days after making the treaty, they learned
that these people actually lived nearby! 17 The Isra-
elites set out at once to investigate and reached their
towns in three days. The names of these towns were
Gibeon, Kephirah, Beeroth, and Kiriath-jearim. 18 But
the Israelites did not attack the towns, for the Israelite
leaders had made a vow to them in the name of the
LORD, the God of Israel.
The people of Israel grumbled against their lead-
ers because of the treaty. 19 But the leaders replied,
"Since we have sworn an oath in the presence of the
LORD, the God of Israel, we cannot touch them. 20 This
is what we must do. We must let them live, for divine
anger would come upon us if we broke our oath. 21 Let
them live." So they made them woodcutters and wa-
ter carriers for the entire community, as the Israelite
leaders directed.
22 Joshua called together the Gibeonites and said,
"Why did you lie to us? Why did you say that you live
in a distant land when you live right here among us?
23 May you be cursed! From now on you will always be
servants who cut wood and carry water for the house
of my God."
24 They replied, "We did it because we—your ser-
vants—were clearly told that the LORD your God
commanded his servant Moses to give you this entire
land and to destroy all the people living in it. So we
feared greatly for our lives because of you. That is
why we have done this. 25 Now we are at your mer-
cy—do to us whatever you think is right."
26 So Joshua did not allow the people of Israel to
kill them. 27 But that day he made the Gibeonites the
woodcutters and water carriers for the community
of Israel and for the altar of the LORD—wherever the
LORD would choose to build it. And that is what they
do to this day.

ISRAEL DEFEATS THE SOUTHERN ARMIES

10 Adoni-zedek, king of Jerusalem, heard that
Joshua had captured and completely de-
stroyed* Ai and killed its king, just as he had de-
stroyed the town of Jericho and killed its king. He
also learned that the Gibeonites had made peace
with Israel and were now their allies. 2 He and his
people became very afraid when they heard all this
because Gibeon was a large town—as large as the
royal cities and larger than Ai. And the Gibeonite
men were strong warriors.
3 So King Adoni-zedek of Jerusalem sent messen-
gers to several other kings: Hoham of Hebron, Piram
of Jarmuth, Japhia of Lachish, and Debir of Eglon.
4 "Come and help me destroy Gibeon," he urged them,
"for they have made peace with Joshua and the peo-
ple of Israel." 5 So these five Amorite kings combined
their armies for a united attack. They moved all their
troops into place and attacked Gibeon.
6 The men of Gibeon quickly sent messengers to
Joshua at his camp in Gilgal. "Don't abandon your
servants now!" they pleaded. "Come at once! Save us!
Help us! For all the Amorite kings who live in the hill
country have joined forces to attack us."
7 So Joshua and his entire army, including his best
warriors, left Gilgal and set out for Gibeon. 8 "Do not
be afraid of them," the LORD said to Joshua, "for I have
given you victory over them. Not a single one of them
will be able to stand up to you."
9 Joshua traveled all night from Gilgal and took
the Amorite armies by surprise. 10 The LORD threw
them into a panic, and the Israelites slaughtered
great numbers of them at Gibeon. Then the Israelites
chased the enemy along the road to Beth-horon, kill-
ing them all along the way to Azekah and Makkedah.
11 As the Amorites retreated down the road from Beth-
horon, the LORD destroyed them with a terrible hail-
storm from heaven that continued until they reached
Azekah. The hail killed more of the enemy than the
Israelites killed with the sword.
12 On the day the LORD gave the Israelites victory
over the Amorites, Joshua prayed to the LORD in front
of all the people of Israel. He said,

"Let the sun stand still over Gibeon,
and the moon over the valley of Aijalon."

13 So the sun stood still and the moon stayed in place
until the nation of Israel had defeated its enemies.
Is this event not recorded in *The Book of Jashar**?
The sun stayed in the middle of the sky, and it did not
set as on a normal day.* 14 There has never been a day
like this one before or since, when the LORD answered

10:1 The Hebrew term used here refers to the complete consecration of things or people to the LORD, either by destroying them or by giving them as an offering; also in 10:28, 35, 37, 39, 40. **10:13a** Or *The Book of the Upright.* **10:13b** Or *did not set for about a whole day.*

9:14 the Israelites . . . did not consult the LORD. The officers who inspected the claims of the Gibeonites did not seek God's direction in this matter.

9:18 people of Israel grumbled against their leaders. It was too late for complaining. A vow had been made. The honorable thing for Israel to do was uphold their agreement with the Gibeonites.

10:2-19 Several Canaanite kings formed a coalition and challenged Israel to a contest for control of the city of Gibeon. God fought for His people, and the Canaanite kings were defeated.

such a prayer. Surely the LORD fought for Israel that
day!
15 Then Joshua and the Israelite army returned to
their camp at Gilgal.

JOSHUA KILLS THE FIVE SOUTHERN KINGS

16 During the battle the five kings escaped and hid in
a cave at Makkedah. 17 When Joshua heard that they
had been found, 18 he issued this command: "Cover
the opening of the cave with large rocks, and place
guards at the entrance to keep the kings inside. 19 The
rest of you continue chasing the enemy and cut them
down from the rear. Don't give them a chance to get
back to their towns, for the LORD your God has given
you victory over them."
20 So Joshua and the Israelite army continued the
slaughter and completely crushed the enemy. They
totally wiped out the five armies except for a tiny
remnant that managed to reach their fortified towns.
21 Then the Israelites returned safely to Joshua in the
camp at Makkedah. After that, no one dared to speak
even a word against Israel.
22 Then Joshua said, "Remove the rocks covering the
opening of the cave, and bring the five kings to me."
23 So they brought the five kings out of the cave—the
kings of Jerusalem, Hebron, Jarmuth, Lachish, and Eg-
lon. 24 When they brought them out, Joshua told the
commanders of his army, "Come and put your feet on
the kings' necks." And they did as they were told.
25 "Don't ever be afraid or discouraged," Joshua told
his men. "Be strong and courageous, for the LORD is
going to do this to all of your enemies." 26 Then Joshua
killed each of the five kings and impaled them on five
sharpened poles, where they hung until evening.
27 As the sun was going down, Joshua gave instruc-
tions for the bodies of the kings to be taken down from
the poles and thrown into the cave where they had
been hiding. Then they covered the opening of the
cave with a pile of large rocks, which remains to this
very day.

ISRAEL DESTROYS THE SOUTHERN TOWNS

28 That same day Joshua captured and destroyed the
town of Makkedah. He killed everyone in it, including
the king, leaving no survivors. He destroyed them all,
and he killed the king of Makkedah as he had killed
the king of Jericho. 29 Then Joshua and the Israelites
went to Libnah and attacked it. 30 There, too, the LORD
gave them the town and its king. He killed everyone
in it, leaving no survivors. Then Joshua killed the king
of Libnah as he had killed the king of Jericho.
31 From Libnah, Joshua and the Israelites went to
Lachish and attacked it. 32 Here again, the LORD gave
them Lachish. Joshua took it on the second day and
killed everyone in it, just as he had done at Libnah.
33 During the attack on Lachish, King Horam of Gezer
arrived with his army to help defend the town. But
Joshua's men killed him and his army, leaving no sur-
vivors.
34 Then Joshua and the Israelite army went on to
Eglon and attacked it. 35 They captured it that day
and killed everyone in it. He completely destroyed
everyone, just as he had done at Lachish. 36 From Eg-
lon, Joshua and the Israelite army went up to Hebron
and attacked it. 37 They captured the town and killed
everyone in it, including its king, leaving no survi-
vors. They did the same thing to all of its surrounding
villages. And just as he had done at Eglon, he com-
pletely destroyed the entire population.
38 Then Joshua and the Israelites turned back and
attacked Debir. 39 He captured the town, its king, and
all of its surrounding villages. He completely de-
stroyed everyone in it, leaving no survivors. He did to
Debir and its king just what he had done to Hebron
and to Libnah and its king.
40 So Joshua conquered the whole region—the
kings and people of the hill country, the Negev, the
western foothills,* and the mountain slopes. He com-
pletely destroyed everyone in the land, leaving no
survivors, just as the LORD, the God of Israel, had com-
manded. 41 Joshua slaughtered them from Kadesh-
barnea to Gaza and from the region around the town
of Goshen up to Gibeon. 42 Joshua conquered all these
kings and their land in a single campaign, for the
LORD, the God of Israel, was fighting for his people.
43 Then Joshua and the Israelite army returned to
their camp at Gilgal.

ISRAEL DEFEATS THE NORTHERN ARMIES

11 When King Jabin of Hazor heard what had hap-
pened, he sent messages to the following kings:
King Jobab of Madon; the king of Shimron; the king
of Acshaph; 2 all the kings of the northern hill coun-
try; the kings in the Jordan Valley south of Galilee*;
the kings in the Galilean foothills*; the kings of Na-
photh-dor on the west; 3 the kings of Canaan, both
east and west; the kings of the Amorites, the Hittites,
the Perizzites, the Jebusites in the hill country, and the
Hivites in the towns on the slopes of Mount Hermon
in the land of Mizpah.
4 All these kings came out to fight. Their combined
armies formed a vast horde. And with all their horses
and chariots, they covered the landscape like the sand
on the seashore. 5 The kings joined forces and estab-
lished their camp around the water near Merom to
fight against Israel.
6 Then the LORD said to Joshua, "Do not be afraid of
them. By this time tomorrow I will hand all of them
over to Israel as dead men. Then you must cripple
their horses and burn their chariots."
7 So Joshua and all his fighting men traveled to the
water near Merom and attacked suddenly. 8 And the
LORD gave them victory over their enemies. The Isra-
elites chased them as far as Greater Sidon and Misre-

10:40 Hebrew *the Shephelah.* **11:2a** Hebrew *in the Arabah south of Kinnereth.* **11:2b** Hebrew *the Shephelah;* also in 11:16.

10:21 Israelites returned . . . no one dared to speak. If one Canaanite city grumbled against Israel often enough, other cities would soon become hostile against them. Silencing its foes quickly proved to be a powerful tactic used by Joshua.

10:28 Joshua . . . destroyed . . . everyone in it. Israel's destruction of its enemies portrayed God's intolerance for sin. When God destroyed sin, He also protected His people from idolatry and impurity.

10:41 Kadesh-barnea to Gaza. From Ai in the central highlands to the Negev desert, the Israelites' string of victories secured the southern half of the promised land.

11:1 King Jabin of Hazor. A brilliant military strategist, this king convinced several nearby cities to amass their troops for one major offensive against the Israelites.

11:6 By this time tomorrow. Considering the size of the combined armies and their mounted chariots, this 24-hour promise seemed almost too good to be true. **horses . . . chariots.** God wanted Israel to rely on Him rather than the "high-powered" weapons of that day (Deut. 17:16; Isa. 31:1).

photh-maim, and eastward into the valley of Mizpah,
until not one enemy warrior was left alive. 9 Then
Joshua crippled the horses and burned all the char-
iots, as the LORD had instructed.
10 Joshua then turned back and captured Hazor and
killed its king. (Hazor had at one time been the capi-
tal of all these kingdoms.) 11 The Israelites completely
destroyed* every living thing in the city, leaving no
survivors. Not a single person was spared. And then
Joshua burned the city.
12 Joshua slaughtered all the other kings and their
people, completely destroying them, just as Moses, the
servant of the LORD, had commanded. 13 But the Isra-
elites did not burn any of the towns built on mounds
except Hazor, which Joshua burned. 14 And the Isra-
elites took all the plunder and livestock of the ravaged
towns for themselves. But they killed all the people,
leaving no survivors. 15 As the LORD had commanded
his servant Moses, so Moses commanded Joshua. And
Joshua did as he was told, carefully obeying all the
commands that the LORD had given to Moses.
16 So Joshua conquered the entire region—the hill
country, the entire Negev, the whole area around the
town of Goshen, the western foothills, the Jordan Valley,*
the mountains of Israel, and the Galilean foothills. 17 The
Israelite territory now extended all the way from Mount
Halak, which leads up to Seir in the south, as far north as
Baal-gad at the foot of Mount Hermon in the valley of
Lebanon. Joshua killed all the kings of those territories,
18 waging war for a long time to accomplish this. 19 No
one in this region made peace with the Israelites except
the Hivites of Gibeon. All the others were defeated. 20 For
the LORD hardened their hearts and caused them to fight
the Israelites. So they were completely destroyed with-
out mercy, as the LORD had commanded Moses.
21 During this period Joshua destroyed all the de-
scendants of Anak, who lived in the hill country of
Hebron, Debir, Anab, and the entire hill country of
Judah and Israel. He killed them all and completely
destroyed their towns. 22 None of the descendants of
Anak were left in all the land of Israel, though some
still remained in Gaza, Gath, and Ashdod.
23 So Joshua took control of the entire land, just as
the LORD had instructed Moses. He gave it to the people
of Israel as their special possession, dividing the land
among the tribes. So the land finally had rest from war.

KINGS DEFEATED EAST OF THE JORDAN

12 These are the kings east of the Jordan River who
had been killed by the Israelites and whose land
was taken. Their territory extended from the Arnon
Gorge to Mount Hermon and included all the land
east of the Jordan Valley.*
2 King Sihon of the Amorites, who lived in Hesh-
bon, was defeated. His kingdom included Aroer, on
the edge of the Arnon Gorge, and extended from the
middle of the Arnon Gorge to the Jabbok River, which
serves as a border for the Ammonites. This territory
included the southern half of the territory of Gilead.
3 Sihon also controlled the Jordan Valley and regions
to the east—from as far north as the Sea of Galilee to
as far south as the Dead Sea,* including the road to
Beth-jeshimoth and southward to the slopes of Pisgah.
4 King Og of Bashan, the last of the Rephaites, lived
at Ashtaroth and Edrei. 5 He ruled a territory stretch-
ing from Mount Hermon to Salecah in the north and
to all of Bashan in the east, and westward to the bor-
ders of the kingdoms of Geshur and Maacah. This ter-
ritory included the northern half of Gilead, as far as
the boundary of King Sihon of Heshbon.
6 Moses, the servant of the LORD, and the Israelites
had destroyed the people of King Sihon and King
Og. And Moses gave their land as a possession to the
tribes of Reuben, Gad, and the half-tribe of Manasseh.

KINGS DEFEATED WEST OF THE JORDAN

7 The following is a list of the kings that Joshua and the
Israelite armies defeated on the west side of the Jordan,
from Baal-gad in the valley of Lebanon to Mount Hal-
ak, which leads up to Seir. (Joshua gave this land to the
tribes of Israel as their possession, 8 including the hill
country, the western foothills,* the Jordan Valley, the
mountain slopes, the Judean wilderness, and the Negev.
The people who lived in this region were the Hittites,
the Amorites, the Canaanites, the Perizzites, the Hivites,
and the Jebusites.) These are the kings Israel defeated:

9 The king of Jericho
The king of Ai, near Bethel
10 The king of Jerusalem
The king of Hebron
11 The king of Jarmuth
The king of Lachish
12 The king of Eglon
The king of Gezer
13 The king of Debir
The king of Geder
14 The king of Hormah
The king of Arad
15 The king of Libnah
The king of Adullam
16 The king of Makkedah
The king of Bethel
17 The king of Tappuah
The king of Hepher
18 The king of Aphek
The king of Lasharon
19 The king of Madon
The king of Hazor
20 The king of Shimron-meron
The king of Acshaph
21 The king of Taanach
The king of Megiddo
22 The king of Kedesh

11:11 The Hebrew term used here refers to the complete consecration of things or people to the LORD, either by destroying them or by giving them as an offering; also in 11:12, 20, 21. **11:16** Hebrew *the Shephelah, the Arabah.* **12:1** Hebrew *the Arabah;* also in 12:3, 8. **12:3** Hebrew *from the Sea of Kinnereth to the Sea of the Arabah, which is the Salt Sea.* **12:8** Hebrew *the Shephelah.*

11:10 Hazor. A large, powerful city that controlled the caravan route from Damascus to the coast of the Mediterranean Sea and on to Egypt.

11:12 just as Moses, the servant of the LORD, had commanded. Joshua destroyed the Canaanite cities and their population to purify the land of pagan idolatry and moral and spiritual pollution (Deut. 7:1-6).

11:18 waging war for a long time. Although he was outnumbered and in unfamiliar territory, Joshua did not give up. He stayed at the task he had been assigned by the Lord.

11:20 harden their hearts. God confirmed that the Canaanites stubbornly resisted His grace. But Rahab showed His willingness to give these pagan people the opportunity to repent (6:25).

12:12 king of Gezer. Although Joshua defeated many Canaanite kings, the record does not necessarily mean their cities were captured as well. The king of Gezer is one example (10:33). With his limited army, Joshua was not able to station troops at all the cities of the Canaanites.

The king of Jokneam in Carmel
23 The king of Dor in the town of Naphoth-dor*
The king of Goyim in Gilgal*
24 The king of Tirzah.

In all, thirty-one kings were defeated.

THE LAND YET TO BE CONQUERED

13 When Joshua was an old man, the LORD said
to him, "You are growing old, and much land
remains to be conquered. 2 This is the territory that
remains: all the regions of the Philistines and the
Geshurites, 3 and the larger territory of the Ca-
naanites, extending from the stream of Shihor on
the border of Egypt, northward to the boundary of
Ekron. It includes the territory of the five Philistine
rulers of Gaza, Ashdod, Ashkelon, Gath, and Ekron.
The land of the Avvites 4 in the south also remains
to be conquered. In the north, the following area
has not yet been conquered: all the land of the Ca-
naanites, including Mearah (which belongs to the
Sidonians), stretching northward to Aphek on the
border of the Amorites; 5 the land of the Gebalites
and all of the Lebanon mountain area to the east,
from Baal-gad below Mount Hermon to Lebo-ha-
math; 6 and all the hill country from Lebanon to
Misrephoth-maim, including all the land of the Si-
donians.

"I myself will drive these people out of the land
ahead of the Israelites. So be sure to give this land to
Israel as a special possession, just as I have command-
ed you. 7 Include all this territory as Israel's posses-
sion when you divide this land among the nine tribes
and the half-tribe of Manasseh."

THE LAND DIVIDED EAST OF THE JORDAN

8 Half the tribe of Manasseh and the tribes of Reuben
and Gad had already received their grants of land on
the east side of the Jordan, for Moses, the servant of
the LORD, had previously assigned this land to them.

9 Their territory extended from Aroer on the edge
of the Arnon Gorge (including the town in the
middle of the gorge) to the plain beyond Medeba,
as far as Dibon. 10 It also included all the towns of
King Sihon of the Amorites, who had reigned in
Heshbon, and extended as far as the borders of
Ammon. 11 It included Gilead, the territory of the
kingdoms of Geshur and Maacah, all of Mount
Hermon, all of Bashan as far as Salecah, 12 and
all the territory of King Og of Bashan, who had
reigned in Ashtaroth and Edrei. King Og was the
last of the Rephaites, for Moses had attacked them
and driven them out. 13 But the Israelites failed to
drive out the people of Geshur and Maacah, so
they continue to live among the Israelites to this
day.

AN ALLOTMENT FOR THE TRIBE OF LEVI

14 Moses did not assign any allotment of land to the
tribe of Levi. Instead, as the LORD had promised them,
their allotment came from the offerings burned on
the altar to the LORD, the God of Israel.

THE LAND GIVEN TO THE TRIBE OF REUBEN

15 Moses had assigned the following area to the clans
of the tribe of Reuben.

16 Their territory extended from Aroer on the edge
of the Arnon Gorge (including the town in the
middle of the gorge) to the plain beyond Medeba.
17 It included Heshbon and the other towns on the
plain—Dibon, Bamoth-baal, Beth-baal-meon, 18 Ja-
haz, Kedemoth, Mephaath, 19 Kiriathaim, Sibmah,
Zereth-shahar on the hill above the valley, 20 Beth-
peor, the slopes of Pisgah, and Beth-jeshimoth.
21 The land of Reuben also included all the towns
of the plain and the entire kingdom of Sihon.
Sihon was the Amorite king who had reigned
in Heshbon and was killed by Moses along with
the leaders of Midian—Evi, Rekem, Zur, Hur, and
Reba—princes living in the region who were
allied with Sihon. 22 The Israelites had also killed
Balaam son of Beor, who used magic to tell the
future. 23 The Jordan River marked the western
boundary for the tribe of Reuben. The towns and
their surrounding villages in this area were given
as a homeland to the clans of the tribe of Reuben.

THE LAND GIVEN TO THE TRIBE OF GAD

24 Moses had assigned the following area to the clans
of the tribe of Gad.

25 Their territory included Jazer, all the towns
of Gilead, and half of the land of Ammon, as far
as the town of Aroer just west of* Rabbah. 26 It
extended from Heshbon to Ramath-mizpeh and
Betonim, and from Mahanaim to the territory
of Lo-debar.* 27 In the valley were Beth-haram,
Beth-nimrah, Succoth, Zaphon, and the rest of the
kingdom of King Sihon of Heshbon. The western
boundary ran along the Jordan River, extended as
far north as the tip of the Sea of Galilee,* and then
turned eastward. 28 The towns and their surround-
ing villages in this area were given as a homeland
to the clans of the tribe of Gad.

THE LAND GIVEN TO THE HALF-TRIBE OF MANASSEH

29 Moses had assigned the following area to the clans
of the half-tribe of Manasseh.

30 Their territory extended from Mahanaim,
including all of Bashan, all the former kingdom of
King Og, and the sixty towns of Jair in Bashan. 31 It

12:23a Hebrew *Naphath-dor,* a variant spelling of Naphoth-dor. **12:23b** Greek version reads *Goyim in Galilee.* **13:25** Hebrew *in front of.* **13:26** Hebrew *Li-debir,* apparently a variant spelling of Lo-debar (compare 2 Sam 9:4; 17:27; Amos 6:13). **13:27** Hebrew *Sea of Kinnereth.*

13:1 Joshua was an old man. At the time of these events, Joshua was about 100 years old.

13:2-6 the territory that remains. At the end of Joshua's conquest of Canaan, two primary territories remained in enemy hands: (1) the southwest coastal strip controlled by the Philistines and Geshurites and (2) the far northern plains associated with Sidon on the coast and Mt. Hermon in the interior.

13:15 tribe of Reuben. These Israelites were cattle herders, and they anxiously awaited possession of the rich grazing land southeast of the Jordan River.

13:24 tribe of Gad. Members of this tribe had settled in the central region east of the Jordan River.

13:29 half-tribe of Manasseh. Although the land northeast of the Jordan River was beautiful, neither Manasseh, Gad, or Reuben had a natural protective border to the east.

also included half of Gilead and King Og's royal cities of Ashtaroth and Edrei. All this was given to the clans of the descendants of Makir, who was Manasseh's son.

32 These are the allotments Moses had made while he was on the plains of Moab, across the Jordan River, east of Jericho. 33 But Moses gave no allotment of land to the tribe of Levi, for the LORD, the God of Israel, had promised that he himself would be their allotment.

THE LAND DIVIDED WEST OF THE JORDAN

14 The remaining tribes of Israel received land in Canaan as allotted by Eleazar the priest, Joshua son of Nun, and the tribal leaders. 2 These nine and a half tribes received their grants of land by means of sacred lots, in accordance with the LORD's command through Moses. 3 Moses had already given a grant of land to the two and a half tribes on the east side of the Jordan River, but he had given the Levites no such allotment. 4 The descendants of Joseph had become two separate tribes—Manasseh and Ephraim. And the Levites were given no land at all, only towns to live in with surrounding pasturelands for their livestock and all their possessions. 5 So the land was distributed in strict accordance with the LORD's commands to Moses.

CALEB REQUESTS HIS LAND

6 A delegation from the tribe of Judah, led by Caleb son of Jephunneh the Kenizzite, came to Joshua at Gilgal. Caleb said to Joshua, "Remember what the LORD said to Moses, the man of God, about you and me when we were at Kadesh-barnea. 7 I was forty years old when Moses, the servant of the LORD, sent me from Kadesh-barnea to explore the land of Canaan. I returned and gave an honest report, 8 but my brothers who went with me frightened the people from entering the Promised Land. For my part, I wholeheartedly followed the LORD my God. 9 So that day Moses solemnly promised me, 'The land of Canaan on which you were just walking will be your grant of land and that of your descendants forever, because you wholeheartedly followed the LORD my God.'

10 "Now, as you can see, the LORD has kept me alive and well as he promised for all these forty-five years since Moses made this promise—even while Israel wandered in the wilderness. Today I am eighty-five years old. 11 I am as strong now as I was when Moses sent me on that journey, and I can still travel and fight as well as I could then. 12 So give me the hill country that the LORD promised me. You will remember that as scouts we found the descendants of Anak living there in great, walled towns. But if the LORD is with me, I will drive them out of the land, just as the LORD said."

13 So Joshua blessed Caleb son of Jephunneh and gave Hebron to him as his portion of land. 14 Hebron still belongs to the descendants of Caleb son of Jephunneh the Kenizzite because he wholeheartedly followed the LORD, the God of Israel. 15 (Previously Hebron had been called Kiriath-arba. It had been named after Arba, a great hero of the descendants of Anak.)

And the land had rest from war.

THE LAND GIVEN TO THE TRIBE OF JUDAH

15 The allotment for the clans of the tribe of Judah reached southward to the border of Edom, as far south as the wilderness of Zin.

2 The southern boundary began at the south bay
of the Dead Sea,* 3 ran south of Scorpion Pass*
into the wilderness of Zin, and then went south of
Kadesh-barnea to Hezron. Then it went up to Addar, where it turned toward Karka. 4 From there it
passed to Azmon until it finally reached the Brook
of Egypt, which it followed to the Mediterranean
Sea.* This was their* southern boundary.

5 The eastern boundary extended along the
Dead Sea to the mouth of the Jordan River.

The northern boundary began at the bay where
the Jordan River empties into the Dead Sea, 6 went
up from there to Beth-hoglah, then proceeded
north of Beth-arabah to the Stone of Bohan.
(Bohan was Reuben's son.) 7 From that point it
went through the valley of Achor to Debir, turning
north toward Gilgal, which is across from the
slopes of Adummim on the south side of the valley.
From there the boundary extended to the springs
at En-shemesh and on to En-rogel. 8 The boundary
then passed through the valley of Ben-Hinnom,
along the southern slopes of the Jebusites, where
the city of Jerusalem is located. Then it went west
to the top of the mountain above the valley of Hinnom, and on up to the northern end of the valley
of Rephaim. 9 From there the boundary extended
from the top of the mountain to the spring at the
waters of Nephtoah,* and from there to the towns
on Mount Ephron. Then it turned toward Baalah
(that is, Kiriath-jearim). 10 The boundary circled
west of Baalah to Mount Seir, passed along to the
town of Kesalon on the northern slope of Mount
Jearim, and went down to Beth-shemesh and on
to Timnah. 11 The boundary then proceeded to the
slope of the hill north of Ekron, where it turned
toward Shikkeron and Mount Baalah. It passed
Jabneel and ended at the Mediterranean Sea.
12 The western boundary was the shoreline of
the Mediterranean Sea.*

These are the boundaries for the clans of the tribe of Judah.

THE LAND GIVEN TO CALEB

13 The LORD commanded Joshua to assign some of Judah's territory to Caleb son of Jephunneh. So Caleb

15:2 Hebrew *the Salt Sea;* also in 15:5. **15:3** Hebrew *Akrabbim.* **15:4a** Hebrew *the sea;* also in 15:11. **15:4b** Hebrew *your.* **15:9** Or *the spring at Me-nephtoah.* **15:12** Hebrew *the Great Sea;* also in 15:47.

14:1 Eleazar. Using the priest Eleazar to divide the land according to lots reemphasized God's role in each tribe's inheritance.

14:4 two separate tribes—Manasseh and Ephraim. These were actually Joseph's children, whom Jacob had adopted to form the twelve tribes. They shared full legal rights of inheritance. Half of Manasseh had already received an allotment of land east of the Jordan River.

14:6-13 Caleb son of Jephunneh. Caleb, one of the original spies sent into Canaan, revealed his plans for securing his inheritance in Hebron. This had been the favored city of Abraham (Gen. 13:18) and the burial place of the patriarchs (Gen. 25:9; 35:27-29; 50:12-13). The 12 spies had visited Hebron (Num. 13:22).

15:1 clans of the tribe of Judah. From this tribe sprang powerful rulers like David and eventually the Messiah.

15:2 The southern boundary. The great detail provided here (vv. 1-12) reveals the importance of the land inheritance to the people and God.

was given the town of Kiriath-arba (that is, Hebron),
which had been named after Anak's ancestor. 14 Ca-
leb drove out the three groups of Anakites—the de-
scendants of Sheshai, Ahiman, and Talmai, the sons
of Anak.
15 From there he went to fight against the people
living in the town of Debir (formerly called Kiriath-
sepher). 16 Caleb said, "I will give my daughter Acsah
in marriage to the one who attacks and captures Kir-
iath-sepher." 17 Othniel, the son of Caleb's brother Ke-
naz, was the one who conquered it, so Acsah became
Othniel's wife.
18 When Acsah married Othniel, she urged him* to
ask her father for a field. As she got down off her don-
key, Caleb asked her, "What's the matter?"
19 She said, "Give me another gift. You have al-
ready given me land in the Negev; now please give
me springs of water, too." So Caleb gave her the upper
and lower springs.

THE TOWNS ALLOTTED TO JUDAH

20 This was the homeland allocated to the clans of the
tribe of Judah.

21 The towns of Judah situated along the borders
of Edom in the extreme south were Kabzeel, Eder,
Jagur, 22 Kinah, Dimonah, Adadah, 23 Kedesh, Hazor,
Ithnan, 24 Ziph, Telem, Bealoth, 25 Hazor-hadattah,
Kerioth-hezron (that is, Hazor), 26 Amam, Shema, Mo-
ladah, 27 Hazar-gaddah, Heshmon, Beth-pelet, 28 Haz-
ar-shual, Beersheba, Biziothiah, 29 Baalah, Iim, Ezem,
30 Eltolad, Kesil, Hormah, 31 Ziklag, Madmannah,
Sansannah, 32 Lebaoth, Shilhim, Ain, and Rimmon—
twenty-nine towns with their surrounding villages.
33 The following towns situated in the western
foothills* were also given to Judah: Eshtaol, Zorah,
Ashnah, 34 Zanoah, En-gannim, Tappuah, Enam,
35 Jarmuth, Adullam, Socoh, Azekah, 36 Shaaraim,
Adithaim, Gederah, and Gederothaim—fourteen
towns with their surrounding villages.
37 Also included were Zenan, Hadashah, Migdal-
gad, 38 Dilean, Mizpeh, Joktheel, 39 Lachish, Bozkath,
Eglon, 40 Cabbon, Lahmam, Kitlish, 41 Gederoth,
Beth-dagon, Naamah, and Makkedah—sixteen
towns with their surrounding villages.
42 Besides these, there were Libnah, Ether,
Ashan, 43 Iphtah, Ashnah, Nezib, 44 Keilah, Aczib,
and Mareshah—nine towns with their surround-
ing villages.
45 The territory of the tribe of Judah also included
Ekron and its surrounding settlements and villages.
46 From Ekron the boundary extended west and
included the towns near Ashdod with their sur-
rounding villages. 47 It also included Ashdod with its
surrounding settlements and villages and Gaza with
its settlements and villages, as far as the Brook of
Egypt and along the coast of the Mediterranean Sea.
48 Judah also received the following towns in
the hill country: Shamir, Jattir, Socoh, 49 Dannah,
Kiriath-sannah (that is, Debir), 50 Anab, Eshtemoh,
Anim, 51 Goshen, Holon, and Giloh—eleven towns
with their surrounding villages.
52 Also included were the towns of Arab, Dumah,
Eshan, 53 Janim, Beth-tappuah, Aphekah, 54 Hum-
tah, Kiriath-arba (that is, Hebron), and Zior—nine
towns with their surrounding villages.
55 Besides these, there were Maon, Carmel, Ziph,
Juttah, 56 Jezreel, Jokdeam, Zanoah, 57 Kain, Gibeah, and
Timnah—ten towns with their surrounding villages.
58 In addition, there were Halhul, Beth-zur,
Gedor, 59 Maarath, Beth-anoth, and Eltekon—six
towns with their surrounding villages.
60 There were also Kiriath-baal (that is, Kiriath-
jearim) and Rabbah—two towns with their
surrounding villages.
61 In the wilderness there were the towns of
Beth-arabah, Middin, Secacah, 62 Nibshan, the
City of Salt, and En-gedi—six towns with their
surrounding villages.

63 But the tribe of Judah could not drive out the Jeb-
usites, who lived in the city of Jerusalem, so the Jebu-
sites live there among the people of Judah to this day.

THE LAND GIVEN TO EPHRAIM AND WEST MANASSEH

16 The allotment for the descendants of Joseph
extended from the Jordan River near Jeri-
cho, east of the springs of Jericho, through the
wilderness and into the hill country of Bethel.
2 From Bethel (that is, Luz)* it ran over to Ataroth
in the territory of the Arkites. 3 Then it descended
westward to the territory of the Japhletites as far
as Lower Beth-horon, then to Gezer and over to the
Mediterranean Sea.*

4 This was the homeland allocated to the families of
Joseph's sons, Manasseh and Ephraim.

THE LAND GIVEN TO EPHRAIM

5 The following territory was given to the clans of the
tribe of Ephraim.

The boundary of their homeland began at At-
aroth-addar in the east. From there it ran to Upper
Beth-horon, 6 then on to the Mediterranean Sea.
From Micmethath on the north, the boundary
curved eastward past Taanath-shiloh to the east
of Janoah. 7 From Janoah it turned southward to
Ataroth and Naarah, touched Jericho, and ended
at the Jordan River. 8 From Tappuah the boundary
extended westward, following the Kanah Ravine
to the Mediterranean Sea. This is the homeland
allocated to the clans of the tribe of Ephraim.
9 In addition, some towns with their surround-
ing villages in the territory allocated to the half-
tribe of Manasseh were set aside for the tribe of
Ephraim. 10 They did not drive the Canaanites out
of Gezer, however, so the people of Gezer live as
slaves among the people of Ephraim to this day.

15:18 Some Greek manuscripts read *he urged her.* **15:33** Hebrew *the Shephelah.* **16:2** As in Greek version (also see 18:13); Hebrew reads *From Bethel to Luz.* **16:3** Hebrew *the sea;* also in 16:6, 8.

15:63 could not drive out the Jebusites. Joshua had conquered Jerusalem (10:1-27; 12:10), but the Jebusites apparently reoccupied the city.

16:1–17:18 Not only did Joseph's tribes, Manasseh and Ephraim, follow Judah in priority; they were also given the beautiful central corridor of Canaan.

16:1 Joseph. Since Joseph played such a key role in the survival of the Israelites during a famine, it was fitting that his sons should be given such prominence.

16:5 Ephraim. His territory became well known because of Shiloh's role as the early location for the tabernacle.

THE LAND GIVEN TO WEST MANASSEH

17 The next allotment of land was given to the half-tribe of Manasseh, the descendants of Joseph's older son. Makir, the firstborn son of Manasseh, was the father of Gilead. Because his descendants were experienced soldiers, the regions of Gilead and Bashan on the east side of the Jordan had already been given to them. 2 So the allotment on the west side of the Jordan was for the remaining families within the clans of the tribe of Manasseh: Abiezer, Helek, Asriel, Shechem, Hepher, and Shemida. These clans represent the male descendants of Manasseh son of Joseph.

3 However, Zelophehad, a descendant of Hepher son of Gilead, son of Makir, son of Manasseh, had no sons. He had only daughters, whose names were Mahlah, Noah, Hoglah, Milcah, and Tirzah. 4 These women came to Eleazar the priest, Joshua son of Nun, and the Israelite leaders and said, "The LORD commanded Moses to give us a grant of land along with the men of our tribe."

So Joshua gave them a grant of land along with their uncles, as the LORD had commanded. 5 As a result, Manasseh's total allocation came to ten parcels of land, in addition to the land of Gilead and Bashan across the Jordan River, 6 because the female descendants of Manasseh received a grant of land along with the male descendants. (The land of Gilead was given to the rest of the male descendants of Manasseh.)

7 The boundary of the tribe of Manasseh extended from the border of Asher to Micmethath, near Shechem. Then the boundary went south from Micmethath to the settlement near the spring of Tappuah. 8 The land surrounding Tappuah belonged to Manasseh, but the town of Tappuah itself, on the border of Manasseh's territory, belonged to the tribe of Ephraim. 9 From the spring of Tappuah, the boundary of Manasseh followed the Kanah Ravine to the Mediterranean Sea.* Several towns south of the ravine were inside Manasseh's territory, but they actually belonged to the tribe of Ephraim. 10 In general, however, the land south of the ravine belonged to Ephraim, and the land north of the ravine belonged to Manasseh. Manasseh's boundary ran along the northern side of the ravine and ended at the Mediterranean Sea. North of Manasseh was the territory of Asher, and to the east was the territory of Issachar.

11 The following towns within the territory of Issachar and Asher, however, were given to Manasseh: Beth-shan,* Ibleam, Dor (that is, Naphoth-dor),* Endor, Taanach, and Megiddo, each with their surrounding settlements.

12 But the descendants of Manasseh were unable to occupy these towns because the Canaanites were determined to stay in that region. 13 Later, however, when the Israelites became strong enough, they forced the Canaanites to work as slaves. But they did not drive them out of the land.

14 The descendants of Joseph came to Joshua and asked, "Why have you given us only one portion of land as our homeland when the LORD has blessed us with so many people?"

15 Joshua replied, "If there are so many of you, and if the hill country of Ephraim is not large enough for you, clear out land for yourselves in the forest where the Perizzites and Rephaites live."

16 The descendants of Joseph responded, "It's true that the hill country is not large enough for us. But all the Canaanites in the lowlands have iron chariots, both those in Beth-shan and its surrounding settlements and those in the valley of Jezreel. They are too strong for us."

17 Then Joshua said to the tribes of Ephraim and Manasseh, the descendants of Joseph, "Since you are so large and strong, you will be given more than one portion. 18 The forests of the hill country will be yours as well. Clear as much of the land as you wish, and take possession of its farthest corners. And you will drive out the Canaanites from the valleys, too, even though they are strong and have iron chariots."

THE ALLOTMENTS OF THE REMAINING LAND

18 Now that the land was under Israelite control, the entire community of Israel gathered at Shiloh and set up the Tabernacle.* 2 But there remained seven tribes who had not yet been allotted their grants of land.

3 Then Joshua asked them, "How long are you going to wait before taking possession of the remaining land the LORD, the God of your ancestors, has given to you? 4 Select three men from each tribe, and I will send them out to explore the land and map it out. They will then return to me with a written report of their proposed divisions of their new homeland. 5 Let them divide the land into seven sections, excluding Judah's territory in the south and Joseph's territory in the north. 6 And when you record the seven divisions of the land and bring them to me, I will cast sacred lots in the presence of the LORD our God to assign land to each tribe.

7 "The Levites, however, will not receive any allotment of land. Their role as priests of the LORD is their

17:9 Hebrew *the sea;* also in 17:10. **17:11a** Hebrew *Beth-shean,* a variant spelling of Beth-shan; also in 17:16. **17:11b** The meaning of the Hebrew here is uncertain. **18:1** Hebrew *Tent of Meeting.*

17:1 Manasseh. The tribe of Manasseh would become Ephraim's northern neighbor and would receive a territory a little smaller than that of Judah.

17:3 Zelophehad. The great-great grandson of Manasseh.

17:5-10 Manasseh's total allocation. Zelophehad's daughters received shares of land along with the male descendants of Manasseh.

17:14 only one portion. One of the larger tribes felt too crowded in its current allotment.

17:15 clear out land . . . in the forest. Joshua instructed this tribe to leverage their size, dominate their enemies, and expand beyond their hill country to gain more territory.

18:1–19:51 Joshua gathered the tribes at the tabernacle in Shiloh for the final divisions of the land. Lots were cast, and a special allotment of land was set aside for Joshua.

18:1 entire community of Israel gathered at Shiloh. The tabernacle was located at Shiloh—a perfect spot for group decisions about what was important in Israel's priorities. Shiloh was in the hill country of Ephraim roughly 15 miles northwest of Jericho and 10 miles north of Bethel.

18:3 taking possession of the remaining land. It was one thing to conquer a rival king. It was quite another to move in and take over—as the tribes would soon find out.

18:6 I will cast sacred lots. The Lord distributed the portions of land to the various tribes by means of lots. No politicking, favoritism, or pressure tactics played any role in who got what territory.

allotment. And the tribes of Gad, Reuben, and the
half-tribe of Manasseh won't receive any more land,
for they have already received their grant of land,
which Moses, the servant of the LORD, gave them on
the east side of the Jordan River."
8 As the men started on their way to map out the
land, Joshua commanded them, "Go and explore the
land and write a description of it. Then return to me,
and I will assign the land to the tribes by casting sa-
cred lots here in the presence of the LORD at Shiloh."
9 The men did as they were told and mapped the en-
tire territory into seven sections, listing the towns in
each section. They made a written record and then
returned to Joshua in the camp at Shiloh. 10 And there
at Shiloh, Joshua cast sacred lots in the presence of
the LORD to determine which tribe should have each
section.

THE LAND GIVEN TO BENJAMIN

11 The first allotment of land went to the clans of the
tribe of Benjamin. It lay between the territory as-
signed to the tribes of Judah and Joseph.

12 The northern boundary of Benjamin's land
began at the Jordan River, went north of the slope
of Jericho, then west through the hill country and
the wilderness of Beth-aven. 13 From there the
boundary went south to Luz (that is, Bethel) and
proceeded down to Ataroth-addar on the hill that
lies south of Lower Beth-horon.
14 The boundary then made a turn and swung
south along the western edge of the hill facing
Beth-horon, ending at the village of Kiriath-baal
(that is, Kiriath-jearim), a town belonging to the
tribe of Judah. This was the western boundary.
15 The southern boundary began at the outskirts
of Kiriath-jearim. From that western point it ran*
to the spring at the waters of Nephtoah,* 16 and
down to the base of the mountain beside the
valley of Ben-Hinnom, at the northern end of
the valley of Rephaim. From there it went down
the valley of Hinnom, crossing south of the slope
where the Jebusites lived, and continued down to
En-rogel. 17 From En-rogel the boundary proceeded
in a northerly direction and came to En-shemesh
and on to Geliloth (which is across from the slopes
of Adummim). Then it went down to the Stone of
Bohan. (Bohan was Reuben's son.) 18 From there it
passed along the north side of the slope over-
looking the Jordan Valley.* The border then went
down into the valley, 19 ran past the north slope
of Beth-hoglah, and ended at the north bay of the
Dead Sea,* which is the southern end of the Jordan
River. This was the southern boundary.
20 The eastern boundary was the Jordan River.

These were the boundaries of the homeland allocated
to the clans of the tribe of Benjamin.

THE TOWNS GIVEN TO BENJAMIN

21 These were the towns given to the clans of the tribe
of Benjamin.

Jericho, Beth-hoglah, Emek-keziz, 22 Beth-ara-
bah, Zemaraim, Bethel, 23 Avvim, Parah, Ophrah,
24 Kephar-ammoni, Ophni, and Geba—twelve
towns with their surrounding villages. 25 Also
Gibeon, Ramah, Beeroth, 26 Mizpah, Kephirah,
Mozah, 27 Rekem, Irpeel, Taralah, 28 Zela, Haeleph,
the Jebusite town (that is, Jerusalem), Gibeah,
and Kiriath-jearim*—fourteen towns with their
surrounding villages.

This was the homeland allocated to the clans of the
tribe of Benjamin.

THE LAND GIVEN TO SIMEON

19 The second allotment of land went to the clans
of the tribe of Simeon. Their homeland was sur-
rounded by Judah's territory.

2 Simeon's homeland included Beersheba, Sheba,
Moladah, 3 Hazar-shual, Balah, Ezem, 4 Eltolad,
Bethul, Hormah, 5 Ziklag, Beth-marcaboth, Haz-
ar-susah, 6 Beth-lebaoth, and Sharuhen—thirteen
towns with their surrounding villages. 7 It also
included Ain, Rimmon, Ether, and Ashan—four
towns with their villages, 8 including all the
surrounding villages as far south as Baalath-beer
(also known as Ramah of the Negev).

This was the homeland allocated to the clans of the
tribe of Simeon. 9 Their allocation of land came from
part of what had been given to Judah because Judah's
territory was too large for them. So the tribe of Simeon
received an allocation within the territory of Judah.

THE LAND GIVEN TO ZEBULUN

10 The third allotment of land went to the clans of the
tribe of Zebulun.

The boundary of Zebulun's homeland started
at Sarid. 11 From there it went west, going past
Maralah, touching Dabbesheth, and proceeding to
the brook east of Jokneam. 12 In the other direction,
the boundary went east from Sarid to the border
of Kisloth-tabor, and from there to Daberath and
up to Japhia. 13 Then it continued east to Gath-he-
pher, Eth-kazin, and Rimmon and turned toward
Neah. 14 The northern boundary of Zebulun passed
Hannathon and ended at the valley of Iphtah-el.
15 The towns in these areas included Kattath, Na-
halal, Shimron, Idalah, and Bethlehem—twelve
towns with their surrounding villages.

16 The homeland allocated to the clans of the tribe of
Zebulun included these towns and their surrounding
villages.

18:15a Or *From there it went to Mozah.* The meaning of the Hebrew is uncertain. **18:15b** Or *the spring at Me-nephtoah.* **18:18** Hebrew *overlooking the Arabah,* or *overlooking Beth-arabah.* **18:19** Hebrew *Salt Sea.* **18:28** As in Greek version; Hebrew reads *Kiriath.*

18:11 first allotment . . . tribe of Benjamin. The territory settled by this tribe was squeezed between the two dominant tribes, Judah and Ephraim, and served as an important link between these two tribes. In the years to come, Benjamin would exert an influence in Israel far beyond its territorial and population size. The following key cities fell within the boundaries of Benjamin: Jericho, Bethel, Gibeon, Mizpah, Ai, and Jerusalem. The temple would be built in the territory of Benjamin. Israel's first king, Saul, would come from the tribe of Benjamin as would another Saul (of Tarsus, Paul), Christ's foremost representative to the Gentile world.

THE LAND GIVEN TO ISSACHAR

17 The fourth allotment of land went to the clans of the tribe of Issachar.

18 Its boundaries included the following towns: Jezreel, Kesulloth, Shunem, 19 Hapharaim, Shion, Anaharath, 20 Rabbith, Kishion, Ebez, 21 Remeth, En-gannim, En-haddah, and Beth-pazzez. 22 The boundary also touched Tabor, Shahazumah, and Beth-shemesh, ending at the Jordan River—sixteen towns with their surrounding villages.

23 The homeland allocated to the clans of the tribe of Issachar included these towns and their surrounding villages.

THE LAND GIVEN TO ASHER

24 The fifth allotment of land went to the clans of the tribe of Asher.

25 Its boundaries included these towns: Helkath, Hali, Beten, Acshaph, 26 Allammelech, Amad, and Mishal. The boundary on the west touched Carmel and Shihor-libnath, 27 then it turned east toward Beth-dagon, and ran as far as Zebulun in the valley of Iphtah-el, going north to Beth-emek and Neiel. It then continued north to Cabul, 28 Abdon,* Rehob, Hammon, Kanah, and as far as Greater Sidon. 29 Then the boundary turned toward Ramah and the fortress of Tyre, where it turned toward Hosah and came to the Mediterranean Sea.* The territory also included Mehebel, Aczib, 30 Ummah, Aphek, and Rehob—twenty-two towns with their surrounding villages.

31 The homeland allocated to the clans of the tribe of Asher included these towns and their surrounding villages.

THE LAND GIVEN TO NAPHTALI

32 The sixth allotment of land went to the clans of the tribe of Naphtali.

33 Its boundary ran from Heleph, from the oak at Zaanannim, and extended across to Adami-nekeb, Jabneel, and as far as Lakkum, ending at the Jordan River. 34 The western boundary ran past Aznoth-tabor, then to Hukkok, and touched the border of Zebulun in the south, the border of Asher on the west, and the Jordan River* on the east. 35 The fortified towns included in this territory were Ziddim, Zer, Hammath, Rakkath, Kinnereth, 36 Adamah, Ramah, Hazor, 37 Kedesh, Edrei, En-hazor, 38 Yiron, Migdal-el, Horem, Beth-anath, and Beth-shemesh—nineteen towns with their surrounding villages.

39 The homeland allocated to the clans of the tribe of Naphtali included these towns and their surrounding villages.

THE LAND GIVEN TO DAN

40 The seventh allotment of land went to the clans of the tribe of Dan.

41 The land allocated as their homeland included the following towns: Zorah, Eshtaol, Ir-shemesh, 42 Shaalabbin, Aijalon, Ithlah, 43 Elon, Timnah, Ekron, 44 Eltekeh, Gibbethon, Baalath, 45 Jehud, Bene-berak, Gath-rimmon, 46 Me-jarkon, Rakkon, and the territory across from Joppa.

47 But the tribe of Dan had trouble taking possession of their land,* so they attacked the town of Laish.* They captured it, slaughtered its people, and settled there. They renamed the town Dan after their ancestor.

48 The homeland allocated to the clans of the tribe of Dan included these towns and their surrounding villages.

THE LAND GIVEN TO JOSHUA

49 After all the land was divided among the tribes, the Israelites gave a piece of land to Joshua as his allocation. 50 For the LORD had said he could have any town he wanted. He chose Timnath-serah in the hill country of Ephraim. He rebuilt the town and lived there.

51 These are the territories that Eleazar the priest, Joshua son of Nun, and the tribal leaders allocated as grants of land to the tribes of Israel by casting sacred lots in the presence of the LORD at the entrance of the Tabernacle* at Shiloh. So the division of the land was completed.

THE CITIES OF REFUGE

20 The LORD said to Joshua, 2 "Now tell the Israelites to designate the cities of refuge, as I instructed Moses. 3 Anyone who kills another person accidentally and unintentionally can run to one of these cities; they will be places of refuge from relatives seeking revenge for the person who was killed.

4 "Upon reaching one of these cities, the one who caused the death will appear before the elders at the city gate and present his case. They must allow him to enter the city and give him a place to live among them. 5 If the relatives of the victim come to avenge the killing, the leaders must not release the slayer to them, for he killed the other person unintentionally and without previous hostility. 6 But the slayer must stay in that city and be tried by the local assembly, which will render a judgment. And he must continue to live in that city until the death of the high priest

19:28 As in some Hebrew manuscripts (see also 21:30); most Hebrew manuscripts read *Ebron*. **19:29** Hebrew *the sea*. **19:34** Hebrew *and Judah at the Jordan River*. **19:47a** Or *had trouble holding on to their land*. **19:47b** Hebrew *Leshem*, a variant spelling of Laish. **19:51** Hebrew *Tent of Meeting*.

19:47 attacked . . . captured. Joshua assigned Dan tribal land between Judah and Benjamin to the east and the Amorites and Philistines to the west. Dan could not conquer its assigned territory (Judg. 1:34; 18:1). Eventually most of the tribe migrated about 100 miles to the far north of Israel and seized undefended towns and land (18:2-31).

19:49 gave a piece of land . . . as his allocation. A true leader, Joshua served his people first. At last, he was rewarded with a land allotment that he wanted and deserved.

20:1-9 Now that Israel was settled in the land, the crime of manslaughter was the first issue addressed. A city of refuge under the supervision of the Levites would provide justice for people accused of this crime.

20:3 places of refuge. A relative of the person who had been killed was responsible for killing the criminal in a murder case.

20:4 at the city gate. The city gate was a place where commerce and trials took place. This gate was more than a doorway. It was a fortress with interior rooms that everyone entering and leaving the city had to pass through.

who was in office at the time of the accident. After that, he is free to return to his own home in the town from which he fled."

7 The following cities were designated as cities of refuge: Kedesh of Galilee, in the hill country of Naphtali; Shechem, in the hill country of Ephraim; and Kiriath-arba (that is, Hebron), in the hill country of Judah. 8 On the east side of the Jordan River, across from Jericho, the following cities were designated: Bezer, in the wilderness plain of the tribe of Reuben; Ramoth in Gilead, in the territory of the tribe of Gad; and Golan in Bashan, in the land of the tribe of Manasseh. 9 These cities were set apart for all the Israelites as well as the foreigners living among them. Anyone who accidentally killed another person could take refuge in one of these cities. In this way, they could escape being killed in revenge prior to standing trial before the local assembly.

THE TOWNS GIVEN TO THE LEVITES

21 Then the leaders of the tribe of Levi came to consult with Eleazar the priest, Joshua son of Nun, and the leaders of the other tribes of Israel. 2 They came to them at Shiloh in the land of Canaan and said, "The LORD commanded Moses to give us towns to live in and pasturelands for our livestock." 3 So by the command of the LORD the people of Israel gave the Levites the following towns and pasturelands out of their own grants of land.

4 The descendants of Aaron, who were members of the Kohathite clan within the tribe of Levi, were allotted thirteen towns that were originally assigned to the tribes of Judah, Simeon, and Benjamin. 5 The other families of the Kohathite clan were allotted ten towns from the tribes of Ephraim, Dan, and the half-tribe of Manasseh.

6 The clan of Gershon was allotted thirteen towns from the tribes of Issachar, Asher, Naphtali, and the half-tribe of Manasseh in Bashan.

7 The clan of Merari was allotted twelve towns from the tribes of Reuben, Gad, and Zebulun.

8 So the Israelites obeyed the LORD's command to Moses and assigned these towns and pasturelands to the Levites by casting sacred lots.

9 The Israelites gave the following towns from the tribes of Judah and Simeon 10 to the descendants of Aaron, who were members of the Kohathite clan within the tribe of Levi, since the sacred lot fell to them first: 11 Kiriath-arba (that is, Hebron), in the hill country of Judah, along with its surrounding pasturelands. (Arba was an ancestor of Anak.) 12 But the open fields beyond the town and the surrounding villages were given to Caleb son of Jephunneh as his possession.

13 The following towns with their pasturelands were given to the descendants of Aaron the priest: Hebron (a city of refuge for those who accidentally killed someone), Libnah, 14 Jattir, Eshtemoa, 15 Holon, Debir, 16 Ain, Juttah, and Beth-shemesh—nine towns from these two tribes.

17 From the tribe of Benjamin the priests were given the following towns with their pasturelands: Gibeon, Geba, 18 Anathoth, and Almon—four towns. 19 So in all, thirteen towns with their pasturelands were given to the priests, the descendants of Aaron.

20 The rest of the Kohathite clan from the tribe of Levi was allotted the following towns and pasturelands from the tribe of Ephraim: 21 Shechem in the hill country of Ephraim (a city of refuge for those who accidentally killed someone), Gezer, 22 Kibzaim, and Beth-horon—four towns.

23 The following towns and pasturelands were allotted to the priests from the tribe of Dan: Eltekeh, Gibbethon, 24 Aijalon, and Gath-rimmon—four towns.

25 The half-tribe of Manasseh allotted the following towns with their pasturelands to the priests: Taanach and Gath-rimmon—two towns. 26 So in all, ten towns with their pasturelands were given to the rest of the Kohathite clan.

27 The descendants of Gershon, another clan within the tribe of Levi, received the following towns with their pasturelands from the half-tribe of Manasseh: Golan in Bashan (a city of refuge for those who accidentally killed someone) and Be-eshterah—two towns.

28 From the tribe of Issachar they received the following towns with their pasturelands: Kishion, Daberath, 29 Jarmuth, and En-gannim—four towns.

30 From the tribe of Asher they received the following towns with their pasturelands: Mishal, Abdon, 31 Helkath, and Rehob—four towns.

32 From the tribe of Naphtali they received the following towns with their pasturelands: Kedesh in Galilee (a city of refuge for those who accidentally killed someone), Hammoth-dor, and Kartan—three towns. 33 So in all, thirteen towns with their pasturelands were allotted to the clan of Gershon.

34 The rest of the Levites—the Merari clan—were given the following towns with their pasturelands from the tribe of Zebulun: Jokneam, Kartah, 35 Dimnah, and Nahalal—four towns.

36 From the tribe of Reuben they received the following towns with their pasturelands: Bezer, Jahaz,* 37 Kedemoth, and Mephaath—four towns.

38 From the tribe of Gad they received the following towns with their pasturelands: Ramoth in Gilead (a city of refuge for those who accidentally killed someone), Mahanaim, 39 Heshbon, and Jazer—four towns. 40 So in all, twelve towns were allotted to the clan of Merari.

41 The total number of towns and pasturelands within Israelite territory given to the Levites came to forty-eight. 42 Every one of these towns had pasturelands surrounding it.

43 So the LORD gave to Israel all the land he had sworn to give their ancestors, and they took possession of it and settled there. 44 And the LORD gave them rest on every side, just as he had solemnly promised their ancestors. None of their enemies could stand against them, for the LORD helped them conquer all

21:36 Hebrew *Jahzah,* a variant spelling of Jahaz.

20:7-8 were designated. Northern, central, and southern cities of refuge were designated on the eastern and western sides of the Jordan River. All citizens had easy access to one of these cities.

21:1-45 The towns and pasturelands given to the Levites were distributed evenly throughout the other tribes. Their priestly service to the Lord was considered the inheritance of the Levites (13:33; 18:7).

21:11-12 Hebron. Caleb was free to shepherd the range of fields and outlying villages of Hebron, the resting place of Sarah and her family (Gen. 23:1-2). But the priests and Levites considered the city of Hebron their home.

21:43-45 as he solemnly promised. God reminded these battle-weary warriors that every victory, every conquest, and every blade of grass in this land was a gift from Him.

their enemies. 45 Not a single one of all the good prom-
ises the LORD had given to the family of Israel was left
unfulfilled; everything he had spoken came true.

THE EASTERN TRIBES RETURN HOME

22 Then Joshua called together the tribes of Reu-
ben, Gad, and the half-tribe of Manasseh. 2 He
told them, "You have done as Moses, the servant of the
LORD, commanded you, and you have obeyed every
order I have given you. 3 During all this time you have
not deserted the other tribes. You have been careful
to obey the commands of the LORD your God right up
to the present day. 4 And now the LORD your God has
given the other tribes rest, as he promised them. So
go back home to the land that Moses, the servant of
the LORD, gave you as your possession on the east side
of the Jordan River. 5 But be very careful to obey all
the commands and the instructions that Moses gave
to you. Love the LORD your God, walk in all his ways,
obey his commands, hold firmly to him, and serve
him with all your heart and all your soul." 6 So Josh-
ua blessed them and sent them away, and they went
home.

7 Moses had given the land of Bashan, east of the
Jordan River, to the half-tribe of Manasseh. (The other
half of the tribe was given land west of the Jordan.)
As Joshua sent them away and blessed them, 8 he
said to them, "Go back to your homes with the great
wealth you have taken from your enemies—the vast
herds of livestock, the silver, gold, bronze, and iron,
and the large supply of clothing. Share the plunder
with your relatives."

9 So the men of Reuben, Gad, and the half-tribe of
Manasseh left the rest of Israel at Shiloh in the land
of Canaan. They started the journey back to their own
land of Gilead, the territory that belonged to them ac-
cording to the LORD's command through Moses.

THE EASTERN TRIBES BUILD AN ALTAR

10 But while they were still in Canaan, and when they
came to a place called Geliloth* near the Jordan River,
the men of Reuben, Gad, and the half-tribe of Manas-
seh stopped to build a large and imposing altar.

11 The rest of Israel heard that the people of Reuben,
Gad, and the half-tribe of Manasseh had built an al-
tar at Geliloth at the edge of the land of Canaan, on
the west side of the Jordan River. 12 So the whole com-
munity of Israel gathered at Shiloh and prepared to
go to war against them. 13 First, however, they sent a
delegation led by Phinehas son of Eleazar, the priest,
to talk with the tribes of Reuben, Gad, and the half-
tribe of Manasseh. 14 In this delegation were ten lead-
ers of Israel, one from each of the ten tribes, and each
the head of his family within the clans of Israel.

15 When they arrived in the land of Gilead, they
said to the tribes of Reuben, Gad, and the half-tribe
of Manasseh, 16 "The whole community of the LORD
demands to know why you are betraying the God of
Israel. How could you turn away from the LORD and
build an altar for yourselves in rebellion against him?
17 Was our sin at Peor not enough? To this day we are
not fully cleansed of it, even after the plague that
struck the entire community of the LORD. 18 And yet
today you are turning away from following the LORD.
If you rebel against the LORD today, he will be angry
with all of us tomorrow.

19 "If you need the altar because the land you pos-
sess is defiled, then join us in the LORD's land, where
the Tabernacle of the LORD is situated, and share our
land with us. But do not rebel against the LORD or
against us by building an altar other than the one
true altar of the LORD our God. 20 Didn't divine anger
fall on the entire community of Israel when Achan, a
member of the clan of Zerah, sinned by stealing the
things set apart for the LORD*? He was not the only
one who died because of his sin."

21 Then the people of Reuben, Gad, and the half-
tribe of Manasseh answered the heads of the clans
of Israel: 22 "The LORD, the Mighty One, is God! The
LORD, the Mighty One, is God! He knows the truth, and
may Israel know it, too! We have not built the altar
in treacherous rebellion against the LORD. If we have
done so, do not spare our lives this day. 23 If we have
built an altar for ourselves to turn away from the
LORD or to offer burnt offerings or grain offerings or
peace offerings, may the LORD himself punish us.

24 "The truth is, we have built this altar because we
fear that in the future your descendants will say to
ours, 'What right do you have to worship the LORD,
the God of Israel? 25 The LORD has placed the Jordan
River as a barrier between our people and you people
of Reuben and Gad. You have no claim to the LORD.' So
your descendants may prevent our descendants from
worshiping the LORD.

26 "So we decided to build the altar, not for burnt
offerings or sacrifices, 27 but as a memorial. It will re-
mind our descendants and your descendants that we,
too, have the right to worship the LORD at his sanc-
tuary with our burnt offerings, sacrifices, and peace
offerings. Then your descendants will not be able to
say to ours, 'You have no claim to the LORD.'

28 "If they say this, our descendants can reply, 'Look
at this copy of the LORD's altar that our ancestors
made. It is not for burnt offerings or sacrifices; it is
a reminder of the relationship both of us have with
the LORD.' 29 Far be it from us to rebel against the LORD
or turn away from him by building our own altar for
burnt offerings, grain offerings, or sacrifices. Only the
altar of the LORD our God that stands in front of the
Tabernacle may be used for that purpose."

30 When Phinehas the priest and the leaders of the
community—the heads of the clans of Israel—heard
this from the tribes of Reuben, Gad, and the half-tribe
of Manasseh, they were satisfied. 31 Phinehas son of

22:10 Or *to the circle of stones;* similarly in 22:11. **22:20** The Hebrew term used here refers to the complete consecration of things or people to the LORD, either by destroying them or by giving them as an offering.

22:2 you have obeyed every order I have given you. Joshua had asked a lot of these warriors. He had separated them from their families on the eastern side of the Jordan River for seven years to fight for their brothers' rights.

22:5 be very carefully to obey. Joshua expressed his concern for the infant nation among such a pagan people.

22:11 The rest of Israel heard . . . built an altar. The story of this altar got passed around from tribe to tribe until it was blown out of proportion. What was meant to be a symbol of a common faith was now rumored to be rebellion against God.

22:12 to go to war against them. Some of the Israelite tribes were actually considering going to war against the tribes on the eastern side of the Jordan River.

22:13-14 ten leaders of Israel. One delegate from each tribe went with Phinehas to investigate the altar erected by the eastern tribes.

22:27 at his sanctuary. The tabernacle at Shiloh housed the one true altar for worship. The law required all the Israelite men to gather there three times a year (Ex. 23:17). The eastern tribes had not intended to worship at the altar they had built—it was just symbolic.

Eleazar, the priest, replied to them, "Today we know
the LORD is among us because you have not commit-
ted this treachery against the LORD as we thought. In-
stead, you have rescued Israel from being destroyed
by the hand of the LORD."
32 Then Phinehas son of Eleazar, the priest, and the
other leaders left the tribes of Reuben and Gad in Gil-
ead and returned to the land of Canaan to tell the Is-
raelites what had happened. 33 And all the Israelites
were satisfied and praised God and spoke no more of
war against Reuben and Gad.
34 The people of Reuben and Gad named the altar
"Witness,"* for they said, "It is a witness between us
and them that the LORD is our God, too."

JOSHUA'S FINAL WORDS TO ISRAEL

23 The years passed, and the LORD had given the
people of Israel rest from all their enemies.
Joshua, who was now very old, 2 called together all
the elders, leaders, judges, and officers of Israel. He
said to them, "I am now a very old man. 3 You have
seen everything the LORD your God has done for you
during my lifetime. The LORD your God has fought for
you against your enemies. 4 I have allotted to you as
your homeland all the land of the nations yet uncon-
quered, as well as the land of those we have already
conquered—from the Jordan River to the Mediterra-
nean Sea* in the west. 5 This land will be yours, for the
LORD your God will himself drive out all the people
living there now. You will take possession of their
land, just as the LORD your God promised you.
6 "So be very careful to follow everything Moses
wrote in the Book of Instruction. Do not deviate from
it, turning either to the right or to the left. 7 Make sure
you do not associate with the other people still re-
maining in the land. Do not even mention the names
of their gods, much less swear by them or serve them
or worship them. 8 Rather, cling tightly to the LORD
your God as you have done until now.
9 "For the LORD has driven out great and powerful
nations for you, and no one has yet been able to defeat
you. 10 Each one of you will put to flight a thousand of
the enemy, for the LORD your God fights for you, just
as he has promised. 11 So be very careful to love the
LORD your God.
12 "But if you turn away from him and cling to the
customs of the survivors of these nations remaining
among you, and if you intermarry with them, 13 then
know for certain that the LORD your God will no lon-
ger drive them out of your land. Instead, they will be
a snare and a trap to you, a whip for your backs and
thorny brambles in your eyes, and you will vanish
from this good land the LORD your God has given you.
14 "Soon I will die, going the way of everything on
earth. Deep in your hearts you know that every prom-
ise of the LORD your God has come true. Not a single
one has failed! 15 But as surely as the LORD your God
has given you the good things he promised, he will
also bring disaster on you if you disobey him. He will
completely destroy you from this good land he has
given you. 16 If you break the covenant of the LORD
your God by worshiping and serving other gods, his
anger will burn against you, and you will quickly
vanish from the good land he has given you."

THE LORD'S COVENANT RENEWED

24 Then Joshua summoned all the tribes of Isra-
el to Shechem, including their elders, leaders,
judges, and officers. So they came and presented
themselves to God.
2 Joshua said to the people, "This is what the LORD,
the God of Israel, says: Long ago your ancestors, in-
cluding Terah, the father of Abraham and Nahor,
lived beyond the Euphrates River,* and they wor-
shiped other gods. 3 But I took your ancestor Abraham
from the land beyond the Euphrates and led him into
the land of Canaan. I gave him many descendants
through his son Isaac. 4 To Isaac I gave Jacob and
Esau. To Esau I gave the mountains of Seir, while Ja-
cob and his children went down into Egypt.
5 "Then I sent Moses and Aaron, and I brought ter-
rible plagues on Egypt; and afterward I brought you
out as a free people. 6 But when your ancestors ar-
rived at the Red Sea,* the Egyptians chased after you
with chariots and charioteers. 7 When your ancestors
cried out to the LORD, I put darkness between you and
the Egyptians. I brought the sea crashing down on
the Egyptians, drowning them. With your very own
eyes you saw what I did. Then you lived in the wilder-
ness for many years.
8 "Finally, I brought you into the land of the Am-
orites on the east side of the Jordan. They fought
against you, but I destroyed them before you. I gave
you victory over them, and you took possession of
their land. 9 Then Balak son of Zippor, king of Moab,
started a war against Israel. He summoned Balaam
son of Beor to curse you, 10 but I would not listen to
him. Instead, I made Balaam bless you, and so I res-
cued you from Balak.
11 "When you crossed the Jordan River and came
to Jericho, the men of Jericho fought against you, as
did the Amorites, the Perizzites, the Canaanites, the
Hittites, the Girgashites, the Hivites, and the Jebusites.
But I gave you victory over them. 12 And I sent terror*
ahead of you to drive out the two kings of the Am-
orites. It was not your swords or bows that brought
you victory. 13 I gave you land you had not worked on,
and I gave you towns you did not build—the towns
where you are now living. I gave you vineyards and
olive groves for food, though you did not plant them.
14 "So fear the LORD and serve him wholeheartedly.
ly. Put away forever the idols your ancestors wor-
shiped when they lived beyond the Euphrates Riv-
er and in Egypt. Serve the LORD alone. 15 But if you

22:34 Some manuscripts lack this word. 23:4 Hebrew *the Great Sea*. 24:2 Hebrew *the river;* also in 24:3, 14, 15. 24:6 Hebrew *sea of reeds*.
24:12 Often rendered *the hornet*. The meaning of the Hebrew is uncertain.

22:31 you have rescued Israel from being destroyed. One tribe's sin would have meant disaster for the entire nation. Phinehas was not exaggerating when he thanked the eastern tribes for sparing their lives as well.

23:1-2 Joshua . . . called together. Sensing the end of his life was near, Joshua summoned the leaders of Israel. He reviewed the past and exhorted the people to continue obeying the Lord.

23:6 be very careful. Joshua's last words to his people were the first words God had spoken to him at the beginning of his command (1:6).

23:12 if you . . . cling to the customs. The temptation to compromise by associating with the pagan people would be strong for the young nation. But Joshua warned the people of Israel to avoid them.

24:14 fear the LORD. To "fear" the Lord means worshipful submission, reverential awe, and obedient respect.

24:15 as for me . . . we will serve. Joshua knew he could not speak for Israel. The commitment to serve God must be an individual, personal decision.

refuse to serve the LORD, then choose today whom
you will serve. Would you prefer the gods your an-
cestors served beyond the Euphrates? Or will it be
the gods of the Amorites in whose land you now
live? But as for me and my family, we will serve the
LORD."
16 The people replied, "We would never abandon the
LORD and serve other gods. 17 For the LORD our God is
the one who rescued us and our ancestors from slav-
ery in the land of Egypt. He performed mighty mir-
acles before our very eyes. As we traveled through
the wilderness among our enemies, he preserved us.
18 It was the LORD who drove out the Amorites and the
other nations living here in the land. So we, too, will
serve the LORD, for he alone is our God."
19 Then Joshua warned the people, "You are not able
to serve the LORD, for he is a holy and jealous God.
He will not forgive your rebellion and your sins. 20 If
you abandon the LORD and serve other gods, he will
turn against you and destroy you, even though he has
been so good to you."
21 But the people answered Joshua, "No, we will
serve the LORD!"
22 "You are a witness to your own decision," Joshua
said. "You have chosen to serve the LORD."
"Yes," they replied, "we are witnesses to what we
have said."
23 "All right then," Joshua said, "destroy the idols
among you, and turn your hearts to the LORD, the God
of Israel."
24 The people said to Joshua, "We will serve the
LORD our God. We will obey him alone."
25 So Joshua made a covenant with the people that
day at Shechem, committing them to follow the de-
crees and regulations of the LORD. 26 Joshua recorded
these things in the Book of God's Instructions. As a re-
minder of their agreement, he took a huge stone and
rolled it beneath the terebinth tree beside the Taber-
nacle of the LORD.
27 Joshua said to all the people, "This stone has
heard everything the LORD said to us. It will be a wit-
ness to testify against you if you go back on your word
to God."
28 Then Joshua sent all the people away to their
own homelands.

LEADERS BURIED IN THE PROMISED LAND

29 After this, Joshua son of Nun, the servant of the
LORD, died at the age of 110. 30 They buried him in the
land he had been allocated, at Timnath-serah in the
hill country of Ephraim, north of Mount Gaash.
31 The people of Israel served the LORD throughout
the lifetime of Joshua and of the elders who outlived
him—those who had personally experienced all that
the LORD had done for Israel.
32 The bones of Joseph, which the Israelites had
brought along with them when they left Egypt, were
buried at Shechem, in the plot of land Jacob had
bought from the sons of Hamor for 100 pieces of sil-
ver.* This land was located in the territory allotted to
the descendants of Joseph.
33 Eleazar son of Aaron also died. He was buried in
the hill country of Ephraim, in the town of Gibeah,
which had been given to his son Phinehas.

24:32 Hebrew *100 kesitahs;* the value or weight of the kesitah is no longer known.

24:17-18 For the LORD our God. What choice could the people make other than to promise to serve the Lord? But their claims of loyalty would return to haunt them in the future when they fell away.

24:19 You are not able to serve the LORD. Joshua did not trust Israel's promise of allegiance to God. He feared they would not keep their commitment when they returned home. **Jealous God.** God is only called jealous when idolatry is mentioned. God burns with possessive, protective anger toward His people when they follow false gods.

24:22 You are a witness. Witnesses could be called to testify in court if one party was charged with breaking an agreement. Joshua made Israel function as their own witnesses to their oath to serve the Lord. They would indict themselves if they were untrue to God.

24:25 Joshua made a covenant with the people. As a symbol of personal commitment, Joshua signed and dated the terms of their agreement "in the Book God's instructions" (v. 26).

24:26 beside the Tabernacle of the LORD. Putting the memorial stone next to the sanctuary indicated that God Himself was witnessing the promise Israel made to remain true to Him.

24:31 throughout the lifetime of Joshua. Joshua was able to keep Israel on course throughout the time when he led the nation.

24:32 bones of Joseph . . . buried at Shechem. In fulfillment of prophecy, Joseph's bones were brought from a land of slavery to a land of freedom (Gen. 50:24-25). His grave was near the border between the territories settled by the descendants of his two sons, Ephraim and Manasseh.

INTRODUCTION TO JUDGES

PERSONAL READING PLAN

☐ Judges 1:1–2:5	☐ Judges 7:1–8:35	☐ Judges 15:1–16:31
☐ Judges 2:6–3:31	☐ Judges 9:1-57	☐ Judges 17:1–18:31
☐ Judges 4:1–5:31	☐ Judges 10:1–11:40	☐ Judges 19:1-30
☐ Judges 6:1-40	☐ Judges 12:1–14:20	☐ Judges 20:1–21:25

AUTHOR

The author of Judges is not designated in the book. Some view Samuel as the author, but this is uncertain.

DATE

The exact date of authorship is unknown, but Judges may have been written during the early period of the reign of David (circa 1000–980 B.C.). The action recorded here spans the period between the conquest and the monarchy of Israel.

THEME

God is merciful and long-suffering despite the sin of His people.

HISTORICAL BACKGROUND

The title of the book describes Israel's leaders from Joshua to the time when Israel had kings. Two to three hundred years lapse between the conquest of Canaan (after Joshua's death) and the rise of Saul (ca 1050 B.C.). During this time Israel was a loose confederation of tribes spread throughout the promised land. This area was heavily influenced by Canaanite culture and religion. Because of this, Israel desires to have a king like her neighbors (17:6; 18:1; 19:1; 21:25).

CHARACTERISTICS

Once in Canaan, all the Israelites needed to do was to obey God; instead, they followed the sinful example of the Canaanites. Their disobedience resulted in a cycle observed throughout the book (see 2:11-19): (1) there is apostasy or rebellion by God's people; (2) God raises up foreign oppressors to chasten His people; (3) a cry of distress goes up from the Israelites; (4) God raises up a "deliverer" or "judge" who takes up arms to defend the homeland and rescue the repentant people. The Lord's covenant faithfulness arises out of these repeated cycles. The book of Judges shows that even in dark, chaotic times, God is in control.

PASSAGES FOR TOPICAL GROUP STUDY

7:1-25 . . . VICTORY WITH GOD. . . . . An Upset Victory
14:1-20 . . YOUR OWN WAY and DATING . . . . . Faith Under Fire
16:1-22 . . WEAKNESSES and CHOICES . . . . A Really Bad Hair Day
16:23-31. . STRENGTH FROM GOD . . . . . The Secret of Strength

JUDGES 1

JUDAH AND SIMEON CONQUER THE LAND

1 After the death of Joshua, the Israelites asked the LORD, "Which tribe should go first to attack the Canaanites?"

2 The LORD answered, "Judah, for I have given them victory over the land."

3 The men of Judah said to their relatives from the tribe of Simeon, "Join with us to fight against the Canaanites living in the territory allotted to us. Then we will help you conquer your territory." So the men of Simeon went with Judah.

4 When the men of Judah attacked, the LORD gave them victory over the Canaanites and Perizzites, and they killed 10,000 enemy warriors at the town of Bezek. 5 While at Bezek they encountered King Adoni-bezek and fought against him, and the Canaanites and Perizzites were defeated. 6 Adoni-bezek escaped, but the Israelites soon captured him and cut off his thumbs and big toes.

7 Adoni-bezek said, "I once had seventy kings with their thumbs and big toes cut off, eating scraps from under my table. Now God has paid me back for what I did to them." They took him to Jerusalem, and he died there.

8 The men of Judah attacked Jerusalem and captured it, killing all its people and setting the city on fire. 9 Then they went down to fight the Canaanites living in the hill country, the Negev, and the western foothills.* 10 Judah marched against the Canaanites in Hebron (formerly called Kiriath-arba), defeating the forces of Sheshai, Ahiman, and Talmai.

11 From there they went to fight against the people living in the town of Debir (formerly called Kiriath-sepher). 12 Caleb said, "I will give my daughter Acsah in marriage to the one who attacks and captures Kiriath-sepher." 13 Othniel, the son of Caleb's younger brother, Kenaz, was the one who conquered it, so Acsah became Othniel's wife.

14 When Acsah married Othniel, she urged him* to ask her father for a field. As she got down off her donkey, Caleb asked her, "What's the matter?"

15 She said, "Let me have another gift. You have already given me land in the Negev; now please give me springs of water, too." So Caleb gave her the upper and lower springs.

16 When the tribe of Judah left Jericho—the city of palms—the Kenites, who were descendants of Moses' father-in-law, traveled with them into the wilderness of Judah. They settled among the people there, near the town of Arad in the Negev.

17 Then Judah joined with Simeon to fight against the Canaanites living in Zephath, and they completely destroyed* the town. So the town was named Hormah.* 18 In addition, Judah captured the towns of Gaza, Ashkelon, and Ekron, along with their surrounding territories.

ISRAEL FAILS TO CONQUER THE LAND

19 The LORD was with the people of Judah, and they took possession of the hill country. But they failed to drive out the people living in the plains, who had iron chariots. 20 The town of Hebron was given to Caleb as Moses had promised. And Caleb drove out the people living there, who were descendants of the three sons of Anak.

21 The tribe of Benjamin, however, failed to drive out the Jebusites, who were living in Jerusalem. So to this day the Jebusites live in Jerusalem among the people of Benjamin.

22 The descendants of Joseph attacked the town of Bethel, and the LORD was with them. 23 They sent men to scout out Bethel (formerly known as Luz). 24 They confronted a man coming out of the town and said to him, "Show us a way into the town, and we will have mercy on you." 25 So he showed them a way in, and they killed everyone in the town except that man and his family. 26 Later the man moved to the land of the Hittites, where he built a town. He named it Luz, which is its name to this day.

27 The tribe of Manasseh failed to drive out the people living in Beth-shan,* Taanach, Dor, Ibleam, Megiddo, and all their surrounding settlements, because the Canaanites were determined to stay in that region. 28 When the Israelites grew stronger, they forced the Canaanites to work as slaves, but they never did drive them completely out of the land.

29 The tribe of Ephraim failed to drive out the Canaanites living in Gezer, so the Canaanites continued to live there among them.

30 The tribe of Zebulun failed to drive out the residents of Kitron and Nahalol, so the Canaanites continued to live among them. But the Canaanites were forced to work as slaves for the people of Zebulun.

31 The tribe of Asher failed to drive out the residents of Acco, Sidon, Ahlab, Aczib, Helbah, Aphik, and Rehob. 32 Instead, the people of Asher moved in among the Canaanites, who controlled the land, for they failed to drive them out.

33 Likewise, the tribe of Naphtali failed to drive out the residents of Beth-shemesh and Beth-anath. Instead, they moved in among the Canaanites, who controlled the land. Nevertheless, the people of Beth-shemesh and Beth-anath were forced to work as slaves for the people of Naphtali.

34 As for the tribe of Dan, the Amorites forced them back into the hill country and would not let them come down into the plains. 35 The Amorites were determined to stay in Mount Heres, Aijalon, and Shaalbim, but when the descendants of Joseph became stronger, they forced the Amorites to work as slaves. 36 The boundary of the Amorites ran from Scorpion Pass* to Sela and continued upward from there.

1:9 Hebrew *the Shephelah.* **1:14** Greek version and Latin Vulgate read *he urged her.* **1:17a** The Hebrew term used here refers to the complete consecration of things or people to the LORD, either by destroying them or by giving them as an offering. **1:17b** *Hormah* means "destruction." **1:27** Hebrew *Beth-shean,* a variant spelling of Beth-shan. **1:36** Hebrew *Akrabbim.*

1:1–3:6 Putting up with idolatry proved easier than putting out the pagans (2:2). Israel repeatedly disobeyed God and experienced defeat. The Lord sent leader-heroes to deliver them.

1:1 After the death of Joshua. Without their leader, Israel hesitated. **go first to attack.** Each tribe wanted the other's help to drive out its enemies.

1:8 set the city on fire. Burning the city made Israel's victory permanent.

1:12 I will give my daughter Achsah in marriage. Caleb gained a city and a son-in-law with this deal.

1:17 fight against the Canaanites. Judah and Simeon were carrying out God's judgment.

1:21 tribe of Benjamin. The tribe of Benjamin dropped the ball. David had to finish the job years later (see 2 Sam. 5:6-9).

1:22 descendants of Joseph. Ephraim and Manasseh were Joseph's sons (see Gen. 48:13).

1:25 except the man and his family. Like Rahab in Jericho (see Josh. 2:1-21), the man who helped the Israelites at Bethel was spared.

1:33 were forced to work as slaves. Inhabitants who were not destroyed were enslaved by the Israelites.

THE LORD'S MESSENGER COMES TO BOKIM

2 The angel of the LORD went up from Gilgal to Bokim and said to the Israelites, "I brought you out of Egypt into this land that I swore to give your ancestors, and I said I would never break my covenant with you. 2 For your part, you were not to make any covenants with the people living in this land; instead, you were to destroy their altars. But you disobeyed my command. Why did you do this? 3 So now I declare that I will no longer drive out the people living in your land. They will be thorns in your sides,* and their gods will be a constant temptation to you."

4 When the angel of the LORD finished speaking to all the Israelites, the people wept loudly. 5 So they called the place Bokim (which means "weeping"), and they offered sacrifices there to the LORD.

THE DEATH OF JOSHUA

6 After Joshua sent the people away, each of the tribes left to take possession of the land allotted to them. 7 And the Israelites served the LORD throughout the lifetime of Joshua and the leaders who outlived him—those who had seen all the great things the LORD had done for Israel.

8 Joshua son of Nun, the servant of the LORD, died at the age of 110. 9 They buried him in the land he had been allocated, at Timnath-serah* in the hill country of Ephraim, north of Mount Gaash.

ISRAEL DISOBEYS THE LORD

10 After that generation died, another generation grew up who did not acknowledge the LORD or remember the mighty things he had done for Israel.

11 The Israelites did evil in the LORD's sight and served the images of Baal. 12 They abandoned the LORD, the God of their ancestors, who had brought them out of Egypt. They went after other gods, worshiping the gods of the people around them. And they angered the LORD. 13 They abandoned the LORD to serve Baal and the images of Ashtoreth. 14 This made the LORD burn with anger against Israel, so he handed them over to raiders who stole their possessions. He turned them over to their enemies all around, and they were no longer able to resist them. 15 Every time Israel went out to battle, the LORD fought against them, causing them to be defeated, just as he had warned. And the people were in great distress.

THE LORD RESCUES HIS PEOPLE

16 Then the LORD raised up judges to rescue the Israelites from their attackers. 17 Yet Israel did not listen to the judges but prostituted themselves by worshiping other gods. How quickly they turned away from the path of their ancestors, who had walked in obedience to the LORD's commands.

18 Whenever the LORD raised up a judge over Israel, he was with that judge and rescued the people from their enemies throughout the judge's lifetime. For the LORD took pity on his people, who were burdened by oppression and suffering. 19 But when the judge died, the people returned to their corrupt ways, behaving worse than those who had lived before them. They went after other gods, serving and worshiping them. And they refused to give up their evil practices and stubborn ways.

20 So the LORD burned with anger against Israel. He said, "Because these people have violated my covenant, which I made with their ancestors, and have ignored my commands, 21 I will no longer drive out the nations that Joshua left unconquered when he died. 22 I did this to test Israel—to see whether or not they would follow the ways of the LORD as their ancestors did." 23 That is why the LORD left those nations in place. He did not quickly drive them out or allow Joshua to conquer them all.

THE NATIONS LEFT IN CANAAN

3 These are the nations that the LORD left in the land to test those Israelites who had not experienced the wars of Canaan. 2 He did this to teach warfare to generations of Israelites who had no experience in battle. 3 These are the nations: the Philistines (those living under the five Philistine rulers), all the Canaanites, the Sidonians, and the Hivites living in the mountains of Lebanon from Mount Baal-hermon to Lebo-hamath. 4 These people were left to test the Israelites—to see whether they would obey the commands the LORD had given to their ancestors through Moses.

5 So the people of Israel lived among the Canaanites, Hittites, Amorites, Perizzites, Hivites, and Jebusites, 6 and they intermarried with them. Israelite sons married their daughters, and Israelite daughters were given in marriage to their sons. And the Israelites served their gods.

OTHNIEL BECOMES ISRAEL'S JUDGE

7 The Israelites did evil in the LORD's sight. They forgot about the LORD their God, and they served the images of Baal and the Asherah poles. 8 Then the LORD burned with anger against Israel, and he turned them over to King Cushan-rishathaim of Aram-naharaim.* And the Israelites served Cushan-rishathaim for eight years.

9 But when the people of Israel cried out to the LORD for help, the LORD raised up a rescuer to save them. His name was Othniel, the son of Caleb's younger brother, Kenaz. 10 The Spirit of the LORD came upon him, and he became Israel's judge. He went to war against King Cushan-rishathaim of Aram, and the LORD gave Othniel victory over him. 11 So there was peace in the land for forty years. Then Othniel son of Kenaz died.

2:3 Hebrew *They will be in your sides;* compare Num 33:55. 2:9 As in parallel text at Josh 24:30; Hebrew reads *Timnath-heres,* a variant spelling of Timnath-serah. 3:8 *Aram-naharaim* means "Aram of the two rivers," thought to have been located between the Euphrates and Balih Rivers in northwestern Mesopotamia.

2:1-5 The Angel of the LORD confronted Israel with their broken vows.
2:6–3:6 Israel's commitment to principle ends, and the cycle of disobedience, defeat, and delivery begins.
2:10 another generation grew up. The new generation knew nothing about the Red Sea or Jordan River miracles.
2:11 images of Baal. God kept the Israelites from winning wars whenever they worshiped the Canaanite idols.
2:16-19 Israel did not listen. The judges were the leader-heroes of the land. Whenever a judge led Israel, relative calm resulted. Whenever Israel was between heroes, however, it soon forgot its priorities.
3:1-6 The Israelites failed God's test, accepting the lifestyle of their pagan neighbors, worshiping their gods, and even intermarrying with them.
3:7-11 Othniel is the first of many judges of Israel.
3:10 The Spirit of the LORD. The judge symbolizes God's presence among the people.

EHUD BECOMES ISRAEL'S JUDGE

12 Once again the Israelites did evil in the LORD's sight,
and the LORD gave King Eglon of Moab control over
Israel because of their evil. 13 Eglon enlisted the Am-
monites and Amalekites as allies, and then he went
out and defeated Israel, taking possession of Jericho,
the city of palms. 14 And the Israelites served Eglon of
Moab for eighteen years.

15 But when the people of Israel cried out to the LORD
for help, the LORD again raised up a rescuer to save
them. His name was Ehud son of Gera, a left-handed
man of the tribe of Benjamin. The Israelites sent Ehud
to deliver their tribute money to King Eglon of Moab.
16 So Ehud made a double-edged dagger that was
about a foot* long, and he strapped it to his right thigh,
keeping it hidden under his clothing. 17 He brought the
tribute money to Eglon, who was very fat.

18 After delivering the payment, Ehud started home
with those who had helped carry the tribute. 19 But
when Ehud reached the stone idols near Gilgal, he
turned back. He came to Eglon and said, "I have a se-
cret message for you."

So the king commanded his servants, "Be quiet!"
and he sent them all out of the room.

20 Ehud walked over to Eglon, who was sitting
alone in a cool upstairs room. And Ehud said, "I have
a message from God for you!" As King Eglon rose from
his seat, 21 Ehud reached with his left hand, pulled out
the dagger strapped to his right thigh, and plunged it
into the king's belly. 22 The dagger went so deep that
the handle disappeared beneath the king's fat. So
Ehud did not pull out the dagger, and the king's bow-
els emptied.* 23 Then Ehud closed and locked the doors
of the room and escaped down the latrine.*

24 After Ehud was gone, the king's servants re-
turned and found the doors to the upstairs room
locked. They thought he might be using the latrine in
the room, 25 so they waited. But when the king didn't
come out after a long delay, they became concerned
and got a key. And when they opened the doors, they
found their master dead on the floor.

26 While the servants were waiting, Ehud escaped,
passing the stone idols on his way to Seirah. 27 When
he arrived in the hill country of Ephraim, Ehud
sounded a call to arms. Then he led a band of Isra-
elites down from the hills.

28 "Follow me," he said, "for the LORD has given you
victory over Moab your enemy." So they followed him.
And the Israelites took control of the shallow cross-
ings of the Jordan River across from Moab, prevent-
ing anyone from crossing.

29 They attacked the Moabites and killed about
10,000 of their strongest and most able-bodied war-
riors. Not one of them escaped. 30 So Moab was con-
quered by Israel that day, and there was peace in the
land for eighty years.

SHAMGAR BECOMES ISRAEL'S JUDGE

31 After Ehud, Shamgar son of Anath rescued Israel.
He once killed 600 Philistines with an ox goad.

DEBORAH BECOMES ISRAEL'S JUDGE

4 After Ehud's death, the Israelites again did evil in
the LORD's sight. 2 So the LORD turned them over
to King Jabin of Hazor, a Canaanite king. The com-
mander of his army was Sisera, who lived in Haro-
sheth-haggoyim. 3 Sisera, who had 900 iron chariots,
ruthlessly oppressed the Israelites for twenty years.
Then the people of Israel cried out to the LORD for
help.

4 Deborah, the wife of Lappidoth, was a prophet
who was judging Israel at that time. 5 She would sit
under the Palm of Deborah, between Ramah and
Bethel in the hill country of Ephraim, and the Isra-
elites would go to her for judgment. 6 One day she
sent for Barak son of Abinoam, who lived in Kedesh
in the land of Naphtali. She said to him, "This is what
the LORD, the God of Israel, commands you: Call out
10,000 warriors from the tribes of Naphtali and Zeb-
ulun at Mount Tabor. 7 And I will call out Sisera, com-
mander of Jabin's army, along with his chariots and
warriors, to the Kishon River. There I will give you
victory over him."

8 Barak told her, "I will go, but only if you go with
me."

9 "Very well," she replied, "I will go with you. But
you will receive no honor in this venture, for the
LORD's victory over Sisera will be at the hands of a
woman." So Deborah went with Barak to Kedesh. 10 At
Kedesh, Barak called together the tribes of Zebulun
and Naphtali, and 10,000 warriors went up with him.
Deborah also went with him.

11 Now Heber the Kenite, a descendant of Moses'
brother-in-law* Hobab, had moved away from the
other members of his tribe and pitched his tent by the
oak of Zaanannim near Kedesh.

12 When Sisera was told that Barak son of Abin-
oam had gone up to Mount Tabor, 13 he called for all
900 of his iron chariots and all of his warriors, and
they marched from Harosheth-haggoyim to the Kis-
hon River.

14 Then Deborah said to Barak, "Get ready! This is
the day the LORD will give you victory over Sisera,
for the LORD is marching ahead of you." So Barak led
his 10,000 warriors down the slopes of Mount Tabor
into battle. 15 When Barak attacked, the LORD threw
Sisera and all his chariots and warriors into a panic.
Sisera leaped down from his chariot and escaped on
foot. 16 Then Barak chased the chariots and the enemy
army all the way to Harosheth-haggoyim, killing all
of Sisera's warriors. Not a single one was left alive.

17 Meanwhile, Sisera ran to the tent of Jael, the wife
of Heber the Kenite, because Heber's family was on

3:16 Hebrew *gomed,* the length of which is uncertain. **3:22** Or *and it came out behind.* **3:23** Or *and went out through the porch;* the meaning of the Hebrew is uncertain. **4:11** Or *father-in-law.*

3:12-30 After murdering the king of Moab, Ehud escapes to Israel and then leads them in destroying the Moabite nation.

3:28 the LORD has given you victory. Ehud realizes he was merely the Lord's tool.

3:31 Shamgar. A rugged fighter, Shamgar is credited with "saving" Israel.

4:1-24 The LORD again demonstrates His power through a deliverer—this time a female judge, Deborah.

4:4 Deborah. As a judge, Deborah settled disputes among the Israelites. As a prophetess, she predicted victory for Israel against the Canaanites.

4:6 Barak. Deborah picked him to command Israel's troops.

4:7 I will call out Sisera. According to God's plan, an ideal battleground for Sisera turned into a muddy disaster.

4:9 at the hands of a woman. When Barak hesitated to go forward, Deborah predicted a woman would help secure the victory (vv. 18-22).

4:11 Heber the Kenite. This Kenite nomad was related to Moses, but he had been sleeping with the enemy (v. 17).

4:14 marching ahead of you. Deborah herself would not go into battle, but the Lord advanced before Barak and his army.

friendly terms with King Jabin of Hazor. 18 Jael went
out to meet Sisera and said to him, "Come into my tent,
sir. Come in. Don't be afraid." So he went into her tent,
and she covered him with a blanket.
19 "Please give me some water," he said. "I'm thirsty."
So she gave him some milk from a leather bag and
covered him again.
20 "Stand at the door of the tent," he told her. "If any-
body comes and asks you if there is anyone here, say
no."
21 But when Sisera fell asleep from exhaustion, Jael
quietly crept up to him with a hammer and tent peg
in her hand. Then she drove the tent peg through his
temple and into the ground, and so he died.
22 When Barak came looking for Sisera, Jael went
out to meet him. She said, "Come, and I will show you
the man you are looking for." So he followed her into
the tent and found Sisera lying there dead, with the
tent peg through his temple.
23 So on that day Israel saw God defeat Jabin, the Ca-
naanite king. 24 And from that time on Israel became
stronger and stronger against King Jabin until they
finally destroyed him.

THE SONG OF DEBORAH

5 On that day Deborah and Barak son of Abinoam
sang this song:

2 "Israel's leaders took charge,
and the people gladly followed.
Praise the LORD!

3 "Listen, you kings!
Pay attention, you mighty rulers!
For I will sing to the LORD.
I will make music to the LORD, the God of Israel.

4 "LORD, when you set out from Seir
and marched across the fields of Edom,
the earth trembled,
and the cloudy skies poured down rain.
5 The mountains quaked in the presence of the LORD,
the God of Mount Sinai—
in the presence of the LORD,
the God of Israel.

6 "In the days of Shamgar son of Anath,
and in the days of Jael,
people avoided the main roads,
and travelers stayed on winding pathways.
7 There were few people left in the villages of Israel*—
until Deborah arose as a mother for Israel.
8 When Israel chose new gods,
war erupted at the city gates.
Yet not a shield or spear could be seen
among forty thousand warriors in Israel!
9 My heart is with the commanders of Israel,
with those who volunteered for war.
Praise the LORD!

10 "Consider this, you who ride on fine donkeys,
you who sit on fancy saddle blankets,
and you who walk along the road.
11 Listen to the village musicians*
gathered at the watering holes.
They recount the righteous victories of the LORD
and the victories of his villagers in Israel.
Then the people of the LORD
marched down to the city gates.

12 "Wake up, Deborah, wake up!
Wake up, wake up, and sing a song!
Arise, Barak!
Lead your captives away, son of Abinoam!

13 "Down from Tabor marched the few against the nobles.
The people of the LORD marched down against mighty warriors.
14 They came down from Ephraim—
a land that once belonged to the Amalekites;
they followed you, Benjamin, with your troops.
From Makir the commanders marched down;
from Zebulun came those who carry a commander's staff.
15 The princes of Issachar were with Deborah and Barak.
They followed Barak, rushing into the valley.
But in the tribe of Reuben
there was great indecision.*
16 Why did you sit at home among the sheepfolds—
to hear the shepherds whistle for their flocks?
Yes, in the tribe of Reuben
there was great indecision.
17 Gilead remained east of the Jordan.
And why did Dan stay home?
Asher sat unmoved at the seashore,
remaining in his harbors.
18 But Zebulun risked his life,
as did Naphtali, on the heights of the battlefield.

19 "The kings of Canaan came and fought,
at Taanach near Megiddo's springs,
but they carried off no silver treasures.
20 The stars fought from heaven.
The stars in their orbits fought against Sisera.
21 The Kishon River swept them away—
that ancient torrent, the Kishon.
March on with courage, my soul!
22 Then the horses' hooves hammered the ground,
the galloping, galloping of Sisera's mighty steeds.
23 'Let the people of Meroz be cursed,' said the angel of the LORD.
'Let them be utterly cursed,

5:7 The meaning of the Hebrew is uncertain. 5:11 The meaning of the Hebrew is uncertain. 5:15 As in some Hebrew manuscripts and Syriac version, which read *searchings of heart;* Masoretic Text reads *resolve of heart.*

4:18 he went into her tent. As a family friend, Sisera did not suspect Jael's warm behavior.

4:21 drove the tent peg through his temple. Accustomed to pitching and tearing down tents, Jael used familiar tools to murder the commander as Deborah had predicted (v. 9).

5:1-31 Deborahs celebrates the great victory over the Canaanites with one of the oldest poems in the Bible.

5:5 Sinai. Deborah reminds the people of their ancestors' commitment to the covenant with God at Mt. Sinai (see Ex. 19:17-20).

5:13-18 Deborah reviews those who contributed to Israel's campaign. Tribes who did not join the united effort are criticized for their indifference.

because they did not come to help the LORD—
to help the LORD against the mighty warriors.'

24 "Most blessed among women is Jael,
the wife of Heber the Kenite.
May she be blessed above all women who live
in tents.
25 Sisera asked for water,
and she gave him milk.
In a bowl fit for nobles,
she brought him yogurt.
26 Then with her left hand she reached for a tent peg,
and with her right hand for the workman's
hammer.
She struck Sisera with the hammer, crushing his
head.
With a shattering blow, she pierced his temples.
27 He sank, he fell,
he lay still at her feet.
And where he sank,
there he died.

28 "From the window Sisera's mother looked out.
Through the window she watched for his
return, saying,
'Why is his chariot so long in coming?
Why don't we hear the sound of chariot
wheels?'

29 "Her wise women answer,
and she repeats these words to herself:
30 'They must be dividing the captured plunder—
with a woman or two for every man.
There will be colorful robes for Sisera,
and colorful, embroidered robes for me.
Yes, the plunder will include
colorful robes embroidered on both sides.'

31 "LORD, may all your enemies die like Sisera!
But may those who love you rise like the sun in
all its power!"

Then there was peace in the land for forty years.

GIDEON BECOMES ISRAEL'S JUDGE

6 The Israelites did evil in the LORD's sight. So the
LORD handed them over to the Midianites for
seven years. 2 The Midianites were so cruel that the
Israelites made hiding places for themselves in the
mountains, caves, and strongholds. 3 Whenever the
Israelites planted their crops, marauders from Mid-
ian, Amalek, and the people of the east would attack
Israel, 4 camping in the land and destroying crops as
far away as Gaza. They left the Israelites with noth-
ing to eat, taking all the sheep, goats, cattle, and don-
keys. 5 These enemy hordes, coming with their live-
stock and tents, were as thick as locusts; they arrived
on droves of camels too numerous to count. And they
stayed until the land was stripped bare. 6 So Israel
was reduced to starvation by the Midianites. Then the
Israelites cried out to the LORD for help.
7 When they cried out to the LORD because of Mid-
ian, 8 the LORD sent a prophet to the Israelites. He
said, "This is what the LORD, the God of Israel, says: I
brought you up out of slavery in Egypt. 9 I rescued you
from the Egyptians and from all who oppressed you.
I drove out your enemies and gave you their land. 10 I
told you, 'I am the LORD your God. You must not wor-
ship the gods of the Amorites, in whose land you now
live.' But you have not listened to me."
11 Then the angel of the LORD came and sat beneath
the great tree at Ophrah, which belonged to Joash of
the clan of Abiezer. Gideon son of Joash was thresh-
ing wheat at the bottom of a winepress to hide the
grain from the Midianites. 12 The angel of the LORD
appeared to him and said, "Mighty hero, the LORD is
with you!"
13 "Sir," Gideon replied, "if the LORD is with us, why
has all this happened to us? And where are all the
miracles our ancestors told us about? Didn't they say,
'The LORD brought us up out of Egypt'? But now the
LORD has abandoned us and handed us over to the
Midianites."
14 Then the LORD turned to him and said, "Go with
the strength you have, and rescue Israel from the
Midianites. I am sending you!"
15 "But Lord," Gideon replied, "how can I rescue Is-
rael? My clan is the weakest in the whole tribe of Ma-
nasseh, and I am the least in my entire family!"
16 The LORD said to him, "I will be with you. And you
will destroy the Midianites as if you were fighting
against one man."
17 Gideon replied, "If you are truly going to help
me, show me a sign to prove that it is really the LORD
speaking to me. 18 Don't go away until I come back and
bring my offering to you."
He answered, "I will stay here until you return."
19 Gideon hurried home. He cooked a young goat,
and with a basket* of flour he baked some bread
without yeast. Then, carrying the meat in a basket
and the broth in a pot, he brought them out and pre-
sented them to the angel, who was under the great
tree.
20 The angel of God said to him, "Place the meat and
the unleavened bread on this rock, and pour the broth
over it." And Gideon did as he was told. 21 Then the an-
gel of the LORD touched the meat and bread with the
tip of the staff in his hand, and fire flamed up from the
rock and consumed all he had brought. And the angel
of the LORD disappeared.

6:19 Hebrew *an ephah* [20 quarts or 22 liters].

5:31 peace. The period of peace completes the cycle the Israelites experienced. Upon the death of Deborah, however, the cycle begins again with Israel's disobedience.

6:1–9:57 Despite a series of judges and their heroic efforts, Israel continued to deteriorate. The account of Gideon's victory shows that Israel had a real opportunity to change its course and return to God. Even Gideon, however, ultimately disobeyed God (8:24-27). Abimelech's self-proclaimed royalty (9:1-57) contributes to the decline.

6:7 because of Midian. The Israelites blamed the Midianites for their problems, but God had used Midian to punish the Israelites' unfaithfulness to Him.

6:11 threshing wheat at the bottom of a winepress. People usually threshed wheat in the open air so the wind could take away the chaff. With the threat of Midianite attack, however, Gideon sought safety in the winepress.

6:12 Mighty hero. The Angel of the LORD saw the potential for a mighty warrior in this laborer.

6:14 I am sending you Gideon did not know it then, but he was being selected as the next judge to deliver Israel.

6:15 how can I rescue Israel? Gideon's focus was not on his faith in God but on his small family. How could he be a hero?

6:17 show me a sign. Gideon's small faith needed more assurance.

22 When Gideon realized that it was the angel of the
LORD, he cried out, "Oh, Sovereign LORD, I'm doomed! I
have seen the angel of the LORD face to face!"
23 "It is all right," the LORD replied. "Do not be
afraid. You will not die." 24 And Gideon built an al-
tar to the LORD there and named it Yahweh-Shalom
(which means "the LORD is peace"). The altar re-
mains in Ophrah in the land of the clan of Abiezer
to this day.
25 That night the LORD said to Gideon, "Take the
second bull from your father's herd, the one that
is seven years old. Pull down your father's altar to
Baal, and cut down the Asherah pole standing be-
side it. 26 Then build an altar to the LORD your God
here on this hilltop sanctuary, laying the stones
carefully. Sacrifice the bull as a burnt offering on
the altar, using as fuel the wood of the Asherah pole
you cut down."
27 So Gideon took ten of his servants and did as the
LORD had commanded. But he did it at night because
he was afraid of the other members of his father's
household and the people of the town.
28 Early the next morning, as the people of the town
began to stir, someone discovered that the altar of
Baal had been broken down and that the Asherah
pole beside it had been cut down. In their place a new
altar had been built, and on it were the remains of
the bull that had been sacrificed. 29 The people said to
each other, "Who did this?" And after asking around
and making a careful search, they learned that it was
Gideon, the son of Joash.
30 "Bring out your son," the men of the town de-
manded of Joash. "He must die for destroying the altar
of Baal and for cutting down the Asherah pole."
31 But Joash shouted to the mob that confronted
him, "Why are you defending Baal? Will you argue
his case? Whoever pleads his case will be put to death
by morning! If Baal truly is a god, let him defend him-
self and destroy the one who broke down his altar!"
32 From then on Gideon was called Jerub-baal, which
means "Let Baal defend himself," because he broke
down Baal's altar.

GIDEON ASKS FOR A SIGN

33 Soon afterward the armies of Midian, Amalek, and
the people of the east formed an alliance against Is-
rael and crossed the Jordan, camping in the valley of
Jezreel. 34 Then the Spirit of the LORD clothed Gideon
with power. He blew a ram's horn as a call to arms,
and the men of the clan of Abiezer came to him. 35 He
also sent messengers throughout Manasseh, Asher,
Zebulun, and Naphtali, summoning their warriors,
and all of them responded.
36 Then Gideon said to God, "If you are truly going
to use me to rescue Israel as you promised, 37 prove
it to me in this way. I will put a wool fleece on the
threshing floor tonight. If the fleece is wet with dew
in the morning but the ground is dry, then I will
know that you are going to help me rescue Israel as
you promised." 38 And that is just what happened.
When Gideon got up early the next morning, he
squeezed the fleece and wrung out a whole bowlful
of water.
39 Then Gideon said to God, "Please don't be angry
with me, but let me make one more request. Let me
use the fleece for one more test. This time let the fleece
remain dry while the ground around it is wet with
dew." 40 So that night God did as Gideon asked. The
fleece was dry in the morning, but the ground was
covered with dew.

GIDEON DEFEATS THE MIDIANITES

7 So Jerub-baal (that is, Gideon) and his army got up
early and went as far as the spring of Harod. The
armies of Midian were camped north of them in the
valley near the hill of Moreh. 2 The LORD said to Gide-
on, "You have too many warriors with you. If I let all
of you fight the Midianites, the Israelites will boast to
me that they saved themselves by their own strength.
3 Therefore, tell the people, 'Whoever is timid or afraid
may leave this mountain* and go home.'" So 22,000 of
them went home, leaving only 10,000 who were will-
ing to fight.
4 But the LORD told Gideon, "There are still too
many! Bring them down to the spring, and I will test
them to determine who will go with you and who
will not." 5 When Gideon took his warriors down to
the water, the LORD told him, "Divide the men into two
groups. In one group put all those who cup water in
their hands and lap it up with their tongues like dogs.
In the other group put all those who kneel down and
drink with their mouths in the stream." 6 Only 300 of
the men drank from their hands. All the others got
down on their knees and drank with their mouths in
the stream.
7 The LORD told Gideon, "With these 300 men I will
rescue you and give you victory over the Midianites.
Send all the others home." 8 So Gideon collected the
provisions and rams' horns of the other warriors
and sent them home. But he kept the 300 men with
him.
The Midianite camp was in the valley just below
Gideon. 9 That night the LORD said, "Get up! Go down
into the Midianite camp, for I have given you vic-
tory over them! 10 But if you are afraid to attack, go
down to the camp with your servant Purah. 11 Lis-
ten to what the Midianites are saying, and you will
be greatly encouraged. Then you will be eager to
attack."
So Gideon took Purah and went down to the edge
of the enemy camp. 12 The armies of Midian, Amalek,
and the people of the east had settled in the valley
like a swarm of locusts. Their camels were like grains
of sand on the seashore—too many to count! 13 Gide-
on crept up just as a man was telling his companion
about a dream. The man said, "I had this dream, and

7:3 Hebrew *may leave Mount Gilead.* The identity of Mount Gilead is uncertain in this context. It is perhaps used here as another name for Mount Gilboa.

6:25 Pull down your father's altar to Baal. Sacrificing the symbol of his father's pagan faith would demonstrate God's superiority and Gideon's new start.

6:34 Spirit of the LORD. God's Spirit empowered Gideon to do His work. He now feels more confident about God's instructions for his life.

7:1-8 Large numbers were not high on God's list of requirements for success. In fact, he shaved thousands of men off Gideon's battle plan and accomplished victory—with only 300 warriors.

7:3 go home. God wanted warriors who were confident in His ability to make them strong.

7:4-8 cup water in their hands and lap it up. Another test weeded the army down from 10,000 to just 300, to go against the Midianites' army of 135,000. God wanted to leave no doubt that the victory was His doing.

7:8-14 Eavesdropping became an important morale booster and battle strategy for Gideon when an enemy's dream was interpreted to predict the Israelites' victory.

AN UPSET VICTORY

1. What is the biggest "upset victory" you have experienced? Were you a winner or loser?

JUDGES 7:1-25

2. Why did God ask Gideon to reduce the size of his army?
3. Why did He select the men who drank water while looking around? What does this suggest about how to be a good "soldier" for Christ?
4. How did God use the man's dream (v. 13) to bring about victory? How has God used circumstances in your own life to bring about His will?
5. Are you facing an overpowering "enemy" in competition? In your life? In your mental attitude? How do you need God's help in fighting the battle?

in my dream a loaf of barley bread came tumbling
down into the Midianite camp. It hit a tent, turned it
over, and knocked it flat!"
14 His companion answered, "Your dream can mean
only one thing—God has given Gideon son of Joash,
the Israelite, victory over Midian and all its allies!"
15 When Gideon heard the dream and its interpreta-
tion, he bowed in worship before the LORD.* Then he
returned to the Israelite camp and shouted, "Get up!
For the LORD has given you victory over the Midianite
hordes!" 16 He divided the 300 men into three groups
and gave each man a ram's horn and a clay jar with
a torch in it.
17 Then he said to them, "Keep your eyes on me.
When I come to the edge of the camp, do just as I do.
18 As soon as I and those with me blow the rams' horns,
blow your horns, too, all around the entire camp, and
shout, 'For the LORD and for Gideon!'"
19 It was just after midnight,* after the changing of
the guard, when Gideon and the 100 men with him
reached the edge of the Midianite camp. Suddenly,
they blew the rams' horns and broke their clay jars.
20 Then all three groups blew their horns and broke
their jars. They held the blazing torches in their left
hands and the horns in their right hands, and they all
shouted, "A sword for the LORD and for Gideon!"
21 Each man stood at his position around the camp
and watched as all the Midianites rushed around in
a panic, shouting as they ran to escape. 22 When the
300 Israelites blew their rams' horns, the LORD caused
the warriors in the camp to fight against each other
with their swords. Those who were not killed fled to
places as far away as Beth-shittah near Zererah and
to the border of Abel-meholah near Tabbath.
23 Then Gideon sent for the warriors of Naphtali,
Asher, and Manasseh, who joined in chasing the army
of Midian. 24 Gideon also sent messengers throughout
the hill country of Ephraim, saying, "Come down to at-
tack the Midianites. Cut them off at the shallow cross-
ings of the Jordan River at Beth-barah."
So all the men of Ephraim did as they were told.
25 They captured Oreb and Zeeb, the two Midianite
commanders, killing Oreb at the rock of Oreb, and
Zeeb at the winepress of Zeeb. And they continued
to chase the Midianites. Afterward the Israelites
brought the heads of Oreb and Zeeb to Gideon, who
was by the Jordan River.

GIDEON KILLS ZEBAH AND ZALMUNNA

8 Then the people of Ephraim asked Gideon, "Why
have you treated us this way? Why didn't you
send for us when you first went out to fight the Midi-
anites?" And they argued heatedly with Gideon.
2 But Gideon replied, "What have I accomplished
compared to you? Aren't even the leftover grapes of
Ephraim's harvest better than the entire crop of my
little clan of Abiezer? 3 God gave you victory over
Oreb and Zeeb, the commanders of the Midianite
army. What have I accomplished compared to that?"
When the men of Ephraim heard Gideon's answer,
their anger subsided.
4 Gideon then crossed the Jordan River with his
300 men, and though exhausted, they continued to
chase the enemy. 5 When they reached Succoth, Gid-
eon asked the leaders of the town, "Please give my
warriors some food. They are very tired. I am chasing
Zebah and Zalmunna, the kings of Midian."
6 But the officials of Succoth replied, "Catch Zebah
and Zalmunna first, and then we will feed your army."
7 So Gideon said, "After the LORD gives me victory
over Zebah and Zalmunna, I will return and tear your
flesh with the thorns and briers from the wilderness."
8 From there Gideon went up to Peniel* and again
asked for food, but he got the same answer. 9 So he said
to the people of Peniel, "After I return in victory, I will
tear down this tower."
10 By this time Zebah and Zalmunna were in Karkor
with about 15,000 warriors—all that remained of
the allied armies of the east, for 120,000 had already
been killed. 11 Gideon circled around by the caravan
route east of Nobah and Jogbehah, taking the Midi-
anite army by surprise. 12 Zebah and Zalmunna, the
two Midianite kings, fled, but Gideon chased them
down and captured all their warriors.
13 After this, Gideon returned from the battle by
way of Heres Pass. 14 There he captured a young man
from Succoth and demanded that he write down the
names of all the seventy-seven officials and elders in
the town. 15 Gideon then returned to Succoth and said

7:15 As in Greek version; Hebrew reads *he bowed.* 7:19 Hebrew *at the beginning of the second watch.* 8:8 Hebrew *Penuel,* a variant spelling of Peniel; also in 8:9, 17.

7:13-14 dream. A loaf of barley bread. A crushed tent. These images in a Midianite's dream spelled victory for the Israelites. While Gideon's confidence increased at the news, a sleepless night awaited the worried Midianite warriors.

7:19 after midnight. Not necessarily midnight in the way we consider time. About 10:00 p.m., according to the Jewish custom of dividing the night into three parts.

7:22 against each other. In the confusion, the Midianites began fighting each other. Gideon's band got into the action only after the Midianite soldiers began to flee.

7:24 Cut them off at the shallow crossings. Gideon knew that streams and oases would be critically important to the fleeing army.

8:1 people of Ephraim. Gideon handles their criticism with grace, averting trouble and even skirting a potential civil war.

8:2 leftover grapes of Ephraim. Gideon expresses his view in language familiar to many of his worker-warriors. Gleanings were the leftovers—we might call it a "mop-up operation."

8:3 their anger subsided. Gideon points out that the mighty Ephraimites have no right to complain. After all, Ephraim took top honors, killing two of the top Midianite officers (7:25).

to the leaders, "Here are Zebah and Zalmunna. When
we were here before, you taunted me, saying, 'Catch
Zebah and Zalmunna first, and then we will feed your
exhausted army.'" 16 Then Gideon took the elders of the
town and taught them a lesson, punishing them with
thorns and briers from the wilderness. 17 He also tore
down the tower of Peniel and killed all the men in the
town.
18 Then Gideon asked Zebah and Zalmunna, "The
men you killed at Tabor—what were they like?"
"Like you," they replied. "They all had the look of a
king's son."
19 "They were my brothers, the sons of my own
mother!" Gideon exclaimed. "As surely as the LORD
lives, I wouldn't kill you if you hadn't killed them."
20 Turning to Jether, his oldest son, he said, "Kill
them!" But Jether did not draw his sword, for he was
only a boy and was afraid.
21 Then Zebah and Zalmunna said to Gideon, "Be
a man! Kill us yourself!" So Gideon killed them both
and took the royal ornaments from the necks of their
camels.

GIDEON'S SACRED EPHOD

22 Then the Israelites said to Gideon, "Be our ruler! You
and your son and your grandson will be our rulers,
for you have rescued us from Midian."
23 But Gideon replied, "I will not rule over you, nor
will my son. The LORD will rule over you! 24 Howev-
er, I do have one request—that each of you give me
an earring from the plunder you collected from your
fallen enemies." (The enemies, being Ishmaelites, all
wore gold earrings.)
25 "Gladly!" they replied. They spread out a cloak,
and each one threw in a gold earring he had gathered
from the plunder. 26 The weight of the gold earrings
was forty-three pounds,* not including the royal or-
naments and pendants, the purple clothing worn by
the kings of Midian, or the chains around the necks of
their camels.
27 Gideon made a sacred ephod from the gold and
put it in Ophrah, his hometown. But soon all the Isra-
elites prostituted themselves by worshiping it, and it
became a trap for Gideon and his family.
28 That is the story of how the people of Israel de-
feated Midian, which never recovered. Throughout
the rest of Gideon's lifetime—about forty years—
there was peace in the land.
29 Then Gideon* son of Joash returned home. 30 He
had seventy sons born to him, for he had many wives.
31 He also had a concubine in Shechem, who gave
birth to a son, whom he named Abimelech. 32 Gideon
died when he was very old, and he was buried in the
grave of his father, Joash, at Ophrah in the land of the
clan of Abiezer.
33 As soon as Gideon died, the Israelites prostituted
themselves by worshiping the images of Baal, mak-
ing Baal-berith their god. 34 They forgot the LORD their
God, who had rescued them from all their enemies
surrounding them. 35 Nor did they show any loyalty
to the family of Jerub-baal (that is, Gideon), despite all
the good he had done for Israel.

ABIMELECH RULES OVER SHECHEM

9 One day Gideon's* son Abimelech went to She-
chem to visit his uncles—his mother's brothers.
He said to them and to the rest of his mother's family,
2 "Ask the leading citizens of Shechem whether they
want to be ruled by all seventy of Gideon's sons or by
one man. And remember that I am your own flesh
and blood!"
3 So Abimelech's uncles gave his message to all the
citizens of Shechem on his behalf. And after listen-
ing to this proposal, the people of Shechem decided
in favor of Abimelech because he was their relative.
4 They gave him seventy silver coins from the temple
of Baal-berith, which he used to hire some reckless
troublemakers who agreed to follow him. 5 He went to
his father's home at Ophrah, and there, on one stone,
they killed all seventy of his half brothers, the sons
of Gideon.* But the youngest brother, Jotham, escaped
and hid.
6 Then all the leading citizens of Shechem and
Beth-millo called a meeting under the oak beside the
pillar* at Shechem and made Abimelech their king.

JOTHAM'S PARABLE

7 When Jotham heard about this, he climbed to the top
of Mount Gerizim and shouted,

"Listen to me, citizens of Shechem!
Listen to me if you want God to listen to you!
8 Once upon a time the trees decided to choose a
king.
First they said to the olive tree,
'Be our king!'
9 But the olive tree refused, saying,
'Should I quit producing the olive oil
that blesses both God and people,
just to wave back and forth over the trees?'

10 "Then they said to the fig tree,
'You be our king!'
11 But the fig tree also refused, saying,
'Should I quit producing my sweet fruit
just to wave back and forth over the trees?'

12 "Then they said to the grapevine,
'You be our king!'
13 But the grapevine also refused, saying,

8:26 Hebrew *1,700 [shekels]* [19.4 kilograms]. 8:29 Hebrew *Jerub-baal;* see 6:32. 9:1 Hebrew *Jerub-baal's* (see 6:32); also in 9:2, 24. 9:5 Hebrew *Jerub-baal* (see 6:32); also in 9:16, 19, 28, 57. 9:6 The meaning of the Hebrew is uncertain.

8:23 The LORD will rule. Although Gideon is theologically correct here, he will quickly fall into idolatry (v. 27).
8:27 ephod. This golden chest piece usually was worn by a priest (see Ex. 28:6-30). However, Gideon and the people worshiped the golden object as an idol.
8:31 gave birth to a son. Gideon had several wives who bore him at least 70 children. **Abimelech.** The mother of Abimelech was Gideon's slave, but her son soon proclaimed himself king (9:2).
8:33 As soon as Gideon died. With their leader gone, the cycle of disobedience starts over again for the Israelites.
9:1-57 Abimelech rises to power by murdering his own family members (v. 5). Renouncing his father's faith, Abimelech looks toward Baal for assistance in his plot. Overcome with evil, Abimelech dies an ignominious death after just three years in power (vv. 52-54).
9:1 Gideon. Gideon is called by another name, Jerubbaal, in the Hebrew text.
9:5 seventy of his half brothers. Abimelech murdered his father's sons in an attempt to secure his royal position.
9:9-13 Jotham used familiar cultural images to make his point.

'Should I quit producing the wine
that cheers both God and people,
just to wave back and forth over the trees?'

14 "Then all the trees finally turned to the thornbush
and said,
'Come, you be our king!'
15 And the thornbush replied to the trees,
'If you truly want to make me your king,
come and take shelter in my shade.
If not, let fire come out from me
and devour the cedars of Lebanon.'"

16 Jotham continued, "Now make sure you have act-
ed honorably and in good faith by making Abimelech
your king, and that you have done right by Gideon
and all of his descendants. Have you treated him with
the honor he deserves for all he accomplished? 17 For
he fought for you and risked his life when he rescued
you from the Midianites. 18 But today you have revolt-
ed against my father and his descendants, killing his
seventy sons on one stone. And you have chosen his
slave woman's son, Abimelech, to be your king just
because he is your relative.
19 "If you have acted honorably and in good faith
toward Gideon and his descendants today, then may
you find joy in Abimelech, and may he find joy in you.
20 But if you have not acted in good faith, then may fire
come out from Abimelech and devour the leading cit-
izens of Shechem and Beth-millo; and may fire come
out from the citizens of Shechem and Beth-millo and
devour Abimelech!"
21 Then Jotham escaped and lived in Beer because
he was afraid of his brother Abimelech.

SHECHEM REBELS AGAINST ABIMELECH

22 After Abimelech had ruled over Israel for three
years, 23 God sent a spirit that stirred up trouble be-
tween Abimelech and the leading citizens of She-
chem, and they revolted. 24 God was punishing Abim-
elech for murdering Gideon's seventy sons, and the
citizens of Shechem for supporting him in this treach-
ery of murdering his brothers. 25 The citizens of She-
chem set an ambush for Abimelech on the hilltops
and robbed everyone who passed that way. But some-
one warned Abimelech about their plot.
26 One day Gaal son of Ebed moved to Shechem with
his brothers and gained the confidence of the leading
citizens of Shechem. 27 During the annual harvest festi-
val at Shechem, held in the temple of the local god, the
wine flowed freely, and everyone began cursing Abim-
elech. 28 "Who is Abimelech?" Gaal shouted. "He's not a
true son of Shechem,* so why should we be his servants?
He's merely the son of Gideon, and this Zebul is merely
his deputy. Serve the true sons of Hamor, the founder of
Shechem. Why should we serve Abimelech? 29 If I were
in charge here, I would get rid of Abimelech. I would
say* to him, 'Get some soldiers, and come out and fight!'"

30 But when Zebul, the leader of the city, heard
what Gaal was saying, he was furious. 31 He sent mes-
sengers to Abimelech in Arumah,* telling him, "Gaal
son of Ebed and his brothers have come to live in
Shechem, and now they are inciting the city to rebel
against you. 32 Come by night with an army and hide
out in the fields. 33 In the morning, as soon as it is day-
light, attack the city. When Gaal and those who are
with him come out against you, you can do with them
as you wish."
34 So Abimelech and all his men went by night and
split into four groups, stationing themselves around
Shechem. 35 Gaal was standing at the city gates when
Abimelech and his army came out of hiding. 36 When
Gaal saw them, he said to Zebul, "Look, there are peo-
ple coming down from the hilltops!"
Zebul replied, "It's just the shadows on the hills that
look like men."
37 But again Gaal said, "No, people are coming down
from the hills.* And another group is coming down
the road past the Diviners' Oak.*"
38 Then Zebul turned on him and asked, "Now
where is that big mouth of yours? Wasn't it you that
said, 'Who is Abimelech, and why should we be his
servants?' The men you mocked are right outside the
city! Go out and fight them!"
39 So Gaal led the leading citizens of Shechem into
battle against Abimelech. 40 But Abimelech chased
him, and many of Shechem's men were wounded and
fell along the road as they retreated to the city gate.
41 Abimelech returned to Arumah, and Zebul drove
Gaal and his brothers out of Shechem.
42 The next day the people of Shechem went out
into the fields to battle. When Abimelech heard
about it, 43 he divided his men into three groups and
set an ambush in the fields. When Abimelech saw
the people coming out of the city, he and his men
jumped up from their hiding places and attacked
them. 44 Abimelech and his group stormed the city
gate to keep the men of Shechem from getting back
in, while Abimelech's other two groups cut them
down in the fields. 45 The battle went on all day be-
fore Abimelech finally captured the city. He killed
the people, leveled the city, and scattered salt all
over the ground.
46 When the leading citizens who lived in the tower
of Shechem heard what had happened, they ran and
hid in the temple of Baal-berith.* 47 Someone report-
ed to Abimelech that the citizens had gathered in the
temple, 48 so he led his forces to Mount Zalmon. He
took an ax and chopped some branches from a tree,
then put them on his shoulder. "Quick, do as I have
done!" he told his men. 49 So each of them cut down
some branches, following Abimelech's example. They
piled the branches against the walls of the temple
and set them on fire. So all the people who had lived
in the tower of Shechem died—about 1,000 men and
women.

9:28 Hebrew *Who is Shechem?* **9:29** As in Greek version; Hebrew reads *And he said.* **9:31** Or *in secret;* Hebrew reads *in Tormah;* compare 9:41. **9:37a** Or *the center of the land.* **9:37b** Hebrew *Elon-meonenim.* **9:46** Hebrew *El-berith,* another name for Baal-berith; compare 9:4.

9:14 thornbush. Thornbushes, sometimes called brambles, are only good for pricking bare heels and kindling fires.

9:15 cedars of Lebanon. The influential men of Shechem saw themselves in this image. The worthless thornbush would summarily destroy the valuable cedars.

9:23 a spirit that stirred up trouble. Unable to escape his deadly deeds, Abimelech has a falling out with his allies.

9:26 Gaal. With Abimelech fallen from grace, Gaal appears on the scene to further deceive the willing people.

9:32 hide out. In a favorite military tactic, the governor recommends an ambush to guarantee Abimelech's success.

9:34 went by night. Although they took their places at night, the attack does not come until the morning light.

50 Then Abimelech attacked the town of Thebez and captured it. 51 But there was a strong tower inside the town, and all the men and women—the entire population—fled to it. They barricaded themselves in and climbed up to the roof of the tower. 52 Abimelech followed them to attack the tower. But as he prepared to set fire to the entrance, 53 a woman on the roof dropped a millstone that landed on Abimelech's head and crushed his skull.

54 He quickly said to his young armor bearer, "Draw your sword and kill me! Don't let it be said that a woman killed Abimelech!" So the young man ran him through with his sword, and he died. 55 When Abimelech's men saw that he was dead, they disbanded and returned to their homes.

56 In this way, God punished Abimelech for the evil he had done against his father by murdering his seventy brothers. 57 God also punished the men of Shechem for all their evil. So the curse of Jotham son of Gideon was fulfilled.

TOLA BECOMES ISRAEL'S JUDGE

10 After Abimelech died, Tola son of Puah, son of Dodo, was the next person to rescue Israel. He was from the tribe of Issachar but lived in the town of Shamir in the hill country of Ephraim. 2 He judged Israel for twenty-three years. When he died, he was buried in Shamir.

JAIR BECOMES ISRAEL'S JUDGE

3 After Tola died, Jair from Gilead judged Israel for twenty-two years. 4 His thirty sons rode around on thirty donkeys, and they owned thirty towns in the land of Gilead, which are still called the Towns of Jair.* 5 When Jair died, he was buried in Kamon.

THE AMMONITES OPPRESS ISRAEL

6 Again the Israelites did evil in the LORD's sight. They served the images of Baal and Ashtoreth, and the gods of Aram, Sidon, Moab, Ammon, and Philistia. They abandoned the LORD and no longer served him at all. 7 So the LORD burned with anger against Israel, and he turned them over to the Philistines and the Ammonites, 8 who began to oppress them that year. For eighteen years they oppressed all the Israelites east of the Jordan River in the land of the Amorites (that is, in Gilead). 9 The Ammonites also crossed to the west side of the Jordan and attacked Judah, Benjamin, and Ephraim.

The Israelites were in great distress. 10 Finally, they cried out to the LORD for help, saying, "We have sinned against you because we have abandoned you as our God and have served the images of Baal."

11 The LORD replied, "Did I not rescue you from the Egyptians, the Amorites, the Ammonites, the Philistines, 12 the Sidonians, the Amalekites, and the Maonites? When they oppressed you, you cried out to me for help, and I rescued you. 13 Yet you have abandoned me and served other gods. So I will not rescue you anymore. 14 Go and cry out to the gods you have chosen! Let them rescue you in your hour of distress!"

15 But the Israelites pleaded with the LORD and said, "We have sinned. Punish us as you see fit, only rescue us today from our enemies." 16 Then the Israelites put aside their foreign gods and served the LORD. And he was grieved by their misery.

17 At that time the armies of Ammon had gathered for war and were camped in Gilead, and the people of Israel assembled and camped at Mizpah. 18 The leaders of Gilead said to each other, "Whoever attacks the Ammonites first will become ruler over all the people of Gilead."

JEPHTHAH BECOMES ISRAEL'S JUDGE

11 Now Jephthah of Gilead was a great warrior. He was the son of Gilead, but his mother was a prostitute. 2 Gilead's wife also had several sons, and when these half brothers grew up, they chased Jephthah off the land. "You will not get any of our father's inheritance," they said, "for you are the son of a prostitute." 3 So Jephthah fled from his brothers and lived in the land of Tob. Soon he had a band of worthless rebels following him.

4 At about this time, the Ammonites began their war against Israel. 5 When the Ammonites attacked, the elders of Gilead sent for Jephthah in the land of Tob. 6 The elders said, "Come and be our commander! Help us fight the Ammonites!"

7 But Jephthah said to them, "Aren't you the ones who hated me and drove me from my father's house? Why do you come to me now when you're in trouble?"

8 "Because we need you," the elders replied. "If you lead us in battle against the Ammonites, we will make you ruler over all the people of Gilead."

9 Jephthah said to the elders, "Let me get this straight. If I come with you and if the LORD gives me victory over the Ammonites, will you really make me ruler over all the people?"

10 "The LORD is our witness," the elders replied. "We promise to do whatever you say."

11 So Jephthah went with the elders of Gilead, and the people made him their ruler and commander of the army. At Mizpah, in the presence of the LORD, Jephthah repeated what he had said to the elders.

12 Then Jephthah sent messengers to the king of Ammon, asking, "Why have you come out to fight against my land?"

13 The king of Ammon answered Jephthah's messengers, "When the Israelites came out of Egypt, they stole my land from the Arnon River to the Jabbok River and all the way to the Jordan. Now then, give back the land peaceably."

14 Jephthah sent this message back to the Ammonite king:

> 15 "This is what Jephthah says: Israel did not steal any land from Moab or Ammon. 16 When the

10:4 Hebrew *Havvoth-jair.*

10:1 Tola. Without foreign oppression, Tola could focus on Israel's spiritual woes.
10:3 from Gilead. Number seven in the line of judges, Jair was from Gilead, within the tribe of Manasseh.
10:6–12:7 Rejected by his own people as a young man (11:3), Jephthah eventually became Israel's judge for six years.
10:12 I rescued you. A series of judges over many decades had represented God's faithfulness by delivering the people from oppression.
10:18 "Whoever attacks." A desperate people looked for military leadership.
11:1 his mother was a prostitute. Jephthah was the illegitimate son of Gilead, a prostitute, and likely half-Canaanite—a social outcast.
11:8 ruler. The elders of Gilead were willing to promise Jephthah leadership of their region if he would lead them militarily.
11:13 stole my land. The king twisted history to make his case.
11:14-27 Jephthah's letter to the Ammonite king clarified Israel's claim to the land: They attained it from the Amorites, not the Ammonites; Israel's God had given them the land; and Israel had occupied the land for many years.

people of Israel arrived at Kadesh on their journey from Egypt after crossing the Red Sea,* 17 they sent messengers to the king of Edom asking for permission to pass through his land. But their request was denied. Then they asked the king of Moab for similar permission, but he wouldn't let them pass through either. So the people of Israel stayed in Kadesh.

18 "Finally, they went around Edom and Moab through the wilderness. They traveled along Moab's eastern border and camped on the other side of the Arnon River. But they never once crossed the Arnon River into Moab, for the Arnon was the border of Moab.

19 "Then Israel sent messengers to King Sihon of the Amorites, who ruled from Heshbon, asking for permission to cross through his land to get to their destination. 20 But King Sihon didn't trust Israel to pass through his land. Instead, he mobilized his army at Jahaz and attacked them. 21 But the LORD, the God of Israel, gave his people victory over King Sihon. So Israel took control of all the land of the Amorites, who lived in that region, 22 from the Arnon River to the Jabbok River, and from the eastern wilderness to the Jordan.

23 "So you see, it was the LORD, the God of Israel, who took away the land from the Amorites and gave it to Israel. Why, then, should we give it back to you? 24 You keep whatever your god Chemosh gives you, and we will keep whatever the LORD our God gives us. 25 Are you any better than Balak son of Zippor, king of Moab? Did he try to make a case against Israel for disputed land? Did he go to war against them?

26 "Israel has been living here for 300 years, inhabiting Heshbon and its surrounding settlements, all the way to Aroer and its settlements, and in all the towns along the Arnon River. Why have you made no effort to recover it before now? 27 Therefore, I have not sinned against you. Rather, you have wronged me by attacking me. Let the LORD, who is judge, decide today which of us is right—Israel or Ammon."

28 But the king of Ammon paid no attention to Jephthah's message.

JEPHTHAH'S VOW

29 At that time the Spirit of the LORD came upon Jephthah, and he went throughout the land of Gilead and Manasseh, including Mizpah in Gilead, and from there he led an army against the Ammonites. 30 And Jephthah made a vow to the LORD. He said, "If you give me victory over the Ammonites, 31 I will give to the LORD whatever comes out of my house to meet me when I return in triumph. I will sacrifice it as a burnt offering."

32 So Jephthah led his army against the Ammonites, and the LORD gave him victory. 33 He crushed the Ammonites, devastating about twenty towns from Aroer to an area near Minnith and as far away as Abel-keramim. In this way Israel defeated the Ammonites.

34 When Jephthah returned home to Mizpah, his daughter came out to meet him, playing on a tambourine and dancing for joy. She was his one and only child; he had no other sons or daughters. 35 When he saw her, he tore his clothes in anguish. "Oh, my daughter!" he cried out. "You have completely destroyed me! You've brought disaster on me! For I have made a vow to the LORD, and I cannot take it back."

36 And she said, "Father, if you have made a vow to the LORD, you must do to me what you have vowed, for the LORD has given you a great victory over your enemies, the Ammonites. 37 But first let me do this one thing: Let me go up and roam in the hills and weep with my friends for two months, because I will die a virgin."

38 "You may go," Jephthah said. And he sent her away for two months. She and her friends went into the hills and wept because she would never have children. 39 When she returned home, her father kept the vow he had made, and she died a virgin.

So it has become a custom in Israel 40 for young Israelite women to go away for four days each year to lament the fate of Jephthah's daughter.

EPHRAIM FIGHTS WITH JEPHTHAH

12 Then the people of Ephraim mobilized an army and crossed over the Jordan River to Zaphon. They sent this message to Jephthah: "Why didn't you call for us to help you fight against the Ammonites? We are going to burn down your house with you in it!"

2 Jephthah replied, "I summoned you at the beginning of the dispute, but you refused to come! You failed to help us in our struggle against Ammon. 3 So when I realized you weren't coming, I risked my life and went to battle without you, and the LORD gave me victory over the Ammonites. So why have you now come to fight me?"

4 The people of Ephraim responded, "You men of Gilead are nothing more than fugitives from Ephraim and Manasseh." So Jephthah gathered all the men of Gilead and attacked the men of Ephraim and defeated them.

5 Jephthah captured the shallow crossings of the Jordan River, and whenever a fugitive from Ephraim tried to go back across, the men of Gilead would challenge him. "Are you a member of the tribe of Ephraim?" they would ask. If the man said, "No, I'm not," 6 they would tell him to say "Shibboleth." If he was from Ephraim, he would say "Sibboleth," because people from Ephraim cannot pronounce the word correctly. Then they would take him and kill him at the shallow crossings of the Jordan. In all, 42,000 Ephraimites were killed at that time.

7 Jephthah judged Israel for six years. When he died, he was buried in one of the towns of Gilead.

11:16 Hebrew *sea of reeds.*

11:30 made a vow. Vows were taken seriously in Israel. Their very existence as a people began with a vow between Abraham and God.

11:34 dancing. The entire community celebrated a military victory. Young girls often led the celebration (see Ex. 15:20, 1 Sam. 18:6).

11:35 tore his clothes. An act of extreme grief.

11:37 roam in the hills. Jephthah's daughter did not defy her father or resist the terrible consequence of his vow. Her father may have offered her as a human sacrifice, or he may simply have kept her from ever marrying.

11:39-40 custom in Israel. This custom is mentioned nowhere else in the Old Testament.

12:2 Jephthah replied. Jephthah's first response to the threat was diplomacy.

12:6 Shibboleth. Gileadites used a verbal test to identify Ephraimites.

IBZAN BECOMES ISRAEL'S JUDGE

8 After Jephthah died, Ibzan from Bethlehem judged
Israel. 9 He had thirty sons and thirty daughters. He
sent his daughters to marry men outside his clan, and
he brought in thirty young women from outside his
clan to marry his sons. Ibzan judged Israel for seven
years. 10 When he died, he was buried at Bethlehem.

ELON BECOMES ISRAEL'S JUDGE

11 After Ibzan died, Elon from the tribe of Zebulun
judged Israel for ten years. 12 When he died, he was
buried at Aijalon in Zebulun.

ABDON BECOMES ISRAEL'S JUDGE

13 After Elon died, Abdon son of Hillel, from Pirathon,
judged Israel. 14 He had forty sons and thirty grand-
sons, who rode on seventy donkeys. He judged Israel
for eight years. 15 When he died, he was buried at Pira-
thon in Ephraim, in the hill country of the Amalekites.

THE BIRTH OF SAMSON

13 Again the Israelites did evil in the LORD's sight,
so the LORD handed them over to the Philistines,
who oppressed them for forty years.
2 In those days a man named Manoah from the
tribe of Dan lived in the town of Zorah. His wife was
unable to become pregnant, and they had no chil-
dren. 3 The angel of the LORD appeared to Manoah's
wife and said, "Even though you have been unable to
have children, you will soon become pregnant and
give birth to a son. 4 So be careful; you must not drink
wine or any other alcoholic drink nor eat any forbid-
den food.* 5 You will become pregnant and give birth
to a son, and his hair must never be cut. For he will
be dedicated to God as a Nazirite from birth. He will
begin to rescue Israel from the Philistines."
6 The woman ran and told her husband, "A man of
God appeared to me! He looked like one of God's an-
gels, terrifying to see. I didn't ask where he was from,
and he didn't tell me his name. 7 But he told me, 'You
will become pregnant and give birth to a son. You
must not drink wine or any other alcoholic drink nor
eat any forbidden food. For your son will be dedicated
to God as a Nazirite from the moment of his birth un-
til the day of his death.'"
8 Then Manoah prayed to the LORD, saying, "Lord,
please let the man of God come back to us again and
give us more instructions about this son who is to be
born."
9 God answered Manoah's prayer, and the angel of
God appeared once again to his wife as she was sit-
ting in the field. But her husband, Manoah, was not
with her. 10 So she quickly ran and told her husband,
"The man who appeared to me the other day is here
again!"
11 Manoah ran back with his wife and asked, "Are
you the man who spoke to my wife the other day?"
"Yes," he replied, "I am."
12 So Manoah asked him, "When your words come
true, what kind of rules should govern the boy's life
and work?"
13 The angel of the LORD replied, "Be sure your wife
follows the instructions I gave her. 14 She must not eat
grapes or raisins, drink wine or any other alcoholic
drink, or eat any forbidden food."
15 Then Manoah said to the angel of the LORD,
"Please stay here until we can prepare a young goat
for you to eat."
16 "I will stay," the angel of the LORD replied, "but I
will not eat anything. However, you may prepare a
burnt offering as a sacrifice to the LORD." (Manoah
didn't realize it was the angel of the LORD.)
17 Then Manoah asked the angel of the LORD, "What
is your name? For when all this comes true, we want
to honor you."
18 "Why do you ask my name?" the angel of the LORD
replied. "It is too wonderful for you to understand."
19 Then Manoah took a young goat and a grain
offering and offered it on a rock as a sacrifice to the
LORD. And as Manoah and his wife watched, the LORD
did an amazing thing. 20 As the flames from the altar
shot up toward the sky, the angel of the LORD ascend-
ed in the fire. When Manoah and his wife saw this,
they fell with their faces to the ground.
21 The angel did not appear again to Manoah and
his wife. Manoah finally realized it was the angel of
the LORD, 22 and he said to his wife, "We will certainly
die, for we have seen God!"
23 But his wife said, "If the LORD were going to kill
us, he wouldn't have accepted our burnt offering and
grain offering. He wouldn't have appeared to us and
told us this wonderful thing and done these miracles."
24 When her son was born, she named him Samson.
And the LORD blessed him as he grew up. 25 And the
Spirit of the LORD began to stir him while he lived in
Mahaneh-dan, which is located between the towns of
Zorah and Eshtaol.

SAMSON'S RIDDLE

14 One day when Samson was in Timnah, one of
the Philistine women caught his eye. 2 When
he returned home, he told his father and mother, "A
young Philistine woman in Timnah caught my eye. I
want to marry her. Get her for me."
3 His father and mother objected. "Isn't there even
one woman in our tribe or among all the Israelites
you could marry?" they asked. "Why must you go to
the pagan Philistines to find a wife?"
But Samson told his father, "Get her for me! She
looks good to me." 4 His father and mother didn't re-

13:4 Hebrew *any unclean thing;* also in 13:7, 14.

13:1–16:31 Like Israel, Samson was blessed by God and consecrated to Him, but he also had an attraction for ungodly things.

13:2 had no children. A woman was not considered complete until she bore children. But compare Manoah's wife with Sarah (Gen. 11:30), Rebekah (Gen. 25:21), and Hannah (1 Sam. 1:2).

13:3 you will . . . give birth to a son. God sent an angel to announce Samson's coming birth; compare Ishmael (Gen. 16:11), John the Baptist (Luke 1:13), and Jesus Christ (Luke 1:31).

13:5 dedicated to God as a Nazirite from birth. Samson was "set apart" by God as a Nazirite for life, and this involved not cutting one's hair, abstaining from fermented beverages, and avoiding contact with dead bodies (see Num. 6:1-21).

13:6 A man of God appeared. Manoah's wife knew something significant had happened, but she was clear only about the Nazirite requirements.

13:8 give us more instructions. Manoah believed his wife about the birth of a child. His concern was that they be prepared to carry out the Lord's will for their child.

13:17 What is your name? Manoah was sure that the promise would come true, so he wanted to know whom to honor.

14:3 pagan. In Israel, calling someone "pagan" implied ungodly behavior.

14:4 creating an opportunity. God used Samson's wrong desire for a Philistine woman to further his work against the enemies of God's people (see Gen. 50:20; Acts 2:23; Rom. 8:28).

FAITH UNDER FIRE

1. In choosing a date, what is more important: Body build? Looks? Brains? Personality? Spirituality?

JUDGES 14:1-20

2. God commanded the Israelites not to marry Gentiles, such as the Philistines. How did Samson demand that his parents help him sin?
3. How did Samson's bad choices cause harm to others? When have you seen your own sins hurt innocent people?
4. What did Samson put his faith in most: God? His strength? His clever wit? His parents? Other?
5. Do you sometimes do things your own way, even though you know it's not God's way? What happened the last time you did this?

alize the LORD was at work in this, creating an opportunity to work against the Philistines, who ruled over Israel at that time.

5 As Samson and his parents were going down to Timnah, a young lion suddenly attacked Samson near the vineyards of Timnah. 6 At that moment the Spirit of the LORD came powerfully upon him, and he ripped the lion's jaws apart with his bare hands. He did it as easily as if it were a young goat. But he didn't tell his father or mother about it. 7 When Samson arrived in Timnah, he talked with the woman and was very pleased with her.

8 Later, when he returned to Timnah for the wedding, he turned off the path to look at the carcass of the lion. And he found that a swarm of bees had made some honey in the carcass. 9 He scooped some of the honey into his hands and ate it along the way. He also gave some to his father and mother, and they ate it. But he didn't tell them he had taken the honey from the carcass of the lion.

10 As his father was making final arrangements for the marriage, Samson threw a party at Timnah, as was the custom for elite young men. 11 When the bride's parents* saw him, they selected thirty young men from the town to be his companions.

12 Samson said to them, "Let me tell you a riddle. If you solve my riddle during these seven days of the celebration, I will give you thirty fine linen robes and thirty sets of festive clothing. 13 But if you can't solve it, then you must give me thirty fine linen robes and thirty sets of festive clothing."

"All right," they agreed, "let's hear your riddle."

14 So he said:

"Out of the one who eats came something to eat;
out of the strong came something sweet."

Three days later they were still trying to figure it out. 15 On the fourth* day they said to Samson's wife, "Entice your husband to explain the riddle for us, or we will burn down your father's house with you in it. Did you invite us to this party just to make us poor?"

16 So Samson's wife came to him in tears and said, "You don't love me; you hate me! You have given my people a riddle, but you haven't told me the answer."

"I haven't even given the answer to my father or mother," he replied. "Why should I tell you?" 17 So she cried whenever she was with him and kept it up for the rest of the celebration. At last, on the seventh day he told her the answer because she was tormenting him with her nagging. Then she explained the riddle to the young men.

18 So before sunset of the seventh day, the men of the town came to Samson with their answer:

"What is sweeter than honey?
What is stronger than a lion?"

Samson replied, "If you hadn't plowed with my heifer, you wouldn't have solved my riddle!"

19 Then the Spirit of the LORD came powerfully upon him. He went down to the town of Ashkelon, killed thirty men, took their belongings, and gave their clothing to the men who had solved his riddle. But Samson was furious about what had happened, and he went back home to live with his father and mother. 20 So his wife was given in marriage to the man who had been Samson's best man at the wedding.

SAMSON'S VENGEANCE ON THE PHILISTINES

15 Later on, during the wheat harvest, Samson took a young goat as a present to his wife. He said, "I'm going into my wife's room to sleep with her," but her father wouldn't let him in.

2 "I truly thought you must hate her," her father explained, "so I gave her in marriage to your best man. But look, her younger sister is even more beautiful than she is. Marry her instead."

3 Samson said, "This time I cannot be blamed for everything I am going to do to you Philistines." 4 Then he went out and caught 300 foxes. He tied their tails together in pairs, and he fastened a torch to each pair of tails. 5 Then he lit the torches and let the foxes run through the grain fields of the Philistines. He burned all their grain to the ground, including the sheaves and the uncut grain. He also destroyed their vineyards and olive groves.

6 "Who did this?" the Philistines demanded.

"Samson," was the reply, "because his father-in-law from Timnah gave Samson's wife to be married to his best man." So the Philistines went and got the woman and her father and burned them to death.

7 "Because you did this," Samson vowed, "I won't rest until I take my revenge on you!" 8 So he attacked the Philistines with great fury and killed many of them. Then he went to live in a cave in the rock of Etam.

14:11 Hebrew *they*. 14:15 As in Greek version; Hebrew reads *seventh*.

14:12 riddle. Riddles were a form of entertainment. Samson was showing off his cleverness.

14:16 You don't love me; you hate me! This accusation was one to which Samson would prove extremely vulnerable.

14:19 came powerfully upon him. The Spirit of God empowered Samson to take revenge against the Philistines.

15:5 burned. Samson struck back at the Philistines by burning their food.

15:7 revenge. Usually revenge led to an escalation of violence as the conflict grew from man against man, to family against family, to tribe against tribe, to nation against nation.

9 The Philistines retaliated by setting up camp in
Judah and spreading out near the town of Lehi. 10 The
men of Judah asked the Philistines, "Why are you at-
tacking us?"
The Philistines replied, "We've come to capture
Samson. We've come to pay him back for what he did
to us."
11 So 3,000 men of Judah went down to get Samson
at the cave in the rock of Etam. They said to Samson,
"Don't you realize the Philistines rule over us? What
are you doing to us?"
But Samson replied, "I only did to them what they
did to me."
12 But the men of Judah told him, "We have come to
tie you up and hand you over to the Philistines."
"All right," Samson said. "But promise that you
won't kill me yourselves."
13 "We will only tie you up and hand you over to the
Philistines," they replied. "We won't kill you." So they
tied him up with two new ropes and brought him up
from the rock.
14 As Samson arrived at Lehi, the Philistines came
shouting in triumph. But the Spirit of the LORD came
powerfully upon Samson, and he snapped the ropes
on his arms as if they were burnt strands of flax, and
they fell from his wrists. 15 Then he found the jawbone
of a recently killed donkey. He picked it up and killed
1,000 Philistines with it. 16 Then Samson said,

"With the jawbone of a donkey,
I've piled them in heaps!
With the jawbone of a donkey,
I've killed a thousand men!"

17 When he finished his boasting, he threw away the
jawbone; and the place was named Jawbone Hill.*
18 Samson was now very thirsty, and he cried out
to the LORD, "You have accomplished this great vic-
tory by the strength of your servant. Must I now die
of thirst and fall into the hands of these pagans?"
19 So God caused water to gush out of a hollow in the
ground at Lehi, and Samson was revived as he drank.
Then he named that place "The Spring of the One Who
Cried Out,"* and it is still in Lehi to this day.
20 Samson judged Israel for twenty years during the
period when the Philistines dominated the land.

SAMSON CARRIES AWAY GAZA'S GATES

16 One day Samson went to the Philistine town
of Gaza and spent the night with a prostitute.
2 Word soon spread* that Samson was there, so the
men of Gaza gathered together and waited all night
at the town gates. They kept quiet during the night,
saying to themselves, "When the light of morning
comes, we will kill him."
3 But Samson stayed in bed only until midnight.
Then he got up, took hold of the doors of the town gate,
including the two posts, and lifted them up, bar and
all. He put them on his shoulders and carried them
all the way to the top of the hill across from Hebron.

SAMSON AND DELILAH

4 Some time later Samson fell in love with a woman
named Delilah, who lived in the valley of Sorek. 5 The
rulers of the Philistines went to her and said, "Entice
Samson to tell you what makes him so strong and
how he can be overpowered and tied up securely.
Then each of us will give you 1,100 pieces* of silver."
6 So Delilah said to Samson, "Please tell me what
makes you so strong and what it would take to tie you
up securely."
7 Samson replied, "If I were tied up with seven new
bowstrings that have not yet been dried, I would be-
come as weak as anyone else."
8 So the Philistine rulers brought Delilah seven
new bowstrings, and she tied Samson up with them.
9 She had hidden some men in one of the inner rooms
of her house, and she cried out, "Samson! The Philis-
tines have come to capture you!" But Samson snapped
the bowstrings as a piece of string snaps when it is
burned by a fire. So the secret of his strength was not
discovered.
10 Afterward Delilah said to him, "You've been mak-
ing fun of me and telling me lies! Now please tell me
how you can be tied up securely."
11 Samson replied, "If I were tied up with brand-
new ropes that had never been used, I would become
as weak as anyone else."
12 So Delilah took new ropes and tied him up with
them. The men were hiding in the inner room as before,
and again Delilah cried out, "Samson! The Philistines

A REALLY BAD HAIR DAY

1. When was your hair the shortest? Longest? Craziest?

JUDGES 16:1-22

2. What caused Samson to go back to Delilah again and again, knowing she would betray him?
3. Samson was probably sleeping with Delilah, though they weren't married. How did Samson's own sinful choices bring about his destruction?
4. Why didn't Samson know that "the LORD had left him" (v. 20)? Is there evidence in your own life of God's Holy Spirit?
5. What one weakness of yours is in danger of taking away your spiritual strength?

15:17 Hebrew *Ramath-lehi.* **15:19** Hebrew *En-hakkore.* **16:2** As in Greek and Syriac versions and Latin Vulgate; Hebrew lacks *Word soon spread.* **16:5** Hebrew *1,100 [shekels],* about 28 pounds or 12.5 kilograms in weight.

15:11 What are you doing to us? The tribe of Judah preferred being under Philistine rule to being the enemy of the Philistines. Samson was upsetting the status quo (13:5).

15:15 killed 1,000 Philistines. Compare this report with Shamgar's killing of 600 Philistines with an oxgoad (3:31).

15:19 water to gush out. As God provided water for the wandering Israelites (Ex. 17:1-7), He provided it for Samson.

16:3 put them on his shoulders and carried them. Samson's act was one of defiance and pride, telling the Philistines their gates couldn't hold him.

16:5 can be overpowered and tied up securely. The Philistines were still out for revenge. They wanted to torture and humiliate Samson.

16:7 seven new bowstrings. Samson tried to deceive the Philistines by repeatedly using the number seven, which was believed to have magical powers.

16:11 brand-new ropes. The Philistines had forgotten that they had tried new ropes before with terrible results (15:13-14).

have come to capture you!" But again Samson snapped
the ropes from his arms as if they were thread.
13 Then Delilah said, "You've been making fun of me
and telling me lies! Now tell me how you can be tied
up securely."
Samson replied, "If you were to weave the seven
braids of my hair into the fabric on your loom and
tighten it with the loom shuttle, I would become as
weak as anyone else."
So while he slept, Delilah wove the seven braids of
his hair into the fabric. 14 Then she tightened it with
the loom shuttle.* Again she cried out, "Samson! The
Philistines have come to capture you!" But Samson
woke up, pulled back the loom shuttle, and yanked his
hair away from the loom and the fabric.
15 Then Delilah pouted, "How can you tell me, 'I love
you,' when you don't share your secrets with me?
You've made fun of me three times now, and you still
haven't told me what makes you so strong!" 16 She tor-
mented him with her nagging day after day until he
was sick to death of it.
17 Finally, Samson shared his secret with her. "My
hair has never been cut," he confessed, "for I was
dedicated to God as a Nazirite from birth. If my head
were shaved, my strength would leave me, and I
would become as weak as anyone else."
18 Delilah realized he had finally told her the truth,
so she sent for the Philistine rulers. "Come back one
more time," she said, "for he has finally told me his
secret." So the Philistine rulers returned with the
money in their hands. 19 Delilah lulled Samson to sleep
with his head in her lap, and then she called in a man
to shave off the seven locks of his hair. In this way she
began to bring him down,* and his strength left him.
20 Then she cried out, "Samson! The Philistines have
come to capture you!"
When he woke up, he thought, "I will do as before
and shake myself free." But he didn't realize the LORD
had left him.
21 So the Philistines captured him and gouged out
his eyes. They took him to Gaza, where he was bound
with bronze chains and forced to grind grain in the
prison.
22 But before long, his hair began to grow back.

SAMSON'S FINAL VICTORY

23 The Philistine rulers held a great festival, offering
sacrifices and praising their god, Dagon. They said,
"Our god has given us victory over our enemy Sam-
son!"
24 When the people saw him, they praised their god,
saying, "Our god has delivered our enemy to us! The
one who killed so many of us is now in our power!"
25 Half drunk by now, the people demanded,
"Bring out Samson so he can amuse us!" So he was
brought from the prison to amuse them, and they
had him stand between the pillars supporting the
roof.
26 Samson said to the young servant who was lead-
ing him by the hand, "Place my hands against the
pillars that hold up the temple. I want to rest against
them." 27 Now the temple was completely filled with
people. All the Philistine rulers were there, and there
were about 3,000 men and women on the roof who
were watching as Samson amused them.
28 Then Samson prayed to the LORD, "Sovereign
LORD, remember me again. O God, please strength-
en me just one more time. With one blow let me pay
back the Philistines for the loss of my two eyes."
29 Then Samson put his hands on the two center pil-
lars that held up the temple. Pushing against them
with both hands, 30 he prayed, "Let me die with the
Philistines." And the temple crashed down on the
Philistine rulers and all the people. So he killed more
people when he died than he had during his entire
lifetime.
31 Later his brothers and other relatives went down
to get his body. They took him back home and buried
him between Zorah and Eshtaol, where his father,
Manoah, was buried. Samson had judged Israel for
twenty years.

THE SECRET OF STRENGTH

1. Who is the strongest (physically, intellectually, emotionally, or spiritually) person you know? What makes that person so strong?

JUDGES 16:21-31

2. What was the real secret of Samson's strength (v. 28)?
3. What caused God to depart from Samson? How might he have avoided this tragic death?
4. How does God's Spirit bring strength to His people today? What is required of us if we are to have His strength in our lives?
5. In what area of your life do you most need the strength of God's Spirit today?

MICAH'S IDOLS

17 There was a man named Micah, who lived in the
hill country of Ephraim. 2 One day he said to his
mother, "I heard you place a curse on the person who
stole 1,100 pieces* of silver from you. Well, I have the
money. I was the one who took it."

16:13-14 As in Greek version and Latin Vulgate; Hebrew lacks *I would become as weak as anyone else. / So while he slept, Delilah wove the seven braids of his hair into the fabric.* [14]*Then she tightened it with the loom shuttle.* **16:19** Or *she began to torment him.* Greek version reads *He began to grow weak.* **17:2** Hebrew *1,100 [shekels],* about 28 pounds or 12.5 kilograms in weight.

16:13 making fun of me and telling me lies. Delilah was correct; Samson had been playing games with her and her people.
16:19-20 his strength left him . . . the LORD had left him. Samson's strength was from the Spirit of the Lord. When he betrayed his vow, he lost that special blessing.
16:21 gouged out his eyes. By blinding Samson the Philistines were able to both control and humiliate him.
16:27 all the Philistine rulers were there. The Philistines had planned a public humiliation of Samson at their pagan temple, but God had other plans.
16:30 he killed more people when he died. He took more than 3,000 Philistines with him.
17:1–18:31 This story tells of theft, curses, idols, the love of money, and abandonment of God's plan. It involved the tribes of Ephraim and Dan and a corrupt young Levite.
17:2 heard you place a curse. Uttering a curse irresponsibly was an immoral act. Both Micah and his mother had lost any real faith and had descended into superstition.

"The LORD bless you for admitting it," his mother replied. 3 He returned the money to her, and she said, "I now dedicate these silver coins to the LORD. In honor of my son, I will have an image carved and an idol cast."

4 So when he returned the money to his mother, she took 200 silver coins and gave them to a silversmith, who made them into an image and an idol. And these were placed in Micah's house. 5 Micah set up a shrine for the idol, and he made a sacred ephod and some household idols. Then he installed one of his sons as his personal priest.

6 In those days Israel had no king; all the people did whatever seemed right in their own eyes.

7 One day a young Levite, who had been living in Bethlehem in Judah, arrived in that area. 8 He had left Bethlehem in search of another place to live, and as he traveled, he came to the hill country of Ephraim. He happened to stop at Micah's house as he was traveling through. 9 "Where are you from?" Micah asked him.

He replied, "I am a Levite from Bethlehem in Judah, and I am looking for a place to live."

10 "Stay here with me," Micah said, "and you can be a father and priest to me. I will give you ten pieces of silver* a year, plus a change of clothes and your food." 11 The Levite agreed to this, and the young man became like one of Micah's sons.

12 So Micah installed the Levite as his personal priest, and he lived in Micah's house. 13 "I know the LORD will bless me now," Micah said, "because I have a Levite serving as my priest."

IDOLATRY IN THE TRIBE OF DAN

18 Now in those days Israel had no king. And the tribe of Dan was trying to find a place where they could settle, for they had not yet moved into the land assigned to them when the land was divided among the tribes of Israel. 2 So the men of Dan chose from their clans five capable warriors from the towns of Zorah and Eshtaol to scout out a land for them to settle in.

When these warriors arrived in the hill country of Ephraim, they came to Micah's house and spent the night there. 3 While at Micah's house, they recognized the young Levite's accent, so they went over and asked him, "Who brought you here, and what are you doing in this place? Why are you here?" 4 He told them about his agreement with Micah and that he had been hired as Micah's personal priest.

5 Then they said, "Ask God whether or not our journey will be successful."

6 "Go in peace," the priest replied. "For the LORD is watching over your journey."

7 So the five men went on to the town of Laish, where they noticed the people living carefree lives, like the Sidonians; they were peaceful and secure.* The people were also wealthy because their land was very fertile. And they lived a great distance from Sidon and had no allies nearby.

8 When the men returned to Zorah and Eshtaol, their relatives asked them, "What did you find?"

9 The men replied, "Come on, let's attack them! We have seen the land, and it is very good. What are you waiting for? Don't hesitate to go and take possession of it. 10 When you get there, you will find the people living carefree lives. God has given us a spacious and fertile land, lacking in nothing!"

11 So 600 men from the tribe of Dan, armed with weapons of war, set out from Zorah and Eshtaol. 12 They camped at a place west of Kiriath-jearim in Judah, which is called Mahaneh-dan* to this day. 13 Then they went on from there into the hill country of Ephraim and came to the house of Micah.

14 The five men who had scouted out the land around Laish explained to the others, "These buildings contain a sacred ephod, as well as some household idols, a carved image, and a cast idol. What do you think you should do?" 15 Then the five men turned off the road and went over to Micah's house, where the young Levite lived, and greeted him kindly. 16 As the 600 armed warriors from the tribe of Dan stood at the entrance of the gate, 17 the five scouts entered the shrine and removed the carved image, the sacred ephod, the household idols, and the cast idol. Meanwhile, the priest was standing at the gate with the 600 armed warriors.

18 When the priest saw the men carrying all the sacred objects out of Micah's shrine, he said, "What are you doing?"

19 "Be quiet and come with us," they said. "Be a father and priest to all of us. Isn't it better to be a priest for an entire tribe and clan of Israel than for the household of just one man?"

20 The young priest was quite happy to go with them, so he took along the sacred ephod, the household idols, and the carved image. 21 They turned and started on their way again, placing their children, livestock, and possessions in front of them.

22 When the people from the tribe of Dan were quite a distance from Micah's house, the people who lived near Micah came chasing after them. 23 They were shouting as they caught up with them. The men of Dan turned around and said to Micah, "What's the matter? Why have you called these men together and chased after us like this?"

24 "What do you mean, 'What's the matter?'" Micah replied. "You've taken away all the gods I have made, and my priest, and I have nothing left!"

25 The men of Dan said, "Watch what you say! There are some short-tempered men around here who might get angry and kill you and your family." 26 So the men of Dan continued on their way. When Micah saw that there were too many of them for him to attack, he turned around and went home.

27 Then, with Micah's idols and his priest, the men of Dan came to the town of Laish, whose people were

17:10 Hebrew *10 [shekels] of silver,* about 4 ounces or 114 grams in weight. **18:7** The meaning of the Hebrew is uncertain. **18:12** *Mahaneh-dan* means "the camp of Dan."

17:3 dedicate these silver coins . . . I will have an image carved and an idol cast. In one breath she wanted to dedicate her wealth to God, and with the next she disobeyed His commands by making a graven image.

17:6 Israel had no king. Most scholars think that the book of Judges was written during Israel's monarchy, partly to show how the monarchy had brought order out of chaos.

17:10 ten pieces of silver. The young Levite's main concerns were exactly what Micah offered: money, clothes, and food.

17:12 installed . . . as his personal priest. Micah wanted his own priest, idols, and all the trappings that imply piety.

18:1 a place where they could settle. Dan had never been able to defeat the Canaanite residents and claim their homeland.

18:3 recognized the . . . accent. At this time Israel was still a loose confederation of tribes, each with its distinct accent and dialect.

18:19 tribe and clan of Israel. The Danites appealed to the young Levite's greed and pride.

peaceful and secure. They attacked with swords and
burned the town to the ground. 28 There was no one to
rescue the people, for they lived a great distance from
Sidon and had no allies nearby. This happened in the
valley near Beth-rehob.
Then the people of the tribe of Dan rebuilt the town
and lived there. 29 They renamed the town Dan after
their ancestor, Israel's son, but it had originally been
called Laish.
30 Then they set up the carved image, and they ap-
pointed Jonathan son of Gershom, son of Moses,* as
their priest. This family continued as priests for the
tribe of Dan until the Exile. 31 So Micah's carved image
was worshiped by the tribe of Dan as long as the Tab-
ernacle of God remained at Shiloh.

THE LEVITE AND HIS CONCUBINE

19 Now in those days Israel had no king. There
was a man from the tribe of Levi living in a re-
mote area of the hill country of Ephraim. One day he
brought home a woman from Bethlehem in Judah to
be his concubine. 2 But she became angry with him*
and returned to her father's home in Bethlehem.
After about four months, 3 her husband set out for
Bethlehem to speak personally to her and persuade
her to come back. He took with him a servant and
a pair of donkeys. When he arrived at* her father's
house, her father saw him and welcomed him. 4 Her
father urged him to stay awhile, so he stayed three
days, eating, drinking, and sleeping there.
5 On the fourth day the man was up early, ready to
leave, but the woman's father said to his son-in-law,
"Have something to eat before you go." 6 So the two
men sat down together and had something to eat and
drink. Then the woman's father said, "Please stay an-
other night and enjoy yourself." 7 The man got up to
leave, but his father-in-law kept urging him to stay, so
he finally gave in and stayed the night.
8 On the morning of the fifth day he was up early
again, ready to leave, and again the woman's father
said, "Have something to eat; then you can leave later
this afternoon." So they had another day of feasting.
9 Later, as the man and his concubine and servant
were preparing to leave, his father-in-law said,
"Look, it's almost evening. Stay the night and enjoy
yourself. Tomorrow you can get up early and be on
your way."
10 But this time the man was determined to leave.
So he took his two saddled donkeys and his concubine
and headed in the direction of Jebus (that is, Jerusa-
lem). 11 It was late in the day when they neared Jebus,
and the man's servant said to him, "Let's stop at this
Jebusite town and spend the night there."
12 "No," his master said, "we can't stay in this foreign
town where there are no Israelites. Instead, we will
go on to Gibeah. 13 Come on, let's try to get as far as
Gibeah or Ramah, and we'll spend the night in one of
those towns." 14 So they went on. The sun was setting
as they came to Gibeah, a town in the land of Benja-
min, 15 so they stopped there to spend the night. They
rested in the town square, but no one took them in for
the night.
16 That evening an old man came home from his
work in the fields. He was from the hill country of
Ephraim, but he was living in Gibeah, where the
people were from the tribe of Benjamin. 17 When he
saw the travelers sitting in the town square, he asked
them where they were from and where they were
going.
18 "We have been in Bethlehem in Judah," the man
replied. "We are on our way to a remote area in the
hill country of Ephraim, which is my home. I traveled
to Bethlehem, and now I'm returning home.* But no
one has taken us in for the night, 19 even though we
have everything we need. We have straw and feed for
our donkeys and plenty of bread and wine for our-
selves."
20 "You are welcome to stay with me," the old man
said. "I will give you anything you might need. But
whatever you do, don't spend the night in the square."
21 So he took them home with him and fed the don-
keys. After they washed their feet, they ate and drank
together.
22 While they were enjoying themselves, a crowd of
troublemakers from the town surrounded the house.
They began beating at the door and shouting to the
old man, "Bring out the man who is staying with you
so we can have sex with him."
23 The old man stepped outside to talk to them. "No,
my brothers, don't do such an evil thing. For this man
is a guest in my house, and such a thing would be
shameful. 24 Here, take my virgin daughter and this
man's concubine. I will bring them out to you, and
you can abuse them and do whatever you like. But
don't do such a shameful thing to this man."
25 But they wouldn't listen to him. So the Levite
took hold of his concubine and pushed her out the
door. The men of the town abused her all night, tak-
ing turns raping her until morning. Finally, at dawn
they let her go. 26 At daybreak the woman returned to
the house where her husband was staying. She col-
lapsed at the door of the house and lay there until it
was light.
27 When her husband opened the door to leave,
there lay his concubine with her hands on the thresh-
old. 28 He said, "Get up! Let's go!" But there was no an-
swer.* So he put her body on his donkey and took her
home.
29 When he got home, he took a knife and cut his
concubine's body into twelve pieces. Then he sent one
piece to each tribe throughout all the territory of Is-
rael.

18:30 As in an ancient Hebrew tradition, some Greek manuscripts, and Latin Vulgate; Masoretic Text reads *son of Manasseh.* 19:2 Or *she was unfaithful to him.* 19:3 As in Greek version; Hebrew reads *When she brought him to.* 19:18 As in Greek version (see also 19:29); Hebrew reads *now I'm going to the Tabernacle of the LORD.* 19:28 Greek version adds *for she was dead.*

18:30 set up the carved image. The Danites based their new city around some stolen idols and a corrupt Levite priest.

19:1–21:25 The second story is one of moral decadence and tribal foolishness. The Gibeah incident is remarkably similar to Lot's experience in Sodom (see Gen. 19:1-13). There are no moral heroes in the story.

19:21 took them home with him and fed the donkeys. The old man showed the Levite the proper hospitality for a fellow Israelite.

19:22 a crowd of troublemakers. The men of Gibeah exhibited perversions usually associated with the pagan Canaanites.

19:23 don't do such an evil thing. Though the owner of the house called their homosexual demands "evil," he also called them "brothers."

19:24 my virgin daughter, and the man's concubine. The old man was willing to sacrifice his daughter and his guest's concubine to the mob, but he refused to violate the code of hospitality covering his guest.

19:29 cut his concubine's body into twelve pieces. The Levite's action of dismembering his concubine's body was meant to send a message to the tribes about Benjamin's morally degenerate state. He did not recognize that by his inaction in protecting his concubine, he virtually condoned her assault.

30 Everyone who saw it said, "Such a horrible crime
has not been committed in all the time since Israel left
Egypt. Think about it! What are we going to do? Who's
going to speak up?"

ISRAEL'S WAR WITH BENJAMIN

20 Then all the Israelites were united as one
man, from Dan in the north to Beersheba in
the south, including those from across the Jordan in
the land of Gilead. The entire community assembled
in the presence of the LORD at Mizpah. 2 The leaders
of all the people and all the tribes of Israel—400,000
warriors armed with swords—took their positions
in the assembly of the people of God. 3 (Word soon
reached the land of Benjamin that the other tribes
had gone up to Mizpah.) The Israelites then asked
how this terrible crime had happened.
4 The Levite, the husband of the woman who had
been murdered, said, "My concubine and I came to
spend the night in Gibeah, a town that belongs to the
people of Benjamin. 5 That night some of the leading
citizens of Gibeah surrounded the house, planning to
kill me, and they raped my concubine until she was
dead. 6 So I cut her body into twelve pieces and sent
the pieces throughout the territory assigned to Israel,
for these men have committed a terrible and shame-
ful crime. 7 Now then, all of you—the entire com-
munity of Israel—must decide here and now what
should be done about this!"
8 And all the people rose to their feet in unison and
declared, "None of us will return home! No, not even
one of us! 9 Instead, this is what we will do to Gibe-
ah; we will draw lots to decide who will attack it.
10 One-tenth of the men* from each tribe will be cho-
sen to supply the warriors with food, and the rest of
us will take revenge on Gibeah* of Benjamin for this
shameful thing they have done in Israel." 11 So all the
Israelites were completely united, and they gathered
together to attack the town.
12 The Israelites sent messengers to the tribe of Ben-
jamin, saying, "What a terrible thing has been done
among you! 13 Give up those evil men, those trouble-
makers from Gibeah, so we can execute them and
purge Israel of this evil."
But the people of Benjamin would not listen. 14 In-
stead, they came from their towns and gathered at
Gibeah to fight the Israelites. 15 In all, 26,000 of their
warriors armed with swords arrived in Gibeah to join
the 700 elite troops who lived there. 16 Among Benja-
min's elite troops, 700 were left-handed, and each
of them could sling a rock and hit a target within a
hairsbreadth without missing. 17 Israel had 400,000
experienced soldiers armed with swords, not count-
ing Benjamin's warriors.
18 Before the battle the Israelites went to Bethel and
asked God, "Which tribe should go first to attack the
people of Benjamin?"
The LORD answered, "Judah is to go first."
19 So the Israelites left early the next morning and
camped near Gibeah. 20 Then they advanced toward
Gibeah to attack the men of Benjamin. 21 But Benja-
min's warriors, who were defending the town, came
out and killed 22,000 Israelites on the battlefield that
day.
22 But the Israelites encouraged each other and
took their positions again at the same place they
had fought the previous day. 23 For they had gone up
to Bethel and wept in the presence of the LORD until
evening. They had asked the LORD, "Should we fight
against our relatives from Benjamin again?"
And the LORD had said, "Go out and fight against
them."
24 So the next day they went out again to fight
against the men of Benjamin, 25 but the men of Benja-
min killed another 18,000 Israelites, all of whom were
experienced with the sword.
26 Then all the Israelites went up to Bethel and wept
in the presence of the LORD and fasted until evening.
They also brought burnt offerings and peace offerings
to the LORD. 27 The Israelites went up seeking direction
from the LORD. (In those days the Ark of the Covenant
of God was in Bethel, 28 and Phinehas son of Eleazar
and grandson of Aaron was the priest.) The Israelites
asked the LORD, "Should we fight against our relatives
from Benjamin again, or should we stop?"
The LORD said, "Go! Tomorrow I will hand them
over to you."
29 So the Israelites set an ambush all around Gibeah.
30 They went out on the third day and took their posi-
tions at the same place as before. 31 When the men of
Benjamin came out to attack, they were drawn away
from the town. And as they had done before, they be-
gan to kill the Israelites. About thirty Israelites died
in the open fields and along the roads, one leading to
Bethel and the other leading back to Gibeah.
32 Then the warriors of Benjamin shouted, "We're
defeating them as we did before!" But the Israelites
had planned in advance to run away so that the men
of Benjamin would chase them along the roads and
be drawn away from the town.
33 When the main group of Israelite warriors
reached Baal-tamar, they turned and took up their
positions. Meanwhile, the Israelites hiding in ambush
to the west* of Gibeah jumped up to fight. 34 There
were 10,000 elite Israelite troops who advanced
against Gibeah. The fighting was so heavy that Ben-
jamin didn't realize the impending disaster. 35 So the
LORD helped Israel defeat Benjamin, and that day the
Israelites killed 25,100 of Benjamin's warriors, all of
whom were experienced swordsmen. 36 Then the men
of Benjamin saw that they were beaten.
The Israelites had retreated from Benjamin's war-
riors in order to give those hiding in ambush more
room to maneuver against Gibeah. 37 Then those
who were hiding rushed in from all sides and killed
everyone in the town. 38 They had arranged to send

20:10a Hebrew *10 men from every hundred, 100 men from every thousand, and 1,000 men from every 10,000.* **20:10b** Hebrew *Geba,* in this case a variant spelling of Gibeah; also in 20:33. **20:33** As in Greek and Syriac versions and Latin Vulgate; Hebrew reads *hiding in the open space.*

20:1-48 The dismembered concubine got Israel's attention and prompted immediate action.
20:1 Dan . . . to Beer-sheba. This phrase indicated that all of Israel was involved in this conflict.
20:10 One-tenth of the men. This method for provisioning an army seemed equitable and possible in the tribal confederation of the time.
20:13 Give up those evil men. Israel made a reasonable demand that the guilty men be turned over for execution. This would have brought a peaceful end to the conflict, but the Benjaminites chose to fight.
20:21 22,000 Israelites. Israel was in the right and had the Lord's guidance, but the Benjaminites scored a big victory in the first battle.
20:35 the LORD helped Israel defeat Benjamin. After two days of heavy losses, Israel prevailed the third day, slaughtering 25,100 Benjaminite warriors.

up a large cloud of smoke from the town as a signal.
39 When the Israelites saw the smoke, they turned and
attacked Benjamin's warriors.
By that time Benjamin's warriors had killed about
thirty Israelites, and they shouted, "We're defeating
them as we did in the first battle!" 40 But when the
warriors of Benjamin looked behind them and saw
the smoke rising into the sky from every part of the
town, 41 the men of Israel turned and attacked. At this
point the men of Benjamin became terrified, because
they realized disaster was close at hand. 42 So they
turned around and fled before the Israelites toward
the wilderness. But they couldn't escape the battle,
and the people who came out of the nearby towns
were also killed.* 43 The Israelites surrounded the
men of Benjamin and chased them relentlessly, final-
ly overtaking them east of Gibeah.* 44 That day 18,000
of Benjamin's strongest warriors died in battle. 45 The
survivors fled into the wilderness toward the rock
of Rimmon, but Israel killed 5,000 of them along the
road. They continued the chase until they had killed
another 2,000 near Gidom.
46 So that day the tribe of Benjamin lost 25,000 strong
warriors armed with swords, 47 leaving only 600 men
who escaped to the rock of Rimmon, where they lived
for four months. 48 And the Israelites returned and
slaughtered every living thing in all the towns—the
people, the livestock, and everything they found. They
also burned down all the towns they came to.

ISRAEL PROVIDES WIVES FOR BENJAMIN

21 The Israelites had vowed at Mizpah, "We will
never give our daughters in marriage to a man
from the tribe of Benjamin." 2 Now the people went to
Bethel and sat in the presence of God until evening,
weeping loudly and bitterly. 3 "O LORD, God of Israel,"
they cried out, "why has this happened in Israel? Now
one of our tribes is missing from Israel!"
4 Early the next morning the people built an altar
and presented their burnt offerings and peace offer-
ings on it. 5 Then they said, "Who among the tribes of
Israel did not join us at Mizpah when we held our
assembly in the presence of the LORD?" At that time
they had taken a solemn oath in the LORD's presence,
vowing that anyone who refused to come would be
put to death.
6 The Israelites felt sorry for their brother Benjamin
and said, "Today one of the tribes of Israel has been
cut off. 7 How can we find wives for the few who re-
main, since we have sworn by the LORD not to give
them our daughters in marriage?"
8 So they asked, "Who among the tribes of Israel did
not join us at Mizpah when we assembled in the pres-
ence of the LORD?" And they discovered that no one
from Jabesh-gilead had attended the assembly. 9 For
after they counted all the people, no one from Jabesh-
gilead was present.
10 So the assembly sent 12,000 of their best war-
riors to Jabesh-gilead with orders to kill everyone
there, including women and children. 11 "This is what
you are to do," they said. "Completely destroy* all
the males and every woman who is not a virgin."
12 Among the residents of Jabesh-gilead they found
400 young virgins who had never slept with a man,
and they brought them to the camp at Shiloh in the
land of Canaan.
13 The Israelite assembly sent a peace delegation to
the remaining people of Benjamin who were living at
the rock of Rimmon. 14 Then the men of Benjamin re-
turned to their homes, and the 400 women of Jabesh-
gilead who had been spared were given to them as
wives. But there were not enough women for all of
them.
15 The people felt sorry for Benjamin because the LORD
had made this gap among the tribes of Israel. 16 So the
elders of the assembly asked, "How can we find wives
for the few who remain, since the women of the tribe
of Benjamin are dead? 17 There must be heirs for the
survivors so that an entire tribe of Israel is not wiped
out. 18 But we cannot give them our own daughters in
marriage because we have sworn with a solemn oath
that anyone who does this will fall under God's curse."
19 Then they thought of the annual festival of the
LORD held in Shiloh, south of Lebonah and north of
Bethel, along the east side of the road that goes from
Bethel to Shechem. 20 They told the men of Benjamin
who still needed wives, "Go and hide in the vineyards.
21 When you see the young women of Shiloh come out
for their dances, rush out from the vineyards, and
each of you can take one of them home to the land of
Benjamin to be your wife! 22 And when their fathers
and brothers come to us in protest, we will tell them,
'Please be sympathetic. Let them have your daugh-
ters, for we didn't find wives for all of them when we
destroyed Jabesh-gilead. And you are not guilty of
breaking the vow since you did not actually give your
daughters to them in marriage.'"
23 So the men of Benjamin did as they were told.
Each man caught one of the women as she danced
in the celebration and carried her off to be his wife.
They returned to their own land, and they rebuilt
their towns and lived in them.
24 Then the people of Israel departed by tribes and
families, and they returned to their own homes.
25 In those days Israel had no king; all the people
did whatever seemed right in their own eyes.

20:42 Or *battle, for the people from the nearby towns also came out and killed them.* **20:43** The meaning of the Hebrew is uncertain.
21:11 The Hebrew term used here refers to the complete consecration of things or people to the LORD, either by destroying them or by giving them as an offering.

20:47 600 men who escaped. If these 600 had not escaped, the tribe of Benjamin would have been wiped out.

21:1-25 The Israelites mourned the loss of their kinsmen and realized that some provision had to be made for the survival of the tribe of Benjamin.

21:1 had vowed. The oath not to allow a daughter to marry a Benjaminite also had a curse attached for anyone who violated it (v. 18).

21:2 weeping loudly and bitterly. Israel had done the right thing, but the consequences of that action were still disastrous. The people wept because "one tribe is missing in Israel today."

21:5 did not join us at Mizpah. The Israelites also had vowed to kill any of their own people who failed to participate in the campaign against the Benjaminites. They discovered that no assistance had come from the city of Jabesh-gilead.

21:11 Completely destroy all the males and every woman who is not a virgin. This punishment seems brutal, but it was what the strict covenant law required.

21:12 brought them to the camp. Israel decided that by providing the Benjaminites with virgins from Jabesh-gilead, they could skirt around the demands of both vows (vv. 1,5).

21:21 take one . . . to be your wife. The Benjaminites still needed another 200 wives, so the Israelites decided to just allow them to "kidnap" women. Since the women weren't actually given to them, the vow was not formally breached.

21:22 when their fathers or brothers come to us in protest. Israel prepared a standard response to the kidnapped girls' family members.

INTRODUCTION TO
RUTH

PERSONAL READING PLAN

☐Ruth 1:1-22
☐Ruth 2:1-23
☐Ruth 3:1-18
☐Ruth 4:1-22

AUTHOR

The author of Ruth is unknown.

DATE

The date of composition is difficult to fix, though it was probably written during the period of the Israelite monarchy (c. 1000–722 B.C.). An early date is likely, as suggested by the fact that the genealogy in 4:17-22 ends with David.

THEME

Divine providence and human loyalty in the life of one family. The legal procedure of kinsman-redeemer also serves to illustrate the larger biblical theme of redemption.

HISTORICAL BACKGROUND

The action of the book of Ruth is set in the tumultuous period of the judges (ca 1100 B.C.). In a time of foreign oppression and spiritual decline, this encouraging story takes place at a temporary time of peace and presents a picture of genuine faith. It may be that the book's original intention was to provide a politically important genealogy for David (4:17-22). The story goes to great lengths to legitimize his Moabite connections. This was important since Moabite women were considered immoral by many in Israel (see Gen. 19:30-38; Num. 25:1-3). Modern readers of Ruth, unfamiliar with the background of the "kinsman-redeemer" motif, will also want to read about the plight of bereft widows and disenfranchised poor people and how the next of kin was obliged to extend the family name (see Deut. 25:5-10) and redeem their lost property (see Lev. 25:23-28).

CHARACTERISTICS

The book of Ruth presents its themes in the form of a dramatic love story. The book is interesting for its contrast to the book of Judges. Though set during the time of the judges, the story of Ruth does not present the dramatic acts of God; in fact, God is not often mentioned in the book. Nonetheless, implied throughout is the quiet and tangible presence of God superintending the action of the story.

Above all, this is a book about a loving and righteous woman. The author takes a foreigner (and one who is not Jewish), Ruth, and shows her to be a person about whom God is vitally concerned. Throughout the book, Ruth displays an unconditional loyalty to her desolate mother-in-law, Naomi. In her love and in Boaz's kindness to these two widows, we see an illustration of God's self-giving love.

ELIMELECH MOVES HIS FAMILY TO MOAB

1 In the days when the judges ruled in Israel, a severe famine came upon the land. So a man from Bethlehem in Judah left his home and went to live in the country of Moab, taking his wife and two sons with him. 2 The man's name was Elimelech, and his wife was Naomi. Their two sons were Mahlon and Kilion. They were Ephrathites from Bethlehem in the land of Judah. And when they reached Moab, they settled there.

3 Then Elimelech died, and Naomi was left with her two sons. 4 The two sons married Moabite women. One married a woman named Orpah, and the other a woman named Ruth. But about ten years later, 5 both Mahlon and Kilion died. This left Naomi alone, without her two sons or her husband.

NAOMI AND RUTH RETURN

6 Then Naomi heard in Moab that the LORD had blessed his people in Judah by giving them good crops again. So Naomi and her daughters-in-law got ready to leave Moab to return to her homeland. 7 With her two daughters-in-law she set out from the place where she had been living, and they took the road that would lead them back to Judah.

8 But on the way, Naomi said to her two daughters-in-law, "Go back to your mothers' homes. And may the LORD reward you for your kindness to your husbands and to me. 9 May the LORD bless you with the security of another marriage." Then she kissed them good-bye, and they all broke down and wept.

10 "No," they said. "We want to go with you to your people."

11 But Naomi replied, "Why should you go on with me? Can I still give birth to other sons who could grow up to be your husbands? 12 No, my daughters, return to your parents' homes, for I am too old to marry again. And even if it were possible, and I were to get married tonight and bear sons, then what? 13 Would you wait for them to grow up and refuse to marry someone else? No, of course not, my daughters! Things are far more bitter for me than for you, because the LORD himself has raised his fist against me."

14 And again they wept together, and Orpah kissed her mother-in-law good-bye. But Ruth clung tightly to Naomi. 15 "Look," Naomi said to her, "your sister-in-law has gone back to her people and to her gods. You should do the same."

16 But Ruth replied, "Don't ask me to leave you and turn back. Wherever you go, I will go; wherever you live, I will live. Your people will be my people, and your God will be my God. 17 Wherever you die, I will die, and there I will be buried. May the LORD punish me severely if I allow anything but death to separate us!" 18 When Naomi saw that Ruth was determined to go with her, she said nothing more.

19 So the two of them continued on their journey. When they came to Bethlehem, the entire town was excited by their arrival. "Is it really Naomi?" the women asked.

20 "Don't call me Naomi," she responded. "Instead, call me Mara,* for the Almighty has made life very bitter for me. 21 I went away full, but the LORD has brought me home empty. Why call me Naomi when the LORD has caused me to suffer* and the Almighty has sent such tragedy upon me?"

22 So Naomi returned from Moab, accompanied by her daughter-in-law Ruth, the young Moabite woman. They arrived in Bethlehem in late spring, at the beginning of the barley harvest.

RUTH WORKS IN BOAZ'S FIELD

2 Now there was a wealthy and influential man in Bethlehem named Boaz, who was a relative of Naomi's husband, Elimelech.

2 One day Ruth the Moabite said to Naomi, "Let me go out into the harvest fields to pick up the stalks of grain left behind by anyone who is kind enough to let me do it."

Naomi replied, "All right, my daughter, go ahead." 3 So Ruth went out to gather grain behind the harvesters. And as it happened, she found herself working in a field that belonged to Boaz, the relative of her father-in-law, Elimelech.

4 While she was there, Boaz arrived from Bethlehem and greeted the harvesters. "The LORD be with you!" he said.

"The LORD bless you!" the harvesters replied.

5 Then Boaz asked his foreman, "Who is that young woman over there? Who does she belong to?"

6 And the foreman replied, "She is the young woman from Moab who came back with Naomi. 7 She asked me this morning if she could gather grain behind the harvesters. She has been hard at work ever since, except for a few minutes' rest in the shelter."

8 Boaz went over and said to Ruth, "Listen, my daughter. Stay right here with us when you gather grain; don't go to any other fields. Stay right behind the young women working in my field. 9 See which part of the field they are harvesting, and then follow them. I have warned the young men not to treat you roughly. And when you are thirsty, help yourself to the water they have drawn from the well."

10 Ruth fell at his feet and thanked him warmly. "What have I done to deserve such kindness?" she asked. "I am only a foreigner."

11 "Yes, I know," Boaz replied. "But I also know about everything you have done for your mother-in-law since the death of your husband. I have heard how you left your father and mother and your own land to live here among complete strangers. 12 May the LORD, the God of Israel, under whose wings you have come to take refuge, reward you fully for what you have done."

1:20 *Naomi* means "pleasant"; *Mara* means "bitter." 1:21 Or *has testified against me.*

1:4 Moabite. The Moabites were descendants of Lot's son Moab (Gen. 19:30-36). Lot was Abraham's nephew. God had forbidden the Hebrews to marry the Canaanites, but not the Moabites.

1:16 I will go. Ruth gave up her national identity, her religion, and her home with no promise for any future or reward except to share in Naomi's sorrow.

1:20 Naomi. This name meant "sweetness" or "pleasantness." **Mara**. This name meant "bitterness." During the Exodus, the Hebrews arrived at a place named "Marah," which was known for its bitter water (Ex. 15:23).

2:1 relative. The Law brought hope for a widowed woman, if a brother or other relative stepped in to carry on some of the deceased husband's responsibilities (Deut. 25:5-6).

2:2 grain left behind. In Leviticus 19:9-10, the Hebrews were instructed to leave grain in their fields and grapes in their vineyards for the poor and widowed to glean from.

2:12 under whose wings. Boaz used a beautiful image of protection to describe his hopes for Ruth. This same image is used by the psalmist in Psalm 91:4 and by Jesus Himself in Matthew 23:37.

13 "I hope I continue to please you, sir," she replied.
"You have comforted me by speaking so kindly to me,
even though I am not one of your workers."
14 At mealtime Boaz called to her, "Come over here,
and help yourself to some food. You can dip your
bread in the sour wine." So she sat with his harvest-
ers, and Boaz gave her some roasted grain to eat. She
ate all she wanted and still had some left over.
15 When Ruth went back to work again, Boaz or-
dered his young men, "Let her gather grain right
among the sheaves without stopping her. 16 And pull
out some heads of barley from the bundles and drop
them on purpose for her. Let her pick them up, and
don't give her a hard time!"
17 So Ruth gathered barley there all day, and when
she beat out the grain that evening, it filled an entire
basket.* 18 She carried it back into town and showed it
to her mother-in-law. Ruth also gave her the roasted
grain that was left over from her meal.
19 "Where did you gather all this grain today?" Na-
omi asked. "Where did you work? May the LORD bless
the one who helped you!"
So Ruth told her mother-in-law about the man in
whose field she had worked. She said, "The man I
worked with today is named Boaz."
20 "May the LORD bless him!" Naomi told her daugh-
ter-in-law. "He is showing his kindness to us as well as
to your dead husband.* That man is one of our closest
relatives, one of our family redeemers."
21 Then Ruth* said, "What's more, Boaz even told me
to come back and stay with his harvesters until the
entire harvest is completed."
22 "Good!" Naomi exclaimed. "Do as he said, my
daughter. Stay with his young women right through
the whole harvest. You might be harassed in other
fields, but you'll be safe with him."
23 So Ruth worked alongside the women in Boaz's
fields and gathered grain with them until the end of
the barley harvest. Then she continued working with
them through the wheat harvest in early summer.
And all the while she lived with her mother-in-law.

RUTH AT THE THRESHING FLOOR

3 One day Naomi said to Ruth, "My daughter, it's
time that I found a permanent home for you, so
that you will be provided for. 2 Boaz is a close relative
of ours, and he's been very kind by letting you gath-
er grain with his young women. Tonight he will be
winnowing barley at the threshing floor. 3 Now do as
I tell you—take a bath and put on perfume and dress
in your nicest clothes. Then go to the threshing floor,
but don't let Boaz see you until he has finished eating
and drinking. 4 Be sure to notice where he lies down;
then go and uncover his feet and lie down there. He
will tell you what to do."
5 "I will do everything you say," Ruth replied. 6 So
she went down to the threshing floor that night and
followed the instructions of her mother-in-law.
7 After Boaz had finished eating and drinking and
was in good spirits, he lay down at the far end of
the pile of grain and went to sleep. Then Ruth came
quietly, uncovered his feet, and lay down. 8 Around
midnight Boaz suddenly woke up and turned over.
He was surprised to find a woman lying at his feet!
9 "Who are you?" he asked.
"I am your servant Ruth," she replied. "Spread the
corner of your covering over me, for you are my fam-
ily redeemer."
10 "The LORD bless you, my daughter!" Boaz ex-
claimed. "You are showing even more family loyalty
now than you did before, for you have not gone after
a younger man, whether rich or poor. 11 Now don't
worry about a thing, my daughter. I will do what
is necessary, for everyone in town knows you are a
virtuous woman. 12 But while it's true that I am one
of your family redeemers, there is another man who
is more closely related to you than I am. 13 Stay here
tonight, and in the morning I will talk to him. If he
is willing to redeem you, very well. Let him marry
you. But if he is not willing, then as surely as the LORD
lives, I will redeem you myself! Now lie down here
until morning."
14 So Ruth lay at Boaz's feet until the morning, but
she got up before it was light enough for people to
recognize each other. For Boaz had said, "No one must
know that a woman was here at the threshing floor."
15 Then Boaz said to her, "Bring your cloak and spread
it out." He measured six scoops* of barley into the
cloak and placed it on her back. Then he* returned to
the town.
16 When Ruth went back to her mother-in-law, Nao-
mi asked, "What happened, my daughter?"
Ruth told Naomi everything Boaz had done for
her, 17 and she added, "He gave me these six scoops of
barley and said, 'Don't go back to your mother-in-law
empty-handed.'"
18 Then Naomi said to her, "Just be patient, my
daughter, until we hear what happens. The man
won't rest until he has settled things today."

BOAZ MARRIES RUTH

4 Boaz went to the town gate and took a seat there.
Just then the family redeemer he had mentioned
came by, so Boaz called out to him, "Come over here
and sit down, friend. I want to talk to you." So they
sat down together. 2 Then Boaz called ten leaders from
the town and asked them to sit as witnesses. 3 And
Boaz said to the family redeemer, "You know Naomi,
who came back from Moab. She is selling the land
that belonged to our relative Elimelech. 4 I thought I
should speak to you about it so that you can redeem it
if you wish. If you want the land, then buy it here in
the presence of these witnesses. But if you don't want
it, let me know right away, because I am next in line
to redeem it after you."
The man replied, "All right, I'll redeem it."

2:17 Hebrew *it was about an ephah* [20 quarts or 22 liters]. 2:20 Hebrew *to the living and to the dead.* 2:21 Hebrew *Ruth the Moabite.*
3:15a Hebrew *six measures,* an unknown quantity. 3:15b Most Hebrew manuscripts read *he;* many Hebrew manuscripts, Syriac version, and Latin Vulgate read *she.*

2:17. an entire basket. About half a bushel—a large amount for one day of gleaning.

3:4 uncover his feet. A request for marriage in that culture.

3:9 Spread the corner of your covering over me. Some translations speak of "the corner of your garment," and the word used for "corner" also means "wings." Boaz's blessing to Ruth earlier had mentioned her being under God's wing. Now Ruth was asking to be under Boaz's wing as well.

3:12 more closely related to you than I am. Here is an example of sophisticated ancient legal customs that involved inheritance and family structure. Boaz knew about a relative closer in bloodline to Ruth's husband than he was. Boaz had to deal with this legal matter before they could move ahead with any plan.

[5]Then Boaz told him, "Of course, your purchase of the land from Naomi also requires that you marry Ruth, the Moabite widow. That way she can have children who will carry on her husband's name and keep the land in the family."

[6]"Then I can't redeem it," the family redeemer replied, "because this might endanger my own estate. You redeem the land; I cannot do it."

[7]Now in those days it was the custom in Israel for anyone transferring a right of purchase to remove his sandal and hand it to the other party. This publicly validated the transaction. [8]So the other family redeemer drew off his sandal as he said to Boaz, "You buy the land."

[9]Then Boaz said to the elders and to the crowd standing around, "You are witnesses that today I have bought from Naomi all the property of Elimelech, Kilion, and Mahlon. [10]And with the land I have acquired Ruth, the Moabite widow of Mahlon, to be my wife. This way she can have a son to carry on the family name of her dead husband and to inherit the family property here in his hometown. You are all witnesses today."

[11]Then the elders and all the people standing in the gate replied, "We are witnesses! May the LORD make this woman who is coming into your home like Rachel and Leah, from whom all the nation of Israel descended! May you prosper in Ephrathah and be famous in Bethlehem. [12]And may the LORD give you descendants by this young woman who will be like those of our ancestor Perez, the son of Tamar and Judah."

THE DESCENDANTS OF BOAZ

[13]So Boaz took Ruth into his home, and she became his wife. When he slept with her, the LORD enabled her to become pregnant, and she gave birth to a son. [14]Then the women of the town said to Naomi, "Praise the LORD, who has now provided a redeemer for your family! May this child be famous in Israel. [15]May he restore your youth and care for you in your old age. For he is the son of your daughter-in-law who loves you and has been better to you than seven sons!"

[16]Naomi took the baby and cuddled him to her breast. And she cared for him as if he were her own. [17]The neighbor women said, "Now at last Naomi has a son again!" And they named him Obed. He became the father of Jesse and the grandfather of David.

[18]This is the genealogical record of their ancestor Perez:

Perez was the father of Hezron.
[19] Hezron was the father of Ram.
Ram was the father of Amminadab.
[20] Amminadab was the father of Nahshon.
Nahshon was the father of Salmon.*
[21] Salmon was the father of Boaz.
Boaz was the father of Obed.
[22] Obed was the father of Jesse.
Jesse was the father of David.

4:20 As in some Greek manuscripts (see also 4:21); Hebrew reads *Salma*.

4:9 I have bought from Naomi. While Naomi was neither part of the proceedings nor the woman in question, ultimately her right to the land was being transferred.

4:13-17 gave birth to a son. At this point, Naomi had come full circle in her journey. She left Bethlehem with a family, then lost them all, and saved Ruth. But through God's provision, Naomi now held again the inheritance of her husband and family.

4:16 cuddled him to her breast. Joseph had done the same thing with his grandchildren as a symbol of ownership (Gen. 50:22-23), to indicate that that they were as real to him as actual sons.

4:18-22 This genealogy stands as a reminder that God's plan reaches beyond generations. From Naomi's sorrow came a grandchild who established the family line of both King David and then Jesus, the Messiah.

INTRODUCTION TO

1 SAMUEL

PERSONAL READING PLAN

- ☐ 1 Samuel 1:1–2:11
- ☐ 1 Samuel 2:12–3:21
- ☐ 1 Samuel 4:1–5:12
- ☐ 1 Samuel 6:1–7:17
- ☐ 1 Samuel 8:1–10:8
- ☐ 1 Samuel 10:9–11:15
- ☐ 1 Samuel 12:1–13:15
- ☐ 1 Samuel 13:16–14:52
- ☐ 1 Samuel 15:1–16:23
- ☐ 1 Samuel 17:1-58
- ☐ 1 Samuel 18:1–19:24
- ☐ 1 Samuel 20:1-42
- ☐ 1 Samuel 21:1–22:23
- ☐ 1 Samuel 23:1–24:22
- ☐ 1 Samuel 25:1-44
- ☐ 1 Samuel 26:1–27:12
- ☐ 1 Samuel 28:1–29:11
- ☐ 1 Samuel 30:1–31:13

AUTHOR

The author of 1 Samuel is not known with certainty. Perhaps a compiler drew from materials written by others such as Samuel, Gad, and Nathan (see 1 Chron. 29:29) in order to produce the final rendition. Note that 1 and 2 Samuel were originally composed as one unit.

DATE

The date of authorship is uncertain, though it is possible that this two-volume book was written around the time of Solomon's death (ca 930 B.C.).

THEME

The king-maker (Samuel) and the first king (Saul).

HISTORICAL BACKGROUND AND CHARACTERISTICS

The first book of Samuel narrates a major transition in the life of Israel—the shift from government under judges to a monarchy. Samuel, the last judge, anoints Saul as Israel's first king (ca 1050 B.C.). He later anoints David as the king who will succeed Saul.

This historical book highlights the lives of three central figures: Samuel, Saul, and David. Sad elements abound: Eli's sons rebel; faithless Israel rejects her great King; Saul self-destructs in his vicious pursuit of David, reaching his lowest point when he consults a witch. But bright notes also punctuate this sordid story: Samuel stands firm and godly as the prophet of God who is ever faithful to his Lord; David (with best friend Jonathan) appears youthful, courageous, popular, and abounding in faith in the mighty God of Israel. In the context of almost constant warfare, trust in God is either conspicuously present or conspicuously absent. God is seen as the rejected King, the revealer of the unknown, the judge of the rebellious, as well as the deliverer of His people.

ELKANAH AND HIS FAMILY

1 There was a man named Elkanah who lived in Ra-
mah in the region of Zuph* in the hill country of
Ephraim. He was the son of Jeroham, son of Elihu, son
of Tohu, son of Zuph, of Ephraim. 2 Elkanah had two
wives, Hannah and Peninnah. Peninnah had chil-
dren, but Hannah did not.
3 Each year Elkanah would travel to Shiloh to wor-
ship and sacrifice to the LORD of Heaven's Armies at
the Tabernacle. The priests of the LORD at that time
were the two sons of Eli—Hophni and Phinehas. 4 On
the days Elkanah presented his sacrifice, he would
give portions of the meat to Peninnah and each of her
children. 5 And though he loved Hannah, he would
give her only one choice portion* because the LORD
had given her no children. 6 So Peninnah would taunt
Hannah and make fun of her because the LORD had
kept her from having children. 7 Year after year it was
the same—Peninnah would taunt Hannah as they
went to the Tabernacle.* Each time, Hannah would be
reduced to tears and would not even eat.
8 "Why are you crying, Hannah?" Elkanah would
ask. "Why aren't you eating? Why be downhearted
just because you have no children? You have me—
isn't that better than having ten sons?"

HANNAH'S PRAYER FOR A SON

9 Once after a sacrificial meal at Shiloh, Hannah got up
and went to pray. Eli the priest was sitting at his cus-
tomary place beside the entrance of the Tabernacle.*
10 Hannah was in deep anguish, crying bitterly as she
prayed to the LORD. 11 And she made this vow: "O LORD
of Heaven's Armies, if you will look upon my sorrow
and answer my prayer and give me a son, then I will
give him back to you. He will be yours for his entire
lifetime, and as a sign that he has been dedicated to
the LORD, his hair will never be cut.*"
12 As she was praying to the LORD, Eli watched her.
13 Seeing her lips moving but hearing no sound, he
thought she had been drinking. 14 "Must you come
here drunk?" he demanded. "Throw away your wine!"
15 "Oh no, sir!" she replied. "I haven't been drinking
wine or anything stronger. But I am very discouraged,
and I was pouring out my heart to the LORD. 16 Don't
think I am a wicked woman! For I have been praying
out of great anguish and sorrow."
17 "In that case," Eli said, "go in peace! May the God
of Israel grant the request you have asked of him."
18 "Oh, thank you, sir!" she exclaimed. Then she went
back and began to eat again, and she was no longer sad.

SAMUEL'S BIRTH AND DEDICATION

19 The entire family got up early the next morning
and went to worship the LORD once more. Then they
returned home to Ramah. When Elkanah slept with
Hannah, the LORD remembered her plea, 20 and in due
time she gave birth to a son. She named him Samuel,*
for she said, "I asked the LORD for him."
21 The next year Elkanah and his family went on
their annual trip to offer a sacrifice to the LORD and
to keep his vow. 22 But Hannah did not go. She told her
husband, "Wait until the boy is weaned. Then I will
take him to the Tabernacle and leave him there with
the LORD permanently.*"
23 "Whatever you think is best," Elkanah agreed.
"Stay here for now, and may the LORD help you keep
your promise.*" So she stayed home and nursed the
boy until he was weaned.
24 When the child was weaned, Hannah took him
to the Tabernacle in Shiloh. They brought along a
three-year-old bull* for the sacrifice and a basket* of
flour and some wine. 25 After sacrificing the bull, they
brought the boy to Eli. 26 "Sir, do you remember me?"
Hannah asked. "I am the very woman who stood here
several years ago praying to the LORD. 27 I asked the
LORD to give me this boy, and he has granted my re-
quest. 28 Now I am giving him to the LORD, and he will
belong to the LORD his whole life." And they* wor-
shiped the LORD there.

HANNAH'S PRAYER OF PRAISE

2 Then Hannah prayed:

"My heart rejoices in the LORD!
The LORD has made me strong.*
Now I have an answer for my enemies;
I rejoice because you rescued me.
2 No one is holy like the LORD!
There is no one besides you;
there is no Rock like our God.

3 "Stop acting so proud and haughty!
Don't speak with such arrogance!
For the LORD is a God who knows what you have
done;
he will judge your actions.
4 The bow of the mighty is now broken,
and those who stumbled are now strong.
5 Those who were well fed are now starving,
and those who were starving are now full.
The childless woman now has seven children,
and the woman with many children wastes
away.
6 The LORD gives both death and life;
he brings some down to the grave* but raises
others up.
7 The LORD makes some poor and others rich;
he brings some down and lifts others up.
8 He lifts the poor from the dust
and the needy from the garbage dump.
He sets them among princes,
placing them in seats of honor.

1:1 As in Greek version; Hebrew reads *in Ramathaim-zophim;* compare 1:19. **1:5** Or *And because he loved Hannah, he would give her a choice portion.* The meaning of the Hebrew is uncertain. **1:7** Hebrew *the house of the LORD;* also in 1:24. **1:9** Hebrew *the Temple of the LORD.* **1:11** Some manuscripts add *He will drink neither wine nor intoxicants.* **1:20** *Samuel* sounds like the Hebrew term for "asked of God" or "heard by God." **1:22** Some manuscripts add *I will offer him as a Nazirite for all time.* **1:23** As in Dead Sea Scrolls and Greek version; Masoretic Text reads *may the LORD keep his promise.* **1:24a** As in Dead Sea Scrolls, Greek and Syriac versions; Masoretic Text reads *three bulls.* **1:24b** Hebrew *and an ephah* [20 quarts or 22 liters]. **1:28** Hebrew *he.* **2:1** Hebrew *has exalted my horn.* **2:6** Hebrew *to Sheol.*

1:1 Ramah. A town about 15 miles north of Jerusalem. Samuel was born and buried here. **of Ephraim.** Elkanah, Samuel's father, was Ephraimite by residence, but his ancestry was through the tribe of Levi. It was appropriate, then, for Samuel to become a priest, even though his family was from Ephraim.

1:3 Each year. Three times a year, Hebrews journeyed to a central location of worship, in this case at Shiloh in Ephraim, to celebrate a national feast. The temple had not yet been built. Joshua had settled the tabernacle there as a more permanent structure (Josh. 18:1). This remained the central place of worship until the ark of the covenant was stolen.

1:5 had given her no children. During this time in history, infertility was always considered a curse from God. To be barren was the greatest shame any woman could bear.

For all the earth is the LORD's,
and he has set the world in order.
9 "He will protect his faithful ones,
but the wicked will disappear in darkness.
No one will succeed by strength alone.
10 Those who fight against the LORD will be
shattered.
He thunders against them from heaven;
the LORD judges throughout the earth.
He gives power to his king;
he increases the strength* of his anointed one."

11 Then Elkanah returned home to Ramah without
Samuel. And the boy served the LORD by assisting Eli
the priest.

ELI'S WICKED SONS

12 Now the sons of Eli were scoundrels who had no
respect for the LORD 13 or for their duties as priests.
Whenever anyone offered a sacrifice, Eli's sons
would send over a servant with a three-pronged
fork. While the meat of the sacrificed animal was still
boiling, 14 the servant would stick the fork into the pot
and demand that whatever it brought up be given to
Eli's sons. All the Israelites who came to worship at
Shiloh were treated this way. 15 Sometimes the ser-
vant would come even before the animal's fat had
been burned on the altar. He would demand raw
meat before it had been boiled so that it could be used
for roasting.

16 The man offering the sacrifice might reply, "Take
as much as you want, but the fat must be burned first."
Then the servant would demand, "No, give it to me
now, or I'll take it by force." 17 So the sin of these young
men was very serious in the LORD's sight, for they
treated the LORD's offerings with contempt.

18 But Samuel, though he was only a boy, served the
LORD. He wore a linen garment like that of a priest.*
19 Each year his mother made a small coat for him and
brought it to him when she came with her husband
for the sacrifice. 20 Before they returned home, Eli
would bless Elkanah and his wife and say, "May the
LORD give you other children to take the place of this
one she gave to the LORD.*" 21 And the LORD blessed
Hannah, and she conceived and gave birth to three
sons and two daughters. Meanwhile, Samuel grew up
in the presence of the LORD.

22 Now Eli was very old, but he was aware of what
his sons were doing to the people of Israel. He knew,
for instance, that his sons were seducing the young
women who assisted at the entrance of the Taber-
nacle.* 23 Eli said to them, "I have been hearing reports
from all the people about the wicked things you are
doing. Why do you keep sinning? 24 You must stop, my
sons! The reports I hear among the LORD's people are
not good. 25 If someone sins against another person,
God* can mediate for the guilty party. But if someone
sins against the LORD, who can intercede?" But Eli's
sons wouldn't listen to their father, for the LORD was
already planning to put them to death.

26 Meanwhile, the boy Samuel grew taller and grew
in favor with the LORD and with the people.

A WARNING FOR ELI'S FAMILY

27 One day a man of God came to Eli and gave him this
message from the LORD: "I revealed myself* to your
ancestors when they were Pharaoh's slaves in Egypt.
28 I chose your ancestor Aaron* from among all the
tribes of Israel to be my priest, to offer sacrifices on
my altar, to burn incense, and to wear the priestly
vest* as he served me. And I assigned the sacrificial
offerings to you priests. 29 So why do you scorn my
sacrifices and offerings? Why do you give your sons
more honor than you give me—for you and they
have become fat from the best offerings of my people
Israel!

30 "Therefore, the LORD, the God of Israel, says: I
promised that your branch of the tribe of Levi* would
always be my priests. But I will honor those who hon-
or me, and I will despise those who think lightly of
me. 31 The time is coming when I will put an end to
your family, so it will no longer serve as my priests.
All the members of your family will die before their
time. None will reach old age. 32 You will watch with
envy as I pour out prosperity on the people of Isra-
el. But no members of your family will ever live out
their days. 33 The few not cut off from serving at my
altar will survive, but only so their eyes can go blind
and their hearts break, and their children will die a
violent death.* 34 And to prove that what I have said
will come true, I will cause your two sons, Hophni and
Phinehas, to die on the same day!

35 "Then I will raise up a faithful priest who will
serve me and do what I desire. I will establish his
family, and they will be priests to my anointed kings
forever. 36 Then all of your surviving family will bow
before him, begging for money and food. 'Please,' they
will say, 'give us jobs among the priests so we will
have enough to eat.'"

THE LORD SPEAKS TO SAMUEL

3 Meanwhile, the boy Samuel served the LORD by
assisting Eli. Now in those days messages from the
LORD were very rare, and visions were quite uncom-
mon.

2:10 Hebrew *he exalts the horn.* **2:18** Hebrew *He wore a linen ephod.* **2:20** As in Dead Sea Scrolls and Greek version; Masoretic Text reads *this one he requested of the LORD.* **2:22** Hebrew *Tent of Meeting.* Some manuscripts lack this entire sentence. **2:25** Or *the judges.* **2:27** As in Greek and Syriac versions; Hebrew reads *Did I reveal myself.* **2:28a** Hebrew *your father.* **2:28b** Hebrew *an ephod.* **2:30** Hebrew *that your house and your father's house.* **2:33** As in Dead Sea Scrolls and Greek version, which read *die by the sword;* Masoretic Text reads *die like mortals.*

2:10 his king. Through Samuel's leadership God would anoint the first and second kings, Saul and David.

2:13-16 The priests lived off *some* of the offerings. The three-pronged fork was a random method of giving the priests some food. Eli's sons chose a method that put the choice in their hands rather than God's.

2:15 even before the animal's fat had been burned. For the priests to take meat before the fat had been boiled or burned off was to claim for themselves what belonged to God by His own decree. It was the ultimate disregard and disrespect.

2:16 I'll take it by force. Sacrifices were to be voluntary to have any meaning at all. This coercion turned an "offering" into a "do it or else."

2:18 like that of a priest. The high priest wore a sacred, ornamental ephod, a sleeveless, tunic-like garment. Samuel's was linen.

2:22 women who assisted. These women are mentioned only one other time (Ex. 38:8) without much detail. Pagan women offered sexual favors at their temples as worship to fertility gods. Eli's sons were blatantly insulting God in mimicking that behavior.

2:35 my anointed kings. Ultimately Jesus Christ, it was fulfilled as well in ancient Israel when the priesthood was taken away from Ithamar's descendants (Eli, etc.) and given to Eleazar's descendants (another son of Aaron).

3:1 messages from the LORD was very rare. Samuel was about to usher in a new day.

A WARNING IN THE NIGHT

1. Are you a light or heavy sleeper? What does it take to wake you?

1 SAMUEL 3:1-14

2. Samuel lived in the Lord's temple, yet "he had never had a message from the LORD before" (v. 7). What does that say about Eli, the high priest?
3. Why is God going to judge Eli's family forever?
4. What might Eli have done to stop his sons? In what way is he responsible for their sins?
5. How are you responsible for speaking out against those who are doing wrong?

2 One night Eli, who was almost blind by now, had gone to bed. 3 The lamp of God had not yet gone out, and Samuel was sleeping in the Tabernacle* near the Ark of God. 4 Suddenly the LORD called out, "Samuel!"

"Yes?" Samuel replied. "What is it?" 5 He got up and ran to Eli. "Here I am. Did you call me?"

"I didn't call you," Eli replied. "Go back to bed." So he did.

6 Then the LORD called out again, "Samuel!"

Again Samuel got up and went to Eli. "Here I am. Did you call me?"

"I didn't call you, my son," Eli said. "Go back to bed."

7 Samuel did not yet know the LORD because he had never had a message from the LORD before. 8 So the LORD called a third time, and once more Samuel got up and went to Eli. "Here I am. Did you call me?"

Then Eli realized it was the LORD who was calling the boy. 9 So he said to Samuel, "Go and lie down again, and if someone calls again, say, 'Speak, LORD, your servant is listening.'" So Samuel went back to bed.

10 And the LORD came and called as before, "Samuel! Samuel!"

And Samuel replied, "Speak, your servant is listening."

11 Then the LORD said to Samuel, "I am about to do a shocking thing in Israel. 12 I am going to carry out all my threats against Eli and his family, from beginning to end. 13 I have warned him that judgment is coming upon his family forever, because his sons are blaspheming God* and he hasn't disciplined them. 14 So I have vowed that the sins of Eli and his sons will never be forgiven by sacrifices or offerings."

SAMUEL SPEAKS FOR THE LORD

15 Samuel stayed in bed until morning, then got up and opened the doors of the Tabernacle* as usual. He was afraid to tell Eli what the LORD had said to him. 16 But Eli called out to him, "Samuel, my son."

"Here I am," Samuel replied.

17 "What did the LORD say to you? Tell me everything. And may God strike you and even kill you if you hide anything from me!" 18 So Samuel told Eli everything; he didn't hold anything back. "It is the LORD's will," Eli replied. "Let him do what he thinks best."

19 As Samuel grew up, the LORD was with him, and everything Samuel said proved to be reliable. 20 And all Israel, from Dan in the north to Beersheba in the south, knew that Samuel was confirmed as a prophet of the LORD. 21 The LORD continued to appear at Shiloh and gave messages to Samuel there at the Tabernacle. 4:1 And Samuel's words went out to all the people of Israel.

THE PHILISTINES CAPTURE THE ARK

4 At that time Israel was at war with the Philistines. The Israelite army was camped near Ebenezer, and the Philistines were at Aphek. 2 The Philistines attacked and defeated the army of Israel, killing 4,000 men. 3 After the battle was over, the troops retreated to their camp, and the elders of Israel asked, "Why did the LORD allow us to be defeated by the Philistines?" Then they said, "Let's bring the Ark of the Covenant of the LORD from Shiloh. If we carry it into battle with us, it* will save us from our enemies."

4 So they sent men to Shiloh to bring the Ark of the Covenant of the LORD of Heaven's Armies, who is enthroned between the cherubim. Hophni and Phinehas, the sons of Eli, were also there with the Ark of the Covenant of God. 5 When all the Israelites saw the Ark of the Covenant of the LORD coming into the camp, their shout of joy was so loud it made the ground shake!

6 "What's going on?" the Philistines asked. "What's all the shouting about in the Hebrew camp?" When they were told it was because the Ark of the LORD had arrived, 7 they panicked. "The gods have* come into their camp!" they cried. "This is a disaster! We have never had to face anything like this before! 8 Help! Who can save us from these mighty gods of Israel? They are the same gods who destroyed the Egyptians with plagues when Israel was in the wilderness. 9 Fight as never before, Philistines! If you don't, we will become the Hebrews' slaves just as they have been ours! Stand up like men and fight!"

10 So the Philistines fought desperately, and Israel was defeated again. The slaughter was great; 30,000 Israelite soldiers died that day. The survivors turned and fled to their tents. 11 The Ark of God was captured, and Hophni and Phinehas, the two sons of Eli, were killed.

THE DEATH OF ELI

12 A man from the tribe of Benjamin ran from the battlefield and arrived at Shiloh later that same day. He had torn his clothes and put dust on his head to show his grief. 13 Eli was waiting beside the road to hear the news of the battle, for his heart trembled for the safety of the Ark of God. When the messenger arrived and told what had happened, an outcry resounded throughout the town.

14 "What is all the noise about?" Eli asked.

3:3 Hebrew *the Temple of the LORD.* **3:13** As in Greek version; Hebrew reads *his sons have made themselves contemptible.* **3:15** Hebrew *the house of the LORD.* **4:3** Or *he.* **4:7** Or *A god has.*

3:17 even kill you. Ruth used this expression when making her vow of loyalty to Naomi (Ruth 1:17). Jonathan used it in committing his loyalty and protection to David (20:12-13). David, Abner, Ben-Hadad, and even Jezebel also spoke these same words.

4:7 The gods. While the ark represented the presence of the One true God, the Philistines thought many gods had come.

4:11 The Ark of God was captured. The ark had not saved them—it was not their lucky charm. **Hophni and Phinehas.** God had prophesied their death because they misused their position as priests (2:25).

The messenger rushed over to Eli, [15] who was ninety-eight years old and blind. [16] He said to Eli, "I have just come from the battlefield—I was there this very day."

"What happened, my son?" Eli demanded.

[17] "Israel has been defeated by the Philistines," the messenger replied. "The people have been slaughtered, and your two sons, Hophni and Phinehas, were also killed. And the Ark of God has been captured."

[18] When the messenger mentioned what had happened to the Ark of God, Eli fell backward from his seat beside the gate. He broke his neck and died, for he was old and overweight. He had been Israel's judge for forty years.

[19] Eli's daughter-in-law, the wife of Phinehas, was pregnant and near her time of delivery. When she heard that the Ark of God had been captured and that her father-in-law and husband were dead, she went into labor and gave birth. [20] She died in childbirth, but before she passed away the midwives tried to encourage her. "Don't be afraid," they said. "You have a baby boy!" But she did not answer or pay attention to them.

[21] She named the child Ichabod (which means "Where is the glory?"), for she said, "Israel's glory is gone." She named him this because the Ark of God had been captured and because her father-in-law and husband were dead. [22] Then she said, "The glory has departed from Israel, for the Ark of God has been captured."

THE ARK IN PHILISTIA

5 After the Philistines captured the Ark of God, they took it from the battleground at Ebenezer to the town of Ashdod. [2] They carried the Ark of God into the temple of Dagon and placed it beside an idol of Dagon. [3] But when the citizens of Ashdod went to see it the next morning, Dagon had fallen with his face to the ground in front of the Ark of the LORD! So they took Dagon and put him in his place again. [4] But the next morning the same thing happened—Dagon had fallen face down before the Ark of the LORD again. This time his head and hands had broken off and were lying in the doorway. Only the trunk of his body was left intact. [5] That is why to this day neither the priests of Dagon nor anyone who enters the temple of Dagon in Ashdod will step on its threshold.

[6] Then the LORD's heavy hand struck the people of Ashdod and the nearby villages with a plague of tumors.* [7] When the people realized what was happening, they cried out, "We can't keep the Ark of the God of Israel here any longer! He is against us! We will all be destroyed along with Dagon, our god." [8] So they called together the rulers of the Philistine towns and asked, "What should we do with the Ark of the God of Israel?"

The rulers discussed it and replied, "Move it to the town of Gath." So they moved the Ark of the God of Israel to Gath. [9] But when the Ark arrived at Gath, the LORD's heavy hand fell on its men, young and old; he struck them with a plague of tumors, and there was a great panic.

[10] So they sent the Ark of God to the town of Ekron, but when the people of Ekron saw it coming they cried out, "They are bringing the Ark of the God of Israel here to kill us, too!" [11] The people summoned the Philistine rulers again and begged them, "Please send the Ark of the God of Israel back to its own country, or it* will kill us all." For the deadly plague from God had already begun, and great fear was sweeping across the town. [12] Those who didn't die were afflicted with tumors; and the cry from the town rose to heaven.

THE PHILISTINES RETURN THE ARK

6 The Ark of the LORD remained in Philistine territory seven months in all. [2] Then the Philistines called in their priests and diviners and asked them, "What should we do about the Ark of the LORD? Tell us how to return it to its own country."

[3] "Send the Ark of the God of Israel back with a gift," they were told. "Send a guilt offering so the plague will stop. Then, if you are healed, you will know it was his hand that caused the plague."

[4] "What sort of guilt offering should we send?" they asked.

And they were told, "Since the plague has struck both you and your five rulers, make five gold tumors and five gold rats, just like those that have ravaged your land. [5] Make these things to show honor to the God of Israel. Perhaps then he will stop afflicting you, your gods, and your land. [6] Don't be stubborn and rebellious as Pharaoh and the Egyptians were. By the time God was finished with them, they were eager to let Israel go.

[7] "Now build a new cart, and find two cows that have just given birth to calves. Make sure the cows have never been yoked to a cart. Hitch the cows to the cart, but shut their calves away from them in a pen. [8] Put the Ark of the LORD on the cart, and beside it place a chest containing the gold rats and gold tumors you are sending as a guilt offering. Then let the cows go wherever they want. [9] If they cross the border of our land and go to Beth-shemesh, we will know it was the LORD who brought this great disaster upon us. If they don't, we will know it was not his hand that caused the plague. It came simply by chance."

[10] So these instructions were carried out. Two cows were hitched to the cart, and their newborn calves were shut up in a pen. [11] Then the Ark of the LORD and the chest containing the gold rats and gold tumors were placed on the cart. [12] And sure enough, without veering off in other directions, the cows went straight along the road toward Beth-shemesh, lowing as they went. The Philistine rulers followed them as far as the border of Beth-shemesh.

5:6 Greek version and Latin Vulgate read *tumors; and rats appeared in their land, and death and destruction were throughout the city.* **5:11** Or *he.*

4:18 forty years. Eli's leadership probably overlapped with several of Israel's judges, including Samson.

5:2 the temple of Dagon. This temple was located 50 miles from Shiloh, the central sanctuary of the Hebrews. Dagon was the mythical father of Baal.

5:8 Gath. A town 12 miles southeast of Israel. The same fate that settled on Ashdod fell on the people of Gath and Ekron.

6:2 diviners. A "yes or no" test was often involved, such as the one Gideon proposed when he laid his fleece before God. For instance, animal livers gave such signs.

6:4 tumors . . . rats. The gold was in the form of the plagues the Philistines had suffered: tumors and mice. The mice may have been carriers of the disease that caused the plague of tumors.

6:7 build a new cart. The Philistines made the "test" as difficult as possible. Cows new to the yoke would not know how to pull together. Leaving calves behind would force cows to go against their natural instincts to return the ark to Israel.

6:9 Beth-shemesh. An Israelite border town about 15 miles west of Jerusalem.

[13] The people of Beth-shemesh were harvesting wheat in the valley, and when they saw the Ark, they were overjoyed! [14] The cart came into the field of a man named Joshua and stopped beside a large rock. So the people broke up the wood of the cart for a fire and killed the cows and sacrificed them to the LORD as a burnt offering. [15] Several men of the tribe of Levi lifted the Ark of the LORD and the chest containing the gold rats and gold tumors from the cart and placed them on the large rock. Many sacrifices and burnt offerings were offered to the LORD that day by the people of Beth-shemesh. [16] The five Philistine rulers watched all this and then returned to Ekron that same day.

[17] The five gold tumors sent by the Philistines as a guilt offering to the LORD were gifts from the rulers of Ashdod, Gaza, Ashkelon, Gath, and Ekron. [18] The five gold rats represented the five Philistine towns and their surrounding villages, which were controlled by the five rulers. The large rock* at Beth-shemesh, where they set the Ark of the LORD, still stands in the field of Joshua as a witness to what happened there.

THE ARK MOVED TO KIRIATH-JEARIM

[19] But the LORD killed seventy men* from Beth-shemesh because they looked into the Ark of the LORD. And the people mourned greatly because of what the LORD had done. [20] "Who is able to stand in the presence of the LORD, this holy God?" they cried out. "Where can we send the Ark from here?"

[21] So they sent messengers to the people at Kiriath-jearim and told them, "The Philistines have returned the Ark of the LORD. Come here and get it!"

7 So the men of Kiriath-jearim came to get the Ark of the LORD. They took it to the hillside home of Abinadab and ordained Eleazar, his son, to be in charge of it. [2] The Ark remained in Kiriath-jearim for a long time—twenty years in all. During that time all Israel mourned because it seemed the LORD had abandoned them.

SAMUEL LEADS ISRAEL TO VICTORY

[3] Then Samuel said to all the people of Israel, "If you want to return to the LORD with all your hearts, get rid of your foreign gods and your images of Ashtoreth. Turn your hearts to the LORD and obey him alone; then he will rescue you from the Philistines." [4] So the Israelites got rid of their images of Baal and Ashtoreth and worshiped only the LORD.

[5] Then Samuel told them, "Gather all of Israel to Mizpah, and I will pray to the LORD for you." [6] So they gathered at Mizpah and, in a great ceremony, drew water from a well and poured it out before the LORD. They also went without food all day and confessed that they had sinned against the LORD. (It was at Mizpah that Samuel became Israel's judge.)

[7] When the Philistine rulers heard that Israel had gathered at Mizpah, they mobilized their army and advanced. The Israelites were badly frightened when they learned that the Philistines were approaching. [8] "Don't stop pleading with the LORD our God to save us from the Philistines!" they begged Samuel. [9] So Samuel took a young lamb and offered it to the LORD as a whole burnt offering. He pleaded with the LORD to help Israel, and the LORD answered him.

[10] Just as Samuel was sacrificing the burnt offering, the Philistines arrived to attack Israel. But the LORD spoke with a mighty voice of thunder from heaven that day, and the Philistines were thrown into such confusion that the Israelites defeated them. [11] The men of Israel chased them from Mizpah to a place below Beth-car, slaughtering them all along the way.

[12] Samuel then took a large stone and placed it between the towns of Mizpah and Jeshanah.* He named it Ebenezer (which means "the stone of help"), for he said, "Up to this point the LORD has helped us!"

[13] So the Philistines were subdued and didn't invade Israel again for some time. And throughout Samuel's lifetime, the LORD's powerful hand was raised against the Philistines. [14] The Israelite villages near Ekron and Gath that the Philistines had captured were restored to Israel, along with the rest of the territory that the Philistines had taken. And there was peace between Israel and the Amorites in those days.

[15] Samuel continued as Israel's judge for the rest of his life. [16] Each year he traveled around, setting up his court first at Bethel, then at Gilgal, and then at Mizpah. He judged the people of Israel at each of these places. [17] Then he would return to his home at Ramah, and he would hear cases there, too. And Samuel built an altar to the LORD at Ramah.

ISRAEL REQUESTS A KING

8 As Samuel grew old, he appointed his sons to be judges over Israel. [2] Joel and Abijah, his oldest sons, held court in Beersheba. [3] But they were not like their father, for they were greedy for money. They accepted bribes and perverted justice.

[4] Finally, all the elders of Israel met at Ramah to discuss the matter with Samuel. [5] "Look," they told him, "you are now old, and your sons are not like you. Give us a king to judge us like all the other nations have."

[6] Samuel was displeased with their request and went to the LORD for guidance. [7] "Do everything they say to you," the LORD replied, "for they are rejecting me, not you. They don't want me to be their king any longer. [8] Ever since I brought them from Egypt they have continually abandoned me and followed other gods. And now they are giving you the same

6:18 As in some Hebrew manuscripts and Greek version; most Hebrew manuscripts read *great meadow* or *Abel-haggedolah.* **6:19** As in a few Hebrew manuscripts; most Hebrew manuscripts read *70 men, 50,000 men.* Perhaps the text should be understood to read *the LORD killed 70 men and 50 oxen.* **7:12** As in Greek and Syriac versions; Hebrew reads *Shen.*

6:19 looked into the Ark. While they were glad to have it their national treasure back, the people still were required to treat the ark with reverence, unlike kids who have found a prize.

7:1 home of Abinadab. The ark stayed in his family for about 100 years. David finally brought the ark to Jerusalem (2 Sam. 6:2-3).

7:5 Mizpah. A common gathering spot for Israel, Mizpah was seven miles north of Jerusalem. It was there that Saul would later be presented as king (10:17-21).

7:10 the Philistines arrived. This battle marked a new phase in relations between the two peoples: the bully would become the beaten because Israel was obeying God.

7:12 took a large stone . . . named it Ebenezer. To commemorate what God had done (see Gen. 28: 16-19).

8:5 like all the other nations have. Israel's real motive for requesting a monarchy was now public: "Everyone else is doing it." Apparently the people expressed concerns about the wickedness of Samuel's sons; this, while valid, was a cover.

8:7 they are rejecting me. God directed Samuel to look at the deeper spiritual issue. Samuel's wounds were understandable. His leadership was being rejected. The more important issue, however, was that God's leadership was rejected.

DETRIMENTAL DESIRES

1. When have you wanted something "just like" someone else had? What was it? Did you get it?

1 SAMUEL 8:1-22

2. Why did the Israelites want a king? Why did Samuel consider their demand sinful (v. 6)?
3. The people wanted a king to fight their battles (v. 20). What seems to be their basic motive in demanding this? Who should they have trusted to fight their battles?
4. Does wanting to be like other people sometimes influence your motives? In what way?
5. Does fear ever motivate your decisions? How can faith in God help?

treatment. 9 Do as they ask, but solemnly warn them about the way a king will reign over them."

SAMUEL WARNS AGAINST A KINGDOM

10 So Samuel passed on the LORD's warning to the people who were asking him for a king. 11 "This is how a king will reign over you," Samuel said. "The king will draft your sons and assign them to his chariots and his charioteers, making them run before his chariots. 12 Some will be generals and captains in his army,* some will be forced to plow in his fields and harvest his crops, and some will make his weapons and chariot equipment. 13 The king will take your daughters from you and force them to cook and bake and make perfumes for him. 14 He will take away the best of your fields and vineyards and olive groves and give them to his own officials. 15 He will take a tenth of your grain and your grape harvest and distribute it among his officers and attendants. 16 He will take your male and female slaves and demand the finest of your cattle* and donkeys for his own use. 17 He will demand a tenth of your flocks, and you will be his slaves. 18 When that day comes, you will beg for relief from this king you are demanding, but then the LORD will not help you."

19 But the people refused to listen to Samuel's warning. "Even so, we still want a king," they said. 20 "We want to be like the nations around us. Our king will judge us and lead us into battle."

21 So Samuel repeated to the LORD what the people had said, 22 and the LORD replied, "Do as they say, and give them a king." Then Samuel agreed and sent the people home.

SAUL MEETS SAMUEL

9 There was a wealthy, influential man named Kish from the tribe of Benjamin. He was the son of Abiel, son of Zeror, son of Becorath, son of Aphiah, of the tribe of Benjamin. 2 His son Saul was the most handsome man in Israel—head and shoulders taller than anyone else in the land.

3 One day Kish's donkeys strayed away, and he told Saul, "Take a servant with you, and go look for the donkeys." 4 So Saul took one of the servants and traveled through the hill country of Ephraim, the land of Shalishah, the Shaalim area, and the entire land of Benjamin, but they couldn't find the donkeys anywhere.

5 Finally, they entered the region of Zuph, and Saul said to his servant, "Let's go home. By now my father will be more worried about us than about the donkeys!"

6 But the servant said, "I've just thought of something! There is a man of God who lives here in this town. He is held in high honor by all the people because everything he says comes true. Let's go find him. Perhaps he can tell us which way to go."

7 "But we don't have anything to offer him," Saul replied. "Even our food is gone, and we don't have a thing to give him."

8 "Well," the servant said, "I have one small silver piece.* We can at least offer it to the man of God and see what happens!" 9 (In those days if people wanted a message from God, they would say, "Let's go and ask the seer," for prophets used to be called seers.)

10 "All right," Saul agreed, "let's try it!" So they started into the town where the man of God lived.

11 As they were climbing the hill to the town, they met some young women coming out to draw water. So Saul and his servant asked, "Is the seer here today?"

12 "Yes," they replied. "Stay right on this road. He is at the town gates. He has just arrived to take part in a public sacrifice up at the place of worship. 13 Hurry and catch him before he goes up there to eat. The guests won't begin eating until he arrives to bless the food."

14 So they entered the town, and as they passed through the gates, Samuel was coming out toward them to go up to the place of worship.

15 Now the LORD had told Samuel the previous day, 16 "About this time tomorrow I will send you a man from the land of Benjamin. Anoint him to be the leader of my people, Israel. He will rescue them from the Philistines, for I have looked down on my people in mercy and have heard their cry."

17 When Samuel saw Saul, the LORD said, "That's the man I told you about! He will rule my people."

18 Just then Saul approached Samuel at the gateway and asked, "Can you please tell me where the seer's house is?"

19 "I am the seer!" Samuel replied. "Go up to the place of worship ahead of me. We will eat there together, and in the morning I'll tell you what you want to know and send you on your way. 20 And don't worry about those donkeys that were lost three days ago, for they have been found. And I am here to tell you that you and your family are the focus of all Israel's hopes."

8:12 Hebrew *commanders of thousands and commanders of fifties.* **8:16** As in Greek version; Hebrew reads *young men.* **9:8** Hebrew *1/4 shekel of silver,* about 0.1 ounces or 3 grams in weight.

9:16 Anoint. Anointing someone was a sign of special power. The ceremony usually involved oil poured over someone's head or placed on the face. Often anointing was accompanied by laying hands on the person. Even today some churches anoint in prayers for healing and lay hands on new leaders as the people pray for wisdom and success (Ex. 28:41; 2 Tim. 1:6; James 5:14).

9:21 tribe of Benjamin. Benjamin was the youngest of Israel's sons. The smallness of Saul's clan and tribe was an issue because in these times those would be his base of support. Gideon voiced similar concerns when asked to lead Israel against the Midianites (Judg. 6:15.)

21 Saul replied, "But I'm only from the tribe of Benjamin, the smallest tribe in Israel, and my family is the least important of all the families of that tribe! Why are you talking like this to me?"

22 Then Samuel brought Saul and his servant into the hall and placed them at the head of the table, honoring them above the thirty special guests. 23 Samuel then instructed the cook to bring Saul the finest cut of meat, the piece that had been set aside for the guest of honor. 24 So the cook brought in the meat and placed it before Saul. "Go ahead and eat it," Samuel said. "I was saving it for you even before I invited these others!" So Saul ate with Samuel that day.

25 When they came down from the place of worship and returned to town, Samuel took Saul up to the roof of the house and prepared a bed for him there.* 26 At daybreak the next morning, Samuel called to Saul, "Get up! It's time you were on your way." So Saul got ready, and he and Samuel left the house together. 27 When they reached the edge of town, Samuel told Saul to send his servant on ahead. After the servant was gone, Samuel said, "Stay here, for I have received a special message for you from God."

SAMUEL ANOINTS SAUL AS KING

10 Then Samuel took a flask of olive oil and poured it over Saul's head. He kissed Saul and said, "I am doing this because the LORD has appointed you to be the ruler over Israel, his special possession.* 2 When you leave me today, you will see two men beside Rachel's tomb at Zelzah, on the border of Benjamin. They will tell you that the donkeys have been found and that your father has stopped worrying about them and is now worried about you. He is asking, 'Have you seen my son?'

3 "When you get to the oak of Tabor, you will see three men coming toward you who are on their way to worship God at Bethel. One will be bringing three young goats, another will have three loaves of bread, and the third will be carrying a wineskin full of wine. 4 They will greet you and offer you two of the loaves, which you are to accept.

5 "When you arrive at Gibeah of God,* where the garrison of the Philistines is located, you will meet a band of prophets coming down from the place of worship. They will be playing a harp, a tambourine, a flute, and a lyre, and they will be prophesying. 6 At that time the Spirit of the LORD will come powerfully upon you, and you will prophesy with them. You will be changed into a different person. 7 After these signs take place, do what must be done, for God is with you. 8 Then go down to Gilgal ahead of me. I will join you there to sacrifice burnt offerings and peace offerings. You must wait for seven days until I arrive and give you further instructions."

SAMUEL'S SIGNS ARE FULFILLED

9 As Saul turned and started to leave, God gave him a new heart, and all Samuel's signs were fulfilled that day. 10 When Saul and his servant arrived at Gibeah, they saw a group of prophets coming toward them. Then the Spirit of God came powerfully upon Saul, and he, too, began to prophesy. 11 When those who knew Saul heard about it, they exclaimed, "What? Is even Saul a prophet? How did the son of Kish become a prophet?"

12 And one of those standing there said, "Can anyone become a prophet, no matter who his father is?"* So that is the origin of the saying "Is even Saul a prophet?"

13 When Saul had finished prophesying, he went up to the place of worship. 14 "Where have you been?" Saul's uncle asked him and his servant.

"We were looking for the donkeys," Saul replied, "but we couldn't find them. So we went to Samuel to ask him where they were."

15 "Oh? And what did he say?" his uncle asked.

16 "He told us that the donkeys had already been found," Saul replied. But Saul didn't tell his uncle what Samuel said about the kingdom.

SAUL IS ACCLAIMED KING

17 Later Samuel called all the people of Israel to meet before the LORD at Mizpah. 18 And he said, "This is what the LORD, the God of Israel, has declared: I brought you from Egypt and rescued you from the Egyptians and from all of the nations that were oppressing you. 19 But though I have rescued you from your misery and distress, you have rejected your God today and have said, 'No, we want a king instead!' Now, therefore, present yourselves before the LORD by tribes and clans."

20 So Samuel brought all the tribes of Israel before the LORD, and the tribe of Benjamin was chosen by lot. 21 Then he brought each family of the tribe of Benjamin before the LORD, and the family of the Matrites was chosen. And finally Saul son of Kish was chosen from among them. But when they looked for him, he had disappeared! 22 So they asked the LORD, "Where is he?"

And the LORD replied, "He is hiding among the baggage." 23 So they found him and brought him out, and he stood head and shoulders above anyone else.

24 Then Samuel said to all the people, "This is the man the LORD has chosen as your king. No one in all Israel is like him!"

And all the people shouted, "Long live the king!"

25 Then Samuel told the people what the rights and duties of a king were. He wrote them down on a scroll and placed it before the LORD. Then Samuel sent the people home again.

26 When Saul returned to his home at Gibeah, a group of men whose hearts God had touched went

9:25 As in Greek version; Hebrew reads *and talked with him there.* **10:1** Greek version reads *over Israel. And you will rule over the LORD's people and save them from their enemies around them. This will be the sign to you that the LORD has appointed you to be leader over his special possession.* **10:5** Hebrew *Gibeath-haelohim.* **10:12** Hebrew *said, "Who is their father?"*

9:24 meat. Saul's receiving the thigh, part of the sacrifice usually kept for the priests (Ex. 29:27; Lev. 7:32), foreshadowed the honor in store for him.

10:1 flask of olive oil and poured it over. Kings were doused with oil as a sign of God's blessing. Jesus later became God's "Anointed One." "Christos" and "Messiah" mean "Anointed One."

10:8 Gilgal. The site of the first Israelite camp after they crossed the Jordan (Josh. 4:19).

10:11 heard about it. Saul's people were shocked at his presumptuous new role. The citizens of Nazareth asked similar questions about Jesus (Matt. 13:54-56).

10:20 chosen. Urim and Thummim were stones used in making decisions like drawing straws or throwing dice (Ex. 28:30).

10:25 rights and duties of a king. Included Moses' instructions about the responsibilities of the king (Deut. 17:14-20).

with him. 27 But there were some scoundrels who
complained, "How can this man save us?" And they
scorned him and refused to bring him gifts. But Saul
ignored them.

[Nahash, king of the Ammonites, had been griev-
ously oppressing the people of Gad and Reuben who
lived east of the Jordan River. He gouged out the right
eye of each of the Israelites living there, and he didn't
allow anyone to come and rescue them. In fact, of all
the Israelites east of the Jordan, there wasn't a single
one whose right eye Nahash had not gouged out. But
there were 7,000 men who had escaped from the Am-
monites, and they had settled in Jabesh-gilead.]*

SAUL DEFEATS THE AMMONITES

11 About a month later,* King Nahash of Ammon
led his army against the Israelite town of Ja-
besh-gilead. But all the citizens of Jabesh asked for
peace. "Make a treaty with us, and we will be your
servants," they pleaded.

2 "All right," Nahash said, "but only on one condi-
tion. I will gouge out the right eye of every one of you
as a disgrace to all Israel!"

3 "Give us seven days to send messengers through-
out Israel!" replied the elders of Jabesh. "If no one
comes to save us, we will agree to your terms."

4 When the messengers came to Gibeah of Saul and
told the people about their plight, everyone broke into
tears. 5 Saul had been plowing a field with his oxen,
and when he returned to town, he asked, "What's the
matter? Why is everyone crying?" So they told him
about the message from Jabesh.

6 Then the Spirit of God came powerfully upon Saul,
and he became very angry. 7 He took two oxen and
cut them into pieces and sent the messengers to car-
ry them throughout Israel with this message: "This is
what will happen to the oxen of anyone who refuses
to follow Saul and Samuel into battle!" And the LORD
made the people afraid of Saul's anger, and all of them
came out together as one. 8 When Saul mobilized them
at Bezek, he found that there were 300,000 men from
Israel and 30,000* men from Judah.

9 So Saul sent the messengers back to Jabesh-gilead
to say, "We will rescue you by noontime tomorrow!"
There was great joy throughout the town when that
message arrived!

10 The men of Jabesh then told their enemies, "To-
morrow we will come out to you, and you can do to
us whatever you wish." 11 But before dawn the next
morning, Saul arrived, having divided his army into
three detachments. He launched a surprise attack
against the Ammonites and slaughtered them the
whole morning. The remnant of their army was so
badly scattered that no two of them were left togeth-
er.

12 Then the people exclaimed to Samuel, "Now
where are those men who said, 'Why should Saul rule
over us?' Bring them here, and we will kill them!"

13 But Saul replied, "No one will be executed today,
for today the LORD has rescued Israel!"

14 Then Samuel said to the people, "Come, let us all
go to Gilgal to renew the kingdom." 15 So they all went
to Gilgal, and in a solemn ceremony before the LORD
they made Saul king. Then they offered peace offer-
ings to the LORD, and Saul and all the Israelites were
filled with joy.

SAMUEL'S FAREWELL ADDRESS

12 Then Samuel addressed all Israel: "I have done
as you asked and given you a king. 2 Your king
is now your leader. I stand here before you—an old,
gray-haired man—and my sons serve you. I have
served as your leader from the time I was a boy to
this very day. 3 Now testify against me in the presence
of the LORD and before his anointed one. Whose ox or
donkey have I stolen? Have I ever cheated any of you?
Have I ever oppressed you? Have I ever taken a bribe
and perverted justice? Tell me and I will make right
whatever I have done wrong."

4 "No," they replied, "you have never cheated or op-
pressed us, and you have never taken even a single
bribe."

5 "The LORD and his anointed one are my witnesses
today," Samuel declared, "that my hands are clean."

"Yes, he is a witness," they replied.

6 "It was the LORD who appointed Moses and Aar-
on," Samuel continued. "He brought your ancestors
out of the land of Egypt. 7 Now stand here quietly be-
fore the LORD as I remind you of all the great things
the LORD has done for you and your ancestors.

8 "When the Israelites were* in Egypt and cried out
to the LORD, he sent Moses and Aaron to rescue them
from Egypt and to bring them into this land. 9 But the
people soon forgot about the LORD their God, so he
handed them over to Sisera, the commander of Ha-
zor's army, and also to the Philistines and to the king
of Moab, who fought against them.

10 "Then they cried to the LORD again and confessed,
'We have sinned by turning away from the LORD and
worshiping the images of Baal and Ashtoreth. But
we will worship you and you alone if you will rescue
us from our enemies.' 11 Then the LORD sent Gideon,*
Bedan,* Jephthah, and Samuel* to save you, and you
lived in safety.

12 "But when you were afraid of Nahash, the king
of Ammon, you came to me and said that you want-

10:27 This paragraph, which is not included in the Masoretic Text, is found in Dead Sea Scroll 4QSam[a]. **11:1** As in Dead Sea Scroll 4QSam[a] and Greek version; Masoretic Text lacks *About a month later.* **11:8** Dead Sea Scrolls and Greek version read *70,000.* **12:8** Hebrew *When Jacob was.* The names "Jacob" and "Israel" are often interchanged throughout the Old Testament, referring sometimes to the individual patriarch and sometimes to the nation. **12:11a** Hebrew *Jerub-baal,* another name for Gideon; see Judg 6:32. **12:11b** Greek and Syriac versions read *Barak.* **12:11c** Greek and Syriac versions read *Samson.*

11:6 Spirit of God. Beginning well, Saul's first official act was prompted by God's power and spirit. Saul's later rule would be characterized by pettiness and indecision.

11:15 they made Saul king. At this confirmation the people formally honored Saul as their choice, as well as God's choice. Now in battle he had proved himself.

12:3 testify against me. When the people first came to Samuel to request a king, they cited the failure of his sons to lead them (8:4-7). Here he defends himself.

12:6 the LORD who appointed Moses and Aaron. Samuel confronted the people on their lack of wisdom in requesting a king. He referred to the history of God's leadership. God had chosen Moses and Aaron (Ex. 4:14-17), but the people chose a king.

12:7 Now stand here quietly. Samuel switched from defending himself to accusing the people. He seems to be playing the role of God's defense attorney. His key point: "God keeps promises. Do the people keep theirs?"

12:11 to save you. During the time of the judges (between Joshua and Samuel), the people had developed a repetitive cycle of drawing close to God when they needed help, then falling away after the crisis cooled.

ed a king to reign over you, even though the LORD
your God was already your king. 13 All right, here is
the king you have chosen. You asked for him, and the
LORD has granted your request.
14 "Now if you fear and worship the LORD and listen
to his voice, and if you do not rebel against the LORD's
commands, then both you and your king will show
that you recognize the LORD as your God. 15 But if you
rebel against the LORD's commands and refuse to lis-
ten to him, then his hand will be as heavy upon you as
it was upon your ancestors.
16 "Now stand here and see the great thing the LORD
is about to do. 17 You know that it does not rain at this
time of the year during the wheat harvest. I will ask
the LORD to send thunder and rain today. Then you
will realize how wicked you have been in asking the
LORD for a king!"
18 So Samuel called to the LORD, and the LORD sent
thunder and rain that day. And all the people were
terrified of the LORD and of Samuel. 19 "Pray to the
LORD your God for us, or we will die!" they all said to
Samuel. "For now we have added to our sins by asking
for a king."
20 "Don't be afraid," Samuel reassured them. "You
have certainly done wrong, but make sure now that
you worship the LORD with all your heart, and don't
turn your back on him. 21 Don't go back to worshiping
worthless idols that cannot help or rescue you—they
are totally useless! 22 The LORD will not abandon his
people, because that would dishonor his great name.
For it has pleased the LORD to make you his very own
people.
23 "As for me, I will certainly not sin against the
LORD by ending my prayers for you. And I will con-
tinue to teach you what is good and right. 24 But be
sure to fear the LORD and faithfully serve him. Think
of all the wonderful things he has done for you. 25 But
if you continue to sin, you and your king will be swept
away."

CONTINUED WAR WITH PHILISTIA

13 Saul was thirty* years old when he became
king, and he reigned for forty-two years.*
2 Saul selected 3,000 special troops from the army
of Israel and sent the rest of the men home. He took
2,000 of the chosen men with him to Micmash and
the hill country of Bethel. The other 1,000 went with
Saul's son Jonathan to Gibeah in the land of Benja-
min.
3 Soon after this, Jonathan attacked and defeated
the garrison of Philistines at Geba. The news spread
quickly among the Philistines. So Saul blew the ram's
horn throughout the land, saying, "Hebrews, hear
this! Rise up in revolt!" 4 All Israel heard the news that
Saul had destroyed the Philistine garrison at Geba
and that the Philistines now hated the Israelites more
than ever. So the entire Israelite army was summoned
to join Saul at Gilgal.
5 The Philistines mustered a mighty army of 3,000*
chariots, 6,000 charioteers, and as many warriors as
the grains of sand on the seashore! They camped at
Micmash east of Beth-aven. 6 The men of Israel saw
what a tight spot they were in; and because they were
hard pressed by the enemy, they tried to hide in caves,
thickets, rocks, holes, and cisterns. 7 Some of them
crossed the Jordan River and escaped into the land of
Gad and Gilead.

SAUL'S DISOBEDIENCE AND SAMUEL'S REBUKE

Meanwhile, Saul stayed at Gilgal, and his men were
trembling with fear. 8 Saul waited there seven days
for Samuel, as Samuel had instructed him earlier, but
Samuel still didn't come. Saul realized that his troops
were rapidly slipping away. 9 So he demanded, "Bring
me the burnt offering and the peace offerings!" And
Saul sacrificed the burnt offering himself.
10 Just as Saul was finishing with the burnt offering,
Samuel arrived. Saul went out to meet and welcome
him, 11 but Samuel said, "What is this you have done?"
Saul replied, "I saw my men scattering from me,
and you didn't arrive when you said you would, and
the Philistines are at Micmash ready for battle. 12 So I
said, 'The Philistines are ready to march against us at
Gilgal, and I haven't even asked for the LORD's help!'
So I felt compelled to offer the burnt offering myself
before you came."
13 "How foolish!" Samuel exclaimed. "You have not
kept the command the LORD your God gave you. Had

"THE DEVIL MADE ME DO IT"

1. How many "tardies" have you had this school year? Are you generally late or on time for your scheduled appointments? For practices?

1 SAMUEL 13:1-15

2. Only the priests were allowed to offer sacrifices, so Saul sinned when he did this. What motivated him to disregard this law?
3. How did Saul excuse himself for his sin? Whose fault was it, according to Saul?
4. Why did Saul say, "I haven't even even asked for the LORD's help" (v. 12)? How do we sometimes make the same excuses to God that Saul made?
5. What commands of God, your teachers, or your coach do you sometimes ignore? How do you make excuses?

13:1a As in a few Greek manuscripts; the number is missing in the Hebrew. 13:1b Hebrew *reigned . . . and two;* the number is incomplete in the Hebrew. Compare Acts 13:21. 13:5 As in Greek and Syriac versions; Hebrew reads *30,000.*

12:14 you and your king . . . recognize the LORD. Samuel reminded the people that establishing a king would not change the original covenant (Deut. 6:1-7) in which God claimed them as His own and established Himself as their provider.

12:17 wheat harvest . . . thunder and rain. These acts of nature were most unusual during the months of the wheat harvest.

12:24 Think of all the wonderful things he has done. Before Moses died, he reminded the people about the exodus and God's miraculous provisions (Deut. 4:10; 5:15; 7:18).

13:5 3,000 chariots. Without chariots, the Israelites were outnumbered and under-equipped.

13:9 Saul sacrificed the burnt offering himself. Saul was from the tribe of Benjamin, not Levi. Offering sacrifices was not his privilege. This choice was the watershed in Saul's reign. From this point, his decisions fail in wisdom and his influence plummets.

you kept it, the LORD would have established your kingdom over Israel forever. 14 But now your kingdom must end, for the LORD has sought out a man after his own heart. The LORD has already appointed him to be the leader of his people, because you have not kept the LORD's command."

ISRAEL'S MILITARY DISADVANTAGE

15 Samuel then left Gilgal and went on his way, but the rest of the troops went with Saul to meet the army. They went up from Gilgal to Gibeah in the land of Benjamin.* When Saul counted the men who were still with him, he found only 600 were left! 16 Saul and Jonathan and the troops with them were staying at Geba in the land of Benjamin. The Philistines set up their camp at Micmash. 17 Three raiding parties soon left the camp of the Philistines. One went north toward Ophrah in the land of Shual, 18 another went west to Beth-horon, and the third moved toward the border above the valley of Zeboim near the wilderness.

19 There were no blacksmiths in the land of Israel in those days. The Philistines wouldn't allow them for fear they would make swords and spears for the Hebrews. 20 So whenever the Israelites needed to sharpen their plowshares, picks, axes, or sickles,* they had to take them to a Philistine blacksmith. 21 The charges were as follows: a quarter of an ounce* of silver for sharpening a plowshare or a pick, and an eighth of an ounce* for sharpening an ax or making the point of an ox goad. 22 So on the day of the battle none of the people of Israel had a sword or spear, except for Saul and Jonathan.

23 The pass at Micmash had meanwhile been secured by a contingent of the Philistine army.

JONATHAN'S DARING PLAN

14 One day Jonathan said to his armor bearer, "Come on, let's go over to where the Philistines have their outpost." But Jonathan did not tell his father what he was doing.

2 Meanwhile, Saul and his 600 men were camped on the outskirts of Gibeah, around the pomegranate tree* at Migron. 3 Among Saul's men was Ahijah the priest, who was wearing the ephod, the priestly vest. Ahijah was the son of Ichabod's brother Ahitub, son of Phinehas, son of Eli, the priest of the LORD who had served at Shiloh.

No one realized that Jonathan had left the Israelite camp. 4 To reach the Philistine outpost, Jonathan had to go down between two rocky cliffs that were called Bozez and Seneh. 5 The cliff on the north was in front of Micmash, and the one on the south was in front of Geba. 6 "Let's go across to the outpost of those pagans," Jonathan said to his armor bearer. "Perhaps the LORD will help us, for nothing can hinder the LORD. He can win a battle whether he has many warriors or only a few!"

7 "Do what you think is best," the armor bearer replied. "I'm with you completely, whatever you decide."

8 "All right, then," Jonathan told him. "We will cross over and let them see us. 9 If they say to us, 'Stay where you are or we'll kill you,' then we will stop and not go up to them. 10 But if they say, 'Come on up and fight,' then we will go up. That will be the LORD's sign that he will help us defeat them."

11 When the Philistines saw them coming, they shouted, "Look! The Hebrews are crawling out of their holes!" 12 Then the men from the outpost shouted to Jonathan, "Come on up here, and we'll teach you a lesson!"

"Come on, climb right behind me," Jonathan said to his armor bearer, "for the LORD will help us defeat them!"

13 So they climbed up using both hands and feet, and the Philistines fell before Jonathan, and his armor bearer killed those who came behind them. 14 They killed some twenty men in all, and their bodies were scattered over about half an acre.*

15 Suddenly, panic broke out in the Philistine army, both in the camp and in the field, including even the outposts and raiding parties. And just then an earthquake struck, and everyone was terrified.

ISRAEL DEFEATS THE PHILISTINES

16 Saul's lookouts in Gibeah of Benjamin saw a strange sight—the vast army of Philistines began to melt away in every direction.* 17 "Call the roll and find out who's missing," Saul ordered. And when they checked, they found that Jonathan and his armor bearer were gone.

18 Then Saul shouted to Ahijah, "Bring the ephod here!" For at that time Ahijah was wearing the ephod in front of the Israelites.* 19 But while Saul was talking to the priest, the confusion in the Philistine camp grew louder and louder. So Saul said to the priest, "Never mind; let's get going!"*

20 Then Saul and all his men rushed out to the battle and found the Philistines killing each other. There was terrible confusion everywhere. 21 Even the Hebrews who had previously gone over to the Philistine army revolted and joined in with Saul, Jonathan, and the rest of the Israelites. 22 Likewise, the men of Israel who were hiding in the hill country of Ephraim joined the chase when they saw the Philistines running away. 23 So the LORD saved Israel that day, and the battle continued to rage even beyond Beth-aven.

SAUL'S FOOLISH OATH

24 Now the men of Israel were pressed to exhaustion that day, because Saul had placed them under an

13:15 As in Greek version; Hebrew reads *Samuel then left Gilgal and went to Gibeah in the land of Benjamin.* **13:20** As in Greek version; Hebrew reads *or plowshares.* **13:21a** Hebrew *1 pim* [8 grams]. **13:21b** Hebrew *1/3 [of a shekel]* [4 grams]. **14:2** Or *around the rock of Rimmon;* compare Judg 20:45, 47; 21:13. **14:14** Hebrew *half a yoke;* a "yoke" was the amount of land plowed by a pair of yoked oxen in one day. **14:16** As in Greek version; Hebrew reads *they went and there.* **14:18** As in some Greek manuscripts; Hebrew reads *"Bring the Ark of God." For at that time the Ark of God was with the Israelites.* **14:19** Hebrew *Withdraw your hand.*

13:14 **your kingdom must end.** Though Saul had three sons, his kingdom never passed through his family line. Because of David's kindness and loyalty, Mephibosheth, Jonathan's son and Saul's grandson, eventually ate at King David's table—the closest any of his descendants came to the monarchy (2 Sam. 9).

13:15 **600 were left.** Saul had 3,000 soldiers at the start, but he lost 2,400 during the war at Gilgal.

13:22 **sword or spear.** The Philistines restricted the Israelites from working with metal. At a large disadvantage, they went to battle with weapons made only from natural substances—bows, arrows, and slingshots.

14:15 **everyone was terrified.** When the Philistines captured the ark, God sent a panic through plagues rather than earthquakes (5:9-10).

14:19 **Never mind.** The priests made decisions by reaching into the pocket of the ephod and pulling out stones. Saul was telling the priest to go ahead and check the stones.

14:24 **I have full revenge.** The conflict with the Philistines had become a personal agenda. Saul no longer represent God's interests.

oath, saying, "Let a curse fall on anyone who eats be-
fore evening—before I have full revenge on my ene-
mies." So no one ate anything all day, 25 even though
they had all found honeycomb on the ground in the
forest. 26 They didn't dare touch the honey because
they all feared the oath they had taken.
27 But Jonathan had not heard his father's com-
mand, and he dipped the end of his stick into a piece
of honeycomb and ate the honey. After he had eaten
it, he felt refreshed.* 28 But one of the men saw him
and said, "Your father made the army take a strict
oath that anyone who eats food today will be cursed.
That is why everyone is weary and faint."
29 "My father has made trouble for us all!" Jonathan
exclaimed. "A command like that only hurts us. See
how refreshed I am now that I have eaten this little
bit of honey. 30 If the men had been allowed to eat free-
ly from the food they found among our enemies, think
how many more Philistines we could have killed!"
31 They chased and killed the Philistines all day from
Micmash to Aijalon, growing more and more faint.
32 That evening they rushed for the battle plunder and
butchered the sheep, goats, cattle, and calves, but they
ate them without draining the blood. 33 Someone re-
ported to Saul, "Look, the men are sinning against the
LORD by eating meat that still has blood in it."
"That is very wrong," Saul said. "Find a large stone
and roll it over here. 34 Then go out among the troops
and tell them, 'Bring the cattle, sheep, and goats here
to me. Kill them here, and drain the blood before you
eat them. Do not sin against the LORD by eating meat
with the blood still in it.'"
So that night all the troops brought their animals
and slaughtered them there. 35 Then Saul built an al-
tar to the LORD; it was the first of the altars he built
to the LORD.
36 Then Saul said, "Let's chase the Philistines all
night and plunder them until sunrise. Let's destroy
every last one of them."
His men replied, "We'll do whatever you think is
best."
But the priest said, "Let's ask God first."
37 So Saul asked God, "Should we go after the Philis-
tines? Will you help us defeat them?" But God made no
reply that day.
38 Then Saul said to the leaders, "Something's
wrong! I want all my army commanders to come here.
We must find out what sin was committed today. 39 I
vow by the name of the LORD who rescued Israel that
the sinner will surely die, even if it is my own son Jon-
athan!" But no one would tell him what the trouble
was.
40 Then Saul said, "Jonathan and I will stand over
here, and all of you stand over there."
And the people responded to Saul, "Whatever you
think is best."
41 Then Saul prayed, "O LORD, God of Israel, please
show us who is guilty and who is innocent.*" Then
they cast sacred lots, and Jonathan and Saul were
chosen as the guilty ones, and the people were de-
clared innocent.
42 Then Saul said, "Now cast lots again and choose
between me and Jonathan." And Jonathan was
shown to be the guilty one.
43 "Tell me what you have done," Saul demanded of
Jonathan.
"I tasted a little honey," Jonathan admitted. "It was
only a little bit on the end of my stick. Does that de-
serve death?"
44 "Yes, Jonathan," Saul said, "you must die! May God
strike me and even kill me if you do not die for this."
45 But the people broke in and said to Saul, "Jona-
than has won this great victory for Israel. Should he
die? Far from it! As surely as the LORD lives, not one
hair on his head will be touched, for God helped him
do a great deed today." So the people rescued Jona-
than, and he was not put to death.
46 Then Saul called back the army from chasing the
Philistines, and the Philistines returned home.

SAUL'S MILITARY SUCCESSES

47 Now when Saul had secured his grasp on Israel's
throne, he fought against his enemies in every direc-
tion—against Moab, Ammon, Edom, the kings of Zo-
bah, and the Philistines. And wherever he turned, he
was victorious.* 48 He performed great deeds and con-
quered the Amalekites, saving Israel from all those
who had plundered them.
49 Saul's sons included Jonathan, Ishbosheth,* and
Malkishua. He also had two daughters: Merab, who
was older, and Michal. 50 Saul's wife was Ahinoam,
the daughter of Ahimaaz. The commander of Saul's
army was Abner, the son of Saul's uncle Ner. 51 Saul's
father, Kish, and Abner's father, Ner, were both sons
of Abiel.
52 The Israelites fought constantly with the Philis-
tines throughout Saul's lifetime. So whenever Saul
observed a young man who was brave and strong, he
drafted him into his army.

SAUL DEFEATS THE AMALEKITES

15 One day Samuel said to Saul, "It was the LORD
who told me to anoint you as king of his people,
Israel. Now listen to this message from the LORD! 2 This
is what the LORD of Heaven's Armies has declared: I
have decided to settle accounts with the nation of
Amalek for opposing Israel when they came from
Egypt. 3 Now go and completely destroy* the entire
Amalekite nation—men, women, children, babies,
cattle, sheep, goats, camels, and donkeys."
4 So Saul mobilized his army at Telaim. There were
200,000 soldiers from Israel and 10,000 men from

14:27 Or *his eyes brightened;* similarly in 14:29. **14:41** Greek version adds *If the fault is with me or my son Jonathan, respond with Urim; but if the men of Israel are at fault, respond with Thummim.* **14:47** As in Greek version; Hebrew reads *he acted wickedly.* **14:49** Hebrew *Ishvi,* a variant name for Ishbosheth; also known as Esh-baal. **15:3** The Hebrew term used here refers to the complete consecration of things or people to the LORD, either by destroying them or by giving them as an offering; also in 15:8, 9, 15, 18, 20, 21.

14:33 eating meat that still has blood on it. The blood represented the life of the person or creature (Gen. 9:4; Lev. 17:11; Deut. 12:16). To this day, draining of blood is an important part of making meat kosher.

14:52 Philistines. The Philistines occupied the land between Israel and the Mediterranean Sea. With no natural boundaries the dividing line was always in dispute.

15:3 completely destroy. Everything—and everyone—that might witness to their values and culture could pollute the values and faith God was seeking to build in Israel and, therefore, must be destroyed. **children and infants.** Most people today have a hard time reconciling such an order with the loving God revealed through Jesus Christ. Still, this was a different era, and we can't always understand from our limited perspective all that was necessary in order to establish Israel and their faith in the true God over against the other cultures around them.

Judah. 5 Then Saul and his army went to a town of the Amalekites and lay in wait in the valley. 6 Saul sent this warning to the Kenites: "Move away from where the Amalekites live, or you will die with them. For you showed kindness to all the people of Israel when they came up from Egypt." So the Kenites packed up and left.

7 Then Saul slaughtered the Amalekites from Havilah all the way to Shur, east of Egypt. 8 He captured Agag, the Amalekite king, but completely destroyed everyone else. 9 Saul and his men spared Agag's life and kept the best of the sheep and goats, the cattle, the fat calves, and the lambs—everything, in fact, that appealed to them. They destroyed only what was worthless or of poor quality.

THE LORD REJECTS SAUL

10 Then the LORD said to Samuel, 11 "I am sorry that I ever made Saul king, for he has not been loyal to me and has refused to obey my command." Samuel was so deeply moved when he heard this that he cried out to the LORD all night.

12 Early the next morning Samuel went to find Saul. Someone told him, "Saul went to the town of Carmel to set up a monument to himself; then he went on to Gilgal."

13 When Samuel finally found him, Saul greeted him cheerfully. "May the LORD bless you," he said. "I have carried out the LORD's command!"

14 "Then what is all the bleating of sheep and goats and the lowing of cattle I hear?" Samuel demanded.

15 "It's true that the army spared the best of the sheep, goats, and cattle," Saul admitted. "But they are going to sacrifice them to the LORD your God. We have destroyed everything else."

16 Then Samuel said to Saul, "Stop! Listen to what the LORD told me last night!"

"What did he tell you?" Saul asked.

17 And Samuel told him, "Although you may think little of yourself, are you not the leader of the tribes of Israel? The LORD has anointed you king of Israel. 18 And the LORD sent you on a mission and told you, 'Go and completely destroy the sinners, the Amalekites, until they are all dead.' 19 Why haven't you obeyed the LORD? Why did you rush for the plunder and do what was evil in the LORD's sight?"

20 "But I did obey the LORD," Saul insisted. "I carried out the mission he gave me. I brought back King Agag, but I destroyed everyone else. 21 Then my troops brought in the best of the sheep, goats, cattle, and plunder to sacrifice to the LORD your God in Gilgal."

22 But Samuel replied,

"What is more pleasing to the LORD:
your burnt offerings and sacrifices
or your obedience to his voice?
Listen! Obedience is better than sacrifice,
and submission is better than offering the fat
of rams.
23 Rebellion is as sinful as witchcraft,
and stubbornness as bad as worshiping idols.
So because you have rejected the command of the
LORD,
he has rejected you as king."

SAUL PLEADS FOR FORGIVENESS

24 Then Saul admitted to Samuel, "Yes, I have sinned. I have disobeyed your instructions and the LORD's command, for I was afraid of the people and did what they demanded. 25 But now, please forgive my sin and come back with me so that I may worship the LORD."

26 But Samuel replied, "I will not go back with you! Since you have rejected the LORD's command, he has rejected you as king of Israel."

27 As Samuel turned to go, Saul tried to hold him back and tore the hem of his robe. 28 And Samuel said to him, "The LORD has torn the kingdom of Israel from you today and has given it to someone else—one who is better than you. 29 And he who is the Glory of Israel will not lie, nor will he change his mind, for he is not human that he should change his mind!"

30 Then Saul pleaded again, "I know I have sinned. But please, at least honor me before the elders of my people and before Israel by coming back with me so that I may worship the LORD your God." 31 So Samuel finally agreed and went back with him, and Saul worshiped the LORD.

SAMUEL EXECUTES KING AGAG

32 Then Samuel said, "Bring King Agag to me." Agag arrived full of hope, for he thought, "Surely the worst is over, and I have been spared!"* 33 But Samuel said, "As your sword has killed the sons of many mothers, now your mother will be childless." And Samuel cut Agag to pieces before the LORD at Gilgal.

34 Then Samuel went home to Ramah, and Saul returned to his house at Gibeah of Saul. 35 Samuel never went to meet with Saul again, but he mourned constantly for him. And the LORD was sorry he had ever made Saul king of Israel.

SAMUEL ANOINTS DAVID AS KING

16 Now the LORD said to Samuel, "You have mourned long enough for Saul. I have rejected him as king of Israel, so fill your flask with olive oil and go to Bethlehem. Find a man named Jesse who lives there, for I have selected one of his sons to be my king."

2 But Samuel asked, "How can I do that? If Saul hears about it, he will kill me."

"Take a heifer with you," the LORD replied, "and say that you have come to make a sacrifice to the LORD. 3 Invite Jesse to the sacrifice, and I will show you which of his sons to anoint for me."

4 So Samuel did as the LORD instructed. When he arrived at Bethlehem, the elders of the town came trembling to meet him. "What's wrong?" they asked. "Do you come in peace?"

15:32 Dead Sea Scrolls and Greek version read *Agag arrived hesitantly, for he thought, "Surely this is the bitterness of death."*

15:13 I have carried out the LORD's command. Saul was already making foolish decisions. Here he lied, intentionally stealing from God and deceiving God's representative.

15:15 the army. Without much subtlety, Saul passed the blame. He blamed his soldiers and took no responsibility himself. Saul was like Adam when he said, "The woman You gave" and Eve saying, "It was the serpent" (Gen. 3:12-13). **the LORD your God.** Saul's choice of pronouns, from "my God" to "your God," is an indication of his shift in loyalty.

15:35 the LORD was. Before Noah and the flood, God was grieved that He had even created humankind (Gen. 6:6-8).

16:2 he will kill me. In order to go where God had commanded, he had to pass through Saul's town. Samuel had already told Saul that his kingdom would be replaced (15:28), so Saul could have been paranoid. Anointing a new king would be seen as an act of treason.

SEEING THE HEART AND SOUL

1. When the elementary kids picked teams on the playground, how long did it usually take you to get chosen?

1 SAMUEL 16:1-13

2. What does "people judge by outward appearance, but the LORD looks at the heart" mean (v. 7)?
3. Why do you think God skipped over the older brothers and chose David?
4. How can outward appearances be misleading? How can you learn to see more the way God sees?
5. When the Lord looks at your heart, what does He see?

5 "Yes," Samuel replied. "I have come to sacrifice to
the LORD. Purify yourselves and come with me to the
sacrifice." Then Samuel performed the purification
rite for Jesse and his sons and invited them to the sac-
rifice, too.
6 When they arrived, Samuel took one look at Eliab
and thought, "Surely this is the LORD's anointed!"
7 But the LORD said to Samuel, "Don't judge by his
appearance or height, for I have rejected him. The
LORD doesn't see things the way you see them. People
judge by outward appearance, but the LORD looks at
the heart."
8 Then Jesse told his son Abinadab to step forward
and walk in front of Samuel. But Samuel said, "This
is not the one the LORD has chosen." 9 Next Jesse sum-
moned Shimea,* but Samuel said, "Neither is this the
one the LORD has chosen." 10 In the same way all seven
of Jesse's sons were presented to Samuel. But Samuel
said to Jesse, "The LORD has not chosen any of these."
11 Then Samuel asked, "Are these all the sons you
have?"
"There is still the youngest," Jesse replied. "But he's
out in the fields watching the sheep and goats."
"Send for him at once," Samuel said. "We will not sit
down to eat until he arrives."
12 So Jesse sent for him. He was dark and handsome,
with beautiful eyes.
And the LORD said, "This is the one; anoint him."
13 So as David stood there among his brothers, Sam-
uel took the flask of olive oil he had brought and
anointed David with the oil. And the Spirit of the
LORD came powerfully upon David from that day on.
Then Samuel returned to Ramah.

DAVID SERVES IN SAUL'S COURT

14 Now the Spirit of the LORD had left Saul, and the
LORD sent a tormenting spirit* that filled him with
depression and fear.
15 Some of Saul's servants said to him, "A tormenting
spirit from God is troubling you. 16 Let us find a good
musician to play the harp whenever the tormenting
spirit troubles you. He will play soothing music, and
you will soon be well again."
17 "All right," Saul said. "Find me someone who
plays well, and bring him here."
18 One of the servants said to Saul, "One of Jesse's
sons from Bethlehem is a talented harp player. Not
only that—he is a brave warrior, a man of war, and
has good judgment. He is also a fine-looking young
man, and the LORD is with him."
19 So Saul sent messengers to Jesse to say, "Send me
your son David, the shepherd." 20 Jesse responded
by sending David to Saul, along with a young goat,
a donkey loaded with bread, and a wineskin full of
wine.
21 So David went to Saul and began serving him.
Saul loved David very much, and David became his
armor bearer.
22 Then Saul sent word to Jesse asking, "Please let
David remain in my service, for I am very pleased
with him."
23 And whenever the tormenting spirit from God
troubled Saul, David would play the harp. Then Saul
would feel better, and the tormenting spirit would go
away.

GOLIATH CHALLENGES THE ISRAELITES

17 The Philistines now mustered their army for
battle and camped between Socoh in Judah and
Azekah at Ephes-dammim. 2 Saul countered by gath-
ering his Israelite troops near the valley of Elah. 3 So
the Philistines and Israelites faced each other on op-
posite hills, with the valley between them.
4 Then Goliath, a Philistine champion from Gath,
came out of the Philistine ranks to face the forc-
es of Israel. He was over nine feet* tall! 5 He wore a
bronze helmet, and his bronze coat of mail weighed
125 pounds.* 6 He also wore bronze leg armor, and he
carried a bronze javelin on his shoulder. 7 The shaft
of his spear was as heavy and thick as a weaver's
beam, tipped with an iron spearhead that weighed
15 pounds.* His armor bearer walked ahead of him
carrying a shield.
8 Goliath stood and shouted a taunt across to the
Israelites. "Why are you all coming out to fight?" he
called. "I am the Philistine champion, but you are only
the servants of Saul. Choose one man to come down
here and fight me! 9 If he kills me, then we will be your
slaves. But if I kill him, you will be our slaves! 10 I defy

16:9 Hebrew *Shammah,* a variant spelling of Shimea; compare 1 Chr 2:13; 20:7. **16:14** Or *an evil spirit;* also in 16:15, 16, 23. **17:4** Hebrew *6 cubits and 1 span* [which totals about 9.75 feet or 3 meters]; Dead Sea Scrolls and Greek version read *4 cubits and 1 span* [which totals about 6.75 feet or 2 meters]. **17:5** Hebrew *5,000 shekels* [57 kilograms]. **17:7** Hebrew *600 shekels* [6.8 kilograms].

16:7 appearance or height. The choice of Saul had been based on distinctive physical attributes. He was the "most handsome man . . . head and shoulders taller than anyone else." (9:2). Now Samuel is instructed to ignore those criteria.

16:11 There is still the youngest. Generally priority went with being the eldest, not the youngest. However, David came to the throne as the youngest of a long line of brothers. This may have resulted in the humility that David often showed. Significantly, Jesus later taught, "whoever is greatest among you must become like the youngest" (Luke 22:26.)

16:14 the LORD sent a tormenting spirit. Evil spirits, like everything else in creation, are ultimately under God's control and cannot move where they are not allowed. **filled him with depression and fear.** Saul was tormented with depression and jealousy.

16:16 good musician to play the harp. David, the future king, calmed Saul's spirit with music. God's Spirit had left Saul and rested on David. And the Spirit, expressed through the music, was the reason Saul felt relief.

16:18-19 David. David was a warrior-musician. Music brought him to the palace, and his fighting skills won the victory against Goliath (17:46-58) and fame among the Israelites. But faith would make him God's choice as king (13:14).

the armies of Israel today! Send me a man who will
fight me!" 11 When Saul and the Israelites heard this,
they were terrified and deeply shaken.

JESSE SENDS DAVID TO SAUL'S CAMP

12 Now David was the son of a man named Jesse, an
Ephrathite from Bethlehem in the land of Judah. Jesse
was an old man at that time, and he had eight sons.
13 Jesse's three oldest sons—Eliab, Abinadab, and
Shimea*—had already joined Saul's army to fight
the Philistines. 14 David was the youngest son. David's
three oldest brothers stayed with Saul's army, 15 but
David went back and forth so he could help his father
with the sheep in Bethlehem.
16 For forty days, every morning and evening, the
Philistine champion strutted in front of the Israelite
army.
17 One day Jesse said to David, "Take this basket* of
roasted grain and these ten loaves of bread, and carry
them quickly to your brothers. 18 And give these ten
cuts of cheese to their captain. See how your broth-
ers are getting along, and bring back a report on how
they are doing.*" 19 David's brothers were with Saul
and the Israelite army at the valley of Elah, fighting
against the Philistines.
20 So David left the sheep with another shepherd
and set out early the next morning with the gifts, as
Jesse had directed him. He arrived at the camp just
as the Israelite army was leaving for the battlefield
with shouts and battle cries. 21 Soon the Israelite
and Philistine forces stood facing each other, army
against army. 22 David left his things with the keeper
of supplies and hurried out to the ranks to greet his
brothers. 23 As he was talking with them, Goliath, the
Philistine champion from Gath, came out from the
Philistine ranks. Then David heard him shout his usu-
al taunt to the army of Israel.
24 As soon as the Israelite army saw him, they began
to run away in fright. 25 "Have you seen the giant?" the
men asked. "He comes out each day to defy Israel. The
king has offered a huge reward to anyone who kills
him. He will give that man one of his daughters for
a wife, and the man's entire family will be exempted
from paying taxes!"
26 David asked the soldiers standing nearby, "What
will a man get for killing this Philistine and ending
his defiance of Israel? Who is this pagan Philistine
anyway, that he is allowed to defy the armies of the
living God?"
27 And these men gave David the same reply. They
said, "Yes, that is the reward for killing him."
28 But when David's oldest brother, Eliab, heard Da-
vid talking to the men, he was angry. "What are you
doing around here anyway?" he demanded. "What
about those few sheep you're supposed to be taking
care of? I know about your pride and deceit. You just
want to see the battle!"
29 "What have I done now?" David replied. "I was
only asking a question!" 30 He walked over to some

TRAINING FOR ACTION

1. Who bullied you when you were a child?

1 SAMUEL 17:20-50

2. How does David consider Goliath to be in "defiance of Israel" (v. 26)?
3. What is David's real motivation in fighting Goliath: Fame? The reward? God's honor? His own glory?
4. How had God prepared David for this battle? How might small events in your life be preparing you for a significant event or challenge in the future? Are you disciplined in practices or preparations for upcoming events?
5. Why did David choose to fight with a sling instead of conventional weapons? How might God be able to use your skills to accomplish great things?

others and asked them the same thing and received
the same answer. 31 Then David's question was report-
ed to King Saul, and the king sent for him.

DAVID KILLS GOLIATH

32 "Don't worry about this Philistine," David told Saul.
"I'll go fight him!"
33 "Don't be ridiculous!" Saul replied. "There's no
way you can fight this Philistine and possibly win!
You're only a boy, and he's been a man of war since
his youth."
34 But David persisted. "I have been taking care of
my father's sheep and goats," he said. "When a lion or
a bear comes to steal a lamb from the flock, 35 I go after
it with a club and rescue the lamb from its mouth. If
the animal turns on me, I catch it by the jaw and club
it to death. 36 I have done this to both lions and bears,
and I'll do it to this pagan Philistine, too, for he has
defied the armies of the living God! 37 The LORD who
rescued me from the claws of the lion and the bear
will rescue me from this Philistine!"
Saul finally consented. "All right, go ahead," he
said. "And may the LORD be with you!"
38 Then Saul gave David his own armor—a bronze
helmet and a coat of mail. 39 David put it on, strapped
the sword over it, and took a step or two to see what
it was like, for he had never worn such things before.
"I can't go in these," he protested to Saul. "I'm not
used to them." So David took them off again. 40 He
picked up five smooth stones from a stream and put
them into his shepherd's bag. Then, armed only with
his shepherd's staff and sling, he started across the
valley to fight the Philistine.
41 Goliath walked out toward David with his shield
bearer ahead of him, 42 sneering in contempt at this rud-
dy-faced boy. 43 "Am I a dog," he roared at David, "that

17:13 Hebrew *Shammah*, a variant spelling of Shimea; compare 1 Chr 2:13; 20:7. **17:17** Hebrew *ephah* [20 quarts or 22 liters]. **17:18** Hebrew *and take their pledge*.

17:28 your pride. The words of Eliab, David's oldest brother, give insight into David's character. While a brother may perceive conceit, it was David's confidence in himself and God that saved Israel that day.

17:33 You're only a boy. By this point, Saul saw only the physical dimensions of the battle. His eyes were blind to the more crucial spiritual battle underway.

17:34 lion. David wasn't the only hero to face lions. Samson fought a young lion (Judg. 14:5-6). Benaiah, one of David's mighty men, was known for killing a lion (2 Sam. 23:20). And Daniel faced lions as punishment for his crime of praying (Dan. 6:22).

you come at me with a stick?" And he cursed David by the names of his gods. 44 "Come over here, and I'll give your flesh to the birds and wild animals!" Goliath yelled.

45 David replied to the Philistine, "You come to me with sword, spear, and javelin, but I come to you in the name of the LORD of Heaven's Armies—the God of the armies of Israel, whom you have defied. 46 Today the LORD will conquer you, and I will kill you and cut off your head. And then I will give the dead bodies of your men to the birds and wild animals, and the whole world will know that there is a God in Israel! 47 And everyone assembled here will know that the LORD rescues his people, but not with sword and spear. This is the LORD's battle, and he will give you to us!"

48 As Goliath moved closer to attack, David quickly ran out to meet him. 49 Reaching into his shepherd's bag and taking out a stone, he hurled it with his sling and hit the Philistine in the forehead. The stone sank in, and Goliath stumbled and fell face down on the ground.

50 So David triumphed over the Philistine with only a sling and a stone, for he had no sword. 51 Then David ran over and pulled Goliath's sword from its sheath. David used it to kill him and cut off his head.

ISRAEL ROUTS THE PHILISTINES

When the Philistines saw that their champion was dead, they turned and ran. 52 Then the men of Israel and Judah gave a great shout of triumph and rushed after the Philistines, chasing them as far as Gath* and the gates of Ekron. The bodies of the dead and wounded Philistines were strewn all along the road from Shaaraim, as far as Gath and Ekron. 53 Then the Israelite army returned and plundered the deserted Philistine camp. 54 (David took the Philistine's head to Jerusalem, but he stored the man's armor in his own tent.)

55 As Saul watched David go out to fight the Philistine, he asked Abner, the commander of his army, "Abner, whose son is this young man?"

"I really don't know," Abner declared.

56 "Well, find out who he is!" the king told him.

57 As soon as David returned from killing Goliath, Abner brought him to Saul with the Philistine's head still in his hand. 58 "Tell me about your father, young man," Saul said.

And David replied, "His name is Jesse, and we live in Bethlehem."

SAUL BECOMES JEALOUS OF DAVID

18 After David had finished talking with Saul, he met Jonathan, the king's son. There was an immediate bond between them, for Jonathan loved David. 2 From that day on Saul kept David with him and wouldn't let him return home. 3 And Jonathan made a solemn pact with David, because he loved him as he loved himself. 4 Jonathan sealed the pact by taking off his robe and giving it to David, together with his tunic, sword, bow, and belt.

5 Whatever Saul asked David to do, David did it successfully. So Saul made him a commander over the men of war, an appointment that was welcomed by the people and Saul's officers alike.

6 When the victorious Israelite army was returning home after David had killed the Philistine, women from all the towns of Israel came out to meet King Saul. They sang and danced for joy with tambourines and cymbals.* 7 This was their song:

"Saul has killed his thousands,
  and David his ten thousands!"

FRIENDS AND FOES

1. Who was your best friend in grade school? Did you ever swap or give each other stuff?

1 SAMUEL 18:1-16

2. Why did Saul try to kill David?
3. Why did Jonathan give these particular gifts to David (v. 4)? As a warrior, how might these gifts have been costly to Jonathan and meaningful to David?
4. Is there jealousy in your life? How is it affecting you? What can you do about it?
5. Are you a generous friend like Jonathan? Who in your group or team has been such a friend to you?

8 This made Saul very angry. "What's this?" he said. "They credit David with ten thousands and me with only thousands. Next they'll be making him their king!" 9 So from that time on Saul kept a jealous eye on David.

10 The very next day a tormenting spirit* from God overwhelmed Saul, and he began to rave in his house like a madman. David was playing the harp, as he did each day. But Saul had a spear in his hand, 11 and he suddenly hurled it at David, intending to pin him to the wall. But David escaped him twice.

12 Saul was then afraid of David, for the LORD was with David and had turned away from Saul. 13 Finally, Saul sent him away and appointed him commander over 1,000 men, and David faithfully led his troops into battle.

14 David continued to succeed in everything he did, for the LORD was with him. 15 When Saul recognized this, he became even more afraid of him. 16 But all Israel and Judah loved David because he was so successful at leading his troops into battle.

DAVID MARRIES SAUL'S DAUGHTER

17 One day Saul said to David, "I am ready to give you my older daughter, Merab, as your wife. But first you must prove yourself to be a real warrior by fighting

17:52 As in some Greek manuscripts; Hebrew reads *a valley.* **18:6** The type of instrument represented by the word *cymbals* is uncertain. **18:10** Or *an evil spirit.*

17:46 the whole world will know. David's motivation for victory is completely different than Saul's. David's ambitions are directed toward glorifying God.

17:54 the man's armor. Later, when hiding from Saul, David was given Goliath's sword for protection. At the time it was in the tabernacle, so David must have dedicated the sword, if not the rest of the weapons, to the Lord.

18:1 Jonathan. David and Jonathan became best friends. Eventually David would be crowned in Jonathan's place as Saul's successor. Their friendship survived even this test. **immediate bond between them.** Jonathan's love for David was like the Law (Lev. 19:18), and later Jesus (Matt. 22:39) said we all should love.

18:13 apointed him. In other words, Saul sent David to war. Saul hoped David would be killed in battle and thus be out of the way. Years later, David would use this same tactic with Uriah, Bathsheba's husband (2 Sam. 11:14-15).

the LORD's battles." For Saul thought, "I'll send him out
against the Philistines and let them kill him rather
than doing it myself."
18 "Who am I, and what is my family in Israel that
I should be the king's son-in-law?" David exclaimed.
"My father's family is nothing!" 19 So* when the time
came for Saul to give his daughter Merab in marriage
to David, he gave her instead to Adriel, a man from
Meholah.
20 In the meantime, Saul's daughter Michal had fall-
en in love with David, and Saul was delighted when
he heard about it. 21 "Here's another chance to see him
killed by the Philistines!" Saul said to himself. But to
David he said, "Today you have a second chance to be-
come my son-in-law!"
22 Then Saul told his men to say to David, "The king
really likes you, and so do we. Why don't you accept
the king's offer and become his son-in-law?"
23 When Saul's men said these things to David, he
replied, "How can a poor man from a humble family
afford the bride price for the daughter of a king?"
24 When Saul's men reported this back to the king,
25 he told them, "Tell David that all I want for the
bride price is 100 Philistine foreskins! Vengeance
on my enemies is all I really want." But what Saul
had in mind was that David would be killed in the
fight.
26 David was delighted to accept the offer. Before
the time limit expired, 27 he and his men went out and
killed 200 Philistines. Then David fulfilled the king's
requirement by presenting all their foreskins to him.
So Saul gave his daughter Michal to David to be his
wife.
28 When Saul realized that the LORD was with David
and how much his daughter Michal loved him, 29 Saul
became even more afraid of him, and he remained
David's enemy for the rest of his life.
30 Every time the commanders of the Philistines at-
tacked, David was more successful against them than
all the rest of Saul's officers. So David's name became
very famous.

SAUL TRIES TO KILL DAVID

19 Saul now urged his servants and his son Jon-
athan to assassinate David. But Jonathan, be-
cause of his strong affection for David, 2 told him
what his father was planning. "Tomorrow morning,"
he warned him, "you must find a hiding place out in
the fields. 3 I'll ask my father to go out there with me,
and I'll talk to him about you. Then I'll tell you every-
thing I can find out."
4 The next morning Jonathan spoke with his father
about David, saying many good things about him.
"The king must not sin against his servant David,"
Jonathan said. "He's never done anything to harm
you. He has always helped you in any way he could.
5 Have you forgotten about the time he risked his life
to kill the Philistine giant and how the LORD brought
a great victory to all Israel as a result? You were cer-
tainly happy about it then. Why should you murder
an innocent man like David? There is no reason for
it at all!"
6 So Saul listened to Jonathan and vowed, "As sure-
ly as the LORD lives, David will not be killed."
7 Afterward Jonathan called David and told him
what had happened. Then he brought David to Saul,
and David served in the court as before.
8 War broke out again after that, and David led his
troops against the Philistines. He attacked them with
such fury that they all ran away.
9 But one day when Saul was sitting at home, with
spear in hand, the tormenting spirit* from the LORD
suddenly came upon him again. As David played
his harp, 10 Saul hurled his spear at David. But David
dodged out of the way, and leaving the spear stuck in
the wall, he fled and escaped into the night.

MICHAL SAVES DAVID'S LIFE

11 Then Saul sent troops to watch David's house. They
were told to kill David when he came out the next
morning. But Michal, David's wife, warned him, "If
you don't escape tonight, you will be dead by morn-
ing." 12 So she helped him climb out through a window,
and he fled and escaped. 13 Then she took an idol* and
put it in his bed, covered it with blankets, and put a
cushion of goat's hair at its head.
14 When the troops came to arrest David, she told
them he was sick and couldn't get out of bed.
15 But Saul sent the troops back to get David. He or-
dered, "Bring him to me in his bed so I can kill him!"
16 But when they came to carry David out, they discov-
ered that it was only an idol in the bed with a cushion
of goat's hair at its head.
17 "Why have you betrayed me like this and let my
enemy escape?" Saul demanded of Michal.
"I had to," Michal replied. "He threatened to kill me
if I didn't help him."
18 So David escaped and went to Ramah to see
Samuel, and he told him all that Saul had done to
him. Then Samuel took David with him to live at Nai-
oth. 19 When the report reached Saul that David was
at Naioth in Ramah, 20 he sent troops to capture him.
But when they arrived and saw Samuel leading a
group of prophets who were prophesying, the Spirit
of God came upon Saul's men, and they also began to
prophesy. 21 When Saul heard what had happened,
he sent other troops, but they, too, prophesied! The
same thing happened a third time. 22 Finally, Saul
himself went to Ramah and arrived at the great well
in Secu. "Where are Samuel and David?" he demand-
ed.
"They are at Naioth in Ramah," someone told him.
23 But on the way to Naioth in Ramah the Spirit of
God came even upon Saul, and he, too, began to proph-
esy all the way to Naioth! 24 He tore off his clothes and
lay naked on the ground all day and all night, prophe-
sying in the presence of Samuel. The people who were
watching exclaimed, "What? Is even Saul a prophet?"

18:19 Or *But.* **19:9** Or *evil spirit.* **19:13** Hebrew *teraphim;* also in 19:16.

18:25 bride price. A future husband brought some wealth to the father of the bride. This practice is still followed in many parts of the world.

18:28 Michal loved him. No matter how Saul tried to get rid of David, God used that very scheme to bring David closer. Rather than falling in battle, David became a national hero, best friend of the king's son, and then husband to the king's daughter. Could Saul be getting a message?

19:1 assassinate David. He was so unaware of the dynamics in his family and court that he shared that news with his son, David's best friend.

19:13 she took an idol. That the family had such idols is disturbing and evidence of the fact that at very least Saul's family had less than full allegiance to the God of Israel. This one was large enough to be mistaken for an adult human being.

JONATHAN HELPS DAVID

20 David now fled from Naioth in Ramah and found Jonathan. "What have I done?" he exclaimed. "What is my crime? How have I offended your father that he is so determined to kill me?"

2 "That's not true!" Jonathan protested. "You're not going to die. He always tells me everything he's going to do, even the little things. I know my father wouldn't hide something like this from me. It just isn't so!"

3 Then David took an oath before Jonathan and said, "Your father knows perfectly well about our friendship, so he has said to himself, 'I won't tell Jonathan—why should I hurt him?' But I swear to you that I am only a step away from death! I swear it by the LORD and by your own soul!"

4 "Tell me what I can do to help you," Jonathan exclaimed.

5 David replied, "Tomorrow we celebrate the new moon festival. I've always eaten with the king on this occasion, but tomorrow I'll hide in the field and stay there until the evening of the third day. 6 If your father asks where I am, tell him I asked permission to go home to Bethlehem for an annual family sacrifice. 7 If he says, 'Fine!' you will know all is well. But if he is angry and loses his temper, you will know he is determined to kill me. 8 Show me this loyalty as my sworn friend—for we made a solemn pact before the LORD—or kill me yourself if I have sinned against your father. But please don't betray me to him!"

9 "Never!" Jonathan exclaimed. "You know that if I had the slightest notion my father was planning to kill you, I would tell you at once."

10 Then David asked, "How will I know whether or not your father is angry?"

11 "Come out to the field with me," Jonathan replied. And they went out there together. 12 Then Jonathan told David, "I promise by the LORD, the God of Israel, that by this time tomorrow, or the next day at the latest, I will talk to my father and let you know at once how he feels about you. If he speaks favorably about you, I will let you know. 13 But if he is angry and wants you killed, may the LORD strike me and even kill me if I don't warn you so you can escape and live. May the LORD be with you as he used to be with my father. 14 And may you treat me with the faithful love of the LORD as long as I live. But if I die, 15 treat my family with this faithful love, even when the LORD destroys all your enemies from the face of the earth."

16 So Jonathan made a solemn pact with David,* saying, "May the LORD destroy all your enemies!" 17 And Jonathan made David reaffirm his vow of friendship again, for Jonathan loved David as he loved himself.

18 Then Jonathan said, "Tomorrow we celebrate the new moon festival. You will be missed when your place at the table is empty. 19 The day after tomorrow, toward evening, go to the place where you hid before, and wait there by the stone pile.* 20 I will come out and shoot three arrows to the side of the stone pile as though I were shooting at a target. 21 Then I will send a boy to bring the arrows back. If you hear me tell him, 'They're on this side,' then you will know, as surely as the LORD lives, that all is well, and there is no trouble. 22 But if I tell him, 'Go farther—the arrows are still ahead of you,' then it will mean that you must leave immediately, for the LORD is sending you away. 23 And may the LORD make us keep our promises to each other, for he has witnessed them."

24 So David hid himself in the field, and when the new moon festival began, the king sat down to eat. 25 He sat at his usual place against the wall, with Jonathan sitting opposite him* and Abner beside him. But David's place was empty. 26 Saul didn't say anything about it that day, for he said to himself, "Something must have made David ceremonially unclean." 27 But when David's place was empty again the next day, Saul asked Jonathan, "Why hasn't the son of Jesse been here for the meal either yesterday or today?"

28 Jonathan replied, "David earnestly asked me if he could go to Bethlehem. 29 He said, 'Please let me go, for we are having a family sacrifice. My brother demanded that I be there. So please let me get away to see my brothers.' That's why he isn't here at the king's table."

30 Saul boiled with rage at Jonathan. "You stupid son of a whore!"* he swore at him. "Do you think I don't know that you want him to be king in your place, shaming yourself and your mother? 31 As long as that son of Jesse is alive, you'll never be king. Now go and get him so I can kill him!"

32 "But why should he be put to death?" Jonathan asked his father. "What has he done?" 33 Then Saul hurled his spear at Jonathan, intending to kill him. So at last Jonathan realized that his father was really determined to kill David.

34 Jonathan left the table in fierce anger and refused to eat on that second day of the festival, for he

OKAY TO DISOBEY

1. What secret ways of communicating have you tried with a friend: Secret handshake? Sign language? Passing notes?

1 SAMUEL 20:1-13,18-42

2. Why did Jonathan take such risks to help David?
3. Was Jonathan right in helping David instead of helping his father? Why?
4. When are Christians justified in disobeying human authorities? When are we not justified?
5. Jonathan and David fled from Saul but didn't fight him. What does that suggest about how to "disobey" ungodly orders?

20:16 Hebrew *with the house of David.* **20:19** Hebrew *the stone Ezel.* The meaning of the Hebrew is uncertain. **20:25** As in Greek version; Hebrew reads *with Jonathan standing.* **20:30** Hebrew *You son of a perverse and rebellious woman.*

20:11 Jonathan's words to David were the same as Cain's to Abel (Gen. 4:8). Yet, Jonathan's motivation was to save the life of his friend.

20:14 may you treat me with the faithful love of the LORD. In Jonathan's mind, as long as descendants of Saul existed, David might fear a rebellion. In fact, it was common for a new monarch to kill any heirs from the previous royal line. Here, Jonathan requested the survival of his family amid the change of kings.

20:15 my family. Many years later, David invited Jonathan's son, Mephibosheth, to eat at the royal table (2 Sam. 9:6-10).

20:31 you'll never be king. Saul saw the end of their legacy and tried to kill the culprit. Jonathan saw the end of their legacy and wanted to be a part of what God was doing.

was crushed by his father's shameful behavior toward David.

35 The next morning, as agreed, Jonathan went out into the field and took a young boy with him to gather his arrows. 36 "Start running," he told the boy, "so you can find the arrows as I shoot them." So the boy ran, and Jonathan shot an arrow beyond him. 37 When the boy had almost reached the arrow, Jonathan shouted, "The arrow is still ahead of you. 38 Hurry, hurry, don't wait." So the boy quickly gathered up the arrows and ran back to his master. 39 He, of course, suspected nothing; only Jonathan and David understood the signal. 40 Then Jonathan gave his bow and arrows to the boy and told him to take them back to town.

41 As soon as the boy was gone, David came out from where he had been hiding near the stone pile.* Then David bowed three times to Jonathan with his face to the ground. Both of them were in tears as they embraced each other and said good-bye, especially David.

42 At last Jonathan said to David, "Go in peace, for we have sworn loyalty to each other in the LORD's name. The LORD is the witness of a bond between us and our children forever." Then David left, and Jonathan returned to the town.*

DAVID RUNS FROM SAUL

21 1* David went to the town of Nob to see Ahimelech the priest. Ahimelech trembled when he saw him. "Why are you alone?" he asked. "Why is no one with you?"

2 "The king has sent me on a private matter," David said. "He told me not to tell anyone why I am here. I have told my men where to meet me later. 3 Now, what is there to eat? Give me five loaves of bread or anything else you have."

4 "We don't have any regular bread," the priest replied. "But there is the holy bread, which you can have if your young men have not slept with any women recently."

5 "Don't worry," David replied. "I never allow my men to be with women when we are on a campaign. And since they stay clean even on ordinary trips, how much more on this one!"

6 Since there was no other food available, the priest gave him the holy bread—the Bread of the Presence that was placed before the LORD in the Tabernacle. It had just been replaced that day with fresh bread.

7 Now Doeg the Edomite, Saul's chief herdsman, was there that day, having been detained before the LORD.*

8 David asked Ahimelech, "Do you have a spear or sword? The king's business was so urgent that I didn't even have time to grab a weapon!"

9 "I only have the sword of Goliath the Philistine, whom you killed in the valley of Elah," the priest replied. "It is wrapped in a cloth behind the ephod. Take that if you want it, for there is nothing else here."

"There is nothing like it!" David replied. "Give it to me!"

10 So David escaped from Saul and went to King Achish of Gath. 11 But the officers of Achish were unhappy about his being there. "Isn't this David, the king of the land?" they asked. "Isn't he the one the people honor with dances, singing,

'Saul has killed his thousands,
and David his ten thousands'?"

12 David heard these comments and was very afraid of what King Achish of Gath might do to him. 13 So he pretended to be insane, scratching on doors and drooling down his beard.

14 Finally, King Achish said to his men, "Must you bring me a madman? 15 We already have enough of them around here! Why should I let someone like this be my guest?"

DAVID AT THE CAVE OF ADULLAM

22 So David left Gath and escaped to the cave of Adullam. Soon his brothers and all his other relatives joined him there. 2 Then others began coming—men who were in trouble or in debt or who were just discontented—until David was the captain of about 400 men.

3 Later David went to Mizpeh in Moab, where he asked the king, "Please allow my father and mother to live here with you until I know what God is going to do for me." 4 So David's parents stayed in Moab with the king during the entire time David was living in his stronghold.

5 One day the prophet Gad told David, "Leave the stronghold and return to the land of Judah." So David went to the forest of Hereth.

6 The news of his arrival in Judah soon reached Saul. At the time, the king was sitting beneath the tamarisk tree on the hill at Gibeah, holding his spear and surrounded by his officers.

7 "Listen here, you men of Benjamin!" Saul shouted to his officers when he heard the news. "Has that son of Jesse promised every one of you fields and vineyards? Has he promised to make you all generals and captains in his army?* 8 Is that why you have conspired against me? For not one of you told me when my own son made a solemn pact with the son of Jesse. You're not even sorry for me. Think of it! My own son—encouraging him to kill me, as he is trying to do this very day!"

9 Then Doeg the Edomite, who was standing there with Saul's men, spoke up. "When I was at Nob," he said, "I saw the son of Jesse talking to the priest, Ahimelech son of Ahitub. 10 Ahimelech consulted the

20:41 As in Greek version; Hebrew reads *near the south edge.* **20:42** This sentence is numbered 21:1 in Hebrew text. **21:1** Verses 21:1-15 are numbered 21:2-16 in Hebrew text. **21:7** The meaning of the Hebrew is uncertain. **22:7** Hebrew *commanders of thousands and commanders of hundreds?*

20:41 both . . . were in tears as they embraced. This was a culture where men were not afraid to show feelings, even showing affection to each other.

21:2 not to tell anyone. David was less than forthcoming with Ahimelech the priest. David's "the-less-you-know-the-better" tactic unraveled when the priest was killed (22:16-18).

21:4 bread. Bread was always kept at the tabernacle. When a fresh supply was made, the old was given to the priests. David's request was contrary to what this bread was supposed to be used for. Jesus referred to this incident in Matthew 12:3-4, implying that some laws and traditions are secondary to human need.

22:4 Moab. David's great-grandmother, Ruth, came from Moab, so he had extended family there.

22:5 Gad. The prophet became a regular among David's entourage. Gad confronted David's sin (2 Sam. 24:11-14) and served as biographer (1 Chron. 29:29) and music arranger for some of David's psalms (2 Chron. 29:25).

LORD for him. Then he gave him food and the sword of Goliath the Philistine."

THE SLAUGHTER OF THE PRIESTS

11 King Saul immediately sent for Ahimelech and all his family, who served as priests at Nob. 12 When they arrived, Saul shouted at him, "Listen to me, you son of Ahitub!"

"What is it, my king?" Ahimelech asked.

13 "Why have you and the son of Jesse conspired against me?" Saul demanded. "Why did you give him food and a sword? Why have you consulted God for him? Why have you encouraged him to kill me, as he is trying to do this very day?"

14 "But sir," Ahimelech replied, "is anyone among all your servants as faithful as David, your son-in-law? Why, he is the captain of your bodyguard and a highly honored member of your household! 15 This was certainly not the first time I had consulted God for him! May the king not accuse me and my family in this matter, for I knew nothing at all of any plot against you."

16 "You will surely die, Ahimelech, along with your entire family!" the king shouted. 17 And he ordered his bodyguards, "Kill these priests of the LORD, for they are allies and conspirators with David! They knew he was running away from me, but they didn't tell me!" But Saul's men refused to kill the LORD's priests.

18 Then the king said to Doeg, "You do it." So Doeg the Edomite turned on them and killed them that day, eighty-five priests in all, still wearing their priestly garments. 19 Then he went to Nob, the town of the priests, and killed the priests' families—men and women, children and babies—and all the cattle, donkeys, sheep, and goats.

20 Only Abiathar, one of the sons of Ahimelech, escaped and fled to David. 21 When he told David that Saul had killed the priests of the LORD, 22 David exclaimed, "I knew it! When I saw Doeg the Edomite there that day, I knew he was sure to tell Saul. Now I have caused the death of all your father's family. 23 Stay here with me, and don't be afraid. I will protect you with my own life, for the same person wants to kill us both."

DAVID PROTECTS THE TOWN OF KEILAH

23 One day news came to David that the Philistines were at Keilah stealing grain from the threshing floors. 2 David asked the LORD, "Should I go and attack them?"

"Yes, go and save Keilah," the LORD told him.

3 But David's men said, "We're afraid even here in Judah. We certainly don't want to go to Keilah to fight the whole Philistine army!"

4 So David asked the LORD again, and again the LORD replied, "Go down to Keilah, for I will help you conquer the Philistines."

5 So David and his men went to Keilah. They slaughtered the Philistines and took all their livestock and rescued the people of Keilah. 6 Now when Abiathar son of Ahimelech fled to David at Keilah, he brought the ephod with him.

7 Saul soon learned that David was at Keilah. "Good!" he exclaimed. "We've got him now! God has handed him over to me, for he has trapped himself in a walled town!" 8 So Saul mobilized his entire army to march to Keilah and besiege David and his men.

9 But David learned of Saul's plan and told Abiathar the priest to bring the ephod and ask the LORD what he should do. 10 Then David prayed, "O LORD, God of Israel, I have heard that Saul is planning to come and destroy Keilah because I am here. 11 Will the leaders of Keilah betray me to him?* And will Saul actually come as I have heard? O LORD, God of Israel, please tell me."

And the LORD said, "He will come."

12 Again David asked, "Will the leaders of Keilah betray me and my men to Saul?"

And the LORD replied, "Yes, they will betray you."

DAVID HIDES IN THE WILDERNESS

13 So David and his men—about 600 of them now—left Keilah and began roaming the countryside. Word soon reached Saul that David had escaped, so he didn't go to Keilah after all. 14 David now stayed in the strongholds of the wilderness and in the hill country of Ziph. Saul hunted him day after day, but God didn't let Saul find him.

15 One day near Horesh, David received the news that Saul was on the way to Ziph to search for him and kill him. 16 Jonathan went to find David and encouraged him to stay strong in his faith in God. 17 "Don't be afraid," Jonathan reassured him. "My father will never find you! You are going to be the king of Israel, and I will be next to you, as my father, Saul, is well aware." 18 So the two of them renewed their solemn pact before the LORD. Then Jonathan returned home, while David stayed at Horesh.

19 But now the men of Ziph went to Saul in Gibeah and betrayed David to him. "We know where David is hiding," they said. "He is in the strongholds of Horesh on the hill of Hakilah, which is in the southern part of Jeshimon. 20 Come down whenever you're ready, O king, and we will catch him and hand him over to you!"

21 "The LORD bless you," Saul said. "At last someone is concerned about me! 22 Go and check again to be sure of where he is staying and who has seen him there, for I know that he is very crafty. 23 Discover his hiding places, and come back when you are sure. Then I'll go with you. And if he is in the area at all, I'll track him down, even if I have to search every hiding place in Judah!" 24 So the men of Ziph returned home ahead of Saul.

Meanwhile, David and his men had moved into the wilderness of Maon in the Arabah Valley south of Jeshimon. 25 When David heard that Saul and his men were searching for him, he went even farther into the

23:11 Some manuscripts lack the first sentence of 23:11.

22:7 Benjamin. Saul's strongest political support was from his own tribe, Benjamin. David was from the tribe of Judah.

22:17 They knew. It is unlikely that the priests knew David's plans, since David was cautious and guarded by Ahimelech. Saul's paranoia was talking louder than his reason.

22:20 Abiathar. Once the priest, Abiathar, joined the group, David's board of advisors was complete, though he had yet to receive the crown.

23:2 asked the LORD. When Abiathar joined David, he brought the ephod with the Urim and Thummim. This gave David access to God's wisdom and direction.

23:18 Jonathan. This was the last meeting of Jonathan and David. Jonathan had been faithful to David as Saul's successor, even though it meant forfeiting his own chance at the top. Jonathan died in battle before David came to the throne, so he never served in David's kingdom (31:2).

wilderness to the great rock, and he remained there
in the wilderness of Maon. But Saul kept after him in
the wilderness.
26 Saul and David were now on opposite sides of a
mountain. Just as Saul and his men began to close in
on David and his men, 27 an urgent message reached
Saul that the Philistines were raiding Israel again.
28 So Saul quit chasing David and returned to fight the
Philistines. Ever since that time, the place where Da-
vid was camped has been called the Rock of Escape.*
29*David then went to live in the strongholds of En-ge-
di.

DAVID SPARES SAUL'S LIFE

24 1*After Saul returned from fighting the Phi-
listines, he was told that David had gone into
the wilderness of En-gedi. 2 So Saul chose 3,000 elite
troops from all Israel and went to search for David
and his men near the rocks of the wild goats.
3 At the place where the road passes some sheep-
folds, Saul went into a cave to relieve himself. But as
it happened, David and his men were hiding farther
back in that very cave!
4 "Now's your opportunity!" David's men whispered
to him. "Today the LORD is telling you, 'I will certain-
ly put your enemy into your power, to do with as you
wish.'" So David crept forward and cut off a piece of
the hem of Saul's robe.
5 But then David's conscience began bothering him
because he had cut Saul's robe. 6 He said to his men,
"The LORD forbid that I should do this to my lord
the king. I shouldn't attack the LORD's anointed one,
for the LORD himself has chosen him." 7 So David re-
strained his men and did not let them kill Saul.
After Saul had left the cave and gone on his way,
8 David came out and shouted after him, "My lord the
king!" And when Saul looked around, David bowed
low before him.
9 Then he shouted to Saul, "Why do you listen to the
people who say I am trying to harm you? 10 This very
day you can see with your own eyes it isn't true. For
the LORD placed you at my mercy back there in the
cave. Some of my men told me to kill you, but I spared
you. For I said, 'I will never harm the king—he is the
LORD's anointed one.' 11 Look, my father, at what I have
in my hand. It is a piece of the hem of your robe! I cut
it off, but I didn't kill you. This proves that I am not
trying to harm you and that I have not sinned against
you, even though you have been hunting for me to kill
me.
12 "May the LORD judge between us. Perhaps the
LORD will punish you for what you are trying to do to
me, but I will never harm you. 13 As that old proverb
says, 'From evil people come evil deeds.' So you can be
sure I will never harm you. 14 Who is the king of Isra-
el trying to catch anyway? Should he spend his time
chasing one who is as worthless as a dead dog or a
single flea? 15 May the LORD therefore judge which of
us is right and punish the guilty one. He is my advo-
cate, and he will rescue me from your power!"
16 When David had finished speaking, Saul called
back, "Is that really you, my son David?" Then he be-
gan to cry. 17 And he said to David, "You are a better
man than I am, for you have repaid me good for evil.
18 Yes, you have been amazingly kind to me today, for
when the LORD put me in a place where you could
have killed me, you didn't do it. 19 Who else would let
his enemy get away when he had him in his power?
May the LORD reward you well for the kindness you
have shown me today. 20 And now I realize that you
are surely going to be king, and that the kingdom of
Israel will flourish under your rule. 21 Now swear to
me by the LORD that when that happens you will not
kill my family and destroy my line of descendants!"
22 So David promised this to Saul with an oath. Then
Saul went home, but David and his men went back to
their stronghold.

RESPECTING AUTHORITY

1. Is there a "hideout" in your neighborhood? Did you go there when you were growing up?

1 SAMUEL 24:1-22

2. How would David have been justified in killing Saul? Why didn't he?
3. What did David mean that Saul was "the LORD's anointed one" (v. 6)? What does this suggest about people who are in positions of authority?
4. What affect did David's action have on Saul?
5. Is there someone in authority over you who is abusing his or her power? How should you respond to that person?

THE DEATH OF SAMUEL

25 Now Samuel died, and all Israel gathered for
his funeral. They buried him at his house in Ra-
mah.

NABAL ANGERS DAVID

Then David moved down to the wilderness of Maon.*
2 There was a wealthy man from Maon who owned
property near the town of Carmel. He had 3,000 sheep
and 1,000 goats, and it was sheep-shearing time. 3 This
man's name was Nabal, and his wife, Abigail, was a
sensible and beautiful woman. But Nabal, a descen-
dant of Caleb, was crude and mean in all his dealings.

23:28 Hebrew *Sela-hammahlekoth.* 23:29 Verse 23:29 is numbered 24:1 in Hebrew text. 24:1 Verses 24:1-22 are numbered 24:2-23 in Hebrew text. 25:1 As in Greek version (see also 25:2); Hebrew reads *Paran.*

24:4 the LORD is telling you. The Bible contains no record of God giving this word to David or his men. It may have been a prophecy not recorded or an inference on the part of his men based on other statements about David.

24:6 the LORD's anointed. David was consistently loyal to God. Building God's kingdom was his priority. Saul had allowed his reign to degenerate into the normal political games of survival, intrigue, and greed. Even so, David would not sink to that level by killing God's anointed king.

24:11 my father. Since David had married Michal, Saul was his father-in-law as well as his king.

24:16 began to cry. Saul operated at both extremes. Before long, he quickly resumed his posse and forced David into flight again.

24:22 stronghold. Saul had just proclaimed David's righteousness, but David knew better than to trust Saul's goodwill. He scampered to a cave or similar hideout.

25:1 Samuel died. Samuel bridged the era of the judges and the kings. His impact on Israel's spiritual life was great, though his sons failed to carry on his work.

25:2-44 Nabal. His name meant "fool." He certainly dealt with David foolishly. This passage describes a husband who was as foolish as his wife was wise. Abigail saved the situation, but Nabal didn't survive it.

4 When David heard that Nabal was shearing his sheep, 5 he sent ten of his young men to Carmel with this message for Nabal: 6 "Peace and prosperity to you, your family, and everything you own! 7 I am told that it is sheep-shearing time. While your shepherds stayed among us near Carmel, we never harmed them, and nothing was ever stolen from them. 8 Ask your own men, and they will tell you this is true. So would you be kind to us, since we have come at a time of celebration? Please share any provisions you might have on hand with us and with your friend David." 9 David's young men gave this message to Nabal in David's name, and they waited for a reply.

10 "Who is this fellow David?" Nabal sneered to the young men. "Who does this son of Jesse think he is? There are lots of servants these days who run away from their masters. 11 Should I take my bread and my water and my meat that I've slaughtered for my shearers and give it to a band of outlaws who come from who knows where?"

12 So David's young men returned and told him what Nabal had said. 13 "Get your swords!" was David's reply as he strapped on his own. Then 400 men started off with David, and 200 remained behind to guard their equipment.

14 Meanwhile, one of Nabal's servants went to Abigail and told her, "David sent messengers from the wilderness to greet our master, but he screamed insults at them. 15 These men have been very good to us, and we never suffered any harm from them. Nothing was stolen from us the whole time they were with us. 16 In fact, day and night they were like a wall of protection to us and the sheep. 17 You need to know this and figure out what to do, for there is going to be trouble for our master and his whole family. He's so ill-tempered that no one can even talk to him!"

18 Abigail wasted no time. She quickly gathered 200 loaves of bread, two wineskins full of wine, five sheep that had been slaughtered, nearly a bushel* of roasted grain, 100 clusters of raisins, and 200 fig cakes. She packed them on donkeys 19 and said to her servants, "Go on ahead. I will follow you shortly." But she didn't tell her husband Nabal what she was doing.

20 As she was riding her donkey into a mountain ravine, she saw David and his men coming toward her. 21 David had just been saying, "A lot of good it did to help this fellow. We protected his flocks in the wilderness, and nothing he owned was lost or stolen. But he has repaid me evil for good. 22 May God strike me and kill me* if even one man of his household is still alive tomorrow morning!"

ABIGAIL INTERCEDES FOR NABAL

23 When Abigail saw David, she quickly got off her donkey and bowed low before him. 24 She fell at his feet and said, "I accept all blame in this matter, my lord. Please listen to what I have to say. 25 I know Nabal is a wicked and ill-tempered man; please don't pay any attention to him. He is a fool, just as his name suggests.* But I never even saw the young men you sent.

26 "Now, my lord, as surely as the LORD lives and you yourself live, since the LORD has kept you from murdering and taking vengeance into your own hands, let all your enemies and those who try to harm you be as cursed as Nabal is. 27 And here is a present that I, your servant, have brought to you and your young men. 28 Please forgive me if I have offended you in any way. The LORD will surely reward you with a lasting dynasty, for you are fighting the LORD's battles. And you have not done wrong throughout your entire life.

29 "Even when you are chased by those who seek to kill you, your life is safe in the care of the LORD your God, secure in his treasure pouch! But the lives of your enemies will disappear like stones shot from a sling! 30 When the LORD has done all he promised and has made you leader of Israel, 31 don't let this be a blemish on your record. Then your conscience won't have to bear the staggering burden of needless bloodshed and vengeance. And when the LORD has done these great things for you, please remember me, your servant!"

32 David replied to Abigail, "Praise the LORD, the God of Israel, who has sent you to meet me today! 33 Thank God for your good sense! Bless you for keeping me from murder and from carrying out vengeance with my own hands. 34 For I swear by the LORD, the God of Israel, who has kept me from hurting you, that if you had not hurried out to meet me, not one of Nabal's men would still be alive tomorrow morning." 35 Then David accepted her present and told her, "Return home in peace. I have heard what you said. We will not kill your husband."

36 When Abigail arrived home, she found that Nabal was throwing a big party and was celebrating like a king. He was very drunk, so she didn't tell him anything about her meeting with David until dawn the next day. 37 In the morning when Nabal was sober, his wife told him what had happened. As a result he had a stroke,* and he lay paralyzed on his bed like a stone. 38 About ten days later, the LORD struck him, and he died.

DAVID MARRIES ABIGAIL

39 When David heard that Nabal was dead, he said, "Praise the LORD, who has avenged the insult I received from Nabal and has kept me from doing it myself. Nabal has received the punishment for his sin." Then David sent messengers to Abigail to ask her to become his wife.

40 When the messengers arrived at Carmel, they told Abigail, "David has sent us to take you back to marry him."

41 She bowed low to the ground and responded, "I, your servant, would be happy to marry David. I would even be willing to become a slave, washing the feet of his servants!" 42 Quickly getting ready, she took along five of her servant girls as attendants, mounted her donkey, and went with David's messengers. And

25:18 Hebrew *5 seahs* [36.5 liters]. **25:22** As in Greek version; Hebrew reads *May God strike and kill the enemies of David.* **25:25** The name *Nabal* means "fool." **25:37** Hebrew *his heart failed him.*

25:22 strike me and kill me. This is a severe Hebrew curse. David's oath of revenge reveals the other side of his leadership: quick, sure, confident, and violent.

25:25 just as his name suggests. "Nabal" meant "fool." Names often reflect the character of a person, especially during this era. Even in the New Testament book of Philemon, Paul makes a request based on the meaning of a name. He asks that Onesimus (whose name means "useful" or "profitable") be made useful again (Philem. 1:10-11).

25:28 have not done wrong. Abigail was a clever diplomat and became David's wife (v. 42).

so she became his wife. 43 David also married Ahinoam from Jezreel, making both of them his wives. 44 Saul, meanwhile, had given his daughter Michal, David's wife, to a man from Gallim named Palti son of Laish.

DAVID SPARES SAUL AGAIN

26 Now some men from Ziph came to Saul at Gibeah to tell him, "David is hiding on the hill of Hakilah, which overlooks Jeshimon."

2 So Saul took 3,000 of Israel's elite troops and went to hunt him down in the wilderness of Ziph. 3 Saul camped along the road beside the hill of Hakilah, near Jeshimon, where David was hiding. When David learned that Saul had come after him into the wilderness, 4 he sent out spies to verify the report of Saul's arrival.

5 David slipped over to Saul's camp one night to look around. Saul and Abner son of Ner, the commander of his army, were sleeping inside a ring formed by the slumbering warriors. 6 "Who will volunteer to go in there with me?" David asked Ahimelech the Hittite and Abishai son of Zeruiah, Joab's brother.

"I'll go with you," Abishai replied. 7 So David and Abishai went right into Saul's camp and found him asleep, with his spear stuck in the ground beside his head. Abner and the soldiers were lying asleep around him.

8 "God has surely handed your enemy over to you this time!" Abishai whispered to David. "Let me pin him to the ground with one thrust of the spear; I won't need to strike twice!"

9 "No!" David said. "Don't kill him. For who can remain innocent after attacking the LORD's anointed one? 10 Surely the LORD will strike Saul down someday, or he will die of old age or in battle. 11 The LORD forbid that I should kill the one he has anointed! But take his spear and that jug of water beside his head, and then let's get out of here!"

12 So David took the spear and jug of water that were near Saul's head. Then he and Abishai got away without anyone seeing them or even waking up, because the LORD had put Saul's men into a deep sleep.

13 David climbed the hill opposite the camp until he was at a safe distance. 14 Then he shouted down to the soldiers and to Abner son of Ner, "Wake up, Abner!"

"Who is it?" Abner demanded.

15 "Well, Abner, you're a great man, aren't you?" David taunted. "Where in all Israel is there anyone as mighty? So why haven't you guarded your master the king when someone came to kill him? 16 This isn't good at all! I swear by the LORD that you and your men deserve to die, because you failed to protect your master, the LORD's anointed! Look around! Where are the king's spear and the jug of water that were beside his head?"

17 Saul recognized David's voice and called out, "Is that you, my son David?"

And David replied, "Yes, my lord the king. 18 Why are you chasing me? What have I done? What is my crime? 19 But now let my lord the king listen to his servant. If the LORD has stirred you up against me, then let him accept my offering. But if this is simply a human scheme, then may those involved be cursed by the LORD. For they have driven me from my home, so I can no longer live among the LORD's people, and they have said, 'Go, worship pagan gods.' 20 Must I die on foreign soil, far from the presence of the LORD? Why has the king of Israel come out to search for a single flea? Why does he hunt me down like a partridge on the mountains?"

21 Then Saul confessed, "I have sinned. Come back home, my son, and I will no longer try to harm you, for you valued my life today. I have been a fool and very, very wrong."

22 "Here is your spear, O king," David replied. "Let one of your young men come over and get it. 23 The LORD gives his own reward for doing good and for being loyal, and I refused to kill you even when the LORD placed you in my power, for you are the LORD's anointed one. 24 Now may the LORD value my life, even as I have valued yours today. May he rescue me from all my troubles."

25 And Saul said to David, "Blessings on you, my son David. You will do many heroic deeds, and you will surely succeed." Then David went away, and Saul returned home.

DAVID AMONG THE PHILISTINES

27 But David kept thinking to himself, "Someday Saul is going to get me. The best thing I can do is escape to the Philistines. Then Saul will stop hunting for me in Israelite territory, and I will finally be safe."

2 So David took his 600 men and went over and joined Achish son of Maoch, the king of Gath. 3 David and his men and their families settled there with Achish at Gath. David brought his two wives along with him—Ahinoam from Jezreel and Abigail, Nabal's widow from Carmel. 4 Word soon reached Saul that David had fled to Gath, so he stopped hunting for him.

5 One day David said to Achish, "If it is all right with you, we would rather live in one of the country towns instead of here in the royal city."

6 So Achish gave him the town of Ziklag (which still belongs to the kings of Judah to this day), 7 and they lived there among the Philistines for a year and four months.

8 David and his men spent their time raiding the Geshurites, the Girzites, and the Amalekites—people who had lived near Shur, toward the land of Egypt, since ancient times. 9 David did not leave one person alive in the villages he attacked. He took the sheep,

---

26:2 3,000 of Israel's elite troops. The size of Saul's posse reveals his priorities: settling personal vendettas rather than fighting enemies or governing the country.

26:5 Abner. Abner and Saul were cousins. Abner was the commander of Saul's army who first brought David to Saul after Goliath was defeated (17:55-58).

26:20 search for a single flea. The allusion to a flea is saying that David is too harmless and insignificant for Saul to be pursuing him in this way.

27:1 to the Philistines. David had fled to Philistia before (21:10-15). On that occasion he had feigned insanity to escape from the home of King Achish, the very king with whom he was about to establish an alliance.

27:2 Achish. The first time David faced Achish, David was afraid he'd be seen as Goliath's killer. This time his position was much safer. If he were seen as Saul's enemy, Achish would easily accept him. If David were living in an outlying town, perhaps Achish would call on him less often.

27:7 among the Philistines. David lived in Ziklag (in Philistia) until Saul's death. Ziklag was thereafter a Judean city.

27:8 Geshurites. Two tribes had this name. The tribe David attacked, south of Philistia on the way to Egypt, were among the settlers Joshua had failed to conquer (Josh. 13:2).

27:9 did not leave one person alive. David's complete destruction fulfilled God's original direction to Joshua, and it covered David's lie to Achish. David had led the king to believe that his fight was against Judah.

goats, cattle, donkeys, camels, and clothing before returning home to see King Achish.

10 "Where did you make your raid today?" Achish would ask.

And David would reply, "Against the south of Judah, the Jerahmeelites, and the Kenites."

11 No one was left alive to come to Gath and tell where he had really been. This happened again and again while he was living among the Philistines. 12 Achish believed David and thought to himself, "By now the people of Israel must hate him bitterly. Now he will have to stay here and serve me forever!"

SAUL CONSULTS A MEDIUM

28 About that time the Philistines mustered their armies for another war with Israel. King Achish told David, "You and your men will be expected to join me in battle."

2 "Very well!" David agreed. "Now you will see for yourself what we can do."

Then Achish told David, "I will make you my personal bodyguard for life."

3 Meanwhile, Samuel had died, and all Israel had mourned for him. He was buried in Ramah, his hometown. And Saul had banned from the land of Israel all mediums and those who consult the spirits of the dead.

4 The Philistines set up their camp at Shunem, and Saul gathered all the army of Israel and camped at Gilboa. 5 When Saul saw the vast Philistine army, he became frantic with fear. 6 He asked the LORD what he should do, but the LORD refused to answer him, either by dreams or by sacred lots* or by the prophets. 7 Saul then said to his advisers, "Find a woman who is a medium, so I can go and ask her what to do."

His advisers replied, "There is a medium at Endor."

8 So Saul disguised himself by wearing ordinary clothing instead of his royal robes. Then he went to the woman's home at night, accompanied by two of his men.

"I have to talk to a man who has died," he said. "Will you call up his spirit for me?"

9 "Are you trying to get me killed?" the woman demanded. "You know that Saul has outlawed all the mediums and all who consult the spirits of the dead. Why are you setting a trap for me?"

10 But Saul took an oath in the name of the LORD and promised, "As surely as the LORD lives, nothing bad will happen to you for doing this."

11 Finally, the woman said, "Well, whose spirit do you want me to call up?"

"Call up Samuel," Saul replied.

12 When the woman saw Samuel, she screamed, "You've deceived me! You are Saul!"

13 "Don't be afraid!" the king told her. "What do you see?"

"I see a god* coming up out of the earth," she said.

14 "What does he look like?" Saul asked.

"He is an old man wrapped in a robe," she replied. Saul realized it was Samuel, and he fell to the ground before him.

15 "Why have you disturbed me by calling me back?" Samuel asked Saul.

"Because I am in deep trouble," Saul replied. "The Philistines are at war with me, and God has left me and won't reply by prophets or dreams. So I have called for you to tell me what to do."

16 But Samuel replied, "Why ask me, since the LORD has left you and has become your enemy? 17 The LORD has done just as he said he would. He has torn the kingdom from you and given it to your rival, David. 18 The LORD has done this to you today because you refused to carry out his fierce anger against the Amalekites. 19 What's more, the LORD will hand you and the army of Israel over to the Philistines tomorrow, and you and your sons will be here with me. The LORD will bring down the entire army of Israel in defeat."

20 Saul fell full length on the ground, paralyzed with fright because of Samuel's words. He was also faint with hunger, for he had eaten nothing all day and all night.

21 When the woman saw how distraught he was, she said, "Sir, I obeyed your command at the risk of my life. 22 Now do what I say, and let me give you a little something to eat so you can regain your strength for the trip back."

23 But Saul refused to eat anything. Then his advisers joined the woman in urging him to eat, so he finally yielded and got up from the ground and sat on the couch.

24 The woman had been fattening a calf, so she hurried out and killed it. She took some flour, kneaded it into dough and baked unleavened bread. 25 She brought the meal to Saul and his advisers, and they ate it. Then they went out into the night.

THE PHILISTINES REJECT DAVID

29 The entire Philistine army now mobilized at Aphek, and the Israelites camped at the spring in Jezreel. 2 As the Philistine rulers were leading out their troops in groups of hundreds and thousands, David and his men marched at the rear with King Achish. 3 But the Philistine commanders demanded, "What are these Hebrews doing here?"

And Achish told them, "This is David, the servant of King Saul of Israel. He's been with me for years, and I've never found a single fault in him from the day he arrived until today."

4 But the Philistine commanders were angry. "Send him back to the town you've given him!" they demanded. "He can't go into the battle with us. What if he turns against us in battle and becomes our adversary? Is there any better way for him to reconcile himself with his master than by handing our heads over to him? 5 Isn't this the same David about whom the women of Israel sing in their dances,

'Saul has killed his thousands,
and David his ten thousands'?"

6 So Achish finally summoned David and said to him, "I swear by the LORD that you have been a trustworthy

28:6 Hebrew *by Urim*. **28:13** Or *gods*.

28:6 the LORD refused to answer. Saul's connections to God as the source of wisdom and strength were dwindling. Samuel was dead (v. 3). The prophet Abiathar had aligned himself with David and taken the official ephod (with its Urim and Thummim for decision making). The prophet Gad had aligned himself with David as well.

29:4 becomes our adversary. The Hebrews had allied with the Philistines before (14:20-22), and their memories of it were not pleasant. In the heat of battle they left the Philistines to join with Saul and Jonathan.

29:6 I swear by the LORD. Whether Achish believed in the Lord or not, he was speaking a language David understood.

ally. I think you should go with me into battle, for I've never found a single flaw in you from the day you arrived until today. But the other Philistine rulers won't hear of it. 7 Please don't upset them, but go back quietly."

8 "What have I done to deserve this treatment?" David demanded. "What have you ever found in your servant, that I can't go and fight the enemies of my lord the king?"

9 But Achish insisted, "As far as I'm concerned, you're as perfect as an angel of God. But the Philistine commanders are afraid to have you with them in the battle. 10 Now get up early in the morning, and leave with your men as soon as it gets light."

11 So David and his men headed back into the land of the Philistines, while the Philistine army went on to Jezreel.

DAVID DESTROYS THE AMALEKITES

30 Three days later, when David and his men arrived home at their town of Ziklag, they found that the Amalekites had made a raid into the Negev and Ziklag; they had crushed Ziklag and burned it to the ground. 2 They had carried off the women and children and everyone else but without killing anyone.

3 When David and his men saw the ruins and realized what had happened to their families, 4 they wept until they could weep no more. 5 David's two wives, Ahinoam from Jezreel and Abigail, the widow of Nabal from Carmel, were among those captured. 6 David was now in great danger because all his men were very bitter about losing their sons and daughters, and they began to talk of stoning him. But David found strength in the LORD his God.

7 Then he said to Abiathar the priest, "Bring me the ephod!" So Abiathar brought it. 8 Then David asked the LORD, "Should I chase after this band of raiders? Will I catch them?"

And the LORD told him, "Yes, go after them. You will surely recover everything that was taken from you!"

9 So David and his 600 men set out, and they came to the brook Besor. 10 But 200 of the men were too exhausted to cross the brook, so David continued the pursuit with 400 men.

11 Along the way they found an Egyptian man in a field and brought him to David. They gave him some bread to eat and water to drink. 12 They also gave him part of a fig cake and two clusters of raisins, for he hadn't had anything to eat or drink for three days and nights. Before long his strength returned.

13 "To whom do you belong, and where do you come from?" David asked him.

"I am an Egyptian—the slave of an Amalekite," he replied. "My master abandoned me three days ago because I was sick. 14 We were on our way back from raiding the Kerethites in the Negev, the territory of Judah, and the land of Caleb, and we had just burned Ziklag."

15 "Will you lead me to this band of raiders?" David asked.

The young man replied, "If you take an oath in God's name that you will not kill me or give me back to my master, then I will guide you to them."

16 So he led David to them, and they found the Amalekites spread out across the fields, eating and drinking and dancing with joy because of the vast amount of plunder they had taken from the Philistines and the land of Judah. 17 David and his men rushed in among them and slaughtered them throughout that night and the entire next day until evening. None of the Amalekites escaped except 400 young men who fled on camels. 18 David got back everything the Amalekites had taken, and he rescued his two wives. 19 Nothing was missing: small or great, son or daughter, nor anything else that had been taken. David brought everything back. 20 He also recovered all the flocks and herds, and his men drove them ahead of the other livestock. "This plunder belongs to David!" they said.

21 Then David returned to the brook Besor and met up with the 200 men who had been left behind because they were too exhausted to go with him. They went out to meet David and his men, and David greeted them joyfully. 22 But some evil troublemakers among David's men said, "They didn't go with us, so they can't have any of the plunder we recovered. Give them their wives and children, and tell them to be gone."

23 But David said, "No, my brothers! Don't be selfish with what the LORD has given us. He has kept us safe and helped us defeat the band of raiders that attacked us. 24 Who will listen when you talk like this? We share and share alike—those who go to battle and those who guard the equipment." 25 From then on David made this a decree and regulation for Israel, and it is still followed today.

26 When he arrived at Ziklag, David sent part of the plunder to the elders of Judah, who were his friends. "Here is a present for you, taken from the LORD's enemies," he said.

27 The gifts were sent to the people of the following towns David had visited: Bethel, Ramoth-negev, Jattir, 28 Aroer, Siphmoth, Eshtemoa, 29 Racal,* the towns of the Jerahmeelites, the towns of the Kenites, 30 Hormah, Bor-ashan, Athach, 31 Hebron, and all the other places David and his men had visited.

THE DEATH OF SAUL

31 Now the Philistines attacked Israel, and the men of Israel fled before them. Many were slaughtered on the slopes of Mount Gilboa. 2 The Philistines closed in on Saul and his sons, and they killed three of his sons—Jonathan, Abinadab, and Malkishua. 3 The fighting grew very fierce around Saul, and the Philistine archers caught up with him and wounded him severely.

4 Saul groaned to his armor bearer, "Take your sword and kill me before these pagan Philistines come to run me through and taunt and torture me."

But his armor bearer was afraid and would not do it. So Saul took his own sword and fell on it. 5 When his

30:29 Greek version reads *Carmel.*

29:8 What have I done. David played along, but this turn of events was fortunate. Saul was still king; David's time had not yet come. Had he fought in this battle, David would have put his sword against his own countrymen.

30:1 Amalekites. These were people south of Philistia that David had raided, while he claimed to be fighting his own tribe of Judah (27:8).

30:26 sent part of the plunder. The Amalekites had plundered Judah, and David was recovering lost goods. Crediting God with the victory gave David reason to spread the spoils evenly and win the people's allegiance in future conflict.

31:2 killed three of his sons. Saul had a fourth son, Ish-Bosheth (2 Sam. 2:8), who was not killed in this battle.

SAUL'S SUICIDE

1. What is your first memory about death: A pet or other animal? A friend or relative? A famous person in the news?

1 SAMUEL 31:1-13

2. Why did Saul commit suicide? Why did his armor-bearer? Were they justified in doing this?
3. How did Saul's suicide affect the Israelites? How does suicide do great harm to innocent people?
4. What should Saul have done instead of killing himself? What should his armor-bearer have done? How might things have ended differently if they had?
5. What is the world's view on assisted suicide? What is God's view?

---

armor bearer realized that Saul was dead, he fell on
his own sword and died beside the king. 6 So Saul, his
three sons, his armor bearer, and his troops all died
together that same day.
7 When the Israelites on the other side of the Jezreel
Valley and beyond the Jordan saw that the Israelite
army had fled and that Saul and his sons were dead,
they abandoned their towns and fled. So the Philis-
tines moved in and occupied their towns.
8 The next day, when the Philistines went out to
strip the dead, they found the bodies of Saul and his
three sons on Mount Gilboa. 9 So they cut off Saul's
head and stripped off his armor. Then they pro-
claimed the good news of Saul's death in their pagan
temple and to the people throughout the land of Phi-
listia. 10 They placed his armor in the temple of the
Ashtoreths, and they fastened his body to the wall of
the city of Beth-shan.
11 But when the people of Jabesh-gilead heard what
the Philistines had done to Saul, 12 all their mighty
warriors traveled through the night to Beth-shan
and took the bodies of Saul and his sons down from
the wall. They brought them to Jabesh, where they
burned the bodies. 13 Then they took their bones and
buried them beneath the tamarisk tree at Jabesh, and
they fasted for seven days.

31:9 cut off Saul's head. Goliath received the same treatment. Decapitation was proof that the adversary had perished. Allies of headless adversaries best take cover.

31:10 Ashtoreths. Idols representing the Philistine and Canaanite goddess—counterpart to Baal. Placing Saul's armor in the temple credited his defeat to a false god.

31:11-12 Jabesh-gilead. Saul had defended these people in his first act as king. **burned the bodies.** Cremation was not the typical burial for an Israelite. Later David exhumed the bones and reburied them in the territory of Benjamin, Saul's tribe.

INTRODUCTION TO

2 SAMUEL

PERSONAL READING PLAN

☐ 2 Samuel 1:1-27
☐ 2 Samuel 2:1–3:5
☐ 2 Samuel 3:6-39
☐ 2 Samuel 4:1–5:25
☐ 2 Samuel 6:1-23
☐ 2 Samuel 7:1–8:18
☐ 2 Samuel 9:1–10:19
☐ 2 Samuel 11:1-27
☐ 2 Samuel 12:1-31
☐ 2 Samuel 13:1-39
☐ 2 Samuel 14:1-33
☐ 2 Samuel 15:1–16:14
☐ 2 Samuel 16:15–17:29
☐ 2 Samuel 18:1–19:8a
☐ 2 Samuel 19:8b–20:25
☐ 2 Samuel 21:1–22:51
☐ 2 Samuel 23:1-39
☐ 2 Samuel 24:1-25

AUTHOR

The author is not known with certainty. Perhaps a compiler drew from materials written by others such as Samuel, Gad, and Nathan (see 1 Chron. 29:29) in order to produce the final rendition. Note that 1 and 2 Samuel were originally composed as one unit.

DATE

The date of authorship is uncertain, though it is possible that this two-volume book was written around the time of Solomon's death (ca 930 B.C.).

THEME

The life and times of King David.

HISTORICAL BACKGROUND

David had been on the run from Saul. Now that Saul is dead, David is able to take his rightful place on the throne over all of Israel, but only after he emerges triumphant from a political power struggle. Surrounding nations, especially the Philistines, still pose the threat of war; however, Israel is militarily strong under David's victorious reign.

CHARACTERISTICS

Second Samuel continues the historical narrative of 1 Samuel, where David's youth and troublesome exile were the focus. Now in "volume two" David reigns as Saul's successor, and he must heal and unify the war-torn country. Chapters 1–10 narrate the prosperous early reign of David. He is anointed king over Judah and then over all Israel. He also sustains victory after victory on the battlefield. David's adultery with Bathsheba (chaps. 11–12), however, marks a turning point in the book. In the chapters that follow, the "sword will never leave" David's house (12:10). Throughout the book, God is seen as the One who establishes David upon the throne of Israel and gives him victory over his enemies.

PASSAGES FOR TOPICAL GROUP STUDY

11:1-27 . . SIN and TURNING TO GOD . . . . Busted!
12:1-14. . . ACCOUNTABILITY. . . . . Nathan's Parable and David's Repentance
13:1-22 . . SEX and DATE RAPE . . . . . .Amnon's Rape of Tamar
13:23-39. . RIVALRY and REVENGE. . . . . .Absalom's Revenge

PASSAGES FOR GENERAL GROUP STUDY

12:15-25. . . . . . Tragic Consequences (David loses his son)

DAVID LEARNS OF SAUL'S DEATH

1 After the death of Saul, David returned from his
victory over the Amalekites and spent two days in
Ziklag. 2 On the third day a man arrived from Saul's
army camp. He had torn his clothes and put dirt on his
head to show that he was in mourning. He fell to the
ground before David in deep respect.
3 "Where have you come from?" David asked.
"I escaped from the Israelite camp," the man re-
plied.
4 "What happened?" David demanded. "Tell me how
the battle went."
The man replied, "Our entire army fled from the
battle. Many of the men are dead, and Saul and his
son Jonathan are also dead."
5 "How do you know Saul and Jonathan are dead?"
David demanded of the young man.
6 The man answered, "I happened to be on Mount
Gilboa, and there was Saul leaning on his spear with
the enemy chariots and charioteers closing in on him.
7 When he turned and saw me, he cried out for me to
come to him. 'How can I help?' I asked him.
8 "He responded, 'Who are you?'
"'I am an Amalekite,' I told him.
9 "Then he begged me, 'Come over here and put me out
of my misery, for I am in terrible pain and want to die.'
10 "So I killed him," the Amalekite told David, "for
I knew he couldn't live. Then I took his crown and his
armband, and I have brought them here to you, my lord."
11 David and his men tore their clothes in sorrow
when they heard the news. 12 They mourned and wept
and fasted all day for Saul and his son Jonathan, and
for the LORD's army and the nation of Israel, because
they had died by the sword that day.
13 Then David said to the young man who had
brought the news, "Where are you from?"
And he replied, "I am a foreigner, an Amalekite,
who lives in your land."
14 "Why were you not afraid to kill the LORD's
anointed one?" David asked.
15 Then David said to one of his men, "Kill him!" So
the man thrust his sword into the Amalekite and
killed him. 16 "You have condemned yourself," David
said, "for you yourself confessed that you killed the
LORD's anointed one."

DAVID'S SONG FOR SAUL AND JONATHAN

17 Then David composed a funeral song for Saul and
Jonathan, 18 and he commanded that it be taught to
the people of Judah. It is known as the Song of the
Bow, and it is recorded in *The Book of Jashar.**

19 Your pride and joy, O Israel, lies dead on the hills!
Oh, how the mighty heroes have fallen!
20 Don't announce the news in Gath,
don't proclaim it in the streets of Ashkelon,
or the daughters of the Philistines will rejoice
and the pagans will laugh in triumph.

21 O mountains of Gilboa,
let there be no dew or rain upon you,
nor fruitful fields producing offerings
of grain.*
For there the shield of the mighty heroes was
defiled;
the shield of Saul will no longer be anointed
with oil.
22 The bow of Jonathan was powerful,
and the sword of Saul did its mighty work.
They shed the blood of their enemies
and pierced the bodies of mighty heroes.

23 How beloved and gracious were Saul and
Jonathan!
They were together in life and in death.
They were swifter than eagles,
stronger than lions.
24 O women of Israel, weep for Saul,
for he dressed you in luxurious scarlet clothing,
in garments decorated with gold.

25 Oh, how the mighty heroes have fallen in battle!
Jonathan lies dead on the hills.
26 How I weep for you, my brother Jonathan!
Oh, how much I loved you!
And your love for me was deep,
deeper than the love of women!

27 Oh, how the mighty heroes have fallen!
Stripped of their weapons, they lie dead.

DAVID ANOINTED KING OF JUDAH

2 After this, David asked the LORD, "Should I move
back to one of the towns of Judah?"
"Yes," the LORD replied.
Then David asked, "Which town should I go to?"
"To Hebron," the LORD answered.
2 David's two wives were Ahinoam from Jezreel
and Abigail, the widow of Nabal from Carmel. So Da-
vid and his wives 3 and his men and their families all
moved to Judah, and they settled in the villages near
Hebron. 4 Then the men of Judah came to David and
anointed him king over the people of Judah.
When David heard that the men of Jabesh-gilead
had buried Saul, 5 he sent them this message: "May
the LORD bless you for being so loyal to your master
Saul and giving him a decent burial. 6 May the LORD
be loyal to you in return and reward you with his
unfailing love! And I, too, will reward you for what
you have done. 7 Now that Saul is dead, I ask you to be
my strong and loyal subjects like the people of Judah,
who have anointed me as their new king."

1:18 Or *The Book of the Upright.* 1:21 The meaning of the Hebrew is uncertain.

1:8 Amalekite. Contrary to 1 Samuel 31:4-6, the Amalekite is providing additional information to the previous account, or he is altering the story because he expects the action he claims to have taken will earn a reward.

1:11 David and his men. King Saul had forced David and his men into hiding. Yet here they wept for their nation's loss.

1:13 Amalekite. David had just rescued his wives from Amalekite kidnappers. He wouldn't welcome an Amalekite deserter into his camp.

1:14 the LORD's anointed one. On two occasions, David could have killed Saul but did not (1 Sam. 24:3-7; 26:9-12). It was not David's (nor anyone else's) right to kill God's selected leader.

1:15 Kill him. Years before, Saul was told he had lost his kingdom for failing to destroy the Amalekites (1 Sam. 15:3-9) as God commanded. Here, an Amalekite lost his life because he claimed to have destroyed Saul.

1:18 Book of Jashar. This lost manuscript is also mentioned in the Book of Joshua (Josh. 10:13).

2:1 asked. More than likely, David inquired with the Urim and Thummin (1 Sam. 10:20; 23:1-6; 28:6).

ISHBOSHETH PROCLAIMED KING OF ISRAEL

8 But Abner son of Ner, the commander of Saul's army, had already gone to Mahanaim with Saul's son Ishbosheth.* 9 There he proclaimed Ishbosheth king over Gilead, Jezreel, Ephraim, Benjamin, the land of the Ashurites, and all the rest of Israel.

10 Ishbosheth, Saul's son, was forty years old when he became king, and he ruled from Mahanaim for two years. Meanwhile, the people of Judah remained loyal to David. 11 David made Hebron his capital, and he ruled as king of Judah for seven and a half years.

WAR BETWEEN ISRAEL AND JUDAH

12 One day Abner led Ishbosheth's troops from Mahanaim to Gibeon. 13 About the same time, Joab son of Zeruiah led David's troops out and met them at the pool of Gibeon. The two groups sat down there, facing each other from opposite sides of the pool.

14 Then Abner suggested to Joab, "Let's have a few of our warriors fight hand to hand here in front of us."

"All right," Joab agreed. 15 So twelve men were chosen to fight from each side—twelve men of Benjamin representing Ishbosheth son of Saul, and twelve representing David. 16 Each one grabbed his opponent by the hair and thrust his sword into the other's side so that all of them died. So this place at Gibeon has been known ever since as the Field of Swords.*

17 A fierce battle followed that day, and Abner and the men of Israel were defeated by the forces of David.

THE DEATH OF ASAHEL

18 Joab, Abishai, and Asahel—the three sons of Zeruiah—were among David's forces that day. Asahel could run like a gazelle, 19 and he began chasing Abner. He pursued him relentlessly, not stopping for anything. 20 When Abner looked back and saw him coming, he called out, "Is that you, Asahel?"

"Yes, it is," he replied.

21 "Go fight someone else!" Abner warned. "Take on one of the younger men, and strip him of his weapons." But Asahel kept right on chasing Abner.

22 Again Abner shouted to him, "Get away from here! I don't want to kill you. How could I ever face your brother Joab again?"

23 But Asahel refused to turn back, so Abner thrust the butt end of his spear through Asahel's stomach, and the spear came out through his back. He stumbled to the ground and died there. And everyone who came by that spot stopped and stood still when they saw Asahel lying there.

24 When Joab and Abishai found out what had happened, they set out after Abner. The sun was just going down as they arrived at the hill of Ammah near Giah, along the road to the wilderness of Gibeon. 25 Abner's troops from the tribe of Benjamin regrouped there at the top of the hill to take a stand.

26 Abner shouted down to Joab, "Must we always be killing each other? Don't you realize that bitterness is the only result? When will you call off your men from chasing their Israelite brothers?"

27 Then Joab said, "God only knows what would have happened if you hadn't spoken, for we would have chased you all night if necessary." 28 So Joab blew the ram's horn, and his men stopped chasing the troops of Israel.

29 All that night Abner and his men retreated through the Jordan Valley.* They crossed the Jordan River, traveling all through the morning,* and didn't stop until they arrived at Mahanaim.

30 Meanwhile, Joab and his men also returned home. When Joab counted his casualties, he discovered that only 19 men were missing in addition to Asahel. 31 But 360 of Abner's men had been killed, all from the tribe of Benjamin. 32 Joab and his men took Asahel's body to Bethlehem and buried him there in his father's tomb. Then they traveled all night and reached Hebron at daybreak.

3 That was the beginning of a long war between those who were loyal to Saul and those loyal to David. As time passed David became stronger and stronger, while Saul's dynasty became weaker and weaker.

DAVID'S SONS BORN IN HEBRON

2 These are the sons who were born to David in Hebron:

The oldest was Amnon, whose mother was
Ahinoam from Jezreel.
3 The second was Daniel,* whose mother was
Abigail, the widow of Nabal from Carmel.
The third was Absalom, whose mother was
Maacah, the daughter of Talmai, king of Geshur.
4 The fourth was Adonijah, whose mother was
Haggith.
The fifth was Shephatiah, whose mother was
Abital.
5 The sixth was Ithream, whose mother was Eglah,
David's wife.

These sons were all born to David in Hebron.

ABNER JOINS FORCES WITH DAVID

6 As the war between the house of Saul and the house of David went on, Abner became a powerful leader among those loyal to Saul. 7 One day Ishbosheth,* Saul's son, accused Abner of sleeping with one of his father's concubines, a woman named Rizpah, daughter of Aiah.

8 Abner was furious. "Am I some Judean dog to be kicked around like this?" he shouted. "After all I have done for your father, Saul, and his family and friends

2:8 *Ishbosheth* is another name for Esh-baal. **2:16** Hebrew *Helkath-hazzurim.* **2:29a** Hebrew *the Arabah.* **2:29b** Or *continued on through the Bithron.* The meaning of the Hebrew is uncertain. **3:3** As in parallel text at 1 Chr 3:1 (see also Greek version, which reads *Daluia,* and possible support by Dead Sea Scrolls); Hebrew reads *Kileab.* **3:7** *Ishbosheth* is another name for Esh-baal.

2:8 Abner. Abner (Saul's cousin and the commander of his army) knew his best play for power was through Saul's one surviving son, Ish-Bosheth.

2:12 Gibeon. David went first to Judah, his own tribe, to establish his sovereignty. Abner took Ish-Bosheth to Gibeon, a town in the region of Benjamin, the tribe of Saul's heritage.

2:13 Joab. Joab, a distant nephew of David, was commander of David's army and had a reputation for ruthlessness that even David eventually criticized (3:39).

2:28 his men stopped. Even though the truce failed, each army had time to retreat to its home base.

3:7 one of his father's concubines. In the ancient Middle East, taking a former king's concubine was often a political statement. Ish-Bosheth worried that it indicated a conspiracy to take over the throne (12:8; 16:21; 1 Kings 2:22).

by not handing you over to David, is this my reward—
that you find fault with me about this woman? 9 May
God strike me and even kill me if I don't do everything I
can to help David get what the LORD has promised him!
10 I'm going to take Saul's kingdom and give it to David.
I will establish the throne of David over Israel as well
as Judah, all the way from Dan in the north to Beershe-
ba in the south." 11 Ishbosheth didn't dare say another
word because he was afraid of what Abner might do.

12 Then Abner sent messengers to David, saying,
"Doesn't the entire land belong to you? Make a solemn
pact with me, and I will help turn over all of Israel to
you."

13 "All right," David replied, "but I will not negoti-
ate with you unless you bring back my wife Michal,
Saul's daughter, when you come."

14 David then sent this message to Ishbosheth, Saul's
son: "Give me back my wife Michal, for I bought her
with the lives* of 100 Philistines."

15 So Ishbosheth took Michal away from her hus-
band, Palti* son of Laish. 16 Palti followed along be-
hind her as far as Bahurim, weeping as he went. Then
Abner told him, "Go back home!" So Palti returned.

17 Meanwhile, Abner had consulted with the elders
of Israel. "For some time now," he told them, "you have
wanted to make David your king. 18 Now is the time!
For the LORD has said, 'I have chosen David to save
my people Israel from the hands of the Philistines
and from all their other enemies.'" 19 Abner also spoke
with the men of Benjamin. Then he went to Hebron to
tell David that all the people of Israel and Benjamin
had agreed to support him.

20 When Abner and twenty of his men came to
Hebron, David entertained them with a great feast.
21 Then Abner said to David, "Let me go and call an as-
sembly of all Israel to support my lord the king. They
will make a covenant with you to make you their king,
and you will rule over everything your heart desires."
So David sent Abner safely on his way.

JOAB MURDERS ABNER

22 But just after David had sent Abner away in safe-
ty, Joab and some of David's troops returned from a
raid, bringing much plunder with them. 23 When Joab
arrived, he was told that Abner had just been there
visiting the king and had been sent away in safety.

24 Joab rushed to the king and demanded, "What
have you done? What do you mean by letting Abner
get away? 25 You know perfectly well that he came to
spy on you and find out everything you're doing!"

26 Joab then left David and sent messengers to catch
up with Abner, asking him to return. They found him
at the well of Sirah and brought him back, though
David knew nothing about it. 27 When Abner arrived
back at Hebron, Joab took him aside at the gateway
as if to speak with him privately. But then he stabbed
Abner in the stomach and killed him in revenge for
killing his brother Asahel.

28 When David heard about it, he declared, "I vow
by the LORD that I and my kingdom are forever inno-
cent of this crime against Abner son of Ner. 29 Joab and
his family are the guilty ones. May the family of Joab
be cursed in every generation with a man who has
open sores or leprosy* or who walks on crutches* or
dies by the sword or begs for food!"

30 So Joab and his brother Abishai killed Abner be-
cause Abner had killed their brother Asahel at the
battle of Gibeon.

DAVID MOURNS ABNER'S DEATH

31 Then David said to Joab and all those who were
with him, "Tear your clothes and put on burlap.
Mourn for Abner." And King David himself walked
behind the procession to the grave. 32 They buried Ab-
ner in Hebron, and the king and all the people wept at
his graveside. 33 Then the king sang this funeral song
for Abner:

"Should Abner have died as fools die?
34 Your hands were not bound;
  your feet were not chained.
No, you were murdered—
  the victim of a wicked plot."

All the people wept again for Abner. 35 David had
refused to eat anything on the day of the funeral, and
now everyone begged him to eat. But David had made
a vow, saying, "May God strike me and even kill me if
I eat anything before sundown."

36 This pleased the people very much. In fact, every-
thing the king did pleased them! 37 So everyone in Ju-
dah and all Israel understood that David was not re-
sponsible for Abner's murder.

38 Then King David said to his officials, "Don't you
realize that a great commander has fallen today in Is-
rael? 39 And even though I am the anointed king, these
two sons of Zeruiah—Joab and Abishai—are too
strong for me to control. So may the LORD repay these
evil men for their evil deeds."

THE MURDER OF ISHBOSHETH

4 When Ishbosheth,* Saul's son, heard about Ab-
ner's death at Hebron, he lost all courage, and all
Israel became paralyzed with fear. 2 Now there were
two brothers, Baanah and Recab, who were cap-
tains of Ishbosheth's raiding parties. They were sons
of Rimmon, a member of the tribe of Benjamin who
lived in Beeroth. The town of Beeroth is now part of
Benjamin's territory 3 because the original people of
Beeroth fled to Gittaim, where they still live as for-
eigners.

4 (Saul's son Jonathan had a son named Mephibo-
sheth,* who was crippled as a child. He was five years
old when the report came from Jezreel that Saul and
Jonathan had been killed in battle. When the child's
nurse heard the news, she picked him up and fled. But

3:14 Hebrew *the foreskins.* **3:15** As in 1 Sam 25:44; Hebrew reads *Paltiel,* a variant spelling of Palti. **3:29a** Or *or a contagious skin disease.* The Hebrew word used here can describe various skin diseases. **3:29b** Or *who is effeminate;* Hebrew reads *who handles a spindle.* **4:1** *Ishbosheth* is another name for Esh-baal. **4:4** *Mephibosheth* is another name for Merib-baal.

3:13 Michal. Michal (1 Sam. 18:27) had been given to another man, Palti (1 Sam. 25:44). If reunited, it would aid David's claim to the throne as Saul's son-in-law.

3:17 to make David your king. Benjamin and Gilead in the Transjordan seemed to provide most of Ish-Bosheth's support (2:8, 15; 1 Sam. 11:9-11; 31:11-13).

3:27 Joab. The murder was unjustified. No state of war existed at this point, and blood revenge (Num. 35:12; Deut. 19:11-13) did not apply because Joab's brother Asahel had been killed in battle (v. 30; 2:21,23). Furthermore, the act occurred in Hebron, a city of refuge (Josh. 20:7) where a blood avenger was not permitted to deal with a murderer without a trial (Num. 35:22-24).

as she hurried away, she dropped him, and he became
crippled.)
5 One day Recab and Baanah, the sons of Rimmon
from Beeroth, went to Ishbosheth's house around
noon as he was taking his midday rest. 6 The door-
keeper, who had been sifting wheat, became drowsy
and fell asleep. So Recab and Baanah slipped past
her.* 7 They went into the house and found Ishbosheth
sleeping on his bed. They struck and killed him and
cut off his head. Then, taking his head with them,
they fled across the Jordan Valley* through the night.
8 When they arrived at Hebron, they presented Ishbo-
sheth's head to David. "Look!" they exclaimed to the
king. "Here is the head of Ishbosheth, the son of your
enemy Saul who tried to kill you. Today the LORD has
given my lord the king revenge on Saul and his entire
family!"
9 But David said to Recab and Baanah, "The LORD,
who saves me from all my enemies, is my witness.
10 Someone once told me, 'Saul is dead,' thinking he
was bringing me good news. But I seized him and
killed him at Ziklag. That's the reward I gave him
for his news! 11 How much more should I reward
evil men who have killed an innocent man in his
own house and on his own bed? Shouldn't I hold
you responsible for his blood and rid the earth of
you?"
12 So David ordered his young men to kill them, and
they did. They cut off their hands and feet and hung
their bodies beside the pool in Hebron. Then they took
Ishbosheth's head and buried it in Abner's tomb in
Hebron.

DAVID BECOMES KING OF ALL ISRAEL

5 Then all the tribes of Israel went to David at He-
bron and told him, "We are your own flesh and
blood. 2 In the past,* when Saul was our king, you
were the one who really led the forces of Israel. And
the LORD told you, 'You will be the shepherd of my
people Israel. You will be Israel's leader.'"
3 So there at Hebron, King David made a covenant
before the LORD with all the elders of Israel. And they
anointed him king of Israel.
4 David was thirty years old when he began to
reign, and he reigned forty years in all. 5 He had
reigned over Judah from Hebron for seven years and
six months, and from Jerusalem he reigned over all
Israel and Judah for thirty-three years.

DAVID CAPTURES JERUSALEM

6 David then led his men to Jerusalem to fight against
the Jebusites, the original inhabitants of the land who
were living there. The Jebusites taunted David, say-
ing, "You'll never get in here! Even the blind and lame
could keep you out!" For the Jebusites thought they
were safe. 7 But David captured the fortress of Zion,
which is now called the City of David.
8 On the day of the attack, David said to his troops,
"I hate those 'lame' and 'blind' Jebusites.* Whoev-
er attacks them should strike by going into the city
through the water tunnel.*" That is the origin of the
saying, "The blind and the lame may not enter the
house."*
9 So David made the fortress his home, and he called
it the City of David. He extended the city, starting at
the supporting terraces* and working inward. 10 And
David became more and more powerful, because the
LORD God of Heaven's Armies was with him.
11 Then King Hiram of Tyre sent messengers to Da-
vid, along with cedar timber and carpenters and
stonemasons, and they built David a palace. 12 And
David realized that the LORD had confirmed him as
king over Israel and had blessed his kingdom for the
sake of his people Israel.
13 After moving from Hebron to Jerusalem, David
married more concubines and wives, and they had
more sons and daughters. 14 These are the names of
David's sons who were born in Jerusalem: Shammua,
Shobab, Nathan, Solomon, 15 Ibhar, Elishua, Nepheg,
Japhia, 16 Elishama, Eliada, and Eliphelet.

DAVID CONQUERS THE PHILISTINES

17 When the Philistines heard that David had been
anointed king of Israel, they mobilized all their
forces to capture him. But David was told they were
coming, so he went into the stronghold. 18 The Phi-
listines arrived and spread out across the valley of
Rephaim. 19 So David asked the LORD, "Should I go out
to fight the Philistines? Will you hand them over to
me?"
The LORD replied to David, "Yes, go ahead. I will cer-
tainly hand them over to you."
20 So David went to Baal-perazim and defeated the
Philistines there. "The LORD did it!" David exclaimed.
"He burst through my enemies like a raging flood!"
So he named that place Baal-perazim (which means
"the Lord who bursts through"). 21 The Philistines had
abandoned their idols there, so David and his men
confiscated them.
22 But after a while the Philistines returned and
again spread out across the valley of Rephaim. 23 And
again David asked the LORD what to do. "Do not at-
tack them straight on," the LORD replied. "Instead, cir-
cle around behind and attack them near the poplar*
trees. 24 When you hear a sound like marching feet in
the tops of the poplar trees, be on the alert! That will
be the signal that the LORD is moving ahead of you to
strike down the Philistine army." 25 So David did what
the LORD commanded, and he struck down the Philis-
tines all the way from Gibeon* to Gezer.

4:6 As in Greek version; Hebrew reads *So they went into the house pretending to fetch wheat, but they stabbed him in the stomach. Then Recab and Baanah escaped.* **4:7** Hebrew *the Arabah.* **5:2** Or *For some time.* **5:8a** Or *Those 'lame' and 'blind' Jebusites hate me.* **5:8b** Or *with scaling hooks.* The meaning of the Hebrew is uncertain. **5:8c** The meaning of this saying is uncertain. **5:9** Hebrew *the millo.* The meaning of the Hebrew is uncertain. **5:23** Or *aspen,* or *balsam;* also in 5:24. The exact identification of this tree is uncertain. **5:25** As in Greek version (see also 1 Chr 14:16); Hebrew reads *Geba.*

5:3 they anointed him. David's third anointing as king. First Samuel privately anointed him with his family (1 Sam. 16:13), the tribe of Judah anointed him publicly (2:4), and finally, the northern tribes anoint him at Hebron.

5:6 Jebusites. The Jebusites (Gen. 10:15, 16; Num. 13:29) could boast because Jerusalem was easy to defend, surrounded on three sides by deep valleys. Its location on the border between the two parts of David's kingdom was strategic, since it favored neither.

5:8 That is the origin of the saying. They were forbidden to offer sacrifices in the temple (Lev. 21:18).

5:13 concubines and wives. The result of treaties and alliances with other nations, concubines were basically wives who did not enjoy the full rights of marriage. God had warned Israel against this practice (Deut. 17:17).

5:24 sound like marching feet. God's angelic soldiers rustled the leaves as they moved in front of David (2 Kings 6:17).

MOVING THE ARK TO JERUSALEM

6 Then David again gathered all the elite troops in Israel, 30,000 in all. 2 He led them to Baalah of Judah* to bring back the Ark of God, which bears the name of the LORD of Heaven's Armies,* who is enthroned between the cherubim. 3 They placed the Ark of God on a new cart and brought it from Abinadab's house, which was on a hill. Uzzah and Ahio, Abinadab's sons, were guiding the cart 4 that carried the Ark of God.* Ahio walked in front of the Ark. 5 David and all the people of Israel were celebrating before the LORD, singing songs* and playing all kinds of musical instruments—lyres, harps, tambourines, castanets, and cymbals.

6 But when they arrived at the threshing floor of Nacon, the oxen stumbled, and Uzzah reached out his hand and steadied the Ark of God. 7 Then the LORD's anger was aroused against Uzzah, and God struck him dead because of this.* So Uzzah died right there beside the Ark of God.

8 David was angry because the LORD's anger had burst out against Uzzah. He named that place Perez-uzzah (which means "to burst out against Uzzah"), as it is still called today.

9 David was now afraid of the LORD, and he asked, "How can I ever bring the Ark of the LORD back into my care?" 10 So David decided not to move the Ark of the LORD into the City of David. Instead, he took it to the house of Obed-edom of Gath. 11 The Ark of the LORD remained there in Obed-edom's house for three months, and the LORD blessed Obed-edom and his entire household.

12 Then King David was told, "The LORD has blessed Obed-edom's household and everything he has because of the Ark of God." So David went there and brought the Ark of God from the house of Obed-edom to the City of David with a great celebration. 13 After the men who were carrying the Ark of the LORD had gone six steps, David sacrificed a bull and a fattened calf. 14 And David danced before the LORD with all his might, wearing a priestly garment.* 15 So David and all the people of Israel brought up the Ark of the LORD with shouts of joy and the blowing of rams' horns.

MICHAL'S CONTEMPT FOR DAVID

16 But as the Ark of the LORD entered the City of David, Michal, the daughter of Saul, looked down from her window. When she saw King David leaping and dancing before the LORD, she was filled with contempt for him.

17 They brought the Ark of the LORD and set it in its place inside the special tent David had prepared for it. And David sacrificed burnt offerings and peace offerings to the LORD. 18 When he had finished his sacrifices, David blessed the people in the name of the LORD of Heaven's Armies. 19 Then he gave to every Israelite man and woman in the crowd a loaf of bread, a cake of dates,* and a cake of raisins. Then all the people returned to their homes.

20 When David returned home to bless his own family, Michal, the daughter of Saul, came out to meet him. She said in disgust, "How distinguished the king of Israel looked today, shamelessly exposing himself to the servant girls like any vulgar person might do!"

21 David retorted to Michal, "I was dancing before the LORD, who chose me above your father and all his family! He appointed me as the leader of Israel, the people of the LORD, so I celebrate before the LORD. 22 Yes, and I am willing to look even more foolish than this, even to be humiliated in my own eyes! But those servant girls you mentioned will indeed think I am distinguished!" 23 So Michal, the daughter of Saul, remained childless throughout her entire life.

THE LORD'S COVENANT PROMISE TO DAVID

7 When King David was settled in his palace and the LORD had given him rest from all the surrounding enemies, 2 the king summoned Nathan the prophet. "Look," David said, "I am living in a beautiful cedar palace,* but the Ark of God is out there in a tent!"

3 Nathan replied to the king, "Go ahead and do whatever you have in mind, for the LORD is with you."

4 But that same night the LORD said to Nathan,

> 5 "Go and tell my servant David, 'This is what the LORD has declared: Are you the one to build a house for me to live in? 6 I have never lived in a house, from the day I brought the Israelites out of Egypt until this very day. I have always moved from one place to another with a tent and a Tabernacle as my dwelling. 7 Yet no matter where I have gone with the Israelites, I have never once complained to Israel's tribal leaders, the shepherds of my people Israel. I have never asked them, "Why haven't you built me a beautiful cedar house?"'
>
> 8 "Now go and say to my servant David, 'This is what the LORD of Heaven's Armies has declared: I took you from tending sheep in the pasture and selected you to be the leader of my people Israel. 9 I have been with you wherever you have gone, and I have destroyed all your enemies before your eyes. Now I will make your name as famous as anyone who has ever lived on the earth! 10 And I will provide a homeland for my people Israel, planting them in a secure place where they will never be disturbed. Evil nations won't oppress them as they've done in the past, 11 starting from the time I appointed judges to rule my people

6:2a Hebrew *Baale of Judah,* another name for Kiriath-jearim; compare 1 Chr 13:6. **6:2b** Or *the Ark of God where the Name is proclaimed—the name of the LORD of Heaven's Armies.* **6:4** As in Dead Sea Scrolls and some Greek manuscripts; Masoretic Text reads *4and they brought it from Abinadab's house, which was on a hill, with the Ark of God.* **6:5** As in Dead Sea Scrolls and Greek version (see also 1 Chr 13:8); Masoretic Text reads *before the LORD with all manner of cypress wood.* **6:7** As in Dead Sea Scrolls; Masoretic Text reads *because of his irreverence.* **6:14** Hebrew *a linen ephod.* **6:19** Or *a portion of meat.* The meaning of the Hebrew is uncertain. **7:2** Hebrew *a house of cedar.*

6:3 new cart. The ark should only be carried by Levites (Exod. 25:12-14; Num. 4:5-15), but David used a cart like the Philistines (1 Sam. 6:7).

6:7 Uzzah. Uzzah broke God's clear command (Ex. 25:12-14; Num. 4:5-15; 1 Chron. 15:13-15).

6:8-9 David was angry. Sometimes David got angry with God for things he didn't understand.

6:12 blessed Obed-Edom's household. God showed he would also bless the ark's correct transportation, while David researched his mistake.

6:20 king of Israel . . . shamelessly exposing himself. Discarding kingly robes, David was performing priestly duties while returning the ark in a linen ephod normally worn by Levites (1 Sam. 2:18)

7:2 tent. David felt that since he had a palace, which represented his reign, God deserved more than a tent (Ps. 132:2-5; Acts 7:46).

7:3 replied to the king. Nathan approved what he assumed made sense.

7:5-7 Are you the one to build a house for me to live in? Living in a stationary house might give the impression that God is limited. As he had allowed a king, God would eventually allow a temple building.

Israel. And I will give you rest from all your
enemies.
11 "'Furthermore, the LORD declares that he will
make a house for you—a dynasty of kings! 12 For
when you die and are buried with your ancestors,
I will raise up one of your descendants, your own
offspring, and I will make his kingdom strong. 13 He
is the one who will build a house—a temple—for
my name. And I will secure his royal throne for-
ever. 14 I will be his father, and he will be my son. If
he sins, I will correct and discipline him with the
rod, like any father would do. 15 But my favor will
not be taken from him as I took it from Saul, whom
I removed from your sight. 16 Your house and your
kingdom will continue before me* for all time, and
your throne will be secure forever.'"

17 So Nathan went back to David and told him every-
thing the LORD had said in this vision.

DAVID'S PRAYER OF THANKS

18 Then King David went in and sat before the LORD
and prayed,

"Who am I, O Sovereign LORD, and what is my fam-
ily, that you have brought me this far? 19 And now,
Sovereign LORD, in addition to everything else, you
speak of giving your servant a lasting dynasty!
Do you deal with everyone this way, O Sovereign
LORD?*

20 "What more can I say to you? You know
what your servant is really like, Sovereign LORD.
21 Because of your promise and according to your
will, you have done all these great things and have
made them known to your servant.

22 "How great you are, O Sovereign LORD! There
is no one like you. We have never even heard of
another God like you! 23 What other nation on
earth is like your people Israel? What other nation,
O God, have you redeemed from slavery to be your
own people? You made a great name for yourself
when you redeemed your people from Egypt. You
performed awesome miracles and drove out the
nations and gods that stood in their way.* 24 You
made Israel your very own people forever, and
you, O LORD, became their God.

25 "And now, O LORD God, I am your servant; do
as you have promised concerning me and my fam-
ily. Confirm it as a promise that will last forever.
26 And may your name be honored forever so that
everyone will say, 'The LORD of Heaven's Armies
is God over Israel!' And may the house of your
servant David continue before you forever.

27 "O LORD of Heaven's Armies, God of Israel, I
have been bold enough to pray this prayer to you
because you have revealed all this to your servant,
saying, 'I will build a house for you—a dynasty of
kings!' 28 For you are God, O Sovereign LORD. Your
words are truth, and you have promised these good
things to your servant. 29 And now, may it please
you to bless the house of your servant, so that it
may continue forever before you. For you have
spoken, and when you grant a blessing to your
servant, O Sovereign LORD, it is an eternal blessing!"

DAVID'S MILITARY VICTORIES

8 After this, David defeated and subdued the Phi-
listines by conquering Gath, their largest town.*
2 David also conquered the land of Moab. He made
the people lie down on the ground in a row, and he
measured them off in groups with a length of rope. He
measured off two groups to be executed for every one
group to be spared. The Moabites who were spared
became David's subjects and paid him tribute money.
3 David also destroyed the forces of Hadadezer son
of Rehob, king of Zobah, when Hadadezer marched
out to strengthen his control along the Euphrates Riv-
er. 4 David captured 1,000 chariots, 7,000 charioteers,*
and 20,000 foot soldiers. He crippled all the chariot
horses except enough for 100 chariots.
5 When Arameans from Damascus arrived to help
King Hadadezer, David killed 22,000 of them. 6 Then
he placed several army garrisons in Damascus, the
Aramean capital, and the Arameans became David's
subjects and paid him tribute money. So the LORD
made David victorious wherever he went.
7 David brought the gold shields of Hadadezer's
officers to Jerusalem, 8 along with a large amount of
bronze from Hadadezer's towns of Tebah* and Bero-
thai.
9 When King Toi of Hamath heard that David had
destroyed the entire army of Hadadezer, 10 he sent his
son Joram to congratulate King David for his success-
ful campaign. Hadadezer and Toi had been enemies
and were often at war. Joram presented David with
many gifts of silver, gold, and bronze.
11 King David dedicated all these gifts to the LORD, as
he did with the silver and gold from the other nations
he had defeated—12 from Edom,* Moab, Ammon, Phi-
listia, and Amalek—and from Hadadezer son of Re-
hob, king of Zobah.
13 So David became even more famous when he re-
turned from destroying 18,000 Edomites* in the Valley
of Salt. 14 He placed army garrisons throughout Edom,
and all the Edomites became David's subjects. In fact,
the LORD made David victorious wherever he went.
15 So David reigned over all Israel and did what was
just and right for all his people. 16 Joab son of Zerui-
ah was commander of the army. Jehoshaphat son of
Ahilud was the royal historian. 17 Zadok son of Ahitub

7:16 As in Greek version and some Hebrew manuscripts; Masoretic Text reads *before you.* **7:19** Or *This is your instruction for all humanity, O Sovereign LORD.* **7:23** As in Greek version (see also 1 Chr 17:21); Hebrew reads *You made a name for yourself and awesome miracles for your land in the sight of your people, whom you redeemed from Egypt, the nations and their gods.* **8:1** Hebrew *by conquering Metheg-ammah,* a name that means "the bridle," possibly referring to the size of the town or the tribute money taken from it. Compare 1 Chr 18:1. **8:4** As in Dead Sea Scrolls and Greek version (see also 1 Chr 18:4); Masoretic Text reads *captured 1,700 charioteers.* **8:8** As in some Greek manuscripts (see also 1 Chr 18:8); Hebrew reads *Betah.* **8:12** As in a few Hebrew manuscripts and Greek and Syriac versions (see also 8:14; 1 Chr 18:11); most Hebrew manuscripts read *Aram.* **8:13** As in a few Hebrew manuscripts and Greek and Syriac versions (see also 8:14; 1 Chr 18:12); most Hebrew manuscripts read *Arameans.*

7:14 If he sins. God promises not to remove his merciful love—as he had done with Saul (1 Sam. 13:13-14; 15:22-23).
7:21 Because of your promise. A reference to God's covenant with Abraham regarding the nation and the land (Gen. 12:2-3; Deut. 7:6-8; 33:26-29).
7:23 made a great name. God chose Israel to spread His glory (Deut. 9:4-5; Isa. 63:12; Jer. 32:20-21; Ezek. 36:22-38).
8:3 to strengthen . . . Euphrates River. Saul had previously defeated Zobah (1 Sam. 14:47), partially fulfilling God's promise of the land from Egypt to the Euphrates (Gen. 15:18).
8:15 all Israel. David now occupies the entire area God promised Abraham.

and Ahimelech son of Abiathar were the priests. Seraiah was the court secretary. 18 Benaiah son of Jehoiada was captain of the king's bodyguard.* And David's sons served as priestly leaders.*

DAVID'S KINDNESS TO MEPHIBOSHETH

9 One day David asked, "Is anyone in Saul's family still alive—anyone to whom I can show kindness for Jonathan's sake?" 2 He summoned a man named Ziba, who had been one of Saul's servants. "Are you Ziba?" the king asked.

"Yes sir, I am," Ziba replied.

3 The king then asked him, "Is anyone still alive from Saul's family? If so, I want to show God's kindness to them."

Ziba replied, "Yes, one of Jonathan's sons is still alive. He is crippled in both feet."

4 "Where is he?" the king asked.

"In Lo-debar," Ziba told him, "at the home of Makir son of Ammiel."

5 So David sent for him and brought him from Makir's home. 6 His name was Mephibosheth*; he was Jonathan's son and Saul's grandson. When he came to David, he bowed low to the ground in deep respect. David said, "Greetings, Mephibosheth."

Mephibosheth replied, "I am your servant."

7 "Don't be afraid!" David said. "I intend to show kindness to you because of my promise to your father, Jonathan. I will give you all the property that once belonged to your grandfather Saul, and you will eat here with me at the king's table!"

8 Mephibosheth bowed respectfully and exclaimed, "Who is your servant, that you should show such kindness to a dead dog like me?"

9 Then the king summoned Saul's servant Ziba and said, "I have given your master's grandson everything that belonged to Saul and his family. 10 You and your sons and servants are to farm the land for him to produce food for your master's household.* But Mephibosheth, your master's grandson, will eat here at my table." (Ziba had fifteen sons and twenty servants.)

11 Ziba replied, "Yes, my lord the king; I am your servant, and I will do all that you have commanded." And from that time on, Mephibosheth ate regularly at David's table,* like one of the king's own sons.

12 Mephibosheth had a young son named Mica. From then on, all the members of Ziba's household were Mephibosheth's servants. 13 And Mephibosheth, who was crippled in both feet, lived in Jerusalem and ate regularly at the king's table.

DAVID DEFEATS THE AMMONITES

10 Some time after this, King Nahash* of the Ammonites died, and his son Hanun became king. 2 David said, "I am going to show loyalty to Hanun just as his father, Nahash, was always loyal to me." So David sent ambassadors to express sympathy to Hanun about his father's death.

But when David's ambassadors arrived in the land of Ammon, 3 the Ammonite commanders said to Hanun, their master, "Do you really think these men are coming here to honor your father? No! David has sent them to spy out the city so they can come in and conquer it!" 4 So Hanun seized David's ambassadors and shaved off half of each man's beard, cut off their robes at the buttocks, and sent them back to David in shame.

5 When David heard what had happened, he sent messengers to tell the men, "Stay at Jericho until your beards grow out, and then come back." For they felt deep shame because of their appearance.

6 When the people of Ammon realized how seriously they had angered David, they sent and hired 20,000 Aramean foot soldiers from the lands of Beth-rehob and Zobah, 1,000 from the king of Maacah, and 12,000 from the land of Tob. 7 When David heard about this, he sent Joab and all his warriors to fight them. 8 The Ammonite troops came out and drew up their battle lines at the entrance of the city gate, while the Arameans from Zobah and Rehob and the men from Tob and Maacah positioned themselves to fight in the open fields.

9 When Joab saw that he would have to fight on both the front and the rear, he chose some of Israel's elite troops and placed them under his personal command to fight the Arameans in the fields. 10 He left the rest of the army under the command of his brother Abishai, who was to attack the Ammonites. 11 "If the Arameans are too strong for me, then come over and help me," Joab told his brother. "And if the Ammonites are too strong for you, I will come and help you. 12 Be courageous! Let us fight bravely for our people and the cities of our God. May the LORD's will be done."

13 When Joab and his troops attacked, the Arameans began to run away. 14 And when the Ammonites saw the Arameans running, they ran from Abishai and retreated into the city. After the battle was over, Joab returned to Jerusalem.

15 The Arameans now realized that they were no match for Israel. So when they regrouped, 16 they were joined by additional Aramean troops summoned by Hadadezer from the other side of the Euphrates River.* These troops arrived at Helam under the command of Shobach, the commander of Hadadezer's forces.

17 When David heard what was happening, he mobilized all Israel, crossed the Jordan River, and led the army to Helam. The Arameans positioned themselves in battle formation and fought against David. 18 But again the Arameans fled from the Israelites. This time David's forces killed 700 charioteers and 40,000 foot soldiers,* in-

8:18a Hebrew *of the Kerethites and Pelethites.* **8:18b** Hebrew *David's sons were priests;* compare parallel text at 1 Chr 18:17. **9:6** *Mephibosheth* is another name for Merib-baal. **9:10** As in Greek version; Hebrew reads *your master's grandson.* **9:11** As in Greek version; Hebrew reads *my table.* **10:1** As in parallel text at 1 Chr 19:1; Hebrew reads *the king.* **10:16** Hebrew *the river.* **10:18** As in some Greek manuscripts (see also 1 Chr 19:18); Hebrew reads *charioteers.*

8:18 the king's bodyguard. Soldiers in David's army (15:18) and elite royal guard (23:22-23).

9:1 can show kindness. David remembered his promise to Jonathan (1 Sam. 20:15, 42).

9:2 Ziba. Ziba was chief steward of Saul's estate: the inheritance of Jonathan's son Mephibosheth, Saul's grandson and primary heir. Saul did have other descendants (21:8).

9:4 Machir. Machir, who later assisted David (17:27), cared for the crippled Mephibosheth.

9:7 Don't be afraid. In the ancient Middle East heirs of previous dynasties were executed to protect new kings.

9:8 a dead dog like me. Mephibosheth, even though he was royalty, would feel despised as dogs were because he was disabled. Disabilities were seen as God's punishment.

9:10 Ziba had fifteen sons and twenty servants. 35 men were required to oversee Saul's estate.

9:13 crippled. Mephibosheth was injured when his nurse fell with him while they fled from Gibeah, after hearing that Saul and Jonathan had been killed (4:4).

cluding Shobach, the commander of their army. 19 When all the kings allied with Hadadezer saw that they had been defeated by Israel, they surrendered to Israel and became their subjects. After that, the Arameans were afraid to help the Ammonites.

DAVID AND BATHSHEBA

11 In the spring of the year,* when kings normally go out to war, David sent Joab and the Israelite army to fight the Ammonites. They destroyed the Ammonite army and laid siege to the city of Rabbah. However, David stayed behind in Jerusalem.

2 Late one afternoon, after his midday rest, David got out of bed and was walking on the roof of the palace. As he looked out over the city, he noticed a woman of unusual beauty taking a bath. 3 He sent someone to find out who she was, and he was told, "She is Bathsheba, the daughter of Eliam and the wife of Uriah the Hittite." 4 Then David sent messengers to get her; and when she came to the palace, he slept with her. She had just completed the purification rites after having her menstrual period. Then she returned home. 5 Later, when Bathsheba discovered that she was pregnant, she sent David a message, saying, "I'm pregnant."

6 Then David sent word to Joab: "Send me Uriah the Hittite." So Joab sent him to David. 7 When Uriah arrived, David asked him how Joab and the army were getting along and how the war was progressing. 8 Then he told Uriah, "Go on home and relax.*" David even sent a gift to Uriah after he had left the palace. 9 But Uriah didn't go home. He slept that night at the palace entrance with the king's palace guard.

10 When David heard that Uriah had not gone home, he summoned him and asked, "What's the matter? Why didn't you go home last night after being away for so long?"

11 Uriah replied, "The Ark and the armies of Israel and Judah are living in tents,* and Joab and my master's men are camping in the open fields. How could I go home to wine and dine and sleep with my wife? I swear that I would never do such a thing."

12 "Well, stay here today," David told him, "and tomorrow you may return to the army." So Uriah stayed in Jerusalem that day and the next. 13 Then David invited him to dinner and got him drunk. But even then he couldn't get Uriah to go home to his wife. Again he slept at the palace entrance with the king's palace guard.

DAVID ARRANGES FOR URIAH'S DEATH

14 So the next morning David wrote a letter to Joab and gave it to Uriah to deliver. 15 The letter instructed Joab, "Station Uriah on the front lines where the battle is fiercest. Then pull back so that he will be killed." 16 So Joab assigned Uriah to a spot close to the city wall where he knew the enemy's strongest men were fighting. 17 And when the enemy soldiers came out of the city to fight, Uriah the Hittite was killed along with several other Israelite soldiers.

18 Then Joab sent a battle report to David. 19 He told his messenger, "Report all the news of the battle to the king. 20 But he might get angry and ask, 'Why did the troops go so close to the city? Didn't they know there would be shooting from the walls? 21 Wasn't Abimelech son of Gideon* killed at Thebez by a woman who threw a millstone down on him from the wall? Why would you get so close to the wall?' Then tell him, 'Uriah the Hittite was killed, too.'"

22 So the messenger went to Jerusalem and gave a complete report to David. 23 "The enemy came out against us in the open fields," he said. "And as we chased them back to the city gate, 24 the archers on the wall shot arrows at us. Some of the king's men were killed, including Uriah the Hittite."

25 "Well, tell Joab not to be discouraged," David said. "The sword devours this one today and that one tomorrow! Fight harder next time, and conquer the city!"

26 When Uriah's wife heard that her husband was dead, she mourned for him. 27 When the period of mourning was over, David sent for her and brought her to the palace, and she became one of his wives. Then she gave birth to a son. But the LORD was displeased with what David had done.

ADULTERY AND MURDER

1. Who is the most beautiful woman you know personally? What makes her so beautiful?

2 SAMUEL 11:1-27

2. David was the leader of his army. Why was he not in battle? How did avoiding his proper duty lead him into deeper sin?
3. Why did Uriah refuse to go home to his wife? How did his actions add even more shame to what David had done?
4. How did David's sins keep leading to more and worse sins? How have you seen this occur in your own life?

NATHAN REBUKES DAVID

12 So the LORD sent Nathan the prophet to tell David this story: "There were two men in a certain town. One was rich, and one was poor. 2 The rich man owned a great many sheep and cattle. 3 The

11:1 Hebrew *At the turn of the year.* The first day of the year in the ancient Hebrew lunar calendar occurred in March or April. 11:8 Hebrew *and wash your feet,* an expression that may also have a connotation of ritualistic washing. 11:11 Or *at Succoth.* 11:21 Hebrew *son of Jerub-besheth.* Jerub-besheth is a variation on the name Jerub-baal, which is another name for Gideon; see Judg 6:32.

11:4. just completed the purification rites. Bathsheba had just become ceremonially clean (following menstruation; Lev. 15:19-30); she could not have been pregnant by her husband Uriah when David slept with her.

11:5 she was pregnant. David and Bathsheba's adultery could not be hidden. The penalty was death for them both (Lev. 20:10; Deut. 22:22).

11:11 Ark. The ark was being kept in a field tent with Israel's army—for blessing and guidance. **Joab and my master's men.** Mindful of his comrades' sacrifice, Uriah would not even sleep with his own wife. While an Israelite king is unfaithful, a non-Israelite soldier is faithful.

11:13 invited him to dinner and got him drunk. David hoped that if Uriah were drunk, he might sleep with Bathsheba.

11:23-24 killed . . . including Uriah the Hittite. Joab pursued a different plan than David had ordered—namely, to have Uriah abandoned. As a cover up, Joab had Uriah's platoon engaged near the city wall where archers' arrows resulted in several fatalities.

12:1 the LORD sent Nathan. God the true King commissions His ambassador to rebuke the chosen king and declare judgment.

BUSTED!

1. Have you ever been caught with your hand in the cookie jar? How did you react?

2 SAMUEL 12:1-14

2. How was David like the man in Nathan's story who stole the sheep?
3. Did the man in Nathan's story deserve to die? Did David?
4. What was David's response when confronted with his sin? How does this reflect what God meant when He said, "David is a man after God's own heart"?
5. How do you respond when someone confronts you with sin? How can you become a man or woman after God's own heart?

poor man owned nothing but one little lamb he had bought. He raised that little lamb, and it grew up with his children. It ate from the man's own plate and drank from his cup. He cuddled it in his arms like a baby daughter. 4 One day a guest arrived at the home of the rich man. But instead of killing an animal from his own flock or herd, he took the poor man's lamb and killed it and prepared it for his guest."

5 David was furious. "As surely as the LORD lives," he vowed, "any man who would do such a thing deserves to die! 6 He must repay four lambs to the poor man for the one he stole and for having no pity."

7 Then Nathan said to David, "You are that man! The LORD, the God of Israel, says: I anointed you king of Israel and saved you from the power of Saul. 8 I gave you your master's house and his wives and the kingdoms of Israel and Judah. And if that had not been enough, I would have given you much, much more. 9 Why, then, have you despised the word of the LORD and done this horrible deed? For you have murdered Uriah the Hittite with the sword of the Ammonites and stolen his wife. 10 From this time on, your family will live by the sword because you have despised me by taking Uriah's wife to be your own.

11 "This is what the LORD says: Because of what you have done, I will cause your own household to rebel against you. I will give your wives to another man before your very eyes, and he will go to bed with them in public view. 12 You did it secretly, but I will make this happen to you openly in the sight of all Israel."

DAVID CONFESSES HIS GUILT

13 Then David confessed to Nathan, "I have sinned against the LORD."

Nathan replied, "Yes, but the LORD has forgiven you, and you won't die for this sin. 14 Nevertheless, because you have shown utter contempt for the word of the LORD* by doing this, your child will die."

15 After Nathan returned to his home, the LORD sent a deadly illness to the child of David and Uriah's wife. 16 David begged God to spare the child. He went without food and lay all night on the bare ground. 17 The elders of his household pleaded with him to get up and eat with them, but he refused.

18 Then on the seventh day the child died. David's advisers were afraid to tell him. "He wouldn't listen to reason while the child was ill," they said. "What drastic thing will he do when we tell him the child is dead?"

19 When David saw them whispering, he realized what had happened. "Is the child dead?" he asked.

"Yes," they replied, "he is dead."

20 Then David got up from the ground, washed himself, put on lotions,* and changed his clothes. He went to the Tabernacle and worshiped the LORD. After that, he returned to the palace and was served food and ate.

21 His advisers were amazed. "We don't understand you," they told him. "While the child was still living, you wept and refused to eat. But now that the child is dead, you have stopped your mourning and are eating again."

22 David replied, "I fasted and wept while the child was alive, for I said, 'Perhaps the LORD will be gracious to me and let the child live.' 23 But why should I fast when he is dead? Can I bring him back again? I will go to him one day, but he cannot return to me."

24 Then David comforted Bathsheba, his wife, and slept with her. She became pregnant and gave birth to

TRAGIC CONSEQUENCES

1. What do you do when you're really upset: Do you eat? Not eat? Not sleep?

2 SAMUEL 12:15-25

2. Why did David react this way when his son became ill? Why did the elders try to make him stop?
3. Why did David get up, wash, and eat after the baby died? What would most people have done?
4. What did David mean when he said, "I'll go to him, but he will never return to me" (v. 23)? What does this suggest about babies who have died?

12:14 As in Dead Sea Scrolls; Masoretic Text reads *the enemies of the LORD.* **12:20** Hebrew *anointed himself.*

12:5 David was furious. David was furious over the injustice and called for the man's death, though not normally a death penalty crime.
12:6 repay four lambs to the poor man. Ironically, David knew God's law (Exod. 22:1).
12:8 I gave you your master's house and. Simply meaning that God had given David Saul's throne and all it entailed (new kings usually kept the prior king's harem).
12:10 your family will live by the sword. This is fulfilled in the violent deaths of three sons: Amnon (13:23-31); Absalom (18:1-18); and Adonijah (1 Kings 2:13-25).
12:11 I will cause your own household to rebel against you. Fulfilled when his son Absalom forced David to flee Jerusalem (15:1-24).
12:13 I have sinned. David joined a list of people of faith who committed heinous crimes and depended on God's grace. Abraham lied about Sarah being his wife, resulting in her almost being taken sexually by another man (Gen. 20:1-5); Peter denied Christ; Paul persecuted Christians. **The LORD has forgiven you.** David sincerely repented (Ps. 32:1,5; 51:8,12).
12:15 the child. No name is given, so apparently the child did not live long enough to be circumcised on the eighth day—the time a son was normally named.

a son, and David* named him Solomon. The LORD loved
the child 25 and sent word through Nathan the proph-
et that they should name him Jedidiah (which means
"beloved of the LORD"), as the LORD had commanded.*

DAVID CAPTURES RABBAH

26 Meanwhile, Joab was fighting against Rabbah, the
capital of Ammon, and he captured the royal fortifi-
cations.* 27 Joab sent messengers to tell David, "I have
fought against Rabbah and captured its water sup-
ply.* 28 Now bring the rest of the army and capture the
city. Otherwise, I will capture it and get credit for the
victory."
29 So David gathered the rest of the army and went
to Rabbah, and he fought against it and captured it.
30 David removed the crown from the king's head,*
and it was placed on his own head. The crown was
made of gold and set with gems, and it weighed sev-
enty-five pounds.* David took a vast amount of plun-
der from the city. 31 He also made slaves of the people
of Rabbah and forced them to labor with* saws, iron
picks, and iron axes, and to work in the brick kilns.*
That is how he dealt with the people of all the Am-
monite towns. Then David and all the army returned
to Jerusalem.

THE RAPE OF TAMAR

13 Now David's son Absalom had a beautiful sis-
ter named Tamar. And Amnon, her half brother,
fell desperately in love with her. 2 Amnon became so
obsessed with Tamar that he became ill. She was a
virgin, and Amnon thought he could never have her.
3 But Amnon had a very crafty friend—his cousin
Jonadab. He was the son of David's brother Shimea.*
4 One day Jonadab said to Amnon, "What's the trou-
ble? Why should the son of a king look so dejected
morning after morning?"
So Amnon told him, "I am in love with Tamar, my
brother Absalom's sister."
5 "Well," Jonadab said, "I'll tell you what to do. Go
back to bed and pretend you are ill. When your fa-
ther comes to see you, ask him to let Tamar come and
prepare some food for you. Tell him you'll feel better
if she prepares it as you watch and feeds you with her
own hands."
6 So Amnon lay down and pretended to be sick. And
when the king came to see him, Amnon asked him,
"Please let my sister Tamar come and cook my favor-
ite dish* as I watch. Then I can eat it from her own
hands." 7 So David agreed and sent Tamar to Amnon's
house to prepare some food for him.
8 When Tamar arrived at Amnon's house, she went
to the place where he was lying down so he could
watch her mix some dough. Then she baked his favor-
ite dish for him. 9 But when she set the serving tray
before him, he refused to eat. "Everyone get out of
here," Amnon told his servants. So they all left.
10 Then he said to Tamar, "Now bring the food into
my bedroom and feed it to me here." So Tamar took his
favorite dish to him. 11 But as she was feeding him, he
grabbed her and demanded, "Come to bed with me,
my darling sister."
12 "No, my brother!" she cried. "Don't be foolish!
Don't do this to me! Such wicked things aren't done
in Israel. 13 Where could I go in my shame? And you
would be called one of the greatest fools in Israel.
Please, just speak to the king about it, and he will let
you marry me."
14 But Amnon wouldn't listen to her, and since he
was stronger than she was, he raped her. 15 Then sud-
denly Amnon's love turned to hate, and he hated her
even more than he had loved her. "Get out of here!" he
snarled at her.
16 "No, no!" Tamar cried. "Sending me away now is
worse than what you've already done to me."
But Amnon wouldn't listen to her. 17 He shouted for
his servant and demanded, "Throw this woman out,
and lock the door behind her!"
18 So the servant put her out and locked the door
behind her. She was wearing a long, beautiful robe,*
as was the custom in those days for the king's virgin
daughters. 19 But now Tamar tore her robe and put
ashes on her head. And then, with her face in her
hands, she went away crying.
20 Her brother Absalom saw her and asked, "Is it
true that Amnon has been with you? Well, my sister,

AMNON'S RAPE OF TAMAR

1. Have you ever been lovesick over someone who didn't like you? How did it affect you?

2 SAMUEL 13:1-22

2. What should Amnon have done if he was in love with Tamar?
3. How did Amnon feel about Tamar after he'd raped her? What does this suggest about his love in the first place?
4. What effect did Amnon's sin have on Tamar? On the family? (See vv. 28-29.)
5. How do sexual sins affect people beyond just those involved?
6. Is someone pressuring you to have sex? Are you pressuring someone? How can you avoid this temptation?

12:24 Hebrew *he;* an alternate Hebrew reading and some Hebrew manuscripts read *she.* **12:25** As in Greek version; Hebrew reads *because of the LORD.* **12:26** Or *the royal city.* **12:27** Or *captured the city of water.* **12:30a** Or *from the head of Milcom* (as in Greek version). Milcom, also called Molech, was the god of the Ammonites. **12:30b** Hebrew *1 talent* [34 kilograms]. **12:31a** Hebrew *He also brought out the people [of Rabbah] and put them under.* **12:31b** Hebrew *and he made them pass through the brick kilns.* **13:3** Hebrew *Shimeah* (also in 13:32), a variant spelling of Shimea; compare 1 Chr 2:13. **13:6** Or *a couple of cakes;* also in 13:8, 10. **13:18** Or *a robe with sleeves,* or *an ornamented robe.* The meaning of the Hebrew is uncertain.

12:25 Jedidiah. Solomon's nickname means "loved by the LORD."
13:1 Amnon. Amnon was David's oldest son (3:2). Tamar was Amnon's half-sister and Absalom's full sister.
13:13 Where could I go in my shame? Amnon's suggestion was wicked (Lev. 18:9; 20:17, Deut. 27:22). Rape would cause her to be unfit for marriage (Deut. 22:13-21) and jeopardize Amnon's right to the throne.
13:16 Sending me away. The law demanded that Amnon marry Tamar (Deut. 22:29), but in sending her away, he rejected her as a bride. No longer a virgin, Tamar was disgraced.

keep quiet for now, since he's your brother. Don't you
worry about it." So Tamar lived as a desolate woman
in her brother Absalom's house.
21 When King David heard what had happened, he
was very angry.* 22 And though Absalom never spoke
to Amnon about this, he hated Amnon deeply because
of what he had done to his sister.

ABSALOM'S REVENGE ON AMNON

23 Two years later, when Absalom's sheep were being
sheared at Baal-hazor near Ephraim, Absalom in-
vited all the king's sons to come to a feast. 24 He went
to the king and said, "My sheep-shearers are now at
work. Would the king and his servants please come to
celebrate the occasion with me?"
25 The king replied, "No, my son. If we all came, we
would be too much of a burden on you." Absalom
pressed him, but the king would not come, though he
gave Absalom his blessing.
26 "Well, then," Absalom said, "if you can't come,
how about sending my brother Amnon with us?"
"Why Amnon?" the king asked. 27 But Absalom kept
on pressing the king until he finally agreed to let all
his sons attend, including Amnon. So Absalom pre-
pared a feast fit for a king.*
28 Absalom told his men, "Wait until Amnon gets
drunk; then at my signal, kill him! Don't be afraid. I'm
the one who has given the command. Take courage
and do it!" 29 So at Absalom's signal they murdered
Amnon. Then the other sons of the king jumped on
their mules and fled.
30 As they were on the way back to Jerusalem, this
report reached David: "Absalom has killed all the
king's sons; not one is left alive!" 31 The king got up,
tore his robe, and threw himself on the ground. His
advisers also tore their clothes in horror and sorrow.
32 But just then Jonadab, the son of David's brother
Shimea, arrived and said, "No, don't believe that all
the king's sons have been killed! It was only Amnon!
Absalom has been plotting this ever since Amnon
raped his sister Tamar. 33 No, my lord the king, your
sons aren't all dead! It was only Amnon." 34 Mean-
while Absalom escaped.
Then the watchman on the Jerusalem wall saw a
great crowd coming down the hill on the road from
the west. He ran to tell the king, "I see a crowd of peo-
ple coming from the Horonaim road along the side of
the hill."*
35 "Look!" Jonadab told the king. "There they are
now! The king's sons are coming, just as I said."
36 They soon arrived, weeping and sobbing, and
the king and all his servants wept bitterly with
them. 37 And David mourned many days for his son
Amnon.
Absalom fled to his grandfather, Talmai son of
Ammihud, the king of Geshur. 38 He stayed there in
Geshur for three years. 39 And King David,* now rec-
onciled to Amnon's death, longed to be reunited with
his son Absalom.*

ABSALOM'S REVENGE

1. Who is your school's biggest rival in sports? Has this competition ever gotten out of control?

2 SAMUEL 13:23-39

2. What motivated Absalom's hatred? Was his anger justified? Were his actions justified?
3. How should Absalom have dealt with the sin of Amnon? How should David have dealt with it?
4. How did Absalom's vengeance injure innocent people? How has your own vengeance injured innocent people?
5. Are you angry with someone who has wronged you? Are you looking for revenge on your rival? What would God have you do about it?

JOAB ARRANGES FOR ABSALOM'S RETURN

14 Joab realized how much the king longed to see
Absalom. 2 So he sent for a woman from Tekoa
who had a reputation for great wisdom. He said to
her, "Pretend you are in mourning; wear mourning
clothes and don't put on lotions.* Act like a woman
who has been mourning for the dead for a long time.
3 Then go to the king and tell him the story I am about
to tell you." Then Joab told her what to say.
4 When the woman from Tekoa approached* the
king, she bowed with her face to the ground in deep
respect and cried out, "O king! Help me!"
5 "What's the trouble?" the king asked.
"Alas, I am a widow!" she replied. "My husband is
dead. 6 My two sons had a fight out in the field. And
since no one was there to stop it, one of them was
killed. 7 Now the rest of the family is demanding, 'Let
us have your son. We will execute him for murdering
his brother. He doesn't deserve to inherit his fami-
ly's property.' They want to extinguish the only coal
I have left, and my husband's name and family will
disappear from the face of the earth."
8 "Leave it to me," the king told her. "Go home, and
I'll see to it that no one touches him."
9 "Oh, thank you, my lord the king," the woman from
Tekoa replied. "If you are criticized for helping me, let

13:21 Dead Sea Scrolls and Greek version add *But he did not punish his son Amnon, because he loved him, for he was his firstborn.* **13:27** As in Greek and Latin versions (compare also Dead Sea Scrolls); the Hebrew text lacks this sentence. **13:34** As in Greek version, Hebrew lacks this sentence. **13:39a** Dead Sea Scrolls and Greek version read *And the spirit of the king.* **13:39b** Or *no longer felt a need to go out after Absalom.* **14:2** Hebrew *don't anoint yourself with oil* **14:4** As in many Hebrew manuscripts and Greek and Syriac versions; Masoretic Text reads *spoke to.*

13:21 he was very angry. Though livid, David did not punish his son as the law prescribed (Lev. 20:17). Perhaps he felt he had lost all moral authority on account of Bathsheba. His failure to discipline his children would cause him much grief.

13:23 invited all the king's sons. It was customary in Israel to host an annual sheep-shearing festival (1 Sam. 25:2,8).

13:26 how about sending my brother Amnon with us? Absalom requested that he send his heir Amnon instead. **Why Amnon?** David was suspicious; well aware of the brothers' feud (v. 22).

13:28 kill him. Absalom's strategy, murdering Amnon when he least expected it—two long years after his sin and during a party he had been invited to—would also secure Absalom's position as successor to the throne.

14:2 he sent. Joab knew David missed Absalom; and was concerned about the political ramifications of David's estrangement from the heir. So he sent a Tekoan woman to tell David a story designed to convince him to pardon Absalom. Here Joab is the most active in restoring Absalom, later he kills him (18:14-15.)

14:7 They want to extinguish the only coal. The death of the woman's remaining son would mean the elimination of her only source of financial support and her dead husband's family name.

the blame fall on me and on my father's house, and let the king and his throne be innocent."

10 "If anyone objects," the king said, "bring him to me. I can assure you he will never harm you again!"

11 Then she said, "Please swear to me by the LORD your God that you won't let anyone take vengeance against my son. I want no more bloodshed."

"As surely as the LORD lives," he replied, "not a hair on your son's head will be disturbed!"

12 "Please allow me to ask one more thing of my lord the king," she said.

"Go ahead and speak," he responded.

13 She replied, "Why don't you do as much for the people of God as you have promised to do for me? You have convicted yourself in making this decision, because you have refused to bring home your own banished son. 14 All of us must die eventually. Our lives are like water spilled out on the ground, which cannot be gathered up again. But God does not just sweep life away; instead, he devises ways to bring us back when we have been separated from him.

15 "I have come to plead with my lord the king because people have threatened me. I said to myself, 'Perhaps the king will listen to me 16 and rescue us from those who would cut us off from the inheritance* God has given us. 17 Yes, my lord the king will give us peace of mind again.' I know that you are like an angel of God in discerning good from evil. May the LORD your God be with you."

18 "I must know one thing," the king replied, "and tell me the truth."

"Yes, my lord the king," she responded.

19 "Did Joab put you up to this?"

And the woman replied, "My lord the king, how can I deny it? Nobody can hide anything from you. Yes, Joab sent me and told me what to say. 20 He did it to place the matter before you in a different light. But you are as wise as an angel of God, and you understand everything that happens among us!"

21 So the king sent for Joab and told him, "All right, go and bring back the young man Absalom."

22 Joab bowed with his face to the ground in deep respect and said, "At last I know that I have gained your approval, my lord the king, for you have granted me this request!"

23 Then Joab went to Geshur and brought Absalom back to Jerusalem. 24 But the king gave this order: "Absalom may go to his own house, but he must never come into my presence." So Absalom did not see the king.

ABSALOM RECONCILED TO DAVID

25 Now Absalom was praised as the most handsome man in all Israel. He was flawless from head to foot. 26 He cut his hair only once a year, and then only because it was so heavy. When he weighed it out, it came to five pounds!* 27 He had three sons and one daughter. His daughter's name was Tamar, and she was very beautiful.

28 Absalom lived in Jerusalem for two years, but he never got to see the king. 29 Then Absalom sent for Joab to ask him to intercede for him, but Joab refused to come. Absalom sent for him a second time, but again Joab refused to come. 30 So Absalom said to his servants, "Go and set fire to Joab's barley field, the field next to mine." So they set his field on fire, as Absalom had commanded.

31 Then Joab came to Absalom at his house and demanded, "Why did your servants set my field on fire?"

32 And Absalom replied, "Because I wanted you to ask the king why he brought me back from Geshur if he didn't intend to see me. I might as well have stayed there. Let me see the king; if he finds me guilty of anything, then let him kill me."

33 So Joab told the king what Absalom had said. Then at last David summoned Absalom, who came and bowed low before the king, and the king kissed him.

ABSALOM'S REBELLION

15 After this, Absalom bought a chariot and horses, and he hired fifty bodyguards to run ahead of him. 2 He got up early every morning and went out to the gate of the city. When people brought a case to the king for judgment, Absalom would ask where in Israel they were from, and they would tell him their tribe. 3 Then Absalom would say, "You've really got a strong case here! It's too bad the king doesn't have anyone to hear it. 4 I wish I were the judge. Then everyone could bring their cases to me for judgment, and I would give them justice!"

5 When people tried to bow before him, Absalom wouldn't let them. Instead, he took them by the hand and kissed them. 6 Absalom did this with everyone who came to the king for judgment, and so he stole the hearts of all the people of Israel.

7 After four years,* Absalom said to the king, "Let me go to Hebron to offer a sacrifice to the LORD and fulfill a vow I made to him. 8 For while your servant was at Geshur in Aram, I promised to sacrifice to the LORD in Hebron* if he would bring me back to Jerusalem."

9 "All right," the king told him. "Go and fulfill your vow."

So Absalom went to Hebron. 10 But while he was there, he sent secret messengers to all the tribes of Israel to stir up a rebellion against the king. "As soon as you hear the ram's horn," his message read, "you are to say, 'Absalom has been crowned king in Hebron.'" 11 He took 200 men from Jerusalem with him as guests, but they knew nothing of his intentions. 12 While Absalom was offering the sacrifices, he sent for Ahith-

14:16 Or *the property;* or *the people.* **14:26** Hebrew *200 shekels* [2.3 kilograms] *by the royal standard.* **15:7** As in Greek and Syriac versions; Hebrew reads *forty years.* **15:8** As in some Greek manuscripts; Hebrew lacks *in Hebron.*

14:24 Absalom may go to his own house, but he must never come into my presence. David refused to grant Absalom access to the palace. In the end, David's coldness toward Absalom drove a wedge between them.

14:26 He cut his hair only once a year. The mention of Absalom's hair is particularly notable because it eventually played a role in his death (18:9).

14:32 Let me see the king. Absalom demanded to either be granted full pardon or be punished by death. He was outraged at how he was treated but gave no sign of repentance for killing Amnon.

14:33 the king kissed him. The kiss was a symbol of David's forgiveness and Absalom's restoration to the royal family. David did not ask for Absalom to repent, thereby further failing to deal with the situation justly. Absalom remained bitter at David's delay in forgiving him.

15:1-2 chariot and horses. Absalom was the first Israelite leader known to have a chariot. **went out to the gate of the city.** Absalom gained popularity by making himself available to hear the complaints of the masses. He even supported their complaints without investigating them. Then he told them that the king would not help them, an ancient version of dirty politics.

15:7 go to Hebron. This important city was 20 miles south of Jerusalem.

ophel, one of David's counselors who lived in Giloh. Soon many others also joined Absalom, and the conspiracy gained momentum.

DAVID ESCAPES FROM JERUSALEM

13 A messenger soon arrived in Jerusalem to tell David, "All Israel has joined Absalom in a conspiracy against you!"

14 "Then we must flee at once, or it will be too late!" David urged his men. "Hurry! If we get out of the city before Absalom arrives, both we and the city of Jerusalem will be spared from disaster."

15 "We are with you," his advisers replied. "Do what you think is best."

16 So the king and all his household set out at once. He left no one behind except ten of his concubines to look after the palace. 17 The king and all his people set out on foot, pausing at the last house 18 to let all the king's men move past to lead the way. There were 600 men from Gath who had come with David, along with the king's bodyguard.*

19 Then the king turned and said to Ittai, a leader of the men from Gath, "Why are you coming with us? Go on back to King Absalom, for you are a guest in Israel, a foreigner in exile. 20 You arrived only recently, and should I force you today to wander with us? I don't even know where we will go. Go on back and take your kinsmen with you, and may the LORD show you his unfailing love and faithfulness.*"

21 But Ittai said to the king, "I vow by the LORD and by your own life that I will go wherever my lord the king goes, no matter what happens—whether it means life or death."

22 David replied, "All right, come with us." So Ittai and all his men and their families went along.

23 Everyone cried loudly as the king and his followers passed by. They crossed the Kidron Valley and then went out toward the wilderness.

24 Zadok and all the Levites also came along, carrying the Ark of the Covenant of God. They set down the Ark of God, and Abiathar offered sacrifices[A] until everyone had passed out of the city.

25 Then the king instructed Zadok to take the Ark of God back into the city. "If the LORD sees fit," David said, "he will bring me back to see the Ark and the Tabernacle* again. 26 But if he is through with me, then let him do what seems best to him."

27 The king also told Zadok the priest, "Look,* here is my plan. You and Abiathar* should return quietly to the city with your son Ahimaaz and Abiathar's son Jonathan. 28 I will stop at the shallows of the Jordan River[A] and wait there for a report from you." 29 So Zadok and Abiathar took the Ark of God back to the city and stayed there.

30 David walked up the road to the Mount of Olives, weeping as he went. His head was covered and his feet were bare as a sign of mourning. And the people who were with him covered their heads and wept as they climbed the hill. 31 When someone told David that his adviser Ahithophel was now backing Absalom, David prayed, "O LORD, let Ahithophel give Absalom foolish advice!"

32 When David reached the summit of the Mount of Olives where people worshiped God, Hushai the Arkite was waiting there for him. Hushai had torn his clothing and put dirt on his head as a sign of mourning. 33 But David told him, "If you go with me, you will only be a burden. 34 Return to Jerusalem and tell Absalom, 'I will now be your adviser, O king, just as I was your father's adviser in the past.' Then you can frustrate and counter Ahithophel's advice. 35 Zadok and Abiathar, the priests, will be there. Tell them about the plans being made in the king's palace, 36 and they will send their sons Ahimaaz and Jonathan to tell me what is going on."

37 So David's friend Hushai returned to Jerusalem, getting there just as Absalom arrived.

DAVID AND ZIBA

16 When David had gone a little beyond the summit of the Mount of Olives, Ziba, the servant of Mephibosheth,[A] was waiting there for him. He had two donkeys loaded with 200 loaves of bread, 100 clusters of raisins, 100 bunches of summer fruit, and a wineskin full of wine.

2 "What are these for?" the king asked Ziba.

Ziba replied, "The donkeys are for the king's people to ride on, and the bread and summer fruit are for the young men to eat. The wine is for those who become exhausted in the wilderness."

3 "And where is Mephibosheth, Saul's grandson?" the king asked him.

"He stayed in Jerusalem," Ziba replied. "He said, 'Today I will get back the kingdom of my grandfather Saul.'"

4 "In that case," the king told Ziba, "I give you everything Mephibosheth owns."

"I bow before you," Ziba replied. "May I always be pleasing to you, my lord the king."

SHIMEI CURSES DAVID

5 As King David came to Bahurim, a man came out of the village cursing them. It was Shimei son of Gera, from the same clan as Saul's family. 6 He threw stones at the king and the king's officers and all the mighty warriors who surrounded him. 7 "Get out of here, you murderer, you scoundrel!" he shouted at David. 8 "The LORD is paying you back for all the bloodshed in Saul's clan. You stole his throne, and now the LORD has given

15:18 Hebrew *the Kerethites and Pelethites.* **15:20** As in Greek version; Hebrew reads *and may unfailing love and faithfulness go with you.* **15:24** Or *Abiathar went up.* **15:25** Hebrew *and his dwelling place.* **15:27a** As in Greek version; Hebrew reads *Are you a seer?* or *Do you see?* **15:27b** Hebrew lacks *and Abiathar;* compare 15:29. **15:28** Hebrew *at the crossing points of the wilderness.* **16:1** *Mephibosheth* is another name for Merib-baal.

15:18 the king's bodyguard. These were elite units of David's army (8:18).

15:25 take the Ark of God. David understood that the Ark of the Covenant was the symbol of God's presence and belonged in the capital city regardless of where the king was.

15:27 return quietly to the city. David wanted the priests to remain in the tabernacle and be available to receive any messages the Lord might give them to tell David.

16:4 I give you everything Mephibosheth owns. David believed Ziba's story, assuming the worst. Later he ran into Mephibosheth (19:24-30), who claimed that Ziba lied.

16:7 you murderer, you scoundrel. While it is possible he was accusing David in the death of Saul or members of Saul's family, David may have taken it as a reference to Uriah's death.

16:8 The LORD is paying you back. Shimei blamed David for the downfall of Saul's family. His accusations were untrue because David did not even strike Saul and made every effort on behalf of his surviving family.

it to your son Absalom. At last you will taste some of your own medicine, for you are a murderer!"

9 "Why should this dead dog curse my lord the king?" Abishai son of Zeruiah demanded. "Let me go over and cut off his head!"

10 "No!" the king said. "Who asked your opinion, you sons of Zeruiah! If the LORD has told him to curse me, who are you to stop him?"

11 Then David said to Abishai and to all his servants, "My own son is trying to kill me. Doesn't this relative of Saul* have even more reason to do so? Leave him alone and let him curse, for the LORD has told him to do it. 12 And perhaps the LORD will see that I am being wronged* and will bless me because of these curses today." 13 So David and his men continued down the road, and Shimei kept pace with them on a nearby hillside, cursing and throwing stones and dirt at David.

14 The king and all who were with him grew weary along the way, so they rested when they reached the Jordan River.*

AHITHOPHEL ADVISES ABSALOM

15 Meanwhile, Absalom and all the army of Israel arrived at Jerusalem, accompanied by Ahithophel. 16 When David's friend Hushai the Arkite arrived, he went immediately to see Absalom. "Long live the king!" he exclaimed. "Long live the king!"

17 "Is this the way you treat your friend David?" Absalom asked him. "Why aren't you with him?"

18 "I'm here because I belong to the man who is chosen by the LORD and by all the men of Israel," Hushai replied. 19 "And anyway, why shouldn't I serve you? Just as I was your father's adviser, now I will be your adviser!"

20 Then Absalom turned to Ahithophel and asked him, "What should I do next?"

21 Ahithophel told him, "Go and sleep with your father's concubines, for he has left them here to look after the palace. Then all Israel will know that you have insulted your father beyond hope of reconciliation, and they will throw their support to you." 22 So they set up a tent on the palace roof where everyone could see it, and Absalom went in and had sex with his father's concubines.

23 Absalom followed Ahithophel's advice, just as David had done. For every word Ahithophel spoke seemed as wise as though it had come directly from the mouth of God.

17 Now Ahithophel urged Absalom, "Let me choose 12,000 men to start out after David tonight. 2 I will catch up with him while he is weary and discouraged. He and his troops will panic, and everyone will run away. Then I will kill only the king, 3 and I will bring all the people back to you as a bride returns to her husband. After all, it is only one man's life that you seek.* Then you will be at peace with all the people." 4 This plan seemed good to Absalom and to all the elders of Israel.

HUSHAI COUNTERS AHITHOPHEL'S ADVICE

5 But then Absalom said, "Bring in Hushai the Arkite. Let's see what he thinks about this." 6 When Hushai arrived, Absalom told him what Ahithophel had said. Then he asked, "What is your opinion? Should we follow Ahithophel's advice? If not, what do you suggest?"

7 "Well," Hushai replied to Absalom, "this time Ahithophel has made a mistake. 8 You know your father and his men; they are mighty warriors. Right now they are as enraged as a mother bear who has been robbed of her cubs. And remember that your father is an experienced man of war. He won't be spending the night among the troops. 9 He has probably already hidden in some pit or cave. And when he comes out and attacks and a few of your men fall, there will be panic among your troops, and the word will spread that Absalom's men are being slaughtered. 10 Then even the bravest soldiers, though they have the heart of a lion, will be paralyzed with fear. For all Israel knows what a mighty warrior your father is and how courageous his men are.

11 "I recommend that you mobilize the entire army of Israel, bringing them from as far away as Dan in the north and Beersheba in the south. That way you will have an army as numerous as the sand on the seashore. And I advise that you personally lead the troops. 12 When we find David, we'll fall on him like dew that falls on the ground. Then neither he nor any of his men will be left alive. 13 And if David were to escape into some town, you will have all Israel there at your command. Then we can take ropes and drag the walls of the town into the nearest valley until every stone is torn down."

14 Then Absalom and all the men of Israel said, "Hushai's advice is better than Ahithophel's." For the LORD had determined to defeat the counsel of Ahithophel, which really was the better plan, so that he could bring disaster on Absalom!

HUSHAI WARNS DAVID TO ESCAPE

15 Hushai told Zadok and Abiathar, the priests, what Ahithophel had said to Absalom and the elders of Israel and what he himself had advised instead. 16 "Quick!" he told them. "Find David and urge him not to stay at the shallows of the Jordan River* tonight. He must go across at once into the wilderness beyond. Otherwise he will die and his entire army with him."

17 Jonathan and Ahimaaz had been staying at En-rogel so as not to be seen entering and leaving the city. Arrangements had been made for a servant girl to bring them the message they were to take to King David. 18 But a boy spotted them at En-rogel, and he told Absalom about it. So they quickly escaped to Bahurim, where a man hid them down inside a well in his courtyard. 19 The man's wife put a cloth over the

16:11 Hebrew *this Benjaminite.* **16:12** As in Greek and Syriac versions; Hebrew reads *see my iniquity.* **16:14** As in Greek version (see also 17:16); Hebrew reads *when they reached their destination.* **17:3** As in Greek version; Hebrew reads *like the return of all is the man whom you seek.* **17:16** Hebrew *at the crossing points of the wilderness.*

16:21 Go and sleep with your father's concubines. This act signified that Absalom was claiming royal power and made it impossible for reconciliation. It also fulfilled Nathan's prophecy (12:11-12).

17:1-3 to start after David tonight. Ahithophel underestimated the loyalty of David's soldiers, assuming that with David absent, his armies would scatter.

17:7-13 Hushai, secretly loyal to David, convinced Absalom to disregard Ahithophel's advice and amass a huge army before attacking, hoping to buy David some time.

17:16 He must go across at once. Hushai warned David to cross the Jordan in case Absalom changed his mind and followed Ahithophel's advice.

top of the well and scattered grain on it to dry in the sun; so no one suspected they were there.

20 When Absalom's men arrived, they asked her, "Have you seen Ahimaaz and Jonathan?"

The woman replied, "They were here, but they crossed over the brook." Absalom's men looked for them without success and returned to Jerusalem.

21 Then the two men crawled out of the well and hurried on to King David. "Quick!" they told him, "cross the Jordan tonight!" And they told him how Ahithophel had advised that he be captured and killed. 22 So David and all the people with him went across the Jordan River during the night, and they were all on the other bank before dawn.

23 When Ahithophel realized that his advice had not been followed, he saddled his donkey, went to his hometown, set his affairs in order, and hanged himself. He died there and was buried in the family tomb.

24 David soon arrived at Mahanaim. By now, Absalom had mobilized the entire army of Israel and was leading his troops across the Jordan River. 25 Absalom had appointed Amasa as commander of his army, replacing Joab, who had been commander under David. (Amasa was Joab's cousin. His father was Jether,* an Ishmaelite.* His mother, Abigail daughter of Nahash, was the sister of Joab's mother, Zeruiah.) 26 Absalom and the Israelite army set up camp in the land of Gilead.

27 When David arrived at Mahanaim, he was warmly greeted by Shobi son of Nahash, who came from Rabbah of the Ammonites, and by Makir son of Ammiel from Lo-debar, and by Barzillai of Gilead from Rogelim. 28 They brought sleeping mats, cooking pots, serving bowls, wheat and barley, flour and roasted grain, beans, lentils, 29 honey, butter, sheep, goats, and cheese for David and those who were with him. For they said, "You must all be very hungry and tired and thirsty after your long march through the wilderness."

ABSALOM'S DEFEAT AND DEATH

18 David now mustered the men who were with him and appointed generals and captains* to lead them. 2 He sent the troops out in three groups, placing one group under Joab, one under Joab's brother Abishai son of Zeruiah, and one under Ittai, the man from Gath. The king told his troops, "I am going out with you."

3 But his men objected strongly. "You must not go," they urged. "If we have to turn and run—and even if half of us die—it will make no difference to Absalom's troops; they will be looking only for you. You are worth 10,000 of us,* and it is better that you stay here in the town and send help if we need it."

4 "If you think that's the best plan, I'll do it," the king answered. So he stood alongside the gate of the town as all the troops marched out in groups of hundreds and of thousands.

5 And the king gave this command to Joab, Abishai, and Ittai: "For my sake, deal gently with young Absalom." And all the troops heard the king give this order to his commanders.

6 So the battle began in the forest of Ephraim, 7 and the Israelite troops were beaten back by David's men. There was a great slaughter that day, and 20,000 men laid down their lives. 8 The battle raged all across the countryside, and more men died because of the forest than were killed by the sword.

9 During the battle, Absalom happened to come upon some of David's men. He tried to escape on his mule, but as he rode beneath the thick branches of a great tree, his hair* got caught in the tree. His mule kept going and left him dangling in the air. 10 One of David's men saw what had happened and told Joab, "I saw Absalom dangling from a great tree."

11 "What?" Joab demanded. "You saw him there and didn't kill him? I would have rewarded you with ten pieces of silver* and a hero's belt!"

12 "I would not kill the king's son for even a thousand pieces of silver,*" the man replied to Joab. "We all heard the king say to you and Abishai and Ittai, 'For my sake, please spare young Absalom.' 13 And if I had betrayed the king by killing his son—and the king would certainly find out who did it—you yourself would be the first to abandon me."

14 "Enough of this nonsense," Joab said. Then he took three daggers and plunged them into Absalom's heart as he dangled, still alive, in the great tree. 15 Ten of Joab's young armor bearers then surrounded Absalom and killed him.

16 Then Joab blew the ram's horn, and his men returned from chasing the army of Israel. 17 They threw Absalom's body into a deep pit in the forest and piled a great heap of stones over it. And all Israel fled to their homes.

18 During his lifetime, Absalom had built a monument to himself in the King's Valley, for he said, "I have no son to carry on my name." He named the monument after himself, and it is known as Absalom's Monument to this day.

DAVID MOURNS ABSALOM'S DEATH

19 Then Zadok's son Ahimaaz said, "Let me run to the king with the good news that the LORD has rescued him from his enemies."

20 "No," Joab told him, "it wouldn't be good news to the king that his son is dead. You can be my messenger another time, but not today."

21 Then Joab said to a man from Ethiopia,* "Go tell the king what you have seen." The man bowed and ran off.

22 But Ahimaaz continued to plead with Joab, "Whatever happens, please let me go, too."

"Why should you go, my son?" Joab replied. "There will be no reward for your news."

17:25a Hebrew *Ithra,* a variant spelling of Jether. **17:25b** As in some Greek manuscripts (see also 1 Chr 2:17); Hebrew reads *an Israelite.* **18:1** Hebrew *appointed commanders of thousands and commanders of hundreds.* **18:3** As in two Hebrew manuscripts and some Greek and Latin manuscripts; most Hebrew manuscripts read *Now there are 10,000 like us.* **18:9** Hebrew *his head.* **18:11** Hebrew *10 [shekels] of silver,* about 4 ounces or 114 grams in weight. **18:12** Hebrew *1,000 [shekels] of silver,* about 25 pounds or 11.4 kilograms in weight. **18:21** Hebrew *from Cush;* similarly in 18:23, 31, 32.

17:23 set his affairs in order, and hanged himself. Ahithophel's suicide comes in response to two realities: (1) he had lost his role as the most respected advisor in the land (16:23), and his advice had been spurned (17:14); and (2) he had cast his unsuccessful lot with Absalom. He faced most certain execution.

18:8 more people died because of the forest. Guerilla tactics favored by David's warriors utilized the rough terrain against superior numbers.

18:9 his hair. Ironically, Absalom's beautiful hair (14:25) became his undoing.

18:13 you . . . would be the first to abandon me. This man knew political reality: lower level people get sacrificed in order to protect the involvement of higher-ups.

18:17 a great heap of stones. The pile of stones may have been a memorial ridiculing the memorial Absalom made for himself (v. 18).

23 "Yes, but let me go anyway," he begged.
Joab finally said, "All right, go ahead." So Ahima-
az took the less demanding route by way of the plain
and ran to Mahanaim ahead of the Ethiopian.
24 While David was sitting between the inner and
outer gates of the town, the watchman climbed to the
roof of the gateway by the wall. As he looked, he saw
a lone man running toward them. 25 He shouted the
news down to David, and the king replied, "If he is
alone, he has news."
As the messenger came closer, 26 the watchman
saw another man running toward them. He shouted
down, "Here comes another one!"
The king replied, "He also will have news."
27 "The first man runs like Ahimaaz son of Zadok,"
the watchman said.
"He is a good man and comes with good news," the
king replied.
28 Then Ahimaaz cried out to the king, "Everything
is all right!" He bowed before the king with his face
to the ground and said, "Praise to the LORD your God,
who has handed over the rebels who dared to stand
against my lord the king."
29 "What about young Absalom?" the king demand-
ed. "Is he all right?"
Ahimaaz replied, "When Joab told me to come,
there was a lot of commotion. But I didn't know what
was happening."
30 "Wait here," the king told him. So Ahimaaz
stepped aside.
31 Then the man from Ethiopia arrived and said, "I
have good news for my lord the king. Today the LORD
has rescued you from all those who rebelled against
you."
32 "What about young Absalom?" the king demand-
ed. "Is he all right?"
And the Ethiopian replied, "May all of your ene-
mies, my lord the king, both now and in the future,
share the fate of that young man!"
33* The king was overcome with emotion. He went
up to the room over the gateway and burst into tears.
And as he went, he cried, "O my son Absalom! My son,
my son Absalom! If only I had died instead of you!
O Absalom, my son, my son."

JOAB REBUKES THE KING

19 1* Word soon reached Joab that the king was
weeping and mourning for Absalom. 2 As all the
people heard of the king's deep grief for his son, the
joy of that day's victory was turned into deep sadness.
3 They crept back into the town that day as though
they were ashamed and had deserted in battle. 4 The
king covered his face with his hands and kept on cry-
ing, "O my son Absalom! O Absalom, my son, my son!"
5 Then Joab went to the king's room and said to
him, "We saved your life today and the lives of your
sons, your daughters, and your wives and concubines.
Yet you act like this, making us feel ashamed of our-
selves. 6 You seem to love those who hate you and hate
those who love you. You have made it clear today that
your commanders and troops mean nothing to you.
It seems that if Absalom had lived and all of us had
died, you would be pleased. 7 Now go out there and
congratulate your troops, for I swear by the LORD that
if you don't go out, not a single one of them will re-
main here tonight. Then you will be worse off than
ever before."
8 So the king went out and took his seat at the town
gate, and as the news spread throughout the town
that he was there, everyone went to him.
Meanwhile, the Israelites who had supported Ab-
salom fled to their homes. 9 And throughout all the
tribes of Israel there was much discussion and ar-
gument going on. The people were saying, "The king
rescued us from our enemies and saved us from the
Philistines, but Absalom chased him out of the coun-
try. 10 Now Absalom, whom we anointed to rule over
us, is dead. Why not ask David to come back and be
our king again?"
11 Then King David sent Zadok and Abiathar, the
priests, to say to the elders of Judah, "Why are you the
last ones to welcome back the king into his palace?
For I have heard that all Israel is ready. 12 You are my
relatives, my own tribe, my own flesh and blood! So
why are you the last ones to welcome back the king?"
13 And David told them to tell Amasa, "Since you are
my own flesh and blood, like Joab, may God strike me
and even kill me if I do not appoint you as commander
of my army in his place."
14 Then Amasa* convinced all the men of Judah,
and they responded unanimously. They sent word
to the king, "Return to us, and bring back all who are
with you."

DAVID'S RETURN TO JERUSALEM

15 So the king started back to Jerusalem. And when he
arrived at the Jordan River, the people of Judah came
to Gilgal to meet him and escort him across the river.
16 Shimei son of Gera, the man from Bahurim in Ben-
jamin, hurried across with the men of Judah to wel-
come King David. 17 A thousand other men from the
tribe of Benjamin were with him, including Ziba, the
chief servant of the house of Saul, and Ziba's fifteen
sons and twenty servants. They rushed down to the
Jordan to meet the king. 18 They crossed the shallows
of the Jordan to bring the king's household across the
river, helping him in every way they could.

DAVID'S MERCY TO SHIMEI

As the king was about to cross the river, Shimei fell
down before him. 19 "My lord the king, please forgive
me," he pleaded. "Forget the terrible thing your ser-
vant did when you left Jerusalem. May the king put it
out of his mind. 20 I know how much I sinned. That is
why I have come here today, the very first person in
all Israel* to greet my lord the king."

18:33 Verse 18:33 is numbered 19:1 in Hebrew text. **19:1** Verses 19:1-43 are numbered 19:2-44 in Hebrew text. **19:14** Or *David;* Hebrew reads *he.* **19:20** Hebrew *in the house of Joseph.*

18:27 a good man . . . with good news. Messengers were chosen based on what type of news was being delivered.

19:9 throughout all the tribes of Israel there was much discussion and argument. On the one hand, David was an effective leader who accomplished great things for them in the past. On the other hand, he fled from the land—not a very kingly thing to do.

19:11 welcome back the king. David appealed to his faithful priests to take the initiative in inviting him back to the throne.

19:13 Amasa. As a further means of gaining support, particularly from Judah, David appointed Amasa as commander of his army in place of Joab. Amasa had been commander of Absalom's army, thus gaining the allegiance of the rebels. Apparently Joab's disagreements with David's policies and killing Absalom made David distrust him.

19:17 from the tribe of Benjamin. This large contingent probably feared that they would be associated with Shimei's cursing. They were a sign to David that Saul's family had at last accepted him as king.

21 Then Abishai son of Zeruiah said, "Shimei should
die, for he cursed the LORD's anointed king!"
22 "Who asked your opinion, you sons of Zeruiah!"
David exclaimed. "Why have you become my adver-
sary* today? This is not a day for execution, for today
I am once again the king of Israel!" 23 Then, turning to
Shimei, David vowed, "Your life will be spared."

DAVID'S KINDNESS TO MEPHIBOSHETH

24 Now Mephibosheth,* Saul's grandson, came down
from Jerusalem to meet the king. He had not cared
for his feet, trimmed his beard, or washed his clothes
since the day the king left Jerusalem. 25 "Why didn't
you come with me, Mephibosheth?" the king asked
him.
26 Mephibosheth replied, "My lord the king, my
servant Ziba deceived me. I told him, 'Saddle my
donkey* so I can go with the king.' For as you know
I am crippled. 27 Ziba has slandered me by saying
that I refused to come. But I know that my lord the
king is like an angel of God, so do what you think is
best. 28 All my relatives and I could expect only death
from you, my lord, but instead you have honored me
by allowing me to eat at your own table! What more
can I ask?"
29 "You've said enough," David replied. "I've decided
that you and Ziba will divide your land equally be-
tween you."
30 "Give him all of it," Mephibosheth said. "I am con-
tent just to have you safely back again, my lord the
king!"

DAVID'S KINDNESS TO BARZILLAI

31 Barzillai of Gilead had come down from Rogelim
to escort the king across the Jordan. 32 He was very
old—eighty years of age—and very wealthy. He was
the one who had provided food for the king during
his stay in Mahanaim. 33 "Come across with me and
live in Jerusalem," the king said to Barzillai. "I will
take care of you there."
34 "No," he replied, "I am far too old to go with the
king to Jerusalem. 35 I am eighty years old today, and
I can no longer enjoy anything. Food and wine are
no longer tasty, and I cannot hear the singers as they
sing. I would only be a burden to my lord the king.
36 Just to go across the Jordan River with the king is all
the honor I need! 37 Then let me return again to die in
my own town, where my father and mother are bur-
ied. But here is your servant, my son Kimham. Let him
go with my lord the king and receive whatever you
want to give him."
38 "Good," the king agreed. "Kimham will go with
me, and I will help him in any way you would like.
And I will do for you anything you want." 39 So all the
people crossed the Jordan with the king. After David
had blessed Barzillai and kissed him, Barzillai re-
turned to his own home.
40 The king then crossed over to Gilgal, taking Kim-
ham with him. All the troops of Judah and half the
troops of Israel escorted the king on his way.

AN ARGUMENT OVER THE KING

41 But all the men of Israel complained to the king,
"The men of Judah stole the king and didn't give us
the honor of helping take you, your household, and all
your men across the Jordan."
42 The men of Judah replied, "The king is one of our
own kinsmen. Why should this make you angry? We
haven't eaten any of the king's food or received any
special favors!"
43 "But there are ten tribes in Israel," the others
replied. "So we have ten times as much right to the
king as you do. What right do you have to treat us
with such contempt? Weren't we the first to speak
of bringing him back to be our king again?" The ar-
gument continued back and forth, and the men of
Judah spoke even more harshly than the men of Is-
rael.

THE REVOLT OF SHEBA

20 There happened to be a troublemaker there
named Sheba son of Bicri, a man from the tribe
of Benjamin. Sheba blew a ram's horn and began to
chant:

"Down with the dynasty of David!
We have no interest in the son of Jesse.
Come on, you men of Israel,
back to your homes!"

2 So all the men of Israel deserted David and fol-
lowed Sheba son of Bicri. But the men of Judah stayed
with their king and escorted him from the Jordan Riv-
er to Jerusalem.
3 When David came to his palace in Jerusalem, he
took the ten concubines he had left to look after the
palace and placed them in seclusion. Their needs
were provided for, but he no longer slept with them.
So each of them lived like a widow until she died.
4 Then the king told Amasa, "Mobilize the army
of Judah within three days, and report back at that
time." 5 So Amasa went out to notify Judah, but it took
him longer than the time he had been given.
6 Then David said to Abishai, "Sheba son of Bicri is
going to hurt us more than Absalom did. Quick, take
my troops and chase after him before he gets into a
fortified town where we can't reach him."
7 So Abishai and Joab,* together with the king's
bodyguard* and all the mighty warriors, set out from
Jerusalem to go after Sheba. 8 As they arrived at the
great stone in Gibeon, Amasa met them. Joab was
wearing his military tunic with a dagger strapped
to his belt. As he stepped forward to greet Amasa, he
slipped the dagger from its sheath.*

19:22 Or *my prosecutor.* **19:24** *Mephibosheth* is another name for Merib-baal. **19:26** As in Greek, Syriac, and Latin versions; Hebrew reads *I will saddle a donkey for myself.* **20:7a** Hebrew *So Joab's men.* **20:7b** Hebrew *the Kerethites and Pelethites;* also in 20:23. **20:8** Hebrew *As he stepped forward, it fell out.*

19:23 Shimei . . . "Your life will be spared." David kept the pledge he made that day. However, Shimei eventually paid for his sin at the hand of Solomon, at David's request (1 Kings 2:8-9,36-46).

19:25 Why didn't you come with me, Mephiboseth? Remembering Ziba's accusations, David questioned Mephibosheth's allegiance (16:3).

19:29 you and Ziba will divide your land. In this way, David did not have to determine whose story was true.

19:43 ten times as much right to the king. Forming 10 of 12 tribes, Israel claimed a greater share in David's kingship despite having just supported Absalom.

20:1 tribe of Benjamin. The royal house had once been Benjamite under Saul, but was forfeited by his actions. **We have no interest in the son of Jessee.** Sheba played on Israel's fear of being treated with contempt (19:43).

20:3 took the ten concubines. The concubines reminded everyone of the tragic consequences of Absalom's sin (15:16; 16:22).

9 "How are you, my cousin?" Joab said and took him by the beard with his right hand as though to kiss him. 10 Amasa didn't notice the dagger in his left hand, and Joab stabbed him in the stomach with it so that his insides gushed out onto the ground. Joab did not need to strike again, and Amasa soon died. Joab and his brother Abishai left him lying there and continued after Sheba.

11 One of Joab's young men shouted to Amasa's troops, "If you are for Joab and David, come and follow Joab." 12 But Amasa lay in his blood in the middle of the road, and Joab's man saw that everyone was stopping to stare at him. So he pulled him off the road into a field and threw a cloak over him. 13 With Amasa's body out of the way, everyone went on with Joab to capture Sheba son of Bicri.

14 Meanwhile, Sheba traveled through all the tribes of Israel and eventually came to the town of Abel-beth-maacah. All the members of his own clan, the Bicrites,* assembled for battle and followed him into the town. 15 When Joab's forces arrived, they attacked Abel-beth-maacah. They built a siege ramp against the town's fortifications and began battering down the wall. 16 But a wise woman in the town called out to Joab, "Listen to me, Joab. Come over here so I can talk to you." 17 As he approached, the woman asked, "Are you Joab?"

"I am," he replied.

So she said, "Listen carefully to your servant."

"I'm listening," he said.

18 Then she continued, "There used to be a saying, 'If you want to settle an argument, ask advice at the town of Abel.' 19 I am one who is peace loving and faithful in Israel. But you are destroying an important town in Israel.* Why do you want to devour what belongs to the LORD?"

20 And Joab replied, "Believe me, I don't want to devour or destroy your town! 21 That's not my purpose. All I want is a man named Sheba son of Bicri from the hill country of Ephraim, who has revolted against King David. If you hand over this one man to me, I will leave the town in peace."

"All right," the woman replied, "we will throw his head over the wall to you." 22 Then the woman went to all the people with her wise advice, and they cut off Sheba's head and threw it out to Joab. So he blew the ram's horn and called his troops back from the attack. They all returned to their homes, and Joab returned to the king at Jerusalem.

23 Now Joab was the commander of the army of Israel. Benaiah son of Jehoiada was captain of the king's bodyguard. 24 Adoniram* was in charge of forced labor. Jehoshaphat son of Ahilud was the royal historian. 25 Sheva was the court secretary. Zadok and Abiathar were the priests. 26 And Ira, a descendant of Jair, was David's personal priest.

DAVID AVENGES THE GIBEONITES

21 There was a famine during David's reign that lasted for three years, so David asked the LORD about it. And the LORD said, "The famine has come because Saul and his family are guilty of murdering the Gibeonites."

2 So the king summoned the Gibeonites. They were not part of Israel but were all that was left of the nation of the Amorites. The people of Israel had sworn not to kill them, but Saul, in his zeal for Israel and Judah, had tried to wipe them out. 3 David asked them, "What can I do for you? How can I make amends so that you will bless the LORD's people again?"

4 "Well, money can't settle this matter between us and the family of Saul," the Gibeonites replied. "Neither can we demand the life of anyone in Israel."

"What can I do then?" David asked. "Just tell me and I will do it for you."

5 Then they replied, "It was Saul who planned to destroy us, to keep us from having any place at all in the territory of Israel. 6 So let seven of Saul's sons be handed over to us, and we will execute them before the LORD at Gibeon, on the mountain of the LORD.*"

"All right," the king said, "I will do it." 7 The king spared Jonathan's son Mephibosheth,* who was Saul's grandson, because of the oath David and Jonathan had sworn before the LORD. 8 But he gave them Saul's two sons Armoni and Mephibosheth, whose mother was Rizpah daughter of Aiah. He also gave them the five sons of Saul's daughter Merab,* the wife of Adriel son of Barzillai from Meholah. 9 The men of Gibeon executed them on the mountain before the LORD. So all seven of them died together at the beginning of the barley harvest.

10 Then Rizpah daughter of Aiah, the mother of two of the men, spread burlap on a rock and stayed there the entire harvest season. She prevented the scavenger birds from tearing at their bodies during the day and stopped wild animals from eating them at night. 11 When David learned what Rizpah, Saul's concubine, had done, 12 he went to the people of Jabesh-gilead and retrieved the bones of Saul and his son Jonathan. (When the Philistines had killed Saul and Jonathan on Mount Gilboa, the people of Jabesh-gilead stole their bodies from the public square of Beth-shan, where the Philistines had hung them.) 13 So David obtained the bones of Saul and Jonathan, as well as the bones of the men the Gibeonites had executed.

14 Then the king ordered that they bury the bones in the tomb of Kish, Saul's father, at the town of Zela in the land of Benjamin. After that, God ended the famine in the land.

BATTLES AGAINST PHILISTINE GIANTS

15 Once again the Philistines were at war with Israel. And when David and his men were in the thick of bat-

20:14 As in Greek and Latin versions; Hebrew reads *All the Berites.* 20:19 Hebrew *a town that is a mother in Israel.* 20:24 As in Greek version (see also 1 Kgs 4:6; 5:14); Hebrew reads *Adoram.* 21:6 As in Greek version (see also 21:9); Hebrew reads *at Gibeah of Saul, the chosen of the LORD.* 21:7 *Mephibosheth* is another name for Merib-baal. 21:8 As in a few Hebrew and Greek manuscripts and Syriac version (see also 1 Sam 18:19); most Hebrew manuscripts read *Michal.*

20:10 Joab stabbed him in the stomach. Joab had a track record for treachery (3:26-30; 18:12-14). David would not let Joab's actions be forgotten or go unpunished (1 Kings 2:5-6).

21:1 because Saul and his family are guilty of murdering the Gibeonites. Saul's zeal for Israel justified ignoring the promises made by God (v. 2). Even though the Gibeonites tricked Joshua into this treaty (Josh. 9:14-15), to God a promise is a promise.

21:3 so that you will bless the LORD's people again. The tables of blessing had been turned. Through Israel all the peoples (nations) would be blessed (Gen. 12:3). Here David asked another nation to bless Israel.

21:4 Just tell me and I will do it for you. Though Saul had given the Gibeonites no rights, David was willing to do all that was necessary to make amends.

21:12 bones of Saul. The people of Jabesh-gilead had rescued the bodies of Saul and his sons from the Philistines and had buried the bones under a tamarisk tree (1 Sam. 31:11-13).

tle, David became weak and exhausted. 16 Ishbi-benob
was a descendant of the giants*; his bronze spearhead
weighed more than seven pounds,* and he was armed
with a new sword. He had cornered David and was
about to kill him. 17 But Abishai son of Zeruiah came to
David's rescue and killed the Philistine. Then David's
men declared, "You are not going out to battle with us
again! Why risk snuffing out the light of Israel?"
18 After this, there was another battle against the
Philistines at Gob. As they fought, Sibbecai from Hu-
shah killed Saph, another descendant of the giants.
19 During another battle at Gob, Elhanan son of Jair*
from Bethlehem killed the brother of Goliath of Gath.*
The handle of his spear was as thick as a weaver's beam!
20 In another battle with the Philistines at Gath,
they encountered a huge man* with six fingers on
each hand and six toes on each foot, twenty-four in
all, who was also a descendant of the giants. 21 But
when he defied and taunted Israel, he was killed by
Jonathan, the son of David's brother Shimea.*
22 These four Philistines were descendants of the gi-
ants of Gath, but David and his warriors killed them.

DAVID'S SONG OF PRAISE

22 David sang this song to the LORD on the day
the LORD rescued him from all his enemies and
from Saul. 2 He sang:

"The LORD is my rock, my fortress, and my savior;
3 my God is my rock, in whom I find protection.
He is my shield, the power that saves me,
and my place of safety.
He is my refuge, my savior,
the one who saves me from violence.
4 I called on the LORD, who is worthy of praise,
and he saved me from my enemies.

5 "The waves of death overwhelmed me;
floods of destruction swept over me.
6 The grave* wrapped its ropes around me;
death laid a trap in my path.
7 But in my distress I cried out to the LORD;
yes, I cried to my God for help.
He heard me from his sanctuary;
my cry reached his ears.

8 "Then the earth quaked and trembled.
The foundations of the heavens shook;
they quaked because of his anger.
9 Smoke poured from his nostrils;
fierce flames leaped from his mouth.
Glowing coals blazed forth from him.
10 He opened the heavens and came down;
dark storm clouds were beneath his feet.
11 Mounted on a mighty angelic being,* he flew,
soaring* on the wings of the wind.
12 He shrouded himself in darkness,
veiling his approach with dense rain clouds.
13 A great brightness shone around him,
and burning coals* blazed forth.
14 The LORD thundered from heaven;
the voice of the Most High resounded.
15 He shot arrows and scattered his enemies;
his lightning flashed, and they were confused.
16 Then at the command of the LORD,
at the blast of his breath,
the bottom of the sea could be seen,
and the foundations of the earth were laid bare.

17 "He reached down from heaven and rescued me;
he drew me out of deep waters.
18 He rescued me from my powerful enemies,
from those who hated me and were too strong
for me.
19 They attacked me at a moment when I was in
distress,
but the LORD supported me.
20 He led me to a place of safety;
he rescued me because he delights in me.
21 The LORD rewarded me for doing right;
he restored me because of my innocence.
22 For I have kept the ways of the LORD;
I have not turned from my God to follow evil.
23 I have followed all his regulations;
I have never abandoned his decrees.
24 I am blameless before God;
I have kept myself from sin.
25 The LORD rewarded me for doing right.
He has seen my innocence.

26 "To the faithful you show yourself faithful;
to those with integrity you show integrity.
27 To the pure you show yourself pure,
but to the crooked you show yourself shrewd.
28 You rescue the humble,
but your eyes watch the proud and humiliate
them.
29 O LORD, you are my lamp.
The LORD lights up my darkness.
30 In your strength I can crush an army;
with my God I can scale any wall.

31 "God's way is perfect.
All the LORD's promises prove true.
He is a shield for all who look to him for
protection.
32 For who is God except the LORD?
Who but our God is a solid rock?

21:16a Or *a descendant of the Rapha;* also in 21:18, 20, 22. **21:16b** Hebrew *300 [shekels]* [3.4 kilograms]. **21:19a** As in parallel text at 1 Chr 20:5; Hebrew reads *son of Jaare-oregim.* **21:19b** As in parallel text at 1 Chr 20:5; Hebrew reads *killed Goliath of Gath.* **21:20** As in parallel text at 1 Chr 20:6; Hebrew reads *a Midianite.* **21:21** As in parallel text at 1 Chr 20:7; Hebrew reads *Shimei,* a variant spelling of Shimea. **22:6** Hebrew *Sheol.* **22:11a** Hebrew *a cherub.* **22:11b** As in some Hebrew manuscripts (see also Ps 18:10); other Hebrew manuscripts read *appearing.* **22:13** Or *and lightning bolts.*

21:16 the giant. The Raphaites were strong, numerous, perhaps up to 8-10 feet tall, and also called Zamzummites (Deut. 2:20-21).

21:19 killed the brother of Goliath of Gath. A relative of the Goliath that David killed at Socoh in Judah (1 Sam. 17:1-3,50-54; 1 Chron. 20:5).

22:1 sang this song. David wrote this song (Ps. 18) soon after God delivered him from Saul's hand (1 Sam. 31:8) and before his humiliation with Bathsheba (12:9-10).

22:2 my rock. Like Moses, David described God as his rock (Deut. 32:4,15,18,30). David often refers to God as his rock, for example, "my rock and my Redeemer" (Ps. 19:14). It is also a prophetic reference to his descendant Jesus Christ.

22:11 Mounted on a mighty angelic being. Heavenly creatures who act as escorts and guards of the God's throne room (Gen. 3:24).

22:14 The LORD thundered from heaven. The voice of God, like thunder, strikes fear in people's hearts (Deut. 5:25-26). By His powerful voice, God created the world (Gen. 1), and by it He can shake the world (Ps. 29).

22:28 the proud and humiliate them. God humbled Nebuchadnezzar and then blessed him with new insight (Dan. 4:33-34).

33 God is my strong fortress,
and he makes my way perfect.
34 He makes me as surefooted as a deer,
enabling me to stand on mountain heights.
35 He trains my hands for battle;
he strengthens my arm to draw a bronze bow.
36 You have given me your shield of victory;
your help* has made me great.
37 You have made a wide path for my feet
to keep them from slipping.

38 "I chased my enemies and destroyed them;
I did not stop until they were conquered.
39 I consumed them;
I struck them down so they did not get up;
they fell beneath my feet.
40 You have armed me with strength for the battle;
you have subdued my enemies under my feet.
41 You placed my foot on their necks.
I have destroyed all who hated me.
42 They looked for help, but no one came to their
rescue.
They even cried to the LORD, but he refused to
answer.
43 I ground them as fine as the dust of the earth;
I trampled them* in the gutter like dirt.

44 "You gave me victory over my accusers.
You preserved me as the ruler over nations;
people I don't even know now serve me.
45 Foreign nations cringe before me;
as soon as they hear of me, they submit.
46 They all lose their courage
and come trembling* from their strongholds.

47 "The LORD lives! Praise to my Rock!
May God, the Rock of my salvation, be exalted!
48 He is the God who pays back those who harm me;
he brings down the nations under me
49 and delivers me from my enemies.
You hold me safe beyond the reach of my
enemies;
you save me from violent opponents.
50 For this, O LORD, I will praise you among the
nations;
I will sing praises to your name.
51 You give great victories to your king;
you show unfailing love to your anointed,
to David and all his descendants forever."

DAVID'S LAST WORDS

23 These are the last words of David:

"David, the son of Jesse, speaks—
David, the man who was raised up so high,
David, the man anointed by the God of Jacob,
David, the sweet psalmist of Israel.*
2 "The Spirit of the LORD speaks through me;
his words are upon my tongue.
3 The God of Israel spoke.
The Rock of Israel said to me:
'The one who rules righteously,
who rules in the fear of God,
4 is like the light of morning at sunrise,
like a morning without clouds,
like the gleaming of the sun
on new grass after rain.'

5 "Is it not my family God has chosen?
Yes, he has made an everlasting covenant with
me.
His agreement is arranged and guaranteed in
every detail.
He will ensure my safety and success.
6 But the godless are like thorns to be thrown away,
for they tear the hand that touches them.
7 One must use iron tools to chop them down;
they will be totally consumed by fire."

DAVID'S MIGHTIEST WARRIORS

8 These are the names of David's mightiest warriors.
The first was Jashobeam the Hacmonite,* who was
leader of the Three*—the three mightiest warriors
among David's men. He once used his spear to kill
800 enemy warriors in a single battle.*
9 Next in rank among the Three was Eleazar son
of Dodai, a descendant of Ahoah. Once Eleazar and
David stood together against the Philistines when the
entire Israelite army had fled.
10 He killed Philistines
until his hand was too tired to lift his sword, and the
LORD gave him a great victory that day. The rest of the
army did not return until it was time to collect the
plunder!
11 Next in rank was Shammah son of Agee from
Harar. One time the Philistines gathered at Lehi and
attacked the Israelites in a field full of lentils. The Is-
raelite army fled,
12 but Shammah* held his ground in
the middle of the field and beat back the Philistines.
So the LORD brought about a great victory.
13 Once during the harvest, when David was at the
cave of Adullam, the Philistine army was camped in
the valley of Rephaim. The Three (who were among
the Thirty—an elite group among David's fighting
men) went down to meet him there.
14 David was stay-
ing in the stronghold at the time, and a Philistine de-
tachment had occupied the town of Bethlehem.
15 David remarked longingly to his men, "Oh, how I
would love some of that good water from the well by
the gate in Bethlehem."
16 So the Three broke through

22:36 As in Dead Sea Scrolls; Masoretic Text reads *your answering.* **22:43** As in Dead Sea Scrolls (see also Ps 18:42); Masoretic Text reads *I crushed and trampled them.* **22:46** As in parallel text at Ps 18:45; Hebrew reads *come girding themselves.* **23:1** Or *the favorite subject of the songs of Israel;* or *the favorite of the Strong One of Israel.* **23:8a** As in parallel text at 1 Chr 11:11; Hebrew reads *Josheb-basshebeth the Tahkemonite.* **23:8b** As in Greek and Latin versions (see also 1 Chr 11:11); the meaning of the Hebrew is uncertain. **23:8c** As in some Greek manuscripts (see also 1 Chr 11:11); the meaning of the Hebrew is uncertain, though it might be rendered *the Three. It was Adino the Eznite who killed 800 men at one time.* **23:12** Hebrew *he.*

22:51 to your anointed. David's third-person reference to himself teaches two lessons: 1) he was saved and blessed because of his position as king, not because he was better than others; 2) all great victories (salvation) are administered by God through David's descendants. Believers declare that all the blessings of salvation come through David's son, Jesus Christ (Rom. 1:3; 2 Tim. 2:8; Rev. 22:16).

23:2 The Spirit of the LORD speaks. David's claim means that God "breathed" His words into and through David, who is credited with 73 of the 150 psalms. Second Peter 1:21 confirms that God gave biblical writers the thoughts He wanted included in His Scripture.

23:13 valley of Rephaim. The Philistines spread out in this valley on the route to Jerusalem to do battle with David's men. The Philistine garrison was at Bethlehem, David's hometown.

the Philistine lines, drew some water from the well by the gate in Bethlehem, and brought it back to David. But he refused to drink it. Instead, he poured it out as an offering to the LORD. [17] "The LORD forbid that I should drink this!" he exclaimed. "This water is as precious as the blood of these men* who risked their lives to bring it to me." So David did not drink it. These are examples of the exploits of the Three.

DAVID'S THIRTY MIGHTY MEN

[18] Abishai son of Zeruiah, the brother of Joab, was the leader of the Thirty.* He once used his spear to kill 300 enemy warriors in a single battle. It was by such feats that he became as famous as the Three. [19] Abishai was the most famous of the Thirty* and was their commander, though he was not one of the Three.

[20] There was also Benaiah son of Jehoiada, a valiant warrior* from Kabzeel. He did many heroic deeds, which included killing two champions* of Moab. Another time, on a snowy day, he chased a lion down into a pit and killed it. [21] Once, armed only with a club, he killed an imposing Egyptian warrior who was armed with a spear. Benaiah wrenched the spear from the Egyptian's hand and killed him with it. [22] Deeds like these made Benaiah as famous as the Three mightiest warriors. [23] He was more honored than the other members of the Thirty, though he was not one of the Three. And David made him captain of his bodyguard.

[24] Other members of the Thirty included:

Asahel, Joab's brother;
Elhanan son of Dodo from Bethlehem;
[25] Shammah from Harod;
Elika from Harod;
[26] Helez from Pelon*;
Ira son of Ikkesh from Tekoa;
[27] Abiezer from Anathoth;
Sibbecai* from Hushah;
[28] Zalmon from Ahoah;
Maharai from Netophah;
[29] Heled* son of Baanah from Netophah;
Ithai* son of Ribai from Gibeah (in the land of Benjamin);
[30] Benaiah from Pirathon;
Hurai* from Nahale-gaash*;
[31] Abi-albon from Arabah;
Azmaveth from Bahurim;
[32] Eliahba from Shaalbon;
the sons of Jashen;
Jonathan [33] son of Shagee* from Harar;
Ahiam son of Sharar from Harar;
[34] Eliphelet son of Ahasbai from Maacah;
Eliam son of Ahithophel from Giloh;
[35] Hezro from Carmel;
Paarai from Arba;
[36] Igal son of Nathan from Zobah;
Bani from Gad;
[37] Zelek from Ammon;
Naharai from Beeroth, the armor bearer of Joab son of Zeruiah;
[38] Ira from Jattir;
Gareb from Jattir;
[39] Uriah the Hittite.

There were thirty-seven in all.

DAVID TAKES A CENSUS

24 Once again the anger of the LORD burned against Israel, and he caused David to harm them by taking a census. "Go and count the people of Israel and Judah," the LORD told him.

[2] So the king said to Joab and the commanders* of the army, "Take a census of all the tribes of Israel—from Dan in the north to Beersheba in the south—so I may know how many people there are."

[3] But Joab replied to the king, "May the LORD your God let you live to see a hundred times as many people as there are now! But why, my lord the king, do you want to do this?"

[4] But the king insisted that they take the census, so Joab and the commanders of the army went out to count the people of Israel. [5] First they crossed the Jordan and camped at Aroer, south of the town in the valley, in the direction of Gad. Then they went on to Jazer, [6] then to Gilead in the land of Tahtim-hodshi* and to Dan-jaan and around to Sidon. [7] Then they came to the fortress of Tyre, and all the towns of the Hivites and Canaanites. Finally, they went south to Judah* as far as Beersheba.

[8] Having gone through the entire land for nine months and twenty days, they returned to Jerusalem. [9] Joab reported the number of people to the king. There were 800,000 capable warriors in Israel who could handle a sword, and 500,000 in Judah.

JUDGMENT FOR DAVID'S SIN

[10] But after he had taken the census, David's conscience began to bother him. And he said to the LORD, "I have sinned greatly by taking this census. Please forgive my guilt, LORD, for doing this foolish thing."

[11] The next morning the word of the LORD came to the prophet Gad, who was David's seer. This was

23:17 Hebrew *Shall I drink the blood of these men?* **23:18** As in a few Hebrew manuscripts and Syriac version; most Hebrew manuscripts read *the Three.* **23:19** As in Syriac version; Hebrew reads *the Three.* **23:20a** Or *son of Jehoiada, son of Ish-hai.* **23:20b** Hebrew *two of Ariel.* **23:26** As in parallel text at 1 Chr 11:27 (see also 1 Chr 27:10); Hebrew reads *from Palti.* **23:27** As in some Greek manuscripts (see also 1 Chr 11:29); Hebrew reads *Mebunnai.* **23:29a** As in some Hebrew manuscripts (see also 1 Chr 11:30); most Hebrew manuscripts read *Heleb.* **23:29b** As in parallel text at 1 Chr 11:31; Hebrew reads *Ittai.* **23:30a** As in some Greek manuscripts (see also 1 Chr 11:32); Hebrew reads *Hiddai.* **23:30b** Or *from the ravines of Gaash.* **23:33** As in parallel text at 1 Chr 11:34; Hebrew reads *Jonathan, Shammah;* some Greek manuscripts read *Jonathan son of Shammah.* **24:2** As in Greek version (see also 24:4 and 1 Chr 21:2); Hebrew reads *Joab the commander.* **24:6** Greek version reads *to Gilead and to Kadesh in the land of the Hittites.* **24:7** Or *they went to the Negev of Judah.*

23:20 Benaiah . . . many heroic deeds. An army commander with a division of 24,000 men, he was also in charge of David's personal bodyguards.

23:34 Eliam. Bathsheba's father and the son of Ahithophel, David's counselor, who joined Absalom's plot.

23:39 Uriah. Not until Nathan confronted David did he admit his sin of killing Uriah and repent (12:11-13).

24:1 Go and count the people of Israel and Judah. Just as God allowed Satan to afflict Job, he also allowed him to tempt David to take a census with sinful motives. It was not the census that displeased God but rather the condition of David's heart, relying on military muscle to defend Israel, rather than on God alone.

24:3 Joab. Joab knew that God was able to provide the necessary manpower, and he believed David should trust God.

24:9 capable warriors. David counted only men of military age. The counters began east of the Jordan River, went counterclockwise until they reached Beersheba in the south, and reported to David in Jerusalem nearly 10 months later.

the message: [12] "Go and say to David, 'This is what the
LORD says: I will give you three choices. Choose one of
these punishments, and I will inflict it on you.'"
[13] So Gad came to David and asked him, "Will you
choose three* years of famine throughout your land,
three months of fleeing from your enemies, or three
days of severe plague throughout your land? Think
this over and decide what answer I should give the
LORD who sent me."
[14] "I'm in a desperate situation!" David replied to
Gad. "But let us fall into the hands of the LORD, for
his mercy is great. Do not let me fall into human
hands."
[15] So the LORD sent a plague upon Israel that morn-
ing, and it lasted for three days.* A total of 70,000 peo-
ple died throughout the nation, from Dan in the north
to Beersheba in the south. [16] But as the angel was pre-
paring to destroy Jerusalem, the LORD relented and
said to the death angel, "Stop! That is enough!" At that
moment the angel of the LORD was by the threshing
floor of Araunah the Jebusite.
[17] When David saw the angel, he said to the LORD,
"I am the one who has sinned and done wrong! But
these people are as innocent as sheep—what have
they done? Let your anger fall against me and my
family."

DAVID BUILDS AN ALTAR

[18] That day Gad came to David and said to him, "Go up
and build an altar to the LORD on the threshing floor
of Araunah the Jebusite."
[19] So David went up to do what the LORD had com-
manded him. [20] When Araunah saw the king and his
men coming toward him, he came and bowed before
the king with his face to the ground. [21] "Why have you
come, my lord the king?" Araunah asked.
David replied, "I have come to buy your threshing
floor and to build an altar to the LORD there, so that he
will stop the plague."
[22] "Take it, my lord the king, and use it as you wish,"
Araunah said to David. "Here are oxen for the burnt
offering, and you can use the threshing boards and ox
yokes for wood to build a fire on the altar. [23] I will give
it all to you, Your Majesty, and may the LORD your God
accept your sacrifice."
[24] But the king replied to Araunah, "No, I insist on buy-
ing it, for I will not present burnt offerings to the LORD
my God that have cost me nothing." So David paid him
fifty pieces of silver* for the threshing floor and the oxen.
[25] David built an altar there to the LORD and sac-
rificed burnt offerings and peace offerings. And
the LORD answered his prayer for the land, and the
plague on Israel was stopped.

24:13 As in Greek version (see also 1 Chr 21:12); Hebrew reads *seven.* **24:15** Hebrew *for the designated time.* **24:24** Hebrew *50 shekels of silver,* about 20 ounces or 570 grams in weight.

24:16 angel was preparing. Angels' duties range from delivering joyful messages ("He isn't here! He is risen from the dead," Matt. 28:6), guarding God's people (Ps. 91:11), caring for Jesus in the desert ("angels came and took care of Jesus," Matt. 4:11), and destroying people (2 Chron. 32:21).

24:21 to buy the threshing floor. A further example of David's acceptance of responsibility for his sin. The property owner offered to give David whatever he needed for the altar and the burnt offerings, but David bought the threshing floor and the oxen. He also bought the land surrounding the threshing floor for 600 shekels, or 15 pounds of gold. This spot, Mount Moriah, was where Abraham had offered Isaac and where Solomon later built his splendid temple.

INTRODUCTION TO

1 KINGS

PERSONAL READING PLAN

- ☐ 1 Kings 1:1-53
- ☐ 1 Kings 2:1-46
- ☐ 1 Kings 3:1–4:19
- ☐ 1 Kings 4:20–5:18
- ☐ 1 Kings 6:1-38
- ☐ 1 Kings 7:1-51
- ☐ 1 Kings 8:1-66
- ☐ 1 Kings 9:1–10:13
- ☐ 1 Kings 10:14–11:25
- ☐ 1 Kings 11:26–12:33
- ☐ 1 Kings 13:1–14:20
- ☐ 1 Kings 14:21–15:32
- ☐ 1 Kings 15:33–16:34
- ☐ 1 Kings 17:1-24
- ☐ 1 Kings 18:1-46
- ☐ 1 Kings 19:1–20:34
- ☐ 1 Kings 20:35–21:29
- ☐ 1 Kings 22:1-53

AUTHOR

The author of 1 and 2 Kings is not known, but the three literary sources that are named suggest multiple authors and editors: The Book of the Acts of Solomon (1 Kings 11:41); The Book of the History of the Kings of Israel (1 Kings 14:19; 2 Kings 15:31); and The Book of the History of the Kings of Judah (1 Kings 14:29; 2 Kings 24:5).

DATE

The account of Jehoiachin's release from prison in 2 Kings 25:27-30 means that the final form of Kings was written after 561 B.C. However, the source materials could have been written at the time of the events they describe. These events span almost 400 years.

THEME

Israel's golden age—its coronation and corrosion.

HISTORICAL BACKGROUND

Solomon reaps the reward of David's military success. He inherits peace and security and so launches Israel's "Golden Age." Following Solomon's death, the country divides into two separate nations: Israel and Judah, bringing an end to this era of strength. Both nations, then, enter a period of decline.

CHARACTERISTICS

The atmosphere in the early chapters of 1 Kings is one of grandeur— displaying Solomon's wealth, wisdom, and fame. But Solomon's end is most pitiful, as he turns to foreign wives and their false gods. Jeroboam follows suit, as do other kings of northern Israel and southern Judah. All told, 19 kings in the north and 20 rulers in the south are alternately profiled in 1 Kings. Tracking the rise and fall of both kingdoms can be confusing, but it helps to remember that none of Israel's kings were faithful to God during this time and only half of Judah's rulers showed any faithfulness.

PASSAGES FOR TOPICAL GROUP STUDY

3:16-28 .... STRUGGLES and WISDOM ... Life and Death Crisis
10:23–11:13 ... TEMPTATIONS ... Overwhelmed by Temptation
12:1-24 .... ADVICE and .... Free Advice
18:16-40 .... FALSE PROPHETS and JUDGEMENT ...... Fire from Heaven

DAVID IN HIS OLD AGE

1 King David was now very old, and no matter how many blankets covered him, he could not keep warm. 2 So his advisers told him, "Let us find a young virgin to wait on you and look after you, my lord. She will lie in your arms and keep you warm."

3 So they searched throughout the land of Israel for a beautiful girl, and they found Abishag from Shunem and brought her to the king. 4 The girl was very beautiful, and she looked after the king and took care of him. But the king had no sexual relations with her.

ADONIJAH CLAIMS THE THRONE

5 About that time David's son Adonijah, whose mother was Haggith, began boasting, "I will make myself king." So he provided himself with chariots and charioteers and recruited fifty men to run in front of him. 6 Now his father, King David, had never disciplined him at any time, even by asking, "Why are you doing that?" Adonijah had been born next after Absalom, and he was very handsome.

7 Adonijah took Joab son of Zeruiah and Abiathar the priest into his confidence, and they agreed to help him become king. 8 But Zadok the priest, Benaiah son of Jehoiada, Nathan the prophet, Shimei, Rei, and David's personal bodyguard refused to support Adonijah.

9 Adonijah went to the Stone of Zoheleth* near the spring of En-rogel, where he sacrificed sheep, cattle, and fattened calves. He invited all his brothers—the other sons of King David—and all the royal officials of Judah. 10 But he did not invite Nathan the prophet or Benaiah or the king's bodyguard or his brother Solomon.

11 Then Nathan went to Bathsheba, Solomon's mother, and asked her, "Haven't you heard that Haggith's son, Adonijah, has made himself king, and our lord David doesn't even know about it? 12 If you want to save your own life and the life of your son Solomon, follow my advice. 13 Go at once to King David and say to him, 'My lord the king, didn't you make a vow and say to me, "Your son Solomon will surely be the next king and will sit on my throne"? Why then has Adonijah become king?' 14 And while you are still talking with him, I will come and confirm everything you have said."

15 So Bathsheba went into the king's bedroom. (He was very old now, and Abishag was taking care of him.) 16 Bathsheba bowed down before the king.

"What can I do for you?" he asked her.

17 She replied, "My lord, you made a vow before the LORD your God when you said to me, 'Your son Solomon will surely be the next king and will sit on my throne.' 18 But instead, Adonijah has made himself king, and my lord the king does not even know about it. 19 He has sacrificed many cattle, fattened calves, and sheep, and he has invited all the king's sons to attend the celebration. He also invited Abiathar the priest and Joab, the commander of the army. But he did not invite your servant Solomon. 20 And now, my lord the king, all Israel is waiting for you to announce who will become king after you. 21 If you do not act, my son Solomon and I will be treated as criminals as soon as my lord the king has died."

22 While she was still speaking with the king, Nathan the prophet arrived. 23 The king's officials told him, "Nathan the prophet is here to see you."

Nathan went in and bowed before the king with his face to the ground. 24 Nathan asked, "My lord the king, have you decided that Adonijah will be the next king and that he will sit on your throne? 25 Today he has sacrificed many cattle, fattened calves, and sheep, and he has invited all the king's sons to attend the celebration. He also invited the commanders of the army and Abiathar the priest. They are feasting and drinking with him and shouting, 'Long live King Adonijah!' 26 But he did not invite me or Zadok the priest or Benaiah or your servant Solomon. 27 Has my lord the king really done this without letting any of his officials know who should be the next king?"

DAVID MAKES SOLOMON KING

28 King David responded, "Call Bathsheba!" So she came back in and stood before the king. 29 And the king repeated his vow: "As surely as the LORD lives, who has rescued me from every danger, 30 your son Solomon will be the next king and will sit on my throne this very day, just as I vowed to you before the LORD, the God of Israel."

31 Then Bathsheba bowed down with her face to the ground before the king and exclaimed, "May my lord King David live forever!"

32 Then King David ordered, "Call Zadok the priest, Nathan the prophet, and Benaiah son of Jehoiada." When they came into the king's presence, 33 the king said to them, "Take Solomon and my officials down to Gihon Spring. Solomon is to ride on my own mule. 34 There Zadok the priest and Nathan the prophet are to anoint him king over Israel. Blow the ram's horn and shout, 'Long live King Solomon!' 35 Then escort him back here, and he will sit on my throne. He will succeed me as king, for I have appointed him to be ruler over Israel and Judah."

36 "Amen!" Benaiah son of Jehoiada replied. "May the LORD, the God of my lord the king, decree that it happen. 37 And may the LORD be with Solomon as he has been with you, my lord the king, and may he make Solomon's reign even greater than yours!"

38 So Zadok the priest, Nathan the prophet, Benaiah son of Jehoiada, and the king's bodyguard* took Solomon down to Gihon Spring, with Solomon riding on King David's own mule. 39 There Zadok the priest took the flask of olive oil from the sacred tent and anointed Solomon with the oil. Then they sounded the ram's

1:9 Or *to the Serpent's Stone;* Greek version supports reading *Zoheleth* as a proper name. **1:38** Hebrew *the Kerethites and Pelethites;* also in 1:44.

1:1 David was now very old. David was about 70 when he died.

1:5 Adonijah. David's fourth son, he was the oldest surviving heir to David's throne. **fifty men to run in front.** Adonijah sought to impress the people. Compare Absalom in 2 Samuel 15:1.

1:6 never disciplined him. Although David was a godly, capable leader, he neglected to properly parent his children.

1:7 Joab. David's nephew, Joab had been a brave warrior but didn't always obey David's orders; for example, he executed David's son Absalom against David's orders.

1:11 Nathan. This prophet had been David's spiritual advisor for years (see 2 Sam. 7:4-17; 12:1-14).

1:12 save your own life. It is likely that Bathsheba and Solomon would be executed if Adonijah became king.

1:14 confirm everything you have said. Nathan arranged for the two witnesses required under Mosaic law.

1:34 anoint him king. See 1 Sam. 16:13.

1:38 king's bodyguard. Originally associated with the Philistines, they became David's bodyguards.

horn and all the people shouted, "Long live King Solomon!" [40] And all the people followed Solomon into Jerusalem, playing flutes and shouting for joy. The celebration was so joyous and noisy that the earth shook with the sound.

[41] Adonijah and his guests heard the celebrating and shouting just as they were finishing their banquet. When Joab heard the sound of the ram's horn, he asked, "What's going on? Why is the city in such an uproar?"

[42] And while he was still speaking, Jonathan son of Abiathar the priest arrived. "Come in," Adonijah said to him, "for you are a good man. You must have good news."

[43] "Not at all!" Jonathan replied. "Our lord King David has just declared Solomon king! [44] The king sent him down to Gihon Spring with Zadok the priest, Nathan the prophet, and Benaiah son of Jehoiada, protected by the king's bodyguard. They had him ride on the king's own mule, [45] and Zadok and Nathan have anointed him at Gihon Spring as the new king. They have just returned, and the whole city is celebrating and rejoicing. That's what all the noise is about. [46] What's more, Solomon is now sitting on the royal throne as king. [47] And all the royal officials have gone to King David and congratulated him, saying, 'May your God make Solomon's fame even greater than your own, and may Solomon's reign be even greater than yours!' Then the king bowed his head in worship as he lay in his bed, [48] and he said, 'Praise the LORD, the God of Israel, who today has chosen a successor to sit on my throne while I am still alive to see it.'"

[49] Then all of Adonijah's guests jumped up in panic from the banquet table and quickly scattered. [50] Adonijah was afraid of Solomon, so he rushed to the sacred tent and grabbed on to the horns of the altar. [51] Word soon reached Solomon that Adonijah had seized the horns of the altar in fear, and that he was pleading, "Let King Solomon swear today that he will not kill me!"

[52] Solomon replied, "If he proves himself to be loyal, not a hair on his head will be touched. But if he makes trouble, he will die." [53] So King Solomon summoned Adonijah, and they brought him down from the altar. He came and bowed respectfully before King Solomon, who dismissed him, saying, "Go on home."

DAVID'S FINAL INSTRUCTIONS TO SOLOMON

2 As the time of King David's death approached, he gave this charge to his son Solomon:

[2] "I am going where everyone on earth must someday go. Take courage and be a man. [3] Observe the requirements of the LORD your God, and follow all his ways. Keep the decrees, commands, regulations, and laws written in the Law of Moses so that you will be successful in all you do and wherever you go. [4] If you do this, then the LORD will keep the promise he made to me. He told me, 'If your descendants live as they should and follow me faithfully with all their heart and soul, one of them will always sit on the throne of Israel.'

[5] "And there is something else. You know what Joab son of Zeruiah did to me when he murdered my two army commanders, Abner son of Ner and Amasa son of Jether. He pretended that it was an act of war, but it was done in a time of peace,* staining his belt and sandals with innocent blood.* [6] Do with him what you think best, but don't let him grow old and go to his grave in peace.*

[7] "Be kind to the sons of Barzillai of Gilead. Make them permanent guests at your table, for they took care of me when I fled from your brother Absalom.

[8] "And remember Shimei son of Gera, the man from Bahurim in Benjamin. He cursed me with a terrible curse as I was fleeing to Mahanaim. When he came down to meet me at the Jordan River, I swore by the LORD that I would not kill him. [9] But that oath does not make him innocent. You are a wise man, and you will know how to arrange a bloody death for him.*"

[10] Then David died and was buried with his ancestors in the City of David. [11] David had reigned over Israel for forty years, seven of them in Hebron and thirty-three in Jerusalem. [12] Solomon became king and sat on the throne of David his father, and his kingdom was firmly established.

SOLOMON ESTABLISHES HIS RULE

[13] One day Adonijah, whose mother was Haggith, came to see Bathsheba, Solomon's mother. "Have you come with peaceful intentions?" she asked him.

"Yes," he said, "I come in peace. [14] In fact, I have a favor to ask of you."

"What is it?" she asked.

[15] He replied, "As you know, the kingdom was rightfully mine; all Israel wanted me to be the next king. But the tables were turned, and the kingdom went to my brother instead; for that is the way the LORD wanted it. [16] So now I have just one favor to ask of you. Please don't turn me down."

"What is it?" she asked.

[17] He replied, "Speak to King Solomon on my behalf, for I know he will do anything you request. Ask him to let me marry Abishag, the girl from Shunem."

[18] "All right," Bathsheba replied. "I will speak to the king for you."

[19] So Bathsheba went to King Solomon to speak on Adonijah's behalf. The king rose from his throne to meet her, and he bowed down before her. When he

2:5a Or *He murdered them during a time of peace as revenge for deaths they had caused in time of war.* **2:5b** As in some Greek and Old Latin manuscripts; Hebrew reads *with the blood of war.* **2:6** Hebrew *don't let his white head go down to Sheol in peace.* **2.9** Hebrew *how to bring his white head down to Sheol in blood.*

1:50 the horns of the altar. The altar was a safe haven for people who had committed unintentional crimes.

1:52 loyal. Although Adonijah's sin was not unintentional, Solomon showed mercy and pardoned him.

2:1 David . . . gave this charge to his son. Giving last instructions to sons was customary (Gen. 49).

2:4 the promise he made to me. God's promise to David was unconditional. He would have a royal dynasty forever, but evil kings would not receive the benefits of walking with God (see Deut. 11:26-28). **one of them will always sit on the throne.** While Israel was divided and exiled because of disobedience to God, ultimately, the promised Messiah, an heir of David, will reign.

2:5 stained his belt . . . with innocent blood. Although Joab had served David well for many years, David instructed Solomon to deal with Joab because of his revengeful act of murdering Amasa and Abner.

2:8 Shimei. He had cursed David and thrown stones at him when David fled from Absalom (2 Sam. 16:5-11).

2:15 the kingdom was rightfully mine. Adonijah believed he should have been king and wanted compensation.

2:17 let me marry Abishag. She was in the royal harem. Adonijah's request to marry her was effectively a claim to the throne.

sat down on his throne again, the king ordered that a throne be brought for his mother, and she sat at his right hand.

20 "I have one small request to make of you," she said. "I hope you won't turn me down."

"What is it, my mother?" he asked. "You know I won't refuse you."

21 "Then let your brother Adonijah marry Abishag, the girl from Shunem," she replied.

22 "How can you possibly ask me to give Abishag to Adonijah?" King Solomon demanded. "You might as well ask me to give him the kingdom! You know that he is my older brother, and that he has Abiathar the priest and Joab son of Zeruiah on his side."

23 Then King Solomon made a vow before the LORD: "May God strike me and even kill me if Adonijah has not sealed his fate with this request. 24 The LORD has confirmed me and placed me on the throne of my father, David; he has established my dynasty as he promised. So as surely as the LORD lives, Adonijah will die this very day!" 25 So King Solomon ordered Benaiah son of Jehoiada to execute him, and Adonijah was put to death.

26 Then the king said to Abiathar the priest, "Go back to your home in Anathoth. You deserve to die, but I will not kill you now, because you carried the Ark of the Sovereign LORD for David my father and you shared all his hardships." 27 So Solomon deposed Abiathar from his position as priest of the LORD, thereby fulfilling the prophecy the LORD had given at Shiloh concerning the descendants of Eli.

28 Joab had not joined Absalom's earlier rebellion, but he had joined Adonijah's rebellion. So when Joab heard about Adonijah's death, he ran to the sacred tent of the LORD and grabbed on to the horns of the altar. 29 When this was reported to King Solomon, he sent Benaiah son of Jehoiada to execute him.

30 Benaiah went to the sacred tent of the LORD and said to Joab, "The king orders you to come out!"

But Joab answered, "No, I will die here."

So Benaiah returned to the king and told him what Joab had said.

31 "Do as he said," the king replied. "Kill him there beside the altar and bury him. This will remove the guilt of Joab's senseless murders from me and from my father's family. 32 The LORD will repay him* for the murders of two men who were more righteous and better than he. For my father knew nothing about the deaths of Abner son of Ner, commander of the army of Israel, and of Amasa son of Jether, commander of the army of Judah. 33 May their blood be on Joab and his descendants forever, and may the LORD grant peace forever to David, his descendants, his dynasty, and his throne."

34 So Benaiah son of Jehoiada returned to the sacred tent and killed Joab, and he was buried at his home in the wilderness. 35 Then the king appointed Benaiah to command the army in place of Joab, and he installed Zadok the priest to take the place of Abiathar.

36 The king then sent for Shimei and told him, "Build a house here in Jerusalem and live there. But don't step outside the city to go anywhere else. 37 On the day you so much as cross the Kidron Valley, you will surely die; and your blood will be on your own head."

38 Shimei replied, "Your sentence is fair; I will do whatever my lord the king commands." So Shimei lived in Jerusalem for a long time.

39 But three years later two of Shimei's slaves ran away to King Achish son of Maacah of Gath. When Shimei learned where they were, 40 he saddled his donkey and went to Gath to search for them. When he found them, he brought them back to Jerusalem.

41 Solomon heard that Shimei had left Jerusalem and had gone to Gath and returned. 42 So the king sent for Shimei and demanded, "Didn't I make you swear by the LORD and warn you not to go anywhere else or you would surely die? And you replied, 'The sentence is fair; I will do as you say.' 43 Then why haven't you kept your oath to the LORD and obeyed my command?"

44 The king also said to Shimei, "You certainly remember all the wicked things you did to my father, David. May the LORD now bring that evil on your own head. 45 But may I, King Solomon, receive the LORD's blessings, and may one of David's descendants always sit on this throne in the presence of the LORD." 46 Then, at the king's command, Benaiah son of Jehoiada took Shimei outside and killed him.

So the kingdom was now firmly in Solomon's grip.

SOLOMON ASKS FOR WISDOM

3 Solomon made an alliance with Pharaoh, the king of Egypt, and married one of his daughters. He brought her to live in the City of David until he could finish building his palace and the Temple of the LORD and the wall around the city. 2 At that time the people of Israel sacrificed their offerings at local places of worship, for a temple honoring the name of the LORD had not yet been built.

3 Solomon loved the LORD and followed all the decrees of his father, David, except that Solomon, too, offered sacrifices and burned incense at the local places of worship. 4 The most important of these places of worship was at Gibeon, so the king went there and sacrificed 1,000 burnt offerings. 5 That night the LORD appeared to Solomon in a dream, and God said, "What do you want? Ask, and I will give it to you!"

6 Solomon replied, "You showed great and faithful love to your servant my father, David, because he was honest and true and faithful to you. And you have continued to show this great and faithful love to him today by giving him a son to sit on his throne.

7 "Now, O LORD my God, you have made me king instead of my father, David, but I am like a little child who doesn't know his way around. 8 And here I am in the midst of your own chosen people, a nation so great and numerous they cannot be counted! 9 Give

2:32 Hebrew *will return his blood on his own head.*

2:22 ask me to give him the kingdom. Solomon perceived the plot.

2:26 Abiathar. The high priest had served David faithfully during Saul's pursuit of David (see 1 Sam. 22:20-23).

2:27 fulfilling the prophecy of the LORD. God had said Eli's line of priests would be cut off because of their wickedness (see 1 Sam. 2:30-35).

2:28 grabbed on to the horns. The refuge was only for those who had committed unintentional sins (see Ex. 21:14).

2:46 took Shimei . . . and killed him. Shimei had violated the terms of his house arrest. He deserved death for his sins against David (see verses 8-9).

3:2 local places of worship. The Law forbade sacrificing anywhere besides the tabernacle, yet Solomon and the Israelites sacrificed at these Canaanite shrines.

3:5 LORD appeared . . . in a dream. God also revealed His will in dreams to Jacob (Gen. 28:10-15; 31:11), Joseph (Gen. 37:5-8), and Nebuchadnezzar (Dan. 2:28-30).

3:7 I am like a little child. Solomon was about 20 when he became king.

me an understanding heart so that I can govern your
people well and know the difference between right
and wrong. For who by himself is able to govern this
great people of yours?"
10 The Lord was pleased that Solomon had asked for
wisdom. 11 So God replied, "Because you have asked
for wisdom in governing my people with justice and
have not asked for a long life or wealth or the death of
your enemies—12 I will give you what you asked for!
I will give you a wise and understanding heart such
as no one else has had or ever will have! 13 And I will
also give you what you did not ask for—riches and
fame! No other king in all the world will be compared
to you for the rest of your life! 14 And if you follow me
and obey my decrees and my commands as your fa-
ther, David, did, I will give you a long life."
15 Then Solomon woke up and realized it had been a
dream. He returned to Jerusalem and stood before the
Ark of the Lord's Covenant, where he sacrificed burnt
offerings and peace offerings. Then he invited all his
officials to a great banquet.

SOLOMON JUDGES WISELY

16 Some time later two prostitutes came to the king
to have an argument settled. 17 "Please, my lord," one
of them began, "this woman and I live in the same
house. I gave birth to a baby while she was with me
in the house. 18 Three days later this woman also had
a baby. We were alone; there were only two of us in
the house.
19 "But her baby died during the night when she
rolled over on it. 20 Then she got up in the night and
took my son from beside me while I was asleep. She
laid her dead child in my arms and took mine to sleep
beside her. 21 And in the morning when I tried to nurse
my son, he was dead! But when I looked more closely
in the morning light, I saw that it wasn't my son at all."
22 Then the other woman interrupted, "It certainly
was your son, and the living child is mine."
"No," the first woman said, "the living child is mine,
and the dead one is yours." And so they argued back
and forth before the king.
23 Then the king said, "Let's get the facts straight.
Both of you claim the living child is yours, and each
says that the dead one belongs to the other. 24 All
right, bring me a sword." So a sword was brought to
the king.
25 Then he said, "Cut the living child in two, and give
half to one woman and half to the other!"
26 Then the woman who was the real mother of the
living child, and who loved him very much, cried out,
"Oh no, my lord! Give her the child—please do not kill
him!"
But the other woman said, "All right, he will be nei-
ther yours nor mine; divide him between us!"
27 Then the king said, "Do not kill the child, but give
him to the woman who wants him to live, for she is
his mother!"

LIFE AND DEATH CRISIS

1. How did your parents settle disputes between you and your brothers or sisters?

1 KINGS 3:16-28

2. Why would the King of Israel bother to settle a dispute between prostitutes? Whose life was actually on the line in this dispute?
3. Why did Solomon suggest cutting the baby in two? What did that suggestion accomplish?
4. How did Solomon know which woman was the real mother of the living baby?
5. For what crisis do you need the wisdom of Solomon?

28 When all Israel heard the king's decision, the
people were in awe of the king, for they saw the wis-
dom God had given him for rendering justice.

SOLOMON'S OFFICIALS AND GOVERNORS

4 King Solomon now ruled over all Israel, 2 and
these were his high officials:

Azariah son of Zadok was the priest.
3 Elihoreph and Ahijah, the sons of Shisha, were
court secretaries.
Jehoshaphat son of Ahilud was the royal historian.
4 Benaiah son of Jehoiada was commander of the
army.
Zadok and Abiathar were priests.
5 Azariah son of Nathan was in charge of the
district governors.
Zabud son of Nathan, a priest, was a trusted
adviser to the king.
6 Ahishar was manager of the palace property.
Adoniram son of Abda was in charge of forced
labor.

7 Solomon also had twelve district governors who
were over all Israel. They were responsible for pro-
viding food for the king's household. Each of them ar-
ranged provisions for one month of the year. 8 These
are the names of the twelve governors:

Ben-hur, in the hill country of Ephraim.
9 Ben-deker, in Makaz, Shaalbim, Beth-shemesh,
and Elon-bethhanan.
10 Ben-hesed, in Arubboth, including Socoh and all
the land of Hepher.
11 Ben-abinadab, in all of Naphoth-dor.* (He
was married to Taphath, one of Solomon's
daughters.)

4:11 Hebrew *Naphath-dor,* a variant spelling of Naphoth-dor.

3:15 stood before the Ark of the LORD's Covenant. Instead of making an offering to God at the high place, Solomon went to the tabernacle. Since only the high priest could approach the ark, the king stood outside facing the ark and made his offerings.

4:4 Benaiah. Commander in chief of the entire army, he did not participate in Adonijah's plots. He had participated in Solomon's anointing at Gihon and had executed Adonijah.

4:5 Azariah. He was in charge of the 12 district officers in verses 8-19. This is not Azariah the priest (verse 2).

4:6 manager of the palace property. Ahishar supervised the servants and other palace workers.

4:7 twelve district governors. Solomon needed revenue to support his military forces. He divided Israel into 12 districts with a governor for each who collected taxes for the royal household. Two of the governors were Solomon's sons-in-law.

12 Baana son of Ahilud, in Taanach and Megiddo,
all of Beth-shan* near Zarethan below Jezreel,
and all the territory from Beth-shan to Abel-
meholah and over to Jokmeam.
13 Ben-geber, in Ramoth-gilead, including the Towns
of Jair (named for Jair of the tribe of Manasseh*)
in Gilead, and in the Argob region of Bashan,
including sixty large fortified towns with
bronze bars on their gates.
14 Ahinadab son of Iddo, in Mahanaim.
15 Ahimaaz, in Naphtali. (He was married to
Basemath, another of Solomon's daughters.)
16 Baana son of Hushai, in Asher and in Aloth.
17 Jehoshaphat son of Paruah, in Issachar.
18 Shimei son of Ela, in Benjamin.
19 Geber son of Uri, in the land of Gilead,* including
the territories of King Sihon of the Amorites and
King Og of Bashan.
There was also one governor over the land of
Judah.*

SOLOMON'S PROSPERITY AND WISDOM

20 The people of Judah and Israel were as numerous as
the sand on the seashore. They were very contented,
with plenty to eat and drink.
21 *Solomon ruled over all
the kingdoms from the Euphrates River* in the north
to the land of the Philistines and the border of Egypt
in the south. The conquered peoples of those lands
sent tribute money to Solomon and continued to serve
him throughout his lifetime.
22 The daily food requirements for Solomon's palace
were 150 bushels of choice flour and 300 bushels of
meal*;
23 also 10 oxen from the fattening pens, 20 pas-
ture-fed cattle, 100 sheep or goats, as well as deer, ga-
zelles, roe deer, and choice poultry.*
24 Solomon's dominion extended over all the king-
doms west of the Euphrates River, from Tiphsah
to Gaza. And there was peace on all his borders.
25 During the lifetime of Solomon, all of Judah and Is-
rael lived in peace and safety. And from Dan in the
north to Beersheba in the south, each family had its
own home and garden.*
26 Solomon had 4,000* stalls for his chariot horses,
and he had 12,000 horses.*
27 The district governors faithfully provided food
for King Solomon and his court; each made sure noth-
ing was lacking during the month assigned to him.
28 They also brought the necessary barley and straw
for the royal horses in the stables.
29 God gave Solomon very great wisdom and under-
standing, and knowledge as vast as the sands of the
seashore.
30 In fact, his wisdom exceeded that of all
the wise men of the East and the wise men of Egypt.
31 He was wiser than anyone else, including Ethan the
Ezrahite and the sons of Mahol—Heman, Calcol, and
Darda. His fame spread throughout all the surround-
ing nations.
32 He composed some 3,000 proverbs and
wrote 1,005 songs.
33 He could speak with authority
about all kinds of plants, from the great cedar of Leb-
anon to the tiny hyssop that grows from cracks in a
wall. He could also speak about animals, birds, small
creatures, and fish.
34 And kings from every nation
sent their ambassadors to listen to the wisdom of Sol-
omon.

PREPARATIONS FOR BUILDING THE TEMPLE

5 1 *King Hiram of Tyre had always been a loyal
friend of David. When Hiram learned that David's
son Solomon was the new king of Israel, he sent am-
bassadors to congratulate him.
2 Then Solomon sent this message back to Hiram:
3 "You know that my father, David, was not able to
build a Temple to honor the name of the LORD his
God because of the many wars waged against him
by surrounding nations. He could not build until
the LORD gave him victory over all his enemies.
4 But now the LORD my God has given me peace
on every side; I have no enemies, and all is well.
5 So I am planning to build a Temple to honor the
name of the LORD my God, just as he had instructed
my father, David. For the LORD told him, 'Your son,
whom I will place on your throne, will build the
Temple to honor my name.'
6 "Therefore, please command that cedars from
Lebanon be cut for me. Let my men work alongside
yours, and I will pay your men whatever wages
you ask. As you know, there is no one among us
who can cut timber like you Sidonians!"

7 When Hiram received Solomon's message, he was
very pleased and said, "Praise the LORD today for giv-
ing David a wise son to be king of the great nation of
Israel."
8 Then he sent this reply to Solomon:

"I have received your message, and I will supply
all the cedar and cypress timber you need.
9 My
servants will bring the logs from the Lebanon
mountains to the Mediterranean Sea* and make
them into rafts and float them along the coast to
whatever place you choose. Then we will break
the rafts apart so you can carry the logs away.
You can pay me by supplying me with food for my
household."

10 So Hiram supplied as much cedar and cypress
timber as Solomon desired.
11 In return, Solomon sent
him an annual payment of 100,000 bushels* of wheat

4:12 Hebrew *Beth-shean,* a variant spelling of Beth-shan; also in 4:12b. **4:13** Hebrew *Jair son of Manasseh;* compare 1 Chr 2:22. **4:19a** Greek version reads *of Gad;* compare 4:13. **4:19b** As in some Greek manuscripts; Hebrew lacks *of Judah.* The meaning of the Hebrew is uncertain. **4:21a** Verses 4:21-34 are numbered 5:1-14 in Hebrew text. **4:21b** Hebrew *the river;* also in 4:24. **4:22** Hebrew *30 cors* [6.6 kiloliters] *of choice flour and 60 cors* [13.2 kiloliters] *of meal.* **4:23** Or *and fattened geese.* **4:25** Hebrew *each family lived under its own grapevine and under its own fig tree.* **4:26a** As in some Greek manuscripts (see also 2 Chr 9:25); Hebrew reads *40,000.* **4:26b** Or *12,000 charioteers.* **5:1** Verses 5:1-18 are numbered 5:15-32 in Hebrew text. **5:9** Hebrew *the sea.* **5:11a** Hebrew *20,000 cors* [4,400 kiloliters].

4:13 sixty large fortified towns. The Israelites had captured these from Og, king of Bashan (see Deut. 3:3-5).
4:21 from the Euphrates River . . . to the land of the Philistines. Solomon's kingdom reached from the Euphrates River on the east, Egypt on the south, and the land of the Philistines on the west.
4:30 the East. Probably Mesopotamia.
4:32 proverbs . . . songs. Some are preserved for us in the books of Proverbs, Ecclesiastes, and the Song of Songs.
5:1 Hiram. An ally of David, he had ruled Tyre for 34 years and had provided workers and supplies, including cedars from Lebanon east of Tyre, to build David's palace.
5:5 Your son . . . will build the Temple. David made preparations for the temple after God promised him that his son would build it (see 2 Sam. 7:1-17).
5:9 supplying me with food for my household. Wheat and olive oil were not plentiful in or around Tyre.

for his household and 110,000 gallons* of pure olive
oil. [12] So the LORD gave wisdom to Solomon, just as he
had promised. And Hiram and Solomon made a for-
mal alliance of peace.
[13] Then King Solomon conscripted a labor force of
30,000 men from all Israel. [14] He sent them to Lebanon
in shifts, 10,000 every month, so that each man would
be one month in Lebanon and two months at home. Ad-
oniram was in charge of this labor force. [15] Solomon also
had 70,000 common laborers, 80,000 quarry workers
in the hill country, [16] and 3,600* foremen to supervise
the work. [17] At the king's command, they quarried large
blocks of high-quality stone and shaped them to make
the foundation of the Temple. [18] Men from the city of
Gebal helped Solomon's and Hiram's builders prepare
the timber and stone for the Temple.

SOLOMON BUILDS THE TEMPLE

6 It was in midspring, in the month of Ziv,* during
the fourth year of Solomon's reign, that he be-
gan to construct the Temple of the LORD. This was
480 years after the people of Israel were rescued from
their slavery in the land of Egypt.
[2] The Temple that King Solomon built for the LORD
was 90 feet long, 30 feet wide, and 45 feet high.* [3] The
entry room at the front of the Temple was 30 feet*
wide, running across the entire width of the Temple.
It projected outward 15 feet* from the front of the
Temple. [4] Solomon also made narrow recessed win-
dows throughout the Temple.
[5] He built a complex of rooms against the outer
walls of the Temple, all the way around the sides and
rear of the building. [6] The complex was three stories
high, the bottom floor being $7\frac{1}{2}$ feet wide, the second
floor 9 feet wide, and the top floor $10\frac{1}{2}$ feet wide.* The
rooms were connected to the walls of the Temple by
beams resting on ledges built out from the wall. So the
beams were not inserted into the walls themselves.
[7] The stones used in the construction of the Temple
were finished at the quarry, so there was no sound of
hammer, ax, or any other iron tool at the building site.
[8] The entrance to the bottom floor* was on the
south side of the Temple. There were winding stairs
going up to the second floor, and another flight of
stairs between the second and third floors. [9] After
completing the Temple structure, Solomon put in a
ceiling made of cedar beams and planks. [10] As already
stated, he built a complex of rooms along the sides of
the building, attached to the Temple walls by cedar
timbers. Each story of the complex was $7\frac{1}{2}$ feet* high.
[11] Then the LORD gave this message to Solomon:
[12] "Concerning this Temple you are building, if you
keep all my decrees and regulations and obey all
my commands, I will fulfill through you the promise
I made to your father, David. [13] I will live among the
Israelites and will never abandon my people Israel."

THE TEMPLE'S INTERIOR

[14] So Solomon finished building the Temple. [15] The
entire inside, from floor to ceiling, was paneled with
wood. He paneled the walls and ceilings with cedar,
and he used planks of cypress for the floors. [16] He
partitioned off an inner sanctuary—the Most Holy
Place—at the far end of the Temple. It was 30 feet
deep and was paneled with cedar from floor to ceil-
ing. [17] The main room of the Temple, outside the Most
Holy Place, was 60 feet* long. [18] Cedar paneling com-
pletely covered the stone walls throughout the Tem-
ple, and the paneling was decorated with carvings of
gourds and open flowers.
[19] He prepared the inner sanctuary at the far end
of the Temple, where the Ark of the LORD's Covenant
would be placed. [20] This inner sanctuary was 30 feet
long, 30 feet wide, and 30 feet high. He overlaid the
inside with solid gold. He also overlaid the altar made
of cedar.* [21] Then Solomon overlaid the rest of the Tem-
ple's interior with solid gold, and he made gold chains
to protect the entrance* to the Most Holy Place. [22] So
he finished overlaying the entire Temple with gold, in-
cluding the altar that belonged to the Most Holy Place.
[23] He made two cherubim of wild olive* wood, each
15 feet* tall, and placed them in the inner sanctuary.
[24] The wingspan of each of the cherubim was 15 feet,
each wing being $7\frac{1}{2}$ feet* long. [25] The two cherubim
were identical in shape and size; [26] each was 15 feet
tall. [27] He placed them side by side in the inner sanc-
tuary of the Temple. Their outspread wings reached
from wall to wall, while their inner wings touched at
the center of the room. [28] He overlaid the two cheru-
bim with gold.
[29] He decorated all the walls of the inner sanctuary
and the main room with carvings of cherubim, palm
trees, and open flowers. [30] He overlaid the floor in
both rooms with gold.
[31] For the entrance to the inner sanctuary, he made
double doors of wild olive wood with five-sided door-
posts.* [32] These double doors were decorated with
carvings of cherubim, palm trees, and open flowers.
The doors, including the decorations of cherubim and
palm trees, were overlaid with gold.
[33] Then he made four-sided doorposts of wild olive
wood for the entrance to the Temple. [34] There were
two folding doors of cypress wood, and each door was
hinged to fold back upon itself. [35] These doors were

5:11b As in Greek version, which reads *20,000 baths* [420 kiloliters] (see also 2 Chr 2:10); Hebrew reads *20 cors,* about 1,000 gallons or 4.4 kiloliters in volume. **5:16** As in some Greek manuscripts (see also 2 Chr 2:2, 18); Hebrew reads *3,300.* **6:1** Hebrew *It was in the month of Ziv, which is the second month.* This month of the ancient Hebrew lunar calendar usually occurs within the months of April and May. **6:2** Hebrew *60 cubits* [27.6 meters] *long, 20 cubits* [9.2 meters] *wide, and 30 cubits* [13.8 meters] *high.* **6:3a** Hebrew *20 cubits* [9.2 meters]; also in 6:16, 20. **6:3b** Hebrew *10 cubits* [4.6 meters]. **6:6** Hebrew *the bottom floor being 5 cubits* [2.3 meters] *wide, the second floor 6 cubits* [2.8 meters] *wide, and the top floor 7 cubits* [3.2 meters] *wide.* **6:8** As in Greek version; Hebrew reads *middle floor.* **6:10** Hebrew *5 cubits* [2.3 meters]. **6:17** Hebrew *40 cubits* [18.4 meters]. **6:20** Or *overlaid the altar with cedar.* The meaning of the Hebrew is uncertain. **6:21** Or *to draw curtains across.* The meaning of the Hebrew is uncertain. **6:23a** Or *pine;* Hebrew reads *oil tree;* also in 6:31, 33. **6:23b** Hebrew *10 cubits* [4.6 meters]; also in 6:24, 26. **6:24** Hebrew *5 cubits* [2.3 meters]. **6:31** The meaning of the Hebrew is uncertain.

5:17 large blocks of . . . stone. Stonecutters cut massive limestone blocks out of the quarry in the hills north of Jerusalem.
6:1 480 years. This helps set the time of the exodus at 1446 B.C.
6:2 Temple. The temple was twice the size of the tabernacle.
6:12 if you keep all my decrees. God reaffirms the promise He had made to David (2 Sam. 7:13). If Solomon would obey God, it would bring blessing on his nation. Israel lost out on some of this fellowship because of Solomon's later sin.
6:19 Ark of the LORD's Covenant. This symbolized God's presence among His people and contained the two stone tablets of the Ten Commandments (see Deut. 10:1-5).
6:23 two cherubim. Creatures with the lions' bodies, human faces, and huge wings.
6:34 doors. The doors folded in half to open.

decorated with carvings of cherubim, palm trees, and open flowers—all overlaid evenly with gold.

36 The walls of the inner courtyard were built so that there was one layer of cedar beams between every three layers of finished stone.

37 The foundation of the LORD's Temple was laid in midspring, in the month of Ziv,* during the fourth year of Solomon's reign. 38 The entire building was completed in every detail by midautumn, in the month of Bul,* during the eleventh year of his reign. So it took seven years to build the Temple.

SOLOMON BUILDS HIS PALACE

7 Solomon also built a palace for himself, and it took him thirteen years to complete the construction.

2 One of Solomon's buildings was called the Palace of the Forest of Lebanon. It was 150 feet long, 75 feet wide, and 45 feet high.* There were four rows of cedar pillars, and great cedar beams rested on the pillars. 3 The hall had a cedar roof. Above the beams on the pillars were forty-five side rooms,* arranged in three tiers of fifteen each. 4 On each end of the long hall were three rows of windows facing each other. 5 All the doorways and doorposts* had rectangular frames and were arranged in sets of three, facing each other.

6 Solomon also built the Hall of Pillars, which was 75 feet long and 45 feet wide.* There was a porch in front, along with a canopy supported by pillars.

7 Solomon also built the throne room, known as the Hall of Justice, where he sat to hear legal matters. It was paneled with cedar from floor to ceiling.* 8 Solomon's living quarters surrounded a courtyard behind this hall, and they were constructed the same way. He also built similar living quarters for Pharaoh's daughter, whom he had married.

9 From foundation to eaves, all these buildings were built from huge blocks of high-quality stone, cut with saws and trimmed to exact measure on all sides. 10 Some of the huge foundation stones were 15 feet long, and some were 12 feet* long. 11 The blocks of high-quality stone used in the walls were also cut to measure, and cedar beams were also used. 12 The walls of the great courtyard were built so that there was one layer of cedar beams between every three layers of finished stone, just like the walls of the inner courtyard of the LORD's Temple with its entry room.

FURNISHINGS FOR THE TEMPLE

13 King Solomon then asked for a man named Huram* to come from Tyre. 14 He was half Israelite, since his mother was a widow from the tribe of Naphtali, and his father had been a craftsman in bronze from Tyre. Huram was extremely skillful and talented in any work in bronze, and he came to do all the metal work for King Solomon.

15 Huram cast two bronze pillars, each 27 feet tall and 18 feet in circumference.* 16 For the tops of the pillars he cast bronze capitals, each 7½ feet* tall. 17 Each capital was decorated with seven sets of latticework and interwoven chains. 18 He also encircled the latticework with two rows of pomegranates to decorate the capitals over the pillars. 19 The capitals on the columns inside the entry room were shaped like water lilies, and they were six feet* tall. 20 The capitals on the two pillars had 200 pomegranates in two rows around them, beside the rounded surface next to the latticework. 21 Huram set the pillars at the entrance of the Temple, one toward the south and one toward the north. He named the one on the south Jakin, and the one on the north Boaz.* 22 The capitals on the pillars were shaped like water lilies. And so the work on the pillars was finished.

23 Then Huram cast a great round basin, 15 feet across from rim to rim, called the Sea. It was 7½ feet deep and about 45 feet in circumference.* 24 It was encircled just below its rim by two rows of decorative gourds. There were about six gourds per foot* all the way around, and they were cast as part of the basin.

25 The Sea was placed on a base of twelve bronze oxen,* all facing outward. Three faced north, three faced west, three faced south, and three faced east, and the Sea rested on them. 26 The walls of the Sea were about three inches* thick, and its rim flared out like a cup and resembled a water lily blossom. It could hold about 11,000 gallons* of water.

27 Huram also made ten bronze water carts, each 6 feet long, 6 feet wide, and 4½ feet tall.* 28 They were constructed with side panels braced with crossbars. 29 Both the panels and the crossbars were decorated with carved lions, oxen, and cherubim. Above and below the lions and oxen were wreath decorations. 30 Each of these carts had four bronze wheels and bronze axles. There were supporting posts for the bronze basins at the corners of the carts; these supports were decorated on each side with carvings of wreaths. 31 The top of each cart had a rounded frame for the basin. It projected 1½ feet* above the cart's top like a round pedestal, and its opening was 2¼ feet* across; it was decorated on the outside with carvings of wreaths. The panels of the carts were square, not

6:37 Hebrew *was laid in the month of Ziv.* This month of the ancient Hebrew lunar calendar usually occurs within the months of April and May. **6:38** Hebrew *by the month of Bul, which is the eighth month.* This month of the ancient Hebrew lunar calendar usually occurs within the months of October and November. **7:2** Hebrew *100 cubits* [46 meters] *long, 50 cubits* [23 meters] *wide, and 30 cubits* [13.8 meters] *high.* **7:3** Or *45 rafters,* or *45 beams,* or *45 pillars.* The architectural details in 7:2-6 can be interpreted in many different ways. **7:5** Greek version reads *windows.* **7:6** Hebrew *50 cubits* [23 meters] *long and 30 cubits* [13.8 meters] *wide.* **7:7** As in Syriac version and Latin Vulgate; Hebrew reads *from floor to floor.* **7:10** Hebrew *10 cubits* [4.6 meters] . . . *8 cubits* [3.7 meters]. **7:13** Hebrew *Hiram* (also in 7:40, 45); compare 2 Chr 2:13. This is not the same person mentioned in 5:1. **7:15** Hebrew *18 cubits* [8.3 meters] *tall and 12 cubits* [5.5 meters] *in circumference.* **7:16** Hebrew *5 cubits* [2.3 meters]. **7:19** Hebrew *4 cubits* [1.8 meters]; also in 7:38. **7:21** *Jakin* probably means "he establishes"; *Boaz* probably means "in him is strength." **7:23** Hebrew *10 cubits* [4.6 meters] *across. . . . 5 cubits* [2.3 meters] *deep and 30 cubits* [13.8 meters] *in circumference.* **7:24** Or *20 gourds per meter;* Hebrew reads *10 per cubit.* **7:25** Hebrew *12 oxen;* compare 2 Kgs 16:17, which specifies *bronze oxen.* **7:26a** Hebrew *a handbreadth* [8 centimeters]. **7:26b** Hebrew *2,000 baths* [42 kiloliters]. **7:27** Hebrew *4 cubits* [1.8 meters] *long, 4 cubits wide, and 3 cubits* [1.4 meters] *high.* **7:31a** Hebrew *a cubit* [46 centimeters]. **7:31b** Hebrew *1½ cubits* [69 centimeters]; also in 7:32.

6:36 inner courtyard. Only the priests could use this courtyard.
7:2 Palace of the Forest of Lebanon. Lebanese cedar was used extensively throughout this palace. It was 11,250 square feet—four times the size of the temple.
7:8 living quarters. Solomon's residence and a residence for Pharaoh's daughter, his wife. They were all attached.
7:9 saws. Limestone can be cut with a saw as it is quarried, but it hardens after exposure to the air.
7:15 bronze pillars. These pillars stood near the temple entrance.
7:23 great round basin. This was a large wash basin for the priests. It also served as a reservoir for the temple.
7:27 10 bronze water carts. The carts were used during the butchering of animal sacrifices (2 Chron. 4:6). A basin holding 220 gallons of water rested on each cart.

round. 32 Under the panels were four wheels that were connected to axles that had been cast as one unit with the cart. The wheels were 2¼ feet in diameter 33 and were similar to chariot wheels. The axles, spokes, rims, and hubs were all cast from molten bronze.

34 There were handles at each of the four corners of the carts, and these, too, were cast as one unit with the cart. 35 Around the top of each cart was a rim nine inches wide.* The corner supports and side panels were cast as one unit with the cart. 36 Carvings of cherubim, lions, and palm trees decorated the panels and corner supports wherever there was room, and there were wreaths all around. 37 All ten water carts were the same size and were made alike, for each was cast from the same mold.

38 Huram also made ten smaller bronze basins, one for each cart. Each basin was six feet across and could hold 220 gallons* of water. 39 He set five water carts on the south side of the Temple and five on the north side. The great bronze basin called the Sea was placed near the southeast corner of the Temple. 40 He also made the necessary washbasins, shovels, and bowls.

So at last Huram completed everything King Solomon had assigned him to make for the Temple of the LORD:

41 the two pillars;
the two bowl-shaped capitals on top of the pillars;
the two networks of interwoven chains that decorated the capitals;
42 the 400 pomegranates that hung from the chains on the capitals (two rows of pomegranates for each of the chain networks that decorated the capitals on top of the pillars);
43 the ten water carts holding the ten basins;
44 the Sea and the twelve oxen under it;
45 the ash buckets, the shovels, and the bowls.

Huram made all these things of burnished bronze for the Temple of the LORD, just as King Solomon had directed. 46 The king had them cast in clay molds in the Jordan Valley between Succoth and Zarethan. 47 Solomon did not weigh all these things because there were so many; the weight of the bronze could not be measured.

48 Solomon also made all the furnishings of the Temple of the LORD:

the gold altar;
the gold table for the Bread of the Presence;
49 the lampstands of solid gold, five on the south and five on the north, in front of the Most Holy Place;
the flower decorations, lamps, and tongs—all of gold;
50 the small bowls, lamp snuffers, bowls, ladles, and incense burners—all of solid gold;
the doors for the entrances to the Most Holy Place and the main room of the Temple, with their fronts overlaid with gold.

51 So King Solomon finished all his work on the Temple of the LORD. Then he brought all the gifts his father, David, had dedicated—the silver, the gold, and the various articles—and he stored them in the treasuries of the LORD's Temple.

THE ARK BROUGHT TO THE TEMPLE

8 Solomon then summoned to Jerusalem the elders of Israel and all the heads of the tribes—the leaders of the ancestral families of the Israelites. They were to bring the Ark of the LORD's Covenant to the Temple from its location in the City of David, also known as Zion. 2 So all the men of Israel assembled before King Solomon at the annual Festival of Shelters, which is held in early autumn in the month of Ethanim.*

3 When all the elders of Israel arrived, the priests picked up the Ark. 4 The priests and Levites brought up the Ark of the LORD along with the special tent* and all the sacred items that had been in it. 5 There, before the Ark, King Solomon and the entire community of Israel sacrificed so many sheep, goats, and cattle that no one could keep count!

6 Then the priests carried the Ark of the LORD's Covenant into the inner sanctuary of the Temple—the Most Holy Place—and placed it beneath the wings of the cherubim. 7 The cherubim spread their wings over the Ark, forming a canopy over the Ark and its carrying poles. 8 These poles were so long that their ends could be seen from the Holy Place, which is in front of the Most Holy Place, but not from the outside. They are still there to this day. 9 Nothing was in the Ark except the two stone tablets that Moses had placed in it at Mount Sinai,* where the LORD made a covenant with the people of Israel when they left the land of Egypt.

10 When the priests came out of the Holy Place, a thick cloud filled the Temple of the LORD. 11 The priests could not continue their service because of the cloud, for the glorious presence of the LORD filled the Temple of the LORD.

SOLOMON PRAISES THE LORD

12 Then Solomon prayed, "O LORD, you have said that you would live in a thick cloud of darkness. 13 Now I have built a glorious Temple for you, a place where you can live forever!*"

7:35 Hebrew *half a cubit wide* [23 centimeters]. **7:38** Hebrew *40 baths* [840 liters]. **8:2** Hebrew *at the festival in the month Ethanim, which is the seventh month.* The Festival of Shelters began on the fifteenth day of the seventh month of the ancient Hebrew lunar calendar. This day occurred in late September, October, or early November. **8:4** Hebrew *the Tent of Meeting;* i.e., the tent mentioned in 2 Sam 6:17 and 1 Chr 16:1. **8:9** Hebrew *at Horeb,* another name for Sinai. **8:13** Some Greek texts add the line *Is this not written in the Book of Jashar?*

7:40 shovels. These were used to remove ashes from the altar.
7:46 Succoth and Zarethan. An area about 35 miles north of the Dead Sea, east of the Jordan River.
7:48 gold altar . . . table. These replaced the altar of incense (Ex. 30:2-4) and the table of the bread of the Presence (Ex. 25:23-30) in the tabernacle.
7:51 gifts . . . dedicated. David had already prepared and dedicated furnishings for the temple (2 Sam. 8:11).
8:1 bring the Ark. The ark was brought from its temporary shelter in Jerusalem. From now on, the temple would be the permanent center of worship.
8:4 priests and Levites. God required that the ark be carried by the priests and Levites (Num. 4:15; Deut. 10:8).
8:8 poles . . . could be seen. The poles by which the priests carried the ark were left in their rings (Ex. 25:15).
8:9 two stone tablets. The tablets containing the Ten Commandments were kept in the ark. The pot of manna (Ex. 16:33-34) and Aaron's rod (Num. 17:10) may have been lost by Solomon's time.
8:10 a thick cloud. Just as a cloud had covered the tabernacle, a cloud, the symbol of God's glory, filled the temple. This is sometimes called "shekinah glory," a visible representation of God's presence with His people.

14 Then the king turned around to the entire com-
munity of Israel standing before him and gave this
blessing: 15 "Praise the LORD, the God of Israel, who has
kept the promise he made to my father, David. For he
told my father, 16 'From the day I brought my people
Israel out of Egypt, I have never chosen a city among
any of the tribes of Israel as the place where a Temple
should be built to honor my name. But I have chosen
David to be king over my people Israel.'"

17 Then Solomon said, "My father, David, wanted to
build this Temple to honor the name of the LORD, the
God of Israel. 18 But the LORD told him, 'You wanted to
build the Temple to honor my name. Your intention
is good, 19 but you are not the one to do it. One of your
own sons will build the Temple to honor me.'

20 "And now the LORD has fulfilled the promise he
made, for I have become king in my father's place,
and now I sit on the throne of Israel, just as the LORD
promised. I have built this Temple to honor the name
of the LORD, the God of Israel. 21 And I have prepared
a place there for the Ark, which contains the cov-
enant that the LORD made with our ancestors when
he brought them out of Egypt."

SOLOMON'S PRAYER OF DEDICATION

22 Then Solomon stood before the altar of the LORD in
front of the entire community of Israel. He lifted his
hands toward heaven, 23 and he prayed,

"O LORD, God of Israel, there is no God like you in
all of heaven above or on the earth below. You
keep your covenant and show unfailing love to all
who walk before you in wholehearted devotion.
24 You have kept your promise to your servant Da-
vid, my father. You made that promise with your
own mouth, and with your own hands you have
fulfilled it today.

25 "And now, O LORD, God of Israel, carry out the
additional promise you made to your servant David,
my father. For you said to him, 'If your descendants
guard their behavior and faithfully follow me as
you have done, one of them will always sit on the
throne of Israel.' 26 Now, O God of Israel, fulfill this
promise to your servant David, my father.

27 "But will God really live on earth? Why, even
the highest heavens cannot contain you. How
much less this Temple I have built! 28 Nevertheless,
listen to my prayer and my plea, O LORD my God.
Hear the cry and the prayer that your servant is
making to you today. 29 May you watch over this
Temple night and day, this place where you have
said, 'My name will be there.' May you always
hear the prayers I make toward this place. 30 May
you hear the humble and earnest requests from
me and your people Israel when we pray toward
this place. Yes, hear us from heaven where you
live, and when you hear, forgive.

31 "If someone wrongs another person and is
required to take an oath of innocence in front of
your altar in this Temple, 32 then hear from heaven
and judge between your servants—the accuser
and the accused. Punish the guilty as they deserve.
Acquit the innocent because of their innocence.

33 "If your people Israel are defeated by their en-
emies because they have sinned against you, and
if they turn to you and acknowledge your name
and pray to you here in this Temple, 34 then hear
from heaven and forgive the sin of your people
Israel and return them to this land you gave their
ancestors.

35 "If the skies are shut up and there is no rain
because your people have sinned against you, and
if they pray toward this Temple and acknowledge
your name and turn from their sins because you
have punished them, 36 then hear from heaven
and forgive the sins of your servants, your people
Israel. Teach them to follow the right path, and
send rain on your land that you have given to your
people as their special possession.

37 "If there is a famine in the land or a plague or
crop disease or attacks of locusts or caterpillars, or
if your people's enemies are in the land besieging
their towns—whatever disaster or disease there
is—38 and if your people Israel pray about their
troubles, raising their hands toward this Temple,
39 then hear from heaven where you live, and for-
give. Give your people what their actions deserve,
for you alone know each human heart. 40 Then
they will fear you as long as they live in the land
you gave to our ancestors.

41 "In the future, foreigners who do not belong to
your people Israel will hear of you. They will come
from distant lands because of your name, 42 for
they will hear of your great name and your strong
hand and your powerful arm. And when they
pray toward this Temple, 43 then hear from heaven
where you live, and grant what they ask of you.
In this way, all the people of the earth will come to
know and fear you, just as your own people Israel
do. They, too, will know that this Temple I have
built honors your name.

44 "If your people go out where you send them
to fight their enemies, and if they pray to the LORD
by turning toward this city you have chosen and
toward this Temple I have built to honor your
name, 45 then hear their prayers from heaven and
uphold their cause.

46 "If they sin against you—and who has never
sinned?—you might become angry with them
and let their enemies conquer them and take
them captive to their land far away or near. 47 But
in that land of exile, they might turn to you in
repentance and pray, 'We have sinned, done evil,
and acted wickedly.' 48 If they turn to you with

8:23 no God like you. This was an especially good reminder in view of the pagan deities of the surrounding Canaanites.

8:25 descendants . . . faithfully follow me. Solomon knew the need for his royal descendants to be faithful to God.

8:27 this Temple I have built. Since God is infinite, no building—not even a magnificent one—can contain Him. And yet God chooses to dwell among His people.

8:33 defeated by their enemies. Sin against God could cause defeat in battle (see Lev. 26:36-39; Josh. 7:11-12).

8:34 Israel . . . to this land. One of the consequences of sin against God was being scattered in foreign lands (see Lev. 26:41-45).

8:37 plague or crop disease. God allows His people to suffer trouble in order to restore relationships and renew their commitment to Him. Good things result from that. Not all disasters or diseases are the result of sin (John 9:3), but this verse lists some of the troubles sin brings.

8:40 fear you. Experiencing God produces a sense of fear or reverence that helps us to obey God.

8:42 your great name. Solomon knew that those who heard of God's power would be impressed and would believe (see Deut. 3:24). In this way, Solomon hoped that news of God's greatness would spread all over the earth.

their whole heart and soul in the land of their
enemies and pray toward the land you gave to
their ancestors—toward this city you have cho-
sen, and toward this Temple I have built to honor
your name—49 then hear their prayers and their
petition from heaven where you live, and uphold
their cause. 50 Forgive your people who have
sinned against you. Forgive all the offenses they
have committed against you. Make their captors
merciful to them, 51 for they are your people—your
special possession—whom you brought out of the
iron-smelting furnace of Egypt.
52 "May your eyes be open to my requests and
to the requests of your people Israel. May you
hear and answer them whenever they cry out
to you. 53 For when you brought our ancestors
out of Egypt, O Sovereign LORD, you told your
servant Moses that you had set Israel apart from
all the nations of the earth to be your own special
possession."

THE DEDICATION OF THE TEMPLE

54 When Solomon finished making these prayers and
petitions to the LORD, he stood up in front of the al-
tar of the LORD, where he had been kneeling with his
hands raised toward heaven. 55 He stood and in a loud
voice blessed the entire congregation of Israel:
56 "Praise the LORD who has given rest to his people
Israel, just as he promised. Not one word has failed
of all the wonderful promises he gave through his
servant Moses. 57 May the LORD our God be with us as
he was with our ancestors; may he never leave us or
abandon us. 58 May he give us the desire to do his will
in everything and to obey all the commands, decrees,
and regulations that he gave our ancestors. 59 And
may these words that I have prayed in the presence
of the LORD be before him constantly, day and night,
so that the LORD our God may give justice to me and
to his people Israel, according to each day's needs.
60 Then people all over the earth will know that the
LORD alone is God and there is no other. 61 And may
you be completely faithful to the LORD our God. May
you always obey his decrees and commands, just as
you are doing today."
62 Then the king and all Israel with him offered
sacrifices to the LORD. 63 Solomon offered to the LORD
a peace offering of 22,000 cattle and 120,000 sheep
and goats. And so the king and all the people of Israel
dedicated the Temple of the LORD.
64 That same day the king consecrated the central
area of the courtyard in front of the LORD's Temple. He
offered burnt offerings, grain offerings, and the fat of
peace offerings there, because the bronze altar in the
LORD's presence was too small to hold all the burnt offer-
ings, grain offerings, and the fat of the peace offerings.
65 Then Solomon and all Israel celebrated the Festi-
val of Shelters* in the presence of the LORD our God. A
large congregation had gathered from as far away as
Lebo-hamath in the north and the Brook of Egypt in
the south. The celebration went on for fourteen days
in all—seven days for the dedication of the altar and
seven days for the Festival of Shelters.* 66 After the
festival was over,* Solomon sent the people home.
They blessed the king and went to their homes joyful
and glad because the LORD had been good to his ser-
vant David and to his people Israel.

THE LORD'S RESPONSE TO SOLOMON

9 So Solomon finished building the Temple of the
LORD, as well as the royal palace. He completed
everything he had planned to do. 2 Then the LORD
appeared to Solomon a second time, as he had done
before at Gibeon. 3 The LORD said to him,

"I have heard your prayer and your petition. I
have set this Temple apart to be holy—this place
you have built where my name will be honored
forever. I will always watch over it, for it is dear to
my heart.
4 "As for you, if you will follow me with integrity
and godliness, as David your father did, obeying
all my commands, decrees, and regulations, 5 then
I will establish the throne of your dynasty over
Israel forever. For I made this promise to your fa-
ther, David: 'One of your descendants will always
sit on the throne of Israel.'
6 "But if you or your descendants abandon me
and disobey the commands and decrees I have
given you, and if you serve and worship other
gods, 7 then I will uproot Israel from this land that
I have given them. I will reject this Temple that
I have made holy to honor my name. I will make
Israel an object of mockery and ridicule among
the nations. 8 And though this Temple is impres-
sive now, all who pass by will be appalled and will
gasp in horror. They will ask, 'Why did the LORD
do such terrible things to this land and to this
Temple?'
9 "And the answer will be, 'Because his people
abandoned the LORD their God, who brought their
ancestors out of Egypt, and they worshiped other
gods instead and bowed down to them. That is
why the LORD has brought all these disasters on
them.'"

SOLOMON'S AGREEMENT WITH HIRAM

10 It took Solomon twenty years to build the LORD's
Temple and his own royal palace. At the end of that
time, 11 he gave twenty towns in the land of Galilee to
King Hiram of Tyre. (Hiram had previously provided
all the cedar and cypress timber and gold that Sol-
omon had requested.) 12 But when Hiram came from
Tyre to see the towns Solomon had given him, he was
not at all pleased with them. 13 "What kind of towns

8:65a Hebrew *the festival;* see note on 8:2. **8:65b** Hebrew *seven days and seven days, fourteen days;* compare parallel text at 2 Chr 7:8-10.
8:66 Hebrew *On the eighth day,* probably referring to the day following the seven-day Festival of Shelters; compare parallel text at 2 Chr 7:9-10.

8:52 whenever they cry out to you. Solomon summarized his prayer by asking God to always listen to His people, despite their sin.

8:53 your own special possession. This is another reference to God's special love for Israel. (See also Ex. 19:5-6; Ps. 135:4.)

8:58 May he give us the desire. Solomon prays for God's sovereign grace (see Ps. 119:36; Jer. 31:33).

9:4-5 if you follow me with integrity. This involved attitudes, actions, and words that were submissive to God's instructions. God said He would provide rulers of Israel through Solomon if he would obey Him.

9:9 Because his people abandoned the LORD their God. People would know that Israel suffered because of its idolatry. God's warnings were clear. He knew how easy it would be for Solomon, his descendants, and the people of Israel to be seduced by other gods.

9:11 he gave . . . to Hiram. Hiram had provided cedar, pine, the equivalent of 9,000 pounds of gold for the temple.

9:12 he was not at all pleased with them. The towns were near unproductive land and did not meet with Hiram's approval.

are these, my brother?" he asked. So Hiram called that
area Cabul (which means "worthless"), as it is still
known today. 14 Nevertheless, Hiram paid* Solomon
9,000 pounds* of gold.

SOLOMON'S MANY ACHIEVEMENTS

15 This is the account of the forced labor that King
Solomon conscripted to build the LORD's Temple, the
royal palace, the supporting terraces,* the wall of Je-
rusalem, and the cities of Hazor, Megiddo, and Gezer.
16 (Pharaoh, the king of Egypt, had attacked and cap-
tured Gezer, killing the Canaanite population and
burning it down. He gave the city to his daughter as
a wedding gift when she married Solomon. 17 So Sol-
omon rebuilt the city of Gezer.) He also built up the
towns of Lower Beth-horon, 18 Baalath, and Tamar*
in the wilderness within his land. 19 He built towns
as supply centers and constructed towns where his
chariots and horses* could be stationed. He built
everything he desired in Jerusalem and Lebanon and
throughout his entire realm.

20 There were still some people living in the land
who were not Israelites, including Amorites, Hit-
tites, Perizzites, Hivites, and Jebusites. 21 These were
descendants of the nations whom the people of Is-
rael had not completely destroyed.* So Solomon
conscripted them as slaves, and they serve as forced
laborers to this day. 22 But Solomon did not conscript
any of the Israelites for forced labor. Instead, he as-
signed them to serve as fighting men, government
officials, officers and captains in his army, command-
ers of his chariots, and charioteers. 23 Solomon ap-
pointed 550 of them to supervise the people working
on his various projects.

24 Solomon moved his wife, Pharaoh's daughter,
from the City of David to the new palace he had built
for her. Then he constructed the supporting terraces.

25 Three times each year Solomon presented burnt
offerings and peace offerings on the altar he had built
for the LORD. He also burned incense to the LORD. And
so he finished the work of building the Temple.

26 King Solomon also built a fleet of ships at Ezion-
geber, a port near Elath* in the land of Edom, along
the shore of the Red Sea.* 27 Hiram sent experienced
crews of sailors to sail the ships with Solomon's men.
28 They sailed to Ophir and brought back to Solomon
some sixteen tons* of gold.

VISIT OF THE QUEEN OF SHEBA

10 When the queen of Sheba heard of Solomon's
fame, which brought honor to the name of the
LORD,* she came to test him with hard questions. 2 She
arrived in Jerusalem with a large group of attendants
and a great caravan of camels loaded with spices,
large quantities of gold, and precious jewels. When
she met with Solomon, she talked with him about
everything she had on her mind. 3 Solomon had an-
swers for all her questions; nothing was too hard for
the king to explain to her. 4 When the queen of Sheba
realized how very wise Solomon was, and when she
saw the palace he had built, 5 she was overwhelmed.
She was also amazed at the food on his tables, the or-
ganization of his officials and their splendid clothing,
the cup-bearers, and the burnt offerings Solomon
made at the Temple of the LORD.

6 She exclaimed to the king, "Everything I heard
in my country about your achievements* and wis-
dom is true! 7 I didn't believe what was said until I
arrived here and saw it with my own eyes. In fact, I
had not heard the half of it! Your wisdom and pros-
perity are far beyond what I was told. 8 How happy
your people* must be! What a privilege for your of-
ficials to stand here day after day, listening to your
wisdom! 9 Praise the LORD your God, who delights
in you and has placed you on the throne of Isra-
el. Because of the LORD's eternal love for Israel, he
has made you king so you can rule with justice and
righteousness."

10 Then she gave the king a gift of 9,000 pounds* of
gold, great quantities of spices, and precious jewels.
Never again were so many spices brought in as those
the queen of Sheba gave to King Solomon.

11 (In addition, Hiram's ships brought gold from
Ophir, and they also brought rich cargoes of red san-
dalwood* and precious jewels. 12 The king used the
sandalwood to make railings for the Temple of the
LORD and the royal palace, and to construct lyres and
harps for the musicians. Never before or since has
there been such a supply of sandalwood.)

13 King Solomon gave the queen of Sheba whatever
she asked for, besides all the customary gifts he had
so generously given. Then she and all her attendants
returned to their own land.

SOLOMON'S WEALTH AND SPLENDOR

14 Each year Solomon received about 25 tons* of gold.
15 This did not include the additional revenue he re-
ceived from merchants and traders, all the kings of
Arabia, and the governors of the land.

16 King Solomon made 200 large shields of ham-
mered gold, each weighing more than fifteen pounds.*
17 He also made 300 smaller shields of hammered gold,
each weighing nearly four pounds.* The king placed
these shields in the Palace of the Forest of Lebanon.

9:14a Or *For Hiram had paid.* **9:14b** Hebrew *120 talents* [4,000 kilograms]. **9:15** Hebrew *the millo;* also in 9:24. The meaning of the Hebrew is uncertain. **9:18** An alternate reading in the Masoretic Text reads *Tadmor.* **9:19** Or *and charioteers.* **9:21** The Hebrew term used here refers to the complete consecration of things or people to the LORD, either by destroying them or by giving them as an offering. **9:26a** As in Greek version (see also 2 Kgs 14:22; 16:6); Hebrew reads *Eloth,* a variant spelling of Elath. **9:26b** Hebrew *sea of reeds.* **9:28** Hebrew *420 talents* [14 metric tons]. **10:1** Or *which was due to the name of the LORD.* The meaning of the Hebrew is uncertain. **10:6** Hebrew *your words.* **10:8** Greek and Syriac versions and Latin Vulgate read *your wives.* **10:10** Hebrew *120 talents* [4,000 kilograms]. **10:11** Hebrew *almug wood;* also in 10:12. **10:14** Hebrew *666 talents* [23 metric tons]. **10:16** Hebrew *600 [shekels] of gold* [6.8 kilograms]. **10:17** Hebrew *3 minas* [1.8 kilograms].

9:15 supporting terraces. Probably large level areas between hills. He also built a wall around Jerusalem that doubled the size of the city.

9:20 not Israelites . . . Amorites . . . Jebusites. These were descendants of the conquered Canaanites.

9:25 Three times each year . . . burnt offerings. The occasions were the Festival of Unleavened Bread, the Festival of Harvest, and the Festival of Booths—the major feasts of Israel (see Ex. 23:14-16). Solomon led his people in worship.

10:1 queen of Sheba. This is modern Yemen in Arabia, about 1,200 miles from Jerusalem. It was a prosperous trading country. Solomon's traders were able to go east and south by water and probably brought him news of this country. **heard of Solomon's fame.** Solomon's legendary wisdom attracted many people. Sages from many countries visited him and learned that his wisdom came from God.

10:9 Praise. The queen of Sheba acknowledged Solomon's God, as Hiram had done in 5:7. Whether she became a worshiper or merely admired Solomon's giftedness is unknown.

18 Then the king made a huge throne, decorated
with ivory and overlaid with fine gold. 19 The throne
had six steps and a rounded back. There were arm-
rests on both sides of the seat, and the figure of a lion
stood on each side of the throne. 20 There were also
twelve other lions, one standing on each end of the
six steps. No other throne in all the world could be
compared with it!
21 All of King Solomon's drinking cups were solid
gold, as were all the utensils in the Palace of the For-
est of Lebanon. They were not made of silver, for sil-
ver was considered worthless in Solomon's day!
22 The king had a fleet of trading ships of Tarshish
that sailed with Hiram's fleet. Once every three years
the ships returned, loaded with gold, silver, ivory,
apes, and peacocks.*
23 So King Solomon became richer and wiser than
any other king on earth. 24 People from every nation
came to consult him and to hear the wisdom God had
given him. 25 Year after year everyone who visited
brought him gifts of silver and gold, clothing, weap-
ons, spices, horses, and mules.
26 Solomon built up a huge force of chariots and
horses.* He had 1,400 chariots and 12,000 horses.
He stationed some of them in the chariot cities and
some near him in Jerusalem. 27 The king made silver
as plentiful in Jerusalem as stone. And valuable ce-
dar timber was as common as the sycamore-fig trees
that grow in the foothills of Judah.* 28 Solomon's hors-
es were imported from Egypt* and from Cilicia*; the
king's traders acquired them from Cilicia at the stan-
dard price. 29 At that time chariots from Egypt could
be purchased for 600 pieces of silver,* and horses for
150 pieces of silver.* They were then exported to the
kings of the Hittites and the kings of Aram.

OVERWHELMED BY TEMPTATION

1. Finish the sentence: "The one with the most toys ________________": (a) wins, (b) sins, (c) is lucky, (d) must be God's favorite.

1 KINGS 10:23–11:13

2. What was Solomon's biggest problem: His wealth? His women? His will? His worship?
3. Where did Solomon's great wisdom come from (10:24)? In what ways was Solomon's success as a king completely dependent upon God?
4. In what ways does your success in life depend upon God? What does God require from you?
5. What things in life tempt you to ignore God's commands? Are you avoiding those temptations or flirting with them?

SOLOMON'S MANY WIVES

11 Now King Solomon loved many foreign women.
Besides Pharaoh's daughter, he married women
from Moab, Ammon, Edom, Sidon, and from among
the Hittites. 2 The LORD had clearly instructed the peo-
ple of Israel, "You must not marry them, because they
will turn your hearts to their gods." Yet Solomon in-
sisted on loving them anyway. 3 He had 700 wives of
royal birth and 300 concubines. And in fact, they did
turn his heart away from the LORD.
4 In Solomon's old age, they turned his heart to wor-
ship other gods instead of being completely faithful
to the LORD his God, as his father, David, had been.
5 Solomon worshiped Ashtoreth, the goddess of the Si-
donians, and Molech,* the detestable god of the Am-
monites. 6 In this way, Solomon did what was evil in
the LORD's sight; he refused to follow the LORD com-
pletely, as his father, David, had done.
7 On the Mount of Olives, east of Jerusalem,* he even
built a pagan shrine for Chemosh, the detestable god
of Moab, and another for Molech, the detestable god
of the Ammonites. 8 Solomon built such shrines for all
his foreign wives to use for burning incense and sac-
rificing to their gods.
9 The LORD was very angry with Solomon, for his
heart had turned away from the LORD, the God of Isra-
el, who had appeared to him twice. 10 He had warned
Solomon specifically about worshiping other gods,
but Solomon did not listen to the LORD's command.
11 So now the LORD said to him, "Since you have not
kept my covenant and have disobeyed my decrees, I
will surely tear the kingdom away from you and give
it to one of your servants. 12 But for the sake of your fa-
ther, David, I will not do this while you are still alive.
I will take the kingdom away from your son. 13 And
even so, I will not take away the entire kingdom; I will
let him be king of one tribe, for the sake of my servant
David and for the sake of Jerusalem, my chosen city."

SOLOMON'S ADVERSARIES

14 Then the LORD raised up Hadad the Edomite, a
member of Edom's royal family, to be Solomon's ad-
versary. 15 Years before, David had defeated Edom.
Joab, his army commander, had stayed to bury some
of the Israelite soldiers who had died in battle. While
there, they killed every male in Edom. 16 Joab and the
army of Israel had stayed there for six months, kill-
ing them.
17 But Hadad and a few of his father's royal officials
escaped and headed for Egypt. (Hadad was just a boy
at the time.) 18 They set out from Midian and went to
Paran, where others joined them. Then they trav-
eled to Egypt and went to Pharaoh, who gave them a
home, food, and some land. 19 Pharaoh grew very fond
of Hadad, and he gave him his wife's sister in mar-
riage—the sister of Queen Tahpenes. 20 She bore him
a son named Genubath. Tahpenes raised him* in Pha-
raoh's palace among Pharaoh's own sons.

10:22 Or *and baboons.* **10:26** Or *charioteers;* also in 10:26b. **10:27** Hebrew *the Shephelah.* **10:28a** Possibly *Muzur,* a district near Cilicia; also in 10:29. **10:28b** Hebrew *Kue,* probably another name for Cilicia. **10:29a** Hebrew *600 [shekels] of silver,* about 15 pounds or 6.8 kilograms in weight. **10:29b** Hebrew *150 [shekels],* about 3.8 pounds or 1.7 kilograms in weight. **11:5** Hebrew *Milcom,* a variant spelling of Molech; also in 11:33. **11:7** Hebrew *On the mountain east of Jerusalem.* **11:20** As in Greek version; Hebrew reads *weaned him.*

11:1 loved many foreign women. God forbade a king multiple wives (see Deut. 17:17). He also forbade marrying foreign women. Solomon's pagan wives led him into idolatry.

11:5 Ashtoreth. Canaanite goddess of fertility and war whose worship involved sexual rites. **Molech.** Worship included child sacrifices, which was strictly forbidden (see Lev. 18:21).

11:6 as his father . . . done. David never worshiped false gods and always repented when he sinned.

21 When the news reached Hadad in Egypt that David and his commander Joab were both dead, he said to Pharaoh, "Let me return to my own country."

22 "Why?" Pharaoh asked him. "What do you lack here that makes you want to go home?"

"Nothing," he replied. "But even so, please let me return home."

23 God also raised up Rezon son of Eliada as Solomon's adversary. Rezon had fled from his master, King Hadadezer of Zobah, 24 and had become the leader of a gang of rebels. After David conquered Hadadezer, Rezon and his men fled to Damascus, where he became king. 25 Rezon was Israel's bitter adversary for the rest of Solomon's reign, and he made trouble, just as Hadad did. Rezon hated Israel intensely and continued to reign in Aram.

JEROBOAM REBELS AGAINST SOLOMON

26 Another rebel leader was Jeroboam son of Nebat, one of Solomon's own officials. He came from the town of Zeredah in Ephraim, and his mother was Zeruah, a widow.

27 This is the story behind his rebellion. Solomon was rebuilding the supporting terraces* and repairing the walls of the city of his father, David. 28 Jeroboam was a very capable young man, and when Solomon saw how industrious he was, he put him in charge of the labor force from the tribes of Ephraim and Manasseh, the descendants of Joseph.

29 One day as Jeroboam was leaving Jerusalem, the prophet Ahijah from Shiloh met him along the way. Ahijah was wearing a new cloak. The two of them were alone in a field, 30 and Ahijah took hold of the new cloak he was wearing and tore it into twelve pieces. 31 Then he said to Jeroboam, "Take ten of these pieces, for this is what the LORD, the God of Israel, says: 'I am about to tear the kingdom from the hand of Solomon, and I will give ten of the tribes to you! 32 But I will leave him one tribe for the sake of my servant David and for the sake of Jerusalem, which I have chosen out of all the tribes of Israel. 33 For Solomon has* abandoned me and worshiped Ashtoreth, the goddess of the Sidonians; Chemosh, the god of Moab; and Molech, the god of the Ammonites. He has not followed my ways and done what is pleasing in my sight. He has not obeyed my decrees and regulations as David his father did.

34 "'But I will not take the entire kingdom from Solomon at this time. For the sake of my servant David, the one whom I chose and who obeyed my commands and decrees, I will keep Solomon as leader for the rest of his life. 35 But I will take the kingdom away from his son and give ten of the tribes to you. 36 His son will have one tribe so that the descendants of David my servant will continue to reign, shining like a lamp in Jerusalem, the city I have chosen to be the place for my name. 37 And I will place you on the throne of Israel, and you will rule over all that your heart desires. 38 If you listen to what I tell you and follow my ways and do whatever I consider to be right, and if you obey my decrees and commands, as my servant David did, then I will always be with you. I will establish an enduring dynasty for you as I did for David, and I will give Israel to you. 39 Because of Solomon's sin I will punish the descendants of David—though not forever.'"

40 Solomon tried to kill Jeroboam, but he fled to King Shishak of Egypt and stayed there until Solomon died.

SUMMARY OF SOLOMON'S REIGN

41 The rest of the events in Solomon's reign, including all his deeds and his wisdom, are recorded in *The Book of the Acts of Solomon.* 42 Solomon ruled in Jerusalem over all Israel for forty years. 43 When he died, he was buried in the City of David, named for his father. Then his son Rehoboam became the next king.

THE NORTHERN TRIBES REVOLT

12 Rehoboam went to Shechem, where all Israel had gathered to make him king. 2 When Jeroboam son of Nebat heard of this, he returned from Egypt,* for he had fled to Egypt to escape from King Solomon. 3 The leaders of Israel summoned him, and Jeroboam and the whole assembly of Israel went to speak with Rehoboam. 4 "Your father was a hard master," they said. "Lighten the harsh labor demands and heavy taxes that your father imposed on us. Then we will be your loyal subjects."

5 Rehoboam replied, "Give me three days to think this over. Then come back for my answer." So the people went away.

6 Then King Rehoboam discussed the matter with the older men who had counseled his father, Solomon. "What is your advice?" he asked. "How should I answer these people?"

7 The older counselors replied, "If you are willing to be a servant to these people today and give them a favorable answer, they will always be your loyal subjects."

8 But Rehoboam rejected the advice of the older men and instead asked the opinion of the young men who had grown up with him and were now his advisers. 9 "What is your advice?" he asked them. "How should I answer these people who want me to lighten the burdens imposed by my father?"

10 The young men replied, "This is what you should tell those complainers who want a lighter burden: 'My little finger is thicker than my father's waist! 11 Yes, my father laid heavy burdens on you, but I'm

11:27 Hebrew *the millo.* The meaning of the Hebrew is uncertain. **11:33** As in Greek, Syriac, and Latin Vulgate; Hebrew reads *For they have.* **12:2** As in Greek version and Latin Vulgate (see also 2 Chr 10:2); Hebrew reads *he lived in Egypt.*

11:26 another rebel leader was Jeroboam. Solomon trusted Jeroboam, who supervised the labor force of Ephraim and Manasseh, but Jeroboam knew of discontent among the laborers.

11:31-32 ten of the tribes. The twelfth tribe may be Simeon, which became part of Judah. Benjamin may have served as a buffer area between Israel and Judah, linked occasionally with the Northern Kingdom.

11:36 David . . . shining like a lamp in Jerusalem. As forerunners of Jesus the kings in ancient Israel were to act as light in a dark pagan world. God remembered His promise to David despite the chastening Solomon had brought on himself.

11:38 I will establish an enduring dynasty. God gave a promise to Jeroboam that was similar to David's, but for Jeroboam it was conditional: only if he obeyed God.

11:39 not forever. Always faithful to His promises, God would restore David's line to the throne in Jesus Christ (see Jer. 30:8-10).

12:1 All Israel had gathered. Shechem was a northern city. The northern tribes were willing to accept Jeroboam, but he had to meet them halfway.

12:4 we will be your loyal subjects. In later years, Solomon weighed the Israelites down with heavy taxes and pressed them into labor gangs (4:27-28; 5:13-16). The northern tribes were willing to accept Solomon's son as their king on the condition that there be less work.

FREE ADVICE

1. What issue divides the students in your school or on your team? Where do you stand on this issue?

1 KINGS 12:1-24

2. Why do you think Rehoboam chose his friends' advice: He didn't trust old people? He gave in to peer pressure? God made him?
3. Do you listen more to the advice of your parents, teachers, and coaches . . . or to your friends? Why?
4. Where do you usually go for advice? What do you do if you don't like what you hear?
5. Since giving your life to God, what has changed in the way you see things? In the way you make decisions?

---

going to make them even heavier! My father beat you
with whips, but I will beat you with scorpions!'"
12 Three days later Jeroboam and all the people re-
turned to hear Rehoboam's decision, just as the king
had ordered. 13 But Rehoboam spoke harshly to the peo-
ple, for he rejected the advice of the older counselors
14 and followed the counsel of his younger advisers. He
told the people, "My father laid heavy burdens on you,
but I'm going to make them even heavier! My father
beat you with whips, but I will beat you with scorpions!"
15 So the king paid no attention to the people. This
turn of events was the will of the LORD, for it fulfilled
the LORD's message to Jeroboam son of Nebat through
the prophet Ahijah from Shiloh.
16 When all Israel realized that the king had refused
to listen to them, they responded,

"Down with the dynasty of David!
We have no interest in the son of Jesse.
Back to your homes, O Israel!
Look out for your own house, O David!"

So the people of Israel returned home. 17 But Re-
hoboam continued to rule over the Israelites who
lived in the towns of Judah.
18 King Rehoboam sent Adoniram,* who was in
charge of forced labor, to restore order, but the peo-
ple of Israel stoned him to death. When this news
reached King Rehoboam, he quickly jumped into his
chariot and fled to Jerusalem. 19 And to this day the
northern tribes of Israel have refused to be ruled by a
descendant of David.
20 When the people of Israel learned of Jeroboam's
return from Egypt, they called an assembly and made
him king over all Israel. So only the tribe of Judah re-
mained loyal to the family of David.

SHEMAIAH'S PROPHECY

21 When Rehoboam arrived at Jerusalem, he mobilized
the men of Judah and the tribe of Benjamin—180,000
select troops—to fight against the men of Israel and
to restore the kingdom to himself.
22 But God said to Shemaiah, the man of God, 23 "Say
to Rehoboam son of Solomon, king of Judah, and to all
the people of Judah and Benjamin, and to the rest of
the people, 24 'This is what the LORD says: Do not fight
against your relatives, the Israelites. Go back home,
for what has happened is my doing!'" So they obeyed
the message of the LORD and went home, as the LORD
had commanded.

JEROBOAM MAKES GOLD CALVES

25 Jeroboam then built up the city of Shechem in the
hill country of Ephraim, and it became his capital.
Later he went and built up the town of Peniel.*
26 Jeroboam thought to himself, "Unless I am care-
ful, the kingdom will return to the dynasty of David.
27 When these people go to Jerusalem to offer sacrific-
es at the Temple of the LORD, they will again give their
allegiance to King Rehoboam of Judah. They will kill
me and make him their king instead."
28 So on the advice of his counselors, the king made
two gold calves. He said to the people,* "It is too much
trouble for you to worship in Jerusalem. Look, Israel,
these are the gods who brought you out of Egypt!"
29 He placed these calf idols in Bethel and in Dan—
at either end of his kingdom. 30 But this became a
great sin, for the people worshiped the idols, traveling
as far north as Dan to worship the one there.
31 Jeroboam also erected buildings at the pagan
shrines and ordained priests from the common peo-
ple—those who were not from the priestly tribe of
Levi. 32 And Jeroboam instituted a religious festival
in Bethel, held on the fifteenth day of the eighth
month,* in imitation of the annual Festival of Shel-
ters in Judah. There at Bethel he himself offered sac-
rifices to the calves he had made, and he appointed
priests for the pagan shrines he had made. 33 So on
the fifteenth day of the eighth month, a day that he
himself had designated, Jeroboam offered sacrifices
on the altar at Bethel. He instituted a religious fes-
tival for Israel, and he went up to the altar to burn
incense.

A PROPHET DENOUNCES JEROBOAM

13 At the LORD's command, a man of God from Ju-
dah went to Bethel, arriving there just as Jer-
oboam was approaching the altar to burn incense.
2 Then at the LORD's command, he shouted, "O altar,
altar! This is what the LORD says: A child named Josi-
ah will be born into the dynasty of David. On you he
will sacrifice the priests from the pagan shrines who
come here to burn incense, and human bones will be
burned on you." 3 That same day the man of God gave
a sign to prove his message. He said, "The LORD has

12:18 As in some Greek manuscripts and Syriac version (see also 4:6; 5:14); Hebrew reads *Adoram*. 12:25 Hebrew *Penuel,* a variant spelling of Peniel. 12:28 Hebrew *to them.* 12:32 This day of the ancient Hebrew lunar calendar occurred in late October or early November, exactly one month after the annual Festival of Shelters in Judah (see Lev 23:34).

12:26 Jeroboam thought to himself. Jeroboam had been promised that God would build him a lasting dynasty (11:37-38), but he did not trust God. He thought that if his people continued making pilgrimages to the temple in Jerusalem, he would lose control over them.

12:31 not from . . . tribe of Levi. Jeroboam rejected and banished God's priests (2 Chron. 11:13-17; 13:9) and made his own.

12:32 instituted a religious festival. The Israelites were required to worship God at the temple in Jerusalem during three great feasts every year. Jeroboam created a substitute festival.

13:3 this sign. When this prophecy was fulfilled, Jeroboam would know that the judgment would also happen.

promised to give this sign: This altar will split apart,
and its ashes will be poured out on the ground."
4 When King Jeroboam heard the man of God
speaking against the altar at Bethel, he pointed at
him and shouted, "Seize that man!" But instantly the
king's hand became paralyzed in that position, and
he couldn't pull it back. 5 At the same time a wide
crack appeared in the altar, and the ashes poured out,
just as the man of God had predicted in his message
from the LORD.
6 The king cried out to the man of God, "Please ask
the LORD your God to restore my hand again!" So the
man of God prayed to the LORD, and the king's hand
was restored and he could move it again.
7 Then the king said to the man of God, "Come to the
palace with me and have something to eat, and I will
give you a gift."
8 But the man of God said to the king, "Even if you
gave me half of everything you own, I would not go
with you. I would not eat or drink anything in this
place. 9 For the LORD gave me this command: 'You must
not eat or drink anything while you are there, and do
not return to Judah by the same way you came.'" 10 So
he left Bethel and went home another way.
11 As it happened, there was an old prophet living
in Bethel, and his sons* came home and told him what
the man of God had done in Bethel that day. They also
told their father what the man had said to the king.
12 The old prophet asked them, "Which way did he go?"
So they showed their father* which road the man of
God had taken. 13 "Quick, saddle the donkey," the old
man said. So they saddled the donkey for him, and he
mounted it.
14 Then he rode after the man of God and found him
sitting under a great tree. The old prophet asked him,
"Are you the man of God who came from Judah?"
"Yes, I am," he replied.
15 Then he said to the man of God, "Come home with
me and eat some food."
16 "No, I cannot," he replied. "I am not allowed to eat
or drink anything here in this place. 17 For the LORD
gave me this command: 'You must not eat or drink
anything while you are there, and do not return to Ju-
dah by the same way you came.'"
18 But the old prophet answered, "I am a prophet,
too, just as you are. And an angel gave me this com-
mand from the LORD: 'Bring him home with you so
he can have something to eat and drink.'" But the old
man was lying to him. 19 So they went back together,
and the man of God ate and drank at the prophet's
home.
20 Then while they were sitting at the table, a com-
mand from the LORD came to the old prophet. 21 He
cried out to the man of God from Judah, "This is what
the LORD says: You have defied the word of the LORD
and have disobeyed the command the LORD your God
gave you. 22 You came back to this place and ate and
drank where he told you not to eat or drink. Because
of this, your body will not be buried in the grave of
your ancestors."
23 After the man of God had finished eating and
drinking, the old prophet saddled his own donkey
for him, 24 and the man of God started off again. But
as he was traveling along, a lion came out and killed
him. His body lay there on the road, with the donkey
and the lion standing beside it. 25 People who passed
by saw the body lying in the road and the lion stand-
ing beside it, and they went and reported it in Bethel,
where the old prophet lived.
26 When the prophet heard the report, he said, "It is
the man of God who disobeyed the LORD's command.
The LORD has fulfilled his word by causing the lion to
attack and kill him."
27 Then the prophet said to his sons, "Saddle a don-
key for me." So they saddled a donkey, 28 and he went
out and found the body lying in the road. The donkey
and lion were still standing there beside it, for the
lion had not eaten the body nor attacked the donkey.
29 So the prophet laid the body of the man of God on
the donkey and took it back to the town to mourn
over him and bury him. 30 He laid the body in his own
grave, crying out in grief, "Oh, my brother!"
31 Afterward the prophet said to his sons, "When
I die, bury me in the grave where the man of God is
buried. Lay my bones beside his bones. 32 For the mes-
sage the LORD told him to proclaim against the altar in
Bethel and against the pagan shrines in the towns of
Samaria will certainly come true."
33 But even after this, Jeroboam did not turn from
his evil ways. He continued to choose priests from the
common people. He appointed anyone who wanted to
become a priest for the pagan shrines. 34 This became
a great sin and resulted in the utter destruction of Jer-
oboam's dynasty from the face of the earth.

AHIJAH'S PROPHECY AGAINST JEROBOAM

14 At that time Jeroboam's son Abijah became
very sick. 2 So Jeroboam told his wife, "Disguise
yourself so that no one will recognize you as my wife.
Then go to the prophet Ahijah at Shiloh—the man
who told me I would become king. 3 Take him a gift
of ten loaves of bread, some cakes, and a jar of honey,
and ask him what will happen to the boy."
4 So Jeroboam's wife went to Ahijah's home at Shi-
loh. He was an old man now and could no longer see.
5 But the LORD had told Ahijah, "Jeroboam's wife will
come here, pretending to be someone else. She will
ask you about her son, for he is very sick. Give her the
answer I give you."
6 So when Ahijah heard her footsteps at the door, he
called out, "Come in, wife of Jeroboam! Why are you
pretending to be someone else?" Then he told her, "I
have bad news for you. 7 Give your husband, Jerobo-
am, this message from the LORD, the God of Israel: 'I

13:11 As in Greek version; Hebrew reads *son*. **13:12** As in Greek version; Hebrew reads *They had seen*.

13:7 a gift. Jeroboam was not repentant (v. 33), but he wanted to placate God. Had the prophet accepted a gift, Jeroboam's guilty conscience would have been eased, so the prophet refused (see 2 Kings 5:13-16).

13:8 I would not go. God did not want His prophet to share a meal in the Northern Kingdom because that would have implied that God was at peace with them.

13:19 went back together. The man of God was tired (v. 14), hungry, and thirsty. He probably wished God hadn't forbidden him to eat or drink. The old prophet said what he wanted to hear.

13:24 a lion . . . killed him. This may seem harsh, but the fate of an entire nation was at stake. The death of the prophet was an example to Israel. **standing beside it.** The donkey didn't flee, and the lion didn't eat the man or attack the donkey. This proved that the young prophet's death was a divine judgment. This story was told in Bethel (v. 25) and served notice to Jeroboam that God would judge him as well.

promoted you from the ranks of the common people
and made you ruler over my people Israel. 8 I ripped
the kingdom away from the family of David and gave
it to you. But you have not been like my servant Da-
vid, who obeyed my commands and followed me
with all his heart and always did whatever I wanted.
9 You have done more evil than all who lived before
you. You have made other gods for yourself and have
made me furious with your gold calves. And since you
have turned your back on me, 10 I will bring disaster
on your dynasty and will destroy every one of your
male descendants, slave and free alike, anywhere in
Israel. I will burn up your royal dynasty as one burns
up trash until it is all gone. 11 The members of Jerobo-
am's family who die in the city will be eaten by dogs,
and those who die in the field will be eaten by vul-
tures. I, the LORD, have spoken.'"
12 Then Ahijah said to Jeroboam's wife, "Go on home,
and when you enter the city, the child will die. 13 All Is-
rael will mourn for him and bury him. He is the only
member of your family who will have a proper burial,
for this child is the only good thing that the LORD, the
God of Israel, sees in the entire family of Jeroboam.
14 "In addition, the LORD will raise up a king over
Israel who will destroy the family of Jeroboam. This
will happen today, even now! 15 Then the LORD will
shake Israel like a reed whipped about in a stream.
He will uproot the people of Israel from this good land
that he gave their ancestors and will scatter them
beyond the Euphrates River,* for they have angered
the LORD with the Asherah poles they have set up for
worship. 16 He will abandon Israel because Jeroboam
sinned and made Israel sin along with him."
17 So Jeroboam's wife returned to Tirzah, and the
child died just as she walked through the door of her
home. 18 And all Israel buried him and mourned for
him, as the LORD had promised through the prophet
Ahijah.
19 The rest of the events in Jeroboam's reign, includ-
ing all his wars and how he ruled, are recorded in *The
Book of the History of the Kings of Israel.* 20 Jeroboam
reigned in Israel twenty-two years. When Jeroboam
died, his son Nadab became the next king.

REHOBOAM RULES IN JUDAH

21 Meanwhile, Rehoboam son of Solomon was king in
Judah. He was forty-one years old when he became
king, and he reigned seventeen years in Jerusalem,
the city the LORD had chosen from among all the tribes
of Israel as the place to honor his name. Rehoboam's
mother was Naamah, an Ammonite woman.
22 During Rehoboam's reign, the people of Judah
did what was evil in the LORD's sight, provoking his
anger with their sin, for it was even worse than that
of their ancestors. 23 For they also built for themselves
pagan shrines and set up sacred pillars and Asherah
poles on every high hill and under every green tree.
24 There were even male and female shrine prosti-
tutes throughout the land. The people imitated the
detestable practices of the pagan nations the LORD
had driven from the land ahead of the Israelites.
25 In the fifth year of King Rehoboam's reign, King
Shishak of Egypt came up and attacked Jerusalem.
26 He ransacked the treasuries of the LORD's Temple
and the royal palace; he stole everything, including
all the gold shields Solomon had made. 27 King Re-
hoboam later replaced them with bronze shields
as substitutes, and he entrusted them to the care of
the commanders of the guard who protected the en-
trance to the royal palace. 28 Whenever the king went
to the Temple of the LORD, the guards would also take
the shields and then return them to the guardroom.
29 The rest of the events in Rehoboam's reign and
everything he did are recorded in *The Book of the
History of the Kings of Judah.* 30 There was constant
war between Rehoboam and Jeroboam. 31 When Re-
hoboam died, he was buried among his ancestors in
the City of David. His mother was Naamah, an Am-
monite woman. Then his son Abijam* became the
next king.

ABIJAM RULES IN JUDAH

15 Abijam* began to rule over Judah in the eigh-
teenth year of Jeroboam's reign in Israel. 2 He
reigned in Jerusalem three years. His mother was
Maacah, the granddaughter of Absalom.*
3 He committed the same sins as his father before
him, and he was not faithful to the LORD his God, as
his ancestor David had been. 4 But for David's sake,
the LORD his God allowed his descendants to continue
ruling, shining like a lamp, and he gave Abijam a son
to rule after him in Jerusalem. 5 For David had done
what was pleasing in the LORD's sight and had obeyed
the LORD's commands throughout his life, except in
the affair concerning Uriah the Hittite.
6 There was war between Abijam and Jeroboam*
throughout Abijam's reign. 7 The rest of the events in
Abijam's reign and everything he did are recorded in
The Book of the History of the Kings of Judah. There
was constant war between Abijam and Jeroboam.
8 When Abijam died, he was buried in the City of Da-
vid. Then his son Asa became the next king.

ASA RULES IN JUDAH

9 Asa began to rule over Judah in the twentieth year
of Jeroboam's reign in Israel. 10 He reigned in Jerusa-
lem forty-one years. His grandmother* was Maacah,
the granddaughter of Absalom.
11 Asa did what was pleasing in the LORD's sight, as
his ancestor David had done. 12 He banished the male
and female shrine prostitutes from the land and got
rid of all the idols* his ancestors had made. 13 He even

14:15 Hebrew *the river.* **14:31** Also known as *Abijah.* **15:1** Also known as *Abijah.* **15:2** Hebrew *Abishalom* (also in 15:10), a variant spelling of Absalom; compare 2 Chr 11:20. **15:6** As in a few Hebrew and Greek manuscripts; most Hebrew manuscripts read *between Rehoboam and Jeroboam.* **15:10** Or *The queen mother;* Hebrew reads *His mother* (also in 15:13); compare 15:2. **15:12** The Hebrew term (literally *round things*) probably alludes to dung.

14:9 turned your back on me. This implies Jeroboam's forceful decision to turn his back on God.

14:14 will destroy the family of Jeroboam. Baasha killed all his descendants (15:27-30).

14:15 He will uproot the people of Israel. God gave Jeroboam an opportunity to have a godly dynasty. When Jeroboam chose evil, the nation's destruction was inevitable.

14:23 sacred pillars. Stone pillars symbolizing a god. **Asherah poles.** Carved wooden poles, images of the goddess Asherah, probably imitating growing trees, full of life.

14:24 male and female shrine prostitutes. Contrary to God's commands, the Israelites imitated the Canaanites whom their forefathers left in the land (see Deut. 18:9-13; 23:17; Ps. 106:34-39).

15:3 not faithful. Abijam tolerated idols but publicly claimed godliness (2 Chron. 13:4, 10-12).

deposed his grandmother Maacah from her position as queen mother because she had made an obscene Asherah pole. He cut down her obscene pole and burned it in the Kidron Valley. 14 Although the pagan shrines were not removed, Asa's heart remained completely faithful to the LORD throughout his life. 15 He brought into the Temple of the LORD the silver and gold and the various items that he and his father had dedicated.

16 There was constant war between King Asa of Judah and King Baasha of Israel. 17 King Baasha of Israel invaded Judah and fortified Ramah in order to prevent anyone from entering or leaving King Asa's territory in Judah.

18 Asa responded by removing all the silver and gold that was left in the treasuries of the Temple of the LORD and the royal palace. He sent it with some of his officials to Ben-hadad son of Tabrimmon, son of Hezion, the king of Aram, who was ruling in Damascus, along with this message:

> 19 "Let there be a treaty* between you and me like the one between your father and my father. See, I am sending you a gift of silver and gold. Break your treaty with King Baasha of Israel so that he will leave me alone."

20 Ben-hadad agreed to King Asa's request and sent the commanders of his army to attack the towns of Israel. They conquered the towns of Ijon, Dan, Abel-beth-maacah, and all Kinnereth, and all the land of Naphtali. 21 As soon as Baasha of Israel heard what was happening, he abandoned his project of fortifying Ramah and withdrew to Tirzah. 22 Then King Asa sent an order throughout Judah, requiring that everyone, without exception, help to carry away the building stones and timbers that Baasha had been using to fortify Ramah. Asa used these materials to fortify the town of Geba in Benjamin and the town of Mizpah.

23 The rest of the events in Asa's reign—the extent of his power, everything he did, and the names of the cities he built—are recorded in *The Book of the History of the Kings of Judah.* In his old age his feet became diseased. 24 When Asa died, he was buried with his ancestors in the City of David.

Then Jehoshaphat, Asa's son, became the next king.

NADAB RULES IN ISRAEL

25 Nadab son of Jeroboam began to rule over Israel in the second year of King Asa's reign in Judah. He reigned in Israel two years. 26 But he did what was evil in the LORD's sight and followed the example of his father, continuing the sins that Jeroboam had led Israel to commit.

27 Then Baasha son of Ahijah, from the tribe of Issachar, plotted against Nadab and assassinated him while he and the Israelite army were laying siege to the Philistine town of Gibbethon. 28 Baasha killed Nadab in the third year of King Asa's reign in Judah, and he became the next king of Israel.

29 He immediately slaughtered all the descendants of King Jeroboam, so that not one of the royal family was left, just as the LORD had promised concerning Jeroboam by the prophet Ahijah from Shiloh. 30 This was done because Jeroboam had provoked the anger of the LORD, the God of Israel, by the sins he had committed and the sins he had led Israel to commit.

31 The rest of the events in Nadab's reign and everything he did are recorded in *The Book of the History of the Kings of Israel.*

BAASHA RULES IN ISRAEL

32 There was constant war between King Asa of Judah and King Baasha of Israel. 33 Baasha son of Ahijah began to rule over all Israel in the third year of King Asa's reign in Judah. Baasha reigned in Tirzah twenty-four years. 34 But he did what was evil in the LORD's sight and followed the example of Jeroboam, continuing the sins that Jeroboam had led Israel to commit.

16 This message from the LORD was delivered to King Baasha by the prophet Jehu son of Hanani: 2 "I lifted you out of the dust to make you ruler of my people Israel, but you have followed the evil example of Jeroboam. You have provoked my anger by causing my people Israel to sin. 3 So now I will destroy you and your family, just as I destroyed the descendants of Jeroboam son of Nebat. 4 The members of Baasha's family who die in the city will be eaten by dogs, and those who die in the field will be eaten by vultures."

5 The rest of the events in Baasha's reign and the extent of his power are recorded in *The Book of the History of the Kings of Israel.* 6 When Baasha died, he was buried in Tirzah. Then his son Elah became the next king.

7 The message from the LORD against Baasha and his family came through the prophet Jehu son of Hanani. It was delivered because Baasha had done what was evil in the LORD's sight (just as the family of Jeroboam had done), and also because Baasha had destroyed the family of Jeroboam. The LORD's anger was provoked by Baasha's sins.

ELAH RULES IN ISRAEL

8 Elah son of Baasha began to rule over Israel in the twenty-sixth year of King Asa's reign in Judah. He reigned in the city of Tirzah for two years.

9 Then Zimri, who commanded half of the royal chariots, made plans to kill him. One day in Tirzah, Elah was getting drunk at the home of Arza, the supervisor of the palace. 10 Zimri walked in and struck

15:19 As in Greek version; Hebrew reads *There is a treaty.*

15:13 grandmother Maacah. Maacah (vv. 2,9) was the queen mother. Her son had followed God only half-heartedly, likely due to her influence. Asa was free from her control.

15:17 deny anyone access. Many godly people of Israel moved south to Judah (see 2 Chron. 11:16-17; 15:8-9). Baasha tried to stop this population drain.

15:19 a treaty. Asa thought Baasha was preparing to invade, so he paid the Arameans to threaten Israel's northern border.

15:21 Baasha . . . abandoned his project. Asa's plan worked, but instead of trusting God to protect him, Asa had relied on a pagan nation (see 2 Chron. 16:7).

15:23 events in Asa's reign. More details are preserved in 2 Chronicles 14–16.

15:25 in the second year of King Asa's reign. The author now backtracks to describe the kings that had ruled in Israel during this same period.

15:29 as the LORD had promised. Ahijah had prophesied the end of Jeroboam's family (13:34; 14:14). In Baasha's mind, he was simply securing his throne.

16:7 Baasha had destroyed. God knew Baasha was going to do this, but Baasha was responsible for his deeds (see Matt. 26:24).

him down and killed him. This happened in the twen-
ty-seventh year of King Asa's reign in Judah. Then
Zimri became the next king.
11 Zimri immediately killed the entire royal family
of Baasha, leaving him not even a single male child.
He even destroyed distant relatives and friends. 12 So
Zimri destroyed the dynasty of Baasha as the LORD
had promised through the prophet Jehu. 13 This hap-
pened because of all the sins Baasha and his son Elah
had committed, and because of the sins they led Israel
to commit. They provoked the anger of the LORD, the
God of Israel, with their worthless idols.
14 The rest of the events in Elah's reign and every-
thing he did are recorded in *The Book of the History
of the Kings of Israel.*

ZIMRI RULES IN ISRAEL

15 Zimri began to rule over Israel in the twenty-sev-
enth year of King Asa's reign in Judah, but his reign
in Tirzah lasted only seven days. The army of Israel
was then attacking the Philistine town of Gibbe-
thon. 16 When they heard that Zimri had committed
treason and had assassinated the king, that very day
they chose Omri, commander of the army, as the new
king of Israel. 17 So Omri led the entire army of Isra-
el up from Gibbethon to attack Tirzah, Israel's capi-
tal. 18 When Zimri saw that the city had been taken,
he went into the citadel of the palace and burned it
down over himself and died in the flames. 19 For he,
too, had done what was evil in the LORD's sight. He
followed the example of Jeroboam in all the sins he
had committed and led Israel to commit.
20 The rest of the events in Zimri's reign and his con-
spiracy are recorded in *The Book of the History of the
Kings of Israel.*

OMRI RULES IN ISRAEL

21 But now the people of Israel were split into two fac-
tions. Half the people tried to make Tibni son of Ginath
their king, while the other half supported Omri. 22 But
Omri's supporters defeated the supporters of Tibni. So
Tibni was killed, and Omri became the next king.
23 Omri began to rule over Israel in the thirty-first
year of King Asa's reign in Judah. He reigned twelve
years in all, six of them in Tirzah. 24 Then Omri bought
the hill now known as Samaria from its owner, She-
mer, for 150 pounds of silver.* He built a city on it and
called the city Samaria in honor of Shemer.
25 But Omri did what was evil in the LORD's sight,
even more than any of the kings before him. 26 He fol-
lowed the example of Jeroboam son of Nebat in all the
sins he had committed and led Israel to commit. The
people provoked the anger of the LORD, the God of Is-
rael, with their worthless idols.
27 The rest of the events in Omri's reign, the ex-
tent of his power, and everything he did are record-
ed in *The Book of the History of the Kings of Israel.*
28 When Omri died, he was buried in Samaria. Then
his son Ahab became the next king.

AHAB RULES IN ISRAEL

29 Ahab son of Omri began to rule over Israel in the
thirty-eighth year of King Asa's reign in Judah. He
reigned in Samaria twenty-two years. 30 But Ahab
son of Omri did what was evil in the LORD's sight,
even more than any of the kings before him. 31 And as
though it were not enough to follow the sinful exam-
ple of Jeroboam, he married Jezebel, the daughter of
King Ethbaal of the Sidonians, and he began to bow
down in worship of Baal. 32 First Ahab built a temple
and an altar for Baal in Samaria. 33 Then he set up an
Asherah pole. He did more to provoke the anger of the
LORD, the God of Israel, than any of the other kings of
Israel before him.
34 It was during his reign that Hiel, a man from
Bethel, rebuilt Jericho. When he laid its foundations,
it cost him the life of his oldest son, Abiram. And
when he completed it and set up its gates, it cost him
the life of his youngest son, Segub.* This all happened
according to the message from the LORD concerning
Jericho spoken by Joshua son of Nun.

ELIJAH FED BY RAVENS

17 Now Elijah, who was from Tishbe in Gilead, told
King Ahab, "As surely as the LORD, the God of Is-
rael, lives—the God I serve—there will be no dew or
rain during the next few years until I give the word!"
2 Then the LORD said to Elijah, 3 "Go to the east and
hide by Kerith Brook, near where it enters the Jordan
River. 4 Drink from the brook and eat what the ravens
bring you, for I have commanded them to bring you
food."
5 So Elijah did as the LORD told him and camped
beside Kerith Brook, east of the Jordan. 6 The ravens
brought him bread and meat each morning and eve-
ning, and he drank from the brook. 7 But after a while
the brook dried up, for there was no rainfall any-
where in the land.

THE WIDOW AT ZAREPHATH

8 Then the LORD said to Elijah, 9 "Go and live in the vil-
lage of Zarephath, near the city of Sidon. I have in-
structed a widow there to feed you."
10 So he went to Zarephath. As he arrived at the
gates of the village, he saw a widow gathering sticks,
and he asked her, "Would you please bring me a little
water in a cup?" 11 As she was going to get it, he called
to her, "Bring me a bite of bread, too."
12 But she said, "I swear by the LORD your God that I
don't have a single piece of bread in the house. And I
have only a handful of flour left in the jar and a little
cooking oil in the bottom of the jug. I was just gather-
ing a few sticks to cook this last meal, and then my son
and I will die."

16:24 Hebrew *for 2 talents* [68 kilograms] *of silver.* **16:34** An ancient Hebrew scribal tradition reads *He killed his oldest son when he laid its foundations, and he killed his youngest son when he set up its gates.*

16:12 as the LORD had promised. Zimri unwittingly fulfilled the prophecy of Jehu (vv. 1-4).

16:19 example of Jeroboam. Not a single king of Israel turned from calf worship.

16:24 hill now known as Samaria. Omri was threatened on three sides, so he needed an easily defended capital.

16:31 married Jezebel. Ahab wanted an alliance with the Phoenicians against Assyria, but Jezebel brought Baal worship.

16:34 rebuilt Jericho. Hiel fulfilled Joshua's prophecy (see Josh. 6:26).

17:1 Elijah. When the Northern Kingdom was in its greatest spiritual darkness, Elijah appeared. Merely human (see Jas. 5:17), his power came from his relationship with God. He immediately obeyed God's commands and was uncompromising in his message.

17:10 Zarephath. Zarephath was only eight miles from Sidon, Jezebel's hometown.

13 But Elijah said to her, "Don't be afraid! Go ahead
and do just what you've said, but make a little bread
for me first. Then use what's left to prepare a meal for
yourself and your son. 14 For this is what the LORD, the
God of Israel, says: There will always be flour and ol-
ive oil left in your containers until the time when the
LORD sends rain and the crops grow again!"
15 So she did as Elijah said, and she and Elijah and
her family continued to eat for many days. 16 There
was always enough flour and olive oil left in the con-
tainers, just as the LORD had promised through Elijah.
17 Some time later the woman's son became sick. He
grew worse and worse, and finally he died. 18 Then
she said to Elijah, "O man of God, what have you done
to me? Have you come here to point out my sins and
kill my son?"
19 But Elijah replied, "Give me your son." And he
took the child's body from her arms, carried him up
the stairs to the room where he was staying, and laid
the body on his bed. 20 Then Elijah cried out to the
LORD, "O LORD my God, why have you brought tragedy
to this widow who has opened her home to me, caus-
ing her son to die?"
21 And he stretched himself out over the child
three times and cried out to the LORD, "O LORD my
God, please let this child's life return to him." 22 The
LORD heard Elijah's prayer, and the life of the child
returned, and he revived! 23 Then Elijah brought him
down from the upper room and gave him to his moth-
er. "Look!" he said. "Your son is alive!"
24 Then the woman told Elijah, "Now I know for
sure that you are a man of God, and that the LORD tru-
ly speaks through you."

THE CONTEST ON MOUNT CARMEL

18 Later on, in the third year of the drought, the
LORD said to Elijah, "Go and present yourself to
King Ahab. Tell him that I will soon send rain!" 2 So
Elijah went to appear before Ahab.
Meanwhile, the famine had become very severe
in Samaria. 3 So Ahab summoned Obadiah, who was
in charge of the palace. (Obadiah was a devoted
follower of the LORD. 4 Once when Jezebel had tried
to kill all the LORD's prophets, Obadiah had hidden
100 of them in two caves. He put fifty prophets in
each cave and supplied them with food and water.)
5 Ahab said to Obadiah, "We must check every spring
and valley in the land to see if we can find enough
grass to save at least some of my horses and mules."
6 So they divided the land between them. Ahab went
one way by himself, and Obadiah went another way
by himself.
7 As Obadiah was walking along, he suddenly saw
Elijah coming toward him. Obadiah recognized him
at once and bowed low to the ground before him. "Is it
really you, my lord Elijah?" he asked.
8 "Yes, it is," Elijah replied. "Now go and tell your
master, 'Elijah is here.'"
9 "Oh, sir," Obadiah protested, "what harm have I
done to you that you are sending me to my death at the
hands of Ahab? 10 For I swear by the LORD your God
that the king has searched every nation and kingdom
on earth from end to end to find you. And each time he
was told, 'Elijah isn't here,' King Ahab forced the king
of that nation to swear to the truth of his claim. 11 And
now you say, 'Go and tell your master, "Elijah is here."'
12 But as soon as I leave you, the Spirit of the LORD will
carry you away to who knows where. When Ahab
comes and cannot find you, he will kill me. Yet I have
been a true servant of the LORD all my life. 13 Has no one
told you, my lord, about the time when Jezebel was
trying to kill the LORD's prophets? I hid 100 of them
in two caves and supplied them with food and water.
14 And now you say, 'Go and tell your master, "Elijah is
here."' Sir, if I do that, Ahab will certainly kill me."
15 But Elijah said, "I swear by the LORD Almighty, in
whose presence I stand, that I will present myself to
Ahab this very day."
16 So Obadiah went to tell Ahab that Elijah had
come, and Ahab went out to meet Elijah. 17 When
Ahab saw him, he exclaimed, "So, is it really you, you
troublemaker of Israel?"
18 "I have made no trouble for Israel," Elijah replied.
"You and your family are the troublemakers, for you
have refused to obey the commands of the LORD and
have worshiped the images of Baal instead. 19 Now
summon all Israel to join me at Mount Carmel, along
with the 450 prophets of Baal and the 400 prophets of
Asherah who are supported by Jezebel.*"
20 So Ahab summoned all the people of Israel and
the prophets to Mount Carmel. 21 Then Elijah stood in
front of them and said, "How much longer will you
waver, hobbling between two opinions? If the LORD is
God, follow him! But if Baal is God, then follow him!"
But the people were completely silent.
22 Then Elijah said to them, "I am the only proph-
et of the LORD who is left, but Baal has 450 prophets.
23 Now bring two bulls. The prophets of Baal may
choose whichever one they wish and cut it into pieces
and lay it on the wood of their altar, but without set-
ting fire to it. I will prepare the other bull and lay it on
the wood on the altar, but not set fire to it. 24 Then call
on the name of your god, and I will call on the name
of the LORD. The god who answers by setting fire to
the wood is the true God!" And all the people agreed.
25 Then Elijah said to the prophets of Baal, "You
go first, for there are many of you. Choose one of the
bulls, and prepare it and call on the name of your god.
But do not set fire to the wood."
26 So they prepared one of the bulls and placed it on
the altar. Then they called on the name of Baal from
morning until noontime, shouting, "O Baal, answer
us!" But there was no reply of any kind. Then they
danced, hobbling around the altar they had made.
27 About noontime Elijah began mocking them.
"You'll have to shout louder," he scoffed, "for surely he

18:19 Hebrew *who eat at Jezebel's table.* **18:27** Or *is busy somewhere else,* or *is engaged in business.*

17:15 as Elijah said. The widow was not only obeying Elijah but God (v. 9). She shared her last meal because she believed that God cared for her.

17:24 Now I know . . . you are a man of God. This miracle increased the widow's faith. This was God's purpose. Jesus raising Lazarus from the dead achieved similar results (see John 11:1-4, 40-45).

18:1 I will soon send rain. During the drought, Israel had prayed in vain to Baal, the god of rain. Love for Baal was at an all-time low. The drought had accomplished God's purpose. Now God would send rain.

18:4 to kill all the LORD's prophets. Soon Elijah would command the Israelites to slay the prophets of Baal (v. 40). That seems harsh, but it must be remembered that they had consented to the murder of God's prophets. They also sacrificed children.

18:20 all the people of Israel. Elijah wanted an audience. Ahab, more than ready for a showdown, complied.

18:22 the only prophet. The other prophets were in hiding (v. 4). Elijah was the only prophet left with the courage to do what a prophet should do.

FIRE FROM HEAVEN

1. Have you ever had an accident involving fire? What happened?

1 KINGS 18:16-40

2. When Elijah told the people to follow either God or Baal, why didn't they answer him (v. 21)? Why did Elijah, then, suggest a contest between God and Baal?
3. Why did Elijah mock the false prophets (v. 27)? What do his taunts ("maybe he is away on a trip," "or is asleep") suggest about the character of God?
4. What does this story suggest about the seriousness of leading people away from God?
5. What "false prophets" lead people away from God today?

is a god! Perhaps he is daydreaming, or is relieving himself.* Or maybe he is away on a trip, or is asleep and needs to be wakened!"

28 So they shouted louder, and following their normal custom, they cut themselves with knives and swords until the blood gushed out. 29 They raved all afternoon until the time of the evening sacrifice, but still there was no sound, no reply, no response.

30 Then Elijah called to the people, "Come over here!" They all crowded around him as he repaired the altar of the LORD that had been torn down. 31 He took twelve stones, one to represent each of the tribes of Israel,* 32 and he used the stones to rebuild the altar in the name of the LORD. Then he dug a trench around the altar large enough to hold about three gallons.* 33 He piled wood on the altar, cut the bull into pieces, and laid the pieces on the wood.*

Then he said, "Fill four large jars with water, and pour the water over the offering and the wood."

34 After they had done this, he said, "Do the same thing again!" And when they were finished, he said, "Now do it a third time!" So they did as he said, 35 and the water ran around the altar and even filled the trench.

36 At the usual time for offering the evening sacrifice, Elijah the prophet walked up to the altar and prayed, "O LORD, God of Abraham, Isaac, and Jacob,* prove today that you are God in Israel and that I am your servant. Prove that I have done all this at your command. 37 O LORD, answer me! Answer me so these people will know that you, O LORD, are God and that you have brought them back to yourself."

38 Immediately the fire of the LORD flashed down from heaven and burned up the young bull, the wood, the stones, and the dust. It even licked up all the water in the trench! 39 And when all the people saw it, they fell face down on the ground and cried out, "The LORD—he is God! Yes, the LORD is God!"

40 Then Elijah commanded, "Seize all the prophets of Baal. Don't let a single one escape!" So the people seized them all, and Elijah took them down to the Kishon Valley and killed them there.

ELIJAH PRAYS FOR RAIN

41 Then Elijah said to Ahab, "Go get something to eat and drink, for I hear a mighty rainstorm coming!"

42 So Ahab went to eat and drink. But Elijah climbed to the top of Mount Carmel and bowed low to the ground and prayed with his face between his knees.

43 Then he said to his servant, "Go and look out toward the sea."

The servant went and looked, then returned to Elijah and said, "I didn't see anything."

Seven times Elijah told him to go and look. 44 Finally the seventh time, his servant told him, "I saw a little cloud about the size of a man's hand rising from the sea."

Then Elijah shouted, "Hurry to Ahab and tell him, 'Climb into your chariot and go back home. If you don't hurry, the rain will stop you!'"

45 And soon the sky was black with clouds. A heavy wind brought a terrific rainstorm, and Ahab left quickly for Jezreel. 46 Then the LORD gave special strength to Elijah. He tucked his cloak into his belt* and ran ahead of Ahab's chariot all the way to the entrance of Jezreel.

ELIJAH FLEES TO SINAI

19 When Ahab got home, he told Jezebel everything Elijah had done, including the way he had killed all the prophets of Baal. 2 So Jezebel sent this message to Elijah: "May the gods strike me and even kill me if by this time tomorrow I have not killed you just as you killed them."

3 Elijah was afraid and fled for his life. He went to Beersheba, a town in Judah, and he left his servant there. 4 Then he went on alone into the wilderness, traveling all day. He sat down under a solitary broom tree and prayed that he might die. "I have had enough, LORD," he said. "Take my life, for I am no better than my ancestors who have already died."

5 Then he lay down and slept under the broom tree. But as he was sleeping, an angel touched him and told him, "Get up and eat!" 6 He looked around and there beside his head was some bread baked on hot stones and a jar of water! So he ate and drank and lay down again.

7 Then the angel of the LORD came again and touched him and said, "Get up and eat some more, or the journey ahead will be too much for you."

18:31 Hebrew *each of the tribes of the sons of Jacob to whom the LORD had said, "Your name will be Israel."* **18:32** Hebrew *2 seahs* [14.6 liters] *of seed.* **18:33** Verse 18:34 in the Hebrew text begins here. **18:36** Hebrew *and Israel.* The names "Jacob" and "Israel" are often interchanged throughout the Old Testament, referring sometimes to the individual patriarch and sometimes to the nation. **18:46** Hebrew *He bound up his loins.*

18:30 the altar of the LORD. The altar was one of many ancient places of worship built before Solomon finished the temple (3:2).

18:36 Elijah . . . prayed. Elijah's brief, simple prayer was in direct contrast to the prophets of Baal, who had prayed, chanted, danced, and mutilated themselves for hours (see Matt. 6:7).

18:40 killed. Idolatrous prophets were to be slain (Deut. 13:12-17).

19:3 Elijah was afraid. With God's victory, Elijah was popular, but when Jezebel threatened, the people deserted Elijah. He had been critical of timid prophets (18:22), but now he felt their fear.

19:4 prayed that he might die. Elijah's entire life's work had culminated in a great victory that seemed poised to cause a national revival. When the victory vaporized, Elijah felt that his work amounted to nothing and his life was futile.

8 So he got up and ate and drank, and the food gave
him enough strength to travel forty days and forty
nights to Mount Sinai,* the mountain of God. 9 There
he came to a cave, where he spent the night.

THE LORD SPEAKS TO ELIJAH

But the LORD said to him, "What are you doing here,
Elijah?"
10 Elijah replied, "I have zealously served the LORD
God Almighty. But the people of Israel have broken
their covenant with you, torn down your altars, and
killed every one of your prophets. I am the only one
left, and now they are trying to kill me, too."
11 "Go out and stand before me on the mountain,"
the LORD told him. And as Elijah stood there, the LORD
passed by, and a mighty windstorm hit the mountain.
It was such a terrible blast that the rocks were torn
loose, but the LORD was not in the wind. After the
wind there was an earthquake, but the LORD was not
in the earthquake. 12 And after the earthquake there
was a fire, but the LORD was not in the fire. And af-
ter the fire there was the sound of a gentle whisper.
13 When Elijah heard it, he wrapped his face in his
cloak and went out and stood at the entrance of the
cave.
And a voice said, "What are you doing here, Elijah?"
14 He replied again, "I have zealously served the
LORD God Almighty. But the people of Israel have bro-
ken their covenant with you, torn down your altars,
and killed every one of your prophets. I am the only
one left, and now they are trying to kill me, too."
15 Then the LORD told him, "Go back the same way
you came, and travel to the wilderness of Damascus.
When you arrive there, anoint Hazael to be king of
Aram. 16 Then anoint Jehu grandson of Nimshi* to
be king of Israel, and anoint Elisha son of Shaphat
from the town of Abel-meholah to replace you as my
prophet. 17 Anyone who escapes from Hazael will be
killed by Jehu, and those who escape Jehu will be
killed by Elisha! 18 Yet I will preserve 7,000 others in
Israel who have never bowed down to Baal or kissed
him!"

THE CALL OF ELISHA

19 So Elijah went and found Elisha son of Shaphat
plowing a field. There were twelve teams of oxen in
the field, and Elisha was plowing with the twelfth
team. Elijah went over to him and threw his cloak
across his shoulders and then walked away. 20 Elisha
left the oxen standing there, ran after Elijah, and said
to him, "First let me go and kiss my father and mother
good-bye, and then I will go with you!"
Elijah replied, "Go on back, but think about what I
have done to you."
21 So Elisha returned to his oxen and slaughtered
them. He used the wood from the plow to build a fire
to roast their flesh. He passed around the meat to the
townspeople, and they all ate. Then he went with Eli-
jah as his assistant.

BEN-HADAD ATTACKS SAMARIA

20 About that time King Ben-hadad of Aram mo-
bilized his army, supported by the chariots
and horses of thirty-two allied kings. They went to
besiege Samaria, the capital of Israel, and launched
attacks against it. 2 Ben-hadad sent messengers into
the city to relay this message to King Ahab of Israel:
"This is what Ben-hadad says: 3 'Your silver and gold
are mine, and so are your wives and the best of your
children!'"
4 "All right, my lord the king," Israel's king replied.
"All that I have is yours!"
5 Soon Ben-hadad's messengers returned again and
said, "This is what Ben-hadad says: 'I have already
demanded that you give me your silver, gold, wives,
and children. 6 But about this time tomorrow I will
send my officials to search your palace and the homes
of your officials. They will take away everything you
consider valuable!'"
7 Then Ahab summoned all the elders of the land
and said to them, "Look how this man is stirring up
trouble! I already agreed with his demand that I give
him my wives and children and silver and gold."
8 "Don't give in to any more demands," all the elders
and the people advised.
9 So Ahab told the messengers from Ben-hadad,
"Say this to my lord the king: 'I will give you every-
thing you asked for the first time, but I cannot accept
this last demand of yours.'" So the messengers re-
turned to Ben-hadad with that response.
10 Then Ben-hadad sent this message to Ahab: "May
the gods strike me and even kill me if there remains
enough dust from Samaria to provide even a handful
for each of my soldiers."
11 The king of Israel sent back this answer: "A war-
rior putting on his sword for battle should not boast
like a warrior who has already won."
12 Ahab's reply reached Ben-hadad and the other
kings as they were drinking in their tents.* "Prepare
to attack!" Ben-hadad commanded his officers. So
they prepared to attack the city.

AHAB'S VICTORY OVER BEN-HADAD

13 Then a certain prophet came to see King Ahab of Is-
rael and told him, "This is what the LORD says: Do you
see all these enemy forces? Today I will hand them all
over to you. Then you will know that I am the LORD."
14 Ahab asked, "How will he do it?"
And the prophet replied, "This is what the LORD
says: The troops of the provincial commanders will
do it."
"Should we attack first?" Ahab asked.

19:8 Hebrew *to Horeb,* another name for Sinai. 19:16 Hebrew *descendant of Nimshi;* compare 2 Kgs 9:2, 14. 20:12 Or *in Succoth;* also in 20:16.

19:10 I have zealously served. Elijah had been driven by intense devotion for God to the point of burnout, but in his uncompromising stand against idolatry, he had lost his patience and empathy. **broken their covenant with you.** The people had sinned, and Elijah wanted God to judge them—now. Elijah knew there were other prophets (18:13), but he had little respect for people who would not take a stand for God.

19:12 a gentle whisper. When God sent wind, earthquake, and fire, He showed He could speak in power and judge His people. But God wanted to touch people's hearts rather than drive them to obey out of fear, and He taught Elijah compassion in the process.

19:15 anoint Hazael to be king of Aram. Hazael would be such a merciless enemy of Israel that Elisha literally wept as he anointed him (2 Kings 8:7-15).

19:16 to replace you as my prophet. Elijah had not finished God's work, but he learned that it didn't depend just on him. God could raise up someone to take his place.

19:19 threw his cloak across his shoulders. This immediately told Elisha that he had been chosen to succeed Elijah in ministry.

20:11 This proverb means, "Save your bragging until after you win."

20:13 you will know that I am the LORD. God's purpose never changes. He wants people to know and honor Him.

"Yes," the prophet answered.

15 So Ahab mustered the troops of the 232 provincial commanders. Then he called out the rest of the army of Israel, some 7,000 men. 16 About noontime, as Ben-hadad and the thirty-two allied kings were still in their tents drinking themselves into a stupor, 17 the troops of the provincial commanders marched out of the city as the first contingent.

As they approached, Ben-hadad's scouts reported to him, "Some troops are coming from Samaria."

18 "Take them alive," Ben-hadad commanded, "whether they have come for peace or for war."

19 But Ahab's provincial commanders and the entire army had now come out to fight. 20 Each Israelite soldier killed his Aramean opponent, and suddenly the entire Aramean army panicked and fled. The Israelites chased them, but King Ben-hadad and a few of his charioteers escaped on horses. 21 However, the king of Israel destroyed the other horses and chariots and slaughtered the Arameans.

22 Afterward the prophet said to King Ahab, "Get ready for another attack. Begin making plans now, for the king of Aram will come back next spring.*"

BEN-HADAD'S SECOND ATTACK

23 After their defeat, Ben-hadad's officers said to him, "The Israelite gods are gods of the hills; that is why they won. But we can beat them easily on the plains. 24 Only this time replace the kings with field commanders! 25 Recruit another army like the one you lost. Give us the same number of horses, chariots, and men, and we will fight against them on the plains. There's no doubt that we will beat them." So King Ben-hadad did as they suggested.

26 The following spring he called up the Aramean army and marched out against Israel, this time at Aphek. 27 Israel then mustered its army, set up supply lines, and marched out for battle. But the Israelite army looked like two little flocks of goats in comparison to the vast Aramean forces that filled the countryside!

28 Then the man of God went to the king of Israel and said, "This is what the LORD says: The Arameans have said, 'The LORD is a god of the hills and not of the plains.' So I will defeat this vast army for you. Then you will know that I am the LORD."

29 The two armies camped opposite each other for seven days, and on the seventh day the battle began. The Israelites killed 100,000 Aramean foot soldiers in one day. 30 The rest fled into the town of Aphek, but the wall fell on them and killed another 27,000. Ben-hadad fled into the town and hid in a secret room.

31 Ben-hadad's officers said to him, "Sir, we have heard that the kings of Israel are merciful. So let's humble ourselves by wearing burlap around our waists and putting ropes on our heads, and surrender to the king of Israel. Then perhaps he will let you live."

32 So they put on burlap and ropes, and they went to the king of Israel and begged, "Your servant Ben-hadad says, 'Please let me live!'"

The king of Israel responded, "Is he still alive? He is my brother!"

33 The men took this as a good sign and quickly picked up on his words. "Yes," they said, "your brother Ben-hadad!"

"Go and get him," the king of Israel told them. And when Ben-hadad arrived, Ahab invited him up into his chariot.

34 Ben-hadad told him, "I will give back the towns my father took from your father, and you may establish places of trade in Damascus, as my father did in Samaria."

Then Ahab said, "I will release you under these conditions." So they made a new treaty, and Ben-hadad was set free.

A PROPHET CONDEMNS AHAB

35 Meanwhile, the LORD instructed one of the group of prophets to say to another man, "Hit me!" But the man refused to hit the prophet. 36 Then the prophet told him, "Because you have not obeyed the voice of the LORD, a lion will kill you as soon as you leave me." And when he had gone, a lion did attack and kill him.

37 Then the prophet turned to another man and said, "Hit me!" So he struck the prophet and wounded him.

38 The prophet placed a bandage over his eyes to disguise himself and then waited beside the road for the king. 39 As the king passed by, the prophet called out to him, "Sir, I was in the thick of battle, and suddenly a man brought me a prisoner. He said, 'Guard this man; if for any reason he gets away, you will either die or pay a fine of seventy-five pounds* of silver!' 40 But while I was busy doing something else, the prisoner disappeared!"

"Well, it's your own fault," the king replied. "You have brought the judgment on yourself."

41 Then the prophet quickly pulled the bandage from his eyes, and the king of Israel recognized him as one of the prophets. 42 The prophet said to him, "This is what the LORD says: Because you have spared the man I said must be destroyed,* now you must die in his place, and your people will die instead of his people." 43 So the king of Israel went home to Samaria angry and sullen.

NABOTH'S VINEYARD

21 Now there was a man named Naboth, from Jezreel, who owned a vineyard in Jezreel beside the palace of King Ahab of Samaria. 2 One day Ahab said to Naboth, "Since your vineyard is so convenient to my palace, I would like to buy it to use as a vegetable garden. I will give you a better vineyard in exchange, or if you prefer, I will pay you for it."

20:22 Hebrew *at the turn of the year;* similarly in 20:26. The first day of the year in the ancient Hebrew lunar calendar occurred in March or April. 20:39 Hebrew *1 talent* [34 kilograms]. 20:42 The Hebrew term used here refers to the complete consecration of things or people to the LORD, either by destroying them or by giving them as an offering.

20:15 7,000. This was not a large army compared to Ben-hadad's. The smaller the army, though, the more obvious it was that victory belonged to the Lord.

20:22 next spring. This was the favorite time for kings to go to war (2 Sam. 11:1).

20:28 man of God. This same prophet talked with Ahab earlier (vv. 13, 22).

20:32 brother. This does not mean a literal brother but "not an enemy."

20:34 your father. This phrase probably did not refer to Ahab's father, Omri, but to his predecessor, Baasha, who once had a treaty with Ben-hadad.

20:35 One of the group of prophets. The prophets were organized into schools where they trained and studied the law of Moses.

20:42 Compare the prophet Nathan, who allowed David to pass judgment on a fictitious man who stole a lamb and then applied the judgment to David, who had stolen another man's wife (see 2 Sam. 12:1-7).

3 But Naboth replied, "The LORD forbid that I should
give you the inheritance that was passed down by my
ancestors."
4 So Ahab went home angry and sullen because of
Naboth's answer. The king went to bed with his face
to the wall and refused to eat!
5 "What's the matter?" his wife Jezebel asked him.
"What's made you so upset that you're not eating?"
6 "I asked Naboth to sell me his vineyard or trade it,
but he refused!" Ahab told her.
7 "Are you the king of Israel or not?" Jezebel de-
manded. "Get up and eat something, and don't worry
about it. I'll get you Naboth's vineyard!"
8 So she wrote letters in Ahab's name, sealed them
with his seal, and sent them to the elders and other
leaders of the town where Naboth lived. 9 In her let-
ters she commanded: "Call the citizens together for
a time of fasting, and give Naboth a place of honor.
10 And then seat two scoundrels across from him who
will accuse him of cursing God and the king. Then
take him out and stone him to death."
11 So the elders and other town leaders followed
the instructions Jezebel had written in the letters.
12 They called for a fast and put Naboth at a promi-
nent place before the people. 13 Then the two scoun-
drels came and sat down across from him. And they
accused Naboth before all the people, saying, "He
cursed God and the king." So he was dragged outside
the town and stoned to death. 14 The town leaders
then sent word to Jezebel, "Naboth has been stoned
to death."
15 When Jezebel heard the news, she said to Ahab,
"You know the vineyard Naboth wouldn't sell you?
Well, you can have it now! He's dead!" 16 So Ahab im-
mediately went down to the vineyard of Naboth to
claim it.
17 But the LORD said to Elijah,* 18 "Go down to meet
King Ahab of Israel, who rules in Samaria. He will be
at Naboth's vineyard in Jezreel, claiming it for him-
self. 19 Give him this message: 'This is what the LORD
says: Wasn't it enough that you killed Naboth? Must
you rob him, too? Because you have done this, dogs
will lick your blood at the very place where they
licked the blood of Naboth!'"
20 "So, my enemy, you have found me!" Ahab ex-
claimed to Elijah.
"Yes," Elijah answered, "I have come because you
have sold yourself to what is evil in the LORD's sight.
21 So now the LORD says,* 'I will bring disaster on you
and consume you. I will destroy every one of your
male descendants, slave and free alike, anywhere in
Israel! 22 I am going to destroy your family as I did the
family of Jeroboam son of Nebat and the family of Ba-
asha son of Ahijah, for you have made me very angry
and have led Israel into sin.'
23 "And regarding Jezebel, the LORD says, 'Dogs will
eat Jezebel's body at the plot of land in Jezreel.*'
24 "The members of Ahab's family who die in the
city will be eaten by dogs, and those who die in the
field will be eaten by vultures."
25 (No one else so completely sold himself to what
was evil in the LORD's sight as Ahab did under the in-
fluence of his wife Jezebel. 26 His worst outrage was
worshiping idols* just as the Amorites had done—
the people whom the LORD had driven out from the
land ahead of the Israelites.)
27 But when Ahab heard this message, he tore his
clothing, dressed in burlap, and fasted. He even slept
in burlap and went about in deep mourning.
28 Then another message from the LORD came to Eli-
jah: 29 "Do you see how Ahab has humbled himself be-
fore me? Because he has done this, I will not do what
I promised during his lifetime. It will happen to his
sons; I will destroy his dynasty."

JEHOSHAPHAT AND AHAB

22 For three years there was no war between
Aram and Israel. 2 Then during the third year,
King Jehoshaphat of Judah went to visit King Ahab of
Israel. 3 During the visit, the king of Israel said to his
officials, "Do you realize that the town of Ramoth-gil-
ead belongs to us? And yet we've done nothing to re-
capture it from the king of Aram!"
4 Then he turned to Jehoshaphat and asked, "Will
you join me in battle to recover Ramoth-gilead?"
Jehoshaphat replied to the king of Israel, "Why,
of course! You and I are as one. My troops are your
troops, and my horses are your horses." 5 Then Jehosh-
aphat added, "But first let's find out what the LORD
says."
6 So the king of Israel summoned the prophets,
about 400 of them, and asked them, "Should I go to
war against Ramoth-gilead, or should I hold back?"
They all replied, "Yes, go right ahead! The Lord will
give the king victory."
7 But Jehoshaphat asked, "Is there not also a proph-
et of the LORD here? We should ask him the same ques-
tion."
8 The king of Israel replied to Jehoshaphat, "There is
one more man who could consult the LORD for us, but
I hate him. He never prophesies anything but trouble
for me! His name is Micaiah son of Imlah."
Jehoshaphat replied, "That's not the way a king
should talk! Let's hear what he has to say."
9 So the king of Israel called one of his officials and
said, "Quick! Bring Micaiah son of Imlah."

MICAIAH PROPHESIES AGAINST AHAB

10 King Ahab of Israel and King Jehoshaphat of Judah,
dressed in their royal robes, were sitting on thrones
at the threshing floor near the gate of Samaria. All
of Ahab's prophets were prophesying there in front
of them. 11 One of them, Zedekiah son of Kenaanah,
made some iron horns and proclaimed, "This is what

21:17 Hebrew *Elijah the Tishbite;* also in 21:28. **21:21** As in Greek version; Hebrew lacks *So now the LORD says.* **21:23** As in several Hebrew manuscripts, Syriac, and Latin Vulgate (see also 2 Kgs 9:26, 36); most Hebrew manuscripts read *at the city wall.* **21:26** The Hebrew term (literally *round things*) probably alludes to dung.

21:7 Jezebel. She treated Ahab the way a mother treats a spoiled child, making evil plans to give him whatever he wanted.

21:10 two scoundrels. The law required two witnesses. **cursing God and the king.** Mosaic law did prescribe death for cursing God but not for cursing the king.

22:2 Jehoshaphat. Jehoshaphat, unlike Ahab, was a godly king.

22:4 Will you join me. Ahab was prepared to create an alliance with Judah against Aram. This switch of loyalties happened generation after generation. Jehoshaphat's father had made an alliance with the king of Aram against Israel.

22:5 what the LORD says. Even though Jehoshaphat gave lip service to confirming his decisions with God, he made a poor choice in this case, as the prophet Jehu pointed out (see 2 Chron. 19:2).

22:8 never prophecies anything but trouble. This was Ahab's rule of thumb for a prophet: Did the prophet tell him good things or bad? Ahab was not interested in truth. He had hated Elijah for this very reason.

the LORD says: With these horns you will gore the Ar-
ameans to death!"
12 All the other prophets agreed. "Yes," they said, "go
up to Ramoth-gilead and be victorious, for the LORD
will give the king victory!"
13 Meanwhile, the messenger who went to get Mi-
caiah said to him, "Look, all the prophets are promis-
ing victory for the king. Be sure that you agree with
them and promise success."
14 But Micaiah replied, "As surely as the LORD lives, I
will say only what the LORD tells me to say."
15 When Micaiah arrived before the king, Ahab
asked him, "Micaiah, should we go to war against Ra-
moth-gilead, or should we hold back?"
Micaiah replied sarcastically, "Yes, go up and be
victorious, for the LORD will give the king victory!"
16 But the king replied sharply, "How many times
must I demand that you speak only the truth to me
when you speak for the LORD?"
17 Then Micaiah told him, "In a vision I saw all Is-
rael scattered on the mountains, like sheep without a
shepherd. And the LORD said, 'Their master has been
killed.* Send them home in peace.'"
18 "Didn't I tell you?" the king of Israel exclaimed
to Jehoshaphat. "He never prophesies anything but
trouble for me."
19 Then Micaiah continued, "Listen to what the LORD
says! I saw the LORD sitting on his throne with all the
armies of heaven around him, on his right and on his
left. 20 And the LORD said, 'Who can entice Ahab to go
into battle against Ramoth-gilead so he can be killed?'
"There were many suggestions, 21 and finally a spir-
it approached the LORD and said, 'I can do it!'
22 "'How will you do this?' the LORD asked.
"And the spirit replied, 'I will go out and inspire all
of Ahab's prophets to speak lies.'
"'You will succeed,' said the LORD. 'Go ahead and do
it.'
23 "So you see, the LORD has put a lying spirit in the
mouths of all your prophets. For the LORD has pro-
nounced your doom."
24 Then Zedekiah son of Kenaanah walked up to Mi-
caiah and slapped him across the face. "Since when
did the Spirit of the LORD leave me to speak to you?"
he demanded.
25 And Micaiah replied, "You will find out soon
enough when you are trying to hide in some secret
room!"
26 "Arrest him!" the king of Israel ordered. "Take
him back to Amon, the governor of the city, and to my
son Joash. 27 Give them this order from the king: 'Put
this man in prison, and feed him nothing but bread
and water until I return safely from the battle!'"
28 But Micaiah replied, "If you return safely, it will
mean that the LORD has not spoken through me!" Then
he added to those standing around, "Everyone mark
my words!"

THE DEATH OF AHAB

29 So King Ahab of Israel and King Jehoshaphat of Ju-
dah led their armies against Ramoth-gilead. 30 The
king of Israel said to Jehoshaphat, "As we go into bat-
tle, I will disguise myself so no one will recognize me,
but you wear your royal robes." So the king of Israel
disguised himself, and they went into battle.
31 Meanwhile, the king of Aram had issued these
orders to his thirty-two chariot commanders: "Attack
only the king of Israel. Don't bother with anyone else!"
32 So when the Aramean chariot commanders saw Je-
hoshaphat in his royal robes, they went after him.
"There is the king of Israel!" they shouted. But when
Jehoshaphat called out, 33 the chariot commanders re-
alized he was not the king of Israel, and they stopped
chasing him.
34 An Aramean soldier, however, randomly shot an
arrow at the Israelite troops and hit the king of Israel
between the joints of his armor. "Turn the horses* and
get me out of here!" Ahab groaned to the driver of his
chariot. "I'm badly wounded!"
35 The battle raged all that day, and the king re-
mained propped up in his chariot facing the Aramе-
ans. The blood from his wound ran down to the floor
of his chariot, and as evening arrived he died. 36 Just
as the sun was setting, the cry ran through his troops:
"We're done for! Run for your lives!"
37 So the king died, and his body was taken to Sa-
maria and buried there. 38 Then his chariot was
washed beside the pool of Samaria, and dogs came
and licked his blood at the place where the prostitutes
bathed,* just as the LORD had promised.
39 The rest of the events in Ahab's reign and every-
thing he did, including the story of the ivory palace
and the towns he built, are recorded in *The Book of
the History of the Kings of Israel.* 40 So Ahab died, and
his son Ahaziah became the next king.

JEHOSHAPHAT RULES IN JUDAH

41 Jehoshaphat son of Asa began to rule over Judah in
the fourth year of King Ahab's reign in Israel. 42 Je-
hoshaphat was thirty-five years old when he became
king, and he reigned in Jerusalem twenty-five years.
His mother was Azubah, the daughter of Shilhi.
43 Jehoshaphat was a good king, following the ex-
ample of his father, Asa. He did what was pleasing in
the LORD's sight. *During his reign, however, he failed
to remove all the pagan shrines, and the people still
offered sacrifices and burned incense there. 44 Jehosh-
aphat also made peace with the king of Israel.
45 The rest of the events in Jehoshaphat's reign,
the extent of his power, and the wars he waged are

22:17 Hebrew *These people have no master.* 22:34 Hebrew *Turn your hand.* 22:38 Or *his blood, and the prostitutes bathed [in it];* or *his blood, and they washed his armor.* 22:43 Verses 22:43b-53 are numbered 22:44-54 in Hebrew text.

22:23 lying spirit. There are other times in the Old Testament when an evil or unrighteous spirit seems to be sent from God (for instance, when King Saul was tormented by an evil spirit, 1 Sam. 16:14).

22:31 the king of Israel. It was (and is) an excellent war strategy to attack the leadership so that the soldiers are disoriented and cannot finish the battle well.

22:34 randomly shot. Ahab's disguise didn't protect him when it counted. The consequences of his actions found him no matter who he was trying to fool. **Ahab groaned to the driver of his chariot.** In those days, one drove and the other fought; a third sometimes commanded the other chariots.

22:38 dogs came and licked. Elijah had pronounced this prophecy (21:19). Ahab would die a death of shame. The dogs would lick his blood; his body would not be carefully prepared for a ceremonial burial.

22:42 became king. Jehoshaphat actually became king while his father (King Asa) was still alive. Because of King Asa's failing health, he and his son shared rule for three years. King David and his son Solomon had shared leadership as well. This was called "co-regency."

22:44 king of Israel. Three kings ruled Israel during Jehoshaphat's reign in Judah: Ahab, Ahaziah, and Joram. This statement probably meant that Jehoshaphat's kingdom lived peaceably with Israel's kingdom, regardless of who was king at the time.

recorded in *The Book of the History of the Kings of*
Judah. 46 He banished from the land the rest of the
male and female shrine prostitutes, who still contin-
ued their practices from the days of his father, Asa.
47 (There was no king in Edom at that time, only a
deputy.)
48 Jehoshaphat also built a fleet of trading ships*
to sail to Ophir for gold. But the ships never set sail,
for they met with disaster in their home port of Ezi-
on-geber. 49 At one time Ahaziah son of Ahab had
proposed to Jehoshaphat, "Let my men sail with
your men in the ships." But Jehoshaphat refused the
request.
50 When Jehoshaphat died, he was buried with his
ancestors in the City of David. Then his son Jehoram
became the next king.

AHAZIAH RULES IN ISRAEL

51 Ahaziah son of Ahab began to rule over Israel in the
seventeenth year of King Jehoshaphat's reign in Judah.
He reigned in Samaria two years. 52 But he did what
was evil in the LORD's sight, following the example of
his father and mother and the example of Jeroboam
son of Nebat, who had led Israel to sin. 53 He served
Baal and worshiped him, provoking the anger of the
LORD, the God of Israel, just as his father had done.

22:48 Hebrew *fleet of ships of Tarshish.*

INTRODUCTION TO

2 KINGS

PERSONAL READING PLAN

☐2 Kings 1:1–2:25
☐2 Kings 3:1-27
☐2 Kings 4:1-44
☐2 Kings 5:1–6:23
☐2 Kings 6:24–8:6
☐2 Kings 8:7–9:13
☐2 Kings 9:14–10:17
☐2 Kings 10:18–11:21
☐2 Kings 12:1–13:25
☐2 Kings 14:1–15:12
☐2 Kings 15:13–16:20
☐2 Kings 17:1-41
☐2 Kings 18:1-37
☐2 Kings 19:1-37
☐2 Kings 20:1–21:26
☐2 Kings 22:1–23:30
☐2 Kings 23:31–24:17
☐2 Kings 24:18–25:30

AUTHOR

The author of 1 and 2 Kings is not known, but the three literary sources that are named suggest multiple authors and editors: The Book of the Acts of Solomon (1 Kings 11:41); The Book of the History of the Kings of Israel (1 Kings 14:19; 2 Kings 15:31); and The Book of the History of the Kings of Judah (1 Kings 14:29; 2 Kings 24:5).

DATE

The account of Jehoiachin's release from prison in 2 Kings 25:27-30 means that the final form of Kings was written after 561 B.C. However, the source materials could have been written at the time of the events they describe. These events span almost 400 years.

THEME

Israel's and Judah's spiral to destruction.

HISTORICAL BACKGROUND

The divided kingdoms of Israel and Judah continue their political and moral decline. They are oppressed by their enemies, particularly Aram (Syria). Second Kings gives witness to the rise of Assyrian power that crushes Israel's capital, Samaria, in 722 B.C. (2 Kings 17). The Babylonians succeeded the Assyrians as the dominant power in the region. It was at their hands, in 586 B.C., that Judah's capital, Jerusalem, suffered a fate similar to that of Samaria (2 Kings 25).

CHARACTERISTICS

Second Kings completes the historical narrative begun in 1 Kings. It chronicles the succession of kings in both the northern kingdom of Israel and the southern kingdom of Judah. The verdict upon most of these kings is sadly repetitive: They did "what was evil in the LORD's sight." But God keeps speaking through Elijah and Elisha who succeeds the great prophet and is doubly blessed" with God's Spirit.

PASSAGES FOR TOPICAL GROUP STUDY

4:1-7 ...... USING YOUR GIFTS AND TALENTS ... Miracles with What You Have
5:1-16 ... HURTING AND HEALING .... Healing Phenomenon
6:8-23 ... MIRACLES and POWER .... Struck Blind

ELIJAH CONFRONTS KING AHAZIAH

1 After King Ahab's death, the land of Moab rebelled against Israel.

2 One day Israel's new king, Ahaziah, fell through the latticework of an upper room at his palace in Samaria and was seriously injured. So he sent messengers to the temple of Baal-zebub, the god of Ekron, to ask whether he would recover.

3 But the angel of the LORD told Elijah, who was from Tishbe, "Go and confront the messengers of the king of Samaria and ask them, 'Is there no God in Israel? Why are you going to Baal-zebub, the god of Ekron, to ask whether the king will recover? 4 Now, therefore, this is what the LORD says: You will never leave the bed you are lying on; you will surely die.'" So Elijah went to deliver the message.

5 When the messengers returned to the king, he asked them, "Why have you returned so soon?"

6 They replied, "A man came up to us and told us to go back to the king and give him this message. 'This is what the LORD says: Is there no God in Israel? Why are you sending men to Baal-zebub, the god of Ekron, to ask whether you will recover? Therefore, because you have done this, you will never leave the bed you are lying on; you will surely die.'"

7 "What sort of man was he?" the king demanded. "What did he look like?"

8 They replied, "He was a hairy man,* and he wore a leather belt around his waist."

"Elijah from Tishbe!" the king exclaimed.

9 Then he sent an army captain with fifty soldiers to arrest him. They found him sitting on top of a hill. The captain said to him, "Man of God, the king has commanded you to come down with us."

10 But Elijah replied to the captain, "If I am a man of God, let fire come down from heaven and destroy you and your fifty men!" Then fire fell from heaven and killed them all.

11 So the king sent another captain with fifty men. The captain said to him, "Man of God, the king demands that you come down at once."

12 Elijah replied, "If I am a man of God, let fire come down from heaven and destroy you and your fifty men!" And again the fire of God fell from heaven and killed them all.

13 Once more the king sent a third captain with fifty men. But this time the captain went up the hill and fell to his knees before Elijah. He pleaded with him, "O man of God, please spare my life and the lives of these, your fifty servants. 14 See how the fire from heaven came down and destroyed the first two groups. But now please spare my life!"

15 Then the angel of the LORD said to Elijah, "Go down with him, and don't be afraid of him." So Elijah got up and went with him to the king.

16 And Elijah said to the king, "This is what the LORD says: Why did you send messengers to Baal-zebub, the god of Ekron, to ask whether you will recover? Is there no God in Israel to answer your question? Therefore, because you have done this, you will never leave the bed you are lying on; you will surely die."

17 So Ahaziah died, just as the LORD had promised through Elijah. Since Ahaziah did not have a son to succeed him, his brother Joram* became the next king. This took place in the second year of the reign of Jehoram son of Jehoshaphat, king of Judah.

18 The rest of the events in Ahaziah's reign and everything he did are recorded in *The Book of the History of the Kings of Israel.*

ELIJAH TAKEN INTO HEAVEN

2 When the LORD was about to take Elijah up to heaven in a whirlwind, Elijah and Elisha were traveling from Gilgal. 2 And Elijah said to Elisha, "Stay here, for the LORD has told me to go to Bethel."

But Elisha replied, "As surely as the LORD lives and you yourself live, I will never leave you!" So they went down together to Bethel.

3 The group of prophets from Bethel came to Elisha and asked him, "Did you know that the LORD is going to take your master away from you today?"

"Of course I know," Elisha answered. "But be quiet about it."

4 Then Elijah said to Elisha, "Stay here, for the LORD has told me to go to Jericho."

But Elisha replied again, "As surely as the LORD lives and you yourself live, I will never leave you." So they went on together to Jericho.

5 Then the group of prophets from Jericho came to Elisha and asked him, "Did you know that the LORD is going to take your master away from you today?"

"Of course I know," Elisha answered. "But be quiet about it."

6 Then Elijah said to Elisha, "Stay here, for the LORD has told me to go to the Jordan River."

But again Elisha replied, "As surely as the LORD lives and you yourself live, I will never leave you." So they went on together.

7 Fifty men from the group of prophets also went and watched from a distance as Elijah and Elisha stopped beside the Jordan River. 8 Then Elijah folded his cloak together and struck the water with it. The river divided, and the two of them went across on dry ground!

9 When they came to the other side, Elijah said to Elisha, "Tell me what I can do for you before I am taken away."

And Elisha replied, "Please let me inherit a double share of your spirit and become your successor."

10 "You have asked a difficult thing," Elijah replied. "If you see me when I am taken from you, then you will get your request. But if not, then you won't."

11 As they were walking along and talking, suddenly a chariot of fire appeared, drawn by horses of fire. It drove between the two men, separating them, and Elijah was carried by a whirlwind into heaven. 12 Elisha saw it and cried out, "My father! My father! I see the chariots and charioteers of Israel!" And as they disappeared from sight, Elisha tore his clothes in distress.

1:8 Or *He was wearing clothing made of hair.* **1:17** Hebrew *Jehoram,* a variant spelling of Joram.

1:10 fire done down from heaven. Elijah called on God to execute a trial by fire as He had done on Mt. Carmel (1 Kings 18:36-39).

1:17 Ahaziah died. Ahaziah's death because of his sin confirmed God's word as the true revelation.

2:2 I will never leave you. Elisha knew that Elijah's work was almost finished and wanted to be at his side until the end.

2:3 group of prophets. Groups or companies of prophets.

2:9 a double share. A double portion was the rightful inheritance of a firstborn son.

2:12 chariots and charioteers. Elisha recognized the chariot of fire as a manifestation of God.

13 Elisha picked up Elijah's cloak, which had fallen
when he was taken up. Then Elisha returned to the
bank of the Jordan River. 14 He struck the water with
Elijah's cloak and cried out, "Where is the LORD, the
God of Elijah?" Then the river divided, and Elisha
went across.
15 When the group of prophets from Jericho saw
from a distance what happened, they exclaimed, "Eli-
jah's spirit rests upon Elisha!" And they went to meet
him and bowed to the ground before him. 16 "Sir," they
said, "just say the word and fifty of our strongest men
will search the wilderness for your master. Perhaps
the Spirit of the LORD has left him on some mountain
or in some valley."
"No," Elisha said, "don't send them." 17 But they kept
urging him until they shamed him into agreeing, and
he finally said, "All right, send them." So fifty men
searched for three days but did not find Elijah. 18 Eli-
sha was still at Jericho when they returned. "Didn't I
tell you not to go?" he asked.

ELISHA'S FIRST MIRACLES

19 One day the leaders of the town of Jericho visited
Elisha. "We have a problem, my lord," they told him.
"This town is located in pleasant surroundings, as you
can see. But the water is bad, and the land is unpro-
ductive."
20 Elisha said, "Bring me a new bowl with salt in it."
So they brought it to him. 21 Then he went out to the
spring that supplied the town with water and threw
the salt into it. And he said, "This is what the LORD
says: I have purified this water. It will no longer cause
death or infertility.*" 22 And the water has remained
pure ever since, just as Elisha said.
23 Elisha left Jericho and went up to Bethel. As he
was walking along the road, a group of boys from
the town began mocking and making fun of him.
"Go away, baldy!" they chanted. "Go away, baldy!"
24 Elisha turned around and looked at them, and he
cursed them in the name of the LORD. Then two bears
came out of the woods and mauled forty-two of them.
25 From there Elisha went to Mount Carmel and final-
ly returned to Samaria.

WAR BETWEEN ISRAEL AND MOAB

3 Ahab's son Joram* began to rule over Israel in
the eighteenth year of King Jehoshaphat's reign
in Judah. He reigned in Samaria twelve years. 2 He
did what was evil in the LORD's sight, but not to the
same extent as his father and mother. He at least tore
down the sacred pillar of Baal that his father had set
up. 3 Nevertheless, he continued in the sins that Jero-
boam son of Nebat had committed and led the people
of Israel to commit.
4 King Mesha of Moab was a sheep breeder. He used
to pay the king of Israel an annual tribute of 100,000
lambs and the wool of 100,000 rams. 5 But after Ahab's
death, the king of Moab rebelled against the king of
Israel. 6 So King Joram promptly mustered the army
of Israel and marched from Samaria. 7 On the way, he
sent this message to King Jehoshaphat of Judah: "The
king of Moab has rebelled against me. Will you join
me in battle against him?"
And Jehoshaphat replied, "Why, of course! You and
I are as one. My troops are your troops, and my hors-
es are your horses." 8 Then Jehoshaphat asked, "What
route will we take?"
"We will attack from the wilderness of Edom," Jo-
ram replied.
9 The king of Edom and his troops joined them, and
all three armies traveled along a roundabout route
through the wilderness for seven days. But there was
no water for the men or their animals.
10 "What should we do?" the king of Israel cried out.
"The LORD has brought the three of us here to let the
king of Moab defeat us."
11 But King Jehoshaphat of Judah asked, "Is there no
prophet of the LORD with us? If there is, we can ask the
LORD what to do through him."
One of King Joram's officers replied, "Elisha son of
Shaphat is here. He used to be Elijah's personal assis-
tant.*"
12 Jehoshaphat said, "Yes, the LORD speaks through
him." So the king of Israel, King Jehoshaphat of Judah,
and the king of Edom went to consult with Elisha.
13 "Why are you coming to me?"* Elisha asked the
king of Israel. "Go to the pagan prophets of your fa-
ther and mother!"
But King Joram of Israel said, "No! For it was the
LORD who called us three kings here—only to be de-
feated by the king of Moab!"
14 Elisha replied, "As surely as the LORD Almighty
lives, whom I serve, I wouldn't even bother with you
except for my respect for King Jehoshaphat of Judah.
15 Now bring me someone who can play the harp."
While the harp was being played, the power* of the
LORD came upon Elisha, 16 and he said, "This is what
the LORD says: This dry valley will be filled with pools
of water! 17 You will see neither wind nor rain, says
the LORD, but this valley will be filled with water. You
will have plenty for yourselves and your cattle and
other animals. 18 But this is only a simple thing for the
LORD, for he will make you victorious over the army
of Moab! 19 You will conquer the best of their towns,
even the fortified ones. You will cut down all their
good trees, stop up all their springs, and ruin all their
good land with stones."
20 The next day at about the time when the morn-
ing sacrifice was offered, water suddenly appeared!
It was flowing from the direction of Edom, and soon
there was water everywhere.
21 Meanwhile, when the people of Moab heard
about the three armies marching against them, they
mobilized every man who was old enough to strap on

2:21 Or *or make the land unproductive;* Hebrew reads *or barrenness.* 3:1 Hebrew *Jehoram,* a variant spelling of Joram; also in 3:6. 3:11 Hebrew *He used to pour water on the hands of Elijah.* 3:13 Hebrew *What is there in common between you and me?* 3:15 Hebrew *the hand.*

2:14 He struck the waters. Elisha's inheritance and right of succession were confirmed when he duplicated Elijah's miracle.

2:16 the Spirit of the LORD has left him. The prophets could not believe that Elijah would be spared the most universal of human experiences—death.

3:2 He did what was evil. King Joram stood in a line of progressively evil kings that had begun with Omri (1 Kings 16:25).

3:3 sins that Jeroboam. King Jeroboam turned the people of Israel away from worship of God to idol worship.

3:7 message to King Jehoshaphat. King Joram hoped the northern and southern kingdoms could form an alliance between them against a common threat, the Moabites.

3:11 Is there no prophet of the LORD with us? The rulers had followed their own wisdom nearly to destruction. Now desperate, they wanted God's help.

3:14 wouldn't even bother . . . except for my respect for. The kings of Israel (northern kingdom) had broken God's covenant. Joram was not as bad as his father and grandfather (v. 2), but neither was he a king after God's heart.

3:19 cut down . . . ruin. God demanded the devastation of rebellious Moab.

a sword, and they stationed themselves along their
border. [22] But when they got up the next morning, the
sun was shining across the water, making it appear
red to the Moabites—like blood. [23] "It's blood!" the
Moabites exclaimed. "The three armies must have at-
tacked and killed each other! Let's go, men of Moab,
and collect the plunder!"
[24] But when the Moabites arrived at the Israelite
camp, the army of Israel rushed out and attacked
them until they turned and ran. The army of Isra-
el chased them into the land of Moab, destroying
everything as they went.* [25] They destroyed the
towns, covered their good land with stones, stopped
up all the springs, and cut down all the good trees.
Finally, only Kir-hareseth and its stone walls were
left, but men with slings surrounded and attacked
it.
[26] When the king of Moab saw that he was losing
the battle, he led 700 of his swordsmen in a desper-
ate attempt to break through the enemy lines near
the king of Edom, but they failed. [27] Then the king of
Moab took his oldest son, who would have been the
next king, and sacrificed him as a burnt offering on
the wall. So there was great anger against Israel,*
and the Israelites withdrew and returned to their
own land.

ELISHA HELPS A POOR WIDOW

4 One day the widow of a member of the group of
prophets came to Elisha and cried out, "My hus-
band who served you is dead, and you know how he
feared the LORD. But now a creditor has come, threat-
ening to take my two sons as slaves."
[2] "What can I do to help you?" Elisha asked. "Tell me,
what do you have in the house?"
"Nothing at all, except a flask of olive oil," she re-
plied.
[3] And Elisha said, "Borrow as many empty jars as
you can from your friends and neighbors. [4] Then go
into your house with your sons and shut the door be-
hind you. Pour olive oil from your flask into the jars,
setting each one aside when it is filled."
[5] So she did as she was told. Her sons kept bringing
jars to her, and she filled one after another. [6] Soon ev-
ery container was full to the brim!
"Bring me another jar," she said to one of her sons.
"There aren't any more!" he told her. And then the
olive oil stopped flowing.
[7] When she told the man of God what had hap-
pened, he said to her, "Now sell the olive oil and pay
your debts, and you and your sons can live on what
is left over."

ELISHA AND THE WOMAN FROM SHUNEM

[8] One day Elisha went to the town of Shunem. A
wealthy woman lived there, and she urged him to
come to her home for a meal. After that, whenever he
passed that way, he would stop there for something
to eat.

MIRACLES WITH WHAT YOU HAVE

1. Do you or have you received an allowance? How does it compare to what your friends get?

2 KINGS 4:1-7

2. This woman didn't know what Elisha was planning when he told her to gather empty containers. Why did she gather so many? How did her faith in God make her rich?
3. Why did God choose to use what the widow already had in the house (a small jar of oil)?
4. How has God used your gifts and talents to bless others?
5. How can you use your gifts and talents even more in God's service?

[9] She said to her husband, "I am sure this man
who stops in from time to time is a holy man of God.
[10] Let's build a small room for him on the roof and
furnish it with a bed, a table, a chair, and a lamp.
Then he will have a place to stay whenever he
comes by."
[11] One day Elisha returned to Shunem, and he went
up to this upper room to rest. [12] He said to his servant
Gehazi, "Tell the woman from Shunem I want to speak
to her." When she appeared, [13] Elisha said to Gehazi,
"Tell her, 'We appreciate the kind concern you have
shown us. What can we do for you? Can we put in a
good word for you to the king or to the commander of
the army?'"
"No," she replied, "my family takes good care of
me."
[14] Later Elisha asked Gehazi, "What can we do for
her?"
Gehazi replied, "She doesn't have a son, and her
husband is an old man."
[15] "Call her back again," Elisha told him. When the
woman returned, Elisha said to her as she stood in the
doorway, [16] "Next year at this time you will be holding
a son in your arms!"
"No, my lord!" she cried. "O man of God, don't de-
ceive me and get my hopes up like that."
[17] But sure enough, the woman soon became preg-
nant. And at that time the following year she had a
son, just as Elisha had said.
[18] One day when her child was older, he went out to
help his father, who was working with the harvest-
ers. [19] Suddenly he cried out, "My head hurts! My head
hurts!"
His father said to one of the servants, "Carry him
home to his mother."
[20] So the servant took him home, and his mother
held him on her lap. But around noontime he died.

3:24 The meaning of the Hebrew is uncertain. 3:27 Or *So Israel's anger was great.* The meaning of the Hebrew is uncertain.

3:23 killed each other. The Moabites saw water that looked like blood. They thought the weak alliance opposing them had come to blows.
3:27 sacrificed him as a burnt offering. The king of Moab sacrificed his own son as a burnt offering to the Moabite god Chemosh. The sight of the sacrifice may have encouraged the Moabites to fight furiously and drive Israel away.
4:14 doesn't have a son . . . husband is an old man. Without a son to help her after her husband was gone, this woman would soon be in a desperate situation.
4:16-17 In spite of her unbelief, the Shunammite woman delivered a child, and she did so exactly as Elisha had predicted.
4:20 he died. The child was a gift from God in response to the woman's faith. His death tested her faith.

21 She carried him up and laid him on the bed of the
man of God, then shut the door and left him there.
22 She sent a message to her husband: "Send one of the
servants and a donkey so that I can hurry to the man
of God and come right back."
23 "Why go today?" he asked. "It is neither a new
moon festival nor a Sabbath."
But she said, "It will be all right."
24 So she saddled the donkey and said to the ser-
vant, "Hurry! Don't slow down unless I tell you to."
25 As she approached the man of God at Mount Car-
mel, Elisha saw her in the distance. He said to Gehazi,
"Look, the woman from Shunem is coming. 26 Run out
to meet her and ask her, 'Is everything all right with
you, your husband, and your child?'"
"Yes," the woman told Gehazi, "everything is fine."
27 But when she came to the man of God at the moun-
tain, she fell to the ground before him and caught
hold of his feet. Gehazi began to push her away, but
the man of God said, "Leave her alone. She is deeply
troubled, but the LORD has not told me what it is."
28 Then she said, "Did I ask you for a son, my lord?
And didn't I say, 'Don't deceive me and get my hopes
up'?"
29 Then Elisha said to Gehazi, "Get ready to travel*;
take my staff and go! Don't talk to anyone along the
way. Go quickly and lay the staff on the child's face."
30 But the boy's mother said, "As surely as the LORD
lives and you yourself live, I won't go home unless you
go with me." So Elisha returned with her.
31 Gehazi hurried on ahead and laid the staff on the
child's face, but nothing happened. There was no sign
of life. He returned to meet Elisha and told him, "The
child is still dead."
32 When Elisha arrived, the child was indeed dead,
lying there on the prophet's bed. 33 He went in alone
and shut the door behind him and prayed to the LORD.
34 Then he lay down on the child's body, placing his
mouth on the child's mouth, his eyes on the child's
eyes, and his hands on the child's hands. And as he
stretched out on him, the child's body began to grow
warm again! 35 Elisha got up, walked back and forth
across the room once, and then stretched himself out
again on the child. This time the boy sneezed seven
times and opened his eyes!
36 Then Elisha summoned Gehazi. "Call the child's
mother!" he said. And when she came in, Elisha said,
"Here, take your son!" 37 She fell at his feet and bowed
before him, overwhelmed with gratitude. Then she
took her son in her arms and carried him downstairs.

MIRACLES DURING A FAMINE

38 Elisha now returned to Gilgal, and there was a famine
in the land. One day as the group of prophets was seat-
ed before him, he said to his servant, "Put a large pot on
the fire, and make some stew for the rest of the group."
39 One of the young men went out into the field to
gather herbs and came back with a pocketful of wild
gourds. He shredded them and put them into the pot
without realizing they were poisonous. 40 Some of the
stew was served to the men. But after they had eaten
a bite or two they cried out, "Man of God, there's poi-
son in this stew!" So they would not eat it.
41 Elisha said, "Bring me some flour." Then he threw
it into the pot and said, "Now it's all right; go ahead
and eat." And then it did not harm them.
42 One day a man from Baal-shalishah brought the
man of God a sack of fresh grain and twenty loaves of
barley bread made from the first grain of his harvest.
Elisha said, "Give it to the people so they can eat."
43 "What?" his servant exclaimed. "Feed a hundred
people with only this?"
But Elisha repeated, "Give it to the people so they
can eat, for this is what the LORD says: Everyone will
eat, and there will even be some left over!" 44 And
when they gave it to the people, there was plenty for
all and some left over, just as the LORD had promised.

THE HEALING OF NAAMAN

5 The king of Aram had great admiration for Naa-
man, the commander of his army, because through
him the LORD had given Aram great victories. But
though Naaman was a mighty warrior, he suffered
from leprosy.*
2 At this time Aramean raiders had invaded the
land of Israel, and among their captives was a young
girl who had been given to Naaman's wife as a maid.
3 One day the girl said to her mistress, "I wish my mas-
ter would go to see the prophet in Samaria. He would
heal him of his leprosy."

HEALING PHENOMENON

1. Does your family have any "home remedies" to cure the hiccups, a cold, or something else?

2 KINGS 5:1-16

2. Why did Elisha heal this great enemy leader (v. 8)?
3. Why did Naaman get angry with Elisha? How did he expect to be healed? What does this show about his character?
4. In what way did God require that Naaman humble himself in order to be healed? What does this show about God's character?
5. When you ask God for help, is your attitude humble or proud? How might God want you to humble yourself before Him?

4:29 Hebrew *Bind up your loins.* 5:1 Or *from a contagious skin disease.* The Hebrew word used here and throughout this passage can describe various skin diseases.

4:21-26 The woman was determined to keep her son's death a private matter until she had spoken to Elisha.
4:29 lay the staff. Elisha assumed that the special powers he had from God could be transferred through his staff.
4:33 shut the door . . . and prayed. Elisha sought God's will in this act of healing and then acted on it.
4:38 famine in the land. Just as God provided for His people, He sometimes showed His displeasure by sending famine and other trouble (see Lev. 26:19-20; Deut. 28:18,23-24).
4:39 wild gourds. Just like Baal worship, the wild gourds was native to the land, but it was poisonous and deadly.
4:42 first grain of his harvest. People in the northern kingdom had lost confidence in a corrupt priesthood, so their offerings went to prophets who still spoke God's truth.
5:2 a young girl. This passage contrasts the corrupt rulers of the northern kingdom with a faithful slave girl who had a compassionate heart.

4 So Naaman told the king what the young girl from Israel had said. 5 "Go and visit the prophet," the king of Aram told him. "I will send a letter of introduction for you to take to the king of Israel." So Naaman started out, carrying as gifts 750 pounds of silver, 150 pounds of gold,* and ten sets of clothing. 6 The letter to the king of Israel said: "With this letter I present my servant Naaman. I want you to heal him of his leprosy."

7 When the king of Israel read the letter, he tore his clothes in dismay and said, "Am I God, that I can give life and take it away? Why is this man asking me to heal someone with leprosy? I can see that he's just trying to pick a fight with me."

8 But when Elisha, the man of God, heard that the king of Israel had torn his clothes in dismay, he sent this message to him: "Why are you so upset? Send Naaman to me, and he will learn that there is a true prophet here in Israel."

9 So Naaman went with his horses and chariots and waited at the door of Elisha's house. 10 But Elisha sent a messenger out to him with this message: "Go and wash yourself seven times in the Jordan River. Then your skin will be restored, and you will be healed of your leprosy."

11 But Naaman became angry and stalked away. "I thought he would certainly come out to meet me!" he said. "I expected him to wave his hand over the leprosy and call on the name of the LORD his God and heal me! 12 Aren't the rivers of Damascus, the Abana and the Pharpar, better than any of the rivers of Israel? Why shouldn't I wash in them and be healed?" So Naaman turned and went away in a rage.

13 But his officers tried to reason with him and said, "Sir,* if the prophet had told you to do something very difficult, wouldn't you have done it? So you should certainly obey him when he says simply, 'Go and wash and be cured!'" 14 So Naaman went down to the Jordan River and dipped himself seven times, as the man of God had instructed him. And his skin became as healthy as the skin of a young child, and he was healed!

15 Then Naaman and his entire party went back to find the man of God. They stood before him, and Naaman said, "Now I know that there is no God in all the world except in Israel. So please accept a gift from your servant."

16 But Elisha replied, "As surely as the LORD lives, whom I serve, I will not accept any gifts." And though Naaman urged him to take the gift, Elisha refused.

17 Then Naaman said, "All right, but please allow me to load two of my mules with earth from this place, and I will take it back home with me. From now on I will never again offer burnt offerings or sacrifices to any other god except the LORD. 18 However, may the LORD pardon me in this one thing: When my master the king goes into the temple of the god Rimmon to worship there and leans on my arm, may the LORD pardon me when I bow, too."

19 "Go in peace," Elisha said. So Naaman started home again.

THE GREED OF GEHAZI

20 But Gehazi, the servant of Elisha, the man of God, said to himself, "My master should not have let this Aramean get away without accepting any of his gifts. As surely as the LORD lives, I will chase after him and get something from him." 21 So Gehazi set off after Naaman.

When Naaman saw Gehazi running after him, he climbed down from his chariot and went to meet him. "Is everything all right?" Naaman asked.

22 "Yes," Gehazi said, "but my master has sent me to tell you that two young prophets from the hill country of Ephraim have just arrived. He would like 75 pounds* of silver and two sets of clothing to give to them."

23 "By all means, take twice as much* silver," Naaman insisted. He gave him two sets of clothing, tied up the money in two bags, and sent two of his servants to carry the gifts for Gehazi. 24 But when they arrived at the citadel,* Gehazi took the gifts from the servants and sent the men back. Then he went and hid the gifts inside the house.

25 When he went in to his master, Elisha asked him, "Where have you been, Gehazi?"

"I haven't been anywhere," he replied.

26 But Elisha asked him, "Don't you realize that I was there in spirit when Naaman stepped down from his chariot to meet you? Is this the time to receive money and clothing, olive groves and vineyards, sheep and cattle, and male and female servants? 27 Because you have done this, you and your descendants will suffer from Naaman's leprosy forever." When Gehazi left the room, he was covered with leprosy; his skin was white as snow.

THE FLOATING AX HEAD

6 One day the group of prophets came to Elisha and told him, "As you can see, this place where we meet with you is too small. 2 Let's go down to the Jordan River, where there are plenty of logs. There we can build a new place for us to meet."

"All right," he told them, "go ahead."

3 "Please come with us," someone suggested.

"I will," he said. 4 So he went with them.

When they arrived at the Jordan, they began cutting down trees. 5 But as one of them was cutting a tree, his ax head fell into the river. "Oh, sir!" he cried. "It was a borrowed ax!"

5:5 Hebrew *10 talents* [340 kilograms] *of silver, 6,000 [shekels]* [68 kilograms] *of gold.* 5:13 Hebrew *My father.* 5:22 Hebrew *1 talent* [34 kilograms]. 5:23 Hebrew *take 2 talents* [150 pounds or 68 kilograms]. 5:24 Hebrew *the Ophel.*

5:8 Why are you so upset? Elisha scolded King Joram for his fear and faithlessness. This was an opportunity to demonstrate God's power to a pagan ruler.

5:10 wash . . . in the Jordan. There was nothing magical about washing in the Jordan River. What Elisha demanded was Naaman's obedience.

5:11-14 When Naaman became a servant of God and acknowledged God's sovereignty, he was healed.

5:15 no God . . . except in Israel. At a time when Israel's people were worshipping other gods, it was left to a pagan to declare the power of the only true God.

5:16 I will not accept any gifts. Elisha recognized Naaman's healing as an act of God. He could not accept a reward for something God had done.

5:22 75 pounds of silver. Gehazi's love of money led to other sins—coveting and lying.

5:26 time to receive money. Gehazi had acted no better than the pagan soothsayers, who were prophets for profit (see Num. 22).

6:1 group of prophets. Several groups of prophets who acknowledged the leadership of Elijah and Elisha clustered around the cities of Bethel, Jericho, and Gilgal (2:1,3,5).

6:5 borrowed. A person who lost an ax head was liable for it, and its loss might mean servitude to repay the debt.

6 "Where did it fall?" the man of God asked. When
he showed him the place, Elisha cut a stick and threw
it into the water at that spot. Then the ax head float-
ed to the surface. 7 "Grab it," Elisha said. And the man
reached out and grabbed it.

ELISHA TRAPS THE ARAMEANS

8 When the king of Aram was at war with Israel, he
would confer with his officers and say, "We will mobi-
lize our forces at such and such a place."

9 But immediately Elisha, the man of God, would
warn the king of Israel, "Do not go near that place, for
the Arameans are planning to mobilize their troops
there." 10 So the king of Israel would send word to the
place indicated by the man of God. Time and again
Elisha warned the king, so that he would be on the
alert there.

11 The king of Aram became very upset over this. He
called his officers together and demanded, "Which of
you is the traitor? Who has been informing the king of
Israel of my plans?"

12 "It's not us, my lord the king," one of the officers
replied. "Elisha, the prophet in Israel, tells the king
of Israel even the words you speak in the privacy of
your bedroom!"

13 "Go and find out where he is," the king command-
ed, "so I can send troops to seize him."

And the report came back: "Elisha is at Dothan."
14 So one night the king of Aram sent a great army
with many chariots and horses to surround the city.

15 When the servant of the man of God got up ear-
ly the next morning and went outside, there were
troops, horses, and chariots everywhere. "Oh, sir,
what will we do now?" the young man cried to Elisha.

16 "Don't be afraid!" Elisha told him. "For there
are more on our side than on theirs!" 17 Then Elisha
prayed, "O LORD, open his eyes and let him see!" The
LORD opened the young man's eyes, and when he
looked up, he saw that the hillside around Elisha was
filled with horses and chariots of fire.

18 As the Aramean army advanced toward him,
Elisha prayed, "O LORD, please make them blind." So
the LORD struck them with blindness as Elisha had
asked.

19 Then Elisha went out and told them, "You have
come the wrong way! This isn't the right city! Follow
me, and I will take you to the man you are looking
for." And he led them to the city of Samaria.

20 As soon as they had entered Samaria, Elisha
prayed, "O LORD, now open their eyes and let them
see." So the LORD opened their eyes, and they discov-
ered that they were in the middle of Samaria.

21 When the king of Israel saw them, he shouted
to Elisha, "My father, should I kill them? Should I kill
them?"

22 "Of course not!" Elisha replied. "Do we kill prison-
ers of war? Give them food and drink and send them
home again to their master."

23 So the king made a great feast for them and then
sent them home to their master. After that, the Ara-
mean raiders stayed away from the land of Israel.

BEN-HADAD BESIEGES SAMARIA

24 Some time later, however, King Ben-hadad of Aram
mustered his entire army and besieged Samaria. 25 As
a result, there was a great famine in the city. The siege
lasted so long that a donkey's head sold for eighty
pieces of silver, and a cup of dove's dung sold for five
pieces* of silver.

26 One day as the king of Israel was walking along
the wall of the city, a woman called to him, "Please
help me, my lord the king!"

27 He answered, "If the LORD doesn't help you, what
can I do? I have neither food from the threshing floor
nor wine from the press to give you." 28 But then the
king asked, "What is the matter?"

She replied, "This woman said to me: 'Come on, let's
eat your son today, then we will eat my son tomorrow.'
29 So we cooked my son and ate him. Then the next day
I said to her, 'Kill your son so we can eat him,' but she
has hidden her son."

30 When the king heard this, he tore his clothes in
despair. And as the king walked along the wall, the
people could see that he was wearing burlap under
his robe next to his skin. 31 "May God strike me and
even kill me if I don't separate Elisha's head from his
shoulders this very day," the king vowed.

32 Elisha was sitting in his house with the elders of
Israel when the king sent a messenger to summon
him. But before the messenger arrived, Elisha said to
the elders, "A murderer has sent a man to cut off my
head. When he arrives, shut the door and keep him
out. We will soon hear his master's steps following
him."

33 While Elisha was still saying this, the messenger
arrived. And the king* said, "All this misery is from
the LORD! Why should I wait for the LORD any longer?"

STRUCK BLIND

1. Recall a time when you got lost. How did you find your way?

2 KINGS 6:8-23

2. To whom was Elisha referring when he said, "there are more on our side than on theirs" (v. 16)?
3. Why did Elisha show mercy to those who were trying to kill him? What was the result?
4. What was God's purpose in working this great miracle: To save Elisha? To show His power to a foreign nation? Other?
5. How can this passage encourage you when you feel outnumbered by the world's forces?

6:25 Hebrew *sold for 80 [shekels]* [2 pounds or 0.9 kilograms] *of silver, and 1/4 of a cab* [0.3 liters] *of dove's dung sold for 5 [shekels]* [2 ounces or 57 grams]. *Dove's dung* may be a variety of wild vegetable. **6:33** Hebrew *he*.

6:9 man of God . . . warn the king. Elisha was a spiritual leader and advisor to the king of Israel. He advised Joram in this situation on military intelligence.
6:13 seize him. The king of Aram wanted to capture Elisha to keep him from offering assistance to King Joram of Israel.
6:24 King Ben-hadad. This Aramean king had besieged Samaria in the past.
6:30 tore his clothes. King Joram was expressing his anger toward Elisha, whom he blamed for the famine that had struck Israel.
6:33 misery is from the LORD. Joram believed that Elisha had deceived him and that God was actually responsible for the famine.

7 Elisha replied, "Listen to this message from the LORD!
This is what the LORD says: By this time tomorrow in
the markets of Samaria, six quarts of choice flour will
cost only one piece of silver,* and twelve quarts of bar-
ley grain will cost only one piece of silver.*"
2 The officer assisting the king said to the man of
God, "That couldn't happen even if the LORD opened
the windows of heaven!"
But Elisha replied, "You will see it happen with
your own eyes, but you won't be able to eat any of it!"

LEPERS VISIT THE ENEMY CAMP

3 Now there were four men with leprosy* sitting at
the entrance of the city gates. "Why should we sit
here waiting to die?" they asked each other. 4 "We
will starve if we stay here, but with the famine in the
city, we will starve if we go back there. So we might
as well go out and surrender to the Aramean army. If
they let us live, so much the better. But if they kill us,
we would have died anyway."
5 So at twilight they set out for the camp of the Ar-
ameans. But when they came to the edge of the camp,
no one was there! 6 For the Lord had caused the Ar-
amean army to hear the clatter of speeding chariots
and the galloping of horses and the sounds of a great
army approaching. "The king of Israel has hired the
Hittites and Egyptians* to attack us!" they cried to one
another. 7 So they panicked and ran into the night,
abandoning their tents, horses, donkeys, and every-
thing else, as they fled for their lives.
8 When the men with leprosy arrived at the edge of
the camp, they went into one tent after another, eating
and drinking wine; and they carried off silver and gold
and clothing and hid it. 9 Finally, they said to each other,
"This is not right. This is a day of good news, and we ar-
en't sharing it with anyone! If we wait until morning,
some calamity will certainly fall upon us. Come on, let's
go back and tell the people at the palace."
10 So they went back to the city and told the gate-
keepers what had happened. "We went out to the Ar-
amean camp," they said, "and no one was there! The
horses and donkeys were tethered and the tents were
all in order, but there wasn't a single person around!"
11 Then the gatekeepers shouted the news to the peo-
ple in the palace.

ISRAEL PLUNDERS THE CAMP

12 The king got out of bed in the middle of the night
and told his officers, "I know what has happened. The
Arameans know we are starving, so they have left
their camp and have hidden in the fields. They are ex-
pecting us to leave the city, and then they will take us
alive and capture the city."
13 One of his officers replied, "We had better send out
scouts to check into this. Let them take five of the remain-
ing horses. If something happens to them, it will be no
worse than if they stay here and die with the rest of us."
14 So two chariots with horses were prepared, and
the king sent scouts to see what had happened to the
Aramean army. 15 They went all the way to the Jordan
River, following a trail of clothing and equipment
that the Arameans had thrown away in their mad
rush to escape. The scouts returned and told the king
about it. 16 Then the people of Samaria rushed out and
plundered the Aramean camp. So it was true that six
quarts of choice flour were sold that day for one piece
of silver, and twelve quarts of barley grain were sold
for one piece of silver, just as the LORD had promised.
17 The king appointed his officer to control the traffic
at the gate, but he was knocked down and trampled to
death as the people rushed out.
So everything happened exactly as the man of God
had predicted when the king came to his house. 18 The
man of God had said to the king, "By this time tomor-
row in the markets of Samaria, six quarts of choice
flour will cost one piece of silver, and twelve quarts of
barley grain will cost one piece of silver."
19 The king's officer had replied, "That couldn't hap-
pen even if the LORD opened the windows of heaven!"
And the man of God had said, "You will see it happen
with your own eyes, but you won't be able to eat any
of it!" 20 And so it was, for the people trampled him to
death at the gate!

THE WOMAN FROM SHUNEM RETURNS HOME

8 Elisha had told the woman whose son he had
brought back to life, "Take your family and move
to some other place, for the LORD has called for a fam-
ine on Israel that will last for seven years." 2 So the
woman did as the man of God instructed. She took
her family and settled in the land of the Philistines for
seven years.
3 After the famine ended she returned from the
land of the Philistines, and she went to see the king
about getting back her house and land. 4 As she came
in, the king was talking with Gehazi, the servant of
the man of God. The king had just said, "Tell me some
stories about the great things Elisha has done." 5 And
Gehazi was telling the king about the time Elisha had
brought a boy back to life. At that very moment, the
mother of the boy walked in to make her appeal to the
king about her house and land.
"Look, my lord the king!" Gehazi exclaimed. "Here
is the woman now, and this is her son—the very one
Elisha brought back to life!"
6 "Is this true?" the king asked her. And she told him
the story. So he directed one of his officials to see that
everything she had lost was restored to her, includ-
ing the value of any crops that had been harvested
during her absence.

HAZAEL MURDERS BEN-HADAD

7 Elisha went to Damascus, the capital of Aram, where
King Ben-hadad lay sick. When someone told the king

7:1a Hebrew *1 seah* [7.3 liters] *of choice flour will cost 1 shekel* [0.4 ounces or 11 grams]; also in 7:16, 18. **7:1b** Hebrew *2 seahs* [14.6 liters] *of barley grain will cost 1 shekel* [0.4 ounces or 11 grams]; also in 7:16, 18. **7:3** Or *with a contagious skin disease.* The Hebrew word used here and throughout this passage can describe various skin diseases. **7:6** Possibly *and the people of Muzur,* a district near Cilicia.

7:12 I know what has happened. Instead of recognizing God's provision and the fulfillment of Elisha's prophecy, Joram saw only deception.

8:2 She . . . settled in the land of the Philistines. The Shunammite woman was obedient to Elisha's warning. Her obedience had saved her from the famine.

8:3 went to see the king about getting back her house and land. In this woman's absence, someone had illegally taken her property.

8:6 everything she had lost was restored. God's blessing was not limited to restoration of lost property but included all the income her property had generated.

8:7 Elisha went. Elisha journeyed to Damascus to anoint Hazael as the new king of Syria in obedience of the instructions he had received earlier from the Lord (1 Kings 19:15-18).

that the man of God had come, 8 the king said to Hazael, "Take a gift to the man of God. Then tell him to ask the LORD, 'Will I recover from this illness?'"

9 So Hazael loaded down forty camels with the finest products of Damascus as a gift for Elisha. He went to him and said, "Your servant Ben-hadad, the king of Aram, has sent me to ask, 'Will I recover from this illness?'"

10 And Elisha replied, "Go and tell him, 'You will surely recover.' But actually the LORD has shown me that he will surely die!" 11 Elisha stared at Hazael* with a fixed gaze until Hazael became uneasy.* Then the man of God started weeping.

12 "What's the matter, my lord?" Hazael asked him.

Elisha replied, "I know the terrible things you will do to the people of Israel. You will burn their fortified cities, kill their young men with the sword, dash their little children to the ground, and rip open their pregnant women!"

13 Hazael responded, "How could a nobody like me* ever accomplish such great things?"

Elisha answered, "The LORD has shown me that you are going to be the king of Aram."

14 When Hazael left Elisha and went back, the king asked him, "What did Elisha tell you?"

And Hazael replied, "He told me that you will surely recover."

15 But the next day Hazael took a blanket, soaked it in water, and held it over the king's face until he died. Then Hazael became the next king of Aram.

JEHORAM RULES IN JUDAH

16 Jehoram son of King Jehoshaphat of Judah began to rule over Judah in the fifth year of the reign of Joram son of Ahab, king of Israel. 17 Jehoram was thirty-two years old when he became king, and he reigned in Jerusalem eight years. 18 But Jehoram followed the example of the kings of Israel and was as wicked as King Ahab, for he had married one of Ahab's daughters. So Jehoram did what was evil in the LORD's sight. 19 But the LORD did not want to destroy Judah, for he had promised his servant David that his descendants would continue to rule, shining like a lamp forever.

20 During Jehoram's reign, the Edomites revolted against Judah and crowned their own king. 21 So Jehoram* went with all his chariots to attack the town of Zair.* The Edomites surrounded him and his chariot commanders, but he went out at night and attacked them* under cover of darkness. But Jehoram's army deserted him and fled to their homes. 22 So Edom has been independent from Judah to this day. The town of Libnah also revolted about that same time.

23 The rest of the events in Jehoram's reign and everything he did are recorded in *The Book of the History of the Kings of Judah.* 24 When Jehoram died, he was buried with his ancestors in the City of David. Then his son Ahaziah became the next king.

AHAZIAH RULES IN JUDAH

25 Ahaziah son of Jehoram began to rule over Judah in the twelfth year of the reign of Joram son of Ahab, king of Israel.

26 Ahaziah was twenty-two years old when he became king, and he reigned in Jerusalem one year. His mother was Athaliah, a granddaughter of King Omri of Israel. 27 Ahaziah followed the evil example of King Ahab's family. He did what was evil in the LORD's sight, just as Ahab's family had done, for he was related by marriage to the family of Ahab.

28 Ahaziah joined Joram son of Ahab in his war against King Hazael of Aram at Ramoth-gilead. When the Arameans wounded King Joram in the battle, 29 he returned to Jezreel to recover from the wounds he had received at Ramoth.* Because Joram was wounded, King Ahaziah of Judah went to Jezreel to visit him.

JEHU ANOINTED KING OF ISRAEL

9 Meanwhile, Elisha the prophet had summoned a member of the group of prophets. "Get ready to travel,"* he told him, "and take this flask of olive oil with you. Go to Ramoth-gilead, 2 and find Jehu son of Jehoshaphat, son of Nimshi. Call him into a private room away from his friends, 3 and pour the oil over his head. Say to him, 'This is what the LORD says: I anoint you to be the king over Israel.' Then open the door and run for your life!"

4 So the young prophet did as he was told and went to Ramoth-gilead. 5 When he arrived there, he found Jehu sitting around with the other army officers. "I have a message for you, Commander," he said.

"For which one of us?" Jehu asked.

"For you, Commander," he replied.

6 So Jehu left the others and went into the house. Then the young prophet poured the oil over Jehu's head and said, "This is what the LORD, the God of Israel, says: I anoint you king over the LORD's people, Israel. 7 You are to destroy the family of Ahab, your master. In this way, I will avenge the murder of my prophets and all the LORD's servants who were killed by Jezebel. 8 The entire family of Ahab must be wiped out. I will destroy every one of his male descendants, slave and free alike, anywhere in Israel. 9 I will destroy the family of Ahab as I destroyed the families of Jeroboam son of Nebat and of Baasha son of Ahijah. 10 Dogs will eat Ahab's wife Jezebel at the plot of land

8:11a Hebrew *He stared at him.* **8:11b** The meaning of the Hebrew is uncertain. **8:13** Hebrew *a dog.* **8:21a** Hebrew *Joram,* a variant spelling of Jehoram; also in 8:23, 24. **8:21b** Greek version reads *Seir.* **8:21c** Or *he went out and escaped.* The meaning of the Hebrew is uncertain. **8:29** Hebrew *Ramah,* a variant spelling of Ramoth. **9:1** Hebrew *Bind up your loins.*

8:8 to ask the LORD. Ironically, as the pagan king Ben-hadad of Aram faced death, he wanted to know his fate from Israel's God. This was the opposite of Ahaziah's actions in 1:1-3.

8:12 I know the terrible things you will do to the people of Israel. Elisha realized that God would use Hazael, an aide of King Ben-hadad, as an instrument of judgment against Israel.

8:15 held it over the king's face. This story illustrates that God is in control of the entire world, not just Israel. He used a brutal pagan man, Hazael, as His instrument of divine judgment against King Ben-hadad (Isa. 10:5-19; Amos 1:4).

8:19 for he had promised . . . David. The Lord spared Judah's unfaithful royal house but only because of the promise made to David that one of his descendants would always rule on the throne of Judah (2 Sam. 7:16).

8:20 Edomites revolted. Judah had ruled over Edom for many years through a governor appointed by Judah's king.

8:21 Jehoram went . . . to attack. The rebel Edomites defeated King Jehoram's army.

8:28 Ahaziah joined . . . war against King Hazael. First Kings 22 tells about King Jehoshaphat of Judah uniting with King Ahab of Israel to fight the Arameans. In a similar situation, the kings of Israel and Judah united their forces to fight the Arameans under Hazael's leadership.

9:7 destroy the family of Ahab. Jehu learned that he was appointed to be king and would be the instrument of God's judgment against King Ahab and his descendants.

in Jezreel, and no one will bury her." Then the young prophet opened the door and ran.

11 Jehu went back to his fellow officers, and one of them asked him, "What did that madman want? Is everything all right?"

"You know how a man like that babbles on," Jehu replied.

12 "You're hiding something," they said. "Tell us."

So Jehu told them, "He said to me, 'This is what the LORD says: I have anointed you to be king over Israel.'"

13 Then they quickly spread out their cloaks on the bare steps and blew the ram's horn, shouting, "Jehu is king!"

JEHU KILLS JORAM AND AHAZIAH

14 So Jehu son of Jehoshaphat, son of Nimshi, led a conspiracy against King Joram. (Now Joram had been with the army at Ramoth-gilead, defending Israel against the forces of King Hazael of Aram. 15 But King Joram* was wounded in the fighting and returned to Jezreel to recover from his wounds.) So Jehu told the men with him, "If you want me to be king, don't let anyone leave town and go to Jezreel to report what we have done."

16 Then Jehu got into a chariot and rode to Jezreel to find King Joram, who was lying there wounded. King Ahaziah of Judah was there, too, for he had gone to visit him. 17 The watchman on the tower of Jezreel saw Jehu and his company approaching, so he shouted to Joram, "I see a company of troops coming!"

"Send out a rider to ask if they are coming in peace," King Joram ordered.

18 So a horseman went out to meet Jehu and said, "The king wants to know if you are coming in peace."

Jehu replied, "What do you know about peace? Fall in behind me!"

The watchman called out to the king, "The messenger has met them, but he's not returning."

19 So the king sent out a second horseman. He rode up to them and said, "The king wants to know if you come in peace."

Again Jehu answered, "What do you know about peace? Fall in behind me!"

20 The watchman exclaimed, "The messenger has met them, but he isn't returning either! It must be Jehu son of Nimshi, for he's driving like a madman."

21 "Quick! Get my chariot ready!" King Joram commanded.

Then King Joram of Israel and King Ahaziah of Judah rode out in their chariots to meet Jehu. They met him at the plot of land that had belonged to Naboth of Jezreel. 22 King Joram demanded, "Do you come in peace, Jehu?"

Jehu replied, "How can there be peace as long as the idolatry and witchcraft of your mother, Jezebel, are all around us?"

23 Then King Joram turned the horses around* and fled, shouting to King Ahaziah, "Treason, Ahaziah!" 24 But Jehu drew his bow and shot Joram between the shoulders. The arrow pierced his heart, and he sank down dead in his chariot.

25 Jehu said to Bidkar, his officer, "Throw him into the plot of land that belonged to Naboth of Jezreel. Do you remember when you and I were riding along behind his father, Ahab? The LORD pronounced this message against him: 26 'I solemnly swear that I will repay him here on this plot of land, says the LORD, for the murder of Naboth and his sons that I saw yesterday.' So throw him out on Naboth's property, just as the LORD said."

27 When King Ahaziah of Judah saw what was happening, he fled along the road to Beth-haggan. Jehu rode after him, shouting, "Shoot him, too!" So they shot Ahaziah* in his chariot at the Ascent of Gur, near Ibleam. He was able to go on as far as Megiddo, but he died there. 28 His servants took him by chariot to Jerusalem, where they buried him with his ancestors in the City of David. 29 Ahaziah had become king over Judah in the eleventh year of the reign of Joram son of Ahab.

THE DEATH OF JEZEBEL

30 When Jezebel, the queen mother, heard that Jehu had come to Jezreel, she painted her eyelids and fixed her hair and sat at a window. 31 When Jehu entered the gate of the palace, she shouted at him, "Have you come in peace, you murderer? You're just like Zimri, who murdered his master!"*

32 Jehu looked up and saw her at the window and shouted, "Who is on my side?" And two or three eunuchs looked out at him. 33 "Throw her down!" Jehu yelled. So they threw her out the window, and her blood spattered against the wall and on the horses. And Jehu trampled her body under his horses' hooves.

34 Then Jehu went into the palace and ate and drank. Afterward he said, "Someone go and bury this cursed woman, for she is the daughter of a king." 35 But when they went out to bury her, they found only her skull, her feet, and her hands.

36 When they returned and told Jehu, he stated, "This fulfills the message from the LORD, which he spoke through his servant Elijah from Tishbe: 'At the plot of land in Jezreel, dogs will eat Jezebel's body. 37 Her remains will be scattered like dung on the plot of land in Jezreel, so that no one will be able to recognize her.'"

JEHU KILLS AHAB'S FAMILY

10 Ahab had seventy sons living in the city of Samaria. So Jehu wrote letters and sent them to Samaria, to the elders and officials of the city,* and to the guardians of King Ahab's sons. He said, 2 "The king's sons are with you, and you have at your disposal chariots, horses, a fortified city, and weapons. As

9:15 Hebrew *Jehoram,* a variant spelling of Joram; also in 9:17, 21, 22, 23, 24. **9:23** Hebrew *turned his hands.* **9:27** As in Greek and Syriac versions; Hebrew lacks *So they shot Ahaziah.* **9:31** See 1 Kgs 16:9-10, where Zimri killed his master, King Elah. **10:1** As in some Greek manuscripts and Latin Vulgate (see also 10:6); Hebrew reads *of Jezreel.*

9:15 don't let anyone leave town. To succeed, Jehu's coup had to be a surprise. The celebration of verse 13 was a means of generating support for Jehu's rebellion.

9:31 Zimri. Jezebel compared Jehu to Zimri, who had killed Elah to become king of Israel.

9:36 This fulfills the message from the LORD. Elijah had prophesied the terrible way that Jezebel would die (1 Kings 21:23). Her death happened just as God had promised (1 Kings 16:31-33; 18:13; 21:7-14.)

10:1-7 Killing the king was just the first step in taking the throne of Israel. Jehu would have to capture Samaria and murder Ahab's 70 sons. He played on the worst traits of the leaders of Samaria—their desire to survive at all costs. They were willing to commit mass murder against all of these sons in order to save themselves.

soon as you receive this letter, 3 select the best quali-
fied of your master's sons to be your king, and prepare
to fight for Ahab's dynasty."
4 But they were paralyzed with fear and said,
"We've seen that two kings couldn't stand against this
man! What can we do?"
5 So the palace and city administrators, together
with the elders and the guardians of the king's sons,
sent this message to Jehu: "We are your servants and
will do anything you tell us. We will not make anyone
king; do whatever you think is best."
6 Jehu responded with a second letter: "If you are on
my side and are going to obey me, bring the heads of
your master's sons to me at Jezreel by this time tomor-
row." Now the seventy sons of the king were being
cared for by the leaders of Samaria, where they had
been raised since childhood. 7 When the letter arrived,
the leaders killed all seventy of the king's sons. They
placed their heads in baskets and presented them to
Jehu at Jezreel.
8 A messenger went to Jehu and said, "They have
brought the heads of the king's sons."
So Jehu ordered, "Pile them in two heaps at the
entrance of the city gate, and leave them there until
morning."
9 In the morning he went out and spoke to the
crowd that had gathered around them. "You are
not to blame," he told them. "I am the one who con-
spired against my master and killed him. But who
killed all these? 10 You can be sure that the message
of the LORD that was spoken concerning Ahab's
family will not fail. The LORD declared through his
servant Elijah that this would happen." 11 Then Jehu
killed all who were left of Ahab's relatives living in
Jezreel and all his important officials, his personal
friends, and his priests. So Ahab was left without a
single survivor.
12 Then Jehu set out for Samaria. Along the way,
while he was at Beth-eked of the Shepherds, 13 he met
some relatives of King Ahaziah of Judah. "Who are
you?" he asked them.
And they replied, "We are relatives of King Ahazi-
ah. We are going to visit the sons of King Ahab and
the sons of the queen mother."
14 "Take them alive!" Jehu shouted to his men.
And they captured all forty-two of them and killed
them at the well of Beth-eked. None of them es-
caped.
15 When Jehu left there, he met Jehonadab son of
Recab, who was coming to meet him. After they had
greeted each other, Jehu said to him, "Are you as loyal
to me as I am to you?"
"Yes, I am," Jehonadab replied.
"If you are," Jehu said, "then give me your hand."
So Jehonadab put out his hand, and Jehu helped him
into the chariot. 16 Then Jehu said, "Now come with
me, and see how devoted I am to the LORD." So Jehon-
adab rode along with him.
17 When Jehu arrived in Samaria, he killed every-
one who was left there from Ahab's family, just as the
LORD had promised through Elijah.

JEHU KILLS THE PRIESTS OF BAAL

18 Then Jehu called a meeting of all the people of the
city and said to them, "Ahab's worship of Baal was
nothing compared to the way I will worship him!
19 Therefore, summon all the prophets and worship-
ers of Baal, and call together all his priests. See to it
that every one of them comes, for I am going to offer a
great sacrifice to Baal. Anyone who fails to come will
be put to death." But Jehu's cunning plan was to de-
stroy all the worshipers of Baal.
20 Then Jehu ordered, "Prepare a solemn assembly
to worship Baal!" So they did. 21 He sent messengers
throughout all Israel summoning those who wor-
shiped Baal. They all came—not a single one re-
mained behind—and they filled the temple of Baal
from one end to the other. 22 And Jehu instructed the
keeper of the wardrobe, "Be sure that every worship-
er of Baal wears one of these robes." So robes were
given to them.
23 Then Jehu went into the temple of Baal with Je-
honadab son of Recab. Jehu said to the worshipers of
Baal, "Make sure no one who worships the LORD is
here—only those who worship Baal." 24 So they were
all inside the temple to offer sacrifices and burnt of-
ferings. Now Jehu had stationed eighty of his men
outside the building and had warned them, "If you
let anyone escape, you will pay for it with your own
life."
25 As soon as Jehu had finished sacrificing the burnt
offering, he commanded his guards and officers, "Go
in and kill all of them. Don't let a single one escape!"
So they killed them all with their swords, and the
guards and officers dragged their bodies outside.*
Then Jehu's men went into the innermost fortress* of
the temple of Baal. 26 They dragged out the sacred pil-
lar* used in the worship of Baal and burned it. 27 They
smashed the sacred pillar and wrecked the temple of
Baal, converting it into a public toilet, as it remains
to this day.
28 In this way, Jehu destroyed every trace of Baal
worship from Israel. 29 He did not, however, destroy
the gold calves at Bethel and Dan, with which Jerobo-
am son of Nebat had caused Israel to sin.
30 Nonetheless the LORD said to Jehu, "You have
done well in following my instructions to destroy the
family of Ahab. Therefore, your descendants will be
kings of Israel down to the fourth generation." 31 But
Jehu did not obey the Law of the LORD, the God of Isra-
el, with all his heart. He refused to turn from the sins
that Jeroboam had led Israel to commit.

THE DEATH OF JEHU

32 At about that time the LORD began to cut down the
size of Israel's territory. King Hazael conquered sev-
eral sections of the country 33 east of the Jordan River,
including all of Gilead, Gad, Reuben, and Manasseh.
He conquered the area from the town of Aroer by the
Arnon Gorge to as far north as Gilead and Bashan.
34 The rest of the events in Jehu's reign—every-
thing he did and all his achievements—are recorded
in *The Book of the History of the Kings of Israel.*

10:25a Or *and they left their bodies lying there;* or *and they threw them out into the outermost court.* **10:25b** Hebrew *city.* **10:26** As in Greek and Syriac versions and Latin Vulgate; Hebrew reads *sacred pillars.*

10:30 You have done well. God had chosen Jehu to carry out His vengeance against the house of Ahab. God blessed Jehu with the longest dynasty (one hundred years) of any leader of the northern kingdom.

10:34 The rest of the events of Jehu's reign. Jehu paid tribute to the Assyrians. Israel's decline affected the balance of power in the region.

35 When Jehu died, he was buried in Samaria. Then his son Jehoahaz became the next king. 36 In all, Jehu reigned over Israel from Samaria for twenty-eight years.

QUEEN ATHALIAH RULES IN JUDAH

11 When Athaliah, the mother of King Ahaziah of Judah, learned that her son was dead, she began to destroy the rest of the royal family. 2 But Ahaziah's sister Jehosheba, the daughter of King Jehoram,* took Ahaziah's infant son, Joash, and stole him away from among the rest of the king's children, who were about to be killed. She put Joash and his nurse in a bedroom, and they hid him from Athaliah, so the child was not murdered. 3 Joash remained hidden in the Temple of the LORD for six years while Athaliah ruled over the land.

REVOLT AGAINST ATHALIAH

4 In the seventh year of Athaliah's reign, Jehoiada the priest summoned the commanders, the Carite mercenaries, and the palace guards to come to the Temple of the LORD. He made a solemn pact with them and made them swear an oath of loyalty there in the LORD's Temple; then he showed them the king's son.

5 Jehoiada told them, "This is what you must do. A third of you who are on duty on the Sabbath are to guard the royal palace itself. 6 Another third of you are to stand guard at the Sur Gate. And the final third must stand guard behind the palace guard. These three groups will all guard the palace. 7 The other two units who are off duty on the Sabbath must stand guard for the king at the LORD's Temple. 8 Form a bodyguard around the king and keep your weapons in hand. Kill anyone who tries to break through. Stay with the king wherever he goes."

9 So the commanders did everything as Jehoiada the priest ordered. The commanders took charge of the men reporting for duty that Sabbath, as well as those who were going off duty. They brought them all to Jehoiada the priest, 10 and he supplied them with the spears and small shields that had once belonged to King David and were stored in the Temple of the LORD. 11 The palace guards stationed themselves around the king, with their weapons ready. They formed a line from the south side of the Temple around to the north side and all around the altar.

12 Then Jehoiada brought out Joash, the king's son, placed the crown on his head, and presented him with a copy of God's laws.* They anointed him and proclaimed him king, and everyone clapped their hands and shouted, "Long live the king!"

THE DEATH OF ATHALIAH

13 When Athaliah heard the noise made by the palace guards and the people, she hurried to the LORD's Temple to see what was happening. 14 When she arrived, she saw the newly crowned king standing in his place of authority by the pillar, as was the custom at times of coronation. The commanders and trumpeters were surrounding him, and people from all over the land were rejoicing and blowing trumpets. When Athaliah saw all this, she tore her clothes in despair and shouted, "Treason! Treason!"

15 Then Jehoiada the priest ordered the commanders who were in charge of the troops, "Take her to the soldiers in front of the Temple,* and kill anyone who tries to rescue her." For the priest had said, "She must not be killed in the Temple of the LORD." 16 So they seized her and led her out to the gate where horses enter the palace grounds, and she was killed there.

JEHOIADA'S RELIGIOUS REFORMS

17 Then Jehoiada made a covenant between the LORD and the king and the people that they would be the LORD's people. He also made a covenant between the king and the people. 18 And all the people of the land went over to the temple of Baal and tore it down. They demolished the altars and smashed the idols to pieces, and they killed Mattan the priest of Baal in front of the altars.

Jehoiada the priest stationed guards at the Temple of the LORD. 19 Then the commanders, the Carite mercenaries, the palace guards, and all the people of the land escorted the king from the Temple of the LORD. They went through the gate of the guards and into the palace, and the king took his seat on the royal throne. 20 So all the people of the land rejoiced, and the city was peaceful because Athaliah had been killed at the king's palace.

21* Joash* was seven years old when he became king.

JOASH REPAIRS THE TEMPLE

12 1* Joash* began to rule over Judah in the seventh year of King Jehu's reign in Israel. He reigned in Jerusalem forty years. His mother was Zibiah from Beersheba. 2 All his life Joash did what was pleasing in the LORD's sight because Jehoiada the priest instructed him. 3 Yet even so, he did not destroy the pagan shrines, and the people still offered sacrifices and burned incense there.

4 One day King Joash said to the priests, "Collect all the money brought as a sacred offering to the LORD's Temple, whether it is a regular assessment, a payment of vows, or a voluntary gift. 5 Let the priests take

11:2 Hebrew *Joram,* a variant spelling of Jehoram. 11:12 Or *a copy of the covenant.* 11:15 Or *Bring her out from between the ranks;* or *Take her out of the Temple precincts.* The meaning of the Hebrew is uncertain. 11:21a Verse 11:21 is numbered 12:1 in Hebrew text. 11:21b Hebrew *Jehoash,* a variant spelling of Joash. 12:1a Verses 12:1-21 are numbered 12:2-22 in Hebrew text. 12:1b Hebrew *Jehoash,* a variant spelling of Joash; also in 12:2, 4, 6, 7, 18.

11:1-2 Athaliah was determined to kill all heirs to the throne of Judah and seize power. But King Joash's young son was hidden away by his supporters.

11:4 commanders. The conspiracy to install Joash as king was organized by a priest, Jehoiada, who enlisted many people to support the coup against Athaliah.

11:12 placed the crown on his head. The coup was staged as an official coronation. Joash was given the symbol of earthly kingship, the crown, and then proclaimed king and anointed.

11:17 covenant between the LORD and the king and the people. The old Mosaic covenant had to be renewed before Judah could move forward as a godly nation under Joash. Also important was a renewal of covenant between king and people.

11:21 seven years old. The new king, who would carry on the lineage of David in the royal house of Judah, was a child who had been hidden away until the time was right for his coronation.

12:2 Joash did what was pleasing. Joash was a good ruler who followed the Lord for a while. But after the priest Jehoiada died, his laxity led to the renewal of Baal worship.

12:4-5 Joash had a new financial plan for the temple. Funds given by the people were handled by assessors who would allocate funds back to priests to keep the temple in good repair.

some of that money to pay for whatever repairs are
needed at the Temple."
6 But by the twenty-third year of Joash's reign, the
priests still had not repaired the Temple. 7 So King
Joash called for Jehoiada and the other priests and
asked them, "Why haven't you repaired the Temple?
Don't use any more money for your own needs. From
now on, it must all be spent on Temple repairs." 8 So
the priests agreed not to accept any more money from
the people, and they also agreed to let others take re-
sponsibility for repairing the Temple.
9 Then Jehoiada the priest bored a hole in the lid
of a large chest and set it on the right-hand side of
the altar at the entrance of the Temple of the LORD.
The priests guarding the entrance put all of the peo-
ple's contributions into the chest. 10 Whenever the
chest became full, the court secretary and the high
priest counted the money that had been brought to
the LORD's Temple and put it into bags. 11 Then they
gave the money to the construction supervisors, who
used it to pay the people working on the LORD's Tem-
ple—the carpenters, the builders, 12 the masons, and
the stonecutters. They also used the money to buy the
timber and the finished stone needed for repairing
the LORD's Temple, and they paid any other expenses
related to the Temple's restoration.
13 The money brought to the Temple was not used
for making silver bowls, lamp snuffers, basins, trum-
pets, or other articles of gold or silver for the Tem-
ple of the LORD. 14 It was paid to the workmen, who
used it for the Temple repairs. 15 No accounting of this
money was required from the construction super-
visors, because they were honest and trustworthy
men. 16 However, the money that was contributed for
guilt offerings and sin offerings was not brought into
the LORD's Temple. It was given to the priests for their
own use.

THE END OF JOASH'S REIGN

17 About this time King Hazael of Aram went to war
against Gath and captured it. Then he turned to at-
tack Jerusalem. 18 King Joash collected all the sacred
objects that Jehoshaphat, Jehoram, and Ahaziah, the
previous kings of Judah, had dedicated, along with
what he himself had dedicated. He sent them all to
Hazael, along with all the gold in the treasuries of the
LORD's Temple and the royal palace. So Hazael called
off his attack on Jerusalem.
19 The rest of the events in Joash's reign and every-
thing he did are recorded in *The Book of the History
of the Kings of Judah.*
20 Joash's officers plotted against him and assas-
sinated him at Beth-millo on the road to Silla. 21 The
assassins were Jozacar* son of Shimeath and Jehoza-
bad son of Shomer—both trusted advisers. Joash was
buried with his ancestors in the City of David. Then
his son Amaziah became the next king.

JEHOAHAZ RULES IN ISRAEL

13 Jehoahaz son of Jehu began to rule over Israel
in the twenty-third year of King Joash's reign in
Judah. He reigned in Samaria seventeen years. 2 But
he did what was evil in the LORD's sight. He followed
the example of Jeroboam son of Nebat, continuing
the sins that Jeroboam had led Israel to commit. 3 So
the LORD was very angry with Israel, and he allowed
King Hazael of Aram and his son Ben-hadad to defeat
them repeatedly.
4 Then Jehoahaz prayed for the LORD's help, and the
LORD heard his prayer, for he could see how severely
the king of Aram was oppressing Israel. 5 So the LORD
provided someone to rescue the Israelites from the
tyranny of the Arameans. Then Israel lived in safety
again as they had in former days.
6 But they continued to sin, following the evil exam-
ple of Jeroboam. They also allowed the Asherah pole
in Samaria to remain standing. 7 Finally, Jehoahaz's
army was reduced to 50 charioteers, 10 chariots, and
10,000 foot soldiers. The king of Aram had killed the
others, trampling them like dust under his feet.
8 The rest of the events in Jehoahaz's reign—every-
thing he did and the extent of his power—are record-
ed in *The Book of the History of the Kings of Israel.*
9 When Jehoahaz died, he was buried in Samaria.
Then his son Jehoash* became the next king.

JEHOASH RULES IN ISRAEL

10 Jehoash son of Jehoahaz began to rule over Israel
in the thirty-seventh year of King Joash's reign in Ju-
dah. He reigned in Samaria sixteen years. 11 But he did
what was evil in the LORD's sight. He refused to turn
from the sins that Jeroboam son of Nebat had led Is-
rael to commit.
12 The rest of the events in Jehoash's reign and
everything he did, including the extent of his power
and his war with King Amaziah of Judah, are record-
ed in *The Book of the History of the Kings of Israel.*
13 When Jehoash died, he was buried in Samaria with
the kings of Israel. Then his son Jeroboam II became
the next king.

ELISHA'S FINAL PROPHECY

14 When Elisha was in his last illness, King Jehoash of
Israel visited him and wept over him. "My father! My
father! I see the chariots and charioteers of Israel!" he
cried.
15 Elisha told him, "Get a bow and some arrows."
And the king did as he was told. 16 Elisha told him,
"Put your hand on the bow," and Elisha laid his own
hands on the king's hands.
17 Then he commanded, "Open that eastern win-
dow," and he opened it. Then he said, "Shoot!" So he
shot an arrow. Elisha proclaimed, "This is the LORD's
arrow, an arrow of victory over Aram, for you will
completely conquer the Arameans at Aphek."

12:21 As in Greek and Syriac versions; Hebrew reads *Jozabad.* **13:9** Hebrew *Joash,* a variant spelling of Jehoash; also in 13:10, 12, 13, 14, 25.

12:9-13 Public confidence in the funding process for the temple grew. So did the offerings.

12:17 he turned to attack Jerusalem. King Hazael of Damascus captured the Philistine city of Gath, and then turned toward Jerusalem.

12:18-20 Joash used the temple treasuries to pay off Hazael and forestall the attack. His outrageous acts led his own officials to assassinate him while he was asleep.

13:3 Ben-hadad. Like his father before him, this Ben-hadad was also used as an instrument of God's punishment against the northern kingdom.

13:5 the LORD provided someone to rescue Israel. Israel was able to break the Aramean stranglehold during the reigns of Jehoash and Jeroboam II.

13:14 the chariots and charioteers of Israel. This exclamation by King Jehoash recognized that God was the real strength of Israel.

13:16 Elisha laid his own hands on the king's hands. By holding the bow with King Jehoash, Elisha demonstrated that God would give him victory over the Arameans.

[18]Then he said, "Now pick up the other arrows and strike them against the ground." So the king picked them up and struck the ground three times. [19]But the man of God was angry with him. "You should have struck the ground five or six times!" he exclaimed. "Then you would have beaten Aram until it was entirely destroyed. Now you will be victorious only three times."

[20]Then Elisha died and was buried.

Groups of Moabite raiders used to invade the land each spring. [21]Once when some Israelites were burying a man, they spied a band of these raiders. So they hastily threw the corpse into the tomb of Elisha and fled. But as soon as the body touched Elisha's bones, the dead man revived and jumped to his feet!

[22]King Hazael of Aram had oppressed Israel during the entire reign of King Jehoahaz. [23]But the LORD was gracious and merciful to the people of Israel, and they were not totally destroyed. He pitied them because of his covenant with Abraham, Isaac, and Jacob. And to this day he still has not completely destroyed them or banished them from his presence.

[24]King Hazael of Aram died, and his son Ben-hadad became the next king. [25]Then Jehoash son of Jehoahaz recaptured from Ben-hadad son of Hazael the towns that had been taken from Jehoash's father, Jehoahaz. Jehoash defeated Ben-hadad on three occasions, and he recovered the Israelite towns.

AMAZIAH RULES IN JUDAH

14 Amaziah son of Joash began to rule over Judah in the second year of the reign of King Jehoash* of Israel. [2]Amaziah was twenty-five years old when he became king, and he reigned in Jerusalem twenty-nine years. His mother was Jehoaddin from Jerusalem. [3]Amaziah did what was pleasing in the LORD's sight, but not like his ancestor David. Instead, he followed the example of his father, Joash. [4]Amaziah did not destroy the pagan shrines, and the people still offered sacrifices and burned incense there.

[5]When Amaziah was well established as king, he executed the officials who had assassinated his father. [6]However, he did not kill the children of the assassins, for he obeyed the command of the LORD as written by Moses in the Book of the Law: "Parents must not be put to death for the sins of their children, nor children for the sins of their parents. Those deserving to die must be put to death for their own crimes."*

[7]Amaziah also killed 10,000 Edomites in the Valley of Salt. He also conquered Sela and changed its name to Joktheel, as it is called to this day.

[8]One day Amaziah sent messengers with this challenge to Israel's king Jehoash, the son of Jehoahaz and grandson of Jehu: "Come and meet me in battle!"*

[9]But King Jehoash of Israel replied to King Amaziah of Judah with this story: "Out in the Lebanon mountains, a thistle sent a message to a mighty cedar tree: 'Give your daughter in marriage to my son.' But just then a wild animal of Lebanon came by and stepped on the thistle, crushing it!

[10]"You have indeed defeated Edom, and you are proud of it. But be content with your victory and stay at home! Why stir up trouble that will only bring disaster on you and the people of Judah?"

[11]But Amaziah refused to listen, so King Jehoash of Israel mobilized his army against King Amaziah of Judah. The two armies drew up their battle lines at Beth-shemesh in Judah. [12]Judah was routed by the army of Israel, and its army scattered and fled for home. [13]King Jehoash of Israel captured Judah's king, Amaziah son of Joash and grandson of Ahaziah, at Beth-shemesh. Then he marched to Jerusalem, where he demolished 600 feet* of Jerusalem's wall, from the Ephraim Gate to the Corner Gate. [14]He carried off all the gold and silver and all the articles from the Temple of the LORD. He also seized the treasures from the royal palace, along with hostages, and then returned to Samaria.

[15]The rest of the events in Jehoash's reign and everything he did, including the extent of his power and his war with King Amaziah of Judah, are recorded in *The Book of the History of the Kings of Israel.* [16]When Jehoash died, he was buried in Samaria with the kings of Israel. And his son Jeroboam II became the next king.

[17]King Amaziah of Judah lived for fifteen years after the death of King Jehoash of Israel. [18]The rest of the events in Amaziah's reign are recorded in *The Book of the History of the Kings of Judah.*

[19]There was a conspiracy against Amaziah's life in Jerusalem, and he fled to Lachish. But his enemies sent assassins after him, and they killed him there. [20]They brought his body back to Jerusalem on a horse, and he was buried with his ancestors in the City of David.

[21]All the people of Judah had crowned Amaziah's sixteen-year-old son, Uzziah,* as king in place of his father, Amaziah. [22]After his father's death, Uzziah rebuilt the town of Elath and restored it to Judah.

JEROBOAM II RULES IN ISRAEL

[23]Jeroboam II, the son of Jehoash, began to rule over Israel in the fifteenth year of King Amaziah's reign in Judah. He reigned in Samaria forty-one years. [24]He did what was evil in the LORD's sight. He refused to turn from the sins that Jeroboam son of Nebat had led Israel to commit. [25]Jeroboam II recovered the territories of Israel between Lebo-hamath and the Dead Sea,* just as the LORD, the God of Israel, had promised through Jonah son of Amittai, the prophet from Gath-hepher.

[26]For the LORD saw the bitter suffering of everyone in Israel, and that there was no one in Israel, slave or free, to help them. [27]And because the LORD

14:1 Hebrew *Joash,* a variant spelling of Jehoash; also in 14:13, 23, 27. **14:6** Deut 24:16. **14:8** Hebrew *Come, let us look one another in the face.* **14:13** Hebrew *400 cubits* [180 meters]. **14:21** Hebrew *Azariah,* a variant spelling of Uzziah. **14:25** Hebrew *the sea of the Arabah.*

13:21 the dead man revived. Even in death, Elisha's bones were able to transmit God's power (4:32-35).

13:23 covenant. Israel deserved the full punishment prescribed in the law for disobedience to the covenant, but God was full of mercy and grace toward His people.

14:3 not like his ancestor David. King Jeroboam promoted idol worship. David was considered the ideal king who was faithful to God in all ways.

14:7 Amaziah also killed 10,000 Edomites. Edom had rebelled successfully against Judah in King Jehoram's time. Amaziah defeated the Edomites.

14:8 Come and meet me in battle. Feeling bold after his victory over the Edomites, Amaziah challenged the northern kingdom to battle. Military mercenaries hired by Israel killed three thousand people of Judah and plundered property (2 Chron. 25:10-17).

had not said he would blot out the name of Israel
completely, he used Jeroboam II, the son of Jehoash,
to save them.
28 The rest of the events in the reign of Jeroboam II
and everything he did—including the extent of his
power, his wars, and how he recovered for Israel
both Damascus and Hamath, which had belonged to
Judah*—are recorded in *The Book of the History of
the Kings of Israel.* 29 When Jeroboam II died, he was
buried in Samaria* with the kings of Israel. Then his
son Zechariah became the next king.

UZZIAH RULES IN JUDAH

15 Uzziah* son of Amaziah began to rule over Ju-
dah in the twenty-seventh year of the reign of
King Jeroboam II of Israel. 2 He was sixteen years old
when he became king, and he reigned in Jerusalem
fifty-two years. His mother was Jecoliah from Jerusa-
lem.
3 He did what was pleasing in the LORD's sight,
just as his father, Amaziah, had done. 4 But he did
not destroy the pagan shrines, and the people still
offered sacrifices and burned incense there. 5 The
LORD struck the king with leprosy,* which lasted
until the day he died. He lived in isolation in a sepa-
rate house. The king's son Jotham was put in charge
of the royal palace, and he governed the people of
the land.
6 The rest of the events in Uzziah's reign and every-
thing he did are recorded in *The Book of the History
of the Kings of Judah.* 7 When Uzziah died, he was
buried with his ancestors in the City of David. And his
son Jotham became the next king.

ZECHARIAH RULES IN ISRAEL

8 Zechariah son of Jeroboam II began to rule over Is-
rael in the thirty-eighth year of King Uzziah's reign
in Judah. He reigned in Samaria six months. 9 Zech-
ariah did what was evil in the LORD's sight, as his
ancestors had done. He refused to turn from the sins
that Jeroboam son of Nebat had led Israel to commit.
10 Then Shallum son of Jabesh conspired against Zech-
ariah, assassinated him in public,* and became the
next king.
11 The rest of the events in Zechariah's reign are re-
corded in *The Book of the History of the Kings of Is-
rael.* 12 So the LORD's message to Jehu came true: "Your
descendants will be kings of Israel down to the fourth
generation."

SHALLUM RULES IN ISRAEL

13 Shallum son of Jabesh began to rule over Israel in
the thirty-ninth year of King Uzziah's reign in Ju-
dah. Shallum reigned in Samaria only one month.
14 Then Menahem son of Gadi went to Samaria from
Tirzah and assassinated him, and he became the
next king.
15 The rest of the events in Shallum's reign, includ-
ing his conspiracy, are recorded in *The Book of the
History of the Kings of Israel.*

MENAHEM RULES IN ISRAEL

16 At that time Menahem destroyed the town of Tap-
puah* and all the surrounding countryside as far as
Tirzah, because its citizens refused to surrender the
town. He killed the entire population and ripped open
the pregnant women.
17 Menahem son of Gadi began to rule over Israel in
the thirty-ninth year of King Uzziah's reign in Judah.
He reigned in Samaria ten years. 18 But Menahem did
what was evil in the LORD's sight. During his entire
reign, he refused to turn from the sins that Jeroboam
son of Nebat had led Israel to commit.
19 Then King Tiglath-pileser* of Assyria invaded the
land. But Menahem paid him thirty-seven tons* of sil-
ver to gain his support in tightening his grip on royal
power. 20 Menahem extorted the money from the rich
of Israel, demanding that each of them pay fifty piec-
es* of silver to the king of Assyria. So the king of As-
syria turned from attacking Israel and did not stay in
the land.
21 The rest of the events in Menahem's reign and
everything he did are recorded in *The Book of the
History of the Kings of Israel.* 22 When Menahem
died, his son Pekahiah became the next king.

PEKAHIAH RULES IN ISRAEL

23 Pekahiah son of Menahem began to rule over Israel
in the fiftieth year of King Uzziah's reign in Judah.
He reigned in Samaria two years. 24 But Pekahiah did
what was evil in the LORD's sight. He refused to turn
from the sins that Jeroboam son of Nebat had led Is-
rael to commit.
25 Then Pekah son of Remaliah, the commander of
Pekahiah's army, conspired against him. With fifty
men from Gilead, Pekah assassinated the king, along
with Argob and Arieh, in the citadel of the palace at
Samaria. And Pekah reigned in his place.
26 The rest of the events in Pekahiah's reign and
everything he did are recorded in *The Book of the
History of the Kings of Israel.*

PEKAH RULES IN ISRAEL

27 Pekah son of Remaliah began to rule over Israel in
the fifty-second year of King Uzziah's reign in Judah.
He reigned in Samaria twenty years. 28 But Pekah did
what was evil in the LORD's sight. He refused to turn
from the sins that Jeroboam son of Nebat had led Is-
rael to commit.
29 During Pekah's reign, King Tiglath-pileser of
Assyria attacked Israel again, and he captured the
towns of Ijon, Abel-beth-maacah, Janoah, Kedesh,
and Hazor. He also conquered the regions of Gilead,
Galilee, and all of Naphtali, and he took the people to

14:28 Or *to Yaudi.* The meaning of the Hebrew is uncertain. **14:29** As in some Greek manuscripts; Hebrew lacks *he was buried in Samaria.* **15:1** Hebrew *Azariah,* a variant spelling of Uzziah; also in 15:6, 7, 8, 17, 23, 27. **15:5** Or *with a contagious skin disease.* The Hebrew word used here and throughout this passage can describe various skin diseases. **15:10** Or *at Ibleam.* **15:16** As in some Greek manuscripts; Hebrew reads *Tiphsah.* **15:19a** Hebrew *Pul,* another name for Tiglath-pileser. **15:19b** Hebrew *1,000 talents* [34 metric tons]. **15:20** Hebrew *50 shekels* [20 ounces or 570 grams].

14:28 recovered for Israel both Damascus and Hamath. These cities had been under David's rule but were lost to Syria. King Jeroboam finally brought them back under Israel's control.

15:6 Uzziah's reign and everything he did. Uzziah increased Judah's military strength and improved the organization of its government.

15:12 message . . . came true. Jehu had destroyed the worshipers of Baal in Ahab's wicked kingdom. God had promised Jehu that his dynasty would continue for four generations, and it did so.

15:20 extorted money from the rich of Israel. Rather than fight the Assyrians, King Menahem of Israel paid them off with a bribe.

Assyria as captives. 30 Then Hoshea son of Elah conspired against Pekah and assassinated him. He began to rule over Israel in the twentieth year of Jotham son of Uzziah.

31 The rest of the events in Pekah's reign and everything he did are recorded in *The Book of the History of the Kings of Israel.*

JOTHAM RULES IN JUDAH

32 Jotham son of Uzziah began to rule over Judah in the second year of King Pekah's reign in Israel. 33 He was twenty-five years old when he became king, and he reigned in Jerusalem sixteen years. His mother was Jerusha, the daughter of Zadok.

34 Jotham did what was pleasing in the LORD's sight. He did everything his father, Uzziah, had done. 35 But he did not destroy the pagan shrines, and the people still offered sacrifices and burned incense there. He rebuilt the upper gate of the Temple of the LORD.

36 The rest of the events in Jotham's reign and everything he did are recorded in *The Book of the History of the Kings of Judah.* 37 In those days the LORD began to send King Rezin of Aram and King Pekah of Israel to attack Judah. 38 When Jotham died, he was buried with his ancestors in the City of David. And his son Ahaz became the next king.

AHAZ RULES IN JUDAH

16 Ahaz son of Jotham began to rule over Judah in the seventeenth year of King Pekah's reign in Israel. 2 Ahaz was twenty years old when he became king, and he reigned in Jerusalem sixteen years. He did not do what was pleasing in the sight of the LORD his God, as his ancestor David had done. 3 Instead, he followed the example of the kings of Israel, even sacrificing his own son in the fire.* In this way, he followed the detestable practices of the pagan nations the LORD had driven from the land ahead of the Israelites. 4 He offered sacrifices and burned incense at the pagan shrines and on the hills and under every green tree.

5 Then King Rezin of Aram and King Pekah of Israel came up to attack Jerusalem. They besieged Ahaz but could not conquer him. 6 At that time the king of Edom* recovered the town of Elath for Edom.* He drove out the people of Judah and sent Edomites* to live there, as they do to this day.

7 King Ahaz sent messengers to King Tiglath-pileser of Assyria with this message: "I am your servant and your vassal.* Come up and rescue me from the attacking armies of Aram and Israel." 8 Then Ahaz took the silver and gold from the Temple of the LORD and the palace treasury and sent it as a payment to the Assyrian king. 9 So the king of Assyria attacked the Aramean capital of Damascus and led its population away as captives, resettling them in Kir. He also killed King Rezin.

10 King Ahaz then went to Damascus to meet with King Tiglath-pileser of Assyria. While he was there, he took special note of the altar. Then he sent a model of the altar to Uriah the priest, along with its design in full detail. 11 Uriah followed the king's instructions and built an altar just like it, and it was ready before the king returned from Damascus. 12 When the king returned, he inspected the altar and made offerings on it. 13 He presented a burnt offering and a grain offering, he poured out a liquid offering, and he sprinkled the blood of peace offerings on the altar.

14 Then King Ahaz removed the old bronze altar from its place in front of the LORD's Temple, between the entrance and the new altar, and placed it on the north side of the new altar. 15 He told Uriah the priest, "Use the new altar* for the morning sacrifices of burnt offering, the evening grain offering, the king's burnt offering and grain offering, and the burnt offerings of all the people, as well as their grain offerings and liquid offerings. Sprinkle the blood from all the burnt offerings and sacrifices on the new altar. The bronze altar will be for my personal use only." 16 Uriah the priest did just as King Ahaz commanded him.

17 Then the king removed the side panels and basins from the portable water carts. He also removed the great bronze basin called the Sea from the backs of the bronze oxen and placed it on the stone pavement. 18 In deference to the king of Assyria, he also removed the canopy that had been constructed inside the palace for use on the Sabbath day,* as well as the king's outer entrance to the Temple of the LORD.

19 The rest of the events in Ahaz's reign and everything he did are recorded in *The Book of the History of the Kings of Judah.* 20 When Ahaz died, he was buried with his ancestors in the City of David. Then his son Hezekiah became the next king.

HOSHEA RULES IN ISRAEL

17 Hoshea son of Elah began to rule over Israel in the twelfth year of King Ahaz's reign in Judah. He reigned in Samaria nine years. 2 He did what was evil in the LORD's sight, but not to the same extent as the kings of Israel who ruled before him.

3 King Shalmaneser of Assyria attacked King Hoshea, so Hoshea was forced to pay heavy tribute to Assyria. 4 But Hoshea stopped paying the annual tribute and conspired against the king of Assyria by asking King So of Egypt* to help him shake free of Assyria's power. When the king of Assyria discovered this treachery, he seized Hoshea and put him in prison.

16:3 Or *even making his son pass through the fire.* **16:6a** As in Latin Vulgate; Hebrew reads *Rezin king of Aram.* **16:6b** As in Latin Vulgate; Hebrew reads *Aram.* **16:6c** As in Greek version, Latin Vulgate, and an alternate reading of the Masoretic Text; the other alternate reads *Arameans.* **16:7** Hebrew *your son.* **16:15** Hebrew *the great altar.* **16:18** The meaning of the Hebrew is uncertain. **17:4** Or *by asking the king of Egypt at Sais.*

15:30 Hoshea. This king of Israel aligned himself with Assyria. In fact, the king of Assyria claimed to have established Hoshea's rule.

15:35 upper gate. The restoration of the temple's Upper Gate was one of Jotham's greatest accomplishments. But he failed to remove the high places—areas designated for the worship of false gods.

15:37 Rezin . . . Pekah. The alliance of King Pekah of Israel with Rezin, king of Aram, strengthened his position against Judah.

16:2 as his ancestor David had done. King David was the standard of excellence for Judah's kings. Ahaz did not measure up.

16:3 sacrificing his son in the fire. God had forbidden His people to participate in child sacrifice, yet the king of Judah succumbed to this terrible sin.

16:7 Ahaz sent messengers. Since Aram and Israel were uniting against Assyria, Assyria was a likely candidate for an alignment with Judah.

16:8 from the LORD's temple. Ahaz followed the example of King Joash, who had used the temple wealth to pay tribute to Hazael of Damascus (12:17-18). The treasures that Ahaz paid to Assyria had probably been restored during Jotham's reign.

16:13-14 King Ahaz placed his new altar in the most prominent place in the temple. This reflected the priority he placed on his alliance with Assyria.

SAMARIA FALLS TO ASSYRIA

5 Then the king of Assyria invaded the entire land, and for three years he besieged the city of Samaria. 6 Finally, in the ninth year of King Hoshea's reign, Samaria fell, and the people of Israel were exiled to Assyria. They were settled in colonies in Halah, along the banks of the Habor River in Gozan, and in the cities of the Medes.

7 This disaster came upon the people of Israel because they worshiped other gods. They sinned against the LORD their God, who had brought them safely out of Egypt and had rescued them from the power of Pharaoh, the king of Egypt. 8 They had followed the practices of the pagan nations the LORD had driven from the land ahead of them, as well as the practices the kings of Israel had introduced. 9 The people of Israel had also secretly done many things that were not pleasing to the LORD their God. They built pagan shrines for themselves in all their towns, from the smallest outpost to the largest walled city. 10 They set up sacred pillars and Asherah poles at the top of every hill and under every green tree. 11 They offered sacrifices on all the hilltops, just like the nations the LORD had driven from the land ahead of them. So the people of Israel had done many evil things, arousing the LORD's anger. 12 Yes, they worshiped idols,* despite the LORD's specific and repeated warnings.

13 Again and again the LORD had sent his prophets and seers to warn both Israel and Judah: "Turn from all your evil ways. Obey my commands and decrees—the entire law that I commanded your ancestors to obey, and that I gave you through my servants the prophets."

14 But the Israelites would not listen. They were as stubborn as their ancestors who had refused to believe in the LORD their God. 15 They rejected his decrees and the covenant he had made with their ancestors, and they despised all his warnings. They worshiped worthless idols, so they became worthless themselves. They followed the example of the nations around them, disobeying the LORD's command not to imitate them.

16 They rejected all the commands of the LORD their God and made two calves from metal. They set up an Asherah pole and worshiped Baal and all the forces of heaven. 17 They even sacrificed their own sons and daughters in the fire.* They consulted fortune-tellers and practiced sorcery and sold themselves to evil, arousing the LORD's anger.

18 Because the LORD was very angry with Israel, he swept them away from his presence. Only the tribe of Judah remained in the land. 19 But even the people of Judah refused to obey the commands of the LORD their God, for they followed the evil practices that Israel had introduced. 20 The LORD rejected all the descendants of Israel. He punished them by handing them over to their attackers until he had banished Israel from his presence.

21 For when the LORD* tore Israel away from the kingdom of David, they chose Jeroboam son of Nebat as their king. But Jeroboam drew Israel away from following the LORD and made them commit a great sin. 22 And the people of Israel persisted in all the evil ways of Jeroboam. They did not turn from these sins 23 until the LORD finally swept them away from his presence, just as all his prophets had warned. So Israel was exiled from their land to Assyria, where they remain to this day.

FOREIGNERS SETTLE IN ISRAEL

24 The king of Assyria transported groups of people from Babylon, Cuthah, Avva, Hamath, and Sepharvaim and resettled them in the towns of Samaria, replacing the people of Israel. They took possession of Samaria and lived in its towns. 25 But since these foreign settlers did not worship the LORD when they first arrived, the LORD sent lions among them, which killed some of them.

26 So a message was sent to the king of Assyria: "The people you have sent to live in the towns of Samaria do not know the religious customs of the God of the land. He has sent lions among them to destroy them because they have not worshiped him correctly."

27 The king of Assyria then commanded, "Send one of the exiled priests back to Samaria. Let him live there and teach the new residents the religious customs of the God of the land." 28 So one of the priests who had been exiled from Samaria returned to Bethel and taught the new residents how to worship the LORD.

29 But these various groups of foreigners also continued to worship their own gods. In town after town where they lived, they placed their idols at the pagan shrines that the people of Samaria had built. 30 Those from Babylon worshiped idols of their god Succoth-benoth. Those from Cuthah worshiped their god Nergal. And those from Hamath worshiped Ashima. 31 The Avvites worshiped their gods Nibhaz and Tartak. And the people from Sepharvaim even burned their own children as sacrifices to their gods Adrammelech and Anammelech.

32 These new residents worshiped the LORD, but they also appointed from among themselves all sorts of people as priests to offer sacrifices at their places of worship. 33 And though they worshiped the LORD, they continued to follow their own gods according to the religious customs of the nations from which they came. 34 And this is still going on today. They continue to follow their former practices instead of truly worshiping the LORD and obeying the decrees, regulations, instructions, and commands he gave the descendants of Jacob, whose name he changed to Israel.

17:12 The Hebrew term (literally *round things*) probably alludes to dung. 17:17 Or *They even made their sons and daughters pass through the fire.* 17:21 Hebrew *he;* compare 1 Kgs 11:31-32.

17:5 besieged the city of Samaria. Samaria, capital of Israel, was fortified with a massive defensive wall.

17:6 exiled. This deportation to a foreign nation had been prophesied to Jeroboam, the first ruler of the northern kingdom (1 Kings 14:5-11).

17:7 they worshiped other gods. Israel's chief betrayal in their covenant with God was worship of pagan gods.

17:16-17 rejected all the commands. God consistently reminded the people not to take on the worship practices of the Canaanites. But they refused to listen.

17:24 replacing the people of Israel. The Assyrians deported the most influential Israelites and replaced them with citizens who were loyal to Assyria.

17:25 lions. The lions, much like the frogs in Egypt (Ex. 8) and the rats in Philista (1 Sam. 5–6), represented a plague of God to the new inhabitants in Samaria.

17:29-33 Samaria became a melting-pot culture, combining the truth of God with popular religions of the day.

35 For the LORD had made a covenant with the descendants of Jacob and commanded them: "Do not worship any other gods or bow before them or serve them or offer sacrifices to them. 36 But worship only the LORD, who brought you out of Egypt with great strength and a powerful arm. Bow down to him alone, and offer sacrifices only to him. 37 Be careful at all times to obey the decrees, regulations, instructions, and commands that he wrote for you. You must not worship other gods. 38 Do not forget the covenant I made with you, and do not worship other gods. 39 You must worship only the LORD your God. He is the one who will rescue you from all your enemies."

40 But the people would not listen and continued to follow their former practices. 41 So while these new residents worshiped the LORD, they also worshiped their idols. And to this day their descendants do the same.

HEZEKIAH RULES IN JUDAH

18 Hezekiah son of Ahaz began to rule over Judah in the third year of King Hoshea's reign in Israel. 2 He was twenty-five years old when he became king, and he reigned in Jerusalem twenty-nine years. His mother was Abijah,* the daughter of Zechariah. 3 He did what was pleasing in the LORD's sight, just as his ancestor David had done. 4 He removed the pagan shrines, smashed the sacred pillars, and cut down the Asherah poles. He broke up the bronze serpent that Moses had made, because the people of Israel had been offering sacrifices to it. The bronze serpent was called Nehushtan.*

5 Hezekiah trusted in the LORD, the God of Israel. There was no one like him among all the kings of Judah, either before or after his time. 6 He remained faithful to the LORD in everything, and he carefully obeyed all the commands the LORD had given Moses. 7 So the LORD was with him, and Hezekiah was successful in everything he did. He revolted against the king of Assyria and refused to pay him tribute. 8 He also conquered the Philistines as far distant as Gaza and its territory, from their smallest outpost to their largest walled city.

9 During the fourth year of Hezekiah's reign, which was the seventh year of King Hoshea's reign in Israel, King Shalmaneser of Assyria attacked the city of Samaria and began a siege against it. 10 Three years later, during the sixth year of King Hezekiah's reign and the ninth year of King Hoshea's reign in Israel, Samaria fell. 11 At that time the king of Assyria exiled the Israelites to Assyria and placed them in colonies in Halah, along the banks of the Habor River in Gozan, and in the cities of the Medes. 12 For they refused to listen to the LORD their God and obey him. Instead, they violated his covenant—all the laws that Moses the LORD's servant had commanded them to obey.

ASSYRIA INVADES JUDAH

13 In the fourteenth year of King Hezekiah's reign,* King Sennacherib of Assyria came to attack the fortified towns of Judah and conquered them. 14 King Hezekiah sent this message to the king of Assyria at Lachish: "I have done wrong. I will pay whatever tribute money you demand if you will only withdraw." The king of Assyria then demanded a settlement of more than eleven tons of silver and one ton of gold.* 15 To gather this amount, King Hezekiah used all the silver stored in the Temple of the LORD and in the palace treasury. 16 Hezekiah even stripped the gold from the doors of the LORD's Temple and from the doorposts he had overlaid with gold, and he gave it all to the Assyrian king.

17 Nevertheless, the king of Assyria sent his commander in chief, his field commander, and his chief of staff* from Lachish with a huge army to confront King Hezekiah in Jerusalem. The Assyrians took up a position beside the aqueduct that feeds water into the upper pool, near the road leading to the field where cloth is washed.* 18 They summoned King Hezekiah, but the king sent these officials to meet with them: Eliakim son of Hilkiah, the palace administrator; Shebna the court secretary; and Joah son of Asaph, the royal historian.

SENNACHERIB THREATENS JERUSALEM

19 Then the Assyrian king's chief of staff told them to give this message to Hezekiah:

"This is what the great king of Assyria says: What are you trusting in that makes you so confident? 20 Do you think that mere words can substitute for military skill and strength? Who are you counting on, that you have rebelled against me? 21 On Egypt? If you lean on Egypt, it will be like a reed that splinters beneath your weight and pierces your hand. Pharaoh, the king of Egypt, is completely unreliable!

22 "But perhaps you will say to me, 'We are trusting in the LORD our God!' But isn't he the one who was insulted by Hezekiah? Didn't Hezekiah tear down his shrines and altars and make everyone in Judah and Jerusalem worship only at the altar here in Jerusalem?

23 "I'll tell you what! Strike a bargain with my master, the king of Assyria. I will give you 2,000 horses if you can find that many men to ride on them! 24 With your tiny army, how can you think of challenging even the weakest contingent of my master's troops, even with the help of Egypt's chariots and charioteers? 25 What's more, do you think we have invaded your land without the LORD's direction? The LORD himself told us, 'Attack this land and destroy it!'"

18:2 As in parallel text at 2 Chr 29:1; Hebrew reads *Abi,* a variant spelling of Abijah. **18:4** *Nehushtan* sounds like the Hebrew terms that mean "snake," "bronze," and "unclean thing." **18:13** The fourteenth year of Hezekiah's reign was 701 B.C. **18:14** Hebrew *300 talents* [10 metric tons] *of silver and 30 talents* [1 metric ton] *of gold.* **18:17a** Or *the rabshakeh;* also in 18:19, 26, 27, 28, 37. **18:17b** Or *bleached.*

17:41 descendants. God commanded His people to teach their children about His deliverance (Deut. 6:4-9). But they continued to participate in idol worship.

18:1-2 Hezekiah. At age 11, Hezekiah began serving as king under his father, Ahaz.

18:4 bronze serpent. Other righteous kings of Judah had destroyed the idols used in false worship. Hezekiah destroyed even this artifact made by Moses. It had become an idol to the Israelites.

18:7 revolted against . . . Assyria. During Ahaz's reign, Judah had become a vassal of Assyria. But Hezekiah refused to pay tribute to Assyria and to recognize its pagan gods.

18:14-16 Hezekiah refused at first to pay tribute to Assyria. But he eventually gave in and raided his own holdings as well as the temple treasures to pacify his Assyrian overseers.

18:23 I will give you 2,000 horses. This statement implies that Judah's army was inferior to the Assyrian army.

26 Then Eliakim son of Hilkiah, Shebna, and Joah
said to the Assyrian chief of staff, "Please speak to us
in Aramaic, for we understand it well. Don't speak in
Hebrew,* for the people on the wall will hear."
27 But Sennacherib's chief of staff replied, "Do you
think my master sent this message only to you and
your master? He wants all the people to hear it, for
when we put this city under siege, they will suffer
along with you. They will be so hungry and thirsty
that they will eat their own dung and drink their own
urine."
28 Then the chief of staff stood and shouted in He-
brew to the people on the wall, "Listen to this message
from the great king of Assyria! 29 This is what the king
says: Don't let Hezekiah deceive you. He will never
be able to rescue you from my power. 30 Don't let him
fool you into trusting in the LORD by saying, 'The LORD
will surely rescue us. This city will never fall into the
hands of the Assyrian king!'
31 "Don't listen to Hezekiah! These are the terms the
king of Assyria is offering: Make peace with me—
open the gates and come out. Then each of you can
continue eating from your own grapevine and fig
tree and drinking from your own well. 32 Then I will
arrange to take you to another land like this one—a
land of grain and new wine, bread and vineyards,
olive groves and honey. Choose life instead of death!
"Don't listen to Hezekiah when he tries to mislead
you by saying, 'The LORD will rescue us!' 33 Have the
gods of any other nations ever saved their people
from the king of Assyria? 34 What happened to the
gods of Hamath and Arpad? And what about the gods
of Sepharvaim, Hena, and Ivvah? Did any god rescue
Samaria from my power? 35 What god of any nation
has ever been able to save its people from my power?
So what makes you think that the LORD can rescue Je-
rusalem from me?"
36 But the people were silent and did not utter a
word because Hezekiah had commanded them, "Do
not answer him."
37 Then Eliakim son of Hilkiah, the palace admin-
istrator; Shebna the court secretary; and Joah son of
Asaph, the royal historian, went back to Hezekiah.
They tore their clothes in despair, and they went in
to see the king and told him what the Assyrian chief
of staff had said.

HEZEKIAH SEEKS THE LORD'S HELP

19 When King Hezekiah heard their report, he tore
his clothes and put on burlap and went into the
Temple of the LORD. 2 And he sent Eliakim the palace
administrator, Shebna the court secretary, and the
leading priests, all dressed in burlap, to the prophet
Isaiah son of Amoz. 3 They told him, "This is what King
Hezekiah says: Today is a day of trouble, insults, and
disgrace. It is like when a child is ready to be born, but
the mother has no strength to deliver the baby. 4 But
perhaps the LORD your God has heard the Assyrian
chief of staff,* sent by the king to defy the living God,
and will punish him for his words. Oh, pray for those
of us who are left!"
5 After King Hezekiah's officials delivered the
king's message to Isaiah, 6 the prophet replied, "Say to
your master, 'This is what the LORD says: Do not be dis-
turbed by this blasphemous speech against me from
the Assyrian king's messengers. 7 Listen! I myself will
move against him,* and the king will receive a mes-
sage that he is needed at home. So he will return to
his land, where I will have him killed with a sword.'"
8 Meanwhile, the Assyrian chief of staff left Jerusa-
lem and went to consult the king of Assyria, who had
left Lachish and was attacking Libnah.
9 Soon afterward King Sennacherib received word
that King Tirhakah of Ethiopia* was leading an army
to fight against him. Before leaving to meet the attack,
he sent messengers back to Hezekiah in Jerusalem
with this message:

10 "This message is for King Hezekiah of Judah.
Don't let your God, in whom you trust, deceive you
with promises that Jerusalem will not be captured
by the king of Assyria. 11 You know perfectly well
what the kings of Assyria have done wherever
they have gone. They have completely destroyed
everyone who stood in their way! Why should
you be any different? 12 Have the gods of other
nations rescued them—such nations as Gozan,
Haran, Rezeph, and the people of Eden who were
in Tel-assar? My predecessors destroyed them all!
13 What happened to the king of Hamath and the
king of Arpad? What happened to the kings of
Sepharvaim, Hena, and Ivvah?"

14 After Hezekiah received the letter from the mes-
sengers and read it, he went up to the LORD's Temple
and spread it out before the LORD. 15 And Hezekiah
prayed this prayer before the LORD: "O LORD, God of
Israel, you are enthroned between the mighty cher-
ubim! You alone are God of all the kingdoms of the
earth. You alone created the heavens and the earth.
16 Bend down, O LORD, and listen! Open your eyes,
O LORD, and see! Listen to Sennacherib's words of defi-
ance against the living God.
17 "It is true, LORD, that the kings of Assyria have
destroyed all these nations. 18 And they have thrown
the gods of these nations into the fire and burned
them. But of course the Assyrians could destroy
them! They were not gods at all—only idols of wood
and stone shaped by human hands. 19 Now, O LORD
our God, rescue us from his power; then all the king-
doms of the earth will know that you alone, O LORD,
are God."

18:26 Hebrew *in the dialect of Judah;* also in 18:28. **19:4** Or *the rabshakeh;* also in 19:8. **19:7** Hebrew *I will put a spirit in him.* **19:9** Hebrew *of Cush.*

18:26 speak to us in Aramaic. Only the most educated people understood Aramaic. The leaders of Judah were hoping that if they switched to Aramaic, the townspeople listening from the wall wouldn't be able to understand the conversation. This might cause them to grow discouraged.

18:27-30 never be able to rescue you from my power. The Assyrian commander's words were intended for all the people of Judah. He wanted to break their confidence so that they would surrender in fear.

19:2 Isaiah. The writer of the book of Isaiah and a prophet during the reigns of Uzziah, Jotham, and Ahaz.

19:3 to deliver the baby. In other words, this was a "do or die" situation—a huge threat.

19:4 defy. King Hezekiah's hope seemed based more on God's protection of his reputation than on God's compassion for Judah.

19:7 I myself will move against him. The report Isaiah described may have been that Tirhakah, king of Egypt, was marching against Assyria (v. 9).

19:18 They were not gods at all. Hezekiah answered the accusations of the Assyrian commander (18:33-35) and affirmed that the Lord is the only true God.

ISAIAH PREDICTS JUDAH'S DELIVERANCE

20 Then Isaiah son of Amoz sent this message to Hez-
ekiah: "This is what the LORD, the God of Israel, says:
I have heard your prayer about King Sennacherib of
Assyria. 21 And the LORD has spoken this word against
him:

"The virgin daughter of Zion
despises you and laughs at you.
The daughter of Jerusalem
shakes her head in derision as you flee.

22 "Whom have you been defying and ridiculing?
Against whom did you raise your voice?
At whom did you look with such haughty eyes?
It was the Holy One of Israel!
23 By your messengers you have defied the Lord.
You have said, 'With my many chariots
I have conquered the highest mountains—
yes, the remotest peaks of Lebanon.
I have cut down its tallest cedars
and its finest cypress trees.
I have reached its farthest corners
and explored its deepest forests.
24 I have dug wells in many foreign lands
and refreshed myself with their water.
With the sole of my foot
I stopped up all the rivers of Egypt!'

25 "But have you not heard?
I decided this long ago.
Long ago I planned it,
and now I am making it happen.
I planned for you to crush fortified cities
into heaps of rubble.
26 That is why their people have so little power
and are so frightened and confused.
They are as weak as grass,
as easily trampled as tender green shoots.
They are like grass sprouting on a housetop,
scorched before it can grow lush and tall.

27 "But I know you well—
where you stay
and when you come and go.
I know the way you have raged against me.
28 And because of your raging against me
and your arrogance, which I have heard for
myself,
I will put my hook in your nose
and my bit in your mouth.
I will make you return
by the same road on which you came."

29 Then Isaiah said to Hezekiah, "Here is the proof that
what I say is true:

"This year you will eat only what grows up by
itself,
and next year you will eat what springs up
from that.
But in the third year you will plant crops and
harvest them;
you will tend vineyards and eat their fruit.
30 And you who are left in Judah,
who have escaped the ravages of the siege,
will put roots down in your own soil
and will grow up and flourish.
31 For a remnant of my people will spread out from
Jerusalem,
a group of survivors from Mount Zion.
The passionate commitment of the LORD of
Heaven's Armies*
will make this happen!

32 "And this is what the LORD says about the king of
Assyria:

"His armies will not enter Jerusalem.
They will not even shoot an arrow at it.
They will not march outside its gates with their
shields
nor build banks of earth against its walls.
33 The king will return to his own country
by the same road on which he came.
He will not enter this city,
says the LORD.
34 For my own honor and for the sake of my servant
David,
I will defend this city and protect it."

35 That night the angel of the LORD went out to the
Assyrian camp and killed 185,000 Assyrian soldiers.
When the surviving Assyrians* woke up the next
morning, they found corpses everywhere. 36 Then
King Sennacherib of Assyria broke camp and re-
turned to his own land. He went home to his capital
of Nineveh and stayed there.
37 One day while he was worshiping in the temple
of his god Nisroch, his sons* Adrammelech and Sha-
rezer killed him with their swords. They then escaped
to the land of Ararat, and another son, Esarhaddon,
became the next king of Assyria.

HEZEKIAH'S SICKNESS AND RECOVERY

20 About that time Hezekiah became deathly ill,
and the prophet Isaiah son of Amoz went to
visit him. He gave the king this message: "This is what
the LORD says: Set your affairs in order, for you are go-
ing to die. You will not recover from this illness."
2 When Hezekiah heard this, he turned his face
to the wall and prayed to the LORD, 3 "Remember,
O LORD, how I have always been faithful to you and
have served you single-mindedly, always doing
what pleases you." Then he broke down and wept
bitterly.
4 But before Isaiah had left the middle courtyard,*
this message came to him from the LORD: 5 "Go back to

19:31 As in Greek and Syriac versions, Latin Vulgate, and an alternate reading of the Masoretic Text (see also Isa 37:32); the other alternate reads *the LORD.* 19:35 Hebrew *When they.* 19:37 As in Greek version and an alternate reading of the Masoretic Text (see also Isa 37:38); the other alternate reading lacks *his sons.* 20:4 As in Greek version and an alternate reading in the Masoretic Text; the other alternate reads *the middle of the city.*

19:22 Holy One of Israel. Assyria's offense was not just against the city of Jerusalem or the nation of Judah. It was against God.

19:28 will put my hook in your nose. Some ancient monuments picture Assyria's enemies being led around with hooks in their noses. Isaiah's prophecy reversed the image.

19:30-31 remnant of my people. Attacks on Samaria and Judah had forced survivors to settle in this last piece of the original nation of Israel.

19:32 will not enter. God sometimes delivered His people through mighty military victories. In this case, a shift in Sennacherib's schedule showed God's provision.

Hezekiah, the leader of my people. Tell him, 'This is
what the LORD, the God of your ancestor David, says:
I have heard your prayer and seen your tears. I will
heal you, and three days from now you will get out
of bed and go to the Temple of the LORD. [6] I will add
fifteen years to your life, and I will rescue you and
this city from the king of Assyria. I will defend this
city for my own honor and for the sake of my servant
David.'"

[7] Then Isaiah said, "Make an ointment from figs."
So Hezekiah's servants spread the ointment over the
boil, and Hezekiah recovered!

[8] Meanwhile, Hezekiah had said to Isaiah, "What
sign will the LORD give to prove that he will heal me
and that I will go to the Temple of the LORD three days
from now?"

[9] Isaiah replied, "This is the sign from the LORD to
prove that he will do as he promised. Would you like
the shadow on the sundial to go forward ten steps or
backward ten steps?*"

[10] "The shadow always moves forward," Hezekiah
replied, "so that would be easy. Make it go ten steps
backward instead." [11] So Isaiah the prophet asked the
LORD to do this, and he caused the shadow to move ten
steps backward on the sundial* of Ahaz!

ENVOYS FROM BABYLON

[12] Soon after this, Merodach-baladan* son of Baladan,
king of Babylon, sent Hezekiah his best wishes and a
gift, for he had heard that Hezekiah had been very
sick. [13] Hezekiah received the Babylonian envoys and
showed them everything in his treasure-houses—the
silver, the gold, the spices, and the aromatic oils. He
also took them to see his armory and showed them
everything in his royal treasuries! There was nothing
in his palace or kingdom that Hezekiah did not show
them.

[14] Then Isaiah the prophet went to King Hezekiah
and asked him, "What did those men want? Where
were they from?"

Hezekiah replied, "They came from the distant land
of Babylon."

[15] "What did they see in your palace?" Isaiah asked.

"They saw everything," Hezekiah replied. "I showed
them everything I own—all my royal treasuries."

[16] Then Isaiah said to Hezekiah, "Listen to this mes-
sage from the LORD: [17] The time is coming when every-
thing in your palace—all the treasures stored up
by your ancestors until now—will be carried off to
Babylon. Nothing will be left, says the LORD. [18] Some
of your very own sons will be taken away into exile.
They will become eunuchs who will serve in the pal-
ace of Babylon's king."

[19] Then Hezekiah said to Isaiah, "This message you
have given me from the LORD is good." For the king
was thinking, "At least there will be peace and securi-
ty during my lifetime."

[20] The rest of the events in Hezekiah's reign, includ-
ing the extent of his power and how he built a pool
and dug a tunnel* to bring water into the city, are re-
corded in *The Book of the History of the Kings of Ju-
dah.* [21] Hezekiah died, and his son Manasseh became
the next king.

MANASSEH RULES IN JUDAH

21 Manasseh was twelve years old when he be-
came king, and he reigned in Jerusalem fif-
ty-five years. His mother was Hephzibah. [2] He did
what was evil in the LORD's sight, following the de-
testable practices of the pagan nations that the LORD
had driven from the land ahead of the Israelites. [3] He
rebuilt the pagan shrines his father, Hezekiah, had de-
stroyed. He constructed altars for Baal and set up an
Asherah pole, just as King Ahab of Israel had done.
He also bowed before all the powers of the heavens
and worshiped them.

[4] He built pagan altars in the Temple of the LORD,
the place where the LORD had said, "My name will re-
main in Jerusalem forever." [5] He built these altars for
all the powers of the heavens in both courtyards of
the LORD's Temple. [6] Manasseh also sacrificed his own
son in the fire.* He practiced sorcery and divination,
and he consulted with mediums and psychics. He did
much that was evil in the LORD's sight, arousing his
anger.

[7] Manasseh even made a carved image of Ashe-
rah and set it up in the Temple, the very place where
the LORD had told David and his son Solomon: "My
name will be honored forever in this Temple and in
Jerusalem—the city I have chosen from among all
the tribes of Israel. [8] If the Israelites will be careful
to obey my commands—all the laws my servant
Moses gave them—I will not send them into exile
from this land that I gave their ancestors." [9] But the
people refused to listen, and Manasseh led them to
do even more evil than the pagan nations that the
LORD had destroyed when the people of Israel en-
tered the land.

[10] Then the LORD said through his servants the
prophets: [11] "King Manasseh of Judah has done
many detestable things. He is even more wicked
than the Amorites, who lived in this land before Is-
rael. He has caused the people of Judah to sin with
his idols.* [12] So this is what the LORD, the God of Is-
rael, says: I will bring such disaster on Jerusalem
and Judah that the ears of those who hear about it
will tingle with horror. [13] I will judge Jerusalem by
the same standard I used for Samaria and the same
measure* I used for the family of Ahab. I will wipe
away the people of Jerusalem as one wipes a dish

20:9 Or *The shadow on the sundial has gone forward ten steps; do you want it to go backward ten steps?* **20:11** Hebrew *the steps.* **20:12** As in some Hebrew manuscripts and Greek and Syriac versions (see also Isa 39:1); Masoretic Text reads *Berodach-baladan.* **20:20** Hebrew *water-course.* **21:6** Or *also made his son pass through the fire.* **21:11** The Hebrew term (literally *round things*) probably alludes to dung; also in 21:21. **21:13** Hebrew *the same plumb line I used for Samaria and the same plumb bob.*

20:6 for the sake of my servant David. King David established Jerusalem as his capital and the site for Solomon's temple. God had made a similar promise to Solomon (1 Kings 11:13).

20:12 Merodach-baladan . . . sent Hezekiah. This was more than a get-well card. This Babylonian king invited Hezekiah to join a political alliance.

20:13 showed them. Hezekiah realized that a wealthy and powerful king would stand a better chance of allying with Babylonia against Assyria.

20:14-17 Hezekiah reported his actions to Isaiah the prophet, but he held back any mention of an alliance. Hezekiah's plan eventually backfired. Judah was exiled to Babylon 115 years later.

20:20 a tunnel. Hezekiah's tunnel through solid rock connected Jerusalem to an outside water source so they could hold on during a long siege.

21:1 reigned . . . fifty-five years. Manasseh's reign was the longest of any king of Israel or Judah.

21:2 evil. Manasseh rebuilt the pagan worship sites that his father, Hezekiah, had torn down and reverted to worship of Canaanite idols.

and turns it upside down. 14 Then I will reject even the remnant of my own people who are left, and I will hand them over as plunder for their enemies. 15 For they have done great evil in my sight and have angered me ever since their ancestors came out of Egypt."

16 Manasseh also murdered many innocent people until Jerusalem was filled from one end to the other with innocent blood. This was in addition to the sin that he caused the people of Judah to commit, leading them to do evil in the LORD's sight.

17 The rest of the events in Manasseh's reign and everything he did, including the sins he committed, are recorded in *The Book of the History of the Kings of Judah.* 18 When Manasseh died, he was buried in the palace garden, the garden of Uzza. Then his son Amon became the next king.

AMON RULES IN JUDAH

19 Amon was twenty-two years old when he became king, and he reigned in Jerusalem two years. His mother was Meshullemeth, the daughter of Haruz from Jotbah. 20 He did what was evil in the LORD's sight, just as his father, Manasseh, had done. 21 He followed the example of his father, worshiping the same idols his father had worshiped. 22 He abandoned the LORD, the God of his ancestors, and he refused to follow the LORD's ways.

23 Then Amon's own officials conspired against him and assassinated him in his palace. 24 But the people of the land killed all those who had conspired against King Amon, and they made his son Josiah the next king.

25 The rest of the events in Amon's reign and what he did are recorded in *The Book of the History of the Kings of Judah.* 26 He was buried in his tomb in the garden of Uzza. Then his son Josiah became the next king.

JOSIAH RULES IN JUDAH

22 Josiah was eight years old when he became king, and he reigned in Jerusalem thirty-one years. His mother was Jedidah, the daughter of Adaiah from Bozkath. 2 He did what was pleasing in the LORD's sight and followed the example of his ancestor David. He did not turn away from doing what was right.

3 In the eighteenth year of his reign, King Josiah sent Shaphan son of Azaliah and grandson of Meshullam, the court secretary, to the Temple of the LORD. He told him, 4 "Go to Hilkiah the high priest and have him count the money the gatekeepers have collected from the people at the LORD's Temple. 5 Entrust this money to the men assigned to supervise the restoration of the LORD's Temple. Then they can use it to pay workers to repair the Temple. 6 They will need to hire carpenters, builders, and masons. Also have them buy the timber and the finished stone needed to repair the Temple. 7 But don't require the construction supervisors to keep account of the money they receive, for they are honest and trustworthy men."

HILKIAH DISCOVERS GOD'S LAW

8 Hilkiah the high priest said to Shaphan the court secretary, "I have found the Book of the Law in the LORD's Temple!" Then Hilkiah gave the scroll to Shaphan, and he read it.

9 Shaphan went to the king and reported, "Your officials have turned over the money collected at the Temple of the LORD to the workers and supervisors at the Temple." 10 Shaphan also told the king, "Hilkiah the priest has given me a scroll." So Shaphan read it to the king.

11 When the king heard what was written in the Book of the Law, he tore his clothes in despair. 12 Then he gave these orders to Hilkiah the priest, Ahikam son of Shaphan, Acbor son of Micaiah, Shaphan the court secretary, and Asaiah the king's personal adviser: 13 "Go to the Temple and speak to the LORD for me and for the people and for all Judah. Inquire about the words written in this scroll that has been found. For the LORD's great anger is burning against us because our ancestors have not obeyed the words in this scroll. We have not been doing everything it says we must do."

14 So Hilkiah the priest, Ahikam, Acbor, Shaphan, and Asaiah went to the New Quarter* of Jerusalem to consult with the prophet Huldah. She was the wife of Shallum son of Tikvah, son of Harhas, the keeper of the Temple wardrobe.

15 She said to them, "The LORD, the God of Israel, has spoken! Go back and tell the man who sent you, 16 'This is what the LORD says: I am going to bring disaster on this city* and its people. All the words written in the scroll that the king of Judah has read will come true. 17 For my people have abandoned me and offered sacrifices to pagan gods, and I am very angry with them for everything they have done. My anger will burn against this place, and it will not be quenched.'

18 "But go to the king of Judah who sent you to seek the LORD and tell him: 'This is what the LORD, the God of Israel, says concerning the message you have just heard: 19 You were sorry and humbled yourself before the LORD when you heard what I said against this city and its people—that this land would be cursed and become desolate. You tore your clothing in despair and wept before me in repentance. And I have indeed heard you, says the LORD. 20 So I will not send the promised disaster until after you have died and been buried in peace. You will not see the disaster I am going to bring on this city.'"

So they took her message back to the king.

22:14 Or *the Second Quarter,* a newer section of Jerusalem. Hebrew reads *the Mishneh.* **22:16** Hebrew *this place;* also in 22:19, 20.

21:14 reject. God let His people suffer the consequences of their own choices.

21:15 they have done great evil. From the time of the exodus, the Hebrews had lived in cycles of obedience and disobedience. Their exile in Babylonia would be the harshest judgment of their history.

22:1 Josiah. The last righteous king from the line of David before Judah's exile.

22:4 the money. This money had been collected specifically for restoration of the temple.

22:8 Book of the Law. Either the complete writings of Moses (Genesis through Deuteronomy) or a portion of the book of Deuteronomy by itself.

22:14 Huldah. A woman with great influence in Judah. The men considered her word a message from God.

22:20 Your eyes will not see. King Josiah received the same comfort as Hezekiah. Judgment was coming, but he would not be around to watch the ax fall.

JOSIAH'S RELIGIOUS REFORMS

23 Then the king summoned all the elders of Judah and Jerusalem. 2 And the king went up to the Temple of the LORD with all the people of Judah and Jerusalem, along with the priests and the prophets—all the people from the least to the greatest. There the king read to them the entire Book of the Covenant that had been found in the LORD's Temple. 3 The king took his place of authority beside the pillar and renewed the covenant in the LORD's presence. He pledged to obey the LORD by keeping all his commands, laws, and decrees with all his heart and soul. In this way, he confirmed all the terms of the covenant that were written in the scroll, and all the people pledged themselves to the covenant.

4 Then the king instructed Hilkiah the high priest and the priests of the second rank and the Temple gatekeepers to remove from the LORD's Temple all the articles that were used to worship Baal, Asherah, and all the powers of the heavens. The king had all these things burned outside Jerusalem on the terraces of the Kidron Valley, and he carried the ashes away to Bethel. 5 He did away with the idolatrous priests, who had been appointed by the previous kings of Judah, for they had offered sacrifices at the pagan shrines throughout Judah and even in the vicinity of Jerusalem. They had also offered sacrifices to Baal, and to the sun, the moon, the constellations, and to all the powers of the heavens. 6 The king removed the Asherah pole from the LORD's Temple and took it outside Jerusalem to the Kidron Valley, where he burned it. Then he ground the ashes of the pole to dust and threw the dust over the graves of the people. 7 He also tore down the living quarters of the male and female shrine prostitutes that were inside the Temple of the LORD, where the women wove coverings for the Asherah pole.

8 Josiah brought to Jerusalem all the priests who were living in other towns of Judah. He also defiled the pagan shrines, where they had offered sacrifices—all the way from Geba to Beersheba. He destroyed the shrines at the entrance to the gate of Joshua, the governor of Jerusalem. This gate was located to the left of the city gate as one enters the city. 9 The priests who had served at the pagan shrines were not allowed to serve at* the LORD's altar in Jerusalem, but they were allowed to eat unleavened bread with the other priests.

10 Then the king defiled the altar of Topheth in the valley of Ben-Hinnom, so no one could ever again use it to sacrifice a son or daughter in the fire* as an offering to Molech. 11 He removed from the entrance of the LORD's Temple the horse statues that the former kings of Judah had dedicated to the sun. They were near the quarters of Nathan-melech the eunuch, an officer of the court.* The king also burned the chariots dedicated to the sun.

12 Josiah tore down the altars that the kings of Judah had built on the palace roof above the upper room of Ahaz. The king destroyed the altars that Manasseh had built in the two courtyards of the LORD's Temple. He smashed them to bits* and scattered the pieces in the Kidron Valley. 13 The king also desecrated the pagan shrines east of Jerusalem, to the south of the Mount of Corruption, where King Solomon of Israel had built shrines for Ashtoreth, the detestable goddess of the Sidonians; and for Chemosh, the detestable god of the Moabites; and for Molech,* the vile god of the Ammonites. 14 He smashed the sacred pillars and cut down the Asherah poles. Then he desecrated these places by scattering human bones over them.

15 The king also tore down the altar at Bethel—the pagan shrine that Jeroboam son of Nebat had made when he caused Israel to sin. He burned down the shrine and ground it to dust, and he burned the Asherah pole. 16 Then Josiah turned around and noticed several tombs in the side of the hill. He ordered that the bones be brought out, and he burned them on the altar at Bethel to desecrate it. (This happened just as the LORD had promised through the man of God when Jeroboam stood beside the altar at the festival.)

Then Josiah turned and looked up at the tomb of the man of God* who had predicted these things. 17 "What is that monument over there?" Josiah asked.

And the people of the town told him, "It is the tomb of the man of God who came from Judah and predicted the very things that you have just done to the altar at Bethel!"

18 Josiah replied, "Leave it alone. Don't disturb his bones." So they did not burn his bones or those of the old prophet from Samaria.

19 Then Josiah demolished all the buildings at the pagan shrines in the towns of Samaria, just as he had done at Bethel. They had been built by the various kings of Israel and had made the LORD* very angry. 20 He executed the priests of the pagan shrines on their own altars, and he burned human bones on the altars to desecrate them. Finally, he returned to Jerusalem.

JOSIAH CELEBRATES PASSOVER

21 King Josiah then issued this order to all the people: "You must celebrate the Passover to the LORD your God, as required in this Book of the Covenant." 22 There had not been a Passover celebration like that since the time when the judges ruled in Israel, nor throughout all the years of the kings of Israel and Judah. 23 But in the eighteenth year of King Josiah's reign, this Passover was celebrated to the LORD in Jerusalem.

24 Josiah also got rid of the mediums and psychics, the household gods, the idols,* and every other kind of detestable practice, both in Jerusalem and throughout

23:9 Hebrew *did not come up to.* **23:10** Or *to make a son or daughter pass through the fire.* **23:11** The meaning of the Hebrew is uncertain. **23:12** Or *He quickly removed them.* **23:13** Hebrew *Milcom,* a variant spelling of Molech. **23:16** As in Greek version; Hebrew lacks *when Jeroboam stood beside the altar at the festival. Then Josiah turned and looked up at the tomb of the man of God.* **23:19** As in Greek and Syriac versions and Latin Vulgate; Hebrew lacks *the LORD.* **23:24** The Hebrew term (literally *round things*) probably alludes to dung.

23:2 entire Book of the Covenant. They probably read sections of Deuteronomy 27–28 where God set the terms of His covenant.

23:9 were not allowed to serve. Josiah honored the priests of the high places (those who led in pagan worship) by allowing them to fraternize with priests who led in the worship of God.

23:15 pagan shrine that Jeroboam . . . had made. When King Jeroboam built this altar, he received a prophecy about its destruction.

23:20 executed the priests. This refers to the pagan priests, not the levitical priests who were incorporated back into Jerusalem.

23:21 as required. Deuteronomy 16:1-8 outlined the Passover as a community celebration at the temple sanctuary instead of a family event held in homes.

23:22 not been a Passover. King Josiah's attention to detail made this Passover special. He made sure that only Levites slaughtered the sacrificial lambs, and he brought people from Israel and Judah together for the celebration.

the land of Judah. He did this in obedience to the laws written in the scroll that Hilkiah the priest had found in the LORD's Temple. 25 Never before had there been a king like Josiah, who turned to the LORD with all his heart and soul and strength, obeying all the laws of Moses. And there has never been a king like him since.

26 Even so, the LORD was very angry with Judah because of all the wicked things Manasseh had done to provoke him. 27 For the LORD said, "I will also banish Judah from my presence just as I have banished Israel. And I will reject my chosen city of Jerusalem and the Temple where my name was to be honored."

28 The rest of the events in Josiah's reign and all his deeds are recorded in *The Book of the History of the Kings of Judah.*

29 While Josiah was king, Pharaoh Neco, king of Egypt, went to the Euphrates River to help the king of Assyria. King Josiah and his army marched out to fight him,* but King Neco* killed him when they met at Megiddo. 30 Josiah's officers took his body back in a chariot from Megiddo to Jerusalem and buried him in his own tomb. Then the people of the land anointed Josiah's son Jehoahaz and made him the next king.

JEHOAHAZ RULES IN JUDAH

31 Jehoahaz was twenty-three years old when he became king, and he reigned in Jerusalem three months. His mother was Hamutal, the daughter of Jeremiah from Libnah. 32 He did what was evil in the LORD's sight, just as his ancestors had done.

33 Pharaoh Neco put Jehoahaz in prison at Riblah in the land of Hamath to prevent him from ruling* in Jerusalem. He also demanded that Judah pay 7,500 pounds of silver and 75 pounds of gold* as tribute.

JEHOIAKIM RULES IN JUDAH

34 Pharaoh Neco then installed Eliakim, another of Josiah's sons, to reign in place of his father, and he changed Eliakim's name to Jehoiakim. Jehoahaz was taken to Egypt as a prisoner, where he died.

35 In order to get the silver and gold demanded as tribute by Pharaoh Neco, Jehoiakim collected a tax from the people of Judah, requiring them to pay in proportion to their wealth.

36 Jehoiakim was twenty-five years old when he became king, and he reigned in Jerusalem eleven years. His mother was Zebidah, the daughter of Pedaiah from Rumah. 37 He did what was evil in the LORD's sight, just as his ancestors had done.

24 During Jehoiakim's reign, King Nebuchadnezzar of Babylon invaded the land of Judah. Jehoiakim surrendered and paid him tribute for three years but then rebelled. 2 Then the LORD sent bands of Babylonian,* Aramean, Moabite, and Ammonite raiders against Judah to destroy it, just as the LORD had promised through his prophets. 3 These disasters happened to Judah because of the LORD's command. He had decided to banish Judah from his presence because of the many sins of Manasseh, 4 who had filled Jerusalem with innocent blood. The LORD would not forgive this.

5 The rest of the events in Jehoiakim's reign and all his deeds are recorded in *The Book of the History of the Kings of Judah.* 6 When Jehoiakim died, his son Jehoiachin became the next king.

7 The king of Egypt did not venture out of his country after that, for the king of Babylon captured the entire area formerly claimed by Egypt—from the Brook of Egypt to the Euphrates River.

JEHOIACHIN RULES IN JUDAH

8 Jehoiachin was eighteen years old when he became king, and he reigned in Jerusalem three months. His mother was Nehushta, the daughter of Elnathan from Jerusalem. 9 Jehoiachin did what was evil in the LORD's sight, just as his father had done.

10 During Jehoiachin's reign, the officers of King Nebuchadnezzar of Babylon came up against Jerusalem and besieged it. 11 Nebuchadnezzar himself arrived at the city during the siege. 12 Then King Jehoiachin, along with the queen mother, his advisers, his commanders, and his officials, surrendered to the Babylonians.

In the eighth year of Nebuchadnezzar's reign, he took Jehoiachin prisoner. 13 As the LORD had said beforehand, Nebuchadnezzar carried away all the treasures from the LORD's Temple and the royal palace. He stripped away* all the gold objects that King Solomon of Israel had placed in the Temple. 14 King Nebuchadnezzar took all of Jerusalem captive, including all the commanders and the best of the soldiers, craftsmen, and artisans—10,000 in all. Only the poorest people were left in the land.

15 Nebuchadnezzar led King Jehoiachin away as a captive to Babylon, along with the queen mother, his wives and officials, and all Jerusalem's elite. 16 He also exiled 7,000 of the best troops and 1,000 craftsmen and artisans, all of whom were strong and fit for war. 17 Then the king of Babylon installed Mattaniah, Jehoiachin's* uncle, as the next king, and he changed Mattaniah's name to Zedekiah.

ZEDEKIAH RULES IN JUDAH

18 Zedekiah was twenty-one years old when he became king, and he reigned in Jerusalem eleven years.

23:29a Or *Josiah went out to meet him.* **23:29b** Hebrew *he.* **23:33a** The meaning of the Hebrew is uncertain. **23:33b** Hebrew *100 talents* [3,400 kilograms] *of silver and 1 talent* [34 kilograms] *of gold.* **24:2** Or *Chaldean.* **24:13** Or *He cut apart.* **24:17** Hebrew *his.*

23:29 King Josiah . . . marched out to fight him. Because Judah was located between Assyria and Egypt, Josiah opposed any alliance between the two nations.

23:30 Jehoahaz. The third son of Josiah, he opposed any alliance with Egypt and won the people's support.

23:33 He also demanded . . . as tribute. When Neco of Egypt killed Josiah of Judah, he took control of Judah.

23:34 Jehoiakim. Jehoahaz was formerly named Shallum; Jehoiakim was formerly named Eliakim.

24:1 King Nebuchadnezzar of Babylon. When Babylon conquered Egypt, Judah came under Nebuchadnezzar's rule. Eventually Nebuchadnezzar took captives, including Daniel, from Judah to Babylon (see Dan. 1).

24:2 Babylonians . . . Ammonite. The Babylonians commanded such power that all these countries were at King Nebuchadnezzar's disposal to launch an attack against Judah.

24:6 When Jehoiakim died. Jeremiah prophesied that Jehoiakim would not be given a royal burial (see Jer. 22:19).

24:7 did not venture out. The Babylonians had become so strong that even Egypt would not take a stand against them.

24:13-16 carried away. Nebuchadnezzar seized the riches of Judah and the most skilled and educated people. He carried them to Babylon, leaving the peasants to till the land.

24:17-19 Mattaniah . . . Zedekiah. When Babylonia came to power, Nebuchadnezzar named Josiah's youngest son as king and changed his name to Zedekiah.

His mother was Hamutal, the daughter of Jeremiah
from Libnah. [19] But Zedekiah did what was evil in
the LORD's sight, just as Jehoiakim had done. [20] These
things happened because of the LORD's anger against
the people of Jerusalem and Judah, until he finally
banished them from his presence and sent them into
exile.

THE FALL OF JERUSALEM

Zedekiah rebelled against the king of Babylon.

25 So on January 15,* during the ninth year of
Zedekiah's reign, King Nebuchadnezzar of
Babylon led his entire army against Jerusalem. They
surrounded the city and built siege ramps against its
walls. [2] Jerusalem was kept under siege until the elev-
enth year of King Zedekiah's reign.
[3] By July 18 in the eleventh year of Zedekiah's
reign,* the famine in the city had become very severe,
and the last of the food was entirely gone. [4] Then a
section of the city wall was broken down. Since the
city was surrounded by the Babylonians,* the sol-
diers waited for nightfall and escaped* through the
gate between the two walls behind the king's garden.
Then they headed toward the Jordan Valley.*
[5] But the Babylonian* troops chased the king and
overtook him on the plains of Jericho, for his men had
all deserted him and scattered. [6] They captured the
king and took him to the king of Babylon at Riblah,
where they pronounced judgment upon Zedekiah.
[7] They made Zedekiah watch as they slaughtered his
sons. Then they gouged out Zedekiah's eyes, bound
him in bronze chains, and led him away to Babylon.

THE TEMPLE DESTROYED

[8] On August 14 of that year,* which was the nineteenth
year of King Nebuchadnezzar's reign, Nebuzaradan,
the captain of the guard and an official of the Bab-
ylonian king, arrived in Jerusalem. [9] He burned down
the Temple of the LORD, the royal palace, and all the
houses of Jerusalem. He destroyed all the important
buildings* in the city. [10] Then he supervised the entire
Babylonian army as they tore down the walls of Jeru-
salem on every side. [11] Then Nebuzaradan, the captain
of the guard, took as exiles the rest of the people who
remained in the city, the defectors who had declared
their allegiance to the king of Babylon, and the rest of
the population. [12] But the captain of the guard allowed
some of the poorest people to stay behind to care for
the vineyards and fields.
[13] The Babylonians broke up the bronze pillars in
front of the LORD's Temple, the bronze water carts,
and the great bronze basin called the Sea, and they
carried all the bronze away to Babylon. [14] They also
took all the ash buckets, shovels, lamp snuffers, ladles,
and all the other bronze articles used for making sac-
rifices at the Temple. [15] The captain of the guard also
took the incense burners and basins, and all the other
articles made of pure gold or silver.
[16] The weight of the bronze from the two pillars,
the Sea, and the water carts was too great to be mea-
sured. These things had been made for the LORD's
Temple in the days of Solomon. [17] Each of the pillars
was 27 feet* tall. The bronze capital on top of each
pillar was 7½ feet* high and was decorated with
a network of bronze pomegranates all the way
around.
[18] Nebuzaradan, the captain of the guard, took with
him as prisoners Seraiah the high priest, Zephaniah
the priest of the second rank, and the three chief gate
keepers. [19] And from among the people still hiding in
the city, he took an officer who had been in charge of
the Judean army; five of the king's personal advisers;
the army commander's chief secretary, who was in
charge of recruitment; and sixty other citizens. [20] Neb-
uzaradan, the captain of the guard, took them all to
the king of Babylon at Riblah. [21] And there at Riblah,
in the land of Hamath, the king of Babylon had them
all put to death. So the people of Judah were sent into
exile from their land.

GEDALIAH GOVERNS IN JUDAH

[22] Then King Nebuchadnezzar appointed Gedaliah
son of Ahikam and grandson of Shaphan as governor
over the people he had left in Judah. [23] When all the
army commanders and their men learned that the
king of Babylon had appointed Gedaliah as governor,
they went to see him at Mizpah. These included Ish-
mael son of Nethaniah, Johanan son of Kareah, Se-
raiah son of Tanhumeth the Netophathite, Jezaniah*
son of the Maacathite, and all their men.
[24] Gedaliah vowed to them that the Babylonian of-
ficials meant them no harm. "Don't be afraid of them.
Live in the land and serve the king of Babylon, and all
will go well for you," he promised.
[25] But in midautumn of that year,* Ishmael son of
Nethaniah and grandson of Elishama, who was a
member of the royal family, went to Mizpah with ten
men and killed Gedaliah. He also killed all the Judeans
and Babylonians who were with him at Mizpah.
[26] Then all the people of Judah, from the least to
the greatest, as well as the army commanders, fled in
panic to Egypt, for they were afraid of what the Bab-
ylonians would do to them.

25:1 Hebrew *on the tenth day of the tenth month,* of the ancient Hebrew lunar calendar. A number of events in 2 Kings can be cross-checked with dates in surviving Babylonian records and related accurately to our modern calendar. This day was January 15, 588 B.C. **25:3** Hebrew *By the ninth day of the [fourth] month* [in the eleventh year of Zedekiah's reign] (compare Jer 39:2; 52:6 and the notes there). This day was July 18, 586 B.C.; also see note on 25:1. **25:4a** Or *the Chaldeans;* also in 25:13, 25, 26. **25:4b** As in Greek version (see also Jer 39:4; 52:7); Hebrew lacks *escaped.* **25:4c** Hebrew *the Arabah.* **25:5** Or *Chaldean*; also in 25:10, 24. **25:8** Hebrew *On the seventh day of the fifth month,* of the ancient Hebrew lunar calendar. This day was August 14, 586 B.C.; also see note on 25:1. **25:9** Or *destroyed the houses of all the important people.* **25:17a** Hebrew *18 cubits* [8.3 meters]. **25:17b** As in parallel texts at 1 Kgs 7:16, 2 Chr 3:15, and Jer 52:22, all of which read *5 cubits* [2.3 meters]; Hebrew reads *3 cubits,* which is 4.5 feet or 1.4 meters. **25:23** As in parallel text at Jer 40:8; Hebrew reads *Jaazaniah*, a variant spelling of Jezaniah. **25:25** Hebrew *in the seventh month,* of the ancient Hebrew lunar calendar. This month occurred within the months of October and November 586 B.C.; also see note on 25:1.

25:7 slaughtered his sons. The prophet Jeremiah had warned Zedekiah to surrender to Babylonia, but Zedekiah did not listen (see Jer. 38:1-28). He suffered greatly for his rebellion.

25:8-10 nineteenth year. In 586 B.C. the temple was burned, and the walls of the city of Jerusalem were torn down. In their exile in Babylon, the people of Judah were cut off from their temple and their sacred city. It was about 50 years before a remnant of the people was allowed to return to Jerusalem.

25:22-23 Gedaliah. A man who had served as King Josiah's secretary of state.

25:24 serve the king of Babylon. Gedaliah heeded Jeremiah's advice that his predecessor, Zedekiah, had ignored (v. 7).

HOPE FOR ISRAEL'S ROYAL LINE

27 In the thirty-seventh year of the exile of King Jehoiachin of Judah, Evil-merodach ascended to the Babylonian throne. He was kind to* Jehoiachin and released him* from prison on April 2 of that year.*
28 He spoke kindly to Jehoiachin and gave him a higher place than all the other exiled kings in Babylon. 29 He supplied Jehoiachin with new clothes to replace his prison garb and allowed him to dine in the king's presence for the rest of his life. 30 So the king gave him a regular food allowance as long as he lived.

25:27a Hebrew *He raised the head of.* **25:27b** As in some Hebrew manuscripts and Greek and Syriac versions (see also Jer 52:31); Masoretic Text lacks *released him.* **25:27c** Hebrew *on the twenty-seventh day of the twelfth month,* of the ancient Hebrew lunar calendar. This day was April 2, 561 B.C.; also see note on 25:1.

INTRODUCTION TO

1 CHRONICLES

PERSONAL READING PLAN

☐ 1 Chronicles 2:1-55
☐ 1 Chronicles 3:1-24
☐ 1 Chronicles 4:1-43
☐ 1 Chronicles 5:1-26
☐ 1 Chronicles 6:1-30
☐ 1 Chronicles 6:31-80
☐ 1 Chronicles 7:1-40
☐ 1 Chronicles 9:1-44
☐ 1 Chronicles 10:1–11:9
☐ 1 Chronicles 11:10-47
☐ 1 Chronicles 12:1-40
☐ 1 Chronicles 13:1–14:17
☐ 1 Chronicles 15:1–16:6
☐ 1 Chronicles 16:7-43
☐ 1 Chronicles 18:1–19:19
☐ 1 Chronicles 20:1–22:1
☐ 1 Chronicles 22:2–23:32
☐ 1 Chronicles 24:1–25:31
☐ 1 Chronicles 26:1–27:34
☐ 1 Chronicles 28:1-21
☐ 1 Chronicles 29:1-30

AUTHOR

Jewish tradition suggests Ezra as author, but there is no firm evidence.

DATE

First Chronicles was probably written toward the end of the fifth century B.C. or a little later. The actions narrated in the book are centered primarily in the reign of David (ca 1011–971 B.C.).

THEME

A family record to remind exiled and returning Israelites of God's chosen king and of their place in the restored Jerusalem.

HISTORICAL BACKGROUND

The reign of David was the golden age of Jewish history. The country was united, and military victories allowed David to enlarge his territory. He introduced new administrative organization, which brought stability and prosperity. He brought the ark of the covenant to Jerusalem and restructured the tabernacle worship.

CHARACTERISTICS

In his recounting of history long past, the author relied on many written sources. About half of his work was taken from Samuel and Kings, and the rest he drew from the Pentateuch, Judges, Ruth, Psalms, Isaiah, Jeremiah, Lamentations, and Zechariah. Chapters 1–9 trace Israel's family record back to Adam. God is evident behind the scenes selecting a people for Himself. Chapters 10–29 record the history of David's reign from the viewpoint of the chronicler's priestly interests. His concern is not the ups and downs of one man, but the lasting achievements of David—the monarchy and the temple. David is seen as God's chosen king around whom the welfare of the nation revolves. The chronicler omits much of the personal and family detail recorded in 2 Samuel. Instead, he records the nature of David's reorganization of worship in Jerusalem—detailing his appointments of not only priests but singers, musicians, and gatekeepers.

FROM ADAM TO NOAH'S SONS

1 The descendants of Adam were Seth, Enosh,
[2] Kenan, Mahalalel, Jared, [3] Enoch, Methuselah,
Lamech, [4] and Noah.
The sons of Noah were* Shem, Ham, and Japheth.

DESCENDANTS OF JAPHETH

[5] The descendants of Japheth were Gomer, Magog,
Madai, Javan, Tubal, Meshech, and Tiras.
[6] The descendants of Gomer were Ashkenaz,
Riphath,* and Togarmah.
[7] The descendants of Javan were Elishah, Tarshish,
Kittim, and Rodanim.

DESCENDANTS OF HAM

[8] The descendants of Ham were Cush, Mizraim,* Put,
and Canaan.
[9] The descendants of Cush were Seba, Havilah,
Sabtah, Raamah, and Sabteca. The descendants of
Raamah were Sheba and Dedan. [10] Cush was also
the ancestor of Nimrod, who was the first heroic
warrior on earth.
[11] Mizraim was the ancestor of the Ludites, Anamites,
Lehabites, Naphtuhites, [12] Pathrusites, Casluhites,
and the Caphtorites, from whom the Philistines
came.*
[13] Canaan's oldest son was Sidon, the ancestor of
the Sidonians. Canaan was also the ancestor of
the Hittites,* [14] Jebusites, Amorites, Girgashites,
[15] Hivites, Arkites, Sinites, [16] Arvadites, Zemarites,
and Hamathites.

DESCENDANTS OF SHEM

[17] The descendants of Shem were Elam, Asshur,
Arphaxad, Lud, and Aram.
The descendants of Aram were* Uz, Hul, Gether, and
Mash.*
[18] Arphaxad was the father of Shelah.
Shelah was the father of Eber.
[19] Eber had two sons. The first was named Peleg
(which means "division"), for during his lifetime
the people of the world were divided into dif-
ferent language groups. His brother's name was
Joktan.
[20] Joktan was the ancestor of Almodad, Sheleph, Haz-
armaveth, Jerah, [21] Hadoram, Uzal, Diklah, [22] Obal,*
Abimael, Sheba, [23] Ophir, Havilah, and Jobab. All
these were descendants of Joktan.

[24] So this is the family line descended from Shem: Ar-
phaxad, Shelah,* [25] Eber, Peleg, Reu, [26] Serug, Nahor,
Terah, [27] and Abram, later known as Abraham.

DESCENDANTS OF ABRAHAM

[28] The sons of Abraham were Isaac and Ishmael.
[29] These are their genealogical records:
The sons of Ishmael were Nebaioth (the oldest),
Kedar, Adbeel, Mibsam, [30] Mishma, Dumah, Massa,
Hadad, Tema, [31] Jetur, Naphish, and Kedemah.
These were the sons of Ishmael.
[32] The sons of Keturah, Abraham's concubine, were
Zimran, Jokshan, Medan, Midian, Ishbak, and
Shuah.
The sons of Jokshan were Sheba and Dedan.
[33] The sons of Midian were Ephah, Epher, Hanoch,
Abida, and Eldaah.
All these were descendants of Abraham through his
concubine Keturah.

DESCENDANTS OF ISAAC

[34] Abraham was the father of Isaac. The sons of Isaac
were Esau and Israel.*

DESCENDANTS OF ESAU

[35] The sons of Esau were Eliphaz, Reuel, Jeush, Jalam,
and Korah.
[36] The descendants of Eliphaz were Teman, Omar,
Zepho,* Gatam, Kenaz, and Amalek, who was born
to Timna.*
[37] The descendants of Reuel were Nahath, Zerah,
Shammah, and Mizzah.

ORIGINAL PEOPLES OF EDOM

[38] The descendants of Seir were Lotan, Shobal, Zi-
beon, Anah, Dishon, Ezer, and Dishan.
[39] The descendants of Lotan were Hori and Hemam.*
Lotan's sister was named Timna.
[40] The descendants of Shobal were Alvan,* Mana-
hath, Ebal, Shepho,* and Onam.
The descendants of Zibeon were Aiah and Anah.
[41] The son of Anah was Dishon.
The descendants of Dishon were Hemdan,* Eshban,
Ithran, and Keran.
[42] The descendants of Ezer were Bilhan, Zaavan, and
Akan.*
The descendants of Dishan* were Uz and Aran.

1:4 As in Greek version (see also Gen 5:3-32); Hebrew lacks *The sons of Noah were.* **1:6** As in some Hebrew manuscripts and Greek version (see also Gen 10:3); most Hebrew manuscripts read *Diphath.* **1:8** Or *Egypt;* also in 1:11. **1:12** Hebrew *Casluhites, from whom the Philistines came, Caphtorites.* See Jer 47:4; Amos 9:7. **1:13** Hebrew *ancestor of Heth.* **1:17a** As in one Hebrew manuscript and some Greek manuscripts (see also Gen 10:23); most Hebrew manuscripts lack *The descendants of Aram were.* **1:17b** As in parallel text at Gen 10:23; Hebrew reads *and Meshech.* **1:22** As in some Hebrew manuscripts and Syriac version (see also Gen 10:28); most Hebrew manuscripts read *Ebal.* **1:24** Some Greek manuscripts read *Arphaxad, Cainan, Shelah.* See notes on Gen 10:24; 11:12-13. **1:34** *Israel* is the name that God gave to Jacob. **1:36a** As in many Hebrew manuscripts and a few Greek manuscripts (see also Gen 36:11); most Hebrew manuscripts read *Zephi.* **1:36b** As in some Greek manuscripts (see also Gen 36:12); Hebrew reads *Kenaz, Timna, and Amalek.* **1:39** As in parallel text at Gen 36:22; Hebrew reads *and Homam.* **1:40a** As in many Hebrew manuscripts and a few Greek manuscripts (see also Gen 36:23); most Hebrew manuscripts read *Alian.* **1:40b** As in some Hebrew manuscripts (see also Gen 36:23); most Hebrew manuscripts read *Shephi.* **1:41** As in many Hebrew manuscripts and some Greek manuscripts (see also Gen 36:26); most Hebrew manuscripts read *Hamran.* **1:42a** As in many Hebrew and Greek manuscripts (see also Gen 36:27); most Hebrew manuscripts read *Jaakan.* **1:42b** Hebrew *Dishon;* compare 1:38 and parallel text at Gen 36:28. **1:43** Or *before an Israelite king ruled over them.*

1:1–9:44 The chronicler uses genealogies to capture volumes of family history, tracing Israel's history from Saul (9:35-44) back to Adam (vv. 1-4). The genealogies show the continuum of God's faithfulness. As the chronicler's contemporaries returned from exile, review of the past helped secure their faith in God's presence. Emphasizing David and the Davidic line is a major theme of both Chronicles.

1:1–2:1 The lineage between Adam and Jacob is a brief stop on the road to the chronicler's ultimate destination—King David. The chronicler leaves out names that do not directly contribute to the royal route between Adam and David.

1:29-36 Abraham's descendants are grouped according to mothers: Hagar, Keturah, Sarah. **Timna.** Eliphaz's concubine; their son, Amalek, led the Amalekites (see 1 Sam. 15).

1:43-51 kings. The chronicler reveals the longstanding relationship between the Edomites and Israel with their appearance here. (See also Gen. 36:31-43.)

RULERS OF EDOM

[43] These are the kings who ruled in the land of Edom
before any king ruled over the Israelites*:

Bela son of Beor, who ruled from his city of Dinhabah.
[44] When Bela died, Jobab son of Zerah from Bozrah
became king in his place.
[45] When Jobab died, Husham from the land of the
Temanites became king in his place.
[46] When Husham died, Hadad son of Bedad became
king in his place and ruled from the city of Avith.
He was the one who destroyed the Midianite army
in the land of Moab.
[47] When Hadad died, Samlah from the city of Mas-
rekah became king in his place.
[48] When Samlah died, Shaul from the city of Reho-
both-on-the-River became king in his place.
[49] When Shaul died, Baal-hanan son of Acbor became
king in his place.
[50] When Baal-hanan died, Hadad became king in his
place and ruled from the city of Pau.* His wife was
Mehetabel, the daughter of Matred and grand-
daughter of Me-zahab. [51] Then Hadad died.

The clan leaders of Edom were Timna, Alvah,* Je-
theth, [52] Oholibamah, Elah, Pinon, [53] Kenaz, Teman,
Mibzar, [54] Magdiel, and Iram. These are the clan
leaders of Edom.

DESCENDANTS OF ISRAEL

2 The sons of Israel* were Reuben, Simeon, Levi,
Judah, Issachar, Zebulun, [2] Dan, Joseph, Benjamin,
Naphtali, Gad, and Asher.

DESCENDANTS OF JUDAH

[3] Judah had three sons from Bathshua, a Canaanite
woman. Their names were Er, Onan, and Shelah.
But the LORD saw that the oldest son, Er, was a
wicked man, so he killed him. [4] Later Judah had
twin sons from Tamar, his widowed daughter-in-
law. Their names were Perez and Zerah. So Judah
had five sons in all.
[5] The sons of Perez were Hezron and Hamul.
[6] The sons of Zerah were Zimri, Ethan, Heman, Calcol,
and Darda*—five in all.
[7] The son of Carmi (a descendant of Zimri) was
Achan,* who brought disaster on Israel by taking
plunder that had been set apart for the LORD.*
[8] The son of Ethan was Azariah.

FROM JUDAH'S GRANDSON HEZRON TO DAVID

[9] The sons of Hezron were Jerahmeel, Ram, and
Caleb.*
[10] Ram was the father of Amminadab.
Amminadab was the father of Nahshon, a leader
of Judah.
[11] Nahshon was the father of Salmon.*
Salmon was the father of Boaz.
[12] Boaz was the father of Obed.
Obed was the father of Jesse.
[13] Jesse's first son was Eliab, his second was Abinad-
ab, his third was Shimea, [14] his fourth was Neth-
anel, his fifth was Raddai, [15] his sixth was Ozem,
and his seventh was David.
[16] Their sisters were named Zeruiah and Abigail.
Zeruiah had three sons named Abishai, Joab, and
Asahel. [17] Abigail married a man named Jether, an
Ishmaelite, and they had a son named Amasa.

OTHER DESCENDANTS OF HEZRON

[18] Hezron's son Caleb had sons from his wife Azubah
and from Jerioth.* Her sons were named Jesher,
Shobab, and Ardon. [19] After Azubah died, Caleb
married Ephrathah,* and they had a son named
Hur. [20] Hur was the father of Uri. Uri was the
father of Bezalel.
[21] When Hezron was sixty years old, he married Gil-
ead's sister, the daughter of Makir. They had a son
named Segub. [22] Segub was the father of Jair, who
ruled twenty-three towns in the land of Gilead.
[23] (But Geshur and Aram captured the Towns of
Jair* and also took Kenath and its sixty surround-
ing villages.) All these were descendants of Makir,
the father of Gilead.
[24] Soon after Hezron died in the town of Caleb-ephra-
thah, his wife Abijah gave birth to a son named
Ashhur (the father of* Tekoa).

DESCENDANTS OF HEZRON'S SON JERAHMEEL

[25] The sons of Jerahmeel, the oldest son of Hezron,
were Ram (the firstborn), Bunah, Oren, Ozem, and
Ahijah. [26] Jerahmeel had a second wife named
Atarah. She was the mother of Onam.
[27] The sons of Ram, the oldest son of Jerahmeel, were
Maaz, Jamin, and Eker.
[28] The sons of Onam were Shammai and Jada.
The sons of Shammai were Nadab and Abishur.
[29] The sons of Abishur and his wife Abihail were
Ahban and Molid.
[30] The sons of Nadab were Seled and Appaim. Seled
died without children, [31] but Appaim had a son
named Ishi. The son of Ishi was Sheshan. Sheshan
had a descendant named Ahlai.
[32] The sons of Jada, Shammai's brother, were Jether
and Jonathan. Jether died without children, [33] but
Jonathan had two sons named Peleth and Zaza.

1:50 As in many Hebrew manuscripts, some Greek manuscripts, Syriac version, and Latin Vulgate (see also Gen 36:39); most Hebrew manuscripts read *Pai.* **1:51** As in an alternate reading of the Masoretic Text (see also Gen 36:40); the other alternate reads *Aliah.* **2:1** *Israel* is the name that God gave to Jacob. **2:6** As in many Hebrew manuscripts, some Greek manuscripts, and Syriac version (see also 1 Kgs 4:31); Hebrew reads *Dara.* **2:7a** Hebrew *Achar;* compare Josh 7:1. *Achar* means "disaster." **2:7b** The Hebrew term used here refers to the complete consecration of things or people to the LORD, either by destroying them or by giving them as an offering. **2:9** Hebrew *Kelubai,* a variant spelling of Caleb; compare 2:18. **2:11** As in Greek version (see also Ruth 4:20); Hebrew reads *Salma.* **2:18** Or *Caleb had a daughter named Jerioth from his wife, Azubah.* The meaning of the Hebrew is uncertain. **2:19** Hebrew *Ephrath,* a variant spelling of Ephrathah; compare 2:50 and 4:4. **2:23** Or *captured Havvoth-jair.* **2:24** Or *the founder of;* also in 2:42, 45, 49.

1:51-54 clan leaders of Edom. These are the military leaders.
2:1-2 sons of Israel. These two verses provide an introductory framework for the next eight chapters. It's interesting to note that not all of the twelve sons of Jacob (Israel) are listed. Dan and Zebulun are missing. One reason that Dan may be missing is the fact that a center of pagan worship was set up at Dan after the United Kingdom divided in 931 B.C. **Joseph.** There is no tribe of Joseph. Tribes are named for his sons, Ephraim and Manasseh
2:3-9 Perez, son of Tamar, emerges to carry on the royal line amid the sordid tales of Judah's other sons.
2:7 Achan. Achan bookmarks a lesson learned from the tragedy of disobedience (see Josh. 7).
2:10–3:24 The chronicler zeroes in on the genealogy related to David. The lineage begins with David's immediate family and half sisters (2:13-17). It concludes with a focus on the sons of David himself (3:1-9).

These were all descendants of Jerahmeel.
34 Sheshan had no sons, though he did have daugh-
ters. He also had an Egyptian servant named
Jarha. 35 Sheshan gave one of his daughters to
be the wife of Jarha, and they had a son named
Attai.
36 Attai was the father of Nathan.
Nathan was the father of Zabad.
37 Zabad was the father of Ephlal.
Ephlal was the father of Obed.
38 Obed was the father of Jehu.
Jehu was the father of Azariah.
39 Azariah was the father of Helez.
Helez was the father of Eleasah.
40 Eleasah was the father of Sismai.
Sismai was the father of Shallum.
41 Shallum was the father of Jekamiah.
Jekamiah was the father of Elishama.

DESCENDANTS OF HEZRON'S SON CALEB

42 The descendants of Caleb, the brother of Jerahmeel,
included Mesha (the firstborn), who became the
father of Ziph. Caleb's descendants also included
the sons of Mareshah, the father of Hebron.*
43 The sons of Hebron were Korah, Tappuah, Rekem,
and Shema. 44 Shema was the father of Raham.
Raham was the father of Jorkeam. Rekem was the
father of Shammai. 45 The son of Shammai was
Maon. Maon was the father of Beth-zur.
46 Caleb's concubine Ephah gave birth to Haran,
Moza, and Gazez. Haran was the father of Gazez.
47 The sons of Jahdai were Regem, Jotham, Geshan,
Pelet, Ephah, and Shaaph.
48 Another of Caleb's concubines, Maacah, gave birth
to Sheber and Tirhanah. 49 She also gave birth to
Shaaph (the father of Madmannah) and Sheva (the
father of Macbenah and Gibea). Caleb also had a
daughter named Acsah.
50 These were all descendants of Caleb.

DESCENDANTS OF CALEB'S SON HUR

The sons of Hur, the oldest son of Caleb's wife Ephra-
thah, were Shobal (the founder of Kiriath-jearim),
51 Salma (the founder of Bethlehem), and Hareph
(the founder of Beth-gader).
52 The descendants of Shobal (the founder of Kiriath-
jearim) were Haroeh, half the Manahathites,
53 and the families of Kiriath-jearim—the Ithrites,
Puthites, Shumathites, and Mishraites, from whom
came the people of Zorah and Eshtaol.
54 The descendants of Salma were the people of
Bethlehem, the Netophathites, Atroth-beth-joab,
the other half of the Manahathites, the Zorites,
55 and the families of scribes living at Jabez—the
Tirathites, Shimeathites, and Sucathites. All these
were Kenites who descended from Hammath, the
father of the family of Recab.*

DESCENDANTS OF DAVID

3 These are the sons of David who were born in He-
bron:

The oldest was Amnon, whose mother was
Ahinoam from Jezreel.
The second was Daniel, whose mother was Abigail
from Carmel.
2 The third was Absalom, whose mother was
Maacah, the daughter of Talmai, king of Geshur.
The fourth was Adonijah, whose mother was
Haggith.
3 The fifth was Shephatiah, whose mother was
Abital.
The sixth was Ithream, whose mother was Eglah,
David's wife.
4 These six sons were born to David in Hebron, where
he reigned seven and a half years.

Then David reigned another thirty-three years in Je-
rusalem. 5 The sons born to David in Jerusalem included
Shammua,* Shobab, Nathan, and Solomon. Their moth-
er was Bathsheba,* the daughter of Ammiel. 6 David
also had nine other sons: Ibhar, Elishua,* Elpelet,* 7 No-
gah, Nepheg, Japhia, 8 Elishama, Eliada, and Eliphelet.
9 These were the sons of David, not including his
sons born to his concubines. Their sister was named
Tamar.

DESCENDANTS OF SOLOMON

10 The descendants of Solomon were Rehoboam, Abi-
jah, Asa, Jehoshaphat, 11 Jehoram,* Ahaziah, Joash,
12 Amaziah, Uzziah,* Jotham, 13 Ahaz, Hezekiah,
Manasseh, 14 Amon, and Josiah.
15 The sons of Josiah were Johanan (the oldest),
Jehoiakim (the second), Zedekiah (the third), and
Jehoahaz* (the fourth).
16 The successors of Jehoiakim were his son Jehoia-
chin and his brother Zedekiah.*

DESCENDANTS OF JEHOIACHIN

17 The sons of Jehoiachin,* who was taken prisoner
by the Babylonians, were Shealtiel, 18 Malkiram,
Pedaiah, Shenazzar, Jekamiah, Hoshama, and
Nedabiah.
19 The sons of Pedaiah were Zerubbabel and Shimei.
The sons of Zerubbabel were Meshullam and Hana-
niah. (Their sister was Shelomith.) 20 His five other
sons were Hashubah, Ohel, Berekiah, Hasadiah,
and Jushab-hesed.
21 The sons of Hananiah were Pelatiah and Jeshaiah.
Jeshaiah's son was Rephaiah. Rephaiah's son was

2:42 Or *who founded Hebron.* The meaning of the Hebrew is uncertain. **2:55** Or *the founder of Beth-recab.* **3:5a** As in Syriac version (see also 14:4; 2 Sam 5:14); Hebrew reads *Shimea.* **3:5b** Hebrew *Bathshua,* a variant spelling of Bathsheba. **3:6a** As in some Hebrew and Greek manuscripts (see also 14:5-7 and 2 Sam 5:15); most Hebrew manuscripts read *Elishama.* **3:6b** Hebrew *Eliphelet;* compare parallel text at 14:5-7. **3:11** Hebrew *Joram,* a variant spelling of Jehoram. **3:12** Hebrew *Azariah,* a variant spelling of Uzziah. **3:15** Hebrew *Shallum,* another name for Jehoahaz. **3:16** Hebrew *The sons of Jehoiakim were his son Jeconiah* [a variant spelling of Jehoiachin] *and his son Zedekiah.* **3:17** Hebrew *Jeconiah,* a variant spelling of Jehoiachin.

2:34-41 Subtle reference to God's favor is implied in the names of those rendered childless (vv. 30, 32). In contrast, Sheshan's initially jeopardized status continues through his daughter's son, Attai (v. 34).

3:1-9 David's complex family unit is recorded. (See also 2 Sam. 3:2-5; 5:13-16; 13:1). Solomon, as the bearer of the royal lineage, stands out among David's other children. Obviously omitted is Bathsheba's son, who died at birth (2 Sam. 12:18).

3:9 Tamar. Only one of David's daughters is listed. She is here because of the injustice done to her by brother Amnon (see 2 Sam. 13:14-16). This sin brought shame on the family and resulted in a murder (see 2 Sam. 13:18-29).

3:17-20 Jehoiachin. None of Jehoiachin's sons succeeded him as king. Babylon took Judah captive at that time.

Arnan. Arnan's son was Obadiah. Obadiah's son
was Shecaniah.
22 The descendants of Shecaniah were Shemaiah
and his sons, Hattush, Igal, Bariah, Neariah, and
Shaphat—six in all.
23 The sons of Neariah were Elioenai, Hizkiah, and
Azrikam—three in all.
24 The sons of Elioenai were Hodaviah, Eliashib,
Pelaiah, Akkub, Johanan, Delaiah, and Anani—
seven in all.

OTHER DESCENDANTS OF JUDAH

4 The descendants of Judah were Perez, Hezron,
Carmi, Hur, and Shobal.
2 Shobal's son Reaiah was the father of Jahath. Jahath
was the father of Ahumai and Lahad. These were
the families of the Zorathites.
3 The descendants of* Etam were Jezreel, Ishma,
Idbash, their sister Hazzelelponi, 4 Penuel (the
father of* Gedor), and Ezer (the father of Hushah).
These were the descendants of Hur (the firstborn
of Ephrathah), the ancestor of Bethlehem.
5 Ashhur (the father of Tekoa) had two wives, named
Helah and Naarah. 6 Naarah gave birth to Ahuz
zam, Hepher, Temeni, and Haahashtari. 7 Helah
gave birth to Zereth, Izhar,* Ethnan, 8 and Koz,
who became the ancestor of Anub, Zobebah, and
all the families of Aharhel son of Harum.
9 There was a man named Jabez who was more
honorable than any of his brothers. His mother
named him Jabez* because his birth had been so
painful. 10 He was the one who prayed to the God
of Israel, "Oh, that you would bless me and expand
my territory! Please be with me in all that I do,
and keep me from all trouble and pain!" And God
granted him his request.
11 Kelub (the brother of Shuhah) was the father of Me-
hir. Mehir was the father of Eshton. 12 Eshton was
the father of Beth-rapha, Paseah, and Tehinnah.
Tehinnah was the father of Ir-nahash. These were
the descendants of Recah.
13 The sons of Kenaz were Othniel and Seraiah.
Othniel's sons were Hathath and Meonothai.*
14 Meonothai was the father of Ophrah. Seraiah
was the father of Joab, the founder of the Valley of
Craftsmen,* so called because they were crafts-
men.
15 The sons of Caleb son of Jephunneh were Iru, Elah,
and Naam. The son of Elah was Kenaz.
16 The sons of Jehallelel were Ziph, Ziphah, Tiria, and
Asarel.
17 The sons of Ezrah were Jether, Mered, Epher, and
Jalon. One of Mered's wives became* the mother
of Miriam, Shammai, and Ishbah (the father of
Eshtemoa). 18 He married a woman from Judah,
who became the mother of Jered (the father of
Gedor), Heber (the father of Soco), and Jekuth-
iel (the father of Zanoah). Mered also married
Bithia, a daughter of Pharaoh, and she bore him
children.
19 Hodiah's wife was the sister of Naham. One of her
sons was the father of Keilah the Garmite, and
another was the father of Eshtemoa the Maa-
cathite.
20 The sons of Shimon were Amnon, Rinnah,
Ben-hanan, and Tilon.
The descendants of Ishi were Zoheth and Ben-zo-
heth.

DESCENDANTS OF JUDAH'S SON SHELAH

21 Shelah was one of Judah's sons. The descendants of
Shelah were Er (the father of Lecah); Laadah (the
father of Mareshah); the families of linen workers
at Beth-ashbea; 22 Jokim; the men of Cozeba; and
Joash and Saraph, who ruled over Moab and
Jashubi-lehem. These names all come from ancient
records. 23 They were the pottery makers who
lived in Netaim and Gederah. They lived there and
worked for the king.

DESCENDANTS OF SIMEON

24 The sons of Simeon were Jemuel,* Jamin, Jarib,
Zohar,* and Shaul.
25 The descendants of Shaul were Shallum, Mibsam,
and Mishma.
26 The descendants of Mishma were Hammuel, Zac-
cur, and Shimei.
27 Shimei had sixteen sons and six daughters,
but none of his brothers had large families. So
Simeon's tribe never grew as large as the tribe of
Judah.
28 They lived in Beersheba, Moladah, Hazar-shual,
29 Bilhah, Ezem, Tolad, 30 Bethuel, Hormah, Ziklag,
31 Beth-marcaboth, Hazar-susim, Beth-biri, and
Shaaraim. These towns were under their control
until the time of King David. 32 Their descendants
also lived in Etam, Ain, Rimmon, Token, and
Ashan—five towns 33 and their surrounding
villages as far away as Baalath.* This was their
territory, and these names are listed in their gene-
alogical records.
34 Other descendants of Simeon included Meshobab,
Jamlech, Joshah son of Amaziah, 35 Joel, Jehu
son of Joshibiah, son of Seraiah, son of Asiel,
36 Elioenai, Jaakobah, Jeshohaiah, Asaiah, Adiel,
Jesimiel, Benaiah, 37 and Ziza son of Shiphi, son
of Allon, son of Jedaiah, son of Shimri, son of
Shemaiah.

4:3 As in Greek version; Hebrew reads *father of.* The meaning of the Hebrew is uncertain. **4:4** Or *the founder of;* also in 4:5, 12, 14, 17, 18, and perhaps other instances where the text reads *the father of.* **4:7** As in an alternate reading in the Masoretic Text (see also Latin Vulgate); the other alternate and the Greek version read *Zohar.* **4:9** *Jabez* sounds like a Hebrew word meaning "distress" or "pain." **4:13** As in some Greek manuscripts and Latin Vulgate; Hebrew lacks *and Meonothai.* **4:14** Or *Joab, the father of Ge-harashim.* **4:17** Or *Jether's wife became;* Hebrew reads *She became.* **4:24a** As in Syriac version (see also Gen 46:10; Exod 6:15); Hebrew reads *Nemuel.* **4:24b** As in parallel texts at Gen 46:10 and Exod 6:15; Hebrew reads *Zerah.* **4:33** As in some Greek manuscripts (see also Josh 19:8); Hebrew reads *Baal.*

4:9-10 Jabez. Jabez depended on God for his needs. Certainly there was some selfishness in his prayer ("extend my border") as well as some lack of realistic expectation. Not only does he want to avoid all harm, but many versions (NIV, RSV, KJV) translate the second half of verse 10 as saying that he wants to even avoid all pain. In a world where the "rain falls on the righteous and the unrighteous" (Matt. 5:45), that is hardly realistic. However, that he took these requests to God, when so many were seeking their answers in other gods, was highly commendable.

4:21-23 descendants . . . linen workers . . . pottery makers. Families passed along trade and craft secrets to their descendants.

4:24-43 The chronicler mentions Simeon as part of the nation of Judah. With no land of their own (Josh. 19:1-9), these people were taken in by the larger tribe of Judah, having lost their own identity by David's time.

[38] These were the names of some of the leaders of Simeon's wealthy clans. Their families grew, [39] and they traveled to the region of Gerar,* in the east part of the valley, seeking pastureland for their flocks. [40] They found lush pastures there, and the land was spacious, quiet, and peaceful.

Some of Ham's descendants had been living in that region. [41] But during the reign of King Hezekiah of Judah, these leaders of Simeon invaded the region and completely destroyed* the homes of the descendants of Ham and of the Meunites. No trace of them remains today. They killed everyone who lived there and took the land for themselves, because they wanted its good pastureland for their flocks. [42] Five hundred of these invaders from the tribe of Simeon went to Mount Seir, led by Pelatiah, Neariah, Rephaiah, and Uzziel—all sons of Ishi. [43] They destroyed the few Amalekites who had survived, and they have lived there ever since.

DESCENDANTS OF REUBEN

5 The oldest son of Israel* was Reuben. But since he dishonored his father by sleeping with one of his father's concubines, his birthright was given to the sons of his brother Joseph. For this reason, Reuben is not listed in the genealogical records as the firstborn son. [2] The descendants of Judah became the most powerful tribe and provided a ruler for the nation,* but the birthright belonged to Joseph.

[3] The sons of Reuben, the oldest son of Israel, were Hanoch, Pallu, Hezron, and Carmi.

[4] The descendants of Joel were Shemaiah, Gog, Shimei, [5] Micah, Reaiah, Baal, [6] and Beerah. Beerah was the leader of the Reubenites when they were taken into captivity by King Tiglath-pileser* of Assyria.

[7] Beerah's* relatives are listed in their genealogical records by their clans: Jeiel (the leader), Zechariah, [8] and Bela son of Azaz, son of Shema, son of Joel.

The Reubenites lived in the area that stretches from Aroer to Nebo and Baal-meon. [9] And since they had so many livestock in the land of Gilead, they spread east toward the edge of the desert that stretches to the Euphrates River.

[10] During the reign of Saul, the Reubenites defeated the Hagrites in battle. Then they moved into the Hagrite settlements all along the eastern edge of Gilead.

DESCENDANTS OF GAD

[11] Next to the Reubenites, the descendants of Gad lived in the land of Bashan as far east as Salecah. [12] Joel was the leader in the land of Bashan, and Shapham was second-in-command, followed by Janai and Shaphat.

[13] Their relatives, the leaders of seven other clans, were Michael, Meshullam, Sheba, Jorai, Jacan, Zia, and Eber. [14] These were all descendants of Abihail son of Huri, son of Jaroah, son of Gilead, son of Michael, son of Jeshishai, son of Jahdo, son of Buz. [15] Ahi son of Abdiel, son of Guni, was the leader of their clans.

[16] The Gadites lived in the land of Gilead, in Bashan and its villages, and throughout all the pasturelands of Sharon. [17] All of these were listed in the genealogical records during the days of King Jotham of Judah and King Jeroboam of Israel.

THE TRIBES EAST OF THE JORDAN

[18] There were 44,760 capable warriors in the armies of Reuben, Gad, and the half-tribe of Manasseh. They were all skilled in combat and armed with shields, swords, and bows. [19] They waged war against the Hagrites, the Jeturites, the Naphishites, and the Nodabites. [20] They cried out to God during the battle, and he answered their prayer because they trusted in him. So the Hagrites and all their allies were defeated. [21] The plunder taken from the Hagrites included 50,000 camels, 250,000 sheep and goats, 2,000 donkeys, and 100,000 captives. [22] Many of the Hagrites were killed in the battle because God was fighting against them. The people of Reuben, Gad, and Manasseh lived in their land until they were taken into exile.

[23] The half-tribe of Manasseh was very large and spread through the land from Bashan to Baal-hermon, Senir, and Mount Hermon. [24] These were the leaders of their clans: Epher,* Ishi, Eliel, Azriel, Jeremiah, Hodaviah, and Jahdiel. These men had a great reputation as mighty warriors and leaders of their clans.

[25] But these tribes were unfaithful to the God of their ancestors. They worshiped the gods of the nations that God had destroyed. [26] So the God of Israel caused King Pul of Assyria (also known as Tiglath-pileser) to invade the land and take away the people of Reuben, Gad, and the half-tribe of Manasseh as captives. The Assyrians exiled them to Halah, Habor, Hara, and the Gozan River, where they remain to this day.

THE PRIESTLY LINE

6 [1]*The sons of Levi were Gershon, Kohath, and Merari.

[2] The descendants of Kohath included Amram, Izhar, Hebron, and Uzziel.

[3] The children of Amram were Aaron, Moses, and Miriam.

The sons of Aaron were Nadab, Abihu, Eleazar, and Ithamar.

[4] Eleazar was the father of Phinehas.
Phinehas was the father of Abishua.

4:39 As in Greek version; Hebrew reads *Gedor.* **4:41** The Hebrew term used here refers to the complete consecration of things or people to the LORD, either by destroying them or by giving them as an offering. **5:1** *Israel* is the name that God gave to Jacob. **5:2** Or *and from Judah came a prince.* **5:6** Hebrew *Tilgath-pilneser,* a variant spelling of Tiglath-pileser; also in 5:26. **5:7** Hebrew *His.* **5:24** As in Greek version and Latin Vulgate; Hebrew reads *and Epher.* **6:1** Verses 6:1-15 are numbered 5:27-41 in Hebrew text.

4:41 completely destroyed the homes of the descendants. Hamites were essentially Canaanites. They were "set apart for destruction" because they were in the land designated for the people of Israel.

5:20 he answered their prayer. Again, the chronicler gives an example of God's faithfulness throughout the generations.

5:25-26 the tribes were unfaithful. Sexual imagery is often used to describe the way that Israel ran after other gods (see for example, Hosea 1:2). **exiled.** Tilgath-pileser III of Assyria carried these northern tribes off into exile. This was God's punishment for their unfaithfulness.

6:1-3 sons of Levi. The office of high priest was a family business—a person had to be born into the role.

6:4-15 Jehozadak. Aaron was the patriarchal priest (Ex. 28:1). His lineage languished when Jehozadak was taken captive (v. 15).

5 Abishua was the father of Bukki.
Bukki was the father of Uzzi.
6 Uzzi was the father of Zerahiah.
Zerahiah was the father of Meraioth.
7 Meraioth was the father of Amariah.
Amariah was the father of Ahitub.
8 Ahitub was the father of Zadok.
Zadok was the father of Ahimaaz.
9 Ahimaaz was the father of Azariah.
Azariah was the father of Johanan.
10 Johanan was the father of Azariah, the high priest at the Temple* built by Solomon in Jerusalem.
11 Azariah was the father of Amariah.
Amariah was the father of Ahitub.
12 Ahitub was the father of Zadok.
Zadok was the father of Shallum.
13 Shallum was the father of Hilkiah.
Hilkiah was the father of Azariah.
14 Azariah was the father of Seraiah.
Seraiah was the father of Jehozadak, 15 who went into exile when the LORD sent the people of Judah and Jerusalem into captivity under Nebuchadnezzar.

THE LEVITE CLANS

16*The sons of Levi were Gershon,* Kohath, and Merari.
17 The descendants of Gershon included Libni and Shimei.
18 The descendants of Kohath included Amram, Izhar, Hebron, and Uzziel.
19 The descendants of Merari included Mahli and Mushi.

The following were the Levite clans, listed according to their ancestral descent:

20 The descendants of Gershon included Libni, Jahath, Zimmah, 21 Joah, Iddo, Zerah, and Jeatherai.
22 The descendants of Kohath included Amminadab, Korah, Assir, 23 Elkanah, Abiasaph,* Assir, 24 Tahath, Uriel, Uzziah, and Shaul.
25 The descendants of Elkanah included Amasai, Ahimoth, 26 Elkanah, Zophai, Nahath, 27 Eliab, Jeroham, Elkanah, and Samuel.*
28 The sons of Samuel were Joel* (the older) and Abijah (the second).
29 The descendants of Merari included Mahli, Libni, Shimei, Uzzah, 30 Shimea, Haggiah, and Asaiah.

THE TEMPLE MUSICIANS

31 David assigned the following men to lead the music at the house of the LORD after the Ark was placed there.
32 They ministered with music at the Tabernacle* until Solomon built the Temple of the LORD in Jerusalem. They carried out their work, following all the regulations handed down to them.
33 These are the men who served, along with their sons:

Heman the musician was from the clan of Kohath. His genealogy was traced back through Joel, Samuel,
34 Elkanah, Jeroham, Eliel, Toah,
35 Zuph, Elkanah, Mahath, Amasai,
36 Elkanah, Joel, Azariah, Zephaniah,
37 Tahath, Assir, Abiasaph, Korah,
38 Izhar, Kohath, Levi, and Israel.*
39 Heman's first assistant was Asaph from the clan of Gershon.* Asaph's genealogy was traced back through Berekiah, Shimea,
40 Michael, Baaseiah, Malkijah,
41 Ethni, Zerah, Adaiah,
42 Ethan, Zimmah, Shimei,
43 Jahath, Gershon, and Levi.
44 Heman's second assistant was Ethan from the clan of Merari. Ethan's genealogy was traced back through Kishi, Abdi, Malluch,
45 Hashabiah, Amaziah, Hilkiah,
46 Amzi, Bani, Shemer,
47 Mahli, Mushi, Merari, and Levi.

48 Their fellow Levites were appointed to various other tasks in the Tabernacle, the house of God.

AARON'S DESCENDANTS

49 Only Aaron and his descendants served as priests. They presented the offerings on the altar of burnt offering and the altar of incense, and they performed all the other duties related to the Most Holy Place. They made atonement for Israel by doing everything that Moses, the servant of God, had commanded them.

50 The descendants of Aaron were Eleazar, Phinehas, Abishua,
51 Bukki, Uzzi, Zerahiah,
52 Meraioth, Amariah, Ahitub,
53 Zadok, and Ahimaaz.

TERRITORY FOR THE LEVITES

54 This is a record of the towns and territory assigned by means of sacred lots to the descendants of Aaron, who were from the clan of Kohath.
55 This territory included Hebron and its surrounding pasturelands in Judah,
56 but the fields and outlying areas belonging to the city were given to Caleb son of Jephunneh.
57 So the descendants of Aaron were given the following towns, each with its pasturelands: Hebron (a city of refuge),* Libnah, Jattir, Eshtemoa,
58 Holon,* Debir,

6:10 Hebrew *the house.* **6:16a** Verses 6:16-81 are numbered 6:1-66 in Hebrew text. **6:16b** Hebrew *Gershom,* a variant spelling of Gershon (see 6:1); also in 6:17, 20, 43, 62, 71. **6:23** Hebrew *Ebiasaph,* a variant spelling of Abiasaph (also in 6:37); compare parallel text at Exod 6:24. **6:27** As in some Greek manuscripts (see also 6:33-34); Hebrew lacks *and Samuel.* **6:28** As in some Greek manuscripts and the Syriac version (see also 6:33 and 1 Sam 8:2); Hebrew lacks *Joel.* **6:32** Hebrew *the Tabernacle, the Tent of Meeting.* **6:38** *Israel* is the name that God gave to Jacob. **6:39** Hebrew lacks *from the clan of Gershon;* see 6:43. **6:57** As in parallel text at Josh 21:13; Hebrew reads *were given the cities of refuge: Hebron, and the following towns, each with its pasturelands.* **6:58** As in parallel text at Josh 21:15; Masoretic Text reads *Hilez;* other manuscripts read *Hilen.*

6:11 Azariah. High priest who led 80 priests to oppose King Uzziah of Judah (792–740 B.C.) when he tried to burn incense in the temple rather than let the priests. God struck Uzziah with a dreaded skin disease (2 Chron. 26:16-21).

6:13 Hilkiah. High priest who aided in Josiah's reform movement (2 Kings 22:4). He supported Josiah by overseeing the repair of the temple. While the temple was being repaired, Josiah found the book of the law in the temple. When Josiah heard the reading from the book of the law, he tore his clothes and was deeply trouble. Josiah commanded Hilkiah and others to remove the pagan articles of worship that had been placed in the LORD's temple.

6:22 Kohath. Leader of rebellion against Moses and Aaron while Israel was camped in the wilderness of Paran (Num. 16). He led a confederacy of 250 princes of the people against Aaron's claim to the priesthood and Moses' claim to authority in general. The rebels contended that the entire congregation was sanctified and therefore qualified to perform priestly functions. As punishment for their insubordination, God caused the earth to open and swallow the leaders.

6:28 sons of Samuel. Samuel faithfully served in the tabernacle as an influential priest and leader. Samuel's family was described as Ephraimites (1 Sam. 1:1). He was clearly a Levite and was dedicated to service in the tabernacle (see 1 Sam. 2:11).

59 Ain,* Juttah,* and Beth-shemesh. 60 And from the
territory of Benjamin they were given Gibeon,* Geba,
Alemeth, and Anathoth, each with its pasturelands.
So thirteen towns were given to the descendants of
Aaron. 61 The remaining descendants of Kohath re-
ceived ten towns from the territory of the half-tribe
of Manasseh by means of sacred lots.
62 The descendants of Gershon received by sacred
lots thirteen towns from the territories of Issachar,
Asher, Naphtali, and from the Bashan area of Manas-
seh, east of the Jordan.
63 The descendants of Merari received by sacred
lots twelve towns from the territories of Reuben, Gad,
and Zebulun.
64 So the people of Israel assigned all these towns
and pasturelands to the Levites. 65 The towns in the
territories of Judah, Simeon, and Benjamin, men-
tioned above, were assigned to them by means of sa-
cred lots.
66 The descendants of Kohath were given the fol-
lowing towns from the territory of Ephraim, each
with its pasturelands: 67 Shechem (a city of refuge in
the hill country of Ephraim),* Gezer, 68 Jokmeam, Beth-
horon, 69 Aijalon, and Gath-rimmon. 70 The remaining
descendants of Kohath were assigned the towns of
Aner and Bileam from the territory of the half-tribe
of Manasseh, each with its pasturelands.
71 The descendants of Gershon received the towns
of Golan (in Bashan) and Ashtaroth from the territory
of the half-tribe of Manasseh, each with its pasture-
lands. 72 From the territory of Issachar, they were giv-
en Kedesh, Daberath, 73 Ramoth, and Anem, each with
its pasturelands. 74 From the territory of Asher, they
received Mashal, Abdon, 75 Hukok, and Rehob, each
with its pasturelands. 76 From the territory of Naph-
tali, they were given Kedesh in Galilee, Hammon, and
Kiriathaim, each with its pasturelands.
77 The remaining descendants of Merari received
the towns of Jokneam, Kartah,* Rimmon,* and Tabor
from the territory of Zebulun, each with its pasture-
lands. 78 From the territory of Reuben, east of the
Jordan River opposite Jericho, they received Bezer
(a desert town), Jahaz,* 79 Kedemoth, and Mephaath,
each with its pasturelands. 80 And from the territory
of Gad, they received Ramoth in Gilead, Mahanaim,
81 Heshbon, and Jazer, each with its pasturelands.

DESCENDANTS OF ISSACHAR

7 The four sons of Issachar were Tola, Puah, Jashub,
and Shimron.
2 The sons of Tola were Uzzi, Rephaiah, Jeriel, Jahmai,
Ibsam, and Shemuel. Each of them was the leader
of an ancestral clan. At the time of King David,
the total number of mighty warriors listed in the
records of these clans was 22,600.
3 The son of Uzzi was Izrahiah. The sons of Izrahiah
were Michael, Obadiah, Joel, and Isshiah. These
five became the leaders of clans. 4 All of them had
many wives and many sons, so the total number
of men available for military service among their
descendants was 36,000.
5 The total number of mighty warriors from all the
clans of the tribe of Issachar was 87,000. All of them
were listed in their genealogical records.

DESCENDANTS OF BENJAMIN

6 Three of Benjamin's sons were Bela, Beker, and
Jediael.
7 The five sons of Bela were Ezbon, Uzzi, Uzziel,
Jerimoth, and Iri. Each of them was the leader
of an ancestral clan. The total number of mighty
warriors from these clans was 22,034, as listed in
their genealogical records.
8 The sons of Beker were Zemirah, Joash, Eliezer,
Elioenai, Omri, Jeremoth, Abijah, Anathoth, and
Alemeth. 9 Each of them was the leader of an an-
cestral clan. The total number of mighty warriors
and leaders from these clans was 20,200, as listed
in their genealogical records.
10 The son of Jediael was Bilhan. The sons of Bilhan
were Jeush, Benjamin, Ehud, Kenaanah, Zethan,
Tarshish, and Ahishahar. 11 Each of them was the
leader of an ancestral clan. From these clans the
total number of mighty warriors ready for war
was 17,200.
12 The sons of Ir were Shuppim and Huppim. Hushim
was the son of Aher.

DESCENDANTS OF NAPHTALI

13 The sons of Naphtali were Jahzeel,* Guni, Jezer,
and Shillem.* They were all descendants of Jacob's
concubine Bilhah.

DESCENDANTS OF MANASSEH

14 The descendants of Manasseh through his Ar-
amean concubine included Asriel. She also bore
Makir, the father of Gilead. 15 Makir found wives
for* Huppim and Shuppim. Makir had a sister
named Maacah. One of his descendants was Zelo-
phehad, who had only daughters.
16 Makir's wife, Maacah, gave birth to a son whom
she named Peresh. His brother's name was
Sheresh. The sons of Peresh were Ulam and
Rakem. 17 The son of Ulam was Bedan. All these
were considered Gileadites, descendants of Makir
son of Manasseh.
18 Makir's sister Hammoleketh gave birth to Ishhod,
Abiezer, and Mahlah.
19 The sons of Shemida were Ahian, Shechem, Likhi,
and Aniam.

DESCENDANTS OF EPHRAIM

20 The descendants of Ephraim were Shuthelah,
Bered, Tahath, Eleadah, Tahath, 21 Zabad,

6:59a As in parallel text at Josh 21:16; Hebrew reads *Ashan.* **6:59b** As in Syriac version (see also Josh 21:16); Hebrew lacks *Juttah.* **6:60** As in parallel text at Josh 21:17; Hebrew lacks *Gibeon.* **6:66-67** As in parallel text at Josh 21:21. Hebrew text reads *were given the cities of refuge: Shechem in the hill country of Ephraim, and the following towns, each with its pasturelands.* **6:77a** As in Greek version (see also Josh 21:34); Hebrew lacks *Jokneam, Kartah.* **6:77b** As in Greek version (see also Josh 19:13); Hebrew reads *Rimmono.* **6:78** Hebrew *Jahzah,* a variant spelling of Jahaz. **7:13a** As in parallel text at Gen 46:24; Hebrew reads *Jahziel,* a variant spelling of Jahzeel. **7:13b** As in some Hebrew and Greek manuscripts (see also Gen 46:24; Num 26:49); most Hebrew manuscripts read *Shallum.* **7:15** Or *Makir took a wife from.* The meaning of the Hebrew is uncertain.

7:1-5 Issachar. The chronicler details Issachar's strength in numbers during its most populated era.

7:6-12 Benjamin's. Other lists give varying figures for the number of Benjamin's sons (see 8:1-2; Gen. 46:21). Genealogies provided various functions for the people, and this is why the chronicler likely slanted his count to include only those in the military.

7:14-19 In a document of this period, highlighting women was an unusual, though legitimate, function of a genealogy.

Shuthelah, Ezer, and Elead. These two were killed
trying to steal livestock from the local farmers
near Gath. 22 Their father, Ephraim, mourned
for them a long time, and his relatives came to
comfort him. 23 Afterward Ephraim slept with his
wife, and she became pregnant and gave birth
to a son. Ephraim named him Beriah* because of
the tragedy his family had suffered. 24 He had a
daughter named Sheerah. She built the towns of
Lower and Upper Beth-horon and Uzzen-sheer-
ah.
25 The descendants of Ephraim included Rephah,
Resheph, Telah, Tahan, 26 Ladan, Ammihud, Elisha-
ma, 27 Nun, and Joshua.

28 The descendants of Ephraim lived in the territory
that included Bethel and its surrounding towns to the
south, Naaran to the east, Gezer and its villages to the
west, and Shechem and its surrounding villages to
the north as far as Ayyah and its towns. 29 Along the
border of Manasseh were the towns of Beth-shan,*
Taanach, Megiddo, Dor, and their surrounding villag-
es. The descendants of Joseph son of Israel* lived in
these towns.

DESCENDANTS OF ASHER

30 The sons of Asher were Imnah, Ishvah, Ishvi, and
Beriah. They had a sister named Serah.
31 The sons of Beriah were Heber and Malkiel (the
father of Birzaith).
32 The sons of Heber were Japhlet, Shomer, and
Hotham. They had a sister named Shua.
33 The sons of Japhlet were Pasach, Bimhal, and
Ashvath.
34 The sons of Shomer were Ahi,* Rohgah, Hubbah,
and Aram.
35 The sons of his brother Helem* were Zophah, Imna,
Shelesh, and Amal.
36 The sons of Zophah were Suah, Harnepher, Shual,
Beri, Imrah, 37 Bezer, Hod, Shamma, Shilshah,
Ithran,* and Beera.
38 The sons of Jether were Jephunneh, Pispah, and
Ara.
39 The sons of Ulla were Arah, Hanniel, and Rizia.
40 Each of these descendants of Asher was the head of
an ancestral clan. They were all select men—mighty
warriors and outstanding leaders. The total number
of men available for military service was 26,000, as
listed in their genealogical records.

DESCENDANTS OF BENJAMIN

8 Benjamin's first son was Bela, the second was
Ashbel, the third was Aharah, 2 the fourth was
Nohah, and the fifth was Rapha.
3 The sons of Bela were Addar, Gera, Abihud,* 4 Abi-
shua, Naaman, Ahoah, 5 Gera, Shephuphan, and
Huram.
6 The sons of Ehud, leaders of the clans living at
Geba, were exiled to Manahath. 7 Ehud's sons were
Naaman, Ahijah, and Gera. Gera, who led them
into exile, was the father of Uzza and Ahihud.*
8 After Shaharaim divorced his wives Hushim and
Baara, he had children in the land of Moab. 9 His
wife Hodesh gave birth to Jobab, Zibia, Mesha,
Malcam, 10 Jeuz, Sakia, and Mirmah. These sons all
became the leaders of clans.
11 Shaharaim's wife Hushim had already given birth
to Abitub and Elpaal. 12 The sons of Elpaal were
Eber, Misham, Shemed (who built the towns of Ono
and Lod and their nearby villages), 13 Beriah, and
Shema. They were the leaders of the clans living in
Aijalon, and they drove out the inhabitants of Gath.
14 Ahio, Shashak, Jeremoth, 15 Zebadiah, Arad, Eder,
16 Michael, Ishpah, and Joha were the sons of
Beriah.
17 Zebadiah, Meshullam, Hizki, Heber, 18 Ishmerai,
Izliah, and Jobab were the sons of Elpaal.
19 Jakim, Zicri, Zabdi, 20 Elienai, Zillethai, Eliel,
21 Adaiah, Beraiah, and Shimrath were the sons of
Shimei.
22 Ishpan, Eber, Eliel, 23 Abdon, Zicri, Hanan, 24 Hana-
niah, Elam, Anthothijah, 25 Iphdeiah, and Penuel
were the sons of Shashak.
26 Shamsherai, Shehariah, Athaliah, 27 Jaareshiah,
Elijah, and Zicri were the sons of Jeroham.
28 These were the leaders of the ancestral clans; they
were listed in their genealogical records, and they all
lived in Jerusalem.

THE FAMILY OF SAUL

29 Jeiel* (the father of* Gibeon) lived in the town of
Gibeon. His wife's name was Maacah, 30 and his
oldest son was named Abdon. Jeiel's other sons
were Zur, Kish, Baal, Ner,* Nadab, 31 Gedor, Ahio,
Zechariah,* 32 and Mikloth, who was the father of
Shimeam.* All these families lived near each other
in Jerusalem.
33 Ner was the father of Kish.
Kish was the father of Saul.
Saul was the father of Jonathan, Malkishua,
Abinadab, and Esh-baal.
34 Jonathan was the father of Merib-baal.
Merib-baal was the father of Micah.
35 Micah was the father of Pithon, Melech, Tahrea,*
and Ahaz.
36 Ahaz was the father of Jadah.*
Jadah was the father of Alemeth, Azmaveth, and
Zimri.

7:23 *Beriah* sounds like a Hebrew term meaning "tragedy" or "misfortune." **7:29a** Hebrew *Beth-shean,* a variant spelling of Beth-shan. **7:29b** *Israel* is the name that God gave to Jacob. **7:34** Or *The sons of Shomer, his brother, were.* **7:35** Possibly another name for *Hotham;* compare 7:32. **7:37** Possibly another name for *Jether;* compare 7:38. **8:3** Possibly *Gera the father of Ehud;* compare 8:6. **8:7** Or *Gera, that is Heglam, was the father of Uzza and Ahihud.* **8:29a** As in some Greek manuscripts (see also 9:35); Hebrew lacks *Jeiel.* **8:29b** Or *the founder of.* **8:30** As in some Greek manuscripts (see also 9:36); Hebrew lacks *Ner.* **8:31** As in parallel text at 9:37; Hebrew reads *Zeker,* a variant spelling of Zechariah. **8:32** As in parallel text at 9:38; Hebrew reads *Shimeah,* a variant spelling of Shimeam. **8:35** As in parallel text at 9:41; Hebrew reads *Tarea,* a variant spelling of Tahrea. **8:36** As in parallel text at 9:42; Hebrew reads *Jehoaddah,* a variant spelling of Jadah.

7:30-40 Asher. Asher stood out from the clan, a tribe of leaders and outstanding warriors (see Gen. 30:9-13). Asher was the son of Jacob. His mother was Leah's servant Zilpah.

8:1-40 Benjamin's tribe, the tribe of Saul, earns a second helping of highlights (7:6-12). Understanding Saul's historical context early on allows the chronicler to pick up the story at Saul's death in chapter ten.

8:28 lived in Jerusalem. Families of Benjamin lived in Jerusalem. It is interesting to note that Jerusalem was not occupied until David's time. With this representation of Saul's tribe Benjamin in Jerusalem, it is evident that David did not exclude Saul's relations from favorable positions in Israel.

8:33 Esh-baal. Also known as Ish-Bosheth, Saul's youngest son who ruled over Israel (see 2 Sam. 2:8-10). Esh-baal was a pagan name and illustrates the influence of paganism in even the best families.

Zimri was the father of Moza.
37 Moza was the father of Binea.
Binea was the father of Rephaiah.*
Rephaiah was the father of Eleasah.
Eleasah was the father of Azel.
38 Azel had six sons: Azrikam, Bokeru, Ishmael,
Sheariah, Obadiah, and Hanan. These were the
sons of Azel.
39 Azel's brother Eshek had three sons: the first was
Ulam, the second was Jeush, and the third was
Eliphelet. 40 Ulam's sons were all mighty warriors
and expert archers. They had many sons and
grandsons—150 in all.

All these were descendants of Benjamin.

9 So all Israel was listed in the genealogical records
in *The Book of the Kings of Israel.*

THE RETURNING EXILES

The people of Judah were exiled to Babylon because
they were unfaithful to the LORD. 2 The first of the ex-
iles to return to their property in their former towns
were priests, Levites, Temple servants, and other Is-
raelites. 3 Some of the people from the tribes of Judah,
Benjamin, Ephraim, and Manasseh came and settled
in Jerusalem.

4 One family that returned was that of Uthai son of
Ammihud, son of Omri, son of Imri, son of Bani, a
descendant of Perez son of Judah.
5 Others returned from the Shilonite clan, including
Asaiah (the oldest) and his sons.
6 From the Zerahite clan, Jeuel returned with his
relatives.
In all, 690 families from the tribe of Judah returned.

7 From the tribe of Benjamin came Sallu son of
Meshullam, son of Hodaviah, son of Hassenuah;
8 Ibneiah son of Jeroham; Elah son of Uzzi, son of
Micri; and Meshullam son of Shephatiah, son of
Reuel, son of Ibnijah.
9 These men were all leaders of clans, and they were
listed in their genealogical records. In all, 956 families
from the tribe of Benjamin returned.

THE RETURNING PRIESTS

10 Among the priests who returned were Jedaiah,
Jehoiarib, Jakin, 11 Azariah son of Hilkiah, son of
Meshullam, son of Zadok, son of Meraioth, son of
Ahitub. Azariah was the chief officer of the house
of God.
12 Other returning priests were Adaiah son of Jero-
ham, son of Pashhur, son of Malkijah, and Maasai
son of Adiel, son of Jahzerah, son of Meshullam,
son of Meshillemith, son of Immer.

13 In all, 1,760 priests returned. They were heads of
clans and very able men. They were responsible for
ministering at the house of God.

THE RETURNING LEVITES

14 The Levites who returned were Shemaiah son of
Hasshub, son of Azrikam, son of Hashabiah, a
descendant of Merari; 15 Bakbakkar; Heresh; Galal;
Mattaniah son of Mica, son of Zicri, son of Asaph;
16 Obadiah son of Shemaiah, son of Galal, son of
Jeduthun; and Berekiah son of Asa, son of Elkanah,
who lived in the area of Netophah.
17 The gatekeepers who returned were Shallum,
Akkub, Talmon, Ahiman, and their relatives.
Shallum was the chief gatekeeper. 18 Prior to this
time, they were responsible for the King's Gate
on the east side. These men served as gatekeepers
for the camps of the Levites. 19 Shallum was the
son of Kore, a descendant of Abiasaph,* from the
clan of Korah. He and his relatives, the Korahites,
were responsible for guarding the entrance to the
sanctuary, just as their ancestors had guarded the
Tabernacle in the camp of the LORD.
20 Phinehas son of Eleazar had been in charge
of the gatekeepers in earlier times, and the LORD
had been with him. 21 And later Zechariah son of
Meshelemiah was responsible for guarding the
entrance to the Tabernacle.*

22 In all, there were 212 gatekeepers in those days,
and they were listed according to the genealogies
in their villages. David and Samuel the seer had ap-
pointed their ancestors because they were reliable
men. 23 These gatekeepers and their descendants, by
their divisions, were responsible for guarding the en-
trance to the house of the LORD when that house was
a tent. 24 The gatekeepers were stationed on all four
sides—east, west, north, and south. 25 Their relatives
in the villages came regularly to share their duties for
seven-day periods.
26 The four chief gatekeepers, all Levites, were trust-
ed officials, for they were responsible for the rooms
and treasuries at the house of God. 27 They would spend
the night around the house of God, since it was their
duty to guard it and to open the gates every morning.
28 Some of the gatekeepers were assigned to care
for the various articles used in worship. They checked
them in and out to avoid any loss. 29 Others were respon-
sible for the furnishings, the items in the sanctuary, and
the supplies, such as choice flour, wine, olive oil, frank-
incense, and spices. 30 But it was the priests who blend-
ed the spices. 31 Mattithiah, a Levite and the oldest son
of Shallum the Korahite, was entrusted with baking the
bread used in the offerings. 32 And some members of the
clan of Kohath were in charge of preparing the bread to
be set on the table each Sabbath day.

8:37 As in parallel text at 9:43; Hebrew reads *Raphah,* a variant spelling of Rephaiah. **9:19** Hebrew *Ebiasaph,* a variant spelling of Abiasaph; compare Exod 6:24. **9:21** Hebrew *Tent of Meeting.*

9:1 The people of Judah were exiled to Babylon because they were unfaithful. As with the northern tribes, Judah was exiled because of unfaithfulness to God (see 5:25-6). Judah, however, did return. The books of 1 and 2 Chronicles were written in an attempt to help them learn from past mistakes.

9:4-6 descendant. The chronicler's records served as an important "who's who" directory for the returnees. Genealogy played a crucial role in restoring individual identities, family roles, and social class to a lost people.

9:10-13 responsible for ministering at the house of God. In Nehemiah 11:10-14 a match was made between historical record (6:12-13) and contemporary record. The people's ties with the past gave them a perspective on the present and hope for the future.

9:19 Korah. These were descendants of Kohath, who were close relations to the priests.

9:22-27 gatekeepers. The gatekeepers served as the neighborhood watch. Refugees rebuilt their lives amid ruin.

33 The musicians, all prominent Levites, lived at the
Temple. They were exempt from other responsibili-
ties since they were on duty at all hours. 34 All these
men lived in Jerusalem. They were the heads of Levite
families and were listed as prominent leaders in their
genealogical records.

KING SAUL'S FAMILY TREE

35 Jeiel (the father of* Gibeon) lived in the town of
Gibeon. His wife's name was Maacah, 36 and his
oldest son was named Abdon. Jeiel's other sons
were Zur, Kish, Baal, Ner, Nadab, 37 Gedor, Ahio,
Zechariah, and Mikloth. 38 Mikloth was the father
of Shimeam. All these families lived near each
other in Jerusalem.

39 Ner was the father of Kish.
Kish was the father of Saul.
Saul was the father of Jonathan, Malkishua,
Abinadab, and Esh-baal.

40 Jonathan was the father of Merib-baal.
Merib-baal was the father of Micah.

41 The sons of Micah were Pithon, Melech, Tahrea,
and Ahaz.*

42 Ahaz was the father of Jadah.*
Jadah was the father of Alemeth, Azmaveth, and
Zimri.
Zimri was the father of Moza.

43 Moza was the father of Binea.
Binea's son was Rephaiah.
Rephaiah's son was Eleasah.
Eleasah's son was Azel.

44 Azel had six sons, whose names were Azrikam,
Bokeru, Ishmael, Sheariah, Obadiah, and Hanan.
These were the sons of Azel.

THE DEATH OF KING SAUL

10 Now the Philistines attacked Israel, and the men
of Israel fled before them. Many were slaugh-
tered on the slopes of Mount Gilboa. 2 The Philistines
closed in on Saul and his sons, and they killed three of
his sons—Jonathan, Abinadab, and Malkishua. 3 The
fighting grew very fierce around Saul, and the Philis-
tine archers caught up with him and wounded him.

4 Saul groaned to his armor bearer, "Take your
sword and kill me before these pagan Philistines
come to taunt and torture me."

But his armor bearer was afraid and would not do
it. So Saul took his own sword and fell on it. 5 When his
armor bearer realized that Saul was dead, he fell on
his own sword and died. 6 So Saul and his three sons
died there together, bringing his dynasty to an end.

7 When all the Israelites in the Jezreel Valley saw
that their army had fled and that Saul and his sons
were dead, they abandoned their towns and fled. So
the Philistines moved in and occupied their towns.

8 The next day, when the Philistines went out to
strip the dead, they found the bodies of Saul and his
sons on Mount Gilboa. 9 So they stripped off Saul's ar-
mor and cut off his head. Then they proclaimed the
good news of Saul's death before their idols and to the
people throughout the land of Philistia. 10 They placed
his armor in the temple of their gods, and they fas-
tened his head to the temple of Dagon.

11 But when everyone in Jabesh-gilead heard about
everything the Philistines had done to Saul, 12 all their
mighty warriors brought the bodies of Saul and his
sons back to Jabesh. Then they buried their bones
beneath the great tree at Jabesh, and they fasted for
seven days.

13 So Saul died because he was unfaithful to the
LORD. He failed to obey the LORD's command, and he
even consulted a medium 14 instead of asking the LORD
for guidance. So the LORD killed him and turned the
kingdom over to David son of Jesse.

DAVID BECOMES KING OF ALL ISRAEL

11 Then all Israel gathered before David at Hebron
and told him, "We are your own flesh and blood.
2 In the past,* even when Saul was king, you were the
one who really led the forces of Israel. And the LORD
your God told you, 'You will be the shepherd of my peo-
ple Israel. You will be the leader of my people Israel.'"

3 So there at Hebron, David made a covenant be-
fore the LORD with all the elders of Israel. And they
anointed him king of Israel, just as the LORD had
promised through Samuel.

DAVID CAPTURES JERUSALEM

4 Then David and all Israel went to Jerusalem (or Je-
bus, as it used to be called), where the Jebusites, the
original inhabitants of the land, were living. 5 The
people of Jebus taunted David, saying, "You'll never
get in here!" But David captured the fortress of Zion,
which is now called the City of David.

6 David had said to his troops, "Whoever is first to
attack the Jebusites will become the commander of
my armies!" And Joab, the son of David's sister Zerui-
ah, was first to attack, so he became the commander
of David's armies.

7 David made the fortress his home, and that is
why it is called the City of David. 8 He extended the
city from the supporting terraces* to the surrounding
area, while Joab rebuilt the rest of Jerusalem. 9 And
David became more and more powerful, because the
LORD of Heaven's Armies was with him.

DAVID'S MIGHTIEST WARRIORS

10 These are the leaders of David's mighty warriors. To-
gether with all Israel, they decided to make David their
king, just as the LORD had promised concerning Israel.

9:35 Or *the founder of.* **9:41** As in Syriac version and Latin Vulgate (see also 8:35); Hebrew lacks *and Ahaz.* **9:42** As in some Hebrew manuscripts and Greek version (see also 8:36); Hebrew reads *Jarah.* **11:2** Or *For some time.* **11:8** Hebrew *the millo.* The meaning of the Hebrew is uncertain.

9:28-34 This division of duties among the Levites consisted of civic duty specialties. Levites cared for the house of God.

10:3-6 Take your sword and kill me. Saul was requesting assisted suicide. The armor-bearer refused to cooperate, most likely because he was trained to respect the king. His whole purpose in life was to assist and protect him. When Saul did himself in, the armor-bearer probably felt he had nothing to live for and followed the king's example. Saul's suicide was a final act of despair by one who had entirely alienated himself from God. **Saul and his three sons died there together.** While three sons of Saul died in this same battle (including Jonathan, David's friend), two sons of Saul, Mephibosheth and Ishbosheth, survived Saul's death.

11:2 You will be the shepherd of my people Israel. David grew up as a shepherd of sheep, and now he would use his skills as a protector of people. This phrase would also apply to the Messiah who would come from David's lineage (see Isa. 40:11; Matt. 2:6).

11:7 it was called the City of David. Bethlehem was the city of David's birth, but Jerusalem was the city of David's triumph. Located near the juncture of the northern tribes of Israel and the southern tribes that became Judah, Jerusalem was an ideal place for a capital city that would bring the nation together under one king.

11 Here is the record of David's mightiest warriors:
The first was Jashobeam the Hacmonite, who was
leader of the Three—the mightiest warriors among
David's men.* He once used his spear to kill 300 ene-
my warriors in a single battle.
12 Next in rank among the Three was Eleazar son of
Dodai,* a descendant of Ahoah. 13 He was with David
when the Philistines gathered for battle at Pas-dam-
mim and attacked the Israelites in a field full of bar-
ley. The Israelite army fled, 14 but Eleazar and David*
held their ground in the middle of the field and beat
back the Philistines. So the LORD saved them by giving
them a great victory.
15 Once when David was at the rock near the cave
of Adullam, the Philistine army was camped in the
valley of Rephaim. The Three (who were among the
Thirty—an elite group among David's fighting men)
went down to meet him there. 16 David was staying in
the stronghold at the time, and a Philistine detach-
ment had occupied the town of Bethlehem.
17 David remarked longingly to his men, "Oh, how I
would love some of that good water from the well by
the gate in Bethlehem." 18 So the Three broke through
the Philistine lines, drew some water from the well by
the gate in Bethlehem, and brought it back to David.
But David refused to drink it. Instead, he poured it out
as an offering to the LORD. 19 "God forbid that I should
drink this!" he exclaimed. "This water is as precious as
the blood of these men* who risked their lives to bring
it to me." So David did not drink it. These are examples
of the exploits of the Three.

DAVID'S THIRTY MIGHTY MEN

20 Abishai, the brother of Joab, was the leader of the
Thirty.* He once used his spear to kill 300 enemy
warriors in a single battle. It was by such feats that
he became as famous as the Three. 21 Abishai was the
most famous of the Thirty and was their commander,
though he was not one of the Three.
22 There was also Benaiah son of Jehoiada, a val-
iant warrior from Kabzeel. He did many heroic
deeds, which included killing two champions* of
Moab. Another time, on a snowy day, he chased a
lion down into a pit and killed it. 23 Once, armed only
with a club, he killed an Egyptian warrior who was
7½ feet* tall and who was armed with a spear as
thick as a weaver's beam. Benaiah wrenched the
spear from the Egyptian's hand and killed him with
it. 24 Deeds like these made Benaiah as famous as the
three mightiest warriors. 25 He was more honored
than the other members of the Thirty, though he was
not one of the Three. And David made him captain of
his bodyguard.
26 David's mighty warriors also included:
Asahel, Joab's brother;
Elhanan son of Dodo from Bethlehem;
27 Shammah from Harod;*
Helez from Pelon;
28 Ira son of Ikkesh from Tekoa;
Abiezer from Anathoth;
29 Sibbecai from Hushah;
Zalmon* from Ahoah;
30 Maharai from Netophah;
Heled son of Baanah from Netophah;
31 Ithai son of Ribai from Gibeah (in the land of
Benjamin);
Benaiah from Pirathon;
32 Hurai from near Nahale-gaash*;
Abi-albon* from Arabah;
33 Azmaveth from Bahurim*;
Eliahba from Shaalbon;
34 the sons of Jashen* from Gizon;
Jonathan son of Shagee from Harar;
35 Ahiam son of Sharar* from Harar;
Eliphal son of Ur;
36 Hepher from Mekerah;
Ahijah from Pelon;
37 Hezro from Carmel;
Paarai* son of Ezbai;
38 Joel, the brother of Nathan;
Mibhar son of Hagri;
39 Zelek from Ammon;
Naharai from Beeroth, the armor bearer of Joab
son of Zeruiah;
40 Ira from Jattir;
Gareb from Jattir;
41 Uriah the Hittite;
Zabad son of Ahlai;
42 Adina son of Shiza, the Reubenite leader who had
thirty men with him;
43 Hanan son of Maacah;
Joshaphat from Mithna;
44 Uzzia from Ashtaroth;
Shama and Jeiel, the sons of Hotham, from Aroer;
45 Jediael son of Shimri;
Joha, his brother, from Tiz;
46 Eliel from Mahavah;
Jeribai and Joshaviah, the sons of Elnaam;
Ithmah from Moab;
47 Eliel and Obed;
Jaasiel from Zobah.*

WARRIORS JOIN DAVID'S ARMY

12 The following men joined David at Ziklag while
he was hiding from Saul son of Kish. They were
among the warriors who fought beside David in bat-
tle. 2 All of them were expert archers, and they could
shoot arrows or sling stones with their left hand as

11:11 As in some Greek manuscripts (see also 2 Sam 23:8); Hebrew reads *leader of the Thirty,* or *leader of the captains.* **11:12** As in parallel text at 2 Sam 23:9 (see also 1 Chr 27:4); Hebrew reads *Dodo,* a variant spelling of Dodai. **11:14** Hebrew *they.* **11:19** Hebrew *Shall I drink the lifeblood of these men?* **11:20** As in Syriac version; Hebrew reads *the Three;* also in 11:21. **11:22** Or *two sons of Ariel.* **11:23** Hebrew *5 cubits* [2.3 meters]. **11:27** As in parallel text at 2 Sam 23:25; Hebrew reads *Shammoth from Haror.* **11:29** As in parallel text at 2 Sam 23:28; Hebrew reads *Ilai.* **11:32a** Or *from the ravines of Gaash.* **11:32b** As in parallel text at 2 Sam 23:31; Hebrew reads *Abiel.* **11:33** As in parallel text at 2 Sam 23:31; Hebrew reads *Baharum.* **11:34** As in parallel text at 2 Sam 23:32; Hebrew reads *sons of Hashem.* **11:35** As in parallel text at 2 Sam 23:33; Hebrew reads *son of Sacar.* **11:37** As in parallel text at 2 Sam 23:35; Hebrew reads *Naarai.* **11:47** Or *the Mezobaite.*

11:15-19 David's warriors demonstrate their unselfish devotion. Their efforts prompt David to demonstrate his ultimate devotion to God.

11:20 Abishai. He was listed as bravest of the brave.

11:39,41,46 At least three of David's thirty were of Gentile origin: Zelek the Ammonite, Uriah the Hittite, and Ithmah the Moabite. This is all the more remarkable since the Ammonites and the Moabites carried a curse on them (Deut. 23:3). Uriah the Hittite was the husband of Bathsheba.

12:2 left hand as well as their right. In the ancient world, left-handedness was usually associated with evil or demons, so many southpaws became ambidextrous. This could be turned to a huge advantage in battle, because when an army attacked from the left, the defenders shields would be facing away in their left hands, thus exposing their right side to immediate danger. Conversely, an ambidextrous attacker could switch their shield to their right hand and attack with their natural left. In the close-up manner in which most battles were decided, this was a decided benefit.

well as their right. They were all relatives of Saul
from the tribe of Benjamin. 3 Their leader was Ahie-
zer son of Shemaah from Gibeah; his brother Joash
was second-in-command. These were the other war-
riors:

Jeziel and Pelet, sons of Azmaveth;
Beracah;
Jehu from Anathoth;
4 Ishmaiah from Gibeon, a famous warrior and
leader among the Thirty;
*Jeremiah, Jahaziel, Johanan, and Jozabad from
Gederah;
5 Eluzai, Jerimoth, Bealiah, Shemariah, and
Shephatiah from Haruph;
6 Elkanah, Isshiah, Azarel, Joezer, and Jashobeam,
who were Korahites;
7 Joelah and Zebadiah, sons of Jeroham from Gedor.

8 Some brave and experienced warriors from the
tribe of Gad also defected to David while he was at
the stronghold in the wilderness. They were expert
with both shield and spear, as fierce as lions and as
swift as deer on the mountains.

9 Ezer was their leader.
Obadiah was second.
Eliab was third.
10 Mishmannah was fourth.
Jeremiah was fifth.
11 Attai was sixth.
Eliel was seventh.
12 Johanan was eighth.
Elzabad was ninth.
13 Jeremiah was tenth.
Macbannai was eleventh.

14 These warriors from Gad were army command-
ers. The weakest among them could take on a hun-
dred regular troops, and the strongest could take on
a thousand! 15 These were the men who crossed the
Jordan River during its seasonal flooding at the be-
ginning of the year and drove out all the people living
in the lowlands on both the east and west banks.
16 Others from Benjamin and Judah came to David
at the stronghold. 17 David went out to meet them and
said, "If you have come in peace to help me, we are
friends. But if you have come to betray me to my en-
emies when I am innocent, then may the God of our
ancestors see it and punish you."
18 Then the Spirit came upon Amasai, the leader of
the Thirty, and he said,

"We are yours, David!
We are on your side, son of Jesse.
Peace and prosperity be with you,
and success to all who help you,
for your God is the one who helps you."

So David let them join him, and he made them officers
over his troops.

19 Some men from Manasseh defected from the Isra-
elite army and joined David when he set out with the
Philistines to fight against Saul. But as it turned out,
the Philistine rulers refused to let David and his men
go with them. After much discussion, they sent them
back, for they said, "It will cost us our heads if David
switches loyalties to Saul and turns against us."
20 Here is a list of the men from Manasseh who de-
fected to David as he was returning to Ziklag: Adnah,
Jozabad, Jediael, Michael, Jozabad, Elihu, and Zille-
thai. Each commanded 1,000 troops from the tribe of
Manasseh. 21 They helped David chase down bands
of raiders, for they were all brave and able warriors
who became commanders in his army. 22 Day after
day more men joined David until he had a great army,
like the army of God.
23 These are the numbers of armed warriors who
joined David at Hebron. They were all eager to see
David become king instead of Saul, just as the LORD
had promised.

24 From the tribe of Judah, there were 6,800 warriors
armed with shields and spears.
25 From the tribe of Simeon, there were 7,100 brave
warriors.
26 From the tribe of Levi, there were 4,600 warriors.
27 This included Jehoiada, leader of the family of
Aaron, who had 3,700 under his command. 28 This
also included Zadok, a brave young warrior, with
22 members of his family who were all officers.
29 From the tribe of Benjamin, Saul's relatives, there
were 3,000 warriors. Most of the men from Benja-
min had remained loyal to Saul until this time.
30 From the tribe of Ephraim, there were 20,800 brave
warriors, each highly respected in his own clan.
31 From the half-tribe of Manasseh west of the Jor-
dan, 18,000 men were designated by name to help
David become king.
32 From the tribe of Issachar, there were 200 leaders
of the tribe with their relatives. All these men
understood the signs of the times and knew the
best course for Israel to take.
33 From the tribe of Zebulun, there were 50,000
skilled warriors. They were fully armed and pre-
pared for battle and completely loyal to David.
34 From the tribe of Naphtali, there were 1,000
officers and 37,000 warriors armed with shields
and spears.
35 From the tribe of Dan, there were 28,600 warriors,
all prepared for battle.
36 From the tribe of Asher, there were 40,000 trained
warriors, all prepared for battle.
37 From the east side of the Jordan River—where
the tribes of Reuben and Gad and the half-tribe
of Manasseh lived—there were 120,000 troops
armed with every kind of weapon.

38 All these men came in battle array to Hebron
with the single purpose of making David the king
over all Israel. In fact, everyone in Israel agreed that
David should be their king. 39 They feasted and drank

12:4 Verses 12:4b-40 are numbered 12:5-41 in Hebrew text.

12:23-37 David warmly received the help of Saul's defectors and made many volunteers leaders of his army (v. 18).

12:38 single purpose. Throughout Israel's history, the people were never of one mind about anything. The ten northern ten tribes (Israel) were always opposed to the two southern tribes (Judah). David's era was a golden era in part because he was able to unite a divided nation.

with David for three days, for preparations had been
made by their relatives for their arrival. 40 And people
from as far away as Issachar, Zebulun, and Naphta-
li brought food on donkeys, camels, mules, and oxen.
Vast supplies of flour, fig cakes, clusters of raisins,
wine, olive oil, cattle, sheep, and goats were brought
to the celebration. There was great joy throughout
the land of Israel.

DAVID ATTEMPTS TO MOVE THE ARK

13 David consulted with all his officials, including
the generals and captains of his army.* 2 Then he
addressed the entire assembly of Israel as follows: "If
you approve and if it is the will of the LORD our God,
let us send messages to all the Israelites throughout
the land, including the priests and Levites in their
towns and pasturelands. Let us invite them to come
and join us. 3 It is time to bring back the Ark of our
God, for we neglected it during the reign of Saul."
4 The whole assembly agreed to this, for the people
could see it was the right thing to do. 5 So David sum-
moned all Israel, from the Shihor Brook of Egypt in
the south all the way to the town of Lebo-hamath in
the north, to join in bringing the Ark of God from Kiri-
ath-jearim. 6 Then David and all Israel went to Baalah
of Judah (also called Kiriath-jearim) to bring back the
Ark of God, which bears the name* of the LORD who
is enthroned between the cherubim. 7 They placed the
Ark of God on a new cart and brought it from Abin-
adab's house. Uzzah and Ahio were guiding the cart.
8 David and all Israel were celebrating before God
with all their might, singing songs and playing all
kinds of musical instruments—lyres, harps, tambou-
rines, cymbals, and trumpets.
9 But when they arrived at the threshing floor of
Nacon,* the oxen stumbled, and Uzzah reached out
his hand to steady the Ark. 10 Then the LORD's anger
was aroused against Uzzah, and he struck him dead
because he had laid his hand on the Ark. So Uzzah
died there in the presence of God.
11 David was angry because the LORD's anger had
burst out against Uzzah. He named that place Perez-
uzzah (which means "to burst out against Uzzah"), as
it is still called today.
12 David was now afraid of God, and he asked, "How
can I ever bring the Ark of God back into my care?"
13 So David did not move the Ark into the City of David.
Instead, he took it to the house of Obed-edom of Gath.
14 The Ark of God remained there in Obed-edom's
house for three months, and the LORD blessed the
household of Obed-edom and everything he owned.

DAVID'S PALACE AND FAMILY

14 Then King Hiram of Tyre sent messengers to
David, along with cedar timber, and stonema-
sons and carpenters to build him a palace. 2 And Da-
vid realized that the LORD had confirmed him as king
over Israel and had greatly blessed his kingdom for
the sake of his people Israel.
3 Then David married more wives in Jerusalem, and
they had more sons and daughters. 4 These are the
names of David's sons who were born in Jerusalem:
Shammua, Shobab, Nathan, Solomon, 5 Ibhar, Elishua,
Elpelet, 6 Nogah, Nepheg, Japhia, 7 Elishama, Eliada,*
and Eliphelet.

DAVID CONQUERS THE PHILISTINES

8 When the Philistines heard that David had been
anointed king over all Israel, they mobilized all their
forces to capture him. But David was told they were
coming, so he marched out to meet them. 9 The Philis-
tines arrived and made a raid in the valley of Repha-
im. 10 So David asked God, "Should I go out to fight the
Philistines? Will you hand them over to me?"
The LORD replied, "Yes, go ahead. I will hand them
over to you."
11 So David and his troops went up to Baal-perazim
and defeated the Philistines there. "God did it!" David
exclaimed. "He used me to burst through my enemies
like a raging flood!" So they named that place Baal-pe-
razim (which means "the Lord who bursts through").
12 The Philistines had abandoned their gods there, so
David gave orders to burn them.
13 But after a while the Philistines returned and
raided the valley again. 14 And once again David
asked God what to do. "Do not attack them straight
on," God replied. "Instead, circle around behind and
attack them near the poplar* trees. 15 When you hear
a sound like marching feet in the tops of the poplar
trees, go out and attack! That will be the signal that
God is moving ahead of you to strike down the Phi-
listine army." 16 So David did what God commanded,
and they struck down the Philistine army all the way
from Gibeon to Gezer.
17 So David's fame spread everywhere, and the LORD
caused all the nations to fear David.

PREPARING TO MOVE THE ARK

15 David now built several buildings for himself in
the City of David. He also prepared a place for
the Ark of God and set up a special tent for it. 2 Then
he commanded, "No one except the Levites may carry
the Ark of God. The LORD has chosen them to carry the
Ark of the LORD and to serve him forever."
3 Then David summoned all Israel to Jerusalem to
bring the Ark of the LORD to the place he had pre-
pared for it. 4 This is the number of the descendants of
Aaron (the priests) and the Levites who were called
together:

5 From the clan of Kohath, 120, with Uriel as their
leader.

13:1 Hebrew *the commanders of thousands and of hundreds.* **13:6** Or *the Ark of God, where the Name is proclaimed—the name.* **13:9** As in parallel text at 2 Sam 6:6; Hebrew reads *Kidon.* **14:7** Hebrew *Beeliada,* a variant spelling of Eliada; compare 3:8 and parallel text at 2 Sam 5:16. **14:14** Or *aspen,* or *balsam;* also in 14:15. The exact identification of this tree is uncertain.

13:1-4 bring back the Ark. The Philistines had captured and then returned the ark years earlier, but it remained forgotten in a warehouse.

13:7 new cart. The ark was irreverently transported on a cart. The Levites alone were allowed to carry the ark. Even then, it could only be transported on poles inserted in its corner rings (see Ex. 25:13-15).

13:10 reached out . . . to steady the Ark. Uzzah's punishment seems harsh, but it impressed the Lord's holiness on the people.

14:10 David asked God. "Asked" reflects the same Hebrew word used to describe Saul's inquiry of the Lord (1 Sam. 28:6). Unlike David, when Saul did not immediately get an answer from God, he "consulted" (a stronger Hebrew word for "inquire") the witch-medium from Endor. How the mighty had fallen! God then replied to Saul that he would be defeated by the Philistines and die the next day; a stark contrast to the thumbs-up given David here. David was, after all, a man after God's own heart.

14:11 Baal-perazim. "Perazim" in Hebrew, means "broken out." Previously, it described God's anger directed towards the Israelites, who were worshiping idols in the wilderness (Ps. 106:29), and Uzzah (13:11). Here, Yahweh once again strikes against those who violate His holiness.

6 From the clan of Merari, 220, with Asaiah as their
leader.
7 From the clan of Gershon,* 130, with Joel as their
leader.
8 From the descendants of Elizaphan, 200, with She-
maiah as their leader.
9 From the descendants of Hebron, 80, with Eliel as
their leader.
10 From the descendants of Uzziel, 112, with Ammi-
nadab as their leader.

11 Then David summoned the priests, Zadok and
Abiathar, and these Levite leaders: Uriel, Asaiah, Joel,
Shemaiah, Eliel, and Amminadab. 12 He said to them,
"You are the leaders of the Levite families. You must
purify yourselves and all your fellow Levites, so you
can bring the Ark of the LORD, the God of Israel, to the
place I have prepared for it. 13 Because you Levites did
not carry the Ark the first time, the anger of the LORD
our God burst out against us. We failed to ask God how
to move it properly." 14 So the priests and the Levites
purified themselves in order to bring the Ark of the
LORD, the God of Israel, to Jerusalem. 15 Then the Lev-
ites carried the Ark of God on their shoulders with its
carrying poles, just as the LORD had instructed Moses.
16 David also ordered the Levite leaders to appoint
a choir of Levites who were singers and musicians to
sing joyful songs to the accompaniment of harps, lyres,
and cymbals. 17 So the Levites appointed Heman son of
Joel along with his fellow Levites: Asaph son of Bereki-
ah, and Ethan son of Kushaiah from the clan of Merari.
18 The following men were chosen as their assistants:
Zechariah, Jaaziel,* Shemiramoth, Jehiel, Unni, Eliab,
Benaiah, Maaseiah, Mattithiah, Eliphelehu, Mikneiah,
and the gatekeepers—Obed-edom and Jeiel.
19 The musicians Heman, Asaph, and Ethan were
chosen to sound the bronze cymbals. 20 Zechariah,
Aziel, Shemiramoth, Jehiel, Unni, Eliab, Maaseiah,
and Benaiah were chosen to play the harps.* 21 Mat-
tithiah, Eliphelehu, Mikneiah, Obed-edom, Jeiel, and
Azaziah were chosen to play the lyres.* 22 Kenaniah,
the head Levite, was chosen as the choir leader be-
cause of his skill.
23 Berekiah and Elkanah were chosen to guard*
the Ark. 24 Shebaniah, Joshaphat, Nethanel, Amasai,
Zechariah, Benaiah, and Eliezer—all of whom were
priests—were chosen to blow the trumpets as they
marched in front of the Ark of God. Obed-edom and
Jehiah were chosen to guard the Ark.

MOVING THE ARK TO JERUSALEM

25 Then David and the elders of Israel and the generals
of the army* went to the house of Obed-edom to bring
the Ark of the LORD's Covenant up to Jerusalem with a
great celebration. 26 And because God was clearly help-
ing the Levites as they carried the Ark of the LORD's
Covenant, they sacrificed seven bulls and seven rams.
27 David was dressed in a robe of fine linen, as were
all the Levites who carried the Ark, and also the sing-
ers, and Kenaniah the choir leader. David was also
wearing a priestly garment.* 28 So all Israel brought
up the Ark of the LORD's Covenant with shouts of joy,
the blowing of rams' horns and trumpets, the crash-
ing of cymbals, and loud playing on harps and lyres.
29 But as the Ark of the LORD's Covenant entered the
City of David, Michal, the daughter of Saul, looked
down from her window. When she saw King David
skipping about and laughing with joy, she was filled
with contempt for him.

16 They brought the Ark of God and placed it in-
side the special tent David had prepared for it.
And they presented burnt offerings and peace offer-
ings to God. 2 When he had finished his sacrifices, Da-
vid blessed the people in the name of the LORD. 3 Then
he gave to every man and woman in all Israel a loaf of
bread, a cake of dates,* and a cake of raisins.
4 David appointed the following Levites to lead
the people in worship before the Ark of the LORD—
to invoke his blessings, to give thanks, and to praise
the LORD, the God of Israel. 5 Asaph, the leader of this
group, sounded the cymbals. Second to him was Zech-
ariah, followed by Jeiel, Shemiramoth, Jehiel, Mat-
tithiah, Eliab, Benaiah, Obed-edom, and Jeiel. They
played the harps and lyres. 6 The priests, Benaiah and
Jahaziel, played the trumpets regularly before the
Ark of God's Covenant.

DAVID'S SONG OF PRAISE

7 On that day David gave to Asaph and his fellow Lev-
ites this song of thanksgiving to the LORD:

8 Give thanks to the LORD and proclaim his greatness.
Let the whole world know what he has done.
9 Sing to him; yes, sing his praises.
Tell everyone about his wonderful deeds.
10 Exult in his holy name;
rejoice, you who worship the LORD.
11 Search for the LORD and for his strength;
continually seek him.
12 Remember the wonders he has performed,
his miracles, and the rulings he has given,
13 you children of his servant Israel,
you descendants of Jacob, his chosen ones.

14 He is the LORD our God.
His justice is seen throughout the land.
15 Remember his covenant forever—
the commitment he made to a thousand
generations.

15:7 Hebrew *Gershom,* a variant spelling of Gershon. 15:18 As in several Hebrew manuscripts and Greek version (see also parallel lists in 15:20; 16:5); Masoretic Text reads *Zechariah ben Jaaziel.* 15:20 Hebrew adds *according to Alamoth,* which is probably a musical term. The meaning of the Hebrew is uncertain. 15:21 Hebrew adds *according to the Sheminith,* which is probably a musical term. The meaning of the Hebrew is uncertain. 15:23 Hebrew *chosen as gatekeepers for;* also in 15:24. 15:25 Hebrew *the commanders of thousands.* 15:27 Hebrew *a linen ephod.* 16:3 Or *a portion of meat.* The meaning of the Hebrew is uncertain.

15:12 purify yourselves. Rather than repeat history, the Levites are to be spiritually prepared for their assignment (see Ex. 29:1-37).

15:27 robe of fine linen. The ephod was a chest covering reserved for the office of priest. As a sort of priest-king, David exercises a new form of spiritual leadership over Israel.

15:29 she was filled with contempt. It seems that Michal's feeling was due to the fact that David was dancing nearly naked, which was beneath David's dignity as king—especially since servant girls were watching (see 2 Sam. 6:16-23.) David, however, was showing an unbridled exuberance, which was appropriate to this moment of celebration. Michal's displeasure also gives example to her disregard for things sacred as her father had before her (1 Sam. 13:8-14).

16:8-36 The chronicler embellishes the celebration in Jerusalem by the addition of a compilation of psalms not found in the book of Samuel (see Pss. 96:1-13; 105:1-15; 106:1,47-48). David compiles events from the past into a merry celebration of the present.

16 This is the covenant he made with Abraham
and the oath he swore to Isaac.
17 He confirmed it to Jacob as a decree,
and to the people of Israel as a never-ending
covenant:
18 "I will give you the land of Canaan
as your special possession."

19 He said this when you were few in number,
a tiny group of strangers in Canaan.
20 They wandered from nation to nation,
from one kingdom to another.
21 Yet he did not let anyone oppress them.
He warned kings on their behalf:
22 "Do not touch my chosen people,
and do not hurt my prophets."

23 Let the whole earth sing to the LORD!
Each day proclaim the good news that he saves.
24 Publish his glorious deeds among the nations.
Tell everyone about the amazing things he does.
25 Great is the LORD! He is most worthy of praise!
He is to be feared above all gods.
26 The gods of other nations are mere idols,
but the LORD made the heavens!
27 Honor and majesty surround him;
strength and joy fill his dwelling.

28 O nations of the world, recognize the LORD,
recognize that the LORD is glorious and strong.
29 Give to the LORD the glory he deserves!
Bring your offering and come into his presence.
Worship the LORD in all his holy splendor.
30 Let all the earth tremble before him.
The world stands firm and cannot be shaken.

31 Let the heavens be glad, and the earth rejoice!
Tell all the nations, "The LORD reigns!"
32 Let the sea and everything in it shout his praise!
Let the fields and their crops burst out with joy!
33 Let the trees of the forest sing for joy before the LORD,
for he is coming to judge the earth.

34 Give thanks to the LORD, for he is good!
His faithful love endures forever.
35 Cry out, "Save us, O God of our salvation!
Gather and rescue us from among the nations,
so we can thank your holy name
and rejoice and praise you."

36 Praise the LORD, the God of Israel,
who lives from everlasting to everlasting!

And all the people shouted "Amen!" and praised the LORD.

WORSHIP AT JERUSALEM AND GIBEON

37 David arranged for Asaph and his fellow Levites
to serve regularly before the Ark of the LORD's Covenant,
doing whatever needed to be done each day.
38 This group included Obed-edom (son of Jeduthun),
Hosah, and sixty-eight other Levites as gatekeepers.
39 Meanwhile, David stationed Zadok the priest
and his fellow priests at the Tabernacle of the LORD
at the place of worship in Gibeon, where they con-
tinued to minister before the LORD. 40 They sacrificed
the regular burnt offerings to the LORD each morning
and evening on the altar set aside for that purpose,
obeying everything written in the Law of the LORD,
as he had commanded Israel. 41 David also appointed
Heman, Jeduthun, and the others chosen by name to
give thanks to the LORD, for "his faithful love endures
forever." 42 They used their trumpets, cymbals, and
other instruments to accompany their songs of praise
to God.* And the sons of Jeduthun were appointed as
gatekeepers.
43 Then all the people returned to their homes, and
David turned and went home to bless his own family.

THE LORD'S COVENANT PROMISE TO DAVID

17 When David was settled in his palace, he sum-
moned Nathan the prophet. "Look," David said,
"I am living in a beautiful cedar palace,* but the Ark
of the LORD's Covenant is out there under a tent!"
2 Nathan replied to David, "Do whatever you have
in mind, for God is with you."
3 But that same night God said to Nathan,

4 "Go and tell my servant David, 'This is what the
LORD has declared: You are not the one to build
a house for me to live in. 5 I have never lived in a
house, from the day I brought the Israelites out
of Egypt until this very day. My home has always
been a tent, moving from one place to another in
a Tabernacle. 6 Yet no matter where I have gone
with the Israelites, I have never once complained
to Israel's leaders, the shepherds of my people. I
have never asked them, "Why haven't you built me
a beautiful cedar house?"'
7 "Now go and say to my servant David, 'This is
what the LORD of Heaven's Armies has declared:
I took you from tending sheep in the pasture and
selected you to be the leader of my people Israel.
8 I have been with you wherever you have gone,
and I have destroyed all your enemies before
your eyes. Now I will make your name as famous
as anyone who has ever lived on the earth! 9 And
I will provide a homeland for my people Israel,
planting them in a secure place where they will
never be disturbed. Evil nations won't oppress
them as they've done in the past, 10 starting from
the time I appointed judges to rule my people
Israel. And I will defeat all your enemies.
"'Furthermore, I declare that the LORD will build a
house for you—a dynasty of kings! 11 For when you
die and join your ancestors, I will raise up one of
your descendants, one of your sons, and I will make
his kingdom strong. 12 He is the one who will build
a house—a temple—for me. And I will secure his

16:42 Or *to accompany the sacred music;* or *to accompany singing to God.* **17:1** Hebrew *a house of cedar.*

17:1 a beautiful cedar palace . . . a tent. Cedars of Lebanon provided the most sought after building material of the time, later used in the temple's construction. In humility, David did not feel he should have a better dwelling than God.

17:5 My home has always been a tent. God resists the idea of being penned up in one building. In the book of Acts Paul declares, "He is the God who made the world and everything in it. . . . he doesn't live in man-made temples" (Acts 17:24).

17:10 the LORD will build a house for you. God counters David's offer to build a house for Him by saying He will build a house for David. God is not talking about a physical house, but a dynasty, the "house" of David.

17:12 He is the one who will build a house . . . for me. God says David's son will build a physical house for Him. Perhaps this was a concession to human weakness—we need a physical place to go in our search for God.

throne forever. [13] I will be his father, and he will be my son. I will never take my favor from him as I took it from the one who ruled before you. [14] I will confirm him as king over my house and my kingdom for all time, and his throne will be secure forever.'"

[15] So Nathan went back to David and told him everything the LORD had said in this vision.

DAVID'S PRAYER OF THANKS

[16] Then King David went in and sat before the LORD and prayed,

"Who am I, O LORD God, and what is my family, that you have brought me this far? [17] And now, O God, in addition to everything else, you speak of giving your servant a lasting dynasty! You speak as though I were someone very great,* O LORD God!

[18] "What more can I say to you about the way you have honored me? You know what your servant is really like. [19] For the sake of your servant, O LORD, and according to your will, you have done all these great things and have made them known.

[20] "O LORD, there is no one like you. We have never even heard of another God like you! [21] What other nation on earth is like your people Israel? What other nation, O God, have you redeemed from slavery to be your own people? You made a great name for yourself when you redeemed your people from Egypt. You performed awesome miracles and drove out the nations that stood in their way. [22] You chose Israel to be your very own people forever, and you, O LORD, became their God.

[23] "And now, O LORD, I am your servant; do as you have promised concerning me and my family. May it be a promise that will last forever. [24] And may your name be established and honored forever so that everyone will say, 'The LORD of Heaven's Armies, the God of Israel, is Israel's God!' And may the house of your servant David continue before you forever.

[25] "O my God, I have been bold enough to pray to you because you have revealed to your servant that you will build a house for him—a dynasty of kings! [26] For you are God, O LORD. And you have promised these good things to your servant. [27] And now, it has pleased you to bless the house of your servant, so that it will continue forever before you. For when you grant a blessing, O LORD, it is an eternal blessing!"

DAVID'S MILITARY VICTORIES

18 After this, David defeated and subdued the Philistines by conquering Gath and its surrounding towns. [2] David also conquered the land of Moab, and the Moabites who were spared became David's subjects and paid him tribute money.

[3] David also destroyed the forces of Hadadezer, king of Zobah, as far as Hamath,* when Hadadezer marched out to strengthen his control along the Euphrates River. [4] David captured 1,000 chariots, 7,000 charioteers, and 20,000 foot soldiers. He crippled all the chariot horses except enough for 100 chariots.

[5] When Arameans from Damascus arrived to help King Hadadezer, David killed 22,000 of them. [6] Then he placed several army garrisons* in Damascus, the Aramean capital, and the Arameans became David's subjects and paid him tribute money. So the LORD made David victorious wherever he went.

[7] David brought the gold shields of Hadadezer's officers to Jerusalem, [8] along with a large amount of bronze from Hadadezer's towns of Tebah* and Cun. Later Solomon melted the bronze and molded it into the great bronze basin called the Sea, the pillars, and the various bronze articles used at the Temple.

[9] When King Toi* of Hamath heard that David had destroyed the entire army of King Hadadezer of Zobah, [10] he sent his son Joram* to congratulate King David for his successful campaign. Hadadezer and Toi had been enemies and were often at war. Joram presented David with many gifts of gold, silver, and bronze.

[11] King David dedicated all these gifts to the LORD, along with the silver and gold he had taken from the other nations—from Edom, Moab, Ammon, Philistia, and Amalek.

[12] Abishai son of Zeruiah destroyed 18,000 Edomites in the Valley of Salt. [13] He placed army garrisons in Edom, and all the Edomites became David's subjects. In fact, the LORD made David victorious wherever he went.

[14] So David reigned over all Israel and did what was just and right for all his people. [15] Joab son of Zeruiah was commander of the army. Jehoshaphat son of Ahilud was the royal historian. [16] Zadok son of Ahitub and Ahimelech* son of Abiathar were the priests. Seraiah* was the court secretary. [17] Benaiah son of Jehoiada was captain of the king's bodyguard.* And David's sons served as the king's chief assistants.

DAVID DEFEATS THE AMMONITES

19 Some time after this, King Nahash of the Ammonites died, and his son Hanun* became king. [2] David said, "I am going to show loyalty to Hanun because his father, Nahash, was always loyal to me." So David sent messengers to express sympathy to Hanun about his father's death.

But when David's ambassadors arrived in the land of Ammon, [3] the Ammonite commanders said to Hanun, "Do you really think these men are coming here to honor your father? No! David has sent them to spy out the land so they can come in and conquer it!" [4] So Hanun seized David's ambassadors and shaved them, cut off their robes at the buttocks, and sent them back to David in shame.

17:17 The meaning of the Hebrew is uncertain. **18:3** The meaning of the Hebrew is uncertain. **18:6** As in Greek version and Latin Vulgate (see also 2 Sam 8:6); Hebrew lacks *several army garrisons.* **18:8** Hebrew reads *Tibhath,* a variant spelling of Tebah; compare parallel text at 2 Sam 8:8. **18:9** As in parallel text at 2 Sam 8:9; Hebrew reads *Tou;* also in 18:10. **18:10** As in parallel text at 2 Sam 8:10; Hebrew reads *Hadoram,* a variant spelling of Joram. **18:16a** As in some Hebrew manuscripts, Syriac version, and Latin Vulgate (see also 2 Sam 8:17); most Hebrew manuscripts read *Abimelech.* **18:16b** As in parallel text at 2 Sam 8:17; Hebrew reads *Shavsha.* **18:17** Hebrew *of the Kerethites and Pelethites.* **19:1** As in parallel text at 2 Sam 10:1; Hebrew lacks *Hanun.*

17:14 secure forever. God implies a heavenly, eternal reign through His own son, Jesus (see Isa. 9:6-7; Luke 1:32-33), a promise made to David (Ps. 89:35-37).

18:1–20:8 David's victories assure God's blessings on his reign. He defeated Israel's archenemies: the Philistines and the Moabites.

19:1–20:3 David's risky battle against the Ammonites and their reinforcements pays off in a secured victory. David began by showing kindness at the death of Nahash, who ruled some 50 years.

19:4-5 shaved them. It was traditional for all adult men to wear beards as a sign of virility; this was a great humiliation.

5 When David heard what had happened to the
men, he sent messengers to tell them, "Stay at Jericho
until your beards grow out, and then come back." For
they felt deep shame because of their appearance.
6 When the people of Ammon realized how seri-
ously they had angered David, Hanun and the Am-
monites sent 75,000 pounds* of silver to hire chariots
and charioteers from Aram-naharaim, Aram-maa-
cah, and Zobah. 7 They also hired 32,000 chariots and
secured the support of the king of Maacah and his
army. These forces camped at Medeba, where they
were joined by the Ammonite troops that Hanun had
recruited from his own towns. 8 When David heard
about this, he sent Joab and all his warriors to fight
them. 9 The Ammonite troops came out and drew up
their battle lines at the entrance of the city, while the
other kings positioned themselves to fight in the open
fields.
10 When Joab saw that he would have to fight on
both the front and the rear, he chose some of Israel's
elite troops and placed them under his personal com-
mand to fight the Arameans in the fields. 11 He left the
rest of the army under the command of his brother
Abishai, who was to attack the Ammonites. 12 "If the
Arameans are too strong for me, then come over and
help me," Joab told his brother. "And if the Ammonites
are too strong for you, I will help you. 13 Be courageous!
Let us fight bravely for our people and the cities of our
God. May the LORD's will be done."
14 When Joab and his troops attacked, the Arameans
began to run away. 15 And when the Ammonites saw
the Arameans running, they also ran from Abishai
and retreated into the city. Then Joab returned to Je-
rusalem.
16 The Arameans now realized that they were no
match for Israel, so they sent messengers and sum-
moned additional Aramean troops from the other
side of the Euphrates River.* These troops were under
the command of Shobach,* the commander of Hadad-
ezer's forces.
17 When David heard what was happening, he
mobilized all Israel, crossed the Jordan River, and
positioned his troops in battle formation. Then Da-
vid engaged the Arameans in battle, and they fought
against him. 18 But again the Arameans fled from the
Israelites. This time David's forces killed 7,000 char-
ioteers and 40,000 foot soldiers, including Shobach,
the commander of their army. 19 When Hadadezer's
allies saw that they had been defeated by Israel, they
surrendered to David and became his subjects. After
that, the Arameans were no longer willing to help the
Ammonites.

DAVID CAPTURES RABBAH

20 In the spring of the year,* when kings normally
go out to war, Joab led the Israelite army in suc-
cessful attacks against the land of the Ammonites. In
the process he laid siege to the city of Rabbah, attack-
ing and destroying it. However, David stayed behind
in Jerusalem.
2 Then David went to Rabbah and removed the
crown from the king's head,* and it was placed on
his own head. The crown was made of gold and set
with gems, and he found that it weighed seventy-five
pounds.* David took a vast amount of plunder from
the city. 3 He also made slaves of the people of Rabbah
and forced them to labor with saws, iron picks, and
iron axes.* That is how David dealt with the people of
all the Ammonite towns. Then David and all the army
returned to Jerusalem.

BATTLES AGAINST PHILISTINE GIANTS

4 After this, war broke out with the Philistines at
Gezer. As they fought, Sibbecai from Hushah killed
Saph,* a descendant of the giants,* and so the Philis-
tines were subdued.
5 During another battle with the Philistines, Elha-
nan son of Jair killed Lahmi, the brother of Goliath of
Gath. The handle of Lahmi's spear was as thick as a
weaver's beam!
6 In another battle with the Philistines at Gath, they
encountered a huge man with six fingers on each
hand and six toes on each foot, twenty-four in all,
who was also a descendant of the giants. 7 But when
he defied and taunted Israel, he was killed by Jona-
than, the son of David's brother Shimea.
8 These Philistines were descendants of the giants
of Gath, but David and his warriors killed them.

DAVID TAKES A CENSUS

21 Satan rose up against Israel and caused Da-
vid to take a census of the people of Israel. 2 So
David said to Joab and the commanders of the army,
"Take a census of all the people of Israel—from Beer-
sheba in the south to Dan in the north—and bring me
a report so I may know how many there are."
3 But Joab replied, "May the LORD increase the num-
ber of his people a hundred times over! But why, my
lord the king, do you want to do this? Are they not all
your servants? Why must you cause Israel to sin?"
4 But the king insisted that they take the census,
so Joab traveled throughout all Israel to count the
people. Then he returned to Jerusalem 5 and reported
the number of people to David. There were 1,100,000
warriors in all Israel who could handle a sword, and
470,000 in Judah. 6 But Joab did not include the tribes
of Levi and Benjamin in the census because he was so
distressed at what the king had made him do.

JUDGMENT FOR DAVID'S SIN

7 God was very displeased with the census, and he
punished Israel for it. 8 Then David said to God, "I have
sinned greatly by taking this census. Please forgive
my guilt for doing this foolish thing."

19:6 Hebrew *1,000 talents* [34,000 kilograms]. **19:16a** Hebrew *the river.* **19:16b** As in parallel text at 2 Sam 10:16; Hebrew reads *Shophach;* also in 19:18. **20:1** Hebrew *At the turn of the year.* The first day of the year in the ancient Hebrew lunar calendar occurred in March or April. **20:2a** Or *from the head of Milcom* (as in Greek version and Latin Vulgate). Milcom, also called Molech, was the god of the Ammonites. **20:2b** Hebrew *1 talent* [34 kilograms]. **20:3** As in parallel text at 2 Sam 12:31; Hebrew reads *and cut them with saws, iron picks, and saws.* **20:4a** As in parallel text at 2 Sam 21:18; Hebrew reads *Sippai.* **20:4b** Hebrew *descendant of the Rephaites;* also in 20:6, 8.

19:9 Ammonite troops. The battlefield consisted of a heavy Ammonite front at the entrance to the city with Arameans' reinforcements waiting in the open fields.

20:2-3 placed on his own head. Crowning himself with an enemy's royalty was the ultimate sign of victory.

21:1–22:1 In the midst of military momentum, David takes stock of his might through the use of a census. David's conceit and foolishness angers God (see 2 Sam. 24:1). The problem with this census is that David is putting his faith in numbers rather than in the promises of God.

21:4 Joab. Joab, ever loyal to David, has the complex job of tallying the totals for David's census.

9 Then the LORD spoke to Gad, David's seer. This was
the message: 10 "Go and say to David, 'This is what the
LORD says: I will give you three choices. Choose one of
these punishments, and I will inflict it on you.'"
11 So Gad came to David and said, "These are the
choices the LORD has given you. 12 You may choose
three years of famine, three months of destruction
by the sword of your enemies, or three days of severe
plague as the angel of the LORD brings devastation
throughout the land of Israel. Decide what answer I
should give the LORD who sent me."
13 "I'm in a desperate situation!" David replied to
Gad. "But let me fall into the hands of the LORD, for
his mercy is very great. Do not let me fall into human
hands."
14 So the LORD sent a plague upon Israel, and 70,000
people died as a result. 15 And God sent an angel to de-
stroy Jerusalem. But just as the angel was preparing
to destroy it, the LORD relented and said to the death
angel, "Stop! That is enough!" At that moment the an-
gel of the LORD was standing by the threshing floor of
Araunah* the Jebusite.
16 David looked up and saw the angel of the LORD
standing between heaven and earth with his sword
drawn, reaching out over Jerusalem. So David and
the leaders of Israel put on burlap to show their deep
distress and fell face down on the ground. 17 And Da-
vid said to God, "I am the one who called for the cen-
sus! I am the one who has sinned and done wrong!
But these people are as innocent as sheep—what
have they done? O LORD my God, let your anger fall
against me and my family, but do not destroy your
people."

DAVID BUILDS AN ALTAR

18 Then the angel of the LORD told Gad to instruct Da-
vid to go up and build an altar to the LORD on the
threshing floor of Araunah the Jebusite. 19 So David
went up to do what the LORD had commanded him
through Gad. 20 Araunah, who was busy threshing
wheat at the time, turned and saw the angel there.
His four sons, who were with him, ran away and hid.
21 When Araunah saw David approaching, he left his
threshing floor and bowed before David with his face
to the ground.
22 David said to Araunah, "Let me buy this thresh-
ing floor from you at its full price. Then I will build
an altar to the LORD there, so that he will stop the
plague."
23 "Take it, my lord the king, and use it as you wish,"
Araunah said to David. "I will give the oxen for the
burnt offerings, and the threshing boards for wood to
build a fire on the altar, and the wheat for the grain
offering. I will give it all to you."
24 But King David replied to Araunah, "No, I insist
on buying it for the full price. I will not take what is
yours and give it to the LORD. I will not present burnt
offerings that have cost me nothing!" 25 So David
gave Araunah 600 pieces of gold* in payment for the
threshing floor.
26 David built an altar there to the LORD and sacri-
ficed burnt offerings and peace offerings. And when
David prayed, the LORD answered him by sending
fire from heaven to burn up the offering on the al-
tar. 27 Then the LORD spoke to the angel, who put the
sword back into its sheath.
28 When David saw that the LORD had answered
his prayer, he offered sacrifices there at Araunah's
threshing floor. 29 At that time the Tabernacle of the
LORD and the altar of burnt offering that Moses had
made in the wilderness were located at the place of
worship in Gibeon. 30 But David was not able to go
there to inquire of God, because he was terrified by
the drawn sword of the angel of the LORD.

22 Then David said, "This will be the location for
the Temple of the LORD God and the place of the
altar for Israel's burnt offerings!"

PREPARATIONS FOR THE TEMPLE

2 So David gave orders to call together the foreigners
living in Israel, and he assigned them the task of pre-
paring finished stone for building the Temple of God.
3 David provided large amounts of iron for the nails
that would be needed for the doors in the gates and
for the clamps, and he gave more bronze than could
be weighed. 4 He also provided innumerable cedar
logs, for the men of Tyre and Sidon had brought vast
amounts of cedar to David.
5 David said, "My son Solomon is still young and
inexperienced. And since the Temple to be built for
the LORD must be a magnificent structure, famous
and glorious throughout the world, I will begin mak-
ing preparations for it now." So David collected vast
amounts of building materials before his death.
6 Then David sent for his son Solomon and instruct-
ed him to build a Temple for the LORD, the God of Is-
rael. 7 "My son, I wanted to build a Temple to honor
the name of the LORD my God," David told him. 8 "But
the LORD said to me, 'You have killed many men in the
battles you have fought. And since you have shed so
much blood in my sight, you will not be the one to
build a Temple to honor my name. 9 But you will have
a son who will be a man of peace. I will give him
peace with his enemies in all the surrounding lands.
His name will be Solomon,* and I will give peace and
quiet to Israel during his reign. 10 He is the one who
will build a Temple to honor my name. He will be
my son, and I will be his father. And I will secure the
throne of his kingdom over Israel forever.'
11 "Now, my son, may the LORD be with you and give
you success as you follow his directions in building

21:15 As in parallel text at 2 Sam 24:16; Hebrew reads *Ornan,* another name for Araunah; also in 21:18-28. **21:25** Hebrew *600 shekels of gold,* about 15 pounds or 6.8 kilograms in weight. **22:9** *Solomon* sounds like and is probably derived from the Hebrew word for "peace."

21:24 offerings that have cost me nothing. Although Araunah was willing to provide a ready-made sacrifice free of charge, David insists on purchasing it. If one's offering doesn't cost him anything, giving it to God cannot really be a sacrifice.

22:2-19 Resigned to the fact that he will not actually build the temple, David makes its spiritual and material preparations. His intimate connection with the temple is a major theme of both 1 and 2 Chronicles.

22:8-9 you have shed so much blood. Here we have a great paradox: while God was the one who called David to make war, the fact that David was a man of war disqualified him from building a temple to God. Even though God's directives are associated with much violence in the Old Testament, God was still working to lessen the amount of violence in the world. He sent the flood to end humanity's trend to violence (see Gen. 6:11). Then later He sent visions of peace through prophets like Isaiah, visions of turning swords into plows and spears into pruning knives (Isa. 2:4) and visions of the wolf living with the lamb and a time when "No one will harm or destroy" (Isa. 11:6,9).

the Temple of the LORD your God. 12 And may the LORD give you wisdom and understanding, that you may obey the Law of the LORD your God as you rule over Israel. 13 For you will be successful if you carefully obey the decrees and regulations that the LORD gave to Israel through Moses. Be strong and courageous; do not be afraid or lose heart!

14 "I have worked hard to provide materials for building the Temple of the LORD—nearly 4,000 tons of gold, 40,000 tons of silver,* and so much iron and bronze that it cannot be weighed. I have also gathered timber and stone for the walls, though you may need to add more. 15 You have a large number of skilled stonemasons and carpenters and craftsmen of every kind. 16 You have expert goldsmiths and silversmiths and workers of bronze and iron. Now begin the work, and may the LORD be with you!"

17 Then David ordered all the leaders of Israel to assist Solomon in this project. 18 "The LORD your God is with you," he declared. "He has given you peace with the surrounding nations. He has handed them over to me, and they are now subject to the LORD and his people. 19 Now seek the LORD your God with all your heart and soul. Build the sanctuary of the LORD God so that you can bring the Ark of the LORD's Covenant and the holy vessels of God into the Temple built to honor the LORD's name."

DUTIES OF THE LEVITES

23 When David was an old man, he appointed his son Solomon to be king over Israel. 2 David summoned all the leaders of Israel, together with the priests and Levites. 3 All the Levites who were thirty years old or older were counted, and the total came to 38,000. 4 Then David said, "From all the Levites, 24,000 will supervise the work at the Temple of the LORD. Another 6,000 will serve as officials and judges. 5 Another 4,000 will work as gatekeepers, and 4,000 will praise the LORD with the musical instruments I have made." 6 Then David divided the Levites into divisions named after the clans descended from the three sons of Levi—Gershon, Kohath, and Merari.

THE GERSHONITES

7 The Gershonite family units were defined by their lines of descent from Libni* and Shimei, the sons of Gershon. 8 Three of the descendants of Libni were Jehiel (the family leader), Zetham, and Joel. 9 These were the leaders of the family of Libni.

Three of the descendants of Shimei were Shelomoth, Haziel, and Haran. 10 Four other descendants of Shimei were Jahath, Ziza,* Jeush, and Beriah.

11 Jahath was the family leader, and Ziza was next. Jeush and Beriah were counted as a single family because neither had many sons.

THE KOHATHITES

12 Four of the descendants of Kohath were Amram, Izhar, Hebron, and Uzziel.

13 The sons of Amram were Aaron and Moses. Aaron and his descendants were set apart to dedicate the most holy things, to offer sacrifices in the LORD's presence, to serve the LORD, and to pronounce blessings in his name forever.

14 As for Moses, the man of God, his sons were included with the tribe of Levi. 15 The sons of Moses were Gershom and Eliezer. 16 The descendants of Gershom included Shebuel, the family leader. 17 Eliezer had only one son, Rehabiah, the family leader. Rehabiah had numerous descendants.

18 The descendants of Izhar included Shelomith, the family leader.

19 The descendants of Hebron included Jeriah (the family leader), Amariah (the second), Jahaziel (the third), and Jekameam (the fourth).

20 The descendants of Uzziel included Micah (the family leader) and Isshiah (the second).

THE MERARITES

21 The descendants of Merari included Mahli and Mushi.

The sons of Mahli were Eleazar and Kish. 22 Eleazar died with no sons, only daughters. His daughters married their cousins, the sons of Kish.

23 Three of the descendants of Mushi were Mahli, Eder, and Jerimoth.

24 These were the descendants of Levi by clans, the leaders of their family groups, registered carefully by name. Each had to be twenty years old or older to qualify for service in the house of the LORD. 25 For David said, "The LORD, the God of Israel, has given us peace, and he will always live in Jerusalem. 26 Now the Levites will no longer need to carry the Tabernacle and its furnishings from place to place." 27 In accordance with David's final instructions, all the Levites twenty years old or older were registered for service.

28 The work of the Levites was to assist the priests, the descendants of Aaron, as they served at the house of the LORD. They also took care of the courtyards and side rooms, helped perform the ceremonies of purification, and served in many other ways in the house of God. 29 They were in charge of the sacred bread that was set out on the table, the choice flour for the grain offerings, the wafers made without yeast, the cakes cooked in olive oil, and the other mixed breads. They were also responsible to check all the weights and measures. 30 And each morning and evening they stood before the LORD to sing songs of thanks and praise to him. 31 They assisted with the burnt offerings that were presented to the LORD on Sabbath days, at new moon celebrations, and at all the appointed festivals. The required number of Levites served in the LORD's presence at all times, following all the procedures they had been given.

32 And so, under the supervision of the priests, the Levites watched over the Tabernacle and the Temple* and faithfully carried out their duties of service at the house of the LORD.

22:14 Hebrew *100,000 talents* [3,400 metric tons] *of gold, 1,000,000 talents* [34,000 metric tons] *of silver.* **23:7** Hebrew *Ladan* (also in 23:8, 9), a variant spelling of Libni; compare 6:17. **23:10** As in Greek version and Latin Vulgate (see also 23:11); Hebrew reads *Zina.* **23:32** Hebrew *the Tent of Meeting and the sanctuary.*

23:1 an old man, he appointed his son Solomon to be king. The chronicler smoothes the tough transition between David and Solomon's reign by leaving out its political implications (1 Kings 1-2).

23:3 Levites. By assembling the Levites, David showed concern for his son's spiritual, as well as royal, readiness.

DUTIES OF THE PRIESTS

24 This is how Aaron's descendants, the priests,
were divided into groups for service. The sons
of Aaron were Nadab, Abihu, Eleazar, and Ithamar.
2 But Nadab and Abihu died before their father, and
they had no sons. So only Eleazar and Ithamar were
left to carry on as priests.
3 With the help of Zadok, who was a descendant
of Eleazar, and of Ahimelech, who was a descen-
dant of Ithamar, David divided Aaron's descen-
dants into groups according to their various duties.
4 Eleazar's descendants were divided into sixteen
groups and Ithamar's into eight, for there were
more family leaders among the descendants of El-
eazar.
5 All tasks were assigned to the various groups by
means of sacred lots so that no preference would be
shown, for there were many qualified officials serv-
ing God in the sanctuary from among the descen-
dants of both Eleazar and Ithamar. 6 Shemaiah son
of Nethanel, a Levite, acted as secretary and wrote
down the names and assignments in the presence of
the king, the officials, Zadok the priest, Ahimelech son
of Abiathar, and the family leaders of the priests and
Levites. The descendants of Eleazar and Ithamar took
turns casting lots.

7 The first lot fell to Jehoiarib.
The second lot fell to Jedaiah.
8 The third lot fell to Harim.
The fourth lot fell to Seorim.
9 The fifth lot fell to Malkijah.
The sixth lot fell to Mijamin.
10 The seventh lot fell to Hakkoz.
The eighth lot fell to Abijah.
11 The ninth lot fell to Jeshua.
The tenth lot fell to Shecaniah.
12 The eleventh lot fell to Eliashib.
The twelfth lot fell to Jakim.
13 The thirteenth lot fell to Huppah.
The fourteenth lot fell to Jeshebeab.
14 The fifteenth lot fell to Bilgah.
The sixteenth lot fell to Immer.
15 The seventeenth lot fell to Hezir.
The eighteenth lot fell to Happizzez.
16 The nineteenth lot fell to Pethahiah.
The twentieth lot fell to Jehezkel.
17 The twenty-first lot fell to Jakin.
The twenty-second lot fell to Gamul.
18 The twenty-third lot fell to Delaiah.
The twenty-fourth lot fell to Maaziah.

19 Each group carried out its appointed duties in the house of the LORD according to the procedures established by their ancestor Aaron in obedience to the commands of the LORD, the God of Israel.

FAMILY LEADERS AMONG THE LEVITES

20 These were the other family leaders descended from Levi:

From the descendants of Amram, the leader was Shebuel.*
From the descendants of Shebuel, the leader was Jehdeiah.
21 From the descendants of Rehabiah, the leader was Isshiah.
22 From the descendants of Izhar, the leader was Shelomith.*
From the descendants of Shelomith, the leader was Jahath.
23 From the descendants of Hebron, Jeriah was the leader,* Amariah was second, Jahaziel was third, and Jekameam was fourth.
24 From the descendants of Uzziel, the leader was Micah.
From the descendants of Micah, the leader was
Shamir, 25 along with Isshiah, the brother of
Micah.
From the descendants of Isshiah, the leader was Zechariah.
26 From the descendants of Merari, the leaders were Mahli and Mushi.
From the descendants of Jaaziah, the leader was Beno.
27 From the descendants of Merari through Jaaziah, the leaders were Beno, Shoham, Zaccur, and Ibri.
28 From the descendants of Mahli, the leader was Eleazar, though he had no sons.
29 From the descendants of Kish, the leader was Jerahmeel.
30 From the descendants of Mushi, the leaders were Mahli, Eder, and Jerimoth.

These were the descendants of Levi in their vari-
ous families. 31 Like the descendants of Aaron, they
were assigned to their duties by means of sacred lots,
without regard to age or rank. Lots were drawn in the
presence of King David, Zadok, Ahimelech, and the
family leaders of the priests and the Levites.

DUTIES OF THE MUSICIANS

25 David and the army commanders then appointed men from the families of Asaph, Heman, and Jeduthun to proclaim God's messages to the accompaniment of lyres, harps, and cymbals. Here is a list of their names and their work:

2 From the sons of Asaph, there were Zaccur, Joseph, Nethaniah, and Asarelah. They worked under the direction of their father, Asaph, who proclaimed God's messages by the king's orders.

24:20 Hebrew *Shubael* (also in 24:20b), a variant spelling of Shebuel; compare 23:16 and 26:24. **24:22** Hebrew *Shelomoth* (also in 24:22b), a variant spelling of Shelomith; compare 23:18. **24:23** Hebrew *From the descendants of Jeriah;* compare 23:19.

24:2 Nadab and Abihu died before their father. Like Uzzah's mishandling of the ark (13:10), Nadab and Abihu had been extinguished for offering unholy fire before the Lord with incense that was not lit from the tabernacle's altar flame (Lev. 10:1-7; Num. 26:61). Since most people would be familiar with this infamous episode and Chronicles is primarily a priestly history of Israel, praise is instead given for the preservation of the Aaronic priesthood through Eleazar and Ithamar.

25:1 and the army commanders. No autocrat, David pulls together a cabinet of decision makers. **to proclaim God's messages.** During David's reign, musically gifted priests were encouraged to add their gifts to the people's worship experience. **lyres, harps, and cymbals.** A popular instrument in the ancient Near East, lyres often accompanied singing (Gen. 31:27; Job 21:12; Ps. 137:2; Isa. 23:16) and worship (1 Sam. 10:5; 2 Sam. 6:5; Pss. 33:2; 43:4; 98:5). It was the instrument David used to calm Saul (1 Sam. 16:16). The harp was an Egyptian favorite with 10-20 strings (Ps. 144:9) used mostly in worship (2 Chron. 29:25; Pss. 33:2; 81:2; 150:3) and was popular at banquets (1 Kings 10:12; 2 Chron. 9:11; Isa. 5:12; 14:11; Amos 5:23). They were also used in the New Testament church (1 Cor. 14:7) and even in heaven as well (Rev. 15:8; 14:2; 15:2).

[3] From the sons of Jeduthun, there were Gedaliah, Zeri, Jeshaiah, Shimei,* Hashabiah, and Mattithiah, six in all. They worked under the direction of their father, Jeduthun, who proclaimed God's messages to the accompaniment of the lyre, offering thanks and praise to the LORD.
[4] From the sons of Heman, there were Bukkiah, Mattaniah, Uzziel, Shubael,* Jerimoth, Hananiah, Hanani, Eliathah, Giddalti, Romamti-ezer, Joshbekashah, Mallothi, Hothir, and Mahazioth.
[5] All these were the sons of Heman, the king's seer, for God had honored him with fourteen sons and three daughters.

[6] All these men were under the direction of their fathers as they made music at the house of the LORD. Their responsibilities included the playing of cymbals, harps, and lyres at the house of God. Asaph, Jeduthun, and Heman reported directly to the king.
[7] They and their families were all trained in making music before the LORD, and each of them—288 in all—was an accomplished musician.
[8] The musicians were appointed to their term of service by means of sacred lots, without regard to whether they were young or old, teacher or student.

[9] The first lot fell to Joseph of the Asaph clan and twelve of his sons and relatives.*
The second lot fell to Gedaliah and twelve of his sons and relatives.
[10] The third lot fell to Zaccur and twelve of his sons and relatives.
[11] The fourth lot fell to Zeri* and twelve of his sons and relatives.
[12] The fifth lot fell to Nethaniah and twelve of his sons and relatives.
[13] The sixth lot fell to Bukkiah and twelve of his sons and relatives.
[14] The seventh lot fell to Asarelah* and twelve of his sons and relatives.
[15] The eighth lot fell to Jeshaiah and twelve of his sons and relatives.
[16] The ninth lot fell to Mattaniah and twelve of his sons and relatives.
[17] The tenth lot fell to Shimei and twelve of his sons and relatives.
[18] The eleventh lot fell to Uzziel* and twelve of his sons and relatives.
[19] The twelfth lot fell to Hashabiah and twelve of his sons and relatives.
[20] The thirteenth lot fell to Shubael and twelve of his sons and relatives.
[21] The fourteenth lot fell to Mattithiah and twelve of his sons and relatives.
[22] The fifteenth lot fell to Jerimoth* and twelve of his sons and relatives.
[23] The sixteenth lot fell to Hananiah and twelve of his sons and relatives.
[24] The seventeenth lot fell to Joshbekashah* and twelve of his sons and relatives.
[25] The eighteenth lot fell to Hanani and twelve of his sons and relatives.
[26] The nineteenth lot fell to Mallothi and twelve of his sons and relatives.
[27] The twentieth lot fell to Eliathah and twelve of his sons and relatives.
[28] The twenty-first lot fell to Hothir and twelve of his sons and relatives.
[29] The twenty-second lot fell to Giddalti and twelve of his sons and relatives.
[30] The twenty-third lot fell to Mahazioth and twelve of his sons and relatives.
[31] The twenty-fourth lot fell to Romamti-ezer and twelve of his sons and relatives.

DUTIES OF THE GATEKEEPERS

26 These are the divisions of the gatekeepers:

From the Korahites, there was Meshelemiah son of Kore, of the family of Abiasaph.*
[2] The sons of Meshelemiah were Zechariah (the oldest), Jediael (the second), Zebadiah (the third), Jathniel (the fourth),
[3] Elam (the fifth), Jehohanan (the sixth), and Eliehoenai (the seventh).
[4] The sons of Obed-edom, also gatekeepers, were Shemaiah (the oldest), Jehozabad (the second), Joah (the third), Sacar (the fourth), Nethanel (the fifth),
[5] Ammiel (the sixth), Issachar (the seventh), and Peullethai (the eighth). God had richly blessed Obed-edom.
[6] Obed-edom's son Shemaiah had sons with great ability who earned positions of great authority in the clan.
[7] Their names were Othni, Rephael, Obed, and Elzabad. Their relatives, Elihu and Semakiah, were also very capable men.
[8] All of these descendants of Obed-edom, including their sons and grandsons—sixty-two of them in all—were very capable men, well qualified for their work.
[9] Meshelemiah's eighteen sons and relatives were also very capable men.

[10] Hosah, of the Merari clan, appointed Shimri as the leader among his sons, though he was not the oldest.
[11] His other sons included Hilkiah (the second), Tebaliah (the third), and Zechariah (the fourth). Hosah's sons and relatives, who served as gatekeepers, numbered thirteen in all.

[12] These divisions of the gatekeepers were named for their family leaders, and like the other Levites, they served at the house of the LORD.
[13] They were assigned by families for guard duty at the various gates,

25:3 As in one Hebrew manuscript and some Greek manuscripts (see also 25:17); most Hebrew manuscripts lack *Shimei*. **25:4** Hebrew *Shebuel*, a variant spelling of Shubael; compare 25:20. **25:9** As in Greek version; Hebrew lacks *and twelve of his sons and relatives*. **25:11** Hebrew *Izri*, a variant spelling of Zeri; compare 25:3. **25:14** Hebrew *Jesarelah*, a variant spelling of Asarelah; compare 25:2. **25:18** Hebrew *Azarel*, a variant spelling of Uzziel; compare 25:4. **25:22** Hebrew *Jeremoth*, a variant spelling of Jerimoth; compare 25:4. **25:24** Hebrew *Joshbekasha*, a variant spelling of Joshbekashah; compare 25:4. **26:1** As in Greek version (see also Exod 6:24); Hebrew reads *Asaph*.

25:10-13 Zaccur . . . Bukkiah. Filling the temple with music of praise was a priority for the nation. Like the tribal leaders, the great warriors, and the priest, the musicians held a place of honor. For the nation to prosper, it needed to be obediently serving God. The future was determined by the devotion of the people to God. Worship was essential.

26:1-15 gatekeepers. The gatekeepers, formed from over 4,000 participants (23:5), served in a group of 22 at a time. The assignments were made through lots, similar to the way musicians were called to perform.

without regard to age or training, for it was all decid-
ed by means of sacred lots.
14 The responsibility for the east gate went to Me-
shelemiah* and his group. The north gate was as-
signed to his son Zechariah, a man of unusual wis-
dom. 15 The south gate went to Obed-edom, and his
sons were put in charge of the storehouse. 16 Shup-
pim and Hosah were assigned the west gate and the
gateway leading up to the Temple.* Guard duties
were divided evenly. 17 Six Levites were assigned
each day to the east gate, four to the north gate, four
to the south gate, and two pairs at the storehouse.
18 Six were assigned each day to the west gate, four
to the gateway leading up to the Temple, and two to
the courtyard.*
19 These were the divisions of the gatekeepers from
the clans of Korah and Merari.

TREASURERS AND OTHER OFFICIALS

20 Other Levites, led by Ahijah, were in charge of the
treasuries of the house of God and the treasuries of
the gifts dedicated to the LORD. 21 From the family of
Libni* in the clan of Gershon, Jehiel* was the leader.
22 The sons of Jehiel, Zetham and his brother Joel, were
in charge of the treasuries of the house of the LORD.
23 These are the leaders that descended from Am-
ram, Izhar, Hebron, and Uzziel:

24 From the clan of Amram, Shebuel was a descen-
dant of Gershom son of Moses. He was the chief
officer of the treasuries. 25 His relatives through
Eliezer were Rehabiah, Jeshaiah, Joram, Zicri, and
Shelomoth.
26 Shelomoth and his relatives were in charge of
the treasuries containing the gifts that King David,
the family leaders, and the generals and captains*
and other officers of the army had dedicated to the
LORD. 27 These men dedicated some of the plunder
they had gained in battle to maintain the house
of the LORD. 28 Shelomoth* and his relatives also
cared for the gifts dedicated to the LORD by Samuel
the seer, Saul son of Kish, Abner son of Ner, and
Joab son of Zeruiah. All the other dedicated gifts
were in their care, too.
29 From the clan of Izhar came Kenaniah. He and his
sons were given administrative responsibilities*
over Israel as officials and judges.
30 From the clan of Hebron came Hashabiah. He and
his relatives—1,700 capable men—were put in
charge of the Israelite lands west of the Jordan
River. They were responsible for all matters relat-
ed to the things of the LORD and the service of the
king in that area.
31 Also from the clan of Hebron came Jeriah,* who
was the leader of the Hebronites according to the
genealogical records. (In the fortieth year of David's
reign, a search was made in the records, and capa-
ble men from the clan of Hebron were found at Jaz-
er in the land of Gilead.) 32 There were 2,700 capable
men among the relatives of Jeriah. King David sent
them to the east side of the Jordan River and put
them in charge of the tribes of Reuben and Gad and
the half-tribe of Manasseh. They were responsible
for all matters related to God and to the king.

MILITARY COMMANDERS AND DIVISIONS

27 This is the list of Israelite generals and cap-
tains,* and their officers, who served the king
by supervising the army divisions that were on duty
each month of the year. Each division served for one
month and had 24,000 troops.

2 Jashobeam son of Zabdiel was commander of the
first division of 24,000 troops, which was on duty
during the first month. 3 He was a descendant of
Perez and was in charge of all the army officers
for the first month.
4 Dodai, a descendant of Ahoah, was commander of
the second division of 24,000 troops, which was
on duty during the second month. Mikloth was his
chief officer.
5 Benaiah son of Jehoiada the priest was commander
of the third division of 24,000 troops, which was
on duty during the third month. 6 This was the
Benaiah who commanded David's elite military
group known as the Thirty. His son Ammizabad
was his chief officer.
7 Asahel, the brother of Joab, was commander of
the fourth division of 24,000 troops, which was
on duty during the fourth month. Asahel was
succeeded by his son Zebadiah.
8 Shammah* the Izrahite was commander of the
fifth division of 24,000 troops, which was on duty
during the fifth month.
9 Ira son of Ikkesh from Tekoa was commander of the
sixth division of 24,000 troops, which was on duty
during the sixth month.
10 Helez, a descendant of Ephraim from Pelon, was
commander of the seventh division of 24,000
troops, which was on duty during the seventh
month.
11 Sibbecai, a descendant of Zerah from Hushah, was
commander of the eighth division of 24,000 troops,
which was on duty during the eighth month.
12 Abiezer from Anathoth in the territory of Ben-
jamin was commander of the ninth division of

26:14 Hebrew *Shelemiah,* a variant spelling of Meshelemiah; compare 26:2. **26:16** Or *the gate of Shalleketh on the upper road* (also in 26:18). The meaning of the Hebrew is uncertain. **26:18** Or *the colonnade.* The meaning of the Hebrew is uncertain. **26:21a** Hebrew *Ladan,* a variant spelling of Libni; compare 6:17. **26:21b** Hebrew *Jehieli* (also in 26:22), a variant spelling of Jehiel; compare 23:8. **26:26** Hebrew *the commanders of thousands and of hundreds.* **26:28** Hebrew *Shelomith,* a variant spelling of Shelomoth. **26:29** Or *were given outside work;* or *were given work away from the Temple area.* **26:31** Hebrew *Jerijah,* a variant spelling of Jeriah; compare 23:19. **27:1** Hebrew *commanders of thousands and of hundreds.* **27:8** Hebrew *Shamhuth,* a variant spelling of Shammah; compare 11:27 and 2 Sam 23:25.

26:16-18 were assigned the . . . gate. The gatekeepers served as the temple police force. One of their jobs was to prevent the access of "unclean" persons to the inner temple area (2 Chron. 23:19). They also guarded the temple treasuries and storehouses 9:26; Neh. 12:25)

26:20 the treasuries of the gifts dedicated. Temple officers served to receive and administrate the plunder from battles. The silver and gold from enemy cities would be dedicated to God's glory.

26:30-32 put in charge. The complexity of the civic arrangements concludes with the role of those who work outside of Jerusalem. These traveling legal experts helped to keep the peace and administer justice throughout the land. That men are still being selected in the last year of David's reign (v. 31) demonstrates that he carefully considered the preparations for the temple-centered administration of his son, Solomon.

27:2-20 David rotated his soldiers in twelve units consisting of 24,000 men. Each went on active duty one month each year. They were commanded by twelve of David's heroic commanders (11:11-47; 2 Sam. 23:8-9). These men were not part of the permanent bodyguard that surrounded the king (2 Sam. 15:18; 23:23).

24,000 troops, which was on duty during the ninth month.
13 Maharai, a descendant of Zerah from Netophah, was commander of the tenth division of 24,000 troops, which was on duty during the tenth month.
14 Benaiah from Pirathon in Ephraim was commander of the eleventh division of 24,000 troops, which was on duty during the eleventh month.
15 Heled,* a descendant of Othniel from Netophah, was commander of the twelfth division of 24,000 troops, which was on duty during the twelfth month.

LEADERS OF THE TRIBES

16 The following were the tribes of Israel and their leaders:

Tribe	*Leader*
Reuben	Eliezer son of Zicri
Simeon	Shephatiah son of Maacah
17 Levi	Hashabiah son of Kemuel
Aaron (the priests)	Zadok
18 Judah	Elihu (a brother of David)
Issachar	Omri son of Michael
19 Zebulun	Ishmaiah son of Obadiah
Naphtali	Jeremoth son of Azriel
20 Ephraim	Hoshea son of Azaziah
Manasseh (west)	Joel son of Pedaiah
21 Manasseh in Gilead (east)	Iddo son of Zechariah
Benjamin	Jaasiel son of Abner
22 Dan	Azarel son of Jeroham

These were the leaders of the tribes of Israel.

23 When David took his census, he did not count
those who were younger than twenty years of age,
because the LORD had promised to make the Israelites
as numerous as the stars in heaven. 24 Joab son of Zer-
uiah began the census but never finished it because*
the anger of God fell on Israel. The total number was
never recorded in King David's official records.

OFFICIALS OF DAVID'S KINGDOM

25 Azmaveth son of Adiel was in charge of the palace treasuries.
Jonathan son of Uzziah was in charge of the regional treasuries throughout the towns, villages, and fortresses of Israel.
26 Ezri son of Kelub was in charge of the field workers who farmed the king's lands.
27 Shimei from Ramah was in charge of the king's vineyards.
Zabdi from Shepham was responsible for the grapes and the supplies of wine.
28 Baal-hanan from Geder was in charge of the king's olive groves and sycamore-fig trees in the foothills of Judah.*
Joash was responsible for the supplies of olive oil.
29 Shitrai from Sharon was in charge of the cattle on the Sharon Plain.
Shaphat son of Adlai was responsible for the cattle in the valleys.
30 Obil the Ishmaelite was in charge of the camels.
Jehdeiah from Meronoth was in charge of the donkeys.
31 Jaziz the Hagrite was in charge of the king's flocks of sheep and goats.
All these officials were overseers of King David's property.

32 Jonathan, David's uncle, was a wise counselor
to the king, a man of great insight, and a scribe. Je-
hiel the Hacmonite was responsible for teaching the
king's sons. 33 Ahithophel was the royal adviser. Hu-
shai the Arkite was the king's friend. 34 Ahithophel
was succeeded by Jehoiada son of Benaiah and by
Abiathar. Joab was commander of the king's army.

DAVID'S INSTRUCTIONS TO SOLOMON

28 David summoned all the officials of Israel to
Jerusalem—the leaders of the tribes, the com-
manders of the army divisions, the other generals
and captains,* the overseers of the royal property
and livestock, the palace officials, the mighty men,
and all the other brave warriors in the kingdom. 2 Da-
vid rose to his feet and said: "My brothers and my
people! It was my desire to build a Temple where the
Ark of the LORD's Covenant, God's footstool, could rest
permanently. I made the necessary preparations for
building it, 3 but God said to me, 'You must not build a
Temple to honor my name, for you are a warrior and
have shed much blood.'

4 "Yet the LORD, the God of Israel, has chosen me
from among all my father's family to be king over
Israel forever. For he has chosen the tribe of Judah
to rule, and from among the families of Judah he
chose my father's family. And from among my fa-
ther's sons the LORD was pleased to make me king
over all Israel. 5 And from among my sons—for the
LORD has given me many—he chose Solomon to
succeed me on the throne of Israel and to rule over
the LORD's kingdom. 6 He said to me, 'Your son Sol-
omon will build my Temple and its courtyards, for I
have chosen him as my son, and I will be his father.
7 And if he continues to obey my commands and
regulations as he does now, I will make his kingdom
last forever.'

8 "So now, with God as our witness, and in the sight
of all Israel—the LORD's assembly—I give you this
charge. Be careful to obey all the commands of the
LORD your God, so that you may continue to possess
this good land and leave it to your children as a per-
manent inheritance.

9 "And Solomon, my son, learn to know the God of
your ancestors intimately. Worship and serve him
with your whole heart and a willing mind. For the
LORD sees every heart and knows every plan and
thought. If you seek him, you will find him. But if you
forsake him, he will reject you forever. 10 So take this

27:15 Hebrew *Heldai,* a variant spelling of Heled; compare 11:30 and 2 Sam 23:29. 27:24 Or *never finished it, and yet.* 27:28 Hebrew *the Shephelah.* 28:1 Hebrew *the commanders of thousands and commanders of hundreds.*

27:16-22 Each tribe of Israel symbolizes its loyalty to King David through the representation of its officer. The tribes are similarly listed in Numbers 1:1-19.
27:23 numerous as the stars. The chronicler's phrase is reminiscent of God's promise to Abraham (see Gen. 12:2). Inspired by God's assurance, David does not need to include the younger warriors in order to boost his confidence.
27:24 total number was never recorded. David's military strength needed no fixed number. David counted on God's assurance.
28:1 David summoned all the officials. David proclaimed the succession of his son Solomon and his plans for the temple and the future of Israel.
28:5 he chose. David emphasized God's selection of the next king. Like his father, Solomon enjoyed the assurance of being divinely appointed to his throne.

seriously. The LORD has chosen you to build a Temple as his sanctuary. Be strong, and do the work."

11 Then David gave Solomon the plans for the Temple and its surroundings, including the entry room, the storerooms, the upstairs rooms, the inner rooms, and the inner sanctuary—which was the place of atonement. 12 David also gave Solomon all the plans he had in mind* for the courtyards of the LORD's Temple, the outside rooms, the treasuries, and the rooms for the gifts dedicated to the LORD. 13 The king also gave Solomon the instructions concerning the work of the various divisions of priests and Levites in the Temple of the LORD. And he gave specifications for the items in the Temple that were to be used for worship.

14 David gave instructions regarding how much gold and silver should be used to make the items needed for service. 15 He told Solomon the amount of gold needed for the gold lampstands and lamps, and the amount of silver for the silver lampstands and lamps, depending on how each would be used. 16 He designated the amount of gold for the table on which the Bread of the Presence would be placed and the amount of silver for other tables.

17 David also designated the amount of gold for the solid gold meat hooks used to handle the sacrificial meat and for the basins, pitchers, and dishes, as well as the amount of silver for every dish. 18 He designated the amount of refined gold for the altar of incense. Finally, he gave him a plan for the LORD's "chariot"—the gold cherubim* whose wings were stretched out over the Ark of the LORD's Covenant. 19 "Every part of this plan," David told Solomon, "was given to me in writing from the hand of the LORD.*"

20 Then David continued, "Be strong and courageous, and do the work. Don't be afraid or discouraged, for the LORD God, my God, is with you. He will not fail you or forsake you. He will see to it that all the work related to the Temple of the LORD is finished correctly. 21 The various divisions of priests and Levites will serve in the Temple of God. Others with skills of every kind will volunteer, and the officials and the entire nation are at your command."

GIFTS FOR BUILDING THE TEMPLE

29 Then King David turned to the entire assembly and said, "My son Solomon, whom God has clearly chosen as the next king of Israel, is still young and inexperienced. The work ahead of him is enormous, for the Temple he will build is not for mere mortals—it is for the LORD God himself! 2 Using every resource at my command, I have gathered as much as I could for building the Temple of my God. Now there is enough gold, silver, bronze, iron, and wood, as well as great quantities of onyx, other precious stones, costly jewels, and all kinds of fine stone and marble.

3 "And now, because of my devotion to the Temple of my God, I am giving all of my own private treasures of gold and silver to help in the construction. This is in addition to the building materials I have already collected for his holy Temple. 4 I am donating more than 112 tons of gold* from Ophir and 262 tons of refined silver* to be used for overlaying the walls of the buildings 5 and for the other gold and silver work to be done by the craftsmen. Now then, who will follow my example and give offerings to the LORD today?"

6 Then the family leaders, the leaders of the tribes of Israel, the generals and captains of the army,* and the king's administrative officers all gave willingly. 7 For the construction of the Temple of God, they gave about 188 tons of gold,* 10,000 gold coins,* 375 tons of silver,* 675 tons of bronze,* and 3,750 tons of iron.* 8 They also contributed numerous precious stones, which were deposited in the treasury of the house of the LORD under the care of Jehiel, a descendant of Gershon. 9 The people rejoiced over the offerings, for they had given freely and wholeheartedly to the LORD, and King David was filled with joy.

DAVID'S PRAYER OF PRAISE

10 Then David praised the LORD in the presence of the whole assembly:

"O LORD, the God of our ancestor Israel,* may you be praised forever and ever! 11 Yours, O LORD, is the greatness, the power, the glory, the victory, and the majesty. Everything in the heavens and on earth is yours, O LORD, and this is your kingdom. We adore you as the one who is over all things. 12 Wealth and honor come from you alone, for you rule over everything. Power and might are in your hand, and at your discretion people are made great and given strength.

13 "O our God, we thank you and praise your glorious name! 14 But who am I, and who are my people, that we could give anything to you? Everything we have has come from you, and we give you only what you first gave us! 15 We are here for only a moment, visitors and strangers in the land as our ancestors were before us. Our days on earth are like a passing shadow, gone so soon without a trace.

16 "O LORD our God, even this material we have gathered to build a Temple to honor your holy name comes from you! It all belongs to you! 17 I know, my God, that you examine our hearts and rejoice when you find integrity there. You know I have done all this with good motives, and I have watched your people offer their gifts willingly and joyously.

28:12 Or *the plans of the spirit that was with him.* **28:18** Hebrew *for the gold cherub chariot.* **28:19** Or *was written under the direction of the* LORD. **29:4a** Hebrew *3,000 talents* [102 metric tons] *of gold.* **29:4b** Hebrew *7,000 talents* [238 metric tons] *of silver.* **29:6** Hebrew *the commanders of thousands and commanders of hundreds.* **29:7a** Hebrew *5,000 talents* [170 metric tons] *of gold.* **29:7b** Hebrew *10,000 darics* [a Persian coin] *of gold,* about 185 pounds or 84 kilograms in weight. **29:7c** Hebrew *10,000 talents* [340 metric tons] *of silver.* **29:7d** Hebrew *18,000 talents* [612 metric tons] *of bronze.* **29:7e** Hebrew *100,000 talents* [3,400 metric tons] *of iron.* **29:10** *Israel* is the name that God gave to Jacob.

28:19 from the hand of the LORD. The plan for the temple was ultimately from God, not David. Hebrews asserts that the original tabernacle was built according to a heavenly pattern (see Heb. 8:5).

29:2-9 The capstone of David's reign was the initiation of the building of the temple. David dedicated his personal wealth to its construction. The people gladly responded to his leadership and voluntarily gave their gifts.

29:15 visitors and strangers. The Hebrew people had spent much of their history as foreigners and sojourners, having spent so many years in Egypt and the wilderness. But here David voices the realization that this is still their status since the land they had occupied was God's. The author of Hebrews may have had David in mind when he wrote of the people of faith who "confessed that they were foreigners and temporary residents on the earth" (Heb 11:13).

18 "O LORD, the God of our ancestors Abraham,
Isaac, and Israel, make your people always want
to obey you. See to it that their love for you never
changes. 19 Give my son Solomon the wholeheart-
ed desire to obey all your commands, laws, and
decrees, and to do everything necessary to build
this Temple, for which I have made these prepa-
rations."

20 Then David said to the whole assembly, "Give
praise to the LORD your God!" And the entire assembly
praised the LORD, the God of their ancestors, and they
bowed low and knelt before the LORD and the king.

SOLOMON NAMED AS KING

21 The next day they brought 1,000 bulls, 1,000 rams,
and 1,000 male lambs as burnt offerings to the LORD.
They also brought liquid offerings and many other
sacrifices on behalf of all Israel. 22 They feasted and
drank in the LORD's presence with great joy that day.
And again they crowned David's son Solomon as
their new king. They anointed him before the LORD as
their leader, and they anointed Zadok as priest. 23 So
Solomon took the throne of the LORD in place of his
father, David, and he succeeded in everything, and
all Israel obeyed him. 24 All the officials, the warriors,
and the sons of King David pledged their loyalty to
King Solomon. 25 And the LORD exalted Solomon in the
sight of all Israel, and he gave Solomon greater royal
splendor than any king in Israel before him.

SUMMARY OF DAVID'S REIGN

26 So David son of Jesse reigned over all Israel. 27 He
reigned over Israel for forty years, seven of them in
Hebron and thirty-three in Jerusalem. 28 He died at
a ripe old age, having enjoyed long life, wealth, and
honor. Then his son Solomon ruled in his place.
29 All the events of King David's reign, from be-
ginning to end, are written in *The Record of Samuel
the Seer, The Record of Nathan the Prophet,* and *The
Record of Gad the Seer.* 30 These accounts include the
mighty deeds of his reign and everything that hap-
pened to him and to Israel and to all the surrounding
kingdoms.

29:22 And again. Nearly two years prior, David had appointed Solomon to be king (23:1). However, the time had come for the official transition of power.

29:24 All the officials, the warriors. David's officers continued the chronicler's theme of unity among Israel in support for the king.

29:29 *The Record of Samuel the Seer, The Record of Nathan the Prophet, and The Record of Gad the Seer.* These annals are apparently lost to history.

INTRODUCTION TO

2 CHRONICLES

PERSONAL READING PLAN

- ☐2 Chronicles 1:1–3:17
- ☐2 Chronicles 4:1–6:11
- ☐2 Chronicles 6:12–7:10
- ☐2 Chronicles 7:11–9:12
- ☐2 Chronicles 9:13–11:4
- ☐2 Chronicles 11:5–14:1
- ☐2 Chronicles 14:2–16:14
- ☐2 Chronicles 17:1–18:27
- ☐2 Chronicles 18:28–20:30
- ☐2 Chronicles 20:31–22:9
- ☐2 Chronicles 22:10–24:16
- ☐2 Chronicles 24:17–25:28
- ☐2 Chronicles 26:1–28:27
- ☐2 Chronicles 29:1-36
- ☐2 Chronicles 30:1–31:21
- ☐2 Chronicles 32:1–33:25
- ☐2 Chronicles 34:1-33
- ☐2 Chronicles 35:1–36:23

AUTHOR

Jewish tradition suggests Ezra as author, but there is no firm evidence.

DATE

Second Chronicles was probably written toward the end of the fifth century B.C. or a little later. The events narrated span 970–538 B.C.

THEME

Kingship and worship in Judah from Solomon to the Exile.

HISTORICAL BACKGROUND

After the glory days of Israel under Solomon, warfare and unrest divide the nation, the people forsake temple worship for idols, and they lose their national identity when Jerusalem is totally destroyed in 586 B.C. Along the way, the southern kingdom of Judah is led into slow decline by evil kings and, alternately, into periods of spiritual reformation and restored national pride by Asa, Jehoshaphat, Uzziah, Hezekiah, and Josiah. Judah's slow decline (and the chronicler's account) ends with the Exile, but a "postscript" gives us a brief glimpse of future restoration.

CHARACTERISTICS

The major interests of 1 Chronicles—the Davidic dynasty and the temple worship—are continued in 2 Chronicles. Compared to the colorful stories in the books of Samuel and Kings, the chronicler has written a blander account. The stains of David's or Solomon's past are not addressed. Instead, the great wealth, worldwide acclaim, political stability, and magnificent temple get primary attention (chaps. 1–9). Each king is evaluated on the basis of his response to God, especially regarding worship of God and obedience to the Law. Those who introduce reforms are given top billing, and the nature of their reforms is described in some detail.

Some of the details included in 2 Chronicles that are not mentioned in Samuel and Kings are: (1) God giving the plans for both the tabernacle and temple; (2) the spoils of war being used as building materials for both tabernacle and temple; (3) the people generously contributing for both structures; and (4) the glory cloud appearing at the dedication of both structures.

SOLOMON ASKS FOR WISDOM

1 Solomon son of David took firm control of his king-
dom, for the LORD his God was with him and made
him very powerful.
2 Solomon called together all the leaders of Isra-
el—the generals and captains of the army,* the judg-
es, and all the political and clan leaders. 3 Then he led
the entire assembly to the place of worship in Gibeon,
for God's Tabernacle* was located there. (This was the
Tabernacle that Moses, the LORD's servant, had made
in the wilderness.)
4 David had already moved the Ark of God from
Kiriath-jearim to the tent he had prepared for it in Je-
rusalem. 5 But the bronze altar made by Bezalel son
of Uri and grandson of Hur was there* at Gibeon in
front of the Tabernacle of the LORD. So Solomon and
the people gathered in front of it to consult the LORD.*
6 There in front of the Tabernacle, Solomon went up to
the bronze altar in the LORD's presence and sacrificed
1,000 burnt offerings on it.
7 That night God appeared to Solomon and said,
"What do you want? Ask, and I will give it to you!"
8 Solomon replied to God, "You showed great and
faithful love to David, my father, and now you have
made me king in his place. 9 O LORD God, please con-
tinue to keep your promise to David my father, for you
have made me king over a people as numerous as the
dust of the earth! 10 Give me the wisdom and knowl-
edge to lead them properly,* for who could possibly
govern this great people of yours?"
11 God said to Solomon, "Because your greatest de-
sire is to help your people, and you did not ask for
wealth, riches, fame, or even the death of your ene-
mies or a long life, but rather you asked for wisdom
and knowledge to properly govern my people—12 I
will certainly give you the wisdom and knowledge
you requested. But I will also give you wealth, riches,
and fame such as no other king has had before you or
will ever have in the future!"
13 Then Solomon returned to Jerusalem from the
Tabernacle at the place of worship in Gibeon, and he
reigned over Israel.
14 Solomon built up a huge force of chariots and
horses.* He had 1,400 chariots and 12,000 horses. He
stationed some of them in the chariot cities and some
near him in Jerusalem. 15 The king made silver and
gold as plentiful in Jerusalem as stone. And valuable
cedar timber was as common as the sycamore-fig
trees that grow in the foothills of Judah.* 16 Solomon's
horses were imported from Egypt* and from Cilicia*;
the king's traders acquired them from Cilicia at the
standard price. 17 At that time chariots from Egypt
could be purchased for 600 pieces of silver,* and hors-
es for 150 pieces of silver.* They were then exported
to the kings of the Hittites and the kings of Aram.

PREPARATIONS FOR BUILDING THE TEMPLE

2 1*Solomon decided to build a Temple to honor the
name of the LORD, and also a royal palace for him-
self. 2*He enlisted a force of 70,000 laborers, 80,000
men to quarry stone in the hill country, and 3,600
foremen.
3 Solomon also sent this message to King Hiram* at
Tyre:

"Send me cedar logs as you did for my father,
David, when he was building his palace. 4 I am
about to build a Temple to honor the name of the
LORD my God. It will be a place set apart to burn
fragrant incense before him, to display the special
sacrificial bread, and to sacrifice burnt offerings
each morning and evening, on the Sabbaths, at
new moon celebrations, and at the other appoint-
ed festivals of the LORD our God. He has command-
ed Israel to do these things forever.
5 "This must be a magnificent Temple because
our God is greater than all other gods. 6 But who
can really build him a worthy home? Not even the
highest heavens can contain him! So who am I to
consider building a Temple for him, except as a
place to burn sacrifices to him?
7 "So send me a master craftsman who can work
with gold, silver, bronze, and iron, as well as with
purple, scarlet, and blue cloth. He must be a skilled
engraver who can work with the craftsmen of
Judah and Jerusalem who were selected by my
father, David.
8 "Also send me cedar, cypress, and red san-
dalwood* logs from Lebanon, for I know that
your men are without equal at cutting timber in
Lebanon. I will send my men to help them. 9 An
immense amount of timber will be needed, for the
Temple I am going to build will be very large and
magnificent. 10 In payment for your woodcutters,
I will send 100,000 bushels of crushed wheat,
100,000 bushels of barley,* 110,000 gallons of
wine, and 110,000 gallons of olive oil.*"

11 King Hiram sent this letter of reply to Solomon:

"It is because the LORD loves his people that he has
made you their king! 12 Praise the LORD, the God of
Israel, who made the heavens and the earth! He
has given King David a wise son, gifted with skill
and understanding, who will build a Temple for
the LORD and a royal palace for himself.

1:2 Hebrew *the commanders of thousands and of hundreds.* **1:3** Hebrew *Tent of Meeting;* also in 1:6, 13. **1:5a** As in Greek version and Latin Vulgate, and some Hebrew manuscripts. Masoretic Text reads *he placed.* **1:5b** Hebrew *to consult him.* **1:10** Hebrew *to go out and come in before this people.* **1:14** Or *charioteers;* also in 1:14b. **1:15** Hebrew *the Shephelah.* **1:16a** Possibly *Muzur,* a district near Cilicia; also in 1:17. **1:16b** Hebrew *Kue,* probably another name for Cilicia. **1:17a** Hebrew *600 [shekels] of silver,* about 15 pounds or 6.8 kilograms in weight. **1:17b** Hebrew *150 [shekels],* about 3.8 pounds or 1.7 kilograms in weight. **2:1** Verse 2:1 is numbered 1:18 in Hebrew text. **2:2** Verses 2:2-18 are numbered 2:1-17 in Hebrew text. **2:3** Hebrew *Huram,* a variant spelling of Hiram; also in 2:11. **2:8** Or *juniper;* Hebrew reads *algum,* perhaps a variant spelling of *almug;* compare 9:10-11 and parallel text at 1 Kgs 10:11-12. **2:10a** Hebrew *20,000 cors* [4,400 kiloliters] *of crushed wheat, 20,000 cors of barley.* **2:10b** Hebrew *20,000 baths* [420 kiloliters] *of wine, and 20,000 baths of olive oil.*

1:1 made him very powerful. Solomon became known as one of the greatest leaders in Israel's history. The nation enjoyed widespread stability and prosperity during his reign. Solomon's wisdom enabled him to accomplish much.

1:7 What do you want? As a sign of His blessing, God tells Solomon that anything he requests will be granted.

2:1 Temple. According to God's promise, Solomon began the construction of the temple. It would be the greatest accomplishment of his reign.

2:3-10 Solomon sent Hiram, king of Tyre, a specific order concerning Hiram's contribution to the construction of the temple. Hiram's participation would have spiritual and material significance. Solomon and Hiram had a close relationship. Both were respected world leaders.

2:6 Not even the highest heavens can contain him! Solomon realizes that in one sense what he has tried to do in building a temple to God is inappropriate. God is bigger than the universe itself. He can't be limited to one building, no matter how ornate it is.

13 "I am sending you a master craftsman named Huram-abi, who is extremely talented. 14 His mother is from the tribe of Dan in Israel, and his father is from Tyre. He is skillful at making things from gold, silver, bronze, and iron, and he also works with stone and wood. He can work with purple, blue, and scarlet cloth and fine linen. He is also an engraver and can follow any design given to him. He will work with your craftsmen and those appointed by my lord David, your father.

15 "Send along the wheat, barley, olive oil, and wine that my lord has mentioned. 16 We will cut whatever timber you need from the Lebanon mountains and will float the logs in rafts down the coast of the Mediterranean Sea* to Joppa. From there you can transport the logs up to Jerusalem."

17 Solomon took a census of all foreigners in the land of Israel, like the census his father had taken, and he counted 153,600. 18 He assigned 70,000 of them as common laborers, 80,000 as quarry workers in the hill country, and 3,600 as foremen.

SOLOMON BUILDS THE TEMPLE

3 So Solomon began to build the Temple of the LORD in Jerusalem on Mount Moriah, where the LORD had appeared to David, his father. The Temple was built on the threshing floor of Araunah* the Jebusite, the site that David had selected. 2 The construction began in midspring,* during the fourth year of Solomon's reign.

3 These are the dimensions Solomon used for the foundation of the Temple of God (using the old standard of measurement).* It was 90 feet long and 30 feet wide.* 4 The entry room at the front of the Temple was 30 feet* wide, running across the entire width of the Temple, and 30 feet* high. He overlaid the inside with pure gold.

5 He paneled the main room of the Temple with cypress wood, overlaid it with fine gold, and decorated it with carvings of palm trees and chains. 6 He decorated the walls of the Temple with beautiful jewels and with gold from the land of Parvaim. 7 He overlaid the beams, thresholds, walls, and doors throughout the Temple with gold, and he carved figures of cherubim on the walls.

8 He made the Most Holy Place 30 feet wide, corresponding to the width of the Temple, and 30 feet deep. He overlaid its interior with 23 tons* of fine gold. 9 The gold nails that were used weighed 20 ounces* each. He also overlaid the walls of the upper rooms with gold.

10 He made two figures shaped like cherubim, overlaid them with gold, and placed them in the Most Holy Place. 11 The total wingspan of the two cherubim standing side by side was 30 feet. One wing of the first figure was 7½ feet* long, and it touched the Temple wall. The other wing, also 7½ feet long, touched one of the wings of the second figure. 12 In the same way, the second figure had one wing 7½ feet long that touched the opposite wall. The other wing, also 7½ feet long, touched the wing of the first figure. 13 So the wingspan of the two cherubim side by side was 30 feet. They stood on their feet and faced out toward the main room of the Temple.

14 Across the entrance of the Most Holy Place he hung a curtain made of fine linen, decorated with blue, purple, and scarlet thread and embroidered with figures of cherubim.

15 For the front of the Temple, he made two pillars that were 27 feet* tall, each topped by a capital extending upward another 7½ feet. 16 He made a network of interwoven chains* and used them to decorate the tops of the pillars. He also made 100 decorative pomegranates and attached them to the chains. 17 Then he set up the two pillars at the entrance of the Temple, one to the south of the entrance and the other to the north. He named the one on the south Jakin, and the one on the north Boaz.*

FURNISHINGS FOR THE TEMPLE

4 Solomon* also made a bronze altar 30 feet long, 30 feet wide, and 15 feet high.* 2 Then he cast a great round basin, 15 feet across from rim to rim, called the Sea. It was 7½ feet deep and about 45 feet in circumference.* 3 It was encircled just below its rim by two rows of figures that resembled oxen. There were about six oxen per foot* all the way around, and they were cast as part of the basin.

4 The Sea was placed on a base of twelve bronze oxen, all facing outward. Three faced north, three faced west, three faced south, and three faced east, and the Sea rested on them. 5 The walls of the Sea were about three inches* thick, and its rim flared out like a cup and resembled a water lily blossom. It could hold about 16,500 gallons* of water.

6 He also made ten smaller basins for washing the utensils for the burnt offerings. He set five on the south side and five on the north. But the priests washed themselves in the Sea.

2:16 Hebrew *the sea.* **3:1** Hebrew reads *Ornan,* a variant spelling of Araunah; compare 2 Sam 24:16. **3:2** Hebrew *on the second [day] of the second month.* This day of the ancient Hebrew lunar calendar occurred in April or May. **3:3a** The "old standard of measurement" was a cubit equal to 18 inches [46 centimeters]. The new standard was a cubit of approximately 21 inches [53 centimeters]. **3:3b** Hebrew *60 cubits* [27.6 meters] *long and 20 cubits* [9.2 meters] *wide.* **3:4a** Hebrew *20 cubits* [9.2 meters]; also in 3:8, 11, 13. **3:4b** As in some Greek and Syriac manuscripts, which read *20 cubits* [9.2 meters]; Hebrew reads *120 [cubits],* which is 180 feet or 55 meters. **3:8** Hebrew *600 talents* [20.4 metric tons]. **3:9** Hebrew *50 shekels* [570 grams]. **3:11** Hebrew *5 cubits* [2.3 meters]; also in 3:11b, 12, 15. **3:15** As in Syriac version (see also 1 Kgs 7:15; 2 Kgs 25:17; Jer 52:21), which reads *18 cubits* [8.3 meters]; Hebrew reads *35 cubits,* which is 52.5 feet or 16.5 meters. **3:16** Hebrew *He made chains in the inner sanctuary.* The meaning of the Hebrew is uncertain. **3:17** *Jakin* probably means "he establishes"; *Boaz* probably means "in him is strength." **4:1a** Or *Huram-abi;* Hebrew reads *He.* **4:1b** Hebrew *20 cubits* [9.2 meters] *long, 20 cubits wide, and 10 cubits* [4.6 meters] *high.* **4:2** Hebrew *10 cubits* [4.6 meters] *across . . . 5 cubits* [2.3 meters] *deep and 30 cubits* [13.8 meters] *in circumference.* **4:3** Or *20 oxen per meter;* Hebrew reads *10 per cubit.* **4:5a** Hebrew *a handbreadth* [8 centimeters]. **4:5b** Hebrew *3,000 baths* [63 kiloliters].

2:17-18 all foreigners in the land of Israel. One way of keeping foreign enemies in the land from rebelling is to occupy them with forced labor.

3:1 the Temple of the LORD. The temple would rise over the spot where Abraham and his son, Isaac, learned the importance of an obedient sacrifice (see Gen. 22).

3:8 Most Holy Place. When imagining the most holy place, think of a perfect cube. This proportionately square room would house the presence of God.

4:1 made a bronze altar. The bronze altar is located in the courtyard. Steps stretch across it in front of the temple.

4:2 cast a great round basin. A huge round basin is erected for ceremonial washings. The reservoir contains about 11,000 gallons of water.

4:4 base of twelve bronze oxen. The twelve tribes are symbolized in the detailed statues, which face all four directions. In this way, Israel could always see itself in worship.

4:6 But the priests washed themselves in the Sea. The great round basin is called the Sea in v. 2. Offering animal sacrifices was messy. This meant that the priests had to have a place to scrub themselves often.

7 He then cast ten gold lampstands according to
the specifications that had been given, and he put
them in the Temple. Five were placed against the
south wall, and five were placed against the north
wall.
8 He also built ten tables and placed them in the
Temple, five along the south wall and five along the
north wall. Then he molded 100 gold basins.
9 He then built a courtyard for the priests, and
also the large outer courtyard. He made doors for
the courtyard entrances and overlaid them with
bronze. 10 The great bronze basin called the Sea
was placed near the southeast corner of the Tem-
ple.
11 Huram-abi also made the necessary washbasins,
shovels, and bowls.
So at last Huram-abi completed everything King
Solomon had assigned him to make for the Temple of
God:

12 the two pillars;
the two bowl-shaped capitals on top of the pillars;
the two networks of interwoven chains that decorated the capitals;
13 the 400 pomegranates that hung from the chains on the capitals (two rows of pomegranates for each of the chain networks that decorated the capitals on top of the pillars);
14 the water carts holding the basins;
15 the Sea and the twelve oxen under it;
16 the ash buckets, the shovels, the meat hooks, and all the related articles.

Huram-abi made all these things of burnished
bronze for the Temple of the LORD, just as King Sol-
omon had directed. 17 The king had them cast in
clay molds in the Jordan Valley between Succoth
and Zarethan.* 18 Solomon used such great quan-
tities of bronze that its weight could not be deter-
mined.
19 Solomon also made all the furnishings for the
Temple of God:

the gold altar;
the tables for the Bread of the Presence;
20 the lampstands and their lamps of solid gold, to burn in front of the Most Holy Place as prescribed;
21 the flower decorations, lamps, and tongs—all of the purest gold;
22 the lamp snuffers, bowls, ladles, and incense burners—all of solid gold;
the doors for the entrances to the Most Holy Place and the main room of the Temple, overlaid with gold.

5 So Solomon finished all his work on the Temple of
the LORD. Then he brought all the gifts his father,
David, had dedicated—the silver, the gold, and the
various articles—and he stored them in the treasur-
ies of the Temple of God.

THE ARK BROUGHT TO THE TEMPLE

2 Solomon then summoned to Jerusalem the elders
of Israel and all the heads of tribes—the leaders of
the ancestral families of Israel. They were to bring
the Ark of the LORD's Covenant to the Temple from
its location in the City of David, also known as Zion.
3 So all the men of Israel assembled before the king at
the annual Festival of Shelters, which is held in early
autumn.*
4 When all the elders of Israel arrived, the Levites
picked up the Ark. 5 The priests and Levites brought
up the Ark along with the special tent* and all the sa-
cred items that had been in it. 6 There, before the Ark,
King Solomon and the entire community of Israel
sacrificed so many sheep, goats, and cattle that no one
could keep count!
7 Then the priests carried the Ark of the LORD's
Covenant into the inner sanctuary of the Tem-
ple—the Most Holy Place—and placed it beneath
the wings of the cherubim. 8 The cherubim spread
their wings over the Ark, forming a canopy over
the Ark and its carrying poles. 9 These poles were
so long that their ends could be seen from the Holy
Place,* which is in front of the Most Holy Place, but
not from the outside. They are still there to this day.
10 Nothing was in the Ark except the two stone tab-
lets that Moses had placed in it at Mount Sinai,*
where the LORD made a covenant with the people of
Israel when they left Egypt.
11 Then the priests left the Holy Place. All the priests
who were present had purified themselves, whether
or not they were on duty that day. 12 And the Levites
who were musicians—Asaph, Heman, Jeduthun,
and all their sons and brothers—were dressed in
fine linen robes and stood at the east side of the altar
playing cymbals, lyres, and harps. They were joined
by 120 priests who were playing trumpets. 13 The
trumpeters and singers performed together in unison
to praise and give thanks to the LORD. Accompanied
by trumpets, cymbals, and other instruments, they
raised their voices and praised the LORD with these
words:

"He is good!
His faithful love endures forever!"

At that moment a thick cloud filled the Temple of
the LORD. 14 The priests could not continue their ser-
vice because of the cloud, for the glorious presence of
the LORD filled the Temple of God.

4:17 As in parallel text at 1 Kgs 7:46; Hebrew reads *Zeredah*. **5:3** Hebrew *at the festival that is in the seventh month.* The Festival of Shelters began on the fifteenth day of the seventh month of the ancient Hebrew lunar calendar. This day occurred in late September, October, or early November. **5:5** Hebrew *the Tent of Meeting;* i.e., the tent mentioned in 2 Sam 6:17 and 1 Chr 16:1. **5:9** As in some Hebrew manuscripts and Greek version (see also 1 Kgs 8:8); Masoretic Text reads *from the Ark.* **5:10** Hebrew *Horeb,* another name for Sinai.

5:2 Solomon then summoned . . . to bring the Ark. For the first time, the ark is housed in a permanent, glorious dwelling. Its significance in the temple makes the seven years of labor worth every moment—God's presence is among them.

5:10 Nothing was in the Ark except the two stone tablets. The Israelites recognize the significance of God's commands on the stone tablets inside the ark (Ex. 32:15-16). Although the ark had changed hands with Israel's enemies, God's commandments are miraculously undisturbed.

5:14 glorious presence of the LORD. A supernatural cloud symbolizes the Lord's presence (Ex. 40:34-35) and God's pleasure with the new "home." This is reminiscent of the pillar of cloud that led the people of Israel in the wilderness.

SOLOMON PRAISES THE LORD

6 Then Solomon prayed, "O LORD, you have said that
you would live in a thick cloud of darkness. 2 Now
I have built a glorious Temple for you, a place where
you can live forever!"
3 Then the king turned around to the entire com-
munity of Israel standing before him and gave this
blessing: 4 "Praise the LORD, the God of Israel, who has
kept the promise he made to my father, David. For he
told my father, 5 'From the day I brought my people
out of the land of Egypt, I have never chosen a city
among any of the tribes of Israel as the place where
a Temple should be built to honor my name. Nor have
I chosen a king to lead my people Israel. 6 But now I
have chosen Jerusalem as the place for my name to be
honored, and I have chosen David to be king over my
people Israel.'"
7 Then Solomon said, "My father, David, wanted to
build this Temple to honor the name of the LORD, the
God of Israel. 8 But the LORD told him, 'You wanted to
build the Temple to honor my name. Your intention
is good, 9 but you are not the one to do it. One of your
own sons will build the Temple to honor me.'
10 "And now the LORD has fulfilled the promise he
made, for I have become king in my father's place,
and now I sit on the throne of Israel, just as the LORD
promised. I have built this Temple to honor the name
of the LORD, the God of Israel. 11 There I have placed
the Ark, which contains the covenant that the LORD
made with the people of Israel."

SOLOMON'S PRAYER OF DEDICATION

12 Then Solomon stood before the altar of the LORD in
front of the entire community of Israel, and he lift-
ed his hands in prayer. 13 Now Solomon had made
a bronze platform 7½ feet long, 7½ feet wide, and
4½ feet high* and had placed it at the center of the
Temple's outer courtyard. He stood on the platform,
and then he knelt in front of the entire community
of Israel and lifted his hands toward heaven. 14 He
prayed,

"O LORD, God of Israel, there is no God like you in
all of heaven and earth. You keep your covenant
and show unfailing love to all who walk before
you in wholehearted devotion. 15 You have kept
your promise to your servant David, my father.
You made that promise with your own mouth, and
with your own hands you have fulfilled it today.
16 "And now, O LORD, God of Israel, carry out
the additional promise you made to your servant
David, my father. For you said to him, 'If your
descendants guard their behavior and faithfully
follow my Law as you have done, one of them will
always sit on the throne of Israel.' 17 Now, O LORD,
God of Israel, fulfill this promise to your servant
David.
18 "But will God really live on earth among
people? Why, even the highest heavens cannot
contain you. How much less this Temple I have
built! 19 Nevertheless, listen to my prayer and my
plea, O LORD my God. Hear the cry and the prayer
that your servant is making to you. 20 May you
watch over this Temple day and night, this place
where you have said you would put your name.
May you always hear the prayers I make toward
this place. 21 May you hear the humble and earnest
requests from me and your people Israel when we
pray toward this place. Yes, hear us from heaven
where you live, and when you hear, forgive.
22 "If someone wrongs another person and is
required to take an oath of innocence in front
of your altar at this Temple, 23 then hear from
heaven and judge between your servants—the
accuser and the accused. Pay back the guilty as
they deserve. Acquit the innocent because of their
innocence.
24 "If your people Israel are defeated by their en-
emies because they have sinned against you, and
if they turn back and acknowledge your name and
pray to you here in this Temple, 25 then hear from
heaven and forgive the sin of your people Israel
and return them to this land you gave to them and
to their ancestors.
26 "If the skies are shut up and there is no rain
because your people have sinned against you, and
if they pray toward this Temple and acknowledge
your name and turn from their sins because you
have punished them, 27 then hear from heaven
and forgive the sins of your servants, your people
Israel. Teach them to follow the right path, and
send rain on your land that you have given to your
people as their special possession.
28 "If there is a famine in the land or a plague or
crop disease or attacks of locusts or caterpillars, or
if your people's enemies are in the land besieging
their towns—whatever disaster or disease there
is—29 and if your people Israel pray about their
troubles or sorrow, raising their hands toward this
Temple, 30 then hear from heaven where you live,
and forgive. Give your people what their actions
deserve, for you alone know each human heart.
31 Then they will fear you and walk in your ways
as long as they live in the land you gave to our
ancestors.
32 "In the future, foreigners who do not belong
to your people Israel will hear of you. They will
come from distant lands when they hear of your
great name and your strong hand and your
powerful arm. And when they pray toward this
Temple, 33 then hear from heaven where you live,
and grant what they ask of you. In this way, all
the people of the earth will come to know and fear
you, just as your own people Israel do. They, too,
will know that this Temple I have built honors
your name.
34 "If your people go out where you send them
to fight their enemies, and if they pray to you by

6:13 Hebrew *5 cubits* [2.3 meters] *long, 5 cubits wide, and 3 cubits* [1.4 meters] *high.*

6:1 live in a thick cloud of darkness. There is a holiness and mystery about God that prevents people from fully comprehending or "seeing" Him.
6:9 you are not the one to do it. In 1 Chronicles 22:8 we are told that David was rejected for this honor because he had been involved in so much violence and warfare.
6:13 in front of the entire community of Israel. Solomon models a spirit of humility and submission before the people. In a time and culture where some kings saw themselves as gods and most thought it more important to encourage people to bow to them, Solomon shows that submission to God is what's important.
6:26-31 As spiritually focused as Solomon's people are at present, a weaker moment for them is on the horizon. Solomon requested God's mercy in advance of their inevitable mistakes. He reminded God that the land is a gift. He called on God to show mercy so all will fear Him.

turning toward this city you have chosen and to-
ward this Temple I have built to honor your name,
35 then hear their prayers from heaven and uphold
their cause.
36 "If they sin against you—and who has never
sinned?—you might become angry with them
and let their enemies conquer them and take them
captive to a foreign land far away or near. 37 But
in that land of exile, they might turn to you in
repentance and pray, 'We have sinned, done evil,
and acted wickedly.' 38 If they turn to you with
their whole heart and soul in the land of their
captivity and pray toward the land you gave to
their ancestors—toward this city you have cho-
sen, and toward this Temple I have built to honor
your name—39 then hear their prayers and their
petitions from heaven where you live, and uphold
their cause. Forgive your people who have sinned
against you.
40 "O my God, may your eyes be open and your
ears attentive to all the prayers made to you in
this place.

41 "And now arise, O LORD God, and enter your
resting place,
along with the Ark, the symbol of your
power.
May your priests, O LORD God, be clothed with
salvation;
may your loyal servants rejoice in your
goodness.
42 O LORD God, do not reject the king you have
anointed.
Remember your unfailing love for your
servant David."

THE DEDICATION OF THE TEMPLE

7 When Solomon finished praying, fire flashed
down from heaven and burned up the burnt offer-
ings and sacrifices, and the glorious presence of the
LORD filled the Temple. 2 The priests could not enter
the Temple of the LORD because the glorious presence
of the LORD filled it. 3 When all the people of Israel saw
the fire coming down and the glorious presence of
the LORD filling the Temple, they fell face down on the
ground and worshiped and praised the LORD, saying,

"He is good!
His faithful love endures forever!"

4 Then the king and all the people offered sacrific-
es to the LORD. 5 King Solomon offered a sacrifice of
22,000 cattle and 120,000 sheep and goats. And so the
king and all the people dedicated the Temple of God.
6 The priests took their assigned positions, and so did
the Levites who were singing, "His faithful love en-
dures forever!" They accompanied the singing with
music from the instruments King David had made for
praising the LORD. Across from the Levites, the priests
blew the trumpets, while all Israel stood.
7 Solomon then consecrated the central area of the
courtyard in front of the LORD's Temple. He offered
burnt offerings and the fat of peace offerings there,
because the bronze altar he had built could not hold
all the burnt offerings, grain offerings, and sacrificial
fat.
8 For the next seven days Solomon and all Israel cel-
ebrated the Festival of Shelters.* A large congregation
had gathered from as far away as Lebo-hamath in the
north and the Brook of Egypt in the south. 9 On the
eighth day they had a closing ceremony, for they had
celebrated the dedication of the altar for seven days
and the Festival of Shelters for seven days. 10 Then at
the end of the celebration,* Solomon sent the people
home. They were all joyful and glad because the LORD
had been so good to David and to Solomon and to his
people Israel.

THE LORD'S RESPONSE TO SOLOMON

11 So Solomon finished the Temple of the LORD, as well
as the royal palace. He completed everything he had
planned to do in the construction of the Temple and
the palace. 12 Then one night the LORD appeared to
Solomon and said,

"I have heard your prayer and have chosen this
Temple as the place for making sacrifices. 13 At
times I might shut up the heavens so that no rain
falls, or command grasshoppers to devour your
crops, or send plagues among you. 14 Then if my
people who are called by my name will humble
themselves and pray and seek my face and turn
from their wicked ways, I will hear from heaven
and will forgive their sins and restore their land.
15 My eyes will be open and my ears attentive to ev-
ery prayer made in this place. 16 For I have chosen
this Temple and set it apart to be holy—a place
where my name will be honored forever. I will
always watch over it, for it is dear to my heart.
17 "As for you, if you faithfully follow me as
David your father did, obeying all my commands,
decrees, and regulations, 18 then I will establish the
throne of your dynasty. For I made this covenant
with your father, David, when I said, 'One of your
descendants will always rule over Israel.'
19 "But if you or your descendants abandon me
and disobey the decrees and commands I have
given you, and if you serve and worship other
gods, 20 then I will uproot the people from this land
that I have given them. I will reject this Temple

7:8 Hebrew *the festival* (also in 7:9); see note on 5:3. **7:10** Hebrew *Then on the twenty-third day of the seventh month.* This day of the ancient Hebrew lunar calendar occurred in October or early November.

6:36 take them captive to a foreign land. This was a military strategy the Assyrians invented some 300 years after Solomon spoke these words. The Assyrians used it against the northern tribes of Israel. Later, the Babylonians used it against the southern kingdom of Judah. The prayer is that God will still listen to Israel even in this worst of all scenarios.

6:40-42 Solomon asked God to come among the Israelites, reminding Him of His promise to David. Solomon had brought the ark to the temple (5:2-14).

7:1-3 God concludes the ceremonies in a firework display of heavenly power. God consumes the sacrifice on the altar, showing He accepts the praise and prayers from His people. God's sending fire as a visible sign of His presence is reminiscent of His sending fire on Sinai (Deut. 4:11; 5:22). He likewise sent fire when Moses and Aaron dedicated the tabernacle (Num. 9:24) and when David set up the altar on the threshing floor of Araunah (1 Chron. 21:26).

7:6 music from instruments. Israel rises to its feet in celebration. The Levites render praise to God for His goodness.

7:14 humble themselves . . . then I will hear from heaven. Earlier, Solomon modeled what God was now calling for, a humility in which the people would pray and seek God whenever they had fallen away. When people honestly acknowledge God, He is attentive to their prayers.

that I have made holy to honor my name. I will
make it an object of mockery and ridicule among
the nations. 21 And though this Temple is impres-
sive now, all who pass by will be appalled. They
will ask, 'Why did the LORD do such terrible things
to this land and to this Temple?'
22 "And the answer will be, 'Because his people
abandoned the LORD, the God of their ances-
tors, who brought them out of Egypt, and they
worshiped other gods instead and bowed down
to them. That is why he has brought all these
disasters on them.'"

SOLOMON'S MANY ACHIEVEMENTS

8 It took Solomon twenty years to build the LORD's
Temple and his own royal palace. At the end of
that time, 2 Solomon turned his attention to rebuilding
the towns that King Hiram* had given him, and he
settled Israelites in them.
3 Solomon also fought against the town of Hamath-
zobah and conquered it. 4 He rebuilt Tadmor in the
wilderness and built towns in the region of Hamath
as supply centers. 5 He fortified the towns of Upper
Beth-horon and Lower Beth-horon, rebuilding their
walls and installing barred gates. 6 He also rebuilt
Baalath and other supply centers and constructed
towns where his chariots and horses* could be sta-
tioned. He built everything he desired in Jerusalem
and Lebanon and throughout his entire realm.
7 There were still some people living in the land
who were not Israelites, including the Hittites, Am-
orites, Perizzites, Hivites, and Jebusites. 8 These were
descendants of the nations whom the people of Israel
had not destroyed. So Solomon conscripted them for
his labor force, and they serve as forced laborers to
this day. 9 But Solomon did not conscript any of the Is-
raelites for his labor force. Instead, he assigned them
to serve as fighting men, officers in his army, com-
manders of his chariots, and charioteers. 10 King Sol-
omon appointed 250 of them to supervise the people.
11 Solomon moved his wife, Pharaoh's daughter,
from the City of David to the new palace he had built
for her. He said, "My wife must not live in King David's
palace, for the Ark of the LORD has been there, and it
is holy ground."
12 Then Solomon presented burnt offerings to the
LORD on the altar he had built for him in front of the
entry room of the Temple. 13 He offered the sacrific-
es for the Sabbaths, the new moon festivals, and the
three annual festivals—the Passover celebration, the
Festival of Harvest,* and the Festival of Shelters—as
Moses had commanded.
14 In assigning the priests to their duties, Solomon
followed the regulations of his father, David. He also
assigned the Levites to lead the people in praise and
to assist the priests in their daily duties. And he as-
signed the gatekeepers to their gates by their divi-
sions, following the commands of David, the man of
God. 15 Solomon did not deviate in any way from Da-
vid's commands concerning the priests and Levites
and the treasuries.
16 So Solomon made sure that all the work related
to building the Temple of the LORD was carried out,
from the day its foundation was laid to the day of its
completion.
17 Later Solomon went to Ezion-geber and Elath,*
ports along the shore of the Red Sea* in the land of
Edom. 18 Hiram sent him ships commanded by his
own officers and manned by experienced crews of
sailors. These ships sailed to Ophir with Solomon's
men and brought back to Solomon almost seventeen
tons* of gold.

VISIT OF THE QUEEN OF SHEBA

9 When the queen of Sheba heard of Solomon's
fame, she came to Jerusalem to test him with hard
questions. She arrived with a large group of atten-
dants and a great caravan of camels loaded with
spices, large quantities of gold, and precious jewels.
When she met with Solomon, she talked with him
about everything she had on her mind. 2 Solomon had
answers for all her questions; nothing was too hard
for him to explain to her. 3 When the queen of Sheba
realized how wise Solomon was, and when she saw
the palace he had built, 4 she was overwhelmed. She
was also amazed at the food on his tables, the organi-
zation of his officials and their splendid clothing, the
cup-bearers and their robes, and the burnt offerings*
Solomon made at the Temple of the LORD.
5 She exclaimed to the king, "Everything I heard in
my country about your achievements* and wisdom is
true! 6 I didn't believe what was said until I arrived
here and saw it with my own eyes. In fact, I had not
heard the half of your great wisdom! It is far beyond
what I was told. 7 How happy your people must be!
What a privilege for your officials to stand here day
after day, listening to your wisdom! 8 Praise the LORD
your God, who delights in you and has placed you on
the throne as king to rule for him. Because God loves
Israel and desires this kingdom to last forever, he has
made you king over them so you can rule with justice
and righteousness."
9 Then she gave the king a gift of 9,000 pounds* of
gold, great quantities of spices, and precious jewels.
Never before had there been spices as fine as those
the queen of Sheba gave to King Solomon.
10 (In addition, the crews of Hiram and Solomon
brought gold from Ophir, and they also brought red

8:2 Hebrew *Huram,* a variant spelling of Hiram; also in 8:18. **8:6** Or *and charioteers.* **8:13** Or *Festival of Weeks.* **8:17a** As in Greek version (see also 2 Kgs 14:22; 16:6); Hebrew reads *Eloth,* a variant spelling of Elath. **8:17b** As in parallel text at 1 Kgs 9:26; Hebrew reads *the sea.* **8:18** Hebrew *450 talents* [15.3 metric tons]. **9:4** As in Greek and Syriac versions (see also 1 Kgs 10:5), Hebrew reads *and the ascent.* **9:5** Hebrew *your words.* **9:9** Hebrew *120 talents* [4,000 kilograms]. **9:10** Hebrew *algum wood* (also in 9:11); perhaps a variant spelling of *almug.* Compare parallel text at 1 Kgs 10:11-12.

8:1-2 In contrast to his battle-weary father, Solomon enjoyed a peaceful reign. Solomon originally gave Hiram 20 cities as partial payment for his help. Hiram wasn't pleased and eventually returned them (see 1 Kings 9:10-14).

8:11 for the Ark of the LORD has been there . . . holy ground. Solomon was all too aware of the spiritual conflict represented in his idol-worshiping Egyptian wife. His care to remove her from David's palace betrayed his better sense (1 Kings 11:1-4).

8:12-16 Solomon demonstrated the detail of his religious success in the form of numerous sacrifices. He kept pace with his father's outward religious acts, though he ultimately failed to replicate David's devotion (1 Kings 11:4).

8:17-18 The chronicler completes Solomon's success profile by including his economic achievements. King Hiram once again proved to be a royal relationship worth keeping. Tyre's navy became an important resource.

9:8 loves . . . he has made you king. The chronicler frames the queen's speech to affirm Solomon's divinely appointed rule. God enabled and enlightened this obscure but resplendent queen to speak courteously of the competition.

sandalwood* and precious jewels. 11 The king used the sandalwood to make steps* for the Temple of the LORD and the royal palace, and to construct lyres and harps for the musicians. Never before had such beautiful things been seen in Judah.)

12 King Solomon gave the queen of Sheba whatever she asked for—gifts of greater value than the gifts she had given him. Then she and all her attendants returned to their own land.

SOLOMON'S WEALTH AND SPLENDOR

13 Each year Solomon received about 25 tons* of gold. 14 This did not include the additional revenue he received from merchants and traders. All the kings of Arabia and the governors of the provinces also brought gold and silver to Solomon.

15 King Solomon made 200 large shields of hammered gold, each weighing more than 15 pounds.* 16 He also made 300 smaller shields of hammered gold, each weighing more than 7½ pounds.* The king placed these shields in the Palace of the Forest of Lebanon.

17 Then the king made a huge throne, decorated with ivory and overlaid with pure gold. 18 The throne had six steps, with a footstool of gold. There were armrests on both sides of the seat, and the figure of a lion stood on each side of the throne. 19 There were also twelve other lions, one standing on each end of the six steps. No other throne in all the world could be compared with it!

20 All of King Solomon's drinking cups were solid gold, as were all the utensils in the Palace of the Forest of Lebanon. They were not made of silver, for silver was considered worthless in Solomon's day!

21 The king had a fleet of trading ships of Tarshish manned by the sailors sent by Hiram.* Once every three years the ships returned, loaded with gold, silver, ivory, apes, and peacocks.*

22 So King Solomon became richer and wiser than any other king on earth. 23 Kings from every nation came to consult him and to hear the wisdom God had given him. 24 Year after year everyone who visited brought him gifts of silver and gold, clothing, weapons, spices, horses, and mules.

25 Solomon had 4,000 stalls for his horses and chariots, and he had 12,000 horses.* He stationed some of them in the chariot cities, and some near him in Jerusalem. 26 He ruled over all the kings from the Euphrates River* in the north to the land of the Philistines and the border of Egypt in the south. 27 The king made silver as plentiful in Jerusalem as stone. And valuable cedar timber was as common as the sycamore-fig trees that grow in the foothills of Judah.* 28 Solomon's horses were imported from Egypt* and many other countries.

SUMMARY OF SOLOMON'S REIGN

29 The rest of the events of Solomon's reign, from beginning to end, are recorded in *The Record of Nathan the Prophet,* and *The Prophecy of Ahijah from Shiloh,* and also in *The Visions of Iddo the Seer,* concerning Jeroboam son of Nebat. 30 Solomon ruled in Jerusalem over all Israel for forty years. 31 When he died, he was buried in the City of David, named for his father. Then his son Rehoboam became the next king.

THE NORTHERN TRIBES REVOLT

10 Rehoboam went to Shechem, where all Israel had gathered to make him king. 2 When Jeroboam son of Nebat heard of this, he returned from Egypt, for he had fled to Egypt to escape from King Solomon. 3 The leaders of Israel summoned him, and Jeroboam and all Israel went to speak with Rehoboam. 4 "Your father was a hard master," they said. "Lighten the harsh labor demands and heavy taxes that your father imposed on us. Then we will be your loyal subjects."

5 Rehoboam replied, "Come back in three days for my answer." So the people went away.

6 Then King Rehoboam discussed the matter with the older men who had counseled his father, Solomon. "What is your advice?" he asked. "How should I answer these people?"

7 The older counselors replied, "If you are good to these people and do your best to please them and give them a favorable answer, they will always be your loyal subjects."

8 But Rehoboam rejected the advice of the older men and instead asked the opinion of the young men who had grown up with him and were now his advisers. 9 "What is your advice?" he asked them. "How should I answer these people who want me to lighten the burdens imposed by my father?"

10 The young men replied, "This is what you should tell those complainers who want a lighter burden: 'My little finger is thicker than my father's waist! 11 Yes, my father laid heavy burdens on you, but I'm going to make them even heavier! My father beat you with whips, but I will beat you with scorpions!'"

12 Three days later Jeroboam and all the people returned to hear Rehoboam's decision, just as the king had ordered. 13 But Rehoboam spoke harshly to them, for he rejected the advice of the older counselors 14 and followed the counsel of his younger advisers. He told the people, "My father laid* heavy burdens

9:11 Or *gateways.* The meaning of the Hebrew is uncertain. **9:13** Hebrew *666 talents* [23 metric tons]. **9:15** Hebrew *600 [shekels] of hammered gold* [6.8 kilograms]. **9:16** Hebrew *300 [shekels] of gold* [3.4 kilograms]. **9:21a** Hebrew *Huram,* a variant spelling of Hiram. **9:21b** Or *and baboons.* **9:25** Or *12,000 charioteers.* **9:26** Hebrew *the river.* **9:27** Hebrew *the Shephelah.* **9:28** Possibly *Muzur,* a district near Cilicia.
10:14 As in Greek version and many Hebrew manuscripts (see also 1 Kgs 12:14); Masoretic Text reads *I will lay.*

9:28 horses were imported from Egypt. Solomon's picture-perfect conclusion conveys the chronicler's biographical bias. The happy ending serves to contrast with the heritage of rebellion that came from his many foreign wives (1 Kings 11:1-40).

10:4 Your father was a hard master. At some point in time, Solomon went from merely conscripting foreign laborers to forcing hard labor on Israelites as well. This uncharacteristically unwise move helped sow the seeds for the division of the kingdom.

10:7 If you are good to these people. Here the advice of the elders points to an important secret of successful rule: being good to your people is the best way to assure their loyalty.

10:13 rejected the advice of the older counselors. Lack of respect for the wisdom of those who have lived a long time often leads to downfall.

10:15 This turn of events was the will of God. The wisdom of God operates through the foolishness of men. Abijah had prophesied to Jeroboam that he would become king over the ten tribes. This was a consequence of Solomon's disobedience to God. (1 Kings 11:3). God used Rehoboam's imperceptiveness to bring about what He had ordained.

on you, but I'm going to make them even heavier! My
father beat you with whips, but I will beat you with
scorpions!"
15 So the king paid no attention to the people. This
turn of events was the will of God, for it fulfilled the
LORD's message to Jeroboam son of Nebat through the
prophet Ahijah from Shiloh.
16 When all Israel realized* that the king had re-
fused to listen to them, they responded,

"Down with the dynasty of David!
We have no interest in the son of Jesse.
Back to your homes, O Israel!
Look out for your own house, O David!"

So all the people of Israel returned home. 17 But
Rehoboam continued to rule over the Israelites who
lived in the towns of Judah.
18 King Rehoboam sent Adoniram,* who was in
charge of forced labor, to restore order, but the peo-
ple of Israel stoned him to death. When this news
reached King Rehoboam, he quickly jumped into his
chariot and fled to Jerusalem. 19 And to this day the
northern tribes of Israel have refused to be ruled by a
descendant of David.

SHEMAIAH'S PROPHECY

11 When Rehoboam arrived at Jerusalem, he mobi-
lized the men of Judah and Benjamin—180,000
select troops—to fight against Israel and to restore
the kingdom to himself.
2 But the LORD said to Shemaiah, the man of God,
3 "Say to Rehoboam son of Solomon, king of Judah,
and to all the Israelites in Judah and Benjamin: 4 'This
is what the LORD says: Do not fight against your rel-
atives. Go back home, for what has happened is my
doing!'" So they obeyed the message of the LORD and
did not fight against Jeroboam.

REHOBOAM FORTIFIES JUDAH

5 Rehoboam remained in Jerusalem and fortified vari-
ous towns for the defense of Judah. 6 He built up Beth-
lehem, Etam, Tekoa, 7 Beth-zur, Soco, Adullam, 8 Gath,
Mareshah, Ziph, 9 Adoraim, Lachish, Azekah, 10 Zo-
rah, Aijalon, and Hebron. These became the fortified
towns of Judah and Benjamin. 11 Rehoboam strength-
ened their defenses and stationed commanders in
them, and he stored supplies of food, olive oil, and
wine. 12 He also put shields and spears in these towns
as a further safety measure. So only Judah and Benja-
min remained under his control.
13 But all the priests and Levites living among the
northern tribes of Israel sided with Rehoboam. 14 The
Levites even abandoned their pasturelands and prop-
erty and moved to Judah and Jerusalem, because Jer-
oboam and his sons would not allow them to serve the
LORD as priests. 15 Jeroboam appointed his own priests
to serve at the pagan shrines, where they worshiped
the goat and calf idols he had made. 16 From all the
tribes of Israel, those who sincerely wanted to wor-
ship the LORD, the God of Israel, followed the Levites
to Jerusalem, where they could offer sacrifices to the
LORD, the God of their ancestors. 17 This strengthened
the kingdom of Judah, and for three years they sup-
ported Rehoboam son of Solomon, for during those
years they faithfully followed in the footsteps of Da-
vid and Solomon.

REHOBOAM'S FAMILY

18 Rehoboam married his cousin Mahalath, the
daughter of David's son Jerimoth and of Abihail, the
daughter of Eliab son of Jesse. 19 Mahalath had three
sons—Jeush, Shemariah, and Zaham.
20 Later Rehoboam married another cousin, Maa-
cah, the granddaughter of Absalom. Maacah gave
birth to Abijah, Attai, Ziza, and Shelomith. 21 Re-
hoboam loved Maacah more than any of his other
wives and concubines. In all, he had eighteen wives
and sixty concubines, and they gave birth to twen-
ty-eight sons and sixty daughters.
22 Rehoboam appointed Maacah's son Abijah as
leader among the princes, making it clear that he
would be the next king. 23 Rehoboam also wisely
gave responsibilities to his other sons and stationed
some of them in the fortified towns throughout the
land of Judah and Benjamin. He provided them with
generous provisions, and he found many wives for
them.

EGYPT INVADES JUDAH

12 But when Rehoboam was firmly established
and strong, he abandoned the Law of the LORD,
and all Israel followed him in this sin. 2 Because they
were unfaithful to the LORD, King Shishak of Egypt
came up and attacked Jerusalem in the fifth year of
King Rehoboam's reign. 3 He came with 1,200 chari-
ots, 60,000 horses,* and a countless army of foot sol-
diers, including Libyans, Sukkites, and Ethiopians.*
4 Shishak conquered Judah's fortified towns and then
advanced to attack Jerusalem.
5 The prophet Shemaiah then met with Rehoboam
and Judah's leaders, who had all fled to Jerusalem be-
cause of Shishak. Shemaiah told them, "This is what
the LORD says: You have abandoned me, so I am aban-
doning you to Shishak."
6 Then the leaders of Israel and the king humbled
themselves and said, "The LORD is right in doing this
to us!"
7 When the LORD saw their change of heart, he gave
this message to Shemaiah: "Since the people have
humbled themselves, I will not completely destroy
them and will soon give them some relief. I will not
use Shishak to pour out my anger on Jerusalem. 8 But
they will become his subjects, so they will know the

10:16 As in Syriac version, Latin Vulgate, and many Hebrew manuscripts (see also 1 Kgs 12:16); Masoretic Text lacks *realized*. **10:18** Hebrew *Hadoram*, a variant spelling of Adoniram; compare 1 Kgs 4:6; 5:14; 12:18. **12:3a** Or *charioteers,* or *horsemen.* **12:3b** Hebrew *and Cushites.*

11:5-10 Rehoboam. Rehoboam faces great opposition but is armed with only two tribes: Benjamin and Judah. Despite great odds, Rehoboam prepares his forces for a fight. He fortified the cities and brought the priests into them. Many supported him and strengthened the kingdom (v. 17).

11:12 Judah and Benjamin . . . under his control. The northern kingdom of Israel was made up of ten tribes, while the southern kingdom of Judah was made up of two tribes: Judah and Benjamin.

11:22 Abijah. Rehoboam thinks ahead to the succession of his favored son, Abijah. His remaining sons are given political prestige.

12:1 abandoned the Law . . . all Israel followed him. The divided kingdom is represented in terms of Judah (to the south) and Israel (to the north). The chronicler implies the reference is to Israelites living in Judah and who abandon God's ways.

difference between serving me and serving earthly
rulers."
9 So King Shishak of Egypt came up and attacked
Jerusalem. He ransacked the treasuries of the LORD's
Temple and the royal palace; he stole everything, in-
cluding all the gold shields Solomon had made. 10 King
Rehoboam later replaced them with bronze shields
as substitutes, and he entrusted them to the care of
the commanders of the guard who protected the en-
trance to the royal palace. 11 Whenever the king went
to the Temple of the LORD, the guards would also take
the shields and then return them to the guardroom.
12 Because Rehoboam humbled himself, the LORD's
anger was turned away, and he did not destroy him
completely. There were still some good things in the
land of Judah.

SUMMARY OF REHOBOAM'S REIGN

13 King Rehoboam firmly established himself in Jeru-
salem and continued to rule. He was forty-one years
old when he became king, and he reigned seventeen
years in Jerusalem, the city the LORD had chosen from
among all the tribes of Israel as the place to honor his
name. Rehoboam's mother was Naamah, a woman
from Ammon. 14 But he was an evil king, for he did not
seek the LORD with all his heart.
15 The rest of the events of Rehoboam's reign, from
beginning to end, are recorded in *The Record of She-
maiah the Prophet* and *The Record of Iddo the Seer,*
which are part of the genealogical record. Rehoboam
and Jeroboam were continually at war with each oth-
er. 16 When Rehoboam died, he was buried in the City
of David. Then his son Abijah became the next king.

ABIJAH'S WAR WITH JEROBOAM

13 Abijah began to rule over Judah in the eigh-
teenth year of Jeroboam's reign in Israel. 2 He
reigned in Jerusalem three years. His mother was
Maacah,* the daughter of Uriel from Gibeah.
Then war broke out between Abijah and Jerobo-
am. 3 Judah, led by King Abijah, fielded 400,000 select
warriors, while Jeroboam mustered 800,000 select
troops from Israel.
4 When the army of Judah arrived in the hill coun-
try of Ephraim, Abijah stood on Mount Zemaraim
and shouted to Jeroboam and all Israel: "Listen to
me! 5 Don't you realize that the LORD, the God of Isra-
el, made a lasting covenant* with David, giving him
and his descendants the throne of Israel forever? 6 Yet
Jeroboam son of Nebat, a mere servant of David's son
Solomon, rebelled against his master. 7 Then a whole
gang of scoundrels joined him, defying Solomon's son
Rehoboam when he was young and inexperienced
and could not stand up to them.
8 "Do you really think you can stand against the
kingdom of the LORD that is led by the descendants
of David? You may have a vast army, and you have
those gold calves that Jeroboam made as your gods.
9 But you have chased away the priests of the LORD
(the descendants of Aaron) and the Levites, and you
have appointed your own priests, just like the pagan
nations. You let anyone become a priest these days!
Whoever comes to be dedicated with a young bull
and seven rams can become a priest of these so-called
gods of yours!
10 "But as for us, the LORD is our God, and we have
not abandoned him. Only the descendants of Aaron
serve the LORD as priests, and the Levites alone may
help them in their work. 11 They present burnt offer-
ings and fragrant incense to the LORD every morning
and evening. They place the Bread of the Presence on
the holy table, and they light the gold lampstand ev-
ery evening. We are following the instructions of the
LORD our God, but you have abandoned him. 12 So you
see, God is with us. He is our leader. His priests blow
their trumpets and lead us into battle against you.
O people of Israel, do not fight against the LORD, the
God of your ancestors, for you will not succeed!"
13 Meanwhile, Jeroboam had secretly sent part of
his army around behind the men of Judah to ambush
them. 14 When Judah realized that they were being
attacked from the front and the rear, they cried out to
the LORD for help. Then the priests blew the trumpets,
15 and the men of Judah began to shout. At the sound
of their battle cry, God defeated Jeroboam and all Is-
rael and routed them before Abijah and the army of
Judah.
16 The Israelite army fled from Judah, and God
handed them over to Judah in defeat. 17 Abijah and his
army inflicted heavy losses on them; 500,000 of Isra-
el's select troops were killed that day. 18 So Judah de-
feated Israel on that occasion because they trusted in
the LORD, the God of their ancestors. 19 Abijah and his
army pursued Jeroboam's troops and captured some
of his towns, including Bethel, Jeshanah, and Ephron,
along with their surrounding villages.
20 So Jeroboam of Israel never regained his power
during Abijah's lifetime, and finally the LORD struck
him down and he died. 21 Meanwhile, Abijah of Judah
grew more and more powerful. He married fourteen
wives and had twenty-two sons and sixteen daugh-
ters.
22 The rest of the events of Abijah's reign, including
his words and deeds, are recorded in *The Commen-
tary of Iddo the Prophet.*

EARLY YEARS OF ASA'S REIGN

14 1* When Abijah died, he was buried in the City of
David. Then his son Asa became the next king.
There was peace in the land for ten years. 2* Asa did
what was pleasing and good in the sight of the LORD
his God. 3 He removed the foreign altars and the pagan
shrines. He smashed the sacred pillars and cut down
the Asherah poles. 4 He commanded the people of Ju-
dah to seek the LORD, the God of their ancestors, and
to obey his law and his commands. 5 Asa also removed
the pagan shrines, as well as the incense altars from
every one of Judah's towns. So Asa's kingdom enjoyed

13:2 As in most Greek manuscripts and Syriac version (see also 2 Chr 11:20-21; 1 Kgs 15:2); Hebrew reads *Micaiah,* a variant spelling of Maacah.
13:5 Hebrew *a covenant of salt.* **14:1** Verse 14:1 is numbered 13:23 in Hebrew text. **14:2** Verses 14:2-15 are numbered 14:1-14 in Hebrew text.

13:1–14:1 The story in 1 Kings 15:1-8 parallels the details of Abijah's reign in 2 Chronicles, only with a different twist. First Kings' more negative portrayal is balanced by the chronicler's illustration of Abijah's battlefield plea.

13:9 Whoever comes to be dedicated. God must call those ordained to a ministry. These false priests were taking it upon themselves to elevate themselves to priesthood.

14:5 removed the pagan shrines, as well as the incense altars. Asa attempted to reform worshiping in Judah. His mission was short-lived in the wake of overwhelming odds (15:17), and he wasn't able to remove the high places (see 1 Kings 15:14).

a period of peace. 6 During those peaceful years, he was able to build up the fortified towns throughout Judah. No one tried to make war against him at this time, for the LORD was giving him rest from his enemies.

7 Asa told the people of Judah, "Let us build towns and fortify them with walls, towers, gates, and bars. The land is still ours because we sought the LORD our God, and he has given us peace on every side." So they went ahead with these projects and brought them to completion.

8 King Asa had an army of 300,000 warriors from the tribe of Judah, armed with large shields and spears. He also had an army of 280,000 warriors from the tribe of Benjamin, armed with small shields and bows. Both armies were composed of well-trained fighting men.

9 Once an Ethiopian* named Zerah attacked Judah with an army of 1,000,000 men* and 300 chariots. They advanced to the town of Mareshah, 10 so Asa deployed his armies for battle in the valley north of Mareshah.* 11 Then Asa cried out to the LORD his God, "O LORD, no one but you can help the powerless against the mighty! Help us, O LORD our God, for we trust in you alone. It is in your name that we have come against this vast horde. O LORD, you are our God; do not let mere men prevail against you!"

12 So the LORD defeated the Ethiopians* in the presence of Asa and the army of Judah, and the enemy fled. 13 Asa and his army pursued them as far as Gerar, and so many Ethiopians fell that they were unable to rally. They were destroyed by the LORD and his army, and the army of Judah carried off a vast amount of plunder.

14 While they were at Gerar, they attacked all the towns in that area, and terror from the LORD came upon the people there. As a result, a vast amount of plunder was taken from these towns, too. 15 They also attacked the camps of herdsmen and captured many sheep, goats, and camels before finally returning to Jerusalem.

ASA'S RELIGIOUS REFORMS

15 Then the Spirit of God came upon Azariah son of Oded, 2 and he went out to meet King Asa as he was returning from the battle. "Listen to me, Asa!" he shouted. "Listen, all you people of Judah and Benjamin! The LORD will stay with you as long as you stay with him! Whenever you seek him, you will find him. But if you abandon him, he will abandon you. 3 For a long time Israel was without the true God, without a priest to teach them, and without the Law to instruct them. 4 But whenever they were in trouble and turned to the LORD, the God of Israel, and sought him out, they found him.

5 "During those dark times, it was not safe to travel. Problems troubled the people of every land. 6 Nation fought against nation, and city against city, for God was troubling them with every kind of problem. 7 But as for you, be strong and courageous, for your work will be rewarded."

8 When Asa heard this message from Azariah the prophet,* he took courage and removed all the detestable idols from the land of Judah and Benjamin and in the towns he had captured in the hill country of Ephraim. And he repaired the altar of the LORD, which stood in front of the entry room of the LORD's Temple.

9 Then Asa called together all the people of Judah and Benjamin, along with the people of Ephraim, Manasseh, and Simeon who had settled among them. For many from Israel had moved to Judah during Asa's reign when they saw that the LORD his God was with him. 10 The people gathered at Jerusalem in late spring,* during the fifteenth year of Asa's reign.

11 On that day they sacrificed to the LORD 700 cattle and 7,000 sheep and goats from the plunder they had taken in the battle. 12 Then they entered into a covenant to seek the LORD, the God of their ancestors, with all their heart and soul. 13 They agreed that anyone who refused to seek the LORD, the God of Israel, would be put to death—whether young or old, man or woman. 14 They shouted out their oath of loyalty to the LORD with trumpets blaring and rams' horns sounding. 15 All in Judah were happy about this covenant, for they had entered into it with all their heart. They earnestly sought after God, and they found him. And the LORD gave them rest from their enemies on every side.

16 King Asa even deposed his grandmother* Maacah from her position as queen mother because she had made an obscene Asherah pole. He cut down her obscene pole, broke it up, and burned it in the Kidron Valley. 17 Although the pagan shrines were not removed from Israel, Asa's heart remained completely faithful throughout his life. 18 He brought into the Temple of God the silver and gold and the various items that he and his father had dedicated.

19 So there was no more war until the thirty-fifth year of Asa's reign.

FINAL YEARS OF ASA'S REIGN

16 In the thirty-sixth year of Asa's reign, King Baasha of Israel invaded Judah and fortified Ramah in order to prevent anyone from entering or leaving King Asa's territory in Judah.

2 Asa responded by removing the silver and gold from the treasuries of the Temple of the LORD and the royal palace. He sent it to King Ben-hadad of Aram, who was ruling in Damascus, along with this message:

3 "Let there be a treaty* between you and me like the one between your father and my father. See, I

14:9a Hebrew *a Cushite.* **14:9b** Or *an army of thousands and thousands;* Hebrew reads *an army of a thousand thousands.* **14:10** As in Greek version; Hebrew reads *valley of Zephathah near Mareshah.* **14:12** Hebrew *Cushites;* also in 14:13. **15:8** As in Syriac version and Latin Vulgate (see also 15:1); Hebrew reads *from Oded the prophet.* **15:10** Hebrew *in the third month.* This month of the ancient Hebrew lunar calendar usually occurs within the months of May and June. **15:16** Hebrew *his mother.* **16:3** As in Greek version; Hebrew reads *There is a treaty.*

15:1-19 A prophet's encouragement goes a long way with Asa. He resumed his search-and-destroy mission against idols with great zeal.

15:13 put to death. Religious expression has significant social and political implications. Rebellion against God is taken as a serious offense against the state. In keeping with the law, all who would not seek the Lord were to be put to death (see Deut. 13:6-9).

15:15 for they had entered into it with all their heart. Christ promises us that those who seek will find (Matt. 7:7-8). To seek with our whole hearts is to seek in a way that isn't debilitated by ulterior motives and conflicting pursuits.

am sending you silver and gold. Break your treaty
with King Baasha of Israel so that he will leave me
alone."

4 Ben-hadad agreed to King Asa's request and sent
the commanders of his army to attack the towns of
Israel. They conquered the towns of Ijon, Dan, Abel-
beth-maacah,* and all the store cities in Naphtali. 5 As
soon as Baasha of Israel heard what was happening,
he abandoned his project of fortifying Ramah and
stopped all work on it. 6 Then King Asa called out all
the men of Judah to carry away the building stones
and timbers that Baasha had been using to fortify Ra-
mah. Asa used these materials to fortify the towns of
Geba and Mizpah.

7 At that time Hanani the seer came to King Asa
and told him, "Because you have put your trust in the
king of Aram instead of in the LORD your God, you
missed your chance to destroy the army of the king
of Aram. 8 Don't you remember what happened to the
Ethiopians* and Libyans and their vast army, with all
of their chariots and charioteers?* At that time you
relied on the LORD, and he handed them over to you.
9 The eyes of the LORD search the whole earth in order
to strengthen those whose hearts are fully committed
to him. What a fool you have been! From now on you
will be at war."

10 Asa became so angry with Hanani for saying this
that he threw him into prison and put him in stocks.
At that time Asa also began to oppress some of his
people.

SUMMARY OF ASA'S REIGN

11 The rest of the events of Asa's reign, from beginning
to end, are recorded in *The Book of the Kings of Ju-
dah and Israel.* 12 In the thirty-ninth year of his reign,
Asa developed a serious foot disease. Yet even with
the severity of his disease, he did not seek the LORD's
help but turned only to his physicians. 13 So he died in
the forty-first year of his reign. 14 He was buried in the
tomb he had carved out for himself in the City of Da-
vid. He was laid on a bed perfumed with sweet spices
and fragrant ointments, and the people built a huge
funeral fire in his honor.

JEHOSHAPHAT RULES IN JUDAH

17 Then Jehoshaphat, Asa's son, became the next
king. He strengthened Judah to stand against
any attack from Israel. 2 He stationed troops in all the
fortified towns of Judah, and he assigned additional
garrisons to the land of Judah and to the towns of
Ephraim that his father, Asa, had captured.

3 The LORD was with Jehoshaphat because he fol-
lowed the example of his father's early years* and
did not worship the images of Baal. 4 He sought his
father's God and obeyed his commands instead of fol-
lowing the evil practices of the kingdom of Israel. 5 So
the LORD established Jehoshaphat's control over the
kingdom of Judah. All the people of Judah brought
gifts to Jehoshaphat, so he became very wealthy and
highly esteemed. 6 He was deeply committed to* the
ways of the LORD. He removed the pagan shrines and
Asherah poles from Judah.

7 In the third year of his reign Jehoshaphat sent his
officials to teach in all the towns of Judah. These offi-
cials included Ben-hail, Obadiah, Zechariah, Nethan-
el, and Micaiah. 8 He sent Levites along with them,
including Shemaiah, Nethaniah, Zebadiah, Asahel,
Shemiramoth, Jehonathan, Adonijah, Tobijah, and
Tob-Adonijah. He also sent out the priests Elishama
and Jehoram. 9 They took copies of the Book of the
Law of the LORD and traveled around through all the
towns of Judah, teaching the people.

10 Then the fear of the LORD fell over all the sur-
rounding kingdoms so that none of them wanted to
declare war on Jehoshaphat. 11 Some of the Philistines
brought him gifts and silver as tribute, and the Arabs
brought 7,700 rams and 7,700 male goats.

12 So Jehoshaphat became more and more powerful
and built fortresses and storage cities throughout Ju-
dah. 13 He stored numerous supplies in Judah's towns
and stationed an army of seasoned troops at Jerusa-
lem. 14 His army was enrolled according to ancestral
clans.

From Judah there were 300,000 troops organized
in units of 1,000, under the command of Adnah.
15 Next in command was Jehohanan, who com-
manded 280,000 troops. 16 Next was Amasiah son
of Zicri, who volunteered for the LORD's service,
with 200,000 troops under his command.
17 From Benjamin there were 200,000 troops
equipped with bows and shields. They were under
the command of Eliada, a veteran soldier. 18 Next
in command was Jehozabad, who commanded
180,000 armed men.

19 These were the troops stationed in Jerusalem to
serve the king, besides those Jehoshaphat stationed in
the fortified towns throughout Judah.

JEHOSHAPHAT AND AHAB

18 Jehoshaphat enjoyed great riches and high es-
teem, and he made an alliance with Ahab of Is-
rael by having his son marry Ahab's daughter. 2 A few
years later he went to Samaria to visit Ahab, who pre-
pared a great banquet for him and his officials. They
butchered great numbers of sheep, goats, and cattle
for the feast. Then Ahab enticed Jehoshaphat to join
forces with him to recover Ramoth-gilead.

3 "Will you go with me to Ramoth-gilead?" King
Ahab of Israel asked King Jehoshaphat of Judah.

16:4 As in parallel text at 1 Kgs 15:20; Hebrew reads *Abel-maim,* another name for Abel-beth-maacah. **16:8a** Hebrew *Cushites.* **16:8b** Or *and horsemen?* **17:3** Some Hebrew manuscripts read *the example of his father, David.* **17:6** Hebrew *His heart was courageous in.*

16:9 The eyes of the LORD search the whole earth . . . committerd to him. Even at this time God did not simply look for faith and allegiance from those who were in Israel. He chose Israel as a light to the people of other nations, but He always wanted to win the allegiance of others too.

17:1–21:3 Jehoshaphat. Jehoshaphat receives high marks from the chronicler for his general devotion to God and his denouncement of idolatrous worship (vv. 3-4,6). The king also instituted a noteworthy emphasis on religious education (vv. 7-9). This account is longer than the parallel in 1 Kings 22:1-46 to emphasize retribution during Jehoshaphat's reign.

17:6 He was deeply committed. Jehoshaphat is lauded for his good intentions. However, like others before him, he fell short of even his own goals. He allowed the idols to be restored during his reign (20:33).

18:1 made an alliance. This subtle reference to a family alliance would prove near disastrous for Judah on more than one occasion. First, Jehoshaphat nearly loses his life, but he learns his lesson and recovers quickly (19:1-3). However, the Davidic line itself would be at stake (22:10–23:21).

Jehoshaphat replied, "Why, of course! You and I are
as one, and my troops are your troops. We will cer-
tainly join you in battle." 4 Then Jehoshaphat added,
"But first let's find out what the LORD says."
5 So the king of Israel summoned the prophets,
400 of them, and asked them, "Should we go to war
against Ramoth-gilead, or should I hold back?"
They all replied, "Yes, go right ahead! God will give
the king victory."
6 But Jehoshaphat asked, "Is there not also a prophet
of the LORD here? We should ask him the same question."
7 The king of Israel replied to Jehoshaphat, "There is
one more man who could consult the LORD for us, but
I hate him. He never prophesies anything but trouble
for me! His name is Micaiah son of Imlah."
Jehoshaphat replied, "That's not the way a king
should talk! Let's hear what he has to say."
8 So the king of Israel called one of his officials and
said, "Quick! Bring Micaiah son of Imlah."

MICAIAH PROPHESIES AGAINST AHAB

9 King Ahab of Israel and King Jehoshaphat of Judah,
dressed in their royal robes, were sitting on thrones
at the threshing floor near the gate of Samaria. All
of Ahab's prophets were prophesying there in front
of them. 10 One of them, Zedekiah son of Kenaanah,
made some iron horns and proclaimed, "This is what
the LORD says: With these horns you will gore the Ar-
ameans to death!"
11 All the other prophets agreed. "Yes," they said, "go
up to Ramoth-gilead and be victorious, for the LORD
will give the king victory!"
12 Meanwhile, the messenger who went to get Mi-
caiah said to him, "Look, all the prophets are promis-
ing victory for the king. Be sure that you agree with
them and promise success."
13 But Micaiah replied, "As surely as the LORD lives,
I will say only what my God says."
14 When Micaiah arrived before the king, Ahab
asked him, "Micaiah, should we go to war against Ra-
moth-gilead, or should I hold back?"
Micaiah replied sarcastically, "Yes, go up and be
victorious, for you will have victory over them!"
15 But the king replied sharply, "How many times
must I demand that you speak only the truth to me
when you speak for the LORD?"
16 Then Micaiah told him, "In a vision I saw all Is-
rael scattered on the mountains, like sheep without a
shepherd. And the LORD said, 'Their master has been
killed.* Send them home in peace.'"
17 "Didn't I tell you?" the king of Israel exclaimed
to Jehoshaphat. "He never prophesies anything but
trouble for me."
18 Then Micaiah continued, "Listen to what the LORD
says! I saw the LORD sitting on his throne with all the
armies of heaven around him, on his right and on his
left. 19 And the LORD said, 'Who can entice King Ahab
of Israel to go into battle against Ramoth-gilead so he
can be killed?'
"There were many suggestions, 20 and finally a spir-
it approached the LORD and said, 'I can do it!'
"'How will you do this?' the LORD asked.
21 "And the spirit replied, 'I will go out and inspire
all of Ahab's prophets to speak lies.'
"'You will succeed,' said the LORD. 'Go ahead and do
it.'
22 "So you see, the LORD has put a lying spirit in
the mouths of your prophets. For the LORD has pro-
nounced your doom."
23 Then Zedekiah son of Kenaanah walked up to Mi-
caiah and slapped him across the face. "Since when
did the Spirit of the LORD leave me to speak to you?"
he demanded.
24 And Micaiah replied, "You will find out soon
enough when you are trying to hide in some secret
room!"
25 "Arrest him!" the king of Israel ordered. "Take
him back to Amon, the governor of the city, and to my
son Joash. 26 Give them this order from the king: 'Put
this man in prison, and feed him nothing but bread
and water until I return safely from the battle!'"
27 But Micaiah replied, "If you return safely, it will
mean that the LORD has not spoken through me!" Then
he added to those standing around, "Everyone mark
my words!"

THE DEATH OF AHAB

28 So King Ahab of Israel and King Jehoshaphat of Ju-
dah led their armies against Ramoth-gilead. 29 The
king of Israel said to Jehoshaphat, "As we go into bat-
tle, I will disguise myself so no one will recognize me,
but you wear your royal robes." So the king of Israel
disguised himself, and they went into battle.
30 Meanwhile, the king of Aram had issued these
orders to his chariot commanders: "Attack only the
king of Israel! Don't bother with anyone else." 31 So
when the Aramean chariot commanders saw Jehosh-
aphat in his royal robes, they went after him. "There
is the king of Israel!" they shouted. But Jehoshaphat
called out, and the LORD saved him. God helped him
by turning the attackers away from him. 32 As soon as
the chariot commanders realized he was not the king
of Israel, they stopped chasing him.
33 An Aramean soldier, however, randomly shot an
arrow at the Israelite troops and hit the king of Israel
between the joints of his armor. "Turn the horses* and
get me out of here!" Ahab groaned to the driver of the
chariot. "I'm badly wounded!"
34 The battle raged all that day, and the king of Is-
rael propped himself up in his chariot facing the Ar-
ameans. In the evening, just as the sun was setting,
he died.

JEHOSHAPHAT APPOINTS JUDGES

19 When King Jehoshaphat of Judah arrived safe-
ly home in Jerusalem, 2 Jehu son of Hanani the
seer went out to meet him. "Why should you help
the wicked and love those who hate the LORD?" he

18:16 Hebrew *These people have no master.* 18:33 Hebrew *Turn your hand.*

18:5 the king of Israel summoned the prophets. These prophets Ahab gathered were prophets of Baal.
18:7 He never prophesies anything but trouble. Micaiah, whose name means "Who is like Yah?", was the only one of Yahweh's prophets left in the region. The 400 prophets of Baal were Ahab's yes-men. They prophesied whatever he wanted.
18:29 disguise myself. Ahab arranges for his rival to become an easy target, and Jehoshaphat falls for it.
18:31 by turning the attackers away. God intervenes despite human foolishness. Jehoshaphat narrowly escapes death.
19:2 Jehu . . . the seer. Jehu carries a precautionary message to Jehoshaphat. The next time he might not be so lucky!

asked the king. "Because of what you have done, the
LORD is very angry with you. 3 Even so, there is some
good in you, for you have removed the Asherah poles
throughout the land, and you have committed your-
self to seeking God."
4 Jehoshaphat lived in Jerusalem, but he went out
among the people, traveling from Beersheba to the
hill country of Ephraim, encouraging the people
to return to the LORD, the God of their ancestors.
5 He appointed judges throughout the nation in all
the fortified towns, 6 and he said to them, "Always
think carefully before pronouncing judgment. Re-
member that you do not judge to please people but
to please the LORD. He will be with you when you
render the verdict in each case. 7 Fear the LORD and
judge with integrity, for the LORD our God does not
tolerate perverted justice, partiality, or the taking
of bribes."
8 In Jerusalem, Jehoshaphat appointed some of the
Levites and priests and clan leaders in Israel to serve
as judges* for cases involving the LORD's regulations
and for civil disputes. 9 These were his instructions to
them: "You must always act in the fear of the LORD,
with faithfulness and an undivided heart. 10 When-
ever a case comes to you from fellow citizens in an
outlying town, whether a murder case or some other
violation of God's laws, commands, decrees, or regula-
tions, you must warn them not to sin against the LORD,
so that he will not be angry with you and them. Do
this and you will not be guilty.
11 "Amariah the high priest will have final say in all
cases involving the LORD. Zebadiah son of Ishmael, a
leader from the tribe of Judah, will have final say in
all civil cases. The Levites will assist you in making
sure that justice is served. Take courage as you fulfill
your duties, and may the LORD be with those who do
what is right."

WAR WITH SURROUNDING NATIONS

20 After this, the armies of the Moabites, Am-
monites, and some of the Meunites* declared
war on Jehoshaphat. 2 Messengers came and told Je-
hoshaphat, "A vast army from Edom* is marching
against you from beyond the Dead Sea.* They are
already at Hazazon-tamar." (This was another name
for En-gedi.)
3 Jehoshaphat was terrified by this news and
begged the LORD for guidance. He also ordered every-
one in Judah to begin fasting. 4 So people from all the
towns of Judah came to Jerusalem to seek the LORD's
help.
5 Jehoshaphat stood before the community of Ju-
dah and Jerusalem in front of the new courtyard at
the Temple of the LORD. 6 He prayed, "O LORD, God
of our ancestors, you alone are the God who is in
heaven. You are ruler of all the kingdoms of the
earth. You are powerful and mighty; no one can
stand against you! 7 O our God, did you not drive out
those who lived in this land when your people Is-
rael arrived? And did you not give this land forever
to the descendants of your friend Abraham? 8 Your
people settled here and built this Temple to honor
your name. 9 They said, 'Whenever we are faced
with any calamity such as war,* plague, or famine,
we can come to stand in your presence before this
Temple where your name is honored. We can cry
out to you to save us, and you will hear us and res-
cue us.'
10 "And now see what the armies of Ammon, Moab,
and Mount Seir are doing. You would not let our an-
cestors invade those nations when Israel left Egypt,
so they went around them and did not destroy them.
11 Now see how they reward us! For they have come
to throw us out of your land, which you gave us as
an inheritance. 12 O our God, won't you stop them? We
are powerless against this mighty army that is about
to attack us. We do not know what to do, but we are
looking to you for help."
13 As all the men of Judah stood before the LORD
with their little ones, wives, and children, 14 the Spirit
of the LORD came upon one of the men standing there.
His name was Jahaziel son of Zechariah, son of Bena-
iah, son of Jeiel, son of Mattaniah, a Levite who was a
descendant of Asaph.
15 He said, "Listen, all you people of Judah and Je-
rusalem! Listen, King Jehoshaphat! This is what the
LORD says: Do not be afraid! Don't be discouraged by
this mighty army, for the battle is not yours, but God's.
16 Tomorrow, march out against them. You will find
them coming up through the ascent of Ziz at the end
of the valley that opens into the wilderness of Jeruel.
17 But you will not even need to fight. Take your posi-
tions; then stand still and watch the LORD's victory. He
is with you, O people of Judah and Jerusalem. Do not
be afraid or discouraged. Go out against them tomor-
row, for the LORD is with you!"
18 Then King Jehoshaphat bowed low with his face
to the ground. And all the people of Judah and Jeru-
salem did the same, worshiping the LORD. 19 Then the
Levites from the clans of Kohath and Korah stood to
praise the LORD, the God of Israel, with a very loud
shout.
20 Early the next morning the army of Judah went
out into the wilderness of Tekoa. On the way Jehosh-
aphat stopped and said, "Listen to me, all you people
of Judah and Jerusalem! Believe in the LORD your
God, and you will be able to stand firm. Believe in his
prophets, and you will succeed."
21 After consulting the people, the king appointed
singers to walk ahead of the army, singing to the LORD
and praising him for his holy splendor. This is what
they sang:

19:8 As in Greek version; the meaning of the Hebrew is uncertain. **20:1** As in some Greek manuscripts (see also 26:7); Hebrew repeats *Ammonites.* **20:2a** As in one Hebrew manuscript; most Hebrew manuscripts and ancient versions read *Aram.* **20:2b** Hebrew *the sea.* **20:9** Or *sword of judgment;* or *sword, judgment.*

19:5 appointed judges . . . in all the fortified cities. The postexilic refugees reading the chronicler's message would refer to Jehoshaphat's system as a model for rebuilding the civil and judicial systems necessary to function as a nation.

19:7 not tolerate perverted justice. God's perfect, personal example is the standard for justice.

19:8 appointed some of the Levites. The Levites would oversee the fairness of this supreme court. Thus, a balance between religion and state would be achieved.

20:1-30 The mere mention of Moab caused worry and fear. A record of Jehoshaphat's decisive victory over the Moabites and Ammonites would be cause for celebration.

20:5-12 Jehoshaphat wrestled in prayer before battling in the field. In answer to his prayer, God granted Judah victory.

20:20 Believe in the LORD your God. As a military leader, Jehoshaphat might have instructed his warriors to hit first and hit hardest. But his military strategy was spiritual.

"Give thanks to the LORD;
his faithful love endures forever!"

[22] At the very moment they began to sing and give praise, the LORD caused the armies of Ammon, Moab, and Mount Seir to start fighting among themselves. [23] The armies of Moab and Ammon turned against their allies from Mount Seir and killed every one of them. After they had destroyed the army of Seir, they began attacking each other. [24] So when the army of Judah arrived at the lookout point in the wilderness, all they saw were dead bodies lying on the ground as far as they could see. Not a single one of the enemy had escaped.

[25] King Jehoshaphat and his men went out to gather the plunder. They found vast amounts of equipment, clothing,* and other valuables—more than they could carry. There was so much plunder that it took them three days just to collect it all! [26] On the fourth day they gathered in the Valley of Blessing,* which got its name that day because the people praised and thanked the LORD there. It is still called the Valley of Blessing today.

[27] Then all the men returned to Jerusalem, with Jehoshaphat leading them, overjoyed that the LORD had given them victory over their enemies. [28] They marched into Jerusalem to the music of harps, lyres, and trumpets, and they proceeded to the Temple of the LORD.

[29] When all the surrounding kingdoms heard that the LORD himself had fought against the enemies of Israel, the fear of God came over them. [30] So Jehoshaphat's kingdom was at peace, for his God had given him rest on every side.

SUMMARY OF JEHOSHAPHAT'S REIGN

[31] So Jehoshaphat ruled over the land of Judah. He was thirty-five years old when he became king, and he reigned in Jerusalem twenty-five years. His mother was Azubah, the daughter of Shilhi.

[32] Jehoshaphat was a good king, following the ways of his father, Asa. He did what was pleasing in the LORD's sight. [33] During his reign, however, he failed to remove all the pagan shrines, and the people never fully committed themselves to follow the God of their ancestors.

[34] The rest of the events of Jehoshaphat's reign, from beginning to end, are recorded in *The Record of Jehu Son of Hanani,* which is included in *The Book of the Kings of Israel.*

[35] Some time later King Jehoshaphat of Judah made an alliance with King Ahaziah of Israel, who was very wicked.* [36] Together they built a fleet of trading ships* at the port of Ezion-geber. [37] Then Eliezer son of Dodavahu from Mareshah prophesied against Jehoshaphat. He said, "Because you have allied yourself with King Ahaziah, the LORD will destroy your work." So the ships met with disaster and never put out to sea.*

JEHORAM RULES IN JUDAH

21 When Jehoshaphat died, he was buried with his ancestors in the City of David. Then his son Jehoram became the next king.

[2] Jehoram's brothers—the other sons of Jehoshaphat—were Azariah, Jehiel, Zechariah, Azariahu, Michael, and Shephatiah; all these were the sons of Jehoshaphat king of Judah.* [3] Their father had given each of them valuable gifts of silver, gold, and costly items, and also some of Judah's fortified towns. However, he designated Jehoram as the next king because he was the oldest. [4] But when Jehoram had become solidly established as king, he killed all his brothers and some of the other leaders of Judah.

[5] Jehoram was thirty-two years old when he became king, and he reigned in Jerusalem eight years. [6] But Jehoram followed the example of the kings of Israel and was as wicked as King Ahab, for he had married one of Ahab's daughters. So Jehoram did what was evil in the LORD's sight. [7] But the LORD did not want to destroy David's dynasty, for he had made a covenant with David and promised that his descendants would continue to rule, shining like a lamp forever.

[8] During Jehoram's reign, the Edomites revolted against Judah and crowned their own king. [9] So Jehoram went out with his full army and all his chariots. The Edomites surrounded him and his chariot commanders, but he went out at night and attacked them* under cover of darkness. [10] Even so, Edom has been independent from Judah to this day. The town of Libnah also revolted about that same time. All this happened because Jehoram had abandoned the LORD, the God of his ancestors. [11] He had built pagan shrines in the hill country of Judah and had led the people of Jerusalem and Judah to give themselves to pagan gods and to go astray.

[12] Then Elijah the prophet wrote Jehoram this letter:

"This is what the LORD, the God of your ancestor David, says: You have not followed the good example of your father, Jehoshaphat, or your grandfather King Asa of Judah. [13] Instead, you have been as evil as the kings of Israel. You have led the people of Jerusalem and Judah to worship idols, just as King Ahab did in Israel. And you have even killed your own brothers, men who were better

20:25 As in some Hebrew manuscripts and Latin Vulgate; most Hebrew manuscripts read *corpses.* **20:26** Hebrew *valley of Beracah.* **20:35** Or *who made him do what was wicked.* **20:36** Hebrew *fleet of ships that could go to Tarshish.* **20:37** Hebrew *never set sail for Tarshish.* **21:2** Masoretic Text reads *of Israel,* also in 21:4. The author of Chronicles sees Judah as representative of the true Israel. (Some Hebrew manuscripts, Greek and Syriac versions, and Latin Vulgate read *of Judah.*) **21:9** Or *he went out and escaped.* The meaning of the Hebrew is uncertain.

20:22 the LORD caused . . . to start fighting. While Judah celebrated, the enemies grew more confused. They ambushed each other, securing the victory for the Israelites who had yet to draw their weapons.

20:30 at peace. After a weaponless victory, Judah's reputation for godly assistance kept the enemy at bay. God's peace signified His blessing on Judah during the king's reign.

20:35-37 Despite Jehoshaphat's battlefield success, he proved to be an inept entrepreneur. He failed to carry godly trust into his business efforts, choosing instead to seek a failed alliance with a pagan partner.

21:4-20 Jehoram. Jehoram tested the limits of God's merciful protection of the line of David. Apart from God's commitment to David, the evil king's family would have been entirely obliterated (2 Kings 8:16-24).

21:4 Jehoram was likely inspired by his wife's evil heritage. He brutally snuffed out all the competition in the false belief that this treachery will secure his empire.

21:10 God of his ancestors. Jehoram's lean toward evil was not consistent with his family tree. He was from David's line, and his propensity toward evil was his own personal choice.

21:12-15 Elijah's wake-up call could not have come at a better time, yet Jehoram ignored this word of warning and suffered the consequences.

than you. 14 So now the LORD is about to strike you, your people, your children, your wives, and all that is yours with a heavy blow. 15 You yourself will suffer with a severe intestinal disease that will get worse each day until your bowels come out."

16 Then the LORD stirred up the Philistines and the Arabs, who lived near the Ethiopians,* to attack Jehoram. 17 They marched against Judah, broke down its defenses, and carried away everything of value in the royal palace, including the king's sons and his wives. Only his youngest son, Ahaziah,* was spared.

18 After all this, the LORD struck Jehoram with an incurable intestinal disease. 19 The disease grew worse and worse, and at the end of two years it caused his bowels to come out, and he died in agony. His people did not build a great funeral fire to honor him as they had done for his ancestors.

20 Jehoram was thirty-two years old when he became king, and he reigned in Jerusalem eight years. No one was sorry when he died. They buried him in the City of David, but not in the royal cemetery.

AHAZIAH RULES IN JUDAH

22 Then the people of Jerusalem made Ahaziah, Jehoram's youngest son, their next king, since the marauding bands who came with the Arabs* had killed all the older sons. So Ahaziah son of Jehoram reigned as king of Judah.

2 Ahaziah was twenty-two* years old when he became king, and he reigned in Jerusalem one year. His mother was Athaliah, a granddaughter of King Omri. 3 Ahaziah also followed the evil example of King Ahab's family, for his mother encouraged him in doing wrong. 4 He did what was evil in the LORD's sight, just as Ahab's family had done. They even became his advisers after the death of his father, and they led him to ruin.

5 Following their evil advice, Ahaziah joined Joram,* the son of King Ahab of Israel, in his war against King Hazael of Aram at Ramoth-gilead. When the Arameans* wounded Joram in the battle, 6 he returned to Jezreel to recover from the wounds he had received at Ramoth.* Because Joram was wounded, King Ahaziah* of Judah went to Jezreel to visit him.

7 But God had decided that this visit would be Ahaziah's downfall. While he was there, Ahaziah went out with Joram to meet Jehu grandson of Nimshi,* whom the LORD had appointed to destroy the dynasty of Ahab.

8 While Jehu was executing judgment against the family of Ahab, he happened to meet some of Judah's officials and Ahaziah's relatives* who were traveling with Ahaziah. So Jehu killed them all. 9 Then Jehu's men searched for Ahaziah, and they found him hiding in the city of Samaria. They brought him to Jehu, who killed him. Ahaziah was given a decent burial because the people said, "He was the grandson of Jehoshaphat—a man who sought the LORD with all his heart." But none of the surviving members of Ahaziah's family was capable of ruling the kingdom.

QUEEN ATHALIAH RULES IN JUDAH

10 When Athaliah, the mother of King Ahaziah of Judah, learned that her son was dead, she began to destroy the rest of Judah's royal family. 11 But Ahaziah's sister Jehosheba,* the daughter of King Jehoram, took Ahaziah's infant son, Joash, and stole him away from among the rest of the king's children, who were about to be killed. She put Joash and his nurse in a bedroom. In this way, Jehosheba, wife of Jehoiada the priest and sister of Ahaziah, hid the child so that Athaliah could not murder him. 12 Joash remained hidden in the Temple of God for six years while Athaliah ruled over the land.

REVOLT AGAINST ATHALIAH

23 In the seventh year of Athaliah's reign, Jehoiada the priest decided to act. He summoned his courage and made a pact with five army commanders: Azariah son of Jeroham, Ishmael son of Jehohanan, Azariah son of Obed, Maaseiah son of Adaiah, and Elishaphat son of Zicri. 2 These men traveled secretly throughout Judah and summoned the Levites and clan leaders in all the towns to come to Jerusalem. 3 They all gathered at the Temple of God, where they made a solemn pact with Joash, the young king.

Jehoiada said to them, "Here is the king's son! The time has come for him to reign! The LORD has promised that a descendant of David will be our king. 4 This is what you must do. When you priests and Levites come on duty on the Sabbath, a third of you will serve as gatekeepers. 5 Another third will go over to the royal palace, and the final third will be at the Foundation Gate. Everyone else should stay in the courtyards of the LORD's Temple. 6 Remember, only the priests and Levites on duty may enter the Temple of the LORD, for they are set apart as holy. The rest of the people must obey the LORD's instructions and stay outside. 7 You Levites, form a bodyguard around the king and keep your weapons in hand. Kill anyone who tries to enter the Temple. Stay with the king wherever he goes."

21:16 Hebrew *the Cushites.* **21:17** Hebrew *Jehoahaz,* a variant spelling of Ahaziah; compare 22:1. **22:1** Or *marauding bands of Arabs.* **22:2** As in some Greek manuscripts and Syriac version (see also 2 Kgs 8:26); Hebrew reads *forty-two.* **22:5a** Hebrew *Jehoram,* a variant spelling of Joram; also in 22:6, 7. **22:5b** As in two Hebrew manuscripts and Latin Vulgate (see also 2 Kgs 8:28); Masoretic Text reads *the archers.* **22:6a** Hebrew *Ramah,* a variant spelling of Ramoth. **22:6b** As in some Hebrew manuscripts, Greek and Syriac versions, and Latin Vulgate (see also 2 Kgs 8:29); most Hebrew manuscripts read *Azariah.* **22:7** Hebrew *descendant of Nimshi;* compare 2 Kgs 9:2, 14. **22:8** As in Greek version (see also 2 Kgs 10:13); Hebrew reads *and sons of the brothers of Ahaziah.* **22:11** As in parallel text at 2 Kgs 11:2; Hebrew lacks *Ahaziah's sister* and reads *Jehoshabeath* [a variant spelling of Jehosheba].

21:20 died . . . not in the royal cemetery. Death has the final word on Jehoram's life. No funeral. No procession. Nothing was done to honor this relentlessly evil king.

22:2 Ahaziah was twenty-two. Ahaziah's youth and inexperience played into his quick demise.

22:3-4 Ahaziah allowed himself to become a puppet of the northern kingdom. Unfortunately, his own mother was pulling the strings.

22:7 Ahaziah's downfall. Jehu, Israel's next king, assassinated Ahaziah, yet all was according to God's plan.

22:9 Ahaziah's end leaves the story in suspense. An occupied tomb leaves an empty throne. The only successor in Judah is a mere infant.

22:10-12 Athaliah, like Jehoram, attempted to eradicate every inch of the Davidic line. However, her efforts were thwarted by the ingenuity of a quick-thinking girl.

23:1–24:27 Joash. Joash leaned on Jehoiada for inspiration. Under his influence, the king restored the temple and combatted idol worship. When Jehoiada died, Joash's success soon soured.

23:1 Jehoiada the priest decided to act. Jehoiada went from zero to hero as he shared the weight of a king's mantle with a seven-year-old. Jehoiada's decisions became royal rule.

8 So the Levites and all the people of Judah did everything as Jehoiada the priest ordered. The commanders took charge of the men reporting for duty that Sabbath, as well as those who were going off duty. Jehoiada the priest did not let anyone go home after their shift ended. 9 Then Jehoiada supplied the commanders with the spears and the large and small shields that had once belonged to King David and were stored in the Temple of God. 10 He stationed all the people around the king, with their weapons ready. They formed a line from the south side of the Temple around to the north side and all around the altar.

11 Then Jehoiada and his sons brought out Joash, the king's son, placed the crown on his head, and presented him with a copy of God's laws.* They anointed him and proclaimed him king, and everyone shouted, "Long live the king!"

THE DEATH OF ATHALIAH

12 When Athaliah heard the noise of the people running and the shouts of praise to the king, she hurried to the LORD's Temple to see what was happening. 13 When she arrived, she saw the newly crowned king standing in his place of authority by the pillar at the Temple entrance. The commanders and trumpeters were surrounding him, and people from all over the land were rejoicing and blowing trumpets. Singers with musical instruments were leading the people in a great celebration. When Athaliah saw all this, she tore her clothes in despair and shouted, "Treason! Treason!"

14 Then Jehoiada the priest ordered the commanders who were in charge of the troops, "Take her to the soldiers in front of the Temple,* and kill anyone who tries to rescue her." For the priest had said, "She must not be killed in the Temple of the LORD." 15 So they seized her and led her out to the entrance of the Horse Gate on the palace grounds, and they killed her there.

JEHOIADA'S RELIGIOUS REFORMS

16 Then Jehoiada made a covenant between himself and the king and the people that they would be the LORD's people. 17 And all the people went over to the temple of Baal and tore it down. They demolished the altars and smashed the idols, and they killed Mattan the priest of Baal in front of the altars.

18 Jehoiada now put the priests and Levites in charge of the Temple of the LORD, following all the directions given by David. He also commanded them to present burnt offerings to the LORD, as prescribed by the Law of Moses, and to sing and rejoice as David had instructed. 19 He also stationed gatekeepers at the gates of the LORD's Temple to keep out those who for any reason were ceremonially unclean.

20 Then the commanders, nobles, rulers, and all the people of the land escorted the king from the Temple of the LORD. They went through the upper gate and into the palace, and they seated the king on the royal throne. 21 So all the people of the land rejoiced, and the city was peaceful because Athaliah had been killed.

JOASH REPAIRS THE TEMPLE

24 Joash was seven years old when he became king, and he reigned in Jerusalem forty years. His mother was Zibiah from Beersheba. 2 Joash did what was pleasing in the LORD's sight throughout the lifetime of Jehoiada the priest. 3 Jehoiada chose two wives for Joash, and he had sons and daughters.

4 At one point Joash decided to repair and restore the Temple of the LORD. 5 He summoned the priests and Levites and gave them these instructions: "Go to all the towns of Judah and collect the required annual offerings, so that we can repair the Temple of your God. Do not delay!" But the Levites did not act immediately.

6 So the king called for Jehoiada the high priest and asked him, "Why haven't you demanded that the Levites go out and collect the Temple taxes from the towns of Judah and from Jerusalem? Moses, the servant of the LORD, levied this tax on the community of Israel in order to maintain the Tabernacle of the Covenant.*"

7 Over the years the followers of wicked Athaliah had broken into the Temple of God, and they had used all the dedicated things from the Temple of the LORD to worship the images of Baal.

8 So now the king ordered a chest to be made and set outside the gate leading to the Temple of the LORD. 9 Then a proclamation was sent throughout Judah and Jerusalem, telling the people to bring to the LORD the tax that Moses, the servant of God, had required of the Israelites in the wilderness. 10 This pleased all the leaders and the people, and they gladly brought their money and filled the chest with it.

11 Whenever the chest became full, the Levites would carry it to the king's officials. Then the court secretary and an officer of the high priest would come and empty the chest and take it back to the Temple again. This went on day after day, and a large amount of money was collected. 12 The king and Jehoiada gave the money to the construction supervisors, who hired masons and carpenters to restore the Temple of the LORD. They also hired metalworkers, who made articles of iron and bronze for the LORD's Temple.

13 The men in charge of the renovation worked hard and made steady progress. They restored the Temple of God according to its original design and strengthened it. 14 When all the repairs were finished, they brought the remaining money to the king and Jehoiada. It was used to make various articles for the Temple of the LORD—articles for worship services and for burnt offerings, including ladles and other articles made of gold and silver. And the burnt offerings were sacrificed continually in the Temple of the LORD during the lifetime of Jehoiada the priest.

15 Jehoiada lived to a very old age, finally dying at 130. 16 He was buried among the kings in the City of

23:11 Or *a copy of the covenant.* **23:14** Or *Bring her out from between the ranks;* or *Take her out of the Temple precincts.* The meaning of the Hebrew is uncertain. **24:6** Hebrew *Tent of the Testimony.*

23:13 Treason! Treason! Athaliah could not believe her ears. The sound of celebration suffocated her dream for royal power. Joash, the boy-king, would take her place. Her plan failed, and God's plan came into play.

24:2 throughout the lifetime of Jehoiada. With Jehoiada in the picture, King Joash could not go wrong. However, he forfeited his borrowed enthusiasm for God at Jehoiada's death.

24:4 Joash . . . restore the Temple of the LORD. Athaliah had left true worship in disarray. Restoring the temple was job number one.

24:5 Joash sent his Levitical priests in search of long overdue tax monies (Ex. 30:12-16).

David, because he had done so much good in Israel for God and his Temple.

JEHOIADA'S REFORMS REVERSED

17 But after Jehoiada's death, the leaders of Judah came and bowed before King Joash and persuaded him to listen to their advice. 18 They decided to abandon the Temple of the LORD, the God of their ancestors, and they worshiped Asherah poles and idols instead! Because of this sin, divine anger fell on Judah and Jerusalem. 19 Yet the LORD sent prophets to bring them back to him. The prophets warned them, but still the people would not listen.

20 Then the Spirit of God came upon Zechariah son of Jehoiada the priest. He stood before the people and said, "This is what God says: Why do you disobey the LORD's commands and keep yourselves from prospering? You have abandoned the LORD, and now he has abandoned you!"

21 Then the leaders plotted to kill Zechariah, and King Joash ordered that they stone him to death in the courtyard of the LORD's Temple. 22 That was how King Joash repaid Jehoiada for his loyalty—by killing his son. Zechariah's last words as he died were, "May the LORD see what they are doing and avenge my death!"

THE END OF JOASH'S REIGN

23 In the spring of the year* the Aramean army marched against Joash. They invaded Judah and Jerusalem and killed all the leaders of the nation. Then they sent all the plunder back to their king in Damascus. 24 Although the Arameans attacked with only a small army, the LORD helped them conquer the much larger army of Judah. The people of Judah had abandoned the LORD, the God of their ancestors, so judgment was carried out against Joash.

25 The Arameans withdrew, leaving Joash severely wounded. But his own officials plotted to kill him for murdering the son* of Jehoiada the priest. They assassinated him as he lay in bed. Then he was buried in the City of David, but not in the royal cemetery. 26 The assassins were Jozacar,* the son of an Ammonite woman named Shimeath, and Jehozabad, the son of a Moabite woman named Shomer.*

27 The account of the sons of Joash, the prophecies about him, and the record of his restoration of the Temple of God are written in *The Commentary on the Book of the Kings.* His son Amaziah became the next king.

AMAZIAH RULES IN JUDAH

25 Amaziah was twenty-five years old when he became king, and he reigned in Jerusalem twenty-nine years. His mother was Jehoaddin* from Jerusalem. 2 Amaziah did what was pleasing in the LORD's sight, but not wholeheartedly.

3 When Amaziah was well established as king, he executed the officials who had assassinated his father. 4 However, he did not kill the children of the assassins, for he obeyed the command of the LORD as written by Moses in the Book of the Law: "Parents must not be put to death for the sins of their children, nor children for the sins of their parents. Those deserving to die must be put to death for their own crimes."*

5 Then Amaziah organized the army, assigning generals and captains* for all Judah and Benjamin. He took a census and found that he had an army of 300,000 select troops, twenty years old and older, all trained in the use of spear and shield. 6 He also paid about 7,500 pounds* of silver to hire 100,000 experienced fighting men from Israel.

7 But a man of God came to him and said, "Your Majesty, do not hire troops from Israel, for the LORD is not with Israel. He will not help those people of Ephraim! 8 If you let them go with your troops into battle, you will be defeated by the enemy no matter how well you fight. God will overthrow you, for he has the power to help you or to trip you up."

9 Amaziah asked the man of God, "But what about all that silver I paid to hire the army of Israel?"

The man of God replied, "The LORD is able to give you much more than this!" 10 So Amaziah discharged the hired troops and sent them back to Ephraim. This made them very angry with Judah, and they returned home in a great rage.

11 Then Amaziah summoned his courage and led his army to the Valley of Salt, where they killed 10,000 Edomite troops from Seir. 12 They captured another 10,000 and took them to the top of a cliff and threw them off, dashing them to pieces on the rocks below.

13 Meanwhile, the hired troops that Amaziah had sent home raided several of the towns of Judah between Samaria and Beth-horon. They killed 3,000 people and carried off great quantities of plunder.

14 When King Amaziah returned from slaughtering the Edomites, he brought with him idols taken from the people of Seir. He set them up as his own gods, bowed down in front of them, and offered sacrifices to them! 15 This made the LORD very angry, and he sent a prophet to ask, "Why do you turn to gods who could not even save their own people from you?"

24:23 Hebrew *At the turn of the year.* The first day of the year in the ancient Hebrew lunar calendar occurred in March or April. **24:25** As in Greek version and Latin Vulgate; Hebrew reads *sons.* **24:26a** As in parallel text at 2 Kgs 12:21; Hebrew reads *Zabad.* **24:26b** As in parallel text at 2 Kgs 12:21; Hebrew reads *Shimrith,* a variant spelling of Shomer. **25:1** As in parallel text at 2 Kgs 14:2; Hebrew reads *Jehoaddan,* a variant spelling of Jehoaddin. **25:4** Deut 24:16. **25:5** Hebrew *commanders of thousands and commanders of hundreds.* **25:6** Hebrew *100 talents* [3,400 kilograms].

24:19 the LORD sent them prophets . . . but still the people would not listen. This is a summary of most of Israel's history. Only when prophets were dead and long gone did the people respect their voice.

24:21 Kin Joash ordered . . . stone him to death. This was the fate of far too many of the prophets. Jesus told the parable of the vineyard owner (Matt. 22:33-46) to condemn the way Israel had so often rejected and killed the prophets. Stephen was stoned for reminding the religious leaders of Israel of this tendency (see Acts 7:51-60).

24:24 judgment was carried out against Joash. The king pays for the sins of the people. Joash suffered an inexplicable defeat at the hands of a smaller army.

24:25 Joash . . . to kill . . . buried . . . not in the royal cemetery. Like Jehoram before him, Joash's undignified burial marks the dishonor of his evil life.

25:1 Amaziah. His reign was basically good but not wholeheartedly godly.

25:2 Amaziah battled idolatry with lesser zeal than he should. Even though he did "what was pleasing in the LORD's sight," he did not do so "wholeheartedly."

25:7 the LORD is not with Israel. Hosting Israel's troops within his ranks would invite a curse. Amaziah wisely dismissed them.

25:14-25 Amaziah was so taken with the spoils of victory that he actually worshiped his plunder. In heavenly irony, God used a taunting northern king to punish Amaziah's foolishness.

16 But the king interrupted him and said, "Since
when have I made you the king's counselor? Be quiet
now before I have you killed!"
So the prophet stopped with this warning: "I know
that God has determined to destroy you because you
have done this and have refused to accept my counsel."
17 After consulting with his advisers, King Amaziah
of Judah sent this challenge to Israel's king Jehoash,*
the son of Jehoahaz and grandson of Jehu: "Come and
meet me in battle!"*
18 But King Jehoash of Israel replied to King Amaziah of Judah with this story: "Out in the Lebanon
mountains, a thistle sent a message to a mighty cedar tree: 'Give your daughter in marriage to my son.'
But just then a wild animal of Lebanon came by and
stepped on the thistle, crushing it!
19 "You are saying, 'I have defeated Edom,' and you
are very proud of it. But my advice is to stay at home.
Why stir up trouble that will only bring disaster on
you and the people of Judah?"
20 But Amaziah refused to listen, for God was determined to destroy him for turning to the gods of
Edom. 21 So King Jehoash of Israel mobilized his army
against King Amaziah of Judah. The two armies drew
up their battle lines at Beth-shemesh in Judah. 22 Judah was routed by the army of Israel, and its army
scattered and fled for home. 23 King Jehoash of Israel captured Judah's king, Amaziah son of Joash and
grandson of Ahaziah, at Beth-shemesh. Then he
brought him to Jerusalem, where he demolished
600 feet* of Jerusalem's wall, from the Ephraim Gate
to the Corner Gate. 24 He carried off all the gold and
silver and all the articles from the Temple of God that
had been in the care of Obed-edom. He also seized the
treasures of the royal palace, along with hostages,
and then returned to Samaria.
25 King Amaziah of Judah lived for fifteen years
after the death of King Jehoash of Israel. 26 The rest
of the events in Amaziah's reign, from beginning to
end, are recorded in *The Book of the Kings of Judah
and Israel.*
27 After Amaziah turned away from the LORD, there
was a conspiracy against his life in Jerusalem, and he
fled to Lachish. But his enemies sent assassins after
him, and they killed him there. 28 They brought his
body back on a horse, and he was buried with his ancestors in the City of David.*

UZZIAH RULES IN JUDAH

26 All the people of Judah had crowned Amaziah's sixteen-year-old son, Uzziah, as king in
place of his father. 2 After his father's death, Uzziah
rebuilt the town of Elath* and restored it to Judah.
3 Uzziah was sixteen years old when he became
king, and he reigned in Jerusalem fifty-two years. His
mother was Jecoliah from Jerusalem. 4 He did what
was pleasing in the LORD's sight, just as his father,
Amaziah, had done. 5 Uzziah sought God during the
days of Zechariah, who taught him to fear God.* And
as long as the king sought guidance from the LORD,
God gave him success.
6 Uzziah declared war on the Philistines and broke
down the walls of Gath, Jabneh, and Ashdod. Then
he built new towns in the Ashdod area and in other
parts of Philistia. 7 God helped him in his wars against
the Philistines, his battles with the Arabs of Gur,* and
his wars with the Meunites. 8 The Meunites* paid
annual tribute to him, and his fame spread even to
Egypt, for he had become very powerful.
9 Uzziah built fortified towers in Jerusalem at the
Corner Gate, at the Valley Gate, and at the angle in
the wall. 10 He also constructed forts in the wilderness
and dug many water cisterns, because he kept great
herds of livestock in the foothills of Judah* and on
the plains. He was also a man who loved the soil. He
had many workers who cared for his farms and vineyards, both on the hillsides and in the fertile valleys.
11 Uzziah had an army of well-trained warriors,
ready to march into battle, unit by unit. This army
had been mustered and organized by Jeiel, the secretary of the army, and his assistant, Maaseiah. They
were under the direction of Hananiah, one of the
king's officials. 12 These regiments of mighty warriors
were commanded by 2,600 clan leaders. 13 The army
consisted of 307,500 men, all elite troops. They were
prepared to assist the king against any enemy.
14 Uzziah provided the entire army with shields,
spears, helmets, coats of mail, bows, and sling stones.
15 And he built structures on the walls of Jerusalem,
designed by experts to protect those who shot arrows
and hurled large stones* from the towers and the corners of the wall. His fame spread far and wide, for the
LORD gave him marvelous help, and he became very
powerful.

UZZIAH'S SIN AND PUNISHMENT

16 But when he had become powerful, he also became
proud, which led to his downfall. He sinned against the
LORD his God by entering the sanctuary of the LORD's
Temple and personally burning incense on the incense
altar. 17 Azariah the high priest went in after him with
eighty other priests of the LORD, all brave men. 18 They
confronted King Uzziah and said, "It is not for you, Uzziah, to burn incense to the LORD. That is the work of
the priests alone, the descendants of Aaron who are set
apart for this work. Get out of the sanctuary, for you
have sinned. The LORD God will not honor you for this!"
19 Uzziah, who was holding an incense burner, became furious. But as he was standing there raging
at the priests before the incense altar in the LORD's
Temple, leprosy* suddenly broke out on his fore

25:17a Hebrew *Joash,* a variant spelling of Jehoash; also in 25:18, 21, 23, 25. **25:17b** Hebrew *Come, let us look one another in the face.* **25:23** Hebrew *400 cubits* [180 meters]. **25:28** As in some Hebrew manuscripts and other ancient versions (see also 2 Kgs 14:20); most Hebrew manuscripts read *the city of Judah.* **26:2** As in Greek version (see also 2 Kgs 14:22; 16:6); Hebrew reads *Eloth,* a variant spelling of Elath. **26:5** As in Syriac and Greek versions; Hebrew reads *who instructed him in divine visions.* **26:7** As in Greek version; Hebrew reads *Gur-baal.* **26:8** As in Greek version; Hebrew reads *Ammonites.* Compare 26:7. **26:10** Hebrew *the Shephelah.* **26:15** Or *to shoot arrows and hurl large stones.* **26:19** Or *a contagious skin disease.* The Hebrew word used here and throughout this passage can describe various skin diseases.

26:1 Uzziah was sixteen. He started his reign as an adolescent and ended as a convalescent, 52 years later.

26:5 as long as the king sought guidance from the LORD. Uzziah's secret to success is no surprise. Obedience is the consistent key in the Davidic line.

26:16 when he had become powerful, he also became proud. How one handles power and success is an important test of character. David remained humble even after his great victories (2 Sam. 6:22), but Uzziah became full of himself.

head. [20] When Azariah the high priest and all the other priests saw the leprosy, they rushed him out. And the king himself was eager to get out because the LORD had struck him. [21] So King Uzziah had leprosy until the day he died. He lived in isolation in a separate house, for he was excluded from the Temple of the LORD. His son Jotham was put in charge of the royal palace, and he governed the people of the land.

[22] The rest of the events of Uzziah's reign, from beginning to end, are recorded by the prophet Isaiah son of Amoz. [23] When Uzziah died, he was buried with his ancestors; his grave was in a nearby burial field belonging to the kings, for the people said, "He had leprosy." And his son Jotham became the next king.

JOTHAM RULES IN JUDAH

27 Jotham was twenty-five years old when he became king, and he reigned in Jerusalem sixteen years. His mother was Jerusha, the daughter of Zadok.

[2] Jotham did what was pleasing in the LORD's sight. He did everything his father, Uzziah, had done, except that Jotham did not sin by entering the Temple of the LORD. But the people continued in their corrupt ways.

[3] Jotham rebuilt the upper gate of the Temple of the LORD. He also did extensive rebuilding on the wall at the hill of Ophel. [4] He built towns in the hill country of Judah and constructed fortresses and towers in the wooded areas. [5] Jotham went to war against the Ammonites and conquered them. Over the next three years he received from them an annual tribute of 7,500 pounds* of silver, 50,000 bushels of wheat, and 50,000 bushels of barley.*

[6] King Jotham became powerful because he was careful to live in obedience to the LORD his God.

[7] The rest of the events of Jotham's reign, including all his wars and other activities, are recorded in *The Book of the Kings of Israel and Judah.* [8] He was twenty-five years old when he became king, and he reigned in Jerusalem sixteen years. [9] When Jotham died, he was buried in the City of David. And his son Ahaz became the next king.

AHAZ RULES IN JUDAH

28 Ahaz was twenty years old when he became king, and he reigned in Jerusalem sixteen years. He did not do what was pleasing in the sight of the LORD, as his ancestor David had done. [2] Instead, he followed the example of the kings of Israel. He cast metal images for the worship of Baal. [3] He offered sacrifices in the valley of Ben-Hinnom, even sacrificing his own sons in the fire.* In this way, he followed the detestable practices of the pagan nations the LORD had driven from the land ahead of the Israelites. [4] He offered sacrifices and burned incense at the pagan shrines and on the hills and under every green tree.

[5] Because of all this, the LORD his God allowed the king of Aram to defeat Ahaz and to exile large numbers of his people to Damascus. The armies of the king of Israel also defeated Ahaz and inflicted many casualties on his army. [6] In a single day Pekah son of Remaliah, Israel's king, killed 120,000 of Judah's troops, all of them experienced warriors, because they had abandoned the LORD, the God of their ancestors. [7] Then Zicri, a warrior from Ephraim, killed Maaseiah, the king's son; Azrikam, the king's palace commander; and Elkanah, the king's second-in-command. [8] The armies of Israel captured 200,000 women and children from Judah and seized tremendous amounts of plunder, which they took back to Samaria.

[9] But a prophet of the LORD named Oded was there in Samaria when the army of Israel returned home. He went out to meet them and said, "The LORD, the God of your ancestors, was angry with Judah and let you defeat them. But you have gone too far, killing them without mercy, and all heaven is disturbed. [10] And now you are planning to make slaves of these people from Judah and Jerusalem. What about your own sins against the LORD your God? [11] Listen to me and return these prisoners you have taken, for they are your own relatives. Watch out, because now the LORD's fierce anger has been turned against you!"

[12] Then some of the leaders of Israel*—Azariah son of Jehohanan, Berekiah son of Meshillemoth, Jehizkiah son of Shallum, and Amasa son of Hadlai—agreed with this and confronted the men returning from battle. [13] "You must not bring the prisoners here!" they declared. "We cannot afford to add to our sins and guilt. Our guilt is already great, and the LORD's fierce anger is already turned against Israel."

[14] So the warriors released the prisoners and handed over the plunder in the sight of the leaders and all the people. [15] Then the four men just mentioned by name came forward and distributed clothes from the plunder to the prisoners who were naked. They provided clothing and sandals to wear, gave them enough food and drink, and dressed their wounds with olive oil. They put those who were weak on donkeys and took all the prisoners back to their own people in Jericho, the city of palms. Then they returned to Samaria.

AHAZ CLOSES THE TEMPLE

[16] At that time King Ahaz of Judah asked the king of Assyria for help. [17] The armies of Edom had again invaded Judah and taken captives. [18] And the Philistines had raided towns located in the foothills of Judah* and in the Negev of Judah. They had already captured and occupied Beth-shemesh, Aijalon, Gederoth, Soco with its villages, Timnah with its villages, and Gimzo with its villages. [19] The LORD was humbling Judah because of King Ahaz of Judah,* for he had encouraged his people to sin and had been utterly unfaithful to the LORD.

27:5a Hebrew *100 talents* [3,400 kilograms]. **27:5b** Hebrew *10,000 cors* [2,200 kiloliters] *of wheat, and 10,000 cors of barley.* **28:3** Or *even making his sons pass through the fire.* **28:12** Hebrew *Ephraim,* referring to the northern kingdom of Israel. **28:18** Hebrew *the Shephelah.* **28:19** Masoretic Text reads *of Israel;* also in 28:23, 27. The author of Chronicles sees Judah as representative of the true Israel. (Some Hebrew manuscripts and Greek version read *of Judah.*)

26:22 Isaiah son of Amoz. Isaiah got his famous call as a prophet "In the year that King Uzziah died" (Isa. 6:1).

27:1 sixteen years. Jotham began his rule alongside his incapacitated father during the last years of his leprosy-ridden reign.

27:6 Jotham became powerful. Because Jotham was a righteous king, God gave him some prosperous and relatively uneventful years.

28:1-27 Ahaz's life was riddled with reprehensible behavior (see 2 Kings 16:1-20). He was more akin to the wretchedness of the northern kingdom.

28:17-18 Just when Ahaz thought things could not get worse, they did. His enemies declared open season on Judah.

20 So when King Tiglath-pileser* of Assyria arrived, he attacked Ahaz instead of helping him. 21 Ahaz took valuable items from the LORD's Temple, the royal palace, and from the homes of his officials and gave them to the king of Assyria as tribute. But this did not help him.

22 Even during this time of trouble, King Ahaz continued to reject the LORD. 23 He offered sacrifices to the gods of Damascus who had defeated him, for he said, "Since these gods helped the kings of Aram, they will help me, too, if I sacrifice to them." But instead, they led to his ruin and the ruin of all Judah.

24 The king took the various articles from the Temple of God and broke them into pieces. He shut the doors of the LORD's Temple so that no one could worship there, and he set up altars to pagan gods in every corner of Jerusalem. 25 He made pagan shrines in all the towns of Judah for offering sacrifices to other gods. In this way, he aroused the anger of the LORD, the God of his ancestors.

26 The rest of the events of Ahaz's reign and everything he did, from beginning to end, are recorded in *The Book of the Kings of Judah and Israel.* 27 When Ahaz died, he was buried in Jerusalem but not in the royal cemetery of the kings of Judah. Then his son Hezekiah became the next king.

HEZEKIAH RULES IN JUDAH

29 Hezekiah was twenty-five years old when he became the king of Judah, and he reigned in Jerusalem twenty-nine years. His mother was Abijah, the daughter of Zechariah. 2 He did what was pleasing in the LORD's sight, just as his ancestor David had done.

HEZEKIAH REOPENS THE TEMPLE

3 In the very first month of the first year of his reign, Hezekiah reopened the doors of the Temple of the LORD and repaired them. 4 He summoned the priests and Levites to meet him at the courtyard east of the Temple. 5 He said to them, "Listen to me, you Levites! Purify yourselves, and purify the Temple of the LORD, the God of your ancestors. Remove all the defiled things from the sanctuary. 6 Our ancestors were unfaithful and did what was evil in the sight of the LORD our God. They abandoned the LORD and his dwelling place; they turned their backs on him. 7 They also shut the doors to the Temple's entry room, and they snuffed out the lamps. They stopped burning incense and presenting burnt offerings at the sanctuary of the God of Israel.

8 "That is why the LORD's anger has fallen upon Judah and Jerusalem. He has made them an object of dread, horror, and ridicule, as you can see with your own eyes. 9 Because of this, our fathers have been killed in battle, and our sons and daughters and wives have been captured. 10 But now I will make a covenant with the LORD, the God of Israel, so that his fierce anger will turn away from us. 11 My sons, do not neglect your duties any longer! The LORD has chosen you to stand in his presence, to minister to him, and to lead the people in worship and present offerings to him."

12 Then these Levites got right to work:

From the clan of Kohath: Mahath son of Amasai and Joel son of Azariah.
From the clan of Merari: Kish son of Abdi and Azariah son of Jehallelel.
From the clan of Gershon: Joah son of Zimmah and Eden son of Joah.
13 From the family of Elizaphan: Shimri and Jeiel.
From the family of Asaph: Zechariah and Mattaniah.
14 From the family of Heman: Jehiel and Shimei.
From the family of Jeduthun: Shemaiah and Uzziel.

15 These men called together their fellow Levites, and they all purified themselves. Then they began to cleanse the Temple of the LORD, just as the king had commanded. They were careful to follow all the LORD's instructions in their work. 16 The priests went into the sanctuary of the Temple of the LORD to cleanse it, and they took out to the Temple courtyard all the defiled things they found. From there the Levites carted it all out to the Kidron Valley.

17 They began the work in early spring, on the first day of the new year,* and in eight days they had reached the entry room of the LORD's Temple. Then they purified the Temple of the LORD itself, which took another eight days. So the entire task was completed in sixteen days.

THE TEMPLE REDEDICATION

18 Then the Levites went to King Hezekiah and gave him this report: "We have cleansed the entire Temple of the LORD, the altar of burnt offering with all its utensils, and the table of the Bread of the Presence with all its utensils. 19 We have also recovered all the items discarded by King Ahaz when he was unfaithful and closed the Temple. They are now in front of the altar of the LORD, purified and ready for use."

20 Early the next morning King Hezekiah gathered the city officials and went to the Temple of the LORD. 21 They brought seven bulls, seven rams, and seven male lambs as a burnt offering, together with seven male goats as a sin offering for the kingdom, for the Temple, and for Judah. The king commanded the priests, who were descendants of Aaron, to sacrifice the animals on the altar of the LORD.

22 So they killed the bulls, and the priests took the blood and sprinkled it on the altar. Next they killed

28:20 Hebrew *Tilgath-pilneser,* a variant spelling of Tiglath-pileser. **29:17** Hebrew *on the first day of the first month.* This day in the ancient Hebrew lunar calendar occurred in March or early April, 715 B.C.

28:20 Tiglath-pileser of Assyria. Assyria answered Ahaz's cry for help but brought more harm than good.

28:24-25 Not only did Ahaz bar the temple shut, but he went one step further. He prohibited worshiping God—the faith of his fathers was now a crime.

28:27 Ahaz . . . buried in Jerusalem. He was ousted from the royal cemetery—a sign that he could not eradicate religion completely.

29:1–32:33 Hezekiah's rule is refreshing. Finally, a king with stamina to stand up against the rule of evil. He is noted for his religious reforms and restoration of the temple worship.

29:1 Hezekiah . . . reigned . . . twenty-nine years. Halfway into his reign Hezekiah became deathly ill (2 Kings 20:1). The Lord was gracious and allowed him to rule another 15 years (2 Kings 20:6).

29:5-11 Hezekiah knew how to read the signs, explaining the simple history lesson in terms of cause and effect.

29:7 burning incense . . . burnt offerings. Solomon's solemn religious orders seem almost like ancient history (2:4; 4:7), but they are just the remedy needed to rejuvenate Judah's languishing faith.

the rams and sprinkled their blood on the altar. And
finally, they did the same with the male lambs. 23 The
male goats for the sin offering were then brought
before the king and the assembly of people, who laid
their hands on them. 24 The priests then killed the
goats as a sin offering and sprinkled their blood on
the altar to make atonement for the sins of all Israel.
The king had specifically commanded that this burnt
offering and sin offering should be made for all Israel.
25 King Hezekiah then stationed the Levites at the
Temple of the LORD with cymbals, lyres, and harps.
He obeyed all the commands that the LORD had giv-
en to King David through Gad, the king's seer, and
the prophet Nathan. 26 The Levites then took their
positions around the Temple with the instruments of
David, and the priests took their positions with the
trumpets.
27 Then Hezekiah ordered that the burnt offering
be placed on the altar. As the burnt offering was pre-
sented, songs of praise to the LORD were begun, ac-
companied by the trumpets and other instruments of
David, the former king of Israel. 28 The entire assembly
worshiped the LORD as the singers sang and the trum-
pets blew, until all the burnt offerings were finished.
29 Then the king and everyone with him bowed down
in worship. 30 King Hezekiah and the officials ordered
the Levites to praise the LORD with the psalms written
by David and by Asaph the seer. So they offered joy-
ous praise and bowed down in worship.
31 Then Hezekiah declared, "Now that you have con-
secrated yourselves to the LORD, bring your sacrifices
and thanksgiving offerings to the Temple of the LORD."
So the people brought their sacrifices and thanks-
giving offerings, and all whose hearts were willing
brought burnt offerings, too. 32 The people brought to
the LORD 70 bulls, 100 rams, and 200 male lambs for
burnt offerings. 33 They also brought 600 cattle and
3,000 sheep and goats as sacred offerings.
34 But there were too few priests to prepare all the
burnt offerings. So their relatives the Levites helped
them until the work was finished and more priests
had been purified, for the Levites had been more
conscientious about purifying themselves than the
priests had been. 35 There was an abundance of burnt
offerings, along with the usual liquid offerings, and a
great deal of fat from the many peace offerings.
So the Temple of the LORD was restored to service.
36 And Hezekiah and all the people rejoiced because of
what God had done for the people, for everything had
been accomplished so quickly.

PREPARATIONS FOR PASSOVER

30 King Hezekiah now sent word to all Israel and
Judah, and he wrote letters of invitation to the
people of Ephraim and Manasseh. He asked every-
one to come to the Temple of the LORD at Jerusalem to
celebrate the Passover of the LORD, the God of Israel.
2 The king, his officials, and all the community of Je-
rusalem decided to celebrate Passover a month later
than usual.* 3 They were unable to celebrate it at the
prescribed time because not enough priests could be
purified by then, and the people had not yet assem-
bled at Jerusalem.
4 This plan for keeping the Passover seemed right
to the king and all the people. 5 So they sent a procla-
mation throughout all Israel, from Beersheba in the
south to Dan in the north, inviting everyone to come
to Jerusalem to celebrate the Passover of the LORD, the
God of Israel. The people had not been celebrating it
in great numbers as required in the Law.
6 At the king's command, runners were sent
throughout Israel and Judah. They carried letters
that said:

"O people of Israel, return to the LORD, the God of
Abraham, Isaac, and Israel,* so that he will return
to the few of us who have survived the conquest of
the Assyrian kings. 7 Do not be like your ancestors
and relatives who abandoned the LORD, the God of
their ancestors, and became an object of derision,
as you yourselves can see. 8 Do not be stubborn,
as they were, but submit yourselves to the LORD.
Come to his Temple, which he has set apart as holy
forever. Worship the LORD your God so that his
fierce anger will turn away from you.
9 "For if you return to the LORD, your relatives
and your children will be treated mercifully by
their captors, and they will be able to return to
this land. For the LORD your God is gracious and
merciful. If you return to him, he will not continue
to turn his face from you."

CELEBRATION OF PASSOVER

10 The runners went from town to town throughout
Ephraim and Manasseh and as far as the territory
of Zebulun. But most of the people just laughed at
the runners and made fun of them. 11 However, some
people from Asher, Manasseh, and Zebulun humbled
themselves and went to Jerusalem.
12 At the same time, God's hand was on the people
in the land of Judah, giving them all one heart to obey
the orders of the king and his officials, who were fol-
lowing the word of the LORD. 13 So a huge crowd as-
sembled at Jerusalem in midspring* to celebrate the
Festival of Unleavened Bread. 14 They set to work and
removed the pagan altars from Jerusalem. They took
away all the incense altars and threw them into the
Kidron Valley.
15 On the fourteenth day of the second month, one
month later than usual,* the people slaughtered the
Passover lamb. This shamed the priests and Levites,
so they purified themselves and brought burnt of-

30:2 Hebrew *in the second month.* Passover was normally observed in the first month (of the ancient Hebrew lunar calendar). 30:6 *Israel* is the name that God gave to Jacob. 30:13 Hebrew *in the second month.* The second month of the ancient Hebrew lunar calendar usually occurs within the months of April and May. 30:15 Hebrew *On the fourteenth day of the second month.* Passover normally began on the fourteenth day of the first month (see Lev 23:5).

29:35 offerings. These personal offerings express the repentance of the individual, not just the corporate response of the nation.

30:1-27 Now Hezekiah is getting somewhere. He celebrates his monumental progress with a Passover feast. The people of Judah and remnants of Israel witness an unprecedented spiritual renewal.

30:2 Passover. The people plan a nationwide unity celebration, inviting refugees of the northern kingdom and Ephraim and Manasseh.

30:9 captors. The Assyrians now dominate the northern kingdom, having captured most of its inhabitants. Those who remain are challenged to demonstrate their allegiance to God by attending the feast.

30:15 priests and Levites. In order to maintain the spiritual momentum, Hezekiah turns to those commissioned to be holy examples among the people.

ferings to the Temple of the LORD. [16] Then they took
their places at the Temple as prescribed in the Law of
Moses, the man of God. The Levites brought the sac-
rificial blood to the priests, who then sprinkled it on
the altar.
[17] Since many of the people had not purified
themselves, the Levites had to slaughter their Pass-
over lamb for them, to set them apart for the LORD.
[18] Most of those who came from Ephraim, Manas-
seh, Issachar, and Zebulun had not purified them-
selves. But King Hezekiah prayed for them, and
they were allowed to eat the Passover meal anyway,
even though this was contrary to the requirements
of the Law. For Hezekiah said, "May the LORD, who
is good, pardon those [19] who decide to follow the
LORD, the God of their ancestors, even though they
are not properly cleansed for the ceremony." [20] And
the LORD listened to Hezekiah's prayer and healed
the people.
[21] So the people of Israel who were present in Jeru-
salem joyously celebrated the Festival of Unleavened
Bread for seven days. Each day the Levites and priests
sang to the LORD, accompanied by loud instruments.*
[22] Hezekiah encouraged all the Levites regarding the
skill they displayed as they served the LORD. The cel-
ebration continued for seven days. Peace offerings
were sacrificed, and the people gave thanks to the
LORD, the God of their ancestors.
[23] The entire assembly then decided to continue the
festival another seven days, so they celebrated joyful-
ly for another week. [24] King Hezekiah gave the people
1,000 bulls and 7,000 sheep and goats for offerings,
and the officials donated 1,000 bulls and 10,000 sheep
and goats. Meanwhile, many more priests purified
themselves.
[25] The entire assembly of Judah rejoiced, including
the priests, the Levites, all who came from the land
of Israel, the foreigners who came to the festival, and
all those who lived in Judah. [26] There was great joy
in the city, for Jerusalem had not seen a celebration
like this one since the days of Solomon, King David's
son. [27] Then the priests and Levites stood and blessed
the people, and God heard their prayer from his holy
dwelling in heaven.

HEZEKIAH'S RELIGIOUS REFORMS

31 When the festival ended, the Israelites who
attended went to all the towns of Judah, Ben-
jamin, Ephraim, and Manasseh, and they smashed
all the sacred pillars, cut down the Asherah poles,
and removed the pagan shrines and altars. After
this, the Israelites returned to their own towns and
homes.
[2] Hezekiah then organized the priests and Levites
into divisions to offer the burnt offerings and peace
offerings, and to worship and give thanks and praise
to the LORD at the gates of the Temple. [3] The king also
made a personal contribution of animals for the dai-
ly morning and evening burnt offerings, the weekly
Sabbath festivals, the monthly new moon festivals,
and the annual festivals as prescribed in the Law of
the LORD. [4] In addition, he required the people in Jeru-
salem to bring a portion of their goods to the priests
and Levites, so they could devote themselves fully to
the Law of the LORD.
[5] When the people of Israel heard these require-
ments, they responded generously by bringing the
first share of their grain, new wine, olive oil, honey,
and all the produce of their fields. They brought a
large quantity—a tithe of all they produced. [6] The
people who had moved to Judah from Israel, and the
people of Judah themselves, brought in the tithes of
their cattle, sheep, and goats and a tithe of the things
that had been dedicated to the LORD their God, and
they piled them up in great heaps. [7] They began pil-
ing them up in late spring, and the heaps continued to
grow until early autumn.* [8] When Hezekiah and his
officials came and saw these huge piles, they thanked
the LORD and his people Israel!
[9] "Where did all this come from?" Hezekiah asked
the priests and Levites.
[10] And Azariah the high priest, from the family of
Zadok, replied, "Since the people began bringing their
gifts to the LORD's Temple, we have had enough to eat
and plenty to spare. The LORD has blessed his people,
and all this is left over."
[11] Hezekiah ordered that storerooms be prepared
in the Temple of the LORD. When this was done, [12] the
people faithfully brought all the gifts, tithes, and oth-
er items dedicated for use in the Temple. Conaniah
the Levite was put in charge, assisted by his brother
Shimei. [13] The supervisors under them were Jehiel,
Azaziah, Nahath, Asahel, Jerimoth, Jozabad, Eliel, Is-
makiah, Mahath, and Benaiah. These appointments
were made by King Hezekiah and Azariah, the chief
official in the Temple of God.
[14] Kore son of Imnah the Levite, who was the gate-
keeper at the East Gate, was put in charge of distribut-
ing the voluntary offerings given to God, the gifts, and
the things that had been dedicated to the LORD. [15] His
faithful assistants were Eden, Miniamin, Jeshua, She-
maiah, Amariah, and Shecaniah. They distributed the
gifts among the families of priests in their towns by
their divisions, dividing the gifts fairly among old and
young alike. [16] They distributed the gifts to all males
three years old or older, regardless of their place
in the genealogical records. The distribution went
to all who would come to the LORD's Temple to per-
form their daily duties according to their divisions.
[17] They distributed gifts to the priests who were listed
by their families in the genealogical records, and to
the Levites twenty years old or older who were list-
ed according to their jobs and their divisions. [18] Food
allotments were also given to the families of all those

30:21 Or *sang to the LORD with all their strength.* **31:7** Hebrew *in the third month . . . until the seventh month.* The third month of the ancient Hebrew lunar calendar usually occurs within the months of May and June; the seventh month usually occurs within September and October.

30:17 Passover lamb. The Levites eagerly serve the people who come to the Passover unprepared. Just like in old times, the Levites slay the lambs for the people's sacrifice.

30:18-19 Hezekiah, ever the diplomat, smoothes the transition from heathen to holiness for those who attend the Passover.

30:26 celebration like this one since the days of Solomon. The chronicler cannot resist drawing the parallels between the overt religious emphasis of Hezekiah and that of Solomon.

31:2 Hezekiah single-handedly motivates the people to an inspired movement. Then he directs the details of the operation among his staff.

31:3 king also made a personal contribution. David showed the power of example (1 Chron. 29:3-9). Hezekiah discovers its motivational strength by giving generously toward his own project.

31:5 by bringing the first share. Tithing (giving a tenth of one's income) is a solid biblical guideline for stewardship.

listed in the genealogical records, including their little babies, wives, sons, and daughters. For they had all been faithful in purifying themselves.
[19] As for the priests, the descendants of Aaron, who were living in the open villages around the towns, men were appointed by name to distribute portions to every male among the priests and to all the Levites listed in the genealogical records.
[20] In this way, King Hezekiah handled the distribution throughout all Judah, doing what was pleasing and good in the sight of the LORD his God. [21] In all that he did in the service of the Temple of God and in his efforts to follow God's laws and commands, Hezekiah sought his God wholeheartedly. As a result, he was very successful.

ASSYRIA INVADES JUDAH

32 After Hezekiah had faithfully carried out this work, King Sennacherib of Assyria invaded Judah. He laid siege to the fortified towns, giving orders for his army to break through their walls. [2] When Hezekiah realized that Sennacherib also intended to attack Jerusalem, [3] he consulted with his officials and military advisers, and they decided to stop the flow of the springs outside the city. [4] They organized a huge work crew to stop the flow of the springs, cutting off the brook that ran through the fields. For they said, "Why should the kings of Assyria come here and find plenty of water?"
[5] Then Hezekiah worked hard at repairing all the broken sections of the wall, erecting towers, and constructing a second wall outside the first. He also reinforced the supporting terraces* in the City of David and manufactured large numbers of weapons and shields. [6] He appointed military officers over the people and assembled them before him in the square at the city gate. Then Hezekiah encouraged them by saying: [7] "Be strong and courageous! Don't be afraid or discouraged because of the king of Assyria or his mighty army, for there is a power far greater on our side! [8] He may have a great army, but they are merely men. We have the LORD our God to help us and to fight our battles for us!" Hezekiah's words greatly encouraged the people.

SENNACHERIB THREATENS JERUSALEM

[9] While King Sennacherib of Assyria was still besieging the town of Lachish, he sent his officers to Jerusalem with this message for Hezekiah and all the people in the city:

[10] "This is what King Sennacherib of Assyria says: What are you trusting in that makes you think you can survive my siege of Jerusalem? [11] Hezekiah has said, 'The LORD our God will rescue us from the king of Assyria.' Surely Hezekiah is misleading you, sentencing you to death by famine and thirst! [12] Don't you realize that Hezekiah is the very person who destroyed all the LORD's shrines and altars? He commanded Judah and Jerusalem to worship only at the altar at the Temple and to offer sacrifices on it alone.
[13] "Surely you must realize what I and the other kings of Assyria before me have done to all the people of the earth! Were any of the gods of those nations able to rescue their people from my power? [14] Which of their gods was able to rescue its people from the destructive power of my predecessors? What makes you think your God can rescue you from me? [15] Don't let Hezekiah deceive you! Don't let him fool you like this! I say it again—no god of any nation or kingdom has ever yet been able to rescue his people from me or my ancestors. How much less will your God rescue you from my power!"

[16] And Sennacherib's officers further mocked the LORD God and his servant Hezekiah, heaping insult upon insult. [17] The king also sent letters scorning the LORD, the God of Israel. He wrote, "Just as the gods of all the other nations failed to rescue their people from my power, so the God of Hezekiah will also fail." [18] The Assyrian officials who brought the letters shouted this in Hebrew* to the people gathered on the walls of the city, trying to terrify them so it would be easier to capture the city. [19] These officers talked about the God of Jerusalem as though he were one of the pagan gods, made by human hands.
[20] Then King Hezekiah and the prophet Isaiah son of Amoz cried out in prayer to God in heaven. [21] And the LORD sent an angel who destroyed the Assyrian army with all its commanders and officers. So Sennacherib was forced to return home in disgrace to his own land. And when he entered the temple of his god, some of his own sons killed him there with a sword.
[22] That is how the LORD rescued Hezekiah and the people of Jerusalem from King Sennacherib of Assyria and from all the others who threatened them. So there was peace throughout the land. [23] From then on King Hezekiah became highly respected among all the surrounding nations, and many gifts for the LORD arrived at Jerusalem, with valuable presents for King Hezekiah, too.

HEZEKIAH'S SICKNESS AND RECOVERY

[24] About that time Hezekiah became deathly ill. He prayed to the LORD, who healed him and gave him a miraculous sign. [25] But Hezekiah did not respond appropriately to the kindness shown him, and he became proud. So the LORD's anger came against him and against Judah and Jerusalem. [26] Then Hezekiah humbled himself and repented of his pride, as did the people of Jerusalem. So the LORD's anger did not fall on them during Hezekiah's lifetime.

32:5 Hebrew *the millo.* The meaning of the Hebrew is uncertain. 32:18 Hebrew *in the dialect of Judah.*

32:1-23 Hezekiah encountered an Assyrian king with an attitude. It is one thing to challenge a godly king. Sennacherib, however, defied God Himself (vv. 10-15). The result was humiliating disaster for Assyria (vv. 20-21).

32:5-8 Then Hezekiah worked hard . . . Then Hezekiah encouraged them. Hezekiah showed himself to be a good military leader by taking both practical steps (rebuilding) and spiritual steps (encouraging his people and pointing them to faith) to be able to resist their enemy.

32:9 Sennacherib. Sennacherib began his battle with a war of words. He insulted Judah's king and Judah's God. His aim was to demoralize his enemy, to intimidate them into submission. The chronicler leaves out Hezekiah's response (2 Kings 18:14-16).

32:14 Which of their gods. Sennacherib was calling the people of Israel to question whether their God was truly different than the gods of those around them. There was in fact an important difference. The gods of other nations were simply objects "made by human hands" (v. 19).

27 Hezekiah was very wealthy and highly honored.
He built special treasury buildings for his silver, gold,
precious stones, and spices, and for his shields and
other valuable items. 28 He also constructed many
storehouses for his grain, new wine, and olive oil; and
he made many stalls for his cattle and pens for his
flocks of sheep and goats. 29 He built many towns and
acquired vast flocks and herds, for God had given him
great wealth. 30 He blocked up the upper spring of Gi-
hon and brought the water down through a tunnel to
the west side of the City of David. And so he succeeded
in everything he did.
31 However, when ambassadors arrived from Bab-
ylon to ask about the remarkable events that had
taken place in the land, God withdrew from Hezekiah
in order to test him and to see what was really in his
heart.

SUMMARY OF HEZEKIAH'S REIGN

32 The rest of the events in Hezekiah's reign and his
acts of devotion are recorded in *The Vision of the
Prophet Isaiah Son of Amoz,* which is included in *The
Book of the Kings of Judah and Israel.* 33 When Hez-
ekiah died, he was buried in the upper area of the
royal cemetery, and all Judah and Jerusalem honored
him at his death. And his son Manasseh became the
next king.

MANASSEH RULES IN JUDAH

33 Manasseh was twelve years old when he be-
came king, and he reigned in Jerusalem fif-
ty-five years. 2 He did what was evil in the LORD's
sight, following the detestable practices of the pagan
nations that the LORD had driven from the land ahead
of the Israelites. 3 He rebuilt the pagan shrines his fa-
ther, Hezekiah, had broken down. He constructed al-
tars for the images of Baal and set up Asherah poles.
He also bowed before all the powers of the heavens
and worshiped them.
4 He built pagan altars in the Temple of the LORD,
the place where the LORD had said, "My name will
remain in Jerusalem forever." 5 He built these altars
for all the powers of the heavens in both courtyards
of the LORD's Temple. 6 Manasseh also sacrificed his
own sons in the fire* in the valley of Ben-Hinnom.
He practiced sorcery, divination, and witchcraft,
and he consulted with mediums and psychics. He
did much that was evil in the LORD's sight, arousing
his anger.
7 Manasseh even took a carved idol he had made
and set it up in God's Temple, the very place where
God had told David and his son Solomon: "My name
will be honored forever in this Temple and in Jerusa-
lem—the city I have chosen from among all the tribes
of Israel. 8 If the Israelites will be careful to obey my
commands—all the laws, decrees, and regulations
given through Moses—I will not send them into ex-
ile from this land that I set aside for your ancestors."
9 But Manasseh led the people of Judah and Jerusalem
to do even more evil than the pagan nations that the
LORD had destroyed when the people of Israel entered
the land.
10 The LORD spoke to Manasseh and his people, but
they ignored all his warnings. 11 So the LORD sent the
commanders of the Assyrian armies, and they took
Manasseh prisoner. They put a ring through his
nose, bound him in bronze chains, and led him away
to Babylon. 12 But while in deep distress, Manasseh
sought the LORD his God and sincerely humbled him-
self before the God of his ancestors. 13 And when he
prayed, the LORD listened to him and was moved by
his request. So the LORD brought Manasseh back to Je-
rusalem and to his kingdom. Then Manasseh finally
realized that the LORD alone is God!
14 After this Manasseh rebuilt the outer wall of
the City of David, from west of the Gihon Spring in
the Kidron Valley to the Fish Gate, and continuing
around the hill of Ophel. He built the wall very high.
And he stationed his military officers in all of the
fortified towns of Judah. 15 Manasseh also removed
the foreign gods and the idol from the LORD's Temple.
He tore down all the altars he had built on the hill
where the Temple stood and all the altars that were
in Jerusalem, and he dumped them outside the city.
16 Then he restored the altar of the LORD and sacri-
ficed peace offerings and thanksgiving offerings on
it. He also encouraged the people of Judah to worship
the LORD, the God of Israel. 17 However, the people still
sacrificed at the pagan shrines, though only to the
LORD their God.
18 The rest of the events of Manasseh's reign, his
prayer to God, and the words the seers spoke to him
in the name of the LORD, the God of Israel, are record-
ed in *The Book of the Kings of Israel.* 19 Manasseh's
prayer, the account of the way God answered him,
and an account of all his sins and unfaithfulness are
recorded in *The Record of the Seers.** It includes a list
of the locations where he built pagan shrines and set
up Asherah poles and idols before he humbled him-
self and repented. 20 When Manasseh died, he was
buried in his palace. Then his son Amon became the
next king.

AMON RULES IN JUDAH

21 Amon was twenty-two years old when he became
king, and he reigned in Jerusalem two years. 22 He did
what was evil in the LORD's sight, just as his father,
Manasseh, had done. He worshiped and sacrificed
to all the idols his father had made. 23 But unlike his
father, he did not humble himself before the LORD. In-
stead, Amon sinned even more.
24 Then Amon's own officials conspired against him
and assassinated him in his palace. 25 But the people
of the land killed all those who had conspired against
King Amon, and they made his son Josiah the next
king.

33:6 Or *also made his sons pass through the fire.* **33:19** Or *The Record of Hozai.*

33:1-20 According to the chronicler, Manasseh was no less evil for having repented. His is the longest evil reign in Judah's history.

33:6 Manasseh also sacrified his sons in the fire. Sacrificing children to the foreign god Molech was one of the evils that God condemned the most. The Valley of Hinnom was infamous for this practice. The name "Valley of Hinnom" was later translated into "Gehenna," the word for "hell."

33:11-17 It took a ring in his nose and bars in front of his face for Manasseh to call on God, who always responds to sincere repentance.

33:11 took Manasseh prisoner . . . to Babylon. Leading prisoners into captivity with hooks was similar to how animals were led to slaughter.

33:20 Manasseh . . . buried in his palace. Manasseh's burial plot is not among the kings. Even in death he remains outside of God's favor. Five kings (Ahaz, Jehoram, Joash, Uzziah, and Manasseh) had this kind of burial.

JOSIAH RULES IN JUDAH

34 Josiah was eight years old when he became king, and he reigned in Jerusalem thirty-one years. 2 He did what was pleasing in the LORD's sight and followed the example of his ancestor David. He did not turn away from doing what was right.

3 During the eighth year of his reign, while he was still young, Josiah began to seek the God of his ancestor David. Then in the twelfth year he began to purify Judah and Jerusalem, destroying all the pagan shrines, the Asherah poles, and the carved idols and cast images. 4 He ordered that the altars of Baal be demolished and that the incense altars which stood above them be broken down. He also made sure that the Asherah poles, the carved idols, and the cast images were smashed and scattered over the graves of those who had sacrificed to them. 5 He burned the bones of the pagan priests on their own altars, and so he purified Judah and Jerusalem.

6 He did the same thing in the towns of Manasseh, Ephraim, and Simeon, even as far as Naphtali, and in the regions* all around them. 7 He destroyed the pagan altars and the Asherah poles, and he crushed the idols into dust. He cut down all the incense altars throughout the land of Israel. Finally, he returned to Jerusalem.

8 In the eighteenth year of his reign, after he had purified the land and the Temple, Josiah appointed Shaphan son of Azaliah, Maaseiah the governor of Jerusalem, and Joah son of Joahaz, the royal historian, to repair the Temple of the LORD his God. 9 They gave Hilkiah the high priest the money that had been collected by the Levites who served as gatekeepers at the Temple of God. The gifts were brought by people from Manasseh, Ephraim, and from all the remnant of Israel, as well as from all Judah, Benjamin, and the people of Jerusalem.

10 He entrusted the money to the men assigned to supervise the restoration of the LORD's Temple. Then they paid the workers who did the repairs and renovation of the Temple. 11 They hired carpenters and builders, who purchased finished stone for the walls and timber for the rafters and beams. They restored what earlier kings of Judah had allowed to fall into ruin.

12 The workers served faithfully under the leadership of Jahath and Obadiah, Levites of the Merarite clan, and Zechariah and Meshullam, Levites of the Kohathite clan. Other Levites, all of whom were skilled musicians, 13 were put in charge of the laborers of the various trades. Still others assisted as secretaries, officials, and gatekeepers.

HILKIAH DISCOVERS GOD'S LAW

14 While they were bringing out the money collected at the LORD's Temple, Hilkiah the priest found the Book of the Law of the LORD that was written by Moses. 15 Hilkiah said to Shaphan the court secretary, "I have found the Book of the Law in the LORD's Temple!" Then Hilkiah gave the scroll to Shaphan.

16 Shaphan took the scroll to the king and reported, "Your officials are doing everything they were assigned to do. 17 The money that was collected at the Temple of the LORD has been turned over to the supervisors and workmen." 18 Shaphan also told the king, "Hilkiah the priest has given me a scroll." So Shaphan read it to the king.

19 When the king heard what was written in the Law, he tore his clothes in despair. 20 Then he gave these orders to Hilkiah, Ahikam son of Shaphan, Acbor son of Micaiah,* Shaphan the court secretary, and Asaiah the king's personal adviser: 21 "Go to the Temple and speak to the LORD for me and for all the remnant of Israel and Judah. Inquire about the words written in the scroll that has been found. For the LORD's great anger has been poured out on us because our ancestors have not obeyed the word of the LORD. We have not been doing everything this scroll says we must do."

22 So Hilkiah and the other men went to the New Quarter* of Jerusalem to consult with the prophet Huldah. She was the wife of Shallum son of Tikvah, son of Harhas,* the keeper of the Temple wardrobe.

23 She said to them, "The LORD, the God of Israel, has spoken! Go back and tell the man who sent you, 24 'This is what the LORD says: I am going to bring disaster on this city* and its people. All the curses written in the scroll that was read to the king of Judah will come true. 25 For my people have abandoned me and offered sacrifices to pagan gods, and I am very angry with them for everything they have done. My anger will be poured out on this place, and it will not be quenched.'

26 "But go to the king of Judah who sent you to seek the LORD and tell him: 'This is what the LORD, the God of Israel, says concerning the message you have just heard: 27 You were sorry and humbled yourself before God when you heard his words against this city and its people. You humbled yourself and tore your clothing in despair and wept before me in repentance. And I have indeed heard you, says the LORD. 28 So I will not send the promised disaster until after you have died and been buried in peace. You yourself will not see the disaster I am going to bring on this city and its people.'"

So they took her message back to the king.

JOSIAH'S RELIGIOUS REFORMS

29 Then the king summoned all the elders of Judah and Jerusalem. 30 And the king went up to the Temple of the LORD with all the people of Judah and Jerusalem, along with the priests and the Levites—all the people from the greatest to the least. There the king read to them the entire Book of the Covenant that had been found in the LORD's Temple. 31 The king took his place of authority beside the pillar and renewed the covenant in the LORD's presence. He pledged to obey the

34:6 As in Syriac version; Hebrew reads *in their temples,* or *in their ruins.* The meaning of the Hebrew is uncertain. **34:20** As in parallel text at 2 Kgs 22:12; Hebrew reads *Abdon son of Micah.* **34:22a** Or *the Second Quarter,* a newer section of Jerusalem. Hebrew reads *the Mishneh.* **34:22b** As in parallel text at 2 Kgs 22:14; Hebrew reads *son of Tokhath, son of Hasrah.* **34:24** Hebrew *this place;* also in 34:27, 28.

34:1–36:1 Josiah. Josiah initiates religious reform that sweeps across the nation of Judah and into Israel (vv. 3-7). When he discovers the book of Moses and its long forgotten laws, his reform becomes revival (vv. 14,29-32).

34:3-7 Josiah follows in great-grandfather Hezekiah's steps. All his national reforms flow from his intimate relationship with God.

34:6 as far as Naphtali. Josiah's zeal knows no bounds. His reforms sweep to the northern borders by sheer spiritual momentum.

34:14 found the Book of the Law of the LORD. This book was probably the Book of Deuteronomy. This finding helped spur Josiah's reforms.

34:19 tore his clothes. This was a sign of mourning. The people of Israel had strayed so far from what God had commanded in the book that Josiah found.

LORD by keeping all his commands, laws, and decrees with all his heart and soul. He promised to obey all the terms of the covenant that were written in the scroll. 32 And he required everyone in Jerusalem and the people of Benjamin to make a similar pledge. The people of Jerusalem did so, renewing their covenant with God, the God of their ancestors.

33 So Josiah removed all detestable idols from the entire land of Israel and required everyone to worship the LORD their God. And throughout the rest of his lifetime, they did not turn away from the LORD, the God of their ancestors.

JOSIAH CELEBRATES PASSOVER

35 Then Josiah announced that the Passover of the LORD would be celebrated in Jerusalem, and so the Passover lamb was slaughtered on the fourteenth day of the first month.* 2 Josiah also assigned the priests to their duties and encouraged them in their work at the Temple of the LORD. 3 He issued this order to the Levites, who were to teach all Israel and who had been set apart to serve the LORD: "Put the holy Ark in the Temple that was built by Solomon son of David, the king of Israel. You no longer need to carry it back and forth on your shoulders. Now spend your time serving the LORD your God and his people Israel. 4 Report for duty according to the family divisions of your ancestors, following the directions of King David of Israel and the directions of his son Solomon.

5 "Then stand in the sanctuary at the place appointed for your family division and help the families assigned to you as they bring their offerings to the Temple. 6 Slaughter the Passover lambs, purify yourselves, and prepare to help those who come. Follow all the directions that the LORD gave through Moses."

7 Then Josiah provided 30,000 lambs and young goats for the people's Passover offerings, along with 3,000 cattle, all from the king's own flocks and herds. 8 The king's officials also made willing contributions to the people, priests, and Levites. Hilkiah, Zechariah, and Jehiel, the administrators of God's Temple, gave the priests 2,600 lambs and young goats and 300 cattle as Passover offerings. 9 The Levite leaders—Conaniah and his brothers Shemaiah and Nethanel, as well as Hashabiah, Jeiel, and Jozabad—gave 5,000 lambs and young goats and 500 cattle to the Levites for their Passover offerings.

10 When everything was ready for the Passover celebration, the priests and the Levites took their places, organized by their divisions, as the king had commanded. 11 The Levites then slaughtered the Passover lambs and presented the blood to the priests, who sprinkled the blood on the altar while the Levites prepared the animals. 12 They divided the burnt offerings among the people by their family groups, so they could offer them to the LORD as prescribed in the Book of Moses. They did the same with the cattle. 13 Then they roasted the Passover lambs as prescribed; and they boiled the holy offerings in pots, kettles, and pans, and brought them out quickly so the people could eat them.

14 Afterward the Levites prepared Passover offerings for themselves and for the priests—the descendants of Aaron—because the priests had been busy from morning till night offering the burnt offerings and the fat portions. The Levites took responsibility for all these preparations.

15 The musicians, descendants of Asaph, were in their assigned places, following the commands that had been given by David, Asaph, Heman, and Jeduthun, the king's seer. The gatekeepers guarded the gates and did not need to leave their posts of duty, for their Passover offerings were prepared for them by their fellow Levites.

16 The entire ceremony for the LORD's Passover was completed that day. All the burnt offerings were sacrificed on the altar of the LORD, as King Josiah had commanded. 17 All the Israelites present in Jerusalem celebrated Passover and the Festival of Unleavened Bread for seven days. 18 Never since the time of the prophet Samuel had there been such a Passover. None of the kings of Israel had ever kept a Passover as Josiah did, involving all the priests and Levites, all the people of Jerusalem, and people from all over Judah and Israel. 19 This Passover was celebrated in the eighteenth year of Josiah's reign.

JOSIAH DIES IN BATTLE

20 After Josiah had finished restoring the Temple, King Neco of Egypt led his army up from Egypt to do battle at Carchemish on the Euphrates River, and Josiah and his army marched out to fight him.* 21 But King Neco sent messengers to Josiah with this message:

> "What do you want with me, king of Judah? I have no quarrel with you today! I am on my way to fight another nation, and God has told me to hurry! Do not interfere with God, who is with me, or he will destroy you."

22 But Josiah refused to listen to Neco, to whom God had indeed spoken, and he would not turn back. Instead, he disguised himself and led his army into battle on the plain of Megiddo. 23 But the enemy archers hit King Josiah with their arrows and wounded him. He cried out to his men, "Take me from the battle, for I am badly wounded!"

24 So they lifted Josiah out of his chariot and placed him in another chariot. Then they brought him back to Jerusalem, where he died. He was buried there in the royal cemetery. And all Judah and Jerusalem mourned for him. 25 The prophet Jeremiah composed funeral songs for Josiah, and to this day choirs still sing these sad songs about his death. These songs of sorrow have become a tradition and are recorded in *The Book of Laments.*

35:1 This day in the ancient Hebrew lunar calendar was April 5, 622 B.C. **35:20** Or *Josiah went out to meet him.*

35:3 Put the holy Ark in the Temple that was built by Solomon. The ark symbolizes God's presence among His people. Placing it back in the temple communicates security and stability.

35:4 following the directions. Josiah is a traditionalist. He takes his orders for religious reform from David and Solomon. Two other passages support this thought (7:10; 11:17).

35:18 Never since the time of the prophet Samuel had there been such a Passover. The people had probably observed a Passover of sorts but not with the pageantry and precise attention to regulation that was done here.

35:21 Do not interfere with God, who is with me. Anyone could claim to be acting according to God's direction. However, Josiah's mistake was that he didn't do anything to consult God to see whether or not this was true.

35:25 The shocking news of Josiah's death caused the prophet Jeremiah to express his emotions in written laments. These laments remained popular even in the chronicler's day.

26 The rest of the events of Josiah's reign and his acts of devotion (carried out according to what was written in the Law of the LORD), 27 from beginning to end—all are recorded in *The Book of the Kings of Israel and Judah.*

JEHOAHAZ RULES IN JUDAH

36 Then the people of the land took Josiah's son Jehoahaz and made him the next king in Jerusalem.

2 Jehoahaz* was twenty-three years old when he became king, and he reigned in Jerusalem three months.

3 Then he was deposed by the king of Egypt, who demanded that Judah pay 7,500 pounds of silver and 75 pounds of gold* as tribute.

JEHOIAKIM RULES IN JUDAH

4 The king of Egypt then installed Eliakim, the brother of Jehoahaz, as the next king of Judah and Jerusalem, and he changed Eliakim's name to Jehoiakim. Then Neco took Jehoahaz to Egypt as a prisoner.

5 Jehoiakim was twenty-five years old when he became king, and he reigned in Jerusalem eleven years. He did what was evil in the sight of the LORD his God. 6 Then King Nebuchadnezzar of Babylon came to Jerusalem and captured it, and he bound Jehoiakim in bronze chains and led him away to Babylon. 7 Nebuchadnezzar also took some of the treasures from the Temple of the LORD, and he placed them in his palace* in Babylon.

8 The rest of the events in Jehoiakim's reign, including all the evil things he did and everything found against him, are recorded in *The Book of the Kings of Israel and Judah.* Then his son Jehoiachin became the next king.

JEHOIACHIN RULES IN JUDAH

9 Jehoiachin was eighteen* years old when he became king, and he reigned in Jerusalem three months and ten days. Jehoiachin did what was evil in the LORD's sight.

10 In the spring of the year* King Nebuchadnezzar took Jehoiachin to Babylon. Many treasures from the Temple of the LORD were also taken to Babylon at that time. And Nebuchadnezzar installed Jehoiachin's uncle,* Zedekiah, as the next king in Judah and Jerusalem.

ZEDEKIAH RULES IN JUDAH

11 Zedekiah was twenty-one years old when he became king, and he reigned in Jerusalem eleven years. 12 But Zedekiah did what was evil in the sight of the LORD his God, and he refused to humble himself when the prophet Jeremiah spoke to him directly from the LORD. 13 He also rebelled against King Nebuchadnezzar, even though he had taken an oath of loyalty in God's name. Zedekiah was a hard and stubborn man, refusing to turn to the LORD, the God of Israel.

14 Likewise, all the leaders of the priests and the people became more and more unfaithful. They followed all the pagan practices of the surrounding nations, desecrating the Temple of the LORD that had been consecrated in Jerusalem.

15 The LORD, the God of their ancestors, repeatedly sent his prophets to warn them, for he had compassion on his people and his Temple. 16 But the people mocked these messengers of God and despised their words. They scoffed at the prophets until the LORD's anger could no longer be restrained and nothing could be done.

THE FALL OF JERUSALEM

17 So the LORD brought the king of Babylon against them. The Babylonians* killed Judah's young men, even chasing after them into the Temple. They had no pity on the people, killing both young men and young women, the old and the infirm. God handed all of them over to Nebuchadnezzar. 18 The king took home to Babylon all the articles, large and small, used in the Temple of God, and the treasures from both the LORD's Temple and from the palace of the king and his officials. 19 Then his army burned the Temple of God, tore down the walls of Jerusalem, burned all the palaces, and completely destroyed everything of value.* 20 The few who survived were taken as exiles to Babylon, and they became servants to the king and his sons until the kingdom of Persia came to power.

21 So the message of the LORD spoken through Jeremiah was fulfilled. The land finally enjoyed its Sabbath rest, lying desolate until the seventy years were fulfilled, just as the prophet had said.

CYRUS ALLOWS THE EXILES TO RETURN

22 In the first year of King Cyrus of Persia,* the LORD fulfilled the prophecy he had given through Jeremiah.* He stirred the heart of Cyrus to put this proclamation in writing and to send it throughout his kingdom:

23 "This is what King Cyrus of Persia says:

"The LORD, the God of heaven, has given me all the kingdoms of the earth. He has appointed me to build him a Temple at Jerusalem, which is in Judah. Any of you who are his people may go there for this task. And may the LORD your God be with you!"

36:2 Hebrew *Joahaz,* a variant spelling of Jehoahaz; also in 36:4. **36:3** Hebrew *100 talents* [3,400 kilograms] *of silver and 1 talent* [34 kilograms] *of gold.* **36:7** Or *temple.* **36:9** As in one Hebrew manuscript, some Greek manuscripts, and Syriac version (see also 2 Kgs 24:8); most Hebrew manuscripts read *eight.* **36:10a** Hebrew *At the turn of the year.* The first day of this year in the ancient Hebrew lunar calendar was April 13, 597 B.C. **36:10b** As in parallel text at 2 Kgs 24:17; Hebrew reads *brother,* or *relative.* **36:17** Or *Chaldeans.* **36:19** Or *destroyed all the valuable articles from the Temple.* **36:22a** The first year of Cyrus's reign over Babylon was 538 B.C. **36:22b** See Jer 25:11-12; 29:10.

36:2-14 Josiah's offspring were neither as righteous nor influential as their ancestor.

36:15 the LORD, the God of their ancestors, repeatedly sent prophets. This is an important summary statement of all that the chronicler had described. God kept sending the people warnings; they kept ignoring them.

36:19 Then his army burned the Temple of God, tore down the walls of Jerusalem. This was the response of God's judgment on what had been described in verse 15. It was the greatest tragedy of Israel's history.

36:20-21 The chronicler concludes with Nebuchadnezzar. This foreigner terminated the royal kingdom, taking Judah's people captive. The authors of 1 and 2 Samuel and 1 and 2 Kings shared these reasons for why Israel was taken into exile, while the chronicler looks at the exile as a new beginning. **The land finally enjoyed its Sabbath.** This was quite a positive spin on what had happened! It was like the land itself enjoyed a little time where it didn't have to bear with the evil that had been done in it. And just as giving land some fallow time can make it more productive, so too did this rest for the land prepare it for the people's return.

36:22-23 The Davidic dynasty did not die. A broken and contrite people arose from the rubble of ruined dreams. The King of Israel would be their newfound hope.

INTRODUCTION TO

EZRA

PERSONAL READING PLAN

☐Ezra 1:1-11
☐Ezra 2:1-70
☐Ezra 3:1–4:24
☐Ezra 5:1-17
☐Ezra 6:1-22
☐Ezra 7:1-28
☐Ezra 8:1-36
☐Ezra 9:1-15
☐Ezra 10:1-44

AUTHOR

The book is named for the principal character, Ezra, but the book does not state its author. This unknown author may have also helped to compile the book of Nehemiah and perhaps 1 and 2 Chronicles, as these books share many common characteristics:

1. A fondness for lists, for the descriptions of religious festivals, and for the phrases "heads of families" and "the house of God."

2. The prominence of Levites and temple personnel.

3. The almost exclusive use of the Hebrew words for "singer," "gatekeeper," and "temple servants."

DATE

With an unstated author, precise dating is difficult to determine. The events narrated cover the years circa 538–458 B.C.

THEME

Beginning again by building the second temple.

HISTORICAL BACKGROUND

Originally this work was one book, united with Nehemiah. In the Latin Bible, Ezra and Nehemiah are entitled 1 and 2 Esdras. This book chronicles the restoration of Israel after 70 years of captivity in Babylon. This is accomplished through the help of three Persian kings (Cyrus, Darius, and Artaxerxes I). Cyrus was an enlightened king who reversed the oppressive policies of his Assyrian and Babylonian predecessors and encouraged the return of the exiles and the rebirth of their religion. The traditional view is that Ezra arrived in Jerusalem in the seventh year of the reign of Artaxerxes I (458 B.C.) and Nehemiah in the twentieth year of the reign (445 B.C.).

CHARACTERISTICS

This book weaves together various lists, the first-person and third-person memoirs of Ezra, and official documents. These include: (1) the decree of Cyrus (1:2-4); (2) the accusation against the Jews (4:11-16); (3) the response of Artaxerxes (4:17-22); (4) the letter of Tattenai to Darius (5:7-17); (5) a memo (6:2b-5); (6) Darius' reply to Tattenai (6:6-12); and (7) a letter from Artaxerxes I to Ezra (7:12-26). God is shown using Persian kings and Jewish leaders both to bless and to discipline His people. Ezra is often seen as the "father of Judaism" because he promotes a way of life renewed by and centered on unswerving allegiance to the Torah (God's Law). Ezra's policies saved Judaism from oblivion in this crucial period of transition.

CYRUS ALLOWS THE EXILES TO RETURN

1 In the first year of King Cyrus of Persia,* the LORD
fulfilled the prophecy he had given through Jere-
miah.* He stirred the heart of Cyrus to put this proc-
lamation in writing and to send it throughout his
kingdom:

2 "This is what King Cyrus of Persia says:
"The LORD, the God of heaven, has given me all
the kingdoms of the earth. He has appointed me
to build him a Temple at Jerusalem, which is in
Judah. 3 Any of you who are his people may go to
Jerusalem in Judah to rebuild this Temple of the
LORD, the God of Israel, who lives in Jerusalem.
And may your God be with you! 4 Wherever this
Jewish remnant is found, let their neighbors
contribute toward their expenses by giving them
silver and gold, supplies for the journey, and
livestock, as well as a voluntary offering for the
Temple of God in Jerusalem."

5 Then God stirred the hearts of the priests and Lev-
ites and the leaders of the tribes of Judah and Benja-
min to go to Jerusalem to rebuild the Temple of the
LORD. 6 And all their neighbors assisted by giving
them articles of silver and gold, supplies for the jour-
ney, and livestock. They gave them many valuable
gifts in addition to all the voluntary offerings.
7 King Cyrus himself brought out the articles that
King Nebuchadnezzar had taken from the LORD's
Temple in Jerusalem and had placed in the temple of
his own gods. 8 Cyrus directed Mithredath, the trea-
surer of Persia, to count these items and present them
to Sheshbazzar, the leader of the exiles returning to
Judah.* 9 This is a list of the items that were returned:

gold basins.......................................30
silver basins...................................1,000
silver incense burners*.........................29
10 gold bowls......................................30
silver bowls....................................410
other items....................................1,000

11 In all, there were 5,400 articles of gold and silver.
Sheshbazzar brought all of these along when the ex-
iles went from Babylon to Jerusalem.

EXILES WHO RETURNED WITH ZERUBBABEL

2 Here is the list of the Jewish exiles of the provinc-
es who returned from their captivity. King Nebu-
chadnezzar had deported them to Babylon, but now
they returned to Jerusalem and the other towns in
Judah where they originally lived. 2 Their leaders
were Zerubbabel, Jeshua, Nehemiah, Seraiah, Reel-
aiah, Mordecai, Bilshan, Mispar, Bigvai, Rehum, and
Baanah.

This is the number of the men of Israel who returned from exile:

3 The family of Parosh.............................2,172
4 The family of Shephatiah.........................372
5 The family of Arah.................................775
6 The family of Pahath-moab (descendants of Jeshua and Joab).............2,812
7 The family of Elam...............................1,254
8 The family of Zattu................................945
9 The family of Zaccai...............................760
10 The family of Bani................................642
11 The family of Bebai...............................623
12 The family of Azgad.............................1,222
13 The family of Adonikam...........................666
14 The family of Bigvai............................2,056
15 The family of Adin.................................454
16 The family of Ater (descendants of Hezekiah)..98
17 The family of Bezai................................323
18 The family of Jorah................................112
19 The family of Hashum.............................223
20 The family of Gibbar...............................95
21 The people of Bethlehem..........................123
22 The people of Netophah............................56
23 The people of Anathoth............................128
24 The people of Beth-azmaveth*......................42
25 The people of Kiriath-jearim,* Kephirah, and Beeroth..........743
26 The people of Ramah and Geba.....................621
27 The people of Micmash.............................122
28 The people of Bethel and Ai.......................223
29 The citizens of Nebo................................52
30 The citizens of Magbish............................156
31 The citizens of West Elam*......................1,254
32 The citizens of Harim..............................320
33 The citizens of Lod, Hadid, and Ono...............725
34 The citizens of Jericho............................345
35 The citizens of Senaah...........................3,630

36 These are the priests who returned from exile:
The family of Jedaiah (through the line of Jeshua).............973
37 The family of Immer..............................1,052
38 The family of Pashhur............................1,247
39 The family of Harim..............................1,017

40 These are the Levites who returned from exile:
The families of Jeshua and Kadmiel (descendants of Hodaviah)................74
41 The singers of the family of Asaph..................128
42 The gatekeepers of the families of Shallum, Ater, Talmon, Akkub, Hatita, and Shobai.........139

43 The descendants of the following Temple servants returned from exile:
Ziha, Hasupha, Tabbaoth,
44 Keros, Siaha, Padon,

1:1a The first year of Cyrus's reign over Babylon was 538 B.C. **1:1b** See Jer 25:11-12; 29:10. **1:8** Hebrew *Sheshbazzar, the prince of Judah.* **1:9** The meaning of this Hebrew word is uncertain. **2:24** As in parallel text at Neh 7:28; Hebrew reads *Azmaveth.* **2:25** As in some Hebrew manuscripts and Greek version (see also Neh 7:29); Hebrew reads *Kiriath-arim.* **2:31** Or *of the other Elam.*

1:1 Cyrus. Cyrus the Great, founder of the greater Persian Empire, conquered Babylon without a struggle in 539 B.C. **given through Jeremiah.** God used Cyrus to fulfill Jeremiah's prophecy that the Jewish captivity in Babylon would last seventy years (Jer. 25:11-12). By the time the people returned and built the altar in 536 B.C., seventy years were nearly fulfilled (2 Chron. 36:22-23; Isa. 44:28).

1:3 rebuild this Temple of the LORD. Isaiah had referred to Cyrus by name 150 years earlier as the one who would allow the rebuilding of Jerusalem's temple (Isa. 44:28).

2:2 Zerubbabel. Listed in the genealogy of David (1 Chron. 3:19). **Jeshua.** This was Joshua, the high priest (Hag. 1:1).

2:40 Levites. During David's reign, 24,000 Levites assisted the temple priests and taught the Law. At the time of the return to Jerusalem, the ratio of Levites to priests was much smaller.

2:42 gatekeepers. The returning group included 139 Levite gatekeepers who prevented unauthorized people from entering the temple's restricted area. During Solomon's reign, there were 4,000 gatekeepers (1 Chron. 23:5; 2 Chron. 8:14).

45 Lebanah, Hagabah, Akkub,
46 Hagab, Shalmai,* Hanan,
47 Giddel, Gahar, Reaiah,
48 Rezin, Nekoda, Gazzam,
49 Uzza, Paseah, Besai,
50 Asnah, Meunim, Nephusim,
51 Bakbuk, Hakupha, Harhur,
52 Bazluth, Mehida, Harsha,
53 Barkos, Sisera, Temah,
54 Neziah, and Hatipha.

55 The descendants of these servants of King Solomon returned from exile:
Sotai, Hassophereth, Peruda,
56 Jaalah, Darkon, Giddel,
57 Shephatiah, Hattil, Pokereth-hazzebaim, and Ami.

58 In all, the Temple servants and the descendants of Solomon's servants numbered 392.

59 Another group returned at this time from the
towns of Tel-melah, Tel-harsha, Kerub, Addan, and
Immer. However, they could not prove that they or
their families were descendants of Israel. 60 This
group included the families of Delaiah, Tobiah, and
Nekoda—a total of 652 people.
61 Three families of priests—Hobaiah, Hakkoz,
and Barzillai—also returned. (This Barzillai had
married a woman who was a descendant of Barzillai of Gilead, and he had taken her family name.)
62 They searched for their names in the genealogical records, but they were not found, so they were
disqualified from serving as priests. 63 The governor
told them not to eat the priests' share of food from
the sacrifices until a priest could consult the LORD
about the matter by using the Urim and Thummim—the sacred lots.
64 So a total of 42,360 people returned to Judah,
65 in addition to 7,337 servants and 200 singers, both
men and women. 66 They took with them 736 horses,
245 mules, 67 435 camels, and 6,720 donkeys.
68 When they arrived at the Temple of the LORD in
Jerusalem, some of the family leaders made voluntary offerings toward the rebuilding of God's Temple
on its original site, 69 and each leader gave as much as
he could. The total of their gifts came to 61,000 gold
coins,* 6,250 pounds* of silver, and 100 robes for the
priests.
70 So the priests, the Levites, the singers, the gatekeepers, the Temple servants, and some of the common people settled in villages near Jerusalem. The rest of the people returned to their own towns throughout Israel.

THE ALTAR IS REBUILT

3 In early autumn,* when the Israelites had settled
in their towns, all the people assembled in Jerusalem with a unified purpose. 2 Then Jeshua son of
Jehozadak* joined his fellow priests and Zerubbabel
son of Shealtiel with his family in rebuilding the altar
of the God of Israel. They wanted to sacrifice burnt
offerings on it, as instructed in the Law of Moses, the
man of God. 3 Even though the people were afraid of
the local residents, they rebuilt the altar at its old site.
Then they began to sacrifice burnt offerings on the
altar to the LORD each morning and evening.
4 They celebrated the Festival of Shelters as prescribed in the Law, sacrificing the number of burnt
offerings specified for each day of the festival. 5 They
also offered the regular burnt offerings and the offerings required for the new moon celebrations and
the annual festivals as prescribed by the LORD. The
people also gave voluntary offerings to the LORD. 6 Fifteen days before the Festival of Shelters began,* the
priests had begun to sacrifice burnt offerings to the
LORD. This was even before they had started to lay the
foundation of the LORD's Temple.

THE PEOPLE BEGIN TO REBUILD THE TEMPLE

7 Then the people hired masons and carpenters and
bought cedar logs from the people of Tyre and Sidon,
paying them with food, wine, and olive oil. The logs
were brought down from the Lebanon mountains and
floated along the coast of the Mediterranean Sea* to
Joppa, for King Cyrus had given permission for this.
8 The construction of the Temple of God began in
midspring,* during the second year after they arrived
in Jerusalem. The work force was made up of everyone who had returned from exile, including Zerubbabel son of Shealtiel, Jeshua son of Jehozadak and
his fellow priests, and all the Levites. The Levites who
were twenty years old or older were put in charge
of rebuilding the LORD's Temple. 9 The workers at
the Temple of God were supervised by Jeshua with
his sons and relatives, and Kadmiel and his sons, all
descendants of Hodaviah.* They were helped in this
task by the Levites of the family of Henadad.
10 When the builders completed the foundation of
the LORD's Temple, the priests put on their robes and
took their places to blow their trumpets. And the Levites, descendants of Asaph, clashed their cymbals to
praise the LORD, just as King David had prescribed.
11 With praise and thanks, they sang this song to the
LORD:

"He is so good!
His faithful love for Israel endures forever!"

2:46 As in an alternate reading of the Masoretic Text (see also Neh 7:48); the other alternate reads *Shamlai.* **2:69a** Hebrew *61,000 darics of gold,* about 1,100 pounds or 500 kilograms in weight. **2:69b** Hebrew *5,000 minas* [3,000 kilograms]. **3:1** Hebrew *In the seventh month.* The year is not specified, so it may have been during Cyrus's first year (538 B.C.) or second year (537 B.C.). The seventh month of the ancient Hebrew lunar calendar occurred within the months of September/October 538 B.C. and October/November 537 B.C. **3:2** Hebrew *Jozadak,* a variant spelling of Jehozadak; also in 3:8. **3:6** Hebrew *On the first day of the seventh month.* This day in the ancient Hebrew lunar calendar occurred in September or October. The Festival of Shelters began on the fifteenth day of the seventh month. **3:7** Hebrew *the sea.* **3:8** Hebrew *in the second month.* This month in the ancient Hebrew lunar calendar occurred within the months of April and May 536 B.C. **3:9** Hebrew *sons of Judah* (i.e., *bene Yehudah*). *Bene* might also be read here as the proper name Binnui; *Yehudah* is probably another name for Hodaviah. Compare 2:40; Neh 7:43; 1 Esdras 5:58.

2:59 they could not prove that they or their families were descendants of Israel. Those who could not prove their Levitical genealogy were excluded from the priesthood. They were, however, allowed to return to Jerusalem.

2:66 736 horses. The large number of horses indicates affluence. Previously, horses were only used for war and ceremonies.

3:2 altar. The first job was to rebuild the altar of burnt offerings essential for reestablishing the sacrificial system that set the Jews apart.

3:7 Tyre and Sidon. Solomon purchased materials for the first temple from Sidon and Tyre in Lebanon: well known for cedar forests and expert woodworkers (2 Chron. 2:10-16). For the rebuilt temple, Cyrus authorized the sale of cedar logs.

3:10 trumpets. When David brought the ark to Jerusalem, priests blew trumpets and Asaph sounded cymbals (1 Chron. 16:5-6). This was repeated when Solomon returned the ark to the temple. Here again descendants of Asaph play cymbals.

Then all the people gave a great shout, praising the LORD because the foundation of the LORD's Temple had been laid.

12 But many of the older priests, Levites, and other leaders who had seen the first Temple wept aloud when they saw the new Temple's foundation. The others, however, were shouting for joy. 13 The joyful shouting and weeping mingled together in a loud noise that could be heard far in the distance.

ENEMIES OPPOSE THE REBUILDING

4 The enemies of Judah and Benjamin heard that the exiles were rebuilding a Temple to the LORD, the God of Israel. 2 So they approached Zerubbabel and the other leaders and said, "Let us build with you, for we worship your God just as you do. We have sacrificed to him ever since King Esarhaddon of Assyria brought us here."

3 But Zerubbabel, Jeshua, and the other leaders of Israel replied, "You may have no part in this work. We alone will build the Temple for the LORD, the God of Israel, just as King Cyrus of Persia commanded us."

4 Then the local residents tried to discourage and frighten the people of Judah to keep them from their work. 5 They bribed agents to work against them and to frustrate their plans. This went on during the entire reign of King Cyrus of Persia and lasted until King Darius of Persia took the throne.*

LATER OPPOSITION UNDER XERXES AND ARTAXERXES

6 Years later when Xerxes* began his reign, the enemies of Judah wrote a letter of accusation against the people of Judah and Jerusalem.

7 Even later, during the reign of King Artaxerxes of Persia,* the enemies of Judah, led by Bishlam, Mithredath, and Tabeel, sent a letter to Artaxerxes in the Aramaic language, and it was translated for the king.

8 *Rehum the governor and Shimshai the court secretary wrote the letter, telling King Artaxerxes about the situation in Jerusalem. 9 They greeted the king for all their colleagues—the judges and local leaders, the people of Tarpel, the Persians, the Babylonians, and the people of Erech and Susa (that is, Elam). 10 They also sent greetings from the rest of the people whom the great and noble Ashurbanipal* had deported and relocated in Samaria and throughout the neighboring lands of the province west of the Euphrates River.* 11 This is a copy of their letter:

"To King Artaxerxes, from your loyal subjects in the province west of the Euphrates River.

12 "The king should know that the Jews who came here to Jerusalem from Babylon are rebuilding this rebellious and evil city. They have already laid the foundation and will soon finish its walls. 13 And the king should know that if this city is rebuilt and its walls are completed, it will be much to your disadvantage, for the Jews will then refuse to pay their tribute, customs, and tolls to you.

14 "Since we are your loyal subjects* and do not want to see the king dishonored in this way, we have sent the king this information. 15 We suggest that a search be made in your ancestors' records, where you will discover what a rebellious city this has been in the past. In fact, it was destroyed because of its long and troublesome history of revolt against the kings and countries who controlled it. 16 We declare to the king that if this city is rebuilt and its walls are completed, the province west of the Euphrates River will be lost to you."

17 Then King Artaxerxes sent this reply:

"To Rehum the governor, Shimshai the court secretary, and their colleagues living in Samaria and throughout the province west of the Euphrates River. Greetings.

18 "The letter you sent has been translated and read to me. 19 I ordered a search of the records and have found that Jerusalem has indeed been a hotbed of insurrection against many kings. In fact, rebellion and revolt are normal there! 20 Powerful kings have ruled over Jerusalem and the entire province west of the Euphrates River, receiving tribute, customs, and tolls. 21 Therefore, issue orders to have these men stop their work. That city must not be rebuilt except at my express command. 22 Be diligent, and don't neglect this matter, for we must not permit the situation to harm the king's interests."

23 When this letter from King Artaxerxes was read to Rehum, Shimshai, and their colleagues, they hurried to Jerusalem. Then, with a show of strength, they forced the Jews to stop building.

THE REBUILDING RESUMES

24 So the work on the Temple of God in Jerusalem had stopped, and it remained at a standstill until the second year of the reign of King Darius of Persia.*

5 At that time the prophets Haggai and Zechariah son of Iddo prophesied to the Jews in Judah and Jerusalem. They prophesied in the name of the God of Israel who was over them. 2 Zerubbabel son of Shealtiel and Jeshua son of Jehozadak* responded by starting again to rebuild the Temple of God in Jeru-

4:5 Darius reigned 521–486 B.C. **4:6** Hebrew *Ahasuerus,* another name for Xerxes. He reigned 486–465 B.C. **4:7** Artaxerxes reigned 465–424 B.C. **4:8** The original text of 4:8–6:18 is in Aramaic. **4:10a** Aramaic *Osnappar,* another name for Ashurbanipal. **4:10b** Aramaic *the province beyond the river;* also in 4:11, 16, 17, 20. **4:14** Aramaic *Since we eat the salt of the palace.* **4:24** The second year of Darius's reign was 520 B.C. The narrative started in 4:1-5 is resumed at verse 24. **5:2** Aramaic *Jozadak,* a variant spelling of Jehozadak.

3:13 weeping. The old men could remember the splendor of Solomon's temple, destroyed fifty years earlier (586 B.C.), and they wept.

4:3 You may have no part in this work. The Samaritans, who opposed rebuilding, offered their help in order to subvert the effort. The Jewish leaders refused since they blended worship of God with idols.

4:10 Ashurbanipal. This Assyrian king had deported people to Samaria (in Israel) during 669–626 B.C. (2 Kings 17:24). Descendants of the deported Babylonians opposed the Jews' return.

4:13 tribute. The letter-writer tried to persuade Artaxerxes (465–424 B.C.) that if Jerusalem's walls were rebuilt, the city would no longer pay taxes and capture part of his territory.

4:21 issue orders. The archival search revealed that the people of Jerusalem had revolted against the Babylonians. Artaxerxes temporarily ordered the rebuilding to stop but left the way open for future completion. When they received his order, the officials stopped the work, probably destroying sections of the wall already repaired (Neh. 2:12-16).

5:1 Haggai and Zechariah. Two important prophets who favored resumption of work on the temple (Hag. 1:1-3; Zech. 1:1, 16).

salem. And the prophets of God were with them and
helped them.
3 But Tattenai, governor of the province west of the
Euphrates River,* and Shethar-bozenai and their col-
leagues soon arrived in Jerusalem and asked, "Who
gave you permission to rebuild this Temple and re-
store this structure?" 4 They also asked for* the names
of all the men working on the Temple. 5 But because
their God was watching over them, the leaders of the
Jews were not prevented from building until a report
was sent to Darius and he returned his decision.

TATTENAI'S LETTER TO KING DARIUS

6 This is a copy of the letter that Tattenai the governor,
Shethar-bozenai, and the other officials of the prov-
ince west of the Euphrates River sent to King Darius:

7 "To King Darius. Greetings.
8 "The king should know that we went to the
construction site of the Temple of the great God
in the province of Judah. It is being rebuilt with
specially prepared stones, and timber is being laid
in its walls. The work is going forward with great
energy and success.
9 "We asked the leaders, 'Who gave you permis-
sion to rebuild this Temple and restore this struc-
ture?' 10 And we demanded their names so that we
could tell you who the leaders were.
11 "This was their answer: 'We are the servants of
the God of heaven and earth, and we are rebuild-
ing the Temple that was built here many years
ago by a great king of Israel. 12 But because our
ancestors angered the God of heaven, he aban-
doned them to King Nebuchadnezzar of Babylon,*
who destroyed this Temple and exiled the people
to Babylonia. 13 However, King Cyrus of Babylon,*
during the first year of his reign, issued a decree
that the Temple of God should be rebuilt. 14 King
Cyrus returned the gold and silver cups that Ne-
buchadnezzar had taken from the Temple of God
in Jerusalem and had placed in the temple of Bab-
ylon. These cups were taken from that temple and
presented to a man named Sheshbazzar, whom
King Cyrus appointed as governor of Judah. 15 The
king instructed him to return the cups to their
place in Jerusalem and to rebuild the Temple of
God there on its original site. 16 So this Sheshbazzar
came and laid the foundations of the Temple of God
in Jerusalem. The people have been working on it
ever since, though it is not yet completed.'
17 "Therefore, if it pleases the king, we request
that a search be made in the royal archives of Bab-
ylon to discover whether King Cyrus ever issued
a decree to rebuild God's Temple in Jerusalem.
And then let the king send us his decision in this
matter."

DARIUS APPROVES THE REBUILDING

6 So King Darius issued orders that a search be
made in the Babylonian archives, which were
stored in the treasury. 2 But it was at the fortress at
Ecbatana in the province of Media that a scroll was
found. This is what it said:

"Memorandum:
3 "In the first year of King Cyrus's reign, a decree
was sent out concerning the Temple of God at
Jerusalem.
"Let the Temple be rebuilt on the site where
Jews used to offer their sacrifices, using the origi-
nal foundations. Its height will be ninety feet, and
its width will be ninety feet.* 4 Every three layers
of specially prepared stones will be topped by a
layer of timber. All expenses will be paid by the
royal treasury. 5 Furthermore, the gold and silver
cups, which were taken to Babylon by Nebuchad-
nezzar from the Temple of God in Jerusalem, must
be returned to Jerusalem and put back where they
belong. Let them be taken back to the Temple of
God."

6 So King Darius sent this message:

"Now therefore, Tattenai, governor of the province
west of the Euphrates River,* and Shethar-boze-
nai, and your colleagues and other officials west
of the Euphrates River—stay away from there!
7 Do not disturb the construction of the Temple of
God. Let it be rebuilt on its original site, and do not
hinder the governor of Judah and the elders of the
Jews in their work.
8 "Moreover, I hereby decree that you are to
help these elders of the Jews as they rebuild this
Temple of God. You must pay the full construction
costs, without delay, from my taxes collected in the
province west of the Euphrates River so that the
work will not be interrupted.
9 "Give the priests in Jerusalem whatever is
needed in the way of young bulls, rams, and male
lambs for the burnt offerings presented to the God
of heaven. And without fail, provide them with as
much wheat, salt, wine, and olive oil as they need
each day. 10 Then they will be able to offer accept-
able sacrifices to the God of heaven and pray for
the welfare of the king and his sons.
11 "Those who violate this decree in any way
will have a beam pulled from their house. Then
they will be lifted up and impaled on it, and their
house will be reduced to a pile of rubble.* 12 May
the God who has chosen the city of Jerusalem as
the place to honor his name destroy any king or
nation that violates this command and destroys
this Temple.

5:3 Aramaic *the province beyond the river;* also in 5:6. **5:4** As in one Hebrew manuscript and Greek and Syriac versions; Masoretic Text reads *Then we told them.* **5:12** Aramaic *Nebuchadnezzar the Chaldean.* **5:13** King Cyrus of Persia is here identified as the king of Babylon because Persia had conquered the Babylonian Empire. **6:3** Aramaic *Its height will be 60 cubits* [27.6 meters], *and its width will be 60 cubits.* It is commonly held that this verse should be emended to read: "Its height will be 30 cubits [45 feet or 13.8 meters], its length will be 60 cubits [90 feet or 27.6 meters], and its width will be 20 cubits [30 feet or 9.2 meters]"; compare 1 Kgs 6:2. The emendation regarding the width is supported by the Syriac version. **6:6** Aramaic *the province beyond the river;* also in 6:6b, 8, 13. **6:11** Aramaic *a dunghill.*

5:6 King Darius. In order to verify the report of the Jewish leaders, the governor inquired whether Darius had authorized the work.
5:11 rebuilding the Temple. The Jews told Tattenai about Solomon and his temple. They said it had been destroyed and that they had been deported because of their sin. They wanted Darius' decree to be found so that the temple could be completed. They were allowed to continue working while waiting.
6:7 Do not disturb. After reading Cyrus's official decree, Darius gave instructions that temple reconstruction be funded by taxes and all necessaries for sacrifices supplied. Work resumed in the second year of his reign (520 B.C.).

"I, Darius, have issued this decree. Let it be
obeyed with all diligence."

THE TEMPLE'S DEDICATION

13 Tattenai, governor of the province west of the Eu-
phrates River, and Shethar-bozenai and their col-
leagues complied at once with the command of King
Darius. 14 So the Jewish elders continued their work,
and they were greatly encouraged by the preaching
of the prophets Haggai and Zechariah son of Iddo. The
Temple was finally finished, as had been command-
ed by the God of Israel and decreed by Cyrus, Dari-
us, and Artaxerxes, the kings of Persia. 15 The Temple
was completed on March 12,* during the sixth year of
King Darius's reign.

16 The Temple of God was then dedicated with great
joy by the people of Israel, the priests, the Levites, and
the rest of the people who had returned from exile.
17 During the dedication ceremony for the Temple of
God, 100 young bulls, 200 rams, and 400 male lambs
were sacrificed. And 12 male goats were presented
as a sin offering for the twelve tribes of Israel. 18 Then
the priests and Levites were divided into their vari-
ous divisions to serve at the Temple of God in Jerusa-
lem, as prescribed in the Book of Moses.

CELEBRATION OF PASSOVER

19 On April 21* the returned exiles celebrated Pass-
over. 20 The priests and Levites had purified them-
selves and were ceremonially clean. So they slaugh-
tered the Passover lamb for all the returned exiles,
for their fellow priests, and for themselves. 21 The
Passover meal was eaten by the people of Israel who
had returned from exile and by the others in the land
who had turned from their corrupt practices to wor-
ship the LORD, the God of Israel. 22 Then they celebrat-
ed the Festival of Unleavened Bread for seven days.
There was great joy throughout the land because the
LORD had caused the king of Assyria* to be favorable
to them, so that he helped them to rebuild the Temple
of God, the God of Israel.

EZRA ARRIVES IN JERUSALEM

7 Many years later, during the reign of King Arta-
xerxes of Persia,* there was a man named Ezra. He
was the son* of Seraiah, son of Azariah, son of Hilki-
ah, 2 son of Shallum, son of Zadok, son of Ahitub, 3 son
of Amariah, son of Azariah, son* of Meraioth, 4 son
of Zerahiah, son of Uzzi, son of Bukki, 5 son of Abish-
ua, son of Phinehas, son of Eleazar, son of Aaron the
high priest.* 6 This Ezra was a scribe who was well
versed in the Law of Moses, which the LORD, the God
of Israel, had given to the people of Israel. He came
up to Jerusalem from Babylon, and the king gave him
everything he asked for, because the gracious hand of
the LORD his God was on him. 7 Some of the people of
Israel, as well as some of the priests, Levites, singers,
gatekeepers, and Temple servants, traveled up to Je-
rusalem with him in the seventh year of King Arta-
xerxes' reign.
8 Ezra arrived in Jerusalem in August* of that year.
9 He had arranged to leave Babylon on April 8, the
first day of the new year,* and he arrived at Jerusa-
lem on August 4,* for the gracious hand of his God
was on him. 10 This was because Ezra had determined
to study and obey the Law of the LORD and to teach
those decrees and regulations to the people of Israel.

ARTAXERXES' LETTER TO EZRA

11 King Artaxerxes had given a copy of the following
letter to Ezra, the priest and scribe who studied and
taught the commands and decrees of the LORD to Is-
rael:

12*"From Artaxerxes, the king of kings, to Ezra the
priest, the teacher of the law of the God of heaven.
Greetings.
13 "I decree that any of the people of Israel in
my kingdom, including the priests and Levites,
may volunteer to return to Jerusalem with you.
14 I and my council of seven hereby instruct you to
conduct an inquiry into the situation in Judah and
Jerusalem, based on your God's law, which is in
your hand. 15 We also commission you to take with
you silver and gold, which we are freely present-
ing as an offering to the God of Israel who lives in
Jerusalem.
16 "Furthermore, you are to take any silver and
gold that you may obtain from the province of
Babylon, as well as the voluntary offerings of the
people and the priests that are presented for the
Temple of their God in Jerusalem. 17 These dona-
tions are to be used specifically for the purchase
of bulls, rams, male lambs, and the appropriate
grain offerings and liquid offerings, all of which
will be offered on the altar of the Temple of your
God in Jerusalem. 18 Any silver and gold that is left
over may be used in whatever way you and your
colleagues feel is the will of your God.
19 "But as for the cups we are entrusting to you
for the service of the Temple of your God, deliver
them all to the God of Jerusalem. 20 If you need

6:15 Aramaic *on the third day of the month Adar,* of the ancient Hebrew lunar calendar. A number of events in Ezra can be cross-checked with dates in surviving Persian records and related accurately to our modern calendar. This day was March 12, 515 B.C. **6:19** Hebrew *On the fourteenth day of the first month,* of the ancient Hebrew lunar calendar. This day was April 21, 515 B.C.; also see note on 6:15. **6:22** King Darius of Persia is here identified as the king of Assyria because Persia had conquered the Babylonian Empire, which included the earlier Assyrian Empire. **7:1a** Artaxerxes reigned 465–424 B.C. **7:1b** Or *descendant;* see 1 Chr 6:14. **7:3** Or *descendant;* see 1 Chr 6:6-10. **7:5** Or *the first priest.* **7:8** Hebrew *in the fifth month.* This month in the ancient Hebrew lunar calendar occurred within the months of August and September 458 B.C. **7:9a** Hebrew *on the first day of the first month,* of the ancient Hebrew lunar calendar. This day was April 8, 458 B.C.; also see note on 6:15. **7:9b** Hebrew *on the first day of the fifth month,* of the ancient Hebrew lunar calendar. This day was August 4, 458 B.C.; also see note on 6:15. **7:12** The original text of 7:12-26 is in Aramaic.

6:15 The Temple was completed. The temple was completed 70.5 years after its destruction and 21 years after reconstruction began (515 B.C.).

6:21 turned from. God's prohibition against marrying foreigners was specifically meant for the Jewish people to keep their race set apart for God. The Jews were only permitted to marry foreigners who truly converted. It was never intended as a timeless prohibition of intermarriage. Later, in New Testament times, the law of grace superseded Old Testament commands so that distinctions between Jews and other races became meaningless (see Eph. 2:11-22; Gal. 3:27-29).

7:1 during the reign of King Artaxerxes. The events in Esther occurred during this 57 year gap.

7:16 voluntary offerings of the people. Voluntary gifts from the Jewish people who remained in Babylon. God accepts gifts from those who do not know Him (the king and his counselors in v. 15 and the people of Babylon in v. 16) and from His followers. But He rejects gifts from people who appear to know Him but whose hearts are far from Him (Isa. 1:10-15).

anything else for your God's Temple or for any similar needs, you may take it from the royal treasury.

21 "I, Artaxerxes the king, hereby send this decree to all the treasurers in the province west of the Euphrates River*: 'You are to give Ezra, the priest and teacher of the law of the God of heaven, whatever he requests of you. 22 You are to give him up to 7,500 pounds* of silver, 500 bushels* of wheat, 550 gallons of wine, 550 gallons of olive oil,* and an unlimited supply of salt. 23 Be careful to provide whatever the God of heaven demands for his Temple, for why should we risk bringing God's anger against the realm of the king and his sons? 24 I also decree that no priest, Levite, singer, gatekeeper, Temple servant, or other worker in this Temple of God will be required to pay tribute, customs, or tolls of any kind.'

25 "And you, Ezra, are to use the wisdom your God has given you to appoint magistrates and judges who know your God's laws to govern all the people in the province west of the Euphrates River. Teach the law to anyone who does not know it. 26 Anyone who refuses to obey the law of your God and the law of the king will be punished immediately, either by death, banishment, confiscation of goods, or imprisonment."

EZRA PRAISES THE LORD

27 Praise the LORD, the God of our ancestors, who made the king want to beautify the Temple of the LORD in Jerusalem! 28 And praise him for demonstrating such unfailing love to me by honoring me before the king, his council, and all his mighty nobles! I felt encouraged because the gracious hand of the LORD my God was on me. And I gathered some of the leaders of Israel to return with me to Jerusalem.

EXILES WHO RETURNED WITH EZRA

8 Here is a list of the family leaders and the genealogies of those who came with me from Babylon during the reign of King Artaxerxes:

2 From the family of Phinehas: Gershom.
From the family of Ithamar: Daniel.
From the family of David: Hattush, 3 a descendant of Shecaniah.
From the family of Parosh: Zechariah and 150 other men were registered.
4 From the family of Pahath-moab: Eliehoenai son of Zerahiah and 200 other men.
5 From the family of Zattu*: Shecaniah son of Jahaziel and 300 other men.
6 From the family of Adin: Ebed son of Jonathan and 50 other men.
7 From the family of Elam: Jeshaiah son of Athaliah and 70 other men.
8 From the family of Shephatiah: Zebadiah son of Michael and 80 other men.
9 From the family of Joab: Obadiah son of Jehiel and 218 other men.
10 From the family of Bani*: Shelomith son of Josiphiah and 160 other men.
11 From the family of Bebai: Zechariah son of Bebai and 28 other men.
12 From the family of Azgad: Johanan son of Hakkatan and 110 other men.
13 From the family of Adonikam, who came later*: Eliphelet, Jeuel, Shemaiah, and 60 other men.
14 From the family of Bigvai: Uthai, Zaccur,* and 70 other men.

EZRA'S JOURNEY TO JERUSALEM

15 I assembled the exiles at the Ahava Canal, and we camped there for three days while I went over the lists of the people and the priests who had arrived. I found that not one Levite had volunteered to come along. 16 So I sent for Eliezer, Ariel, Shemaiah, Elnathan, Jarib, Elnathan, Nathan, Zechariah, and Meshullam, who were leaders of the people. I also sent for Joiarib and Elnathan, who were men of discernment. 17 I sent them to Iddo, the leader of the Levites at Casiphia, to ask him and his relatives and the Temple servants to send us ministers for the Temple of God at Jerusalem.

18 Since the gracious hand of our God was on us, they sent us a man named Sherebiah, along with eighteen of his sons and brothers. He was a very astute man and a descendant of Mahli, who was a descendant of Levi son of Israel.* 19 They also sent Hashabiah, together with Jeshaiah from the descendants of Merari, and twenty of his sons and brothers, 20 and 220 Temple servants. The Temple servants were assistants to the Levites—a group of Temple workers first instituted by King David and his officials. They were all listed by name.

21 And there by the Ahava Canal, I gave orders for all of us to fast and humble ourselves before our God. We prayed that he would give us a safe journey and protect us, our children, and our goods as we traveled. 22 For I was ashamed to ask the king for soldiers and horsemen* to accompany us and protect us from enemies along the way. After all, we had told the king, "Our God's hand of protection is on all who worship him, but his fierce anger rages against those who abandon him." 23 So we fasted and earnestly prayed

7:21 Aramaic *the province beyond the river;* also in 7:25. 7:22a Aramaic *100 talents* [3,400 kilograms]. 7:22b Aramaic *100 cors* [22 kiloliters]. 7:22c Aramaic *100 baths* [2.1 kiloliters] *of wine, 100 baths of olive oil.* 8:5 As in some Greek manuscripts (see also 1 Esdras 8:32); Hebrew lacks *Zattu.* 8:10 As in some Greek manuscripts (see also 1 Esdras 8:36); Hebrew lacks *Bani.* 8:13 Or *who were the last of his family.* 8:14 As in Greek and Syriac versions and an alternate reading of the Masoretic Text; the other alternate reads *Zabbud.* 8:18 *Israel* is the name that God gave to Jacob. 8:22 Or *charioteers.*

7:26 Anyone who refused to obey the law . . . death, banishment, confiscation of goods, or imprisonment. The king gave Ezra authority to administer justice to the Jews in Jerusalem, Syria, Phoenicia, and Palestine. Ezra later used this authority to punish sin.

8:1 list of family leaders. There were 1,496 heads of families who returned to Jerusalem with Ezra. Including women and children, the group probably numbered 5,000 people—far fewer than the 50,000 on the first return.

8:15 found that not one Levite. Ezra discovered that the group lacked Levites to conduct temple ministry and teach the Law. Levites were also responsible for taking the precious metals and utensils back to Jerusalem.

8:17 send us ministers for the Temple of God. Ezra sent a group of leaders to Casiphia, a place probably on the Tigris River near modern Baghdad, to recruit Levites and temple servants. There may have been a Jewish temple in Casiphia.

8:18 Sherebiah. They found 38 Levites from the families of Sherebiah and Jeshaiah and 220 temple servants willing to go to Jerusalem.

8:22 I was ashamed to ask the king. Ezra did not want to ask for soldiers and horsemen to protect the group because he had publicly said that God would take care of His people. Later Nehemiah accepted a military escort for his return to Jerusalem.

that our God would take care of us, and he heard our prayer.

24 I appointed twelve leaders of the priests—Sherebiah, Hashabiah, and ten other priests—25 to be in charge of transporting the silver, the gold, the gold bowls, and the other items that the king, his council, his officials, and all the people of Israel had presented for the Temple of God. 26 I weighed the treasure as I gave it to them and found the totals to be as follows:

24 tons* of silver,
7,500 pounds* of silver articles,
7,500 pounds of gold,
27 20 gold bowls, equal in value to 1,000 gold coins,*
2 fine articles of polished bronze, as precious as gold.

28 And I said to these priests, "You and these treasures have been set apart as holy to the LORD. This silver and gold is a voluntary offering to the LORD, the God of our ancestors. 29 Guard these treasures well until you present them to the leading priests, the Levites, and the leaders of Israel, who will weigh them at the storerooms of the LORD's Temple in Jerusalem." 30 So the priests and the Levites accepted the task of transporting these treasures of silver and gold to the Temple of our God in Jerusalem.

31 We broke camp at the Ahava Canal on April 19* and started off to Jerusalem. And the gracious hand of our God protected us and saved us from enemies and bandits along the way. 32 So we arrived safely in Jerusalem, where we rested for three days.

33 On the fourth day after our arrival, the silver, gold, and other valuables were weighed at the Temple of our God and entrusted to Meremoth son of Uriah the priest and to Eleazar son of Phinehas, along with Jozabad son of Jeshua and Noadiah son of Binnui—both of whom were Levites. 34 Everything was accounted for by number and weight, and the total weight was officially recorded.

35 Then the exiles who had come out of captivity sacrificed burnt offerings to the God of Israel. They presented twelve bulls for all the people of Israel, as well as ninety-six rams and seventy-seven male lambs. They also offered twelve male goats as a sin offering. All this was given as a burnt offering to the LORD. 36 The king's decrees were delivered to his highest officers and the governors of the province west of the Euphrates River,* who then cooperated by supporting the people and the Temple of God.

EZRA'S PRAYER CONCERNING INTERMARRIAGE

9 When these things had been done, the Jewish leaders came to me and said, "Many of the people of Israel, and even some of the priests and Levites, have not kept themselves separate from the other peoples living in the land. They have taken up the detestable practices of the Canaanites, Hittites, Perizzites, Jebusites, Ammonites, Moabites, Egyptians, and Amorites. 2 For the men of Israel have married women from these people and have taken them as wives for their sons. So the holy race has become polluted by these mixed marriages. Worse yet, the leaders and officials have led the way in this outrage."

3 When I heard this, I tore my cloak and my shirt, pulled hair from my head and beard, and sat down utterly shocked. 4 Then all who trembled at the words of the God of Israel came and sat with me because of this outrage committed by the returned exiles. And I sat there utterly appalled until the time of the evening sacrifice.

5 At the time of the sacrifice, I stood up from where I had sat in mourning with my clothes torn. I fell to my knees and lifted my hands to the LORD my God. 6 I prayed,

"O my God, I am utterly ashamed; I blush to lift up my face to you. For our sins are piled higher than our heads, and our guilt has reached to the heavens. 7 From the days of our ancestors until now, we have been steeped in sin. That is why we and our kings and our priests have been at the mercy of the pagan kings of the land. We have been killed, captured, robbed, and disgraced, just as we are today.

8 "But now we have been given a brief moment of grace, for the LORD our God has allowed a few of us to survive as a remnant. He has given us security in this holy place. Our God has brightened our eyes and granted us some relief from our slavery. 9 For we were slaves, but in his unfailing love our God did not abandon us in our slavery. Instead, he caused the kings of Persia to treat us favorably. He revived us so we could rebuild the Temple of our God and repair its ruins. He has given us a protective wall in Judah and Jerusalem.

10 "And now, O our God, what can we say after all of this? For once again we have abandoned your commands! 11 Your servants the prophets warned us when they said, 'The land you are entering to possess is totally defiled by the detestable practices of the people living there. From one end to the other, the land is filled with corruption. 12 Don't let your daughters marry their sons! Don't take their daughters as wives for your sons. Don't ever promote the peace and prosperity of those nations. If you follow these instructions, you will be strong and will enjoy the good things the land produces, and you will leave this prosperity to your children forever.'

13 "Now we are being punished because of our wickedness and our great guilt. But we have actually been punished far less than we deserve, for you, our God, have allowed some of us to survive as a remnant. 14 But even so, we are again breaking your commands and intermarrying with people who do these detestable things. Won't your anger be enough to destroy us, so that even this little remnant no longer survives? 15 O LORD, God of Israel, you are just. We come before you in our

8:26a Hebrew *650 talents* [22 metric tons]. **8:26b** Hebrew *100 talents* [3,400 kilograms]; also in 8:26c. **8:27** Hebrew *1,000 darics,* about 19 pounds or 8.6 kilograms in weight. **8:31** Hebrew *on the twelfth day of the first month,* of the ancient Hebrew lunar calendar. This day was April 19, 458 B.C.; also see note on 6:15. **8:36** Hebrew *the province beyond the river.*

9:2 leaders . . . have led the way. The Law expressly forbade marrying Israel's pagan neighbors (Ex. 34:16). This practice often led Jews to worship the gods of their spouses (Neh. 13:23-27). Leaders, if anyone, should have known better.

9:6 sins. Ezra feared that God would send the people into captivity again.

9:8 brightened our eyes. God gave the light of His will to those in sin's darkness. Not only were they free from the Babylonian captivity but also from sin's bondage. Ezra warned against choosing to become its slave again.

guilt as nothing but an escaped remnant, though in such a condition none of us can stand in your presence."

THE PEOPLE CONFESS THEIR SIN

10 While Ezra prayed and made this confession, weeping and lying face down on the ground in front of the Temple of God, a very large crowd of people from Israel—men, women, and children—gathered and wept bitterly with him. 2 Then Shecaniah son of Jehiel, a descendant of Elam, said to Ezra, "We have been unfaithful to our God, for we have married these pagan women of the land. But in spite of this there is hope for Israel. 3 Let us now make a covenant with our God to divorce our pagan wives and to send them away with their children. We will follow the advice given by you and by the others who respect the commands of our God. Let it be done according to the Law of God. 4 Get up, for it is your duty to tell us how to proceed in setting things straight. We are behind you, so be strong and take action."

5 So Ezra stood up and demanded that the leaders of the priests and the Levites and all the people of Israel swear that they would do as Shecaniah had said. And they all swore a solemn oath. 6 Then Ezra left the front of the Temple of God and went to the room of Jehohanan son of Eliashib. He spent the night* there without eating or drinking anything. He was still in mourning because of the unfaithfulness of the returned exiles.

7 Then a proclamation was made throughout Judah and Jerusalem that all the exiles should come to Jerusalem. 8 Those who failed to come within three days would, if the leaders and elders so decided, forfeit all their property and be expelled from the assembly of the exiles.

9 Within three days, all the people of Judah and Benjamin had gathered in Jerusalem. This took place on December 19,* and all the people were sitting in the square before the Temple of God. They were trembling both because of the seriousness of the matter and because it was raining. 10 Then Ezra the priest stood and said to them: "You have committed a terrible sin. By marrying pagan women, you have increased Israel's guilt. 11 So now confess your sin to the LORD, the God of your ancestors, and do what he demands. Separate yourselves from the people of the land and from these pagan women."

12 Then the whole assembly raised their voices and answered, "Yes, you are right; we must do as you say!" 13 Then they added, "This isn't something that can be done in a day or two, for many of us are involved in this extremely sinful affair. And this is the rainy season, so we cannot stay out here much longer. 14 Let our leaders act on behalf of us all. Let everyone who has a pagan wife come at a scheduled time, accompanied by the leaders and judges of his city, so that the fierce anger of our God concerning this affair may be turned away from us."

15 Only Jonathan son of Asahel and Jahzeiah son of Tikvah opposed this course of action, and they were supported by Meshullam and Shabbethai the Levite.

16 So this was the plan they followed. Ezra selected leaders to represent their families, designating each of the representatives by name. On December 29,* the leaders sat down to investigate the matter. 17 By March 27, the first day of the new year,* they had finished dealing with all the men who had married pagan wives.

THOSE GUILTY OF INTERMARRIAGE

18 These are the priests who had married pagan wives:

From the family of Jeshua son of Jehozadak* and his brothers: Maaseiah, Eliezer, Jarib, and Gedaliah. 19 They vowed to divorce their wives, and they each acknowledged their guilt by offering a ram as a guilt offering.

20 From the family of Immer: Hanani and Zebadiah.

21 From the family of Harim: Maaseiah, Elijah, Shemaiah, Jehiel, and Uzziah.

22 From the family of Pashhur: Elioenai, Maaseiah, Ishmael, Nethanel, Jozabad, and Elasah.

23 These are the Levites who were guilty: Jozabad, Shimei, Kelaiah (also called Kelita), Pethahiah, Judah, and Eliezer.

24 This is the singer who was guilty: Eliashib.

These are the gatekeepers who were guilty: Shallum, Telem, and Uri.

25 These are the other people of Israel who were guilty:

From the family of Parosh: Ramiah, Izziah, Malkijah, Mijamin, Eleazar, Hashabiah,* and Benaiah.

26 From the family of Elam: Mattaniah, Zechariah, Jehiel, Abdi, Jeremoth, and Elijah.

27 From the family of Zattu: Elioenai, Eliashib, Mattaniah, Jeremoth, Zabad, and Aziza.

28 From the family of Bebai: Jehohanan, Hananiah, Zabbai, and Athlai.

29 From the family of Bani: Meshullam, Malluch, Adaiah, Jashub, Sheal, and Jeremoth.

30 From the family of Pahath-moab: Adna, Kelal, Benaiah, Maaseiah, Mattaniah, Bezalel, Binnui, and Manasseh.

31 From the family of Harim: Eliezer, Ishijah, Malkijah, Shemaiah, Shimeon, 32 Benjamin, Malluch, and Shemariah.

33 From the family of Hashum: Mattenai, Mattattah, Zabad, Eliphelet, Jeremai, Manasseh, and Shimei.

10:6 As in parallel text at 1 Esdras 9:2; Hebrew reads *He went.* **10:9** Hebrew *on the twentieth day of the ninth month,* of the ancient Hebrew lunar calendar. This day was December 19, 458 B.C.; also see note on 6:15. **10:16** Hebrew *On the first day of the tenth month,* of the ancient Hebrew lunar calendar. This day was December 29, 458 B.C.; also see note on 6:15. **10:17** Hebrew *By the first day of the first month,* of the ancient Hebrew lunar calendar. This day was March 27, 457 B.C.; also see note on 6:15. **10:18** Hebrew *Jozadak,* a variant spelling of Jehozadak. **10:25** As in parallel text at 1 Esdras 9:26; Hebrew reads *Malkijah.*

10:5 Ezra . . . the leaders of the priests . . . swear. A covenant was the most binding form of agreement. While God clearly prohibits and even "hates" divorce (Mal. 2:16), intermarriage led the Israelites into worship of false deities and seduced them away from God. The Law permitted marriage with outside women only if they converted.

10:7 proclamation. Whoever ignored the proclamation would be stripped of legal rights.

10:8 within three days. Even though it was the rainy season, the people gathered in the square east of the temple. They feared both God's wrath and family breakups. **forfeit.** Confiscated property was sold; proceeds went into the temple treasury.

10:16 investigate the matter. The elders and judges of each town knew whether the women worshiped the Lord or idols. All the marriages were examined within three months.

[34] From the family of Bani: Maadai, Amram, Uel,
[35] Benaiah, Bedeiah, Keluhi, [36] Vaniah, Meremoth,
Eliashib, [37] Mattaniah, Mattenai, and Jaasu.
[38] From the family of Binnui*: Shimei, [39] Shelemiah,
Nathan, Adaiah, [40] Macnadebai, Shashai, Sharai,
[41] Azarel, Shelemiah, Shemariah, [42] Shallum, Amariah, and Joseph.
[43] From the family of Nebo: Jeiel, Mattithiah, Zabad,
Zebina, Jaddai, Joel, and Benaiah.

[44] Each of these men had a pagan wife, and some
even had children by these wives.*

10:37-38 As in Greek version; Hebrew reads *Jaasu,* [38]*Bani, Binnui.* **10:44** Or *and they sent them away with their children.* The meaning of the Hebrew is uncertain.

INTRODUCTION TO

NEHEMIAH

PERSONAL READING PLAN

☐Nehemiah 1:1–2:20
☐Nehemiah 3:1-32
☐Nehemiah 4:1-23
☐Nehemiah 5:1–6:14
☐Nehemiah 6:15–7:73a
☐Nehemiah 7:73b–8:18
☐Nehemiah 9:1-37
☐Nehemiah 9:38–10:39
☐Nehemiah 11:1-36
☐Nehemiah 12:1-26
☐Nehemiah 12:27-47
☐Nehemiah 13:1-31

AUTHOR

The book is named for the principal character, Nehemiah, but the book does not state its author. This unknown author may have also helped to compile the book of Ezra and perhaps 1 and 2 Chronicles as these books share many common characteristics:

1. A fondness for lists, for the descriptions of religious festivals, and for the phrases "heads of families" and "the house of God."
2. The prominence of Levites and temple personnel.
3. The almost exclusive use of the Hebrew words for "singer," "gatekeeper," and "temple servants."

DATE

With an unstated author, precise dating is difficult to determine. The events narrated cover the years *circa* 445–432 B.C.

THEME

Restoration of the second temple and revival of the people, providing a legacy of God-given leadership principles.

HISTORICAL BACKGROUND

Originally this work was one book, united with Ezra. In the Latin Bible, Ezra and Nehemiah are entitled 1 and 2 Esdras. This book complements Ezra in reporting the restoration of Israel after 70 years of captivity in Babylon. Nehemiah's distress over the broken-down walls of Jerusalem (1:3) is probably caused by the episode in Ezra 4:7-23. Ezra's return had revived spiritual and nationalistic fervor in God's people so that they worked to rebuild the walls of Jerusalem (chaps. 8–9). But the completion of that task apparently fell to governor Nehemiah, a man dedicated to God.

CHARACTERISTICS

This book weaves together various lists with first-person and third-person memoirs of Nehemiah, who is the lead actor in this drama. Some of the most moving prayers outside the Psalms are found here (1:5-11; 9:5b-37). Sounding like a modern dramatic story, Nehemiah describes the rebuilding of the Jerusalem walls. The physical condition of the walls (chaps. 1–7) parallels the spiritual condition of the people. As the walls are restored, the people are rehabilitated (chaps. 8–13). As Nehemiah follows God wholeheartedly, he models invaluable, God-given leadership principles for all types of situations.

1 These are the memoirs of Nehemiah son of Hacaliah.

NEHEMIAH'S CONCERN FOR JERUSALEM

In late autumn, in the month of Kislev, in the twentieth year of King Artaxerxes' reign,* I was at the fortress of Susa. 2 Hanani, one of my brothers, came to visit me with some other men who had just arrived from Judah. I asked them about the Jews who had returned there from captivity and about how things were going in Jerusalem.

3 They said to me, "Things are not going well for those who returned to the province of Judah. They are in great trouble and disgrace. The wall of Jerusalem has been torn down, and the gates have been destroyed by fire."

4 When I heard this, I sat down and wept. In fact, for days I mourned, fasted, and prayed to the God of heaven. 5 Then I said,

"O LORD, God of heaven, the great and awesome God who keeps his covenant of unfailing love with those who love him and obey his commands, 6 listen to my prayer! Look down and see me praying night and day for your people Israel. I confess that we have sinned against you. Yes, even my own family and I have sinned! 7 We have sinned terribly by not obeying the commands, decrees, and regulations that you gave us through your servant Moses.

8 "Please remember what you told your servant Moses: 'If you are unfaithful to me, I will scatter you among the nations. 9 But if you return to me and obey my commands and live by them, then even if you are exiled to the ends of the earth,* I will bring you back to the place I have chosen for my name to be honored.'

10 "The people you rescued by your great power and strong hand are your servants. 11 O Lord, please hear my prayer! Listen to the prayers of those of us who delight in honoring you. Please grant me success today by making the king favorable to me.* Put it into his heart to be kind to me."

In those days I was the king's cup-bearer.

NEHEMIAH GOES TO JERUSALEM

2 Early the following spring, in the month of Nisan,* during the twentieth year of King Artaxerxes' reign, I was serving the king his wine. I had never before appeared sad in his presence. 2 So the king asked me, "Why are you looking so sad? You don't look sick to me. You must be deeply troubled."

Then I was terrified, 3 but I replied, "Long live the king! How can I not be sad? For the city where my ancestors are buried is in ruins, and the gates have been destroyed by fire."

4 The king asked, "Well, how can I help you?"

With a prayer to the God of heaven, 5 I replied, "If it please the king, and if you are pleased with me, your servant, send me to Judah to rebuild the city where my ancestors are buried."

6 The king, with the queen sitting beside him, asked, "How long will you be gone? When will you return?" After I told him how long I would be gone, the king agreed to my request.

7 I also said to the king, "If it please the king, let me have letters addressed to the governors of the province west of the Euphrates River,* instructing them to let me travel safely through their territories on my way to Judah. 8 And please give me a letter addressed to Asaph, the manager of the king's forest, instructing him to give me timber. I will need it to make beams for the gates of the Temple fortress, for the city walls, and for a house for myself." And the king granted these requests, because the gracious hand of God was on me.

9 When I came to the governors of the province west of the Euphrates River, I delivered the king's letters to them. The king, I should add, had sent along army officers and horsemen* to protect me. 10 But when Sanballat the Horonite and Tobiah the Ammonite official heard of my arrival, they were very displeased that someone had come to help the people of Israel.

NEHEMIAH INSPECTS JERUSALEM'S WALL

11 So I arrived in Jerusalem. Three days later, 12 I slipped out during the night, taking only a few others with me. I had not told anyone about the plans God had put in my heart for Jerusalem. We took no pack animals with us except the donkey I was riding. 13 After dark I went out through the Valley Gate, past the Jackal's Well,* and over to the Dung Gate to inspect the broken walls and burned gates. 14 Then I went to the Fountain Gate and to the King's Pool, but my donkey couldn't get through the rubble. 15 So, though it was still dark, I went up the Kidron Valley* instead, inspecting the wall before I turned back and entered again at the Valley Gate.

16 The city officials did not know I had been out there or what I was doing, for I had not yet said anything to anyone about my plans. I had not yet spoken to the Jewish leaders—the priests, the nobles, the officials, or anyone else in the administration. 17 But now I said to them, "You know very well what trouble we are in. Jerusalem lies in ruins, and its gates have been destroyed by fire. Let us rebuild the wall of Jerusalem

1:1 Hebrew *In the month of Kislev of the twentieth year.* A number of dates in the book of Nehemiah can be cross-checked with dates in surviving Persian records and related accurately to our modern calendar. This month of the ancient Hebrew lunar calendar occurred within the months of November and December 446 B.C. The *twentieth year* probably refers to the reign of King Artaxerxes I; compare 2:1; 5:14. **1:9** Hebrew *of the heavens.* **1:11** Hebrew *today in the sight of this man.* **2:1** Hebrew *In the month of Nisan.* This month of the ancient Hebrew lunar calendar occurred within the months of April and May 445 B.C. **2:7** Hebrew *the province beyond the river;* also in 2:9. **2:9** Or *charioteers.* **2:13** Or *Serpent's Well.* **2:15** Hebrew *the valley.*

1:1 Nehemiah. Nehemiah served as personal cupbearer to King Artaxerxes.
1:2 Hanani. Nehemiah's brother brought him a disturbing report that Jerusalem's wall was broken down and its gates were burned.
1:6 listen to my prayer! Nehemiah wept, fasted, and prayed over the condition of Jerusalem.
1:10 by your great power. Recalling God's work on behalf of His people in the past (Ex. 32:11), Nehemiah asked Him to help them again.
2:3-6 Nehemiah received permission from the king to go to Jerusalem to rebuild its walls.
2:11 Three days later. When he arrived in the city, Nehemiah prepared himself with prayer and research before trusting a few men with his plans.
2:13 inspect the broken walls. He surveyed the walls at night, perhaps to make plans before informing others about his intentions.
2:15 Valley Gate. This was Nehemiah's starting point in the southwest wall of Jerusalem.
2:17 Jerusalem lies in ruins. The walls and gates of the city had been destroyed by the Babylonian army in 586 B.C.

and end this disgrace!" [18] Then I told them about how the gracious hand of God had been on me, and about my conversation with the king.

They replied at once, "Yes, let's rebuild the wall!" So they began the good work.

[19] But when Sanballat, Tobiah, and Geshem the Arab heard of our plan, they scoffed contemptuously. "What are you doing? Are you rebelling against the king?" they asked.

[20] I replied, "The God of heaven will help us succeed. We, his servants, will start rebuilding this wall. But you have no share, legal right, or historic claim in Jerusalem."

REBUILDING THE WALL OF JERUSALEM

3 Then Eliashib the high priest and the other priests started to rebuild at the Sheep Gate. They dedicated it and set up its doors, building the wall as far as the Tower of the Hundred, which they dedicated, and the Tower of Hananel. [2] People from the town of Jericho worked next to them, and beyond them was Zaccur son of Imri.

[3] The Fish Gate was built by the sons of Hassenaah. They laid the beams, set up its doors, and installed its bolts and bars. [4] Meremoth son of Uriah and grandson of Hakkoz repaired the next section of wall. Beside him were Meshullam son of Berekiah and grandson of Meshezabel, and then Zadok son of Baana. [5] Next were the people from Tekoa, though their leaders refused to work with the construction supervisors.

[6] The Old City Gate* was repaired by Joiada son of Paseah and Meshullam son of Besodeiah. They laid the beams, set up its doors, and installed its bolts and bars. [7] Next to them were Melatiah from Gibeon, Jadon from Meronoth, people from Gibeon, and people from Mizpah, the headquarters of the governor of the province west of the Euphrates River.* [8] Next was Uzziel son of Harhaiah, a goldsmith by trade, who also worked on the wall. Beyond him was Hananiah, a manufacturer of perfumes. They left out a section of Jerusalem as they built the Broad Wall.*

[9] Rephaiah son of Hur, the leader of half the district of Jerusalem, was next to them on the wall. [10] Next Jedaiah son of Harumaph repaired the wall across from his own house, and next to him was Hattush son of Hashabneiah. [11] Then came Malkijah son of Harim and Hasshub son of Pahath-moab, who repaired another section of the wall and the Tower of the Ovens. [12] Shallum son of Hallohesh and his daughters repaired the next section. He was the leader of the other half of the district of Jerusalem.

[13] The Valley Gate was repaired by the people from Zanoah, led by Hanun. They set up its doors and installed its bolts and bars. They also repaired the 1,500 feet* of wall to the Dung Gate.

[14] The Dung Gate was repaired by Malkijah son of Recab, the leader of the Beth-hakkerem district. He rebuilt it, set up its doors, and installed its bolts and bars.

[15] The Fountain Gate was repaired by Shallum* son of Col-hozeh, the leader of the Mizpah district. He rebuilt it, roofed it, set up its doors, and installed its bolts and bars. Then he repaired the wall of the pool of Siloam* near the king's garden, and he rebuilt the wall as far as the stairs that descend from the City of David. [16] Next to him was Nehemiah son of Azbuk, the leader of half the district of Beth-zur. He rebuilt the wall from a place across from the tombs of David's family as far as the water reservoir and the House of the Warriors.

[17] Next to him, repairs were made by a group of Levites working under the supervision of Rehum son of Bani. Then came Hashabiah, the leader of half the district of Keilah, who supervised the building of the wall on behalf of his own district. [18] Next down the line were his countrymen led by Binnui* son of Henadad, the leader of the other half of the district of Keilah.

[19] Next to them, Ezer son of Jeshua, the leader of Mizpah, repaired another section of wall across from the ascent to the armory near the angle in the wall. [20] Next to him was Baruch son of Zabbai, who zealously repaired an additional section from the angle to the door of the house of Eliashib the high priest. [21] Meremoth son of Uriah and grandson of Hakkoz rebuilt another section of the wall extending from the door of Eliashib's house to the end of the house.

[22] The next repairs were made by the priests from the surrounding region. [23] After them, Benjamin and Hasshub repaired the section across from their house, and Azariah son of Maaseiah and grandson of Ananiah repaired the section across from his house. [24] Next was Binnui son of Henadad, who rebuilt another section of the wall from Azariah's house to the angle and the corner. [25] Palal son of Uzai carried on the work from a point opposite the angle and the tower that projects up from the king's upper house beside the court of the guard. Next to him were Pedaiah son of Parosh, [26] with the Temple servants living on the hill of Ophel, who repaired the wall as far as a point across from the Water Gate to the east and the projecting tower. [27] Then came the people of Tekoa, who repaired another section across from the great projecting tower and over to the wall of Ophel.

[28] Above the Horse Gate, the priests repaired the wall. Each one repaired the section immediately across from his own house. [29] Next Zadok son of Immer also rebuilt the wall across from his own house, and beyond him was Shemaiah son of Shecaniah, the gatekeeper of the East Gate. [30] Next Hananiah son of Shelemiah and Hanun, the sixth son of Zalaph, repaired another section, while Meshullam son of Berekiah rebuilt the wall across from where he lived. [31] Malkijah, one of the goldsmiths, repaired the wall as far as the housing for the Temple servants and merchants, across from the Inspection Gate. Then he continued as far as the upper room at the corner. [32] The other goldsmiths and merchants repaired the wall from that corner to the Sheep Gate.

3:6 Or *The Mishneh Gate,* or *The Jeshanah Gate.* **3:7** Hebrew *the province beyond the river.* **3:8** Or *They fortified Jerusalem up to the Broad Wall.* **3:13** Hebrew *1,000 cubits* [460 meters]. **3:15a** As in Syriac version; Hebrew reads *Shallun.* **3:15b** Hebrew *pool of Shelah,* another name for the pool of Siloam. **3:18** As in a few Hebrew manuscripts, some Greek manuscripts, and Syriac version (see also 3:24; 10:9); most Hebrew manuscripts read *Bavvai.*

2:18 gracious hand of God. Nehemiah urged the people to rebuild the wall, noting its disgraceful condition.

3:1 Eliashib . . . and the other priests. Eliashib and the other priests started rebuilding the walls under Nehemiah's supervision.

3:10 Jedaiah . . . repaired the wall across from his own house. It was sensible to have the workers make repairs near their homes.

ENEMIES OPPOSE THE REBUILDING

4 1*Sanballat was very angry when he learned
that we were rebuilding the wall. He flew into
a rage and mocked the Jews, 2 saying in front of his
friends and the Samarian army officers, "What does
this bunch of poor, feeble Jews think they're doing? Do
they think they can build the wall in a single day by
just offering a few sacrifices?* Do they actually think
they can make something of stones from a rubbish
heap—and charred ones at that?"
3 Tobiah the Ammonite, who was standing beside
him, remarked, "That stone wall would collapse if
even a fox walked along the top of it!"
4 Then I prayed, "Hear us, our God, for we are be-
ing mocked. May their scoffing fall back on their own
heads, and may they themselves become captives in
a foreign land! 5 Do not ignore their guilt. Do not blot
out their sins, for they have provoked you to anger
here in front of* the builders."
6 At last the wall was completed to half its height
around the entire city, for the people had worked
with enthusiasm.
7*But when Sanballat and Tobiah and the Arabs,
Ammonites, and Ashdodites heard that the work was
going ahead and that the gaps in the wall of Jerusa-
lem were being repaired, they were furious. 8 They
all made plans to come and fight against Jerusalem
and throw us into confusion. 9 But we prayed to our
God and guarded the city day and night to protect
ourselves.
10 Then the people of Judah began to complain, "The
workers are getting tired, and there is so much rubble
to be moved. We will never be able to build the wall
by ourselves."
11 Meanwhile, our enemies were saying, "Before
they know what's happening, we will swoop down
on them and kill them and end their work."
12 The Jews who lived near the enemy came and
told us again and again, "They will come from all di-
rections and attack us!"* 13 So I placed armed guards
behind the lowest parts of the wall in the exposed ar-
eas. I stationed the people to stand guard by families,
armed with swords, spears, and bows.
14 Then as I looked over the situation, I called to-
gether the nobles and the rest of the people and said
to them, "Don't be afraid of the enemy! Remember the
Lord, who is great and glorious, and fight for your
brothers, your sons, your daughters, your wives, and
your homes!"
15 When our enemies heard that we knew of their
plans and that God had frustrated them, we all re-
turned to our work on the wall. 16 But from then on,
only half my men worked while the other half stood
guard with spears, shields, bows, and coats of mail.
The leaders stationed themselves behind the people
of Judah 17 who were building the wall. The laborers
carried on their work with one hand supporting their
load and one hand holding a weapon. 18 All the build-
ers had a sword belted to their side. The trumpeter
stayed with me to sound the alarm.
19 Then I explained to the nobles and officials and
all the people, "The work is very spread out, and we
are widely separated from each other along the wall.
20 When you hear the blast of the trumpet, rush to
wherever it is sounding. Then our God will fight for
us!"
21 We worked early and late, from sunrise to sun-
set. And half the men were always on guard. 22 I also
told everyone living outside the walls to stay in Jeru-
salem. That way they and their servants could help
with guard duty at night and work during the day.
23 During this time, none of us—not I, nor my rel-
atives, nor my servants, nor the guards who were
with me—ever took off our clothes. We carried our
weapons with us at all times, even when we went for
water.*

NEHEMIAH DEFENDS THE OPPRESSED

5 About this time some of the men and their wives
raised a cry of protest against their fellow Jews.
2 They were saying, "We have such large families. We
need more food to survive."
3 Others said, "We have mortgaged our fields, vine-
yards, and homes to get food during the famine."
4 And others said, "We have had to borrow money
on our fields and vineyards to pay our taxes. 5 We be-
long to the same family as those who are wealthy, and
our children are just like theirs. Yet we must sell our
children into slavery just to get enough money to live.
We have already sold some of our daughters, and we
are helpless to do anything about it, for our fields and
vineyards are already mortgaged to others."
6 When I heard their complaints, I was very angry.
7 After thinking it over, I spoke out against these no-
bles and officials. I told them, "You are hurting your
own relatives by charging interest when they borrow
money!" Then I called a public meeting to deal with
the problem.
8 At the meeting I said to them, "We are doing all we
can to redeem our Jewish relatives who have had to
sell themselves to pagan foreigners, but you are sell-
ing them back into slavery again. How often must we
redeem them?" And they had nothing to say in their
defense.

4:1 Verses 4:1-6 are numbered 3:33-38 in Hebrew text. 4:2 The meaning of the Hebrew is uncertain. 4:5 Or *for they have thrown insults in the face of.* 4:7 Verses 4:7-23 are numbered 4:1-17 in Hebrew text. 4:12 The meaning of the Hebrew is uncertain. 4:23 Or *Each carried his weapon in his right hand.* Hebrew reads *Each his weapon the water.* The meaning of the Hebrew is uncertain.

4:1-4 Sanballat accused the Jews of rebelling against the king of Persia. He may have objected to the rebuilding because he wanted to gain control of Judah.

4:9 prayed to our God and guarded the city. The workers joined in Nehemiah's prayer and prepared to resist any attack.

4:10 workers are getting tired. Posting a guard did not end the problem. The workers were exhausted, and the job was only half done. Discouragement set in.

4:11 our enemies were saying. Nehemiah's enemies started rumors to produce fear and weaken the people's resolve to complete the task.

4:13 stationed the people to stand guard by families. Placing families together was dangerous, but Nehemiah knew that fathers would fight to protect their families.

4:14 Don't be afraid of the enemy! Nehemiah encouraged the people to remember God's strength and power.

4:17 work with one hand. Armed by Nehemiah, the laborers held their weapons in one hand and worked with the other.

4:20 our God will fight for us! Nehemiah combined faith and effort, trusting God to protect them.

4:23 even when we went for water. The urgency of the project required the workers to work night and day and remain armed at all times.

5:1 some of the men and their wives. Stress caused the people to complain. These complaints were as hard to deal with as outside opposition.

5:3-9 Nehemiah got angry when he learned that some of the Jews were charging their fellow Jews exorbitant interest rates and then foreclosing on their property. He put a stop to the practice.

9 Then I pressed further, "What you are doing is not
right! Should you not walk in the fear of our God in
order to avoid being mocked by enemy nations? 10 I
myself, as well as my brothers and my workers, have
been lending the people money and grain, but now
let us stop this business of charging interest. 11 You
must restore their fields, vineyards, olive groves, and
homes to them this very day. And repay the interest
you charged when you lent them money, grain, new
wine, and olive oil."

12 They replied, "We will give back everything and
demand nothing more from the people. We will do as
you say." Then I called the priests and made the nobles
and officials swear to do what they had promised.

13 I shook out the folds of my robe and said, "If you
fail to keep your promise, may God shake you like this
from your homes and from your property!"

The whole assembly responded, "Amen," and they
praised the LORD. And the people did as they had
promised.

14 For the entire twelve years that I was governor of
Judah—from the twentieth year to the thirty-second
year of the reign of King Artaxerxes*—neither I nor
my officials drew on our official food allowance. 15 The
former governors, in contrast, had laid heavy bur-
dens on the people, demanding a daily ration of food
and wine, besides forty pieces* of silver. Even their
assistants took advantage of the people. But because I
feared God, I did not act that way.

16 I also devoted myself to working on the wall and
refused to acquire any land. And I required all my
servants to spend time working on the wall. 17 I asked
for nothing, even though I regularly fed 150 Jewish
officials at my table, besides all the visitors from oth-
er lands! 18 The provisions I paid for each day included
one ox, six choice sheep or goats, and a large number
of poultry. And every ten days we needed a large sup-
ply of all kinds of wine. Yet I refused to claim the gov-
ernor's food allowance because the people already
carried a heavy burden.

19 Remember, O my God, all that I have done for
these people, and bless me for it.

CONTINUED OPPOSITION TO REBUILDING

6 Sanballat, Tobiah, Geshem the Arab, and the
rest of our enemies found out that I had finished
rebuilding the wall and that no gaps remained—
though we had not yet set up the doors in the gates.
2 So Sanballat and Geshem sent a message asking me
to meet them at one of the villages* in the plain of Ono.

But I realized they were plotting to harm me, 3 so
I replied by sending this message to them: "I am en-
gaged in a great work, so I can't come. Why should I
stop working to come and meet with you?"

4 Four times they sent the same message, and each
time I gave the same reply. 5 The fifth time, Sanballat's
servant came with an open letter in his hand, 6 and
this is what it said:

"There is a rumor among the surrounding nations,
and Geshem* tells me it is true, that you and the
Jews are planning to rebel and that is why you
are building the wall. According to his reports,
you plan to be their king. 7 He also reports that you
have appointed prophets in Jerusalem to proclaim
about you, 'Look! There is a king in Judah!'

"You can be very sure that this report will get
back to the king, so I suggest that you come and
talk it over with me."

8 I replied, "There is no truth in any part of your sto-
ry. You are making up the whole thing."

9 They were just trying to intimidate us, imagining
that they could discourage us and stop the work. So I
continued the work with even greater determination.*

10 Later I went to visit Shemaiah son of Delaiah
and grandson of Mehetabel, who was confined to his
home. He said, "Let us meet together inside the Temple
of God and bolt the doors shut. Your enemies are com-
ing to kill you tonight."

11 But I replied, "Should someone in my position
run from danger? Should someone in my position en-
ter the Temple to save his life? No, I won't do it!" 12 I
realized that God had not spoken to him, but that he
had uttered this prophecy against me because Tobiah
and Sanballat had hired him. 13 They were hoping to
intimidate me and make me sin. Then they would be
able to accuse and discredit me.

14 Remember, O my God, all the evil things that
Tobiah and Sanballat have done. And remember
Noadiah the prophet and all the prophets like her
who have tried to intimidate me.

THE BUILDERS COMPLETE THE WALL

15 So on October 2* the wall was finished—just fif-
ty-two days after we had begun. 16 When our enemies
and the surrounding nations heard about it, they
were frightened and humiliated. They realized this
work had been done with the help of our God.

17 During those fifty-two days, many letters went
back and forth between Tobiah and the nobles of Ju-
dah. 18 For many in Judah had sworn allegiance to
him because his father-in-law was Shecaniah son
of Arah, and his son Jehohanan was married to the
daughter of Meshullam son of Berekiah. 19 They kept
telling me about Tobiah's good deeds, and then they
told him everything I said. And Tobiah kept sending
threatening letters to intimidate me.

5:14 That is, 445–433 B.C. **5:15** Hebrew *40 shekels* [1 pound or 456 grams]. **6:2** As in Greek version; Hebrew reads *at Kephirim.* **6:6** Hebrew *Gashmu,* a variant spelling of Geshem. **6:9** As in Greek version; Hebrew reads *But now to strengthen my hands.* **6:15** Hebrew *on the twenty-fifth day of the month Elul,* of the ancient Hebrew lunar calendar. This day was October 2, 445 B.C.; also see note on 1:1.

5:14-16 During his years as governor of Jerusalem, Nehemiah could have lent money and then foreclosed when the people could not repay their debts. But he would not abuse his position as governor.

6:2-3 Nehemiah's enemies tried to trap him by luring him away from Jerusalem for a meeting. But he refused to leave.

6:5-8 His enemies then accused Nehemiah of planning to overthrow King Artaxerxes. But he explained the lie to the Jewish workers and prayed for strength.

6:10-12 Nehemiah's enemies enlisted Shemaiah, a priest, in their plan to frighten Nehemiah into hiding from assassins in the holy place, which was forbidden by the Law (Num. 3:10; 18:7). But Nehemiah knew that a true priest or prophet would not advise someone to desecrate the sanctuary by disobeying the Law.

6:15 wall was finished. After lying in ruins for almost 150 years, the walls of Jerusalem were rebuilt in less than two months.

6:17 Tobiah. Many Jews traded with Tobiah and tried to convince Nehemiah of his loyalty to the project. But Tobiah actually opposed the work.

7 After the wall was finished and I had set up the
doors in the gates, the gatekeepers, singers, and
Levites were appointed. 2 I gave the responsibility of
governing Jerusalem to my brother Hanani, along
with Hananiah, the commander of the fortress, for
he was a faithful man who feared God more than
most. 3 I said to them, "Do not leave the gates open
during the hottest part of the day.* And even while
the gatekeepers are on duty, have them shut and bar
the doors. Appoint the residents of Jerusalem to act as
guards, everyone on a regular watch. Some will serve
at sentry posts and some in front of their own homes."

NEHEMIAH REGISTERS THE PEOPLE

4 At that time the city was large and spacious, but
the population was small, and none of the houses
had been rebuilt. 5 So my God gave me the idea to call
together all the nobles and leaders of the city, along
with the ordinary citizens, for registration. I had
found the genealogical record of those who had first
returned to Judah. This is what was written there:

6 Here is the list of the Jewish exiles of the prov-
inces who returned from their captivity. King
Nebuchadnezzar had deported them to Babylon,
but now they returned to Jerusalem and the other
towns in Judah where they originally lived. 7 Their
leaders were Zerubbabel, Jeshua, Nehemiah, Se-
raiah,* Reelaiah,* Nahamani, Mordecai, Bilshan,
Mispar,* Bigvai, Rehum,* and Baanah.

This is the number of the men of Israel who re-
turned from exile:

8 The family of Parosh........................2,172
9 The family of Shephatiah...................372
10 The family of Arah...........................652
11 The family of Pahath-moab
(descendants of Jeshua and Joab).......2,818
12 The family of Elam...........................1,254
13 The family of Zattu..........................845
14 The family of Zaccai.........................760
15 The family of Bani*..........................648
16 The family of Bebai..........................628
17 The family of Azgad.........................2,322
18 The family of Adonikam....................667
19 The family of Bigvai.........................2,067
20 The family of Adin............................655
21 The family of Ater (descendants of Hezekiah)..98
22 The family of Hashum.......................328
23 The family of Bezai..........................324
24 The family of Jorah*.........................112
25 The family of Gibbar*.......................95
26 The people of Bethlehem and Netophah....188
27 The people of Anathoth....................128
28 The people of Beth-azmaveth.............42
29 The people of Kiriath-jearim, Kephirah,
and Beeroth.......................................743
30 The people of Ramah and Geba...........621
31 The people of Micmash.......................122
32 The people of Bethel and Ai.................123
33 The people of West Nebo*....................52
34 The citizens of West Elam*..................1,254
35 The citizens of Harim........................320
36 The citizens of Jericho......................345
37 The citizens of Lod, Hadid, and Ono.......721
38 The citizens of Senaah.......................3,930

39 These are the priests who returned from exile:
The family of Jedaiah
(through the line of Jeshua)..............973
40 The family of Immer..........................1,052
41 The family of Pashhur........................1,247
42 The family of Harim...........................1,017

43 These are the Levites who returned from exile:
The families of Jeshua and Kadmiel (descendants
of Hodaviah*)....................................74
44 The singers of the family of Asaph.........148
45 The gatekeepers of the families of Shallum, Ater,
Talmon, Akkub, Hatita, and Shobai......138

46 The descendants of the following Temple ser-
vants returned from exile:
Ziha, Hasupha, Tabbaoth,
47 Keros, Siaha,* Padon,
48 Lebanah, Hagabah, Shalmai,
49 Hanan, Giddel, Gahar,
50 Reaiah, Rezin, Nekoda,
51 Gazzam, Uzza, Paseah,
52 Besai, Meunim, Nephusim,*
53 Bakbuk, Hakupha, Harhur,
54 Bazluth,* Mehida, Harsha,
55 Barkos, Sisera, Temah,
56 Neziah, and Hatipha.

57 The descendants of these servants of King Solo-
mon returned from exile:
Sotai, Hassophereth, Peruda,*
58 Jaalah,* Darkon, Giddel,
59 Shephatiah, Hattil, Pokereth-hazzebaim, and Ami.*

60 In all, the Temple servants and the descendants
of Solomon's servants numbered 392.

61 Another group returned at this time from the
towns of Tel-melah, Tel-harsha, Kerub, Addan,*
and Immer. However, they could not prove that
they or their families were descendants of Israel.
62 This group included the families of Delaiah,
Tobiah, and Nekoda—a total of 642 people.

7:3 Or *Keep the gates of Jerusalem closed until the sun is hot.* **7:7a** As in parallel text at Ezra 2:2; Hebrew reads *Azariah.* **7:7b** As in parallel text at Ezra 2:2; Hebrew reads *Raamiah.* **7:7c** As in parallel text at Ezra 2:2; Hebrew reads *Mispereth.* **7:7d** As in parallel text at Ezra 2:2; Hebrew reads *Nehum.* **7:15** As in parallel text at Ezra 2:10; Hebrew reads *Binnui.* **7:24** As in parallel text at Ezra 2:18; Hebrew reads *Hariph.* **7:25** As in parallel text at Ezra 2:20; Hebrew reads *Gibeon.* **7:33** Or *of the other Nebo.* **7:34** Or *of the other Elam.* **7:43** As in parallel text at Ezra 2:40; Hebrew reads *Hodevah.* **7:47** As in parallel text at Ezra 2:44; Hebrew reads *Sia.* **7:52** As in parallel text at Ezra 2:50; Hebrew reads *Nephushesim.* **7:54** As in parallel text at Ezra 2:52; Hebrew reads *Bazlith.* **7:57** As in parallel text at Ezra 2:55; Hebrew reads *Sotai, Sophereth, Perida.* **7:58** As in parallel text at Ezra 2:56; Hebrew reads *Jaala.* **7:59** As in parallel text at Ezra 2:57; Hebrew reads *Amon.* **7:61** As in parallel text at Ezra 2:59; Hebrew reads *Addon.*

7:2 he was a faithful man. This is one of the major lessons in Nehemiah: God brings success to those who are faithful to carry out His work.

7:3 have them shut and bar the doors. Nehemiah took sensible precautions by closing the city gates. Depending on God's protection does not excuse irresponsible behavior.

7:5 So my God gave me the idea. While taking action and using his common sense, Nehemiah relied on God's leadership. This combination of faithful work and prayerful obedience made him a great leader.

63 Three families of priests—Hobaiah, Hakkoz,
and Barzillai—also returned. (This Barzillai
had married a woman who was a descendant of
Barzillai of Gilead, and he had taken her family
name.) 64 They searched for their names in the
genealogical records, but they were not found, so
they were disqualified from serving as priests.
65 The governor told them not to eat the priests'
share of food from the sacrifices until a priest
could consult the LORD about the matter by using
the Urim and Thummim—the sacred lots.
66 So a total of 42,360 people returned to Judah,
67 in addition to 7,337 servants and 245 singers,
both men and women. 68 They took with them
736 horses, 245 mules,* 69 435 camels, and 6,720
donkeys.
70 Some of the family leaders gave gifts for the
work. The governor gave to the treasury 1,000
gold coins,* 50 gold basins, and 530 robes for the
priests. 71 The other leaders gave to the treasury a
total of 20,000 gold coins* and some 2,750 pounds*
of silver for the work. 72 The rest of the people gave
20,000 gold coins, about 2,500 pounds* of silver,
and 67 robes for the priests.
73 So the priests, the Levites, the gatekeepers,
the singers, the Temple servants, and some of the
common people settled near Jerusalem. The rest of
the people returned to their own towns through-
out Israel.

EZRA READS THE LAW

8 In October,* when the Israelites had settled in
their towns, 8:1 all the people assembled with a
unified purpose at the square just inside the Water
Gate. They asked Ezra the scribe to bring out the Book
of the Law of Moses, which the LORD had given for Is-
rael to obey.
2 So on October 8* Ezra the priest brought the Book
of the Law before the assembly, which included the
men and women and all the children old enough
to understand. 3 He faced the square just inside the
Water Gate from early morning until noon and read
aloud to everyone who could understand. All the peo-
ple listened closely to the Book of the Law.
4 Ezra the scribe stood on a high wooden platform
that had been made for the occasion. To his right
stood Mattithiah, Shema, Anaiah, Uriah, Hilkiah,
and Maaseiah. To his left stood Pedaiah, Mishael,
Malkijah, Hashum, Hashbaddanah, Zechariah, and
Meshullam. 5 Ezra stood on the platform in full view
of all the people. When they saw him open the book,
they all rose to their feet.
6 Then Ezra praised the LORD, the great God, and
all the people chanted, "Amen! Amen!" as they lifted
their hands. Then they bowed down and worshiped
the LORD with their faces to the ground.
7 The Levites—Jeshua, Bani, Sherebiah, Jamin, Ak-
kub, Shabbethai, Hodiah, Maaseiah, Kelita, Azariah,
Jozabad, Hanan, and Pelaiah—then instructed the
people in the Law while everyone remained in their
places. 8 They read from the Book of the Law of God
and clearly explained the meaning of what was being
read, helping the people understand each passage.
9 Then Nehemiah the governor, Ezra the priest and
scribe, and the Levites who were interpreting for the
people said to them, "Don't mourn or weep on such a
day as this! For today is a sacred day before the LORD
your God." For the people had all been weeping as
they listened to the words of the Law.
10 And Nehemiah* continued, "Go and celebrate
with a feast of rich foods and sweet drinks, and share
gifts of food with people who have nothing prepared.
This is a sacred day before our Lord. Don't be dejected
and sad, for the joy of the LORD is your strength!"
11 And the Levites, too, quieted the people, telling
them, "Hush! Don't weep! For this is a sacred day."
12 So the people went away to eat and drink at a fes-
tive meal, to share gifts of food, and to celebrate with
great joy because they had heard God's words and
understood them.

THE FESTIVAL OF SHELTERS

13 On October 9* the family leaders of all the people, to-
gether with the priests and Levites, met with Ezra the
scribe to go over the Law in greater detail. 14 As they
studied the Law, they discovered that the LORD had com-
manded through Moses that the Israelites should live in
shelters during the festival to be held that month.* 15 He
had said that a proclamation should be made through-
out their towns and in Jerusalem, telling the people to
go to the hills to get branches from olive, wild olive,*
myrtle, palm, and other leafy trees. They were to use
these branches to make shelters in which they would
live during the festival, as prescribed in the Law.
16 So the people went out and cut branches and used
them to build shelters on the roofs of their houses, in
their courtyards, in the courtyards of God's Temple,
or in the squares just inside the Water Gate and the
Ephraim Gate. 17 So everyone who had returned from
captivity lived in these shelters during the festival,

7:68 As in some Hebrew manuscripts (see also Ezra 2:66); most Hebrew manuscripts lack this verse. Verses 7:69-73 are numbered 7:68-72 in Hebrew text. **7:70** Hebrew *1,000 darics of gold,* about 19 pounds or 8.6 kilograms in weight. **7:71a** Hebrew *20,000 darics of gold,* about 375 pounds or 170 kilograms in weight; also in 7:72. **7:71b** Hebrew *2,200 minas* [1,300 kilograms]. **7:72** Hebrew *2,000 minas* [1,200 kilograms]. **7:73** Hebrew *In the seventh month.* This month of the ancient Hebrew lunar calendar occurred within the months of October and November 445 B.C. **8:2** Hebrew *on the first day of the seventh month,* of the ancient Hebrew lunar calendar. This day was October 8, 445 B.C.; also see note on 1:1. **8:10** Hebrew *he.* **8:13** Hebrew *On the second day,* of the seventh month of the ancient Hebrew lunar calendar. This day was October 9, 445 B.C.; also see notes on 1:1 and 8:2. **8:14** Hebrew *in the seventh month.* This month of the ancient Hebrew lunar calendar usually occurs within the months of September and October. See Lev 23:39-43. **8:15** Or *pine;* Hebrew reads *oil tree.*

8:1 all the people assembled with a unified purpose. The people from throughout Judah gathered to hear Ezra read and teach the Law from the five books of Moses (Deut. 31:11-12).

8:2 October 8. Taking place in the September-October period, the Feast of Trumpets was a time when work stopped and a sacred assembly was observed.

8:3 From early morning until noon and read aloud. Adults and children who were old enough to understand (vv. 2-3) listened attentively all morning as Ezra read from the Law.

8:10 Go and celebrate with a feast of rich foods. When the people heard the Law read and explained, they wept and repented of their sins. Pleased by their response, Nehemiah reminded them that it was a time to celebrate with feasting.

8:16 courtyards . . . squares. The priests and Levites built their booths to celebrate this feast in the courts of the temple. Residents of the cities built booths (temporary shelters for the feast) on the roofs of their houses or in the courtyards. People from the countryside set up huts in the streets. Booths commemorated the time of wandering in the wilderness when the people had no permanent homes (Lev. 23:43).

8:17 since the days of Joshua. Such joy in this celebration had not been expressed since Joshua's day because the people themselves had helped rebuild the walls.

and they were all filled with great joy! The Israelites
had not celebrated like this since the days of Joshua*
son of Nun.
18 Ezra read from the Book of the Law of God on
each of the seven days of the festival. Then on the
eighth day they held a solemn assembly, as was required by law.

THE PEOPLE CONFESS THEIR SINS

9 On October 31* the people assembled again, and
this time they fasted and dressed in burlap and
sprinkled dust on their heads. 2 Those of Israelite
descent separated themselves from all foreigners as
they confessed their own sins and the sins of their ancestors. 3 They remained standing in place for three
hours* while the Book of the Law of the LORD their
God was read aloud to them. Then for three more
hours they confessed their sins and worshiped the
LORD their God. 4 The Levites—Jeshua, Bani, Kadmiel, Shebaniah, Bunni, Sherebiah, Bani, and Kenani—
stood on the stairway of the Levites and cried out to
the LORD their God with loud voices.
5 Then the leaders of the Levites—Jeshua, Kadmiel, Bani, Hashabneiah, Sherebiah, Hodiah, Shebaniah,
and Pethahiah—called out to the people: "Stand up
and praise the LORD your God, for he lives from everlasting to everlasting!" Then they prayed:

"May your glorious name be praised! May it be
exalted above all blessing and praise!
6 "You alone are the LORD. You made the skies
and the heavens and all the stars. You made
the earth and the seas and everything in them.
You preserve them all, and the angels of heaven
worship you.
7 "You are the LORD God, who chose Abram
and brought him from Ur of the Chaldeans and
renamed him Abraham. 8 When he had proved
himself faithful, you made a covenant with him
to give him and his descendants the land of the
Canaanites, Hittites, Amorites, Perizzites, Jebusites,
and Girgashites. And you have done what you
promised, for you are always true to your word.
9 "You saw the misery of our ancestors in
Egypt, and you heard their cries from beside the
Red Sea.* 10 You displayed miraculous signs and
wonders against Pharaoh, his officials, and all his
people, for you knew how arrogantly they were
treating our ancestors. You have a glorious reputation that has never been forgotten. 11 You divided
the sea for your people so they could walk through
on dry land! And then you hurled their enemies
into the depths of the sea. They sank like stones beneath the mighty waters. 12 You led our ancestors
by a pillar of cloud during the day and a pillar of
fire at night so that they could find their way.
13 "You came down at Mount Sinai and spoke to
them from heaven. You gave them regulations and
instructions that were just, and decrees and commands that were good. 14 You instructed them concerning your holy Sabbath. And you commanded
them, through Moses your servant, to obey all
your commands, decrees, and instructions.
15 "You gave them bread from heaven when they
were hungry and water from the rock when they
were thirsty. You commanded them to go and take
possession of the land you had sworn to give them.
16 "But our ancestors were proud and stubborn,
and they paid no attention to your commands.
17 They refused to obey and did not remember the
miracles you had done for them. Instead, they
became stubborn and appointed a leader to take
them back to their slavery in Egypt.* But you are
a God of forgiveness, gracious and merciful, slow
to become angry, and rich in unfailing love. You
did not abandon them, 18 even when they made an
idol shaped like a calf and said, 'This is your god
who brought you out of Egypt!' They committed
terrible blasphemies.
19 "But in your great mercy you did not abandon
them to die in the wilderness. The pillar of cloud
still led them forward by day, and the pillar of fire
showed them the way through the night. 20 You
sent your good Spirit to instruct them, and you did
not stop giving them manna from heaven or water
for their thirst. 21 For forty years you sustained
them in the wilderness, and they lacked nothing.
Their clothes did not wear out, and their feet did
not swell!
22 "Then you helped our ancestors conquer kingdoms and nations, and you placed your people in
every corner of the land.* They took over the land
of King Sihon of Heshbon and the land of King
Og of Bashan. 23 You made their descendants as
numerous as the stars in the sky and brought them
into the land you had promised to their ancestors.
24 "They went in and took possession of the land.
You subdued whole nations before them. Even the
Canaanites, who inhabited the land, were powerless! Your people could deal with these nations
and their kings as they pleased. 25 Our ancestors
captured fortified cities and fertile land. They
took over houses full of good things, with cisterns
already dug and vineyards and olive groves and

8:17 Hebrew *Jeshua,* a variant spelling of Joshua. **9:1** Hebrew *On the twenty-fourth day of that same month,* the seventh month of the ancient Hebrew lunar calendar. This day was October 31, 445 B.C.; also see notes on 1:1 and 8:2. **9:3** Hebrew *for a quarter of a day.* **9:9** Hebrew *sea of reeds.* **9:17** As in Greek version; Hebrew reads *in their rebellion.* **9:22** The meaning of the Hebrew is uncertain.

9:1 fasted . . . burlap . . . dust. These actions symbolized remorse over sin. Sackcloth was a dark, coarse cloth made from goat's hair (Pss. 30:11; 35:13). Dust refers to ashes (1 Sam. 4:12).

9:5 your glorious name. The importance of God's name is spelled out in the Law. The Levites recalled times when God showed His goodness to the Jews. They called attention to the covenant and its requirement of obedience.

9:13 You gave . . . instructions that were just. God took the initiative in calling Israel and giving them laws and instructions that would raise the quality of life for them as individuals and a society and would reflect God's glory through them to the other nations. Those who have lived in societies with the rule of law may not be able to appreciate how much more desirable life is in such a society than in societies where might makes right.

9:14 You instructed them concerning your holy Sabbath. God's day of rest is a gift born of grace and wisdom. Religious leaders have often made Sabbath a burden—a set of rules to be followed. Jesus' interpretation was that Sabbath was made for man—designed as a gift to bring blessing, thus enhancing life.

9:15 You gave them bread . . . and water. God not only gave instruction but supplied the most basic provisions of life, bread and water. **the land you had sworn to give them.** God's gifts were daily reminders that He was going to provide the land He had long promised. These generous gifts daily revealed the character of this One who is the very Source of truthworthiness and reliability. How awesome that the Creator of the universe has sworn to give a small group of freed slaves a land!

9:16 our ancestors were proud and stubborn. The Levites' prayer extolled God's graciousness and compassion, even in the face of disobedience and idol worship (Ex. 32). The priests emphasized that although God's people had rebelled, God mercifully forgave them and restored them to the land.

fruit trees in abundance. So they ate until they
were full and grew fat and enjoyed themselves in
all your blessings.
26 "But despite all this, they were disobedient
and rebelled against you. They turned their backs
on your Law, they killed your prophets who
warned them to return to you, and they committed
terrible blasphemies. 27 So you handed them over
to their enemies, who made them suffer. But in
their time of trouble they cried to you, and you
heard them from heaven. In your great mercy, you
sent them liberators who rescued them from their
enemies.
28 "But as soon as they were at peace, your
people again committed evil in your sight, and
once more you let their enemies conquer them.
Yet whenever your people turned and cried to
you again for help, you listened once more from
heaven. In your wonderful mercy, you rescued
them many times!
29 "You warned them to return to your Law, but
they became proud and obstinate and disobeyed
your commands. They did not follow your regu-
lations, by which people will find life if only they
obey. They stubbornly turned their backs on you
and refused to listen. 30 In your love, you were
patient with them for many years. You sent your
Spirit, who warned them through the prophets.
But still they wouldn't listen! So once again you
allowed the peoples of the land to conquer them.
31 But in your great mercy, you did not destroy
them completely or abandon them forever. What a
gracious and merciful God you are!
32 "And now, our God, the great and mighty and
awesome God, who keeps his covenant of unfailing
love, do not let all the hardships we have suffered
seem insignificant to you. Great trouble has come
upon us and upon our kings and leaders and
priests and prophets and ancestors—all of your
people—from the days when the kings of Assyria
first triumphed over us until now. 33 Every time
you punished us you were being just. We have
sinned greatly, and you gave us only what we de-
served. 34 Our kings, leaders, priests, and ancestors
did not obey your Law or listen to the warnings in
your commands and laws. 35 Even while they had
their own kingdom, they did not serve you, though
you showered your goodness on them. You gave
them a large, fertile land, but they refused to turn
from their wickedness.
36 "So now today we are slaves in the land of
plenty that you gave our ancestors for their enjoy-
ment! We are slaves here in this good land. 37 The
lush produce of this land piles up in the hands of
the kings whom you have set over us because of
our sins. They have power over us and our live-
stock. We serve them at their pleasure, and we are
in great misery."

THE PEOPLE AGREE TO OBEY

38*The people responded, "In view of all this,* we are
making a solemn promise and putting it in writing.
On this sealed document are the names of our leaders
and Levites and priests."

10 1*The document was ratified and sealed with
the following names:

The governor:
Nehemiah son of Hacaliah, and also Zedekiah.
2 The following priests:
Seraiah, Azariah, Jeremiah, 3 Pashhur, Amariah,
Malkijah, 4 Hattush, Shebaniah, Malluch, 5 Harim,
Meremoth, Obadiah, 6 Daniel, Ginnethon, Baruch,
7 Meshullam, Abijah, Mijamin, 8 Maaziah, Bilgai,
and Shemaiah. These were the priests.
9 The following Levites:
Jeshua son of Azaniah, Binnui from the family
of Henadad, Kadmiel, 10 and their fellow Levites:
Shebaniah, Hodiah, Kelita, Pelaiah, Hanan, 11 Mica,
Rehob, Hashabiah, 12 Zaccur, Sherebiah, Shebani-
ah, 13 Hodiah, Bani, and Beninu.
14 The following leaders:
Parosh, Pahath-moab, Elam, Zattu, Bani, 15 Bunni,
Azgad, Bebai, 16 Adonijah, Bigvai, Adin, 17 Ater,
Hezekiah, Azzur, 18 Hodiah, Hashum, Bezai, 19 Har-
iph, Anathoth, Nebai, 20 Magpiash, Meshullam,
Hezir, 21 Meshezabel, Zadok, Jaddua, 22 Pelatiah,
Hanan, Anaiah, 23 Hoshea, Hananiah, Hasshub,
24 Hallohesh, Pilha, Shobek, 25 Rehum, Hashabnah,
Maaseiah, 26 Ahiah, Hanan, Anan, 27 Malluch,
Harim, and Baanah.

THE VOW OF THE PEOPLE

28 Then the rest of the people—the priests, Levites,
gatekeepers, singers, Temple servants, and all who
had separated themselves from the pagan people of
the land in order to obey the Law of God, together
with their wives, sons, daughters, and all who were
old enough to understand—29 joined their leaders
and bound themselves with an oath. They swore a
curse on themselves if they failed to obey the Law of
God as issued by his servant Moses. They solemnly
promised to carefully follow all the commands, regu-
lations, and decrees of the LORD our Lord:

30 "We promise not to let our daughters marry the
pagan people of the land, and not to let our sons
marry their daughters.
31 "We also promise that if the people of the land
should bring any merchandise or grain to be sold
on the Sabbath or on any other holy day, we will
refuse to buy it. Every seventh year we will let our
land rest, and we will cancel all debts owed to us.
32 "In addition, we promise to obey the command
to pay the annual Temple tax of one-eighth of an
ounce of silver* for the care of the Temple of our

9:38a Verse 9:38 is numbered 10:1 in Hebrew text. **9:38b** Or *In spite of all this.* **10:1** Verses 10:1-39 are numbered 10:2-40 in Hebrew text. **10:32** Hebrew *tax of* $^{1}/_{3}$ *of a shekel* [4 grams].

10:1-8 sealed with the following names. Twenty-four heads of families signed the agreement to obey the Law. A distinctive seal authenticating the document was pressed into soft clay, similar to the use of sealing wax in later years.

10:31-33 Sabbath. The agreement spelled out the leaders' commitment to avoid intermarriage: keep the Sabbath by refraining from work (Ex. 20:10) and provide for the needs of the temple. The commitment to avoid intermarriage was not racially but spiritually motivated. Marriage to Canaanite women had been a key factor in leading Israel away from walking in the ways of God. These families sought to avoid the paths of their forefathers. **seventh year . . . cancel all debts.** Fields were to be left uncultivated, and debts forgiven every seventh year (Lev. 25:1-7). The word Sabbath literally means cessation or rest. The various periods of rest were design to help God's people depend on Him to supply their needs, even in these times of cessation. Also, it served to remind them that the earth is the Lord's and they are only temporary stewards of it.

God. 33 This will provide for the Bread of the Pres-
ence; for the regular grain offerings and burnt
offerings; for the offerings on the Sabbaths, the
new moon celebrations, and the annual festivals;
for the holy offerings; and for the sin offerings
to make atonement for Israel. It will provide for
everything necessary for the work of the Temple
of our God.

34 "We have cast sacred lots to determine
when—at regular times each year—the families
of the priests, Levites, and the common people
should bring wood to God's Temple to be burned
on the altar of the LORD our God, as is written in
the Law.

35 "We promise to bring the first part of every
harvest to the LORD's Temple year after year—
whether it be a crop from the soil or from our
fruit trees. 36 We agree to give God our oldest sons
and the firstborn of all our herds and flocks, as
prescribed in the Law. We will present them to
the priests who minister in the Temple of our God.
37 We will store the produce in the storerooms of
the Temple of our God. We will bring the best of
our flour and other grain offerings, the best of our
fruit, and the best of our new wine and olive oil.
And we promise to bring to the Levites a tenth of
everything our land produces, for it is the Levites
who collect the tithes in all our rural towns.

38 "A priest—a descendant of Aaron—will be
with the Levites as they receive these tithes. And
a tenth of all that is collected as tithes will be
delivered by the Levites to the Temple of our God
and placed in the storerooms. 39 The people and the
Levites must bring these offerings of grain, new
wine, and olive oil to the storerooms and place
them in the sacred containers near the minister-
ing priests, the gatekeepers, and the singers.

"We promise together not to neglect the Temple
of our God."

THE PEOPLE OCCUPY JERUSALEM

11 The leaders of the people were living in Jeru-
salem, the holy city. A tenth of the people from
the other towns of Judah and Benjamin were chosen
by sacred lots to live there, too, while the rest stayed
where they were. 2 And the people commended every-
one who volunteered to resettle in Jerusalem.

3 Here is a list of the names of the provincial officials
who came to live in Jerusalem. (Most of the people,
priests, Levites, Temple servants, and descendants of Sol-
omon's servants continued to live in their own homes in
the various towns of Judah, 4 but some of the people from
Judah and Benjamin resettled in Jerusalem.)

From the tribe of Judah:

Athaiah son of Uzziah, son of Zechariah, son of
Amariah, son of Shephatiah, son of Mahalalel, of
the family of Perez. 5 Also Maaseiah son of Baruch,
son of Col-hozeh, son of Hazaiah, son of Adaiah,
son of Joiarib, son of Zechariah, of the family of
Shelah.* 6 There were 468 descendants of Perez
who lived in Jerusalem—all outstanding men.

7 From the tribe of Benjamin:

Sallu son of Meshullam, son of Joed, son of
Pedaiah, son of Kolaiah, son of Maaseiah, son of
Ithiel, son of Jeshaiah. 8 After him were Gabbai
and Sallai and a total of 928 relatives. 9 Their chief
officer was Joel son of Zicri, who was assisted by
Judah son of Hassenuah, second-in-command over
the city.

10 From the priests:

Jedaiah son of Joiarib; Jakin; 11 and Seraiah son
of Hilkiah, son of Meshullam, son of Zadok, son
of Meraioth, son of Ahitub, the supervisor of the
Temple of God. 12 Also 822 of their associates, who
worked at the Temple. Also Adaiah son of Jero-
ham, son of Pelaliah, son of Amzi, son of Zechari-
ah, son of Pashhur, son of Malkijah, 13 along with
242 of his associates, who were heads of their fam-
ilies. Also Amashsai son of Azarel, son of Ahzai,
son of Meshillemoth, son of Immer, 14 and 128 of
his* outstanding associates. Their chief officer was
Zabdiel son of Haggedolim.

15 From the Levites:

Shemaiah son of Hasshub, son of Azrikam, son of
Hashabiah, son of Bunni. 16 Also Shabbethai and
Jozabad, who were in charge of the work outside
the Temple of God. 17 Also Mattaniah son of Mica,
son of Zabdi, a descendant of Asaph, who led in
thanksgiving and prayer. Also Bakbukiah, who
was Mattaniah's assistant, and Abda son of Sham-
mua, son of Galal, son of Jeduthun. 18 In all, there
were 284 Levites in the holy city.

19 From the gatekeepers:

Akkub, Talmon, and 172 of their associates, who
guarded the gates.

20 The other priests, Levites, and the rest of the Isra-
elites lived wherever their family inheritance was lo-
cated in any of the towns of Judah. 21 The Temple ser-
vants, however, whose leaders were Ziha and Gishpa,
all lived on the hill of Ophel.

22 The chief officer of the Levites in Jerusalem was
Uzzi son of Bani, son of Hashabiah, son of Mattaniah,
son of Mica, a descendant of Asaph, whose family
served as singers at God's Temple. 23 Their daily re-
sponsibilities were carried out according to the terms
of a royal command.

24 Pethahiah son of Meshezabel, a descendant of
Zerah son of Judah, was the royal adviser in all mat-
ters of public administration.

25 As for the surrounding villages with their open
fields, some of the people of Judah lived in Kiriath-
arba with its settlements, Dibon with its settlements,
and Jekabzeel with its villages. 26 They also lived in
Jeshua, Moladah, Beth-pelet, 27 Hazar-shual, Beer-

11:5 Hebrew *son of the Shilonite.* **11:14** As in Greek version; Hebrew reads *their.*

10:35 first part of every harvest. This means giving to the Lord from the first and best crops to acknowledge that God owns the land. Firstfruits of the trees meant giving over and above what the Law required to provide wood to keep the altar fire burning constantly (Lev. 6:12-13). The people cast lots to put together a schedule by which families would be responsible for providing the wood for the altar.

10:37 in the storerooms. The precious metals and temple articles were stored in rooms in the temple courts.

11:1 tenth of the people. Along with the leaders, one-tenth of the people were to settle in Jerusalem to make it a strong and vital city.

11:10-18 priests . . . Levites. The priests, from six family heads, totaled 1,192 (vv. 10-14). The number given in 1 Chronicles 9:13 is 1,760. There were fewer Levites, only 284 (vv. 15-18). Many Levites did not return to Judah from the exile.

sheba with its settlements, 28 Ziklag, and Meconah
with its settlements. 29 They also lived in En-rimmon,
Zorah, Jarmuth, 30 Zanoah, and Adullam with their
surrounding villages. They also lived in Lachish with
its nearby fields and Azekah with its surrounding vil-
lages. So the people of Judah were living all the way
from Beersheba in the south to the valley of Hinnom.
31 Some of the people of Benjamin lived at Geba,
Micmash, Aija, and Bethel with its settlements.
32 They also lived in Anathoth, Nob, Ananiah, 33 Ha-
zor, Ramah, Gittaim, 34 Hadid, Zeboim, Neballat, 35 Lod,
Ono, and the Valley of Craftsmen.* 36 Some of the Lev-
ites who lived in Judah were sent to live with the tribe
of Benjamin.

A HISTORY OF THE PRIESTS AND LEVITES

12 Here is the list of the priests and Levites who
returned with Zerubbabel son of Shealtiel and
Jeshua the high priest:

Seraiah, Jeremiah, Ezra,
2 Amariah, Malluch, Hattush,
3 Shecaniah, Harim,* Meremoth,
4 Iddo, Ginnethon,* Abijah,
5 Miniamin, Moadiah,* Bilgah,
6 Shemaiah, Joiarib, Jedaiah,
7 Sallu, Amok, Hilkiah, and Jedaiah.
These were the leaders of the priests and their associ-
ates in the days of Jeshua.

8 The Levites who returned with them were Jeshua,
Binnui, Kadmiel, Sherebiah, Judah, and Mattaniah,
who with his associates was in charge of the songs of
thanksgiving. 9 Their associates, Bakbukiah and Unni,
stood opposite them during the service.

10 Jeshua the high priest was the father of Joiakim.
Joiakim was the father of Eliashib.
Eliashib was the father of Joiada.
11 Joiada was the father of Johanan.*
Johanan was the father of Jaddua.

12 Now when Joiakim was high priest, the family lead-
ers of the priests were as follows:

Meraiah was leader of the family of Seraiah.
Hananiah was leader of the family of Jeremiah.
13 Meshullam was leader of the family of Ezra.
Jehohanan was leader of the family of Amariah.
14 Jonathan was leader of the family of Malluch.*
Joseph was leader of the family of Shecaniah.*
15 Adna was leader of the family of Harim.
Helkai was leader of the family of Meremoth.*
16 Zechariah was leader of the family of Iddo.
Meshullam was leader of the family of Ginnethon.
17 Zicri was leader of the family of Abijah.
There was also a* leader of the family of Miniamin.
Piltai was leader of the family of Moadiah.
18 Shammua was leader of the family of Bilgah.
Jehonathan was leader of the family of Shemaiah.
19 Mattenai was leader of the family of Joiarib.
Uzzi was leader of the family of Jedaiah.
20 Kallai was leader of the family of Sallu.*
Eber was leader of the family of Amok.
21 Hashabiah was leader of the family of Hilkiah.
Nethanel was leader of the family of Jedaiah.

22 A record of the Levite families was kept during
the years when Eliashib, Joiada, Johanan, and Jaddua
served as high priest. Another record of the priests
was kept during the reign of Darius the Persian.* 23 A
record of the heads of the Levite families was kept in
The Book of History down to the days of Johanan, the
grandson* of Eliashib.
24 These were the family leaders of the Levites:
Hashabiah, Sherebiah, Jeshua, Binnui,* Kadmiel, and
other associates, who stood opposite them during the
ceremonies of praise and thanksgiving, one section
responding to the other, as commanded by David, the
man of God. 25 This included Mattaniah, Bakbukiah,
and Obadiah.
Meshullam, Talmon, and Akkub were the gate-
keepers in charge of the storerooms at the gates.
26 These all served in the days of Joiakim son of Jeshua,
son of Jehozadak,* and in the days of Nehemiah the
governor and of Ezra the priest and scribe.

DEDICATION OF JERUSALEM'S WALL

27 For the dedication of the new wall of Jerusalem, the
Levites throughout the land were asked to come to
Jerusalem to assist in the ceremonies. They were to
take part in the joyous occasion with their songs of
thanksgiving and with the music of cymbals, harps,
and lyres. 28 The singers were brought together from
the region around Jerusalem and from the villages of
the Netophathites. 29 They also came from Beth-gilgal
and the rural areas near Geba and Azmaveth, for the
singers had built their own settlements around Jeru-
salem. 30 The priests and Levites first purified them-
selves; then they purified the people, the gates, and
the wall.
31 I led the leaders of Judah to the top of the wall
and organized two large choirs to give thanks. One
of the choirs proceeded southward* along the top of
the wall to the Dung Gate. 32 Hoshaiah and half the
leaders of Judah followed them, 33 along with Azari-
ah, Ezra, Meshullam, 34 Judah, Benjamin, Shemaiah,
and Jeremiah. 35 Then came some priests who played
trumpets, including Zechariah son of Jonathan, son
of Shemaiah, son of Mattaniah, son of Micaiah, son
of Zaccur, a descendant of Asaph. 36 And Zechariah's
colleagues were Shemaiah, Azarel, Milalai, Gilalai,
Maai, Nethanel, Judah, and Hanani. They used the
musical instruments prescribed by David, the man
of God. Ezra the scribe led this procession. 37 At the
Fountain Gate they went straight up the steps on the
ascent of the city wall toward the City of David. They
passed the house of David and then proceeded to the
Water Gate on the east.

11:35 Or *and Ge-harashim.* **12:3** Hebrew *Rehum;* compare 7:42; 12:15; Ezra 2:39. **12:4** As in some Hebrew manuscripts and Latin Vulgate (see also 12:16); most Hebrew manuscripts read *Ginnethoi.* **12:5** Hebrew *Mijamin, Maadiah;* compare 12:17. **12:11** Hebrew *Jonathan;* compare 12:22. **12:14a** As in Greek version (see also 10:4; 12:2); Hebrew reads *Malluchi.* **12:14b** As in many Hebrew manuscripts, some Greek manuscripts, and Syriac version (see also 12:3); most Hebrew manuscripts read *Shebaniah.* **12:15** As in some Greek manuscripts (see also 12:3); Hebrew reads *Meraioth.* **12:17** Hebrew lacks the name of this family leader. **12:20** Hebrew *Sallai;* compare 12:7. **12:22** *Darius the Persian* is probably Darius II, who reigned 423–404 B.C., or possibly Darius III, who reigned 336–331 B.C. **12:23** Hebrew *descendant;* compare 12:10-11. **12:24** Hebrew *son of* (i.e., *ben*), which should probably be read here as the proper name Binnui; compare Ezra 3:9 and the note there. **12:26** Hebrew *Jozadak,* a variant spelling of Jehozadak. **12:31** Hebrew *to the right.*

38 The second choir giving thanks went northward* around the other way to meet them. I followed them, together with the other half of the people, along the top of the wall past the Tower of the Ovens to the Broad Wall, 39 then past the Ephraim Gate to the Old City Gate,* past the Fish Gate and the Tower of Hananel, and on to the Tower of the Hundred. Then we continued on to the Sheep Gate and stopped at the Guard Gate.

40 The two choirs that were giving thanks then proceeded to the Temple of God, where they took their places. So did I, together with the group of leaders who were with me. 41 We went together with the trumpet-playing priests—Eliakim, Maaseiah, Miniamin, Micaiah, Elioenai, Zechariah, and Hananiah—42 and the singers—Maaseiah, Shemaiah, Eleazar, Uzzi, Jehohanan, Malkijah, Elam, and Ezer. They played and sang loudly under the direction of Jezrahiah the choir director.

43 Many sacrifices were offered on that joyous day, for God had given the people cause for great joy. The women and children also participated in the celebration, and the joy of the people of Jerusalem could be heard far away.

PROVISIONS FOR TEMPLE WORSHIP

44 On that day men were appointed to be in charge of the storerooms for the offerings, the first part of the harvest, and the tithes. They were responsible to collect from the fields outside the towns the portions required by the Law for the priests and Levites. For all the people of Judah took joy in the priests and Levites and their work. 45 They performed the service of their God and the service of purification, as commanded by David and his son Solomon, and so did the singers and the gatekeepers. 46 The custom of having choir directors to lead the choirs in hymns of praise and thanksgiving to God began long ago in the days of David and Asaph. 47 So now, in the days of Zerubbabel and of Nehemiah, all Israel brought a daily supply of food for the singers, the gatekeepers, and the Levites. The Levites, in turn, gave a portion of what they received to the priests, the descendants of Aaron.

NEHEMIAH'S VARIOUS REFORMS

13 On that same day, as the Book of Moses was being read to the people, the passage was found that said no Ammonite or Moabite should ever be permitted to enter the assembly of God.* 2 For they had not provided the Israelites with food and water in the wilderness. Instead, they hired Balaam to curse them, though our God turned the curse into a blessing. 3 When this passage of the Law was read, all those of foreign descent were immediately excluded from the assembly.

4 Before this had happened, Eliashib the priest, who had been appointed as supervisor of the storerooms of the Temple of our God and who was also a relative of Tobiah, 5 had converted a large storage room and placed it at Tobiah's disposal. The room had previously been used for storing the grain offerings, the frankincense, various articles for the Temple, and the tithes of grain, new wine, and olive oil (which were prescribed for the Levites, the singers, and the gatekeepers), as well as the offerings for the priests.

6 I was not in Jerusalem at that time, for I had returned to King Artaxerxes of Babylon in the thirty-second year of his reign,* though I later asked his permission to return. 7 When I arrived back in Jerusalem, I learned about Eliashib's evil deed in providing Tobiah with a room in the courtyards of the Temple of God. 8 I became very upset and threw all of Tobiah's belongings out of the room. 9 Then I demanded that the rooms be purified, and I brought back the articles for God's Temple, the grain offerings, and the frankincense.

10 I also discovered that the Levites had not been given their prescribed portions of food, so they and the singers who were to conduct the worship services had all returned to work their fields. 11 I immediately confronted the leaders and demanded, "Why has the Temple of God been neglected?" Then I called all the Levites back again and restored them to their proper duties. 12 And once more all the people of Judah began bringing their tithes of grain, new wine, and olive oil to the Temple storerooms.

13 I assigned supervisors for the storerooms: Shelemiah the priest, Zadok the scribe, and Pedaiah, one of the Levites. And I appointed Hanan son of Zaccur and grandson of Mattaniah as their assistant. These men had an excellent reputation, and it was their job to make honest distributions to their fellow Levites.

14 Remember this good deed, O my God, and do not forget all that I have faithfully done for the Temple of my God and its services.

15 In those days I saw men of Judah treading out their winepresses on the Sabbath. They were also bringing in grain, loading it on donkeys, and bringing their wine, grapes, figs, and all sorts of produce to Jerusalem to sell on the Sabbath. So I rebuked them for selling their produce on that day. 16 Some men from Tyre, who lived in Jerusalem, were bringing in fish and all kinds of merchandise. They were selling it on the Sabbath to the people of Judah—and in Jerusalem at that!

17 So I confronted the nobles of Judah. "Why are you profaning the Sabbath in this evil way?" I asked. 18 "Wasn't it just this sort of thing that your ancestors did that caused our God to bring all this trouble upon us and our city? Now you are bringing even more

12:38 Hebrew *to the left.* **12:39** Or *the Mishneh Gate,* or *the Jeshanah Gate.* **13:1** See Deut 23:3-6. **13:6** King Artaxerxes of Persia is here identified as the king of Babylon because Persia had conquered the Babylonian Empire. The thirty-second year of Artaxerxes was 433 B.C.

12:44 Judah took joy in the priests and Levites. The joy of the celebration overflowed into generous provision for the temple. The priests and Levites followed the pattern of worship that David had established (1 Chron. 22–26), including the prominent role of music.

12:47 all Israel brought . . . food. Giving firstfruits and tithes was to be a continual practice rather than a one-time event. Everyone participated in this contribution.

13:5-8 When Nehemiah returned to Jerusalem after an absence of several months, he discovered that the high priest had allowed Tobiah to occupy one of the temple storerooms. Tobiah had opposed the rebuilding of Jerusalem's walls, so Nehemiah threw out his belongings and refilled the storeroom with grain.

13:10-13 Nehemiah discovered that the people had not brought their tithes and offerings to support the temple. He reprimanded them for their laxity and then appointed several people to oversee these tithes. He realized that neglect could undo the reforms already accomplished.

13:17-19 Nehemiah stopped commercial activity on the Sabbath by shutting the city gates on Friday evening and posting guards.

wrath upon Israel by permitting the Sabbath to be
desecrated in this way!"
19 Then I commanded that the gates of Jerusalem
should be shut as darkness fell every Friday evening,*
not to be opened until the Sabbath ended. I sent some
of my own servants to guard the gates so that no
merchandise could be brought in on the Sabbath day.
20 The merchants and tradesmen with a variety of
wares camped outside Jerusalem once or twice. 21 But
I spoke sharply to them and said, "What are you do-
ing out here, camping around the wall? If you do this
again, I will arrest you!" And that was the last time
they came on the Sabbath. 22 Then I commanded the
Levites to purify themselves and to guard the gates in
order to preserve the holiness of the Sabbath.

Remember this good deed also, O my God! Have
compassion on me according to your great and
unfailing love.

23 About the same time I realized that some of the
men of Judah had married women from Ashdod, Am-
mon, and Moab. 24 Furthermore, half their children
spoke the language of Ashdod or of some other people
and could not speak the language of Judah at all. 25 So
I confronted them and called down curses on them. I
beat some of them and pulled out their hair. I made
them swear in the name of God that they would not
let their children intermarry with the pagan people
of the land.
26 "Wasn't this exactly what led King Solomon of Is-
rael into sin?" I demanded. "There was no king from
any nation who could compare to him, and God loved
him and made him king over all Israel. But even he was
led into sin by his foreign wives. 27 How could you even
think of committing this sinful deed and acting unfaith-
fully toward God by marrying foreign women?"
28 One of the sons of Joiada son of Eliashib the high
priest had married a daughter of Sanballat the Horo-
nite, so I banished him from my presence.

29 Remember them, O my God, for they have defiled
the priesthood and the solemn vows of the priests
and Levites.

30 So I purged out everything foreign and assigned
tasks to the priests and Levites, making certain that
each knew his work. 31 I also made sure that the sup-
ply of wood for the altar and the first portions of the
harvest were brought at the proper times.

Remember this in my favor, O my God.

13:19 Hebrew *on the day before the Sabbath.*

13:23 some of the men of Judah had married women from Ashdod, Ammon, and Moab. Ezra had dealt with the problem of intermarriage thirty years earlier (Ezra 9:1-4), and the people had made a vow not to marry foreign wives.

13:25 they would not let their children intermarry with the pagan people. Nehemiah did not dissolve the foreign marriages as Ezra had done, but he reacted passionately, realizing that intermarriage had led to Israel's captivity by Babylon.

13:26 King Solomon. Nehemiah reminded the people of this king of Israel, who drifted away from God when he married foreign women (1 Kings 11:1-8). Solomon worshipped his foreign wives' idols, which drew his heart away from God. He even built high places to the false gods (1 Kings 11:7).

INTRODUCTION TO

ESTHER

PERSONAL READING PLAN

☐Esther 1:1-22
☐Esther 2:1-23
☐Esther 3:1–4:17
☐Esther 5:1–6:14
☐Esther 7:1–8:17
☐Esther 9:1–10:3

AUTHOR

The author is unknown but was most likely a Jewish nationalist who was a resident of a Persian city. Some suggest that Mordecai was the author.

DATE

The writing of Esther was no earlier than the reign of Xerxes (ca 486–465 B.C.), and probably no later than 331 B.C., when the Persian Empire fell to Greece.

THEME

The providence of God in the free decisions of people, especially in delivering the Jews under Xerxes — also a profile in human courage.

HISTORICAL BACKGROUND

More than a generation had passed since Cyrus defeated the Babylonians and allowed the Jews to return to Israel. Still, many Jews remained scattered throughout the known world, making their home among their captors. The book of Esther features some of these expatriates. It is noteworthy that Artaxerxes, the son of Xerxes, was king during Nehemiah's time. He may have been influenced by Queen Esther in his handling of the Jews (see Neh. 2:6).

CHARACTERISTICS

The book of Esther recounts how the feast of Purim came to be celebrated—a feast still observed today by Jews in memory of God's sovereign, providential care of His people. The story revolves around 10 banquets (1:3-4; 1:5-8; 1:9; 2:18; 3:15; 5:1-8; 7:1-10; 8:17; 9:17; 9:18-32). The banquets culminate in the double celebration of the feast of Purim. Interestingly, the book of Esther does not directly name God. This conspicuous lack of any reference to God focuses attention on what He is doing, behind the scenes, to effect deliverance for the Jews. Esther is a literary masterpiece that reads like a modern suspense novel, complete with plot twists, coincidence, irony, intrigue, revenge, and plenty of feasting.

PASSAGES FOR TOPICAL GROUP STUDY

2:1-18 . . . POPULARITY and RISK . . . . A Beauty Contest

THE KING'S BANQUET

1 These events happened in the days of King Xerx-
es,* who reigned over 127 provinces stretching
from India to Ethiopia.* [2]At that time Xerxes ruled
his empire from his royal throne at the fortress of
Susa. [3]In the third year of his reign, he gave a ban-
quet for all his nobles and officials. He invited all the
military officers of Persia and Media as well as the
princes and nobles of the provinces. [4]The celebration
lasted 180 days—a tremendous display of the opu-
lent wealth of his empire and the pomp and splendor
of his majesty.

[5]When it was all over, the king gave a banquet
for all the people, from the greatest to the least, who
were in the fortress of Susa. It lasted for seven days
and was held in the courtyard of the palace garden.
[6]The courtyard was beautifully decorated with
white cotton curtains and blue hangings, which
were fastened with white linen cords and purple
ribbons to silver rings embedded in marble pillars.
Gold and silver couches stood on a mosaic pavement
of porphyry, marble, mother-of-pearl, and other
costly stones.

[7]Drinks were served in gold goblets of many de-
signs, and there was an abundance of royal wine, re-
flecting the king's generosity. [8]By edict of the king, no
limits were placed on the drinking, for the king had
instructed all his palace officials to serve each man as
much as he wanted.

[9]At the same time, Queen Vashti gave a banquet for
the women in the royal palace of King Xerxes.

QUEEN VASHTI DEPOSED

[10]On the seventh day of the feast, when King Xerx-
es was in high spirits because of the wine, he told
the seven eunuchs who attended him—Mehuman,
Biztha, Harbona, Bigtha, Abagtha, Zethar, and Car-
cas—[11]to bring Queen Vashti to him with the royal
crown on her head. He wanted the nobles and all the
other men to gaze on her beauty, for she was a very
beautiful woman. [12]But when they conveyed the
king's order to Queen Vashti, she refused to come.
This made the king furious, and he burned with an-
ger.

[13]He immediately consulted with his wise advisers,
who knew all the Persian laws and customs, for he
always asked their advice. [14]The names of these men
were Carshena, Shethar, Admatha, Tarshish, Meres,
Marsena, and Memucan—seven nobles of Persia and
Media. They met with the king regularly and held the
highest positions in the empire.

[15]"What must be done to Queen Vashti?" the king
demanded. "What penalty does the law provide for a
queen who refuses to obey the king's orders, properly
sent through his eunuchs?"

[16]Memucan answered the king and his nobles,
"Queen Vashti has wronged not only the king but
also every noble and citizen throughout your em-
pire. [17]Women everywhere will begin to despise
their husbands when they learn that Queen Vash-
ti has refused to appear before the king. [18]Before
this day is out, the wives of all the king's nobles
throughout Persia and Media will hear what the
queen did and will start treating their husbands the
same way. There will be no end to their contempt
and anger.

[19]"So if it please the king, we suggest that you issue
a written decree, a law of the Persians and Medes that
cannot be revoked. It should order that Queen Vash-
ti be forever banished from the presence of King Xe-
rxes, and that the king should choose another queen
more worthy than she. [20]When this decree is pub-
lished throughout the king's vast empire, husbands
everywhere, whatever their rank, will receive proper
respect from their wives!"

[21]The king and his nobles thought this made good
sense, so he followed Memucan's counsel. [22]He sent
letters to all parts of the empire, to each province in
its own script and language, proclaiming that every
man should be the ruler of his own home and should
say whatever he pleases.*

ESTHER BECOMES QUEEN

2 But after Xerxes' anger had subsided, he began
thinking about Vashti and what she had done and
the decree he had made. [2]So his personal attendants
suggested, "Let us search the empire to find beauti-
ful young virgins for the king. [3]Let the king appoint
agents in each province to bring these beautiful
young women into the royal harem at the fortress of
Susa. Hegai, the king's eunuch in charge of the harem,
will see that they are all given beauty treatments.
[4]After that, the young woman who most pleases the
king will be made queen instead of Vashti." This ad-
vice was very appealing to the king, so he put the plan
into effect.

[5]At that time there was a Jewish man in the for-
tress of Susa whose name was Mordecai son of Jair.
He was from the tribe of Benjamin and was a de-
scendant of Kish and Shimei. [6]His family* had been
among those who, with King Jehoiachin* of Judah,
had been exiled from Jerusalem to Babylon by King
Nebuchadnezzar. [7]This man had a very beautiful
and lovely young cousin, Hadassah, who was also
called Esther. When her father and mother died,
Mordecai adopted her into his family and raised her
as his own daughter.

[8]As a result of the king's decree, Esther, along with
many other young women, was brought to the king's
harem at the fortress of Susa and placed in Hegai's
care. [9]Hegai was very impressed with Esther and
treated her kindly. He quickly ordered a special menu
for her and provided her with beauty treatments. He
also assigned her seven maids specially chosen from
the king's palace, and he moved her and her maids
into the best place in the harem.

1:1a Hebrew *Ahasuerus,* another name for Xerxes; also throughout the book of Esther. Xerxes reigned 486–465 B.C. **1:1b** Hebrew *to Cush.* **1:22** Or *and should speak in the language of his own people.* **2:6a** Hebrew *He.* **2:6b** Hebrew *Jeconiah,* a variant spelling of Jehoiachin.

1:1 King Xerxes, who reigned. His name is also written as Xerxes. Ahasuerus succeeded his father, Darius, as king. Ahasuerus ruled the Persian Empire for 21 years from 486 to 465 B.C.

1:13 consulted with his wise advisers. Astrologers and magicians served in the court by giving advice and attempting to predict the future. God's prophets viewed them with scorn (Isa. 44:24-25).

1:19 Vashti be forever banished from the presence of King Xerxes. One of Ahasuerus' wise men suggested deposing the queen so that the women of the kingdom would not follow Vashti's example and disobey their husbands. The king issued a royal decree demoting Vashti from her position of queen and banishing her from his sight.

2:7 young cousin, Hadassah. Esther's Hebrew name means "myrtle." Esther is a Persian name, meaning "star." Her parents died when she was young.

A BEAUTY CONTEST

1. Who is the most beautiful or handsome person you know? How has that person's looks affected him or her?

ESTHER 2:1-18

2. Besides being beautiful, what else did Esther have going for her?
3. What makes a person beautiful to God (1 Sam. 16:7)? How is this different from the world's standard?
4. God used Esther's beauty to put her in a position of power. Why would He have chosen her for that role?
5. Later, Esther risked everything to save God's people from murder. Are you willing to risk all that you have to serve God?

[10] Esther had not told anyone of her nationality and family background, because Mordecai had directed her not to do so. [11] Every day Mordecai would take a walk near the courtyard of the harem to find out about Esther and what was happening to her.

[12] Before each young woman was taken to the king's bed, she was given the prescribed twelve months of beauty treatments—six months with oil of myrrh, followed by six months with special perfumes and ointments. [13] When it was time for her to go to the king's palace, she was given her choice of whatever clothing or jewelry she wanted to take from the harem. [14] That evening she was taken to the king's private rooms, and the next morning she was brought to the second harem,* where the king's wives lived. There she would be under the care of Shaashgaz, the king's eunuch in charge of the concubines. She would never go to the king again unless he had especially enjoyed her and requested her by name.

[15] Esther was the daughter of Abihail, who was Mordecai's uncle. (Mordecai had adopted his younger cousin Esther.) When it was Esther's turn to go to the king, she accepted the advice of Hegai, the eunuch in charge of the harem. She asked for nothing except what he suggested, and she was admired by everyone who saw her.

[16] Esther was taken to King Xerxes at the royal palace in early winter* of the seventh year of his reign. [17] And the king loved Esther more than any of the other young women. He was so delighted with her that he set the royal crown on her head and declared her queen instead of Vashti. [18] To celebrate the occasion, he gave a great banquet in Esther's honor for all his nobles and officials, declaring a public holiday for the provinces and giving generous gifts to everyone.

[19] Even after all the young women had been transferred to the second harem* and Mordecai had become a palace official,* [20] Esther continued to keep her family background and nationality a secret. She was still following Mordecai's directions, just as she did when she lived in his home.

MORDECAI'S LOYALTY TO THE KING

[21] One day as Mordecai was on duty at the king's gate, two of the king's eunuchs, Bigthana* and Teresh—who were guards at the door of the king's private quarters—became angry at King Xerxes and plotted to assassinate him. [22] But Mordecai heard about the plot and gave the information to Queen Esther. She then told the king about it and gave Mordecai credit for the report. [23] When an investigation was made and Mordecai's story was found to be true, the two men were impaled on a sharpened pole. This was all recorded in *The Book of the History of King Xerxes' Reign.*

HAMAN'S PLOT AGAINST THE JEWS

3 Some time later King Xerxes promoted Haman son of Hammedatha the Agagite over all the other nobles, making him the most powerful official in the empire. [2] All the king's officials would bow down before Haman to show him respect whenever he passed by, for so the king had commanded. But Mordecai refused to bow down or show him respect.

[3] Then the palace officials at the king's gate asked Mordecai, "Why are you disobeying the king's command?" [4] They spoke to him day after day, but still he refused to comply with the order. So they spoke to Haman about this to see if he would tolerate Mordecai's conduct, since Mordecai had told them he was a Jew.

[5] When Haman saw that Mordecai would not bow down or show him respect, he was filled with rage. [6] He had learned of Mordecai's nationality, so he decided it was not enough to lay hands on Mordecai alone. Instead, he looked for a way to destroy all the Jews throughout the entire empire of Xerxes.

[7] So in the month of April,* during the twelfth year of King Xerxes' reign, lots were cast in Haman's presence (the lots were called *purim*) to determine the best day and month to take action. And the day selected was March 7, nearly a year later.*

2:14 Or *to another part of the harem.* **2:16** Hebrew *in the tenth month, the month of Tebeth.* A number of dates in the book of Esther can be cross-checked with dates in surviving Persian records and related accurately to our modern calendar. This month of the ancient Hebrew lunar calendar occurred within the months of December 479 B.C. and January 478 B.C. **2:19a** The meaning of the Hebrew is uncertain. **2:19b** Hebrew *and Mordecai was sitting in the gate of the king.* **2:21** Hebrew *Bigthan;* compare 6:2. **3:7a** Hebrew *in the first month, the month of Nisan.* This month of the ancient Hebrew lunar calendar occurred within the months of April and May 474 B.C.; also see note on 2:16. **3:7b** As in 3:13, which reads *the thirteenth day of the twelfth month, the month of Adar;* Hebrew reads *in the twelfth month,* of the ancient Hebrew lunar calendar. The date selected was March 7, 473 B.C.; also see note on 2:16.

2:10 nationality or family background. Mordecai had warned Esther not to reveal her nationality. Jews were forbidden to marry pagans (Deut. 7:1-4) or to have sexual relations outside of marriage (Ex. 20:14). Joining the king's harem violated these rules, but God protected and used Esther and Mordecai to save their people.

2:19 had become a palace official. The gate was where commercial and legal transactions were made. Mordecai probably held an official position in the judicial system that helped him uncover the assassination plot against the king.

3:1 Some time later. Four years after Mordecai saved the king from assassination, Haman was promoted to the highest position in the land. **Haman . . . the Agagite.** Haman was an Amalekite, a group of people descended from Esau. Ever since Saul had captured an Amalekite king, hostility between Jews and Amalekites was common.

3:7 in the month of April . . . twelfth year. This description corresponds to April or May, 474 B.C., the fifth year after Esther became queen. **lots were cast.** A Babylonian word for "the lot," this was the system used by Haman to decide when the Jews should be killed.

8 Then Haman approached King Xerxes and said,
"There is a certain race of people scattered through
all the provinces of your empire who keep themselves
separate from everyone else. Their laws are differ-
ent from those of any other people, and they refuse
to obey the laws of the king. So it is not in the king's
interest to let them live. 9 If it please the king, issue a
decree that they be destroyed, and I will give 10,000
large sacks* of silver to the government administra-
tors to be deposited in the royal treasury."

10 The king agreed, confirming his decision by re-
moving his signet ring from his finger and giving it to
Haman son of Hammedatha the Agagite, the enemy of
the Jews. 11 The king said, "The money and the people
are both yours to do with as you see fit."

12 So on April 17* the king's secretaries were sum-
moned, and a decree was written exactly as Haman
dictated. It was sent to the king's highest officers, the
governors of the respective provinces, and the nobles
of each province in their own scripts and languages.
The decree was written in the name of King Xerxes
and sealed with the king's signet ring. 13 Dispatches
were sent by swift messengers into all the provinces
of the empire, giving the order that all Jews—young
and old, including women and children—must be
killed, slaughtered, and annihilated on a single day.
This was scheduled to happen on March 7 of the next
year.* The property of the Jews would be given to
those who killed them.

14 A copy of this decree was to be issued as law in
every province and proclaimed to all peoples, so that
they would be ready to do their duty on the appointed
day. 15 At the king's command, the decree went out by
swift messengers, and it was also proclaimed in the
fortress of Susa. Then the king and Haman sat down
to drink, but the city of Susa fell into confusion.

MORDECAI REQUESTS ESTHER'S HELP

4 When Mordecai learned about all that had been
done, he tore his clothes, put on burlap and ash-
es, and went out into the city, crying with a loud and
bitter wail. 2 He went as far as the gate of the pal-
ace, for no one was allowed to enter the palace gate
while wearing clothes of mourning. 3 And as news
of the king's decree reached all the provinces, there
was great mourning among the Jews. They fasted,
wept, and wailed, and many people lay in burlap
and ashes.

4 When Queen Esther's maids and eunuchs came
and told her about Mordecai, she was deeply dis-
tressed. She sent clothing to him to replace the bur-
lap, but he refused it. 5 Then Esther sent for Hathach,
one of the king's eunuchs who had been appointed as
her attendant. She ordered him to go to Mordecai and
find out what was troubling him and why he was in
mourning. 6 So Hathach went out to Mordecai in the
square in front of the palace gate.

7 Mordecai told him the whole story, including the
exact amount of money Haman had promised to pay
into the royal treasury for the destruction of the Jews.
8 Mordecai gave Hathach a copy of the decree issued
in Susa that called for the death of all Jews. He asked
Hathach to show it to Esther and explain the situation
to her. He also asked Hathach to direct her to go to the
king to beg for mercy and plead for her people. 9 So
Hathach returned to Esther with Mordecai's message.

10 Then Esther told Hathach to go back and relay
this message to Mordecai: 11 "All the king's officials
and even the people in the provinces know that any-
one who appears before the king in his inner court
without being invited is doomed to die unless the king
holds out his gold scepter. And the king has not called
for me to come to him for thirty days." 12 So Hathach*
gave Esther's message to Mordecai.

13 Mordecai sent this reply to Esther: "Don't think
for a moment that because you're in the palace you
will escape when all other Jews are killed. 14 If you
keep quiet at a time like this, deliverance and relief
for the Jews will arise from some other place, but you
and your relatives will die. Who knows if perhaps you
were made queen for just such a time as this?"

15 Then Esther sent this reply to Mordecai: 16 "Go and
gather together all the Jews of Susa and fast for me.
Do not eat or drink for three days, night or day. My
maids and I will do the same. And then, though it is
against the law, I will go in to see the king. If I must
die, I must die." 17 So Mordecai went away and did
everything as Esther had ordered him.

ESTHER'S REQUEST TO THE KING

5 On the third day of the fast, Esther put on her roy-
al robes and entered the inner court of the palace,
just across from the king's hall. The king was sitting
on his royal throne, facing the entrance. 2 When he
saw Queen Esther standing there in the inner court,
he welcomed her and held out the gold scepter to her.
So Esther approached and touched the end of the
scepter.

3 Then the king asked her, "What do you want,
Queen Esther? What is your request? I will give it to
you, even if it is half the kingdom!"

4 And Esther replied, "If it please the king, let the
king and Haman come today to a banquet I have pre-
pared for the king."

5 The king turned to his attendants and said, "Tell
Haman to come quickly to a banquet, as Esther has
requested." So the king and Haman went to Esther's
banquet.

6 And while they were drinking wine, the king said
to Esther, "Now tell me what you really want. What is
your request? I will give it to you, even if it is half the
kingdom!"

7 Esther replied, "This is my request and deepest
wish. 8 If I have found favor with the king, and if it

3:9 Hebrew *10,000 talents*, about 375 tons or 340 metric tons in weight. 3:12 Hebrew *On the thirteenth day of the first month*, of the ancient Hebrew lunar calendar. This day was April 17, 474 B.C.; also see note on 2:16. 3:13 Hebrew *on the thirteenth day of the twelfth month, the month of Adar*, of the ancient Hebrew lunar calendar. The date selected was March 7, 473 B.C.; also see note on 2:16. 4:12 As in Greek version; Hebrew reads *they*.

3:9 I will give 10,000 large sacks of silver. Haman's offer to pay the equivalent of millions of dollars to crush the supposed rebellion was meant to show his devotion to the king.

3:13 all Jews . . . must be killed, slaugthered, and annihilated. The proclamation was sent to all the provinces in various languages. The order included all Jewish men, women, and children.

4:16 fast. Esther asked her people to support her by fasting for three days before she approached the king. She didn't mention praying, but fasting normally included earnestly seeking God in prayer.

5:2 she won his approval. Although Esther had not seen the king in a month, he held out the gold scepter toward her, granting permission to approach him.

pleases the king to grant my request and do what I ask, please come with Haman tomorrow to the banquet I will prepare for you. Then I will explain what this is all about."

HAMAN'S PLAN TO KILL MORDECAI

9 Haman was a happy man as he left the banquet! But when he saw Mordecai sitting at the palace gate, not standing up or trembling nervously before him, Haman became furious. 10 However, he restrained himself and went on home.

Then Haman gathered together his friends and Zeresh, his wife, 11 and boasted to them about his great wealth and his many children. He bragged about the honors the king had given him and how he had been promoted over all the other nobles and officials.

12 Then Haman added, "And that's not all! Queen Esther invited only me and the king himself to the banquet she prepared for us. And she has invited me to dine with her and the king again tomorrow!" 13 Then he added, "But this is all worth nothing as long as I see Mordecai the Jew just sitting there at the palace gate."

14 So Haman's wife, Zeresh, and all his friends suggested, "Set up a sharpened pole that stands seventy-five feet* tall, and in the morning ask the king to impale Mordecai on it. When this is done, you can go on your merry way to the banquet with the king." This pleased Haman, and he ordered the pole set up.

THE KING HONORS MORDECAI

6 That night the king had trouble sleeping, so he ordered an attendant to bring the book of the history of his reign so it could be read to him. 2 In those records he discovered an account of how Mordecai had exposed the plot of Bigthana and Teresh, two of the eunuchs who guarded the door to the king's private quarters. They had plotted to assassinate King Xerxes.

3 "What reward or recognition did we ever give Mordecai for this?" the king asked.

His attendants replied, "Nothing has been done for him."

4 "Who is that in the outer court?" the king inquired. As it happened, Haman had just arrived in the outer court of the palace to ask the king to impale Mordecai on the pole he had prepared.

5 So the attendants replied to the king, "Haman is out in the court."

"Bring him in," the king ordered. 6 So Haman came in, and the king said, "What should I do to honor a man who truly pleases me?"

Haman thought to himself, "Whom would the king wish to honor more than me?" 7 So he replied, "If the king wishes to honor someone, 8 he should bring out one of the king's own royal robes, as well as a horse that the king himself has ridden—one with a royal emblem on its head. 9 Let the robes and the horse be handed over to one of the king's most noble officials. And let him see that the man whom the king wishes to honor is dressed in the king's robes and led through the city square on the king's horse. Have the official shout as they go, 'This is what the king does for someone he wishes to honor!'"

10 "Excellent!" the king said to Haman. "Quick! Take the robes and my horse, and do just as you have said for Mordecai the Jew, who sits at the gate of the palace. Leave out nothing you have suggested!"

11 So Haman took the robes and put them on Mordecai, placed him on the king's own horse, and led him through the city square, shouting, "This is what the king does for someone he wishes to honor!" 12 Afterward Mordecai returned to the palace gate, but Haman hurried home dejected and completely humiliated.

13 When Haman told his wife, Zeresh, and all his friends what had happened, his wise advisers and his wife said, "Since Mordecai—this man who has humiliated you—is of Jewish birth, you will never succeed in your plans against him. It will be fatal to continue opposing him."

14 While they were still talking, the king's eunuchs arrived and quickly took Haman to the banquet Esther had prepared.

THE KING EXECUTES HAMAN

7 So the king and Haman went to Queen Esther's banquet. 2 On this second occasion, while they were drinking wine, the king again said to Esther, "Tell me what you want, Queen Esther. What is your request? I will give it to you, even if it is half the kingdom!"

3 Queen Esther replied, "If I have found favor with the king, and if it pleases the king to grant my request, I ask that my life and the lives of my people will be spared. 4 For my people and I have been sold to those who would kill, slaughter, and annihilate us. If we had merely been sold as slaves, I could remain quiet, for that would be too trivial a matter to warrant disturbing the king."

5 "Who would do such a thing?" King Xerxes demanded. "Who would be so presumptuous as to touch you?"

6 Esther replied, "This wicked Haman is our adversary and our enemy." Haman grew pale with fright before the king and queen. 7 Then the king jumped to his feet in a rage and went out into the palace garden.

Haman, however, stayed behind to plead for his life with Queen Esther, for he knew that the king intended to kill him. 8 In despair he fell on the couch where Queen Esther was reclining, just as the king was returning from the palace garden.

The king exclaimed, "Will he even assault the queen right here in the palace, before my very eyes?" And as soon as the king spoke, his attendants covered Haman's face, signaling his doom.

9 Then Harbona, one of the king's eunuchs, said, "Haman has set up a sharpened pole that stands seventy-five feet* tall in his own courtyard. He intended

5:14 Hebrew *50 cubits* [23 meters]. 7:9 Hebrew *50 cubits* [23 meters].

5:10 Zeresh. Haman and his wife were well suited to each other. After Haman's whining about Mordecai and his boasting about his favor with the king, Haman's wife encouraged him to murder Mordecai as an example to everyone that Haman was in control.

6:3 reward or recognition. God used a sleepless night to accomplish His purpose. The king read the official records and discovered that Mordecai had never been honored for saving his life five years before.

7:8 he fell on the couch where Queen Esther was reclining. The reason the king went out into the palace garden is not known. But Haman begged her for his life after the king left. He was not assaulting her, but he may have been grasping at her in desperation.

7:9 sharpened pole. The eunuch informed the king of Haman's plot and reminded the king of Mordecai's bravery. The tables were turned as Haman was executed on the gallows he had prepared for Mordecai.

to use it to impale Mordecai, the man who saved the
king from assassination."
"Then impale Haman on it!" the king ordered. 10 So
they impaled Haman on the pole he had set up for
Mordecai, and the king's anger subsided.

A DECREE TO HELP THE JEWS

8 On that same day King Xerxes gave the property
of Haman, the enemy of the Jews, to Queen Esther.
Then Mordecai was brought before the king, for Esther
had told the king how they were related. 2 The king took
off his signet ring—which he had taken back from Ha-
man—and gave it to Mordecai. And Esther appointed
Mordecai to be in charge of Haman's property.
3 Then Esther went again before the king, falling
down at his feet and begging him with tears to stop
the evil plot devised by Haman the Agagite against
the Jews. 4 Again the king held out the gold scepter to
Esther. So she rose and stood before him.
5 Esther said, "If it please the king, and if I have
found favor with him, and if he thinks it is right, and
if I am pleasing to him, let there be a decree that re-
verses the orders of Haman son of Hammedatha the
Agagite, who ordered that Jews throughout all the
king's provinces should be destroyed. 6 For how can
I endure to see my people and my family slaughtered
and destroyed?"
7 Then King Xerxes said to Queen Esther and Mor-
decai the Jew, "I have given Esther the property of
Haman, and he has been impaled on a pole because
he tried to destroy the Jews. 8 Now go ahead and send
a message to the Jews in the king's name, telling them
whatever you want, and seal it with the king's signet
ring. But remember that whatever has already been
written in the king's name and sealed with his signet
ring can never be revoked."
9 So on June 25* the king's secretaries were sum-
moned, and a decree was written exactly as Morde-
cai dictated. It was sent to the Jews and to the high-
est officers, the governors, and the nobles of all the
127 provinces stretching from India to Ethiopia.* The
decree was written in the scripts and languages of all
the peoples of the empire, including that of the Jews.
10 The decree was written in the name of King Xerxes
and sealed with the king's signet ring. Mordecai sent
the dispatches by swift messengers, who rode fast
horses especially bred for the king's service.
11 The king's decree gave the Jews in every city
authority to unite to defend their lives. They were
allowed to kill, slaughter, and annihilate anyone of
any nationality or province who might attack them
or their children and wives, and to take the proper-
ty of their enemies. 12 The day chosen for this event
throughout all the provinces of King Xerxes was
March 7 of the next year.*
13 A copy of this decree was to be issued as law
in every province and proclaimed to all peoples, so
that the Jews would be ready to take revenge on
their enemies on the appointed day. 14 So urged on
by the king's command, the messengers rode out
swiftly on fast horses bred for the king's service.
The same decree was also proclaimed in the fortress
of Susa.
15 Then Mordecai left the king's presence, wearing
the royal robe of blue and white, the great crown of
gold, and an outer cloak of fine linen and purple. And
the people of Susa celebrated the new decree. 16 The
Jews were filled with joy and gladness and were hon-
ored everywhere. 17 In every province and city, wher-
ever the king's decree arrived, the Jews rejoiced and
had a great celebration and declared a public festival
and holiday. And many of the people of the land be-
came Jews themselves, for they feared what the Jews
might do to them.

THE VICTORY OF THE JEWS

9 So on March 7* the two decrees of the king were
put into effect. On that day, the enemies of the Jews
had hoped to overpower them, but quite the opposite
happened. It was the Jews who overpowered their
enemies. 2 The Jews gathered in their cities through-
out all the king's provinces to attack anyone who
tried to harm them. But no one could make a stand
against them, for everyone was afraid of them. 3 And
all the nobles of the provinces, the highest officers, the
governors, and the royal officials helped the Jews for
fear of Mordecai. 4 For Mordecai had been promoted
in the king's palace, and his fame spread throughout
all the provinces as he became more and more pow-
erful.
5 So the Jews went ahead on the appointed day
and struck down their enemies with the sword. They
killed and annihilated their enemies and did as they
pleased with those who hated them. 6 In the fortress
of Susa itself, the Jews killed 500 men. 7 They also
killed Parshandatha, Dalphon, Aspatha, 8 Poratha,
Adalia, Aridatha, 9 Parmashta, Arisai, Aridai, and
Vaizatha—10 the ten sons of Haman son of Hamme-
datha, the enemy of the Jews. But they did not take
any plunder.
11 That very day, when the king was informed of the
number of people killed in the fortress of Susa, 12 he
called for Queen Esther. He said, "The Jews have killed
500 men in the fortress of Susa alone, as well as Ha-
man's ten sons. If they have done that here, what has
happened in the rest of the provinces? But now, what
more do you want? It will be granted to you; tell me
and I will do it."
13 Esther responded, "If it please the king, give the
Jews in Susa permission to do again tomorrow as they

8:9a Hebrew *on the twenty-third day of the third month, the month of Sivan,* of the ancient Hebrew lunar calendar. This day was June 25, 474 B.C.; also see note on 2:16. **8:9b** Hebrew *to Cush.* **8:12** Hebrew *the thirteenth day of the twelfth month, the month of Adar,* of the ancient Hebrew lunar calendar. The date selected was March 7, 473 B.C.; also see note on 2:16. **9:1** Hebrew *on the thirteenth day of the twelfth month, the month of Adar,* of the ancient Hebrew lunar calendar. This day was March 7, 473 B.C.; also see note on 2:16.

8:1 gave the property of Haman . . . to Queen Esther. Ironically, all of Haman's property was given to the Jews whom Haman had planned to strip of their property.

8:3 the evil plot. Although Haman was dead, his decree was still in effect. When Esther again approached the king without permission, he held out his gold scepter to her.

8:8 seal it with the king's signet ring. While Haman's decree could not be revoked, a second one could override it. The new decree gave the Jews the right to protect themselves against anyone who sought to attack them. God had used Esther to help her people.

9:5 struck down their enemies with the sword. The Jews gathered in various cities to face their attackers, and government authorities helped them. On the day of battle they killed 500 men plus Haman's ten sons. The Jews took no plunder, though the king had given them permission to do so.

have done today, and let the bodies of Haman's ten sons be impaled on a pole."
[14]So the king agreed, and the decree was announced in Susa. And they impaled the bodies of Haman's ten sons. [15]Then the Jews at Susa gathered together on March 8* and killed 300 more men, and again they took no plunder.
[16]Meanwhile, the other Jews throughout the king's provinces had gathered together to defend their lives. They gained relief from all their enemies, killing 75,000 of those who hated them. But they did not take any plunder. [17]This was done throughout the provinces on March 7, and on March 8 they rested,* celebrating their victory with a day of feasting and gladness. [18](The Jews at Susa killed their enemies on March 7 and again on March 8, then rested on March 9,* making that their day of feasting and gladness.) [19]So to this day, rural Jews living in remote villages celebrate an annual festival and holiday on the appointed day in late winter,* when they rejoice and send gifts of food to each other.

THE FESTIVAL OF PURIM

[20]Mordecai recorded these events and sent letters to the Jews near and far, throughout all the provinces of King Xerxes, [21]calling on them to celebrate an annual festival on these two days.* [22]He told them to celebrate these days with feasting and gladness and by giving gifts of food to each other and presents to the poor. This would commemorate a time when the Jews gained relief from their enemies, when their sorrow was turned into gladness and their mourning into joy.
[23]So the Jews accepted Mordecai's proposal and adopted this annual custom. [24]Haman son of Hammedatha the Agagite, the enemy of the Jews, had plotted to crush and destroy them on the date determined by casting lots (the lots were called *purim*). [25]But when Esther came before the king, he issued a decree causing Haman's evil plot to backfire, and Haman and his sons were impaled on a sharpened pole. [26]That is why this celebration is called Purim, because it is the ancient word for casting lots.

So because of Mordecai's letter and because of what they had experienced, [27]the Jews throughout the realm agreed to inaugurate this tradition and to pass it on to their descendants and to all who became Jews. They declared they would never fail to celebrate these two prescribed days at the appointed time each year. [28]These days would be remembered and kept from generation to generation and celebrated by every family throughout the provinces and cities of the empire. This Festival of Purim would never cease to be celebrated among the Jews, nor would the memory of what happened ever die out among their descendants.
[29]Then Queen Esther, the daughter of Abihail, along with Mordecai the Jew, wrote another letter putting the queen's full authority behind Mordecai's letter to establish the Festival of Purim. [30]Letters wishing peace and security were sent to the Jews throughout the 127 provinces of the empire of Xerxes. [31]These letters established the Festival of Purim—an annual celebration of these days at the appointed time, decreed by both Mordecai the Jew and Queen Esther. (The people decided to observe this festival, just as they had decided for themselves and their descendants to establish the times of fasting and mourning.) [32]So the command of Esther confirmed the practices of Purim, and it was all written down in the records.

THE GREATNESS OF XERXES AND MORDECAI

10 King Xerxes imposed a tribute throughout his empire, even to the distant coastlands. [2]His great achievements and the full account of the greatness of Mordecai, whom the king had promoted, are recorded in *The Book of the History of the Kings of Media and Persia.* [3]Mordecai the Jew became the prime minister, with authority next to that of King Xerxes himself. He was very great among the Jews, who held him in high esteem, because he continued to work for the good of his people and to speak up for the welfare of all their descendants.

9:15 Hebrew *the fourteenth day of the month of Adar,* of the ancient Hebrew lunar calendar. This day was March 8, 473 B.C.; also see note on 2:16. **9:17** Hebrew *on the thirteenth day of the month of Adar, and on the fourteenth day they rested.* These days were March 7 and 8, 473 B.C.; also see note on 2:16. **9:18** Hebrew *killed their enemies on the thirteenth day and the fourteenth day, and then rested on the fifteenth day,* of the Hebrew month of Adar. **9:19** Hebrew *on the fourteenth day of the month of Adar.* This day of the ancient Hebrew lunar calendar occurs in February or March. **9:21** Hebrew *on the fourteenth and fifteenth days of Adar,* of the ancient Hebrew lunar calendar.

9:16 to defend their lives . . . gained relief from all their enemies. After defeating their enemies, the Jews experienced peace, and Mordecai became a powerful leader. In Deuteronomy 25:17-19, Moses linked rest from their enemies with the command to blot out the Amalekites, Haman's people.

9:19 rejoice and send gifts of food. The Feast of Purim was commanded by Mordecai and Esther to commemorate God's goodness in protecting His people from destruction. It was to be an annual event celebrated with eating, rejoicing, and sharing with the poor. It was called Purim because of Haman's use of the *pur* (the lot) to determine the time for the Jews' execution (3:7). The *pur* became a symbol of God's rescue from desperate and dangerous events.

INTRODUCTION TO
JOB

PERSONAL READING PLAN

☐Job 1:1–2:13
☐Job 3:1–5:27
☐Job 6:1–7:21
☐Job 8:1-22
☐Job 9:1–11:20
☐Job 12:1–14:22
☐Job 15:1–17:16
☐Job 18:1–19:29
☐Job 20:1–21:34
☐Job 22:1-30
☐Job 23:1–25:6
☐Job 26:1–28:28
☐Job 29:1–30:31
☐Job 31:1-40
☐Job 32:1–33:33
☐Job 34:1-37
☐Job 35:1–37:24
☐Job 38:1-41
☐Job 39:1-30
☐Job 40:1–41:34
☐Job 42:1-17

AUTHOR

The writer is not likely Job himself, but an Israelite who is otherwise unknown.

DATE

The events described may have taken place in the patriarchal age, but the book was probably not written in its present form until much later, possibly 600–400 B.C.

THEME

The justice of God in the light of human suffering.

HISTORICAL BACKGROUND

Since there is little significant detail given, the precise situation cannot be established with certainty.

CHARACTERISTICS

The opening verses set the stage for this well-crafted drama. Job is a wealthy, leading citizen, reputed to be very wise. When he loses herds, house, and family and is struck down with a painful illness, we see in Job's life the suffering that afflicts so many in our world. As a clue to Job's apparent alienation from God, the reader is shown that Satan, as accuser, is actively driving a wedge between God and His beloved. If Job proves to be righteous only because "it pays," then Satan wins his bet with God. Job's friends do not have the benefit of this insight and their counsel does not comfort Job. They focus on three arguments:

1. God is almighty.

2. God is just.

3. No human is entirely innocent in God's eyes.

Therefore, say his friends, Job's suffering must be punishment for some sin—a logical answer, but not at all consoling to Job in his despair. Finally, all are silenced, as God breaks in, but He gives no "solution" except to point to His greatness, glory, and power. For the most profound insight, we look ahead to Jesus' death on the cross. There God takes on Himself human suffering and thus defeats it forever—a solution only hinted at in the book of Job.

PASSAGES FOR TOPICAL GROUP STUDY

1:6-22 . . . TRAGEDY and DISASTER . . . . . . Losing Everything

PROLOGUE

1 There once was a man named Job who lived in
the land of Uz. He was blameless—a man of
complete integrity. He feared God and stayed away
from evil. 2 He had seven sons and three daughters.
3 He owned 7,000 sheep, 3,000 camels, 500 teams of
oxen, and 500 female donkeys. He also had many
servants. He was, in fact, the richest person in that
entire area.
4 Job's sons would take turns preparing feasts in
their homes, and they would also invite their three
sisters to celebrate with them. 5 When these celebra-
tions ended—sometimes after several days—Job
would purify his children. He would get up early in
the morning and offer a burnt offering for each of
them. For Job said to himself, "Perhaps my children
have sinned and have cursed God in their hearts."
This was Job's regular practice.

JOB'S FIRST TEST

6 One day the members of the heavenly court* came to
present themselves before the LORD, and the Accus-
er, Satan,* came with them. 7 "Where have you come
from?" the LORD asked Satan.
Satan answered the LORD, "I have been patrolling
the earth, watching everything that's going on."
8 Then the LORD asked Satan, "Have you noticed my
servant Job? He is the finest man in all the earth. He is
blameless—a man of complete integrity. He fears God
and stays away from evil."
9 Satan replied to the LORD, "Yes, but Job has good
reason to fear God. 10 You have always put a wall of
protection around him and his home and his proper-
ty. You have made him prosper in everything he does.
Look how rich he is! 11 But reach out and take away
everything he has, and he will surely curse you to
your face!"
12 "All right, you may test him," the LORD said to Sa-
tan. "Do whatever you want with everything he pos-
sesses, but don't harm him physically." So Satan left
the LORD's presence.
13 One day when Job's sons and daughters were
feasting at the oldest brother's house, 14 a messenger
arrived at Job's home with this news: "Your oxen
were plowing, with the donkeys feeding beside them,
15 when the Sabeans raided us. They stole all the ani-
mals and killed all the farmhands. I am the only one
who escaped to tell you."
16 While he was still speaking, another messenger
arrived with this news: "The fire of God has fallen
from heaven and burned up your sheep and all the
shepherds. I am the only one who escaped to tell
you."
17 While he was still speaking, a third messenger
arrived with this news: "Three bands of Chaldean
raiders have stolen your camels and killed your
servants. I am the only one who escaped to tell
you."

LOSING EVERYTHING

1. Do you know anyone who has lost all he or she owned? How did that person react?

JOB 1:6-22

2. Why did Satan urge God to make Job suffer? Why did God agree?
3. If you suddenly lost all your money, possessions, and family, what would be your first response: Anger at God? Anger at Satan? Loss of faith? Peaceful acceptance?
4. Read Job's response in verse 21. Why did he respond that way? Why did he worship God?
5. How do you respond when tragedy strikes? How can you be like Job and learn to trust God?

18 While he was still speaking, another messenger
arrived with this news: "Your sons and daughters
were feasting in their oldest brother's home. 19 Sud-
denly, a powerful wind swept in from the wilderness
and hit the house on all sides. The house collapsed,
and all your children are dead. I am the only one who
escaped to tell you."
20 Job stood up and tore his robe in grief. Then he
shaved his head and fell to the ground to worship.
21 He said,

"I came naked from my mother's womb,
  and I will be naked when I leave.
The LORD gave me what I had,
  and the LORD has taken it away.
Praise the name of the LORD!"

22 In all of this, Job did not sin by blaming God.

JOB'S SECOND TEST

2 One day the members of the heavenly court* came
again to present themselves before the LORD, and
the Accuser, Satan,* came with them. 2 "Where have
you come from?" the LORD asked Satan.
Satan answered the LORD, "I have been patrolling
the earth, watching everything that's going on."
3 Then the LORD asked Satan, "Have you noticed my
servant Job? He is the finest man in all the earth. He
is blameless—a man of complete integrity. He fears
God and stays away from evil. And he has maintained
his integrity, even though you urged me to harm him
without cause."
4 Satan replied to the LORD, "Skin for skin! A man
will give up everything he has to save his life. 5 But
reach out and take away his health, and he will surely
curse you to your face!"

1:6a Hebrew *the sons of God.* 1:6b Hebrew *and the satan;* similarly throughout this chapter. 2:1a Hebrew *the sons of God.* 2:1b Hebrew *and the satan;* similarly throughout this chapter.

1:1 land of Uz. Some scholars believe that Uz was in Bashan, south of Damascus; others say Uz was east of Edom in northern Arabia.

1:6-7 members of the heavenly court. Sometimes called the "hosts" of heaven, they act as God's messengers by patrolling the earth (Zech. 1:10ff and 6:5ff) and are active in human affairs (though invisible).

1:7 Where have you come from? At this point in Old Testament history, Satan was merely known as the adversary who delights in the downfall of God's people. (See also 2:2)

1:10 put a wall of protection. God is *aware* of every detail in our lives.

1:11 he will surely curse you to your face. Satan said man's only motive in loving God is selfish because human love is bought with good gifts.

1:20 tore his robe . . . shaved his head. Job grieved greatly over his overwhelming losses and yet bowed in worship to God.

2:4-5 Skin for skin! Satan reasoned that personal, physical suffering would break Job if losing his children and wealth didn't.

6 "All right, do with him as you please," the LORD said to Satan. "But spare his life." 7 So Satan left the LORD's presence, and he struck Job with terrible boils from head to foot.

8 Job scraped his skin with a piece of broken pottery as he sat among the ashes. 9 His wife said to him, "Are you still trying to maintain your integrity? Curse God and die."

10 But Job replied, "You talk like a foolish woman. Should we accept only good things from the hand of God and never anything bad?" So in all this, Job said nothing wrong.

JOB'S THREE FRIENDS SHARE HIS ANGUISH

11 When three of Job's friends heard of the tragedy he had suffered, they got together and traveled from their homes to comfort and console him. Their names were Eliphaz the Temanite, Bildad the Shuhite, and Zophar the Naamathite.
12 When they saw Job from a distance, they scarcely recognized him. Wailing loudly, they tore their robes and threw dust into the air over their heads to show their grief.
13 Then they sat on the ground with him for seven days and nights. No one said a word to Job, for they saw that his suffering was too great for words.

JOB'S FIRST SPEECH

3 At last Job spoke, and he cursed the day of his birth. 2 He said:

3 "Let the day of my birth be erased,
and the night I was conceived.
4 Let that day be turned to darkness.
Let it be lost even to God on high,
and let no light shine on it.
5 Let the darkness and utter gloom claim that day
for its own.
Let a black cloud overshadow it,
and let the darkness terrify it.
6 Let that night be blotted off the calendar,
never again to be counted among the days of
the year,
never again to appear among the months.
7 Let that night be childless.
Let it have no joy.
8 Let those who are experts at cursing—
whose cursing could rouse Leviathan*—
curse that day.
9 Let its morning stars remain dark.
Let it hope for light, but in vain;
may it never see the morning light.
10 Curse that day for failing to shut my mother's womb,
for letting me be born to see all this trouble.

11 "Why wasn't I born dead?
Why didn't I die as I came from the womb?
12 Why was I laid on my mother's lap?
Why did she nurse me at her breasts?
13 Had I died at birth, I would now be at peace.
I would be asleep and at rest.
14 I would rest with the world's kings and prime
ministers,
whose great buildings now lie in ruins.
15 I would rest with princes, rich in gold,
whose palaces were filled with silver.
16 Why wasn't I buried like a stillborn child,
like a baby who never lives to see the light?
17 For in death the wicked cause no trouble,
and the weary are at rest.
18 Even captives are at ease in death,
with no guards to curse them.
19 Rich and poor are both there,
and the slave is free from his master.

20 "Oh, why give light to those in misery,
and life to those who are bitter?
21 They long for death, and it won't come.
They search for death more eagerly than for
hidden treasure.
22 They're filled with joy when they finally die,
and rejoice when they find the grave.
23 Why is life given to those with no future,
those God has surrounded with difficulties?
24 I cannot eat for sighing;
my groans pour out like water.
25 What I always feared has happened to me.
What I dreaded has come true.
26 I have no peace, no quietness.
I have no rest; only trouble comes."

ELIPHAZ'S FIRST RESPONSE TO JOB

4 Then Eliphaz the Temanite replied to Job:

2 "Will you be patient and let me say a word?
For who could keep from speaking out?

3 "In the past you have encouraged many people;
you have strengthened those who were weak.
4 Your words have supported those who were falling;
you encouraged those with shaky knees.
5 But now when trouble strikes, you lose heart.
You are terrified when it touches you.
6 Doesn't your reverence for God give you
confidence?
Doesn't your life of integrity give you hope?

7 "Stop and think! Do the innocent die?
When have the upright been destroyed?
8 My experience shows that those who plant
trouble
and cultivate evil will harvest the same.

3:8 The identification of Leviathan is disputed, ranging from an earthly creature to a mythical sea monster in ancient literature.

2:7 terrible boils. The two Hebrew words used for "terrible boils" were used to describe the plague of festering boils in Egypt (Ex. 9:8-11). "Painful boils" is one of the curses for disobedience and refers to an incurable disease (Deut. 28:35).
2:12 scarcely recognized him. His maladies included ulcerous sores, itching, degenerative changes in facial skin, loss of appetite, depression, worms in the boils, weight loss, running sores, and difficulty breathing.
2:13 sat . . . with him. This silence was the best response of Job's friends.
3:13 rest. Job merely longs for relief from what he saw as the judgment he was already living, not judgment after death.
3:23 has surrounded. While earlier God's hedge produced bounty and all good things, now it kept Job trapped in pain.
4:1 Eliphaz. Eliphaz, probably the oldest of the three friends, begins their counsel (which some suggest is Satanic).
4:3-6 you have encouraged many. Eliphaz reminds Job how he advised others to be patient under trial and should do likewise.
4:8 those who plant trouble . . . will harvest the same. "You reap what you sow" appears throughout the Bible (Ps. 7:14-16; Prov. 11:18). God sometimes disciplines people (Heb. 12:7), yet Scripture is also clear that not all suffering is the result of personal sin (John 9:1-3; 1 Peter 2:19-20). Eliphaz encouraged Job to submit to his punishment since God shows mercy to the humble (1 Sam. 2:7).

9 A breath from God destroys them.
They vanish in a blast of his anger.
10 The lion roars and the wildcat snarls,
but the teeth of strong lions will be broken.
11 The fierce lion will starve for lack of prey,
and the cubs of the lioness will be scattered.

12 "This truth was given to me in secret,
as though whispered in my ear.
13 It came to me in a disturbing vision at night,
when people are in a deep sleep.
14 Fear gripped me,
and my bones trembled.
15 A spirit* swept past my face,
and my hair stood on end.*
16 The spirit stopped, but I couldn't see its shape.
There was a form before my eyes.
In the silence I heard a voice say,
17 'Can a mortal be innocent before God?
Can anyone be pure before the Creator?'

18 "If God does not trust his own angels
and has charged his messengers with foolishness,
19 how much less will he trust people made of clay!
They are made of dust, crushed as easily as a moth.
20 They are alive in the morning but dead by evening,
gone forever without a trace.
21 Their tent-cords are pulled and the tent collapses,
and they die in ignorance.

ELIPHAZ'S RESPONSE CONTINUES

5 1 "Cry for help, but will anyone answer you?
Which of the angels* will help you?
2 Surely resentment destroys the fool,
and jealousy kills the simple.
3 I have seen that fools may be successful for the moment,
but then comes sudden disaster.
4 Their children are abandoned far from help;
they are crushed in court with no one to defend them.
5 The hungry devour their harvest,
even when it is guarded by brambles.*
The thirsty pant after their wealth.*
6 But evil does not spring from the soil,
and trouble does not sprout from the earth.
7 People are born for trouble
as readily as sparks fly up from a fire.

8 "If I were you, I would go to God
and present my case to him.
9 He does great things too marvelous to understand.
He performs countless miracles.
10 He gives rain for the earth
and water for the fields.
11 He gives prosperity to the poor
and protects those who suffer.
12 He frustrates the plans of schemers
so the work of their hands will not succeed.
13 He traps the wise in their own cleverness
so their cunning schemes are thwarted.
14 They find it is dark in the daytime,
and they grope at noon as if it were night.
15 He rescues the poor from the cutting words of the strong,
and rescues them from the clutches of the powerful.
16 And so at last the poor have hope,
and the snapping jaws of the wicked are shut.

17 "But consider the joy of those corrected by God!
Do not despise the discipline of the Almighty when you sin.
18 For though he wounds, he also bandages.
He strikes, but his hands also heal.
19 From six disasters he will rescue you;
even in the seventh, he will keep you from evil.
20 He will save you from death in time of famine,
from the power of the sword in time of war.
21 You will be safe from slander
and have no fear when destruction comes.
22 You will laugh at destruction and famine;
wild animals will not terrify you.
23 You will be at peace with the stones of the field,
and its wild animals will be at peace with you.
24 You will know that your home is safe.
When you survey your possessions, nothing will be missing.
25 You will have many children;
your descendants will be as plentiful as grass!
26 You will go to the grave at a ripe old age,
like a sheaf of grain harvested at the proper time!

27 "We have studied life and found all this to be true.
Listen to my counsel, and apply it to yourself."

JOB'S SECOND SPEECH: A RESPONSE TO ELIPHAZ

6 Then Job spoke again:
2 "If my misery could be weighed
and my troubles be put on the scales,
3 they would outweigh all the sands of the sea.
That is why I spoke impulsively.
4 For the Almighty has struck me down with his arrows.
Their poison infects my spirit.
God's terrors are lined up against me.
5 Don't I have a right to complain?
Don't wild donkeys bray when they find no grass,
and oxen bellow when they have no food?
6 Don't people complain about unsalted food?
Does anyone want the tasteless white of an egg?*

4:15a Or *wind;* also in 4:16. **4:15b** Or *its wind sent shivers up my spine.* **5:1** Hebrew *the holy ones.* **5:5a** The meaning of the Hebrew for this phrase is uncertain. **5:5b** As in Greek and Syriac versions; Hebrew reads *A snare snatches their wealth.* **6:6** Or *the tasteless juice of the mallow plant?*

5:1 angels. Eliphaz warned Job that angels would not intervene. Job later desired a mediator between himself and God (9:33; 16:19-21).
5:17 Almighty. The divine title *Shaddai* is found 31 times in Job and only 17 times in the rest of the Old Testament.
5:27 Listen to my counsel, and apply it to yourself. In other words, the final word!
6:1 If my misery could be weighed. Job's lofty response makes it seem like a speech contest.
6:5-6 wild donkeys . . . oxen . . . unsalted food. Rhetorical questions are often used in Wisdom Literature to point out something absurd.

7 My appetite disappears when I look at it;
I gag at the thought of eating it!

8 "Oh, that I might have my request,
that God would grant my desire.
9 I wish he would crush me.
I wish he would reach out his hand and kill me.
10 At least I can take comfort in this:
Despite the pain,
I have not denied the words of the Holy One.
11 But I don't have the strength to endure.
I have nothing to live for.
12 Do I have the strength of a stone?
Is my body made of bronze?
13 No, I am utterly helpless,
without any chance of success.

14 "One should be kind to a fainting friend,
but you accuse me without any fear of the Almighty.*
15 My brothers, you have proved as unreliable as a seasonal brook
that overflows its banks in the spring
16 when it is swollen with ice and melting snow.
17 But when the hot weather arrives, the water disappears.
The brook vanishes in the heat.
18 The caravans turn aside to be refreshed,
but there is nothing to drink, so they die.
19 The caravans from Tema search for this water;
the travelers from Sheba hope to find it.
20 They count on it but are disappointed.
When they arrive, their hopes are dashed.
21 You, too, have given no help.
You have seen my calamity, and you are afraid.
22 But why? Have I ever asked you for a gift?
Have I begged for anything of yours for myself?
23 Have I asked you to rescue me from my enemies,
or to save me from ruthless people?
24 Teach me, and I will keep quiet.
Show me what I have done wrong.
25 Honest words can be painful,
but what do your criticisms amount to?
26 Do you think your words are convincing
when you disregard my cry of desperation?
27 You would even send an orphan into slavery*
or sell a friend.
28 Look at me!
Would I lie to your face?
29 Stop assuming my guilt,
for I have done no wrong.
30 Do you think I am lying?
Don't I know the difference between right and wrong?

7 1 "Is not all human life a struggle?
Our lives are like that of a hired hand,
2 like a worker who longs for the shade,
like a servant waiting to be paid.
3 I, too, have been assigned months of futility,
long and weary nights of misery.
4 Lying in bed, I think, 'When will it be morning?'
But the night drags on, and I toss till dawn.
5 My body is covered with maggots and scabs.
My skin breaks open, oozing with pus.

JOB CRIES OUT TO GOD

6 "My days fly faster than a weaver's shuttle.
They end without hope.
7 O God, remember that my life is but a breath,
and I will never again feel happiness.
8 You see me now, but not for long.
You will look for me, but I will be gone.
9 Just as a cloud dissipates and vanishes,
those who die* will not come back.
10 They are gone forever from their home—
never to be seen again.

11 "I cannot keep from speaking.
I must express my anguish.
My bitter soul must complain.
12 Am I a sea monster or a dragon
that you must place me under guard?
13 I think, 'My bed will comfort me,
and sleep will ease my misery,'
14 but then you shatter me with dreams
and terrify me with visions.
15 I would rather be strangled—
rather die than suffer like this.
16 I hate my life and don't want to go on living.
Oh, leave me alone for my few remaining days.

17 "What are people, that you should make so much of us,
that you should think of us so often?
18 For you examine us every morning
and test us every moment.
19 Why won't you leave me alone,
at least long enough for me to swallow!
20 If I have sinned, what have I done to you,
O watcher of all humanity?
Why make me your target?
Am I a burden to you?*
21 Why not just forgive my sin
and take away my guilt?
For soon I will lie down in the dust and die.
When you look for me, I will be gone."

BILDAD'S FIRST RESPONSE TO JOB

8 Then Bildad the Shuhite replied to Job:
2 "How long will you go on like this?
You sound like a blustering wind.
3 Does God twist justice?
Does the Almighty twist what is right?
4 Your children must have sinned against him,
so their punishment was well deserved.

6:14 Or *friend, / or he might lose his fear of the Almighty.* 6:27 Hebrew *even gamble over an orphan.* 7:9 Hebrew *who go down to Sheol.* 7:20 As in Greek version; Hebrew reads *target, so that I am a burden to myself?*

6:8-10 I wish he would crush me. Job longs for death to release him from the struggle of proving to (God and) his friends that he is innocent of sin.
6:15 My brothers. Job's friends supported him in good times, but in adversity their support "evaporates" (v. 17; see also vv. 20-21).
6:22-23 Job could not expect friends to remove his pain, but he needed them to "be there" for him in his suffering (12:1-3; 21:1-6; 26:1-4).
6:27 sell a friend. Job exaggerates their cruelty to make his point.
7:13 My bed will comfort. Job can't even get a good night's sleep.
7:20-21 If I have sinned. Job, allowing for the possibility of sinning without realizing it, longs for release from his suffering through forgiveness or death.
8:1 Bildad the Shuhite. Job's second friend arrives to speak "truth." Bildad quickly points out that Job is only getting his due.

5 But if you pray to God
and seek the favor of the Almighty,
6 and if you are pure and live with integrity,
he will surely rise up and restore your happy home.
7 And though you started with little,
you will end with much.

8 "Just ask the previous generation.
Pay attention to the experience of our ancestors.
9 For we were born but yesterday and know nothing.
Our days on earth are as fleeting as a shadow.
10 But those who came before us will teach you.
They will teach you the wisdom of old.

11 "Can papyrus reeds grow tall without a marsh?
Can marsh grass flourish without water?
12 While they are still flowering, not ready to be cut,
they begin to wither more quickly than grass.
13 The same happens to all who forget God.
The hopes of the godless evaporate.
14 Their confidence hangs by a thread.
They are leaning on a spider's web.
15 They cling to their home for security, but it won't last.
They try to hold it tight, but it will not endure.
16 The godless seem like a lush plant growing in the sunshine,
its branches spreading across the garden.
17 Its roots grow down through a pile of stones;
it takes hold on a bed of rocks.
18 But when it is uprooted,
it's as though it never existed!
19 That's the end of its life,
and others spring up from the earth to replace it.

20 "But look, God will not reject a person of integrity,
nor will he lend a hand to the wicked.
21 He will once again fill your mouth with laughter
and your lips with shouts of joy.
22 Those who hate you will be clothed with shame,
and the home of the wicked will be destroyed."

JOB'S THIRD SPEECH: A RESPONSE TO BILDAD

9 Then Job spoke again:
2 "Yes, I know all this is true in principle.
But how can a person be declared innocent in God's sight?
3 If someone wanted to take God to court,*
would it be possible to answer him even once in a thousand times?
4 For God is so wise and so mighty.
Who has ever challenged him successfully?

5 "Without warning, he moves the mountains,
overturning them in his anger.
6 He shakes the earth from its place,
and its foundations tremble.
7 If he commands it, the sun won't rise
and the stars won't shine.
8 He alone has spread out the heavens
and marches on the waves of the sea.
9 He made all the stars—the Bear and Orion,
the Pleiades and the constellations of the southern sky.
10 He does great things too marvelous to understand.
He performs countless miracles.

11 "Yet when he comes near, I cannot see him.
When he moves by, I do not see him go.
12 If he snatches someone in death, who can stop him?
Who dares to ask, 'What are you doing?'
13 And God does not restrain his anger.
Even the monsters of the sea* are crushed beneath his feet.

14 "So who am I, that I should try to answer God
or even reason with him?
15 Even if I were right, I would have no defense.
I could only plead for mercy.
16 And even if I summoned him and he responded,
I'm not sure he would listen to me.
17 For he attacks me with a storm
and repeatedly wounds me without cause.
18 He will not let me catch my breath,
but fills me instead with bitter sorrows.
19 If it's a question of strength, he's the strong one.
If it's a matter of justice, who dares to summon him* to court?
20 Though I am innocent, my own mouth would pronounce me guilty.
Though I am blameless, it* would prove me wicked.

21 "I am innocent,
but it makes no difference to me—
I despise my life.
22 Innocent or wicked, it is all the same to God.
That's why I say, 'He destroys both the blameless and the wicked.'
23 When a plague* sweeps through,
he laughs at the death of the innocent.
24 The whole earth is in the hands of the wicked,
and God blinds the eyes of the judges.
If he's not the one who does it, who is?

9:3 Or *If God wanted to take someone to court.* 9:13 Hebrew *the helpers of Rahab,* the name of a mythical sea monster that represents chaos in ancient literature. 9:19 As in Greek version; Hebrew reads *me.* 9:20 Or *he.* 9:23 Or *disaster.*

8:5-6 if you earnestly seek God. Bildad's focus is on God's power and unwavering justice. However, Bildad's God is inflexible and without mercy.
8:6 if you are pure and live with integrity. A sliver of sarcasm: If Job were really innocent, his healing would not be delayed.
8:8 previous generation. Where Eliphaz turned to mysticism for insight (4:12-21), Bildad found straightforward wisdom in the pages of history. Bildad truly believes he KNOWS the answer for Job. He uses illustrations from nature in verses 11-19 to point out the logic of his "truth."
8:20 not reject a person of integrity. Bildad invited Job to read between the lines and recognize himself as a hypocrite or a liar.
9:2-3 Job recognized that Bildad was right: the wicked do deserve punishment. If only he had sinned.
9:3 take God to court. In an imaginary courtroom, Job "lawyers up" in describing his plight in legal terms (vv. 3,15-16,20,24,32).
9:17 without cause. Job is unaware of the heavenly drama that preceded all his troubles (1:6-12).
9:22-24 If he's not the one who does it, who is? Without realizing it, Job is on the right track.

25 "My life passes more swiftly than a runner.
It flees away without a glimpse of happiness.
26 It disappears like a swift papyrus boat,
like an eagle swooping down on its prey.
27 If I decided to forget my complaints,
to put away my sad face and be cheerful,
28 I would still dread all the pain,
for I know you will not find me innocent,
O God.
29 Whatever happens, I will be found guilty.
So what's the use of trying?
30 Even if I were to wash myself with soap
and clean my hands with lye,
31 you would plunge me into a muddy ditch,
and my own filthy clothing would hate me.

32 "God is not a mortal like me,
so I cannot argue with him or take him to trial.
33 If only there were a mediator between us,
someone who could bring us together.
34 The mediator could make God stop beating me,
and I would no longer live in terror of his
punishment.
35 Then I could speak to him without fear,
but I cannot do that in my own strength.

JOB FRAMES HIS PLEA TO GOD

10 1 "I am disgusted with my life.
Let me complain freely.
My bitter soul must complain.
2 I will say to God, 'Don't simply condemn me—
tell me the charge you are bringing against me.
3 What do you gain by oppressing me?
Why do you reject me, the work of your own
hands,
while smiling on the schemes of the wicked?
4 Are your eyes like those of a human?
Do you see things only as people see them?
5 Is your lifetime only as long as ours?
Is your life so short
6 that you must quickly probe for my guilt
and search for my sin?
7 Although you know I am not guilty,
no one can rescue me from your hands.

8 "'You formed me with your hands; you made me,
yet now you completely destroy me.
9 Remember that you made me from dust—
will you turn me back to dust so soon?
10 You guided my conception
and formed me in the womb.*
11 You clothed me with skin and flesh,
and you knit my bones and sinews together.
12 You gave me life and showed me your unfailing
love.
My life was preserved by your care.

13 "'Yet your real motive—
your true intent—
14 was to watch me, and if I sinned,
you would not forgive my guilt.
15 If I am guilty, too bad for me;
and even if I'm innocent, I can't hold my head
high,
because I am filled with shame and misery.
16 And if I hold my head high, you hunt me like a lion
and display your awesome power against me.
17 Again and again you witness against me.
You pour out your growing anger on me
and bring fresh armies against me.

18 "'Why, then, did you deliver me from my mother's
womb?
Why didn't you let me die at birth?
19 It would be as though I had never existed,
going directly from the womb to the grave.
20 I have only a few days left, so leave me alone,
that I may have a moment of comfort
21 before I leave—never to return—
for the land of darkness and utter gloom.
22 It is a land as dark as midnight,
a land of gloom and confusion,
where even the light is dark as midnight.'"

ZOPHAR'S FIRST RESPONSE TO JOB

11 Then Zophar the Naamathite replied to Job:
2 "Shouldn't someone answer this torrent of words?
Is a person proved innocent just by a lot of
talking?
3 Should I remain silent while you babble on?
When you mock God, shouldn't someone make
you ashamed?
4 You claim, 'My beliefs are pure,'
and 'I am clean in the sight of God.'
5 If only God would speak;
if only he would tell you what he thinks!
6 If only he would tell you the secrets of wisdom,
for true wisdom is not a simple matter.
Listen! God is doubtless punishing you
far less than you deserve!

7 "Can you solve the mysteries of God?
Can you discover everything about the
Almighty?
8 Such knowledge is higher than the heavens—
and who are you?
It is deeper than the underworld*—
what do you know?
9 It is broader than the earth
and wider than the sea.
10 If God comes and puts a person in prison
or calls the court to order, who can stop him?

10:10 Hebrew *You poured me out like milk / and curdled me like cheese.*

11:8 Hebrew *than Sheol.*

9:32-3 God is not a mortal like me. Job sought in vain for an impartial arbiter. Who better than God Himself? Job has arrived at the painful place of admitting that God appears to be his "enemy," and yet there is no one else to whom he can go.

10:3 reject me, the work of your own hands. Job assigned cruel intentions to God. Depressed and utterly discouraged, Job began to believe his rantings, though his ideas denied everything that Job had always believed about God.

10:8-17 As if addressing the witness stand, Job questions God's character by attributing to God the evil done to him (see v. 8).

11:1-20 Eliphaz started it. Bildad elaborated on it. Now, Zophar reiterates their condemnation.

11:5 speak . . . tell you what he thinks! Zophar wanted to put words in God's mouth, presuming he knew God's mind. Instead, God eventually spoke against Zophar himself (42:7).

11:8-9 higher than the heavens. Zophar's (partial) portrait of God resembles God's self-description (38:1–42:6). Knowing about God is not the same as knowing God.

[11] For he knows those who are false,
and he takes note of all their sins.
[12] An empty-headed person won't become wise
any more than a wild donkey can bear a human child.*

[13] "If only you would prepare your heart
and lift up your hands to him in prayer!
[14] Get rid of your sins,
and leave all iniquity behind you.
[15] Then your face will brighten with innocence.
You will be strong and free of fear.
[16] You will forget your misery;
it will be like water flowing away.
[17] Your life will be brighter than the noonday.
Even darkness will be as bright as morning.
[18] Having hope will give you courage.
You will be protected and will rest in safety.
[19] You will lie down unafraid,
and many will look to you for help.
[20] But the wicked will be blinded.
They will have no escape.
Their only hope is death."

JOB'S FOURTH SPEECH: A RESPONSE TO ZOPHAR

12 Then Job spoke again:
[2] "You people really know everything, don't you?
And when you die, wisdom will die with you!
[3] Well, I know a few things myself—
and you're no better than I am.
Who doesn't know these things you've been saying?
[4] Yet my friends laugh at me,
for I call on God and expect an answer.
I am a just and blameless man,
yet they laugh at me.
[5] People who are at ease mock those in trouble.
They give a push to people who are stumbling.
[6] But robbers are left in peace,
and those who provoke God live in safety—
though God keeps them in his power.*

[7] "Just ask the animals, and they will teach you.
Ask the birds of the sky, and they will tell you.
[8] Speak to the earth, and it will instruct you.
Let the fish in the sea speak to you.
[9] For they all know
that my disaster* has come from the hand of the LORD.
[10] For the life of every living thing is in his hand,
and the breath of every human being.
[11] The ear tests the words it hears
just as the mouth distinguishes between foods.
[12] Wisdom belongs to the aged,
and understanding to the old.

[13] "But true wisdom and power are found in God;
counsel and understanding are his.
[14] What he destroys cannot be rebuilt.
When he puts someone in prison, there is no escape.
[15] If he holds back the rain, the earth becomes a desert.
If he releases the waters, they flood the earth.
[16] Yes, strength and wisdom are his;
deceivers and deceived are both in his power.
[17] He leads counselors away, stripped of good judgment;
wise judges become fools.
[18] He removes the royal robe of kings.
They are led away with ropes around their waist.
[19] He leads priests away, stripped of status;
he overthrows those with long years in power.
[20] He silences the trusted adviser
and removes the insight of the elders.
[21] He pours disgrace upon princes
and disarms the strong.

[22] "He uncovers mysteries hidden in darkness;
he brings light to the deepest gloom.
[23] He builds up nations, and he destroys them.
He expands nations, and he abandons them.
[24] He strips kings of understanding
and leaves them wandering in a pathless wasteland.
[25] They grope in the darkness without a light.
He makes them stagger like drunkards.

JOB WANTS TO ARGUE HIS CASE WITH GOD

13 [1] "Look, I have seen all this with my own eyes
and heard it with my own ears, and now I understand.
[2] I know as much as you do.
You are no better than I am.
[3] As for me, I would speak directly to the Almighty.
I want to argue my case with God himself.
[4] As for you, you smear me with lies.
As physicians, you are worthless quacks.
[5] If only you could be silent!
That's the wisest thing you could do.
[6] Listen to my charge;
pay attention to my arguments.

[7] "Are you defending God with lies?
Do you make your dishonest arguments for his sake?
[8] Will you slant your testimony in his favor?
Will you argue God's case for him?
[9] What will happen when he finds out what you are doing?
Can you fool him as easily as you fool people?

11:12 Or *than a wild male donkey can bear a tame colt.* **12:6** Or *safety—those who try to manipulate God.* The meaning of the Hebrew is uncertain. **12:9** Hebrew *that this.*

11:11-12 an empty-headed person. Zophar mocks Job's feeble understanding.
11:13-20 Despite Zophar's formula for happiness (vv. 16-17), a relationship with God is not a formula.
12:1–14:22 Job's longest speech thus far (12:1–13:19). Finally, his attention turns again to God (13:20–14:22).
12:2 wisdom will die with you. Job sneered at his friends' supposed monopoly on wisdom.
12:6 robbers are left in peace. Job repeatedly ponders why those who have committed real evil are not suffering as he is.
12:9-10 hand of the LORD. Not only is God's hand skillful in what He has created (Isa. 66:2; Jer. 14:22), but his hand sustains human life and provides its direction.
12:12,20 Wisdom belongs to the aged. Job insinuates that wisdom has not accompanied age in the case of his friends.
13:3 I would speak directly to the Almighty. Job still waits to hear his verdict from God's mouth rather than his friends' (see also v. 15).
13:7 defending God with lies. That the friends could be wrong doesn't seem to have occurred to them.

10 No, you will be in trouble with him
if you secretly slant your testimony in his favor.
11 Doesn't his majesty terrify you?
Doesn't your fear of him overwhelm you?
12 Your platitudes are as valuable as ashes.
Your defense is as fragile as a clay pot.

13 "Be silent now and leave me alone.
Let me speak, and I will face the consequences.
14 Why should I put myself in mortal danger*
and take my life in my own hands?
15 God might kill me, but I have no other hope.*
I am going to argue my case with him.
16 But this is what will save me—I am not godless.
If I were, I could not stand before him.

17 "Listen closely to what I am about to say.
Hear me out.
18 I have prepared my case;
I will be proved innocent.
19 Who can argue with me over this?
And if you prove me wrong, I will remain silent and die.

JOB ASKS HOW HE HAS SINNED

20 "O God, grant me these two things,
and then I will be able to face you.
21 Remove your heavy hand from me,
and don't terrify me with your awesome presence.
22 Now summon me, and I will answer!
Or let me speak to you, and you reply.
23 Tell me, what have I done wrong?
Show me my rebellion and my sin.
24 Why do you turn away from me?
Why do you treat me as your enemy?
25 Would you terrify a leaf blown by the wind?
Would you chase dry straw?

26 "You write bitter accusations against me
and bring up all the sins of my youth.
27 You put my feet in stocks.
You examine all my paths.
You trace all my footprints.
28 I waste away like rotting wood,
like a moth-eaten coat.

14 1 "How frail is humanity!
How short is life, how full of trouble!
2 We blossom like a flower and then wither.
Like a passing shadow, we quickly disappear.
3 Must you keep an eye on such a frail creature
and demand an accounting from me?
4 Who can bring purity out of an impure person?
No one!
5 You have decided the length of our lives.
You know how many months we will live,
and we are not given a minute longer.
6 So leave us alone and let us rest!
We are like hired hands, so let us finish our work in peace.

7 "Even a tree has more hope!
If it is cut down, it will sprout again
and grow new branches.
8 Though its roots have grown old in the earth
and its stump decays,
9 at the scent of water it will bud
and sprout again like a new seedling.

10 "But when people die, their strength is gone.
They breathe their last, and then where are they?
11 As water evaporates from a lake
and a river disappears in drought,
12 people are laid to rest and do not rise again.
Until the heavens are no more, they will not wake up
nor be roused from their sleep.

13 "I wish you would hide me in the grave*
and forget me there until your anger has passed.
But mark your calendar to think of me again!
14 Can the dead live again?
If so, this would give me hope through all my years of struggle,
and I would eagerly await the release of death.
15 You would call and I would answer,
and you would yearn for me, your handiwork.
16 For then you would guard my steps,
instead of watching for my sins.
17 My sins would be sealed in a pouch,
and you would cover my guilt.

18 "But instead, as mountains fall and crumble
and as rocks fall from a cliff,
19 as water wears away the stones
and floods wash away the soil,
so you destroy people's hope.
20 You always overpower them, and they pass from the scene.
You disfigure them in death and send them away.
21 They never know if their children grow up in honor
or sink to insignificance.
22 They suffer painfully;
their life is full of trouble."

13:14 Hebrew *Why should I take my flesh in my teeth.* **13:15** An alternate reading in the Masoretic Text reads *God might kill me, but I hope in him.* **14:13** Hebrew *in Sheol.*

13:15 I have no other hope. The climax of the book, Job asserts ultimate faith in God's character and will die proclaiming it.
13:20-22 grant me these two things. Here Job asked for relief from his torment (v. 21), if not at least a fair trial. Then Job would know that he and God were still communicating.
13:26 write bitter accusations. Job supposed that God had meticulously recorded His vendetta against him (7:19-20; 10:14; 31:4).
14:2-6 Job tried a bit of poetic psychology, suggesting that a mere mortal is not worth the time or effort of a magnificent God. So why doesn't God just leave him alone (v. 6)?
14:13-17 Death would be a safe, hiding place until God chose to revive him.
14:18-22 Hope may await Job at death, but what about the here and now? Worn out, Job searched for any sign of hope in life.

ELIPHAZ'S SECOND RESPONSE TO JOB

15 Then Eliphaz the Temanite replied:

2 "A wise man wouldn't answer with such empty
talk!
You are nothing but a windbag.
3 The wise don't engage in empty chatter.
What good are such words?
4 Have you no fear of God,
no reverence for him?
5 Your sins are telling your mouth what to say.
Your words are based on clever deception.
6 Your own mouth condemns you, not I.
Your own lips testify against you.

7 "Were you the first person ever born?
Were you born before the hills were made?
8 Were you listening at God's secret council?
Do you have a monopoly on wisdom?
9 What do you know that we don't?
What do you understand that we do not?
10 On our side are aged, gray-haired men
much older than your father!

11 "Is God's comfort too little for you?
Is his gentle word not enough?
12 What has taken away your reason?
What has weakened your vision,*
13 that you turn against God
and say all these evil things?
14 Can any mortal be pure?
Can anyone born of a woman be just?
15 Look, God does not even trust the angels.*
Even the heavens are not absolutely pure in his
sight.
16 How much less pure is a corrupt and sinful person
with a thirst for wickedness!

17 "If you will listen, I will show you.
I will answer you from my own experience.
18 And it is confirmed by the reports of wise men
who have heard the same thing from their
fathers—
19 from those to whom the land was given
long before any foreigners arrived.

20 "The wicked writhe in pain throughout their lives.
Years of trouble are stored up for the ruthless.
21 The sound of terror rings in their ears,
and even on good days they fear the attack of
the destroyer.
22 They dare not go out into the darkness
for fear they will be murdered.
23 They wander around, saying, 'Where can I find
bread?'*
They know their day of destruction is near.
24 That dark day terrifies them.
They live in distress and anguish,
like a king preparing for battle.
25 For they shake their fists at God,
defying the Almighty.
26 Holding their strong shields,
they defiantly charge against him.

27 "These wicked people are heavy and prosperous;
their waists bulge with fat.
28 But their cities will be ruined.
They will live in abandoned houses
that are ready to tumble down.
29 Their riches will not last,
and their wealth will not endure.
Their possessions will no longer spread across
the horizon.

30 "They will not escape the darkness.
The burning sun will wither their shoots,
and the breath of God will destroy them.
31 Let them no longer fool themselves by trusting in
empty riches,
for emptiness will be their only reward.
32 They will be cut down in the prime of life;
their branches will never again be green.
33 They will be like a vine whose grapes are
harvested too early,
like an olive tree that loses its blossoms before
the fruit can form.
34 For the godless are barren.
Their homes, enriched through bribery, will
burn.
35 They conceive trouble and give birth to evil.
Their womb produces deceit."

JOB'S FIFTH SPEECH: A RESPONSE TO ELIPHAZ

16 Then Job spoke again:

2 "I have heard all this before.
What miserable comforters you are!
3 Won't you ever stop blowing hot air?
What makes you keep on talking?
4 I could say the same things if you were in my
place.
I could spout off criticism and shake my head
at you.
5 But if it were me, I would encourage you.
I would try to take away your grief.
6 Instead, I suffer if I defend myself,
and I suffer no less if I refuse to speak.

7 "O God, you have ground me down
and devastated my family.
8 As if to prove I have sinned, you've reduced me to
skin and bones.
My gaunt flesh testifies against me.
9 God hates me and angrily tears me apart.

15:12 Or *Why do your eyes flash with anger;* Hebrew reads *Why do your eyes blink.* 15:15 Hebrew *the holy ones.* 15:23 Greek version reads *He is appointed to be food for a vulture.*

15:1-6 Eliphaz serves a second helping of advice. He is less compassionate and more impatient this time around.
15:7-10 When it came to wisdom, Job claimed equality with his elders, not superiority (12:3; 13:2). However, Eliphaz was indignant. Who did Job think he was, anyway? Did he know more than they did?
15:10 gray-haired. Eliphaz relied on seniority for his right to speak.
15:12 taken away your reason. Apparently Job fails to realize the good fortune that his friends are God's consolations.
15:14-16 Can any mortal. Once more, Eliphaz attempts to force Job to a confession (4:17). How can a man be pure compared to God, if even angels are not pure? How much more sinful Job must be than the angels!
15:20-35 Eliphaz describes a clear-cut moral world of cause and effect. Calamity befalls only the wicked (vv. 20-24); Job must be blind or stubborn not to see it.

He snaps his teeth at me
and pierces me with his eyes.
10 People jeer and laugh at me.
They slap my cheek in contempt.
A mob gathers against me.
11 God has handed me over to sinners.
He has tossed me into the hands of the wicked.

12 "I was living quietly until he shattered me.
He took me by the neck and broke me in pieces.
Then he set me up as his target,
13 and now his archers surround me.
His arrows pierce me without mercy.
The ground is wet with my blood.*
14 Again and again he smashes against me,
charging at me like a warrior.
15 I wear burlap to show my grief.
My pride lies in the dust.
16 My eyes are red with weeping;
dark shadows circle my eyes.
17 Yet I have done no wrong,
and my prayer is pure.

18 "O earth, do not conceal my blood.
Let it cry out on my behalf.
19 Even now my witness is in heaven.
My advocate is there on high.
20 My friends scorn me,
but I pour out my tears to God.
21 I need someone to mediate between God and me,
as a person mediates between friends.
22 For soon I must go down that road
from which I will never return.

JOB CONTINUES TO DEFEND HIS INNOCENCE

17 1 "My spirit is crushed,
and my life is nearly snuffed out.
The grave is ready to receive me.
2 I am surrounded by mockers.
I watch how bitterly they taunt me.

3 "You must defend my innocence, O God,
since no one else will stand up for me.
4 You have closed their minds to understanding,
but do not let them triumph.
5 They betray their friends for their own advantage,
so let their children faint with hunger.

6 "God has made a mockery of me among the people;
they spit in my face.
7 My eyes are swollen with weeping,
and I am but a shadow of my former self.
8 The virtuous are horrified when they see me.
The innocent rise up against the ungodly.
9 The righteous keep moving forward,
and those with clean hands become stronger and stronger.
10 "As for all of you, come back with a better argument,
though I still won't find a wise man among you.
11 My days are over.
My hopes have disappeared.
My heart's desires are broken.
12 These men say that night is day;
they claim that the darkness is light.
13 What if I go to the grave*
and make my bed in darkness?
14 What if I call the grave my father,
and the maggot my mother or my sister?
15 Where then is my hope?
Can anyone find it?
16 No, my hope will go down with me to the grave.
We will rest together in the dust!"

BILDAD'S SECOND RESPONSE TO JOB

18 Then Bildad the Shuhite replied:
2 "How long before you stop talking?
Speak sense if you want us to answer!
3 Do you think we are mere animals?
Do you think we are stupid?
4 You may tear out your hair in anger,
but will that destroy the earth?
Will it make the rocks tremble?

5 "Surely the light of the wicked will be snuffed out.
The sparks of their fire will not glow.
6 The light in their tent will grow dark.
The lamp hanging above them will be quenched.
7 The confident stride of the wicked will be shortened.
Their own schemes will be their downfall.
8 The wicked walk into a net.
They fall into a pit.
9 A trap grabs them by the heel.
A snare holds them tight.
10 A noose lies hidden on the ground.
A rope is stretched across their path.

11 "Terrors surround the wicked
and trouble them at every step.
12 Hunger depletes their strength,
and calamity waits for them to stumble.
13 Disease eats their skin;
death devours their limbs.
14 They are torn from the security of their homes
and are brought down to the king of terrors.
15 The homes of the wicked will burn down;
burning sulfur rains on their houses.
16 Their roots will dry up,
and their branches will wither.
17 All memory of their existence will fade from the earth;
no one will remember their names.

16:13 Hebrew *my gall.* **17:13** Hebrew *to Sheol;* also in 17:16.

16:10-14 Despite Eliphaz's accusation, Job did not see himself on the offensive with God (15:25). God was on the offensive against *him*.
16:18-21 cry out on my behalf. Is there anyone who will be a true friend and testify to his innocence (9:33)?
17:3 must defend. Job asks God to post bail for him as a sign of Job's innocence (Ps. 119:121-122). He certainly cannot ask his friends.
17:5 betray their friends. Job quotes an ancient proverb in predicting that his friends' children would become blind on account of their parents' sin.
17:15 Where then is my hope? Job could not see any other ending to the story than the certain darkness of death (v. 13).
18:1-4 Bildad was incensed at Job's insults that said the animals were smarter than these friends (12:7-9).
18:5-21 In Bildad's universe all people receive their due: the wicked suffer, the righteous prosper.

18 They will be thrust from light into darkness,
driven from the world.
19 They will have neither children nor
grandchildren,
nor any survivor in the place where they lived.
20 People in the west are appalled at their fate;
people in the east are horrified.
21 They will say, 'This was the home of a wicked
person,
the place of one who rejected God.'"

JOB'S SIXTH SPEECH: A RESPONSE TO BILDAD

19 Then Job spoke again:
2 "How long will you torture me?
How long will you try to crush me with your
words?
3 You have already insulted me ten times.
You should be ashamed of treating me so badly.
4 Even if I have sinned,
that is my concern, not yours.
5 You think you're better than I am,
using my humiliation as evidence of my sin.
6 But it is God who has wronged me,
capturing me in his net.*

7 "I cry out, 'Help!' but no one answers me.
I protest, but there is no justice.
8 God has blocked my way so I cannot move.
He has plunged my path into darkness.
9 He has stripped me of my honor
and removed the crown from my head.
10 He has demolished me on every side, and I am
finished.
He has uprooted my hope like a fallen tree.
11 His fury burns against me;
he counts me as an enemy.
12 His troops advance.
They build up roads to attack me.
They camp all around my tent.

13 "My relatives stay far away,
and my friends have turned against me.
14 My family is gone,
and my close friends have forgotten me.
15 My servants and maids consider me a stranger.
I am like a foreigner to them.
16 When I call my servant, he doesn't come;
I have to plead with him!
17 My breath is repulsive to my wife.
I am rejected by my own family.
18 Even young children despise me.
When I stand to speak, they turn their backs on
me.
19 My close friends detest me.
Those I loved have turned against me.
20 I have been reduced to skin and bones
and have escaped death by the skin of my teeth.

21 "Have mercy on me, my friends, have mercy,
for the hand of God has struck me.
22 Must you also persecute me, like God does?
Haven't you chewed me up enough?

23 "Oh, that my words could be recorded.
Oh, that they could be inscribed on a monument,
24 carved with an iron chisel and filled with lead,
engraved forever in the rock.

25 "But as for me, I know that my Redeemer lives,
and he will stand upon the earth at last.
26 And after my body has decayed,
yet in my body I will see God!*
27 I will see him for myself.
Yes, I will see him with my own eyes.
I am overwhelmed at the thought!

28 "How dare you go on persecuting me,
saying, 'It's his own fault'?
29 You should fear punishment yourselves,
for your attitude deserves punishment.
Then you will know that there is indeed a
judgment."

ZOPHAR'S SECOND RESPONSE TO JOB

20 Then Zophar the Naamathite replied:
2 "I must reply
because I am greatly disturbed.
3 I've had to endure your insults,
but now my spirit prompts me to reply.

4 "Don't you realize that from the beginning of time,
ever since people were first placed on the earth,
5 the triumph of the wicked has been short lived
and the joy of the godless has been only
temporary?
6 Though the pride of the godless reaches to the
heavens
and their heads touch the clouds,
7 yet they will vanish forever,
thrown away like their own dung.
Those who knew them will ask,
'Where are they?'
8 They will fade like a dream and not be found.
They will vanish like a vision in the night.
9 Those who once saw them will see them no more.
Their families will never see them again.
10 Their children will beg from the poor,
for they must give back their stolen riches.
11 Though they are young,
their bones will lie in the dust.

19:6 Or *for I am like a city under siege.* **19:26** Or *without my body I will see God.* The meaning of the Hebrew is uncertain.

19:4 that is my concern, not yours. Job politely told his friends he didn't need their advice.
19:8-12 Job felt like God's enemy since God no longer honored him or his former faithfulness.
19:23-27 From the bottom, Job suddenly rallies to express confidence. His sorry situation had caused him to rely on God alone for deliverance (v. 26).
19:25 I know my Redeemer lives. Although Job was ready to die, he confidently proclaimed that God would vindicate his innocence in the end. Job was referring to the end of his physical life.
19:26 after my skin has decayed, . . . I will see God. Job expects to see God after his flesh is destroyed. This was an amazing insight for anyone of his time, not to mention someone in those circumstances.
20:4-11 According to Zophar, wickedness always gets punished immediately (v. 5). Job would soon perish if he did not repent (v. 8).
20:10,19 the poor. At least they agreed on this: Oppressing the poor is wicked (31:16-23). The Jews were commanded to take care of the poor.

12 "They enjoyed the sweet taste of wickedness,
letting it melt under their tongue.
13 They savored it,
holding it long in their mouths.
14 But suddenly the food in their bellies turns sour,
a poisonous venom in their stomach.
15 They will vomit the wealth they swallowed.
God won't let them keep it down.
16 They will suck the poison of cobras.
The viper will kill them.
17 They will never again enjoy streams of olive oil
or rivers of milk and honey.
18 They will give back everything they worked for.
Their wealth will bring them no joy.
19 For they oppressed the poor and left them
destitute.
They foreclosed on their homes.
20 They were always greedy and never satisfied.
Nothing remains of all the things they dreamed
about.
21 Nothing is left after they finish gorging
themselves.
Therefore, their prosperity will not endure.

22 "In the midst of plenty, they will run into trouble
and be overcome by misery.
23 May God give them a bellyful of trouble.
May God rain down his anger upon them.
24 When they try to escape an iron weapon,
a bronze-tipped arrow will pierce them.
25 The arrow is pulled from their back,
and the arrowhead glistens with blood.*
The terrors of death are upon them.
26 Their treasures will be thrown into deepest
darkness.
A wildfire will devour their goods,
consuming all they have left.
27 The heavens will reveal their guilt,
and the earth will testify against them.
28 A flood will sweep away their house.
God's anger will descend on them in torrents.
29 This is the reward that God gives the wicked.
It is the inheritance decreed by God."

JOB'S SEVENTH SPEECH: A RESPONSE TO ZOPHAR

21 Then Job spoke again:
2 "Listen closely to what I am saying.
That's one consolation you can give me.
3 Bear with me, and let me speak.
After I have spoken, you may resume mocking me.

4 "My complaint is with God, not with people.
I have good reason to be so impatient.
5 Look at me and be stunned.
Put your hand over your mouth in shock.
6 When I think about what I am saying, I shudder.
My body trembles.
7 "Why do the wicked prosper,
growing old and powerful?
8 They live to see their children grow up and settle
down,
and they enjoy their grandchildren.
9 Their homes are safe from every fear,
and God does not punish them.
10 Their bulls never fail to breed.
Their cows bear calves and never miscarry.
11 They let their children frisk about like lambs.
Their little ones skip and dance.
12 They sing with tambourine and harp.
They celebrate to the sound of the flute.
13 They spend their days in prosperity,
then go down to the grave* in peace.
14 And yet they say to God, 'Go away.
We want no part of you and your ways.
15 Who is the Almighty, and why should we obey
him?
What good will it do us to pray?'
16 (They think their prosperity is of their own doing,
but I will have nothing to do with that kind of
thinking.)

17 "Yet the light of the wicked never seems to be
extinguished.
Do they ever have trouble?
Does God distribute sorrows to them in anger?
18 Are they driven before the wind like straw?
Are they carried away by the storm like chaff?
Not at all!

19 "'Well,' you say, 'at least God will punish their
children!'
But I say he should punish the ones who sin,
so that they understand his judgment.
20 Let them see their destruction with their own eyes.
Let them drink deeply of the anger of the
Almighty.
21 For they will not care what happens to their family
after they are dead.

22 "But who can teach a lesson to God,
since he judges even the most powerful?
23 One person dies in prosperity,
completely comfortable and secure,
24 the picture of good health,
vigorous and fit.
25 Another person dies in bitter poverty,
never having tasted the good life.
26 But both are buried in the same dust,
both eaten by the same maggots.

27 "Look, I know what you're thinking.
I know the schemes you plot against me.
28 You will tell me of rich and wicked people
whose houses have vanished because of their
sins.

20:25 Hebrew *with gall.* **21:13** Hebrew *to Sheol.*

20:20-25 Zophar implied that since Job has been wealthy, perhaps this was his sin—that he had not cared adequately for the poor.
20:29 inheritance decreed by God. Zophar sounded very pleased at how God would repay the oppressors of the poor (despite the fact that he has just included Job in that group).
21:7-15 Contrary to the theology of his companions, Job acknowledged that indeed the wicked do grow powerful (v. 7), not powerless (20:11). They may be blessed with offspring (v. 8, 11), not barren (18:19). Outwardly, the righteous and wicked may share a common happiness (5:17-27).
21:20 destruction. Job knew the fate of the wicked. This Hebrew word for "demise" means to strike, crush, or destroy. Job felt this was exactly what had happened to him—unjustly.

29 But ask those who have been around,
and they will tell you the truth.
30 Evil people are spared in times of calamity
and are allowed to escape disaster.
31 No one criticizes them openly
or pays them back for what they have done.
32 When they are carried to the grave,
an honor guard keeps watch at their tomb.
33 A great funeral procession goes to the cemetery.
Many pay their respects as the body is laid to rest,
and the earth gives sweet repose.

34 "How can your empty clichés comfort me?
All your explanations are lies!"

ELIPHAZ'S THIRD RESPONSE TO JOB

22 Then Eliphaz the Temanite replied:
2 "Can a person do anything to help God?
Can even a wise person be helpful to him?
3 Is it any advantage to the Almighty if you are righteous?
Would it be any gain to him if you were perfect?
4 Is it because you're so pious that he accuses you
and brings judgment against you?
5 No, it's because of your wickedness!
There's no limit to your sins.

6 "For example, you must have lent money to your friend
and demanded clothing as security.
Yes, you stripped him to the bone.
7 You must have refused water for the thirsty
and food for the hungry.
8 You probably think the land belongs to the powerful
and only the privileged have a right to it!
9 You must have sent widows away empty-handed
and crushed the hopes of orphans.
10 That is why you are surrounded by traps
and tremble from sudden fears.
11 That is why you cannot see in the darkness,
and waves of water cover you.

12 "God is so great—higher than the heavens,
higher than the farthest stars.
13 But you reply, 'That's why God can't see what I am doing!
How can he judge through the thick darkness?
14 For thick clouds swirl about him, and he cannot see us.
He is way up there, walking on the vault of heaven.'

15 "Will you continue on the old paths
where evil people have walked?
16 They were snatched away in the prime of life,
the foundations of their lives washed away.
17 For they said to God, 'Leave us alone!
What can the Almighty do to us?'
18 Yet he was the one who filled their homes with good things,
so I will have nothing to do with that kind of thinking.

19 "The righteous will be happy to see the wicked destroyed,
and the innocent will laugh in contempt.
20 They will say, 'See how our enemies have been destroyed.
The last of them have been consumed in the fire.'

21 "Submit to God, and you will have peace;
then things will go well for you.
22 Listen to his instructions,
and store them in your heart.
23 If you return to the Almighty, you will be restored—
so clean up your life.
24 If you give up your lust for money
and throw your precious gold into the river,
25 the Almighty himself will be your treasure.
He will be your precious silver!

26 "Then you will take delight in the Almighty
and look up to God.
27 You will pray to him, and he will hear you,
and you will fulfill your vows to him.
28 You will succeed in whatever you choose to do,
and light will shine on the road ahead of you.
29 If people are in trouble and you say, 'Help them,'
God will save them.
30 Even sinners will be rescued;
they will be rescued because your hands are pure."

JOB'S EIGHTH SPEECH: A RESPONSE TO ELIPHAZ

23 Then Job spoke again:
2 "My complaint today is still a bitter one,
and I try hard not to groan aloud.
3 If only I knew where to find God,
I would go to his court.
4 I would lay out my case
and present my arguments.
5 Then I would listen to his reply
and understand what he says to me.
6 Would he use his great power to argue with me?
No, he would give me a fair hearing.
7 Honest people can reason with him,
so I would be forever acquitted by my judge.
8 I go east, but he is not there.
I go west, but I cannot find him.
9 I do not see him in the north, for he is hidden.
I look to the south, but he is concealed.

10 "But he knows where I am going.
And when he tests me, I will come out as pure as gold.

22:1–26:14 For the third and final round of speeches, Eliphaz gave it his best shot, Bildad came up short, and Zophar gave up entirely. Neither Job nor his friends were willing to concede. The friends resorted to specific accusations, which Job resolutely refuted.

22:2-4 gain. Eliphaz erroneously concluded that God is indifferent to personal purity. In fact, the purity of the worshiper was at the heart of the heavenly question behind Job's suffering (1:8-12; 2:3-6).

22:5-11 Agreeing with Zophar (20:10), Eliphaz concludes that Job is guilty of oppressing the poor. But Job's reputation refuted the accusation (1:1-5).

22:12-20 Concern turned to callousness. Eliphaz assigned Job a dishonorable place in the evil hall of fame (v. 15).

23:3 If only I knew where to find God. This verse may well summarize the main message of the book and the strongest cry of Job's heart. He bears bravely with physical suffering and material loss. But his loss of relationship with God cannot be assuaged.

23:10 he knows where I am going. God alone knows his heart. Job is beginning to hope that God will yet find him blameless.

11 For I have stayed on God's paths;
I have followed his ways and not turned aside.
12 I have not departed from his commands,
but have treasured his words more than daily food.
13 But once he has made his decision, who can change his mind?
Whatever he wants to do, he does.
14 So he will do to me whatever he has planned.
He controls my destiny.
15 No wonder I am so terrified in his presence.
When I think of it, terror grips me.
16 God has made me sick at heart;
the Almighty has terrified me.
17 Darkness is all around me;
thick, impenetrable darkness is everywhere.

JOB ASKS WHY THE WICKED ARE NOT PUNISHED

24 1 "Why doesn't the Almighty bring the wicked to judgment?
Why must the godly wait for him in vain?
2 Evil people steal land by moving the boundary markers.
They steal livestock and put them in their own pastures.
3 They take the orphan's donkey
and demand the widow's ox as security for a loan.
4 The poor are pushed off the path;
the needy must hide together for safety.
5 Like wild donkeys in the wilderness,
the poor must spend all their time looking for food,
searching even in the desert for food for their children.
6 They harvest a field they do not own,
and they glean in the vineyards of the wicked.
7 All night they lie naked in the cold,
without clothing or covering.
8 They are soaked by mountain showers,
and they huddle against the rocks for want of a home.

9 "The wicked snatch a widow's child from her breast,
taking the baby as security for a loan.
10 The poor must go about naked, without any clothing.
They harvest food for others while they themselves are starving.
11 They press out olive oil without being allowed to taste it,
and they tread in the winepress as they suffer from thirst.
12 The groans of the dying rise from the city,
and the wounded cry for help,
yet God ignores their moaning.

13 "Wicked people rebel against the light.
They refuse to acknowledge its ways
or stay in its paths.
14 The murderer rises in the early dawn
to kill the poor and needy;
at night he is a thief.
15 The adulterer waits for the twilight,
saying, 'No one will see me then.'
He hides his face so no one will know him.
16 Thieves break into houses at night
and sleep in the daytime.
They are not acquainted with the light.
17 The black night is their morning.
They ally themselves with the terrors of the darkness.

18 "But they disappear like foam down a river.
Everything they own is cursed,
and they are afraid to enter their own vineyards.
19 The grave* consumes sinners
just as drought and heat consume snow.
20 Their own mothers will forget them.
Maggots will find them sweet to eat.
No one will remember them.
Wicked people are broken like a tree in the storm.
21 They cheat the woman who has no son to help her.
They refuse to help the needy widow.

22 "God, in his power, drags away the rich.
They may rise high, but they have no assurance of life.
23 They may be allowed to live in security,
but God is always watching them.
24 And though they are great now,
in a moment they will be gone like all others,
cut off like heads of grain.
25 Can anyone claim otherwise?
Who can prove me wrong?"

BILDAD'S THIRD RESPONSE TO JOB

25 Then Bildad the Shuhite replied:
2 "God is powerful and dreadful.
He enforces peace in the heavens.
3 Who is able to count his heavenly army?
Doesn't his light shine on all the earth?
4 How can a mortal be innocent before God?
Can anyone born of a woman be pure?
5 God is more glorious than the moon;
he shines brighter than the stars.
6 In comparison, people are maggots;
we mortals are mere worms."

24:19 Hebrew *Sheol.*

23:13 Whatever he wants to do, he does. Job may not have understood God's mysterious ways, but He still trusted his history with God.
23:17 Darkness. Job discovered that the darkness has not destroyed him and his spiritual eyes are adjusting to it.
24:1-12 Job outlined several outlandish injustices. Orphans and widows were robbed of their minimal possessions, leaving them hungry and homeless. However, the gap between the actual crime and the punishment made a mockery of justice.
24:17 black night is their morning. Job listed criminal activities that are conducted in the dark. Therefore, morning's light makes them highly visible. The mistake of evildoers was thinking that the darkness could hide their crimes from God.
24:18-25 The only justice Job could see was that death would finally triumph over evildoers (see also 21:23-26).
25:1-6 Bildad made one last speech to convince Job of his folly.
25:6 maggots. Bildad's meaning is clear: there is no way for a mere human to be pure when compared to God.

JOB'S NINTH SPEECH: A RESPONSE TO BILDAD

26 Then Job spoke again:

2 "How you have helped the powerless!
How you have saved the weak!
3 How you have enlightened my stupidity!
What wise advice you have offered!
4 Where have you gotten all these wise sayings?
Whose spirit speaks through you?

5 "The dead tremble—
those who live beneath the waters.
6 The underworld* is naked in God's presence.
The place of destruction* is uncovered.
7 God stretches the northern sky over empty space
and hangs the earth on nothing.
8 He wraps the rain in his thick clouds,
and the clouds don't burst with the weight.
9 He covers the face of the moon,*
shrouding it with his clouds.
10 He created the horizon when he separated the waters;
he set the boundary between day and night.
11 The foundations of heaven tremble;
they shudder at his rebuke.
12 By his power the sea grew calm.
By his skill he crushed the great sea monster.*
13 His Spirit made the heavens beautiful,
and his power pierced the gliding serpent.
14 These are just the beginning of all that he does,
merely a whisper of his power.
Who, then, can comprehend the thunder of his power?"

JOB'S FINAL SPEECH

27 Job continued speaking:

2 "I vow by the living God, who has taken away my rights,
by the Almighty who has embittered my soul—
3 As long as I live,
while I have breath from God,
4 my lips will speak no evil,
and my tongue will speak no lies.
5 I will never concede that you are right;
I will defend my integrity until I die.
6 I will maintain my innocence without wavering.
My conscience is clear for as long as I live.

7 "May my enemy be punished like the wicked,
my adversary like those who do evil.
8 For what hope do the godless have when God cuts them off
and takes away their life?
9 Will God listen to their cry
when trouble comes upon them?
10 Can they take delight in the Almighty?
Can they call to God at any time?
11 I will teach you about God's power.
I will not conceal anything concerning the Almighty.
12 But you have seen all this,
yet you say all these useless things to me.

13 "This is what the wicked will receive from God;
this is their inheritance from the Almighty.
14 They may have many children,
but the children will die in war or starve to death.
15 Those who survive will die of a plague,
and not even their widows will mourn them.

16 "Evil people may have piles of money
and may store away mounds of clothing.
17 But the righteous will wear that clothing,
and the innocent will divide that money.
18 The wicked build houses as fragile as a spider's web,*
as flimsy as a shelter made of branches.
19 The wicked go to bed rich
but wake to find that all their wealth is gone.
20 Terror overwhelms them like a flood,
and they are blown away in the storms of the night.
21 The east wind carries them away, and they are gone.
It sweeps them away.
22 It whirls down on them without mercy.
They struggle to flee from its power.
23 But everyone jeers at them
and mocks them.

JOB SPEAKS OF WISDOM AND UNDERSTANDING

28 1 "People know where to mine silver
and how to refine gold.
2 They know where to dig iron from the earth
and how to smelt copper from rock.
3 They know how to shine light in the darkness
and explore the farthest regions of the earth
as they search in the dark for ore.
4 They sink a mine shaft into the earth
far from where anyone lives.
They descend on ropes, swinging back and forth.
5 Food is grown on the earth above,
but down below, the earth is melted as by fire.
6 Here the rocks contain precious lapis lazuli,
and the dust contains gold.
7 These are treasures no bird of prey can see,
no falcon's eye observe.

26:6a Hebrew *Sheol.* **26:6b** Hebrew *Abaddon.* **26:9** Or *covers his throne.* **26:12** Hebrew *Rahab,* the name of a mythical sea monster that represents chaos in ancient literature. **27:18** As in Greek and Syriac versions (see also 8:14); Hebrew reads *a moth.*

26:2-14 Job launched into the longest speech in the entire book. This chapter is united with chapters 27–28 in theme. Job can speak at length now that the three friends have completed their arguments.

26:6 underworld. This Hebrew word means perishing or destruction. *Abaddon* is another word for *Sheol* or the place of the dead.

26:14 the beginning of all that he does. Job doesn't claim to understand God but he knows enough to know that if God revealed all his glory, the experience would be thunderous and overwhelming.

27:1-6 His companions may question his innocence, but they could not doubt Job's convictions about his innocence (vv. 2-6).

27:2-4 by the living God . . . my lips will speak no evil. Notice that Job still swore by God ; "As God lives" was the preface to his oath taking. He still claimed God was just even when he could not see justice being applied to his own case before God.

27:13-23 Job's list of calamities that befall the wicked are a jumble of metaphors ranging from moths to floods to windstorms. They convey the retribution due evildoers.

28:1-28 Chapter 28 defines wisdom as a mystery at best. This abstract description of wisdom foreshadows God's own response (38:1–41:34).

8 No wild animal has walked upon these treasures;
no lion has ever set his paw there.
9 People know how to tear apart flinty rocks
and overturn the roots of mountains.
10 They cut tunnels in the rocks
and uncover precious stones.
11 They dam up the trickling streams
and bring to light the hidden treasures.

12 "But do people know where to find wisdom?
Where can they find understanding?
13 No one knows where to find it,*
for it is not found among the living.
14 'It is not here,' says the ocean.
'Nor is it here,' says the sea.
15 It cannot be bought with gold.
It cannot be purchased with silver.
16 It's worth more than all the gold of Ophir,
greater than precious onyx or lapis lazuli.
17 Wisdom is more valuable than gold and crystal.
It cannot be purchased with jewels mounted in fine gold.
18 Coral and jasper are worthless in trying to get it.
The price of wisdom is far above rubies.
19 Precious peridot from Ethiopia* cannot be exchanged for it.
It's worth more than the purest gold.

20 "But do people know where to find wisdom?
Where can they find understanding?
21 It is hidden from the eyes of all humanity.
Even the sharp-eyed birds in the sky cannot discover it.
22 Destruction* and Death say,
'We've heard only rumors of where wisdom can be found.'

23 "God alone understands the way to wisdom;
he knows where it can be found,
24 for he looks throughout the whole earth
and sees everything under the heavens.
25 He decided how hard the winds should blow
and how much rain should fall.
26 He made the laws for the rain
and laid out a path for the lightning.
27 Then he saw wisdom and evaluated it.
He set it in place and examined it thoroughly.
28 And this is what he says to all humanity:
'The fear of the Lord is true wisdom;
to forsake evil is real understanding.'"

JOB SPEAKS OF HIS FORMER BLESSINGS

29 Job continued speaking:
2 "I long for the years gone by
when God took care of me,
3 when he lit up the way before me
and I walked safely through the darkness.
4 When I was in my prime,
God's friendship was felt in my home.
5 The Almighty was still with me,
and my children were around me.
6 My steps were awash in cream,
and the rocks gushed olive oil for me.

7 "Those were the days when I went to the city gate
and took my place among the honored leaders.
8 The young stepped aside when they saw me,
and even the aged rose in respect at my coming.
9 The princes stood in silence
and put their hands over their mouths.
10 The highest officials of the city stood quietly,
holding their tongues in respect.

11 "All who heard me praised me.
All who saw me spoke well of me.
12 For I assisted the poor in their need
and the orphans who required help.
13 I helped those without hope, and they blessed me.
And I caused the widows' hearts to sing for joy.
14 Everything I did was honest.
Righteousness covered me like a robe,
and I wore justice like a turban.
15 I served as eyes for the blind
and feet for the lame.
16 I was a father to the poor
and assisted strangers who needed help.
17 I broke the jaws of godless oppressors
and plucked their victims from their teeth.

18 "I thought, 'Surely I will die surrounded by my family
after a long, good life.*
19 For I am like a tree whose roots reach the water,
whose branches are refreshed with the dew.
20 New honors are constantly bestowed on me,
and my strength is continually renewed.'

21 "Everyone listened to my advice.
They were silent as they waited for me to speak.
22 And after I spoke, they had nothing to add,
for my counsel satisfied them.
23 They longed for me to speak as people long for rain.
They drank my words like a refreshing spring rain.
24 When they were discouraged, I smiled at them.
My look of approval was precious to them.
25 Like a chief, I told them what to do.
I lived like a king among his troops
and comforted those who mourned.

JOB SPEAKS OF HIS ANGUISH

30 1 "But now I am mocked by people younger than I,
by young men whose fathers are not worthy to run with my sheepdogs.

28:13 As in Greek version; Hebrew reads *knows its value.* **28:19** Hebrew *from Cush.* **28:22** Hebrew *Abaddon.* **29:18** Hebrew *after I have counted my days like sand.*

28:28 fear of the LORD is true wisdom. This profound verse is found in several other places in Scripture (Ps. 111:10; Prov. 1:7; 9:10; Eccles. 12:13).
29:1–31:40 This long speech of Job's are his last words in this book. He first recalled his former happy state, then his calamities, and finally a checklist of potential sins he might have committed. Once again, he proclaimed himself innocent.
29:4 God's friendship. Job's relationship with God still existed. However, his circumstances had prevented his feeling God's presence as in the past.
29:12-13 poor . . . orphans. Job summarized his claims of innocence. Chief among his claims was that he never oppressed the poor.
29:21-25 Job recalled past respect given to him. People listened and were blessed (vv. 21-23).
30:1-31 The haunting contrast of past and present (vv. 1-19) made reliving the agony all the more painful for Job (vv. 20-31).

2 A lot of good they are to me—
those worn-out wretches!
3 They are gaunt from poverty and hunger.
They claw the dry ground in desolate
wastelands.
4 They pluck wild greens from among the bushes
and eat from the roots of broom trees.
5 They are driven from human society,
and people shout at them as if they were
thieves.
6 So now they live in frightening ravines,
in caves and among the rocks.
7 They sound like animals howling among the
bushes,
huddled together beneath the nettles.
8 They are nameless fools,
outcasts from society.

9 "And now they mock me with vulgar songs!
They taunt me!
10 They despise me and won't come near me,
except to spit in my face.
11 For God has cut my bowstring.
He has humbled me,
so they have thrown off all restraint.
12 These outcasts oppose me to my face.
They send me sprawling
and lay traps in my path.
13 They block my road
and do everything they can to destroy me.
They know I have no one to help me.
14 They come at me from all directions.
They jump on me when I am down.
15 I live in terror now.
My honor has blown away in the wind,
and my prosperity has vanished like a cloud.

16 "And now my life seeps away.
Depression haunts my days.
17 At night my bones are filled with pain,
which gnaws at me relentlessly.
18 With a strong hand, God grabs my shirt.*
He grips me by the collar of my coat.
19 He has thrown me into the mud.
I'm nothing more than dust and ashes.

20 "I cry to you, O God, but you don't answer.
I stand before you, but you don't even look.
21 You have become cruel toward me.
You use your power to persecute me.
22 You throw me into the whirlwind
and destroy me in the storm.
23 And I know you are sending me to my death—
the destination of all who live.

24 "Surely no one would turn against the needy
when they cry for help in their trouble.
25 Did I not weep for those in trouble?
Was I not deeply grieved for the needy?
26 So I looked for good, but evil came instead.
I waited for the light, but darkness fell.
27 My heart is troubled and restless.
Days of suffering torment me.
28 I walk in gloom, without sunlight.
I stand in the public square and cry for
help.
29 Instead, I am considered a brother to jackals
and a companion to owls.
30 My skin has turned dark,
and my bones burn with fever.
31 My harp plays sad music,
and my flute accompanies those who
weep.

JOB'S FINAL PROTEST OF INNOCENCE

31 1 "I made a covenant with my eyes
not to look with lust at a young woman.
2 For what has God above chosen for us?
What is our inheritance from the Almighty on
high?
3 Isn't it calamity for the wicked
and misfortune for those who do evil?
4 Doesn't he see everything I do
and every step I take?

5 "Have I lied to anyone
or deceived anyone?
6 Let God weigh me on the scales of justice,
for he knows my integrity.
7 If I have strayed from his pathway,
or if my heart has lusted for what my eyes have
seen,
or if I am guilty of any other sin,
8 then let someone else eat the crops I have
planted.
Let all that I have planted be uprooted.

9 "If my heart has been seduced by a woman,
or if I have lusted for my neighbor's wife,
10 then let my wife serve* another man;
let other men sleep with her.
11 For lust is a shameful sin,
a crime that should be punished.
12 It is a fire that burns all the way to hell.*
It would wipe out everything I own.

13 "If I have been unfair to my male or female
servants
when they brought their complaints to me,
14 how could I face God?
What could I say when he questioned me?
15 For God created both me and my servants.
He created us both in the womb.

16 "Have I refused to help the poor,
or crushed the hopes of widows?
17 Have I been stingy with my food
and refused to share it with orphans?

30:18 As in Greek version; Hebrew reads *hand, my garment is disfigured.* **31:10** Hebrew *grind for.* **31:12** Hebrew *to Abaddon.*

30:8 nameless. Since a name bespoke dignity in the sense that Job was known to have perfect integrity (1:1), the nameless (whose animal behaviors are listed in vv. 2-8) were especially infamous; lacking all character.

30:20-23 you don't answer. If only Job could have known the prologue (1:6-12). God's power was responsible for restraining further suffering, not causing it (1:12; 2:6).

30:29 companion to owls. Better jackals and owls than the nameless (v. 8).

31:1-40 Job issued his strongest denial yet. If he were guilty of any listed sin, he would gladly accept the consequence, but he cannot deny the truth of his own conscience. The list of sins includes: lust, dishonesty, adultery, oppression, stinginess, greed, idolatry, vindictiveness, hypocrisy, and exploitation.

31:1-12 Job denied sexual longing (vv. 1-4) as well as sexual immorality (vv. 9-12). He professed upright business practices as well (vv. 5-8).

18 No, from childhood I have cared for orphans like a father,
and all my life I have cared for widows.
19 Whenever I saw the homeless without clothes
and the needy with nothing to wear,
20 did they not praise me
for providing wool clothing to keep them warm?

21 "If I raised my hand against an orphan,
knowing the judges would take my side,
22 then let my shoulder be wrenched out of place!
Let my arm be torn from its socket!
23 That would be better than facing God's judgment.
For if the majesty of God opposes me, what hope is there?

24 "Have I put my trust in money
or felt secure because of my gold?
25 Have I gloated about my wealth
and all that I own?

26 "Have I looked at the sun shining in the skies,
or the moon walking down its silver pathway,
27 and been secretly enticed in my heart
to throw kisses at them in worship?
28 If so, I should be punished by the judges,
for it would mean I had denied the God of heaven.

29 "Have I ever rejoiced when disaster struck my enemies,
or become excited when harm came their way?
30 No, I have never sinned by cursing anyone
or by asking for revenge.

31 "My servants have never said,
'He let others go hungry.'
32 I have never turned away a stranger
but have opened my doors to everyone.

33 "Have I tried to hide my sins like other people do,
concealing my guilt in my heart?
34 Have I feared the crowd
or the contempt of the masses,
so that I kept quiet and stayed indoors?

35 "If only someone would listen to me!
Look, I will sign my name to my defense.
Let the Almighty answer me.
Let my accuser write out the charges against me.
36 I would face the accusation proudly.
I would wear it like a crown.
37 For I would tell him exactly what I have done.
I would come before him like a prince.

38 "If my land accuses me
and all its furrows cry out together,
39 or if I have stolen its crops
or murdered its owners,
40 then let thistles grow on that land instead of wheat,
and weeds instead of barley."

Job's words are ended.

ELIHU RESPONDS TO JOB'S FRIENDS

32 Job's three friends refused to reply further to
him because he kept insisting on his innocence.
2 Then Elihu son of Barakel the Buzite, of the clan
of Ram, became angry. He was angry because Job re-
fused to admit that he had sinned and that God was
right in punishing him. 3 He was also angry with Job's
three friends, for they made God* appear to be wrong
by their inability to answer Job's arguments. 4 Elihu
had waited for the others to speak to Job because they
were older than he. 5 But when he saw that they had
no further reply, he spoke out angrily. 6 Elihu son of
Barakel the Buzite said,

"I am young and you are old,
so I held back from telling you what I think.
7 I thought, 'Those who are older should speak,
for wisdom comes with age.'
8 But there is a spirit* within people,
the breath of the Almighty within them,
that makes them intelligent.
9 Sometimes the elders are not wise.
Sometimes the aged do not understand justice.
10 So listen to me,
and let me tell you what I think.

11 "I have waited all this time,
listening very carefully to your arguments,
listening to you grope for words.
12 I have listened,
but not one of you has refuted Job
or answered his arguments.
13 And don't tell me, 'He is too wise for us.
Only God can convince him.'
14 If Job had been arguing with me,
I would not answer with your kind of logic!
15 You sit there baffled,
with nothing more to say.
16 Should I continue to wait, now that you are silent?
Must I also remain silent?
17 No, I will say my piece.
I will speak my mind.
18 For I am full of pent-up words,
and the spirit within me urges me on.
19 I am like a cask of wine without a vent,
like a new wineskin ready to burst!
20 I must speak to find relief,
so let me give my answers.

32:3 As in ancient Hebrew scribal tradition; the Masoretic Text reads *Job*. 32:8 Or *Spirit;* also in 32:18.

31:24-28 Job's friends had accused him of secret covetousness (22:24), though he had forthrightly denounced greed.
32:1–37:24 Elihu, to this point silent before his elders, now spoke. His tone was tactful, compared to the exasperated trio who had rushed to judgment (or so he thought) without fully considering the facts of Job's case (32:12). Job, for his part, seemed prideful in his pronouncements against God (40:2). Elihu addressed the different sides through four levels of speeches (32:5–33:33; chapters 34–35; chapters 36–37).
32:6,10,17 what I think. As the youngest, it is interesting that he claimed three times to *know* what no one else has been able to explain. So he confidently added his perspective.

21 I won't play favorites
or try to flatter anyone.
22 For if I tried flattery,
my Creator would soon destroy me.

ELIHU PRESENTS HIS CASE AGAINST JOB

33 1 "Listen to my words, Job;
pay attention to what I have to say.
2 Now that I have begun to speak,
let me continue.
3 I speak with all sincerity;
I speak the truth.
4 For the Spirit of God has made me,
and the breath of the Almighty gives me
life.
5 Answer me, if you can;
make your case and take your stand.
6 Look, you and I both belong to God.
I, too, was formed from clay.
7 So you don't need to be afraid of me.
I won't come down hard on you.

8 "You have spoken in my hearing,
and I have heard your very words.
9 You said, 'I am pure; I am without sin;
I am innocent; I have no guilt.
10 God is picking a quarrel with me,
and he considers me his enemy.
11 He puts my feet in the stocks
and watches my every move.'

12 "But you are wrong, and I will show you why.
For God is greater than any human being.
13 So why are you bringing a charge against him?
Why say he does not respond to people's
complaints?
14 For God speaks again and again,
though people do not recognize it.
15 He speaks in dreams, in visions of the night,
when deep sleep falls on people
as they lie in their beds.
16 He whispers in their ears
and terrifies them with warnings.
17 He makes them turn from doing wrong;
he keeps them from pride.
18 He protects them from the grave,
from crossing over the river of death.

19 "Or God disciplines people with pain on their
sickbeds,
with ceaseless aching in their bones.
20 They lose their appetite
for even the most delicious food.
21 Their flesh wastes away,
and their bones stick out.
22 They are at death's door;
the angels of death wait for them.

23 "But if an angel from heaven appears—
a special messenger to intercede for a person
and declare that he is upright—
24 he will be gracious and say,
'Rescue him from the grave,
for I have found a ransom for his life.'
25 Then his body will become as healthy as a child's,
firm and youthful again.
26 When he prays to God,
he will be accepted.
And God will receive him with joy
and restore him to good standing.
27 He will declare to his friends,
'I sinned and twisted the truth,
but it was not worth it.*
28 God rescued me from the grave,
and now my life is filled with light.'

29 "Yes, God does these things
again and again for people.
30 He rescues them from the grave
so they may enjoy the light of life.
31 Mark this well, Job. Listen to me,
for I have more to say.
32 But if you have anything to say, go ahead.
Speak, for I am anxious to see you justified.
33 But if not, then listen to me.
Keep silent and I will teach you wisdom!"

ELIHU ACCUSES JOB OF ARROGANCE

34 Then Elihu said:

2 "Listen to me, you wise men.
Pay attention, you who have knowledge.
3 Job said, 'The ear tests the words it hears
just as the mouth distinguishes between
foods.'
4 So let us discern for ourselves what is right;
let us learn together what is good.
5 For Job also said, 'I am innocent,
but God has taken away my rights.
6 I am innocent, but they call me a liar.
My suffering is incurable, though I have not
sinned.'

7 "Tell me, has there ever been a man like Job,
with his thirst for irreverent talk?
8 He chooses evil people as companions.
He spends his time with wicked men.
9 He has even said, 'Why waste time
trying to please God?'

10 "Listen to me, you who have understanding.
Everyone knows that God doesn't sin!
The Almighty can do no wrong.
11 He repays people according to their deeds.
He treats people as they deserve.

33:27 Greek version reads *but he* [God] *did not punish me as my sin deserved.*

32:21-22 In a twist of irony, the Hebrew text implies, "I am not partial to you with flattery because if I flattered you, God would not be partial to me."
33:1-33 In his speeches, Elihu addressed all of Job's major points. He began by refuting Job's charge concerning God's apparent silence. In fact, God sometimes speaks through dreams (v. 15) and personal pain (v. 19).
33:7 afraid of me. Elihu was clearly full of his own importance. He almost sounded as if he were speaking for God in his overemphasis of equality, while implying superior power (terror).
33:23-28 Eliphaz thought Job was a lost cause (5:1). Elihu, however, envisioned an angel mediating on Job's behalf.
33:33 I will teach you wisdom. Satisfied that he has convinced Job of his opening argument, Elihu rambles on for the next four chapters. Only God ultimately answers (38:1).
34:1-37 Satisfied that he had defended God's silence, Elihu next took on the issue of God's fairness, or lack thereof. He systematically addressed the so-called wise companions (vv. 2-15), then Job (vv. 16-33), and then himself (vv. 34-37).

12 Truly, God will not do wrong.
The Almighty will not twist justice.
13 Did someone else put the world in his care?
Who set the whole world in place?
14 If God were to take back his spirit
and withdraw his breath,
15 all life would cease,
and humanity would turn again to dust.

16 "Now listen to me if you are wise.
Pay attention to what I say.
17 Could God govern if he hated justice?
Are you going to condemn the almighty judge?
18 For he says to kings, 'You are wicked,'
and to nobles, 'You are unjust.'
19 He doesn't care how great a person may be,
and he pays no more attention to the rich than
to the poor.
He made them all.
20 In a moment they die.
In the middle of the night they pass away;
the mighty are removed without human hand.

21 "For God watches how people live;
he sees everything they do.
22 No darkness is thick enough
to hide the wicked from his eyes.
23 We don't set the time
when we will come before God in judgment.
24 He brings the mighty to ruin without asking
anyone,
and he sets up others in their place.
25 He knows what they do,
and in the night he overturns and destroys
them.
26 He strikes them down because they are wicked,
doing it openly for all to see.
27 For they turned away from following him.
They have no respect for any of his ways.
28 They cause the poor to cry out, catching God's
attention.
He hears the cries of the needy.
29 But if he chooses to remain quiet,
who can criticize him?
When he hides his face, no one can find him,
whether an individual or a nation.
30 He prevents the godless from ruling
so they cannot be a snare to the people.

31 "Why don't people say to God, 'I have sinned,
but I will sin no more'?
32 Or 'I don't know what evil I have done—tell me.
If I have done wrong, I will stop at once'?

33 "Must God tailor his justice to your demands?
But you have rejected him!
The choice is yours, not mine.
Go ahead, share your wisdom with us.
34 After all, bright people will tell me,
and wise people will hear me say,
35 'Job speaks out of ignorance;
his words lack insight.'
36 Job, you deserve the maximum penalty
for the wicked way you have talked.
37 For you have added rebellion to your sin;
you show no respect,
and you speak many angry words against
God."

ELIHU REMINDS JOB OF GOD'S JUSTICE

35 Then Elihu said:
2 "Do you think it is right for you to claim,
'I am righteous before God'?
3 For you also ask, 'What's in it for me?
What's the use of living a righteous life?'

4 "I will answer you
and all your friends, too.
5 Look up into the sky,
and see the clouds high above you.
6 If you sin, how does that affect God?
Even if you sin again and again,
what effect will it have on him?
7 If you are good, is this some great gift to him?
What could you possibly give him?
8 No, your sins affect only people like yourself,
and your good deeds also affect only humans.

9 "People cry out when they are oppressed.
They groan beneath the power of the mighty.
10 Yet they don't ask, 'Where is God my Creator,
the one who gives songs in the night?
11 Where is the one who makes us smarter than the
animals
and wiser than the birds of the sky?'
12 And when they cry out, God does not answer
because of their pride.
13 But it is wrong to say God doesn't listen,
to say the Almighty isn't concerned.
14 You say you can't see him,
but he will bring justice if you will only wait.*
15 You say he does not respond to sinners with anger
and is not greatly concerned about
wickedness.*
16 But you are talking nonsense, Job.
You have spoken like a fool."

36 Elihu continued speaking:
2 "Let me go on, and I will show you the truth.
For I have not finished defending God!
3 I will present profound arguments
for the righteousness of my Creator.
4 I am telling you nothing but the truth,
for I am a man of great knowledge.

35:13-14 These verses can also be translated as follows: [13]*Indeed, God doesn't listen to their empty plea; / the Almighty is not concerned. /* [14]*How much less will he listen when you say you don't see him, / and that your case is before him and you're waiting for justice.* **35:15** As in Greek and Latin versions; the meaning of this Hebrew word is uncertain.

34:14-15 If God were to take back his spirit. Elihu's arguments centered around God's right to use His power at His discretion. What he did not consider was that choices are based on His goodness.

34:35 lack insight. Each person has part of the puzzle, but God alone fits the pieces together (38:2; 42:3).

35:1-3,12-15 Elihu has misunderstood Job to mean that he is seeking God's acquittal, while at the same time claiming that God does not punish the wicked.

35:5 Look up into the sky. Like Bildad (18:4), Elihu encouraged Job to see the big picture. God is so above it all that Job's sins cause their own consequences.

5 "God is mighty, but he does not despise anyone!
He is mighty in both power and
understanding.
6 He does not let the wicked live
but gives justice to the afflicted.
7 He never takes his eyes off the innocent,
but he sets them on thrones with kings
and exalts them forever.
8 If they are bound in chains
and caught up in a web of trouble,
9 he shows them the reason.
He shows them their sins of pride.
10 He gets their attention
and commands that they turn from evil.

11 "If they listen and obey God,
they will be blessed with prosperity throughout
their lives.
All their years will be pleasant.
12 But if they refuse to listen to him,
they will cross over the river of death,
dying from lack of understanding.
13 For the godless are full of resentment.
Even when he punishes them,
they refuse to cry out to him for help.
14 They die when they are young,
after wasting their lives in immoral living.
15 But by means of their suffering, he rescues those
who suffer.
For he gets their attention through adversity.

16 "God is leading you away from danger, Job,
to a place free from distress.
He is setting your table with the best food.
17 But you are obsessed with whether the godless
will be judged.
Don't worry, judgment and justice will be
upheld.
18 But watch out, or you may be seduced by
wealth.*
Don't let yourself be bribed into sin.
19 Could all your wealth*
or all your mighty efforts
keep you from distress?
20 Do not long for the cover of night,
for that is when people will be destroyed.*
21 Be on guard! Turn back from evil,
for God sent this suffering
to keep you from a life of evil.

ELIHU REMINDS JOB OF GOD'S POWER

22 "Look, God is all-powerful.
Who is a teacher like him?
23 No one can tell him what to do,
or say to him, 'You have done wrong.'
24 Instead, glorify his mighty works,
singing songs of praise.
25 Everyone has seen these things,
though only from a distance.
26 "Look, God is greater than we can understand.
His years cannot be counted.
27 He draws up the water vapor
and then distills it into rain.
28 The rain pours down from the clouds,
and everyone benefits.
29 Who can understand the spreading of the
clouds
and the thunder that rolls forth from
heaven?
30 See how he spreads the lightning around him
and how it lights up the depths of the sea.
31 By these mighty acts he nourishes* the people,
giving them food in abundance.
32 He fills his hands with lightning bolts
and hurls each at its target.
33 The thunder announces his presence;
the storm announces his indignant anger.*

37 1 "My heart pounds as I think of this.
It trembles within me.
2 Listen carefully to the thunder of God's voice
as it rolls from his mouth.
3 It rolls across the heavens,
and his lightning flashes in every direction.
4 Then comes the roaring of the thunder—
the tremendous voice of his majesty.
He does not restrain it when he speaks.
5 God's voice is glorious in the thunder.
We can't even imagine the greatness of his
power.

6 "He directs the snow to fall on the earth
and tells the rain to pour down.
7 Then everyone stops working
so they can watch his power.
8 The wild animals take cover
and stay inside their dens.
9 The stormy wind comes from its chamber,
and the driving winds bring the cold.
10 God's breath sends the ice,
freezing wide expanses of water.
11 He loads the clouds with moisture,
and they flash with his lightning.
12 The clouds churn about at his direction.
They do whatever he commands throughout
the earth.
13 He makes these things happen either to punish
people
or to show his unfailing love.

14 "Pay attention to this, Job.
Stop and consider the wonderful miracles of
God!
15 Do you know how God controls the storm
and causes the lightning to flash from his
clouds?
16 Do you understand how he moves the clouds
with wonderful perfection and skill?

36:18 Or *But don't let your anger lead you to mockery.* **36:19** Or *Could all your cries for help.* **36:16-20** The meaning of the Hebrew in this passage is uncertain. **36:31** Or *he governs.* **36:33** Or *even the cattle know when a storm is coming.* The meaning of the Hebrew is uncertain.

36:10 gets their attention. Elihu posed his only original idea in his speeches: God uses discipline to teach us about Himself. He implied that Job had not yet learned his lesson (see also v. 15).

36:16-21 Elihu encouraged Job not to miss God's purpose: opportunities for growth in his affliction.

36:26 greater than we can understand. Elihu returned to his claim from 33:12. He moved the argument from God's justice to God's wisdom—for the rightness of an action could be proved by wisdom, even if it did not satisfy the standards of justice.

37:1-13 Elihu affirms God's power and sovereignty over nature. This focus sets the reader up for God's own words about creation in chapters 38–41.

17 When you are sweltering in your clothes
and the south wind dies down and everything
is still,
18 he makes the skies reflect the heat like a bronze
mirror.
Can you do that?

19 "So teach the rest of us what to say to God.
We are too ignorant to make our own
arguments.
20 Should God be notified that I want to speak?
Can people even speak when they are confused?*
21 We cannot look at the sun,
for it shines brightly in the sky
when the wind clears away the clouds.
22 So also, golden splendor comes from the mountain
of God.*
He is clothed in dazzling splendor.
23 We cannot imagine the power of the Almighty;
but even though he is just and righteous,
he does not destroy us.
24 No wonder people everywhere fear him.
All who are wise show him reverence.*"

THE LORD CHALLENGES JOB

38 Then the LORD answered Job from the whirlwind:

2 "Who is this that questions my wisdom
with such ignorant words?
3 Brace yourself like a man,
because I have some questions for you,
and you must answer them.

4 "Where were you when I laid the foundations of
the earth?
Tell me, if you know so much.
5 Who determined its dimensions
and stretched out the surveying line?
6 What supports its foundations,
and who laid its cornerstone
7 as the morning stars sang together
and all the angels* shouted for joy?

8 "Who kept the sea inside its boundaries
as it burst from the womb,
9 and as I clothed it with clouds
and wrapped it in thick darkness?
10 For I locked it behind barred gates,
limiting its shores.
11 I said, 'This far and no farther will you come.
Here your proud waves must stop!'

12 "Have you ever commanded the morning to appear
and caused the dawn to rise in the east?
13 Have you made daylight spread to the ends of the
earth,
to bring an end to the night's wickedness?
14 As the light approaches,
the earth takes shape like clay pressed beneath
a seal;
it is robed in brilliant colors.*
15 The light disturbs the wicked
and stops the arm that is raised in violence.

16 "Have you explored the springs from which the
seas come?
Have you explored their depths?
17 Do you know where the gates of death are
located?
Have you seen the gates of utter gloom?
18 Do you realize the extent of the earth?
Tell me about it if you know!

19 "Where does light come from,
and where does darkness go?
20 Can you take each to its home?
Do you know how to get there?
21 But of course you know all this!
For you were born before it was all created,
and you are so very experienced!

22 "Have you visited the storehouses of the snow
or seen the storehouses of hail?
23 (I have reserved them as weapons for the time of
trouble,
for the day of battle and war.)
24 Where is the path to the source of light?
Where is the home of the east wind?

25 "Who created a channel for the torrents of rain?
Who laid out the path for the lightning?
26 Who makes the rain fall on barren land,
in a desert where no one lives?
27 Who sends rain to satisfy the parched ground
and make the tender grass spring up?

28 "Does the rain have a father?
Who gives birth to the dew?
29 Who is the mother of the ice?
Who gives birth to the frost from the heavens?
30 For the water turns to ice as hard as rock,
and the surface of the water freezes.

31 "Can you direct the movement of the stars—
binding the cluster of the Pleiades
or loosening the cords of Orion?
32 Can you direct the constellations through the
seasons
or guide the Bear with her cubs across the
heavens?
33 Do you know the laws of the universe?
Can you use them to regulate the earth?

34 "Can you shout to the clouds
and make it rain?

37:20 Or *speak without being swallowed up?* **37:22** Or *from the north;* or *from the abode.* **37:24** As in Greek version; Hebrew reads *He is not impressed by the wise.* **38:7** Hebrew *the sons of God.* **38:14** Or *its features stand out like folds in a robe.*

38:1–40:2 In these three chapters God questioned Job on at least 20 creatures as well as the cosmos. Obviously, Job did not know any answers.
38:1 whirlwind. A windstorm took away Job's children (1:19), and now God speaks from a whirlwind.
38:3 Brace yourself like a man. Through all Job's sufferings, his hope had been that God would one day answer him, proving His concern for Job. At last God spoke, and Job knew that their relationship was still intact.
38:7 morning stars. Morning stars here stand in parallel to "the sons of God." Rather than the stars which were created on the fourth day, both terms refer to angels who existed with God prior to creation.
38:8-11 sea. God points out to Job how impossible it would be for Job to control the seas.
38:19-21 light . . . darkness. Light and darkness were personified and pictured as having homes. How could Job know where they "lived"?

35 Can you make lightning appear
and cause it to strike as you direct?
36 Who gives intuition to the heart
and instinct to the mind?
37 Who is wise enough to count all the clouds?
Who can tilt the water jars of heaven
38 when the parched ground is dry
and the soil has hardened into clods?

39 "Can you stalk prey for a lioness
and satisfy the young lions' appetites
40 as they lie in their dens
or crouch in the thicket?
41 Who provides food for the ravens
when their young cry out to God
and wander about in hunger?

THE LORD'S CHALLENGE CONTINUES

39 1 "Do you know when the wild goats give birth?
Have you watched as deer are born in the wild?
2 Do you know how many months they carry their young?
Are you aware of the time of their delivery?
3 They crouch down to give birth to their young
and deliver their offspring.
4 Their young grow up in the open fields,
then leave home and never return.

5 "Who gives the wild donkey its freedom?
Who untied its ropes?
6 I have placed it in the wilderness;
its home is the wasteland.
7 It hates the noise of the city
and has no driver to shout at it.
8 The mountains are its pastureland,
where it searches for every blade of grass.

9 "Will the wild ox consent to being tamed?
Will it spend the night in your stall?
10 Can you hitch a wild ox to a plow?
Will it plow a field for you?
11 Given its strength, can you trust it?
Can you leave and trust the ox to do your work?
12 Can you rely on it to bring home your grain
and deliver it to your threshing floor?

13 "The ostrich flaps her wings grandly,
but they are no match for the feathers of the stork.
14 She lays her eggs on top of the earth,
letting them be warmed in the dust.
15 She doesn't worry that a foot might crush them
or a wild animal might destroy them.
16 She is harsh toward her young,
as if they were not her own.
She doesn't care if they die.
17 For God has deprived her of wisdom.
He has given her no understanding.
18 But whenever she jumps up to run,
she passes the swiftest horse with its rider.

19 "Have you given the horse its strength
or clothed its neck with a flowing mane?
20 Did you give it the ability to leap like a locust?
Its majestic snorting is terrifying!
21 It paws the earth and rejoices in its strength
when it charges out to battle.
22 It laughs at fear and is unafraid.
It does not run from the sword.
23 The arrows rattle against it,
and the spear and javelin flash.
24 It paws the ground fiercely
and rushes forward into battle when the ram's horn blows.
25 It snorts at the sound of the horn.
It senses the battle in the distance.
It quivers at the captain's commands and the noise of battle.

26 "Is it your wisdom that makes the hawk soar
and spread its wings toward the south?
27 Is it at your command that the eagle rises
to the heights to make its nest?
28 It lives on the cliffs,
making its home on a distant, rocky crag.
29 From there it hunts its prey,
keeping watch with piercing eyes.
30 Its young gulp down blood.
Where there's a carcass, there you'll find it."

40 Then the LORD said to Job,
2 "Do you still want to argue with the Almighty?
You are God's critic, but do you have the answers?"

JOB RESPONDS TO THE LORD

3 Then Job replied to the LORD,

4 "I am nothing—how could I ever find the answers?
I will cover my mouth with my hand.
5 I have said too much already.
I have nothing more to say."

THE LORD CHALLENGES JOB AGAIN

6 Then the LORD answered Job from the whirlwind:

7 "Brace yourself like a man,
because I have some questions for you,
and you must answer them.

8 "Will you discredit my justice
and condemn me just to prove you are right?
9 Are you as strong as God?
Can you thunder with a voice like his?

38:36 Who gives intuition to the heart? God clearly announced that only the One who possessed such wisdom as One who created rain (v. 28) and stars (vv. 31-32) could also give that wisdom to human creatures.

39:1-4 wild goats . . . deer. God mentioned the creatures that lived in hiding to highlight the mysteries of nature that we never see. God, the Creator, has thought up multitudes of natural wonders we may never discover.

39:9-12 wild ox. The wild ox referred to here may have been the aurochs (extinct since 1627). It was larger than a hippo and terrifyingly dangerous.

39:18-25 horse . . . strength. Highlighted by God, perhaps again to point out His own strength.

40:1-2 do you have the answers? This is the end of the first speech by God. Job's request returned to haunt him. He now received his longed-for opportunity to dialogue with God.

40:3-5 I will cover my mouth. Job has learned there was was no suitable reply to the grandeur of God. It was enough that God spoke with him.

40:6-9 discredit my justice. God still didn't rebuke Job; He simply asked what right Job had to assume he understood God's ways.

10 All right, put on your glory and splendor,
your honor and majesty.
11 Give vent to your anger.
Let it overflow against the proud.
12 Humiliate the proud with a glance;
walk on the wicked where they stand.
13 Bury them in the dust.
Imprison them in the world of the dead.
14 Then even I would praise you,
for your own strength would save you.

15 "Take a look at Behemoth,*
which I made, just as I made you.
It eats grass like an ox.
16 See its powerful loins
and the muscles of its belly.
17 Its tail is as strong as a cedar.
The sinews of its thighs are knit tightly
together.
18 Its bones are tubes of bronze.
Its limbs are bars of iron.
19 It is a prime example of God's handiwork,
and only its Creator can threaten it.
20 The mountains offer it their best food,
where all the wild animals play.
21 It lies under the lotus plants,*
hidden by the reeds in the marsh.
22 The lotus plants give it shade
among the willows beside the stream.
23 It is not disturbed by the raging river,
not concerned when the swelling Jordan rushes
around it.
24 No one can catch it off guard
or put a ring in its nose and lead it away.

THE LORD'S CHALLENGE CONTINUES

41 1*"Can you catch Leviathan* with a hook
or put a noose around its jaw?
2 Can you tie it with a rope through the nose
or pierce its jaw with a spike?
3 Will it beg you for mercy
or implore you for pity?
4 Will it agree to work for you,
to be your slave for life?
5 Can you make it a pet like a bird,
or give it to your little girls to play with?
6 Will merchants try to buy it
to sell it in their shops?
7 Will its hide be hurt by spears
or its head by a harpoon?
8 If you lay a hand on it,
you will certainly remember the battle that
follows.
You won't try that again!
9*No, it is useless to try to capture it.
The hunter who attempts it will be knocked
down.
10 And since no one dares to disturb it,
who then can stand up to me?
11 Who has given me anything that I need to pay
back?
Everything under heaven is mine.

12 "I want to emphasize Leviathan's limbs
and its enormous strength and graceful form.
13 Who can strip off its hide,
and who can penetrate its double layer of
armor?*
14 Who could pry open its jaws?
For its teeth are terrible!
15 The scales on its back are like* rows of shields
tightly sealed together.
16 They are so close together
that no air can get between them.
17 Each scale sticks tight to the next.
They interlock and cannot be penetrated.

18 "When it sneezes, it flashes light!
Its eyes are like the red of dawn.
19 Lightning leaps from its mouth;
flames of fire flash out.
20 Smoke streams from its nostrils
like steam from a pot heated over burning
rushes.
21 Its breath would kindle coals,
for flames shoot from its mouth.

22 "The tremendous strength in Leviathan's neck
strikes terror wherever it goes.
23 Its flesh is hard and firm
and cannot be penetrated.
24 Its heart is hard as rock,
hard as a millstone.
25 When it rises, the mighty are afraid,
gripped by terror.
26 No sword can stop it,
no spear, dart, or javelin.
27 Iron is nothing but straw to that creature,
and bronze is like rotten wood.
28 Arrows cannot make it flee.
Stones shot from a sling are like bits of grass.
29 Clubs are like a blade of grass,
and it laughs at the swish of javelins.
30 Its belly is covered with scales as sharp as glass.
It plows up the ground as it drags through the
mud.

31 "Leviathan makes the water boil with its
commotion.
It stirs the depths like a pot of ointment.

40:15 The identification of Behemoth is disputed, ranging from an earthly creature to a mythical sea monster in ancient literature. **40:21** Or *bramble bushes;* also in 40:22. **41:1a** Verses 41:1-8 are numbered 40:25-32 in Hebrew text. **41:1b** The identification of Leviathan is disputed, ranging from an earthly creature to a mythical sea monster in ancient literature. **41:9** Verses 41:9-34 are numbered 41:1-26 in Hebrew text. **41:13** As in Greek version; Hebrew reads *its bridle?* **41:15** As in some Greek manuscripts and Latin Vulgate; Hebrew reads *Its pride is in its.*

40:15,23 Behemoth. What was the behemoth? Suggestions include hippopotamus, elephant, or dinosaur. The identity is unclear, but the word means "great beast."

41:1 Leviathan. Meaning "sea serpent" and considered more ferocious than the behemoth in Job's time, this vicious marine animal commonly symbolized chaos and evil. Some suggest it could be a crocodile or whale. Both illustrate the human folly of attempting to wrestle (including trying to wrestle God) something immensely more powerful than man. That an entire chapter is devoted to describing it emphasizes its overwhelming power.

41:2-5 Perhaps the "Croc Hunter" would be briefly able to get the upper hand on a crocodile, but he couldn't take him home and make him his pet. In other words, Job is unqualified to take over God's job of dealing with evil, which makes man its pet.

41:34 king of beasts. Even a lion or tiger would hesitate to go swimming near a crocodile.

41:27 Ancient weapons made of bronze or iron had little effect on a crocodile's hide.

32 The water glistens in its wake,
making the sea look white.
33 Nothing on earth is its equal,
no other creature so fearless.
34 Of all the creatures, it is the proudest.
It is the king of beasts."

JOB RESPONDS TO THE LORD

42 Then Job replied to the LORD:
2 "I know that you can do anything,
and no one can stop you.
3 You asked, 'Who is this that questions my wisdom
with such ignorance?'
It is I—and I was talking about things I knew
nothing about,
things far too wonderful for me.
4 You said, 'Listen and I will speak!
I have some questions for you,
and you must answer them.'
5 I had only heard about you before,
but now I have seen you with my own eyes.
6 I take back everything I said,
and I sit in dust and ashes to show my
repentance."

CONCLUSION: THE LORD BLESSES JOB

7 After the LORD had finished speaking to Job, he
said to Eliphaz the Temanite: "I am angry with you
and your two friends, for you have not spoken ac-
curately about me, as my servant Job has. 8 So take
seven bulls and seven rams and go to my servant
Job and offer a burnt offering for yourselves. My
servant Job will pray for you, and I will accept his
prayer on your behalf. I will not treat you as you de-
serve, for you have not spoken accurately about me,
as my servant Job has." 9 So Eliphaz the Temanite,
Bildad the Shuhite, and Zophar the Naamathite did
as the LORD commanded them, and the LORD accept-
ed Job's prayer.

10 When Job prayed for his friends, the LORD re-
stored his fortunes. In fact, the LORD gave him twice
as much as before! 11 Then all his brothers, sisters,
and former friends came and feasted with him in his
home. And they consoled him and comforted him be-
cause of all the trials the LORD had brought against
him. And each of them brought him a gift of money*
and a gold ring.

12 So the LORD blessed Job in the second half of his
life even more than in the beginning. For now he had
14,000 sheep, 6,000 camels, 1,000 teams of oxen, and
1,000 female donkeys. 13 He also gave Job seven more
sons and three more daughters. 14 He named his first
daughter Jemimah, the second Keziah, and the third
Keren-happuch. 15 In all the land no women were as
lovely as the daughters of Job. And their father put
them into his will along with their brothers.

16 Job lived 140 years after that, living to see four
generations of his children and grandchildren. 17 Then
he died, an old man who had lived a long, full life.

42:11 Hebrew *a kesitah;* the value or weight of the kesitah is no longer known.

42:5 I had only heard rumors about you. Speaking of the God he thought he knew before his trials, Job realizes how little he understood.
42:3 Who is this. After a litany of more than 70 rhetorical questions, Job's ears still burned with God's initial inquiry (38:2).
42:7 I am angry with you and your two friends. God was angry at those who claimed He was angry at Job!
42:7-8 my servant Job. Unlike his friends, God lavished the well-deserved title on Job (1:8; 2:3).
42:12 So the LORD blessed. Satan's scheme had failed (1:6-12). Job continued to love and trust God throughout the sufferings. And God chose to multiply Job's blessings beyond what he had lost.
42:13 seven more sons and three more daughters. Children, particularly sons, were considered a blessing from God. Job would have someone to take care of him in his old age (see also verse 16).

INTRODUCTION TO

PSALMS

PERSONAL READING PLAN

☐Psalms 1–7
☐Psalms 8–14
☐Psalms 15–18
☐Psalms 19–23
☐Psalms 24–29
☐Psalms 30–33
☐Psalms 34–36
☐Psalms 37–39
☐Psalms 40–44
☐Psalms 45–49
☐Psalms 50–54
☐Psalms 55–60
☐Psalms 61–66
☐Psalms 67–69
☐Psalms 70–72
☐Psalms 73–77
☐Psalms 78–79
☐Psalms 80–83
☐Psalms 84–88
☐Psalms 89–90
☐Psalms 91–95
☐Psalms 96–100
☐Psalms 101–103
☐Psalms 104–105
☐Psalms 106–107
☐Psalms 108–112
☐Psalms 113–118
☐Psalm 119:1-88
☐Psalm 119:89-176
☐Psalms 120–129
☐Psalms 130–137
☐Psalms 138–144
☐Psalms 145–150

AUTHOR

King David (Pss. 3; 7 and many others), King Solomon (Pss. 72; 127), the sons of Korah (Pss. 42–49; 84–85; 87–88), Asaph (Pss. 50; 73–83), Heman (Ps. 88), Ethan (Ps. 89), and Moses (Ps. 90) all have psalms attributed to them. Many psalms are anonymous.

DATE

Although composed over centuries (ca 1400–400 B.C.), the Psalms may well have been collected and arranged in their present form as the "hymn book" of Israel sometime in the fourth or third century B.C.

THEME

The range of human response to God and His world.

HISTORICAL BACKGROUND

The book of Psalms is a collection of various smaller groupings of psalms that were used in Israel's worship over the centuries. Some psalms were associated with certain feasts (Ps. 130, Yom Kippur; Ps. 135, Passover), others with the Sabbath (Pss. 92–100), and others for confession (Pss. 32; 51) or praise (Pss. 111–118; 146–150).

CHARACTERISTICS

The moods of the various psalms embrace the whole range of human experience from exuberant praise (Ps. 145) to despair (Ps. 42); from intense anger (Ps. 137) and doubt about God's care (Ps. 73) to hope for a future based precisely upon God's care (Ps. 23). The Psalms help us express and pray with all our emotions. The Psalms capture the reality of our up-and-down relationship with God, but they also move us steadily along the path of knowing God.

PASSAGES FOR TOPICAL GROUP STUDY

17:1-15 . . ENEMIES . . . . Enemy Outlook
23:1-6 . . GOD'S RESCUE AND CARE. . . . . The Great Shepherd
46:1-11 . . FIGHTING and REFUGE . . . . God, Our Refuge
139:1-24 . . GOD'S PRESENCE and ABORTION . . . . . God's Perpetual Presence

BOOK ONE (PSALMS 1–41)

1

1 Oh, the joys of those who do not
follow the advice of the wicked,
or stand around with sinners,
or join in with mockers.
2 But they delight in the law of the LORD,
meditating on it day and night.
3 They are like trees planted along the riverbank,
bearing fruit each season.
Their leaves never wither,
and they prosper in all they do.

4 But not the wicked!
They are like worthless chaff, scattered by the wind.
5 They will be condemned at the time of judgment.
Sinners will have no place among the godly.
6 For the LORD watches over the path of the godly,
but the path of the wicked leads to destruction.

2

1 Why are the nations so angry?
Why do they waste their time with futile plans?
2 The kings of the earth prepare for battle;
the rulers plot together
against the LORD
and against his anointed one.
3 "Let us break their chains," they cry,
"and free ourselves from slavery to God."

4 But the one who rules in heaven laughs.
The Lord scoffs at them.
5 Then in anger he rebukes them,
terrifying them with his fierce fury.
6 For the Lord declares, "I have placed my chosen king on the throne
in Jerusalem,* on my holy mountain."

7 The king proclaims the LORD's decree:
"The LORD said to me, 'You are my son.*
Today I have become your Father.*
8 Only ask, and I will give you the nations as your inheritance,
the whole earth as your possession.
9 You will break* them with an iron rod
and smash them like clay pots.'"

10 Now then, you kings, act wisely!
Be warned, you rulers of the earth!
11 Serve the LORD with reverent fear,
and rejoice with trembling.
12 Submit to God's royal son,* or he will become angry,
and you will be destroyed in the midst of all your activities—
for his anger flares up in an instant.
But what joy for all who take refuge in him!

3

A psalm of David, regarding the time David fled from his son Absalom.

1 O LORD, I have so many enemies;
so many are against me.
2 So many are saying,
"God will never rescue him!"
*Interlude**

3 But you, O LORD, are a shield around me;
you are my glory, the one who holds my head high.
4 I cried out to the LORD,
and he answered me from his holy mountain.
Interlude

5 I lay down and slept,
yet I woke up in safety,
for the LORD was watching over me.
6 I am not afraid of ten thousand enemies
who surround me on every side.

7 Arise, O LORD!
Rescue me, my God!
Slap all my enemies in the face!
Shatter the teeth of the wicked!
8 Victory comes from you, O LORD.
May you bless your people.
Interlude

4

For the choir director: A psalm of David, to be accompanied by stringed instruments.

1 Answer me when I call to you,
O God who declares me innocent.
Free me from my troubles.
Have mercy on me and hear my prayer.

2 How long will you people ruin my reputation?
How long will you make groundless accusations?
How long will you continue your lies?
Interlude
3 You can be sure of this:
The LORD set apart the godly for himself.
The LORD will answer when I call to him.

4 Don't sin by letting anger control you.
Think about it overnight and remain silent.
Interlude

2:6 Hebrew *on Zion.* **2:7a** Or *Son;* also in 2:12. **2:7b** Or *Today I reveal you as my son.* **2:9** Greek version reads *rule.* Compare Rev 2:27. **2:12** The meaning of the Hebrew is uncertain. **3:2** Hebrew *Selah.* The meaning of this word is uncertain, though it is probably a musical or literary term. It is rendered *Interlude* throughout the Psalms.

1:2 meditating on it day and night. The blessed person relishes God's law (Word). God's ways are a necessary part of daily living.
1:3 they prosper in all they do. The psalmist describes the rewards of godly living: strength, security, and prosperity. The picture of a godly person's life is like a tree blessing others with fruit and shade.
2:7 my son . . . become your father. The king recognized God as his higher authority. This verse also points to God's proclamation of Christ as both Son and servant at His baptism and transfiguration. (See Matt. 3:17; 17:5.)
Ps. 3 David penned this psalm while running from his son Absalom (2 Sam. 15:13-30). First he focuses on the urgency of his problem (vv. 1-2). Then he asserts his unfailing trust (vv. 3-6), all the while soliciting God's help (vv. 7-8). Fourteen Psalms recount specific events in David's life: 3, 7, 18, 30, 34, 51, 56, 57, 59, 60, 63, and 142.
3:2 *Interlude*. This word occurs often in the Psalms, and its meaning has been debated. It may indicate a pause for the singers and musicians when the Psalms were being sung.
4:2-3 The LORD will answer. David criticizes his enemies who are intent on ruining his reputation. He reminds them the Lord will respond to his cries for help.
4:4 Don't sin by letting anger . . . Think about it. Anger is inappropriate when it substitutes for trust in God (Eph. 4:26).

5 Offer sacrifices in the right spirit,
and trust the LORD.

6 Many people say, "Who will show us better times?"
Let your face smile on us, LORD.
7 You have given me greater joy
than those who have abundant harvests of
grain and new wine.
8 In peace I will lie down and sleep,
for you alone, O LORD, will keep me safe.

5 *For the choir director: A psalm of David, to be accompanied by the flute.*

1 O LORD, hear me as I pray;
pay attention to my groaning.
2 Listen to my cry for help, my King and my God,
for I pray to no one but you.
3 Listen to my voice in the morning, LORD.
Each morning I bring my requests to you and
wait expectantly.

4 O God, you take no pleasure in wickedness;
you cannot tolerate the sins of the wicked.
5 Therefore, the proud may not stand in your presence,
for you hate all who do evil.
6 You will destroy those who tell lies.
The LORD detests murderers and deceivers.

7 Because of your unfailing love, I can enter your
house;
I will worship at your Temple with deepest awe.
8 Lead me in the right path, O LORD,
or my enemies will conquer me.
Make your way plain for me to follow.

9 My enemies cannot speak a truthful word.
Their deepest desire is to destroy others.
Their talk is foul, like the stench from an open grave.
Their tongues are filled with flattery.*
10 O God, declare them guilty.
Let them be caught in their own traps.
Drive them away because of their many sins,
for they have rebelled against you.

11 But let all who take refuge in you rejoice;
let them sing joyful praises forever.
Spread your protection over them,
that all who love your name may be filled with
joy.
12 For you bless the godly, O LORD;
you surround them with your shield of love.

6 *For the choir director: A psalm of David, to be accompanied by an eight-stringed instrument.*

1 O LORD, don't rebuke me in your anger
or discipline me in your rage.
2 Have compassion on me, LORD, for I am weak.
Heal me, LORD, for my bones are in agony.
3 I am sick at heart.
How long, O LORD, until you restore me?

4 Return, O LORD, and rescue me.
Save me because of your unfailing love.
5 For the dead do not remember you.
Who can praise you from the grave?*

6 I am worn out from sobbing.
All night I flood my bed with weeping,
drenching it with my tears.
7 My vision is blurred by grief;
my eyes are worn out because of all my
enemies.

8 Go away, all you who do evil,
for the LORD has heard my weeping.
9 The LORD has heard my plea;
the LORD will answer my prayer.
10 May all my enemies be disgraced and terrified.
May they suddenly turn back in shame.

7 *A psalm* of David, which he sang to the Lord concerning Cush of the tribe of Benjamin.*

1 I come to you for protection, O LORD my God.
Save me from my persecutors—rescue me!
2 If you don't, they will maul me like a lion,
tearing me to pieces with no one to rescue me.
3 O LORD my God, if I have done wrong
or am guilty of injustice,
4 if I have betrayed a friend
or plundered my enemy without cause,
5 then let my enemies capture me.
Let them trample me into the ground
and drag my honor in the dust.
Interlude

6 Arise, O LORD, in anger!
Stand up against the fury of my enemies!
Wake up, my God, and bring justice!
7 Gather the nations before you.
Rule over them from on high.
8 The LORD judges the nations.
Declare me righteous, O LORD,
for I am innocent, O Most High!
9 End the evil of those who are wicked,
and defend the righteous.
For you look deep within the mind and heart,
O righteous God.

10 God is my shield,
saving those whose hearts are true and
right.
11 God is an honest judge.
He is angry with the wicked every day.

5:9 Greek version reads *with lies*. Compare Rom 3:13. 6:TITLE Hebrew *with stringed instruments; according to the sheminith.* 6:5 Hebrew *from Sheol?* 7:TITLE Hebrew *A shiggaion*, probably indicating a musical setting for the psalm.

Ps. 5 I pray. When his enemies verbally assault him, David turns to prayer. David begins his morning with a petition for the Lord's help. Notice David habitually prays morning and night.

6:1-10 This is the first of David's seven 'penitential' psalms. (See also 32, 38, 51, 102, 130, and 142.) They follow a pattern of spoken fears, weeping, and a burst of faith.

6:7 eyes are worn out. David has wept until he can barely see. He strains to see God's deliverance, but foes fill his vision.

6:8-10 the LORD has heard... May all my enemies... suddenly turn back. Regaining his second wind, David defiantly addresses his enemies. His concluding confidence in God is a common theme in many psalms (7:10-17; 10:16-18; 12:7).

7:11 judge. This image is of a judge bringing a swift sentence (See also 7:8, 11; 68:18).

12 If a person does not repent,
God* will sharpen his sword;
he will bend and string his bow.
13 He will prepare his deadly weapons
and shoot his flaming arrows.

14 The wicked conceive evil;
they are pregnant with trouble
and give birth to lies.
15 They dig a deep pit to trap others,
then fall into it themselves.
16 The trouble they make for others backfires on them.
The violence they plan falls on their own heads.

17 I will thank the LORD because he is just;
I will sing praise to the name of the LORD Most
High.

8 *For the choir director: A psalm of David, to be accompanied by a stringed instrument.**

1 O LORD, our Lord, your majestic name fills the
earth!
Your glory is higher than the heavens.
2 You have taught children and infants
to tell of your strength,*
silencing your enemies
and all who oppose you.

3 When I look at the night sky and see the work of
your fingers—
the moon and the stars you set in place—
4 what are mere mortals that you should think
about them,
human beings that you should care for them?*
5 Yet you made them only a little lower than God*
and crowned them* with glory and honor.
6 You gave them charge of everything you made,
putting all things under their authority—
7 the flocks and the herds
and all the wild animals,
8 the birds in the sky, the fish in the sea,
and everything that swims the ocean currents.

9 O LORD, our Lord, your majestic name fills the
earth!

9 *For the choir director: A psalm of David, to be sung to the tune "Death of the Son."*

1 I will praise you, LORD, with all my heart;
I will tell of all the marvelous things you have
done.
2 I will be filled with joy because of you.
I will sing praises to your name, O Most High.

3 My enemies retreated;
they staggered and died when you appeared.
4 For you have judged in my favor;
from your throne you have judged with
fairness.
5 You have rebuked the nations and destroyed the
wicked;
you have erased their names forever.
6 The enemy is finished, in endless ruins;
the cities you uprooted are now forgotten.

7 But the LORD reigns forever,
executing judgment from his throne.
8 He will judge the world with justice
and rule the nations with fairness.
9 The LORD is a shelter for the oppressed,
a refuge in times of trouble.
10 Those who know your name trust in you,
for you, O LORD, do not abandon those who
search for you.

11 Sing praises to the LORD who reigns in Jerusalem.*
Tell the world about his unforgettable deeds.
12 For he who avenges murder cares for the helpless.
He does not ignore the cries of those who suffer.

13 LORD, have mercy on me.
See how my enemies torment me.
Snatch me back from the jaws of death.
14 Save me so I can praise you publicly at Jerusalem's
gates,
so I can rejoice that you have rescued me.

15 The nations have fallen into the pit they dug for
others.
Their own feet have been caught in the trap
they set.
16 The LORD is known for his justice.
The wicked are trapped by their own deeds.
*Quiet Interlude**

17 The wicked will go down to the grave.*
This is the fate of all the nations who ignore God.
18 But the needy will not be ignored forever;
the hopes of the poor will not always be
crushed.

19 Arise, O LORD!
Do not let mere mortals defy you!
Judge the nations!

7:12 Hebrew *he.* 8:TITLE Hebrew *according to the gittith.* 8:2 Greek version reads *to give you praise.* Compare Matt 21:16. 8:4 Hebrew *what is man that you should think of him, / the son of man that you should care for him?* 8:5a Or *Yet you made them only a little lower than the angels;* Hebrew reads *Yet you made him* [i.e., man] *a little lower than Elohim.* 8:5b Hebrew *him* [i.e., man]; similarly in 8:6. 9:11 Hebrew *Zion;* also in 9:14. 9:16 Hebrew *Higgaion Selah.* The meaning of this phrase is uncertain. 9:17 Hebrew *to Sheol.*

7:16 The violence they plan falls on their own heads. Disobedience to God's ways always results in unpleasant consequences of our own making!

8:1-5 your magnificent name. This psalm exemplifies how God should be praised: for who He is and for all He does.

8:3-4 what are mere mortals. God has built a universe for us to live in. How we deserve His wondrous love and concern is beyond David's comprehension.

8:6-8 You gave them charge. The psalmist applies the job description given in the Garden of Eden (Gen. 1:28; 2:15). Also quoted in Heb. 2:6-8.

9:1 tell . . . marvelous things. "Marvelous things" is a single word in Hebrew that is used to praise God's redemptive miracles. (See also Ps. 106:7,22.)

9:3-6 Each victory carried national as well as personal meaning. David praises God for rescue and for justice.

9:7-10 the LORD reigns forever. Before the psalm concludes, David extols God's continuous, righteous judgment.

9:18 the needy will not be ignored forever. David speaks prophetically of the reign of God's justice in the future.

9:19-20 Let the nations know. David prompts God to awaken his enemies to a harsh reality. The original word used here for "human" emphasizes human frailty.

20 Make them tremble in fear, O LORD.
Let the nations know they are merely human.
Interlude

10

1 O LORD, why do you stand so far away?
Why do you hide when I am in trouble?
2 The wicked arrogantly hunt down the poor.
Let them be caught in the evil they plan for others.
3 For they brag about their evil desires;
they praise the greedy and curse the LORD.

4 The wicked are too proud to seek God.
They seem to think that God is dead.
5 Yet they succeed in everything they do.
They do not see your punishment awaiting them.
They sneer at all their enemies.
6 They think, "Nothing bad will ever happen to us!
We will be free of trouble forever!"

7 Their mouths are full of cursing, lies, and threats.*
Trouble and evil are on the tips of their tongues.
8 They lurk in ambush in the villages,
waiting to murder innocent people.
They are always searching for helpless victims.
9 Like lions crouched in hiding,
they wait to pounce on the helpless.
Like hunters they capture the helpless
and drag them away in nets.
10 Their helpless victims are crushed;
they fall beneath the strength of the wicked.
11 The wicked think, "God isn't watching us!
He has closed his eyes and won't even see what we do!"

12 Arise, O LORD!
Punish the wicked, O God!
Do not ignore the helpless!
13 Why do the wicked get away with despising God?
They think, "God will never call us to account."
14 But you see the trouble and grief they cause.
You take note of it and punish them.
The helpless put their trust in you.
You defend the orphans.

15 Break the arms of these wicked, evil people!
Go after them until the last one is destroyed.
16 The LORD is king forever and ever!
The godless nations will vanish from the land.
17 LORD, you know the hopes of the helpless.
Surely you will hear their cries and comfort them.
18 You will bring justice to the orphans and the oppressed,
so mere people can no longer terrify them.

11

For the choir director: A psalm of David.

1 I trust in the LORD for protection.
So why do you say to me,
"Fly like a bird to the mountains for safety!
2 The wicked are stringing their bows
and fitting their arrows on the bowstrings.
They shoot from the shadows
at those whose hearts are right.
3 The foundations of law and order have collapsed.
What can the righteous do?"

4 But the LORD is in his holy Temple;
the LORD still rules from heaven.
He watches everyone closely,
examining every person on earth.
5 The LORD examines both the righteous and the wicked.
He hates those who love violence.
6 He will rain down blazing coals and burning sulfur on the wicked,
punishing them with scorching winds.
7 For the righteous LORD loves justice.
The virtuous will see his face.

12

*For the choir director: A psalm of David, to be accompanied by an eight-stringed instrument.**

1 Help, O LORD, for the godly are fast disappearing!
The faithful have vanished from the earth!
2 Neighbors lie to each other,
speaking with flattering lips and deceitful hearts.
3 May the LORD cut off their flattering lips
and silence their boastful tongues.
4 They say, "We will lie to our hearts' content.
Our lips are our own—who can stop us?"

5 The LORD replies, "I have seen violence done to the helpless,
and I have heard the groans of the poor.
Now I will rise up to rescue them,
as they have longed for me to do."
6 The LORD's promises are pure,
like silver refined in a furnace,
purified seven times over.
7 Therefore, LORD, we know you will protect the oppressed,
preserving them forever from this lying generation,
8 even though the wicked strut about,
and evil is praised throughout the land.

13

For the choir director: A psalm of David.

1 O LORD, how long will you forget me? Forever?
How long will you look the other way?
2 How long must I struggle with anguish in my soul,
with sorrow in my heart every day?
How long will my enemy have the upper hand?

3 Turn and answer me, O LORD my God!
Restore the sparkle to my eyes, or I will die.

10:7 Greek version reads *cursing and bitterness.* Compare Rom 3:14. **12:TITLE** Hebrew *according to the sheminith.*

10:11 God isn't watching us. Wicked people wink at evil and erroneously believe God does the same. God may not act immediately, but He is not indifferent to injustice (v. 14).

10:16-18 Nations are destroyed and prideful people are humbled—as in the previous psalm (9:19-20). The two psalms link together, portraying the whole of God's awesome power.

Ps. 13 Similar to other psalms of lament, this one details David's distress (vv. 1-2), asks for deliverance (vv. 3-4), and ends on a confident note (vv. 5-6).

13:1-2 how long will you forget me? David feels as if his prayers are going nowhere. Four times he asks God: "How long" must I survive without Your presence—personally and militarily?

4 Don't let my enemies gloat, saying, "We have
defeated him!"
Don't let them rejoice at my downfall.

5 But I trust in your unfailing love.
I will rejoice because you have rescued me.
6 I will sing to the LORD
because he is good to me.

14 *For the choir director: A psalm of David.*

1 Only fools say in their hearts,
"There is no God."
They are corrupt, and their actions are evil;
not one of them does good!

2 The LORD looks down from heaven
on the entire human race;
he looks to see if anyone is truly wise,
if anyone seeks God.
3 But no, all have turned away;
all have become corrupt.*
No one does good,
not a single one!

4 Will those who do evil never learn?
They eat up my people like bread
and wouldn't think of praying to the LORD.
5 Terror will grip them,
for God is with those who obey him.
6 The wicked frustrate the plans of the oppressed,
but the LORD will protect his people.

7 Who will come from Mount Zion to rescue Israel?
When the LORD restores his people,
Jacob will shout with joy, and Israel will
rejoice.

15 *A psalm of David.*

1 Who may worship in your sanctuary, LORD?
Who may enter your presence on your holy hill?
2 Those who lead blameless lives and do what is
right,
speaking the truth from sincere hearts.
3 Those who refuse to gossip
or harm their neighbors
or speak evil of their friends.
4 Those who despise flagrant sinners,
and honor the faithful followers of the LORD,
and keep their promises even when it hurts.
5 Those who lend money without charging interest,
and who cannot be bribed to lie about the
innocent.
Such people will stand firm forever.

16 *A psalm* of David.*

1 Keep me safe, O God,
for I have come to you for refuge.

2 I said to the LORD, "You are my Master!
Every good thing I have comes from you."
3 The godly people in the land
are my true heroes!
I take pleasure in them!
4 Troubles multiply for those who chase after other
gods.
I will not take part in their sacrifices of
blood
or even speak the names of their gods.

5 LORD, you alone are my inheritance, my cup of
blessing.
You guard all that is mine.
6 The land you have given me is a pleasant land.
What a wonderful inheritance!

7 I will bless the LORD who guides me;
even at night my heart instructs me.
8 I know the LORD is always with me.
I will not be shaken, for he is right beside me.

9 No wonder my heart is glad, and I rejoice.*
My body rests in safety.
10 For you will not leave my soul among the dead*
or allow your holy one* to rot in the grave.
11 You will show me the way of life,
granting me the joy of your presence
and the pleasures of living with you
forever.*

17 *A prayer of David.*

1 O LORD, hear my plea for justice.
Listen to my cry for help.
Pay attention to my prayer,
for it comes from honest lips.
2 Declare me innocent,
for you see those who do right.

3 You have tested my thoughts and examined my
heart in the night.
You have scrutinized me and found nothing
wrong.
I am determined not to sin in what I say.
4 I have followed your commands,
which keep me from following cruel and evil
people.
5 My steps have stayed on your path;
I have not wavered from following you.

14:3 Greek version reads *have become useless.* Compare Rom 3:12. **16:TITLE** Hebrew *miktam.* This may be a literary or musical term. **16:9** Greek version reads *and my tongue shouts his praises.* Compare Acts 2:26. **16:10a** Hebrew *in Sheol.* **16:10b** Or *your Holy One.* **16:11** Greek version reads *You have shown me the way of life, / and you will fill me with the joy of your presence.* Compare Acts 2:28.

13:5 trust in your unfailing love. These honest expressions of emotions before God make the Psalms a comfort to people in every age.

14:1 fools. The Hebrew word for fool, *nabal,* implies aggressiveness and perversity such as seen in Nabal's story in 1 Samuel 25:25. This kind of fool believes God is irrelevant to the practicality of life (10:4).

14:4 eat up. David is amazed at the audacity of evil. Wicked people attack God's people, disregarding their value to God.

15:1 worship in you sanctuary? The Psalms provide two images: one of formal worship and sacrifice and the other of simple hospitality. God desires His people to be at home when worshipping Him.

15:5 lend money without charging interest. Using excessive interest as a means to get ahead was condemned (Lev. 25:35-38).

16:9-11 way of life . . . presence. This "way of life" provides both physical security and eternity in God's presence.

17:1-6 hear my plea for justice. David's first concern is to plead his innocence as a prelude to asking for God's protection again in the second half of this prayer (vv. 7-15).

17:3-5 You have . . . found nothing. David contrasts the purity of his life with the evil people around him (vv. 9-12). He asks God to vindicate his innocence, to "test his heart."

ENEMY OUTLOOK

1. Have you ever had an eye injury? What happened? How did you react?

PSALM 17

2. When David prayed, "Guard me as you would guard your own eyes" (v. 8), what was he asking of God? How does this show David's value to God?
3. Why did David ask God to destroy his enemies? How might an ungodly man have responded to his enemies rather than praying?
4. What did David mean when he prayed, "I will see you . . . and be satisfied" (v. 15)?
5. What lesson can you learn from David's attitude toward his enemies?

6 I am praying to you because I know you will
answer, O God.
Bend down and listen as I pray.
7 Show me your unfailing love in wonderful
ways.
By your mighty power you rescue
those who seek refuge from their enemies.
8 Guard me as you would guard your own
eyes.*
Hide me in the shadow of your wings.
9 Protect me from wicked people who attack me,
from murderous enemies who surround me.
10 They are without pity.
Listen to their boasting!
11 They track me down and surround me,
watching for the chance to throw me to the
ground.
12 They are like hungry lions, eager to tear me
apart—
like young lions hiding in ambush.

13 Arise, O LORD!
Stand against them, and bring them to their
knees!
Rescue me from the wicked with your
sword!
14 By the power of your hand, O LORD,
destroy those who look to this world for their
reward.
But satisfy the hunger of your treasured
ones.
May their children have plenty,
leaving an inheritance for their descendants.
15 Because I am righteous, I will see you.
When I awake, I will see you face to face and be
satisfied.

18

For the choir director: A psalm of David, the servant of the Lord. He sang this song to the Lord on the day the Lord rescued him from all his enemies and from Saul. He sang:

1 I love you, LORD;
you are my strength.
2 The LORD is my rock, my fortress, and my savior;
my God is my rock, in whom I find protection.
He is my shield, the power that saves me,
and my place of safety.
3 I called on the LORD, who is worthy of praise,
and he saved me from my enemies.

4 The ropes of death entangled me;
floods of destruction swept over me.
5 The grave* wrapped its ropes around me;
death laid a trap in my path.
6 But in my distress I cried out to the LORD;
yes, I prayed to my God for help.
He heard me from his sanctuary;
my cry to him reached his ears.

7 Then the earth quaked and trembled.
The foundations of the mountains shook;
they quaked because of his anger.
8 Smoke poured from his nostrils;
fierce flames leaped from his mouth.
Glowing coals blazed forth from him.
9 He opened the heavens and came down;
dark storm clouds were beneath his feet.
10 Mounted on a mighty angelic being,* he flew,
soaring on the wings of the wind.
11 He shrouded himself in darkness,
veiling his approach with dark rain clouds.
12 Thick clouds shielded the brightness around him
and rained down hail and burning coals.*
13 The LORD thundered from heaven;
the voice of the Most High resounded
amid the hail and burning coals.
14 He shot his arrows and scattered his enemies;
great bolts of lightning flashed, and they were
confused.
15 Then at your command, O LORD,
at the blast of your breath,
the bottom of the sea could be seen,
and the foundations of the earth were laid bare.

16 He reached down from heaven and rescued me;
he drew me out of deep waters.
17 He rescued me from my powerful enemies,
from those who hated me and were too strong
for me.
18 They attacked me at a moment when I was in
distress,
but the LORD supported me.
19 He led me to a place of safety;
he rescued me because he delights in me.

17:8 Hebrew *as the pupil of your eye.* **18:5** Hebrew *Sheol.* **18:10** Hebrew *a cherub.* **18:12** Or *and lightning bolts;* also in 18:13.

17:15 When I awake. Sleep was a euphemism for death. He will awake to the glorious presence of God at the resurrection. (Dan. 12:2; Isa. 26:19).
18:4-6 David penned this psalm when King Saul's army was closing in. Much of its content, with a few variations, is also quoted in 2 Sam. 22.
18:4-5 ropes of death. David describes his near death experience.
18:8 Smoke . . . fierce flames. Smoke in Isaiah. 6:4 depicts the reaction of God's holiness to sin. "Fierce flames" is also used in Deuteronomy 4:24 when God is described as being jealously eager for the people to keep the covenant.
18:16-19 rescued . . . delights in me. After the powerful images of God's might in the previous verses, the contrast here highlights the love and tenderness with which God cares for each of us. God's holiness paradoxically and simultaneously contains both wrath at our sin and love for us.

20 The LORD rewarded me for doing right;
he restored me because of my innocence.
21 For I have kept the ways of the LORD;
I have not turned from my God to follow evil.
22 I have followed all his regulations;
I have never abandoned his decrees.
23 I am blameless before God;
I have kept myself from sin.
24 The LORD rewarded me for doing right.
He has seen my innocence.

25 To the faithful you show yourself faithful;
to those with integrity you show integrity.
26 To the pure you show yourself pure,
but to the crooked you show yourself shrewd.
27 You rescue the humble,
but you humiliate the proud.
28 You light a lamp for me.
The LORD, my God, lights up my darkness.
29 In your strength I can crush an army;
with my God I can scale any wall.

30 God's way is perfect.
All the LORD's promises prove true.
He is a shield for all who look to him for protection.
31 For who is God except the LORD?
Who but our God is a solid rock?
32 God arms me with strength,
and he makes my way perfect.
33 He makes me as surefooted as a deer,
enabling me to stand on mountain heights.
34 He trains my hands for battle;
he strengthens my arm to draw a bronze bow.
35 You have given me your shield of victory.
Your right hand supports me;
your help* has made me great.
36 You have made a wide path for my feet
to keep them from slipping.

37 I chased my enemies and caught them;
I did not stop until they were conquered.
38 I struck them down so they could not get up;
they fell beneath my feet.
39 You have armed me with strength for the battle;
you have subdued my enemies under my feet.
40 You placed my foot on their necks.
I have destroyed all who hated me.
41 They called for help, but no one came to their rescue.
They even cried to the LORD, but he refused to answer.
42 I ground them as fine as dust in the wind.
I swept them into the gutter like dirt.
43 You gave me victory over my accusers.
You appointed me ruler over nations;
people I don't even know now serve me.
44 As soon as they hear of me, they submit;
foreign nations cringe before me.
45 They all lose their courage
and come trembling from their strongholds.

46 The LORD lives! Praise to my Rock!
May the God of my salvation be exalted!
47 He is the God who pays back those who harm me;
he subdues the nations under me
48 and rescues me from my enemies.
You hold me safe beyond the reach of my enemies;
you save me from violent opponents.
49 For this, O LORD, I will praise you among the nations;
I will sing praises to your name.
50 You give great victories to your king;
you show unfailing love to your anointed,
to David and all his descendants forever.

19 *For the choir director: A psalm of David.*

1 The heavens proclaim the glory of God.
The skies display his craftsmanship.
2 Day after day they continue to speak;
night after night they make him known.
3 They speak without a sound or word;
their voice is never heard.*
4 Yet their message has gone throughout the earth,
and their words to all the world.

God has made a home in the heavens for the sun.
5 It bursts forth like a radiant bridegroom after his wedding.
It rejoices like a great athlete eager to run the race.
6 The sun rises at one end of the heavens
and follows its course to the other end.
Nothing can hide from its heat.

7 The instructions of the LORD are perfect,
reviving the soul.
The decrees of the LORD are trustworthy,
making wise the simple.
8 The commandments of the LORD are right,
bringing joy to the heart.
The commands of the LORD are clear,
giving insight for living.
9 Reverence for the LORD is pure,
lasting forever.
The laws of the LORD are true;
each one is fair.
10 They are more desirable than gold,
even the finest gold.
They are sweeter than honey,
even honey dripping from the comb.
11 They are a warning to your servant,
a great reward for those who obey them.

12 How can I know all the sins lurking in my heart?
Cleanse me from these hidden faults.
13 Keep your servant from deliberate sins!
Don't let them control me.
Then I will be free of guilt
and innocent of great sin.

18:35 Hebrew *your humility;* compare 2 Sam 22:36. **19:3** Or *There is no speech or language where their voice is not heard.*

18:25-35 you . . . God. David offers a catalog of the attributes of God's character.

19:1-4 proclaim . . . they continue to speak. Though the heavens seem to be silent, they speak of God's glory through sheer beauty.

19:11-13 reward . . . obey them. God gave us divine law as both warning and promise. It warns that certain actions require forgiveness. It promises that faithfulness to the Law brings reward. Willful disregard for the Law results in separation from God.

14 May the words of my mouth
and the meditation of my heart
be pleasing to you,
O LORD, my rock and my redeemer.

20 *For the choir director: A psalm of David.*

1 In times of trouble, may the LORD answer your cry.
May the name of the God of Jacob keep you safe
from all harm.
2 May he send you help from his sanctuary
and strengthen you from Jerusalem.*
3 May he remember all your gifts
and look favorably on your burnt offerings.
Interlude

4 May he grant your heart's desires
and make all your plans succeed.
5 May we shout for joy when we hear of your
victory
and raise a victory banner in the name of our
God.
May the LORD answer all your prayers.

6 Now I know that the LORD rescues his anointed
king.
He will answer him from his holy heaven
and rescue him by his great power.
7 Some nations boast of their chariots and horses,
but we boast in the name of the LORD our
God.
8 Those nations will fall down and collapse,
but we will rise up and stand firm.

9 Give victory to our king, O LORD!
Answer our cry for help.

21 *For the choir director: A psalm of David.*

1 How the king rejoices in your strength, O LORD!
He shouts with joy because you give him
victory.
2 For you have given him his heart's desire;
you have withheld nothing he requested.
Interlude

3 You welcomed him back with success and
prosperity.
You placed a crown of finest gold on his head.
4 He asked you to preserve his life,
and you granted his request.
The days of his life stretch on forever.
5 Your victory brings him great honor,
and you have clothed him with splendor and
majesty.
6 You have endowed him with eternal blessings
and given him the joy of your presence.
7 For the king trusts in the LORD.
The unfailing love of the Most High will keep
him from stumbling.

8 You will capture all your enemies.
Your strong right hand will seize all who hate
you.
9 You will throw them in a flaming furnace
when you appear.
The LORD will consume them in his anger;
fire will devour them.
10 You will wipe their children from the face of the
earth;
they will never have descendants.
11 Although they plot against you,
their evil schemes will never succeed.
12 For they will turn and run
when they see your arrows aimed at them.
13 Rise up, O LORD, in all your power.
With music and singing we celebrate your
mighty acts.

22 *For the choir director: A psalm of David, to be sung to the tune "Doe of the Dawn."*

1 My God, my God, why have you abandoned me?
Why are you so far away when I groan for help?
2 Every day I call to you, my God, but you do not
answer.
Every night I lift my voice, but I find no relief.

3 Yet you are holy,
enthroned on the praises of Israel.
4 Our ancestors trusted in you,
and you rescued them.
5 They cried out to you and were saved.
They trusted in you and were never disgraced.

6 But I am a worm and not a man.
I am scorned and despised by all!
7 Everyone who sees me mocks me.
They sneer and shake their heads, saying,
8 "Is this the one who relies on the LORD?
Then let the LORD save him!
If the LORD loves him so much,
let the LORD rescue him!"

9 Yet you brought me safely from my mother's
womb
and led me to trust you at my mother's breast.
10 I was thrust into your arms at my birth.
You have been my God from the moment I was
born.

11 Do not stay so far from me,
for trouble is near,
and no one else can help me.

20:2 Hebrew *Zion.*

Ps. 20 This psalm was sung by the people to encourage their king to face the enemy in battle. Verses 1-5 ask God's blessing and success for the king. The second part, verses 6-9, is a confession of faith in God's willingness and power to answer.

21:1-2 your strength. "Your strength" and "your victory" are the same word in Hebrew. To have God's help is to have victory secured. Verse 6 repeats this thought.

Ps. 22 why have you abandoned me? David is under siege from God's enemies, feeling hopeless and deserted by God who has helped him in the past. This psalm is the cry of a righteous sufferer. Gospel writers find striking parallels between David in this psalm and Christ at His crucifixion (Matt. 27:35,39,43; John 19:23-24).

22:1 Jesus quotes this verse (and perhaps the entire Psalm) during His crucifixion (Matt. 27:46; Mark 15:34).

22:3-5 you are holy. These verses show us that true prayer is all about God's faithfulness.

22:9-10 from my mother's womb. God chose David in the same manner that He chose Jeremiah and Paul—before their births.

12 My enemies surround me like a herd of bulls;
fierce bulls of Bashan have hemmed me in!
13 Like lions they open their jaws against me,
roaring and tearing into their prey.
14 My life is poured out like water,
and all my bones are out of joint.
My heart is like wax,
melting within me.
15 My strength has dried up like sunbaked clay.
My tongue sticks to the roof of my mouth.
You have laid me in the dust and left me for dead.
16 My enemies surround me like a pack of dogs;
an evil gang closes in on me.
They have pierced* my hands and feet.
17 I can count all my bones.
My enemies stare at me and gloat.
18 They divide my garments among themselves
and throw dice* for my clothing.

19 O LORD, do not stay far away!
You are my strength; come quickly to my aid!
20 Save me from the sword;
spare my precious life from these dogs.
21 Snatch me from the lion's jaws
and from the horns of these wild oxen.

22 I will proclaim your name to my brothers and sisters.*
I will praise you among your assembled people.
23 Praise the LORD, all you who fear him!
Honor him, all you descendants of Jacob!
Show him reverence, all you descendants of Israel!
24 For he has not ignored or belittled the suffering of the needy.
He has not turned his back on them,
but has listened to their cries for help.

25 I will praise you in the great assembly.
I will fulfill my vows in the presence of those who worship you.
26 The poor will eat and be satisfied.
All who seek the LORD will praise him.
Their hearts will rejoice with everlasting joy.
27 The whole earth will acknowledge the LORD and return to him.
All the families of the nations will bow down before him.
28 For royal power belongs to the LORD.
He rules all the nations.

29 Let the rich of the earth feast and worship.
Bow before him, all who are mortal,
all whose lives will end as dust.
30 Our children will also serve him.
Future generations will hear about the wonders of the Lord.
31 His righteous acts will be told to those not yet born.
They will hear about everything he has done.

23 *A psalm of David.*

1 The LORD is my shepherd;
I have all that I need.
2 He lets me rest in green meadows;
he leads me beside peaceful streams.
3 He renews my strength.
He guides me along right paths,
bringing honor to his name.
4 Even when I walk
through the darkest valley,*
I will not be afraid,
for you are close beside me.
Your rod and your staff
protect and comfort me.
5 You prepare a feast for me
in the presence of my enemies.
You honor me by anointing my head with oil.
My cup overflows with blessings.
6 Surely your goodness and unfailing love will pursue me
all the days of my life,
and I will live in the house of the LORD
forever.

THE GREAT SHEPHERD

1. Have you ever been around sheep? What are they like?

PSALM 23

2. What does it mean to "rest in green meadows" and to be led "beside peaceful streams" (v. 2)?
3. A shepherd used his rod and staff to guide, discipline, protect, and rescue sheep. How is this a picture of God's care for His people? How are we like sheep?
4. Why would God's "rod and staff" actually comfort David instead of making him afraid?
5. How have you experienced God's "rod and staff" in your life?

24 *A psalm of David.*

1 The earth is the LORD's, and everything in it.
The world and all its people belong to him.
2 For he laid the earth's foundation on the seas
and built it on the ocean depths.

22:16 As in some Hebrew manuscripts and Greek and Syriac versions; most Hebrew manuscripts read *They are like a lion at.* 22:18 Hebrew *cast lots.* 22:22 Hebrew *my brothers.* 23:4 Or *the dark valley of death.*

22:12-18 bulls . . . dogs. The psalmist uses a series of powerful images to portray his enemies (bulls, lions, dogs, and evil men). Bashan bulls were the heaviest breed of their day. "Dog" was a term used for barbarians.

22:14-17 poured out like water. David is exhausted from fighting off powerful enemies. He likens his weakness to water that has been poured out (gone), melting wax, baked clay (too hard for use), and dust (What can be done with dust?). These are strong images illustrating that he has come to the end of his human ability to fight back.

23:1 shepherd. In the Psalms, the shepherd was a widely used metaphor for the king (78:71-72; 2 Sam. 5:2).

23:6 goodness and unfailing love. The Hebrew word *hesed* combines mercy and love with eternal qualities to capture the nature of God's love for us.

Ps. 24 This Psalm celebrates the Lord's entrance into Zion. Three thousand years old, this Psalm is recited by Jews on the first day of each week as an act of worship.

3 Who may climb the mountain of the LORD?
Who may stand in his holy place?
4 Only those whose hands and hearts are pure,
who do not worship idols
and never tell lies.
5 They will receive the LORD's blessing
and have a right relationship with God their
savior.
6 Such people may seek you
and worship in your presence, O God of Jacob.*
Interlude

7 Open up, ancient gates!
Open up, ancient doors,
and let the King of glory enter.
8 Who is the King of glory?
The LORD, strong and mighty;
the LORD, invincible in battle.
9 Open up, ancient gates!
Open up, ancient doors,
and let the King of glory enter.
10 Who is the King of glory?
The LORD of Heaven's Armies—
he is the King of glory.
Interlude

25 *A psalm of David.

1 O LORD, I give my life to you.
2 I trust in you, my God!
Do not let me be disgraced,
or let my enemies rejoice in my defeat.
3 No one who trusts in you will ever be disgraced,
but disgrace comes to those who try to deceive
others.

4 Show me the right path, O LORD;
point out the road for me to follow.
5 Lead me by your truth and teach me,
for you are the God who saves me.
All day long I put my hope in you.
6 Remember, O LORD, your compassion and unfailing
love,
which you have shown from long ages past.
7 Do not remember the rebellious sins of my youth.
Remember me in the light of your unfailing
love,
for you are merciful, O LORD.

8 The LORD is good and does what is right;
he shows the proper path to those who go
astray.
9 He leads the humble in doing right,
teaching them his way.
10 The LORD leads with unfailing love and
faithfulness
all who keep his covenant and obey his
demands.

11 For the honor of your name, O LORD,
forgive my many, many sins.
12 Who are those who fear the LORD?
He will show them the path they should choose.
13 They will live in prosperity,
and their children will inherit the land.
14 The LORD is a friend to those who fear him.
He teaches them his covenant.
15 My eyes are always on the LORD,
for he rescues me from the traps of my
enemies.

16 Turn to me and have mercy,
for I am alone and in deep distress.
17 My problems go from bad to worse.
Oh, save me from them all!
18 Feel my pain and see my trouble.
Forgive all my sins.
19 See how many enemies I have
and how viciously they hate me!
20 Protect me! Rescue my life from them!
Do not let me be disgraced, for in you I take
refuge.
21 May integrity and honesty protect me,
for I put my hope in you.

22 O God, ransom Israel
from all its troubles.

26 *A psalm of David.*

1 Declare me innocent, O LORD,
for I have acted with integrity;
I have trusted in the LORD without wavering.
2 Put me on trial, LORD, and cross-examine me.
Test my motives and my heart.
3 For I am always aware of your unfailing love,
and I have lived according to your truth.
4 I do not spend time with liars
or go along with hypocrites.
5 I hate the gatherings of those who do evil,
and I refuse to join in with the wicked.
6 I wash my hands to declare my innocence.
I come to your altar, O LORD,
7 singing a song of thanksgiving
and telling of all your wonders.
8 I love your sanctuary, LORD,
the place where your glorious presence dwells.

9 Don't let me suffer the fate of sinners.
Don't condemn me along with murderers.
10 Their hands are dirty with evil schemes,
and they constantly take bribes.

24:6 As in two Hebrew manuscripts and Greek and Syriac versions; most Hebrew manuscripts read *O Jacob.* 25 This psalm is a Hebrew acrostic poem; each verse begins with a successive letter of the Hebrew alphabet.

24:4 hearts are pure. Having a pure heart does not imply moral perfection. "Heart," in Hebrew, encompassed thoughts, attitudes, affections, and will. (See also Matt. 5:8).

24:5 the LORD's blessing. The products of righteousness ("clean hands and a pure heart") are blessings from God. The righteous person is the one who desires righteousness and cooperates with God, but only God can impart righteousness.

24:7-10 Open up . . . gates . . . doors. The pilgrims sing and praise God as they, with God, enter the gates of Jerusalem.

25:7 Do not remember. He prays that his past sins might be swallowed up in the *chesed* (loving-kindness) of God's great heart.

26:1 acted with integrity. Integrity does not mean moral perfection. Here "integrity" refers to the writer's passionate and lifelong devotion to God. Verse 6 illustrates his continual presence at God's altar.

26:8 glorious presence dwells. The tabernacle was originally built as a tangible sign of the presence of the Lord among the Israelites. God's glory dwelt in the tent (Ex. 40:35) and later in the temple (1 Kings 8:11). The glory of God dwelling in the tabernacle assures Israel that God's covenant with them is still in place.

11 But I am not like that; I live with integrity.
So redeem me and show me mercy.
12 Now I stand on solid ground,
and I will publicly praise the LORD.

27 *A psalm of David.*

1 The LORD is my light and my salvation—
so why should I be afraid?
The LORD is my fortress, protecting me from danger,
so why should I tremble?
2 When evil people come to devour me,
when my enemies and foes attack me,
they will stumble and fall.
3 Though a mighty army surrounds me,
my heart will not be afraid.
Even if I am attacked,
I will remain confident.
4 The one thing I ask of the LORD—
the thing I seek most—
is to live in the house of the LORD all the days of my life,
delighting in the LORD's perfections
and meditating in his Temple.
5 For he will conceal me there when troubles come;
he will hide me in his sanctuary.
He will place me out of reach on a high rock.
6 Then I will hold my head high
above my enemies who surround me.
At his sanctuary I will offer sacrifices with shouts of joy,
singing and praising the LORD with music.

7 Hear me as I pray, O LORD.
Be merciful and answer me!
8 My heart has heard you say, "Come and talk with me."
And my heart responds, "LORD, I am coming."
9 Do not turn your back on me.
Do not reject your servant in anger.
You have always been my helper.
Don't leave me now; don't abandon me,
O God of my salvation!
10 Even if my father and mother abandon me,
the LORD will hold me close.

11 Teach me how to live, O LORD.
Lead me along the right path,
for my enemies are waiting for me.
12 Do not let me fall into their hands.
For they accuse me of things I've never done;
with every breath they threaten me with violence.
13 Yet I am confident I will see the LORD's goodness
while I am here in the land of the living.

14 Wait patiently for the LORD.
Be brave and courageous.
Yes, wait patiently for the LORD.

28 *A psalm of David.*

1 I pray to you, O LORD, my rock.
Do not turn a deaf ear to me.
For if you are silent,
I might as well give up and die.
2 Listen to my prayer for mercy
as I cry out to you for help,
as I lift my hands toward your holy sanctuary.
3 Do not drag me away with the wicked—
with those who do evil—
those who speak friendly words to their neighbors
while planning evil in their hearts.
4 Give them the punishment they so richly deserve!
Measure it out in proportion to their wickedness.
Pay them back for all their evil deeds!
Give them a taste of what they have done to others.
5 They care nothing for what the LORD has done
or for what his hands have made.
So he will tear them down,
and they will never be rebuilt!

6 Praise the LORD!
For he has heard my cry for mercy.
7 The LORD is my strength and shield.
I trust him with all my heart.
He helps me, and my heart is filled with joy.
I burst out in songs of thanksgiving.
8 The LORD gives his people strength.
He is a safe fortress for his anointed king.
9 Save your people!
Bless Israel, your special possession.*
Lead them like a shepherd,
and carry them in your arms forever.

29 *A psalm of David.*

1 Honor the LORD, you heavenly beings*;
honor the LORD for his glory and strength.
2 Honor the LORD for the glory of his name.
Worship the LORD in the splendor of his holiness.

3 The voice of the LORD echoes above the sea.
The God of glory thunders.
The LORD thunders over the mighty sea.
4 The voice of the LORD is powerful;
the voice of the LORD is majestic.
5 The voice of the LORD splits the mighty cedars;
the LORD shatters the cedars of Lebanon.
6 He makes Lebanon's mountains skip like a calf;
he makes Mount Hermon* leap like a young wild ox.
7 The voice of the LORD strikes
with bolts of lightning.

28:9 Hebrew *Bless your inheritance.* **29:1** Hebrew *you sons of God.* **29:6** Hebrew *Sirion,* another name for Mount Hermon.

27:4-6 live in the house of the LORD. "To live" was to literally sit. Four postures for prayer were practiced: sitting, kneeling, bowing flat on the ground, and standing.

27:7-12 Hear me. He asks God to show him the right way to handle his problem. The Lord has already answered.

27:11 Teach me how to live. Notice that the psalmist's prayers are dialogue, as if he is asking a human teacher for guidance. The writer is also aware that learning God's ways will take years, and he is willing to wait. (See also vv. 13-14.)

[8] The voice of the LORD makes the barren wilderness
quake;
the LORD shakes the wilderness of Kadesh.
[9] The voice of the LORD twists mighty oaks*
and strips the forests bare.
In his Temple everyone shouts, "Glory!"
[10] The LORD rules over the floodwaters.
The LORD reigns as king forever.
[11] The LORD gives his people strength.
The LORD blesses them with peace.

30 *A psalm of David. A song for the dedication of the Temple.*

[1] I will exalt you, LORD, for you rescued me.
You refused to let my enemies triumph over me.
[2] O LORD my God, I cried to you for help,
and you restored my health.
[3] You brought me up from the grave,* O LORD.
You kept me from falling into the pit of death.

[4] Sing to the LORD, all you godly ones!
Praise his holy name.
[5] For his anger lasts only a moment,
but his favor lasts a lifetime!
Weeping may last through the night,
but joy comes with the morning.

[6] When I was prosperous, I said,
"Nothing can stop me now!"
[7] Your favor, O LORD, made me as secure as a mountain.
Then you turned away from me, and I was
shattered.

[8] I cried out to you, O LORD.
I begged the Lord for mercy, saying,
[9] "What will you gain if I die,
if I sink into the grave?
Can my dust praise you?
Can it tell of your faithfulness?
[10] Hear me, LORD, and have mercy on me.
Help me, O LORD."

[11] You have turned my mourning into joyful dancing.
You have taken away my clothes of mourning
and clothed me with joy,
[12] that I might sing praises to you and not be silent.
O LORD my God, I will give you thanks forever!

31 *For the choir director: A psalm of David.*

[1] O LORD, I have come to you for protection;
don't let me be disgraced.
Save me, for you do what is right.
[2] Turn your ear to listen to me;
rescue me quickly.
Be my rock of protection,
a fortress where I will be safe.
[3] You are my rock and my fortress.
For the honor of your name, lead me out of this
danger.
[4] Pull me from the trap my enemies set for me,
for I find protection in you alone.
[5] I entrust my spirit into your hand.
Rescue me, LORD, for you are a faithful God.

[6] I hate those who worship worthless idols.
I trust in the LORD.
[7] I will be glad and rejoice in your unfailing love,
for you have seen my troubles,
and you care about the anguish of my soul.
[8] You have not handed me over to my enemies
but have set me in a safe place.

[9] Have mercy on me, LORD, for I am in distress.
Tears blur my eyes.
My body and soul are withering away.
[10] I am dying from grief;
my years are shortened by sadness.
Sin has drained my strength;
I am wasting away from within.
[11] I am scorned by all my enemies
and despised by my neighbors—
even my friends are afraid to come near me.
When they see me on the street,
they run the other way.
[12] I am ignored as if I were dead,
as if I were a broken pot.
[13] I have heard the many rumors about me,
and I am surrounded by terror.
My enemies conspire against me,
plotting to take my life.

[14] But I am trusting you, O LORD,
saying, "You are my God!"
[15] My future is in your hands.
Rescue me from those who hunt me down
relentlessly.
[16] Let your favor shine on your servant.
In your unfailing love, rescue me.
[17] Don't let me be disgraced, O LORD,
for I call out to you for help.
Let the wicked be disgraced;
let them lie silent in the grave.*
[18] Silence their lying lips—
those proud and arrogant lips that accuse the
godly.

[19] How great is the goodness
you have stored up for those who fear you.
You lavish it on those who come to you for
protection,
blessing them before the watching world.

29:9 Or *causes the deer to writhe in labor.* 30:3 Hebrew *from Sheol.* 31:17 Hebrew *in Sheol.*

29:9 Temple. The temple can be understood on three levels: the faithful who worship at the temple (tabernacle) in Jerusalem, the heavenly temple of God (Isa. 6:1), or all of creation.

30:1-3 rescued me. David has been healed by God (v. 2) from some illness he thought would kill him.

30:11-12 You have turned . . . taken away . . . clothed. God answers David's cries. The Lord turns lament into dancing. Despair ("sackcloth") becomes gladness. David, reminded that God is the source of all blessings, vows to praise God forever.

31:1 what is right. In the feminine form of this Hebrew word, righteousness takes on the connotation of the transformation that God creates in us, making us into loving, creative personalities.

31:5 I entrust my spirit into your hand. In Hebrew, "entrust" literally means "to deposit." David gives up control of his life and places it in God's hands for safekeeping. This phrase is quoted by Jesus just before He dies (see Luke 23:46).

20 You hide them in the shelter of your presence,
safe from those who conspire against them.
You shelter them in your presence,
far from accusing tongues.

21 Praise the LORD,
for he has shown me the wonders of his
unfailing love.
He kept me safe when my city was under attack.
22 In panic I cried out,
"I am cut off from the LORD!"
But you heard my cry for mercy
and answered my call for help.

23 Love the LORD, all you godly ones!
For the LORD protects those who are loyal to
him,
but he harshly punishes the arrogant.
24 So be strong and courageous,
all you who put your hope in the LORD!

32 *A psalm* of David.*

1 Oh, what joy for those
whose disobedience is forgiven,
whose sin is put out of sight!
2 Yes, what joy for those
whose record the LORD has cleared of guilt,*
whose lives are lived in complete honesty!
3 When I refused to confess my sin,
my body wasted away,
and I groaned all day long.
4 Day and night your hand of discipline was heavy
on me.
My strength evaporated like water in the
summer heat.
Interlude

5 Finally, I confessed all my sins to you
and stopped trying to hide my guilt.
I said to myself, "I will confess my rebellion to the
LORD."
And you forgave me! All my guilt is gone.
Interlude

6 Therefore, let all the godly pray to you while there
is still time,
that they may not drown in the floodwaters of
judgment.
7 For you are my hiding place;
you protect me from trouble.
You surround me with songs of victory.
Interlude

8 The LORD says, "I will guide you along the best
pathway for your life.
I will advise you and watch over you.
9 Do not be like a senseless horse or mule
that needs a bit and bridle to keep it under
control."

10 Many sorrows come to the wicked,
but unfailing love surrounds those who trust
the LORD.
11 So rejoice in the LORD and be glad, all you who
obey him!
Shout for joy, all you whose hearts are
pure!

33

1 Let the godly sing for joy to the LORD;
it is fitting for the pure to praise him.
2 Praise the LORD with melodies on the lyre;
make music for him on the ten-stringed harp.
3 Sing a new song of praise to him;
play skillfully on the harp, and sing with joy.
4 For the word of the LORD holds true,
and we can trust everything he does.
5 He loves whatever is just and good;
the unfailing love of the LORD fills the earth.

6 The LORD merely spoke,
and the heavens were created.
He breathed the word,
and all the stars were born.
7 He assigned the sea its boundaries
and locked the oceans in vast reservoirs.
8 Let the whole world fear the LORD,
and let everyone stand in awe of him.
9 For when he spoke, the world began!
It appeared at his command.

10 The LORD frustrates the plans of the nations
and thwarts all their schemes.
11 But the LORD's plans stand firm forever;
his intentions can never be shaken.

12 What joy for the nation whose God is the LORD,
whose people he has chosen as his
inheritance.

13 The LORD looks down from heaven
and sees the whole human race.
14 From his throne he observes
all who live on the earth.
15 He made their hearts,
so he understands everything they do.
16 The best-equipped army cannot save a king,
nor is great strength enough to save a
warrior.
17 Don't count on your warhorse to give you
victory—
for all its strength, it cannot save you.

32:TITLE Hebrew *maskil.* This may be a literary or musical term. **32:2** Greek version reads *of sin.* Compare Rom 4:8.

32:3-5 trying to hide . . . confess. The psalmist shares his personal experience with hidden sin. The sin itself is not specified, but the effects of it drain life away.
32:4 strength evaporated. God's disapproval of the psalmist's sin is like a heavy hand that holds him down. Though he might fight against it, that heavy hand is a burden he must carry. Under that burden he wilts like a plant in the hot summer sun.
32:9 mule. Mules are symbols of stubbornness and resistance to the master. We are exhorted to mature in spiritual understanding and not be like mules.
33:1-3 lyre . . . harp. The instructions for the musicians and instruments in these verses require a more sophisticated orchestra and choir, like the one mentioned in Daniel 3:5.
33:12-19 the nation. Israel is the blessed beneficiary of God's plan, chosen as a witness of His saving power. God's protection of Israel is assured, for He is the Lord of creation, and He will not be frustrated (vv. 6-11).
33:16-17 army . . . warhorse . . . cannot save. These verses regarding military might have always been ignored by warring men who do not truly believe in God's sovereignty.

18 But the LORD watches over those who fear him,
those who rely on his unfailing love.
19 He rescues them from death
and keeps them alive in times of famine.

20 We put our hope in the LORD.
He is our help and our shield.
21 In him our hearts rejoice,
for we trust in his holy name.
22 Let your unfailing love surround us, LORD,
for our hope is in you alone.

34

34 **A psalm of David, regarding the time he pretended to be insane in front of Abimelech, who sent him away.*

1 I will praise the LORD at all times.
I will constantly speak his praises.
2 I will boast only in the LORD;
let all who are helpless take heart.
3 Come, let us tell of the LORD's greatness;
let us exalt his name together.

4 I prayed to the LORD, and he answered me.
He freed me from all my fears.
5 Those who look to him for help will be radiant
with joy;
no shadow of shame will darken their faces.
6 In my desperation I prayed, and the LORD listened;
he saved me from all my troubles.
7 For the angel of the LORD is a guard;
he surrounds and defends all who fear him.

8 Taste and see that the LORD is good.
Oh, the joys of those who take refuge in him!
9 Fear the LORD, you his godly people,
for those who fear him will have all they need.
10 Even strong young lions sometimes go hungry,
but those who trust in the LORD will lack no
good thing.

11 Come, my children, and listen to me,
and I will teach you to fear the LORD.
12 Does anyone want to live a life
that is long and prosperous?
13 Then keep your tongue from speaking evil
and your lips from telling lies!
14 Turn away from evil and do good.
Search for peace, and work to maintain it.

15 The eyes of the LORD watch over those who do
right;
his ears are open to their cries for help.
16 But the LORD turns his face against those who do
evil;
he will erase their memory from the earth.
17 The LORD hears his people when they call to him
for help.
He rescues them from all their troubles.
18 The LORD is close to the brokenhearted;
he rescues those whose spirits are crushed.

19 The righteous person faces many troubles,
but the LORD comes to the rescue each time.
20 For the LORD protects the bones of the righteous;
not one of them is broken!

21 Calamity will surely destroy the wicked,
and those who hate the righteous will be
punished.
22 But the LORD will redeem those who serve him.
No one who takes refuge in him will be
condemned.

35

A psalm of David.

1 O LORD, oppose those who oppose me.
Fight those who fight against me.
2 Put on your armor, and take up your shield.
Prepare for battle, and come to my aid.
3 Lift up your spear and javelin
against those who pursue me.
Let me hear you say,
"I will give you victory!"
4 Bring shame and disgrace on those trying to kill
me;
turn them back and humiliate those who want
to harm me.
5 Blow them away like chaff in the wind—
a wind sent by the angel of the LORD.
6 Make their path dark and slippery,
with the angel of the LORD pursuing them.
7 I did them no wrong, but they laid a trap for me.
I did them no wrong, but they dug a pit to catch
me.
8 So let sudden ruin come upon them!
Let them be caught in the trap they set for me!
Let them be destroyed in the pit they dug for me.

9 Then I will rejoice in the LORD.
I will be glad because he rescues me.
10 With every bone in my body I will praise him:
"LORD, who can compare with you?
Who else rescues the helpless from the strong?
Who else protects the helpless and poor from
those who rob them?"

11 Malicious witnesses testify against me.
They accuse me of crimes I know nothing about.
12 They repay me evil for good.
I am sick with despair.
13 Yet when they were ill, I grieved for them.
I denied myself by fasting for them,
but my prayers returned unanswered.
14 I was sad, as though they were my friends or family,
as if I were grieving for my own mother.

34 This psalm is a Hebrew acrostic poem; each verse begins with a successive letter of the Hebrew alphabet.

33:18,22 unfailing love. The love described here is God's continual passion for His covenant people.

34:8-14 I will teach you. The psalmist moves from praise to instruction, concentrating on human senses and emotions. By tasting (v. 8), fearing (v. 9), listening (v. 11), wanting to live (v. 12), and speaking well (v. 13), a person learns to fear God and do His will.

34:15-18 eyes of the LORD watch over those who do right. The Lord sees the righteous (v. 15) and hears their cry (vv. 15,17). To hear their cry implies rescue.

34:19-22 Calamity will surely destroy the wicked. A righteous person can be delivered from troubles and saved from sin. The wicked must suffer the consequence of sin: death (Rom. 6:23).

35:1-3 shield . . . spear and javelin. David mentions military gear figuratively to emphasize his need of God's might to save him.

15 But they are glad now that I am in trouble;
they gleefully join together against me.
I am attacked by people I don't even know;
they slander me constantly.
16 They mock me and call me names;
they snarl at me.
17 How long, O Lord, will you look on and do nothing?
Rescue me from their fierce attacks.
Protect my life from these lions!
18 Then I will thank you in front of the great assembly.
I will praise you before all the people.
19 Don't let my treacherous enemies rejoice over my defeat.
Don't let those who hate me without cause gloat over my sorrow.
20 They don't talk of peace;
they plot against innocent people who mind their own business.
21 They shout, "Aha! Aha!
With our own eyes we saw him do it!"

22 O LORD, you know all about this.
Do not stay silent.
Do not abandon me now, O Lord.
23 Wake up! Rise to my defense!
Take up my case, my God and my Lord.
24 Declare me not guilty, O LORD my God, for you give justice.
Don't let my enemies laugh about me in my troubles.
25 Don't let them say, "Look, we got what we wanted!
Now we will eat him alive!"

26 May those who rejoice at my troubles
be humiliated and disgraced.
May those who triumph over me
be covered with shame and dishonor.
27 But give great joy to those who came to my defense.
Let them continually say, "Great is the LORD,
who delights in blessing his servant with peace!"
28 Then I will proclaim your justice,
and I will praise you all day long.

36 *For the choir director: A psalm of David, the servant of the Lord.*

1 Sin whispers to the wicked, deep within their hearts.*
They have no fear of God at all.
2 In their blind conceit,
they cannot see how wicked they really are.
3 Everything they say is crooked and deceitful.
They refuse to act wisely or do good.
4 They lie awake at night, hatching sinful plots.
Their actions are never good.
They make no attempt to turn from evil.

5 Your unfailing love, O LORD, is as vast as the heavens;
your faithfulness reaches beyond the clouds.
6 Your righteousness is like the mighty mountains,
your justice like the ocean depths.
You care for people and animals alike, O LORD.
7 How precious is your unfailing love, O God!
All humanity finds shelter
in the shadow of your wings.
8 You feed them from the abundance of your own house,
letting them drink from your river of delights.
9 For you are the fountain of life,
the light by which we see.

10 Pour out your unfailing love on those who love you;
give justice to those with honest hearts.
11 Don't let the proud trample me
or the wicked push me around.
12 Look! Those who do evil have fallen!
They are thrown down, never to rise again.

37 **A psalm of David.*

1 Don't worry about the wicked
or envy those who do wrong.
2 For like grass, they soon fade away.
Like spring flowers, they soon wither.

3 Trust in the LORD and do good.
Then you will live safely in the land and prosper.
4 Take delight in the LORD,
and he will give you your heart's desires.

5 Commit everything you do to the LORD.
Trust him, and he will help you.
6 He will make your innocence radiate like the dawn,
and the justice of your cause will shine like the noonday sun.

7 Be still in the presence of the LORD,
and wait patiently for him to act.
Don't worry about evil people who prosper
or fret about their wicked schemes.

8 Stop being angry!
Turn from your rage!
Do not lose your temper—
it only leads to harm.
9 For the wicked will be destroyed,
but those who trust in the LORD will possess the land.

10 Soon the wicked will disappear.
Though you look for them, they will be gone.
11 The lowly will possess the land
and will live in peace and prosperity.

36:1 As in some Hebrew manuscripts and Syriac version, which read *in his heart.* Masoretic Text reads *in my heart.* 37 This psalm is a Hebrew acrostic poem; each stanza begins with a successive letter of the Hebrew alphabet.

35:27-28 give great joy. David ends his prayer with shouts of joy to the faithful God he trusts to rescue him—again.
36:1-4 the wicked. The wicked do not fear the Lord. They judge their own behavior (See "in their blind conceit," v. 2) and so act as their own god.
36:4 lie awake. A wicked person even uses leisure time to plot wickedness. Why waste time meditating on God's law (1:2) or praying (42:8) when evil is your goal?
36:5-6 unfailing love . . . faithfulness . . . righteousness . . . justice. The psalmist sees these four virtues, which are central to God's character, evident in all of nature.
37:11 lowly will possess the land. This phrase is quoted by Jesus in the Beatitudes (Matt. 5:5). The meek are those who are humble before the Lord, acknowledging their dependence on God.

12 The wicked plot against the godly;
they snarl at them in defiance.
13 But the Lord just laughs,
for he sees their day of judgment coming.

14 The wicked draw their swords
and string their bows
to kill the poor and the oppressed,
to slaughter those who do right.
15 But their swords will stab their own hearts,
and their bows will be broken.

16 It is better to be godly and have little
than to be evil and rich.
17 For the strength of the wicked will be shattered,
but the LORD takes care of the godly.

18 Day by day the LORD takes care of the innocent,
and they will receive an inheritance that lasts
forever.
19 They will not be disgraced in hard times;
even in famine they will have more than enough.

20 But the wicked will die.
The LORD's enemies are like flowers in a field—
they will disappear like smoke.

21 The wicked borrow and never repay,
but the godly are generous givers.
22 Those the LORD blesses will possess the land,
but those he curses will die.

23 The LORD directs the steps of the godly.
He delights in every detail of their lives.
24 Though they stumble, they will never fall,
for the LORD holds them by the hand.

25 Once I was young, and now I am old.
Yet I have never seen the godly abandoned
or their children begging for bread.
26 The godly always give generous loans to others,
and their children are a blessing.

27 Turn from evil and do good,
and you will live in the land forever.
28 For the LORD loves justice,
and he will never abandon the godly.

He will keep them safe forever,
but the children of the wicked will die.
29 The godly will possess the land
and will live there forever.

30 The godly offer good counsel;
they teach right from wrong.
31 They have made God's law their own,
so they will never slip from his path.

32 The wicked wait in ambush for the godly,
looking for an excuse to kill them.
33 But the LORD will not let the wicked
succeed
or let the godly be condemned when they are
put on trial.

34 Put your hope in the LORD.
Travel steadily along his path.
He will honor you by giving you the land.
You will see the wicked destroyed.

35 I have seen wicked and ruthless people
flourishing like a tree in its native soil.
36 But when I looked again, they were gone!
Though I searched for them, I could not find
them!

37 Look at those who are honest and good,
for a wonderful future awaits those who love
peace.
38 But the rebellious will be destroyed;
they have no future.

39 The LORD rescues the godly;
he is their fortress in times of trouble.
40 The LORD helps them,
rescuing them from the wicked.
He saves them,
and they find shelter in him.

38 *A psalm of David, asking God to remember him.*

1 O LORD, don't rebuke me in your anger
or discipline me in your rage!
2 Your arrows have struck deep,
and your blows are crushing me.
3 Because of your anger, my whole body is sick;
my health is broken because of my sins.
4 My guilt overwhelms me—
it is a burden too heavy to bear.
5 My wounds fester and stink
because of my foolish sins.
6 I am bent over and racked with pain.
All day long I walk around filled with grief.
7 A raging fever burns within me,
and my health is broken.
8 I am exhausted and completely crushed.
My groans come from an anguished heart.

9 You know what I long for, Lord;
you hear my every sigh.
10 My heart beats wildly, my strength fails,
and I am going blind.
11 My loved ones and friends stay away, fearing my
disease.
Even my own family stands at a distance.
12 Meanwhile, my enemies lay traps to kill me.
Those who wish me harm make plans to ruin
me.
All day long they plan their treachery.

37:22 blessed . . . cursed. Four times in this psalm a choice of two ways is given: God's way or our own (wicked) way. (See also v. 9, 11; 29).
37:29 forever. God's blessings to His people are eternal. In contrast, the prosperity of the wicked is temporary (vv. 10,28).
37:32 wait in ambush . . . looking for an excuse to kill. The wicked are predatory but cowardly. They prefer ambush tactics to steal the blessings of the righteous (10:8-9), even bringing false charges against them in court (v. 33).
37:39-40 He saves them. Despite all the efforts of the wicked, the righteous will prevail. The Lord helps, delivers, and saves them.
Ps. 38 wounds . . . burns . . . disease. David begs the Lord to heal him of a serious illness. David interprets the illness as a rebuke from God. He suffers pain and anguish (vv. 3-8), social alienation (v. 11), and political turmoil (v. 12).
38:11 loved ones . . . stay away. David often finds himself undeservedly abandoned by friends and under attack by enemies (31:11-12).

13 But I am deaf to all their threats.
I am silent before them as one who cannot speak.
14 I choose to hear nothing,
and I make no reply.
15 For I am waiting for you, O LORD.
You must answer for me, O Lord my God.
16 I prayed, "Don't let my enemies gloat over me
or rejoice at my downfall."

17 I am on the verge of collapse,
facing constant pain.
18 But I confess my sins;
I am deeply sorry for what I have done.
19 I have many aggressive enemies;
they hate me without reason.
20 They repay me evil for good
and oppose me for pursuing good.
21 Do not abandon me, O LORD.
Do not stand at a distance, my God.
22 Come quickly to help me,
O Lord my savior.

39 *For Jeduthun, the choir director: A psalm of David.*

1 I said to myself, "I will watch what I do
and not sin in what I say.
I will hold my tongue
when the ungodly are around me."
2 But as I stood there in silence—
not even speaking of good things—
the turmoil within me grew worse.
3 The more I thought about it,
the hotter I got,
igniting a fire of words:
4 "LORD, remind me how brief my time on earth will be.
Remind me that my days are numbered—
how fleeting my life is.
5 You have made my life no longer than the width of my hand.
My entire lifetime is just a moment to you;
at best, each of us is but a breath."
Interlude

6 We are merely moving shadows,
and all our busy rushing ends in nothing.
We heap up wealth,
not knowing who will spend it.
7 And so, Lord, where do I put my hope?
My only hope is in you.
8 Rescue me from my rebellion.
Do not let fools mock me.
9 I am silent before you; I won't say a word,
for my punishment is from you.
10 But please stop striking me!
I am exhausted by the blows from your hand.
11 When you discipline us for our sins,
you consume like a moth what is precious to us.
Each of us is but a breath.
Interlude

12 Hear my prayer, O LORD!
Listen to my cries for help!
Don't ignore my tears.
For I am your guest—
a traveler passing through,
as my ancestors were before me.
13 Leave me alone so I can smile again
before I am gone and exist no more.

40 *For the choir director: A psalm of David.*

1 I waited patiently for the LORD to help me,
and he turned to me and heard my cry.
2 He lifted me out of the pit of despair,
out of the mud and the mire.
He set my feet on solid ground
and steadied me as I walked along.
3 He has given me a new song to sing,
a hymn of praise to our God.
Many will see what he has done and be amazed.
They will put their trust in the LORD.

4 Oh, the joys of those who trust the LORD,
who have no confidence in the proud
or in those who worship idols.
5 O LORD my God, you have performed many wonders for us.
Your plans for us are too numerous to list.
You have no equal.
If I tried to recite all your wonderful deeds,
I would never come to the end of them.

6 You take no delight in sacrifices or offerings.
Now that you have made me listen, I finally understand*—
you don't require burnt offerings or sin offerings.
7 Then I said, "Look, I have come.
As is written about me in the Scriptures:
8 I take joy in doing your will, my God,
for your instructions are written on my heart."

9 I have told all your people about your justice.
I have not been afraid to speak out,
as you, O LORD, well know.
10 I have not kept the good news of your justice hidden in my heart;
I have talked about your faithfulness and saving power.
I have told everyone in the great assembly
of your unfailing love and faithfulness.

11 LORD, don't hold back your tender mercies from me.

40:6 Greek version reads *You have given me a body.* Compare Heb 10:5.

38:17-20 verge of collapse. David grows weaker because of his illness and guilt. His cries to God are reminiscent of Job's.
39:1 sin in what I say. As spiritual leader and king, David must control his anger and not speak evil words that would give the wicked even more ammunition against him, while betraying the righteous (73:15).
39:4-6 remind me. David prays for understanding. He recognizes the brevity of human life and wants to understand what is most important from God's point of view.
40:6 no delight . . . don't require. Though the Law demands sacrifice and offerings, they are actually tools to teach us obedience (see 1 Sam. 15:22).
40:8 take joy. David has learned true obedience, desiring and delighting in the things God desires and delights in.

Let your unfailing love and faithfulness always
protect me.
12 For troubles surround me—
too many to count!
My sins pile up so high
I can't see my way out.
They outnumber the hairs on my head.
I have lost all courage.

13 Please, LORD, rescue me!
Come quickly, LORD, and help me.
14 May those who try to destroy me
be humiliated and put to shame.
May those who take delight in my trouble
be turned back in disgrace.
15 Let them be horrified by their shame,
for they said, "Aha! We've got him now!"

16 But may all who search for you
be filled with joy and gladness in you.
May those who love your salvation
repeatedly shout, "The LORD is great!"
17 As for me, since I am poor and needy,
let the Lord keep me in his thoughts.
You are my helper and my savior.
O my God, do not delay.

41 *For the choir director: A psalm of David.*

1 Oh, the joys of those who are kind to the poor!
The LORD rescues them when they are in
trouble.
2 The LORD protects them
and keeps them alive.
He gives them prosperity in the land
and rescues them from their enemies.
3 The LORD nurses them when they are sick
and restores them to health.

4 "O LORD," I prayed, "have mercy on me.
Heal me, for I have sinned against you."
5 But my enemies say nothing but evil about me.
"How soon will he die and be forgotten?" they
ask.
6 They visit me as if they were my friends,
but all the while they gather gossip,
and when they leave, they spread it
everywhere.
7 All who hate me whisper about me,
imagining the worst.
8 "He has some fatal disease," they say.
"He will never get out of that bed!"
9 Even my best friend, the one I trusted
completely,
the one who shared my food, has turned against
me.
10 LORD, have mercy on me.
Make me well again, so I can pay them back!
11 I know you are pleased with me,
for you have not let my enemies triumph over me.
12 You have preserved my life because I am innocent;
you have brought me into your presence
forever.

13 Praise the LORD, the God of Israel,
who lives from everlasting to everlasting.
Amen and amen!

BOOK TWO (PSALMS 42–72)

42 *For the choir director: A psalm* of the descendants of Korah.*

1 As the deer longs for streams of water,
so I long for you, O God.
2 I thirst for God, the living God.
When can I go and stand before him?
3 Day and night I have only tears for food,
while my enemies continually taunt me, saying,
"Where is this God of yours?"

4 My heart is breaking
as I remember how it used to be:
I walked among the crowds of worshipers,
leading a great procession to the house of God,
singing for joy and giving thanks
amid the sound of a great celebration!

5 Why am I discouraged?
Why is my heart so sad?
I will put my hope in God!
I will praise him again—
my Savior and 6 my God!

Now I am deeply discouraged,
but I will remember you—
even from distant Mount Hermon, the source of
the Jordan,
from the land of Mount Mizar.
7 I hear the tumult of the raging seas
as your waves and surging tides sweep over me.
8 But each day the LORD pours his unfailing love
upon me,
and through each night I sing his songs,
praying to God who gives me life.

9 "O God my rock," I cry,
"Why have you forgotten me?
Why must I wander around in grief,
oppressed by my enemies?"
10 Their taunts break my bones.
They scoff, "Where is this God of yours?"

42:TITLE Hebrew *maskil.* This may be a literary or musical term.

40:12 troubles . . . sins. David's troubles are products of sin. David claims his sins and troubles are more numerous than the hairs on his head.
40:16-17 repeatedly shout. These two verses compose the chorus to be sung, praising God's deliverance.
41:1-3 The Psalms are divided into books. This Psalm ends Book I with "Praise the LORD." This book of Psalms began with "the joys of those." Worship always moves from human orientation God-ward.
41:9 friend . . . shared my food. Sharing meals together implies intimacy. One of David's inner circle has betrayed him. In John 13:18, Jesus quotes this passage to predict His own betrayal by Judas.
41:13 Praise the LORD. This psalm ends with a doxology of praise.
42:1 deer longs for streams of water. Drought is implied here as David's long spiritual ordeal has exhausted him and spiritually dehydrated him. He longs for God's restoring power to stand against oppressors.
42:5 hope in God. This stanza, repeated in verse 11, serves as the refrain of the psalm. Its theme: To overcome difficulty, praise God.

11 Why am I discouraged?
Why is my heart so sad?
I will put my hope in God!
I will praise him again—
my Savior and my God!

43

1 Declare me innocent, O God!
Defend me against these ungodly people.
Rescue me from these unjust liars.
2 For you are God, my only safe haven.
Why have you tossed me aside?
Why must I wander around in grief,
oppressed by my enemies?
3 Send out your light and your truth;
let them guide me.
Let them lead me to your holy mountain,
to the place where you live.
4 There I will go to the altar of God,
to God—the source of all my joy.
I will praise you with my harp,
O God, my God!

5 Why am I discouraged?
Why is my heart so sad?
I will put my hope in God!
I will praise him again—
my Savior and my God!

44

For the choir director: A psalm of the descendants of Korah.*

1 O God, we have heard it with our own ears—
our ancestors have told us
of all you did in their day,
in days long ago:
2 You drove out the pagan nations by your power
and gave all the land to our ancestors.
You crushed their enemies
and set our ancestors free.
3 They did not conquer the land with their swords;
it was not their own strong arm that gave them victory.
It was your right hand and strong arm
and the blinding light from your face that helped them,
for you loved them.

4 You are my King and my God.
You command victories for Israel.*
5 Only by your power can we push back our enemies;
only in your name can we trample our foes.
6 I do not trust in my bow;
I do not count on my sword to save me.
7 You are the one who gives us victory over our enemies;
you disgrace those who hate us.
8 O God, we give glory to you all day long
and constantly praise your name. *Interlude*

9 But now you have tossed us aside in dishonor.
You no longer lead our armies to battle.
10 You make us retreat from our enemies
and allow those who hate us to plunder our land.
11 You have butchered us like sheep
and scattered us among the nations.
12 You sold your precious people for a pittance,
making nothing on the sale.
13 You let our neighbors mock us.
We are an object of scorn and derision to those around us.
14 You have made us the butt of their jokes;
they shake their heads at us in scorn.
15 We can't escape the constant humiliation;
shame is written across our faces.
16 All we hear are the taunts of our mockers.
All we see are our vengeful enemies.

17 All this has happened though we have not forgotten you.
We have not violated your covenant.
18 Our hearts have not deserted you.
We have not strayed from your path.
19 Yet you have crushed us in the jackal's desert home.
You have covered us with darkness and death.
20 If we had forgotten the name of our God
or spread our hands in prayer to foreign gods,
21 God would surely have known it,
for he knows the secrets of every heart.
22 But for your sake we are killed every day;
we are being slaughtered like sheep.

23 Wake up, O Lord! Why do you sleep?
Get up! Do not reject us forever.
24 Why do you look the other way?
Why do you ignore our suffering and oppression?
25 We collapse in the dust,
lying face down in the dirt.
26 Rise up! Help us!
Ransom us because of your unfailing love.

45

For the choir director: A love song to be sung to the tune "Lilies." A psalm of the descendants of Korah.*

1 Beautiful words stir my heart.
I will recite a lovely poem about the king,
for my tongue is like the pen of a skillful poet.

2 You are the most handsome of all.
Gracious words stream from your lips.

44:TITLE Hebrew *maskil.* This may be a literary or musical term. **44:4** Hebrew *for Jacob.* The names "Jacob" and "Israel" are often interchanged throughout the Old Testament, referring sometimes to the individual patriarch and sometimes to the nation. **45:TITLE** Hebrew *maskil.* This may be a literary or musical term.

43:1-4 The psalmist prays for deliverance from enemies who are "deceitful and unjust." He longs to return safely to the temple where God dwells, so he can properly commune with God and praise Him.

43:3 light . . . truth. God's light and truth are personified as messengers who will guide the psalmist back to the temple where restoration will take place.

44:1-8 These words compose a communal lament upon Israel's defeat. Before crying out for help, the psalmist reviews how God has helped the Israelites in the past. Verses 1-3 recall how God aided the Israelites in capturing the promised land. Verses 4-8 review how He has helped them keep the land given them.

45:1 lovely poem. This psalm was recited at a royal wedding. Two other wedding poems in the Old Testament can be found in I Kings 16:31 and I Samuel 18:27. This is a love song sung to the tune: "The lilies." It sounds somewhat like Song of Solomon (v.2).

God himself has blessed you forever.
3 Put on your sword, O mighty warrior!
You are so glorious, so majestic!
4 In your majesty, ride out to victory,
defending truth, humility, and justice.
Go forth to perform awe-inspiring deeds!
5 Your arrows are sharp, piercing your enemies' hearts.
The nations fall beneath your feet.

6 Your throne, O God,* endures forever and ever.
You rule with a scepter of justice.
7 You love justice and hate evil.
Therefore God, your God, has anointed you,
pouring out the oil of joy on you more than on anyone else.
8 Myrrh, aloes, and cassia perfume your robes.
In ivory palaces the music of strings entertains you.
9 Kings' daughters are among your noble women.
At your right side stands the queen,
wearing jewelry of finest gold from Ophir!

10 Listen to me, O royal daughter; take to heart what I say.
Forget your people and your family far away.
11 For your royal husband delights in your beauty;
honor him, for he is your lord.
12 The princess of Tyre* will shower you with gifts.
The wealthy will beg your favor.
13 The bride, a princess, looks glorious
in her golden gown.
14 In her beautiful robes, she is led to the king,
accompanied by her bridesmaids.
15 What a joyful and enthusiastic procession
as they enter the king's palace!

16 Your sons will become kings like their father.
You will make them rulers over many lands.
17 I will bring honor to your name in every generation.
Therefore, the nations will praise you forever and ever.

46

For the choir director: A song of the descendants of Korah, to be sung by soprano voices.

1 God is our refuge and strength,
always ready to help in times of trouble.
2 So we will not fear when earthquakes come
and the mountains crumble into the sea.
3 Let the oceans roar and foam.
Let the mountains tremble as the waters surge!
Interlude

4 A river brings joy to the city of our God,
the sacred home of the Most High.

GOD, OUR REFUGE

1. What is the worst disaster you've been in: Earthquake? Tornado? Hurricane? Flood? Your room?

PSALM 46

2. How is God "our refuge and strength" (v. 1)?
3. Why does God say that we must "Be still" in order to know that He is God (v. 10)?
4. Is there someone you've been fighting with lately? How can you stop fighting and spend time with God?
5. In what way do you need to find refuge in God? How can His strength rescue you from trouble?

5 God dwells in that city; it cannot be destroyed.
From the very break of day, God will protect it.
6 The nations are in chaos,
and their kingdoms crumble!
God's voice thunders,
and the earth melts!
7 The LORD of Heaven's Armies is here among us;
the God of Israel* is our fortress.
Interlude

8 Come, see the glorious works of the LORD:
See how he brings destruction upon the world.
9 He causes wars to end throughout the earth.
He breaks the bow and snaps the spear;
he burns the shields with fire.

10 "Be still, and know that I am God!
I will be honored by every nation.
I will be honored throughout the world."

11 The LORD of Heaven's Armies is here among us;
the God of Israel is our fortress.
Interlude

47

For the choir director: A psalm of the descendants of Korah.

1 Come, everyone! Clap your hands!
Shout to God with joyful praise!
2 For the LORD Most High is awesome.
He is the great King of all the earth.
3 He subdues the nations before us,
putting our enemies beneath our feet.
4 He chose the Promised Land as our inheritance,
the proud possession of Jacob's descendants,
whom he loves.
Interlude

45:6 Or *Your divine throne.* 45:12 Hebrew *The daughter of Tyre.* 46:TITLE Hebrew *according to alamoth.* 46:7 Hebrew *of Jacob;* also in 46:11. See note on 44:4.

45:3-5 Put on your sword. The psalmist encourages the king to be a warrior for good, to go out and fight on behalf of "truth, humility, and justice."
45:16 like their father. The psalmist pronounces a subtle blessing on the king by assuming his new bride will bear him sons.
46:1-3 we will not fear. The psalmist confesses his complete trust in God as his personal and national refuge. The powerful imagery here is reminiscent of the creation process itself. He claims that even if creation were to fall apart, God would still stand.
46:4-6 river. The psalmist continues the water images of verses 1-3. Jerusalem has no actual river, but it sits on top of a natural spring just outside the city wall.
46:10 Be still, and know that I am God. God interrupts the psalmist and commands the people to quit fighting and be still long enough to perceive His presence. This is a frequent theme in Psalms (47:9; 65:8; 66:1-7).
47:1-4 everyone. These verses expand on the idea in 46:10 that God will be exalted among all nations.

5 God has ascended with a mighty shout.
The LORD has ascended with trumpets blaring.
6 Sing praises to God, sing praises;
sing praises to our King, sing praises!
7 For God is the King over all the earth.
Praise him with a psalm.*
8 God reigns above the nations,
sitting on his holy throne.
9 The rulers of the world have gathered together
with the people of the God of Abraham.
For all the kings of the earth belong to God.
He is highly honored everywhere.

48 *A song. A psalm of the descendants of Korah.*

1 How great is the LORD,
how deserving of praise,
in the city of our God,
which sits on his holy mountain!
2 It is high and magnificent;
the whole earth rejoices to see it!
Mount Zion, the holy mountain,*
is the city of the great King!
3 God himself is in Jerusalem's towers,
revealing himself as its defender.

4 The kings of the earth joined forces
and advanced against the city.
5 But when they saw it, they were stunned;
they were terrified and ran away.
6 They were gripped with terror
and writhed in pain like a woman in labor.
7 You destroyed them like the mighty ships of Tarshish
shattered by a powerful east wind.

8 We had heard of the city's glory,
but now we have seen it ourselves—
the city of the LORD of Heaven's Armies.
It is the city of our God;
he will make it safe forever.
Interlude

9 O God, we meditate on your unfailing love
as we worship in your Temple.
10 As your name deserves, O God,
you will be praised to the ends of the earth.
Your strong right hand is filled with victory.
11 Let the people on Mount Zion rejoice.
Let all the towns of Judah be glad
because of your justice.

12 Go, inspect the city of Jerusalem.*
Walk around and count the many towers.
13 Take note of the fortified walls,
and tour all the citadels,
that you may describe them
to future generations.
14 For that is what God is like.
He is our God forever and ever,
and he will guide us until we die.

49 *For the choir director: A psalm of the descendants of Korah.*

1 Listen to this, all you people!
Pay attention, everyone in the world!
2 High and low,
rich and poor—listen!
3 For my words are wise,
and my thoughts are filled with insight.
4 I listen carefully to many proverbs
and solve riddles with inspiration from a harp.

5 Why should I fear when trouble comes,
when enemies surround me?
6 They trust in their wealth
and boast of great riches.
7 Yet they cannot redeem themselves from death*
by paying a ransom to God.
8 Redemption does not come so easily,
for no one can ever pay enough
9 to live forever
and never see the grave.

10 Those who are wise must finally die,
just like the foolish and senseless,
leaving all their wealth behind.
11 The grave* is their eternal home,
where they will stay forever.
They may name their estates after themselves,
12 but their fame will not last.
They will die, just like animals.
13 This is the fate of fools,
though they are remembered as being wise.*
Interlude

14 Like sheep, they are led to the grave,*
where death will be their shepherd.
In the morning the godly will rule over them.
Their bodies will rot in the grave,
far from their grand estates.
15 But as for me, God will redeem my life.
He will snatch me from the power of the grave.
Interlude

16 So don't be dismayed when the wicked grow rich
and their homes become ever more splendid.
17 For when they die, they take nothing with them.
Their wealth will not follow them into the grave.
18 In this life they consider themselves fortunate
and are applauded for their success.
19 But they will die like all before them
and never again see the light of day.
20 People who boast of their wealth don't understand;
they will die, just like animals.

47:7 Hebrew *maskil.* This may be a literary or musical term. **48:2** Or *Mount Zion, in the far north;* Hebrew reads *Mount Zion, the heights of Zaphon.* **48:12** Hebrew *Zion.* **49:7** Some Hebrew manuscripts read *no one can redeem the life of another.* **49:11** As in Greek and Syriac versions; Hebrew reads *Their inward [thought].* **49:13** The meaning of the Hebrew is uncertain. **49:14** Hebrew *Sheol;* also in 49:14b, 15.

47:9 all the kings of the earth belong to God. In fulfillment of the promise to Abraham (Gen. 12:2-3), all nations will be blessed through Israel.
48:1 his holy mountain. Jerusalem commands a wide view, which makes it difficult to attack.
49:1 all you people. Knowledge of God is for all nations, not just the Jews.
49:15 God will redeem my life. Is there hope anywhere? Can the cycle of life and death be broken and meaning to life restored? Only God holds the keys to Sheol.
49:16-19 Their wealth will not follow them. We cannot take it with us, though some followers of pagan religions tried to.

50 *A psalm of Asaph.*

1 The LORD, the Mighty One, is God,
and he has spoken;
he has summoned all humanity
from where the sun rises to where it sets.
2 From Mount Zion, the perfection of beauty,
God shines in glorious radiance.
3 Our God approaches,
and he is not silent.
Fire devours everything in his way,
and a great storm rages around him.
4 He calls on the heavens above and earth below
to witness the judgment of his people.
5 "Bring my faithful people to me—
those who made a covenant with me by giving
sacrifices."
6 Then let the heavens proclaim his justice,
for God himself will be the judge.
Interlude

7 "O my people, listen as I speak.
Here are my charges against you, O Israel:
I am God, your God!
8 I have no complaint about your sacrifices
or the burnt offerings you constantly offer.
9 But I do not need the bulls from your barns
or the goats from your pens.
10 For all the animals of the forest are mine,
and I own the cattle on a thousand hills.
11 I know every bird on the mountains,
and all the animals of the field are mine.
12 If I were hungry, I would not tell you,
for all the world is mine and everything in it.
13 Do I eat the meat of bulls?
Do I drink the blood of goats?
14 Make thankfulness your sacrifice to God,
and keep the vows you made to the Most High.
15 Then call on me when you are in trouble,
and I will rescue you,
and you will give me glory."

16 But God says to the wicked:
"Why bother reciting my decrees
and pretending to obey my covenant?
17 For you refuse my discipline
and treat my words like trash.
18 When you see thieves, you approve of them,
and you spend your time with adulterers.
19 Your mouth is filled with wickedness,
and your tongue is full of lies.
20 You sit around and slander your brother—
your own mother's son.
21 While you did all this, I remained silent,
and you thought I didn't care.
But now I will rebuke you,
listing all my charges against you.
22 Repent, all of you who forget me,
or I will tear you apart,
and no one will help you.
23 But giving thanks is a sacrifice that truly honors
me.
If you keep to my path,
I will reveal to you the salvation of God."

51 *For the choir director: A psalm of David, regarding the time Nathan the prophet came to him after David had committed adultery with Bathsheba.*

1 Have mercy on me, O God,
because of your unfailing love.
Because of your great compassion,
blot out the stain of my sins.
2 Wash me clean from my guilt.
Purify me from my sin.
3 For I recognize my rebellion;
it haunts me day and night.
4 Against you, and you alone, have I sinned;
I have done what is evil in your sight.
You will be proved right in what you say,
and your judgment against me is just.*
5 For I was born a sinner—
yes, from the moment my mother conceived me.
6 But you desire honesty from the womb,*
teaching me wisdom even there.

7 Purify me from my sins,* and I will be clean;
wash me, and I will be whiter than snow.
8 Oh, give me back my joy again;
you have broken me—
now let me rejoice.
9 Don't keep looking at my sins.
Remove the stain of my guilt.
10 Create in me a clean heart, O God.
Renew a loyal spirit within me.
11 Do not banish me from your presence,
and don't take your Holy Spirit* from me.

12 Restore to me the joy of your salvation,
and make me willing to obey you.
13 Then I will teach your ways to rebels,
and they will return to you.
14 Forgive me for shedding blood, O God who saves;
then I will joyfully sing of your forgiveness.
15 Unseal my lips, O Lord,
that my mouth may praise you.

16 You do not desire a sacrifice, or I would offer one.
You do not want a burnt offering.

51:4 Greek version reads *and you will win your case in court.* Compare Rom 3:4. **51:6** Or *from the heart;* Hebrew reads *in the inward parts.* **51:7** Hebrew *Purify me with the hyssop branch.* **51:11** Or *your spirit of holiness.*

50:1 the Mighty One. The many titles for God in this psalm serve to accent His ability and right to judge Israel.

50:7-15 sacrifices . . . you will give me glory. The people have come to believe that they can legalistically offer sacrifices while disobeying God in other ways, but they can't keep sinning and still keep the law.

50:14-15 Make thankfulness your sacrifice. One way Israel acknowledged its total dependence on God—an acknowledgment God desires.

50:16-23 to the wicked. The Lord reproves the wicked for sinful behavior, especially their hypocrisy (vv. 16-17), thievery (v. 18), adultery (v. 18), and lying (vv. 19-20).

Ps. 51 This psalm is David's prayer for forgiveness after Nathan the prophet confronts him regarding his adultery with Bathsheba (see 2 Samuel 11:2-17).

51:5 born a sinner. David cannot claim that his sin is a one-time failure. His nature is to be sinful. He feels deeply that he has grieved the heart of God.

51:6 honesty from the womb. David realizes that he cannot keep God's laws without God's help.

51:10 Create in me a clean heart. Only God is described in the Old Testament as creating. The psalmist wants to be a new man, free of the burden and stain of sin.

17 The sacrifice you desire is a broken spirit.
You will not reject a broken and repentant heart, O God.
18 Look with favor on Zion and help her;
rebuild the walls of Jerusalem.
19 Then you will be pleased with sacrifices offered in the right spirit—
with burnt offerings and whole burnt offerings.
Then bulls will again be sacrificed on your altar.

52

For the choir director: A psalm of David, regarding the time Doeg the Edomite said to Saul, "David has gone to see Ahimelech."*

1 Why do you boast about your crimes, great warrior?
Don't you realize God's justice continues forever?
2 All day long you plot destruction.
Your tongue cuts like a sharp razor;
you're an expert at telling lies.
3 You love evil more than good
and lies more than truth.
Interlude

4 You love to destroy others with your words,
you liar!
5 But God will strike you down once and for all.
He will pull you from your home
and uproot you from the land of the living.
Interlude

6 The righteous will see it and be amazed.
They will laugh and say,
7 "Look what happens to mighty warriors
who do not trust in God.
They trust their wealth instead
and grow more and more bold in their wickedness."

8 But I am like an olive tree, thriving in the house of God.
I will always trust in God's unfailing love.
9 I will praise you forever, O God,
for what you have done.
I will trust in your good name
in the presence of your faithful people.

53

For the choir director: A meditation; a psalm of David.*

1 Only fools say in their hearts,
"There is no God."
They are corrupt, and their actions are evil;
not one of them does good!

2 God looks down from heaven
on the entire human race;
he looks to see if anyone is truly wise,
if anyone seeks God.
3 But no, all have turned away;
all have become corrupt.*
No one does good,
not a single one!

4 Will those who do evil never learn?
They eat up my people like bread
and wouldn't think of praying to God.
5 Terror will grip them,
terror like they have never known before.
God will scatter the bones of your enemies.
You will put them to shame, for God has rejected them.

6 Who will come from Mount Zion to rescue Israel?
When God restores his people,
Jacob will shout with joy, and Israel will rejoice.

54

For the choir director: A psalm of David, regarding the time the Ziphites came and said to Saul, "We know where David is hiding." To be accompanied by stringed instruments.*

1 Come with great power, O God, and rescue me!
Defend me with your might.
2 Listen to my prayer, O God.
Pay attention to my plea.
3 For strangers are attacking me;
violent people are trying to kill me.
They care nothing for God.
Interlude

4 But God is my helper.
The Lord keeps me alive!
5 May the evil plans of my enemies be turned against them.
Do as you promised and put an end to them.

6 I will sacrifice a voluntary offering to you;
I will praise your name, O LORD,
for it is good.
7 For you have rescued me from my troubles
and helped me to triumph over my enemies.

55

For the choir director: A psalm of David, to be accompanied by stringed instruments.*

1 Listen to my prayer, O God.
Do not ignore my cry for help!
2 Please listen and answer me,
for I am overwhelmed by my troubles.
3 My enemies shout at me,
making loud and wicked threats.
They bring trouble on me
and angrily hunt me down.

52:TITLE Hebrew *maskil.* This may be a literary or musical term. **53:TITLE** Hebrew *According to mahalath; a maskil.* These may be literary or musical terms. **53:3** Greek version reads *have become useless.* Compare Rom 3:12. **54:TITLE** Hebrew *maskil.* This may be a literary or musical term. **55:TITLE** Hebrew *maskil.* This may be a literary or musical term.

Ps. 52 This passage relates one of David's bitterest experiences. While fleeing Saul, David asks help of a priest, Ahimelech. The priest is massacred along with his whole town for helping David (see 1 Sam. 21:7-22:23).

52:8 like an olive tree. Olive trees live for hundreds of years and can withstand harsh conditions (v. 5). As an olive tree produces good fruit, the righteous person produces praise for God.

53:4-6 Will those who do evil never learn? Verses 4 and 6 are identical to 14:4,7. Verse 5, however, is quite different. In 14:5 the psalmist portrays evildoers as afraid because of the presence of God. In verse 5 here, evildoers are afraid without reason. They lack security because they lack faith.

4 My heart pounds in my chest.
The terror of death assaults me.
5 Fear and trembling overwhelm me,
and I can't stop shaking.
6 Oh, that I had wings like a dove;
then I would fly away and rest!
7 I would fly far away
to the quiet of the wilderness.
Interlude

8 How quickly I would escape—
far from this wild storm of hatred.

9 Confuse them, Lord, and frustrate their plans,
for I see violence and conflict in the city.
10 Its walls are patrolled day and night against
invaders,
but the real danger is wickedness within the
city.
11 Everything is falling apart;
threats and cheating are rampant in the
streets.

12 It is not an enemy who taunts me—
I could bear that.
It is not my foes who so arrogantly insult me—
I could have hidden from them.
13 Instead, it is you—my equal,
my companion and close friend.
14 What good fellowship we once enjoyed
as we walked together to the house of God.

15 Let death stalk my enemies;
let the grave* swallow them alive,
for evil makes its home within them.

16 But I will call on God,
and the LORD will rescue me.
17 Morning, noon, and night
I cry out in my distress,
and the LORD hears my voice.
10 He ransoms me and keeps me safe
from the battle waged against me,
though many still oppose me.
19 God, who has ruled forever,
will hear me and humble them.
Interlude
For my enemies refuse to change their ways;
they do not fear God.

20 As for my companion, he betrayed his friends;
he broke his promises.
21 His words are as smooth as butter,
but in his heart is war.
His words are as soothing as lotion,
but underneath are daggers!

22 Give your burdens to the LORD,
and he will take care of you.
He will not permit the godly to slip and fall.
23 But you, O God, will send the wicked
down to the pit of destruction.
Murderers and liars will die young,
but I am trusting you to save me.

56

For the choir director: A psalm of David, regarding the time the Philistines seized him in Gath. To be sung to the tune "Dove on Distant Oaks."*

1 O God, have mercy on me,
for people are hounding me.
My foes attack me all day long.
2 I am constantly hounded by those who slander
me,
and many are boldly attacking me.
3 But when I am afraid,
I will put my trust in you.
4 I praise God for what he has promised.
I trust in God, so why should I be afraid?
What can mere mortals do to me?

5 They are always twisting what I say;
they spend their days plotting to harm me.
6 They come together to spy on me—
watching my every step, eager to kill me.
7 Don't let them get away with their wickedness;
in your anger, O God, bring them down.

8 You keep track of all my sorrows.*
You have collected all my tears in your bottle.
You have recorded each one in your book.

9 My enemies will retreat when I call to you for
help.
This I know: God is on my side!
10 I praise God for what he has promised;
yes, I praise the LORD for what he has promised.
11 I trust in God, so why should I be afraid?
What can mere mortals do to me?

12 I will fulfill my vows to you, O God,
and will offer a sacrifice of thanks for your help.
13 For you have rescued me from death;
you have kept my feet from slipping.
So now I can walk in your presence, O God,
in your life-giving light.

57

For the choir director: A psalm of David, regarding the time he fled from Saul and went into the cave. To be sung to the tune "Do Not Destroy!"*

1 Have mercy on me, O God, have mercy!
I look to you for protection.
I will hide beneath the shadow of your wings
until the danger passes by.
2 I cry out to God Most High,*
to God who will fulfill his purpose for me.

55:15 Hebrew *let Sheol.* **56:TITLE** Hebrew *miktam.* This may be a literary or musical term. **56:8** Or *my wanderings.* **57:TITLE** Hebrew *miktam.* This may be a literary or musical term. **57:2** Hebrew *Elohim-Elyon.*

55:4-8 My heart pounds. His present enemy is a former friend. David feels betrayed and fears for his life (v. 4). And he fears that the present conflict will destroy all the work he has done as king (vv. 9-11). His first thought is just to escape and have some peace.

55:9 confuse them. At the center of any conspiracy, plans are discussed, and plots are hatched. David prays that God will disrupt enemy communication and render conspiracy harmless as happened at the Tower of Babel (Gen. 11:5-9).

57:2 God Most High . . . who will fulfill his purpose for me. God appointed David as king with a divine purpose. He will not allow Saul to kill David (see 1 Samuel 22 and 24).

3 He will send help from heaven to rescue me,
disgracing those who hound me.
Interlude
My God will send forth his unfailing love and faithfulness.
4 I am surrounded by fierce lions
who greedily devour human prey—
whose teeth pierce like spears and arrows,
and whose tongues cut like swords.

5 Be exalted, O God, above the highest heavens!
May your glory shine over all the earth.

6 My enemies have set a trap for me.
I am weary from distress.
They have dug a deep pit in my path,
but they themselves have fallen into it.
Interlude

7 My heart is confident in you, O God;
my heart is confident.
No wonder I can sing your praises!
8 Wake up, my heart!
Wake up, O lyre and harp!
I will wake the dawn with my song.
9 I will thank you, Lord, among all the people.
I will sing your praises among the nations.
10 For your unfailing love is as high as the heavens.
Your faithfulness reaches to the clouds.

11 Be exalted, O God, above the highest heavens.
May your glory shine over all the earth.

58 *For the choir director: A psalm* of David, to be sung to the tune "Do Not Destroy!"*

1 Justice—do you rulers* know the meaning of the word?
Do you judge the people fairly?
2 No! You plot injustice in your hearts.
You spread violence throughout the land.
3 These wicked people are born sinners;
even from birth they have lied and gone their own way.
4 They spit venom like deadly snakes;
they are like cobras that refuse to listen,
5 ignoring the tunes of the snake charmers,
no matter how skillfully they play.

6 Break off their fangs, O God!
Smash the jaws of these lions, O LORD!
7 May they disappear like water into thirsty ground.
Make their weapons useless in their hands.*
8 May they be like snails that dissolve into slime,
like a stillborn child who will never see the sun.
9 God will sweep them away, both young and old,
faster than a pot heats over burning thorns.

10 The godly will rejoice when they see injustice avenged.
They will wash their feet in the blood of the wicked.
11 Then at last everyone will say,
"There truly is a reward for those who live for God;
surely there is a God who judges justly here on earth."

59 *For the choir director: A psalm* of David, regarding the time Saul sent soldiers to watch David's house in order to kill him. To be sung to the tune "Do Not Destroy!"*

1 Rescue me from my enemies, O God.
Protect me from those who have come to destroy me.
2 Rescue me from these criminals;
save me from these murderers.
3 They have set an ambush for me.
Fierce enemies are out there waiting, LORD,
though I have not sinned or offended them.
4 I have done nothing wrong,
yet they prepare to attack me.
Wake up! See what is happening and help me!
5 O LORD God of Heaven's Armies, the God of Israel,
wake up and punish those hostile nations.
Show no mercy to wicked traitors.
Interlude

6 They come out at night,
snarling like vicious dogs
as they prowl the streets.
7 Listen to the filth that comes from their mouths;
their words cut like swords.
"After all, who can hear us?" they sneer.
8 But LORD, you laugh at them.
You scoff at all the hostile nations.
9 You are my strength; I wait for you to rescue me,
for you, O God, are my fortress.
10 In his unfailing love, my God will stand with me.
He will let me look down in triumph on all my enemies.

11 Don't kill them, for my people soon forget such lessons;
stagger them with your power, and bring them to their knees,
O Lord our shield.
12 Because of the sinful things they say,
because of the evil that is on their lips,
let them be captured by their pride,
their curses, and their lies.
13 Destroy them in your anger!
Wipe them out completely!

58:TITLE Hebrew *miktam.* This may be a literary or musical term. 58:1 Or *you gods.* 58:7 Or *Let them be trodden down and wither like grass.* The meaning of the Hebrew is uncertain. 59:TITLE Hebrew *miktam.* This may be a literary or musical term. 59:13 Hebrew *in Jacob.* See note on 44:4.

57:6 dug a deep pit. The psalmist described his enemies as lions (v. 4). Here those enemies had set a net and dug a pit as if they were hunters and David the lion. But God changes the roles, and the enemies fall into the trap. The lions fall prey to David and to God.

58:6-8 Break . . . Smash. David prays that Israel will be purged of such evil judges. The tone of the verses is much more like a curse than a prayer.

59:1 Rescue me. The Hebrew words for this phrase literally mean "raise me to a high, secure place." David prays for a safe deliverance from Saul's soldiers who have surrounded David's house in an effort to kill him. (See also 1 Samuel 19:11-17.)

59:3-5 For no fault of mine. Though others lie (v. 12) and slander (v. 10), the psalmist proclaims innocence. He asks God to judge these enemies and to punish them for wickedness.

Then the whole world will know
that God reigns in Israel.*
Interlude

14 My enemies come out at night,
snarling like vicious dogs
as they prowl the streets.
15 They scavenge for food
but go to sleep unsatisfied.*

16 But as for me, I will sing about your power.
Each morning I will sing with joy about your unfailing love.
For you have been my refuge,
a place of safety when I am in distress.
17 O my Strength, to you I sing praises,
for you, O God, are my refuge,
the God who shows me unfailing love.

60

For the choir director: A psalm of David useful for teaching, regarding the time David fought Aram-naharaim and Aram-zobah, and Joab returned and killed 12,000 Edomites in the Valley of Salt. To be sung to the tune "Lily of the Testimony."*

1 You have rejected us, O God, and broken our defenses.
You have been angry with us; now restore us to your favor.
2 You have shaken our land and split it open.
Seal the cracks, for the land trembles.
3 You have been very hard on us,
making us drink wine that sent us reeling.
4 But you have raised a banner for those who fear you—
a rallying point in the face of attack.
Interlude

5 Now rescue your beloved people.
Answer and save us by your power.
6 God has promised this by his holiness*:
"I will divide up Shechem with joy.
I will measure out the valley of Succoth.
7 Gilead is mine,
and Manasseh, too.
Ephraim, my helmet, will produce my warriors,
and Judah, my scepter, will produce my kings.
8 But Moab, my washbasin, will become my servant,
and I will wipe my feet on Edom
and shout in triumph over Philistia."

9 Who will bring me into the fortified city?
Who will bring me victory over Edom?
10 Have you rejected us, O God?
Will you no longer march with our armies?
11 Oh, please help us against our enemies,
for all human help is useless.
12 With God's help we will do mighty things,
for he will trample down our foes.

61

For the choir director: A psalm of David, to be accompanied by stringed instruments.

1 O God, listen to my cry!
Hear my prayer!
2 From the ends of the earth,
I cry to you for help
when my heart is overwhelmed.
Lead me to the towering rock of safety,
3 for you are my safe refuge,
a fortress where my enemies cannot reach me.
4 Let me live forever in your sanctuary,
safe beneath the shelter of your wings!
Interlude

5 For you have heard my vows, O God.
You have given me an inheritance reserved for those who fear your name.
6 Add many years to the life of the king!
May his years span the generations!
7 May he reign under God's protection forever.
May your unfailing love and faithfulness watch over him.
8 Then I will sing praises to your name forever
as I fulfill my vows each day.

62

For Jeduthun, the choir director: A psalm of David.

1 I wait quietly before God,
for my victory comes from him.
2 He alone is my rock and my salvation,
my fortress where I will never be shaken.

3 So many enemies against one man—
all of them trying to kill me.
To them I'm just a broken-down wall
or a tottering fence.
4 They plan to topple me from my high position.
They delight in telling lies about me.
They praise me to my face
but curse me in their hearts.
Interlude

5 Let all that I am wait quietly before God,
for my hope is in him.
6 He alone is my rock and my salvation,
my fortress where I will not be shaken.
7 My victory and honor come from God alone.
He is my refuge, a rock where no enemy can reach me.

59:15 Or *and growl if they don't get enough.* **60:TITLE** Hebrew *miktam.* This may be a literary or musical term. **60:6** Or *in his sanctuary.*

60:1 Aram-naharaim. In the superscription, this is the Hebrew word for Mesopotamia, the area and people that have just defeated Israel. The Valley of Ghor was a flat area south of the Dead Sea where they lost 12,000 in battle.
60:4 banner. In the middle of battle, flags were used to establish a rallying point, a place where an army could regroup and counterattack.
60:6-8 Shechem . . . Ephraim. Shechem was comprised of patriarchal settlements (Gen. 33:17-20). Although they were far from Jerusalem and the temple, God has not forgotten them. Ephraim became the name for the northern tribes of Israel.
61:2 towering rock. God is pictured as solid rock—an image first used by Moses (Deut. 32:4) and echoed elsewhere in the Psalms (62:2; 71:3; 91:1,2; 144:1).
Ps. 62 If the writer was David, the events prompting this wisdom psalm could be the attempt of Saul's family to remove David from the throne. The writer feels weak (v. 3), perhaps due to his age, and seeks God's strength. Structurally the psalm has three parts: reliance on God, trust and hope, and an explanation of why those are possible.

[8] O my people, trust in him at all times.
Pour out your heart to him,
for God is our refuge.
Interlude

[9] Common people are as worthless as a puff of wind,
and the powerful are not what they appear to be.
If you weigh them on the scales,
together they are lighter than a breath of air.

[10] Don't make your living by extortion
or put your hope in stealing.
And if your wealth increases,
don't make it the center of your life.

[11] God has spoken plainly,
and I have heard it many times:
Power, O God, belongs to you;
[12] unfailing love, O Lord, is yours.
Surely you repay all people
according to what they have done.

63 *A psalm of David, regarding a time when David was in the wilderness of Judah.*

[1] O God, you are my God;
I earnestly search for you.
My soul thirsts for you;
my whole body longs for you
in this parched and weary land
where there is no water.
[2] I have seen you in your sanctuary
and gazed upon your power and glory.
[3] Your unfailing love is better than life itself;
how I praise you!
[4] I will praise you as long as I live,
lifting up my hands to you in prayer.
[5] You satisfy me more than the richest feast.
I will praise you with songs of joy.

[6] I lie awake thinking of you,
meditating on you through the night.
[7] Because you are my helper,
I sing for joy in the shadow of your wings.
[8] I cling to you;
your strong right hand holds me securely.

[9] But those plotting to destroy me will come to ruin.
They will go down into the depths of the earth.
[10] They will die by the sword
and become the food of jackals.
[11] But the king will rejoice in God.
All who swear to tell the truth will praise him,
while liars will be silenced.

64 *For the choir director: A psalm of David.*

[1] O God, listen to my complaint.
Protect my life from my enemies' threats.
[2] Hide me from the plots of this evil mob,
from this gang of wrongdoers.
[3] They sharpen their tongues like swords
and aim their bitter words like arrows.
[4] They shoot from ambush at the innocent,
attacking suddenly and fearlessly.
[5] They encourage each other to do evil
and plan how to set their traps in secret.
"Who will ever notice?" they ask.
[6] As they plot their crimes, they say,
"We have devised the perfect plan!"
Yes, the human heart and mind are cunning.

[7] But God himself will shoot them with his arrows,
suddenly striking them down.
[8] Their own tongues will ruin them,
and all who see them will shake their heads in scorn.
[9] Then everyone will be afraid;
they will proclaim the mighty acts of God
and realize all the amazing things he does.
[10] The godly will rejoice in the LORD
and find shelter in him.
And those who do what is right
will praise him.

65 *For the choir director: A song. A psalm of David.*

[1] What mighty praise, O God,
belongs to you in Zion.
We will fulfill our vows to you,
[2] for you answer our prayers.
All of us must come to you.
[3] Though we are overwhelmed by our sins,
you forgive them all.
[4] What joy for those you choose to bring near,
those who live in your holy courts.
What festivities await us
inside your holy Temple.

[5] You faithfully answer our prayers with awesome deeds,
O God our savior.
You are the hope of everyone on earth,
even those who sail on distant seas.
[6] You formed the mountains by your power
and armed yourself with mighty strength.
[7] You quieted the raging oceans
with their pounding waves
and silenced the shouting of the nations.
[8] Those who live at the ends of the earth
stand in awe of your wonders.

62:12 repay all people. Ultimately God will judge each person according to his actions.
63:2 the sanctuary. David had sought God's presence at Nob (1 Sam. 21:1). Later the sanctuary was moved to Jerusalem.
63:6 lie awake. In the darkness the psalmist turns to God and anticipates the morning when God will rescue him. **through the night.** The Jews divided the night into three watches.
63:8 your strong right hand. The right hand of God refers to His power and authority—the same power that delivered Israel from Egypt (Ex. 15:6).
63:9-10 food of jackals. Bodies left on battlefields were eaten by jackals.
64:3 tongues. Psalmists often complain about slanderous tongues, which are more painful than the sword (5:9). They are called swords and deadly arrows for the curses and lies they tell (59:7, 12).
64:7-8 But God himself will. The psalmist expresses his certain trust in God's justice. God will surely act with righteousness, doing to them what they planned to do to him (63:9, 10).
Ps. 65 This psalm was sung at the harvest thanksgiving service (end of September) and at the celebration of a new year during an eight day festival.
65:3 you forgive them all. The people offered God the prescribed sacrifices for atonement. As a result, God forgave them (32:1, 2; 78:38; 79:9).

From where the sun rises to where it sets,
you inspire shouts of joy.

9 You take care of the earth and water it,
making it rich and fertile.
The river of God has plenty of water;
it provides a bountiful harvest of grain,
for you have ordered it so.
10 You drench the plowed ground with rain,
melting the clods and leveling the ridges.
You soften the earth with showers
and bless its abundant crops.
11 You crown the year with a bountiful harvest;
even the hard pathways overflow with abundance.
12 The grasslands of the wilderness become a lush pasture,
and the hillsides blossom with joy.
13 The meadows are clothed with flocks of sheep,
and the valleys are carpeted with grain.
They all shout and sing for joy!

66 *For the choir director: A song. A psalm.*

1 Shout joyful praises to God, all the earth!
2 Sing about the glory of his name!
Tell the world how glorious he is.
3 Say to God, "How awesome are your deeds!
Your enemies cringe before your mighty power.
4 Everything on earth will worship you;
they will sing your praises,
shouting your name in glorious songs."
Interlude

5 Come and see what our God has done,
what awesome miracles he performs for people!
6 He made a dry path through the Red Sea,*
and his people went across on foot.
There we rejoiced in him.
7 For by his great power he rules forever.
He watches every movement of the nations;
let no rebel rise in defiance.
Interlude

8 Let the whole world bless our God
and loudly sing his praises.
9 Our lives are in his hands,
and he keeps our feet from stumbling.
10 You have tested us, O God;
you have purified us like silver.
11 You captured us in your net
and laid the burden of slavery on our backs.
12 Then you put a leader over us.*
We went through fire and flood,
but you brought us to a place of great abundance.

13 Now I come to your Temple with burnt offerings
to fulfill the vows I made to you—
14 yes, the sacred vows that I made
when I was in deep trouble.
15 That is why I am sacrificing burnt offerings to you—
the best of my rams as a pleasing aroma,
and a sacrifice of bulls and male goats.
Interlude

16 Come and listen, all you who fear God,
and I will tell you what he did for me.
17 For I cried out to him for help,
praising him as I spoke.
18 If I had not confessed the sin in my heart,
the Lord would not have listened.
19 But God did listen!
He paid attention to my prayer.
20 Praise God, who did not ignore my prayer
or withdraw his unfailing love from me.

67 *For the choir director: A song. A psalm, to be accompanied by stringed instruments.*

1 May God be merciful and bless us.
May his face smile with favor on us.
Interlude

2 May your ways be known throughout the earth,
your saving power among people everywhere.
3 May the nations praise you, O God.
Yes, may all the nations praise you.
4 Let the whole world sing for joy,
because you govern the nations with justice
and guide the people of the whole world.
Interlude

5 May the nations praise you, O God.
Yes, may all the nations praise you.
6 Then the earth will yield its harvests,
and God, our God, will richly bless us.
7 Yes, God will bless us,
and people all over the world will fear him.

68 *For the choir director: A song. A psalm of David.*

1 Rise up, O God, and scatter your enemies.
Let those who hate God run for their lives.
2 Blow them away like smoke.
Melt them like wax in a fire.
Let the wicked perish in the presence of God.
3 But let the godly rejoice.
Let them be glad in God's presence.
Let them be filled with joy.
4 Sing praises to God and to his name!
Sing loud praises to him who rides the clouds.*
His name is the LORD—
rejoice in his presence!

5 Father to the fatherless, defender of widows—
this is God, whose dwelling is holy.
6 God places the lonely in families;
he sets the prisoners free and gives them joy.

66:6 Hebrew *the sea.* 66:12 Or *You made people ride over our heads.* 68:4 Or *rides through the deserts.*

66:10 tested . . . purified. Precious metals were refined by fire to remove any impurities and increase their value. The psalmist uses the metaphor to describe spiritual maturing (12:6; 17:3).

66:17 praising. Old Testament believers praised God even in the face of the difficulties from which they were seeking deliverance (Phil. 4:6; 1 Tim. 2:1).

67:1 May God be merciful and bless us. The psalmist uses Aaron's benediction (Num. 6:24-26).

68:4 rides the clouds. This description, used often of the Canaanite god Baal, is applied to the true God who rules over all (v. 33; 104:3; Matt. 26:64).

But he makes the rebellious live in a sun-scorched
land.

7 O God, when you led your people out from Egypt,
when you marched through the dry wasteland,
Interlude
8 the earth trembled, and the heavens poured down
rain
before you, the God of Sinai,
before God, the God of Israel.
9 You sent abundant rain, O God,
to refresh the weary land.
10 There your people finally settled,
and with a bountiful harvest, O God,
you provided for your needy people.

11 The Lord gives the word,
and a great army* brings the good news.
12 Enemy kings and their armies flee,
while the women of Israel divide the plunder.
13 Even those who lived among the sheepfolds found
treasures—
doves with wings of silver
and feathers of gold.
14 The Almighty scattered the enemy kings
like a blowing snowstorm on Mount Zalmon.
15 The mountains of Bashan are majestic,
with many peaks stretching high into the sky.
16 Why do you look with envy, O rugged mountains,
at Mount Zion, where God has chosen to live,
where the LORD himself will live forever?

17 Surrounded by unnumbered thousands of
chariots,
the Lord came from Mount Sinai into his
sanctuary.
18 When you ascended to the heights,
you led a crowd of captives.
You received gifts from the people,
even from those who rebelled against you.
Now the LORD God will live among us there.

19 Praise the Lord; praise God our savior!
For each day he carries us in his arms.
Interlude
20 Our God is a God who saves!
The Sovereign LORD rescues us from death.

21 But God will smash the heads of his enemies,
crushing the skulls of those who love their
guilty ways.
22 The Lord says, "I will bring my enemies down from
Bashan;
I will bring them up from the depths of the sea.
23 You, my people, will wash* your feet in their blood,
and even your dogs will get their share!"

24 Your procession has come into view, O God—
the procession of my God and King as he goes
into the sanctuary.
25 Singers are in front, musicians behind;
between them are young women playing
tambourines.
26 Praise God, all you people of Israel;
praise the LORD, the source of Israel's life.
27 Look, the little tribe of Benjamin leads the way.
Then comes a great throng of rulers from Judah
and all the rulers of Zebulun and Naphtali.

28 Summon your might, O God.*
Display your power, O God, as you have in the
past.
29 The kings of the earth are bringing tribute
to your Temple in Jerusalem.
30 Rebuke these enemy nations—
these wild animals lurking in the reeds,
this herd of bulls among the weaker calves.
Make them bring bars of silver in humble tribute.
Scatter the nations that delight in war.
31 Let Egypt come with gifts of precious metals*;
let Ethiopia* bring tribute to God.
32 Sing to God, you kingdoms of the earth.
Sing praises to the Lord.
Interlude
33 Sing to the one who rides across the ancient
heavens,
his mighty voice thundering from the sky.
34 Tell everyone about God's power.
His majesty shines down on Israel;
his strength is mighty in the heavens.
35 God is awesome in his sanctuary.
The God of Israel gives power and strength to
his people.

Praise be to God!

69

For the choir director: A psalm of David, to be sung to the tune "Lilies."

1 Save me, O God,
for the floodwaters are up to my neck.
2 Deeper and deeper I sink into the mire;
I can't find a foothold.
I am in deep water,
and the floods overwhelm me.
3 I am exhausted from crying for help;
my throat is parched.
My eyes are swollen with weeping,
waiting for my God to help me.

68:11 Or *a host of women.* **68:23** As in Greek and Syriac versions; Hebrew reads *shatter.* **68:28** As in some Hebrew manuscripts and Greek and Syriac versions; most Hebrew manuscripts read *Your God has commanded your strength.* **68:31a** Or *of rich cloth.* **68:31b** Hebrew *Cush.*

68:11 brings the good news. God clearly revealed beforehand that He would defeat the Canaanites in order to give His people the land (Ex. 23:22-31; Deut. 7:10-24).
68:14 the Almighty. The Hebrew name is *Shaddai*, referring to God's strength and majesty (91:1).
68:15-16 mountains of Bashan. Bashan was a fertile area to the northeast of the Sea of Galilee. Mt. Bashan is pictured here as being envious over God's choice of Mt. Zion as His throne—thus making it the "highest" of all mountains (48:2).
68:17 chariots. A reference to the vast host of God's angelic beings likened to a powerful force of charioteers (2 Kings 6:17; Hab. 3:8).
68:29 bringing tribute. Gifts of homage were made to Solomon (1 Kings 10:1-10), but this also may look forward to the time when kings would bring gifts to the baby Jesus (Matt. 2:1-12).
Ps. 69 A lament psalm with messianic references similar to Psalm 22, foreshadowing Christ's agony.
69:1-2 floodwaters . . . floods. This figurative language is used to describe deep pain and distress. The cause of the pain is enemy attacks (vv. 14, 15, 29), but also God's own "wounding" of the psalmist (v. 26).

4 Those who hate me without cause
outnumber the hairs on my head.
Many enemies try to destroy me with lies,
demanding that I give back what I didn't steal.

5 O God, you know how foolish I am;
my sins cannot be hidden from you.
6 Don't let those who trust in you be ashamed
because of me,
O Sovereign LORD of Heaven's Armies.
Don't let me cause them to be humiliated,
O God of Israel.
7 For I endure insults for your sake;
humiliation is written all over my face.
8 Even my own brothers pretend they don't know
me;
they treat me like a stranger.

9 Passion for your house has consumed me,
and the insults of those who insult you have
fallen on me.
10 When I weep and fast,
they scoff at me.
11 When I dress in burlap to show sorrow,
they make fun of me.
12 I am the favorite topic of town gossip,
and all the drunks sing about me.

13 But I keep praying to you, LORD,
hoping this time you will show me favor.
In your unfailing love, O God,
answer my prayer with your sure salvation.
14 Rescue me from the mud;
don't let me sink any deeper!
Save me from those who hate me,
and pull me from these deep waters.
15 Don't let the floods overwhelm me,
or the deep waters swallow me,
or the pit of death devour me.

16 Answer my prayers, O LORD,
for your unfailing love is wonderful.
Take care of me,
for your mercy is so plentiful.
17 Don't hide from your servant;
answer me quickly, for I am in deep trouble!
18 Come and redeem me;
free me from my enemies.

19 You know of my shame, scorn, and disgrace.
You see all that my enemies are doing.
20 Their insults have broken my heart,
and I am in despair.
If only one person would show some pity;
if only one would turn and comfort me.
21 But instead, they give me poison* for food;
they offer me sour wine for my thirst.

22 Let the bountiful table set before them become a
snare
and their prosperity become a trap.*
23 Let their eyes go blind so they cannot see,
and make their bodies shake continually.*
24 Pour out your fury on them;
consume them with your burning anger.
25 Let their homes become desolate
and their tents be deserted.
26 To the one you have punished, they add insult to
injury;
they add to the pain of those you have hurt.
27 Pile their sins up high,
and don't let them go free.
28 Erase their names from the Book of Life;
don't let them be counted among the righteous.

29 I am suffering and in pain.
Rescue me, O God, by your saving power.

30 Then I will praise God's name with singing,
and I will honor him with thanksgiving.
31 For this will please the LORD more than sacrificing
cattle,
more than presenting a bull with its horns and
hooves.
32 The humble will see their God at work and be
glad.
Let all who seek God's help be encouraged.
33 For the LORD hears the cries of the needy;
he does not despise his imprisoned people.

34 Praise him, O heaven and earth,
the seas and all that move in them.
35 For God will save Jerusalem*
and rebuild the towns of Judah.
His people will live there
and settle in their own land.
36 The descendants of those who obey him will
inherit the land,
and those who love him will live there in safety.

70 *For the choir director: A psalm of David, asking God to remember him.*

1 Please, God, rescue me!
Come quickly, LORD, and help me.
2 May those who try to kill me
be humiliated and put to shame.
May those who take delight in my trouble
be turned back in disgrace.
3 Let them be horrified by their shame,
for they said, "Aha! We've got him now!"
4 But may all who search for you
be filled with joy and gladness in you.
May those who love your salvation
repeatedly shout, "God is great!"

69:21 Or *gall.* **69:22** Greek version reads *Let their bountiful table set before them become a snare, / a trap that makes them think all is well. / Let their blessings cause them to stumble, / and let them get what they deserve.* Compare Rom 11:9. **69:23** Greek version reads *and let their backs be bent forever.* Compare Rom 11:10. **69:35** Hebrew *Zion.*

69:13-15 Rescue. The psalmist refers to "rescue" as answered prayer.
69:23 eyes . . . bodies. The psalmist's enemies made fun of him because of his pain. Now he asks God to give them the same painful blind eyes (v. 3) and bent backs (38:5-8).
69:24-28 with your burning anger. The writer asks God to judge his enemies in a display of anger. Verse 25 was fulfilled by Judas Iscariot (Acts 1:20 combines these words with those of 109:8).
69:28 Book of Life. God's divine list of all the righteous who enjoy His blessing of life (37:17,29; 55:22; 75:10). The New Testament use of the term includes those who have received God's gift of eternal life (Phil. 4:3; Rev. 3:5).

5 But as for me, I am poor and needy;
please hurry to my aid, O God.
You are my helper and my savior;
O LORD, do not delay.

71

1 O LORD, I have come to you for protection;
don't let me be disgraced.
2 Save me and rescue me,
for you do what is right.
Turn your ear to listen to me,
and set me free.
3 Be my rock of safety
where I can always hide.
Give the order to save me,
for you are my rock and my fortress.
4 My God, rescue me from the power of the wicked,
from the clutches of cruel oppressors.
5 O Lord, you alone are my hope.
I've trusted you, O LORD, from childhood.
6 Yes, you have been with me from birth;
from my mother's womb you have cared for me.
No wonder I am always praising you!

7 My life is an example to many,
because you have been my strength and protection.
8 That is why I can never stop praising you;
I declare your glory all day long.
9 And now, in my old age, don't set me aside.
Don't abandon me when my strength is failing.
10 For my enemies are whispering against me.
They are plotting together to kill me.
11 They say, "God has abandoned him.
Let's go and get him,
for no one will help him now."

12 O God, don't stay away.
My God, please hurry to help me.
13 Bring disgrace and destruction on my accusers.
Humiliate and shame those who want to harm me.
14 But I will keep on hoping for your help;
I will praise you more and more.
15 I will tell everyone about your righteousness.
All day long I will proclaim your saving power,
though I am not skilled with words.*
16 I will praise your mighty deeds, O Sovereign LORD.
I will tell everyone that you alone are just.

17 O God, you have taught me from my earliest childhood,
and I constantly tell others about the wonderful things you do.
18 Now that I am old and gray,
do not abandon me, O God.
Let me proclaim your power to this new generation,
your mighty miracles to all who come after me.

19 Your righteousness, O God, reaches to the highest heavens.
You have done such wonderful things.
Who can compare with you, O God?
20 You have allowed me to suffer much hardship,
but you will restore me to life again
and lift me up from the depths of the earth.
21 You will restore me to even greater honor
and comfort me once again.

22 Then I will praise you with music on the harp,
because you are faithful to your promises, O my God.
I will sing praises to you with a lyre,
O Holy One of Israel.
23 I will shout for joy and sing your praises,
for you have ransomed me.
24 I will tell about your righteous deeds
all day long,
for everyone who tried to hurt me
has been shamed and humiliated.

72

A psalm of Solomon.

1 Give your love of justice to the king, O God,
and righteousness to the king's son.
2 Help him judge your people in the right way;
let the poor always be treated fairly.
3 May the mountains yield prosperity for all,
and may the hills be fruitful.
4 Help him to defend the poor,
to rescue the children of the needy,
and to crush their oppressors.
5 May they fear you* as long as the sun shines,
as long as the moon remains in the sky.
Yes, forever!

6 May the king's rule be refreshing like spring rain
on freshly cut grass,
like the showers that water the earth.
7 May all the godly flourish during his reign.
May there be abundant prosperity until the moon is no more.
8 May he reign from sea to sea,
and from the Euphrates River* to the ends of the earth.
9 Desert nomads will bow before him;
his enemies will fall before him in the dust.
10 The western kings of Tarshish and other distant lands
will bring him tribute.
The eastern kings of Sheba and Seba
will bring him gifts.
11 All kings will bow before him,
and all nations will serve him.

12 He will rescue the poor when they cry to him;
he will help the oppressed, who have no one to

71:15 Or *though I cannot count it.* **72:5** Greek version reads *May they endure.* **72:8** Hebrew *the river.*

Ps. 71 Psalm 71 may be a continuation of Psalm 70 since there is no inscription, and it carries the same theme.

71:1-3 These verses are duplicates of Psalm 31:1-3. But they are developed in a different way since now the psalmist is an old man with a memory of a long life of grace.

71:14 keep on hoping. This verse marks the turning point of the psalm. After his plea for help in verses 1-13, the psalmist here determines to hope in God as he has since his youth.

71:20 depths of the earth. This metaphor expresses the psalmist's desperation. He feels as though he were in the realm of the dead, cast down beyond the grave.

72:1 justice . . . righteousness. The entire prayer may be summed up in this verse.

defend them.
13 He feels pity for the weak and the needy,
and he will rescue them.
14 He will redeem them from oppression and violence,
for their lives are precious to him.

15 Long live the king!
May the gold of Sheba be given to him.
May the people always pray for him
and bless him all day long.
16 May there be abundant grain throughout the land,
flourishing even on the hilltops.
May the fruit trees flourish like the trees of Lebanon,
and may the people thrive like grass in a field.
17 May the king's name endure forever;
may it continue as long as the sun shines.
May all nations be blessed through him
and bring him praise.

18 Praise the LORD God, the God of Israel,
who alone does such wonderful things.
19 Praise his glorious name forever!
Let the whole earth be filled with his glory.
Amen and amen!

20 (This ends the prayers of David son of Jesse.)

BOOK THREE (PSALMS 73–89)

73 *A psalm of Asaph.*

1 Truly God is good to Israel,
to those whose hearts are pure.
2 But as for me, I almost lost my footing.
My feet were slipping, and I was almost gone.
3 For I envied the proud
when I saw them prosper despite their wickedness.
4 They seem to live such painless lives;
their bodies are so healthy and strong.
5 They don't have troubles like other people;
they're not plagued with problems like everyone else.
6 They wear pride like a jeweled necklace
and clothe themselves with cruelty.
7 These fat cats have everything
their hearts could ever wish for!
8 They scoff and speak only evil;
in their pride they seek to crush others.
9 They boast against the very heavens,
and their words strut throughout the earth.
10 And so the people are dismayed and confused,
drinking in all their words.
11 "What does God know?" they ask.
"Does the Most High even know what's happening?"
12 Look at these wicked people—
enjoying a life of ease while their riches multiply.
13 Did I keep my heart pure for nothing?
Did I keep myself innocent for no reason?
14 I get nothing but trouble all day long;
every morning brings me pain.

15 If I had really spoken this way to others,
I would have been a traitor to your people.
16 So I tried to understand why the wicked prosper.
But what a difficult task it is!
17 Then I went into your sanctuary, O God,
and I finally understood the destiny of the wicked.
18 Truly, you put them on a slippery path
and send them sliding over the cliff to destruction.
19 In an instant they are destroyed,
completely swept away by terrors.
20 When you arise, O Lord,
you will laugh at their silly ideas
as a person laughs at dreams in the morning.

21 Then I realized that my heart was bitter,
and I was all torn up inside.
22 I was so foolish and ignorant—
I must have seemed like a senseless animal to you.
23 Yet I still belong to you;
you hold my right hand.
24 You guide me with your counsel,
leading me to a glorious destiny.
25 Whom have I in heaven but you?
I desire you more than anything on earth.
26 My health may fail, and my spirit may grow weak,
but God remains the strength of my heart;
he is mine forever.

27 Those who desert him will perish,
for you destroy those who abandon you.
28 But as for me, how good it is to be near God!
I have made the Sovereign LORD my shelter,
and I will tell everyone about the wonderful things you do.

74 *A psalm* of Asaph.*

1 O God, why have you rejected us so long?
Why is your anger so intense against the sheep of your own pasture?
2 Remember that we are the people you chose long ago,
the tribe you redeemed as your own special possession!
And remember Jerusalem,* your home here on earth.
3 Walk through the awful ruins of the city;

74:TITLE Hebrew *maskil.* This may be a literary or musical term. **74:2** Hebrew *Mount Zion.*

Ps. 73 This is the first of eleven psalms (73–83) attributed to Asaph. He and his descendants were the leaders of one of David's Levitical choirs.

Ps. 74. This psalm is a communal lament such as was prayed when Israel was exiled, the promised land devastated, and the temple lay in ruins.(See also Zech. 7:1-6, 8:18-19.)

74:1 why. The first word of the psalm introduces a lament—a cry to God.

74:2 Remember. The psalm is punctuated with pleas for God to "remember." The wording of this verse and verses 12-17 recalls the victory song of Exodus 15.

74:3-8 destroyed. These verses detail the Babylonians' methods for destroying the temple.

see how the enemy has destroyed your
sanctuary.

4 There your enemies shouted their victorious battle
cries;
there they set up their battle standards.
5 They swung their axes
like woodcutters in a forest.
6 With axes and picks,
they smashed the carved paneling.
7 They burned your sanctuary to the ground.
They defiled the place that bears your name.
8 Then they thought, "Let's destroy everything!"
So they burned down all the places where God
was worshiped.

9 We no longer see your miraculous signs.
All the prophets are gone,
and no one can tell us when it will end.
10 How long, O God, will you allow our enemies to
insult you?
Will you let them dishonor your name
forever?
11 Why do you hold back your strong right hand?
Unleash your powerful fist and destroy them.

12 You, O God, are my king from ages past,
bringing salvation to the earth.
13 You split the sea by your strength
and smashed the heads of the sea monsters.
14 You crushed the heads of Leviathan*
and let the desert animals eat him.
15 You caused the springs and streams to gush forth,
and you dried up rivers that never run dry.
16 Both day and night belong to you;
you made the starlight* and the sun.
17 You set the boundaries of the earth,
and you made both summer and winter.

18 See how these enemies insult you, LORD.
A foolish nation has dishonored your name.
19 Don't let these wild beasts destroy your
turtledoves.
Don't forget your suffering people forever.

20 Remember your covenant promises,
for the land is full of darkness and violence!
21 Don't let the downtrodden be humiliated again.
Instead, let the poor and needy praise your name.

22 Arise, O God, and defend your cause.
Remember how these fools insult you all day
long.
23 Don't overlook what your enemies have said
or their growing uproar.

75 *For the choir director: A psalm of Asaph. A song to be sung to the tune "Do Not Destroy!"*

1 We thank you, O God!
We give thanks because you are near.
People everywhere tell of your wonderful
deeds.

2 God says, "At the time I have planned,
I will bring justice against the wicked.
3 When the earth quakes and its people live in
turmoil,
I am the one who keeps its foundations firm.
Interlude

4 "I warned the proud, 'Stop your boasting!'
I told the wicked, 'Don't raise your fists!
5 Don't raise your fists in defiance at the
heavens
or speak with such arrogance.'"
6 For no one on earth—from east or west,
or even from the wilderness—
should raise a defiant fist.*
7 It is God alone who judges;
he decides who will rise and who will fall.
8 For the LORD holds a cup in his hand
that is full of foaming wine mixed with spices.
He pours out the wine in judgment,
and all the wicked must drink it,
draining it to the dregs.

9 But as for me, I will always proclaim what God has
done;
I will sing praises to the God of Jacob.
10 For God says, "I will break the strength of the
wicked,
but I will increase the power of the godly."

76 *For the choir director: A psalm of Asaph. A song to be accompanied by stringed instruments.*

1 God is honored in Judah;
his name is great in Israel.
2 Jerusalem* is where he lives;
Mount Zion is his home.
3 There he has broken the fiery arrows of the
enemy,
the shields and swords and weapons of war.
Interlude

74:14 The identification of Leviathan is disputed, ranging from an earthly creature to a mythical sea monster in ancient literature. **74:16** Or *moon;* Hebrew reads *light.* **75:6** Hebrew *should lift.* **76:2** Hebrew *Salem,* another name for Jerusalem.

74:9 All the prophets are gone. Most troubling to Asaph was the absence of prophets to speak God's words to them and tell them when these troubles would end. During the exile, Jeremiah was taken to Egypt (Jer. 43:6-7), and Ezekiel was deported to Babylon (Ezek. 1:1).

74:13-14 sea monsters. Asaph recalls God's deliverance of His people from Egypt. The sea monster concept comes from Near Eastern creation myths, in which the creator battled a many-headed sea monster before establishing order in creation. **Leviathan.** This may be a symbol for Satan; it may refer to the Egyptians—the monster of their captivity. God opened the Red Sea for the Hebrews but destroyed the Egyptians when they tried to follow.

74:15 springs and streams. God performed many water miracles. He gave the Israelites water in the wilderness (Ex. 17:5, 6; Num. 20:8-13), and enabled them to cross the Red Sea (Ex. 14) and the Jordan River (Josh. 3).

74:22-23 defend your cause. Asaph thinks God should save His people for His own glory. Israel is His nation, so its suffering causes God's name to be mocked. Israel's enemies are God's enemies.

75:2 At the time I have planned. God will judge all people, but His judgment comes in His time, not ours. When He judges, no one on earth can help those under His wrath (v. 6).

75:4 boasting . . . wicked. God warns those who misinterpret His delay. Make no mistake—judgment will come. The wicked are described in Psalm 73:4-12.

76:1 God is honored. The good news of God's truth and power will be honored particularly after the defeat of the enemies of Judah and Israel, His covenant people. See Isaiah 36–37.

4 You are glorious and more majestic
than the everlasting mountains.*
5 Our boldest enemies have been plundered.
They lie before us in the sleep of death.
No warrior could lift a hand against us.
6 At the blast of your breath, O God of Jacob,
their horses and chariots lay still.

7 No wonder you are greatly feared!
Who can stand before you when your anger
explodes?
8 From heaven you sentenced your enemies;
the earth trembled and stood silent before you.
9 You stand up to judge those who do evil, O God,
and to rescue the oppressed of the earth.
Interlude
10 Human defiance only enhances your glory,
for you use it as a weapon.*

11 Make vows to the LORD your God, and keep them.
Let everyone bring tribute to the Awesome One.
12 For he breaks the pride of princes,
and the kings of the earth fear him.

77 *For Jeduthun, the choir director: A psalm of Asaph.*

1 I cry out to God; yes, I shout.
Oh, that God would listen to me!
2 When I was in deep trouble,
I searched for the Lord.
All night long I prayed, with hands lifted toward
heaven,
but my soul was not comforted.
3 I think of God, and I moan,
overwhelmed with longing for his help.
Interlude
4 You don't let me sleep.
I am too distressed even to pray!
5 I think of the good old days,
long since ended,
6 when my nights were filled with joyful songs.
I search my soul and ponder the difference now.
7 Has the Lord rejected me forever?
Will he never again be kind to me?
8 Is his unfailing love gone forever?
Have his promises permanently failed?
9 Has God forgotten to be gracious?
Has he slammed the door on his compassion?
Interlude
10 And I said, "This is my fate;
the Most High has turned his hand against me."
11 But then I recall all you have done, O LORD;
I remember your wonderful deeds of long ago.
12 They are constantly in my thoughts.
I cannot stop thinking about your mighty works.
13 O God, your ways are holy.
Is there any god as mighty as you?
14 You are the God of great wonders!
You demonstrate your awesome power among
the nations.
15 By your strong arm, you redeemed your people,
the descendants of Jacob and Joseph.
Interlude
16 When the Red Sea* saw you, O God,
its waters looked and trembled!
The sea quaked to its very depths.
17 The clouds poured down rain;
the thunder rumbled in the sky.
Your arrows of lightning flashed.
18 Your thunder roared from the whirlwind;
the lightning lit up the world!
The earth trembled and shook.
19 Your road led through the sea,
your pathway through the mighty waters—
a pathway no one knew was there!
20 You led your people along that road like a flock of
sheep,
with Moses and Aaron as their shepherds.

78 *A psalm* of Asaph.*

1 O my people, listen to my instructions.
Open your ears to what I am saying,
2 for I will speak to you in a parable.
I will teach you hidden lessons from our past—
3 stories we have heard and known,
stories our ancestors handed down to us.
4 We will not hide these truths from our children;
we will tell the next generation
about the glorious deeds of the LORD,
about his power and his mighty wonders.
5 For he issued his laws to Jacob;
he gave his instructions to Israel.
He commanded our ancestors
to teach them to their children,
6 so the next generation might know them—
even the children not yet born—
and they in turn will teach their own children.
7 So each generation should set its hope anew on God,
not forgetting his glorious miracles
and obeying his commands.
8 Then they will not be like their ancestors—
stubborn, rebellious, and unfaithful,
refusing to give their hearts to God.

9 The warriors of Ephraim, though armed with
bows,
turned their backs and fled on the day of battle.
10 They did not keep God's covenant
and refused to live by his instructions.
11 They forgot what he had done—
the great wonders he had shown them,

76:4 As in Greek version; Hebrew reads *than mountains filled with beasts of prey.* **76:10** The meaning of the Hebrew is uncertain. **77:16** Hebrew *the waters.* **78:TITLE** Hebrew *maskil.* This may be a literary or musical term.

Ps. 77 A picture of ordinary self-centered prayers—full of "I" references. I cry, I think, I groan. But at verse 11 Asaph changes his focus to God and is encouraged by remembering God's past deliverances.
77:16-19 trembled . . . quaked . . . flashed. In vivid language, the poet describes God's display of power in delivering the Israelites from the Egyptians at the Red Sea (see Ex. 14).
78:2 parable. The Hebrew word for parable, *mashal,* also included the idea that the saying was concrete enough to be pictured in the mind's eye. Also used were dark sayings or secrets (*hidoth*). What he means here is that God's words make sense only to those whose eyes see the truth.
78:9-16 They forgot. The northern kingdom had forgotten God's miraculous acts and had broken God's covenantal law.

[12] the miracles he did for their ancestors
on the plain of Zoan in the land of Egypt.
[13] For he divided the sea and led them through,
making the water stand up like walls!
[14] In the daytime he led them by a cloud,
and all night by a pillar of fire.
[15] He split open the rocks in the wilderness
to give them water, as from a gushing spring.
[16] He made streams pour from the rock,
making the waters flow down like a river!

[17] Yet they kept on sinning against him,
rebelling against the Most High in the desert.
[18] They stubbornly tested God in their hearts,
demanding the foods they craved.
[19] They even spoke against God himself, saying,
"God can't give us food in the wilderness.
[20] Yes, he can strike a rock so water gushes out,
but he can't give his people bread and meat."
[21] When the LORD heard them, he was furious.
The fire of his wrath burned against Jacob.
Yes, his anger rose against Israel,
[22] for they did not believe God
or trust him to care for them.
[23] But he commanded the skies to open;
he opened the doors of heaven.
[24] He rained down manna for them to eat;
he gave them bread from heaven.
[25] They ate the food of angels!
God gave them all they could hold.
[26] He released the east wind in the heavens
and guided the south wind by his mighty
power.
[27] He rained down meat as thick as dust—
birds as plentiful as the sand on the seashore!
[28] He caused the birds to fall within their camp
and all around their tents.
[29] The people ate their fill.
He gave them what they craved.
[30] But before they satisfied their craving,
while the meat was yet in their mouths,
[31] the anger of God rose against them,
and he killed their strongest men.
He struck down the finest of Israel's young men.

[32] But in spite of this, the people kept sinning.
Despite his wonders, they refused to trust him.
[33] So he ended their lives in failure,
their years in terror.
[34] When God began killing them,
they finally sought him.
They repented and took God seriously.
[35] Then they remembered that God was their rock,
that God Most High* was their redeemer.
[36] But all they gave him was lip service;
they lied to him with their tongues.
[37] Their hearts were not loyal to him.
They did not keep his covenant.
[38] Yet he was merciful and forgave their sins
and did not destroy them all.
Many times he held back his anger
and did not unleash his fury!
[39] For he remembered that they were merely
mortal,
gone like a breath of wind that never returns.

[40] Oh, how often they rebelled against him in the
wilderness
and grieved his heart in that dry wasteland.
[41] Again and again they tested God's patience
and provoked the Holy One of Israel.
[42] They did not remember his power
and how he rescued them from their enemies.
[43] They did not remember his miraculous signs in
Egypt,
his wonders on the plain of Zoan.
[44] For he turned their rivers into blood,
so no one could drink from the streams.
[45] He sent vast swarms of flies to consume them
and hordes of frogs to ruin them.
[46] He gave their crops to caterpillars;
their harvest was consumed by locusts.
[47] He destroyed their grapevines with hail
and shattered their sycamore-figs with sleet.
[48] He abandoned their cattle to the hail,
their livestock to bolts of lightning.
[49] He loosed on them his fierce anger—
all his fury, rage, and hostility.
He dispatched against them
a band of destroying angels.
[50] He turned his anger against them;
he did not spare the Egyptians' lives
but ravaged them with the plague.
[51] He killed the oldest son in each Egyptian family,
the flower of youth throughout the land of
Egypt.*
[52] But he led his own people like a flock of sheep,
guiding them safely through the wilderness.
[53] He kept them safe so they were not afraid;
but the sea covered their enemies.
[54] He brought them to the border of his holy land,
to this land of hills he had won for them.
[55] He drove out the nations before them;
he gave them their inheritance by lot.
He settled the tribes of Israel into their homes.

[56] But they kept testing and rebelling against God
Most High.
They did not obey his laws.
[57] They turned back and were as faithless as their
parents.
They were as undependable as a crooked bow.
[58] They angered God by building shrines to other
gods;
they made him jealous with their idols.
[59] When God heard them, he was very angry,
and he completely rejected Israel.
[60] Then he abandoned his dwelling at Shiloh,
the Tabernacle where he had lived among the
people.

78:35 Hebrew *El-Elyon.* **78:51** Hebrew *in the tents of Ham.*

78:17-72 This passage is a long history lesson of God's gracious acts among His people. These lessons were repeated from one generation to the next to teach them the kind of God they worshiped.

78:44-51 blood . . . flies . . . frogs. These verses recount the plagues God brought on Egypt (Ex. 7-12).

78:60 Shiloh. Located in Ephraim, Shiloh was the center of worship during the latter period of the judges until it was destroyed, most likely by the Philistines.

61 He allowed the Ark of his might to be captured;
he surrendered his glory into enemy hands.
62 He gave his people over to be butchered by the sword,
because he was so angry with his own people—his special possession.
63 Their young men were killed by fire;
their young women died before singing their wedding songs.
64 Their priests were slaughtered,
and their widows could not mourn their deaths.

65 Then the Lord rose up as though waking from sleep,
like a warrior aroused from a drunken stupor.
66 He routed his enemies
and sent them to eternal shame.
67 But he rejected Joseph's descendants;
he did not choose the tribe of Ephraim.
68 He chose instead the tribe of Judah,
and Mount Zion, which he loved.
69 There he built his sanctuary as high as the heavens,
as solid and enduring as the earth.
70 He chose his servant David,
calling him from the sheep pens.
71 He took David from tending the ewes and lambs
and made him the shepherd of Jacob's descendants—
God's own people, Israel.
72 He cared for them with a true heart
and led them with skillful hands.

79 *A psalm of Asaph.*

1 O God, pagan nations have conquered your land,
your special possession.
They have defiled your holy Temple
and made Jerusalem a heap of ruins.
2 They have left the bodies of your servants
as food for the birds of heaven.
The flesh of your godly ones
has become food for the wild animals.
3 Blood has flowed like water all around Jerusalem;
no one is left to bury the dead.
4 We are mocked by our neighbors,
an object of scorn and derision to those around us.

5 O Lord, how long will you be angry with us? Forever?
How long will your jealousy burn like fire?
6 Pour out your wrath on the nations that refuse to acknowledge you—
on kingdoms that do not call upon your name.
7 For they have devoured your people Israel,*
making the land a desolate wilderness.
8 Do not hold us guilty for the sins of our ancestors!
Let your compassion quickly meet our needs,
for we are on the brink of despair.

9 Help us, O God of our salvation!
Help us for the glory of your name.
Save us and forgive our sins
for the honor of your name.
10 Why should pagan nations be allowed to scoff,
asking, "Where is their God?"
Show us your vengeance against the nations,
for they have spilled the blood of your servants.
11 Listen to the moaning of the prisoners.
Demonstrate your great power by saving those condemned to die.

12 O Lord, pay back our neighbors seven times
for the scorn they have hurled at you.
13 Then we your people, the sheep of your pasture,
will thank you forever and ever,
praising your greatness from generation to generation.

80 *For the choir director: A psalm of Asaph, to be sung to the tune "Lilies of the Covenant."*

1 Please listen, O Shepherd of Israel,
you who lead Joseph's descendants like a flock.
O God, enthroned above the cherubim,
display your radiant glory
2 to Ephraim, Benjamin, and Manasseh.
Show us your mighty power.
Come to rescue us!

3 Turn us again to yourself, O God.
Make your face shine down upon us.
Only then will we be saved.
4 O Lord God of Heaven's Armies,
how long will you be angry with our prayers?
5 You have fed us with sorrow
and made us drink tears by the bucketful.
6 You have made us the scorn* of neighboring nations.
Our enemies treat us as a joke.

7 Turn us again to yourself, O God of Heaven's Armies.
Make your face shine down upon us.
Only then will we be saved.
8 You brought us from Egypt like a grapevine;
you drove away the pagan nations and transplanted us into your land.
9 You cleared the ground for us,
and we took root and filled the land.

79:7 Hebrew *devoured Jacob.* See note on 44:4. **80:6** As in Syriac version; Hebrew reads *the strife.*

79:1-4 Jerusalem . . . ruins. The psalm opens with a review of the nations' sin. Asaph laments the devastation of Jerusalem by foreign nations. God's temple had been defiled and destroyed. God's people lay slaughtered; their bodies eaten by animals because no one was alive to bury the dead.
79:6 Pour out your wrath. A prayer for curses on one's enemies is often part of psalms of lament. These prayers are based on God's covenant promise to Abraham to curse those who curse him (Gen. 12:2–3).
79:9-11 Save us. This is a prayer for God to help, to forgive His people, and to punish their enemies. The appeal claims God is not being true to Himself; He should present Himself as a God of vengeance to the nations.
80:1 Shepherd. God is portrayed as a shepherd of Israel as in Psalm 23. Sheep have a tendency to wander and get lost without a shepherd to lead them. See also John 10.
80:3 Make your face shine down upon us. The phrasing of this verse echoes the priestly benediction "May the Lord smile" (Num. 6:25).
80:5 fed us with sorrow. This is a reference to the manna and water that God provided for Israel in the wilderness (Ex. 16:4; Num. 20:1-13).
80:8-16 grapevine . . . transplanted. This passage shows God as a gardener caring for Israel, the vine (Isa. 5:1-7; Hos. 10:1; John 15).

10 Our shade covered the mountains;
our branches covered the mighty cedars.
11 We spread our branches west to the Mediterranean Sea;
our shoots spread east to the Euphrates River.*
12 But now, why have you broken down our walls
so that all who pass by may steal our fruit?
13 The wild boar from the forest devours it,
and the wild animals feed on it.

14 Come back, we beg you, O God of Heaven's Armies.
Look down from heaven and see our plight.
Take care of this grapevine
15 that you yourself have planted,
this son you have raised for yourself.
16 For we are chopped up and burned by our enemies.
May they perish at the sight of your frown.
17 Strengthen the man you love,
the son of your choice.
18 Then we will never abandon you again.
Revive us so we can call on your name once more.

19 Turn us again to yourself, O LORD God of Heaven's Armies.
Make your face shine down upon us.
Only then will we be saved.

81 *For the choir director: A psalm of Asaph, to be accompanied by a stringed instrument.**

1 Sing praises to God, our strength.
Sing to the God of Jacob.
2 Sing! Beat the tambourine.
Play the sweet lyre and the harp.
3 Blow the ram's horn at new moon,
and again at full moon to call a festival!
4 For this is required by the decrees of Israel;
it is a regulation of the God of Jacob.
5 He made it a law for Israel*
when he attacked Egypt to set us free.

I heard an unknown voice say,
6 "Now I will take the load from your shoulders;
I will free your hands from their heavy tasks.
7 You cried to me in trouble, and I saved you;
I answered out of the thundercloud
and tested your faith when there was no water at Meribah.
Interlude

8 "Listen to me, O my people, while I give you stern warnings.
O Israel, if you would only listen to me!
9 You must never have a foreign god;
you must not bow down before a false god.
10 For it was I, the LORD your God,
who rescued you from the land of Egypt.
Open your mouth wide, and I will fill it with good things.

11 "But no, my people wouldn't listen.
Israel did not want me around.
12 So I let them follow their own stubborn desires,
living according to their own ideas.
13 Oh, that my people would listen to me!
Oh, that Israel would follow me, walking in my paths!
14 How quickly I would then subdue their enemies!
How soon my hands would be upon their foes!
15 Those who hate the LORD would cringe before him;
they would be doomed forever.
16 But I would feed you with the finest wheat.
I would satisfy you with wild honey from the rock."

82 *A psalm of Asaph.*

1 God presides over heaven's court;
he pronounces judgment on the heavenly beings:
2 "How long will you hand down unjust decisions
by favoring the wicked?
Interlude

3 "Give justice to the poor and the orphan;
uphold the rights of the oppressed and the destitute.
4 Rescue the poor and helpless;
deliver them from the grasp of evil people.
5 But these oppressors know nothing;
they are so ignorant!
They wander about in darkness,
while the whole world is shaken to the core.
6 I say, 'You are gods;
you are all children of the Most High.
7 But you will die like mere mortals
and fall like every other ruler.'"
8 Rise up, O God, and judge the earth,
for all the nations belong to you.

83 *A song. A psalm of Asaph.*

1 O God, do not be silent!
Do not be deaf.
Do not be quiet, O God.
2 Don't you hear the uproar of your enemies?
Don't you see that your arrogant enemies are rising up?

80:11 Hebrew *west to the sea, . . . east to the river.* **81:TITLE** Hebrew *according to the gittith.* **81:5** Hebrew *for Joseph.*

80:12 broken down our walls. The Lord removed His hand of protection from Israel.
Ps. 81 This festival psalm begins as a psalm of praise and becomes a call to obedience. It was probably used at the Feast of Tabernacles (v. 3) that commemorated God's care of His people during the desert journey.
81:6 take the load . . . heavy tasks. God delivered His people from forced labor in Egypt where they made and hauled bricks (Ex. 1).
81:16 finest wheat . . . wild honey from the rock. God promised prosperity for obedience. Wheat and honey (which often came from hives built among rocks) were symbols of prosperity.
82:1 heaven's court. This is the psalmist's vision of God presiding over the court of judgment in heaven. The rulers and judges of the earth are called before Him to give account of their judgments.
83:1-4 Asaph calls on God to judge the wicked and to protect Israel in the face of grave danger. The Jews took God for granted, believing He would automatically answer any time they prayed.

[3] They devise crafty schemes against your people;
they conspire against your precious ones.
[4] "Come," they say, "let us wipe out Israel as a nation.
We will destroy the very memory of its existence."
[5] Yes, this was their unanimous decision.
They signed a treaty as allies against you—
[6] these Edomites and Ishmaelites;
Moabites and Hagrites;
[7] Gebalites, Ammonites, and Amalekites;
and people from Philistia and Tyre.
[8] Assyria has joined them, too,
and is allied with the descendants of Lot.
Interlude

[9] Do to them as you did to the Midianites
and as you did to Sisera and Jabin at the Kishon River.
[10] They were destroyed at Endor,
and their decaying corpses fertilized the soil.
[11] Let their mighty nobles die as Oreb and Zeeb did.
Let all their princes die like Zebah and Zalmunna,
[12] for they said, "Let us seize for our own use
these pasturelands of God!"
[13] O my God, scatter them like tumbleweed,
like chaff before the wind!
[14] As a fire burns a forest
and as a flame sets mountains ablaze,
[15] chase them with your fierce storm;
terrify them with your tempest.
[16] Utterly disgrace them
until they submit to your name, O LORD.
[17] Let them be ashamed and terrified forever.
Let them die in disgrace.
[18] Then they will learn that you alone are called the LORD,
that you alone are the Most High,
supreme over all the earth.

84

*For the choir director: A psalm of the descendants of Korah, to be accompanied by a stringed instrument.**

[1] How lovely is your dwelling place,
O LORD of Heaven's Armies.
[2] I long, yes, I faint with longing
to enter the courts of the LORD.
With my whole being, body and soul,
I will shout joyfully to the living God.
[3] Even the sparrow finds a home,
and the swallow builds her nest and raises her young
at a place near your altar,
O LORD of Heaven's Armies, my King and my God!
[4] What joy for those who can live in your house,
always singing your praises.
Interlude

[5] What joy for those whose strength comes from the LORD,
who have set their minds on a pilgrimage to Jerusalem.
[6] When they walk through the Valley of Weeping,*
it will become a place of refreshing springs.
The autumn rains will clothe it with blessings.
[7] They will continue to grow stronger,
and each of them will appear before God in Jerusalem.*

[8] O LORD God of Heaven's Armies, hear my prayer.
Listen, O God of Jacob.
Interlude

[9] O God, look with favor upon the king, our shield!
Show favor to the one you have anointed.

[10] A single day in your courts
is better than a thousand anywhere else!
I would rather be a gatekeeper in the house of my God
than live the good life in the homes of the wicked.
[11] For the LORD God is our sun and our shield.
He gives us grace and glory.
The LORD will withhold no good thing
from those who do what is right.
[12] O LORD of Heaven's Armies,
what joy for those who trust in you.

85

For the choir director: A psalm of the descendants of Korah.

[1] LORD, you poured out blessings on your land!
You restored the fortunes of Israel.*
[2] You forgave the guilt of your people—
yes, you covered all their sins.
Interlude
[3] You held back your fury.
You kept back your blazing anger.

[4] Now restore us again, O God of our salvation.
Put aside your anger against us once more.
[5] Will you be angry with us always?
Will you prolong your wrath to all generations?
[6] Won't you revive us again,
so your people can rejoice in you?
[7] Show us your unfailing love, O LORD,
and grant us your salvation.

[8] I listen carefully to what God the LORD is saying,
for he speaks peace to his faithful people.
But let them not return to their foolish ways.
[9] Surely his salvation is near to those who fear him,
so our land will be filled with his glory.

84:TITLE Hebrew *according to the gittith.* See note on 44:4. **84:6** Or *Valley of Poplars;* Hebrew reads *valley of Baca.* **84:7** Hebrew *Zion.* **85:1** Hebrew *of Jacob.*

83:15 fierce storm . . . tempest. God, pictured here as a heavenly warrior, uses natural disasters as a weapon against enemies.
83:18 they will learn. Asaph's motive in asking God to wipe out Israel's enemies is that God's name will be glorified.
84:5 whose strength comes from the LORD. Happy are the people who love God and come to Zion, not so much from obligation as for joy at drawing near to God.
84:6 Valley of Weeping. Literally "Valley of Baca," this phrase refers to the difficulties pilgrims face on their journey through life.
85:9 glory. The manifestation of God's presence is called His glory. Recall that Moses could only see the back of God's glory lest it kill him (Ex. 33).

10 Unfailing love and truth have met together.
Righteousness and peace have kissed!
11 Truth springs up from the earth,
and righteousness smiles down from heaven.
12 Yes, the LORD pours down his blessings.
Our land will yield its bountiful harvest.
13 Righteousness goes as a herald before him,
preparing the way for his steps.

86 *A prayer of David.*

1 Bend down, O LORD, and hear my prayer;
answer me, for I need your help.
2 Protect me, for I am devoted to you.
Save me, for I serve you and trust you.
You are my God.
3 Be merciful to me, O Lord,
for I am calling on you constantly.
4 Give me happiness, O Lord,
for I give myself to you.
5 O Lord, you are so good, so ready to forgive,
so full of unfailing love for all who ask for your help.
6 Listen closely to my prayer, O LORD;
hear my urgent cry.
7 I will call to you whenever I'm in trouble,
and you will answer me.

8 No pagan god is like you, O Lord.
None can do what you do!
9 All the nations you made
will come and bow before you, Lord;
they will praise your holy name.
10 For you are great and perform wonderful deeds.
You alone are God.

11 Teach me your ways, O LORD,
that I may live according to your truth!
Grant me purity of heart,
so that I may honor you.
12 With all my heart I will praise you, O Lord my God.
I will give glory to your name forever,
13 for your love for me is very great.
You have rescued me from the depths of death.*

14 O God, insolent people rise up against me;
a violent gang is trying to kill me.
You mean nothing to them.
15 But you, O Lord,
are a God of compassion and mercy,
slow to get angry
and filled with unfailing love and faithfulness.
16 Look down and have mercy on me.
Give your strength to your servant;
save me, the son of your servant.
17 Send me a sign of your favor.
Then those who hate me will be put to shame,
for you, O LORD, help and comfort me.

87 *A song. A psalm of the descendants of Korah.*

1 On the holy mountain
stands the city founded by the LORD.
2 He loves the city of Jerusalem
more than any other city in Israel.*
3 O city of God,
what glorious things are said of you! *Interlude*

4 I will count Egypt* and Babylon among those who know me—
also Philistia and Tyre, and even distant Ethiopia.*
They have all become citizens of Jerusalem!
5 Regarding Jerusalem* it will be said,
"Everyone enjoys the rights of citizenship there."
And the Most High will personally bless this city.
6 When the LORD registers the nations, he will say,
"They have all become citizens of Jerusalem." *Interlude*

7 The people will play flutes* and sing,
"The source of my life springs from Jerusalem!"

88 *For the choir director: A psalm of the descendants of Korah. A song to be sung to the tune "The Suffering of Affliction." A psalm* of Heman the Ezrahite.*

1 O LORD, God of my salvation,
I cry out to you by day.
I come to you at night.
2 Now hear my prayer;
listen to my cry.
3 For my life is full of troubles,
and death* draws near.
4 I am as good as dead,
like a strong man with no strength left.
5 They have left me among the dead,
and I lie like a corpse in a grave.
I am forgotten,
cut off from your care.

86:13 Hebrew *of Sheol.* **87:2** Hebrew *He loves the gates of Zion more than all the dwellings of Jacob.* See note on 44:4. **87:4a** Hebrew *Rahab,* the name of a mythical sea monster that represents chaos in ancient literature. The name is used here as a poetic name for Egypt. **87:4b** Hebrew *Cush.* **87:5** Hebrew *Zion.* **87:7** Or *will dance.* **88:TITLE** Hebrew *maskil.* This may be a literary or musical term. **88:3** Hebrew *Sheol.*

86:1 I need your help. Here the psalmist expresses that he is totally dependent on God (see 34:6; 35:10).
86:5-7 I will call . . . you will answer. In the middle of trouble David trusts God. Clearly, David knows the meaning of praying without ceasing.
86:9 All the nations. God's work on behalf of Israel will cause the whole world to acknowledge Him—a prominent theme throughout Psalms (22:27; 47:9; 66:1-7; 86:9) and the Old Testament (Ex. 7:5; Lev. 26:45; 1 Sam. 17:46; 1 Kings 8:41-43; Ezek. 20:41).
86:14 violent gang. The Hebrew word includes the concept of ferocious violence that has no regard for God (Jer. 20:11). Throughout the Psalms, God is described as the enemy of the proud and the helper of the humble (138:6; 147:6).
87:1 city founded by the LORD. God Himself established the foundations of the city on a mountain, Mt. Zion (48:2; 68:15-16; Isa. 14:32). The city included the temple Solomon built.
87:5 Everyone. Wherever God's people are scattered in the world, their "home" is in God's covenant and His holy city, Zion.
87:7 life springs. Zion is a refreshing spring, the only source of God and salvation.
88:1-2 I cry out. The psalmist cries out to God for salvation. The verb indicates a loud scream or desperate weeping.
88:5 I am forgotten. God's care appears to end at death, after which God no longer needs to rescue the suffering one (25:7; 106:4).

6 You have thrown me into the lowest pit,
into the darkest depths.
7 Your anger weighs me down;
with wave after wave you have engulfed me.
Interlude

8 You have driven my friends away
by making me repulsive to them.
I am in a trap with no way of escape.
9 My eyes are blinded by my tears.
Each day I beg for your help, O LORD;
I lift my hands to you for mercy.
10 Are your wonderful deeds of any use to the dead?
Do the dead rise up and praise you?
Interlude

11 Can those in the grave declare your unfailing love?
Can they proclaim your faithfulness in the place of destruction?*
12 Can the darkness speak of your wonderful deeds?
Can anyone in the land of forgetfulness talk about your righteousness?
13 O LORD, I cry out to you.
I will keep on pleading day by day.
14 O LORD, why do you reject me?
Why do you turn your face from me?

15 I have been sick and close to death since my youth.
I stand helpless and desperate before your terrors.
16 Your fierce anger has overwhelmed me.
Your terrors have paralyzed me.
17 They swirl around me like floodwaters all day long.
They have engulfed me completely.
18 You have taken away my companions and loved ones.
Darkness is my closest friend.

89 *A psalm* of Ethan the Ezrahite.*

1 I will sing of the LORD's unfailing love forever!
Young and old will hear of your faithfulness.
2 Your unfailing love will last forever.
Your faithfulness is as enduring as the heavens.

3 The LORD said, "I have made a covenant with David, my chosen servant.
I have sworn this oath to him:
4 'I will establish your descendants as kings forever;
they will sit on your throne from now until eternity.'"
Interlude
5 All heaven will praise your great wonders, LORD;
myriads of angels will praise you for your faithfulness.
6 For who in all of heaven can compare with the LORD?
What mightiest angel is anything like the LORD?
7 The highest angelic powers stand in awe of God.
He is far more awesome than all who surround his throne.
8 O LORD God of Heaven's Armies!
Where is there anyone as mighty as you, O LORD?
You are entirely faithful.

9 You rule the oceans.
You subdue their storm-tossed waves.
10 You crushed the great sea monster.*
You scattered your enemies with your mighty arm.
11 The heavens are yours, and the earth is yours;
everything in the world is yours—you created it all.
12 You created north and south.
Mount Tabor and Mount Hermon praise your name.
13 Powerful is your arm!
Strong is your hand!
Your right hand is lifted high in glorious strength.
14 Righteousness and justice are the foundation of your throne.
Unfailing love and truth walk before you as attendants.
15 Happy are those who hear the joyful call to worship,
for they will walk in the light of your presence, LORD.
16 They rejoice all day long in your wonderful reputation.
They exult in your righteousness.
17 You are their glorious strength.
It pleases you to make us strong.
18 Yes, our protection comes from the LORD,
and he, the Holy One of Israel, has given us our king.

19 Long ago you spoke in a vision to your faithful people.
You said, "I have raised up a warrior.
I have selected him from the common people to be king.
20 I have found my servant David.
I have anointed him with my holy oil.
21 I will steady him with my hand;
with my powerful arm I will make him strong.
22 His enemies will not defeat him,
nor will the wicked overpower him.
23 I will beat down his adversaries before him
and destroy those who hate him.
24 My faithfulness and unfailing love will be with him,
and by my authority he will grow in power.
25 I will extend his rule over the sea,
his dominion over the rivers.
26 And he will call out to me, 'You are my Father,
my God, and the Rock of my salvation.'
27 I will make him my firstborn son,
the mightiest king on earth.
28 I will love him and be kind to him forever;
my covenant with him will never end.

88:11 Hebrew *in Abaddon?* 89:TITLE Hebrew *maskil.* This may be a literary or musical term. 89:10 Hebrew *Rahab,* the name of a mythical sea monster that represents chaos in ancient literature.

89:19-29 my servant David. The psalmist recounts God's eternal covenant with David as king and steward of God's people.

89:27 firstborn son. This verse prefigures Christ as God's firstborn.

29 I will preserve an heir for him;
his throne will be as endless as the days of heaven.
30 But if his descendants forsake my instructions
and fail to obey my regulations,
31 if they do not obey my decrees
and fail to keep my commands,
32 then I will punish their sin with the rod,
and their disobedience with beating.
33 But I will never stop loving him
nor fail to keep my promise to him.
34 No, I will not break my covenant;
I will not take back a single word I said.
35 I have sworn an oath to David,
and in my holiness I cannot lie:
36 His dynasty will go on forever;
his kingdom will endure as the sun.
37 It will be as eternal as the moon,
my faithful witness in the sky!"
Interlude

38 But now you have rejected him and cast him off.
You are angry with your anointed king.
39 You have renounced your covenant with him;
you have thrown his crown in the dust.
40 You have broken down the walls protecting him
and ruined every fort defending him.
41 Everyone who comes along has robbed him,
and he has become a joke to his neighbors.
42 You have strengthened his enemies
and made them all rejoice.
43 You have made his sword useless
and refused to help him in battle.
44 You have ended his splendor
and overturned his throne.
45 You have made him old before his time
and publicly disgraced him.
Interlude

46 O LORD, how long will this go on?
Will you hide yourself forever?
How long will your anger burn like fire?
47 Remember how short my life is,
how empty and futile this human existence!
48 No one can live forever; all will die.
No one can escape the power of the grave.*
Interlude

49 Lord, where is your unfailing love?
You promised it to David with a faithful pledge.
50 Consider, Lord, how your servants are disgraced!
I carry in my heart the insults of so many people.
51 Your enemies have mocked me, O LORD;
they mock your anointed king wherever he goes.

52 Praise the LORD forever!
Amen and amen!

89:48 Hebrew *of Sheol.*

BOOK FOUR (PSALMS 90–106)

90 *A prayer of Moses, the man of God.*

1 Lord, through all the generations
you have been our home!
2 Before the mountains were born,
before you gave birth to the earth and the world,
from beginning to end, you are God.

3 You turn people back to dust, saying,
"Return to dust, you mortals!"
4 For you, a thousand years are as a passing day,
as brief as a few night hours.
5 You sweep people away like dreams that disappear.
They are like grass that springs up in the morning.
6 In the morning it blooms and flourishes,
but by evening it is dry and withered.
7 We wither beneath your anger;
we are overwhelmed by your fury.
8 You spread out our sins before you—
our secret sins—and you see them all.
9 We live our lives beneath your wrath,
ending our years with a groan.

10 Seventy years are given to us!
Some even live to eighty.
But even the best years are filled with pain and trouble;
soon they disappear, and we fly away.
11 Who can comprehend the power of your anger?
Your wrath is as awesome as the fear you deserve.
12 Teach us to realize the brevity of life,
so that we may grow in wisdom.

13 O LORD, come back to us!
How long will you delay?
Take pity on your servants!
14 Satisfy us each morning with your unfailing love,
so we may sing for joy to the end of our lives.
15 Give us gladness in proportion to our former misery!
Replace the evil years with good.
16 Let us, your servants, see you work again;
let our children see your glory.
17 And may the Lord our God show us his approval
and make our efforts successful.
Yes, make our efforts successful!

91

1 Those who live in the shelter of the Most High
will find rest in the shadow of the Almighty.
2 This I declare about the LORD:
He alone is my refuge, my place of safety;
he is my God, and I trust him.
3 For he will rescue you from every trap
and protect you from deadly disease.

89:52 Amen. This verse was probably added later to conclude Book III of the Psalms on a note of praise.

Ps. 90 Several characteristics of God are highlighted in this psalm: a home (v. 1); creative (v. 2); eternal (v. 4); present (v. 8); angry at sin (vv. 7, 11); compassionate (v. 13); loving (v. 14); splendid (v. 16). Only this psalm is attributed to Moses, who wrote two other poems in the Pentateuch (Ex. 15; Deut. 32).

90:10 seventy . . . eighty. Human life is brief, and death is inevitable.

91:3 every trap. The trap depicted danger from any enemy. "Refuge" and "place of safety" (v. 2) present the opposite image for God, making it clear that security resides only in a right relationship with Him.

4 He will cover you with his feathers.
He will shelter you with his wings.
His faithful promises are your armor and protection.
5 Do not be afraid of the terrors of the night,
nor the arrow that flies in the day.
6 Do not dread the disease that stalks in darkness,
nor the disaster that strikes at midday.
7 Though a thousand fall at your side,
though ten thousand are dying around you,
these evils will not touch you.
8 Just open your eyes,
and see how the wicked are punished.

9 If you make the LORD your refuge,
if you make the Most High your shelter,
10 no evil will conquer you;
no plague will come near your home.
11 For he will order his angels
to protect you wherever you go.
12 They will hold you up with their hands
so you won't even hurt your foot on a stone.
13 You will trample upon lions and cobras;
you will crush fierce lions and serpents under your feet!

14 The LORD says, "I will rescue those who love me.
I will protect those who trust in my name.
15 When they call on me, I will answer;
I will be with them in trouble.
I will rescue and honor them.
16 I will reward them with a long life
and give them my salvation."

92 *A psalm. A song to be sung on the Sabbath Day.*

1 It is good to give thanks to the LORD,
to sing praises to the Most High.
2 It is good to proclaim your unfailing love in the morning,
your faithfulness in the evening,
3 accompanied by a ten-stringed instrument,
a harp,
and the melody of a lyre.

4 You thrill me, LORD, with all you have done for me!
I sing for joy because of what you have done.
5 O LORD, what great works you do!
And how deep are your thoughts.
6 Only a simpleton would not know,
and only a fool would not understand this:
7 Though the wicked sprout like weeds
and evildoers flourish,
they will be destroyed forever.
8 But you, O LORD, will be exalted forever.
9 Your enemies, LORD, will surely perish;
all evildoers will be scattered.
10 But you have made me as strong as a wild ox.
You have anointed me with the finest oil.
11 My eyes have seen the downfall of my enemies;
my ears have heard the defeat of my wicked opponents.
12 But the godly will flourish like palm trees
and grow strong like the cedars of Lebanon.
13 For they are transplanted to the LORD's own house.
They flourish in the courts of our God.
14 Even in old age they will still produce fruit;
they will remain vital and green.
15 They will declare, "The LORD is just!
He is my rock!
There is no evil in him!"

93

1 The LORD is king! He is robed in majesty.
Indeed, the LORD is robed in majesty and armed with strength.
The world stands firm
and cannot be shaken.

2 Your throne, O LORD, has stood from time immemorial.
You yourself are from the everlasting past.
3 The floods have risen up, O LORD.
The floods have roared like thunder;
the floods have lifted their pounding waves.
4 But mightier than the violent raging of the seas,
mightier than the breakers on the shore—
the LORD above is mightier than these!
5 Your royal laws cannot be changed.
Your reign, O LORD, is holy forever and ever.

94

1 O LORD, the God of vengeance,
O God of vengeance, let your glorious justice shine forth!
2 Arise, O Judge of the earth.
Give the proud what they deserve.
3 How long, O LORD?
How long will the wicked be allowed to gloat?
4 How long will they speak with arrogance?
How long will these evil people boast?
5 They crush your people, LORD,
hurting those you claim as your own.
6 They kill widows and foreigners
and murder orphans.
7 "The LORD isn't looking," they say,
"and besides, the God of Israel* doesn't care."

8 Think again, you fools!
When will you finally catch on?
9 Is he deaf—the one who made your ears?
Is he blind—the one who formed your eyes?

94:7 Hebrew *of Jacob*. See note on 44:4.

91:12 on a stone. God constantly watches over His people, sending angels to guard and protect them even from common mishaps. This does not mean believers won't ever have difficulties; instead, it reminds us of God's constant awareness and concern for us.
91:13 lions and cobras . . . fierce lions and serpents. Lions, cobras, and snakes are common in the Middle East and posed an unpredictable and deadly threat to people. God is not unaware of attack and can protect us.
Ps. 92 on the Sabbath day. Psalm 92 is a song to be sung at morning worship on the Sabbath. Every day of the week had a psalm designated for morning worship.
92:4-5 I sing for joy. God's works are worthy of being joyfully shouted to the whole world. These verses are more exclamations or shouts than mere words to recite.
92:12-13 palm trees . . . cedars. Palms were valued for their straightness and height. Cedars of Lebanon were magnificent trees that grew up to 120 feet tall and 40 feet in circumference. Supposedly there are cedars growing there today which are 2,000 years old.
93:1-2 The LORD . . . is robed. To help the people connect to an invisible God, He is pictured as wearing a robe and crown (see 47 and 95-99).
94:1 vengeance. Vengeance is God's privilege because only God is holy and wise enough to mete out true justice. (Deut. 32:35,41; Rom. 12:19; Heb. 10:30).

10 He punishes the nations—won't he also punish
you?
He knows everything—doesn't he also know
what you are doing?
11 The LORD knows people's thoughts;
he knows they are worthless!

12 Joyful are those you discipline, LORD,
those you teach with your instructions.
13 You give them relief from troubled times
until a pit is dug to capture the wicked.
14 The LORD will not reject his people;
he will not abandon his special possession.
15 Judgment will again be founded on justice,
and those with virtuous hearts will pursue it.

16 Who will protect me from the wicked?
Who will stand up for me against evildoers?
17 Unless the LORD had helped me,
I would soon have settled in the silence of the
grave.
18 I cried out, "I am slipping!"
but your unfailing love, O LORD, supported me.
19 When doubts filled my mind,
your comfort gave me renewed hope and cheer.

20 Can unjust leaders claim that God is on their
side—
leaders whose decrees permit injustice?
21 They gang up against the righteous
and condemn the innocent to death.
22 But the LORD is my fortress;
my God is the mighty rock where I hide.
23 God will turn the sins of evil people back on
them.
He will destroy them for their sins.
The LORD our God will destroy them.

95 1 Come, let us sing to the LORD!
Let us shout joyfully to the Rock of our
salvation.
2 Let us come to him with thanksgiving.
Let us sing psalms of praise to him.
3 For the LORD is a great God,
a great King above all gods.
4 He holds in his hands the depths of the earth
and the mightiest mountains.
5 The sea belongs to him, for he made it.
His hands formed the dry land, too.

6 Come, let us worship and bow down.
Let us kneel before the LORD our maker,
7 for he is our God.
We are the people he watches over,
the flock under his care.

If only you would listen to his voice today!
8 The LORD says, "Don't harden your hearts as Israel
did at Meribah,
as they did at Massah in the wilderness.
9 For there your ancestors tested and tried my
patience,
even though they saw everything I did.
10 For forty years I was angry with them, and I said,
'They are a people whose hearts turn away from
me.
They refuse to do what I tell them.'
11 So in my anger I took an oath:
'They will never enter my place of rest.'"

96 1 Sing a new song to the LORD!
Let the whole earth sing to the LORD!
2 Sing to the LORD; praise his name.
Each day proclaim the good news that he saves.
3 Publish his glorious deeds among the nations.
Tell everyone about the amazing things he does.
4 Great is the LORD! He is most worthy of praise!
He is to be feared above all gods.
5 The gods of other nations are mere idols,
but the LORD made the heavens!
6 Honor and majesty surround him;
strength and beauty fill his sanctuary.

7 O nations of the world, recognize the LORD;
recognize that the LORD is glorious and strong.
8 Give to the LORD the glory he deserves!
Bring your offering and come into his courts.
9 Worship the LORD in all his holy splendor.
Let all the earth tremble before him.
10 Tell all the nations, "The LORD reigns!"
The world stands firm and cannot be shaken.
He will judge all peoples fairly.

11 Let the heavens be glad, and the earth rejoice!
Let the sea and everything in it shout his
praise!
12 Let the fields and their crops burst out with joy!
Let the trees of the forest sing for joy
13 before the LORD, for he is coming!
He is coming to judge the earth.
He will judge the world with justice,
and the nations with his truth.

97 1 The LORD is king!
Let the earth rejoice!
Let the farthest coastlands be glad.
2 Dark clouds surround him.
Righteousness and justice are the foundation of
his throne.
3 Fire spreads ahead of him
and burns up all his foes.
4 His lightning flashes out across the world.
The earth sees and trembles.
5 The mountains melt like wax before the LORD,
before the Lord of all the earth.
6 The heavens proclaim his righteousness;
every nation sees his glory.
7 Those who worship idols are disgraced—
all who brag about their worthless gods—
for every god must bow to him.

94:12-15 discipline . . . teach. Our entire lives are to be spent learning the ways of God.
95:3-5 in his hands. God holds all of creation in His hand. Many ancient religions had gods that ruled over various aspects of creation (the sea, fire, the skies).
95:6-11 worship. True worship of God involves obedience.
95:8 Meribah . . . Massah. The psalmist reminds the readers of their ancestors' disobedience against God. After all the miracles in Egypt, the people complained. At Meribah and Massah, God told Moses to strike a rock with his staff and give water to the people (Ex. 17:1-7).
95:10 forty years. The people's lack of faith in God was evident throughout the travels to the promised land. They feared and rebelled (Num. 14:1-38) until God was so angry that He sent them to wander forty years in the desert.
97:1 coastlands. The Lord reigns not just in the land of Israel but beyond.
97:3 Fire. Fire may represent destruction of enemies, but it can also be a refining and cleansing agent.

[8] Jerusalem* has heard and rejoiced,
and all the towns of Judah are glad
because of your justice, O LORD!
[9] For you, O LORD, are supreme over all the earth;
you are exalted far above all gods.

[10] You who love the LORD, hate evil!
He protects the lives of his godly people
and rescues them from the power of the wicked.
[11] Light shines on the godly,
and joy on those whose hearts are right.
[12] May all who are godly rejoice in the LORD
and praise his holy name!

98 *A psalm.*

[1] Sing a new song to the LORD,
for he has done wonderful deeds.
His right hand has won a mighty victory;
his holy arm has shown his saving power!
[2] The LORD has announced his victory
and has revealed his righteousness to every nation!
[3] He has remembered his promise to love and be faithful to Israel.
The ends of the earth have seen the victory of our God.

[4] Shout to the LORD, all the earth;
break out in praise and sing for joy!
[5] Sing your praise to the LORD with the harp,
with the harp and melodious song,
[6] with trumpets and the sound of the ram's horn.
Make a joyful symphony before the LORD, the King!

[7] Let the sea and everything in it shout his praise!
Let the earth and all living things join in.
[8] Let the rivers clap their hands in glee!
Let the hills sing out their songs of joy
[9] before the LORD,
for he is coming to judge the earth.
He will judge the world with justice,
and the nations with fairness.

99

[1] The LORD is king!
Let the nations tremble!
He sits on his throne between the cherubim.
Let the whole earth quake!
[2] The LORD sits in majesty in Jerusalem,*
exalted above all the nations.
[3] Let them praise your great and awesome name.
Your name is holy!
[4] Mighty King, lover of justice,
you have established fairness.
You have acted with justice
and righteousness throughout Israel.*
[5] Exalt the LORD our God!
Bow low before his feet, for he is holy!

[6] Moses and Aaron were among his priests;
Samuel also called on his name.
They cried to the LORD for help,
and he answered them.
[7] He spoke to Israel from the pillar of cloud,
and they followed the laws and decrees he gave them.
[8] O LORD our God, you answered them.
You were a forgiving God to them,
but you punished them when they went wrong.

[9] Exalt the LORD our God,
and worship at his holy mountain in Jerusalem,
for the LORD our God is holy!

100 *A psalm of thanksgiving.*

[1] Shout with joy to the LORD, all the earth!
[2] Worship the LORD with gladness.
Come before him, singing with joy.
[3] Acknowledge that the LORD is God!
He made us, and we are his.*
We are his people, the sheep of his pasture.
[4] Enter his gates with thanksgiving;
go into his courts with praise.
Give thanks to him and praise his name.
[5] For the LORD is good.
His unfailing love continues forever,
and his faithfulness continues to each generation.

101 *A psalm of David.*

[1] I will sing of your love and justice, LORD.
I will praise you with songs.
[2] I will be careful to live a blameless life—
when will you come to help me?
I will lead a life of integrity
in my own home.
[3] I will refuse to look at
anything vile and vulgar.
I hate all who deal crookedly;
I will have nothing to do with them.
[4] I will reject perverse ideas
and stay away from every evil.
[5] I will not tolerate people who slander their neighbors.
I will not endure conceit and pride.

97:8 Hebrew *Zion.* **99:2** Hebrew *Zion.* **99:4** Hebrew *Jacob.* See note on 44:4. **100:3** As in an alternate reading in the Masoretic Text; the other alternate and some ancient versions read *and not we ourselves.*

97:8-12 Jerusalem. They will rejoice when God is exalted there.
98:9 judge the earth. For God's people, the day when He judges will not bring sorrow. It will be a day of rejoicing because He will judge in righteousness and fairness.
99:6 Moses . . . Aaron . . . Samuel. These three men had served as priests to the nation of Israel. Moses served as the first priest, anointing Aaron to serve as Israel's high priest (Ex. 24:1-7; 28:1). Samuel was both a priest and a prophet who served Israel during a time when they had no strong leaders (1 Sam. 7:2-17).
99:7 pillar of cloud. This image recalls the desert when God led His people with a pillar of cloud by day and a pillar of fire by night. God's presence was in the cloud, and He spoke to Moses (Ex. 33:9) and Aaron (Num. 12:5-6).
100:1 all the earth. The psalmist sends out a call to pagan nations to acknowledge God as the supreme God.
101:2-5 life of integrity. David understood that obedience is a matter of the heart, so he carefully guarded his heart from sin. Old Testament believers understood sinful actions to result from following their hearts (inward compulsion) or eyes (external influences). (See Num. 15:39; Job 31:7; Prov. 21:4.)
101:5-8 David made seven pledges: to be loyal to God's way; to stop people from speaking evil behind backs; to have peace reign in the court; to encourage stability in the community; to encourage godliness; to not tolerate deceit; and to convene court first thing every morning.

6 I will search for faithful people
to be my companions.
Only those who are above reproach
will be allowed to serve me.
7 I will not allow deceivers to serve in my house,
and liars will not stay in my presence.
8 My daily task will be to ferret out the wicked
and free the city of the LORD from their grip.

102 *A prayer of one overwhelmed with trouble, pouring out problems before the Lord.*

1 LORD, hear my prayer!
Listen to my plea!
2 Don't turn away from me
in my time of distress.
Bend down to listen,
and answer me quickly when I call to you.
3 For my days disappear like smoke,
and my bones burn like red-hot coals.
4 My heart is sick, withered like grass,
and I have lost my appetite.
5 Because of my groaning,
I am reduced to skin and bones.
6 I am like an owl in the desert,
like a little owl in a far-off wilderness.
7 I lie awake,
lonely as a solitary bird on the roof.
8 My enemies taunt me day after day.
They mock and curse me.
9 I eat ashes for food.
My tears run down into my drink
10 because of your anger and wrath.
For you have picked me up and thrown me out.
11 My life passes as swiftly as the evening shadows.
I am withering away like grass.

12 But you, O LORD, will sit on your throne forever.
Your fame will endure to every generation.
13 You will arise and have mercy on Jerusalem*—
and now is the time to pity her,
now is the time you promised to help.
14 For your people love every stone in her walls
and cherish even the dust in her streets.
15 Then the nations will tremble before the LORD.
The kings of the earth will tremble before his
glory.
16 For the LORD will rebuild Jerusalem.
He will appear in his glory.
17 He will listen to the prayers of the destitute.
He will not reject their pleas.

18 Let this be recorded for future generations,
so that a people not yet born will praise the LORD.
19 Tell them the LORD looked down
from his heavenly sanctuary.
He looked down to earth from heaven
20 to hear the groans of the prisoners,
to release those condemned to die.
21 And so the LORD's fame will be celebrated in Zion,
his praises in Jerusalem,
22 when multitudes gather together
and kingdoms come to worship the LORD.

23 He broke my strength in midlife,
cutting short my days.
24 But I cried to him, "O my God, who lives forever,
don't take my life while I am so young!
25 Long ago you laid the foundation of the earth
and made the heavens with your hands.
26 They will perish, but you remain forever;
they will wear out like old clothing.
You will change them like a garment
and discard them.
27 But you are always the same;
you will live forever.
28 The children of your people
will live in security.
Their children's children
will thrive in your presence."

103 *A psalm of David.*

1 Let all that I am praise the LORD;
with my whole heart, I will praise his holy
name.
2 Let all that I am praise the LORD;
may I never forget the good things he does for
me.
3 He forgives all my sins
and heals all my diseases.
4 He redeems me from death
and crowns me with love and tender mercies.
5 He fills my life with good things.
My youth is renewed like the eagle's!

6 The LORD gives righteousness
and justice to all who are treated unfairly.
7 He revealed his character to Moses
and his deeds to the people of Israel.
8 The LORD is compassionate and merciful,
slow to get angry and filled with unfailing love.
9 He will not constantly accuse us,
nor remain angry forever.
10 He does not punish us for all our sins;
he does not deal harshly with us, as we deserve.
11 For his unfailing love toward those who fear him
is as great as the height of the heavens above
the earth.
12 He has removed our sins as far from us
as the east is from the west.
13 The LORD is like a father to his children,
tender and compassionate to those who fear him.
14 For he knows how weak we are;
he remembers we are only dust.
15 Our days on earth are like grass;
like wildflowers, we bloom and die.
16 The wind blows, and we are gone—
as though we had never been here.
17 But the love of the LORD remains forever
with those who fear him.

102:13 Hebrew *Zion;* also in 102:16.

102:14 love every stone in her walls. Jerusalem (Zion) symbolized the nation's prosperity and relationship with God (2 Sam. 5:6-12; Ps. 48).

103:10-12 as the east is from the west. So great is God's grace that when He forgives, He also forgets our sins.

103:17 forever. God's love is infinite; it extends beyond our finite lives across all generations and into eternity.

His salvation extends to the children's children
18 of those who are faithful to his covenant,
of those who obey his commandments!

19 The LORD has made the heavens his throne;
from there he rules over everything.

20 Praise the LORD, you angels,
you mighty ones who carry out his plans,
listening for each of his commands.
21 Yes, praise the LORD, you armies of angels
who serve him and do his will!
22 Praise the LORD, everything he has created,
everything in all his kingdom.

Let all that I am praise the LORD.

104

1 Let all that I am praise the LORD.

O LORD my God, how great you are!
You are robed with honor and majesty.
2 You are dressed in a robe of light.
You stretch out the starry curtain of the heavens;
3 you lay out the rafters of your home in the rain
clouds.
You make the clouds your chariot;
you ride upon the wings of the wind.
4 The winds are your messengers;
flames of fire are your servants.*

5 You placed the world on its foundation
so it would never be moved.
6 You clothed the earth with floods of water,
water that covered even the mountains.
7 At your command, the water fled;
at the sound of your thunder, it hurried away.
8 Mountains rose and valleys sank
to the levels you decreed.
9 Then you set a firm boundary for the seas,
so they would never again cover the earth.

10 You make springs pour water into the ravines,
so streams gush down from the mountains.
11 They provide water for all the animals,
and the wild donkeys quench their thirst.
12 The birds nest beside the streams
and sing among the branches of the trees.
13 You send rain on the mountains from your
heavenly home,
and you fill the earth with the fruit of your
labor.
14 You cause grass to grow for the livestock
and plants for people to use.
You allow them to produce food from the earth—
15 wine to make them glad,
olive oil to soothe their skin,
and bread to give them strength.
16 The trees of the LORD are well cared for—
the cedars of Lebanon that he planted.
17 There the birds make their nests,
and the storks make their homes in the
cypresses.
18 High in the mountains live the wild goats,
and the rocks form a refuge for the hyraxes.*

19 You made the moon to mark the seasons,
and the sun knows when to set.
20 You send the darkness, and it becomes night,
when all the forest animals prowl about.
21 Then the young lions roar for their prey,
stalking the food provided by God.
22 At dawn they slink back
into their dens to rest.
23 Then people go off to their work,
where they labor until evening.

24 O LORD, what a variety of things you have
made!
In wisdom you have made them all.
The earth is full of your creatures.
25 Here is the ocean, vast and wide,
teeming with life of every kind,
both large and small.
26 See the ships sailing along,
and Leviathan,* which you made to play in the
sea.

27 They all depend on you
to give them food as they need it.
28 When you supply it, they gather it.
You open your hand to feed them,
and they are richly satisfied.
29 But if you turn away from them, they panic.
When you take away their breath,
they die and turn again to dust.
30 When you give them your breath,* life is created,
and you renew the face of the earth.

31 May the glory of the LORD continue forever!
The LORD takes pleasure in all he has made!
32 The earth trembles at his glance;
the mountains smoke at his touch.

33 I will sing to the LORD as long as I live.
I will praise my God to my last breath!
34 May all my thoughts be pleasing to him,
for I rejoice in the LORD.
35 Let all sinners vanish from the face of the
earth;
let the wicked disappear forever.

Let all that I am praise the LORD.

Praise the LORD!

104:4 Greek version reads *He sends his angels like the winds, / his servants like flames of fire.* Compare Heb 1:7. **104:18** Or *coneys*, or *rock badgers.* **104:26** The identification of Leviathan is disputed, ranging from an earthly creature to a mythical sea monster in ancient literature. **104:30** Or *When you send your Spirit.*

104:2 light. The reference to light pictures that first day of creation when God said, "Let there be light" (Gen. 1:3). The stretching out of the heavens pictures that second day of creation when God separated the sky from the water (Gen. 1:6-8).

104:9 set a firm boundary. God set in place boundaries for the waters so that they would never again flood the earth (see Genesis 9:15).

104:14-15 food . . . wine . . . bread. God's extravagant blessings are illustrated by grapes to make wine, olives to make the oil, and grain to make bread—all of which make His people glow with health.

104:31 glory of the LORD. Here glory refers to all of creation. God's glory is visible in His creation.

104:35 wicked . . . disappear forever. Creation, for all its beauty, has been marred by sin. The writer longs for the day when all sin will vanish from the earth.

105 1 Give thanks to the LORD and proclaim his greatness.
Let the whole world know what he has done.
2 Sing to him; yes, sing his praises.
Tell everyone about his wonderful deeds.
3 Exult in his holy name;
rejoice, you who worship the LORD.
4 Search for the LORD and for his strength;
continually seek him.
5 Remember the wonders he has performed,
his miracles, and the rulings he has given,
6 you children of his servant Abraham,
you descendants of Jacob, his chosen ones.

7 He is the LORD our God.
His justice is seen throughout the land.
8 He always stands by his covenant—
the commitment he made to a thousand generations.
9 This is the covenant he made with Abraham
and the oath he swore to Isaac.
10 He confirmed it to Jacob as a decree,
and to the people of Israel as a never-ending covenant:
11 "I will give you the land of Canaan
as your special possession."

12 He said this when they were few in number,
a tiny group of strangers in Canaan.
13 They wandered from nation to nation,
from one kingdom to another.
14 Yet he did not let anyone oppress them.
He warned kings on their behalf:
15 "Do not touch my chosen people,
and do not hurt my prophets."

16 He called for a famine on the land of Canaan,
cutting off its food supply.
17 Then he sent someone to Egypt ahead of them—
Joseph, who was sold as a slave.
18 They bruised his feet with fetters
and placed his neck in an iron collar.
19 Until the time came to fulfill his dreams,*
the LORD tested Joseph's character.
20 Then Pharaoh sent for him and set him free;
the ruler of the nation opened his prison door.
21 Joseph was put in charge of all the king's household;
he became ruler over all the king's possessions.
22 He could instruct* the king's aides as he pleased
and teach the king's advisers.

23 Then Israel arrived in Egypt;
Jacob lived as a foreigner in the land of Ham.
24 And the LORD multiplied the people of Israel
until they became too mighty for their enemies.
25 Then he turned the Egyptians against the Israelites,
and they plotted against the LORD's servants.

26 But the LORD sent his servant Moses,
along with Aaron, whom he had chosen.
27 They performed miraculous signs among the Egyptians,
and wonders in the land of Ham.
28 The LORD blanketed Egypt in darkness,
for they had defied* his commands to let his people go.
29 He turned their water into blood,
poisoning all the fish.
30 Then frogs overran the land
and even invaded the king's bedrooms.
31 When the LORD spoke, flies descended on the Egyptians,
and gnats swarmed across Egypt.
32 He sent them hail instead of rain,
and lightning flashed over the land.
33 He ruined their grapevines and fig trees
and shattered all the trees.
34 He spoke, and hordes of locusts came—
young locusts beyond number.
35 They ate up everything green in the land,
destroying all the crops in their fields.
36 Then he killed the oldest son in each Egyptian home,
the pride and joy of each family.

37 The LORD brought his people out of Egypt, loaded with silver and gold;
and not one among the tribes of Israel even stumbled.
38 Egypt was glad when they were gone,
for they feared them greatly.
39 The LORD spread a cloud above them as a covering
and gave them a great fire to light the darkness.
40 They asked for meat, and he sent them quail;
he satisfied their hunger with manna—bread from heaven.
41 He split open a rock, and water gushed out
to form a river through the dry wasteland.
42 For he remembered his sacred promise
to his servant Abraham.
43 So he brought his people out of Egypt with joy,
his chosen ones with rejoicing.
44 He gave his people the lands of pagan nations,
and they harvested crops that others had planted.
45 All this happened so they would follow his decrees
and obey his instructions.

Praise the LORD!

105:19 Hebrew *his word.* **105:22** As in Greek and Syriac versions; Hebrew reads *bind* or *imprison.* **105:28** As in Greek and Syriac versions; Hebrew reads *had not defied.*

Ps. 105 Remember . . . wonders . . . miracles. This psalm was composed by David (1 Chron. 16:7) to sing at one of the festivals. The first 15 verses of the psalm are the same as the song recorded in 1 Chronicles 16:8-22. The entire psalm rehearses Israel's history, giving thanks to the Lord for all he has done on the nation's behalf. (See also 78; 106.)
105:8-11 covenant. God's covenant with Abraham is recorded in Genesis 15:9-21. This covenant promised that Abraham would receive the land of Canaan, which Israel possessed at the time this psalm was written.
105:12-41 my chosen people. This section of the psalm describes God's fulfillment of His covenant to Abraham—from the days of the patriarchs, who were nomads in the land, to the days of God's protection of the people through the leadership of Moses. God never failed to keep His covenant promises.
105:25 he turned the Egyptians against. This is probably a reference to Pharaoh, whose heart God hardened so that he would not let the people go (Ex. 4:21). This allowed God to show the Egyptians His powerful signs and wonders on behalf of His enslaved people.
105:45 decrees. This is from the same Hebrew word translated "decree" in verse 10. God's work of redeeming the Israelites through fulfilling His covenant promises was also to teach them to love Him and conform their lives to His will.

106

[1] Praise the LORD!
Give thanks to the LORD, for he is good!
His faithful love endures forever.
[2] Who can list the glorious miracles of the LORD?
Who can ever praise him enough?
[3] There is joy for those who deal justly with others
and always do what is right.

[4] Remember me, LORD, when you show favor to your people;
come near and rescue me.
[5] Let me share in the prosperity of your chosen ones.
Let me rejoice in the joy of your people;
let me praise you with those who are your heritage.

[6] Like our ancestors, we have sinned.
We have done wrong! We have acted wickedly!
[7] Our ancestors in Egypt
were not impressed by the LORD's miraculous deeds.
They soon forgot his many acts of kindness to them.
Instead, they rebelled against him at the Red Sea.*
[8] Even so, he saved them—
to defend the honor of his name
and to demonstrate his mighty power.
[9] He commanded the Red Sea* to dry up.
He led Israel across the sea as if it were a desert.
[10] So he rescued them from their enemies
and redeemed them from their foes.
[11] Then the water returned and covered their enemies;
not one of them survived.
[12] Then his people believed his promises.
Then they sang his praise.

[13] Yet how quickly they forgot what he had done!
They wouldn't wait for his counsel!
[14] In the wilderness their desires ran wild,
testing God's patience in that dry wasteland.
[15] So he gave them what they asked for,
but he sent a plague along with it.
[16] The people in the camp were jealous of Moses
and envious of Aaron, the LORD's holy priest.
[17] Because of this, the earth opened up;
it swallowed Dathan
and buried Abiram and the other rebels.
[18] Fire fell upon their followers;
a flame consumed the wicked.

[19] The people made a calf at Mount Sinai*;
they bowed before an image made of gold.
[20] They traded their glorious God
for a statue of a grass-eating bull.
[21] They forgot God, their savior,
who had done such great things in Egypt—
[22] such wonderful things in the land of Ham,
such awesome deeds at the Red Sea.
[23] So he declared he would destroy them.
But Moses, his chosen one, stepped between the LORD and the people.
He begged him to turn from his anger and not destroy them.

[24] The people refused to enter the pleasant land,
for they wouldn't believe his promise to care for them.
[25] Instead, they grumbled in their tents
and refused to obey the LORD.
[26] Therefore, he solemnly swore
that he would kill them in the wilderness,
[27] that he would scatter their descendants* among the nations,
exiling them to distant lands.

[28] Then our ancestors joined in the worship of Baal at Peor;
they even ate sacrifices offered to the dead!
[29] They angered the LORD with all these things,
so a plague broke out among them.
[30] But Phinehas had the courage to intervene,
and the plague was stopped.
[31] So he has been regarded as a righteous man
ever since that time.

[32] At Meribah, too, they angered the LORD,
causing Moses serious trouble.
[33] They made Moses angry,*
and he spoke foolishly.

[34] Israel failed to destroy the nations in the land,
as the LORD had commanded them.
[35] Instead, they mingled among the pagans
and adopted their evil customs.
[36] They worshiped their idols,
which led to their downfall.
[37] They even sacrificed their sons
and their daughters to the demons.
[38] They shed innocent blood,
the blood of their sons and daughters.
By sacrificing them to the idols of Canaan,
they polluted the land with murder.
[39] They defiled themselves by their evil deeds,
and their love of idols was adultery in the LORD's sight.

[40] That is why the LORD's anger burned against his people,
and he abhorred his own special possession.
[41] He handed them over to pagan nations,
and they were ruled by those who hated them.
[42] Their enemies crushed them
and brought them under their cruel power.

106:7 Hebrew *at the sea, the sea of reeds.* **106:9** Hebrew *sea of reeds;* also in 106:22. **106:19** Hebrew *at Horeb,* another name for Sinai. **106:27** As in Syriac version; Hebrew reads *he would cause their descendants to fall.* **106:33** Hebrew *They embittered his spirit.*

106:6-43 The previous psalm focused on God's great works on behalf of Israel; this psalm chronicles Israel's history of rebellion that occurred despite God's care for the nation.
106:13 wait for his counsel. Not long after Israel had experienced deliverance from Egypt at the Red Sea, the people began to complain against God. They did not wait for God's "counsel" (His divine plan and power) but gave in to fear and rebelled.
106:34-39 worshiped their idols. Rebellion took the form of idol worship and even child-sacrifice to Canaanite gods. Ultimately, worshipping other gods (breaking the first commandment and God's heart) resulted in exile.
106:40-43 the LORD's anger burned. Because of their constant idol worship, God caused the Babylonians to overpower them. Eventually they were exiled to Babylon, who destroyed their temple and cities and took the people into captivity.

[43] Again and again he rescued them,
but they chose to rebel against him,
and they were finally destroyed by their sin.
[44] Even so, he pitied them in their distress
and listened to their cries.
[45] He remembered his covenant with them
and relented because of his unfailing love.
[46] He even caused their captors
to treat them with kindness.

[47] Save us, O LORD our God!
Gather us back from among the nations,
so we can thank your holy name
and rejoice and praise you.

[48] Praise the LORD, the God of Israel,
who lives from everlasting to everlasting!
Let all the people say, "Amen!"

Praise the LORD!

BOOK FIVE (107–150)

107

[1] Give thanks to the LORD, for he is good!
His faithful love endures forever.
[2] Has the LORD redeemed you? Then speak out!
Tell others he has redeemed you from your enemies.
[3] For he has gathered the exiles from many lands,
from east and west,
from north and south.*

[4] Some wandered in the wilderness,
lost and homeless.
[5] Hungry and thirsty,
they nearly died.
[6] "LORD, help!" they cried in their trouble,
and he rescued them from their distress.
[7] He led them straight to safety,
to a city where they could live.
[8] Let them praise the LORD for his great love
and for the wonderful things he has done for them.
[9] For he satisfies the thirsty
and fills the hungry with good things.

[10] Some sat in darkness and deepest gloom,
imprisoned in iron chains of misery.
[11] They rebelled against the words of God,
scorning the counsel of the Most High.
[12] That is why he broke them with hard labor;
they fell, and no one was there to help them.
[13] "LORD, help!" they cried in their trouble,
and he saved them from their distress.
[14] He led them from the darkness and deepest gloom;
he snapped their chains.
[15] Let them praise the LORD for his great love
and for the wonderful things he has done for them.
[16] For he broke down their prison gates of bronze;
he cut apart their bars of iron.

[17] Some were fools; they rebelled
and suffered for their sins.
[18] They couldn't stand the thought of food,
and they were knocking on death's door.
[19] "LORD, help!" they cried in their trouble,
and he saved them from their distress.
[20] He sent out his word and healed them,
snatching them from the door of death.
[21] Let them praise the LORD for his great love
and for the wonderful things he has done for them.
[22] Let them offer sacrifices of thanksgiving
and sing joyfully about his glorious acts.

[23] Some went off to sea in ships,
plying the trade routes of the world.
[24] They, too, observed the LORD's power in action,
his impressive works on the deepest seas.
[25] He spoke, and the winds rose,
stirring up the waves.
[26] Their ships were tossed to the heavens
and plunged again to the depths;
the sailors cringed in terror.
[27] They reeled and staggered like drunkards
and were at their wits' end.
[28] "LORD, help!" they cried in their trouble,
and he saved them from their distress.
[29] He calmed the storm to a whisper
and stilled the waves.
[30] What a blessing was that stillness
as he brought them safely into harbor!
[31] Let them praise the LORD for his great love
and for the wonderful things he has done for them.
[32] Let them exalt him publicly before the congregation
and before the leaders of the nation.

[33] He changes rivers into deserts,
and springs of water into dry, thirsty land.
[34] He turns the fruitful land into salty wastelands,
because of the wickedness of those who live there.
[35] But he also turns deserts into pools of water,
the dry land into springs of water.
[36] He brings the hungry to settle there
and to build their cities.
[37] They sow their fields, plant their vineyards,
and harvest their bumper crops.
[38] How he blesses them!
They raise large families there,
and their herds of livestock increase.

[39] When they decrease in number and become impoverished
through oppression, trouble, and sorrow,

107:3 Hebrew *and sea.*

107:3 has gathered the exiles. The writer rejoices in Israel's return from the Babylonian Exile. The people who had been dispersed were gathered and returned to rebuild the land, the city of Jerusalem, and the temple (Ezra 2; Neh. 1:8-9; Isa. 11:12; 43:5-6).

107:24 his impressive works on the deepest seas. Probably the Mediterranean Sea.

107:33-42 thirsty land . . . fruitful land. The Lord sometimes disciplined His wayward people by causing drought (v. 34). When the people repented, He restored the land and made it prosperous so that it would yield a crop (v. 37). Repeatedly, sin led to judgment, and God would discipline the people through oppression, calamity, and sorrow (v. 39), through powerful enemy armies that destroyed the land and cities, and through deportation.

40 the LORD pours contempt on their princes,
causing them to wander in trackless wastelands.
41 But he rescues the poor from trouble
and increases their families like flocks of sheep.
42 The godly will see these things and be glad,
while the wicked are struck silent.
43 Those who are wise will take all this to heart;
they will see in our history the faithful love of the LORD.

108 *A song. A psalm of David.*

1 My heart is confident in you, O God;
no wonder I can sing your praises with all my heart!
2 Wake up, lyre and harp!
I will wake the dawn with my song.
3 I will thank you, LORD, among all the people.
I will sing your praises among the nations.
4 For your unfailing love is higher than the heavens.
Your faithfulness reaches to the clouds.
5 Be exalted, O God, above the highest heavens.
May your glory shine over all the earth.

6 Now rescue your beloved people.
Answer and save us by your power.
7 God has promised this by his holiness*:
"I will divide up Shechem with joy.
I will measure out the valley of Succoth.
8 Gilead is mine,
and Manasseh, too.
Ephraim, my helmet, will produce my warriors,
and Judah, my scepter, will produce my kings.
9 But Moab, my washbasin, will become my servant,
and I will wipe my feet on Edom
and shout in triumph over Philistia."

10 Who will bring me into the fortified city?
Who will bring me victory over Edom?
11 Have you rejected us, O God?
Will you no longer march with our armies?
12 Oh, please help us against our enemies,
for all human help is useless.
13 With God's help we will do mighty things,
for he will trample down our foes.

109 *For the choir director: A psalm of David.*

1 O God, whom I praise,
don't stand silent and aloof
2 while the wicked slander me
and tell lies about me.
3 They surround me with hateful words
and fight against me for no reason.
4 I love them, but they try to destroy me with accusations
even as I am praying for them!
5 They repay evil for good,
and hatred for my love.

6 They say,* "Get an evil person to turn against him.
Send an accuser to bring him to trial.
7 When his case comes up for judgment,
let him be pronounced guilty.
Count his prayers as sins.
8 Let his years be few;
let someone else take his position.
9 May his children become fatherless,
and his wife a widow.
10 May his children wander as beggars
and be driven from* their ruined homes.
11 May creditors seize his entire estate,
and strangers take all he has earned.
12 Let no one be kind to him;
let no one pity his fatherless children.
13 May all his offspring die.
May his family name be blotted out in the next generation.
14 May the LORD never forget the sins of his fathers;
may his mother's sins never be erased from the record.
15 May the LORD always remember these sins,
and may his name disappear from human memory.
16 For he refused all kindness to others;
he persecuted the poor and needy,
and he hounded the brokenhearted to death.
17 He loved to curse others;
now you curse him.
He never blessed others;
now don't you bless him.
18 Cursing is as natural to him as his clothing,
or the water he drinks,
or the rich food he eats.
19 Now may his curses return and cling to him like clothing;
may they be tied around him like a belt."

20 May those curses become the LORD's punishment
for my accusers who speak evil of me.
21 But deal well with me, O Sovereign LORD,
for the sake of your own reputation!
Rescue me
because you are so faithful and good.
22 For I am poor and needy,
and my heart is full of pain.
23 I am fading like a shadow at dusk;
I am brushed off like a locust.
24 My knees are weak from fasting,
and I am skin and bones.

108:7 Or *in his sanctuary.* **109:6** Hebrew lacks *They say.* **109:10** As in Greek version; Hebrew reads *and seek.*

107:40 princes. The corruption of Israel's leaders led to the downfall of both the northern and southern kingdoms (2 Kings 17:1-18; 24:18-20).

Ps. 108 The psalmist praises God for love and faithfulness and then prays for God to deliver His people from their enemies. The psalm combines sections from other psalms (57:7-11; 60:5-12).

108:1-5 higher than the heavens. God's love toward His people is not just for earth but reaches the heavens—spanning life and eternity (v. 4).

109:4 I am praying. David begins by praising God and cursing his "enemies." Scholars debate whether the enemies were real persons or enemies within himself. Imprecatory psalms make for difficult reading as we have the benefit of Jesus' teaching to love our enemies. But David's curses are generally offered on behalf of God's reputation.

109:14-15 sins of his fathers. The Old Testament placed the guilt for sin not only on the sinner but also on all his or her family and possessions (Josh. 7:24). Punishment was often extended to the family (Ex. 20:5).

109:17-18 curse. This referred not to swearing but to pronouncements of evil upon someone. David asks that his enemy's curses would return on his enemy's own head.

25 I am a joke to people everywhere;
when they see me, they shake their heads in scorn.
26 Help me, O LORD my God!
Save me because of your unfailing love.
27 Let them see that this is your doing,
that you yourself have done it, LORD.
28 Then let them curse me if they like,
but you will bless me!
When they attack me, they will be disgraced!
But I, your servant, will go right on rejoicing!
29 May my accusers be clothed with disgrace;
may their humiliation cover them like a cloak.
30 But I will give repeated thanks to the LORD,
praising him to everyone.
31 For he stands beside the needy,
ready to save them from those who condemn
them.

110 *A psalm of David.*

1 The LORD said to my Lord,*
"Sit in the place of honor at my right hand
until I humble your enemies,
making them a footstool under your feet."
2 The LORD will extend your powerful kingdom
from Jerusalem*;
you will rule over your enemies.
3 When you go to war,
your people will serve you willingly.
You are arrayed in holy garments,
and your strength will be renewed each day
like the morning dew.

4 The LORD has taken an oath and will not break his
vow:
"You are a priest forever in the order of
Melchizedek."

5 The Lord stands at your right hand to protect you.
He will strike down many kings when his anger
erupts.
6 He will punish the nations
and fill their lands with corpses;
he will shatter heads over the whole earth.
7 But he himself will be refreshed from brooks
along the way.
He will be victorious.

111 * 1 Praise the LORD!

I will thank the LORD with all my heart
as I meet with his godly people.
2 How amazing are the deeds of the LORD!
All who delight in him should ponder them.
3 Everything he does reveals his glory and majesty.
His righteousness never fails.
4 He causes us to remember his wonderful works.
How gracious and merciful is our LORD!
5 He gives food to those who fear him;
he always remembers his covenant.
6 He has shown his great power to his people
by giving them the lands of other nations.
7 All he does is just and good,
and all his commandments are trustworthy.
8 They are forever true,
to be obeyed faithfully and with integrity.
9 He has paid a full ransom for his people.
He has guaranteed his covenant with them
forever.
What a holy, awe-inspiring name he has!
10 Fear of the LORD is the foundation of true wisdom.
All who obey his commandments will grow in
wisdom.

Praise him forever!

112 * 1 Praise the LORD!

How joyful are those who fear the LORD
and delight in obeying his commands.
2 Their children will be successful everywhere;
an entire generation of godly people will be
blessed.
3 They themselves will be wealthy,
and their good deeds will last forever.
4 Light shines in the darkness for the godly.
They are generous, compassionate, and
righteous.
5 Good comes to those who lend money generously
and conduct their business fairly.
6 Such people will not be overcome by evil.
Those who are righteous will be long
remembered.
7 They do not fear bad news;
they confidently trust the LORD to care for
them.
8 They are confident and fearless
and can face their foes triumphantly.
9 They share freely and give generously to those in
need.
Their good deeds will be remembered forever.
They will have influence and honor.
10 The wicked will see this and be infuriated.
They will grind their teeth in anger;
they will slink away, their hopes thwarted.

113 1 Praise the LORD!

Yes, give praise, O servants of the LORD.
Praise the name of the LORD!
2 Blessed be the name of the LORD
now and forever.
3 Everywhere—from east to west—
praise the name of the LORD.

110:1 Or *my lord.* **110:2** Hebrew *Zion.* **111** This psalm is a Hebrew acrostic poem; after the introductory note of praise, each line begins with a successive letter of the Hebrew alphabet. **112** This psalm is a Hebrew acrostic poem; after the introductory note of praise, each line begins with a successive letter of the Hebrew alphabet.

Ps. 110 This psalm, written by David, is a prophetic picture of the coming Messiah (King). Verses 1 and 4 are quoted in the New Testament as referring to Jesus Christ (Matt. 22:41-46; Mark 12:35-37; Luke 20:41-44; Heb. 1:13; 5:6; 7:11-28).

111:2 Psalms 111–118 are a collection of "hallelujah" psalms expressing praise to the Lord.

112:7-8 confidently trust. No matter how people's circumstances are affecting them, they can remain steadfast in faith.

Ps. 113 Praise. Psalm 113, being a Hallel Psalm and containing the word "Hallelujah," focuses on praising God. These Hallel Psalms are still sung in the synagogues on great festival days such as Passover.

[4] For the LORD is high above the nations;
his glory is higher than the heavens.
[5] Who can be compared with the LORD our God,
who is enthroned on high?
[6] He stoops to look down
on heaven and on earth.
[7] He lifts the poor from the dust
and the needy from the garbage dump.
[8] He sets them among princes,
even the princes of his own people!
[9] He gives the childless woman a family,
making her a happy mother.

Praise the LORD!

114 [1] When the Israelites escaped from Egypt—
when the family of Jacob left that foreign land—
[2] the land of Judah became God's sanctuary,
and Israel became his kingdom.

[3] The Red Sea* saw them coming and hurried out of their way!
The water of the Jordan River turned away.
[4] The mountains skipped like rams,
the hills like lambs!
[5] What's wrong, Red Sea, that made you hurry out of their way?
What happened, Jordan River, that you turned away?
[6] Why, mountains, did you skip like rams?
Why, hills, like lambs?

[7] Tremble, O earth, at the presence of the Lord,
at the presence of the God of Jacob.
[8] He turned the rock into a pool of water;
yes, a spring of water flowed from solid rock.

115 [1] Not to us, O LORD, not to us,
but to your name goes all the glory
for your unfailing love and faithfulness.
[2] Why let the nations say,
"Where is their God?"
[3] Our God is in the heavens,
and he does as he wishes.
[4] Their idols are merely things of silver and gold,
shaped by human hands.
[5] They have mouths but cannot speak,
and eyes but cannot see.
[6] They have ears but cannot hear,
and noses but cannot smell.
[7] They have hands but cannot feel,
and feet but cannot walk,
and throats but cannot make a sound.
[8] And those who make idols are just like them,
as are all who trust in them.

[9] O Israel, trust the LORD!
He is your helper and your shield.
[10] O priests, descendants of Aaron, trust the LORD!
He is your helper and your shield.
[11] All you who fear the LORD, trust the LORD!
He is your helper and your shield.

[12] The LORD remembers us and will bless us.
He will bless the people of Israel
and bless the priests, the descendants of Aaron.
[13] He will bless those who fear the LORD,
both great and lowly.

[14] May the LORD richly bless
both you and your children.
[15] May you be blessed by the LORD,
who made heaven and earth.
[16] The heavens belong to the LORD,
but he has given the earth to all humanity.
[17] The dead cannot sing praises to the LORD,
for they have gone into the silence of the grave.
[18] But we can praise the LORD
both now and forever!

Praise the LORD!

116 [1] I love the LORD because he hears my voice
and my prayer for mercy.
[2] Because he bends down to listen,
I will pray as long as I have breath!
[3] Death wrapped its ropes around me;
the terrors of the grave* overtook me.
I saw only trouble and sorrow.
[4] Then I called on the name of the LORD:
"Please, LORD, save me!"
[5] How kind the LORD is! How good he is!
So merciful, this God of ours!
[6] The LORD protects those of childlike faith;
I was facing death, and he saved me.
[7] Let my soul be at rest again,
for the LORD has been good to me.
[8] He has saved me from death,
my eyes from tears,
my feet from stumbling.
[9] And so I walk in the LORD's presence
as I live here on earth!
[10] I believed in you, so I said,
"I am deeply troubled, LORD."
[11] In my anxiety I cried out to you,
"These people are all liars!"
[12] What can I offer the LORD
for all he has done for me?
[13] I will lift up the cup of salvation
and praise the LORD's name for saving me.
[14] I will keep my promises to the LORD
in the presence of all his people.

114:3 Hebrew *the sea;* also in 114:5. 116:3 Hebrew *of Sheol.*

113:4 is high. God's name tells us what God is like. To say that God's name is exalted above the heavens is to assert His supremacy over everything we know.
113:9 childless woman. In ancient cultures, childlessness was the greatest of tragedies (Gen. 30:1; 1 Sam. 1:2-8). Some even thought barrenness indicated God's displeasure with the woman or her family. God, who controls all of creation, can provide a barren woman with children as with Sarah (Gen. 21:2), Rebekah (Gen. 25:21), Rachel (Gen. 30:23), Hannah (1 Sam. 1:19-20) and Elizabeth (Luke 1:7, 13).
Ps. 114 This psalm celebrates God's works in creating the nation of Israel (1-2); and delivering them as a nation from bondage in Egypt.
114:3 Red Sea . . . Jordan. The parting of the Red Sea (Ex. 14:21-22) and the parting of the Jordan River to allow entrance to the promised land are recalled (Josh. 3:14-17).

15 The LORD cares deeply
when his loved ones die.
16 O LORD, I am your servant;
yes, I am your servant, born into your
household;
you have freed me from my chains.
17 I will offer you a sacrifice of thanksgiving
and call on the name of the LORD.
18 I will fulfill my vows to the LORD
in the presence of all his people—
19 in the house of the LORD
in the heart of Jerusalem.

Praise the LORD!

117 1 Praise the LORD, all you nations.
Praise him, all you people of the earth.
2 For his unfailing love for us is powerful;
the LORD's faithfulness endures forever.

Praise the LORD!

118 1 Give thanks to the LORD, for he is good!
His faithful love endures forever.

2 Let all Israel repeat:
"His faithful love endures forever."
3 Let Aaron's descendants, the priests, repeat:
"His faithful love endures forever."
4 Let all who fear the LORD repeat:
"His faithful love endures forever."

5 In my distress I prayed to the LORD,
and the LORD answered me and set me free.
6 The LORD is for me, so I will have no fear.
What can mere people do to me?
7 Yes, the LORD is for me; he will help me.
I will look in triumph at those who hate me.
8 It is better to take refuge in the LORD
than to trust in people.
9 It is better to take refuge in the LORD
than to trust in princes.

10 Though hostile nations surrounded me,
I destroyed them all with the authority of the
LORD.
11 Yes, they surrounded and attacked me,
but I destroyed them all with the authority of
the LORD.
12 They swarmed around me like bees;
they blazed against me like a crackling fire.
But I destroyed them all with the authority of
the LORD.
13 My enemies did their best to kill me,
but the LORD rescued me.
14 The LORD is my strength and my song;
he has given me victory.
15 Songs of joy and victory are sung in the camp of
the godly.
The strong right arm of the LORD has done
glorious things!
16 The strong right arm of the LORD is raised in triumph.
The strong right arm of the LORD has done
glorious things!
17 I will not die; instead, I will live
to tell what the LORD has done.
18 The LORD has punished me severely,
but he did not let me die.

19 Open for me the gates where the righteous enter,
and I will go in and thank the LORD.
20 These gates lead to the presence of the LORD,
and the godly enter there.
21 I thank you for answering my prayer
and giving me victory!

22 The stone that the builders rejected
has now become the cornerstone.
23 This is the LORD's doing,
and it is wonderful to see.
24 This is the day the LORD has made.
We will rejoice and be glad in it.
25 Please, LORD, please save us.
Please, LORD, please give us success.
26 Bless the one who comes in the name of the LORD.
We bless you from the house of the LORD.
27 The LORD is God, shining upon us.
Take the sacrifice and bind it with cords on the
altar.
28 You are my God, and I will praise you!
You are my God, and I will exalt you!

29 Give thanks to the LORD, for he is good!
His faithful love endures forever.

ALEPH

119 * 1 Joyful are people of integrity,
who follow the instructions of the LORD.
2 Joyful are those who obey his laws
and search for him with all their hearts.
3 They do not compromise with evil,
and they walk only in his paths.
4 You have charged us
to keep your commandments carefully.
5 Oh, that my actions would consistently
reflect your decrees!

119 This psalm is a Hebrew acrostic poem; there are twenty-two stanzas, one for each successive letter of the Hebrew alphabet. Each of the eight verses within each stanza begins with the Hebrew letter named in its heading.

116:3 Death wrapped its ropes. This could refer to a severe sickness or to the fear of death experienced in times of war or bondage.
116:15 The LORD cares deeply. The phrase "cares deeply" suggests that God carefully watches over His people, caring for them as precious ones at the time of their death and receiving them into His presence (72:14).
Ps. 117 This is the shortest psalm and the shortest chapter in the Bible.
Ps. 118 Give thanks. This is the last of the Hallel psalms (Ps. 111–118). As the last song of that liturgy, this may have been the hymn sung by Jesus and the disciples at the conclusion of the Last Supper (Matt. 26:30).
118:5 set me free. The Hebrew word for "set free" literally means a "spacious place," as opposed to being in bondage.
118:19-20 gates where the righteous enter. This song, situated at the end of the hallelujah psalms, may have been the final song sung as pilgrims approached the city of Jerusalem on festival days (v. 27). The call to "open the gates" could be a call to open the gates of the city and of the temple.
118:22 The stone that the builders rejected. This was the stone at the corner of a building's foundation which supports the greatest weight. (See also Matt. 21:42-44; Acts 4:8-12; 1 Peter 2:7).
Ps. 119 This is the longest psalm and the longest chapter in the Bible as well as an outstanding example of an acrostic (alphabetical) poem. This carefully constructed psalm has 22 stanzas containing eight verses each. The repetitive structure of this psalm, with built-in memory aids, allowed for easy memorization.

6 Then I will not be ashamed
when I compare my life with your commands.
7 As I learn your righteous regulations,
I will thank you by living as I should!
8 I will obey your decrees.
Please don't give up on me!

BETH

9 How can a young person stay pure?
By obeying your word.
10 I have tried hard to find you—
don't let me wander from your commands.
11 I have hidden your word in my heart,
that I might not sin against you.
12 I praise you, O LORD;
teach me your decrees.
13 I have recited aloud
all the regulations you have given us.
14 I have rejoiced in your laws
as much as in riches.
15 I will study your commandments
and reflect on your ways.
16 I will delight in your decrees
and not forget your word.

GIMEL

17 Be good to your servant,
that I may live and obey your word.
18 Open my eyes to see
the wonderful truths in your instructions.
19 I am only a foreigner in the land.
Don't hide your commands from me!
20 I am always overwhelmed
with a desire for your regulations.
21 You rebuke the arrogant;
those who wander from your commands are
cursed.
22 Don't let them scorn and insult me,
for I have obeyed your laws.
23 Even princes sit and speak against me,
but I will meditate on your decrees.
24 Your laws please me;
they give me wise advice.

DALETH

25 I lie in the dust;
revive me by your word.
26 I told you my plans, and you answered.
Now teach me your decrees.
27 Help me understand the meaning of your
commandments,
and I will meditate on your wonderful deeds.
28 I weep with sorrow;
encourage me by your word.
29 Keep me from lying to myself;
give me the privilege of knowing your
instructions.
30 I have chosen to be faithful;
I have determined to live by your regulations.
31 I cling to your laws.
LORD, don't let me be put to shame!
32 I will pursue your commands,
for you expand my understanding.

HE

33 Teach me your decrees, O LORD;
I will keep them to the end.
34 Give me understanding and I will obey your
instructions;
I will put them into practice with all my heart.
35 Make me walk along the path of your
commands,
for that is where my happiness is found.
36 Give me an eagerness for your laws
rather than a love for money!
37 Turn my eyes from worthless things,
and give me life through your word.*
38 Reassure me of your promise,
made to those who fear you.
39 Help me abandon my shameful ways;
for your regulations are good.
40 I long to obey your commandments!
Renew my life with your goodness.

WAW

41 LORD, give me your unfailing love,
the salvation that you promised me.
42 Then I can answer those who taunt me,
for I trust in your word.
43 Do not snatch your word of truth from me,
for your regulations are my only hope.
44 I will keep on obeying your instructions
forever and ever.
45 I will walk in freedom,
for I have devoted myself to your
commandments.
46 I will speak to kings about your laws,
and I will not be ashamed.
47 How I delight in your commands!
How I love them!
48 I honor and love your commands.
I meditate on your decrees.

ZAYIN

49 Remember your promise to me;
it is my only hope.
50 Your promise revives me;
it comforts me in all my troubles.
51 The proud hold me in utter contempt,
but I do not turn away from your instructions.
52 I meditate on your age-old regulations;
O LORD, they comfort me.
53 I become furious with the wicked,
because they reject your instructions.

119:37 Some manuscripts read *in your ways.*

119:13 have recited aloud. The Jews committed great portions of Scripture to memory.
119:29 lying. In Hebrew, "the way of lying." The writer prays to not be like those who deceive themselves and depart from God's law.
119:32 expand my understanding. Literally "enlarge my heart," or "cause my heart to swell with joy." The writer had gone from being "weary from grief" (v. 28) to bursting with joy.
119:41 unfailing love. The Law repeatedly stated God's unfailing love for His covenant people. It composed the foundation of life for Hebrew believers. Whatever else they might have to face, God's love would get them through.
119:42 Then I can answer. The writer did not seek prosperity and security. He merely wanted to be able to stand and say, "God has provided for me and protected me just as He promised He would if I trusted Him."
119:53 I become furious. He did not burn with anger at the wicked for oppressing him nor for their proud boasts; he was indignant because they were mocking the Word of God.

54 Your decrees have been the theme of my songs
wherever I have lived.
55 I reflect at night on who you are, O LORD;
therefore, I obey your instructions.
56 This is how I spend my life:
obeying your commandments.

HETH

57 LORD, you are mine!
I promise to obey your words!
58 With all my heart I want your blessings.
Be merciful as you promised.
59 I pondered the direction of my life,
and I turned to follow your laws.
60 I will hurry, without delay,
to obey your commands.
61 Evil people try to drag me into sin,
but I am firmly anchored to your instructions.
62 I rise at midnight to thank you
for your just regulations.
63 I am a friend to anyone who fears you—
anyone who obeys your commandments.
64 O LORD, your unfailing love fills the earth;
teach me your decrees.

TETH

65 You have done many good things for me, LORD,
just as you promised.
66 I believe in your commands;
now teach me good judgment and knowledge.
67 I used to wander off until you disciplined me;
but now I closely follow your word.
68 You are good and do only good;
teach me your decrees.
69 Arrogant people smear me with lies,
but in truth I obey your commandments with
all my heart.
70 Their hearts are dull and stupid,
but I delight in your instructions.
71 My suffering was good for me,
for it taught me to pay attention to your decrees.
72 Your instructions are more valuable to me
than millions in gold and silver.

YODH

73 You made me; you created me.
Now give me the sense to follow your
commands.
74 May all who fear you find in me a cause for joy,
for I have put my hope in your word.
75 I know, O LORD, that your regulations are fair;
you disciplined me because I needed it.
76 Now let your unfailing love comfort me,
just as you promised me, your servant.
77 Surround me with your tender mercies so I may live,
for your instructions are my delight.
78 Bring disgrace upon the arrogant people who lied
about me;
meanwhile, I will concentrate on your
commandments.
79 Let me be united with all who fear you,
with those who know your laws.
80 May I be blameless in keeping your decrees;
then I will never be ashamed.

KAPH

81 I am worn out waiting for your rescue,
but I have put my hope in your word.
82 My eyes are straining to see your promises come true.
When will you comfort me?
83 I am shriveled like a wineskin in the smoke,
but I have not forgotten to obey your decrees.
84 How long must I wait?
When will you punish those who persecute me?
85 These arrogant people who hate your instructions
have dug deep pits to trap me.
86 All your commands are trustworthy.
Protect me from those who hunt me down
without cause.
87 They almost finished me off,
but I refused to abandon your commandments.
88 In your unfailing love, spare my life;
then I can continue to obey your laws.

LAMEDH

89 Your eternal word, O LORD,
stands firm in heaven.
90 Your faithfulness extends to every generation,
as enduring as the earth you created.
91 Your regulations remain true to this day,
for everything serves your plans.
92 If your instructions hadn't sustained me with joy,
I would have died in my misery.
93 I will never forget your commandments,
for by them you give me life.
94 I am yours; rescue me!
For I have worked hard at obeying your
commandments.
95 Though the wicked hide along the way to kill me,
I will quietly keep my mind on your laws.
96 Even perfection has its limits,
but your commands have no limit.

MEM

97 Oh, how I love your instructions!
I think about them all day long.
98 Your commands make me wiser than my enemies,
for they are my constant guide.
99 Yes, I have more insight than my teachers,
for I am always thinking of your laws.
100 I am even wiser than my elders,
for I have kept your commandments.
101 I have refused to walk on any evil path,
so that I may remain obedient to your word.
102 I haven't turned away from your regulations,
for you have taught me well.
103 How sweet your words taste to me;
they are sweeter than honey.
104 Your commandments give me understanding;
no wonder I hate every false way of life.

NUN

105 Your word is a lamp to guide my feet
and a light for my path.

119:83 like a wineskin in the smoke. The psalmist felt as if he had been dried out and shriveled through as would happen to an old wineskin left hanging by a fire.

119:99 teachers. His teachers had been able scholars, but the writer had given himself completely to the Word all day long (v. 97).

119:105 light for my path. This verse echoes Proverbs 6:23, which says that God's commands show clearly which moral choices lead to life and which do not.

106 I've promised it once, and I'll promise it again:
I will obey your righteous regulations.
107 I have suffered much, O LORD;
restore my life again as you promised.
108 LORD, accept my offering of praise,
and teach me your regulations.
109 My life constantly hangs in the balance,
but I will not stop obeying your instructions.
110 The wicked have set their traps for me,
but I will not turn from your commandments.
111 Your laws are my treasure;
they are my heart's delight.
112 I am determined to keep your decrees
to the very end.

SAMEKH

113 I hate those with divided loyalties,
but I love your instructions.
114 You are my refuge and my shield;
your word is my source of hope.
115 Get out of my life, you evil-minded people,
for I intend to obey the commands of my God.
116 LORD, sustain me as you promised, that I may live!
Do not let my hope be crushed.
117 Sustain me, and I will be rescued;
then I will meditate continually on your decrees.
118 But you have rejected all who stray from your decrees.
They are only fooling themselves.
119 You skim off the wicked of the earth like scum;
no wonder I love to obey your laws!
120 I tremble in fear of you;
I stand in awe of your regulations.

AYIN

121 Don't leave me to the mercy of my enemies,
for I have done what is just and right.
122 Please guarantee a blessing for me.
Don't let the arrogant oppress me!
123 My eyes strain to see your rescue,
to see the truth of your promise fulfilled.
124 I am your servant; deal with me in unfailing love,
and teach me your decrees.
125 Give discernment to me, your servant;
then I will understand your laws.
126 LORD, it is time for you to act,
for these evil people have violated your instructions.
127 Truly, I love your commands
more than gold, even the finest gold.
128 Each of your commandments is right.
That is why I hate every false way.

PE

129 Your laws are wonderful.
No wonder I obey them!
130 The teaching of your word gives light,
so even the simple can understand.
131 I pant with expectation,
longing for your commands.
132 Come and show me your mercy,
as you do for all who love your name.
133 Guide my steps by your word,
so I will not be overcome by evil.
134 Ransom me from the oppression of evil people;
then I can obey your commandments.
135 Look upon me with love;
teach me your decrees.
136 Rivers of tears gush from my eyes
because people disobey your instructions.

TSADE

137 O LORD, you are righteous,
and your regulations are fair.
138 Your laws are perfect
and completely trustworthy.
139 I am overwhelmed with indignation,
for my enemies have disregarded your words.
140 Your promises have been thoroughly tested;
that is why I love them so much.
141 I am insignificant and despised,
but I don't forget your commandments.
142 Your justice is eternal,
and your instructions are perfectly true.
143 As pressure and stress bear down on me,
I find joy in your commands.
144 Your laws are always right;
help me to understand them so I may live.

QOPH

145 I pray with all my heart; answer me, LORD!
I will obey your decrees.
146 I cry out to you; rescue me,
that I may obey your laws.
147 I rise early, before the sun is up;
I cry out for help and put my hope in your words.
148 I stay awake through the night,
thinking about your promise.
149 In your faithful love, O LORD, hear my cry;
let me be revived by following your regulations.
150 Lawless people are coming to attack me;
they live far from your instructions.
151 But you are near, O LORD,
and all your commands are true.
152 I have known from my earliest days
that your laws will last forever.

RESH

153 Look upon my suffering and rescue me,
for I have not forgotten your instructions.
154 Argue my case; take my side!
Protect my life as you promised.
155 The wicked are far from rescue,
for they do not bother with your decrees.
156 LORD, how great is your mercy;
let me be revived by following your regulations.
157 Many persecute and trouble me,
yet I have not swerved from your laws.
158 Seeing these traitors makes me sick at heart,
because they care nothing for your word.
159 See how I love your commandments, LORD.
Give back my life because of your unfailing love.
160 The very essence of your words is truth;
all your just regulations will stand forever.

119:113 divided loyalties. Such a person lacks integrity, wholeness. He is fickle and so is undependable. He wants to serve God and the world and so violates the first commandment.

119:130 teaching of your word. God's Word is simple and straightforward. Only those who refuse to understand are confounded.

SHIN

161 Powerful people harass me without cause,
but my heart trembles only at your word.
162 I rejoice in your word
like one who discovers a great treasure.
163 I hate and abhor all falsehood,
but I love your instructions.
164 I will praise you seven times a day
because all your regulations are just.
165 Those who love your instructions have great
peace
and do not stumble.
166 I long for your rescue, LORD,
so I have obeyed your commands.
167 I have obeyed your laws,
for I love them very much.
168 Yes, I obey your commandments and laws
because you know everything I do.

TAW

169 O LORD, listen to my cry;
give me the discerning mind you promised.
170 Listen to my prayer;
rescue me as you promised.
171 Let praise flow from my lips,
for you have taught me your decrees.
172 Let my tongue sing about your word,
for all your commands are right.
173 Give me a helping hand,
for I have chosen to follow your
commandments.
174 O LORD, I have longed for your rescue,
and your instructions are my delight.
175 Let me live so I can praise you,
and may your regulations help me.
176 I have wandered away like a lost sheep;
come and find me,
for I have not forgotten your commands.

120 *A song for pilgrims ascending to Jerusalem.*

1 I took my troubles to the LORD;
I cried out to him, and he answered my
prayer.
2 Rescue me, O LORD, from liars
and from all deceitful people.
3 O deceptive tongue, what will God do to you?
How will he increase your punishment?
4 You will be pierced with sharp arrows
and burned with glowing coals.

5 How I suffer in far-off Meshech.
It pains me to live in distant Kedar.
6 I am tired of living
among people who hate peace.
7 I search for peace;
but when I speak of peace, they want war!

121 *A song for pilgrims ascending to Jerusalem.*

1 I look up to the mountains—
does my help come from there?
2 My help comes from the LORD,
who made heaven and earth!

3 He will not let you stumble;
the one who watches over you will not
slumber.
4 Indeed, he who watches over Israel
never slumbers or sleeps.

5 The LORD himself watches over you!
The LORD stands beside you as your protective
shade.
6 The sun will not harm you by day,
nor the moon at night.
7 The LORD keeps you from all harm
and watches over your life.
8 The LORD keeps watch over you as you come and
go,
both now and forever.

122 *A song for pilgrims ascending to Jerusalem. A psalm of David.*

1 I was glad when they said to me,
"Let us go to the house of the LORD."
2 And now here we are,
standing inside your gates, O Jerusalem.
3 Jerusalem is a well-built city;
its seamless walls cannot be breached.
4 All the tribes of Israel—the LORD's people—
make their pilgrimage here.
They come to give thanks to the name of the
LORD,
as the law requires of Israel.
5 Here stand the thrones where judgment is
given,
the thrones of the dynasty of David.

6 Pray for peace in Jerusalem.
May all who love this city prosper.
7 O Jerusalem, may there be peace within your
walls
and prosperity in your palaces.
8 For the sake of my family and friends, I will say,
"May you have peace."
9 For the sake of the house of the LORD our God,
I will seek what is best for you, O Jerusalem.

119:164 seven times a day. Seven is a number signifying completeness. The psalmist was in constant communion with God, praising Him throughout the activities of his day.
119:176 I have wandered away like a lost sheep. He prayed, "Don't let me wonder" (v. 10), but he had longed for the wealth that others enjoyed. The proud had strayed from God's law in their scramble for things (v. 113), and the psalmist recognizes that he sinned in similar ways.
Ps. 120 A song of pilgrims ascending. This psalm is the first of a group of psalms (120 –134) which have this heading. Some take "ascents" to mean the stairs leading up to the temple or that they were sung by pilgrims as they "ascended " to the temple in Jerusalem for the annual Jewish festivals (Ex. 23:14-17; Micah 4:2). Crowds of pilgrims traveling to Jerusalem often rejoiced, sang, and played musical instruments as they traveled (Isa. 30:29).
120:5 Meshech . . . Kedar. After the Exile, Jews lived throughout the Persian Empire (Est. 3:8). They lived from Meshech (central Asia Minor) in the north to Kedar in Arabia to the south.
121:1 mountains. Refers to the group of hills on which Jerusalem is situated. Because the temple was there, help was to come from the temple, from God.
121:3 not let you stumble. This could refer to physical protection (91:9-12) as well as spiritual protection.
122:3-5 Jerusalem. To the scattered Jews, Jerusalem was a holy city, the center of their faith. God's presence resided in the temple.
122:6 love. In Hebrew a beautiful wordplay unites the words "pray," "peace," "Jerusalem," and "prosper." To *love* Jerusalem meant to love God and to love the nation—which were all one in the minds of the Jews.

123 *A song for pilgrims ascending to Jerusalem.*

1 I lift my eyes to you,
O God, enthroned in heaven.
2 We keep looking to the LORD our God for his mercy,
just as servants keep their eyes on their master,
as a slave girl watches her mistress for the
slightest signal.
3 Have mercy on us, LORD, have mercy,
for we have had our fill of contempt.
4 We have had more than our fill of the scoffing of
the proud
and the contempt of the arrogant.

124 *A song for pilgrims ascending to Jerusalem. A psalm of David.*

1 What if the LORD had not been on our side?
Let all Israel repeat:
2 What if the LORD had not been on our side
when people attacked us?
3 They would have swallowed us alive
in their burning anger.
4 The waters would have engulfed us;
a torrent would have overwhelmed us.
5 Yes, the raging waters of their fury
would have overwhelmed our very lives.

6 Praise the LORD,
who did not let their teeth tear us apart!
7 We escaped like a bird from a hunter's trap.
The trap is broken, and we are free!
8 Our help is from the LORD,
who made heaven and earth.

125 *A song for pilgrims ascending to Jerusalem.*

1 Those who trust in the LORD are as secure as
Mount Zion;
they will not be defeated but will endure
forever.
2 Just as the mountains surround Jerusalem,
so the LORD surrounds his people, both now and
forever.
3 The wicked will not rule the land of the godly,
for then the godly might be tempted to do wrong.
4 O LORD, do good to those who are good,
whose hearts are in tune with you.
5 But banish those who turn to crooked ways, O LORD.
Take them away with those who do evil.

May Israel have peace!

126 *A song for pilgrims ascending to Jerusalem.*

1 When the LORD brought back his exiles to
Jerusalem,[*]
it was like a dream!
2 We were filled with laughter,
and we sang for joy.
And the other nations said,
"What amazing things the LORD has done for
them."
3 Yes, the LORD has done amazing things for us!
What joy!

4 Restore our fortunes, LORD,
as streams renew the desert.
5 Those who plant in tears
will harvest with shouts of joy.
6 They weep as they go to plant their seed,
but they sing as they return with the harvest.

127 *A song for pilgrims ascending to Jerusalem. A psalm of Solomon.*

1 Unless the LORD builds a house,
the work of the builders is wasted.
Unless the LORD protects a city,
guarding it with sentries will do no good.
2 It is useless for you to work so hard
from early morning until late at night,
anxiously working for food to eat;
for God gives rest to his loved ones.

3 Children are a gift from the LORD;
they are a reward from him.
4 Children born to a young man
are like arrows in a warrior's hands.
5 How joyful is the man whose quiver is full of them!
He will not be put to shame when he confronts
his accusers at the city gates.

128 *A song for pilgrims ascending to Jerusalem.*

1 How joyful are those who fear the LORD—
all who follow his ways!
2 You will enjoy the fruit of your labor.
How joyful and prosperous you will be!
3 Your wife will be like a fruitful grapevine,
flourishing within your home.
Your children will be like vigorous young olive trees
as they sit around your table.
4 That is the LORD's blessing
for those who fear him.

5 May the LORD continually bless you from Zion.
May you see Jerusalem prosper as long as you live.
6 May you live to enjoy your grandchildren.
May Israel have peace!

129 *A song for pilgrims ascending to Jerusalem.*

1 From my earliest youth my enemies have
persecuted me.
Let all Israel repeat this:

126:1 Hebrew *Zion*.

123:2 servants. Humble, faithful men and women of God are utterly dependent upon Him. Just as slaves and maids look to their masters, God's people look to Him for mercy.

125:1–2 Those who trust in the LORD. Foreign oppressors tried to push the Jews around, but trusting in God made Israel as unmovable as a mountain. The Lord surrounded His people by placing a ring of protection and blessing around them that the enemy could not penetrate (Job 1:10).

126:2 filled with laughter. As the returning exiles caught sight of Mt. Zion, they were filled with joy to be back in their own land. The surrounding nations knew what had happened to the Jews. Now they looked on in awe as God fulfilled his Word and brought His people back.

127:1–2 Unless the LORD builds. If God's people fail to trust Him as their ultimate source of shelter, security, and food, their efforts result in failure.

128:3 Your wife. Psalm 128 is called the marriage prayer as it was often sung at Jewish weddings. Culturally, a woman's role was to provide children.

2 From my earliest youth my enemies have
persecuted me,
but they have never defeated me.
3 My back is covered with cuts,
as if a farmer had plowed long furrows.
4 But the LORD is good;
he has cut me free from the ropes of the ungodly.

5 May all who hate Jerusalem*
be turned back in shameful defeat.
6 May they be as useless as grass on a rooftop,
turning yellow when only half grown,
7 ignored by the harvester,
despised by the binder.
8 And may those who pass by
refuse to give them this blessing:
"The LORD bless you;
we bless you in the LORD's name."

130 *A song for pilgrims ascending to Jerusalem.*

1 From the depths of despair, O LORD,
I call for your help.
2 Hear my cry, O Lord.
Pay attention to my prayer.

3 LORD, if you kept a record of our sins,
who, O Lord, could ever survive?
4 But you offer forgiveness,
that we might learn to fear you.

5 I am counting on the LORD;
yes, I am counting on him.
I have put my hope in his word.
6 I long for the Lord
more than sentries long for the dawn,
yes, more than sentries long for the dawn.

7 O Israel, hope in the LORD;
for with the LORD there is unfailing love.
His redemption overflows.
8 He himself will redeem Israel
from every kind of sin.

131 *A song for pilgrims ascending to Jerusalem. A psalm of David.*

1 LORD, my heart is not proud;
my eyes are not haughty.
I don't concern myself with matters too great
or too awesome for me to grasp.
2 Instead, I have calmed and quieted myself,
like a weaned child who no longer cries for its
mother's milk.
Yes, like a weaned child is my soul within me.

3 O Israel, put your hope in the LORD—
now and always.

132 *A song for pilgrims ascending to Jerusalem.*

1 LORD, remember David
and all that he suffered.
2 He made a solemn promise to the LORD.
He vowed to the Mighty One of Israel,*
3 "I will not go home;
I will not let myself rest.
4 I will not let my eyes sleep
nor close my eyelids in slumber
5 until I find a place to build a house for the LORD,
a sanctuary for the Mighty One of Israel."

6 We heard that the Ark was in Ephrathah;
then we found it in the distant countryside of
Jaar.
7 Let us go to the sanctuary of the LORD;
let us worship at the footstool of his throne.
8 Arise, O LORD, and enter your resting place,
along with the Ark, the symbol of your
power.
9 May your priests be clothed in godliness;
may your loyal servants sing for joy.
10 For the sake of your servant David,
do not reject the king you have anointed.
11 The LORD swore an oath to David
with a promise he will never take back:
"I will place one of your descendants
on your throne.
12 If your descendants obey the terms of my
covenant
and the laws that I teach them,
then your royal line
will continue forever and ever."

13 For the LORD has chosen Jerusalem*;
he has desired it for his home.
14 "This is my resting place forever," he said.
"I will live here, for this is the home I desired.
15 I will bless this city and make it prosperous;
I will satisfy its poor with food.
16 I will clothe its priests with godliness;
its faithful servants will sing for joy.
17 Here I will increase the power of David;
my anointed one will be a light for my
people.
18 I will clothe his enemies with shame,
but he will be a glorious king."

133 *A song for pilgrims ascending to Jerusalem. A psalm of David.*

1 How wonderful and pleasant it is
when brothers live together in harmony!
2 For harmony is as precious as the anointing oil
that was poured over Aaron's head,
that ran down his beard
and onto the border of his robe.

129:5 Hebrew *Zion.* **132:2** Hebrew *of Jacob;* also in 132:5. See note on 44:4. **132:13** Hebrew *Zion.*

129:6 as useless as grass on a rooftop. Grass cannot take deep root on a hard, sun baked roof. It is scorched before it bears fruit.

132:2 He made a solemn promise. David had a special relationship with God. When God committed Himself to David and his descendants (v. 11), David responded by committing himself to the work of God (v. 8). (See also 2 Sam. 6-7).

132:6 We heard. David was a youth in Ephrathah (Bethlehem) when he heard of the ark not having a "house." The ark spent twenty years in "the fields of Jaar" (Kiriath Jearim). David moved it from there to Jerusalem (1 Sam. 7:1-2; 2 Sam. 6:1-3).

132:12 obey the terms of my covenant. This covenant was the law of Moses, given at Mt. Sinai. When the Israelites agreed to obey it, the terms of this "contract" were made binding upon them and blessing resulted (see I Kings 2:3-4).

133:1 wonderful and pleasant. God desires that His people love one another and live in peace with one another (1 Cor. 1:10). In Israel, this unity was most evident when the entire nation came together to celebrate the feasts.

3 Harmony is as refreshing as the dew from Mount Hermon
that falls on the mountains of Zion.
And there the LORD has pronounced his blessing,
even life everlasting.

134 *A song for pilgrims ascending to Jerusalem.*

1 Oh, praise the LORD, all you servants of the LORD,
you who serve at night in the house of the LORD.
2 Lift your hands toward the sanctuary,
and praise the LORD.

3 May the LORD, who made heaven and earth,
bless you from Jerusalem.*

135

1 Praise the LORD!

Praise the name of the LORD!
Praise him, you who serve the LORD,
2 you who serve in the house of the LORD,
in the courts of the house of our God.

3 Praise the LORD, for the LORD is good;
celebrate his lovely name with music.
4 For the LORD has chosen Jacob for himself,
Israel for his own special treasure.

5 I know the greatness of the LORD—
that our Lord is greater than any other god.
6 The LORD does whatever pleases him
throughout all heaven and earth,
and on the seas and in their depths.
7 He causes the clouds to rise over the whole earth.
He sends the lightning with the rain
and releases the wind from his storehouses.

8 He destroyed the firstborn in each Egyptian home,
both people and animals.
9 He performed miraculous signs and wonders in Egypt
against Pharaoh and all his people.
10 He struck down great nations
and slaughtered mighty kings—
11 Sihon king of the Amorites,
Og king of Bashan,
and all the kings of Canaan.
12 He gave their land as an inheritance,
a special possession to his people Israel.

13 Your name, O LORD, endures forever;
your fame, O LORD, is known to every generation.
14 For the LORD will give justice to his people
and have compassion on his servants.

15 The idols of the nations are merely things of silver and gold,
shaped by human hands.
16 They have mouths but cannot speak,
and eyes but cannot see.
17 They have ears but cannot hear,
and mouths but cannot breathe.
18 And those who make idols are just like them,
as are all who trust in them.

19 O Israel, praise the LORD!
O priests—descendants of Aaron—praise the LORD!
20 O Levites, praise the LORD!
All you who fear the LORD, praise the LORD!
21 The LORD be praised from Zion,
for he lives here in Jerusalem.

Praise the LORD!

136

1 Give thanks to the LORD, for he is good!
His faithful love endures forever.
2 Give thanks to the God of gods.
His faithful love endures forever.
3 Give thanks to the Lord of lords.
His faithful love endures forever.

4 Give thanks to him who alone does mighty miracles.
His faithful love endures forever.
5 Give thanks to him who made the heavens so skillfully.
His faithful love endures forever.
6 Give thanks to him who placed the earth among the waters.
His faithful love endures forever.
7 Give thanks to him who made the heavenly lights—
His faithful love endures forever.
8 the sun to rule the day,
His faithful love endures forever.
9 and the moon and stars to rule the night.
His faithful love endures forever.

10 Give thanks to him who killed the firstborn of Egypt.
His faithful love endures forever.
11 He brought Israel out of Egypt.
His faithful love endures forever.
12 He acted with a strong hand and powerful arm.
His faithful love endures forever.
13 Give thanks to him who parted the Red Sea.*
His faithful love endures forever.
14 He led Israel safely through,
His faithful love endures forever.
15 but he hurled Pharaoh and his army into the Red Sea.
His faithful love endures forever.
16 Give thanks to him who led his people through the wilderness.
His faithful love endures forever.

17 Give thanks to him who struck down mighty kings.
His faithful love endures forever.

134:3 Hebrew *Zion.* 136:13 Hebrew *sea of reeds;* also in 136:15.

133:3 dew from Mount Hermon . . . Zion. Israel was a dry land, and the Jews depended on dew to water the ground and sustain life. Dew was therefore a symbol of the blessing of God on Israel (Gen. 27:28; Hos. 14:5). Mt. Hermon was a tall, cold mountain, so heavy dew fell upon it. God compared that to the blessings which drenched Mt. Zion.

Ps. 136 In Jewish tradition, this psalm is known as the Great Hallel, repeating many of the themes of Psalm 135. It is intended for public worship. A Levite or song leader would sing one verse after another, and the choir or worshipers would respond with, "His love endures forever" (see 2 Chron. 5:12-14). God's love for His people is the reason He blesses and protects them.

18 He killed powerful kings—
His faithful love endures forever.
19 Sihon king of the Amorites,
His faithful love endures forever.
20 and Og king of Bashan.
His faithful love endures forever.
21 God gave the land of these kings as an inheritance—
His faithful love endures forever.
22 a special possession to his servant Israel.
His faithful love endures forever.

23 He remembered us in our weakness.
His faithful love endures forever.
24 He saved us from our enemies.
His faithful love endures forever.
25 He gives food to every living thing.
His faithful love endures forever.
26 Give thanks to the God of heaven.
His faithful love endures forever.

137

1 Beside the rivers of Babylon, we sat and wept
as we thought of Jerusalem.*
2 We put away our harps,
hanging them on the branches of poplar trees.
3 For our captors demanded a song from us.
Our tormentors insisted on a joyful hymn:
"Sing us one of those songs of Jerusalem!"
4 But how can we sing the songs of the LORD
while in a pagan land?

5 If I forget you, O Jerusalem,
let my right hand forget how to play the harp.
6 May my tongue stick to the roof of my mouth
if I fail to remember you,
if I don't make Jerusalem my greatest joy.

7 O LORD, remember what the Edomites did
on the day the armies of Babylon captured Jerusalem.
"Destroy it!" they yelled.
"Level it to the ground!"
8 O Babylon, you will be destroyed.
Happy is the one who pays you back
for what you have done to us.
9 Happy is the one who takes your babies
and smashes them against the rocks!

138

A psalm of David.

1 I give you thanks, O LORD, with all my heart;
I will sing your praises before the gods.
2 I bow before your holy Temple as I worship.
I praise your name for your unfailing love and faithfulness;
for your promises are backed
by all the honor of your name.
3 As soon as I pray, you answer me;
you encourage me by giving me strength.

4 Every king in all the earth will thank you, LORD,
for all of them will hear your words.
5 Yes, they will sing about the LORD's ways,
for the glory of the LORD is very great.
6 Though the LORD is great, he cares for the humble,
but he keeps his distance from the proud.

7 Though I am surrounded by troubles,
you will protect me from the anger of my enemies.
You reach out your hand,
and the power of your right hand saves me.
8 The LORD will work out his plans for my life—
for your faithful love, O LORD, endures forever.
Don't abandon me, for you made me.

139

For the choir director: A psalm of David.

1 O LORD, you have examined my heart
and know everything about me.
2 You know when I sit down or stand up.
You know my thoughts even when I'm far away.
3 You see me when I travel
and when I rest at home.
You know everything I do.
4 You know what I am going to say
even before I say it, LORD.
5 You go before me and follow me.
You place your hand of blessing on my head.
6 Such knowledge is too wonderful for me,
too great for me to understand!

7 I can never escape from your Spirit!
I can never get away from your presence!
8 If I go up to heaven, you are there;
if I go down to the grave,* you are there.
9 If I ride the wings of the morning,
if I dwell by the farthest oceans,
10 even there your hand will guide me,
and your strength will support me.
11 I could ask the darkness to hide me
and the light around me to become night—
12 but even in darkness I cannot hide from you.
To you the night shines as bright as day.
Darkness and light are the same to you.

13 You made all the delicate, inner parts of my body
and knit me together in my mother's womb.

137:1 Hebrew *Zion;* also in 137:3. **139:8** Hebrew *to Sheol.*

137:1 rivers of Babylon. This refers to the Tigris and Euphrates Rivers and the great network of canals between them.
137:2,3 put away our harps. Overcome with grief, the exiled Jews had no heart for music (Lam. 5:14-18). The songs of Zion were worship songs sung in the temple on Mount Zion. The Israelites could not bring themselves to sing happy songs of victory and praise.
137:7 Edomites. Like the Israelites, the Edomites descended from Abraham and Isaac. God had told the Israelites to respect the Edomites as brothers (Deut. 23:7), so it was especially painful to know that the Edomites had urged the Babylonians to mercilessly attack the Israelites (Obad. 8-15).
Ps. 138 This psalm begins a collection of eight Davidic Psalms, including six prayers and two songs in Psalms 138—145.
138:2 your name. Out of the many so-called gods, Yahweh's name rises above all others—Yahweh, the God of Israel. The Law was God's Word, His covenant with Israel. Within the Law are many promises of blessing. God's name and God's Word were the same in Jewish thinking.
Ps. 139 God is aware of and cares for the birth and life of each individual.
139:7-12 I can never escape from your Spirit! No place in all creation is a hiding place from God. Even complete darkness hides nothing from Him.
139:13 You made. God is the One who creates the unique mental and physical attributes of each individual. This implies loving care for each detail of our own complexity.

GOD'S PERPETUAL PRESENCE

1. Who knows you so well that they know what you are going to say before you even say it?

PSALM 139

2. How is it a comfort that you cannot "escape" God? How is it sobering?
3. What do verses 13-16 suggest about abortion? If God knits us together in the womb and plans all our days, what are we doing if we abort a baby?
4. Why does David say that he hates those who hate God (v. 21)?
5. Have you been walking more in a way that "offends" or an "everlasting" way (v. 24)? How do you need God's help to change?

14 Thank you for making me so wonderfully
complex!
Your workmanship is marvelous—how well I
know it.
15 You watched me as I was being formed in utter
seclusion,
as I was woven together in the dark of the
womb.
16 You saw me before I was born.
Every day of my life was recorded in your book.
Every moment was laid out
before a single day had passed.

17 How precious are your thoughts about me,* O God.
They cannot be numbered!
18 I can't even count them;
they outnumber the grains of sand!
And when I wake up,
you are still with me!

19 O God, if only you would destroy the wicked!
Get out of my life, you murderers!
20 They blaspheme you;
your enemies misuse your name.
21 O LORD, shouldn't I hate those who hate you?
Shouldn't I despise those who oppose you?
22 Yes, I hate them with total hatred,
for your enemies are my enemies.

23 Search me, O God, and know my heart;
test me and know my anxious thoughts.
24 Point out anything in me that offends you,
and lead me along the path of everlasting life.

140 *For the choir director: A psalm of David.*

1 O LORD, rescue me from evil people.
Protect me from those who are violent,
2 those who plot evil in their hearts
and stir up trouble all day long.
3 Their tongues sting like a snake;
the venom of a viper drips from their lips.
Interlude

4 O LORD, keep me out of the hands of the wicked.
Protect me from those who are violent,
for they are plotting against me.
5 The proud have set a trap to catch me;
they have stretched out a net;
they have placed traps all along the way.
Interlude

6 I said to the LORD, "You are my God!"
Listen, O LORD, to my cries for mercy!
7 O Sovereign LORD, the strong one who rescued me,
you protected me on the day of battle.
8 LORD, do not let evil people have their way.
Do not let their evil schemes succeed,
or they will become proud.
Interlude

9 Let my enemies be destroyed
by the very evil they have planned for me.
10 Let burning coals fall down on their heads.
Let them be thrown into the fire
or into watery pits from which they can't escape.
11 Don't let liars prosper here in our land.
Cause great disasters to fall on the violent.

12 But I know the LORD will help those they
persecute;
he will give justice to the poor.
13 Surely righteous people are praising your name;
the godly will live in your presence.

141 *A psalm of David.*

1 O LORD, I am calling to you. Please hurry!
Listen when I cry to you for help!
2 Accept my prayer as incense offered to you,
and my upraised hands as an evening offering.

3 Take control of what I say, O LORD,
and guard my lips.
4 Don't let me drift toward evil
or take part in acts of wickedness.
Don't let me share in the delicacies
of those who do wrong.

5 Let the godly strike me!
It will be a kindness!
If they correct me, it is soothing medicine.
Don't let me refuse it.

But I pray constantly
against the wicked and their deeds.
6 When their leaders are thrown down from a cliff,
the wicked will listen to my words and find
them true.
7 Like rocks brought up by a plow,
the bones of the wicked will lie scattered
without burial.*

139:17 Or *How precious to me are your thoughts.* 141:7 Hebrew *our bones will be scattered at the mouth of Sheol.*

139:16 You saw me. God sees every human being as he or she is being formed in the womb. He has determined the length of each person's life.

140:10 fire . . . watery pits. This is similar to the fiery coals and burning sulfur (11:6) which God rains on the wicked. It foreshadows the final place of punishment for the wicked (Rev. 19:20).

8 I look to you for help, O Sovereign LORD.
You are my refuge; don't let them kill me.
9 Keep me from the traps they have set for me,
from the snares of those who do wrong.
10 Let the wicked fall into their own nets,
but let me escape.

142 *A psalm* of David, regarding his experience in the cave. A prayer.*

1 I cry out to the LORD;
I plead for the LORD's mercy.
2 I pour out my complaints before him
and tell him all my troubles.
3 When I am overwhelmed,
you alone know the way I should turn.
Wherever I go,
my enemies have set traps for me.
4 I look for someone to come and help me,
but no one gives me a passing thought!
No one will help me;
no one cares a bit what happens to me.
5 Then I pray to you, O LORD.
I say, "You are my place of refuge.
You are all I really want in life.
6 Hear my cry,
for I am very low.
Rescue me from my persecutors,
for they are too strong for me.
7 Bring me out of prison
so I can thank you.
The godly will crowd around me,
for you are good to me."

143 *A psalm of David.*

1 Hear my prayer, O LORD;
listen to my plea!
Answer me because you are faithful and righteous.
2 Don't put your servant on trial,
for no one is innocent before you.
3 My enemy has chased me.
He has knocked me to the ground
and forces me to live in darkness like those in the grave.
4 I am losing all hope;
I am paralyzed with fear.
5 I remember the days of old.
I ponder all your great works
and think about what you have done.
6 I lift my hands to you in prayer.
I thirst for you as parched land thirsts for rain.

Interlude

7 Come quickly, LORD, and answer me,
for my depression deepens.
Don't turn away from me,
or I will die.
8 Let me hear of your unfailing love each morning,
for I am trusting you.
Show me where to walk,
for I give myself to you.
9 Rescue me from my enemies, LORD;
I run to you to hide me.
10 Teach me to do your will,
for you are my God.
May your gracious Spirit lead me forward
on a firm footing.
11 For the glory of your name, O LORD, preserve my life.
Because of your faithfulness, bring me out of this distress.
12 In your unfailing love, silence all my enemies
and destroy all my foes,
for I am your servant.

144 *A psalm of David.*

1 Praise the LORD, who is my rock.
He trains my hands for war
and gives my fingers skill for battle.
2 He is my loving ally and my fortress,
my tower of safety, my rescuer.
He is my shield, and I take refuge in him.
He makes the nations* submit to me.

3 O LORD, what are human beings that you should notice them,
mere mortals that you should think about them?
4 For they are like a breath of air;
their days are like a passing shadow.

5 Open the heavens, LORD, and come down.
Touch the mountains so they billow smoke.
6 Hurl your lightning bolts and scatter your enemies!
Shoot your arrows and confuse them!
7 Reach down from heaven and rescue me;
rescue me from deep waters,
from the power of my enemies.
8 Their mouths are full of lies;
they swear to tell the truth, but they lie instead.

9 I will sing a new song to you, O God!
I will sing your praises with a ten-stringed harp.
10 For you grant victory to kings!
You rescued your servant David from the fatal sword.
11 Save me!
Rescue me from the power of my enemies.
Their mouths are full of lies;
they swear to tell the truth, but they lie instead.

12 May our sons flourish in their youth
like well-nurtured plants.

142:TITLE Hebrew *maskil.* This may be a literary or musical term. 144:2 Some manuscripts read *my people.*

142:3 overwhelmed. David was overwhelmed from being daily beset with "troubles" (v. 2), plots, and danger. David knew that enemies were all around and didn't know which way to turn. He needed God's wisdom to proceed.

143:2 no one is innocent. This is one of David's most beautiful prayers and begins with an honest admission of his own sinfulness. David asks God to answer him, not because David is righteous or for the fact that David deserves God's righteousness, but because God is righteous.

143:12 for I am your servant. David could ask God to destroy his foes because he stood for the principles of God. Those who fought him made themselves enemies of the God he served.

144:2 He is my loving ally. In the midst of battle, David declared that the source of his strength was God's unfailing love.

144:3-4 what are human beings. David marveled that a God so powerful cared for insignificant humans, for creatures whose entire life is like a fleeting shadow (see Psalm 8:4).

May our daughters be like graceful pillars,
carved to beautify a palace.
13 May our barns be filled
with crops of every kind.
May the flocks in our fields multiply by the thousands,
even tens of thousands,
14 and may our oxen be loaded down with produce.
May there be no enemy breaking through our walls,
no going into captivity,
no cries of alarm in our town squares.
15 Yes, joyful are those who live like this!
Joyful indeed are those whose God is the LORD.

145

**A psalm of praise of David.*

1 I will exalt you, my God and King,
and praise your name forever and ever.
2 I will praise you every day;
yes, I will praise you forever.
3 Great is the LORD! He is most worthy of praise!
No one can measure his greatness.
4 Let each generation tell its children of your mighty acts;
let them proclaim your power.
5 I will meditate on your majestic, glorious splendor
and your wonderful miracles.
6 Your awe-inspiring deeds will be on every tongue;
I will proclaim your greatness.
7 Everyone will share the story of your wonderful goodness;
they will sing with joy about your righteousness.
8 The LORD is merciful and compassionate,
slow to get angry and filled with unfailing love.
9 The LORD is good to everyone.
He showers compassion on all his creation.
10 All of your works will thank you, LORD,
and your faithful followers will praise you.
11 They will speak of the glory of your kingdom;
they will give examples of your power.
12 They will tell about your mighty deeds
and about the majesty and glory of your reign.
13 For your kingdom is an everlasting kingdom.
You rule throughout all generations.

The LORD always keeps his promises;
he is gracious in all he does.*
14 The LORD helps the fallen
and lifts those bent beneath their loads.
15 The eyes of all look to you in hope;
you give them their food as they need it.
16 When you open your hand,
you satisfy the hunger and thirst of every living thing.
17 The LORD is righteous in everything he does;
he is filled with kindness.
18 The LORD is close to all who call on him,
yes, to all who call on him in truth.
19 He grants the desires of those who fear him;
he hears their cries for help and rescues them.
20 The LORD protects all those who love him,
but he destroys the wicked.
21 I will praise the LORD,
and may everyone on earth bless his holy name
forever and ever.

146

1 Praise the LORD!

Let all that I am praise the LORD.
2 I will praise the LORD as long as I live.
I will sing praises to my God with my dying breath.

3 Don't put your confidence in powerful people;
there is no help for you there.
4 When they breathe their last, they return to the earth,
and all their plans die with them.
5 But joyful are those who have the God of Israel* as their helper,
whose hope is in the LORD their God.
6 He made heaven and earth,
the sea, and everything in them.
He keeps every promise forever.
7 He gives justice to the oppressed
and food to the hungry.
The LORD frees the prisoners.
8 The LORD opens the eyes of the blind.
The LORD lifts up those who are weighed down.
The LORD loves the godly.
9 The LORD protects the foreigners among us.
He cares for the orphans and widows,
but he frustrates the plans of the wicked.

10 The LORD will reign forever.
He will be your God, O Jerusalem,* throughout the generations.

Praise the LORD!

147

1 Praise the LORD!

How good to sing praises to our God!
How delightful and how fitting!
2 The LORD is rebuilding Jerusalem
and bringing the exiles back to Israel.
3 He heals the brokenhearted
and bandages their wounds.
4 He counts the stars
and calls them all by name.
5 How great is our Lord! His power is absolute!
His understanding is beyond comprehension!
6 The LORD supports the humble,
but he brings the wicked down into the dust.

145 This psalm is a Hebrew acrostic poem; each verse (including 13b) begins with a successive letter of the Hebrew alphabet. 145:13 As in Dead Sea Scrolls and Greek and Syriac versions; the Masoretic Text lacks the final two lines of this verse. 146:5 Hebrew *of Jacob.* See note on 44:4. 146:10 Hebrew *Zion.*

145:3-7 Let each generation tell. Israel's history was a long list of miracles that God had done to protect them. Jewish parents were instructed to tell God's mighty acts to their children, so they too would be in awe of God (Ex. 13:14-15).

146:5-9 God alone has power to truly help. God's infinite compassion motivates His use of power to stop oppressors and help the oppressed.

Ps. 147 This joyful psalm was likely composed and sung when Nehemiah and the Jews finished rebuilding the walls of Jerusalem (vv. 2, 13; Neh. 12:27-43).

147:4-6 stars . . . calls them all by name. Untold numbers of galaxies comprise the universe, each one containing billions of stars. God created and knows each one by name.

7 Sing out your thanks to the LORD;
sing praises to our God with a harp.
8 He covers the heavens with clouds,
provides rain for the earth,
and makes the grass grow in mountain
pastures.
9 He gives food to the wild animals
and feeds the young ravens when they cry.
10 He takes no pleasure in the strength of a horse
or in human might.
11 No, the LORD's delight is in those who fear him,
those who put their hope in his unfailing love.

12 Glorify the LORD, O Jerusalem!
Praise your God, O Zion!
13 For he has strengthened the bars of your gates
and blessed your children within your walls.
14 He sends peace across your nation
and satisfies your hunger with the finest wheat.
15 He sends his orders to the world—
how swiftly his word flies!
16 He sends the snow like white wool;
he scatters frost upon the ground like ashes.
17 He hurls the hail like stones.*
Who can stand against his freezing cold?
18 Then, at his command, it all melts.
He sends his winds, and the ice thaws.
19 He has revealed his words to Jacob,
his decrees and regulations to Israel.
20 He has not done this for any other nation;
they do not know his regulations.

Praise the LORD!

148

1 Praise the LORD!

Praise the LORD from the heavens!
Praise him from the skies!
2 Praise him, all his angels!
Praise him, all the armies of heaven!
3 Praise him, sun and moon!
Praise him, all you twinkling stars!
4 Praise him, skies above!
Praise him, vapors high above the clouds!
5 Let every created thing give praise to the LORD,
for he issued his command, and they came into
being.
6 He set them in place forever and ever.
His decree will never be revoked.

7 Praise the LORD from the earth,
you creatures of the ocean depths,
8 fire and hail, snow and clouds,*
wind and weather that obey him,
9 mountains and all hills,
fruit trees and all cedars,
10 wild animals and all livestock,
small scurrying animals and birds,
11 kings of the earth and all people,
rulers and judges of the earth,
12 young men and young women,
old men and children.

13 Let them all praise the name of the LORD.
For his name is very great;
his glory towers over the earth and heaven!
14 He has made his people strong,
honoring his faithful ones—
the people of Israel who are close to him.

Praise the LORD!

149

1 Praise the LORD!

Sing to the LORD a new song.
Sing his praises in the assembly of the faithful.

2 O Israel, rejoice in your Maker.
O people of Jerusalem,* exult in your King.
3 Praise his name with dancing,
accompanied by tambourine and harp.
4 For the LORD delights in his people;
he crowns the humble with victory.
5 Let the faithful rejoice that he honors them.
Let them sing for joy as they lie on their beds.

6 Let the praises of God be in their mouths,
and a sharp sword in their hands—
7 to execute vengeance on the nations
and punishment on the peoples,
8 to bind their kings with shackles
and their leaders with iron chains,
9 to execute the judgment written against them.
This is the glorious privilege of his faithful ones.

Praise the LORD!

150

1 Praise the LORD!

Praise God in his sanctuary;
praise him in his mighty heaven!
2 Praise him for his mighty works;
praise his unequaled greatness!
3 Praise him with a blast of the ram's horn;
praise him with the lyre and harp!
4 Praise him with the tambourine and dancing;
praise him with strings and flutes!
5 Praise him with a clash of cymbals;
praise him with loud clanging cymbals.
6 Let everything that breathes sing praises to the LORD!

Praise the LORD!

147:17 Hebrew *like bread crumbs.* **148:8** Or *mist,* or *smoke.* **149:2** Hebrew *Zion.*

147:19-20 any other nation. God chose Israel, gave them His law, and made a covenant with them. God did not create this relationship with any other nation (Ezra 4:1-4). Through Israel, salvation would come to all (John 4:22).

148:8-10 clouds. All of nature praises God by declaring His glory (19:1-4). Likewise, all living things, by their very existence, praise God. Their complex design declares the existence of an intelligent Creator.

149:4 delights . . . with victory. Here these words mean deliverance or victory, both physically and spiritually. They also have the deeper spiritual meaning of eternal life (Matt. 5:3; James 1:12).

149:5 on their beds. For the people, being able to lie down on their beds and sleep without fear resulted from God's protection.

149:6-9 When battling enemies, the Israelites knew that strength was not primarily in the swords they held but in the God they trusted and praised (Rev. 19:14-15).

150:1-2 Praise God. This triumphant, joyous psalm gives a rousing call to believers to praise God. It is a fitting finale to the book of Psalms. We should praise God for the miracles He has done, for His surpassing greatness, and because He is powerful, great, and glorious.

150:3 Praise him with. Worship here is depicted as a rousing, loud celebration accompanied by a full array of musical instruments.

INTRODUCTION TO PROVERBS

PERSONAL READING PLAN

☐Proverbs 1:1–2:22	☐Proverbs 11:1–12:28	☐Proverbs 21:1–22:29
☐Proverbs 3:1–4:27	☐Proverbs 13:1–14:35	☐Proverbs 23:1–24:29
☐Proverbs 5:1–6:35	☐Proverbs 15:1–16:33	☐Proverbs 25:1–26:28
☐Proverbs 7:1–8:36	☐Proverbs 17:1–18:24	☐Proverbs 27:1–28:28
☐Proverbs 9:1–10:32	☐Proverbs 19:1–20:30	☐Proverbs 29:1–31:31

AUTHOR

Proverbs has multiple authors and compilers who are named in the section subtitles. Solomon (1:1–22:16; 25:1–29:27) is the most prominent of these, and the introduction to the work (1:1-7) is attributed to him. The group of authors entitled "the wise" (22:17–24:34) may have been royal scribes. The sayings of Agur (chap. 30) and Lemuel (chap. 31) conclude the book.

DATE

Solomon reigned in Israel *circa* 970–930 B.C. During that time he wrote thousands of proverbs and songs (1 Kings 4:32). The final compilation of this work occurred after Hezekiah's time (25:1), more than 200 years later, possibly as late as 500 B.C.

THEME

To impart moral wisdom and uncommon sense for right living.

HISTORICAL BACKGROUND

Following Solomon's ascension to the throne of Israel, the Lord appeared to him in a dream and offered him the desire of his heart (1 Kings 3:1-28; 4:29-34). Solomon chose wisdom. The book of Proverbs collects this God-given wisdom in poetic figures of speech, along with the trusted sayings of wise men, accumulated over 200-plus years. Given the international nature of Solomon's court and Israel's mixing with its neighbors, it is not surprising that many parallels to the Proverbs have been found in extra-biblical texts.

CHARACTERISTICS

Following the book of Psalms, which focuses on our devotional lives, we find the book of Proverbs, which focuses on our practical lives. The English word "proverb" means a brief saying in place of many words. The Hebrew word for proverb, however, has a much broader meaning, including longer sentences and discourses. The book of Proverbs is a part of the Wisdom Literature of the Hebrews. Drawn from the everyday life of common people, these proverbs are couched in figurative, poetic speech laced with analogies and word pictures. Therefore, the book of Proverbs leaves a visual as well as a verbal impact on the reader.

As the introduction states, Proverbs was written to give "insight to the simple" (1:4). The repeated references to "my child" (1:8, 10; 2:1; 3:1; 4:1; 5:1) focus on guiding the young to make righteous and moral choices. Because these proverbs were written particularly for instruction, they are frequently given in the form of commands.

PASSAGES FOR TOPICAL GROUP STUDY

3:1-8 .... TRUSTING GOD ...... Health for Body and Mind

THE PURPOSE OF PROVERBS

1 These are the proverbs of Solomon, David's son, king of Israel.

2 Their purpose is to teach people wisdom and discipline,
to help them understand the insights of the wise.
3 Their purpose is to teach people to live disciplined and successful lives,
to help them do what is right, just, and fair.
4 These proverbs will give insight to the simple,
knowledge and discernment to the young.

5 Let the wise listen to these proverbs and become even wiser.
Let those with understanding receive guidance
6 by exploring the meaning in these proverbs and parables,
the words of the wise and their riddles.

7 Fear of the LORD is the foundation of true knowledge,
but fools despise wisdom and discipline.

A FATHER'S EXHORTATION: ACQUIRE WISDOM

8 My child,* listen when your father corrects you.
Don't neglect your mother's instruction.
9 What you learn from them will crown you with grace
and be a chain of honor around your neck.

10 My child, if sinners entice you,
turn your back on them!
11 They may say, "Come and join us.
Let's hide and kill someone!
Just for fun, let's ambush the innocent!
12 Let's swallow them alive, like the grave*;
let's swallow them whole, like those who go down to the pit of death.
13 Think of the great things we'll get!
We'll fill our houses with all the stuff we take.
14 Come, throw in your lot with us;
we'll all share the loot."

15 My child, don't go along with them!
Stay far away from their paths.
16 They rush to commit evil deeds.
They hurry to commit murder.
17 If a bird sees a trap being set,
it knows to stay away.
18 But these people set an ambush for themselves;
they are trying to get themselves killed.
19 Such is the fate of all who are greedy for money;
it robs them of life.

WISDOM SHOUTS IN THE STREETS

20 Wisdom shouts in the streets.
She cries out in the public square.
21 She calls to the crowds along the main street,
to those gathered in front of the city gate:
22 "How long, you simpletons,
will you insist on being simpleminded?
How long will you mockers relish your mocking?
How long will you fools hate knowledge?
23 Come and listen to my counsel.
I'll share my heart with you
and make you wise.

24 "I called you so often, but you wouldn't come.
I reached out to you, but you paid no attention.
25 You ignored my advice
and rejected the correction I offered.
26 So I will laugh when you are in trouble!
I will mock you when disaster overtakes you—
27 when calamity overtakes you like a storm,
when disaster engulfs you like a cyclone,
and anguish and distress overwhelm you.

28 "When they cry for help, I will not answer.
Though they anxiously search for me, they will not find me.
29 For they hated knowledge
and chose not to fear the LORD.
30 They rejected my advice
and paid no attention when I corrected them.
31 Therefore, they must eat the bitter fruit of living their own way,
choking on their own schemes.
32 For simpletons turn away from me—to death.
Fools are destroyed by their own complacency.
33 But all who listen to me will live in peace,
untroubled by fear of harm."

THE BENEFITS OF WISDOM

2 1 My child,* listen to what I say,
and treasure my commands.
2 Tune your ears to wisdom,
and concentrate on understanding.
3 Cry out for insight,
and ask for understanding.
4 Search for them as you would for silver;
seek them like hidden treasures.
5 Then you will understand what it means to fear the LORD,
and you will gain knowledge of God.
6 For the LORD grants wisdom!
From his mouth come knowledge and understanding.
7 He grants a treasure of common sense to the honest.
He is a shield to those who walk with integrity.

1:8 Hebrew *My son;* also in 1:10, 15. **1:12** Hebrew *like Sheol.* **2:1** Hebrew *My son.*

1:2 teach . . . wisdom. True wisdom begins with fearing the Lord (v. 7).
1:7 Fear of the LORD. The fear of the Lord involves acknowledging God's power and sovereignty.
1:13 great things we'll get. Thieves disregard what truly matters for stolen trinkets and wasted lives.
1:18 ambush . . . get themselves killed. Those who live apart from God are like people who set a trap, only to catch themselves in it.
1:26 laugh . . . mock. Wisdom derives joy from the works of God and condemns those who reject His will.
1:32 to death . . . destroyed. Living outside of God's wisdom brings destruction—a message repeated throughout the New Testament (Rom. 6:23).
1:33 live in peace. Obedience may seem like a burden, but consider the difference between honesty and deception—living openly before others as opposed to having to keep track of lies and half-truths.
2:4 Tune . . . concentrate. A person must focus on gaining wisdom in order to grow in it.

8 He guards the paths of the just
and protects those who are faithful to him.

9 Then you will understand what is right, just, and fair,
and you will find the right way to go.
10 For wisdom will enter your heart,
and knowledge will fill you with joy.
11 Wise choices will watch over you.
Understanding will keep you safe.

12 Wisdom will save you from evil people,
from those whose words are twisted.
13 These men turn from the right way
to walk down dark paths.
14 They take pleasure in doing wrong,
and they enjoy the twisted ways of evil.
15 Their actions are crooked,
and their ways are wrong.

16 Wisdom will save you from the immoral woman,
from the seductive words of the promiscuous woman.
17 She has abandoned her husband
and ignores the covenant she made before God.
18 Entering her house leads to death;
it is the road to the grave.*
19 The man who visits her is doomed.
He will never reach the paths of life.

20 Follow the steps of good men instead,
and stay on the paths of the righteous.
21 For only the godly will live in the land,
and those with integrity will remain in it.
22 But the wicked will be removed from the land,
and the treacherous will be uprooted.

TRUSTING IN THE LORD

3 1 My child,* never forget the things I have taught you.
Store my commands in your heart.
2 If you do this, you will live many years,
and your life will be satisfying.
3 Never let loyalty and kindness leave you!
Tie them around your neck as a reminder.
Write them deep within your heart.
4 Then you will find favor with both God and people,
and you will earn a good reputation.

5 Trust in the LORD with all your heart;
do not depend on your own understanding.
6 Seek his will in all you do,
and he will show you which path to take.

HEALTH FOR BODY AND MIND

1. What's your favorite "health food?" What's your least favorite?

PROVERBS 3:1-8

2. What does it mean to tie "loyalty and kindness . . . around your neck" and to "write them deep within your heart" (v. 3)? How do we do accomplish this?
3. How does relying on our own understanding interfere with trusting God (v. 5)?
4. In what ways do you sometimes consider yourself wise? How has this gotten you in trouble?
5. Are you relying more on your own wisdom or on God's guidance?

7 Don't be impressed with your own wisdom.
Instead, fear the LORD and turn away from evil.
8 Then you will have healing for your body
and strength for your bones.

9 Honor the LORD with your wealth
and with the best part of everything you produce.
10 Then he will fill your barns with grain,
and your vats will overflow with good wine.

11 My child, don't reject the LORD's discipline,
and don't be upset when he corrects you.
12 For the LORD corrects those he loves,
just as a father corrects a child in whom he delights.*

13 Joyful is the person who finds wisdom,
the one who gains understanding.
14 For wisdom is more profitable than silver,
and her wages are better than gold.
15 Wisdom is more precious than rubies;
nothing you desire can compare with her.
16 She offers you long life in her right hand,
and riches and honor in her left.
17 She will guide you down delightful paths;
all her ways are satisfying.
18 Wisdom is a tree of life to those who embrace her;
happy are those who hold her tightly.

19 By wisdom the LORD founded the earth;
by understanding he created the heavens.
20 By his knowledge the deep fountains of the earth burst forth,
and the dew settles beneath the night sky.

2:18 Hebrew *to the spirits of the dead.* **3:1** Hebrew *My son;* also in 3:11, 21. **3:12** Greek version reads *loves, / and he punishes those he accepts as his children.* Compare Heb 12:6.

2:10-19 Wisdom is our protection against evil people who would lure us into self-destruction.
2:12 twisted. The original word translated as "twisted" means "to turn away from the upright." Throughout Proverbs this word describes a person who chooses wickedness over wisdom, or self over God (see 8:13; 10:31).
2:21 only the godly will live in the land. The Jews' history involved a journey back to the land God had promised their ancestor Abraham—their reward for following God.
3:2 satisfying. This word is often translated "peace." It suggests wholeness, health, and harmony.
3:5 with all your heart. The Bible uses this phrase to express total commitment. The Shema in Deuteronomy 6:5 calls us to love God with all our hearts, minds, and souls. Jesus described this as the first and greatest commandment.
3:6 will show . . . path. This implies more than guidance. It means God removes obstacles from our path.
3:10 vats will overflow. Plenty of wine meant prosperity to Old Testament worshippers. Often the wealth of a land was described in terms of its vineyards, grapes, or wine.
3:11-12 discipline. The Lord corrects those whom He loves.

21 My child, don't lose sight of common sense and discernment.
Hang on to them,
22 for they will refresh your soul.
They are like jewels on a necklace.
23 They keep you safe on your way,
and your feet will not stumble.
24 You can go to bed without fear;
you will lie down and sleep soundly.
25 You need not be afraid of sudden disaster
or the destruction that comes upon the wicked,
26 for the LORD is your security.
He will keep your foot from being caught in a trap.

27 Do not withhold good from those who deserve it
when it's in your power to help them.
28 If you can help your neighbor now, don't say,
"Come back tomorrow, and then I'll help you."

29 Don't plot harm against your neighbor,
for those who live nearby trust you.
30 Don't pick a fight without reason,
when no one has done you harm.

31 Don't envy violent people
or copy their ways.
32 Such wicked people are detestable to the LORD,
but he offers his friendship to the godly.

33 The LORD curses the house of the wicked,
but he blesses the home of the upright.

34 The LORD mocks the mockers
but is gracious to the humble.*

35 The wise inherit honor,
but fools are put to shame!

A FATHER'S WISE ADVICE

4 1 My children,* listen when your father corrects you.
Pay attention and learn good judgment,
2 for I am giving you good guidance.
Don't turn away from my instructions.
3 For I, too, was once my father's son,
tenderly loved as my mother's only child.
4 My father taught me,
"Take my words to heart.
Follow my commands, and you will live.
5 Get wisdom; develop good judgment.
Don't forget my words or turn away from them.
6 Don't turn your back on wisdom, for she will protect you.
Love her, and she will guard you.
7 Getting wisdom is the wisest thing you can do!
And whatever else you do, develop good judgment.
8 If you prize wisdom, she will make you great.
Embrace her, and she will honor you.
9 She will place a lovely wreath on your head;
she will present you with a beautiful crown."

10 My child,* listen to me and do as I say,
and you will have a long, good life.
11 I will teach you wisdom's ways
and lead you in straight paths.
12 When you walk, you won't be held back;
when you run, you won't stumble.
13 Take hold of my instructions; don't let them go.
Guard them, for they are the key to life.

14 Don't do as the wicked do,
and don't follow the path of evildoers.
15 Don't even think about it; don't go that way.
Turn away and keep moving.
16 For evil people can't sleep until they've done their evil deed for the day.
They can't rest until they've caused someone to stumble.
17 They eat the food of wickedness
and drink the wine of violence!

18 The way of the righteous is like the first gleam of dawn,
which shines ever brighter until the full light of day.
19 But the way of the wicked is like total darkness.
They have no idea what they are stumbling over.

20 My child, pay attention to what I say.
Listen carefully to my words.
21 Don't lose sight of them.
Let them penetrate deep into your heart,
22 for they bring life to those who find them,
and healing to their whole body.

23 Guard your heart above all else,
for it determines the course of your life.

24 Avoid all perverse talk;
stay away from corrupt speech.

25 Look straight ahead,
and fix your eyes on what lies before you.
26 Mark out a straight path for your feet;
stay on the safe path.
27 Don't get sidetracked;
keep your feet from following evil.

AVOID IMMORAL WOMEN

5 1 My son, pay attention to my wisdom;
listen carefully to my wise counsel.
2 Then you will show discernment,
and your lips will express what you've learned.

3:34 Greek version reads *The LORD opposes the proud / but gives grace to the humble.* Compare Jas 4:6; 1 Pet 5:5. **4:1** Hebrew *My sons.* **4:10** Hebrew *My son;* also in 4:20.

4:3 my father's son. Solomon's father was King David. Because Solomon was "young and inexperienced" (1 Chron. 22:5), David envisioned a temple whose construction became Solomon's great achievement.
4:4 My father taught me. Solomon transfers the wisdom of his father David to his own sons as was the Hebrew custom.

4:10 have a long, good life. The Bible often equates obedience with long life, but a long life is measured by quality of life as well as number of years.
4:18-19 Throughout the Bible righteousness and wickedness are compared to light and darkness. God's presence and guidance are described in terms of light. Jesus called Himself "the Light of the World" (see John 8:12).

3 For the lips of an immoral woman are as sweet as
honey,
and her mouth is smoother than oil.
4 But in the end she is as bitter as poison,
as dangerous as a double-edged sword.
5 Her feet go down to death;
her steps lead straight to the grave.*
6 For she cares nothing about the path to life.
She staggers down a crooked trail and doesn't
realize it.

7 So now, my sons, listen to me.
Never stray from what I am about to say:
8 Stay away from her!
Don't go near the door of her house!
9 If you do, you will lose your honor
and will lose to merciless people all you have
achieved.
10 Strangers will consume your wealth,
and someone else will enjoy the fruit of your
labor.
11 In the end you will groan in anguish
when disease consumes your body.
12 You will say, "How I hated discipline!
If only I had not ignored all the warnings!
13 Oh, why didn't I listen to my teachers?
Why didn't I pay attention to my instructors?
14 I have come to the brink of utter ruin,
and now I must face public disgrace."

15 Drink water from your own well—
share your love only with your wife.*
16 Why spill the water of your springs in the streets,
having sex with just anyone?*
17 You should reserve it for yourselves.
Never share it with strangers.

18 Let your wife be a fountain of blessing for you.
Rejoice in the wife of your youth.
19 She is a loving deer, a graceful doe.
Let her breasts satisfy you always.
May you always be captivated by her love.
20 Why be captivated, my son, by an immoral woman,
or fondle the breasts of a promiscuous woman?

21 For the LORD sees clearly what a man does,
examining every path he takes.
22 An evil man is held captive by his own sins;
they are ropes that catch and hold him.
23 He will die for lack of self-control;
he will be lost because of his great foolishness.

LESSONS FOR DAILY LIFE

6 1 My child,* if you have put up security for a
friend's debt
or agreed to guarantee the debt of a stranger—
2 if you have trapped yourself by your agreement
and are caught by what you said—
3 follow my advice and save yourself,
for you have placed yourself at your friend's
mercy.
Now swallow your pride;
go and beg to have your name erased.
4 Don't put it off; do it now!
Don't rest until you do.
5 Save yourself like a gazelle escaping from a
hunter,
like a bird fleeing from a net.

6 Take a lesson from the ants, you lazybones.
Learn from their ways and become wise!
7 Though they have no prince
or governor or ruler to make them work,
8 they labor hard all summer,
gathering food for the winter.
9 But you, lazybones, how long will you sleep?
When will you wake up?
10 A little extra sleep, a little more slumber,
a little folding of the hands to rest—
11 then poverty will pounce on you like a bandit;
scarcity will attack you like an armed robber.

12 What are worthless and wicked people like?
They are constant liars,
13 signaling their deceit with a wink of the eye,
a nudge of the foot, or the wiggle of fingers.
14 Their perverted hearts plot evil,
and they constantly stir up trouble.
15 But they will be destroyed suddenly,
broken in an instant beyond all hope of healing.

16 There are six things the LORD hates—
no, seven things he detests:
17 haughty eyes,
a lying tongue,
hands that kill the innocent,
18 a heart that plots evil,
feet that race to do wrong,
19 a false witness who pours out lies,
a person who sows discord in a family.

20 My son, obey your father's commands,
and don't neglect your mother's instruction.
21 Keep their words always in your heart.
Tie them around your neck.
22 When you walk, their counsel will lead you.
When you sleep, they will protect you.
When you wake up, they will advise you.
23 For their command is a lamp
and their instruction a light;
their corrective discipline
is the way to life.

5:5 Hebrew *to Sheol.* 5:15 Hebrew *Drink water from your own cistern, / flowing water from your own well.* 5:16 Hebrew *Why spill your springs in the streets, / your streams in the city squares?* 6:1 Hebrew *My son.*

5:3 honey . . . oil. Honey was the sweetest substance, and olive oil was the smoothest substance in Hebrew culture. Both are metaphors for folly.
5:7-14 Sexual infidelity carries a price. It costs a person dearly, including self-respect.
5:11 you will groan. "Groan" may refer to old age, but more likely it refers to the cumulative, debilitating effects of living immorally.
5:13 my teachers. This phrase could refer to parents or teachers of the law.
6:1 security . . . agreed to guarantee. The equivalent of cosigning a loan and being responsible for someone else's debt. Charging interest on loans to fellow countrymen was not considered honorable among the Hebrews.
6:6 lazybones. A lazybones was a lazy and shiftless person who chose a lifestyle of irresponsibility over actively doing the right things.
6:12 worthless and wicked. A worthless and wicked person (Judg. 19:22; 1 Sam. 25:25) was also a troublemaker. Eventually this term became associated with Satan (2 Cor. 6:14-15).
6:17 haughty eyes. A proud look. God does not reward pride or arrogance. Pride leads to destruction (16:18; 18:12).
6:23 lamp . . . light. This writer describes parents teaching truth to their children in the same way the psalmist describes the Word of God: "a lamp to guide my feet and a light for my path" (Ps. 119:105).

24 It will keep you from the immoral woman,
from the smooth tongue of a promiscuous woman.
25 Don't lust for her beauty.
Don't let her coy glances seduce you.
26 For a prostitute will bring you to poverty,*
but sleeping with another man's wife will cost you your life.
27 Can a man scoop a flame into his lap
and not have his clothes catch on fire?
28 Can he walk on hot coals
and not blister his feet?
29 So it is with the man who sleeps with another man's wife.
He who embraces her will not go unpunished.

30 Excuses might be found for a thief
who steals because he is starving.
31 But if he is caught, he must pay back seven times what he stole,
even if he has to sell everything in his house.
32 But the man who commits adultery is an utter fool,
for he destroys himself.
33 He will be wounded and disgraced.
His shame will never be erased.
34 For the woman's jealous husband will be furious,
and he will show no mercy when he takes revenge.
35 He will accept no compensation,
nor be satisfied with a payoff of any size.

ANOTHER WARNING ABOUT IMMORAL WOMEN

7 1 Follow my advice, my son;
always treasure my commands.
2 Obey my commands and live!
Guard my instructions as you guard your own eyes.*
3 Tie them on your fingers as a reminder.
Write them deep within your heart.

4 Love wisdom like a sister;
make insight a beloved member of your family.
5 Let them protect you from an affair with an immoral woman,
from listening to the flattery of a promiscuous woman.

6 While I was at the window of my house,
looking through the curtain,
7 I saw some naive young men,
and one in particular who lacked common sense.
8 He was crossing the street near the house of an immoral woman,
strolling down the path by her house.
9 It was at twilight, in the evening,
as deep darkness fell.
10 The woman approached him,
seductively dressed and sly of heart.
11 She was the brash, rebellious type,
never content to stay at home.
12 She is often in the streets and markets,
soliciting at every corner.
13 She threw her arms around him and kissed him,
and with a brazen look she said,
14 "I've just made my peace offerings
and fulfilled my vows.
15 You're the one I was looking for!
I came out to find you, and here you are!
16 My bed is spread with beautiful blankets,
with colored sheets of Egyptian linen.
17 I've perfumed my bed
with myrrh, aloes, and cinnamon.
18 Come, let's drink our fill of love until morning.
Let's enjoy each other's caresses,
19 for my husband is not home.
He's away on a long trip.
20 He has taken a wallet full of money with him
and won't return until later this month.*"

21 So she seduced him with her pretty speech
and enticed him with her flattery.
22 He followed her at once,
like an ox going to the slaughter.
He was like a stag caught in a trap,*
23 awaiting the arrow that would pierce its heart.
He was like a bird flying into a snare,
little knowing it would cost him his life.

24 So listen to me, my sons,
and pay attention to my words.
25 Don't let your hearts stray away toward her.
Don't wander down her wayward path.
26 For she has been the ruin of many;
many men have been her victims.
27 Her house is the road to the grave.*
Her bedroom is the den of death.

WISDOM CALLS FOR A HEARING

8 1 Listen as Wisdom calls out!
Hear as understanding raises her voice!
2 On the hilltop along the road,
she takes her stand at the crossroads.
3 By the gates at the entrance to the town,
on the road leading in, she cries aloud,
4 "I call to you, to all of you!
I raise my voice to all people.
5 You simple people, use good judgment.
You foolish people, show some understanding.
6 Listen to me! For I have important things to tell you.
Everything I say is right,
7 for I speak the truth
and detest every kind of deception.
8 My advice is wholesome.
There is nothing devious or crooked in it.
9 My words are plain to anyone with understanding,
clear to those with knowledge.

6:26 Hebrew *to a loaf of bread.* **7:2** Hebrew *as the pupil of your eye.* **7:20** Hebrew *until the moon is full.* **7:22** As in Greek and Syriac versions; Hebrew reads *slaughter, as shackles are for the discipline of a fool.* **7:27** Hebrew *to Sheol.*

6:31 seven times. Seven is a number representing completion. Hebrew law did not require more than a fivefold restitution for stolen property. "Seven times" implies full restoration or "whatever it takes." No penalty could pardon adultery.

7:3 Tie them. Moses' last charge to the Israelites was to bind God's Law to their foreheads and hands (Deut. 6:8). Solomon echoes Moses' command here.

7:21 enticed. An accurate picture of sin and temptation. The immoral woman sets out deliberately to cause a man to fall into sin.

10 Choose my instruction rather than silver,
and knowledge rather than pure gold.
11 For wisdom is far more valuable than rubies.
Nothing you desire can compare with it.

12 "I, Wisdom, live together with good judgment.
I know where to discover knowledge and
discernment.
13 All who fear the LORD will hate evil.
Therefore, I hate pride and arrogance,
corruption and perverse speech.
14 Common sense and success belong to me.
Insight and strength are mine.
15 Because of me, kings reign,
and rulers make just decrees.
16 Rulers lead with my help,
and nobles make righteous judgments.*

17 "I love all who love me.
Those who search will surely find me.
18 I have riches and honor,
as well as enduring wealth and justice.
19 My gifts are better than gold, even the purest gold,
my wages better than sterling silver!
20 I walk in righteousness,
in paths of justice.
21 Those who love me inherit wealth.
I will fill their treasuries.

22 "The LORD formed me from the beginning,
before he created anything else.
23 I was appointed in ages past,
at the very first, before the earth began.
24 I was born before the oceans were created,
before the springs bubbled forth their waters.
25 Before the mountains were formed,
before the hills, I was born—
26 before he had made the earth and fields
and the first handfuls of soil.
27 I was there when he established the heavens,
when he drew the horizon on the oceans.
28 I was there when he set the clouds above,
when he established springs deep in the earth.
29 I was there when he set the limits of the seas,
so they would not spread beyond their
boundaries.
And when he marked off the earth's foundations,
30 I was the architect at his side.
I was his constant delight,
rejoicing always in his presence.
31 And how happy I was with the world he created;
how I rejoiced with the human family!

32 "And so, my children,* listen to me,
for all who follow my ways are joyful.
33 Listen to my instruction and be wise.
Don't ignore it.
34 Joyful are those who listen to me,
watching for me daily at my gates,
waiting for me outside my home!
35 For whoever finds me finds life
and receives favor from the LORD.
36 But those who miss me injure themselves.
All who hate me love death."

9 1 Wisdom has built her house;
she has carved its seven columns.
2 She has prepared a great banquet,
mixed the wines, and set the table.
3 She has sent her servants to invite everyone to
come.
She calls out from the heights overlooking the city.
4 "Come in with me," she urges the simple.
To those who lack good judgment, she says,
5 "Come, eat my food,
and drink the wine I have mixed.
6 Leave your simple ways behind, and begin to live;
learn to use good judgment."

7 Anyone who rebukes a mocker will get an insult
in return.
Anyone who corrects the wicked will get hurt.
8 So don't bother correcting mockers;
they will only hate you.
But correct the wise,
and they will love you.
9 Instruct the wise,
and they will be even wiser.
Teach the righteous,
and they will learn even more.

10 Fear of the LORD is the foundation of wisdom.
Knowledge of the Holy One results in good
judgment.

11 Wisdom will multiply your days
and add years to your life.
12 If you become wise, you will be the one to benefit.
If you scorn wisdom, you will be the one to
suffer.

FOLLY CALLS FOR A HEARING

13 The woman named Folly is brash.
She is ignorant and doesn't know it.
14 She sits in her doorway
on the heights overlooking the city.
15 She calls out to men going by
who are minding their own business.
16 "Come in with me," she urges the simple.
To those who lack good judgment, she says,

8:16 Some Hebrew manuscripts and Greek version read *and nobles are judges over the earth.* **8:32** Hebrew *my sons.*

8:14 Wisdom is highlighted here as a source of strength. This chapter draws a stark contrast between the wise person and the helpless victim caught in the web of sin.
8:22-31 Wisdom is personified in this hymn-like passage. New Testament writers describe Jesus in similar terms. He was the Word that was with God during creation (John 1:1-3) as well as the wisdom of God (1 Cor. 1:24,30).
8:32 all who follow my ways are joyful. Blessings that follow wisdom are not so much mystical rewards as the natural consequences of good choices and a life well-lived.
8:36 injure themselves. The Bible equates sin, choosing our own way over God's, with self-destruction.
9:1 house . . . seven columns. "Seven columns" could refer to the seven days of creation or to the seven constellations in the heavens.
9:5 eat . . . drink. Wisdom is like wine and food.
9:7 mocker. A wicked person will lash out at correction and retaliate against discipline.
9:8 they will love you. Even a rebuke is a pleasant thing because a wise person will learn from it.
9:11 add years. Generally speaking, wisdom adds to the quality and longevity of life.
9:12 The rewards of wisdom and folly work on the same principle that Paul described in Galatians 6:7. What a person sows will yield consequences.

[17] "Stolen water is refreshing;
food eaten in secret tastes the best!"
[18] But little do they know that the dead are there.
Her guests are in the depths of the grave.*

THE PROVERBS OF SOLOMON

10 The proverbs of Solomon:

A wise child* brings joy to a father;
a foolish child brings grief to a mother.

[2] Tainted wealth has no lasting value,
but right living can save your life.

[3] The LORD will not let the godly go hungry,
but he refuses to satisfy the craving of the wicked.

[4] Lazy people are soon poor;
hard workers get rich.

[5] A wise youth harvests in the summer,
but one who sleeps during harvest is a disgrace.

[6] The godly are showered with blessings;
the words of the wicked conceal violent
intentions.

[7] We have happy memories of the godly,
but the name of a wicked person rots away.

[8] The wise are glad to be instructed,
but babbling fools fall flat on their faces.

[9] People with integrity walk safely,
but those who follow crooked paths will be
exposed.

[10] People who wink at wrong cause trouble,
but a bold reproof promotes peace.*

[11] The words of the godly are a life-giving fountain;
the words of the wicked conceal violent
intentions.

[12] Hatred stirs up quarrels,
but love makes up for all offenses.

[13] Wise words come from the lips of people with
understanding,
but those lacking sense will be beaten with a
rod.

[14] Wise people treasure knowledge,
but the babbling of a fool invites disaster.

[15] The wealth of the rich is their fortress;
the poverty of the poor is their destruction.

[16] The earnings of the godly enhance their lives,
but evil people squander their money on sin.

[17] People who accept discipline are on the pathway
to life,
but those who ignore correction will go astray.

[18] Hiding hatred makes you a liar;
slandering others makes you a fool.

[19] Too much talk leads to sin.
Be sensible and keep your mouth shut.

[20] The words of the godly are like sterling silver;
the heart of a fool is worthless.

[21] The words of the godly encourage many,
but fools are destroyed by their lack of common
sense.

[22] The blessing of the LORD makes a person rich,
and he adds no sorrow with it.

[23] Doing wrong is fun for a fool,
but living wisely brings pleasure to the sensible.

[24] The fears of the wicked will be fulfilled;
the hopes of the godly will be granted.

[25] When the storms of life come, the wicked are
whirled away,
but the godly have a lasting foundation.

[26] Lazy people irritate their employers,
like vinegar to the teeth or smoke in the eyes.

[27] Fear of the LORD lengthens one's life,
but the years of the wicked are cut short.

[28] The hopes of the godly result in happiness,
but the expectations of the wicked come to
nothing.

[29] The way of the LORD is a stronghold to those with
integrity,
but it destroys the wicked.

[30] The godly will never be disturbed,
but the wicked will be removed from the land.

[31] The mouth of the godly person gives wise advice,
but the tongue that deceives will be cut off.

[32] The lips of the godly speak helpful words,
but the mouth of the wicked speaks perverse
words.

11 [1] The LORD detests the use of dishonest scales,
but he delights in accurate weights.

[2] Pride leads to disgrace,
but with humility comes wisdom.

9:18 Hebrew *in Sheol.* 10:1 Hebrew *son;* also in 10:1b. 10:10 As in Greek version; Hebrew reads *but babbling fools fall flat on their faces.*

10:1 proverbs of Solomon. Chapters 10–22 are collections of individual proverbs that do not have a common theme.
10:4 poor. In Proverbs poverty is associated with laziness or a lack of discipline.
10:5 harvests. Solomon often uses the image of harvest to illustrate a person who understands the discipline of taking care of himself.
10:13 rod. Beatings were a form of punishment in Solomon's time. Even in Jesus' day, beatings accompanied capital punishment (Matt. 27:26).
10:25 Jesus may have had this proverb in mind when He told the parable of the wise man who built his house on a rock and thus withstood a fierce storm, while the foolish man built on the unstable sand (Matt. 7:24-29).

[3] Honesty guides good people;
dishonesty destroys treacherous people.

[4] Riches won't help on the day of judgment,
but right living can save you from death.

[5] The godly are directed by honesty;
the wicked fall beneath their load of sin.

[6] The godliness of good people rescues them;
the ambition of treacherous people traps them.

[7] When the wicked die, their hopes die with them,
for they rely on their own feeble strength.

[8] The godly are rescued from trouble,
and it falls on the wicked instead.

[9] With their words, the godless destroy their friends,
but knowledge will rescue the righteous.

[10] The whole city celebrates when the godly
succeed;
they shout for joy when the wicked die.

[11] Upright citizens are good for a city and make it
prosper,
but the talk of the wicked tears it apart.

[12] It is foolish to belittle one's neighbor;
a sensible person keeps quiet.

[13] A gossip goes around telling secrets,
but those who are trustworthy can keep a
confidence.

[14] Without wise leadership, a nation falls;
there is safety in having many advisers.

[15] There's danger in putting up security for a
stranger's debt;
it's safer not to guarantee another person's debt.

[16] A gracious woman gains respect,
but ruthless men gain only wealth.

[17] Your kindness will reward you,
but your cruelty will destroy you.

[18] Evil people get rich for the moment,
but the reward of the godly will last.

[19] Godly people find life;
evil people find death.

[20] The LORD detests people with crooked hearts,
but he delights in those with integrity.

[21] Evil people will surely be punished,
but the children of the godly will go free.

[22] A beautiful woman who lacks discretion
is like a gold ring in a pig's snout.

[23] The godly can look forward to a reward,
while the wicked can expect only judgment.

[24] Give freely and become more wealthy;
be stingy and lose everything.

[25] The generous will prosper;
those who refresh others will themselves be
refreshed.

[26] People curse those who hoard their grain,
but they bless the one who sells in time of need.

[27] If you search for good, you will find favor;
but if you search for evil, it will find you!

[28] Trust in your money and down you go!
But the godly flourish like leaves in spring.

[29] Those who bring trouble on their families inherit
the wind.
The fool will be a servant to the wise.

[30] The seeds of good deeds become a tree of life;
a wise person wins friends.*

[31] If the righteous are rewarded here on earth,
what will happen to wicked sinners?*

12

[1] To learn, you must love discipline;
it is stupid to hate correction.

[2] The LORD approves of those who are good,
but he condemns those who plan wickedness.

[3] Wickedness never brings stability,
but the godly have deep roots.

[4] A worthy wife is a crown for her husband,
but a disgraceful woman is like cancer in his
bones.

[5] The plans of the godly are just;
the advice of the wicked is treacherous.

[6] The words of the wicked are like a murderous
ambush,
but the words of the godly save lives.

[7] The wicked die and disappear,
but the family of the godly stands firm.

11:30 Or *and those who win souls are wise.* **11:31** Greek version reads *If the righteous are barely saved, / what will happen to godless sinners?* Compare 1 Pet 4:18.

11:4 day of judgment. It is righteousness, not wealth, that will save us when we face God's judgment at the end of our lives.
11:7 hopes die with them. Beyond this life, wealth and power mean nothing. To trade righteousness or wisdom for either is a futile attempt at happiness. This passage is reminiscent of the teaching of Ecclesiastes on futility or meaninglessness. Only hope built on Christ and His teachings will last.
11:16 This proverb makes its point by comparing the value of respect to material wealth. The reader is not left to doubt which is the prize. Riches cannot buy good relationships, contentment, and respect from others.
11:24 Give freely and become more wealthy. Generosity toward others, not hoarding what we own, is the path to prosperity.
11:28 Trust. The problem is not having riches but trusting in them. Jesus touched on this topic (Matt. 19:23-24). The second half of this verse refers to attitude more than material wealth.
11:31 rewarded. This phrase can be interpreted both in terms of blessings and consequences. David suffered because of his sin with Bathsheba (2 Sam. 12:7-10). Moses suffered because of his lack of trust in the Lord (Num. 20:9-12).

8 A sensible person wins admiration,
but a warped mind is despised.

9 Better to be an ordinary person with a servant
than to be self-important but have no food.

10 The godly care for their animals,
but the wicked are always cruel.

11 A hard worker has plenty of food,
but a person who chases fantasies has no sense.

12 Thieves are jealous of each other's loot,
but the godly are well rooted and bear their own fruit.

13 The wicked are trapped by their own words,
but the godly escape such trouble.

14 Wise words bring many benefits,
and hard work brings rewards.

15 Fools think their own way is right,
but the wise listen to others.

16 A fool is quick-tempered,
but a wise person stays calm when insulted.

17 An honest witness tells the truth;
a false witness tells lies.

18 Some people make cutting remarks,
but the words of the wise bring healing.

19 Truthful words stand the test of time,
but lies are soon exposed.

20 Deceit fills hearts that are plotting evil;
joy fills hearts that are planning peace!

21 No harm comes to the godly,
but the wicked have their fill of trouble.

22 The LORD detests lying lips,
but he delights in those who tell the truth.

23 The wise don't make a show of their knowledge,
but fools broadcast their foolishness.

24 Work hard and become a leader;
be lazy and become a slave.

25 Worry weighs a person down;
an encouraging word cheers a person up.

26 The godly give good advice to their friends;*
the wicked lead them astray.

27 Lazy people don't even cook the game they catch,
but the diligent make use of everything they find.

28 The way of the godly leads to life;
that path does not lead to death.

13

1 A wise child accepts a parent's discipline;*
a mocker refuses to listen to correction.

2 Wise words will win you a good meal,
but treacherous people have an appetite for violence.

3 Those who control their tongue will have a long life;
opening your mouth can ruin everything.

4 Lazy people want much but get little,
but those who work hard will prosper.

5 The godly hate lies;
the wicked cause shame and disgrace.

6 Godliness guards the path of the blameless,
but the evil are misled by sin.

7 Some who are poor pretend to be rich;
others who are rich pretend to be poor.

8 The rich can pay a ransom for their lives,
but the poor won't even get threatened.

9 The life of the godly is full of light and joy,
but the light of the wicked will be snuffed out.

10 Pride leads to conflict;
those who take advice are wise.

11 Wealth from get-rich-quick schemes quickly disappears;
wealth from hard work grows over time.

12 Hope deferred makes the heart sick,
but a dream fulfilled is a tree of life.

13 People who despise advice are asking for trouble;
those who respect a command will succeed.

14 The instruction of the wise is like a life-giving fountain;
those who accept it avoid the snares of death.

15 A person with good sense is respected;
a treacherous person is headed for destruction.*

16 Wise people think before they act;
fools don't—and even brag about their foolishness.

12:26 Or *The godly are cautious in friendship;* or *The godly are freed from evil.* The meaning of the Hebrew is uncertain. 13:1 Hebrew *A wise son accepts his father's discipline.* 13:15 As in Greek version; Hebrew reads *the way of the treacherous is lasting.*

12:11 who chases fantasies. Consistent, constructive work, not daydreaming or fantasizing, yields the provisions we need for daily living.

12:14 wise words. Literally, "the words he speaks" (25:11). The good things we do and say bring rewards.

12:16 stays calm. Sometimes this word is translated "covers." The concept here is diplomacy and tact rather than avoidance.

12:27 cook. This may refer to the preparation of food or to preparation for the hunt. A lazy person doesn't provide adequately for himself and his family.

13:3 control their tongue. Words produce consequences. James reinforced the wisdom of taming the tongue (James 3:5-9).

13:8 Which is the greater protection—to have the money to ransom yourself or to have so little property that no thief would try to steal from you?

13:11 get-rich-quick schemes. This refers to money gained illegally (10:2, Jer. 17:11), by extortion (Ps. 62:10) or deceit (Prov. 21:6).

17 An unreliable messenger stumbles into trouble,
but a reliable messenger brings healing.

18 If you ignore criticism, you will end in poverty and disgrace;
if you accept correction, you will be honored.

19 It is pleasant to see dreams come true,
but fools refuse to turn from evil to attain them.

20 Walk with the wise and become wise;
associate with fools and get in trouble.

21 Trouble chases sinners,
while blessings reward the righteous.

22 Good people leave an inheritance to their grandchildren,
but the sinner's wealth passes to the godly.

23 A poor person's farm may produce much food,
but injustice sweeps it all away.

24 Those who spare the rod of discipline hate their children.
Those who love their children care enough to discipline them.

25 The godly eat to their hearts' content,
but the belly of the wicked goes hungry.

14 1 A wise woman builds her home,
but a foolish woman tears it down with her own hands.

2 Those who follow the right path fear the LORD;
those who take the wrong path despise him.

3 A fool's proud talk becomes a rod that beats him,
but the words of the wise keep them safe.

4 Without oxen a stable stays clean,
but you need a strong ox for a large harvest.

5 An honest witness does not lie;
a false witness breathes lies.

6 A mocker seeks wisdom and never finds it,
but knowledge comes easily to those with understanding.

7 Stay away from fools,
for you won't find knowledge on their lips.

8 The prudent understand where they are going,
but fools deceive themselves.

9 Fools make fun of guilt,
but the godly acknowledge it and seek reconciliation.

10 Each heart knows its own bitterness,
and no one else can fully share its joy.

11 The house of the wicked will be destroyed,
but the tent of the godly will flourish.

12 There is a path before each person that seems right,
but it ends in death.

13 Laughter can conceal a heavy heart,
but when the laughter ends, the grief remains.

14 Backsliders get what they deserve;
good people receive their reward.

15 Only simpletons believe everything they're told!
The prudent carefully consider their steps.

16 The wise are cautious* and avoid danger;
fools plunge ahead with reckless confidence.

17 Short-tempered people do foolish things,
and schemers are hated.

18 Simpletons are clothed with foolishness,*
but the prudent are crowned with knowledge.

19 Evil people will bow before good people;
the wicked will bow at the gates of the godly.

20 The poor are despised even by their neighbors,
while the rich have many "friends."

21 It is a sin to belittle one's neighbor;
blessed are those who help the poor.

22 If you plan to do evil, you will be lost;
if you plan to do good, you will receive unfailing love and faithfulness.

23 Work brings profit,
but mere talk leads to poverty!

24 Wealth is a crown for the wise;
the effort of fools yields only foolishness.

25 A truthful witness saves lives,
but a false witness is a traitor.

26 Those who fear the LORD are secure;
he will be a refuge for their children.

27 Fear of the LORD is a life-giving fountain;
it offers escape from the snares of death.

28 A growing population is a king's glory;
a prince without subjects has nothing.

29 People with understanding control their anger;
a hot temper shows great foolishness.

14:16 Hebrew *The wise fear.* 14:18 Or *inherit foolishness.*

13:22 inheritance. Throughout Proverbs the long-term legacy of the righteous is compared to the short life of the unrighteous (10:27).
13:24 the rod. The rod was used for spanking. Proverbs consistently reinforces the importance of discipline, especially for children
14:4 large harvest. In order to realize a harvest, the farmer must invest money and work. **stable.** An empty manger implies laziness.
14:21 belittle. Holds in contempt, belittles, ridicules. God made it clear that His people should show concern for the poor.
14:22 unfailing love and faithfulness. The New Testament equivalent would be grace and truth.
14:29 hot temper. Quick-tempered people often act before thinking. James encouraged his readers to be slow to speak and slow to anger (James 1:19).

30 A peaceful heart leads to a healthy body;
jealousy is like cancer in the bones.

31 Those who oppress the poor insult their Maker,
but helping the poor honors him.

32 The wicked are crushed by disaster,
but the godly have a refuge when they die.

33 Wisdom is enshrined in an understanding heart;
wisdom is not* found among fools.

34 Godliness makes a nation great,
but sin is a disgrace to any people.

35 A king rejoices in wise servants
but is angry with those who disgrace him.

15 1 A gentle answer deflects anger,
but harsh words make tempers flare.

2 The tongue of the wise makes knowledge
appealing,
but the mouth of a fool belches out
foolishness.

3 The LORD is watching everywhere,
keeping his eye on both the evil and the good.

4 Gentle words are a tree of life;
a deceitful tongue crushes the spirit.

5 Only a fool despises a parent's* discipline;
whoever learns from correction is wise.

6 There is treasure in the house of the godly,
but the earnings of the wicked bring trouble.

7 The lips of the wise give good advice;
the heart of a fool has none to give.

8 The LORD detests the sacrifice of the wicked,
but he delights in the prayers of the upright.

9 The LORD detests the way of the wicked,
but he loves those who pursue godliness.

10 Whoever abandons the right path will be severely
disciplined;
whoever hates correction will die.

11 Even Death and Destruction* hold no secrets from
the LORD.
How much more does he know the human
heart!

12 Mockers hate to be corrected,
so they stay away from the wise.

13 A glad heart makes a happy face;
a broken heart crushes the spirit.

14 A wise person is hungry for knowledge,
while the fool feeds on trash.

15 For the despondent, every day brings trouble;
for the happy heart, life is a continual feast.

16 Better to have little, with fear for the LORD,
than to have great treasure and inner
turmoil.

17 A bowl of vegetables with someone you love
is better than steak with someone you hate.

18 A hot-tempered person starts fights;
a cool-tempered person stops them.

19 A lazy person's way is blocked with briers,
but the path of the upright is an open
highway.

20 Sensible children bring joy to their father;
foolish children despise their mother.

21 Foolishness brings joy to those with no sense;
a sensible person stays on the right path.

22 Plans go wrong for lack of advice;
many advisers bring success.

23 Everyone enjoys a fitting reply;
it is wonderful to say the right thing at the right
time!

24 The path of life leads upward for the wise;
they leave the grave* behind.

25 The LORD tears down the house of the proud,
but he protects the property of widows.

26 The LORD detests evil plans,
but he delights in pure words.

27 Greed brings grief to the whole family,
but those who hate bribes will live.

28 The heart of the godly thinks carefully before
speaking;
the mouth of the wicked overflows with evil
words.

29 The LORD is far from the wicked,
but he hears the prayers of the righteous.

30 A cheerful look brings joy to the heart;
good news makes for good health.

14:33 As in Greek and Syriac versions; Hebrew lacks *not.* **15:5** Hebrew *father's.* **15:11** Hebrew *Sheol and Abaddon.* **15:24** Hebrew *Sheol.*

14:31 God protects the poor (22:22-23). Our actions toward the poor reflect our attitude toward God.

15:1 The way we use speech says a lot about what kind of people we are (James 3:5-8). Whether we use gentle or harsh words, our conversation reflects our character.

15:3 is watching. That God sees everything we do evokes different responses from people: to the righteous this brings comfort; to the wicked a threat.

15:4 deceitful tongue. Our words have the power to influence people around us for good or evil.

15:8 sacrifice. God wants devoted hearts—not cold obedience.

15:11 Death and Destruction. This is probably an allusion to the fact that God sees the dead in their graves or in their eternal homes. How much more is God able to see the hearts of living people?

15:15 the despondent. People bowed down by affliction who cannot overcome their circumstances.

31 If you listen to constructive criticism,
you will be at home among the wise.

32 If you reject discipline, you only harm yourself;
but if you listen to correction, you grow in
understanding.

33 Fear of the LORD teaches wisdom;
humility precedes honor.

16 1 We can make our own plans,
but the LORD gives the right answer.

2 People may be pure in their own eyes,
but the LORD examines their motives.

3 Commit your actions to the LORD,
and your plans will succeed.

4 The LORD has made everything for his own
purposes,
even the wicked for a day of disaster.

5 The LORD detests the proud;
they will surely be punished.

6 Unfailing love and faithfulness make atonement
for sin.
By fearing the LORD, people avoid evil.

7 When people's lives please the LORD,
even their enemies are at peace with them.

8 Better to have little, with godliness,
than to be rich and dishonest.

9 We can make our plans,
but the LORD determines our steps.

10 The king speaks with divine wisdom;
he must never judge unfairly.

11 The LORD demands accurate scales and
balances;
he sets the standards for fairness.

12 A king detests wrongdoing,
for his rule is built on justice.

13 The king is pleased with words from righteous
lips;
he loves those who speak honestly.

14 The anger of the king is a deadly threat;
the wise will try to appease it.

15 When the king smiles, there is life;
his favor refreshes like a spring rain.

16 How much better to get wisdom than gold,
and good judgment than silver!

17 The path of the virtuous leads away from
evil;
whoever follows that path is safe.

18 Pride goes before destruction,
and haughtiness before a fall.

19 Better to live humbly with the poor
than to share plunder with the proud.

20 Those who listen to instruction will prosper;
those who trust the LORD will be joyful.

21 The wise are known for their understanding,
and pleasant words are persuasive.

22 Discretion is a life-giving fountain to those who
possess it,
but discipline is wasted on fools.

23 From a wise mind comes wise speech;
the words of the wise are persuasive.

24 Kind words are like honey—
sweet to the soul and healthy for the
body.

25 There is a path before each person that seems
right,
but it ends in death.

26 It is good for workers to have an appetite;
an empty stomach drives them on.

27 Scoundrels create trouble;
their words are a destructive blaze.

28 A troublemaker plants seeds of strife;
gossip separates the best of friends.

29 Violent people mislead their companions,
leading them down a harmful path.

30 With narrowed eyes, people plot evil;
with a smirk, they plan their mischief.

31 Gray hair is a crown of glory;
it is gained by living a godly life.

32 Better to be patient than powerful;
better to have self-control than to conquer a
city.

33 We may throw the dice,*
but the LORD determines how they fall.

16:33 Hebrew *We may cast lots.*

15:32 discipline. God's discipline or moral correction is a part of His love for us (Heb. 12:7-11).
16:4 disaster. God's justice includes punishment for wickedness as well as rewards for righteousness.
16:6 unfailing love and faithfulness. This is God's loyalty and God's faithfulness. We avoid evil through God's saving grace and our relationship with Him.
16:7 please the LORD. Habits that please God include pure thoughts (15:26) and honesty (20:23).
16:9 make our plans. God's sovereignty should not keep us from planning and setting goals. But we need God's wisdom to guide us as we make these plans.
16:10 king. Originally the nation of Israel was a theocracy governed by God. Later, Israel was ruled by judges and finally by kings. The first two kings, Saul and David (Solomon's father), were chosen by God. Even though these early kings were political rulers, they were also God's representatives.

17

[1] Better a dry crust eaten in peace
than a house filled with feasting—and
conflict.

[2] A wise servant will rule over the master's
disgraceful son
and will share the inheritance of the master's
children.

[3] Fire tests the purity of silver and gold,
but the LORD tests the heart.

[4] Wrongdoers eagerly listen to gossip;
liars pay close attention to slander.

[5] Those who mock the poor insult their Maker;
those who rejoice at the misfortune of others
will be punished.

[6] Grandchildren are the crowning glory of the
aged;
parents* are the pride of their children.

[7] Eloquent words are not fitting for a fool;
even less are lies fitting for a ruler.

[8] A bribe is like a lucky charm;
whoever gives one will prosper!

[9] Love prospers when a fault is forgiven,
but dwelling on it separates close friends.

[10] A single rebuke does more for a person of
understanding
than a hundred lashes on the back of a fool.

[11] Evil people are eager for rebellion,
but they will be severely punished.

[12] It is safer to meet a bear robbed of her cubs
than to confront a fool caught in foolishness.

[13] If you repay good with evil,
evil will never leave your house.

[14] Starting a quarrel is like opening a floodgate,
so stop before a dispute breaks out.

[15] Acquitting the guilty and condemning the
innocent—
both are detestable to the LORD.

[16] It is senseless to pay to educate a fool,
since he has no heart for learning.

[17] A friend is always loyal,
and a brother is born to help in time of
need.

[18] It's poor judgment to guarantee another person's
debt
or put up security for a friend.

[19] Anyone who loves to quarrel loves sin;
anyone who trusts in high walls invites disaster.

[20] The crooked heart will not prosper;
the lying tongue tumbles into trouble.

[21] It is painful to be the parent of a fool;
there is no joy for the father of a rebel.

[22] A cheerful heart is good medicine,
but a broken spirit saps a person's strength.

[23] The wicked take secret bribes
to pervert the course of justice.

[24] Sensible people keep their eyes glued on wisdom,
but a fool's eyes wander to the ends of the earth.

[25] Foolish children* bring grief to their father
and bitterness to the one who gave them birth.

[26] It is wrong to punish the godly for being good
or to flog leaders for being honest.

[27] A truly wise person uses few words;
a person with understanding is even-tempered.

[28] Even fools are thought wise when they keep silent;
with their mouths shut, they seem intelligent.

18

[1] Unfriendly people care only about themselves;
they lash out at common sense.

[2] Fools have no interest in understanding;
they only want to air their own opinions.

[3] Doing wrong leads to disgrace,
and scandalous behavior brings contempt.

[4] Wise words are like deep waters;
wisdom flows from the wise like a bubbling
brook.

[5] It is not right to acquit the guilty
or deny justice to the innocent.

[6] Fools' words get them into constant quarrels;
they are asking for a beating.

[7] The mouths of fools are their ruin;
they trap themselves with their lips.

[8] Rumors are dainty morsels
that sink deep into one's heart.

17:6 Hebrew *fathers.* **17:25** Hebrew *A foolish son.*

17:2 wise servant. The truth of this proverb is revealed in Solomon's own life. His son Rehoboam was rejected by the northern tribes, which broke away into Israel, or the northern kingdom.

17:17 friend . . . brother. This verse does not focus on the difference between a friend and a brother but on the commitment required in both relationships. Solomon likely heard stories about his father David's friendship with Jonathan (see 1 Sam. 18:1).

17:19 high walls. Either a door that is tall to show off wealth or a symbol for boasting.

18:8 dainty morsels. An apt description of a "juicy" piece of gossip. Just as a rich and delicious food is digested, gossip becomes a part of us and affects our attitudes.

9 A lazy person is as bad as
someone who destroys things.

10 The name of the LORD is a strong fortress;
the godly run to him and are safe.

11 The rich think of their wealth as a strong defense;
they imagine it to be a high wall of safety.

12 Haughtiness goes before destruction;
humility precedes honor.

13 Spouting off before listening to the facts
is both shameful and foolish.

14 The human spirit can endure a sick body,
but who can bear a crushed spirit?

15 Intelligent people are always ready to learn.
Their ears are open for knowledge.

16 Giving a gift can open doors;
it gives access to important people!

17 The first to speak in court sounds right—
until the cross-examination begins.

18 Flipping a coin* can end arguments;
it settles disputes between powerful
opponents.

19 An offended friend is harder to win back than a
fortified city.
Arguments separate friends like a gate locked
with bars.

20 Wise words satisfy like a good meal;
the right words bring satisfaction.

21 The tongue can bring death or life;
those who love to talk will reap the
consequences.

22 The man who finds a wife finds a treasure,
and he receives favor from the LORD.

23 The poor plead for mercy;
the rich answer with insults.

24 There are "friends" who destroy each other,
but a real friend sticks closer than a brother.

19

1 Better to be poor and honest
than to be dishonest and a fool.

2 Enthusiasm without knowledge is no good;
haste makes mistakes.

3 People ruin their lives by their own foolishness
and then are angry at the LORD.

4 Wealth makes many "friends";
poverty drives them all away.

5 A false witness will not go unpunished,
nor will a liar escape.

6 Many seek favors from a ruler;
everyone is the friend of a person who gives
gifts!

7 The relatives of the poor despise them;
how much more will their friends avoid them!
Though the poor plead with them,
their friends are gone.

8 To acquire wisdom is to love yourself;
people who cherish understanding will prosper.

9 A false witness will not go unpunished,
and a liar will be destroyed.

10 It isn't right for a fool to live in luxury
or for a slave to rule over princes!

11 Sensible people control their temper;
they earn respect by overlooking wrongs.

12 The king's anger is like a lion's roar,
but his favor is like dew on the grass.

13 A foolish child* is a calamity to a father;
a quarrelsome wife is as annoying as constant
dripping.

14 Fathers can give their sons an inheritance of
houses and wealth,
but only the LORD can give an understanding
wife.

15 Lazy people sleep soundly,
but idleness leaves them hungry.

16 Keep the commandments and keep your life;
despising them leads to death.

17 If you help the poor, you are lending to the LORD—
and he will repay you!

18 Discipline your children while there is hope.
Otherwise you will ruin their lives.

19 Hot-tempered people must pay the penalty.
If you rescue them once, you will have to do it
again.

20 Get all the advice and instruction you can,
so you will be wise the rest of your life.

21 You can make many plans,
but the LORD's purpose will prevail.

18:18 Hebrew *Casting lots.* **19:13** Hebrew *son;* also in 19:27.

18:11 a high wall. Cities were surrounded with walls to provide protection; money is also viewed by many people as a form of security. Jesus addressed this security issue with the rich young ruler (Matt. 19:21-24).

18:17 Hearing both sides of the story before making a decision is wisdom that extends beyond the courtroom.

19:3 are angry at the LORD. God did not accept Cain's sacrifice. He became angry with God and killed his brother (Heb. 11:4; 1 John 3:12).

19:13 quarrelsome. Sometimes translated as "trouble" (10:12) or "fighting" (23:29), this word is used more in Proverbs than in any other Old Testament book.

[22] Loyalty makes a person attractive.
It is better to be poor than dishonest.

[23] Fear of the LORD leads to life,
bringing security and protection from harm.

[24] Lazy people take food in their hand
but don't even lift it to their mouth.

[25] If you punish a mocker, the simpleminded will
learn a lesson;
if you correct the wise, they will be all the wiser.

[26] Children who mistreat their father or chase away
their mother
are an embarrassment and a public disgrace.

[27] If you stop listening to instruction, my child,
you will turn your back on knowledge.

[28] A corrupt witness makes a mockery of justice;
the mouth of the wicked gulps down evil.

[29] Punishment is made for mockers,
and the backs of fools are made to be beaten.

20 [1] Wine produces mockers; alcohol leads to
brawls.
Those led astray by drink cannot be wise.

[2] The king's fury is like a lion's roar;
to rouse his anger is to risk your life.

[3] Avoiding a fight is a mark of honor;
only fools insist on quarreling.

[4] Those too lazy to plow in the right season
will have no food at the harvest.

[5] Though good advice lies deep within the heart,
a person with understanding will draw it out.

[6] Many will say they are loyal friends,
but who can find one who is truly reliable?

[7] The godly walk with integrity;
blessed are their children who follow them.

[8] When a king sits in judgment, he weighs all the
evidence,
distinguishing the bad from the good.

[9] Who can say, "I have cleansed my heart;
I am pure and free from sin"?

[10] False weights and unequal measures*—
the LORD detests double standards of every kind.

[11] Even children are known by the way they act,
whether their conduct is pure, and whether it
is right.

[12] Ears to hear and eyes to see—
both are gifts from the LORD.

[13] If you love sleep, you will end in poverty.
Keep your eyes open, and there will be plenty
to eat!

[14] The buyer haggles over the price, saying, "It's
worthless,"
then brags about getting a bargain!

[15] Wise words are more valuable
than much gold and many rubies.

[16] Get security from someone who guarantees a
stranger's debt.
Get a deposit if he does it for foreigners.*

[17] Stolen bread tastes sweet,
but it turns to gravel in the mouth.

[18] Plans succeed through good counsel;
don't go to war without wise advice.

[19] A gossip goes around telling secrets,
so don't hang around with chatterers.

[20] If you insult your father or mother,
your light will be snuffed out in total
darkness.

[21] An inheritance obtained too early in life
is not a blessing in the end.

[22] Don't say, "I will get even for this wrong."
Wait for the LORD to handle the matter.

[23] The LORD detests double standards;
he is not pleased by dishonest scales.

[24] The LORD directs our steps,
so why try to understand everything along the
way?

[25] Don't trap yourself by making a rash promise to
God
and only later counting the cost.

[26] A wise king scatters the wicked like wheat,
then runs his threshing wheel over them.

[27] The LORD's light penetrates the human spirit,*
exposing every hidden motive.

20:10 Hebrew *A stone and a stone, an ephah and an ephah.* 20:16 An alternate reading in the Masoretic Text is *for a promiscuous woman.* 20:27 Or *The human spirit is the LORD's light.*

20:1 Wine . . . alcohol. Wine refers to fermented grape juice. Beer was made from barley, dates, or pomegranates. Priests were forbidden to drink alcohol.
20:3 Avoiding a fight. The wise person avoids arguments.
20:9 pure and free from sin. Before Christ's once-for-all sacrifice, cleansing from sin was gained through sacrificial offerings. These had to be repeated for each new sin or offense, so a person could not stay cleansed for long.
20:20 total darkness. Cursing one's parents was punishable by death (see Lev. 20:9).
20:21 obtained too early in life. The inheritance described here could be gained by deceit, or by request, as in the case of the prodigal son (Luke 15:12-13).
20:25 making a rash promise. Jephthah promised God that he would sacrifice the first thing he saw at his house. Because of his rash vow, He was forced to take the life of his own daughter (see Judg. 11:34-35).

28 Unfailing love and faithfulness protect the king;
his throne is made secure through love.

29 The glory of the young is their strength;
the gray hair of experience is the splendor of the old.

30 Physical punishment cleanses away evil;*
such discipline purifies the heart.

21 1 The king's heart is like a stream of water directed by the LORD;
he guides it wherever he pleases.

2 People may be right in their own eyes,
but the LORD examines their heart.

3 The LORD is more pleased when we do what is right and just
than when we offer him sacrifices.

4 Haughty eyes, a proud heart,
and evil actions are all sin.

5 Good planning and hard work lead to prosperity,
but hasty shortcuts lead to poverty.

6 Wealth created by a lying tongue
is a vanishing mist and a deadly trap.*

7 The violence of the wicked sweeps them away,
because they refuse to do what is just.

8 The guilty walk a crooked path;
the innocent travel a straight road.

9 It's better to live alone in the corner of an attic
than with a quarrelsome wife in a lovely home.

10 Evil people desire evil;
their neighbors get no mercy from them.

11 If you punish a mocker, the simpleminded become wise;
if you instruct the wise, they will be all the wiser.

12 The Righteous One* knows what is going on in the homes of the wicked;
he will bring disaster on them.

13 Those who shut their ears to the cries of the poor
will be ignored in their own time of need.

14 A secret gift calms anger;
a bribe under the table pacifies fury.

15 Justice is a joy to the godly,
but it terrifies evildoers.

16 The person who strays from common sense
will end up in the company of the dead.

17 Those who love pleasure become poor;
those who love wine and luxury will never be rich.

18 The wicked are punished in place of the godly,
and traitors in place of the honest.

19 It's better to live alone in the desert
than with a quarrelsome, complaining wife.

20 The wise have wealth and luxury,
but fools spend whatever they get.

21 Whoever pursues righteousness and unfailing love
will find life, righteousness, and honor.

22 The wise conquer the city of the strong
and level the fortress in which they trust.

23 Watch your tongue and keep your mouth shut,
and you will stay out of trouble.

24 Mockers are proud and haughty;
they act with boundless arrogance.

25 Despite their desires, the lazy will come to ruin,
for their hands refuse to work.

26 Some people are always greedy for more,
but the godly love to give!

27 The sacrifice of an evil person is detestable,
especially when it is offered with wrong motives.

28 A false witness will be cut off,
but a credible witness will be allowed to speak.

29 The wicked bluff their way through,
but the virtuous think before they act.

30 No human wisdom or understanding or plan
can stand against the LORD.

31 The horse is prepared for the day of battle,
but the victory belongs to the LORD.

22 1 Choose a good reputation over great riches;
being held in high esteem is better than silver or gold.

2 The rich and poor have this in common:
The LORD made them both.

3 A prudent person foresees danger and takes precautions.

20:30 The meaning of the Hebrew is uncertain. **21:6** As in Greek version; Hebrew reads *mist for those who seek death.* **21:12** Or *The righteous man.*

21:1 stream of water. Just as a farmer controls the direction and amount of water that runs into irrigation canals, God also controls government.

21:3 sacrifices. While the sacrificial system was an important part of Hebrew life, God's greatest desire was for His people to honor Him through their righteousness and justice.

21:13 in their own time. We reap what we sow. People will receive the same treatment they give to the poor.

21:14 secret gift. The purpose of this verse is not to condone bribery but to emphasize a gift's ability to ease a tense situation (18:16; 19:6).

22:1 good reputation. An honorable reputation was highly esteemed. It comes through love and faithfulness (3:3-4).

The simpleton goes blindly on and suffers the consequences.

4 True humility and fear of the LORD
lead to riches, honor, and long life.

5 Corrupt people walk a thorny, treacherous road;
whoever values life will avoid it.

6 Direct your children onto the right path,
and when they are older, they will not leave it.

7 Just as the rich rule the poor,
so the borrower is servant to the lender.

8 Those who plant injustice will harvest disaster,
and their reign of terror will come to an end.*

9 Blessed are those who are generous,
because they feed the poor.

10 Throw out the mocker, and fighting goes, too.
Quarrels and insults will disappear.

11 Whoever loves a pure heart and gracious speech
will have the king as a friend.

12 The LORD preserves those with knowledge,
but he ruins the plans of the treacherous.

13 The lazy person claims, "There's a lion out there!
If I go outside, I might be killed!"

14 The mouth of an immoral woman is a dangerous trap;
those who make the LORD angry will fall into it.

15 A youngster's heart is filled with foolishness,
but physical discipline will drive it far away.

16 A person who gets ahead by oppressing the poor
or by showering gifts on the rich will end in poverty.

SAYINGS OF THE WISE

17 Listen to the words of the wise;
apply your heart to my instruction.
18 For it is good to keep these sayings in your heart
and always ready on your lips.
19 I am teaching you today—yes, you—
so you will trust in the LORD.
20 I have written thirty sayings* for you,
filled with advice and knowledge.
21 In this way, you may know the truth
and take an accurate report to those who sent you.

22 Don't rob the poor just because you can,
or exploit the needy in court.
23 For the LORD is their defender.
He will ruin anyone who ruins them.

24 Don't befriend angry people
or associate with hot-tempered people,
25 or you will learn to be like them
and endanger your soul.

26 Don't agree to guarantee another person's debt
or put up security for someone else.
27 If you can't pay it,
even your bed will be snatched from under you.

28 Don't cheat your neighbor by moving the ancient boundary markers
set up by previous generations.

29 Do you see any truly competent workers?
They will serve kings
rather than working for ordinary people.

23 1 While dining with a ruler,
pay attention to what is put before you.
2 If you are a big eater,
put a knife to your throat;
3 don't desire all the delicacies,
for he might be trying to trick you.

4 Don't wear yourself out trying to get rich.
Be wise enough to know when to quit.
5 In the blink of an eye wealth disappears,
for it will sprout wings
and fly away like an eagle.

6 Don't eat with people who are stingy;
don't desire their delicacies.
7 They are always thinking about how much it costs.*
"Eat and drink," they say, but they don't mean it.
8 You will throw up what little you've eaten,
and your compliments will be wasted.

9 Don't waste your breath on fools,
for they will despise the wisest advice.

10 Don't cheat your neighbor by moving the ancient boundary markers;
don't take the land of defenseless orphans.
11 For their Redeemer* is strong;
he himself will bring their charges against you.

22:8 The Greek version includes an additional proverb: *God blesses a man who gives cheerfully, / but his worthless deeds will come to an end.* Compare 2 Cor 9:7. 22:20 Or *excellent sayings;* the meaning of the Hebrew is uncertain. 23:7 The meaning of the Hebrew is uncertain. 23:11 Or *redeemer.*

22:7 servant. In Bible times people often had to sell themselves into slavery to pay off their debts.
22:9 they feed the poor. Stewardship is more than giving; it also involves a compassionate attitude that reaches out to people in need.
22:13 lazy person. A lazy, irresponsible person. A slacker will go to any length to avoid work and justify his laziness.
22:14 mouth. Not just the immoral woman's kisses but also her empty promises endanger anyone who believes her.
22:17 apply your heart. Believers should be open to wisdom and truth from the Lord and His appointed leaders.
23:1-3 A guest should show restraint in order to honor his host.
23:5 fly away like an eagle. Accumulating earthly wealth is foolish. It can take wings and fly away at any moment.
23:6 stingy. While a stingy host will offer food to appear generous, he is more concerned with counting the cost.
23:10 moving the ancient boundary markers. Moving property lines was a form of stealing a neighbor's land. **don't take the land.** Not leaving grain in the fields for the poor after gathering the harvest was also considered stealing (see Ruth 2:1-3).
23:11 Redeemer is strong. God is a defender of the fatherless and a redeemer of widows. This passage also alludes to a kinsman-redeemer, a person who cares for the family of a dead relative (see Ruth 2:20).

12 Commit yourself to instruction;
listen carefully to words of knowledge.
13 Don't fail to discipline your children.
The rod of punishment won't kill them.
14 Physical discipline
may well save them from death.*
15 My child,* if your heart is wise,
my own heart will rejoice!
16 Everything in me will celebrate
when you speak what is right.
17 Don't envy sinners,
but always continue to fear the LORD.
18 You will be rewarded for this;
your hope will not be disappointed.
19 My child, listen and be wise:
Keep your heart on the right course.
20 Do not carouse with drunkards
or feast with gluttons,
21 for they are on their way to poverty,
and too much sleep clothes them in rags.
22 Listen to your father, who gave you life,
and don't despise your mother when she is old.
23 Get the truth and never sell it;
also get wisdom, discipline, and good judgment.
24 The father of godly children has cause for joy.
What a pleasure to have children who are wise.*
25 So give your father and mother joy!
May she who gave you birth be happy.
26 O my son, give me your heart.
May your eyes take delight in following my ways.
27 A prostitute is a dangerous trap;
a promiscuous woman is as dangerous as falling into a narrow well.
28 She hides and waits like a robber,
eager to make more men unfaithful.
29 Who has anguish? Who has sorrow?
Who is always fighting? Who is always complaining?
Who has unnecessary bruises? Who has bloodshot eyes?
30 It is the one who spends long hours in the taverns,
trying out new drinks.
31 Don't gaze at the wine, seeing how red it is,
how it sparkles in the cup, how smoothly it goes down.
32 For in the end it bites like a poisonous snake;
it stings like a viper.
33 You will see hallucinations,
and you will say crazy things.
34 You will stagger like a sailor tossed at sea,
clinging to a swaying mast.
35 And you will say, "They hit me, but I didn't feel it.
I didn't even know it when they beat me up.
When will I wake up
so I can look for another drink?"

24 1 Don't envy evil people
or desire their company.
2 For their hearts plot violence,
and their words always stir up trouble.
3 A house is built by wisdom
and becomes strong through good sense.
4 Through knowledge its rooms are filled
with all sorts of precious riches and valuables.
5 The wise are mightier than the strong,*
and those with knowledge grow stronger and stronger.
6 So don't go to war without wise guidance;
victory depends on having many advisers.
7 Wisdom is too lofty for fools.
Among leaders at the city gate, they have nothing to say.
8 A person who plans evil
will get a reputation as a troublemaker.
9 The schemes of a fool are sinful;
everyone detests a mocker.
10 If you fail under pressure,
your strength is too small.
11 Rescue those who are unjustly sentenced to die;
save them as they stagger to their death.
12 Don't excuse yourself by saying, "Look, we didn't know."
For God understands all hearts, and he sees you.
He who guards your soul knows you knew.
He will repay all people as their actions deserve.
13 My child,* eat honey, for it is good,
and the honeycomb is sweet to the taste.
14 In the same way, wisdom is sweet to your soul.
If you find it, you will have a bright future,
and your hopes will not be cut short.
15 Don't wait in ambush at the home of the godly,
and don't raid the house where the godly live.
16 The godly may trip seven times, but they will get up again.
But one disaster is enough to overthrow the wicked.
17 Don't rejoice when your enemies fall;
don't be happy when they stumble.
18 For the LORD will be displeased with you
and will turn his anger away from them.
19 Don't fret because of evildoers;
don't envy the wicked.
20 For evil people have no future;
the light of the wicked will be snuffed out.

23:14 Hebrew *from Sheol.* 23:15 Hebrew *My son;* also in 23:19. 23:24 Hebrew *to have a wise son.* 24:5 As in Greek version; Hebrew reads *A wise man is strength.* 24:13 Hebrew *My son;* also in 24:21.

24:11 unjustly sentenced to die. This probably refers to people who have been unjustly accused.

24:12 we didn't know. God judges those who are aware of injustice but do not oppose it.

24:17-18 Don't rejoice. God detests an attitude of superiority.

24:20 evil people have no future. No matter how prosperous the wicked may seem, their future without God is dismal and hopeless.

21 My child, fear the LORD and the king.
Don't associate with rebels,
22 for disaster will hit them suddenly.
Who knows what punishment will come
from the LORD and the king?

MORE SAYINGS OF THE WISE

23 Here are some further sayings of the wise:

It is wrong to show favoritism when passing
judgment.
24 A judge who says to the wicked, "You are innocent,"
will be cursed by many people and denounced
by the nations.
25 But it will go well for those who convict the guilty;
rich blessings will be showered on them.

26 An honest answer
is like a kiss of friendship.

27 Do your planning and prepare your fields
before building your house.

28 Don't testify against your neighbors without
cause;
don't lie about them.
29 And don't say, "Now I can pay them back for what
they've done to me!
I'll get even with them!"

30 I walked by the field of a lazy person,
the vineyard of one with no common sense.
31 I saw that it was overgrown with nettles.
It was covered with weeds,
and its walls were broken down.
32 Then, as I looked and thought about it,
I learned this lesson:
33 A little extra sleep, a little more slumber,
a little folding of the hands to rest—
34 then poverty will pounce on you like a bandit;
scarcity will attack you like an armed robber.

MORE PROVERBS OF SOLOMON

25 These are more proverbs of Solomon, collected
by the advisers of King Hezekiah of Judah.

2 It is God's privilege to conceal things
and the king's privilege to discover them.

3 No one can comprehend the height of heaven, the
depth of the earth,
or all that goes on in the king's mind!

4 Remove the impurities from silver,
and the sterling will be ready for the
silversmith.
5 Remove the wicked from the king's court,
and his reign will be made secure by justice.

6 Don't demand an audience with the king
or push for a place among the great.
7 It's better to wait for an invitation to the head
table
than to be sent away in public disgrace.

Just because you've seen something,
8 don't be in a hurry to go to court.
For what will you do in the end
if your neighbor deals you a shameful defeat?

9 When arguing with your neighbor,
don't betray another person's secret.
10 Others may accuse you of gossip,
and you will never regain your good reputation.

11 Timely advice is lovely,
like golden apples in a silver basket.

12 To one who listens, valid criticism
is like a gold earring or other gold jewelry.

13 Trustworthy messengers refresh like snow in
summer.
They revive the spirit of their employer.

14 A person who promises a gift but doesn't give it
is like clouds and wind that bring no rain.

15 Patience can persuade a prince,
and soft speech can break bones.

16 Do you like honey?
Don't eat too much, or it will make you sick!

17 Don't visit your neighbors too often,
or you will wear out your welcome.

18 Telling lies about others
is as harmful as hitting them with an ax,
wounding them with a sword,
or shooting them with a sharp arrow.

19 Putting confidence in an unreliable person in
times of trouble
is like chewing with a broken tooth or walking
on a lame foot.

20 Singing cheerful songs to a person with a heavy
heart
is like taking someone's coat in cold weather
or pouring vinegar in a wound.*

21 If your enemies are hungry, give them food to eat.
If they are thirsty, give them water to drink.
22 You will heap burning coals of shame on their
heads,
and the LORD will reward you.

25:20 As in Greek version; Hebrew reads *pouring vinegar on soda.*

24:27 before building your house. The first priority in an agricultural society was preparing the land and planting the seed. After that the people could build houses and establish families.

25:4 impurities. Impurities must be removed from silver before it can be made into beautiful and useful things.

25:8 a hurry. Before going to court, a person should ask if this is sensible. He should consider the possibility of losing and the consequences of an unfavorable decision.

25:9-10 arguing. When you make your accusation public, the court of public opinion will make its judgment, and you will be held accountable.

25:11 Timely advice. This advice can be an encouragement or a rebuke spoken in good timing and the right spirit. Used correctly, words make us appear wise. Used incorrectly, they make us appear foolish.

23 As surely as a north wind brings rain,
so a gossiping tongue causes anger!

24 It's better to live alone in the corner of an attic
than with a quarrelsome wife in a lovely home.

25 Good news from far away
is like cold water to the thirsty.

26 If the godly give in to the wicked,
it's like polluting a fountain or muddying a spring.

27 It's not good to eat too much honey,
and it's not good to seek honors for yourself.

28 A person without self-control
is like a city with broken-down walls.

26 1 Honor is no more associated with fools
than snow with summer or rain with harvest.

2 Like a fluttering sparrow or a darting swallow,
an undeserved curse will not land on its intended victim.

3 Guide a horse with a whip, a donkey with a bridle,
and a fool with a rod to his back!

4 Don't answer the foolish arguments of fools,
or you will become as foolish as they are.

5 Be sure to answer the foolish arguments of fools,
or they will become wise in their own estimation.

6 Trusting a fool to convey a message
is like cutting off one's feet or drinking poison!

7 A proverb in the mouth of a fool
is as useless as a paralyzed leg.

8 Honoring a fool
is as foolish as tying a stone to a slingshot.

9 A proverb in the mouth of a fool
is like a thorny branch brandished by a drunk.

10 An employer who hires a fool or a bystander
is like an archer who shoots at random.

11 As a dog returns to its vomit,
so a fool repeats his foolishness.

12 There is more hope for fools
than for people who think they are wise.

13 The lazy person claims, "There's a lion on the road!
Yes, I'm sure there's a lion out there!"

14 As a door swings back and forth on its hinges,
so the lazy person turns over in bed.

15 Lazy people take food in their hand
but don't even lift it to their mouth.

16 Lazy people consider themselves smarter
than seven wise counselors.

17 Interfering in someone else's argument
is as foolish as yanking a dog's ears.

18 Just as damaging
as a madman shooting a deadly weapon
19 is someone who lies to a friend
and then says, "I was only joking."

20 Fire goes out without wood,
and quarrels disappear when gossip stops.

21 A quarrelsome person starts fights
as easily as hot embers light charcoal or fire lights wood.

22 Rumors are dainty morsels
that sink deep into one's heart.

23 Smooth* words may hide a wicked heart,
just as a pretty glaze covers a clay pot.

24 People may cover their hatred with pleasant words,
but they're deceiving you.
25 They pretend to be kind, but don't believe them.
Their hearts are full of many evils.*
26 While their hatred may be concealed by trickery,
their wrongdoing will be exposed in public.

27 If you set a trap for others,
you will get caught in it yourself.
If you roll a boulder down on others,
it will crush you instead.

28 A lying tongue hates its victims,
and flattering words cause ruin.

27 1 Don't brag about tomorrow,
since you don't know what the day will bring.

2 Let someone else praise you, not your own mouth—
a stranger, not your own lips.

3 A stone is heavy and sand is weighty,
but the resentment caused by a fool is even heavier.

4 Anger is cruel, and wrath is like a flood,
but jealousy is even more dangerous.

5 An open rebuke
is better than hidden love!

26:23 As in Greek version; Hebrew reads *Burning*. 26:25 Hebrew *seven evils*.

26:14 door swings back and forth on its hinges. The point is not the way a slacker twists and turns but the fact that a slacker never gets up.
26:18-19 I was only joking. Pranks and practical jokes can cause serious damage.
26:27 Haman prepared a gallows on which to execute Mordecai. But in a twist of fate, he died on it instead (Esth. 9:24-25).
26:28 A lying tongue hates. Lying and hating are connected. When we lie, we disrespect the people to whom we lie.

6 Wounds from a sincere friend
are better than many kisses from an enemy.

7 A person who is full refuses honey,
but even bitter food tastes sweet to the hungry.

8 A person who strays from home
is like a bird that strays from its nest.

9 The heartfelt counsel of a friend
is as sweet as perfume and incense.

10 Never abandon a friend—
either yours or your father's.
When disaster strikes, you won't have to ask your brother for assistance.
It's better to go to a neighbor than to a brother who lives far away.

11 Be wise, my child,* and make my heart glad.
Then I will be able to answer my critics.

12 A prudent person foresees danger and takes precautions.
The simpleton goes blindly on and suffers the consequences.

13 Get security from someone who guarantees a stranger's debt.
Get a deposit if he does it for foreigners.*

14 A loud and cheerful greeting early in the morning
will be taken as a curse!

15 A quarrelsome wife is as annoying
as constant dripping on a rainy day.
16 Stopping her complaints is like trying to stop the wind
or trying to hold something with greased hands.

17 As iron sharpens iron,
so a friend sharpens a friend.

18 As workers who tend a fig tree are allowed to eat the fruit,
so workers who protect their employer's interests will be rewarded.

19 As a face is reflected in water,
so the heart reflects the real person.

20 Just as Death and Destruction* are never satisfied,
so human desire is never satisfied.

21 Fire tests the purity of silver and gold,
but a person is tested by being praised.*

22 You cannot separate fools from their foolishness,
even though you grind them like grain with mortar and pestle.

23 Know the state of your flocks,
and put your heart into caring for your herds,
24 for riches don't last forever,
and the crown might not be passed to the next generation.
25 After the hay is harvested and the new crop appears
and the mountain grasses are gathered in,
26 your sheep will provide wool for clothing,
and your goats will provide the price of a field.
27 And you will have enough goats' milk for yourself,
your family, and your servant girls.

28

1 The wicked run away when no one is chasing them,
but the godly are as bold as lions.

2 When there is moral rot within a nation, its government topples easily.
But wise and knowledgeable leaders bring stability.

3 A poor person who oppresses the poor
is like a pounding rain that destroys the crops.

4 To reject the law is to praise the wicked;
to obey the law is to fight them.

5 Evil people don't understand justice,
but those who follow the LORD understand completely.

6 Better to be poor and honest
than to be dishonest and rich.

7 Young people who obey the law are wise;
those with wild friends bring shame to their parents.*

8 Income from charging high interest rates
will end up in the pocket of someone who is kind to the poor.

9 God detests the prayers
of a person who ignores the law.

10 Those who lead good people along an evil path
will fall into their own trap,
but the honest will inherit good things.

11 Rich people may think they are wise,
but a poor person with discernment can see right through them.

27:11 Hebrew *my son.* **27:13** As in Greek and Latin versions (see also 20:16); Hebrew reads *for a promiscuous woman.* **27:20** Hebrew *Sheol and Abaddon.* **27:21** Or *by flattery.* **28:7** Hebrew *their father.*

27:10. Family ties are important, but close friends are our family in times of need.
27:17 iron sharpens iron. Good relationships are tools that God uses to develop our character.
27:23-27 This passage celebrates the security and the cycle of an agricultural society.
28:5 Wickedness perverts a person's sense of justice and fairness. When Solomon became king, he prayed for wisdom and the ability to distinguish between right and wrong (1 Kings 3:9).
28:11 think they are wise. To be unteachable or proud. Proverbs describes the fool (26:5) and the sluggard (26:16) as people who refuse instruction and learning.

12 When the godly succeed, everyone is glad.
When the wicked take charge, people go into hiding.

13 People who conceal their sins will not prosper,
but if they confess and turn from them, they will receive mercy.

14 Blessed are those who fear to do wrong,*
but the stubborn are headed for serious trouble.

15 A wicked ruler is as dangerous to the poor
as a roaring lion or an attacking bear.

16 A ruler with no understanding will oppress his people,
but one who hates corruption will have a long life.

17 A murderer's tormented conscience will drive him into the grave.
Don't protect him!

18 The blameless will be rescued from harm,
but the crooked will be suddenly destroyed.

19 A hard worker has plenty of food,
but a person who chases fantasies ends up in poverty.

20 The trustworthy person will get a rich reward,
but a person who wants quick riches will get into trouble.

21 Showing partiality is never good,
yet some will do wrong for a mere piece of bread.

22 Greedy people try to get rich quick
but don't realize they're headed for poverty.

23 In the end, people appreciate honest criticism
far more than flattery.

24 Anyone who steals from his father and mother
and says, "What's wrong with that?"
is no better than a murderer.

25 Greed causes fighting;
trusting the LORD leads to prosperity.

26 Those who trust their own insight are foolish,
but anyone who walks in wisdom is safe.

27 Whoever gives to the poor will lack nothing,
but those who close their eyes to poverty will be cursed.

28 When the wicked take charge, people go into hiding.
When the wicked meet disaster, the godly flourish.

29

1 Whoever stubbornly refuses to accept criticism
will suddenly be destroyed beyond recovery.

2 When the godly are in authority, the people rejoice.
But when the wicked are in power, they groan.

3 The man who loves wisdom brings joy to his father,
but if he hangs around with prostitutes, his wealth is wasted.

4 A just king gives stability to his nation,
but one who demands bribes destroys it.

5 To flatter friends
is to lay a trap for their feet.

6 Evil people are trapped by sin,
but the righteous escape, shouting for joy.

7 The godly care about the rights of the poor;
the wicked don't care at all.

8 Mockers can get a whole town agitated,
but the wise will calm anger.

9 If a wise person takes a fool to court,
there will be ranting and ridicule but no satisfaction.

10 The bloodthirsty hate blameless people,
but the upright seek to help them.*

11 Fools vent their anger,
but the wise quietly hold it back.

12 If a ruler pays attention to liars,
all his advisers will be wicked.

13 The poor and the oppressor have this in common—
the LORD gives sight to the eyes of both.

14 If a king judges the poor fairly,
his throne will last forever.

15 To discipline a child produces wisdom,
but a mother is disgraced by an undisciplined child.

16 When the wicked are in authority, sin flourishes,
but the godly will live to see their downfall.

28:14 Or *those who fear the LORD;* Hebrew reads *those who fear.* **29:10** Or *The bloodthirsty hate blameless people, / and they seek to kill the upright;* Hebrew reads *The bloodthirsty hate blameless people; / as for the upright, they seek their life.*

28:13 conceal their sins. David, after committing adultery with Bathsheba, tried to hide his sin by murdering her husband (2 Sam. 12:7-9).

28:15 A wicked ruler . . . as a roaring lion. A ruler like this does not realize that his security as king depends on the well-being of those over whom he rules.

28:20 get a rich reward. Get-rich-quick schemes are contrasted with being faithful to God. Proverbs listed those who will not go unpunished, including the adulterer (6:29), the wicked (11:21), the proud (16:5), the person who mocks the poor (17:5), and the false witness (19:9).

28:23 Rebukes are welcomed by the wise. But flattery is never effective with those who are wise and discerning.

29:7 poor. Feeble or helpless. A righteous person demonstrates concern for others. A wicked person has no such compassion.

29:9 ranting and ridicule. Fools love turmoil and strife more than resolving problems and living peaceably with others.

17 Discipline your children, and they will give you peace of mind
and will make your heart glad.

18 When people do not accept divine guidance, they run wild.
But whoever obeys the law is joyful.

19 Words alone will not discipline a servant;
the words may be understood, but they are not heeded.

20 There is more hope for a fool
than for someone who speaks without thinking.

21 A servant pampered from childhood
will become a rebel.

22 An angry person starts fights;
a hot-tempered person commits all kinds of sin.

23 Pride ends in humiliation,
while humility brings honor.

24 If you assist a thief, you only hurt yourself.
You are sworn to tell the truth, but you dare not testify.

25 Fearing people is a dangerous trap,
but trusting the LORD means safety.

26 Many seek the ruler's favor,
but justice comes from the LORD.

27 The righteous despise the unjust;
the wicked despise the godly.

THE SAYINGS OF AGUR

30 The sayings of Agur son of Jakeh contain this message.*

I am weary, O God;
I am weary and worn out, O God.*
2 I am too stupid to be human,
and I lack common sense.
3 I have not mastered human wisdom,
nor do I know the Holy One.

4 Who but God goes up to heaven and comes back down?
Who holds the wind in his fists?
Who wraps up the oceans in his cloak?
Who has created the whole wide world?
What is his name—and his son's name?
Tell me if you know!

5 Every word of God proves true.
He is a shield to all who come to him for protection.
6 Do not add to his words,
or he may rebuke you and expose you as a liar.

7 O God, I beg two favors from you;
let me have them before I die.
8 First, help me never to tell a lie.
Second, give me neither poverty nor riches!
Give me just enough to satisfy my needs.
9 For if I grow rich, I may deny you and say, "Who is the LORD?"
And if I am too poor, I may steal and thus insult God's holy name.

10 Never slander a worker to the employer,
or the person will curse you, and you will pay for it.

11 Some people curse their father
and do not thank their mother.
12 They are pure in their own eyes,
but they are filthy and unwashed.
13 They look proudly around,
casting disdainful glances.
14 They have teeth like swords
and fangs like knives.
They devour the poor from the earth
and the needy from among humanity.

15 The leech has two suckers
that cry out, "More, more!"*

There are three things that are never satisfied—
no, four that never say, "Enough!":
16 the grave,*
the barren womb,
the thirsty desert,
the blazing fire.

17 The eye that mocks a father
and despises a mother's instructions
will be plucked out by ravens of the valley
and eaten by vultures.

18 There are three things that amaze me—
no, four things that I don't understand:
19 how an eagle glides through the sky,
how a snake slithers on a rock,
how a ship navigates the ocean,
how a man loves a woman.

20 An adulterous woman consumes a man,
then wipes her mouth and says, "What's wrong with that?"

30:1a Or *son of Jakeh from Massa;* or *son of Jakeh, an oracle.* **30:1b** The Hebrew can also be translated *The man declares this to Ithiel, / to Ithiel and to Ucal.* **30:15** Hebrew *two daughters who cry out, "Give, give!"* **30:16** Hebrew *Sheol.*

29:18 divine guidance. When people do not hear God's truth, they live lawless lives.
30:2-3 too stupid. Agur comes up lacking when he compares his knowledge with God's (9:10).
30:6 Do not add. Let God's Word stand on its own authority and serve as its own interpreter.
30:9 Who is the LORD? When Israel prospered, the people strayed from God, thinking they were self-sufficient.
30:12 pure in their own eyes. People who believe they are morally pure are blind to the danger of self-righteousness.
30:16 the grave, the barren womb. In Solomon's day, being barren was compared to Sheol (the place of the dead) because it caused a feeling of emptiness.
30:20 What's wrong with that? The sexual appetite of the adulteress is no more sinful to her than eating a meal.

21 There are three things that make the earth tremble—
no, four it cannot endure:
22 a slave who becomes a king,
an overbearing fool who prospers,
23 a bitter woman who finally gets a husband,
a servant girl who supplants her mistress.

24 There are four things on earth that are small but unusually wise:
25 Ants—they aren't strong,
but they store up food all summer.
26 Hyraxes*—they aren't powerful,
but they make their homes among the rocks.
27 Locusts—they have no king,
but they march in formation.
28 Lizards—they are easy to catch,
but they are found even in kings' palaces.

29 There are three things that walk with stately stride—
no, four that strut about:
30 the lion, king of animals, who won't turn aside for anything,
31 the strutting rooster,
the male goat,
a king as he leads his army.

32 If you have been a fool by being proud or plotting evil,
cover your mouth in shame.

33 As the beating of cream yields butter
and striking the nose causes bleeding,
so stirring up anger causes quarrels.

THE SAYINGS OF KING LEMUEL

31 The sayings of King Lemuel contain this message,* which his mother taught him.

2 O my son, O son of my womb,
O son of my vows,
3 do not waste your strength on women,
on those who ruin kings.

4 It is not for kings, O Lemuel, to guzzle wine.
Rulers should not crave alcohol.
5 For if they drink, they may forget the law
and not give justice to the oppressed.
6 Alcohol is for the dying,
and wine for those in bitter distress.
7 Let them drink to forget their poverty
and remember their troubles no more.

8 Speak up for those who cannot speak for themselves;
ensure justice for those being crushed.
9 Yes, speak up for the poor and helpless,
and see that they get justice.

A WIFE OF NOBLE CHARACTER

10*Who can find a virtuous and capable wife?
She is more precious than rubies.
11 Her husband can trust her,
and she will greatly enrich his life.
12 She brings him good, not harm,
all the days of her life.

13 She finds wool and flax
and busily spins it.
14 She is like a merchant's ship,
bringing her food from afar.
15 She gets up before dawn to prepare breakfast for her household
and plan the day's work for her servant girls.

16 She goes to inspect a field and buys it;
with her earnings she plants a vineyard.
17 She is energetic and strong,
a hard worker.
18 She makes sure her dealings are profitable;
her lamp burns late into the night.

19 Her hands are busy spinning thread,
her fingers twisting fiber.
20 She extends a helping hand to the poor
and opens her arms to the needy.
21 She has no fear of winter for her household,
for everyone has warm* clothes.

22 She makes her own bedspreads.
She dresses in fine linen and purple gowns.
23 Her husband is well known at the city gates,
where he sits with the other civic leaders.
24 She makes belted linen garments
and sashes to sell to the merchants.

25 She is clothed with strength and dignity,
and she laughs without fear of the future.
26 When she speaks, her words are wise,
and she gives instructions with kindness.
27 She carefully watches everything in her household
and suffers nothing from laziness.

28 Her children stand and bless her.
Her husband praises her:

30:26 Or *Coneys,* or *Rock badgers.* **31:1** Or *of Lemuel, king of Massa;* or *of King Lemuel, an oracle.* **31:10** Verses 10-31 comprise a Hebrew acrostic poem; each verse begins with a successive letter of the Hebrew alphabet. **31:21** As in Greek and Latin versions; Hebrew reads *scarlet.*

30:27 Locusts. Locusts are capable of destroying crops with the precision of a military invasion.
30:28 Lizards. Lizards had the run of the palace—illustrating that strength comes in many forms.
31:2 vows. Perhaps his mother had committed Lemuel to God—much as Hannah had done with Samuel (1 Sam. 1:11).
31:3 do not waste your strength. A king's strength would be foolishly spent if all he did was chase women.
31:4-7 An alcoholic king posed a double danger. His people and his politics depended on judgment and clear thinking.
31:8-9 Speak up for. Jewish law required that the king also represent those who had nothing to give in return.
31:14 merchant's ship. The ideal wife in this verse is a wise consumer.
31:15 gets up before dawn. This woman is the opposite of the sluggard who loves to sleep (6:9; 20:13).
31:18 her lamp burns late into the night. The ideal wife manages her resources well so she does not run out of oil for her lamp.
31:22 fine linen and purple gowns. The clothes worn by this woman reflect her family's high position. Purple was a color worn by royalty.
31:23 known at the city gates. The wise men of the town gathered here to share wisdom, settle disputes, and transact business. Their reputations were enhanced by the skills of their wives.
31:24 makes . . . to sell. The ideal wife not only supplies her home, but she is productive enough to supply merchants with her wares.
31:26 words are wise . . . instructions with kindness. This woman's wisdom is shared with her children and servants.

[29] "There are many virtuous and capable women in
the world,
but you surpass them all!"

[30] Charm is deceptive, and beauty does not last;
but a woman who fears the LORD will be greatly
praised.

[31] Reward her for all she has done.
Let her deeds publicly declare her praise.

31:28-29 capable. This wise wife enjoys a good reputation in the community and in her own household.
31:30 praised. Beauty and charm are temporary, but a life lived for the Lord is worthy of praise.

31:31 publicly. A place where only men received recognition. Good character and wisdom surpass gender and cultural bias.

INTRODUCTION TO

ECCLESIASTES

PERSONAL READING PLAN

☐Ecclesiastes 1:1–2:16
☐Ecclesiastes 2:17–4:12
☐Ecclesiastes 4:13–6:12
☐Ecclesiastes 7:1–8:17
☐Ecclesiastes 9:1–10:20
☐Ecclesiastes 11:1–12:14

AUTHOR

The writing of Ecclesiastes is traditionally attributed to Solomon because of references to "son of David" and "king over Israel" (see 1:1,12). No writer is named in the book, and Ecclesiastes may have been the product of a writer from a later period who sought to emulate Solomon's wisdom.

DATE

The book may perhaps be dated after the return from exile, in the fifth century B.C. If Solomon were the author, the book would date from *circa* 950 B.C.

THEME

Life not focused on God is purposeless and meaningless. Without Him, nothing can satisfy (2:25). With Him, all of life is to be enjoyed to the full (2:26; 11:8).

HISTORICAL BACKGROUND

With so little information available about the author or date, it is difficult to place Ecclesiastes into a historical context. One possibility is that it was produced by a wisdom movement in Judaism that was responsible for collecting stories and sayings.

CHARACTERISTICS

Ecclesiastes has always raised questions concerning its appropriateness in the Old Testament canon (the authoritative list of books accepted as Holy Scripture). Its philosophical attitude of questioning beliefs central to Judaism and Christianity has led many to dismiss it. It may be, however, that the work is a foil against which we discern our tendency to overestimate or over-spiritualize our relationship with God. The book is unsparingly forthright in recording the author's desperate search for meaning. While he might be accused of overstating his case, hints of his true piety are evident (see 7:29), and the conclusion challenges the reader to obey God (12:13-14).

Near the end of the book, young people are specifically addressed (11:7–12:8). Youth are challenged to "it's wonderful to be young! Enjoy every minute of it." (11:9). The author exhorts to "Honor him [God] in your youth" (12:1)—because without focusing on God, "Everything is meaningless" (12:8). The book climaxes in 12:13-14 where the message is finally spelled out: Life without God and the fear of God is futility.

1 These are the words of the Teacher,* King David's son, who ruled in Jerusalem.

EVERYTHING IS MEANINGLESS

2 "Everything is meaningless," says the Teacher, "completely meaningless!"

3 What do people get for all their hard work under the sun? 4 Generations come and generations go, but the earth never changes. 5 The sun rises and the sun sets, then hurries around to rise again. 6 The wind blows south, and then turns north. Around and around it goes, blowing in circles. 7 Rivers run into the sea, but the sea is never full. Then the water returns again to the rivers and flows out again to the sea. 8 Everything is wearisome beyond description. No matter how much we see, we are never satisfied. No matter how much we hear, we are not content.

9 History merely repeats itself. It has all been done before. Nothing under the sun is truly new. 10 Sometimes people say, "Here is something new!" But actually it is old; nothing is ever truly new. 11 We don't remember what happened in the past, and in future generations, no one will remember what we are doing now.

THE TEACHER SPEAKS: THE FUTILITY OF WISDOM

12 I, the Teacher, was king of Israel, and I lived in Jerusalem. 13 I devoted myself to search for understanding and to explore by wisdom everything being done under heaven. I soon discovered that God has dealt a tragic existence to the human race. 14 I observed everything going on under the sun, and really, it is all meaningless—like chasing the wind.

15 What is wrong cannot be made right.
What is missing cannot be recovered.

16 I said to myself, "Look, I am wiser than any of the kings who ruled in Jerusalem before me. I have greater wisdom and knowledge than any of them." 17 So I set out to learn everything from wisdom to madness and folly. But I learned firsthand that pursuing all this is like chasing the wind.

18 The greater my wisdom, the greater my grief.
To increase knowledge only increases sorrow.

THE FUTILITY OF PLEASURE

2 I said to myself, "Come on, let's try pleasure. Let's look for the 'good things' in life." But I found that this, too, was meaningless. 2 So I said, "Laughter is silly. What good does it do to seek pleasure?" 3 After much thought, I decided to cheer myself with wine. And while still seeking wisdom, I clutched at foolishness. In this way, I tried to experience the only happiness most people find during their brief life in this world.

4 I also tried to find meaning by building huge homes for myself and by planting beautiful vineyards. 5 I made gardens and parks, filling them with all kinds of fruit trees. 6 I built reservoirs to collect the water to irrigate my many flourishing groves. 7 I bought slaves, both men and women, and others were born into my household. I also owned large herds and flocks, more than any of the kings who had lived in Jerusalem before me. 8 I collected great sums of silver and gold, the treasure of many kings and provinces. I hired wonderful singers, both men and women, and had many beautiful concubines. I had everything a man could desire!

9 So I became greater than all who had lived in Jerusalem before me, and my wisdom never failed me. 10 Anything I wanted, I would take. I denied myself no pleasure. I even found great pleasure in hard work, a reward for all my labors. 11 But as I looked at everything I had worked so hard to accomplish, it was all so meaningless—like chasing the wind. There was nothing really worthwhile anywhere.

THE WISE AND THE FOOLISH

12 So I decided to compare wisdom with foolishness and madness (for who can do this better than I, the king?*). 13 I thought, "Wisdom is better than foolishness, just as light is better than darkness. 14 For the wise can see where they are going, but fools walk in the dark." Yet I saw that the wise and the foolish share the same fate. 15 Both will die. So I said to myself, "Since I will end up the same as the fool, what's the value of all my wisdom? This is all so meaningless!" 16 For the wise and the foolish both die. The wise will not be remembered any longer than the fool. In the days to come, both will be forgotten.

17 So I came to hate life because everything done here under the sun is so troubling. Everything is meaningless—like chasing the wind.

THE FUTILITY OF WORK

18 I came to hate all my hard work here on earth, for I must leave to others everything I have earned. 19 And who can tell whether my successors will be wise or foolish? Yet they will control everything I have gained by my skill and hard work under the sun. How meaningless! 20 So I gave up in despair, questioning the value of all my hard work in this world.

21 Some people work wisely with knowledge and skill, then must leave the fruit of their efforts to someone who hasn't worked for it. This, too, is meaningless, a great tragedy. 22 So what do people get in this life for all their hard work and anxiety? 23 Their days of labor are filled with pain and grief; even at night their minds cannot rest. It is all meaningless.

1:1 Hebrew *Qoheleth;* this term is rendered "the Teacher" throughout this book. **2:12** The meaning of the Hebrew is uncertain.

1:2 meaningless. This concept is the main theme of Ecclesiastes. Occurring 38 times in the book, "absolute futility" emphasizes the uselessness of life apart from God. In Hebrew, futility (or vanity) means "breath" or "vapor." Thus, Ecclesiastes repeats the theme of wisdom literature—that all our concerns are temporary as the morning mist.

1:3 under the sun. This key phrase is used 29 times in this book to refer to our limited view of life.

1:8 Everything is wearisome. Many things God created are wonderful, but we are not to find our meaning in creation itself. This search for meaning in the creation rather than the Creator becomes unbearably wearisome.

1:13 God. The name used for God throughout Ecclesiastes (*Elohim*, used 40 times) emphasizes divine sovereignty over all things.

1:17 wisdom . . . knowledge. Even vast wisdom and knowledge are insufficient to provide meaning in life. In fact, wisdom and knowledge increase the seeker's sorrow rather than providing elusive happiness.

2:1 pleasure. In its simplest form, the Hebrew word for pleasure (*towb*) means "to be good"—not in a moral sense but through blessing or prosperity. Related words are bounty, cheer, joy, gladness, prosperity, wealth, love, and mercy. The writer tried the best life had to offer and found it lacking meaning.

24 So I decided there is nothing better than to enjoy
food and drink and to find satisfaction in work. Then
I realized that these pleasures are from the hand
of God. 25 For who can eat or enjoy anything apart
from him?* 26 God gives wisdom, knowledge, and joy
to those who please him. But if a sinner becomes
wealthy, God takes the wealth away and gives it to
those who please him. This, too, is meaningless—like
chasing the wind.

A TIME FOR EVERYTHING

3 1 For everything there is a season,
a time for every activity under heaven.
2 A time to be born and a time to die.
A time to plant and a time to harvest.
3 A time to kill and a time to heal.
A time to tear down and a time to build up.
4 A time to cry and a time to laugh.
A time to grieve and a time to dance.
5 A time to scatter stones and a time to gather
stones.
A time to embrace and a time to turn away.
6 A time to search and a time to quit searching.
A time to keep and a time to throw away.
7 A time to tear and a time to mend.
A time to be quiet and a time to speak.
8 A time to love and a time to hate.
A time for war and a time for peace.

9 What do people really get for all their hard work?
10 I have seen the burden God has placed on us all.
11 Yet God has made everything beautiful for its own
time. He has planted eternity in the human heart, but
even so, people cannot see the whole scope of God's
work from beginning to end. 12 So I concluded there is
nothing better than to be happy and enjoy ourselves
as long as we can. 13 And people should eat and drink
and enjoy the fruits of their labor, for these are gifts
from God.
14 And I know that whatever God does is final.
Nothing can be added to it or taken from it. God's
purpose is that people should fear him. 15 What is
happening now has happened before, and what will
happen in the future has happened before, because
God makes the same things happen over and over
again.

THE INJUSTICES OF LIFE

16 I also noticed that under the sun there is evil
in the courtroom. Yes, even the courts of law are
corrupt! 17 I said to myself, "In due season God will
judge everyone, both good and bad, for all their
deeds."
18 I also thought about the human condition—
how God proves to people that they are like animals.
19 For people and animals share the same fate—both
breathe* and both must die. So people have no real
advantage over the animals. How meaningless!
20 Both go to the same place—they came from dust
and they return to dust. 21 For who can prove that the
human spirit goes up and the spirit of animals goes
down into the earth? 22 So I saw that there is nothing
better for people than to be happy in their work. That
is our lot in life. And no one can bring us back to see
what happens after we die.

4 Again, I observed all the oppression that takes
place under the sun. I saw the tears of the op-
pressed, with no one to comfort them. The oppressors
have great power, and their victims are helpless. 2 So I
concluded that the dead are better off than the living.
3 But most fortunate of all are those who are not yet
born. For they have not seen all the evil that is done
under the sun.
4 Then I observed that most people are motivated to
success because they envy their neighbors. But this,
too, is meaningless—like chasing the wind.

5 "Fools fold their idle hands,
leading them to ruin."

6 And yet,

"Better to have one handful with quietness
than two handfuls with hard work
and chasing the wind."

THE ADVANTAGES OF COMPANIONSHIP

7 I observed yet another example of something mean-
ingless under the sun. 8 This is the case of a man who
is all alone, without a child or a brother, yet who
works hard to gain as much wealth as he can. But
then he asks himself, "Who am I working for? Why am
I giving up so much pleasure now?" It is all so mean-
ingless and depressing.
9 Two people are better off than one, for they can
help each other succeed. 10 If one person falls, the
other can reach out and help. But someone who
falls alone is in real trouble. 11 Likewise, two people
lying close together can keep each other warm. But
how can one be warm alone? 12 A person standing
alone can be attacked and defeated, but two can
stand back-to-back and conquer. Three are even
better, for a triple-braided cord is not easily bro-
ken.

THE FUTILITY OF POLITICAL POWER

13 It is better to be a poor but wise youth than an old
and foolish king who refuses all advice. 14 Such a
youth could rise from poverty and succeed. He might
even become king, though he has been in prison.
15 But then everyone rushes to the side of yet anoth-
er youth* who replaces him. 16 Endless crowds stand
around him,* but then another generation grows up
and rejects him, too. So it is all meaningless—like
chasing the wind.

2:25 As in Greek and Syriac versions; Hebrew reads *apart from me?* **3:19** Or *both have the same spirit.* **4:15** Hebrew *the second youth.* **4:16** Hebrew *There is no end to all the people, to all those who are before them.*

2:24 enjoy food and drink . . . find satisfaction in work. The Teacher concludes that there is pleasure and joy in eating, drinking, and work. But we must be careful not to expect more from simple pleasures than they can give. (See also 5:18; 8:17.)

3:11 He has planted eternity in the human heart. Humans are made for eternity.

3:16-18 proves to people that they are like animals. This verse implies that we all need to recognize our own unjust acts. We are part of the problem.

4:5 Fools fold their idle hands. The idle person (fool) is consistently portrayed in Scripture as coming to ruin (10:18; Prov. 6:6-11; 24:30-34).

4:9-12 Two people are better off than one. The human solution to life's misery is companionship. Life is better with a companion, but even with intimate friendship one still experiences the troubles life brings.

APPROACHING GOD WITH CARE

5 1*As you enter the house of God, keep your ears
open and your mouth shut. It is evil to make mind-
less offerings to God. 2*Don't make rash promises, and
don't be hasty in bringing matters before God. After
all, God is in heaven, and you are here on earth. So let
your words be few.
3 Too much activity gives you restless dreams; too
many words make you a fool.
4 When you make a promise to God, don't delay in
following through, for God takes no pleasure in fools.
Keep all the promises you make to him. 5 It is better to
say nothing than to make a promise and not keep it.
6 Don't let your mouth make you sin. And don't defend
yourself by telling the Temple messenger that the
promise you made was a mistake. That would make
God angry, and he might wipe out everything you
have achieved.
7 Talk is cheap, like daydreams and other useless
activities. Fear God instead.

THE FUTILITY OF WEALTH

8 Don't be surprised if you see a poor person being op-
pressed by the powerful and if justice is being miscar-
ried throughout the land. For every official is under
orders from higher up, and matters of justice get lost
in red tape and bureaucracy. 9 Even the king milks the
land for his own profit!*
10 Those who love money will never have enough.
How meaningless to think that wealth brings true
happiness! 11 The more you have, the more people
come to help you spend it. So what good is wealth—
except perhaps to watch it slip through your fingers!
12 People who work hard sleep well, whether they
eat little or much. But the rich seldom get a good
night's sleep.
13 There is another serious problem I have seen un-
der the sun. Hoarding riches harms the saver. 14 Mon-
ey is put into risky investments that turn sour, and
everything is lost. In the end, there is nothing left to
pass on to one's children. 15 We all come to the end of
our lives as naked and empty-handed as on the day
we were born. We can't take our riches with us.
16 And this, too, is a very serious problem. People
leave this world no better off than when they came.
All their hard work is for nothing—like working for
the wind. 17 Throughout their lives, they live under a
cloud—frustrated, discouraged, and angry.
18 Even so, I have noticed one thing, at least, that
is good. It is good for people to eat, drink, and enjoy
their work under the sun during the short life God
has given them, and to accept their lot in life. 19 And
it is a good thing to receive wealth from God and the
good health to enjoy it. To enjoy your work and accept
your lot in life—this is indeed a gift from God. 20 God
keeps such people so busy enjoying life that they take
no time to brood over the past.

6 1 There is another serious tragedy I have seen un-
der the sun, and it weighs heavily on humanity.
2 God gives some people great wealth and honor and
everything they could ever want, but then he doesn't
give them the chance to enjoy these things. They die,
and someone else, even a stranger, ends up enjoying
their wealth! This is meaningless—a sickening trag-
edy.
3 A man might have a hundred children and live
to be very old. But if he finds no satisfaction in life
and doesn't even get a decent burial, it would have
been better for him to be born dead. 4 His birth would
have been meaningless, and he would have ended in
darkness. He wouldn't even have had a name, 5 and
he would never have seen the sun or known of its
existence. Yet he would have had more peace than in
growing up to be an unhappy man. 6 He might live a
thousand years twice over but still not find content-
ment. And since he must die like everyone else—well,
what's the use?
7 All people spend their lives scratching for food,
but they never seem to have enough. 8 So are wise
people really better off than fools? Do poor people
gain anything by being wise and knowing how to act
in front of others?
9 Enjoy what you have rather than desiring what
you don't have. Just dreaming about nice things is
meaningless—like chasing the wind.

THE FUTURE—DETERMINED AND UNKNOWN

10 Everything has already been decided. It was known
long ago what each person would be. So there's no use
arguing with God about your destiny.
11 The more words you speak, the less they mean. So
what good are they?
12 In the few days of our meaningless lives, who
knows how our days can best be spent? Our lives are
like a shadow. Who can tell what will happen on this
earth after we are gone?

WISDOM FOR LIFE

7 1 A good reputation is more valuable than costly
perfume.
And the day you die is better than the day you
are born.
2 Better to spend your time at funerals than at
parties.
After all, everyone dies—
so the living should take this to heart.
3 Sorrow is better than laughter,
for sadness has a refining influence on us.
4 A wise person thinks a lot about death,
while a fool thinks only about having a good
time.
5 Better to be criticized by a wise person
than to be praised by a fool.

5:1 Verse 5:1 is numbered 4:17 in Hebrew text. **5:2** Verses 5:2-20 are numbered 5:1-19 in Hebrew text. **5:9** The meaning of the Hebrew in verses 8 and 9 is uncertain.

5:1-7 This more up-beat section of the book gives commands about how to worship God properly. The writer encourages readers to worship God sincerely, not merely to talk of faith but to humbly obey the Lord. He also warns that vows made to God must be promptly kept.

5:2 Don't make rash promises. We should not be hasty to make vows to the Lord. Jesus gave this same advice in Matthew 5:33-37.

5:7 Fear God. Fearing, or reverencing, God is the main theme of the Wisdom literature.

5:20 God keeps such people so busy enjoying life. The person whose heart is caught up in enjoying God and His good gifts will find life fulfilling and enjoyable.

6:12 who knows how our days can best be spent? We don't have the ability to change ourselves; without God we don't even know what we should aim to become.

[6] A fool's laughter is quickly gone,
like thorns crackling in a fire.
This also is meaningless.

[7] Extortion turns wise people into fools,
and bribes corrupt the heart.

[8] Finishing is better than starting.
Patience is better than pride.

[9] Control your temper,
for anger labels you a fool.

[10] Don't long for "the good old days."
This is not wise.

[11] Wisdom is even better when you have money.
Both are a benefit as you go through life.
[12] Wisdom and money can get you almost anything,
but only wisdom can save your life.

[13] Accept the way God does things,
for who can straighten what he has made
crooked?
[14] Enjoy prosperity while you can,
but when hard times strike, realize that both
come from God.
Remember that nothing is certain in this life.

THE LIMITS OF HUMAN WISDOM

[15] I have seen everything in this meaningless life,
including the death of good young people and the
long life of wicked people. [16] So don't be too good or
too wise! Why destroy yourself? [17] On the other hand,
don't be too wicked either. Don't be a fool! Why die be-
fore your time? [18] Pay attention to these instructions,
for anyone who fears God will avoid both extremes.*
[19] One wise person is stronger than ten leading cit-
izens of a town!
[20] Not a single person on earth is always good and
never sins.
[21] Don't eavesdrop on others—you may hear your
servant curse you. [22] For you know how often you
yourself have cursed others.
[23] I have always tried my best to let wisdom guide my
thoughts and actions. I said to myself, "I am determined
to be wise." But it didn't work. [24] Wisdom is always dis-
tant and difficult to find. [25] I searched everywhere, de-
termined to find wisdom and to understand the reason
for things. I was determined to prove to myself that
wickedness is stupid and that foolishness is madness.
[26] I discovered that a seductive woman* is a trap
more bitter than death. Her passion is a snare, and
her soft hands are chains. Those who are pleasing to
God will escape her, but sinners will be caught in her
snare.
[27] "This is my conclusion," says the Teacher. "I dis-
covered this after looking at the matter from every
possible angle. [28] Though I have searched repeatedly, I
have not found what I was looking for. Only one out of
a thousand men is virtuous, but not one woman! [29] But
I did find this: God created people to be virtuous, but
they have each turned to follow their own downward
path."

8

[1] How wonderful to be wise,
to analyze and interpret things.
Wisdom lights up a person's face,
softening its harshness.

OBEDIENCE TO THE KING

[2] Obey the king since you vowed to God that you
would. [3] Don't try to avoid doing your duty, and don't
stand with those who plot evil, for the king can do
whatever he wants. [4] His command is backed by great
power. No one can resist or question it. [5] Those who
obey him will not be punished. Those who are wise
will find a time and a way to do what is right, [6] for
there is a time and a way for everything, even when a
person is in trouble.
[7] Indeed, how can people avoid what they don't
know is going to happen? [8] None of us can hold back
our spirit from departing. None of us has the power
to prevent the day of our death. There is no escaping
that obligation, that dark battle. And in the face of
death, wickedness will certainly not rescue the wick-
ed.

THE WICKED AND THE RIGHTEOUS

[9] I have thought deeply about all that goes on here
under the sun, where people have the power to hurt
each other. [10] I have seen wicked people buried with
honor. Yet they were the very ones who frequent-
ed the Temple and are now praised* in the same
city where they committed their crimes! This, too, is
meaningless. [11] When a crime is not punished quickly,
people feel it is safe to do wrong. [12] But even though
a person sins a hundred times and still lives a long
time, I know that those who fear God will be better
off. [13] The wicked will not prosper, for they do not fear
God. Their days will never grow long like the evening
shadows.
[14] And this is not all that is meaningless in our
world. In this life, good people are often treated as
though they were wicked, and wicked people are
often treated as though they were good. This is so
meaningless!
[15] So I recommend having fun, because there is
nothing better for people in this world than to eat,

7:18 Or *will follow them both.* 7:26 Hebrew *a woman.* 8:10 As in some Hebrew manuscripts and Greek version; many Hebrew manuscripts read *and are forgotten.*

7:9-10 temper . . . "the good old days". Neither anger nor nostalgia are proper responses to life's sorrows.

7:13-14 what he has made crooked? Crooked refers to the twists and turns of life. Rather than fighting against our circumstances, we are to trust that God is present in them and will take care of our needs.

7:27-28 Only one . . . not one woman. The writer says of relationships that he has only found one man he could trust and no trustworthy women. Why? We all lack wisdom and understanding. (See also v. 20.)

7:29 God created people to be virtuous, but. God is not to blame for troubles on earth. He created humans perfectly, but we chose to disobey.

8:1 How wonderful to be wise. The Hebrew word for "wise" involves intelligence, cunning, subtlety, and the skillful use of wisdom. It brings to mind a thinking person—one who doesn't simply react but reflects on a situation and considers the best response.

8:10-14 The writer poses a problem and then offers a solution. The problem (vv. 10-11) is that wicked people are often praised, and punishment is often delayed. The solution (vv. 12-13) is that in the end, the right thing will be done in every case. God knows our hearts.

8:15 having fun. Here, again man is encouraged to "eat, drink, and enjoy himself." This is not a license for thoughtless Hedonism but is encouragement for humbly enjoying the life God has given us, whatever it holds. (See also 2:24 and 5:18.)

drink, and enjoy life. That way they will experience
some happiness along with all the hard work God
gives them under the sun.
16 In my search for wisdom and in my observation
of people's burdens here on earth, I discovered that
there is ceaseless activity, day and night. 17 I realized
that no one can discover everything God is doing
under the sun. Not even the wisest people discover
everything, no matter what they claim.

DEATH COMES TO ALL

9 This, too, I carefully explored: Even though the
actions of godly and wise people are in God's
hands, no one knows whether God will show them
favor. 2 The same destiny ultimately awaits everyone,
whether righteous or wicked, good or bad,* ceremo-
nially clean or unclean, religious or irreligious. Good
people receive the same treatment as sinners, and
people who make promises to God are treated like
people who don't.
3 It seems so wrong that everyone under the sun
suffers the same fate. Already twisted by evil, people
choose their own mad course, for they have no hope.
There is nothing ahead but death anyway. 4 There is
hope only for the living. As they say, "It's better to be a
live dog than a dead lion!"
5 The living at least know they will die, but the dead
know nothing. They have no further reward, nor
are they remembered. 6 Whatever they did in their
lifetime—loving, hating, envying—is all long gone.
They no longer play a part in anything here on earth.
7 So go ahead. Eat your food with joy, and drink your
wine with a happy heart, for God approves of this!
8 Wear fine clothes, with a splash of cologne!
9 Live happily with the woman you love through all
the meaningless days of life that God has given you
under the sun. The wife God gives you is your reward
for all your earthly toil. 10 Whatever you do, do well.
For when you go to the grave,* there will be no work
or planning or knowledge or wisdom.
11 I have observed something else under the sun.
The fastest runner doesn't always win the race, and
the strongest warrior doesn't always win the battle.
The wise sometimes go hungry, and the skillful are
not necessarily wealthy. And those who are educated
don't always lead successful lives. It is all decided by
chance, by being in the right place at the right time.
12 People can never predict when hard times might
come. Like fish in a net or birds in a trap, people are
caught by sudden tragedy.

THOUGHTS ON WISDOM AND FOLLY

13 Here is another bit of wisdom that has impressed
me as I have watched the way our world works.
14 There was a small town with only a few people, and
a great king came with his army and besieged it. 15 A
poor, wise man knew how to save the town, and so it
was rescued. But afterward no one thought to thank
him. 16 So even though wisdom is better than strength,
those who are wise will be despised if they are poor.
What they say will not be appreciated for long.

17 Better to hear the quiet words of a wise person
than the shouts of a foolish king.
18 Better to have wisdom than weapons of war,
but one sinner can destroy much that is good.

10 1 As dead flies cause even a bottle of perfume
to stink,
so a little foolishness spoils great wisdom and
honor.

2 A wise person chooses the right road;
a fool takes the wrong one.

3 You can identify fools
just by the way they walk down the street!

4 If your boss is angry at you, don't quit!
A quiet spirit can overcome even great
mistakes.

THE IRONIES OF LIFE

5 There is another evil I have seen under the sun.
Kings and rulers make a grave mistake 6 when they
give great authority to foolish people and low posi-
tions to people of proven worth. 7 I have even seen
servants riding horseback like princes—and princes
walking like servants!

8 When you dig a well,
you might fall in.
When you demolish an old wall,
you could be bitten by a snake.
9 When you work in a quarry,
stones might fall and crush you.
When you chop wood,
there is danger with each stroke of your ax.

10 Using a dull ax requires great strength,
so sharpen the blade.
That's the value of wisdom;
it helps you succeed.

11 If a snake bites before you charm it,
what's the use of being a snake charmer?
12 Wise words bring approval,
but fools are destroyed by their own words.
13 Fools base their thoughts on foolish assumptions,
so their conclusions will be wicked madness;
14 they chatter on and on.

No one really knows what is going to happen;
no one can predict the future.

9:2 As in Greek and Syriac versions and Latin Vulgate; Hebrew lacks *or bad.* 9:10 Hebrew *to Sheol.*

8:17 no one can. God allows humans to understand a little, but we are limited by our finite minds.
9:2 same destiny . . . awaits everyone. Through a series of opposites, we see that all people—no matter how privileged or oppressed they were in life—share the common destiny of death.
9:10 grave. Life after death is a rare concept in the Old Testament. Here the literal word is *Sheol*, which is the shadowy idea of the place of the dead.
10:2 chooses the right road. The right may refer to the right hand, the place of protection, or may simply be a contrast between the way of good and the way of evil.
10:12-14 words. Here the writer reminds us of the importance of being wise in our choice of words. The book of James gives us instructions in taming our tongues.

15 Fools are so exhausted by a little work
that they can't even find their way home.

16 What sorrow for the land ruled by a servant,*
the land whose leaders feast in the morning.
17 Happy is the land whose king is a noble leader
and whose leaders feast at the proper time
to gain strength for their work, not to get drunk.

18 Laziness leads to a sagging roof;
idleness leads to a leaky house.

19 A party gives laughter,
wine gives happiness,
and money gives everything!

20 Never make light of the king, even in your
thoughts.
And don't make fun of the powerful, even in
your own bedroom.
For a little bird might deliver your message
and tell them what you said.

THE UNCERTAINTIES OF LIFE

11 1 Send your grain across the seas,
and in time, profits will flow back to you.*
2 But divide your investments among many places,*
for you do not know what risks might lie ahead.

3 When clouds are heavy, the rains come down.
Whether a tree falls north or south, it stays
where it falls.

4 Farmers who wait for perfect weather never
plant.
If they watch every cloud, they never harvest.

5 Just as you cannot understand the path of the
wind or the mystery of a tiny baby growing in its
mother's womb,* so you cannot understand the activ-
ity of God, who does all things.
6 Plant your seed in the morning and keep busy all
afternoon, for you don't know if profit will come from
one activity or another—or maybe both.

ADVICE FOR YOUNG AND OLD

7 Light is sweet; how pleasant to see a new day dawn-
ing.
8 When people live to be very old, let them rejoice
in every day of life. But let them also remember there
will be many dark days. Everything still to come is
meaningless.
9 Young people,* it's wonderful to be young! Enjoy
every minute of it. Do everything you want to do; take
it all in. But remember that you must give an account
to God for everything you do. 10 So refuse to worry, and
keep your body healthy. But remember that youth,
with a whole life before you, is meaningless.

12 Don't let the excitement of youth cause you to
forget your Creator. Honor him in your youth
before you grow old and say, "Life is not pleasant
anymore." 2 Remember him before the light of the
sun, moon, and stars is dim to your old eyes, and rain
clouds continually darken your sky. 3 Remember him
before your legs—the guards of your house—start
to tremble; and before your shoulders—the strong
men—stoop. Remember him before your teeth—
your few remaining servants—stop grinding; and
before your eyes—the women looking through the
windows—see dimly.
4 Remember him before the door to life's opportu-
nities is closed and the sound of work fades. Now you
rise at the first chirping of the birds, but then all their
sounds will grow faint.
5 Remember him before you become fearful of fall-
ing and worry about danger in the streets; before
your hair turns white like an almond tree in bloom,
and you drag along without energy like a dying
grasshopper, and the caperberry no longer inspires
sexual desire. Remember him before you near the
grave, your everlasting home, when the mourners
will weep at your funeral.
6 Yes, remember your Creator now while you are
young, before the silver cord of life snaps and the
golden bowl is broken. Don't wait until the water jar
is smashed at the spring and the pulley is broken at
the well. 7 For then the dust will return to the earth,
and the spirit will return to God who gave it.

CONCLUDING THOUGHTS ABOUT THE TEACHER

8 "Everything is meaningless," says the Teacher, "com-
pletely meaningless."
9 Keep this in mind: The Teacher was considered
wise, and he taught the people everything he knew.
He listened carefully to many proverbs, studying and
classifying them. 10 The Teacher sought to find just the
right words to express truths clearly.*
11 The words of the wise are like cattle prods—
painful but helpful. Their collected sayings are like a

10:16 Or *a child.* **11:1** Or *Give generously, / for your gifts will return to you later.* Hebrew reads *Throw your bread on the waters, / for after many days you will find it again.* **11:2** Hebrew *among seven or even eight.* **11:5** Some manuscripts read *Just as you cannot understand how breath comes to a tiny baby in its mother's womb.* **11:9** Hebrew *Young man.* **12:10** Or *sought to write what was upright and true.*

11:2 divide your investments among many places. Since wealth is meaningless and uncertain, be generous with money. Since disaster is always possible, make investments in people instead of hoarding your resources for a "rainy day."
11:8 many dark days. Darkness may involve misery, destruction, sorrow, or death. It is inevitable that all will know their share of dark days as well as "light" (v. 7).
11:9 it's wonderful to be young. Young people are urged to enjoy whatever their hearts desire but should temper their desires with an awareness of God's commands. Ignoring them results in judgment.
12:1-8 The writer uses a variety of images to describe old age.
12:2 darken your sky. Darkness and clouds may be metaphors for weakening eyesight as well as the darkened ideals of youth (see v. 1).
12:3-4 Age is compared to a disintegrating house. The writer describes the trembling hands, stooping shoulders, lost teeth, poor eyesight, loss of hearing, sleeplessness, and confused speech of the elderly.
12:5 become fearful. Old people fear going out, partly because their waning vigor and feebleness make movement dangerous. **almond tree in blossom.** This refers to the white hair of the aging. **dying grasshopper.** People previously as agile as grasshoppers become stiff and frail in old age. **caperberry.** These berries were used to stimulate sexual desire when sex no longer appealed. All these images capture the fragility of human life.
12:6 cord . . . bowl . . . jar. Remember God before your life is broken and comes to an end like the household objects described in this verse.
12:8 meaningless. The writer repeats the theme of the book. Life apart from God is futile.
12:9-10 listened carefully. The writer diligently sought true wisdom; he studied and classified many proverbs, seeking out meaning and truth.
12:11-12 a shepherd drives the sheep. The writer affirms that Scripture, unlike any other book, is full of wisdom. Earthly wisdom, which comes through the study of many books, is tiring. But the Bible is full of spiritual wisdom and does not lack.

nail-studded stick with which a shepherd* drives the sheep.
[12] But, my child,* let me give you some further advice: Be careful, for writing books is endless, and much study wears you out.
[13] That's the whole story. Here now is my final conclusion: Fear God and obey his commands, for this is everyone's duty. [14] God will judge us for everything we do, including every secret thing, whether good or bad.

12:11 Or *one shepherd.* 12:12 Hebrew *my son.*

12:13-14 Fear God and obey his commands. All the Teacher's investigations have led to this truth: life's meaning is found in God alone. God's commands provide all the meaning and truth we desire.

INTRODUCTION TO

SONG OF SONGS

PERSONAL READING PLAN

☐Song of Songs 1:1–2:13
☐Song of Songs 2:14–3:11
☐Song of Songs 4:1-16
☐Song of Songs 5:1-16
☐Song of Songs 6:1–7:9a
☐Song of Songs 7:9b–8:14

AUTHOR

Traditionally, Song of Songs is attributed to King Solomon. However, its title, "Solomon's song of songs" (1:1), can mean a song by, for, or about Solomon. Thus, the identity of the author remains an open question.

DATE

Song of Songs was perhaps written during Solomon's reign, *circa* 970–930 B.C., but the presence of non-Hebrew words or expressions suggests a later date for the final editing.

THEME

A celebration of love between a man and woman, a love akin to God's love for His people.

HISTORICAL BACKGROUND

Solomon's dynasty, his unsurpassed wisdom and wealth, and his many wives and concubines are thought-provoking contrasts to the simple, rustic purity of the Song of Songs.

CHARACTERISTICS

Interpretations of this "best of all songs" vary widely. Some view it literally, as a human love poem about King Solomon and his bride. Others see a third character in a triangle of relationships: a shepherd-figure who is the true lover and who wins the Shulammite girl's hand over against the advances of Solomon. Some understand the book to be an anthology of unrelated love poems, with no overall story to tell. Others interpret this lovers' song as an allegory, depicting either God's love for Israel or Christ's love for His bride, the church. Still others think it is natural to extol the wonders of human love. Readers are sometimes surprised to find an explicit love song in the Bible, hence the many attempts to spiritualize away its sensual lyrics. Another problem in understanding the Song of Songs has to do with the frequent change of voice and scene. The captions in the text are designed to help follow the lovers' dialogue.

PASSAGES FOR TOPICAL GROUP STUDY

1:1–2:7 .. LOVE and ROMANCE .... Love Song

1 This is Solomon's song of songs, more wonderful than any other.

YOUNG WOMAN*

2 Kiss me and kiss me again,
for your love is sweeter than wine.
3 How pleasing is your fragrance;
your name is like the spreading fragrance of scented oils.
No wonder all the young women love you!
4 Take me with you; come, let's run!
The king has brought me into his bedroom.

YOUNG WOMEN OF JERUSALEM

How happy we are for you, O king.
We praise your love even more than wine.

YOUNG WOMAN

How right they are to adore you.

5 I am dark but beautiful,
O women of Jerusalem—
dark as the tents of Kedar,
dark as the curtains of Solomon's tents.
6 Don't stare at me because I am dark—
the sun has darkened my skin.
My brothers were angry with me;
they forced me to care for their vineyards,
so I couldn't care for myself—my own vineyard.

7 Tell me, my love, where are you leading your flock today?
Where will you rest your sheep at noon?
For why should I wander like a prostitute*
among your friends and their flocks?

YOUNG MAN

8 If you don't know, O most beautiful woman,
follow the trail of my flock,
and graze your young goats by the shepherds' tents.
9 You are as exciting, my darling,
as a mare among Pharaoh's stallions.
10 How lovely are your cheeks;
your earrings set them afire!
How lovely is your neck,
enhanced by a string of jewels.
11 We will make for you earrings of gold
and beads of silver.

YOUNG WOMAN

12 The king is lying on his couch,
enchanted by the fragrance of my perfume.
13 My lover is like a sachet of myrrh
lying between my breasts.
14 He is like a bouquet of sweet henna blossoms
from the vineyards of En-gedi.

LOVE SONG

1. Ladies: What celebrity fits your idea of a "Prince Charming"? Guys: What celebrity fits your idea of a "Dream Girl"?

SONG OF SONGS 1:1–2:7

2. What does the woman find attractive in the man? The man in the woman?
3. What does this love song suggest about God's views on love and romance?
4. What do you think the beloved meant when she said, "Promise me . . . not to awaken love until the time is right" (2:7)?
5. What or who can help you to wait until "the time is right" when you're in a romantic relationship?

YOUNG MAN

15 How beautiful you are, my darling,
how beautiful!
Your eyes are like doves.

YOUNG WOMAN

16 You are so handsome, my love,
pleasing beyond words!
The soft grass is our bed;
17 fragrant cedar branches are the beams of our house,
and pleasant smelling firs are the rafters.

YOUNG WOMAN

2 1 I am the spring crocus blooming on the Sharon Plain,*
the lily of the valley.

YOUNG MAN

2 Like a lily among thistles
is my darling among young women.

YOUNG WOMAN

3 Like the finest apple tree in the orchard
is my lover among other young men.
I sit in his delightful shade
and taste his delicious fruit.
4 He escorts me to the banquet hall;
it's obvious how much he loves me.
5 Strengthen me with raisin cakes,
refresh me with apples,
for I am weak with love.
6 His left arm is under my head,
and his right arm embraces me.

1:1 The headings identifying the speakers are not in the original text, though the Hebrew usually gives clues by means of the gender of the person speaking. **1:7** Hebrew *like a veiled woman.* **2:1** Traditionally rendered *I am the rose of Sharon.* Sharon Plain is a region in the coastal plain of Palestine.

1:1 Solomon's song of songs. Solomon (the assumed lover here) wrote more than 1,000 songs (1 Kings 4:32). This is a poetic description of joyful, marital sexual love.
1:2 Kiss me . . . again. Illustrates greater desire. Nose kisses were common in the Ancient Near East.
1:5 I am dark. Deeply tanned skin was not considered attractive compared to the court's pale maidens.
1:7 like a prostitute. Prostitutes wore veils. She fears shepherds would mistake her for one if she pursued her lover among his flocks.
1:9 mare. Solomon purchased the best horses from Pharaoh (1 Kings 10:28).
1:13 sachet of myrrh. Aromatic sap from balsam trees that grew in Arabia, Ethiopia, and India kept in a small pouch around a woman's neck for perfume (Esth. 2:12; Prov. 7:17). Royal wedding clothes were also perfumed with myrrh (3:6; Ps. 45:8). Myrrh was not found in Israel, increasing its value.

7 Promise me, O women of Jerusalem,
by the gazelles and wild deer,
not to awaken love until the time is
right.*

8 Ah, I hear my lover coming!
He is leaping over the mountains,
bounding over the hills.
9 My lover is like a swift gazelle
or a young stag.
Look, there he is behind the wall,
looking through the window,
peering into the room.

10 My lover said to me,
"Rise up, my darling!
Come away with me, my fair one!
11 Look, the winter is past,
and the rains are over and gone.
12 The flowers are springing up,
the season of singing birds* has come,
and the cooing of turtledoves fills the air.
13 The fig trees are forming young fruit,
and the fragrant grapevines are blossoming.
Rise up, my darling!
Come away with me, my fair one!"

YOUNG MAN

14 My dove is hiding behind the rocks,
behind an outcrop on the cliff.
Let me see your face;
let me hear your voice.
For your voice is pleasant,
and your face is lovely.

YOUNG WOMEN OF JERUSALEM

15 Catch all the foxes,
those little foxes,
before they ruin the vineyard of love,
for the grapevines are blossoming!

YOUNG WOMAN

16 My lover is mine, and I am his.
He browses among the lilies.
17 Before the dawn breezes blow
and the night shadows flee,
return to me, my love, like a gazelle
or a young stag on the rugged mountains.*

YOUNG WOMAN

3 1 One night as I lay in bed, I yearned for my lover.
I yearned for him, but he did not come.
2 So I said to myself, "I will get up and roam the city,
searching in all its streets and squares.
I will search for the one I love."
So I searched everywhere but did not find him.
3 The watchmen stopped me as they made their
rounds,
and I asked, "Have you seen the one I love?"
4 Then scarcely had I left them
when I found my love!
I caught and held him tightly,
then I brought him to my mother's house,
into my mother's bed, where I had been
conceived.

5 Promise me, O women of Jerusalem,
by the gazelles and wild deer,
not to awaken love until the time is right.*

YOUNG WOMEN OF JERUSALEM

6 Who is this sweeping in from the wilderness
like a cloud of smoke?
Who is it, fragrant with myrrh and frankincense
and every kind of spice?
7 Look, it is Solomon's carriage,
surrounded by sixty heroic men,
the best of Israel's soldiers.
8 They are all skilled swordsmen,
experienced warriors.
Each wears a sword on his thigh,
ready to defend the king against an attack in
the night.
9 King Solomon's carriage is built
of wood imported from Lebanon.
10 Its posts are silver,
its canopy gold;
its cushions are purple.
It was decorated with love
by the young women of Jerusalem.

YOUNG WOMAN

11 Come out to see King Solomon,
young women of Jerusalem.*
He wears the crown his mother gave him on his
wedding day,
his most joyous day.

YOUNG MAN

4 1 You are beautiful, my darling,
beautiful beyond words.
Your eyes are like doves
behind your veil.
Your hair falls in waves,
like a flock of goats winding down the slopes of
Gilead.
2 Your teeth are as white as sheep,
recently shorn and freshly washed.
Your smile is flawless,
each tooth matched with its twin.*
3 Your lips are like scarlet ribbon;
your mouth is inviting.
Your cheeks are like rosy pomegranates
behind your veil.
4 Your neck is as beautiful as the tower of David,
jeweled with the shields of a thousand heroes.

2:7 Or *not to awaken love until it is ready.* **2:12** Or *the season of pruning vines.* **2:17** Or *on the hills of Bether.* **3:5** Or *not to awaken love until it is ready.* **3:11** Hebrew *of Zion.* **4:2** Hebrew *Not one is missing; each has a twin.*

2:15 foxes . . . vineyards. Foxes were common pests in vineyards but here are probably symbols of threats to their relationship, perhaps other admirers.
3:5 not to awaken love. This is a poetic warning against premarital relations, against opening the fragrant garden of sexual love before a commitment to marriage is sealed (2:7).
3:7-10 carriage. A specially built sedan chair on which bearers carried the beloved to the wedding.
4:1 a flock of goats. Goats in Canaan were generally black; the lover sees his beloved's dark hair cascading down.
4:2 newly shorn. The sheep would thus have been clean and white.
4:3 Your lips . . . scarlet. Egyptian women often painted their lips, and her beautiful lips incite the lover's desire to kiss her.
4:4 Your neck is . . . as the tower. Her neck, adorned with beautiful necklaces, was strong and straight as David's military tower.

5 Your breasts are like two fawns,
twin fawns of a gazelle grazing among the lilies.
6 Before the dawn breezes blow
and the night shadows flee,
I will hurry to the mountain of myrrh
and to the hill of frankincense.
7 You are altogether beautiful, my darling,
beautiful in every way.

8 Come with me from Lebanon, my bride,
come with me from Lebanon.
Come down* from Mount Amana,
from the peaks of Senir and Hermon,
where the lions have their dens
and leopards live among the hills.
9 You have captured my heart,
my treasure,* my bride.
You hold it hostage with one glance of
your eyes,
with a single jewel of your necklace.
10 Your love delights me,
my treasure, my bride.
Your love is better than wine,
your perfume more fragrant than spices.
11 Your lips are as sweet as nectar, my bride.
Honey and milk are under your tongue.
Your clothes are scented
like the cedars of Lebanon.

12 You are my private garden, my treasure, my bride,
a secluded spring, a hidden fountain.
13 Your thighs shelter a paradise of pomegranates
with rare spices—
henna with nard,
14 nard and saffron,
fragrant calamus and cinnamon,
with all the trees of frankincense, myrrh, and
aloes,
and every other lovely spice.
15 You are a garden fountain,
a well of fresh water
streaming down from Lebanon's mountains.

YOUNG WOMAN

16 Awake, north wind!
Rise up, south wind!
Blow on my garden
and spread its fragrance all around.
Come into your garden, my love;
taste its finest fruits.

YOUNG MAN

5 1 I have entered my garden, my treasure,* my
bride!
I gather myrrh with my spices
and eat honeycomb with my honey.
I drink wine with my milk.

YOUNG WOMEN OF JERUSALEM

Oh, lover and beloved, eat and drink!
Yes, drink deeply of your love!

YOUNG WOMAN

2 I slept, but my heart was awake,
when I heard my lover knocking and calling:
"Open to me, my treasure, my darling,
my dove, my perfect one.
My head is drenched with dew,
my hair with the dampness of the night."

3 But I responded,
"I have taken off my robe.
Should I get dressed again?
I have washed my feet.
Should I get them soiled?"

4 My lover tried to unlatch the door,
and my heart thrilled within me.
5 I jumped up to open the door for my love,
and my hands dripped with perfume.
My fingers dripped with lovely myrrh
as I pulled back the bolt.
6 I opened to my lover,
but he was gone!
My heart sank.
I searched for him
but could not find him anywhere.
I called to him,
but there was no reply.
7 The night watchmen found me
as they made their rounds.
They beat and bruised me
and stripped off my veil,
those watchmen on the walls.

8 Make this promise, O women of Jerusalem—
If you find my lover,
tell him I am weak with love.

YOUNG WOMEN OF JERUSALEM

9 Why is your lover better than all others,
O woman of rare beauty?
What makes your lover so special
that we must promise this?

YOUNG WOMAN

10 My lover is dark and dazzling,
better than ten thousand others!
11 His head is finest gold,
his wavy hair is black as a raven.
12 His eyes sparkle like doves
beside springs of water;
they are set like jewels
washed in milk.
13 His cheeks are like gardens of spices
giving off fragrance.

4:8 Or *Look down.* **4:9** Hebrew *my sister;* also in 4:10, 12. **5:1** Hebrew *my sister;* also in 5:2.

4:9 captured my heart, my treasure. The word "treasure" is literally "sister" in Hebrew. Lovers often call each other "brother" and "sister" (vv. 10, 12; 5:1) as terms of endearment.

4:12 private garden. A garden is full of beauty, refreshment, and sensual delight—a beautiful description of love (v. 16; 5:1; 6:2). The private garden may refer to the beloved's virginity.

4:16 Come into your garden, my love. An invitation to enjoy sexual intimacy for the first time. He expresses his complete satisfaction as a result in 5:1.

5:5 My fingers dripped with lovely myrrh. The beloved's hands are oiled with perfume for her lover's arrival. Other interpretations suggest that myrrh may also symbolize her readiness for sexual encounter. But he has left by the time she opens the door (5:6).

5:8 Make this promise. This refrain (used also in 2:7; 3:5) comprises an oath to wait for a love such as this before entering into intimacy.

His lips are like lilies,
perfumed with myrrh.
14 His arms are like rounded bars of gold,
set with beryl.
His body is like bright ivory,
glowing with lapis lazuli.
15 His legs are like marble pillars
set in sockets of finest gold.
His posture is stately,
like the noble cedars of Lebanon.
16 His mouth is sweetness itself;
he is desirable in every way.
Such, O women of Jerusalem,
is my lover, my friend.

YOUNG WOMEN OF JERUSALEM

6 1 Where has your lover gone,
O woman of rare beauty?
Which way did he turn
so we can help you find him?

YOUNG WOMAN

2 My lover has gone down to his garden,
to his spice beds,
to browse in the gardens
and gather the lilies.
3 I am my lover's, and my lover is mine.
He browses among the lilies.

YOUNG MAN

4 You are beautiful, my darling,
like the lovely city of Tirzah.
Yes, as beautiful as Jerusalem,
as majestic as an army with billowing banners.
5 Turn your eyes away,
for they overpower me.
Your hair falls in waves,
like a flock of goats winding down the slopes of Gilead.
6 Your teeth are as white as sheep
that are freshly washed.
Your smile is flawless,
each tooth matched with its twin.*
7 Your cheeks are like rosy pomegranates
behind your veil.

8 Even among sixty queens
and eighty concubines
and countless young women,
9 I would still choose my dove, my perfect one—
the favorite of her mother,
dearly loved by the one who bore her.
The young women see her and praise her;
even queens and royal concubines sing her praises:
10 "Who is this, arising like the dawn,
as fair as the moon,
as bright as the sun,
as majestic as an army with billowing banners?"

YOUNG WOMAN

11 I went down to the grove of walnut trees
and out to the valley to see the new spring growth,
to see whether the grapevines had budded
or the pomegranates were in bloom.
12 Before I realized it,
my strong desires had taken me to the chariot of a noble man.*

YOUNG WOMEN OF JERUSALEM

13*Return, return to us, O maid of Shulam.
Come back, come back, that we may see you again.

YOUNG MAN

Why do you stare at this young woman of Shulam,
as she moves so gracefully between two lines of dancers?*

7 1*How beautiful are your sandaled feet,
O queenly maiden.
Your rounded thighs are like jewels,
the work of a skilled craftsman.
2 Your navel is perfectly formed
like a goblet filled with mixed wine.
Between your thighs lies a mound of wheat
bordered with lilies.
3 Your breasts are like two fawns,
twin fawns of a gazelle.
4 Your neck is as beautiful as an ivory tower.
Your eyes are like the sparkling pools in Heshbon
by the gate of Bath-rabbim.
Your nose is as fine as the tower of Lebanon
overlooking Damascus.
5 Your head is as majestic as Mount Carmel,
and the sheen of your hair radiates royalty.
The king is held captive by its tresses.
6 Oh, how beautiful you are!
How pleasing, my love, how full of delights!
7 You are slender like a palm tree,
and your breasts are like its clusters of fruit.
8 I said, "I will climb the palm tree
and take hold of its fruit."
May your breasts be like grape clusters,
and the fragrance of your breath like apples.

6:6 Hebrew *Not one is missing; each has a twin.* **6:12** Or *to the royal chariots of my people,* or *to the chariots of Amminadab.* The meaning of the Hebrew is uncertain. **6:13a** Verse 6:13 is numbered 7:1 in Hebrew text. **6:13b** Or *as you would at the movements of two armies?* or *as you would at the dance of Mahanaim?* The meaning of the Hebrew is uncertain. **7:1** Verses 7:1-13 are numbered 7:2-14 in Hebrew text.

6:2-3 gather the lilies. Imaginative language that portrays the lover as a gazelle (2:7) nibbling on the alluring lilies in the exotic garden, thus enjoying intimate moments with his beloved.
6:4 Tirzah. Tirzah was the capitol of Israel's northern kingdom, known for its grand architecture.
6:5 Turn your eyes. The lover is captivated by the deep love he sees through his beloved's eyes—it is almost too wonderful to bear (4:9).
6:8-9 queens . . . concubines . . . young women. Naming the notable women in the kingdom, or even compared to all the women in the kingdom, his lover is still "unique."
6:13 maid of Shulam. This name is ambiguous, either referring to her origin as a girl from Shulam ("Shunammite," 1 Kings 1:3), or as a feminine version of Solomon's name meaning, "Solomon's girl." Or even perhaps an oblique reference to a Mesopotamian goddess of love, Sulmanitu.
7:4 neck . . . ivory tower. Ivory is used to describe the shape, color, and smoothness of the beloved's neck.
7:7 palm tree. This reference likely refers to her tall, slim appearance with breasts like clusters of fruit at the top of the tree.

9 May your kisses be as exciting as the best
wine—

YOUNG WOMAN

Yes, wine that goes down smoothly for my
lover,
flowing gently over lips and teeth.*
10 I am my lover's,
and he claims me as his own.
11 Come, my love, let us go out to the fields
and spend the night among the
wildflowers.*
12 Let us get up early and go to the vineyards
to see if the grapevines have budded,
if the blossoms have opened,
and if the pomegranates have bloomed.
There I will give you my love.
13 There the mandrakes give off their fragrance,
and the finest fruits are at our door,
new delights as well as old,
which I have saved for you, my lover.

YOUNG WOMAN

8 1 Oh, I wish you were my brother,
who nursed at my mother's breasts.
Then I could kiss you no matter who was
watching,
and no one would criticize me.
2 I would bring you to my childhood home,
and there you would teach me.*
I would give you spiced wine to drink,
my sweet pomegranate wine.
3 Your left arm would be under my head,
and your right arm would embrace me.

4 Promise me, O women of Jerusalem,
not to awaken love until the time is right.*

YOUNG WOMEN OF JERUSALEM

5 Who is this sweeping in from the desert,
leaning on her lover?

YOUNG WOMAN

I aroused you under the apple tree,
where your mother gave you birth,
where in great pain she delivered you.
6 Place me like a seal over your heart,
like a seal on your arm.
For love is as strong as death,
its jealousy* as enduring as the grave.*
Love flashes like fire,
the brightest kind of flame.
7 Many waters cannot quench love,
nor can rivers drown it.
If a man tried to buy love
with all his wealth,
his offer would be utterly scorned.

THE YOUNG WOMAN'S BROTHERS

8 We have a little sister
too young to have breasts.
What will we do for our sister
if someone asks to marry her?
9 If she is a virgin, like a wall,
we will protect her with a silver tower.
But if she is promiscuous, like a swinging
door,
we will block her door with a cedar bar.

YOUNG WOMAN

10 I was a virgin, like a wall;
now my breasts are like towers.
When my lover looks at me,
he is delighted with what he sees.

11 Solomon has a vineyard at Baal-hamon,
which he leases out to tenant farmers.
Each of them pays a thousand pieces of
silver
for harvesting its fruit.
12 But my vineyard is mine to give,
and Solomon need not pay a thousand pieces of
silver.
But I will give two hundred pieces
to those who care for its vines.

YOUNG MAN

13 O my darling, lingering in the gardens,
your companions are fortunate to hear your
voice.
Let me hear it, too!

YOUNG WOMAN

14 Come away, my love! Be like a gazelle
or a young stag on the mountains of
spices.

7:9 As in Greek and Syriac versions and Latin Vulgate; Hebrew reads *over lips of sleepers.* 7:11 Or *in the villages.* 8:2 Or *there she will teach me.* 8:4 Or *not to awaken love until it is ready.* 8:6a Or *its passion.* 8:6b Hebrew *as Sheol.*

7:13 mandrakes. These flowering herbs with a pungent fragrance were used for fertility (see Gen. 30:14-16).

8:1 like my brother. She longs to be as free and affectionate in public as she could be with a brother (though unacceptable between lovers in that culture).

8:12 my vineyard is mine to give. A poetic reference to her own body (1:6).

8:13 lingering in the gardens. The beloved had earlier invited Solomon to her vineyards in the country (7:11-12).

8:14 like a gazelle or a young stag. The beloved desires her lover to be graceful, virile, and strong, and he return quickly to her (1:13; 4:6).

INTRODUCTION TO

ISAIAH

PERSONAL READING PLAN

☐Isaiah 1:1–2:22
☐Isaiah 3:1–5:30
☐Isaiah 6:1–8:22
☐Isaiah 9:1–10:34
☐Isaiah 11:1–14:23
☐Isaiah 14:24–18:7
☐Isaiah 19:1–22:25
☐Isaiah 23:1–25:12
☐Isaiah 26:1–28:29
☐Isaiah 29:1–30:33
☐Isaiah 31:1–34:17
☐Isaiah 35:1–37:38
☐Isaiah 38:1–40:31
☐Isaiah 41:1–42:25
☐Isaiah 43:1–44:23
☐Isaiah 44:24–47:15
☐Isaiah 48:1–49:26
☐Isaiah 50:1–52:12
☐Isaiah 52:13–55:13
☐Isaiah 56:1–58:14
☐Isaiah 59:1–60:22
☐Isaiah 61:1–63:6
☐Isaiah 63:7–65:16
☐Isaiah 65:17–66:24

AUTHOR

In the opening verse of the book, the author is declared to be Isaiah son of Amoz (see also 2:1; 13:1). Chapters 1–39 ("The Book of Judgment") reflect the kingdom of Isaiah's day, but chapters 40–66 ("The Book of Comfort") envision the return from exile (536 B.C.) and the coming kingdom of God. There are some who believe that these visionary chapters may have been written later by other prophets.

DATE

Isaiah ministered in Judah *circa* 740–681 B.C.

THEME

The sovereign Lord, judging and redeeming the whole earth.

HISTORICAL BACKGROUND

Assyria, the invincible superpower of the day, was threatening Jerusalem with conquest (2 Kings 15–20; 2 Chron. 26–32). Isaiah saw in this the culmination of God's judgment against the widespread apostasy of Judah under King Ahaz. He predicted the fall of Jerusalem (which occurred in 586 B.C.). The only hope for escape, Isaiah declared, was God's intervention, not political alliances, material wealth, or religious pretense. Chapters 40–66 focus on events 150–200 years after Isaiah's day, foretelling God's deliverance of His people from their Babylonian captors (In 538 B.C.) and pointing ahead to the greater deliverance from sin through Christ.

CHARACTERISTICS

As a prophet, poet, and politician, Isaiah was a giant in his day, respected in royal circles despite his unpopular message. Known for his beautiful images and profound insights into the nature of God (whom Isaiah calls "The Holy One of Israel"), the prophet Isaiah is quoted in the New Testament more than all other prophets combined. Isaiah's use of fire as a symbol of punishment (1:31), his references to the "mountain" of Jerusalem (2:2-4), and his mention of the highway to Jerusalem (11:16) are images that recur throughout the book.

PASSAGES FOR TOPICAL GROUP STUDY

40:25-31 . . . . . . GOD'S HELP . . . . . . The Source of All Strength
52:13–53:12 . . PROPHECY OF JESUS . . The Suffering Servant

1 These are the visions that Isaiah son of Amoz saw concerning Judah and Jerusalem. He saw these visions during the years when Uzziah, Jotham, Ahaz, and Hezekiah were kings of Judah.*

A MESSAGE FOR REBELLIOUS JUDAH

2 Listen, O heavens! Pay attention, earth!
This is what the LORD says:
"The children I raised and cared for
have rebelled against me.
3 Even an ox knows its owner,
and a donkey recognizes its master's care—
but Israel doesn't know its master.
My people don't recognize my care for them."
4 Oh, what a sinful nation they are—
loaded down with a burden of guilt.
They are evil people,
corrupt children who have rejected the LORD.
They have despised the Holy One of Israel
and turned their backs on him.
5 Why do you continue to invite punishment?
Must you rebel forever?
Your head is injured,
and your heart is sick.
6 You are battered from head to foot—
covered with bruises, welts, and infected wounds—
without any soothing ointments or bandages.
7 Your country lies in ruins,
and your towns are burned.
Foreigners plunder your fields before your eyes
and destroy everything they see.
8 Beautiful Jerusalem* stands abandoned
like a watchman's shelter in a vineyard,
like a lean-to in a cucumber field after the harvest,
like a helpless city under siege.
9 If the LORD of Heaven's Armies
had not spared a few of us,*
we would have been wiped out like Sodom,
destroyed like Gomorrah.

10 Listen to the LORD, you leaders of "Sodom."
Listen to the law of our God, people of "Gomorrah."
11 "What makes you think I want all your sacrifices?"
says the LORD.
"I am sick of your burnt offerings of rams
and the fat of fattened cattle.
I get no pleasure from the blood
of bulls and lambs and goats.
12 When you come to worship me,
who asked you to parade through my courts
with all your ceremony?
13 Stop bringing me your meaningless gifts;
the incense of your offerings disgusts me!
As for your celebrations of the new moon and the Sabbath
and your special days for fasting—
they are all sinful and false.
I want no more of your pious meetings.
14 I hate your new moon celebrations and your annual festivals.
They are a burden to me. I cannot stand them!
15 When you lift up your hands in prayer, I will not look.
Though you offer many prayers, I will not listen,
for your hands are covered with the blood of innocent victims.
16 Wash yourselves and be clean!
Get your sins out of my sight.
Give up your evil ways.
17 Learn to do good.
Seek justice.
Help the oppressed.
Defend the cause of orphans.
Fight for the rights of widows.

18 "Come now, let's settle this,"
says the LORD.
"Though your sins are like scarlet,
I will make them as white as snow.
Though they are red like crimson,
I will make them as white as wool.
19 If you will only obey me,
you will have plenty to eat.
20 But if you turn away and refuse to listen,
you will be devoured by the sword of your enemies.
I, the LORD, have spoken!"

UNFAITHFUL JERUSALEM

21 See how Jerusalem, once so faithful,
has become a prostitute.
Once the home of justice and righteousness,
she is now filled with murderers.
22 Once like pure silver,
you have become like worthless slag.
Once so pure,
you are now like watered-down wine.
23 Your leaders are rebels,
the companions of thieves.
All of them love bribes
and demand payoffs,
but they refuse to defend the cause of orphans
or fight for the rights of widows.

24 Therefore, the Lord, the LORD of Heaven's Armies,
the Mighty One of Israel, says,
"I will take revenge on my enemies
and pay back my foes!
25 I will raise my fist against you.

1:1 These kings reigned from 792 to 686 B.C. **1:8** Hebrew *The daughter of Zion.* **1:9** Greek version reads *a few of our children.* Compare Rom 9:29.

1:1 kings of Judah. The nation of Israel had been divided into Judah in the south and Israel in the north. Isaiah focuses his message on Judah, listing the four kings who ruled from 792 to 686 B.C., during the time when he received God's prophetic visions and words.

1:9-10 Sodom . . . Gomorrah. So far Judah has escaped total destruction, but the precedent has already been set by these sinful cities God utterly destroyed (see 3:9; Gen. 13:13; 18:20,21; 19:5,24,25). God compares the Judeans to the depraved people of Sodom and Gomorrah.

1:17 Defend . . . orphans. Fight for rights of the widows. This guidance is echoed in Jeremiah 22:16 and James 1:27. These types of people are symbolic of all oppressed peoples in society. Their treatment by the nation as a whole was a barometer for the nation's spiritual and moral health; rulers were not to take advantage of them (see v. 23; 10:2; Jer. 22:3).

1:18 let's settle this. This was not an invitation to compromise but a call to come to a legal decision in alignment with God's perfect will regarding their sin. **scarlet.** God has caught His people "red handed." Blood covers their hands as it would a murderer's (vv. 15,21). **as snow.** God's forgiveness provides complete cleansing (Ps. 51:7), but the offer depends on the people's receptiveness and true repentance (v. 19).

I will melt you down and skim off your slag.
I will remove all your impurities.
26 Then I will give you good judges again
and wise counselors like you used to have.
Then Jerusalem will again be called the Home of Justice
and the Faithful City."

27 Zion will be restored by justice;
those who repent will be revived by righteousness.
28 But rebels and sinners will be completely destroyed,
and those who desert the LORD will be consumed.

29 You will be ashamed of your idol worship
in groves of sacred oaks.
You will blush because you worshiped
in gardens dedicated to idols.
30 You will be like a great tree with withered leaves,
like a garden without water.
31 The strongest among you will disappear like straw;
their evil deeds will be the spark that sets it on fire.
They and their evil works will burn up together,
and no one will be able to put out the fire.

THE LORD'S FUTURE REIGN

2 This is a vision that Isaiah son of Amoz saw concerning Judah and Jerusalem:

2 In the last days, the mountain of the LORD's house
will be the highest of all—
the most important place on earth.
It will be raised above the other hills,
and people from all over the world will stream there to worship.
3 People from many nations will come and say,
"Come, let us go up to the mountain of the LORD,
to the house of Jacob's God.
There he will teach us his ways,
and we will walk in his paths."
For the LORD's teaching will go out from Zion;
his word will go out from Jerusalem.
4 The LORD will mediate between nations
and will settle international disputes.
They will hammer their swords into plowshares
and their spears into pruning hooks.
Nation will no longer fight against nation,
nor train for war anymore.

A WARNING OF JUDGMENT

5 Come, descendants of Jacob,
let us walk in the light of the LORD!
6 For the LORD has rejected his people,
the descendants of Jacob,
because they have filled their land with practices from the East
and with sorcerers, as the Philistines do.
They have made alliances with pagans.
7 Israel is full of silver and gold;
there is no end to its treasures.
Their land is full of warhorses;
there is no end to its chariots.
8 Their land is full of idols;
the people worship things they have made
with their own hands.
9 So now they will be humbled,
and all will be brought low—
do not forgive them.
10 Crawl into caves in the rocks.
Hide in the dust
from the terror of the LORD
and the glory of his majesty.
11 Human pride will be brought down,
and human arrogance will be humbled.
Only the LORD will be exalted
on that day of judgment.

12 For the LORD of Heaven's Armies
has a day of reckoning.
He will punish the proud and mighty
and bring down everything that is exalted.
13 He will cut down the tall cedars of Lebanon
and all the mighty oaks of Bashan.
14 He will level all the high mountains
and all the lofty hills.
15 He will break down every high tower
and every fortified wall.
16 He will destroy all the great trading ships*
and every magnificent vessel.
17 Human pride will be humbled,
and human arrogance will be brought down.
Only the LORD will be exalted
on that day of judgment.

18 Idols will completely disappear.
19 When the LORD rises to shake the earth,
his enemies will crawl into holes in the ground.
They will hide in caves in the rocks
from the terror of the LORD
and the glory of his majesty.
20 On that day of judgment they will abandon the gold and silver idols
they made for themselves to worship.
They will leave their gods to the rodents and bats,
21 while they crawl away into caverns
and hide among the jagged rocks in the cliffs.
They will try to escape the terror of the LORD
and the glory of his majesty
as he rises to shake the earth.
22 Don't put your trust in mere humans.
They are as frail as breath.
What good are they?

JUDGMENT AGAINST JUDAH

3 1 The Lord, the LORD of Heaven's Armies,
will take away from Jerusalem and Judah
everything they depend on:
every bit of bread
and every drop of water,

2:16 Hebrew *every ship of Tarshish.*

2:2-4 Isaiah often refers to the "mountain of the LORD," which is quite similar to Micah 4:1-3.
2:7 silver and gold . . . warhorses . . . chariots. Kings were specifically forbidden to accumulate these things (see Deut. 17:16-17) because they tended to cause the king, and the nation, to put their trust in money rather than in God (31:1).
3:1-3 God would remove the nation's leaders, either through death or exile (2 Kings 24:14; 25:18-21).

2 all their heroes and soldiers,
judges and prophets,
fortune-tellers and elders,
3 army officers and high officials,
advisers, skilled sorcerers, and astrologers.

4 I will make boys their leaders,
and toddlers their rulers.
5 People will oppress each other—
man against man,
neighbor against neighbor.
Young people will insult their elders,
and vulgar people will sneer at the honorable.

6 In those days a man will say to his brother,
"Since you have a coat, you be our leader!
Take charge of this heap of ruins!"
7 But he will reply,
"No! I can't help.
I don't have any extra food or clothes.
Don't put me in charge!"

8 For Jerusalem will stumble,
and Judah will fall,
because they speak out against the LORD and refuse to obey him.
They provoke him to his face.
9 The very look on their faces gives them away.
They display their sin like the people of Sodom
and don't even try to hide it.
They are doomed!
They have brought destruction upon themselves.

10 Tell the godly that all will be well for them.
They will enjoy the rich reward they have earned!
11 But the wicked are doomed,
for they will get exactly what they deserve.

12 Childish leaders oppress my people,
and women rule over them.
O my people, your leaders mislead you;
they send you down the wrong road.

13 The LORD takes his place in court
and presents his case against his people.*
14 The LORD comes forward to pronounce judgment
on the elders and rulers of his people:
"You have ruined Israel, my vineyard.
Your houses are filled with things stolen from the poor.
15 How dare you crush my people,
grinding the faces of the poor into the dust?"
demands the Lord, the LORD of Heaven's Armies.

A WARNING TO JERUSALEM

16 The LORD says, "Beautiful Zion* is haughty:
craning her elegant neck,
flirting with her eyes,
walking with dainty steps,
tinkling her ankle bracelets.
17 So the Lord will send scabs on her head;
the LORD will make beautiful Zion bald."

18 On that day of judgment
the Lord will strip away everything that makes her beautiful:
ornaments, headbands, crescent necklaces,
19 earrings, bracelets, and veils;
20 scarves, ankle bracelets, sashes,
perfumes, and charms;
21 rings, jewels,
22 party clothes, gowns, capes, and purses;
23 mirrors, fine linen garments,
head ornaments, and shawls.

24 Instead of smelling of sweet perfume, she will stink.
She will wear a rope for a sash,
and her elegant hair will fall out.
She will wear rough burlap instead of rich robes.
Shame will replace her beauty.*
25 The men of the city will be killed with the sword,
and her warriors will die in battle.
26 The gates of Zion will weep and mourn.
The city will be like a ravaged woman,
huddled on the ground.

4 In that day so few men will be left that seven
women will fight for each man, saying, "Let us all
marry you! We will provide our own food and cloth-
ing. Only let us take your name so we won't be mocked
as old maids."

A PROMISE OF RESTORATION

2 But in that day, the branch* of the LORD
will be beautiful and glorious;
the fruit of the land will be the pride and glory
of all who survive in Israel.
3 All who remain in Zion
will be a holy people—
those who survive the destruction of Jerusalem
and are recorded among the living.
4 The Lord will wash the filth from beautiful Zion*
and cleanse Jerusalem of its bloodstains
with the hot breath of fiery judgment.
5 Then the LORD will provide shade for Mount Zion
and all who assemble there.
He will provide a canopy of cloud during the day
and smoke and flaming fire at night,
covering the glorious land.

3:13 As in Greek and Syriac versions; Hebrew reads *against the peoples.* **3:16** Or *The women of Zion* (with corresponding changes to plural forms through verse 24); Hebrew reads *The daughters of Zion;* also in 3:17. **3:24** As in Dead Sea Scrolls; Masoretic Text reads *robes / because instead of beauty.* **4:2** Or *the Branch.* **4:4** Or *from the women of Zion;* Hebrew reads *from the daughters of Zion.*

3:12 women rule. Ancient Near Eastern culture looked down on the exercise of leadership by women or youth.

3:15 crush . . . grinding. Just as grain was crushed by millstones, the nation's poor have been ground down by their leaders.

3:21 rings, jewels. Signet rings, worn by those in authority, featured an official seal (see Gen. 41:42). Nose rings made of gold or other precious metals were worn by brides.

3:24 rope . . . shame. Those taken captive would be herded and treated like cattle—a far cry from the opulent ease they were accustomed to.

4:2 branch of the LORD. This title is used of the Messiah because He will be the "branch" that will grow from "the stump" (11:1; 53:2; Jer. 23:5), a descendant of David. However, some scholars take this reference to be Judah rather than the Messiah.

4:5-6 canopy . . . smoke. God's glory in the wilderness was enshrouded in a cloud. In the Messianic kingdom of Christ, Israel will be restored, and a canopy will cover Jerusalem. This is the same word used for a wedding canopy, a *khuppah*. The picture is of God reunited with his bride, Israel.

6 It will be a shelter from daytime heat
and a hiding place from storms and rain.

A SONG ABOUT THE LORD'S VINEYARD

5 1 Now I will sing for the one I love
a song about his vineyard:
My beloved had a vineyard
on a rich and fertile hill.
2 He plowed the land, cleared its stones,
and planted it with the best vines.
In the middle he built a watchtower
and carved a winepress in the nearby
rocks.
Then he waited for a harvest of sweet grapes,
but the grapes that grew were bitter.

3 Now, you people of Jerusalem and Judah,
you judge between me and my vineyard.
4 What more could I have done for my vineyard
that I have not already done?
When I expected sweet grapes,
why did my vineyard give me bitter grapes?
5 Now let me tell you
what I will do to my vineyard:
I will tear down its hedges
and let it be destroyed.
I will break down its walls
and let the animals trample it.
6 I will make it a wild place
where the vines are not pruned and the ground
is not hoed,
a place overgrown with briers and thorns.
I will command the clouds
to drop no rain on it.

7 The nation of Israel is the vineyard of the LORD of
Heaven's Armies.
The people of Judah are his pleasant garden.
He expected a crop of justice,
but instead he found oppression.
He expected to find righteousness,
but instead he heard cries of violence.

JUDAH'S GUILT AND JUDGMENT

8 What sorrow for you who buy up house after
house and field after field,
until everyone is evicted and you live alone in
the land.
9 But I have heard the LORD of Heaven's Armies
swear a solemn oath:
"Many houses will stand deserted;
even beautiful mansions will be empty.
10 Ten acres* of vineyard will not produce even six
gallons* of wine.
Ten baskets of seed will yield only one basket*
of grain."

11 What sorrow for those who get up early in the
morning
looking for a drink of alcohol
and spend long evenings drinking wine
to make themselves flaming drunk.
12 They furnish wine and lovely music at their grand
parties—
lyre and harp, tambourine and flute—
but they never think about the LORD
or notice what he is doing.

13 So my people will go into exile far away
because they do not know me.
Those who are great and honored will starve,
and the common people will die of thirst.
14 The grave* is licking its lips in anticipation,
opening its mouth wide.
The great and the lowly
and all the drunken mob will be swallowed up.
15 Humanity will be destroyed, and people brought
down;
even the arrogant will lower their eyes in
humiliation.
16 But the LORD of Heaven's Armies will be exalted
by his justice.
The holiness of God will be displayed by his
righteousness.
17 In that day lambs will find good pastures,
and fattened sheep and young goats* will feed
among the ruins.

18 What sorrow for those who drag their sins behind
them
with ropes made of lies,
who drag wickedness behind them like a cart!
19 They even mock God and say,
"Hurry up and do something!
We want to see what you can do.
Let the Holy One of Israel carry out his plan,
for we want to know what it is."
20 What sorrow for those who say
that evil is good and good is evil,
that dark is light and light is dark,
that bitter is sweet and sweet is bitter.
21 What sorrow for those who are wise in their own
eyes
and think themselves so clever.
22 What sorrow for those who are heroes at drinking
wine
and boast about all the alcohol they can hold.
23 They take bribes to let the wicked go free,
and they punish the innocent.

24 Therefore, just as fire licks up stubble
and dry grass shrivels in the flame,
so their roots will rot
and their flowers wither.
For they have rejected the law of the LORD of
Heaven's Armies;
they have despised the word of the Holy One of
Israel.

5:10a Hebrew *A ten yoke,* that is, the area of land plowed by ten teams of oxen in one day. **5:10b** Hebrew *a bath* [21 liters]. **5:10c** Hebrew *A homer* [5 bushels or 220 liters] *of seed will yield only an ephah* [20 quarts or 22 liters]. **5:14** Hebrew *Sheol.* **5:17** As in Greek version; Hebrew reads *and strangers.*

5:7 vineyard of the LORD. This verse provides the interpretation of verses 1-6, the "Song of the Vineyard."
5:8 house after house . . . field after field until everyone is evicted. The land of Israel had been given permanently to specific families, so it could only be rented to others, not sold (see Num. 27:7-11; 1 Kings 21:1-3). God declared the land "Mine" (Lev. 25:23), but greedy landowners sought to control the best plots of land in Israel for themselves.

25 That is why the LORD's anger burns against his
people,
and why he has raised his fist to crush them.
The mountains tremble,
and the corpses of his people litter the streets
like garbage.
But even then the LORD's anger is not satisfied.
His fist is still poised to strike!

26 He will send a signal to distant nations far
away
and whistle to those at the ends of the earth.
They will come racing toward Jerusalem.
27 They will not get tired or stumble.
They will not stop for rest or sleep.
Not a belt will be loose,
not a sandal strap broken.
28 Their arrows will be sharp
and their bows ready for battle.
Sparks will fly from their horses' hooves,
and the wheels of their chariots will spin like a
whirlwind.
29 They will roar like lions,
like the strongest of lions.
Growling, they will pounce on their victims and
carry them off,
and no one will be there to rescue them.
30 They will roar over their victims on that day of
destruction
like the roaring of the sea.
If someone looks across the land,
only darkness and distress will be seen;
even the light will be darkened by clouds.

ISAIAH'S CLEANSING AND CALL

6 It was in the year King Uzziah died* that I saw
the Lord. He was sitting on a lofty throne, and
the train of his robe filled the Temple. 2 Attending
him were mighty seraphim, each having six wings.
With two wings they covered their faces, with two
they covered their feet, and with two they flew. 3 They
were calling out to each other,

"Holy, holy, holy is the LORD of Heaven's Armies!
The whole earth is filled with his glory!"

4 Their voices shook the Temple to its foundations, and
the entire building was filled with smoke.
5 Then I said, "It's all over! I am doomed, for I am a
sinful man. I have filthy lips, and I live among a peo-
ple with filthy lips. Yet I have seen the King, the LORD
of Heaven's Armies."
6 Then one of the seraphim flew to me with a burn-
ing coal he had taken from the altar with a pair of
tongs. 7 He touched my lips with it and said, "See, this
coal has touched your lips. Now your guilt is removed,
and your sins are forgiven."
8 Then I heard the Lord asking, "Whom should I
send as a messenger to this people? Who will go for
us?"
I said, "Here I am. Send me."
9 And he said, "Yes, go, and say to this people,

'Listen carefully, but do not understand.
Watch closely, but learn nothing.'
10 Harden the hearts of these people.
Plug their ears and shut their eyes.
That way, they will not see with their eyes,
nor hear with their ears,
nor understand with their hearts
and turn to me for healing."*

11 Then I said, "Lord, how long will this go on?"
And he replied,

"Until their towns are empty,
their houses are deserted,
and the whole country is a wasteland;
12 until the LORD has sent everyone away,
and the entire land of Israel lies deserted.
13 If even a tenth—a remnant—survive,
it will be invaded again and burned.
But as a terebinth or oak tree leaves a stump when
it is cut down,
so Israel's stump will be a holy seed."

A MESSAGE FOR AHAZ

7 When Ahaz, son of Jotham and grandson of Uz-
ziah, was king of Judah, King Rezin of Syria* and
Pekah son of Remaliah, the king of Israel, set out to
attack Jerusalem. However, they were unable to carry
out their plan.
2 The news had come to the royal court of Judah:
"Syria is allied with Israel* against us!" So the hearts
of the king and his people trembled with fear, like
trees shaking in a storm.
3 Then the LORD said to Isaiah, "Take your son
Shear-jashub* and go out to meet King Ahaz. You will
find him at the end of the aqueduct that feeds water
into the upper pool, near the road leading to the field
where cloth is washed.* 4 Tell him to stop worrying.
Tell him he doesn't need to fear the fierce anger of
those two burned-out embers, King Rezin of Syria
and Pekah son of Remaliah. 5 Yes, the kings of Syria
and Israel are plotting against him, saying, 6 'We will
attack Judah and capture it for ourselves. Then we
will install the son of Tabeel as Judah's king.' 7 But this
is what the Sovereign LORD says:

"This invasion will never happen;
it will never take place;
8 for Syria is no stronger than its capital, Damascus,
and Damascus is no stronger than its king,
Rezin.

6:1 King Uzziah died in 740 B.C. **6:9-10** Greek version reads *And he said, "Go and say to this people, / 'When you hear what I say, you will not understand. / When you see what I do, you will not comprehend.' / For the hearts of these people are hardened, / and their ears cannot hear, and they have closed their eyes— / so their eyes cannot see, / and their ears cannot hear, / and their hearts cannot understand, / and they cannot turn to me and let me heal them."* Compare Matt 13:14-15; Mark 4:12; Luke 8:10; Acts 28:26-27. **7:1** Hebrew *Aram;* also in 7:2, 4, 5, 8. **7:2** Hebrew *Ephraim,* referring to the northern kingdom of Israel; also in 7:5, 8, 9, 17. **7:3a** *Shear-jashub* means "A remnant will return." **7:3b** Or *bleached.*

6:1 King Uzziah died. Uzziah, a good king who ruled well, reigned from 792 until he died in 740 B.C. He contracted leprosy as a judgment upon his insistence on burning incense in God's temple and died with that condition (2 Chron. 26:16-21).

6:2 seraphim. These angels are mentioned by name only here in the Bible. Their name comes from a Hebrew word meaning "burn," possibly speaking of God's purity (v. 6; Rev. 4:6-9). Note the contrast between their worship of God and the rebellious pride of humanity.

As for Israel, within sixty-five years
it will be crushed and completely destroyed.
9 Israel is no stronger than its capital, Samaria,
and Samaria is no stronger than its king, Pekah
son of Remaliah.
Unless your faith is firm,
I cannot make you stand firm."

THE SIGN OF IMMANUEL

10 Later, the LORD sent this message to King Ahaz:
11 "Ask the LORD your God for a sign of confirmation,
Ahaz. Make it as difficult as you want—as high as
heaven or as deep as the place of the dead.*"
12 But the king refused. "No," he said, "I will not test
the LORD like that."
13 Then Isaiah said, "Listen well, you royal fam-
ily of David! Isn't it enough to exhaust human pa-
tience? Must you exhaust the patience of my God as
well? 14 All right then, the Lord himself will give you
the sign. Look! The virgin* will conceive a child! She
will give birth to a son and will call him Immanuel
(which means 'God is with us'). 15 By the time this child
is old enough to choose what is right and reject what
is wrong, he will be eating yogurt* and honey. 16 For
before the child is that old, the lands of the two kings
you fear so much will both be deserted.
17 "Then the LORD will bring things on you, your
nation, and your family unlike anything since Israel
broke away from Judah. He will bring the king of As-
syria upon you!"
18 In that day the LORD will whistle for the army of
southern Egypt and for the army of Assyria. They will
swarm around you like flies and bees. 19 They will come
in vast hordes and settle in the fertile areas and also in
the desolate valleys, caves, and thorny places. 20 In that
day the Lord will hire a "razor" from beyond the Euphra-
tes River*—the king of Assyria—and use it to shave off
everything: your land, your crops, and your people.*
21 In that day a farmer will be fortunate to have a cow
and two sheep or goats left. 22 Nevertheless, there will
be enough milk for everyone because so few people
will be left in the land. They will eat their fill of yogurt
and honey. 23 In that day the lush vineyards, now worth
1,000 pieces of silver,* will become patches of briers and
thorns. 24 The entire land will become a vast expanse of
briers and thorns, a hunting ground overrun by wild-
life. 25 No one will go to the fertile hillsides where the
gardens once grew, for briers and thorns will cover
them. Cattle, sheep, and goats will graze there.

THE COMING ASSYRIAN INVASION

8 Then the LORD said to me, "Make a large signboard
and clearly write this name on it: Maher-shalal-
hash-baz.*" 2 I asked Uriah the priest and Zechariah
son of Jeberekiah, both known as honest men, to wit-
ness my doing this.
3 Then I slept with my wife, and she became preg-
nant and gave birth to a son. And the LORD said, "Call
him Maher-shalal-hash-baz. 4 For before this child is
old enough to say 'Papa' or 'Mama,' the king of Assyr-
ia will carry away both the abundance of Damascus
and the riches of Samaria."
5 Then the LORD spoke to me again and said, 6 "My
care for the people of Judah is like the gently flowing
waters of Shiloah, but they have rejected it. They are
rejoicing over what will happen to* King Rezin and
King Pekah.* 7 Therefore, the Lord will overwhelm
them with a mighty flood from the Euphrates Riv-
er*—the king of Assyria and all his glory. This flood
will overflow all its channels 8 and sweep into Judah
until it is chin deep. It will spread its wings, submerg-
ing your land from one end to the other, O Immanuel.

9 "Huddle together, you nations, and be terrified.
Listen, all you distant lands.
Prepare for battle, but you will be crushed!
Yes, prepare for battle, but you will be crushed!
10 Call your councils of war, but they will be worthless.
Develop your strategies, but they will not
succeed.
For God is with us!*"

A CALL TO TRUST THE LORD

11 The LORD has given me a strong warning not to
think like everyone else does. He said,

12 "Don't call everything a conspiracy, like they do,
and don't live in dread of what frightens them.
13 Make the LORD of Heaven's Armies holy in your
life.
He is the one you should fear.
He is the one who should make you tremble.
14 He will keep you safe.
But to Israel and Judah
he will be a stone that makes people stumble,
a rock that makes them fall.
And for the people of Jerusalem
he will be a trap and a snare.
15 Many will stumble and fall,
never to rise again.
They will be snared and captured."

16 Preserve the teaching of God;
entrust his instructions to those who follow me.
17 I will wait for the LORD,
who has turned away from the descendants of
Jacob.
I will put my hope in him.

7:11 Hebrew *as deep as Sheol.* **7:14** Or *young woman.* **7:15** Or *curds;* also in 7:22. **7:20a** Hebrew *the river.* **7:20b** Hebrew *shave off the head, the hair of the legs, and the beard.* **7:23** Hebrew *1,000 [shekels] of silver,* about 25 pounds or 11.4 kilograms in weight. **8:1** *Maher-shalal-hash-baz* means "Swift to plunder and quick to carry away." **8:6a** Or *They are rejoicing because of.* **8:6b** Hebrew *and the son of Remaliah.* **8:7** Hebrew *the river.* **8:10** Hebrew *Immanuel!*

7:14 will give you the sign . . . virgin. There are two possible interpretations for this verse. First, that this was a direct prophecy of the virgin birth of Jesus or second, that this was a sign given in the days of King Ahaz. For a sign to help Ahaz's faith, it would seemingly have to happen in his days. Matthew 1:23 seems to say that Isaiah 7:14 is a prophecy of Jesus' virgin birth. Yet, Matthew 1:23 can be understood as comparing Jesus' birth to the announcement in Isaiah 7:14: a special messenger (prophet/angel) announces a special child whose birth will signify God's presence with us. It is possible that Isaiah's verse referred to a child in his day and also to Jesus (double fulfillment). **Immanuel.** The name means "God is with us," assuring King Ahaz that God would protect him from enemy nations (see Num. 14:9; 2 Chron. 13:12; Ps. 46:7). The same name appears in 8:8,10, perhaps in reference to Maher-Shalal-Hash-Baz, whose name literally means "quick to the plunder, swift to the spoil" (8:3). Of course, the final application of the name is to Jesus Christ who truly became "God with us" (9:6-7; Matt. 1:23).

8:11 The LORD has given me a strong warning. The prophets were clearly aware that their word was inspired and that God was using them for divine purposes (see Ezek. 1:3; 37:1; 40:1).

8:17 wait. Isaiah still hopes in God, confidently expecting that the people will ultimately be delivered.

18 I and the children the LORD has given me serve as
signs and warnings to Israel from the LORD of Heaven's Armies who dwells in his Temple on Mount Zion.
19 Someone may say to you, "Let's ask the mediums
and those who consult the spirits of the dead. With their whisperings and mutterings, they will tell us what to do." But shouldn't people ask God for guidance? Should the living seek guidance from the dead?
20 Look to God's instructions and teachings! People
who contradict his word are completely in the dark.
21 They will go from one place to another, weary and
hungry. And because they are hungry, they will rage and curse their king and their God. They will look up
to heaven 22 and down at the earth, but wherever they
look, there will be trouble and anguish and dark despair. They will be thrown out into the darkness.

HOPE IN THE MESSIAH

9 1*Nevertheless, that time of darkness and despair will not go on forever. The land of Zebulun and Naphtali will be humbled, but there will be a time in the future when Galilee of the Gentiles, which lies along the road that runs between the Jordan and the sea, will be filled with glory.

2*The people who walk in darkness
will see a great light.
For those who live in a land of deep darkness,*
a light will shine.
3 You will enlarge the nation of Israel,
and its people will rejoice.
They will rejoice before you
as people rejoice at the harvest
and like warriors dividing the plunder.
4 For you will break the yoke of their slavery
and lift the heavy burden from their shoulders.
You will break the oppressor's rod,
just as you did when you destroyed the army of Midian.
5 The boots of the warrior
and the uniforms bloodstained by war
will all be burned.
They will be fuel for the fire.

6 For a child is born to us,
a son is given to us.
The government will rest on his shoulders.
And he will be called:
Wonderful Counselor,* Mighty God,
Everlasting Father, Prince of Peace.
7 His government and its peace
will never end.
He will rule with fairness and justice from the throne of his ancestor David
for all eternity.
The passionate commitment of the LORD of Heaven's Armies
will make this happen!

THE LORD'S ANGER AGAINST ISRAEL

8 The Lord has spoken out against Jacob;
his judgment has fallen upon Israel.
9 And the people of Israel* and Samaria,
who spoke with such pride and arrogance,
will soon know it.
10 They said, "We will replace the broken bricks of our ruins with finished stone,
and replant the felled sycamore-fig trees with cedars."

11 But the LORD will bring Rezin's enemies against Israel
and stir up all their foes.
12 The Syrians* from the east and the Philistines from the west
will bare their fangs and devour Israel.
But even then the LORD's anger will not be satisfied.
His fist is still poised to strike.

13 For after all this punishment, the people will still not repent.
They will not seek the LORD of Heaven's Armies.
14 Therefore, in a single day the LORD will destroy
both the head and the tail,
the noble palm branch and the lowly reed.
15 The leaders of Israel are the head,
and the lying prophets are the tail.
16 For the leaders of the people have misled them.
They have led them down the path of destruction.
17 That is why the Lord takes no pleasure in the young men
and shows no mercy even to the widows and orphans.
For they are all wicked hypocrites,
and they all speak foolishness.
But even then the LORD's anger will not be satisfied.
His fist is still poised to strike.

18 This wickedness is like a brushfire.
It burns not only briers and thorns
but also sets the forests ablaze.
Its burning sends up clouds of smoke.
19 The land will be blackened
by the fury of the LORD of Heaven's Armies.
The people will be fuel for the fire,
and no one will spare even his own brother.
20 They will attack their neighbor on the right
but will still be hungry.

9:1 Verse 9:1 is numbered 8:23 in Hebrew text. **9:2a** Verses 9:2-21 are numbered 9:1-20 in Hebrew text. **9:2b** Greek version reads *a land where death casts its shadow.* Compare Matt 4:16. **9:6** Or *Wonderful, Counselor.* **9:9** Hebrew *of Ephraim,* referring to the northern kingdom of Israel. **9:12** Hebrew *Arameans.* **9:20** Or *eat their own arms.*

8:19 mediums and those who consult the spirits of the dead. In crises the people sometimes sought help through the practice of necromancy (contact with the spirits of dead people in an effort to influence present reality). King Saul consulted the deceased Samuel to ascertain what would happen to him (see 1 Sam. 28:8-11). God abhors this practice because it demonstrated a lack of trust in Him.

9:1-2 Galilee of the Gentiles . . . will see a great light. At times in Israel's history, Galilee has had a mixed population of Jews and Gentiles. God would reveal His person and blessing to the people of Galilee in the days of Jesus. Later Isaiah would refer to the Messiah as a "light for the nations" (42:6).

9:6 a child is born to us. This is a prophecy about Messiah Jesus. **Wonderful Counselor.** Like other names in Isaiah, this one should be made into a sentence: "A Wonderful Counselor is Almighty God, the Eternal Father is a Prince of Peace." God has a plan and nothing takes Him by surprise. He is all-powerful and eternal. Under His reign the people will experience "shalom," peace, well-being, and wholeness.

9:7 throne of . . . David . . . for all eternity. Unlike the human kings of Israel—even the good ones like Ahaz—Messiah Jesus will eternally rule with perfect wisdom, justice, and righteousness (11:3-5; 2 Sam. 7:12, 13, 16; Jer. 33:15, 20-22).

They will devour their neighbor on the left
but will not be satisfied.
In the end they will even eat their own children.*
21 Manasseh will feed on Ephraim,
Ephraim will feed on Manasseh,
and both will devour Judah.
But even then the LORD's anger will not be satisfied.
His fist is still poised to strike.

10 1 What sorrow awaits the unjust judges
and those who issue unfair laws.
2 They deprive the poor of justice
and deny the rights of the needy among my people.
They prey on widows
and take advantage of orphans.
3 What will you do when I punish you,
when I send disaster upon you from a distant land?
To whom will you turn for help?
Where will your treasures be safe?
4 You will stumble along as prisoners
or lie among the dead.
But even then the LORD's anger will not be satisfied.
His fist is still poised to strike.

JUDGMENT AGAINST ASSYRIA

5 "What sorrow awaits Assyria, the rod of my anger.
I use it as a club to express my anger.
6 I am sending Assyria against a godless nation,
against a people with whom I am angry.
Assyria will plunder them,
trampling them like dirt beneath its feet.
7 But the king of Assyria will not understand that he is my tool;
his mind does not work that way.
His plan is simply to destroy,
to cut down nation after nation.
8 He will say,
'Each of my princes will soon be a king.
9 We destroyed Calno just as we did Carchemish.
Hamath fell before us as Arpad did.
And we destroyed Samaria just as we did Damascus.
10 Yes, we have finished off many a kingdom
whose gods were greater than those in Jerusalem and Samaria.
11 So we will defeat Jerusalem and her gods,
just as we destroyed Samaria with hers.'"

12 After the Lord has used the king of Assyria to ac-
complish his purposes on Mount Zion and in Jerusa-
lem, he will turn against the king of Assyria and pun-
ish him—for he is proud and arrogant. 13 He boasts,

"By my own powerful arm I have done this.
With my own shrewd wisdom I planned it.
I have broken down the defenses of nations
and carried off their treasures.
I have knocked down their kings like a bull.
14 I have robbed their nests of riches
and gathered up kingdoms as a farmer gathers eggs.
No one can even flap a wing against me
or utter a peep of protest."

15 But can the ax boast greater power than the person who uses it?
Is the saw greater than the person who saws?
Can a rod strike unless a hand moves it?
Can a wooden cane walk by itself?
16 Therefore, the Lord, the LORD of Heaven's Armies,
will send a plague among Assyria's proud troops,
and a flaming fire will consume its glory.
17 The LORD, the Light of Israel, will be a fire;
the Holy One will be a flame.
He will devour the thorns and briers with fire,
burning up the enemy in a single night.
18 The LORD will consume Assyria's glory
like a fire consumes a forest in a fruitful land;
it will waste away like sick people in a plague.
19 Of all that glorious forest, only a few trees will survive—
so few that a child could count them!

HOPE FOR THE LORD'S PEOPLE

20 In that day the remnant left in Israel,
the survivors in the house of Jacob,
will no longer depend on allies
who seek to destroy them.
But they will faithfully trust the LORD,
the Holy One of Israel.
21 A remnant will return;*
yes, the remnant of Jacob will return to the Mighty God.
22 But though the people of Israel are as numerous
as the sand of the seashore,
only a remnant of them will return.
The LORD has rightly decided to destroy his people.
23 Yes, the Lord, the LORD of Heaven's Armies,
has already decided to destroy the entire land.*

24 So this is what the Lord, the LORD of Heaven's Ar-
mies, says: "O my people in Zion, do not be afraid of
the Assyrians when they oppress you with rod and
club as the Egyptians did long ago. 25 In a little while
my anger against you will end, and then my anger
will rise up to destroy them." 26 The LORD of Heaven's
Armies will lash them with his whip, as he did when
Gideon triumphed over the Midianites at the rock of
Oreb, or when the LORD's staff was raised to drown
the Egyptian army in the sea.

10:21 Hebrew *Shear-jashub;* see 7:3; 8:18. 10:22-23 Greek version reads *only a remnant of them will be saved. / For he will carry out his sentence quickly and with finality and righteousness; / for God will carry out his sentence upon all the world with finality.* Compare Rom 9:27-28.

10:5 rod of my anger. God will ultimately destroy the weapons of the oppressor, Assyria (9:4). Babylon also was used by God as a club of punishment against rebellious nations (see Jer. 50:23; 51:20; Hab. 1:6).

10:10 gods. Despite God's clear word concerning idols, Israelites routinely worshiped them (2:8). Just as God had chastened Samaria because of idolatry (through defeat by Shalmaneser V and Sargon II in 722–21 B.C.), God would be forced to do the same to Israel.

10:16 will send a plague. This probably refers to a plague, as happened to Sennacherib when 185,000 Assyrian soldiers were put to death by an angel of God in 701 B.C. (See also 37:36; 2 Sam. 24:15,16; 1 Chron. 21:22,27.)

10:25 In a little while. From a human point of view the present difficulty would be long and hard, but in the context of eternity, the time would be very brief.

[27] In that day the LORD will end the bondage of his
people.
He will break the yoke of slavery
and lift it from their shoulders.*
[28] Look, the Assyrians are now at Aiath.
They are passing through Migron
and are storing their equipment at Micmash.
[29] They are crossing the pass
and are camping at Geba.
Fear strikes the town of Ramah.
All the people of Gibeah, the hometown of Saul,
are running for their lives.
[30] Scream in terror,
you people of Gallim!
Shout out a warning to Laishah.
Oh, poor Anathoth!
[31] There go the people of Madmenah, all fleeing.
The citizens of Gebim are trying to hide.
[32] The enemy stops at Nob for the rest of that day.
He shakes his fist at beautiful Mount Zion, the
mountain of Jerusalem.

[33] But look! The Lord, the LORD of Heaven's Armies,
will chop down the mighty tree of Assyria with
great power!
He will cut down the proud.
That lofty tree will be brought down.
[34] He will cut down the forest trees with an ax.
Lebanon will fall to the Mighty One.*

A BRANCH FROM DAVID'S LINE

11 [1] Out of the stump of David's family* will grow
a shoot—
yes, a new Branch bearing fruit from the old
root.
[2] And the Spirit of the LORD will rest on him—
the Spirit of wisdom and understanding,
the Spirit of counsel and might,
the Spirit of knowledge and the fear of the
LORD.
[3] He will delight in obeying the LORD.
He will not judge by appearance
nor make a decision based on hearsay.
[4] He will give justice to the poor
and make fair decisions for the exploited.
The earth will shake at the force of his word,
and one breath from his mouth will destroy the
wicked.
[5] He will wear righteousness like a belt
and truth like an undergarment.
[6] In that day the wolf and the lamb will live
together;
the leopard will lie down with the baby goat.
The calf and the yearling will be safe with the
lion,
and a little child will lead them all.
[7] The cow will graze near the bear.
The cub and the calf will lie down together.
The lion will eat hay like a cow.
[8] The baby will play safely near the hole of a
cobra.
Yes, a little child will put its hand in a nest of
deadly snakes without harm.
[9] Nothing will hurt or destroy in all my holy
mountain,
for as the waters fill the sea,
so the earth will be filled with people who
know the LORD.

[10] In that day the heir to David's throne*
will be a banner of salvation to all the world.
The nations will rally to him,
and the land where he lives will be a glorious
place.*
[11] In that day the Lord will reach out his hand a
second time
to bring back the remnant of his people—
those who remain in Assyria and northern
Egypt;
in southern Egypt, Ethiopia,* and Elam;
in Babylonia,* Hamath, and all the distant
coastlands.
[12] He will raise a flag among the nations
and assemble the exiles of Israel.
He will gather the scattered people of Judah
from the ends of the earth.

[13] Then at last the jealousy between Israel* and
Judah will end.
They will not be rivals anymore.
[14] They will join forces to swoop down on Philistia to
the west.
Together they will attack and plunder the
nations to the east.
They will occupy the lands of Edom and Moab,
and Ammon will obey them.
[15] The LORD will make a dry path through the gulf of
the Red Sea.*
He will wave his hand over the Euphrates
River,*
sending a mighty wind to divide it into seven
streams
so it can easily be crossed on foot.
[16] He will make a highway for the remnant of his
people,
the remnant coming from Assyria,
just as he did for Israel long ago
when they returned from Egypt.

10:27 As in Greek version; Hebrew reads *The yoke will be broken, / for you have grown so fat.* **10:34** Or *with an ax / as even the mighty trees of Lebanon fall.* **11:1** Hebrew *the stump of the line of Jesse.* Jesse was King David's father. **11:10a** Hebrew *the root of Jesse.* **11:10b** Greek version reads *In that day the heir to David's throne* [literally *the root of Jesse*] *will come, / and he will rule over the Gentiles. / They will place their hopes on him.* Compare Rom 15:12. **11:11a** Hebrew *in Pathros, Cush.* **11:11b** Hebrew *in Shinar.* **11:13** Hebrew *Ephraim,* referring to the northern kingdom of Israel. **11:15a** Hebrew *will destroy the tongue of the sea of Egypt.* **11:15b** Hebrew *the river.*

11:1 stump of David's family. The figurative stump of David's father Jesse is all that remained of David's dynasty after Judah was exiled to Babylon in 586 B.C. Yet just as a shoot will come up from a stump and make a new tree, so too would a branch from David's line rise: Jesus the Messiah. (See also Zech. 6:12; Acts 13:23.)

11:2 the Spirit of the LORD will rest on him. Like David, the Messiah would be empowered by the Holy Spirit (see Luke 3:22; John 1:32-34) and characterized by wisdom, understanding, counsel, power, knowledge, and fear of the Lord, making Him the Wonderful Counselor of 9:6. With Judah's history of bad kings, this promise of a Spirit-empowered king was significant. Isaiah refers to the Holy Spirit more than any other Old Testament prophet (16 times).

SONGS OF PRAISE FOR SALVATION

12 [1] In that day you will sing:
"I will praise you, O LORD!
You were angry with me, but not any more.
Now you comfort me.
[2] See, God has come to save me.
I will trust in him and not be afraid.
The LORD GOD is my strength and my song;
he has given me victory."

[3] With joy you will drink deeply
from the fountain of salvation!
[4] In that wonderful day you will sing:
"Thank the LORD! Praise his name!
Tell the nations what he has done.
Let them know how mighty he is!
[5] Sing to the LORD, for he has done wonderful things.
Make known his praise around the world.
[6] Let all the people of Jerusalem* shout his praise with joy!
For great is the Holy One of Israel who lives among you."

A MESSAGE ABOUT BABYLON

13 Isaiah son of Amoz received this message concerning the destruction of Babylon:

[2] "Raise a signal flag on a bare hilltop.
Call up an army against Babylon.
Wave your hand to encourage them
as they march into the palaces of the high and mighty.
[3] I, the LORD, have dedicated these soldiers for this task.
Yes, I have called mighty warriors to express my anger,
and they will rejoice when I am exalted."

[4] Hear the noise on the mountains!
Listen, as the vast armies march!
It is the noise and shouting of many nations.
The LORD of Heaven's Armies has called this army together.
[5] They come from distant countries,
from beyond the farthest horizons.
They are the LORD's weapons to carry out his anger.
With them he will destroy the whole land.

[6] Scream in terror, for the day of the LORD has arrived—
the time for the Almighty to destroy.
[7] Every arm is paralyzed with fear.
Every heart melts,
[8] and people are terrified.
Pangs of anguish grip them,
like those of a woman in labor.
They look helplessly at one another,
their faces aflame with fear.
[9] For see, the day of the LORD is coming—
the terrible day of his fury and fierce anger.
The land will be made desolate,
and all the sinners destroyed with it.
[10] The heavens will be black above them;
the stars will give no light.
The sun will be dark when it rises,
and the moon will provide no light.
[11] "I, the LORD, will punish the world for its evil
and the wicked for their sin.
I will crush the arrogance of the proud
and humble the pride of the mighty.
[12] I will make people scarcer than gold—
more rare than the fine gold of Ophir.
[13] For I will shake the heavens.
The earth will move from its place
when the LORD of Heaven's Armies displays his wrath
in the day of his fierce anger."

[14] Everyone in Babylon will run about like a hunted gazelle,
like sheep without a shepherd.
They will try to find their own people
and flee to their own land.
[15] Anyone who is captured will be cut down—
run through with a sword.
[16] Their little children will be dashed to death before their eyes.
Their homes will be sacked, and their wives will be raped.

[17] "Look, I will stir up the Medes against Babylon.
They cannot be tempted by silver
or bribed with gold.
[18] The attacking armies will shoot down the young men with arrows.
They will have no mercy on helpless babies
and will show no compassion for children."

[19] Babylon, the most glorious of kingdoms,
the flower of Chaldean pride,
will be devastated like Sodom and Gomorrah
when God destroyed them.
[20] Babylon will never be inhabited again.
It will remain empty for generation after generation.
Nomads will refuse to camp there,
and shepherds will not bed down their sheep.
[21] Desert animals will move into the ruined city,
and the houses will be haunted by howling creatures.

12:6 Hebrew *Zion*.

12:3 fountain of salvation. Water is salvation in the desert and in the dry climate of the Middle East. God's salvation is like a spring in the desert. Drawing water from this spring means living according to God's Instructions and enjoying the blessings God provides.

13:1 message concerning . . . Babylon. Sometimes translated "burden," as in a weighty message to deliver. Isaiah's oracle concerned Babylon, which had been a pagan city ever since Genesis 11:1-9. This is significant because Isaiah made this prophecy before the fall of Babylon occurred. The Book of Isaiah takes a major turn at 13:1 and focuses on God's judgments against the nations.

13:3 I . . . have dedicated these soldiers. God calls this army from many places. The army's purpose is to serve as an instrument of His judgment upon sinful nations (see Joel 3:11).

13:6 the day of the LORD has arrived. This refers to the time of God's judgment on the wicked and deliverance of His people. The political upheaval resulting in the fall of Babylon to the Assyrians in 689 B.C. parallels the turmoil coming upon the world just before God establishes a kingdom of peace.

Owls will live among the ruins,
and wild goats will go there to dance.
22 Hyenas will howl in its fortresses,
and jackals will make dens in its luxurious palaces.
Babylon's days are numbered;
its time of destruction will soon arrive.

A TAUNT FOR BABYLON'S KING

14 But the LORD will have mercy on the descendants of Jacob. He will choose Israel as his special people once again. He will bring them back to settle once again in their own land. And people from many different nations will come and join them there and unite with the people of Israel.*
2 The nations of the world will help the people of Israel to return, and those who come to live in the LORD's land will serve them. Those who captured Israel will themselves be captured, and Israel will rule over its enemies.
3 In that wonderful day when the LORD gives his people rest from sorrow and fear, from slavery and chains,
4 you will taunt the king of Babylon. You will say,

"The mighty man has been destroyed.
Yes, your insolence* is ended.
5 For the LORD has crushed your wicked power
and broken your evil rule.
6 You struck the people with endless blows of rage
and held the nations in your angry grip
with unrelenting tyranny.
7 But finally the earth is at rest and quiet.
Now it can sing again!
8 Even the trees of the forest—
the cypress trees and the cedars of Lebanon—
sing out this joyous song:
'Since you have been cut down,
no one will come now to cut us down!'

9 "In the place of the dead* there is excitement
over your arrival.
The spirits of world leaders and mighty kings long dead
stand up to see you.
10 With one voice they all cry out,
'Now you are as weak as we are!
11 Your might and power were buried with you.*
The sound of the harp in your palace has ceased.
Now maggots are your sheet,
and worms your blanket.'

12 "How you are fallen from heaven,
O shining star, son of the morning!
You have been thrown down to the earth,
you who destroyed the nations of the world.
13 For you said to yourself,
'I will ascend to heaven and set my throne
above God's stars.
I will preside on the mountain of the gods
far away in the north.*
14 I will climb to the highest heavens
and be like the Most High.'
15 Instead, you will be brought down to the place of the dead,
down to its lowest depths.
16 Everyone there will stare at you and ask,
'Can this be the one who shook the earth
and made the kingdoms of the world tremble?
17 Is this the one who destroyed the world
and made it into a wasteland?
Is this the king who demolished the world's greatest cities
and had no mercy on his prisoners?'

18 "The kings of the nations lie in stately glory,
each in his own tomb,
19 but you will be thrown out of your grave
like a worthless branch.
Like a corpse trampled underfoot,
you will be dumped into a mass grave
with those killed in battle.
You will descend to the pit.
20 You will not be given a proper burial,
for you have destroyed your nation
and slaughtered your people.
The descendants of such an evil person
will never again receive honor.
21 Kill this man's children!
Let them die because of their father's sins!
They must not rise and conquer the earth,
filling the world with their cities."

22 This is what the LORD of Heaven's Armies says:
"I, myself, have risen against Babylon!
I will destroy its children and its children's children,"
says the LORD.
23 "I will make Babylon a desolate place of owls,
filled with swamps and marshes.
I will sweep the land with the broom of destruction.
I, the LORD of Heaven's Armies, have spoken!"

A MESSAGE ABOUT ASSYRIA

24 The LORD of Heaven's Armies has sworn this oath:

"It will all happen as I have planned.
It will be as I have decided.
25 I will break the Assyrians when they are in Israel;
I will trample them on my mountains.
My people will no longer be their slaves
nor bow down under their heavy loads.
26 I have a plan for the whole earth,
a hand of judgment upon all the nations.
27 The LORD of Heaven's Armies has spoken—
who can change his plans?
When his hand is raised,
who can stop him?"

14:1 Hebrew *the house of Jacob.* The names "Jacob" and "Israel" are often interchanged throughout the Old Testament, referring sometimes to the individual patriarch and sometimes to the nation. **14:4** As in Dead Sea Scrolls; the meaning of the Masoretic Text is uncertain. **14:9** Hebrew *Sheol;* also in 14:15. **14:11** Hebrew *were brought down to Sheol.* **14:13** Or *on the heights of Zaphon.*

14:12 A shining star. Many people see this as a description of Satan, who fell from heaven (see Luke 10:18). Others see this as the Babylonian king (v. 4) or perhaps the Babylonian king under Satan's influence. The language here does not need to be taken literally but could refer to the Babylonian king's own mythological beliefs about himself and the gods.

14:17 had no mercy on his prisoners. King Cyrus would send the exiles home, but the king of Babylon kept them in captivity.

A MESSAGE ABOUT PHILISTIA

28 This message came to me the year King Ahaz died:*

29 Do not rejoice, you Philistines,
that the rod that struck you is broken—
that the king who attacked you is dead.
For from that snake a more poisonous snake will be born,
a fiery serpent to destroy you!
30 I will feed the poor in my pasture;
the needy will lie down in peace.
But as for you, I will wipe you out with famine
and destroy the few who remain.
31 Wail at the gates! Weep in the cities!
Melt with fear, you Philistines!
A powerful army comes like smoke from the north.
Each soldier rushes forward eager to fight.
32 What should we tell the Philistine messengers?
Tell them,

"The LORD has built Jerusalem*;
its walls will give refuge to his oppressed people."

A MESSAGE ABOUT MOAB

15 This message came to me concerning Moab:

In one night the town of Ar will be leveled,
and the city of Kir will be destroyed.
2 Your people will go to their temple in Dibon to mourn.
They will go to their sacred shrines to weep.
They will wail for the fate of Nebo and Medeba,
shaving their heads in sorrow and cutting off their beards.
3 They will wear burlap as they wander the streets.
From every home and public square will come
the sound of wailing.
4 The people of Heshbon and Elealeh will cry out;
their voices will be heard as far away as Jahaz!
The bravest warriors of Moab will cry out in utter terror.
They will be helpless with fear.

5 My heart weeps for Moab.
Its people flee to Zoar and Eglath-shelishiyah.
Weeping, they climb the road to Luhith.
Their cries of distress can be heard all along the road to Horonaim.
6 Even the waters of Nimrim are dried up!
The grassy banks are scorched.
The tender plants are gone;
nothing green remains.
7 The people grab their possessions
and carry them across the Ravine of Willows.
8 A cry of distress echoes through the land of Moab
from one end to the other—
from Eglaim to Beer-elim.
9 The stream near Dibon* runs red with blood,
but I am still not finished with Dibon!
Lions will hunt down the survivors—
both those who try to escape
and those who remain behind.

16 1 Send lambs from Sela as tribute
to the ruler of the land.
Send them through the desert
to the mountain of beautiful Zion.
2 The women of Moab are left like homeless birds
at the shallow crossings of the Arnon River.
3 "Help us," they cry.
"Defend us against our enemies.
Protect us from their relentless attack.
Do not betray us now that we have escaped.
4 Let our refugees stay among you.
Hide them from our enemies until the terror is past."
When oppression and destruction have ended
and enemy raiders have disappeared,
5 then God will establish one of David's descendants as king.
He will rule with mercy and truth.
He will always do what is just
and be eager to do what is right.

6 We have heard about proud Moab—
about its pride and arrogance and rage.
But all that boasting has disappeared.
7 The entire land of Moab weeps.
Yes, everyone in Moab mourns
for the cakes of raisins from Kir-hareseth.
They are all gone now.
8 The farms of Heshbon are abandoned;
the vineyards at Sibmah are deserted.
The rulers of the nations have broken down Moab—
that beautiful grapevine.
Its tendrils spread north as far as the town of Jazer
and trailed eastward into the wilderness.
Its shoots reached so far west
that they crossed over the Dead Sea.*
9 So now I weep for Jazer and the vineyards of Sibmah;
my tears will flow for Heshbon and Elealeh.
There are no more shouts of joy
over your summer fruits and harvest.
10 Gone now is the gladness,
gone the joy of harvest.
There will be no singing in the vineyards,
no more happy shouts,
no treading of grapes in the winepresses.
I have ended all their harvest joys.

14:28 King Ahaz died in 715 B.C. **14:32** Hebrew *Zion.* **15:9** As in Dead Sea Scrolls, some Greek manuscripts, and Latin Vulgate; Masoretic Text reads *Dimon;* also in 15:9b. **16:8** Hebrew *the sea.*

15:2 shaving . . . cutting off. Shaving one's head and cutting off one's beard were signs of humiliation. Wearing sackcloth (coarse, dark cloth) symbolized mourning. The Moabities were lamenting the destruction of their cities.

15:9 stream near Dibon . . . blood. So much death and destruction had occurred there that the water supply ran with blood.

16:1 Send lambs. The Moabites fled to strongholds 50 miles away, but they should have fled to Jerusalem, sending lambs on ahead as gifts. Isaiah had already prophesied that Jerusalem would be saved from attacks by Assyria.

16:6 heard about proud Moab. Moab was a small, boastful country whose people thought they could defeat the Assyrians without God's help (see Jer. 48:29).

16:9 weep for . . . the vineyards. Due to the people's pride, Moab's harvests would be lost. The combination of the invading army and drought would wipe out its crops and orchards. Isaiah had compassion for them as they experienced judgment.

11 My heart's cry for Moab is like a lament on a harp.
I am filled with anguish for Kir-hareseth.*
12 The people of Moab will worship at their pagan shrines,
but it will do them no good.
They will cry to the gods in their temples,
but no one will be able to save them.

13 The LORD has already said these things about Moab in the past. 14 But now the LORD says, "Within three years, counting each day,* the glory of Moab will be ended. From its great population, only a feeble few will be left alive."

A MESSAGE ABOUT DAMASCUS AND ISRAEL

17 This message came to me concerning Damascus:
"Look, the city of Damascus will disappear!
It will become a heap of ruins.
2 The towns of Aroer will be deserted.
Flocks will graze in the streets and lie down undisturbed,
with no one to chase them away.
3 The fortified towns of Israel* will also be destroyed,
and the royal power of Damascus will end.
All that remains of Syria*
will share the fate of Israel's departed glory,"
declares the LORD of Heaven's Armies.

4 "In that day Israel's* glory will grow dim;
its robust body will waste away.
5 The whole land will look like a grainfield
after the harvesters have gathered the grain.
It will be desolate,
like the fields in the valley of Rephaim after the harvest.
6 Only a few of its people will be left,
like stray olives left on a tree after the harvest.
Only two or three remain in the highest branches,
four or five scattered here and there on the limbs,"
declares the LORD, the God of Israel.

7 Then at last the people will look to their Creator
and turn their eyes to the Holy One of Israel.
8 They will no longer look to their idols for help
or worship what their own hands have made.
They will never again bow down to their Asherah poles
or worship at the pagan shrines they have built.
9 Their largest cities will be like a deserted forest,
like the land the Hivites and Amorites abandoned*
when the Israelites came here so long ago.
It will be utterly desolate.
10 Why? Because you have turned from the God who can save you.
You have forgotten the Rock who can hide you.
So you may plant the finest grapevines
and import the most expensive seedlings.
11 They may sprout on the day you set them out;
yes, they may blossom on the very morning you plant them,
but you will never pick any grapes from them.
Your only harvest will be a load of grief and unrelieved pain.

12 Listen! The armies of many nations
roar like the roaring of the sea.
Hear the thunder of the mighty forces
as they rush forward like thundering waves.
13 But though they thunder like breakers on a beach,
God will silence them, and they will run away.
They will flee like chaff scattered by the wind,
like a tumbleweed whirling before a storm.
14 In the evening Israel waits in terror,
but by dawn its enemies are dead.
This is the just reward of those who plunder us,
a fitting end for those who destroy us.

A MESSAGE ABOUT ETHIOPIA

18 1 Listen, Ethiopia*—land of fluttering sails*
that lies at the headwaters of the Nile,
2 that sends ambassadors
in swift boats down the river.

Go, swift messengers!
Take a message to a tall, smooth-skinned people,
who are feared far and wide
for their conquests and destruction,
and whose land is divided by rivers.

3 All you people of the world,
everyone who lives on the earth—
when I raise my battle flag on the mountain, look!
When I blow the ram's horn, listen!
4 For the LORD has told me this:
"I will watch quietly from my dwelling place—
as quietly as the heat rises on a summer day,
or as the morning dew forms during the harvest."
5 Even before you begin your attack,
while your plans are ripening like grapes,
the LORD will cut off your new growth with pruning shears.
He will snip off and discard your spreading branches.
6 Your mighty army will be left dead in the fields
for the mountain vultures and wild animals.
The vultures will tear at the corpses all summer.
The wild animals will gnaw at the bones all winter.

16:11 Hebrew *Kir-heres,* a variant spelling of Kir-hareseth. **16:14** Hebrew *Within three years, as a servant bound by contract would count them.* **17:3a** Hebrew *of Ephraim,* referring to the northern kingdom of Israel. **17:3b** Hebrew *Aram.* **17:4** Hebrew *Jacob's.* See note on 14:1. **17:9** As in Greek version; Hebrew reads *like places of the wood and the highest bough.* **18:1a** Hebrew *Cush.* **18:1b** Or *land of many locusts;* Hebrew reads *land of whirring wings.*

17:3 Israel. This refers to northern Israel, which was allied with Damascus, Syria's capital. Isaiah predicted judgment against both nations. Assyria defeated Damascus in 732 B.C. and Israel in 722 B.C.
17:5 in the valley of Rephaim. A fertile area west of Jerusalem where David had defeated the Philistines twice (see 2 Sam. 5:18-20,22-25). Rephaim is the Hebrew word for *ghosts*, so this is the Valley of Death.
17:8 Asherah poles. Wooden symbols of the Canaanite fertility goddess in the Baal worship system. Many Asherah-worshipers lived in the northern kingdom of Israel. But under Assyrian attack, Israel would realize that wooden idols could not help them.
17:13 chaff. Chaff is the lightweight and useless part of grain that blows away during threshing, leaving the valuable wheat behind. The enemies of Israel would become insignificant and easily defeated.

7 At that time the LORD of Heaven's Armies will
receive gifts
from this land divided by rivers,
from this tall, smooth-skinned people,
who are feared far and wide for their conquests
and destruction.
They will bring the gifts to Jerusalem,*
where the LORD of Heaven's Armies dwells.

A MESSAGE ABOUT EGYPT

19 This message came to me concerning Egypt:

Look! The LORD is advancing against Egypt,
riding on a swift cloud.
The idols of Egypt tremble.
The hearts of the Egyptians melt with fear.

2 "I will make Egyptian fight against Egyptian—
brother against brother,
neighbor against neighbor,
city against city,
province against province.
3 The Egyptians will lose heart,
and I will confuse their plans.
They will plead with their idols for wisdom
and call on spirits, mediums, and those who
consult the spirits of the dead.
4 I will hand Egypt over
to a hard, cruel master.
A fierce king will rule them,"
says the Lord, the LORD of Heaven's Armies.

5 The waters of the Nile will fail to rise and flood the
fields.
The riverbed will be parched and dry.
6 The canals of the Nile will dry up,
and the streams of Egypt will stink
with rotting reeds and rushes.
7 All the greenery along the riverbank
and all the crops along the river
will dry up and blow away.
8 The fishermen will lament for lack of work.
Those who cast hooks into the Nile will groan,
and those who use nets will lose heart.
9 There will be no flax for the harvesters,
no thread for the weavers.
10 They will be in despair,
and all the workers will be sick at heart.

11 What fools are the officials of Zoan!
Their best counsel to the king of Egypt is stupid
and wrong.
Will they still boast to Pharaoh of their wisdom?
Will they dare brag about all their wise
ancestors?
12 Where are your wise counselors, Pharaoh?
Let them tell you what God plans,
what the LORD of Heaven's Armies is going to do
to Egypt.
13 The officials of Zoan are fools,
and the officials of Memphis* are deluded.
The leaders of the people
have led Egypt astray.
14 The LORD has sent a spirit of foolishness on them,
so all their suggestions are wrong.
They cause Egypt to stagger
like a drunk in his vomit.
15 There is nothing Egypt can do.
All are helpless—
the head and the tail,
the noble palm branch and the lowly reed.

16 In that day the Egyptians will be as weak as
women. They will cower in fear beneath the upraised
fist of the LORD of Heaven's Armies. 17 Just to speak
the name of Israel will terrorize them, for the LORD of
Heaven's Armies has laid out his plans against them.
18 In that day five of Egypt's cities will follow the
LORD of Heaven's Armies. They will even begin to
speak Hebrew, the language of Canaan. One of these
cities will be Heliopolis, the City of the Sun.*
19 In that day there will be an altar to the LORD in
the heart of Egypt, and there will be a monument to
the LORD at its border. 20 It will be a sign and a wit-
ness that the LORD of Heaven's Armies is worshiped
in the land of Egypt. When the people cry to the LORD
for help against those who oppress them, he will send
them a savior who will rescue them. 21 The LORD will
make himself known to the Egyptians. Yes, they will
know the LORD and will give their sacrifices and of-
ferings to him. They will make a vow to the LORD and
will keep it. 22 The LORD will strike Egypt, and then he
will bring healing. For the Egyptians will turn to the
LORD, and he will listen to their pleas and heal them.
23 In that day Egypt and Assyria will be connected
by a highway. The Egyptians and Assyrians will move
freely between their lands, and they will both worship
God. 24 In that day Israel will be the third, along with
Egypt and Assyria, a blessing in the midst of the earth.
25 For the LORD of Heaven's Armies will say, "Blessed be
Egypt, my people. Blessed be Assyria, the land I have
made. Blessed be Israel, my special possession!"

A MESSAGE ABOUT EGYPT AND ETHIOPIA

20 In the year when King Sargon of Assyria sent
his commander in chief to capture the Phi-
listine city of Ashdod,* 2 the LORD told Isaiah son of
Amoz, "Take off the burlap you have been wearing,
and remove your sandals." Isaiah did as he was told
and walked around naked and barefoot.

18:7 Hebrew *to Mount Zion.* **19:13** Hebrew *Noph.* **19:18** Or *will be the City of Destruction.* **20:1** Ashdod was captured by Assyria in 711 B.C. **20:3** Hebrew *Cush;* also in 20:5. **20:4** Hebrew *Cushites.*

19:3 plead with their idols. Some Israelites hoped that Egypt would help against Assyria, but God announced His judgment on Egypt. Its idols and mediums would be unable to help this once cruel master of the Israelites. Now Egypt would have its own cruel master in the Assyrian Empire.

19:19 altar to the LORD. This promise must have been remarkable to Israelites who considered Egypt a perpetual enemy.

19:20 those who oppress them . . . savior. When the Egyptians turn to God and ask for help, God will give it. This will take place after the Messiah has returned and established His millennial kingdom (43:11).

19:23 highway. Egypt and Assyria had been enemies for centuries. People from both nations and from Israel will worship together peacefully in the millennial kingdom. This will fulfill part of God's promise to Abraham that all peoples would be blessed through him (Gen. 12:3).

19:25 my people . . . the land I have made . . . my special possession. Here these titles for Israel are applied to nations typically considered enemies. God will restore other nations besides Israel in the Messianic kingdom.

20:1 Ashdod. The capture of this Philistine city by Assyrian King Sargon II demonstrated to Israel that foreign alliances could not protect them.

20:2 naked and barefoot. To represent exile and captivity, Isaiah probably did not wear clothing. This showed how Egypt and Cush would be treated by a victorious Assyria, a warning that Israel should not look to foreign allies for protection.

[3] Then the LORD said, "My servant Isaiah has been
walking around naked and barefoot for the last
three years. This is a sign—a symbol of the terri-
ble troubles I will bring upon Egypt and Ethiopia.*
[4] For the king of Assyria will take away the Egyp-
tians and Ethiopians* as prisoners. He will make
them walk naked and barefoot, both young and old,
their buttocks bared, to the shame of Egypt. [5] Then
the Philistines will be thrown into panic, for they
counted on the power of Ethiopia and boasted of
their allies in Egypt! [6] They will say, 'If this can hap-
pen to Egypt, what chance do we have? We were
counting on Egypt to protect us from the king of As-
syria.'"

A MESSAGE ABOUT BABYLON

21 This message came to me concerning Babylon—the desert by the sea*:

Disaster is roaring down on you from the desert,
like a whirlwind sweeping in from the Negev.
[2] I see a terrifying vision:
I see the betrayer betraying,
the destroyer destroying.
Go ahead, you Elamites and Medes,
attack and lay siege.
I will make an end
to all the groaning Babylon caused.
[3] My stomach aches and burns with pain.
Sharp pangs of anguish are upon me,
like those of a woman in labor.
I grow faint when I hear what God is planning;
I am too afraid to look.
[4] My mind reels and my heart races.
I longed for evening to come,
but now I am terrified of the dark.

[5] Look! They are preparing a great feast.
They are spreading rugs for people to sit on.
Everyone is eating and drinking.
But quick! Grab your shields and prepare for battle.
You are being attacked!

[6] Meanwhile, the Lord said to me,
"Put a watchman on the city wall.
Let him shout out what he sees.
[7] He should look for chariots
drawn by pairs of horses,
and for riders on donkeys and camels.
Let the watchman be fully alert."

[8] Then the watchman* called out,
"Day after day I have stood on the watchtower, my lord.
Night after night I have remained at my post.
[9] Now at last—look!
Here comes a man in a chariot
with a pair of horses!"
Then the watchman said,
"Babylon is fallen, fallen!
All the idols of Babylon
lie broken on the ground!"
[10] O my people, threshed and winnowed,
I have told you everything the LORD of Heaven's Armies has said,
everything the God of Israel has told me.

A MESSAGE ABOUT EDOM

[11] This message came to me concerning Edom*:

Someone from Edom* keeps calling to me,
"Watchman, how much longer until morning?
When will the night be over?"
[12] The watchman replies,
"Morning is coming, but night will soon return.
If you wish to ask again, then come back and ask."

A MESSAGE ABOUT ARABIA

[13] This message came to me concerning Arabia:

O caravans from Dedan,
hide in the deserts of Arabia.
[14] O people of Tema,
bring water to these thirsty people,
food to these weary refugees.
[15] They have fled from the sword,
from the drawn sword,
from the bent bow
and the terrors of battle.

[16] The Lord said to me, "Within a year, counting
each day,* all the glory of Kedar will come to an end.
[17] Only a few of its courageous archers will survive. I,
the LORD, the God of Israel, have spoken!"

A MESSAGE ABOUT JERUSALEM

22 This message came to me concerning Jerusalem—the Valley of Vision*:

What is happening?
Why is everyone running to the rooftops?
[2] The whole city is in a terrible uproar.
What do I see in this reveling city?
Bodies are lying everywhere,
killed not in battle but by famine and disease.
[3] All your leaders have fled.
They surrendered without resistance.
The people tried to slip away,
but they were captured, too.
[4] That's why I said, "Leave me alone to weep;
do not try to comfort me.
Let me cry for my people
as I watch them being destroyed."

[5] Oh, what a day of crushing defeat!
What a day of confusion and terror
brought by the Lord, the LORD of Heaven's Armies,
upon the Valley of Vision!
The walls of Jerusalem have been broken,
and cries of death echo from the mountainsides.

21:1 Hebrew *concerning the desert by the sea.* 21:8 As in Dead Sea Scrolls and Syriac version; Masoretic Text reads *a lion.* 21:11a Hebrew *Dumah,* which means "silence" or "stillness." It is a wordplay on the word *Edom.* 21:11b Hebrew *Seir,* another name for Edom. 21:16 Hebrew *Within a year, as a servant bound by contract would count it.* Some ancient manuscripts read *Within three years,* as in 16:14. 22:1 Hebrew *concerning the Valley of Vision.*

21:5 eating and drinking. The Babylonians were living in confident self-assurance, but Isaiah warned them of coming battle (Dan. 5:4-5). **But quick! Grab.** He urged them to stop feasting and prepare for war.

21:9 Babylon is fallen. Israel hoped that Babylon would defeat the Assyrians, so this news was devastating (see Jer. 51:8).

[6] Elamites are the archers,
with their chariots and charioteers.
The men of Kir hold up the shields.
[7] Chariots fill your beautiful valleys,
and charioteers storm your gates.
[8] Judah's defenses have been stripped away.
You run to the armory* for your weapons.
[9] You inspect the breaks in the walls of Jerusalem.*
You store up water in the lower pool.
[10] You survey the houses and tear some down
for stone to strengthen the walls.
[11] Between the city walls, you build a reservoir
for water from the old pool.
But you never ask for help from the One who did
all this.
You never considered the One who planned this
long ago.

[12] At that time the Lord, the LORD of Heaven's Armies,
called you to weep and mourn.
He told you to shave your heads in sorrow for your
sins
and to wear clothes of burlap to show your
remorse.
[13] But instead, you dance and play;
you slaughter cattle and kill sheep.
You feast on meat and drink wine.
You say, "Let's feast and drink,
for tomorrow we die!"

[14] The LORD of Heaven's Armies has revealed this to me: "Till the day you die, you will never be forgiven for this sin." That is the judgment of the Lord, the LORD of Heaven's Armies.

A MESSAGE FOR SHEBNA

[15] This is what the Lord, the LORD of Heaven's Armies, said to me: "Confront Shebna, the palace administrator, and give him this message:

[16] "Who do you think you are,
and what are you doing here,
building a beautiful tomb for yourself—
a monument high up in the rock?
[17] For the LORD is about to hurl you away, mighty
man.
He is going to grab you,
[18] crumple you into a ball,
and toss you away into a distant, barren land.
There you will die,
and your glorious chariots will be broken and
useless.
You are a disgrace to your master!

[19] "Yes, I will drive you out of office," says the LORD. "I will pull you down from your high position. [20] And then I will call my servant Eliakim son of Hilkiah to replace you. [21] I will dress him in your royal robes and will give him your title and your authority. And he will be a father to the people of Jerusalem and Judah. [22] I will give him the key to the house of David—the highest position in the royal court. When he opens doors, no one will be able to close them; when he closes doors, no one will be able to open them. [23] He will bring honor to his family name, for I will drive him firmly in place like a nail in the wall. [24] They will give him great responsibility, and he will bring honor to even the lowliest members of his family.*"

[25] But the LORD of Heaven's Armies also says: "The time will come when I will pull out the nail that seemed so firm. It will come out and fall to the ground. Everything it supports will fall with it. I, the LORD, have spoken!"

A MESSAGE ABOUT TYRE

23 This message came to me concerning Tyre:

Wail, you trading ships of Tarshish,
for the harbor and houses of Tyre are gone!
The rumors you heard in Cyprus*
are all true.
[2] Mourn in silence, you people of the coast
and you merchants of Sidon.
Your traders crossed the sea,*
[3] sailing over deep waters.
They brought you grain from Egypt*
and harvests from along the Nile.
You were the marketplace of the world.
[4] But now you are put to shame, city of Sidon,
for Tyre, the fortress of the sea, says,*
"Now I am childless;
I have no sons or daughters."
[5] When Egypt hears the news about Tyre,
there will be great sorrow.
[6] Send word now to Tarshish!
Wail, you people who live in distant lands!
[7] Is this silent ruin all that is left of your once joyous
city?
What a long history was yours!
Think of all the colonists you sent to distant places.

[8] Who has brought this disaster on Tyre,
that great creator of kingdoms?
Her traders were all princes,
her merchants were nobles.
[9] The LORD of Heaven's Armies has done it
to destroy your pride
and bring low all earth's nobility.
[10] Come, people of Tarshish,
sweep over the land like the flooding Nile,
for Tyre is defenseless.*

22:8 Hebrew *to the House of the Forest;* see 1 Kgs 7:2-5. **22:9** Hebrew *the city of David.* **22:24** Hebrew *They will hang on him all the glory of his father's house: its offspring and offshoots, all its lesser vessels, from the bowls to all the jars.* **23:1** Hebrew *Kittim;* also in 23:12. **23:2** As in Dead Sea Scrolls and Greek version; Masoretic Text reads *Those who have gone over the sea have filled you.* **23:3** Hebrew *from Shihor,* a branch of the Nile River. **23:4** Or *for the god of the sea says;* Hebrew reads *for the sea, the fortress of the sea, says.* **23:10** The meaning of the Hebrew in this verse is uncertain.

22:9 Jerusalem. The defense of the city depended upon available water. Hezekiah had repaired broken sections of the wall and also preserved the water supply (2 Chron. 32:1-5). **lower pool.** A reservoir in Jerusalem's southwestern valley. Hezekiah connected it, by a 1,777-foot tunnel carved out of rock under the city, to the Old Pool, the water source in the eastern valley.
22:11 the One who did all this. Hezekiah's tunnel was insufficient to protect the people. They refused to turn to God, who alone could save them.
22:25 nail . . . will fall with it. Eliakim was the palace administrator and a godly man. He would be a respected leader and a firm and stable foundation for the nation. But even he would come to an end, and the kingdom of Judah would be taken into captivity.
23:1 Tyre. This seaport city was captured several times over a period of 400 years before being destroyed by Alexander the Great in 332 B.C. King Hiram of Tyre supplied the cedars and craftsmen for Solomon's temple.

11 The LORD held out his hand over the sea
and shook the kingdoms of the earth.
He has spoken out against Phoenicia,*
ordering that her fortresses be destroyed.
12 He says, "Never again will you rejoice,
O daughter of Sidon, for you have been crushed.
Even if you flee to Cyprus,
you will find no rest."

13 Look at the land of Babylonia*—
the people of that land are gone!
The Assyrians have handed Babylon over
to the wild animals of the desert.
They have built siege ramps against its walls,
torn down its palaces,
and turned it to a heap of rubble.

14 Wail, you ships of Tarshish,
for your harbor is destroyed!

15 For seventy years, the length of a king's life, Tyre will be forgotten. But then the city will come back to life as in the song about the prostitute:

16 Take a harp and walk the streets,
you forgotten harlot.
Make sweet melody and sing your songs
so you will be remembered again.

17 Yes, after seventy years the LORD will revive Tyre. But she will be no different than she was before. She will again be a prostitute to all kingdoms around the world. 18 But in the end her profits will be given to the LORD. Her wealth will not be hoarded but will provide good food and fine clothing for the LORD's priests.

DESTRUCTION OF THE EARTH

24 1 Look! The LORD is about to destroy the earth
and make it a vast wasteland.
He devastates the surface of the earth
and scatters the people.
2 Priests and laypeople,
servants and masters,
maids and mistresses,
buyers and sellers,
lenders and borrowers,
bankers and debtors—none will be spared.
3 The earth will be completely emptied and looted.
The LORD has spoken!

4 The earth mourns and dries up,
and the land wastes away and withers.
Even the greatest people on earth waste away.
5 The earth suffers for the sins of its people,
for they have twisted God's instructions,
violated his laws,
and broken his everlasting covenant.
6 Therefore, a curse consumes the earth.
Its people must pay the price for their sin.
They are destroyed by fire,
and only a few are left alive.
7 The grapevines waste away,
and there is no new wine.
All the merrymakers sigh and mourn.
8 The cheerful sound of tambourines is stilled;
the happy cries of celebration are heard no more.
The melodious chords of the harp are silent.
9 Gone are the joys of wine and song;
alcoholic drink turns bitter in the mouth.
10 The city writhes in chaos;
every home is locked to keep out intruders.
11 Mobs gather in the streets, crying out for wine.
Joy has turned to gloom.
Gladness has been banished from the land.
12 The city is left in ruins,
its gates battered down.
13 Throughout the earth the story is the same—
only a remnant is left,
like the stray olives left on the tree
or the few grapes left on the vine after harvest.

14 But all who are left shout and sing for joy.
Those in the west praise the LORD's majesty.
15 In eastern lands, give glory to the LORD.
In the lands beyond the sea, praise the name of the LORD, the God of Israel.
16 We hear songs of praise from the ends of the earth,
songs that give glory to the Righteous One!

But my heart is heavy with grief.
Weep for me, for I wither away.
Deceit still prevails,
and treachery is everywhere.
17 Terror and traps and snares will be your lot,
you people of the earth.
18 Those who flee in terror will fall into a trap,
and those who escape the trap will be caught in a snare.

Destruction falls like rain from the heavens;
the foundations of the earth shake.
19 The earth has broken up.
It has utterly collapsed;
it is violently shaken.
20 The earth staggers like a drunk.
It trembles like a tent in a storm.
It falls and will not rise again,
for the guilt of its rebellion is very heavy.

21 In that day the LORD will punish the gods in the heavens
and the proud rulers of the nations on earth.
22 They will be rounded up and put in prison.
They will be shut up in prison
and will finally be punished.
23 Then the glory of the moon will wane,
and the brightness of the sun will fade,
for the LORD of Heaven's Armies will rule on Mount Zion.

23:11 Hebrew *Canaan.* 23:13 Or *Chaldea.*

23:15 For seventy years . . . will be forgotten. This represented a king's lifetime. The period referred to was probably from about 700 to 630 B.C. when Phoenicia's trade was reduced by the Assyrians. After 630 B.C. Assyria declined, and Tyre rebuilt its successful trading operations.

23:17 prostitute. Tyre's reestablished (and profitable) trade activities, often conducted with unethical partners, is compared to a prostitute who stops her trade in illicit sex but returns to it more successful than ever.

24:6 a curse consumes the earth. God's judgment in consequence of sin. **only a few survive.** A remnant will be preserved (10:20).

He will rule in great glory in Jerusalem,
in the sight of all the leaders of his people.

PRAISE FOR JUDGMENT AND SALVATION

25 1 O LORD, I will honor and praise your name,
for you are my God.
You do such wonderful things!
You planned them long ago,
and now you have accomplished them.
2 You turn mighty cities into heaps of ruins.
Cities with strong walls are turned to rubble.
Beautiful palaces in distant lands disappear
and will never be rebuilt.
3 Therefore, strong nations will declare your glory;
ruthless nations will fear you.

4 But you are a tower of refuge to the poor, O LORD,
a tower of refuge to the needy in distress.
You are a refuge from the storm
and a shelter from the heat.
For the oppressive acts of ruthless people
are like a storm beating against a wall,
5 or like the relentless heat of the desert.
But you silence the roar of foreign nations.
As the shade of a cloud cools relentless heat,
so the boastful songs of ruthless people are stilled.

6 In Jerusalem,* the LORD of Heaven's Armies
will spread a wonderful feast
for all the people of the world.
It will be a delicious banquet
with clear, well-aged wine and choice meat.
7 There he will remove the cloud of gloom,
the shadow of death that hangs over the earth.
8 He will swallow up death forever!
The Sovereign LORD will wipe away all tears.
He will remove forever all insults and mockery
against his land and people.
The LORD has spoken!

9 In that day the people will proclaim,
"This is our God!
We trusted in him, and he saved us!
This is the LORD, in whom we trusted.
Let us rejoice in the salvation he brings!"
10 For the LORD's hand of blessing will rest on Jerusalem.
But Moab will be crushed.
It will be like straw trampled down and left to rot.
11 God will push down Moab's people
as a swimmer pushes down water with his hands.
He will end their pride
and all their evil works.
12 The high walls of Moab will be demolished.
They will be brought down to the ground,
down into the dust.

A SONG OF PRAISE TO THE LORD

26 1 In that day, everyone in the land of Judah will sing this song:

Our city is strong!
We are surrounded by the walls of God's salvation.
2 Open the gates to all who are righteous;
allow the faithful to enter.
3 You will keep in perfect peace
all who trust in you,
all whose thoughts are fixed on you!
4 Trust in the LORD always,
for the LORD GOD is the eternal Rock.
5 He humbles the proud
and brings down the arrogant city.
He brings it down to the dust.
6 The poor and oppressed trample it underfoot,
and the needy walk all over it.

7 But for those who are righteous,
the way is not steep and rough.
You are a God who does what is right,
and you smooth out the path ahead of them.
8 LORD, we show our trust in you by obeying your laws;
our heart's desire is to glorify your name.
9 In the night I search for you;
in the morning* I earnestly seek you.
For only when you come to judge the earth
will people learn what is right.
10 Your kindness to the wicked
does not make them do good.
Although others do right, the wicked keep doing wrong
and take no notice of the LORD's majesty.
11 O LORD, they pay no attention to your upraised fist.
Show them your eagerness to defend your people.
Then they will be ashamed.
Let your fire consume your enemies.

12 LORD, you will grant us peace;
all we have accomplished is really from you.
13 O LORD our God, others have ruled us,
but you alone are the one we worship.
14 Those we served before are dead and gone.
Their departed spirits will never return!
You attacked them and destroyed them,
and they are long forgotten.
15 O LORD, you have made our nation great;
yes, you have made us great.
You have extended our borders,
and we give you the glory!

16 LORD, in distress we searched for you.
We prayed beneath the burden of your discipline.
17 Just as a pregnant woman
writhes and cries out in pain as she gives birth,
so were we in your presence, LORD.

25:6 Hebrew *On this mountain;* also in 25:10. 26:9 Hebrew *within me.*

25:4 tower of refuge to the poor . . . the needy. God's protection was described as a shelter and a shade (Ps. 91:1-3). He protects the needy from the storm and stills the storms created by the ruthless.

25:6 wonderful feast . . . delicious banquet. There will be a banquet on Mt. Zion for those who will be saved (Dan. 7:14). Perhaps this is similar to the wedding supper of the Lamb (see Rev. 19:9).

26:1 Our city is strong. Refers to Jerusalem where the Messiah will reign. The humble will be exalted, and oppressors vanquished, a reversal of the world's wicked system.

26:13 others have ruled us. This included rulers of Egypt in the past, Assyria in the present, and Babylon in the future (2 Chron. 12:8).

18 We, too, writhe in agony,
but nothing comes of our suffering.
We have not given salvation to the earth,
nor brought life into the world.
19 But those who die in the LORD will live;
their bodies will rise again!
Those who sleep in the earth
will rise up and sing for joy!
For your life-giving light will fall like dew
on your people in the place of the dead!

RESTORATION FOR ISRAEL

20 Go home, my people,
and lock your doors!
Hide yourselves for a little while
until the LORD's anger has passed.
21 Look! The LORD is coming from heaven
to punish the people of the earth for their sins.
The earth will no longer hide those who have been killed.
They will be brought out for all to see.

27 In that day the LORD will take his terrible, swift
sword and punish Leviathan,* the swiftly mov-
ing serpent, the coiling, writhing serpent. He will kill
the dragon of the sea.

2 "In that day,
sing about the fruitful vineyard.
3 I, the LORD, will watch over it,
watering it carefully.
Day and night I will watch so no one can harm it.
4 My anger will be gone.
If I find briers and thorns growing,
I will attack them;
I will burn them up—
5 unless they turn to me for help.
Let them make peace with me;
yes, let them make peace with me."
6 The time is coming when Jacob's descendants will take root.
Israel will bud and blossom
and fill the whole earth with fruit!

7 Has the LORD struck Israel
as he struck her enemies?
Has he punished her
as he punished them?
8 No, but he exiled Israel to call her to account.
She was exiled from her land
as though blown away in a storm from the east.
9 The LORD did this to purge Israel's* wickedness,
to take away all her sin.
As a result, all the pagan altars will be crushed to dust.
No Asherah pole or pagan shrine will be left standing.
10 The fortified towns will be silent and empty,
the houses abandoned, the streets overgrown with weeds.
Calves will graze there,
chewing on twigs and branches.
11 The people are like the dead branches of a tree,
broken off and used for kindling beneath the cooking pots.
Israel is a foolish and stupid nation,
for its people have turned away from God.
Therefore, the one who made them
will show them no pity or mercy.

12 Yet the time will come when the LORD will gather
them together like handpicked grain. One by one he
will gather them—from the Euphrates River* in the
east to the Brook of Egypt in the west.
13 In that day
the great trumpet will sound. Many who were dying
in exile in Assyria and Egypt will return to Jerusalem
to worship the LORD on his holy mountain.

A MESSAGE ABOUT SAMARIA

28 1 What sorrow awaits the proud city of Samaria—
the glorious crown of the drunks of Israel.*
It sits at the head of a fertile valley,
but its glorious beauty will fade like a flower.
It is the pride of a people
brought down by wine.
2 For the Lord will send a mighty army against it.
Like a mighty hailstorm and a torrential rain,
they will burst upon it like a surging flood
and smash it to the ground.
3 The proud city of Samaria—
the glorious crown of the drunks of Israel*—
will be trampled beneath its enemies' feet.
4 It sits at the head of a fertile valley,
but its glorious beauty will fade like a flower.
Whoever sees it will snatch it up,
as an early fig is quickly picked and eaten.

5 Then at last the LORD of Heaven's Armies
will himself be Israel's glorious crown.
He will be the pride and joy
of the remnant of his people.
6 He will give a longing for justice
to their judges.
He will give great courage
to their warriors who stand at the gates.

27:1 The identification of Leviathan is disputed, ranging from an earthly creature to a mythical sea monster in ancient literature. **27:9** Hebrew *Jacob's.* See note on 14:1. **27:12** Hebrew *the river.* **28:1** Hebrew *What sorrow awaits the crowning glory of the drunks of Ephraim,* referring to Samaria, capital of the northern kingdom of Israel. **28:3** Hebrew *The crowning glory of the drunks of Ephraim;* see note on 28:1.

26:19 those who die . . . will live . . . their bodies will rise. God made a promise here for the first time: assuring the people that the believing dead will rise to life at Christ's second coming (Dan. 12:2). **dew.** As dew refreshes grass, so will believers experience new life along with God's blessing at the resurrection (Ps. 133:3).

26:20 Hide . . . a little while . . . anger. Isaiah urged the future believing remnant to hide during the tribulation when God pours out His anger. They should wait for God to deliver them.

26:21 to punish. God will judge people for both open and secret sins. **hide those . . . killed.** Since God knows all the bloodshed and evil on earth and will judge its perpetrators, this statement encourages believers to completely obey God.

27:1 sword . . . Leviathan. God will triumph over all who oppose Him, including this large sea creature, which symbolizes the chaos and evil in the world (Ps. 74:13-14).

27:2 vineyard. Israel (see Isa. 5).

27:5 turn . . . for help . . . peace. While God must judge sin, He prefers that believers repent and obey Him, living in the proper covenant relationship and receiving His blessings (Job 22:21).

27:10 empty . . . abandoned . . . overgrown. Because of Israel's sin, Jerusalem was destroyed in 586 B.C.

27:12 the LORD will gather. Like the oxen that thresh wheat and gather it from the fields, God will bring the Israelites from Assyria and Egypt to Jerusalem where the Messiah will reign.

7 Now, however, Israel is led by drunks
who reel with wine and stagger with alcohol.
The priests and prophets stagger with alcohol
and lose themselves in wine.
They reel when they see visions
and stagger as they render decisions.
8 Their tables are covered with vomit;
filth is everywhere.
9 "Who does the LORD think we are?" they ask.
"Why does he speak to us like this?
Are we little children,
just recently weaned?
10 He tells us everything over and over—
one line at a time,
one line at a time,
a little here,
and a little there!"

11 So now God will have to speak to his people
through foreign oppressors who speak a strange language!
12 God has told his people,
"Here is a place of rest;
let the weary rest here.
This is a place of quiet rest."
But they would not listen.
13 So the LORD will spell out his message for them again,
one line at a time,
one line at a time,
a little here,
and a little there,
so that they will stumble and fall.
They will be injured, trapped, and captured.

14 Therefore, listen to this message from the LORD,
you scoffing rulers in Jerusalem.
15 You boast, "We have struck a bargain to cheat death
and have made a deal to dodge the grave.*
The coming destruction can never touch us,
for we have built a strong refuge made of lies and deception."

16 Therefore, this is what the Sovereign LORD says:
"Look! I am placing a foundation stone in Jerusalem,*
a firm and tested stone.
It is a precious cornerstone that is safe to build on.
Whoever believes need never be shaken.*
17 I will test you with the measuring line of justice
and the plumb line of righteousness.
Since your refuge is made of lies,
a hailstorm will knock it down.
Since it is made of deception,
a flood will sweep it away.
18 I will cancel the bargain you made to cheat death,
and I will overturn your deal to dodge the grave.
When the terrible enemy sweeps through,
you will be trampled into the ground.
19 Again and again that flood will come,
morning after morning,
day and night,
until you are carried away."

This message will bring terror to your people.
20 The bed you have made is too short to lie on.
The blankets are too narrow to cover you.
21 The LORD will come as he did against the Philistines at Mount Perazim
and against the Amorites at Gibeon.
He will come to do a strange thing;
he will come to do an unusual deed:
22 For the Lord, the LORD of Heaven's Armies,
has plainly said that he is determined to crush the whole land.
So scoff no more,
or your punishment will be even greater.

23 Listen to me;
listen, and pay close attention.
24 Does a farmer always plow and never sow?
Is he forever cultivating the soil and never planting?
25 Does he not finally plant his seeds—
black cumin, cumin, wheat, barley, and emmer wheat—
each in its proper way,
and each in its proper place?
26 The farmer knows just what to do,
for God has given him understanding.
27 A heavy sledge is never used to thresh black cumin;
rather, it is beaten with a light stick.
A threshing wheel is never rolled on cumin;
instead, it is beaten lightly with a flail.
28 Grain for bread is easily crushed,
so he doesn't keep on pounding it.
He threshes it under the wheels of a cart,
but he doesn't pulverize it.
29 The LORD of Heaven's Armies is a wonderful teacher,
and he gives the farmer great wisdom.

A MESSAGE ABOUT JERUSALEM

29 1 "What sorrow awaits Ariel,* the City of David.
Year after year you celebrate your feasts.
2 Yet I will bring disaster upon you,
and there will be much weeping and sorrow.

28:15 Hebrew *Sheol;* also in 28:18. **28:16a** Hebrew *in Zion.* **28:16b** Greek version reads *Look! I am placing a stone in the foundation of Jerusalem* [literally *Zion*], */ a precious cornerstone for its foundation, chosen for great honor. / Anyone who trusts in him will never be disgraced.* Compare Rom 9:33; 1 Pet 2:6. **29:1** *Ariel* sounds like a Hebrew term that means "hearth" or "altar."

28:12 let the weary rest. Although God had offered Israel peace and rest, they refused to listen.

28:15,18 bargain to cheat death. Isaiah's way of describing Israel's covenant with Egypt. Jerusalem's leaders trusted in other gods, such as the god of the underworld, to save them.

28:20 bed . . . cover. Looking for protection from false gods was as futile as trying to sleep in a small, uncomfortable bed with only a thin blanket to keep out the cold.

28:24 farmer. Isaiah compared God's judgment to the work of a farmer who must grind certain of his crops to get out the small seeds. Though God will judge sin, He will also save and restore.

29:1–2,7 Ariel. Means "lion of God" and is a fitting name for Jerusalem, the capital of Judah who is a lion (Gen. 49:9). Yet the name also means altar hearth (Ezek. 43:15) and refers to Jerusalem, where so much bloodshed would make the city appear like an altar where sacrifices had been slain (see Ezek. 24:6,9).

For Jerusalem will become what her name Ariel
means—
an altar covered with blood.
3 I will be your enemy,
surrounding Jerusalem and attacking its walls.
I will build siege towers
and destroy it.
4 Then deep from the earth you will speak;
from low in the dust your words will come.
Your voice will whisper from the ground
like a ghost conjured up from the grave.

5 "But suddenly, your ruthless enemies will be
crushed
like the finest of dust.
Your many attackers will be driven away
like chaff before the wind.
Suddenly, in an instant,
6 I, the LORD of Heaven's Armies, will act for you
with thunder and earthquake and great noise,
with whirlwind and storm and consuming fire.
7 All the nations fighting against Jerusalem*
will vanish like a dream!
Those who are attacking her walls
will vanish like a vision in the night.
8 A hungry person dreams of eating
but wakes up still hungry.
A thirsty person dreams of drinking
but is still faint from thirst when morning comes.
So it will be with your enemies,
with those who attack Mount Zion."

9 Are you amazed and incredulous?
Don't you believe it?
Then go ahead and be blind.
You are stupid, but not from wine!
You stagger, but not from liquor!
10 For the LORD has poured out on you a spirit of deep
sleep.
He has closed the eyes of your prophets and
visionaries.

11 All the future events in this vision are like a
sealed book to them. When you give it to those who
can read, they will say, "We can't read it because it is
sealed." 12 When you give it to those who cannot read,
they will say, "We don't know how to read."

13 And so the Lord says,
"These people say they are mine.
They honor me with their lips,
but their hearts are far from me.
And their worship of me
is nothing but man-made rules learned by rote.*
14 Because of this, I will once again astound these
hypocrites
with amazing wonders.
The wisdom of the wise will pass away,
and the intelligence of the intelligent will
disappear."

15 What sorrow awaits those who try to hide their
plans from the LORD,
who do their evil deeds in the dark!
"The LORD can't see us," they say.
"He doesn't know what's going on!"
16 How foolish can you be?
He is the Potter, and he is certainly greater than
you, the clay!
Should the created thing say of the one who made it,
"He didn't make me"?
Does a jar ever say,
"The potter who made me is stupid"?

17 Soon—and it will not be very long—
the forests of Lebanon will become a fertile field,
and the fertile field will yield bountiful crops.
18 In that day the deaf will hear words read from a
book,
and the blind will see through the gloom and
darkness.
19 The humble will be filled with fresh joy from the
LORD.
The poor will rejoice in the Holy One of Israel.
20 The scoffer will be gone,
the arrogant will disappear,
and those who plot evil will be killed.
21 Those who convict the innocent
by their false testimony will disappear.
A similar fate awaits those who use trickery to
pervert justice
and who tell lies to destroy the innocent.

22 That is why the LORD, who redeemed Abraham,
says to the people of Israel,*

"My people will no longer be ashamed
or turn pale with fear.
23 For when they see their many children
and all the blessings I have given them,
they will recognize the holiness of the Holy One
of Jacob.
They will stand in awe of the God of Israel.
24 Then the wayward will gain understanding,
and complainers will accept instruction.

JUDAH'S WORTHLESS TREATY WITH EGYPT

30 1 "What sorrow awaits my rebellious children,"
says the LORD.
"You make plans that are contrary to mine.
You make alliances not directed by my Spirit,
thus piling up your sins.

29:7 Hebrew *Ariel.* 29:13 Greek version reads *Their worship is a farce, / for they teach man-made ideas as commands from God.* Compare Mark 7:7.
29:22 Hebrew *of Jacob.* See note on 14:1.

29:4 voice will whisper from the ground. Refers to the deceptive "voices" of the dead who supposedly spoke through mediums. A humbled Jerusalem will only be able to speak in a whisper.
29:6 I . . . will act for you. As God intervened and spared Jerusalem from destruction by Assyrian soldiers, He will come and destroy the nations attacking His people (see Zech. 14:1-3).
29:13 their hearts are far from me. Professing to know God or engaging in acts of worship do not necessarily mean that a person's heart is turned toward Him.
29:22 the LORD, who redeemed. God renewed His covenant with Abraham, promising to deliver and bless Israel (see Josh. 24:3; Acts 7:2-4). **no longer be ashamed.** God's deliverance from the Assyrian army was a preview of a future day when God's people will no longer be dominated by either foreign oppression or their own sin.
30:1 alliances. King Hezekiah's advisors wanted to join Egypt to fight against the Assyrians, though Egypt was then a weak player on the Near East scene.

2 For without consulting me,
you have gone down to Egypt for help.
You have put your trust in Pharaoh's protection.
You have tried to hide in his shade.
3 But by trusting Pharaoh, you will be humiliated,
and by depending on him, you will be disgraced.
4 For though his power extends to Zoan
and his officials have arrived in Hanes,
5 all who trust in him will be ashamed.
He will not help you.
Instead, he will disgrace you."

6 This message came to me concerning the animals in the Negev:

The caravan moves slowly
across the terrible desert to Egypt—
donkeys weighed down with riches
and camels loaded with treasure—
all to pay for Egypt's protection.
They travel through the wilderness,
a place of lionesses and lions,
a place where vipers and poisonous snakes live.
All this, and Egypt will give you nothing in return.
7 Egypt's promises are worthless!
Therefore, I call her Rahab—
the Harmless Dragon.*

A WARNING FOR REBELLIOUS JUDAH

8 Now go and write down these words.
Write them in a book.
They will stand until the end of time
as a witness
9 that these people are stubborn rebels
who refuse to pay attention to the LORD's instructions.
10 They tell the seers,
"Stop seeing visions!"
They tell the prophets,
"Don't tell us what is right.
Tell us nice things.
Tell us lies.
11 Forget all this gloom.
Get off your narrow path.
Stop telling us about your
'Holy One of Israel.'"

12 This is the reply of the Holy One of Israel:

"Because you despise what I tell you
and trust instead in oppression and lies,
13 calamity will come upon you suddenly—
like a bulging wall that bursts and falls.
In an instant it will collapse
and come crashing down.
14 You will be smashed like a piece of pottery—
shattered so completely that
there won't be a piece big enough
to carry coals from a fireplace
or a little water from the well."

15 This is what the Sovereign LORD,
the Holy One of Israel, says:
"Only in returning to me
and resting in me will you be saved.
In quietness and confidence is your strength.
But you would have none of it.
16 You said, 'No, we will get our help from Egypt.
They will give us swift horses for riding into battle.'
But the only swiftness you are going to see
is the swiftness of your enemies chasing you!
17 One of them will chase a thousand of you.
Five of them will make all of you flee.
You will be left like a lonely flagpole on a hill
or a tattered banner on a distant mountaintop."

BLESSINGS FOR THE LORD'S PEOPLE

18 So the LORD must wait for you to come to him
so he can show you his love and compassion.
For the LORD is a faithful God.
Blessed are those who wait for his help.

19 O people of Zion, who live in Jerusalem,
you will weep no more.
He will be gracious if you ask for help.
He will surely respond to the sound of your cries.
20 Though the Lord gave you adversity for food
and suffering for drink,
he will still be with you to teach you.
You will see your teacher with your own eyes.
21 Your own ears will hear him.
Right behind you a voice will say,
"This is the way you should go,"
whether to the right or to the left.
22 Then you will destroy all your silver idols
and your precious gold images.
You will throw them out like filthy rags,
saying to them, "Good riddance!"

23 Then the LORD will bless you with rain at planting
time. There will be wonderful harvests and plenty of
pastureland for your livestock. 24 The oxen and don-
keys that till the ground will eat good grain, its chaff
blown away by the wind. 25 In that day, when your en-
emies are slaughtered and the towers fall, there will
be streams of water flowing down every mountain
and hill. 26 The moon will be as bright as the sun, and
the sun will be seven times brighter—like the light of
seven days in one! So it will be when the LORD begins
to heal his people and cure the wounds he gave them.

27 Look! The LORD is coming from far away,
burning with anger,
surrounded by thick, rising smoke.

30:7 Hebrew *Rahab who sits still.* Rahab is the name of a mythical sea monster that represents chaos in ancient literature. The name is used here as a poetic name for Egypt.

30:8 write down . . . Write them. Even though the people would not obey God's instructions, Isaiah was to write them down so the people could not say they had never heard them.

30:13 calamity . . . like a bulging wall. The simile meant that judgment would come suddenly and completely (see Jer. 19:11).

30:15 quietness and confidence. The peace and confidence available to people who trust totally in God's strength are part of the promise of the new life of faith.

30:18 the LORD must wait for you to come to him. Although God judges the unrepentant, His desire is for all men to be saved. He is waiting to show mercy, if Israel will repent.

30:26 heal his people . . . cure the wounds. God will restore and bless His people after purging and judging their sin. God will heal the people from their wickedness.

His lips are filled with fury;
his words consume like fire.
28 His hot breath pours out like a flood
up to the neck of his enemies.
He will sift out the proud nations for destruction.
He will bridle them and lead them away to ruin.

29 But the people of God will sing a song of joy,
like the songs at the holy festivals.
You will be filled with joy,
as when a flutist leads a group of pilgrims
to Jerusalem, the mountain of the LORD—
to the Rock of Israel.
30 And the LORD will make his majestic voice heard.
He will display the strength of his mighty arm.
It will descend with devouring flames,
with cloudbursts, thunderstorms, and huge hailstones.
31 At the LORD's command, the Assyrians will be shattered.
He will strike them down with his royal scepter.
32 And as the LORD strikes them with his rod of punishment,*
his people will celebrate with tambourines and harps.
Lifting his mighty arm, he will fight the Assyrians.
33 Topheth—the place of burning—
has long been ready for the Assyrian king;
the pyre is piled high with wood.
The breath of the LORD, like fire from a volcano,
will set it ablaze.

THE FUTILITY OF RELYING ON EGYPT

31 1 What sorrow awaits those who look to Egypt for help,
trusting their horses, chariots, and charioteers
and depending on the strength of human armies
instead of looking to the LORD,
the Holy One of Israel.
2 In his wisdom, the LORD will send great disaster;
he will not change his mind.
He will rise against the wicked
and against their helpers.
3 For these Egyptians are mere humans, not God!
Their horses are puny flesh, not mighty spirits!
When the LORD raises his fist against them,
those who help will stumble,
and those being helped will fall.
They will all fall down and die together.

4 But this is what the LORD has told me:

"When a strong young lion
stands growling over a sheep it has killed,
it is not frightened by the shouts and noise
of a whole crowd of shepherds.
In the same way, the LORD of Heaven's Armies
will come down and fight on Mount Zion.
5 The LORD of Heaven's Armies will hover over Jerusalem
and protect it like a bird protecting its nest.
He will defend and save the city;
he will pass over it and rescue it."

6 Though you are such wicked rebels, my people,
come and return to the LORD. 7 I know the glorious day
will come when each of you will throw away the gold
idols and silver images your sinful hands have made.

8 "The Assyrians will be destroyed,
but not by the swords of men.
The sword of God will strike them,
and they will panic and flee.
The strong young Assyrians
will be taken away as captives.
9 Even the strongest will quake with terror,
and princes will flee when they see your battle flags,"
says the LORD, whose fire burns in Zion,
whose flame blazes from Jerusalem.

ISRAEL'S ULTIMATE DELIVERANCE

32 1 Look, a righteous king is coming!
And honest princes will rule under him.
2 Each one will be like a shelter from the wind
and a refuge from the storm,
like streams of water in the desert
and the shadow of a great rock in a parched land.

3 Then everyone who has eyes will be able to see the truth,
and everyone who has ears will be able to hear it.
4 Even the hotheads will be full of sense and understanding.
Those who stammer will speak out plainly.
5 In that day ungodly fools will not be heroes.
Scoundrels will not be respected.
6 For fools speak foolishness
and make evil plans.
They practice ungodliness
and spread false teachings about the LORD.
They deprive the hungry of food
and give no water to the thirsty.
7 The smooth tricks of scoundrels are evil.
They plot crooked schemes.
They lie to convict the poor,
even when the cause of the poor is just.
8 But generous people plan to do what is generous,
and they stand firm in their generosity.

9 Listen, you women who lie around in ease.
Listen to me, you who are so smug.

30:32 As in some Hebrew manuscripts and Syriac version; Masoretic Text reads *with the founded rod.*

31:4 lion. God was not intimidated by the Assyrians, just as a lion is not afraid of shepherds (see Hos. 11:10).
31:5 like a bird . . . will defend . . . the city. A picture of God's protection of Jerusalem against the enemy.
31:9 battle flags. A banner serving as the rallying point for battle. The Assyrian commanders would be terrified when they saw Judah's banner and the slaughter of their soldiers by God's angel.
32:1 a righteous king. The Messiah will reign in righteousness when God's justice is finally won over all the earth (see Jer. 23:5).
32:5 fools. A senseless person who teaches falsehood and gives no thought to the needs of others. **Scoundrels.** A person who plots to take advantage of the poor and needy (see Prov. 24:7-9).
32:8 generous people . . . what is generous . . . generosity. The righteous king will be generous. Literally, the word is "noble," which has the connotation of generous in Hebrew. Isaiah didn't live to see this ideal king.
32:9 women. A warning to the women of Judah who thought that judgment would not come (3:16-23). **in ease . . . so smug.** The wicked relied on Egypt for security, while the righteous trusted in the Lord.

10 In a short time—just a little more than a year—
you careless ones will suddenly begin to care.
For your fruit crops will fail,
and the harvest will never take place.
11 Tremble, you women of ease;
throw off your complacency.
Strip off your pretty clothes,
and put on burlap to show your grief.
12 Beat your breasts in sorrow for your bountiful farms
and your fruitful grapevines.
13 For your land will be overgrown with thorns and briers.
Your joyful homes and happy towns will be gone.
14 The palace and the city will be deserted,
and busy towns will be empty.
Wild donkeys will frolic and flocks will graze
in the empty forts* and watchtowers
15 until at last the Spirit is poured out
on us from heaven.
Then the wilderness will become a fertile field,
and the fertile field will yield bountiful crops.

16 Justice will rule in the wilderness
and righteousness in the fertile field.
17 And this righteousness will bring peace.
Yes, it will bring quietness and confidence forever.
18 My people will live in safety, quietly at home.
They will be at rest.
19 Even if the forest should be destroyed
and the city torn down,
20 the LORD will greatly bless his people.
Wherever they plant seed, bountiful crops will spring up.
Their cattle and donkeys will graze freely.

A MESSAGE ABOUT ASSYRIA

33 1 What sorrow awaits you Assyrians, who have destroyed others*
but have never been destroyed yourselves.
You betray others,
but you have never been betrayed.
When you are done destroying,
you will be destroyed.
When you are done betraying,
you will be betrayed.
2 But LORD, be merciful to us,
for we have waited for you.
Be our strong arm each day
and our salvation in times of trouble.
3 The enemy runs at the sound of your voice.
When you stand up, the nations flee!
4 Just as caterpillars and locusts strip the fields and vines,
so the fallen army of Assyria will be stripped!

5 Though the LORD is very great and lives in heaven,
he will make Jerusalem* his home of justice and righteousness.
6 In that day he will be your sure foundation,
providing a rich store of salvation, wisdom, and knowledge.
The fear of the LORD will be your treasure.

7 But now your brave warriors weep in public.
Your ambassadors of peace cry in bitter disappointment.
8 Your roads are deserted;
no one travels them anymore.
The Assyrians have broken their peace treaty
and care nothing for the promises they made before witnesses.*
They have no respect for anyone.
9 The land of Israel wilts in mourning.
Lebanon withers with shame.
The plain of Sharon is now a wilderness.
Bashan and Carmel have been plundered.

10 But the LORD says: "Now I will stand up.
Now I will show my power and might.
11 You Assyrians produce nothing but dry grass and stubble.
Your own breath will turn to fire and consume you.
12 Your people will be burned up completely,
like thornbushes cut down and tossed in a fire.
13 Listen to what I have done, you nations far away!
And you that are near, acknowledge my might!"

14 The sinners in Jerusalem shake with fear.
Terror seizes the godless.
"Who can live with this devouring fire?"
they cry.
"Who can survive this all-consuming fire?"
15 Those who are honest and fair,
who refuse to profit by fraud,
who stay far away from bribes,
who refuse to listen to those who plot murder,
who shut their eyes to all enticement to do wrong—
16 these are the ones who will dwell on high.
The rocks of the mountains will be their fortress.
Food will be supplied to them,
and they will have water in abundance.

17 Your eyes will see the king in all his splendor,
and you will see a land that stretches into the distance.
18 You will think back to this time of terror, asking,
"Where are the Assyrian officers
who counted our towers?
Where are the bookkeepers
who recorded the plunder taken from our fallen city?"
19 You will no longer see these fierce, violent people
with their strange, unknown language.

32:14 Hebrew *the Ophel.* **33:1** Hebrew *What sorrow awaits you, O destroyer.* The Hebrew text does not specifically name Assyria as the object of the prophecy in this chapter. **33:5** Hebrew *Zion;* also in 33:14. **33:8** As in Dead Sea Scrolls; Masoretic Text reads *care nothing for the cities.*

32:15 until . . . the Spirit. The outpouring of God's Spirit will bring fertility, justice, productivity, and security, as promised in the Deuteronomic covenant. But the people must obey God (see Deut. 5:2-3; 29:9; Joel 2:28).

33:2 our strong arm . . . our salvation. Isaiah and the believing remnant longed for God's deliverance and defeat of their opponents. God has shown His power by defeating their opponents many times before.

33:16 on high . . . their fortress. God will make Jerusalem into a fortress, protected not by walls but by His power.

20 Instead, you will see Zion as a place of holy
festivals.
You will see Jerusalem, a city quiet and secure.
It will be like a tent whose ropes are taut
and whose stakes are firmly fixed.
21 The LORD will be our Mighty One.
He will be like a wide river of protection
that no enemy can cross,
that no enemy ship can sail upon.
22 For the LORD is our judge,
our lawgiver, and our king.
He will care for us and save us.
23 The enemies' sails hang loose
on broken masts with useless tackle.
Their treasure will be divided by the people of God.
Even the lame will take their share!
24 The people of Israel will no longer say,
"We are sick and helpless,"
for the LORD will forgive their sins.

A MESSAGE FOR THE NATIONS

34 1 Come here and listen, O nations of the earth.
Let the world and everything in it hear my
words.
2 For the LORD is enraged against the nations.
His fury is against all their armies.
He will completely destroy* them,
dooming them to slaughter.
3 Their dead will be left unburied,
and the stench of rotting bodies will fill the land.
The mountains will flow with their blood.
4 The heavens above will melt away
and disappear like a rolled-up scroll.
The stars will fall from the sky
like withered leaves from a grapevine,
or shriveled figs from a fig tree.

5 And when my sword has finished its work in the
heavens,
it will fall upon Edom,
the nation I have marked for destruction.
6 The sword of the LORD is drenched with blood
and covered with fat—
with the blood of lambs and goats,
with the fat of rams prepared for sacrifice.
Yes, the LORD will offer a sacrifice in the city of
Bozrah.
He will make a mighty slaughter in Edom.
7 Even men as strong as wild oxen will die—
the young men alongside the veterans.
The land will be soaked with blood
and the soil enriched with fat.

8 For it is the day of the LORD's revenge,
the year when Edom will be paid back for all it
did to Israel.*
9 The streams of Edom will be filled with burning
pitch,
and the ground will be covered with fire.
10 This judgment on Edom will never end;
the smoke of its burning will rise forever.
The land will lie deserted from generation to
generation.
No one will live there anymore.
11 It will be haunted by the desert owl and the
screech owl,
the great owl and the raven.*
For God will measure that land carefully;
he will measure it for chaos and destruction.
12 It will be called the Land of Nothing,
and all its nobles will soon be gone.*
13 Thorns will overrun its palaces;
nettles and thistles will grow in its forts.
The ruins will become a haunt for jackals
and a home for owls.
14 Desert animals will mingle there with hyenas,
their howls filling the night.
Wild goats will bleat at one another among the
ruins,
and night creatures* will come there to rest.
15 There the owl will make her nest and lay her eggs.
She will hatch her young and cover them with
her wings.
And the buzzards will come,
each one with its mate.

16 Search the book of the LORD,
and see what he will do.
Not one of these birds and animals will be missing,
and none will lack a mate,
for the LORD has promised this.
His Spirit will make it all come true.
17 He has surveyed and divided the land
and deeded it over to those creatures.
They will possess it forever,
from generation to generation.

HOPE FOR RESTORATION

35 1 Even the wilderness and desert will be glad
in those days.
The wasteland will rejoice and blossom with
spring crocuses.
2 Yes, there will be an abundance of flowers
and singing and joy!
The deserts will become as green as the mountains
of Lebanon,
as lovely as Mount Carmel or the plain of
Sharon.
There the LORD will display his glory,
the splendor of our God.
3 With this news, strengthen those who have tired
hands,

34:2 The Hebrew term used here refers to the complete consecration of things or people to the LORD, either by destroying them or by giving them as an offering; similarly in 34:5. **34:8** Hebrew *to Zion.* **34:11** The identification of some of these birds is uncertain. **34:12** The meaning of the Hebrew is uncertain. **34:14** Hebrew *Lilith,* possibly a reference to a mythical demon of the night.

33:24 will forgive their sins. Both sickness and sin will be removed in the coming kingdom (see Jer. 31:34). The Messiah will be judge, lawgiver, and king.

34:2 is enraged . . . fury. God responds to sin by destroying it (13:5). Even the stars will be dissolved in His final judgment.

34:7 wild oxen. May symbolize Edom's soldiers or leaders who will attack Israel. God will destroy them at Bozrah, about 25 miles southeast of the Dead Sea.

34:9 pitch . . . fire. Pitch is a tar like substance that seems to burn forever. Fire burns with great heat and intensity. This may refer to the destruction of Sodom and Gomorrah.

34:16 Search the book. This book of the Lord may refer to the prophecy in verses 1-15 where God will judge all nations hostile to Israel (Mal. 3:16).

35:3 strengthen those who have tired hands. Isaiah encouraged the believing remnant to live by God's instructions and to encourage the faint-hearted and weak (see Josh. 1:6; Heb. 12:12).

and encourage those who have weak knees.
4 Say to those with fearful hearts,
"Be strong, and do not fear,
for your God is coming to destroy your enemies.
He is coming to save you."

5 And when he comes, he will open the eyes of the blind
and unplug the ears of the deaf.
6 The lame will leap like a deer,
and those who cannot speak will sing for joy!
Springs will gush forth in the wilderness,
and streams will water the wasteland.
7 The parched ground will become a pool,
and springs of water will satisfy the thirsty land.
Marsh grass and reeds and rushes will flourish
where desert jackals once lived.

8 And a great road will go through that once deserted land.
It will be named the Highway of Holiness.
Evil-minded people will never travel on it.
It will be only for those who walk in God's ways;
fools will never walk there.
9 Lions will not lurk along its course,
nor any other ferocious beasts.
There will be no other dangers.
Only the redeemed will walk on it.
10 Those who have been ransomed by the LORD will return.
They will enter Jerusalem* singing,
crowned with everlasting joy.
Sorrow and mourning will disappear,
and they will be filled with joy and gladness.

ASSYRIA INVADES JUDAH

36 In the fourteenth year of King Hezekiah's
reign,* King Sennacherib of Assyria came to
attack the fortified towns of Judah and conquered
them. 2 Then the king of Assyria sent his chief of staff*
from Lachish with a huge army to confront King Hez-
ekiah in Jerusalem. The Assyrians took up a position
beside the aqueduct that feeds water into the upper
pool, near the road leading to the field where cloth
is washed.*
3 These are the officials who went out to meet with
them: Eliakim son of Hilkiah, the palace adminis-
trator; Shebna the court secretary; and Joah son of
Asaph, the royal historian.

SENNACHERIB THREATENS JERUSALEM

4 Then the Assyrian king's chief of staff told them to
give this message to Hezekiah:
"This is what the great king of Assyria says: What
are you trusting in that makes you so confident?
5 Do you think* that mere words can substitute for
military skill and strength? Who are you counting
on, that you have rebelled against me? 6 On Egypt?
If you lean on Egypt, it will be like a reed that
splinters beneath your weight and pierces your
hand. Pharaoh, the king of Egypt, is completely
unreliable!
7 "But perhaps you will say to me, 'We are trust-
ing in the LORD our God!' But isn't he the one who
was insulted by Hezekiah? Didn't Hezekiah tear
down his shrines and altars and make everyone
in Judah and Jerusalem worship only at the altar
here in Jerusalem?
8 "I'll tell you what! Strike a bargain with my
master, the king of Assyria. I will give you 2,000
horses if you can find that many men to ride on
them! 9 With your tiny army, how can you think
of challenging even the weakest contingent of
my master's troops, even with the help of Egypt's
chariots and charioteers? 10 What's more, do you
think we have invaded your land without the
LORD's direction? The LORD himself told us, 'Attack
this land and destroy it!'"
11 Then Eliakim, Shebna, and Joah said to the Assyr-
ian chief of staff, "Please speak to us in Aramaic, for
we understand it well. Don't speak in Hebrew,* for the
people on the wall will hear."
12 But Sennacherib's chief of staff replied, "Do you
think my master sent this message only to you and
your master? He wants all the people to hear it, for
when we put this city under siege, they will suffer
along with you. They will be so hungry and thirsty
that they will eat their own dung and drink their own
urine."
13 Then the chief of staff stood and shouted in He-
brew to the people on the wall, "Listen to this message
from the great king of Assyria! 14 This is what the king
says: Don't let Hezekiah deceive you. He will never be
able to rescue you. 15 Don't let him fool you into trust-
ing in the LORD by saying, 'The LORD will surely rescue
us. This city will never fall into the hands of the As-
syrian king!'
16 "Don't listen to Hezekiah! These are the terms
the king of Assyria is offering: Make peace with
me—open the gates and come out. Then each of you
can continue eating from your own grapevine and
fig tree and drinking from your own well. 17 Then
I will arrange to take you to another land like this
one—a land of grain and new wine, bread and vine-
yards.

35:10 Hebrew *Zion.* **36:1** The fourteenth year of Hezekiah's reign was 701 B.C. **36:2a** Or *the rabshakeh;* also in 36:4, 11, 12, 22. **36:2b** Or *bleached.* **36:5** As in Dead Sea Scrolls (see also 2 Kgs 18:20); Masoretic Text reads *Do I think.* **36:11** Hebrew *in the dialect of Judah;* also in 36:13.

35:5 open the eyes . . . unplug the ears. The Messiah will heal the people and the land. Jesus accomplished both spiritual and physical healing during His life on earth. He alluded to this verse when answering John the Baptist (see Matt. 11:5).

35:8 road . . . named the Highway of Holiness. This highway will lead to God's city, Jerusalem, where His ways will be followed (Joel 3:17). Only the righteous will travel on this road.

36:4 king of Assyria. Sennacherib and his proud army believed themselves invincible. They believed they were gods. The field commander did not even acknowledge Hezekiah as king in this message.

36:7 shrines and altars. Shrines, or high places, were the locations of pagan worship. The Assyrian commander knew that Hezekiah had removed many pagan sites that his father Ahaz had built in Judah (2 Chron. 31:1-3). The commander may have thought Hezekiah had stopped trusting in any god altogether.

36:10 The LORD . . . told us, "Attack this land." Ancient conquerors often claimed that the gods of their defeated enemies had joined their side (2 Chron. 35:21). The commander used this tactic to intimidate the Israelites.

36:11 Don't speak in Hebrew. The negotiators thought panic might spread if the people heard the Assyrian demands in Hebrew. The confident commander went ahead and spoke in Hebrew anyway.

36:12 eat their own dung. The commander predicted that the Assyrian siege would cause famine in Judah. Famine would cause people to do horrific things.

18 "Don't let Hezekiah mislead you by saying, 'The LORD will rescue us!' Have the gods of any other nations ever saved their people from the king of Assyria? 19 What happened to the gods of Hamath and Arpad? And what about the gods of Sepharvaim? Did any god rescue Samaria from my power? 20 What god of any nation has ever been able to save its people from my power? So what makes you think that the LORD can rescue Jerusalem from me?"

21 But the people were silent and did not utter a word because Hezekiah had commanded them, "Do not answer him."

22 Then Eliakim son of Hilkiah, the palace administrator; Shebna the court secretary; and Joah son of Asaph, the royal historian, went back to Hezekiah. They tore their clothes in despair, and they went in to see the king and told him what the Assyrian chief of staff had said.

HEZEKIAH SEEKS THE LORD'S HELP

37 When King Hezekiah heard their report, he tore his clothes and put on burlap and went into the Temple of the LORD. 2 And he sent Eliakim the palace administrator, Shebna the court secretary, and the leading priests, all dressed in burlap, to the prophet Isaiah son of Amoz. 3 They told him, "This is what King Hezekiah says: Today is a day of trouble, insults, and disgrace. It is like when a child is ready to be born, but the mother has no strength to deliver the baby. 4 But perhaps the LORD your God has heard the Assyrian chief of staff,* sent by the king to defy the living God, and will punish him for his words. Oh, pray for those of us who are left!"

5 After King Hezekiah's officials delivered the king's message to Isaiah, 6 the prophet replied, "Say to your master, 'This is what the LORD says: Do not be disturbed by this blasphemous speech against me from the Assyrian king's messengers. 7 Listen! I myself will move against him,* and the king will receive a message that he is needed at home. So he will return to his land, where I will have him killed with a sword.'"

8 Meanwhile, the Assyrian chief of staff left Jerusalem and went to consult the king of Assyria, who had left Lachish and was attacking Libnah.

9 Soon afterward King Sennacherib received word that King Tirhakah of Ethiopia* was leading an army to fight against him. Before leaving to meet the attack, he sent messengers back to Hezekiah in Jerusalem with this message:

10 "This message is for King Hezekiah of Judah. Don't let your God, in whom you trust, deceive you with promises that Jerusalem will not be captured by the king of Assyria. 11 You know perfectly well what the kings of Assyria have done wherever they have gone. They have completely destroyed everyone who stood in their way! Why should you be any different? 12 Have the gods of other nations rescued them—such nations as Gozan, Haran, Rezeph, and the people of Eden who were in Tel-assar? My predecessors destroyed them all! 13 What happened to the king of Hamath and the king of Arpad? What happened to the kings of Sepharvaim, Hena, and Ivvah?"

14 After Hezekiah received the letter from the messengers and read it, he went up to the LORD's Temple and spread it out before the LORD. 15 And Hezekiah prayed this prayer before the LORD: 16 "O LORD of Heaven's Armies, God of Israel, you are enthroned between the mighty cherubim! You alone are God of all the kingdoms of the earth. You alone created the heavens and the earth. 17 Bend down, O LORD, and listen! Open your eyes, O LORD, and see! Listen to Sennacherib's words of defiance against the living God.

18 "It is true, LORD, that the kings of Assyria have destroyed all these nations. 19 And they have thrown the gods of these nations into the fire and burned them. But of course the Assyrians could destroy them! They were not gods at all—only idols of wood and stone shaped by human hands. 20 Now, O LORD our God, rescue us from his power; then all the kingdoms of the earth will know that you alone, O LORD, are God.*"

ISAIAH PREDICTS JUDAH'S DELIVERANCE

21 Then Isaiah son of Amoz sent this message to Hezekiah: "This is what the LORD, the God of Israel, says: Because you prayed about King Sennacherib of Assyria, 22 the LORD has spoken this word against him:

"The virgin daughter of Zion
despises you and laughs at you.
The daughter of Jerusalem
shakes her head in derision as you flee.

23 "Whom have you been defying and ridiculing?
Against whom did you raise your voice?
At whom did you look with such haughty eyes?
It was the Holy One of Israel!
24 By your messengers you have defied the Lord.
You have said, 'With my many chariots
I have conquered the highest mountains—
yes, the remotest peaks of Lebanon.
I have cut down its tallest cedars
and its finest cypress trees.
I have reached its farthest heights
and explored its deepest forests.
25 I have dug wells in many foreign lands*
and refreshed myself with their water.
With the sole of my foot,
I stopped up all the rivers of Egypt!'

26 "But have you not heard?
I decided this long ago.
Long ago I planned it,
and now I am making it happen.
I planned for you to crush fortified cities
into heaps of rubble.
27 That is why their people have so little power
and are so frightened and confused.

37:4 Or *the rabshakeh;* also in 37:8. 37:7 Hebrew *I will put a spirit in him.* 37:9 Hebrew *of Cush.* 37:20 As in Dead Sea Scrolls (see also 2 Kgs 19:19); Masoretic Text reads *you alone are the LORD.* 37:25 As in Dead Sea Scrolls (see also 2 Kgs 19:24); Masoretic Text lacks *in many foreign lands.* 37:27 As in Dead Sea Scrolls and some Greek manuscripts (see also 2 Kgs 19:26); most Hebrew manuscripts read *like a terraced field.*

36:18 Hezekiah mislead you. The commander tried to undermine the king of Judah by tempting the people with prosperity if they surrendered to Assyria. He reasoned that since the gods of other nations had not been able to protect them from Assyria, God could not protect His people either.

37:23 did you look. In response to Hezekiah's prayer, God said that the Assyrians would be defeated because of their blasphemy and pride.

They are as weak as grass,
as easily trampled as tender green shoots.
They are like grass sprouting on a housetop,
scorched* before it can grow lush and tall.

28 "But I know you well—
where you stay
and when you come and go.
I know the way you have raged against me.
29 And because of your raging against me
and your arrogance, which I have heard for myself,
I will put my hook in your nose
and my bit in your mouth.
I will make you return
by the same road on which you came."

30 Then Isaiah said to Hezekiah, "Here is the proof that
what I say is true:

"This year you will eat only what grows up by itself,
and next year you will eat what springs up from that.
But in the third year you will plant crops and harvest them;
you will tend vineyards and eat their fruit.
31 And you who are left in Judah,
who have escaped the ravages of the siege,
will put roots down in your own soil
and grow up and flourish.
32 For a remnant of my people will spread out from Jerusalem,
a group of survivors from Mount Zion.
The passionate commitment of the LORD of Heaven's Armies
will make this happen!

33 "And this is what the LORD says about the king of
Assyria:

"'His armies will not enter Jerusalem.
They will not even shoot an arrow at it.
They will not march outside its gates with their shields
nor build banks of earth against its walls.
34 The king will return to his own country
by the same road on which he came.
He will not enter this city,'
says the LORD.
35 'For my own honor and for the sake of my servant David,
I will defend this city and protect it.'"

36 That night the angel of the LORD went out to the
Assyrian camp and killed 185,000 Assyrian soldiers.
When the surviving Assyrians* woke up the next
morning, they found corpses everywhere. 37 Then
King Sennacherib of Assyria broke camp and re-
turned to his own land. He went home to his capital
of Nineveh and stayed there.

38 One day while he was worshiping in the temple
of his god Nisroch, his sons Adrammelech and Share-
zer killed him with their swords. They then escaped
to the land of Ararat, and another son, Esarhaddon,
became the next king of Assyria.

HEZEKIAH'S SICKNESS AND RECOVERY

38 About that time Hezekiah became deathly ill,
and the prophet Isaiah son of Amoz went to
visit him. He gave the king this message: "This is what
the LORD says: 'Set your affairs in order, for you are
going to die. You will not recover from this illness.'"
2 When Hezekiah heard this, he turned his face
to the wall and prayed to the LORD, 3 "Remember,
O LORD, how I have always been faithful to you and
have served you single-mindedly, always doing what
pleases you." Then he broke down and wept bitterly.
4 Then this message came to Isaiah from the LORD:
5 "Go back to Hezekiah and tell him, 'This is what the
LORD, the God of your ancestor David, says: I have
heard your prayer and seen your tears. I will add fif-
teen years to your life, 6 and I will rescue you and this
city from the king of Assyria. Yes, I will defend this city.
7 "'And this is the sign from the LORD to prove that
he will do as he promised: 8 I will cause the sun's
shadow to move ten steps backward on the sundial*
of Ahaz!'" So the shadow on the sundial moved back-
ward ten steps.

HEZEKIAH'S POEM OF PRAISE

9 When King Hezekiah was well again, he wrote this
poem:

10 I said, "In the prime of my life,
must I now enter the place of the dead?*
Am I to be robbed of the rest of my years?"
11 I said, "Never again will I see the LORD GOD
while still in the land of the living.
Never again will I see my friends
or be with those who live in this world.
12 My life has been blown away
like a shepherd's tent in a storm.
It has been cut short,
as when a weaver cuts cloth from a loom.
Suddenly, my life was over.
13 I waited patiently all night,
but I was torn apart as though by lions.
Suddenly, my life was over.
14 Delirious, I chattered like a swallow or a crane,
and then I moaned like a mourning dove.
My eyes grew tired of looking to heaven for help.
I am in trouble, Lord. Help me!"

15 But what could I say?
For he himself sent this sickness.
Now I will walk humbly throughout my years
because of this anguish I have felt.
16 Lord, your discipline is good,
for it leads to life and health.
You restore my health

37:36 Hebrew *When they.* 38:8 Hebrew *the steps.* 38:10 Hebrew *enter the gates of Sheol?*

37:30 next year . . . third year. Any part of a year was counted as a year, so the third year could have been 13 to 15 months from that time. The third year is the normal time it takes for a vineyard to begin producing grapes.

37:38 worshiping in the temple. God slaughtered the Assyrians overnight, as Isaiah had predicted. Sennacherib was assassinated twenty years later in 681 B.C. by two of his sons.

38:3 been faithful . . . served you singlemindedly. He asked God to remember the good things he had done.

and allow me to live!
17 Yes, this anguish was good for me,
for you have rescued me from death
and forgiven all my sins.
18 For the dead* cannot praise you;
they cannot raise their voices in praise.
Those who go down to the grave
can no longer hope in your faithfulness.
19 Only the living can praise you as I do today.
Each generation tells of your faithfulness to the next.
20 Think of it—the LORD is ready to heal me!
I will sing his praises with instruments
every day of my life
in the Temple of the LORD.

21 Isaiah had said to Hezekiah's servants, "Make an
ointment from figs and spread it over the boil, and
Hezekiah will recover."
22 And Hezekiah had asked, "What sign will prove
that I will go to the Temple of the LORD?"

ENVOYS FROM BABYLON

39 Soon after this, Merodach-baladan son of Baladan, king of Babylon, sent Hezekiah his best wishes and a gift. He had heard that Hezekiah had been very sick and that he had recovered.
2 Hezekiah was delighted with the Babylonian envoys and showed them everything in his treasure-houses—the silver, the gold, the spices, and the aromatic oils. He also took them to see his armory and showed them everything in his royal treasuries! There was nothing in his palace or kingdom that Hezekiah did not show them.
3 Then Isaiah the prophet went to King Hezekiah and asked him, "What did those men want? Where were they from?"

Hezekiah replied, "They came from the distant land of Babylon."
4 "What did they see in your palace?" asked Isaiah.

"They saw everything," Hezekiah replied. "I showed them everything I own—all my royal treasuries."
5 Then Isaiah said to Hezekiah, "Listen to this message from the LORD of Heaven's Armies:
6 'The time is coming when everything in your palace—all the treasures stored up by your ancestors until now—will be carried off to Babylon. Nothing will be left,' says the LORD.
7 'Some of your very own sons will be taken away into exile. They will become eunuchs who will serve in the palace of Babylon's king.'"
8 Then Hezekiah said to Isaiah, "This message you have given me from the LORD is good." For the king was thinking, "At least there will be peace and security during my lifetime."

COMFORT FOR GOD'S PEOPLE

40 1 "Comfort, comfort my people,"
says your God.
2 "Speak tenderly to Jerusalem.
Tell her that her sad days are gone
and her sins are pardoned.
Yes, the LORD has punished her twice over
for all her sins."

3 Listen! It's the voice of someone shouting,
"Clear the way through the wilderness
for the LORD!
Make a straight highway through the wasteland
for our God!
4 Fill in the valleys,
and level the mountains and hills.
Straighten the curves,
and smooth out the rough places.
5 Then the glory of the LORD will be revealed,
and all people will see it together.
The LORD has spoken!"*

6 A voice said, "Shout!"
I asked, "What should I shout?"

"Shout that people are like the grass.
Their beauty fades as quickly
as the flowers in a field.
7 The grass withers and the flowers fade
beneath the breath of the LORD.
And so it is with people.
8 The grass withers and the flowers fade,
but the word of our God stands forever."

9 O Zion, messenger of good news,
shout from the mountaintops!
Shout it louder, O Jerusalem.*
Shout, and do not be afraid.
Tell the towns of Judah,
"Your God is coming!"
10 Yes, the Sovereign LORD is coming in power.
He will rule with a powerful arm.
See, he brings his reward with him as he comes.
11 He will feed his flock like a shepherd.
He will carry the lambs in his arms,
holding them close to his heart.
He will gently lead the mother sheep with their young.

THE LORD HAS NO EQUAL

12 Who else has held the oceans in his hand?
Who has measured off the heavens with his fingers?

38:18 Hebrew *Sheol.* **40:3-5** Greek version reads *He is a voice shouting in the wilderness, / "Prepare the way for the LORD's coming! / Clear a road for our God! / Fill in the valleys, / and level the mountains and hills. / And then the glory of the LORD will be revealed, / and all people will see the salvation sent from God. / The LORD has spoken!"* Compare Matt 3:3; Mark 1:3; Luke 3:4-6. **40:9** Or *O messenger of good news, shout to Zion from the mountaintops! Shout it louder to Jerusalem.*

38:17 forgiven all my sins. Apparently Hezekiah's illness was connected to his sin. Not all sickness is the result of a personal sin (see John 9:2-3).
38:21 Make an oinment from figs. God used medical procedures of that day to heal Hezekiah.
39:2 treasure-houses. Hezekiah proudly showed his riches, perhaps because he was trusting in his wealth and the foreign armies he could hire.
39:6 carried off to Babylon. Since the enemy at the time was Assyria, this prediction was surprising (Jer. 20:4). Babylon hardly seemed a threat.
40:1 Comfort, comfort my people. The last part of Isaiah (chapters 40–66) is even more Messianic and future-oriented than the first. Many of the promises were for those who would return from exile about 200 years after Isaiah's lifetime. Many of the prophecies are still to come in the millennial reign of Christ.
40:2 Jerusalem. That is, the exiles who would return there. **twice over for all her sins.** God had punished Israel enough in the exile and was ready to restore her.
40:3 voice of someone shouting. Each Gospel writer applied this verse to John the Baptist who prepared the way for Jesus Christ (see Matt. 3:1-4; Mark 1:1-4; Luke 1:76-78; John 1:23). **a straight highway.** The image is of a highway through the desert, leading people straight back from Assyria and Babylon to Israel.
40:5 the glory of the LORD. When God restores Israel, the world will see His glory.

Who else knows the weight of the earth
or has weighed the mountains and hills on a scale?
13 Who is able to advise the Spirit of the LORD?*
Who knows enough to give him advice or teach him?
14 Has the LORD ever needed anyone's advice?
Does he need instruction about what is good?
Did someone teach him what is right
or show him the path of justice?

15 No, for all the nations of the world
are but a drop in the bucket.
They are nothing more
than dust on the scales.
He picks up the whole earth
as though it were a grain of sand.
16 All the wood in Lebanon's forests
and all Lebanon's animals would not be enough
to make a burnt offering worthy of our God.
17 The nations of the world are worth nothing to him.
In his eyes they count for less than nothing—
mere emptiness and froth.

18 To whom can you compare God?
What image can you find to resemble him?
19 Can he be compared to an idol formed in a mold,
overlaid with gold, and decorated with silver chains?
20 Or if people are too poor for that,
they might at least choose wood that won't decay
and a skilled craftsman
to carve an image that won't fall down!

21 Haven't you heard? Don't you understand?
Are you deaf to the words of God—
the words he gave before the world began?
Are you so ignorant?
22 God sits above the circle of the earth.
The people below seem like grasshoppers to him!
He spreads out the heavens like a curtain
and makes his tent from them.
23 He judges the great people of the world
and brings them all to nothing.
24 They hardly get started, barely taking root,
when he blows on them and they wither.
The wind carries them off like chaff.

25 "To whom will you compare me?
Who is my equal?" asks the Holy One.

26 Look up into the heavens.
Who created all the stars?
He brings them out like an army, one after another,
calling each by its name.
Because of his great power and incomparable strength,
not a single one is missing.
27 O Jacob, how can you say the LORD does not see your troubles?
O Israel, how can you say God ignores your rights?
28 Have you never heard?
Have you never understood?
The LORD is the everlasting God,
the Creator of all the earth.
He never grows weak or weary.
No one can measure the depths of his understanding.
29 He gives power to the weak
and strength to the powerless.
30 Even youths will become weak and tired,
and young men will fall in exhaustion.
31 But those who trust in the LORD will find new strength.
They will soar high on wings like eagles.
They will run and not grow weary.
They will walk and not faint.

THE SOURCE OF ALL STRENGTH

1. Who is the strongest person you know? The smartest?

ISAIAH 40:25-31

2. What does it mean in verse 26 that God "brings them [the stars] out like an army"? Then "calling each by its name"? That "not a single one is missing"?
3. When have you felt like, "the Lord does not see your troubles" and "you say God ignores your rights" (v. 27)?
4. Are you feeling powerless right now? How can God strengthen you for an event or performance ahead?
5. Do you feel that God is ignoring you? How can He show you His great understanding?

GOD'S HELP FOR ISRAEL

41 1 "Listen in silence before me, you lands beyond the sea.
Bring your strongest arguments.
Come now and speak.
The court is ready for your case.

2 "Who has stirred up this king from the east,
rightly calling him to God's service?
Who gives this man victory over many nations
and permits him to trample their kings underfoot?
With his sword, he reduces armies to dust.
With his bow, he scatters them like chaff before the wind.

40:13 Greek version reads *Who can know the LORD's thoughts?* Compare Rom 11:34; 1 Cor 2:16.

40:17 nothing. This word is translated "formless" in Genesis 1:2.
40:27 Jacob . . . Israel. That is, all 12 tribes. God's people should never think He does not see or remember them or fail to keep His promises.
40:31 trust in the LORD. Implies confident expectation rather than passive resignation (see Ps. 40:1). Faith brings spiritual transformation. Weary captives returning from the exile would be emotionally uplifted.
41:2 from the east. Cyrus, king of Persia from 559–530 B.C. **rightly calling.** Because of God's promise to Abraham, He brought the exiles back. Cyrus was to carry out God's righteous plan, fulfilling God's will, even if he was unaware of it.

3 He chases them away and goes on safely,
though he is walking over unfamiliar ground.
4 Who has done such mighty deeds,
summoning each new generation from the beginning of time?
It is I, the LORD, the First and the Last.
I alone am he."

5 The lands beyond the sea watch in fear.
Remote lands tremble and mobilize for war.
6 The idol makers encourage one another,
saying to each other, "Be strong!"
7 The carver encourages the goldsmith,
and the molder helps at the anvil.
"Good," they say. "It's coming along fine."
Carefully they join the parts together,
then fasten the thing in place so it won't fall over.

8 "But as for you, Israel my servant,
Jacob my chosen one,
descended from Abraham my friend,
9 I have called you back from the ends of the earth,
saying, 'You are my servant.'
For I have chosen you
and will not throw you away.
10 Don't be afraid, for I am with you.
Don't be discouraged, for I am your God.
I will strengthen you and help you.
I will hold you up with my victorious right hand.

11 "See, all your angry enemies lie there,
confused and humiliated.
Anyone who opposes you will die
and come to nothing.
12 You will look in vain
for those who tried to conquer you.
Those who attack you
will come to nothing.
13 For I hold you by your right hand—
I, the LORD your God.
And I say to you,
'Don't be afraid. I am here to help you.
14 Though you are a lowly worm, O Jacob,
don't be afraid, people of Israel, for I will help you.
I am the LORD, your Redeemer.
I am the Holy One of Israel.'
15 You will be a new threshing instrument
with many sharp teeth.
You will tear your enemies apart,
making chaff of mountains.
16 You will toss them into the air,
and the wind will blow them all away;
a whirlwind will scatter them.
Then you will rejoice in the LORD.
You will glory in the Holy One of Israel.

17 "When the poor and needy search for water and there is none,
and their tongues are parched from thirst,
then I, the LORD, will answer them.
I, the God of Israel, will never abandon them.
18 I will open up rivers for them on the high plateaus.
I will give them fountains of water in the valleys.
I will fill the desert with pools of water.
Rivers fed by springs will flow across the parched ground.
19 I will plant trees in the barren desert—
cedar, acacia, myrtle, olive, cypress, fir, and pine.
20 I am doing this so all who see this miracle
will understand what it means—
that it is the LORD who has done this,
the Holy One of Israel who created it.

21 "Present the case for your idols,"
says the LORD.
"Let them show what they can do,"
says the King of Israel.*
22 "Let them try to tell us what happened long ago
so that we may consider the evidence.
Or let them tell us what the future holds,
so we can know what's going to happen.
23 Yes, tell us what will occur in the days ahead.
Then we will know you are gods.
In fact, do anything—good or bad!
Do something that will amaze and frighten us.
24 But no! You are less than nothing and can do nothing at all.
Those who choose you pollute themselves.

25 "But I have stirred up a leader who will approach from the north.
From the east he will call on my name.
I will give him victory over kings and princes.
He will trample them as a potter treads on clay.

26 "Who told you from the beginning
that this would happen?
Who predicted this,
making you admit that he was right?
No one said a word!
27 I was the first to tell Zion,
'Look! Help is on the way!'*
I will send Jerusalem a messenger with good news.
28 Not one of your idols told you this.
Not one gave any answer when I asked.
29 See, they are all foolish, worthless things.
All your idols are as empty as the wind.

THE LORD'S CHOSEN SERVANT

42 1 "Look at my servant, whom I strengthen.
He is my chosen one, who pleases me.
I have put my Spirit upon him.
He will bring justice to the nations.

41:21 Hebrew *the King of Jacob*. See note on 14:1. 41:27 Or *'Look! They are coming home.'*

41:14 your Redeemer. Isaiah used this title for God 13 times. The redeemer was the family protector who helped distressed relatives, avenged murders, and reclaimed indentured slaves.

41:19 barren desert. In the millennial kingdom, the climate will be changed so that even the desert is fertile.

41:20 Holy One of Israel who created it. Only God can truly create.

41:25 a leader . . . from the north. This refers to King Cyrus of Persia whose territories were both to the north and east of Israel. **will call on my name.** Although Cyrus did not know God, he called on God's name (2 Chron. 36:23).

42:1 my servant . . . strengthen. Jesus Christ will bring universal justice and peace in the millennium. These verses are quoted in Matt. 12:15-21.

2 He will not shout
or raise his voice in public.
3 He will not crush the weakest reed
or put out a flickering candle.
He will bring justice to all who have been wronged.
4 He will not falter or lose heart
until justice prevails throughout the earth.
Even distant lands beyond the sea will wait for his instruction.*"

5 God, the LORD, created the heavens and stretched them out.
He created the earth and everything in it.
He gives breath to everyone,
life to everyone who walks the earth.
And it is he who says,
6 "I, the LORD, have called you to demonstrate my righteousness.
I will take you by the hand and guard you,
and I will give you to my people, Israel,
as a symbol of my covenant with them.
And you will be a light to guide the nations.
7 You will open the eyes of the blind.
You will free the captives from prison,
releasing those who sit in dark dungeons.

8 "I am the LORD; that is my name!
I will not give my glory to anyone else,
nor share my praise with carved idols.
9 Everything I prophesied has come true,
and now I will prophesy again.
I will tell you the future before it happens."

A SONG OF PRAISE TO THE LORD

10 Sing a new song to the LORD!
Sing his praises from the ends of the earth!
Sing, all you who sail the seas,
all you who live in distant coastlands.
11 Join in the chorus, you desert towns;
let the villages of Kedar rejoice!
Let the people of Sela sing for joy;
shout praises from the mountaintops!
12 Let the whole world glorify the LORD;
let it sing his praise.
13 The LORD will march forth like a mighty hero;
he will come out like a warrior, full of fury.
He will shout his battle cry
and crush all his enemies.

14 He will say, "I have long been silent;
yes, I have restrained myself.
But now, like a woman in labor,
I will cry and groan and pant.
15 I will level the mountains and hills
and blight all their greenery.
I will turn the rivers into dry land
and will dry up all the pools.
16 I will lead blind Israel down a new path,
guiding them along an unfamiliar way.
I will brighten the darkness before them
and smooth out the road ahead of them.
Yes, I will indeed do these things;
I will not forsake them.
17 But those who trust in idols,
who say, 'You are our gods,'
will be turned away in shame.

ISRAEL'S FAILURE TO LISTEN AND SEE

18 "Listen, you who are deaf!
Look and see, you blind!
19 Who is as blind as my own people, my servant?
Who is as deaf as my messenger?
Who is as blind as my chosen people,
the servant of the LORD?
20 You see and recognize what is right
but refuse to act on it.
You hear with your ears,
but you don't really listen."

21 Because he is righteous,
the LORD has exalted his glorious law.
22 But his own people have been robbed and plundered,
enslaved, imprisoned, and trapped.
They are fair game for anyone
and have no one to protect them,
no one to take them back home.

23 Who will hear these lessons from the past
and see the ruin that awaits you in the future?
24 Who allowed Israel to be robbed and hurt?
It was the LORD, against whom we sinned,
for the people would not walk in his path,
nor would they obey his law.
25 Therefore, he poured out his fury on them
and destroyed them in battle.
They were enveloped in flames,
but they still refused to understand.
They were consumed by fire,
but they did not learn their lesson.

THE SAVIOR OF ISRAEL

43 1 But now, O Jacob, listen to the LORD who created you.
O Israel, the one who formed you says,
"Do not be afraid, for I have ransomed you.
I have called you by name; you are mine.
2 When you go through deep waters,
I will be with you.
When you go through rivers of difficulty,
you will not drown.
When you walk through the fire of oppression,
you will not be burned up;
the flames will not consume you.

42:4 Greek version reads *And his name will be the hope of all the world.* Compare Matt 12:21.

42:3 weakest reed. The promise points to Christ who will be gentle to those who are hurting, poor, and needy. **flickering candle.** People who have nearly lost their faith in God. Jesus will restore their hope.
42:13 warrior. God will be a conquering warrior on behalf of His people, just as He was when He fought for them at the Red Sea (Ex. 15:3).
42:15 mountains and hills. Obstacles that could prevent Israel's return to Jerusalem. **blight.** Recalled the passage through the Red Sea on dry land (Ex. 14:16-29). God can cause land to become barren.
42:24 Who allowed Israel to be robbed? Since Israel was blind to her sin, God allowed her to be plundered and taken into captivity. The Messiah will open the people's eyes to their sin and to God's salvation.
42:25 poured out his anger. God's anger against sin would destroy Jerusalem with flames; God's people already had a taste of His wrath (2 Kings 25:9; Jer. 10:25).

3 For I am the LORD, your God,
the Holy One of Israel, your Savior.
I gave Egypt as a ransom for your freedom;
I gave Ethiopia* and Seba in your place.
4 Others were given in exchange for you.
I traded their lives for yours
because you are precious to me.
You are honored, and I love you.

5 "Do not be afraid, for I am with you.
I will gather you and your children from east and west.
6 I will say to the north and south,
'Bring my sons and daughters back to Israel
from the distant corners of the earth.
7 Bring all who claim me as their God,
for I have made them for my glory.
It was I who created them.'"

8 Bring out the people who have eyes but are blind,
who have ears but are deaf.
9 Gather the nations together!
Assemble the peoples of the world!
Which of their idols has ever foretold such things?
Which can predict what will happen tomorrow?
Where are the witnesses of such predictions?
Who can verify that they spoke the truth?

10 "But you are my witnesses, O Israel!" says the LORD.
"You are my servant.
You have been chosen to know me, believe in me,
and understand that I alone am God.
There is no other God—
there never has been, and there never will be.
11 I, yes I, am the LORD,
and there is no other Savior.
12 First I predicted your rescue,
then I saved you and proclaimed it to the world.
No foreign god has ever done this.
You are witnesses that I am the only God,"
says the LORD.
13 "From eternity to eternity I am God.
No one can snatch anyone out of my hand.
No one can undo what I have done."

THE LORD'S PROMISE OF VICTORY

14 This is what the LORD says—your Redeemer, the Holy One of Israel:

"For your sakes I will send an army against Babylon,
forcing the Babylonians* to flee in those ships
they are so proud of.
15 I am the LORD, your Holy One,
Israel's Creator and King.
16 I am the LORD, who opened a way through the waters,
making a dry path through the sea.
17 I called forth the mighty army of Egypt
with all its chariots and horses.
I drew them beneath the waves, and they drowned,
their lives snuffed out like a smoldering candlewick.

18 "But forget all that—
it is nothing compared to what I am going to do.
19 For I am about to do something new.
See, I have already begun! Do you not see it?
I will make a pathway through the wilderness.
I will create rivers in the dry wasteland.
20 The wild animals in the fields will thank me,
the jackals and owls, too,
for giving them water in the desert.
Yes, I will make rivers in the dry wasteland
so my chosen people can be refreshed.
21 I have made Israel for myself,
and they will someday honor me before the whole world.

22 "But, dear family of Jacob, you refuse to ask for my help.
You have grown tired of me, O Israel!
23 You have not brought me sheep or goats for burnt offerings.
You have not honored me with sacrifices,
though I have not burdened and wearied you
with requests for grain offerings and frankincense.
24 You have not brought me fragrant calamus
or pleased me with the fat from sacrifices.
Instead, you have burdened me with your sins
and wearied me with your faults.

25 "I—yes, I alone—will blot out your sins for my own sake
and will never think of them again.
26 Let us review the situation together,
and you can present your case to prove your innocence.
27 From the very beginning, your first ancestor
sinned against me;
all your leaders broke my laws.
28 That is why I have disgraced your priests;
I have decreed complete destruction* for Jacob
and shame for Israel.

44 1 "But now, listen to me, Jacob my servant,
Israel my chosen one.
2 The LORD who made you and helps you says:
Do not be afraid, O Jacob, my servant,
O dear Israel,* my chosen one.

43:3 Hebrew *Cush.* 43:14 Or *Chaldeans.* 43:28 The Hebrew term used here refers to the complete consecration of things or people to the LORD, either by destroying them or by giving them as an offering. 44:2 Hebrew *Jeshurun,* a term of endearment for Israel.

43:3 your Savior. The name Jesus is derived from the Hebrew word for Savior. Israel is precious because of God's love and protection, because God chose to favor this people. **Egypt . . . Ethiopia and Seba.** To reward Cyrus for releasing the Jewish captives, God allowed Persia to conquer these lands. Ethiopia here consisted of modern-day Sudan, southern Egypt, and northern Ethiopia. Seba may be Sheba in southern Arabia.

43:14 forcing the Babylonians to flee in those ships. God would turn the Babylonians into conquered people, rather than conquerors (see Jer. 51:1-44). The ships may have been trading vessels.

43:20 jackals and owls. Although Israel would travel through desolate areas on the way back to Jerusalem, God would provide refreshment even in the desert.

43:22 refuse to ask . . . grown tired. The people had worshiped God only half-heartedly without troubling themselves with the sacrificial system God required.

43:25 for my own sake. Through grace God loves people even though we do not deserve it.

44:1 Jacob My servant. Many times in Isaiah, "servant" refers to Israel. Other times it refers to the Messiah. There is a relationship: Jesus the Messiah fulfills Israel's calling, living as Israel was supposed to as God's servant.

3 For I will pour out water to quench your thirst
and to irrigate your parched fields.
And I will pour out my Spirit on your descendants,
and my blessing on your children.
4 They will thrive like watered grass,
like willows on a riverbank.
5 Some will proudly claim, 'I belong to the LORD.'
Others will say, 'I am a descendant of Jacob.'
Some will write the LORD's name on their hands
and will take the name of Israel as their own."

THE FOOLISHNESS OF IDOLS

6 This is what the LORD says—Israel's King and Redeemer, the LORD of Heaven's Armies:

"I am the First and the Last;
there is no other God.
7 Who is like me?
Let him step forward and prove to you his power.
Let him do as I have done since ancient times
when I established a people and explained its future.
8 Do not tremble; do not be afraid.
Did I not proclaim my purposes for you long ago?
You are my witnesses—is there any other God?
No! There is no other Rock—not one!"

9 How foolish are those who manufacture idols.
These prized objects are really worthless.
The people who worship idols don't know this,
so they are all put to shame.
10 Who but a fool would make his own god—
an idol that cannot help him one bit?
11 All who worship idols will be disgraced
along with all these craftsmen—mere humans—
who claim they can make a god.
They may all stand together,
but they will stand in terror and shame.

12 The blacksmith stands at his forge to make a sharp tool,
pounding and shaping it with all his might.
His work makes him hungry and weak.
It makes him thirsty and faint.
13 Then the wood-carver measures a block of wood
and draws a pattern on it.
He works with chisel and plane
and carves it into a human figure.
He gives it human beauty
and puts it in a little shrine.
14 He cuts down cedars;
he selects the cypress and the oak;
he plants the pine in the forest
to be nourished by the rain.
15 Then he uses part of the wood to make a fire.
With it he warms himself and bakes his bread.
Then—yes, it's true—he takes the rest of it
and makes himself a god to worship!
He makes an idol
and bows down in front of it!
16 He burns part of the tree to roast his meat
and to keep himself warm.
He says, "Ah, that fire feels good."
17 Then he takes what's left
and makes his god: a carved idol!
He falls down in front of it,
worshiping and praying to it.
"Rescue me!" he says.
"You are my god!"

18 Such stupidity and ignorance!
Their eyes are closed, and they cannot see.
Their minds are shut, and they cannot think.
19 The person who made the idol never stops to reflect,
"Why, it's just a block of wood!
I burned half of it for heat
and used it to bake my bread and roast my meat.
How can the rest of it be a god?
Should I bow down to worship a piece of wood?"
20 The poor, deluded fool feeds on ashes.
He trusts something that can't help him at all.
Yet he cannot bring himself to ask,
"Is this idol that I'm holding in my hand a lie?"

RESTORATION FOR JERUSALEM

21 "Pay attention, O Jacob,
for you are my servant, O Israel.
I, the LORD, made you,
and I will not forget you.
22 I have swept away your sins like a cloud.
I have scattered your offenses like the morning mist.
Oh, return to me,
for I have paid the price to set you free."

23 Sing, O heavens, for the LORD has done this wondrous thing.
Shout for joy, O depths of the earth!
Break into song,
O mountains and forests and every tree!
For the LORD has redeemed Jacob
and is glorified in Israel.

24 This is what the LORD says—
your Redeemer and Creator:
"I am the LORD, who made all things.
I alone stretched out the heavens.
Who was with me
when I made the earth?
25 I expose the false prophets as liars
and make fools of fortune-tellers.
I cause the wise to give bad advice,
thus proving them to be fools.
26 But I carry out the predictions of my prophets!
By them I say to Jerusalem, 'People will live here again,'
and to the towns of Judah, 'You will be rebuilt;
I will restore all your ruins!'

44:4 thrive like watered grass. A symbol of prosperity. When the Messiah comes, God will pour water on the land and pour His Holy Spirit on the people.
44:5 I belong to the LORD. Israel will want to be known as the Lord's obedient people. **write . . . on their hands.** Signified ownership.
44:6 First . . . Last. God is sovereign over time, and He is eternal.
44:9 foolish . . . worthless. This warning to future generations condemned idolatry and noted the foolishness of worshiping a stone or metal image.
44:17 makes his god. The idolater prayed to an inanimate object incapable of helping him. Anything that comes before God in a person's life is an idol.
44:22 swept away your sins like a cloud. God offers total forgiveness (40:2; 43:25). Israel's punishment made forgiveness and restoration possible. **paid the price.** God will buy back His people.

[27] When I speak to the rivers and say, 'Dry up!'
they will be dry.
[28] When I say of Cyrus, 'He is my shepherd,'
he will certainly do as I say.
He will command, 'Rebuild Jerusalem';
he will say, 'Restore the Temple.'"

CYRUS, THE LORD'S CHOSEN ONE

45 [1] This is what the LORD says to Cyrus, his anointed one,
whose right hand he will empower.
Before him, mighty kings will be paralyzed with fear.
Their fortress gates will be opened,
never to shut again.
[2] This is what the LORD says:

"I will go before you, Cyrus,
and level the mountains.*
I will smash down gates of bronze
and cut through bars of iron.
[3] And I will give you treasures hidden in the darkness—
secret riches.
I will do this so you may know that I am the LORD,
the God of Israel, the one who calls you by name.

[4] "And why have I called you for this work?
Why did I call you by name when you did not know me?
It is for the sake of Jacob my servant,
Israel my chosen one.
[5] I am the LORD;
there is no other God.
I have equipped you for battle,
though you don't even know me,
[6] so all the world from east to west
will know there is no other God.
I am the LORD, and there is no other.
[7] I create the light and make the darkness.
I send good times and bad times.
I, the LORD, am the one who does these things.

[8] "Open up, O heavens,
and pour out your righteousness.
Let the earth open wide
so salvation and righteousness can sprout up together.
I, the LORD, created them.

[9] "What sorrow awaits those who argue with their Creator.
Does a clay pot argue with its maker?
Does the clay dispute with the one who shapes it, saying,
'Stop, you're doing it wrong!'
Does the pot exclaim,
'How clumsy can you be?'
[10] How terrible it would be if a newborn baby said to its father,
'Why was I born?'
or if it said to its mother,
'Why did you make me this way?'"

[11] This is what the LORD says—
the Holy One of Israel and your Creator:
"Do you question what I do for my children?
Do you give me orders about the work of my hands?
[12] I am the one who made the earth
and created people to live on it.
With my hands I stretched out the heavens.
All the stars are at my command.
[13] I will raise up Cyrus to fulfill my righteous purpose,
and I will guide his actions.
He will restore my city and free my captive people—
without seeking a reward!
I, the LORD of Heaven's Armies, have spoken!"

FUTURE CONVERSION OF GENTILES

[14] This is what the LORD says:

"You will rule the Egyptians,
the Ethiopians,* and the Sabeans.
They will come to you with all their merchandise,
and it will all be yours.
They will follow you as prisoners in chains.
They will fall to their knees in front of you and say,
'God is with you, and he is the only God.
There is no other.'"

[15] Truly, O God of Israel, our Savior,
you work in mysterious ways.
[16] All craftsmen who make idols will be humiliated.
They will all be disgraced together.
[17] But the LORD will save the people of Israel
with eternal salvation.
Throughout everlasting ages,
they will never again be humiliated and disgraced.

[18] For the LORD is God,
and he created the heavens and earth
and put everything in place.
He made the world to be lived in,
not to be a place of empty chaos.
"I am the LORD," he says,
"and there is no other.
[19] I publicly proclaim bold promises.
I do not whisper obscurities in some dark corner.
I would not have told the people of Israel* to seek me
if I could not be found.

45:2 As in Dead Sea Scrolls and Greek version; Masoretic Text reads *the swellings.* 45:14 Hebrew *Cushites.* 45:19 Hebrew *of Jacob.* See note on 14:1.

45:1 his anointed one. Hebrew *messiah*. Anointing was a ceremony of pouring fragrant oil over a king or priest being appointed. Cyrus is not the Messiah, but a messiah, one anointed by God for an important task. As the Persian king (who lived over 200 years after Isaiah), he would decree Israel's freedom to return from exile.

45:9 clay pot. The thing created by another has no right to question its creator (see Jer. 18:6).

45:14 come to you . . . fall to their knees. People from Egypt and Cush would acknowledge the God of Israel as Lord and would bow down to Israel. They would submit to God's truth and worship Him (1 Cor. 14:25).

I, the LORD, speak only what is true
and declare only what is right.

20 "Gather together and come,
you fugitives from surrounding nations.
What fools they are who carry around their
wooden idols
and pray to gods that cannot save!
21 Consult together, argue your case.
Get together and decide what to say.
Who made these things known so long ago?
What idol ever told you they would happen?
Was it not I, the LORD?
For there is no other God but me,
a righteous God and Savior.
There is none but me.
22 Let all the world look to me for salvation!
For I am God; there is no other.
23 I have sworn by my own name;
I have spoken the truth,
and I will never go back on my word:
Every knee will bend to me,
and every tongue will declare allegiance to
me.*"
24 The people will declare,
"The LORD is the source of all my righteousness
and strength."
And all who were angry with him
will come to him and be ashamed.
25 In the LORD all the generations of Israel will be
justified,
and in him they will boast.

BABYLON'S FALSE GODS

46 1 Bel and Nebo, the gods of Babylon,
bow as they are lowered to the ground.
They are being hauled away on ox carts.
The poor beasts stagger under the weight.
2 Both the idols and their owners are bowed down.
The gods cannot protect the people,
and the people cannot protect the gods.
They go off into captivity together.

3 "Listen to me, descendants of Jacob,
all you who remain in Israel.
I have cared for you since you were born.
Yes, I carried you before you were born.
4 I will be your God throughout your lifetime—
until your hair is white with age.
I made you, and I will care for you.
I will carry you along and save you.

5 "To whom will you compare me?
Who is my equal?
6 Some people pour out their silver and gold
and hire a craftsman to make a god from it.
Then they bow down and worship it!
7 They carry it around on their shoulders,
and when they set it down, it stays there.
It can't even move!
And when someone prays to it, there is no answer.
It can't rescue anyone from trouble.

8 "Do not forget this! Keep it in mind!
Remember this, you guilty ones.
9 Remember the things I have done in the past.
For I alone am God!
I am God, and there is none like me.
10 Only I can tell you the future
before it even happens.
Everything I plan will come to pass,
for I do whatever I wish.
11 I will call a swift bird of prey from the east—
a leader from a distant land to come and do my
bidding.
I have said what I would do,
and I will do it.

12 "Listen to me, you stubborn people
who are so far from doing right.
13 For I am ready to set things right,
not in the distant future, but right now!
I am ready to save Jerusalem*
and show my glory to Israel.

PREDICTION OF BABYLON'S FALL

47 1 "Come down, virgin daughter of Babylon,
and sit in the dust.
For your days of sitting on a throne have ended.
O daughter of Babylonia,* never again will you be
the lovely princess, tender and delicate.
2 Take heavy millstones and grind flour.
Remove your veil, and strip off your robe.
Expose yourself to public view.*
3 You will be naked and burdened with shame.
I will take vengeance against you without pity."

4 Our Redeemer, whose name is the LORD of
Heaven's Armies,
is the Holy One of Israel.

5 "O beautiful Babylon, sit now in darkness and
silence.
Never again will you be known as the queen of
kingdoms.
6 For I was angry with my chosen people
and punished them by letting them fall into
your hands.
But you, Babylon, showed them no mercy.
You oppressed even the elderly.
7 You said, 'I will reign forever as queen of the world!'
You did not reflect on your actions
or think about their consequences.

8 "Listen to this, you pleasure-loving kingdom,
living at ease and feeling secure.
You say, 'I am the only one, and there is no other.
I will never be a widow or lose my children.'

45:23 Hebrew *will confess;* Greek version reads *will declare allegiance to God.* Compare Rom 14:11. **46:13** Hebrew *Zion.* **47:1** Or *Chaldea;* also in 47:5. **47:2** Hebrew *Bare your legs; pass through the rivers.*

45:24 all who were angry with him. Everyone is invited by God to repent of sin, yet many will continue to angrily oppose Him. These people will have no part in His eternal kingdom.

46:2 They go off into captivity together. The idols were heavy burdens to carry around, and they could not help the Babylonians escape defeat. Instead, they were carried off into captivity along with the people.

46:12 Listen . . . stubborn. God is calling Israel to repent of their sin by telling them the great things He will do for them in the future.

47:3 naked. Indicated disgrace, vulnerability, and impropriety (Gen. 9:22-23). Babylon will be humbled and shamed. She will be like a prostitute caught in the act.

9 Well, both these things will come upon you in a moment:
widowhood and the loss of your children.
Yes, these calamities will come upon you,
despite all your witchcraft and magic.

10 "You felt secure in your wickedness.
'No one sees me,' you said.
But your 'wisdom' and 'knowledge' have led you astray,
and you said, 'I am the only one, and there is no other.'
11 So disaster will overtake you,
and you won't be able to charm it away.
Calamity will fall upon you,
and you won't be able to buy your way out.
A catastrophe will strike you suddenly,
one for which you are not prepared.

12 "Now use your magical charms!
Use the spells you have worked at all these years!
Maybe they will do you some good.
Maybe they can make someone afraid of you.
13 All the advice you receive has made you tired.
Where are all your astrologers,
those stargazers who make predictions each month?
Let them stand up and save you from what the future holds.
14 But they are like straw burning in a fire;
they cannot save themselves from the flame.
You will get no help from them at all;
their hearth is no place to sit for warmth.
15 And all your friends,
those with whom you've done business since childhood,
will go their own ways,
turning a deaf ear to your cries.

GOD'S STUBBORN PEOPLE

48 1 "Listen to me, O family of Jacob,
you who are called by the name of Israel
and born into the family of Judah.
Listen, you who take oaths in the name of the LORD
and call on the God of Israel.
You don't keep your promises,
2 even though you call yourself the holy city
and talk about depending on the God of Israel,
whose name is the LORD of Heaven's Armies.
3 Long ago I told you what was going to happen.
Then suddenly I took action,
and all my predictions came true.
4 For I know how stubborn and obstinate you are.
Your necks are as unbending as iron.
Your heads are as hard as bronze.
5 That is why I told you what would happen;
I told you beforehand what I was going to do.
Then you could never say, 'My idols did it.
My wooden image and metal god commanded it to happen!'
6 You have heard my predictions and seen them fulfilled,
but you refuse to admit it.
Now I will tell you new things,
secrets you have not yet heard.
7 They are brand new, not things from the past.
So you cannot say, 'We knew that all the time!'

8 "Yes, I will tell you of things that are entirely new,
things you never heard of before.
For I know so well what traitors you are.
You have been rebels from birth.
9 Yet for my own sake and for the honor of my name,
I will hold back my anger and not wipe you out.
10 I have refined you, but not as silver is refined.
Rather, I have refined you in the furnace of suffering.
11 I will rescue you for my sake—
yes, for my own sake!
I will not let my reputation be tarnished,
and I will not share my glory with idols!

FREEDOM FROM BABYLON

12 "Listen to me, O family of Jacob,
Israel my chosen one!
I alone am God,
the First and the Last.
13 It was my hand that laid the foundations of the earth,
my right hand that spread out the heavens above.
When I call out the stars,
they all appear in order."

14 Have any of your idols ever told you this?
Come, all of you, and listen:
The LORD has chosen Cyrus as his ally.
He will use him to put an end to the empire of Babylon
and to destroy the Babylonian* armies.

15 "I have said it: I am calling Cyrus!
I will send him on this errand and will help him succeed.
16 Come closer, and listen to this.
From the beginning I have told you plainly what would happen."

And now the Sovereign LORD and his Spirit
have sent me with this message.
17 This is what the LORD says—
your Redeemer, the Holy One of Israel:

48:14 Or *Chaldean.*

47:9 widowhood and loss of your children. Boastful Babylon believed she would never be defeated. But God would judge her, causing desolation in a single day.

47:10 wickedness . . . wisdom . . . knowledge. The leaders of Babylon believed they would rule forever. Babylon's religions included sorcery and magic, practices forbidden by God (8:19; 44:24-25).

47:14 cannot save themselves. Astrologers could not save Babylon any more than idols could. Some idols were carved out of firewood.

47:15 done business since childhood. Referred to the merchants whose trade made Babylon wealthy.

48:6 tell you new things. The new things included Cyrus' activities, the fall of Babylon, and Israel's restoration. The new era of God's kingdom that the Messiah would usher in is also in view here.

48:10 furnace of suffering. The captivity in Babylon purified the people like gold and silver are refined in high heat.

48:16 Sovereign LORD and his Spirit have sent me. Just as God helped Cyrus accomplish his task, the Messiah, with the Holy Spirit on Him, will accomplish God's mission.

"I am the LORD your God,
who teaches you what is good for you
and leads you along the paths you should follow.
18 Oh, that you had listened to my commands!
Then you would have had peace flowing like a gentle river
and righteousness rolling over you like waves in the sea.
19 Your descendants would have been like the sands along the seashore—
too many to count!
There would have been no need for your destruction,
or for cutting off your family name."

20 Yet even now, be free from your captivity!
Leave Babylon and the Babylonians.*
Sing out this message!
Shout it to the ends of the earth!
The LORD has redeemed his servants,
the people of Israel.*
21 They were not thirsty
when he led them through the desert.
He divided the rock,
and water gushed out for them to drink.
22 "But there is no peace for the wicked,"
says the LORD.

THE LORD'S SERVANT COMMISSIONED

49 1 Listen to me, all you in distant lands!
Pay attention, you who are far away!
The LORD called me before my birth;
from within the womb he called me by name.
2 He made my words of judgment as sharp as a sword.
He has hidden me in the shadow of his hand.
I am like a sharp arrow in his quiver.

3 He said to me, "You are my servant, Israel,
and you will bring me glory."

4 I replied, "But my work seems so useless!
I have spent my strength for nothing and to no purpose.
Yet I leave it all in the LORD's hand;
I will trust God for my reward."

5 And now the LORD speaks—
the one who formed me in my mother's womb to be his servant,
who commissioned me to bring Israel back to him.
The LORD has honored me,
and my God has given me strength.
6 He says, "You will do more than restore the people of Israel to me.
I will make you a light to the Gentiles,
and you will bring my salvation to the ends of the earth."

7 The LORD, the Redeemer
and Holy One of Israel,
says to the one who is despised and rejected by the nations,
to the one who is the servant of rulers:
"Kings will stand at attention when you pass by.
Princes will also bow low
because of the LORD, the faithful one,
the Holy One of Israel, who has chosen you."

PROMISES OF ISRAEL'S RESTORATION

8 This is what the LORD says:

"At just the right time, I will respond to you.*
On the day of salvation I will help you.
I will protect you and give you to the people
as my covenant with them.
Through you I will reestablish the land of Israel
and assign it to its own people again.
9 I will say to the prisoners, 'Come out in freedom,'
and to those in darkness, 'Come into the light.'
They will be my sheep, grazing in green pastures
and on hills that were previously bare.
10 They will neither hunger nor thirst.
The searing sun will not reach them anymore.
For the LORD in his mercy will lead them;
he will lead them beside cool waters.
11 And I will make my mountains into level paths for them.
The highways will be raised above the valleys.
12 See, my people will return from far away,
from lands to the north and west,
and from as far south as Egypt.*"

13 Sing for joy, O heavens!
Rejoice, O earth!
Burst into song, O mountains!
For the LORD has comforted his people
and will have compassion on them in their suffering.

14 Yet Jerusalem* says, "The LORD has deserted us;
the Lord has forgotten us."

15 "Never! Can a mother forget her nursing child?
Can she feel no love for the child she has borne?
But even if that were possible,
I would not forget you!

48:20a Or *the Chaldeans.* **48:20b** Hebrew *his servant, Jacob.* See note on 14:1. **49:8** Greek version reads *I heard you.* Compare 2 Cor 6:2. **49:12** As in Dead Sea Scrolls, which read *from the region of Aswan,* which is in southern Egypt. Masoretic Text reads *from the region of Sinim.* **49:14** Hebrew *Zion.*

48:18 peace . . . like a gentle river. The Israelites could have avoided captivity by obeying God's law (Ps. 81:11-16).
48:21 He divided the rock, and water gushed. After the Hebrews left Egypt, God provided water in the desert out of a rock (Ex. 17:1-7). God would provide for them as they left Babylon too.
49:2 my words . . . as sharp as a sword. Jesus Christ will conquer the earth through the word of the gospel (Rev. 1:16; 2:12). God's Word is also depicted as a sword (Eph. 6:17; Heb. 4:12).
49:3 my servant, Israel. The Messiah is called Israel because He epitomizes the nation, fulfilling what it failed to do (Zech. 3:8).
49:4 spent my strength for nothing. This pointed to Christ's rejection by the nation of Israel and His suffering. **Yet I leave it all in the LORD's hand.** Jesus' vindication was His resurrection.
49:6 restore the people of Israel . . . light to the Gentiles. Jesus' mission is twofold: He will restore Israel and already has brought the light of God's truth to the Gentiles.
49:7 despised and rejected. Although rejected by Israel (John 1:10-11), the Servant would succeed in His ministry to the Gentiles.
49:8 the right time . . . day of salvation. God's offer of salvation is always current.

[16] See, I have written your name on the palms of my hands.
Always in my mind is a picture of Jerusalem's walls in ruins.
[17] Soon your descendants will come back,
and all who are trying to destroy you will go away.
[18] Look around you and see,
for all your children will come back to you.
As surely as I live," says the LORD,
"they will be like jewels or bridal ornaments for you to display.
[19] "Even the most desolate parts of your abandoned land
will soon be crowded with your people.
Your enemies who enslaved you
will be far away.
[20] The generations born in exile will return and say,
'We need more room! It's crowded here!'
[21] Then you will think to yourself,
'Who has given me all these descendants?
For most of my children were killed,
and the rest were carried away into exile.
I was left here all alone.
Where did all these people come from?
Who bore these children?
Who raised them for me?'"

[22] This is what the Sovereign LORD says:
"See, I will give a signal to the godless nations.
They will carry your little sons back to you in their arms;
they will bring your daughters on their shoulders.
[23] Kings and queens will serve you
and care for all your needs.
They will bow to the earth before you
and lick the dust from your feet.
Then you will know that I am the LORD.
Those who trust in me will never be put to shame."

[24] Who can snatch the plunder of war from the hands of a warrior?
Who can demand that a tyrant* let his captives go?
[25] But the LORD says,
"The captives of warriors will be released,
and the plunder of tyrants will be retrieved.
For I will fight those who fight you,
and I will save your children.
[26] I will feed your enemies with their own flesh.
They will be drunk with rivers of their own blood.
All the world will know that I, the LORD,
am your Savior and your Redeemer,
the Mighty One of Israel.*"

50

[1] This is what the LORD says:
"Was your mother sent away because I divorced her?
Did I sell you as slaves to my creditors?
No, you were sold because of your sins.
And your mother, too, was taken because of your sins.
[2] Why was no one there when I came?
Why didn't anyone answer when I called?
Is it because I have no power to rescue?
No, that is not the reason!
For I can speak to the sea and make it dry up!
I can turn rivers into deserts covered with dying fish.
[3] I dress the skies in darkness,
covering them with clothes of mourning."

THE LORD'S OBEDIENT SERVANT

[4] The Sovereign LORD has given me his words of wisdom,
so that I know how to comfort the weary.
Morning by morning he wakens me
and opens my understanding to his will.
[5] The Sovereign LORD has spoken to me,
and I have listened.
I have not rebelled or turned away.
[6] I offered my back to those who beat me
and my cheeks to those who pulled out my beard.
I did not hide my face
from mockery and spitting.

[7] Because the Sovereign LORD helps me,
I will not be disgraced.
Therefore, I have set my face like a stone,
determined to do his will.
And I know that I will not be put to shame.
[8] He who gives me justice is near.
Who will dare to bring charges against me now?
Where are my accusers?
Let them appear!
[9] See, the Sovereign LORD is on my side!
Who will declare me guilty?
All my enemies will be destroyed
like old clothes that have been eaten by moths!

[10] Who among you fears the LORD
and obeys his servant?
If you are walking in darkness,
without a ray of light,
trust in the LORD
and rely on your God.
[11] But watch out, you who live in your own light
and warm yourselves by your own fires.
This is the reward you will receive from me:
You will soon fall down in great torment.

49:24 As in Dead Sea Scrolls, Syriac version, and Latin Vulgate (also see 49:25); Masoretic Text reads *a righteous person*. See note on 14:1. **49:26** Hebrew *of Jacob*.

49:22 will carry your little sons . . . in their arms. Gentiles will support Israel in the millennium and will bring Jews into the land at the beginning of Christ's rule.

50:1 Was your mother sent away . . . Did I sell you? God denies that He has given His people a divorce certificate or that he has sold his children to pay His debts.

50:6 offered my back to those who beat me. Yet another prophecy of Messiah. Isaiah is speaking as though he is the Servant (42:1), the Messiah who will be rejected before He takes His throne.

A CALL TO TRUST THE LORD

51 1 "Listen to me, all who hope for deliverance—
all who seek the LORD!
Consider the rock from which you were cut,
the quarry from which you were mined.
2 Yes, think about Abraham, your ancestor,
and Sarah, who gave birth to your nation.
Abraham was only one man when I called him.
But when I blessed him, he became a great nation."

3 The LORD will comfort Israel* again
and have pity on her ruins.
Her desert will blossom like Eden,
her barren wilderness like the garden of the LORD.
Joy and gladness will be found there.
Songs of thanksgiving will fill the air.

4 "Listen to me, my people.
Hear me, Israel,
for my law will be proclaimed,
and my justice will become a light to the nations.
5 My mercy and justice are coming soon.
My salvation is on the way.
My strong arm will bring justice to the nations.
All distant lands will look to me
and wait in hope for my powerful arm.
6 Look up to the skies above,
and gaze down on the earth below.
For the skies will disappear like smoke,
and the earth will wear out like a piece of clothing.
The people of the earth will die like flies,
but my salvation lasts forever.
My righteous rule will never end!

7 "Listen to me, you who know right from wrong,
you who cherish my law in your hearts.
Do not be afraid of people's scorn,
nor fear their insults.
8 For the moth will devour them as it devours clothing.
The worm will eat at them as it eats wool.
But my righteousness will last forever.
My salvation will continue from generation to generation."

9 Wake up, wake up, O LORD! Clothe yourself with strength!
Flex your mighty right arm!
Rouse yourself as in the days of old
when you slew Egypt, the dragon of the Nile.*
10 Are you not the same today,
the one who dried up the sea,
making a path of escape through the depths
so that your people could cross over?
11 Those who have been ransomed by the LORD will return.
They will enter Jerusalem* singing,
crowned with everlasting joy.
Sorrow and mourning will disappear,
and they will be filled with joy and gladness.

12 "I, yes I, am the one who comforts you.
So why are you afraid of mere humans,
who wither like the grass and disappear?
13 Yet you have forgotten the LORD, your Creator,
the one who stretched out the sky like a canopy
and laid the foundations of the earth.
Will you remain in constant dread of human oppressors?
Will you continue to fear the anger of your enemies?
Where is their fury and anger now?
It is gone!
14 Soon all you captives will be released!
Imprisonment, starvation, and death will not be your fate!
15 For I am the LORD your God,
who stirs up the sea, causing its waves to roar.
My name is the LORD of Heaven's Armies.
16 And I have put my words in your mouth
and hidden you safely in my hand.
I stretched out* the sky like a canopy
and laid the foundations of the earth.
I am the one who says to Israel,
'You are my people!'"

17 Wake up, wake up, O Jerusalem!
You have drunk the cup of the LORD's fury.
You have drunk the cup of terror,
tipping out its last drops.
18 Not one of your children is left alive
to take your hand and guide you.
19 These two calamities have fallen on you:
desolation and destruction, famine and war.
And who is left to sympathize with you?
Who is left to comfort you?*
20 For your children have fainted and lie in the streets,
helpless as antelopes caught in a net.
The LORD has poured out his fury;
God has rebuked them.

21 But now listen to this, you afflicted ones
who sit in a drunken stupor,
though not from drinking wine.
22 This is what the Sovereign LORD,
your God and Defender, says:
"See, I have taken the terrible cup from your hands.
You will drink no more of my fury.

51:3 Hebrew *Zion;* also in 51:16. **51:9** Hebrew *You slew Rahab; you pierced the dragon.* Rahab is the name of a mythical sea monster that represents chaos in ancient literature. The name is used here as a poetic name for Egypt. **51:11** Hebrew *Zion.* **51:16** As in Syriac version (see also 51:13); Hebrew reads *planted.* **51:19** As in Dead Sea Scrolls and Greek, Latin, and Syriac versions; Masoretic Text reads *How can I comfort you?*

51:3 Israel . . . Eden. Both referred to places of fellowship with God that were free from sin and guarded by angels (see Gen. 3:24). Zion will be fruitful and lush like the garden of Eden.

51:4 my law . . . my justice will become a light to the nations. The word for instruction is Torah, the law of God. God's law will be known, and justice will prevail all over the world. God's law will be light for the world in the millennial reign of Christ.

51:9 Wake up. While it appeared to the Israelites that God was asleep, God is ever vigilant on behalf of His people (see Ps. 121:3-4).

51:14 Soon . . . captives will be released. These were captives in exile in Babylon, yet meaning extends to everyone living in the darkness of sin and alienated from God.

51:17 cup . . . its last drops. The empty cup referred to suffering God's judgment. While in exile, the Israelites truly felt God's punishment (see Jer. 25:15-29; Lam. 4:21).

51:18 Not one . . . to take your hand. Many young men of Jerusalem were killed during the destruction of the city. This phrase depicted Jerusalem as a sick woman with no sons to care for her.

23 Instead, I will hand that cup to your tormentors,
those who said, 'We will trample you into the
dust
and walk on your backs.'"

DELIVERANCE FOR JERUSALEM

52 1 Wake up, wake up, O Zion!
Clothe yourself with strength.
Put on your beautiful clothes, O holy city of
Jerusalem,
for unclean and godless people will enter your
gates no longer.
2 Rise from the dust, O Jerusalem.
Sit in a place of honor.
Remove the chains of slavery from your neck,
O captive daughter of Zion.
3 For this is what the LORD says:
"When I sold you into exile,
I received no payment.
Now I can redeem you
without having to pay for you."

4 This is what the Sovereign LORD says: "Long ago my
people chose to live in Egypt. Now they are oppressed
by Assyria. 5 What is this?" asks the LORD. "Why are my
people enslaved again? Those who rule them shout
in exultation.* My name is blasphemed all day long.*
6 But I will reveal my name to my people, and they will
come to know its power. Then at last they will recog-
nize that I am the one who speaks to them."

7 How beautiful on the mountains
are the feet of the messenger who brings good
news,
the good news of peace and salvation,
the news that the God of Israel* reigns!
8 The watchmen shout and sing with joy,
for before their very eyes
they see the LORD returning to Jerusalem.*
9 Let the ruins of Jerusalem break into joyful song,
for the LORD has comforted his people.
He has redeemed Jerusalem.
10 The LORD has demonstrated his holy power
before the eyes of all the nations.
All the ends of the earth will see
the victory of our God.

11 Get out! Get out and leave your captivity,
where everything you touch is unclean.
Get out of there and purify yourselves,
you who carry home the sacred objects of the
LORD.
12 You will not leave in a hurry,
running for your lives.
For the LORD will go ahead of you;
yes, the God of Israel will protect you from
behind.

THE SUFFERING SERVANT

1. When have you suffered for someone else's misbehavior? When has someone else suffered because of your misbehavior?

ISAIAH 52:13–53:12

2. Who is the "Servant" to whom this passage is referring? Why did He suffer? What did His suffering accomplish?
3. What does it mean that "All of us, like sheep, have strayed away. We have left God's path to follow our own" (53:6)? Why did the Lord punish the Servant for us all?
4. What does it mean that God made the Servant a "an offering for sin" (53:10)?
5. How does this passage teach that Jesus is the only way to finding peace with God?

THE LORD'S SUFFERING SERVANT

13 See, my servant will prosper;
he will be highly exalted.
14 But many were amazed when they saw him.*
His face was so disfigured he seemed hardly
human,
and from his appearance, one would scarcely
know he was a man.
15 And he will startle* many nations.
Kings will stand speechless in his presence.
For they will see what they had not been told;
they will understand what they had not heard
about.*

53 1 Who has believed our message?
To whom has the LORD revealed his powerful
arm?
2 My servant grew up in the LORD's presence like a
tender green shoot,
like a root in dry ground.
There was nothing beautiful or majestic about his
appearance,
nothing to attract us to him.
3 He was despised and rejected—
a man of sorrows, acquainted with deepest
grief.
We turned our backs on him and looked the other
way.
He was despised, and we did not care.

4 Yet it was our weaknesses he carried;
it was our sorrows* that weighed him down.

52:5a As in Dead Sea Scrolls; Masoretic Text reads *Those who rule them wail.* 52:5b Greek version reads *The Gentiles continually blaspheme my name because of you.* Compare Rom 2:24. 52:7 Hebrew *of Zion.* 52:8 Hebrew *to Zion.* 52:14 As in Syriac version; Hebrew reads *you.* 52:15a Or *cleanse.* 52:15b Greek version reads *Those who have never been told about him will see, / and those who have never heard of him will understand.* Compare Rom 15:21. 53:4 Or *Yet it was our sicknesses he carried; / it was our diseases.*

52:7 feet of the messenger. Messengers ran with news of battles (2 Sam. 18:26). **the God of Israel reigns!** The gospel is the good news that God is king (see Mark 1:14-15).

52:13 will prosper . . . be highly exalted. From here to 53:12 the Servant's death for the sins of His people is predicted. This phrase referred to His resurrection and glorification (Rom. 4:24-25).

52:14 amazed. Many were shocked at Israel's exile, so would many be surprised at Jesus' humiliation.

52:15 stand speechless. Stunned respect. **they will see.** The nations will finally understand that the Messiah is Lord (Rom. 15:21).

53:2 tender green shoot. He will seem frail before His exaltation.

53:4 our weaknessess he carried. Sickness is used as a metaphor for spiritual sickness: sin. Christ was punished for our sins.

And we thought his troubles were a punishment
from God,
a punishment for his own sins!
5 But he was pierced for our rebellion,
crushed for our sins.
He was beaten so we could be whole.
He was whipped so we could be healed.
6 All of us, like sheep, have strayed away.
We have left God's paths to follow our own.
Yet the LORD laid on him
the sins of us all.

7 He was oppressed and treated harshly,
yet he never said a word.
He was led like a lamb to the slaughter.
And as a sheep is silent before the shearers,
he did not open his mouth.
8 Unjustly condemned,
he was led away.*
No one cared that he died without descendants,
that his life was cut short in midstream.*
But he was struck down
for the rebellion of my people.
9 He had done no wrong
and had never deceived anyone.
But he was buried like a criminal;
he was put in a rich man's grave.

10 But it was the LORD's good plan to crush him
and cause him grief.
Yet when his life is made an offering for sin,
he will have many descendants.
He will enjoy a long life,
and the LORD's good plan will prosper in his
hands.
11 When he sees all that is accomplished by his
anguish,
he will be satisfied.
And because of his experience,
my righteous servant will make it possible
for many to be counted righteous,
for he will bear all their sins.
12 I will give him the honors of a victorious soldier,
because he exposed himself to death.
He was counted among the rebels.
He bore the sins of many and interceded for
rebels.

FUTURE GLORY FOR JERUSALEM

54 1 "Sing, O childless woman,
you who have never given birth!
Break into loud and joyful song, O Jerusalem,
you who have never been in labor.
For the desolate woman now has more children
than the woman who lives with her husband,"
says the LORD.
2 "Enlarge your house; build an addition.
Spread out your home, and spare no expense!
3 For you will soon be bursting at the seams.
Your descendants will occupy other nations
and resettle the ruined cities.

4 "Fear not; you will no longer live in shame.
Don't be afraid; there is no more disgrace for
you.
You will no longer remember the shame of your
youth
and the sorrows of widowhood.
5 For your Creator will be your husband;
the LORD of Heaven's Armies is his name!
He is your Redeemer, the Holy One of Israel,
the God of all the earth.
6 For the LORD has called you back from your grief—
as though you were a young wife abandoned by
her husband,"
says your God.
7 "For a brief moment I abandoned you,
but with great compassion I will take you back.
8 In a burst of anger I turned my face away for a
little while.
But with everlasting love I will have
compassion on you,"
says the LORD, your Redeemer.

9 "Just as I swore in the time of Noah
that I would never again let a flood cover the
earth,
so now I swear
that I will never again be angry and punish you.
10 For the mountains may move
and the hills disappear,
but even then my faithful love for you will remain.
My covenant of blessing will never be broken,"
says the LORD, who has mercy on you.

11 "O storm-battered city,
troubled and desolate!
I will rebuild you with precious jewels
and make your foundations from lapis lazuli.
12 I will make your towers of sparkling rubies,
your gates of shining gems,
and your walls of precious stones.
13 I will teach all your children,
and they will enjoy great peace.
14 You will be secure under a government that is just
and fair.
Your enemies will stay far away.
You will live in peace,
and terror will not come near.
15 If any nation comes to fight you,
it is not because I sent them.
Whoever attacks you will go down in defeat.

16 "I have created the blacksmith
who fans the coals beneath the forge
and makes the weapons of destruction.

53:8a Greek version reads *He was humiliated and received no justice.* Compare Acts 8:33. **53:8b** Or *As for his contemporaries, / who cared that his life was cut short in midstream?* Greek version reads *Who can speak of his descendants? / For his life was taken from the earth.* Compare Acts 8:33.

53:5 crushed for our sins. The Servant suffered in our place in order to reconcile us with God. **beaten so we could be whole.** The punishment Jesus received brought peace (wholeness) for us.

53:6 laid on him the sins of us all. God punished Jesus for our sins so that we won't have to be punished for them.

53:9 criminal . . . rich man's. Jesus was crucified as a criminal but was buried by a wealthy man, Joseph of Arimathea (see Matt. 27:57-60). This is a remarkable detail showing that this prophecy from over 700 years before the time of Jesus is truly from God.

53:10 good plan to crush him. God gladly took on Himself the punishment we deserve.

And I have created the armies that destroy.
17 But in that coming day
no weapon turned against you will succeed.
You will silence every voice
raised up to accuse you.
These benefits are enjoyed by the servants of the LORD;
their vindication will come from me.
I, the LORD, have spoken!

INVITATION TO THE LORD'S SALVATION

55 1 "Is anyone thirsty?
Come and drink—
even if you have no money!
Come, take your choice of wine or milk—
it's all free!
2 Why spend your money on food that does not give you strength?
Why pay for food that does you no good?
Listen to me, and you will eat what is good.
You will enjoy the finest food.

3 "Come to me with your ears wide open.
Listen, and you will find life.
I will make an everlasting covenant with you.
I will give you all the unfailing love I promised to David.
4 See how I used him to display my power among the peoples.
I made him a leader among the nations.
5 You also will command nations you do not know,
and peoples unknown to you will come running to obey,
because I, the LORD your God,
the Holy One of Israel, have made you glorious."

6 Seek the LORD while you can find him.
Call on him now while he is near.
7 Let the wicked change their ways
and banish the very thought of doing wrong.
Let them turn to the LORD that he may have mercy on them.
Yes, turn to our God, for he will forgive generously.

8 "My thoughts are nothing like your thoughts," says the LORD.
"And my ways are far beyond anything you could imagine.
9 For just as the heavens are higher than the earth,
so my ways are higher than your ways
and my thoughts higher than your thoughts.

10 "The rain and snow come down from the heavens
and stay on the ground to water the earth.
They cause the grain to grow,
producing seed for the farmer
and bread for the hungry.
11 It is the same with my word.
I send it out, and it always produces fruit.
It will accomplish all I want it to,
and it will prosper everywhere I send it.
12 You will live in joy and peace.
The mountains and hills will burst into song,
and the trees of the field will clap their hands!
13 Where once there were thorns, cypress trees will grow.
Where nettles grew, myrtles will sprout up.
These events will bring great honor to the LORD's name;
they will be an everlasting sign of his power and love."

BLESSINGS FOR ALL NATIONS

56 This is what the LORD says:
"Be just and fair to all.
Do what is right and good,
for I am coming soon to rescue you
and to display my righteousness among you.
2 Blessed are all those
who are careful to do this.
Blessed are those who honor my Sabbath days of rest
and keep themselves from doing wrong.

3 "Don't let foreigners who commit themselves to the LORD say,
'The LORD will never let me be part of his people.'
And don't let the eunuchs say,
'I'm a dried-up tree with no children and no future.'
4 For this is what the LORD says:
I will bless those eunuchs
who keep my Sabbath days holy
and who choose to do what pleases me
and commit their lives to me.
5 I will give them—within the walls of my house—
a memorial and a name
far greater than sons and daughters could give.
For the name I give them is an everlasting one.
It will never disappear!

6 "I will also bless the foreigners who commit themselves to the LORD,
who serve him and love his name,
who worship him and do not desecrate the Sabbath day of rest,
and who hold fast to my covenant.
7 I will bring them to my holy mountain of Jerusalem
and will fill them with joy in my house of prayer.
I will accept their burnt offerings and sacrifices,
because my Temple will be called a house of

55:1 thirsty? come and drink. Thirst speaks of the desire for spiritual answers to life's mysteries. Waters represent the satisfaction of knowing God as Savior and Provider (John 4:10-14).

55:2 spend your money . . . food that does you no good? Throughout history, people have tried to find satisfaction through many things other than God. But the joy of salvation cannot be obtained except through God's free gift.

55:5 nations you do not know. Many nations will recognize the splendor of the Lord and will go to Israel to worship Him. This is a reversal of the exile when Israel was taken to a foreign nation.

56:2 those who honor my Sabbath. Keeping the Sabbath was an important part of the law because it signified God's covenant with Israel. Refraining from work on that day showed trust in God's ability to provide.

56:3 foreigners. Gentiles, who were not part of the covenant, would also find God's peace if they turned to God in faith. **eunuchs.** Eunuchs were excluded from entry into the temple under the Mosaic law (Deut. 23:1), but they will be part of Christ's kingdom.

56:7 house of prayer. Being included in the covenantal family of Israel will mean access to the temple, which will be rebuilt before Christ returns.

prayer for all nations.
8 For the Sovereign LORD,
who brings back the outcasts of Israel, says:
I will bring others, too,
besides my people Israel."

SINFUL LEADERS CONDEMNED

9 Come, wild animals of the field!
Come, wild animals of the forest!
Come and devour my people!
10 For the leaders of my people—
the LORD's watchmen, his shepherds—
are blind and ignorant.
They are like silent watchdogs
that give no warning when danger comes.
They love to lie around, sleeping and dreaming.
11 Like greedy dogs, they are never satisfied.
They are ignorant shepherds,
all following their own path
and intent on personal gain.
12 "Come," they say, "let's get some wine and have a party.
Let's all get drunk.
Then tomorrow we'll do it again
and have an even bigger party!"

57 1 Good people pass away;
the godly often die before their time.
But no one seems to care or wonder why.
No one seems to understand
that God is protecting them from the evil to come.
2 For those who follow godly paths
will rest in peace when they die.

IDOLATROUS WORSHIP CONDEMNED

3 "But you—come here, you witches' children,
you offspring of adulterers and prostitutes!
4 Whom do you mock,
making faces and sticking out your tongues?
You children of sinners and liars!
5 You worship your idols with great passion
beneath the oaks and under every green tree.
You sacrifice your children down in the valleys,
among the jagged rocks in the cliffs.
6 Your gods are the smooth stones in the valleys.
You worship them with liquid offerings and grain offerings.
They, not I, are your inheritance.
Do you think all this makes me happy?
7 You have committed adultery on every high mountain.
There you have worshiped idols
and have been unfaithful to me.
8 You have put pagan symbols
on your doorposts and behind your doors.
You have left me
and climbed into bed with these detestable gods.
You have committed yourselves to them.
You love to look at their naked bodies.
9 You have gone to Molech*
with olive oil and many perfumes,
sending your agents far and wide,
even to the world of the dead.*
10 You grew weary in your search,
but you never gave up.
Desire gave you renewed strength,
and you did not grow weary.

11 "Are you afraid of these idols?
Do they terrify you?
Is that why you have lied to me
and forgotten me and my words?
Is it because of my long silence
that you no longer fear me?
12 Now I will expose your so-called good deeds.
None of them will help you.
13 Let's see if your idols can save you
when you cry to them for help.
Why, a puff of wind can knock them down!
If you just breathe on them, they fall over!
But whoever trusts in me will inherit the land
and possess my holy mountain."

GOD FORGIVES THE REPENTANT

14 God says, "Rebuild the road!
Clear away the rocks and stones
so my people can return from captivity."
15 The high and lofty one who lives in eternity,
the Holy One, says this:
"I live in the high and holy place
with those whose spirits are contrite and humble.
I restore the crushed spirit of the humble
and revive the courage of those with repentant hearts.
16 For I will not fight against you forever;
I will not always be angry.
If I were, all people would pass away—
all the souls I have made.
17 I was angry,
so I punished these greedy people.
I withdrew from them,
but they kept going on their own stubborn way.
18 I have seen what they do,
but I will heal them anyway!
I will lead them.
I will comfort those who mourn,
19 bringing words of praise to their lips.
May they have abundant peace, both near and far,"
says the LORD, who heals them.
20 "But those who still reject me are like the restless sea,
which is never still
but continually churns up mud and dirt.

57:9a Or *to the king.* **57:9b** Hebrew *to Sheol.*

56:8 brings back . . . others. God promised Abraham that through him all peoples of the world would be blessed (see Gen. 12:3). People everywhere who repent and come to God are welcomed into His kingdom with joy.

57:3 adulterers and prostitutes. This referred to the Canaanite fertility rites in which some Israelites participated. Supposedly, engaging in sexual relations with prostitutes in the temple helped guarantee fertility in crops, animals, and families.

57:10 you never gave up. The people continued in sin, refusing to give up their false religious practices (Jer. 2:25).

57:11 Is it because of my long silence. Israel appeared to forget God because He seemed silent to them (Ps. 50:21).

57:15 high and holy place with those . . . contrite and humble. Though God is transcendent (above everything), He is present with us. His presence is even stronger with the lowly, because God helps the needy and exalts the humble.

21 There is no peace for the wicked,"
says my God.

TRUE AND FALSE WORSHIP

58 1 "Shout with the voice of a trumpet blast.
Shout aloud! Don't be timid.
Tell my people Israel* of their sins!
2 Yet they act so pious!
They come to the Temple every day
and seem delighted to learn all about me.
They act like a righteous nation
that would never abandon the laws of its God.
They ask me to take action on their behalf,
pretending they want to be near me.
3 'We have fasted before you!' they say.
'Why aren't you impressed?
We have been very hard on ourselves,
and you don't even notice it!'

"I will tell you why!" I respond.
"It's because you are fasting to please yourselves.
Even while you fast,
you keep oppressing your workers.
4 What good is fasting
when you keep on fighting and quarreling?
This kind of fasting
will never get you anywhere with me.
5 You humble yourselves
by going through the motions of penance,
bowing your heads
like reeds bending in the wind.
You dress in burlap
and cover yourselves with ashes.
Is this what you call fasting?
Do you really think this will please the LORD?

6 "No, this is the kind of fasting I want:
Free those who are wrongly imprisoned;
lighten the burden of those who work for you.
Let the oppressed go free,
and remove the chains that bind people.
7 Share your food with the hungry,
and give shelter to the homeless.
Give clothes to those who need them,
and do not hide from relatives who need your help.

8 "Then your salvation will come like the dawn,
and your wounds will quickly heal.
Your godliness will lead you forward,
and the glory of the LORD will protect you from behind.
9 Then when you call, the LORD will answer.
'Yes, I am here,' he will quickly reply.
"Remove the heavy yoke of oppression.
Stop pointing your finger and spreading vicious rumors!
10 Feed the hungry,
and help those in trouble.
Then your light will shine out from the darkness,
and the darkness around you will be as bright as noon.
11 The LORD will guide you continually,
giving you water when you are dry
and restoring your strength.
You will be like a well-watered garden,
like an ever-flowing spring.
12 Some of you will rebuild the deserted ruins of your cities.
Then you will be known as a rebuilder of walls
and a restorer of homes.

13 "Keep the Sabbath day holy.
Don't pursue your own interests on that day,
but enjoy the Sabbath
and speak of it with delight as the LORD's holy day.
Honor the Sabbath in everything you do on that day,
and don't follow your own desires or talk idly.
14 Then the LORD will be your delight.
I will give you great honor
and satisfy you with the inheritance I promised to your ancestor Jacob.
I, the LORD, have spoken!"

WARNINGS AGAINST SIN

59 1 Listen! The LORD's arm is not too weak to save you,
nor is his ear too deaf to hear you call.
2 It's your sins that have cut you off from God.
Because of your sins, he has turned away
and will not listen anymore.
3 Your hands are the hands of murderers,
and your fingers are filthy with sin.
Your lips are full of lies,
and your mouth spews corruption.

4 No one cares about being fair and honest.
The people's lawsuits are based on lies.
They conceive evil deeds
and then give birth to sin.
5 They hatch deadly snakes
and weave spiders' webs.
Whoever eats their eggs will die;
whoever cracks them will hatch a viper.
6 Their webs can't be made into clothing,
and nothing they do is productive.
All their activity is filled with sin,
and violence is their trademark.

58:1 Hebrew *Jacob.* See note on 14:1.

58:2 They come to the Temple every day. God is speaking sarcastically. The people seem to be religious, but He knows their motives are not right.
58:3 fasted . . . been very hard on ourselves. Refraining from food, repenting of sin, and praying signified a humble people before God in times of national calamity. Here the people continued in sin, going through the religious motions, without truly turning their hearts and minds toward God.
58:5 think this will please the LORD? God exposed their hypocrisy. Their self-righteous behavior did not hide their exploitation of employees. Religious activity without obedience is never acceptable to God.
58:7 Share your food. Inner righteousness manifests itself in a concern for others and in acts of justice and mercy.
59:4 No one cares about being fair and honest. The poor received no fairness in the courts. This was evidence of the nation's spiritual depravity.
59:7 Their feet run . . . to commit murder. Used in Romans 3:15-17 to demonstrate the universality of sin. **think only about sinning.** Sin begins in the mind (James 1:14-15).

7 Their feet run to do evil,
and they rush to commit murder.
They think only about sinning.
Misery and destruction always follow them.
8 They don't know where to find peace
or what it means to be just and good.
They have mapped out crooked roads,
and no one who follows them knows a
moment's peace.

9 So there is no justice among us,
and we know nothing about right living.
We look for light but find only darkness.
We look for bright skies but walk in gloom.
10 We grope like the blind along a wall,
feeling our way like people without eyes.
Even at brightest noontime,
we stumble as though it were dark.
Among the living,
we are like the dead.
11 We growl like hungry bears;
we moan like mournful doves.
We look for justice, but it never comes.
We look for rescue, but it is far away from us.
12 For our sins are piled up before God
and testify against us.
Yes, we know what sinners we are.
13 We know we have rebelled and have denied the
LORD.
We have turned our backs on our God.
We know how unfair and oppressive we have
been,
carefully planning our deceitful lies.
14 Our courts oppose the righteous,
and justice is nowhere to be found.
Truth stumbles in the streets,
and honesty has been outlawed.
15 Yes, truth is gone,
and anyone who renounces evil is attacked.

The LORD looked and was displeased
to find there was no justice.
16 He was amazed to see that no one intervened
to help the oppressed.
So he himself stepped in to save them with his
strong arm,
and his justice sustained him.
17 He put on righteousness as his body armor
and placed the helmet of salvation on his head.
He clothed himself with a robe of vengeance
and wrapped himself in a cloak of divine
passion.
18 He will repay his enemies for their evil deeds.
His fury will fall on his foes.
He will pay them back even to the ends of the
earth.
19 In the west, people will respect the name of the
LORD;
in the east, they will glorify him.
For he will come like a raging flood tide
driven by the breath of the LORD.*

20 "The Redeemer will come to Jerusalem
to buy back those in Israel
who have turned from their sins,"*
says the LORD.

21 "And this is my covenant with them," says the
LORD. "My Spirit will not leave them, and neither will
these words I have given you. They will be on your
lips and on the lips of your children and your chil-
dren's children forever. I, the LORD, have spoken!

FUTURE GLORY FOR JERUSALEM

60 1 "Arise, Jerusalem! Let your light shine for
all to see.
For the glory of the LORD rises to shine on you.
2 Darkness as black as night covers all the nations
of the earth,
but the glory of the LORD rises and appears over
you.
3 All nations will come to your light;
mighty kings will come to see your radiance.

4 "Look and see, for everyone is coming home!
Your sons are coming from distant lands;
your little daughters will be carried home.
5 Your eyes will shine,
and your heart will thrill with joy,
for merchants from around the world will come
to you.
They will bring you the wealth of many lands.
6 Vast caravans of camels will converge on you,
the camels of Midian and Ephah.
The people of Sheba will bring gold and
frankincense
and will come worshiping the LORD.
7 The flocks of Kedar will be given to you,
and the rams of Nebaioth will be brought for
my altars.
I will accept their offerings,
and I will make my Temple glorious.

8 "And what do I see flying like clouds to Israel,
like doves to their nests?
9 They are ships from the ends of the earth,
from lands that trust in me,
led by the great ships of Tarshish.
They are bringing the people of Israel home from
far away,
carrying their silver and gold.
They will honor the LORD your God,

59:19 Or *When the enemy comes like a raging flood tide, / the Spirit of the LORD will drive him back.* **59:20** Hebrew *The Redeemer will come to Zion / to buy back those in Jacob / who have turned from their sins.* Greek version reads *The one who rescues will come on behalf of Zion, / and he will turn Jacob away from ungodliness.* Compare Rom 11:26.

59:10 like the blind. This was part of the covenant curse on the disobedient (Deut. 28:29). Without God's light in our lives, we live in spiritual darkness.

59:11 growl like hungry bears. Expressed frustration and despair.

59:17 put on righteousness as his body armor. God fights for His people like a warrior. Believers need to put on Christ's armor in the fight against Satan (see Eph. 6:14-17).

59:20 who have turned from their sins. Jesus Christ will save all who turn from sin and put their faith in Him (see Rom. 11:26).

59:21 my covenant. The Messiah will return in judgment and enter into a new covenant with believing Israel (Jer. 31:31), pouring His Spirit on them.

60:1 Arise . . . shine. Jerusalem will both receive and reflect God's light and blessing. God is the light—His light will endure forever.

60:5 wealth of many lands. At the beginning of the Millennium when Israel is restored to her land, redeemed people from other nations will bring great wealth to Israel.

the Holy One of Israel,
for he has filled you with splendor.

10 "Foreigners will come to rebuild your towns,
and their kings will serve you.
For though I have destroyed you in my anger,
I will now have mercy on you through my grace.
11 Your gates will stay open day and night
to receive the wealth of many lands.
The kings of the world will be led as captives
in a victory procession.
12 For the nations that refuse to serve you
will be destroyed.

13 "The glory of Lebanon will be yours—
the forests of cypress, fir, and pine—
to beautify my sanctuary.
My Temple will be glorious!
14 The descendants of your tormentors
will come and bow before you.
Those who despised you
will kiss your feet.
They will call you the City of the LORD,
and Zion of the Holy One of Israel.

15 "Though you were once despised and hated,
with no one traveling through you,
I will make you beautiful forever,
a joy to all generations.
16 Powerful kings and mighty nations
will satisfy your every need,
as though you were a child
nursing at the breast of a queen.
You will know at last that I, the LORD,
am your Savior and your Redeemer,
the Mighty One of Israel.*
17 I will exchange your bronze for gold,
your iron for silver,
your wood for bronze,
and your stones for iron.
I will make peace your leader
and righteousness your ruler.
18 Violence will disappear from your land;
the desolation and destruction of war will end.
Salvation will surround you like city walls,
and praise will be on the lips of all who enter there.

19 "No longer will you need the sun to shine by day,
nor the moon to give its light by night,
for the LORD your God will be your everlasting light,
and your God will be your glory.
20 Your sun will never set;
your moon will not go down.
For the LORD will be your everlasting light.
Your days of mourning will come to an end.
21 All your people will be righteous.
They will possess their land forever,
for I will plant them there with my own hands
in order to bring myself glory.
22 The smallest family will become a thousand people,
and the tiniest group will become a mighty nation.
At the right time, I, the LORD, will make it happen."

GOOD NEWS FOR THE OPPRESSED

61 1 The Spirit of the Sovereign LORD is upon me,
for the LORD has anointed me
to bring good news to the poor.
He has sent me to comfort the brokenhearted
and to proclaim that captives will be released
and prisoners will be freed.*
2 He has sent me to tell those who mourn
that the time of the LORD's favor has come,*
and with it, the day of God's anger against their enemies.
3 To all who mourn in Israel,*
he will give a crown of beauty for ashes,
a joyous blessing instead of mourning,
festive praise instead of despair.
In their righteousness, they will be like great oaks
that the LORD has planted for his own glory.

4 They will rebuild the ancient ruins,
repairing cities destroyed long ago.
They will revive them,
though they have been deserted for many generations.
5 Foreigners will be your servants.
They will feed your flocks
and plow your fields
and tend your vineyards.
6 You will be called priests of the LORD,
ministers of our God.
You will feed on the treasures of the nations
and boast in their riches.
7 Instead of shame and dishonor,
you will enjoy a double share of honor.
You will possess a double portion of prosperity in your land,
and everlasting joy will be yours.

8 "For I, the LORD, love justice.
I hate robbery and wrongdoing.
I will faithfully reward my people for their suffering
and make an everlasting covenant with them.
9 Their descendants will be recognized
and honored among the nations.
Everyone will realize that they are a people
the LORD has blessed."

60:16 Hebrew *of Jacob.* See note on 14:1. 61:1 Greek version reads *and the blind will see.* Compare Luke 4:18. 61:2 Or *to proclaim the acceptable year of the LORD.* 61:3 Hebrew *in Zion.*

60:11 gates will stay open day and night. Zion will be secure and won't need locked gates for protection.
61:1 to bring good news. Jesus read these verses from a scroll in the synagogue (see Luke 4:16-21). All who heard knew these verses to be a prophecy of the Messiah. Jesus said that He was fulfilling them.
61:3 a crown of beauty. In place of the ashes that signify mourning, the Israelites will wear a crown symbolizing joy (Ps. 30:11). This is to be a time of celebration—the mourning period is over.
61:4 rebuild the ancient ruins. The cities of Israel, destroyed many years ago, will be rebuilt after the exile.
61:6 priests. Israel will finally fulfill the calling given to them at Mt. Sinai. They will be God's priests to the world (see Ex. 19:6).

10 I am overwhelmed with joy in the LORD my God!
For he has dressed me with the clothing of salvation
and draped me in a robe of righteousness.
I am like a bridegroom dressed for his wedding
or a bride with her jewels.
11 The Sovereign LORD will show his justice to the nations of the world.
Everyone will praise him!
His righteousness will be like a garden in early spring,
with plants springing up everywhere.

ISAIAH'S PRAYER FOR JERUSALEM

62 1 Because I love Zion,
I will not keep still.
Because my heart yearns for Jerusalem,
I cannot remain silent.
I will not stop praying for her
until her righteousness shines like the dawn,
and her salvation blazes like a burning torch.
2 The nations will see your righteousness.
World leaders will be blinded by your glory.
And you will be given a new name
by the LORD's own mouth.
3 The LORD will hold you in his hand for all to see—
a splendid crown in the hand of God.
4 Never again will you be called "The Forsaken City"*
or "The Desolate Land."*
Your new name will be "The City of God's Delight"*
and "The Bride of God,"*
for the LORD delights in you
and will claim you as his bride.
5 Your children will commit themselves to you, O Jerusalem,
just as a young man commits himself to his bride.
Then God will rejoice over you
as a bridegroom rejoices over his bride.

6 O Jerusalem, I have posted watchmen on your walls;
they will pray day and night, continually.
Take no rest, all you who pray to the LORD.
7 Give the LORD no rest until he completes his work,
until he makes Jerusalem the pride of the earth.
8 The LORD has sworn to Jerusalem by his own strength:
"I will never again hand you over to your enemies.
Never again will foreign warriors come
and take away your grain and new wine.
9 You raised the grain, and you will eat it,
praising the LORD.
Within the courtyards of the Temple,
you yourselves will drink the wine you have pressed."

10 Go out through the gates!
Prepare the highway for my people to return!
Smooth out the road; pull out the boulders;
raise a flag for all the nations to see.
11 The LORD has sent this message to every land:
"Tell the people of Israel,*
'Look, your Savior is coming.
See, he brings his reward with him as he comes.'"
12 They will be called "The Holy People"
and "The People Redeemed by the LORD."
And Jerusalem will be known as "The Desirable Place"
and "The City No Longer Forsaken."

JUDGMENT AGAINST THE LORD'S ENEMIES

63 1 Who is this who comes from Edom,
from the city of Bozrah,
with his clothing stained red?
Who is this in royal robes,
marching in his great strength?

"It is I, the LORD, announcing your salvation!
It is I, the LORD, who has the power to save!"

2 Why are your clothes so red,
as if you have been treading out grapes?

3 "I have been treading the winepress alone;
no one was there to help me.
In my anger I have trampled my enemies
as if they were grapes.
In my fury I have trampled my foes.
Their blood has stained my clothes.
4 For the time has come for me to avenge my people,
to ransom them from their oppressors.
5 I was amazed to see that no one intervened
to help the oppressed.
So I myself stepped in to save them with my strong arm,
and my wrath sustained me.
6 I crushed the nations in my anger
and made them stagger and fall to the ground,
spilling their blood upon the earth."

PRAISE FOR DELIVERANCE

7 I will tell of the LORD's unfailing love.
I will praise the LORD for all he has done.
I will rejoice in his great goodness to Israel,
which he has granted according to his mercy and love.
8 He said, "They are my very own people.
Surely they will not betray me again."
And he became their Savior.
9 In all their suffering he also suffered,
and he personally* rescued them.
In his love and mercy he redeemed them.

62:4a Hebrew *Azubah,* which means "forsaken." **62:4b** Hebrew *Shemamah,* which means "desolate." **62:4c** Hebrew *Hephzibah,* which means "my delight is in her." **62:4d** Hebrew *Beulah,* which means "married." **62:11** Hebrew *Tell the daughter of Zion.* **63:9** Hebrew *and the angel of his presence.*

62:2 new name. Signified a new status and a new righteous character. Names often represented one's anticipated or present character.
62:6 watchmen on your walls. Guards stationed on city walls looked for any approaching enemy. Here it refers to prophets who call on the Lord. **no rest.** The prophets are like watchmen who keep waiting for God to do what He promised. God's promises give Him no rest until He fulfills them.
63:1 Bozrah. The main town of Edom, an enemy of Israel that God would judge.
63:5 wrath sustained me. In the final battle of Armageddon, God will defeat His enemies. Sin produces anger in God because it offends His holiness.
63:7 I will tell. As a representative of the people, Isaiah publicly proclaimed God's mercy, love, and goodness. Recalling God's loving actions in the past helps believers to trust in His provision for the present and future.

He lifted them up and carried them
through all the years.
10 But they rebelled against him
and grieved his Holy Spirit.
So he became their enemy
and fought against them.

11 Then they remembered those days of old
when Moses led his people out of Egypt.
They cried out, "Where is the one who brought
Israel through the sea,
with Moses as their shepherd?
Where is the one who sent his Holy Spirit
to be among his people?
12 Where is the one whose power was displayed
when Moses lifted up his hand—
the one who divided the sea before them,
making himself famous forever?
13 Where is the one who led them through the
bottom of the sea?
They were like fine stallions
racing through the desert, never stumbling.
14 As with cattle going down into a peaceful valley,
the Spirit of the LORD gave them rest.
You led your people, LORD,
and gained a magnificent reputation."

PRAYER FOR MERCY AND PARDON

15 LORD, look down from heaven;
look from your holy, glorious home, and see us.
Where is the passion and the might
you used to show on our behalf?
Where are your mercy and compassion now?
16 Surely you are still our Father!
Even if Abraham and Jacob* would disown us,
LORD, you would still be our Father.
You are our Redeemer from ages past.
17 LORD, why have you allowed us to turn from your
path?
Why have you given us stubborn hearts so we
no longer fear you?
Return and help us, for we are your servants,
the tribes that are your special possession.
18 How briefly your holy people possessed your holy
place,
and now our enemies have destroyed it.
19 Sometimes it seems as though we never belonged
to you,
as though we had never been known as your
people.

64 1*Oh, that you would burst from the heavens
and come down!
How the mountains would quake in your presence!
2*As fire causes wood to burn
and water to boil,
your coming would make the nations tremble.
Then your enemies would learn the reason for
your fame!
3 When you came down long ago,
you did awesome deeds beyond our highest
expectations.
And oh, how the mountains quaked!
4 For since the world began,
no ear has heard
and no eye has seen a God like you,
who works for those who wait for him!
5 You welcome those who gladly do good,
who follow godly ways.
But you have been very angry with us,
for we are not godly.
We are constant sinners;
how can people like us be saved?
6 We are all infected and impure with sin.
When we display our righteous deeds,
they are nothing but filthy rags.
Like autumn leaves, we wither and fall,
and our sins sweep us away like the wind.
7 Yet no one calls on your name
or pleads with you for mercy.
Therefore, you have turned away from us
and turned us over* to our sins.

8 And yet, O LORD, you are our Father.
We are the clay, and you are the potter.
We all are formed by your hand.
9 Don't be so angry with us, LORD.
Please don't remember our sins forever.
Look at us, we pray,
and see that we are all your people.
10 Your holy cities are destroyed.
Zion is a wilderness;
yes, Jerusalem is a desolate ruin.
11 The holy and beautiful Temple
where our ancestors praised you
has been burned down,
and all the things of beauty are destroyed.
12 After all this, LORD, must you still refuse to help us?
Will you continue to be silent and punish us?

JUDGMENT AND FINAL SALVATION

65 The LORD says,
"I was ready to respond, but no one asked for help.
I was ready to be found, but no one was looking
for me.
I said, 'Here I am, here I am!'
to a nation that did not call on my name.*
2 All day long I opened my arms to a rebellious
people.*
But they follow their own evil paths
and their own crooked schemes.
3 All day long they insult me to my face
by worshiping idols in their sacred gardens.

63:16 Hebrew *Israel.* See note on 14:1. **64:1** In the Hebrew text this verse is included in 63:19. **64:2** Verses 64:2-12 are numbered 64:1-11 in Hebrew text. **64:7** As in Greek, Syriac, and Aramaic versions; Hebrew reads *melted us.* **65:1** Or *to a nation that did not bear my name.* **65:1-2** Greek version reads *I was found by people who were not looking for me. / I showed myself to those who were not asking for me. / All day long I opened my arms to them, / but they were disobedient and rebellious.* Compare Rom 10:20-21.

63:17 allowed us to turn from your path. As with Pharaoh, God allowed Israel's heart to harden further once they started straying.
64:1 burst from the heavens and come down. The sky was depicted as a piece of cloth God would tear as He came to destroy Israel's enemies.
64:6 righteous deeds . . . nothing but filthy rags. Sins were described as the color red—a warning of loss, of hurt, of defeat—in 1:18. Compared to God's righteousness, even our good behavior is worthless.
65:1 no one asked . . . no one was looking. God allowed Himself to be found as He continually reached out in love to Israel. He was ready to help them, but they did not respond to His voice.
65:3 All day long they insult me. The people disobeyed God by worshiping idols and consulting mediums and spiritists. **to my face.** They did not hide their shameful activities, but they defiantly and boldly sacrificed to idols.

They burn incense on pagan altars.
4 At night they go out among the graves,
worshiping the dead.
They eat the flesh of pigs
and make stews with other forbidden foods.
5 Yet they say to each other,
'Don't come too close or you will defile me!
I am holier than you!'
These people are a stench in my nostrils,
an acrid smell that never goes away.

6 "Look, my decree is written out* in front of me:
I will not stand silent;
I will repay them in full!
Yes, I will repay them—
7 both for their own sins
and for those of their ancestors,"
says the LORD.
"For they also burned incense on the mountains
and insulted me on the hills.
I will pay them back in full!

8 "But I will not destroy them all,"
says the LORD.
"For just as good grapes are found among a cluster of bad ones
(and someone will say, 'Don't throw them all away—
some of those grapes are good!'),
so I will not destroy all Israel.
For I still have true servants there.
9 I will preserve a remnant of the people of Israel*
and of Judah to possess my land.
Those I choose will inherit it,
and my servants will live there.
10 The plain of Sharon will again be filled with flocks
for my people who have searched for me,
and the valley of Achor will be a place to pasture herds.

11 "But because the rest of you have forsaken the LORD
and have forgotten his Temple,
and because you have prepared feasts to honor the god of Fate
and have offered mixed wine to the god of Destiny,
12 now I will 'destine' you for the sword.
All of you will bow down before the executioner.
For when I called, you did not answer.
When I spoke, you did not listen.
You deliberately sinned—before my very eyes—
and chose to do what you know I despise."

13 Therefore, this is what the Sovereign LORD says:
"My servants will eat,
but you will starve.
My servants will drink,
but you will be thirsty.
My servants will rejoice,
but you will be sad and ashamed.
14 My servants will sing for joy,
but you will cry in sorrow and despair.
15 Your name will be a curse word among my people,
for the Sovereign LORD will destroy you
and will call his true servants by another name.
16 All who invoke a blessing or take an oath
will do so by the God of truth.
For I will put aside my anger
and forget the evil of earlier days.

17 "Look! I am creating new heavens and a new earth,
and no one will even think about the old ones anymore.
18 Be glad; rejoice forever in my creation!
And look! I will create Jerusalem as a place of happiness.
Her people will be a source of joy.
19 I will rejoice over Jerusalem
and delight in my people.
And the sound of weeping and crying
will be heard in it no more.

20 "No longer will babies die when only a few days old.
No longer will adults die before they have lived a full life.
No longer will people be considered old at one hundred!
Only the cursed will die that young!
21 In those days people will live in the houses they build
and eat the fruit of their own vineyards.
22 Unlike the past, invaders will not take their houses
and confiscate their vineyards.
For my people will live as long as trees,
and my chosen ones will have time to enjoy their hard-won gains.
23 They will not work in vain,
and their children will not be doomed to misfortune.
For they are people blessed by the LORD,
and their children, too, will be blessed.
24 I will answer them before they even call to me.
While they are still talking about their needs,
I will go ahead and answer their prayers!
25 The wolf and the lamb will feed together.
The lion will eat hay like a cow.
But the snakes will eat dust.
In those days no one will be hurt or destroyed on my holy mountain.
I, the LORD, have spoken!"

65:6 Or *their sins are written out;* Hebrew reads *it stands written.* **65:9** Hebrew *remnant of Jacob.* See note on 14:1.

65:5 I am holier than you! Idolaters are like the New Testament Pharisees whom Jesus called children of the Devil (see John 8:44). They thought of themselves as better than others.
65:13 my servants will eat but you will starve. The call for God to tear open the heavens and come down (64:1) is a call to blessing and judgment. Verses 13-16 describe the very different results of God's coming.
65:15 a curse word among my people. Believers will refer to rebellious Israelites as an example of those receiving judgment. The name of evil King Ahab was used as a curse. The restored remnant would receive both a new name and a new character as a blessing.
65:18 create Jerusalem as a place of happiness. As God created the earth and heavens, so will He create a new world for the enjoyment of His people when Christ returns (Rev. 21:1).
65:24 I will answer them before they even call. Some refuse to pray because God knows everything. But prayer is God's appointed means for bringing His blessings.

66 This is what the LORD says:
"Heaven is my throne,
and the earth is my footstool.
Could you build me a temple as good as that?
Could you build me such a resting place?
2 My hands have made both heaven and earth;
they and everything in them are mine.*
I, the LORD, have spoken!

"I will bless those who have humble and contrite hearts,
who tremble at my word.
3 But those who choose their own ways—
delighting in their detestable sins—
will not have their offerings accepted.
When such people sacrifice a bull,
it is no more acceptable than a human sacrifice.
When they sacrifice a lamb,
it's as though they had sacrificed a dog!
When they bring an offering of grain,
they might as well offer the blood of a pig.
When they burn frankincense,
it's as if they had blessed an idol.
4 I will send them great trouble—
all the things they feared.
For when I called, they did not answer.
When I spoke, they did not listen.
They deliberately sinned before my very eyes
and chose to do what they know I despise."

5 Hear this message from the LORD,
all you who tremble at his words:
"Your own people hate you
and throw you out for being loyal to my name.
'Let the LORD be honored!' they scoff.
'Be joyful in him!'
But they will be put to shame.
6 What is all the commotion in the city?
What is that terrible noise from the Temple?
It is the voice of the LORD
taking vengeance against his enemies.

7 "Before the birth pains even begin,
Jerusalem gives birth to a son.
8 Who has ever seen anything as strange as this?
Who ever heard of such a thing?
Has a nation ever been born in a single day?
Has a country ever come forth in a mere moment?
But by the time Jerusalem's* birth pains begin,
her children will be born.
9 Would I ever bring this nation to the point of birth
and then not deliver it?" asks the LORD.
"No! I would never keep this nation from being born,"
says your God.

10 "Rejoice with Jerusalem!
Be glad with her, all you who love her
and all you who mourn for her.
11 Drink deeply of her glory
even as an infant drinks at its mother's comforting breasts."

12 This is what the LORD says:
"I will give Jerusalem a river of peace and prosperity.
The wealth of the nations will flow to her.
Her children will be nursed at her breasts,
carried in her arms, and held on her lap.
13 I will comfort you there in Jerusalem
as a mother comforts her child."

14 When you see these things, your heart will rejoice.
You will flourish like the grass!
Everyone will see the LORD's hand of blessing on his servants—
and his anger against his enemies.
15 See, the LORD is coming with fire,
and his swift chariots roar like a whirlwind.
He will bring punishment with the fury of his anger
and the flaming fire of his hot rebuke.
16 The LORD will punish the world by fire
and by his sword.
He will judge the earth,
and many will be killed by him.

17 "Those who 'consecrate' and 'purify' themselves
in a sacred garden with its idol in the center—feast-
ing on pork and rats and other detestable meats—
will come to a terrible end," says the LORD.
18 "I can see what they are doing, and I know what
they are thinking. So I will gather all nations and
peoples together, and they will see my glory. 19 I will
perform a sign among them. And I will send those
who survive to be messengers to the nations—to Tar-
shish, to the Libyans* and Lydians* (who are famous
as archers), to Tubal and Greece,* and to all the lands
beyond the sea that have not heard of my fame or
seen my glory. There they will declare my glory to the
nations. 20 They will bring the remnant of your peo-
ple back from every nation. They will bring them to
my holy mountain in Jerusalem as an offering to the
LORD. They will ride on horses, in chariots and wag-
ons, and on mules and camels," says the LORD. 21 "And
I will appoint some of them to be my priests and Lev-
ites. I, the LORD, have spoken!

22 "As surely as my new heavens and earth will remain,
so will you always be my people,
with a name that will never disappear,"
says the LORD.

66:2 As in Greek, Latin, and Syriac versions; Hebrew reads *these things are.* **66:8** Hebrew *Zion's.* **66:19a** As in some Greek manuscripts, which read *Put* [that is, *Libya*]; Hebrew reads *Pul.* **66:19b** Hebrew *Lud.* **66:19c** Hebrew *Javan.*

66:1 a temple as good as that . . . such a resting place. God cannot be contained in any building (1 Kings 8:27). Jesus told the Samaritan woman "the time is coming—indeed it's here now—when true worshipers will worship the Father in spirit and in truth. . . . God is Spirit, so those who worship him must worship in spirit and in truth" (John 4:23-24).

66:7 Before the birth pains even begin. Israel's return to the land will happen so quickly that it will occur without pain. Jerusalem here is pictured as the mother of Israel, which is also the Messiah.

66:11 Drink deeply of her glory. The people in Jerusalem will enjoy the city as an infant enjoys food provided by its mother. Everyone will rejoice.

66:20 They will bring. The Gentiles will bring Jews into the land at the beginning of the millennium. Gentiles too will worship God in the land in those days (56:6-7).

23 "All humanity will come to worship me
from week to week
and from month to month.
24 And as they go out, they will see
the dead bodies of those who have rebelled
against me.
For the worms that devour them will never die,
and the fire that burns them will never go out.
All who pass by
will view them with utter horror."

66:23 All humanity. Referred to believing Jews and Gentiles from all nations, in contrast to those who reject God (Zech. 14:16). **from month to month.** Many provisions of the law of Moses will be practiced in the millennium.

66:24 the fire . . . will never go out. Jesus quoted this verse from the end of Isaiah as the destiny of the lost who are confined to hell (Mark 9:48). Hell is eternal torment and separation from God.

INTRODUCTION TO

JEREMIAH

PERSONAL READING PLAN

- ☐Jeremiah 1:1–3:5
- ☐Jeremiah 3:6–4:31
- ☐Jeremiah 5:1–6:30
- ☐Jeremiah 7:1–9:26
- ☐Jeremiah 10:1–12:17
- ☐Jeremiah 13:1–15:21
- ☐Jeremiah 16:1–17:27
- ☐Jeremiah 18:1–20:18
- ☐Jeremiah 21:1–23:8
- ☐Jeremiah 23:9–25:14
- ☐Jeremiah 25:15–26:24
- ☐Jeremiah 27:1–29:32
- ☐Jeremiah 30:1–31:40
- ☐Jeremiah 32:1–33:26
- ☐Jeremiah 34:1–35:19
- ☐Jeremiah 36:1–37:21
- ☐Jeremiah 38:1–40:6
- ☐Jeremiah 40:7–43:13
- ☐Jeremiah 44:1–46:28
- ☐Jeremiah 47:1–48:47
- ☐Jeremiah 49:1-39
- ☐Jeremiah 50:1-46
- ☐Jeremiah 51:1-64
- ☐Jeremiah 52:1-34

AUTHOR

These are the words of Jeremiah, who was both a prophet and a priest. They were written down by his secretary, Baruch (36:4-32), who may have finalized Jeremiah's prophecies in written form.

DATE

Events recorded here span the years 626–585 B.C. The book was compiled sometime later. Jeremiah's ministry was immediately preceded by that of Zephaniah. Habakkuk, Obadiah, and Ezekiel were all possible contemporaries of Jeremiah.

THEME

God is just and must punish sin. But God in His grace promises Israel restoration and covenant renewal.

HISTORICAL BACKGROUND

The prophet Jeremiah ministered in the context of three major kings. Under King Josiah (640–609 B.C.), Jeremiah was free to preach and join in Josiah's reform movement. Under King Jehoiakim (609–598 B.C.), Jeremiah fell out of royal favor and experienced frequent imprisonments. Under King Zedekiah (597–586 B.C.), Jeremiah was treated more kindly but still feared for his life. The judgment that Jeremiah announced was brought about by King Nebuchadnezzar of Babylon. He besieged Jerusalem three times, culminating in the sacking of Jerusalem in 586 B.C. and a full-scale exile of Jews to Babylon. Jewish tradition asserts that while Jeremiah was living in exile in Egypt, he was stoned to death (see Heb. 11:37).

CHARACTERISTICS

The book is constructed thematically, not chronologically. In it, Jeremiah speaks God's words, and he is obviously distressed. He complains to God about the job allotted to him more than any other prophet. Jeremiah denounces Judah's kings for their folly and weakness and the people for going their own way. Equally a part of his message, however, is a God of love who is determined to mold a people worthy of His name. Jeremiah is allowed to see that the divine wrath had a 70-year limit. After that, forgiveness and cleansing would come, bringing a new day in which all expectations would be fulfilled in a manner transcending all God's mercies of old.

1 These are the words of Jeremiah son of Hilkiah,
one of the priests from the town of Anathoth in
the land of Benjamin. 2 The LORD first gave messages
to Jeremiah during the thirteenth year of the reign of
Josiah son of Amon, king of Judah.* 3 The LORD's mes-
sages continued throughout the reign of King Jehoia-
kim, Josiah's son, until the eleventh year of the reign
of King Zedekiah, another of Josiah's sons. In August*
of that eleventh year the people of Jerusalem were
taken away as captives.

JEREMIAH'S CALL AND FIRST VISIONS

4 The LORD gave me this message:

5 "I knew you before I formed you in your mother's
womb.
Before you were born I set you apart
and appointed you as my prophet to the
nations."

6 "O Sovereign LORD," I said, "I can't speak for you!
I'm too young!"
7 The LORD replied, "Don't say, 'I'm too young,' for
you must go wherever I send you and say whatever
I tell you. 8 And don't be afraid of the people, for I will
be with you and will protect you. I, the LORD, have
spoken!" 9 Then the LORD reached out and touched my
mouth and said,

"Look, I have put my words in your mouth!
10 Today I appoint you to stand up
against nations and kingdoms.
Some you must uproot and tear down,
destroy and overthrow.
Others you must build up
and plant."

11 Then the LORD said to me, "Look, Jeremiah! What
do you see?"
And I replied, "I see a branch from an almond tree."
12 And the LORD said, "That's right, and it means that
I am watching,* and I will certainly carry out all my
plans."
13 Then the LORD spoke to me again and asked,
"What do you see now?"
And I replied, "I see a pot of boiling water, spilling
from the north."
14 "Yes," the LORD said, "for terror from the north
will boil out on the people of this land. 15 Listen! I am
calling the armies of the kingdoms of the north to
come to Jerusalem. I, the LORD, have spoken!

"They will set their thrones
at the gates of the city.
They will attack its walls
and all the other towns of Judah.
16 I will pronounce judgment
on my people for all their evil—
for deserting me and burning incense to other
gods.
Yes, they worship idols made with their own
hands!

17 "Get up and prepare for action.
Go out and tell them everything I tell you to say.
Do not be afraid of them,
or I will make you look foolish in front of them.
18 For see, today I have made you strong
like a fortified city that cannot be captured,
like an iron pillar or a bronze wall.
You will stand against the whole land—
the kings, officials, priests, and people of Judah.
19 They will fight you, but they will fail.
For I am with you, and I will take care of you.
I, the LORD, have spoken!"

THE LORD'S CASE AGAINST HIS PEOPLE

2 The LORD gave me another message. He said, 2 "Go
and shout this message to Jerusalem. This is what
the LORD says:

"I remember how eager you were to please me
as a young bride long ago,
how you loved me and followed me
even through the barren wilderness.
3 In those days Israel was holy to the LORD,
the first of his children.*
All who harmed his people were declared guilty,
and disaster fell on them.
I, the LORD, have spoken!"

4 Listen to the word of the LORD, people of Jacob—
all you families of Israel! 5 This is what the LORD says:

"What did your ancestors find wrong with me
that led them to stray so far from me?
They worshiped worthless idols,
only to become worthless themselves.
6 They did not ask, 'Where is the LORD
who brought us safely out of Egypt
and led us through the barren wilderness—
a land of deserts and pits,
a land of drought and death,
where no one lives or even travels?'

7 "And when I brought you into a fruitful land
to enjoy its bounty and goodness,
you defiled my land and
corrupted the possession I had promised you.
8 The priests did not ask,
'Where is the LORD?'
Those who taught my word ignored me,

1:2 The thirteenth year of Josiah's reign was 627 B.C. **1:3** Hebrew *In the fifth month,* of the ancient Hebrew lunar calendar. A number of events in Jeremiah can be cross-checked with dates in surviving Babylonian records and related accurately to our modern calendar. The fifth month in the eleventh year of Zedekiah's reign occurred within the months of August and September 586 B.C. Also see 52:12 and the note there. **1:12** The Hebrew word for "watching" *(shoqed)* sounds like the word for "almond tree" *(shaqed).* **2:3** Hebrew *the firstfruits of his harvest.*

1:2 Josiah. Josiah, the last godly king of Judah, became king at age eight. When he matured, he realized Israel had drifted from obedience to the Law and initiated reforms (2 Kings 22:11). The subsequent spiritual deterioration of Judah gave rise to Jeremiah.

1:3 Jehoiakim. After Josiah was killed by Pharaoh Neco (2 Kings 23:29), pharaoh named his evil son Jehoiakim as king.

1:6 I can't speak. Jeremiah tried the same excuse as Moses (Ex. 4:10).

1:9 touched my mouth. When Moses bemoaned his lack of speaking skill, God appointed Aaron his spokesman (Ex. 4:10-16). For Jeremiah, God simply reached down and placed His words in the prophet's mouth.

2:2 young bride. Marriage often illustrated the relationship between God and His people (Isa. 54:5; Hos. 2:16). In the New Testament, Paul compared the husband/wife relationship to that of Jesus and His church (Eph. 5:23).

the rulers turned against me,
and the prophets spoke in the name of Baal,
wasting their time on worthless idols.
9 Therefore, I will bring my case against you,"
says the LORD.
"I will even bring charges against your children's children
in the years to come.

10 "Go west and look in the land of Cyprus*;
go east and search through the land of Kedar.
Has anyone ever heard of anything
as strange as this?
11 Has any nation ever traded its gods for new ones,
even though they are not gods at all?
Yet my people have exchanged their glorious God*
for worthless idols!
12 The heavens are shocked at such a thing
and shrink back in horror and dismay,"
says the LORD.
13 "For my people have done two evil things:
They have abandoned me—
the fountain of living water.
And they have dug for themselves cracked cisterns
that can hold no water at all!

THE RESULTS OF ISRAEL'S SIN

14 "Why has Israel become a slave?
Why has he been carried away as plunder?
15 Strong lions have roared against him,
and the land has been destroyed.
The towns are now in ruins,
and no one lives in them anymore.
16 Egyptians, marching from their cities of Memphis* and Tahpanhes,
have destroyed Israel's glory and power.
17 And you have brought this upon yourselves
by rebelling against the LORD your God,
even though he was leading you on the way!

18 "What have you gained by your alliances with Egypt
and your covenants with Assyria?
What good to you are the streams of the Nile*
or the waters of the Euphrates River?*
19 Your wickedness will bring its own punishment.
Your turning from me will shame you.
You will see what an evil, bitter thing it is
to abandon the LORD your God and not to fear him.
I, the Lord, the LORD of Heaven's Armies, have spoken!

20 "Long ago I broke the yoke that oppressed you
and tore away the chains of your slavery,
but still you said,
'I will not serve you.'
On every hill and under every green tree,
you have prostituted yourselves by bowing down to idols.
21 But I was the one who planted you,
choosing a vine of the purest stock—the very best.
How did you grow into this corrupt wild vine?
22 No amount of soap or lye can make you clean.
I still see the stain of your guilt.
I, the Sovereign LORD, have spoken!

ISRAEL, AN UNFAITHFUL WIFE

23 "You say, 'That's not true!
I haven't worshiped the images of Baal!'
But how can you say that?
Go and look in any valley in the land!
Face the awful sins you have done.
You are like a restless female camel
desperately searching for a mate.
24 You are like a wild donkey,
sniffing the wind at mating time.
Who can restrain her lust?
Those who desire her don't need to search,
for she goes running to them!
25 When will you stop running?
When will you stop panting after other gods?
But you say, 'Save your breath.
I'm in love with these foreign gods,
and I can't stop loving them now!'

26 "Israel is like a thief
who feels shame only when he gets caught.
They, their kings, officials, priests, and prophets—
all are alike in this.
27 To an image carved from a piece of wood they say,
'You are my father.'
To an idol chiseled from a block of stone they say,
'You are my mother.'
They turn their backs on me,
but in times of trouble they cry out to me,
'Come and save us!'
28 But why not call on these gods you have made?
When trouble comes, let them save you if they can!
For you have as many gods
as there are towns in Judah.
29 Why do you accuse me of doing wrong?
You are the ones who have rebelled,"
says the LORD.
30 "I have punished your children,
but they did not respond to my discipline.
You yourselves have killed your prophets
as a lion kills its prey.

31 "O my people, listen to the words of the LORD!
Have I been like a desert to Israel?
Have I been to them a land of darkness?
Why then do my people say, 'At last we are free from God!

2:10 Hebrew *Kittim.* 2:11 Hebrew *their glory.* 2:16 Hebrew *Noph.* 2:18a Hebrew *of Shihor,* a branch of the Nile River. 2:18b Hebrew *the river?*

2:13 cracked cisterns. Note the contrast between God and the pagan deities represented by idols. God was the source of life-sustaining water while cisterns could not hold even a drop for the people to drink.

2:18 What good . . . the waters. Jeremiah returned to the illustration of verse 13. God had provided spiritual and physical food in the desert (v. 6), yet the people turned away and looked to enemies for political and spiritual guidance.

2:19 evil . . . abandon. The Hebrew word translated "abandon" implied repeated descents into backsliding. Other passages further demonstrate Jeremiah's understanding of apostasy (3:22; 5:6; 14:7).

2:20 broke the yoke. Jeremiah compared Judah to a stubborn draft animal that rebelled against its master. Judah was more than willing to degrade itself as a prostitute serves her customer.

2:22 make you clean . . . stain. The stain of sin is only removed by the grace and forgiveness of God.

We don't need him anymore!'
32 Does a young woman forget her jewelry,
or a bride her wedding dress?
Yet for years on end
my people have forgotten me.

33 "How you plot and scheme to win your lovers.
Even an experienced prostitute could learn
from you!
34 Your clothing is stained with the blood of the
innocent and the poor,
though you didn't catch them breaking into
your houses!
35 And yet you say,
'I have done nothing wrong.
Surely God isn't angry with me!'
But now I will punish you severely
because you claim you have not sinned.
36 First here, then there—
you flit from one ally to another asking for help.
But your new friends in Egypt will let you down,
just as Assyria did before.
37 In despair, you will be led into exile
with your hands on your heads,
for the LORD has rejected the nations you trust.
They will not help you at all.

3 1 "If a man divorces a woman
and she goes and marries someone else,
he will not take her back again,
for that would surely corrupt the land.
But you have prostituted yourself with many
lovers,
so why are you trying to come back to me?"
says the LORD.
2 "Look at the shrines on every hilltop.
Is there any place you have not been defiled
by your adultery with other gods?
You sit like a prostitute beside the road waiting for
a customer.
You sit alone like a nomad in the desert.
You have polluted the land with your prostitution
and your wickedness.
3 That's why even the spring rains have failed.
For you are a brazen prostitute and completely
shameless.
4 Yet you say to me,
'Father, you have been my guide since my youth.
5 Surely you won't be angry forever!
Surely you can forget about it!'
So you talk,
but you keep on doing all the evil you can."

JUDAH FOLLOWS ISRAEL'S EXAMPLE

6 During the reign of King Josiah, the LORD said to me,
"Have you seen what fickle Israel has done? Like a wife
who commits adultery, Israel has worshiped other gods
on every hill and under every green tree. 7 I thought,
'After she has done all this, she will return to me.' But
she did not return, and her faithless sister Judah saw
this. 8 She saw* that I divorced faithless Israel because
of her adultery. But that treacherous sister Judah had
no fear, and now she, too, has left me and given her-
self to prostitution. 9 Israel treated it all so lightly—she
thought nothing of committing adultery by worship-
ing idols made of wood and stone. So now the land has
been polluted. 10 But despite all this, her faithless sister
Judah has never sincerely returned to me. She has only
pretended to be sorry. I, the LORD, have spoken!"

HOPE FOR WAYWARD ISRAEL

11 Then the LORD said to me, "Even faithless Israel is less
guilty than treacherous Judah! 12 Therefore, go and
give this message to Israel.* This is what the LORD says:

"O Israel, my faithless people,
come home to me again,
for I am merciful.
I will not be angry with you forever.
13 Only acknowledge your guilt.
Admit that you rebelled against the LORD your
God
and committed adultery against him
by worshiping idols under every green tree.
Confess that you refused to listen to my voice.
I, the LORD, have spoken!

14 "Return home, you wayward children,"
says the LORD,
"for I am your master.
I will bring you back to the land of Israel*—
one from this town and two from that family—
from wherever you are scattered.
15 And I will give you shepherds after my own heart,
who will guide you with knowledge and
understanding.

16 "And when your land is once more filled with
people," says the LORD, "you will no longer wish for
'the good old days' when you possessed the Ark of the
LORD's Covenant. You will not miss those days or even
remember them, and there will be no need to rebuild
the Ark. 17 In that day Jerusalem will be known as
'The Throne of the LORD.' All nations will come there
to honor the LORD. They will no longer stubbornly fol-
low their own evil desires. 18 In those days the people
of Judah and Israel will return together from exile in
the north. They will return to the land I gave your an-
cestors as an inheritance forever.

19 "I thought to myself,
'I would love to treat you as my own children!'
I wanted nothing more than to give you this
beautiful land—
the finest possession in the world.

3:8 As in Dead Sea Scrolls, one Greek manuscript, and Syriac version; Masoretic Text reads *I saw.* **3:12** Hebrew *toward the north.* **3:14** Hebrew *to Zion.*

3:1 come back to me. Jeremiah reminded the people that the covenant relationship was not only contractual, it was personal at its core. The faithlessness of Israel was bad enough (v. 8), but Judah's sin was worse. She had prostituted herself with other gods. Would Judah's men forgive and take back an unfaithful wife?

3:7 faithless sister. Ezekiel expanded on this metaphor of Judah and Israel as unfaithful sisters (Ezek. 23).

3:8 no fear. Judah had watched the decline and fall of Israel (2 Kings 15:17–17:41). Yet the southern kingdom never seemed to worry that the same fate might befall them.

3:10 only pretended. Judah had only pretended to embrace Josiah's reforms (2 Kings 23:1-25).

3:12 to Israel. Many of Israel's citizens had been taken into exile by Assyria and removed to that empire's northern provinces. Those who remained in Israel lived north of Judah.

3:16 when . . . you will no longer wish. Even the ark of the covenant will be irrelevant and forgotten. Jeremiah did not imply that this coming Messianic age would be godless but rather that the old covenant would be superseded by something better.

I looked forward to your calling me 'Father,'
and I wanted you never to turn from me.
20 But you have been unfaithful to me, you people of Israel!
You have been like a faithless wife who leaves her husband.
I, the LORD, have spoken."

21 Voices are heard high on the windswept mountains,
the weeping and pleading of Israel's people.
For they have chosen crooked paths
and have forgotten the LORD their God.

22 "My wayward children," says the LORD,
"come back to me, and I will heal your wayward hearts."

"Yes, we're coming," the people reply,
"for you are the LORD our God.
23 Our worship of idols on the hills
and our religious orgies on the mountains
are a delusion.
Only in the LORD our God
will Israel ever find salvation.
24 From childhood we have watched
as everything our ancestors worked for—
their flocks and herds, their sons and daughters—
was squandered on a delusion.
25 Let us now lie down in shame
and cover ourselves with dishonor,
for we and our ancestors have sinned
against the LORD our God.
From our childhood to this day
we have never obeyed him."

4 1 "O Israel," says the LORD,
"if you wanted to return to me, you could.
You could throw away your detestable idols
and stray away no more.
2 Then when you swear by my name, saying,
'As surely as the LORD lives,'
you could do so
with truth, justice, and righteousness.
Then you would be a blessing to the nations of the world,
and all people would come and praise my name."

COMING JUDGMENT AGAINST JUDAH

3 This is what the LORD says to the people of Judah and Jerusalem:

"Plow up the hard ground of your hearts!
Do not waste your good seed among thorns.
4 O people of Judah and Jerusalem,
surrender your pride and power.
Change your hearts before the LORD,*
or my anger will burn like an unquenchable fire
because of all your sins.

5 "Shout to Judah, and broadcast to Jerusalem!
Tell them to sound the alarm throughout the land:
'Run for your lives!
Flee to the fortified cities!'
6 Raise a signal flag as a warning for Jerusalem*:
'Flee now! Do not delay!'
For I am bringing terrible destruction upon you
from the north."

7 A lion stalks from its den,
a destroyer of nations.
It has left its lair and is headed your way.
It's going to devastate your land!
Your towns will lie in ruins,
with no one living in them anymore.
8 So put on clothes of mourning
and weep with broken hearts,
for the fierce anger of the LORD
is still upon us.

9 "In that day," says the LORD,
"the king and the officials will tremble in fear.
The priests will be struck with horror,
and the prophets will be appalled."

10 Then I said, "O Sovereign LORD,
the people have been deceived by what you said,
for you promised peace for Jerusalem.
But the sword is held at their throats!"

11 The time is coming when the LORD will say
to the people of Jerusalem,
"My dear people, a burning wind is blowing in
from the desert,
and it's not a gentle breeze useful for
winnowing grain.
12 It is a roaring blast sent by me!
Now I will pronounce your destruction!"

13 Our enemy rushes down on us like storm clouds!
His chariots are like whirlwinds.
His horses are swifter than eagles.
How terrible it will be, for we are doomed!
14 O Jerusalem, cleanse your heart
that you may be saved.
How long will you harbor
your evil thoughts?
15 Your destruction has been announced
from Dan and the hill country of Ephraim.

4:4 Hebrew *Circumcise yourselves to the LORD, and take away the foreskins of your heart.* 4:6 Hebrew *Zion.*

3:17 known as 'The Throne of the LORD.' The ark of the covenant had contained the atonement cover. Golden cherubim sat on each end, and God was enthroned between the cherubim (see 2 Chron. 5:8). In the Messianic age, however, Jesus' throne will be in Jerusalem instead of the ark.
3:18 people of Judah and Israel . . . together. God's people had become a divided nation (1 Kings 11–12). In the Messianic age, God's people would be united again.
4:2 a blessing to the nations. God promised to make Abram's descendants into a great nation and that other nations would be blessed by his descendants (Gen. 12:2-3).
4:10 the people have been deceived. God had not directly deceived but allowed false prophets to promulgate untruths for various reasons (see 1 Kings 22:20-23).
4:11 burning wind is blowing. The Babylonians were speedily approaching with the goal of destroying Israel.
4:12 a roaring blast. A light breeze separates good (wheat) and bad (chaff) (Ps. 35:5.) The Lord will soon send a wind that destroys.

16 "Warn the surrounding nations
and announce this to Jerusalem:
The enemy is coming from a distant land,
raising a battle cry against the towns of Judah.
17 They surround Jerusalem like watchmen around a field,
for my people have rebelled against me,"
says the LORD.
18 "Your own actions have brought this upon you.
This punishment is bitter, piercing you to the heart!"

JEREMIAH WEEPS FOR HIS PEOPLE

19 My heart, my heart—I writhe in pain!
My heart pounds within me! I cannot be still.
For I have heard the blast of enemy trumpets
and the roar of their battle cries.
20 Waves of destruction roll over the land,
until it lies in complete desolation.
Suddenly my tents are destroyed;
in a moment my shelters are crushed.
21 How long must I see the battle flags
and hear the trumpets of war?

22 "My people are foolish
and do not know me," says the LORD.
"They are stupid children
who have no understanding.
They are clever enough at doing wrong,
but they have no idea how to do right!"

JEREMIAH'S VISION OF COMING DISASTER

23 I looked at the earth, and it was empty and formless.
I looked at the heavens, and there was no light.
24 I looked at the mountains and hills,
and they trembled and shook.
25 I looked, and all the people were gone.
All the birds of the sky had flown away.
26 I looked, and the fertile fields had become a wilderness.
The towns lay in ruins,
crushed by the LORD's fierce anger.

27 This is what the LORD says:
"The whole land will be ruined,
but I will not destroy it completely.
28 The earth will mourn
and the heavens will be draped in black
because of my decree against my people.
I have made up my mind and will not change it."

29 At the noise of charioteers and archers,
the people flee in terror.
They hide in the bushes
and run for the mountains.
All the towns have been abandoned—
not a person remains!
30 What are you doing,
you who have been plundered?
Why do you dress up in beautiful clothing
and put on gold jewelry?
Why do you brighten your eyes with mascara?
Your primping will do you no good!
The allies who were your lovers
despise you and seek to kill you.

31 I hear a cry, like that of a woman in labor,
the groans of a woman giving birth to her first child.
It is beautiful Jerusalem*
gasping for breath and crying out,
"Help! I'm being murdered!"

THE SINS OF JUDAH

5 1 "Run up and down every street in Jerusalem,"
says the LORD.
"Look high and low; search throughout the city!
If you can find even one just and honest person,
I will not destroy the city.
2 But even when they are under oath,
saying, 'As surely as the LORD lives,'
they are still telling lies!"

3 LORD, you are searching for honesty.
You struck your people,
but they paid no attention.
You crushed them,
but they refused to be corrected.
They are determined, with faces set like stone;
they have refused to repent.

4 Then I said, "But what can we expect from the poor?
They are ignorant.
They don't know the ways of the LORD.
They don't understand God's laws.
5 So I will go and speak to their leaders.
Surely they know the ways of the LORD
and understand God's laws."
But the leaders, too, as one man,
had thrown off God's yoke
and broken his chains.
6 So now a lion from the forest will attack them;
a wolf from the desert will pounce on them.
A leopard will lurk near their towns,
tearing apart any who dare to venture out.
For their rebellion is great,
and their sins are many.

7 "How can I pardon you?
For even your children have turned from me.

4:31 Hebrew *the daughter of Zion.*

4:23 earth . . . was empty and formless. Israel and Judah's destruction would return the world to the state of pre-creation chaos. Genesis 1:2 is the only other use of this phrase in the Bible.
4:25-26 I looked, and all the people were gone. The world reduced to the state which existed before God had created life (Gen. 1:1-10).
4:27 I will not destroy it completely. The coming devastation would be terrible, but God's judgment would be tempered with mercy.
5:1 find even one just and honest person. Like His challenge to Abraham at Sodom (Gen. 18:26-33), God would spare Jerusalem for only one just and honest person.
5:6 lion . . . wolf . . . leopard. Not only has the ox broken from his yoke, he has wandered beyond the farmer's protection (5:5). Some see lions, wolves, and leopards as literal animals of God's judgment (Lev. 26:22; 2 Kings 2:24; 17:25; Ezek. 14:15). Yet, it is easier to see them as the nations referred to in chapters 4 and 6 (2:15; 4:7; 6:3; Hosea 13:7-8; Hab. 1:8; Zeph. 3:3). While the text says "will attack . . . pounce . . . tearing apart," the verbs used are in the perfect tense (in Hebrew). The prophetic writings regularly used this tense to underscore that prophecies were as good as done (Amos 5:2).

They have sworn by gods that are not gods at all!
I fed my people until they were full.
But they thanked me by committing adultery
and lining up at the brothels.
8 They are well-fed, lusty stallions,
each neighing for his neighbor's wife.
9 Should I not punish them for this?" says the LORD.
"Should I not avenge myself against such a nation?

10 "Go down the rows of the vineyards and destroy the grapevines,
leaving a scattered few alive.
Strip the branches from the vines,
for these people do not belong to the LORD.
11 The people of Israel and Judah
are full of treachery against me,"
says the LORD.
12 "They have lied about the LORD
and said, 'He won't bother us!
No disasters will come upon us.
There will be no war or famine.
13 God's prophets are all windbags
who don't really speak for him.
Let their predictions of disaster fall on themselves!'"

14 Therefore, this is what the LORD God of Heaven's Armies says:

"Because the people are talking like this,
my messages will flame out of your mouth
and burn the people like kindling wood.
15 O Israel, I will bring a distant nation against you,"
says the LORD.
"It is a mighty nation,
an ancient nation,
a people whose language you do not know,
whose speech you cannot understand.
16 Their weapons are deadly;
their warriors are mighty.
17 They will devour the food of your harvest;
they will devour your sons and daughters.
They will devour your flocks and herds;
they will devour your grapes and figs.
And they will destroy your fortified towns,
which you think are so safe.

18 "Yet even in those days I will not blot you out completely," says the LORD. 19 "And when your people ask, 'Why did the LORD our God do all this to us?' you must reply, 'You rejected him and gave yourselves to foreign gods in your own land. Now you will serve foreigners in a land that is not your own.'

A WARNING FOR GOD'S PEOPLE

20 "Make this announcement to Israel,*
and say this to Judah:
21 Listen, you foolish and senseless people,
with eyes that do not see
and ears that do not hear.
22 Have you no respect for me?
Why don't you tremble in my presence?
I, the LORD, define the ocean's sandy shoreline
as an everlasting boundary that the waters cannot cross.
The waves may toss and roar,
but they can never pass the boundaries I set.
23 But my people have stubborn and rebellious hearts.
They have turned away and abandoned me.
24 They do not say from the heart,
'Let us live in awe of the LORD our God,
for he gives us rain each spring and fall,
assuring us of a harvest when the time is right.'
25 Your wickedness has deprived you of these wonderful blessings.
Your sin has robbed you of all these good things.

26 "Among my people are wicked men
who lie in wait for victims like a hunter hiding in a blind.
They continually set traps
to catch people.
27 Like a cage filled with birds,
their homes are filled with evil plots.
And now they are great and rich.
28 They are fat and sleek,
and there is no limit to their wicked deeds.
They refuse to provide justice to orphans
and deny the rights of the poor.
29 Should I not punish them for this?" says the LORD.
"Should I not avenge myself against such a nation?
30 A horrible and shocking thing
has happened in this land—
31 the prophets give false prophecies,
and the priests rule with an iron hand.
Worse yet, my people like it that way!
But what will you do when the end comes?

JERUSALEM'S LAST WARNING

6 1 "Run for your lives, you people of Benjamin!
Get out of Jerusalem!
Sound the alarm in Tekoa!
Send up a signal at Beth-hakkerem!
A powerful army is coming from the north,
coming with disaster and destruction.
2 O Jerusalem,* you are my beautiful and delicate daughter—
but I will destroy you!
3 Enemies will surround you, like shepherds
camped around the city.
Each chooses a place for his troops to devour.
4 They shout, 'Prepare for battle!
Attack at noon!'

5:20 Hebrew *to the house of Jacob.* The names "Jacob" and "Israel" are often interchanged throughout the Old Testament, referring sometimes to the individual patriarch and sometimes to the nation. 6:2 Hebrew *Daughter of Zion.*

5:12 no war or famine. Jeremiah mentions two of God's weapons. The third was plague. (14:12).
5:23 stubborn and rebellious hearts. Israel and Judah "refused to accept discipline" (v. 3) and kept on sinning (adultery and idolatry, v. 7).
5:28 no limit to their wicked deeds. The sins of the people are doubly terrible because they not only committed sins but also neglected to do right for the poor and unfortunate.
6:1 out of Jerusalem. There was a certain safety implied in the "fortified cities" (4:5), but even that refuge would be swept away by the onslaught of Babylonians serving as the Lord's instruments of judgment. The Babylonians served without knowing better, while the Israelites should have known.

'No, it's too late; the day is fading,
and the evening shadows are falling.'
5 'Well then, let's attack at night
and destroy her palaces!'"

6 This is what the LORD of Heaven's Armies says:
"Cut down the trees for battering rams.
Build siege ramps against the walls of Jerusalem.
This is the city to be punished,
for she is wicked through and through.
7 She spouts evil like a fountain.
Her streets echo with the sounds of violence and destruction.
I always see her sickness and sores.
8 Listen to this warning, Jerusalem,
or I will turn from you in disgust.
Listen, or I will turn you into a heap of ruins,
a land where no one lives."

9 This is what the LORD of Heaven's Armies says:
"Even the few who remain in Israel
will be picked over again,
as when a harvester checks each vine a second time
to pick the grapes that were missed."

JUDAH'S CONSTANT REBELLION

10 To whom can I give warning?
Who will listen when I speak?
Their ears are closed,
and they cannot hear.
They scorn the word of the LORD.
They don't want to listen at all.
11 So now I am filled with the LORD's fury.
Yes, I am tired of holding it in!

"I will pour out my fury on children playing in the streets
and on gatherings of young men,
on husbands and wives
and on those who are old and gray.
12 Their homes will be turned over to their enemies,
as will their fields and their wives.
For I will raise my powerful fist
against the people of this land,"
says the LORD.
13 "From the least to the greatest,
their lives are ruled by greed.
From prophets to priests,
they are all frauds.
14 They offer superficial treatments
for my people's mortal wound.
They give assurances of peace
when there is no peace.
15 Are they ashamed of their disgusting actions?
Not at all—they don't even know how to blush!
Therefore, they will lie among the slaughtered.
They will be brought down when I punish them,"
says the LORD.

JUDAH REJECTS THE LORD'S WAY

16 This is what the LORD says:
"Stop at the crossroads and look around.
Ask for the old, godly way, and walk in it.
Travel its path, and you will find rest for your souls.
But you reply, 'No, that's not the road we want!'
17 I posted watchmen over you who said,
'Listen for the sound of the alarm.'
But you replied,
'No! We won't pay attention!'

18 "Therefore, listen to this, all you nations.
Take note of my people's situation.
19 Listen, all the earth!
I will bring disaster on my people.
It is the fruit of their own schemes,
because they refuse to listen to me.
They have rejected my word.
20 There's no use offering me sweet frankincense from Sheba.
Keep your fragrant calamus imported from distant lands!
I will not accept your burnt offerings.
Your sacrifices have no pleasing aroma for me."

21 Therefore, this is what the LORD says:
"I will put obstacles in my people's path.
Fathers and sons will both fall over them.
Neighbors and friends will die together."

AN INVASION FROM THE NORTH

22 This is what the LORD says:
"Look! A great army coming from the north!
A great nation is rising against you from far-off lands.
23 They are armed with bows and spears.
They are cruel and show no mercy.
They sound like a roaring sea
as they ride forward on horses.
They are coming in battle formation,
planning to destroy you, beautiful Jerusalem.*"

24 We have heard reports about the enemy,
and we wring our hands in fright.
Pangs of anguish have gripped us,
like those of a woman in labor.
25 Don't go out to the fields!
Don't travel on the roads!
The enemy's sword is everywhere
and terrorizes us at every turn!

6:23 Hebrew *daughter of Zion.*

6:4 Prepare for battle! The Babylonians speak in verses 4 and 5. In contrast to the panic felt by the people of Judah (v. 1), the invaders were calm and calculating. The Babylonians prepared themselves for war, but the people of Judah looked only to escape.
6:10 ears are closed. The people were so caught up in their sin that they would not listen. Though the people could physically hear, they could not spiritually and acted like pagans.
6:11 filled with th LORD's fury. Jeremiah had "ingested" the Word of God through visions and is filled with the Lord's righteous anger.
6:14 assurances of peace when there is no peace. Corrupt priests and prophets taught a "feel-good" message that aimed to treat the symptoms of the people's spiritual disease instead of treating the disease itself. Instead of calling for repentance, they tried to console the people with lies.
6:17 posted watchmen. God appointed true prophets to serve His people so that His Word could be heard and His warnings understood. (Ezek. 3:17.)
6:20 I will not accept your burnt offerings. God would rather see a spirit of repentance than hardened people doing rituals.

26 Oh, my people, dress yourselves in burlap
and sit among the ashes.
Mourn and weep bitterly, as for the loss of an only son.
For suddenly the destroying armies will be upon you!

27 "Jeremiah, I have made you a tester of metals,*
that you may determine the quality of my people.
28 They are the worst kind of rebel,
full of slander.
They are as hard as bronze and iron,
and they lead others into corruption.
29 The bellows fiercely fan the flames
to burn out the corruption.
But it does not purify them,
for the wickedness remains.
30 I will label them 'Rejected Silver,'
for I, the LORD, am discarding them."

JEREMIAH SPEAKS AT THE TEMPLE

7 The LORD gave another message to Jeremiah. He
said, 2 "Go to the entrance of the LORD's Temple,
and give this message to the people: 'O Judah, listen
to this message from the LORD! Listen to it, all of you
who worship here! 3 This is what the LORD of Heaven's
Armies, the God of Israel, says:
"'Even now, if you quit your evil ways, I will let you
stay in your own land. 4 But don't be fooled by those
who promise you safety simply because the LORD's
Temple is here. They chant, "The LORD's Temple is
here! The LORD's Temple is here!" 5 But I will be mer-
ciful only if you stop your evil thoughts and deeds
and start treating each other with justice; 6 only if
you stop exploiting foreigners, orphans, and widows;
only if you stop your murdering; and only if you stop
harming yourselves by worshiping idols. 7 Then I will
let you stay in this land that I gave to your ancestors
to keep forever.
8 "'Don't be fooled into thinking that you will never
suffer because the Temple is here. It's a lie! 9 Do you
really think you can steal, murder, commit adultery,
lie, and burn incense to Baal and all those other new
gods of yours, 10 and then come here and stand before
me in my Temple and chant, "We are safe!"—only
to go right back to all those evils again? 11 Don't you
yourselves admit that this Temple, which bears my
name, has become a den of thieves? Surely I see all
the evil going on there. I, the LORD, have spoken!
12 "'Go now to the place at Shiloh where I once put
the Tabernacle that bore my name. See what I did
there because of all the wickedness of my people,
the Israelites. 13 While you were doing these wicked
things, says the LORD, I spoke to you about it repeat-
edly, but you would not listen. I called out to you, but
you refused to answer. 14 So just as I destroyed Shiloh,
I will now destroy this Temple that bears my name,
this Temple that you trust in for help, this place that I
gave to you and your ancestors. 15 And I will send you
out of my sight into exile, just as I did your relatives,
the people of Israel.*'

JUDAH'S PERSISTENT IDOLATRY

16 "Pray no more for these people, Jeremiah. Do not
weep or pray for them, and don't beg me to help them,
for I will not listen to you. 17 Don't you see what they
are doing throughout the towns of Judah and in the
streets of Jerusalem? 18 No wonder I am so angry!
Watch how the children gather wood and the fathers
build sacrificial fires. See how the women knead
dough and make cakes to offer to the Queen of Heav-
en. And they pour out liquid offerings to their other
idol gods! 19 Am I the one they are hurting?" asks the
LORD. "Most of all, they hurt themselves, to their own
shame."
20 So this is what the Sovereign LORD says: "I will
pour out my terrible fury on this place. Its people, an-
imals, trees, and crops will be consumed by the un-
quenchable fire of my anger."
21 This is what the LORD of Heaven's Armies, the God
of Israel, says: "Take your burnt offerings and your
other sacrifices and eat them yourselves! 22 When I
led your ancestors out of Egypt, it was not burnt of-
ferings and sacrifices I wanted from them. 23 This is
what I told them: 'Obey me, and I will be your God,
and you will be my people. Do everything as I say, and
all will be well!'
24 "But my people would not listen to me. They kept
doing whatever they wanted, following the stubborn
desires of their evil hearts. They went backward in-
stead of forward. 25 From the day your ancestors left
Egypt until now, I have continued to send my ser-
vants, the prophets—day in and day out. 26 But my
people have not listened to me or even tried to hear.
They have been stubborn and sinful—even worse
than their ancestors.
27 "Tell them all this, but do not expect them to lis-
ten. Shout out your warnings, but do not expect them
to respond. 28 Say to them, 'This is the nation whose
people will not obey the LORD their God and who re-
fuse to be taught. Truth has vanished from among
them; it is no longer heard on their lips. 29 Shave your
head in mourning, and weep alone on the mountains.
For the LORD has rejected and forsaken this genera-
tion that has provoked his fury.'

THE VALLEY OF SLAUGHTER

30 "The people of Judah have sinned before my very
eyes," says the LORD. "They have set up their abomina-

6:27 As in Greek version; Hebrew reads *a tester of my people a fortress.* **7:15** Hebrew *of Ephraim,* referring to the northern kingdom of Israel.

6:29-30 it does not purify them. To refine silver, the refiner would add lead which would oxidize and remove other impurities. The result was pure silver. In this refining, however, the ore was so corrupt that its impurities couldn't be purged.
7:4 don't be fooled by those who promise . . . the LORD's temple. The corrupt priests and prophets proclaimed that Jerusalem would not be destroyed because of God's temple.
7:12 place at Shiloh. After the conquest of Canaan, the tabernacle was set up at Shiloh (Josh. 18:1) and remained there through the period of the judges (1 Sam. 1:9). Though 1 Samuel 1–4 does not actually record Shiloh's destruction by the Philistines, Jeremiah implies this historical precedent. Later, the tabernacle is at Gibeon in David's reign (1 Chron. 21:29).
7:25 my servants, the prophets. Jeremiah was part of a long roster specially chosen for this role (see Deut. 18:15-22).
7:30 set up their abominable idols right in the Temple that bears my name. King Hezekiah tried to end paganism among the people (2 Kings 18:3-4). His son Manasseh, however, built altars in the temple to pagan gods (2 Kings 21:4). During Jeremiah's time, Josiah renewed the covenant (2 Kings 23) and tried to stop idolatry (2 Kings 23:24). These reforms failed as well. Less than 20 years after Jeremiah's death, Ezekiel reported that idols again occupied the temple courts (see Ezek. 8:3,5-6).

ble idols right in the Temple that bears my name, de-
filing it. 31 They have built pagan shrines at Topheth,
the garbage dump in the valley of Ben Hinnom, and
there they burn their sons and daughters in the fire. I
have never commanded such a horrible deed; it nev-
er even crossed my mind to command such a thing!
32 So beware, for the time is coming," says the LORD,
"when that garbage dump will no longer be called
Topheth or the valley of Ben-Hinnom, but the Valley
of Slaughter. They will bury the bodies in Topheth
until there is no more room for them. 33 The bodies
of my people will be food for the vultures and wild
animals, and no one will be left to scare them away.
34 I will put an end to the happy singing and laugh-
ter in the streets of Jerusalem. The joyful voices of
bridegrooms and brides will no longer be heard in
the towns of Judah. The land will lie in complete des-
olation.

8 "In that day," says the LORD, "the enemy will break
open the graves of the kings and officials of Judah,
and the graves of the priests, prophets, and common
people of Jerusalem. 2 They will spread out their bones
on the ground before the sun, moon, and stars—the
gods my people have loved, served, and worshiped.
Their bones will not be gathered up again or buried
but will be scattered on the ground like manure. 3 And
the people of this evil nation who survive will wish
to die rather than live where I will send them. I, the
LORD of Heaven's Armies, have spoken!

DECEPTION BY FALSE PROPHETS

4 "Jeremiah, say to the people, 'This is what the LORD
says:

"'When people fall down, don't they get up again?
When they discover they're on the wrong road,
don't they turn back?
5 Then why do these people stay on their self-
destructive path?
Why do the people of Jerusalem refuse to turn
back?
They cling tightly to their lies
and will not turn around.
6 I listen to their conversations
and don't hear a word of truth.
Is anyone sorry for doing wrong?
Does anyone say, "What a terrible thing I have
done"?
No! All are running down the path of sin
as swiftly as a horse galloping into battle!
7 Even the stork that flies across the sky
knows the time of her migration,
as do the turtledove, the swallow, and the crane.*
They all return at the proper time each year.
But not my people!
They do not know the LORD's laws.

8 "'How can you say, "We are wise because we have
the word of the LORD,"
when your teachers have twisted it by writing
lies?
9 These wise teachers will fall
into the trap of their own foolishness,
for they have rejected the word of the LORD.
Are they so wise after all?
10 I will give their wives to others
and their farms to strangers.
From the least to the greatest,
their lives are ruled by greed.
Yes, even my prophets and priests are like that.
They are all frauds.
11 They offer superficial treatments
for my people's mortal wound.
They give assurances of peace
when there is no peace.
12 Are they ashamed of these disgusting actions?
Not at all—they don't even know how to blush!
Therefore, they will lie among the slaughtered.
They will be brought down when I punish them,
says the LORD.
13 I will surely consume them.
There will be no more harvests of figs and
grapes.
Their fruit trees will all die.
Whatever I gave them will soon be gone.
I, the LORD, have spoken!'

14 "Then the people will say,
'Why should we wait here to die?
Come, let's go to the fortified towns and die there.
For the LORD our God has decreed our
destruction
and has given us a cup of poison to drink
because we sinned against the LORD.
15 We hoped for peace, but no peace came.
We hoped for a time of healing, but found only
terror.'

16 "The snorting of the enemies' warhorses can be
heard
all the way from the land of Dan in the north!
The neighing of their stallions makes the whole
land tremble.
They are coming to devour the land and
everything in it—
cities and people alike.
17 I will send these enemy troops among you
like poisonous snakes you cannot charm.
They will bite you, and you will die.
I, the LORD, have spoken!"

JEREMIAH WEEPS FOR SINFUL JUDAH

18 My grief is beyond healing;
my heart is broken.
19 Listen to the weeping of my people;
it can be heard all across the land.
"Has the LORD abandoned Jerusalem?*" the people
ask.
"Is her King no longer there?"

8:7 The identification of some of these birds is uncertain. 8:19 Hebrew *Zion?*

7:31 burn their sons and daughters. Here trash was dumped and children were sacrificed to pagan gods. Though prohibited by the Law (Lev. 18:21), child sacrifice was practiced by Ahaz (2 Kings 16:2-3) and Manasseh (2 Kings 21:1,6). The Hebrew name for the Valley of Hinnom (*ge' hinnom*) became "Gehenna," which was translated in the New Testament as "hell" (Matt. 18:9).

8:19 Has the LORD abandoned Jerusalem? The people wondered how their sovereign God-King could allow such a terrible fate to befall them. The correct answer: God had always been with them, but they had not been "with" God.

"Oh, why have they provoked my anger with their
carved idols
and their worthless foreign gods?" says the
LORD.

20 "The harvest is finished,
and the summer is gone," the people cry,
"yet we are not saved!"

21 I hurt with the hurt of my people.
I mourn and am overcome with grief.
22 Is there no medicine in Gilead?
Is there no physician there?
Why is there no healing
for the wounds of my people?

9 1*If only my head were a pool of water
and my eyes a fountain of tears,
I would weep day and night
for all my people who have been slaughtered.
2*Oh, that I could go away and forget my people
and live in a travelers' shack in the desert.
For they are all adulterers—
a pack of treacherous liars.

JUDGMENT FOR DISOBEDIENCE

3 "My people bend their tongues like bows
to shoot out lies.
They refuse to stand up for the truth.
They only go from bad to worse.
They do not know me,"
says the LORD.

4 "Beware of your neighbor!
Don't even trust your brother!
For brother takes advantage of brother,
and friend slanders friend.
5 They all fool and defraud each other;
no one tells the truth.
With practiced tongues they tell lies;
they wear themselves out with all their
sinning.
6 They pile lie upon lie
and utterly refuse to acknowledge me,"
says the LORD.

7 Therefore, this is what the LORD of Heaven's
Armies says:
"See, I will melt them down in a crucible
and test them like metal.
What else can I do with my people?*
8 For their tongues shoot lies like poisoned
arrows.
They speak friendly words to their neighbors
while scheming in their heart to kill them.
9 Should I not punish them for this?" says the LORD.
"Should I not avenge myself against such a
nation?"

10 I will weep for the mountains
and wail for the wilderness pastures.
For they are desolate and empty of life;
the lowing of cattle is heard no more;
the birds and wild animals have all fled.

11 "I will make Jerusalem into a heap of ruins," says
the LORD.
"It will be a place haunted by jackals.
The towns of Judah will be ghost towns,
with no one living in them."

12 Who is wise enough to understand all this? Who
has been instructed by the LORD and can explain it to
others? Why has the land been so ruined that no one
dares to travel through it?
13 The LORD replies, "This has happened because my
people have abandoned my instructions; they have
refused to obey what I said.
14 Instead, they have stubbornly followed their own desires and worshiped the
images of Baal, as their ancestors taught them.
15 So now, this is what the LORD of Heaven's Armies, the God
of Israel, says: Look! I will feed them with bitterness
and give them poison to drink.
16 I will scatter them
around the world, in places they and their ancestors
never heard of, and even there I will chase them with
the sword until I have destroyed them completely."

WEEPING IN JERUSALEM

17 This is what the LORD of Heaven's Armies says:
"Consider all this, and call for the mourners.
Send for the women who mourn at funerals.
18 Quick! Begin your weeping!
Let the tears flow from your eyes.
19 Hear the people of Jerusalem* crying in despair,
'We are ruined! We are completely humiliated!
We must leave our land,
because our homes have been torn down.'"

20 Listen, you women, to the words of the LORD;
open your ears to what he has to say.
Teach your daughters to wail;
teach one another how to lament.
21 For death has crept in through our windows
and has entered our mansions.
It has killed off the flower of our youth:
Children no longer play in the streets,
and young men no longer gather in the squares.

22 This is what the LORD says:
"Bodies will be scattered across the fields like
clumps of manure,
like bundles of grain after the harvest.
No one will be left to bury them."

23 This is what the LORD says:
"Don't let the wise boast in their wisdom,

9:1 Verse 9:1 is numbered 8:23 in Hebrew text. 9:2 Verses 9:2-26 are numbered 9:1-25 in Hebrew text. 9:7 Hebrew *with the daughter of my people?* Greek version reads *with the evil daughter of my people?* 9:19 Hebrew *Zion.*

9:1 my eyes a fountain of tears. Jeremiah, the "weeping prophet," was a tenderhearted man (see 9:10; 13:17, and the book of Lamentations).

9:2 go away and forget my people. Jeremiah wanted to get away from his wicked countrymen. He despised their unfaithfulness, and even used the term "adulterers" to describe their sin of desiring other gods.

9:12 Who . . . Who . . . Why. The first two questions are rhetorical. God's answer could only be "You, Jeremiah." Jeremiah's task was to be wise about God's ways, to be instructed by Him, and to explain His Word to the people. Verses 13-16 are God's answer to the third question.

9:13 abandoned my instructions. Ongoing disobedience without repentance was a breach in the covenant between God and Israel—with terrible consequences for the nation (11:9-13).

9:17 Send for the women who mourn. These were professionals who led funeral processions.

or the powerful boast in their power,
or the rich boast in their riches.
24 But those who wish to boast
should boast in this alone:
that they truly know me and understand that I am the LORD
who demonstrates unfailing love
and who brings justice and righteousness to the earth,
and that I delight in these things.
I, the LORD, have spoken!

25 "A time is coming," says the LORD, "when I will
punish all those who are circumcised in body but
not in spirit—26 the Egyptians, Edomites, Ammonites,
Moabites, the people who live in the desert in remote
places,* and yes, even the people of Judah. And like
all these pagan nations, the people of Israel also have
uncircumcised hearts."

IDOLATRY BRINGS DESTRUCTION

10 Hear the word that the LORD speaks to you, O Israel! 2 This is what the LORD says:

"Do not act like the other nations,
who try to read their future in the stars.
Do not be afraid of their predictions,
even though other nations are terrified by them.
3 Their ways are futile and foolish.
They cut down a tree, and a craftsman carves an idol.
4 They decorate it with gold and silver
and then fasten it securely with hammer and nails
so it won't fall over.
5 Their gods are like
helpless scarecrows in a cucumber field!
They cannot speak,
and they need to be carried because they cannot walk.
Do not be afraid of such gods,
for they can neither harm you nor do you any good."

6 LORD, there is no one like you!
For you are great, and your name is full of power.
7 Who would not fear you, O King of nations?
That title belongs to you alone!
Among all the wise people of the earth
and in all the kingdoms of the world,
there is no one like you.

8 People who worship idols are stupid and foolish.
The things they worship are made of wood!
9 They bring beaten sheets of silver from Tarshish
and gold from Uphaz,
and they give these materials to skillful craftsmen
who make their idols.
Then they dress these gods in royal blue and purple robes
made by expert tailors.
10 But the LORD is the only true God.
He is the living God and the everlasting King!
The whole earth trembles at his anger.
The nations cannot stand up to his wrath.

11 Say this to those who worship other gods: "Your
so-called gods, who did not make the heavens and
earth, will vanish from the earth and from under the
heavens."*

12 But the LORD made the earth by his power,
and he preserves it by his wisdom.
With his own understanding
he stretched out the heavens.
13 When he speaks in the thunder,
the heavens roar with rain.
He causes the clouds to rise over the earth.
He sends the lightning with the rain
and releases the wind from his storehouses.
14 The whole human race is foolish and has no knowledge!
The craftsmen are disgraced by the idols they make,
for their carefully shaped works are a fraud.
These idols have no breath or power.
15 Idols are worthless; they are ridiculous lies!
On the day of reckoning they will all be destroyed.
16 But the God of Israel* is no idol!
He is the Creator of everything that exists,
including Israel, his own special possession.
The LORD of Heaven's Armies is his name!

THE COMING DESTRUCTION

17 Pack your bags and prepare to leave;
the siege is about to begin.
18 For this is what the LORD says:
"Suddenly, I will fling out
all you who live in this land.
I will pour great troubles upon you,
and at last you will feel my anger."

19 My wound is severe,
and my grief is great.
My sickness is incurable,
but I must bear it.
20 My home is gone,
and no one is left to help me rebuild it.

9:26 Or *in the desert and clip the corners of their hair.* See note on 5:20. **10:11** The original text of this verse is in Aramaic. **10:16** Hebrew *the Portion of Jacob.*

9:24 boast . . . that they truly know me and understand. Boasting is risky, but if one is going to boast, let it be in knowing and understanding the eternal God. (See also 1 Corinthians 1:31.)

10:1-25 In the last of these temple messages, Jeremiah contrasts the powerlessness of idols with the might of God. Idolatry creates a breach in the covenant (9:13) by forsaking trust in God alone (2:11)—a violation of the divine law and a personal betrayal (3:9).

10:4 decorate it with gold and silver. Wooden idols, often plated with silver or gold to preserve them and make them more beautiful, would still rot away—pretty packages with no permanence.

10:11 those. This verse was written in Aramaic (other examples include Ezra 4:8–6:18; 7:12–26; and Dan. 2:4b–7:28), the common language during that period, and may have been inserted (and spoken) for emphasis. The message was clear: since idols were worthless in God's eyes, so were idolmakers. Idols were valueless not only for God's people but also for the pagans who built and worshiped them.

10:19-20 Jeremiah evoked the image of the old, pastoral-nomadic lifestyle to illustrate the disappearance of the culture the Israelites had planted in the promised land. Towns would become empty with no one left to even pitch a tent (v. 25).

My children have been taken away,
and I will never see them again.
21 The shepherds of my people have lost their senses.
They no longer seek wisdom from the LORD.
Therefore, they fail completely,
and their flocks are scattered.
22 Listen! Hear the terrifying roar of great armies
as they roll down from the north.
The towns of Judah will be destroyed
and become a haunt for jackals.

JEREMIAH'S PRAYER

23 I know, LORD, that our lives are not our own.
We are not able to plan our own course.
24 So correct me, LORD, but please be gentle.
Do not correct me in anger, for I would die.
25 Pour out your wrath on the nations that refuse to
acknowledge you—
on the peoples that do not call upon your name.
For they have devoured your people Israel*;
they have devoured and consumed them,
making the land a desolate wilderness.

JUDAH'S BROKEN COVENANT

11 The LORD gave another message to Jeremiah.
He said, 2 "Remind the people of Judah and Je-
rusalem about the terms of my covenant with them.
3 Say to them, 'This is what the LORD, the God of Israel,
says: Cursed is anyone who does not obey the terms
of my covenant! 4 For I said to your ancestors when
I brought them out of the iron-smelting furnace of
Egypt, "If you obey me and do whatever I command
you, then you will be my people, and I will be your
God." 5 I said this so I could keep my promise to your
ancestors to give you a land flowing with milk and
honey—the land you live in today."'

Then I replied, "Amen, LORD! May it be so."

6 Then the LORD said, "Broadcast this message in the
streets of Jerusalem. Go from town to town through-
out the land and say, 'Remember the ancient cov-
enant, and do everything it requires. 7 For I solemnly
warned your ancestors when I brought them out of
Egypt, "Obey me!" I have repeated this warning over
and over to this day, 8 but your ancestors did not lis-
ten or even pay attention. Instead, they stubbornly
followed their own evil desires. And because they
refused to obey, I brought upon them all the curses
described in this covenant."'

9 Again the LORD spoke to me and said, "I have dis-
covered a conspiracy against me among the people
of Judah and Jerusalem. 10 They have returned to the
sins of their ancestors. They have refused to listen to
me and are worshiping other gods. Israel and Judah
have both broken the covenant I made with their an-
cestors. 11 Therefore, this is what the LORD says: I am
going to bring calamity upon them, and they will not
escape. Though they beg for mercy, I will not listen to
their cries. 12 Then the people of Judah and Jerusalem
will pray to their idols and burn incense before them.
But the idols will not save them when disaster strikes!
13 Look now, people of Judah; you have as many gods as
you have towns. You have as many altars of shame—
altars for burning incense to your god Baal—as there
are streets in Jerusalem.

14 "Pray no more for these people, Jeremiah. Do not
weep or pray for them, for I will not listen to them
when they cry out to me in distress.

15 "What right do my beloved people have to come to
my Temple,
when they have done so many immoral things?
Can their vows and sacrifices prevent their
destruction?
They actually rejoice in doing evil!
16 I, the LORD, once called them a thriving olive tree,
beautiful to see and full of good fruit.
But now I have sent the fury of their enemies
to burn them with fire,
leaving them charred and broken.

17 "I, the LORD of Heaven's Armies, who planted this
olive tree, have ordered it destroyed. For the people of
Israel and Judah have done evil, arousing my anger
by burning incense to Baal."

A PLOT AGAINST JEREMIAH

18 Then the LORD told me about the plots my enemies
were making against me. 19 I was like a lamb being led
to the slaughter. I had no idea that they were plan-
ning to kill me! "Let's destroy this man and all his
words," they said. "Let's cut him down, so his name
will be forgotten forever."

20 O LORD of Heaven's Armies,
you make righteous judgments,
and you examine the deepest thoughts and
secrets.
Let me see your vengeance against them,
for I have committed my cause to you.

21 This is what the LORD says about the men of Ana-
thoth who wanted me dead. They had said, "We will
kill you if you do not stop prophesying in the LORD's
name." 22 So this is what the LORD of Heaven's Armies
says about them: "I will punish them! Their young
men will die in battle, and their boys and girls will
starve to death. 23 Not one of these plotters from Ana-
thoth will survive, for I will bring disaster upon them
when their time of punishment comes."

JEREMIAH QUESTIONS THE LORD'S JUSTICE

12 1 LORD, you always give me justice
when I bring a case before you.
So let me bring you this complaint:
Why are the wicked so prosperous?
Why are evil people so happy?
2 You have planted them,
and they have taken root and prospered.
Your name is on their lips,
but you are far from their hearts.

10:25 Hebrew *devoured Jacob.* See note on 5:20.

11:3 Cursed is anyone who does not obey. Moses used this phrase 12 times in Deuteronomy 27:15-26. There, Moses instructed the people that obedience resulted in blessings (Deut. 28:1-14), and disobedience in curses (Deut. 28:15-68).

11:21 Anathoth. A priestly city in Benjamin, which was Jeremiah's hometown (1:1).

11:23 Not one . . . will survive. Only the conspirators of Anathoth were annihilated. After the exile, 128 other men returned to the village (Ezra 2:23).

12:1 Why are the wicked so prosperous? Jeremiah was not alone in asking this question (see Job 21:7-15, Mal. 3:15). God answered that the wicked *seem* to prosper but will perish (v. 7-13), and the invaders who seem to benefit from his people's misery will surely be destroyed.

3 But as for me, LORD, you know my heart.
You see me and test my thoughts.
Drag these people away like sheep to be butchered!
Set them aside to be slaughtered!

4 How long must this land mourn?
Even the grass in the fields has withered.
The wild animals and birds have disappeared
because of the evil in the land.
For the people have said,
"The LORD doesn't see what's ahead for us!"

THE LORD'S REPLY TO JEREMIAH

5 "If racing against mere men makes you tired,
how will you race against horses?
If you stumble and fall on open ground,
what will you do in the thickets near the Jordan?
6 Even your brothers, members of your own family,
have turned against you.
They plot and raise complaints against you.
Do not trust them,
no matter how pleasantly they speak.

7 "I have abandoned my people, my special possession.
I have surrendered my dearest ones to their enemies.
8 My chosen people have roared at me like a lion of the forest,
so I have treated them with contempt.
9 My chosen people act like speckled vultures,*
but they themselves are surrounded by vultures.
Bring on the wild animals to pick their corpses clean!

10 "Many rulers have ravaged my vineyard,
trampling down the vines
and turning all its beauty into a barren wilderness.
11 They have made it an empty wasteland;
I hear its mournful cry.
The whole land is desolate,
and no one even cares.
12 On all the bare hilltops,
destroying armies can be seen.
The sword of the LORD devours people
from one end of the nation to the other.
No one will escape!
13 My people have planted wheat
but are harvesting thorns.
They have worn themselves out,
but it has done them no good.
They will harvest a crop of shame
because of the fierce anger of the LORD."

A MESSAGE FOR ISRAEL'S NEIGHBORS

14 Now this is what the LORD says: "I will uproot from
their land all the evil nations reaching out for the pos-
session I gave my people Israel. And I will uproot Ju-
dah from among them. 15 But afterward I will return
and have compassion on all of them. I will bring them
home to their own lands again, each nation to its
own possession. 16 And if these nations truly learn the
ways of my people, and if they learn to swear by my
name, saying, 'As surely as the LORD lives' (just as they
taught my people to swear by the name of Baal), then
they will be given a place among my people. 17 But any
nation who refuses to obey me will be uprooted and
destroyed. I, the LORD, have spoken!"

JEREMIAH'S LINEN LOINCLOTH

13 This is what the LORD said to me: "Go and buy
a linen loincloth and put it on, but do not wash
it." 2 So I bought the loincloth as the LORD directed me,
and I put it on.

3 Then the LORD gave me another message: 4 "Take
the linen loincloth you are wearing, and go to the Eu-
phrates River.* Hide it there in a hole in the rocks." 5 So
I went and hid it by the Euphrates as the LORD had
instructed me.

6 A long time afterward the LORD said to me, "Go back
to the Euphrates and get the loincloth I told you to hide
there." 7 So I went to the Euphrates and dug it out of the
hole where I had hidden it. But now it was rotting and
falling apart. The loincloth was good for nothing.

8 Then I received this message from the LORD: 9 "This
is what the LORD says: This shows how I will rot away
the pride of Judah and Jerusalem. 10 These wicked
people refuse to listen to me. They stubbornly follow
their own desires and worship other gods. Therefore,
they will become like this loincloth—good for noth-
ing! 11 As a loincloth clings to a man's waist, so I creat-
ed Judah and Israel to cling to me, says the LORD. They
were to be my people, my pride, my glory—an honor
to my name. But they would not listen to me.

12 "So tell them, 'This is what the LORD, the God of Is-
rael, says: May all your jars be filled with wine.' And
they will reply, 'Of course! Jars are made to be filled
with wine!'

13 "Then tell them, 'No, this is what the LORD means:
I will fill everyone in this land with drunkenness—
from the king sitting on David's throne to the priests
and the prophets, right down to the common people
of Jerusalem. 14 I will smash them against each other,
even parents against children, says the LORD. I will
not let my pity or mercy or compassion keep me from
destroying them.'"

A WARNING AGAINST PRIDE

15 Listen and pay attention!
Do not be arrogant, for the LORD has spoken.
16 Give glory to the LORD your God
before it is too late.

12:9 Or *speckled hyenas.* **13:4** Hebrew *Perath;* also in 13:5, 6, 7.

12:3 sheep to be butchered. Jeremiah requested that the same fate be given the wicked in Judah as his enemies planned for him (11:19).
12:6 Even your brothers. Members of Jeremiah's own family were conspiring to kill him. (God said in v. 5 that things would get worse—they just did.) There is a direct connection to verse 7 in which Jeremiah disavows his family.
13:1 linen loincloth. The priests' garments, made of linen, symbolized the nation as a "kingdom of priests" (Ex. 19:6). Putting on a priestly garment must have been hard for Jeremiah, since he was a descendant of the deposed priest Abiathar. Jeremiah's family was not allowed to officiate in the temple.
13:7 Falling apart . . . good for nothing. The linen underwear was meant to be worn, symbolizing the close connection between God and His people. When taken off and hidden (exiled), it became ruined by the elements.
13:13 fill . . . with drunkenness. Instead of continuing to be prospered by God as his vessels, he would cause them to become defenseless before their enemies as vessels of destruction.

Acknowledge him before he brings darkness upon
you,
causing you to stumble and fall on the
darkening mountains.
For then, when you look for light,
you will find only terrible darkness and
gloom.
17 And if you still refuse to listen,
I will weep alone because of your pride.
My eyes will overflow with tears,
because the LORD's flock will be led away into
exile.

18 Say to the king and his mother,
"Come down from your thrones
and sit in the dust,
for your glorious crowns
will soon be snatched from your heads."
19 The towns of the Negev will close their gates,
and no one will be able to open them.
The people of Judah will be taken away as
captives.
All will be carried into exile.

20 Open up your eyes and see
the armies marching down from the north!
Where is your flock—
your beautiful flock—
that he gave you to care for?
21 What will you say when the LORD takes the allies
you have cultivated
and appoints them as your rulers?
Pangs of anguish will grip you,
like those of a woman in labor!
22 You may ask yourself,
"Why is all this happening to me?"
It is because of your many sins!
That is why you have been stripped
and raped by invading armies.
23 Can an Ethiopian* change the color of his skin?
Can a leopard take away its spots?
Neither can you start doing good,
for you have always done evil.

24 "I will scatter you like chaff
that is blown away by the desert winds.
25 This is your allotment,
the portion I have assigned to you,"
says the LORD,
"for you have forgotten me,
putting your trust in false gods.
26 I myself will strip you
and expose you to shame.
27 I have seen your adultery and lust,
and your disgusting idol worship out in the
fields and on the hills.
What sorrow awaits you, Jerusalem!
How long before you are pure?"

JUDAH'S TERRIBLE DROUGHT

14 This message came to Jeremiah from the LORD,
explaining why he was holding back the rain:

2 "Judah wilts;
commerce at the city gates grinds to a halt.
All the people sit on the ground in mourning,
and a great cry rises from Jerusalem.
3 The nobles send servants to get water,
but all the wells are dry.
The servants return with empty pitchers,
confused and desperate,
covering their heads in grief.
4 The ground is parched
and cracked for lack of rain.
The farmers are deeply troubled;
they, too, cover their heads.
5 Even the doe abandons her newborn fawn
because there is no grass in the field.
6 The wild donkeys stand on the bare hills
panting like thirsty jackals.
They strain their eyes looking for grass,
but there is none to be found."

7 The people say, "Our wickedness has caught up
with us, LORD,
but help us for the sake of your own
reputation.
We have turned away from you
and sinned against you again and again.
8 O Hope of Israel, our Savior in times of trouble,
why are you like a stranger to us?
Why are you like a traveler passing through the
land,
stopping only for the night?
9 Are you also confused?
Is our champion helpless to save us?
You are right here among us, LORD.
We are known as your people.
Please don't abandon us now!"

10 So this is what the LORD says to his people:
"You love to wander far from me
and do not restrain yourselves.
Therefore, I will no longer accept you as my
people.
Now I will remember all your wickedness
and will punish you for your sins."

THE LORD FORBIDS JEREMIAH TO INTERCEDE

11 Then the LORD said to me, "Do not pray for these peo-
ple anymore. 12 When they fast, I will pay no attention.
When they present their burnt offerings and grain of-
ferings to me, I will not accept them. Instead, I will
devour them with war, famine, and disease."
13 Then I said, "O Sovereign LORD, their prophets
are telling them, 'All is well—no war or famine will
come. The LORD will surely send you peace.'"

13:23 Hebrew *a Cushite.*

13:18 king and his mother. If this refers to king and queen Jehoiachin and Nehushta (2 Kings 24:8), then it was just before Nebuchadnezzar laid siege to Jerusalem in 597 B.C.

13:22 have been stripped. Defeat by the Babylonians would mean total humiliation. Judah and Babylon had been allies in the past (v. 21), but now defeat would reduce Judah to a prostitute's status. This was a proper fate because Judah had acted like a prostitute in adultery with other gods.

14:1 holding back the rain. Drought was one of the curses of disobedience (Lev. 26:19-20). This drought was especially terrible because it came during the Babylonian invasion. No food, no water, no safety (v. 18).

14:4 ground is parched. Judah and Israel occupy arid land. Normally enough rain falls to sustain life, but Israel and Judah were dependent on rainfall to fill wells and cisterns to keep their water supply adequate.

14:10-11 these people . . . wander. God rejected His people for a time. They might offer sacrifices, but God would not accept them.

14 Then the LORD said, "These prophets are telling
lies in my name. I did not send them or tell them to
speak. I did not give them any messages. They proph-
esy of visions and revelations they have never seen
or heard. They speak foolishness made up in their
own lying hearts. 15 Therefore, this is what the LORD
says: I will punish these lying prophets, for they have
spoken in my name even though I never sent them.
They say that no war or famine will come, but they
themselves will die by war and famine! 16 As for the
people to whom they prophesy—their bodies will
be thrown out into the streets of Jerusalem, victims
of famine and war. There will be no one left to bury
them. Husbands, wives, sons, and daughters—all will
be gone. For I will pour out their own wickedness on
them. 17 Now, Jeremiah, say this to them:

"Night and day my eyes overflow with tears.
 I cannot stop weeping,
for my virgin daughter—my precious people—
 has been struck down
 and lies mortally wounded.
18 If I go out into the fields,
 I see the bodies of people slaughtered by the enemy.
If I walk the city streets,
 I see people who have died of starvation.
The prophets and priests continue with their work,
 but they don't know what they're doing."

A PRAYER FOR HEALING

19 LORD, have you completely rejected Judah?
 Do you really hate Jerusalem?*
Why have you wounded us past all hope of healing?
 We hoped for peace, but no peace came.
 We hoped for a time of healing, but found only terror.
20 LORD, we confess our wickedness
 and that of our ancestors, too.
 We all have sinned against you.
21 For the sake of your reputation, LORD, do not abandon us.
 Do not disgrace your own glorious throne.
Please remember us,
 and do not break your covenant with us.

22 Can any of the worthless foreign gods send us rain?
 Does it fall from the sky by itself?
No, you are the one, O LORD our God!
 Only you can do such things.
 So we will wait for you to help us.

JUDAH'S INEVITABLE DOOM

15 Then the LORD said to me, "Even if Moses and
Samuel stood before me pleading for these peo-
ple, I wouldn't help them. Away with them! Get them
out of my sight! 2 And if they say to you, 'But where
can we go?' tell them, 'This is what the LORD says:

"'Those who are destined for death, to death;
 those who are destined for war, to war;
those who are destined for famine, to famine;
 those who are destined for captivity, to captivity.'

3 "I will send four kinds of destroyers against them,"
says the LORD. "I will send the sword to kill, the dogs
to drag away, the vultures to devour, and the wild an-
imals to finish up what is left. 4 Because of the wicked
things Manasseh son of Hezekiah, king of Judah, did
in Jerusalem, I will make my people an object of hor-
ror to all the kingdoms of the earth.

5 "Who will feel sorry for you, Jerusalem?
 Who will weep for you?
 Who will even bother to ask how you are?
6 You have abandoned me
 and turned your back on me,"
 says the LORD.
"Therefore, I will raise my fist to destroy you.
 I am tired of always giving you another chance.
7 I will winnow you like grain at the gates of your cities
 and take away the children you hold dear.
I will destroy my own people,
 because they refuse to change their evil ways.
8 There will be more widows
 than the grains of sand on the seashore.
At noontime I will bring a destroyer
 against the mothers of young men.
I will cause anguish and terror
 to come upon them suddenly.
9 The mother of seven grows faint and gasps for breath;
 her sun has gone down while it is still day.
She sits childless now,
 disgraced and humiliated.
And I will hand over those who are left
 to be killed by the enemy.
 I, the LORD, have spoken!"

JEREMIAH'S COMPLAINT

10 Then I said,

"What sorrow is mine, my mother.
 Oh, that I had died at birth!
 I am hated everywhere I go.
I am neither a lender who threatens to foreclose
 nor a borrower who refuses to pay—
 yet they all curse me."

11 The LORD replied,

"I will take care of you, Jeremiah.
 Your enemies will ask you to plead on their behalf

14:19 Hebrew *Zion?*

14:16 no one left to bury them. For an Israelite to remain unburied was a terrible violation of dignity, a sign of awful calamity (Ezek. 6:5; 37:1; Amos 2:1). Even today, natural and other disasters are so overwhelming that it often takes days to deal with all the corpses. That is what is pictured here.

14:21 do not break your covenant with us. Jeremiah desperately pleaded with God to fulfill His part of the covenant. Judah had forsaken the Law, and God's punishment was intensely felt (9:13).

15:2 destined for death . . . war . . . famine . . . captivity. The people had failed to worship and serve God, and now punishment had arrived.

15:5-9 Much of this poem (vv. 8-9) about the destruction of Jerusalem (in 586 B.C.) focuses on widows and mothers. Even these miserable survivors, who would normally receive special consideration, would be treated without mercy.

in times of trouble and distress.
12 Can a man break a bar of iron from the north,
or a bar of bronze?
13 At no cost to them,
I will hand over your wealth and treasures
as plunder to your enemies,
for sin runs rampant in your land.
14 I will tell your enemies to take you
as captives to a foreign land.
For my anger blazes like a fire
that will burn forever.*"

15 Then I said,

"LORD, you know what's happening to me.
Please step in and help me. Punish my
persecutors!
Please give me time; don't let me die young.
It's for your sake that I am suffering.
16 When I discovered your words, I devoured them.
They are my joy and my heart's delight,
for I bear your name,
O LORD God of Heaven's Armies.
17 I never joined the people in their merry feasts.
I sat alone because your hand was on me.
I was filled with indignation at their sins.
18 Why then does my suffering continue?
Why is my wound so incurable?
Your help seems as uncertain as a seasonal brook,
like a spring that has gone dry."

19 This is how the LORD responds:

"If you return to me, I will restore you
so you can continue to serve me.
If you speak good words rather than worthless
ones,
you will be my spokesman.
You must influence them;
do not let them influence you!
20 They will fight against you like an attacking army,
but I will make you as secure as a fortified wall
of bronze.
They will not conquer you,
for I am with you to protect and rescue you.
I, the LORD, have spoken!
21 Yes, I will certainly keep you safe from these
wicked men.
I will rescue you from their cruel hands."

JEREMIAH FORBIDDEN TO MARRY

16 The LORD gave me another message. He said,
2 "Do not get married or have children in this
place. 3 For this is what the LORD says about the chil-
dren born here in this city and about their mothers
and fathers: 4 They will die from terrible diseases. No
one will mourn for them or bury them, and they will
lie scattered on the ground like manure. They will die
from war and famine, and their bodies will be food
for the vultures and wild animals."

JUDAH'S COMING PUNISHMENT

5 This is what the LORD says: "Do not go to funerals
to mourn and show sympathy for these people, for I
have removed my protection and peace from them.
I have taken away my unfailing love and my mercy.
6 Both the great and the lowly will die in this land. No
one will bury them or mourn for them. Their friends
will not cut themselves in sorrow or shave their heads
in sadness. 7 No one will offer a meal to comfort those
who mourn for the dead—not even at the death of a
mother or father. No one will send a cup of wine to
console them.
8 "And do not go to their feasts and parties. Do not
eat and drink with them at all. 9 For this is what the
LORD of Heaven's Armies, the God of Israel, says: In
your own lifetime, before your very eyes, I will put an
end to the happy singing and laughter in this land.
The joyful voices of bridegrooms and brides will no
longer be heard.
10 "When you tell the people all these things, they
will ask, 'Why has the LORD decreed such terrible
things against us? What have we done to deserve such
treatment? What is our sin against the LORD our God?'
11 "Then you will give them the LORD's reply: 'It is
because your ancestors were unfaithful to me. They
worshiped other gods and served them. They aban-
doned me and did not obey my word. 12 And you are
even worse than your ancestors! You stubbornly fol-
low your own evil desires and refuse to listen to me.
13 So I will throw you out of this land and send you
into a foreign land where you and your ancestors
have never been. There you can worship idols day
and night—and I will grant you no favors!'

HOPE DESPITE THE DISASTER

14 "But the time is coming," says the LORD, "when peo-
ple who are taking an oath will no longer say, 'As
surely as the LORD lives, who rescued the people of
Israel from the land of Egypt.' 15 Instead, they will say,
'As surely as the LORD lives, who brought the people
of Israel back to their own land from the land of the
north and from all the countries to which he had ex-
iled them.' For I will bring them back to this land that
I gave their ancestors.
16 "But now I am sending for many fishermen who
will catch them," says the LORD. "I am sending for
hunters who will hunt them down in the mountains,
hills, and caves. 17 I am watching them closely, and I
see every sin. They cannot hope to hide from me. 18 I
will double their punishment for all their sins, be-
cause they have defiled my land with lifeless images
of their detestable gods and have filled my territory
with their evil deeds."

15:14 As in some Hebrew manuscripts (see also 17:4); most Hebrew manuscripts read *will burn against you.*

15:15 you know . . . Please step in. Judah had lost its connection with God, but Jeremiah called on his own relationship with the Lord to support his request for vengeance against his enemies.

15:19-21 If you return to me, I will restore you. Jeremiah was neither exempt from the temptation to sin nor immune to sin's consequences. God called him to repent for doubting God. He understood Jeremiah (v. 15) and encouraged him by promising protection from enemies and salvation from the wicked.

16:2 Do not get married. God prohibited Jeremiah from marrying and having children. The language here is the same as the absolute commands of the Ten Commandments (Ex. 20:3-4, 7, 13-17).

16:5 Do not go to funerals. The times would become so bad that Jeremiah was not to participate in either mourning or feasting. The present mourning was only a shadow of what was to come, and nothing warranted celebrating.

16:14 the time is coming. Mirroring Isaiah 40–55, the Lord announces that a new exodus will take place (23:7-8).

16:16 many fishermen . . . hunters. Like these, conquerors snare their victims in a net (Ezek. 12:13) or hook the jaws of enemies (Ezek. 29:4).

JEREMIAH'S PRAYER OF CONFIDENCE

19 LORD, you are my strength and fortress,
my refuge in the day of trouble!
Nations from around the world
will come to you and say,
"Our ancestors left us a foolish heritage,
for they worshiped worthless idols.
20 Can people make their own gods?
These are not real gods at all!"

21 The LORD says,
"Now I will show them my power;
now I will show them my might.
At last they will know and understand
that I am the LORD.

JUDAH'S SIN AND PUNISHMENT

17 1 "The sin of Judah
is inscribed with an iron chisel—
engraved with a diamond point on their stony
hearts
and on the corners of their altars.
2 Even their children go to worship
at their pagan altars and Asherah poles,
beneath every green tree
and on every high hill.
3 So I will hand over my holy mountain—
along with all your wealth and treasures
and your pagan shrines—
as plunder to your enemies,
for sin runs rampant in your land.
4 The wonderful possession I have reserved for you
will slip from your hands.
I will tell your enemies to take you
as captives to a foreign land.
For my anger blazes like a fire
that will burn forever."

WISDOM FROM THE LORD

5 This is what the LORD says:
"Cursed are those who put their trust in mere
humans,
who rely on human strength
and turn their hearts away from the LORD.
6 They are like stunted shrubs in the desert,
with no hope for the future.
They will live in the barren wilderness,
in an uninhabited salty land.

7 "But blessed are those who trust in the LORD
and have made the LORD their hope and
confidence.
8 They are like trees planted along a riverbank,
with roots that reach deep into the water.
Such trees are not bothered by the heat
or worried by long months of drought.
Their leaves stay green,
and they never stop producing fruit.

9 "The human heart is the most deceitful of all
things,
and desperately wicked.
Who really knows how bad it is?
10 But I, the LORD, search all hearts
and examine secret motives.
I give all people their due rewards,
according to what their actions deserve."

JEREMIAH'S TRUST IN THE LORD

11 Like a partridge that hatches eggs she has not laid,
so are those who get their wealth by unjust
means.
At midlife they will lose their riches;
in the end, they will become poor old fools.
12 But we worship at your throne—
eternal, high, and glorious!
13 O LORD, the hope of Israel,
all who turn away from you will be disgraced.
They will be buried in the dust of the earth,
for they have abandoned the LORD, the fountain
of living water.

14 O LORD, if you heal me, I will be truly healed;
if you save me, I will be truly saved.
My praises are for you alone!
15 People scoff at me and say,
"What is this 'message from the LORD' you talk about?
Why don't your predictions come true?"

16 LORD, I have not abandoned my job
as a shepherd for your people.
I have not urged you to send disaster.
You have heard everything I've said.
17 LORD, don't terrorize me!
You alone are my hope in the day of disaster.
18 Bring shame and dismay on all who persecute me,
but don't let me experience shame and dismay.
Bring a day of terror on them.
Yes, bring double destruction upon them!

OBSERVING THE SABBATH

19 This is what the LORD said to me: "Go and stand in
the gates of Jerusalem, first in the gate where the king
goes in and out, and then in each of the other gates.
20 Say to all the people, 'Listen to this message from the
LORD, you kings of Judah and all you people of Judah
and everyone living in Jerusalem. 21 This is what the
LORD says: Listen to my warning! Stop carrying on
your trade at Jerusalem's gates on the Sabbath day.
22 Do not do your work on the Sabbath, but make it a
holy day. I gave this command to your ancestors, 23 but
they did not listen or obey. They stubbornly refused to
pay attention or accept my discipline.
24 "'But if you obey me, says the LORD, and do not
carry on your trade at the gates or work on the Sab-
bath day, and if you keep it holy, 25 then kings and their
officials will go in and out of these gates forever. There
will always be a descendant of David sitting on the
throne here in Jerusalem. Kings and their officials will
always ride in and out among the people of Judah in
chariots and on horses, and this city will remain forev-
er. 26 And from all around Jerusalem, from the towns of
Judah and Benjamin, from the western foothills* and
the hill country and the Negev, the people will come

17:26 Hebrew *the Shephelah.*

17:1 their stony hearts. When God writes his law on human hearts in the new covenant (31:31-34), obedience rather than rebellion becomes possible for those who confess Jesus as Lord (Luke 22:20; 1 Cor. 11:15; Heb. 8:8–9:28).

17:2 Asherah poles. During King Josiah's time, the worship of Asherah had gotten so bad that an Asherah pole was brought into the temple precinct. Josiah had it removed and burned in the Kidron Valley (2 Kings 23:6).

with their burnt offerings and sacrifices. They will
bring their grain offerings, frankincense, and thanks-
giving offerings to the LORD's Temple.
27 "'But if you do not listen to me and refuse to keep
the Sabbath holy, and if on the Sabbath day you bring
loads of merchandise through the gates of Jerusalem
just as on other days, then I will set fire to these gates.
The fire will spread to the palaces, and no one will be
able to put out the roaring flames.'"

THE POTTER AND THE CLAY

18 The LORD gave another message to Jeremiah.
He said, 2 "Go down to the potter's shop, and I
will speak to you there." 3 So I did as he told me and
found the potter working at his wheel. 4 But the jar
he was making did not turn out as he had hoped, so
he crushed it into a lump of clay again and started
over.
5 Then the LORD gave me this message: 6 "O Israel,
can I not do to you as this potter has done to his clay?
As the clay is in the potter's hand, so are you in my
hand. 7 If I announce that a certain nation or kingdom
is to be uprooted, torn down, and destroyed, 8 but then
that nation renounces its evil ways, I will not destroy
it as I had planned. 9 And if I announce that I will
plant and build up a certain nation or kingdom, 10 but
then that nation turns to evil and refuses to obey me, I
will not bless it as I said I would.
11 "Therefore, Jeremiah, go and warn all Judah and
Jerusalem. Say to them, 'This is what the LORD says:
I am planning disaster for you instead of good. So
turn from your evil ways, each of you, and do what
is right.'"
12 But the people replied, "Don't waste your breath.
We will continue to live as we want to, stubbornly fol-
lowing our own evil desires."
13 So this is what the LORD says:

"Has anyone ever heard of such a thing,
even among the pagan nations?
My virgin daughter Israel
has done something terrible!
14 Does the snow ever disappear from the
mountaintops of Lebanon?
Do the cold streams flowing from those distant
mountains ever run dry?
15 But my people are not so reliable, for they have
deserted me;
they burn incense to worthless idols.
They have stumbled off the ancient highways
and walk in muddy paths.
16 Therefore, their land will become desolate,
a monument to their stupidity.
All who pass by will be astonished
and will shake their heads in amazement.
17 I will scatter my people before their enemies
as the east wind scatters dust.
And in all their trouble I will turn my back on
them
and refuse to notice their distress."

A PLOT AGAINST JEREMIAH

18 Then the people said, "Come on, let's plot a way to
stop Jeremiah. We have plenty of priests and wise
men and prophets. We don't need him to teach the
word and give us advice and prophecies. Let's spread
rumors about him and ignore what he says."

19 LORD, hear me and help me!
Listen to what my enemies are saying.
20 Should they repay evil for good?
They have dug a pit to kill me,
though I pleaded for them
and tried to protect them from your anger.
21 So let their children starve!
Let them die by the sword!
Let their wives become childless widows.
Let their old men die in a plague,
and let their young men be killed in battle!
22 Let screaming be heard from their homes
as warriors come suddenly upon them.
For they have dug a pit for me
and have hidden traps along my path.
23 LORD, you know all about their murderous plots
against me.
Don't forgive their crimes and blot out their
sins.
Let them die before you.
Deal with them in your anger.

JEREMIAH'S SHATTERED JAR

19 This is what the LORD said to me: "Go and buy a
clay jar. Then ask some of the leaders of the peo-
ple and of the priests to follow you. 2 Go out through
the Gate of Broken Pots to the garbage dump in the
valley of Ben-Hinnom, and give them this message.
3 Say to them, 'Listen to this message from the LORD,
you kings of Judah and citizens of Jerusalem! This is
what the LORD of Heaven's Armies, the God of Israel,
says: I will bring a terrible disaster on this place, and
the ears of those who hear about it will ring!
4 "'For Israel has forsaken me and turned this valley
into a place of wickedness. The people burn incense
to foreign gods—idols never before acknowledged by
this generation, by their ancestors, or by the kings of
Judah. And they have filled this place with the blood
of innocent children. 5 They have built pagan shrines
to Baal, and there they burn their sons as sacrifices
to Baal. I have never commanded such a horrible
deed; it never even crossed my mind to command
such a thing! 6 So beware, for the time is coming, says
the LORD, when this garbage dump will no longer be
called Topheth or the valley of Ben-Hinnom, but the
Valley of Slaughter.
7 "'For I will upset the careful plans of Judah and Je-
rusalem. I will allow the people to be slaughtered by
invading armies, and I will leave their dead bodies as
food for the vultures and wild animals. 8 I will reduce
Jerusalem to ruins, making it a monument to their
stupidity. All who pass by will be astonished and will
gasp at the destruction they see there. 9 I will see to

18:14-15 While nature behaved as prescribed, Judah wandered from the path God set for the people.

19:1-15 In chapter 18, a clay pot illustrated how God, the master potter, could reshape a repentant person. Here, however, the pot was useless. God would smash Judah.

19:1 leaders of the people . . . priests. Since leaders of the nation disregarded God's warning to urge a covenant renewal, all levels of the culture would feel the heat of punishment.

19:7 upset the careful plans. The Hebrew verb means "to empty." Judah and Jerusalem had made plans without concern for God's will and commands. Jeremiah may have poured water out of the clay jar to illustrate the point that plans turn to nothing without God.

it that your enemies lay siege to the city until all the
food is gone. Then those trapped inside will eat their
own sons and daughters and friends. They will be
driven to utter despair.'
10 "As these men watch you, Jeremiah, smash the jar
you brought. 11 Then say to them, 'This is what the LORD
of Heaven's Armies says: As this jar lies shattered, so
I will shatter the people of Judah and Jerusalem be-
yond all hope of repair. They will bury the bodies here
in Topheth, the garbage dump, until there is no more
room for them. 12 This is what I will do to this place
and its people, says the LORD. I will cause this city to
become defiled like Topheth. 13 Yes, all the houses in Je-
rusalem, including the palace of Judah's kings, will be-
come like Topheth—all the houses where you burned
incense on the rooftops to your star gods, and where
liquid offerings were poured out to your idols.'"
14 Then Jeremiah returned from Topheth, the gar-
bage dump where he had delivered this message,
and he stopped in front of the Temple of the LORD. He
said to the people there, 15 "This is what the LORD of
Heaven's Armies, the God of Israel, says: 'I will bring
disaster upon this city and its surrounding towns as
I promised, because you have stubbornly refused to
listen to me.'"

JEREMIAH AND PASHHUR

20 Now Pashhur son of Immer, the priest in
charge of the Temple of the LORD, heard what
Jeremiah was prophesying. 2 So he arrested Jeremiah
the prophet and had him whipped and put in stocks
at the Benjamin Gate of the LORD's Temple.
3 The next day, when Pashhur finally released him,
Jeremiah said, "Pashhur, the LORD has changed your
name. From now on you are to be called 'The Man
Who Lives in Terror.'* 4 For this is what the LORD says:
'I will send terror upon you and all your friends, and
you will watch as they are slaughtered by the swords
of the enemy. I will hand the people of Judah over to
the king of Babylon. He will take them captive to Bab-
ylon or run them through with the sword. 5 And I will
let your enemies plunder Jerusalem. All the famed
treasures of the city—the precious jewels and gold
and silver of your kings—will be carried off to Bab-
ylon. 6 As for you, Pashhur, you and all your house-
hold will go as captives to Babylon. There you will die
and be buried, you and all your friends to whom you
prophesied that everything would be all right.'"

JEREMIAH'S COMPLAINT

7 O LORD, you misled me,
and I allowed myself to be misled.
You are stronger than I am,
and you overpowered me.
Now I am mocked every day;
everyone laughs at me.
8 When I speak, the words burst out.
"Violence and destruction!" I shout.
So these messages from the LORD
have made me a household joke.
9 But if I say I'll never mention the LORD
or speak in his name,
his word burns in my heart like a fire.
It's like a fire in my bones!
I am worn out trying to hold it in!
I can't do it!
10 I have heard the many rumors about me.
They call me "The Man Who Lives in Terror."
They threaten, "If you say anything, we will report
it."
Even my old friends are watching me,
waiting for a fatal slip.
"He will trap himself," they say,
"and then we will get our revenge on him."

11 But the LORD stands beside me like a great warrior.
Before him my persecutors will stumble.
They cannot defeat me.
They will fail and be thoroughly humiliated.
Their dishonor will never be forgotten.
12 O LORD of Heaven's Armies,
you test those who are righteous,
and you examine the deepest thoughts and
secrets.
Let me see your vengeance against them,
for I have committed my cause to you.
13 Sing to the LORD!
Praise the LORD!
For though I was poor and needy,
he rescued me from my oppressors.

14 Yet I curse the day I was born!
May no one celebrate the day of my birth.
15 I curse the messenger who told my father,
"Good news—you have a son!"
16 Let him be destroyed like the cities of old
that the LORD overthrew without mercy.
Terrify him all day long with battle shouts,
17 because he did not kill me at birth.
Oh, that I had died in my mother's womb,
that her body had been my grave!
18 Why was I ever born?
My entire life has been filled
with trouble, sorrow, and shame.

NO DELIVERANCE FROM BABYLON

21 The LORD spoke through Jeremiah when King
Zedekiah sent Pashhur son of Malkijah and
Zephaniah son of Maaseiah, the priest, to speak with
him. They begged Jeremiah, 2 "Please speak to the
LORD for us and ask him to help us. King Nebuchad-
nezzar* of Babylon is attacking Judah. Perhaps the

20:3 Hebrew *Magor-missabib,* which means "surrounded by terror"; also in 20:10. 21:2 Hebrew *Nebuchadrezzar,* a variant spelling of Nebuchadnezzar; also in 21:7.

19:11 As this jar lies shattered . . . shatter the people. The elders had seen many terrible things—drought, disease, and military defeat—but never irreparable devastation.
20:2 Jeremiah . . . whipped. Pashur probably had Jeremiah beaten in accordance with the law covering disputes (Deut. 25:1-3).
20:6 you prophesied. Pashur was a priest but not a true prophet. Perhaps he was among the false prophets who proclaimed peace (6:14). His prophecies failed the test; they did not come about; they were lies (Deut. 18:22).
20:8-9 When I speak . . . I'll never mention the LORD. Jeremiah was caught in a paradox. Both options brought misery.
20:14 curse the day. Jeremiah's calling as a prophet began before he was conceived (1:5). Therefore, he saw his conception day as misery. In that way, he was like Job who regarded birth as the beginning of sorrow (Job 3:3).
21:2 ask him to help us. Whether the king requested the Lord's help would depend on other factors, including the information he received (Gen. 25:22; 2 Kings 22:13). In many ways, this inquiry resembled seeking the advice of a fortuneteller, not the will of God.

LORD will be gracious and do a mighty miracle as he
has done in the past. Perhaps he will force Nebuchad-
nezzar to withdraw his armies."
3 Jeremiah replied, "Go back to King Zedekiah and
tell him, 4 'This is what the LORD, the God of Israel,
says: I will make your weapons useless against the
king of Babylon and the Babylonians* who are out-
side your walls attacking you. In fact, I will bring
your enemies right into the heart of this city. 5 I my-
self will fight against you with a strong hand and a
powerful arm, for I am very angry. You have made me
furious! 6 I will send a terrible plague upon this city,
and both people and animals will die. 7 And after all
that, says the LORD, I will hand over King Zedekiah,
his staff, and everyone else in the city who survives
the disease, war, and famine. I will hand them over to
King Nebuchadnezzar of Babylon and to their other
enemies. He will slaughter them and show them no
mercy, pity, or compassion.'
8 "Tell all the people, 'This is what the LORD says:
Take your choice of life or death! 9 Everyone who stays
in Jerusalem will die from war, famine, or disease, but
those who go out and surrender to the Babylonians
will live. Their reward will be life! 10 For I have decid-
ed to bring disaster and not good upon this city, says
the LORD. It will be handed over to the king of Bab-
ylon, and he will reduce it to ashes.'

JUDGMENT ON JUDAH'S KINGS

11 "Say to the royal family of Judah, 'Listen to this mes-
sage from the LORD! 12 This is what the LORD says to the
dynasty of David:

"'Give justice each morning to the people you
judge!
Help those who have been robbed;
rescue them from their oppressors.
Otherwise, my anger will burn like an
unquenchable fire
because of all your sins.
13 I will personally fight against the people in
Jerusalem,
that mighty fortress—
the people who boast, "No one can touch us here.
No one can break in here."
14 And I myself will punish you for your sinfulness,
says the LORD.
I will light a fire in your forests
that will burn up everything around you."'

A MESSAGE FOR JUDAH'S KINGS

22 This is what the LORD said to me: "Go over and
speak directly to the king of Judah. Say to him,
2 'Listen to this message from the LORD, you king of
Judah, sitting on David's throne. Let your attendants
and your people listen, too. 3 This is what the LORD
says: Be fair-minded and just. Do what is right! Help
those who have been robbed; rescue them from their
oppressors. Quit your evil deeds! Do not mistreat for-
eigners, orphans, and widows. Stop murdering the
innocent! 4 If you obey me, there will always be a de-
scendant of David sitting on the throne here in Jeru-
salem. The king will ride through the palace gates in
chariots and on horses, with his parade of attendants
and subjects. 5 But if you refuse to pay attention to this
warning, I swear by my own name, says the LORD,
that this palace will become a pile of rubble.'"

A MESSAGE ABOUT THE PALACE

6 Now this is what the LORD says concerning Judah's
royal palace:

"I love you as much as fruitful Gilead
and the green forests of Lebanon.
But I will turn you into a desert,
with no one living within your walls.
7 I will call for wreckers,
who will bring out their tools to dismantle you.
They will tear out all your fine cedar beams
and throw them on the fire.

8 "People from many nations will pass by the ruins
of this city and say to one another, 'Why did the LORD
destroy such a great city?' 9 And the answer will be,
'Because they violated their covenant with the LORD
their God by worshiping other gods.'"

A MESSAGE ABOUT JEHOAHAZ

10 Do not weep for the dead king or mourn his loss.
Instead, weep for the captive king being led
away!
For he will never return to see his native land
again.

11 For this is what the LORD says about Jehoahaz,*
who succeeded his father, King Josiah, and was tak-
en away as a captive: "He will never return. 12 He will
die in a distant land and will never again see his own
country."

A MESSAGE ABOUT JEHOIAKIM

13 And the LORD says, "What sorrow awaits
Jehoiakim,*
who builds his palace with forced labor.*
He builds injustice into its walls,
for he makes his neighbors work for nothing.
He does not pay them for their labor.
14 He says, 'I will build a magnificent palace
with huge rooms and many windows.
I will panel it throughout with fragrant cedar
and paint it a lovely red.'
15 But a beautiful cedar palace does not make a great
king!
Your father, Josiah, also had plenty to eat and
drink.
But he was just and right in all his dealings.

21:4 Or *Chaldeans;* also in 21:9. **22:11** Hebrew *Shallum,* another name for Jehoahaz. **22:13a** The brother and successor of the exiled Jehoahaz. See 22:18. **22:13b** Hebrew *by unrighteousness.*

21:8 choice of life or death. God did not condemn the Israelites to death but offered them the opportunity to live, albeit in captivity. At least choosing life brought opportunity to love God and be loved by Him (Deut. 30:19-20).

21:9 go out and surrender. Jeremiah was branded a traitor for advising surrender to the Babylonians (37:13). But he was not a traitor at all. He was simply explaining to the people their choice of living or dying. Jeremiah himself wanted to remain in Judah even after Jerusalem was destroyed (37:14; 40:6).

22:2 king of Judah . . . on the throne of David. The king was likely Zedekiah (21:3). The dynasty founded by David had endured, though the path was strewn with failures.

22:10 Do not weep for the dead. Though his reforms were quickly reversed, the beloved King Josiah was mourned (2 Chron. 35:25).

That is why God blessed him.
16 He gave justice and help to the poor and needy,
and everything went well for him.
Isn't that what it means to know me?"
says the LORD.
17 "But you! You have eyes only for greed and
dishonesty!
You murder the innocent,
oppress the poor, and reign ruthlessly."

18 Therefore, this is what the LORD says about Jehoiakim, son of King Josiah:

"The people will not mourn for him, crying to one
another,
'Alas, my brother! Alas, my sister!'
His subjects will not mourn for him, crying,
'Alas, our master is dead! Alas, his splendor is
gone!'
19 He will be buried like a dead donkey—
dragged out of Jerusalem and dumped outside
the gates!
20 Weep for your allies in Lebanon.
Shout for them in Bashan.
Search for them in the regions east of the river.*
See, they are all destroyed.
Not one is left to help you.
21 I warned you when you were prosperous,
but you replied, 'Don't bother me.'
You have been that way since childhood—
you simply will not obey me!
22 And now the wind will blow away your allies.
All your friends will be taken away as
captives.
Surely then you will see your wickedness and
be ashamed.
23 It may be nice to live in a beautiful palace
paneled with wood from the cedars of Lebanon,
but soon you will groan with pangs of anguish—
anguish like that of a woman in labor.

A MESSAGE FOR JEHOIACHIN

24 "As surely as I live," says the LORD, "I will abandon you, Jehoiachin* son of Jehoiakim, king of Judah. Even if you were the signet ring on my right hand, I would pull you off.
25 I will hand you over to those who seek to kill you, those you so desperately fear—to King Nebuchadnezzar* of Babylon and the mighty Babylonian* army.
26 I will expel you and your mother from this land, and you will die in a foreign country, not in your native land.
27 You will never again return to the land you yearn for.

28 "Why is this man Jehoiachin like a discarded,
broken jar?
Why are he and his children to be exiled to a
foreign land?
29 O earth, earth, earth!
Listen to this message from the LORD!
30 This is what the LORD says:
'Let the record show that this man Jehoiachin was
childless.
He is a failure,
for none of his children will succeed him on the
throne of David
to rule over Judah.'

THE RIGHTEOUS DESCENDANT

23 "What sorrow awaits the leaders of my people—the shepherds of my sheep—for they have destroyed and scattered the very ones they were expected to care for," says the LORD.
2 Therefore, this is what the LORD, the God of Israel, says to these shepherds: "Instead of caring for my flock and leading them to safety, you have deserted them and driven them to destruction. Now I will pour out judgment on you for the evil you have done to them.
3 But I will gather together the remnant of my flock from the countries where I have driven them. I will bring them back to their own sheepfold, and they will be fruitful and increase in number.
4 Then I will appoint responsible shepherds who will care for them, and they will never be afraid again. Not a single one will be lost or missing. I, the LORD, have spoken!

5 "For the time is coming,"
says the LORD,
"when I will raise up a righteous descendant*
from King David's line.
He will be a King who rules with wisdom.
He will do what is just and right throughout the
land.
6 And this will be his name:
'The LORD Is Our Righteousness.'*
In that day Judah will be saved,
and Israel will live in safety.

7 "In that day," says the LORD, "when people are taking an oath, they will no longer say, 'As surely as the LORD lives, who rescued the people of Israel from the land of Egypt.'
8 Instead, they will say, 'As surely as the LORD lives, who brought the people of Israel back to their own land from the land of the north and from all the countries to which he had exiled them.' Then they will live in their own land."

JUDGMENT ON FALSE PROPHETS

9 My heart is broken because of the false prophets,
and my bones tremble.
I stagger like a drunkard,
like someone overcome by wine,
because of the holy words
the LORD has spoken against them.

22:20 Or *in Abarim.* 22:24 Hebrew *Coniah,* a variant spelling of Jehoiachin; also in 22:28. 22:25a Hebrew *Nebuchadrezzar,* a variant spelling of Nebuchadnezzar. 22:25b Or *Chaldean.* 23:5 Hebrew *a righteous branch.* 23:6 Hebrew *Yahweh Tsidqenu.*

22:28 a discarded, broken jar. Jeremiah returned to an image used in 18:1-10 and 19:1-15. Jehoiachin was "cast away" and taken into exile where he became utterly irrelevant.

22:30 was childless . . . none of his children. Although Jehoiachin had at least seven children, none of them sat on the throne of Judah. Thus, Jehoiachin was the last king of the Davidic line. Jehoiachin's line was restored, however, in the time of Zerubbabel. Christ came from his restored line (Matt. 1:12).

23:5 a righteous descendant from King David's line. One of Messiah's titles. The title signifies that Messiah is a branch from David's line (Isa. 11:1), which would be cut off for centuries and restored in the person of Jesus Christ.

23:6 will be his name: 'The LORD Is Our Righteousness.' The Messiah will represent the fact that our righteousness does not come from ourselves but from God.

[10] For the land is full of adultery,
and it lies under a curse.
The land itself is in mourning—
its wilderness pastures are dried up.
For they all do evil
and abuse what power they have.

[11] "Even the priests and prophets
are ungodly, wicked men.
I have seen their despicable acts
right here in my own Temple,"
says the LORD.
[12] "Therefore, the paths they take
will become slippery.
They will be chased through the dark,
and there they will fall.
For I will bring disaster upon them
at the time fixed for their punishment.
I, the LORD, have spoken!
[13] "I saw that the prophets of Samaria were terribly evil,
for they prophesied in the name of Baal
and led my people of Israel into sin.
[14] But now I see that the prophets of Jerusalem are even worse!
They commit adultery and love dishonesty.
They encourage those who are doing evil
so that no one turns away from their sins.
These prophets are as wicked
as the people of Sodom and Gomorrah once were."

[15] Therefore, this is what the LORD of Heaven's Armies says concerning the prophets:

"I will feed them with bitterness
and give them poison to drink.
For it is because of Jerusalem's prophets
that wickedness has filled this land."

[16] This is what the LORD of Heaven's Armies says to his people:

"Do not listen to these prophets when they prophesy to you,
filling you with futile hopes.
They are making up everything they say.
They do not speak for the LORD!
[17] They keep saying to those who despise my word,
'Don't worry! The LORD says you will have peace!'
And to those who stubbornly follow their own desires,
they say, 'No harm will come your way!'

[18] "Have any of these prophets been in the LORD's presence
to hear what he is really saying?
Has even one of them cared enough to listen?
[19] Look! The LORD's anger bursts out like a storm,
a whirlwind that swirls down on the heads of the wicked.
[20] The anger of the LORD will not diminish
until it has finished all he has planned.
In the days to come
you will understand all this very clearly.

[21] "I have not sent these prophets,
yet they run around claiming to speak for me.
I have given them no message,
yet they go on prophesying.
[22] If they had stood before me and listened to me,
they would have spoken my words,
and they would have turned my people
from their evil ways and deeds.
[23] Am I a God who is only close at hand?" says the LORD.
"No, I am far away at the same time.
[24] Can anyone hide from me in a secret place?
Am I not everywhere in all the heavens and earth?"
says the LORD.

[25] "I have heard these prophets say, 'Listen to the
dream I had from God last night.' And then they pro-
ceed to tell lies in my name. [26] How long will this go
on? If they are prophets, they are prophets of deceit,
inventing everything they say. [27] By telling these false
dreams, they are trying to get my people to forget me,
just as their ancestors did by worshiping the idols of
Baal.

[28] "Let these false prophets tell their dreams,
but let my true messengers faithfully proclaim my every word.
There is a difference between straw and grain!
[29] Does not my word burn like fire?"
says the LORD.
"Is it not like a mighty hammer
that smashes a rock to pieces?

[30] "Therefore," says the LORD, "I am against these
prophets who steal messages from each other and
claim they are from me. [31] I am against these smooth-
tongued prophets who say, 'This prophecy is from the
LORD!' [32] I am against these false prophets. Their imagi-
nary dreams are flagrant lies that lead my people into
sin. I did not send or appoint them, and they have no
message at all for my people. I, the LORD, have spoken!

FALSE PROPHECIES AND FALSE PROPHETS

[33] "Suppose one of the people or one of the prophets or
priests asks you, 'What prophecy has the LORD bur-
dened you with now?' You must reply, 'You are the
burden!* The LORD says he will abandon you!'
[34] "If any prophet, priest, or anyone else says, 'I have
a prophecy from the LORD,' I will punish that person
along with his entire family. [35] You should keep asking

23:33 As in Greek version and Latin Vulgate; Hebrew reads *What burden?*

23:14 Sodom . . . Gomorrah. The relationship of false prophets (Sodom) to Jerusalem (Gomorrah) replicates the connection of the false prophets of the northern kingdom to the fall of Samaria in 722 B.C. (23:27). Though the people did not need a prophet to cause them to sin, those who presume to speak for God will incur stricter judgment (Jas. 3:1).
23:16 They are making up everything they say. True prophets were God's messengers. False prophets spoke their own mind, not God's mind.
23:17 you will have peace . . . No harm. False prophets lulled their listeners into a false assurance. God would punish them for their foolishness.
23:23 close at hand . . . far away. There was nowhere to hide. God heard every word of their deceit.
23:31 smooth-tongued prophets. The false prophets enjoyed a prophetic position without heeding principles. They declared lies as "feel good" truths.

each other, 'What is the LORD's answer?' or 'What is the
LORD saying?' 36 But stop using this phrase, 'prophecy
from the LORD.' For people are using it to give authority
to their own ideas, turning upside down the words of
our God, the living God, the LORD of Heaven's Armies.
37 "This is what you should say to the prophets: 'What
is the LORD's answer?' or 'What is the LORD saying?'
38 But suppose they respond, 'This is a prophecy from the
LORD!' Then you should say, 'This is what the LORD says:
Because you have used this phrase, "prophecy from the
LORD," even though I warned you not to use it, 39 I will
forget you completely.* I will expel you from my pres-
ence, along with this city that I gave to you and your
ancestors. 40 And I will make you an object of ridicule,
and your name will be infamous throughout the ages.'"

GOOD AND BAD FIGS

24 After King Nebuchadnezzar* of Babylon ex-
iled Jehoiachin* son of Jehoiakim, king of Ju-
dah, to Babylon along with the officials of Judah and
all the craftsmen and artisans, the LORD gave me this
vision. I saw two baskets of figs placed in front of the
LORD's Temple in Jerusalem. 2 One basket was filled
with fresh, ripe figs, while the other was filled with
bad figs that were too rotten to eat.
3 Then the LORD said to me, "What do you see, Jer-
emiah?"
I replied, "Figs, some very good and some very bad,
too rotten to eat."
4 Then the LORD gave me this message: 5 "This is what
the LORD, the God of Israel, says: The good figs repre-
sent the exiles I sent from Judah to the land of the Bab-
ylonians.* 6 I will watch over and care for them, and
I will bring them back here again. I will build them
up and not tear them down. I will plant them and not
uproot them. 7 I will give them hearts that recognize
me as the LORD. They will be my people, and I will be
their God, for they will return to me wholeheartedly.
8 "But the bad figs," the LORD said, "represent King
Zedekiah of Judah, his officials, all the people left in
Jerusalem, and those who live in Egypt. I will treat
them like bad figs, too rotten to eat. 9 I will make them
an object of horror and a symbol of evil to every na-
tion on earth. They will be disgraced and mocked,
taunted and cursed, wherever I scatter them. 10 And
I will send war, famine, and disease until they have
vanished from the land of Israel, which I gave to them
and their ancestors."

SEVENTY YEARS OF CAPTIVITY

25 This message for all the people of Judah came
to Jeremiah from the LORD during the fourth
year of Jehoiakim's reign over Judah.* This was the
year when King Nebuchadnezzar* of Babylon began
his reign.
2 Jeremiah the prophet said to all the people in
Judah and Jerusalem, 3 "For the past twenty-three
years—from the thirteenth year of the reign of Josi-
ah son of Amon,* king of Judah, until now—the LORD
has been giving me his messages. I have faithfully
passed them on to you, but you have not listened.
4 "Again and again the LORD has sent you his ser-
vants, the prophets, but you have not listened or even
paid attention. 5 Each time the message was this:
'Turn from the evil road you are traveling and from
the evil things you are doing. Only then will I let you
live in this land that the LORD gave to you and your
ancestors forever. 6 Do not provoke my anger by wor-
shiping idols you made with your own hands. Then I
will not harm you.'
7 "But you would not listen to me," says the LORD.
"You made me furious by worshiping idols you made
with your own hands, bringing on yourselves all the
disasters you now suffer. 8 And now the LORD of Heav-
en's Armies says: Because you have not listened to me,
9 I will gather together all the armies of the north un-
der King Nebuchadnezzar of Babylon, whom I have
appointed as my deputy. I will bring them all against
this land and its people and against the surrounding
nations. I will completely destroy* you and make you
an object of horror and contempt and a ruin forever. 10 I
will take away your happy singing and laughter. The
joyful voices of bridegrooms and brides will no longer
be heard. Your millstones will fall silent, and the lights
in your homes will go out. 11 This entire land will be-
come a desolate wasteland. Israel and her neighboring
lands will serve the king of Babylon for seventy years.
12 "Then, after the seventy years of captivity are
over, I will punish the king of Babylon and his people
for their sins," says the LORD. "I will make the coun-
try of the Babylonians* a wasteland forever. 13 I will
bring upon them all the terrors I have promised in
this book—all the penalties announced by Jeremiah
against the nations. 14 Many nations and great kings
will enslave the Babylonians, just as they enslaved
my people. I will punish them in proportion to the
suffering they cause my people."

THE CUP OF THE LORD'S ANGER

15 This is what the LORD, the God of Israel, said to me:
"Take from my hand this cup filled to the brim with my
anger, and make all the nations to whom I send you
drink from it. 16 When they drink from it, they will stag-
ger, crazed by the warfare I will send against them."
17 So I took the cup of anger from the LORD and made
all the nations drink from it—every nation to which

23:39 Some Hebrew manuscripts and Greek version read *I will surely lift you up.* **24:1a** Hebrew *Nebuchadrezzar,* a variant spelling of Nebuchadnezzar. **24:1b** Hebrew *Jeconiah,* a variant spelling of Jehoiachin. **24:5** Or *Chaldeans.* **25:1a** The fourth year of Jehoiakim's reign and the accession year of Nebuchadnezzar's reign was 605 B.C. **25:1b** Hebrew *Nebuchadrezzar,* a variant spelling of Nebuchadnezzar; also in 25:9. **25:3** The thirteenth year of Josiah's reign was 627 B.C. **25:9** The Hebrew term used here refers to the complete consecration of things or people to the LORD, either by destroying them or by giving them as an offering. **25:12** Or *Chaldeans.*

24:1 exiled. Babylon selectively captured the influential leaders of Judah. **gave me.** Jeremiah had a prophetic vision from God.

24:5-6 Figs were a favored, oft-preserved delicacy of this culture. God's people were a similar delight—well worth saving.

25:3 I have faithfully passed . . . you have not listened. Jeremiah's message had not changed for over two decades. Yet his warnings were unheeded.

25:9 Nebuchadnezzar. The king of Babylon was decidedly pagan. However, in God's grand scheme, even a pagan can be used as a tool to accomplish His will.

25:11-12 neighboring lands will serve . . . seventy years. Jeremiah's warnings concerned an extensive exile. The Babylonians punished the exiled people for over half a century.

25:12 punish. God used the Babylonians; He did not favor them. He would eventually punish them for brutalizing His people.

25:15 drink from it. God's wrath is unavoidable. His enemies will experience it.

25:17 the cup. The book of Numbers speaks of a drink of bitter water a husband would give his wife as a test for adultery (Num. 5:22-28). Here, such a cup is applied to the many nations. Though it refers to Babylon in 51:7, it usually is directly related to God and His judgment (49:12; Pss. 60:3; 75:9; Isa. 51:17-23; Lam. 4:21; Ezek. 23:31-34; Hab. 2:16). As host, God offers this cup to Judah first, then those who have persecuted her. Jeremiah probably offered the actual cup (though symbolic) to each nation's representative in Jerusalem (27:3).

the LORD sent me. 18 I went to Jerusalem and the other
towns of Judah, and their kings and officials drank
from the cup. From that day until this, they have been
a desolate ruin, an object of horror, contempt, and
cursing. 19 I gave the cup to Pharaoh, king of Egypt,
his attendants, his officials, and all his people, 20 along
with all the foreigners living in that land. I also gave
it to all the kings of the land of Uz and the kings of the
Philistine cities of Ashkelon, Gaza, Ekron, and what
remains of Ashdod. 21 Then I gave the cup to the na-
tions of Edom, Moab, and Ammon, 22 and the kings of
Tyre and Sidon, and the kings of the regions across
the sea. 23 I gave it to Dedan, Tema, and Buz, and to the
people who live in distant places.* 24 I gave it to the
kings of Arabia, the kings of the nomadic tribes of the
desert, 25 and to the kings of Zimri, Elam, and Media.
26 And I gave it to the kings of the northern countries,
far and near, one after the other—all the kingdoms of
the world. And finally, the king of Babylon* himself
drank from the cup of the LORD's anger.

27 Then the LORD said to me, "Now tell them, 'This is
what the LORD of Heaven's Armies, the God of Israel,
says: Drink from this cup of my anger. Get drunk and
vomit; fall to rise no more, for I am sending terrible
wars against you.' 28 And if they refuse to accept the
cup, tell them, 'The LORD of Heaven's Armies says: You
have no choice but to drink from it. 29 I have begun to
punish Jerusalem, the city that bears my name. Now
should I let you go unpunished? No, you will not escape
disaster. I will call for war against all the nations of the
earth. I, the LORD of Heaven's Armies, have spoken!'

30 "Now prophesy all these things, and say to them,

"'The LORD will roar against his own land
from his holy dwelling in heaven.
He will shout like those who tread grapes;
he will shout against everyone on earth.
31 His cry of judgment will reach the ends of the
earth,
for the LORD will bring his case against all the
nations.
He will judge all the people of the earth,
slaughtering the wicked with the sword.
I, the LORD, have spoken!'"

32 This is what the LORD of Heaven's Armies says:
"Look! Disaster will fall upon nation after
nation!
A great whirlwind of fury is rising
from the most distant corners of the earth!"

33 In that day those the LORD has slaughtered will
fill the earth from one end to the other. No one will
mourn for them or gather up their bodies to bury
them. They will be scattered on the ground like ma-
nure.

34 Weep and moan, you evil shepherds!
Roll in the dust, you leaders of the flock!
The time of your slaughter has arrived;
you will fall and shatter like a fragile vase.
35 You will find no place to hide;
there will be no way to escape.
36 Listen to the frantic cries of the shepherds.
The leaders of the flock are wailing in despair,
for the LORD is ruining their pastures.
37 Peaceful meadows will be turned into a wasteland
by the LORD's fierce anger.
38 He has left his den like a strong lion seeking its
prey,
and their land will be made desolate
by the sword* of the enemy
and the LORD's fierce anger.

JEREMIAH'S ESCAPE FROM DEATH

26 This message came to Jeremiah from the LORD
early in the reign of Jehoiakim son of Josiah,*
king of Judah. 2 "This is what the LORD says: Stand in
the courtyard in front of the Temple of the LORD, and
make an announcement to the people who have come
there to worship from all over Judah. Give them my
entire message; include every word. 3 Perhaps they
will listen and turn from their evil ways. Then I will
change my mind about the disaster I am ready to
pour out on them because of their sins.

4 "Say to them, 'This is what the LORD says: If you
will not listen to me and obey my word I have giv-
en you, 5 and if you will not listen to my servants, the
prophets—for I sent them again and again to warn
you, but you would not listen to them— 6 then I will
destroy this Temple as I destroyed Shiloh, the place
where the Tabernacle was located. And I will make
Jerusalem an object of cursing in every nation on
earth.'"

7 The priests, the prophets, and all the people lis-
tened to Jeremiah as he spoke in front of the LORD's
Temple. 8 But when Jeremiah had finished his mes-
sage, saying everything the LORD had told him to say,
the priests and prophets and all the people at the
Temple mobbed him. "Kill him!" they shouted. 9 "What
right do you have to prophesy in the LORD's name that
this Temple will be destroyed like Shiloh? What do
you mean, saying that Jerusalem will be destroyed
and left with no inhabitants?" And all the people
threatened him as he stood in front of the Temple.

10 When the officials of Judah heard what was
happening, they rushed over from the palace and sat
down at the New Gate of the Temple to hold court.
11 The priests and prophets presented their accusa-
tions to the officials and the people. "This man should
die!" they said. "You have heard with your own ears
what a traitor he is, for he has prophesied against this
city."

12 Then Jeremiah spoke to the officials and the peo-
ple in his own defense. "The LORD sent me to prophesy
against this Temple and this city," he said. "The LORD
gave me every word that I have spoken. 13 But if you
stop your sinning and begin to obey the LORD your
God, he will change his mind about this disaster that
he has announced against you. 14 As for me, I am in
your hands—do with me as you think best. 15 But if
you kill me, rest assured that you will be killing an

25:23 Or *who clip the corners of their hair.* **25:26** Hebrew *of Sheshach,* a code name for Babylon. **25:38** As in some Hebrew manuscripts and Greek version; Masoretic Text reads *by the anger.* **26:1** The first year of Jehoiakim's reign was 608 B.C.

25:18 Judah. God's own people drink first (see Ezek. 9:6; 1 Pet. 4:17).
25:19-26 Though Babylon performs as God's "cup of wrath," it would drink too.
25:30 will roar against. God is said to roar like a lion (Hos. 11:10; Amos 3:8).

innocent man! The responsibility for such a deed will lie on you, on this city, and on every person living in it. For it is absolutely true that the LORD sent me to speak every word you have heard."

16 Then the officials and the people said to the priests and prophets, "This man does not deserve the death sentence, for he has spoken to us in the name of the LORD our God."

17 Then some of the wise old men stood and spoke to all the people assembled there. 18 They said, "Remember when Micah of Moresheth prophesied during the reign of King Hezekiah of Judah. He told the people of Judah,

> 'This is what the LORD of Heaven's Armies says:
> Mount Zion will be plowed like an open field;
> Jerusalem will be reduced to ruins!
> A thicket will grow on the heights
> where the Temple now stands.'*

19 But did King Hezekiah and the people kill him for saying this? No, they turned from their sins and worshiped the LORD. They begged him for mercy. Then the LORD changed his mind about the terrible disaster he had pronounced against them. So we are about to do ourselves great harm."

20 At this time Uriah son of Shemaiah from Kiriath-jearim was also prophesying for the LORD. And he predicted the same terrible disaster against the city and nation as Jeremiah did. 21 When King Jehoiakim and the army officers and officials heard what he was saying, the king sent someone to kill him. But Uriah heard about the plan and escaped in fear to Egypt. 22 Then King Jehoiakim sent Elnathan son of Acbor to Egypt along with several other men to capture Uriah. 23 They took him prisoner and brought him back to King Jehoiakim. The king then killed Uriah with a sword and had him buried in an unmarked grave.

24 Nevertheless, Ahikam son of Shaphan stood up for Jeremiah and persuaded the court not to turn him over to the mob to be killed.

JEREMIAH WEARS AN OX YOKE

27 This message came to Jeremiah from the LORD early in the reign of Zedekiah* son of Josiah, king of Judah.

2 This is what the LORD said to me: "Make a yoke, and fasten it on your neck with leather straps. 3 Then send messages to the kings of Edom, Moab, Ammon, Tyre, and Sidon through their ambassadors who have come to see King Zedekiah in Jerusalem. 4 Give them this message for their masters: 'This is what the LORD of Heaven's Armies, the God of Israel, says: 5 With my great strength and powerful arm I made the earth and all its people and every animal. I can give these things of mine to anyone I choose. 6 Now I will give your countries to King Nebuchadnezzar of Babylon, who is my servant. I have put everything, even the wild animals, under his control. 7 All the nations will serve him, his son, and his grandson until his time is up. Then many nations and great kings will conquer and rule over Babylon. 8 So you must submit to Babylon's king and serve him; put your neck under Babylon's yoke! I will punish any nation that refuses to be his slave, says the LORD. I will send war, famine, and disease upon that nation until Babylon has conquered it.

9 "'Do not listen to your false prophets, fortune-tellers, interpreters of dreams, mediums, and sorcerers who say, "The king of Babylon will not conquer you." 10 They are all liars, and their lies will lead to your being driven out of your land. I will drive you out and send you far away to die. 11 But the people of any nation that submits to the king of Babylon will be allowed to stay in their own country to farm the land as usual. I, the LORD, have spoken!'"

12 Then I repeated this same message to King Zedekiah of Judah. "If you want to live, submit to the yoke of the king of Babylon and his people. 13 Why do you insist on dying—you and your people? Why should you choose war, famine, and disease, which the LORD will bring against every nation that refuses to submit to Babylon's king? 14 Do not listen to the false prophets who keep telling you, 'The king of Babylon will not conquer you.' They are liars. 15 This is what the LORD says: 'I have not sent these prophets! They are telling you lies in my name, so I will drive you from this land. You will all die—you and all these prophets, too.'"

16 Then I spoke to the priests and the people and said, "This is what the LORD says: 'Do not listen to your prophets who claim that soon the gold articles taken from my Temple will be returned from Babylon. It is all a lie! 17 Do not listen to them. Surrender to the king of Babylon, and you will live. Why should this whole city be destroyed? 18 If they really are prophets and speak the LORD's messages, let them pray to the LORD of Heaven's Armies. Let them pray that the articles remaining in the LORD's Temple and in the king's palace and in the palaces of Jerusalem will not be carried away to Babylon!'

19 "For the LORD of Heaven's Armies has spoken about the pillars in front of the Temple, the great bronze basin called the Sea, the water carts, and all the other ceremonial articles. 20 King Nebuchadnezzar of Babylon left them here when he exiled Jehoiachin* son of Jehoiakim, king of Judah, to Babylon, along with all the other nobles of Judah and Jerusalem. 21 Yes, this is what the LORD of Heaven's Armies, the God of Israel, says about the precious things still in the Temple, in the palace of Judah's king, and in Jerusalem: 22 'They will all be carried away to Babylon and will stay there until I send for them,' says the LORD. 'Then I will bring them back to Jerusalem again.'"

26:18 Mic 3:12. **27:1** As in some Hebrew manuscripts and Syriac version (see also 27:3, 12); most Hebrew manuscripts read *Jehoiakim*. **27:20** Hebrew *Jeconiah*, a variant spelling of Jehoiachin.

26:16 he has spoken. The people and their elders were more obedient to God than the priests and so-called prophets of the land in acquitting Jeremiah. Obedience, not opposition, was the proper response to a prophet's message.

26:17-19 Some elders gave the priests and prophets a history lesson. Because of Hezekiah's repentance in 701 B.C., judgment on Jerusalem was averted (Micah 3:12; 4:12).

26:20-23 God's judgment was not news. King Jehoiakim's disrespect for the messenger could not silence the message.

26:20 Uriah ... prophesying. Uriah responded to the Lord and spoke boldly of God's prophecy with fear and reverence.

27:2 Make a yoke. Fetters were restraints for prisoners, and yokes were used to keep oxen in line while plowing. God used Jeremiah as a human word-picture. Judah and other rebellious nations would not listen to his warnings; perhaps they would pay attention to his example.

27:12 submit to the yoke. Jeremiah told the king that God had handed the people over to Babylon's domination and the king should submit like an ox under a yoke.

JEREMIAH CONDEMNS HANANIAH

28 One day in late summer* of that same year—the fourth year of the reign of Zedekiah, king of Judah—Hananiah son of Azzur, a prophet from Gibeon, addressed me publicly in the Temple while all the priests and people listened. He said, 2 "This is what the LORD of Heaven's Armies, the God of Israel, says: 'I will remove the yoke of the king of Babylon from your necks. 3 Within two years I will bring back all the Temple treasures that King Nebuchadnezzar carried off to Babylon. 4 And I will bring back Jehoiachin* son of Jehoiakim, king of Judah, and all the other captives that were taken to Babylon. I will surely break the yoke that the king of Babylon has put on your necks. I, the LORD, have spoken!'"

5 Jeremiah responded to Hananiah as they stood in front of all the priests and people at the Temple. 6 He said, "Amen! May your prophecies come true! I hope the LORD does everything you say. I hope he does bring back from Babylon the treasures of this Temple and all the captives. 7 But listen now to the solemn words I speak to you in the presence of all these people. 8 The ancient prophets who preceded you and me spoke against many nations, always warning of war, disaster, and disease. 9 So a prophet who predicts peace must show he is right. Only when his predictions come true can we know that he is really from the LORD."

10 Then Hananiah the prophet took the yoke off Jeremiah's neck and broke it in pieces. 11 And Hananiah said again to the crowd that had gathered, "This is what the LORD says: 'Just as this yoke has been broken, within two years I will break the yoke of oppression from all the nations now subject to King Nebuchadnezzar of Babylon.'" With that, Jeremiah left the Temple area.

12 Soon after this confrontation with Hananiah, the LORD gave this message to Jeremiah: 13 "Go and tell Hananiah, 'This is what the LORD says: You have broken a wooden yoke, but you have replaced it with a yoke of iron. 14 The LORD of Heaven's Armies, the God of Israel, says: I have put a yoke of iron on the necks of all these nations, forcing them into slavery under King Nebuchadnezzar of Babylon. I have put everything, even the wild animals, under his control.'"

15 Then Jeremiah the prophet said to Hananiah, "Listen, Hananiah! The LORD has not sent you, but the people believe your lies. 16 Therefore, this is what the LORD says: 'You must die. Your life will end this very year because you have rebelled against the LORD.'"

17 Two months later* the prophet Hananiah died.

A LETTER TO THE EXILES

29 Jeremiah wrote a letter from Jerusalem to the elders, priests, prophets, and all the people who had been exiled to Babylon by King Nebuchadnezzar. 2 This was after King Jehoiachin,* the queen mother, the court officials, the other officials of Judah, and all the craftsmen and artisans had been deported from Jerusalem. 3 He sent the letter with Elasah son of Shaphan and Gemariah son of Hilkiah when they went to Babylon as King Zedekiah's ambassadors to Nebuchadnezzar. This is what Jeremiah's letter said:

4 This is what the LORD of Heaven's Armies, the God of Israel, says to all the captives he has exiled to Babylon from Jerusalem: 5 "Build homes, and plan to stay. Plant gardens, and eat the food they produce. 6 Marry and have children. Then find spouses for them so that you may have many grandchildren. Multiply! Do not dwindle away! 7 And work for the peace and prosperity of the city where I sent you into exile. Pray to the LORD for it, for its welfare will determine your welfare."

8 This is what the LORD of Heaven's Armies, the God of Israel, says: "Do not let your prophets and fortune-tellers who are with you in the land of Babylon trick you. Do not listen to their dreams, 9 because they are telling you lies in my name. I have not sent them," says the LORD.

10 This is what the LORD says: "You will be in Babylon for seventy years. But then I will come and do for you all the good things I have promised, and I will bring you home again. 11 For I know the plans I have for you," says the LORD. "They are plans for good and not for disaster, to give you a future and a hope. 12 In those days when you pray, I will listen. 13 If you look for me wholeheartedly, you will find me. 14 I will be found by you," says the LORD. "I will end your captivity and restore your fortunes. I will gather you out of the nations where I sent you and will bring you home again to your own land."

15 You claim that the LORD has raised up prophets for you in Babylon. 16 But this is what the LORD says about the king who sits on David's throne and all those still living here in Jerusalem—your relatives who were not exiled to Babylon. 17 This is what the LORD of Heaven's Armies says: "I will send war, famine, and disease upon them and make them like bad figs, too rotten to eat. 18 Yes, I will pursue them with war, famine, and disease, and I will scatter them around the world. In every nation where I send them, I will make them an object of damnation, horror, contempt, and mock-

28:1 Hebrew *In the fifth month,* of the ancient Hebrew lunar calendar. The fifth month in the fourth year of Zedekiah's reign occurred within the months of August and September 593 B.C. Also see note on 1:3. **28:4** Hebrew *Jeconiah,* a variant spelling of Jehoiachin. **28:17** Hebrew *In the seventh month of that same year.* See 28:1 and the note there. **29:2** Hebrew *Jeconiah,* a variant spelling of Jehoiachin.

28:1 Hananiah . . . a prophet. This prophet's name means, "The LORD is gracious." However, Hananiah exhibited wishful thinking rather than a true revelation of God's plans. He may have been falsely encouraged by a revolt Nebuchadnezzar was dealing with at the time and recorded in the Babylonian Chronicles. Human reasoning would suggest a return in two years under such circumstances (v. 3).

28:8 prophets who preceded you. Hananiah's predictions went against the tide. How could all the prior prophets of doom and destruction be wrong?

28:10 broke it. Hananiah came up with his own word-picture. He broke the yoke around Jeremiah's neck—a vivid symbol of Babylon's dominance being broken. Hananiah predicted this would happen within two years.

28:16 you have rebelled against. Hananiah preached what the people wanted to hear: good news. However, his message was falsely delivered in God's name—a sin that required the death penalty (see Deut. 18:20).

28:17 Two months later . . . died. Jeremiah proved trustworthy once again. His prediction came true within the allotted time.

29:4 The exiles received a message from God Himself. He delivered encouragement to their Babylonian doorstep.

29:8 trick you. False prophets were eager to draw an audience with their message of false hope.

29:13 look for me . . . you will find me. God's promise is still for the Jewish people scattered in every nation. Though they were scattered from the land, they would find God again, if they sought Him (see Deut. 30:1-6; Rom. 11:26).

ery. 19 For they refuse to listen to me, though I have
spoken to them repeatedly through the prophets
I sent. And you who are in exile have not listened
either," says the LORD.
20 Therefore, listen to this message from the
LORD, all you captives there in Babylon. 21 This
is what the LORD of Heaven's Armies, the God of
Israel, says about your prophets—Ahab son of
Kolaiah and Zedekiah son of Maaseiah—who are
telling you lies in my name: "I will turn them over
to Nebuchadnezzar* for execution before your
eyes. 22 Their terrible fate will become proverbial,
so that the Judean exiles will curse someone by
saying, 'May the LORD make you like Zedekiah and
Ahab, whom the king of Babylon burned alive!'
23 For these men have done terrible things among
my people. They have committed adultery with
their neighbors' wives and have lied in my name,
saying things I did not command. I am a witness
to this. I, the LORD, have spoken."

A MESSAGE FOR SHEMAIAH

24 The LORD sent this message to Shemaiah the Nehel-
amite in Babylon: 25 "This is what the LORD of Heaven's
Armies, the God of Israel, says: You wrote a letter on
your own authority to Zephaniah son of Maaseiah,
the priest, and you sent copies to the other priests and
people in Jerusalem. You wrote to Zephaniah,

26 "The LORD has appointed you to replace Jehoiada
as the priest in charge of the house of the LORD.
You are responsible to put into stocks and neck
irons any crazy man who claims to be a prophet.
27 So why have you done nothing to stop Jeremiah
from Anathoth, who pretends to be a prophet
among you? 28 Jeremiah sent a letter here to Bab-
ylon, predicting that our captivity will be a long
one. He said, 'Build homes, and plan to stay. Plant
gardens, and eat the food they produce.'"

29 But when Zephaniah the priest received She-
maiah's letter, he took it to Jeremiah and read it to
him. 30 Then the LORD gave this message to Jeremiah:
31 "Send an open letter to all the exiles in Babylon. Tell
them, 'This is what the LORD says concerning She-
maiah the Nehelamite: Since he has prophesied to
you when I did not send him and has tricked you into
believing his lies, 32 I will punish him and his fami-
ly. None of his descendants will see the good things
I will do for my people, for he has incited you to rebel
against me. I, the LORD, have spoken!'"

PROMISES OF DELIVERANCE

30 The LORD gave another message to Jeremiah.
He said, 2 "This is what the LORD, the God of
Israel, says: Write down for the record everything I
have said to you, Jeremiah. 3 For the time is coming
when I will restore the fortunes of my people of Israel
and Judah. I will bring them home to this land that I
gave to their ancestors, and they will possess it again.
I, the LORD, have spoken!"
4 This is the message the LORD gave concerning Is-
rael and Judah. 5 This is what the LORD says:

"I hear cries of fear;
there is terror and no peace.
6 Now let me ask you a question:
Do men give birth to babies?
Then why do they stand there, ashen-faced,
hands pressed against their sides
like a woman in labor?
7 In all history there has never been such a time of
terror.
It will be a time of trouble for my people Israel.*
Yet in the end they will be saved!
8 For in that day,"
says the LORD of Heaven's Armies,
"I will break the yoke from their necks
and snap their chains.
Foreigners will no longer be their masters.
9 For my people will serve the LORD their God
and their king descended from David—
the king I will raise up for them.

10 "So do not be afraid, Jacob, my servant;
do not be dismayed, Israel,"
says the LORD.
"For I will bring you home again from distant lands,
and your children will return from their exile.
Israel will return to a life of peace and quiet,
and no one will terrorize them.
11 For I am with you and will save you,"
says the LORD.
"I will completely destroy the nations where I
have scattered you,
but I will not completely destroy you.
I will discipline you, but with justice;
I cannot let you go unpunished."

12 This is what the LORD says:
"Your injury is incurable—
a terrible wound.
13 There is no one to help you
or to bind up your injury.
No medicine can heal you.
14 All your lovers—your allies—have left you
and do not care about you anymore.
I have wounded you cruelly,
as though I were your enemy.
For your sins are many,
and your guilt is great.
15 Why do you protest your punishment—
this wound that has no cure?
I have had to punish you
because your sins are many
and your guilt is great.

29:21 Hebrew *Nebuchadrezzar,* a variant spelling of Nebuchadnezzar. **30:7** Hebrew *Jacob;* also in 30:10b, 18. See note on 5:20.

29:21 turn them over to Nebuchadnezzar. Once again, a pagan king was God's tool for assigning punishment. The false prophets were finally silenced.

29:31-32 God made it easier for His people to understand His true intentions. He identified and silenced false prophets like Shemaiah.

30:1–33:26 Jeremiah balanced his message of doom with that of hope. He described a postexilic day of restoration that would serve as an encouraging reminder to the returning exiles.

30:1–31:40 Jeremiah used poetic language to describe the people's physical deliverance (30:1-11). Additionally, he described the ensuing spiritual healing (30:12-17) and joyful results (31:2-40).

30:3 time is coming. The first exiles would not return to their homeland until many years later (537 B.C.). Yet even then, God's full promise was not fulfilled. In the days of Christ's kingdom, Israel will possess the land and be fully restored.

30:9 their king. David is the king whose line leads to the Messiah. Jesus Christ is the Son of David who will rule physically in Israel during the Millennium.

16 "But all who devour you will be devoured,
and all your enemies will be sent into exile.
All who plunder you will be plundered,
and all who attack you will be attacked.
17 I will give you back your health
and heal your wounds," says the LORD.
"For you are called an outcast—
'Jerusalem* for whom no one cares.'"

18 This is what the LORD says:
"When I bring Israel home again from captivity
and restore their fortunes,
Jerusalem will be rebuilt on its ruins,
and the palace reconstructed as before.
19 There will be joy and songs of thanksgiving,
and I will multiply my people, not diminish
them;
I will honor them, not despise them.
20 Their children will prosper as they did long ago.
I will establish them as a nation before me,
and I will punish anyone who hurts them.
21 They will have their own ruler again,
and he will come from their own people.
I will invite him to approach me," says the LORD,
"for who would dare to come unless invited?
22 You will be my people,
and I will be your God."

23 Look! The LORD's anger bursts out like a storm,
a driving wind that swirls down on the heads of
the wicked.
24 The fierce anger of the LORD will not diminish
until it has finished all he has planned.
In the days to come
you will understand all this.

HOPE FOR RESTORATION

31 "In that day," says the LORD, "I will be the God
of all the families of Israel, and they will be my
people. 2 This is what the LORD says:

"Those who survive the coming destruction
will find blessings even in the barren land,
for I will give rest to the people of Israel."

3 Long ago the LORD said to Israel:
"I have loved you, my people, with an everlasting
love.
With unfailing love I have drawn you to myself.
4 I will rebuild you, my virgin Israel.
You will again be happy
and dance merrily with your tambourines.
5 Again you will plant your vineyards on the
mountains of Samaria
and eat from your own gardens there.
6 The day will come when watchmen will shout
from the hill country of Ephraim,
'Come, let us go up to Jerusalem*
to worship the LORD our God.'"

7 Now this is what the LORD says:
"Sing with joy for Israel.*
Shout for the greatest of nations!
Shout out with praise and joy:
'Save your people, O LORD,
the remnant of Israel!'
8 For I will bring them from the north
and from the distant corners of the earth.
I will not forget the blind and lame,
the expectant mothers and women in labor.
A great company will return!
9 Tears of joy will stream down their faces,
and I will lead them home with great care.
They will walk beside quiet streams
and on smooth paths where they will not
stumble.
For I am Israel's father,
and Ephraim is my oldest child.

10 "Listen to this message from the LORD,
you nations of the world;
proclaim it in distant coastlands:
The LORD, who scattered his people,
will gather them and watch over them
as a shepherd does his flock.
11 For the LORD has redeemed Israel
from those too strong for them.
12 They will come home and sing songs of joy on the
heights of Jerusalem.
They will be radiant because of the LORD's good
gifts—
the abundant crops of grain, new wine, and olive
oil,
and the healthy flocks and herds.
Their life will be like a watered garden,
and all their sorrows will be gone.
13 The young women will dance for joy,
and the men—old and young—will join in the
celebration.
I will turn their mourning into joy.
I will comfort them and exchange their sorrow
for rejoicing.
14 The priests will enjoy abundance,
and my people will feast on my good gifts.
I, the LORD, have spoken!"

RACHEL'S SADNESS TURNS TO JOY

15 This is what the LORD says:

"A cry is heard in Ramah—
deep anguish and bitter weeping.
Rachel weeps for her children,
refusing to be comforted—
for her children are gone."

30:17 Hebrew *Zion.* 31:6 Hebrew *Zion;* also in 31:12. 31:7 Hebrew *Jacob;* also in 31:11. See note on 5:20.

30:20 as . . . long ago. In the midst of such a chaotic state, thoughts of David's reign inspired a desire for a future restoration characterized by the peace and stability that David's rule brought to their nation.

30:22 You will be my people. This is the traditional covenant formula (7:23; 11:4; Gen. 17:7-8; Exod. 6:7; 19:6; Lev. 26:12; Deut. 7:26; Ezek. 36:28). Looking ahead, the basis for this will not be the Mosaic covenant but a new relationship (31:31-34).

31:6 Jerusalem. This verse anticipates when the inhabitants of the northern kingdom will once again worship in Jerusalem.

31:7 Shout for the greatest. Israel is the "greatest of the nations" by God's favor (Deut. 7:6-8). Israel was chosen to bring God's story to the world.

31:11 those too strong. God redeemed Israel from Babylon, a power far stronger than Israel but not stronger than God.

31:15 Rachel weeps. Jeremiah described the disappearance of the tribes of Manasseh and Ephraim (Rachel's grandchildren, Gen. 46:19). Their defeat by Assyria symbolized true heartache among the people. Yet God promised to restore Ephraim in the future (v. 17-20).

16 But now this is what the LORD says:
"Do not weep any longer,
for I will reward you," says the LORD.
"Your children will come back to you
from the distant land of the enemy.
17 There is hope for your future," says the LORD.
"Your children will come again to their own land.
18 I have heard Israel* saying,
'You disciplined me severely,
like a calf that needs training for the yoke.
Turn me again to you and restore me,
for you alone are the LORD my God.
19 I turned away from God,
but then I was sorry.
I kicked myself for my stupidity!
I was thoroughly ashamed of all I did in my
younger days.'
20 "Is not Israel still my son,
my darling child?" says the LORD.
"I often have to punish him,
but I still love him.
That's why I long for him
and surely will have mercy on him.
21 Set up road signs;
put up guideposts.
Mark well the path
by which you came.
Come back again, my virgin Israel;
return to your towns here.
22 How long will you wander,
my wayward daughter?
For the LORD will cause something new to happen—
Israel will embrace her God.*"

23 This is what the LORD of Heaven's Armies, the God
of Israel, says: "When I bring them back from captiv-
ity, the people of Judah and its towns will again say,
'The LORD bless you, O righteous home, O holy moun-
tain!'
24 Townspeople and farmers and shepherds alike
will live together in peace and happiness.
25 For I have
given rest to the weary and joy to the sorrowing."
26 At this, I woke up and looked around. My sleep
had been very sweet.
27 "The day is coming," says the LORD, "when I will
greatly increase the human population and the num-
ber of animals here in Israel and Judah.
28 In the past
I deliberately uprooted and tore down this nation. I
overthrew it, destroyed it, and brought disaster upon
it. But in the future I will just as deliberately plant it
and build it up. I, the LORD, have spoken!
29 "The people will no longer quote this proverb:

'The parents have eaten sour grapes,
but their children's mouths pucker at the taste.'

30 All people will die for their own sins—those who
eat the sour grapes will be the ones whose mouths
will pucker.
31 "The day is coming," says the LORD, "when I will
make a new covenant with the people of Israel and
Judah.
32 This covenant will not be like the one I made
with their ancestors when I took them by the hand
and brought them out of the land of Egypt. They
broke that covenant, though I loved them as a hus-
band loves his wife," says the LORD.
33 "But this is the new covenant I will make with the
people of Israel after those days," says the LORD. "I will
put my instructions deep within them, and I will write
them on their hearts. I will be their God, and they will
be my people.
34 And they will not need to teach their
neighbors, nor will they need to teach their relatives,
saying, 'You should know the LORD.' For everyone,
from the least to the greatest, will know me already,"
says the LORD. "And I will forgive their wickedness,
and I will never again remember their sins."

35 It is the LORD who provides the sun to light the day
and the moon and stars to light the night,
and who stirs the sea into roaring waves.
His name is the LORD of Heaven's Armies,
and this is what he says:
36 "I am as likely to reject my people Israel
as I am to abolish the laws of nature!"
37 This is what the LORD says:
"Just as the heavens cannot be measured
and the foundations of the earth cannot be
explored,
so I will not consider casting them away
for the evil they have done.
I, the LORD, have spoken!

38 "The day is coming," says the LORD, "when all
Jerusalem will be rebuilt for me, from the Tower of
Hananel to the Corner Gate.
39 A measuring line will
be stretched out over the hill of Gareb and across to
Goah.
40 And the entire area—including the grave-
yard and ash dump in the valley, and all the fields out
to the Kidron Valley on the east as far as the Horse
Gate—will be holy to the LORD. The city will never
again be captured or destroyed."

JEREMIAH'S LAND PURCHASE

32 The following message came to Jeremiah from
the LORD in the tenth year of the reign of Zed-
ekiah,* king of Judah. This was also the eighteenth
year of the reign of King Nebuchadnezzar.*
2 Jerusa-
lem was then under siege from the Babylonian army,
and Jeremiah was imprisoned in the courtyard of the
guard in the royal palace.
3 King Zedekiah had put
him there, asking why he kept giving this prophecy:

31:18 Hebrew *Ephraim,* referring to the northern kingdom of Israel; also in 31:20. **31:22** Hebrew *a woman will surround a man.* **32:1a** The tenth year of Zedekiah's reign and the eighteenth year of Nebuchadnezzar's reign was 587 B.C. **32:1b** Hebrew *Nebuchadrezzar,* a variant spelling of Nebuchadnezzar; also in 32:28.

31:29 no longer quote. A common complaint in Jeremiah's day, the people falsely accused God of unfairly assigning consequence of their ancestors' sins on them (Ezek. 18:2-4).

31:30 God justly assigned blame to individuals for their sins (Deut. 24:16). The exile was prompted by the sheer extent of apostasy, and so the punishment appeared to be on the nation as a whole.

31:31 I will make a new covenant. God said He would make a new covenant with Israel and Judah (Gentiles are included by faith in this covenant). This promise is very significant, for it shows that God's revelation through Moses was not the end but the beginning. The New Covenant was inaugurated by Jesus' death (see 1 Cor. 11:25; 2 Cor. 3:6; Heb. 9:15).

31:33 put my instructions deep within them. Far from being rendered obsolete, God's law is being internalized in those who have the indwelling Holy Spirit that enables one to obey it in spirit. Ezekiel speaks of God replacing hearts of stone with hearts of flesh—hearts that want to do God's will. This is parallel to Jesus' statement in the Sermon on the Mount that He did not come to destroy the law but to fulfill it (Matt. 5:17-20).

32:1 tenth year. Jeremiah carefully noted the dates of his messages. The destruction of Judah was quickly approaching within a year.

"This is what the LORD says: 'I am about to hand this city over to the king of Babylon, and he will take it. 4 King Zedekiah will be captured by the Babylonians* and taken to meet the king of Babylon face to face. 5 He will take Zedekiah to Babylon, and I will deal with him there,' says the LORD. 'If you fight against the Babylonians, you will never succeed.'"

6 At that time the LORD sent me a message. He said, 7 "Your cousin Hanamel son of Shallum will come and say to you, 'Buy my field at Anathoth. By law you have the right to buy it before it is offered to anyone else.'"

8 Then, just as the LORD had said he would, my cousin Hanamel came and visited me in the prison. He said, "Please buy my field at Anathoth in the land of Benjamin. By law you have the right to buy it before it is offered to anyone else, so buy it for yourself." Then I knew that the message I had heard was from the LORD.

9 So I bought the field at Anathoth, paying Hanamel seventeen pieces* of silver for it. 10 I signed and sealed the deed of purchase before witnesses, weighed out the silver, and paid him. 11 Then I took the sealed deed and an unsealed copy of the deed, which contained the terms and conditions of the purchase, 12 and I handed them to Baruch son of Neriah and grandson of Mahseiah. I did all this in the presence of my cousin Hanamel, the witnesses who had signed the deed, and all the men of Judah who were there in the courtyard of the guardhouse.

13 Then I said to Baruch as they all listened, 14 "This is what the LORD of Heaven's Armies, the God of Israel, says: 'Take both this sealed deed and the unsealed copy, and put them into a pottery jar to preserve them for a long time.' 15 For this is what the LORD of Heaven's Armies, the God of Israel, says: 'Someday people will again own property here in this land and will buy and sell houses and vineyards and fields.'"

JEREMIAH'S PRAYER

16 Then after I had given the papers to Baruch, I prayed to the LORD:

17 "O Sovereign LORD! You made the heavens and earth by your strong hand and powerful arm. Nothing is too hard for you! 18 You show unfailing love to thousands, but you also bring the consequences of one generation's sin upon the next. You are the great and powerful God, the LORD of Heaven's Armies. 19 You have all wisdom and do great and mighty miracles. You see the conduct of all people, and you give them what they deserve. 20 You performed miraculous signs and wonders in the land of Egypt—things still remembered to this day! And you have continued to do great miracles in Israel and all around the world. You have made your name famous to this day.

21 "You brought Israel out of Egypt with mighty signs and wonders, with a strong hand and powerful arm, and with overwhelming terror. 22 You gave the people of Israel this land that you had promised their ancestors long before—a land flowing with milk and honey. 23 Our ancestors came and conquered it and lived in it, but they refused to obey you or follow your word. They have not done anything you commanded. That is why you have sent this terrible disaster upon them.

24 "See how the siege ramps have been built against the city walls! Through war, famine, and disease, the city will be handed over to the Babylonians, who will conquer it. Everything has happened just as you said. 25 And yet, O Sovereign LORD, you have told me to buy the field—paying good money for it before these witnesses—even though the city will soon be handed over to the Babylonians."

A PREDICTION OF JERUSALEM'S FALL

26 Then this message came to Jeremiah from the LORD: 27 "I am the LORD, the God of all the peoples of the world. Is anything too hard for me? 28 Therefore, this is what the LORD says: I will hand this city over to the Babylonians and to Nebuchadnezzar, king of Babylon, and he will capture it. 29 The Babylonians outside the walls will come in and set fire to the city. They will burn down all these houses where the people provoked my anger by burning incense to Baal on the rooftops and by pouring out liquid offerings to other gods. 30 Israel and Judah have done nothing but wrong since their earliest days. They have infuriated me with all their evil deeds," says the LORD. 31 "From the time this city was built until now, it has done nothing but anger me, so I am determined to get rid of it.

32 "The sins of Israel and Judah—the sins of the people of Jerusalem, the kings, the officials, the priests, and the prophets—have stirred up my anger. 33 My people have turned their backs on me and have refused to return. Even though I diligently taught them, they would not receive instruction or obey. 34 They have set up their abominable idols right in my own Temple, defiling it. 35 They have built pagan shrines to Baal in the valley of Ben-Hinnom, and there they sacrifice their sons and daughters to Molech. I have never commanded such a horrible deed; it never even crossed my mind to command such a thing. What an incredible evil, causing Judah to sin so greatly!

A PROMISE OF RESTORATION

36 "Now I want to say something more about this city. You have been saying, 'It will fall to the king of Babylon through war, famine, and disease.' But this is what the LORD, the God of Israel, says: 37 I will certainly bring my people back again from all the countries where I will scatter them in my fury. I will bring them back to this very city and let them live in peace and safety. 38 They will be my people, and I will be their God. 39 And I will give them one heart and one purpose: to worship me forever, for their own good and for the good of all their descendants. 40 And I will

32:4 Or *Chaldeans;* also in 32:5, 24, 25, 28, 29, 43. **32:9** Hebrew *17 shekels,* about 7 ounces or 194 grams in weight.

32:7 right to buy it. Jeremiah followed an ancient law (Lev. 25:23-25). It required him to buy land from a financially struggling relative in order to keep it within the family.

32:25 buy the field. Despite the city's inevitable fate, Jeremiah purchased the land as another word-picture. He put a down payment on Judah's eventual return to their homeland.

32:39 worship me. Literally "fear me." The Lord complains of the lack of fear three times in Jeremiah (2:27; 5:22-24; 44:10). "Fear of the LORD" in the Old Testament can be variously defined as dread (Deut. 1:29), respect (Ps. 19:9), worship (2 Kings 17:7), love (Deut. 10:12,20), wisdom (Prov. 1:29), service (Deut. 6:13), or obedience (Gen. 20:11; Job 1:8). Rather than isolate a single meaning, perhaps "fear of the LORD" should encapsulate all of these. The Israelites wish they knew, and "new covenanters" would come to learn, that total reverence of the Lord obliterates human fear (1 John 4:18).

make an everlasting covenant with them: I will never
stop doing good for them. I will put a desire in their
hearts to worship me, and they will never leave me.
41 I will find joy doing good for them and will faith-
fully and wholeheartedly replant them in this land.
42 "This is what the LORD says: Just as I have brought
all these calamities on them, so I will do all the good
I have promised them. 43 Fields will again be bought
and sold in this land about which you now say, 'It has
been ravaged by the Babylonians, a desolate land
where people and animals have all disappeared.'
44 Yes, fields will once again be bought and sold—
deeds signed and sealed and witnessed—in the land
of Benjamin and here in Jerusalem, in the towns of Ju-
dah and in the hill country, in the foothills of Judah*
and in the Negev, too. For someday I will restore pros-
perity to them. I, the LORD, have spoken!"

PROMISES OF PEACE AND PROSPERITY

33 While Jeremiah was still confined in the court-
yard of the guard, the LORD gave him this sec-
ond message: 2 "This is what the LORD says—the LORD
who made the earth, who formed and established it,
whose name is the LORD: 3 Ask me and I will tell you
remarkable secrets you do not know about things to
come. 4 For this is what the LORD, the God of Israel,
says: You have torn down the houses of this city and
even the king's palace to get materials to strengthen
the walls against the siege ramps and swords of the
enemy. 5 You expect to fight the Babylonians,* but the
men of this city are already as good as dead, for I have
determined to destroy them in my terrible anger. I
have abandoned them because of all their wickedness.
6 "Nevertheless, the time will come when I will
heal Jerusalem's wounds and give it prosperity and
true peace. 7 I will restore the fortunes of Judah and
Israel and rebuild their towns. 8 I will cleanse them
of their sins against me and forgive all their sins of
rebellion. 9 Then this city will bring me joy, glory, and
honor before all the nations of the earth! The people
of the world will see all the good I do for my people,
and they will tremble with awe at the peace and pros-
perity I provide for them.
10 "This is what the LORD says: You have said, 'This
is a desolate land where people and animals have
all disappeared.' Yet in the empty streets of Jeru-
salem and Judah's other towns, there will be heard
once more 11 the sounds of joy and laughter. The joy-
ful voices of bridegrooms and brides will be heard
again, along with the joyous songs of people bringing
thanksgiving offerings to the LORD. They will sing,

'Give thanks to the LORD of Heaven's Armies,
for the LORD is good.
His faithful love endures forever!'

For I will restore the prosperity of this land to what it
was in the past, says the LORD.
12 "This is what the LORD of Heaven's Armies says:
This land—though it is now desolate and has no
people and animals—will once more have pastures
where shepherds can lead their flocks. 13 Once again
shepherds will count their flocks in the towns of the
hill country, the foothills of Judah,* the Negev, the
land of Benjamin, the vicinity of Jerusalem, and all
the towns of Judah. I, the LORD, have spoken!
14 "The day will come, says the LORD, when I will do
for Israel and Judah all the good things I have prom-
ised them.

15 "In those days and at that time
I will raise up a righteous descendant* from
King David's line.
He will do what is just and right throughout the
land.
16 In that day Judah will be saved,
and Jerusalem will live in safety.
And this will be its name:
'The LORD Is Our Righteousness.'*

17 For this is what the LORD says: David will have a de-
scendant sitting on the throne of Israel forever. 18 And
there will always be Levitical priests to offer burnt
offerings and grain offerings and sacrifices to me."
19 Then this message came to Jeremiah from the
LORD: 20 "This is what the LORD says: If you can break
my covenant with the day and the night so that one
does not follow the other, 21 only then will my cov-
enant with my servant David be broken. Only then
will he no longer have a descendant to reign on his
throne. The same is true for my covenant with the Le-
vitical priests who minister before me. 22 And as the
stars of the sky cannot be counted and the sand on
the seashore cannot be measured, so I will multiply
the descendants of my servant David and the Levites
who minister before me."
23 The LORD gave another message to Jeremiah.
He said, 24 "Have you noticed what people are say-
ing?—'The LORD chose Judah and Israel and then
abandoned them!' They are sneering and saying that
Israel is not worthy to be counted as a nation. 25 But
this is what the LORD says: I would no more reject
my people than I would change my laws that govern
night and day, earth and sky. 26 I will never abandon
the descendants of Jacob or David, my servant, or
change the plan that David's descendants will rule
the descendants of Abraham, Isaac, and Jacob. In-
stead, I will restore them to their land and have mer-
cy on them."

A WARNING FOR ZEDEKIAH

34 King Nebuchadnezzar* of Babylon came with
all the armies from the kingdoms he ruled,
and he fought against Jerusalem and the towns of
Judah. At that time this message came to Jeremiah
from the LORD: 2 "Go to King Zedekiah of Judah, and

32:44 Hebrew *the Shephelah.* **33:5** Or *Chaldeans.* **33:13** Hebrew *the Shephelah.* **33:15** Hebrew *a righteous branch.* **33:16** Hebrew *Yahweh Tsidqenu.* **34:1** Hebrew *Nebuchadrezzar,* a variant spelling of Nebuchadnezzar.

33:4 torn down. Babylon's relentless siege required entire homes to be dismantled. The materials were then reassembled to fill gaps in the city walls.

33:8 cleanse. God promised what His people needed most: forgiveness. His grace would wash away their unrighteousness and provide a new start.

33:18 When God restores Israel, the temple will be rebuilt, and the priests will again function (Ezek. 40–48). This will continue throughout Christ's millennial reign.

33:22 cannot be counted. God used a phrase that was familiar throughout the generations of His people (see Gen. 22:17). God will not fail to keep His promises made to Abraham and the patriarchs.

33:24 abandoned them. Other nations were not oblivious to the plight of Judah and Israel. However, they did not realize God's plan to use apparent rejection as a preface to Israel's restoration.

tell him, 'This is what the LORD, the God of Israel, says:
I am about to hand this city over to the king of Bab-
ylon, and he will burn it down. 3 You will not escape
his grasp but will be captured and taken to meet the
king of Babylon face to face. Then you will be exiled
to Babylon.
4 "'But listen to this promise from the LORD, O Zed-
ekiah, king of Judah. This is what the LORD says: You
will not be killed in war 5 but will die peacefully. Peo-
ple will burn incense in your memory, just as they did
for your ancestors, the kings who preceded you. They
will mourn for you, crying, "Alas, our master is dead!"
This I have decreed, says the LORD.'"
6 So Jeremiah the prophet delivered the message to
King Zedekiah of Judah. 7 At this time the Babylonian
army was besieging Jerusalem, Lachish, and Aze-
kah—the only fortified cities of Judah not yet cap-
tured.

FREEDOM FOR HEBREW SLAVES

8 This message came to Jeremiah from the LORD af-
ter King Zedekiah made a covenant with the people,
proclaiming freedom for the slaves. 9 He had ordered
all the people to free their Hebrew slaves—both men
and women. No one was to keep a fellow Judean in
bondage. 10 The officials and all the people had obeyed
the king's command, 11 but later they changed their
minds. They took back the men and women they had
freed, forcing them to be slaves again.
12 So the LORD gave them this message through
Jeremiah: 13 "This is what the LORD, the God of Israel,
says: I made a covenant with your ancestors long ago
when I rescued them from their slavery in Egypt. 14 I
told them that every Hebrew slave must be freed after
serving six years. But your ancestors paid no atten-
tion to me. 15 Recently you repented and did what was
right, following my command. You freed your slaves
and made a solemn covenant with me in the Temple
that bears my name. 16 But now you have shrugged off
your oath and defiled my name by taking back the
men and women you had freed, forcing them to be
slaves once again.
17 "Therefore, this is what the LORD says: Since
you have not obeyed me by setting your country-
men free, I will set you free to be destroyed by war,
disease, and famine. You will be an object of hor-
ror to all the nations of the earth. 18 Because you
have broken the terms of our covenant, I will cut
you apart just as you cut apart the calf when you
walked between its halves to solemnize your vows.
19 Yes, I will cut you apart, whether you are officials
of Judah or Jerusalem, court officials, priests, or
common people—for you have broken your oath.
20 I will give you to your enemies, and they will kill
you. Your bodies will be food for the vultures and
wild animals.
21 "I will hand over King Zedekiah of Judah and his
officials to the army of the king of Babylon. And al-
though they have left Jerusalem for a while, 22 I will
call the Babylonian armies back again. They will
fight against this city and will capture it and burn it
down. I will see to it that all the towns of Judah are
destroyed, with no one living there."

THE FAITHFUL RECABITES

35 This is the message the LORD gave Jeremiah
when Jehoiakim son of Josiah was king of Ju-
dah: 2 "Go to the settlement where the families of the
Recabites live, and invite them to the LORD's Temple.
Take them into one of the inner rooms, and offer them
some wine."
3 So I went to see Jaazaniah son of Jeremiah and
grandson of Habazziniah and all his brothers and
sons—representing all the Recabite families. 4 I took
them to the Temple, and we went into the room as-
signed to the sons of Hanan son of Igdaliah, a man of
God. This room was located next to the one used by
the Temple officials, directly above the room of Maa-
seiah son of Shallum, the Temple gatekeeper.
5 I set cups and jugs of wine before them and invit-
ed them to have a drink, 6 but they refused. "No," they
said, "we don't drink wine, because our ancestor Je-
honadab* son of Recab gave us this command: 'You
and your descendants must never drink wine. 7 And
do not build houses or plant crops or vineyards, but
always live in tents. If you follow these commands,
you will live long, good lives in the land.' 8 So we have
obeyed him in all these things. We have never had a
drink of wine to this day, nor have our wives, our sons,
or our daughters. 9 We haven't built houses or owned
vineyards or farms or planted crops. 10 We have lived
in tents and have fully obeyed all the commands of
Jehonadab, our ancestor. 11 But when King Nebuchad-
nezzar* of Babylon attacked this country, we were
afraid of the Babylonian and Syrian* armies. So we
decided to move to Jerusalem. That is why we are
here."
12 Then the LORD gave this message to Jeremiah:
13 "This is what the LORD of Heaven's Armies, the God
of Israel, says: Go and say to the people in Judah and
Jerusalem, 'Come and learn a lesson about how to
obey me. 14 The Recabites do not drink wine to this
day because their ancestor Jehonadab told them not
to. But I have spoken to you again and again, and you
refuse to obey me. 15 Time after time I sent you proph-
ets, who told you, "Turn from your wicked ways, and
start doing things right. Stop worshiping other gods
so that you might live in peace here in the land I have
given to you and your ancestors." But you would not
listen to me or obey me. 16 The descendants of Jehon-
adab son of Recab have obeyed their ancestor com-
pletely, but you have refused to listen to me.'

35:6 Hebrew *Jonadab*, a variant spelling of Jehonadab; also in 35:10, 19. See 2 Kgs 10:15. **35:11a** Hebrew *Nebuchadrezzar*, a variant spelling of Nebuchadnezzar. **35:11b** Or *Chaldean and Aramean*.

34:5 will die peacefully. Zedekiah's rebellion against Nebuchadnezzar was worthy of execution. However, God graciously sustained his life as a sign of hope to Israel that His favor was not gone forever.

34:8 freedom. In accordance with the law of the year of Jubilee (Lev. 25:10), Zedekiah proclaimed freedom for the Hebrews who were slaves of their own people.

34:14 paid no attention to. Unfortunately, Judah's attempts to reinstate the Law were halfhearted at best (see Deut. 15:12). They eventually recaptured their slaves (v. 16).

34:18 as you cut apart calf. God had passed through the sacrifice in making the covenant (Gen. 15:8-11, 17). Judah's punishment was to be treated like the original sacrifice.

35:2 families of the Recabites. Fiercely loyal to the Lord, the Rechabites were nomads who joined Israel in the wilderness and took a special vow of holiness with God, including abstention from alcohol. They helped Jehu destroy the Baal worshippers in 2 Kings 10.

35:6 we don't drink wine. An object lesson of faithfulness to Judah, the Rechabites steadfastly refused the wine prohibited by their forefather.

[17] "Therefore, this is what the LORD God of Heaven's Armies, the God of Israel, says: 'Because you refuse to listen or answer when I call, I will send upon Judah and Jerusalem all the disasters I have threatened.'"

[18] Then Jeremiah turned to the Recabites and said, "This is what the LORD of Heaven's Armies, the God of Israel, says: 'You have obeyed your ancestor Jehonadab in every respect, following all his instructions.' [19] Therefore, this is what the LORD of Heaven's Armies, the God of Israel, says: 'Jehonadab son of Recab will always have descendants who serve me.'"

BARUCH READS THE LORD'S MESSAGES

36 During the fourth year that Jehoiakim son of Josiah was king in Judah,* the LORD gave this message to Jeremiah: [2] "Get a scroll, and write down all my messages against Israel, Judah, and the other nations. Begin with the first message back in the days of Josiah, and write down every message, right up to the present time. [3] Perhaps the people of Judah will repent when they hear again all the terrible things I have planned for them. Then I will be able to forgive their sins and wrongdoings."

[4] So Jeremiah sent for Baruch son of Neriah, and as Jeremiah dictated all the prophecies that the LORD had given him, Baruch wrote them on a scroll. [5] Then Jeremiah said to Baruch, "I am a prisoner here and unable to go to the Temple. [6] So you go to the Temple on the next day of fasting, and read the messages from the LORD that I have had you write on this scroll. Read them so the people who are there from all over Judah will hear them. [7] Perhaps even yet they will turn from their evil ways and ask the LORD's forgiveness before it is too late. For the LORD has threatened them with his terrible anger."

[8] Baruch did as Jeremiah told him and read these messages from the LORD to the people at the Temple. [9] He did this on a day of sacred fasting held in late autumn,* during the fifth year of the reign of Jehoiakim son of Josiah. People from all over Judah had come to Jerusalem to attend the services at the Temple on that day. [10] Baruch read Jeremiah's words on the scroll to all the people. He stood in front of the Temple room of Gemariah, son of Shaphan the secretary. This room was just off the upper courtyard of the Temple, near the New Gate entrance.

[11] When Micaiah son of Gemariah and grandson of Shaphan heard the messages from the LORD, [12] he went down to the secretary's room in the palace where the administrative officials were meeting. Elishama the secretary was there, along with Delaiah son of Shemaiah, Elnathan son of Acbor, Gemariah son of Shaphan, Zedekiah son of Hananiah, and all the other officials. [13] When Micaiah told them about the messages Baruch was reading to the people, [14] the officials sent Jehudi son of Nethaniah, grandson of Shelemiah and great-grandson of Cushi, to ask Baruch to come and read the messages to them, too. So Baruch took the scroll and went to them. [15] "Sit down and read the scroll to us," the officials said, and Baruch did as they requested.

[16] When they heard all the messages, they looked at one another in alarm. "We must tell the king what we have heard," they said to Baruch. [17] "But first, tell us how you got these messages. Did they come directly from Jeremiah?"

[18] So Baruch explained, "Jeremiah dictated them, and I wrote them down in ink, word for word, on this scroll."

[19] "You and Jeremiah should both hide," the officials told Baruch. "Don't tell anyone where you are!" [20] Then the officials left the scroll for safekeeping in the room of Elishama the secretary and went to tell the king what had happened.

KING JEHOIAKIM BURNS THE SCROLL

[21] The king sent Jehudi to get the scroll. Jehudi brought it from Elishama's room and read it to the king as all his officials stood by. [22] It was late autumn, and the king was in a winterized part of the palace, sitting in front of a fire to keep warm. [23] Each time Jehudi finished reading three or four columns, the king took a knife and cut off that section of the scroll. He then threw it into the fire, section by section, until the whole scroll was burned up. [24] Neither the king nor his attendants showed any signs of fear or repentance at what they heard. [25] Even when Elnathan, Delaiah, and Gemariah begged the king not to burn the scroll, he wouldn't listen.

[26] Then the king commanded his son Jerahmeel, Seraiah son of Azriel, and Shelemiah son of Abdeel to arrest Baruch and Jeremiah. But the LORD had hidden them.

JEREMIAH REWRITES THE SCROLL

[27] After the king had burned the scroll on which Baruch had written Jeremiah's words, the LORD gave Jeremiah another message. He said, [28] "Get another scroll, and write everything again just as you did on the scroll King Jehoiakim burned. [29] Then say to the king, 'This is what the LORD says: You burned the scroll because it said the king of Babylon would destroy this land and empty it of people and animals. [30] Now this is what the LORD says about King Jehoiakim of Judah: He will have no heirs to sit on the throne of David. His dead body will be thrown out to lie unburied—exposed to the heat of the day and the frost of the night. [31] I will punish him and his family and his attendants for their sins. I will pour out on them and on all the people of Jerusalem and Judah all the disasters I promised, for they would not listen to my warnings.'"

36:1 The fourth year of Jehoiakim's reign was 605 B.C. **36:9** Hebrew *in the ninth month,* of the ancient Hebrew lunar calendar (also in 36:22). The ninth month in the fifth year of Jehoiakim's reign occurred within the months of November and December 604 B.C. Also see note on 1:3.

36:1 The fourth year of Jehoiakim's reign marks the beginning of the Babylonian siege.

36:2 scroll. This was Jeremiah's first attempt to pen his prophecies. A written record could be read aloud, hopefully warning more people.

36:5 I am a prisoner. Despite having been threatened (20:2), the unpopular Jeremiah found a way to propagate his message (26:7-11). His assistant, Baruch, took the message to the temple.

36:19 should both hide. The news was so disturbing, the officials instructed Baruch to run for safety. They feared the king would react to the messenger as well as the message.

36:23 threw it into the fire. Jeremiah's message was all but wasted on Judah's King Jehoiakim, who demonstrated his disdain by burning the message instead of heeding it.

36:30 no heirs to sit on the throne of David. Although God eliminated Jehoiakim's line from the Davidic throne succession, his line was restored after the exile when Zerubbabel was placed as a signet ring on God's hand (see Hag. 2:23). Jesus was descended from Zerubbabel and thus from Jehoiakim (see Matt. 1:11-12).

32 So Jeremiah took another scroll and dictated again to his secretary, Baruch. He wrote everything that had been on the scroll King Jehoiakim had burned in the fire. Only this time he added much more!

ZEDEKIAH CALLS FOR JEREMIAH

37 Zedekiah son of Josiah succeeded Jehoiachin* son of Jehoiakim as the king of Judah. He was appointed by King Nebuchadnezzar* of Babylon. 2 But neither King Zedekiah nor his attendants nor the people who were left in the land listened to what the LORD said through Jeremiah.

3 Nevertheless, King Zedekiah sent Jehucal son of Shelemiah, and Zephaniah the priest, son of Maaseiah, to ask Jeremiah, "Please pray to the LORD our God for us." 4 Jeremiah had not yet been imprisoned, so he could come and go among the people as he pleased.

5 At this time the army of Pharaoh Hophra* of Egypt appeared at the southern border of Judah. When the Babylonian* army heard about it, they withdrew from their siege of Jerusalem.

6 Then the LORD gave this message to Jeremiah: 7 "This is what the LORD, the God of Israel, says: The king of Judah sent you to ask me what is going to happen. Tell him, 'Pharaoh's army is about to return to Egypt, though he came here to help you. 8 Then the Babylonians* will come back and capture this city and burn it to the ground.'

9 "This is what the LORD says: Do not fool yourselves into thinking that the Babylonians are gone for good. They aren't! 10 Even if you were to destroy the entire Babylonian army, leaving only a handful of wounded survivors, they would still stagger from their tents and burn this city to the ground!"

JEREMIAH IS IMPRISONED

11 When the Babylonian army left Jerusalem because of Pharaoh's approaching army, 12 Jeremiah started to leave the city on his way to the territory of Benjamin, to claim his share of the property among his relatives there.* 13 But as he was walking through the Benjamin Gate, a sentry arrested him and said, "You are defecting to the Babylonians!" The sentry making the arrest was Irijah son of Shelemiah, grandson of Hananiah.

14 "That's not true!" Jeremiah protested. "I had no intention of doing any such thing." But Irijah wouldn't listen, and he took Jeremiah before the officials. 15 They were furious with Jeremiah and had him flogged and imprisoned in the house of Jonathan the secretary. Jonathan's house had been converted into a prison. 16 Jeremiah was put into a dungeon cell, where he remained for many days.

17 Later King Zedekiah secretly requested that Jeremiah come to the palace, where the king asked him, "Do you have any messages from the LORD?"

"Yes, I do!" said Jeremiah. "You will be defeated by the king of Babylon."

18 Then Jeremiah asked the king, "What crime have I committed? What have I done against you, your attendants, or the people that I should be imprisoned like this? 19 Where are your prophets now who told you the king of Babylon would not attack you or this land? 20 Listen, my lord the king, I beg you. Don't send me back to the dungeon in the house of Jonathan the secretary, for I will die there."

21 So King Zedekiah commanded that Jeremiah not be returned to the dungeon. Instead, he was imprisoned in the courtyard of the guard in the royal palace. The king also commanded that Jeremiah be given a loaf of fresh bread every day as long as there was any left in the city. So Jeremiah was put in the palace prison.

JEREMIAH IN A CISTERN

38 Now Shephatiah son of Mattan, Gedaliah son of Pashhur, Jehucal* son of Shelemiah, and Pashhur son of Malkijah heard what Jeremiah had been telling the people. He had been saying, 2 "This is what the LORD says: 'Everyone who stays in Jerusalem will die from war, famine, or disease, but those who surrender to the Babylonians* will live. Their reward will be life. They will live!' 3 The LORD also says: 'The city of Jerusalem will certainly be handed over to the army of the king of Babylon, who will capture it.'"

4 So these officials went to the king and said, "Sir, this man must die! That kind of talk will undermine the morale of the few fighting men we have left, as well as that of all the people. This man is a traitor!"

5 King Zedekiah agreed. "All right," he said. "Do as you like. I can't stop you."

6 So the officials took Jeremiah from his cell and lowered him by ropes into an empty cistern in the prison yard. It belonged to Malkijah, a member of the royal family. There was no water in the cistern, but there was a thick layer of mud at the bottom, and Jeremiah sank down into it.

7 But Ebed-melech the Ethiopian,* an important court official, heard that Jeremiah was in the cistern. At that time the king was holding court at the Benjamin Gate, 8 so Ebed-melech rushed from the palace to speak with him. 9 "My lord the king," he said, "these men have done a very evil thing in putting Jeremiah the prophet into the cistern. He will soon die of hunger, for almost all the bread in the city is gone."

10 So the king told Ebed-melech, "Take thirty of my men with you, and pull Jeremiah out of the cistern before he dies."

37:1a Hebrew *Coniah,* a variant spelling of Jehoiachin. **37:1b** Hebrew *Nebuchadrezzar,* a variant spelling of Nebuchadnezzar. **37:5a** Hebrew *army of Pharaoh;* see 44:30. **37:5b** Or *Chaldean;* also in 37:10, 11. **37:8** Or *Chaldeans;* also in 37:9, 13. **37:12** Hebrew *to separate from there in the midst of the people.* **38:1** Hebrew *Jucal,* a variant spelling of Jehucal; see 37:3. **38:2** Or *Chaldeans;* also in 38:18, 19, 23. **38:7** Hebrew *the Cushite.*

37:1–38:28 With the threat of Babylon closing in on the inhabitants of Jerusalem, the unpopular prophet was imprisoned for treason (37:11-16). King Zedekiah tried protecting the prisoner (37:17-21); however, Jeremiah ended up in a dark cistern (38:1-6). Jeremiah's rescue proved to be a timely turn of events (38:7-13).

37:3 Please pray. Zedekiah enjoyed a cafeteria-style relationship with Jeremiah—picking and choosing what he wanted to hear (v. 2).

37:5 they withdrew from their seige of Jerusalem. The Babylonians were drawn away from smaller prey to pursue the powerful pharaoh. The Egyptians proved an insufficient ally against the Babylonians.

38:5 Do as you like. Zedekiah eagerly released himself from responsibility in a potentially volatile situation.

38:7 Ebed-melech the Ethiopian. His name means "king's servant." He actually became a servant by helping Jeremiah, who was about 60 years old at the time. Jeremiah would have died at the hands of unjust men apart from the protests of this appalled official. Ebed-melech was rewarded for acting justly and rescuing Jeremiah (39:15-18).

11 So Ebed-melech took the men with him and went
to a room in the palace beneath the treasury, where he
found some old rags and discarded clothing. He carried
these to the cistern and lowered them to Jeremiah on
a rope. 12 Ebed-melech called down to Jeremiah, "Put
these rags under your armpits to protect you from the
ropes." Then when Jeremiah was ready, 13 they pulled
him out. So Jeremiah was returned to the courtyard of
the guard—the palace prison—where he remained.

ZEDEKIAH QUESTIONS JEREMIAH

14 One day King Zedekiah sent for Jeremiah and had
him brought to the third entrance of the LORD's Temple. "I want to ask you something," the king said. "And
don't try to hide the truth."

15 Jeremiah said, "If I tell you the truth, you will kill
me. And if I give you advice, you won't listen to me
anyway."

16 So King Zedekiah secretly promised him, "As
surely as the LORD our Creator lives, I will not kill you
or hand you over to the men who want you dead."

17 Then Jeremiah said to Zedekiah, "This is what
the LORD God of Heaven's Armies, the God of Israel,
says: 'If you surrender to the Babylonian officers,
you and your family will live, and the city will not
be burned down. 18 But if you refuse to surrender,
you will not escape! This city will be handed over
to the Babylonians, and they will burn it to the
ground.'"

19 "But I am afraid to surrender," the king said, "for
the Babylonians may hand me over to the Judeans
who have defected to them. And who knows what
they will do to me!"

20 Jeremiah replied, "You won't be handed over to
them if you choose to obey the LORD. Your life will be
spared, and all will go well for you. 21 But if you refuse
to surrender, this is what the LORD has revealed to me:
22 All the women left in your palace will be brought
out and given to the officers of the Babylonian army.
Then the women will taunt you, saying,

'What fine friends you have!
    They have betrayed and misled you.
When your feet sank in the mud,
    they left you to your fate!'

23 All your wives and children will be led out to the
Babylonians, and you will not escape. You will be
seized by the king of Babylon, and this city will be
burned down."

24 Then Zedekiah said to Jeremiah, "Don't tell anyone you told me this, or you will die! 25 My officials
may hear that I spoke to you, and they may say, 'Tell
us what you and the king were talking about. If you
don't tell us, we will kill you.' 26 If this happens, just
tell them you begged me not to send you back to Jonathan's dungeon, for fear you would die there."

27 Sure enough, it wasn't long before the king's
officials came to Jeremiah and asked him why the
king had called for him. But Jeremiah followed the
king's instructions, and they left without finding out
the truth. No one had overheard the conversation
between Jeremiah and the king. 28 And Jeremiah remained a prisoner in the courtyard of the guard until
the day Jerusalem was captured.

THE FALL OF JERUSALEM

39 In January* of the ninth year of King Zedekiah's reign, King Nebuchadnezzar* of Babylon
came with his entire army to besiege Jerusalem. 2 Two
and a half years later, on July 18* in the eleventh year
of Zedekiah's reign, a section of the city wall was broken down. 3 All the officers of the Babylonian army
came in and sat in triumph at the Middle Gate: Nergal-sharezer of Samgar, and Nebo-sarsekim,* a chief
officer, and Nergal-sharezer, the king's adviser, and
all the other officers of the king of Babylon.

4 When King Zedekiah of Judah and all the soldiers saw that the Babylonians had broken into the
city, they fled. They waited for nightfall and then
slipped through the gate between the two walls behind the king's garden and headed toward the Jordan Valley.*

5 But the Babylonian* troops chased them and
overtook Zedekiah on the plains of Jericho. They captured him and took him to King Nebuchadnezzar of
Babylon, who was at Riblah in the land of Hamath.
There the king of Babylon pronounced judgment
upon Zedekiah. 6 The king of Babylon made Zedekiah
watch as he slaughtered his sons at Riblah. The king
of Babylon also slaughtered all the nobles of Judah.
7 Then he gouged out Zedekiah's eyes and bound him
in bronze chains to lead him away to Babylon.

8 Meanwhile, the Babylonians burned Jerusalem,
including the royal palace and the houses of the people, and they tore down the walls of the city. 9 Then
Nebuzaradan, the captain of the guard, took as exiles
to Babylon the rest of the people who remained in the
city, those who had defected to him, and everyone else
who remained. 10 But Nebuzaradan allowed some of
the poorest people to stay behind in the land of Judah, and he assigned them to care for the vineyards
and fields.

JEREMIAH REMAINS IN JUDAH

11 King Nebuchadnezzar had told Nebuzaradan, the
captain of the guard, to find Jeremiah. 12 "See that he
isn't hurt," he said. "Look after him well, and give him
anything he wants." 13 So Nebuzaradan, the captain
of the guard; Nebushazban, a chief officer; Nergal-sharezer, the king's adviser; and the other officers of
Babylon's king 14 sent messengers to bring Jeremiah
out of the prison. They put him under the care of Gedaliah son of Ahikam and grandson of Shaphan, who

39:1a Hebrew *In the tenth month,* of the ancient Hebrew lunar calendar. A number of events in Jeremiah can be cross-checked with dates in surviving Babylonian records and related accurately to our modern calendar. This event occurred on January 15, 588 B.C.; see 52:4a and the note there. **39:1b** Hebrew *Nebuchadrezzar,* a variant spelling of Nebuchadnezzar; also in 39:5, 11. **39:2** Hebrew *On the ninth day of the fourth month.* This day was July 18, 586 B.C.; also see note on 39:1a. **39:3** Or *Nergal-sharezer, Samgar-nebo, Sarsekim.* **39:4** Hebrew *the Arabah.* **39:5** Or *Chaldean;* similarly in 39:8.

38:12 Ebed-melech exercised extra-mile effort. He managed the process with concern for Jeremiah's safety and comfort.
38:19 I am afraid. Zedekiah was right to be afraid. Before his eyes were put out (2 Kings 25:7), his sons would be put to death before his eyes.

38:27 No one had overheard. Zedekiah instructed Jeremiah not to disclose their private conversation. When asked about this by the officials, Jeremiah backtracked to his earlier pleas to Zedekiah regarding his safekeeping (37:20).
39:2 A pile of rubble marked the beginning of the end for Jerusalem. After a two-month siege, the Babylonians captured the stalwart city.

took him back to his home. So Jeremiah stayed in Judah among his own people.

[15] The LORD had given the following message to Jeremiah while he was still in prison: [16] "Say to Ebed-melech the Ethiopian,* 'This is what the LORD of Heaven's Armies, the God of Israel, says: I will do to this city everything I have threatened. I will send disaster, not prosperity. You will see its destruction, [17] but I will rescue you from those you fear so much. [18] Because you trusted me, I will give you your life as a reward. I will rescue you and keep you safe. I, the LORD, have spoken!'"

40 The LORD gave a message to Jeremiah after Nebuzaradan, the captain of the guard, had released him at Ramah. He had found Jeremiah bound in chains among all the other captives of Jerusalem and Judah who were being sent to exile in Babylon.

[2] The captain of the guard called for Jeremiah and said, "The LORD your God has brought this disaster on this land, [3] just as he said he would. For these people have sinned against the LORD and disobeyed him. That is why it happened. [4] But I am going to take off your chains and let you go. If you want to come with me to Babylon, you are welcome. I will see that you are well cared for. But if you don't want to come, you may stay here. The whole land is before you—go wherever you like. [5] If you decide to stay, then return to Gedaliah son of Ahikam and grandson of Shaphan. He has been appointed governor of Judah by the king of Babylon. Stay there with the people he rules. But it's up to you; go wherever you like."

Then Nebuzaradan, the captain of the guard, gave Jeremiah some food and money and let him go. [6] So Jeremiah returned to Gedaliah son of Ahikam at Mizpah, and he lived in Judah with the few who were still left in the land.

GEDALIAH GOVERNS IN JUDAH

[7] The leaders of the Judean military groups in the countryside heard that the king of Babylon had appointed Gedaliah son of Ahikam as governor over the poor people who were left behind in Judah—the men, women, and children who hadn't been exiled to Babylon. [8] So they went to see Gedaliah at Mizpah. These included: Ishmael son of Nethaniah, Johanan and Jonathan sons of Kareah, Seraiah son of Tanhumeth, the sons of Ephai the Netophathite, Jezaniah son of the Maacathite, and all their men.

[9] Gedaliah vowed to them that the Babylonians* meant them no harm. "Don't be afraid to serve them. Live in the land and serve the king of Babylon, and all will go well for you," he promised. [10] "As for me, I will stay at Mizpah to represent you before the Babylonians who come to meet with us. Settle in the towns you have taken, and live off the land. Harvest the grapes and summer fruits and olives, and store them away."

[11] When the Judeans in Moab, Ammon, Edom, and the other nearby countries heard that the king of Babylon had left a few people in Judah and that Gedaliah was the governor, [12] they began to return to Judah from the places to which they had fled. They stopped at Mizpah to meet with Gedaliah and then went into the Judean countryside to gather a great harvest of grapes and other crops.

A PLOT AGAINST GEDALIAH

[13] Soon after this, Johanan son of Kareah and the other military leaders came to Gedaliah at Mizpah. [14] They said to him, "Did you know that Baalis, king of Ammon, has sent Ishmael son of Nethaniah to assassinate you?" But Gedaliah refused to believe them.

[15] Later Johanan had a private conference with Gedaliah and volunteered to kill Ishmael secretly. "Why should we let him come and murder you?" Johanan asked. "What will happen then to the Judeans who have returned? Why should the few of us who are still left be scattered and lost?"

[16] But Gedaliah said to Johanan, "I forbid you to do any such thing, for you are lying about Ishmael."

THE MURDER OF GEDALIAH

41 But in midautumn of that year,* Ishmael son of Nethaniah and grandson of Elishama, who was a member of the royal family and had been one of the king's high officials, went to Mizpah with ten men to meet Gedaliah. While they were eating together, [2] Ishmael and his ten men suddenly jumped up, drew their swords, and killed Gedaliah, whom the king of Babylon had appointed governor. [3] Ishmael also killed all the Judeans and the Babylonian* soldiers who were with Gedaliah at Mizpah.

[4] The next day, before anyone had heard about Gedaliah's murder, [5] eighty men arrived from Shechem, Shiloh, and Samaria to worship at the Temple of the LORD. They had shaved off their beards, torn their clothes, and cut themselves, and had brought along grain offerings and frankincense. [6] Ishmael left Mizpah to meet them, weeping as he went. When he reached them, he said, "Oh, come and see what has happened to Gedaliah!"

[7] But as soon as they were all inside the town, Ishmael and his men killed all but ten of them and

39:16 Hebrew *the Cushite.* **40:9** Or *Chaldeans;* also in 40:10. **41:1** Hebrew *in the seventh month,* of the ancient Hebrew lunar calendar. This month occurred within the months of October and November 586 B.C.; also see note on 39:1a. **41:3** Or *Chaldean.*

39:14 among his own people. In the midst of deportation, Jeremiah was identified and released from his political imprisonment.

39:18 trusted me. Ebed-melech's past heroism proved to be invaluable (38:7-13). He escaped certain death.

40:1 gave a message to Jeremiah. Jeremiah began another chapter of post-prison prophecies. His job was not yet over. He continued the task at hand, even though he had just been given freedom.

40:2-3 Jeremiah's insightful prophecies against Judah were not lost on the pagan officials of Babylon. The first exiles likely spread the word as his predictions came true.

40:5 Gedaliah. An impression from a royal seal reading "Belonging to Gedaliah, Over the House," was found at Lachish. It is dated from the early sixth century B.C.

40:10 represent you before the Babylonians. As governor, Gedaliah served as a national link between the remnants of Jews in Judah and the powerful Babylon.

40:16 I forbid you. The last thing Gedaliah wanted was to upset his peacekeeping position. Little did he know his advisers were right, and he would soon be killed by Ishmael (41:1-3). Gedaliah serves as a reminder that one should not assume that everyone sees things alike or aspires to the same lofty goals.

41:1 eating together. Gedaliah's first feast would be his last official event. Ishmael's mealtime murder caught him off guard, though he had been warned that Ishmael was involved in a plot to assassinate him (40:13-16). Fearing Babylonian reprisal, the Jewish remnant fled to Egypt (vv. 16-18). The Holy Land would be bereft of Jews until their return from exile. Thereafter, they remembered the anniversary of Gedaliah's death (Zech. 7:5; 8:19).

threw their bodies into a cistern. [8] The other ten had talked Ishmael into letting them go by promising to bring him their stores of wheat, barley, olive oil, and honey that they had hidden away. [9] The cistern where Ishmael dumped the bodies of the men he murdered was the large one* dug by King Asa when he fortified Mizpah to protect himself against King Baasha of Israel. Ishmael son of Nethaniah filled it with corpses.

[10] Then Ishmael made captives of the king's daughters and the other people who had been left under Gedaliah's care in Mizpah by Nebuzaradan, the captain of the guard. Taking them with him, he started back toward the land of Ammon.

[11] But when Johanan son of Kareah and the other military leaders heard about Ishmael's crimes, [12] they took all their men and set out to stop him. They caught up with him at the large pool near Gibeon. [13] The people Ishmael had captured shouted for joy when they saw Johanan and the other military leaders. [14] And all the captives from Mizpah escaped and began to help Johanan. [15] Meanwhile, Ishmael and eight of his men escaped from Johanan into the land of Ammon.

[16] Then Johanan son of Kareah and the other military leaders took all the people they had rescued in Gibeon—the soldiers, women, children, and court officials* whom Ishmael had captured after he killed Gedaliah. [17] They took them all to the village of Geruth-kimham near Bethlehem, where they prepared to leave for Egypt. [18] They were afraid of what the Babylonians* would do when they heard that Ishmael had killed Gedaliah, the governor appointed by the Babylonian king.

WARNING TO STAY IN JUDAH

42 Then all the military leaders, including Johanan son of Kareah and Jezaniah* son of Hoshaiah, and all the people, from the least to the greatest, approached [2] Jeremiah the prophet. They said, "Please pray to the LORD your God for us. As you can see, we are only a tiny remnant compared to what we were before. [3] Pray that the LORD your God will show us what to do and where to go."

[4] "All right," Jeremiah replied. "I will pray to the LORD your God, as you have asked, and I will tell you everything he says. I will hide nothing from you."

[5] Then they said to Jeremiah, "May the LORD your God be a faithful witness against us if we refuse to obey whatever he tells us to do! [6] Whether we like it or not, we will obey the LORD our God to whom we are sending you with our plea. For if we obey him, everything will turn out well for us."

[7] Ten days later the LORD gave his reply to Jeremiah. [8] So he called for Johanan son of Kareah and the other military leaders, and for all the people, from the least to the greatest. [9] He said to them, "You sent me to the LORD, the God of Israel, with your request, and this is his reply: [10] 'Stay here in this land. If you do, I will build you up and not tear you down; I will plant you and not uproot you. For I am sorry about all the punishment I have had to bring upon you. [11] Do not fear the king of Babylon anymore,' says the LORD. 'For I am with you and will save you and rescue you from his power. [12] I will be merciful to you by making him kind, so he will let you stay here in your land.'

[13] "But if you refuse to obey the LORD your God, and if you say, 'We will not stay here; [14] instead, we will go to Egypt where we will be free from war, the call to arms, and hunger,' [15] then hear the LORD's message to the remnant of Judah. This is what the LORD of Heaven's Armies, the God of Israel, says: 'If you are determined to go to Egypt and live there, [16] the very war and famine you fear will catch up to you, and you will die there. [17] That is the fate awaiting every one of you who insists on going to live in Egypt. Yes, you will die from war, famine, and disease. None of you will escape the disaster I will bring upon you there.'

[18] "This is what the LORD of Heaven's Armies, the God of Israel, says: 'Just as my anger and fury have been poured out on the people of Jerusalem, so they will be poured out on you when you enter Egypt. You will be an object of damnation, horror, cursing, and mockery. And you will never see your homeland again.'

[19] "Listen, you remnant of Judah. The LORD has told you: 'Do not go to Egypt!' Don't forget this warning I have given you today. [20] For you were not being honest when you sent me to pray to the LORD your God for you. You said, 'Just tell us what the LORD our God says, and we will do it!' [21] And today I have told you exactly what he said, but you will not obey the LORD your God any better now than you have in the past. [22] So you can be sure that you will die from war, famine, and disease in Egypt, where you insist on going."

JEREMIAH TAKEN TO EGYPT

43 When Jeremiah had finished giving this message from the LORD their God to all the people, [2] Azariah son of Hoshaiah and Johanan son of Kareah and all the other proud men said to Jeremiah, "You lie! The LORD our God hasn't forbidden us to go to Egypt! [3] Baruch son of Neriah has convinced you to say this, because he wants us to stay here and be killed by the Babylonians* or be carried off into exile."

[4] So Johanan and the other military leaders and all the people refused to obey the LORD's command to stay in Judah. [5] Johanan and the other leaders took with them all the people who had returned from the nearby countries to which they had fled. [6] In the crowd were men, women, and children, the king's daughters, and all those whom Nebuzaradan, the captain of the guard, had left with Gedaliah. The prophet Jeremiah and Baruch were also included. [7] The people refused to obey the voice of the LORD and went to Egypt, going as far as the city of Tahpanhes.

41:9 As in Greek version; Hebrew reads *murdered because of Gedaliah was one.* **41:16** Or *eunuchs.* **41:18** Or *Chaldeans.* **42:1** Greek version reads *Azariah;* compare 43:2. **43:3** Or *Chaldeans.*

42:6 We will obey. The army officers' good intentions prove to be short-lived. Like many in the prophet's presence, they heard only what they wanted (43:2).

42:7 Ten days later. Jeremiah spent 10 days in prayer for the people. His message came as a result of his persistence.

43:1-3 Since the Jewish remnant did not like the message (even though Jeremiah's predictions had proven to be incredibly accurate), they once again blamed the messenger. Jeremiah's message was exactly opposite of what they had planned, even if their plan contradicted the Lord's promise to bless and protect them (42:9-12) and disregarded His warning that they would be severely punished by choosing to go to Egypt (42:13-18).

8 Then at Tahpanhes, the LORD gave another message
to Jeremiah. He said, 9 "While the people of Judah are
watching, take some large rocks and bury them under
the pavement stones at the entrance of Pharaoh's pal-
ace here in Tahpanhes. 10 Then say to the people of Ju-
dah, 'This is what the LORD of Heaven's Armies, the God
of Israel, says: I will certainly bring my servant Neb-
uchadnezzar,* king of Babylon, here to Egypt. I will
set his throne over these stones that I have hidden. He
will spread his royal canopy over them. 11 And when he
comes, he will destroy the land of Egypt. He will bring
death to those destined for death, captivity to those
destined for captivity, and war to those destined for
war. 12 He will set fire to the temples of Egypt's gods; he
will burn the temples and carry the idols away as plun-
der. He will pick clean the land of Egypt as a shepherd
picks fleas from his cloak. And he himself will leave
unharmed. 13 He will break down the sacred pillars
standing in the temple of the sun* in Egypt, and he will
burn down the temples of Egypt's gods.'"

JUDGMENT FOR IDOLATRY

44 This is the message Jeremiah received con-
cerning the Judeans living in northern Egypt
in the cities of Migdol, Tahpanhes, and Memphis,*
and in southern Egypt* as well: 2 "This is what the
LORD of Heaven's Armies, the God of Israel, says: You
saw the calamity I brought on Jerusalem and all the
towns of Judah. They now lie deserted and in ruins.
3 They provoked my anger with all their wickedness.
They burned incense and worshiped other gods—
gods that neither they nor you nor any of your ances-
tors had ever even known.

4 "Again and again I sent my servants, the proph-
ets, to plead with them, 'Don't do these horrible things
that I hate so much.' 5 But my people would not listen
or turn back from their wicked ways. They kept on
burning incense to these gods. 6 And so my fury boiled
over and fell like fire on the towns of Judah and into
the streets of Jerusalem, and they are still a desolate
ruin today.

7 "And now the LORD God of Heaven's Armies, the
God of Israel, asks you: Why are you destroying your-
selves? For not one of you will survive—not a man,
woman, or child among you who has come here from
Judah, not even the babies in your arms. 8 Why pro-
voke my anger by burning incense to the idols you
have made here in Egypt? You will only destroy your-
selves and make yourselves an object of cursing and
mockery for all the nations of the earth. 9 Have you
forgotten the sins of your ancestors, the sins of the
kings and queens of Judah, and the sins you and your
wives committed in Judah and Jerusalem? 10 To this
very hour you have shown no remorse or reverence.
No one has chosen to follow my word and the decrees
I gave to you and your ancestors before you.

11 "Therefore, this is what the LORD of Heaven's Ar-
mies, the God of Israel, says: I am determined to de-
stroy every one of you! 12 I will take this remnant of
Judah—those who were determined to come here
and live in Egypt—and I will consume them. They
will fall here in Egypt, killed by war and famine. All
will die, from the least to the greatest. They will be an
object of damnation, horror, cursing, and mockery. 13 I
will punish them in Egypt just as I punished them in
Jerusalem, by war, famine, and disease. 14 Of that rem-
nant who fled to Egypt, hoping someday to return to
Judah, there will be no survivors. Even though they
long to return home, only a handful will do so."

15 Then all the women present and all the men who
knew that their wives had burned incense to idols—a
great crowd of all the Judeans living in northern
Egypt and southern Egypt*—answered Jeremiah,
16 "We will not listen to your messages from the LORD!
17 We will do whatever we want. We will burn incense
and pour out liquid offerings to the Queen of Heaven
just as much as we like—just as we, and our ancestors,
and our kings and officials have always done in the
towns of Judah and in the streets of Jerusalem. For in
those days we had plenty to eat, and we were well off
and had no troubles! 18 But ever since we quit burning
incense to the Queen of Heaven and stopped worship-
ing her with liquid offerings, we have been in great
trouble and have been dying from war and famine."

19 "Besides," the women added, "do you suppose
that we were burning incense and pouring out liquid
offerings to the Queen of Heaven, and making cakes
marked with her image, without our husbands know-
ing it and helping us? Of course not!"

20 Then Jeremiah said to all of them, men and wom-
en alike, who had given him that answer, 21 "Do you
think the LORD did not know that you and your an-
cestors, your kings and officials, and all the people
were burning incense to idols in the towns of Judah
and in the streets of Jerusalem? 22 It was because the
LORD could no longer bear all the disgusting things
you were doing that he made your land an object of
cursing—a desolate ruin without inhabitants—as it
is today. 23 All these terrible things happened to you
because you have burned incense to idols and sinned
against the LORD. You have refused to obey him and
have not followed his instructions, his decrees, and
his laws."

24 Then Jeremiah said to them all, including the
women, "Listen to this message from the LORD, all you
citizens of Judah who live in Egypt. 25 This is what the
LORD of Heaven's Armies, the God of Israel, says: 'You
and your wives have said, "We will keep our prom-
ises to burn incense and pour out liquid offerings to
the Queen of Heaven," and you have proved by your
actions that you meant it. So go ahead and carry out
your promises and vows to her!'

43:10 Hebrew *Nebuchadrezzar,* a variant spelling of Nebuchadnezzar. 43:13 Or *in Heliopolis.* 44:1a Hebrew *Noph.* 44:1b Hebrew *in Pathros.* 44:15 Hebrew *in Egypt, in Pathros.*

43:8 Tahpanhes. Tahpanhes was a frontier town in the eastern Nile delta. Having once reached the Egyptian border in 601 B.C., Nebuchadnezzar's army returned there in 567 B.C. (46:14; Ezek. 29:17-20).

43:13 temple of the sun. Just as Nebuchadnezzar had demolished the temple in Jerusalem, he would destroy the temple of the sun god *Re* in the Egyptian worship center at Heliopolis.

44:1 Migdol. Previously mentioned as near the exodus route (Ex. 14:2) and a place where some Jewish refugees fled, Egypt's doom was proclaimed there (46:13-14).

44:18 Queen of Heaven. The people refused to believe the truth of their calamity by choosing to return to the worship of the queen of heaven (7:18; perhaps the Assyrian-Babylonian-Canaanite goddess of love and fertility, *Astarte*). Reasoning that they had been reasonably well off prior to Josiah's reforms (2 Kings 23:4-20), worshipping the queen (once again) was to be preferred over the Lord. Instead of believing that their punishment was the result of their disobedience (vv. 20-23), they decided that they had offended *Astarte* and needed to renew their vows to her (vv. 24-25).

26 "But listen to this message from the LORD, all you
Judeans now living in Egypt: 'I have sworn by my great
name,' says the LORD, 'that my name will no longer be
spoken by any of the Judeans in the land of Egypt.
None of you may invoke my name or use this oath: "As
surely as the Sovereign LORD lives." 27 For I will watch
over you to bring you disaster and not good. Everyone
from Judah who is now living in Egypt will suffer war
and famine until all of you are dead. 28 Only a small
number will escape death and return to Judah from
Egypt. Then all those who came to Egypt will find out
whose words are true—mine or theirs!

29 "'And this is the proof I give you,' says the LORD, 'that
all I have threatened will happen to you and that I will
punish you here.' 30 This is what the LORD says: 'I will
turn Pharaoh Hophra, king of Egypt, over to his enemies
who want to kill him, just as I turned King Zedekiah of
Judah over to King Nebuchadnezzar* of Babylon.'"

A MESSAGE FOR BARUCH

45 The prophet Jeremiah gave a message to Bar-
uch son of Neriah in the fourth year of the reign
of Jehoiakim son of Josiah,* after Baruch had written
down everything Jeremiah had dictated to him. He
said, 2 "This is what the LORD, the God of Israel, says to
you, Baruch: 3 You have said, 'I am overwhelmed with
trouble! Haven't I had enough pain already? And now
the LORD has added more! I am worn out from sighing
and can find no rest.'

4 "Baruch, this is what the LORD says: 'I will destroy
this nation that I built. I will uproot what I planted.
5 Are you seeking great things for yourself? Don't do
it! I will bring great disaster upon all these people; but
I will give you your life as a reward wherever you go.
I, the LORD, have spoken!'"

MESSAGES FOR THE NATIONS

46 The following messages were given to Jeremi-
ah the prophet from the LORD concerning for-
eign nations.

MESSAGES ABOUT EGYPT

2 This message concerning Egypt was given in the
fourth year of the reign of Jehoiakim son of Josiah,
the king of Judah, on the occasion of the battle of Car-
chemish* when Pharaoh Neco, king of Egypt, and his
army were defeated beside the Euphrates River by
King Nebuchadnezzar* of Babylon.

3 "Prepare your shields,
and advance into battle!
4 Harness the horses,
and mount the stallions.
Take your positions.
Put on your helmets.
Sharpen your spears,
and prepare your armor.
5 But what do I see?
The Egyptian army flees in terror.
The bravest of its fighting men run
without a backward glance.
They are terrorized at every turn,"
says the LORD.
6 "The swiftest runners cannot flee;
the mightiest warriors cannot escape.
By the Euphrates River to the north,
they stumble and fall.

7 "Who is this, rising like the Nile at floodtime,
overflowing all the land?
8 It is the Egyptian army,
overflowing all the land,
boasting that it will cover the earth like a flood,
destroying cities and their people.
9 Charge, you horses and chariots;
attack, you mighty warriors of Egypt!
Come, all you allies from Ethiopia, Libya, and Lydia*
who are skilled with the shield and bow!
10 For this is the day of the Lord, the LORD of Heaven's
Armies,
a day of vengeance on his enemies.
The sword will devour until it is satisfied,
yes, until it is drunk with your blood!
The Lord, the LORD of Heaven's Armies, will
receive a sacrifice today
in the north country beside the Euphrates River.

11 "Go up to Gilead to get medicine,
O virgin daughter of Egypt!
But your many treatments
will bring you no healing.
12 The nations have heard of your shame.
The earth is filled with your cries of despair.
Your mightiest warriors will run into each other
and fall down together."

13 Then the LORD gave the prophet Jeremiah this
message about King Nebuchadnezzar's plans to at-
tack Egypt.

14 "Shout it out in Egypt!
Publish it in the cities of Migdol, Memphis,* and
Tahpanhes!
Mobilize for battle,

44:30 Hebrew *Nebuchadrezzar,* a variant spelling of Nebuchadnezzar. **45:1** The fourth year of Jehoiakim's reign was 605 B.C. **46:2a** This event occurred in 605 B.C., during the fourth year of Jehoiakim's reign (according to the calendar system in which the new year begins in the spring). **46:2b** Hebrew *Nebuchadrezzar,* a variant spelling of Nebuchadnezzar; also in 46:13, 26. **46:9** Hebrew *from Cush, Put, and Lud.* **46:14** Hebrew *Noph;* also in 46:19.

45:1-4 Baruch. Perhaps because the fate of the Jewish exiles in Egypt (including Baruch) was hanging in the balance, these verses are a flashback to 605 B.C. (36:9-32). At that time, Baruch had been instructed to read a scroll of judgment which was so poorly received at the temple that he was forced into hiding (36:19,26) and later accused of being a liar and traitor (43:1-3). Baruch was feeling sorry for himself. God's response (v. 4) was to remind him of the message of judgment he had been given. In Egypt, God was not yet through. Thus, Baruch's original message uttered in chapter 36 is placed here as a reminder.

45:5 Don't do it! Rather than seeking reward for faithfulness, Baruch should be grateful that his life was spared. A similar promise had been made to Ebed-melech (39:15-18). Thorough judgment would precede complete restoration (1:10; 31:28; 42:10).

46:1-51:64 Just as chapters 36–45 are largely concerned with the judgment against Judah commencing in 605 B.C. and running to Babylon's catching up with the Jewish exiles in Egypt (567 B B.C.), chapter 46 begins with the original judgment of Egypt through its defeat by Nebuchadnezzar at the battle of Carchemish in 605 B.C. and ending with the Babylonian onslaught within Egypt itself (567 B.C.). Proceeding from the southwest to the distant east, the oracles continue. They concern the other nations that surround and had oppressed Israel (chaps. 47–49) and conclude with the 539 B.C. fall of the Lord's instrument in these judgments, Babylon (chaps. 50–51). This final judgment ultimately resulted in Israel's return from exile.

for the sword will devour everyone around you.
15 Why have your warriors fallen?
They cannot stand, for the LORD has knocked them down.
16 They stumble and fall over each other
and say among themselves,
'Come, let's go back to our people,
to the land of our birth.
Let's get away from the sword of the enemy!'
17 There they will say,
'Pharaoh, the king of Egypt, is a loudmouth
who missed his opportunity!'

18 "As surely as I live," says the King,
whose name is the LORD of Heaven's Armies,
"one is coming against Egypt
who is as tall as Mount Tabor,
or as Mount Carmel by the sea!
19 Pack up! Get ready to leave for exile,
you citizens of Egypt!
The city of Memphis will be destroyed,
without a single inhabitant.
20 Egypt is as sleek as a beautiful heifer,
but a horsefly from the north is on its way!
21 Egypt's mercenaries have become like fattened calves.
They, too, will turn and run,
for it is a day of great disaster for Egypt,
a time of great punishment.
22 Egypt flees, silent as a serpent gliding away.
The invading army marches in;
they come against her with axes like woodsmen.
23 They will cut down her people like trees," says the LORD,
"for they are more numerous than locusts.
24 Egypt will be humiliated;
she will be handed over to people from the north."

25 The LORD of Heaven's Armies, the God of Israel,
says: "I will punish Amon, the god of Thebes,* and all
the other gods of Egypt. I will punish its rulers and
Pharaoh, too, and all who trust in him. 26 I will hand
them over to those who want them killed—to King
Nebuchadnezzar of Babylon and his army. But after-
ward the land will recover from the ravages of war. I,
the LORD, have spoken!

27 "But do not be afraid, Jacob, my servant;
do not be dismayed, Israel.
For I will bring you home again from distant lands,
and your children will return from their exile.
Israel* will return to a life of peace and quiet,
and no one will terrorize them.
28 Do not be afraid, Jacob, my servant,
for I am with you," says the LORD.
"I will completely destroy the nations to which I have exiled you,
but I will not completely destroy you.
I will discipline you, but with justice;
I cannot let you go unpunished."

A MESSAGE ABOUT PHILISTIA

47 This is the LORD's message to the prophet Jere-
miah concerning the Philistines of Gaza, before
it was captured by the Egyptian army. 2 This is what
the LORD says:

"A flood is coming from the north
to overflow the land.
It will destroy the land and everything in it—
cities and people alike.
People will scream in terror,
and everyone in the land will wail.
3 Hear the clatter of stallions' hooves
and the rumble of wheels as the chariots rush by.
Terrified fathers run madly,
without a backward glance at their helpless children.

4 "The time has come for the Philistines to be destroyed,
along with their allies from Tyre and Sidon.
Yes, the LORD is destroying the remnant of the Philistines,
those colonists from the island of Crete.*
5 Gaza will be humiliated, its head shaved bald;
Ashkelon will lie silent.
You remnant from the Mediterranean coast,*
how long will you cut yourselves in mourning?

6 "Now, O sword of the LORD,
when will you be at rest again?
Go back into your sheath;
rest and be still.

7 "But how can it be still
when the LORD has sent it on a mission?
For the city of Ashkelon
and the people living along the sea
must be destroyed."

A MESSAGE ABOUT MOAB

48 This message was given concerning Moab.
This is what the LORD of Heaven's Armies, the
God of Israel, says:

"What sorrow awaits the city of Nebo;
it will soon lie in ruins.
The city of Kiriathaim will be humiliated and captured;
the fortress will be humiliated and broken down.

46:25 Hebrew *of No.* **46:27** Hebrew *Jacob.* See note on 5:20. **47:4** Hebrew *from Caphtor.* **47:5** Hebrew *the plain.*

46:16 to our people. Warriors from smaller, nearby nations would turn their backs on the losing Egyptian army. They would rather return home alive with what they had than end up with nothing.

48:1 concerning Moab. Tracing its ancestry to Lot (Gen. 19:37) and assigned to Reuben's tribe (Num. 32; Josh. 13:15-23) Moab was located east of the Dead Sea. David subjected the Moabites (2 Sam 8:2,12), and Solomon continued control. After Ahab's death, Moab rebelled against Israel and regained independence (2 Kgs 1:1; 3:4-27), Afterwards its influence waned, and it became Assyria's vassal (734 B.C.). In 605 it came under Babylonian control and aided Nebuchadnezzar against Judah's rebellion under Jehoiakim (2 Kings 24:2). Along with Ammon, Moab lost its freedom to Nebuchadnezzar in 582. Soon after an Arab invasion from the east eliminated Moab as a nation. Except for Babylon, Moab received more attention from Jeremiah than any other nation, including Egypt (Jer. 9:26; 25:21). It was a favorite target of other prophets as well (Isa. 15–16; Ezek. 25:8-11; Amos 2:1-3; Zeph. 2:8-11).

2 No one will ever brag about Moab again,
for in Heshbon there is a plot to destroy her.
'Come,' they say, 'we will cut her off from being a nation.'
The town of Madmen,* too, will be silenced;
the sword will follow you there.
3 Listen to the cries from Horonaim,
cries of devastation and great destruction.
4 All Moab is destroyed.
Her little ones will cry out.*
5 Her refugees weep bitterly,
climbing the slope to Luhith.
They cry out in terror,
descending the slope to Horonaim.
6 Flee for your lives!
Hide* in the wilderness!
7 Because you have trusted in your wealth and skill,
you will be taken captive.
Your god Chemosh, with his priests and officials,
will be hauled off to distant lands!

8 "All the towns will be destroyed,
and no one will escape—
either on the plateaus or in the valleys,
for the LORD has spoken.
9 Oh, that Moab had wings
so she could fly away,*
for her towns will be left empty,
with no one living in them.
10 Cursed are those who refuse to do the LORD's work,
who hold back their swords from shedding blood!

11 "From his earliest history, Moab has lived in peace,
never going into exile.
He is like wine that has been allowed to settle.
He has not been poured from flask to flask,
and he is now fragrant and smooth.
12 But the time is coming soon," says the LORD,
"when I will send men to pour him from his jar.
They will pour him out,
then shatter the jar!
13 At last Moab will be ashamed of his idol Chemosh,
as the people of Israel were ashamed of their gold calf at Bethel.*

14 "You used to boast, 'We are heroes,
mighty men of war.'
15 But now Moab and his towns will be destroyed.
His most promising youth are doomed to slaughter,"
says the King, whose name is the LORD of Heaven's Armies.
16 "Destruction is coming fast for Moab;
calamity threatens ominously.
17 You friends of Moab,
weep for him and cry!
See how the strong scepter is broken,
how the beautiful staff is shattered!

18 "Come down from your glory
and sit in the dust, you people of Dibon,
for those who destroy Moab will shatter Dibon, too.
They will tear down all your towers.
19 You people of Aroer,
stand beside the road and watch.
Shout to those who flee from Moab,
'What has happened there?'
20 "And the reply comes back,
'Moab lies in ruins, disgraced;
weep and wail!
Tell it by the banks of the Arnon River:
Moab has been destroyed!'
21 Judgment has been poured out on the towns of the plateau—
on Holon and Jahaz* and Mephaath,
22 on Dibon and Nebo and Beth-diblathaim,
23 on Kiriathaim and Beth-gamul and Beth-meon,
24 on Kerioth and Bozrah—
all the towns of Moab, far and near.

25 "The strength of Moab has ended.
His arm has been broken," says the LORD.
26 "Let him stagger and fall like a drunkard,
for he has rebelled against the LORD.
Moab will wallow in his own vomit,
ridiculed by all.
27 Did you not ridicule the people of Israel?
Were they caught in the company of thieves
that you should despise them as you do?

28 "You people of Moab,
flee from your towns and live in the caves.
Hide like doves that nest
in the clefts of the rocks.
29 We have all heard of the pride of Moab,
for his pride is very great.
We know of his lofty pride,
his arrogance, and his haughty heart.
30 I know about his insolence,"
says the LORD,
"but his boasts are empty—
as empty as his deeds.
31 So now I wail for Moab;
yes, I will mourn for Moab.
My heart is broken for the men of Kir-hareseth.*
32 "You people of Sibmah, rich in vineyards,
I will weep for you even more than I did for Jazer.
Your spreading vines once reached as far as the Dead Sea,*

48:2 *Madmen* sounds like the Hebrew word for "silence"; it should not be confused with the English word *madmen.* **48:4** Greek version reads *Her cries are heard as far away as Zoar.* **48:6** Or *Hide like a wild donkey;* or *Hide like a juniper shrub;* or *Be like* [the town of] *Aroer.* The meaning of the Hebrew is uncertain. **48:9** Or *Put salt on Moab, / for she will be laid waste.* **48:13** Hebrew *ashamed when they trusted in Bethel.* **48:21** Hebrew *Jahzah,* a variant spelling of Jahaz. **48:31** Hebrew *Kir-heres,* a variant spelling of Kir-hareseth; also in 48:36. **48:32** Hebrew *the sea of Jazer.*

48:26 stagger and fall like a drunkard. The mighty Moab once brought fear to Judah's inhabitants. Now, God would numb the nation with His wrath (49:12; Pss. 60:3; 75:9; Isa. 51:17-23; Lam. 4:21; Ezek. 23:31-34; Hab. 2:16).
48:27 ridicule. Apparently Moab joined Edom in jeering the captives of Jerusalem as they were taken to Babylon in exile (Lam. 2:15-16).

48:29 We have all heard. Moab's pride brought God to bitter tears (see Isa. 16:7, 11). Ultimately, the nation's arrogance incurred God's wrath as well. Like-sounding Hebrew verbs emphasize God's condemnation: pride (*ga'on*), great pride (*ge'eh*), insolence (*gaboah*), and arrogance (*ga'awa*). These words rightly hiss in succession.

but the destroyer has stripped you bare!
He has harvested your grapes and summer fruits.
33 Joy and gladness are gone from fruitful Moab.
The presses yield no wine.
No one treads the grapes with shouts of joy.
There is shouting, yes, but not of joy.

34 "Instead, their awful cries of terror can be heard
from Heshbon clear across to Elealeh and Jahaz; from
Zoar all the way to Horonaim and Eglath-shelishiyah.
Even the waters of Nimrim are dried up now.
35 "I will put an end to Moab," says the LORD, "for the
people offer sacrifices at the pagan shrines and burn
incense to their false gods. 36 My heart moans like a
flute for Moab and Kir-hareseth, for all their wealth
has disappeared. 37 The people shave their heads and
beards in mourning. They slash their hands and put
on clothes made of burlap. 38 There is crying and sor-
row in every Moabite home and on every street. For I
have smashed Moab like an old, unwanted jar. 39 How
it is shattered! Hear the wailing! See the shame of
Moab! It has become an object of ridicule, an example
of ruin to all its neighbors."
40 This is what the LORD says:

"Look! The enemy swoops down like an eagle,
spreading his wings over Moab.
41 Its cities will fall,
and its strongholds will be seized.
Even the mightiest warriors will be in anguish
like a woman in labor.
42 Moab will no longer be a nation,
for it has boasted against the LORD.

43 "Terror and traps and snares will be your lot,
O Moab," says the LORD.
44 "Those who flee in terror will fall into a trap,
and those who escape the trap will step into a snare.
I will see to it that you do not get away,
for the time of your judgment has come,"
says the LORD.
45 "The people flee as far as Heshbon
but are unable to go on.
For a fire comes from Heshbon,
King Sihon's ancient home,
to devour the entire land
with all its rebellious people.

46 "What sorrow awaits you, O people of Moab!
The people of the god Chemosh are destroyed!
Your sons and your daughters
have been taken away as captives.
47 But I will restore the fortunes of Moab
in days to come.
I, the LORD, have spoken!"

This is the end of Jeremiah's prophecy concerning Moab.

A MESSAGE ABOUT AMMON

49 This message was given concerning the Ammonites. This is what the LORD says:

"Are there no descendants of Israel
to inherit the land of Gad?
Why are you, who worship Molech,*
living in its towns?
2 In the days to come," says the LORD,
"I will sound the battle cry against your city of Rabbah.
It will become a desolate heap of ruins,
and the neighboring towns will be burned.
Then Israel will take back the land
you took from her," says the LORD.

3 "Cry out, O Heshbon,
for the town of Ai is destroyed.
Weep, O people of Rabbah!
Put on your clothes of mourning.
Weep and wail, hiding in the hedges,
for your god Molech, with his priests and officials,
will be hauled off to distant lands.
4 You are proud of your fertile valleys,
but they will soon be ruined.
You trusted in your wealth,
you rebellious daughter,
and thought no one could ever harm you.
5 But look! I will bring terror upon you,"
says the Lord, the LORD of Heaven's Armies.
"Your neighbors will chase you from your land,
and no one will help your exiles as they flee.
6 But I will restore the fortunes of the Ammonites
in days to come.
I, the LORD, have spoken."

MESSAGES ABOUT EDOM

7 This message was given concerning Edom. This is what the LORD of Heaven's Armies says:

"Is there no wisdom in Teman?
Is no one left to give wise counsel?
8 Turn and flee!
Hide in deep caves, you people of Dedan!
For when I bring disaster on Edom,*
I will punish you, too!
9 Those who harvest grapes
always leave a few for the poor.
If thieves came at night,
they would not take everything.
10 But I will strip bare the land of Edom,
and there will be no place left to hide.
Its children, its brothers, and its neighbors

49:1 Hebrew *Malcam,* a variant spelling of Molech; also in 49:3. **49:8** Hebrew *Esau;* also in 49:10.

48:43 Terror and traps and snares. God's wrath would sweep throughout Moab and trap His enemy like a hunter.
48:44 Those who flee. There was no place to hide from God's wrath—all escape attempts would be thwarted (see Amos 5:18-20). There would be no turning back.
49:1 concerning the Ammonites. Like Moab, Ammon descended from Lot (Gen. 19:30-38). Solomon married an Ammonite princess and built a pagan temple on the temple mount (1 Kings 11:7). Their king Baalis was instrumental in the Gedaliah's murder (chaps. 40–41). Ammon had taken territory from the tribe of Gad after the deportation of northern Israel in 733 B.C. The Lord intended to reclaim it. The Babylonians initially accomplished this in 582 B.C. Eventually the Jewish Maccabeans reclaimed it for Israel from 149–63 B.C. until the Romans took over. A large portion of Ammon is presently occupied by Israel on the West Bank.
49:7 concerning Edom. The Edomites, related to Israel through Esau (Gen. 36), were eventually destroyed by Arabs (Mal. 1:2-5). Many moved to Idumea in southern Judah and may have been Herod the Great's ancestors. **no wisdom.** Edomites were known for their wisdom (Job 2:11).

will all be destroyed,
and Edom itself will be no more.
11 But I will protect the orphans who remain among you.
Your widows, too, can depend on me for help."

12 And this is what the LORD says: "If the innocent must suffer, how much more must you! You will not go unpunished! You must drink this cup of judgment!
13 For I have sworn by my own name," says the LORD, "that Bozrah will become an object of horror and a heap of ruins; it will be mocked and cursed. All its towns and villages will be desolate forever."

14 I have heard a message from the LORD
that an ambassador was sent to the nations to say,
"Form a coalition against Edom,
and prepare for battle!"

15 The LORD says to Edom,
"I will cut you down to size among the nations.
You will be despised by all.
16 You have been deceived
by the fear you inspire in others
and by your own pride.
You live in a rock fortress
and control the mountain heights.
But even if you make your nest among the peaks with the eagles,
I will bring you crashing down,"
says the LORD.

17 "Edom will be an object of horror.
All who pass by will be appalled
and will gasp at the destruction they see there.
18 It will be like the destruction of Sodom and Gomorrah
and their neighboring towns," says the LORD.
"No one will live there;
no one will inhabit it.
19 I will come like a lion from the thickets of the Jordan,
leaping on the sheep in the pasture.
I will chase Edom from its land,
and I will appoint the leader of my choice.
For who is like me, and who can challenge me?
What ruler can oppose my will?"

20 Listen to the LORD's plans against Edom
and the people of Teman.
Even the little children will be dragged off like sheep,
and their homes will be destroyed.
21 The earth will shake with the noise of Edom's fall,
and its cry of despair will be heard all the way to the Red Sea.*
22 Look! The enemy swoops down like an eagle,
spreading his wings over Bozrah.
Even the mightiest warriors will be in anguish
like a woman in labor.

A MESSAGE ABOUT DAMASCUS

23 This message was given concerning Damascus. This is what the LORD says:

"The towns of Hamath and Arpad are struck with fear,
for they have heard the news of their destruction.
Their hearts are troubled
like a wild sea in a raging storm.
24 Damascus has become feeble,
and all her people turn to flee.
Fear, anguish, and pain have gripped her
as they grip a woman in labor.
25 That famous city, a city of joy,
will be forsaken!
26 Her young men will fall in the streets and die.
Her soldiers will all be killed,"
says the LORD of Heaven's Armies.
27 "And I will set fire to the walls of Damascus
that will burn up the palaces of Ben-hadad."

A MESSAGE ABOUT KEDAR AND HAZOR

28 This message was given concerning Kedar and the kingdoms of Hazor, which were attacked by King Nebuchadnezzar* of Babylon. This is what the LORD says:

"Advance against Kedar!
Destroy the warriors from the East!
29 Their flocks and tents will be captured,
and their household goods and camels will be taken away.
Everywhere shouts of panic will be heard:
'We are terrorized at every turn!'
30 Run for your lives," says the LORD.
"Hide yourselves in deep caves, you people of Hazor,
for King Nebuchadnezzar of Babylon has plotted against you
and is preparing to destroy you.

31 "Go up and attack that complacent nation,"
says the LORD.
"Its people live alone in the desert
without walls or gates.
32 Their camels and other livestock will all be yours.
I will scatter to the winds these people
who live in remote places.*
I will bring calamity upon them
from every direction," says the LORD.
33 "Hazor will be inhabited by jackals,
and it will be desolate forever.

49:21 Hebrew *sea of reeds.* **49:28** Hebrew *Nebuchadrezzar,* a variant spelling of Nebuchadnezzar; also in 49:30. **49:32** Or *who clip the corners of their hair.*

49:12 unpunished. Some see Edom's punishment as relating to her alliance with Philistia against Judah's King Jehoram (2 Chron. 21:15-16; Amos 1:9, 11; Obad. 10). Esau (Edom) was supposed to be Jacob's brother.
49:13 Bozrah. Edom's capital was located 25 miles southeast of the Dead Sea. The terms used to describe its destruction usually refer to Judah (15:4; 21:7; 25:9; 29:18; 34:17; Deut. 28:37; Ps. 44:14-15).
49:16 been deceived. Edom was a powerful and respected nation. However, these well-intentioned accolades proved to be a disastrous disservice. Pride was one downfall that led to her defeat.
49:17 appalled. The Edomites jeered Jerusalem's defeated residents in 586 B.C. (Ps. 137:7; Lam. 2:15-16) and would be repaid in kind.
49:22 eagle. God used a bird of prey to illustrate His watchful gaze over his enemy. God seemed remote and removed, yet soon He would swoop down upon Edom like an eagle.

No one will live there;
no one will inhabit it."

A MESSAGE ABOUT ELAM

34 This message concerning Elam came to the prophet
Jeremiah from the LORD at the beginning of the reign
of King Zedekiah of Judah. 35 This is what the LORD of
Heaven's Armies says:

"I will destroy the archers of Elam—
the best of their forces.
36 I will bring enemies from all directions,
and I will scatter the people of Elam to the four winds.
They will be exiled to countries around the world.
37 I myself will go with Elam's enemies to shatter it.
In my fierce anger, I will bring great disaster
upon the people of Elam," says the LORD.
"Their enemies will chase them with the sword
until I have destroyed them completely.
38 I will set my throne in Elam," says the LORD,
"and I will destroy its king and officials.
39 But I will restore the fortunes of Elam
in days to come.
I, the LORD, have spoken!"

A MESSAGE ABOUT BABYLON

50 The LORD gave Jeremiah the prophet this mes-
sage concerning Babylon and the land of the
Babylonians.* 2 This is what the LORD says:

"Tell the whole world,
and keep nothing back.
Raise a signal flag
to tell everyone that Babylon will fall!
Her images and idols* will be shattered.
Her gods Bel and Marduk will be utterly disgraced.
3 For a nation will attack her from the north
and bring such destruction that no one will live there again.
Everything will be gone;
both people and animals will flee.

HOPE FOR ISRAEL AND JUDAH

4 "In those coming days,"
says the LORD,
"the people of Israel will return home
together with the people of Judah.
They will come weeping
and seeking the LORD their God.
5 They will ask the way to Jerusalem*
and will start back home again.
They will bind themselves to the LORD
with an eternal covenant that will never be forgotten.
6 "My people have been lost sheep.
Their shepherds have led them astray
and turned them loose in the mountains.
They have lost their way
and can't remember how to get back to the sheepfold.
7 All who found them devoured them.
Their enemies said,
'We did nothing wrong in attacking them,
for they sinned against the LORD,
their true place of rest,
and the hope of their ancestors.'
8 "But now, flee from Babylon!
Leave the land of the Babylonians.
Like male goats at the head of the flock,
lead my people home again.
9 For I am raising up an army
of great nations from the north.
They will join forces to attack Babylon,
and she will be captured.
The enemies' arrows will go straight to the mark;
they will not miss!
10 Babylonia* will be looted
until the attackers are glutted with loot.
I, the LORD, have spoken!

BABYLON'S SURE FALL

11 "You rejoice and are glad,
you who plundered my chosen people.
You frisk about like a calf in a meadow
and neigh like a stallion.
12 But your homeland* will be overwhelmed
with shame and disgrace.
You will become the least of nations—
a wilderness, a dry and desolate land.
13 Because of the LORD's anger,
Babylon will become a deserted wasteland.
All who pass by will be horrified
and will gasp at the destruction they see there.
14 "Yes, prepare to attack Babylon,
all you surrounding nations.
Let your archers shoot at her; spare no arrows.
For she has sinned against the LORD.
15 Shout war cries against her from every side.
Look! She surrenders!
Her walls have fallen.
It is the LORD's vengeance,
so take vengeance on her.
Do to her as she has done to others!
16 Take from Babylon all those who plant crops;
send all the harvesters away.
Because of the sword of the enemy,
everyone will run away and rush back to their own lands.

50:1 Or *Chaldeans;* also in 50:8, 25, 35, 45. **50:2** The Hebrew term (literally *round things*) probably alludes to dung. **50:5** Hebrew *Zion;* also in 50:28. **50:10** Or *Chaldea.* **50:12** Hebrew *your mother.*

49:34 concerning Elam. Jeremiah predicted Elam's defeat in 597 B.C. The capital of Elam, Susa, became the center of the Persian Empire after 539 B.C. (Neh. 1:1; Dan. 8:2).

49:35 bow. Modern Iran—a nation of notable archers—continues Elam's legacy.

49:38 set my throne. In 567 B.C., the Lord set up Nebuchadnezzar's throne at Tahpanhes (Egypt). He may have done likewise to Elam just one year after Jeremiah's prophecy (596 B.C.).

49:39 restore the fortunes of Elam. Like other nations, Elam is promised restoration in the last days (Isa. 19:21,25).

50:2 Babylon. Finally, the conqueror gets conquered. The nation that enjoyed seemingly endless conquests was temporarily halted by many northern nations. All of Babylon was doomed to eventual defeat.

50:11 plundered my chosen people. God resented Babylon's indifference to His chosen people's plight. The people's inheritance was promised by God Himself. Babylon would suffer for its harshness.

HOPE FOR GOD'S PEOPLE

17 "The Israelites are like sheep
that have been scattered by lions.
First the king of Assyria ate them up.
Then King Nebuchadnezzar* of Babylon
cracked their bones."
18 Therefore, this is what the LORD of Heaven's
Armies,
the God of Israel, says:
"Now I will punish the king of Babylon and his
land,
just as I punished the king of Assyria.
19 And I will bring Israel home again to its own land,
to feed in the fields of Carmel and Bashan,
and to be satisfied once more
in the hill country of Ephraim and Gilead.
20 In those days," says the LORD,
"no sin will be found in Israel or in Judah,
for I will forgive the remnant I preserve.

THE LORD'S JUDGMENT ON BABYLON

21 "Go up, my warriors, against the land of
Merathaim
and against the people of Pekod.
Pursue, kill, and completely destroy* them,
as I have commanded you," says the LORD.
22 "Let the battle cry be heard in the land,
a shout of great destruction.
23 Babylon, the mightiest hammer in all the earth,
lies broken and shattered.
Babylon is desolate among the nations!
24 Listen, Babylon, for I have set a trap for you.
You are caught, for you have fought against the
LORD.
25 The LORD has opened his armory
and brought out weapons to vent his fury.
The terror that falls upon the Babylonians
will be the work of the Sovereign LORD of
Heaven's Armies.
26 Yes, come against her from distant lands.
Break open her granaries.
Crush her walls and houses into heaps of rubble.
Destroy her completely, and leave nothing!
27 Destroy even her young bulls—
it will be terrible for them, too!
Slaughter them all!
For Babylon's day of reckoning has come.
28 Listen to the people who have escaped from
Babylon,
as they tell in Jerusalem
how the LORD our God has taken vengeance
against those who destroyed his Temple.
29 "Send out a call for archers to come to Babylon.
Surround the city so none can escape.
Do to her as she has done to others,
for she has defied the LORD, the Holy One of
Israel.
30 Her young men will fall in the streets and die.
Her soldiers will all be killed,"
says the LORD.
31 "See, I am your enemy, you arrogant people,"
says the Lord, the LORD of Heaven's Armies.
"Your day of reckoning has arrived—
the day when I will punish you.
32 O land of arrogance, you will stumble and fall,
and no one will raise you up.
For I will light a fire in the cities of Babylon
that will burn up everything around them."

33 This is what the LORD of Heaven's Armies says:
"The people of Israel and Judah have been
wronged.
Their captors hold them and refuse to let them
go.
34 But the one who redeems them is strong.
His name is the LORD of Heaven's Armies.
He will defend them
and give them rest again in Israel.
But for the people of Babylon
there will be no rest!

35 "The sword of destruction will strike the
Babylonians,"
says the LORD.
"It will strike the people of Babylon—
her officials and wise men, too.
36 The sword will strike her wise counselors,
and they will become fools.
The sword will strike her mightiest warriors,
and panic will seize them.
37 The sword will strike her horses and chariots
and her allies from other lands,
and they will all become like women.
The sword will strike her treasures,
and they all will be plundered.
38 A drought* will strike her water supply,
causing it to dry up.
And why? Because the whole land is filled with idols,
and the people are madly in love with them.

39 "Soon Babylon will be inhabited by desert animals
and hyenas.
It will be a home for owls.
Never again will people live there;
it will lie desolate forever.
40 I will destroy it as I* destroyed Sodom and
Gomorrah
and their neighboring towns," says the LORD.
"No one will live there;
no one will inhabit it.

50:17 Hebrew *Nebuchadrezzar,* a variant spelling of Nebuchadnezzar. 50:21 The Hebrew term used here refers to the complete consecration of things or people to the LORD, either by destroying them or by giving them as an offering. 50:38 Or *sword;* the Hebrew words for *drought* and *sword* are very similar. 50:40 Hebrew *as God.*

50:17-18 Assyria had conquered the northern kingdom in 722 B.C. Babylon had conquered the southern kingdom in 586 B.C. As Assyria had passed into the horizon, to be replaced by Babylon, so too would Babylon come to pass, to be replaced by another (Persia) who would allow the Israelites to return to their homeland.

50:19 Carmel . . . Bashan . . . Gilead. Originally granted to Moses (Num. 21:33; Josh. 13:29-31) but lost to Assyria during Micah's time (2 Kings 14:25), Jeremiah prophesies that Israel will be returned to its initial prosperity (Ezek. 34:13-14; Micah 7:14). The ultimate realization of this prophecy is yet future.

50:20 no sin . . . in Judah. God has forgiven (31:31-34) the remnant (39:10; 52:16).

50:25 weapons to vent his fury. A great coalition of neighboring northern nations would bring God's punishment on Babylon. Those who Babylon had once fought would now be turning to conquer her.

50:32 burn up. God's anger burns hot (15:14; Lam. 4:11; Amos 1:4-14; 2:2-5).

41 "Look! A great army is coming from the north.
A great nation and many kings
are rising against you from far-off lands.
42 They are armed with bows and spears.
They are cruel and show no mercy.
As they ride forward on horses,
they sound like a roaring sea.
They are coming in battle formation,
planning to destroy you, Babylon.
43 The king of Babylon has heard reports about the enemy,
and he is weak with fright.
Pangs of anguish have gripped him,
like those of a woman in labor.

44 "I will come like a lion from the thickets of the Jordan,
leaping on the sheep in the pasture.
I will chase Babylon from its land,
and I will appoint the leader of my choice.
For who is like me, and who can challenge me?
What ruler can oppose my will?"

45 Listen to the LORD's plans against Babylon
and the land of the Babylonians.
Even the little children will be dragged off like sheep,
and their homes will be destroyed.
46 The earth will shake with the shout, "Babylon has been taken!"
and its cry of despair will be heard around the world.

51 1 This is what the LORD says:
"I will stir up a destroyer against Babylon
and the people of Babylonia.*
2 Foreigners will come and winnow her,
blowing her away as chaff.
They will come from every side
to rise against her in her day of trouble.
3 Don't let the archers put on their armor
or draw their bows.
Don't spare even her best soldiers!
Let her army be completely destroyed.*
4 They will fall dead in the land of the Babylonians,*
slashed to death in her streets.
5 For the LORD of Heaven's Armies
has not abandoned Israel and Judah.
He is still their God,
even though their land was filled with sin
against the Holy One of Israel."

6 Flee from Babylon! Save yourselves!
Don't get trapped in her punishment!
It is the LORD's time for vengeance;
he will repay her in full.
7 Babylon has been a gold cup in the LORD's hands,
a cup that made the whole earth drunk.
The nations drank Babylon's wine,
and it drove them all mad.
8 But suddenly Babylon, too, has fallen.
Weep for her.
Give her medicine.
Perhaps she can yet be healed.
9 We would have helped her if we could,
but nothing can save her now.
Let her go; abandon her.
Return now to your own land.
For her punishment reaches to the heavens;
it is so great it cannot be measured.
10 The LORD has vindicated us.
Come, let us announce in Jerusalem*
everything the LORD our God has done.

11 Sharpen the arrows!
Lift up the shields!*
For the LORD has inspired the kings of the Medes
to march against Babylon and destroy her.
This is his vengeance against those
who desecrated his Temple.
12 Raise the battle flag against Babylon!
Reinforce the guard and station the watchmen.
Prepare an ambush,
for the LORD will fulfill all his plans against Babylon.
13 You are a city by a great river,
a great center of commerce,
but your end has come.
The thread of your life is cut.
14 The LORD of Heaven's Armies has taken this vow
and has sworn to it by his own name:
"Your cities will be filled with enemies,
like fields swarming with locusts,
and they will shout in triumph over you."

A HYMN OF PRAISE TO THE LORD

15 The LORD made the earth by his power,
and he preserves it by his wisdom.
With his own understanding
he stretched out the heavens.
16 When he speaks in the thunder,
the heavens roar with rain.
He causes the clouds to rise over the earth.
He sends the lightning with the rain
and releases the wind from his storehouses.

51:1 Hebrew *of Leb-kamai,* a code name for Babylonia. **51:3** The Hebrew term used here refers to the complete consecration of things or people to the LORD, either by destroying them or by giving them as an offering. **51:4** Or *Chaldeans;* also in 51:54. **51:10** Hebrew *Zion;* also in 51:24. **51:11** Greek version reads *Fill up the quivers.*

50:43 a woman in labor. The prophets commonly pictured Daughter Zion crying out in such agony (4:31; 6:24; 13:21; 22:23; 30:6; Isa. 26:17; Micah 4:9-10). In the oracles against the nations (chap. 46–51), Israel's oppressors are pictured in the same way (48:41; 49:22; 50:43; Ps. 48:6; Isa. 13:8; 21:3) In contrast to Daughter Zion's pangs, Daughter of Babylon (v. 42) suffers here. Similar language is often used to describe the terrifying aspects of the Day of the Lord (Dan. 12:1; Zeph. 1:14-15), whose fury will be unsurpassed, and gives a picture of the kind of torments the nations who oppose God will experience in Jeremiah. Birth pangs can also be the occasion for joy when seen as introductory to the crowning of Messiah and the renewal of Israel (Isa. 66:6-9; Micah 5:3; John 16:21; Rev. 12:2).

51:6 Flee from Babylon. Earlier, Jeremiah instructed the people of Judah to surrender to Babylon. Even though God was going to discipline His people, He had a plan for restoration after the exile.

51:11-12 God's avengers are to prepare for battle. Babylon will be vanquished for its destruction of the Lord's temple (50:28; Ps 74:3-8). The avengers are identified as the "kings of the Medes." This is the first mention of Media as the agent of Babylon's destruction. Media, an ancient kingdom northwest of Persia, was conquered by Cyrus in 550 B.C. (Isa. 44:28; 45:1). His mother was a Mede. The "kings" referred to here could be those who served under Cyrus as vassals (v. 27; Ararat, Minni, and Ashkenaz). Cyrus' decree (2 Chron. 36:22-23; Ezra 1:1-4) allowed the Jews to return to Israel. Thus, Cyrus was not only God's avenger but His redeemer as well.

[17] The whole human race is foolish and has no
knowledge!
The craftsmen are disgraced by the idols they
make,
for their carefully shaped works are a fraud.
These idols have no breath or power.
[18] Idols are worthless; they are ridiculous lies!
On the day of reckoning they will all be
destroyed.
[19] But the God of Israel* is no idol!
He is the Creator of everything that exists,
including his people, his own special possession.
The LORD of Heaven's Armies is his name!

BABYLON'S GREAT PUNISHMENT

[20] "You* are my battle-ax and sword,"
says the LORD.
"With you I will shatter nations
and destroy many kingdoms.
[21] With you I will shatter armies—
destroying the horse and rider,
the chariot and charioteer.
[22] With you I will shatter men and women,
old people and children,
young men and young women.
[23] With you I will shatter shepherds and flocks,
farmers and oxen,
captains and officers.

[24] "I will repay Babylon
and the people of Babylonia*
for all the wrong they have done
to my people in Jerusalem," says the LORD.
[25] "Look, O mighty mountain, destroyer of the earth!
I am your enemy," says the LORD.
"I will raise my fist against you,
to knock you down from the heights.
When I am finished,
you will be nothing but a heap of burnt rubble.
[26] You will be desolate forever.
Even your stones will never again be used for
building.
You will be completely wiped out,"
says the LORD.

[27] Raise a signal flag to the nations.
Sound the battle cry!
Mobilize them all against Babylon.
Prepare them to fight against her!
Bring out the armies of Ararat, Minni, and
Ashkenaz.
Appoint a commander,
and bring a multitude of horses like swarming
locusts!
[28] Bring against her the armies of the nations—
led by the kings of the Medes
and all their captains and officers.
[29] The earth trembles and writhes in pain,
for everything the LORD has planned against
Babylon stands unchanged.
Babylon will be left desolate without a single
inhabitant.
[30] Her mightiest warriors no longer fight.
They stay in their barracks, their courage gone.
They have become like women.
The invaders have burned the houses
and broken down the city gates.
[31] The news is passed from one runner to the next
as the messengers hurry to tell the king
that his city has been captured.
[32] All the escape routes are blocked.
The marshes have been set aflame,
and the army is in a panic.

[33] This is what the LORD of Heaven's Armies,
the God of Israel, says:
"Babylon is like wheat on a threshing floor,
about to be trampled.
In just a little while
her harvest will begin."

[34] "King Nebuchadnezzar* of Babylon has eaten and
crushed us
and drained us of strength.
He has swallowed us like a great monster
and filled his belly with our riches.
He has thrown us out of our own country.
[35] Make Babylon suffer as she made us suffer,"
say the people of Zion.
"Make the people of Babylonia pay for spilling our
blood,"
says Jerusalem.

THE LORD'S VENGEANCE ON BABYLON

[36] This is what the LORD says to Jerusalem:

"I will be your lawyer to plead your case,
and I will avenge you.
I will dry up her river,
as well as her springs,
[37] and Babylon will become a heap of ruins,
haunted by jackals.
She will be an object of horror and contempt,
a place where no one lives.
[38] Her people will roar together like strong lions.
They will growl like lion cubs.
[39] And while they lie inflamed with all their wine,
I will prepare a different kind of feast for
them.
I will make them drink until they fall asleep,
and they will never wake up again,"
says the LORD.
[40] "I will bring them down
like lambs to the slaughter,
like rams and goats to be sacrificed.

51:19 Hebrew *the Portion of Jacob.* See note on 5:20. **51:20** Possibly Cyrus, whom God used to conquer Babylon. Compare Isa 44:28; 45:1. **51:24** Or *Chaldea;* also in 51:35. **51:34** Hebrew *Nebuchadrezzar,* a variant spelling of Nebuchadnezzar.

50:34-44 As in Lamentations, Jerusalem itself speaks of the terror inflicted upon her by Babylon. Babylon's gods are also judged, specifically Bel (v. 44; Isa. 46:1-2).

51:36 case. The Lord presented Jerusalem's case against Babylon. "Case" is often used in the context of God's judgments. Jeremiah pleads his case (12:1; 20:12), then the Lord pleads His case (25:31).

51:39. I will make them drink. It might seem strange for God to throw a party for a defendant. But, sure enough, the ancient historians Herodotus and Xenophon reported that one of Cyrus' commanders, Gobrius, took advantage of a drunken party held in the palace by Belshazzar in 539 B.C. Gobryus and his soldiers had been able to slip under Babylon's impressive walls because a dam they built suitably lowered the Euphrates' water-level. As God said, the celebrants in the palace did not awake (Dan. 5:30-31).

41 "How Babylon* is fallen—
great Babylon, praised throughout the earth!
Now she has become an object of horror
among the nations.
42 The sea has risen over Babylon;
she is covered by its crashing waves.
43 Her cities now lie in ruins;
she is a dry wasteland
where no one lives or even passes by.
44 And I will punish Bel, the god of Babylon,
and make him vomit up all he has eaten.
The nations will no longer come and worship him.
The wall of Babylon has fallen!

A MESSAGE FOR THE EXILES

45 "Come out, my people, flee from Babylon.
Save yourselves! Run from the LORD's fierce
anger.
46 But do not panic; don't be afraid
when you hear the first rumor of approaching
forces.
For rumors will keep coming year by year.
Violence will erupt in the land
as the leaders fight against each other.
47 For the time is surely coming
when I will punish this great city and all her
idols.
Her whole land will be disgraced,
and her dead will lie in the streets.
48 Then the heavens and earth will rejoice,
for out of the north will come destroying
armies
against Babylon," says the LORD.
49 "Just as Babylon killed the people of Israel
and others throughout the world,
so must her people be killed.
50 Get out, all you who have escaped the sword!
Do not stand and watch—flee while you can!
Remember the LORD, though you are in a far-off
land,
and think about your home in Jerusalem."

51 "We are ashamed," the people say.
"We are insulted and disgraced
because the LORD's Temple
has been defiled by foreigners."

52 "Yes," says the LORD, "but the time is coming
when I will destroy Babylon's idols.
The groans of her wounded people
will be heard throughout the land.
53 Though Babylon reaches as high as the heavens
and makes her fortifications incredibly
strong,
I will still send enemies to plunder her.
I, the LORD, have spoken!

BABYLON'S COMPLETE DESTRUCTION

54 "Listen! Hear the cry of Babylon,
the sound of great destruction from the land of
the Babylonians.
55 For the LORD is destroying Babylon.
He will silence her loud voice.
Waves of enemies pound against her;
the noise of battle rings through the city.
56 Destroying armies come against Babylon.
Her mighty men are captured,
and their weapons break in their hands.
For the LORD is a God who gives just punishment;
he always repays in full.
57 I will make her officials and wise men drunk,
along with her captains, officers, and warriors.
They will fall asleep
and never wake up again!"
says the King, whose name is
the LORD of Heaven's Armies.

58 This is what the LORD of Heaven's Armies says:
"The thick walls of Babylon will be leveled to the
ground,
and her massive gates will be burned.
The builders from many lands have worked in
vain,
for their work will be destroyed by fire!"

JEREMIAH'S MESSAGE SENT TO BABYLON

59 The prophet Jeremiah gave this message to Se-
raiah son of Neriah and grandson of Mahseiah, a
staff officer, when Seraiah went to Babylon with
King Zedekiah of Judah. This was during the fourth
year of Zedekiah's reign.* 60 Jeremiah had recorded
on a scroll all the terrible disasters that would soon
come upon Babylon—all the words written here.
61 He said to Seraiah, "When you get to Babylon, read
aloud everything on this scroll. 62 Then say, 'LORD,
you have said that you will destroy Babylon so that
neither people nor animals will remain here. She
will lie empty and abandoned forever.' 63 When you
have finished reading the scroll, tie it to a stone and
throw it into the Euphrates River. 64 Then say, 'In this
same way Babylon and her people will sink, never
again to rise, because of the disasters I will bring
upon her.'"

This is the end of Jeremiah's messages.

THE FALL OF JERUSALEM

52 Zedekiah was twenty-one years old when he
became king, and he reigned in Jerusalem elev-
en years. His mother was Hamutal, the daughter of
Jeremiah from Libnah. 2 But Zedekiah did what was
evil in the LORD's sight, just as Jehoiakim had done.
3 These things happened because of the LORD's anger
against the people of Jerusalem and Judah, until he fi-

51:41 Hebrew *Sheshach*, a code name for Babylon. 51:59 The fourth year of Zedekiah's reign was 593 B.C.

51:46 when you hear the first rumor. God warned His people not to be discouraged by false information (see Matt. 24:6). Babylon's end was certain. They only needed to take Him at His word.

51:51 the LORD's temple . . . defiled by foreigners. The physical conquest of Jerusalem was not as shameful as the spiritual toll on the people. Seeing their temple defiled by pagan warriors was heartbreaking.

52:1-34 Chapter 52 parallels the account given at the end of 2 Kings (2 Kings 24:20–25:30). Israel, who had badly wanted a king back in the day of Saul (a man known for his stature), ended with a king whose stature did not exceed the walls of Jerusalem within which he was enclosed (586 B.C.). Saul faced a giant (Goliath) and won (through David). Zedekiah faced a giant without God's blessing and ended up imprisoned, blinded, and dead in a foreign land (52:11). One day the true King would restore them.

52:1-27,31-34 Baruch probably penned the addendum to Jeremiah's prophecies (see the parallel in 2 Kings 24:18–25:21,27-30). Hindsight validated Jeremiah's prophecies against Jerusalem. The eventual fulfillment of his prophecies regarding the exiles' return was an encouragement to them. The plan of God was a help to the people as they endured in a foreign land.

52:1 Zedekiah. Baruch framed Zedekiah's ambition in the bigger picture of God's plan. Zedekiah's attempted heroism resulted in rebellion against God's design for His people.

nally banished them from his presence and sent them into exile.

Zedekiah rebelled against the king of Babylon. 4 So on January 15,* during the ninth year of Zedekiah's reign, King Nebuchadnezzar* of Babylon led his entire army against Jerusalem. They surrounded the city and built siege ramps against its walls. 5 Jerusalem was kept under siege until the eleventh year of King Zedekiah's reign.

6 By July 18 in the eleventh year of Zedekiah's reign,* the famine in the city had become very severe, and the last of the food was entirely gone. 7 Then a section of the city wall was broken down, and all the soldiers fled. Since the city was surrounded by the Babylonians,* they waited for nightfall. Then they slipped through the gate between the two walls behind the king's garden and headed toward the Jordan Valley.*

8 But the Babylonian troops chased King Zedekiah and overtook him on the plains of Jericho, for his men had all deserted him and scattered. 9 They captured the king and took him to the king of Babylon at Riblah in the land of Hamath. There the king of Babylon pronounced judgment upon Zedekiah. 10 The king of Babylon made Zedekiah watch as he slaughtered his sons. He also slaughtered all the officials of Judah at Riblah. 11 Then he gouged out Zedekiah's eyes and bound him in bronze chains, and the king of Babylon led him away to Babylon. Zedekiah remained there in prison until the day of his death.

THE TEMPLE DESTROYED

12 On August 17 of that year,* which was the nineteenth year of King Nebuchadnezzar's reign, Nebuzaradan, the captain of the guard and an official of the Babylonian king, arrived in Jerusalem. 13 He burned down the Temple of the LORD, the royal palace, and all the houses of Jerusalem. He destroyed all the important buildings* in the city. 14 Then he supervised the entire Babylonian* army as they tore down the walls of Jerusalem on every side. 15 Then Nebuzaradan, the captain of the guard, took as exiles some of the poorest of the people, the rest of the people who remained in the city, the defectors who had declared their allegiance to the king of Babylon, and the rest of the craftsmen. 16 But Nebuzaradan allowed some of the poorest people to stay behind to care for the vineyards and fields.

17 The Babylonians broke up the bronze pillars in front of the LORD's Temple, the bronze water carts, and the great bronze basin called the Sea, and they carried all the bronze away to Babylon. 18 They also took all the ash buckets, shovels, lamp snuffers, basins, dishes, and all the other bronze articles used for making sacrifices at the Temple. 19 The captain of the guard also took the small bowls, incense burners, basins, pots, lampstands, ladles, bowls used for liquid offerings, and all the other articles made of pure gold or silver.

20 The weight of the bronze from the two pillars, the Sea with the twelve bronze oxen beneath it, and the water carts was too great to be measured. These things had been made for the LORD's Temple in the days of King Solomon. 21 Each of the pillars was 27 feet tall and 18 feet in circumference.* They were hollow, with walls 3 inches thick.* 22 The bronze capital on top of each pillar was 7½ feet* high and was decorated with a network of bronze pomegranates all the way around. 23 There were 96 pomegranates on the sides, and a total of 100 pomegranates on the network around the top.

24 Nebuzaradan, the captain of the guard, took with him as prisoners Seraiah the high priest, Zephaniah the priest of the second rank, and the three chief gatekeepers. 25 And from among the people still hiding in the city, he took an officer who had been in charge of the Judean army; seven of the king's personal advisers; the army commander's chief secretary, who was in charge of recruitment; and sixty other citizens. 26 Nebuzaradan, the captain of the guard, took them all to the king of Babylon at Riblah. 27 And there at Riblah, in the land of Hamath, the king of Babylon had them all put to death. So the people of Judah were sent into exile from their land.

28 The number of captives taken to Babylon in the seventh year of Nebuchadnezzar's reign* was 3,023. 29 Then in Nebuchadnezzar's eighteenth year* he took 832 more. 30 In Nebuchadnezzar's twenty-third year* he sent Nebuzaradan, the captain of the guard, who took 745 more—a total of 4,600 captives in all.

HOPE FOR ISRAEL'S ROYAL LINE

31 In the thirty-seventh year of the exile of King Jehoiachin of Judah, Evil-merodach ascended to the Babylonian throne. He was kind to* Jehoiachin and released him from prison on March 31 of that year.* 32 He spoke kindly to Jehoiachin and gave him a higher place than all the other exiled kings in Babylon. 33 He supplied Jehoiachin with new clothes to replace his prison garb and allowed him to dine in the king's presence for the rest of his life. 34 So the Babylonian king gave him a regular food allowance as long as he lived. This continued until the day of his death.

52:4a Hebrew *on the tenth day of the tenth month,* of the ancient Hebrew lunar calendar. A number of events in Jeremiah can be cross-checked with dates in surviving Babylonian records and related accurately to our modern calendar. This day was January 15, 588 B.C. **52:4b** Hebrew *Nebuchadrezzar,* a variant spelling of Nebuchadnezzar; also in 52:12, 28, 29, 30. **52:6** Hebrew *By the ninth day of the fourth month* [in the eleventh year of Zedekiah's reign]. This day was July 18, 586 B.C.; also see note on 52:4a. **52:7a** Or *the Chaldeans;* similarly in 52:8, 17. **52:7b** Hebrew *the Arabah.* **52:12** Hebrew *On the tenth day of the fifth month,* of the ancient Hebrew lunar calendar. This day was August 17, 586 B.C.; also see note on 52:4a. **52:13** Or *destroyed the houses of all the important people.* **52:14** Or *Chaldean.* **52:21a** Hebrew *18 cubits* [8.3 meters] *tall and 12 cubits* [5.5 meters] *in circumference.* **52:21b** Hebrew *4 fingers thick* [8 centimeters]. **52:22** Hebrew *5 cubits* [2.3 meters]. **52:28** This exile in the seventh year of Nebuchadnezzar's reign occurred in 597 B.C. **52:29** This exile in the eighteenth year of Nebuchadnezzar's reign occurred in 586 B.C. **52:30** This exile in the twenty-third year of Nebuchadnezzar's reign occurred in 581 B.C. **52:31a** Hebrew *He raised the head of.* **52:31b** Hebrew *on the twenty-fifth day of the twelfth month,* of the ancient Hebrew lunar calendar. This day was March 31, 561 B.C.; also see note on 52:4a.

52:28 The number of captives. The staged deportation represented the Babylonian's systematic conquest. Piece by piece, the nation of Judah was disassembled and taken away.

52:30 twenty-third year. This second deportation was probably a result of the governor Gedaliah's assassination (41:1-3). The numbers likely represent only males. The few Jews left fled to Egypt (chap. 44).

52:31 Jehoiachin. Jehoiachin represented the hope of the people. His release and restoration kindled the exiles' belief in Jeremiah's prophecies of future prosperity. Jehoiachin was treated well until his death.

INTRODUCTION TO

LAMENTATIONS

PERSONAL READING PLAN

- ☐Lamentations 1:1-22
- ☐Lamentations 2:1-22
- ☐Lamentations 3:1-33
- ☐Lamentations 3:34-66
- ☐Lamentations 4:1-22
- ☐Lamentations 5:1-22

AUTHOR

Early Jewish and Christian tradition ascribes this anonymous book to Jeremiah. Although this is likely, the evidence for this view is not certain. It is clear, however, that the author was an eyewitness to the fall of Jerusalem and Judah's forced exile to Babylon.

DATE

Lamentations was probably written between 586 B.C. (the fall of Jerusalem) and 516 B.C. (the dedication of the rebuilt temple).

THEME

Grief over Judah's fall and Jerusalem's destruction.

HISTORICAL BACKGROUND

Jerusalem lay under siege by Babylon for 18 months. Outside the city, the Babylonians captured and killed many of the people of Judah. While inside the city, disease and famine claimed many more. Reflecting on these stark days and then the fall of Jerusalem, Lamentations depicts the incredible grief and loss accompanying the invasion and destruction of Jerusalem—including the temple—and the exile of Judah's residents.

CHARACTERISTICS

Lamentations is a good example of ancient Near Eastern "dirge" poetry that was read aloud at funerals. It is used by Jews praying at the western (wailing) wall, even to this day. The author of this book crafted his theological lessons and channeled his emotions to fit his lament into an "acrostic" poem. (An acrostic poem is one in which the verses each begin with the successive 22 letters of the Hebrew alphabet.) An interesting thematic parallel to Lamentations is the book of Job (see the introduction page for Job). Job grieves over the calamity that has struck him on a personal level, while the author of Lamentations pours out his grief over the destruction of the city of Jerusalem. Whereas Job has done nothing to deserve his disaster and thus wonders how God can be just, the poet of Lamentations readily confesses that Judah is guilty and that God is just. Lamentations provides a sad "post-mortem" on the prophetic warnings that Judah had repeatedly ignored. Although appalled at the severity of the national destruction, the poet still trusts God. Having confessed the people's sin, the poet desperately hopes that the God who brings grief will also renew mercy (see 3:21-33; 5:21-22). Because of its profound reflection on the problem of suffering, Lamentations, like Job (which finds no easy answers, but is content to trust God's mercy), has inspired Christian devotion and hymn-writing.

SORROW IN JERUSALEM

1 * 1 Jerusalem, once so full of people,
is now deserted.
She who was once great among the nations
now sits alone like a widow.
Once the queen of all the earth,
she is now a slave.

2 She sobs through the night;
tears stream down her cheeks.
Among all her lovers,
there is no one left to comfort her.
All her friends have betrayed her
and become her enemies.

3 Judah has been led away into captivity,
oppressed with cruel slavery.
She lives among foreign nations
and has no place of rest.
Her enemies have chased her down,
and she has nowhere to turn.

4 The roads to Jerusalem* are in mourning,
for crowds no longer come to celebrate the
festivals.
The city gates are silent,
her priests groan,
her young women are crying—
how bitter is her fate!

5 Her oppressors have become her masters,
and her enemies prosper,
for the LORD has punished Jerusalem
for her many sins.
Her children have been captured
and taken away to distant lands.

6 All the majesty of beautiful Jerusalem*
has been stripped away.
Her princes are like starving deer
searching for pasture.
They are too weak to run
from the pursuing enemy.

7 In the midst of her sadness and wandering,
Jerusalem remembers her ancient splendor.
But now she has fallen to her enemy,
and there is no one to help her.
Her enemy struck her down
and laughed as she fell.

8 Jerusalem has sinned greatly,
so she has been tossed away like a filthy rag.
All who once honored her now despise her,
for they have seen her stripped naked and
humiliated.
All she can do is groan
and hide her face.

9 She defiled herself with immorality
and gave no thought to her future.
Now she lies in the gutter
with no one to lift her out.
"LORD, see my misery," she cries.
"The enemy has triumphed."

10 The enemy has plundered her completely,
taking every precious thing she owns.
She has seen foreigners violate her sacred Temple,
the place the LORD had forbidden them to enter.

11 Her people groan as they search for bread.
They have sold their treasures for food to stay
alive.
"O LORD, look," she mourns,
"and see how I am despised.

12 "Does it mean nothing to you, all you who pass by?
Look around and see if there is any suffering
like mine,
which the LORD brought on me
when he erupted in fierce anger.

13 "He has sent fire from heaven that burns in my
bones.
He has placed a trap in my path and turned me
back.
He has left me devastated,
racked with sickness all day long.

14 "He wove my sins into ropes
to hitch me to a yoke of captivity.
The Lord sapped my strength and turned me over
to my enemies;
I am helpless in their hands.

15 "The Lord has treated my mighty men
with contempt.
At his command a great army has come
to crush my young warriors.
The Lord has trampled his beloved city*
like grapes are trampled in a winepress.

16 "For all these things I weep;
tears flow down my cheeks.
No one is here to comfort me;

1 Each of the first four chapters of this book is an acrostic, laid out in the order of the Hebrew alphabet. The first word of each verse begins with a successive Hebrew letter. Chapters 1, 2, and 4 have one verse for each of the 22 Hebrew letters. Chapter 3 contains 22 stanzas of three verses each. Though chapter 5 has 22 verses, it is not an acrostic. **1:4** Hebrew *Zion;* also in 1:17. **1:6** Hebrew *of the daughter of Zion.* **1:15** Hebrew *the virgin daughter of Judah.*

1:1 now sits alone. Jerusalem has been devastated by Babylon, and this poetic lament beautifully and woefully portrays the tragedy of God's Holy City as deserted and desolate. The first four chapters follow an acrostic pattern; each verse begins with the Hebrew letter that corresponds to A-Z. Chapter 5 is a scrambled alphabet, perhaps symbolizing despair. **princess.** The Hebrew word used here (Sara) is also the name given Abraham's wife and the mother of the nation. As such, it illustrates Jerusalem's preeminence.

1:2 among all her lovers. Such destruction befell Judah as a consequence of the nation's passionate idolatry. Now, in Judah's time of need, her gods proved useless.

1:9 defiled . . . with immorality. The image is gruesome. Jerusalem is compared to a woman in her time of uncleanness who does not seclude herself or even stem the flow of blood (see Lev. 15:19). Jerusalem was obvious about its idolatry.

1:16-17 No one . . . to comfort. A frequent refrain (see also vv. 2,9,21) in chapter one, hope actually exists (Isa. 40:1-2). Yet in the near-context, it would appear that the possibility of such consolation is beyond possibility (2:13; Jer. 19:10-11). This is also true of tragedy in our own lives, when God's purposes initially appear inscrutable. Even when God harshly disciplines us, there is yet hope. God meant to purify his people, and exile accomplished it well.

any who might encourage me are far away.
My children have no future,
for the enemy has conquered us."

17 Jerusalem reaches out for help,
but no one comforts her.
Regarding his people Israel,*
the LORD has said,
"Let their neighbors be their enemies!
Let them be thrown away like a filthy rag!"

18 "The LORD is right," Jerusalem says,
"for I rebelled against him.
Listen, people everywhere;
look upon my anguish and despair,
for my sons and daughters
have been taken captive to distant lands.

19 "I begged my allies for help,
but they betrayed me.
My priests and leaders
starved to death in the city,
even as they searched for food
to save their lives.

20 "LORD, see my anguish!
My heart is broken
and my soul despairs,
for I have rebelled against you.
In the streets the sword kills,
and at home there is only death.

21 "Others heard my groans,
but no one turned to comfort me.
When my enemies heard about my troubles,
they were happy to see what you had done.
Oh, bring the day you promised,
when they will suffer as I have suffered.

22 "Look at all their evil deeds, LORD.
Punish them,
as you have punished me
for all my sins.
My groans are many,
and I am sick at heart."

GOD'S ANGER AT SIN

2 1 The Lord in his anger
has cast a dark shadow over beautiful
Jerusalem.*
The fairest of Israel's cities lies in the dust,
thrown down from the heights of heaven.
In his day of great anger,
the Lord has shown no mercy even to his
Temple.*

2 Without mercy the Lord has destroyed
every home in Israel.*
In his anger he has broken down
the fortress walls of beautiful
Jerusalem.*
He has brought them to the ground,
dishonoring the kingdom and its rulers.

3 All the strength of Israel
vanishes beneath his fierce anger.
The Lord has withdrawn his protection
as the enemy attacks.
He consumes the whole land of Israel
like a raging fire.

4 He bends his bow against his people,
as though he were their enemy.
His strength is used against them
to kill their finest youth.
His fury is poured out like fire
on beautiful Jerusalem.*

5 Yes, the Lord has vanquished Israel
like an enemy.
He has destroyed her palaces
and demolished her fortresses.
He has brought unending sorrow and tears
upon beautiful Jerusalem.

6 He has broken down his Temple
as though it were merely a garden shelter.
The LORD has blotted out all memory
of the holy festivals and Sabbath days.
Kings and priests fall together
before his fierce anger.

7 The Lord has rejected his own altar;
he despises his own sanctuary.
He has given Jerusalem's palaces
to her enemies.
They shout in the LORD's Temple
as though it were a day of celebration.

8 The LORD was determined
to destroy the walls of beautiful Jerusalem.
He made careful plans for their destruction,
then did what he had planned.
Therefore, the ramparts and walls
have fallen down before him.

9 Jerusalem's gates have sunk into the ground.
He has smashed their locks and bars.
Her kings and princes have been exiled to distant
lands;
her law has ceased to exist.

1:17 Hebrew *Jacob.* The names "Jacob" and "Israel" are often interchanged throughout the Old Testament, referring sometimes to the individual patriarch and sometimes to the nation. **2:1a** Hebrew *the daughter of Zion;* also in 2:8, 10, 18. **2:1b** Hebrew *his footstool.* **2:2a** Hebrew *Jacob;* also in 2:3b. See note on 1:17. **2:2b** Hebrew *the daughter of Judah;* also in 2:5. **2:4** Hebrew *on the tent of the daughter of Zion.*

1:20 In the streets . . . at home there is only death. Judah was in a no-win situation. For 18 months, the city was under Nebuchadnezzar's attack. Certain death awaited any escapees, while starvation stifled those within the city walls.

1:21 day you promised. The author selfishly wished their Babylonian captor would share Judah's same fate—that God's judgment would be severe (Jer. 25:15-38). He understood the impartiality of divine retribution for disobedience.

2:6 broken down his Temple. Judah recognized the temple as a sign of God's presence among them. Their spiritual indifference resulted in its destruction. **LORD has blotted out . . . holy festivals.** The festivals of Leviticus 23 were signs of great joy that God had removed.

2:7 they shout. The pilfering pagans struck the author with sadness. Their irreverent and mocking shouts of victory in the temple added insult to injury.

2:9 prophets receive no more visions from the LORD. God stopped sending the people warning or hope through the prophets. The only message left for Judah was that of mass destruction. However, during the exile, God would continue to encourage his people through the prophet Daniel.

Her prophets receive
no more visions from the LORD.

10 The leaders of beautiful Jerusalem
sit on the ground in silence.
They are clothed in burlap
and throw dust on their heads.
The young women of Jerusalem
hang their heads in shame.

11 I have cried until the tears no longer come;
my heart is broken.
My spirit is poured out in agony
as I see the desperate plight of my people.
Little children and tiny babies
are fainting and dying in the streets.

12 They cry out to their mothers,
"We need food and drink!"
Their lives ebb away in the streets
like the life of a warrior wounded in battle.
They gasp for life
as they collapse in their mothers' arms.

13 What can I say about you?
Who has ever seen such sorrow?
O daughter of Jerusalem,
to what can I compare your anguish?
O virgin daughter of Zion,
how can I comfort you?
For your wound is as deep as the sea.
Who can heal you?

14 Your prophets have said
so many foolish things, false to the core.
They did not save you from exile
by pointing out your sins.
Instead, they painted false pictures,
filling you with false hope.

15 All who pass by jeer at you.
They scoff and insult beautiful Jerusalem,* saying,
"Is this the city called 'Most Beautiful in All the World'
and 'Joy of All the Earth'?"

16 All your enemies mock you.
They scoff and snarl and say,
"We have destroyed her at last!
We have long waited for this day,
and it is finally here!"

17 But it is the LORD who did just as he planned.
He has fulfilled the promises of disaster
he made long ago.
He has destroyed Jerusalem without mercy.
He has caused her enemies to gloat over her
and has given them power over her.

18 Cry aloud* before the Lord,
O walls of beautiful Jerusalem!
Let your tears flow like a river
day and night.
Give yourselves no rest;
give your eyes no relief.

19 Rise during the night and cry out.
Pour out your hearts like water to the Lord.
Lift up your hands to him in prayer,
pleading for your children,
for in every street
they are faint with hunger.

20 "O LORD, think about this!
Should you treat your own people this way?
Should mothers eat their own children,
those they once bounced on their knees?
Should priests and prophets be killed
within the Lord's Temple?

21 "See them lying in the streets—
young and old,
boys and girls,
killed by the swords of the enemy.
You have killed them in your anger,
slaughtering them without mercy.

22 "You have invited terrors from all around,
as though you were calling them to a day of feasting.
In the day of the LORD's anger,
no one has escaped or survived.
The enemy has killed all the children
whom I carried and raised."

HOPE IN THE LORD'S FAITHFULNESS

3 1 I am the one who has seen the afflictions
that come from the rod of the LORD's anger.
2 He has led me into darkness,
shutting out all light.
3 He has turned his hand against me
again and again, all day long.

4 He has made my skin and flesh grow old.
He has broken my bones.
5 He has besieged and surrounded me
with anguish and distress.
6 He has buried me in a dark place,
like those long dead.

7 He has walled me in, and I cannot escape.
He has bound me in heavy chains.
8 And though I cry and shout,
he has shut out my prayers.
9 He has blocked my way with a high stone wall;
he has made my road crooked.

2:15 Hebrew *the daughter of Jerusalem.* **2:18** Hebrew *Their heart cried.*

2:14 false pictures . . . false hope. A true prophet, like Jeremiah, spoke only God's message. False prophets encouraged the kind of covenantal disobedience that Scripture calls spiritual adultery (Jer. 2–6; Ezek. 16,20,23; Hosea 1–3).
2:15 jeer . . . scoff and insult. "The perfection of beauty" (Ps. 50:2; Ezek. 27:3; 28:12) and "the joy of the whole earth" (Ps. 48:2) that was Jerusalem was now laid waste. They "jeer" utilizes the same words used to describe the hostile scorn that God places on the wicked (Job 27:23). Similarly "hiss" (1 Kings 9:8; Job 27:23; Jer. 19:8) and "scoff and insult" also implies scornful derision (Job 16:4; Pss. 22:7; 109:25; Isa. 37:22). Such may have been the case with Edom, Israel's archrival since the days of Exodus. Edom is said to have aided Babylon against Jerusalem in 586 B.C. and even exploited Judah to its own benefit (4:21; Ps. 137:7; Jer. 49:7-22; Ezek. 25:12-14; Obad.). There's nothing worse than being laughed at while in misery (Jer. 18:18-23).
2:19 Pour out your hearts like water. The image pictures a full confession here (Ps. 62:8).

[10] He has hidden like a bear or a lion,
waiting to attack me.
[11] He has dragged me off the path and torn me in pieces,
leaving me helpless and devastated.
[12] He has drawn his bow
and made me the target for his arrows.

[13] He shot his arrows
deep into my heart.
[14] My own people laugh at me.
All day long they sing their mocking songs.
[15] He has filled me with bitterness
and given me a bitter cup of sorrow to drink.

[16] He has made me chew on gravel.
He has rolled me in the dust.
[17] Peace has been stripped away,
and I have forgotten what prosperity is.
[18] I cry out, "My splendor is gone!
Everything I had hoped for from the LORD is lost!"

[19] The thought of my suffering and homelessness
is bitter beyond words.*
[20] I will never forget this awful time,
as I grieve over my loss.
[21] Yet I still dare to hope
when I remember this:

[22] The faithful love of the LORD never ends!*
His mercies never cease.
[23] Great is his faithfulness;
his mercies begin afresh each morning.
[24] I say to myself, "The LORD is my inheritance;
therefore, I will hope in him!"

[25] The LORD is good to those who depend on him,
to those who search for him.
[26] So it is good to wait quietly
for salvation from the LORD.
[27] And it is good for people to submit at an early age
to the yoke of his discipline:

[28] Let them sit alone in silence
beneath the LORD's demands.
[29] Let them lie face down in the dust,
for there may be hope at last.
[30] Let them turn the other cheek to those who strike them
and accept the insults of their enemies.

[31] For no one is abandoned
by the Lord forever.
[32] Though he brings grief, he also shows compassion
because of the greatness of his unfailing love.
[33] For he does not enjoy hurting people
or causing them sorrow.

[34] If people crush underfoot
all the prisoners of the land,
[35] if they deprive others of their rights
in defiance of the Most High,
[36] if they twist justice in the courts—
doesn't the Lord see all these things?

[37] Who can command things to happen
without the Lord's permission?
[38] Does not the Most High
send both calamity and good?
[39] Then why should we, mere humans, complain
when we are punished for our sins?

[40] Instead, let us test and examine our ways.
Let us turn back to the LORD.
[41] Let us lift our hearts and hands
to God in heaven and say,
[42] "We have sinned and rebelled,
and you have not forgiven us.

[43] "You have engulfed us with your anger, chased us down,
and slaughtered us without mercy.
[44] You have hidden yourself in a cloud
so our prayers cannot reach you.
[45] You have discarded us as refuse and garbage
among the nations.

[46] "All our enemies
have spoken out against us.
[47] We are filled with fear,
for we are trapped, devastated, and ruined."
[48] Tears stream from my eyes
because of the destruction of my people!

[49] My tears flow endlessly;
they will not stop
[50] until the LORD looks down
from heaven and sees.
[51] My heart is breaking
over the fate of all the women of Jerusalem.

[52] My enemies, whom I have never harmed,
hunted me down like a bird.
[53] They threw me into a pit
and dropped stones on me.
[54] The water rose over my head,
and I cried out, "This is the end!"

[55] But I called on your name, LORD,
from deep within the pit.
[56] You heard me when I cried, "Listen to my pleading!
Hear my cry for help!"

3:19 Or *is wormwood and gall.* 3:22 As in Syriac version; Hebrew reads *of the LORD keeps us from destruction.*

3:15 bitterness . . . bitter cup of sorrow. The pungent taste of punishment plagued the nation of Judah (Jer. 9:15). Even food, their source for life, was bitterly unsatisfying. At Passover, bitter herbs such as these remind of hardship.
3:23 Great is his faithfulness . . . begin afresh each morning. The basis of a popular hymn, this verse beautifully describes the kindness of God even in judgment.
3:24 inheritance. With nothing but rubble to call their own, Judah's only valuable belonging was God (Num. 18:20). **I will hope in him.** No hope for a second wind. No will for fighting back. There was nothing else Judah could do but wait on God.
3:27 submit . . . to the yoke. The author realized this overbearing trial (v. 1) might turn out for their good.
3:36 twist justice in the courts. The author built a case for God's compassion through rhetorical questions. Judah could hardly call her situation unjust.
3:46-47 Verse 46 repeats the thought of 2:16. Verse 47 summarizes the destruction that had devastated Jerusalem (Isa 24:17-18; Jer 48:43-44).

57 Yes, you came when I called;
you told me, "Do not fear."
58 Lord, you have come to my defense;
you have redeemed my life.
59 You have seen the wrong they have done to me,
LORD.
Be my judge, and prove me right.
60 You have seen the vengeful plots
my enemies have laid against me.

61 LORD, you have heard the vile names they call
me.
You know all about the plans they have made.
62 My enemies whisper and mutter
as they plot against me all day long.
63 Look at them! Whether they sit or stand,
I am the object of their mocking songs.

64 Pay them back, LORD,
for all the evil they have done.
65 Give them hard and stubborn hearts,
and then let your curse fall on them!
66 Chase them down in your anger,
destroying them beneath the LORD's heavens.

GOD'S ANGER SATISFIED

4 1 How the gold has lost its luster!
Even the finest gold has become dull.
The sacred gemstones
lie scattered in the streets!

2 See how the precious children of Jerusalem,*
worth their weight in fine gold,
are now treated like pots of clay
made by a common potter.

3 Even the jackals feed their young,
but not my people Israel.
They ignore their children's cries,
like ostriches in the desert.

4 The parched tongues of their little ones
stick to the roofs of their mouths in thirst.
The children cry for bread,
but no one has any to give them.
5 The people who once ate the richest foods
now beg in the streets for anything they
can get.
Those who once wore the finest clothes
now search the garbage dumps for food.

6 The guilt* of my people
is greater than that of Sodom,
where utter disaster struck in a moment
and no hand offered help.

7 Our princes once glowed with health—
brighter than snow, whiter than milk.
Their faces were as ruddy as rubies,
their appearance like fine jewels.*

8 But now their faces are blacker than soot.
No one recognizes them in the streets.
Their skin sticks to their bones;
it is as dry and hard as wood.

9 Those killed by the sword are better off
than those who die of hunger.
Starving, they waste away
for lack of food from the fields.
10 Tenderhearted women
have cooked their own children.
They have eaten them
to survive the siege.

11 But now the anger of the LORD is satisfied.
His fierce anger has been poured out.
He started a fire in Jerusalem*
that burned the city to its foundations.

12 Not a king in all the earth—
no one in all the world—
would have believed that an enemy
could march through the gates of
Jerusalem.

13 Yet it happened because of the sins of her
prophets
and the sins of her priests,
who defiled the city
by shedding innocent blood.

14 They wandered blindly
through the streets,
so defiled by blood
that no one dared touch them.

15 "Get away!" the people shouted at them.
"You're defiled! Don't touch us!"
So they fled to distant lands
and wandered among foreign nations,
but none would let them stay.

16 The LORD himself has scattered them,
and he no longer helps them.
People show no respect for the priests
and no longer honor the leaders.

17 We looked in vain for our allies
to come and save us,
but we were looking to nations
that could not help us.

4:2 Hebrew *precious sons of Zion.* **4:6** Or *punishment.* **4:7** Hebrew *like lapis lazuli.* **4:11** Hebrew *in Zion.*

3:57 when I called. Jeremiah looks back to his personal experience and gives testimony to God's faithfulness. Crisis was met with compassion. God is real to those He loves (Ps. 145:18).
3:63 their mocking songs. In dire straits, Judah was the joke of many nations (vv. 46-47). Where was Judah's God now?
4:1 finest gold has become dull. Jerusalem was a tragic before-and-after comparison. Before their calamity, the people were priceless. Now, sin devalued them (v. 2). The temple valuables are gone, and even the people, the greater treasure, are now almost worthless (v. 2).
4:6 Sodom . . . disaster struck in a moment. God's punishment on Sodom, although equally thorough, was mercifully quick (Gen. 19:24-29). By contrast, Jerusalem's painful siege went on month after month.
4:10 cooked their own children. The Israelites fulfill the curse of eating their own children as a result of disobedience to the Lord and breaking His covenant (Lev. 26:29; Deut. 28:53-57). It is also reminiscent of cannibalism during the siege of Samaria in Elisha's time (2 Kings 6:28-29).
4:17 nations that could not help. Egypt proved to be an impotent ally against God's plan to use Babylon against Jerusalem.

18 We couldn't go into the streets
without danger to our lives.
Our end was near; our days were numbered.
We were doomed!

19 Our enemies were swifter than eagles in flight.
If we fled to the mountains, they found us.
If we hid in the wilderness,
they were waiting for us there.

20 Our king—the LORD's anointed, the very life of our nation—
was caught in their snares.
We had thought that his shadow
would protect us against any nation on earth!

21 Are you rejoicing in the land of Uz,
O people of Edom?
But you, too, must drink from the cup of the LORD's anger.
You, too, will be stripped naked in your drunkenness.

22 O beautiful Jerusalem,* your punishment will end;
you will soon return from exile.
But Edom, your punishment is just beginning;
soon your many sins will be exposed.

PRAYER FOR RESTORATION

5 1 LORD, remember what has happened to us.
See how we have been disgraced!
2 Our inheritance has been turned over to strangers,
our homes to foreigners.
3 We are orphaned and fatherless.
Our mothers are widowed.
4 We have to pay for water to drink,
and even firewood is expensive.
5 Those who pursue us are at our heels;
we are exhausted but are given no rest.
6 We submitted to Egypt and Assyria
to get enough food to survive.
7 Our ancestors sinned, but they have died—
and we are suffering the punishment they deserved!
8 Slaves have now become our masters;
there is no one left to rescue us.
9 We hunt for food at the risk of our lives,
for violence rules the countryside.
10 The famine has blackened our skin
as though baked in an oven.
11 Our enemies rape the women in Jerusalem*
and the young girls in all the towns of Judah.
12 Our princes are being hanged by their thumbs,
and our elders are treated with contempt.
13 Young men are led away to work at millstones,
and boys stagger under heavy loads of wood.
14 The elders no longer sit in the city gates;
the young men no longer dance and sing.
15 Joy has left our hearts;
our dancing has turned to mourning.
16 The garlands have* fallen from our heads.
Weep for us because we have sinned.
17 Our hearts are sick and weary,
and our eyes grow dim with tears.
18 For Jerusalem* is empty and desolate,
a place haunted by jackals.

19 But LORD, you remain the same forever!
Your throne continues from generation to generation.
20 Why do you continue to forget us?
Why have you abandoned us for so long?
21 Restore us, O LORD, and bring us back to you again!
Give us back the joys we once had!
22 Or have you utterly rejected us?
Are you angry with us still?

4:22 Hebrew *O daughter of Zion.* **5:11** Hebrew *in Zion.* **5:16** Or *The crown has.* **5:18** Hebrew *Mount Zion.*

4:21 people of Edom. The poet mocks Edom in return (see note on 2:15), telling them to enjoy it while it lasts, because it won't last long. She will endure the same kind of humiliation that Jerusalem endured.

4:22 beautiful Jerusalem, your punishment will end. In the end, Judah's sole hope was in God's covenant with His people (Gen. 12:2-3; Deut. 28–30) and His assurance of a new covenant (Jer. 31:31). Because of God's promises, the nation would be restored.

5:1 LORD, remember. The people failed to remember their obligations as covenant people, and God failed to remember them (1:9; 2:1). In 3:19, the poet asked the Lord to remember him. Here he emphatically begs the Lord to remember His people.

5:7 punishment. The people of Judah realized their present condition was the result of years of sin. Their heritage was one of pain and disobedience.

5:16 garlands have fallen. Jerusalem's royal destiny was displaced by rebellion. Thus, the golden city was ruined.

5:19 throne continues from generation to generation. Despite the destruction of God's throne room in the temple, the Lord still reigned as everlasting king.

5:20 abandoned. For the last time, the poet asks God why He has abandoned them.

5:22 utterly rejected. The author feared the one thing God would never do (Jer. 31:37; Rom. 11:2). Despite Judah's rebellious streak, God would never abandon them completely. He was always near (Ps. 145:18).

INTRODUCTION TO

EZEKIEL

PERSONAL READING PLAN

☐Ezekiel 1:1–3:15
☐Ezekiel 3:16–5:17
☐Ezekiel 6:1–8:18
☐Ezekiel 9:1–11:25
☐Ezekiel 12:1–13:23
☐Ezekiel 14:1–15:8
☐Ezekiel 16:1-63
☐Ezekiel 17:1–18:32
☐Ezekiel 19:1–20:49
☐Ezekiel 21:1–22:31
☐Ezekiel 23:1-49
☐Ezekiel 24:1–25:17
☐Ezekiel 26:1–27:36
☐Ezekiel 28:1–29:21
☐Ezekiel 30:1–31:18
☐Ezekiel 32:1–33:33
☐Ezekiel 34:1–35:15
☐Ezekiel 36:1–37:14
☐Ezekiel 37:15–39:29
☐Ezekiel 40:1-47
☐Ezekiel 40:48–42:20
☐Ezekiel 43:1–44:31
☐Ezekiel 45:1–46:24
☐Ezekiel 47:1–48:35

AUTHOR

The writer was Ezekiel, a Jewish priest and prophet, exiled in Babylon. He was a man of broad knowledge, not only of his own traditions but also of international affairs and history.

DATE

Ezekiel's prophecies can be dated with precision, more easily than any other prophet. His first dates from 593 B.C., seven years before the fall of Jerusalem, and his last dates from 571 B.C. The book of Ezekiel contains more dates than any other Old Testament prophetic book. In addition, archaeologists (from Babylonian records) and astronomers (from accurate dating of eclipses referred to in ancient archives) provide precise modern calendar equivalents.

THEME

God acts in the events of human history so that everyone may come to know Him and find new life.

HISTORICAL BACKGROUND

Like his contemporary, Jeremiah, Ezekiel prophesied in politically volatile times. After Israel was destroyed by the Assyrians in 722 B.C., only the southern kingdom of Judah was left. Assyria lost its domination in 612 B.C. and was replaced as a world power by Babylon. Judah was a subservient state of Babylon but rebelled, hoping for Egypt's support. Egypt proved unreliable, and Judah was subdued by King Nebuchadnezzar of Babylon in 605 and again in 598–597 B.C. He took thousands of Jews captive each time; Ezekiel was among those in the second wave of exiles.

CHARACTERISTICS

Ezekiel is a book of heavenly visions, poems, parables, and dramatically acted-out prophetic symbolism. However, to get the people's attention, God uses more than Ezekiel's vivid images and symbolic actions. He allows the people to suffer. Fortunately, Ezekiel's message of imminent doom turns to ultimate hope in the end. There is symmetry in the book with (1) the vision of the desecrated temple balanced by that of the restored temple, (2) the message of God's anger balanced by the truth of God's mercy, and (3) the appointment of Ezekiel as a watchman of judgment balanced by his role as a watchman of consolation. In writing to the Jews in exile, Ezekiel communicated that the God of Israel was God even in idolatrous Babylon. Ezekiel warned the people that their own idolatry would be judged and offered them the encouragement that the Lord would return them to their homeland.

A VISION OF LIVING BEINGS

1 On July 31* of my thirtieth year,* while I was with the Judean exiles beside the Kebar River in Babylon, the heavens were opened and I saw visions of God. 2 This happened during the fifth year of King Jehoiachin's captivity. 3 (The LORD gave this message to Ezekiel son of Buzi, a priest, beside the Kebar River in the land of the Babylonians,* and he felt the hand of the LORD take hold of him.)

4 As I looked, I saw a great storm coming from the north, driving before it a huge cloud that flashed with lightning and shone with brilliant light. There was fire inside the cloud, and in the middle of the fire glowed something like gleaming amber.* 5 From the center of the cloud came four living beings that looked human, 6 except that each had four faces and four wings. 7 Their legs were straight, and their feet had hooves like those of a calf and shone like burnished bronze. 8 Under each of their four wings I could see human hands. So each of the four beings had four faces and four wings. 9 The wings of each living being touched the wings of the beings beside it. Each one moved straight forward in any direction without turning around.

10 Each had a human face in the front, the face of a lion on the right side, the face of an ox on the left side, and the face of an eagle at the back. 11 Each had two pairs of outstretched wings—one pair stretched out to touch the wings of the living beings on either side of it, and the other pair covered its body. 12 They went in whatever direction the spirit chose, and they moved straight forward in any direction without turning around.

13 The living beings looked like bright coals of fire or brilliant torches, and lightning seemed to flash back and forth among them. 14 And the living beings darted to and fro like flashes of lightning.

15 As I looked at these beings, I saw four wheels touching the ground beside them, one wheel belonging to each. 16 The wheels sparkled as if made of beryl. All four wheels looked alike and were made the same; each wheel had a second wheel turning crosswise within it. 17 The beings could move in any of the four directions they faced, without turning as they moved. 18 The rims of the four wheels were tall and frightening, and they were covered with eyes all around.

19 When the living beings moved, the wheels moved with them. When they flew upward, the wheels went up, too. 20 The spirit of the living beings was in the wheels. So wherever the spirit went, the wheels and the living beings also went. 21 When the beings moved, the wheels moved. When the beings stopped, the wheels stopped. When the beings flew upward, the wheels rose up, for the spirit of the living beings was in the wheels.

22 Spread out above them was a surface like the sky, glittering like crystal. 23 Beneath this surface the wings of each living being stretched out to touch the others' wings, and each had two wings covering its body. 24 As they flew, their wings sounded to me like waves crashing against the shore or like the voice of the Almighty* or like the shouting of a mighty army. When they stopped, they let down their wings. 25 As they stood with wings lowered, a voice spoke from beyond the crystal surface above them.

26 Above this surface was something that looked like a throne made of blue lapis lazuli. And on this throne high above was a figure whose appearance resembled a man. 27 From what appeared to be his waist up, he looked like gleaming amber, flickering like a fire. And from his waist down, he looked like a burning flame, shining with splendor. 28 All around him was a glowing halo, like a rainbow shining in the clouds on a rainy day. This is what the glory of the LORD looked like to me. When I saw it, I fell face down on the ground, and I heard someone's voice speaking to me.

EZEKIEL'S CALL AND COMMISSION

2 "Stand up, son of man," said the voice. "I want to speak with you." 2 The Spirit came into me as he spoke, and he set me on my feet. I listened carefully to his words. 3 "Son of man," he said, "I am sending you to the nation of Israel, a rebellious nation that has rebelled against me. They and their ancestors have been rebelling against me to this very day. 4 They are a stubborn and hard-hearted people. But I am sending you to say to them, 'This is what the Sovereign LORD says!' 5 And whether they listen or refuse to listen—for remember, they are rebels—at least they will know they have had a prophet among them.

6 "Son of man, do not fear them or their words. Don't be afraid even though their threats surround you like nettles and briers and stinging scorpions. Do not be dismayed by their dark scowls, even though they are rebels. 7 You must give them my messages whether they listen or not. But they won't listen, for they are completely rebellious! 8 Son of man, listen to what I say to you. Do not join them in their rebellion. Open your mouth, and eat what I give you."

9 Then I looked and saw a hand reaching out to me. It held a scroll, 10 which he unrolled. And I saw that both sides were covered with funeral songs, words of sorrow, and pronouncements of doom.

3 The voice said to me, "Son of man, eat what I am giving you—eat this scroll! Then go and give its message to the people of Israel." 2 So I opened my mouth, and he fed me the scroll. 3 "Fill your stomach with this," he said. And when I ate it, it tasted as sweet as honey in my mouth.

4 Then he said, "Son of man, go to the people of Israel and give them my messages. 5 I am not sending you to a foreign people whose language you cannot

1:1a Hebrew *On the fifth day of the fourth month,* of the ancient Hebrew lunar calendar. A number of dates in Ezekiel can be cross-checked with dates in surviving Babylonian records and related accurately to our modern calendar. This event occurred on July 31, 593 B.C. **1:1b** Or *in the thirtieth year.* **1:3** Or *Chaldeans.* **1:4** Or *like burnished metal;* also in 1:27. **1:24** Hebrew *Shaddai.*

1:1 thirtieth year. Ezekiel celebrated his thirtieth birthday, which ordinarily would have marked the beginning of his priesthood (see Num. 4:3) in Babylonian exile.

1:2 fifth year of King Jehoiachin's captivity. In 597 B.C., the Babylonians captured Jehoiachin, Ezekiel, and many other Jews. Ezekiel's prophetic role began in the fifth year of their exile.

1:5-6 four living beings . . . and four wings. They are identified as cherubim—special angelic beings (chap. 10).

1:12 the spirit. The chariot-throne (God's Spirit) moves wherever God wants. Ezekiel is communicating to the exiles that God is not limited to Israel.

2:1 son of man. Expression used in these ways: (1) as a poetic synonym for "man" or "human," as in Pss. 8:4 and 80:17; (2) in Ezekiel as the title by which God regularly addresses the prophet (2:1,3; 3:1,3); and (3) in Dan. 7 as the identity of the glorious person whom the prophet sees coming with the clouds of heaven to approach the Ancient of Days. "The Son of Man" is a designation of Christ found frequently in the NT.

understand. 6 No, I am not sending you to people with strange and difficult speech. If I did, they would listen! 7 But the people of Israel won't listen to you any more than they listen to me! For the whole lot of them are hard-hearted and stubborn. 8 But look, I have made you as obstinate and hard-hearted as they are. 9 I have made your forehead as hard as the hardest rock! So don't be afraid of them or fear their angry looks, even though they are rebels."

10 Then he added, "Son of man, let all my words sink deep into your own heart first. Listen to them carefully for yourself. 11 Then go to your people in exile and say to them, 'This is what the Sovereign LORD says!' Do this whether they listen to you or not."

12 Then the Spirit lifted me up, and I heard a loud rumbling sound behind me. (May the glory of the LORD be praised in his place!)* 13 It was the sound of the wings of the living beings as they brushed against each other and the rumbling of their wheels beneath them.

14 The Spirit lifted me up and took me away. I went in bitterness and turmoil, but the LORD's hold on me was strong. 15 Then I came to the colony of Judean exiles in Tel-abib, beside the Kebar River. I was overwhelmed and sat among them for seven days.

A WATCHMAN FOR ISRAEL

16 After seven days the LORD gave me a message. He said, 17 "Son of man, I have appointed you as a watchman for Israel. Whenever you receive a message from me, warn people immediately. 18 If I warn the wicked, saying, 'You are under the penalty of death,' but you fail to deliver the warning, they will die in their sins. And I will hold you responsible for their deaths. 19 If you warn them and they refuse to repent and keep on sinning, they will die in their sins. But you will have saved yourself because you obeyed me.

20 "If righteous people turn away from their righteous behavior and ignore the obstacles I put in their way, they will die. And if you do not warn them, they will die in their sins. None of their righteous acts will be remembered, and I will hold you responsible for their deaths. 21 But if you warn righteous people not to sin and they listen to you and do not sin, they will live, and you will have saved yourself, too."

22 Then the LORD took hold of me and said, "Get up and go out into the valley, and I will speak to you there." 23 So I got up and went, and there I saw the glory of the LORD, just as I had seen in my first vision by the Kebar River. And I fell face down on the ground.

24 Then the Spirit came into me and set me on my feet. He spoke to me and said, "Go to your house and shut yourself in. 25 There, son of man, you will be tied with ropes so you cannot go out among the people. 26 And I will make your tongue stick to the roof of your mouth so that you will be speechless and unable to rebuke them, for they are rebels. 27 But when I give you a message, I will loosen your tongue and let you speak. Then you will say to them, 'This is what the Sovereign LORD says!' Those who choose to listen will listen, but those who refuse will refuse, for they are rebels.

A SIGN OF THE COMING SIEGE

4 "And now, son of man, take a large clay brick and set it down in front of you. Then draw a map of the city of Jerusalem on it. 2 Show the city under siege. Build a wall around it so no one can escape. Set up the enemy camp, and surround the city with siege ramps and battering rams. 3 Then take an iron griddle and place it between you and the city. Turn toward the city and demonstrate how harsh the siege will be against Jerusalem. This will be a warning to the people of Israel.

4 "Now lie on your left side and place the sins of Israel on yourself. You are to bear their sins for the number of days you lie there on your side. 5 I am requiring you to bear Israel's sins for 390 days—one day for each year of their sin. 6 After that, turn over and lie on your right side for 40 days—one day for each year of Judah's sin.

7 "Meanwhile, keep staring at the siege of Jerusalem. Lie there with your arm bared and prophesy her destruction. 8 I will tie you up with ropes so you won't be able to turn from side to side until the days of your siege have been completed.

9 "Now go and get some wheat, barley, beans, lentils, millet, and emmer wheat, and mix them together in a storage jar. Use them to make bread for yourself during the 390 days you will be lying on your side. 10 Ration this out to yourself, eight ounces* of food for each day, and eat it at set times. 11 Then measure out a jar* of water for each day, and drink it at set times. 12 Prepare and eat this food as you would barley cakes. While all the people are watching, bake it over a fire using dried human dung as fuel and then eat the bread." 13 Then the LORD said, "This is how Israel will eat defiled bread in the Gentile lands to which I will banish them!"

14 Then I said, "O Sovereign LORD, must I be defiled by using human dung? For I have never been defiled before. From the time I was a child until now I have never eaten any animal that died of sickness or was killed by other animals. I have never eaten any meat forbidden by the law."

15 "All right," the LORD said. "You may bake your bread with cow dung instead of human dung." 16 Then he told me, "Son of man, I will make food very scarce in Jerusalem. It will be weighed out with great care and eaten fearfully. The water will be rationed out drop by drop, and the people will drink it with dismay. 17 Lacking food and water, people will look at one another in terror, and they will waste away under their punishment.

3:12 A possible reading for this verse is *Then the Spirit lifted me up, and as the glory of the LORD rose from its place, I heard a loud rumbling sound behind me.* **4:10** Hebrew *20 shekels* [228 grams]. **4:11** Hebrew *1/6 of a hin* [about 1 pint or 0.6 liters].

3:9 forehead . . . hardest rock. The forehead represented a person's determination or stubbornness (see Isa. 48:4). Ezekiel needed to toughen up in order to deliver bad news to an unreceptive people.

3:11 whether they listen to you or not. A prophet's success was not in a receptive hearing but a faithful delivery of God's message.

3:17 a watchman. Ezekiel was like one positioned on the city walls to warn of impending physical danger.

4:5 to bear Israel's sins. Ezekiel was commanded to lie down for 430 days as a word-picture of Judah and Israel's guilt, which corresponded to the 430 years of Israel's bondage in Egypt (see Ex. 12:41).

4:9 Some call it Ezekiel bread. Because wheat was sparse in times of famine, bread had to be supplemented with inferior grains and legumes.

4:15 cow dung. Manure could be used as a fuel for cooking. Ezekiel requested cow dung rather than human waste that is regarded as ritually impure. Ezekiel's concern for purity especially reflects his priestly role.

A SIGN OF THE COMING JUDGMENT

5 "Son of man, take a sharp sword and use it as a
razor to shave your head and beard. Use a scale to
weigh the hair into three equal parts. 2 Place a third
of it at the center of your map of Jerusalem. After act-
ing out the siege, burn it there. Scatter another third
across your map and chop it with a sword. Scatter
the last third to the wind, for I will scatter my people
with the sword. 3 Keep just a bit of the hair and tie it
up in your robe. 4 Then take some of these hairs out
and throw them into the fire, burning them up. A fire
will then spread from this remnant and destroy all of
Israel.
5 "This is what the Sovereign LORD says: This is an il-
lustration of what will happen to Jerusalem. I placed
her at the center of the nations, 6 but she has rebelled
against my regulations and decrees and has been
even more wicked than the surrounding nations. She
has refused to obey the regulations and decrees I gave
her to follow.
7 "Therefore, this is what the Sovereign LORD says:
You people have behaved worse than your neighbors
and have refused to obey my decrees and regulations.
You have not even lived up to the standards of the na-
tions around you. 8 Therefore, I myself, the Sovereign
LORD, am now your enemy. I will punish you publicly
while all the nations watch. 9 Because of your detest-
able idols, I will punish you like I have never pun-
ished anyone before or ever will again. 10 Parents will
eat their own children, and children will eat their
parents. I will punish you and scatter to the winds the
few who survive.
11 "As surely as I live, says the Sovereign LORD, I will
cut you off completely. I will show you no pity at all
because you have defiled my Temple with your vile
images and detestable sins. 12 A third of your people
will die in the city from disease and famine. A third
of them will be slaughtered by the enemy outside
the city walls. And I will scatter a third to the winds,
chasing them with my sword. 13 Then at last my anger
will be spent, and I will be satisfied. And when my
fury against them has subsided, all Israel will know
that I, the LORD, have spoken to them in my jealous
anger.
14 "So I will turn you into a ruin, a mockery in the
eyes of the surrounding nations and to all who pass
by. 15 You will become an object of mockery and taunt-
ing and horror. You will be a warning to all the na-
tions around you. They will see what happens when
the LORD punishes a nation in anger and rebukes it,
says the LORD.
16 "I will shower you with the deadly arrows of fam-
ine to destroy you. The famine will become more and
more severe until every crumb of food is gone. 17 And
along with the famine, wild animals will attack you
and rob you of your children. Disease and war will
stalk your land, and I will bring the sword of the ene-
my against you. I, the LORD, have spoken!"

JUDGMENT AGAINST ISRAEL'S MOUNTAINS

6 Again a message came to me from the LORD:
2 "Son of man, turn and face the mountains of Is-
rael and prophesy against them. 3 Proclaim this mes-
sage from the Sovereign LORD against the mountains
of Israel. This is what the Sovereign LORD says to the
mountains and hills and to the ravines and valleys:
I am about to bring war upon you, and I will smash
your pagan shrines. 4 All your altars will be demol-
ished, and your places of worship will be destroyed.
I will kill your people in front of your idols.* 5 I will
lay your corpses in front of your idols and scatter
your bones around your altars. 6 Wherever you live
there will be desolation, and I will destroy your pa-
gan shrines. Your altars will be demolished, your
idols will be smashed, your places of worship will
be torn down, and all the religious objects you have
made will be destroyed. 7 The place will be littered
with corpses, and you will know that I alone am the
LORD.
8 "But I will let a few of my people escape destruc-
tion, and they will be scattered among the nations of
the world. 9 Then when they are exiled among the
nations, they will remember me. They will recognize
how hurt I am by their unfaithful hearts and lustful
eyes that long for their idols. Then at last they will
hate themselves for all their detestable sins. 10 They
will know that I alone am the LORD and that I was
serious when I said I would bring this calamity on
them.
11 "This is what the Sovereign LORD says: Clap your
hands in horror, and stamp your feet. Cry out because
of all the detestable sins the people of Israel have
committed. Now they are going to die from war and
famine and disease. 12 Disease will strike down those
who are far away in exile. War will destroy those who
are nearby. And anyone who survives will be killed
by famine. So at last I will spend my fury on them.
13 They will know that I am the LORD when their dead
lie scattered among their idols and altars on every
hill and mountain and under every green tree and ev-
ery great shade tree—the places where they offered
sacrifices to their idols. 14 I will crush them and make
their cities desolate from the wilderness in the south
to Riblah* in the north. Then they will know that I am
the LORD."

THE COMING OF THE END

7 Then this message came to me from the LORD:
2 "Son of man, this is what the Sovereign LORD says
to Israel:

6:4 The Hebrew term (literally *round things*) probably alludes to dung; also in 6:5, 6, 9, 13. **6:14** As in some Hebrew manuscripts; most Hebrew manuscripts read *Diblah*.

5:1 sharp sword. Conquering armies sometimes humiliated enemies by forcibly shaving them.

5:10 Parents will eat their own children. During sieges, starvation kills children and the elderly first. Sometimes survivors eat the deceased to stay alive (see 2 Kings 6:29). God had warned Israel that rejecting His law would bring this very punishment (see Deut. 28:53).

6:3 smash your pagan shrines. Israel and Judah disobeyed God by building shrines, some to God and some to foreign gods, on the same hilltops pagan Canaanites used as shrines.

6:11 Clap your hands. This kind of clapping usually resembles the hostile, taunting jeers of opponents and rival crowds at athletic contests. It describes how spectators treated captives being marched away in disgrace (25:6; Job 27:23; Lam. 2:15; Nah. 3:19). Here, however, it is not a smug gesture. Ezekiel is instructed to act as God's agent in expressing His extreme anger over their abominations (21:14, 17; 22:13).

7:2 end . . . east, west, north, or south. Enough was enough! No one would escape God's punishment. "Four" is used throughout Ezekiel to represent the four directions. God's power moves freely about in all directions and is not limited by boundaries or obstacles.

"The end is here!
Wherever you look—
east, west, north, or south—
your land is finished.
3 No hope remains,
for I will unleash my anger against you.
I will call you to account
for all your detestable sins.
4 I will turn my eyes away and show no pity.
I will repay you for all your detestable sins.
Then you will know that I am the LORD.

5 "This is what the Sovereign LORD says:
Disaster after disaster
is coming your way!
6 The end has come.
It has finally arrived.
Your final doom is waiting!
7 O people of Israel, the day of your destruction is dawning.
The time has come; the day of trouble is near.
Shouts of anguish will be heard on the mountains,
not shouts of joy.
8 Soon I will pour out my fury on you
and unleash my anger against you.
I will call you to account
for all your detestable sins.
9 I will turn my eyes away and show no pity.
I will repay you for all your detestable sins.
Then you will know that it is I, the LORD,
who is striking the blow.

10 "The day of judgment is here;
your destruction awaits!
The people's wickedness and pride
have blossomed to full flower.
11 Their violence has grown into a rod
that will beat them for their wickedness.
None of these proud and wicked people will survive.
All their wealth and prestige will be swept away.
12 Yes, the time has come;
the day is here!
Buyers should not rejoice over bargains,
nor sellers grieve over losses,
for all of them will fall
under my terrible anger.
13 Even if the merchants survive,
they will never return to their business.
For what God has said applies to everyone—
it will not be changed!
Not one person whose life is twisted by sin
will ever recover.

THE DESOLATION OF ISRAEL

14 "The trumpet calls Israel's army to mobilize,
but no one listens,
for my fury is against them all.
15 There is war outside the city
and disease and famine within.
Those outside the city walls
will be killed by enemy swords.
Those inside the city
will die of famine and disease.
16 The survivors who escape to the mountains
will moan like doves, weeping for their sins.
17 Their hands will hang limp,
their knees will be weak as water.
18 They will dress themselves in burlap;
horror and shame will cover them.
They will shave their heads
in sorrow and remorse.

19 "They will throw their money in the streets,
tossing it out like worthless trash.
Their silver and gold won't save them
on that day of the LORD's anger.
It will neither satisfy nor feed them,
for their greed can only trip them up.
20 They were proud of their beautiful jewelry
and used it to make detestable idols and vile images.
Therefore, I will make all their wealth
disgusting to them.
21 I will give it as plunder to foreigners,
to the most wicked of nations,
and they will defile it.
22 I will turn my eyes from them
as these robbers invade and defile my treasured land.

23 "Prepare chains for my people,
for the land is bloodied by terrible crimes.
Jerusalem is filled with violence.
24 I will bring the most ruthless of nations
to occupy their homes.
I will break down their proud fortresses
and defile their sanctuaries.
25 Terror and trembling will overcome my people.
They will look for peace but not find it.
26 Calamity will follow calamity;
rumor will follow rumor.
They will look in vain
for a vision from the prophets.
They will receive no teaching from the priests
and no counsel from the leaders.
27 The king and the prince will stand helpless,
weeping in despair,
and the people's hands
will tremble with fear.
I will bring on them
the evil they have done to others,
and they will receive the punishment
they so richly deserve.
Then they will know that I am the LORD."

IDOLATRY IN THE TEMPLE

8 Then on September 17,* during the sixth year
of King Jehoiachin's captivity, while the leaders
of Judah were in my home, the Sovereign LORD took
hold of me. 2 I saw a figure that appeared to be a man.*

8:1 Hebrew *on the fifth [day] of the sixth month,* of the ancient Hebrew lunar calendar. This event occurred on September 17, 592 B.C.; also see note on 1:1. **8:2a** As in Greek version; Hebrew reads *appeared to be fire.* **8:2b** Or *like burnished metal.*

7:14 The trumpet calls. The devastation will be so complete they will not be able to defend themselves. No one will be able to respond to the trumpet call to war.

From what appeared to be his waist down, he looked
like a burning flame. From the waist up he looked like
gleaming amber.* 3 He reached out what seemed to be
a hand and took me by the hair. Then the Spirit lifted
me up into the sky and transported me to Jerusalem
in a vision from God. I was taken to the north gate of
the inner courtyard of the Temple, where there is a
large idol that has made the LORD very jealous. 4 Sud-
denly, the glory of the God of Israel was there, just as I
had seen it before in the valley.
5 Then the LORD said to me, "Son of man, look to-
ward the north." So I looked, and there to the north,
beside the entrance to the gate near the altar, stood
the idol that had made the LORD so jealous.
6 "Son of man," he said, "do you see what they are
doing? Do you see the detestable sins the people of Is-
rael are committing to drive me from my Temple? But
come, and you will see even more detestable sins than
these!" 7 Then he brought me to the door of the Temple
courtyard, where I could see a hole in the wall. 8 He
said to me, "Now, son of man, dig into the wall." So I
dug into the wall and found a hidden doorway.
9 "Go in," he said, "and see the wicked and detestable
sins they are committing in there!" 10 So I went in and
saw the walls covered with engravings of all kinds of
crawling animals and detestable creatures. I also saw
the various idols* worshiped by the people of Israel.
11 Seventy leaders of Israel were standing there with
Jaazaniah son of Shaphan in the center. Each of them
held an incense burner, from which a cloud of incense
rose above their heads.
12 Then the LORD said to me, "Son of man, have you
seen what the leaders of Israel are doing with their
idols in dark rooms? They are saying, 'The LORD
doesn't see us; he has deserted our land!'" 13 Then the
LORD added, "Come, and I will show you even more
detestable sins than these!"
14 He brought me to the north gate of the LORD's
Temple, and some women were sitting there, weeping
for the god Tammuz. 15 "Have you seen this?" he asked.
"But I will show you even more detestable sins than
these!"
16 Then he brought me into the inner courtyard of
the LORD's Temple. At the entrance to the sanctuary,
between the entry room and the bronze altar, there
were about twenty-five men with their backs to the
sanctuary of the LORD. They were facing east, bowing
low to the ground, worshiping the sun!
17 "Have you seen this, son of man?" he asked. "Is
it nothing to the people of Judah that they commit
these detestable sins, leading the whole nation into
violence, thumbing their noses at me, and provoking
my anger? 18 Therefore, I will respond in fury. I will
neither pity nor spare them. And though they cry for
mercy, I will not listen."

THE SLAUGHTER OF IDOLATERS

9 Then the LORD thundered, "Bring on the men ap-
pointed to punish the city! Tell them to bring their
weapons with them!" 2 Six men soon appeared from
the upper gate that faces north, each carrying a dead-
ly weapon in his hand. With them was a man dressed
in linen, who carried a writer's case at his side. They
all went into the Temple courtyard and stood beside
the bronze altar.
3 Then the glory of the God of Israel rose up from
between the cherubim, where it had rested, and
moved to the entrance of the Temple. And the LORD
called to the man dressed in linen who was carrying
the writer's case. 4 He said to him, "Walk through the
streets of Jerusalem and put a mark on the foreheads
of all who weep and sigh because of the detestable
sins being committed in their city."
5 Then I heard the LORD say to the other men, "Fol-
low him through the city and kill everyone whose
forehead is not marked. Show no mercy; have no
pity! 6 Kill them all—old and young, girls and women
and little children. But do not touch anyone with the
mark. Begin right here at the Temple." So they began
by killing the seventy leaders.
7 "Defile the Temple!" the LORD commanded. "Fill its
courtyards with corpses. Go!" So they went and began
killing throughout the city.
8 While they were out killing, I was all alone. I fell
face down on the ground and cried out, "O Sovereign
LORD! Will your fury against Jerusalem wipe out
everyone left in Israel?"
9 Then he said to me, "The sins of the people of Isra-
el and Judah are very, very great. The entire land is
full of murder; the city is filled with injustice. They are
saying, 'The LORD doesn't see it! The LORD has aban-
doned the land!' 10 So I will not spare them or have any
pity on them. I will fully repay them for all they have
done."
11 Then the man in linen clothing, who carried the
writer's case, reported back and said, "I have done as
you commanded."

THE LORD'S GLORY LEAVES THE TEMPLE

10 In my vision I saw what appeared to be a throne
of blue lapis lazuli above the crystal surface
over the heads of the cherubim. 2 Then the LORD spoke
to the man in linen clothing and said, "Go between
the whirling wheels beneath the cherubim, and take
a handful of burning coals and scatter them over the
city." He did this as I watched.
3 The cherubim were standing at the south end of the
Temple when the man went in, and the cloud of glory
filled the inner courtyard. 4 Then the glory of the LORD
rose up from above the cherubim and went over to the
entrance of the Temple. The Temple was filled with

8:10 The Hebrew term (literally *round things*) probably alludes to dung.

8:3 transported me to Jerusalem. In a dream-vision, God showed Ezekiel the idolatry practiced in the temple by those still living in Jerusalem.

8:11 Seventy elders. Ezekiel was disgusted to find 70 Jewish elders worshipping the animal gods of Egypt while seeking release from Babylonian domination. Ironically, seventy leaders had confirmed the Mosaic Covenant that delivered the Hebrews from bondage to Egyptian gods (Exod 24:1,9). Facing slavery once again, they appealed to Egypt's gods for help. Such an incredible flip-flop goes to show just how far downhill the people had gone (cp. Deut 4:16-19; Lev 11:40-42). Having lost faith in God, they concluded that, because Babylon had conquered Judah, God had forsaken them (9:9). Furthermore, this passage shows that what people do in secret shows their real character. The elders claimed to be believers but acted exactly like unbelievers in the Lord.

8:14 Tammuz. According to Mesopotamian religion, Tammuz was a god who died every winter and was reborn every spring. The pagan ceremony of weeping for Tammuz was believed to aid the arrival of a fertile spring.

9:8 your fury. Ezekiel, like Moses, interceded with God to ease the severity of His punishment (Ezek. 4:14; 11:13).

10:2 take a handful of burning coals. In the temple, hot coals from the altar were used with incense to form a cloud that separated the people from God's glory. Angels—much like priests—perform the same ceremony in heaven to create a cloud of smoke around God's throne (v. 1). Here, God is about to remove His glory from the temple because of Israel's sins. The spreading of these coals anticipates Jerusalem's burning (2 Kings 25:9), a visible sign of God's departure.

this cloud of glory, and the courtyard glowed brightly with the glory of the LORD. 5 The moving wings of the cherubim sounded like the voice of God Almighty* and could be heard even in the outer courtyard.

6 The LORD said to the man in linen clothing, "Go between the cherubim and take some burning coals from between the wheels." So the man went in and stood beside one of the wheels. 7 Then one of the cherubim reached out his hand and took some live coals from the fire burning among them. He put the coals into the hands of the man in linen clothing, and the man took them and went out. 8 (All the cherubim had what looked like human hands under their wings.)

9 I looked, and each of the four cherubim had a wheel beside him, and the wheels sparkled like beryl. 10 All four wheels looked alike and were made the same; each wheel had a second wheel turning crosswise within it. 11 The cherubim could move in any of the four directions they faced, without turning as they moved. They went straight in the direction they faced, never turning aside. 12 Both the cherubim and the wheels were covered with eyes. The cherubim had eyes all over their bodies, including their hands, their backs, and their wings. 13 I heard someone refer to the wheels as "the whirling wheels." 14 Each of the four cherubim had four faces: the first was the face of an ox,* the second was a human face, the third was the face of a lion, and the fourth was the face of an eagle.

15 Then the cherubim rose upward. These were the same living beings I had seen beside the Kebar River. 16 When the cherubim moved, the wheels moved with them. When they lifted their wings to fly, the wheels stayed beside them. 17 When the cherubim stopped, the wheels stopped. When they flew upward, the wheels rose up, for the spirit of the living beings was in the wheels.

18 Then the glory of the LORD moved out from the entrance of the Temple and hovered above the cherubim. 19 And as I watched, the cherubim flew with their wheels to the east gate of the LORD's Temple. And the glory of the God of Israel hovered above them.

20 These were the same living beings I had seen beneath the God of Israel when I was by the Kebar River. I knew they were cherubim, 21 for each had four faces and four wings and what looked like human hands under their wings. 22 And their faces were just like the faces of the beings I had seen at the Kebar, and they traveled straight ahead, just as the others had.

JUDGMENT ON ISRAEL'S LEADERS

11 Then the Spirit lifted me and brought me to the east gateway of the LORD's Temple, where I saw twenty-five prominent men of the city. Among them were Jaazaniah son of Azzur and Pelatiah son of Benaiah, who were leaders among the people.

2 The Spirit said to me, "Son of man, these are the men who are planning evil and giving wicked counsel in this city. 3 They say to the people, 'Is it not a good time to build houses? This city is like an iron pot. We are safe inside it like meat in a pot.*' 4 Therefore, son of man, prophesy against them loudly and clearly."

5 Then the Spirit of the LORD came upon me, and he told me to say, "This is what the LORD says to the people of Israel: I know what you are saying, for I know every thought that comes into your minds. 6 You have murdered many in this city and filled its streets with the dead.

7 "Therefore, this is what the Sovereign LORD says: This city is an iron pot all right, but the pieces of meat are the victims of your injustice. As for you, I will soon drag you from this pot. 8 I will bring on you the sword of war you so greatly fear, says the Sovereign LORD. 9 I will drive you out of Jerusalem and hand you over to foreigners, who will carry out my judgments against you. 10 You will be slaughtered all the way to the borders of Israel. I will execute judgment on you, and you will know that I am the LORD. 11 No, this city will not be an iron pot for you, and you will not be like meat safe inside it. I will judge you even to the borders of Israel, 12 and you will know that I am the LORD. For you have refused to obey my decrees and regulations; instead, you have copied the standards of the nations around you."

13 While I was still prophesying, Pelatiah son of Benaiah suddenly died. Then I fell face down on the ground and cried out, "O Sovereign LORD, are you going to kill everyone in Israel?"

HOPE FOR EXILED ISRAEL

14 Then this message came to me from the LORD: 15 "Son of man, the people still left in Jerusalem are talking about you and your relatives and all the people of Israel who are in exile. They are saying, 'Those people are far away from the LORD, so now he has given their land to us!'

16 "Therefore, tell the exiles, 'This is what the Sovereign LORD says: Although I have scattered you in the countries of the world, I will be a sanctuary to you during your time in exile. 17 I, the Sovereign LORD, will gather you back from the nations where you have been scattered, and I will give you the land of Israel once again.'

18 "When the people return to their homeland, they will remove every trace of their vile images and detestable idols. 19 And I will give them singleness of heart and put a new spirit within them. I will take away their stony, stubborn heart and give them a tender, responsive heart,* 20 so they will obey my decrees and regulations. Then they will truly be my people, and I will be their God. 21 But as for those who long for vile images and detestable idols, I will repay them fully for their sins. I, the Sovereign LORD, have spoken!"

10:5 Hebrew *El-Shaddai.* **10:14** Hebrew *the face of a cherub;* compare 1:10. **11:3** Hebrew *This city is the pot, and we are the meat.* **11:19** Hebrew *a heart of flesh.*

10:19 glory of the God of Israel hovered above them. Israel and Judah failed to keep the land holy, so God's glory left the temple and moved above the chariot-throne.

11:3 city is like an iron pot. Wishful thinkers believed that Jerusalem's walls were all the protection they needed. Not so (v. 11).

11:16 sanctuary. The people's prior conception of God's presence was tied to a place—the temple. Now, God made it clear that His presence went outside the temple's physical limitations.

11:19 give them singleness of heart and put a new spirit within them. God will bring the exiles back and will one day revive them to a spiritual depth the nation had never held. God will give new spirits, making them new creations (see 2 Cor. 5:17).

11:20 obey my decrees. When God restores Israel and Judah, the people will obey the Law of Moses.

THE LORD'S GLORY LEAVES JERUSALEM

22 Then the cherubim lifted their wings and rose into the air with their wheels beside them, and the glory of the God of Israel hovered above them. 23 Then the glory of the LORD went up from the city and stopped above the mountain to the east.

24 Afterward the Spirit of God carried me back again to Babylonia,* to the people in exile there. And so ended the vision of my visit to Jerusalem. 25 And I told the exiles everything the LORD had shown me.

SIGNS OF THE COMING EXILE

12 Again a message came to me from the LORD: 2 "Son of man, you live among rebels who have eyes but refuse to see. They have ears but refuse to hear. For they are a rebellious people.

3 "So now, son of man, pretend you are being sent into exile. Pack the few items an exile could carry, and leave your home to go somewhere else. Do this right in front of the people so they can see you. For perhaps they will pay attention to this, even though they are such rebels. 4 Bring your baggage outside during the day so they can watch you. Then in the evening, as they are watching, leave your house as captives do when they begin a long march to distant lands. 5 Dig a hole through the wall while they are watching and go out through it. 6 As they watch, lift your pack to your shoulders and walk away into the night. Cover your face so you cannot see the land you are leaving. For I have made you a sign for the people of Israel."

7 So I did as I was told. In broad daylight I brought my pack outside, filled with the things I might carry into exile. Then in the evening while the people looked on, I dug through the wall with my hands and went out into the night with my pack on my shoulder.

8 The next morning this message came to me from the LORD: 9 "Son of man, these rebels, the people of Israel, have asked you what all this means. 10 Say to them, 'This is what the Sovereign LORD says: These actions contain a message for King Zedekiah in Jerusalem* and for all the people of Israel.' 11 Explain that your actions are a sign to show what will soon happen to them, for they will be driven into exile as captives.

12 "Even Zedekiah will leave Jerusalem at night through a hole in the wall, taking only what he can carry with him. He will cover his face, and his eyes will not see the land he is leaving. 13 Then I will throw my net over him and capture him in my snare. I will bring him to Babylon, the land of the Babylonians,* though he will never see it, and he will die there. 14 I will scatter his servants and warriors to the four winds and send the sword after them. 15 And when I scatter them among the nations, they will know that I am the LORD. 16 But I will spare a few of them from death by war, famine, or disease, so they can confess all their detestable sins to their captors. Then they will know that I am the LORD."

17 Then this message came to me from the LORD: 18 "Son of man, tremble as you eat your food. Shake with fear as you drink your water. 19 Tell the people, 'This is what the Sovereign LORD says concerning those living in Israel and Jerusalem: They will eat their food with trembling and sip their water in despair, for their land will be stripped bare because of their violence. 20 The cities will be destroyed and the farmland made desolate. Then you will know that I am the LORD.'"

A NEW PROVERB FOR ISRAEL

21 Again a message came to me from the LORD: 22 "Son of man, you've heard that proverb they quote in Israel: 'Time passes, and prophecies come to nothing.' 23 Tell the people, 'This is what the Sovereign LORD says: I will put an end to this proverb, and you will soon stop quoting it.' Now give them this new proverb to replace the old one: 'The time has come for every prophecy to be fulfilled!'

24 "There will be no more false visions and flattering predictions in Israel. 25 For I am the LORD! If I say it, it will happen. There will be no more delays, you rebels of Israel. I will fulfill my threat of destruction in your own lifetime. I, the Sovereign LORD, have spoken!"

26 Then this message came to me from the LORD: 27 "Son of man, the people of Israel are saying, 'He's talking about the distant future. His visions won't come true for a long, long time.' 28 Therefore, tell them, 'This is what the Sovereign LORD says: No more delay! I will now do everything I have threatened. I, the Sovereign LORD, have spoken!'"

JUDGMENT AGAINST FALSE PROPHETS

13 Then this message came to me from the LORD: 2 "Son of man, prophesy against the false prophets of Israel who are inventing their own prophecies. Say to them, 'Listen to the word of the LORD. 3 This is what the Sovereign LORD says: What sorrow awaits the false prophets who are following their own imaginations and have seen nothing at all!'

4 "O people of Israel, these prophets of yours are like jackals digging in the ruins. 5 They have done nothing to repair the breaks in the walls around the nation. They have not helped it to stand firm in battle on the day of the LORD. 6 Instead, they have told lies and made false predictions. They say, 'This message is from the LORD,' even though the LORD never sent them. And yet they expect him to fulfill their prophecies! 7 Can your visions be anything but false if you claim, 'This message is from the LORD,' when I have not even spoken to you?

8 "Therefore, this is what the Sovereign LORD says: Because what you say is false and your visions are a lie, I will stand against you, says the Sovereign LORD. 9 I will raise my fist against all the prophets who see false visions and make lying predictions, and they will be banished from the community of Israel. I will

11:24 Or *Chaldea.* 12:10 Hebrew *the prince in Jerusalem;* similarly in 12:12. 12:13 Or *Chaldeans.*

12:2 eyes but refuse to see. The central theme of chapters 8 and 9 is the Israelites' claim that "The Lord doesn't see us; he has deserted our land!" (8:12; 9:9). In chapters 10 and 11, Ezekiel not only sees what the Lord sees, but forwards the message. Still, they dogmatically stick to their defenses, even though they have been told that these are no defenses at all. It is important to remember that the Lord not only sees us now, but he sees how we will respond in the future to what He graciously allows.

12:8 The next morning this message came to me. The very next day God evaluated the success of Ezekiel's unusual demonstration of obedience. Ezekiel had followed God's instruction (v. 7).

12:27 the distant future. The people thought the prophecy's fulfillment was far off; it wasn't.

13:6 to fulfill their prophecies. Accuracy was the mark of true prophets. False prophets spoke lies.

blot their names from Israel's record books, and they will never again set foot in their own land. Then you will know that I am the Sovereign LORD.

[10] "This will happen because these evil prophets deceive my people by saying, 'All is peaceful' when there is no peace at all! It's as if the people have built a flimsy wall, and these prophets are trying to reinforce it by covering it with whitewash! [11] Tell these whitewashers that their wall will soon fall down. A heavy rainstorm will undermine it; great hailstones and mighty winds will knock it down. [12] And when the wall falls, the people will cry out, 'What happened to your whitewash?'

[13] "Therefore, this is what the Sovereign LORD says: I will sweep away your whitewashed wall with a storm of indignation, with a great flood of anger, and with hailstones of fury. [14] I will break down your wall right to its foundation, and when it falls, it will crush you. Then you will know that I am the LORD. [15] At last my anger against the wall and those who covered it with whitewash will be satisfied. Then I will say to you: 'The wall and those who whitewashed it are both gone. [16] They were lying prophets who claimed peace would come to Jerusalem when there was no peace. I, the Sovereign LORD, have spoken!'

JUDGMENT AGAINST FALSE WOMEN PROPHETS

[17] "Now, son of man, speak out against the women who prophesy from their own imaginations. [18] This is what the Sovereign LORD says: What sorrow awaits you women who are ensnaring the souls of my people, young and old alike. You tie magic charms on their wrists and furnish them with magic veils. Do you think you can trap others without bringing destruction on yourselves? [19] You bring shame on me among my people for a few handfuls of barley or a piece of bread. By lying to my people who love to listen to lies, you kill those who should not die, and you promise life to those who should not live.

[20] "This is what the Sovereign LORD says: I am against all your magic charms, which you use to ensnare my people like birds. I will tear them from your arms, setting my people free like birds set free from a cage. [21] I will tear off the magic veils and save my people from your grasp. They will no longer be your victims. Then you will know that I am the LORD. [22] You have discouraged the righteous with your lies, but I didn't want them to be sad. And you have encouraged the wicked by promising them life, even though they continue in their sins. [23] Because of all this, you will no longer talk of seeing visions that you never saw, nor will you make predictions. For I will rescue my people from your grasp. Then you will know that I am the LORD."

THE IDOLATRY OF ISRAEL'S LEADERS

14 Then some of the leaders of Israel visited me, and while they were sitting with me, [2] this message came to me from the LORD: [3] "Son of man, these leaders have set up idols* in their hearts. They have embraced things that will make them fall into sin. Why should I listen to their requests? [4] Tell them, 'This is what the Sovereign LORD says: The people of Israel have set up idols in their hearts and fallen into sin, and then they go to a prophet asking for a message. So I, the LORD, will give them the kind of answer their great idolatry deserves. [5] I will do this to capture the minds and hearts of all my people who have turned from me to worship their detestable idols.'

[6] "Therefore, tell the people of Israel, 'This is what the Sovereign LORD says: Repent and turn away from your idols, and stop all your detestable sins. [7] I, the LORD, will answer all those, both Israelites and foreigners, who reject me and set up idols in their hearts and so fall into sin, and who then come to a prophet asking for my advice. [8] I will turn against such people and make a terrible example of them, eliminating them from among my people. Then you will know that I am the LORD.

[9] "'And if a prophet is deceived into giving a message, it is because I, the LORD, have deceived that prophet. I will lift my fist against such prophets and cut them off from the community of Israel. [10] False prophets and those who seek their guidance will all be punished for their sins. [11] In this way, the people of Israel will learn not to stray from me, polluting themselves with sin. They will be my people, and I will be their God. I, the Sovereign LORD, have spoken!'"

THE CERTAINTY OF THE LORD'S JUDGMENT

[12] Then this message came to me from the LORD: [13] "Son of man, suppose the people of a country were to sin against me, and I lifted my fist to crush them, cutting off their food supply and sending a famine to destroy both people and animals. [14] Even if Noah, Daniel, and Job were there, their righteousness would save no one but themselves, says the Sovereign LORD.

[15] "Or suppose I were to send wild animals to invade the country, kill the people, and make the land too desolate and dangerous to pass through. [16] As surely as I live, says the Sovereign LORD, even if those three men were there, they wouldn't be able to save their own sons or daughters. They alone would be saved, but the land would be made desolate.

[17] "Or suppose I were to bring war against the land, and I sent enemy armies to destroy both people and animals. [18] As surely as I live, says the Sovereign LORD, even if those three men were there, they wouldn't be able to save their own sons or daughters. They alone would be saved.

[19] "Or suppose I were to pour out my fury by sending an epidemic into the land, and the disease killed people and animals alike. [20] As surely as I live, says the Sovereign LORD, even if Noah, Daniel, and Job were there, they wouldn't be able to save their own sons or daughters. They alone would be saved by their righteousness.

14:3 The Hebrew term (literally *round things*) probably alludes to dung; also in 14:4, 5, 6, 7.

13:10 by covering it with whitewash. A laborer used white paste to cover inconsistencies in a rock-hewn wall. Likewise, God's people focused on appearances rather than the condition of their hearts. God is concerned about the heart (see 1 Sam. 16:7).

13:11 A heavy rainstorm will undermine it . . . hailstones. Reverting back to the storm imagery, Ezekiel described how their sin would be exposed (1:4).

14:3 Why should I listen to their requests? Pagans seeking advice from Ezekiel seemed hypocritical. Why consult two opposing sources?

14:4 fall into sin. The idolatrous people tripped on their own sins—a costly mistake that resulted in death.

14:6 Repent and turn away. Ezekiel urged repentance while there was still time. Repentance is turning from sin to God. Without repentance, there is no real faith in God or Jesus.

14:14,20 Noah, Daniel, and Job. Even biblical characters who sought after God's heart would have no saving influence over such a wicked society. They could save only themselves.

21 "Now this is what the Sovereign LORD says: How
terrible it will be when all four of these dreadful pun-
ishments fall upon Jerusalem—war, famine, wild
animals, and disease—destroying all her people and
animals. 22 Yet there will be survivors, and they will
come here to join you as exiles in Babylon. You will
see with your own eyes how wicked they are, and
then you will feel better about what I have done to
Jerusalem. 23 When you meet them and see their be-
havior, you will understand that these things are not
being done to Israel without cause. I, the Sovereign
LORD, have spoken!"

JERUSALEM—A USELESS VINE

15 Then this message came to me from the LORD:
2 "Son of man, how does a grapevine compare to
a tree? Is a vine's wood as useful as the wood of a tree?
3 Can its wood be used for making things, like pegs to
hang up pots and pans? 4 No, it can only be used for
fuel, and even as fuel, it burns too quickly. 5 Vines are
useless both before and after being put into the fire!
6 "And this is what the Sovereign LORD says: The
people of Jerusalem are like grapevines growing
among the trees of the forest. Since they are useless,
I have thrown them on the fire to be burned. 7 And I
will see to it that if they escape from one fire, they will
fall into another. When I turn against them, you will
know that I am the LORD. 8 And I will make the land
desolate because my people have been unfaithful to
me. I, the Sovereign LORD, have spoken!"

JERUSALEM—AN UNFAITHFUL WIFE

16 Then another message came to me from the
LORD: 2 "Son of man, confront Jerusalem with
her detestable sins. 3 Give her this message from the
Sovereign LORD: You are nothing but a Canaanite!
Your father was an Amorite and your mother a Hit-
tite. 4 On the day you were born, no one cared about
you. Your umbilical cord was not cut, and you were
never washed, rubbed with salt, and wrapped in
cloth. 5 No one had the slightest interest in you; no one
pitied you or cared for you. On the day you were born,
you were unwanted, dumped in a field and left to die.
6 "But I came by and saw you there, helplessly kick-
ing about in your own blood. As you lay there, I said,
'Live!' 7 And I helped you to thrive like a plant in the
field. You grew up and became a beautiful jewel. Your
breasts became full, and your body hair grew, but you
were still naked. 8 And when I passed by again, I saw
that you were old enough for love. So I wrapped my
cloak around you to cover your nakedness and de-
clared my marriage vows. I made a covenant with
you, says the Sovereign LORD, and you became mine.
9 "Then I bathed you and washed off your blood,
and I rubbed fragrant oils into your skin. 10 I gave you
expensive clothing of fine linen and silk, beautiful-
ly embroidered, and sandals made of fine goatskin
leather. 11 I gave you lovely jewelry, bracelets, beauti-
ful necklaces, 12 a ring for your nose, earrings for your
ears, and a lovely crown for your head. 13 And so you
were adorned with gold and silver. Your clothes were
made of fine linen and costly fabric and were beau-
tifully embroidered. You ate the finest foods—choice
flour, honey, and olive oil—and became more beau-
tiful than ever. You looked like a queen, and so you
were! 14 Your fame soon spread throughout the world
because of your beauty. I dressed you in my splendor
and perfected your beauty, says the Sovereign LORD.
15 "But you thought your fame and beauty were
your own. So you gave yourself as a prostitute to ev-
ery man who came along. Your beauty was theirs for
the asking. 16 You used the lovely things I gave you to
make shrines for idols, where you played the prosti-
tute. Unbelievable! How could such a thing ever hap-
pen? 17 You took the very jewels and gold and silver
ornaments I had given you and made statues of men
and worshiped them. This is adultery against me!
18 You used the beautifully embroidered clothes I gave
you to dress your idols. Then you used my special oil
and my incense to worship them. 19 Imagine it! You set
before them as a sacrifice the choice flour, olive oil,
and honey I had given you, says the Sovereign LORD.
20 "Then you took your sons and daughters—the
children you had borne to me—and sacrificed them
to your gods. Was your prostitution not enough?
21 Must you also slaughter my children by sacrificing
them to idols? 22 In all your years of adultery and de-
testable sin, you have not once remembered the days
long ago when you lay naked in a field, kicking about
in your own blood.
23 "What sorrow awaits you, says the Sovereign
LORD. In addition to all your other wickedness, 24 you
built a pagan shrine and put altars to idols in every
town square. 25 On every street corner you defiled
your beauty, offering your body to every passerby in
an endless stream of prostitution. 26 Then you added
lustful Egypt to your lovers, provoking my anger with
your increasing promiscuity. 27 That is why I struck
you with my fist and reduced your boundaries. I
handed you over to your enemies, the Philistines, and
even they were shocked by your lewd conduct. 28 You
have prostituted yourself with the Assyrians, too. It
seems you can never find enough new lovers! And af-
ter your prostitution there, you still were not satisfied.
29 You added to your lovers by embracing Babylonia,*
the land of merchants, but you still weren't satisfied.
30 "What a sick heart you have, says the Sovereign
LORD, to do such things as these, acting like a shame-
less prostitute. 31 You build your pagan shrines on
every street corner and your altars to idols in every
square. In fact, you have been worse than a prostitute,
so eager for sin that you have not even demanded

16:29 Or *Chaldea.*

15:2 vine's wood. Isaiah called Israel God's vineyard (see also John 15), but Ezekiel sarcastically pointed out that God would burn the branches.

15:7 they will fall into another. Jerusalem's remaining inhabitants considered escaping the initial wave of capture in 597 B.C. Yet, total destruction was only a few years away.

16:3 Jerusalem. This city was also called the fortress of Zion and remained a Canaanite hotspot until David completely conquered it (1 Chron. 11:4-9).

16:8 wrapped my cloak around you. God's relationship with Israel, as with the church, is analogous to marriage (see Eph. 5:22-32). He found an orphan girl, Jerusalem, and loved her as His wife.

16:15 fame and beauty were your own. God's gift to Jerusalem became a pitfall as the city asserted its independence.

16:16-19 You took. Israel, the Lord's precious wife, took everything that He had provided (the best clothing, food, and even precious jewelry) and pawned it in service to her idols. The imagery of melting precious metal into idols recalls episodes in Israel's past when it similarly prostituted itself (Exod. 32:2-4; Judg. 8:24-27).

payment. 32 Yes, you are an adulterous wife who takes in strangers instead of her own husband. 33 Prostitutes charge for their services—but not you! You give gifts to your lovers, bribing them to come and have sex with you. 34 So you are the opposite of other prostitutes. You pay your lovers instead of their paying you!

JUDGMENT ON JERUSALEM'S PROSTITUTION

35 "Therefore, you prostitute, listen to this message from the LORD! 36 This is what the Sovereign LORD says: Because you have poured out your lust and exposed yourself in prostitution to all your lovers, and because you have worshiped detestable idols,* and because you have slaughtered your children as sacrifices to your gods, 37 this is what I am going to do. I will gather together all your allies—the lovers with whom you have sinned, both those you loved and those you hated—and I will strip you naked in front of them so they can stare at you. 38 I will punish you for your murder and adultery. I will cover you with blood in my jealous fury. 39 Then I will give you to these many nations who are your lovers, and they will destroy you. They will knock down your pagan shrines and the altars to your idols. They will strip you and take your beautiful jewels, leaving you stark naked. 40 They will band together in a mob to stone you and cut you up with swords. 41 They will burn your homes and punish you in front of many women. I will stop your prostitution and end your payments to your many lovers.

42 "Then at last my fury against you will be spent, and my jealous anger will subside. I will be calm and will not be angry with you anymore. 43 But first, because you have not remembered your youth but have angered me by doing all these evil things, I will fully repay you for all of your sins, says the Sovereign LORD. For you have added lewd acts to all your detestable sins. 44 Everyone who makes up proverbs will say of you, 'Like mother, like daughter.' 45 For your mother loathed her husband and her children, and so do you. And you are exactly like your sisters, for they despised their husbands and their children. Truly your mother was a Hittite and your father an Amorite.

46 "Your older sister was Samaria, who lived with her daughters in the north. Your younger sister was Sodom, who lived with her daughters in the south. 47 But you have not merely sinned as they did. You quickly surpassed them in corruption. 48 As surely as I live, says the Sovereign LORD, Sodom and her daughters were never as wicked as you and your daughters. 49 Sodom's sins were pride, gluttony, and laziness, while the poor and needy suffered outside her door. 50 She was proud and committed detestable sins, so I wiped her out, as you have seen.*

51 "Even Samaria did not commit half your sins. You have done far more detestable things than your sisters ever did. They seem righteous compared to you. 52 Shame on you! Your sins are so terrible that you make your sisters seem righteous, even virtuous.

53 "But someday I will restore the fortunes of Sodom and Samaria, and I will restore you, too. 54 Then you will be truly ashamed of everything you have done, for your sins make them feel good in comparison. 55 Yes, your sisters, Sodom and Samaria, and all their people will be restored, and at that time you also will be restored. 56 In your proud days you held Sodom in contempt. 57 But now your greater wickedness has been exposed to all the world, and you are the one who is scorned—by Edom* and all her neighbors and by Philistia. 58 This is your punishment for all your lewdness and detestable sins, says the LORD.

59 "Now this is what the Sovereign LORD says: I will give you what you deserve, for you have taken your solemn vows lightly by breaking your covenant. 60 Yet I will remember the covenant I made with you when you were young, and I will establish an everlasting covenant with you. 61 Then you will remember with shame all the evil you have done. I will make your sisters, Samaria and Sodom, to be your daughters, even though they are not part of our covenant. 62 And I will reaffirm my covenant with you, and you will know that I am the LORD. 63 You will remember your sins and cover your mouth in silent shame when I forgive you of all that you have done. I, the Sovereign LORD, have spoken!"

A STORY OF TWO EAGLES

17 Then this message came to me from the LORD: 2 "Son of man, give this riddle, and tell this story to the people of Israel. 3 Give them this message from the Sovereign LORD:

"A great eagle with broad wings and long feathers,
covered with many-colored plumage,
came to Lebanon.
He seized the top of a cedar tree
4 and plucked off its highest branch.
He carried it away to a city filled with merchants.
He planted it in a city of traders.
5 He also took a seedling from the land
and planted it in fertile soil.
He placed it beside a broad river,
where it could grow like a willow tree.
6 It took root there and
grew into a low, spreading vine.
Its branches turned up toward the eagle,
and its roots grew down into the ground.
It produced strong branches
and put out shoots.
7 But then another great eagle came
with broad wings and full plumage.

16:36 The Hebrew term (literally *round things*) probably alludes to dung. **16:50** As in a few Hebrew manuscripts and Greek version; Masoretic Text reads *as I have seen.* **16:57** As in many Hebrew manuscripts and Syriac version; Masoretic Text reads *Aram.*

16:37 I will gather together. God's sovereignty over the scenario allowed Him to turn Jerusalem's so-called lovers into enemies.

16:44 proverbs. The Lord is fond of turning Israel's proverbs on their heads (12:21-25; 14:8; 18:2). Jerusalem shared a common bond and a common fate with the rebellious Canaanite people who first inhabited the land (v. 45) and were banished by Joshua (Gen. 15:16; Josh. 3:10). Yet, the Lord will remember His covenant with them (v. 60).

16:47 surpassed . . . in corruption. Comparing a city to Sodom was the ultimate insult (Jer. 23:14).

16:49 poor and needy suffered. Sodom focused completely on her own needs and didn't care for those who needed help.

16:56 held Sodom in contempt. Ezekiel reminisced about Jerusalem's sense of superiority over Sodom. The people never even mentioned the name Sodom for fear of lowering themselves to Sodom's standards.

17:2-10 The prophet contrasted the imagery of a vine (Judah) with that of two powerful eagles: Babylon (v. 3) and Egypt (v. 7). He demonstrated how Judah's varying allegiances played a role in Judah's downfall. King Zedekiah (v. 15) recruited Egypt to help rebel against Babylon (2 Kings 24:20); that proved to be a total failure. Ezekiel predicted the king's revolt and the resulting Babylonian retribution nearly three years in advance (vv. 19-21).

So the vine now sent its roots and branches
toward him for water,
8 even though it was already planted in good soil
and had plenty of water
so it could grow into a splendid vine
and produce rich leaves and luscious fruit.

9 "So now the Sovereign LORD asks:
Will this vine grow and prosper?
No! I will pull it up, roots and all!
I will cut off its fruit
and let its leaves wither and die.
I will pull it up easily
without a strong arm or a large army.
10 But when the vine is transplanted,
will it thrive?
No, it will wither away
when the east wind blows against it.
It will die in the same good soil
where it had grown so well."

THE RIDDLE EXPLAINED

11 Then this message came to me from the LORD: 12 "Say
to these rebels of Israel: Don't you understand the
meaning of this riddle of the eagles? The king of
Babylon came to Jerusalem, took away her king and
princes, and brought them to Babylon. 13 He made a
treaty with a member of the royal family and forced
him to take an oath of loyalty. He also exiled Israel's
most influential leaders, 14 so Israel would not become
strong again and revolt. Only by keeping her treaty
with Babylon could Israel survive.
15 "Nevertheless, this man of Israel's royal family
rebelled against Babylon, sending ambassadors to
Egypt to request a great army and many horses. Can
Israel break her sworn treaties like that and get away
with it? 16 No! For as surely as I live, says the Sovereign
LORD, the king of Israel will die in Babylon, the land of
the king who put him in power and whose treaty he
disregarded and broke. 17 Pharaoh and all his mighty
army will fail to help Israel when the king of Bab-
ylon lays siege to Jerusalem again and destroys many
lives. 18 For the king of Israel disregarded his treaty
and broke it after swearing to obey; therefore, he will
not escape.
19 "So this is what the Sovereign LORD says: As sure-
ly as I live, I will punish him for breaking my cov-
enant and disregarding the solemn oath he made in
my name. 20 I will throw my net over him and capture
him in my snare. I will bring him to Babylon and put
him on trial for this treason against me. 21 And all his
best warriors* will be killed in battle, and those who
survive will be scattered to the four winds. Then you
will know that I, the LORD, have spoken.
22 "This is what the Sovereign LORD says: I will take
a branch from the top of a tall cedar, and I will plant
it on the top of Israel's highest mountain. 23 It will
become a majestic cedar, sending forth its branches
and producing seed. Birds of every sort will nest in
it, finding shelter in the shade of its branches. 24 And
all the trees will know that it is I, the LORD, who cuts
the tall tree down and makes the short tree grow tall.
It is I who makes the green tree wither and gives the
dead tree new life. I, the LORD, have spoken, and I will
do what I said!"

THE JUSTICE OF A RIGHTEOUS GOD

18 Then another message came to me from the
LORD: 2 "Why do you quote this proverb con-
cerning the land of Israel: 'The parents have eaten
sour grapes, but their children's mouths pucker at the
taste'? 3 As surely as I live, says the Sovereign LORD,
you will not quote this proverb anymore in Israel.
4 For all people are mine to judge—both parents and
children alike. And this is my rule: The person who
sins is the one who will die.
5 "Suppose a certain man is righteous and does
what is just and right. 6 He does not feast in the
mountains before Israel's idols* or worship them.
He does not commit adultery or have intercourse
with a woman during her menstrual period. 7 He is
a merciful creditor, not keeping the items given as
security by poor debtors. He does not rob the poor
but instead gives food to the hungry and provides
clothes for the needy. 8 He grants loans without
interest, stays away from injustice, is honest and
fair when judging others, 9 and faithfully obeys my
decrees and regulations. Anyone who does these
things is just and will surely live, says the Sovereign
LORD.
10 "But suppose that man has a son who grows up
to be a robber or murderer and refuses to do what is
right. 11 And that son does all the evil things his father
would never do—he worships idols on the moun-
tains, commits adultery, 12 oppresses the poor and
helpless, steals from debtors by refusing to let them
redeem their security, worships idols, commits de-
testable sins, 13 and lends money at excessive interest.
Should such a sinful person live? No! He must die and
must take full blame.
14 "But suppose that sinful son, in turn, has a son
who sees his father's wickedness and decides against
that kind of life. 15 This son refuses to worship idols
on the mountains and does not commit adultery.
16 He does not exploit the poor, but instead is fair to
debtors and does not rob them. He gives food to the
hungry and provides clothes for the needy. 17 He helps
the poor,* does not lend money at interest, and obeys
all my regulations and decrees. Such a person will
not die because of his father's sins; he will surely live.
18 But the father will die for his many sins—for being
cruel, robbing people, and doing what was clearly
wrong among his people.
19 "'What?' you ask. 'Doesn't the child pay for the
parent's sins?' No! For if the child does what is just
and right and keeps my decrees, that child will surely

17:21 As in many Hebrew manuscripts; Masoretic Text reads *his fleeing warriors.* The meaning is uncertain. 18:6 The Hebrew term (literally *round things*) probably alludes to dung; also in 18:12, 15. 18:17 Greek version reads *He refuses to do evil.*

17:22 I will plant it on the top of Israel's highest mountain. In the last days, God will restore Jerusalem as chief of the world's cities. The high mountain is Zion, the mount on which Jerusalem rests. The cedar tree in the image represents the beauty and majesty of the city when God restores it.

18:2 sour grapes. This was a popular saying that implied that it was inevitable that a child would suffer blame for a parent's sins. Once again, God turns this proverb upside down (12:21; 14:8; 16:44).

18:4 all people are mine to judge. God contrasted a common saying with His sovereign command. Individuals would be accountable for their own sins.

18:9 will surely live. Ezekiel gave God's decree about the physical, not eternal, context of life and death (Deut. 30:15-20). He further illustrated how righteousness is rewarded on its own merit despite family history.

live. 20 The person who sins is the one who will die.
The child will not be punished for the parent's sins,
and the parent will not be punished for the child's
sins. Righteous people will be rewarded for their own
righteous behavior, and wicked people will be pun-
ished for their own wickedness. 21 But if wicked peo-
ple turn away from all their sins and begin to obey my
decrees and do what is just and right, they will surely
live and not die. 22 All their past sins will be forgot-
ten, and they will live because of the righteous things
they have done.
23 "Do you think that I like to see wicked people die?
says the Sovereign LORD. Of course not! I want them
to turn from their wicked ways and live. 24 However, if
righteous people turn from their righteous behavior
and start doing sinful things and act like other sin-
ners, should they be allowed to live? No, of course not!
All their righteous acts will be forgotten, and they
will die for their sins.
25 "Yet you say, 'The Lord isn't doing what's right!'
Listen to me, O people of Israel. Am I the one not do-
ing what's right, or is it you? 26 When righteous peo-
ple turn from their righteous behavior and start do-
ing sinful things, they will die for it. Yes, they will die
because of their sinful deeds. 27 And if wicked people
turn from their wickedness, obey the law, and do what
is just and right, they will save their lives. 28 They will
live because they thought it over and decided to turn
from their sins. Such people will not die. 29 And yet
the people of Israel keep saying, 'The Lord isn't doing
what's right!' O people of Israel, it is you who are not
doing what's right, not I.
30 "Therefore, I will judge each of you, O people of
Israel, according to your actions, says the Sovereign
LORD. Repent, and turn from your sins. Don't let them
destroy you! 31 Put all your rebellion behind you, and
find yourselves a new heart and a new spirit. For
why should you die, O people of Israel? 32 I don't want
you to die, says the Sovereign LORD. Turn back and
live!

A FUNERAL SONG FOR ISRAEL'S KINGS

19 "Sing this funeral song for the princes of Israel:

2 "What is your mother?
A lioness among lions!
She lay down among the young lions
and reared her cubs.
3 She raised one of her cubs
to become a strong young lion.
He learned to hunt and devour prey,
and he became a man-eater.
4 Then the nations heard about him,
and he was trapped in their pit.
They led him away with hooks
to the land of Egypt.

5 "When the lioness saw
that her hopes for him were gone,
she took another of her cubs
and taught him to be a strong young lion.
6 He prowled among the other lions
and stood out among them in his strength.
He learned to hunt and devour prey,
and he, too, became a man-eater.
7 He demolished fortresses*
and destroyed their towns and cities.
Their farms were desolated,
and their crops were destroyed.
The land and its people trembled in fear
when they heard him roar.
8 Then the armies of the nations attacked him,
surrounding him from every direction.
They threw a net over him
and captured him in their pit.
9 With hooks, they dragged him into a cage
and brought him before the king of Babylon.
They held him in captivity,
so his voice could never again be heard
on the mountains of Israel.

10 "Your mother was like a vine
planted by the water's edge.
It had lush, green foliage
because of the abundant water.
11 Its branches became strong—
strong enough to be a ruler's scepter.
It grew very tall,
towering above all others.
It stood out because of its height
and its many lush branches.
12 But the vine was uprooted in fury
and thrown down to the ground.
The desert wind dried up its fruit
and tore off its strong branches,
so that it withered
and was destroyed by fire.
13 Now the vine is transplanted to the wilderness,
where the ground is hard and dry.
14 A fire has burst out from its branches
and devoured its fruit.
Its remaining limbs are not
strong enough to be a ruler's scepter.

"This is a funeral song, and it will be used in a funer-
al."

THE REBELLION OF ISRAEL

20 On August 14,* during the seventh year of King
Jehoiachin's captivity, some of the leaders of Is-
rael came to request a message from the LORD. They
sat down in front of me to wait for his reply. 2 Then
this message came to me from the LORD: 3 "Son of man,

19:7 As in Greek version; Hebrew reads *He knew widows.* **20:1** Hebrew *In the fifth month, on the tenth day,* of the ancient Hebrew lunar calendar. This day was August 14, 591 B.C.; also see note on 1:1.

18:21 he will surely live and not die. Through repentance, a wicked person changes course.

18:32 I don't want you to die. In this summary statement, Ezekiel revealed an important aspect of God's character. God is consistent, not capricious, in His judgment. He is not willing for any to perish (see 2 Peter 3:9).

19:1 princes of Israel. Ezekiel, lamenting the fate of all the wicked people in Jerusalem, rehearsed a mournful poem.

19:3-14 Ezekiel used a pair of analogies to illustrate Jerusalem's demise. The cubs symbolized Kings Jehoahaz (v. 3) and Zedekiah (v. 5). They were full brothers (2 Kings 23:31; 24:18; Jer. 52:1). Their reigns were separated by Jehoiakim and Jehoiachin's reigns. Both died in captivity—Jehoahaz in Egypt (2 Kings 23:34) and Zedekiah in Babylon (2 Kings 25:7). The story of the vine (vv. 10-14) parallels Judah's rebellion that led to its uprooting.

20:1 August 14. The summer of 591 B.C., five years away from Jerusalem's fall. It had been almost eleven months since the last date given by Ezekiel (8:1). God will not dignify the elders request with an answer (cp. 14:3) other than an extended history lesson (vv. 5-45). To understand the present, the elders need to be reminded of God's gracious choice of Israel in spite of their rebellion during their years in Egypt and throughout their history to the present.

tell the leaders of Israel, 'This is what the Sovereign
LORD says: How dare you come to ask me for a mes-
sage? As surely as I live, says the Sovereign LORD, I
will tell you nothing!'
4 "Son of man, bring charges against them and con-
demn them. Make them realize how detestable the
sins of their ancestors really were. 5 Give them this
message from the Sovereign LORD: When I chose Is-
rael—when I revealed myself to the descendants
of Jacob in Egypt—I took a solemn oath that I, the
LORD, would be their God. 6 I took a solemn oath that
day that I would bring them out of Egypt to a land I
had discovered and explored for them—a good land,
a land flowing with milk and honey, the best of all
lands anywhere. 7 Then I said to them, 'Each of you,
get rid of the vile images you are so obsessed with. Do
not defile yourselves with the idols* of Egypt, for I am
the LORD your God.'
8 "But they rebelled against me and would not lis-
ten. They did not get rid of the vile images they were
obsessed with, or forsake the idols of Egypt. Then I
threatened to pour out my fury on them to satisfy my
anger while they were still in Egypt. 9 But I didn't do
it, for I acted to protect the honor of my name. I would
not allow shame to be brought on my name among
the surrounding nations who saw me reveal myself
by bringing the Israelites out of Egypt. 10 So I brought
them out of Egypt and led them into the wilderness.
11 There I gave them my decrees and regulations so
they could find life by keeping them. 12 And I gave
them my Sabbath days of rest as a sign between them
and me. It was to remind them that I am the LORD,
who had set them apart to be holy.
13 "But the people of Israel rebelled against me, and
they refused to obey my decrees there in the wilder-
ness. They wouldn't obey my regulations even though
obedience would have given them life. They also vi-
olated my Sabbath days. So I threatened to pour out
my fury on them, and I made plans to utterly consume
them in the wilderness. 14 But again I held back in or-
der to protect the honor of my name before the na-
tions who had seen my power in bringing Israel out
of Egypt. 15 But I took a solemn oath against them in
the wilderness. I swore I would not bring them into
the land I had given them, a land flowing with milk
and honey, the most beautiful place on earth. 16 For
they had rejected my regulations, refused to follow
my decrees, and violated my Sabbath days. Their
hearts were given to their idols. 17 Nevertheless, I took
pity on them and held back from destroying them in
the wilderness.
18 "Then I warned their children not to follow in
their parents' footsteps, defiling themselves with
their idols. 19 'I am the LORD your God,' I told them.
'Follow my decrees, pay attention to my regulations,
20 and keep my Sabbath days holy, for they are a sign
to remind you that I am the LORD your God.'
21 "But their children, too, rebelled against me. They
refused to keep my decrees and follow my regula-
tions, even though obedience would have given them
life. And they also violated my Sabbath days. So again
I threatened to pour out my fury on them in the wil-
derness. 22 Nevertheless, I withdrew my judgment
against them to protect the honor of my name be-
fore the nations that had seen my power in bringing
them out of Egypt. 23 But I took a solemn oath against
them in the wilderness. I swore I would scatter them
among all the nations 24 because they did not obey my
regulations. They scorned my decrees by violating my
Sabbath days and longing for the idols of their ances-
tors. 25 I gave them over to worthless decrees and reg-
ulations that would not lead to life. 26 I let them pollute
themselves* with the very gifts I had given them, and
I allowed them to give their firstborn children as of-
ferings to their gods—so I might devastate them and
remind them that I alone am the LORD.

JUDGMENT AND RESTORATION

27 "Therefore, son of man, give the people of Israel this
message from the Sovereign LORD: Your ancestors
continued to blaspheme and betray me, 28 for when
I brought them into the land I had promised them,
they offered sacrifices on every high hill and under
every green tree they saw! They roused my fury as
they offered up sacrifices to their gods. They brought
their perfumes and incense and poured out their liq-
uid offerings to them. 29 I said to them, 'What is this
high place where you are going?' (This kind of pagan
shrine has been called Bamah—'high place'—ever
since.)
30 "Therefore, give the people of Israel this mes-
sage from the Sovereign LORD: Do you plan to pollute
yourselves just as your ancestors did? Do you intend
to keep prostituting yourselves by worshiping vile
images? 31 For when you offer gifts to them and give
your little children to be burned as sacrifices,* you
continue to pollute yourselves with idols to this day.
Should I allow you to ask for a message from me,
O people of Israel? As surely as I live, says the Sover-
eign LORD, I will tell you nothing.
32 "You say, 'We want to be like the nations all
around us, who serve idols of wood and stone.' But
what you have in mind will never happen. 33 As surely
as I live, says the Sovereign LORD, I will rule over you
with an iron fist in great anger and with awesome
power. 34 And in anger I will reach out with my strong
hand and powerful arm, and I will bring you back*
from the lands where you are scattered. 35 I will bring
you into the wilderness of the nations, and there I will
judge you face to face. 36 I will judge you there just as
I did your ancestors in the wilderness after bringing
them out of Egypt, says the Sovereign LORD. 37 I will
examine you carefully and hold you to the terms of
the covenant. 38 I will purge you of all those who reb-
el and revolt against me. I will bring them out of the
countries where they are in exile, but they will never
enter the land of Israel. Then you will know that I am
the LORD.

20:7 The Hebrew term (literally *round things*) probably alludes to dung; also in 20:8, 16, 18, 24, 31, 39. **20:25-26** Or *I gave them worthless decrees and regulations. . . . I polluted them.* **20:31** Or *and make your little children pass through the fire.* **20:34** Greek version reads *I will welcome you.* Compare 2 Cor 6:17.

20:25 I gave them over to worthless decrees . . . would not lead to life. This does not refer to God's law, which is good (Rom. 7:12), but to the Canaanite statutes that Israel followed.

20:26 to give . . . as offerings. Child sacrifice is the ultimate example of a Canaanite statute that was not good.

20:32 will never happen. Forget it! God would not release His people from His loving grip.

20:33 iron fist. Reminiscent of the delivery language used to describe God's rescue of Israel through the Exodus (Exod. 6:6; 32:11; Deut. 4:34; 5:15; 7:19; 11:2; Ps. 132:12), God's hand and arm will now purify Israel of rebels once again.

39 "As for you, O people of Israel, this is what the
Sovereign LORD says: Go right ahead and worship
your idols, but sooner or later you will obey me
and will stop bringing shame on my holy name by
worshiping idols. 40 For on my holy mountain, the
great mountain of Israel, says the Sovereign LORD,
the people of Israel will someday worship me, and I
will accept them. There I will require that you bring
me all your offerings and choice gifts and sacrifices.
41 When I bring you home from exile, you will be like
a pleasing sacrifice to me. And I will display my ho-
liness through you as all the nations watch. 42 Then
when I have brought you home to the land I prom-
ised with a solemn oath to give to your ancestors, you
will know that I am the LORD. 43 You will look back
on all the ways you defiled yourselves and will hate
yourselves because of the evil you have done. 44 You
will know that I am the LORD, O people of Israel,
when I have honored my name by treating you mer-
cifully in spite of your wickedness. I, the Sovereign
LORD, have spoken!"

JUDGMENT AGAINST THE NEGEV

45* Then this message came to me from the LORD:
46 "Son of man, turn and face the south* and speak
out against it; prophesy against the brushlands of the
Negev. 47 Tell the southern wilderness, 'This is what
the Sovereign LORD says: Hear the word of the LORD!
I will set you on fire, and every tree, both green and
dry, will be burned. The terrible flames will not be
quenched and will scorch everything from south to
north. 48 And everyone in the world will see that I, the
LORD, have set this fire. It will not be put out.'"

49 Then I said, "O Sovereign LORD, they are saying of
me, 'He only talks in riddles!'"

THE LORD'S SWORD OF JUDGMENT

21 1* Then this message came to me from the LORD:
2 "Son of man, turn and face Jerusalem and
prophesy against Israel and her sanctuaries. 3 Tell her,
'This is what the LORD says: I am your enemy, O Israel,
and I am about to unsheath my sword to destroy your
people—the righteous and the wicked alike. 4 Yes, I
will cut off both the righteous and the wicked! I will
draw my sword against everyone in the land from
south to north. 5 Everyone in the world will know that
I am the LORD. My sword is in my hand, and it will not
return to its sheath until its work is finished.'

6 "Son of man, groan before the people! Groan be-
fore them with bitter anguish and a broken heart.
7 When they ask why you are groaning, tell them, 'I
groan because of the terrifying news I have heard.
When it comes true, the boldest heart will melt with
fear; all strength will disappear. Every spirit will
faint; strong knees will become as weak as water. And
the Sovereign LORD says: It is coming! It's on its way!'"

8 Then the LORD said to me, 9 "Son of man, give the
people this message from the Lord:

"A sword, a sword
 is being sharpened and polished.
10 It is sharpened for terrible slaughter
 and polished to flash like lightning!
Now will you laugh?
 Those far stronger than you have fallen beneath
 its power!*
11 Yes, the sword is now being sharpened and
 polished;
 it is being prepared for the executioner.

12 "Son of man, cry out and wail;
 pound your thighs in anguish,
for that sword will slaughter my people and their
 leaders—
 everyone will die!
13 It will put them all to the test.
 What chance do they have?*
 says the Sovereign LORD.

14 "Son of man, prophesy to them
 and clap your hands.
Then take the sword and brandish it twice,
 even three times,
to symbolize the great massacre,
 the great massacre facing them on every side.
15 Let their hearts melt with terror,
 for the sword glitters at every gate.
It flashes like lightning
 and is polished for slaughter!
16 O sword, slash to the right,
 then slash to the left,
wherever you will,
 wherever you want.
17 I, too, will clap my hands,
 and I will satisfy my fury.
 I, the LORD, have spoken!"

OMENS FOR BABYLON'S KING

18 Then this message came to me from the LORD: 19 "Son
of man, make a map and trace two routes on it for the
sword of Babylon's king to follow. Put a signpost on
the road that comes out of Babylon where the road
forks into two— 20 one road going to Ammon and its
capital, Rabbah, and the other to Judah and fortified
Jerusalem. 21 The king of Babylon now stands at the
fork, uncertain whether to attack Jerusalem or Rab-
bah. He calls his magicians to look for omens. They
cast lots by shaking arrows from the quiver. They
inspect the livers of animal sacrifices. 22 The omen in
his right hand says, 'Jerusalem!' With battering rams
his soldiers will go against the gates, shouting for the
kill. They will put up siege towers and build ramps

20:45 Verses 20:45-49 are numbered 21:1-5 in Hebrew text. **20:46** Hebrew *toward Teman.* **21:1** Verses 21:1-32 are numbered 21:6-37 in Hebrew text. **21:10** The meaning of the Hebrew is uncertain. **21:13** The meaning of the Hebrew is uncertain.

20:39 But sooner or later. At the end of this age, God will end Israel's rebellious streak, and all Israel will be saved (see Rom. 11:26). At that time, Israel will acknowledge their Lord as a faithful God who forgives His people (vv. 42-44).

21:3 My sword . . . destroy . . . the wicked. God would soon use Babylon to carry out His discipline on His people—both righteous and wicked.

21:9 sword. Ezekiel referenced battle imagery to indicate Jerusalem's pending siege and destruction. This was actually written as a song.

21:10 Those far stronger. The people of Judah should not place false hope in their king (those far stronger) for God's judgment (with fire and sword) would destroy both the righteous and wicked (20:47; 21:3-4).

21:21 inspect the livers. At Damascus, Nebuchadnezzar is undecided on which road to take: towards Rabbah in Ammon or towards Jerusalem. For this he consulted two marked arrows shaken up (one picked). Then he turned to his household idols. Finally, sheep were slaughtered so as to observe spots or irregularities on their livers. Apparently, the livers said Jerusalem, and the arrow and idols agreed.

against the walls. 23 The people of Jerusalem will
think it is a false omen, because of their treaty with
the Babylonians. But the king of Babylon will remind
the people of their rebellion. Then he will attack and
capture them.
24 "Therefore, this is what the Sovereign LORD says:
Again and again you remind me of your sin and your
guilt. You don't even try to hide it! In everything you
do, your sins are obvious for all to see. So now the time
of your punishment has come!
25 "O you corrupt and wicked prince of Israel, your
final day of reckoning is here! 26 This is what the Sov-
ereign LORD says:

"Take off your jeweled crown,
for the old order changes.
Now the lowly will be exalted,
and the mighty will be brought down.
27 Destruction! Destruction!
I will surely destroy the kingdom.
And it will not be restored until the one appears
who has the right to judge it.
Then I will hand it over to him.

A MESSAGE FOR THE AMMONITES

28 "And now, son of man, prophesy concerning the
Ammonites and their mockery. Give them this mes-
sage from the Sovereign LORD:

"A sword, a sword
is drawn for your slaughter.
It is polished to destroy,
flashing like lightning!
29 Your prophets have given false visions,
and your fortune-tellers have told lies.
The sword will fall on the necks of the wicked
for whom the day of final reckoning has come.

30 "Now return the sword to its sheath,
for in your own country,
the land of your birth,
I will pass judgment upon you.
31 I will pour out my fury on you
and blow on you with the fire of my anger.
I will hand you over to cruel men
who are skilled in destruction.
32 You will be fuel for the fire,
and your blood will be spilled in your own land.
You will be utterly wiped out,
your memory lost to history,
for I, the LORD, have spoken!"

THE SINS OF JERUSALEM

22 Now this message came to me from the LORD:
2 "Son of man, are you ready to judge Jerusa-
lem? Are you ready to judge this city of murderers?
Publicly denounce her detestable sins, 3 and give her
this message from the Sovereign LORD: O city of mur-
derers, doomed and damned—city of idols,* filthy
and foul—4 you are guilty because of the blood you
have shed. You are defiled because of the idols you
have made. Your day of destruction has come! You
have reached the end of your years. I will make you
an object of mockery throughout the world. 5 O infa-
mous city, filled with confusion, you will be mocked
by people far and near.
6 "Every leader in Israel who lives within your
walls is bent on murder. 7 Fathers and mothers are
treated with contempt. Foreigners are forced to pay
for protection. Orphans and widows are wronged
and oppressed among you. 8 You despise my holy
things and violate my Sabbath days of rest. 9 People
accuse others falsely and send them to their death.
You are filled with idol worshipers and people who
do obscene things. 10 Men sleep with their fathers'
wives and force themselves on women who are men-
struating. 11 Within your walls live men who commit
adultery with their neighbors' wives, who defile
their daughters-in-law, or who rape their own sisters.
12 There are hired murderers, loan racketeers, and ex-
tortioners everywhere. They never even think of me
and my commands, says the Sovereign LORD.
13 "But now I clap my hands in indignation over
your dishonest gain and bloodshed. 14 How strong and
courageous will you be in my day of reckoning? I, the
LORD, have spoken, and I will do what I said. 15 I will
scatter you among the nations and purge you of your
wickedness. 16 And when I have been dishonored
among the nations because of you,* you will know
that I am the LORD."

THE LORD'S REFINING FURNACE

17 Then this message came to me from the LORD: 18 "Son
of man, the people of Israel are the worthless slag that
remains after silver is smelted. They are the dross that
is left over—a useless mixture of copper, tin, iron, and
lead. 19 So tell them, 'This is what the Sovereign LORD
says: Because you are all worthless slag, I will bring
you to my crucible in Jerusalem. 20 Just as silver, cop-
per, iron, lead, and tin are melted down in a furnace,
I will melt you down in the heat of my fury. 21 I will
gather you together and blow the fire of my anger
upon you, 22 and you will melt like silver in fierce heat.
Then you will know that I, the LORD, have poured out
my fury on you.'"

THE SINS OF ISRAEL'S LEADERS

23 Again a message came to me from the LORD: 24 "Son
of man, give the people of Israel this message: In the
day of my indignation, you will be like a polluted
land, a land without rain. 25 Your princes* plot con-
spiracies just as lions stalk their prey. They devour

22:3 The Hebrew term (literally *round things*) probably alludes to dung; also in 22:4. 22:16 As in one Hebrew manuscript and Greek and Syriac versions; Masoretic Text reads *when you have been dishonored among the nations.* 22:25 As in Greek version; Hebrew reads *prophets.*

21:25 final day . . . is here. Zedekiah would be king at the time of Jerusalem's fall.
21:27 Destruction! . . . until the one appears. God will restore Jerusalem at the second coming of Jesus.
21:28 Ammonites. Evil nations were standing in line for judgment. The Ammonites were next.
22:13 clap My hands. Returning to the judgment motif of clapped hands (6:11; 21:14), the sentence on Judah is formally pronounced because of their disregard for Moses' warning (Lev. 26:27-39; Deut. 28:64-68) that disobedience would result in exile (12:15; 20:23; 36:19). God cared less that His reputation would be tarnished by Israel's failure than He cares that Israel acts like His people. Earlier, he had condemned false prophets for whitewashing their messages (13:10-15) and does so again (22:28). Similarly, Jesus condemns phony Pharisees for being more concerned with outward appearance than inner holiness (Matt. 23:27). God would much rather have us publicly fail as Christians than to be privately hypocritical in our activities.
22:30 stand in the gap. The great divide between a holy God and His rebellious people was often bridged by a prophet's pleas (see Jer. 37:3; 42:2).

innocent people, seizing treasures and extorting wealth. They make many widows in the land. 26 Your priests have violated my instructions and defiled my holy things. They make no distinction between what is holy and what is not. And they do not teach my people the difference between what is ceremonially clean and unclean. They disregard my Sabbath days so that I am dishonored among them. 27 Your leaders are like wolves who tear apart their victims. They actually destroy people's lives for money! 28 And your prophets cover up for them by announcing false visions and making lying predictions. They say, 'My message is from the Sovereign LORD,' when the LORD hasn't spoken a single word to them. 29 Even common people oppress the poor, rob the needy, and deprive foreigners of justice.

30 "I looked for someone who might rebuild the wall of righteousness that guards the land. I searched for someone to stand in the gap in the wall so I wouldn't have to destroy the land, but I found no one. 31 So now I will pour out my fury on them, consuming them with the fire of my anger. I will heap on their heads the full penalty for all their sins. I, the Sovereign LORD, have spoken!"

THE ADULTERY OF TWO SISTERS

23 This message came to me from the LORD: 2 "Son of man, once there were two sisters who were daughters of the same mother. 3 They became prostitutes in Egypt. Even as young girls, they allowed men to fondle their breasts. 4 The older girl was named Oholah, and her sister was Oholibah. I married them, and they bore me sons and daughters. I am speaking of Samaria and Jerusalem, for Oholah is Samaria and Oholibah is Jerusalem.

5 "Then Oholah lusted after other lovers instead of me, and she gave her love to the Assyrian officers. 6 They were all attractive young men, captains and commanders dressed in handsome blue, charioteers driving their horses. 7 And so she prostituted herself with the most desirable men of Assyria, worshiping their idols* and defiling herself. 8 For when she left Egypt, she did not leave her spirit of prostitution behind. She was still as lewd as in her youth, when the Egyptians slept with her, fondled her breasts, and used her as a prostitute.

9 "And so I handed her over to her Assyrian lovers, whom she desired so much. 10 They stripped her, took away her children as their slaves, and then killed her. After she received her punishment, her reputation was known to every woman in the land.

11 "Yet even though Oholibah saw what had happened to Oholah, her sister, she followed right in her footsteps. And she was even more depraved, abandoning herself to her lust and prostitution. 12 She fawned over all the Assyrian officers—those captains and commanders in handsome uniforms, those charioteers driving their horses—all of them attractive young men. 13 I saw the way she was going, defiling herself just like her older sister.

14 "Then she carried her prostitution even further. She fell in love with pictures that were painted on a wall—pictures of Babylonian* military officers, outfitted in striking red uniforms. 15 Handsome belts encircled their waists, and flowing turbans crowned their heads. They were dressed like chariot officers from the land of Babylonia.* 16 When she saw these paintings, she longed to give herself to them, so she sent messengers to Babylonia to invite them to come to her. 17 So they came and committed adultery with her, defiling her in the bed of love. After being defiled, however, she rejected them in disgust.

18 "In the same way, I became disgusted with Oholibah and rejected her, just as I had rejected her sister, because she flaunted herself before them and gave herself to satisfy their lusts. 19 Yet she turned to even greater prostitution, remembering her youth when she was a prostitute in Egypt. 20 She lusted after lovers with genitals as large as a donkey's and emissions like those of a horse. 21 And so, Oholibah, you relived your former days as a young girl in Egypt, when you first allowed your breasts to be fondled.

THE LORD'S JUDGMENT OF OHOLIBAH

22 "Therefore, Oholibah, this is what the Sovereign LORD says: I will send your lovers against you from every direction—those very nations from which you turned away in disgust. 23 For the Babylonians will come with all the Chaldeans from Pekod and Shoa and Koa. And all the Assyrians will come with them—handsome young captains, commanders, chariot officers, and other high-ranking officers, all riding their horses. 24 They will all come against you from the north* with chariots, wagons, and a great army prepared for attack. They will take up positions on every side, surrounding you with men armed with shields and helmets. And I will hand you over to them for punishment so they can do with you as they please. 25 I will turn my jealous anger against you, and they will deal harshly with you. They will cut off your nose and ears, and any survivors will then be slaughtered by the sword. Your children will be taken away as captives, and everything that is left will be burned. 26 They will strip you of your beautiful clothes and jewels. 27 In this way, I will put a stop to the lewdness and prostitution you brought from Egypt. You will never again cast longing eyes on those things or fondly remember your time in Egypt.

28 "For this is what the Sovereign LORD says: I will surely hand you over to your enemies, to those you loathe, those you rejected. 29 They will treat you with hatred and rob you of all you own, leaving you stark naked. The shame of your prostitution will be exposed to all the world. 30 You brought all this on yourself by prostituting yourself to other nations, defiling yourself with all their idols. 31 Because you have followed

23:7 The Hebrew term (literally *round things*) probably alludes to dung; also in 23:30, 37, 39, 49. **23:14** Or *Chaldean.* **23:15** Or *Chaldea;* also in 23:16. **23:24** As in Greek version; the meaning of the Hebrew is uncertain.

23:5 lusted. Judah relied on foreign alliances instead of her true love, God.

23:8 did not leave her spirit of prostitution. God's people pursued a political relationship with Egypt, though she proved to be an ineffective ally (see Ex. 17:3; Num. 11:5,18,20).

23:19 in Egypt. From 600–586 B.C., Judah twice attempted to enlist Egypt's aid against Babylon. In the first instance, King Jehoiakim rebelled in 600 B.C. after Egypt defeated Babylon in battle (2 Kings 24:1). In the second instance, Zedekiah relied on Egypt's promises of help in 588 B.C. (29:6-7; 2 Kings 25:1; Jer. 37:5-8).

23:31 same cup. The cup of intoxicating strong drink that a guilty party drank left them reeling because God's judgment was contained in the cup (see Jer. 25:15-29; Hab. 2:15). This cup of wrath is a theme also found in the New Testament (Mark 14:36).

in your sister's footsteps, I will force you to drink the
same cup of terror she drank.
32 "Yes, this is what the Sovereign LORD says:

"You will drink from your sister's cup of terror,
a cup that is large and deep.
It is filled to the brim
with scorn and derision.
33 Drunkenness and anguish will fill you,
for your cup is filled to the brim with distress
and desolation,
the same cup your sister Samaria drank.
34 You will drain that cup of terror
to the very bottom.
Then you will smash it to pieces
and beat your breast in anguish.
I, the Sovereign LORD, have spoken!

35 "And because you have forgotten me and turned
your back on me, this is what the Sovereign LORD says:
You must bear the consequences of all your lewdness
and prostitution."

THE LORD'S JUDGMENT ON BOTH SISTERS

36 The LORD said to me, "Son of man, you must accuse
Oholah and Oholibah of all their detestable sins.
37 They have committed both adultery and murder—
adultery by worshiping idols and murder by burning
as sacrifices the children they bore to me.
38 Further-
more, they have defiled my Temple and violated my
Sabbath day!
39 On the very day that they sacrificed
their children to their idols, they boldly came into
my Temple to worship! They came in and defiled my
house.
40 "You sisters sent messengers to distant lands to get
men. Then when they arrived, you bathed yourselves,
painted your eyelids, and put on your finest jewels for
them.
41 You sat with them on a beautifully embroi-
dered couch and put my incense and my special oil on
a table that was spread before you.
42 From your room
came the sound of many men carousing. They were
lustful men and drunkards* from the wilderness, who
put bracelets on your wrists and beautiful crowns on
your heads.
43 Then I said, 'If they really want to have
sex with old worn-out prostitutes like these, let them!'
44 And that is what they did. They had sex with Oholah
and Oholibah, these shameless prostitutes.
45 But righ-
teous people will judge these sister cities for what they
really are—adulterers and murderers.
46 "Now this is what the Sovereign LORD says: Bring
an army against them and hand them over to be ter-
rorized and plundered.
47 For their enemies will stone
them and kill them with swords. They will butcher
their sons and daughters and burn their homes.
48 In
this way, I will put an end to lewdness and idolatry in
the land, and my judgment will be a warning to all
women not to follow your wicked example.
49 You will
be fully repaid for all your prostitution—your wor-
ship of idols. Yes, you will suffer the full penalty. Then
you will know that I am the Sovereign LORD."

THE SIGN OF THE COOKING POT

24 On January 15,* during the ninth year of King
Jehoiachin's captivity, this message came to
me from the LORD:
2 "Son of man, write down today's
date, because on this very day the king of Babylon is
beginning his attack against Jerusalem.
3 Then give
these rebels an illustration with this message from
the Sovereign LORD:

"Put a pot on the fire,
and pour in some water.
4 Fill it with choice pieces of meat—
the rump and the shoulder
and all the most tender cuts.
5 Use only the best sheep from the flock,
and heap fuel on the fire beneath the pot.
Bring the pot to a boil,
and cook the bones along with the meat.

6 "Now this is what the Sovereign LORD says:
What sorrow awaits Jerusalem,
the city of murderers!
She is a cooking pot
whose corruption can't be cleaned out.
Take the meat out in random order,
for no piece is better than another.
7 For the blood of her murders
is splashed on the rocks.
It isn't even spilled on the ground,
where the dust could cover it!
8 So I will splash her blood on a rock
for all to see,
an expression of my anger
and vengeance against her.

9 "This is what the Sovereign LORD says:
What sorrow awaits Jerusalem,
the city of murderers!
I myself will pile up the fuel beneath her.
10 Yes, heap on the wood!
Let the fire roar to make the pot boil.
Cook the meat with many spices,
and afterward burn the bones.
11 Now set the empty pot on the coals.
Heat it red hot!
Burn away the filth and corruption.
12 But it's hopeless;
the corruption can't be cleaned out.
So throw it into the fire.
13 Your impurity is your lewdness
and the corruption of your idolatry.
I tried to cleanse you,
but you refused.
So now you will remain in your filth
until my fury against you has been satisfied.

23:42 Or *Sabeans.* **24:1** Hebrew *On the tenth day of the tenth month,* of the ancient Hebrew lunar calendar. This event occurred on January 15, 588 B.C.; also see note on 1:1.

23:37-38 burning as sacrifies the children they bore me. The people would not give up their pagan practices of idolatry and child sacrifice, even committing these sins in God's temple.

24:2 beginning his attack. While hundreds of miles away in Babylon, Ezekiel received the news of Jerusalem's siege through a vision.

24:3 rebels. The house would soon receive its dues. It would be cooked like meat in a pot.

24:4 Fill it with choice pieces of meat. Those arrogant leaders who remained from the first exile thought they had opted out of judgment. However, God revealed they were indeed special—special enough to be included on the menu (11:3).

24:6 Take the meat out in random order. In the previous deportation, the Babylonians had cast lots to determine who would go. Now, nobody would wait for unlucky names to be called. This time, *everyone* would be deported.

14 "I, the LORD, have spoken! The time has come, and
I won't hold back. I will not change my mind, and I
will have no pity on you. You will be judged on the
basis of all your wicked actions, says the Sovereign
LORD."

THE DEATH OF EZEKIEL'S WIFE

15 Then this message came to me from the LORD: 16 "Son
of man, with one blow I will take away your dearest
treasure. Yet you must not show any sorrow at her
death. Do not weep; let there be no tears. 17 Groan si-
lently, but let there be no wailing at her grave. Do not
uncover your head or take off your sandals. Do not
perform the usual rituals of mourning or accept any
food brought to you by consoling friends."

18 So I proclaimed this to the people the next morn-
ing, and in the evening my wife died. The next morn-
ing I did everything I had been told to do. 19 Then the
people asked, "What does all this mean? What are you
trying to tell us?"

20 So I said to them, "A message came to me from
the LORD, 21 and I was told to give this message to
the people of Israel. This is what the Sovereign LORD
says: I will defile my Temple, the source of your secu-
rity and pride, the place your heart delights in. Your
sons and daughters whom you left behind in Judah
will be slaughtered by the sword. 22 Then you will
do as Ezekiel has done. You will not mourn in public
or console yourselves by eating the food brought by
friends. 23 Your heads will remain covered, and your
sandals will not be taken off. You will not mourn or
weep, but you will waste away because of your sins.
You will groan among yourselves for all the evil you
have done. 24 Ezekiel is an example for you; you will
do just as he has done. And when that time comes, you
will know that I am the Sovereign LORD."

25 Then the LORD said to me, "Son of man, on the day
I take away their stronghold—their joy and glory,
their heart's desire, their dearest treasure—I will
also take away their sons and daughters. 26 And on
that day a survivor from Jerusalem will come to you
in Babylon and tell you what has happened. 27 And
when he arrives, your voice will suddenly return so
you can talk to him, and you will be a symbol for these
people. Then they will know that I am the LORD."

A MESSAGE FOR AMMON

25 Then this message came to me from the LORD:
2 "Son of man, turn and face the land of Am-
mon and prophesy against its people. 3 Give the Am-
monites this message from the Sovereign LORD: Hear
the word of the Sovereign LORD! Because you cheered
when my Temple was defiled, mocked Israel in her
desolation, and laughed at Judah as she went away
into exile, 4 I will allow nomads from the eastern des-
erts to overrun your country. They will set up their
camps among you and pitch their tents on your land.
They will harvest all your fruit and drink the milk
from your livestock. 5 And I will turn the city of Rab-
bah into a pasture for camels, and all the land of the
Ammonites into a resting place for sheep and goats.
Then you will know that I am the LORD.

6 "This is what the Sovereign LORD says: Because
you clapped and danced and cheered with glee at
the destruction of my people, 7 I will raise my fist of
judgment against you. I will give you as plunder to
many nations. I will cut you off from being a nation
and destroy you completely. Then you will know that
I am the LORD.

A MESSAGE FOR MOAB

8 "This is what the Sovereign LORD says: Because the
people of Moab* have said that Judah is just like all
the other nations, 9 I will open up their eastern flank
and wipe out their glorious frontier towns—Beth-
jeshimoth, Baal-meon, and Kiriathaim. 10 And I will
hand Moab over to nomads from the eastern deserts,
just as I handed over Ammon. Yes, the Ammonites
will no longer be counted among the nations. 11 In
the same way, I will bring my judgment down on the
Moabites. Then they will know that I am the LORD.

A MESSAGE FOR EDOM

12 "This is what the Sovereign LORD says: The people
of Edom have sinned greatly by avenging themselves
against the people of Judah. 13 Therefore, says the Sov-
ereign LORD, I will raise my fist of judgment against
Edom. I will wipe out its people and animals with the
sword. I will make a wasteland of everything from
Teman to Dedan. 14 I will accomplish this by the hand
of my people of Israel. They will carry out my ven-
geance with anger, and Edom will know that this ven-
geance is from me. I, the Sovereign LORD, have spoken!

A MESSAGE FOR PHILISTIA

15 "This is what the Sovereign LORD says: The people
of Philistia have acted against Judah out of bitter re-
venge and long-standing contempt. 16 Therefore, this
is what the Sovereign LORD says: I will raise my fist
of judgment against the land of the Philistines. I will
wipe out the Kerethites and utterly destroy the peo-
ple who live by the sea. 17 I will execute terrible ven-
geance against them to punish them for what they
have done. And when I have inflicted my revenge,
they will know that I am the LORD."

A MESSAGE FOR TYRE

26 On February 3, during the twelfth year of King
Jehoiachin's captivity,* this message came to
me from the LORD: 2 "Son of man, Tyre has rejoiced
over the fall of Jerusalem, saying, 'Ha! She who was
the gateway to the rich trade routes to the east has
been broken, and I am the heir! Because she has been
made desolate, I will become wealthy!'

25:8 As in Greek version; Hebrew reads *Moab and Seir.* **26:1** Hebrew *In the eleventh year, on the first day of the month,* of the ancient Hebrew lunar calendar year. Since an element is missing in the date formula here, scholars have reconstructed this probable reading: *In the eleventh [month of the twelfth] year, on the first day of the month.* This reading would put this message on February 3, 585 B.C.; also see note on 1:1.

24:27 you will be a symbol for these people. Ezekiel, the widower (his wife was taken in an instant by God—24:15-19), offered a living picture of the agony and grief that awaited Judah. Just as Ezekiel was told not to mourn for his wife (v. 17), the exiles would be so stunned by news of Jerusalem's fall that they would be unable to mourn (vv. 22-27).

25:1-32:18. Just as Jeremiah devoted much of his prophecy to a section of oracles concerning God's judgment of the nations surrounding Israel (Jer. 46–51), so Ezekiel prophesies against surrounding nations. The first five nations in Ezekiel's oracles match Jeremiah, while Tyre and Sidon to the northwest of Israel are added in Ezekiel. Syria, Elam, and Babylon, lands to the north and east, are addressed in Jeremiah. Tyre was overthrown by Nebuchadnezzar in 572 B.C. Babylon itself was defeated by Persia in 539 B.C.

26:2 Ha! Tyre wasted no time laying claim to the monopoly of trade opportunities that became available after Jerusalem's demise.

3 "Therefore, this is what the Sovereign LORD says:
I am your enemy, O Tyre, and I will bring many na-
tions against you, like the waves of the sea crashing
against your shoreline. 4 They will destroy the walls
of Tyre and tear down its towers. I will scrape away
its soil and make it a bare rock! 5 It will be just a rock
in the sea, a place for fishermen to spread their nets,
for I have spoken, says the Sovereign LORD. Tyre will
become the prey of many nations, 6 and its mainland
villages will be destroyed by the sword. Then they
will know that I am the LORD.
7 "This is what the Sovereign LORD says: From the
north I will bring King Nebuchadnezzar* of Babylon
against Tyre. He is king of kings and brings his horses,
chariots, charioteers, and great army. 8 First he will de-
stroy your mainland villages. Then he will attack you
by building a siege wall, constructing a ramp, and rais-
ing a roof of shields against you. 9 He will pound your
walls with battering rams and demolish your towers
with sledgehammers. 10 The hooves of his horses will
choke the city with dust, and the noise of the chari-
oteers and chariot wheels will shake your walls as
they storm through your broken gates. 11 His horsemen
will trample through every street in the city. They will
butcher your people, and your strong pillars will topple.
12 "They will plunder all your riches and merchan-
dise and break down your walls. They will destroy
your lovely homes and dump your stones and timbers
and even your dust into the sea. 13 I will stop the mu-
sic of your songs. No more will the sound of harps be
heard among your people. 14 I will make your island a
bare rock, a place for fishermen to spread their nets.
You will never be rebuilt, for I, the LORD, have spoken.
Yes, the Sovereign LORD has spoken!

THE EFFECT OF TYRE'S DESTRUCTION

15 "This is what the Sovereign LORD says to Tyre: The
whole coastline will tremble at the sound of your fall,
as the screams of the wounded echo in the continu-
ing slaughter. 16 All the seaport rulers will step down
from their thrones and take off their royal robes and
beautiful clothing. They will sit on the ground trem-
bling with horror at your destruction. 17 Then they
will wail for you, singing this funeral song:

"O famous island city,
once ruler of the sea,
how you have been destroyed!
Your people, with their naval power,
once spread fear around the world.
18 Now the coastlands tremble at your fall.
The islands are dismayed as you disappear.

19 "This is what the Sovereign LORD says: I will
make Tyre an uninhabited ruin, like many others. I
will bury you beneath the terrible waves of enemy
attack. Great seas will swallow you. 20 I will send you
to the pit to join those who descended there long ago.
Your city will lie in ruins, buried beneath the earth,
like those in the pit who have entered the world of
the dead. You will have no place of respect here in the
land of the living. 21 I will bring you to a terrible end,
and you will exist no more. You will be looked for, but
you will never again be found. I, the Sovereign LORD,
have spoken!"

THE END OF TYRE'S GLORY

27 Then this message came to me from the LORD:
2 "Son of man, sing a funeral song for Tyre, 3 that
mighty gateway to the sea, the trading center of the
world. Give Tyre this message from the Sovereign
LORD:

"You boasted, O Tyre,
'My beauty is perfect!'
4 You extended your boundaries into the sea.
Your builders made your beauty perfect.
5 You were like a great ship
built of the finest cypress from Senir.*
They took a cedar from Lebanon
to make a mast for you.
6 They carved your oars
from the oaks of Bashan.
Your deck of pine from the coasts of Cyprus*
was inlaid with ivory.
7 Your sails were made of Egypt's finest linen,
and they flew as a banner above you.
You stood beneath blue and purple awnings
made bright with dyes from the coasts of
Elishah.
8 Your oarsmen came from Sidon and Arvad;
your helmsmen were skilled men from Tyre
itself.
9 Wise old craftsmen from Gebal did the caulking.
Ships from every land came with goods to
barter for your trade.

10 "Men from distant Persia, Lydia, and Libya*
served in your great army. They hung their shields
and helmets on your walls, giving you great honor.
11 Men from Arvad and Helech stood on your walls.
Your towers were manned by men from Gammad.
Their shields hung on your walls, completing your
beauty.
12 "Tarshish sent merchants to buy your wares in
exchange for silver, iron, tin, and lead. 13 Merchants
from Greece,* Tubal, and Meshech brought slaves and
articles of bronze to trade with you.
14 "From Beth-togarmah came riding horses, chari-
ot horses, and mules, all in exchange for your goods.

26:7 Hebrew *Nebuchadrezzar*, a variant spelling of Nebuchadnezzar. **27:5** Or *Hermon*. **27:6** Hebrew *Kittim*. **27:10** Hebrew *Paras, Lud, and Put*. **27:13** Hebrew *Javan*.

26:5 a place for fisherman to spread their nets. Much later than Ezekiel, Alexander the Great completed Tyre's doom, destroying the city completely. Today, only a land bridge exists where Tyre once was—a land bridge used by fishermen.

26:8 building a siege wall. Babylon besieged the nation of Tyre for 15 years. Tyre was able to hold out because of its navy.

27:3 Tyre . . . My beauty is perfect! Tyre was a city located on the coast and was known for its great navy, variety of goods, and trading port. The city of Tyre believed it was invincible—even against a formidable foe such as Babylon. Chapter 28 refers to Tyre as a city of beauty and pride.

27:10-24 Mercenaries "hung their shields and helmets" on the walls to signal that they were on the job and ready to go. For Tyre, mercenaries would have been easy to come by in the normal order of trade. The scope of Tyre's commerce was extensive. Ammon sold wheat to Judah and Israel to use in trade with Tyre (v. 17). Helbon, a wine center northwest of Damascus, and Zahar, a desert area also northwest of Damascus, traded wine and wool with Damascus for use in trade with Tyre (v. 18). Many nations that traded with Tyre still exist today by the same name. Others have changed their names or no longer exist. Examples of these are the regions of Togarmah (Armenia); Aram (Syria); Kedar in Arabia; Dedan, northwest of Edom; and Haran, Cannah, and Eden in Mesopotamia.

15 Merchants came to you from Dedan.* Numerous
coastlands were your captive markets; they brought
payment in ivory tusks and ebony wood.
16 "Syria* sent merchants to buy your rich variety
of goods. They traded turquoise, purple dyes, embroi-
dery, fine linen, and jewelry of coral and rubies. 17 Ju-
dah and Israel traded for your wares, offering wheat
from Minnith, figs,* honey, olive oil, and balm.
18 "Damascus sent merchants to buy your rich va-
riety of goods, bringing wine from Helbon and white
wool from Zahar. 19 Greeks from Uzal* came to trade
for your merchandise. Wrought iron, cassia, and fra-
grant calamus were bartered for your wares.
20 "Dedan sent merchants to trade their expensive
saddle blankets with you. 21 The Arabians and the
princes of Kedar sent merchants to trade lambs and
rams and male goats in exchange for your goods.
22 The merchants of Sheba and Raamah came with all
kinds of spices, jewels, and gold in exchange for your
wares.
23 "Haran, Canneh, Eden, Sheba, Asshur, and Kilmad
came with their merchandise, too. 24 They brought
choice fabrics to trade—blue cloth, embroidery, and
multicolored carpets rolled up and bound with cords.
25 The ships of Tarshish were your ocean caravans.
Your island warehouse was filled to the brim!

THE DESTRUCTION OF TYRE

26 "But look! Your oarsmen
have taken you into stormy seas!
A mighty eastern gale
has wrecked you in the heart of the sea!
27 Everything is lost—
your riches and wares,
your sailors and pilots,
your ship builders, merchants, and warriors.
On the day of your ruin,
everyone on board sinks into the depths of the sea.
28 Your cities by the sea tremble
as your pilots cry out in terror.
29 All the oarsmen abandon their ships;
the sailors and pilots stand on the shore.
30 They cry aloud over you
and weep bitterly.
They throw dust on their heads
and roll in ashes.
31 They shave their heads in grief for you
and dress themselves in burlap.
They weep for you with bitter anguish
and deep mourning.
32 As they wail and mourn over you,
they sing this sad funeral song:
'Was there ever such a city as Tyre,
now silent at the bottom of the sea?
33 The merchandise you traded
satisfied the desires of many nations.
Kings at the ends of the earth
were enriched by your trade.
34 Now you are a wrecked ship,
broken at the bottom of the sea.
All your merchandise and crew
have gone down with you.
35 All who live along the coastlands
are appalled at your terrible fate.
Their kings are filled with horror
and look on with twisted faces.
36 The merchants among the nations
shake their heads at the sight of you,*
for you have come to a horrible end
and will exist no more.'"

A MESSAGE FOR TYRE'S KING

28 Then this message came to me from the LORD:
2 "Son of man, give the prince of Tyre this mes-
sage from the Sovereign LORD:

"In your great pride you claim, 'I am a god!
I sit on a divine throne in the heart of the sea.'
But you are only a man and not a god,
though you boast that you are a god.
3 You regard yourself as wiser than Daniel
and think no secret is hidden from you.
4 With your wisdom and understanding you have amassed great wealth—
gold and silver for your treasuries.
5 Yes, your wisdom has made you very rich,
and your riches have made you very proud.
6 "Therefore, this is what the Sovereign LORD says:
Because you think you are as wise as a god,
7 I will now bring against you a foreign army,
the terror of the nations.
They will draw their swords against your marvelous wisdom
and defile your splendor!
8 They will bring you down to the pit,
and you will die in the heart of the sea,
pierced with many wounds.
9 Will you then boast, 'I am a god!'
to those who kill you?
To them you will be no god
but merely a man!
10 You will die like an outcast*
at the hands of foreigners.
I, the Sovereign LORD, have spoken!"

11 Then this further message came to me from the
LORD: 12 "Son of man, sing this funeral song for the
king of Tyre. Give him this message from the Sover-
eign LORD:

"You were the model of perfection,
full of wisdom and exquisite in beauty.
13 You were in Eden,
the garden of God.
Your clothing was adorned with every precious stone*—

27:15 Greek version reads *Rhodes.* 27:16 Hebrew *Aram;* some manuscripts read *Edom.* 27:17 The meaning of the Hebrew is uncertain. 27:19 Hebrew *Vedan and Javan from Uzal.* The meaning of the Hebrew is uncertain. 27:36 Hebrew *hiss at you.* 28:10 Hebrew *will die the death of the uncircumcised.* 28:13 The identification of some of these gemstones is uncertain.

27:17 Judah and Israel also traded with Tyre.
28:7 ruthless men from the nations. Babylon, the unchallenged superpower among all nations, would besiege Tyre. Centuries later, Alexander the Great would besiege the city too.

28:13 Eden, the garden of God. Many see this lament as a song about Satan, who likewise empowered wicked kings like the one in Tyre as he empowered the serpent in the garden of Eden. Others see here poetic language drawn from the very mythology the pagan kings believed—stories which had many parallels to the Genesis account of Eden.

red carnelian, pale-green peridot, white
moonstone,
blue-green beryl, onyx, green jasper,
blue lapis lazuli, turquoise, and emerald—
all beautifully crafted for you
and set in the finest gold.
They were given to you
on the day you were created.
14 I ordained and anointed you
as the mighty angelic guardian.*
You had access to the holy mountain of God
and walked among the stones of fire.

15 "You were blameless in all you did
from the day you were created
until the day evil was found in you.
16 Your rich commerce led you to violence,
and you sinned.
So I banished you in disgrace
from the mountain of God.
I expelled you, O mighty guardian,
from your place among the stones of fire.
17 Your heart was filled with pride
because of all your beauty.
Your wisdom was corrupted
by your love of splendor.
So I threw you to the ground
and exposed you to the curious gaze of kings.
18 You defiled your sanctuaries
with your many sins and your dishonest trade.
So I brought fire out from within you,
and it consumed you.
I reduced you to ashes on the ground
in the sight of all who were watching.
19 All who knew you are appalled at your fate.
You have come to a terrible end,
and you will exist no more."

A MESSAGE FOR SIDON

20 Then another message came to me from the LORD:
21 "Son of man, turn and face the city of Sidon and
prophesy against it. 22 Give the people of Sidon this
message from the Sovereign LORD:

"I am your enemy, O Sidon,
and I will reveal my glory by what I do to you.
When I bring judgment against you
and reveal my holiness among you,
everyone watching will know
that I am the LORD.
23 I will send a plague against you,
and blood will be spilled in your streets.
The attack will come from every direction,
and your people will lie slaughtered within
your walls.
Then everyone will know
that I am the LORD.
24 No longer will Israel's scornful neighbors
prick and tear at her like briers and thorns.
For then they will know
that I am the Sovereign LORD.

RESTORATION FOR ISRAEL

25 "This is what the Sovereign LORD says: The people
of Israel will again live in their own land, the land I
gave my servant Jacob. For I will gather them from
the distant lands where I have scattered them. I will
reveal to the nations of the world my holiness among
my people. 26 They will live safely in Israel and build
homes and plant vineyards. And when I punish the
neighboring nations that treated them with con-
tempt, they will know that I am the LORD their God."

A MESSAGE FOR EGYPT

29 On January 7,* during the tenth year of King
Jehoiachin's captivity, this message came to me
from the LORD: 2 "Son of man, turn and face Egypt and
prophesy against Pharaoh the king and all the people
of Egypt. 3 Give them this message from the Sovereign
LORD:

"I am your enemy, O Pharaoh, king of Egypt—
you great monster, lurking in the streams of the
Nile.
For you have said, 'The Nile River is mine;
I made it for myself.'
4 I will put hooks in your jaws
and drag you out on the land
with fish sticking to your scales.
5 I will leave you and all your fish
stranded in the wilderness to die.
You will lie unburied on the open ground,
for I have given you as food to the wild animals
and birds.
6 All the people of Egypt will know that I am the LORD,
for to Israel you were just a staff made of reeds.
7 When Israel leaned on you,
you splintered and broke
and stabbed her in the armpit.
When she put her weight on you,
you collapsed, and her legs gave way.

8 "Therefore, this is what the Sovereign LORD says: I
will bring an army against you, O Egypt, and destroy
both people and animals. 9 The land of Egypt will be-
come a desolate wasteland, and the Egyptians will
know that I am the LORD.
"Because you said, 'The Nile River is mine; I made
it,' 10 I am now the enemy of both you and your riv-
er. I will make the land of Egypt a totally desolate

28:14 Hebrew *guardian cherub;* similarly in 28:16. 29:1 Hebrew *On the twelfth day of the tenth month,* of the ancient Hebrew lunar calendar. This event occurred on January 7, 587 B.C.; also see note on 1:1.

28:14 guardian cherub. Cherubim were angelic beings with flaming swords that guarded the entrance to Eden (Gen. 3:24).
28:17 threw you down to the earth. God cannot tolerate pride in His presence and drove the king of Tyre out.
28:21 Sidon. A sister city to Tyre. Sidon was both a center of commercial vitality and a place of sin.
28:24 prickling briers and painful thorns. Pagan nations would no longer be allowed to torment Israel.
28:25 demonstrate My holiness. God would redeem His reputation before the nations by redeeming His people.
29:3 Pharaoh . . . great monster. Ezekiel portrayed Egypt as a menacing force lying wait in the peaceful Nile.
29:1–32:32 As Jeremiah had focused on the judgment against Babylon, Ezekiel occupies himself here with the judgment of Egypt in these four chapters. Six of seven oracles concerning Egypt date from 587–585 B.C., while 29:17-21 dates to 571 B.C. This oracle, which predicted Babylon's destruction of Egypt in 567 B.C., was placed here as a logical extension of the first oracle (vv. 1-16).
29:1 In the tenth year. This prophecy is dated to January 587 B.C., about a year after the siege of Jerusalem began and about a year and a half before she fell.

wasteland, from Migdol to Aswan, as far south as the
border of Ethiopia.* 11 For forty years not a soul will
pass that way, neither people nor animals. It will be
completely uninhabited. 12 I will make Egypt desolate,
and it will be surrounded by other desolate nations.
Its cities will be empty and desolate for forty years,
surrounded by other ruined cities. I will scatter the
Egyptians to distant lands.

13 "But this is what the Sovereign LORD also says: At
the end of the forty years I will bring the Egyptians
home again from the nations to which they have been
scattered. 14 I will restore the prosperity of Egypt and
bring its people back to the land of Pathros in south-
ern Egypt from which they came. But Egypt will re-
main an unimportant, minor kingdom. 15 It will be the
lowliest of all the nations, never again great enough
to rise above its neighbors.

16 "Then Israel will no longer be tempted to trust
in Egypt for help. Egypt's shattered condition will
remind Israel of how sinful she was to trust Egypt
in earlier days. Then Israel will know that I am the
Sovereign LORD."

NEBUCHADNEZZAR TO CONQUER EGYPT

17 On April 26, the first day of the new year,* during the
twenty-seventh year of King Jehoiachin's captivity, this
message came to me from the LORD: 18 "Son of man, the
army of King Nebuchadnezzar* of Babylon fought so
hard against Tyre that the warriors' heads were rubbed
bare and their shoulders were raw and blistered. Yet
Nebuchadnezzar and his army won no plunder to com-
pensate them for all their work. 19 Therefore, this is what
the Sovereign LORD says: I will give the land of Egypt
to Nebuchadnezzar, king of Babylon. He will carry off
its wealth, plundering everything it has so he can pay
his army. 20 Yes, I have given him the land of Egypt as a
reward for his work, says the Sovereign LORD, because
he was working for me when he destroyed Tyre.

21 "And the day will come when I will cause the an-
cient glory of Israel to revive,* and then, Ezekiel, your
words will be respected. Then they will know that I
am the LORD."

A SAD DAY FOR EGYPT

30 This is another message that came to me from
the LORD: 2 "Son of man, prophesy and give this
message from the Sovereign LORD:

"Weep and wail
for that day,
3 for the terrible day is almost here—
the day of the LORD!
It is a day of clouds and gloom,
a day of despair for the nations.
4 A sword will come against Egypt,
and those who are slaughtered will cover the
ground.
Its wealth will be carried away
and its foundations destroyed.
The land of Ethiopia* will be ravished.
5 Ethiopia, Libya, Lydia, all Arabia,*
and all their other allies
will be destroyed in that war.

6 "For this is what the LORD says:
All of Egypt's allies will fall,
and the pride of her power will end.
From Migdol to Aswan*
they will be slaughtered by the sword,
says the Sovereign LORD.
7 Egypt will be desolate,
surrounded by desolate nations,
and its cities will be in ruins,
surrounded by other ruined cities.
8 And the people of Egypt will know that I am the
LORD
when I have set Egypt on fire
and destroyed all their allies.
9 At that time I will send swift messengers in ships
to terrify the complacent Ethiopians.
Great panic will come upon them
on that day of Egypt's certain destruction.
Watch for it!
It is sure to come!

10 "For this is what the Sovereign LORD says:
By the power of King Nebuchadnezzar* of
Babylon,
I will destroy the hordes of Egypt.
11 He and his armies—the most ruthless of all—
will be sent to demolish the land.
They will make war against Egypt
until slaughtered Egyptians cover the ground.
12 I will dry up the Nile River
and sell the land to wicked men.
I will destroy the land of Egypt and everything
in it
by the hands of foreigners.
I, the LORD, have spoken!

13 "This is what the Sovereign LORD says:
I will smash the idols* of Egypt
and the images at Memphis.*
There will be no rulers left in Egypt;
terror will sweep the land.
14 I will destroy southern Egypt,*
set fire to Zoan,
and bring judgment against Thebes.*
15 I will pour out my fury on Pelusium,*
the strongest fortress of Egypt,
and I will stamp out
the hordes of Thebes.
16 Yes, I will set fire to all Egypt!
Pelusium will be racked with pain;

29:10 Hebrew *from Migdol to Syene as far as the border of Cush.* **29:17** Hebrew *On the first day of the first month,* of the ancient Hebrew lunar calendar. This event occurred on April 26, 571 B.C.; also see note on 1:1. **29:18** Hebrew *Nebuchadrezzar,* a variant spelling of Nebuchadnezzar; also in 29:19. **29:21** Hebrew *I will cause a horn to sprout for the house of Israel.* **30:4** Hebrew *Cush;* similarly in 30:9. **30:5** Hebrew *Cush, Put, Lud, all Arabia, Cub. Cub* is otherwise unknown and may be another spelling for *Lub* (Libya). **30:6** Hebrew *to Syene.* **30:10** Hebrew *Nebuchadrezzar,* a variant spelling of Nebuchadnezzar. **30:13a** The Hebrew term (literally *round things*) probably alludes to dung. **30:13b** Hebrew *Noph;* also in 30:16. **30:14a** Hebrew *Pathros.* **30:14b** Hebrew *No;* also in 30:15, 16. **30:15** Hebrew *Sin;* also in 30:16.

30:3 a day is near. The "day of the LORD" is sometimes used generally to mean a day of judgment. Sometimes it is used to refer to God's judgment on the nations at the end of human history. Sometimes it refers to a day of blessing and deliverance for Israel (v. 3). Ezekiel's prior prophecies (7:19; 13:15) that refer to the "day of the LORD" are in the context of the imminent destruction of Judah. Here it refers to the imminent destruction of Egypt. Other prophets like Joel refer to "day of the LORD" as close at hand (Joel 1:15–2:11), and a future context (2:28:32; 3:1-21) when all nations are judged and the covenant with Israel is restored.

Thebes will be torn apart;
Memphis will live in constant terror.
17 The young men of Heliopolis and Bubastis* will
die in battle,
and the women* will be taken away as slaves.
18 When I come to break the proud strength of Egypt,
it will be a dark day for Tahpanhes, too.
A dark cloud will cover Tahpanhes,
and its daughters will be led away as captives.
19 And so I will greatly punish Egypt,
and they will know that I am the LORD."

THE BROKEN ARMS OF PHARAOH

20 On April 29,* during the eleventh year of King Je-
hoiachin's captivity, this message came to me from
the LORD: 21 "Son of man, I have broken the arm of Pha-
raoh, the king of Egypt. His arm has not been put in a
cast so that it may heal. Neither has it been bound up
with a splint to make it strong enough to hold a sword.
22 Therefore, this is what the Sovereign LORD says:
I am the enemy of Pharaoh, the king of Egypt! I will
break both of his arms—the good arm along with the
broken one—and I will make his sword clatter to the
ground. 23 I will scatter the Egyptians to many lands
throughout the world. 24 I will strengthen the arms
of Babylon's king and put my sword in his hand. But
I will break the arms of Pharaoh, king of Egypt, and
he will lie there mortally wounded, groaning in pain.
25 I will strengthen the arms of the king of Babylon,
while the arms of Pharaoh fall useless to his sides. And
when I put my sword in the hand of Babylon's king
and he brings it against the land of Egypt, Egypt will
know that I am the LORD. 26 I will scatter the Egyptians
among the nations, dispersing them throughout the
earth. Then they will know that I am the LORD."

EGYPT COMPARED TO FALLEN ASSYRIA

31 On June 21,* during the eleventh year of King
Jehoiachin's captivity, this message came to me
from the LORD: 2 "Son of man, give this message to Pha-
raoh, king of Egypt, and all his hordes:

"To whom would you compare your greatness?
3 You are like mighty Assyria,
which was once like a cedar of Lebanon,
with beautiful branches that cast deep forest
shade
and with its top high among the clouds.
4 Deep springs watered it
and helped it to grow tall and luxuriant.
The water flowed around it like a river,
streaming to all the trees nearby.
5 This great tree towered high,
higher than all the other trees around it.
It prospered and grew long thick branches
because of all the water at its roots.
6 The birds nested in its branches,
and in its shade all the wild animals gave birth.
All the great nations of the world
lived in its shadow.
7 It was strong and beautiful,
with wide-spreading branches,
for its roots went deep
into abundant water.
8 No other cedar in the garden of God
could rival it.
No cypress had branches to equal it;
no plane tree had boughs to compare.
No tree in the garden of God
came close to it in beauty.
9 Because I made this tree so beautiful,
and gave it such magnificent foliage,
it was the envy of all the other trees of Eden,
the garden of God.

10 "Therefore, this is what the Sovereign LORD says:
Because Egypt* became proud and arrogant, and
because it set itself so high above the others, with its
top reaching to the clouds, 11 I will hand it over to a
mighty nation that will destroy it as its wickedness
deserves. I have already discarded it. 12 A foreign
army—the terror of the nations—has cut it down
and left it fallen on the ground. Its branches are scat-
tered across the mountains and valleys and ravines of
the land. All those who lived in its shadow have gone
away and left it lying there.

13 "The birds roost on its fallen trunk,
and the wild animals lie among its branches.
14 Let the tree of no other nation
proudly exult in its own prosperity,
though it be higher than the clouds
and it be watered from the depths.
For all are doomed to die,
to go down to the depths of the earth.
They will land in the pit
along with everyone else on earth.

15 "This is what the Sovereign LORD says: When
Assyria went down to the grave,* I made the deep
springs mourn. I stopped its rivers and dried up its
abundant water. I clothed Lebanon in black and
caused the trees of the field to wilt. 16 I made the na-
tions shake with fear at the sound of its fall, for I sent
it down to the grave with all the others who descend
to the pit. And all the other proud trees of Eden, the
most beautiful and the best of Lebanon, the ones
whose roots went deep into the water, took comfort to
find it there with them in the depths of the earth. 17 Its
allies, too, were all destroyed and had passed away.
They had gone down to the grave—all those nations
that had lived in its shade.

30:17a Hebrew *of Awen and Pi-beseth.* **30:17b** Or *and her cities.* **30:20** Hebrew *On the seventh day of the first month,* of the ancient Hebrew lunar calendar. This event occurred on April 29, 587 B.C.; also see note on 1:1. **31:1** Hebrew *On the first day of the third month,* of the ancient Hebrew lunar calendar. This event occurred on June 21, 587 B.C.; also see note on 1:1. **31:10** Hebrew *you.* **31:15** Hebrew *to Sheol;* also in 31:16, 17.

30:21 not been bandaged. A prior defeat by Nebuchadnezzar was only the beginning of Egypt's pain and suffering. Soon, Babylon would crush every bone.

30:23, 26 disperse the Egyptians. Egypt followed Judah into exile (29:12) and was likewise allowed to return by Cyrus.

31:3 Assyria. In case Egypt needed more proof of its pending punishment, God encouraged them to consider once-powerful Assyria. It came to ruin by the hand of Babylon.

31:12 Babylon felled the mighty cedar of Assyria.

31:16 the trees of Eden . . . were comforted. Trees are used in this passage to represent nations. "Trees of Eden" represent the beautiful nations that were consoled by the fact that even the mightiest nation could not withstand Babylon.

31:17 slain by the sword. Smaller nations preceded Assyria in defeat. They shared the same murderous fate.

[18]"O Egypt, to which of the trees of Eden will you compare your strength and glory? You, too, will be brought down to the depths with all these other nations. You will lie there among the outcasts* who have died by the sword. This will be the fate of Pharaoh and all his hordes. I, the Sovereign LORD, have spoken!"

A WARNING FOR PHARAOH

32 On March 3,* during the twelfth year of King Jehoiachin's captivity, this message came to me from the LORD: [2]"Son of man, mourn for Pharaoh, king of Egypt, and give him this message:

"You think of yourself as a strong young lion among
the nations,
but you are really just a sea monster,
heaving around in your own rivers,
stirring up mud with your feet.
[3] Therefore, this is what the Sovereign LORD says:
I will send many people
to catch you in my net
and haul you out of the water.
[4] I will leave you stranded on the land to die.
All the birds of the heavens will land on you,
and the wild animals of the whole earth
will gorge themselves on you.
[5] I will scatter your flesh on the hills
and fill the valleys with your bones.
[6] I will drench the earth with your gushing blood
all the way to the mountains,
filling the ravines to the brim.
[7] When I blot you out,
I will veil the heavens and darken the stars.
I will cover the sun with a cloud,
and the moon will not give you its light.
[8] I will darken the bright stars overhead
and cover your land in darkness.
I, the Sovereign LORD, have spoken!

[9]"I will disturb many hearts when I bring news of
your downfall to distant nations you have never seen.
[10]Yes, I will shock many lands, and their kings will
be terrified at your fate. They will shudder in fear for
their lives as I brandish my sword before them on the
day of your fall. [11]For this is what the Sovereign LORD
says:

"The sword of the king of Babylon
will come against you.
[12] I will destroy your hordes with the swords of
mighty warriors—
the terror of the nations.
They will shatter the pride of Egypt,
and all its hordes will be destroyed.
[13] I will destroy all your flocks and herds
that graze beside the streams.
Never again will people or animals
muddy those waters with their feet.
[14] Then I will let the waters of Egypt become calm
again,
and they will flow as smoothly as olive oil,
says the Sovereign LORD.
[15] And when I destroy Egypt
and strip you of everything you own
and strike down all your people,
then you will know that I am the LORD.
[16] Yes, this is the funeral song
they will sing for Egypt.
Let all the nations mourn.
Let them mourn for Egypt and its hordes.
I, the Sovereign LORD, have spoken!"

EGYPT FALLS INTO THE PIT

[17]On March 17,* during the twelfth year, another mes-
sage came to me from the LORD: [18]"Son of man, weep for
the hordes of Egypt and for the other mighty nations.*
For I will send them down to the world below in com-
pany with those who descend to the pit. [19]Say to them,

'O Egypt, are you lovelier than the other nations?
No! So go down to the pit and lie there among
the outcasts.*'

[20]The Egyptians will fall with the many who have
died by the sword, for the sword is drawn against
them. Egypt and its hordes will be dragged away to
their judgment. [21]Down in the grave* mighty leaders
will mockingly welcome Egypt and its allies, saying,
'They have come down; they lie among the outcasts,
hordes slaughtered by the sword.'
[22]"Assyria lies there surrounded by the graves of
its army, those who were slaughtered by the sword.
[23]Their graves are in the depths of the pit, and they
are surrounded by their allies. They struck terror in
the hearts of people everywhere, but now they have
been slaughtered by the sword.
[24]"Elam lies there surrounded by the graves of all
its hordes, those who were slaughtered by the sword.
They struck terror in the hearts of people everywhere,
but now they have descended as outcasts to the world
below. Now they lie in the pit and share the shame of
those who have gone before them. [25]They have a rest-
ing place among the slaughtered, surrounded by the
graves of all their hordes. Yes, they terrorized the na-
tions while they lived, but now they lie in shame with
others in the pit, all of them outcasts, slaughtered by
the sword.

31:18 Hebrew *among the uncircumcised.* **32:1** Hebrew *On the first day of the twelfth month,* of the ancient Hebrew lunar calendar. This event occurred on March 3, 585 B.C.; also see note on 1:1. **32:17** Hebrew *On the fifteenth day of the month,* presumably in the twelfth month of the ancient Hebrew lunar calendar (see 32:1). This would put this message at the end of King Jehoiachin's twelfth year of captivity, on March 17, 585 B.C.; also see note on 1:1. Greek version reads *On the fifteenth day of the first month,* which would put this message on April 27, 586 B.C., at the beginning of Jehoiachin's twelfth year. **32:18** The meaning of the Hebrew is uncertain. **32:19** Hebrew *the uncircumcised;* also in 32:21, 24, 25, 26, 28, 29, 30, 32. **32:21** Hebrew *in Sheol.*

31:18 God made sure the pharaoh got the message. His end was near.
32:2 lion. Lions were symbols of strength and dominance (cp. Judah's kings, 19:23-9). Such was the apparent power of the pharaoh.
32:17-25 In Ezekiel's final message against Egypt (April 585 B.C.), he recounts all the powers fallen under the Lord's hand and reminds Egypt that she is next. Egypt will join the "uncircumcised" nations already in the "pit" (v. 18) who suffer God's judgment for their oppression of Israel. Egypt would join Assyria in the pit.
32:24 Elam. Elam, located east of Babylon, was devastated by the Assyrians in the late seventh century B.C. Jeremiah also prophesied against Elam in 597 B.C. (Jer. 49:34-39), probably because she had joined Assyria in the conquest of Israel's northern kingdom (Isa. 22:6). Elam was invaded by Nebuchadnezzar in 596. Later she joined Babylon in the destruction and exile of Jerusalem (Ezra 2:7,31; 8:7). Elam was taken over by the Medo-Persians (sixth century B.C.), but full judgment was still to come.

26 "Meshech and Tubal are there, surrounded by the graves of all their hordes. They once struck terror in the hearts of people everywhere. But now they are outcasts, all slaughtered by the sword. 27 They are not buried in honor like their fallen heroes, who went down to the grave* with their weapons—their shields covering their bodies* and their swords beneath their heads. Their guilt rests upon them because they brought terror to everyone while they were still alive.

28 "You too, Egypt, will lie crushed and broken among the outcasts, all slaughtered by the sword.

29 "Edom is there with its kings and princes. Mighty as they were, they also lie among those slaughtered by the sword, with the outcasts who have gone down to the pit.

30 "All the princes of the north and the Sidonians are there with others who have died. Once a terror, they have been put to shame. They lie there as outcasts with others who were slaughtered by the sword. They share the shame of all who have descended to the pit.

31 "When Pharaoh and his entire army arrive, he will take comfort that he is not alone in having his hordes killed, says the Sovereign LORD. 32 Although I have caused his terror to fall upon all the living, Pharaoh and his hordes will lie there among the outcasts who were slaughtered by the sword. I, the Sovereign LORD, have spoken!"

EZEKIEL AS ISRAEL'S WATCHMAN

33 Once again a message came to me from the LORD: 2 "Son of man, give your people this message: 'When I bring an army against a country, the people of that land choose one of their own to be a watchman. 3 When the watchman sees the enemy coming, he sounds the alarm to warn the people. 4 Then if those who hear the alarm refuse to take action, it is their own fault if they die. 5 They heard the alarm but ignored it, so the responsibility is theirs. If they had listened to the warning, they could have saved their lives. 6 But if the watchman sees the enemy coming and doesn't sound the alarm to warn the people, he is responsible for their captivity. They will die in their sins, but I will hold the watchman responsible for their deaths.'

7 "Now, son of man, I am making you a watchman for the people of Israel. Therefore, listen to what I say and warn them for me. 8 If I announce that some wicked people are sure to die and you fail to tell them to change their ways, then they will die in their sins, and I will hold you responsible for their deaths. 9 But if you warn them to repent and they don't repent, they will die in their sins, but you will have saved yourself.

THE WATCHMAN'S MESSAGE

10 "Son of man, give the people of Israel this message: You are saying, 'Our sins are heavy upon us; we are wasting away! How can we survive?' 11 As surely as I live, says the Sovereign LORD, I take no pleasure in the death of wicked people. I only want them to turn from their wicked ways so they can live. Turn! Turn from your wickedness, O people of Israel! Why should you die?

12 "Son of man, give your people this message: The righteous behavior of righteous people will not save them if they turn to sin, nor will the wicked behavior of wicked people destroy them if they repent and turn from their sins. 13 When I tell righteous people that they will live, but then they sin, expecting their past righteousness to save them, then none of their righteous acts will be remembered. I will destroy them for their sins. 14 And suppose I tell some wicked people that they will surely die, but then they turn from their sins and do what is just and right. 15 For instance, they might give back a debtor's security, return what they have stolen, and obey my life-giving laws, no longer doing what is evil. If they do this, then they will surely live and not die. 16 None of their past sins will be brought up again, for they have done what is just and right, and they will surely live.

17 "Your people are saying, 'The Lord isn't doing what's right,' but it is they who are not doing what's right. 18 For again I say, when righteous people turn away from their righteous behavior and turn to evil, they will die. 19 But if wicked people turn from their wickedness and do what is just and right, they will live. 20 O people of Israel, you are saying, 'The Lord isn't doing what's right.' But I judge each of you according to your deeds."

EXPLANATION OF JERUSALEM'S FALL

21 On January 8,* during the twelfth year of our captivity, a survivor from Jerusalem came to me and said, "The city has fallen!" 22 The previous evening the LORD had taken hold of me and given me back my voice. So I was able to speak when this man arrived the next morning.

23 Then this message came to me from the LORD: 24 "Son of man, the scattered remnants of Israel living among the ruined cities keep saying, 'Abraham was only one man, yet he gained possession of the entire land. We are many; surely the land has been given to us as a possession.' 25 So tell these people, 'This is what the Sovereign LORD says: You eat meat with blood in it, you worship idols,* and you murder the innocent. Do you really think the land should be yours? 26 Murderers! Idolaters! Adulterers! Should the land belong to you?'

32:27a Hebrew *to Sheol.* **32:27b** The meaning of the Hebrew is uncertain. **33:21** Hebrew *On the fifth day of the tenth month,* of the ancient Hebrew lunar calendar. This event occurred on January 8, 585 B.C.; also see note on 1:1. **33:25** The Hebrew term (literally *round things*) probably alludes to dung.

33:1–48:35 The last section of Ezekiel's prophecy is concerned with the fulfillment of God's covenant ideal for Israel. He would renew his commitment with them (chap. 33), raise a new David to shepherd them (chap. 34), defeat their enemies and return them to prosperity (chaps. 35–36), resurrect the covenant community (chap. 37), defeat the last-ditch efforts of nations hostile to Israel (chaps. 38–39), and dwell with His people in a renewed Jerusalem (chaps. 40–48).

33:6 responsible for their captivity. The watchman was held responsible for the safety of all the inhabitants inside the city walls. The spiritual condition of Jerusalem was of vital importance.

33:10 Our sins are heavy upon us. The exiles finally made a significant spiritual breakthrough. They recognized their weighty sinfulness.

33:11 to turn from their wicked ways. God's remedy is sincere repentance without which there is not true faith.

33:12-20 In God's justice system, every person is held accountable for personal choices (18:21-29). Judgment is meted out on a fair and equitable scale (vv. 17-20).

33:22 I was able to speak. When Babylon finally took over Jerusalem, God's restrictions on Ezekiel were lifted (see 3:26).

33:24 only one man . . . We are many. The remaining Jews appealed to strength in numbers, hoping to change God's plans. Like homesick children, they wanted to stay in their homeland.

27 "Say to them, 'This is what the Sovereign LORD
says: As surely as I live, those living in the ruins will
die by the sword. And I will send wild animals to eat
those living in the open fields. Those hiding in the
forts and caves will die of disease. 28 I will complete-
ly destroy the land and demolish her pride. Her ar-
rogant power will come to an end. The mountains of
Israel will be so desolate that no one will even travel
through them. 29 When I have completely destroyed
the land because of their detestable sins, then they
will know that I am the LORD.'
30 "Son of man, your people talk about you in their
houses and whisper about you at the doors. They say
to each other, 'Come on, let's go hear the prophet tell
us what the LORD is saying!' 31 So my people come pre-
tending to be sincere and sit before you. They listen to
your words, but they have no intention of doing what
you say. Their mouths are full of lustful words, and
their hearts seek only after money. 32 You are very en-
tertaining to them, like someone who sings love songs
with a beautiful voice or plays fine music on an in-
strument. They hear what you say, but they don't act
on it! 33 But when all these terrible things happen to
them—as they certainly will—then they will know
a prophet has been among them."

THE SHEPHERDS OF ISRAEL

34 Then this message came to me from the LORD:
2 "Son of man, prophesy against the shepherds,
the leaders of Israel. Give them this message from the
Sovereign LORD: What sorrow awaits you shepherds
who feed yourselves instead of your flocks. Shouldn't
shepherds feed their sheep? 3 You drink the milk, wear
the wool, and butcher the best animals, but you let your
flocks starve. 4 You have not taken care of the weak.
You have not tended the sick or bound up the injured.
You have not gone looking for those who have wan-
dered away and are lost. Instead, you have ruled them
with harshness and cruelty. 5 So my sheep have been
scattered without a shepherd, and they are easy prey
for any wild animal. 6 They have wandered through all
the mountains and all the hills, across the face of the
earth, yet no one has gone to search for them.
7 "Therefore, you shepherds, hear the word of the
LORD: 8 As surely as I live, says the Sovereign LORD, you
abandoned my flock and left them to be attacked by ev-
ery wild animal. And though you were my shepherds,
you didn't search for my sheep when they were lost.
You took care of yourselves and left the sheep to starve.
9 Therefore, you shepherds, hear the word of the LORD.
10 This is what the Sovereign LORD says: I now consider
these shepherds my enemies, and I will hold them re-
sponsible for what has happened to my flock. I will take
away their right to feed the flock, and I will stop them
from feeding themselves. I will rescue my flock from
their mouths; the sheep will no longer be their prey.

THE GOOD SHEPHERD

11 "For this is what the Sovereign LORD says: I my-
self will search and find my sheep. 12 I will be like a
shepherd looking for his scattered flock. I will find
my sheep and rescue them from all the places where
they were scattered on that dark and cloudy day. 13 I
will bring them back home to their own land of Is-
rael from among the peoples and nations. I will feed
them on the mountains of Israel and by the rivers and
in all the places where people live. 14 Yes, I will give
them good pastureland on the high hills of Israel.
There they will lie down in pleasant places and feed
in the lush pastures of the hills. 15 I myself will tend my
sheep and give them a place to lie down in peace, says
the Sovereign LORD. 16 I will search for my lost ones
who strayed away, and I will bring them safely home
again. I will bandage the injured and strengthen the
weak. But I will destroy those who are fat and power-
ful. I will feed them, yes—feed them justice!
17 "And as for you, my flock, this is what the Sov-
ereign LORD says to his people: I will judge between
one animal of the flock and another, separating the
sheep from the goats. 18 Isn't it enough for you to keep
the best of the pastures for yourselves? Must you also
trample down the rest? Isn't it enough for you to drink
clear water for yourselves? Must you also muddy the
rest with your feet? 19 Why must my flock eat what
you have trampled down and drink water you have
fouled?
20 "Therefore, this is what the Sovereign LORD says:
I will surely judge between the fat sheep and the
scrawny sheep. 21 For you fat sheep pushed and butt-
ed and crowded my sick and hungry flock until you
scattered them to distant lands. 22 So I will rescue my
flock, and they will no longer be abused. I will judge
between one animal of the flock and another. 23 And
I will set over them one shepherd, my servant David.
He will feed them and be a shepherd to them. 24 And
I, the LORD, will be their God, and my servant David
will be a prince among my people. I, the LORD, have
spoken!

THE LORD'S COVENANT OF PEACE

25 "I will make a covenant of peace with my people
and drive away the dangerous animals from the land.
Then they will be able to camp safely in the wildest
places and sleep in the woods without fear. 26 I will
bless my people and their homes around my holy
hill. And in the proper season I will send the showers
they need. There will be showers of blessing. 27 The
orchards and fields of my people will yield bumper
crops, and everyone will live in safety. When I have
broken their chains of slavery and rescued them from
those who enslaved them, then they will know that I
am the LORD. 28 They will no longer be prey for oth-
er nations, and wild animals will no longer devour
them. They will live in safety, and no one will frighten
them.
29 "And I will make their land famous for its crops,
so my people will never again suffer from famines or
the insults of foreign nations. 30 In this way, they will
know that I, the LORD their God, am with them. And
they will know that they, the people of Israel, are my

34:2 leaders of Israel. Leaders were often regarded as shepherds (Num 27:17; Isa. 44:28; Jer. 23:2). These misfit shepherds disregarded the physical well-being and spiritual condition of the people under their care.

34:5 scattered without a shepherd. As a result of their leaders' selfishness, the entire flock would suffer. Ezekiel referred to the divide-and-conquer strategy of the exile as a flock without a shepherd (see Mark 6:34).

34:16 fat and powerful. The tables were turned. The selfish leaders would now be destroyed. Then God would respond and tend to the discarded sheep Himself.

34:17 I will judge. God turned His attention to the individuals represented in the flock. Judgment would be handed out to each.

34:23-24 my servant David. Ezekiel described a future united kingdom with a king who would truly care for the sheep. Some see this as a reference to Jesus' rule of the kingdom, while others believe David will rule under Jesus.

people, says the Sovereign LORD. [31] You are my flock, the sheep of my pasture. You are my people, and I am your God. I, the Sovereign LORD, have spoken!"

A MESSAGE FOR EDOM

35 Again a message came to me from the LORD: [2] "Son of man, turn and face Mount Seir, and prophesy against its people. [3] Give them this message from the Sovereign LORD:

"I am your enemy, O Mount Seir,
and I will raise my fist against you
to destroy you completely.
[4] I will demolish your cities
and make you desolate.
Then you will know that I am the LORD.

[5] "Your eternal hatred for the people of Israel led you to butcher them when they were helpless, when I had already punished them for all their sins. [6] As surely as I live, says the Sovereign LORD, since you show no distaste for blood, I will give you a bloodbath of your own. Your turn has come! [7] I will make Mount Seir utterly desolate, killing off all who try to escape and any who return. [8] I will fill your mountains with the dead. Your hills, your valleys, and your ravines will be filled with people slaughtered by the sword. [9] I will make you desolate forever. Your cities will never be rebuilt. Then you will know that I am the LORD.

[10] "For you said, 'The lands of Israel and Judah will be ours. We will take possession of them. What do we care that the LORD is there!' [11] Therefore, as surely as I live, says the Sovereign LORD, I will pay back your angry deeds with my own. I will punish you for all your acts of anger, envy, and hatred. And I will make myself known to Israel* by what I do to you. [12] Then you will know that I, the LORD, have heard every contemptuous word you spoke against the mountains of Israel. For you said, 'They are desolate; they have been given to us as food to eat!' [13] In saying that, you boasted proudly against me, and I have heard it all!

[14] "This is what the Sovereign LORD says: The whole world will rejoice when I make you desolate. [15] You rejoiced at the desolation of Israel's territory. Now I will rejoice at yours! You will be wiped out, you people of Mount Seir and all who live in Edom! Then you will know that I am the LORD.

RESTORATION FOR ISRAEL

36 "Son of man, prophesy to Israel's mountains. Give them this message: O mountains of Israel, hear the word of the LORD! [2] This is what the Sovereign LORD says: Your enemies have taunted you, saying, 'Aha! Now the ancient heights belong to us!' [3] Therefore, son of man, give the mountains of Israel this message from the Sovereign LORD: Your enemies have attacked you from all directions, making you the property of many nations and the object of much mocking and slander. [4] Therefore, O mountains of Israel, hear the word of the Sovereign LORD. He speaks to the hills and mountains, ravines and valleys, and to ruined wastes and long-deserted cities that have been destroyed and mocked by the surrounding nations. [5] This is what the Sovereign LORD says: My jealous anger burns against these nations, especially Edom, because they have shown utter contempt for me by gleefully taking my land for themselves as plunder.

[6] "Therefore, prophesy to the hills and mountains, the ravines and valleys of Israel. This is what the Sovereign LORD says: I am furious that you have suffered shame before the surrounding nations. [7] Therefore, this is what the Sovereign LORD says: I have taken a solemn oath that those nations will soon have their own shame to endure.

[8] "But the mountains of Israel will produce heavy crops of fruit for my people—for they will be coming home again soon! [9] See, I care about you, and I will pay attention to you. Your ground will be plowed and your crops planted. [10] I will greatly increase the population of Israel, and the ruined cities will be rebuilt and filled with people. [11] I will increase not only the people, but also your animals. O mountains of Israel, I will bring people to live on you once again. I will make you even more prosperous than you were before. Then you will know that I am the LORD. [12] I will cause my people to walk on you once again, and you will be their territory. You will never again rob them of their children.

[13] "This is what the Sovereign LORD says: The other nations taunt you, saying, 'Israel is a land that devours its own people and robs them of their children!' [14] But you will never again devour your people or rob them of their children, says the Sovereign LORD. [15] I will not let you hear those other nations insult you, and you will no longer be mocked by them. You will not be a land that causes its nation to fall, says the Sovereign LORD."

[16] Then this further message came to me from the LORD: [17] "Son of man, when the people of Israel were living in their own land, they defiled it by the evil way they lived. To me their conduct was as unclean as a woman's menstrual cloth. [18] They polluted the land with murder and the worship of idols,* so I poured out my fury on them. [19] I scattered them to many lands to punish them for the evil way they had lived. [20] But when they were scattered among the nations, they brought shame on my holy name. For the nations said, 'These are the people of the LORD, but he couldn't keep them safe in his own land!' [21] Then I was concerned for my holy name, on which my people brought shame among the nations.

[22] "Therefore, give the people of Israel this message from the Sovereign LORD: I am bringing you back, but not because you deserve it. I am doing it to protect

35:11 Hebrew *to them;* Greek version reads *to you.* **36:18** The Hebrew term (literally *round things*) probably alludes to dung; also in 36:25.

35:2 Mount Seir. While on the subject of peace, God encouraged His people by judging one of their worst enemies, Edom (see Gen. 32–33).
35:5 eternal hatred. The Edomites showed their true colors when they raided the weakened Jerusalem (Obad. 12-14). They cheered when Nebuchadnezzar destroyed the city (Ps. 137; Joel 3:19).
36:1,4 mountains. Earlier, the prophet pronounced judgment on the mountains of Israel because of Israel's worship of idols in the "high places" (6:1-14). After this judgment had been fulfilled, Ezekiel then pronounced a double judgment on Edom's Mount Seir (35:1-3, 14) for Edom's role in reducing Israel's Holy Mount (Jerusalem). Now the prophet again speaks to the mountains of Israel, but this time to announce judgment on the "rest of the nations" the Lord employed to chastise His daughter Israel. Israel's mountains would flourish once more as she is brought back from exile and enjoys prosperity and security (vv. 8-15).
36:22 not because you deserve it. God's restoration of his people was not a personal favor to the people. He recovered His nation for His own sake to demonstrate His glory. This is the reason He gave for withholding wrath (20:9).

my holy name, on which you brought shame while
you were scattered among the nations. 23 I will show
how holy my great name is—the name on which you
brought shame among the nations. And when I re-
veal my holiness through you before their very eyes,
says the Sovereign LORD, then the nations will know
that I am the LORD. 24 For I will gather you up from all
the nations and bring you home again to your land.
25 "Then I will sprinkle clean water on you, and you
will be clean. Your filth will be washed away, and you
will no longer worship idols. 26 And I will give you a
new heart, and I will put a new spirit in you. I will
take out your stony, stubborn heart and give you a
tender, responsive heart.* 27 And I will put my Spirit in
you so that you will follow my decrees and be careful
to obey my regulations.
28 "And you will live in Israel, the land I gave your
ancestors long ago. You will be my people, and I will
be your God. 29 I will cleanse you of your filthy behav-
ior. I will give you good crops of grain, and I will send
no more famines on the land. 30 I will give you great
harvests from your fruit trees and fields, and never
again will the surrounding nations be able to scoff
at your land for its famines. 31 Then you will remem-
ber your past sins and despise yourselves for all the
detestable things you did. 32 But remember, says the
Sovereign LORD, I am not doing this because you de-
serve it. O my people of Israel, you should be utterly
ashamed of all you have done!
33 "This is what the Sovereign LORD says: When
I cleanse you from your sins, I will repopulate your
cities, and the ruins will be rebuilt. 34 The fields that
used to lie empty and desolate in plain view of every-
one will again be farmed. 35 And when I bring you
back, people will say, 'This former wasteland is now
like the Garden of Eden! The abandoned and ruined
cities now have strong walls and are filled with peo-
ple!' 36 Then the surrounding nations that survive will
know that I, the LORD, have rebuilt the ruins and re-
planted the wasteland. For I, the LORD, have spoken,
and I will do what I say.
37 "This is what the Sovereign LORD says: I am ready
to hear Israel's prayers and to increase their numbers
like a flock. 38 They will be as numerous as the sacred
flocks that fill Jerusalem's streets at the time of her festi-
vals. The ruined cities will be crowded with people once
more, and everyone will know that I am the LORD."

A VALLEY OF DRY BONES

37 The LORD took hold of me, and I was carried
away by the Spirit of the LORD to a valley filled
with bones. 2 He led me all around among the bones
that covered the valley floor. They were scattered
everywhere across the ground and were completely
dried out. 3 Then he asked me, "Son of man, can these
bones become living people again?"
"O Sovereign LORD," I replied, "you alone know the
answer to that."
4 Then he said to me, "Speak a prophetic message
to these bones and say, 'Dry bones, listen to the word
of the LORD! 5 This is what the Sovereign LORD says:
Look! I am going to put breath into you and make you
live again! 6 I will put flesh and muscles on you and
cover you with skin. I will put breath into you, and
you will come to life. Then you will know that I am
the LORD.'"
7 So I spoke this message, just as he told me. Sud-
denly as I spoke, there was a rattling noise all across
the valley. The bones of each body came together and
attached themselves as complete skeletons. 8 Then as
I watched, muscles and flesh formed over the bones.
Then skin formed to cover their bodies, but they still
had no breath in them.
9 Then he said to me, "Speak a prophetic message
to the winds, son of man. Speak a prophetic message
and say, 'This is what the Sovereign LORD says: Come,
O breath, from the four winds! Breathe into these
dead bodies so they may live again.'"
10 So I spoke the message as he commanded me, and
breath came into their bodies. They all came to life
and stood up on their feet—a great army.
11 Then he said to me, "Son of man, these bones rep-
resent the people of Israel. They are saying, 'We have
become old, dry bones—all hope is gone. Our nation
is finished.' 12 Therefore, prophesy to them and say,
'This is what the Sovereign LORD says: O my people, I
will open your graves of exile and cause you to rise
again. Then I will bring you back to the land of Isra-
el. 13 When this happens, O my people, you will know
that I am the LORD. 14 I will put my Spirit in you, and
you will live again and return home to your own land.
Then you will know that I, the LORD, have spoken, and
I have done what I said. Yes, the LORD has spoken!'"

REUNION OF ISRAEL AND JUDAH

15 Again a message came to me from the LORD: 16 "Son
of man, take a piece of wood and carve on it these
words: 'This represents Judah and its allied tribes.'
Then take another piece and carve these words on
it: 'This represents Ephraim and the northern tribes
of Israel.'* 17 Now hold them together in your hand as
if they were one piece of wood. 18 When your people
ask you what your actions mean, 19 say to them, 'This
is what the Sovereign LORD says: I will take Ephraim
and the northern tribes and join them to Judah. I will
make them one piece of wood in my hand.'
20 "Then hold out the pieces of wood you have in-
scribed, so the people can see them. 21 And give them
this message from the Sovereign LORD: I will gather
the people of Israel from among the nations. I will
bring them home to their own land from the places
where they have been scattered. 22 I will unify them
into one nation on the mountains of Israel. One king
will rule them all; no longer will they be divided into
two nations or into two kingdoms. 23 They will never
again pollute themselves with their idols* and vile

36:26 Hebrew *a heart of flesh.* **37:16** Hebrew *This is Ephraim's wood, representing Joseph and all the house of Israel;* similarly in 37:19.
37:23a The Hebrew term (literally *round things*) probably alludes to dung.

36:26-27 new heart . . . new spirit . . . my Spirit . . . obey my regulations. In the New Covenant promise, all Israel will be saved (Rom. 11:26), and God's law will be written on their hearts (Jer. 31:33). In that day, Israel will finally obey the Law and have faith in God.
37:8 but they still had no breath. Similar to an airless balloon, the lifeless shape lacked the mysterious and divine quality needed to bring it to life (see also Gen. 2:7). Ezekiel saw Israel's restoration in stages, first in belief and later when God's Spirit was poured into them.
37:17 together. Although Israel had been divided into two kingdoms for centuries, Ezekiel illustrated a united future.

images and rebellion, for I will save them from their
sinful apostasy.* I will cleanse them. Then they will
truly be my people, and I will be their God.
24 "My servant David will be their king, and they
will have only one shepherd. They will obey my reg-
ulations and be careful to keep my decrees. 25 They
will live in the land I gave my servant Jacob, the land
where their ancestors lived. They and their children
and their grandchildren after them will live there
forever, generation after generation. And my servant
David will be their prince forever. 26 And I will make
a covenant of peace with them, an everlasting cov-
enant. I will give them their land and increase their
numbers,* and I will put my Temple among them
forever. 27 I will make my home among them. I will be
their God, and they will be my people. 28 And when my
Temple is among them forever, the nations will know
that I am the LORD, who makes Israel holy."

A MESSAGE FOR GOG

38 This is another message that came to me from
the LORD: 2 "Son of man, turn and face Gog of the
land of Magog, the prince who rules over the nations
of Meshech and Tubal, and prophesy against him.
3 Give him this message from the Sovereign LORD: Gog,
I am your enemy! 4 I will turn you around and put
hooks in your jaws to lead you out with your whole
army—your horses and charioteers in full armor
and a great horde armed with shields and swords.
5 Persia, Ethiopia, and Libya* will join you, too, with
all their weapons. 6 Gomer and all its armies will also
join you, along with the armies of Beth-togarmah
from the distant north, and many others.
7 "Get ready; be prepared! Keep all the armies around
you mobilized, and take command of them. 8 A long
time from now you will be called into action. In the dis-
tant future you will swoop down on the land of Israel,
which will be enjoying peace after recovering from
war and after its people have returned from many
lands to the mountains of Israel. 9 You and all your al-
lies—a vast and awesome army—will roll down on
them like a storm and cover the land like a cloud.
10 "This is what the Sovereign LORD says: At that
time evil thoughts will come to your mind, and you
will devise a wicked scheme. 11 You will say, 'Israel is
an unprotected land filled with unwalled villages! I
will march against her and destroy these people who
live in such confidence! 12 I will go to those formerly
desolate cities that are now filled with people who
have returned from exile in many nations. I will cap-
ture vast amounts of plunder, for the people are rich
with livestock and other possessions now. They think
the whole world revolves around them!' 13 But Sheba
and Dedan and the merchants of Tarshish will ask,
'Do you really think the armies you have gathered
can rob them of silver and gold? Do you think you can
drive away their livestock and seize their goods and
carry off plunder?'
14 "Therefore, son of man, prophesy against Gog.
Give him this message from the Sovereign LORD:
When my people are living in peace in their land,
then you will rouse yourself.* 15 You will come from
your homeland in the distant north with your vast
cavalry and your mighty army, 16 and you will attack
my people Israel, covering their land like a cloud. At
that time in the distant future, I will bring you against
my land as everyone watches, and my holiness will be
displayed by what happens to you, Gog. Then all the
nations will know that I am the LORD.
17 "This is what the Sovereign LORD asks: Are you
the one I was talking about long ago, when I an-
nounced through Israel's prophets that in the future
I would bring you against my people? 18 But this is
what the Sovereign LORD says: When Gog invades the
land of Israel, my fury will boil over! 19 In my jealou-
sy and blazing anger, I promise a mighty shaking in
the land of Israel on that day. 20 All living things—the
fish in the sea, the birds of the sky, the animals of the
field, the small animals that scurry along the ground,
and all the people on earth—will quake in terror at
my presence. Mountains will be thrown down; cliffs
will crumble; walls will fall to the earth. 21 I will sum-
mon the sword against you on all the hills of Israel,
says the Sovereign LORD. Your men will turn their
swords against each other. 22 I will punish you and
your armies with disease and bloodshed; I will send
torrential rain, hailstones, fire, and burning sulfur!
23 In this way, I will show my greatness and holiness,
and I will make myself known to all the nations of the
world. Then they will know that I am the LORD.

THE SLAUGHTER OF GOG'S HORDES

39 "Son of man, prophesy against Gog. Give him
this message from the Sovereign LORD: I am
your enemy, O Gog, ruler of the nations of Meshech
and Tubal. 2 I will turn you around and drive you
toward the mountains of Israel, bringing you from
the distant north. 3 I will knock the bow from your
left hand and the arrows from your right hand, and
I will leave you helpless. 4 You and your army and
your allies will all die on the mountains. I will feed
you to the vultures and wild animals. 5 You will fall in
the open fields, for I have spoken, says the Sovereign
LORD. 6 And I will rain down fire on Magog and on all
your allies who live safely on the coasts. Then they
will know that I am the LORD.

37:23b As in many Hebrew manuscripts and Greek version; Masoretic Text reads *from all their dwelling places where they sinned.* **37:26** Hebrew reads *I will give them and increase their numbers;* Greek version lacks the entire phrase. **38:5** Hebrew *Paras, Cush, and Put.* **38:14** As in Greek version; Hebrew reads *then you will know.*

37:24 David. David was Israel's ultimate king because he obeyed God's law and had great faith. In the millennial kingdom Jesus will rule and perhaps David will rule under Him.

38:8 called into action. Gog would be summoned to battle against Israel once God's people were finally resettled. Some see this as coming after Israel's physical regathering but before the spiritual restoration. Others picture Gog and Magog as participants in the final battle at the end of the millennial kingdom (Rev. 20:8).

38:11 unwalled villages. A peaceful and restored Israel would have no use for protective barriers. In this surreal future battle, Gog would take advantage of its vulnerability.

38:17 Are you the one. Gog is identified as the subject of similar prophecies of days gone by (Joel 3:9-14).

38:19 mighty shaking in the land. God would intervene, announcing His presence in the form of a thunderous earthquake. He would shatter Gog's plans for victory.

38:22 The enemy's internal confusion (v. 21) would be compounded by God's use of supernatural plagues and storms. Israel did not even need an army.

39:4 feed you to the vultures and wild animals. The worst curse imaginable was not to receive proper burial and so be vulnerable to weather and animals. To a Hebrew, there was no clear distinction between body and soul. Those not buried were thought to be aware of such an awful fate and were restless until they were properly buried.

7 "In this way, I will make known my holy name among my people of Israel. I will not let anyone bring shame on it. And the nations, too, will know that I am the LORD, the Holy One of Israel. 8 That day of judgment will come, says the Sovereign LORD. Everything will happen just as I have declared it.

9 "Then the people in the towns of Israel will go out and pick up your small and large shields, bows and arrows, javelins and spears, and they will use them for fuel. There will be enough to last them seven years! 10 They won't need to cut wood from the fields or forests, for these weapons will give them all the fuel they need. They will plunder those who planned to plunder them, and they will rob those who planned to rob them, says the Sovereign LORD.

11 "And I will make a vast graveyard for Gog and his hordes in the Valley of the Travelers, east of the Dead Sea.* It will block the way of those who travel there, and they will change the name of the place to the Valley of Gog's Hordes. 12 It will take seven months for the people of Israel to bury the bodies and cleanse the land. 13 Everyone in Israel will help, for it will be a glorious victory for Israel when I demonstrate my glory on that day, says the Sovereign LORD.

14 "After seven months, teams of men will be appointed to search the land for skeletons to bury, so the land will be made clean again. 15 Whenever bones are found, a marker will be set up so the burial crews will take them to be buried in the Valley of Gog's Hordes. 16 (There will be a town there named Hamonah, which means 'horde.') And so the land will finally be cleansed.

17 "And now, son of man, this is what the Sovereign LORD says: Call all the birds and wild animals. Say to them: Gather together for my great sacrificial feast. Come from far and near to the mountains of Israel, and there eat flesh and drink blood! 18 Eat the flesh of mighty men and drink the blood of princes as though they were rams, lambs, goats, and bulls—all fattened animals from Bashan! 19 Gorge yourselves with flesh until you are glutted; drink blood until you are drunk. This is the sacrificial feast I have prepared for you. 20 Feast at my banquet table—feast on horses and charioteers, on mighty men and all kinds of valiant warriors, says the Sovereign LORD.

21 "In this way, I will demonstrate my glory to the nations. Everyone will see the punishment I have inflicted on them and the power of my fist when I strike. 22 And from that time on the people of Israel will know that I am the LORD their God. 23 The nations will then know why Israel was sent away to exile—it was punishment for sin, for they were unfaithful to their God. Therefore, I turned away from them and let their enemies destroy them. 24 I turned my face away and punished them because of their defilement and their sins.

RESTORATION FOR GOD'S PEOPLE

25 "So now, this is what the Sovereign LORD says: I will end the captivity of my people*; I will have mercy on all Israel, for I jealously guard my holy reputation! 26 They will accept responsibility for* their past shame and unfaithfulness after they come home to live in peace in their own land, with no one to bother them. 27 When I bring them home from the lands of their enemies, I will display my holiness among them for all the nations to see. 28 Then my people will know that I am the LORD their God, because I sent them away to exile and brought them home again. I will leave none of my people behind. 29 And I will never again turn my face from them, for I will pour out my Spirit upon the people of Israel. I, the Sovereign LORD, have spoken!"

THE NEW TEMPLE AREA

40 On April 28,* during the twenty-fifth year of our captivity—fourteen years after the fall of Jerusalem—the LORD took hold of me. 2 In a vision from God he took me to the land of Israel and set me down on a very high mountain. From there I could see toward the south what appeared to be a city. 3 As he brought me nearer, I saw a man whose face shone like bronze standing beside a gateway entrance. He was holding in his hand a linen measuring cord and a measuring rod.

4 He said to me, "Son of man, watch and listen. Pay close attention to everything I show you. You have been brought here so I can show you many things. Then you will return to the people of Israel and tell them everything you have seen."

THE EAST GATEWAY

5 I could see a wall completely surrounding the Temple area. The man took a measuring rod that was 10½ feet* long and measured the wall, and the wall was 10½ feet* thick and 10½ feet high.

6 Then he went over to the eastern gateway. He climbed the steps and measured the threshold of the gateway; it was 10½ feet front to back.* 7 There were guard alcoves on each side built into the gateway passage. Each of these alcoves was 10½ feet square, with a distance between them of 8¾ feet* along the passage wall. The gateway's inner threshold, which led to the entry room at the inner end of the gateway passage, was 10½ feet front to back. 8 He also measured the entry room of the gateway.* 9 It was

39:11 Hebrew *the sea.* **39:25** Hebrew *of Jacob.* **39:26** A few Hebrew manuscripts read *They will forget.* **40:1** Hebrew *At the beginning of the year, on the tenth day of the month,* of the ancient Hebrew lunar calendar. This event occurred on April 28, 573 B.C.; also see note on 1:1. **40:5a** Hebrew *6 long cubits* [3.2 meters], *each being a cubit* [18 inches or 45 centimeters] *and a handbreadth* [3 inches or 8 centimeters] *in length.* **40:5b** Hebrew *1 rod* [3.2 meters]; also in 40:5c, 7. **40:6** As in Greek version, which reads *1 rod* [3.2 meters] *deep;* Hebrew reads *1 rod deep, and 1 threshold, 1 rod deep.* **40:7** Hebrew *5 cubits* [2.7 meters]; also in 40:48. **40:8** As in many Hebrew manuscripts and Syriac version; other Hebrew manuscripts add *which faced inward toward the Temple; it was 1 rod* [10.5 feet or 3.2 meters] *deep.* [9]*Then he measured the entry room of the gateway.*

39:12 seven months. In Israel, it required seven days to be cleansed from touching a dead body (Num. 19:11-22). That the contamination here will take a week of months, rather than a regular week, not only implies the sheer number of dead bodies but the time it would take to purify the land.

39:22-23 God's reputation is one of justice and mercy (v. 25) when it comes to His own people. He showed compassion and safeguarded His name.

40:2 a very high mountain. A reference to Mt. Zion in a restored Jerusalem of the future.

40:4 Pay close attention to everything I show you. Some interpreters feel the temple God showed Ezekiel is symbolic and not a literal temple. Others point out that the description is very specific and must refer to a temple not yet built: the temple of the millennial kingdom of Christ.

40:6 eastern gate. God's glory left the temple through the east gate (10:19) and would likewise return through it (43:1-5). The restoration of the temple would be the capstone of Israel's reemergence (37:26-27). It's magnificence would exceed Solomon's and then Herod's temple. The temple of the last days would be a beacon and sign to the world that God once again dwelt in the midst of Israel (48:35; Rev. 21:3-4; 22:1-4).

14 feet* across, with supporting columns 3½ feet* thick. This entry room was at the inner end of the gateway structure, facing toward the Temple.

10 There were three guard alcoves on each side of the gateway passage. Each had the same measurements, and the dividing walls separating them were also identical. 11 The man measured the gateway entrance, which was 17½ feet* wide at the opening and 22¾ feet* wide in the gateway passage. 12 In front of each of the guard alcoves was a 21-inch* curb. The alcoves themselves were 10½ feet* on each side.

13 Then he measured the entire width of the gateway, measuring the distance between the back walls of facing guard alcoves; this distance was 43¾ feet.* 14 He measured the dividing walls all along the inside of the gateway up to the entry room of the gateway; this distance was 105 feet.* 15 The full length of the gateway passage was 87½ feet* from one end to the other. 16 There were recessed windows that narrowed inward through the walls of the guard alcoves and their dividing walls. There were also windows in the entry room. The surfaces of the dividing walls were decorated with carved palm trees.

THE OUTER COURTYARD

17 Then the man brought me through the gateway into the outer courtyard of the Temple. A stone pavement ran along the walls of the courtyard, and thirty rooms were built against the walls, opening onto the pavement. 18 This pavement flanked the gates and extended out from the walls into the courtyard the same distance as the gateway entrance. This was the lower pavement. 19 Then the man measured across the Temple's outer courtyard between the outer and inner gateways; the distance was 175 feet.*

THE NORTH GATEWAY

20 The man measured the gateway on the north just like the one on the east. 21 Here, too, there were three guard alcoves on each side, with dividing walls and an entry room. All the measurements matched those of the east gateway. The gateway passage was 87½ feet long and 43¾ feet wide between the back walls of facing guard alcoves. 22 The windows, the entry room, and the palm tree decorations were identical to those in the east gateway. There were seven steps leading up to the gateway entrance, and the entry room was at the inner end of the gateway passage. 23 Here on the north side, just as on the east, there was another gateway leading to the Temple's inner courtyard directly opposite this outer gateway. The distance between the two gateways was 175 feet.

THE SOUTH GATEWAY

24 Then the man took me around to the south gateway and measured its various parts, and they were exactly the same as in the others. 25 It had windows along the walls as the others did, and there was an entry room where the gateway passage opened into the outer courtyard. And like the others, the gateway passage was 87½ feet long and 43¾ feet wide between the back walls of facing guard alcoves. 26 This gateway also had a stairway of seven steps leading up to it, and an entry room at the inner end, and palm tree decorations along the dividing walls. 27 And here again, directly opposite the outer gateway, was another gateway that led into the inner courtyard. The distance between the two gateways was 175 feet.

GATEWAYS TO THE INNER COURTYARD

28 Then the man took me to the south gateway leading into the inner courtyard. He measured it, and it had the same measurements as the other gateways. 29 Its guard alcoves, dividing walls, and entry room were the same size as those in the others. It also had windows along its walls and in the entry room. And like the others, the gateway passage was 87½ feet long and 43¾ feet wide. 30 (The entry rooms of the gateways leading into the inner courtyard were 14 feet* across and 43¾ feet wide.) 31 The entry room to the south gateway faced into the outer courtyard. It had palm tree decorations on its columns, and there were eight steps leading to its entrance.

32 Then he took me to the east gateway leading to the inner courtyard. He measured it, and it had the same measurements as the other gateways. 33 Its guard alcoves, dividing walls, and entry room were the same size as those of the others, and there were windows along the walls and in the entry room. The gateway passage measured 87½ feet long and 43¾ feet wide. 34 Its entry room faced into the outer courtyard. It had palm tree decorations on its columns, and there were eight steps leading to its entrance.

35 Then he took me around to the north gateway leading to the inner courtyard. He measured it, and it had the same measurements as the other gateways. 36 The guard alcoves, dividing walls, and entry room of this gateway had the same measurements as in the others and the same window arrangements. The gateway passage measured 87½ feet long and 43¾ feet wide. 37 Its entry room* faced into the outer courtyard, and it had palm tree decorations on the columns. There were eight steps leading to its entrance.

ROOMS FOR PREPARING SACRIFICES

38 A door led from the entry room of one of the inner gateways into a side room, where the meat for sacrifices was washed. 39 On each side of this entry room were two tables, where the sacrificial animals were slaughtered for the burnt offerings, sin offerings, and guilt offerings. 40 Outside the entry room, on each side of the stairs going up to the north entrance, were two more tables. 41 So there were eight tables in all—four inside and four outside—where the sacrifices were cut up and prepared. 42 There were also four tables of finished stone for preparation of the burnt offerings, each 31½ inches square and 21 inches high.* On these

40:9a Hebrew *8 cubits* [4.2 meters]. **40:9b** Hebrew *2 cubits* [1.1 meters]. **40:11a** Hebrew *10 cubits* [5.3 meters]. **40:11b** Hebrew *13 cubits* [6.9 meters]. **40:12a** Hebrew *1 cubit* [53 centimeters]. **40:12b** Hebrew *6 cubits* [3.2 meters]. **40:13** Hebrew *25 cubits* [13.3 meters]; also in 40:21, 25, 29, 30, 33, 36. **40:14** Hebrew *60 cubits* [31.8 meters]. Greek version reads *20 cubits* [35 feet or 10.6 meters]. The meaning of the Hebrew in this verse is uncertain. **40:15** Hebrew *50 cubits* [26.5 meters]; also in 40:21, 25, 29, 33, 36. **40:19** Hebrew *100 cubits* [53 meters]; also in 40:23, 27, 47. **40:30** As in 40:9, which reads *8 cubits* [14 feet or 4.2 meters]; here the Hebrew reads *5 cubits* [83/4 feet or 2.7 meters]. Some Hebrew manuscripts and the Greek version lack this entire verse. **40:37** As in Greek version (compare parallels at 40:26, 31, 34); Hebrew reads *Its dividing wall.* **40:42** Hebrew *1½ cubits* [80 centimeters] *long and 1½ cubits wide and 1 cubit* [53 centimeters] *high.*

40:15 was 87 ½ feet. The gate excavated at Lachish is nearly eighty-two feet deep.

tables were placed the butchering knives and other
implements for slaughtering the sacrificial animals.
43 There were hooks, each 3 inches* long, fastened all
around the foyer walls. The sacrificial meat was laid
on the tables.

ROOMS FOR THE PRIESTS

44 Inside the inner courtyard were two rooms,* one
beside the north gateway, facing south, and the oth-
er beside the south* gateway, facing north. 45 And the
man said to me, "The room beside the north inner gate
is for the priests who supervise the Temple mainte-
nance. 46 The room beside the south inner gate is for
the priests in charge of the altar—the descendants
of Zadok—for they alone of all the Levites may ap-
proach the LORD to minister to him."

THE INNER COURTYARD AND TEMPLE

47 Then the man measured the inner courtyard, and it
was a square, 175 feet wide and 175 feet across. The
altar stood in the courtyard in front of the Temple.
48 Then he brought me to the entry room of the Tem-
ple. He measured the walls on either side of the open-
ing to the entry room, and they were 8¾ feet thick.
The entrance itself was 24½ feet wide, and the walls
on each side of the entrance were an additional 5¼
feet long.* 49 The entry room was 35 feet* wide and
21 feet* deep. There were ten steps* leading up to it,
with a column on each side.

41 After that, the man brought me into the sanc-
tuary of the Temple. He measured the walls on
either side of its doorway,* and they were 10½ feet*
thick. 2 The doorway was 17½ feet* wide, and the
walls on each side of it were 8¾ feet* long. The sanc-
tuary itself was 70 feet long and 35 feet wide.*
3 Then he went beyond the sanctuary into the in-
ner room. He measured the walls on either side of its
entrance, and they were 3½ feet* thick. The entrance
was 10½ feet wide, and the walls on each side of the
entrance were 12¼ feet* long. 4 The inner room of the
sanctuary was 35 feet* long and 35 feet wide. "This,"
he told me, "is the Most Holy Place."
5 Then he measured the wall of the Temple, and it
was 10½ feet thick. There was a row of rooms along
the outside wall; each room was 7 feet* wide. 6 These
side rooms were built in three levels, one above the
other, with thirty rooms on each level. The supports
for these side rooms rested on exterior ledges on the
Temple wall; they did not extend into the wall. 7 Each
level was wider than the one below it, corresponding
to the narrowing of the Temple wall as it rose higher.
A stairway led up from the bottom level through the
middle level to the top level.
8 I saw that the Temple was built on a terrace,
which provided a foundation for the side rooms. This
terrace was 10½ feet* high. 9 The outer wall of the
Temple's side rooms was 8¾ feet thick. This left an
open area between these side rooms 10 and the row
of rooms along the outer wall of the inner courtyard.
This open area was 35 feet wide, and it went all the
way around the Temple. 11 Two doors opened from the
side rooms into the terrace yard, which was 8¾ feet
wide. One door faced north and the other south.
12 A large building stood on the west, facing the
Temple courtyard. It was 122½ feet wide and 157½
feet long, and its walls were 8¾ feet* thick. 13 Then
the man measured the Temple, and it was 175 feet*
long. The courtyard around the building, including
its walls, was an additional 175 feet in length. 14 The
inner courtyard to the east of the Temple was also
175 feet wide. 15 The building to the west, including its
two walls, was also 175 feet wide.
The sanctuary, the inner room, and the entry
room of the Temple 16 were all paneled with wood,
as were the frames of the recessed windows. The
inner walls of the Temple were paneled with wood
above and below the windows. 17 The space above
the door leading into the inner room, and its walls
inside and out, were also paneled. 18 All the walls
were decorated with carvings of cherubim, each
with two faces, and there was a carving of a palm
tree between each of the cherubim. 19 One face—
that of a man—looked toward the palm tree on one
side. The other face—that of a young lion—looked
toward the palm tree on the other side. The figures
were carved all along the inside of the Temple,
20 from the floor to the top of the walls, including the
outer wall of the sanctuary.
21 There were square columns at the entrance to the
sanctuary, and the ones at the entrance of the Most
Holy Place were similar. 22 There was an altar made
of wood, 5¼ feet high and 3½ feet across.* Its corners,
base, and sides were all made of wood. "This," the man
told me, "is the table that stands in the LORD's presence."
23 Both the sanctuary and the Most Holy Place had
double doorways, 24 each with two swinging doors.
25 The doors leading into the sanctuary were decorat-
ed with carved cherubim and palm trees, just as on
the walls. And there was a wooden roof at the front
of the entry room to the Temple. 26 On both sides of the
entry room were recessed windows decorated with
carved palm trees. The side rooms along the outside
wall also had roofs.

40:43 Hebrew *a handbreadth* [8 centimeters]. **40:44a** As in Greek version; Hebrew reads *rooms for singers.* **40:44b** As in Greek version; Hebrew reads *east.* **40:48** As in Greek version, which reads *The entrance was 14 cubits* [7.4 meters] *wide, and the walls of the entrance were 3 cubits* [1.6 meters] *on each side;* Hebrew lacks *14 cubits wide, and the walls of the entrance were.* **40:49a** Hebrew *20 cubits* [10.6 meters]. **40:49b** As in Greek version, which reads *12 cubits* [21 feet or 6.4 meters]; Hebrew reads *11 cubits* [19 1/4 feet or 5.8 meters]. **40:49c** As in Greek version; Hebrew reads *There were steps that were.* **41:1a** As in Greek version; the meaning of the Hebrew is uncertain. **41.1b** Hebrew *6 cubits* [3.2 meters]; also in 41:3, 5. **41:2a** Hebrew *10 cubits* [5.3 meters]. **41:2b** Hebrew *5 cubits* [2.7 meters]; also in 41:9, 11. **41:2c** Hebrew *40 cubits* [21.2 meters] *long and 20 cubits* [10.6 meters] *wide.* **41:3a** Hebrew *2 cubits* [1.1 meters]. **41:3b** Hebrew *7 cubits* [3.7 meters]. **41:4** Hebrew *20 cubits* [10.6 meters]; also in 41:4b, 10. **41:5** Hebrew *4 cubits* [2.1 meters]. **41:8** Hebrew *1 rod, 6 cubits* [3.2 meters]. **41:12** Hebrew *70 cubits* [37.1 meters] *wide and 90 cubits* [47.7 meters] *long, and its walls were 5 cubits* [2.7 meters] *thick.* **41:13** Hebrew *100 cubits* [53 meters]; also in 41:13b, 14, 15. **41:22** Hebrew *3 cubits* [1.6 meters] *high and 2 cubits* [1.1 meters] *across.*

41:1-12 The guide speaks little in these chapters, letting God's awesomeness speak for itself (40:4,45; 41:22; 42:13; 43:18; 46:20,24; 47:8). His description of the temple is reminiscent of the Solomonic temple (1 Kings 6:5-8). The temple sanctuary had three divisions: (1) a porch, (2) an outer "holy place", and (3) an inner sanctuary known as the "holy of holies". This inner sanctuary was inaccessible to ordinary mortals (not even Ezekiel in his vision) and symbolized God's divine presence in Israel's heart. In the real temple, only the high priest could enter the innermost sanctuary, and that only once a year on the Day of Atonement. God, who is transcendent (above it all), cannot really be limited to a single place. Ezekiel's vision strikes a balance. God is indeed present in the world as a holy presence and should be treated with appropriate awe.

41:22 altar. This wooden altar, the only furniture listed, may be where the bread of Presence was placed (see Ex. 25:30).

ROOMS FOR THE PRIESTS

42 Then the man led me out of the Temple court-
yard by way of the north gateway. We en-
tered the outer courtyard and came to a group of
rooms against the north wall of the inner courtyard.
2 This structure, whose entrance opened toward the
north, was 175 feet* long and 87½ feet* wide. 3 One
block of rooms overlooked the 35-foot* width of the
inner courtyard. Another block of rooms looked out
onto the pavement of the outer courtyard. The two
blocks were built three levels high and stood across
from each other. 4 Between the two blocks of rooms
ran a walkway 17½ feet* wide. It extended the en-
tire 175 feet of the complex,* and all the doors faced
north. 5 Each of the two upper levels of rooms was
narrower than the one beneath it because the upper
levels had to allow space for walkways in front of
them. 6 Since there were three levels and they did not
have supporting columns as in the courtyards, each of
the upper levels was set back from the level beneath
it. 7 There was an outer wall that separated the rooms
from the outer courtyard; it was 87½ feet long. 8 This
wall added length to the outer block of rooms, which
extended for only 87½ feet, while the inner block—
the rooms toward the Temple—extended for 175 feet.
9 There was an eastern entrance from the outer court-
yard to these rooms.

10 On the south* side of the Temple there were two
blocks of rooms just south of the inner courtyard
between the Temple and the outer courtyard. These
rooms were arranged just like the rooms on the north.
11 There was a walkway between the two blocks of
rooms just like the complex on the north side of the
Temple. This complex of rooms was the same length
and width as the other one, and it had the same en-
trances and doors. The dimensions of each were iden-
tical. 12 So there was an entrance in the wall facing the
doors of the inner block of rooms, and another on the
east at the end of the interior walkway.

13 Then the man told me, "These rooms that overlook
the Temple from the north and south are holy. Here the
priests who offer sacrifices to the LORD will eat the most
holy offerings. And because these rooms are holy, they
will be used to store the sacred offerings—the grain
offerings, sin offerings, and guilt offerings. 14 When the
priests leave the sanctuary, they must not go directly to
the outer courtyard. They must first take off the clothes
they wore while ministering, because these clothes are
holy. They must put on other clothes before entering the
parts of the building complex open to the public."

15 When the man had finished measuring the inside
of the Temple area, he led me out through the east
gateway to measure the entire perimeter. 16 He mea-
sured the east side with his measuring rod, and it was
875 feet long.* 17 Then he measured the north side, and
it was also 875 feet. 18 The south side was also 875 feet,
19 and the west side was also 875 feet. 20 So the area
was 875 feet on each side with a wall all around it to
separate what was holy from what was common.

THE LORD'S GLORY RETURNS

43 After this, the man brought me back around
to the east gateway. 2 Suddenly, the glory of
the God of Israel appeared from the east. The sound
of his coming was like the roar of rushing waters,
and the whole landscape shone with his glory. 3 This
vision was just like the others I had seen, first by the
Kebar River and then when he came* to destroy Je-
rusalem. I fell face down on the ground. 4 And the
glory of the LORD came into the Temple through the
east gateway.

5 Then the Spirit took me up and brought me into
the inner courtyard, and the glory of the LORD filled
the Temple. 6 And I heard someone speaking to me
from within the Temple, while the man who had
been measuring stood beside me. 7 The LORD said to
me, "Son of man, this is the place of my throne and the
place where I will rest my feet. I will live here forever
among the people of Israel. They and their kings will
not defile my holy name any longer by their adulter-
ous worship of other gods or by honoring the relics
of their kings who have died.* 8 They put their idol
altars right next to mine with only a wall between
them and me. They defiled my holy name by such de-
testable sin, so I consumed them in my anger. 9 Now
let them stop worshiping other gods and honoring
the relics of their kings, and I will live among them
forever.

10 "Son of man, describe to the people of Israel the
Temple I have shown you, so they will be ashamed of
all their sins. Let them study its plan, 11 and they will
be ashamed* of what they have done. Describe to
them all the specifications of the Temple—including
its entrances and exits—and everything else about it.
Tell them about its decrees and laws. Write down all
these specifications and decrees as they watch so they
will be sure to remember and follow them. 12 And this
is the basic law of the Temple: absolute holiness! The
entire top of the mountain where the Temple is built
is holy. Yes, this is the basic law of the Temple.

THE ALTAR

13 "These are the measurements of the altar*: There
is a gutter all around the altar 21 inches deep and

42:2a Hebrew *100 cubits* [53 meters]; also in 42:8. 42:2b Hebrew *50 cubits* [26.5 meters]; also in 42:7, 8. 42:3 Hebrew *20[-cubit]* [10.6-meter]. 42:4a Hebrew *10 cubits* [5.3 meters]. 42:4b As in Greek and Syriac versions, which read *Its length was 100 cubits* [53 meters]; Hebrew reads *and a passage 1 cubit* [21 inches or 53 centimeters] *wide.* 42:10 As in Greek version; Hebrew reads *east.* 42:16 As in 45:2 and in Greek version at 42:17, which reads *500 cubits* [265 meters]; Hebrew reads *500 rods* [5,250 feet or 1,590 meters]; similarly in 42:17, 18, 19, 20. 43:3 As in some Hebrew manuscripts and Latin Vulgate; Masoretic Text reads *I came.* 43:7 Or *kings on their high places.* 43:11 As in Greek version; Hebrew reads *if they are ashamed.* 43:13a Hebrew *measurements of the altar in long cubits, each being a cubit* [18 inches or 45 centimeters] *and a handbreadth* [3 inches or 8 centimeters] *in length.*

42:1 group of rooms. These two buildings served three purposes: (a) the priests ate offering portions there, (b) offerings were stored there, and (c) the priests changed from their official vestments back to street clothes there. According to the Law, the priests received a portion of some offerings. From the whole burnt offering they received only the animal's skin (Lev. 7:8). A memorial portion of grain offerings was burned on the altar and the remainder given to the priests (Lev. 2:3, 10; 6:16-18; 7:14-15). The priests received the brisket and right thigh from the peace offering (Lev. 7:30-34). Finally, the fat of the sin and trespass offerings were burned on the altar and the remainder eaten by the priests (Lev. 6:26; 7:6-7).

43:2 God, who previously abandoned the defiled temple in Jerusalem (11:22-23), will return in triumphant procession to reclaim His place among His people. God's glory was not in the second temple built by Herod but will be in the third.

43:5 glory. The long-awaited day finally came. God's presence, symbolized by splendor and glory, filled the temple (v. 4).

43:8 Solomon built his palace close to the temple, blurring the distinction between what was holy and what was his (1 Kings 7:1-12). God resented the confusion.

43:13-15 Ezekiel describes the future temple whose altar will be considerably larger than Solomon's.

21 inches wide,* with a curb 9 inches* wide around its edge. And this is the height* of the altar: 14 From the gutter the altar rises 3½ feet* to a lower ledge that surrounds the altar and is 21 inches* wide. From the lower ledge the altar rises 7 feet* to the upper ledge that is also 21 inches wide. 15 The top of the altar, the hearth, rises another 7 feet higher, with a horn rising up from each of the four corners. 16 The top of the altar is square, measuring 21 feet by 21 feet.* 17 The upper ledge also forms a square, measuring 24½ feet by 24½ feet,* with a 21-inch gutter and a 10½-inch curb* all around the edge. There are steps going up the east side of the altar."

18 Then he said to me, "Son of man, this is what the Sovereign LORD says: These will be the regulations for the burning of offerings and the sprinkling of blood when the altar is built. 19 At that time, the Levitical priests of the family of Zadok, who minister before me, are to be given a young bull for a sin offering, says the Sovereign LORD. 20 You will take some of its blood and smear it on the four horns of the altar, the four corners of the upper ledge, and the curb that runs around that ledge. This will cleanse and make atonement for the altar. 21 Then take the young bull for the sin offering and burn it at the appointed place outside the Temple area.

22 "On the second day, sacrifice as a sin offering a young male goat that has no physical defects. Then cleanse and make atonement for the altar again, just as you did with the young bull. 23 When you have finished the cleansing ceremony, offer another young bull that has no defects and a perfect ram from the flock. 24 You are to present them to the LORD, and the priests are to sprinkle salt on them and offer them as a burnt offering to the LORD.

25 "Every day for seven days a male goat, a young bull, and a ram from the flock will be sacrificed as a sin offering. None of these animals may have physical defects of any kind. 26 Do this each day for seven days to cleanse and make atonement for the altar, thus setting it apart for holy use. 27 On the eighth day, and on each day afterward, the priests will sacrifice on the altar the burnt offerings and peace offerings of the people. Then I will accept you. I, the Sovereign LORD, have spoken!"

THE PRINCE, LEVITES, AND PRIESTS

44 Then the man brought me back to the east gateway in the outer wall of the Temple area, but it was closed. 2 And the LORD said to me, "This gate must remain closed; it will never again be opened. No one will ever open it and pass through, for the LORD, the God of Israel, has entered here. Therefore, it must always remain shut. 3 Only the prince himself may sit inside this gateway to feast in the LORD's presence. But he may come and go only through the entry room of the gateway."

4 Then the man brought me through the north gateway to the front of the Temple. I looked and saw that the glory of the LORD filled the Temple of the LORD, and I fell face down on the ground.

5 And the LORD said to me, "Son of man, take careful notice. Use your eyes and ears, and listen to everything I tell you about the regulations concerning the LORD's Temple. Take careful note of the procedures for using the Temple's entrances and exits. 6 And give these rebels, the people of Israel, this message from the Sovereign LORD: O people of Israel, enough of your detestable sins! 7 You have brought uncircumcised foreigners into my sanctuary—people who have no heart for God. In this way, you defiled my Temple even as you offered me my food, the fat and blood of sacrifices. In addition to all your other detestable sins, you have broken my covenant. 8 Instead of safeguarding my sacred rituals, you have hired foreigners to take charge of my sanctuary.

9 "So this is what the Sovereign LORD says: No foreigners, including those who live among the people of Israel, will enter my sanctuary if they have not been circumcised and have not surrendered themselves to the LORD. 10 And the men of the tribe of Levi who abandoned me when Israel strayed away from me to worship idols* must bear the consequences of their unfaithfulness. 11 They may still be Temple guards and gatekeepers, and they may slaughter the animals brought for burnt offerings and be present to help the people. 12 But they encouraged my people to worship idols, causing Israel to fall into deep sin. So I have taken a solemn oath that they must bear the consequences for their sins, says the Sovereign LORD. 13 They may not approach me to minister as priests. They may not touch any of my holy things or the holy offerings, for they must bear the shame of all the detestable sins they have committed. 14 They are to serve as the Temple caretakers, taking charge of the maintenance work and performing general duties.

15 "However, the Levitical priests of the family of Zadok continued to minister faithfully in the Temple when Israel abandoned me for idols. These men will serve as my ministers. They will stand in my presence and offer the fat and blood of the sacrifices, says the Sovereign LORD. 16 They alone will enter my sanctuary and approach my table to serve me. They will fulfill all my requirements.

17 "When they enter the gateway to the inner courtyard, they must wear only linen clothing. They must wear no wool while on duty in the inner courtyard or in the Temple itself. 18 They must wear linen turbans and linen undergarments. They must not wear anything that would cause them to perspire. 19 When they

43:13b Hebrew *a cubit* [53 centimeters] *deep and a cubit wide.* **43:13c** Hebrew *1 span* [23 centimeters]. **43:13d** As in Greek version; Hebrew reads *base.* **43:14a** Hebrew *2 cubits* [1.1 meters]. **43:14b** Hebrew *1 cubit* [53 centimeters]; also in 43:14d. **43:14c** Hebrew *4 cubits* [2.1 meters]; also in 43:15. **43:16** Hebrew *12 [cubits]* [6.4 meters] *long and 12 [cubits] wide.* **43:17a** Hebrew *14 [cubits]* [7.4 meters] *long and 14 [cubits] wide.* **43:17b** Hebrew *a gutter of 1 cubit* [53 centimeters] *and a curb of ½ a cubit* [27 centimeters]. **44:10** The Hebrew term (literally *round things*) probably alludes to dung; also in 44:12.

43:19 the Levitical priests . . . given . . . for a sin offering. After it is built, the temple must be cleansed and purified with blood.

43:21 The blood of the sacrifice is necessary to accomplish the offering. The animal carcasses are burned outside of the temple (see Lev. 4:12,21).

44:2 gate. No one else could enter the sealed gate (symbolic of God's holiness) as God had when He first entered the temple (43:4).

44:7 defiled my Temple. God would forbid history repeating itself by allowing faithless foreigners to enter the sanctuary.

44:10 bear the consequences. The Levites were supposed to be the spiritual leader-priests (Deut. 33:8-11). As a result of their sins, they (except those related to Zadok) would be limited in their future role (vv. 13-15).

44:15 the Levitical priests. Zadok's descendants will be allowed full access to the temple as a reward for their devotion and purity (see 1 Sam. 2:27-36).

44:17 linen clothing. Linen, representing holiness and distinction (9:2), produced less sweat and odor than wool.

return to the outer courtyard where the people are, they must take off the clothes they wear while ministering to me. They must leave them in the sacred rooms and put on other clothes so they do not endanger anyone by transmitting holiness to them through this clothing.

20 "They must neither shave their heads nor let their hair grow too long. Instead, they must trim it regularly. 21 The priests must not drink wine before entering the inner courtyard. 22 They may choose their wives only from among the virgins of Israel or the widows of the priests. They may not marry other widows or divorced women. 23 They will teach my people the difference between what is holy and what is common, what is ceremonially clean and unclean.

24 "They will serve as judges to resolve any disagreements among my people. Their decisions must be based on my regulations. And the priests themselves must obey my instructions and decrees at all the sacred festivals, and see to it that the Sabbaths are set apart as holy days.

25 "A priest must not defile himself by being in the presence of a dead person unless it is his father, mother, child, brother, or unmarried sister. In such cases it is permitted. 26 Even then, he can return to his Temple duties only after being ceremonially cleansed and then waiting for seven days. 27 The first day he returns to work and enters the inner courtyard and the sanctuary, he must offer a sin offering for himself, says the Sovereign LORD.

28 "The priests will not have any property or possession of land, for I alone am their special possession. 29 Their food will come from the gifts and sacrifices brought to the Temple by the people—the grain offerings, the sin offerings, and the guilt offerings. Whatever anyone sets apart* for the LORD will belong to the priests. 30 The first of the ripe fruits and all the gifts brought to the LORD will go to the priests. The first batch of dough must also be given to the priests so the LORD will bless your homes. 31 The priests may not eat meat from any bird or animal that dies a natural death or that dies after being attacked by another animal.

DIVISION OF THE LAND

45 "When you divide the land among the tribes of Israel, you must set aside a section for the LORD as his holy portion. This piece of land will be $8\frac{1}{3}$ miles long and $6\frac{2}{3}$ miles wide.* The entire area will be holy. 2 A section of this land, measuring 875 feet by 875 feet,* will be set aside for the Temple. An additional strip of land $87\frac{1}{2}$ feet* wide is to be left empty all around it. 3 Within the larger sacred area, measure out a portion of land $8\frac{1}{3}$ miles long and $3\frac{1}{3}$ miles wide.* Within it the sanctuary of the Most Holy Place will be located. 4 This area will be holy, set aside for the priests who minister to the LORD in the sanctuary. They will use it for their homes, and my Temple will be located within it. 5 The strip of sacred land next to it, also $8\frac{1}{3}$ miles long and $3\frac{1}{3}$ miles wide, will be a living area for the Levites who work at the Temple. It will be their possession and a place for their towns.*

6 "Adjacent to the larger sacred area will be a section of land $8\frac{1}{3}$ miles long and $1\frac{2}{3}$ miles wide.* This will be set aside for a city where anyone in Israel can live.

7 "Two special sections of land will be set apart for the prince. One section will share a border with the east side of the sacred lands and city, and the second section will share a border on the west side. Then the far eastern and western borders of the prince's lands will line up with the eastern and western boundaries of the tribal areas. 8 These sections of land will be the prince's allotment. Then my princes will no longer oppress and rob my people; they will assign the rest of the land to the people, giving an allotment to each tribe.

RULES FOR THE PRINCES

9 "For this is what the Sovereign LORD says: Enough, you princes of Israel! Stop your violence and oppression and do what is just and right. Quit robbing and cheating my people out of their land. Stop expelling them from their homes, says the Sovereign LORD. 10 Use only honest weights and scales and honest measures, both dry and liquid.* 11 The homer* will be your standard unit for measuring volume. The ephah and the bath* will each measure one-tenth of a homer. 12 The standard unit for weight will be the silver shekel.* One shekel will consist of twenty gerahs, and sixty shekels will be equal to one mina.*

SPECIAL OFFERINGS AND CELEBRATIONS

13 "You must give this tax to the prince: one bushel of wheat or barley for every 60* you harvest, 14 one percent of your olive oil,* 15 and one sheep or goat for every 200 in your flocks in Israel. These will be the grain offerings, burnt offerings, and peace offerings that will make atonement for the people who bring them, says the Sovereign LORD. 16 All the people of

44:29 The Hebrew term used here refers to the complete consecration of things or people to the LORD, either by destroying them or by giving them as an offering. **45:1** As in Greek version, which reads *25,000 [cubits]* [13.3 kilometers] *long and 20,000 [cubits]* [10.6 kilometers] *wide;* Hebrew reads *25,000 [cubits] long and 10,000 [cubits]* [3 1/3 miles or 5.3 kilometers] *wide.* Compare 45:3, 5; 48:9. **45:2a** Hebrew *500 [cubits]* [265 meters] *by 500 [cubits], a square.* **45:2b** Hebrew *50 cubits* [26.5 meters]. **45:3** Hebrew *25,000 [cubits]* [13.3 kilometers] *long and 10,000 [cubits]* [5.3 kilometers] *wide;* also in 45:5. **45:5** As in Greek version; Hebrew reads *They will have as their possession 20 rooms.* **45:6** Hebrew *25,000 [cubits]* [13.3 kilometers] *long and 5,000 [cubits]* [2.65 kilometers] *wide.* **45:10** Hebrew *Use honest scales, an honest ephah, and an honest bath.* **45:11a** The *homer* measures about 50 gallons or 220 liters. **45:11b** The *ephah* is a dry measure; the *bath* is a liquid measure. **45:12a** The *shekel* weighs about 0.4 ounces or 11 grams. **45:12b** Elsewhere the *mina* is equated to 50 shekels. **45:13** Hebrew *1/6 of an ephah from each homer of wheat and 1/6 of an ephah from each homer of barley.* **45:14** Hebrew *the portion of oil, measured by the bath, is 1/10 of a bath from each cor, which consists of 10 baths or 1 homer, for 10 baths are equivalent to a homer.*

44:23 difference between what is holy and what is common. With the temple system having been defunct for centuries, the Israelites would need to relearn the laws.

45:2 left empty. No building permits would be given out for the area around the sanctuary this time! God's holiness would be set apart.

45:4 This area will be holy, set aside for the priests. In Israel's history, the priests were scattered throughout the land as references of religious service and justice (Josh. 21:1-42). In the new temple era, they would be centralized around the sanctuary.

45:5 In the Old Testament, priests lived in special "holy" areas they did not own. In the new temple era, however, the Levites would be allowed to own property.

45:7 set apart for the prince. Unlike that of Solomon's time, the new palace would be separate from the new temple.

45:10 only honest weights. God established common ground rules to guard against fraud. Following these guidelines, the people would not find themselves relearning old lessons against greed.

Israel must join in bringing these offerings to the prince. 17 The prince will be required to provide offerings that are given at the religious festivals, the new moon celebrations, the Sabbath days, and all other similar occasions. He will provide the sin offerings, burnt offerings, grain offerings, liquid offerings, and peace offerings to purify the people of Israel, making them right with the LORD.*

18 "This is what the Sovereign LORD says: In early spring, on the first day of each new year,* sacrifice a young bull with no defects to purify the Temple. 19 The priest will take blood from this sin offering and put it on the doorposts of the Temple, the four corners of the upper ledge of the altar, and the gateposts at the entrance to the inner courtyard. 20 Do this also on the seventh day of the new year for anyone who has sinned through error or ignorance. In this way, you will purify* the Temple.

21 "On the fourteenth day of the first month,* you must celebrate the Passover. This festival will last for seven days. The bread you eat during that time must be made without yeast. 22 On the day of Passover the prince will provide a young bull as a sin offering for himself and the people of Israel. 23 On each of the seven days of the feast he will prepare a burnt offering to the LORD, consisting of seven young bulls and seven rams without defects. A male goat will also be given each day for a sin offering. 24 The prince will provide a basket of flour as a grain offering and a gallon of olive oil* with each young bull and ram.

25 "During the seven days of the Festival of Shelters, which occurs every year in early autumn,* the prince will provide these same sacrifices for the sin offering, the burnt offering, and the grain offering, along with the required olive oil.

46 "This is what the Sovereign LORD says: The east gateway of the inner courtyard will be closed during the six workdays each week, but it will be open on Sabbath days and the days of new moon celebrations. 2 The prince will enter the entry room of the gateway from the outside. Then he will stand by the gatepost while the priest offers his burnt offering and peace offering. He will bow down in worship inside the gateway passage and then go back out the way he came. The gateway will not be closed until evening. 3 The common people will bow down and worship the LORD in front of this gateway on Sabbath days and the days of new moon celebrations.

4 "Each Sabbath day the prince will present to the LORD a burnt offering of six lambs and one ram, all with no defects. 5 He will present a grain offering of a basket of choice flour to go with the ram and whatever amount of flour he chooses to go with each lamb, and he is to offer one gallon of olive oil* for each basket of flour. 6 At the new moon celebrations, he will bring one young bull, six lambs, and one ram, all with no defects. 7 With the young bull he must bring a basket of choice flour for a grain offering. With the ram he must bring another basket of flour. And with each lamb he is to bring whatever amount of flour he chooses to give. With each basket of flour he must offer one gallon of olive oil.

8 "The prince must enter the gateway through the entry room, and he must leave the same way. 9 But when the people come in through the north gateway to worship the LORD during the religious festivals, they must leave by the south gateway. And those who entered through the south gateway must leave by the north gateway. They must never leave by the same gateway they came in, but must always use the opposite gateway. 10 The prince will enter and leave with the people on these occasions.

11 "So at the special feasts and sacred festivals, the grain offering will be a basket of choice flour with each young bull, another basket of flour with each ram, and as much flour as the worshiper chooses to give with each lamb. Give one gallon of olive oil with each basket of flour. 12 When the prince offers a voluntary burnt offering or peace offering to the LORD, the east gateway to the inner courtyard will be opened for him, and he will offer his sacrifices as he does on Sabbath days. Then he will leave, and the gateway will be shut behind him.

13 "Each morning you must sacrifice a one-year-old lamb with no defects as a burnt offering to the LORD. 14 With the lamb, a grain offering must also be given to the LORD—about three quarts of flour with a third of a gallon of olive oil* to moisten the choice flour. This will be a permanent law for you. 15 The lamb, the grain offering, and the olive oil must be given as a daily sacrifice every morning without fail.

16 "This is what the Sovereign LORD says: If the prince gives a gift of land to one of his sons as his inheritance, it will belong to him and his descendants forever. 17 But if the prince gives a gift of land from his inheritance to one of his servants, the servant may keep it only until the Year of Jubilee, which comes every fiftieth year.* At that time the land will return to the prince. But when the prince gives gifts to his sons, those gifts will be permanent. 18 And the prince may never take anyone's property by force. If he gives property to his sons, it must be from his own land, for I do not want any of my people unjustly evicted from their property."

THE TEMPLE KITCHENS

19 In my vision, the man brought me through the entrance beside the gateway and led me to the sacred

45:17 Or *to make atonement for the people of Israel.* **45:18** Hebrew *On the first day of the first month,* of the Hebrew calendar. This day in the ancient Hebrew lunar calendar occurred in March or April. **45:20** Or *will make atonement for.* **45:21** This day in the ancient Hebrew lunar calendar occurred in late March, April, or early May. **45:24** Hebrew *an ephah* [20 quarts or 22 liters] *of flour . . . and a hin* [3.8 liters] *of olive oil.* **45:25** Hebrew *the festival which begins on the fifteenth day of the seventh month* (see Lev 23:34). This day in the ancient Hebrew lunar calendar occurred in late September, October, or early November. **46:5** Hebrew *an ephah* [20 quarts or 22 liters] *of choice flour . . . a hin* [3.8 liters] *of olive oil;* similarly in 46:7, 11. **46:14** Hebrew ¹/₆ *of an ephah* [3.7 liters] *of flour with* ¹/₃ *of a hin* [1.3 liters] *of olive oil.* **46:17** Hebrew *until the Year of Release;* see Lev 25:8-17.

45:25 Festival. The Festival of Shelters, or Tabernacles, was a seven-day celebration at the end of the year (see Num. 29:12; Deut. 16:16). Sacrifices were made on each of these seven days.

46:3 worship . . . Sabbath days. One of the few references to Old Testament worship on the Sabbath. Usually referred to in terms of proscribed limitations, this Sabbath had its limits too. The people usually worshipped in the outer court; they could look through the eastern gate to the altar in the inner court where the sacrifices were offered but were not permitted to enter it. The prince could pass through the eastern gate but was only allowed to stand by the inner gatepost and watch.

46:16 gift of land . . . as his inheritance. Since the Law required land be kept within clans and tribes (Lev. 25:1-13), servants of a different clan had to return land at the Jubilee.

rooms assigned to the priests, which faced toward
the north. He showed me a place at the extreme west
end of these rooms. 20 He explained, "This is where the
priests will cook the meat from the guilt offerings and
sin offerings and bake the flour from the grain offer-
ings into bread. They will do it here to avoid carrying
the sacrifices through the outer courtyard and endan-
gering the people by transmitting holiness to them."
21 Then he brought me back to the outer courtyard
and led me to each of its four corners. In each corner
I saw an enclosure. 22 Each of these enclosures was
70 feet long and 52½ feet wide,* surrounded by walls.
23 Along the inside of these walls was a ledge of stone
with fireplaces under the ledge all the way around.
24 The man said to me, "These are the kitchens to be
used by the Temple assistants to boil the sacrifices of-
fered by the people."

THE RIVER OF HEALING

47 In my vision, the man brought me back to the
entrance of the Temple. There I saw a stream
flowing east from beneath the door of the Temple and
passing to the right of the altar on its south side. 2 The
man brought me outside the wall through the north
gateway and led me around to the eastern entrance.
There I could see the water flowing out through the
south side of the east gateway.
3 Measuring as he went, he took me along the stream
for 1,750 feet* and then led me across. The water was
up to my ankles. 4 He measured off another 1,750 feet
and led me across again. This time the water was up
to my knees. After another 1,750 feet, it was up to my
waist. 5 Then he measured another 1,750 feet, and the
river was too deep to walk across. It was deep enough
to swim in, but too deep to walk through.
6 He asked me, "Have you been watching, son of
man?" Then he led me back along the riverbank.
7 When I returned, I was surprised by the sight of many
trees growing on both sides of the river. 8 Then he said
to me, "This river flows east through the desert into
the valley of the Dead Sea.* The waters of this stream
will make the salty waters of the Dead Sea fresh and
pure. 9 There will be swarms of living things wherever
the water of this river flows.* Fish will abound in the
Dead Sea, for its waters will become fresh. Life will
flourish wherever this water flows. 10 Fishermen will
stand along the shores of the Dead Sea. All the way
from En-gedi to En-eglaim, the shores will be covered
with nets drying in the sun. Fish of every kind will
fill the Dead Sea, just as they fill the Mediterranean.*
11 But the marshes and swamps will not be purified;
they will still be salty. 12 Fruit trees of all kinds will
grow along both sides of the river. The leaves of these
trees will never turn brown and fall, and there will al-
ways be fruit on their branches. There will be a new
crop every month, for they are watered by the river
flowing from the Temple. The fruit will be for food and
the leaves for healing."

BOUNDARIES FOR THE LAND

13 This is what the Sovereign LORD says: "Divide the
land in this way for the twelve tribes of Israel: The de-
scendants of Joseph will be given two shares of land.*
14 Otherwise each tribe will receive an equal share. I
took a solemn oath and swore that I would give this
land to your ancestors, and it will now come to you as
your possession.

15 "These are the boundaries of the land: The
northern border will run from the Mediterranean
toward Hethlon, then on through Lebo-hamath to
Zedad; 16 then it will run to Berothah and Sibraim,*
which are on the border between Damascus and
Hamath, and finally to Hazer-hatticon, on the
border of Hauran. 17 So the northern border will
run from the Mediterranean to Hazar-enan, on
the border between Hamath to the north and
Damascus to the south.
18 "The eastern border starts at a point between
Hauran and Damascus and runs south along the
Jordan River between Israel and Gilead, past the
Dead Sea* and as far south as Tamar.* This will be
the eastern border.
19 "The southern border will go west from Tamar
to the waters of Meribah at Kadesh* and then
follow the course of the Brook of Egypt to the Med-
iterranean. This will be the southern border.
20 "On the west side, the Mediterranean itself
will be your border from the southern border
to the point where the northern border begins,
opposite Lebo-hamath.

21 "Divide the land within these boundaries among
the tribes of Israel. 22 Distribute the land as an allot-
ment for yourselves and for the foreigners who have
joined you and are raising their families among you.
They will be like native-born Israelites to you and
will receive an allotment among the tribes. 23 These
foreigners are to be given land within the territory
of the tribe with whom they now live. I, the Sovereign
LORD, have spoken!

DIVISION OF THE LAND

48 "Here is the list of the tribes of Israel and the
territory each is to receive. The territory of
Dan is in the extreme north. Its boundary line follows
the Hethlon road to Lebo-hamath and then runs on
to Hazar-enan on the border of Damascus, with Ha-

46:22 Hebrew *40 [cubits]* [21.2 meters] *long and 30 [cubits]* [15.9 meters] *wide.* 47:3 Hebrew *1,000 cubits* [530 meters]; also in 47:4, 5. 47:8 Hebrew *the sea.* 47:9 As in Greek and Syriac versions; Hebrew reads *of these two rivers flow.* 47:10 Hebrew *the Great Sea;* also in 47:15, 17, 19, 20. 47:13 It was important to retain twelve portions of land. Since Levi had no portion, the descendants of Joseph's sons, Ephraim and Manasseh, received land as two tribes. 47:15-16 As in Greek version; Masoretic Text reads *then on through Lebo to Zedad; 16then it will run to Hamath, Berothah, and Sibraim.* 47:18a Hebrew *the eastern sea.* 47:18b As in Greek version; Hebrew reads *you will measure.* 47:19 Hebrew *waters of Meribath-kadesh.*

47:1 stream. A river will flow from Messiah's temple to the Dead Sea that will become alive (see Rev. 22:1). Freshwater marine life will thrive inside it. Vegetation and trees will grow beside it.

47:10 with nets drying in the sun. For the first time, fishermen will find their livelihood on the banks of the former Dead Sea.

47:14 equal share. God has pre-apportioned the land to be divided amongst the Israelites in the millennial kingdom.

47:15 These are the boundaries of the land. The boundaries of the future allotment will be greater than even the borders in David and Solomon's days. Future Israel will include Lebanon and part of Syria. Also, the land will undergo geographical changes, probably making it larger in other ways.

47:22 foreigners who have joined you. Some non-Jews will live in the land peacefully in the days of Messiah's kingdom.

48:1 The land will be divided according to the names of the tribes of Israel—Jacob's descendants. All of the tribes are listed, proving that there are no lost tribes.

math to the north. Dan's territory extends all the way
across the land of Israel from east to west.
2 "Asher's territory lies south of Dan's and also ex-
tends from east to west. 3 Naphtali's land lies south
of Asher's, also extending from east to west. 4 Then
comes Manasseh south of Naphtali, and its territory
also extends from east to west. 5 South of Manasseh is
Ephraim, 6 and then Reuben, 7 and then Judah, all of
whose boundaries extend from east to west.
8 "South of Judah is the land set aside for a special
purpose. It will be $8\frac{1}{3}$ miles* wide and will extend
as far east and west as the tribal territories, with the
Temple at the center.
9 "The area set aside for the LORD's Temple will be
$8\frac{1}{3}$ miles long and $6\frac{2}{3}$ miles wide.* 10 For the priests
there will be a strip of land measuring $8\frac{1}{3}$ miles long
by $3\frac{1}{3}$ miles wide,* with the LORD's Temple at the cen-
ter. 11 This area is set aside for the ordained priests, the
descendants of Zadok who served me faithfully and
did not go astray with the people of Israel and the rest
of the Levites. 12 It will be their special portion when
the land is distributed, the most sacred land of all.
Next to the priests' territory will lie the land where
the other Levites will live.
13 "The land allotted to the Levites will be the same
size and shape as that belonging to the priests—$8\frac{1}{3}$
miles long and $3\frac{1}{3}$ miles wide. Together these por-
tions of land will measure $8\frac{1}{3}$ miles long by $6\frac{2}{3}$ miles
wide.* 14 None of this special land may ever be sold or
traded or used by others, for it belongs to the LORD; it
is set apart as holy.
15 "An additional strip of land $8\frac{1}{3}$ miles long by $1\frac{2}{3}$
miles wide,* south of the sacred Temple area, will be
allotted for public use—homes, pasturelands, and
common lands, with a city at the center. 16 The city
will measure $1\frac{1}{2}$ miles* on each side—north, south,
east, and west. 17 Open lands will surround the city
for 150 yards* in every direction. 18 Outside the city
there will be a farming area that stretches $3\frac{1}{3}$ miles
to the east and $3\frac{1}{3}$ miles to the west* along the border
of the sacred area. This farmland will produce food
for the people working in the city. 19 Those who come
from the various tribes to work in the city may farm
it. 20 This entire area—including the sacred lands and
the city—is a square that measures $8\frac{1}{3}$ miles* on
each side.
21 "The areas that remain, to the east and to the
west of the sacred lands and the city, will belong
to the prince. Each of these areas will be $8\frac{1}{3}$ miles
wide, extending in opposite directions to the eastern
and western borders of Israel, with the sacred lands
and the sanctuary of the Temple in the center. 22 So
the prince's land will include everything between
the territories allotted to Judah and Benjamin, ex-
cept for the areas set aside for the sacred lands and
the city.
23 "These are the territories allotted to the rest of
the tribes. Benjamin's territory lies just south of the
prince's lands, and it extends across the entire land of
Israel from east to west. 24 South of Benjamin's territo-
ry lies that of Simeon, also extending across the land
from east to west. 25 Next is the territory of Issachar
with the same eastern and western boundaries.
26 "Then comes the territory of Zebulun, which also
extends across the land from east to west. 27 The ter-
ritory of Gad is just south of Zebulun with the same
borders to the east and west. 28 The southern border
of Gad runs from Tamar to the waters of Meribah at
Kadesh* and then follows the Brook of Egypt to the
Mediterranean.*
29 "These are the allotments that will be set aside
for each tribe's exclusive possession. I, the Sovereign
LORD, have spoken!

THE GATES OF THE CITY

30 "These will be the exits to the city: On the north
wall, which is $1\frac{1}{2}$ miles long, 31 there will be three
gates, each one named after a tribe of Israel. The first
will be named for Reuben, the second for Judah, and
the third for Levi. 32 On the east wall, also $1\frac{1}{2}$ miles
long, the gates will be named for Joseph, Benjamin,
and Dan. 33 The south wall, also $1\frac{1}{2}$ miles long, will
have gates named for Simeon, Issachar, and Zebulun.
34 And on the west wall, also $1\frac{1}{2}$ miles long, the gates
will be named for Gad, Asher, and Naphtali.
35 "The distance around the entire city will be
6 miles.* And from that day the name of the city will
be 'The LORD Is There.'*"

48:8 Hebrew *25,000 [cubits]* [13.3 kilometers]. **48:9** As in one Greek manuscript and the Greek reading in 45:1: *25,000 [cubits]* [13.3 kilometers] *long and 20,000 [cubits]* [10.6 kilometers] *wide;* Hebrew reads *25,000 [cubits] long and 10,000 [cubits]* [3 1/3 miles or 5.3 kilometers] *wide.* Similarly in 48:13b. Compare 45:1-5; 48:10-13. **48:10** Hebrew *25,000 [cubits]* [13.3 kilometers] *long by 10,000 [cubits]* [5.3 kilometers] *wide;* also in 48:13a. **48:13** See note on 48:9. **48:15** Hebrew *25,000 [cubits]* [13.3 kilometers] *long by 5,000 [cubits]* [2.65 kilometers] *wide.* **48:16** Hebrew *4,500 [cubits]* [2.4 kilometers]; also in 48:30, 32, 33, 34. **48:17** Hebrew *250 [cubits]* [133 meters]. **48:18** Hebrew *10,000 [cubits]* [5.3 kilometers] *to the east and 10,000 [cubits] to the west.* **48:20** Hebrew *25,000 [cubits]* [13.3 kilometers]; also in 48:21. **48:28a** Hebrew *waters of Meribath-kadesh.* **48:28b** Hebrew *the Great Sea.* **48:35a** Hebrew *18,000 [cubits]* [9.6 kilometers]. **48:35b** Hebrew *Yahweh Shammah.*

48:2 Asher's territory. Asher will receive the most northern section of land—away from the sanctuary. Six other tribes will live in the north.

48:7 Judah. As the tribe of the Messianic royal line, this tribe would take a privileged position next to God's own portion. Four other tribes will live in the south.

48:14 special land. The sacred district at the geographical center of the land. **belongs to the LORD.** The remaining portion of land will function as a "national park" for all the holy city's residents, who represent every tribe.

48:31 gates. Ezekiel's description is similar to John's vision in Revelation 21 (Rev. 21:12-14). Twelve gates will surround the millennial Jerusalem. Israel's future restoration will be complete. In cities of the ancient world such as Babylon the gates were often named after the gods. The more common practice in Israel, however, was for gates to be named for where they led. In the end, Ezekiel demonstrates what has been true all along. The gateway to God is through His twelve tribes, first in his covenant with them, then through the New Covenant in which the twelve tribes are representative of all the people of God (11:19; 16:60; 36:26-27; Jer. 31:31; Luke 22:20; Rom. 11:27; 2 Cor. 3:6; Heb. 7:22; 9:15). God keeps His covenant promises, even beyond the end.

INTRODUCTION TO

DANIEL

PERSONAL READING PLAN

☐Daniel 1:1–2:49
☐Daniel 3:1–4:37
☐Daniel 5:1–6:28
☐Daniel 7:1–8:27
☐Daniel 9:1–11:1
☐Daniel 11:2–12:13

AUTHOR

Daniel (whose name means "God is my judge") was an exiled Israelite statesman in the dominating empires of his time.

DATE

The date for the writing of this book has been vigorously debated. Scholars who regard the book as genuine predictive prophecy date it *circa* 530 B.C., near the end of Daniel's life. The events depicted in the life of Daniel and his friends (chaps. 1–6) are set in the time of the Babylonian captivity (605–538 B.C.) and the onset of the Persian Empire. The visions (chaps. 7–12) look ahead to succeeding history, at least to 160 B.C., and perhaps to events still in the future even today.

THEME

God is sovereign over the kingdoms of men (2:21; 5:21).

HISTORICAL BACKGROUND

In 605 B.C. Nebuchadnezzar took Daniel and other captives to Babylon. Daniel rose quickly to prominence under Nebuchadnezzar. After the king's death, Daniel seems to have fallen from favor only to regain it by interpreting the handwriting on the wall at Belshazzar's feast (5:13-29). With the capture of Babylon by Darius, Daniel maintained his official position, serving under both Darius and Cyrus, the king of Persia.

CHARACTERISTICS

Daniel was written in the context of the exile. It called for a commitment to God's law amongst the people of God who were suffering persecution (even unto death). Daniel appeals to them to awaken and be prepared for the unexpected intervention of God into world affairs. Jesus referred to Daniel in His teachings (Matt. 24:15) and quoted from 9:27, 11:31, and 12:11. The book of Revelation draws heavily from Daniel's apocalyptic imagery (chaps. 7–12).

PASSAGES FOR TOPICAL GROUP STUDY

1:1-21 .... PEER PRESSURE and DISCIPLINE .. Pure Discipline
3:1-12, 19-27 .. PERSECUTION and FAITH .... A Fiery Test
6:1-24 ...... COURAGE and PRAYER .... The Den of Lions

DANIEL IN NEBUCHADNEZZAR'S COURT

1 During the third year of King Jehoiakim's reign in Judah,* King Nebuchadnezzar of Babylon came to Jerusalem and besieged it. 2 The Lord gave him victory over King Jehoiakim of Judah and permitted him to take some of the sacred objects from the Temple of God. So Nebuchadnezzar took them back to the land of Babylonia* and placed them in the treasure-house of his god.

3 Then the king ordered Ashpenaz, his chief of staff, to bring to the palace some of the young men of Judah's royal family and other noble families, who had been brought to Babylon as captives. 4 "Select only strong, healthy, and good-looking young men," he said. "Make sure they are well versed in every branch of learning, are gifted with knowledge and good judgment, and are suited to serve in the royal palace. Train these young men in the language and literature of Babylon.*" 5 The king assigned them a daily ration of food and wine from his own kitchens. They were to be trained for three years, and then they would enter the royal service.

6 Daniel, Hananiah, Mishael, and Azariah were four of the young men chosen, all from the tribe of Judah. 7 The chief of staff renamed them with these Babylonian names:

Daniel was called Belteshazzar.
Hananiah was called Shadrach.
Mishael was called Meshach.
Azariah was called Abednego.

8 But Daniel was determined not to defile himself by eating the food and wine given to them by the king. He asked the chief of staff for permission not to eat these unacceptable foods. 9 Now God had given the chief of staff both respect and affection for Daniel. 10 But he responded, "I am afraid of my lord the king, who has ordered that you eat this food and wine. If you become pale and thin compared to the other youths your age, I am afraid the king will have me beheaded."

11 Daniel spoke with the attendant who had been appointed by the chief of staff to look after Daniel, Hananiah, Mishael, and Azariah. 12 "Please test us for ten days on a diet of vegetables and water," Daniel said. 13 "At the end of the ten days, see how we look compared to the other young men who are eating the king's food. Then make your decision in light of what you see." 14 The attendant agreed to Daniel's suggestion and tested them for ten days.

15 At the end of the ten days, Daniel and his three friends looked healthier and better nourished than the young men who had been eating the food assigned by the king. 16 So after that, the attendant fed them only vegetables instead of the food and wine provided for the others.

17 God gave these four young men an unusual aptitude for understanding every aspect of literature and wisdom. And God gave Daniel the special ability to interpret the meanings of visions and dreams.

18 When the training period ordered by the king was completed, the chief of staff brought all the young men to King Nebuchadnezzar. 19 The king talked with them, and no one impressed him as much as Daniel, Hananiah, Mishael, and Azariah. So they entered the royal service. 20 Whenever the king consulted them in any matter requiring wisdom and balanced judgment, he found them ten times more capable than any of the magicians and enchanters in his entire kingdom.

21 Daniel remained in the royal service until the first year of the reign of King Cyrus.*

PURE DISCIPLINE

1. What is your favorite food? Your favorite drink?

DANIEL 1:1-21

2. Why did Daniel refuse to eat some of the food he was given? How might food have "defiled" him?
3. How did Daniel handle this difficult situation? How can you be like Daniel when you're asked to do something that violates your conscience?
4. What are some things in the world that might "defile" you? How do your peers pressure you to defile yourself?
5. What were the results of Daniel's obedience (vv. 17-20)? How might obedient discipline make you a better student? Athlete?

NEBUCHADNEZZAR'S DREAM

2 One night during the second year of his reign,* Nebuchadnezzar had such disturbing dreams that he couldn't sleep. 2 He called in his magicians, enchanters, sorcerers, and astrologers,* and he demanded that they tell him what he had dreamed. As they stood before the king, 3 he said, "I have had a dream that deeply troubles me, and I must know what it means."

4 Then the astrologers answered the king in Aramaic,* "Long live the king! Tell us the dream, and we will tell you what it means."

5 But the king said to the astrologers, "I am serious about this. If you don't tell me what my dream

1:1 This event occurred in 605 B.C., during the third year of Jehoiakim's reign (according to the calendar system in which the new year begins in the spring). **1:2** Hebrew *the land of Shinar.* **1:4** Or *of the Chaldeans.* **1:21** Cyrus began his reign (over Babylon) in 539 B.C. **2:1** The second year of Nebuchadnezzar's reign was 603 B.C. **2:2** Or *Chaldeans;* also in 2:4, 5, 10. **2:4** The original text from this point through chapter 7 is in Aramaic.

1:1 Jehoiakim. Jehoiakim reigned from 609-598 B.C. Babylonian texts claim that Nebuchadnezzar attacked Israel in 605 B.C. when Daniel and his three friends were captured. Jehoikim was Nebuchadnezzar's vassal for three years and then rebelled. Jerusalem was finally overrun by the Babylonians in 586 B.C.

1:8 determined not to defile himself. The food served at the king's table was unclean according to Mosaic law. It had been prepared by Gentiles, probably included things that the Jews were forbidden to eat, and had been sacrificed to idols. Daniel decided not to eat these things that would displease God—even though to refuse royal food would endanger his position and perhaps his life.

1:9-10 I am afraid. The official liked Daniel, but he feared that granting Daniel's request would put his own career at risk. He was responsible for keeping his captives in good physical shape to prepare them for whatever tasks the king would assign them.

1:12 diet of vegetables and water. The four Hebrews didn't eat the meat or drink the wine because they had most likely been offered to idols.

1:17 ability to interpret . . . visions and dreams. God gave these four young men knowledge and understanding. But the most important gift was Daniel's ability to understand visions and dreams—a talent that no earthly knowledge or training could give.

was and what it means, you will be torn limb from
limb, and your houses will be turned into heaps of
rubble! 6 But if you tell me what I dreamed and what
the dream means, I will give you many wonderful
gifts and honors. Just tell me the dream and what it
means!"
7 They said again, "Please, Your Majesty. Tell us the
dream, and we will tell you what it means."
8 The king replied, "I know what you are doing!
You're stalling for time because you know I am se-
rious when I say, 9 'If you don't tell me the dream,
you are doomed.' So you have conspired to tell me
lies, hoping I will change my mind. But tell me the
dream, and then I'll know that you can tell me what
it means."
10 The astrologers replied to the king, "No one on
earth can tell the king his dream! And no king, how-
ever great and powerful, has ever asked such a thing
of any magician, enchanter, or astrologer! 11 The king's
demand is impossible. No one except the gods can tell
you your dream, and they do not live here among peo-
ple."
12 The king was furious when he heard this, and he
ordered that all the wise men of Babylon be executed.
13 And because of the king's decree, men were sent to
find and kill Daniel and his friends.
14 When Arioch, the commander of the king's guard,
came to kill them, Daniel handled the situation with
wisdom and discretion. 15 He asked Arioch, "Why has
the king issued such a harsh decree?" So Arioch told
him all that had happened. 16 Daniel went at once to
see the king and requested more time to tell the king
what the dream meant.
17 Then Daniel went home and told his friends Han-
aniah, Mishael, and Azariah what had happened.
18 He urged them to ask the God of heaven to show
them his mercy by telling them the secret, so they
would not be executed along with the other wise
men of Babylon. 19 That night the secret was revealed
to Daniel in a vision. Then Daniel praised the God of
heaven. 20 He said,

"Praise the name of God forever and ever,
  for he has all wisdom and power.
21 He controls the course of world events;
  he removes kings and sets up other kings.
He gives wisdom to the wise
  and knowledge to the scholars.
22 He reveals deep and mysterious things
  and knows what lies hidden in darkness,
  though he is surrounded by light.
23 I thank and praise you, God of my ancestors,
  for you have given me wisdom and strength.
You have told me what we asked of you
  and revealed to us what the king demanded."

DANIEL INTERPRETS THE DREAM

24 Then Daniel went in to see Arioch, whom the king
had ordered to execute the wise men of Babylon. Dan-
iel said to him, "Don't kill the wise men. Take me to the
king, and I will tell him the meaning of his dream."
25 Arioch quickly took Daniel to the king and said, "I
have found one of the captives from Judah who will
tell the king the meaning of his dream!"
26 The king said to Daniel (also known as Belteshaz-
zar), "Is this true? Can you tell me what my dream was
and what it means?"
27 Daniel replied, "There are no wise men, enchant-
ers, magicians, or fortune-tellers who can reveal the
king's secret. 28 But there is a God in heaven who re-
veals secrets, and he has shown King Nebuchadnez-
zar what will happen in the future. Now I will tell
you your dream and the visions you saw as you lay
on your bed.
29 "While Your Majesty was sleeping, you dreamed
about coming events. He who reveals secrets has
shown you what is going to happen. 30 And it is not
because I am wiser than anyone else that I know the
secret of your dream, but because God wants you to
understand what was in your heart.
31 "In your vision, Your Majesty, you saw standing
before you a huge, shining statue of a man. It was a
frightening sight. 32 The head of the statue was made
of fine gold. Its chest and arms were silver, its belly
and thighs were bronze, 33 its legs were iron, and its
feet were a combination of iron and baked clay. 34 As
you watched, a rock was cut from a mountain,* but
not by human hands. It struck the feet of iron and
clay, smashing them to bits. 35 The whole statue was
crushed into small pieces of iron, clay, bronze, silver,
and gold. Then the wind blew them away without a
trace, like chaff on a threshing floor. But the rock that
knocked the statue down became a great mountain
that covered the whole earth.
36 "That was the dream. Now we will tell the king
what it means. 37 Your Majesty, you are the greatest of
kings. The God of heaven has given you sovereignty,
power, strength, and honor. 38 He has made you the
ruler over all the inhabited world and has put even
the wild animals and birds under your control. You
are the head of gold.
39 "But after your kingdom comes to an end, another
kingdom, inferior to yours, will rise to take your place.
After that kingdom has fallen, yet a third kingdom,
represented by bronze, will rise to rule the world.
40 Following that kingdom, there will be a fourth one,
as strong as iron. That kingdom will smash and crush
all previous empires, just as iron smashes and crushes
everything it strikes. 41 The feet and toes you saw were
a combination of iron and baked clay, showing that
this kingdom will be divided. Like iron mixed with
clay, it will have some of the strength of iron. 42 But
while some parts of it will be as strong as iron, other
parts will be as weak as clay. 43 This mixture of iron
and clay also shows that these kingdoms will try to
strengthen themselves by forming alliances with
each other through intermarriage. But they will not
hold together, just as iron and clay do not mix.

2:34 As in Greek version (see also 2:45); Hebrew lacks *from a mountain.*

2:18 ask the God of heaven to show them mercy. Even though Daniel was well educated and had great abilities, he asked his friends to join him in prayer concerning this secret of what the king's dream meant. A vision was the answer to the secret.

2:31-43 a huge, shining statue. Nebuchadnezzar's dream had four empires that can be interpreted as Babylon (gold head), Medo-Persia (silver chest and arms), Greece (bronze belly and thighs) and Rome (iron legs and feet).

2:44-45 kingdom that will never be destroyed. This kingdom is the kingdom of God. Jesus is the rock not made by human hands that will conquer all other political powers and have authority over all things. Amillennialists believe that this is a spiritual kingdom that was introduced by Jesus at His first coming. Premillennialists believe that this is a literal kingdom that will be established at the second coming.

[44]"During the reigns of those kings, the God of heaven will set up a kingdom that will never be destroyed or conquered. It will crush all these kingdoms into nothingness, and it will stand forever. [45]That is the meaning of the rock cut from the mountain, though not by human hands, that crushed to pieces the statue of iron, bronze, clay, silver, and gold. The great God was showing the king what will happen in the future. The dream is true, and its meaning is certain."

NEBUCHADNEZZAR REWARDS DANIEL

[46]Then King Nebuchadnezzar threw himself down before Daniel and worshiped him, and he commanded his people to offer sacrifices and burn sweet incense before him. [47]The king said to Daniel, "Truly, your God is the greatest of gods, the Lord over kings, a revealer of mysteries, for you have been able to reveal this secret."

[48]Then the king appointed Daniel to a high position and gave him many valuable gifts. He made Daniel ruler over the whole province of Babylon, as well as chief over all his wise men. [49]At Daniel's request, the king appointed Shadrach, Meshach, and Abednego to be in charge of all the affairs of the province of Babylon, while Daniel remained in the king's court.

NEBUCHADNEZZAR'S GOLD STATUE

3 King Nebuchadnezzar made a gold statue ninety feet tall and nine feet wide* and set it up on the plain of Dura in the province of Babylon. [2]Then he sent messages to the high officers, officials, governors, advisers, treasurers, judges, magistrates, and all the provincial officials to come to the dedication of the statue he had set up. [3]So all these officials* came and stood before the statue King Nebuchadnezzar had set up.

[4]Then a herald shouted out, "People of all races and nations and languages, listen to the king's command! [5]When you hear the sound of the horn, flute, zither, lyre, harp, pipes, and other musical instruments,* bow to the ground to worship King Nebuchadnezzar's gold statue. [6]Anyone who refuses to obey will immediately be thrown into a blazing furnace."

[7]So at the sound of the musical instruments,* all the people, whatever their race or nation or language, bowed to the ground and worshiped the gold statue that King Nebuchadnezzar had set up.

[8]But some of the astrologers* went to the king and informed on the Jews. [9]They said to King Nebuchadnezzar, "Long live the king! [10]You issued a decree requiring all the people to bow down and worship the gold statue when they hear the sound of the horn, flute, zither, lyre, harp, pipes, and other musical instruments. [11]That decree also states that those who refuse to obey must be thrown into a blazing furnace.

A FIERY TEST

1. What's the worst experience you've had with fire?
2. What idols do you face in your school? How do fellow students treat people at your school who do not "bow down" to them?

DANIEL 3:1-12,19-27

3. Why did these three young men refuse to bow down to the idol? What did they risk by refusing?
4. Who was the "fourth man" who appeared in the furnace (v. 25)? What does this teach us about God's intervention for those who are faithful to Him?
5. When you are persecuted for your faith, how do you respond?

[12]But there are some Jews—Shadrach, Meshach, and Abednego—whom you have put in charge of the province of Babylon. They pay no attention to you, Your Majesty. They refuse to serve your gods and do not worship the gold statue you have set up."

[13]Then Nebuchadnezzar flew into a rage and ordered that Shadrach, Meshach, and Abednego be brought before him. When they were brought in, [14]Nebuchadnezzar said to them, "Is it true, Shadrach, Meshach, and Abednego, that you refuse to serve my gods or to worship the gold statue I have set up? [15]I will give you one more chance to bow down and worship the statue I have made when you hear the sound of the musical instruments.* But if you refuse, you will be thrown immediately into the blazing furnace. And then what god will be able to rescue you from my power?"

[16]Shadrach, Meshach, and Abednego replied, "O Nebuchadnezzar, we do not need to defend ourselves before you. [17]If we are thrown into the blazing furnace, the God whom we serve is able to save us. He will rescue us from your power, Your Majesty. [18]But even if he doesn't, we want to make it clear to you, Your Majesty, that we will never serve your gods or worship the gold statue you have set up."

THE BLAZING FURNACE

[19]Nebuchadnezzar was so furious with Shadrach, Meshach, and Abednego that his face became distorted with rage. He commanded that the furnace be heated seven times hotter than usual. [20]Then he ordered some of the strongest men of his army to bind Shadrach, Meshach, and Abednego and throw them

3:1 Aramaic *60 cubits* [27 meters] *tall and 6 cubits* [2.7 meters] *wide.* **3:3** Aramaic *the high officers, officials, governors, advisers, treasurers, judges, magistrates, and all the provincial officials.* **3:5** The identification of some of these musical instruments is uncertain. **3:7** Aramaic *the horn, flute, zither, lyre, harp, pipes, and other musical instruments.* **3:8** Aramaic *Chaldeans.* **3:15** Aramaic *the horn, flute, zither, lyre, harp, pipes, and other musical instruments.*

3:1 a gold statue. After hearing that he would play a significant role in Gentile history, Nebuchadnezzar built a 90-foot gold statue to symbolize the greatness of Babylon under his rule. He hoped that this impressive structure would unify the nation.

3:2 dedication. Nebuchadnezzar called together officials of every rank in the kingdom. He wanted the officials to swear allegiance to him and publicly recognize his absolute authority in the kingdom.

3:12 They pay no attention to you. Shadrach, Meshach, and Abednego chose to obey God rather than the king. The officials who pointed this out to Nebuchadnezzar were probably trying to gain favor with the king by contrasting their worship of the golden image with the disobedience of the three Jews.

3:18 even if he doesn't. As they faced the fiery furnace, Nebuchadnezzar gave the three Jews another chance to bow down to the golden image. But the Jews were obedient to God—even in the face of death. They were confident that God could rescue them but were willing to obey, even if rescue did not come. This was a test of their faith.

into the blazing furnace. 21 So they tied them up and
threw them into the furnace, fully dressed in their
pants, turbans, robes, and other garments. 22 And
because the king, in his anger, had demanded such a
hot fire in the furnace, the flames killed the soldiers
as they threw the three men in. 23 So Shadrach, Me-
shach, and Abednego, securely tied, fell into the roar-
ing flames.

24 But suddenly, Nebuchadnezzar jumped up in
amazement and exclaimed to his advisers, "Didn't we
tie up three men and throw them into the furnace?"

"Yes, Your Majesty, we certainly did," they replied.

25 "Look!" Nebuchadnezzar shouted. "I see four men,
unbound, walking around in the fire unharmed! And
the fourth looks like a god*!"

26 Then Nebuchadnezzar came as close as he could
to the door of the flaming furnace and shouted: "Sha-
drach, Meshach, and Abednego, servants of the Most
High God, come out! Come here!"

So Shadrach, Meshach, and Abednego stepped out
of the fire. 27 Then the high officers, officials, gover-
nors, and advisers crowded around them and saw
that the fire had not touched them. Not a hair on
their heads was singed, and their clothing was not
scorched. They didn't even smell of smoke!

28 Then Nebuchadnezzar said, "Praise to the God of
Shadrach, Meshach, and Abednego! He sent his angel
to rescue his servants who trusted in him. They defied
the king's command and were willing to die rather
than serve or worship any god except their own God.
29 Therefore, I make this decree: If any people, what-
ever their race or nation or language, speak a word
against the God of Shadrach, Meshach, and Abedne-
go, they will be torn limb from limb, and their houses
will be turned into heaps of rubble. There is no other
god who can rescue like this!"

30 Then the king promoted Shadrach, Meshach, and
Abednego to even higher positions in the province of
Babylon.

NEBUCHADNEZZAR'S DREAM ABOUT A TREE

4 1*King Nebuchadnezzar sent this message to the
people of every race and nation and language
throughout the world:

"Peace and prosperity to you!

2 "I want you all to know about the miraculous
signs and wonders the Most High God has per-
formed for me.

3 How great are his signs,
how powerful his wonders!
His kingdom will last forever,
his rule through all generations.

4*"I, Nebuchadnezzar, was living in my palace
in comfort and prosperity. 5 But one night I had
a dream that frightened me; I saw visions that
terrified me as I lay in my bed. 6 So I issued an
order calling in all the wise men of Babylon, so
they could tell me what my dream meant. 7 When
all the magicians, enchanters, astrologers,* and
fortune-tellers came in, I told them the dream, but
they could not tell me what it meant. 8 At last Dan-
iel came in before me, and I told him the dream.
(He was named Belteshazzar after my god, and the
spirit of the holy gods is in him.)

9 "I said to him, 'Belteshazzar, chief of the ma-
gicians, I know that the spirit of the holy gods is
in you and that no mystery is too great for you to
solve. Now tell me what my dream means.

10 "'While I was lying in my bed, this is what I
dreamed. I saw a large tree in the middle of the
earth. 11 The tree grew very tall and strong, reach-
ing high into the heavens for all the world to see.
12 It had fresh green leaves, and it was loaded with
fruit for all to eat. Wild animals lived in its shade,
and birds nested in its branches. All the world was
fed from this tree.

13 "'Then as I lay there dreaming, I saw a mes-
senger,* a holy one, coming down from heaven.
14 The messenger shouted,

"Cut down the tree and lop off its branches!
Shake off its leaves and scatter its fruit!
Chase the wild animals from its shade
and the birds from its branches.
15 But leave the stump and the roots in the ground,
bound with a band of iron and bronze
and surrounded by tender grass.
Now let him be drenched with the dew of
heaven,
and let him live with the wild animals among
the plants of the field.
16 For seven periods of time,
let him have the mind of a wild animal
instead of the mind of a human.
17 For this has been decreed by the messengers*;
it is commanded by the holy ones,
so that everyone may know
that the Most High rules over the kingdoms
of the world.
He gives them to anyone he chooses—
even to the lowliest of people."

18 "'Belteshazzar, that was the dream that I, King
Nebuchadnezzar, had. Now tell me what it means,
for none of the wise men of my kingdom can do so.
But you can tell me because the spirit of the holy
gods is in you.'

DANIEL EXPLAINS THE DREAM

19 "Upon hearing this, Daniel (also known as Belte-
shazzar) was overcome for a time, frightened by

3:25 Aramaic *like a son of the gods.* **4:1** Verses 4:1-3 are numbered 3:31-33 in Aramaic text. **4:4** Verses 4:4-37 are numbered 4:1-34 in Aramaic text. **4:7** Or *Chaldeans.* **4:13** Aramaic *a watcher;* also in 4:23. **4:17** Aramaic *the watchers.*

4:1-3 To those . . . to generation. Nebuchadnezzar issued this official proclamation of God's greatness in response to the events described in verses 4-37.

4:5 I had a dream. This was 30 years after the dream in chapter 2.

4:11-12 tree. The tree in Nebuchadnezzar's dream represents Nebuchadnezzar himself, whose kingdom spread farther than any kingdom before it.

4:13 a messenger, a holy one. Nebuchadnezzar didn't recognize the messenger, but Jews knew that this was an angel from heaven.

4:15 leave the stump and the roots in the ground. The fact that the stump and roots remained in the ground suggested that the tree would be revived later. There would eventually be new growth.

4:17 the Most High rules over the kingdoms. The lesson that Nebuchadnezzar was supposed to learn from his experience was that God is sovereign over all rulers of the earth. It is God who chooses to set rulers over the people, and God has the power to take away their authority.

the meaning of the dream. Then the king said to him, 'Belteshazzar, don't be alarmed by the dream and what it means.'

"Belteshazzar replied, 'I wish the events foreshadowed in this dream would happen to your enemies, my lord, and not to you! 20 The tree you saw was growing very tall and strong, reaching high into the heavens for all the world to see. 21 It had fresh green leaves and was loaded with fruit for all to eat. Wild animals lived in its shade, and birds nested in its branches. 22 That tree, Your Majesty, is you. For you have grown strong and great; your greatness reaches up to heaven, and your rule to the ends of the earth.

23 "'Then you saw a messenger, a holy one, coming down from heaven and saying, "Cut down the tree and destroy it. But leave the stump and the roots in the ground, bound with a band of iron and bronze and surrounded by tender grass. Let him be drenched with the dew of heaven. Let him live with the animals of the field for seven periods of time."

24 "'This is what the dream means, Your Majesty, and what the Most High has declared will happen to my lord the king. 25 You will be driven from human society, and you will live in the fields with the wild animals. You will eat grass like a cow, and you will be drenched with the dew of heaven. Seven periods of time will pass while you live this way, until you learn that the Most High rules over the kingdoms of the world and gives them to anyone he chooses. 26 But the stump and roots of the tree were left in the ground. This means that you will receive your kingdom back again when you have learned that heaven rules.

27 "'King Nebuchadnezzar, please accept my advice. Stop sinning and do what is right. Break from your wicked past and be merciful to the poor. Perhaps then you will continue to prosper.'

THE DREAM'S FULFILLMENT

28 "But all these things did happen to King Nebuchadnezzar. 29 Twelve months later he was taking a walk on the flat roof of the royal palace in Babylon. 30 As he looked out across the city, he said, 'Look at this great city of Babylon! By my own mighty power, I have built this beautiful city as my royal residence to display my majestic splendor.'

31 "While these words were still in his mouth, a voice called down from heaven, 'O King Nebuchadnezzar, this message is for you! You are no longer ruler of this kingdom. 32 You will be driven from human society. You will live in the fields with the wild animals, and you will eat grass like a cow. Seven periods of time will pass while you live this way, until you learn that the Most High rules over the kingdoms of the world and gives them to anyone he chooses.'

33 "That same hour the judgment was fulfilled, and Nebuchadnezzar was driven from human society. He ate grass like a cow, and he was drenched with the dew of heaven. He lived this way until his hair was as long as eagles' feathers and his nails were like birds' claws.

NEBUCHADNEZZAR PRAISES GOD

34 "After this time had passed, I, Nebuchadnezzar, looked up to heaven. My sanity returned, and I praised and worshiped the Most High and honored the one who lives forever.

His rule is everlasting,
  and his kingdom is eternal.
35 All the people of the earth
  are nothing compared to him.
He does as he pleases
  among the angels of heaven
  and among the people of the earth.
No one can stop him or say to him,
  'What do you mean by doing these things?'

36 "When my sanity returned to me, so did my honor and glory and kingdom. My advisers and nobles sought me out, and I was restored as head of my kingdom, with even greater honor than before.

37 "Now I, Nebuchadnezzar, praise and glorify and honor the King of heaven. All his acts are just and true, and he is able to humble the proud."

THE WRITING ON THE WALL

5 Many years later King Belshazzar gave a great feast for 1,000 of his nobles, and he drank wine with them. 2 While Belshazzar was drinking the wine, he gave orders to bring in the gold and silver cups that his predecessor,* Nebuchadnezzar, had taken from the Temple in Jerusalem. He wanted to drink from them with his nobles, his wives, and his concubines. 3 So they brought these gold cups taken from the Temple, the house of God in Jerusalem, and the king and his nobles, his wives, and his concubines drank from them. 4 While they drank from them they praised their idols made of gold, silver, bronze, iron, wood, and stone.

5 Suddenly, they saw the fingers of a human hand writing on the plaster wall of the king's palace, near the lampstand. The king himself saw the hand as it wrote, 6 and his face turned pale with fright. His knees knocked together in fear and his legs gave way beneath him.

7 The king shouted for the enchanters, astrologers,* and fortune-tellers to be brought before him. He said to these wise men of Babylon, "Whoever can read this writing and tell me what it means will be dressed in purple robes of royal honor and will have a gold

5:2 Aramaic *father;* also in 5:11, 13, 18. 5:7 Or *Chaldeans;* also in 5:11.

4:26 heaven rules. This is similar to "kingdom of heaven" used by Jesus in Matthew.

4:28 all these things did happen to . . . Nebuchadnezzar. Daniel's prophecy came true because Nebuchadnezzar refused to heed his warning and acknowledge God's sovereignty. God had given Nebuchadnezzar the opportunity to turn from his ways.

5:1 Belshazzar. Here Belshazzar is said to be Nebuchadnezzar's son. This could also mean grandson or heir. Other documents tell us that Belshazzar, a descendant of Nebuchadnezzar, was the oldest son of Nabonidus, the reigning king. Nabonidus appointed Belshazzar co-regent, so he was called a king and thus exercised the authority of a king.

5:5 king's palace. Remarkably, this palace in the southern citadel was discovered by German archaeologist R. Koldewey in the early twentieth century. Indeed, most scholars agree with his identification of the very same throne room with walls covered in script-friendly white gypsum.

chain placed around his neck. He will become the
third highest ruler in the kingdom!"
8 But when all the king's wise men had come in,
none of them could read the writing or tell him what
it meant. 9 So the king grew even more alarmed, and
his face turned pale. His nobles, too, were shaken.
10 But when the queen mother heard what was
happening, she hurried to the banquet hall. She said
to Belshazzar, "Long live the king! Don't be so pale and
frightened. 11 There is a man in your kingdom who
has within him the spirit of the holy gods. During
Nebuchadnezzar's reign, this man was found to have
insight, understanding, and wisdom like that of the
gods. Your predecessor, the king—your predecessor
King Nebuchadnezzar—made him chief over all the
magicians, enchanters, astrologers, and fortune-tell-
ers of Babylon. 12 This man Daniel, whom the king
named Belteshazzar, has exceptional ability and is
filled with divine knowledge and understanding. He
can interpret dreams, explain riddles, and solve dif-
ficult problems. Call for Daniel, and he will tell you
what the writing means."

DANIEL EXPLAINS THE WRITING

13 So Daniel was brought in before the king. The king
asked him, "Are you Daniel, one of the exiles brought
from Judah by my predecessor, King Nebuchadnez-
zar? 14 I have heard that you have the spirit of the
gods within you and that you are filled with insight,
understanding, and wisdom. 15 My wise men and en-
chanters have tried to read the words on the wall and
tell me their meaning, but they cannot do it. 16 I am
told that you can give interpretations and solve dif-
ficult problems. If you can read these words and tell
me their meaning, you will be clothed in purple robes
of royal honor, and you will have a gold chain placed
around your neck. You will become the third highest
ruler in the kingdom."
17 Daniel answered the king, "Keep your gifts or
give them to someone else, but I will tell you what
the writing means. 18 Your Majesty, the Most High
God gave sovereignty, majesty, glory, and honor to
your predecessor, Nebuchadnezzar. 19 He made him
so great that people of all races and nations and lan-
guages trembled before him in fear. He killed those he
wanted to kill and spared those he wanted to spare.
He honored those he wanted to honor and disgraced
those he wanted to disgrace. 20 But when his heart
and mind were puffed up with arrogance, he was
brought down from his royal throne and stripped
of his glory. 21 He was driven from human society. He
was given the mind of a wild animal, and he lived
among the wild donkeys. He ate grass like a cow, and
he was drenched with the dew of heaven, until he
learned that the Most High God rules over the king-
doms of the world and appoints anyone he desires to
rule over them.
22 "You are his successor,* O Belshazzar, and you
knew all this, yet you have not humbled yourself.
23 For you have proudly defied the Lord of heaven and
have had these cups from his Temple brought before
you. You and your nobles and your wives and con-
cubines have been drinking wine from them while
praising gods of silver, gold, bronze, iron, wood, and
stone—gods that neither see nor hear nor know any-
thing at all. But you have not honored the God who
gives you the breath of life and controls your destiny!
24 So God has sent this hand to write this message.
25 "This is the message that was written: MENE,
MENE, TEKEL, and PARSIN. 26 This is what these words
mean:

Mene means 'numbered'—God has numbered the
days of your reign and has brought it to an end.
27 *Tekel* means 'weighed'—you have been weighed
on the balances and have not measured up.
28 *Parsin** means 'divided'—your kingdom has been
divided and given to the Medes and Persians."

29 Then at Belshazzar's command, Daniel was
dressed in purple robes, a gold chain was hung
around his neck, and he was proclaimed the third
highest ruler in the kingdom.
30 That very night Belshazzar, the Babylonian*
king, was killed.*
31* And Darius the Mede took over the kingdom at
the age of sixty-two.

DANIEL IN THE LIONS' DEN

6 1*Darius the Mede decided to divide the kingdom
into 120 provinces, and he appointed a high offi-
cer to rule over each province. 2 The king also chose
Daniel and two others as administrators to super-
vise the high officers and protect the king's interests.
3 Daniel soon proved himself more capable than all
the other administrators and high officers. Because
of Daniel's great ability, the king made plans to place
him over the entire empire.
4 Then the other administrators and high officers
began searching for some fault in the way Daniel was
handling government affairs, but they couldn't find
anything to criticize or condemn. He was faithful,
always responsible, and completely trustworthy. 5 So
they concluded, "Our only chance of finding grounds
for accusing Daniel will be in connection with the
rules of his religion."
6 So the administrators and high officers went to the
king and said, "Long live King Darius! 7 We are all in
agreement—we administrators, officials, high officers,
advisers, and governors—that the king should make a

5:22 Aramaic *son*. **5:28** Aramaic *Peres*, the singular of *Parsin*. **5:30a** Or *Chaldean*. **5:30b** The Persians and Medes conquered Babylon in October 539 B.C. **5:31** Verse 5:31 is numbered 6:1 in Aramaic text. **6:1** Verses 6:1-28 are numbered 6:2-29 in Aramaic text.

5:13 exiles brought from Judah. It is now over 60 years from the opening of the book. Daniel is possibly over 80 years old.

5:22-23 You . . . Belshazzar . . . have not humbled yourself. Belshazzar knew all that had happened to Nebuchadnezzar, but he failed to learn from his predecessor's experience. He openly defied God by drinking from the temple goblets and worshiping idols.

5:25-28 The inscription on the wall is a play on words. *Mene* is from a verb meaning "to number, to reckon" and refers to a weight of fifty shekels (a mina). *Tekel* is from the verb "to weigh" and refers to a shekel. *Parsin* is from the verb "to break in two, to divide" and refers to a half-mina.

5:27 Tekel. Belshazzar's moral and spiritual life did not measure up to the standard of God's righteousness, so he was rejected as unacceptable. As a result, his reign would come to an end, and his kingdom would be divided between the Medes and the Persians.

6:7 Certainly not all the royal administrators agreed to this edict, since Daniel was not even aware of it and would not support it. The conspirators lied in order to get the king to agree to their scheme. The tables would be turned on them shortly (v. 24).

THE DEN OF LIONS

1. Have you ever been close to a real lion? Where? What was it like?

DANIEL 6:1-24

2. Why were the king's officials out to get Daniel (v. 3)?
3. Why were they unable to find any charge to bring against Daniel (v. 4)? Why did they decide to accuse him "in connection with the rules of his religion" (v. 5)? What does this say about Daniel's character?
4. What saved Daniel: His faith? His innocence? His prayers? The king's prayers? God's faithfulness? Lazy lions?
5. What can you learn from Daniel's prayer habits? From his courage in obeying God?

law that will be strictly enforced. Give orders that for the next thirty days any person who prays to anyone, divine or human—except to you, Your Majesty—will be thrown into the den of lions. 8 And now, Your Majesty, issue and sign this law so it cannot be changed, an official law of the Medes and Persians that cannot be revoked." 9 So King Darius signed the law.

10 But when Daniel learned that the law had been signed, he went home and knelt down as usual in his upstairs room, with its windows open toward Jerusalem. He prayed three times a day, just as he had always done, giving thanks to his God. 11 Then the officials went together to Daniel's house and found him praying and asking for God's help. 12 So they went straight to the king and reminded him about his law. "Did you not sign a law that for the next thirty days any person who prays to anyone, divine or human—except to you, Your Majesty—will be thrown into the den of lions?"

"Yes," the king replied, "that decision stands; it is an official law of the Medes and Persians that cannot be revoked."

13 Then they told the king, "That man Daniel, one of the captives from Judah, is ignoring you and your law. He still prays to his God three times a day."

14 Hearing this, the king was deeply troubled, and he tried to think of a way to save Daniel. He spent the rest of the day looking for a way to get Daniel out of this predicament.

15 In the evening the men went together to the king and said, "Your Majesty, you know that according to the law of the Medes and the Persians, no law that the king signs can be changed."

16 So at last the king gave orders for Daniel to be arrested and thrown into the den of lions. The king said to him, "May your God, whom you serve so faithfully, rescue you."

17 A stone was brought and placed over the mouth of the den. The king sealed the stone with his own royal seal and the seals of his nobles, so that no one could rescue Daniel. 18 Then the king returned to his palace and spent the night fasting. He refused his usual entertainment and couldn't sleep at all that night.

19 Very early the next morning, the king got up and hurried out to the lions' den. 20 When he got there, he called out in anguish, "Daniel, servant of the living God! Was your God, whom you serve so faithfully, able to rescue you from the lions?"

21 Daniel answered, "Long live the king! 22 My God sent his angel to shut the lions' mouths so that they would not hurt me, for I have been found innocent in his sight. And I have not wronged you, Your Majesty."

23 The king was overjoyed and ordered that Daniel be lifted from the den. Not a scratch was found on him, for he had trusted in his God.

24 Then the king gave orders to arrest the men who had maliciously accused Daniel. He had them thrown into the lions' den, along with their wives and children. The lions leaped on them and tore them apart before they even hit the floor of the den.

25 Then King Darius sent this message to the people of every race and nation and language throughout the world:

"Peace and prosperity to you!

26 "I decree that everyone throughout my kingdom should tremble with fear before the God of Daniel.

For he is the living God,
and he will endure forever.
His kingdom will never be destroyed,
and his rule will never end.
27 He rescues and saves his people;
he performs miraculous signs and wonders
in the heavens and on earth.
He has rescued Daniel
from the power of the lions."

28 So Daniel prospered during the reign of Darius and the reign of Cyrus the Persian.*

DANIEL'S VISION OF FOUR BEASTS

7 Earlier, during the first year of King Belshazzar's reign in Babylon,* Daniel had a dream and saw visions as he lay in his bed. He wrote down the dream, and this is what he saw.

2 In my vision that night, I, Daniel, saw a great storm churning the surface of a great sea, with strong winds blowing from every direction. 3 Then four huge beasts came up out of the water, each different from the others.

4 The first beast was like a lion with eagles' wings. As I watched, its wings were pulled off, and it was left standing with its two hind feet on the ground, like a human being. And it was given a human mind.

6:28 Or *of Darius, that is, the reign of Cyrus the Persian.* **7:1** The first year of Belshazzar's reign (who was co-regent with his father, Nabonidus) was 556 B.C. (or perhaps as late as 553 B.C.).

6:20 he called out in anguish. That Darius was in anguish indicates his distress at having been hoodwinked by his administrators and the unlikelihood that Daniel had survived.

6:23 Not a scratch . . . for he trusted in his God. The king was fully expecting to find Daniel devoured. Not only was Daniel's life miraculously preserved, but he did not even have a single scratch from his night with the ravenous lions. God proved His power to save believers.

7:1-8 Daniel had a dream and saw visions. They have been seen by some to represent Babylon, Medo-Persia, Greece, and Rome. Chapter 2:36-43 refers to another dream with four statues.

5 Then I saw a second beast, and it looked like a
bear. It was rearing up on one side, and it had three
ribs in its mouth between its teeth. And I heard a
voice saying to it, "Get up! Devour the flesh of many
people!"
6 Then the third of these strange beasts appeared,
and it looked like a leopard. It had four bird's wings
on its back, and it had four heads. Great authority was
given to this beast.
7 Then in my vision that night, I saw a fourth
beast—terrifying, dreadful, and very strong. It de-
voured and crushed its victims with huge iron teeth
and trampled their remains beneath its feet. It was
different from any of the other beasts, and it had ten
horns.
8 As I was looking at the horns, suddenly another
small horn appeared among them. Three of the first
horns were torn out by the roots to make room for it.
This little horn had eyes like human eyes and a mouth
that was boasting arrogantly.

9 I watched as thrones were put in place
    and the Ancient One* sat down to judge.
His clothing was as white as snow,
    his hair like purest wool.
He sat on a fiery throne
    with wheels of blazing fire,
10 and a river of fire was pouring out,
    flowing from his presence.
Millions of angels ministered to him;
    many millions stood to attend him.
Then the court began its session,
    and the books were opened.

11 I continued to watch because I could hear the lit-
tle horn's boastful speech. I kept watching until the
fourth beast was killed and its body was destroyed by
fire. 12 The other three beasts had their authority tak-
en from them, but they were allowed to live a while
longer.*
13 As my vision continued that night, I saw someone
like a son of man* coming with the clouds of heaven.
He approached the Ancient One and was led into his
presence. 14 He was given authority, honor, and sover-
eignty over all the nations of the world, so that people
of every race and nation and language would obey
him. His rule is eternal—it will never end. His king-
dom will never be destroyed.

THE VISION IS EXPLAINED

15 I, Daniel, was troubled by all I had seen, and my
visions terrified me. 16 So I approached one of those
standing beside the throne and asked him what it all
meant. He explained it to me like this: 17 "These four
huge beasts represent four kingdoms that will arise
from the earth. 18 But in the end, the holy people of the
Most High will be given the kingdom, and they will
rule forever and ever."
19 Then I wanted to know the true meaning of the
fourth beast, the one so different from the others
and so terrifying. It had devoured and crushed its
victims with iron teeth and bronze claws, trampling
their remains beneath its feet. 20 I also asked about
the ten horns on the fourth beast's head and the little
horn that came up afterward and destroyed three of
the other horns. This horn had seemed greater than
the others, and it had human eyes and a mouth that
was boasting arrogantly. 21 As I watched, this horn
was waging war against God's holy people and was
defeating them, 22 until the Ancient One—the Most
High—came and judged in favor of his holy people.
Then the time arrived for the holy people to take over
the kingdom.
23 Then he said to me, "This fourth beast is the
fourth world power that will rule the earth. It will be
different from all the others. It will devour the whole
world, trampling and crushing everything in its path.
24 Its ten horns are ten kings who will rule that em-
pire. Then another king will arise, different from the
other ten, who will subdue three of them. 25 He will
defy the Most High and oppress the holy people of the
Most High. He will try to change their sacred festivals
and laws, and they will be placed under his control
for a time, times, and half a time.
26 "But then the court will pass judgment, and all his
power will be taken away and completely destroyed.
27 Then the sovereignty, power, and greatness of all
the kingdoms under heaven will be given to the holy
people of the Most High. His kingdom will last forev-
er, and all rulers will serve and obey him."
28 That was the end of the vision. I, Daniel, was ter-
rified by my thoughts and my face was pale with fear,
but I kept these things to myself.

DANIEL'S VISION OF A RAM AND GOAT

8 1*During the third year of King Belshazzar's
reign, I, Daniel, saw another vision, following the
one that had already appeared to me. 2 In this vision
I was at the fortress of Susa, in the province of Elam,
standing beside the Ulai River.*
3 As I looked up, I saw a ram with two long horns
standing beside the river.* One of the horns was lon-
ger than the other, even though it had grown later
than the other one. 4 The ram butted everything out of
his way to the west, to the north, and to the south, and
no one could stand against him or help his victims. He
did as he pleased and became very great.
5 While I was watching, suddenly a male goat ap-
peared from the west, crossing the land so swiftly
that he didn't even touch the ground. This goat, which

7:9 Aramaic *an Ancient of Days;* also in 7:13, 22. **7:12** Aramaic *for a season and a time.* **7:13** Or *like a Son of Man.* **8:1** The original text from this point through chapter 12 is in Hebrew. See note at 2:4. **8:2** Or *the Ulai Gate;* also in 8:16. **8:3** Or *the gate;* also in 8:6.

7:13-14 son of man. This is the first time this title is used for the Messiah. Here Christ approaches the Ancient of Days and is given all the authority, glory, and sovereign power that had previously been given to earthly rulers.

7:18 holy people of the Most High. Those who believe in Christ will inherit the kingdom. (see Matt. 19:28-29; Rev. 20:4-6.)

7:24-26 another king will arise. After the ten divided kings, one king will take over three of the ten. But he will oppose God's authority, oppress the saints, and abandon old laws to institute his own governmental system. This king will persecute Israel for three and a half years (a time that may be figurative or could refer to the three and one-half years of the Great Tribulation, Rev. 12:14). After that Jesus will sit as judge, remove him from power, and set up His eternal kingdom.

8:3 a ram with two horns. The ram represents the Medo-Persian Empire with the longer horn signifying the superior position of Persia. The Medo-Persian Empire would charge in all directions until it dominated the entire area.

8:5-7 one very large horn. The goat represents Greece with the prominent horn as a symbol for Alexander the Great. Greece would crush the Medo-Persian Empire.

had one very large horn between its eyes, 6 headed to-
ward the two-horned ram that I had seen standing
beside the river, rushing at him in a rage. 7 The goat
charged furiously at the ram and struck him, break-
ing off both his horns. Now the ram was helpless, and
the goat knocked him down and trampled him. No
one could rescue the ram from the goat's power.
8 The goat became very powerful. But at the height
of his power, his large horn was broken off. In the
large horn's place grew four prominent horns point-
ing in the four directions of the earth. 9 Then from
one of the prominent horns came a small horn whose
power grew very great. It extended toward the south
and the east and toward the glorious land of Israel.
10 Its power reached to the heavens, where it attacked
the heavenly army, throwing some of the heaven-
ly beings and some of the stars to the ground and
trampling them. 11 It even challenged the Command-
er of heaven's army by canceling the daily sacrifices
offered to him and by destroying his Temple. 12 The
army of heaven was restrained from responding to
this rebellion. So the daily sacrifice was halted, and
truth was overthrown. The horn succeeded in every-
thing it did.*
13 Then I heard two holy ones talking to each other.
One of them asked, "How long will the events of this
vision last? How long will the rebellion that causes
desecration stop the daily sacrifices? How long will
the Temple and heaven's army be trampled on?"
14 The other replied, "It will take 2,300 evenings and
mornings; then the Temple will be made right again."

GABRIEL EXPLAINS THE VISION

15 As I, Daniel, was trying to understand the meaning
of this vision, someone who looked like a man stood in
front of me. 16 And I heard a human voice calling out
from the Ulai River, "Gabriel, tell this man the mean-
ing of his vision."
17 As Gabriel approached the place where I was
standing, I became so terrified that I fell with my face
to the ground. "Son of man," he said, "you must un-
derstand that the events you have seen in your vision
relate to the time of the end."
18 While he was speaking, I fainted and lay there
with my face to the ground. But Gabriel roused me
with a touch and helped me to my feet.
19 Then he said, "I am here to tell you what will hap-
pen later in the time of wrath. What you have seen
pertains to the very end of time. 20 The two-horned
ram represents the kings of Media and Persia. 21 The
shaggy male goat represents the king of Greece,* and
the large horn between his eyes represents the first
king of the Greek Empire. 22 The four prominent horns
that replaced the one large horn show that the Greek
Empire will break into four kingdoms, but none as
great as the first.
23 "At the end of their rule, when their sin is at its
height, a fierce king, a master of intrigue, will rise
to power. 24 He will become very strong, but not by
his own power. He will cause a shocking amount
of destruction and succeed in everything he does.
He will destroy powerful leaders and devastate the
holy people. 25 He will be a master of deception and
will become arrogant; he will destroy many without
warning. He will even take on the Prince of princes
in battle, but he will be broken, though not by human
power.
26 "This vision about the 2,300 evenings and morn-
ings* is true. But none of these things will happen for
a long time, so keep this vision a secret."
27 Then I, Daniel, was overcome and lay sick for
several days. Afterward I got up and performed my
duties for the king, but I was greatly troubled by the
vision and could not understand it.

DANIEL'S PRAYER FOR HIS PEOPLE

9 It was the first year of the reign of Darius the
Mede, the son of Ahasuerus, who became king of
the Babylonians.^A 2 During the first year of his reign,
I, Daniel, learned from reading the word of the LORD,
as revealed to Jeremiah the prophet, that Jerusalem
must lie desolate for seventy years.* 3 So I turned to
the Lord God and pleaded with him in prayer and
fasting. I also wore rough burlap and sprinkled my-
self with ashes.
4 I prayed to the LORD my God and confessed:

"O Lord, you are a great and awesome God! You al-
ways fulfill your covenant and keep your promises
of unfailing love to those who love you and obey
your commands. 5 But we have sinned and done
wrong. We have rebelled against you and scorned
your commands and regulations. 6 We have re-
fused to listen to your servants the prophets, who
spoke on your authority to our kings and princes
and ancestors and to all the people of the land.
7 "Lord, you are in the right; but as you see, our
faces are covered with shame. This is true of all of
us, including the people of Judah and Jerusalem
and all Israel, scattered near and far, wherever
you have driven us because of our disloyalty
to you. 8 O LORD, we and our kings, princes, and
ancestors are covered with shame because we
have sinned against you. 9 But the Lord our God is
merciful and forgiving, even though we have re-
belled against him. 10 We have not obeyed the LORD
our God, for we have not followed the instructions
he gave us through his servants the prophets. 11 All
Israel has disobeyed your instruction and turned
away, refusing to listen to your voice.
"So now the solemn curses and judgments writ-
ten in the Law of Moses, the servant of God, have
been poured down on us because of our sin. 12 You
have kept your word and done to us and our rulers
exactly as you warned. Never has there been such
a disaster as happened in Jerusalem. 13 Every curse
written against us in the Law of Moses has come
true. Yet we have refused to seek mercy from the
LORD our God by turning from our sins and recog-
nizing his truth. 14 Therefore, the LORD has brought

8:11-12 The meaning of the Hebrew for these verses is uncertain. 8:21 Hebrew *of Javan.* 8:26 Hebrew *about the evenings and mornings;* compare 8:14. 9:1 Or *the Chaldeans.* 9:2 See Jer 25:11-12; 29:10.

8:8 large horn was broken off. Alexander died at the height of power. The four prominent horns are his four generals who carved up the Macedonian Empire.

8:9-12 The horn that started small but grew in power was Antiochus IV Epiphanes. Antiochus took control of Israel, refused to allow the Jews to make sacrifices, and killed many for their faith. Then he declared himself to be God's equal and was eventually defeated by Judas Maccabeus, who rededicated the temple to the Lord and began the Feast of Hanukkah.

upon us the disaster he prepared. The LORD our
God was right to do all of these things, for we did
not obey him.
15 "O Lord our God, you brought lasting honor to
your name by rescuing your people from Egypt
in a great display of power. But we have sinned
and are full of wickedness. 16 In view of all your
faithful mercies, Lord, please turn your furious
anger away from your city Jerusalem, your holy
mountain. All the neighboring nations mock Jeru-
salem and your people because of our sins and the
sins of our ancestors.
17 "O our God, hear your servant's prayer! Listen
as I plead. For your own sake, Lord, smile again on
your desolate sanctuary.
18 "O my God, lean down and listen to me. Open
your eyes and see our despair. See how your
city—the city that bears your name—lies in
ruins. We make this plea, not because we deserve
help, but because of your mercy.
19 "O Lord, hear. O Lord, forgive. O Lord, listen and
act! For your own sake, do not delay, O my God, for
your people and your city bear your name."

GABRIEL'S MESSAGE ABOUT THE ANOINTED ONE

20 I went on praying and confessing my sin and the sin
of my people, pleading with the LORD my God for Jeru-
salem, his holy mountain. 21 As I was praying, Gabriel,
whom I had seen in the earlier vision, came swiftly to
me at the time of the evening sacrifice. 22 He explained
to me, "Daniel, I have come here to give you insight
and understanding. 23 The moment you began pray-
ing, a command was given. And now I am here to tell
you what it was, for you are very precious to God. Lis-
ten carefully so that you can understand the meaning
of your vision.
24 "A period of seventy sets of seven* has been de-
creed for your people and your holy city to finish their
rebellion, to put an end to their sin, to atone for their
guilt, to bring in everlasting righteousness, to con-
firm the prophetic vision, and to anoint the Most Holy
Place.* 25 Now listen and understand! Seven sets of
seven plus sixty-two sets of seven* will pass from the
time the command is given to rebuild Jerusalem until
a ruler—the Anointed One*—comes. Jerusalem will
be rebuilt with streets and strong defenses,* despite
the perilous times.
26 "After this period of sixty-two sets of seven,*
the Anointed One will be killed, appearing to have
accomplished nothing, and a ruler will arise whose
armies will destroy the city and the Temple. The end
will come with a flood, and war and its miseries are
decreed from that time to the very end. 27 The ruler
will make a treaty with the people for a period of one
set of seven,* but after half this time, he will put an
end to the sacrifices and offerings. And as a climax
to all his terrible deeds,* he will set up a sacrilegious
object that causes desecration,* until the fate decreed
for this defiler is finally poured out on him."

DANIEL'S VISION OF A MESSENGER

10 In the third year of the reign of King Cyrus of
Persia,* Daniel (also known as Belteshazzar)
had another vision. He understood that the vision
concerned events certain to happen in the future—
times of war and great hardship.
2 When this vision came to me, I, Daniel, had been
in mourning for three whole weeks. 3 All that time I
had eaten no rich food. No meat or wine crossed my
lips, and I used no fragrant lotions until those three
weeks had passed.
4 On April 23,* as I was standing on the bank of the
great Tigris River, 5 I looked up and saw a man dressed
in linen clothing, with a belt of pure gold around his
waist. 6 His body looked like a precious gem. His face
flashed like lightning, and his eyes flamed like torch-
es. His arms and feet shone like polished bronze, and
his voice roared like a vast multitude of people.
7 Only I, Daniel, saw this vision. The men with
me saw nothing, but they were suddenly terrified
and ran away to hide. 8 So I was left there all alone
to see this amazing vision. My strength left me, my
face grew deathly pale, and I felt very weak. 9 Then I
heard the man speak, and when I heard the sound of
his voice, I fainted and lay there with my face to the
ground.
10 Just then a hand touched me and lifted me, still
trembling, to my hands and knees. 11 And the man said
to me, "Daniel, you are very precious to God, so listen
carefully to what I have to say to you. Stand up, for
I have been sent to you." When he said this to me, I
stood up, still trembling.
12 Then he said, "Don't be afraid, Daniel. Since the
first day you began to pray for understanding and to
humble yourself before your God, your request has
been heard in heaven. I have come in answer to your
prayer. 13 But for twenty-one days the spirit prince* of
the kingdom of Persia blocked my way. Then Michael,
one of the archangels,* came to help me, and I left him
there with the spirit prince of the kingdom of Persia.*

9:24a Hebrew *seventy sevens.* **9:24b** Or *the Most Holy One.* **9:25a** Hebrew *Seven sevens plus sixty-two sevens.* **9:25b** Or *an anointed one;* similarly in 9:26. Hebrew reads *a messiah.* **9:25c** Or *and a moat,* or *and trenches.* **9:26** Hebrew *After sixty-two sevens.* **9:27a** Hebrew *for one seven.* **9:27b** Hebrew *And on the wing;* the meaning of the Hebrew is uncertain. **9:27c** Hebrew *an abomination of desolation.* **10:1** The third year of Cyrus's reign was 536 B.C. **10:4** Hebrew *On the twenty-fourth day of the first month,* of the ancient Hebrew lunar calendar. This date in the book of Daniel can be cross-checked with dates in surviving Persian records and can be related accurately to our modern calendar. This event occurred on April 23, 536 B.C. **10:13a** Hebrew *the prince;* also in 10:13c, 20. **10:13b** Hebrew *the chief princes.* **10:13c** As in one Greek version; Hebrew reads *and I was left there with the kings of Persia.* The meaning of the Hebrew is uncertain.

9:18 because of your mercy. Daniel based his requests on God's character, not on Israel's worthiness. Daniel was asking God for His mercy. God answers prayer because He is gracious, not because we deserve it.

9:25 the command is given. There are several possibilities as to the identity of this command: by Cyrus (Ezra 1:2-4), the decree by Darius (Ezra 6:3-12), the decree by Artaxerxes (Ezra 7:13-26), or the decree by Artaxerxes (Neh. 2:7-9). This most likely refers to the decree by Artaxerxes Longimanus in 444 B.C. that allowed the Jews permission to rebuild Jerusalem's city walls. Sixty-nine "sevens" (7 plus 62), the equivalent of 483 years, elapsed between this decree and the crucifixion of the Messiah.

9:26 the Anointed One will be killed. This is a reference to the crucifixion of Christ.

9:27 make a treaty. A ruler will come who will guarantee Israel's safety, but he will break the covenant after only three and a half years. Many believe that this is a reference to the Antichrist, who will set up an abomination against God until the end. Others see this as a reference to the Messiah's instituting a new covenant and putting an end to the Old Testament sacrificial system.

10:5 a man dressed in linen. This is either an angel or, as some think, a pre-incarnate appearance of Christ.

10:13 spirit prince of the kingdom of Persia. Possibly a reference to a demonic figure because of the lengthy battle with the angel, Michael.

14 Now I am here to explain what will happen to your people in the future, for this vision concerns a time yet to come."

15 While he was speaking to me, I looked down at the ground, unable to say a word. 16 Then the one who looked like a man* touched my lips, and I opened my mouth and began to speak. I said to the one standing in front of me, "I am filled with anguish because of the vision I have seen, my lord, and I am very weak. 17 How can someone like me, your servant, talk to you, my lord? My strength is gone, and I can hardly breathe."

18 Then the one who looked like a man touched me again, and I felt my strength returning. 19 "Don't be afraid," he said, "for you are very precious to God. Peace! Be encouraged! Be strong!"

As he spoke these words to me, I suddenly felt stronger and said to him, "Please speak to me, my lord, for you have strengthened me."

20 He replied, "Do you know why I have come? Soon I must return to fight against the spirit prince of the kingdom of Persia, and after that the spirit prince of the kingdom of Greece* will come. 21 Meanwhile, I will tell you what is written in the Book of Truth. (No one helps me against these spirit princes except Michael, your spirit prince.* 11:1 I have been standing beside Michael* to support and strengthen him since the first year of the reign of Darius the Mede.)

KINGS OF THE SOUTH AND NORTH

11 2 "Now then, I will reveal the truth to you. Three more Persian kings will reign, to be succeeded by a fourth, far richer than the others. He will use his wealth to stir up everyone to fight against the kingdom of Greece.*

3 "Then a mighty king will rise to power who will rule with great authority and accomplish everything he sets out to do. 4 But at the height of his power, his kingdom will be broken apart and divided into four parts. It will not be ruled by the king's descendants, nor will the kingdom hold the authority it once had. For his empire will be uprooted and given to others.

5 "The king of the south will increase in power, but one of his own officials will become more powerful than he and will rule his kingdom with great strength.

6 "Some years later an alliance will be formed between the king of the north and the king of the south. The daughter of the king of the south will be given in marriage to the king of the north to secure the alliance, but she will lose her influence over him, and so will her father. She will be abandoned along with her supporters. 7 But when one of her relatives* becomes king of the south, he will raise an army and enter the fortress of the king of the north and defeat him. 8 When he returns to Egypt, he will carry back their idols with him, along with priceless articles of gold and silver. For some years afterward he will leave the king of the north alone.

9 "Later the king of the north will invade the realm of the king of the south but will soon return to his own land. 10 However, the sons of the king of the north will assemble a mighty army that will advance like a flood and carry the battle as far as the enemy's fortress.

11 "Then, in a rage, the king of the south will rally against the vast forces assembled by the king of the north and will defeat them. 12 After the enemy army is swept away, the king of the south will be filled with pride and will execute many thousands of his enemies. But his success will be short lived.

13 "A few years later the king of the north will return with a fully equipped army far greater than before. 14 At that time there will be a general uprising against the king of the south. Violent men among your own people will join them in fulfillment of this vision, but they will not succeed. 15 Then the king of the north will come and lay siege to a fortified city and capture it. The best troops of the south will not be able to stand in the face of the onslaught.

16 "The king of the north will march onward unopposed; none will be able to stop him. He will pause in the glorious land of Israel,* intent on destroying it. 17 He will make plans to come with the might of his entire kingdom and will form an alliance with the king of the south. He will give him a daughter in marriage in order to overthrow the kingdom from within, but his plan will fail.

18 "After this, he will turn his attention to the coastland and conquer many cities. But a commander from another land will put an end to his insolence and cause him to retreat in shame. 19 He will take refuge in his own fortresses but will stumble and fall and be seen no more.

20 "His successor will send out a tax collector to maintain the royal splendor. But after a very brief reign, he will die, though not from anger or in battle.

21 "The next to come to power will be a despicable man who is not in line for royal succession. He will slip in when least expected and take over the kingdom by flattery and intrigue. 22 Before him great armies will be swept away, including a covenant prince. 23 With deceitful promises, he will make various alliances. He will become strong despite having only a handful of followers. 24 Without warning he will enter the richest areas of the land. Then he will distribute among his followers the plunder and wealth of the rich—something his predecessors had never done. He will plot the overthrow of strongholds, but this will last for only a short while.

25 "Then he will stir up his courage and raise a great army against the king of the south. The king of the south will go to battle with a mighty army, but to no avail, for there will be plots against him. 26 His own household will cause his downfall. His army will

10:16 As in most manuscripts of the Masoretic Text; one manuscript of the Masoretic Text and one Greek version read *Then something that looked like a human hand.* **10:20** Hebrew *of Javan.* **10:21** Hebrew *against these except Michael, your prince.* **11:1** Hebrew *him.* **11:2** Hebrew *of Javan.* **11:7** Hebrew *a branch from her roots.* **11:16** Hebrew *the glorious land.*

10:21 Book of Truth. This is a reference to God's absolute authority over all of mankind's history—past, present, and future.

11:1 first year of . . . Darius. This is still the same year since chapter nine. This is the year 539 B.C. when Cyrus was appointed as administrator of Babylon.

11:16 king of the north. After the Egyptian defeat at the battle of Sidon, Antiochus III was welcomed by Jerusalem's inhabitants in 198 B.C. This change in government set up the brutal reign of his son, Antiochus Epiphanes IV, 23 years later.

11:21-35 Gabriel, the master angel (8:16; 9:21) who will eventually announce the birth of Jesus 530 years later (Lk. 1:19,26), has set the stage (vv. 2-20) for the appearance of the "little horn" (8:9-12,23-25), Antiochus Epiphanes (175–163 B.C.). The profound effect he would have on Israel makes this section especially climactic.

be swept away, and many will be killed. 27 Seeking nothing but each other's harm, these kings will plot against each other at the conference table, attempting to deceive each other. But it will make no difference, for the end will come at the appointed time.

28 "The king of the north will then return home with great riches. On the way he will set himself against the people of the holy covenant, doing much damage before continuing his journey.

29 "Then at the appointed time he will once again invade the south, but this time the result will be different. 30 For warships from western coastlands* will scare him off, and he will withdraw and return home. But he will vent his anger against the people of the holy covenant and reward those who forsake the covenant.

31 "His army will take over the Temple fortress, pollute the sanctuary, put a stop to the daily sacrifices, and set up the sacrilegious object that causes desecration.* 32 He will flatter and win over those who have violated the covenant. But the people who know their God will be strong and will resist him.

33 "Wise leaders will give instruction to many, but these teachers will die by fire and sword, or they will be jailed and robbed. 34 During these persecutions, little help will arrive, and many who join them will not be sincere. 35 And some of the wise will fall victim to persecution. In this way, they will be refined and cleansed and made pure until the time of the end, for the appointed time is still to come.

36 "The king will do as he pleases, exalting himself and claiming to be greater than every god, even blaspheming the God of gods. He will succeed, but only until the time of wrath is completed. For what has been determined will surely take place. 37 He will have no respect for the gods of his ancestors, or for the god loved by women, or for any other god, for he will boast that he is greater than them all. 38 Instead of these, he will worship the god of fortresses—a god his ancestors never knew—and lavish on him gold, silver, precious stones, and expensive gifts. 39 Claiming this foreign god's help, he will attack the strongest fortresses. He will honor those who submit to him, appointing them to positions of authority and dividing the land among them as their reward.*

40 "Then at the time of the end, the king of the south will attack the king of the north. The king of the north will storm out with chariots, charioteers, and a vast navy. He will invade various lands and sweep through them like a flood. 41 He will enter the glorious land of Israel,* and many nations will fall, but Moab, Edom, and the best part of Ammon will escape. 42 He will conquer many countries, and even Egypt will not escape. 43 He will gain control over the gold, silver, and treasures of Egypt, and the Libyans and Ethiopians* will be his servants.

44 "But then news from the east and the north will alarm him, and he will set out in great anger to destroy and obliterate many. 45 He will stop between the glorious holy mountain and the sea and will pitch his royal tents. But while he is there, his time will suddenly run out, and no one will help him.

THE TIME OF THE END

12 "At that time Michael, the archangel* who stands guard over your nation, will arise. Then there will be a time of anguish greater than any since nations first came into existence. But at that time every one of your people whose name is written in the book will be rescued. 2 Many of those whose bodies lie dead and buried will rise up, some to everlasting life and some to shame and everlasting disgrace. 3 Those who are wise will shine as bright as the sky, and those who lead many to righteousness will shine like the stars forever. 4 But you, Daniel, keep this prophecy a secret; seal up the book until the time of the end, when many will rush here and there, and knowledge will increase."

5 Then I, Daniel, looked and saw two others standing on opposite banks of the river. 6 One of them asked the man dressed in linen, who was now standing above the river, "How long will it be until these shocking events are over?"

7 The man dressed in linen, who was standing above the river, raised both his hands toward heaven and took a solemn oath by the One who lives forever, saying, "It will go on for a time, times, and half a time. When the shattering of the holy people has finally come to an end, all these things will have happened."

8 I heard what he said, but I did not understand what he meant. So I asked, "How will all this finally end, my lord?"

9 But he said, "Go now, Daniel, for what I have said is kept secret and sealed until the time of the end. 10 Many will be purified, cleansed, and refined by these trials. But the wicked will continue in their wickedness, and none of them will understand. Only those who are wise will know what it means.

11 "From the time the daily sacrifice is stopped and the sacrilegious object that causes desecration* is set up to be worshiped, there will be 1,290 days. 12 And blessed are those who wait and remain until the end of the 1,335 days!

13 "As for you, go your way until the end. You will rest, and then at the end of the days, you will rise again to receive the inheritance set aside for you."

11:30 Hebrew *from Kittim.* **11:31** Hebrew *the abomination of desolation.* **11:39** Or *at a price.* **11:41** Hebrew *the glorious land.* **11:43** Hebrew *Cushites.* **12:1** Hebrew *the great prince.* **12:11** Hebrew *the abomination of desolation.*

11:31 pollute the sanctuary. Antiochus polluted the temple with a pagan altar in 168 B.C.

11:36 The king will do as he pleases. From here to the end of chapter 11, the king referred to is the Antichrist. He will set himself up completely independent of any power, even exalting himself above God.

11:40-45 Just before Christ's return, the Antichrist will battle his political enemies. At the battle of Armageddon he will be killed on the "beautiful holy mountain," Jerusalem's temple mount (Rev. 19:11-21).

12:1 Michael. Michael (10:13,21) reappears in a big way in the New Testament (Jude 9; Rev. 12:7,14), where once again he will be arrayed against the forces of evil.

12:2 those who sleep in the dust. This is the first clear scriptural reference to a resurrection. The godly will rise to everlasting life, while the wicked will be resurrected to eternal shame and contempt.

12:13 rise to your destiny. Daniel would die before many of the events he prophesied took place. But he would be raised from the dead according to the promise to receive his reward and inheritance for his service to God.

INTRODUCTION TO

HOSEA

PERSONAL READING PLAN

☐Hosea 1:1–2:23
☐Hosea 3:1–5:15
☐Hosea 6:1–8:14
☐Hosea 9:1–10:15
☐Hosea 11:1–12:14
☐Hosea 13:1–14:9

AUTHOR

The author is identified as Hosea, son of Beeri—a prophet to the northern kingdom (Israel). He was the only one of the writing prophets to come from Israel, and his prophecy is mainly directed to them

DATE

Hosea's prophetic career spanned four decades, from the prosperous latter years of Jeroboam II (793–753 B.C.) to the 720s shortly before the fall of Samaria and the exile of Israel.

THEME

God's undying love for His people.

HISTORICAL BACKGROUND

The dominant faith of Israel during Hosea's time was not Mosaic Judaism but a mixture of the worship of the Lord and the local polytheistic Baal religions. Israel was prosperous and complacent under Jeroboam II, but after his death, and a succession of six kings in 30 years, life became increasingly insecure and the nation's resources weakened. Israel stubbornly sought help from other nations instead of from the Lord.

CHARACTERISTICS

Hosea's language relies heavily upon the covenant stipulations of blessings and curses (see Lev. 26; Deut. 28–32). While reciting the case against Israel and the consequential curses she will face, Hosea interjects God's promise to restore her to the land and to Himself in covenant faithfulness.

The beginning of the book (chaps. 1–3) tells the story of Hosea's intriguing family situation, which demonstrates his message from God to Israel. First, Hosea obeys the Lord's command to marry an adulterous woman, Gomer. They have three children—each given a name symbolic of Hosea's message. Then, even though Hosea and Gomer are separated by her unfaithfulness, the Lord says to Hosea, "Go and love your wife again, even though she commits adultery with another lover" (3:1). This unusual story raises questions. Is the story allegorical, or is it meant to be taken literally? The precise nature of Gomer's relationship to Hosea cannot be established with certainty. God's purpose in this "enacted" prophecy is clear, however. Bound to the Lord by covenant, Israel still "prostitutes" herself and bears "illegitimate children." In word and deed, the book of Hosea communicates that despite Israel's faithlessness, God remains faithful and longs to take them back just as Hosea forgives Gomer. This reunion is described with imagery recalling the exodus from Egypt and settlement in Canaan (see 1:11; 3:5; 14:4-7).

1 The LORD gave this message to Hosea son of Beeri
during the years when Uzziah, Jotham, Ahaz, and
Hezekiah were kings of Judah, and Jeroboam son of
Jehoash* was king of Israel.

HOSEA'S WIFE AND CHILDREN

2 When the LORD first began speaking to Israel
through Hosea, he said to him, "Go and marry a pros-
titute,* so that some of her children will be conceived
in prostitution. This will illustrate how Israel has act-
ed like a prostitute by turning against the LORD and
worshiping other gods."
3 So Hosea married Gomer, the daughter of Dibla-
im, and she became pregnant and gave Hosea a son.
4 And the LORD said, "Name the child Jezreel, for I am
about to punish King Jehu's dynasty to avenge the
murders he committed at Jezreel. In fact, I will bring
an end to Israel's independence. 5 I will break its mili-
tary power in the Jezreel Valley."
6 Soon Gomer became pregnant again and gave
birth to a daughter. And the LORD said to Hosea,
"Name your daughter Lo-ruhamah—'Not loved'—
for I will no longer show love to the people of Is-
rael or forgive them. 7 But I will show love to the
people of Judah. I will free them from their ene-
mies—not with weapons and armies or horses
and charioteers, but by my power as the LORD their
God."
8 After Gomer had weaned Lo-ruhamah, she again
became pregnant and gave birth to a second son.
9 And the LORD said, "Name him Lo-ammi—'Not my
people'—for Israel is not my people, and I am not
their God.
10* "Yet the time will come when Israel's people
will be like the sands of the seashore—too many
to count! Then, at the place where they were told,
'You are not my people,' it will be said, 'You are chil-
dren of the living God.' 11 Then the people of Judah
and Israel will unite together. They will choose one
leader for themselves, and they will return from
exile together. What a day that will be—the day of
Jezreel*—when God will again plant his people in
his land.
2:1* "In that day you will call your brothers Am-
mi—'My people.' And you will call your sisters Ruha-
mah—'The ones I love.'

CHARGES AGAINST AN UNFAITHFUL WIFE

2 2 "But now bring charges against Israel—your
mother—
for she is no longer my wife,
and I am no longer her husband.
Tell her to remove the prostitute's makeup from
her face
and the clothing that exposes her breasts.
3 Otherwise, I will strip her as naked
as she was on the day she was born.
I will leave her to die of thirst,
as in a dry and barren wilderness.
4 And I will not love her children,
for they were conceived in prostitution.
5 Their mother is a shameless prostitute
and became pregnant in a shameful way.
She said, 'I'll run after other lovers
and sell myself to them for food and water,
for clothing of wool and linen,
and for olive oil and drinks.'

6 "For this reason I will fence her in with
thornbushes.
I will block her path with a wall
to make her lose her way.
7 When she runs after her lovers,
she won't be able to catch them.
She will search for them
but not find them.
Then she will think,
'I might as well return to my husband,
for I was better off with him than I am now.'
8 She doesn't realize it was I who gave her
everything she has—
the grain, the new wine, the olive oil;
I even gave her silver and gold.
But she gave all my gifts to Baal.

9 "But now I will take back the ripened grain and
new wine
I generously provided each harvest season.
I will take away the wool and linen clothing
I gave her to cover her nakedness.
10 I will strip her naked in public,
while all her lovers look on.
No one will be able
to rescue her from my hands.
11 I will put an end to her annual festivals,
her new moon celebrations, and her Sabbath
days—
all her appointed festivals.
12 I will destroy her grapevines and fig trees,
things she claims her lovers gave her.
I will let them grow into tangled thickets,
where only wild animals will eat the fruit.
13 I will punish her for all those times
when she burned incense to her images of
Baal,
when she put on her earrings and jewels
and went out to look for her lovers
but forgot all about me,"
says the LORD.

1:1 Hebrew *Joash,* a variant spelling of Jehoash. **1:2** Or *a promiscuous woman.* **1:10** Verses 1:10-11 are numbered 2:1-2 in Hebrew text. **1:11** *Jezreel* means "God plants." **2:1** Verses 2:1-23 are numbered 2:3-25 in Hebrew text.

1:1 Hosea. Hosea's message was good news for Israel; his name means "salvation."

1:3 Gomer, the daughter of Diblaim. It is debatable whether Hosea's wife was unfaithful at the time he married her or that the child she bore is not Hosea's.

1:6 Name your daugher Lo-ruhamah. Or "Not Loved." God emphasized the seriousness of the breach in the love relationship with His people by naming one of the children "Not Loved."

1:9 Name him Lo-ammi. Or "Not my people." Their third child's name carried the ultimate insult. God dared to disown His people.

1:11 the people of Judah and Israel will unite. The Lord foresaw a future time when the two kingdoms would be ruled under His own leadership.

2:2 no longer my wife . . . no longer her husband. Hosea spoke about Gomer as God felt about Israel.

2:10 No one will be able to rescue her from my hands. None of Israel's false gods could save the nation from punishment.

2:12 destroy her grapevines . . . things she claims her lovers gave her. Although the Lord had abundantly blessed Israel, Israel credited its harvests to other gods.

THE LORD'S LOVE FOR UNFAITHFUL ISRAEL

14 "But then I will win her back once again.
I will lead her into the desert
and speak tenderly to her there.
15 I will return her vineyards to her
and transform the Valley of Trouble* into a gateway of hope.
She will give herself to me there,
as she did long ago when she was young,
when I freed her from her captivity in Egypt.
16 When that day comes," says the LORD,
"you will call me 'my husband'
instead of 'my master.'*
17 O Israel, I will wipe the many names of Baal from your lips,
and you will never mention them again.
18 On that day I will make a covenant
with all the wild animals and the birds of the sky
and the animals that scurry along the ground
so they will not harm you.
I will remove all weapons of war from the land,
all swords and bows,
so you can live unafraid
in peace and safety.
19 I will make you my wife forever,
showing you righteousness and justice,
unfailing love and compassion.
20 I will be faithful to you and make you mine,
and you will finally know me as the LORD.

21 "In that day, I will answer,"
says the LORD.
"I will answer the sky as it pleads for clouds.
And the sky will answer the earth with rain.
22 Then the earth will answer the thirsty cries
of the grain, the grapevines, and the olive trees.
And they in turn will answer,
'Jezreel'—'God plants!'
23 At that time I will plant a crop of Israelites
and raise them for myself.
I will show love
to those I called 'Not loved.'*
And to those I called 'Not my people,'*
I will say, 'Now you are my people.'
And they will reply, 'You are our God!'"

HOSEA'S WIFE IS REDEEMED

3 Then the LORD said to me, "Go and love your wife again, even though she* commits adultery with another lover. This will illustrate that the LORD still loves Israel, even though the people have turned to other gods and love to worship them.*"

2 So I bought her back for fifteen pieces of silver*
and five bushels of barley and a measure of wine.*
3 Then I said to her, "You must live in my house for
many days and stop your prostitution. During this
time, you will not have sexual relations with anyone,
not even with me.*"
4 This shows that Israel will go a long time without
a king or prince, and without sacrifices, sacred pillars, priests,* or even idols!
5 But afterward the people
will return and devote themselves to the LORD their
God and to David's descendant, their king.* In the last
days, they will tremble in awe of the LORD and of his
goodness.

THE LORD'S CASE AGAINST ISRAEL

4 1 Hear the word of the LORD, O people of Israel!
The LORD has brought charges against you, saying:
"There is no faithfulness, no kindness,
no knowledge of God in your land.
2 You make vows and break them;
you kill and steal and commit adultery.
There is violence everywhere—
one murder after another.
3 That is why your land is in mourning,
and everyone is wasting away.
Even the wild animals, the birds of the sky,
and the fish of the sea are disappearing.

4 "Don't point your finger at someone else
and try to pass the blame!
My complaint, you priests,
is with you.*
5 So you will stumble in broad daylight,
and your false prophets will fall with you in the night.
And I will destroy Israel, your mother.
6 My people are being destroyed
because they don't know me.
Since you priests refuse to know me,
I refuse to recognize you as my priests.
Since you have forgotten the laws of your God,
I will forget to bless your children.
7 The more priests there are,
the more they sin against me.
They have exchanged the glory of God
for the shame of idols.*

8 "When the people bring their sin offerings, the priests get fed.
So the priests are glad when the people sin!
9 'And what the priests do, the people also do.'
So now I will punish both priests and people
for their wicked deeds.

2:15 Hebrew *valley of Achor.* **2:16** Hebrew *'my baal.'* **2:23a** Hebrew *Lo-ruhamah;* see 1:6. **2:23b** Hebrew *Lo-ammi;* see 1:9. **3:1a** Or *Go and love a woman who.* **3:1b** Hebrew *love their raisin cakes.* **3:2a** Hebrew *15 [shekels] of silver,* about 6 ounces or 171 grams in weight. **3:2b** As in Greek version, which reads *a homer of barley and a wineskin full of wine;* Hebrew reads *a homer* [5 bushels or 220 liters] *of barley and a lethek* [2.5 bushels or 110 liters] *of barley.* **3:3** Or *and I will live with you.* **3:4** Hebrew *ephod,* the vest worn by the priest. **3:5** Hebrew *to David their king.* **4:4** Hebrew *Your people are like those with a complaint against the priests.* **4:7** As in Syriac version and an ancient Hebrew tradition; Masoretic Text reads *I will turn their glory into shame.*

2:16-17 my husband . . . my master. Ironically, the Hebrew word for Baal is "master." The Lord predicted that Israel would disassociate from its current "master" as a sign of repentance.

2:20 I will be faithful to you. The context of Hosea's story illustrates the unfaithfulness of a nation portrayed as a wayward wife. In contrast, God was consistently characterized as stubbornly faithful.

3:3 You must live in my house. Hosea risked heartbreak by inviting an adulterous woman into his household.

4:2 violence everywhere. Israel broke every law in the Ten Commandments with reckless enthusiasm (Ex. 20:13-16).

4:4-9 Don't point your finger at someone else. The priests, responsible for the nation's religious life, could not blame the people for Israel's dilemma. They too were sinners.

4:8 priests are glad when the people sin. The priests cheerfully led the people in idol worship and received part of their offerings as a bonus.

10 They will eat and still be hungry.
They will play the prostitute and gain nothing
from it,
for they have deserted the LORD
11 to worship other gods.

"Wine has robbed my people
of their understanding.
12 They ask a piece of wood for advice!
They think a stick can tell them the future!
Longing after idols
has made them foolish.
They have played the prostitute,
serving other gods and deserting their God.
13 They offer sacrifices to idols on the mountaintops.
They go up into the hills to burn incense
in the pleasant shade of oaks, poplars, and
terebinth trees.

"That is why your daughters turn to prostitution,
and your daughters-in-law commit adultery.
14 But why should I punish them
for their prostitution and adultery?
For your men are doing the same thing,
sinning with whores and shrine prostitutes.
O foolish people! You refuse to understand,
so you will be destroyed.

15 "Though you, Israel, are a prostitute,
may Judah not be guilty of such things.
Do not join the false worship at Gilgal or Beth-aven,*
and do not take oaths there in the LORD's name.
16 Israel is stubborn,
like a stubborn heifer.
So should the LORD feed her
like a lamb in a lush pasture?
17 Leave Israel* alone,
because she is married to idolatry.
18 When the rulers of Israel finish their drinking,
off they go to find some prostitutes.
They love shame more than honor.*
19 So a mighty wind will sweep them away.
Their sacrifices to idols will bring them shame.

THE FAILURE OF ISRAEL'S LEADERS

5 1 "Hear this, you priests.
Pay attention, you leaders of Israel.
Listen, you members of the royal family.
Judgment has been handed down against you.
For you have led the people into a snare
by worshiping the idols at Mizpah and Tabor.
2 You have dug a deep pit to trap them at Acacia
Grove.*
But I will settle with you for what you have done.
3 I know what you are like, O Ephraim.
You cannot hide yourself from me, O Israel.
You have left me as a prostitute leaves her husband;
you are utterly defiled.
4 Your deeds won't let you return to your God.
You are a prostitute through and through,
and you do not know the LORD.

5 "The arrogance of Israel testifies against her;
Israel and Ephraim will stumble under their
load of guilt.
Judah, too, will fall with them.
6 When they come with their flocks and herds
to offer sacrifices to the LORD,
they will not find him,
because he has withdrawn from them.
7 They have betrayed the honor of the LORD,
bearing children that are not his.
Now their false religion will devour them
along with their wealth.*

8 "Sound the alarm in Gibeah!
Blow the trumpet in Ramah!
Raise the battle cry in Beth-aven*!
Lead on into battle, O warriors of Benjamin!
9 One thing is certain, Israel*:
On your day of punishment,
you will become a heap of rubble.

10 "The leaders of Judah have become like thieves.*
So I will pour my anger on them like a waterfall.
11 The people of Israel will be crushed and broken by
my judgment
because they are determined to worship idols.*
12 I will destroy Israel as a moth consumes wool.
I will make Judah as weak as rotten wood.

13 "When Israel and Judah saw how sick they were,
Israel turned to Assyria—
to the great king there—
but he could neither help nor cure them.
14 I will be like a lion to Israel,
like a strong young lion to Judah.
I will tear them to pieces!
I will carry them off,
and no one will be left to rescue them.
15 Then I will return to my place
until they admit their guilt and turn to me.
For as soon as trouble comes,
they will earnestly search for me."

A CALL TO REPENTANCE

6 1 "Come, let us return to the LORD.
He has torn us to pieces;
now he will heal us.
He has injured us;
now he will bandage our wounds.
2 In just a short time he will restore us,

4:15 *Beth-aven* means "house of wickedness"; it is being used as another name for Bethel, which means "house of God." 4:17 Hebrew *Ephraim*, referring to the northern kingdom of Israel. 4:18 As in Greek version; the meaning of the Hebrew is uncertain. 5:2 Hebrew *at Shittim*. The meaning of the Hebrew for this sentence is uncertain. 5:7 The meaning of the Hebrew is uncertain. 5:8 *Beth-aven* means "house of wickedness"; it is being used as another name for Bethel, which means "house of God." 5:9 Hebrew *Ephraim*, referring to the northern kingdom of Israel; also in 5:11, 12, 13, 14. 5:10 Hebrew *like those who move a boundary marker*. 5:11 Or *determined to follow human commands*. The meaning of the Hebrew is uncertain.

4:19 wind. Although Israel felt invincible at the time, God would soon ordain Assyria to destroy Israel's sense of security (9:3).
5:5 Judah. The southern kingdom fell prey to spiritual adultery as well, worshiping Canaanite gods.
5:7 bearing children that are not his. Concerns the legitimacy of Hosea fathering Gomer's children (4:13-15).
5:10 become like thieves. Judah took over some of Israel's territory with complete disregard for God's law (Deut. 19:14).
5:13 Israel turned to Assyria. Instead of turning to God for help, Israel sought aid from a pagan nation.
6:2 a short time. Perhaps an example of wishful thinking—Israel predicted that its punishment would not last long.

so that we may live in his presence.
3 Oh, that we might know the LORD!
Let us press on to know him.
He will respond to us as surely as the arrival of dawn
or the coming of rains in early spring."

4 "O Israel* and Judah,
what should I do with you?" asks the LORD.
"For your love vanishes like the morning mist
and disappears like dew in the sunlight.
5 I sent my prophets to cut you to pieces—
to slaughter you with my words,
with judgments as inescapable as light.
6 I want you to show love,*
not offer sacrifices.
I want you to know me*
more than I want burnt offerings.
7 But like Adam,* you broke my covenant
and betrayed my trust.

8 "Gilead is a city of sinners,
tracked with footprints of blood.
9 Priests form bands of robbers,
waiting in ambush for their victims.
They murder travelers along the road to Shechem
and practice every kind of sin.
10 Yes, I have seen something horrible in Ephraim
and Israel:
My people are defiled by prostituting
themselves with other gods!

11 "O Judah, a harvest of punishment is also waiting
for you,
though I wanted to restore the fortunes of my
people.

ISRAEL'S LOVE FOR WICKEDNESS

7 1 "I want to heal Israel, but its* sins are too great.
Samaria is filled with liars.
Thieves are on the inside
and bandits on the outside!
2 Its people don't realize
that I am watching them.
Their sinful deeds are all around them,
and I see them all.

3 "The people entertain the king with their
wickedness,
and the princes laugh at their lies.
4 They are all adulterers,
always aflame with lust.
They are like an oven that is kept hot
while the baker is kneading the dough.
5 On royal holidays, the princes get drunk with wine,
carousing with those who mock them.
6 Their hearts are like an oven
blazing with intrigue.
Their plot smolders* through the night,
and in the morning it breaks out like a raging
fire.
7 Burning like an oven,
they consume their leaders.
They kill their kings one after another,
and no one cries to me for help.

8 "The people of Israel mingle with godless
foreigners,
making themselves as worthless as a half-baked
cake!
9 Worshiping foreign gods has sapped their
strength,
but they don't even know it.
Their hair is gray,
but they don't realize they're old and weak.
10 Their arrogance testifies against them,
yet they don't return to the LORD their God
or even try to find him.

11 "The people of Israel have become like silly, witless
doves,
first calling to Egypt, then flying to Assyria for
help.
12 But as they fly about,
I will throw my net over them
and bring them down like a bird from the sky.
I will punish them for all the evil they do.*

13 "What sorrow awaits those who have deserted
me!
Let them die, for they have rebelled against me.
I wanted to redeem them,
but they have told lies about me.
14 They do not cry out to me with sincere hearts.
Instead, they sit on their couches and wail.
They cut themselves,* begging foreign gods for
grain and new wine,
and they turn away from me.
15 I trained them and made them strong,
yet now they plot evil against me.
16 They look everywhere except to the Most High.
They are as useless as a crooked bow.
Their leaders will be killed by their enemies
because of their insolence toward me.
Then the people of Egypt
will laugh at them.

ISRAEL HARVESTS THE WHIRLWIND

8 1 "Sound the alarm!
The enemy descends like an eagle on the people
of the LORD,

6:4 Hebrew *Ephraim*, referring to the northern kingdom of Israel. 6:6a Greek version translates this Hebrew term as *to show mercy*. Compare Matt 9:13; 12:7. 6:6b Hebrew *to know God*. 6:7 Or *But at Adam*. 7:1 Hebrew *Ephraim's*, referring to the northern kingdom of Israel; similarly in 7:8, 11. 7:6 Hebrew *Their baker sleeps*. 7:12 Hebrew *I will punish them because of what was reported against them in the assembly*. 7:14 As in Greek version; Hebrew reads *They gather together*.

6:6 to know me. God was looking for more than lip service. Israel must demonstrate its love for Him by adhering to covenant promises of obedience (Josh. 24:16-27).

7:2 I see them all. Like Gomer, Israel thought it sinned in secret. However, God saw and remembered every misdeed.

7:5 On royal holidays. Most likely an innocent celebration that had turned into a disgrace.

7:8 half-baked cakes. Using baker's imagery, Hosea showed that Israel's foolish political intentions were half-baked at best.

7:9 sapped their strength. Israel bought protection with lavish tributes to foreign kings. (See Tiglath-Pileser as an example in 2 Kings 15:19-20,29.)

7:11 silly, witless doves. Hosea showed the ignorance involved in Israel's fickle political policies. Israel relied on whatever country seemed strong at the moment.

7:15 I trained them and made them strong. Israel had taken the credit for its military endeavors.

7:16 crooked bow. A faulty bow would consistently miss its target just as Israel consistently failed to understand God's purposes.

8:1 eagle. The eagle represented the eagerness of Israel's enemy, Assyria.

for they have broken my covenant
and revolted against my law.
2 Now Israel pleads with me,
'Help us, for you are our God!'
3 But it is too late.
The people of Israel have rejected what is good,
and now their enemies will chase after them.
4 The people have appointed kings without my consent,
and princes without my approval.
By making idols for themselves from their silver and gold,
they have brought about their own destruction.

5 "O Samaria, I reject this calf—
this idol you have made.
My fury burns against you.
How long will you be incapable of innocence?
6 This calf you worship, O Israel,
was crafted by your own hands!
It is not God!
Therefore, it must be smashed to bits.

7 "They have planted the wind
and will harvest the whirlwind.
The stalks of grain wither
and produce nothing to eat.
And even if there is any grain,
foreigners will eat it.
8 The people of Israel have been swallowed up;
they lie among the nations like an old discarded pot.
9 Like a wild donkey looking for a mate,
they have gone up to Assyria.
The people of Israel* have sold themselves—
sold themselves to many lovers.
10 But though they have sold themselves to many allies,
I will now gather them together for judgment.
Then they will writhe
under the burden of the great king.

11 "Israel has built many altars to take away sin,
but these very altars became places for sinning!
12 Even though I gave them all my laws,
they act as if those laws don't apply to them.
13 The people love to offer sacrifices to me,
feasting on the meat,
but I do not accept their sacrifices.
I will hold my people accountable for their sins,
and I will punish them.
They will return to Egypt.
14 Israel has forgotten its Maker and built great palaces,
and Judah has fortified its cities.
Therefore, I will send down fire on their cities
and will burn up their fortresses."

HOSEA ANNOUNCES ISRAEL'S PUNISHMENT

9 1 O people of Israel,
do not rejoice as other nations do.
For you have been unfaithful to your God,
hiring yourselves out like prostitutes,
worshiping other gods on every threshing floor.
2 So now your harvests will be too small to feed you.
There will be no grapes for making new wine.
3 You may no longer stay here in the LORD's land.
Instead, you will return to Egypt,
and in Assyria you will eat food
that is ceremonially unclean.
4 There you will make no offerings of wine to the LORD.
None of your sacrifices there will please him.
They will be unclean, like food touched by a person in mourning.
All who present such sacrifices will be defiled.
They may eat this food themselves,
but they may not offer it to the LORD.
5 What then will you do on festival days?
How will you observe the LORD's festivals?
6 Even if you escape destruction from Assyria,
Egypt will conquer you, and Memphis* will bury you.
Nettles will take over your treasures of silver;
thistles will invade your ruined homes.

7 The time of Israel's punishment has come;
the day of payment is here.
Soon Israel will know this all too well.
Because of your great sin and hostility,
you say, "The prophets are crazy
and the inspired men are fools!"
8 The prophet is a watchman over Israel* for my God,
yet traps are laid for him wherever he goes.
He faces hostility even in the house of God.
9 The things my people do are as depraved
as what they did in Gibeah long ago.
God will not forget.
He will surely punish them for their sins.

10 The LORD says, "O Israel, when I first found you,
it was like finding fresh grapes in the desert.
When I saw your ancestors,
it was like seeing the first ripe figs of the season.
But then they deserted me for Baal-peor,
giving themselves to that shameful idol.
Soon they became vile,
as vile as the god they worshiped.

8:9 Hebrew *Ephraim,* referring to the northern kingdom of Israel; also in 8:11. 9:6 Memphis was the capital of northern Egypt. 9:8 Hebrew *Ephraim,* referring to the northern kingdom of Israel; also in 9:11, 13, 16.

8:5 calf—this idol. Jeroboam had fashioned a golden image for the people of Israel to worship (1 Kings 12:26-30).
8:8 discarded pottery. Israel's people were not the successful nation God once envisioned and commanded them to be (Ex. 19:5). They had become as useless as broken pottery.
8:13 Egypt. Egypt could only mean one thing: captivity. Assyria would be the actual site of Israel's torture (11:5).
9:3 may no longer stay here in the LORD's land. Like tenants kicked out by the landlord, Israel would be removed from the promised land. The land promised to the Israelites belonged to the Lord (Josh. 22:19).
9:5 festival days. The point being, Israel will be too far removed from Jerusalem to have any opportunity to celebrate its festivals (i.e., Passover, Unleavened Bread, Weeks, and Booths). So, technically, they would be unable to observe the law (which they were rampantly breaking away). Eventually, in A.D. 70, this change of circumstance became permanent.
9:9 in Gibeah long ago. Compared to a brutal rape and murder in its past, Israel's present sins were worse (Judg. 19-20).
9:10 grapes in the desert. Sweet grapes amid desolation would be a rare find indeed! In the same way, God had once prized Israel for her purity among the nations.

[11] The glory of Israel will fly away like a bird,
for your children will not be born
or grow in the womb
or even be conceived.
[12] Even if you do have children who grow up,
I will take them from you.
It will be a terrible day when I turn away
and leave you alone.
[13] I have watched Israel become as beautiful as Tyre.
But now Israel will bring out her children for slaughter."

[14] O LORD, what should I request for your people?
I will ask for wombs that don't give birth
and breasts that give no milk.

[15] The LORD says, "All their wickedness began at Gilgal;
there I began to hate them.
I will drive them from my land
because of their evil actions.
I will love them no more
because all their leaders are rebels.
[16] The people of Israel are struck down.
Their roots are dried up,
and they will bear no more fruit.
And if they give birth,
I will slaughter their beloved children."

[17] My God will reject the people of Israel
because they will not listen or obey.
They will be wanderers,
homeless among the nations.

THE LORD'S JUDGMENT AGAINST ISRAEL

10 [1] How prosperous Israel is—
a luxuriant vine loaded with fruit.
But the richer the people get,
the more pagan altars they build.
The more bountiful their harvests,
the more beautiful their sacred pillars.
[2] The hearts of the people are fickle;
they are guilty and must be punished.
The LORD will break down their altars
and smash their sacred pillars.
[3] Then they will say, "We have no king
because we didn't fear the LORD.
But even if we had a king,
what could he do for us anyway?"
[4] They spout empty words
and make covenants they don't intend to keep.
So injustice springs up among them
like poisonous weeds in a farmer's field.

[5] The people of Samaria tremble in fear
for their calf idol at Beth-aven,*
and they mourn for it.
Though its priests rejoice over it,
its glory will be stripped away.*
[6] This idol will be carted away to Assyria,
a gift to the great king there.
Ephraim will be ridiculed and Israel will be shamed,
because its people have trusted in this idol.
[7] Samaria and its king will be cut off;
they will float away like driftwood on an ocean wave.
[8] And the pagan shrines of Aven,* the place of Israel's sin, will crumble.
Thorns and thistles will grow up around their altars.
They will beg the mountains, "Bury us!"
and plead with the hills, "Fall on us!"

[9] The LORD says, "O Israel, ever since Gibeah,
there has been only sin and more sin!
You have made no progress whatsoever.
Was it not right that the wicked men of Gibeah
were attacked?
[10] Now whenever it fits my plan,
I will attack you, too.
I will call out the armies of the nations
to punish you for your multiplied sins.

[11] "Israel* is like a trained heifer treading out the grain—
an easy job she loves.
But I will put a heavy yoke on her tender neck.
I will force Judah to pull the plow
and Israel* to break up the hard ground.
[12] I said, 'Plant the good seeds of righteousness,
and you will harvest a crop of love.
Plow up the hard ground of your hearts,
for now is the time to seek the LORD,
that he may come
and shower righteousness upon you.'

[13] "But you have cultivated wickedness
and harvested a thriving crop of sins.
You have eaten the fruit of lies—
trusting in your military might,
believing that great armies
could make your nation safe.
[14] Now the terrors of war
will rise among your people.
All your fortifications will fall,
just as when Shalman destroyed Beth-arbel.
Even mothers and children
were dashed to death there.
[15] You will share that fate, Bethel,
because of your great wickedness.
When the day of judgment dawns,
the king of Israel will be completely destroyed.

THE LORD'S LOVE FOR ISRAEL

11 [1] "When Israel was a child, I loved him,
and I called my son out of Egypt.
[2] But the more I called to him,
the farther he moved from me,*

10:5a *Beth-aven* means "house of wickedness"; it is being used as another name for Bethel, which means "house of God." **10:5b** Or *will be taken away into exile.* **10:8** *Aven* is a reference to Beth-aven; see 10:5a and the note there. **10:11a** Hebrew *Ephraim,* referring to the northern kingdom of Israel. **10:11b** Hebrew *Jacob.* The names "Jacob" and "Israel" are often interchanged throughout the Old Testament, referring sometimes to the individual patriarch and sometimes to the nation. **11:2** As in Greek version; Hebrew reads *the more they called to him, the farther he moved from them.*

10:1 a luxuriant vine. Before its idolatry, Israel was full of promise and hope like a vine full of fruit.

10:4 make covenants. Israel knew when it was in political trouble. However, its kings turned to the wrong power for help.

10:9 Gibeah. Like Gibeah (9:9), Israel would endure war and hardship as a consequence of sin (Judg. 19:12-30).

11:1 called my son. God went back to Israel's past when He and Israel were like Father and son (Ex. 4:22-23).

offering sacrifices to the images of Baal
and burning incense to idols.
3 I myself taught Israel* how to walk,
leading him along by the hand.
But he doesn't know or even care
that it was I who took care of him.
4 I led Israel along
with my ropes of kindness and love.
I lifted the yoke from his neck,
and I myself stooped to feed him.

5 "But since my people refuse to return to me,
they will return to Egypt
and will be forced to serve Assyria.
6 War will swirl through their cities;
their enemies will crash through their gates.
They will destroy them,
trapping them in their own evil plans.
7 For my people are determined to desert me.
They call me the Most High,
but they don't truly honor me.

8 "Oh, how can I give you up, Israel?
How can I let you go?
How can I destroy you like Admah
or demolish you like Zeboiim?
My heart is torn within me,
and my compassion overflows.
9 No, I will not unleash my fierce anger.
I will not completely destroy Israel,
for I am God and not a mere mortal.
I am the Holy One living among you,
and I will not come to destroy.
10 For someday the people will follow me.
I, the LORD, will roar like a lion.
And when I roar,
my people will return trembling from the west.
11 Like a flock of birds, they will come from Egypt.
Trembling like doves, they will return from
Assyria.
And I will bring them home again,"
says the LORD.

CHARGES AGAINST ISRAEL AND JUDAH

12*Israel surrounds me with lies and deceit,
but Judah still obeys God
and is faithful to the Holy One.*

12 1*The people of Israel* feed on the wind;
they chase after the east wind all day long.
They pile up lies and violence;
they are making an alliance with Assyria
while sending olive oil to buy support from
Egypt.
2 Now the LORD is bringing charges against Judah.
He is about to punish Jacob* for all his deceitful
ways,
and pay him back for all he has done.
3 Even in the womb,
Jacob struggled with his brother;
when he became a man,
he even fought with God.
4 Yes, he wrestled with the angel and won.
He wept and pleaded for a blessing from him.
There at Bethel he met God face to face,
and God spoke to him*—
5 the LORD God of Heaven's Armies,
the LORD is his name!
6 So now, come back to your God.
Act with love and justice,
and always depend on him.

7 But no, the people are like crafty merchants
selling from dishonest scales—
they love to cheat.
8 Israel boasts, "I am rich!
I've made a fortune all by myself!
No one has caught me cheating!
My record is spotless!"

9 "But I am the LORD your God,
who rescued you from slavery in Egypt.
And I will make you live in tents again,
as you do each year at the Festival of Shelters.*
10 I sent my prophets to warn you
with many visions and parables."

11 But the people of Gilead are worthless
because of their idol worship.
And in Gilgal, too, they sacrifice bulls;
their altars are lined up like the heaps of stone
along the edges of a plowed field.
12 Jacob fled to the land of Aram,
and there he* earned a wife by tending sheep.
13 Then by a prophet
the LORD brought Jacob's descendants* out of
Egypt;
and by that prophet
they were protected.
14 But the people of Israel
have bitterly provoked the LORD,
so their Lord will now sentence them to death
in payment for their sins.

THE LORD'S ANGER AGAINST ISRAEL

13 1 When the tribe of Ephraim spoke,
the people shook with fear,
for that tribe was important in Israel.

11:3 Hebrew *Ephraim,* referring to the northern kingdom of Israel; also in 11:8, 9, 12. **11:12a** Verse 11:12 is numbered 12:1 in Hebrew text. **11:12b** Or *and Judah is unruly against God, the faithful Holy One.* The meaning of the Hebrew is uncertain. **12:1a** Verses 12:1-14 are numbered 12:2-15 in Hebrew text. **12:1b** Hebrew *Ephraim,* referring to the northern kingdom of Israel; also in 12:8, 14. **12:2** *Jacob* sounds like the Hebrew word for "deceiver." **12:4** As in Greek and Syriac versions; Hebrew reads *to us.* **12:9** Hebrew *as in the days of your appointed feast.* **12:12** Hebrew *Israel.* See note on 10:11b. **12:13** Hebrew *brought Israel.* See note on 10:11b.

11:4 ropes of kindness. A compassionate farmer repositioned the yoke on a work animal so that it can enjoy its food.
11:5 they will return to Egypt. Returning to Egypt was a major step backward: from freedom to slavery, blessing to punishment, success to inferiority.
11:8 God compared Israel's fate to that of cities overthrown by the destruction of Sodom (Deut. 29:23).
11:9 for I am God and not a mere mortal. A father may punish a child and then regret it. However, God was grieved by the punishment before it began.
12:1 while sending olive oil. Israel gave olive oil in hopes of endearing themselves to the Egyptians.
12:6 come back. Jacob turned his life around after encountering God (Gen. 32:24-30), and Israel could choose the same.
12:8 Israel. Literally, "Ephraim." Hosea interchanged "Ephraim" (the most influential northern tribe) and "Israel" for the same northern kingdom.
12:12 Jacob fled. God reminded Israel of its humble beginnings through the story of Jacob. Jacob tended sheep and worked faithfully for his prosperity (Gen. 29:20-28).

But the people of Ephraim sinned by worshiping
Baal
and thus sealed their destruction.
2 Now they continue to sin by making silver
idols,
images shaped skillfully with human hands.
"Sacrifice to these," they cry,
"and kiss the calf idols!"
3 Therefore, they will disappear like the morning
mist,
like dew in the morning sun,
like chaff blown by the wind,
like smoke from a chimney.

4 "I have been the LORD your God
ever since I brought you out of Egypt.
You must acknowledge no God but me,
for there is no other savior.
5 I took care of you in the wilderness,
in that dry and thirsty land.
6 But when you had eaten and were satisfied,
you became proud and forgot me.
7 So now I will attack you like a lion,
like a leopard that lurks along the road.
8 Like a bear whose cubs have been taken away,
I will tear out your heart.
I will devour you like a hungry lioness
and mangle you like a wild animal.

9 "You are about to be destroyed, O Israel—
yes, by me, your only helper.
10 Now where is* your king?
Let him save you!
Where are all the leaders of the land,
the king and the officials you demanded
of me?
11 In my anger I gave you kings,
and in my fury I took them away.

12 "Ephraim's guilt has been collected,
and his sin has been stored up for
punishment.
13 Pain has come to the people
like the pain of childbirth,
but they are like a child
who resists being born.
The moment of birth has arrived,
but they stay in the womb!

14 "Should I ransom them from the grave*?
Should I redeem them from death?
O death, bring on your terrors!
O grave, bring on your plagues!*
For I will not take pity on them.

15 Ephraim was the most fruitful of all his brothers,
but the east wind—a blast from the LORD—
will arise in the desert.
All their flowing springs will run dry,
and all their wells will disappear.
Every precious thing they own
will be plundered and carried away.
16*The people of Samaria
must bear the consequences of their guilt
because they rebelled against their God.
They will be killed by an invading army,
their little ones dashed to death against the
ground,
their pregnant women ripped open by
swords."

HEALING FOR THE REPENTANT

14 1*Return, O Israel, to the LORD your God,
for your sins have brought you down.
2 Bring your confessions, and return to the LORD.
Say to him,
"Forgive all our sins and graciously receive us,
so that we may offer you our praises.*
3 Assyria cannot save us,
nor can our warhorses.
Never again will we say to the idols we have
made,
'You are our gods.'
No, in you alone
do the orphans find mercy."

4 The LORD says,
"Then I will heal you of your faithlessness;
my love will know no bounds,
for my anger will be gone forever.
5 I will be to Israel
like a refreshing dew from heaven.
Israel will blossom like the lily;
it will send roots deep into the soil
like the cedars in Lebanon.
6 Its branches will spread out like beautiful olive
trees,
as fragrant as the cedars of Lebanon.
7 My people will again live under my shade.
They will flourish like grain and blossom like
grapevines.
They will be as fragrant as the wines of
Lebanon.

8 "O Israel,* stay away from idols!
I am the one who answers your prayers and
cares for you.
I am like a tree that is always green;
all your fruit comes from me."

13:10 As in Greek and Syriac versions and Latin Vulgate; Hebrew reads *I will be.* **13:14a** Hebrew *Sheol;* also in 13:14b. **13:14b** Greek version reads *O death, where is your punishment? / O grave* [Hades], *where is your sting?* Compare 1 Cor 15:55. **13:16** Verse 16 is numbered 14:1 in Hebrew text. **14:1** Verses 14:1-9 are numbered 14:2-10 in Hebrew text. **14:2** As in Greek and Syriac versions, which read *may repay the fruit of our lips;* Hebrew reads *may repay the bulls of our lips.* **14:8** Hebrew *Ephraim,* referring to the northern kingdom of Israel.

13:3 will disappear. Although Ephraim thrived for a brief moment, its self-destructive practices would bring the nation down forever.

13:7-8 wild animal. From shepherd to predator, the imagery shifts to express God's frustration with His people. If Israel did not acknowledge His tender mercy, His justice would have to get their attention.

13:10 Now where is your king? Hosea wrote at a time when kings were assassinated as quickly as they were inaugurated. This also implies that the nation needed to seek their help from God, not human rulers.

13:15 east wind. According to God's plan, Assyria blew onto the scene at the right time, destroyed Israel, and took her people captive.

13:16 Samaria. The description of the fall of the capital city of the northern kingdom is similar to language used by other prophets (Isa. 13:6; Amos 1:13; Nahum 3:10). This prediction is fulfilled in 2 Kings 17:5.

14:1 Return, O Israel. God's command has a greater context at the conclusion of His message than earlier references (10:12; 12:6). Lip service will not suffice. Genuine repentance is the only acceptable means for returning to God.

14:8 your fruit comes from me. God revealed the secret of success to a farming community whose existence was tied to the fruit of a harvest. God alone blesses the bounty.

9 Let those who are wise understand these things.
Let those with discernment listen carefully.
The paths of the LORD are true and right,
and righteous people live by walking in them.
But in those paths sinners stumble and fall.

14:9 paths of the LORD are true and right. Hosea concludes with a cause and effect lesson. Rebellion leads to stumbling: righteousness provides a clear path to God.

INTRODUCTION TO
JOEL

PERSONAL READING PLAN

☐Joel 1:1-20 ☐Joel 2:18-32
☐Joel 2:1-17 ☐Joel 3:1-21

AUTHOR

The author is identified as the prophet Joel, son of Pethuel (1:1). While there are 12 other Old Testament characters with this name, none of them can be identified with this prophet.

DATE

The date is uncertain. Joel could have been written as early as the ninth and as late as the fourth century B.C. Since Joel uses quotes or paraphrases from several other prophets and does not refer to either the Babylonian or Assyrian Empire, a later date seems probable—sometime during the Persian period (539–331 B.C.).

THEME

A plague of locusts is a sign of the coming Day of the Lord.

HISTORICAL BACKGROUND

The occasion for Joel's prophetic ministry was a plague of locusts that was consuming Judah. The fact that no historical record of such a plague has endured does not mean this event was simply an allegorical device of the writer. Rather, this underscores the truth that even the worst natural or national disasters fade from memory when attention is turned to something that endures forever— an eternal God and His future kingdom (see 2:28–3:21).

CHARACTERISTICS

The literary genius of Joel shines throughout the book's structure; each section flows into the next. Hence, it helps to read the whole book in one sitting before studying its parts. The focus of the book is twofold:

(1) The ever-present, practical problem of what to do about the locust plague (1:1–2:27); and

(2) The future Day of the Lord, of which the current plague is a sign (2:28–3:21).

In combining the two—event plus interpretation—Joel is performing the classic function of an Old Testament prophet, that of conveying God's revelation. Likewise, the borrowing of phrases from other prophets to speak a "new word" from the Lord in a new setting shows that Joel was probably an educated person. Joel had perhaps heard the prophecies of Micah, Jeremiah, and Isaiah. In 2:28–3:21, Joel expands the apocalyptic dimensions of these prophets. In Acts 2, the Apostle Peter expounds the meaning of Joel's prophecy. Specifically, Joel's prediction about the outpouring of the Holy Spirit was fulfilled on the Day of Pentecost.

1 The LORD gave this message to Joel son of Pethuel.

MOURNING OVER THE LOCUST PLAGUE

2 Hear this, you leaders of the people.
Listen, all who live in the land.
In all your history,
has anything like this happened before?
3 Tell your children about it in the years to come,
and let your children tell their children.
Pass the story down from generation to generation.
4 After the cutting locusts finished eating the crops,
the swarming locusts took what was left!
After them came the hopping locusts,
and then the stripping locusts,* too!

5 Wake up, you drunkards, and weep!
Wail, all you wine-drinkers!
All the grapes are ruined,
and all your sweet wine is gone.
6 A vast army of locusts* has invaded my land,
a terrible army too numerous to count.
Its teeth are like lions' teeth,
its fangs like those of a lioness.
7 It has destroyed my grapevines
and ruined my fig trees,
stripping their bark and destroying it,
leaving the branches white and bare.
8 Weep like a bride dressed in black,
mourning the death of her husband.
9 For there is no grain or wine
to offer at the Temple of the LORD.
So the priests are in mourning.
The ministers of the LORD are weeping.
10 The fields are ruined,
the land is stripped bare.
The grain is destroyed,
the grapes have shriveled,
and the olive oil is gone.

11 Despair, all you farmers!
Wail, all you vine growers!
Weep, because the wheat and barley—
all the crops of the field—are ruined.
12 The grapevines have dried up,
and the fig trees have withered.
The pomegranate trees, palm trees, and apple trees—
all the fruit trees—have dried up.
And the people's joy has dried up with them.

13 Dress yourselves in burlap and weep, you priests!
Wail, you who serve before the altar!
Come, spend the night in burlap,
you ministers of my God.
For there is no grain or wine
to offer at the Temple of your God.
14 Announce a time of fasting;
call the people together for a solemn meeting.
Bring the leaders
and all the people of the land
into the Temple of the LORD your God,
and cry out to him there.
15 The day of the LORD is near,
the day when destruction comes from the Almighty.
How terrible that day will be!

16 Our food disappears before our very eyes.
No joyful celebrations are held in the house of our God.
17 The seeds die in the parched ground,
and the grain crops fail.
The barns stand empty,
and granaries are abandoned.
18 How the animals moan with hunger!
The herds of cattle wander about confused,
because they have no pasture.
The flocks of sheep and goats bleat in misery.

19 LORD, help us!
The fire has consumed the wilderness pastures,
and flames have burned up all the trees.
20 Even the wild animals cry out to you
because the streams have dried up,
and fire has consumed the wilderness pastures.

LOCUSTS INVADE LIKE AN ARMY

2 1 Sound the trumpet in Jerusalem*!
Raise the alarm on my holy mountain!
Let everyone tremble in fear
because the day of the LORD is upon us.
2 It is a day of darkness and gloom,
a day of thick clouds and deep blackness.
Suddenly, like dawn spreading across the mountains,
a great and mighty army appears.
Nothing like it has been seen before
or will ever be seen again.

3 Fire burns in front of them,
and flames follow after them.
Ahead of them the land lies
as beautiful as the Garden of Eden.
Behind them is nothing but desolation;
not one thing escapes.
4 They look like horses;
they charge forward like warhorses.*
5 Look at them as they leap along the mountaintops.
Listen to the noise they make—like the rumbling of chariots,

1:4 The precise identification of the four kinds of locusts mentioned here is uncertain. **1:6** Hebrew *A nation.* **2:1** Hebrew *Zion;* also in 2:15, 23. **2:4** Or *like charioteers.*

1:1 Joel. Joel's prophetic message focuses on God's supreme power and might. As if to emphasize his point, Joel's name means, "The Lord is God."
1:6 invaded. Locusts had invaded the land. Joel uses locusts as a metaphor for God's judgment of their sin. In great numbers locusts can create large-scale devastation (see Ex 10:13-15).
1:14 cry out to him. Joel encouraged the people to cry out to the Lord in repentance, humility, and desperation (see also Judg. 20:26).
1:15 day of the LORD is near. The Day of the Lord signifies both a present event and foreshadowing of a final future event.
2:2 darkness and gloom. Darkness symbolizes a day of destruction, wrath, and judgment on sin. During the time Jesus hung on the cross, darkness descended on the earth, even though it was the middle of the day (see Matt. 27:44-46).
2:10 sun and moon . . . stars. Joel extended God's judgment to the cosmos. Even the sun, moon, and stars were dimmed by the massive destruction (see Isa. 13:10).

like the roar of fire sweeping across a field of
stubble,
or like a mighty army moving into battle.

6 Fear grips all the people;
every face grows pale with terror.
7 The attackers march like warriors
and scale city walls like soldiers.
Straight forward they march,
never breaking rank.
8 They never jostle each other;
each moves in exactly the right position.
They break through defenses
without missing a step.
9 They swarm over the city
and run along its walls.
They enter all the houses,
climbing like thieves through the windows.
10 The earth quakes as they advance,
and the heavens tremble.
The sun and moon grow dark,
and the stars no longer shine.

11 The LORD is at the head of the column.
He leads them with a shout.
This is his mighty army,
and they follow his orders.
The day of the LORD is an awesome, terrible thing.
Who can possibly survive?

A CALL TO REPENTANCE

12 That is why the LORD says,
"Turn to me now, while there is time.
Give me your hearts.
Come with fasting, weeping, and mourning.
13 Don't tear your clothing in your grief,
but tear your hearts instead."
Return to the LORD your God,
for he is merciful and compassionate,
slow to get angry and filled with unfailing love.
He is eager to relent and not punish.
14 Who knows? Perhaps he will give you a reprieve,
sending you a blessing instead of this curse.
Perhaps you will be able to offer grain and wine
to the LORD your God as before.

15 Blow the ram's horn in Jerusalem!
Announce a time of fasting;
call the people together
for a solemn meeting.
16 Gather all the people—
the elders, the children, and even the babies.
Call the bridegroom from his quarters
and the bride from her private room.
17 Let the priests, who minister in the LORD's
presence,
stand and weep between the entry room to the
Temple and the altar.
Let them pray, "Spare your people, LORD!
Don't let your special possession become an
object of mockery.
Don't let them become a joke for unbelieving
foreigners who say,
'Has the God of Israel left them?'"

THE LORD'S PROMISE OF RESTORATION

18 Then the LORD will pity his people
and jealously guard the honor of his land.
19 The LORD will reply,
"Look! I am sending you grain and new wine and
olive oil,
enough to satisfy your needs.
You will no longer be an object of mockery
among the surrounding nations.
20 I will drive away these armies from the north.
I will send them into the parched wastelands.
Those in the front will be driven into the Dead Sea,
and those at the rear into the Mediterranean.*
The stench of their rotting bodies will rise over the
land."

Surely the LORD has done great things!
21 Don't be afraid, O land.
Be glad now and rejoice,
for the LORD has done great things.
22 Don't be afraid, you animals of the field,
for the wilderness pastures will soon be green.
The trees will again be filled with fruit;
fig trees and grapevines will be loaded down
once more.
23 Rejoice, you people of Jerusalem!
Rejoice in the LORD your God!
For the rain he sends demonstrates his
faithfulness.
Once more the autumn rains will come,
as well as the rains of spring.
24 The threshing floors will again be piled high with
grain,
and the presses will overflow with new wine
and olive oil.

25 The LORD says, "I will give you back what you lost
to the swarming locusts, the hopping locusts,
the stripping locusts, and the cutting locusts.*
It was I who sent this great destroying army
against you.
26 Once again you will have all the food you want,
and you will praise the LORD your God,
who does these miracles for you.
Never again will my people be disgraced.
27 Then you will know that I am among my people
Israel,
that I am the LORD your God, and there is no
other.
Never again will my people be disgraced.

THE LORD'S PROMISE OF HIS SPIRIT

28*"Then, after doing all those things,
I will pour out my Spirit upon all people.
Your sons and daughters will prophesy.
Your old men will dream dreams,
and your young men will see visions.

2:20 Hebrew *into the eastern sea, . . . into the western sea.* **2:25** The precise identification of the four kinds of locusts mentioned here is uncertain. **2:28** Verses 2:28-32 are numbered 3:1-5 in Hebrew text.

2:13 compassionate. God's wrath and might are tempered by grace, compassion, slowness to anger, and faithful love. Those who love and obey God will experience His compassion, while those who defy God will experience wrath.

2:21-23 Everything came to life again as a symbol of God's restorative power. Animals (v. 22) and people (v. 23) enjoy the rebirth of the land (v. 21).

2:27 I am the LORD . . . there is no other. The blessings (vv. 25-26) were a sign of God's presence among His people.

29 In those days I will pour out my Spirit
even on servants—men and women alike.
30 And I will cause wonders in the heavens and on the earth—
blood and fire and columns of smoke.
31 The sun will become dark,
and the moon will turn blood red
before that great and terrible* day of the LORD arrives.
32 But everyone who calls on the name of the LORD
will be saved,
for some on Mount Zion in Jerusalem will escape,
just as the LORD has said.
These will be among the survivors
whom the LORD has called.

JUDGMENT AGAINST ENEMY NATIONS

3 1*"At the time of those events," says the LORD,
"when I restore the prosperity of Judah and Jerusalem,
2 I will gather the armies of the world
into the valley of Jehoshaphat.*
There I will judge them
for harming my people, my special possession,
for scattering my people among the nations,
and for dividing up my land.
3 They threw dice* to decide which of my people
would be their slaves.
They traded boys to obtain prostitutes
and sold girls for enough wine to get drunk.

4"What do you have against me, Tyre and Sidon
and you cities of Philistia? Are you trying to take re-
venge on me? If you are, then watch out! I will strike
swiftly and pay you back for everything you have
done. 5You have taken my silver and gold and all my
precious treasures, and have carried them off to your
pagan temples. 6You have sold the people of Judah
and Jerusalem to the Greeks,* so they could take them
far from their homeland.
7"But I will bring them back from all the places
to which you sold them, and I will pay you back for
everything you have done. 8I will sell your sons and
daughters to the people of Judah, and they will sell
them to the people of Arabia,* a nation far away. I, the
LORD, have spoken!"

9 Say to the nations far and wide:
"Get ready for war!
Call out your best warriors.
Let all your fighting men advance for the attack.
10 Hammer your plowshares into swords
and your pruning hooks into spears.
Train even your weaklings to be warriors.
11 Come quickly, all you nations everywhere.
Gather together in the valley."

And now, O LORD, call out your warriors!

12 "Let the nations be called to arms.
Let them march to the valley of Jehoshaphat.
There I, the LORD, will sit
to pronounce judgment on them all.
13 Swing the sickle,
for the harvest is ripe.*
Come, tread the grapes,
for the winepress is full.
The storage vats are overflowing
with the wickedness of these people."

14 Thousands upon thousands are waiting in the valley of decision.
There the day of the LORD will soon arrive.
15 The sun and moon will grow dark,
and the stars will no longer shine.
16 The LORD's voice will roar from Zion
and thunder from Jerusalem,
and the heavens and the earth will shake.
But the LORD will be a refuge for his people,
a strong fortress for the people of Israel.

BLESSINGS FOR GOD'S PEOPLE

17 "Then you will know that I, the LORD your God,
live in Zion, my holy mountain.
Jerusalem will be holy forever,
and foreign armies will never conquer her again.
18 In that day the mountains will drip with sweet wine,
and the hills will flow with milk.
Water will fill the streambeds of Judah,
and a fountain will burst forth from the LORD's Temple,
watering the arid valley of acacias.*
19 But Egypt will become a wasteland
and Edom will become a wilderness,
because they attacked the people of Judah
and killed innocent people in their land.

20 "But Judah will be filled with people forever,
and Jerusalem will endure through all generations.
21 I will pardon my people's crimes,
which I have not yet pardoned;
and I, the LORD, will make my home
in Jerusalem* with my people."

2:31 Greek version reads *glorious.* **3:1** Verses 3:1-21 are numbered 4:1-21 in Hebrew text. **3:2** *Jehoshaphat* means "the LORD judges." **3:3** Hebrew *They cast lots.* **3:6** Hebrew *to the peoples of Javan.* **3:8** Hebrew *to the Sabeans.* **3:13** Greek version reads *for the harvest time has come.* Compare Mark 4:29. **3:18** Hebrew *valley of Shittim.* **3:21** Hebrew *Zion.*

2:30-31 wonders. These cosmic wonders, formerly a scene of destruction (v. 10), now proclaimed God's provision through His Spirit. Joel described it as both a day of judgment for sin and a time of deliverance for God's people.
3:1 At the time of those events. God offers a plan of hope to the Israelites. Their enemies will be judged, and Israel's fortunes will be restored.
3:2 I will judge them. In this supernatural event, evil will ultimately be judged, and the righteous delivered (see also Rev. 20:8-10).
3:4-8 Specific nations were summoned before the Lord for their destructive attitudes toward God.
3:9-11 Get ready for war! The mighty assembly of the Lord's army gears up for battle (see also Rev. 19:14). Joel exhorted the Lord to reveal His protection and provision (v. 11).
3:10 plowshares into swords. Instead of enjoying peace, the nations prepared for war by turning tools for plowing into battle weapons, foreshadowing their inevitable defeat (Isa. 2:4, Mic. 4:3).
3:14 in the valley of decision. All of humankind was represented in this decision that all must make: repent or continue to rebel and sin against God.
3:16 refuge . . . strong fortress. The Day of the Lord will be a place of safety for the righteous and bring delight to those who are saved by faith in God.
3:18 In that day. Joel looked forward to a day when God's people would fully experience the fullness of God's creation forever (2:28–3:1).
3:21 I, the LORD, will make my home. At the close of the prophecy, Joel emphasized God's presence among His people; God's covenant will finally be the rule of the day. This, as many of Joel's prophecies, foreshadows future events at the end of the age.

INTRODUCTION TO
AMOS

PERSONAL READING PLAN

☐Amos 1:1–2:5
☐Amos 2:6–3:15
☐Amos 4:1–5:17
☐Amos 5:18–6:14
☐Amos 7:1–8:14
☐Amos 9:1-15

AUTHOR

Amos, who came from the small town of Tekoa (six miles south of Bethlehem and 11 miles from Jerusalem), was a citizen of the southern state of Judah but ministered in the northern state of Israel alongside the prophet Hosea. Amos was a shepherd (1:1) and fruit farmer (7:14), not a professional prophet. However, his skill with words and the strikingly broad range of his general knowledge of history and the world indicate that he was not an ignorant peasant.

DATE

Amos ministered during the reigns of Uzziah, king of Judah (783–742 B.C.), and Jeroboam II, king of Israel (786–746 B.C.), possibly *circa* 760–750 B.C.

THEME

God's judgment on injustice.

HISTORICAL BACKGROUND

By 800 B.C. both the northern kingdom (Israel) and the southern kingdom (Judah) had reached new political and military heights. Peace reigned, and business was booming. Even religion was on the rise. However, the exterior calm belied Israel's inner disease. Idolatry, extravagant indulgence, and a corrupt judicial system ran beneath the surface. In this context, Amos calls for justice—particularly social justice as the foundation for true piety (5:24).

CHARACTERISTICS

Whereas his contemporary, Hosea, focuses on the love of God and spiritual adultery, Amos focuses on the righteousness of God and social injustice. He often makes his points by use of a simple rhetorical question (e.g., 5:25). Amos speaks as a simple Judean farmer burdened for the materialistic nation of Israel. His prayer averts the total destruction of Israel (7:1-6), and yet his message was most unpopular. However, social acceptance didn't matter to one whose job was not on the line (7:12-15). In Amos, God roars like a lion (1:2) and brings hope only at the end (9:11-15). The book of Amos is constantly shadowed by clouds of judgment as the Lord reacts to the cruel social behaviors in the land. Amos passionately declares both God's concern for the poor and His wrath on those who would exploit them. His message is an uncomfortable one in any age as he challenges followers of God to examine themselves and their society, confronting injustice wherever it exists.

1 This message was given to Amos, a shepherd from
the town of Tekoa in Judah. He received this message in visions two years before the earthquake,
when Uzziah was king of Judah and Jeroboam II, the
son of Jehoash,* was king of Israel.
2 This is what he saw and heard:

"The LORD's voice will roar from Zion
and thunder from Jerusalem!
The lush pastures of the shepherds will dry up;
the grass on Mount Carmel will wither and die."

GOD'S JUDGMENT ON ISRAEL'S NEIGHBORS

3 This is what the LORD says:

"The people of Damascus have sinned again and again,*
and I will not let them go unpunished!
They beat down my people in Gilead
as grain is threshed with iron sledges.
4 So I will send down fire on King Hazael's palace,
and the fortresses of King Ben-hadad will be destroyed.
5 I will break down the gates of Damascus
and slaughter the people in the valley of Aven.
I will destroy the ruler in Beth-eden,
and the people of Aram will go as captives to Kir,"
says the LORD.

6 This is what the LORD says:

"The people of Gaza have sinned again and again,
and I will not let them go unpunished!
They sent whole villages into exile,
selling them as slaves to Edom.
7 So I will send down fire on the walls of Gaza,
and all its fortresses will be destroyed.
8 I will slaughter the people of Ashdod
and destroy the king of Ashkelon.
Then I will turn to attack Ekron,
and the few Philistines still left will be killed,"
says the Sovereign LORD.

9 This is what the LORD says:

"The people of Tyre have sinned again and again,
and I will not let them go unpunished!
They broke their treaty of brotherhood with Israel,
selling whole villages as slaves to Edom.
10 So I will send down fire on the walls of Tyre,
and all its fortresses will be destroyed."

11 This is what the LORD says:

"The people of Edom have sinned again and again,
and I will not let them go unpunished!
They chased down their relatives, the Israelites,
with swords,
showing them no mercy.
In their rage, they slashed them continually
and were unrelenting in their anger.
12 So I will send down fire on Teman,
and the fortresses of Bozrah will be destroyed."

13 This is what the LORD says:

"The people of Ammon have sinned again and again,
and I will not let them go unpunished!
When they attacked Gilead to extend their borders,
they ripped open pregnant women with their swords.
14 So I will send down fire on the walls of Rabbah,
and all its fortresses will be destroyed.
The battle will come upon them with shouts,
like a whirlwind in a mighty storm.
15 And their king* and his princes will go into exile together,"
says the LORD.

2 This is what the LORD says:

"The people of Moab have sinned again and again,*
and I will not let them go unpunished!
They desecrated the bones of Edom's king,
burning them to ashes.
2 So I will send down fire on the land of Moab,
and all the fortresses in Kerioth will be destroyed.
The people will fall in the noise of battle,
as the warriors shout and the ram's horn sounds.
3 And I will destroy their king
and slaughter all their princes,"
says the LORD.

GOD'S JUDGMENT ON JUDAH AND ISRAEL

4 This is what the LORD says:

"The people of Judah have sinned again and again,
and I will not let them go unpunished!
They have rejected the instruction of the LORD,
refusing to obey his decrees.
They have been led astray by the same lies
that deceived their ancestors.
5 So I will send down fire on Judah,
and all the fortresses of Jerusalem will be destroyed."

6 This is what the LORD says:

"The people of Israel have sinned again and again,
and I will not let them go unpunished!
They sell honorable people for silver
and poor people for a pair of sandals.

1:1 Hebrew *Joash,* a variant spelling of Jehoash. **1:3** Hebrew *have committed three sins, even four;* also in 1:6, 9, 11, 13. **1:15** Hebrew *malcam,* possibly referring to their god Molech. **2:1** Hebrew *have committed three sins, even four;* also in 2:4, 6.

1:1 Tekoa. Tekoa was in a desolate area 12 miles south of Jerusalem. There Amos was a shepherd and a keeper of fig trees around 750 B.C.
1:2 roar. God's words were as fearful as a lion's roar. As a shepherd, Amos knew the power of God's words of judgment (see 3:4).
1:3 sinned again and again. Amos pictured God losing patience over repeated disobedience (vv. 6,9,11,13; 2:1,4,6).
2:6 sell honorable people. Amos admonished the Israelites for devaluing human life. God's policy of working off a debt (Deut. 15:12) was stretched into extortion.

7 They trample helpless people in the dust
and shove the oppressed out of the way.
Both father and son sleep with the same woman,
corrupting my holy name.
8 At their religious festivals,
they lounge in clothing their debtors put up as security.
In the house of their gods,*
they drink wine bought with unjust fines.

9 "But as my people watched,
I destroyed the Amorites,
though they were as tall as cedars
and as strong as oaks.
I destroyed the fruit on their branches
and dug out their roots.
10 It was I who rescued you from Egypt
and led you through the desert for forty years,
so you could possess the land of the Amorites.
11 I chose some of your sons to be prophets
and others to be Nazirites.
Can you deny this, my people of Israel?"
asks the LORD.
12 "But you caused the Nazirites to sin by making them drink wine,
and you commanded the prophets, 'Shut up!'
13 "So I will make you groan
like a wagon loaded down with sheaves of grain.
14 Your fastest runners will not get away.
The strongest among you will become weak.
Even mighty warriors will be unable to save themselves.
15 The archers will not stand their ground.
The swiftest runners won't be fast enough to escape.
Even those riding horses won't be able to save themselves.
16 On that day the most courageous of your fighting men
will drop their weapons and run for their lives,"
says the LORD.

3 Listen to this message that the LORD has spoken against you, O people of Israel—against the entire family I rescued from Egypt:

2 "From among all the families on the earth,
I have been intimate with you alone.
That is why I must punish you
for all your sins."

WITNESSES AGAINST GUILTY ISRAEL

3 Can two people walk together
without agreeing on the direction?
4 Does a lion ever roar in a thicket
without first finding a victim?
Does a young lion growl in its den
without first catching its prey?
5 Does a bird ever get caught in a trap
that has no bait?
Does a trap spring shut
when there's nothing to catch?
6 When the ram's horn blows a warning,
shouldn't the people be alarmed?
Does disaster come to a city
unless the LORD has planned it?
7 Indeed, the Sovereign LORD never does anything
until he reveals his plans to his servants the prophets.

8 The lion has roared—
so who isn't frightened?
The Sovereign LORD has spoken—
so who can refuse to proclaim his message?
9 Announce this to the leaders of Philistia*
and to the great ones of Egypt:
"Take your seats now on the hills around Samaria,
and witness the chaos and oppression in Israel."

10 "My people have forgotten how to do right,"
says the LORD.
"Their fortresses are filled with wealth
taken by theft and violence.
11 Therefore," says the Sovereign LORD,
"an enemy is coming!
He will surround them and shatter their defenses.
Then he will plunder all their fortresses."

12 This is what the LORD says:

"A shepherd who tries to rescue a sheep from a lion's mouth
will recover only two legs or a piece of an ear.
So it will be for the Israelites in Samaria lying on luxurious beds,
and for the people of Damascus reclining on couches.*
13 "Now listen to this, and announce it throughout all Israel,*" says the Lord, the LORD God of Heaven's Armies.

14 "On the very day I punish Israel for its sins,
I will destroy the pagan altars at Bethel.
The horns of the altar will be cut off
and fall to the ground.
15 And I will destroy the beautiful homes of the wealthy—

2:8 Or *their God.* 3:9 Hebrew *Ashdod.* 3:12 The meaning of the Hebrew in this sentence is uncertain. 3:13 Hebrew *the house of Jacob.* The names "Jacob" and "Israel" are often interchanged throughout the Old Testament, referring sometimes to the individual patriarch and sometimes to the nation.

2:8 they lounge. Sinful Israel slept soundly on its own guilty conscience near places of pagan idol worship.
2:9 I destroyed the Amorites. God reminded Israel that they did not arrive at success by their own efforts. God had uprooted and destroyed Israel's enemies in Canaan, represented here by the formidable Amorites.
2:10 rescued you . . . led you. God reminded the people of their roots. They are a chosen people with high hopes and a high calling.
2:11 chose . . . prophets. Amos was a living example of God's guidance. Rebelliously, Israel ignored God's messengers and would now suffer the consequences.
2:16 On that day. Little did Israel know that Assyria would soon conquer Israel and take the nation captive.
3:2 From among all the families on the earth. God specifically and lovingly chose Israel as His own people to be a witness to the nations. How then could Israel be so blind to its privileges and responsibilities?
3:8 lion. The lion reappears as an image of the Lord's vengeance on Israel (see also 1:2).
3:12 couches. Amos' warnings of a lion attack fell on the lazy ears of those lounging in luxury.

their winter mansions and their summer
houses, too—
all their palaces filled with ivory,"
says the LORD.

ISRAEL'S FAILURE TO LEARN

4 1 Listen to me, you fat cows*
living in Samaria,
you women who oppress the poor
and crush the needy,
and who are always calling to your husbands,
"Bring us another drink!"
2 The Sovereign LORD has sworn this by his holiness:
"The time will come when you will be led away
with hooks in your noses.
Every last one of you will be dragged away
like a fish on a hook!
3 You will be led out through the ruins of the wall;
you will be thrown from your fortresses,*"
says the LORD.

4 "Go ahead and offer sacrifices to the idols at
Bethel.
Keep on disobeying at Gilgal.
Offer sacrifices each morning,
and bring your tithes every three days.
5 Present your bread made with yeast
as an offering of thanksgiving.
Then give your extra voluntary offerings
so you can brag about it everywhere!
This is the kind of thing you Israelites love to do,"
says the Sovereign LORD.

6 "I brought hunger to every city
and famine to every town.
But still you would not return to me,"
says the LORD.

7 "I kept the rain from falling
when your crops needed it the most.
I sent rain on one town
but withheld it from another.
Rain fell on one field,
while another field withered away.
8 People staggered from town to town looking for
water,
but there was never enough.
But still you would not return to me,"
says the LORD.

9 "I struck your farms and vineyards with blight
and mildew.
Locusts devoured all your fig and olive trees.
But still you would not return to me,"
says the LORD.

10 "I sent plagues on you
like the plagues I sent on Egypt long ago.
I killed your young men in war
and led all your horses away.*
The stench of death filled the air!
But still you would not return to me,"
says the LORD.

11 "I destroyed some of your cities,
as I destroyed* Sodom and Gomorrah.
Those of you who survived
were like charred sticks pulled from a fire.
But still you would not return to me,"
says the LORD.

12 "Therefore, I will bring upon you all the disasters I
have announced.
Prepare to meet your God in judgment, you
people of Israel!"

13 For the LORD is the one who shaped the mountains,
stirs up the winds, and reveals his thoughts to
mankind.
He turns the light of dawn into darkness
and treads on the heights of the earth.
The LORD God of Heaven's Armies is his name!

A CALL TO REPENTANCE

5 Listen, you people of Israel! Listen to this funeral
song I am singing:

2 "The virgin Israel has fallen,
never to rise again!
She lies abandoned on the ground,
with no one to help her up."

3 The Sovereign LORD says:

"When a city sends a thousand men to battle,
only a hundred will return.
When a town sends a hundred,
only ten will come back alive."

4 Now this is what the LORD says to the family of Israel:

"Come back to me and live!
5 Don't worship at the pagan altars at Bethel;
don't go to the shrines at Gilgal or Beersheba.
For the people of Gilgal will be dragged off into
exile,
and the people of Bethel will be reduced to
nothing."
6 Come back to the LORD and live!
Otherwise, he will roar through Israel* like a fire,
devouring you completely.
Your gods in Bethel
won't be able to quench the flames.
7 You twist justice, making it a bitter pill for the
oppressed.
You treat the righteous like dirt.

4:1 Hebrew *you cows of Bashan.* **4:3** Or *thrown out toward Harmon,* possibly a reference to Mount Hermon. **4:10** Or *and slaughtered your captured horses.* **4:11** Hebrew *as when God destroyed.* **5:6** Hebrew *the house of Joseph.*

4:1 fat cows. Bashan, a lush pastureland, catered to its cattle (Ps. 22:12). Likewise, the men of Israel pampered the needs of these luxury-loving women.
4:4 Go ahead . . . at Bethel . . . Gilgal. Amos pinpointed holy places for worshipping Yahweh (God's self-proclaimed name). However, Israel shamelessly used them as sites for engaging in sinful idol worship.
4:5 This is the kind of thing you Israelites love to do. Israel wanted a pick-and-choose religion rather than obeying the whole law of God.
4:6-11 Amos described five disasters in Israel's past: shortage of food (6); drought (vv. 7-8); blight and mildew (v. 9); locusts (v. 9); plagues (v. 10); God's direct judgments (v. 11). But Israel stubbornly refused to repent even after these disasters.
4:13 Amos listed God's credentials in order to remind Israel that God was fully able and prepared to carry out all He had decreed.

8 It is the LORD who created the stars,
the Pleiades and Orion.
He turns darkness into morning
and day into night.
He draws up water from the oceans
and pours it down as rain on the land.
The LORD is his name!
9 With blinding speed and power he destroys the strong,
crushing all their defenses.

10 How you hate honest judges!
How you despise people who tell the truth!
11 You trample the poor,
stealing their grain through taxes and unfair rent.
Therefore, though you build beautiful stone houses,
you will never live in them.
Though you plant lush vineyards,
you will never drink wine from them.
12 For I know the vast number of your sins
and the depth of your rebellions.
You oppress good people by taking bribes
and deprive the poor of justice in the courts.
13 So those who are smart keep their mouths shut,
for it is an evil time.

14 Do what is good and run from evil
so that you may live!
Then the LORD God of Heaven's Armies will be your helper,
just as you have claimed.
15 Hate evil and love what is good;
turn your courts into true halls of justice.
Perhaps even yet the LORD God of Heaven's Armies
will have mercy on the remnant of his people.*

16 Therefore, this is what the Lord, the LORD God of
Heaven's Armies, says:

"There will be crying in all the public squares
and mourning in every street.
Call for the farmers to weep with you,
and summon professional mourners to wail.
17 There will be wailing in every vineyard,
for I will destroy them all,"
says the LORD.

WARNING OF COMING JUDGMENT

18 What sorrow awaits you who say,
"If only the day of the LORD were here!"
You have no idea what you are wishing for.
That day will bring darkness, not light.
19 In that day you will be like a man who runs from a lion—
only to meet a bear.
Escaping from the bear, he leans his hand against
a wall in his house—
and he's bitten by a snake.
20 Yes, the day of the LORD will be dark and hopeless,
without a ray of joy or hope.

21 "I hate all your show and pretense—
the hypocrisy of your religious festivals and
solemn assemblies.
22 I will not accept your burnt offerings and grain offerings.
I won't even notice all your choice peace offerings.
23 Away with your noisy hymns of praise!
I will not listen to the music of your harps.
24 Instead, I want to see a mighty flood of justice,
an endless river of righteous living.

25 "Was it to me you were bringing sacrifices and of-
ferings during the forty years in the wilderness, Isra-
el? 26 No, you served your pagan gods—Sakkuth your
king god and Kaiwan your star god—the images you
made for yourselves. 27 So I will send you into exile, to
a land east of Damascus,*" says the LORD, whose name
is the God of Heaven's Armies.

6 1 What sorrow awaits you who lounge in luxury
in Jerusalem,*
and you who feel secure in Samaria!
You are famous and popular in Israel,
and people go to you for help.
2 But go over to Calneh
and see what happened there.
Then go to the great city of Hamath
and down to the Philistine city of Gath.
You are no better than they were,
and look at how they were destroyed.
3 You push away every thought of coming disaster,
but your actions only bring the day of judgment closer.
4 How terrible for you who sprawl on ivory beds
and lounge on your couches,
eating the meat of tender lambs from the flock
and of choice calves fattened in the stall.
5 You sing trivial songs to the sound of the harp
and fancy yourselves to be great musicians like David.
6 You drink wine by the bowlful
and perfume yourselves with fragrant lotions.
You care nothing about the ruin of your nation.*
7 Therefore, you will be the first to be led away as captives.
Suddenly, all your parties will end.

8 The Sovereign LORD has sworn by his own name, and
this is what he, the LORD God of Heaven's Armies, says:

5:15 Hebrew *the remnant of Joseph.* **5:26-27** Greek version reads *No, you carried your pagan gods—the shrine of Molech, the star of your god Rephan, and the images you made for yourselves. So I will send you into exile, to a land east of Damascus.* Compare Acts 7:43. **6:1** Hebrew *in Zion.* **6:6** Hebrew *of Joseph.* **6:8** Hebrew *Jacob.* See note on 3:13.

5:8-9 It is the LORD. Amos beautifully reminds the people of God's incredible power—the omnipotence with which they were dealing.

5:11 trample the poor. Amos exposed the social injustice against the poor (2:7).

5:16-17 crying . . . mourning. Vineyards, which typically represented bounty and gladness, would now be sites of sorrow (Isa. 16:10). God's presence among them would bring sadness over their plight and not comfort.

5:18 day of the LORD. Amos describes a future day of God's ultimate victory over evil (Isa. 5:19). **darkness.** A day that Israel thought would bring reward to God's people would instead bring unexpected doom (Joel 2:1-2).

5:21-23 hypocrisy . . . noisy hymns. Even Israel's intentions were not pure. Hypocrisy tainted every religious effort.

5:24 an endless stream. Israel's dried-up enthusiasm for its religious traditions should have been replaced by a recommitment to justice to the poor, a recommitment which could have brought peaceful living.

"I despise the arrogance of Israel,*
and I hate their fortresses.
I will give this city
and everything in it to their enemies."

9 (If there are ten men left in one house, they will all
die. 10 And when a relative who is responsible to dis-
pose of the dead* goes into the house to carry out the
bodies, he will ask the last survivor, "Is anyone else
with you?" When the person begins to swear, "No,
by...," he will interrupt and say, "Stop! Don't even
mention the name of the LORD.")

11 When the LORD gives the command,
homes both great and small will be smashed to
pieces.

12 Can horses gallop over boulders?
Can oxen be used to plow them?
But that's how foolish you are when you turn
justice into poison
and the sweet fruit of righteousness into
bitterness.
13 And you brag about your conquest of Lo-debar.*
You boast, "Didn't we take Karnaim* by our own
strength?"

14 "O people of Israel, I am about to bring an enemy
nation against you,"
says the LORD God of Heaven's Armies.
"They will oppress you throughout your land—
from Lebo-hamath in the north
to the Arabah Valley in the south."

A VISION OF LOCUSTS

7 The Sovereign LORD showed me a vision. I saw him
preparing to send a vast swarm of locusts over the
land. This was after the king's share had been har-
vested from the fields and as the main crop was com-
ing up. 2 In my vision the locusts ate every green plant
in sight. Then I said, "O Sovereign LORD, please forgive
us or we will not survive, for Israel* is so small."
3 So the LORD relented from this plan. "I will not do
it," he said.

A VISION OF FIRE

4 Then the Sovereign LORD showed me another vision.
I saw him preparing to punish his people with a great
fire. The fire had burned up the depths of the sea and
was devouring the entire land. 5 Then I said, "O Sover-
eign LORD, please stop or we will not survive, for Isra-
el is so small."
6 Then the LORD relented from this plan, too. "I will
not do that either," said the Sovereign LORD.

A VISION OF A PLUMB LINE

7 Then he showed me another vision. I saw the Lord
standing beside a wall that had been built using a
plumb line. He was using a plumb line to see if it was
still straight. 8 And the LORD said to me, "Amos, what
do you see?"
I answered, "A plumb line."
And the Lord replied, "I will test my people with
this plumb line. I will no longer ignore all their sins.
9 The pagan shrines of your ancestors* will be ruined,
and the temples of Israel will be destroyed; I will
bring the dynasty of King Jeroboam to a sudden end."

AMOS AND AMAZIAH

10 Then Amaziah, the priest of Bethel, sent a message
to Jeroboam, king of Israel: "Amos is hatching a plot
against you right here on your very doorstep! What
he is saying is intolerable. 11 He is saying, 'Jeroboam
will soon be killed, and the people of Israel will be
sent away into exile.'"
12 Then Amaziah sent orders to Amos: "Get out of
here, you prophet! Go on back to the land of Judah,
and earn your living by prophesying there! 13 Don't
bother us with your prophecies here in Bethel. This
is the king's sanctuary and the national place of wor-
ship!"
14 But Amos replied, "I'm not a professional prophet,
and I was never trained to be one.* I'm just a shep-
herd, and I take care of sycamore-fig trees. 15 But the
LORD called me away from my flock and told me, 'Go
and prophesy to my people in Israel.' 16 Now then, lis-
ten to this message from the LORD:

"You say,
'Don't prophesy against Israel.
Stop preaching against my people.*'
17 But this is what the LORD says:
'Your wife will become a prostitute in this city,
and your sons and daughters will be killed.
Your land will be divided up,
and you yourself will die in a foreign land.
And the people of Israel will certainly become
captives in exile,
far from their homeland.'"

A VISION OF RIPE FRUIT

8 Then the Sovereign LORD showed me another
vision. In it I saw a basket filled with ripe fruit.
2 "What do you see, Amos?" he asked.
I replied, "A basket full of ripe fruit."
Then the LORD said, "Like this fruit, Israel is ripe for
punishment! I will not delay their punishment again.
3 In that day the singing in the temple will turn to
wailing. Dead bodies will be scattered everywhere.

6:10 Or *to burn the dead.* The meaning of the Hebrew is uncertain. **6:13a** *Lo-debar* means "nothing." **6:13b** *Karnaim* means "horns," a term that symbolizes strength. **7:2** Hebrew *Jacob;* also in 7:5. See note on 3:13. **7:9** Hebrew *of Isaac.* **7:14** Or *I'm not a prophet nor the son of a prophet.* **7:16** Hebrew *against the house of Isaac.*

6:10-11 dead . . . smashed to pieces. Amos described devastating vengeance on the citizens of the northern kingdom.

6:10 don't even mention. The Lord's destruction would be so severe even a survivor would not be allowed to mention the Lord's name. Doing so might incur God's wrath.

6:13 by our own strength. Israel may have won the battles in nearby cities, but it would soon lose the war to conquering Assyria.

7:1 The Sovereign LORD showed me. God spoke to Amos in a dramatic vision, which Amos communicated to the people: doom for their next crops. Remember that they lived in dependency on each year's crop.

7:8 plumb line. A plumb line is an essential carpenter's tool, composed of a weighted string used to accurately create a straight wall. This symbol highlights Israel's crookedness versus God's holiness (straightness).

7:11 Jeroboam will soon be killed. Amaziah mistook Amos' spiritual exhortation as a political threat against the king.

7:17 prostitute in the city. In the end, Amaziah's intolerance for Amos' warnings would result in his total loss. Amaziah's abandoned wife would resort to prostitution in order to support herself. His children would die violently, and his land would be scattered. Amaziah had repeated these same words in verse 11.

8:2 basket full of ripe fruit. What seemed an innocent image of ready-to-eat fruit was actually a picture of impending punishment.

They will be carried out of the city in silence. I, the Sovereign LORD, have spoken!"

4 Listen to this, you who rob the poor
and trample down the needy!
5 You can't wait for the Sabbath day to be over
and the religious festivals to end
so you can get back to cheating the helpless.
You measure out grain with dishonest measures
and cheat the buyer with dishonest scales.*
6 And you mix the grain you sell
with chaff swept from the floor.
Then you enslave poor people
for one piece of silver or a pair of sandals.

7 Now the LORD has sworn this oath
by his own name, the Pride of Israel*:
"I will never forget
the wicked things you have done!
8 The earth will tremble for your deeds,
and everyone will mourn.
The ground will rise like the Nile River at floodtime;
it will heave up, then sink again.

9 "In that day," says the Sovereign LORD,
"I will make the sun go down at noon
and darken the earth while it is still day.
10 I will turn your celebrations into times of mourning
and your singing into weeping.
You will wear funeral clothes
and shave your heads to show your sorrow—
as if your only son had died.
How very bitter that day will be!

11 "The time is surely coming," says the Sovereign LORD,
"when I will send a famine on the land—
not a famine of bread or water
but of hearing the words of the LORD.
12 People will stagger from sea to sea
and wander from border to border*
searching for the word of the LORD,
but they will not find it.
13 Beautiful girls and strong young men
will grow faint in that day,
thirsting for the LORD's word.
14 And those who swear by the shameful idols of Samaria—
who take oaths in the name of the god of Dan
and make vows in the name of the god of Beersheba*—
they will all fall down,
never to rise again."

A VISION OF GOD AT THE ALTAR

9 Then I saw a vision of the Lord standing beside the
altar. He said,

"Strike the tops of the Temple columns,
so that the foundation will shake.
Bring down the roof
on the heads of the people below.
I will kill with the sword those who survive.
No one will escape!

2 "Even if they dig down to the place of the dead,*
I will reach down and pull them up.
Even if they climb up into the heavens,
I will bring them down.
3 Even if they hide at the very top of Mount Carmel,
I will search them out and capture them.
Even if they hide at the bottom of the ocean,
I will send the sea serpent after them to bite them.
4 Even if their enemies drive them into exile,
I will command the sword to kill them there.
I am determined to bring disaster upon them
and not to help them."

5 The Lord, the LORD of Heaven's Armies,
touches the land and it melts,
and all its people mourn.
The ground rises like the Nile River at floodtime,
and then it sinks again.
6 The LORD's home reaches up to the heavens,
while its foundation is on the earth.
He draws up water from the oceans
and pours it down as rain on the land.
The LORD is his name!

7 "Are you Israelites more important to me
than the Ethiopians?*" asks the LORD.
"I brought Israel out of Egypt,
but I also brought the Philistines from Crete*
and led the Arameans out of Kir.

8 "I, the Sovereign LORD,
am watching this sinful nation of Israel.
I will destroy it
from the face of the earth.
But I will never completely destroy the family of Israel,*"
says the LORD.
9 "For I will give the command
and will shake Israel along with the other nations
as grain is shaken in a sieve,
yet not one true kernel will be lost.
10 But all the sinners will die by the sword—
all those who say, 'Nothing bad will happen to us.'

8:5 Hebrew *You make the ephah* [a unit for measuring grain] *small and the shekel* [a unit of weight] *great, and you deal falsely by using deceitful balances.* **8:7** Hebrew *the pride of Jacob.* See note on 3:13. **8:12** Hebrew *from north to east.* **8:14** Hebrew *the way of Beersheba.* **9:2** Hebrew *to Sheol.* **9:7a** Hebrew *the Cushites?* **9:7b** Hebrew *Caphtor.* **9:8** Hebrew *the house of Jacob.* See note on 3:13.

8:6 enslave poor people. God reiterated the oppressive situation Israel's extortion among the poor had caused. Crimes against a seemingly insignificant sector of society resulted in large-scale devastation (2:6). God's concern for the poor and justice are strong themes seen throughout the entire Bible.

9:1 I saw a vision. Amos' final vision is one of destruction (vv. 1-10) and hope for what is yet to come (vv. 11-15).

9:2-4 if they hide. The fugitives in this vision instinctively hide. However, there is no refuge from God's wrath (See also Ps. 139:7-8).

9:8 never completely destroy. What was only hinted at earlier (5:15) was now confirmed. A remnant of people would remain as a symbol of hope.

A PROMISE OF RESTORATION

11 "In that day I will restore the fallen house* of
David.
I will repair its damaged walls.
From the ruins I will rebuild it
and restore its former glory.
12 And Israel will possess what is left of Edom
and all the nations I have called to be mine.*"
The LORD has spoken,
and he will do these things.

13 "The time will come," says the LORD,
"when the grain and grapes will grow faster
than they can be harvested.
Then the terraced vineyards on the hills of
Israel
will drip with sweet wine!
14 I will bring my exiled people of Israel
back from distant lands,
and they will rebuild their ruined cities
and live in them again.
They will plant vineyards and gardens;
they will eat their crops and drink their wine.
15 I will firmly plant them there
in their own land.
They will never again be uprooted
from the land I have given them,"
says the LORD your God.

9:11a Or *kingdom;* Hebrew reads *tent.* 9:11b-12 Greek version reads *and restore its former glory, / so that the rest of humanity, including the Gentiles— / all those I have called to be mine—might seek me.* Compare Acts 15:16-17.

9:11 I will repair. Amos' words are pure refreshment to those who would repent and turn back to God's ways.
9:12 Edom. Edom was Israel's greatest enemy at the time as far as Israel was concerned. Conquering Edom represented complete victory for Israel.
9:13-15 grain and grapes will grow faster than they can be harvested. Contrasting an earlier description of agricultural disaster (4:6-11), Amos now portrays a farmer's fantasy. God restores the land so that the people could hardly keep up with its bounty.
9:14 rebuild. A once devastated people, God would rebuild their lives from the ground up as a symbol of their restoration.

INTRODUCTION TO

OBADIAH

PERSONAL READING PLAN

☐Obadiah 1-21

AUTHOR

This short book is referred to as the "vision of Obadiah" (v. 1). This prophet's name means "the servant of the Lord." While there are 11 other Old Testament characters with this name, none of them can be identified with this prophet.

DATE

The date of composition is uncertain, depending upon which of these two events in Israel's history correlates with verses 11-14:

(1) The Philistine invasion of Jerusalem during the reign of Jehoram (853–841 B.C.; see 2 Chron. 21:8-20). If this event is referred to, Obadiah would be a ninth-century contemporary of Elisha.

(2) The Babylonian campaign against Jerusalem (605–585 B.C.), in which case Obadiah would be a sixth-century contemporary of Jeremiah. The latter seems more likely.

THEME

God's judgment of proud Edom and the restoration of Israel.

HISTORICAL BACKGROUND

The Edomites apparently took advantage of the fall of Jerusalem to Babylon in 586 B.C. They plundered the land and looted the homes of survivors. Obadiah speaks God's judgment on Edom for the way they took advantage of "brother Jacob" in his moment of weakness. The term "Edom" is used in the Old Testament for the name of Esau (the brother of Jacob) and for the race made up of his descendants. The area this tribe occupied was originally the land of Seir. It was a rugged, mountainous region that extended from the Dead Sea south to the Gulf of Aqabah. The hatred and hostility between Edom and Israel was long-standing. The history of the blood feud between the two peoples can be traced by a study of the relevant Old Testament passages (see Gen. 27:41-45; 32:1-21; 33; Num. 20:14-21; Deut. 2:1-6; 2 Sam. 8:13-14; 2 Kings 8:20-22; Ezek. 35).

Edom was known for sitting smugly in her fortified cities atop rocky clefts, and Obadiah prophesies against her for relying on this for her sense of security. In the fifth century the Edomites were driven out of their own land by the Nabateans. After this, many Edomites moved into southern Palestine.

CHARACTERISTICS

Obadiah is the shortest book in all of the Old Testament. While other prophets often announced oracles directed at other nations (along with their words for Israel), nearly the whole book of Obadiah consists of the words of a Jewish prophet to another country. In this respect Obadiah is like Nahum, who preached against Nineveh. With respect to language, Obadiah is like Jeremiah (compare vv. 1-9 with Jer. 49:7-22), which suggests interdependence on an unknown third source. The language of this book is characterized by vivid and striking metaphors (see vv. 4,5,16,18).

This is the vision that the Sovereign LORD revealed to Obadiah concerning the land of Edom.

EDOM'S JUDGMENT ANNOUNCED

We have heard a message from the LORD
that an ambassador was sent to the nations to say,
"Get ready, everyone!
Let's assemble our armies and attack Edom!"

2 The LORD says to Edom,
"I will cut you down to size among the nations;
you will be greatly despised.
3 You have been deceived by your own pride
because you live in a rock fortress
and make your home high in the mountains.
'Who can ever reach us way up here?'
you ask boastfully.
4 But even if you soar as high as eagles
and build your nest among the stars,
I will bring you crashing down,"
says the LORD.

5 "If thieves came at night and robbed you
(what a disaster awaits you!),
they would not take everything.
Those who harvest grapes
always leave a few for the poor.
But your enemies will wipe you out completely!
6 Every nook and cranny of Edom*
will be searched and looted.
Every treasure will be found and taken.

7 "All your allies will turn against you.
They will help to chase you from your land.
They will promise you peace
while plotting to deceive and destroy you.
Your trusted friends will set traps for you,
and you won't even know about it.
8 At that time not a single wise person
will be left in the whole land of Edom,"
says the LORD.
"For on the mountains of Edom
I will destroy everyone who has understanding.
9 The mightiest warriors of Teman
will be terrified,
and everyone on the mountains of Edom
will be cut down in the slaughter.

REASONS FOR EDOM'S PUNISHMENT

10 "Because of the violence you did
to your close relatives in Israel,*
you will be filled with shame
and destroyed forever.
11 When they were invaded,
you stood aloof, refusing to help them.
Foreign invaders carried off their wealth
and cast lots to divide up Jerusalem,
but you acted like one of Israel's enemies.

12 "You should not have gloated
when they exiled your relatives to distant lands.
You should not have rejoiced
when the people of Judah suffered such misfortune.
You should not have spoken arrogantly
in that terrible time of trouble.
13 You should not have plundered the land of Israel
when they were suffering such calamity.
You should not have gloated over their destruction
when they were suffering such calamity.
You should not have seized their wealth
when they were suffering such calamity.
14 You should not have stood at the crossroads,
killing those who tried to escape.
You should not have captured the survivors
and handed them over in their terrible time of trouble.

EDOM DESTROYED, ISRAEL RESTORED

15 "The day is near when I, the LORD,
will judge all godless nations!
As you have done to Israel,
so it will be done to you.
All your evil deeds
will fall back on your own heads.
16 Just as you swallowed up my people
on my holy mountain,
so you and the surrounding nations
will swallow the punishment I pour out on you.
Yes, all you nations will drink and stagger
and disappear from history.
17 "But Jerusalem* will become a refuge for those who escape;
it will be a holy place.
And the people of Israel* will come back
to reclaim their inheritance.
18 The people of Israel will be a raging fire,
and Edom a field of dry stubble.
The descendants of Joseph will be a flame
roaring across the field, devouring everything.
There will be no survivors in Edom.
I, the LORD, have spoken!

19 "Then my people living in the Negev
will occupy the mountains of Edom.
Those living in the foothills of Judah*

6 Hebrew *Esau;* also in 8b, 9, 18, 19, 21. 10 Hebrew *your brother Jacob.* The names "Jacob" and "Israel" are often interchanged throughout the Old Testament, referring sometimes to the individual patriarch and sometimes to the nation. 17a Hebrew *Mount Zion.* 17b Hebrew *house of Jacob;* also in 18. See note on 10. 19 Hebrew *the Shephelah.*

---

1 Let's assemble our armies. An envoy had been sent to the nations, urging them to rise up against the nation of Edom. The prophet, Obadiah, announces that God is stirring up other nations to judge Edom for its arrogance and hostility toward Israel.

4 as eagles. Eagles symbolized strength and pride. Edom was considered a powerful and even invincible nation.

5-6 Esau. Another name used for Edom because the nation descended from Esau, Jacob's older brother (Gen. 25ff). Edom would be completely desolated because of their attacks against Israel. Although Israelites were commanded to leave a little bit behind for the poor, all of Edom's hidden treasures would be carried away.

15 day is near when I, the LORD. The Day of the Lord will bring judgment for all nations, not just Edom. Edom's imminent humiliation foreshadows God's judgment on all nations.

16 swallowed up . . . on My holy mountain. The Lord was angry with the Edomites for holding a drunken celebration in Jerusalem, God's holy habitation. But all the other nations who have opposed Israel will also feel God's wrath.

19 occupy the mountains. Other peoples will occupy Edom's land, probably the remnant of Israel described in verse 20.

will possess the Philistine plains
and take over the fields of Ephraim and
Samaria.
And the people of Benjamin
will occupy the land of Gilead.
20 The exiles of Israel will return to their land
and occupy the Phoenician coast as far north as
Zarephath.
The captives from Jerusalem exiled in the
north*
will return home and resettle the towns of the
Negev.
21 Those who have been rescued* will go up to*
Mount Zion in Jerusalem
to rule over the mountains of Edom.
And the LORD himself will be king!"

20 Hebrew *in Sepharad.* **21a** As in Greek and Syriac versions; Hebrew reads *Rescuers.* **21b** Or *from.*

21 Those who have been rescued. Also could be translated as "forces." The Hebrews who have been taken away as captives will return as victors and rule over Edom. **the LORD himself will be king.** Edom will not be beyond the reach of God despite their arrogance. Once Israel returns to overcome Edom, God will rule.

INTRODUCTION TO

JONAH

PERSONAL READING PLAN

☐Jonah 1:1-17
☐Jonah 2:1-10
☐Jonah 3:1-10
☐Jonah 4:1-11

AUTHOR

The prophet Jonah originally told the story of this book, though others may have written it down. The author is not identified in the text.

DATE

The book was written sometime after Jonah's ministry *circa* 800–770 B.C., before Nineveh's destruction (612 B.C.) and Samaria's fall (722–721 B.C.).

THEME

God's love for the Gentiles, even Nineveh.

HISTORICAL BACKGROUND

Israel had just restored her northern borders under King Jeroboam II (793–753 B.C.) as Jonah had prophesied (2 Kings 14:25). At this time, Israel was politically secure, spiritually smug, and morally corrupt. Nineveh, the city to which Jonah was sent by God, was the capital of Assyria. Assyria was a ruthless empire that threatened tiny Israel and eventually conquered it in 722 B.C. Nineveh was 500 miles east of Joppa, but Jonah boarded a ship heading 2,000 miles west, revealing how desperately Jonah wanted to get away from a people he despised. The Israelites had many reasons to hate the proud Ninevites as Nahum points out in a prophecy dedicated exclusively to the Ninevites (see the Introduction to Nahum). Nineveh's repentance and revival under Jonah was short-lived. The second time around for proud, cruel Nineveh resulted in her fall in 612 B.C., and they were never heard from again.

CHARACTERISTICS

Unlike most other Old Testament prophetic books, Jonah gives an account of a single incident in the life of the prophet. The story is briefly told in some 40 verses. His prayer consumes the remaining eight verses. Some regard this book as an imaginative tale, akin to a modern "fish story." Others view Jonah as an allegory or parable, teaching God's universal love. However, the Jews accepted this book as reflecting the experience of the actual prophet Jonah. And Jesus' refers to Jonah (Matt. 12:38-41), substantiating that the book recounts actual events. Jonah's missionary message finds later parallels in the message of Peter (see Acts 10:1–11:18) and Paul (see Rom. 9–11). The theological emphases in Jonah are on God's universal love, sovereignty, and redemption, all equally applicable today.

PASSAGES FOR TOPICAL GROUP STUDY

1:1-17 . . . RUNNING FROM GOD . . . . Running Away
2:1–3:10. . OBEYING GOD . . . . A Big Fish Story
4:1-11 . . . SELF FOCUS and ANGER. . . To Pout or Not to Pout?

JONAH RUNS FROM THE LORD

1 The LORD gave this message to Jonah son of Amit-
tai: 2 "Get up and go to the great city of Nineveh.
Announce my judgment against it because I have
seen how wicked its people are."
3 But Jonah got up and went in the opposite direc-
tion to get away from the LORD. He went down to the
port of Joppa, where he found a ship leaving for Tar-
shish. He bought a ticket and went on board, hoping
to escape from the LORD by sailing to Tarshish.
4 But the LORD hurled a powerful wind over the sea,
causing a violent storm that threatened to break the
ship apart. 5 Fearing for their lives, the desperate sail-
ors shouted to their gods for help and threw the cargo
overboard to lighten the ship.
But all this time Jonah was sound asleep down in
the hold. 6 So the captain went down after him. "How
can you sleep at a time like this?" he shouted. "Get up
and pray to your god! Maybe he will pay attention to
us and spare our lives."
7 Then the crew cast lots to see which of them had
offended the gods and caused the terrible storm.
When they did this, the lots identified Jonah as the
culprit. 8 "Why has this awful storm come down on
us?" they demanded. "Who are you? What is your line
of work? What country are you from? What is your
nationality?"
9 Jonah answered, "I am a Hebrew, and I worship
the LORD, the God of heaven, who made the sea and
the land."
10 The sailors were terrified when they heard this, for
he had already told them he was running away from the
LORD. "Oh, why did you do it?" they groaned. 11 And since
the storm was getting worse all the time, they asked him,
"What should we do to you to stop this storm?"

RUNNING AWAY

1. Did you ever try to run away from home? How far did you get?

JONAH 1:1-17

2. Why did Jonah try to run away from God?
3. How did Jonah's disobedience endanger innocent people? In what way did the sailors, who didn't know God, act in a more godly way than Jonah?
4. When have you tried to run away from God? With what results?
5. When have you acted less godly than people who aren't even Christians? How did that damage God's reputation in your school or community?
6. How did God show grace toward Jonah? How has He shown grace toward you?

12 "Throw me into the sea," Jonah said, "and it will
become calm again. I know that this terrible storm is
all my fault."
13 Instead, the sailors rowed even harder to get the
ship to the land. But the stormy sea was too violent
for them, and they couldn't make it. 14 Then they cried
out to the LORD, Jonah's God. "O LORD," they pleaded,
"don't make us die for this man's sin. And don't hold
us responsible for his death. O LORD, you have sent
this storm upon him for your own good reasons."
15 Then the sailors picked Jonah up and threw him
into the raging sea, and the storm stopped at once!
16 The sailors were awestruck by the LORD's great
power, and they offered him a sacrifice and vowed to
serve him.
17* Now the LORD had arranged for a great fish to
swallow Jonah. And Jonah was inside the fish for
three days and three nights.

JONAH'S PRAYER

2 1* Then Jonah prayed to the LORD his God from in-
side the fish. 2 He said,

"I cried out to the LORD in my great trouble,
and he answered me.
I called to you from the land of the dead,*
and LORD, you heard me!
3 You threw me into the ocean depths,
and I sank down to the heart of the sea.
The mighty waters engulfed me;
I was buried beneath your wild and stormy
waves.
4 Then I said, 'O LORD, you have driven me from your
presence.
Yet I will look once more toward your holy
Temple.'

5 "I sank beneath the waves,
and the waters closed over me.
Seaweed wrapped itself around my head.
6 I sank down to the very roots of the mountains.
I was imprisoned in the earth,
whose gates lock shut forever.
But you, O LORD my God,
snatched me from the jaws of death!
7 As my life was slipping away,
I remembered the LORD.
And my earnest prayer went out to you
in your holy Temple.
8 Those who worship false gods
turn their backs on all God's mercies.
9 But I will offer sacrifices to you with songs of
praise,
and I will fulfill all my vows.
For my salvation comes from the LORD alone."

10 Then the LORD ordered the fish to spit Jonah out
onto the beach.

1:17 Verse 1:17 is numbered 2:1 in Hebrew text. **2:1** Verses 2:1-10 are numbered 2:2-11 in Hebrew text. **2:2** Hebrew *from Sheol.*

1:2 how wicked. Nineveh's wickedness is described in generic terms, but elsewhere we learn that they were "self-assured" (Zeph. 2:15), arrogantly declaring themselves to be invincible. Nahum later wrote that the city was brutal to war captives and full of prostitution, witchcraft, and idolatry (Nah. 3:1-4).

1:3 leaving for Tarshish. Many scholars locate this city in the south of Spain. It was the most distant place known to the Israelites in the opposite direction from Nineveh. Jonah was trying to get as far away from God's call as he could.

1:4 hurled a powerful wind over the sea. Jonah attempted unsuccessfully to run away from God's presence.

1:16 The sailors were awestruck. The pagan sailors who worshiped many gods could see that the God of Israel was more powerful. Note the contrast between Jonah's disobedience and the pagan sailors' respect for God.

2:9 all my vows. In response to God's salvation, Jonah made a vow to praise and obey God.

A BIG FISH STORY

1. What is the biggest fish you have ever caught?

JONAH 2:1–3:10

2. How did Jonah react when he found himself inside the belly of a fish? How does this demonstrate that God allowed this for Jonah's own good?
3. How did Nineveh respond when they heard God's commands? How did this compare with Jonah's response?
4. Why did God "relent" from the disaster He was going to send to Nineveh? What did He want from those people in the first place (3:10)?
5. Is God asking you for obedience in some area of your life? How are you responding?

JONAH GOES TO NINEVEH

3 Then the LORD spoke to Jonah a second time: 2 "Get
up and go to the great city of Nineveh, and deliver
the message I have given you."
3 This time Jonah obeyed the LORD's command and
went to Nineveh, a city so large that it took three days
to see it all.* 4 On the day Jonah entered the city, he
shouted to the crowds: "Forty days from now Nineveh
will be destroyed!" 5 The people of Nineveh believed
God's message, and from the greatest to the least, they
declared a fast and put on burlap to show their sorrow.
6 When the king of Nineveh heard what Jonah was
saying, he stepped down from his throne and took off
his royal robes. He dressed himself in burlap and sat
on a heap of ashes. 7 Then the king and his nobles sent
this decree throughout the city:

> "No one, not even the animals from your herds
> and flocks, may eat or drink anything at all.
> 8 People and animals alike must wear garments of
> mourning, and everyone must pray earnestly to
> God. They must turn from their evil ways and stop
> all their violence. 9 Who can tell? Perhaps even yet
> God will change his mind and hold back his fierce
> anger from destroying us."

10 When God saw what they had done and how they
had put a stop to their evil ways, he changed his mind
and did not carry out the destruction he had threatened.

JONAH'S ANGER AT THE LORD'S MERCY

4 This change of plans greatly upset Jonah, and
he became very angry. 2 So he complained to the
LORD about it: "Didn't I say before I left home that
you would do this, LORD? That is why I ran away to
Tarshish! I knew that you are a merciful and compassionate God, slow to get angry and filled with
unfailing love. You are eager to turn back from destroying people. 3 Just kill me now, LORD! I'd rather
be dead than alive if what I predicted will not happen."
4 The LORD replied, "Is it right for you to be angry
about this?"
5 Then Jonah went out to the east side of the city
and made a shelter to sit under as he waited to see
what would happen to the city. 6 And the LORD God
arranged for a leafy plant to grow there, and soon it
spread its broad leaves over Jonah's head, shading
him from the sun. This eased his discomfort, and Jonah was very grateful for the plant.
7 But God also arranged for a worm! The next
morning at dawn the worm ate through the stem of
the plant so that it withered away. 8 And as the sun
grew hot, God arranged for a scorching east wind to
blow on Jonah. The sun beat down on his head until
he grew faint and wished to die. "Death is certainly
better than living like this!" he exclaimed.
9 Then God said to Jonah, "Is it right for you to be
angry because the plant died?"
"Yes," Jonah retorted, "even angry enough to die!"
10 Then the LORD said, "You feel sorry about the
plant, though you did nothing to put it there. It came
quickly and died quickly. 11 But Nineveh has more
than 120,000 people living in spiritual darkness,* not
to mention all the animals. Shouldn't I feel sorry for
such a great city?"

TO POUT OR NOT TO POUT?

1. Who is your biggest rival in school sports? Would you be happy if God started to do a great work among the players on that team?

JONAH 4:1-11

2. Why was Jonah angry that God spared Nineveh? Why did he react by pouting?
3. Why did God create a plant to give Jonah shade and then kill the plant?
4. Summarize in your own words what God said to Jonah in verses 10 and 11.
5. In what situations do you sometimes care more about your own comfort and blessings than about other people—friends or rivals?

3:3 Hebrew *a great city to God, of three days' journey.* **4:11** Hebrew *people who don't know their right hand from their left.*

3:5 The people of Nineveh believed. Much to Jonah's astonishment, the Ninevites repented. People from all classes of society put on sackcloth as a symbol of repentance. Their repentance was short-lived, however, since they soon violently destroyed Israel.

3:9 Perhaps . . . God will change his mind. The king knew that Nineveh's future lay in God's hands. Repentance did not guarantee survival, however, because the final decision was up to God.

4:1 plans greatly upset Jonah. God's compassion on Nineveh angered Jonah. God should punish this evil city, Jonah surmised. He preached reluctantly, hoping that the obstinate Ninevites would get the punishment they deserved . . . with no mercy.

4:3 rather be dead than alive. Jonah was so disappointed in God's mercy to the Ninevites that he wanted to die. Perhaps he thought that Israel had lost its favored standing with God since Nineveh was such an enemy to Israel. Or he may have been embarrassed that his threats were not carried out.

4:10-11 You feel sorry about the plant, though you did nothing to put it there. God uses the vine to show Jonah how misplaced his affections were. Jonah did not truly care for the plant but only for the physical comfort it gave him. A gardener who cared for a plant would have reason to regret its loss. Likewise God, whose love extends to all people, had even more reason to show compassion on Nineveh. Jonah had to acknowledge God's missionary heart: repentance and salvation are for all people.

INTRODUCTION TO
MICAH

PERSONAL READING PLAN

☐Micah 1:1-16	☐Micah 3:1–4:5	☐Micah 6:1-16
☐Micah 2:1-13	☐Micah 4:6–5:15	☐Micah 7:1-20

AUTHOR

The author is identified as Micah, a contemporary of Isaiah and Hosea, who was probably from Moresheth-gath (1:14).

DATE

These prophecies were given during the reigns of Jotham, Ahaz, and Hezekiah (1:1)—kings of Judah who reigned *circa* 750–686 B.C. Since Micah predicted the fall of Israel's capital, Samaria (1:6-7), which occurred in *circa* 722 B.C., these prophecies would date from before that time.

THEME

A just and merciful God delivers His people from darkness. The lives of God's covenant people should reflect God's standards.

HISTORICAL BACKGROUND

It is helpful to understand the life and times during which Micah prophesied (1:1; see 2 Kings 15:32–20:21). During this dark time, when the sins of the northern kingdom of Israel were being punished by Assyrian invaders, Micah could see that these same activities (idolatry, Baal worship, child sacrifice, sorcery) were creeping south to Judah and Jerusalem. As in the northern kingdom, this led to an increasing gap between the rich and the poor. The poor were oppressed with no recourse in the courts because of corrupt judges, so Micah championed their cause. Religious life flourished but had little depth or reality. Micah draws a sharp contrast between this "pop religion" and true faith, which involves justice, faithfulness, and walking with God (6:8).

CHARACTERISTICS

Against this background, judgment is inevitable, says Micah. He stresses that God hates idolatry, injustice, rebellion, and empty ritualism. However, judgment will be followed by restoration, which will prepare the way for a new future. Micah emphasizes God's undeserved grace toward His people and His unstoppable initiative. Micah holds a long view of history, looking ahead several thousand years, and intersperses this futuristic view in his prophecies. One moment he is talking about the promised Messiah; in the next fragment of verses he may focus on the imminent invasion of Assyria. Reading these short speeches with their rapid shifts of focus can be confusing. Furthermore, the book of Micah shifts voices frequently—from God to Micah to the rebellious people and back again. Micah and Isaiah have similar literary styles. Both prophets use very descriptive language and many figures of speech. Micah also has a passion for punning, as seen in 1:10-15.

1 The LORD gave this message to Micah of Moresheth during the years when Jotham, Ahaz, and Hezekiah were kings of Judah. The visions he saw concerned both Samaria and Jerusalem.

GRIEF OVER SAMARIA AND JERUSALEM

2 Attention! Let all the people of the world listen!
Let the earth and everything in it hear.
The Sovereign LORD is making accusations against you;
the Lord speaks from his holy Temple.
3 Look! The LORD is coming!
He leaves his throne in heaven
and tramples the heights of the earth.
4 The mountains melt beneath his feet
and flow into the valleys
like wax in a fire,
like water pouring down a hill.
5 And why is this happening?
Because of the rebellion of Israel*—
yes, the sins of the whole nation.
Who is to blame for Israel's rebellion?
Samaria, its capital city!
Where is the center of idolatry in Judah?
In Jerusalem, its capital!

6 "So I, the LORD, will make the city of Samaria
a heap of ruins.
Her streets will be plowed up
for planting vineyards.
I will roll the stones of her walls into the valley below,
exposing her foundations.
7 All her carved images will be smashed.
All her sacred treasures will be burned.
These things were bought with the money
earned by her prostitution,
and they will now be carried away
to pay prostitutes elsewhere."

8 Therefore, I will mourn and lament.
I will walk around barefoot and naked.
I will howl like a jackal
and moan like an owl.
9 For my people's wound
is too deep to heal.
It has reached into Judah,
even to the gates of Jerusalem.

10 Don't tell our enemies in Gath*;
don't weep at all.
You people in Beth-leaphrah,*
roll in the dust to show your despair.
11 You people in Shaphir,*
go as captives into exile—naked and ashamed.
The people of Zaanan*
dare not come outside their walls.
The people of Beth-ezel* mourn,
for their house has no support.
12 The people of Maroth* anxiously wait for relief,
but only bitterness awaits them
as the LORD's judgment reaches
even to the gates of Jerusalem.

13 Harness your chariot horses and flee,
you people of Lachish.*
You were the first city in Judah
to follow Israel in her rebellion,
and you led Jerusalem* into sin.
14 Send farewell gifts to Moresheth-gath*;
there is no hope of saving it.
The town of Aczib*
has deceived the kings of Israel.
15 O people of Mareshah,*
I will bring a conqueror to capture your town.
And the leaders* of Israel
will go to Adullam.

16 Oh, people of Judah, shave your heads in sorrow,
for the children you love will be snatched away.
Make yourselves as bald as a vulture,
for your little ones will be exiled to distant lands.

JUDGMENT AGAINST WEALTHY OPPRESSORS

2 1 What sorrow awaits you who lie awake at night,
thinking up evil plans.
You rise at dawn and hurry to carry them out,
simply because you have the power to do so.
2 When you want a piece of land,
you find a way to seize it.
When you want someone's house,
you take it by fraud and violence.
You cheat a man of his property,
stealing his family's inheritance.

3 But this is what the LORD says:
"I will reward your evil with evil;
you won't be able to pull your neck out of the noose.
You will no longer walk around proudly,
for it will be a terrible time."

4 In that day your enemies will make fun of you
by singing this song of despair about you:
"We are finished,
completely ruined!
God has confiscated our land,
taking it from us.

1:5 Hebrew *Jacob;* also in 1:5b. The names "Jacob" and "Israel" are often interchanged throughout the Old Testament, referring sometimes to the individual patriarch and sometimes to the nation. **1:10a** *Gath* sounds like the Hebrew term for "tell." **1:10b** *Beth-leaphrah* means "house of dust." **1:11a** *Shaphir* means "pleasant." **1:11b** *Zaanan* sounds like the Hebrew term for "come out." **1:11c** *Beth-ezel* means "adjoining house." **1:12** *Maroth* sounds like the Hebrew term for "bitter." **1:13a** *Lachish* sounds like the Hebrew term for "team of horses." **1:13b** Hebrew *the daughter of Zion.* **1:14a** *Moresheth* sounds like the Hebrew term for "gift" or "dowry." **1:14b** *Aczib* means "deception." **1:15a** *Mareshah* sounds like the Hebrew term for "conqueror." **1:15b** Hebrew *the glory.* **2:4** Or *to those who took us captive.*

1:1 Samaria and Jerusalem. The capitals of the northern kingdom (Israel) and the southern kingdom (Judah) represent all 12 tribes of Israel.

1:2-7 The prophet's synopsis urges all nations to hear God's judgment against them (v. 2), God's punishment (vv. 3-4), the reason (v. 5), and its results (vv. 6-7).

1:3 the heights of the earth. A common phrase for idol worship sites, this refers to Jerusalem and Samaria's mountain locations.

1:6-7 Micah saw this prophecy fulfilled in 722 B.C. when the Assyrians captured Samaria (2 Kings 17:6).

1:11 Shaphir. The name Shaphir meant "beautiful or pleasant," but the town would soon be naked and ashamed, not beautiful. Nakedness here suggests captives with nowhere to hide.

2:2-3 you want. The people would certainly perish because of their violation of the 10th commandment.

He has given our fields
to those who betrayed us.'"
5 Others will set your boundaries then,
and the LORD's people will have no say
in how the land is divided.

TRUE AND FALSE PROPHETS

6 "Don't say such things,"
the people respond.*
"Don't prophesy like that.
Such disasters will never come our way!"

7 Should you talk that way, O family of Israel?*
Will the LORD's Spirit have patience with such
behavior?
If you would do what is right,
you would find my words comforting.
8 Yet to this very hour
my people rise against me like an enemy!
You steal the shirts right off the backs
of those who trusted you,
making them as ragged as men
returning from battle.
9 You have evicted women from their pleasant homes
and forever stripped their children of all that
God would give them.
10 Up! Begone!
This is no longer your land and home,
for you have filled it with sin
and ruined it completely.

11 Suppose a prophet full of lies would say to you,
"I'll preach to you the joys of wine and alcohol!"
That's just the kind of prophet you would like!

HOPE FOR RESTORATION

12 "Someday, O Israel, I will gather you;
I will gather the remnant who are left.
I will bring you together again like sheep in a pen,
like a flock in its pasture.
Yes, your land will again
be filled with noisy crowds!
13 Your leader will break out
and lead you out of exile,
out through the gates of the enemy cities,
back to your own land.
Your king will lead you;
the LORD himself will guide you."

JUDGMENT AGAINST ISRAEL'S LEADERS

3 1 I said, "Listen, you leaders of Israel!
You are supposed to know right from wrong,
2 but you are the very ones
who hate good and love evil.
You skin my people alive
and tear the flesh from their bones.
3 Yes, you eat my people's flesh,
strip off their skin,
and break their bones.
You chop them up
like meat for the cooking pot.
4 Then you beg the LORD for help in times of trouble!
Do you really expect him to answer?
After all the evil you have done,
he won't even look at you!"

5 This is what the LORD says:
"You false prophets are leading my people
astray!
You promise peace for those who give you food,
but you declare war on those who refuse to feed
you.
6 Now the night will close around you,
cutting off all your visions.
Darkness will cover you,
putting an end to your predictions.
The sun will set for you prophets,
and your day will come to an end.
7 Then you seers will be put to shame,
and you fortune-tellers will be disgraced.
And you will cover your faces
because there is no answer from God."

8 But as for me, I am filled with power—
with the Spirit of the LORD.
I am filled with justice and strength
to boldly declare Israel's sin and rebellion.
9 Listen to me, you leaders of Israel!
You hate justice and twist all that is right.
10 You are building Jerusalem
on a foundation of murder and corruption.
11 You rulers make decisions based on bribes;
you priests teach God's laws only for a price;
you prophets won't prophesy unless you are paid.
Yet all of you claim to depend on the LORD.
"No harm can come to us," you say,
"for the LORD is here among us."
12 Because of you, Mount Zion will be plowed like an
open field;
Jerusalem will be reduced to ruins!
A thicket will grow on the heights
where the Temple now stands.

THE LORD'S FUTURE REIGN

4 1 In the last days, the mountain of the LORD's
house
will be the highest of all—
the most important place on earth.
It will be raised above the other hills,
and people from all over the world will stream
there to worship.
2 People from many nations will come and say,
"Come, let us go up to the mountain of the LORD,
to the house of Jacob's God.
There he will teach us his ways,
and we will walk in his paths."

2:6 Or *the prophets respond;* Hebrew reads *they prophesy.* 2:7 Hebrew *O house of Jacob?* See note on 1:5a.

2:6-7 False prophets, believing God incapable of anger against His people, urged Micah not to prophesy judgment.
2:11 wine and alcohol. Like his contemporaries, Isaiah (5:11-12, 22; 28:7-8; 56:12) and Amos (4:1; 6:4-6), Micah speaks against excess as demonstrated by the affluent's overindulgence of wine and beer. He mocks them for even applauding prophets who praise the virtues of their favorite vices. Such prophets become drunk themselves (Isa. 28:7; Amos 2:12). Other sages go further in denunciating the disadvantages of such vices (Prov. 20:1; 21:17; 23:20-21,29-35; 31:4-7). Such is the folly of rejecting God's Word.
2:12-13 remnant. God will keep His covenant promises to Abraham and will gather and bless a remnant of Israel (Isa. 1:9; 4:3).
3:1-3 leaders of Israel. In Micah's words, their leaders were like hunters devouring their own people.
4:1-8 Micah prophesies that in the last days God will exalt Jerusalem as the center of Christ's rule. God will keep His promise to bless the world through Israel.

For the LORD's teaching will go out from Zion;
his word will go out from Jerusalem.
3 The LORD will mediate between peoples
and will settle disputes between strong nations far away.
They will hammer their swords into plowshares
and their spears into pruning hooks.
Nation will no longer fight against nation,
nor train for war anymore.
4 Everyone will live in peace and prosperity,
enjoying their own grapevines and fig trees,
for there will be nothing to fear.
The LORD of Heaven's Armies
has made this promise!
5 Though the nations around us follow their idols,
we will follow the LORD our God forever and ever.

ISRAEL'S RETURN FROM EXILE

6 "In that coming day," says the LORD,
"I will gather together those who are lame,
those who have been exiles,
and those whom I have filled with grief.
7 Those who are weak will survive as a remnant;
those who were exiles will become a strong nation.
Then I, the LORD, will rule from Jerusalem*
as their king forever."
8 As for you, Jerusalem,
the citadel of God's people,*
your royal might and power
will come back to you again.
The kingship will be restored
to my precious Jerusalem.

9 But why are you now screaming in terror?
Have you no king to lead you?
Have your wise people all died?
Pain has gripped you like a woman in childbirth.
10 Writhe and groan like a woman in labor,
you people of Jerusalem,*
for now you must leave this city
to live in the open country.
You will soon be sent in exile
to distant Babylon.
But the LORD will rescue you there;
he will redeem you from the grip of your enemies.

11 Now many nations have gathered against you.
"Let her be desecrated," they say.
"Let us see the destruction of Jerusalem.*"
12 But they do not know the LORD's thoughts
or understand his plan.
These nations don't know
that he is gathering them together
to be beaten and trampled
like sheaves of grain on a threshing floor.
13 "Rise up and crush the nations, O Jerusalem!"*
says the LORD.
"For I will give you iron horns and bronze hooves,
so you can trample many nations to pieces.
You will present their stolen riches to the LORD,
their wealth to the Lord of all the earth."

5 1*Mobilize! Marshal your troops!
The enemy is laying siege to Jerusalem.
They will strike Israel's leader
in the face with a rod.

A RULER FROM BETHLEHEM

2*But you, O Bethlehem Ephrathah,
are only a small village among all the people of Judah.
Yet a ruler of Israel,
whose origins are in the distant past,
will come from you on my behalf.
3 The people of Israel will be abandoned to their enemies
until the woman in labor gives birth.
Then at last his fellow countrymen
will return from exile to their own land.
4 And he will stand to lead his flock with the LORD's strength,
in the majesty of the name of the LORD his God.
Then his people will live there undisturbed,
for he will be highly honored around the world.
5 And he will be the source of peace.

When the Assyrians invade our land
and break through our defenses,
we will appoint seven rulers to watch over us,
eight princes to lead us.
6 They will rule Assyria with drawn swords
and enter the gates of the land of Nimrod.
He will rescue us from the Assyrians
when they pour over the borders to invade our land.

THE REMNANT PURIFIED

7 Then the remnant left in Israel*
will take their place among the nations.
They will be like dew sent by the LORD
or like rain falling on the grass,
which no one can hold back
and no one can restrain.
8 The remnant left in Israel
will take their place among the nations.
They will be like a lion among the animals of the forest,

4:7 Hebrew *Mount Zion.* **4:8** Hebrew *As for you, Migdal-eder, / the Ophel of the daughter of Zion.* **4:10** Hebrew *O daughter of Zion.* **4:11** Hebrew *of Zion.* **4:13** Hebrew *"Rise up and thresh, O daughter of Zion."* **5:1** Verse 5:1 is numbered 4:14 in Hebrew text. **5:2** Verses 5:2-15 are numbered 5:1-14 in Hebrew text. **5:7** Hebrew *in Jacob;* also in 5:8. See note on 1:5a.

4:4 their own grapevines. Grapevines symbolize harvests in times of peace and security.

4:7 Those who are weak. Micah contrasts those who walk after foreign gods (v. 5) with the Israelites who know their weakness (lameness) and dependency on Yahweh. Though Israel is spiritually lame and faces exile, God will save a remnant to rebuild a strong nation under His rule.

4:9-13 Verses 9 and 10 may reflect Isaiah's rebuke of Hezekiah for showing the Babylonian king his treasure in 705 B.C. (2 Kings 20; Isa. 39), an action which eventually resulted in the Babylonian exile in 586 B.C. The Lord's lifting of the Assyrian siege of Jerusalem in 701 B.C. (vv. 11-13) was a postponement of Jerusalem's destruction due to Hezekiah's prior repentance (2 Kings 19; Jer. 26:17-19).

5:2 Bethlehem. This prophecy of Christ's coming was used by the wise men as a guide to find Jesus (see also Matt. 2:1-6).

5:7 the remnant of Jacob. Micah goes into elaborate detail, describing the restoration and refreshment of believing Israelites who will take their rightful place over the enemies of God. Israel will then be all that God intended.

5:8-9 Like a lion who fears no other animal, the remnant of Israel will dominate other nations. Jesus is also called the Lion of Judah.

like a strong young lion among flocks of sheep
and goats,
pouncing and tearing as they go
with no rescuer in sight.
9 The people of Israel will stand up to their foes,
and all their enemies will be wiped out.

10 "In that day," says the LORD,
"I will slaughter your horses
and destroy your chariots.
11 I will tear down your walls
and demolish your defenses.
12 I will put an end to all witchcraft,
and there will be no more fortune-tellers.
13 I will destroy all your idols and sacred pillars,
so you will never again worship the work of
your own hands.
14 I will abolish your idol shrines with their Asherah
poles
and destroy your pagan cities.
15 I will pour out my vengeance
on all the nations that refuse to obey me."

THE LORD'S CASE AGAINST ISRAEL

6 Listen to what the LORD is saying:

"Stand up and state your case against me.
Let the mountains and hills be called to witness
your complaints.
2 And now, O mountains,
listen to the LORD's complaint!
He has a case against his people.
He will bring charges against Israel.

3 "O my people, what have I done to you?
What have I done to make you tired of me?
Answer me!
4 For I brought you out of Egypt
and redeemed you from slavery.
I sent Moses, Aaron, and Miriam to help you.
5 Don't you remember, my people,
how King Balak of Moab tried to have you
cursed
and how Balaam son of Beor blessed you
instead?
And remember your journey from Acacia Grove*
to Gilgal,
when I, the LORD, did everything I could
to teach you about my faithfulness."

6 What can we bring to the LORD?
Should we bring him burnt offerings?
Should we bow before God Most High
with offerings of yearling calves?
7 Should we offer him thousands of rams
and ten thousand rivers of olive oil?
Should we sacrifice our firstborn children
to pay for our sins?
8 No, O people, the LORD has told you what is good,
and this is what he requires of you:
to do what is right, to love mercy,
and to walk humbly with your God.

ISRAEL'S GUILT AND PUNISHMENT

9 Fear the LORD if you are wise!
His voice calls to everyone in Jerusalem:
"The armies of destruction are coming;
the LORD is sending them.*
10 What shall I say about the homes of the wicked
filled with treasures gained by cheating?
What about the disgusting practice
of measuring out grain with dishonest
measures?*
11 How can I tolerate your merchants
who use dishonest scales and weights?
12 The rich among you have become wealthy
through extortion and violence.
Your citizens are so used to lying
that their tongues can no longer tell the truth.

13 "Therefore, I will wound you!
I will bring you to ruin for all your sins.
14 You will eat but never have enough.
Your hunger pangs and emptiness will remain.
And though you try to save your money,
it will come to nothing in the end.
You will save a little,
but I will give it to those who conquer you.
15 You will plant crops
but not harvest them.
You will press your olives
but not get enough oil to anoint yourselves.
You will trample the grapes
but get no juice to make your wine.
16 You keep only the laws of evil King Omri;
you follow only the example of wicked King
Ahab!
Therefore, I will make an example of you,
bringing you to complete ruin.
You will be treated with contempt,
mocked by all who see you."

MISERY TURNED TO HOPE

7 1 How miserable I am!
I feel like the fruit picker after the harvest
who can find nothing to eat.
Not a cluster of grapes or a single early fig
can be found to satisfy my hunger.
2 The godly people have all disappeared;
not one honest person is left on the earth.
They are all murderers,
setting traps even for their own brothers.
3 Both their hands are equally skilled at doing evil!
Officials and judges alike demand bribes.
The people with influence get what they want,
and together they scheme to twist justice.

6:5 Hebrew *Shittim.* **6:9** Hebrew *"Listen to the rod. / Who appointed it?"* **6:10** Hebrew *of using the short ephah?* The ephah was a unit for measuring grain.

5:10-11 slaughter your horses. God will remove Israel's self-reliance. He will take away their military hardware and any other idols that keep them from depending upon Him.

6:4 out of Egypt. The prophets frequently reminded Israel of this deliverance (7:15; Hosea 2:15; 13:4; Amos 2:10; 3:1).

6:6-8 Micah asks what the people can do to regain God's favor. Then he answers his own question: God desires obedience that offers justice and mercy toward others and to humbly fellowship with Him. (See also 1 Sam. 15:22; Isa. 1:11-15.)

6:16 laws of evil King Omri . . . example of wicked King Ahab. These were the worst kings of the northern kingdom; they ruled by idolatry and cruel violence.

7:2 godly people have all disappeared. While Israelites thought they were obeying God, they held their own definitions of obedience, not those in Scripture. Godly people were as rare as summer fruit after the harvest.

4 Even the best of them is like a brier;
the most honest is as dangerous as a hedge of thorns.
But your judgment day is coming swiftly now.
Your time of punishment is here, a time of confusion.
5 Don't trust anyone—
not your best friend or even your wife!
6 For the son despises his father.
The daughter defies her mother.
The daughter-in-law defies her mother-in-law.
Your enemies are right in your own household!

7 As for me, I look to the LORD for help.
I wait confidently for God to save me,
and my God will certainly hear me.
8 Do not gloat over me, my enemies!
For though I fall, I will rise again.
Though I sit in darkness,
the LORD will be my light.
9 I will be patient as the LORD punishes me,
for I have sinned against him.
But after that, he will take up my case
and give me justice for all I have suffered from my enemies.
The LORD will bring me into the light,
and I will see his righteousness.
10 Then my enemies will see that the LORD is on my side.
They will be ashamed that they taunted me, saying,
"So where is the LORD—
that God of yours?"
With my own eyes I will see their downfall;
they will be trampled like mud in the streets.

11 In that day, Israel, your cities will be rebuilt,
and your borders will be extended.
12 People from many lands will come and honor you—
from Assyria all the way to the towns of Egypt,
from Egypt all the way to the Euphrates River,*
and from distant seas and mountains.
13 But the land* will become empty and desolate
because of the wickedness of those who live there.

THE LORD'S COMPASSION ON ISRAEL

14 O LORD, protect your people with your shepherd's staff;
lead your flock, your special possession.
Though they live alone in a thicket
on the heights of Mount Carmel,*
let them graze in the fertile pastures of Bashan and Gilead
as they did long ago.

15 "Yes," says the LORD,
"I will do mighty miracles for you,
like those I did when I rescued you
from slavery in Egypt."

16 All the nations of the world will stand amazed
at what the LORD will do for you.
They will be embarrassed
at their feeble power.
They will cover their mouths in silent awe,
deaf to everything around them.
17 Like snakes crawling from their holes,
they will come out to meet the LORD our God.
They will fear him greatly,
trembling in terror at his presence.

18 Where is another God like you,
who pardons the guilt of the remnant,
overlooking the sins of his special people?
You will not stay angry with your people forever,
because you delight in showing unfailing love.
19 Once again you will have compassion on us.
You will trample our sins under your feet
and throw them into the depths of the ocean!
20 You will show us your faithfulness and unfailing love
as you promised to our ancestors Abraham and Jacob long ago.

7:12 Hebrew *the river.* **7:13** Or *earth.* **7:14** Or *surrounded by a fruitful land.*

7:7 As for me. In contrast to the prophets who watched for judgment on a corrupt nation overseen by corrupt officials (vv. 1-6), Micah and the remnant "watch" for their future deliverance and salvation (vv. 8-16). God keeps both promises: the nation is judged, but its faithful are saved.

7:15-17 Micah's hope for the salvation of Israel rests on the promise of a Messiah. When Christ comes, He will return Israel to her land. Nations will see this deliverance and be overwhelmed by fear of the Lord.

7:20 faithfulness. God's deliverance is certain because of the covenant with Jacob and Abraham (Gen. 22:17). God will bless their descendants and fulfill His promise of blessing (Gen. 17:5).

INTRODUCTION TO

NAHUM

PERSONAL READING PLAN

☐Nahum 1:1-15 ☐Nahum 2:1-13 ☐Nahum 3:1-19

Nahum, "the Elkoshite," was probably from Judah. Nahum means "comfort" and is related to the name Nehemiah, meaning "The Lord comforts."

DATE

Nahum's oracle is dated between the overthrow of Thebes (in 663 B.C.; see 3:8-10) and the fall of Nineveh (in 612 B.C.). It is perhaps near the end of this period since he prophesies the fall of Nineveh as imminent (2:1; 3:14,19). This would place Nahum during the reign of Josiah and make him a contemporary of Zephaniah and a young Jeremiah.

THEME

The Lord's judgment of Nineveh.

HISTORICAL BACKGROUND

The northern kingdom of Israel had fallen to the Assyrians *circa* 722 B.C. The Assyrians were brutally cruel, their kings often pictured as gloating over the gruesome punishments inflicted on conquered peoples. No wonder the fear and dread of Assyria fell on all her neighbors! About 700 B.C., the Assyrian king Sennacherib made Nineveh, which was the greatest city of its day, the capital of the empire. Jonah had announced Nineveh's doom, but the people repented and were given a "stay of execution" (see the Introduction to Jonah). However, they quickly returned to their evil ways. Poetic justice and Nineveh's destruction is the focus of Nahum's prophecy. Within a few years, Nahum's prophecies came true. Proud Nineveh fell so hard that it never rose again. The site of the city was obliterated; it was only rediscovered some 2,500 years later!

CHARACTERISTICS

Like Obadiah, but unlike the other minor prophets, Nahum does not address his homeland at all but a foreign city—Nineveh. Still, the book was intended for Jewish readers. While the style of Nahum is that of traditional judgment oracles, the language is poetic, with many metaphors and similes as well as other vivid images. Each of the three chapters in Nahum is a complete unit in itself. Chapter 1 is in the form of a poem in which Nahum declares the judgment that is to come. Chapter 2 describes the siege and subsequent sack of Nineveh. In chapter 3, Nineveh is described and compared to Thebes. Thebes, the capital of Upper Egypt, was a city like Nineveh that was strong and proud, and yet its destruction had come. Thus Nahum shows that the God of Israel is, in fact, the God who controls the fate of all the nations. Nahum's purpose is to lift up the great God of Israel and thus bring comfort to his people. This book is a powerful indictment of a nation that seeks glory by aggression and oppression. The God of Israel hates violence and pride, and "he never lets the guilty go unpunished" (1:3).

1 This message concerning Nineveh came as a vision to Nahum, who lived in Elkosh.

THE LORD'S ANGER AGAINST NINEVEH

2 The LORD is a jealous God,
filled with vengeance and rage.
He takes revenge on all who oppose him
and continues to rage against his enemies!
3 The LORD is slow to get angry, but his power is great,
and he never lets the guilty go unpunished.
He displays his power in the whirlwind and the storm.
The billowing clouds are the dust beneath his feet.
4 At his command the oceans dry up,
and the rivers disappear.
The lush pastures of Bashan and Carmel fade,
and the green forests of Lebanon wither.
5 In his presence the mountains quake,
and the hills melt away;
the earth trembles,
and its people are destroyed.
6 Who can stand before his fierce anger?
Who can survive his burning fury?
His rage blazes forth like fire,
and the mountains crumble to dust in his presence.

7 The LORD is good,
a strong refuge when trouble comes.
He is close to those who trust in him.
8 But he will sweep away his enemies*
in an overwhelming flood.
He will pursue his foes
into the darkness of night.
9 Why are you scheming against the LORD?
He will destroy you with one blow;
he won't need to strike twice!
10 His enemies, tangled like thornbushes
and staggering like drunks,
will be burned up like dry stubble in a field.
11 Who is this wicked counselor of yours
who plots evil against the LORD?

12 This is what the LORD says:
"Though the Assyrians have many allies,
they will be destroyed and disappear.
O my people, I have punished you before,
but I will not punish you again.
13 Now I will break the yoke of bondage from your neck
and tear off the chains of Assyrian oppression."

14 And this is what the LORD says concerning the Assyrians in Nineveh:
"You will have no more children to carry on your name.
I will destroy all the idols in the temples of your gods.
I am preparing a grave for you
because you are despicable!"

15*Look! A messenger is coming over the mountains
with good news!
He is bringing a message of peace.
Celebrate your festivals, O people of Judah,
and fulfill all your vows,
for your wicked enemies will never invade your land again.
They will be completely destroyed!

THE FALL OF NINEVEH

2 1*Your enemy is coming to crush you, Nineveh.
Man the ramparts! Watch the roads!
Prepare your defenses! Call out your forces!

2 Even though the destroyer has destroyed Judah,
the LORD will restore its honor.
Israel's vine has been stripped of branches,
but he will restore its splendor.

3 Shields flash red in the sunlight!
See the scarlet uniforms of the valiant troops!
Watch as their glittering chariots move into position,
with a forest of spears waving above them.*
4 The chariots race recklessly along the streets
and rush wildly through the squares.
They flash like firelight
and move as swiftly as lightning.
5 The king shouts to his officers;
they stumble in their haste,
rushing to the walls to set up their defenses.
6 The river gates have been torn open!
The palace is about to collapse!
7 Nineveh's exile has been decreed,
and all the servant girls mourn its capture.
They moan like doves
and beat their breasts in sorrow.
8 Nineveh is like a leaking water reservoir!
The people are slipping away.
"Stop, stop!" someone shouts,
but no one even looks back.
9 Loot the silver!
Plunder the gold!
There's no end to Nineveh's treasures—
its vast, uncounted wealth.
10 Soon the city is plundered, empty, and ruined.
Hearts melt and knees shake.
The people stand aghast,
their faces pale and trembling.

11 Where now is that great Nineveh,
that den filled with young lions?

1:8 As in Greek version; Hebrew reads *sweep away her place.* **1:15** Verse 1:15 is numbered 2:1 in Hebrew text. **2:1** Verses 2:1-13 are numbered 2:2-14 in Hebrew text. **2:3** Greek and Syriac versions read *into position, / the horses whipped into a frenzy.*

1:3 slow to get angry. The vengeance described in verse 2 is slow in coming. God withholds judgment to give the people a chance to repent. Similarly, the Lord had previously sent Jonah to Nineveh to urge its people to repent.
1:15 A messenger . . . with good news. Nahum speaks of one who brings news of deliverance from Assyria. In Isaiah 52:7, this phrase is used of one who brings news of deliverance from exile in Babylon. Paul uses this phrase in Romans 10:15 to refer to those who tell about Christ and the good news of salvation.
2:3-4 Shields . . . uniforms . . . chariots. The equipment and speed of Assyria's attackers are described. Red may have been the color of the attackers' shields and armor or a reference to blood on them from battle. Their chariots and swords move like lightning as they approach the city for battle.
2:8 like a leaking water reservoir. With their city flooded by attackers, Ninevites would flee, leaving their possessions behind to be plundered. They would flee in panic as rapidly as water flowed out of a tank.
2:11-12 den filled with young lions. Using the metaphor of a lion's pride, Nahum taunts Assyria. They had fought as brutally as a lion hunting for his lioness and cubs. Yet now their capital, or lions' lair, was wasted by war.

It was a place where people—like lions and their
cubs—
walked freely and without fear.
12 The lion tore up meat for his cubs
and strangled prey for his mate.
He filled his den with prey,
his caverns with his plunder.

13 "I am your enemy!"
says the LORD of Heaven's Armies.
"Your chariots will soon go up in smoke.
Your young men* will be killed in battle.
Never again will you plunder conquered nations.
The voices of your proud messengers will be
heard no more."

THE LORD'S JUDGMENT AGAINST NINEVEH

3 1 What sorrow awaits Nineveh,
the city of murder and lies!
She is crammed with wealth
and is never without victims.
2 Hear the crack of whips,
the rumble of wheels!
Horses' hooves pound,
and chariots clatter wildly.
3 See the flashing swords and glittering spears
as the charioteers charge past!
There are countless casualties,
heaps of bodies—
so many bodies that
people stumble over them.
4 All this because Nineveh,
the beautiful and faithless city,
mistress of deadly charms,
enticed the nations with her beauty.
She taught them all her magic,
enchanting people everywhere.

5 "I am your enemy!"
says the LORD of Heaven's Armies.
"And now I will lift your skirts
and show all the earth your nakedness and
shame.
6 I will cover you with filth
and show the world how vile you really are.
7 All who see you will shrink back and say,
'Nineveh lies in ruins.
Where are the mourners?'
Does anyone regret your destruction?"

8 Are you any better than the city of Thebes,*
situated on the Nile River, surrounded by
water?
She was protected by the river on all sides,
walled in by water.
9 Ethiopia* and the land of Egypt
gave unlimited assistance.
The nations of Put and Libya
were among her allies.
10 Yet Thebes fell,
and her people were led away as captives.
Her babies were dashed to death
against the stones of the streets.
Soldiers threw dice* to get Egyptian officers as
servants.
All their leaders were bound in chains.

11 And you, Nineveh, will also stagger like a
drunkard.
You will hide for fear of the attacking enemy.
12 All your fortresses will fall.
They will be devoured like the ripe figs
that fall into the mouths
of those who shake the trees.
13 Your troops will be as weak
and helpless as women.
The gates of your land will be opened wide to the
enemy
and set on fire and burned.
14 Get ready for the siege!
Store up water!
Strengthen the defenses!
Go into the pits to trample clay,
and pack it into molds,
making bricks to repair the walls.

15 But the fire will devour you;
the sword will cut you down.
The enemy will consume you like locusts,
devouring everything they see.
There will be no escape,
even if you multiply like swarming locusts.
16 Your merchants have multiplied
until they outnumber the stars.
But like a swarm of locusts,
they strip the land and fly away.
17 Your guards* and officials are also like swarming
locusts
that crowd together in the hedges on a cold day.
But like locusts that fly away when the sun comes
up,
all of them will fly away and disappear.

18 Your shepherds are asleep, O Assyrian king;
your princes lie dead in the dust.
Your people are scattered across the mountains
with no one to gather them together.
19 There is no healing for your wound;
your injury is fatal.
All who hear of your destruction
will clap their hands for joy.
Where can anyone be found
who has not suffered from your continual
cruelty?

2:13 Hebrew *young lions.* **3:8** Hebrew *No-amon;* also in 3:10. **3:9** Hebrew *Cush.* **3:10** Hebrew *They cast lots.* **3:17** Or *princes.*

3:4 enticed nations with her beauty. Nineveh had lusted for power it didn't deserve just as a harlot lusts for men. They sold their military services to gain control over other nations. This may also be a reference to Nineveh's goddess of sex and war.

3:7 Nineveh lies in ruins. On Nineveh's judgment day, she would lie in ruins with no one to comfort her. The atrocities committed by the people of Nineveh would catch up with them.

3:15 multiply like swarming locusts. This is a command to the Ninevites to increase their numbers so they can defend themselves against inevitable attack.

3:16 they strip the land. The merchants (locusts), who were once numerous in Nineveh, would strip the land until it had no more wealth.

3:17 locusts. The leaders in the city exploited Nineveh like locusts devouring a crop. But during Nineveh's destruction, they would panic and flee overnight.

INTRODUCTION TO

HABAKKUK

PERSONAL READING PLAN

☐Habakkuk 1:1-11
☐Habakkuk 1:12–2:1
☐Habakkuk 2:2-20
☐Habakkuk 3:1-19

AUTHOR

The book was written by the prophet Habakkuk, a contemporary of Jeremiah. He was a man of deep faith and rooted in the religious traditions of Israel.

DATE

Habakkuk was written in the latter part of the seventh century B.C., probably *circa* 610–605 B.C. Habakkuk, like Jeremiah, probably lived to see the beginning of the fulfillment of his prophecy when Jerusalem was attacked by the Babylonians in 597 B.C.

THEME

Faith triumphs over doubt. Habakkuk wrestles with a problem that faces every age: Why does God seem inactive in the face of evil and injustice?

HISTORICAL BACKGROUND

The northern kingdom (Israel) had fallen to Assyria *circa* 722 B.C., and now the rising Chaldean Empire (i.e., the second Babylonian Empire) was threatening on the horizon. In Habakkuk's day, the rulers of the southern kingdom (Judah) were known to "do what was evil in the Lord's sight" (see 2 Kings 23:31–24:7). As an agent of judgment in God's hand, the Chaldeans invaded Judah in 605 B.C. The king of Babylon, Nebuchadnezzar, made the Judean king, Jehoiakim, his vassal or puppet ruler. Chapters 1 and 2 of Habakkuk are historically rooted in the events preceding and following the 605 B.C. invasion under Nebuchadnezzar's leadership. While 3:1 contains Habakkuk's name, it is less certain whether this chapter should be dated at the time of the invasion or later in the prophet's life.

CHARACTERISTICS

Habakkuk is unusual in that it contains no prophecy directed to Israel. Instead, it is a dialogue between the prophet and God. The book shares some of the structural and thematic traits of the psalms of lament (e.g. Pss. 13; 44; 74; 80). Complaint and petition are followed by the divine perspective on the problem. Like the psalmist, Habakkuk uses stark poetic images to color and convey his message. Like the psalmist, and unlike all other prophets (who mostly speak on God's behalf to the people), Habakkuk speaks for himself and on behalf of his people directly and only to God. Like Job, he receives no answer except that God is God. God is holy, does care, and will act as He sees fit but only in His time.

Habakkuk 2:4—"the righteous will live by their faithfulness"—is quoted by several New Testament authors who use it in speaking of faith (see Rom. 1:17; Gal. 3:11; Heb. 10:38). The book of Habakkuk was popular during the time between the Old and New Testaments. A complete commentary on its first two chapters has been found among the Dead Sea Scrolls.

1 This is the message that the prophet Habakkuk received in a vision.

HABAKKUK'S COMPLAINT

2 How long, O LORD, must I call for help?
But you do not listen!
"Violence is everywhere!" I cry,
but you do not come to save.
3 Must I forever see these evil deeds?
Why must I watch all this misery?
Wherever I look,
I see destruction and violence.
I am surrounded by people
who love to argue and fight.
4 The law has become paralyzed,
and there is no justice in the courts.
The wicked far outnumber the righteous,
so that justice has become perverted.

THE LORD'S REPLY

5 The LORD replied,

"Look around at the nations;
look and be amazed!*
For I am doing something in your own day,
something you wouldn't believe
even if someone told you about it.
6 I am raising up the Babylonians,*
a cruel and violent people.
They will march across the world
and conquer other lands.
7 They are notorious for their cruelty
and do whatever they like.
8 Their horses are swifter than cheetahs*
and fiercer than wolves at dusk.
Their charioteers charge from far away.
Like eagles, they swoop down to devour their prey.

9 "On they come, all bent on violence.
Their hordes advance like a desert wind,
sweeping captives ahead of them like sand.
10 They scoff at kings and princes
and scorn all their fortresses.
They simply pile ramps of earth
against their walls and capture them!
11 They sweep past like the wind
and are gone.
But they are deeply guilty,
for their own strength is their god."

HABAKKUK'S SECOND COMPLAINT

12 O LORD my God, my Holy One, you who are eternal—
surely you do not plan to wipe us out?
O LORD, our Rock, you have sent these Babylonians
to correct us,
to punish us for our many sins.
13 But you are pure and cannot stand the sight of evil.
Will you wink at their treachery?
Should you be silent while the wicked
swallow up people more righteous than they?

14 Are we only fish to be caught and killed?
Are we only sea creatures that have no leader?
15 Must we be strung up on their hooks
and caught in their nets while they rejoice and celebrate?
16 Then they will worship their nets
and burn incense in front of them.
"These nets are the gods who have made us rich!"
they will claim.
17 Will you let them get away with this forever?
Will they succeed forever in their heartless conquests?

2 1 I will climb up to my watchtower
and stand at my guardpost.
There I will wait to see what the LORD says
and how he* will answer my complaint.

THE LORD'S SECOND REPLY

2 Then the LORD said to me,

"Write my answer plainly on tablets,
so that a runner can carry the correct message to others.
3 This vision is for a future time.
It describes the end, and it will be fulfilled.
If it seems slow in coming, wait patiently,
for it will surely take place.
It will not be delayed.

4 "Look at the proud!
They trust in themselves, and their lives are crooked.
But the righteous will live by their faithfulness to God.*
5 Wealth* is treacherous,
and the arrogant are never at rest.
They open their mouths as wide as the grave,*
and like death, they are never satisfied.
In their greed they have gathered up many nations
and swallowed many peoples.

6 "But soon their captives will taunt them.
They will mock them, saying,
'What sorrow awaits you thieves!
Now you will get what you deserve!

1:5 Greek version reads *Look, you mockers; / look and be amazed and die.* Compare Acts 13:41. 1:6 Or *Chaldeans.* 1:8 Or *leopards.* 2:1 As in Syriac version; Hebrew reads *I.* 2:3b-4 Greek version reads *If the vision is delayed, wait patiently, / for it will surely come and not delay. / 4I will take no pleasure in anyone who turns away. / But the righteous person will live by my faith.* Compare Rom 1:17; Gal 3:11; Heb 10:37-38. 2:5a As in Dead Sea Scroll 1QpHab; other Hebrew manuscripts read *Wine.* 2:5b Hebrew *as Sheol.*

1:1-17 How long. Habakkuk asks God why evil goes unpunished, and God's response is that he is going to punish Judah by allowing Babylon (the Chaldeans) to conquer it. Habakkuk questions how God can use Babylon, which is even more wicked than Judah.

1:3 Must I forever see. Habakkuk saw the injustice around him and was appalled. Even worse, the righteous God seems to tolerate this evil.

1:12 who are eternal. Habakkuk finds comfort and confidence in God's faithfulness.

1:13 Should you be silent. Although he accepts that Judah must be punished, Habakkuk wonders why God would use such an evil nation to administer the discipline.

2:4 righteous will live by their faithfulness to God. In contrast to the arrogant Chaldeans, the righteous follower of God will live by faith, patiently experiencing God's blessing and trusting God's promises. (See also Rom. 1:17; Gal. 3:11; Heb. 10:38).

2:6-8 What sorrow awaits. This is the first of five woes that foretell Babylon's destruction.

You've become rich by extortion,
but how much longer can this go on?'
7 Suddenly, your debtors will take action.
They will turn on you and take all you have,
while you stand trembling and helpless.
8 Because you have plundered many nations,
now all the survivors will plunder you.
You committed murder throughout the countryside
and filled the towns with violence.

9 "What sorrow awaits you who build big houses
with money gained dishonestly!
You believe your wealth will buy security,
putting your family's nest beyond the reach of danger.
10 But by the murders you committed,
you have shamed your name and forfeited your lives.
11 The very stones in the walls cry out against you,
and the beams in the ceilings echo the complaint.

12 "What sorrow awaits you who build cities
with money gained through murder and corruption!
13 Has not the LORD of Heaven's Armies promised
that the wealth of nations will turn to ashes?
They work so hard,
but all in vain!
14 For as the waters fill the sea,
the earth will be filled with an awareness
of the glory of the LORD.

15 "What sorrow awaits you who make your neighbors drunk!
You force your cup on them
so you can gloat over their shameful nakedness.
16 But soon it will be your turn to be disgraced.
Come, drink and be exposed!*
Drink from the cup of the LORD's judgment,
and all your glory will be turned to shame.
17 You cut down the forests of Lebanon.
Now you will be cut down.
You destroyed the wild animals,
so now their terror will be yours.
You committed murder throughout the countryside
and filled the towns with violence.

18 "What good is an idol carved by man,
or a cast image that deceives you?
How foolish to trust in your own creation—
a god that can't even talk!
19 What sorrow awaits you who say to wooden idols,
'Wake up and save us!'
To speechless stone images you say,
'Rise up and teach us!'
Can an idol tell you what to do?
They may be overlaid with gold and silver,
but they are lifeless inside.
20 But the LORD is in his holy Temple.
Let all the earth be silent before him."

HABAKKUK'S PRAYER

3 This prayer was sung by the prophet Habakkuk*:

2 I have heard all about you, LORD.
I am filled with awe by your amazing works.
In this time of our deep need,
help us again as you did in years gone by.
And in your anger,
remember your mercy.

3 I see God moving across the deserts from Edom,*
the Holy One coming from Mount Paran.*
His brilliant splendor fills the heavens,
and the earth is filled with his praise.
4 His coming is as brilliant as the sunrise.
Rays of light flash from his hands,
where his awesome power is hidden.
5 Pestilence marches before him;
plague follows close behind.
6 When he stops, the earth shakes.
When he looks, the nations tremble.
He shatters the everlasting mountains
and levels the eternal hills.
He is the Eternal One!*
7 I see the people of Cushan in distress,
and the nation of Midian trembling in terror.

8 Was it in anger, LORD, that you struck the rivers
and parted the sea?
Were you displeased with them?
No, you were sending your chariots of salvation!
9 You brandished your bow
and your quiver of arrows.
You split open the earth with flowing rivers.
10 The mountains watched and trembled.
Onward swept the raging waters.
The mighty deep cried out,
lifting its hands in submission.
11 The sun and moon stood still in the sky
as your brilliant arrows flew
and your glittering spear flashed.

12 You marched across the land in anger
and trampled the nations in your fury.
13 You went out to rescue your chosen people,
to save your anointed ones.
You crushed the heads of the wicked
and stripped their bones from head to toe.
14 With his own weapons,
you destroyed the chief of those
who rushed out like a whirlwind,

2:16 Dead Sea Scrolls and Greek and Syriac versions read *and stagger!* **3:1** Hebrew adds *according to shigionoth,* probably indicating the musical setting for the prayer. **3:3a** Hebrew *Teman.* **3:3b** Hebrew adds *selah;* also in 3:9, 13. The meaning of this Hebrew term is uncertain; it is probably a musical or literary term. **3:6** Or *The ancient paths belong to him.*

2:9-11 money gained dishonestly. The Chaldeans are compared to eagles building nests on mountainsides for protection from predators. The Babylonians used their stolen goods to build a seemingly invincible empire.
2:11 stones in the walls cry out. The materials used to build the Babylonian Empire were purchased with plundered wealth.

2:12-14 They work so hard, but all in vain. To Babylon's greed and pride, add its love of sin. The Lord declares that this empire's labor is in vain because the people follow evil, not God.
2:14 earth will be filled. God's judgment of evil will illustrate how much greater God's glory is than anything greed can assemble.

thinking Israel would be easy prey.
15 You trampled the sea with your horses,
and the mighty waters piled high.

16 I trembled inside when I heard this;
my lips quivered with fear.
My legs gave way beneath me,*
and I shook in terror.
I will wait quietly for the coming day
when disaster will strike the people who invade
us.
17 Even though the fig trees have no blossoms,
and there are no grapes on the vines;
even though the olive crop fails,
and the fields lie empty and barren;
even though the flocks die in the fields,
and the cattle barns are empty,
18 yet I will rejoice in the LORD!
I will be joyful in the God of my
salvation!
19 The Sovereign LORD is my strength!
He makes me as surefooted as a deer,*
able to tread upon the heights.

(For the choir director: This prayer is to be accompanied by stringed instruments.)

3:16 Hebrew *Decay entered my bones.* **3:19** Or *He gives me the speed of a deer.*

2:15-17 make your neighbors drunk. Babylon's inhumanity and violence is condemned. The nation is compared to someone who gives a neighbor alcohol to indulge in lustful behavior.

3:16 I will wait quietly. After seeing God's might in Israel's past, Habakkuk is left physically weak from his encounter with God. But he has greater confidence and peace as he waits for Judah's invasion and Babylon's subsequent fall.

3:18-19 yet I will rejoice. Even if the suffering is hard and relief many years away, Habakkuk will rejoice in the LORD. God gives strength to face any circumstance that will come along the way.

INTRODUCTION TO

ZEPHANIAH

PERSONAL READING PLAN

☐Zephaniah 1:1–2:3 ☐Zephaniah 2:4-15 ☐Zephaniah 3:1-20

AUTHOR

Zephaniah was an aristocrat and a great-great grandson of Hezekiah, the king of Judah from 715 to 686 B.C. (see 1:1).

DATE

Zephaniah prophesied during the reign of Josiah (640–609 B.C.). His preaching as recorded here may have contributed to Josiah's reforms, which took place in 621 B.C. This makes Zephaniah an older contemporary and kindred spirit of Jeremiah.

THEME

The coming Day of the Lord.

HISTORICAL BACKGROUND

Zephaniah's twofold message—"gloom and doom" for Judah and its neighbors (1:1–3:8), then the Lord's purging and purifying of a faithful remnant (3:9-20)—is best appreciated within the context of what necessitated their judgment. The historical situation that he addressed is the same pervasive decadence that triggered King Josiah's reform movement (see 2 Chron. 34–35). Josiah was spurred on by the evils of King Manasseh and King Amon, by the rediscovery of Moses' Law, by hearing Jeremiah's early preaching, and quite possibly by Zephaniah's preaching. Thus it was that Josiah removed the pagan centers of idol worship. The immediate occasion for Zephaniah's prophecy may have been a century-long invasion of Canaan by the Scythians (a fierce nomadic people). Fulfillment of Zephaniah's prophecy (destruction of Judah) came at the hands of King Nebuchadnezzar of Babylon, who defeated the Assyrians in 612 B.C., thus establishing Babylonian supremacy in the Near East.

CHARACTERISTICS

Zephaniah consists of several brief oracles or utterances, heavy with an emphasis on judgment. The prophet foresaw a worldwide catastrophe, but he also saw beyond it. In the prophetic tradition, Zephaniah delivers his message with lament, exhortation, and hope. Zephaniah presents a beautiful picture of a God who delights in His people (3:14-20). The prophecies of Zephaniah against the nations are listed below:

Judah:	1:4–2:3
Philistia:	2:4-7
Ammon:	2:8-11
Moab:	2:8-11
Cush:	2:12
Assyria:	2:13-15

1 The LORD gave this message to Zephaniah when Josiah son of Amon was king of Judah. Zephaniah was the son of Cushi, son of Gedaliah, son of Amariah, son of Hezekiah.

COMING JUDGMENT AGAINST JUDAH

2 "I will sweep away everything
from the face of the earth," says the LORD.
3 "I will sweep away people and animals alike.
I will sweep away the birds of the sky and the fish in the sea.
I will reduce the wicked to heaps of rubble,*
and I will wipe humanity from the face of the earth," says the LORD.
4 "I will crush Judah and Jerusalem with my fist
and destroy every last trace of their Baal worship.
I will put an end to all the idolatrous priests,
so that even the memory of them will disappear.
5 For they go up to their roofs
and bow down to the sun, moon, and stars.
They claim to follow the LORD,
but then they worship Molech,* too.
6 And I will destroy those who used to worship me
but now no longer do.
They no longer ask for the LORD's guidance
or seek my blessings."

7 Stand in silence in the presence of the Sovereign LORD,
for the awesome day of the LORD's judgment is near.
The LORD has prepared his people for a great slaughter
and has chosen their executioners.*
8 "On that day of judgment,"
says the LORD,
"I will punish the leaders and princes of Judah
and all those following pagan customs.
9 Yes, I will punish those who participate in pagan worship ceremonies,
and those who fill their masters' houses with violence and deceit.

10 "On that day," says the LORD,
"a cry of alarm will come from the Fish Gate
and echo throughout the New Quarter of the city.*
And a great crash will sound from the hills.
11 Wail in sorrow, all you who live in the market area,*
for all the merchants and traders will be destroyed.

12 "I will search with lanterns in Jerusalem's darkest corners
to punish those who sit complacent in their sins.
They think the LORD will do nothing to them,
either good or bad.
13 So their property will be plundered,
their homes will be ransacked.
They will build new homes
but never live in them.
They will plant vineyards
but never drink wine from them.

14 "That terrible day of the LORD is near.
Swiftly it comes—
a day of bitter tears,
a day when even strong men will cry out.
15 It will be a day when the LORD's anger is poured out—
a day of terrible distress and anguish,
a day of ruin and desolation,
a day of darkness and gloom,
a day of clouds and blackness,
16 a day of trumpet calls and battle cries.
Down go the walled cities
and the strongest battlements!

17 "Because you have sinned against the LORD,
I will make you grope around like the blind.
Your blood will be poured into the dust,
and your bodies will lie rotting on the ground."

18 Your silver and gold will not save you
on that day of the LORD's anger.
For the whole land will be devoured
by the fire of his jealousy.
He will make a terrifying end
of all the people on earth.*

A CALL TO REPENTANCE

2 1 Gather together—yes, gather together,
you shameless nation.
2 Gather before judgment begins,
before your time to repent is blown away like chaff.
Act now, before the fierce fury of the LORD falls
and the terrible day of the LORD's anger begins.
3 Seek the LORD, all who are humble,
and follow his commands.
Seek to do what is right
and to live humbly.
Perhaps even yet the LORD will protect you—
protect you from his anger on that day of destruction.

JUDGMENT AGAINST PHILISTIA

4 Gaza and Ashkelon will be abandoned,
Ashdod and Ekron torn down.
5 And what sorrow awaits you Philistines*
who live along the coast and in the land of Canaan,

1:3 The meaning of the Hebrew is uncertain. 1:5 Hebrew *Malcam,* a variant spelling of Molech; or it could possibly mean *their king.* 1:7 Hebrew *has prepared a sacrifice and sanctified his guests.* 1:10 Or *the Second Quarter,* a newer section of Jerusalem. Hebrew reads *the Mishneh.* 1:11 Or *in the valley,* a lower section of Jerusalem. Hebrew reads *the Maktesh.* 1:18 Or *the people living in the land.* 2:5 Hebrew *Kerethites.*

1:4-7 Judah is condemned for its idolatry, particularly the worship of Baal, a Canaanite fertility god. Some scholars argue that these threats place Zephaniah's prophecy before the reign of Josiah since his reforms destroyed the altars of Baal (2 Kings 23:4-16). Another alternative is that Josiah's reforms did not last and the people of Judah were again worshiping Baal.
1:5-6 Zephaniah chastises three groups of idolaters: those who worshiped the sun, moon, and stars; those who combined worship of God with Molech, the Ammonite deity to which children were sacrificed; and those who didn't worship any god, including the true God.
1:18 will not save you. Riches can save people from many of life's issues, but are totally worthless when God's wrath comes.
2:1-3 terrible day of the LORD's anger begins. Zephaniah's point in all these dire warnings: repentance is the only hope for Judah.

for this judgment is against you, too!
The LORD will destroy you
until not one of you is left.
6 The Philistine coast will become a wilderness pasture,
a place of shepherd camps
and enclosures for sheep and goats.
7 The remnant of the tribe of Judah will pasture there.
They will rest at night in the abandoned houses in Ashkelon.
For the LORD their God will visit his people in kindness
and restore their prosperity again.

JUDGMENT AGAINST MOAB AND AMMON

8 "I have heard the taunts of the Moabites
and the insults of the Ammonites,
mocking my people
and invading their borders.
9 Now, as surely as I live,"
says the LORD of Heaven's Armies, the God of Israel,
"Moab and Ammon will be destroyed—
destroyed as completely as Sodom and Gomorrah.
Their land will become a place of stinging nettles,
salt pits, and eternal desolation.
The remnant of my people will plunder them
and take their land."
10 They will receive the wages of their pride,
for they have scoffed at the people of the LORD of Heaven's Armies.
11 The LORD will terrify them
as he destroys all the gods in the land.
Then nations around the world will worship the LORD,
each in their own land.

JUDGMENT AGAINST ETHIOPIA AND ASSYRIA

12 "You Ethiopians* will also be slaughtered
by my sword," says the LORD.

13 And the LORD will strike the lands of the north with his fist,
destroying the land of Assyria.
He will make its great capital, Nineveh, a desolate wasteland,
parched like a desert.
14 The proud city will become a pasture for flocks and herds,
and all sorts of wild animals will settle there.
The desert owl and screech owl will roost on its ruined columns,
their calls echoing through the gaping windows.
Rubble will block all the doorways,
and the cedar paneling will be exposed to the weather.
15 This is the boisterous city,
once so secure.
"I am the greatest!" it boasted.
"No other city can compare with me!"
But now, look how it has become an utter ruin,
a haven for wild animals.
Everyone passing by will laugh in derision
and shake a defiant fist.

JERUSALEM'S REBELLION AND REDEMPTION

3 1 What sorrow awaits rebellious, polluted Jerusalem,
the city of violence and crime!
2 No one can tell it anything;
it refuses all correction.
It does not trust in the LORD
or draw near to its God.
3 Its leaders are like roaring lions
hunting for their victims.
Its judges are like ravenous wolves at evening time,
who by dawn have left no trace of their prey.
4 Its prophets are arrogant liars seeking their own gain.
Its priests defile the Temple by disobeying God's instructions.
5 But the LORD is still there in the city,
and he does no wrong.
Day by day he hands down justice,
and he does not fail.
But the wicked know no shame.

6 "I have wiped out many nations,
devastating their fortress walls and towers.
Their streets are now deserted;
their cities lie in silent ruin.
There are no survivors—
none at all.
7 I thought, 'Surely they will have reverence for me now!
Surely they will listen to my warnings.
Then I won't need to strike again,
destroying their homes.'
But no, they get up early
to continue their evil deeds.
8 Therefore, be patient," says the LORD.
"Soon I will stand and accuse these evil nations.
For I have decided to gather the kingdoms of the earth
and pour out my fiercest anger and fury on them.
All the earth will be devoured
by the fire of my jealousy.

2:12 Hebrew *Cushites.* 3:10 Hebrew *Cush.*

2:9-10 Moab and Ammon. Because of Moab's and Ammon's taunting, Judah's remnant (faithful few who survive) will conquer them and inhabit their lands.
2:12 Ethiopians will also be slaughtered. The Ethiopians lived in what is today Egypt, Sudan, and northern Ethiopia, the southernmost point known to the people of Judah. Zephaniah may have intended that God would judge the whole earth.
2:15 boisterous city. For about 200 years Nineveh was the world's strongest city, so the claim "No other city can compare with me!" was partially accurate. But eventually the city lay in ruins; its haughtiness silenced.
3:3-4 leaders . . . judges . . . prophets . . . priests. The rulers and judges were so greedy that by dawn they had devoured prey caught the previous evening. Arrogant prophets twisted God's law for their own gain. Idolatrous priests profaned the places of worship, when they should have been teaching the law.
3:8 All the earth will be devoured by the fire of my jealousy. This section ends with a declaration of God's universal judgment on all nations, fueled by His jealous love.

9 "Then I will purify the speech of all people,
so that everyone can worship the LORD together.
10 My scattered people who live beyond the rivers of Ethiopia*
will come to present their offerings.
11 On that day you will no longer need to be ashamed,
for you will no longer be rebels against me.
I will remove all proud and arrogant people from among you.
There will be no more haughtiness on my holy mountain.
12 Those who are left will be the lowly and humble,
for it is they who trust in the name of the LORD.
13 The remnant of Israel will do no wrong;
they will never tell lies or deceive one another.
They will eat and sleep in safety,
and no one will make them afraid."

14 Sing, O daughter of Zion;
shout aloud, O Israel!
Be glad and rejoice with all your heart,
O daughter of Jerusalem!
15 For the LORD will remove his hand of judgment
and will disperse the armies of your enemy.
And the LORD himself, the King of Israel,
will live among you!
At last your troubles will be over,
and you will never again fear disaster.
16 On that day the announcement to Jerusalem will be,
"Cheer up, Zion! Don't be afraid!
17 For the LORD your God is living among you.
He is a mighty savior.
He will take delight in you with gladness.
With his love, he will calm all your fears.*
He will rejoice over you with joyful songs."

18 "I will gather you who mourn for the appointed festivals;
you will be disgraced no more.*
19 And I will deal severely with all who have oppressed you.
I will save the weak and helpless ones;
I will bring together
those who were chased away.
I will give glory and fame to my former exiles,
wherever they have been mocked and shamed.
20 On that day I will gather you together
and bring you home again.
I will give you a good name, a name of distinction,
among all the nations of the earth,
as I restore your fortunes before their very eyes.
I, the LORD, have spoken!"

3:17 Or *He will be silent in his love.* Greek and Syriac versions read *He will renew you with his love.* **3:18** The meaning of the Hebrew for this verse is uncertain.

3:9 Then I will purify. After God punishes, God promises restoration and peace. God's judgment aims to purify the nations so they call on His name and serve Him.

3:15 The King of Israel. Israel's redeemer and Messiah King will dwell among them (Isa. 9:7; Zech. 14:9). No longer must Israel face God's wrath or her enemies (vv. 8, 19).

3:17-20 Zephaniah concludes his prophetic message with encouragement and hope. He reminds the Israelites that they are God's chosen people and God still loves them. Then Zephaniah offers a series of promises of restoration from God. These would give hope to those that trusted in Yahweh, the almighty yet loving God who keeps His promises.

INTRODUCTION TO

HAGGAI

PERSONAL READING PLAN

☐Haggai 1:1-15 ☐Haggai 2:1-23

AUTHOR

The author is not identified, though the book tells of Haggai's ministry and records his oracles. Haggai means "festal," which may suggest that the prophet was born during one of the three Jewish feasts (Unleavened Bread, Pentecost [or Weeks] or Tabernacles; see Deut. 16:16).

DATE

Haggai is quite specific as to the year, month, and day of his messages: August 29 (1:1); September 15 (1:15); October 17 (2:1); December 18 (2:10 and 2:20), 520 B.C.

THEME

Rebuilding the nation—the blessing is in the doing.

HISTORICAL BACKGROUND

This book is set in the context of the return of the Jews from the Babylonian exile and the subsequent rebuilding of Jerusalem and the temple (see the Introductions to Ezra and Nehemiah). It was through the ministry of Haggai (along with Zechariah) that the rebuilding of the temple began (see Ezra 5:1-2). The problem with getting the building started, it seems, was not just with the neighboring Samaritans who opposed the rebuilding projects (fearing that this would lead to a renewed and politically powerful Jewish state). The real problem had to do with the lethargy of the people. Haggai's aim was to get the people enthusiastic about the project. The temple was completed and dedicated four years later in 516 B.C. No other prophet had results as direct, immediate, and identifiable as Haggai!

CHARACTERISTICS

There is only one book in the Old Testament that is shorter than Haggai (Obadiah). Yet in just 38 verses Haggai is able to show the contrasting consequences of disobedience vs. obedience, as well as point to the coming of the Messiah. Haggai was an older contemporary of Zechariah. Both dealt with the same themes, though in quite different ways (see the Introduction to Zechariah). Haggai was a practical doer, while Zechariah was an apocalyptic visionary. Haggai did not mince words, while Zechariah mixed metaphors in a memorable way. Haggai exhorted the people to get to work on the project at hand (the rebuilding of the temple), while Zechariah encouraged them to put their hope in what lay ahead for them in the distant future (which also served to motivate the people to rebuild the temple, though in a different way). Haggai records not only his oracles but also his ministry and the response of the people to it, while Zechariah emphasizes the prophecies.

Several times Haggai seems to echo other Scriptures (compare 1:6 with Deut. 28:38-39 and 2:17 with Deut. 28:22). The use of "be strong" three times in 2:4 corresponds with the encouragement given in Joshua 1:6-7,9,18.

A CALL TO REBUILD THE TEMPLE

1 On August 29* of the second year of King Darius's reign, the LORD gave a message through the prophet Haggai to Zerubbabel son of Shealtiel, governor of Judah, and to Jeshua* son of Jehozadak, the high priest.

2 "This is what the LORD of Heaven's Armies says: The people are saying, 'The time has not yet come to rebuild the house of the LORD.'"

3 Then the LORD sent this message through the prophet Haggai: 4 "Why are you living in luxurious houses while my house lies in ruins? 5 This is what the LORD of Heaven's Armies says: Look at what's happening to you! 6 You have planted much but harvest little. You eat but are not satisfied. You drink but are still thirsty. You put on clothes but cannot keep warm. Your wages disappear as though you were putting them in pockets filled with holes!

7 "This is what the LORD of Heaven's Armies says: Look at what's happening to you! 8 Now go up into the hills, bring down timber, and rebuild my house. Then I will take pleasure in it and be honored, says the LORD. 9 You hoped for rich harvests, but they were poor. And when you brought your harvest home, I blew it away. Why? Because my house lies in ruins, says the LORD of Heaven's Armies, while all of you are busy building your own fine houses. 10 It's because of you that the heavens withhold the dew and the earth produces no crops. 11 I have called for a drought on your fields and hills—a drought to wither the grain and grapes and olive trees and all your other crops, a drought to starve you and your livestock and to ruin everything you have worked so hard to get."

OBEDIENCE TO GOD'S CALL

12 Then Zerubbabel son of Shealtiel, and Jeshua son of Jehozadak, the high priest, and the whole remnant of God's people began to obey the message from the LORD their God. When they heard the words of the prophet Haggai, whom the LORD their God had sent, the people feared the LORD. 13 Then Haggai, the LORD's messenger, gave the people this message from the LORD: "I am with you, says the LORD!"

14 So the LORD sparked the enthusiasm of Zerubbabel son of Shealtiel, governor of Judah, and the enthusiasm of Jeshua son of Jehozadak, the high priest, and the enthusiasm of the whole remnant of God's people. They began to work on the house of their God, the LORD of Heaven's Armies, 15 on September 21* of the second year of King Darius's reign.

THE NEW TEMPLE'S DIMINISHED SPLENDOR

2 Then on October 17 of that same year,* the LORD sent another message through the prophet Haggai. 2 "Say this to Zerubbabel son of Shealtiel, governor of Judah, and to Jeshua* son of Jehozadak, the high priest, and to the remnant of God's people there in the land: 3 'Does anyone remember this house—this Temple—in its former splendor? How, in comparison, does it look to you now? It must seem like nothing at all! 4 But now the LORD says: Be strong, Zerubbabel. Be strong, Jeshua son of Jehozadak, the high priest. Be strong, all you people still left in the land. And now get to work, for I am with you, says the LORD of Heaven's Armies. 5 My Spirit remains among you, just as I promised when you came out of Egypt. So do not be afraid.'

6 "For this is what the LORD of Heaven's Armies says: In just a little while I will again shake the heavens and the earth, the oceans and the dry land. 7 I will shake all the nations, and the treasures of all the nations will be brought to this Temple. I will fill this place with glory, says the LORD of Heaven's Armies. 8 The silver is mine, and the gold is mine, says the LORD of Heaven's Armies. 9 The future glory of this Temple will be greater than its past glory, says the LORD of Heaven's Armies. And in this place I will bring peace. I, the LORD of Heaven's Armies, have spoken!"

BLESSINGS PROMISED FOR OBEDIENCE

10 On December 18* of the second year of King Darius's reign, the LORD sent this message to the prophet Haggai: 11 "This is what the LORD of Heaven's Armies says. Ask the priests this question about the law: 12 'If one of you is carrying some meat from a holy sacrifice in his robes and his robe happens to brush against some bread or stew, wine or olive oil, or any other kind of food, will it also become holy?'"

The priests replied, "No."

13 Then Haggai asked, "If someone becomes ceremonially unclean by touching a dead person and then touches any of these foods, will the food be defiled?"

And the priests answered, "Yes."

14 Then Haggai responded, "That is how it is with this people and this nation, says the LORD. Everything they do and everything they offer is defiled by their sin. 15 Look at what was happening to you before you began to lay the foundation of the LORD's Temple. 16 When you hoped for a twenty-bushel crop, you

1:1a Hebrew *On the first day of the sixth month,* of the ancient Hebrew lunar calendar. A number of dates in Haggai can be cross-checked with dates in surviving Persian records and related accurately to our modern calendar. This event occurred on August 29, 520 B.C. **1:1b** Hebrew *Joshua,* a variant spelling of Jeshua; also in 1:12, 14. **1:15** Hebrew *on the twenty-fourth day of the sixth month,* of the ancient Hebrew lunar calendar. This event occurred on September 21, 520 B.C.; also see note on 1:1a. **2:1** Hebrew *on the twenty-first day of the seventh month,* of the ancient Hebrew lunar calendar. This event (in the second year of Darius's reign) occurred on October 17, 520 B.C.; also see note on 1:1a. **2:2** Hebrew *Joshua,* a variant spelling of Jeshua; also in 2:4. **2:10** Hebrew *On the twenty-fourth day of the ninth month,* of the ancient Hebrew lunar calendar (similarly in 2:18). This event occurred on December 18, 520 B.C.; also see note on 1:1a.

1:2 The people. The Israelites are called "the people," rather than the usual "my people," to emphasize that sin had separated them from God. They were making excuses for not building the temple as God had commanded.

1:3-4 living in luxurious houses. Haggai rebukes the people for their selfishness and misplaced priorities. They were building comfortable houses for themselves but neglecting to build the house of God.

1:5-6,9-10 Look at what's happening to you! The people's apathy about building the temple has caused God to withhold blessings, so that they will "think carefully" about their ways.

1:14 The LORD sparked enthusiasm. God moved the hearts of his people, giving them a desire to return home and work on the temple.

2:1 On Oct 17. This was the final day of the weeklong Feast of Tabernacles, a time of celebration for the summer harvest.

2:3 former splendor. The people were discouraged as they compared the inferior rebuilt temple to Solomon's glorious temple.

2:7 I will fill this place with glory. To encourage the people, God promises that glory will fill the house of the Lord. This Messianic prophecy foretells Christ's coming (He is the radiance of God's glory, Heb. 1:3) and points toward the glory of God's kingdom fully realized at the end of time.

2:13-14 is defiled. Just as ceremonial uncleanness is transferred from an "unclean" person to anything he touches, so the disobedience of a worshiper is transferred onto sacrifices, which renders them unacceptable to God.

2:15-19 Look at . . . before you began. To convince the people to obey God, Haggai reminds them of the economic hardships God used to punish their sin. He then affirms that God has promised blessing for faithful obedience.

harvested only ten. When you expected to draw fifty
gallons from the winepress, you found only twenty.
17 I sent blight and mildew and hail to destroy every-
thing you worked so hard to produce. Even so, you
refused to return to me, says the LORD.

18 "Think about this eighteenth day of December,
the day* when the foundation of the LORD's Temple
was laid. Think carefully. 19 I am giving you a prom-
ise now while the seed is still in the barn.* You have
not yet harvested your grain, and your grapevines,
fig trees, pomegranates, and olive trees have not yet
produced their crops. But from this day onward I will
bless you."

PROMISES FOR ZERUBBABEL

20 On that same day, December 18,* the LORD sent this
second message to Haggai: 21 "Tell Zerubbabel, the
governor of Judah, that I am about to shake the heav-
ens and the earth. 22 I will overthrow royal thrones
and destroy the power of foreign kingdoms. I will
overturn their chariots and riders. The horses will
fall, and their riders will kill each other.

23 "But when this happens, says the LORD of Heav-
en's Armies, I will honor you, Zerubbabel son of She-
altiel, my servant. I will make you like a signet ring on
my finger, says the LORD, for I have chosen you. I, the
LORD of Heaven's Armies, have spoken!"

2:18 Or *On this eighteenth day of December, think about the day.* **2:19** Hebrew *Is the seed yet in the barn?* **2:20** Hebrew *On the twenty-fourth day of the [ninth] month;* see note on 2:10.

INTRODUCTION TO

ZECHARIAH

PERSONAL READING PLAN

☐Zechariah 1:1–2:13
☐Zechariah 3:1–5:11
☐Zechariah 6:1–7:14
☐Zechariah 8:1–9:17
☐Zechariah 10:1–11:17
☐Zechariah 12:1–13:6
☐Zechariah 13:7–14:21

AUTHOR

The writer is Zechariah, the prophet and priest who was born in exile and returned from Babylon to Judah in 538 B.C. (1:1; see Ezra 5:1; 6:14).

DATE

Zechariah is specific as to the year, month, and day of the messages recorded in chapters 1–8. They span the years from 520 to 518 B.C. The date of his final prophecy (chaps. 9–14) is uncertain, though it was probably not given until some 40 years later (e.g., after 480 B.C.).

THEME

Rebuilding the temple and the nation of Judah; the Lord's return.

HISTORICAL BACKGROUND

Zechariah tells of the return of the Jews from the Babylonian exile and the subsequent rebuilding of Jerusalem and the temple (see the Introductions to Ezra and Nehemiah). It was through the ministry of Zechariah (along with Haggai) that the rebuilding of the temple began (see Ezra 5:1-2). The temple was completed and dedicated four years later in 516 B.C.

CHARACTERISTICS

Zechariah was a younger contemporary of Haggai, with a ministry extending well beyond Haggai's, possibly Into the reign of Artaxerxes I (465–424 B.C.). Both prophets dealt with the same theme (rebuilding the temple) but in contrasting ways (see the Introduction to Haggai). Zechariah was an apocalyptic visionary, while Haggai was a practical doer. The Book of Zechariah poses a study in contrast between Part I (chaps. 1–8) and Part II (chaps. 9–14), written some 40 years later. In Part I, Zechariah tries to instill enthusiasm for the rebuilding of the temple as the people begin to see how things ultimately result in their deliverance and God's greater glory. In Part II, he proclaims that rebuilding the temple will create the future transformation of God's people into a holy nation. The visions of Zechariah are listed below:

Horseman –	1:7-11
Four Horns and Craftsmen –	1:18-21
Surveyor –	2:1-13
High Priest and Branch –	3:1-10
Gold Lampstand –	4:1-14
Flying Scroll –	5:1-4
Woman in the Basket –	5:5-11
Four Chariots –	6:1-8

A CALL TO RETURN TO THE LORD

1 In November* of the second year of King Darius's
reign, the LORD gave this message to the prophet
Zechariah son of Berekiah and grandson of Iddo:
2 "I, the LORD, was very angry with your ancestors.
3 Therefore, say to the people, 'This is what the LORD of
Heaven's Armies says: Return to me, and I will return
to you, says the LORD of Heaven's Armies.' 4 Don't be
like your ancestors who would not listen or pay at-
tention when the earlier prophets said to them, 'This
is what the LORD of Heaven's Armies says: Turn from
your evil ways, and stop all your evil practices.'
5 "Where are your ancestors now? They and the
prophets are long dead. 6 But everything I said
through my servants the prophets happened to your
ancestors, just as I said. As a result, they repented and
said, 'We have received what we deserved from the
LORD of Heaven's Armies. He has done what he said
he would do.'"

A MAN AMONG THE MYRTLE TREES

7 Three months later, on February 15,* the LORD sent
another message to the prophet Zechariah son of Ber-
ekiah and grandson of Iddo.
8 In a vision during the night, I saw a man sitting
on a red horse that was standing among some myr-
tle trees in a small valley. Behind him were riders on
red, brown, and white horses. 9 I asked the angel who
was talking with me, "My lord, what do these horses
mean?"
"I will show you," the angel replied.
10 The rider standing among the myrtle trees then
explained, "They are the ones the LORD has sent out to
patrol the earth."
11 Then the other riders reported to the angel of the
LORD, who was standing among the myrtle trees, "We
have been patrolling the earth, and the whole earth
is at peace."
12 Upon hearing this, the angel of the LORD prayed
this prayer: "O LORD of Heaven's Armies, for seventy
years now you have been angry with Jerusalem and
the towns of Judah. How long until you again show
mercy to them?" 13 And the LORD spoke kind and com-
forting words to the angel who talked with me.
14 Then the angel said to me, "Shout this message
for all to hear: 'This is what the LORD of Heaven's Ar-
mies says: My love for Jerusalem and Mount Zion is
passionate and strong. 15 But I am very angry with the
other nations that are now enjoying peace and secu-
rity. I was only a little angry with my people, but the
nations inflicted harm on them far beyond my inten-
tions.
16 "'Therefore, this is what the LORD says: I have re-
turned to show mercy to Jerusalem. My Temple will
be rebuilt, says the LORD of Heaven's Armies, and
measurements will be taken for the reconstruction of
Jerusalem.*'
17 "Say this also: 'This is what the LORD of Heaven's
Armies says: The towns of Israel will again overflow
with prosperity, and the LORD will again comfort Zion
and choose Jerusalem as his own.'"

FOUR HORNS AND FOUR BLACKSMITHS

18* Then I looked up and saw four animal horns.
19 "What are these?" I asked the angel who was talking
with me.
He replied, "These horns represent the nations that
scattered Judah, Israel, and Jerusalem."
20 Then the LORD showed me four blacksmiths.
21 "What are these men coming to do?" I asked.
The angel replied, "These four horns—these na-
tions—scattered and humbled Judah. Now these
blacksmiths have come to terrify those nations and
throw them down and destroy them."

FUTURE PROSPERITY OF JERUSALEM

2 1* When I looked again, I saw a man with a mea-
suring line in his hand. 2 "Where are you going?"
I asked.
He replied, "I am going to measure Jerusalem, to see
how wide and how long it is."
3 Then the angel who was with me went to meet
a second angel who was coming toward him. 4 The
other angel said, "Hurry, and say to that young man,
'Jerusalem will someday be so full of people and live-
stock that there won't be room enough for everyone!
Many will live outside the city walls. 5 Then I, myself,
will be a protective wall of fire around Jerusalem,
says the LORD. And I will be the glory inside the city!'"

THE EXILES ARE CALLED HOME

6 The LORD says, "Come away! Flee from Babylon in
the land of the north, for I have scattered you to the
four winds. 7 Come away, people of Zion, you who are
exiled in Babylon!"
8 After a period of glory, the LORD of Heaven's Ar-
mies sent me* against the nations who plundered
you. For he said, "Anyone who harms you harms
my most precious possession.* 9 I will raise my fist to
crush them, and their own slaves will plunder them."
Then you will know that the LORD of Heaven's Armies
has sent me.
10 The LORD says, "Shout and rejoice, O beautiful Je-
rusalem,* for I am coming to live among you. 11 Many
nations will join themselves to the LORD on that day,
and they, too, will be my people. I will live among you,
and you will know that the LORD of Heaven's Armies
sent me to you. 12 The land of Judah will be the LORD's
special possession in the holy land, and he will once
again choose Jerusalem to be his own city. 13 Be silent

1:1 Hebrew *In the eighth month.* A number of dates in Zechariah can be cross-checked with dates in surviving Persian records and related accurately to our modern calendar. This month of the ancient Hebrew lunar calendar occurred within the months of October and November 520 B.C. **1:7** Hebrew *On the twenty-fourth day of the eleventh month, the month of Shebat, in the second year of Darius.* This event occurred on February 15, 519 B.C.; also see note on 1:1. **1:16** Hebrew *and the measuring line will be stretched out over Jerusalem.* **1:18** Verses 1:18-21 are numbered 2:1-4 in Hebrew text. **2:1** Verses 2:1-13 are numbered 2:5-17 in Hebrew text. **2:8a** The meaning of the Hebrew is uncertain. **2:8b** Hebrew *Anyone who touches you touches the pupil of his eye.* **2:10** Hebrew *O daughter of Zion.*

1:7-17 Zechariah's first vision of a rider among myrtle trees was a reassuring message. It soothed Israel's fears and inspired hope. The accompanying angel explained that their enemies would be punished (vv. 14-15) and Israel's prosperity would be restored (v. 17).

1:8 during the night I saw. Zechariah experienced eight visions concerning the restoration of Israel, all in a single night.

2:1-13 The renovation projected in the third vision concerned the expansion of the restored city of Jerusalem (vv. 1-2). A city "without walls" was a symbol of the peace and prosperity that awaited the Jews in their future dwelling (v. 4).

2:5 will be a protective wall of fire. This new nation would celebrate their stake in the glory of God.

2:12 in the holy land. Ordinary dirt became holy ground due to the presence of God as God again chooses Jerusalem for His residence.

before the LORD, all humanity, for he is springing into
action from his holy dwelling."

CLEANSING FOR THE HIGH PRIEST

3 Then the angel showed me Jeshua* the high priest
standing before the angel of the LORD. The Accus-
er, Satan,* was there at the angel's right hand, mak-
ing accusations against Jeshua. 2 And the LORD said
to Satan, "I, the LORD, reject your accusations, Satan.
Yes, the LORD, who has chosen Jerusalem, rebukes
you. This man is like a burning stick that has been
snatched from the fire."
3 Jeshua's clothing was filthy as he stood there be-
fore the angel. 4 So the angel said to the others stand-
ing there, "Take off his filthy clothes." And turning to
Jeshua he said, "See, I have taken away your sins, and
now I am giving you these fine new clothes."
5 Then I said, "They should also place a clean tur-
ban on his head." So they put a clean priestly turban
on his head and dressed him in new clothes while the
angel of the LORD stood by.
6 Then the angel of the LORD spoke very solemnly
to Jeshua and said, 7 "This is what the LORD of Heav-
en's Armies says: If you follow my ways and carefully
serve me, then you will be given authority over my
Temple and its courtyards. I will let you walk among
these others standing here.
8 "Listen to me, O Jeshua the high priest, and all you
other priests. You are symbols of things to come. Soon
I am going to bring my servant, the Branch. 9 Now
look at the jewel I have set before Jeshua, a single
stone with seven facets.* I will engrave an inscription
on it, says the LORD of Heaven's Armies, and I will re-
move the sins of this land in a single day.
10 "And on that day, says the LORD of Heaven's Armies,
each of you will invite your neighbor to sit with you
peacefully under your own grapevine and fig tree."

A LAMPSTAND AND TWO OLIVE TREES

4 Then the angel who had been talking with me re-
turned and woke me, as though I had been asleep.
2 "What do you see now?" he asked.
I answered, "I see a solid gold lampstand with a
bowl of oil on top of it. Around the bowl are seven
lamps, each having seven spouts with wicks. 3 And
I see two olive trees, one on each side of the bowl."
4 Then I asked the angel, "What are these, my lord?
What do they mean?"
5 "Don't you know?" the angel asked.
"No, my lord," I replied.
6 Then he said to me, "This is what the LORD says to
Zerubbabel: It is not by force nor by strength, but by
my Spirit, says the LORD of Heaven's Armies. 7 Nothing,
not even a mighty mountain, will stand in Zerubba-
bel's way; it will become a level plain before him! And
when Zerubbabel sets the final stone of the Temple
in place, the people will shout: 'May God bless it! May
God bless it!'*"
8 Then another message came to me from the LORD:
9 "Zerubbabel is the one who laid the foundation of
this Temple, and he will complete it. Then you will
know that the LORD of Heaven's Armies has sent me.
10 Do not despise these small beginnings, for the LORD
rejoices to see the work begin, to see the plumb line in
Zerubbabel's hand."
(The seven lamps* represent the eyes of the LORD
that search all around the world.)
11 Then I asked the angel, "What are these two ol-
ive trees on each side of the lampstand, 12 and what
are the two olive branches that pour out golden oil
through two gold tubes?"
13 "Don't you know?" he asked.
"No, my lord," I replied.
14 Then he said to me, "They represent the two
anointed ones* who stand in the court of the Lord of
all the earth."

A FLYING SCROLL

5 I looked up again and saw a scroll flying through
the air.
2 "What do you see?" the angel asked.
"I see a flying scroll," I replied. "It appears to be
about 30 feet long and 15 feet wide.*"
3 Then he said to me, "This scroll contains the curse
that is going out over the entire land. One side of the
scroll says that those who steal will be banished from
the land; the other side says that those who swear
falsely will be banished from the land. 4 And this is
what the LORD of Heaven's Armies says: I am send-
ing this curse into the house of every thief and into
the house of everyone who swears falsely using my
name. And my curse will remain in that house and
completely destroy it—even its timbers and stones."

A WOMAN IN A BASKET

5 Then the angel who was talking with me came for-
ward and said, "Look up and see what's coming."
6 "What is it?" I asked.
He replied, "It is a basket for measuring grain,* and
it's filled with the sins* of everyone throughout the
land."
7 Then the heavy lead cover was lifted off the bas-
ket, and there was a woman sitting inside it. 8 The an-
gel said, "The woman's name is Wickedness," and he

3:1a Hebrew *Joshua,* a variant spelling of Jeshua; also in 3:3, 4, 6, 8, 9. **3:1b** Hebrew *The satan;* similarly in 3:2. **3:9** Hebrew *seven eyes.* **4:7** Hebrew *'Grace, grace to it.'* **4:10** Or *The seven facets* (see 3:9); Hebrew reads *These seven.* **4:14** Or *two heavenly beings;* Hebrew reads *two sons of fresh oil.* **5:2** Hebrew *20 cubits* [9.2 meters] *long and 10 cubits* [4.6 meters] *wide.* **5:6a** Hebrew *an ephah* [20 quarts or 22 liters]; also in 5:7, 8, 9, 10, 11. **5:6b** As in Greek version; Hebrew reads *the appearance.*

3:8-9 Branch . . . stone. Christ is represented here in two forms: as is a servant of God, a Branch from the King David's line, and the stone associated with the removal of sin.

4:1-14 Zechariah's fifth vision was the motivational force behind the Jews' temple restoration. The people would soon resume the groundbreaking from years earlier (vv. 7-8). God's Spirit would serve as the construction manager (v. 6).

4:2 gold lampstand. The gold lampstand, with a bowl of oil and channels supplying the lights, was significant due to its continual flow. God's presence, symbolized in familiar items from the temple, would never be snuffed out.

4:3 two olive trees. The key players in the temple reconstruction were symbolized in the stately trees. Judah's governor, Zerubbabel, and the high priest, Joshua, would lead the people in their efforts.

5:1-4 Zechariah's fifth vision held no tolerance for sin. The flying scroll portrayed swift judgment on all those who rejected God's commands.

5:2 flying scroll. The scroll served as God's giant billboard, announcing His judgment against sin—large enough that nobody could miss the message.

5:6 basket. A super-sized basket (big enough to hold a person) carried a weighty mission. The corporate sins of all the people would be carried away in it.

5:7 a woman sitting inside it. Her presence had less to do with her gender than it did the animated image of wickedness as alive and well. The wickedness must be destroyed.

pushed her back into the basket and closed the heavy lid again.

9 Then I looked up and saw two women flying toward us, gliding on the wind. They had wings like a stork, and they picked up the basket and flew into the sky.

10 "Where are they taking the basket?" I asked the angel.

11 He replied, "To the land of Babylonia,* where they will build a temple for the basket. And when the temple is ready, they will set the basket there on its pedestal."

FOUR CHARIOTS

6 Then I looked up again and saw four chariots coming from between two bronze mountains. 2 The first chariot was pulled by red horses, the second by black horses, 3 the third by white horses, and the fourth by powerful dappled-gray horses. 4 "And what are these, my lord?" I asked the angel who was talking with me.

5 The angel replied, "These are the four spirits* of heaven who stand before the Lord of all the earth. They are going out to do his work. 6 The chariot with black horses is going north, the chariot with white horses is going west,* and the chariot with dappled-gray horses is going south."

7 The powerful horses were eager to set out to patrol the earth. And the LORD said, "Go and patrol the earth!" So they left at once on their patrol.

8 Then the LORD summoned me and said, "Look, those who went north have vented the anger of my Spirit* there in the land of the north."

THE CROWNING OF JESHUA

9 Then I received another message from the LORD: 10 "Heldai, Tobijah, and Jedaiah will bring gifts of silver and gold from the Jews exiled in Babylon. As soon as they arrive, meet them at the home of Josiah son of Zephaniah. 11 Accept their gifts, and make a crown from the silver and gold. Then put the crown on the head of Jeshua* son of Jehozadak, the high priest. 12 Tell him, 'This is what the LORD of Heaven's Armies says: Here is the man called the Branch. He will branch out from where he is and build the Temple of the LORD. 13 Yes, he will build the Temple of the LORD. Then he will receive royal honor and will rule as king from his throne. He will also serve as priest from his throne,* and there will be perfect harmony between his two roles.'

14 "The crown will be a memorial in the Temple of the LORD to honor those who gave it—Heldai,* Tobijah, Jedaiah, and Josiah* son of Zephaniah."

15 People will come from distant lands to rebuild the Temple of the LORD. And when this happens, you will know that my messages have been from the LORD of Heaven's Armies. All this will happen if you carefully obey what the LORD your God says.

A CALL TO JUSTICE AND MERCY

7 On December 7* of the fourth year of King Darius's reign, another message came to Zechariah from the LORD. 2 The people of Bethel had sent Sharezer and Regemmelech,* along with their attendants, to seek the LORD's favor. 3 They were to ask this question of the prophets and the priests at the Temple of the LORD of Heaven's Armies: "Should we continue to mourn and fast each summer on the anniversary of the Temple's destruction,* as we have done for so many years?"

4 The LORD of Heaven's Armies sent me this message in reply: 5 "Say to all your people and your priests, 'During these seventy years of exile, when you fasted and mourned in the summer and in early autumn,* was it really for me that you were fasting? 6 And even now in your holy festivals, aren't you eating and drinking just to please yourselves? 7 Isn't this the same message the LORD proclaimed through the prophets in years past when Jerusalem and the towns of Judah were bustling with people, and the Negev and the foothills of Judah* were well populated?'"

8 Then this message came to Zechariah from the LORD: 9 "This is what the LORD of Heaven's Armies says: Judge fairly, and show mercy and kindness to one another. 10 Do not oppress widows, orphans, foreigners, and the poor. And do not scheme against each other.

11 "Your ancestors refused to listen to this message. They stubbornly turned away and put their fingers in their ears to keep from hearing. 12 They made their hearts as hard as stone, so they could not hear the instructions or the messages that the LORD of Heaven's Armies had sent them by his Spirit through the earlier prophets. That is why the LORD of Heaven's Armies was so angry with them.

13 "Since they refused to listen when I called to them, I would not listen when they called to me, says the LORD of Heaven's Armies. 14 As with a whirlwind, I scattered them among the distant nations, where they lived as strangers. Their land became so desolate that no one even traveled through it. They turned their pleasant land into a desert."

PROMISED BLESSINGS FOR JERUSALEM

8 Then another message came to me from the LORD of Heaven's Armies: 2 "This is what the LORD of Heaven's Armies says: My love for Mount Zion is passionate and strong; I am consumed with passion for Jerusalem!

3 "And now the LORD says: I am returning to Mount Zion, and I will live in Jerusalem. Then Jerusalem will be called the Faithful City; the mountain of the LORD of Heaven's Armies will be called the Holy Mountain.

4 "This is what the LORD of Heaven's Armies says: Once again old men and women will walk Jerusalem's streets with their canes and will sit together in the city squares. 5 And the streets of the city will be filled with boys and girls at play.

5:11 Hebrew *the land of Shinar.* **6:5** Or *the four winds.* **6:6** Hebrew *is going after them.* **6:8** Hebrew *have given my Spirit rest.* **6:11** Hebrew *Joshua,* a variant spelling of Jeshua. **6:13** Or *There will be a priest by his throne.* **6:14a** As in Syriac version (compare 6:10); Hebrew reads *Helem.* **6:14b** As in Syriac version (compare 6:10); Hebrew reads *Hen.* **7:1** Hebrew *On the fourth day of the ninth month, the month of Kislev,* of the ancient Hebrew lunar calendar. This event occurred on December 7, 518 B.C.; also see note on 1:1. **7:2** Or *Bethel-sharezer had sent Regemmelech.* **7:3** Hebrew *mourn and fast in the fifth month.* The Temple had been destroyed in the fifth month of the ancient Hebrew lunar calendar (August 586 B.C.); see 2 Kgs 25:8. **7:5** Hebrew *fasted and mourned in the fifth and seventh months.* The fifth month of the ancient Hebrew lunar calendar usually occurs within the months of July and August. The seventh month usually occurs within the months of September and October; both the Day of Atonement and the Festival of Shelters were celebrated in the seventh month. **7:7** Hebrew *the Shephelah.*

6:1-8 The eighth vision fulfilled the punishment ordained in the first vision (1:7-17).

8:1-23 Zechariah itemized the blessings promised in his earlier visions (1:7–6:8). If the Lord Almighty said it, they could count on God delivering what He had promised.

6 "This is what the LORD of Heaven's Armies says:
All this may seem impossible to you now, a small rem-
nant of God's people. But is it impossible for me? says
the LORD of Heaven's Armies.
7 "This is what the LORD of Heaven's Armies says:
You can be sure that I will rescue my people from the
east and from the west. 8 I will bring them home again
to live safely in Jerusalem. They will be my people,
and I will be faithful and just toward them as their
God.
9 "This is what the LORD of Heaven's Armies says:
Be strong and finish the task! Ever since the laying of
the foundation of the Temple of the LORD of Heaven's
Armies, you have heard what the prophets have been
saying about completing the building. 10 Before the
work on the Temple began, there were no jobs and no
money to hire people or animals. No traveler was safe
from the enemy, for there were enemies on all sides. I
had turned everyone against each other.
11 "But now I will not treat the remnant of my peo-
ple as I treated them before, says the LORD of Heav-
en's Armies. 12 For I am planting seeds of peace and
prosperity among you. The grapevines will be heavy
with fruit. The earth will produce its crops, and the
heavens will release the dew. Once more I will cause
the remnant in Judah and Israel to inherit these
blessings. 13 Among the other nations, Judah and Isra-
el became symbols of a cursed nation. But no longer!
Now I will rescue you and make you both a symbol
and a source of blessing. So don't be afraid. Be strong,
and get on with rebuilding the Temple!
14 "For this is what the LORD of Heaven's Armies
says: I was determined to punish you when your an-
cestors angered me, and I did not change my mind,
says the LORD of Heaven's Armies. 15 But now I am de-
termined to bless Jerusalem and the people of Judah.
So don't be afraid. 16 But this is what you must do: Tell
the truth to each other. Render verdicts in your courts
that are just and that lead to peace. 17 Don't scheme
against each other. Stop your love of telling lies that
you swear are the truth. I hate all these things, says
the LORD."
18 Here is another message that came to me from the
LORD of Heaven's Armies. 19 "This is what the LORD of
Heaven's Armies says: The traditional fasts and times
of mourning you have kept in early summer, midsum-
mer, autumn, and winter* are now ended. They will
become festivals of joy and celebration for the people
of Judah. So love truth and peace.
20 "This is what the LORD of Heaven's Armies says:
People from nations and cities around the world will
travel to Jerusalem. 21 The people of one city will say
to the people of another, 'Come with us to Jerusalem
to ask the LORD to bless us. Let's worship the LORD of
Heaven's Armies. I'm determined to go.' 22 Many peo-
ples and powerful nations will come to Jerusalem to
seek the LORD of Heaven's Armies and to ask for his
blessing.
23 "This is what the LORD of Heaven's Armies says:
In those days ten men from different nations and lan-
guages of the world will clutch at the sleeve of one
Jew. And they will say, 'Please let us walk with you,
for we have heard that God is with you.'"

JUDGMENT AGAINST ISRAEL'S ENEMIES

9 This is the message* from the LORD against the
land of Aram* and the city of Damascus, for the
eyes of humanity, including all the tribes of Israel, are
on the LORD.

2 Doom is certain for Hamath,
near Damascus,
and for the cities of Tyre and Sidon,
though they are so clever.
3 Tyre has built a strong fortress
and has made silver and gold
as plentiful as dust in the streets!
4 But now the Lord will strip away Tyre's
possessions
and hurl its fortifications into the sea,
and it will be burned to the ground.
5 The city of Ashkelon will see Tyre fall
and will be filled with fear.
Gaza will shake with terror,
as will Ekron, for their hopes will be dashed.
Gaza's king will be killed,
and Ashkelon will be deserted.
6 Foreigners will occupy the city of Ashdod.
I will destroy the pride of the Philistines.
7 I will grab the bloody meat from their mouths
and snatch the detestable sacrifices from their
teeth.
Then the surviving Philistines will worship our
God
and become like a clan in Judah.*
The Philistines of Ekron will join my people,
as the ancient Jebusites once did.
8 I will guard my Temple
and protect it from invading armies.
I am watching closely to ensure
that no more foreign oppressors overrun my
people's land.

ZION'S COMING KING

9 Rejoice, O people of Zion!*
Shout in triumph, O people of Jerusalem!
Look, your king is coming to you.
He is righteous and victorious,*

8:19 Hebrew *in the fourth, fifth, seventh, and tenth months.* The fourth month of the ancient Hebrew lunar calendar usually occurs within the months of June and July. The fifth month usually occurs within the months of July and August. The seventh month usually occurs within the months of September and October. The tenth month usually occurs within the months of December and January. **9:1a** Hebrew *An Oracle: The message.* **9:1b** Hebrew *land of Hadrach.* **9:7** Hebrew *like a leader in Judah.* **9:9a** Hebrew *O daughter of Zion!* **9:9b** Hebrew *and is being vindicated.*

8:9,13 Be strong and finish the task! This exhortation of the Lord both opens and closes His word recorded in 8:9-13. Because God had promised His favor and protection to the inhabitants of Judah, they were encouraged to look to the future with confidence and a commitment to complete the construction of the temple. This description contrasts strikingly with the description of their forebears, who refused to pay attention, turned a stubborn shoulder, stopped their ears from hearing, and made their hearts like flint (7:11-12). Now Judah would be blessed and be a blessing to others.

8:11 But now. Zechariah emphasized the contrast between their present state of disobedience and God's coming restoration (see 8:12).

8:19 fasts. God would turn the deprivations of the past into future feasts. What were once annual seasons of mourning would turn into celebrations.

8:20-23 Yahweh's reputation would inspire many nations. As a result, previously pagan nations would gravitate toward Jerusalem to worship God (Isa. 2:3).

9:9 Chapter 9 marks the second half of Zechariah's prophecies. The concluding five chapters focus on the coming King: Jesus Christ. **Rejoice, O people of Zion!** Jerusalem's citizens are to prepare to receive their King, who will come riding on a donkey. **riding on a donkey.** Here, Zechariah prophesies Christ's peaceful entry into the city of Jerusalem (Matt. 21:5), an entry which sets the stage for His eventual return.

yet he is humble, riding on a donkey—
riding on a donkey's colt.
10 I will remove the battle chariots from Israel*
and the warhorses from Jerusalem.
I will destroy all the weapons used in battle,
and your king will bring peace to the nations.
His realm will stretch from sea to sea
and from the Euphrates River* to the ends of the earth.*
11 Because of the covenant I made with you,
sealed with blood,
I will free your prisoners
from death in a waterless dungeon.
12 Come back to the place of safety,
all you prisoners who still have hope!
I promise this very day
that I will repay two blessings for each of your troubles.
13 Judah is my bow,
and Israel is my arrow.
Jerusalem* is my sword,
and like a warrior, I will brandish it against the Greeks.*

14 The LORD will appear above his people;
his arrows will fly like lightning!
The Sovereign LORD will sound the ram's horn
and attack like a whirlwind from the southern desert.
15 The LORD of Heaven's Armies will protect his people,
and they will defeat their enemies by hurling great stones.
They will shout in battle as though drunk with wine.
They will be filled with blood like a bowl,
drenched with blood like the corners of the altar.
16 On that day the LORD their God will rescue his people,
just as a shepherd rescues his sheep.
They will sparkle in his land
like jewels in a crown.
17 How wonderful and beautiful they will be!
The young men will thrive on abundant grain,
and the young women will flourish on new wine.

THE LORD WILL RESTORE HIS PEOPLE

10 1 Ask the LORD for rain in the spring,
for he makes the storm clouds.
And he will send showers of rain
so every field becomes a lush pasture.
2 Household gods give worthless advice,
fortune-tellers predict only lies,
and interpreters of dreams pronounce
falsehoods that give no comfort.
So my people are wandering like lost sheep;
they are attacked because they have no shepherd.

3 "My anger burns against your shepherds,
and I will punish these leaders.*
For the LORD of Heaven's Armies has arrived
to look after Judah, his flock.
He will make them strong and glorious,
like a proud warhorse in battle.
4 From Judah will come the cornerstone,
the tent peg,
the bow for battle,
and all the rulers.
5 They will be like mighty warriors in battle,
trampling their enemies in the mud under their feet.
Since the LORD is with them as they fight,
they will overthrow even the enemy's horsemen.

6 "I will strengthen Judah and save Israel*;
I will restore them because of my compassion.
It will be as though I had never rejected them,
for I am the LORD their God, who will hear their cries.
7 The people of Israel* will become like mighty warriors,
and their hearts will be made happy as if by wine.
Their children, too, will see it and be glad;
their hearts will rejoice in the LORD.
8 When I whistle to them, they will come running,
for I have redeemed them.
From the few who are left,
they will grow as numerous as they were before.
9 Though I have scattered them like seeds among the nations,
they will still remember me in distant lands.
They and their children will survive
and return again to Israel.
10 I will bring them back from Egypt
and gather them from Assyria.
I will resettle them in Gilead and Lebanon
until there is no more room for them all.
11 They will pass safely through the sea of distress,*
for the waves of the sea will be held back,
and the waters of the Nile will dry up.
The pride of Assyria will be crushed,
and the rule of Egypt will end.
12 By my power* I will make my people strong,
and by my authority they will go wherever they wish.
I, the LORD, have spoken!"

11 1 Open your doors, Lebanon,
so that fire may devour your cedar forests.
2 Weep, you cypress trees, for all the ruined cedars;
the most majestic ones have fallen.
Weep, you oaks of Bashan,
for the thick forests have been cut down.
3 Listen to the wailing of the shepherds,
for their rich pastures are destroyed.
Hear the young lions roaring,
for their thickets in the Jordan Valley are ruined.

THE GOOD AND EVIL SHEPHERDS

4 This is what the LORD my God says: "Go and care for
the flock that is intended for slaughter. 5 The buyers

9:10a Hebrew *Ephraim,* referring to the northern kingdom of Israel; also in 9:13. 9:10b Hebrew *the river.* 9:10c Or *the end of the land.* 9:13a Hebrew *Zion.* 9:13b Hebrew *the sons of Javan.* 10:3 Or *these male goats.* 10:6 Hebrew *save the house of Joseph.* 10:7 Hebrew *of Ephraim.* 10:11 Or *the sea of Egypt,* referring to the Red Sea. 10:12 Hebrew *In the LORD.*

slaughter their sheep without remorse. The sellers
say, 'Praise the LORD! Now I'm rich!' Even the shep-
herds have no compassion for them. 6 Likewise, I will
no longer have pity on the people of the land," says
the LORD. "I will let them fall into each other's hands
and into the hands of their king. They will turn the
land into a wilderness, and I will not rescue them."

7 So I cared for the flock intended for slaughter—
the flock that was oppressed. Then I took two shep-
herd's staffs and named one Favor and the other
Union. 8 I got rid of their three evil shepherds in a
single month.

But I became impatient with these sheep, and they
hated me, too. 9 So I told them, "I won't be your shep-
herd any longer. If you die, you die. If you are killed,
you are killed. And let those who remain devour each
other!"

10 Then I took my staff called Favor and cut it in
two, showing that I had revoked the covenant I had
made with all the nations. 11 That was the end of my
covenant with them. The suffering flock was watch-
ing me, and they knew that the LORD was speaking
through my actions.

12 And I said to them, "If you like, give me my wages,
whatever I am worth; but only if you want to." So they
counted out for my wages thirty pieces of silver.

13 And the LORD said to me, "Throw it to the pot-
ter*"—this magnificent sum at which they valued
me! So I took the thirty coins and threw them to the
potter in the Temple of the LORD.

14 Then I took my other staff, Union, and cut it in
two, showing that the bond of unity between Judah
and Israel was broken.

15 Then the LORD said to me, "Go again and play the
part of a worthless shepherd. 16 This illustrates how
I will give this nation a shepherd who will not care
for those who are dying, nor look after the young, nor
heal the injured, nor feed the healthy. Instead, this
shepherd will eat the meat of the fattest sheep and
tear off their hooves.

17 "What sorrow awaits this worthless shepherd
  who abandons the flock!
The sword will cut his arm
  and pierce his right eye.
His arm will become useless,
  and his right eye completely blind."

FUTURE DELIVERANCE FOR JERUSALEM

12 This* message concerning the fate of Israel
came from the LORD: "This message is from the
LORD, who stretched out the heavens, laid the foun-
dations of the earth, and formed the human spirit. 2 I
will make Jerusalem like an intoxicating drink that
makes the nearby nations stagger when they send
their armies to besiege Jerusalem and Judah. 3 On that
day I will make Jerusalem an immovable rock. All
the nations will gather against it to try to move it, but
they will only hurt themselves.

4 "On that day," says the LORD, "I will cause every
horse to panic and every rider to lose his nerve. I will
watch over the people of Judah, but I will blind all the
horses of their enemies. 5 And the clans of Judah will
say to themselves, 'The people of Jerusalem have found
strength in the LORD of Heaven's Armies, their God.'

6 "On that day I will make the clans of Judah like
a flame that sets a woodpile ablaze or like a burning
torch among sheaves of grain. They will burn up all
the neighboring nations right and left, while the peo-
ple living in Jerusalem remain secure.

7 "The LORD will give victory to the rest of Judah
first, before Jerusalem, so that the people of Jerusalem
and the royal line of David will not have greater hon-
or than the rest of Judah. 8 On that day the LORD will
defend the people of Jerusalem; the weakest among
them will be as mighty as King David! And the roy-
al descendants will be like God, like the angel of the
LORD who goes before them! 9 For on that day I will
begin to destroy all the nations that come against Je-
rusalem.

10 "Then I will pour out a spirit[A] of grace and prayer
on the family of David and on the people of Jerusalem.
They will look on me whom they have pierced and
mourn for him as for an only son. They will grieve
bitterly for him as for a firstborn son who has died.
11 The sorrow and mourning in Jerusalem on that day
will be like the great mourning for Hadad-rimmon in
the valley of Megiddo.

12 "All Israel will mourn, each clan by itself, and
with the husbands separate from their wives. The
clan of David will mourn alone, as will the clan of Na-
than, 13 the clan of Levi, and the clan of Shimei. 14 Each
of the surviving clans from Judah will mourn sepa-
rately, and with the husbands separate from their
wives.

A FOUNTAIN OF CLEANSING

13 "On that day a fountain will be opened for the
dynasty of David and for the people of Jerusa-
lem, a fountain to cleanse them from all their sins and
impurity.

2 "And on that day," says the LORD of Heaven's Ar-
mies, "I will erase idol worship throughout the land,
so that even the names of the idols will be forgotten. I
will remove from the land both the false prophets and
the spirit of impurity that came with them. 3 If anyone
continues to prophesy, his own father and mother will
tell him, 'You must die, for you have prophesied lies in
the name of the LORD.' And as he prophesies, his own
father and mother will stab him.

4 "On that day people will be ashamed to claim the
prophetic gift. No one will pretend to be a prophet

11:13 Syriac version reads *into the treasury;* also in 11:13b. Compare Matt 27:6-10. **12:1** Hebrew *An Oracle: This.* **12:10** Or *the Spirit.*

11:5 buyers . . . sellers. God's people had been and would yet be oppressed by other nations who got rich at their expense. **Even the shepherds.** Their own leaders, those who had been called to exercise compassion, cared only for themselves.

11:7 So I cared for the flock. In the midst of this nation with abusive and self-serving shepherds, Zechariah is sent as good shepherd, one who foreshadows the Good Shepherd. Like the Messiah, he was rejected. **two shepherd's staffs.** Middle Eastern shepherds often carried two staffs: one to use against predatory animals and one designed to enable the shepherd to retrieve a lost sheep from a hard to reach place. **Favor and the other Union.** Symbolic names of the two staffs. Favor spoke of God's grace toward His oppressed people, and Union symbolized the reuniting of the divided kingdom.

11:12 thirty pieces of silver. The price of a slave gored by an ox, the amount for which Jesus was betrayed.

11:14 bond of unity . . . was broken. The Jews' history was one of family hostility, not harmony. The role of the future Messiah-Shepherd would be to reunite the splintered flock (Ezek. 37:16-28).

11:15 worthless shepherd. In the absence of God's Shepherd, a deceiver would arrive on the scene. He would wound many (v. 17).

12:1 message . . . from the LORD. Zechariah put God's message in the context of His powerful works. God's deeds were powerful, but His declaration was more so.

by wearing prophet's clothes. 5 He will say, 'I'm no prophet; I'm a farmer. I began working for a farmer as a boy.' 6 And if someone asks, 'Then what about those wounds on your chest?*' he will say, 'I was wounded at my friends' house!'

THE SCATTERING OF THE SHEEP

7 "Awake, O sword, against my shepherd,
  the man who is my partner,"
  says the LORD of Heaven's Armies.
"Strike down the shepherd,
  and the sheep will be scattered,
  and I will turn against the lambs.
8 Two-thirds of the people in the land
  will be cut off and die," says the LORD.
  "But one-third will be left in the land.
9 I will bring that group through the fire
  and make them pure.
I will refine them like silver
  and purify them like gold.
They will call on my name,
  and I will answer them.
I will say, 'These are my people,'
  and they will say, 'The LORD is our God.'"

THE LORD WILL RULE THE EARTH

14 Watch, for the day of the LORD is coming when your possessions will be plundered right in front of you! 2 I will gather all the nations to fight against Jerusalem. The city will be taken, the houses looted, and the women raped. Half the population will be taken into captivity, and the rest will be left among the ruins of the city.

3 Then the LORD will go out to fight against those nations, as he has fought in times past. 4 On that day his feet will stand on the Mount of Olives, east of Jerusalem. And the Mount of Olives will split apart, making a wide valley running from east to west. Half the mountain will move toward the north and half toward the south. 5 You will flee through this valley, for it will reach across to Azal.* Yes, you will flee as you did from the earthquake in the days of King Uzziah of Judah. Then the LORD my God will come, and all his holy ones with him.*

6 On that day the sources of light will no longer shine,* 7 yet there will be continuous day! Only the LORD knows how this could happen. There will be no normal day and night, for at evening time it will still be light.

8 On that day life-giving waters will flow out from Jerusalem, half toward the Dead Sea and half toward the Mediterranean,* flowing continuously in both summer and winter.

9 And the LORD will be king over all the earth. On that day there will be one LORD—his name alone will be worshiped.

10 All the land from Geba, north of Judah, to Rimmon, south of Jerusalem, will become one vast plain. But Jerusalem will be raised up in its original place and will be inhabited all the way from the Benjamin Gate over to the site of the old gate, then to the Corner Gate, and from the Tower of Hananel to the king's winepresses. 11 And Jerusalem will be filled, safe at last, never again to be cursed and destroyed.

12 And the LORD will send a plague on all the nations that fought against Jerusalem. Their people will become like walking corpses, their flesh rotting away. Their eyes will rot in their sockets, and their tongues will rot in their mouths. 13 On that day they will be terrified, stricken by the LORD with great panic. They will fight their neighbors hand to hand. 14 Judah, too, will be fighting at Jerusalem. The wealth of all the neighboring nations will be captured—great quantities of gold and silver and fine clothing. 15 This same plague will strike the horses, mules, camels, donkeys, and all the other animals in the enemy camps.

16 In the end, the enemies of Jerusalem who survive the plague will go up to Jerusalem each year to worship the King, the LORD of Heaven's Armies, and to celebrate the Festival of Shelters. 17 Any nation in the world that refuses to come to Jerusalem to worship the King, the LORD of Heaven's Armies, will have no rain. 18 If the people of Egypt refuse to attend the festival, the LORD will punish* them with the same plague that he sends on the other nations who refuse to go. 19 Egypt and the other nations will all be punished if they don't go to celebrate the Festival of Shelters.

20 On that day even the harness bells of the horses will be inscribed with these words: HOLY TO THE LORD. And the cooking pots in the Temple of the LORD will be as sacred as the basins used beside the altar. 21 In fact, every cooking pot in Jerusalem and Judah will be holy to the LORD of Heaven's Armies. All who come to worship will be free to use any of these pots to boil their sacrifices. And on that day there will no longer be traders* in the Temple of the LORD of Heaven's Armies.

13:6 Hebrew *wounds between your hands?* **14:5a** The meaning of the Hebrew is uncertain. **14:5b** As in Greek version; Hebrew reads *with you.* **14:6** Hebrew *the precious ones shall diminish;* or *the precious ones and frost.* The meaning of the Hebrew is uncertain. **14:8** Hebrew *half toward the eastern sea and half toward the western sea.* **14:18** As in some Hebrew manuscripts and Greek and Syriac versions; Masoretic Text reads *will not punish.* **14:21** Hebrew *Canaanites.*

13:7 Sword. This sword, representing death, would be employed to bring God's vengeance—first on the Shepherd, then on even the little ones . . . Without the Shepherd, God's people would be vulnerable and defenseless as history attests (see Matt. 26:31,56).

14:3 The LORD will give victory. The Lord will fight on behalf of Jerusalem.

14:18 punish . . . with the same plague. Only those who worshiped God would enjoy His blessings.

14:20 HOLY TO THE LORD. This phrase summarizes God's desire: that all may know God as holy and recognize that there is no other god.

INTRODUCTION TO

MALACHI

PERSONAL READING PLAN

- ☐Malachi 1:1-14
- ☐Malachi 2:1-16
- ☐Malachi 2:17–3:18
- ☐Malachi 4:1-6

AUTHOR

This book is ascribed to Malachi, a contemporary of Ezra and Nehemiah. Since the word "Malachi" means "my messenger," some think that this is a title rather than the name of a person. The Greek translation of the Old Testament (the Septuagint) renders "Malachi" in 1:1 as "my messenger." However, the evidence is not conclusive, and there may well have been a specific prophet by this name.

DATE

The sins denounced by Nehemiah (see Neh. 13:6-31) correspond closely to the denunciation of Malachi (see 1:6-14; 2:14-16; 3:8-11). Hence, a date may be inferred any time after Nehemiah returned to Jerusalem the second time, that is, some time later than 433 B.C.

THEME

Repentance as a prescription to cure spiritual skepticism and indifference.

HISTORICAL BACKGROUND

In the face of stern opposition, the exiles finished the temple in 516 B.C. under the leadership of Zerubbabel and the prophecy of Haggai. The community was strengthened through the restoration of temple worship by Ezra in 458 B.C. In 445 B.C., Nehemiah returned to Jerusalem, rebuilt the walls, and brought many religious reforms.

Twelve years later, Nehemiah returned to serve the Persian king. With success behind them, the people lapsed into religious indifference. Malachi claims the people are "just going through the motions" of their faith, doubting the love and justice of God. Malachi was most likely the last prophet until the time of Christ, some 400 years later.

CHARACTERISTICS

Malachi uses a question-and-answer form of dialogue to develop his themes. Seven questions or complaints raised by the people are recorded. However, the book is dominated by God's voice—the voice of a loving father (1:6) having to discipline His children with "tough love". Malachi is written in forceful, lofty prose. He uses repetition (the name "Lord of Hosts" occurs 20 times) and vivid images to help the people he is addressing to sense the attitudes of God. When He judges, God will be "like a blazing fire . . . or a strong soap" (3:2), but for the righteous "the Sun of Righteousness will rise with healing in his wings. And you will go free, leaping with joy like calves let out to pasture" (4:2).

1 This is the message* that the LORD gave to Israel through the prophet Malachi.*

THE LORD'S LOVE FOR ISRAEL

2 "I have always loved you," says the LORD.

But you retort, "Really? How have you loved us?"

And the LORD replies, "This is how I showed my love for you: I loved your ancestor Jacob, 3 but I rejected his brother, Esau, and devastated his hill country. I turned Esau's inheritance into a desert for jackals."

4 Esau's descendants in Edom may say, "We have been shattered, but we will rebuild the ruins."

But the LORD of Heaven's Armies replies, "They may try to rebuild, but I will demolish them again. Their country will be known as 'The Land of Wickedness,' and their people will be called 'The People with Whom the LORD Is Forever Angry.' 5 When you see the destruction for yourselves, you will say, 'Truly, the LORD's greatness reaches far beyond Israel's borders!'"

UNWORTHY SACRIFICES

6 The LORD of Heaven's Armies says to the priests: "A son honors his father, and a servant respects his master. If I am your father and master, where are the honor and respect I deserve? You have shown contempt for my name!

"But you ask, 'How have we ever shown contempt for your name?'

7 "You have shown contempt by offering defiled sacrifices on my altar.

"Then you ask, 'How have we defiled the sacrifices?'*

"You defile them by saying the altar of the LORD deserves no respect. 8 When you give blind animals as sacrifices, isn't that wrong? And isn't it wrong to offer animals that are crippled and diseased? Try giving gifts like that to your governor, and see how pleased he is!" says the LORD of Heaven's Armies.

9 "Go ahead, beg God to be merciful to you! But when you bring that kind of offering, why should he show you any favor at all?" asks the LORD of Heaven's Armies.

10 "How I wish one of you would shut the Temple doors so that these worthless sacrifices could not be offered! I am not pleased with you," says the LORD of Heaven's Armies, "and I will not accept your offerings. 11 But my name is honored* by people of other nations from morning till night. All around the world they offer* sweet incense and pure offerings in honor of my name. For my name is great among the nations," says the LORD of Heaven's Armies.

12 "But you dishonor my name with your actions. By bringing contemptible food, you are saying it's all right to defile the Lord's table. 13 You say, 'It's too hard to serve the LORD,' and you turn up your noses at my commands," says the LORD of Heaven's Armies. "Think of it! Animals that are stolen and crippled and sick are being presented as offerings! Should I accept from you such offerings as these?" asks the LORD.

14 "Cursed is the cheat who promises to give a fine ram from his flock but then sacrifices a defective one to the Lord. For I am a great king," says the LORD of Heaven's Armies, "and my name is feared among the nations!

A WARNING TO THE PRIESTS

2 "Listen, you priests—this command is for you! 2 Listen to me and make up your minds to honor my name," says the LORD of Heaven's Armies, "or I will bring a terrible curse against you. I will curse even the blessings you receive. Indeed, I have already cursed them, because you have not taken my warning to heart. 3 I will punish your descendants and splatter your faces with the manure from your festival sacrifices, and I will throw you on the manure pile. 4 Then at last you will know it was I who sent you this warning so that my covenant with the Levites can continue," says the LORD of Heaven's Armies.

5 "The purpose of my covenant with the Levites was to bring life and peace, and that is what I gave them. This required reverence from them, and they greatly revered me and stood in awe of my name. 6 They passed on to the people the truth of the instructions they received from me. They did not lie or cheat; they walked with me, living good and righteous lives, and they turned many from lives of sin.

7 "The words of a priest's lips should preserve knowledge of God, and people should go to him for instruction, for the priest is the messenger of the LORD of Heaven's Armies. 8 But you priests have left God's paths. Your instructions have caused many to stumble into sin. You have corrupted the covenant I made with the Levites," says the LORD of Heaven's Armies. 9 "So I have made you despised and humiliated in the eyes of all the people. For you have not obeyed me but have shown favoritism in the way you carry out my instructions."

A CALL TO FAITHFULNESS

10 Are we not all children of the same Father? Are we not all created by the same God? Then why do we betray each other, violating the covenant of our ancestors?

11 Judah has been unfaithful, and a detestable thing has been done in Israel and in Jerusalem. The men of Judah have defiled the LORD's beloved sanctuary by marrying women who worship idols. 12 May the LORD cut off from the nation of Israel* every last man who has done this and yet brings an offering to the LORD of Heaven's Armies.

13 Here is another thing you do. You cover the LORD's altar with tears, weeping and groaning because he pays no attention to your offerings and doesn't accept them with pleasure. 14 You cry out, "Why doesn't the LORD accept my worship?" I'll tell you why! Because

1:1a Hebrew *An Oracle: The message.* **1:1b** *Malachi* means "my messenger." **1:7** As in Greek version; Hebrew reads *defiled you?* **1:11a** Or *will be honored.* **1:11b** Or *will offer.* **2:12** Hebrew *from the tents of Jacob.* The names "Jacob" and "Israel" are often interchanged throughout the Old Testament, referring sometimes to the individual patriarch and sometimes to the nation.

1:7 defiled sacrifices. God gave the priests specific instructions in Leviticus 22:17-30 on how to make acceptable sacrifices. To offer sacrifices wrongly was to profane God's name (Lev. 22:2,32).

2:2 I will curse even the blessings. Words spoken as a blessing or curse in biblical times were understood as bringing into reality whatever was spoken. So to revoke a blessing was unheard of.

2:10 violating the covenant. Malachi condemns the people for breaking the great covenant, which dictated true worship of God and kind, fair treatment of others.

the LORD witnessed the vows you and your wife made when you were young. But you have been unfaithful to her, though she remained your faithful partner, the wife of your marriage vows.

15 Didn't the LORD make you one with your wife? In body and spirit you are his.* And what does he want? Godly children from your union. So guard your heart; remain loyal to the wife of your youth. 16 "For I hate divorce!"* says the LORD, the God of Israel. "To divorce your wife is to overwhelm her with cruelty,*" says the LORD of Heaven's Armies. "So guard your heart; do not be unfaithful to your wife."

17 You have wearied the LORD with your words.

"How have we wearied him?" you ask.

You have wearied him by saying that all who do evil are good in the LORD's sight, and he is pleased with them. You have wearied him by asking, "Where is the God of justice?"

THE COMING DAY OF JUDGMENT

3 "Look! I am sending my messenger, and he will prepare the way before me. Then the Lord you are seeking will suddenly come to his Temple. The messenger of the covenant, whom you look for so eagerly, is surely coming," says the LORD of Heaven's Armies.

2 "But who will be able to endure it when he comes? Who will be able to stand and face him when he appears? For he will be like a blazing fire that refines metal, or like a strong soap that bleaches clothes. 3 He will sit like a refiner of silver, burning away the dross. He will purify the Levites, refining them like gold and silver, so that they may once again offer acceptable sacrifices to the LORD. 4 Then once more the LORD will accept the offerings brought to him by the people of Judah and Jerusalem, as he did in the past.

5 "At that time I will put you on trial. I am eager to witness against all sorcerers and adulterers and liars. I will speak against those who cheat employees of their wages, who oppress widows and orphans, or who deprive the foreigners living among you of justice, for these people do not fear me," says the LORD of Heaven's Armies.

A CALL TO REPENTANCE

6 "I am the LORD, and I do not change. That is why you descendants of Jacob are not already destroyed. 7 Ever since the days of your ancestors, you have scorned my decrees and failed to obey them. Now return to me, and I will return to you," says the LORD of Heaven's Armies.

"But you ask, 'How can we return when we have never gone away?'

8 "Should people cheat God? Yet you have cheated me!

"But you ask, 'What do you mean? When did we ever cheat you?'

"You have cheated me of the tithes and offerings due to me. 9 You are under a curse, for your whole nation has been cheating me. 10 Bring all the tithes into the storehouse so there will be enough food in my Temple. If you do," says the LORD of Heaven's Armies, "I will open the windows of heaven for you. I will pour out a blessing so great you won't have enough room to take it in! Try it! Put me to the test! 11 Your crops will be abundant, for I will guard them from insects and disease.* Your grapes will not fall from the vine before they are ripe," says the LORD of Heaven's Armies. 12 "Then all nations will call you blessed, for your land will be such a delight," says the LORD of Heaven's Armies.

13 "You have said terrible things about me," says the LORD.

"But you say, 'What do you mean? What have we said against you?'

14 "You have said, 'What's the use of serving God? What have we gained by obeying his commands or by trying to show the LORD of Heaven's Armies that we are sorry for our sins? 15 From now on we will call the arrogant blessed. For those who do evil get rich, and those who dare God to punish them suffer no harm.'"

THE LORD'S PROMISE OF MERCY

16 Then those who feared the LORD spoke with each other, and the LORD listened to what they said. In his presence, a scroll of remembrance was written to record the names of those who feared him and always thought about the honor of his name.

17 "They will be my people," says the LORD of Heaven's Armies. "On the day when I act in judgment, they will be my own special treasure. I will spare them as a father spares an obedient child. 18 Then you will again see the difference between the righteous and the wicked, between those who serve God and those who do not."

THE COMING DAY OF JUDGMENT

4 1*The LORD of Heaven's Armies says, "The day of judgment is coming, burning like a furnace. On that day the arrogant and the wicked will be burned up like straw. They will be consumed—roots, branches, and all.

2 "But for you who fear my name, the Sun of Righteousness will rise with healing in his wings.* And you will go free, leaping with joy like calves let out to pasture. 3 On the day when I act, you will tread upon the wicked as if they were dust under your feet," says the LORD of Heaven's Armies.

2:15 Or *Didn't the one* Lord *make us and preserve our life and breath?* or *Didn't the one* Lord *make her, both flesh and spirit?* The meaning of the Hebrew is uncertain. **2:16a** Hebrew *For he hates divorcing.* **2:16b** Hebrew *to cover one's garment with violence.* **3:11** Hebrew *from the devourer.* **4:1** Verses 4:1-6 are numbered 3:19-24 in Hebrew text. **4:2** Or *the sun of righteousness will rise with healing in its wings.*

2:15 your wife. God clearly views being treacherous to one's wife (or husband), as well as divorce, as unjust and in violation of His plan for marriage. Marriage is used here as an illustration of the covenant God made with His "bride," the nation of Israel. God is faithful to His covenants and desires that we be people of fidelity as well.

3:1 my messenger . . . he will prepare the way. The word for "messenger" in Hebrew means "prophet" or "priest." But scholars interpret this as a prophecy of John the Baptist. In fact, Jesus later identified the messenger as John the Baptist (Matt. 11:7-10), whose ministry signaled the coming of the Lord.

3:10-12 Bring all the tithes into the storehouse. Malachi reaffirms the Mosaic covenant of Deuteronomy 28. God had promised Israel that if Israel obeyed, they would be blessed; if they disobeyed, they would be cursed. They were currently experiencing curses. However, if they would obey the Lord and bring offerings to the temple, God promised to pour blessing "without measure" on them.

4:2 Sun of Righteousness will rise with healing. This refers to the Day of the Lord, when righteousness and healing will fill the new heavens and new earth like the bright morning sun.

4 "Remember to obey the Law of Moses, my ser-
vant—all the decrees and regulations that I gave him
on Mount Sinai* for all Israel.
5 "Look, I am sending you the prophet Elijah be-
fore the great and dreadful day of the LORD arrives.
6 His preaching will turn the hearts of fathers to
their children, and the hearts of children to their
fathers. Otherwise I will come and strike the land
with a curse."

4:4 Hebrew *Horeb*, another name for Sinai.

4:4 Remember to obey the Law of Moses. This command, used many times throughout the Old Testament, can mean (1) pay attention to something mentally, (2) meditate as well as obey, or (3) recite the Law. Here the emphasis is on recalling the people to obey.

4:5 I am sending you the prophet Elijah. John the Baptist fulfilled this prophecy in part when he prepared the way for the Messiah. After Elijah appeared in the transfiguration, Christ told His disciples that another Elijah would come. Israel did not accept John the Baptist, so another forerunner will come before the Day of the Lord (Matt. 11:7-14; 17:10-13). Some scholars believe that Elijah is one of the two witnesses in Revelation 11:1-13.

THE NEW
TESTAMENT

INTRODUCTION TO

MATTHEW

PERSONAL READING PLAN

☐Matthew 1:1–2:23
☐Matthew 3:1–4:25
☐Matthew 5:1-48
☐Matthew 6:1-34
☐Matthew 7:1–8:17
☐Matthew 8:18–9:26
☐Matthew 9:27–10:42
☐Matthew 11:1–12:21
☐Matthew 12:22–13:23
☐Matthew 13:24-58
☐Matthew 14:1-36
☐Matthew 15:1–16:12
☐Matthew 16:13–17:27
☐Matthew 18:1–19:15
☐Matthew 19:16–20:34
☐Matthew 21:1-46
☐Matthew 22:1-46
☐Matthew 23:1-39
☐Matthew 24:1-51
☐Matthew 25:1-46
☐Matthew 26:1-46
☐Matthew 26:47–27:26
☐Matthew 27:27-66
☐Matthew 28:1-20

AUTHOR

Nowhere is the author named within the first Gospel. There is, however, a long tradition that has assigned it to Matthew. Little is known about Matthew, except that he was a tax collector. As such, he would have been bitterly hated by the general populace in Israel—with good reason. For one thing, tax collectors worked for Rome, the oppressor, and therefore were seen as traitors to Israel. For another, tax collectors made their living—and many were quite wealthy—by charging above and beyond what Rome required (only the tax collector knew what was owed). Matthew, the tax collector, stands in contrast to the poor and middle-class fishermen who composed the main body of the disciples.

DATE

When Matthew was written is uncertain, but it was probably between A.D. 50–70.

THEME

Jesus is the long-promised Messiah and authoritative teacher.

THE SYNOPTIC GOSPELS

The word "synoptic" literally means "able to be seen together." It refers to the first three Gospels—Matthew, Mark, and Luke—which cover the same events in Jesus' life, often in the same way. A parallel reading of the first three Gospels makes it clear that there is some sort of literary connection between them. The nature of this connection is not absolutely certain, but generally it is assumed that Mark was the first Gospel, that Matthew and Luke had Mark's text before them when they wrote, and that they included some of Mark's material in their own compositions. One reason scholars conclude this is that of the 105 sections of Mark, all but four occur in Matthew or Luke. In fact, Matthew uses 93 of these 105 sections (nearly 90%), including not just the general story but also Mark's very words in 51% of the cases. However, Matthew and Luke also share some 200 verses not found in Mark, most of which consist of the teachings of Jesus. This material may have come from an early (but now lost) collection of Jesus' teachings.

In whatever order they were written, it is clear that when each of the Gospel writers put together their accounts, they did so with a definite purpose in mind. Each selected some stories and left out others to produce an account of Jesus' life that would answer the questions and concerns of a particular audience. Mark probably wrote for Christians in Rome who were suffering under Nero's persecution, and so he told about Jesus who was the Suffering Servant. Luke wrote about the Son of Man who came to seek and to save the needy, the lost, and the outcasts. Matthew wrote to a Jewish audience and told the story of King Jesus, the Son of David, who came as the long-promised Messiah to claim His throne.

CHARACTERISTICS

Matthew is the most Jewish of all the Gospels. It was written by a Jew to other Jews to convince them that Jesus was, indeed, the Messiah foretold by Old Testament Scripture. Thus, the author cites numerous Old Testament prophecies that were fulfilled by Jesus. He uses phrases similar to "all this has happened so that the prophetic Scriptures might be fulfilled" 16 times.

The Jewishness of the Gospel is also seen in the fact that Matthew mentions Jewish customs without explanation (e.g., "phylacteries" in 23:5), that he has a very high view of the law (5:17–20), and that even when recording Jesus' public rebukes, he shows more respect for the teachers of the law and the Pharisees than any other Gospel writer (23:2).

Yet one of the most interesting features of Matthew is that, although he is so Jewish in his concerns, his book clearly portrays the universal nature of the Gospel—that it is for all the peoples of the world. This emphasis emerges right at the beginning when the Gentile wise men bring gifts to the baby Jesus, and it runs through to the end when Jesus sends His followers out to "make disciples of all nations."

Other features of Matthew include his interests in the church (this is the only Gospel to use the word "church") and his concern about the end times—the second coming of Jesus, the end of the world, and the final judgment (his is the fullest account).

STRUCTURE

Matthew is the most orderly in structure of the four Gospel accounts. After an introductory section, the material is organized into five blocks of narrative alternated with five blocks of discourse, or teaching. We can see that this is not an accidental arrangement because Matthew ends each teaching section with a similar statement (compare 7:28; 11:1; 13:53; 19:1; and 26:1).

PASSAGES FOR TOPICAL GROUP STUDY

1:18-25 .. THE GOD-MAN and DIVORCE .... God with Us
3:1-17 ... RECEIVING THE HOLY SPIRIT .... Baptized with Spirit and Fire

PASSAGES FOR GENERAL GROUP STUDY

THE ANCESTORS OF JESUS THE MESSIAH

1 This is a record of the ancestors of Jesus the Messiah, a descendant of David and of Abraham*:

2 Abraham was the father of Isaac.
Isaac was the father of Jacob.
Jacob was the father of Judah and his brothers.
3 Judah was the father of Perez and Zerah (whose mother was Tamar).
Perez was the father of Hezron.
Hezron was the father of Ram.*
4 Ram was the father of Amminadab.
Amminadab was the father of Nahshon.
Nahshon was the father of Salmon.
5 Salmon was the father of Boaz (whose mother was Rahab).
Boaz was the father of Obed (whose mother was Ruth).
Obed was the father of Jesse.
6 Jesse was the father of King David.
David was the father of Solomon (whose mother was Bathsheba, the widow of Uriah).
7 Solomon was the father of Rehoboam.
Rehoboam was the father of Abijah.
Abijah was the father of Asa.*
8 Asa was the father of Jehoshaphat.
Jehoshaphat was the father of Jehoram.*
Jehoram was the father* of Uzziah.
9 Uzziah was the father of Jotham.
Jotham was the father of Ahaz.
Ahaz was the father of Hezekiah.
10 Hezekiah was the father of Manasseh.
Manasseh was the father of Amon.*
Amon was the father of Josiah.
11 Josiah was the father of Jehoiachin* and his brothers (born at the time of the exile to Babylon).
12 After the Babylonian exile:
Jehoiachin was the father of Shealtiel.
Shealtiel was the father of Zerubbabel.
13 Zerubbabel was the father of Abiud.
Abiud was the father of Eliakim.
Eliakim was the father of Azor.
14 Azor was the father of Zadok.
Zadok was the father of Akim.
Akim was the father of Eliud.
15 Eliud was the father of Eleazar.
Eleazar was the father of Matthan.
Matthan was the father of Jacob.
16 Jacob was the father of Joseph, the husband of Mary.
Mary gave birth to Jesus, who is called the Messiah.

17 All those listed above include fourteen generations from Abraham to David, fourteen from David to the Babylonian exile, and fourteen from the Babylonian exile to the Messiah.

THE BIRTH OF JESUS THE MESSIAH

18 This is how Jesus the Messiah was born. His mother, Mary, was engaged to be married to Joseph. But before the marriage took place, while she was still a virgin, she became pregnant through the power of the Holy Spirit.
19 Joseph, to whom she was engaged, was a righteous man and did not want to disgrace her publicly, so he decided to break the engagement* quietly.
20 As he considered this, an angel of the Lord appeared to him in a dream. "Joseph, son of David," the

GOD WITH US

1. Do you know how your parents picked your name? What does your name mean?
2. What age do you think is a good age to get married? How long should you be engaged before getting married?

MATTHEW 1:18-25

3. Why did Joseph decide not to "break the engagement quietly" with Mary? What does this teach us of his character?
4. Why was Jesus born from a virgin? Why is that miracle important to our Christian faith?
5. What does "God is with us" mean? In what ways have you experienced God with you?
6. When did Jesus really become your "Immanuel"—God with you? How are you experiencing Jesus "with you" in your life now?

1:1 Greek *Jesus the Messiah, Son of David and son of Abraham.* **1:3** Greek *Aram,* a variant spelling of Ram; also in 1:4. See 1 Chr 2:9-10. **1:7** Greek *Asaph,* a variant spelling of Asa; also in 1:8. See 1 Chr 3:10. **1:8a** Greek *Joram,* a variant spelling of Jehoram; also in 1:8b. See 1 Kgs 22:50 and note at 1 Chr 3:11. **1:8b** Or *ancestor;* also in 1:11. **1:10** Greek *Amos,* a variant spelling of Amon; also in 1:10b. See 1 Chr 3:14. **1:11** Greek *Jeconiah,* a variant spelling of Jehoiachin; also in 1:12. See 2 Kgs 24:6 and note at 1 Chr 3:16. **1:19** Greek *to divorce her.*

1:1 **This is the record.** It seems curious to the modern reader that Matthew would begin his Gospel with a long list of names. However, this makes perfect sense given that he was writing to a Jewish audience. By tracing the line of Jesus back to Abraham, Matthew was indicating that Jesus was a true Jew.
1:3-6 Only four women are mentioned in these verses. It is surprising that women are mentioned at all in the genealogy since a man's line was never traced through his mother. All four were non-Jews, and in each case, there was something suspect about them and their marriages. Although unlikely to be named as part of the Messiah's line, they draw attention to the fact that God works in unusual ways. **Tamar.** Tamar was a Canaanite who tricked Judah, her father-in-law, into sleeping with her. From this union came the twins, Perez and Zerah (Gen. 38). **Rahab.** She was a prostitute who assisted Joshua's spies when they were in Jericho (Josh. 2:1-21). **Ruth.** A Moabitess who married a Jew named Boaz. She is included in the royal line, although Deuteronomy 23:3 forbids any Moabite from entering "the Lord's assembly." **widow of Uriah.** David seduced Bathsheba, the eventual mother of Solomon, and got her pregnant. He then arranged for her husband Uriah to be killed in battle (2 Sam. 11–12). Bathsheba may have been an Israelite, but she was married to a Hittite.

1:18-25 Matthew and Luke record different aspects of the birth of Jesus.
1:18 **engaged.** A first-century Jewish marriage had three parts to it: the engagement (which often took place when the two people were children and was usually arranged by a marriage broker); the betrothal (a one-year period in which the couple was considered virtually "married," although they did not have sexual relations); and the marriage. Mary and Joseph were at the second stage in their relationship. **she became pregnant.** The penalty in the Old Testament for sleeping with a woman betrothed to another was death by stoning for both parties (Deut. 22:23-24). By this time, however, the breaking of the engagement was the course that was followed. **through the power of the Holy Spirit.** The agent in Jesus' birth was the Holy Spirit (Luke 1:35).
1:20 **a dream.** Dreams were often the means by which God revealed Himself to people. Matthew records four other occasions when dreams were crucial during the birth and childhood of Jesus (2:12, 13, 19, 22). **son of David.** The crucial link between Joseph and David is made quite clear by the angel. **take Mary as your wife.** The marriage was completed when the husband took his betrothed from her parents' home (where she lived during the betrothal) to his own home.

angel said, "do not be afraid to take Mary as your
wife. For the child within her was conceived by the
Holy Spirit. 21 And she will have a son, and you are
to name him Jesus,* for he will save his people from
their sins."
22 All of this occurred to fulfill the Lord's message
through his prophet:

23 "Look! The virgin will conceive a child!
She will give birth to a son,
and they will call him Immanuel,*
which means 'God is with us.'"

24 When Joseph woke up, he did as the angel of the
Lord commanded and took Mary as his wife. 25 But he
did not have sexual relations with her until her son
was born. And Joseph named him Jesus.

VISITORS FROM THE EAST

2 Jesus was born in Bethlehem in Judea, during
the reign of King Herod. About that time some
wise men* from eastern lands arrived in Jerusalem,
asking, 2 "Where is the newborn king of the Jews?
We saw his star as it rose,* and we have come to
worship him."
3 King Herod was deeply disturbed when he heard
this, as was everyone in Jerusalem. 4 He called a meet-
ing of the leading priests and teachers of religious
law and asked, "Where is the Messiah supposed to be
born?"
5 "In Bethlehem in Judea," they said, "for this is
what the prophet wrote:

6 'And you, O Bethlehem in the land of Judah,
are not least among the ruling cities* of
Judah,
for a ruler will come from you
who will be the shepherd for my people
Israel.'*"

7 Then Herod called for a private meeting with the
wise men, and he learned from them the time when
the star first appeared. 8 Then he told them, "Go to
Bethlehem and search carefully for the child. And
when you find him, come back and tell me so that I
can go and worship him, too!"
9 After this interview the wise men went their way.
And the star they had seen in the east guided them
to Bethlehem. It went ahead of them and stopped
over the place where the child was. 10 When they saw
the star, they were filled with joy! 11 They entered the
house and saw the child with his mother, Mary, and
they bowed down and worshiped him. Then they
opened their treasure chests and gave him gifts of
gold, frankincense, and myrrh.
12 When it was time to leave, they returned to their
own country by another route, for God had warned
them in a dream not to return to Herod.

THE ESCAPE TO EGYPT

13 After the wise men were gone, an angel of the Lord
appeared to Joseph in a dream. "Get up! Flee to Egypt
with the child and his mother," the angel said. "Stay
there until I tell you to return, because Herod is going
to search for the child to kill him."
14 That night Joseph left for Egypt with the child
and Mary, his mother, 15 and they stayed there un-
til Herod's death. This fulfilled what the Lord had
spoken through the prophet: "I called my Son out of
Egypt."*
16 Herod was furious when he realized that the
wise men had outwitted him. He sent soldiers to kill
all the boys in and around Bethlehem who were two
years old and under, based on the wise men's report
of the star's first appearance. 17 Herod's brutal action
fulfilled what God had spoken through the prophet
Jeremiah:

18 "A cry was heard in Ramah—
weeping and great mourning.
Rachel weeps for her children,
refusing to be comforted,
for they are dead."*

THE RETURN TO NAZARETH

19 When Herod died, an angel of the Lord appeared in
a dream to Joseph in Egypt. 20 "Get up!" the angel said.
"Take the child and his mother back to the land of Is-
rael, because those who were trying to kill the child
are dead."
21 So Joseph got up and returned to the land of Israel
with Jesus and his mother. 22 But when he learned that
the new ruler of Judea was Herod's son Archelaus, he
was afraid to go there. Then, after being warned in a
dream, he left for the region of Galilee. 23 So the family
went and lived in a town called Nazareth. This ful-
filled what the prophets had said: "He will be called
a Nazarene."

JOHN THE BAPTIST PREPARES THE WAY

3 In those days John the Baptist came to the Judean
wilderness and began preaching. His message

1:21 *Jesus* means "The LORD saves." 1:23 Isa 7:14; 8:8, 10 (Greek version). 2:1 Or *royal astrologers;* Greek reads *magi;* also in 2:7, 16. 2:2 Or *star in the east.* 2:6a Greek *the rulers.* 2:6b Mic 5:2; 2 Sam 5:2. 2:15 Hos 11:1. 2:18 Jer 31:15.

1:21 name him. It was necessary for Joseph to name Jesus and thus formally accept Him as his son. **Jesus.** A common name and the Greek form of the Hebrew name Joshua which meant, "God is salvation."
2:1 King Herod. Herod the Great was a shrewd but cruel monarch who was appointed by Rome to rule over Palestine. His reign lasted from 40 B.C. to 4 B.C. **wise men.** These were astrologers who probably came from Babylon and may have been influenced by Daniel's prophecies.
2:8 worship Him. This was either a cynical or deceptive statement from Herod, statement which contrasts with the genuine worship of the wise men (v. 11). By allowing the wise men to search for the child, he had a better chance of finding Him than if he were to send troops.
2:11 gave him gifts. The giving of gifts signified allegiance. **gold.** A metal of great value; the currency of kings. **frankincense.** A sweet-smelling gum that was burned during worship. **myrrh.** Another gum, used as a perfume and as medicine. It was also used to embalm bodies. Taken together, the gifts represent the identity of Jesus as the royal Son of God who gave His life for His people.
2:16 two years old. This indicates that some time had elapsed since Jesus' actual birth. That Herod was capable of killing children is testified to by another deed he did before his death. He arrested a number of leading people that were executed at the time of his death to assure that genuine mourning would occur when he died!
2:23 He will be called a Nazarene. There is no such quote in the Old Testament. Matthew may have been alluding in general terms to the prophets foretelling the contempt that men would have for Jesus (e.g. Isa. 52:13–53:12). The designation "Jesus of Nazareth" was at first a term of scorn and derision as illustrated in John 1:45-46.
3:1 John the Baptist. There is a gap of 25 to 30 years between the events in chapters 1–2 and the start of Jesus' ministry. John the Baptist was an extremely popular figure whose influence spread from Alexandria in Egypt to Asia Minor.

BAPTIZED WITH SPIRIT AND FIRE

1. Who is the craziest looking man of God you have ever met? Who is the wildest preacher you have heard?

MATTHEW 3:1-17

2. What does John mean by "every tree that does not produce good fruit?" What would that look like in your life?
3. How does Jesus "baptize you with the Holy Spirit?" How does He baptize you with "fire?"
4. Have you been baptized with the Holy Spirit? How does that affect your life?
5. Are you being "baptized with fire" lately? How can your group help?

was, 2 "Repent of your sins and turn to God, for the
Kingdom of Heaven is near.*" 3 The prophet Isaiah
was speaking about John when he said,

> "He is a voice shouting in the wilderness,
> 'Prepare the way for the LORD's coming!
> Clear the road for him!'"*

4 John's clothes were woven from coarse camel
hair, and he wore a leather belt around his waist. For
food he ate locusts and wild honey. 5 People from Je-
rusalem and from all of Judea and all over the Jor-
dan Valley went out to see and hear John. 6 And when
they confessed their sins, he baptized them in the Jor-
dan River.

7 But when he saw many Pharisees and Sadducees
coming to watch him baptize,* he denounced them.
"You brood of snakes!" he exclaimed. "Who warned
you to flee the coming wrath? 8 Prove by the way you
live that you have repented of your sins and turned
to God. 9 Don't just say to each other, 'We're safe, for
we are descendants of Abraham.' That means noth-
ing, for I tell you, God can create children of Abraham
from these very stones. 10 Even now the ax of God's
judgment is poised, ready to sever the roots of the
trees. Yes, every tree that does not produce good fruit
will be chopped down and thrown into the fire.

11 "I baptize with* water those who repent of their
sins and turn to God. But someone is coming soon who
is greater than I am—so much greater that I'm not
worthy even to be his slave and carry his sandals. He
will baptize you with the Holy Spirit and with fire.*
12 He is ready to separate the chaff from the wheat
with his winnowing fork. Then he will clean up the
threshing area, gathering the wheat into his barn but
burning the chaff with never-ending fire."

THE BAPTISM OF JESUS

13 Then Jesus went from Galilee to the Jordan River to
be baptized by John. 14 But John tried to talk him out of
it. "I am the one who needs to be baptized by you," he
said, "so why are you coming to me?"

15 But Jesus said, "It should be done, for we must
carry out all that God requires.*" So John agreed to
baptize him.

16 After his baptism, as Jesus came up out of the wa-
ter, the heavens were opened* and he saw the Spirit of
God descending like a dove and settling on him. 17 And
a voice from heaven said, "This is my dearly loved
Son, who brings me great joy."

THE TEMPTATION OF JESUS

4 Then Jesus was led by the Spirit into the wilder-
ness to be tempted there by the devil. 2 For forty
days and forty nights he fasted and became very hun-
gry.

3 During that time the devil* came and said to him,
"If you are the Son of God, tell these stones to become
loaves of bread."

4 But Jesus told him, "No! The Scriptures say,

> 'People do not live by bread alone,
> but by every word that comes from the mouth
> of God.'*"

5 Then the devil took him to the holy city, Jerusalem,
to the highest point of the Temple, 6 and said, "If you
are the Son of God, jump off! For the Scriptures say,

3:2 Or *has come*, or *is coming soon*. 3:3 Isa 40:3 (Greek version). 3:7 Or *coming to be baptized*. 3:11a Or *in*. 3:11b Or *in the Holy Spirit and in fire*. 3:15 Or *for we must fulfill all righteousness*. 3:16 Some manuscripts read *opened to him*. 4:3 Greek *the tempter*. 4:4 Deut 8:3.

3:2 Kingdom of Heaven. Pious Jews did not mention God's name. To speak of God, they referred to His abode—heaven. Most believe this phrase has the same meaning as the phrase "kingdom of God" in Mark (Mark 1:15). It refers to the messianic age that is yet to come in which God will reign.

3:3 Prepare the way. This is a quotation from Isaiah 40:3. The Jews expected that an Elijah-like figure would precede the Messiah and announce His coming (Mal. 3:1; 4:5; see also Matt. 17:3). This "voice" who would pave the way for the Lord was John the Baptist. Ancient roads were notoriously bad, and the only time they tended to be smoothed out was in preparation for a royal visit.

3:4 locusts and wild honey. This description is similar to that of Old Testament prophets, in particular Elijah (2 Kings 1:8; Zech. 13:4). The locusts John ate could have been either an insect (Lev. 11:22-23) or a kind of bean from the locust tree. Honey could refer either to what bees produce or to the sap of a certain tree. In either case, this was the food eaten by the poorest of people.

3:11 I'm not worthy even to be his slave and carry his sandals. This would be the task of a slave. **fire.** Fire is a symbol of judgment that Matthew refers to a number of times (5:22; 7:19; 13:40,42; 18:8; 25:41).

3:12 gathering the wheat. In the harvesting of wheat, after the grain is separated from the straw, the mixture is tossed up in the air. The heavier kernels fall to the ground, while the straw and chaff blow away and are later burned. This is an image of the judgment that will take place at the future return of Jesus.

3:13 baptized. By allowing Himself to be baptized, Jesus identifies with the people of Israel and with their sin, modeling an act of genuine repentance (although He Himself was without sin as 1 Pet. 2:22 indicates).

3:16 like a dove. Matthew uses a dove as a symbol of the coming of the Holy Spirit

4:1 led by the Spirit into the wilderness to be tempted. Jesus' victory over temptation would demonstrate three things: His sinless character; an example of endurance through times of testing; and how to use Scripture as a means of defense against the devil and a support in the face of evil.

4:2 forty days. Moses fasted 40 days on Mount Sinai while receiving the commandments (Ex. 34:28), and Israel was in the wilderness 40 years (Deut. 8:2).

4:3 the devil came. The Spirit led Jesus into the wilderness, but it was Satan who tested Him. His challenges to Jesus came only after Jesus had entered a condition of physical weakness because of His fast. **If you are the Son of God.** This was a temptation to verify the truth of what God had declared (3:17).

4:4 The Scriptures say. Jesus' response is drawn from Deuteronomy 8:3. Originally this was a reflection on the meaning of the manna in the desert. True life involves not just the physical, but also the spiritual (which the word of God feeds). Jesus will not heed Satan but listens only to His Father, God.

4:5 Temple. The Devil's challenge for Jesus is to prove this love and power of God by creating a peril from which God alone can rescue Him.

'He will order his angels to protect you.
And they will hold you up with their hands
so you won't even hurt your foot on a stone.'*"

[7] Jesus responded, "The Scriptures also say, 'You
must not test the LORD your God.'*"
[8] Next the devil took him to the peak of a very high
mountain and showed him all the kingdoms of the
world and their glory. [9] "I will give it all to you," he
said, "if you will kneel down and worship me."
[10] "Get out of here, Satan," Jesus told him. "For the
Scriptures say,

'You must worship the LORD your God
and serve only him.'*"

[11] Then the devil went away, and angels came and
took care of Jesus.

THE MINISTRY OF JESUS BEGINS

[12] When Jesus heard that John had been arrested, he
left Judea and returned to Galilee. [13] He went first to
Nazareth, then left there and moved to Capernaum,
beside the Sea of Galilee, in the region of Zebulun and
Naphtali. [14] This fulfilled what God said through the
prophet Isaiah:

[15] "In the land of Zebulun and of Naphtali,
beside the sea, beyond the Jordan River,
in Galilee where so many Gentiles live,
[16] the people who sat in darkness
have seen a great light.
And for those who lived in the land where death
casts its shadow,
a light has shined."*

[17] From then on Jesus began to preach, "Repent of
your sins and turn to God, for the Kingdom of Heaven
is near.*"

THE FIRST DISCIPLES

[18] One day as Jesus was walking along the shore of
the Sea of Galilee, he saw two brothers—Simon, also
called Peter, and Andrew—throwing a net into the
water, for they fished for a living. [19] Jesus called out to
them, "Come, follow me, and I will show you how to
fish for people!" [20] And they left their nets at once and
followed him.
[21] A little farther up the shore he saw two other
brothers, James and John, sitting in a boat with their
father, Zebedee, repairing their nets. And he called
them to come, too. [22] They immediately followed him,
leaving the boat and their father behind.

CROWDS FOLLOW JESUS

[23] Jesus traveled throughout the region of Galilee, teach-
ing in the synagogues and announcing the Good News
about the Kingdom. And he healed every kind of disease
and illness. [24] News about him spread as far as Syria, and
people soon began bringing to him all who were sick.
And whatever their sickness or disease, or if they were
demon possessed or epileptic or paralyzed—he healed
them all. [25] Large crowds followed him wherever he
went—people from Galilee, the Ten Towns,* Jerusalem,
from all over Judea, and from east of the Jordan River.

THE SERMON ON THE MOUNT

5 One day as he saw the crowds gathering, Jesus
went up on the mountainside and sat down. His
disciples gathered around him, [2] and he began to
teach them.

THE BEATITUDES

[3] "God blesses those who are poor and realize their
need for him,*
for the Kingdom of Heaven is theirs.
[4] God blesses those who mourn,
for they will be comforted.
[5] God blesses those who are humble,
for they will inherit the whole earth.

ATTITUDE ADJUSTMENT

1. Do you pray or "say a blessing" before you eat meals? Why or why not?

MATTHEW 5:1-12

2. What does it mean to be "humble"? How can a humble person be a good competitor?
3. What does "hearts are pure" mean to you? What things in school, sports, or the rest of life make it hard for you to be pure in heart?
4. On a scale of 1 (not at all) to 10 (totally), how much do you hunger and thirst for righteousness?
5. If God gave you an attitude adjustment, which of the eight "attitudes" in these verses would need the most work?

4:6 Ps 91:11-12. **4:7** Deut 6:16. **4:10** Deut 6:13. **4:15-16** Isa 9:1-2 (Greek version). **4:17** Or *has come*, or *is coming soon*. **4:25** Greek *Decapolis*. **5:3** Greek *poor in spirit*.

4:7 The Scriptures also say. Jesus responds that people are not to test God, as Deuteronomy 6:16 clearly states, but to trust Him.
4:8-9 I will give it all to you. The final temptation has to do with gaining the kingdoms of the world without suffering the coming agonies of the cross.
4:12 John had been arrested. John's arrest and imprisonment are described in more detail in 14:1-12. **Galilee.** This was the northern province of Palestine. It was small, about 25 by 35 miles in size, but quite densely populated. In the time of Jesus, approximately 350,000 people lived there—100,000 of whom were Jews. It was a rich farming and fishing region.
4:13 Nazareth. This was a village located in the hill country of Galilee, 20 miles southwest of Capernaum.
4:20 they left their nets at once. According to 4:12-17, Jesus had been living and preaching in Capernaum. These fishermen probably had the chance to hear His message prior to their call. Still, what they did was an act of great faith and courage.
5:1 on the mountainside. To the original Jewish readers, this would have been an inescapable allusion to when Moses delivered the Law to Israel from Mount Sinai (Deut. 18:15). **sat down.** When rabbis taught, they would sit rather than stand. This accents Jesus' authoritative position.
5:3 God blesses. The Greek word *makarios* refers to people who are to be congratulated. It does not necessarily mean they are happy or prospering. Instead, whether they feel it or not, they are fortunate because their condition reflects that they are in a right relationship to God. **those who are poor and realize their need for him.** This phrase does not refer to those who are poor in the material sense but to those who acknowledge their need of God.
5:5 those who are humble. This involves a lifestyle marked by thoughtfulness, humility, and courteousness. **inherit the whole earth.** The irony of God's reign is that, despite the efforts of those who grasp for the world, it will one day be given not to those who have been covetous but to those who have been generous.

6 God blesses those who hunger and thirst for
justice,*
for they will be satisfied.
7 God blesses those who are merciful,
for they will be shown mercy.
8 God blesses those whose hearts are pure,
for they will see God.
9 God blesses those who work for peace,
for they will be called the children of God.
10 God blesses those who are persecuted for doing
right,
for the Kingdom of Heaven is theirs.

11 "God blesses you when people mock you and
persecute you and lie about you and say all sorts of
evil things against you because you are my followers.
12 Be happy about it! Be very glad! For a great reward
awaits you in heaven. And remember, the ancient
prophets were persecuted in the same way.

TEACHING ABOUT SALT AND LIGHT

13 "You are the salt of the earth. But what good is salt
if it has lost its flavor? Can you make it salty again? It
will be thrown out and trampled underfoot as worth-
less.
14 "You are the light of the world—like a city on a
hilltop that cannot be hidden. 15 No one lights a lamp
and then puts it under a basket. Instead, a lamp is
placed on a stand, where it gives light to everyone
in the house. 16 In the same way, let your good deeds
shine out for all to see, so that everyone will praise
your heavenly Father.

TEACHING ABOUT THE LAW

17 "Don't misunderstand why I have come. I did not
come to abolish the law of Moses or the writings of
the prophets. No, I came to accomplish their purpose.
18 I tell you the truth, until heaven and earth disap-
pear, not even the smallest detail of God's law will
disappear until its purpose is achieved. 19 So if you
ignore the least commandment and teach others to
do the same, you will be called the least in the King-
dom of Heaven. But anyone who obeys God's laws and
teaches them will be called great in the Kingdom of
Heaven.
20 "But I warn you—unless your righteousness is
better than the righteousness of the teachers of reli-
gious law and the Pharisees, you will never enter the
Kingdom of Heaven!

TEACHING ABOUT ANGER

21 "You have heard that our ancestors were told, 'You
must not murder. If you commit murder, you are sub-
ject to judgment.'* 22 But I say, if you are even angry
with someone,* you are subject to judgment! If you
call someone an idiot,* you are in danger of being
brought before the court. And if you curse someone,*
you are in danger of the fires of hell.*
23 "So if you are presenting a sacrifice* at the altar
in the Temple and you suddenly remember that some-
one has something against you, 24 leave your sacrifice
there at the altar. Go and be reconciled to that person.
Then come and offer your sacrifice to God.
25 "When you are on the way to court with your
adversary, settle your differences quickly. Other-
wise, your accuser may hand you over to the judge,
who will hand you over to an officer, and you will be
thrown into prison. 26 And if that happens, you surely
won't be free again until you have paid the last pen-
ny.*

TEACHING ABOUT ADULTERY

27 "You have heard the commandment that says, 'You
must not commit adultery.'* 28 But I say, anyone who
even looks at a woman with lust has already commit-
ted adultery with her in his heart. 29 So if your eye—
even your good eye*—causes you to lust, gouge it out

GOUGE OUT YOUR EYES

1. Who told you about the "birds and the bees"? Was the situation awkward? Boring? Interesting? Funny?

MATTHEW 5:27-30

2. What is "lust?" What is adultery? Why does Jesus speak so strongly against these two sins?
3. How can a person commit adultery in his heart just by lusting after someone else? What is Jesus saying here?
4. Does Jesus really want you to gouge out your eyes if you look lustfully at another person (or picture)?
5. What is one thing that you would like your group to hold you accountable to in the next week?

5:6 Or *for righteousness.* **5:21** Exod 20:13; Deut 5:17. **5:22a** Some manuscripts add *without cause.* **5:22b** Greek uses an Aramaic term of contempt: *If you say to your brother, 'Raca.'* **5:22c** Greek *if you say, 'You fool.'* **5:22d** Greek *Gehenna;* also in 5:29, 30. **5:23** Greek *gift;* also in 5:24. **5:26** Greek *the last kodrantes* [i.e., quadrans]. **5:27** Exod 20:14; Deut 5:18. **5:29** Greek *your right eye.*

5:8 those whose hearts are pure. The call is for single-minded pursuit of God's way with every facet of our being. **see God.** In the Old Testament, this term described what it meant to experience God's favor.

5:13 salt. Salt was a very valuable commodity in ancient times. It was not only used to flavor foods, but it was indispensable in preserving them. The disciples are to flavor the world around them with God's love and direction, and they are to preserve that which is valuable in life from the spoilage of sin and hate.

5:17 the law of Moses or the writings of the prophets. The Law referred to the first five books of the Old Testament, while the Prophets referred to the Major and Minor Prophets as well as the Historical Books.

5:18 I tell you the truth. Literally, this is "for truly I say to you," a phrase characteristic of Jesus. No other teacher of His era was known to say this. **the smallest detail of God's law.** Some Hebrew and Aramaic letters are distinguishable only by a small line or dot. Jesus accents the validity of the Law as the ethical norm for all God's people.

5:22 angry. The Greek word used here describes deep-seated, smoldering, inner anger rather than a flash of anger. **idiot.** An Aramaic term of contempt: "You good-for-nothing" or "I spit on you." **court.** The Sanhedrin (a group of 70 Jewish men) was the official ruling body of the Jews. This body was responsible for administering justice in matters related to Jewish law. **fires of hell.** Literally, *Gehenna*, a ravine outside Jerusalem where children were once sacrificed to the god Molech (1 Kings 11:7). Jews considered it a defiled place, good only as a garbage dump, which was continually burning. Gehenna became a symbol for the place of punishment and spiritual death.

5:23 altar. The primary responsibility for initiating reconciliation lies with the one who, whether on purpose or by accident, has offended another member of the community.

5:25 thrown into prison. The Romans threw debtors into jail where it was impossible for them to earn money to pay off their debt. Jesus uses this image to describe the situation before God of the person who refuses to seek reconciliation.

5:28 with lust. Just as anger is at the root of murder, so too lust is at the root of adultery. This does not condemn sexual attraction as such but rather the deliberate harboring of desire for an illicit relationship.

and throw it away. It is better for you to lose one part of your body than for your whole body to be thrown into hell. 30 And if your hand—even your stronger hand*—causes you to sin, cut it off and throw it away. It is better for you to lose one part of your body than for your whole body to be thrown into hell.

TEACHING ABOUT DIVORCE

31 "You have heard the law that says, 'A man can divorce his wife by merely giving her a written notice of divorce.'* 32 But I say that a man who divorces his wife, unless she has been unfaithful, causes her to commit adultery. And anyone who marries a divorced woman also commits adultery.

TEACHING ABOUT VOWS

33 "You have also heard that our ancestors were told, 'You must not break your vows; you must carry out the vows you make to the LORD.'* 34 But I say, do not make any vows! Do not say, 'By heaven!' because heaven is God's throne. 35 And do not say, 'By the earth!' because the earth is his footstool. And do not say, 'By Jerusalem!' for Jerusalem is the city of the great King. 36 Do not even say, 'By my head!' for you can't turn one hair white or black. 37 Just say a simple, 'Yes, I will,' or 'No, I won't.' Anything beyond this is from the evil one.

TEACHING ABOUT REVENGE

38 "You have heard the law that says the punishment must match the injury: 'An eye for an eye, and a tooth for a tooth.'* 39 But I say, do not resist an evil person! If someone slaps you on the right cheek, offer the other cheek also. 40 If you are sued in court and your shirt is taken from you, give your coat, too. 41 If a soldier demands that you carry his gear for a mile,* carry it two miles. 42 Give to those who ask, and don't turn away from those who want to borrow.

TEACHING ABOUT LOVE FOR ENEMIES

43 "You have heard the law that says, 'Love your neighbor'* and hate your enemy. 44 But I say, love your enemies!* Pray for those who persecute you! 45 In that way, you will be acting as true children of your Father in heaven. For he gives his sunlight to both the evil and the good, and he sends rain on the just and the unjust alike. 46 If you love only those who love you, what reward is there for that? Even corrupt tax collectors do that much. 47 If you are kind only to your friends,* how are you different from anyone else? Even pagans do that. 48 But you are to be perfect, even as your Father in heaven is perfect.

TURN THE OTHER CHEEK

1. What causes you to reach the boiling point: A slow driver in the fast lane? "Technical problems" during your favorite TV show?
2. If someone attacks you, verbally, physically, or some other way, how do you usually respond?

MATTHEW 5:38-48

3. What does it mean, in practical terms, to "offer the other cheek also"? To "go the extra mile"?
4. How can you both love your enemies and still be a good competitor?
5. Who do you need to forgive today? In what situation is God asking you to go an extra mile?

TEACHING ABOUT GIVING TO THE NEEDY

6 "Watch out! Don't do your good deeds publicly, to be admired by others, for you will lose the reward from your Father in heaven. 2 When you give to someone in need, don't do as the hypocrites do—blowing trumpets in the synagogues and streets to call attention to their acts of charity! I tell you the truth, they have received all the reward they will ever get. 3 But when you give to someone in need, don't let your left hand know what your right hand is doing. 4 Give your gifts in private, and your Father, who sees everything, will reward you.

TEACHING ABOUT PRAYER AND FASTING

5 "When you pray, don't be like the hypocrites who love to pray publicly on street corners and in the synagogues where everyone can see them. I tell you the truth, that is all the reward they will ever get. 6 But when you pray, go away by yourself, shut the door behind you, and pray to your Father in private. Then your Father, who sees everything, will reward you.

5:30 Greek *your right hand.* **5:31** Deut 24:1. **5:33** Num 30:2. **5:38** Greek *the law that says: 'An eye for an eye and a tooth for a tooth.'* Exod 21:24; Lev 24:20; Deut 19:21. **5:41** Greek *milion* [4,854 feet or 1,478 meters]. **5:43** Lev 19:18. **5:44** Some manuscripts add *Bless those who curse you. Do good to those who hate you.* Compare Luke 6:27-28. **5:47** Greek *your brothers.*

5:31-32 divorces his wife. As seen from Matthew 19 and Mark 10, divorce and remarriage is a departure from God's intention for marriage.

5:38 An eye for an eye. This is said to be the oldest law in the world. It is found in the codes of Hammurabi, a king who lived in the 18th century B.C. , as well as three times in the Old Testament (Ex. 21:23-24; Lev. 24:20; Deut. 19:21). The Law's original intent was not to require an "an eye for an eye" but to limit punishment to the extent of the crime.

5:40 coat. The Law (Ex. 22:25-26; Deut. 24:10-13) prohibited a person from seizing a person's cloak as the payment of a debt, since this woolen outer robe was used as a blanket at night. Jesus' call here is for His followers to give beyond what even the Law would require.

5:41 demands that you carry . . . for a mile. Roman soldiers had the right to press civilians into service to carry their gear for a distance up to one mile. The word used here is a technical term for such compulsory conscription.

5:43 Love your neighbor. Jesus quotes Leviticus 19:18. **hate your enemy.** This command is found neither in the Old Testament nor in the Talmud but must have been a current saying.

5:44 love your enemies. The word used here is *agape*. This is love that shows itself not by what a person feels but by what the person chooses to do. It is love done on the behalf of another without the expectation of reward. **Pray.** One way this love is demonstrated is by prayer for those who harass you.

5:46 tax collectors. Tax collectors grew rich by charging people more than what was required, keeping the excess for themselves. That they were doing this as agents of Rome made the offense even more grievous.

5:48 be perfect. This means "having attained the end or purpose" or "being complete." People can be "perfect" if they realize that for which they were made, which is to reflect God's image, and hence to love.

6:1 publicly. In general terms, Jesus makes it clear that His followers are not to seek to make themselves look good by making a public display of religious devotion.

6:2 the hypocrites. It was not their lack of inner conviction that Jesus is faulting (they undoubtedly believed they ought to give to the poor), but their desire to make sure their observance of the traditions was seen by others.

PRAYER UPLINK

1. When do you pray: Before meals? In a crisis? Daily in devotions? Before a test? Other?

MATTHEW 6:5-18

2. What does "your name be kept holy" mean? Why does Jesus open His prayer this way?
3. How is God's will done in heaven? If His will were done that way in your life, how would your life be different?
4. According to verses 12-15, just how much is God going to forgive you your debts? How well do you forgive the debts (or injuries) of others?
5. What is the purpose of fasting? Is there a situation in your life right now that would be helped by fasting?

7 "When you pray, don't babble on and on as the
Gentiles do. They think their prayers are answered
merely by repeating their words again and again.
8 Don't be like them, for your Father knows exactly
what you need even before you ask him! 9 Pray like
this:

Our Father in heaven,
  may your name be kept holy.
10 May your Kingdom come soon.
May your will be done on earth,
  as it is in heaven.
11 Give us today the food we need,*
12 and forgive us our sins,
  as we have forgiven those who sin against us.
13 And don't let us yield to temptation,*
  but rescue us from the evil one.*

14 "If you forgive those who sin against you, your
heavenly Father will forgive you. 15 But if you refuse to
forgive others, your Father will not forgive your sins.
16 "And when you fast, don't make it obvious, as the
hypocrites do, for they try to look miserable and di-
sheveled so people will admire them for their fasting.
I tell you the truth, that is the only reward they will
ever get. 17 But when you fast, comb your hair* and
wash your face. 18 Then no one will notice that you are
fasting, except your Father, who knows what you do
in private. And your Father, who sees everything, will
reward you.

TEACHING ABOUT MONEY AND POSSESSIONS

19 "Don't store up treasures here on earth, where
moths eat them and rust destroys them, and where
thieves break in and steal. 20 Store your treasures in
heaven, where moths and rust cannot destroy, and
thieves do not break in and steal. 21 Wherever your
treasure is, there the desires of your heart will also be.
22 "Your eye is like a lamp that provides light for
your body. When your eye is healthy, your whole
body is filled with light. 23 But when your eye is un-
healthy, your whole body is filled with darkness. And
if the light you think you have is actually darkness,
how deep that darkness is!
24 "No one can serve two masters. For you will hate
one and love the other; you will be devoted to one
and despise the other. You cannot serve God and be
enslaved to money.
25 "That is why I tell you not to worry about every-
day life—whether you have enough food and drink,
or enough clothes to wear. Isn't life more than food,
and your body more than clothing? 26 Look at the birds.

DON'T SWEAT IT!

1. What clothes are you most comfortable in? Are you a "fashion guru?" "Casual dresser?" "Neat freak?" "Slob?"
2. What things do you worry about most? Winning? Grades? Your love life? Other?

MATTHEW 6:25-34

3. Why does Jesus only address worrying about food and clothing? What about winning in sports, doing well in school, getting married? How does Jesus' teaching here apply to those things?
4. Does not worrying about tomorrow mean not planning ahead? How do you balance responsibility with faith?
5. What does it mean to "seek the Kingdom of God above all else"? How can you do that this coming week?

6:11 Or *Give us today our food for the day;* or *Give us today our food for tomorrow.* **6:13a** Or *And keep us from being tested.* **6:13b** Or *from evil.* Some manuscripts add *For yours is the kingdom and the power and the glory forever. Amen.* **6:17** Greek *anoint your head.*

6:7 babble on and on as people of other religions do. A common practice of pagan prayer was to recite a long list of divine names in hopes of invoking a god to action.

6:9 Our Father in heaven. This does not locate God somewhere beyond space but stresses His majesty and dignity. **may your name be kept holy.** The first petition is that God's character and nature be held in great esteem by all.

6:10 May your Kingdom come soon. God's kingdom is in evidence whenever His will is being followed. John the Baptist has already preached that "the kingdom of heaven has come near." But it will come in its fullness when all submit to the will of God. **on earth as it is in heaven.** God does not want to rule over just one part of His creation (heaven) but all of it.

6:11 the food we need. This is a reminder that God is not just concerned about our "spiritual side" but our everyday physical needs as well.

6:13 temptation. The request is not a plea to be exempt from the common moral struggles of life but that God would empower the disciple to have the moral strength to resist giving in to evil during such struggles.

6:16 only reward they will ever get. Once again, as with giving and with prayer (6:2,5), those who play to the crowds and are admired by them for being "righteous" have received all the reward they will get.

6:19 moths . . . rust. The irony of building one's life around one's possessions was that even the most valuable treasures on earth were vulnerable to destruction by insignificant creatures and elements.

6:20 treasures in heaven. These would include relationships made eternal (1 Thess. 4:13-18) and a spiritual wholeness that comes from God's approval of us.

6:22 Your eye is a lamp. Both eye and heart are sometimes used in the Bible as metaphors to describe the motivating principle that guides the way a person lives (Ps. 119:36-37). To have a good eye is to have a pure heart.

6:24 hate. This is using dramatic overstatement to express the fact that loyalty to one master makes loyalty to another master impossible. **money.** Dividing our loyalty between God and money turns money into a god.

6:25 not to worry. When we are focused on that which cannot be taken away from us (treasures in heaven), we don't have to worry about what is essential.

They don't plant or harvest or store food in barns, for
your heavenly Father feeds them. And aren't you far
more valuable to him than they are? 27 Can all your
worries add a single moment to your life?
28 "And why worry about your clothing? Look at the
lilies of the field and how they grow. They don't work
or make their clothing, 29 yet Solomon in all his glo-
ry was not dressed as beautifully as they are. 30 And
if God cares so wonderfully for wildflowers that are
here today and thrown into the fire tomorrow, he will
certainly care for you. Why do you have so little faith?
31 "So don't worry about these things, saying, 'What
will we eat? What will we drink? What will we wear?'
32 These things dominate the thoughts of unbelievers,
but your heavenly Father already knows all your needs.
33 Seek the Kingdom of God* above all else, and live righ-
teously, and he will give you everything you need.
34 "So don't worry about tomorrow, for tomorrow
will bring its own worries. Today's trouble is enough
for today.

DO NOT JUDGE OTHERS

7 "Do not judge others, and you will not be judged.
2 For you will be treated as you treat others.* The
standard you use in judging is the standard by which
you will be judged.*
3 "And why worry about a speck in your friend's
eye* when you have a log in your own? 4 How can
you think of saying to your friend,* 'Let me help you
get rid of that speck in your eye,' when you can't see
past the log in your own eye? 5 Hypocrite! First get
rid of the log in your own eye; then you will see well
enough to deal with the speck in your friend's eye.
6 "Don't waste what is holy on people who are un-
holy.* Don't throw your pearls to pigs! They will tram-
ple the pearls, then turn and attack you.

EFFECTIVE PRAYER

7 "Keep on asking, and you will receive what you ask
for. Keep on seeking, and you will find. Keep on knock-
ing, and the door will be opened to you. 8 For everyone
who asks, receives. Everyone who seeks, finds. And to
everyone who knocks, the door will be opened.
9 "You parents—if your children ask for a loaf of
bread, do you give them a stone instead? 10 Or if they
ask for a fish, do you give them a snake? Of course not!
11 So if you sinful people know how to give good gifts
to your children, how much more will your heavenly
Father give good gifts to those who ask him.

THE GOLDEN RULE

12 "Do to others whatever you would like them to do to
you. This is the essence of all that is taught in the law
and the prophets.

THE NARROW GATE

13 "You can enter God's Kingdom only through the
narrow gate. The highway to hell* is broad, and its
gate is wide for the many who choose that way. 14 But
the gateway to life is very narrow and the road is dif-
ficult, and only a few ever find it.

THE TREE AND ITS FRUIT

15 "Beware of false prophets who come disguised as
harmless sheep but are really vicious wolves. 16 You
can identify them by their fruit, that is, by the way
they act. Can you pick grapes from thornbushes, or
figs from thistles? 17 A good tree produces good fruit,
and a bad tree produces bad fruit. 18 A good tree can't
produce bad fruit, and a bad tree can't produce good
fruit. 19 So every tree that does not produce good fruit
is chopped down and thrown into the fire. 20 Yes, just
as you can identify a tree by its fruit, so you can iden-
tify people by their actions.

TRUE DISCIPLES

21 "Not everyone who calls out to me, 'Lord! Lord!' will
enter the Kingdom of Heaven. Only those who actual-
ly do the will of my Father in heaven will enter. 22 On
judgment day many will say to me, 'Lord! Lord! We
prophesied in your name and cast out demons in your
name and performed many miracles in your name.'
23 But I will reply, 'I never knew you. Get away from
me, you who break God's laws.'

BUILDING ON A SOLID FOUNDATION

24 "Anyone who listens to my teaching and follows it
is wise, like a person who builds a house on solid rock.
25 Though the rain comes in torrents and the flood-
waters rise and the winds beat against that house,

6:33 Some manuscripts do not include *of God.* **7:2a** Or *For God will judge you as you judge others.* **7:2b** Or *The measure you give will be the measure you get back.* **7:3** Greek *your brother's eye;* also in 7:5. **7:4** Greek *your brother.* **7:6** Greek *Don't give the sacred to dogs.* **7:13** Greek *The road that leads to destruction.*

6:27 a single moment. If all the worry in the world cannot add height to a person, what is the purpose of worrying? (Modern medicine might add that worry actually will probably *reduce* one's stature and life span through stress-related diseases!)

6:33 Seek the Kingdom of God above all else. The supreme ambition of the Christian is that all he or she thinks, says, and does be for the glory of God.

6:34 tomorrow. Worry generally has to do with the future, about what lies ahead. The disciple is to live one day at a time.

7:1-2 Do not judge. This is not to say that disciples are never to make moral judgments about the actions of others (7:15-20 requires them to do so in certain instances); rather, it condemns a harsh and censorious attitude toward others.

7:12 Do to others whatever you would like them to do to you. This is the so-called Golden Rule. The negative form of this rule was widely known in the ancient world: "Do not do to others what you do not wish them to do to you." Jesus alters this statement in a slight but highly significant way. He shifts the statement from the negative to the positive. Whereas the negative rule was fulfilled by inaction (not bothering others), the positive rule requires active benevolence. **the law and the prophets.** That love is the summary of the Law is one of Jesus' central themes (Mark 12:30-31). Paul had a similar focus (Rom. 13:8-10).

7:13 broad . . . wide. This is the way of the secular world that stands in contrast to the values taught in the Sermon on the Mount. This is where the "natural" way of the secular world leads. While ultimately such a lifestyle leads to the judgment of God against sin (Rom. 1:18), it also leads to destruction here and now in the sense of estranged relationships and inner chaos.

7:14 narrow . . . difficult. The narrower way is the way of life advocated by the Sermon. This way leads to an inner wholeness marked by the presence of God and fulfilling human relationships.

7:15 disguised as harmless sheep. Prophets often wore animal skins (3:4; 2 Kings 1:8). People might dress in this fashion and claim to be prophets. Or, metaphorically, they might act as innocent as sheep, while their true nature is that of vicious wolves who feed off others.

7:20 by its fruit. One important way to discern if a person is a genuine spokesperson for God is by considering what he or she does. Does the person reflect the values of the Sermon on the Mount in what he or she does?

7:21 Not everyone who calls out to me, 'Lord! Lord!' The earliest Christian confession was "Jesus is Lord." However, Jesus emphasizes actions over words (25:31-46; James 1:19-27; 2:14-26).

7:22 On judgment day. This is the final day of judgment. Throughout the Bible, there is a clear expectation of a final accounting of humanity by God.

7:24-27 on solid rock. In the autumn, rains produced flash floods that swept down ravines. While the two houses in the flood's path look alike, only the one built on a solid foundation will stand. Only those who build their lives on the foundation of the words of Jesus will stand.

PRACTICING THE RIGHT STUFF

1. What is the first thing you ever built? Did it last?
2. What happens when you ignore what your coach tells you to do? What happens when you practice what he teaches?

MATTHEW 7:24-29

3. What does it mean to hear Jesus' words and put them into practice? To hear, but not practice?
4. How will obedience to Jesus' words affect a person's life? How about disobedience?
5. What words of Jesus are you putting into action? What words do you need to get going on?

---

it won't collapse because it is built on bedrock. 26 But anyone who hears my teaching and doesn't obey it is foolish, like a person who builds a house on sand. 27 When the rains and floods come and the winds beat against that house, it will collapse with a mighty crash."

28 When Jesus had finished saying these things, the crowds were amazed at his teaching, 29 for he taught with real authority—quite unlike their teachers of religious law.

JESUS HEALS A MAN WITH LEPROSY

8 Large crowds followed Jesus as he came down the mountainside. 2 Suddenly, a man with leprosy approached him and knelt before him. "Lord," the man said, "if you are willing, you can heal me and make me clean."

3 Jesus reached out and touched him. "I am willing," he said. "Be healed!" And instantly the leprosy disappeared. 4 Then Jesus said to him, "Don't tell anyone about this. Instead, go to the priest and let him examine you. Take along the offering required in the law of Moses for those who have been healed of leprosy.* This will be a public testimony that you have been cleansed."

THE FAITH OF A ROMAN OFFICER

5 When Jesus returned to Capernaum, a Roman officer* came and pleaded with him, 6 "Lord, my young servant* lies in bed, paralyzed and in terrible pain."

7 Jesus said, "I will come and heal him."

8 But the officer said, "Lord, I am not worthy to have you come into my home. Just say the word from where you are, and my servant will be healed. 9 I know this because I am under the authority of my superior officers, and I have authority over my soldiers. I only need to say, 'Go,' and they go, or 'Come,' and they come. And if I say to my slaves, 'Do this,' they do it."

10 When Jesus heard this, he was amazed. Turning to those who were following him, he said, "I tell you the truth, I haven't seen faith like this in all Israel! 11 And I tell you this, that many Gentiles will come from all over the world—from east and west—and sit down with Abraham, Isaac, and Jacob at the feast in the Kingdom of Heaven. 12 But many Israelites—those for whom the Kingdom was prepared—will be thrown into outer darkness, where there will be weeping and gnashing of teeth."

13 Then Jesus said to the Roman officer, "Go back home. Because you believed, it has happened." And the young servant was healed that same hour.

JESUS HEALS MANY PEOPLE

14 When Jesus arrived at Peter's house, Peter's mother-in-law was sick in bed with a high fever. 15 But when Jesus touched her hand, the fever left her. Then she got up and prepared a meal for him.

16 That evening many demon-possessed people were brought to Jesus. He cast out the evil spirits with a simple command, and he healed all the sick. 17 This fulfilled the word of the Lord through the prophet Isaiah, who said,

"He took our sicknesses
and removed our diseases."*

THE COST OF FOLLOWING JESUS

18 When Jesus saw the crowd around him, he instructed his disciples to cross to the other side of the lake.

19 Then one of the teachers of religious law said to him, "Teacher, I will follow you wherever you go."

20 But Jesus replied, "Foxes have dens to live in, and birds have nests, but the Son of Man* has no place even to lay his head."

21 Another of his disciples said, "Lord, first let me return home and bury my father."

22 But Jesus told him, "Follow me now. Let the spiritually dead bury their own dead.*"

8:4 See Lev 14:2-32. **8:5** Greek *a centurion;* similarly in 8:8, 13. **8:6** Or *child;* also in 8:13. **8:17** Isa 53:4. **8:20** "Son of Man" is a title Jesus used for himself. **8:22** Greek *Let the dead bury their own dead.*

8:2 leprosy. No disease was more dreaded since it brought not only physical disfigurement but also social banishment.

8:3 touched him. Actually touching a leper was unimaginable to most first century Jews. Not only did one risk contracting the disease, but such contact also made the person ritually impure and thus unable to participate in the religious life of the community (Lev 5:3-6).

8:4 Don't tell anyone. Jesus had to prevent the crowds from proclaiming Him Messiah before they knew what kind of Messiah He was (one who would suffer and die, not the conquering hero they hoped for).

8:5 Roman officer. A Roman military officer, the commander of 100 men. To most Jews, such a soldier would be a hated symbol of Rome.

8:7 I will come. According to rabbinical law, if Jesus were to enter a Gentile's home, he would be made unclean. This does not create concern for Jesus, however.

8:13 Because you believed, it has happened. The testimony of New Testament Scripture is that belief is a powerful force when centered on God. The power of God is released into the world when people believe that "with God all things are possible" (19:26; Mark 10:27; 14:36; Luke 18:27).

8:15 touched her hand. This is the only healing recorded by Matthew that is initiated by Jesus.

8:16 cast out the evil spirits with a simple command. First-century exorcists used elaborate incantations, spells, and magic apparatus to cast out demons—in contrast to Jesus whose word alone carried incredible power.

8:19 one of the teachers of religious law. Typically these teachers of the Law were opposed to Jesus because of His disregard for the oral law or tradition that was so important to them. However, individual scribes became followers of Jesus.

8:20 Son of Man. This is the title Jesus prefers for Himself. In the first century it was a rather colorless, indeterminate title with only some messianic overtones (based on Scriptures such as Dan. 7:13-14). This phrase could be translated as "man" or simply "I." This title is used 29 times in Matthew, always by Jesus, and never by others.

8:21 bury my father. The obligation of a son to bury his father was so important that it normally took precedence over other religious obligations.

8:22 Let the spiritually dead bury their own. Jesus told people that to be His followers, they had to put following Him above all other obligations.

JESUS CALMS THE STORM

23 Then Jesus got into the boat and started across the lake with his disciples. 24 Suddenly, a fierce storm struck the lake, with waves breaking into the boat. But Jesus was sleeping. 25 The disciples went and woke him up, shouting, "Lord, save us! We're going to drown!"

26 Jesus responded, "Why are you afraid? You have so little faith!" Then he got up and rebuked the wind and waves, and suddenly there was a great calm.

27 The disciples were amazed. "Who is this man?" they asked. "Even the winds and waves obey him!"

JESUS HEALS TWO DEMON-POSSESSED MEN

28 When Jesus arrived on the other side of the lake, in the region of the Gadarenes,* two men who were possessed by demons met him. They came out of the tombs and were so violent that no one could go through that area.

29 They began screaming at him, "Why are you interfering with us, Son of God? Have you come here to torture us before God's appointed time?"

30 There happened to be a large herd of pigs feeding in the distance. 31 So the demons begged, "If you cast us out, send us into that herd of pigs."

32 "All right, go!" Jesus commanded them. So the demons came out of the men and entered the pigs, and the whole herd plunged down the steep hillside into the lake and drowned in the water.

33 The herdsmen fled to the nearby town, telling everyone what happened to the demon-possessed men. 34 Then the entire town came out to meet Jesus, but they begged him to go away and leave them alone.

JESUS HEALS A PARALYZED MAN

9 Jesus climbed into a boat and went back across the lake to his own town. 2 Some people brought to him a paralyzed man on a mat. Seeing their faith, Jesus said to the paralyzed man, "Be encouraged, my child! Your sins are forgiven."

3 But some of the teachers of religious law said to themselves, "That's blasphemy! Does he think he's God?"

4 Jesus knew* what they were thinking, so he asked them, "Why do you have such evil thoughts in your hearts? 5 Is it easier to say 'Your sins are forgiven,' or 'Stand up and walk'? 6 So I will prove to you that the Son of Man* has the authority on earth to forgive sins." Then Jesus turned to the paralyzed man and said, "Stand up, pick up your mat, and go home!"

7 And the man jumped up and went home! 8 Fear swept through the crowd as they saw this happen. And they praised God for giving humans such authority.

JESUS CALLS MATTHEW

9 As Jesus was walking along, he saw a man named Matthew sitting at his tax collector's booth. "Follow me and be my disciple," Jesus said to him. So Matthew got up and followed him.

10 Later, Matthew invited Jesus and his disciples to his home as dinner guests, along with many tax collectors and other disreputable sinners. 11 But when the Pharisees saw this, they asked his disciples, "Why does your teacher eat with such scum?*"

12 When Jesus heard this, he said, "Healthy people don't need a doctor—sick people do." 13 Then he added, "Now go and learn the meaning of this Scripture: 'I want you to show mercy, not offer sacrifices.'* For I have come to call not those who think they are righteous, but those who know they are sinners."

A DISCUSSION ABOUT FASTING

14 One day the disciples of John the Baptist came to Jesus and asked him, "Why don't your disciples fast* like we do and the Pharisees do?"

15 Jesus replied, "Do wedding guests mourn while celebrating with the groom? Of course not. But someday the groom will be taken away from them, and then they will fast.

16 "Besides, who would patch old clothing with new cloth? For the new patch would shrink and rip away from the old cloth, leaving an even bigger tear than before.

17 "And no one puts new wine into old wineskins. For the old skins would burst from the pressure, spilling the wine and ruining the skins. New wine is stored in new wineskins so that both are preserved."

JESUS HEALS IN RESPONSE TO FAITH

18 As Jesus was saying this, the leader of a synagogue came and knelt before him. "My daughter has just died," he said, "but you can bring her back to life again if you just come and lay your hand on her."

19 So Jesus and his disciples got up and went with him. 20 Just then a woman who had suffered for

8:28 Other manuscripts read *Gerasenes;* still others read *Gergesenes.* Compare Mark 5:1; Luke 8:26. **9:4** Some manuscripts read *saw.* **9:6** "Son of Man" is a title Jesus used for himself. **9:11** Greek *with tax collectors and sinners?* **9:13** Hos 6:6 (Greek version). **9:14** Some manuscripts read *fast often.*

8:24 a fierce storm. The Sea of Galilee was a deep, freshwater lake, 13 miles long and 8 miles across at its widest point. It was pear-shaped and ringed by mountains, though open at its north and south ends. Fierce winds blew into this bowl-shaped lake, creating savage and unpredictable storms.

8:28 the region of the Gadarenes. Matthew, Mark, and Luke use different terms to describe the place where Jesus landed.

8:34 they begged him to go away. This may have been in part out of fear of His power but also because He had destroyed part of their livelihood (the pigs). To these townspeople, their pigs were worth more than the lives of the two madmen.

9:2 Your sins are forgiven. Jesus repudiates the teaching that all illness and misfortune is an indication that a person had committed a worse sin than others (John 9:1-3).

9:3 blasphemy. Blasphemy is "contempt for God," and under Jewish law its penalty was death (Lev. 24:16). Jesus' was equating Himself with God, and in the scribes' view this was blasphemy.

9:5 Is it easier. It is far easier to say, "Your sins are forgiven" than it is to heal a person. There is no way to verify whether sins have been forgiven, but it is obvious whether a lame person walks or not.

9:8 authority. The issue here, as in each of the three stories in 8:23–9:8, is Jesus' authority. He has authority over the elements, demons, and even sin.

9:9 Matthew. Presumably the author of this Gospel. Matthew would have been hated by both the religious establishment and the common people because he was working for the Romans.

9:11 Why does your teacher eat with such scum? The Pharisees could not understand how a truly religious person could eat with people whose moral life was disreputable and who violated the practices regarding ritual cleanliness.

9:12 Healthy people don't need a doctor—sick people do. Jesus was not necessarily saying that the Pharisees were spiritually healthy, only that they perceived themselves to be so.

9:15 the groom. In the Old Testament, God is often referred to as the groom of Israel. **the groom will be taken away from them.** This is a foreshadowing of Jesus' death. It will be as if the groom is suddenly, violently abducted just prior to his wedding.

9:20 a woman who had suffered . . . with contant bleeding. She was probably undergoing a period of menstruation, which rendered her ritually impure (Lev. 15:25-33). As a result, she should not have been there in the crowd. She was considered "unclean," and if anyone touched her, that person too would become "unclean."

twelve years with constant bleeding came up behind him. She touched the fringe of his robe, [21] for she thought, "If I can just touch his robe, I will be healed."

[22] Jesus turned around, and when he saw her he said, "Daughter, be encouraged! Your faith has made you well." And the woman was healed at that moment.

[23] When Jesus arrived at the official's home, he saw the noisy crowd and heard the funeral music. [24] "Get out!" he told them. "The girl isn't dead; she's only asleep." But the crowd laughed at him. [25] After the crowd was put outside, however, Jesus went in and took the girl by the hand, and she stood up! [26] The report of this miracle swept through the entire countryside.

JESUS HEALS THE BLIND

[27] After Jesus left the girl's home, two blind men followed along behind him, shouting, "Son of David, have mercy on us!"

[28] They went right into the house where he was staying, and Jesus asked them, "Do you believe I can make you see?"

"Yes, Lord," they told him, "we do."

[29] Then he touched their eyes and said, "Because of your faith, it will happen." [30] Then their eyes were opened, and they could see! Jesus sternly warned them, "Don't tell anyone about this." [31] But instead, they went out and spread his fame all over the region.

[32] When they left, a demon-possessed man who couldn't speak was brought to Jesus. [33] So Jesus cast out the demon, and then the man began to speak. The crowds were amazed. "Nothing like this has ever happened in Israel!" they exclaimed.

[34] But the Pharisees said, "He can cast out demons because he is empowered by the prince of demons."

THE NEED FOR WORKERS

[35] Jesus traveled through all the towns and villages of that area, teaching in the synagogues and announcing the Good News about the Kingdom. And he healed every kind of disease and illness. [36] When he saw the crowds, he had compassion on them because they were confused and helpless, like sheep without a shepherd. [37] He said to his disciples, "The harvest is great, but the workers are few. [38] So pray to the Lord who is in charge of the harvest; ask him to send more workers into his fields."

JESUS SENDS OUT THE TWELVE APOSTLES

10 Jesus called his twelve disciples together and gave them authority to cast out evil* spirits and to heal every kind of disease and illness. [2] Here are the names of the twelve apostles:

first, Simon (also called Peter),
then Andrew (Peter's brother),
James (son of Zebedee),
John (James's brother),
[3] Philip,
Bartholomew,
Thomas,
Matthew (the tax collector),
James (son of Alphaeus),
Thaddaeus,*
[4] Simon (the zealot*),
Judas Iscariot (who later betrayed him).

[5] Jesus sent out the twelve apostles with these instructions: "Don't go to the Gentiles or the Samaritans, [6] but only to the people of Israel—God's lost sheep. [7] Go and announce to them that the Kingdom of Heaven is near.* [8] Heal the sick, raise the dead, cure those with leprosy, and cast out demons. Give as freely as you have received!

[9] "Don't take any money in your money belts—no gold, silver, or even copper coins. [10] Don't carry a traveler's bag with a change of clothes and sandals or even a walking stick. Don't hesitate to accept hospitality, because those who work deserve to be fed.

[11] "Whenever you enter a city or village, search for a worthy person and stay in his home until you leave town. [12] When you enter the home, give it your blessing. [13] If it turns out to be a worthy home, let your blessing stand; if it is not, take back the blessing. [14] If any household or town refuses to welcome you or listen to your message, shake its dust from your feet as you leave. [15] I tell you the truth, the wicked cities of Sodom and Gomorrah will be better off than such a town on the judgment day.

[16] "Look, I am sending you out as sheep among wolves. So be as shrewd as snakes and harmless as doves. [17] But beware! For you will be handed over to the courts and will be flogged with whips in the synagogues. [18] You will stand trial before governors and kings because you are my followers. But this will

10:1 Greek *unclean.* 10:3 Other manuscripts read *Lebbaeus;* still others read *Lebbaeus who is called Thaddaeus.* 10:4 Greek *the Cananean,* an Aramaic term for Jewish nationalists. 10:7 Or *has come,* or *is coming soon.* 10:18 Or *But this will be your testimony against the rulers and other unbelievers.*

9:23 noisy crowd . . . funeral music. These were in all likelihood professional mourners. Even the poorest person was required to hire no less than two flutes and one wailing woman to mourn a death.

9:24 The girl isn't dead; she's only sleeping. Jesus uses the same expression in reference to Lazarus who also died (John 11:11-15). What He means is that she is not permanently dead.

9:27 two blind men. Blindness was common in the ancient world, often due to infection. **Son of David.** There was a strong expectation that the Messiah would be a king in the line of David.

9:34 by the prince of demons. The Pharisees dismiss Jesus' healings by attributing them to Satan.

10:1 twelve disciples. This is the first time in Matthew that the 12 disciples are mentioned. The number 12 is significant. There were 12 sons of Jacob, and they became the patriarchs of the 12 tribes of the old Israel.

10:5 Don't go to the Gentiles. The first mission of the Twelve was to the people of Israel. After the death and resurrection of Jesus, their mission expanded to include all nations (28:19).

10:7 the Kingdom of Heaven is near. This is the same message that John the Baptist gave (3:2).

10:11 stay . . . until you leave. They are not to dishonor their hosts by accepting better accommodations.

10:14 shake its dust from your feet. When pious Jews left a Gentile region and returned to Israel, they shook off the dust of the land through which they had traveled to disassociate themselves from the coming judgment against the Gentiles.

10:16 shrewd as snakes . . . harmless as doves. While Jesus' disciples are to use cleverness—not force—to survive, they are to be honest and holy.

10:17-23 when they hand you over. This passage seems to have more applicability to the time after Jesus' resurrection and ascension. At that time, the early church certainly faced all the perils mentioned here.

10:17 courts . . . synagogues. Jewish courts were called sanhedrins, which were where religious troublemakers were tried and then beaten publicly in the synagogues.

10:18 governors and kings. Some of Jesus' disciples will stand before Roman provincial governors and kings.

be your opportunity to tell the rulers and other unbelievers about me.* 19 When you are arrested, don't worry about how to respond or what to say. God will give you the right words at the right time. 20 For it is not you who will be speaking—it will be the Spirit of your Father speaking through you.

21 "A brother will betray his brother to death, a father will betray his own child, and children will rebel against their parents and cause them to be killed. 22 And all nations will hate you because you are my followers.* But everyone who endures to the end will be saved. 23 When you are persecuted in one town, flee to the next. I tell you the truth, the Son of Man* will return before you have reached all the towns of Israel.

24 "Students* are not greater than their teacher, and slaves are not greater than their master. 25 Students are to be like their teacher, and slaves are to be like their master. And since I, the master of the household, have been called the prince of demons,* the members of my household will be called by even worse names!

26 "But don't be afraid of those who threaten you. For the time is coming when everything that is covered will be revealed, and all that is secret will be made known to all. 27 What I tell you now in the darkness, shout abroad when daybreak comes. What I whisper in your ear, shout from the housetops for all to hear!

28 "Don't be afraid of those who want to kill your body; they cannot touch your soul. Fear only God, who can destroy both soul and body in hell.* 29 What is the price of two sparrows—one copper coin*? But not a single sparrow can fall to the ground without your Father knowing it. 30 And the very hairs on your head are all numbered. 31 So don't be afraid; you are more valuable to God than a whole flock of sparrows.

32 "Everyone who acknowledges me publicly here on earth, I will also acknowledge before my Father in heaven. 33 But everyone who denies me here on earth, I will also deny before my Father in heaven.

34 "Don't imagine that I came to bring peace to the earth! I came not to bring peace, but a sword.

35 'I have come to set a man against his father,
a daughter against her mother,
and a daughter-in-law against her mother-in-law.
36 Your enemies will be right in your own
household!'*

37 "If you love your father or mother more than you love me, you are not worthy of being mine; or if you love your son or daughter more than me, you are not worthy of being mine. 38 If you refuse to take up your cross and follow me, you are not worthy of being mine. 39 If you cling to your life, you will lose it; but if you give up your life for me, you will find it.

40 "Anyone who receives you receives me, and anyone who receives me receives the Father who sent me. 41 If you receive a prophet as one who speaks for God,* you will be given the same reward as a prophet. And if you receive righteous people because of their righteousness, you will be given a reward like theirs. 42 And if you give even a cup of cold water to one of the least of my followers, you will surely be rewarded."

JESUS AND JOHN THE BAPTIST

11 When Jesus had finished giving these instructions to his twelve disciples, he went out to teach and preach in towns throughout the region.

2 John the Baptist, who was in prison, heard about all the things the Messiah was doing. So he sent his disciples to ask Jesus, 3 "Are you the Messiah we've been expecting,* or should we keep looking for someone else?"

4 Jesus told them, "Go back to John and tell him what you have heard and seen—5 the blind see, the lame walk, those with leprosy are cured, the deaf hear, the dead are raised to life, and the Good News is being preached to the poor." 6 And he added, "God blesses those who do not fall away because of me.*"

7 As John's disciples were leaving, Jesus began talking about him to the crowds. "What kind of man

10:22 Greek *on account of my name.* **10:23** "Son of Man" is a title Jesus used for himself. **10:24** Or *Disciples.* **10:25** Greek *Beelzeboul;* other manuscripts read *Beezeboul;* Latin version reads *Beelzebub.* **10:28** Greek *Gehenna.* **10:29** Greek *one assarion* [i.e., one "as," a Roman coin equal to 1/16 of a denarius]. **10:35-36** Mic 7:6. **10:41** Greek *receive a prophet in the name of a prophet.* **11:3** Greek *Are you the one who is coming?* **11:6** Or *who are not offended by me.*

10:22 everyone who endures to the end will be saved. His disciples will not be spared persecution, but they are guaranteed entrance into the kingdom of God.

10:23 before you have reached all the towns of Israel. The early church expected an early return of Christ.

10:25 prince of demons. Literally Beelzebub, which is probably a slang expression for a demon-prince, meaning something like "The Lord of Dung."

10:27 from the housetops. Important announcements would often be made from the roof of a building. What Jesus taught the disciples in private was to be broadcast to all.

10:28 Don't be afraid. They are not to fear death, since those who have the power to kill them have no power over their souls. **Fear only God.** This is not meant to imply that the motive for following Jesus is only fear of God's wrath but that believers' lives are to be marked by a greater regard for God than for human opinion.

10:29 sparrows. Sparrows are worth next to nothing (two for a penny) and yet not one of them dies without God knowing it. **copper coin.** A penny was worth one sixteenth of a denarius. A denarius was the average day's wage of a manual laborer.

10:34 Don't imagine that I came to bring peace to the earth. This should not be taken to mean that Jesus was in favor of war. Jesus turned away from the militaristic expectations of the Messiah. He also proclaimed that "all who take up a sword will perish by a sword" (26:52). He was saying that the demands He would make would create conflicts between people, even people in the same family. Jesus did not seek to avoid conflict when conflict was necessary.

10:37 If you love your father or mother. Jesus was not being anti-family here. He was saying that family ties can work against faithful discipleship, and that God's claim must be our clear and first loyalty.

10:38 cross. It would evoke for His hearers the image of a Roman execution.

10:39 you will find it. This is putting one's own natural inclinations ahead of loyalty to Christ.

10:40 receives. To receive someone is to offer hospitality (vv. 11-14). In a time of persecution this could be dangerous. Welcoming the disciple probably means that the host accepts the teaching of the disciple.

10:42 a cup of cold water. In the hot Middle-Eastern climate, cold water was a gift of life-sustaining importance.

11:2 in prison. Herod arrested John at the instigation of his wife Herodias, who was angry with John for denouncing their marriage (14:1-12).

11:4-6 Go back . . . tell. Jesus responds by inviting John's disciples to report what they have seen with their own eyes and heard with their own ears. His actions and His teaching are all the "proof" that is necessary to identify Him from Old Testament prophecies.

11:7-8 a weak reed. John was not a weak and vacillating reed who was affected by every wind of opinion, nor was he a finely dressed courtier in the halls of King Herod.

did you go into the wilderness to see? Was he a weak
reed, swayed by every breath of wind? 8 Or were you
expecting to see a man dressed in expensive clothes?
No, people with expensive clothes live in palaces.
9 Were you looking for a prophet? Yes, and he is more
than a prophet. 10 John is the man to whom the Scrip-
tures refer when they say,

'Look, I am sending my messenger ahead of you,
and he will prepare your way before you.'*

11 "I tell you the truth, of all who have ever lived,
none is greater than John the Baptist. Yet even the
least person in the Kingdom of Heaven is greater
than he is! 12 And from the time John the Baptist be-
gan preaching until now, the Kingdom of Heaven has
been forcefully advancing,* and violent people are
attacking it. 13 For before John came, all the prophets
and the law of Moses looked forward to this present
time. 14 And if you are willing to accept what I say,
he is Elijah, the one the prophets said would come.*
15 Anyone with ears to hear should listen and under-
stand!

16 "To what can I compare this generation? It is like
children playing a game in the public square. They
complain to their friends,

17 'We played wedding songs,
and you didn't dance,
so we played funeral songs,
and you didn't mourn.'

18 For John didn't spend his time eating and drinking,
and you say, 'He's possessed by a demon.' 19 The Son of
Man,* on the other hand, feasts and drinks, and you
say, 'He's a glutton and a drunkard, and a friend of tax
collectors and other sinners!' But wisdom is shown to
be right by its results."

JUDGMENT FOR THE UNBELIEVERS

20 Then Jesus began to denounce the towns where he
had done so many of his miracles, because they hadn't
repented of their sins and turned to God. 21 "What sor-
row awaits you, Korazin and Bethsaida! For if the
miracles I did in you had been done in wicked Tyre
and Sidon, their people would have repented of their
sins long ago, clothing themselves in burlap and
throwing ashes on their heads to show their remorse.
22 I tell you, Tyre and Sidon will be better off on judg-
ment day than you.

23 "And you people of Capernaum, will you be hon-
ored in heaven? No, you will go down to the place of
the dead.* For if the miracles I did for you had been
done in wicked Sodom, it would still be here today. 24 I
tell you, even Sodom will be better off on judgment
day than you."

JESUS' PRAYER OF THANKSGIVING

25 At that time Jesus prayed this prayer: "O Father,
Lord of heaven and earth, thank you for hiding these
things from those who think themselves wise and
clever, and for revealing them to the childlike. 26 Yes,
Father, it pleased you to do it this way!

27 "My Father has entrusted everything to me. No
one truly knows the Son except the Father, and no one
truly knows the Father except the Son and those to
whom the Son chooses to reveal him."

28 Then Jesus said, "Come to me, all of you who are
weary and carry heavy burdens, and I will give you
rest. 29 Take my yoke upon you. Let me teach you, be-
cause I am humble and gentle at heart, and you will
find rest for your souls. 30 For my yoke is easy to bear,
and the burden I give you is light."

A DISCUSSION ABOUT THE SABBATH

12 At about that time Jesus was walking through
some grainfields on the Sabbath. His disciples
were hungry, so they began breaking off some heads
of grain and eating them. 2 But some Pharisees saw
them do it and protested, "Look, your disciples are
breaking the law by harvesting grain on the Sab-
bath."

3 Jesus said to them, "Haven't you read in the
Scriptures what David did when he and his com-
panions were hungry? 4 He went into the house
of God, and he and his companions broke the law
by eating the sacred loaves of bread that only the
priests are allowed to eat. 5 And haven't you read
in the law of Moses that the priests on duty in the
Temple may work on the Sabbath? 6 I tell you, there
is one here who is even greater than the Temple!
7 But you would not have condemned my innocent
disciples if you knew the meaning of this Scripture:
'I want you to show mercy, not offer sacrifices.'*
8 For the Son of Man* is Lord, even over the Sab-
bath!"

11:10 Mal 3:1. **11:12** Or *the Kingdom of Heaven has suffered from violence.* **11:14** See Mal 4:5. **11:19** "Son of Man" is a title Jesus used for himself. **11:23** Greek *to Hades.* **12:7** Hos 6:6 (Greek version). **12:8** "Son of Man" is a title Jesus used for himself.

11:9-10 more than a prophet. John was a very special prophet. He had been foretold by Old Testament prophecy. His role, as the quotation from Malachi 3:1 shows, was to prepare for the coming of the Messiah.

11:19 wisdom is shown to be right by its results. Despite the leaders' rejection of Jesus and John, God's wisdom in sending them is demonstrated in that both will ultimately bear evidence to the kingdom of God at work.

11:20 repented. To repent is to change your mind about the direction in which you are going.

11:21 Korazin. Apart from this reference (and the parallel in Luke 10:13) and one reference in rabbinic writing, there is no other mention of Chorazin. **Bethsaida.** The home of Peter, Andrew, and Philip (John 1:44; 12:21). **Tyre and Sidon.** These were two Phoenician port cities inhabited by Gentiles. **burlap and throwing ashes.** As a sign of mourning and repentance from sin, people would wear rough clothing and cover themselves with ashes.

11:23 Capernaum. The village where Jesus performed many of His first miracles (8:5-17). **Sodom.** This city, destroyed by God because of its evil, was legendary for its wickedness (Gen. 18:20–19:29).

11:25 wise and clever. The scribes and Pharisees, though educated and supposedly wise, are blind to God's plan (1 Cor. 1:19-20).

11:27 My Father. Jesus here defines His relationship with the One He calls "Father" in verse 25. This is one of the most explicit statements in the Gospels about who Jesus is. Three points are made: (1) All things are shared between the Father and the Son; (2) There is an intimate relationship between the two; (3) It is Jesus who reveals the Father to people (John 3:34-35; 10:15).

11:30 burden. The demands of discipleship, while costly in one way (5-7; 8:18-22), are "light" in comparison with the demands of ceremonial law.

12:1 Sabbath. The seventh day of the week (Saturday) begins Friday at sunset and ends Saturday at sunset. The fourth Commandment is to rest from all labor on the Sabbath (Ex. 20:8-11). By the first century, scores of laws had evolved which defined what could not be done on the Sabbath. **breaking off some heads of grain and eating them.** It was permissible for hungry travelers to pluck and eat grain from a field (Deut. 23:25).

12:4 eating the sacred loaves of bread. Each Sabbath, 12 fresh loaves of bread were put in the Holy Place (Ex. 25:30; Num. 4:7). Only the priests were to eat the old bread. David did what was unlawful, providing a precedent that human need supersedes ceremonial law.

JESUS HEALS ON THE SABBATH

9 Then Jesus went over to their synagogue, 10 where
he noticed a man with a deformed hand. The Phar-
isees asked Jesus, "Does the law permit a person to
work by healing on the Sabbath?" (They were hoping
he would say yes, so they could bring charges against
him.)
11 And he answered, "If you had a sheep that fell
into a well on the Sabbath, wouldn't you work to pull
it out? Of course you would. 12 And how much more
valuable is a person than a sheep! Yes, the law per-
mits a person to do good on the Sabbath."
13 Then he said to the man, "Hold out your hand." So
the man held out his hand, and it was restored, just
like the other one! 14 Then the Pharisees called a meet-
ing to plot how to kill Jesus.

JESUS, GOD'S CHOSEN SERVANT

15 But Jesus knew what they were planning. So he left
that area, and many people followed him. He healed
all the sick among them, 16 but he warned them not
to reveal who he was. 17 This fulfilled the prophecy of
Isaiah concerning him:

18 "Look at my Servant, whom I have chosen.
He is my Beloved, who pleases me.
I will put my Spirit upon him,
and he will proclaim justice to the nations.
19 He will not fight or shout
or raise his voice in public.
20 He will not crush the weakest reed
or put out a flickering candle.
Finally he will cause justice to be victorious.
21 And his name will be the hope
of all the world."*

JESUS AND THE PRINCE OF DEMONS

22 Then a demon-possessed man, who was blind and
couldn't speak, was brought to Jesus. He healed the
man so that he could both speak and see. 23 The crowd
was amazed and asked, "Could it be that Jesus is the
Son of David, the Messiah?"
24 But when the Pharisees heard about the miracle,
they said, "No wonder he can cast out demons. He gets
his power from Satan,* the prince of demons."
25 Jesus knew their thoughts and replied, "Any
kingdom divided by civil war is doomed. A town or
family splintered by feuding will fall apart. 26 And if
Satan is casting out Satan, he is divided and fighting
against himself. His own kingdom will not survive.
27 And if I am empowered by Satan, what about your
own exorcists? They cast out demons, too, so they
will condemn you for what you have said. 28 But if I
am casting out demons by the Spirit of God, then the
Kingdom of God has arrived among you. 29 For who is
powerful enough to enter the house of a strong man
and plunder his goods? Only someone even stron-
ger—someone who could tie him up and then plun-
der his house.
30 "Anyone who isn't with me opposes me, and any-
one who isn't working with me is actually working
against me.
31 "So I tell you, every sin and blasphemy can be
forgiven—except blasphemy against the Holy Spirit,
which will never be forgiven. 32 Anyone who speaks
against the Son of Man can be forgiven, but anyone
who speaks against the Holy Spirit will never be for-
given, either in this world or in the world to come.
33 "A tree is identified by its fruit. If a tree is good, its
fruit will be good. If a tree is bad, its fruit will be bad.
34 You brood of snakes! How could evil men like you
speak what is good and right? For whatever is in your
heart determines what you say. 35 A good person pro-
duces good things from the treasury of a good heart,
and an evil person produces evil things from the trea-
sury of an evil heart. 36 And I tell you this, you must
give an account on judgment day for every idle word
you speak. 37 The words you say will either acquit you
or condemn you."

THE SIGN OF JONAH

38 One day some teachers of religious law and Phari-
sees came to Jesus and said, "Teacher, we want you to
show us a miraculous sign to prove your authority."
39 But Jesus replied, "Only an evil, adulterous gener-
ation would demand a miraculous sign; but the only
sign I will give them is the sign of the prophet Jonah.
40 For as Jonah was in the belly of the great fish for
three days and three nights, so will the Son of Man
be in the heart of the earth for three days and three
nights.
41 "The people of Nineveh will stand up against this
generation on judgment day and condemn it, for they
repented of their sins at the preaching of Jonah. Now
someone greater than Jonah is here—but you refuse
to repent. 42 The queen of Sheba* will also stand up
against this generation on judgment day and con-
demn it, for she came from a distant land to hear the
wisdom of Solomon. Now someone greater than Sol-
omon is here—but you refuse to listen.

12:18-21 Isa 42:1-4 (Greek version for 42:4). **12:24** Greek *Beelzeboul;* also in 12:27. Other manuscripts read *Beezeboul;* Latin version reads *Beelzebub.* **12:42** Greek *The queen of the south.*

12:10 deformed hand. Rabbinic law allowed healing on the Sabbath only if there was danger to life. Clearly a paralyzed hand (which had probably been that way for some time) did not constitute an emergency.

12:13 Hold out your hand. Just as He deliberately declared the paralytic's sins forgiven, knowing that this would be considered blasphemy by the teachers of the Law (9:1-8). Here He deliberately heals on the Sabbath, knowing that this too is anathema to His critics.

12:24 from Satan. Here literally Beelzebul, which was the Canaanite name for the chief god Baal. In Jewish terminology, this became identified as the chief among the demons. To be possessed by this demon meant to be controlled and empowered by him, which is how the teachers of the Law explained Jesus' miracles

12:31 blasphemy against the Holy Spirit. This is to resist the Spirit's convicting work, and so not to see one's sin. Therefore rendering the person unable to experience forgiveness of sin and, ultimately, eternal life.

12:32 will never be forgiven. It might be excusable to utter a word against the Son of Man, since who He is, at this point, is somewhat hidden. Even John the Baptist is not sure about Jesus' identity (11:3). To resist the insights brought by the Holy Spirit, who is the revealer of truth, is to put one's self deliberately outside the orbit of God's revelation.

12:40 three days and three nights. Jesus' death and resurrection took place over a three-day period (Friday, Saturday, and Sunday).

12:41 people of Nineveh. The people of Nineveh repented when Jonah preached to them.

12:42 queen of Sheba. This queen came all the way from Arabia to listen to the wisdom of Solomon (1 Kings 10:1-13). In both examples, Gentiles heeded the words of a Jew, but the Jews of this generation will not heed One greater than both Jonah and Solomon.

12:43-45 this evil generation. Jesus tells a parable about the spiritual state of His generation. By His message of healing, Jesus had swept out the demon that possessed the people. But the new Spirit, the Holy Spirit, is not invited to take up residence in their hearts. So, evil returns in much greater power.

43 "When an evil* spirit leaves a person, it goes
into the desert, seeking rest but finding none. 44 Then
it says, 'I will return to the person I came from.' So it
returns and finds its former home empty, swept, and
in order. 45 Then the spirit finds seven other spirits
more evil than itself, and they all enter the person
and live there. And so that person is worse off than
before. That will be the experience of this evil generation."

THE TRUE FAMILY OF JESUS

46 As Jesus was speaking to the crowd, his mother
and brothers stood outside, asking to speak to him.
47 Someone told Jesus, "Your mother and your brothers are standing outside, and they want to speak to
you."*
48 Jesus asked, "Who is my mother? Who are my
brothers?" 49 Then he pointed to his disciples and said,
"Look, these are my mother and brothers. 50 Anyone
who does the will of my Father in heaven is my brother and sister and mother!"

PARABLE OF THE FARMER SCATTERING SEED

13 Later that same day Jesus left the house and
sat beside the lake. 2 A large crowd soon gathered around him, so he got into a boat. Then he sat
there and taught as the people stood on the shore.
3 He told many stories in the form of parables, such
as this one:
"Listen! A farmer went out to plant some seeds. 4 As
he scattered them across his field, some seeds fell on
a footpath, and the birds came and ate them. 5 Other
seeds fell on shallow soil with underlying rock. The
seeds sprouted quickly because the soil was shallow.
6 But the plants soon wilted under the hot sun, and
since they didn't have deep roots, they died. 7 Other
seeds fell among thorns that grew up and choked out
the tender plants. 8 Still other seeds fell on fertile soil,
and they produced a crop that was thirty, sixty, and
even a hundred times as much as had been planted!
9 Anyone with ears to hear should listen and understand."
10 His disciples came and asked him, "Why do you
use parables when you talk to the people?"
11 He replied, "You are permitted to understand
the secrets* of the Kingdom of Heaven, but others
are not. 12 To those who listen to my teaching, more
understanding will be given, and they will have an
abundance of knowledge. But for those who are not

FOUR SOILS

1. Have you ever planted a garden? What kind? How did it do?

MATTHEW 13:1-23

2. Who first planted the "seed" of the kingdom of heaven in your life? What happened to this seed?
3. What are the "the worries of this life and the lure of wealth" (v. 22)? How do these things "choke" the word of God?
4. Which of the four soils best describes the condition of your heart right now?
5. What "fertilizer" would help your spiritual "soil" right now? What "weeds" need to be pulled?

listening, even what little understanding they have
will be taken away from them. 13 That is why I use
these parables,

For they look, but they don't really see.
They hear, but they don't really listen or
understand.

14 This fulfills the prophecy of Isaiah that says,

'When you hear what I say,
you will not understand.
When you see what I do,
you will not comprehend.
15 For the hearts of these people are hardened,
and their ears cannot hear,
and they have closed their eyes—
so their eyes cannot see,
and their ears cannot hear,
and their hearts cannot understand,
and they cannot turn to me
and let me heal them.'*

16 "But blessed are your eyes, because they see;
and your ears, because they hear. 17 I tell you the
truth, many prophets and righteous people longed
to see what you see, but they didn't see it. And they
longed to hear what you hear, but they didn't hear
it.

12:43 Greek *unclean.* 12:47 Some manuscripts do not include verse 47. Compare Mark 3:32 and Luke 8:20. 13:11 Greek *the mysteries.* 13:14-15 Isa 6:9-10 (Greek version).

12:46 stood outside. According to Mark, Jesus' family thinks that He is "out of His mind" and so they go to "restrain Him" (Mark 3:21). When the family arrives, they find Him surrounded by the crowd. Not wanting to confront Him in that setting, they wait outside.

13:3 parables. Parables are comparisons that draw upon common experience in order to teach about kingdom realities. **plant.** Farmers would throw seed into the soil using a broadcast method.

13:4 a footpath. There were long, hard pathways between the various plots of land. The soil was so packed down that seed could not penetrate the soil and germinate.

13:5 shallow soil with underlying rock. Some of the soil covered a limestone base a few inches beneath the surface. Seed that fell here would germinate, but it would not last since a proper root system could not develop because of the rock.

13:7 thorns. In other parts of the plot there were the roots of weeds. When the seed grew up, so did the weeds, which invariably stunted the growth of the good seed. Although it lived, such seed would not bear fruit.

13:8 fertile ground. However, some of the seed did fall where it was intended. **some thirty, sixty, and even a hundred times.** The good soil yielded a spectacular crop. The normal yield for a Palestinian field is seven and a half times what is sown, while 10 times is an especially good harvest. This is where the emphasis in the parable lies: Not with the unproductive soil but with the miracle crop.

13:9 Anyone with ears to hear should listen. Jesus urges His hearers to ponder His parable. Part of the power of a parable lies in the fact that people must reflect on it in order to understand it.

13:10 Why do you use parables. The disciples ask why Jesus uses parables. Behind this question lies the fact that parables do not always act as simple illustrations that illuminate spiritual truth. They can be hard to understand (13:36).

13:11 secrets. A secret in the New Testament is not something that is hidden as much as it is a mystery that is unclear to the outsider but clear to the truth-seeking insider to whom its meaning has been revealed.

13:13-15 those who are not listening. The problem the Pharisees had with parables was not that they could not understand the parables—they understood them all too well but resisted their truth (21:43-46).

18 "Now listen to the explanation of the parable
about the farmer planting seeds: 19 The seed that fell
on the footpath represents those who hear the mes-
sage about the Kingdom and don't understand it.
Then the evil one comes and snatches away the seed
that was planted in their hearts. 20 The seed on the
rocky soil represents those who hear the message and
immediately receive it with joy. 21 But since they don't
have deep roots, they don't last long. They fall away
as soon as they have problems or are persecuted for
believing God's word. 22 The seed that fell among the
thorns represents those who hear God's word, but all
too quickly the message is crowded out by the wor-
ries of this life and the lure of wealth, so no fruit is
produced. 23 The seed that fell on good soil represents
those who truly hear and understand God's word and
produce a harvest of thirty, sixty, or even a hundred
times as much as had been planted!"

PARABLE OF THE WHEAT AND WEEDS

24 Here is another story Jesus told: "The Kingdom of
Heaven is like a farmer who planted good seed in his
field. 25 But that night as the workers slept, his ene-
my came and planted weeds among the wheat, then
slipped away. 26 When the crop began to grow and
produce grain, the weeds also grew.

27 "The farmer's workers went to him and said, 'Sir,
the field where you planted that good seed is full of
weeds! Where did they come from?'

28 "'An enemy has done this!' the farmer exclaimed.
"'Should we pull out the weeds?' they asked.

29 "'No,' he replied, 'you'll uproot the wheat if you do.
30 Let both grow together until the harvest. Then I will
tell the harvesters to sort out the weeds, tie them into
bundles, and burn them, and to put the wheat in the
barn.'"

PARABLE OF THE MUSTARD SEED

31 Here is another illustration Jesus used: "The King-
dom of Heaven is like a mustard seed planted in a
field. 32 It is the smallest of all seeds, but it becomes
the largest of garden plants; it grows into a tree, and
birds come and make nests in its branches."

PARABLE OF THE YEAST

33 Jesus also used this illustration: "The Kingdom of
Heaven is like the yeast a woman used in making
bread. Even though she put only a little yeast in three
measures of flour, it permeated every part of the
dough."

34 Jesus always used stories and illustrations like
these when speaking to the crowds. In fact, he nev-
er spoke to them without using such parables. 35 This
fulfilled what God had spoken through the prophet:

"I will speak to you in parables.
I will explain things hidden since the creation
of the world.*"

PARABLE OF THE WHEAT AND WEEDS EXPLAINED

36 Then, leaving the crowds outside, Jesus went into
the house. His disciples said, "Please explain to us the
story of the weeds in the field."

37 Jesus replied, "The Son of Man* is the farmer who
plants the good seed. 38 The field is the world, and the
good seed represents the people of the Kingdom. The
weeds are the people who belong to the evil one. 39 The
enemy who planted the weeds among the wheat is
the devil. The harvest is the end of the world,* and the
harvesters are the angels.

40 "Just as the weeds are sorted out and burned in
the fire, so it will be at the end of the world. 41 The Son
of Man will send his angels, and they will remove
from his Kingdom everything that causes sin and all
who do evil. 42 And the angels will throw them into
the fiery furnace, where there will be weeping and
gnashing of teeth. 43 Then the righteous will shine like
the sun in their Father's Kingdom. Anyone with ears
to hear should listen and understand!

PARABLES OF THE HIDDEN TREASURE AND THE PEARL

44 "The Kingdom of Heaven is like a treasure that a
man discovered hidden in a field. In his excitement,
he hid it again and sold everything he owned to get
enough money to buy the field.

45 "Again, the Kingdom of Heaven is like a mer-
chant on the lookout for choice pearls. 46 When he dis-
covered a pearl of great value, he sold everything he
owned and bought it!

PARABLE OF THE FISHING NET

47 "Again, the Kingdom of Heaven is like a fishing net
that was thrown into the water and caught fish of ev-
ery kind. 48 When the net was full, they dragged it up
onto the shore, sat down, and sorted the good fish into
crates, but threw the bad ones away. 49 That is the way
it will be at the end of the world. The angels will come
and separate the wicked people from the righteous,
50 throwing the wicked into the fiery furnace, where

13:35 Some manuscripts do not include *of the world.* Ps 78:2. **13:37** "Son of Man" is a title Jesus used for himself. **13:39** Or *the age;* also in 13:40, 49.

13:19 snatches away. The seed is the message about the kingdom. Some are so hardened (like the soil on the paths between farm plots) that the seed of the Word never even penetrates. It is, instead, snatched away by Satan. **hear . . . doesn't understand.** This person merely hears the message; there is no understanding of what is heard. To understand is to grasp the meaning of the message and then make it your own.

13:22 among the thorns. Still others allow the wrong concerns (specifically worries and wealth) to squeeze out their interest in Jesus and His way. **no fruit is produced.** The weeds do not kill the plant (in contrast to the seeds sown on hard ground or on rocky soil, which do not survive). But they do not allow it to bring forth fruit.

13:31 mustard seed. The mustard plant, which grows to about 10 feet, has the smallest seed. Its shade and tasty brown seeds attract flocks of birds.

13:33 yeast. A small piece of dough would be saved from the previous baking and allowed to ferment. It would then be added to the new bread mixture, causing it to rise. **three measures of flour.** This would be almost 160 cups of flour, enough to make bread for about 100 people!

13:38 people of the Kingdom. To be a "son" of something or someone meant to be a person who reflected the characteristics of that particular thing or person. The "sons of the kingdom" are people whose lives are in conformity to the values of that kingdom. The "sons of the evil one" are those whose character reflects that of Satan.

13:40 burned in the fire. God's judgment was often described in terms of a consuming fire that would purify the world of all evil (2 Thess. 1:7; Heb. 12:28-29; 2 Peter 3:10; Rev. 19:20).

13:42 weeping and gnashing of teeth. This was a common phrase used to indicate extreme horror and suffering (8:12; 13:50; 22:13; 24:51; 25:30).

13:43 Anyone with ears to hear should listen. This is one common phrase used to call people to think about what they have heard: What does it mean? What are its implications? How are we to respond to this story (v. 9)?

13:44 treasure . . . hidden in a field. People would often hide their valuables in jars, which they buried in the ground. **that a man discovered.** Probably a day laborer hired to till the field. **sold everything he owned.** It was not a sacrifice on the part of the man to do this. He knew what he was getting was worth all he had.

there will be weeping and gnashing of teeth. 51 Do you
understand all these things?"
"Yes," they said, "we do."
52 Then he added, "Every teacher of religious law
who becomes a disciple in the Kingdom of Heaven
is like a homeowner who brings from his storeroom
new gems of truth as well as old."

JESUS REJECTED AT NAZARETH

53 When Jesus had finished telling these stories
and illustrations, he left that part of the country.
54 He returned to Nazareth, his hometown. When
he taught there in the synagogue, everyone was
amazed and said, "Where does he get this wisdom
and the power to do miracles?" 55 Then they scoffed,
"He's just the carpenter's son, and we know Mary,
his mother, and his brothers—James, Joseph,* Si-
mon, and Judas. 56 All his sisters live right here
among us. Where did he learn all these things?"
57 And they were deeply offended and refused to
believe in him.
Then Jesus told them, "A prophet is honored every-
where except in his own hometown and among his
own family." 58 And so he did only a few miracles
there because of their unbelief.

THE DEATH OF JOHN THE BAPTIST

14 When Herod Antipas, the ruler of Galilee,*
heard about Jesus, 2 he said to his advisers, "This
must be John the Baptist raised from the dead! That is
why he can do such miracles."
3 For Herod had arrested and imprisoned John as a
favor to his wife Herodias (the former wife of Herod's
brother Philip). 4 John had been telling Herod, "It is
against God's law for you to marry her." 5 Herod want-
ed to kill John, but he was afraid of a riot, because all
the people believed John was a prophet.
6 But at a birthday party for Herod, Herodias's
daughter performed a dance that greatly pleased
him, 7 so he promised with a vow to give her anything
she wanted. 8 At her mother's urging, the girl said, "I
want the head of John the Baptist on a tray!" 9 Then
the king regretted what he had said; but because of
the vow he had made in front of his guests, he issued
the necessary orders. 10 So John was beheaded in the
prison, 11 and his head was brought on a tray and giv-
en to the girl, who took it to her mother. 12 Later, John's
disciples came for his body and buried it. Then they
went and told Jesus what had happened.

JESUS FEEDS FIVE THOUSAND

13 As soon as Jesus heard the news, he left in a boat to a
remote area to be alone. But the crowds heard where
he was headed and followed on foot from many towns.
14 Jesus saw the huge crowd as he stepped from the boat,
and he had compassion on them and healed their sick.
15 That evening the disciples came to him and said,
"This is a remote place, and it's already getting late.
Send the crowds away so they can go to the villages
and buy food for themselves."
16 But Jesus said, "That isn't necessary—you feed
them."
17 "But we have only five loaves of bread and two
fish!" they answered.
18 "Bring them here," he said. 19 Then he told the peo-
ple to sit down on the grass. Jesus took the five loaves
and two fish, looked up toward heaven, and blessed
them. Then, breaking the loaves into pieces, he gave
the bread to the disciples, who distributed it to the
people. 20 They all ate as much as they wanted, and
afterward, the disciples picked up twelve baskets of
leftovers. 21 About 5,000 men were fed that day, in ad-
dition to all the women and children!

JESUS WALKS ON WATER

22 Immediately after this, Jesus insisted that his disci-
ples get back into the boat and cross to the other side
of the lake, while he sent the people home. 23 After
sending them home, he went up into the hills by him-
self to pray. Night fell while he was there alone.
24 Meanwhile, the disciples were in trouble far
away from land, for a strong wind had risen, and they
were fighting heavy waves. 25 About three o'clock in
the morning* Jesus came toward them, walking on
the water. 26 When the disciples saw him walking on
the water, they were terrified. In their fear, they cried
out, "It's a ghost!"
27 But Jesus spoke to them at once. "Don't be afraid,"
he said. "Take courage. I am here!*"
28 Then Peter called to him, "Lord, if it's really you,
tell me to come to you, walking on the water."
29 "Yes, come," Jesus said.
So Peter went over the side of the boat and walked
on the water toward Jesus. 30 But when he saw the

13:55 Other manuscripts read *Joses;* still others read *John.* **14:1** Greek *Herod the tetrarch.* Herod Antipas was a son of King Herod and was ruler over Galilee. **14:25** Greek *In the fourth watch of the night.* **14:27** Or *The 'I Am' is here;* Greek reads *I am.* See Exod 3:14.

13:52 what is new and what is old. Jesus challenges people to draw not only from the Law and the Prophets but also from His teachings. The coming of Jesus breathes fresh air into those writings.

13:54 his hometown. This was Nazareth, located in the hill country of Galilee.

13:57 except in his own hometown. Familiarity often prevents people from acknowledging the accomplishments or wisdom of one they assume they know.

14:1 Herod. Herod Antipas was the ruler of the Roman provinces of Galilee and Perea from 4 B.C. to A.D. 39. He was the son of Herod the Great, who had ordered the slaughter of the babies at the time of Jesus' birth.

14:2 This must be John the Baptist. Herod was suffering from a guilty conscience. He was afraid that the holy man he had executed had come back with supernatural powers.

14:16 That isn't necessary—you feed them. Jesus' statement, and the entire scene, is similar to when Elisha miraculously provided food for 100 people from 20 loaves of bread (2 Kings 4:42-44). Since that act authenticated Elisha's commission from God, how much more should this miracle demonstrate Jesus' innate divine power?

14:17 five loaves. These would have been small round cakes made of wheat or barley. **two fish.** These could have been smoked or pickled fish.

14:20 as much as they wanted. As it will be at the messianic feast, the needs of God's people are abundantly met. **twelve.** This is the number of tribes of Israel. The number 12 connotes completeness, reinforcing the idea that this scene is meant to demonstrate how Jesus the Messiah provides nourishment for all God's people. **baskets.** Small wicker containers carried by the Jews.

14:21 in addition to all the women and children. Women and children in this culture were generally not counted.

14:22 while he sent the people home. According to John 6:14-15, the crowd, which saw the feeding as a sign that Jesus was the messianic King, tried in its enthusiasm to get Jesus to lead a revolt against Rome.

14:25 three o'clock in the morning. Referred to as the fourth watch, this period ran from 3 a.m. to 6 a.m. **walking on the water.** In no other situation did the pre-resurrection Jesus take a supernatural shortcut to expedite His travel plans. This event was intended to provide the disciples with further insight into His divine identity and compassionate motivation.

14:26 It's a ghost! The sea, especially at night, was thought at that time to be a dwelling place for demons.

WALKING ON WATER

1. What is the most daring thing you have ever done?

MATTHEW 14:22-33

2. Why were the disciples afraid when they saw someone walking on the water? How would you have felt?
3. Why did Peter ask to walk on the water? Why did he sink? Would you have stepped out? Would you have sunk?
4. When have you asked God for a miracle? What happened? Did you begin to doubt afterward?
5. What are you facing in your life where you need Jesus to remind you, "Don't be afraid"?

strong* wind and the waves, he was terrified and be-
gan to sink. "Save me, Lord!" he shouted.
31 Jesus immediately reached out and grabbed him.
"You have so little faith," Jesus said. "Why did you
doubt me?"
32 When they climbed back into the boat, the wind
stopped. 33 Then the disciples worshiped him. "You
really are the Son of God!" they exclaimed.
34 After they had crossed the lake, they landed at
Gennesaret. 35 When the people recognized Jesus,
the news of his arrival spread quickly throughout
the whole area, and soon people were bringing all
their sick to be healed. 36 They begged him to let the
sick touch at least the fringe of his robe, and all who
touched him were healed.

JESUS TEACHES ABOUT INNER PURITY

15 Some Pharisees and teachers of religious law
now arrived from Jerusalem to see Jesus. They
asked him, 2 "Why do your disciples disobey our age-
old tradition? For they ignore our tradition of ceremo-
nial hand washing before they eat."
3 Jesus replied, "And why do you, by your tradi-
tions, violate the direct commandments of God? 4 For
instance, God says, 'Honor your father and mother,'*
and 'Anyone who speaks disrespectfully of father or
mother must be put to death.'* 5 But you say it is all
right for people to say to their parents, 'Sorry, I can't
help you. For I have vowed to give to God what I
would have given to you.' 6 In this way, you say they
don't need to honor their parents.* And so you cancel
the word of God for the sake of your own tradition.
7 You hypocrites! Isaiah was right when he prophe-
sied about you, for he wrote,

8 'These people honor me with their lips,
but their hearts are far from me.
9 Their worship is a farce,
for they teach man-made ideas as commands
from God.'*"

10 Then Jesus called to the crowd to come and hear.
"Listen," he said, "and try to understand. 11 It's not
what goes into your mouth that defiles you; you are
defiled by the words that come out of your mouth."
12 Then the disciples came to him and asked, "Do
you realize you offended the Pharisees by what you
just said?"
13 Jesus replied, "Every plant not planted by my heav-
enly Father will be uprooted, 14 so ignore them. They
are blind guides leading the blind, and if one blind
person guides another, they will both fall into a ditch."
15 Then Peter said to Jesus, "Explain to us the para-
ble that says people aren't defiled by what they eat."
16 "Don't you understand yet?" Jesus asked. 17 "Any-
thing you eat passes through the stomach and then
goes into the sewer. 18 But the words you speak come
from the heart—that's what defiles you. 19 For from
the heart come evil thoughts, murder, adultery, all
sexual immorality, theft, lying, and slander. 20 These
are what defile you. Eating with unwashed hands
will never defile you."

THE FAITH OF A GENTILE WOMAN

21 Then Jesus left Galilee and went north to the region
of Tyre and Sidon. 22 A Gentile* woman who lived
there came to him, pleading, "Have mercy on me,
O Lord, Son of David! For my daughter is possessed by
a demon that torments her severely."

14:30 Some manuscripts do not include *strong*. **15:4a** Exod 20:12; Deut 5:16. **15:4b** Exod 21:17 (Greek version); Lev 20:9 (Greek version). **15:6** Greek *their father;* other manuscripts read *their father or their mother.* **15:8-9** Isa 29:13 (Greek version). **15:22** Greek *Canaanite.*

14:27 Don't be afraid . . . Take courage. I am here! This is the language of God (Isa. 41:10; 43:5; Jer. 1:8). **I am here.** Literally, "I am." In the Old Testament this is a phrase used by God to describe Himself (Ex. 3:1-14). In the context of Jesus' ongoing revelation of Himself to the disciples, this is another indication of His divine identity.

14:33 You really are the Son of God! In the other Gospels, this identification by the disciples does not happen until the incident at Caesarea Philippi (16:13-20). **the Son of God.** In the Old Testament, this term described God's appointed king who reigned over Israel in God's stead (Ps. 2:7). In the New Testament, this title is often connected with the title "Messiah."

14:34 Gennesaret. This was a thickly populated, fertile plain four miles southwest of Capernaum.

14:36 fringe of his robe. This recalls the healing of the bleeding woman (9:20-22).

15:2 the tradition. There were literally thousands of unwritten rules that developed over time in an attempt to define how the Old Testament Law applied in everyday life. **hand washing.** The issue here is ceremonial holiness, not personal hygiene.

15:4 God says. Jesus cites two commands in the Law regarding how parents are to be treated with respect (Ex. 20:12; 21:17). **put to death.** Jesus was not advocating putting people to death for such an action but rather underlining the issue of respect taught by the Law.

15:5 But you say. The Law was clear. Before pension plans and Social Security, one aspect of that principle was providing for one's parents when they were too old or too sick to work. However, the traditions taught that if people dedicated some money to God, it was thereafter not considered their property. Thus, a child could declare property or money as given over to God and therefore unavailable for his or her parents' support.

15:8 but their hearts. This is the essence of what Jesus had against the Pharisees. They obeyed the laws, but their hearts were not in tune with the love of God. They were not yet part of that New Covenant spoken of by Jeremiah where God's law of love was written "on their hearts" (Jer. 31:33).

15:11 defiles. Those who came into contact with something considered taboo were thought to be unfit to worship or to have physical contact with others. For the Jew, unclean or defiled things included certain animals, dead bodies, lepers, Gentiles, and, as demonstrated here, certain food.

15:13 Every plant. God's people were commonly described as "planted by the LORD" (Isa. 60:21; 61:3). Jesus is declaring that the Pharisees, in spite of their pretense to holiness, had not been divinely planted. They were more like weeds that will be uprooted and cast away.

15:22 Gentile woman. The woman was a Syro-phoenician (Mark 7:26). The Canaanites were ancient archetypal enemies of the Jews. By specifically referring to her as a Canaanite, Matthew accents how far removed she was from those normally considered God's people.

23 But Jesus gave her no reply, not even a word. Then his disciples urged him to send her away. "Tell her to go away," they said. "She is bothering us with all her begging."

24 Then Jesus said to the woman, "I was sent only to help God's lost sheep—the people of Israel."

25 But she came and worshiped him, pleading again, "Lord, help me!"

26 Jesus responded, "It isn't right to take food from the children and throw it to the dogs."

27 She replied, "That's true, Lord, but even dogs are allowed to eat the scraps that fall beneath their masters' table."

28 "Dear woman," Jesus said to her, "your faith is great. Your request is granted." And her daughter was instantly healed.

JESUS HEALS MANY PEOPLE

29 Jesus returned to the Sea of Galilee and climbed a hill and sat down. 30 A vast crowd brought to him people who were lame, blind, crippled, those who couldn't speak, and many others. They laid them before Jesus, and he healed them all. 31 The crowd was amazed! Those who hadn't been able to speak were talking, the crippled were made well, the lame were walking, and the blind could see again! And they praised the God of Israel.

JESUS FEEDS FOUR THOUSAND

32 Then Jesus called his disciples and told them, "I feel sorry for these people. They have been here with me for three days, and they have nothing left to eat. I don't want to send them away hungry, or they will faint along the way."

33 The disciples replied, "Where would we get enough food here in the wilderness for such a huge crowd?"

34 Jesus asked, "How much bread do you have?"

They replied, "Seven loaves, and a few small fish."

35 So Jesus told all the people to sit down on the ground. 36 Then he took the seven loaves and the fish, thanked God for them, and broke them into pieces. He gave them to the disciples, who distributed the food to the crowd.

37 They all ate as much as they wanted. Afterward, the disciples picked up seven large baskets of leftover food. 38 There were 4,000 men who were fed that day, in addition to all the women and children. 39 Then Jesus sent the people home, and he got into a boat and crossed over to the region of Magadan.

LEADERS DEMAND A MIRACULOUS SIGN

16 One day the Pharisees and Sadducees came to test Jesus, demanding that he show them a miraculous sign from heaven to prove his authority.

2 He replied, "You know the saying, 'Red sky at night means fair weather tomorrow; 3 red sky in the morning means foul weather all day.' You know how to interpret the weather signs in the sky, but you don't know how to interpret the signs of the times!* 4 Only an evil, adulterous generation would demand a miraculous sign, but the only sign I will give them is the sign of the prophet Jonah.*" Then Jesus left them and went away.

YEAST OF THE PHARISEES AND SADDUCEES

5 Later, after they crossed to the other side of the lake, the disciples discovered they had forgotten to bring any bread. 6 "Watch out!" Jesus warned them. "Beware of the yeast of the Pharisees and Sadducees."

7 At this they began to argue with each other because they hadn't brought any bread. 8 Jesus knew what they were saying, so he said, "You have so little faith! Why are you arguing with each other about having no bread? 9 Don't you understand even yet? Don't you remember the 5,000 I fed with five loaves, and the baskets of leftovers you picked up? 10 Or the 4,000 I fed with seven loaves, and the large baskets of leftovers you picked up? 11 Why can't you understand that I'm not talking about bread? So again I say, 'Beware of the yeast of the Pharisees and Sadducees.'"

12 Then at last they understood that he wasn't speaking about the yeast in bread, but about the deceptive teaching of the Pharisees and Sadducees.

PETER'S DECLARATION ABOUT JESUS

13 When Jesus came to the region of Caesarea Philippi, he asked his disciples, "Who do people say that the Son of Man is?"*

14 "Well," they replied, "some say John the Baptist, some say Elijah, and others say Jeremiah or one of the other prophets."

15 Then he asked them, "But who do you say I am?"

16 Simon Peter answered, "You are the Messiah,* the Son of the living God."

16:2-3 Several manuscripts do not include any of the words in 16:2-3 after *He replied.* **16:4** Greek *the sign of Jonah.* **16:13** "Son of Man" is a title Jesus used for himself. **16:16** Or *the Christ. Messiah* (a Hebrew term) and *Christ* (a Greek term) both mean "anointed one."

15:24 I was sent only. This seemingly callous statement by Jesus has caused much debate. Could Jesus really have been this ethnocentric? Likely, His actions here, however, are that He was voicing the predominant view of His time precisely with the idea in mind that it could be shown as shallow in light of this faithful foreigner.

15:26 dogs. There is a play on words here. While Jews commonly used a word that referred to wild street dogs when they discussed Gentiles, the word used here refers to a household pet dog.

15:28 your faith is great. Once again Jesus points out the faith of a foreigner (8:5-13) in contrast to the lack of faith of the people of His hometown (13:58) and even the disciples (14:31; 16:8).

15:32-39 4,000. The main difference between the feeding of the 4,000 and the feeding of the 5,000 (14:15-21) is the difference in audience. Just as the feeding of the 5,000 anticipated the coming salvation for Israel, so the feeding of the 4,000 promises this same salvation to Gentiles.

15:32 three days. The crowd had been with Him for a few days in contrast to the 5,000 who were fed on the day they gathered.

15:39 Magadan. It is not certain where this town is located. The point, however, is that Jesus left the Gentile region for Jewish soil at this time.

16:1 Sadducees. While prominent in the early chapters of Acts, the Sadducees (whose main area of concern was with the worship at the temple in Jerusalem) are rarely mentioned in the Gospels. It seems that they were a small but highly influential party of Jews composed mainly of wealthy, aristocratic priests.

16:4 An evil, adulterous generation. The Old Testament prophets often used adultery as a metaphor for the way Israel strayed from fidelity to God (Ezek. 16; Hos. 2:2).

16:6 yeast. Jews connected yeast with the process of fermentation, which they saw as a form of rotting. Hence, yeast became a metaphor for the profound effects of even a little bit of evil.

16:13 Caesarea Philippi. A beautiful city on the slopes of Mount Hermon, 25 miles north of Bethsaida. It had once been called Balinas when it was a center for Baal worship. It was later called Paneas because it was said that the god Pan had his birth in a nearby cave. At the time of Jesus, it was the location of a temple dedicated to the godhead of Caesar.

DENY YOURSELF

1. If your best friends were asked what one word best describes you, what would they say? What would you say?

MATTHEW 16:13-28

2. Who do you say Jesus is? Who does Jesus Himself say that He is (see v. 20)?
3. What does it mean to "turn from your selfish ways"? To "take up your cross"?
4. What does it mean to "lose your life" for Jesus? Give practical examples of times when you or someone you know "lost his life" to obey God.
5. How much is your soul worth? Are there things in your life that are endangering your soul?

17 Jesus replied, "You are blessed, Simon son of John,* because my Father in heaven has revealed this to you. You did not learn this from any human being. 18 Now I say to you that you are Peter (which means 'rock'),* and upon this rock I will build my church, and all the powers of hell* will not conquer it. 19 And I will give you the keys of the Kingdom of Heaven. Whatever you forbid* on earth will be forbidden in heaven, and whatever you permit* on earth will be permitted in heaven."

20 Then he sternly warned the disciples not to tell anyone that he was the Messiah.

JESUS PREDICTS HIS DEATH

21 From then on Jesus* began to tell his disciples plainly that it was necessary for him to go to Jerusalem, and that he would suffer many terrible things at the hands of the elders, the leading priests, and the teachers of religious law. He would be killed, but on the third day he would be raised from the dead.

22 But Peter took him aside and began to reprimand him* for saying such things. "Heaven forbid, Lord," he said. "This will never happen to you!"

23 Jesus turned to Peter and said, "Get away from me, Satan! You are a dangerous trap to me. You are seeing things merely from a human point of view, not from God's."

24 Then Jesus said to his disciples, "If any of you wants to be my follower, you must give up your own way, take up your cross, and follow me. 25 If you try to hang on to your life, you will lose it. But if you give up your life for my sake, you will save it. 26 And what do you benefit if you gain the whole world but lose your own soul?* Is anything worth more than your soul? 27 For the Son of Man will come with his angels in the glory of his Father and will judge all people according to their deeds. 28 And I tell you the truth, some standing here right now will not die before they see the Son of Man coming in his Kingdom."

THE TRANSFIGURATION

17 Six days later Jesus took Peter and the two brothers, James and John, and led them up a high mountain to be alone. 2 As the men watched, Jesus' appearance was transformed so that his face shone like the sun, and his clothes became as white as light. 3 Suddenly, Moses and Elijah appeared and began talking with Jesus.

4 Peter exclaimed, "Lord, it's wonderful for us to be here! If you want, I'll make three shelters as memorials*—one for you, one for Moses, and one for Elijah."

5 But even as he spoke, a bright cloud overshadowed them, and a voice from the cloud said, "This is my dearly loved Son, who brings me great joy. Listen to him." 6 The disciples were terrified and fell face down on the ground.

7 Then Jesus came over and touched them. "Get up," he said. "Don't be afraid." 8 And when they looked up, Moses and Elijah were gone, and they saw only Jesus.

9 As they went back down the mountain, Jesus commanded them, "Don't tell anyone what you have seen until the Son of Man* has been raised from the dead."

10 Then his disciples asked him, "Why do the teachers of religious law insist that Elijah must return before the Messiah comes?*"

11 Jesus replied, "Elijah is indeed coming first to get everything ready. 12 But I tell you, Elijah has already come, but he wasn't recognized, and they chose to

16:17 Greek *Simon bar-Jonah;* see John 1:42; 21:15-17. **16:18a** Greek *that you are Peter.* **16:18b** Greek *and the gates of Hades.* **16:19a** Or *bind,* or *lock.* **16:19b** Or *loose,* or *open.* **16:21** Some manuscripts read *Jesus the Messiah.* **16:22** Or *began to correct him.* **16:26** Or *your self?* also in 16:26b. **17:4** Greek *three tabernacles.* **17:9** "Son of Man" is a title Jesus used for himself. **17:10** Greek *that Elijah must come first?*

16:17 You did not learn this from any human being. Jesus told the disciples that it was not by reason that people came to faith, but rather it was by revelation. The Father granted knowledge or revelation to the seeker (John 6:65). Peter responded in belief in Jesus as the Messiah (6:68-69).

16:18 Peter. Peter (a nickname meaning "rock") by way of his confession articulates the central truth, forming the foundation upon which the new people of God will be built.

16:19 keys of the Kingdom of Heaven. This is an allusion to Isaiah 22:15-24 in which God declared that he would give the "key to the house of David" to a new steward who would replace the old one who had been irresponsible.

16:23 Get away from me, Satan! By urging Jesus to back away from His teaching about suffering, Peter, like Satan, is tempting Jesus with the promise that He can have the whole world without pain (4:8-10).

16:24 turn from your selfish ways. This means to regard one's ambitions as irrelevant in light of the kingdom of God. **take up your cross.** This symbolized the grisly method of Roman execution as the only people who bore crosses were prisoners on their way to their death. This would have startled the original hearers as they thought the Messiah would overthrow Rome. **follow me.** This is a call for the disciples to imitate the lifestyle and embrace the values of their Teacher.

16:28 see the Son of Man coming. Jesus had already said that the kingdom of God was near (4:17; 10:23; 12:28). While some see this as a prediction of His imminent Second Coming, it can also be seen as referring to either to the transfiguration (17:1-13) or to Christ's death and resurrection.

17:1 Six days later. This phrase connects the transfiguration with Jesus' prediction that there are "some standing here right now will not die before until they see the Son of Man coming in his kingdom" (16:28). **Peter . . . James and John.** These three emerge as the inner circle around Jesus. **a high mountain.** This may well be Mount Hermon, a 9,000-foot mountain located 12 miles from Caesarea Philippi (though early tradition says it is Mount Tabor located southwest of the Sea of Galilee).

17:2 transformed. The description of Jesus here is similar to that used to picture the appearance of God when He appeared in a vision to Daniel (Dan. 7:9). In Revelation 1:9-18 the resurrected, glorified Jesus is described in these same terms.

17:3 Moses. Moses was the greatest figure in the Old Testament. It was to him God gave the Law, which became the very heart of the nation. **Elijah.** The Jews expected that Elijah, one of the most esteemed prophets, would return just prior to the coming of the salvation they had been promised. These two figures together represent the Law and the Prophets, the whole of scriptural tradition.

17:4 shelters as memorials. Peter might have had in mind the huts of intertwined branches that were put up at the Festival of Tabernacles to commemorate Israel's time in the wilderness.

17:9 Don't tell. Jesus commands silence because the meaning of this event cannot be understood until Jesus dies and rises again. Only then it will be clear what kind of Messiah He is.

abuse him. And in the same way they will also make
the Son of Man suffer." 13 Then the disciples realized
he was talking about John the Baptist.

JESUS HEALS A DEMON-POSSESSED BOY

14 At the foot of the mountain, a large crowd was wait-
ing for them. A man came and knelt before Jesus and
said, 15 "Lord, have mercy on my son. He has seizures
and suffers terribly. He often falls into the fire or into
the water. 16 So I brought him to your disciples, but
they couldn't heal him."
17 Jesus said, "You faithless and corrupt people! How
long must I be with you? How long must I put up with
you? Bring the boy here to me." 18 Then Jesus rebuked
the demon in the boy, and it left him. From that mo-
ment the boy was well.
19 Afterward the disciples asked Jesus privately,
"Why couldn't we cast out that demon?"
20 "You don't have enough faith," Jesus told them. "I
tell you the truth, if you had faith even as small as a
mustard seed, you could say to this mountain, 'Move
from here to there,' and it would move. Nothing
would be impossible.*"

JESUS AGAIN PREDICTS HIS DEATH

22 After they gathered again in Galilee, Jesus told
them, "The Son of Man is going to be betrayed into the
hands of his enemies. 23 He will be killed, but on the
third day he will be raised from the dead." And the
disciples were filled with grief.

PAYMENT OF THE TEMPLE TAX

24 On their arrival in Capernaum, the collectors of the
Temple tax* came to Peter and asked him, "Doesn't
your teacher pay the Temple tax?"
25 "Yes, he does," Peter replied. Then he went into
the house.
But before he had a chance to speak, Jesus asked
him, "What do you think, Peter?* Do kings tax their
own people or the people they have conquered?*"
26 "They tax the people they have conquered," Peter
replied.
"Well, then," Jesus said, "the citizens are free!
27 However, we don't want to offend them, so go
down to the lake and throw in a line. Open the
mouth of the first fish you catch, and you will find
a large silver coin.* Take it and pay the tax for both
of us."

THE GREATEST IN THE KINGDOM

18 About that time the disciples came to Jesus and
asked, "Who is greatest in the Kingdom of Heaven?"
2 Jesus called a little child to him and put the child
among them. 3 Then he said, "I tell you the truth,
unless you turn from your sins and become like lit-
tle children, you will never get into the Kingdom of
Heaven. 4 So anyone who becomes as humble as this
little child is the greatest in the Kingdom of Heaven.
5 "And anyone who welcomes a little child like this on
my behalf* is welcoming me. 6 But if you cause one of
these little ones who trusts in me to fall into sin, it would
be better for you to have a large millstone tied around
your neck and be drowned in the depths of the sea.
7 "What sorrow awaits the world, because it tempts
people to sin. Temptations are inevitable, but what
sorrow awaits the person who does the tempting. 8 So
if your hand or foot causes you to sin, cut it off and
throw it away. It's better to enter eternal life with
only one hand or one foot than to be thrown into eter-
nal fire with both of your hands and feet. 9 And if your
eye causes you to sin, gouge it out and throw it away.
It's better to enter eternal life with only one eye than
to have two eyes and be thrown into the fire of hell.*
10 "Beware that you don't look down on any of these
little ones. For I tell you that in heaven their angels
are always in the presence of my heavenly Father.*

PARABLE OF THE LOST SHEEP

12 "If a man has a hundred sheep and one of them
wanders away, what will he do? Won't he leave the
ninety-nine others on the hills and go out to search
for the one that is lost? 13 And if he finds it, I tell you
the truth, he will rejoice over it more than over the
ninety-nine that didn't wander away! 14 In the same
way, it is not my heavenly Father's will that even one
of these little ones should perish.

CORRECTING ANOTHER BELIEVER

15 "If another believer* sins against you,* go privately
and point out the offense. If the other person listens
and confesses it, you have won that person back. 16 But
if you are unsuccessful, take one or two others with
you and go back again, so that everything you say may
be confirmed by two or three witnesses. 17 If the per-
son still refuses to listen, take your case to the church.
Then if he or she won't accept the church's decision,
treat that person as a pagan or a corrupt tax collector.

17:20 Some manuscripts add verse 21, *But this kind of demon won't leave except by prayer and fasting.* Compare Mark 9:29. **17:24** Greek *the two-drachma [tax]*; also in 17:24b. See Exod 30:13-16; Neh 10:32-33. **17:25a** Greek *Simon?* **17:25b** Greek *their sons or others?* **17:27** Greek *a stater* [a Greek coin equivalent to four drachmas]. **18:5** Greek *in my name.* **18:9** Greek *the Gehenna of fire.* **18:10** Some manuscripts add verse 11, *And the Son of Man came to save those who are lost.* Compare Luke 19:10. **18:15a** Greek *If your brother.* **18:15b** Some manuscripts do not include *against you.*

17:16 they couldn't heal him. Based on the response of Jesus, it appears that the faith of the disciples is shown once again to be incomplete.
17:20 this mountain. "Removing mountains" is the overcoming of difficulties. **Nothing would be impossible.** This power is subject to acting with God's direction.
17:24 collectors. These were not the "tax collectors" vilified by the Jewish community as traitors because they worked for Rome. Rather, they collected the temple tax. **Doesn't your teacher pay the Temple tax?** If Jesus did not, it could be misconstrued as a scandalous rejection of a common duty. If He did, it could be misconstrued as an endorsement of the temple system that He generally seemed to reject (21:12-13).
17:27 However, we don't want to offend them. Since such freedom would be interpreted by others as disrespect for God and the temple, it is appropriate to pay the tax.
18:2 a little child. Children held little value among adult males in this society. To hold up a child as a model for an adult to emulate was unheard of.
18:3 unless you turn from your sins. Literally, "turn around."
18:4 as humble as this little child. In the Bible, humility is not a denial of one's strengths, nor an attitude of passivity or timidity, but an attitude that values the interests of others above one's own.
18:6 cause . . . to fall into sin. The influence of false teachers is probably in view (2 John 7-15), but it could also refer to disciples who abuse their freedom by refusing to be sensitive to the tender consciences of others (Rom. 14:1–15:2). **a large millstone.** The millstone in view here is the huge upper stone of a community grist mill, so big it had to be drawn around by a donkey.
18:7 What sorrow. A strong warning to false teachers and those who are not careful about how their lives affect others.
18:10 in heaven their angels. The picture is one of angels reporting to God on the condition of those in their charge. Disdain for others has no place in the Christian community since even those people who appear insignificant are divinely watched-over and cared for.
18:13 he will rejoice over it more than over the ninety-nine. This is not to minimize the shepherd's gladness over those sheep that remained in the fold but to accent his joy over the recovery of the one who had strayed away.

18 "I tell you the truth, whatever you forbid* on
earth will be forbidden in heaven, and whatever you
permit* on earth will be permitted in heaven.
19 "I also tell you this: If two of you agree here on
earth concerning anything you ask, my Father in
heaven will do it for you. 20 For where two or three
gather together as my followers,* I am there among
them."

PARABLE OF THE UNFORGIVING DEBTOR

21 Then Peter came to him and asked, "Lord, how of-
ten should I forgive someone* who sins against me?
Seven times?"
22 "No, not seven times," Jesus replied, "but seventy
times seven!*
23 "Therefore, the Kingdom of Heaven can be com-
pared to a king who decided to bring his accounts
up to date with servants who had borrowed money
from him. 24 In the process, one of his debtors was
brought in who owed him millions of dollars.* 25 He
couldn't pay, so his master ordered that he be sold—
along with his wife, his children, and everything he
owned—to pay the debt.
26 "But the man fell down before his master and
begged him, 'Please, be patient with me, and I will pay
it all.' 27 Then his master was filled with pity for him,
and he released him and forgave his debt.
28 "But when the man left the king, he went to a fel-
low servant who owed him a few thousand dollars.*
He grabbed him by the throat and demanded instant
payment.
29 "His fellow servant fell down before him and
begged for a little more time. 'Be patient with me, and
I will pay it,' he pleaded. 30 But his creditor wouldn't
wait. He had the man arrested and put in prison until
the debt could be paid in full.
31 "When some of the other servants saw this, they
were very upset. They went to the king and told him
everything that had happened. 32 Then the king called
in the man he had forgiven and said, 'You evil ser-
vant! I forgave you that tremendous debt because you
pleaded with me. 33 Shouldn't you have mercy on your
fellow servant, just as I had mercy on you?' 34 Then the
angry king sent the man to prison to be tortured until
he had paid his entire debt.
35 "That's what my heavenly Father will do to you if
you refuse to forgive your brothers and sisters* from
your heart."

FORGIVE HIM OR CHOKE HIM?

1. What's the most money you've ever owed? Been owed?
2. Are you quick or slow to forgive when you're hurt?

MATTHEW 18:21-35

3. Why did the master treat the unforgiving slave so harshly? What does this tell us about how God will treat us when we are unforgiving?
4. Why should the slave have forgiven the other man's debt? Why should we forgive others who hurt us?
5. Are you more like the forgiving master (v. 27) or the slave (v. 30)?
6. Who do you need to forgive? What's keeping you from forgiving them?

DISCUSSION ABOUT DIVORCE AND MARRIAGE

19 When Jesus had finished saying these things, he
left Galilee and went down to the region of Ju-
dea east of the Jordan River. 2 Large crowds followed
him there, and he healed their sick.
3 Some Pharisees came and tried to trap him with
this question: "Should a man be allowed to divorce his
wife for just any reason?"
4 "Haven't you read the Scriptures?" Jesus replied.
"They record that from the beginning 'God made
them male and female.'* 5 And he said, "'This explains
why a man leaves his father and mother and is joined
to his wife, and the two are united into one.'* 6 Since
they are no longer two but one, let no one split apart
what God has joined together."
7 "Then why did Moses say in the law that a man
could give his wife a written notice of divorce and
send her away?"* they asked.

18:18a Or *bind*, or *lock*. **18:18b** Or *loose*, or *open*. **18:20** Greek *gather together in my name*. **18:21** Greek *my brother*. **18:22** Or *seventy-seven times*. **18:24** Greek *10,000 talents* [375 tons or 340 metric tons of silver]. **18:28** Greek *100 denarii*. A denarius was equivalent to a laborer's full day's wage. **18:35** Greek *your brother*. **19:4** Gen 1:27; 5:2. **19:5** Gen 2:24. **19:7** See Deut 24:1.

18:21 how often should I forgive. The rabbis taught that a person ought to be forgiven for a particular offense up to three times. After that, the offended person was under no obligation to grant forgiveness.

18:22 seventy times seven. Some translate this as "seventy seven times." Whichever reading is correct, Jesus underscores the idea that learning to bestow the kind of forgiveness He has for us on others is a lifetime pursuit of choosing the health of the relationship over adherence to regulation.

18:24 millions of dollars. Herod the Great, who ruled over Palestine at the time of Jesus' birth, had an annual revenue of only about 900 talents. The crowd listening to Jesus would have gasped at the thought of having to pay someone such a fantastically large amount of money.

18:25 he . . . along with his wife, his children. A Middle Eastern king had total power. Thus, he decided to sell the man and the servant's family into slavery to recoup at least a fraction of his losses.

18:26 I will pay it all. This was an impossible promise, given the amount. While it may reflect the slave's sincere desire to save himself and his family, he was so far in debt that he could never hope to repay the king.

18:27 released him. The man was free. The impossible burden that must have crushed him with fear (while he wondered what would happen to him when his mismanagement was discovered) was suddenly gone. There was no judgment, no debt-restructuring to keep him in perpetual bondage, no more fear. Likewise, the disciple of Jesus is free from the punishment of sin (Rom. 8:1-2).

18:28 a few thousand dollars. Since a denarius was a day's wage for a laborer, this was a reasonably large amount. However, at the rate of one denarius a day, it would have taken the first servant 15 years to pay back the king a single talent!

18:30 his creditor wouldn't wait. Under the circumstances, this man would have been expected to forego the debt. Instead, he insists on carrying out the full weight of the law against the slave indebted to him. The mercy he received from the king does not produce any moral change in this man.

18:33 Shouldn't you have mercy . . . as I had mercy on you? This is the point of the parable.

18:34 to prison. Prisoners were often tortured to make them reveal hidden sources of money. The man will now be pressed for every cent he has. **until he had paid his entire debt.** Given the amount owed, the man would be in prison until death.

18:35 from his heart. The depth and breadth of forgiveness is drawn from the limitless heavenly supply in the heart of the forgiven follower. To do this, we must be in touch with how much God in Christ has forgiven us and invite that same Spirit of Christ into our heart, so it will flow to others.

DIVORCE . . . LIFE SHREDDER

1. Describe your ideal husband or wife. What things are most important to you in finding the right person?

MATTHEW 19:1-12

2. What does it mean that a married couple "united into one"? If the two have become one, then what is divorce like?
3. When does Jesus allow for divorce?
4. How does Jesus' teaching differ from our culture's views on marriage and divorce? Who is right: Jesus? Modern culture? Somewhere in between?
5. How has your life been affected by divorce? How might Jesus' teaching help you to prepare for a "divorce-free" marriage?

---

8 Jesus replied, "Moses permitted divorce only as a
concession to your hard hearts, but it was not what
God had originally intended. 9 And I tell you this, who-
ever divorces his wife and marries someone else com-
mits adultery—unless his wife has been unfaithful.*"
10 Jesus' disciples then said to him, "If this is the case,
it is better not to marry!"
11 "Not everyone can accept this statement," Jesus
said. "Only those whom God helps. 12 Some are born
as eunuchs, some have been made eunuchs by others,
and some choose not to marry* for the sake of the
Kingdom of Heaven. Let anyone accept this who can."

JESUS BLESSES THE CHILDREN

13 One day some parents brought their children to Jesus
so he could lay his hands on them and pray for them.
But the disciples scolded the parents for bothering him.
14 But Jesus said, "Let the children come to me. Don't
stop them! For the Kingdom of Heaven belongs to
those who are like these children." 15 And he placed his
hands on their heads and blessed them before he left.

THE RICH MAN

16 Someone came to Jesus with this question: "Teach-
er,* what good deed must I do to have eternal life?"
17 "Why ask me about what is good?" Jesus replied.
"There is only One who is good. But to answer your
question—if you want to receive eternal life, keep*
the commandments."
18 "Which ones?" the man asked.
And Jesus replied: "'You must not murder. You must
not commit adultery. You must not steal. You must not
testify falsely. 19 Honor your father and mother. Love
your neighbor as yourself.'*"
20 "I've obeyed all these commandments," the young
man replied. "What else must I do?"
21 Jesus told him, "If you want to be perfect, go and
sell all your possessions and give the money to the
poor, and you will have treasure in heaven. Then
come, follow me."
22 But when the young man heard this, he went
away sad, for he had many possessions.
23 Then Jesus said to his disciples, "I tell you the
truth, it is very hard for a rich person to enter the
Kingdom of Heaven. 24 I'll say it again—it is easier for
a camel to go through the eye of a needle than for a
rich person to enter the Kingdom of God!"
25 The disciples were astounded. "Then who in the
world can be saved?" they asked.
26 Jesus looked at them intently and said, "Humanly
speaking, it is impossible. But with God everything is
possible."
27 Then Peter said to him, "We've given up every-
thing to follow you. What will we get?"
28 Jesus replied, "I assure you that when the world is
made new* and the Son of Man* sits upon his glorious
throne, you who have been my followers will also sit
on twelve thrones, judging the twelve tribes of Israel.
29 And everyone who has given up houses or brothers
or sisters or father or mother or children or property,
for my sake, will receive a hundred times as much in
return and will inherit eternal life. 30 But many who
are the greatest now will be least important then,
and those who seem least important now will be the
greatest then.*

PARABLE OF THE VINEYARD WORKERS

20 "For the Kingdom of Heaven is like the land-
owner who went out early one morning to hire
workers for his vineyard. 2 He agreed to pay the nor-
mal daily wage* and sent them out to work.
3 "At nine o'clock in the morning he was passing
through the marketplace and saw some people stand-
ing around doing nothing. 4 So he hired them, telling

19:9 Some manuscripts add *And anyone who marries a divorced woman commits adultery.* Compare Matt 5:32. **19:12** Greek *and some make themselves eunuchs.* **19:16** Some manuscripts read *Good Teacher.* **19:17** Some manuscripts read *continue to keep.* **19:18-19** Exod 20:12-16; Deut 5:16-20; Lev 19:18. **19:28a** Or *in the regeneration.* **19:28b** "Son of Man" is a title Jesus used for himself. **19:30** Greek *But many who are first will be last; and the last, first.* **20:2** Greek *a denarius,* the payment for a full day's labor; similarly in 20:9, 10, 13.

19:8 Moses permitted. Moses' concession was an accommodation to human sinfulness, not part of God's intention.

19:9 marries someone else. Commentators differ as to whether remarriage was prohibited regardless of whether or not the divorce was for reasons of marital unfaithfulness.

19:20 What else must I do? He seems to know that he is lacking something. When we seek a status based on our own works, we always feel like we are short of what we need.

19:21 sell all your possessions. By telling the young man to sell all his goods, Jesus exposed that the man's heart was gripped by his possessions rather than by God.

19:24 eye of a needle. Jesus uses an exaggerated form of speech (hyperbole) to make His point. The camel was the largest animal in Palestine and certainly could not get through the tiny opening of a needle.

19:25 Then who in the world can be saved? The radical nature of Jesus' statement causes them to think about their own destiny. If the rich (who they believed were especially favored of God) will find it difficult to enter the kingdom, then what chance do they have?

19:26 with God everything is possible. This is asserted many times in the New Testament (Mark 9:23; 10:27; 14:36; Luke 1:37). Only the power of atonement and the persuasive pull of the Holy Spirit can overcome man's largest obstacles.

19:30 many who are the greatest now will be least. Jesus often makes the point that those who expect to be part of the kingdom will not necessarily be part of it, and those who expect to be excluded will not necessarily be excluded. Jesus said the tax collectors and the prostitutes were entering the kingdom of heaven ahead of many who considered themselves to be pious (21:31).

20:2 normal daily wage. This was a subsistence wage that would meet one's daily needs but not allow for any excess to be saved for the following day. It was considered a fair wage for a day's work.

20:3 nine o'clock in the morning. Probably the first workers were hired at daybreak (about 6 a.m).

HEY—THAT'S NOT FAIR!

1. When you were a child, what chores were you expected to do? Were you paid?

MATTHEW 20:1-16

2. If you were hired in this story at 5 p.m., how would you have felt at pay time (vv. 8-9)? If you were hired at 9 a.m., how would you have felt (vv. 10-12)?
3. Why did the employer pay everyone the same regardless of how much work they'd done? Is this fair? What might this teach us about God's attitude toward those who serve Him?
4. Do you find yourself resenting it when God blesses people that you think don't deserve it? What does this passage teach you about that attitude?

them he would pay them whatever was right at the end of the day. 5 So they went to work in the vineyard. At noon and again at three o'clock he did the same thing.

6 "At five o'clock that afternoon he was in town again and saw some more people standing around. He asked them, 'Why haven't you been working today?'

7 "They replied, 'Because no one hired us.'

"The landowner told them, 'Then go out and join the others in my vineyard.'

8 "That evening he told the foreman to call the workers in and pay them, beginning with the last workers first. 9 When those hired at five o'clock were paid, each received a full day's wage. 10 When those hired first came to get their pay, they assumed they would receive more. But they, too, were paid a day's wage. 11 When they received their pay, they protested to the owner, 12 'Those people worked only one hour, and yet you've paid them just as much as you paid us who worked all day in the scorching heat.'

13 "He answered one of them, 'Friend, I haven't been unfair! Didn't you agree to work all day for the usual wage? 14 Take your money and go. I wanted to pay this last worker the same as you. 15 Is it against the law for me to do what I want with my money? Should you be jealous because I am kind to others?'

16 "So those who are last now will be first then, and those who are first will be last."

JESUS AGAIN PREDICTS HIS DEATH

17 As Jesus was going up to Jerusalem, he took the twelve disciples aside privately and told them what was going to happen to him. 18 "Listen," he said, "we're going up to Jerusalem, where the Son of Man* will be betrayed to the leading priests and the teachers of religious law. They will sentence him to die. 19 Then they will hand him over to the Romans* to be mocked, flogged with a whip, and crucified. But on the third day he will be raised from the dead."

JESUS TEACHES ABOUT SERVING OTHERS

20 Then the mother of James and John, the sons of Zebedee, came to Jesus with her sons. She knelt respectfully to ask a favor. 21 "What is your request?" he asked.

She replied, "In your Kingdom, please let my two sons sit in places of honor next to you, one on your right and the other on your left."

22 But Jesus answered by saying to them, "You don't know what you are asking! Are you able to drink from the bitter cup of suffering I am about to drink?"

"Oh yes," they replied, "we are able!"

23 Jesus told them, "You will indeed drink from my bitter cup. But I have no right to say who will sit on my right or my left. My Father has prepared those places for the ones he has chosen."

24 When the ten other disciples heard what James and John had asked, they were indignant. 25 But Jesus

SERVE OTHERS

1. What do your parents want you to be "when you grow up"?

MATTHEW 20:20-28

2. What exactly are the guys requesting of Jesus in this passage?
3. How does a person become great in God's kingdom? How is this different from becoming great in sports or business or school?
4. How did Jesus Himself set the example for serving others?
5. How can you serve the people on your team or in your group? How might that attitude help you all in the long run?

20:18 "Son of Man" is a title Jesus used for himself. **20:19** Greek *the Gentiles.*

20:6 five o'clock. So near the end of the workday, it is unusual that they are there at all. They certainly were not expecting work to be offered. This also is a parallel of God's grace, given not when it is expected but when it is least expected.
20:8 That evening. The laborer's day went from sunrise to sunset. According to the Old Testament Law, workers were to be paid their wages at the end of the day so that they would not have to go hungry (Deut. 24:14-15).
20:9-12 they assumed they would receive more. As those hired last receive a denarius for an hour's work, they would have been joyfully surprised. Quite naturally, the spirits of the others in line suddenly rise—if those who worked only one hour received a denarius, what might those who worked all day receive? As the foreman continues to pay each one a denarius, the earlier workers grow angry. What at first seemed like a fair wage (v. 2), now appeared to be unjust and insulting.
20:13 Friend. In the other places where this form of address is used (22:12; 26:50), it has an ironic twist. The laborers are not relating to the landowner as a friend but as an unjust man. **I haven't been unfair!** His actions were not unjust since he was paying them what they had agreed to in the beginning.
20:15 to do what I want with my money. In light of the ongoing conflict with the Pharisees regarding Jesus' interest in the religious outcasts of His time, Jesus, by means of this parable, declares that God's grace is not unjust.
20:20 the mother of James and John. In Mark's account, James and John approach Jesus directly. Regardless of the role their mother played in this incident, it is clear that they are held responsible for it (v. 24).
20:22 drink from the bitter cup. This phrase means to share the same fate. In the Old Testament, drinking the cup is a metaphor for experiencing God's wrath (Ps. 75:8; Isa. 51:17-22). Here, the cup refers to Jesus' suffering and death for the sins of the world. **we are able!** Despite their bold assertion, they do not grasp what Jesus means by the question. They probably assumed He was referring to being willing to share in His future, which they imagine to be one of power and prestige.
20:24 they were indignant. All 12 share the view that the kingdom will be earthly and political with Jesus as the reigning king and them as His chief lieutenants.

called them together and said, "You know that the
rulers in this world lord it over their people, and of-
ficials flaunt their authority over those under them.
26 But among you it will be different. Whoever wants
to be a leader among you must be your servant, 27 and
whoever wants to be first among you must become
your slave. 28 For even the Son of Man came not to be
served but to serve others and to give his life as a ran-
som for many."

JESUS HEALS TWO BLIND MEN

29 As Jesus and the disciples left the town of Jericho, a
large crowd followed behind. 30 Two blind men were
sitting beside the road. When they heard that Jesus
was coming that way, they began shouting, "Lord, Son
of David, have mercy on us!"
31 "Be quiet!" the crowd yelled at them.
But they only shouted louder, "Lord, Son of David,
have mercy on us!"
32 When Jesus heard them, he stopped and called,
"What do you want me to do for you?"
33 "Lord," they said, "we want to see!" 34 Jesus felt
sorry for them and touched their eyes. Instantly they
could see! Then they followed him.

JESUS' TRIUMPHANT ENTRY

21 As Jesus and the disciples approached Jerusa-
lem, they came to the town of Bethphage on
the Mount of Olives. Jesus sent two of them on ahead.
2 "Go into the village over there," he said. "As soon as
you enter it, you will see a donkey tied there, with its
colt beside it. Untie them and bring them to me. 3 If
anyone asks what you are doing, just say, 'The Lord
needs them,' and he will immediately let you take
them."
4 This took place to fulfill the prophecy that said,

5 "Tell the people of Jerusalem,*
'Look, your King is coming to you.
He is humble, riding on a donkey—
riding on a donkey's colt.'"*

6 The two disciples did as Jesus commanded. 7 They
brought the donkey and the colt to him and threw
their garments over the colt, and he sat on it.*
8 Most of the crowd spread their garments on the
road ahead of him, and others cut branches from the
trees and spread them on the road. 9 Jesus was in the
center of the procession, and the people all around
him were shouting,

"Praise God* for the Son of David!
Blessings on the one who comes in the name of
the LORD!
Praise God in highest heaven!"*

10 The entire city of Jerusalem was in an uproar as
he entered. "Who is this?" they asked.
11 And the crowds replied, "It's Jesus, the prophet
from Nazareth in Galilee."

JESUS CLEARS THE TEMPLE

12 Jesus entered the Temple and began to drive out
all the people buying and selling animals for sacri-
fice. He knocked over the tables of the money chang-
ers and the chairs of those selling doves. 13 He said
to them, "The Scriptures declare, 'My Temple will be
called a house of prayer,' but you have turned it into
a den of thieves!"*
14 The blind and the lame came to him in the Tem-
ple, and he healed them. 15 The leading priests and the
teachers of religious law saw these wonderful mira-
cles and heard even the children in the Temple shout-
ing, "Praise God for the Son of David."
But the leaders were indignant. 16 They asked Jesus,
"Do you hear what these children are saying?"
"Yes," Jesus replied. "Haven't you ever read the
Scriptures? For they say, 'You have taught children
and infants to give you praise.'*" 17 Then he returned
to Bethany, where he stayed overnight.

JESUS CURSES THE FIG TREE

18 In the morning, as Jesus was returning to Jerusalem,
he was hungry, 19 and he noticed a fig tree beside the
road. He went over to see if there were any figs, but
there were only leaves. Then he said to it, "May you
never bear fruit again!" And immediately the fig tree
withered up.
20 The disciples were amazed when they saw this
and asked, "How did the fig tree wither so quickly?"

21:5a Greek *Tell the daughter of Zion.* Isa 62:11. **21:5b** Zech 9:9. **21:7** Greek *over them, and he sat on them.* **21:9a** Greek *Hosanna,* an exclamation of praise that literally means "save now"; also in 21:9b, 15. **21:9b** Pss 118:25-26; 148:1. **21:13** Isa 56:7; Jer 7:11. **21:16** Ps 8:2 (Greek version).

20:28 ransom. "Ransom" was a word used generally to describe the act of freeing people from bondage, whether through the literal payment of a purchase price or through some act of deliverance.

20:29 Jericho. The journey begun in 19:1 is almost complete. Jericho, about 18 miles east of Jerusalem, was the place where travelers recrossed the Jordan back into Israel. **a large crowd.** These were pilgrims on their way to Jerusalem for the Passover Feast. Every male over 12 years of age was expected to attend.

20:30 Two blind men. Mark and Luke only mention one. **Lord, Son of David.** This is clearly a messianic title by which the men hail Jesus. The blind truly see who He is, while the Twelve still had not fully grasped this.

21:3 The Lord. Thus far in Matthew's Gospel, Jesus has not referred to Himself by this title. While it can simply be a formal term for a master, the context of this occasion indicates He was implying divine authority as well.

21:8 spread their garments. This was a gesture of respect, given to kings (2 Kings 9:12-13), prophets, and other holy men.

21:9 Praise God. Literally, "Save now!" This was commonly used as an expression of praise to God or as a greeting.

21:12 Temple. Built by Herod the Great in 20 B.C., this magnificent structure covered about 30 acres. **buying and selling.** Temple worship required the sacrifice of an unblemished lamb or (for the poor) a dove. However, inspectors approved only those animals bought from certified vendors employed by the high priest's family. There was great profiteering, as such animals were sold at a huge markup. **money changers.** At Passover each Jew was required to pay a temple tax of nearly two days' wages. Since only a relatively rare currency was acceptable, money changers set up business in the temple to provide people with the correct currency. They charged exorbitant fees for this service.

21:15 children . . . shouting. In contrast to the bitterness created in the worshipers by the exploitation allowed in the temple, Jesus transforms it into a place where children celebrate His presence (18:2-4; 19:14).

21:17 Bethany, where he stayed overnight. Jesus left the city of Jerusalem at night possibly because such opposition to Him was building among the authorities.

21:18-22 a fig tree. Fig trees were a common prophetic symbol associated with Israel and with judgment (Jer. 8:13; Hos. 9:10; Mic. 7:1; Nah. 3:12). Just as the tree was judged for its failure to have fruit, so Israel, and the temple as a symbol of Israel's faith, was judged for its failure to have "fruit"—works that honored God.

21:19 there were only leaves. The tree symbolized Israel. It had the outward appearance of life (bustling activity at the temple) but no fruit (the qualities of justice, love, and godliness that were to mark God's people). **immediately the fig tree withered up.** The immediacy of the event points out the divine power of Jesus and also the authority of Jesus as judge.

21 Then Jesus told them, "I tell you the truth, if you have faith and don't doubt, you can do things like this and much more. You can even say to this mountain, 'May you be lifted up and thrown into the sea,' and it will happen. 22 You can pray for anything, and if you have faith, you will receive it."

THE AUTHORITY OF JESUS CHALLENGED

23 When Jesus returned to the Temple and began teaching, the leading priests and elders came up to him. They demanded, "By what authority are you doing all these things? Who gave you the right?"

24 "I'll tell you by what authority I do these things if you answer one question," Jesus replied. 25 "Did John's authority to baptize come from heaven, or was it merely human?"

They talked it over among themselves. "If we say it was from heaven, he will ask us why we didn't believe John. 26 But if we say it was merely human, we'll be mobbed because the people believe John was a prophet." 27 So they finally replied, "We don't know."

And Jesus responded, "Then I won't tell you by what authority I do these things.

PARABLE OF THE TWO SONS

28 "But what do you think about this? A man with two sons told the older boy, 'Son, go out and work in the vineyard today.' 29 The son answered, 'No, I won't go,' but later he changed his mind and went anyway. 30 Then the father told the other son, 'You go,' and he said, 'Yes, sir, I will.' But he didn't go.

31 "Which of the two obeyed his father?"

They replied, "The first."*

Then Jesus explained his meaning: "I tell you the truth, corrupt tax collectors and prostitutes will get into the Kingdom of God before you do. 32 For John the Baptist came and showed you the right way to live, but you didn't believe him, while tax collectors and prostitutes did. And even when you saw this happening, you refused to believe him and repent of your sins.

PARABLE OF THE EVIL FARMERS

33 "Now listen to another story. A certain landowner planted a vineyard, built a wall around it, dug a pit for pressing out the grape juice, and built a lookout tower. Then he leased the vineyard to tenant farmers and moved to another country. 34 At the time of the grape harvest, he sent his servants to collect his share of the crop. 35 But the farmers grabbed his servants, beat one, killed one, and stoned another. 36 So the landowner sent a larger group of his servants to collect for him, but the results were the same.

37 "Finally, the owner sent his son, thinking, 'Surely they will respect my son.'

38 "But when the tenant farmers saw his son coming, they said to one another, 'Here comes the heir to this estate. Come on, let's kill him and get the estate for ourselves!' 39 So they grabbed him, dragged him out of the vineyard, and murdered him.

40 "When the owner of the vineyard returns," Jesus asked, "what do you think he will do to those farmers?"

41 The religious leaders replied, "He will put the wicked men to a horrible death and lease the vineyard to others who will give him his share of the crop after each harvest."

42 Then Jesus asked them, "Didn't you ever read this in the Scriptures?

'The stone that the builders rejected
  has now become the cornerstone.
This is the LORD's doing,
  and it is wonderful to see.'*

43 I tell you, the Kingdom of God will be taken away from you and given to a nation that will produce the proper fruit. 44 Anyone who stumbles over that stone will be broken to pieces, and it will crush anyone it falls on.*"

45 When the leading priests and Pharisees heard this parable, they realized he was telling the story against them—they were the wicked farmers. 46 They wanted to arrest him, but they were afraid of the crowds, who considered Jesus to be a prophet.

PARABLE OF THE GREAT FEAST

22 Jesus also told them other parables. He said, 2 "The Kingdom of Heaven can be illustrated by the story of a king who prepared a great wedding feast for his son. 3 When the banquet was ready, he sent his servants to notify those who were invited. But they all refused to come!

4 "So he sent other servants to tell them, 'The feast has been prepared. The bulls and fattened cattle have been killed, and everything is ready. Come to the banquet!' 5 But the guests he had invited ignored them and went their own way, one to his farm, another to

21:29-31 Other manuscripts read *"The second."* In still other manuscripts the first son says "Yes" but does nothing, the second son says "No" but then repents and goes, and the answer to Jesus' question is that the second son obeyed his father. **21:42** Ps 118:22-23. **21:44** This verse is not included in some early manuscripts. Compare Luke 20:18.

21:23 the leading priests and elders. The chief priests were the key officers of the temple, just below the high priest in rank. The elders were powerful and (reputedly) wise leaders of Israel. They were generally not priests, but administrators. These were representatives from the Sanhedrin, the Jewish ruling council.

21:31 tax collectors and prostitutes. In this society, these two groups of people represented the lowest depths to which men and women respectively could sink. The tax collectors were Jewish men viewed as exploiting their own people for their own gain as they worked for Rome. Yet Jesus says that these along with prostitutes would be entering the kingdom ahead of the religious authorities!

21:32 the right way to live. John declared that the way to enter God's kingdom was through repentance—a change of heart and life.

21:33 vineyard. This vineyard was built with a wall around it to keep out animals, a pit in which to crush grapes to make wine, and a tower where the farmer kept a lookout for robbers and also where he slept during harvest.

21:37 sent his son. The landowner assumed the tenants would acknowledge the authority of his own son, the heir of the vineyard.

21:38 get the estate. The arrival of the son was mistakenly understood by the servants as a sign that the landowner must have died. By law, a piece of ownerless property could be kept by those who first occupied and cultivated it. Since the tenants assumed the land would be ownerless if the son was dead, they killed him in order to lay claim to the land for themselves.

21:41 lease the vineyard to others. Landowners would rent the vineyard to people who would meet the terms of their contracts. The implication of the parable is that God will raise up new leaders to care for His people.

21:42 The stone that the builders rejected has now become the cornerstone. Here the stone is Jesus (the Messiah) whom the builders (the leaders) fail to recognize. The identification here of the Messiah (the stone) with the Son of God (v. 37) was unique to Jesus.

22:3 sent his servants to notify those who were invited. In well-to-do circles, invitations for banquets were issued well in advance, but the specific time to arrive was communicated on the day of the event when everything was ready (Est. 5:8; 6:14).

his business. 6 Others seized his messengers and in-
sulted them and killed them.
7 "The king was furious, and he sent out his army
to destroy the murderers and burn their town. 8 And
he said to his servants, 'The wedding feast is ready,
and the guests I invited aren't worthy of the honor.
9 Now go out to the street corners and invite everyone
you see.' 10 So the servants brought in everyone they
could find, good and bad alike, and the banquet hall
was filled with guests.
11 "But when the king came in to meet the guests,
he noticed a man who wasn't wearing the proper
clothes for a wedding. 12 'Friend,' he asked, 'how is it
that you are here without wedding clothes?' But the
man had no reply. 13 Then the king said to his aides,
'Bind his hands and feet and throw him into the outer
darkness, where there will be weeping and gnashing
of teeth.'
14 "For many are called, but few are chosen."

TAXES FOR CAESAR

15 Then the Pharisees met together to plot how to trap
Jesus into saying something for which he could be ar-
rested. 16 They sent some of their disciples, along with
the supporters of Herod, to meet with him. "Teacher,"
they said, "we know how honest you are. You teach
the way of God truthfully. You are impartial and don't
play favorites. 17 Now tell us what you think about
this: Is it right to pay taxes to Caesar or not?"
18 But Jesus knew their evil motives. "You hyp-
ocrites!" he said. "Why are you trying to trap me?
19 Here, show me the coin used for the tax." When they
handed him a Roman coin,* 20 he asked, "Whose pic-
ture and title are stamped on it?"
21 "Caesar's," they replied.
"Well, then," he said, "give to Caesar what belongs
to Caesar, and give to God what belongs to God."
22 His reply amazed them, and they went away.

DISCUSSION ABOUT RESURRECTION

23 That same day Jesus was approached by some
Sadducees—religious leaders who say there is no
resurrection from the dead. They posed this ques-
tion: 24 "Teacher, Moses said, 'If a man dies without
children, his brother should marry the widow and
have a child who will carry on the brother's name.'*
25 Well, suppose there were seven brothers. The old-
est one married and then died without children, so
his brother married the widow. 26 But the second
brother also died, and the third brother married her.
This continued with all seven of them. 27 Last of all,
the woman also died. 28 So tell us, whose wife will she
be in the resurrection? For all seven were married to
her."
29 Jesus replied, "Your mistake is that you don't
know the Scriptures, and you don't know the power
of God. 30 For when the dead rise, they will neither
marry nor be given in marriage. In this respect they
will be like the angels in heaven.
31 "But now, as to whether there will be a resurrec-
tion of the dead—haven't you ever read about this in
the Scriptures? Long after Abraham, Isaac, and Jacob
had died, God said,* 32 'I am the God of Abraham, the
God of Isaac, and the God of Jacob.'* So he is the God of
the living, not the dead."
33 When the crowds heard him, they were astound-
ed at his teaching.

THE MOST IMPORTANT COMMANDMENT

34 But when the Pharisees heard that he had silenced
the Sadducees with his reply, they met together to
question him again. 35 One of them, an expert in re-
ligious law, tried to trap him with this question:
36 "Teacher, which is the most important command-
ment in the law of Moses?"
37 Jesus replied, "'You must love the LORD your God
with all your heart, all your soul, and all your mind.'*
38 This is the first and greatest commandment. 39 A
second is equally important: 'Love your neighbor as
yourself.'* 40 The entire law and all the demands of the
prophets are based on these two commandments."

WHOSE SON IS THE MESSIAH?

41 Then, surrounded by the Pharisees, Jesus asked
them a question: 42 "What do you think about the Mes-
siah? Whose son is he?"
They replied, "He is the son of David."
43 Jesus responded, "Then why does David, speaking
under the inspiration of the Spirit, call the Messiah
'my Lord'? For David said,

22:19 Greek *a denarius.* 22:24 Deut 25:5-6. 22:31 Greek *read about this? God said.* 22:32 Exod 3:6. 22:37 Deut 6:5. 22:39 Lev 19:18.

22:9 street corners. These are the public squares where beggars gathered hoping for handouts.

22:11-12 proper clothes for a wedding. In this allegorical parable, the wedding clothes represent the robes of righteousness God provides for His people (Zech. 3:3-5; Rev. 3:4, 5, 18). Without God-given righteousness, one has no part in the kingdom. The false disciple, like the religious leaders (v. 34), is silenced before the king. He has no excuse.

22:13 weeping and gnashing of teeth. This is a common phrase used to indicate the extreme horror and suffering of God's judgment (8:12; 13:42,50).

22:16 supporters of Herod. A political group made up of influential Jewish sympathizers of King Herod. Normally despised by the Pharisees as traitors who worked with Rome and associated with Gentiles, the Pharisees needed this group's assistance to secure the civil authority's opposition to Jesus.

22:17 taxes. An annual poll tax had to be paid to the Romans by all adult Jews. Many Jews felt that paying taxes to Caesar denied the belief that God was the rightful ruler of Israel.

22:18 Why are you trying to trap me? If the authorities can get Jesus to say that the people should not pay taxes to Caesar, then the Roman guard would have grounds to arrest Him. On the other hand, if Jesus says they should pay taxes, then He would lose the support of the crowds who resented being taxed by an occupying force.

22:19 the coin. Only the denarius, a small silver coin, could be used to pay the poll tax. Since it bore the picture of Tiberius Caesar and a description of him as "Son of the Divine Augustine," these coins were offensive to strict Jews, who would not even handle them.

22:23 Sadducees. A small but highly influential party of Jews composed mainly of wealthy, aristocratic priests. Up to this point Jesus has been no threat to the Sadducees since His ministry had been largely in Galilee, far from the temple they controlled. **resurrection.** Most Jews believed that at the end of history God would bring the dead to life for judgment. The Sadducees did not believe in the resurrection.

22:34-40 to try to trap him. In Mark's version, the scribe appears to ask Jesus a sincere question (Mark 12:28-34).

22:36 which is the most important commandment in the law of Moses? The Pharisees, who generally regarded all the laws of God as equally important, probably hoped Jesus would isolate one law and thus provide them with the opportunity to discredit Him for ignoring other laws.

22:37 Love the LORD. This is part of the *Shema* (Deut. 6:4-5). This passage, recited by pious Jews each morning and evening, captures what was essential about the people's relationship to God.

22:42 the Messiah. This title identifies Jesus as the expected deliverer of Israel.

44 'The LORD said to my Lord,
Sit in the place of honor at my right hand
until I humble your enemies beneath your feet.'*

45 Since David called the Messiah 'my Lord,' how can the Messiah be his son?"

46 No one could answer him. And after that, no one dared to ask him any more questions.

JESUS CRITICIZES THE RELIGIOUS LEADERS

23 Then Jesus said to the crowds and to his disciples, 2 "The teachers of religious law and the Pharisees are the official interpreters of the law of Moses.* 3 So practice and obey whatever they tell you, but don't follow their example. For they don't practice what they teach. 4 They crush people with unbearable religious demands and never lift a finger to ease the burden.

5 "Everything they do is for show. On their arms they wear extra wide prayer boxes with Scripture verses inside, and they wear robes with extra long tassels.* 6 And they love to sit at the head table at banquets and in the seats of honor in the synagogues. 7 They love to receive respectful greetings as they walk in the marketplaces, and to be called 'Rabbi.'*

8 "Don't let anyone call you 'Rabbi,' for you have only one teacher, and all of you are equal as brothers and sisters.* 9 And don't address anyone here on earth as 'Father,' for only God in heaven is your Father. 10 And don't let anyone call you 'Teacher,' for you have only one teacher, the Messiah. 11 The greatest among you must be a servant. 12 But those who exalt themselves will be humbled, and those who humble themselves will be exalted.

13 "What sorrow awaits you teachers of religious law and you Pharisees. Hypocrites! For you shut the door of the Kingdom of Heaven in people's faces. You won't go in yourselves, and you don't let others enter either.*

15 "What sorrow awaits you teachers of religious law and you Pharisees. Hypocrites! For you cross land and sea to make one convert, and then you turn that person into twice the child of hell* you yourselves are!

16 "Blind guides! What sorrow awaits you! For you say that it means nothing to swear 'by God's Temple,' but that it is binding to swear 'by the gold in the Temple.' 17 Blind fools! Which is more important—the gold or the Temple that makes the gold sacred? 18 And you say that to swear 'by the altar' is not binding, but to swear 'by the gifts on the altar' is binding. 19 How blind! For which is more important—the gift on the altar or the altar that makes the gift sacred? 20 When you swear 'by the altar,' you are swearing by it and by everything on it. 21 And when you swear 'by the Temple,' you are swearing by it and by God, who lives in it. 22 And when you swear 'by heaven,' you are swearing by the throne of God and by God, who sits on the throne.

23 "What sorrow awaits you teachers of religious law and you Pharisees. Hypocrites! For you are careful to tithe even the tiniest income from your herb gardens,* but you ignore the more important aspects of the law—justice, mercy, and faith. You should tithe, yes, but do not neglect the more important things. 24 Blind guides! You strain your water so you won't accidentally swallow a gnat, but you swallow a camel!*

25 "What sorrow awaits you teachers of religious law and you Pharisees. Hypocrites! For you are so careful to clean the outside of the cup and the dish, but inside you are filthy—full of greed and self-indulgence! 26 You blind Pharisee! First wash the inside of the cup and the dish,* and then the outside will become clean, too.

27 "What sorrow awaits you teachers of religious law and you Pharisees. Hypocrites! For you are like whitewashed tombs—beautiful on the outside but filled on the inside with dead people's bones and all sorts of impurity. 28 Outwardly you look like righteous people, but inwardly your hearts are filled with hypocrisy and lawlessness.

29 "What sorrow awaits you teachers of religious law and you Pharisees. Hypocrites! For you build tombs for the prophets your ancestors killed, and you decorate the monuments of the godly people your ancestors destroyed. 30 Then you say, 'If we had lived in the days of our ancestors, we would never have joined them in killing the prophets.'

31 "But in saying that, you testify against yourselves that you are indeed the descendants of those who murdered the prophets. 32 Go ahead and finish what your ancestors started. 33 Snakes! Sons of vipers! How will you escape the judgment of hell?

22:44 Ps 110:1. **23:2** Greek *and the Pharisees sit in the seat of Moses.* **23:5** Greek *They enlarge their phylacteries and lengthen their tassels.* **23:7** *Rabbi,* from Aramaic, means "master" or "teacher." **23:8** Greek *brothers.* **23:13** Some manuscripts add verse 14, *What sorrow awaits you teachers of religious law and you Pharisees. Hypocrites! You shamelessly cheat widows out of their property and then pretend to be pious by making long prayers in public. Because of this, you will be severely punished.* Compare Mark 12:40 and Luke 20:47. **23:15** Greek *of Gehenna;* also in 23:33. **23:23** Greek *tithe the mint, the dill, and the cumin.* **23:24** See Lev 11:4, 23, where gnats and camels are both forbidden as food. **23:26** Some manuscripts do not include *and the dish.*

23:5 prayer boxes. These were small cases containing passages of the Law. They were tied to the forehead and left arm (Ex. 13:9, 16; Deut. 6:8; 11:18). **tassels.** Jews were to tie tassels on the corners of their robes to remind them of God's commands (Num. 15:37-39). The Pharisees wore these things in an ornamental way to draw attention to themselves.

23:6 in the seats of honor in the synagogues. The choice seat was up front, with its back to the box containing the sacred Scriptures and its front facing the congregation, so that all would see who sat there.

23:7 greetings. Out of respect for the authority of the teachers of the Law, people rose and called out titles of respect when they passed by. **Rabbi.** This official title for the scribes literally meant "my master."

23:13 you shut the door of the Kingdom of Heaven in people's faces. Instead of unlocking the Scriptures, the traditions and rules of the scribes have the effect of securely locking away such knowledge from the people.

23:16 Blind guides! The Pharisees prided themselves on being "guides for the blind." Instead, Jesus asserts they are blind themselves.

23:24 You strain your water so you won't accidentally swallow a gnat, but you swallow a camel! This is an example of Jesus' use of humorous irony to make His point.

23:25 greed and self-indulgence. Jesus says it is as if they think using ritually "clean" utensils makes the consumption of food and drink gained by greed and violence acceptable. While concerned for the external demands of their tradition, they fail to consider what is going on inside of themselves.

23:26 wash the inside. Following the metaphor of the cup and dish, this is a call to self-examination and repentance. True holiness before God comes from the inside out, not from the outside in. A clean heart, not a clean dish, is required.

23:27 whitewashed tombs. Tombs would often be whitewashed. While this gave them an attractive appearance, it could do nothing about the decay inside the tomb.

23:28 lawlessness. Literally, "wickedness."

23:33 Snakes! Sons of vipers! The image painted by these words is of snakes slithering through the undergrowth trying to escape the oncoming fire.

34 "Therefore, I am sending you prophets and wise men and teachers of religious law. But you will kill some by crucifixion, and you will flog others with whips in your synagogues, chasing them from city to city. 35 As a result, you will be held responsible for the murder of all godly people of all time—from the murder of righteous Abel to the murder of Zechariah son of Berekiah, whom you killed in the Temple between the sanctuary and the altar. 36 I tell you the truth, this judgment will fall on this very generation.

JESUS GRIEVES OVER JERUSALEM

37 "O Jerusalem, Jerusalem, the city that kills the prophets and stones God's messengers! How often I have wanted to gather your children together as a hen protects her chicks beneath her wings, but you wouldn't let me. 38 And now, look, your house is abandoned and desolate.* 39 For I tell you this, you will never see me again until you say, 'Blessings on the one who comes in the name of the LORD!'*"

JESUS SPEAKS ABOUT THE FUTURE

24 As Jesus was leaving the Temple grounds, his disciples pointed out to him the various Temple buildings. 2 But he responded, "Do you see all these buildings? I tell you the truth, they will be completely demolished. Not one stone will be left on top of another!"

3 Later, Jesus sat on the Mount of Olives. His disciples came to him privately and said, "Tell us, when will all this happen? What sign will signal your return and the end of the world?*"

4 Jesus told them, "Don't let anyone mislead you, 5 for many will come in my name, claiming, 'I am the Messiah.' They will deceive many. 6 And you will hear of wars and threats of wars, but don't panic. Yes, these things must take place, but the end won't follow immediately. 7 Nation will go to war against nation, and kingdom against kingdom. There will be famines and earthquakes in many parts of the world. 8 But all this is only the first of the birth pains, with more to come.

9 "Then you will be arrested, persecuted, and killed. You will be hated all over the world because you are my followers.* 10 And many will turn away from me and betray and hate each other. 11 And many false prophets will appear and will deceive many people. 12 Sin will be rampant everywhere, and the love of many will grow cold. 13 But the one who endures to the end will be saved. 14 And the Good News about the Kingdom will be preached throughout the whole world, so that all nations* will hear it; and then the end will come.

15 "The day is coming when you will see what Daniel the prophet spoke about—the sacrilegious object that causes desecration* standing in the Holy Place." (Reader, pay attention!) 16 "Then those in Judea must flee to the hills. 17 A person out on the deck of a roof must not go down into the house to pack. 18 A person out in the field must not return even to get a coat. 19 How terrible it will be for pregnant women and for nursing mothers in those days. 20 And pray that your flight will not be in winter or on the Sabbath. 21 For there will be greater anguish than at any time since the world began. And it will never be so great again. 22 In fact, unless that time of calamity is shortened, not a single person will survive. But it will be shortened for the sake of God's chosen ones.

23 "Then if anyone tells you, 'Look, here is the Messiah,' or 'There he is,' don't believe it. 24 For false messiahs and false prophets will rise up and perform great signs and wonders so as to deceive, if possible, even God's chosen ones. 25 See, I have warned you about this ahead of time.

26 "So if someone tells you, 'Look, the Messiah is out in the desert,' don't bother to go and look. Or, 'Look, he is hiding here,' don't believe it! 27 For as the lightning flashes in the east and shines to the west, so it will be when the Son of Man* comes. 28 Just as the gathering of vultures shows there is a carcass nearby, so these signs indicate that the end is near.*

29 "Immediately after the anguish of those days,

the sun will be darkened,
  the moon will give no light,
the stars will fall from the sky,
  and the powers in the heavens will be shaken.*

30 And then at last, the sign that the Son of Man is coming will appear in the heavens, and there will be deep mourning among all the peoples of the earth.

23:38 Some manuscripts do not include *and desolate.* 23:39 Ps 118:26. 24:3 Or *the age?* 24:9 Greek *on account of my name.* 24:14 Or *all peoples.* 24:15 Greek *the abomination of desolation.* See Dan 9:27; 11:31; 12:11. 24:27 "Son of Man" is a title Jesus used for himself. 24:28 Greek *Wherever the carcass is, the vultures gather.* 24:29 See Isa 13:10; 34:4; Joel 2:10. 24:30 See Dan 7:13.

23:34 crucifixion. The Jews did not practice crucifixion. This may be a reference to how the Jewish authorities eventually led the Romans to carry out the execution of Jesus Himself.

23:35 Abel. Abel, the first person to be killed, was murdered by his brother, who, like these leaders, refused to listen to God (Gen. 4:3-8). **Zechariah son of Berekiah.** There were two known Zechariahs who were sons of men named Berechiah. One was the author of the Old Testament book by his name, but there is no record of how he died. The other was a man murdered by Jewish zealots in the temple in A.D. 67. This was contemporary to Matthew's writing but after Jesus' earthly ministry.

23:38 your house. This is the temple from which the presence of God will depart because of the people's rejection of the Messiah (Jer. 12:7; Ezek. 10:18-19).

24:2 Not one stone will be left. The temple was destroyed by Rome in A.D. 70.

24:6-8 you will hear. Some feel that apocalyptic language uses graphic imagery to describe historical events. Others see this as a description of future events.

24:9-13 arrested, persecuted, and killed. The focus shifts from the woes experienced by people in general to those Christians will face. Many will fall away, but Jesus calls for faithfulness (v. 13).

24:14 the Good News. Despite the persecution, the mission of Jesus' disciples is to preach the gospel and make disciples of all nations (28:18-20).

24:15 the sacrilegious object that causes desecration. This phrase (from Dan. 9:27; 11:31; 12:11) refers to an event so awful that Jews will flee from the temple in horror. Such an event occurred in 168 B.C. when Antiochus Epiphanes, a Syrian king, set up an altar to Zeus in the temple. Jesus warns that when that type of desecration occurs again, the fall of Jerusalem would be imminent (2 Thess. 2:1-4). Luke's version includes armies surrounding Jerusalem as a further sign (Luke 21:20).

24:21 greater anguish. The destruction of Jerusalem in A.D. 70 was an unparalleled disaster for Israel. Some consider this the fulfillment of Jesus' words. Others are still looking for the completion of this prophecy.

24:22 chosen ones. These are the people God has called into His kingdom. They are akin to the survivors of God's wrath spoken of in Isaiah 1:9 and 4:2-4.

24:24 great signs and wonders. Miracles in themselves are no proof of a person's divine authority. Pharaoh's magicians in Egypt were able to imitate many of the miracles performed by Moses (Ex. 7:20-22).

24:30 the sign. Jesus uses common military imagery to describe His coming. A "sign" was a banner, flag, or standard under which an army would march. Isaiah 11:10 compares the Messiah to a banner that will be raised as a rallying point for all God's people.

And they will see the Son of Man coming on the
clouds of heaven with power and great glory.* 31 And
he will send out his angels with the mighty blast of a
trumpet, and they will gather his chosen ones from
all over the world*—from the farthest ends of the
earth and heaven.
32 "Now learn a lesson from the fig tree. When its
branches bud and its leaves begin to sprout, you
know that summer is near. 33 In the same way, when
you see all these things, you can know his return is
very near, right at the door. 34 I tell you the truth, this
generation* will not pass from the scene until all
these things take place. 35 Heaven and earth will dis-
appear, but my words will never disappear.
36 "However, no one knows the day or hour when
these things will happen, not even the angels in heav-
en or the Son himself.* Only the Father knows.
37 "When the Son of Man returns, it will be like it
was in Noah's day. 38 In those days before the flood,
the people were enjoying banquets and parties and
weddings right up to the time Noah entered his boat.
39 People didn't realize what was going to happen un-
til the flood came and swept them all away. That is the
way it will be when the Son of Man comes.
40 "Two men will be working together in the field;
one will be taken, the other left. 41 Two women will be
grinding flour at the mill; one will be taken, the other
left.
42 "So you, too, must keep watch! For you don't know
what day your Lord is coming. 43 Understand this: If a
homeowner knew exactly when a burglar was com-
ing, he would keep watch and not permit his house to
be broken into. 44 You also must be ready all the time,
for the Son of Man will come when least expected.
45 "A faithful, sensible servant is one to whom the
master can give the responsibility of managing his
other household servants and feeding them. 46 If the
master returns and finds that the servant has done a
good job, there will be a reward. 47 I tell you the truth,
the master will put that servant in charge of all he
owns. 48 But what if the servant is evil and thinks,
'My master won't be back for a while,' 49 and he be-
gins beating the other servants, partying, and getting
drunk? 50 The master will return unannounced and
unexpected, 51 and he will cut the servant to pieces
and assign him a place with the hypocrites. In that
place there will be weeping and gnashing of teeth.

PARABLE OF THE TEN BRIDESMAIDS

25 "Then the Kingdom of Heaven will be like ten
bridesmaids* who took their lamps and went
to meet the bridegroom. 2 Five of them were foolish,
and five were wise. 3 The five who were foolish didn't
take enough olive oil for their lamps, 4 but the other
five were wise enough to take along extra oil. 5 When
the bridegroom was delayed, they all became drowsy
and fell asleep.
6 "At midnight they were roused by the shout, 'Look,
the bridegroom is coming! Come out and meet him!'
7 "All the bridesmaids got up and prepared their
lamps. 8 Then the five foolish ones asked the others,
'Please give us some of your oil because our lamps are
going out.'
9 "But the others replied, 'We don't have enough for
all of us. Go to a shop and buy some for yourselves.'
10 "But while they were gone to buy oil, the bride-
groom came. Then those who were ready went in with
him to the marriage feast, and the door was locked.
11 Later, when the other five bridesmaids returned, they
stood outside, calling, 'Lord! Lord! Open the door for us!'
12 "But he called back, 'Believe me, I don't know you!'
13 "So you, too, must keep watch! For you do not
know the day or hour of my return.

BE PREPARED

1. What happened the last time your electricity went off? How prepared were you?

MATTHEW 25:1-13

2. Why does Jesus describe five of these girls as foolish? What did they do that was foolish?
3. What would you call the refusal of the five girls in this parable to share their oil: Wise? Selfish? Fair? Unfair?
4. What is the meaning of this parable? What will happen to those people who are not prepared when Jesus returns?
5. If you knew Jesus would return next week, how would you live your life differently?

24:31 Greek *from the four winds.* **24:34** Or *this age,* or *this nation.* **24:36** Some manuscripts do not include *or the Son himself.* **25:1** Or *virgins;* also in 25:7, 11.

24:31 a mighty blast of a trumpet. Trumpets were used to communicate orders to the army. Isaiah 27:13 uses the image of a trumpet blast to describe how God's people will be gathered together when God comes to bring judgment upon their enemies.

24:32 lesson from the fig tree. They knew that the fig tree only got its leaves in late spring. When the leaves came, it was a sure sign that summer was near.

24:33 these things. Jesus evidently refers to those things that will occur prior to the fall of Jerusalem and as a possible foreshadowing of things to come prior to the final judgment (vv. 4-15).

24:45-51 faithful, sensible servant. When the master was away, one slave would be appointed as the head of the household. If he abused this position for his own indulgence, the sudden appearance of his master would bring judgment.

25:1 ten virgins. There is no special meaning here to the numbers ten or five. They simply reflect two categories of people. **took their lamps.** Weddings typically occurred at night. The lamps, probably small earthen jars with a wick inserted to draw the oil used as fuel, would be held up on poles to brighten the way for the procession. **to meet the bridegroom.** Prior to a wedding, the groom would go to the bride's home and lead her in a procession to his house where the wedding took place. These 10 women were probably either at the bride's house or somewhere along the processional route waiting for the groom to come.

25:6 At midnight. This emphasizes the unexpected delay of the groom, since this would have been long after most people would have expected him to come. **Come out and meet him!** People would gather around the groom to escort him to the bride's home and then back to the actual site of the wedding. The unexpected arrival of the groom, the shout of proclamation, and the people coming out to meet him all echo themes of the return of Christ as described in 1 Thessalonians 4:16-17.

25:8 our lamps are going out. Once the time for the procession arrived, the foolish women realized they were short on oil.

25:9 We don't have enough. The refusal to share was not selfish but simply prudent. They carried only enough for themselves. This aspect of the story is thought to show that each person needs his or her own relationship with the Lord; such a relationship cannot be obtained by simply being around those who demonstrate faith. **Go to a shop and buy.** Since it is so late, it would be difficult to find a shopkeeper willing to open shop and sell them oil. Likewise, at the time of the Lord's return, it is too late to try to make up for one's lack of preparation.

PARABLE OF THE THREE SERVANTS

14 "Again, the Kingdom of Heaven can be illustrated by the story of a man going on a long trip. He called together his servants and entrusted his money to them while he was gone. 15 He gave five bags of silver* to one, two bags of silver to another, and one bag of silver to the last—dividing it in proportion to their abilities. He then left on his trip.

16 "The servant who received the five bags of silver began to invest the money and earned five more. 17 The servant with two bags of silver also went to work and earned two more. 18 But the servant who received the one bag of silver dug a hole in the ground and hid the master's money.

19 "After a long time their master returned from his trip and called them to give an account of how they had used his money. 20 The servant to whom he had entrusted the five bags of silver came forward with five more and said, 'Master, you gave me five bags of silver to invest, and I have earned five more.'

21 "The master was full of praise. 'Well done, my good and faithful servant. You have been faithful in handling this small amount, so now I will give you many more responsibilities. Let's celebrate together!*'

22 "The servant who had received the two bags of silver came forward and said, 'Master, you gave me two bags of silver to invest, and I have earned two more.'

23 "The master said, 'Well done, my good and faithful servant. You have been faithful in handling this small amount, so now I will give you many more responsibilities. Let's celebrate together!'

24 "Then the servant with the one bag of silver came and said, 'Master, I knew you were a harsh man, harvesting crops you didn't plant and gathering crops you didn't cultivate. 25 I was afraid I would lose your money, so I hid it in the earth. Look, here is your money back.'

26 "But the master replied, 'You wicked and lazy servant! If you knew I harvested crops I didn't plant and gathered crops I didn't cultivate, 27 why didn't you deposit my money in the bank? At least I could have gotten some interest on it.'

28 "Then he ordered, 'Take the money from this servant, and give it to the one with the ten bags of silver. 29 To those who use well what they are given, even more will be given, and they will have an abundance. But from those who do nothing, even what little they have will be taken away. 30 Now throw this useless servant into outer darkness, where there will be weeping and gnashing of teeth.'

MAKING A PROFIT

1. When you were little, did you receive an allowance? How much? How did you usually spend it?

MATTHEW 25:14-30

2. In this parable, a "bag of silver" is money. Why does the master praise those who earned him money and condemn the guy who buried his?
3. Why was the master so hard on the slave with one bag? After all, he didn't steal or lose it. What principle is Jesus teaching about how we use what we are given for His service?
4. The master was looking for a profit on his investments. How are you making a "profit" for the kingdom of heaven?
5. What areas in your life are you "burying" rather than using for God?

THE FINAL JUDGMENT

31 "But when the Son of Man* comes in his glory, and all the angels with him, then he will sit upon his glorious throne. 32 All the nations* will be gathered in his presence, and he will separate the people as a shepherd separates the sheep from the goats. 33 He will place the sheep at his right hand and the goats at his left.

34 "Then the King will say to those on his right, 'Come, you who are blessed by my Father, inherit the Kingdom prepared for you from the creation of the world. 35 For I was hungry, and you fed me. I was thirsty, and you gave me a drink. I was a stranger, and you invited me into your home. 36 I was naked, and you gave me clothing. I was sick, and you cared for me. I was in prison, and you visited me.'

37 "Then these righteous ones will reply, 'Lord, when did we ever see you hungry and feed you? Or thirsty and give you something to drink? 38 Or a stranger and show you hospitality? Or naked and give you clothing? 39 When did we ever see you sick or in prison and visit you?'

25:15 Greek *talents;* also throughout the story. A talent is equal to 75 pounds or 34 kilograms. **25:21** Greek *Enter into the joy of your master* [or *your Lord*]; also in 25:23. **25:31** "Son of Man" is a title Jesus used for himself. **25:32** Or *peoples.*

25:15 bags of silver. Originally this was a unit of weight. However, it was also used as the highest denomination of coinage. It would take a laborer almost 20 years to earn the equivalent of one talent.

25:16 earned five more. High interest rates in that time could make a thousand percent return possible (though undoubtedly difficult).

25:19 After a long time. The indefinite time reference hints that Christ's own return may be far off. After Jesus ascended to heaven, much of the church was expecting His early return (Heb. 10:37; 1 Peter 4:7; Rev. 1:3). When this did not happen, they had to be taught how to wait. Parables such as this helped as did teachings (1 Thess. 4:13-18; 2 Peter 3:3-10).

25:21 Let's celebate together! The servants are not only given more responsibility; they are invited into a new relationship with the master. No longer simply servants, they now enjoy his friendship and respect. Jesus spoke of this same change in relationship in John 15:15 when He told the disciples, "I no longer call you slaves . . . Now you are my friends."

25:24 a harsh man. Literally, this is "exacting." He was generous in his original entrustment of his property to his servants. He was generous to the first and second servants upon his return. It would raise the question in the listeners' minds whether the problem was with the third servant's perceptions.

25:25 I was afraid. The servant implies that his lack of having anything to show for having been entrusted with the talent is really the fault of the master: he expects too much, and he is too frightening.

25:32 All the nations. This is a universal, worldwide judgment. All people will be present at this judgment scene. **separates the sheep from the goats.** These animals grazed in common herds during the day. At night, however, they were separated because the goats needed to be in shelters to be protected from the elements.

25:34 prepared for you from the creation of the world. Contrast this with the punishment of the wicked in the eternal fire "prepared for the devil and his demons" (v. 41).

25:36 in prison. Probably in view are those (like John the Baptist) who were in prison because they resisted the government out of fidelity to God. Visiting such a prisoner would put the visitor at risk since he or she might be identified as a sympathizer.

SHEEP AND GOATS

1. Have you ever been stopped by someone begging in the street? What did you do?

MATTHEW 25:31-46

2. Who will stand before God to be judged? What will happen after the judgment? Who will go to heaven, and who will go to hell?
3. What principle is Jesus teaching in this passage?
4. Who are "the least of these" that Jesus refers to?
5. When was the last time you did something for someone hungry, alone, poor, sick, or imprisoned?
6. What can your group can do to help someone in need?

40 "And the King will say, 'I tell you the truth, when
you did it to one of the least of these my brothers and
sisters,* you were doing it to me!'
41 "Then the King will turn to those on the left and
say, 'Away with you, you cursed ones, into the eternal
fire prepared for the devil and his demons.* 42 For I
was hungry, and you didn't feed me. I was thirsty, and
you didn't give me a drink. 43 I was a stranger, and you
didn't invite me into your home. I was naked, and you
didn't give me clothing. I was sick and in prison, and
you didn't visit me.'
44 "Then they will reply, 'Lord, when did we ever see
you hungry or thirsty or a stranger or naked or sick or
in prison, and not help you?'
45 "And he will answer, 'I tell you the truth, when
you refused to help the least of these my brothers and
sisters, you were refusing to help me.'
46 "And they will go away into eternal punishment,
but the righteous will go into eternal life."

THE PLOT TO KILL JESUS

26 When Jesus had finished saying all these
things, he said to his disciples, 2 "As you know,
Passover begins in two days, and the Son of Man* will
be handed over to be crucified."
3 At that same time the leading priests and elders
were meeting at the residence of Caiaphas, the high
priest, 4 plotting how to capture Jesus secretly and kill
him. 5 "But not during the Passover celebration," they
agreed, "or the people may riot."

JESUS ANOINTED AT BETHANY

6 Meanwhile, Jesus was in Bethany at the home of Si-
mon, a man who had previously had leprosy. 7 While
he was eating,* a woman came in with a beautiful al-
abaster jar of expensive perfume and poured it over
his head.
8 The disciples were indignant when they saw this.
"What a waste!" they said. 9 "It could have been sold
for a high price and the money given to the poor."
10 But Jesus, aware of this, replied, "Why criticize
this woman for doing such a good thing to me? 11 You
will always have the poor among you, but you will
not always have me. 12 She has poured this perfume
on me to prepare my body for burial. 13 I tell you the
truth, wherever the Good News is preached through-
out the world, this woman's deed will be remembered
and discussed."

JUDAS AGREES TO BETRAY JESUS

14 Then Judas Iscariot, one of the twelve disciples,
went to the leading priests 15 and asked, "How much
will you pay me to betray Jesus to you?" And they
gave him thirty pieces of silver. 16 From that time on,
Judas began looking for an opportunity to betray
Jesus.

THE LAST SUPPER

17 On the first day of the Festival of Unleavened Bread,
the disciples came to Jesus and asked, "Where do you
want us to prepare the Passover meal for you?"
18 "As you go into the city," he told them, "you will
see a certain man. Tell him, 'The Teacher says: My
time has come, and I will eat the Passover meal with
my disciples at your house.'" 19 So the disciples did as
Jesus told them and prepared the Passover meal there.
20 When it was evening, Jesus sat down at the table*
with the Twelve. 21 While they were eating, he said, "I
tell you the truth, one of you will betray me."
22 Greatly distressed, each one asked in turn, "Am I
the one, Lord?"
23 He replied, "One of you who has just eaten from
this bowl with me will betray me. 24 For the Son of
Man must die, as the Scriptures declared long ago. But
how terrible it will be for the one who betrays him. It
would be far better for that man if he had never been
born!"

25:40 Greek *my brothers.* **25:41** Greek *his angels.* **26:2** "Son of Man" is a title Jesus used for himself. **26:7** Or *reclining.* **26:20** Or *Jesus reclined.*

25:41 the eternal fire. The idea of hell, a place of eternal punishment by fire, reflects Israel's experience with the valley of Gehenna, a ravine outside Jerusalem where children were once sacrificed to the god Molech (1 Kings 11:7). Gehenna became a symbol for the place of punishment and spiritual death. **prepared for the devil and his demons.** Satan, the Devil, led a rebellion of angels against God, and they have all been condemned for it (2 Peter 2:4; Rev. 19:20; 20:10).

25:44 Lord, when did we ever see you. With this teaching Jesus condemned those who look past the suffering of the world as they seek a detached religiosity. The New Testament is consistent in saying that love of God and love of people, especially people who are in need, must go together.

25:45 when you refused to help. It is not enough simply to avoid doing bad things—people will be judged also for the good things they neglect to do.

26:2 the Passover. This feast was a celebration of God's deliverance of Israel from Egypt (Ex. 12).

26:3 the high priest. This was the religious and civic head of the Jews.

26:5 not during the Passover celebration. During Passover, Jerusalem's population rose from 50,000 to 250,000. Jesus' popularity with the crowds meant He could not be arrested publicly for fear that this might spark a riot that would lead to harsh Roman repression.

26:7 a woman came in. A woman would not be present at a meal like this except to serve. Her entrance would have been thought scandalous. **poured it over his head.** Typically, this perfume was used very sparingly and only for special occasions. This was a lavish gesture indicating the high regard this woman had for Jesus.

26:15 thirty pieces of silver. This was not a very large amount, but aligns with the prophecy in Zechariah 11:12.

26:17 On the first day of the Festival of Unleavened Bread. This feast did not officially start until the day after Passover. However, in the first century the day on which the lambs were sacrificed was sometimes referred to as the first day of the Feast of Unleavened Bread.

26:20 When it was evening. The Passover could be eaten only after sunset.

26:23 eaten from this bowl with me. To share a meal was a sign of friendship, making the betrayal even more scandalous.

26:24 as the Scriptures declared. Passages such as Isaiah 53:1-6 point to the suffering of God's chosen servant.

25 Judas, the one who would betray him, also asked,
"Rabbi, am I the one?"
And Jesus told him, "You have said it."
26 As they were eating, Jesus took some bread and
blessed it. Then he broke it in pieces and gave it to the
disciples, saying, "Take this and eat it, for this is my body."
27 And he took a cup of wine and gave thanks to God
for it. He gave it to them and said, "Each of you drink
from it, 28 for this is my blood, which confirms the cov-
enant* between God and his people. It is poured out
as a sacrifice to forgive the sins of many. 29 Mark my
words—I will not drink wine again until the day I
drink it new with you in my Father's Kingdom."
30 Then they sang a hymn and went out to the
Mount of Olives.

JESUS PREDICTS PETER'S DENIAL

31 On the way, Jesus told them, "Tonight all of you will
desert me. For the Scriptures say,

'God will strike* the Shepherd,
and the sheep of the flock will be scattered.'

32 But after I have been raised from the dead, I will go
ahead of you to Galilee and meet you there."
33 Peter declared, "Even if everyone else deserts you,
I will never desert you."
34 Jesus replied, "I tell you the truth, Peter—this
very night, before the rooster crows, you will deny
three times that you even know me."
35 "No!" Peter insisted. "Even if I have to die with
you, I will never deny you!" And all the other disciples
vowed the same.

JESUS PRAYS IN GETHSEMANE

36 Then Jesus went with them to the olive grove called
Gethsemane, and he said, "Sit here while I go over there
to pray." 37 He took Peter and Zebedee's two sons, James
and John, and he became anguished and distressed.
38 He told them, "My soul is crushed with grief to the
point of death. Stay here and keep watch with me."
39 He went on a little farther and bowed with his
face to the ground, praying, "My Father! If it is possi-
ble, let this cup of suffering be taken away from me.
Yet I want your will to be done, not mine."
40 Then he returned to the disciples and found them
asleep. He said to Peter, "Couldn't you watch with me
even one hour? 41 Keep watch and pray, so that you
will not give in to temptation. For the spirit is willing,
but the body is weak!"
42 Then Jesus left them a second time and prayed,
"My Father! If this cup cannot be taken away* unless
I drink it, your will be done." 43 When he returned to
them again, he found them sleeping, for they couldn't
keep their eyes open.
44 So he went to pray a third time, saying the same
things again. 45 Then he came to the disciples and said,
"Go ahead and sleep. Have your rest. But look—the time
has come. The Son of Man is betrayed into the hands of
sinners. 46 Up, let's be going. Look, my betrayer is here!"

JESUS IS BETRAYED AND ARRESTED

47 And even as Jesus said this, Judas, one of the twelve
disciples, arrived with a crowd of men armed with
swords and clubs. They had been sent by the leading
priests and elders of the people. 48 The traitor, Judas,
had given them a prearranged signal: "You will know
which one to arrest when I greet him with a kiss."
49 So Judas came straight to Jesus. "Greetings, Rabbi!"
he exclaimed and gave him the kiss.
50 Jesus said, "My friend, go ahead and do what you
have come for."
Then the others grabbed Jesus and arrested him.
51 But one of the men with Jesus pulled out his sword

BETRAYED BY A KISS

1. What is the closest you have come to getting arrested? What happened? Were you guilty?

MATTHEW 26:47-56

2. Why is Jesus being arrested here? What has He done to deserve it?
3. Why does Judas betray Jesus by kissing him? How does Jesus respond to that betrayal?
4. Why does Jesus insist that His disciples not fight back? What had to be "fulfilled" in Jesus' death?
5. How should we respond when we are betrayed by someone close to us? Why?
6. Why did Jesus' disciples run away? With that in mind, who should we turn to in times of trials?

26:28 Some manuscripts read *the new covenant.* **26:31** Greek *I will strike.* Zech 13:7. **26:42** Greek *If this cannot pass.*

26:26 this is my body. Jesus introduces a new meaning for the Passover bread. While it used to represent God's provision of food for His people while they wandered in the desert after the Exodus, now it is to represent Jesus' body that was brutally treated and nailed to the cross, later to be remembered in the bread at Communion.
26:27 cup. Jesus relates the Passover cup of red wine to the renewal of the covenant of God with His people by His sacrificial death.
26:28 covenant. This New Covenant is based upon the promise of Jeremiah 31:31-34 that one day God would initiate a covenant which would result in a deep, inner change in people's character and in the forgiveness of sin. This covenant is dependent upon Jesus' sacrificial death rather than on human effort.
26:29 I will not drink. This may mean that Jesus chose to abstain from the fourth Passover cup, which was passed around at the close of the meal, indicating that the meal will only be consummated when the kingdom comes in its fullness.
26:34 before the rooster crows. The Romans called the watch from midnight to 3 a.m. "cock crow."
26:36 Gethsemane. This was an olive orchard in an estate at the foot of the Mount of Olives just outside the eastern wall of Jerusalem. The name literally means "an oil press" (for making olive oil).
26:39 praying. He would have prayed aloud, as was customary for people at the time, so the disciples could hear His prayer as long as they were awake. **My Father!** This was not a title for God that was used in prayer in the first century. It expressed an intimacy that would have been considered inappropriate. **this cup.** In the Old Testament, drinking a cup of bitter wine was often used as a symbol for experiencing God's judgment (Ps. 75:8; Isa. 51:17-22).
26:41 the spirit . . . the body. Probably as in Psalm 51:12, the spirit is the human spirit energized by God. The problem is that the disciples allowed their physical condition to dictate their response to an impending spiritual crisis.
26:50 arrested him. No charge is given. Perhaps it was blasphemy (9:3), violation of the Sabbath (12:2,10,14), or the practice of sorcery (9:34).
26:51 one of the men with Jesus. According to John's Gospel (John 18:10), this was Peter. **his sword.** That Peter should have a sword is not unusual. Travelers carried them as protection against robbers. **slashing off his ear.** Why he was not seized for this act of aggression is unknown. Luke adds the detail that Jesus immediately healed the man (Luke 22:51).

and struck the high priest's slave, slashing off his ear.
52 "Put away your sword," Jesus told him. "Those
who use the sword will die by the sword. 53 Don't you
realize that I could ask my Father for thousands* of
angels to protect us, and he would send them instant-
ly? 54 But if I did, how would the Scriptures be fulfilled
that describe what must happen now?"
55 Then Jesus said to the crowd, "Am I some dan-
gerous revolutionary, that you come with swords and
clubs to arrest me? Why didn't you arrest me in the
Temple? I was there teaching every day. 56 But this is
all happening to fulfill the words of the prophets as
recorded in the Scriptures." At that point, all the disci-
ples deserted him and fled.

JESUS BEFORE THE COUNCIL

57 Then the people who had arrested Jesus led him
to the home of Caiaphas, the high priest, where the
teachers of religious law and the elders had gathered.
58 Meanwhile, Peter followed him at a distance and
came to the high priest's courtyard. He went in and
sat with the guards and waited to see how it would
all end.
59 Inside, the leading priests and the entire high
council* were trying to find witnesses who would
lie about Jesus, so they could put him to death. 60 But
even though they found many who agreed to give
false witness, they could not use anyone's testimony.
Finally, two men came forward 61 who declared, "This
man said, 'I am able to destroy the Temple of God and
rebuild it in three days.'"
62 Then the high priest stood up and said to Jesus,
"Well, aren't you going to answer these charges?
What do you have to say for yourself?" 63 But Jesus
remained silent. Then the high priest said to him, "I
demand in the name of the living God—tell us if you
are the Messiah, the Son of God."
64 Jesus replied, "You have said it. And in the future
you will see the Son of Man seated in the place of
power at God's right hand* and coming on the clouds
of heaven."*
65 Then the high priest tore his clothing to show his
horror and said, "Blasphemy! Why do we need other
witnesses? You have all heard his blasphemy. 66 What
is your verdict?"
"Guilty!" they shouted. "He deserves to die!"
67 Then they began to spit in Jesus' face and beat
him with their fists. And some slapped him, 68 jeering,
"Prophesy to us, you Messiah! Who hit you that time?"

PETER DENIES JESUS

69 Meanwhile, Peter was sitting outside in the court-
yard. A servant girl came over and said to him, "You
were one of those with Jesus the Galilean."
70 But Peter denied it in front of everyone. "I don't
know what you're talking about," he said.
71 Later, out by the gate, another servant girl noticed
him and said to those standing around, "This man
was with Jesus of Nazareth.*"
72 Again Peter denied it, this time with an oath. "I
don't even know the man," he said.
73 A little later some of the other bystanders came
over to Peter and said, "You must be one of them; we
can tell by your Galilean accent."
74 Peter swore, "A curse on me if I'm lying—I don't
know the man!" And immediately the rooster crowed.
75 Suddenly, Jesus' words flashed through Peter's
mind: "Before the rooster crows, you will deny three
times that you even know me." And he went away,
weeping bitterly.

JUDAS HANGS HIMSELF

27 Very early in the morning the leading priests
and the elders of the people met again to lay
plans for putting Jesus to death. 2 Then they bound
him, led him away, and took him to Pilate, the Roman
governor.
3 When Judas, who had betrayed him, realized that
Jesus had been condemned to die, he was filled with
remorse. So he took the thirty pieces of silver back to
the leading priests and the elders. 4 "I have sinned," he
declared, "for I have betrayed an innocent man."
"What do we care?" they retorted. "That's your
problem."
5 Then Judas threw the silver coins down in the
Temple and went out and hanged himself.

26:53 Greek *twelve legions.* **26:59** Greek *the Sanhedrin.* **26:64a** Greek *seated at the right hand of the power.* See Ps 110:1. **26:64b** See Dan 7:13. **26:71** Or *Jesus the Nazarene.*

26:53 thousands of angels. If force were to be used to establish God's kingdom, Jesus would not be relying on the talents of 12 untrained men to do the job! Instead, more than 12 legions of angels could be at His disposal.

26:54 the Scriptures. Jesus is probably referring to Zechariah 13:7: "God will strike the Shepherd, and the sheep will be scattered" (Mark 14:27).

26:57 the high priest. The high priest oversaw the Sanhedrin, which was the highest Jewish court, made up of 71 leaders, both priests and laymen.

26:59 false witness. To convict someone of a capital crime required the unanimous testimony of at least two witnesses (Deut. 19:15).

26:61 I am able to destroy the Temple of God and rebuild it in three days. Although Matthew does not record it, John's Gospel puts a statement much like this on the lips of Jesus (John 2:19). However, Jesus did not say He would destroy the temple; simply that it would one day be destroyed. In addition, He was referring to the temple of His body being destroyed (John 2:21) and being restored after three days, which was very different from how it was understood here.

26:63-64 the Messiah . . . the Son of God . . . the Son of Man. These are the three main titles that reveal who Jesus is. The time for secrecy is past. He is the Messiah, God's royal King. Jesus' statement (v. 64) is a combination of Psalm 110:1 and Daniel 7:13-14, passages with strong messianic implications.

26:64 You have said it. Jesus uses an ambiguous statement that places the responsibility of affirming it on the questioner. **seated . . . at God's right hand.** To sit at the right hand of a sovereign was to be in a place of honor and power.

26:65 tore his clothing. By tearing his clothes, the high priest signaled that he was profoundly disturbed by Jesus' statement. **Blasphemy!** This is the act of dishonoring or slandering God. Under the Law, its penalty was death by stoning (Lev. 24:10-16).

26:67 spit . . . beat . . . slapped. These were traditional ways of expressing abhorrence and repudiation for someone (Num. 12:14; Deut. 25:9; Job 30:10; Isa. 50:6). These actions reflected the council's fierce opposition to what Jesus said.

26:68 Prophesy. Mark 14:65 says Jesus was first blindfolded. They are mocking His claim to be the Messiah by taunting Him to name who it was that had struck Him while He was unable to see.

27:1 Very early in the morning. The Roman court began at daybreak, which made it necessary for the Sanhedrin to meet in an all-night session. They were anxious to get a quick conviction before the people found out what they had done. **to lay plans.** Legally, the Sanhedrin had no authority to order the death of Jesus (John 18:31). However, under Roman law blasphemy was not a capital offense. Consequently, they needed to work out how to present the case to Pilate to ensure Jesus' conviction. Their decision was to charge Him with high treason.

27:2 Pilate. Pontius Pilate was the fifth procurator of Judea. He served from A.D. 26–36. While the Gospels present him as a fair-minded man, pressured by the Sanhedrin to do its bidding, historians of the time called him an "inflexible, merciless, and obstinate" man who was continually ignoring Jewish customs in his harsh leadership.

[6]The leading priests picked up the coins. "It
wouldn't be right to put this money in the Temple
treasury," they said, "since it was payment for mur-
der."* [7]After some discussion they finally decided to
buy the potter's field, and they made it into a ceme-
tery for foreigners. [8]That is why the field is still called
the Field of Blood. [9]This fulfilled the prophecy of Jer-
emiah that says,

"They took* the thirty pieces of silver—
the price at which he was valued by the people
of Israel,
[10] and purchased the potter's field,
as the LORD directed."*

JESUS' TRIAL BEFORE PILATE

[11]Now Jesus was standing before Pilate, the Roman
governor. "Are you the king of the Jews?" the gover-
nor asked him.
Jesus replied, "You have said it."
[12]But when the leading priests and the elders made their
accusations against him, Jesus remained silent. [13]"Don't
you hear all these charges they are bringing against you?"
Pilate demanded. [14]But Jesus made no response to any of
the charges, much to the governor's surprise.
[15]Now it was the governor's custom each year
during the Passover celebration to release one pris-
oner to the crowd—anyone they wanted. [16]This year
there was a notorious prisoner, a man named Barab-
bas.* [17]As the crowds gathered before Pilate's house
that morning, he asked them, "Which one do you
want me to release to you—Barabbas, or Jesus who
is called the Messiah?" [18](He knew very well that the
religious leaders had arrested Jesus out of envy.)
[19]Just then, as Pilate was sitting on the judgment
seat, his wife sent him this message: "Leave that inno-
cent man alone. I suffered through a terrible night-
mare about him last night."
[20]Meanwhile, the leading priests and the elders
persuaded the crowd to ask for Barabbas to be re-
leased and for Jesus to be put to death. [21]So the gover-
nor asked again, "Which of these two do you want me
to release to you?"
The crowd shouted back, "Barabbas!"
[22]Pilate responded, "Then what should I do with
Jesus who is called the Messiah?"
They shouted back, "Crucify him!"
[23]"Why?" Pilate demanded. "What crime has he
committed?"
But the mob roared even louder, "Crucify him!"
[24]Pilate saw that he wasn't getting anywhere and
that a riot was developing. So he sent for a bowl of
water and washed his hands before the crowd, say-
ing, "I am innocent of this man's blood. The responsi-
bility is yours!"
[25]And all the people yelled back, "We will take re-
sponsibility for his death—we and our children!"*
[26]So Pilate released Barabbas to them. He ordered
Jesus flogged with a lead-tipped whip, then turned
him over to the Roman soldiers to be crucified.

THE SOLDIERS MOCK JESUS

[27]Some of the governor's soldiers took Jesus into their
headquarters* and called out the entire regiment.
[28]They stripped him and put a scarlet robe on him.
[29]They wove thorn branches into a crown and put it on
his head, and they placed a reed stick in his right hand
as a scepter. Then they knelt before him in mockery
and taunted, "Hail! King of the Jews!" [30]And they spit on
him and grabbed the stick and struck him on the head
with it. [31]When they were finally tired of mocking him,
they took off the robe and put his own clothes on him
again. Then they led him away to be crucified.

THE CRUCIFIXION

[32]Along the way, they came across a man named Si-
mon, who was from Cyrene,* and the soldiers forced
him to carry Jesus' cross. [33]And they went out to a
place called Golgotha (which means "Place of the
Skull"). [34]The soldiers gave Jesus wine mixed with
bitter gall, but when he had tasted it, he refused to
drink it.

A CROWN OF THORNS

1. Growing up, who were the "bullies" in your life? How did they pick on you? Did you stand up for yourself or someone else who was being bullied?

MATTHEW 27:26-31

2. Why did the soldiers mock Jesus?
3. What's the truth about Jesus' kingship? Why is it so fitting that His crown be made of thorns?
4. Why did Jesus put up with these things?
5. What was Jesus' response to His torturers (see Luke 23:34)? Is there anybody you need to forgive?
6. How do your sufferings compare to what Jesus went through? How does your response compare with His?

27:6 Greek *since it is the price for blood.* 27:9 Or *I took.* 27:9-10 Greek *as the LORD directed me.* Zech 11:12-13; Jer 32:6-9. 27:16 Some manuscripts read *Jesus Barabbas;* also in 27:17. 27:25 Greek *"His blood be on us and on our children."* 27:27 Or *into the Praetorium.* 27:32 *Cyrene* was a city in northern Africa.

27:6 It wouldn't be right. The irony is intense. The priests will not put the money back into the temple treasury since it was defiled by having been used as bounty on a person's life. However, they make no reflection upon the fact that they are the ones who used the money for this purpose.

27:16 Barabbas. Barabbas was a genuine resistance leader who had led an armed insurrection against Rome. It was probably in relationship to this rebellion that he also had committed murder (Luke 23:19).

27:18 He knew. While Pilate could have simply thrown the charges out of court, John's Gospel hints that the Sanhedrin made a not-too-subtle threat to Pilate that, if he should do, so they would bring charges to Caesar against him for releasing a man who claimed to be a rival king (John 19:12).

27:24 washed his hands. This was a Jewish custom used as a way to disassociate oneself from a criminal act (Deut. 21:1-9). Since it was not a practice of the Romans, Matthew took special note of this as a way of focusing the responsibility upon the Sanhedrin.

27:26 released Barabbas. The death of Jesus (who is innocent) in the place of Barabbas (who is guilty) is a visual statement on the meaning of substitutionary atonement. **flogged.** This was a terrible punishment. Soldiers would lash a naked and bound prisoner with a leather thong with pieces of bone and lead woven into it. The flesh would be cut to shreds. In itself, this punishment sometimes led to death due to shock and loss of blood.

27:32 Simon. This man was probably a Jew who had come on a pilgrimage to Jerusalem for the Passover feast. Cyrene was a Greek city on the north shore of Africa.

27:33 Golgotha. This is the Aramaic word for a "skull."

27:34 wine mixed with bitter gall. It was a custom to offer a pain-deadening narcotic to prisoners about to be killed.

35 After they had nailed him to the cross, the soldiers gambled for his clothes by throwing dice.* 36 Then they sat around and kept guard as he hung there. 37 A sign was fastened above Jesus' head, announcing the charge against him. It read: "This is Jesus, the King of the Jews." 38 Two revolutionaries* were crucified with him, one on his right and one on his left.

39 The people passing by shouted abuse, shaking their heads in mockery. 40 "Look at you now!" they yelled at him. "You said you were going to destroy the Temple and rebuild it in three days. Well then, if you are the Son of God, save yourself and come down from the cross!"

41 The leading priests, the teachers of religious law, and the elders also mocked Jesus. 42 "He saved others," they scoffed, "but he can't save himself! So he is the King of Israel, is he? Let him come down from the cross right now, and we will believe in him! 43 He trusted God, so let God rescue him now if he wants him! For he said, 'I am the Son of God.'" 44 Even the revolutionaries who were crucified with him ridiculed him in the same way.

THE DEATH OF JESUS

45 At noon, darkness fell across the whole land until three o'clock. 46 At about three o'clock, Jesus called out with a loud voice, *"Eli, Eli,* lema sabachthani?"* which means "My God, my God, why have you abandoned me?"*

47 Some of the bystanders misunderstood and thought he was calling for the prophet Elijah. 48 One of them ran and filled a sponge with sour wine, holding it up to him on a reed stick so he could drink. 49 But the rest said, "Wait! Let's see whether Elijah comes to save him."*

50 Then Jesus shouted out again, and he released his spirit. 51 At that moment the curtain in the sanctuary of the Temple was torn in two, from top to bottom. The earth shook, rocks split apart, 52 and tombs opened. The bodies of many godly men and women who had died were raised from the dead. 53 They left the cemetery after Jesus' resurrection, went into the holy city of Jerusalem, and appeared to many people.

54 The Roman officer* and the other soldiers at the crucifixion were terrified by the earthquake and all that had happened. They said, "This man truly was the Son of God!"

55 And many women who had come from Galilee with Jesus to care for him were watching from a distance. 56 Among them were Mary Magdalene, Mary (the mother of James and Joseph), and the mother of James and John, the sons of Zebedee.

THE BURIAL OF JESUS

57 As evening approached, Joseph, a rich man from Arimathea who had become a follower of Jesus, 58 went to Pilate and asked for Jesus' body. And Pilate issued an order to release it to him. 59 Joseph took the body and wrapped it in a long sheet of clean linen cloth. 60 He placed it in his own new tomb, which had been carved out of the rock. Then he rolled a great stone across the entrance and left. 61 Both Mary Magdalene and the other Mary were sitting across from the tomb and watching.

THE GUARD AT THE TOMB

62 The next day, on the Sabbath,* the leading priests and Pharisees went to see Pilate. 63 They told him, "Sir, we remember what that deceiver once said while he was still alive: 'After three days I will rise from the dead.' 64 So we request that you seal the tomb until the third day. This will prevent his disciples from coming and stealing his body and then telling everyone he was raised from the dead! If that happens, we'll be worse off than we were at first."

65 Pilate replied, "Take guards and secure it the best you can." 66 So they sealed the tomb and posted guards to protect it.

THE RESURRECTION

28 Early on Sunday morning,* as the new day was dawning, Mary Magdalene and the other Mary went out to visit the tomb.

2 Suddenly there was a great earthquake! For an angel of the Lord came down from heaven, rolled aside the stone, and sat on it. 3 His face shone like lightning, and his clothing was as white as snow. 4 The guards

27:35 Greek *by casting lots.* A few late manuscripts add *This fulfilled the word of the prophet: "They divided my garments among themselves and cast lots for my robe."* See Ps 22:18. **27:38** Or *criminals;* also in 27:44. **27:46a** Some manuscripts read *Eloi, Eloi.* **27:46b** Ps 22:1. **27:49** Some manuscripts add *And another took a spear and pierced his side, and out flowed water and blood.* Compare John 19:34. **27:54** Greek *The centurion.* **27:62** Or *On the next day, which is after the Preparation.* **28:1** Greek *After the Sabbath, on the first day of the week.*

27:35 nailed . . . to the cross. Crucifixion was the most feared of all punishments in the first-century world. It was cruel in the extreme and totally degrading. **gambled for his clothes.** This fulfills the prophecy of the suffering of God's righteous servant in Psalm 22:18.

27:40 if you are the Son of God, save yourself. This taunt is reminiscent of the temptations in 4:1-11.

27:46 Eli, Eli. This cry has the exact words of Psalm 22:1. While Jesus was bearing the sins of all people throughout all the ages, God the Father withdrew from Him. He ultimately experiences God's deliverance and is resurrected to life giving all believers new life (Ps. 22:19-31).

27:50 shouted out. Generally a victim of crucifixion would be exhausted and unconscious at the point of death. While Jesus' cry reveals His agony, it is likely from the description of the strange incidents in verses 51-53 that it is a cry of victory.

27:51 curtain in the sanctuary . . . was torn in two. This was likely the curtain in the temple that stood between the people and God in the holy of holies. Only the high priest could go behind the curtain into God's presence. Jesus' death and God's tearing of the curtain from the top has opened the way for people to freely enter the presence of God (Heb. 10:19-20). **The earth shook, rocks split apart.** Jewish thought held that at the end of the age the Mount of Olives would split in two and the righteous dead would emerge to live forever. Earthquakes were also seen as signs of God's judgment. They are referred to often in the Old Testament as a metaphor for political or social events that have a major effect upon God's people (Hab. 3:9-10).

27:55 many women. Mary Magdalene was from the fishing village of Magdala on the west coast of Galilee (Luke 8:2). The other Mary had well-known sons in the early church. Zebedee's wife was probably Salome, the mother of James and John. In contrast to these women, all the male disciples had fled.

27:60 tomb. Isaiah 53:9 said God's servant would be laid to rest in the tomb of a rich man.

27:62 The next day. Jesus died on Friday about 3 p.m. The Sabbath began at 6 p.m., after which no work could be done. Yet it was on this day that the Sanhedrin met with Pilate in violation of its own tradition.

27:66 sealed the tomb. This was the insignia of Pilate. It would be a capital offense to remove the stone without Pilate's approval. The seal and the guard represent the most powerful human forces available to keep Jesus' body in the tomb.

28:1 Early on Sunday morning, as the new day was dawning. The Sabbath was considered over at 6 p.m. on Saturday. This scene takes place early on Sunday morning. This is why Christians developed the tradition of worshiping on Sunday instead of on the Sabbath (Saturday).

28:2 great earthquake. Earthquakes were often associated with manifestations of God's power (Hab. 3:6).

HE IS RISEN!

1. What was the biggest or best surprise you've ever had?

MATTHEW 28:1-20

2. How would you react if told a dead friend was suddenly alive again?
3. What did Jesus prove beyond any doubt by rising from the dead? What or who has He gained final victory over?
4. How does the resurrection set Jesus apart from all other religious figures, such as Buddha or Confucius or Mohammed?
5. What story did the Romans invent to explain Jesus' resurrection? What stories have people invented in our own lifetime?
6. What does Jesus' resurrection mean to you? Have you received His gift of eternal life?

---

shook with fear when they saw him, and they fell into
a dead faint.
5 Then the angel spoke to the women. "Don't be
afraid!" he said. "I know you are looking for Jesus,
who was crucified. 6 He isn't here! He is risen from the
dead, just as he said would happen. Come, see where
his body was lying. 7 And now, go quickly and tell his
disciples that he has risen from the dead, and he is
going ahead of you to Galilee. You will see him there.
Remember what I have told you."
8 The women ran quickly from the tomb. They were
very frightened but also filled with great joy, and they
rushed to give the disciples the angel's message. 9 And
as they went, Jesus met them and greeted them. And
they ran to him, grasped his feet, and worshiped him.
10 Then Jesus said to them, "Don't be afraid! Go tell my
brothers to leave for Galilee, and they will see me
there."

THE REPORT OF THE GUARD

11 As the women were on their way, some of the
guards went into the city and told the leading priests
what had happened. 12 A meeting with the elders was
called, and they decided to give the soldiers a large
bribe. 13 They told the soldiers, "You must say, 'Jesus'
disciples came during the night while we were sleep-
ing, and they stole his body.' 14 If the governor hears
about it, we'll stand up for you so you won't get in
trouble." 15 So the guards accepted the bribe and said
what they were told to say. Their story spread widely
among the Jews, and they still tell it today.

THE GREAT COMMISSION

16 Then the eleven disciples left for Galilee, going to the
mountain where Jesus had told them to go. 17 When
they saw him, they worshiped him—but some of
them doubted!
18 Jesus came and told his disciples, "I have been
given all authority in heaven and on earth. 19 There-
fore, go and make disciples of all the nations,* bap-
tizing them in the name of the Father and the Son
and the Holy Spirit. 20 Teach these new disciples to
obey all the commands I have given you. And be
sure of this: I am with you always, even to the end
of the age."

28:19 Or *all peoples.*

28:5 Don't be afraid! This is a standard reply of an angel to the people to whom the angel is sent (Dan. 10:12; Luke 1:12,30; 2:10).

28:7 go . . . tell. Under Jewish law, women were not considered reliable witnesses. That they were the first to know of Jesus' resurrection was somewhat of an embarrassment to the early followers of Christ (Luke 24:11,22-24). Inclusion of this detail reinforces that this is historically accurate. (They certainly would not have invented the story this way!)

28:12 decided to give the soldiers a large bribe. The Sanhedrin bought off the guards so that they would not tell what really happened.

28:13 while we were sleeping, and they stole his body. This attempt at "damage control" was weak. The very reason the guards were posted was to keep the disciples from stealing the body and concocting a story about resurrection. It would be hard to believe that the disciples who had stolen Jesus' body—and hence knew that the resurrection was a hoax—would then go on to die for their faith, often in painful ways.

28:14 If the governor hears about it. For a Roman guard to fall asleep on duty was an offense meriting execution.

28:16 to the mountain. Mountains were the places in times past where God revealed Himself in special ways to the leaders of Israel, such as when He revealed Himself to Moses in Exodus 24 and to Elijah in 1 Kings 19.

28:17 some of them doubted. So stupendous is the resurrection of Jesus that right from the beginning His disciples had difficulty accepting it. When the women reported what had happened at the tomb, the Eleven said that it sounded like nonsense (Luke 24:9-11). After 10 of the disciples (all but Thomas) met the resurrected Jesus and believed (Luke 24:36-48), Thomas still doubted (John 20:24-29).

28:18-20 Jesus came and told his disciples. Because all authority in heaven and earth now belongs to Jesus, He sends His disciples to spread His message everywhere with the promise that He Himself is with them to the end of time.

28:18 I have been given all authority in heaven and on earth. This is the meaning of the statement "Jesus is Lord." Since there is no power greater than His (Rom. 8:38-39; Phil. 2:9-11; Col. 1:15-20), there is no other loyalty to which His disciples can give their absolute allegiance.

28:20 I am with you always. This is the climactic promise of the New Covenant. The presence of God with His people was always the goal toward which Israel looked under the Old Covenant. In Jesus, that presence is assured through the indwelling of Christ's Spirit (John 14:16-17). **even to the end of the age.** This covers all time until the return of Christ when the new heaven and the new earth will be revealed.

INTRODUCTION TO

MARK

PERSONAL READING PLAN

☐Mark 1:1-45
☐Mark 2:1–3:6
☐Mark 3:7-35
☐Mark 4:1-20
☐Mark 4:21-41
☐Mark 5:1-20
☐Mark 5:21-43
☐Mark 6:1-29
☐Mark 6:30-56
☐Mark 7:1-37
☐Mark 8:1-26
☐Mark 8:27–9:1
☐Mark 9:2-32
☐Mark 9:33–10:12
☐Mark 10:13-31
☐Mark 10:32-52
☐Mark 11:1-25
☐Mark 11:27–12:12
☐Mark 12:13-44
☐Mark 13:1-37
☐Mark 14:1-31
☐Mark 14:32-72
☐Mark 15:1-41
☐Mark 15:42–16:20

AUTHOR

In Mark's Gospel, we discover that Mark's full name was John Mark, that his mother's name was Mary, and that their home was used as a meeting place by the disciples. Peter went there directly after his miraculous release from prison (Acts 12:1-17). Consequently, as a young man, Mark was immersed in the life of the newly forming church.

We also learn that Mark was close to Peter as Peter referred to him as "my son Mark" (1 Peter 5:13). Many believe that Mark was Peter's secretary and that his Gospel reflects Peter's view of the events. Writing in A.D. 140, Bishop Papias says: "Mark, having become the interpreter of Peter, wrote down accurately all that he remembered of the things said and done by our Lord, but not, however, in order."

Mark was also closely connected with Paul. Along with his cousin, Barnabas, Mark accompanied the great apostle on the first missionary journey. Mark, for unknown reasons, left the party at Perga when they turned inland to Asia. Because of this, Paul refused to allow Mark to go on the second missionary journey. Thus, Barnabas went with Mark to Cyprus, while Paul teamed up with Silas. For years Mark dropped out of sight. Tradition says he founded the church at Alexandria, Egypt. Eventually, Paul and Mark were reconciled, and Mark became Paul's companion during Paul's imprisonment in a Roman jail.

DATE

Mark was written sometime between A.D. 50–70, probably in the mid-60s.

THEME

Jesus the Messiah, the Son of God.

HISTORICAL BACKGROUND

The 10 years between A.D. 60 and A.D. 70 when Mark wrote his Gospel were years of persecution for Christians living in Rome. Previously, they were regarded as an exotic religious sect. But after Nero burned Rome in A.D. 64, he blamed the Christians, and an era of persecution began. Nero fed them to the lions in the colosseum and burned them as human torches at his garden parties. Mark directed his Gospel to these Christians, who were dying for Jesus' name.

This was the first written account of Jesus' life. Thus it was, according to William Barclay, "the most important book in the world." Mark's collection of previously unrecorded stories was widely circulated and was used by Matthew and Luke when they wrote their Gospels. In fact, all but 24 verses of Mark's Gospel are found in their accounts.

CHARACTERISTICS

In the shortest of the Gospels, Mark races breathlessly through Jesus' life by linking a series of short stories. Despite the way Mark hurries through the material, his account is the richest and most vivid in eyewitness detail. For example, when speaking of Jesus blessing the children, Mark alone tells us that Jesus first took them in his arms (Mark 10:13-16).

Mark's Gospel carefully orders the stories, resulting in a skillfully crafted outline. In fact, he tells the story of Jesus in a remarkably sophisticated way, considering that Mark could not alter well-known stories, witnessed by many people. He was merely the chronicler of the tradition, not the creator of it. The church would not have used his Gospel if it had been inaccurate. Mark's creativity, under the guidance of the Holy Spirit, came in his sequencing of the stories. As you read through the Gospel, be alert to the significance of the sequencing.

Mark does not place his stories in chronological order as we might expect; instead, he groups his stories thematically. Mark uses several themes, simultaneously. However, it is clear that he has structured his story geographically. Jesus' ministry begins to the north in Galilee and then moves down to Jerusalem, where he is finally killed. Mark structures the story in terms of Jesus' unfolding ministry: preparation, proclamation, and completion. There is also an unfolding vision of who Jesus is. Generally, the first half of the book focuses on the discovery of Jesus as the Messiah, and the second half on the discovery of Jesus as the Son of God. Regarding the disciples' growing awareness, they move from experiencing Jesus as an exceptional rabbi to seeing him as a man of power and then as the healer of hardened hearts. After Caesarea Philippi and their realization that he is the Messiah, they know him as a teacher. In Jerusalem during the final week of his life, they come to realize that he is the Son of God.

PASSAGES FOR TOPICAL GROUP STUDY

1:29-39 . . . TIME WITH GOD . . . . Perfect Priorities
2:1-12 . . . JESUS THE HEALER . . . . Healing Forgiveness
3:20-35 . . . IN JESUS' FAMILY . . . . Eternal Family Ties
4:35-41 . . . FEARS and STRUGGLES . . . . Calming the Storm
5:24-34 . . . FAITH and HEALING . . . . Miraculous Faith
6:14-29 . . . MEDIA / ENTERTAINMENT . . . . Losing Your Head
6:30-44 . . . USING FREE TIME . . . . Rest and Refreshment
9:2-13 . . . TIME WITH JESUS . . . . Precious Time
9:14-29 . . . LACK OF FAITH . . . . Help My Unbelief
10:17-31 . POSSESSIONS and PRIORITIES . . Perilous Possessions
10:35-45 . AMBITION and COMPETITION . . . . Fierce Competition

11:12-19 . . . ANGER and STANDING UP . . . . Taking a Stand
12:13-17 . . . RELATING TO AUTHORITY . . . . Money Matters
12:41-44 . . . GIVING MONEY AND TIME . . . . Meaningful Giving
14:32-42 . . . HELPING OTHERS . . . . Stay Awake
15:1-15 . . . . ACCEPTING JESUS . . . . Sacrificing for Us!

PASSAGES FOR GENERAL GROUP STUDY

2:23–3:6. . . Remember the What? The Sabbath

JOHN THE BAPTIST PREPARES THE WAY

1 This is the Good News about Jesus the Messiah, the
Son of God.* It began 2 just as the prophet Isaiah
had written:

"Look, I am sending my messenger ahead of you,
and he will prepare your way.*
3 He is a voice shouting in the wilderness,
'Prepare the way for the LORD's coming!
Clear the road for him!'*"

4 This messenger was John the Baptist. He was in the
wilderness and preached that people should be bap-
tized to show that they had repented of their sins and
turned to God to be forgiven. 5 All of Judea, including
all the people of Jerusalem, went out to see and hear
John. And when they confessed their sins, he baptized
them in the Jordan River. 6 His clothes were woven from
coarse camel hair, and he wore a leather belt around
his waist. For food he ate locusts and wild honey.
7 John announced: "Someone is coming soon who is
greater than I am—so much greater that I'm not even
worthy to stoop down like a slave and untie the straps
of his sandals. 8 I baptize you with* water, but he will
baptize you with the Holy Spirit!"

THE BAPTISM AND TEMPTATION OF JESUS

9 One day Jesus came from Nazareth in Galilee, and
John baptized him in the Jordan River. 10 As Jesus
came up out of the water, he saw the heavens split-
ting apart and the Holy Spirit descending on him* like
a dove. 11 And a voice from heaven said, "You are my
dearly loved Son, and you bring me great joy."
12 The Spirit then compelled Jesus to go into the wil-
derness, 13 where he was tempted by Satan for forty
days. He was out among the wild animals, and angels
took care of him.
14 Later on, after John was arrested, Jesus went
into Galilee, where he preached God's Good News.*
15 "The time promised by God has come at last!" he an-
nounced. "The Kingdom of God is near! Repent of your
sins and believe the Good News!"

THE FIRST DISCIPLES

16 One day as Jesus was walking along the shore of the
Sea of Galilee, he saw Simon* and his brother Andrew
throwing a net into the water, for they fished for a liv-
ing. 17 Jesus called out to them, "Come, follow me, and I
will show you how to fish for people!" 18 And they left
their nets at once and followed him.
19 A little farther up the shore Jesus saw Zebedee's
sons, James and John, in a boat repairing their nets.
20 He called them at once, and they also followed him,
leaving their father, Zebedee, in the boat with the
hired men.

JESUS CASTS OUT AN EVIL SPIRIT

21 Jesus and his companions went to the town of Ca-
pernaum. When the Sabbath day came, he went into
the synagogue and began to teach. 22 The people
were amazed at his teaching, for he taught with real
authority—quite unlike the teachers of religious
law.
23 Suddenly, a man in the synagogue who was pos-
sessed by an evil* spirit cried out, 24 "Why are you in-
terfering with us, Jesus of Nazareth? Have you come
to destroy us? I know who you are—the Holy One of
God!"
25 Jesus cut him short. "Be quiet! Come out of the
man," he ordered. 26 At that, the evil spirit screamed,
threw the man into a convulsion, and then came out
of him.
27 Amazement gripped the audience, and they be-
gan to discuss what had happened. "What sort of new
teaching is this?" they asked excitedly. "It has such au-
thority! Even evil spirits obey his orders!" 28 The news
about Jesus spread quickly throughout the entire re-
gion of Galilee.

JESUS HEALS MANY PEOPLE

29 After Jesus left the synagogue with James and John,
they went to Simon and Andrew's home. 30 Now Si-
mon's mother-in-law was sick in bed with a high
fever. They told Jesus about her right away. 31 So he
went to her bedside, took her by the hand, and helped
her sit up. Then the fever left her, and she prepared a
meal for them.
32 That evening after sunset, many sick and de-
mon-possessed people were brought to Jesus. 33 The
whole town gathered at the door to watch. 34 So Jesus
healed many people who were sick with various dis-
eases, and he cast out many demons. But because the
demons knew who he was, he did not allow them to
speak.

JESUS PREACHES IN GALILEE

35 Before daybreak the next morning, Jesus got up and
went out to an isolated place to pray. 36 Later Simon
and the others went out to find him. 37 When they
found him, they said, "Everyone is looking for you."

1:1 Some manuscripts do not include *the Son of God.* **1:2** Mal 3:1. **1:3** Isa 40:3 (Greek version). **1:8** Or *in;* also in 1:8b. **1:10** Or *toward him,* or *into him.* **1:14** Some manuscripts read *the Good News of the Kingdom of God.* **1:16** *Simon* is called "Peter" in 3:16 and thereafter. **1:23** Greek *unclean;* also in 1:26, 27.

1:3 clear the road for him. When a king was planning to visit or pass through a town, a messenger was sent ahead of the royal entourage so that the towns along the way could get things ready for his coming, literally straightening and smoothing the roads. In this context, making straight paths for the Lord implies repentance from sin (v. 15).

1:5 All of Judea. Mark uses hyperbole to show John's popularity. **all the people of Jerusalem.** It was a difficult 20-mile trip from Jerusalem to where John was baptizing, and yet the crowds came. **the Jordan River.** John's ministry of baptism had a special meaning in this particular river which had an important place in Israel's history. After the exodus from Egypt, it was the miraculous crossing of this river that brought the people of Israel into the land God promised them (Josh. 3).

1:13 forty days. It is possible that this is a symbolic reference to the 40 years Israel spent in the wilderness. The reason for their experience was unbelief; Jesus voluntarily entered His trial. **wild animals.** For the Christians to whom this letter was written (who were facing wild beasts in the Roman Colosseum), it must have been comforting to know that Jesus had also faced such beasts and was sustained by angels.

1:14 after John was arrested. There is a gap of perhaps a year between the incidents recorded in verses 9-13 and those recorded here. The story of John's imprisonment is told in 6:17-29. **Galilee.** The northern province of Palestine, considered by people from Jerusalem as a cultural backwater populated by unsophisticated, uneducated country folk who spoke with an accent.

1:23 an evil spirit. Malignant, supernatural beings that were able to harm and even possess people: these were Satan's legions.

1:25 Be quiet! At the beginning of his ministry, Jesus did not want His identity or power spoken about, probably because people would have misunderstood the meaning of His ministry. **cut him short.** The same word is used in Mark 4:39 when Jesus orders the tumult of the sea and wind to be still. **come out of the man.** In Jesus' day there were exorcists who used a combination of religious and magical practices to try to release people. In contrast, Jesus issues a simple word of command which is immediately obeyed.

PERFECT PRIORITIES

1. Are you a morning person or an evening person?

MARK 1:29-39

2. Why did Simon's mother-in-law begin to serve Jesus and His disciples as soon as she was healed (v. 31)?
3. Why did Jesus spend so much time healing people? What response did people have to this (v. 33)?
4. Why did Jesus go off to "an isolated place" by Himself (v. 35)? What does this show of His priorities?
5. How often do you spend time alone with God? How can you make this more of a priority?

38 But Jesus replied, "We must go on to other towns
as well, and I will preach to them, too. That is why
I came." 39 So he traveled throughout the region of
Galilee, preaching in the synagogues and casting out
demons.

JESUS HEALS A MAN WITH LEPROSY

40 A man with leprosy came and knelt in front of Jesus,
begging to be healed. "If you are willing, you can heal
me and make me clean," he said.
41 Moved with compassion,* Jesus reached out and
touched him. "I am willing," he said. "Be healed!" 42 In-
stantly the leprosy disappeared, and the man was
healed. 43 Then Jesus sent him on his way with a stern
warning: 44 "Don't tell anyone about this. Instead, go
to the priest and let him examine you. Take along the
offering required in the law of Moses for those who
have been healed of leprosy.* This will be a public tes-
timony that you have been cleansed."
45 But the man went and spread the word, pro-
claiming to everyone what had happened. As a result,
large crowds soon surrounded Jesus, and he couldn't
publicly enter a town anywhere. He had to stay out in
the secluded places, but people from everywhere kept
coming to him.

JESUS HEALS A PARALYZED MAN

2 When Jesus returned to Capernaum several days
later, the news spread quickly that he was back
home. 2 Soon the house where he was staying was so
packed with visitors that there was no more room,
even outside the door. While he was preaching God's
word to them, 3 four men arrived carrying a para-
lyzed man on a mat. 4 They couldn't bring him to Jesus
because of the crowd, so they dug a hole through the
roof above his head. Then they lowered the man on
his mat, right down in front of Jesus. 5 Seeing their
faith, Jesus said to the paralyzed man, "My child, your
sins are forgiven."
6 But some of the teachers of religious law who
were sitting there thought to themselves, 7 "What is he
saying? This is blasphemy! Only God can forgive sins!"
8 Jesus knew immediately what they were thinking,
so he asked them, "Why do you question this in your
hearts? 9 Is it easier to say to the paralyzed man 'Your
sins are forgiven,' or 'Stand up, pick up your mat, and
walk'? 10 So I will prove to you that the Son of Man*
has the authority on earth to forgive sins." Then Jesus
turned to the paralyzed man and said, 11 "Stand up,
pick up your mat, and go home!"

HEALING FORGIVENESS

1. When was the last time you had to go to the emergency room? Who took you?
2. Do you have a friend with a disability? How do you help this person?

MARK 2:1-12

3. Why did Jesus forgive the paralyzed man before healing him?
4. What does it show us about Jesus that He could forgive the man's sins?
5. Who are the friends in your life that cared enough to bring you to Jesus? Who do you need to help "carry" to Jesus?

1:41 Some manuscripts read *Moved with anger.* **1:44** See Lev 14:2-32. **2:10** "Son of Man" is a title Jesus used for himself.

1:40 leprosy. No disease was dreaded more than leprosy, since it brought not only physical disfigurement but social banishment. **came and knelt in front of him.** What the leper did was forbidden by law. The leper should have sought to avoid drawing near Jesus. The rabbis taught that if a leper passed by a clean man, the clean man would not become unclean. However, if the leper stopped, then the clean man would become unclean. **If you are willing.** The leper had no doubt about Jesus' ability. However, since leprosy was considered a sign of God's judgment against a person because of sin, the man was uncertain of Jesus' willingness.

1:41 Moved with compassion. Human suffering evoked a deep, affective response from Jesus. He was not afraid of strong emotions. **touched.** Actually touching a leper was unimaginable to most first-century people. From the leper's perspective, the effect of Jesus' touch must have been overwhelming. He had come to think of himself as untouchable and unlovable. This touch affirmed him as a fellow human in spite of his disease.

1:44 offering required in the law of Moses. In Leviticus 14:1-32 the ritual is outlined whereby a leper is declared "clean." Such certification was vital to a leper: it was that person's way back into normal contact with human society.

2:4 dug a hole through the roof. The roof of a typical Palestinian house was flat (it was often used for sleeping) and was reached by an outside ladder or stairway. It was constructed of earth and brushwood that was packed between wooden beams set about three feet apart. The roof was easily breached (and easily repaired). A rather large opening would have been required to lower a man on a mat. While this was going on, with the noise and falling dirt, all attention inside would have been diverted from Jesus' sermon to the ever-growing hole.

2:5 faith. This is the first time in Mark that this word is used. It increasingly becomes the quality Jesus looks for in those to whom He ministers. **your sins are forgiven.** The friends, the man, and the crowd expected a healing; sin was a whole new issue that had not yet been raised by Jesus.

2:6 teachers of the law. Literally, teachers and religious lawyers who interpreted Jewish law.

2:7 blasphemy. Blasphemy is "contempt for God," and under Jewish law its penalty is death (Lev. 24:16). The teachers of the law believed that illness was the direct result of sin (John 9:2), so the sick could not recover until their sin had been forgiven by God.

2:9 Is it easier. Jesus responds to their question (v. 7) in rabbinic fashion: He asks them a question. The answer to His question is obvious. It is far easier to say, "Your sins are forgiven," than it is to heal the man right then and there. There is no way to verify whether sins have been forgiven, but it is obvious whether a lame man walks or not.

2:10 So I will prove to you. If Jesus is able to heal the paralytic in terms of their own theology, which linked forgiveness and healing, the scribes would have to admit that the man's sins had been forgiven.

12 And the man jumped up, grabbed his mat, and
walked out through the stunned onlookers. They
were all amazed and praised God, exclaiming, "We've
never seen anything like this before!"

JESUS CALLS LEVI (MATTHEW)

13 Then Jesus went out to the lakeshore again and
taught the crowds that were coming to him. 14 As he
walked along, he saw Levi son of Alphaeus sitting at
his tax collector's booth. "Follow me and be my disci-
ple," Jesus said to him. So Levi got up and followed him.
15 Later, Levi invited Jesus and his disciples to his
home as dinner guests, along with many tax col-
lectors and other disreputable sinners. (There were
many people of this kind among Jesus' followers.)
16 But when the teachers of religious law who were
Pharisees* saw him eating with tax collectors and
other sinners, they asked his disciples, "Why does he
eat with such scum?*"
17 When Jesus heard this, he told them, "Healthy
people don't need a doctor—sick people do. I have
come to call not those who think they are righteous,
but those who know they are sinners."

A DISCUSSION ABOUT FASTING

18 Once when John's disciples and the Pharisees were
fasting, some people came to Jesus and asked, "Why
don't your disciples fast like John's disciples and the
Pharisees do?"
19 Jesus replied, "Do wedding guests fast while cel-
ebrating with the groom? Of course not. They can't
fast while the groom is with them. 20 But someday the
groom will be taken away from them, and then they
will fast.
21 "Besides, who would patch old clothing with new
cloth? For the new patch would shrink and rip away
from the old cloth, leaving an even bigger tear than
before.
22 "And no one puts new wine into old wineskins.
For the wine would burst the wineskins, and the wine
and the skins would both be lost. New wine calls for
new wineskins."

A DISCUSSION ABOUT THE SABBATH

23 One Sabbath day as Jesus was walking through
some grainfields, his disciples began breaking off
heads of grain to eat. 24 But the Pharisees said to Jesus,
"Look, why are they breaking the law by harvesting
grain on the Sabbath?"

REMEMBER THE WHAT?

1. When you were a kid, what were you not allowed to do on Sunday because it was the "Sabbath"?

MARK 2:23–3:6

2. Why did the Pharisees get angry with the disciples for eating grain from a field? (It was not considered stealing in Jesus' time.)
3. Read Exodus 20:8-11. Is Jesus disobeying Scripture by healing the man? If not, how have the Pharisees misused Scripture to accuse Jesus?
4. How should we "remember to dedicate the Sabbath" today? Are you doing that in your life at present

25 Jesus said to them, "Haven't you ever read in the
Scriptures what David did when he and his compan-
ions were hungry? 26 He went into the house of God
(during the days when Abiathar was high priest) and
broke the law by eating the sacred loaves of bread
that only the priests are allowed to eat. He also gave
some to his companions."
27 Then Jesus said to them, "The Sabbath was made
to meet the needs of people, and not people to meet
the requirements of the Sabbath. 28 So the Son of Man
is Lord, even over the Sabbath!"

JESUS HEALS ON THE SABBATH

3 Jesus went into the synagogue again and noticed a
man with a deformed hand. 2 Since it was the Sab-
bath, Jesus' enemies watched him closely. If he healed
the man's hand, they planned to accuse him of work-
ing on the Sabbath.
3 Jesus said to the man with the deformed hand,
"Come and stand in front of everyone." 4 Then he
turned to his critics and asked, "Does the law permit
good deeds on the Sabbath, or is it a day for doing
evil? Is this a day to save life or to destroy it?" But they
wouldn't answer him.
5 He looked around at them angrily and was deep-
ly saddened by their hard hearts. Then he said to the
man, "Hold out your hand." So the man held out his

2:16a Greek *the scribes of the Pharisees.* 2:16b Greek *with tax collectors and sinners?*

2:14 Levi. Elsewhere he is identified as Matthew (Matt. 9:9), the disciple who wrote one of the Gospels. In his role as a tax collector, Matthew would have been hated by both the religious establishment and the common people.

2:15 invited Jesus to his home as dinner guests. Here speaks of sharing a meal with another, which was a significant event implying acceptance of that person. In this way, Jesus extends His forgiveness (v. 10) to those who were outside orthodox religious life. **tax collectors.** They were hated by the Jews for collecting taxes on behalf of pagan Rome and for growing rich by collecting more than was actually required.

2:20 taken away. An ominous note predicting Jesus' death.

2:22 new wine. New wine continues to ferment. Hence, no one would have poured it into a leather container which was old, dry, and crusty. New wine required new skins which were supple and flexible, able to expand as the wine fermented.

2:23 Sabbath. The seventh day of the week (Saturday), which begins Friday at sunset and ends Saturday at sunset. The fourth Commandment is to rest from all labor on the Sabbath (Ex. 20:8-11). By the first century scores of regulations had evolved which defined what could and could not be done on the Sabbath. **breaking off heads of grain.** It was permissible for hungry travelers to pluck and eat grain from a field (Deut. 23:25). The issue is not stealing. What the Pharisees objected to was the "work" this involved.

3:2 enemies watched him closely. Here the religious leaders were refraining, from questioning Jesus. Now they simply watched to see if His actions betrayed a disregard for the law so they might accuse Him. **they planned to accuse him of working on the Sabbath.** The issue is not healing, but whether Jesus would do so on the Sabbath.

3:5 angrily and was deeply saddened. Jesus felt strongly about the injustice of a system that sacrificed the genuine needs of people for religious traditions that had nothing to do with God. **their hard hearts.** The Greek word, sometimes translated "stubborn," is also used to describe a gallstone or a tooth. **Hold out your hand.** Just as He deliberately declared the paralytic's sins forgiven (knowing that this was blasphemy to the teachers of the law), here He deliberately heals on the Sabbath (knowing that this too was anathema to His critics).

hand, and it was restored! [6] At once the Pharisees went away and met with the supporters of Herod to plot how to kill Jesus.

CROWDS FOLLOW JESUS

[7] Jesus went out to the lake with his disciples, and a large crowd followed him. They came from all over Galilee, Judea, [8] Jerusalem, Idumea, from east of the Jordan River, and even from as far north as Tyre and Sidon. The news about his miracles had spread far and wide, and vast numbers of people came to see him. [9] Jesus instructed his disciples to have a boat ready so the crowd would not crush him. [10] He had healed many people that day, so all the sick people eagerly pushed forward to touch him. [11] And whenever those possessed by evil* spirits caught sight of him, the spirits would throw them to the ground in front of him shrieking, "You are the Son of God!" [12] But Jesus sternly commanded the spirits not to reveal who he was.

JESUS CHOOSES THE TWELVE APOSTLES

[13] Afterward Jesus went up on a mountain and called out the ones he wanted to go with him. And they came to him. [14] Then he appointed twelve of them and called them his apostles.* They were to accompany him, and he would send them out to preach, [15] giving them authority to cast out demons. [16] These are the twelve he chose:

Simon (whom he named Peter),
[17] James and John (the sons of Zebedee, but Jesus nicknamed them "Sons of Thunder"*),
[18] Andrew,
Philip,
Bartholomew,
Matthew,
Thomas,
James (son of Alphaeus),
Thaddaeus,
Simon (the zealot*),
[19] Judas Iscariot (who later betrayed him).

JESUS AND THE PRINCE OF DEMONS

[20] One time Jesus entered a house, and the crowds began to gather again. Soon he and his disciples couldn't even find time to eat. [21] When his family heard what was happening, they tried to take him away. "He's out of his mind," they said.

[22] But the teachers of religious law who had arrived from Jerusalem said, "He's possessed by Satan,* the prince of demons. That's where he gets the power to cast out demons."

[23] Jesus called them over and responded with an illustration. "How can Satan cast out Satan?" he asked. [24] "A kingdom divided by civil war will collapse. [25] Similarly, a family splintered by feuding will fall apart. [26] And if Satan is divided and fights against himself, how can he stand? He would never survive. [27] Let me illustrate this further. Who is powerful enough to enter the house of a strong man and plunder his goods? Only someone even stronger—someone who could tie him up and then plunder his house.

[28] "I tell you the truth, all sin and blasphemy can be forgiven, [29] but anyone who blasphemes the Holy Spirit will never be forgiven. This is a sin with eternal consequences." [30] He told them this because they were saying, "He's possessed by an evil spirit."

THE TRUE FAMILY OF JESUS

[31] Then Jesus' mother and brothers came to see him. They stood outside and sent word for him to come out and talk with them. [32] There was a crowd sitting around Jesus, and someone said, "Your mother and your brothers* are outside asking for you."

[33] Jesus replied, "Who is my mother? Who are my brothers?" [34] Then he looked at those around him and said, "Look, these are my mother and brothers. [35] Anyone who does God's will is my brother and sister and mother."

ETERNAL FAMILY TIES

1. What's something you've done that made your family or friends wonder if you were crazy?

MARK 3:20-35

2. Why do you think Jesus' family thought he was "out of his mind" (v. 21)?
3. What did Jesus mean that we need to "enter the house of a strong man . . . and plunder his goods" (v. 27)? Who is that strong man? How do we tie him up?
4. Who did Jesus say are His true brothers and sisters? Are you a true brother or sister of Jesus? How do you know?

3:11 Greek *unclean;* also in 3:30. **3:14** Some manuscripts do not include *and called them his apostles.* **3:17** Greek *whom he named Boanerges, which means Sons of Thunder.* **3:18** Greek *the Cananean,* an Aramaic term for Jewish nationalists. **3:22** Greek *Beelzeboul;* other manuscripts read *Beezeboul;* Latin version reads *Beelzebub.* **3:32** Some manuscripts add *and sisters.*

3:6 supporters of Herod. A political group made up of influential Jewish sympathizers of King Herod. They were normally despised by the Pharisees, who considered them traitors (for working with Rome) and irreligious (unclean as a result of their association with Gentiles). However, the Pharisees had no power to kill Jesus. Only the civil authority could do this, and hence the collaboration. **to plot how to kill Jesus.** The Pharisees believed Jesus violated the Sabbath by healing on that day but failed to see that they were violating the Sabbath law by plotting how to kill Him on that day!

3:8 a large crowd followed him. They came from near (Galilee) and far, from the north (Tyre and Sidon), south (Idumea), and east (the region across the Jordan was called Perea). They came from Jewish and from Gentile regions. They came from the country regions (Galilee) and from the heart of the nation (Jerusalem).

3:21 they tried to take. They undertook the 30-mile journey from Nazareth to Capernaum. **to him away.** Their intent was to forcibly take Him home (6:17, the same word is translated "arrested"). **out of his mind.** Literally, "he is beside himself." His family concluded that He was suffering from some sort of ecstatic, religiously- induced mental illness.

3:22 He's possessed by Satan. Beelzebub was the Canaanite name for the chief god Baal. The religious leaders equated Beelzebub with Satan. To be possessed by this demon meant to be controlled by him, and this is how the teachers of the law explained Jesus' power over demons.

3:29 but anyone who blasphemes the Holy Spirit will never be forgiven. The first three Gospels (Matt. 12:31-32; Luke 12:10) refer to this concept. In light of the context, the unpardonable sin can be defined as rejecting the power and authority of the Holy Spirit working in Jesus and crediting that authority to Satan. Such a person calls absolute good—the work of the Holy Spirit—absolute evil. No one wanting to repent of sin has committed this sin. No born again person can commit this sin.

3:34-35 my mother and brothers. Jesus gives a new definition of family. Kinship is not a matter of heredity; it is a matter of spirit—doing God's will. Eventually His family will move from doubt to faith (John 19:25-27; Acts 1:14; 1 Cor. 15:7).

PARABLE OF THE FARMER SCATTERING SEED

4 Once again Jesus began teaching by the lakeshore. A very large crowd soon gathered around him, so he got into a boat. Then he sat in the boat while all the people remained on the shore. 2 He taught them by telling many stories in the form of parables, such as this one:

3 "Listen! A farmer went out to plant some seed. 4 As he scattered it across his field, some of the seed fell on a footpath, and the birds came and ate it. 5 Other seed fell on shallow soil with underlying rock. The seed sprouted quickly because the soil was shallow. 6 But the plant soon wilted under the hot sun, and since it didn't have deep roots, it died. 7 Other seed fell among thorns that grew up and choked out the tender plants so they produced no grain. 8 Still other seeds fell on fertile soil, and they sprouted, grew, and produced a crop that was thirty, sixty, and even a hundred times as much as had been planted!" 9 Then he said, "Anyone with ears to hear should listen and understand."

10 Later, when Jesus was alone with the twelve disciples and with the others who were gathered around, they asked him what the parables meant.

11 He replied, "You are permitted to understand the secret* of the Kingdom of God. But I use parables for everything I say to outsiders, 12 so that the Scriptures might be fulfilled:

'When they see what I do,
they will learn nothing.
When they hear what I say,
they will not understand.
Otherwise, they will turn to me
and be forgiven.'*"

13 Then Jesus said to them, "If you can't understand the meaning of this parable, how will you understand all the other parables? 14 The farmer plants seed by taking God's word to others. 15 The seed that fell on the footpath represents those who hear the message, only to have Satan come at once and take it away. 16 The seed on the rocky soil represents those who hear the message and immediately receive it with joy. 17 But since they don't have deep roots, they don't last long. They fall away as soon as they have problems or are persecuted for believing God's word. 18 The seed that fell among the thorns represents others who hear God's word, 19 but all too quickly the message is crowded out by the worries of this life, the lure of wealth, and the desire for other things, so no fruit is produced. 20 And the seed that fell on good soil represents those who hear and accept God's word and produce a harvest of thirty, sixty, or even a hundred times as much as had been planted!"

PARABLE OF THE LAMP

21 Then Jesus asked them, "Would anyone light a lamp and then put it under a basket or under a bed? Of course not! A lamp is placed on a stand, where its light will shine. 22 For everything that is hidden will eventually be brought into the open, and every secret will be brought to light. 23 Anyone with ears to hear should listen and understand."

24 Then he added, "Pay close attention to what you hear. The closer you listen, the more understanding you will be given*—and you will receive even more. 25 To those who listen to my teaching, more understanding will be given. But for those who are not listening, even what little understanding they have will be taken away from them."

PARABLE OF THE GROWING SEED

26 Jesus also said, "The Kingdom of God is like a farmer who scatters seed on the ground. 27 Night and day, while he's asleep or awake, the seed sprouts and grows, but he does not understand how it happens. 28 The earth produces the crops on its own. First a leaf blade pushes through, then the heads of wheat are formed, and finally the grain ripens. 29 And as soon as the grain is ready, the farmer comes and harvests it with a sickle, for the harvest time has come."

PARABLE OF THE MUSTARD SEED

30 Jesus said, "How can I describe the Kingdom of God? What story should I use to illustrate it? 31 It is like a mustard seed planted in the ground. It is the smallest of all seeds, 32 but it becomes the largest of all garden plants; it grows long branches, and birds can make nests in its shade."

33 Jesus used many similar stories and illustrations to teach the people as much as they could understand. 34 In fact, in his public ministry he never taught without using parables; but afterward, when he was alone with his disciples, he explained everything to them.

JESUS CALMS THE STORM

35 As evening came, Jesus said to his disciples, "Let's cross to the other side of the lake." 36 So they took Jesus

4:11 Greek *mystery*. **4:12** Isa 6:9-10 (Greek version). **4:24** Or *The measure you give will be the measure you get back.*

4:1 very large crowd. The scene is similar to that described in 3:7-9. This crowd was probably also drawn to Jesus in hopes of seeking healing and exorcism. However, this time Jesus speaks from a boat in order that all of the people might hear Him.

4:2 parables. Parables are comparisons that draw upon common experience in order to teach the realities of God's kingdom. These metaphors or analogies are often presented in story form; they draw upon the known to explain the unknown.

4:3 Listen! Pay attention! There is more to this story than appears at first. **sow.** Farmers would throw seed into the soil by a broad cast method.

4:4 footpath. The soil of the pathways was so hard packed that seed could not penetrate the soil to germinate.

4:5 shallow soil with underlying rock. Some soil covered a limestone base which was a few inches beneath the surface. Seed that fell here would germinate but not last, since a proper root system could not develop.

4:7 thorns. In other places, there were the roots of weeds. When the seed grew up, so did the weeds, which invariably stunted the growth of the good seed.

4:8 fertile soil. Some of the seed did fall where it could germinate, grow, and produce a crop. **thirty, sixty, and even a hundred times.** The good soil yielded a spectacular crop. While 10 times is an especially good harvest, this is a miracle crop.

4:11 The secret. A secret in the New Testament is something which was previously unknown but has now been revealed to all who will hear. The secret given the disciples is that the kingdom of God is with them. **the kingdom of God.** How God establishes His reign in human affairs is what Jesus' parables in this section are all about. **you are permitted to understand.** Not even the disciples who have been given "the secret" perceive fully what is going on (v. 13). It is as the disciples follow Jesus that they will come to understand more fully what He means

4:12 see what I do. . . hear what I say. This quote is from Isaiah 6:9-10 in which God called the prophet to speak His word even, though Israel would not listen. Although they saw God's messenger and heard his word, they refused to heed his message. **turn to me and be forgiven.** In order to be forgiven, people must repent (turn). In order to repent, they must understand their true situation.

CALMING THE STORM

1. When you were little, what did you do when there was a big storm?

MARK 4:35-41

2. Why was Jesus sleeping while a dangerous storm was raging?
3. Why were the disciples so afraid during the storm? How did their fear show they lacked faith?
4. If "even the wind and waves obey him" (v. 41), what does that teach you about Jesus' power in your life?
5. What "storms" are raging in your life right now? How can Jesus calm them?

in the boat and started out, leaving the crowds behind
(although other boats followed). 37 But soon a fierce
storm came up. High waves were breaking into the
boat, and it began to fill with water.
38 Jesus was sleeping at the back of the boat with
his head on a cushion. The disciples woke him up,
shouting, "Teacher, don't you care that we're going to
drown?"
39 When Jesus woke up, he rebuked the wind and
said to the waves, "Silence! Be still!" Suddenly the
wind stopped, and there was a great calm. 40 Then he
asked them, "Why are you afraid? Do you still have
no faith?"
41 The disciples were absolutely terrified. "Who is
this man?" they asked each other. "Even the wind and
waves obey him!"

JESUS HEALS A DEMON-POSSESSED MAN

5 So they arrived at the other side of the lake, in the
region of the Gerasenes.* 2 When Jesus climbed
out of the boat, a man possessed by an evil* spir-
it came out from the tombs to meet him. 3 This man
lived in the burial caves and could no longer be re-
strained, even with a chain. 4 Whenever he was put
into chains and shackles—as he often was—he
snapped the chains from his wrists and smashed the
shackles. No one was strong enough to subdue him.
5 Day and night he wandered among the burial caves
and in the hills, howling and cutting himself with
sharp stones.
6 When Jesus was still some distance away, the man
saw him, ran to meet him, and bowed low before him.
7 With a shriek, he screamed, "Why are you interfer-
ing with me, Jesus, Son of the Most High God? In the
name of God, I beg you, don't torture me!" 8 For Jesus
had already said to the spirit, "Come out of the man,
you evil spirit."
9 Then Jesus demanded, "What is your name?"
And he replied, "My name is Legion, because there
are many of us inside this man." 10 Then the evil spirits
begged him again and again not to send them to some
distant place.
11 There happened to be a large herd of pigs feeding
on the hillside nearby. 12 "Send us into those pigs," the
spirits begged. "Let us enter them."
13 So Jesus gave them permission. The evil spirits
came out of the man and entered the pigs, and the en-
tire herd of about 2,000 pigs plunged down the steep
hillside into the lake and drowned in the water.
14 The herdsmen fled to the nearby town and the
surrounding countryside, spreading the news as they
ran. People rushed out to see what had happened.
15 A crowd soon gathered around Jesus, and they saw
the man who had been possessed by the legion of de-
mons. He was sitting there fully clothed and perfect-
ly sane, and they were all afraid. 16 Then those who
had seen what happened told the others about the
demon-possessed man and the pigs. 17 And the crowd
began pleading with Jesus to go away and leave them
alone.
18 As Jesus was getting into the boat, the man who
had been demon possessed begged to go with him.
19 But Jesus said, "No, go home to your family, and tell
them everything the Lord has done for you and how
merciful he has been." 20 So the man started off to visit
the Ten Towns* of that region and began to proclaim
the great things Jesus had done for him; and everyone
was amazed at what he told them.

5:1 Other manuscripts read *Gadarenes;* still others read *Gergesenes.* See Matt 8:28; Luke 8:26. **5:2** Greek *unclean;* also in 5:8, 13.

4:37 A fierce storm. The Sea of Galilee was pear-shaped and ringed by mountains, though open at its northern and southern ends. Fierce winds blew into this bowl-shaped sea, creating savage and unpredictable storms.

4:39 Instead of bailing, Jesus commands the wind and the waves to be still, and so they are. He has power over the very elements—in the same way God does (Ps. 65:7; 106:9). This was something no ordinary rabbi could do. **Silence! Be still!** This is literally, "Be muzzled!" as if the storm were some wild beast needing to be subdued. Pictured in this account is Jesus' divine power to calm the storms of life.

4:40 afraid. Once Jesus displays His power, their fear of the storm turns into fear of Him. This is the fear of the unknown and the unexplainable. This miracle would force the disciples to reconsider all they had heard and seen from Jesus.

4:41 absolutely terrified. Terror replaced fear. Terror is felt in the presence of an unknown force or power. **Who then is this man?** This is the key question in Mark's Gospel. The congregation in the synagogue wondered about this (1:27). The religious leaders asked this question (2:7; 3:22). Now his disciples discover that they do not understand who He is. The rest of Mark describes how the disciples discover His true nature.

5:1 the region of the Gerasenes. The location of their landing is not clear. However, it is on the other side of the lake from Capernaum, in Gentile territory, probably near the lower end of the Sea of Galilee.

5:2 Jesus climbed out of the boat. No mention is made of the disciples in this story. **a man possessed by an evil spirit.** There was widespread belief that demons could enter and take control of a person's body, speaking and acting through that person. The demons were understood to be Satan's legions. In overcoming them, Jesus was demonstrating His power over Satan and his work. **burial caves.** The ragged limestone cliffs with their caves and depressions provided a natural burial site. The demoniac occupied the place of the dead, indicating the nature of the evil that was at work in him.

5:6 bowed low. Thus, the demons acknowledge Jesus' power over them. Likewise, in verse 7 they request that He not torture them, again acknowledging His superior power.

5:7 Son of the Most High God. The demons ask who Jesus is (4:41). The demon-filled man, with supernatural insight, points out Jesus' deity (1:11). Interestingly, this is how God was often referred to by the Gentiles (Gen. 14:17-24; Dan. 4:17). **I beg you, don't torment me!** It is not clear what they feared.

5:9 Legion. The name for a company of 6,000 Roman soldiers. The man was occupied not by one but by a huge number of demons.

5:15 they were all afraid. It might be expected that they would rejoice that this man who had terrorized them (and whom they could no longer restrain) was now healed. But instead, they are fearful of Jesus, who had the power to overcome the demons and destroy their herd.

5:20 the Ten Towns. This was a league of 10 Gentile cities patterned after the Greek way of life. This is the first of several ventures by Jesus into Gentile areas, demonstrating what Mark later points out (13:10; 14:9). The gospel is to be preached to all nations.

JESUS HEALS IN RESPONSE TO FAITH

21 Jesus got into the boat again and went back to the
other side of the lake, where a large crowd gathered
around him on the shore. 22 Then a leader of the local
synagogue, whose name was Jairus, arrived. When he
saw Jesus, he fell at his feet, 23 pleading fervently with
him. "My little daughter is dying," he said. "Please
come and lay your hands on her; heal her so she can
live."
24 Jesus went with him, and all the people followed,
crowding around him. 25 A woman in the crowd had
suffered for twelve years with constant bleeding.
26 She had suffered a great deal from many doctors,
and over the years she had spent everything she had
to pay them, but she had gotten no better. In fact, she
had gotten worse. 27 She had heard about Jesus, so she
came up behind him through the crowd and touched
his robe. 28 For she thought to herself, "If I can just
touch his robe, I will be healed." 29 Immediately the
bleeding stopped, and she could feel in her body that
she had been healed of her terrible condition.

MIRACULOUS FAITH

1. How do you feel about a trip to the doctor's office? Would you rather suffer with pain than go see a doctor?

MARK 5:24-34

2. Why did the woman touch Jesus' robe? Why didn't she just ask Him for healing?
3. Why did Jesus ask who had touched Him? What did this force the woman to do?
4. What "faith" did the woman have? How did it make her well?
5. What needs healing in your own life—physically, spiritually, emotionally, or otherwise?

30 Jesus realized at once that healing power had
gone out from him, so he turned around in the crowd
and asked, "Who touched my robe?"
31 His disciples said to him, "Look at this crowd press-
ing around you. How can you ask, 'Who touched me?'"
32 But he kept on looking around to see who had done
it. 33 Then the frightened woman, trembling at the real-
ization of what had happened to her, came and fell to
her knees in front of him and told him what she had
done. 34 And he said to her, "Daughter, your faith has
made you well. Go in peace. Your suffering is over."
35 While he was still speaking to her, messengers
arrived from the home of Jairus, the leader of the
synagogue. They told him, "Your daughter is dead.
There's no use troubling the Teacher now."
36 But Jesus overheard* them and said to Jairus,
"Don't be afraid. Just have faith."
37 Then Jesus stopped the crowd and wouldn't let
anyone go with him except Peter, James, and John
(the brother of James). 38 When they came to the home
of the synagogue leader, Jesus saw much commo-
tion and weeping and wailing. 39 He went inside and
asked, "Why all this commotion and weeping? The
child isn't dead; she's only asleep."
40 The crowd laughed at him. But he made them
all leave, and he took the girl's father and mother
and his three disciples into the room where the girl
was lying. 41 Holding her hand, he said to her, *"Tali-
tha koum,"* which means "Little girl, get up!" 42 And
the girl, who was twelve years old, immediately stood
up and walked around! They were overwhelmed and
totally amazed. 43 Jesus gave them strict orders not
to tell anyone what had happened, and then he told
them to give her something to eat.

JESUS REJECTED AT NAZARETH

6 Jesus left that part of the country and returned
with his disciples to Nazareth, his hometown.
2 The next Sabbath he began teaching in the syna-
gogue, and many who heard him were amazed. They
asked, "Where did he get all this wisdom and the
power to perform such miracles?" 3 Then they scoffed,
"He's just a carpenter, the son of Mary* and the broth-
er of James, Joseph,* Judas, and Simon. And his sisters
live right here among us." They were deeply offended
and refused to believe in him.
4 Then Jesus told them, "A prophet is honored
everywhere except in his own hometown and among
his relatives and his own family." 5 And because of
their unbelief, he couldn't do any miracles among
them except to place his hands on a few sick people
and heal them. 6 And he was amazed at their unbelief.

5:20 Greek *Decapolis.* **5:36** Or *ignored.* **6:3a** Some manuscripts read *He's just the son of the carpenter and of Mary.* **6:3b** Most manuscripts read *Joses;* see Matt 13:55.

5:22 leader of the local synagogue. In first-century Israel, synagogues were found in each city and town. People met there weekly on the Sabbath for worship and instruction. Synagogues were run by a committee of lay people (the rulers).

5:25 a woman. This woman should not have been in the crowd. Because of the nature of her illness, she was considered "ceremonially unclean" (Lev. 15:25-30). **suffered for twelve years with constant bleeding.** Probably hemorrhaging from the womb. Since many people assumed that chronic problems like this were God's judgment upon a person for their sin, she undoubtedly experienced some measure of condemnation from others.

5:28 If I can just touch his robe, I'll be healed. There is no attempt on her part to establish genuine contact with Jesus: she simply wants to brush up against Him so that she can be brought in contact with His power. Nonetheless, by this action the woman showed that she had "ears to hear" (4:9) and had faith that Jesus could indeed heal her.

5:30 Who touched my robe? Jesus desired a relationship with those He helped: He was not an impersonal power source.

5:34 your faith has made you well. It was her faith that compelled her to reach out to Jesus—the source of healing power. **Go in peace.** This phrase means "be complete, be whole."

5:38 weeping and wailing. These were in all likelihood professional mourners. Even the poorest person was required to hire not less than two flutes and one wailing woman to mourn a death.

6:1-2 His hometown. Nazareth, which was located in the hill country of Galilee some 20 miles southwest of Capernaum (Luke 4:14-30).

6:2 Where did he get all this wisdom? The townspeople do not deny Jesus' wisdom or power to do miracles. But they are puzzled as to the origin of such abilities.

6:3 carpenter. The Greek word refers to a general craftsman who worked not only with wood but also with stone and metal. **son of Mary.** A man was never described as the son of his mother except as an insult. The townsfolk may have heard rumors of Jesus' unusual birth and may have taken Him to be illegitimate. **brother of James, Joseph, Judas, and Simon . . . sisters.** Mark names four brothers and indicates Jesus had sisters too. **they were deeply offended.** They could not get past His humble and familiar origins—therefore, they couldn't give credence to who He really was.

JESUS SENDS OUT THE TWELVE DISCIPLES

Then Jesus went from village to village, teaching the
people. 7 And he called his twelve disciples together
and began sending them out two by two, giving them
authority to cast out evil* spirits. 8 He told them to take
nothing for their journey except a walking stick—no
food, no traveler's bag, no money.* 9 He allowed them
to wear sandals but not to take a change of clothes.
10 "Wherever you go," he said, "stay in the same
house until you leave town. 11 But if any place refuses
to welcome you or listen to you, shake its dust from
your feet as you leave to show that you have aban-
doned those people to their fate."
12 So the disciples went out, telling everyone they
met to repent of their sins and turn to God. 13 And they
cast out many demons and healed many sick people,
anointing them with olive oil.

THE DEATH OF JOHN THE BAPTIST

14 Herod Antipas, the king, soon heard about Jesus,
because everyone was talking about him. Some were
saying,* "This must be John the Baptist raised from the
dead. That is why he can do such miracles." 15 Others
said, "He's the prophet Elijah." Still others said, "He's
a prophet like the other great prophets of the past."
16 When Herod heard about Jesus, he said, "John, the
man I beheaded, has come back from the dead."
17 For Herod had sent soldiers to arrest and im-
prison John as a favor to Herodias. She had been his
brother Philip's wife, but Herod had married her.
18 John had been telling Herod, "It is against God's law
for you to marry your brother's wife." 19 So Herodias
bore a grudge against John and wanted to kill him.
But without Herod's approval she was powerless,
20 for Herod respected John; and knowing that he was
a good and holy man, he protected him. Herod was
greatly disturbed whenever he talked with John, but
even so, he liked to listen to him.
21 Herodias's chance finally came on Herod's birth-
day. He gave a party for his high government officials,
army officers, and the leading citizens of Galilee.
22 Then his daughter, also named Herodias,* came in
and performed a dance that greatly pleased Herod
and his guests. "Ask me for anything you like," the
king said to the girl, "and I will give it to you." 23 He
even vowed, "I will give you whatever you ask, up to
half my kingdom!"

LOSING YOUR HEAD

1. When have you recently "lost your head?" What made you upset? What did you do?

MARK 6:14-29

2. Why did Herodias, Herod's wife, want to kill John the Baptist? Why did Herod not want to kill him?
3. What caused Herod to change his mind and kill John? How did his environment get him into trouble?
4. What sorts of "environments" can get you into trouble? Specifically, where do you draw the line when it comes to movies, music, etc. with sexual or violent content?

24 She went out and asked her mother, "What should
I ask for?"
Her mother told her, "Ask for the head of John the
Baptist!"
25 So the girl hurried back to the king and told him,
"I want the head of John the Baptist, right now, on a
tray!"
26 Then the king deeply regretted what he had said;
but because of the vows he had made in front of his
guests, he couldn't refuse her. 27 So he immediate-
ly sent an executioner to the prison to cut off John's
head and bring it to him. The soldier beheaded John
in the prison, 28 brought his head on a tray, and gave
it to the girl, who took it to her mother. 29 When John's
disciples heard what had happened, they came to get
his body and buried it in a tomb.

JESUS FEEDS FIVE THOUSAND

30 The apostles returned to Jesus from their minis-
try tour and told him all they had done and taught.
31 Then Jesus said, "Let's go off by ourselves to a qui-
et place and rest awhile." He said this because there
were so many people coming and going that Jesus
and his apostles didn't even have time to eat.
32 So they left by boat for a quiet place, where they
could be alone. 33 But many people recognized them

6:7 Greek *unclean.* **6:8** Greek *no copper coins in their money belts.* **6:14** Some manuscripts read *He was saying.* **6:22** Some manuscripts read *the daughter of Herodias herself.*

6:7 began sending them out. To go out on a ministry tour is not the idea or plan of the Twelve. Jesus does the sending. **two by two.** He does not send them alone—perhaps as a protection against robbers; perhaps because two witnesses have more credibility than one (Deut. 17:6); perhaps so that they will support one another as they learn to minister. The parallel accounts in Matthew and Luke indicate their mission was to announce and demonstrate the fact that God's kingdom was now at hand (1:15). **giving them authority.** He empowers them to do battle with evil. It is in His name and power that they minister.

6:8 told them. These instructions cause the Twelve to pare down to the bare minimum. They take only the clothes on their backs and a staff, the tool of a shepherd. By faith they must trust that God will provide the rest of their needs as they go about His work.

6:10 They are not to dishonor their host by accepting better accommodations.

6:14 Herod Antipas. Herod Antipas was the ruler of the Roman provinces of Galilee and Perea from 4 B.C. to A.D. 39. He was the son of Herod the Great, the Jewish ruler who ordered the slaughter of the babies after Jesus' birth. Herod Antipas was not, in fact, the "king." When he went to Rome some years later to request this title, his power was taken away and he was banished.

6:18 It is against God's law. According to Leviticus 18:16 and 20:21, it was not lawful for a man to marry his brother's wife while that brother was still alive. Herod, a Jew himself, scandalized his people by divorcing the Nabatean Princess Aretas to marry Herodias who was his niece (the daughter of his half-brother) and his sister-in-law (the wife of a different brother).

6:21 chance finally came. Herodias was plotting a way to kill John (v. 19) because of his criticism of her marriage. **a party.** The sparseness of the lifestyle of the Twelve (vv. 8-11) would have contrasted greatly with the opulence of Herod's birthday party. The men in attendance would have been wealthy landowners, those in high government positions, and military officials.

6:22 his daughter, also named Herodius. This is Herodias' teenage daughter (from her first marriage), whose name is Salome.

6:25 the head of John the Baptist, right now, on a tray! This was a gruesome act: serving John's head on a platter as if it were another course in the banquet.

6:33 ran ahead along the shore. The crowds are now wise to the disciples' tactic of sailing off across the lake and leaving them standing on the shore (4:35-36). So they follow on foot. The distances would not have been great since the lake was only eight miles at its widest. They could probably see where they were sailing to.

REST AND REFRESHMENT

1. How do you unwind after a busy day?

MARK 6:30-44

2. Why did the disciples need a rest? How were they intending to spend their rest time?
3. How did Jesus actually provide rest and refreshment for everyone around Him?
4. The disciples thought they were getting a break (v. 31), but they ended up serving. What does this passage say to you about the use of your free time?
5. How can you use your free time this week in a God-pleasing way?

---

and saw them leaving, and people from many towns
ran ahead along the shore and got there ahead of
them. 34 Jesus saw the huge crowd as he stepped from
the boat, and he had compassion on them because
they were like sheep without a shepherd. So he began
teaching them many things.

35 Late in the afternoon his disciples came to him
and said, "This is a remote place, and it's already get-
ting late. 36 Send the crowds away so they can go to the
nearby farms and villages and buy something to eat."

37 But Jesus said, "You feed them."

"With what?" they asked. "We'd have to work for
months to earn enough money* to buy food for all
these people!"

38 "How much bread do you have?" he asked. "Go
and find out."

They came back and reported, "We have five loaves
of bread and two fish."

39 Then Jesus told the disciples to have the people
sit down in groups on the green grass. 40 So they sat
down in groups of fifty or a hundred.

41 Jesus took the five loaves and two fish, looked up
toward heaven, and blessed them. Then, breaking the
loaves into pieces, he kept giving the bread to the dis-
ciples so they could distribute it to the people. He also
divided the fish for everyone to share. 42 They all ate
as much as they wanted, 43 and afterward, the disci-
ples picked up twelve baskets of leftover bread and
fish. 44 A total of 5,000 men and their families were
fed.*

JESUS WALKS ON WATER

45 Immediately after this, Jesus insisted that his disci-
ples get back into the boat and head across the lake
to Bethsaida, while he sent the people home. 46 After
telling everyone good-bye, he went up into the hills
by himself to pray.

47 Late that night, the disciples were in their boat in
the middle of the lake, and Jesus was alone on land.
48 He saw that they were in serious trouble, rowing
hard and struggling against the wind and waves.
About three o'clock in the morning* Jesus came to-
ward them, walking on the water. He intended to
go past them, 49 but when they saw him walking on
the water, they cried out in terror, thinking he was a
ghost. 50 They were all terrified when they saw him.

But Jesus spoke to them at once. "Don't be afraid,"
he said. "Take courage! I am here!*" 51 Then he climbed
into the boat, and the wind stopped. They were totally
amazed, 52 for they still didn't understand the signifi-
cance of the miracle of the loaves. Their hearts were
too hard to take it in.

53 After they had crossed the lake, they landed at
Gennesaret. They brought the boat to shore 54 and
climbed out. The people recognized Jesus at once,
55 and they ran throughout the whole area, carrying
sick people on mats to wherever they heard he was.
56 Wherever he went—in villages, cities, or the coun-
tryside—they brought the sick out to the market-
places. They begged him to let the sick touch at least
the fringe of his robe, and all who touched him were
healed.

JESUS TEACHES ABOUT INNER PURITY

7 One day some Pharisees and teachers of religious
law arrived from Jerusalem to see Jesus. 2 They
noticed that some of his disciples failed to follow
the Jewish ritual of hand washing before eating.

6:37 Greek *It would take 200 denarii.* A denarius was equivalent to a laborer's full day's wage. **6:44** Some manuscripts read *fed from the loaves.* **6:48** Greek *About the fourth watch of the night.* **6:50** Or *The 'I AM' is here;* Greek reads *I am.* See Exod 3:14.

6:41 five loaves. These were small round cakes made of wheat or barley. **two fish.** These were probably smoked or pickled fish that were used as a sauce for the bread.

6:42 ate as much as they wanted. Miraculously, five loaves and two fish fed everyone, not meagerly but abundantly, so that they were filled.

6:43 twelve The number of the tribes of Israel, reinforcing the idea that what Jesus is doing here has prophetic significance as a demonstration that Jesus provides nourishment for all God's people. **baskets.** Small wicker containers carried by all Jews. Each disciple returned with his full. The word used for basket describes a distinctly Jewish type of basket. **leftover.** The law required that the scraps of a meal be collected. **bread.** Bread and eating are recurring themes in these two cycles of stories (6:30–8:26).

6:44 men. Literally, "males" (Matt. 14:21). When all the women and children are taken into account, this was a huge crowd.

6:45 The reason for Jesus' abrupt dismissal of the disciples and the crowd is explained in the Gospel of John (John 6:14-15). Apparently the crowd wanted to make Jesus the king by force. **Bethsaida.** Literally, "house of the fisher." This is a village on the northern shore of the Sea of Galilee, several miles east of Capernaum. This was the birthplace of Philip, Andrew, and Peter.

6:46 himself to pray. In the midst of great success and popular acclaim, once again Jesus goes off to pray.

6:48 struggling against the wind and the waves. Once again (4:37), the elements work against the disciples. This time the problem is not a storm but a strong headwind that would make rowing difficult. **three o'clock in the morning.** This was the way Roman soldiers told time. The fourth watch ran from 3:00 to 6:00 a.m. Assuming the disciples set out to sea in the late afternoon, they had been struggling at the oars for probably seven or more hours. **walking on the water.** It has already been established that Jesus is Lord over the wind and the water (4:39,41). **intended to go pass by them.** This could be translated: "for He intended to pass their way," presumably to reveal His presence and remind them of His power in the midst of their distress.

6:49 a ghost. The sea, especially at night, was thought to be a dwelling place for demons. Hence the response of the disciples.

6:50 terrified. Once before on this lake they were terrified by an event they did not expect and did not understand (4:41). This is the terror of experiencing something that defies all categories of understanding. **I am here!** Literally, "I Am." This phrase is used by God to describe himself (Ex. 3:1-14).

6:52 their hearts were too hard to take it in. This is the problem. Like the Pharisees in the synagogue (3:5), the disciples' hearts are like calcified stone (the same Greek word is used here and in 3:5).

6:53 Gennesaret. Since the wind frustrated their plan to go north, they instead cross the lake to a thickly populated, fertile plain some four miles southwest of Capernaum. There, crowds again flock to Him as a healer.

3 (The Jews, especially the Pharisees, do not eat until they have poured water over their cupped hands,* as required by their ancient traditions. 4 Similarly, they don't eat anything from the market until they immerse their hands* in water. This is but one of many traditions they have clung to—such as their ceremonial washing of cups, pitchers, and kettles.*)

5 So the Pharisees and teachers of religious law asked him, "Why don't your disciples follow our age-old tradition? They eat without first performing the hand-washing ceremony."

6 Jesus replied, "You hypocrites! Isaiah was right when he prophesied about you, for he wrote,

'These people honor me with their lips,
but their hearts are far from me.
7 Their worship is a farce,
for they teach man-made ideas as commands from God.'*

8 For you ignore God's law and substitute your own tradition."

9 Then he said, "You skillfully sidestep God's law in order to hold on to your own tradition. 10 For instance, Moses gave you this law from God: 'Honor your father and mother,'* and 'Anyone who speaks disrespectfully of father or mother must be put to death.'* 11 But you say it is all right for people to say to their parents, 'Sorry, I can't help you. For I have vowed to give to God what I would have given to you.'* 12 In this way, you let them disregard their needy parents. 13 And so you cancel the word of God in order to hand down your own tradition. And this is only one example among many others."

14 Then Jesus called to the crowd to come and hear. "All of you listen," he said, "and try to understand. 15 It's not what goes into your body that defiles you; you are defiled by what comes from your heart.*"

17 Then Jesus went into a house to get away from the crowd, and his disciples asked him what he meant by the parable he had just used. 18 "Don't you understand either?" he asked. "Can't you see that the food you put into your body cannot defile you? 19 Food doesn't go into your heart, but only passes through the stomach and then goes into the sewer." (By saying this, he declared that every kind of food is acceptable in God's eyes.)

20 And then he added, "It is what comes from inside that defiles you. 21 For from within, out of a person's heart, come evil thoughts, sexual immorality, theft, murder, 22 adultery, greed, wickedness, deceit, lustful desires, envy, slander, pride, and foolishness. 23 All these vile things come from within; they are what defile you."

THE FAITH OF A GENTILE WOMAN

24 Then Jesus left Galilee and went north to the region of Tyre.* He didn't want anyone to know which house he was staying in, but he couldn't keep it a secret. 25 Right away a woman who had heard about him came and fell at his feet. Her little girl was possessed by an evil* spirit, 26 and she begged him to cast out the demon from her daughter.

Since she was a Gentile, born in Syrian Phoenicia, 27 Jesus told her, "First I should feed the children—my own family, the Jews.* It isn't right to take food from the children and throw it to the dogs."

28 She replied, "That's true, Lord, but even the dogs under the table are allowed to eat the scraps from the children's plates."

29 "Good answer!" he said. "Now go home, for the demon has left your daughter." 30 And when she arrived home, she found her little girl lying quietly in bed, and the demon was gone.

JESUS HEALS A DEAF MAN

31 Jesus left Tyre and went up to Sidon before going back to the Sea of Galilee and the region of the Ten Towns.* 32 A deaf man with a speech impediment was brought to him, and the people begged Jesus to lay his hands on the man to heal him.

33 Jesus led him away from the crowd so they could be alone. He put his fingers into the man's ears. Then, spitting on his own fingers, he touched the man's tongue. 34 Looking up to heaven, he sighed and said, *"Ephphatha,"* which means, "Be opened!" 35 Instantly the man could hear perfectly, and his tongue was freed so he could speak plainly!

36 Jesus told the crowd not to tell anyone, but the more he told them not to, the more they spread the news. 37 They were completely amazed and said again and again, "Everything he does is wonderful. He even makes the deaf to hear and gives speech to those who cannot speak."

7:3 Greek *have washed with the fist.* **7:4a** Some manuscripts read *sprinkle themselves.* **7:4b** Some manuscripts add *and dining couches.* **7:7** Isa 29:13 (Greek version). **7:10a** Exod 20:12; Deut 5:16. **7:10b** Exod 21:17 (Greek version); Lev 20:9 (Greek version). **7:11** Greek *'What I would have given to you is Corban' (that is, a gift).* **7:15** Some manuscripts add verse 16, *Anyone with ears to hear should listen and understand.* Compare 4:9, 23. **7:24** Some manuscripts add *and Sidon.* **7:25** Greek *unclean.* **7:27** Greek *Let the children eat first.* **7:31** Greek *Decapolis.*

7:3 poured water over their cupped hands. The issue was holiness, not hygiene (germs were unknown in the first century). Before each meal the hands were washed with special water in a particular way.

7:11 vowed to give God. An oath, which when invoked, dedicated an item to God, rendering it thereafter unavailable for normal use. A son might declare his property "Corban" with the result that his parents would have no further claim on his support, even though the oath neither required him to transfer his property to the temple nor to cease using it himself.

7:15 defile you. This means "to render someone impure in a ritual sense."

7:20 what comes from inside. Jesus calls the people to focus on what comes out of a person's heart and mind. Thoughts and actions reveal true uncleanness.

7:26 Gentile, born in Syrian Phoenicia. This woman is described first by her religion, language, and culture. She is a Greek-speaking Gentile. Then she is described by her nationality. She came from Phoenicia (modern-day Lebanon).

7:27 first. Jesus' primary mission was to the children of Israel. By the use of the word "first," He implies that a mission to the Gentiles was intended from the beginning.

7:28 Instead of being insulted by His metaphor, she catches on to His wordplay and replies, in essence, "Carry on with the meal You are serving Israel, but allow us a few scraps."

7:29 Good answer! Jesus is impressed with the depth of her understanding as well as her clever and witty reply. In fact, this Gentile woman seems to understand more about Jesus than either the Twelve (6:45-56) or the Pharisees (vv. 1-13).

7:33 spitting. This was regarded by Jews and Greeks as a healing agent.

7:36 not to tell anyone. This command stands in sharp contrast to what Jesus said on His previous visit to the region of the Decapolis. On that occasion, He told the ex-demoniac to "go and tell" the story of what the Lord had done for him (5:18-20). On this trip, Jesus sees the results of that man's witness. Instead of urgently requesting Jesus to leave as they had done on his previous visit (5:17), now not only do the townspeople bring a man to be healed, but they have developed expectations about who Jesus is and what He can do. This is why Jesus now commanded silence.

JESUS FEEDS FOUR THOUSAND

8 About this time another large crowd had gath-
ered, and the people ran out of food again. Jesus
called his disciples and told them, 2 "I feel sorry for
these people. They have been here with me for three
days, and they have nothing left to eat. 3 If I send them
home hungry, they will faint along the way. For some
of them have come a long distance."
4 His disciples replied, "How are we supposed to
find enough food to feed them out here in the wilder-
ness?"
5 Jesus asked, "How much bread do you have?"
"Seven loaves," they replied.
6 So Jesus told all the people to sit down on the
ground. Then he took the seven loaves, thanked God
for them, and broke them into pieces. He gave them to
his disciples, who distributed the bread to the crowd.
7 A few small fish were found, too, so Jesus also blessed
these and told the disciples to distribute them.
8 They ate as much as they wanted. Afterward, the
disciples picked up seven large baskets of leftover food.
9 There were about 4,000 people in the crowd that day,
and Jesus sent them home after they had eaten. 10 Im-
mediately after this, he got into a boat with his disci-
ples and crossed over to the region of Dalmanutha.

PHARISEES DEMAND A MIRACULOUS SIGN

11 When the Pharisees heard that Jesus had arrived,
they came and started to argue with him. Testing
him, they demanded that he show them a miraculous
sign from heaven to prove his authority.
12 When he heard this, he sighed deeply in his spirit
and said, "Why do these people keep demanding a mi-
raculous sign? I tell you the truth, I will not give this
generation any such sign." 13 So he got back into the
boat and left them, and he crossed to the other side
of the lake.

YEAST OF THE PHARISEES AND HEROD

14 But the disciples had forgotten to bring any food.
They had only one loaf of bread with them in the
boat. 15 As they were crossing the lake, Jesus warned
them, "Watch out! Beware of the yeast of the Phari-
sees and of Herod."
16 At this they began to argue with each other be-
cause they hadn't brought any bread. 17 Jesus knew
what they were saying, so he said, "Why are you ar-
guing about having no bread? Don't you know or un-
derstand even yet? Are your hearts too hard to take it
in? 18 'You have eyes—can't you see? You have ears—
can't you hear?'* Don't you remember anything at all?
19 When I fed the 5,000 with five loaves of bread, how
many baskets of leftovers did you pick up afterward?"
"Twelve," they said.
20 "And when I fed the 4,000 with seven loaves, how
many large baskets of leftovers did you pick up?"
"Seven," they said.
21 "Don't you understand yet?" he asked them.

JESUS HEALS A BLIND MAN

22 When they arrived at Bethsaida, some people
brought a blind man to Jesus, and they begged him
to touch the man and heal him. 23 Jesus took the blind
man by the hand and led him out of the village. Then,
spitting on the man's eyes, he laid his hands on him
and asked, "Can you see anything now?"
24 The man looked around. "Yes," he said, "I see peo-
ple, but I can't see them very clearly. They look like
trees walking around."
25 Then Jesus placed his hands on the man's eyes
again, and his eyes were opened. His sight was com-
pletely restored, and he could see everything clearly.
26 Jesus sent him away, saying, "Don't go back into the
village on your way home."

PETER'S DECLARATION ABOUT JESUS

27 Jesus and his disciples left Galilee and went up to
the villages near Caesarea Philippi. As they were
walking along, he asked them, "Who do people say I
am?"
28 "Well," they replied, "some say John the Baptist,
some say Elijah, and others say you are one of the oth-
er prophets."
29 Then he asked them, "But who do you say I am?"
Peter replied, "You are the Messiah.*"
30 But Jesus warned them not to tell anyone about
him.

JESUS PREDICTS HIS DEATH

31 Then Jesus began to tell them that the Son of Man*
must suffer many terrible things and be rejected by
the elders, the leading priests, and the teachers of re-
ligious law. He would be killed, but three days later he
would rise from the dead. 32 As he talked about this
openly with his disciples, Peter took him aside and be-
gan to reprimand him for saying such things.*
33 Jesus turned around and looked at his disciples,
then reprimanded Peter. "Get away from me, Satan!"

8:18 Jer 5:21. **8:29** Or *the Christ. Messiah* (a Hebrew term) and *Christ* (a Greek term) both mean "anointed one." **8:31** "Son of Man" is a title Jesus used for himself. **8:32** Or *began to correct him.*

8:1-10 another large crowd. The major difference between the feeding of the four thousand and the feeding of the five thousand is the difference in audience. This feeding included Gentiles (as well as Jews), whereas the earlier feeding involved Jews only.

8:10 Dalmanutha. It is not certain where this town is located. Possibly it is Magdala, a town near Tiberias on the west side of the lake. The point is clear. At this time Jesus left the Gentile region where He was ministering and returned to Jewish soil.

8:15 yeast. To the Jew, yeast was connected with fermentation, which they saw as a form of rotting. So yeast became a metaphor for evil and its expansion.

8:17 Don't you know or understand even yet? Jesus asks this question twice in these verses (vv. 14-21). This is the issue: although exposed to ample evidence of who Jesus is, they still fail to put it all together. **hearts too hard?** This is the problem (3:5; 6:52). Their hearts are stone-like. The seed of the Word can't penetrate (4:15).

8:22 Bethsaida. This was a town at the mouth of the Jordan River on the shore of the Sea of Galilee.

8:25 Then. This is the only healing that requires a second action on the part of Jesus. Mark's placement of this story right after the disciples' incomprehension of the meaning of the feedings, and just prior to their confession of faith in Him as the Messiah, indicates he is using this story to illustrate how difficult it was for the disciples to grasp Jesus' identity.

8:27 Caesarea Philippi. When Jesus and His disciples visited this city, there was a gleaming white marble temple dedicated to the godhead of Caesar. It is fitting that in this place with rich associations to the religions of the world, Jesus, the Galilean, asks His disciples if they understand that He is the Anointed One sent by God.

8:29 who do you say I am? This is the crucial question in Mark's Gospel. By it the author challenges his readers to consider how they will answer the question as well.

8:33 Get away from me, Satan! By urging Jesus to back away from His teaching about suffering and death, Peter is doing what Satan did: tempting Jesus with the promise that He can have the whole world without pain (Matt. 4:8-10).

he said. "You are seeing things merely from a human point of view, not from God's."

34 Then, calling the crowd to join his disciples, he said, "If any of you wants to be my follower, you must give up your own way, take up your cross, and follow me. 35 If you try to hang on to your life, you will lose it. But if you give up your life for my sake and for the sake of the Good News, you will save it. 36 And what do you benefit if you gain the whole world but lose your own soul?* 37 Is anything worth more than your soul? 38 If anyone is ashamed of me and my message in these adulterous and sinful days, the Son of Man will be ashamed of that person when he returns in the glory of his Father with the holy angels."

9 Jesus went on to say, "I tell you the truth, some standing here right now will not die before they see the Kingdom of God arrive in great power!"

THE TRANSFIGURATION

2 Six days later Jesus took Peter, James, and John, and led them up a high mountain to be alone. As the men watched, Jesus' appearance was transformed, 3 and his clothes became dazzling white, far whiter than any earthly bleach could ever make them. 4 Then Elijah and Moses appeared and began talking with Jesus.

5 Peter exclaimed, "Rabbi, it's wonderful for us to be here! Let's make three shelters as memorials*—one for you, one for Moses, and one for Elijah." 6 He said this because he didn't really know what else to say, for they were all terrified.

7 Then a cloud overshadowed them, and a voice from the cloud said, "This is my dearly loved Son. Listen to him." 8 Suddenly, when they looked around, Moses and Elijah were gone, and they saw only Jesus with them.

9 As they went back down the mountain, he told them not to tell anyone what they had seen until the Son of Man* had risen from the dead. 10 So they kept it to themselves, but they often asked each other what he meant by "rising from the dead."

11 Then they asked him, "Why do the teachers of religious law insist that Elijah must return before the Messiah comes?*"

12 Jesus responded, "Elijah is indeed coming first to get everything ready. Yet why do the Scriptures say that the Son of Man must suffer greatly and be treated with utter contempt? 13 But I tell you, Elijah has already come, and they chose to abuse him, just as the Scriptures predicted."

PRECIOUS TIME

1. What's the highest place you've ever climbed?

MARK 9:2-13

2. Why did Jesus wait until He was alone with His disciples to be "transformed" before them?
3. How did Peter react to this awesome event (vv. 5-6)? How would you have reacted?
4. When did you last spend an hour alone with Jesus?
5. Why is it so important that Christians spend time alone with Jesus?
6. How can you make time alone with Jesus a higher priority in your life?

JESUS HEALS A DEMON-POSSESSED BOY

14 When they returned to the other disciples, they saw a large crowd surrounding them, and some teachers of religious law were arguing with them. 15 When the crowd saw Jesus, they were overwhelmed with awe, and they ran to greet him.

16 "What is all this arguing about?" Jesus asked.

17 One of the men in the crowd spoke up and said, "Teacher, I brought my son so you could heal him. He is possessed by an evil spirit that won't let him talk. 18 And whenever this spirit seizes him, it throws him violently to the ground. Then he foams at the mouth and grinds his teeth and becomes rigid.* So I asked your disciples to cast out the evil spirit, but they couldn't do it."

19 Jesus said to them,* "You faithless people! How long must I be with you? How long must I put up with you? Bring the boy to me."

20 So they brought the boy. But when the evil spirit saw Jesus, it threw the child into a violent convulsion, and he fell to the ground, writhing and foaming at the mouth.

21 "How long has this been happening?" Jesus asked the boy's father.

He replied, "Since he was a little boy. 22 The spirit often throws him into the fire or into water, trying to kill him. Have mercy on us and help us, if you can."

23 "What do you mean, 'If I can'?" Jesus asked. "Anything is possible if a person believes."

24 The father instantly cried out, "I do believe, but help me overcome my unbelief!"

8:36 Or *your self?* also in 8:37. 9:5 Greek *three tabernacles.* 9:9 "Son of Man" is a title Jesus used for himself. 9:11 Greek *that Elijah must come first?* 9:18 Or *becomes weak.* 9:19 Or *said to his disciples.* 9:25 Greek *unclean.*

8:34 turn from his selfish ways, take up his cross, and follow me. These words would certainly have special meaning to those in the situation faced by the original recipients of the gospel.

8:38 ashamed of me. This would be indicated by failing to persist in one's Christian testimony in times of persecution.

9:2 Six days later. By this phrase Mark connects the Transfiguration with Jesus' prediction that "some who are standing here will not taste death before they see the kingdom of God come with power" (9:1).

9:4 The presence of both Moses and Elijah on the mountain is meant to indicate that the Old Testament law and the prophets endorse Jesus as God's appointed Messiah.

9:5 shelters. Peter might have had in mind the huts of intertwined branches which were put up at the Festival of Tabernacles to commemorate Israel's time in the wilderness. Or he might be thinking of the "Tent of Meeting" where God met with Moses.

9:6 terrified. Throughout the Bible, whenever God is manifested before people the human response is one of fear (Ex. 3:5-6; Judg. 6:20-23; Isa. 6:5; Dan. 10:7-8; Rev. 1:17).

9:11 Elijah must return before the Messiah comes? The Jews believed God would send Elijah back before the Messiah appeared to again call Israel to faithfulness (Mal. 4:5).

9:18 The symptoms closely resemble those of a certain form of epilepsy.

9:19 faithless people! This is the cry of anguish and loneliness of one who knows so clearly the way things really are and yet is constantly confronted with disbelief in various forms.

9:23 If I can? The question is not whether Jesus has the ability to heal (which has been amply demonstrated); the issue is the man's faith.

HELP MY UNBELIEF

1. What was something you did as a child that drove your parents crazy?

MARK 9:14-29

2. Why did Jesus say "bring the boy to me" (v. 19) when His disciples had failed to heal the boy?
3. Why did Jesus challenge the father who had said, "help us, if you can" (vv. 22-23)? What did the father's wording show about his lack of faith?
4. How did the father overcome his lack of faith? How can Jesus help you overcome your own lack of faith?

25 When Jesus saw that the crowd of onlookers was
growing, he rebuked the evil* spirit. "Listen, you spir-
it that makes this boy unable to hear and speak," he
said. "I command you to come out of this child and
never enter him again!"
26 Then the spirit screamed and threw the boy into
another violent convulsion and left him. The boy ap-
peared to be dead. A murmur ran through the crowd
as people said, "He's dead." 27 But Jesus took him by the
hand and helped him to his feet, and he stood up.
28 Afterward, when Jesus was alone in the house
with his disciples, they asked him, "Why couldn't we
cast out that evil spirit?"
29 Jesus replied, "This kind can be cast out only by
prayer.*"

JESUS AGAIN PREDICTS HIS DEATH

30 Leaving that region, they traveled through Galilee.
Jesus didn't want anyone to know he was there, 31 for
he wanted to spend more time with his disciples and
teach them. He said to them, "The Son of Man is going
to be betrayed into the hands of his enemies. He will be
killed, but three days later he will rise from the dead."
32 They didn't understand what he was saying, howev-
er, and they were afraid to ask him what he meant.

THE GREATEST IN THE KINGDOM

33 After they arrived at Capernaum and settled in a
house, Jesus asked his disciples, "What were you dis-
cussing out on the road?" 34 But they didn't answer,
because they had been arguing about which of them
was the greatest. 35 He sat down, called the twelve
disciples over to him, and said, "Whoever wants to be
first must take last place and be the servant of every-
one else."
36 Then he put a little child among them. Taking the
child in his arms, he said to them, 37 "Anyone who wel-
comes a little child like this on my behalf* welcomes
me, and anyone who welcomes me welcomes not only
me but also my Father who sent me."

USING THE NAME OF JESUS

38 John said to Jesus, "Teacher, we saw someone using
your name to cast out demons, but we told him to stop
because he wasn't in our group."
39 "Don't stop him!" Jesus said. "No one who per-
forms a miracle in my name will soon be able to speak
evil of me. 40 Anyone who is not against us is for us.
41 If anyone gives you even a cup of water because you
belong to the Messiah, I tell you the truth, that person
will surely be rewarded.
42 "But if you cause one of these little ones who
trusts in me to fall into sin, it would be better for
you to be thrown into the sea with a large millstone
hung around your neck. 43 If your hand causes you to
sin, cut it off. It's better to enter eternal life with only
one hand than to go into the unquenchable fires of
hell* with two hands.* 45 If your foot causes you to
sin, cut it off. It's better to enter eternal life with only
one foot than to be thrown into hell with two feet.*
47 And if your eye causes you to sin, gouge it out. It's
better to enter the Kingdom of God with only one
eye than to have two eyes and be thrown into hell,
48 'where the maggots never die and the fire never
goes out.'*
49 "For everyone will be tested with fire.* 50 Salt is
good for seasoning. But if it loses its flavor, how do
you make it salty again? You must have the qualities
of salt among yourselves and live in peace with each
other."

DISCUSSION ABOUT DIVORCE AND MARRIAGE

10 Then Jesus left Capernaum and went down to
the region of Judea and into the area east of the
Jordan River. Once again crowds gathered around
him, and as usual he was teaching them.

9:29 Some manuscripts read *by prayer and fasting.* 9:37 Greek *in my name.* 9:43a Greek *Gehenna;* also in 9:45, 47. 9:43b Some manuscripts add verse 44, *'where the maggots never die and the fire never goes out.'* See 9:48. 9:45 Some manuscripts add verse 46, *'where the maggots never die and the fire never goes out.'* See 9:48. 9:48 Isa 66:24. 9:49 Greek *salted with fire;* other manuscripts add *and every sacrifice will be salted with salt.*

9:24 unbelief. The problem here is one of *doubt* (being of two minds about an issue) not one of *disbelief* (certainty that something is not true). The father did not disbelieve. After all, he had brought his son to Jesus to be healed (v. 17). His faith has been shaken by the failure of the disciples to heal his son (v. 18) so that now, even though he desperately wants his child to be free of this demon, he wonders if it is possible (v. 22).

9:29 prayer. The disciples have been given the authority to cast out demons (6:7) and have, in fact, done so (6:13). However, as this incident makes clear, this power was not their own. It required continuing dependence upon God.

9:30 they traveled through Galilee. They leave Herod Philip's territory, but they do not return to Galilee as they have done in the past. Instead, they pass through enroute to Jerusalem and Jesus' death.

9:31 betrayed. This is a new note in His teaching. It is not just that He will be rejected by the leaders of Israel. There will be an element of treachery involved.

9:34 greatest. Once again the disciples have missed the point. In the face of Jesus' teaching about suffering and death, they are concerned about their position and personal power.

9:42 fall into sin. Literally, something which snares a person or animal, causing them to trip up or enticing them to stray. **these little ones who trust in me.** The reference is to Jesus' followers (v. 37). **a large millstone.** There are two words for millstone. One refers to a small hand mill used in a home; the other (which Jesus uses here) refers to the huge upper stone of a community mill, so big that it had to be drawn around by a donkey. **the sea.** Jews were terrified of the sea.

9:43 life. Spiritual life; life in the kingdom of God (v. 47). **hell.** Literally, Gehenna—a ravine outside Jerusalem where children were once sacrificed and garbage was burned during the time of Jesus.

9:50 Salt. Salt does not normally lose its taste, but salt from the Dead Sea was mixed with impurities and over time could acquire a stale taste. **live in peace with each other.** When His followers have a sense of service, peace is the outcome. Had the disciples grasped this concept of servanthood instead of opting for power and greatness, they would not have been arguing on the road (v. 33).

10:1 left Capernaum. He begins His journey to Jerusalem in Capernaum (9:33), the place where His ministry began in the Gospel of Mark (1:16-45). **Judea.** A Roman province in the south of Palestine, similar in size and location to the land of Judah in the Old Testament. **east of the Jordan River.** This is a reference to a specific region called Perea, which was a narrow corridor on the east side of the Jordan. Pious Jews would cross over the Jordan into Perea to avoid traveling through Samaria. This is the territory of Herod Antipas, the ruler who beheaded John the Baptist.

2 Some Pharisees came and tried to trap him with
this question: "Should a man be allowed to divorce his
wife?"
3 Jesus answered them with a question: "What did
Moses say in the law about divorce?"
4 "Well, he permitted it," they replied. "He said a
man can give his wife a written notice of divorce and
send her away."*
5 But Jesus responded, "He wrote this commandment
only as a concession to your hard hearts. 6 But 'God
made them male and female'* from the beginning of
creation. 7 'This explains why a man leaves his father
and mother and is joined to his wife,* 8 and the two are
united into one.'* Since they are no longer two but one,
9 let no one split apart what God has joined together."
10 Later, when he was alone with his disciples in
the house, they brought up the subject again. 11 He
told them, "Whoever divorces his wife and marries
someone else commits adultery against her. 12 And if
a woman divorces her husband and marries someone
else, she commits adultery."

JESUS BLESSES THE CHILDREN

13 One day some parents brought their children to
Jesus so he could touch and bless them. But the disci-
ples scolded the parents for bothering him.
14 When Jesus saw what was happening, he was an-
gry with his disciples. He said to them, "Let the chil-
dren come to me. Don't stop them! For the Kingdom
of God belongs to those who are like these children.
15 I tell you the truth, anyone who doesn't receive
the Kingdom of God like a child will never enter it."
16 Then he took the children in his arms and placed his
hands on their heads and blessed them.

THE RICH MAN

17 As Jesus was starting out on his way to Jerusalem, a
man came running up to him, knelt down, and asked,
"Good Teacher, what must I do to inherit eternal life?"
18 "Why do you call me good?" Jesus asked. "Only
God is truly good. 19 But to answer your question, you
know the commandments: 'You must not murder. You
must not commit adultery. You must not steal. You
must not testify falsely. You must not cheat anyone.
Honor your father and mother.'*"

PERILOUS POSSESSIONS

1. What is the most valuable thing you own?

MARK 10:17-31

2. If God asked you to give up all your possessions and be a missionary in a distant land, what would you say?
3. Why is it so hard (v. 23) for a rich man to enter the kingdom of heaven?
4. What things in life can make it hard for people to serve God? What things in your life hinder you?
5. If Jesus said to you, "There is still one thing you haven't done" (v. 21), what would be that one thing?

20 "Teacher," the man replied, "I've obeyed all these
commandments since I was young."
21 Looking at the man, Jesus felt genuine love for
him. "There is still one thing you haven't done," he
told him. "Go and sell all your possessions and give
the money to the poor, and you will have treasure in
heaven. Then come, follow me."
22 At this the man's face fell, and he went away sad,
for he had many possessions.
23 Jesus looked around and said to his disciples,
"How hard it is for the rich to enter the Kingdom of
God!" 24 This amazed them. But Jesus said again, "Dear
children, it is very hard* to enter the Kingdom of God.
25 In fact, it is easier for a camel to go through the eye
of a needle than for a rich person to enter the King-
dom of God!"
26 The disciples were astounded. "Then who in the
world can be saved?" they asked.
27 Jesus looked at them intently and said, "Humanly
speaking, it is impossible. But not with God. Every-
thing is possible with God."
28 Then Peter began to speak up. "We've given up
everything to follow you," he said.
29 "Yes," Jesus replied, "and I assure you that every-
one who has given up house or brothers or sisters or

10:4 See Deut 24:1. **10:6** Gen 1:27; 5:2. **10:7** Some manuscripts do not include *and is joined to his wife.* **10:7-8** Gen 2:24. **10:19** Exod 20:12-16; Deut 5:16-20. **10:24** Some manuscripts read *very hard for those who trust in riches.*

10:2 trap him. It is not by chance that the Pharisees question Jesus about divorce. It was this issue that led to John the Baptist's death (6:17-28). If Jesus responded that divorce was lawful, then the leaders could criticize Him as being in opposition to John the Baptist whom the people greatly respected for his courage in opposing Herod's sin. If Jesus said it was not lawful, then the leaders might be able to get Herod to arrest Him as well. **divorce.** All the Jewish parties agreed (on the basis of Deut. 24:1) that divorce was allowed. The issue in this debate concerned the grounds on which such divorce was permissible. It was only the husband who had the right of divorce. The most that a wife could do was to ask her husband to divorce her.

10:4 written notice of divorce. These were issued to the woman as a form of protection, verifying her release from marriage and giving her the right to remarry.

10:11 commits adultery against her. In the Jewish law of that era, adultery was considered to be an offense against the man. Jesus asserts the responsibility of the husband to be faithful to his wife under God's command.

10:13 children. The age is uncertain. The term was used to describe infants and children up to 12 years old. **disciples scolded the parents.** The demands on Jesus were ceaseless. The disciples wanted to protect Him, and so in an era when children were expected to be kept in the background, it was not unreasonable that they would attempt to curb this particular demand.

10:14 the Kingdom of God belongs to those who are like these children. Jesus says this humble inner disposition of soul must be evident in members of his kingdom.

10:20 obeyed all these commandments since I was young. The man believes he has kept the commandments, and yet he is unsure whether he has gained eternal life. This was the fallacy of a system based on works/righteousness. People were struggling to be counted among the righteous until the judgment (and then it was too late). There was no hope for all failed.

10:21 genuine love for him. Mark is the only Gospel to note Jesus' affection for this earnest and sincere young man. **Go and sell all your possessions.** It was felt in the Old Testament that riches by themselves were no hindrance to spiritual pursuit. But Jesus points out that accumulation of wealth can hinder participation in God's kingdom. **follow me.** The weight of emphasis is not on selling all but on following Jesus. The man's possessions are in the way of his discipleship to Jesus.

10:24 amazed. The disciples are astonished because traditional Jewish wisdom saw wealth as a sign of God's favor; it was thought to be a verification that one had led a godly life (Job 1:10; 42:10; Ps. 128:1-2).

10:26 Then who in the world can be saved? They realize the radical nature of Jesus' statement and wonder about their own fate. If it is difficult for anyone to enter the kingdom, even the rich who they had always assumed were favored by God, then what chance do they have?

mother or father or children or property, for my sake and for the Good News, 30 will receive now in return a hundred times as many houses, brothers, sisters, mothers, children, and property—along with persecution. And in the world to come that person will have eternal life. 31 But many who are the greatest now will be least important then, and those who seem least important now will be the greatest then.*"

JESUS AGAIN PREDICTS HIS DEATH

32 They were now on the way up to Jerusalem, and Jesus was walking ahead of them. The disciples were filled with awe, and the people following behind were overwhelmed with fear. Taking the twelve disciples aside, Jesus once more began to describe everything that was about to happen to him. 33 "Listen," he said, "we're going up to Jerusalem, where the Son of Man* will be betrayed to the leading priests and the teachers of religious law. They will sentence him to die and hand him over to the Romans.* 34 They will mock him, spit on him, flog him with a whip, and kill him, but after three days he will rise again."

JESUS TEACHES ABOUT SERVING OTHERS

35 Then James and John, the sons of Zebedee, came over and spoke to him. "Teacher," they said, "we want you to do us a favor."

36 "What is your request?" he asked.

37 They replied, "When you sit on your glorious throne, we want to sit in places of honor next to you, one on your right and the other on your left."

38 But Jesus said to them, "You don't know what you are asking! Are you able to drink from the bitter cup of suffering I am about to drink? Are you able to be baptized with the baptism of suffering I must be baptized with?"

39 "Oh yes," they replied, "we are able!"

Then Jesus told them, "You will indeed drink from my bitter cup and be baptized with my baptism of suffering. 40 But I have no right to say who will sit on my right or my left. God has prepared those places for the ones he has chosen."

41 When the ten other disciples heard what James and John had asked, they were indignant. 42 So Jesus called them together and said, "You know that the rulers in this world lord it over their people, and officials flaunt their authority over those under them. 43 But among you it will be different. Whoever wants to be a leader among you must be your servant, 44 and whoever wants to be first among you must be the slave of everyone else. 45 For even the Son of Man came not to be served but to serve others and to give his life as a ransom for many."

FIERCE COMPETITION

1. Who is the most competitive person in your family? Do you see competitiveness as a positive or negative quality?

MARK 10:35-45

2. What were James and John asking of Jesus? How were their priorities wrong?
3. How is Christ's teaching about how to be great (v. 43) different from what the world teaches?
4. What does it mean to be a servant to others? Do you tend most often to be a servant or the one served?
5. How can you work this week to serve others?

JESUS HEALS BLIND BARTIMAEUS

46 Then they reached Jericho, and as Jesus and his disciples left town, a large crowd followed him. A blind beggar named Bartimaeus (son of Timaeus) was sitting beside the road. 47 When Bartimaeus heard that Jesus of Nazareth was nearby, he began to shout, "Jesus, Son of David, have mercy on me!"

48 "Be quiet!" many of the people yelled at him.

But he only shouted louder, "Son of David, have mercy on me!"

49 When Jesus heard him, he stopped and said, "Tell him to come here."

So they called the blind man. "Cheer up," they said. "Come on, he's calling you!" 50 Bartimaeus threw aside his coat, jumped up, and came to Jesus.

51 "What do you want me to do for you?" Jesus asked.

"My Rabbi,*" the blind man said, "I want to see!"

52 And Jesus said to him, "Go, for your faith has healed you." Instantly the man could see, and he followed Jesus down the road.*

10:31 Greek *But many who are first will be last; and the last, first.* **10:33a** "Son of Man" is a title Jesus used for himself. **10:33b** Greek *the Gentiles.* **10:51** Greek uses the Hebrew term *Rabboni.* **10:52** Or *on the way.*

10:32 Jerusalem. Jesus' destination is now revealed, as is the site of His betrayal, death, and resurrection (v. 33). **awe . . . fear.** Given the increasingly hostile response toward Jesus by the leaders, it was frightening that Jesus headed directly into a confrontation with them.

10:37 They interpret Jesus' heading toward Jerusalem as a sign that He will initiate His new kingdom in Jerusalem, over which He will rule as the new king of Israel.

10:38 drink from the bitter cup. This is a phrase which means "share the same fate." In the Old Testament, the cup is a metaphor for wrath (Ps. 75:8; Isa. 51: 17-22). **baptized.** In the Old Testament, the image of a deluge or flood overwhelming one is used as a metaphor for disaster (Ps. 42:7; Isa. 43:2). Both the cup and the baptism refer to Jesus' suffering and death for the sins of the world.

10:39 we are able! The disciples answer too readily Jesus' question as to whether they can share His cup and His baptism. They do not grasp what He means by this question, thinking perhaps that it is referring to being in fellowship with Him. Their leadership will not be expressed through positions of authority but through suffering and death.

10:43 servant. Rather than become masters (and exercise authority), they are to become servants (and meet the needs of others).

10:45 ransom. In the first century, a slave or a prisoner could gain freedom if a purchase price (ransom) was paid. Jesus would pay the ransom price "for many" by His death (Titus 2:14; 1 Pet. 1:18-19).

10:46 Jericho. They've almost completed their journey from Galilee. Jericho is a city some 18 miles east of Jerusalem and is the place where travelers recrossed the Jordan back into Israel. **a large crowd.** These were pilgrims on their way to Jerusalem for the Passover Feast. Every male over 12 years of age was expected to attend.

10:47 Jesus, Son of David. A debate was going on as to who the Messiah would be. Would he come from the tribe of Levi, or was he a king in the line of David? Clearly this is a messianic title by which Bartimaeus hails Jesus. Interestingly, Jesus does not silence him as He has done so often in the past when His identity is revealed. The time for secrecy is past. He accepts the title. This is the only use in Mark of this title, on the eve of Jesus' entry into Jerusalem as messianic King.

10:52 Your faith has healed you. Bartimaeus demonstrated his faith in several ways: by his title for Jesus (showing he grasped who Jesus was), by his persistence (he will not let this opportunity go by), and by his request for healing (showing that he believed Jesus could do so).

JESUS' TRIUMPHANT ENTRY

11 As Jesus and his disciples approached Jerusalem,
they came to the towns of Bethphage and Betha-
ny on the Mount of Olives. Jesus sent two of them on
ahead. 2 "Go into that village over there," he told them.
"As soon as you enter it, you will see a young donkey
tied there that no one has ever ridden. Untie it and
bring it here. 3 If anyone asks, 'What are you doing?'
just say, 'The Lord needs it and will return it soon.'"
4 The two disciples left and found the colt standing
in the street, tied outside the front door. 5 As they were
untying it, some bystanders demanded, "What are
you doing, untying that colt?" 6 They said what Jesus
had told them to say, and they were permitted to take
it. 7 Then they brought the colt to Jesus and threw
their garments over it, and he sat on it.
8 Many in the crowd spread their garments on the
road ahead of him, and others spread leafy branches
they had cut in the fields. 9 Jesus was in the center of
the procession, and the people all around him were
shouting,

"Praise God!*
Blessings on the one who comes in the name of
the LORD!
10 Blessings on the coming Kingdom of our ancestor
David!
Praise God in highest heaven!"*

11 So Jesus came to Jerusalem and went into the
Temple. After looking around carefully at everything,
he left because it was late in the afternoon. Then he
returned to Bethany with the twelve disciples.

JESUS CURSES THE FIG TREE

12 The next morning as they were leaving Bethany,
Jesus was hungry. 13 He noticed a fig tree in full leaf
a little way off, so he went over to see if he could find
any figs. But there were only leaves because it was
too early in the season for fruit. 14 Then Jesus said to
the tree, "May no one ever eat your fruit again!" And
the disciples heard him say it.

JESUS CLEARS THE TEMPLE

15 When they arrived back in Jerusalem, Jesus entered
the Temple and began to drive out the people buying
and selling animals for sacrifices. He knocked over

TAKING A STAND

1. What does it take to get you to clean your room? How clean is it right now?

MARK 11:12-19

2. In what way had the temple area been made into "a den of thieves" (v. 17)?
3. Why did Jesus get so angry about it? Why did He react so violently?
4. If Jesus came to your town today, what might make Him react in anger?
5. Where do you need to take a righteous stand? How can you go about this?

the tables of the money changers and the chairs of
those selling doves, 16 and he stopped everyone from
using the Temple as a marketplace.* 17 He said to them,
"The Scriptures declare, 'My Temple will be called a
house of prayer for all nations,' but you have turned it
into a den of thieves.'"*
18 When the leading priests and teachers of reli-
gious law heard what Jesus had done, they began
planning how to kill him. But they were afraid of him
because the people were so amazed at his teaching.
19 That evening Jesus and the disciples left* the city.
20 The next morning as they passed by the fig tree
he had cursed, the disciples noticed it had withered
from the roots up. 21 Peter remembered what Jesus
had said to the tree on the previous day and ex-
claimed, "Look, Rabbi! The fig tree you cursed has
withered and died!"
22 Then Jesus said to the disciples, "Have faith in
God. 23 I tell you the truth, you can say to this moun-
tain, 'May you be lifted up and thrown into the sea,'
and it will happen. But you must really believe it will
happen and have no doubt in your heart. 24 I tell you,
you can pray for anything, and if you believe that
you've received it, it will be yours. 25 But when you
are praying, first forgive anyone you are holding a
grudge against, so that your Father in heaven will
forgive your sins, too."*

11:9 Greek *Hosanna*, an exclamation of praise that literally means "save now"; also in 11:10. **11:9-10** Pss 118:25-26; 148:1. **11:16** Or *from carrying merchandise through the Temple.* **11:17** Isa 56:7; Jer 7:11. **11:19** Greek *they left;* other manuscripts read *he left.* **11:25** Some manuscripts add verse 26, *But if you refuse to forgive, your Father in heaven will not forgive your sins.* Compare Matt 6:15.

11:2 a young donkey. According to Zechariah 9:9, the King would come riding on a colt. Jesus will not simply enter Jerusalem. He will come as the messianic King. He will not come as a warrior-king (as the people expected) riding a war horse. Matthew 21:2 states this was a donkey, specifically fulfilling Zechariah's prophecy and emphasizing the peaceful, gentle nature of the Messiah.
11:8 spread their garments. This was a gesture of respect, given to kings (2 Kin. 9:12-13).
11:9 Praise God! Literally, "Save now." **Blessings on the one.** While the psalm from which this cry is taken (Ps. 118:26) originally served as a tribute to the king of Israel, it was applied to any pilgrim who traveled to Jerusalem for the feasts. It was later understood by the rabbis to be a messianic psalm, referring to the final redemption that would be ushered in by the Messiah.
11:11 Temple. This was the third temple to be built on Mount Zion. It was built by Herod the Great in 20 B.C. and was a magnificent structure covering some 30 acres. The temple consisted of four concentric courts ringed by enormous walls.
11:13 fig tree. On the Mount of Olives, fig trees are in leaf by early April, but they would not have ripe fruit until June, long after the Passover. Fig trees were a common prophetic symbol. They were associated with Israel and with judgment (Jer. 8:13; Hos. 9:10-11; Mic. 7:1).
11:15 buying and selling. Worship in the temple centered on sacrifice. Those wishing to participate were required to offer an unblemished animal, and apparently temple inspectors approved only those animals bought from certified vendors (who sold animals at a huge markup). **money changers.** At Passover, each Jew was required to pay a temple tax of one-half shekel (nearly two days' wages). No other currency was acceptable, necessitating money changers to exchange the money of pilgrims coming from outside. The money changers charged exorbitant amounts for the simple act of exchanging currency, up to one-half day's wages of working people. **those selling doves.** A dove was the lowliest of all sacrifices. While a lamb was normally required, the law had a provision that those too poor to afford a lamb could offer two doves instead (Lev. 5:7). While this provision was still observed, temple vendors charged 20 times what it cost to buy a dove outside the temple.
11:17 a house of prayer for all nations. The outermost area of the temple where all these activities were taking place was called the Court of the Gentiles. It was intended to be a place where pious Gentiles could pray.
11:23 this mountain. This is probably the Mount of Olives overlooking Jerusalem. **the sea.** The Dead Sea is visible from the Mount of Olives.

THE AUTHORITY OF JESUS CHALLENGED

27 Again they entered Jerusalem. As Jesus was walking through the Temple area, the leading priests, the teachers of religious law, and the elders came up to him.
28 They demanded, "By what authority are you doing all these things? Who gave you the right to do them?"

29 "I'll tell you by what authority I do these things if you answer one question," Jesus replied. 30 "Did John's authority to baptize come from heaven, or was it merely human? Answer me!"

31 They talked it over among themselves. "If we say it was from heaven, he will ask why we didn't believe John. 32 But do we dare say it was merely human?" For they were afraid of what the people would do, because everyone believed that John was a prophet.
33 So they finally replied, "We don't know."

And Jesus responded, "Then I won't tell you by what authority I do these things."

PARABLE OF THE EVIL FARMERS

12 Then Jesus began teaching them with stories: "A man planted a vineyard. He built a wall around it, dug a pit for pressing out the grape juice, and built a lookout tower. Then he leased the vineyard to tenant farmers and moved to another country. 2 At the time of the grape harvest, he sent one of his servants to collect his share of the crop. 3 But the farmers grabbed the servant, beat him up, and sent him back empty-handed. 4 The owner then sent another servant, but they insulted him and beat him over the head. 5 The next servant he sent was killed. Others he sent were either beaten or killed, 6 until there was only one left—his son whom he loved dearly. The owner finally sent him, thinking, 'Surely they will respect my son.'

7 "But the tenant farmers said to one another, 'Here comes the heir to this estate. Let's kill him and get the estate for ourselves!' 8 So they grabbed him and murdered him and threw his body out of the vineyard.

9 "What do you suppose the owner of the vineyard will do?" Jesus asked. "I'll tell you—he will come and kill those farmers and lease the vineyard to others.
10 Didn't you ever read this in the Scriptures?

'The stone that the builders rejected
has now become the cornerstone.
11 This is the LORD's doing,
and it is wonderful to see.'*"

12 The religious leaders* wanted to arrest Jesus because they realized he was telling the story against them—they were the wicked farmers. But they were afraid of the crowd, so they left him and went away.

TAXES FOR CAESAR

13 Later the leaders sent some Pharisees and supporters of Herod to trap Jesus into saying something for which he could be arrested. 14 "Teacher," they said, "we know how honest you are. You are impartial and don't play favorites. You teach the way of God truthfully. Now tell us—is it right to pay taxes to Caesar or not? 15 Should we pay them, or shouldn't we?"

Jesus saw through their hypocrisy and said, "Why are you trying to trap me? Show me a Roman coin,* and I'll tell you." 16 When they handed it to him, he asked, "Whose picture and title are stamped on it?"

"Caesar's," they replied.

17 "Well, then," Jesus said, "give to Caesar what belongs to Caesar, and give to God what belongs to God."

His reply completely amazed them.

MONEY MATTERS

1. Whose picture appears on a five-dollar bill? Ten? Twenty? Fifty? Hundred?

MARK 12:13-17

2. How were the Pharisees trying to trap Jesus with their questions about paying taxes?
3. What did Jesus mean when he said, "give to Caesar what belongs to Caesar, and give to God what belongs to God" (v. 17)?
4. Who is Caesar today? What things belong to "Caesar"? What things belong to God?
5. What do you need to give to God? Are you doing this?

DISCUSSION ABOUT RESURRECTION

18 Then Jesus was approached by some Sadducees—religious leaders who say there is no resurrection from the dead. They posed this question: 19 "Teacher,

12:10-11 Ps 118:22-23. 12:12 Greek *They.* 12:15 Greek *a denarius.* 12:19 See Deut 25:5-6.

11:27 the leading priests, the teachers of religious law, and the elders. The chief priests were the key officers of the temple, just below the high priest in rank. The elders were powerful and (reputedly) wise leaders of Israel. They were generally not priests but instead were administrators, judges, and military leaders of Israel. The teachers of the law were religious lawyers. Taken together, these three groups comprised the Sanhedrin—the ruling Jewish council—who opposed Him as Jesus prophesied they would (8:31).

12:1 A man planted a vineyard . . . dug a pit . . . built a lookout tower. For the religious leaders, Jesus' use of these phrases would surely call to mind the well-known imagery found in a poem originally delivered by the prophet Isaiah centuries before (Isa. 5:1-7). In Isaiah's song, the symbol of the vineyard was used to describe Israel. Although planted and cultivated by God, Israel was compared to a vineyard that produced only bad fruit. In this parable God is the landlord who leaves his vineyard in the care of others who are responsible to Him. It produces fruit, but the tenants refuse to give Him His share of the produce.

12:6 a son . . . loved dearly. The crowd didn't know the identity of the Son, yet Mark's readers know that it is Jesus. A central theme in chapters 11–16 is the discovery that Jesus is the Son of God.

12:10 cornerstone. The reference is to a stone that was rejected in the building of Solomon's temple, which was later found to be the keystone to the porch (a keystone held an arch in place).

12:13-17 to trap Jesus. Beaten badly in their first two confrontations with Jesus, the leaders regroup and consider their strategy. They decide to send representatives from two groups with a trick question they hope will trap Jesus. The question deals with the explosive issue of taxes.

12:13 Pharisees and supporters of Herod. The origin of this unusual alliance is described in 3:1-6. The plan to destroy Jesus had now matured and was gaining momentum in Jerusalem.

12:14 honest you are. By these and other flattering words they hoped to catch Jesus off guard. **taxes.** A poll tax had to be paid to the Romans each year by all adult Jews. This tax was deeply resented.

12:15 Show me a Roman coin. A denarius was a small, silver coin (worth about 25 cents today) bearing the picture of Tiberius Caesar. The denarius was the only coin that could be used to pay the poll tax.

12:18 Sadducees. There is relatively little information available about this group. It seems they were a small but highly influential party of wealthy, aristocratic priests. Jesus had been no threat to the Sadducees. However, when He cleared the temple, He invaded their sphere of influence and so became their enemy. **resurrection.** The belief that at the end of the age God would bring the dead back to life for judgment. The Sadducees did not accept this belief.

Moses gave us a law that if a man dies, leaving a wife
without children, his brother should marry the wid-
ow and have a child who will carry on the brother's
name.* 20 Well, suppose there were seven brothers.
The oldest one married and then died without chil-
dren. 21 So the second brother married the widow, but
he also died without children. Then the third brother
married her. 22 This continued with all seven of them,
and still there were no children. Last of all, the wom-
an also died. 23 So tell us, whose wife will she be in the
resurrection? For all seven were married to her."
24 Jesus replied, "Your mistake is that you don't
know the Scriptures, and you don't know the power
of God. 25 For when the dead rise, they will neither
marry nor be given in marriage. In this respect they
will be like the angels in heaven.
26 "But now, as to whether the dead will be raised—
haven't you ever read about this in the writings of
Moses, in the story of the burning bush? Long after
Abraham, Isaac, and Jacob had died, God said to
Moses,* 'I am the God of Abraham, the God of Isaac,
and the God of Jacob.'* 27 So he is the God of the living,
not the dead. You have made a serious error."

THE MOST IMPORTANT COMMANDMENT

28 One of the teachers of religious law was standing
there listening to the debate. He realized that Jesus
had answered well, so he asked, "Of all the command-
ments, which is the most important?"
29 Jesus replied, "The most important command-
ment is this: 'Listen, O Israel! The LORD our God is the
one and only LORD. 30 And you must love the LORD
your God with all your heart, all your soul, all your
mind, and all your strength.'* 31 The second is equally
important: 'Love your neighbor as yourself.'* No other
commandment is greater than these."
32 The teacher of religious law replied, "Well said,
Teacher. You have spoken the truth by saying that
there is only one God and no other. 33 And I know it
is important to love him with all my heart and all my
understanding and all my strength, and to love my
neighbor as myself. This is more important than to
offer all of the burnt offerings and sacrifices required
in the law."
34 Realizing how much the man understood, Jesus
said to him, "You are not far from the Kingdom of
God." And after that, no one dared to ask him any
more questions.

WHOSE SON IS THE MESSIAH?

35 Later, as Jesus was teaching the people in the Tem-
ple, he asked, "Why do the teachers of religious law
claim that the Messiah is the son of David? 36 For Da-
vid himself, speaking under the inspiration of the
Holy Spirit, said,

'The LORD said to my Lord,
Sit in the place of honor at my right hand
until I humble your enemies beneath your feet.'*

37 Since David himself called the Messiah 'my Lord,'
how can the Messiah be his son?" The large crowd
listened to him with great delight.
38 Jesus also taught: "Beware of these teachers of re-
ligious law! For they like to parade around in flowing
robes and receive respectful greetings as they walk
in the marketplaces. 39 And how they love the seats of
honor in the synagogues and the head table at ban-
quets. 40 Yet they shamelessly cheat widows out of
their property and then pretend to be pious by mak-
ing long prayers in public. Because of this, they will
be more severely punished."

THE WIDOW'S OFFERING

41 Jesus sat down near the collection box in the Temple
and watched as the crowds dropped in their money.
Many rich people put in large amounts. 42 Then a poor
widow came and dropped in two small coins.*

MEANINGFUL GIVING

1. What is your most priceless possession? What makes it so special?

MARK 12:41-44

2. What did Jesus mean that this poor widow had given more than all the others (v. 43)?
3. What did Jesus mean that other people had given "part of their surplus" (v. 44)?
4. Do you give to God out of your surplus or out of your poverty?
5. If you really get serious about God, what will have to change in the way you spend your money? Your time?

12:26a Greek *in the story of the bush? God said to him.* 12:26b Exod 3:6. 12:29-30 Deut 6:4-5. 12:31 Lev 19:18. 12:36 Ps 110:1.
12:42 Greek *two lepta, which is a kodrantes* [i.e., a quadrans].

12:24-27 Jesus replied. Jesus takes their question seriously (although it is not a sincere question, since they did not believe in the resurrection) and answers them directly. In so doing, He affirms that life after death is real.

12:28 One of the teachers of religious law. Jesus has answered successfully the Herodians, the Pharisees, and the Sadducees. It is now a scribe's turn to ask a question. His attitude toward Jesus is different from the others. He asks a genuine question. **realized that Jesus had answered well.** This teacher of the law is very impressed with the way Jesus answered the questions, so he asks an important question for Him personally. **Of all the commandments, which is the most important?** This phrase is, literally, "which is the chief (or first) commandment" (i.e., what commandment summarizes all the commandments?).

12:29 Listen, O Israel!. The Shema (a statement of faith taken from Deut. 6:4) is recited by pious Jews each morning and evening. This affirmation captures what was clearly distinctive about Israel's God.

12:30 love. In Greek, this is *agape*. It means an active, benevolent giving to others without expectation of reward. **heart.** The inner life; the center of personality; where God reveals Himself to a person. **soul.** The seat of life itself; the personality or ego. **mind.** The organ of knowledge; the intellect. **strength.** The power of a living being; the total effort behind heart, soul, and mind.

12:38 flowing robes. Long, white linen garments fringed with tassels that touched the ground. In such a stately garment, a person could not run or work and would be reckoned to be one of leisure and importance. **respectful greetings.** People considered the teachers of the law to be men of great insight and authority, and so they rose when they passed by and called out titles of respect.

12:39 the seats of honor in the synagogues. The choice seat was up front, with its back to the box which contained the sacred Scriptures and its front facing the congregation so that all would see who sat there.

12:40 they shamelessly cheat widows out of their property. Since the teachers of the law were forbidden to receive pay for their teaching, they lived off others, including, it seems, poor widows who were little able to support them.

12:41 collection box in the Temple. This was located in the court of women (which was the first of the inner courts of the temple). It consisted of 13 trumpet-shaped receptacles used to collect donations for the temple.

43 Jesus called his disciples to him and said, "I tell
you the truth, this poor widow has given more than
all the others who are making contributions. 44 For
they gave a tiny part of their surplus, but she, poor as
she is, has given everything she had to live on."

JESUS FORETELLS THE FUTURE

13 As Jesus was leaving the Temple that day, one of
his disciples said, "Teacher, look at these magnif-
icent buildings! Look at the impressive stones in the
walls."
2 Jesus replied, "Yes, look at these great buildings.
But they will be completely demolished. Not one
stone will be left on top of another!"
3 Later, Jesus sat on the Mount of Olives across the
valley from the Temple. Peter, James, John, and An-
drew came to him privately and asked him, 4 "Tell us,
when will all this happen? What sign will show us
that these things are about to be fulfilled?"
5 Jesus replied, "Don't let anyone mislead you, 6 for
many will come in my name, claiming, 'I am the Mes-
siah.'* They will deceive many. 7 And you will hear of
wars and threats of wars, but don't panic. Yes, these
things must take place, but the end won't follow im-
mediately. 8 Nation will go to war against nation, and
kingdom against kingdom. There will be earthquakes
in many parts of the world, as well as famines. But
this is only the first of the birth pains, with more to
come.
9 "When these things begin to happen, watch out!
You will be handed over to the local councils and
beaten in the synagogues. You will stand trial before
governors and kings because you are my followers.
But this will be your opportunity to tell them about
me.* 10 For the Good News must first be preached to
all nations.* 11 But when you are arrested and stand
trial, don't worry in advance about what to say. Just
say what God tells you at that time, for it is not you
who will be speaking, but the Holy Spirit.
12 "A brother will betray his brother to death, a fa-
ther will betray his own child, and children will reb-
el against their parents and cause them to be killed.
13 And everyone will hate you because you are my
followers.* But the one who endures to the end will
be saved.
14 "The day is coming when you will see the sacrile-
gious object that causes desecration* standing where
he* should not be." (Reader, pay attention!) "Then
those in Judea must flee to the hills. 15 A person out on
the deck of a roof must not go down into the house to
pack. 16 A person out in the field must not return even
to get a coat. 17 How terrible it will be for pregnant
women and for nursing mothers in those days. 18 And
pray that your flight will not be in winter. 19 For there
will be greater anguish in those days than at any time
since God created the world. And it will never be so
great again. 20 In fact, unless the Lord shortens that
time of calamity, not a single person will survive. But
for the sake of his chosen ones he has shortened those
days.
21 "Then if anyone tells you, 'Look, here is the Messi-
ah,' or 'There he is,' don't believe it. 22 For false messi-
ahs and false prophets will rise up and perform signs
and wonders so as to deceive, if possible, even God's
chosen ones. 23 Watch out! I have warned you about
this ahead of time!
24 "At that time, after the anguish of those days,

the sun will be darkened,
  the moon will give no light,
25 the stars will fall from the sky,
  and the powers in the heavens will be shaken.*

26 Then everyone will see the Son of Man* coming on
the clouds with great power and glory.* 27 And he will
send out his angels to gather his chosen ones from all
over the world*—from the farthest ends of the earth
and heaven.
28 "Now learn a lesson from the fig tree. When its
branches bud and its leaves begin to sprout, you
know that summer is near. 29 In the same way, when
you see all these things taking place, you can know
that his return is very near, right at the door. 30 I tell
you the truth, this generation* will not pass from the
scene before all these things take place. 31 Heaven and
earth will disappear, but my words will never disap-
pear.
32 "However, no one knows the day or hour when
these things will happen, not even the angels in heav-
en or the Son himself. Only the Father knows. 33 And

13:6 Greek *claiming, 'I am.'* **13:9** Or *But this will be your testimony against them.* **13:10** Or *all peoples.* **13:13** Greek *on account of my name.* **13:14a** Greek *the abomination of desolation.* See Dan 9:27; 11:31; 12:11. **13:14b** Or *it.* **13:24-25** See Isa 13:10; 34:4; Joel 2:10. **13:26a** "Son of Man" is a title Jesus used for himself. **13:26b** See Dan 7:13. **13:27** Greek *from the four winds.* **13:30** Or *this age,* or *this nation.*

12:42 two small coins. The smallest coins in circulation, worth 1/400 shekel, or about 1/8 of a cent.

13:1 look at these magnificent buildings! The temple was, indeed, a wonder to behold. It was built with huge white stones, some measuring 37 feet long by 12 feet high by 18 feet wide. At a distance the temple appeared to strangers like a mountain covered with snow.

13:3-4 The disciples once again come to Jesus, privately asking Him to explain His teaching. To them, an event as cataclysmic as the temple's destruction must be one of the events that would usher in the new age (Matt. 24:3).

13:5 Don't let anyone mislead you. This is a key theme in this section (vv. 21-23,33-37). Vigilance against being deceived by those who claim that the end times have begun or claim that they are prophets is essential.

13:14 the sacrilegious object that causes desecration. This phrase appears in the book of Daniel (Dan. 9:27; 11:31; 12:11). It refers to an event so awful that Jews will flee from the temple in horror. A similar event happened in 168 B.C. when Antiochus Epiphanes, a Syrian king, captured Jerusalem. He set up an altar to Zeus in the temple and sacrificed a pig there. He also put public brothels in the temple courts. Jesus warns that when such an event occurs again, the fall of Jerusalem is imminent (2 Thess. 2:1-4). **those in Judea must flee.** When the armies march against the city, Jesus' disciples are to recognize that this is the sign that God's judgment against Israel has come to a head. Instead of flocking to the city in anticipation of a dramatic messianic victory, they must run for their lives.

13:23 I have warned you about this ahead of time! Some see the fulfillment of Jesus' words in the fall of Jerusalem in A.D. 70. Others are still looking for the "Great Tribulation" yet to come (Rev. 7:14).

13:24-27 Jesus now describes the second coming of the Son of Man in power and glory. The destruction of Jerusalem is the result of human failure and evil. It will bring suffering and hardship. The second coming will bring salvation and blessing to the people of God.

13:27 gather his chosen ones. It is God who will do this (Deut. 30:3-4; Ps. 50:4-5; Isa. 43:5-6). Jesus makes it quite clear who He is: the Son of God (vv. 26-27).

13:28 lesson from the fig tree. They knew that the fig tree only got its leaves in late spring. When the leaves came, it was a sure sign that summer was near. This is a reference to the rather mysterious cursing of the fig tree by Jesus in 11:12-14,20-21 and has to do with the judgment on Jerusalem, as Jesus' teaching here shows.

13:28-37 With all this as background (vv. 5-27), Jesus can now respond to the disciples' original question (v. 4). His response is that one event (the fall of Jerusalem) will occur within their lifetime, but they are not to be deceived. This will not usher in the end time. The final event (the second coming) will be at a future, unspecified date known only to God the Father (v. 32). Jesus encourages the disciples to be vigilant but not to worry about when all this will take place.

since you don't know when that time will come, be on guard! Stay alert*!

34 "The coming of the Son of Man can be illustrated by the story of a man going on a long trip. When he left home, he gave each of his slaves instructions about the work they were to do, and he told the gatekeeper to watch for his return. 35 You, too, must keep watch! For you don't know when the master of the household will return—in the evening, at midnight, before dawn, or at daybreak. 36 Don't let him find you sleeping when he arrives without warning. 37 I say to you what I say to everyone: Watch for him!"

JESUS ANOINTED AT BETHANY

14 It was now two days before Passover and the Festival of Unleavened Bread. The leading priests and the teachers of religious law were still looking for an opportunity to capture Jesus secretly and kill him. 2 "But not during the Passover celebration," they agreed, "or the people may riot."

3 Meanwhile, Jesus was in Bethany at the home of Simon, a man who had previously had leprosy. While he was eating,* a woman came in with a beautiful alabaster jar of expensive perfume made from essence of nard. She broke open the jar and poured the perfume over his head.

4 Some of those at the table were indignant. "Why waste such expensive perfume?" they asked. 5 "It could have been sold for a year's wages* and the money given to the poor!" So they scolded her harshly.

6 But Jesus replied, "Leave her alone. Why criticize her for doing such a good thing to me? 7 You will always have the poor among you, and you can help them whenever you want to. But you will not always have me. 8 She has done what she could and has anointed my body for burial ahead of time. 9 I tell you the truth, wherever the Good News is preached throughout the world, this woman's deed will be remembered and discussed."

JUDAS AGREES TO BETRAY JESUS

10 Then Judas Iscariot, one of the twelve disciples, went to the leading priests to arrange to betray Jesus to them. 11 They were delighted when they heard why he had come, and they promised to give him money. So he began looking for an opportunity to betray Jesus.

THE LAST SUPPER

12 On the first day of the Festival of Unleavened Bread, when the Passover lamb is sacrificed, Jesus' disciples asked him, "Where do you want us to go to prepare the Passover meal for you?"

13 So Jesus sent two of them into Jerusalem with these instructions: "As you go into the city, a man carrying a pitcher of water will meet you. Follow him. 14 At the house he enters, say to the owner, 'The Teacher asks: Where is the guest room where I can eat the Passover meal with my disciples?' 15 He will take you upstairs to a large room that is already set up. That is where you should prepare our meal." 16 So the two disciples went into the city and found everything just as Jesus had said, and they prepared the Passover meal there.

17 In the evening Jesus arrived with the Twelve. 18 As they were at the table* eating, Jesus said, "I tell you the truth, one of you eating with me here will betray me."

19 Greatly distressed, each one asked in turn, "Am I the one?"

20 He replied, "It is one of you twelve who is eating from this bowl with me. 21 For the Son of Man* must die, as the Scriptures declared long ago. But how terrible it will be for the one who betrays him. It would be far better for that man if he had never been born!"

22 As they were eating, Jesus took some bread and blessed it. Then he broke it in pieces and gave it to the disciples, saying, "Take it, for this is my body."

23 And he took a cup of wine and gave thanks to God for it. He gave it to them, and they all drank from it. 24 And he said to them, "This is my blood, which confirms the covenant* between God and his people. It is poured out as a sacrifice for many. 25 I tell you the truth, I will not drink wine again until the day I drink it new in the Kingdom of God."

26 Then they sang a hymn and went out to the Mount of Olives.

JESUS PREDICTS PETER'S DENIAL

27 On the way, Jesus told them, "All of you will desert me. For the Scriptures say,

'God will strike* the Shepherd,
  and the sheep will be scattered.'

28 But after I am raised from the dead, I will go ahead of you to Galilee and meet you there."

29 Peter said to him, "Even if everyone else deserts you, I never will."

30 Jesus replied, "I tell you the truth, Peter—this very night, before the rooster crows twice, you will deny three times that you even know me."

13:33 Some manuscripts add *and pray.* 14:3 Or *reclining.* 14:5 Greek *for 300 denarii.* A denarius was equivalent to a laborer's full day's wage. 14:18 Or *As they reclined.* 14:21 "Son of Man" is a title Jesus used for himself. 14:24 Some manuscripts read *the new covenant.* 14:27 Greek *I will strike.* Zech 13:7.

14:1 Passover. A feast in which the people of Israel celebrated God's deliverance of their nation from Egypt where they had been held as slaves (Ex. 12). **the Festival of Unleavened Bread.** By the time of the first century, this feast was coupled with the Passover so that there was a week of feasting.

14:3 a woman came. A woman would not be present at a meal like this except to serve. Her entrance would have been scandalous.

14:12 the Passover lamb is sacrificed. Each pilgrim sacrificed his own lamb in the temple. A priest caught the blood in a bowl, and this was thrown on the altar. After removing certain parts of the lamb for sacrifice, the carcass was returned to the pilgrim to be roasted and eaten for Passover.

14:13-16 Follow him. Instructions for Jesus' arrest had already been issued (John 11:57). He knew that the officials were looking for Him in places away from the crowd. To guard against being arrested before His time, He would generally sleep in Bethany, which was outside the jurisdiction of the priests. But the law required that He eat the Passover meal in Jerusalem itself, hence the need for secret arrangements.

14:18 at the table eating. People would eat festive meals by lying on couches or cushions arranged around a low table. **one of you eating with me.** These words recall the prophecy in Psalm 41:9.

14:20 eating from this bowl with me. To share in a meal was a sign of friendship, accenting the act of betrayal.

14:22-26 bread . . . cup. Jesus provides the model for how the church now celebrates communion (1 Cor. 11:23-26).

14:24 covenant. A treaty between two parties. Such an agreement was often sealed by the sacrifice of an animal. It refers to the arrangement that God made with Israel (Ex. 24:1-8) which was dependent on Israel's obedience. Now (as anticipated in Jer. 31:31-34) a new covenant is established, which is made dependent on Jesus' obedience (His sacrificial death). A covenant of law becomes a covenant of love. **poured out.** Blood which was poured out symbolized a violent death (Gen. 4:10-11; Deut. 19:10; Matt. 23:35). This phrase points to the type of death Jesus would experience.

[31]"No!" Peter declared emphatically. "Even if I have
to die with you, I will never deny you!" And all the
others vowed the same.

JESUS PRAYS IN GETHSEMANE

[32]They went to the olive grove called Gethsemane,
and Jesus said, "Sit here while I go and pray." [33]He
took Peter, James, and John with him, and he became
deeply troubled and distressed. [34]He told them, "My
soul is crushed with grief to the point of death. Stay
here and keep watch with me."
[35]He went on a little farther and fell to the ground.
He prayed that, if it were possible, the awful hour
awaiting him might pass him by. [36]"Abba, Father,"* he
cried out, "everything is possible for you. Please take
this cup of suffering away from me. Yet I want your
will to be done, not mine."
[37]Then he returned and found the disciples asleep.
He said to Peter, "Simon, are you asleep? Couldn't you
watch with me even one hour? [38]Keep watch and
pray, so that you will not give in to temptation. For the
spirit is willing, but the body is weak."
[39]Then Jesus left them again and prayed the same
prayer as before. [40]When he returned to them again,
he found them sleeping, for they couldn't keep their
eyes open. And they didn't know what to say.
[41]When he returned to them the third time, he said,
"Go ahead and sleep. Have your rest. But no—the
time has come. The Son of Man is betrayed into the
hands of sinners. [42]Up, let's be going. Look, my betray-
er is here!"

STAY AWAKE

1. When have you fallen asleep at an embarrassing moment: In church? In class? On a date?

MARK 14:32-42

2. Why was Jesus so upset? What did He choose to do at this moment of personal crisis?
3. What does this teach us about how we should handle times of crisis?
4. Jesus told Peter, "Keep watch and pray" because "the spirit is willing, but the body is weak" (v. 38). How do these words apply to you?
5. Is someone in your group or team facing a time of crisis? How can you "stay awake" to help that person?

JESUS IS BETRAYED AND ARRESTED

[43]And immediately, even as Jesus said this, Judas, one of
the twelve disciples, arrived with a crowd of men armed
with swords and clubs. They had been sent by the lead-
ing priests, the teachers of religious law, and the elders.
[44]The traitor, Judas, had given them a prearranged sig-
nal: "You will know which one to arrest when I greet
him with a kiss. Then you can take him away under
guard." [45]As soon as they arrived, Judas walked up to
Jesus. "Rabbi!" he exclaimed, and gave him the kiss.
[46]Then the others grabbed Jesus and arrested him.
[47]But one of the men with Jesus pulled out his sword
and struck the high priest's slave, slashing off his ear.
[48]Jesus asked them, "Am I some dangerous revolu-
tionary, that you come with swords and clubs to ar-
rest me? [49]Why didn't you arrest me in the Temple? I
was there among you teaching every day. But these
things are happening to fulfill what the Scriptures
say about me."
[50]Then all his disciples deserted him and ran away.
[51]One young man following behind was clothed only
in a long linen shirt. When the mob tried to grab him,
[52]he slipped out of his shirt and ran away naked.

JESUS BEFORE THE COUNCIL

[53]They took Jesus to the high priest's home where the
leading priests, the elders, and the teachers of reli-
gious law had gathered. [54]Meanwhile, Peter followed
him at a distance and went right into the high priest's
courtyard. There he sat with the guards, warming
himself by the fire.
[55]Inside, the leading priests and the entire high
council* were trying to find evidence against Jesus,
so they could put him to death. But they couldn't find
any. [56]Many false witnesses spoke against him, but
they contradicted each other. [57]Finally, some men
stood up and gave this false testimony: [58]"We heard
him say, 'I will destroy this Temple made with human

14:36 *Abba* is an Aramaic term for "father." 14:55 Greek *the Sanhedrin.*

14:32 Gethsemane. An olive orchard in an estate at the foot of the Mount of Olives, just outside the eastern wall of Jerusalem. The name means literally "an oil press" (for making olive oil).

14:33 Peter, James, and John. Once again, these three men accompany Jesus during a time of great significance. Interestingly, neither the rebuke by Peter (8:32) nor the self-centered request of James and John (10:35-40) has damaged their relationship with Jesus. Also note each of these men has vowed to stay with Jesus through thick and thin (10:38-39; 14:29, 31). What Jesus asks them to share with Him here is not glory (which they wanted) but sorrow (which they kept denying would come). **crushed with grief.** Literally, filled with "shuddering awe." Jesus is filled with deep sorrow as the impact of submitting to His father's will hits Him.

14:35 fell to the ground. This accents the emotional distress He was feeling. **the awful hour.** This word is often used to refer to an event that represents a crucial turning point in God's plan for a person or for the world. In reference to Jesus, it specifically refers to His crucifixion (John 12:23).

14:36 Abba. This is how a child would address his father: "Daddy." This was not a title that was used in prayer in the first century. **this cup.** Like the word "hour," "cup" was also used as an image referring to the destiny God had in store for a person.

14:43 a crowd of men armed. The Sanhedrin commanded the services of the temple police (who were Levites) and of an auxiliary police force (servants of the court) who maintained order outside the temple area.

14:44 kiss. The intensive form of the verb used here indicates that Judas' actual kiss was a warm and affectionate greeting and not merely perfunctory.

14:45 Rabbi! This title was a form of respect. It meant literally, "My Great One." By his greeting, by his kiss, and by sharing the same bowl (v. 20—to eat together was a sign of friendship), Judas conveys the sense of a warm relationship with Jesus.

14:47 one of the men with Jesus. According to John's Gospel (John 18:10), this was Peter. **pulled out his sword.** That Peter should have a sword is not unusual. Travelers carried them as protection against robbers, and the disciples had just completed a journey from Jerusalem to Galilee (Luke 22:36-38).

14:51 young man. It has been suggested that this is Mark himself. He lived in Jerusalem (Acts 12:12), and there is a tradition that the Last Supper was held in the upper room of his mother's house. **linen shirt.** Probably a bed sheet. The fact that it was linen means that he came from a wealthy family.

14:55 the high council. A council consisting of 71 leaders, both priests and laymen, who made up the highest Jewish court. They were given authority by Rome to rule in matters of religious law. **testimony.** To convict someone of a capital crime required the unanimous testimony of at least two witnesses. Each witness gave his testimony individually to the judge in the presence of the accused. If two witnesses differed in their accounts, their testimony was thrown out of court (Deut. 19:15-18).

hands, and in three days I will build another, made
without human hands.'" 59 But even then they didn't
get their stories straight!
60 Then the high priest stood up before the others
and asked Jesus, "Well, aren't you going to answer
these charges? What do you have to say for yourself?"
61 But Jesus was silent and made no reply. Then the
high priest asked him, "Are you the Messiah, the Son
of the Blessed One?"
62 Jesus said, "I AM.* And you will see the Son of
Man seated in the place of power at God's right hand*
and coming on the clouds of heaven.*"
63 Then the high priest tore his clothing to show his
horror and said, "Why do we need other witnesses?
64 You have all heard his blasphemy. What is your ver-
dict?"
"Guilty!" they all cried. "He deserves to die!"
65 Then some of them began to spit at him, and they
blindfolded him and beat him with their fists. "Proph-
esy to us," they jeered. And the guards slapped him as
they took him away.

PETER DENIES JESUS

66 Meanwhile, Peter was in the courtyard below. One
of the servant girls who worked for the high priest
came by 67 and noticed Peter warming himself at the
fire. She looked at him closely and said, "You were one
of those with Jesus of Nazareth.*"
68 But Peter denied it. "I don't know what you're
talking about," he said, and he went out into the en-
tryway. Just then, a rooster crowed.*
69 When the servant girl saw him standing there,
she began telling the others, "This man is definitely
one of them!" 70 But Peter denied it again.
A little later some of the other bystanders confront-
ed Peter and said, "You must be one of them, because
you are a Galilean."
71 Peter swore, "A curse on me if I'm lying—I don't
know this man you're talking about!" 72 And immedi-
ately the rooster crowed the second time.
Suddenly, Jesus' words flashed through Peter's
mind: "Before the rooster crows twice, you will deny
three times that you even know me." And he broke
down and wept.

JESUS' TRIAL BEFORE PILATE

15 Very early in the morning the leading priests,
the elders, and the teachers of religious law—
the entire high council*—met to discuss their next
step. They bound Jesus, led him away, and took him to
Pilate, the Roman governor.
2 Pilate asked Jesus, "Are you the king of the Jews?"
Jesus replied, "You have said it."

SACRIFICING FOR US!

1. When someone accuses you of something you didn't do, how do you react?

MARK 15:1-15

2. Why do you think Jesus didn't answer the charges against him (v. 5)?
3. Why did the people ask for Barabbas instead of Jesus? What does this show about the human race?
4. How does the story of Barabbas illustrate what Christ did for you?
5. Have you come to the point in your life where you've asked Jesus to forgive your sins, realizing that He died for you? If not, why are you waiting?

3 Then the leading priests kept accusing him of
many crimes, 4 and Pilate asked him, "Aren't you go-
ing to answer them? What about all these charges
they are bringing against you?" 5 But Jesus said noth-
ing, much to Pilate's surprise.
6 Now it was the governor's custom each year during
the Passover celebration to release one prisoner—any-
one the people requested. 7 One of the prisoners at that
time was Barabbas, a revolutionary who had commit-
ted murder in an uprising. 8 The crowd went to Pilate
and asked him to release a prisoner as usual.
9 "Would you like me to release to you this 'King of
the Jews'?" Pilate asked. 10 (For he realized by now that
the leading priests had arrested Jesus out of envy.)
11 But at this point the leading priests stirred up the
crowd to demand the release of Barabbas instead of
Jesus. 12 Pilate asked them, "Then what should I do
with this man you call the king of the Jews?"
13 They shouted back, "Crucify him!"
14 "Why?" Pilate demanded. "What crime has he
committed?"
But the mob roared even louder, "Crucify him!"
15 So to pacify the crowd, Pilate released Barabbas
to them. He ordered Jesus flogged with a lead-tipped
whip, then turned him over to the Roman soldiers to
be crucified.

THE SOLDIERS MOCK JESUS

16 The soldiers took Jesus into the courtyard of the
governor's headquarters (called the Praetorium) and
called out the entire regiment. 17 They dressed him
in a purple robe, and they wove thorn branches into

14:62a Or *The 'I AM' is here;* or *I am the LORD.* See Exod 3:14. **14:62b** Greek *seated at the right hand of the power.* See Ps 110:1. **14:62c** See Dan 7:13. **14:67** Or *Jesus the Nazarene.* **14:68** Some manuscripts do not include *Just then, a rooster crowed.* **15:1** Greek *the Sanhedrin;* also in 15:43.

14:62 This is the first time in Mark that Jesus openly and unequivocally declares His Messiahship.

14:64 blasphemy. Dishonoring or slandering another. The penalty for blaspheming God was death by stoning (Lev. 24:10-16). **deserves to die!** At that point in history, the Sanhedrin did not have power to carry out a death sentence. Only the Roman procurator could do that.

14:71 a curse on me. Peter goes so far as to call down on himself the wrath of God if he is not telling the truth (which he knows he is not)! **I don't know this man.** This, like his previous denial (v. 68), is an outright lie. **you're talking about!** Peter does not use Jesus' name (8:38).

14:72 a rooster crowed the second time. Roosters in Palestine crowed first at about 12:30 a.m., then again at about 1:30 a.m., and for a third time at about 2:30 a.m. As a result of this peculiar habit, the watch kept by soldiers in Palestine from midnight until 3 a.m. was called "cock-crow." Peter's denials were therefore spread over the early hours.

15:1 Pilate. Pontius Pilate was the fifth procurator of Judea. He served from A.D. 26-36. Historians of the time called him an "inflexible, merciless and obstinate" man who disliked the Jews and their customs.

15:8 The crowd. At the beginning of the week the crowd hailed Jesus as "the one who comes in the name of the LORD" (11:9).

15:15 released Barabbas. The death of Jesus (who is innocent) in the place of Barabbas (who is guilty) is a visual statement of the meaning of substitutionary atonement. It explains what Jesus meant in 10:45 when He said that He came to "give his life as a ransom for many."

a crown and put it on his head. 18 Then they saluted him and taunted, "Hail! King of the Jews!" 19 And they struck him on the head with a reed stick, spit on him, and dropped to their knees in mock worship. 20 When they were finally tired of mocking him, they took off the purple robe and put his own clothes on him again. Then they led him away to be crucified.

THE CRUCIFIXION

21 A passerby named Simon, who was from Cyrene,* was coming in from the countryside just then, and the soldiers forced him to carry Jesus' cross. (Simon was the father of Alexander and Rufus.) 22 And they brought Jesus to a place called Golgotha (which means "Place of the Skull"). 23 They offered him wine drugged with myrrh, but he refused it.

24 Then the soldiers nailed him to the cross. They divided his clothes and threw dice* to decide who would get each piece. 25 It was nine o'clock in the morning when they crucified him. 26 A sign announced the charge against him. It read, "The King of the Jews." 27 Two revolutionaries* were crucified with him, one on his right and one on his left.*

29 The people passing by shouted abuse, shaking their heads in mockery. "Ha! Look at you now!" they yelled at him. "You said you were going to destroy the Temple and rebuild it in three days. 30 Well then, save yourself and come down from the cross!"

31 The leading priests and teachers of religious law also mocked Jesus. "He saved others," they scoffed, "but he can't save himself! 32 Let this Messiah, this King of Israel, come down from the cross so we can see it and believe him!" Even the men who were crucified with Jesus ridiculed him.

THE DEATH OF JESUS

33 At noon, darkness fell across the whole land until three o'clock. 34 Then at three o'clock Jesus called out with a loud voice, *"Eloi, Eloi, lema sabachthani?"* which means "My God, my God, why have you abandoned me?"*

35 Some of the bystanders misunderstood and thought he was calling for the prophet Elijah. 36 One of them ran and filled a sponge with sour wine, holding it up to him on a reed stick so he could drink. "Wait!" he said. "Let's see whether Elijah comes to take him down!"

37 Then Jesus uttered another loud cry and breathed his last. 38 And the curtain in the sanctuary of the Temple was torn in two, from top to bottom.

39 When the Roman officer* who stood facing him* saw how he had died, he exclaimed, "This man truly was the Son of God!"

40 Some women were there, watching from a distance, including Mary Magdalene, Mary (the mother of James the younger and of Joseph*), and Salome. 41 They had been followers of Jesus and had cared for him while he was in Galilee. Many other women who had come with him to Jerusalem were also there.

THE BURIAL OF JESUS

42 This all happened on Friday, the day of preparation,* the day before the Sabbath. As evening approached, 43 Joseph of Arimathea took a risk and went to Pilate and asked for Jesus' body. (Joseph was an honored member of the high council, and he was waiting for the Kingdom of God to come.) 44 Pilate couldn't believe that Jesus was already dead, so he called for the Roman officer and asked if he had died yet. 45 The officer confirmed that Jesus was dead, so Pilate told Joseph he could have the body. 46 Joseph bought a long sheet of linen cloth. Then he took Jesus' body down from the cross, wrapped it in the cloth, and laid it in a tomb that had been carved out of the rock. Then he rolled a stone in front of the entrance. 47 Mary Magdalene and Mary the mother of Joseph saw where Jesus' body was laid.

THE RESURRECTION

16 Saturday evening, when the Sabbath ended, Mary Magdalene, Mary the mother of James, and Salome went out and purchased burial spices so

15:21 *Cyrene* was a city in northern Africa. **15:24** Greek *cast lots.* See Ps 22:18. **15:27a** Or *Two criminals.* **15:27b** Some manuscripts add verse 28, *And the Scripture was fulfilled that said, "He was counted among those who were rebels."* See Isa 53:12; also compare Luke 22:37. **15:34** Ps 22:1. **15:39a** Greek *the centurion;* similarly in 15:44, 45. **15:39b** Some manuscripts add *heard his cry and.* **15:40** Greek *Joses;* also in 15:47. See Matt 27:56. **15:42** Greek *It was the day of preparation.*

15:21 Simon. Possibly a Jew, from a Greek city on the north shore of Africa, who had come to Jerusalem for the Passover feast. **Rufus.** Romans 16:13 mentions a Rufus. Mark wrote this Gospel for the church at Rome, and if this is the same Rufus, he would be able to verify this detail about his father. **carry Jesus' cross.** The prisoner carried the heavy cross-beam through the winding streets as an example to others. Jesus, however, had already been without sleep for at least 24 hours and been beaten, flogged, and beaten again. He was physically unable to bear the weight of the cross-beam.

15:22 Golgotha. In Aramaic, "a skull." This was probably a round, bare hill outside Jerusalem.

15:23 wine drugged with myrrh. A pain-deadening narcotic offered to prisoners about to be crucified (Ps. 69:21).

15:24 divided his clothes. The clothes of the condemned person belonged to the four soldiers who carried out the crucifixion (Ps. 22:18; John 19:23-24).

15:26 The King of the Jews. By posting this sign on the cross, Pilate was simply attempting to further humiliate the Jews. The intent was to communicate that Jesus' fate would be shared by anyone else who tried to assert their authority against Rome.

15:27 one on his right and one on his left. Earlier on, James and John had asked for the honor to sit at Jesus' right and left-hand when He came into his kingdom (10:37), a request Jesus denied. Now these two criminals are given the positions on either side of Jesus as He completes His earthly mission.

15:31 He saved others . . . he can't save himself! This is just the point! Because He is saving others, His own life is forfeited.

15:33 darkness. A supernatural event showing the significance of this death (Amos 8:9). There is darkness for three hours.

15:36 sour wine. Wine vinegar was considered a refreshing drink (Ruth 2:14).

15:38 curtain of the sanctuary. There were two curtains in the temple sanctuary. An outer curtain separated the sanctuary from the courtyard. The inner curtain covered the Holy of Holies where only the high priest was admitted. It is most likely it was the latter curtain that was torn by God to allow all access to the Father through Jesus Christ.

15:39 officer. The supervising officer, a pagan soldier who may not have been aware of the significance of what he observed.

15:42 day of preparation. Jesus died on Friday at 3 p.m. The Sabbath began at 6 p.m., after which no work could be done. Great haste was required.

15:43 Joseph. Little is known of him, except that he was from a wealthy and prominent family and was a member of the Sanhedrin.

15:44 Pilate couldn't believe. It often took two or three days for a person to die from crucifixion.

15:46 The body was washed, quickly wrapped, and then placed in a tomb. The tomb was then sealed against robbers or animals by means of a large stone. These stones were set in grooves which would guide the stone to the tomb's entrance. Elevated above the tomb's entrance, it would not be too difficult to set the stone in motion to roll against the entrance. It would be extremely difficult to remove the stone from the entrance since it would have to be pushed uphill.

15:47 saw. Two of the three women at the crucifixion saw clearly where Jesus was entombed.

they could anoint Jesus' body. 2 Very early on Sunday
morning,* just at sunrise, they went to the tomb. 3 On
the way they were asking each other, "Who will roll
away the stone for us from the entrance to the tomb?"
4 But as they arrived, they looked up and saw that the
stone, which was very large, had already been rolled
aside.

5 When they entered the tomb, they saw a young
man clothed in a white robe sitting on the right
side. The women were shocked, 6 but the angel
said, "Don't be alarmed. You are looking for Jesus
of Nazareth,* who was crucified. He isn't here! He
is risen from the dead! Look, this is where they laid
his body. 7 Now go and tell his disciples, including
Peter, that Jesus is going ahead of you to Galilee.
You will see him there, just as he told you before
he died."

8 The women fled from the tomb, trembling and
bewildered, and they said nothing to anyone because
they were too frightened.*

[The most ancient manuscripts of Mark conclude with verse 16:8. Later manuscripts add one or both of the following endings.]

[Shorter Ending of Mark]

Then they briefly reported all this to Peter and his companions. Afterward Jesus himself sent them out from east to west with the sacred and unfailing message of salvation that gives eternal life. Amen.

[Longer Ending of Mark]

9 After Jesus rose from the dead early on Sunday
morning, the first person who saw him was Mary
Magdalene, the woman from whom he had cast out
seven demons. 10 She went to the disciples, who were
grieving and weeping, and told them what had hap-
pened. 11 But when she told them that Jesus was alive
and she had seen him, they didn't believe her.

12 Afterward he appeared in a different form to two
of his followers who were walking from Jerusalem
into the country. 13 They rushed back to tell the others,
but no one believed them.

14 Still later he appeared to the eleven disciples as
they were eating together. He rebuked them for their
stubborn unbelief because they refused to believe
those who had seen him after he had been raised
from the dead.*

15 And then he told them, "Go into all the world and
preach the Good News to everyone. 16 Anyone who
believes and is baptized will be saved. But anyone
who refuses to believe will be condemned. 17 These
miraculous signs will accompany those who believe:
They will cast out demons in my name, and they will
speak in new languages.* 18 They will be able to han-
dle snakes with safety, and if they drink anything poi-
sonous, it won't hurt them. They will be able to place
their hands on the sick, and they will be healed."

19 When the Lord Jesus had finished talking with
them, he was taken up into heaven and sat down in
the place of honor at God's right hand. 20 And the dis-
ciples went everywhere and preached, and the Lord
worked through them, confirming what they said by
many miraculous signs.

16:2 Greek *on the first day of the week;* also in 16:9. 16:6 Or *Jesus the Nazarene.* 16:8 The most reliable early manuscripts of the Gospel of Mark end at verse 8. Other manuscripts include various endings to the Gospel. A few include both the "shorter ending" and the "longer ending." The majority of manuscripts include the "longer ending" immediately after verse 8. 16:14 Some early manuscripts add: *And they excused themselves, saying, "This age of lawlessness and unbelief is under Satan, who does not permit God's truth and power to conquer the evil [unclean] spirits. Therefore, reveal your justice now." This is what they said to Christ. And Christ replied to them, "The period of years of Satan's power has been fulfilled, but other dreadful things will happen soon. And I was handed over to death for those who have sinned, so that they may return to the truth and sin no more, and so they may inherit the spiritual, incorruptible, and righteous glory in heaven."* 16:17 Or *new tongues;* some manuscripts do not include *new.*

16:5 shocked. A rare Greek word used in the New Testament only by Mark (9:15; 14:33), indicating great astonishment in the face of the supernatural.

16:6 He is risen from the dead! In the same way that Mark reports the crucifixion of Jesus in simple, stark terms (15:24), so too he describes his resurrection in a plain, unadorned way. The phrase is literally "he has been raised," showing that God is the One who accomplished this great act.

16:8 they said nothing. Eventually, of course, the women did report what happened (Matt. 28:8; Luke 24:10). **they were frightened.** This was the same sort of fear that the disciples felt on the Sea of Galilee when they discovered that Jesus had power over the elements themselves (4:41). This is how human beings respond in the face of the supernatural. Thus the Gospel of Mark ends on this note of astonishment and fear, which was so characteristic of how he described people's reaction.

INTRODUCTION TO

LUKE

PERSONAL READING PLAN

☐Luke 1:1-38	☐Luke 8:1-39	☐Luke 16:1–17:19
☐Luke 1:39-80	☐Luke 8:40–9:36	☐Luke 17:20–18:43
☐Luke 2:1-52	☐Luke 9:37–10:24	☐Luke 19:1-48
☐Luke 3:1–4:13	☐Luke 10:25–11:28	☐Luke 20:1-47
☐Luke 4:14–5:16	☐Luke 11:29–12:21	☐Luke 21:1-38
☐Luke 5:17–6:11	☐Luke 12:22-59	☐Luke 22:1-53
☐Luke 6:12–7:10	☐Luke 13:1–14:14	☐Luke 22:54–23:56
☐Luke 7:11-50	☐Luke 14:15–15:32	☐Luke 24:1-53

AUTHOR

Although no author is named in the third Gospel, a second century tradition attributes it to Luke. Since Luke was not an apostle and he was a Gentile, it is unlikely that he would have received credit for it if he had not written it.

Internal evidence supports Luke's authorship. It is clear that the same person wrote both the third Gospel and the book of Acts; both books are dedicated to Theophilus. Both books are similar in style, language, and interests. The author of Acts begins by saying, "In my first book," which is surely the Gospel of Luke. Since Acts was traditionally credited to Luke, we assume Luke did indeed write this Gospel.

Additionally, the author of the third Gospel uses the language we would expect from a doctor (Luke was a physician). He describes illnesses with more precision than is found in Matthew and Mark (4:38; 5:12). He also omits the comment in Mark 5:26 that the woman who was subject to bleeding "had suffered a great deal from many doctors ... spent everything ... she had gotten no better."

Little is known about Luke from the New Testament except that he was a doctor beloved by Paul (Col. 4:14) and a coworker with Paul (2 Tim. 4:11; Philem. 24). In the book of Acts, Luke describes experiences while traveling with Paul. One early non-canonical document (writings not included in Holy Scripture), the Prologue to Luke, states that Luke was a physician, that he was unmarried and childless, and that he died at the age of 84. Beyond this, we know Luke only through his two eloquent documents.

DATE

There is no strong evidence as to when Luke's Gospel was written. Many scholars date it between A.D. 75 and 85, although this is by no means conclusive. In fact, since Acts ends with Paul awaiting trial in Rome (probably before A.D. 67), if Luke wrote his Gospel before he wrote Acts, then a date in the early A.D. 60s is likely.

The place of writing was most likely Rome, though Achaia, Ephesus, and Caesarea are also possibilities. The place to which it was sent depends on where Theophilus lived. By its details about Palestine, the Gospel seems to be written for readers who were unfamiliar with that land. The Christians in Antioch, Achaia, and Ephesus are possible recipients of this Gospel.

THEME

Jesus is the Savior of the whole world.

HISTORICAL BACKGROUND

Luke was a Gentile who wrote the story of Jesus for other Gentiles. Luke dedicates the book to Theophilus, probably a high-ranking Roman government official (the title "most honorable" was normally reserved for such officials). Theophilus was a common name among both Greeks and Jews in New Testament times. It means "friend of God."

Luke then dates the conception and birth of John the Baptist and Jesus with reference to the Roman rulers governing at the time (1:5; 2:1-2). Luke makes a habit of translating Hebrew words into their Greek equivalents so that his Gentile readers will understand. For example, Luke never refers to Jesus as "Rabbi," the Hebrew title for a teacher, but always by the Greek equivalent, "Master." Luke identifies the place where Jesus was crucified not as Golgotha (Hebrew) but as Kranion, the Greek equivalent for "the place of the skull."

The Gentile character of the third Gospel is also seen in its identification of Jesus' lineage. Luke traces Him back to Adam, the founder of the human race, and not, as Matthew does, back to Abraham, the founder of the Jewish race. Also, Luke seldom quotes the Old Testament or demonstrates how Jesus fulfills Old Testament prophecy. This is a Gentile book about the Jewish Messiah who died for all people.

CHARACTERISTICS

Luke's account of Jesus' life is the longest book in the New Testament, and it is extraordinarily joyful. It begins and ends with rejoicing (1:46-47 and 24:52-53). Luke uses the words "joy" (6:23), "laugh" (6:21), and "celebrate" (15:23,32). Luke is the only writer to record the four great canticles of joy and worship: *Magnificat* (1:46-55), *Benedictus* (1:68-79), *Gloria in Excelsis* (2:14), and *Nunc dimittis* (2:29-32).

STYLE

Despite Luke's meticulous documentation, his Gospel is no dry, academic document. It sparkles with life and vitality. Luke's portraits of people are particularly vivid and compassionate. People like Zacchaeus, Mary and Martha, Elizabeth, and the mother of Jesus all spring to life through his talented pen.

PASSAGES FOR TOPICAL GROUP STUDY

1:26-38	VIRGIN BIRTH	Miracle Birth
2:1-20	JESUS' PURPOSE	Heavenly Purpose
2:41-52	SPIRITUAL GROWTH	In Dad's House
4:1-13	TEMPTATION	That's Tempting
5:1-11	GOD'S CALL	Giving It All Up
7:36-50	GUILT and FORGIVENESS	Guilty as Charged
8:26-39	DEMONS and JESUS POWER	Dealing with Demons

10:25-37...OUTCASTS and HELPING OTHERS .... The Good Samaritan
10:38-42...PRIORITIES and the MAIN THING.. One Necessary Thing
12:13-21...MONEY and HAVING IT ALL.. Building True Wealth
12:22-34...POSSESSIONS and PASSIONS .... Where's Your Treasure
14:15-24...ACCEPTING/REJECTING JESUS .... The Best Invitation Ever
14:25-35...MAKING A DIFFERENCE .... Salt of the Earth
15:11-32...FAMILY CONFLICTS and LOVE... The Wasteful Son
16:19-31...HEAVEN AND HELL .... Heaven and Hell
17:11-19...THANKFULNESS .... An Attitude of Gratitude
18:9-14...SELF-IMAGE .... Going Down to Go Up
19:1-10....MAKING THINGS RIGHT .... Out on a Limb
19:28-44...JESUS HURTS WITH PEOPLE ... Weeping for Others
22:54-62...FAILURE; BLOWING IT .... Confronting Sin
23:26-49...FORGIVENESS and PARADISE .... On the Cross
24:13-35...SEEING REALITY.... An Eye-Opening Experience

PASSAGES FOR GENERAL GROUP STUDY

4:14-30 .... Get Out of Town — the Rejection of Jesus
22:7-23 .... Celebrating the Lord's Supper (Communion, Eucharist)

INTRODUCTION

1 Many people have set out to write accounts about the events that have been fulfilled among us. 2 They used the eyewitness reports circulating among us from the early disciples.* 3 Having carefully investigated everything from the beginning, I also have decided to write an accurate account for you, most honorable Theophilus, 4 so you can be certain of the truth of everything you were taught.

THE BIRTH OF JOHN THE BAPTIST FORETOLD

5 When Herod was king of Judea, there was a Jewish priest named Zechariah. He was a member of the priestly order of Abijah, and his wife, Elizabeth, was also from the priestly line of Aaron. 6 Zechariah and Elizabeth were righteous in God's eyes, careful to obey all of the Lord's commandments and regulations. 7 They had no children because Elizabeth was unable to conceive, and they were both very old.

8 One day Zechariah was serving God in the Temple, for his order was on duty that week. 9 As was the custom of the priests, he was chosen by lot to enter the sanctuary of the Lord and burn incense. 10 While the incense was being burned, a great crowd stood outside, praying.

11 While Zechariah was in the sanctuary, an angel of the Lord appeared to him, standing to the right of the incense altar. 12 Zechariah was shaken and overwhelmed with fear when he saw him. 13 But the angel said, "Don't be afraid, Zechariah! God has heard your prayer. Your wife, Elizabeth, will give you a son, and you are to name him John. 14 You will have great joy and gladness, and many will rejoice at his birth, 15 for he will be great in the eyes of the Lord. He must never touch wine or other alcoholic drinks. He will be filled with the Holy Spirit, even before his birth.* 16 And he will turn many Israelites to the Lord their God. 17 He will be a man with the spirit and power of Elijah. He will prepare the people for the coming of the Lord. He will turn the hearts of the fathers to their children,* and he will cause those who are rebellious to accept the wisdom of the godly."

18 Zechariah said to the angel, "How can I be sure this will happen? I'm an old man now, and my wife is also well along in years."

19 Then the angel said, "I am Gabriel! I stand in the very presence of God. It was he who sent me to bring you this good news! 20 But now, since you didn't believe what I said, you will be silent and unable to speak until the child is born. For my words will certainly be fulfilled at the proper time."

21 Meanwhile, the people were waiting for Zechariah to come out of the sanctuary, wondering why he was taking so long. 22 When he finally did come out, he couldn't speak to them. Then they realized from his gestures and his silence that he must have seen a vision in the sanctuary.

23 When Zechariah's week of service in the Temple was over, he returned home. 24 Soon afterward his wife, Elizabeth, became pregnant and went into seclusion for five months. 25 "How kind the Lord is!" she exclaimed. "He has taken away my disgrace of having no children."

THE BIRTH OF JESUS FORETOLD

26 In the sixth month of Elizabeth's pregnancy, God sent the angel Gabriel to Nazareth, a village in Galilee, 27 to a virgin named Mary. She was engaged to be married to a man named Joseph, a descendant of King David. 28 Gabriel appeared to her and said, "Greetings,* favored woman! The Lord is with you!*"

29 Confused and disturbed, Mary tried to think what the angel could mean. 30 "Don't be afraid, Mary," the angel told her, "for you have found favor with God! 31 You will conceive and give birth to a son, and you will name him Jesus. 32 He will be very great and will be called the Son of the Most High. The Lord God will give him the throne of his ancestor David. 33 And he will reign over Israel* forever; his Kingdom will never end!"

34 Mary asked the angel, "But how can this happen? I am a virgin."

1:2 Greek *from those who from the beginning were servants of the word.* **1:15** Or *even from birth.* **1:17** See Mal 4:5-6. **1:28a** Or *Rejoice.* **1:28b** Some manuscripts add *Blessed are you among women.* **1:33** Greek *over the house of Jacob.*

1:1 Many. Mark and Luke contain similar material. Most of Mark is included in Luke. Unknown writers also recorded some of the teachings and stories about Jesus that Luke incorporated into his Gospel as well.

1:2 eyewitness reports. "The word" is a shorthand way of referring to the whole of Jesus' life and teaching (Acts 1:21-22; 2 Peter 1:16; 1 John 1:1). The stories that form the Gospels were passed on by those who were personally acquainted with and dedicated to Jesus.

1:3 carefully investigated. While Luke was not an eyewitness, his association with Paul and Mark (Col. 4:10-14; 2 Tim. 4:11), his travels to Judea (Acts 21), and his familiarity with other eyewitnesses afforded him ample opportunity to collect information from reliable witnesses. **Theophilus.** An unknown figure. He may have been Luke's patron who underwrote the cost of writing the Gospel, or a Roman official (Acts 1:1).

1:7 Elizabeth was unable to conceive. Barrenness was seen as a tragedy and a valid reason for divorce.

1:12 overwhelmed with fear. The fear of the angel he experienced is similar to that experienced other places in Scripture when an angel comes to an individual (vv. 29-30; Ex. 3:2-6; Dan. 10:7).

1:15 he . . . never touch wine . . . he will be filled with the Holy Spirit. The first statement connects John to the Old Testament order of Nazirites (Num. 6); the second statement shows him to be the forerunner of the new era of the Messiah when God's Spirit would indwell His people.

1:17 with the spirit and power of Elijah. Elijah was one of the first great Old Testament prophets. Malachi, the last prophet to speak to the Jews, foresaw a time when Elijah would come again to prepare people for the Lord (Mal. 4:5). While Jewish tradition anticipated the literal return of Elijah, the angel's message is that John would be inspired by the same divine energy that led Elijah.

1:19 Gabriel. Literally, "man of God." In Jewish tradition, he was one of the select few angels who represent God as His special servants (Dan. 8:16; 9:21).

1:20 unable to speak. Old Testament saints questioned God without rebuke or punishment (Gen. 15:8; Judg. 6:13). Here, Zechariah's inability to speak is tied to his lack of trust. It may have also been a confirmation of Gabriel's words.

1:26 In the sixth month. This is the sixth month of Elizabeth's pregnancy. **to Nazareth, a village in Galilee.** Nazareth was an insignificant little village (John 1:46) in the province of Galilee. God often uses what others see as small or insignificant, as with the "little town of Bethlehem."

1:27 a virgin . . . engaged . . . to a man. Betrothal, usually lasting for about a year, could occur as young as 12 years old. This was a far more binding arrangement than engagements today. Although sexual relations were not permitted, the woman had the legal status of a wife, and the relationship could only be broken by divorce. The virgin birth of Jesus, although only mentioned in Matthew and Luke in the entire New Testament, traces its roots to the prophecy of the child spoken of in Isaiah 7:14. **Joseph, a descendant of David.** The Messiah was to come through the line of David, the most famous king of Israel's history (2 Sam. 7:16; Ps. 132:11).

1:28 favored woman! The angel is not commending her virtue but recognizing the reality of God's grace to her. **The Lord is with you!** This phrase is often used as a statement of God's special intention to equip a person for His service (Josh. 1:5; Judg. 6:12; Matt. 28:20).

1:34 How can this happen? Zechariah asked a similar question of the angel when informed that he and his wife Elizabeth would have a child (v. 18). He asked out of doubt that such a thing could come to pass. Mary, however, is not registering doubt as much as wonder.

MIRACLE BIRTH

1. How old were your parents when you were born?

LUKE 1:26-38

2. Mary was young, perhaps only 14, when the angel appeared to her. How would you have reacted in her position?
3. What does Mary mean, "I am the Lord's servant" (v. 38)? What does her response show about her character?
4. Why was Jesus born from a woman who'd never had sex? Why was that important?
5. Mary was completely willing to follow God's plan for her life. How can you be more like her?

35 The angel replied, "The Holy Spirit will come upon you, and the power of the Most High will overshadow you. So the baby to be born will be holy, and he will be called the Son of God. 36 What's more, your relative Elizabeth has become pregnant in her old age! People used to say she was barren, but she has conceived a son and is now in her sixth month. 37 For the word of God will never fail.*"

38 Mary responded, "I am the Lord's servant. May everything you have said about me come true." And then the angel left her.

MARY VISITS ELIZABETH

39 A few days later Mary hurried to the hill country of Judea, to the town 40 where Zechariah lived. She entered the house and greeted Elizabeth. 41 At the sound of Mary's greeting, Elizabeth's child leaped within her, and Elizabeth was filled with the Holy Spirit.

42 Elizabeth gave a glad cry and exclaimed to Mary, "God has blessed you above all women, and your child is blessed. 43 Why am I so honored, that the mother of my Lord should visit me? 44 When I heard your greeting, the baby in my womb jumped for joy. 45 You are blessed because you believed that the Lord would do what he said."

THE MAGNIFICAT: MARY'S SONG OF PRAISE

46 Mary responded,

"Oh, how my soul praises the Lord.
47 How my spirit rejoices in God my Savior!
48 For he took notice of his lowly servant girl,
and from now on all generations will call me blessed.
49 For the Mighty One is holy,
and he has done great things for me.
50 He shows mercy from generation to generation
to all who fear him.
51 His mighty arm has done tremendous things!
He has scattered the proud and haughty ones.
52 He has brought down princes from their thrones
and exalted the humble.
53 He has filled the hungry with good things
and sent the rich away with empty hands.
54 He has helped his servant Israel
and remembered to be merciful.
55 For he made this promise to our ancestors,
to Abraham and his children forever."

56 Mary stayed with Elizabeth about three months and then went back to her own home.

THE BIRTH OF JOHN THE BAPTIST

57 When it was time for Elizabeth's baby to be born, she gave birth to a son. 58 And when her neighbors and relatives heard that the Lord had been very merciful to her, everyone rejoiced with her.

59 When the baby was eight days old, they all came for the circumcision ceremony. They wanted to name him Zechariah, after his father. 60 But Elizabeth said, "No! His name is John!"

61 "What?" they exclaimed. "There is no one in all your family by that name." 62 So they used gestures to ask the baby's father what he wanted to name him. 63 He motioned for a writing tablet, and to everyone's surprise he wrote, "His name is John." 64 Instantly Zechariah could speak again, and he began praising God.

65 Awe fell upon the whole neighborhood, and the news of what had happened spread throughout the Judean hills. 66 Everyone who heard about it reflected on these events and asked, "What will this child turn out to be?" For the hand of the Lord was surely upon him in a special way.

ZECHARIAH'S PROPHECY

67 Then his father, Zechariah, was filled with the Holy Spirit and gave this prophecy:

68 "Praise the Lord, the God of Israel,
because he has visited and redeemed his people.
69 He has sent us a mighty Savior*
from the royal line of his servant David,
70 just as he promised
through his holy prophets long ago.
71 Now we will be saved from our enemies
and from all who hate us.
72 He has been merciful to our ancestors
by remembering his sacred covenant—
73 the covenant he swore with an oath
to our ancestor Abraham.
74 We have been rescued from our enemies
so we can serve God without fear,
75 in holiness and righteousness
for as long as we live.

76 "And you, my little son,
will be called the prophet of the Most High,
because you will prepare the way for the Lord.

1:37 Some manuscripts read *For nothing is impossible with God.* 1:69 Greek *has raised up a horn of salvation for us.*

1:43 my Lord. Elizabeth recognizes the sovereignty and power of Mary's child even prior to His birth.

1:45 You are blessed because you believed. In general, the Bible has many more male role models than female, but it is Mary's belief that has made her a model of faith for women through the centuries. Her faith contrasts with the doubt of Zechariah in verse 18.

1:46-55 And Mary responded. Mary's song (known as the *Magnificat* after its first words in the Latin Vulgate translation) may have been used as a hymn by the early church as a means of describing the mission of Mary's Son. It celebrates God's action on behalf of Israel as the fulfillment of the enduring hopes of the nation.

[77] You will tell his people how to find salvation
through forgiveness of their sins.
[78] Because of God's tender mercy,
the morning light from heaven is about to break
upon us,*
[79] to give light to those who sit in darkness and in
the shadow of death,
and to guide us to the path of peace."

[80] John grew up and became strong in spirit. And he lived in the wilderness until he began his public ministry to Israel.

THE BIRTH OF JESUS

2 At that time the Roman emperor, Augustus, decreed that a census should be taken throughout the Roman Empire. [2](This was the first census taken when Quirinius was governor of Syria.) [3]All returned to their own ancestral towns to register for this census. [4]And because Joseph was a descendant of King David, he had to go to Bethlehem in Judea, David's ancient home. He traveled there from the village of Nazareth in Galilee. [5]He took with him Mary, to whom he was engaged, who was now expecting a child.

[6]And while they were there, the time came for her baby to be born. [7]She gave birth to her firstborn son. She wrapped him snugly in strips of cloth and laid him in a manger, because there was no lodging available for them.

THE SHEPHERDS AND ANGELS

[8]That night there were shepherds staying in the fields nearby, guarding their flocks of sheep. [9]Suddenly, an angel of the Lord appeared among them, and the radiance of the Lord's glory surrounded them. They were terrified, [10]but the angel reassured them. "Don't be afraid!" he said. "I bring you good news that will bring great joy to all people. [11]The Savior—yes, the Messiah, the Lord—has been born today in Bethlehem, the city of David! [12]And you will recognize him by this sign: You will find a baby wrapped snugly in strips of cloth, lying in a manger."

[13]Suddenly, the angel was joined by a vast host of others—the armies of heaven—praising God and saying,

[14] "Glory to God in highest heaven,
and peace on earth to those with whom God is
pleased."

[15]When the angels had returned to heaven, the shepherds said to each other, "Let's go to Bethlehem! Let's see this thing that has happened, which the Lord has told us about."

HEAVENLY PURPOSE

1. What's your favorite thing about Christmas?

LUKE 2:1-20

2. Why were the shepherds terrified (v. 9)? How would you have reacted in their situation?
3. Why was Jesus sleeping "in the manger" (v. 16)? Why would the Son of God be born into such poverty?
4. Why was Jesus born in the first place? What was His purpose on earth? What did He accomplish?
5. Have you personally been "born again" into the family of Jesus? If so, what does it mean to you to be part of that family?

1:78 Or *the Morning Light from Heaven is about to visit us.*

2:1 Augustus. Luke roots Jesus' birth firmly in history. Augustus ruled the Roman Empire from B.C. 30 to A.D. 14. Originally known as Gaius Octavius (or Octavian), he was awarded the title Augustus (which means "majestic" or "highly revered") by the Roman senate and became known thereafter as Caesar Augustus. Augustus was a wise ruler who encouraged the arts and built many fine projects. He also brought an unprecedented period of peace to the world. **register.** From about 30 B.C. onward, the Caesars ordered people in the various Roman provinces to be registered every 14 years for a census for purposes of taxation. Resistance from the population and from local rulers sometimes meant census-taking required several years to complete. While there is firm evidence of a census after King Herod's death in A.D. 6, there is no external source that allows us to know whether the census mentioned here was a separate, earlier one or the beginning stages of the census completed at that date.

2:3 All returned to their own ancestral towns. Since Joseph and Mary lived in Galilee, they must have owned some property in Bethlehem. Roman custom required people who owned property in another location from where they lived to register there as well. Bethlehem, a three to four-day journey from Galilee, was the village where King David, through whose line the Messiah was to come, had lived.

2:5 to be registered along with Mary. In some provinces, the Romans charged a poll tax on women 12 years of age or older. **his fiancée, who was now obviously pregnant.** Their betrothal had not yet been consummated by intercourse (Matt. 1:24-25).

2:7 first child. The firstborn of every Jewish family was dedicated to God in a special way (Ex. 13:12). **She wrapped him snugly in strips of cloth.** The tradition of the time was to wrap a baby in strips of cloth. Such cloths would give the child the feeling of being securely held. **manger.** A feeding trough for animals. **lodging.** This is either a building used for the accommodation of travelers or a spare room in a private home. Either way, there was no space for the couple, who stayed with the animals. A tradition dating back to the second century maintains this was in a cave on the site of which today is the Church of the Nativity.

2:8 shepherds. Since temple authorities kept flocks of sheep for sacrificial purposes pastured near Bethlehem, it might be that the shepherds of these flocks were the ones visited by the angels. This happened at a time of year when sheep could still be kept in the field, which was sometime between April and November. The date of December 25 as the birth of Christ was selected in the fourth century.

2:9 an angel of the Lord. In some Old Testament passages, the angel of the Lord is identified as God himself (Gen. 16:7; Ex. 3:2; Judg. 6:11), indicating His divine authority and splendor. Throughout the Bible, angels serve as God's agents of instruction, judgment, and deliverance. **radiance of the Lord's glory.** The overwhelmingly powerful light that accompanies the presence of God (Ps. 104:1-2; Ezek. 1:4). **they were terrified.** Often in the Bible when an angel appears to a person, the response is one of terror. It is the fear of being in the presence of something supernatural, powerful, and totally foreign to one's experience (1:29-30; Dan. 10:7).

2:10 to all people. Another emphasis on the universality of the gospel, especially as presented by Luke.

2:11 The Savior . . .the Messiah, the Lord. "Savior," a term in the Old Testament which only applies to God, is one who delivers his people from evil and harm. "Messiah" means one anointed by God. "Lord" implies both His authority and Deity.

2:12 this sign. In the Old Testament, God sometimes granted signs that pointed out to people the reliability of His message. The "sign" of the Lord is, ironically, that of a baby wrapped in cloths and lying in an animal's feeding trough.

2:13 armies of heaven. At a birth, neighbors and friends would gather to celebrate. At this birth, the angels fulfill this function.

2:14 peace on earth to those with whom God is pleased. While older versions divide this phrase into two clauses (peace on earth / good will toward men), the NLT, with its single clause accenting God's promise of peace to His people, is to be preferred.

16 They hurried to the village and found Mary and
Joseph. And there was the baby, lying in the manger.
17 After seeing him, the shepherds told everyone what
had happened and what the angel had said to them
about this child. 18 All who heard the shepherds' story
were astonished, 19 but Mary kept all these things in
her heart and thought about them often. 20 The shep-
herds went back to their flocks, glorifying and prais-
ing God for all they had heard and seen. It was just as
the angel had told them.

JESUS IS PRESENTED IN THE TEMPLE

21 Eight days later, when the baby was circumcised, he
was named Jesus, the name given him by the angel
even before he was conceived.
22 Then it was time for their purification offering, as
required by the law of Moses after the birth of a child;
so his parents took him to Jerusalem to present him
to the Lord. 23 The law of the Lord says, "If a woman's
first child is a boy, he must be dedicated to the LORD."*
24 So they offered the sacrifice required in the law of
the Lord—"either a pair of turtledoves or two young
pigeons."*

THE PROPHECY OF SIMEON

25 At that time there was a man in Jerusalem named
Simeon. He was righteous and devout and was eager-
ly waiting for the Messiah to come and rescue Israel.
The Holy Spirit was upon him 26 and had revealed to
him that he would not die until he had seen the Lord's
Messiah. 27 That day the Spirit led him to the Temple. So
when Mary and Joseph came to present the baby Jesus
to the Lord as the law required, 28 Simeon was there. He
took the child in his arms and praised God, saying,

29 "Sovereign Lord, now let your servant die in peace,
as you have promised.
30 I have seen your salvation,
31 which you have prepared for all people.
32 He is a light to reveal God to the nations,
and he is the glory of your people Israel!"

33 Jesus' parents were amazed at what was being
said about him. 34 Then Simeon blessed them, and he
said to Mary, the baby's mother, "This child is destined
to cause many in Israel to fall, and many others to
rise. He has been sent as a sign from God, but many
will oppose him. 35 As a result, the deepest thoughts
of many hearts will be revealed. And a sword will
pierce your very soul."

THE PROPHECY OF ANNA

36 Anna, a prophet, was also there in the Temple. She
was the daughter of Phanuel from the tribe of Asher,
and she was very old. Her husband died when they
had been married only seven years. 37 Then she lived
as a widow to the age of eighty-four.* She never left
the Temple but stayed there day and night, worship-
ing God with fasting and prayer. 38 She came along
just as Simeon was talking with Mary and Joseph,
and she began praising God. She talked about the
child to everyone who had been waiting expectantly
for God to rescue Jerusalem.
39 When Jesus' parents had fulfilled all the require-
ments of the law of the Lord, they returned home
to Nazareth in Galilee. 40 There the child grew up
healthy and strong. He was filled with wisdom, and
God's favor was on him.

JESUS SPEAKS WITH THE TEACHERS

41 Every year Jesus' parents went to Jerusalem for the
Passover festival. 42 When Jesus was twelve years old,
they attended the festival as usual. 43 After the cele-
bration was over, they started home to Nazareth, but
Jesus stayed behind in Jerusalem. His parents didn't
miss him at first, 44 because they assumed he was
among the other travelers. But when he didn't show
up that evening, they started looking for him among
their relatives and friends.

IN DAD'S HOUSE

1. Describe a time when you got lost, ran away, or were separated from your parents.

LUKE 2:41-52

2. Why had "Jesus stayed behind" in Jerusalem after His parents had left?
3. Why would Jesus, the Son of God, sit and ask questions about the Bible?
4. How did Joseph and Mary react? What would your parents have said?
5. What did Jesus mean when He said, "I must be in my Father's house" (v. 49)?
6. Jesus grew "in favor with God" (v. 52). What can you do to grow in your relationship with God?

2:23 Exod 13:2. **2:24** Lev 12:8. **2:37** Or *She had been a widow for eighty-four years.*

2:21 eight days later, when the baby was circumcised. The Old Testament Law required that male infants be circumcised on the eighth day (Lev. 12:3). **Jesus.** Jesus was a common Jewish name meaning "God saves."

2:29 let your servant die in peace. The thought is that of a slave requesting leave after fulfilling a task his master had given him. Simeon can approach death easily now, not only because God had kept His promise (v. 26) but because he could be assured that this child would "destroy death." (2 Tim. 1:10).

2:33 Jesus' parents were amazed. The references to Joseph as Jesus' father should be read simply as a shorthand way of referring to Joseph, not as an implied denial of the virgin birth. While Joseph and Mary had already heard many strange things about their Son, they would certainly not be immune to such a startling declaration as Simeon's.

2:34-35 said to Mary. Simeon foreshadows the rest of the Gospel by warning Mary that in the process of fulfilling Jesus' mission there will be great pain for her.

2:36 Asher. One of the 10 tribes "lost" in the Assyrian invasion of Israel in 722 B.C.

2:37 She never left the temple. Since it is unlikely that she could have lived at the temple, the stress is on her great devotion to God as she, like Simeon, prayed and waited for God to fulfill His promises to Israel.

2:39 returned to home to Nazareth in Galilee. In contrast, Matthew reports the family stayed much longer in Bethlehem and then left for Egypt when threatened by Herod. Only after Herod's death did they return to Nazareth in Galilee (Matt. 2:13-23).

2:42 When Jesus was twelve years old. At age 13, a Jewish boy was expected to take his place in the religious community of Israel. Age 12 would be a time of preparation for assuming responsibilities of adulthood.

2:43-44 Jesus stayed behind . . . but his parents didn't miss him. Jewish pilgrims from outside Jerusalem traveled to and from the feast in large caravans. Typically, the women and children would be up front, while the men and older boys traveled along behind. In the evenings, when the caravan stopped for the night, families would regroup. It would have been easy during the day for Mary and Joseph to each assume that Jesus was with the other parent or with friends.

45 When they couldn't find him, they went back to
Jerusalem to search for him there. 46 Three days lat-
er they finally discovered him in the Temple, sitting
among the religious teachers, listening to them and
asking questions. 47 All who heard him were amazed
at his understanding and his answers.
48 His parents didn't know what to think. "Son," his
mother said to him, "why have you done this to us?
Your father and I have been frantic, searching for you
everywhere."
49 "But why did you need to search?" he asked.
"Didn't you know that I must be in my Father's
house?"* 50 But they didn't understand what he meant.
51 Then he returned to Nazareth with them and
was obedient to them. And his mother stored all these
things in her heart.
52 Jesus grew in wisdom and in stature and in favor
with God and all the people.

JOHN THE BAPTIST PREPARES THE WAY

3 It was now the fifteenth year of the reign of Tiber-
ius, the Roman emperor. Pontius Pilate was gover-
nor over Judea; Herod Antipas was ruler* over Galilee;
his brother Philip was ruler* over Iturea and Traconi-
tis; Lysanias was ruler over Abilene. 2 Annas and Ca-
iaphas were the high priests. At this time a message
from God came to John son of Zechariah, who was
living in the wilderness. 3 Then John went from place
to place on both sides of the Jordan River, preaching
that people should be baptized to show that they had
repented of their sins and turned to God to be forgiven.
4 Isaiah had spoken of John when he said,

"He is a voice shouting in the wilderness,
'Prepare the way for the LORD's coming!
Clear the road for him!
5 The valleys will be filled,
and the mountains and hills made level.
The curves will be straightened,
and the rough places made smooth.
6 And then all people will see
the salvation sent from God.'"*

7 When the crowds came to John for baptism, he
said, "You brood of snakes! Who warned you to flee
the coming wrath? 8 Prove by the way you live that
you have repented of your sins and turned to God.
Don't just say to each other, 'We're safe, for we are de-
scendants of Abraham.' That means nothing, for I tell
you, God can create children of Abraham from these
very stones. 9 Even now the ax of God's judgment is
poised, ready to sever the roots of the trees. Yes, every
tree that does not produce good fruit will be chopped
down and thrown into the fire."
10 The crowds asked, "What should we do?"
11 John replied, "If you have two shirts, give one to
the poor. If you have food, share it with those who are
hungry."
12 Even corrupt tax collectors came to be baptized
and asked, "Teacher, what should we do?"
13 He replied, "Collect no more taxes than the gov-
ernment requires."
14 "What should we do?" asked some soldiers.
John replied, "Don't extort money or make false ac-
cusations. And be content with your pay."
15 Everyone was expecting the Messiah to come soon,
and they were eager to know whether John might be
the Messiah. 16 John answered their questions by say-
ing, "I baptize you with* water; but someone is com-
ing soon who is greater than I am—so much greater
that I'm not even worthy to be his slave and untie the
straps of his sandals. He will baptize you with the
Holy Spirit and with fire.* 17 He is ready to separate the
chaff from the wheat with his winnowing fork. Then
he will clean up the threshing area, gathering the
wheat into his barn but burning the chaff with nev-
er-ending fire." 18 John used many such warnings as he
announced the Good News to the people.
19 John also publicly criticized Herod Antipas, the rul-
er of Galilee,* for marrying Herodias, his brother's wife,
and for many other wrongs he had done. 20 So Herod put
John in prison, adding this sin to his many others.

THE BAPTISM OF JESUS

21 One day when the crowds were being baptized,
Jesus himself was baptized. As he was praying, the
heavens opened, 22 and the Holy Spirit, in bodily form,
descended on him like a dove. And a voice from heav-
en said, "You are my dearly loved Son, and you bring
me great joy."*

2:49 Or *"Didn't you realize that I should be involved with my Father's affairs?"* **3:1a** Greek *Herod was tetrarch.* Herod Antipas was a son of King Herod. **3:1b** Greek *tetrarch;* also in 3:1c. **3:4-6** Isa 40:3-5 (Greek version). **3:16a** Or *in.* **3:16b** Or *in the Holy Spirit and in fire.* **3:19** Greek *Herod the tetrarch.* **3:22** Some manuscripts read *my Son, and today I have become your Father.*

2:46 Three days later. This does not mean they spent three days in Jerusalem looking for Jesus. Day one was the trip out of the city with the caravan—probably a walk of about 25 miles. Day two was their trip back to the city. Day three was when they found Him in the temple. **sitting among the religious teachers.** It was common for the rabbis to discuss theology in the temple courts. Interested listeners would sit with them and converse about questions that arose from their discussions. **asking questions.** Even Jesus had to develop as a boy. We learn from this account that He was much different than any other child.

2:47 all those who heard him were amazed. This seems to be the first reason why Luke included this story. Jesus' insight into the Law drew the respect and wonder of His elders.

2:48 Mary's response is not amazement at Jesus' insight into the Law but a motherly one of frustration and concern because of the worry Jesus' absence caused. **Your father and I.** Even though the infant narratives describe Jesus' birth as a virgin birth, Joseph took Jesus as his own child and acted as father to Him.

2:49 I must be. Luke records several statements which reflect Jesus' sense of the necessity of His mission and the steps required to fulfill it (4:43; 9:22; 24:7). Mary and Joseph's inability to comprehend what He meant is paralleled later on by his family's misunderstanding of Him (8:19-21).

2:51 was obedient to them. Jesus may have had an awareness that He was God's unique Son, but that didn't keep Him from being obedient to His human parents.

2:52 grew. Jesus' growth was not one-dimensional. Jesus grew along several dimensions. He grew physically (in stature). He grew intellectually (in wisdom). He grew socially (in favor with men). But most of all He grew spiritually (in favor with God).

3:7 brood of snakes! The image painted by these words is of snakes slithering through the undergrowth, trying to escape the oncoming fire.

3:8 descendants of Abraham. John warns that they cannot retreat into an easy assumption that they will be spared judgment just because they are members of God's chosen race.

3:16 not even worthy to be his slave and untie the straps of his sandals. The task of removing the master's sandals was that of the lowest ranking slave in the household. The Messiah is so great that John feels unworthy to perform even that lowly function for Him.

3:21-22 Jesus himself was baptized. This scene really belongs with verses 1-20 as it briefly records the baptism of Jesus by John. Unlike Matthew's longer account, which includes His conversation with John, Luke's stress is that the importance of this event lay in Jesus' reception of the Spirit and the divine declaration of His status as Son.

THE ANCESTORS OF JESUS

23 Jesus was about thirty years old when he began his public ministry.

Jesus was known as the son of Joseph.
Joseph was the son of Heli.
24 Heli was the son of Matthat.
Matthat was the son of Levi.
Levi was the son of Melki.
Melki was the son of Jannai.
Jannai was the son of Joseph.
25 Joseph was the son of Mattathias.
Mattathias was the son of Amos.
Amos was the son of Nahum.
Nahum was the son of Esli.
Esli was the son of Naggai.
26 Naggai was the son of Maath.
Maath was the son of Mattathias.
Mattathias was the son of Semein.
Semein was the son of Josech.
Josech was the son of Joda.
27 Joda was the son of Joanan.
Joanan was the son of Rhesa.
Rhesa was the son of Zerubbabel.
Zerubbabel was the son of Shealtiel.
Shealtiel was the son of Neri.
28 Neri was the son of Melki.
Melki was the son of Addi.
Addi was the son of Cosam.
Cosam was the son of Elmadam.
Elmadam was the son of Er.
29 Er was the son of Joshua.
Joshua was the son of Eliezer.
Eliezer was the son of Jorim.
Jorim was the son of Matthat.
Matthat was the son of Levi.
30 Levi was the son of Simeon.
Simeon was the son of Judah.
Judah was the son of Joseph.
Joseph was the son of Jonam.
Jonam was the son of Eliakim.
31 Eliakim was the son of Melea.
Melea was the son of Menna.
Menna was the son of Mattatha.
Mattatha was the son of Nathan.
Nathan was the son of David.
32 David was the son of Jesse.
Jesse was the son of Obed.
Obed was the son of Boaz.
Boaz was the son of Salmon.*
Salmon was the son of Nahshon.
33 Nahshon was the son of Amminadab.
Amminadab was the son of Admin.
Admin was the son of Arni.*
Arni was the son of Hezron.
Hezron was the son of Perez.
Perez was the son of Judah.
34 Judah was the son of Jacob.
Jacob was the son of Isaac.
Isaac was the son of Abraham.
Abraham was the son of Terah.
Terah was the son of Nahor.
35 Nahor was the son of Serug.
Serug was the son of Reu.
Reu was the son of Peleg.
Peleg was the son of Eber.
Eber was the son of Shelah.
36 Shelah was the son of Cainan.
Cainan was the son of Arphaxad.
Arphaxad was the son of Shem.
Shem was the son of Noah.
Noah was the son of Lamech.
37 Lamech was the son of Methuselah.
Methuselah was the son of Enoch.
Enoch was the son of Jared.
Jared was the son of Mahalalel.
Mahalalel was the son of Kenan.
38 Kenan was the son of Enosh.*
Enosh was the son of Seth.
Seth was the son of Adam.
Adam was the son of God.

THE TEMPTATION OF JESUS

4 Then Jesus, full of the Holy Spirit, returned from
the Jordan River. He was led by the Spirit in the
wilderness,* 2 where he was tempted by the devil for
forty days. Jesus ate nothing all that time and became
very hungry.
3 Then the devil said to him, "If you are the Son of
God, tell this stone to become a loaf of bread."
4 But Jesus told him, "No! The Scriptures say, 'People
do not live by bread alone.'*"
5 Then the devil took him up and revealed to him
all the kingdoms of the world in a moment of time. 6 "I
will give you the glory of these kingdoms and authority over them," the devil said, "because they are mine
to give to anyone I please. 7 I will give it all to you if
you will worship me."
8 Jesus replied, "The Scriptures say,

'You must worship the LORD your God
and serve only him.'*"

3:32 Greek *Sala,* a variant spelling of Salmon; also in 3:32b. See Ruth 4:20-21. 3:33 Some manuscripts read *Amminadab was the son of Aram. Arni* and *Aram* are alternate spellings of Ram. See 1 Chr 2:9-10. 3:38 Greek *Enos,* a variant spelling of Enosh; also in 3:38b. See Gen 5:6. 4:1 Some manuscripts read *into the wilderness.* 4:4 Deut 8:3. 4:8 Deut 6:13.

3:32 Matthew's genealogy agrees with Luke's from David to Abraham (1 Chron. 2:1-15).

4:1 full of the Holy Spirit . . . led by the Spirit. The work of the Holy Spirit is a major concern for Luke both in his Gospel and in Acts. Satan's confrontation of Jesus was not a result of being apart from the Spirit but an integral part of the Spirit's preparing Him for His mission.

4:2 tempted … forty days. Moses fasted 40 days on Mount Sinai while receiving the commandments (Ex. 34:28). **Jesus ate nothing.** Fasting was a means of communion with God. It was this communion that Satan sought to destroy as he tempted Jesus.

4:3 If you are the Son of God. Satan challenges Jesus at the point of His identity and authority. Surely it must have seemed ironic that the Son of God should be tired, hungry, and apparently alone in such a desolate area. **bread.** While there is nothing inherently wrong with turning stones to bread, the appeal of the temptation was for Jesus to use His power to meet His own needs instead of trusting His Father to do so.

4:5-7 kingdoms of the world. The second temptation is an appeal to ambition and glory. Probably through some form of vision Satan enabled Jesus to see the splendor, wealth, and power that is represented by the world's political authorities. For the price tag of rejecting God, Satan offers Jesus a painless, immediate way to power and fame. It was only by His obedience to the Father Jesus would become the King of kings, possessing all authority and power (Ps. 2:8-9; Dan. 7:14).

4:8 Jesus replied. Jesus quotes Deuteronomy 6:13, again affirming His loyalty to God and God's ways.

THAT'S TEMPTING!

1. What is the longest you have gone without food? What food did you miss most?

LUKE 4:1-13

2. What ways did the devil use to tempt Jesus? How did Jesus resist those temptations?
3. Why would Jesus have even been tempted to throw Himself off the top of the temple? To what was the devil trying to appeal?
4. What areas of temptation are you facing lately? How would giving in to those temptations affect your life and the lives of those around you?
5. How can you follow Jesus' example in resisting those temptations?

9 Then the devil took him to Jerusalem, to the high-
est point of the Temple, and said, "If you are the Son of
God, jump off! 10 For the Scriptures say,

'He will order his angels to protect and guard
you.
11 And they will hold you up with their hands
so you won't even hurt your foot on a stone.'*"

12 Jesus responded, "The Scriptures also say, 'You
must not test the LORD your God.'*"
13 When the devil had finished tempting Jesus, he
left him until the next opportunity came.

JESUS REJECTED AT NAZARETH

14 Then Jesus returned to Galilee, filled with the Holy
Spirit's power. Reports about him spread quickly
through the whole region. 15 He taught regularly in
their synagogues and was praised by everyone.
16 When he came to the village of Nazareth, his
boyhood home, he went as usual to the synagogue
on the Sabbath and stood up to read the Scriptures.
17 The scroll of Isaiah the prophet was handed to him.
He unrolled the scroll and found the place where this
was written:

18 "The Spirit of the LORD is upon me,
for he has anointed me to bring Good News to
the poor.
He has sent me to proclaim that captives will be
released,
that the blind will see,
that the oppressed will be set free,
19 and that the time of the LORD's favor has come.*"

20 He rolled up the scroll, handed it back to the at-
tendant, and sat down. All eyes in the synagogue
looked at him intently. 21 Then he began to speak to
them. "The Scripture you've just heard has been ful-
filled this very day!"
22 Everyone spoke well of him and was amazed by
the gracious words that came from his lips. "How can
this be?" they asked. "Isn't this Joseph's son?"
23 Then he said, "You will undoubtedly quote me
this proverb: 'Physician, heal yourself'—meaning, 'Do
miracles here in your hometown like those you did in
Capernaum.' 24 But I tell you the truth, no prophet is
accepted in his own hometown.
25 "Certainly there were many needy widows in Is-
rael in Elijah's time, when the heavens were closed for
three and a half years, and a severe famine devastated

GET OUT OF TOWN

1. Where did you grow up? What did you like best/least about your hometown?

LUKE 4:14-30

2. Why did Jesus choose this particular passage from Isaiah to read (vv. 18-19)?
3. What did Jesus mean by suggesting that He had come "to proclaim that captives will be released" (v. 18)?
4. Why did the people get so angry that they "forced him" out of town and tried to murder Him (v. 29)?
5. Jesus' words about Elijah meant that God would not heal those who rejected Him. Have you accepted Jesus or rejected Him?

4:10-11 Ps 91:11-12. **4:12** Deut 6:16. **4:18-19** Or *and to proclaim the acceptable year of the LORD.* Isa 61:1-2 (Greek version); 58:6.

4:9 the highest point of the temple. Barclay says this would have been a point 450 feet above the Kidron Valley. **If you are the Son of God.** Once again Jesus' identity as the Messiah is being attacked (v. 3).

4:12 The Scriptures also say. Jesus quotes Deuteronomy 6:16 and again asserts His complete trust in His Father. His Word does not need to be tested in foolish ways in order to find out it is true.

4:13 he left him. Having been resisted in his appeals to self-interest, power, and pride, Satan left Jesus. His opposition to Jesus surfaces again in Jesus' conflicts with demons later on and ultimately in his influence upon Judas, in the events leading to the betrayal of Jesus (22:3).

4:14 Galilee. From chapters 4:14–9:50, Luke records Jesus' ministry in Galilee, a province about 50 miles long and 25 miles wide in the north of Palestine. **filled with the Holy Spirit's power.** Just as the Spirit led Jesus into His time of testing (4:1; Matt. 4:1), so the Spirit now empowers Jesus' ministry.

4:15 synagogues. While the temple in Jerusalem was the religious center for all Jews, the community synagogue was the focal point of weekly worship and teaching. Jesus' initial ministry was as a well-received itinerant preacher.

4:16 stood up to read. As a sign of reverence for God, men would stand as they read the Scripture and then sit down to teach.

4:17 the scroll. Since Nazareth was a small village, it is unlikely that the synagogue would have been able to afford to have scrolls of the entire sacred writings. The Isaiah scroll was undoubtedly a prized possession of the synagogue.

4:18 The passage Jesus read was from Isaiah 61:1-2 (with the addition of a phrase from 58:6). Using the metaphors of people in prison, blindness, and slavery, the prophet speaks of his God-given mission to proclaim freedom and pardon to people who are oppressed and burdened.

4:19 the time of the LORD's favor. This refers to the Jubilee Year of Leviticus 25. Every 50 years, the Jews were to release their slaves, cancel all debts, and return land to the families of its original owners. In this context it became a symbol of the deliverance and new order of justice that God intended to bring about.

4:21 The Scripture . . . has been fulfilled this very day. The phrase is reminiscent of Mark 1:15 with its announcement that the "kingdom of God has come near." In both cases, Jesus asserts that the new era foretold by Isaiah has begun because He has come to bring it about.

4:22 Joseph's son. This may be a slur, alluding to rumors of Jesus' illegitimacy (Mark 6:3). In stark contrast to God's declaration in 3:22 (Matt. 3:17) that Jesus is God's Son, the hometown people could only see Jesus as Joseph's boy.

4:24 No prophet is accepted in his own hometown. This proverb also has Greek parallels.

the land. 26 Yet Elijah was not sent to any of them. He was sent instead to a foreigner—a widow of Zarephath in the land of Sidon. 27 And many in Israel had leprosy in the time of the prophet Elisha, but the only one healed was Naaman, a Syrian."

28 When they heard this, the people in the synagogue were furious. 29 Jumping up, they mobbed him and forced him to the edge of the hill on which the town was built. They intended to push him over the cliff, 30 but he passed right through the crowd and went on his way.

JESUS CASTS OUT A DEMON

31 Then Jesus went to Capernaum, a town in Galilee, and taught there in the synagogue every Sabbath day. 32 There, too, the people were amazed at his teaching, for he spoke with authority.

33 Once when he was in the synagogue, a man possessed by a demon—an evil* spirit—cried out, shouting, 34 "Go away! Why are you interfering with us, Jesus of Nazareth? Have you come to destroy us? I know who you are—the Holy One of God!"

35 Jesus cut him short. "Be quiet! Come out of the man," he ordered. At that, the demon threw the man to the floor as the crowd watched; then it came out of him without hurting him further.

36 Amazed, the people exclaimed, "What authority and power this man's words possess! Even evil spirits obey him, and they flee at his command!" 37 The news about Jesus spread through every village in the entire region.

JESUS HEALS MANY PEOPLE

38 After leaving the synagogue that day, Jesus went to Simon's home, where he found Simon's mother-in-law very sick with a high fever. "Please heal her," everyone begged. 39 Standing at her bedside, he rebuked the fever, and it left her. And she got up at once and prepared a meal for them.

40 As the sun went down that evening, people throughout the village brought sick family members to Jesus. No matter what their diseases were, the touch of his hand healed every one. 41 Many were possessed by demons; and the demons came out at his command, shouting, "You are the Son of God!" But because they knew he was the Messiah, he rebuked them and refused to let them speak.

JESUS CONTINUES TO PREACH

42 Early the next morning Jesus went out to an isolated place. The crowds searched everywhere for him, and when they finally found him, they begged him not to leave them. 43 But he replied, "I must preach the Good News of the Kingdom of God in other towns, too, because that is why I was sent." 44 So he continued to travel around, preaching in synagogues throughout Judea.*

THE FIRST DISCIPLES

5 One day as Jesus was preaching on the shore of the Sea of Galilee,* great crowds pressed in on him to listen to the word of God. 2 He noticed two empty boats at the water's edge, for the fishermen had left them and were washing their nets. 3 Stepping into one of the boats, Jesus asked Simon,* its owner, to push it out into the water. So he sat in the boat and taught the crowds from there.

4 When he had finished speaking, he said to Simon, "Now go out where it is deeper, and let down your nets to catch some fish."

5 "Master," Simon replied, "we worked hard all last night and didn't catch a thing. But if you say so, I'll let the nets down again." 6 And this time their nets were so full of fish they began to tear! 7 A shout for help brought their partners in the other boat, and soon both boats were filled with fish and on the verge of sinking.

8 When Simon Peter realized what had happened, he fell to his knees before Jesus and said, "Oh, Lord, please leave me—I'm such a sinful man." 9 For he was awestruck by the number of fish they had caught, as were the others with him. 10 His partners, James and John, the sons of Zebedee, were also amazed.

Jesus replied to Simon, "Don't be afraid! From now on you'll be fishing for people!" 11 And as soon as they landed, they left everything and followed Jesus.

JESUS HEALS A MAN WITH LEPROSY

12 In one of the villages, Jesus met a man with an advanced case of leprosy. When the man saw Jesus, he bowed with his face to the ground, begging to be healed. "Lord," he said, "if you are willing, you can heal me and make me clean."

13 Jesus reached out and touched him. "I am willing," he said. "Be healed!" And instantly the leprosy

4:33 Greek *unclean;* also in 4:36. 4:44 Some manuscripts read *Galilee.* 5:1 Greek *Lake Gennesaret,* another name for the Sea of Galilee. 5:3 *Simon* is called "Peter" in 6:14 and thereafter.

4:32 he spoke with authority. Most rabbis taught the Law through quoting what other rabbis had said about it. In contrast, Jesus' teaching impressed His hearers with its relevancy, power, and directness.

4:33 an evil spirit. These were seen as malignant, supernatural agents of Satan, able to harm and possess people. In overcoming the demon, Jesus demonstrated His power over the Devil.

4:34 I know who you are. The demon clearly identified Jesus. He knew the person Jesus, the man from Nazareth, and he knew the nature of God, the "Holy One," recognizing that Jesus had the power to destroy him.

4:41 You are the Son of God! While Satan attacked Jesus at the point of His divine nature (vv. 3,9), the defeated demons acknowledged His Deity. **refused to let them speak.** Jesus silenced the demons. He did not want their witness, and it was not yet time for this general announcement.

5:2 washing their nets. In the morning, fishermen would clean and repair their nets..

5:3 two empty boats. While one belonged to Simon Peter, the other boat may have been owned by James and John (Mark 1:19), Simon's partners in the fishing business (v. 10). A fishing boat was an open craft about 20 to 30 feet long.

5:4-5 let down your nets. Jesus' command seemed foolish since mid-morning was not the time fish would be feeding. Picture tired and hungry men who have worked unsuccessfully all night. Why in the world should they listen to a religious teacher when it comes to their fishing business? Yet, Simon Peter decides to go along with Him and was rewarded for it.

5:6-7 they began to tear. In contrast to Simon's doubt, Luke underscores the magnitude of the catch, so large that it tore the nets and threatened to sink Simon's boat as well as that of his partners!

5:8 he fell to his knees before Jesus. Just what Simon Peter recognized about Jesus' identity at this point is unclear since "Lord" can be a title for God or a title of respect for an esteemed person. In any case, it is apparent that Peter was thoroughly convinced that Jesus was at least a rabbi.

5:12 leprosy. Often identified as leprosy, the term was used to cover a wide range of skin diseases besides the true leprosy of Hanson's Disease; no diagnosis was dreaded more than leprosy since it led not only to physical disfigurement and a slow death but social banishment as well.

5:13 touched him. Since touching a leper was unimaginable due to the risk of contracting the disease and the violation of the Law that prohibited such contact, Jesus' touch of this leper communicated the tremendous extent of Jesus' compassion as well as His power.

GIVING IT ALL UP

1. Where is the best fishing spot in your area? What is the biggest fish you've ever caught?

LUKE 5:1-11

2. Jesus was not a professional fisherman, while Simon and the others were. How might you have reacted to Jesus telling you how to do your job?
3. Consider verse 8. Why did Simon Peter tell Jesus to "leave me"? Why did he suddenly realize that he was "too much of a sinner"?
4. Peter, James, and John "left everything and followed Jesus" (v. 11). Where is Jesus asking you to follow Him? What must you give up to follow Him?

disappeared. 14 Then Jesus instructed him not to tell
anyone what had happened. He said, "Go to the priest
and let him examine you. Take along the offering re-
quired in the law of Moses for those who have been
healed of leprosy.* This will be a public testimony that
you have been cleansed."
15 But despite Jesus' instructions, the report of his
power spread even faster, and vast crowds came to
hear him preach and to be healed of their diseases.
16 But Jesus often withdrew to the wilderness for prayer.

JESUS HEALS A PARALYZED MAN

17 One day while Jesus was teaching, some Pharisees
and teachers of religious law were sitting nearby. (It
seemed that these men showed up from every village
in all Galilee and Judea, as well as from Jerusalem.)
And the Lord's healing power was strongly with
Jesus.
18 Some men came carrying a paralyzed man on a
sleeping mat. They tried to take him inside to Jesus,
19 but they couldn't reach him because of the crowd.
So they went up to the roof and took off some tiles.
Then they lowered the sick man on his mat down into
the crowd, right in front of Jesus. 20 Seeing their faith,
Jesus said to the man, "Young man, your sins are for-
given."
21 But the Pharisees and teachers of religious law
said to themselves, "Who does he think he is? That's
blasphemy! Only God can forgive sins!"
22 Jesus knew what they were thinking, so he asked
them, "Why do you question this in your hearts? 23 Is it
easier to say 'Your sins are forgiven,' or 'Stand up and
walk'? 24 So I will prove to you that the Son of Man*
has the authority on earth to forgive sins." Then Jesus
turned to the paralyzed man and said, "Stand up, pick
up your mat, and go home!"
25 And immediately, as everyone watched, the man
jumped up, picked up his mat, and went home prais-
ing God. 26 Everyone was gripped with great wonder
and awe, and they praised God, exclaiming, "We have
seen amazing things today!"

JESUS CALLS LEVI (MATTHEW)

27 Later, as Jesus left the town, he saw a tax collector
named Levi sitting at his tax collector's booth. "Follow
me and be my disciple," Jesus said to him. 28 So Levi got
up, left everything, and followed him.
29 Later, Levi held a banquet in his home with Jesus
as the guest of honor. Many of Levi's fellow tax col-
lectors and other guests also ate with them. 30 But the
Pharisees and their teachers of religious law com-
plained bitterly to Jesus' disciples, "Why do you eat
and drink with such scum?*"
31 Jesus answered them, "Healthy people don't need
a doctor—sick people do. 32 I have come to call not
those who think they are righteous, but those who
know they are sinners and need to repent."

A DISCUSSION ABOUT FASTING

33 One day some people said to Jesus, "John the Bap-
tist's disciples fast and pray regularly, and so do the
disciples of the Pharisees. Why are your disciples al-
ways eating and drinking?"
34 Jesus responded, "Do wedding guests fast while
celebrating with the groom? Of course not. 35 But
someday the groom will be taken away from them,
and then they will fast."
36 Then Jesus gave them this illustration: "No one
tears a piece of cloth from a new garment and uses
it to patch an old garment. For then the new garment
would be ruined, and the new patch wouldn't even
match the old garment.
37 "And no one puts new wine into old wineskins.
For the new wine would burst the wineskins, spilling
the wine and ruining the skins. 38 New wine must be
stored in new wineskins. 39 But no one who drinks the
old wine seems to want the new wine. 'The old is just
fine,' they say."

A DISCUSSION ABOUT THE SABBATH

6 One Sabbath day as Jesus was walking through
some grainfields, his disciples broke off heads of
grain, rubbed off the husks in their hands, and ate the

5:14 See Lev 14:2-32. 5:24 "Son of Man" is a title Jesus used for himself. 5:30 Greek *with tax collectors and sinners?*

5:14 instructed him not to tell anyone. There has been much speculation as to why Jesus in many instances discouraged people from telling others what He has done or who He is (Matt. 16:20; Mark 3:12; 5:43; 7:36). The most prevalent view of why He urged this "messianic secret" was that Jesus had to prevent the crowds from proclaiming Him Messiah before they knew what kind of Messiah He was (one who would suffer and die, not the conquering hero of popular imagination).

5:17 Pharisees. A small, powerful religious sect whose prime concern was keeping the law. Since their standards were too high for most Jews to keep in daily life, they were respected as especially devout, godly people. **teachers of religious law.** Literally, "scribes." Originally, it was their job to make copies of the Old Testament. Because of their familiarity with Scripture, their role evolved into that of teachers of the law.

5:21 blasphemy. Blasphemy is "contempt for God" punishable by death (Lev. 24:16). Since the teachers of the law believed that illness was the direct result of sin (John 9:2), they assumed that the sick could not recover until their sin had been forgiven by God, who alone could offer forgiveness. Hence they are distressed that Jesus pronounced forgiveness since this was tantamount to a claim of Deity.

5:23 Is it easier? There are certainly instances where paralysis has been related to unresolved guilt. That is not to say, however, that in *every* instance paralysis or disease is the result of sin. See Luke 13:1-5 and John 9:1-5.

5:27 Levi. Generally thought to be Matthew, referred to in Matthew 9:9.

5:33 fast. Fasting, almsgiving, and prayer were three traditional practices followed by all Jewish sects.

6:1 Sabbath. By Jesus' time the scribes had developed scores of laws that obscured the point that the Sabbath was meant to be a welcome day of rest. **broke off heads of grain.** Not considered stealing since it was permissible for hungry travelers to pluck and eat grain from a field (Deut. 23:25).

grain. 2 But some Pharisees said, "Why are you break-
ing the law by harvesting grain on the Sabbath?"
3 Jesus replied, "Haven't you read in the Scriptures
what David did when he and his companions were
hungry? 4 He went into the house of God and broke
the law by eating the sacred loaves of bread that only
the priests can eat. He also gave some to his compan-
ions." 5 And Jesus added, "The Son of Man* is Lord,
even over the Sabbath."

JESUS HEALS ON THE SABBATH

6 On another Sabbath day, a man with a deformed right
hand was in the synagogue while Jesus was teach-
ing. 7 The teachers of religious law and the Pharisees
watched Jesus closely. If he healed the man's hand,
they planned to accuse him of working on the Sabbath.
8 But Jesus knew their thoughts. He said to the man
with the deformed hand, "Come and stand in front
of everyone." So the man came forward. 9 Then Jesus
said to his critics, "I have a question for you. Does the
law permit good deeds on the Sabbath, or is it a day
for doing evil? Is this a day to save life or to destroy
it?"
10 He looked around at them one by one and then
said to the man, "Hold out your hand." So the man
held out his hand, and it was restored! 11 At this, the
enemies of Jesus were wild with rage and began to
discuss what to do with him.

JESUS CHOOSES THE TWELVE APOSTLES

12 One day soon afterward Jesus went up on a moun-
tain to pray, and he prayed to God all night. 13 At day-
break he called together all of his disciples and chose
twelve of them to be apostles. Here are their names:

14 Simon (whom he named Peter),
Andrew (Peter's brother),
James,
John,
Philip,
Bartholomew,
15 Matthew,
Thomas,
James (son of Alphaeus),
Simon (who was called the zealot),
16 Judas (son of James),
Judas Iscariot (who later betrayed him).

CROWDS FOLLOW JESUS

17 When they came down from the mountain, the
disciples stood with Jesus on a large, level area, sur-
rounded by many of his followers and by the crowds.
There were people from all over Judea and from Jeru-
salem and from as far north as the seacoasts of Tyre
and Sidon. 18 They had come to hear him and to be
healed of their diseases; and those troubled by evil*
spirits were healed. 19 Everyone tried to touch him,
because healing power went out from him, and he
healed everyone.

THE BEATITUDES

20 Then Jesus turned to his disciples and said,
"God blesses you who are poor,
for the Kingdom of God is yours.
21 God blesses you who are hungry now,
for you will be satisfied.
God blesses you who weep now,
for in due time you will laugh.

22 What blessings await you when people hate you
and exclude you and mock you and curse you as
evil because you follow the Son of Man. 23 When
that happens, be happy! Yes, leap for joy! For a great
reward awaits you in heaven. And remember, their
ancestors treated the ancient prophets that same
way.

SORROWS FORETOLD

24 "What sorrow awaits you who are rich,
for you have your only happiness now.
25 What sorrow awaits you who are fat and
prosperous now,
for a time of awful hunger awaits you.
What sorrow awaits you who laugh now,
for your laughing will turn to mourning and
sorrow.
26 What sorrow awaits you who are praised by the
crowds,
for their ancestors also praised false prophets.

LOVE FOR ENEMIES

27 "But to you who are willing to listen, I say, love
your enemies! Do good to those who hate you. 28 Bless
those who curse you. Pray for those who hurt you.

6:5 "Son of Man" is a title Jesus used for himself. 6:18 Greek *unclean.*

6:3 Haven't you read . . . David. . . ? By comparing His actions with those of David's, Jesus gave the first of several hints that He is the long-expected Son of David, the Messiah (Mark 10:46-48; 11:6-10; 12:35-37).

6:4 went into the house of God . . . eating the sacred loaves of bread. This was technically unlawful since only the priests were allowed to eat this bread (Lev. 24:5-9).

6:7 if he would heal . . . on the Sabbath. The issue is not healing, but whether Jesus would do so on the Sabbath in defiance of the oral tradition, which allowed healing on that day only if there was danger to life.

6:9 Does the law permit . . . ? Jesus points out that the Pharisees' concern for their traditions wrongfully overshadowed God's clear call for love and mercy.

6:17 level area. As a matter of contrast, Matthew has Jesus saying many of the same things recorded here (such as the Beatitudes and the Lord's Prayer) on a mountaintop (Matt. 5:1). **from all over Judea.** Luke emphasizes the breadth of Jesus' ministry. Judea and Jerusalem, known for Jewish orthodoxy, were to the south, while Tyre and Sidon, Gentile areas, were to the north.

6:20 God blesses. Refers to people who are to be congratulated, not necessarily meaning they are happy or prospering. Instead, whether they feel it or not, they are fortunate because their condition reflects that they are in a right relationship to God. **poor.** The Beatitudes in Luke differ slightly from those reported in Matthew 5. Those who are materially poor are generally seen in the New Testament to be more receptive to God (18:18-25; James 2:5-7). **the Kingdom of God.** Those who maintain loyalty to God, even if it means poverty rather than the wealth they might gain if they compromised their integrity, are assured an inheritance in His kingdom.

6:21 are hungry. In the Old Testament hunger and thirst are used as a way of describing the desire for spiritual fullness experienced by those who truly seek God (Ps. 42:1-2; Isa. 55:1; Amos 8:11). **will be satisfied.** The story of the rich man and Lazarus in chapter 16:19 illustrates future rewards for those who follow Christ.

6:23 their ancestors treated the ancient prophets. Elijah, Jeremiah, Ezekiel, and other Old Testament prophets faced consistent rejection, ridicule, and abuse from the people of their day.

6:24 What sorrow. Like "blessed," this is God's pronouncement on the peoples' real state of affairs regardless of what external circumstances feel like. Unless they repent, God's judgment is the only future they have.

6:25 laugh now. Sometimes in the Old Testament, joy and laughter are the spontaneous responses of people blessed by God (Isa. 51:11; 66:10; Jer. 31:13; 33:11). This is the meaning intended in verse 21.

6:27 love. The orthodox Jew of the time only regarded fellow Jews as his neighbor, but Jesus makes it clear that there is no one to whom love is not owed. The word used for love is *agape*, benevolent action done for another without the expectation of reward.

29 If someone slaps you on one cheek, offer the other cheek also. If someone demands your coat, offer your shirt also. 30 Give to anyone who asks; and when things are taken away from you, don't try to get them back. 31 Do to others as you would like them to do to you.

32 "If you love only those who love you, why should you get credit for that? Even sinners love those who love them! 33 And if you do good only to those who do good to you, why should you get credit? Even sinners do that much! 34 And if you lend money only to those who can repay you, why should you get credit? Even sinners will lend to other sinners for a full return.

35 "Love your enemies! Do good to them. Lend to them without expecting to be repaid. Then your reward from heaven will be very great, and you will truly be acting as children of the Most High, for he is kind to those who are unthankful and wicked. 36 You must be compassionate, just as your Father is compassionate.

DO NOT JUDGE OTHERS

37 "Do not judge others, and you will not be judged. Do not condemn others, or it will all come back against you. Forgive others, and you will be forgiven. 38 Give, and you will receive. Your gift will return to you in full—pressed down, shaken together to make room for more, running over, and poured into your lap. The amount you give will determine the amount you get back.*"

39 Then Jesus gave the following illustration: "Can one blind person lead another? Won't they both fall into a ditch? 40 Students* are not greater than their teacher. But the student who is fully trained will become like the teacher.

41 "And why worry about a speck in your friend's eye* when you have a log in your own? 42 How can you think of saying, 'Friend,* let me help you get rid of that speck in your eye,' when you can't see past the log in your own eye? Hypocrite! First get rid of the log in your own eye; then you will see well enough to deal with the speck in your friend's eye.

THE TREE AND ITS FRUIT

43 "A good tree can't produce bad fruit, and a bad tree can't produce good fruit. 44 A tree is identified by its fruit. Figs are never gathered from thornbushes, and grapes are not picked from bramble bushes. 45 A good person produces good things from the treasury of a good heart, and an evil person produces evil things from the treasury of an evil heart. What you say flows from what is in your heart.

BUILDING ON A SOLID FOUNDATION

46 "So why do you keep calling me 'Lord, Lord!' when you don't do what I say? 47 I will show you what it's like when someone comes to me, listens to my teaching, and then follows it. 48 It is like a person building a house who digs deep and lays the foundation on solid rock. When the floodwaters rise and break against that house, it stands firm because it is well built. 49 But anyone who hears and doesn't obey is like a person who builds a house right on the ground, without a foundation. When the floods sweep down against that house, it will collapse into a heap of ruins."

THE FAITH OF A ROMAN OFFICER

7 When Jesus had finished saying all this to the people, he returned to Capernaum. 2 At that time the highly valued slave of a Roman officer* was sick and near death. 3 When the officer heard about Jesus, he sent some respected Jewish elders to ask him to come and heal his slave. 4 So they earnestly begged Jesus to help the man. "If anyone deserves your help, he does," they said, 5 "for he loves the Jewish people and even built a synagogue for us."

6 So Jesus went with them. But just before they arrived at the house, the officer sent some friends to say, "Lord, don't trouble yourself by coming to my home, for I am not worthy of such an honor. 7 I am not even worthy to come and meet you. Just say the word from where you are, and my servant will be healed. 8 I know this because I am under the authority of my superior officers, and I have authority over my soldiers. I only need to say, 'Go,' and they go, or 'Come,' and they come. And if I say to my slaves, 'Do this,' they do it."

9 When Jesus heard this, he was amazed. Turning to the crowd that was following him, he said, "I tell you, I haven't seen faith like this in all Israel!" 10 And when the officer's friends returned to his house, they found the slave completely healed.

JESUS RAISES A WIDOW'S SON

11 Soon afterward Jesus went with his disciples to the village of Nain, and a large crowd followed him. 12 A funeral procession was coming out as he approached the village gate. The young man who had died was a widow's only son, and a large crowd from the village was with her. 13 When the Lord saw her, his heart overflowed with compassion. "Don't cry!" he said. 14 Then he walked over to the coffin and touched it, and the bearers stopped. "Young man," he said, "I tell you, get up." 15 Then the dead boy sat up and began to talk! And Jesus gave him back to his mother.

6:38 Or *The measure you give will be the measure you get back.* 6:40 Or *Disciples.* 6:41 Greek *your brother's eye;* also in 6:42. 6:42 Greek *Brother.* 7:2 Greek *a centurion;* similarly in 7:6.

6:29 coat. An outer robe made of wool, used as a blanket at night. **shirt.** The close-fitting under-robe. Jesus used the humorous picture of a robber being encouraged to take even more than he intended to steal in order to emphasize the spirit of giving that ought to characterize His followers (v. 30).

6:31 would like them to do for you. This is the so-called Golden Rule. The negative form of this rule was widely known in the ancient world: "Do not do to others what you do not wish them to do to you." Jesus alters this statement in a slight but highly significant way.

6:36 be compassionate. The same principle found in the Lord's Prayer where we are told that if we expect God to forgive us of the offenses we have committed, we need to forgive others for their offenses against us (Matt. 6:14-15).

6:37 Do not judge. Moral discernment is not forbidden, but only God is righteous enough to pass final judgment without partiality or error. **you will not be judged.** Not that such people will escape judgment but that they will be treated mercifully when judgment comes.

6:47–49 the floodwaters rise. Palestine was dry most of the year. In the autumn, heavy rains would turn what appeared to be dry land into a raging river as flash floods swept down the ravines. Only lives built on a solid foundation will withstand the trials of life.

7:1 Capernaum. This was a town on the north end of the Sea of Galilee, three miles west of the Jordan River. This was where Jesus often stayed during His ministry in Galilee.

7:2 officer. A commander of over 100 soldiers.

7:11 Nain. The modern-day town of Nen, six miles southeast of Nazareth and within a mile of where Elisha raised another woman's son centuries before (2 Kings 4:18-37).

7:12 widow's only son. This woman's situation was serious: children provided the only "Social Security" available for parents in their old age, and this woman had no more children and no husband. Thus, she faced both loneliness and poverty. **a large crowd.** Mourners accompanied the woman to the burial site.

[16] Great fear swept the crowd, and they praised God, saying, "A mighty prophet has risen among us," and "God has visited his people today." [17] And the news about Jesus spread throughout Judea and the surrounding countryside.

JESUS AND JOHN THE BAPTIST

[18] The disciples of John the Baptist told John about everything Jesus was doing. So John called for two of his disciples, [19] and he sent them to the Lord to ask him, "Are you the Messiah we've been expecting,* or should we keep looking for someone else?"

[20] John's two disciples found Jesus and said to him, "John the Baptist sent us to ask, 'Are you the Messiah we've been expecting, or should we keep looking for someone else?'"

[21] At that very time, Jesus cured many people of their diseases, illnesses, and evil spirits, and he restored sight to many who were blind. [22] Then he told John's disciples, "Go back to John and tell him what you have seen and heard—the blind see, the lame walk, those with leprosy are cured, the deaf hear, the dead are raised to life, and the Good News is being preached to the poor." [23] And he added, "God blesses those who do not fall away because of me.*"

[24] After John's disciples left, Jesus began talking about him to the crowds. "What kind of man did you go into the wilderness to see? Was he a weak reed, swayed by every breath of wind? [25] Or were you expecting to see a man dressed in expensive clothes? No, people who wear beautiful clothes and live in luxury are found in palaces. [26] Were you looking for a prophet? Yes, and he is more than a prophet. [27] John is the man to whom the Scriptures refer when they say,

'Look, I am sending my messenger ahead of you,
 and he will prepare your way before you.'*

[28] I tell you, of all who have ever lived, none is greater than John. Yet even the least person in the Kingdom of God is greater than he is!"

[29] When they heard this, all the people—even the tax collectors—agreed that God's way was right,* for they had been baptized by John. [30] But the Pharisees and experts in religious law rejected God's plan for them, for they had refused John's baptism.

[31] "To what can I compare the people of this generation?" Jesus asked. "How can I describe them? [32] They are like children playing a game in the public square. They complain to their friends,

'We played wedding songs,
 and you didn't dance,
so we played funeral songs,
 and you didn't weep.'

[33] For John the Baptist didn't spend his time eating bread or drinking wine, and you say, 'He's possessed by a demon.' [34] The Son of Man,* on the other hand, feasts and drinks, and you say, 'He's a glutton and a drunkard, and a friend of tax collectors and other sinners!' [35] But wisdom is shown to be right by the lives of those who follow it.*"

JESUS ANOINTED BY A SINFUL WOMAN

[36] One of the Pharisees asked Jesus to have dinner with him, so Jesus went to his home and sat down to eat.* [37] When a certain immoral woman from that city heard he was eating there, she brought a beautiful alabaster jar filled with expensive perfume. [38] Then she knelt behind him at his feet, weeping. Her tears fell on his feet, and she wiped them off with her hair. Then she kept kissing his feet and putting perfume on them.

[39] When the Pharisee who had invited him saw this, he said to himself, "If this man were a prophet, he would know what kind of woman is touching him. She's a sinner!"

[40] Then Jesus answered his thoughts. "Simon," he said to the Pharisee, "I have something to say to you."

"Go ahead, Teacher," Simon replied.

[41] Then Jesus told him this story: "A man loaned money to two people—500 pieces of silver* to one and 50 pieces to the other. [42] But neither of them could repay him, so he kindly forgave them both, canceling their debts. Who do you suppose loved him more after that?"

7:19 Greek *Are you the one who is coming?* Also in 7:20. **7:23** Or *who are not offended by me.* **7:27** Mal 3:1. **7:29** Or *praised God for his justice.* **7:34** "Son of Man" is a title Jesus used for himself. **7:35** Or *But wisdom is justified by all her children.* **7:36** Or *and reclined.* **7:41** Greek *500 denarii.* A denarius was equivalent to a laborer's full day's wage.

7:16 Great fear swept the crowd. The response of both fear and praise is characteristic of people throughout the Bible when God's power is manifest.

7:18-20 Are you the Messiah . . .? The parallel passage in Matthew 11:1-19 indicates that at this point John was in Herod's prison. John's question as to whether Jesus was "the one" comes from confusion over the role of the Messiah. John preached of a Messiah who would come to execute God's wrath and judgment upon the unrighteous in Israel (3:17). Jesus' actions, while empowered by God, did not match John's expectation.

7:21-23 He told John's disciples. Jesus did not answer their question directly but invited them to watch and reflect upon what He did as He healed and taught. The recovery of sight, the healing of the lame, the restoration of hearing to the deaf, the raising of the dead, and the preaching of the good news of God's mercy to the poor and oppressed are all marks of the Messiah's mission according to Isaiah (Isa. 26:19; 29:18-19; 35:5-6; 61:1).

7:24 A weak reed, swayed by every breath of wind? John, who stood firmly for God, was not a man to be swayed by the currents of popular opinion or pressure.

7:25 a man dressed in expensive clothes? Jesus accented how John's ascetic demeanor was in marked contrast to the indulgence and wastefulness that characterized those who served King Herod. One can imagine the crowd's smiles as they caught Jesus' irony in these two comparisons.

7:28 I tell you . . .greater than he is. This sentence was not in the least meant to disparage John or to diminish his place in the kingdom of God but to emphasize the new order that Jesus was beginning. To play the least part in the kingdom of God is greater than to have the lead role in the old order represented by John and the Old Testament prophets—those who could only look forward to the Messiah.

7:36 sat down to eat. People ate by reclining on their left side on low couches arranged around a table, such that their feet would be stretched out behind them.

7:38 tears fell on his feet. The woman's tears show her extreme conviction of her sin as she stood by the feet of Jesus. For a woman to loose her hair in public was scandalous; using it to dry her tears from Jesus' feet marked her great humility before Him. Normally, a person's head would be anointed as a sign of honor. (The Hebrew word *Messiah* means "anointed one.") Like John the Baptist, who felt unworthy to undo the straps of the Messiah's sandals (3:16), perhaps this woman felt she was so unworthy that she dare only anoint Jesus' feet. That Jesus accepted these acts shows much about His character. He did not let what people might think dictate how He related to people. He saw her love and penitence and responded to that instead of public opinion.

7:41-43 500 pieces of silver . . .fifty. The difference here is between owing what one could earn in 18 months versus owing what could be earned in less than two months. Then, as now, it would be the rare moneylender who would cancel either debt! Part of what Jesus was saying was that God cancels debts (in the form of sins) that are far greater than most humans would cancel. A similar point is made in the parable of the unmerciful servant, where the amount the master forgave was greater still (Matt. 18:23-35). Simon rightly gets the point that the man with the greatest debt would be most grateful.

GUILTY AS CHARGED

1. What's something you are guilty of: Speeding? Breaking curfew? Borrowing clothes without asking? Other?

LUKE 7:36-50

2. Why did the woman pour perfume on Jesus' feet, wipe His feet with her hair, and kiss His feet?
3. Why did the Pharisee react the way he did?
4. Who had more sin forgiven: The Pharisee? The woman? Both the same?
5. The point of Jesus' parable is not how much sin He forgives for each person but how each person responds to Jesus' forgiveness. How have you responded to His forgiveness?

43 Simon answered, "I suppose the one for whom he canceled the larger debt."

"That's right," Jesus said. 44 Then he turned to the woman and said to Simon, "Look at this woman kneeling here. When I entered your home, you didn't offer me water to wash the dust from my feet, but she has washed them with her tears and wiped them with her hair. 45 You didn't greet me with a kiss, but from the time I first came in, she has not stopped kissing my feet. 46 You neglected the courtesy of olive oil to anoint my head, but she has anointed my feet with rare perfume.

47 "I tell you, her sins—and they are many—have been forgiven, so she has shown me much love. But a person who is forgiven little shows only little love." 48 Then Jesus said to the woman, "Your sins are forgiven."

49 The men at the table said among themselves, "Who is this man, that he goes around forgiving sins?"

50 And Jesus said to the woman, "Your faith has saved you; go in peace."

WOMEN WHO FOLLOWED JESUS

8 Soon afterward Jesus began a tour of the nearby towns and villages, preaching and announcing the Good News about the Kingdom of God. He took his twelve disciples with him, 2 along with some women who had been cured of evil spirits and diseases. Among them were Mary Magdalene, from whom he had cast out seven demons; 3 Joanna, the wife of Chuza, Herod's business manager; Susanna; and many others who were contributing from their own resources to support Jesus and his disciples.

PARABLE OF THE FARMER SCATTERING SEED

4 One day Jesus told a story in the form of a parable to a large crowd that had gathered from many towns to hear him: 5 "A farmer went out to plant his seed. As he scattered it across his field, some seed fell on a footpath, where it was stepped on, and the birds ate it. 6 Other seed fell among rocks. It began to grow, but the plant soon wilted and died for lack of moisture. 7 Other seed fell among thorns that grew up with it and choked out the tender plants. 8 Still other seed fell on fertile soil. This seed grew and produced a crop that was a hundred times as much as had been planted!" When he had said this, he called out, "Anyone with ears to hear should listen and understand."

9 His disciples asked him what this parable meant. 10 He replied, "You are permitted to understand the secrets* of the Kingdom of God. But I use parables to teach the others so that the Scriptures might be fulfilled:

'When they look, they won't really see.
When they hear, they won't understand.'*

11 "This is the meaning of the parable: The seed is God's word. 12 The seeds that fell on the footpath represent those who hear the message, only to have the devil come and take it away from their hearts and prevent them from believing and being saved. 13 The seeds on the rocky soil represent those who hear the message and receive it with joy. But since they don't have deep roots, they believe for a while, then they fall away when they face temptation. 14 The seeds that fell among the thorns represent those who hear the message, but all too quickly the message is crowded out by the cares and riches and pleasures of this life. And so they never grow into maturity. 15 And the seeds that fell on the good soil represent honest, good-hearted people who hear God's word, cling to it, and patiently produce a huge harvest.

PARABLE OF THE LAMP

16 "No one lights a lamp and then covers it with a bowl or hides it under a bed. A lamp is placed on a stand, where its light can be seen by all who enter the house.

8:10a Greek *mysteries.* **8:10b** Isa 6:9 (Greek version).

7:47 Jesus is not saying that the woman is forgiven *because* she has shown such extravagant love, but her love expresses her gratitude for the forgiveness she has received.

7:50 go in peace. Jesus utters this common saying not simply as a wish but as an expression of fact.

8:2-3 some women. Jesus' band was supported by these women who helped in gratitude for the healing they had received from Jesus. Mary and Joanna are mentioned at the resurrection (24:10). The presence of Joanna, who was married to the man charged with the responsibility for managing Herod's affairs, shows that Jesus' influence had reached to the higher social and economic classes. That women traveled with Jesus shows the difference between Him and other rabbis who often held women in low esteem.

8:5 plant his seed. Farmers sowed their fields by scattering seed with broad sweeping motions of the hand as they walked along the paths in their fields. Afterward, they would go through the field to plow the seed under. **a footpath.** There were hard pathways between the various plots of land. These were packed so hard that seed could not even penetrate the soil, thus making it easy for the birds to simply eat it.

8:6 among rocks. Some of the soil covered a limestone base a few inches beneath the surface. Seed that fell here would germinate, but it would not last since the roots could not penetrate deeply enough into the ground to draw moisture during hot, dry times.

8:7 thorns. In other parts of the plot there were the roots of weeds that grew faster than the seedlings, stunting their growth. Although it lived, such seed would not bear fruit.

8:8 fertile soil. This was the soil in which the seed could grow and flourish. **a hundred times as much as had been planted.** A spectacular crop! A tenfold crop was considered an especially good harvest.

8:10 secrets of the Kingdom of God. In the New Testament a secret is something hidden until God chooses to reveal it. The quote from Isaiah 6:9 does not mean Jesus spoke in parables to keep people from understanding but that their lack of spiritual openness prevented them from understanding.

8:16 lamp. A pottery vessel filled with olive oil.

17 For all that is secret will eventually be brought into
the open, and everything that is concealed will be
brought to light and made known to all.
18 "So pay attention to how you hear. To those who
listen to my teaching, more understanding will be
given. But for those who are not listening, even what
they think they understand will be taken away from
them."

THE TRUE FAMILY OF JESUS

19 Then Jesus' mother and brothers came to see
him, but they couldn't get to him because of the
crowd. 20 Someone told Jesus, "Your mother and
your brothers are standing outside, and they want
to see you."
21 Jesus replied, "My mother and my brothers are all
those who hear God's word and obey it."

JESUS CALMS THE STORM

22 One day Jesus said to his disciples, "Let's cross to
the other side of the lake." So they got into a boat and
started out. 23 As they sailed across, Jesus settled down
for a nap. But soon a fierce storm came down on the
lake. The boat was filling with water, and they were
in real danger.
24 The disciples went and woke him up, shouting,
"Master, Master, we're going to drown!"
When Jesus woke up, he rebuked the wind and
the raging waves. Suddenly the storm stopped and
all was calm. 25 Then he asked them, "Where is your
faith?"
The disciples were terrified and amazed. "Who is
this man?" they asked each other. "When he gives a
command, even the wind and waves obey him!"

JESUS HEALS A DEMON-POSSESSED MAN

26 So they arrived in the region of the Gerasenes,*
across the lake from Galilee. 27 As Jesus was climbing
out of the boat, a man who was possessed by demons
came out to meet him. For a long time he had been
homeless and naked, living in the tombs outside the
town.
28 As soon as he saw Jesus, he shrieked and fell
down in front of him. Then he screamed, "Why are
you interfering with me, Jesus, Son of the Most High
God? Please, I beg you, don't torture me!" 29 For Jesus
had already commanded the evil* spirit to come
out of him. This spirit had often taken control of the
man. Even when he was placed under guard and put
in chains and shackles, he simply broke them and
rushed out into the wilderness, completely under the
demon's power.

DEALING WITH DEMONS

1. What is the scariest place or situation you've ever been in?

LUKE 8:26-39

2. What was wrong with the man who met Jesus? How had he gotten that way?
3. Why did Jesus send the demons into the herd of pigs? Why didn't He just send them to "the bottomless pit" (v. 31)?
4. Why would Jesus tell this grateful man that he couldn't stay with Him but had to go back home? What was the result of his return home?
5. How do you proclaim Jesus' healing power to the people you know?

30 Jesus demanded, "What is your name?"
"Legion," he replied, for he was filled with many
demons. 31 The demons kept begging Jesus not to send
them into the bottomless pit.*
32 There happened to be a large herd of pigs feeding
on the hillside nearby, and the demons begged him to
let them enter into the pigs.
So Jesus gave them permission. 33 Then the demons
came out of the man and entered the pigs, and the en-
tire herd plunged down the steep hillside into the lake
and drowned.
34 When the herdsmen saw it, they fled to the near-
by town and the surrounding countryside, spreading
the news as they ran. 35 People rushed out to see what
had happened. A crowd soon gathered around Jesus,
and they saw the man who had been freed from the
demons. He was sitting at Jesus' feet, fully clothed and
perfectly sane, and they were all afraid. 36 Then those
who had seen what happened told the others how the
demon-possessed man had been healed. 37 And all the
people in the region of the Gerasenes begged Jesus
to go away and leave them alone, for a great wave of
fear swept over them.
So Jesus returned to the boat and left, crossing back
to the other side of the lake. 38 The man who had been
freed from the demons begged to go with him. But
Jesus sent him home, saying, 39 "No, go back to your
family, and tell them everything God has done for
you." So he went all through the town proclaiming
the great things Jesus had done for him.

8:26 Other manuscripts read *Gadarenes;* still others read *Gergesenes;* also in 8:37. See Matt 8:28; Mark 5:1. **8:29** Greek *unclean.* **8:31** Or *the abyss,* or *the underworld.*

8:23 a fierce storm. The Sea of Galilee was a deep, freshwater lake, 13 miles long and 8 miles wide. It was pear-shaped and ringed by mountains, though open at its north and south ends. Fierce winds often blew into this bowl-shaped lake, creating savage and unpredictable storms.
8:24 Master. A common term of address for a rabbi.
8:25 Where is your faith? This may not be so much a rebuke as an invitation for them to take a fresh look at who they think He is. Have they been listening (vv. 4-21)? **terrified and amazed.** The disciples' fear of the storm gives way to fear of the One who has power over that storm! It is the fear of an unknown force or power. **Who is this man?** This is the key question that emerges in these stories of Jesus' divine power. No rabbi could do what they have just seen Jesus do!
8:26 the region of the Gerasenes. The precise location of their landing is not clear. However, it is on the other side of the lake from Capernaum in a burial ground in Gentile territory, probably near the lower end of the Sea of Galilee.
8:27 As Jesus was climbing out of the boat .... cemetery. The ragged limestone cliffs with caves and depressions provided natural tombs.
8:28 don't torture me! The plea not to be tortured comes from the demons. Their plea is ironic in light of their effect on the man whom they possessed.
8:30 Legion. The term for a company of Roman soldiers consisting of 6,000 men. The man was occupied by a huge number of demons.
8:31 the bottomless pit. Despite popular belief that the underworld is the place where Satan and his demons have free reign, the Bible declares it to be the place of punishment for these evil beings (2 Peter 2:4).
8:32 pigs. This herd belonged to Gentiles since Jews considered pigs unclean animals. To associate with them would defile them before God (Lev. 11:1-8).
8:35 they were all afraid. It might be expected that the people would rejoice that this man who had terrorized them was now healed. Instead they are fearful of Jesus who had the power to overcome the demons.

JESUS HEALS IN RESPONSE TO FAITH

40 On the other side of the lake the crowds welcomed
Jesus, because they had been waiting for him. 41 Then
a man named Jairus, a leader of the local synagogue,
came and fell at Jesus' feet, pleading with him to come
home with him. 42 His only daughter,* who was about
twelve years old, was dying.

As Jesus went with him, he was surrounded by the
crowds. 43 A woman in the crowd had suffered for
twelve years with constant bleeding,* and she could
find no cure. 44 Coming up behind Jesus, she touched
the fringe of his robe. Immediately, the bleeding
stopped.

45 "Who touched me?" Jesus asked.

Everyone denied it, and Peter said, "Master, this
whole crowd is pressing up against you."

46 But Jesus said, "Someone deliberately touched
me, for I felt healing power go out from me." 47 When
the woman realized that she could not stay hidden,
she began to tremble and fell to her knees in front of
him. The whole crowd heard her explain why she
had touched him and that she had been immediately
healed. 48 "Daughter," he said to her, "your faith has
made you well. Go in peace."

49 While he was still speaking to her, a messenger
arrived from the home of Jairus, the leader of the syn-
agogue. He told him, "Your daughter is dead. There's
no use troubling the Teacher now."

50 But when Jesus heard what had happened, he
said to Jairus, "Don't be afraid. Just have faith, and she
will be healed."

51 When they arrived at the house, Jesus wouldn't
let anyone go in with him except Peter, John, James,
and the little girl's father and mother. 52 The house
was filled with people weeping and wailing, but he
said, "Stop the weeping! She isn't dead; she's only
asleep."

53 But the crowd laughed at him because they all
knew she had died. 54 Then Jesus took her by the hand
and said in a loud voice, "My child, get up!" 55 And at
that moment her life* returned, and she immediately
stood up! Then Jesus told them to give her something
to eat. 56 Her parents were overwhelmed, but Jesus in-
sisted that they not tell anyone what had happened.

JESUS SENDS OUT THE TWELVE DISCIPLES

9 One day Jesus called together his twelve dis-
ciples* and gave them power and authority to
cast out all demons and to heal all diseases. 2 Then
he sent them out to tell everyone about the Kingdom
of God and to heal the sick. 3 "Take nothing for your
journey," he instructed them. "Don't take a walking
stick, a traveler's bag, food, money,* or even a change
of clothes. 4 Wherever you go, stay in the same house
until you leave town. 5 And if a town refuses to wel-
come you, shake its dust from your feet as you leave
to show that you have abandoned those people to
their fate."

6 So they began their circuit of the villages, preach-
ing the Good News and healing the sick.

HEROD'S CONFUSION

7 When Herod Antipas, the ruler of Galilee,* heard
about everything Jesus was doing, he was puzzled.
Some were saying that John the Baptist had been
raised from the dead. 8 Others thought Jesus was Eli-
jah or one of the other prophets risen from the dead.

9 "I beheaded John," Herod said, "so who is this man
about whom I hear such stories?" And he kept trying
to see him.

JESUS FEEDS FIVE THOUSAND

10 When the apostles returned, they told Jesus every-
thing they had done. Then he slipped quietly away
with them toward the town of Bethsaida. 11 But the
crowds found out where he was going, and they
followed him. He welcomed them and taught them
about the Kingdom of God, and he healed those who
were sick.

12 Late in the afternoon the twelve disciples came to
him and said, "Send the crowds away to the nearby
villages and farms, so they can find food and lodging
for the night. There is nothing to eat here in this re-
mote place."

13 But Jesus said, "You feed them."

"But we have only five loaves of bread and two
fish," they answered. "Or are you expecting us to go
and buy enough food for this whole crowd?" 14 For
there were about 5,000 men there.

Jesus replied, "Tell them to sit down in groups
of about fifty each." 15 So the people all sat down.
16 Jesus took the five loaves and two fish, looked up
toward heaven, and blessed them. Then, breaking
the loaves into pieces, he kept giving the bread and
fish to the disciples so they could distribute it to the
people. 17 They all ate as much as they wanted, and
afterward, the disciples picked up twelve baskets of
leftovers!

8:42 Or *His only child, a daughter.* 8:43 Some manuscripts add *having spent everything she had on doctors.* 8:55 Or *her spirit.* 9:1 Greek *the Twelve;* other manuscripts read *the twelve apostles.* 9:3 Or *silver coins.* 9:7 Greek *Herod the tetrarch.* Herod Antipas was a son of King Herod and was ruler over Galilee.

8:43 A woman . . .had suffered. The woman should not have been there because her illness made her ceremonially "unclean" (Lev. 15:25-30), thus cutting her off from contact with other people, including her husband.

8:48 your faith has made you well. Spiritual as well as physical healing is in view here.

8:51 Peter, John, and James. These three disciples become a sort of inner circle around Jesus.

8:52 house was filled with people weeping. These were in all likelihood professional mourners. Even the poorest person was expected to hire not less than two flutes and one wailing woman to mourn a death. They were a sign that all knew the child was dead.

9:5 shake its dust from your feet. When leaving Gentile areas, Jews would wipe off their feet as a symbolic action of cleansing themselves from the judgment of God that was to come. For the disciples to do this to Jewish villages would indicate that the village was not part of the true Israel.

9:7 Herod. Before his death in 4 B.C., Herod the Great divided his territory between three of his sons: Herod (Antipas) and Philip ruled over their areas until A.D. 39 and 33 respectively. The third son, Archelaus, was given Judea, Samaria, and Edom but was soon removed because of a petition by the Jews he ruled. **John the Baptist had been raised.** Mark 6:14-29 tells the gruesome story of John's death.

9:8 Elijah. It was commonly believed that just prior to the coming of the Messiah, God would raise up Israel's famous prophet to prepare the way (Mal. 4:5).

9:10 Bethsaida. A town north of the Sea of Galilee.

9:12 in this remote place. The disciples pointed out to Jesus that it would soon be too late for the crowd to find hospitality. It may be that they were in the predominately Gentile area on the east side of the Sea of Galilee where Jews could not be assured of being welcomed.

9:13 five loaves of bread and two fish. If three loaves of bread was considered a generous meal for a guest (11:5-8), then the disciples' provision here was barely adequate for their own needs.

9:14 5000 men. Literally, "males" (Matt. 14:21). When all the women and children are added in, this was truly a huge crowd.

PETER'S DECLARATION ABOUT JESUS

18 One day Jesus left the crowds to pray alone. Only his
disciples were with him, and he asked them, "Who do
people say I am?"
19 "Well," they replied, "some say John the Baptist,
some say Elijah, and others say you are one of the oth-
er ancient prophets risen from the dead."
20 Then he asked them, "But who do you say I am?"
Peter replied, "You are the Messiah* sent from God!"

JESUS PREDICTS HIS DEATH

21 Jesus warned his disciples not to tell anyone who
he was. 22 "The Son of Man* must suffer many terrible
things," he said. "He will be rejected by the elders, the
leading priests, and the teachers of religious law. He
will be killed, but on the third day he will be raised
from the dead."
23 Then he said to the crowd, "If any of you wants to
be my follower, you must give up your own way, take
up your cross daily, and follow me. 24 If you try to hang
on to your life, you will lose it. But if you give up your
life for my sake, you will save it. 25 And what do you
benefit if you gain the whole world but are yourself
lost or destroyed? 26 If anyone is ashamed of me and
my message, the Son of Man will be ashamed of that
person when he returns in his glory and in the glory
of the Father and the holy angels. 27 I tell you the truth,
some standing here right now will not die before they
see the Kingdom of God."

THE TRANSFIGURATION

28 About eight days later Jesus took Peter, John, and
James up on a mountain to pray. 29 And as he was
praying, the appearance of his face was trans-
formed, and his clothes became dazzling white.
30 Suddenly, two men, Moses and Elijah, appeared
and began talking with Jesus. 31 They were glorious
to see. And they were speaking about his exodus
from this world, which was about to be fulfilled in
Jerusalem.
32 Peter and the others had fallen asleep. When
they woke up, they saw Jesus' glory and the two men
standing with him. 33 As Moses and Elijah were start-
ing to leave, Peter, not even knowing what he was
saying, blurted out, "Master, it's wonderful for us to
be here! Let's make three shelters as memorials*—
one for you, one for Moses, and one for Elijah." 34 But
even as he was saying this, a cloud overshadowed
them, and terror gripped them as the cloud covered
them.
35 Then a voice from the cloud said, "This is my Son,
my Chosen One.* Listen to him." 36 When the voice fin-
ished, Jesus was there alone. They didn't tell anyone
at that time what they had seen.

JESUS HEALS A DEMON-POSSESSED BOY

37 The next day, after they had come down the moun-
tain, a large crowd met Jesus. 38 A man in the crowd
called out to him, "Teacher, I beg you to look at my son,
my only child. 39 An evil spirit keeps seizing him, mak-
ing him scream. It throws him into convulsions so
that he foams at the mouth. It batters him and hard-
ly ever leaves him alone. 40 I begged your disciples to
cast out the spirit, but they couldn't do it."
41 Jesus said, "You faithless and corrupt people! How
long must I be with you and put up with you?" Then
he said to the man, "Bring your son here."
42 As the boy came forward, the demon knocked
him to the ground and threw him into a violent con-
vulsion. But Jesus rebuked the evil* spirit and healed
the boy. Then he gave him back to his father. 43 Awe
gripped the people as they saw this majestic display
of God's power.

JESUS AGAIN PREDICTS HIS DEATH

While everyone was marveling at everything he
was doing, Jesus said to his disciples, 44 "Listen to me
and remember what I say. The Son of Man is going
to be betrayed into the hands of his enemies." 45 But
they didn't know what he meant. Its significance was
hidden from them, so they couldn't understand it, and
they were afraid to ask him about it.

THE GREATEST IN THE KINGDOM

46 Then his disciples began arguing about which
of them was the greatest. 47 But Jesus knew their
thoughts, so he brought a little child to his side.
48 Then he said to them, "Anyone who welcomes a
little child like this on my behalf* welcomes me, and
anyone who welcomes me also welcomes my Father
who sent me. Whoever is the least among you is the
greatest."

9:20 Or *the Christ. Messiah* (a Hebrew term) and *Christ* (a Greek term) both mean "anointed one." 9:22 "Son of Man" is a title Jesus used for himself. 9:33 Greek *three tabernacles.* 9:35 Some manuscripts read *This is my dearly loved Son.* 9:42 Greek *unclean.* 9:48 Greek *in my name.*

9:20 who do you say I am? This is *the* critical question. Have the disciples heeded what they have seen and heard of Jesus (8:18)? **the Messiah!** This is a Hebrew word meaning "the Anointed One"; that is, the prophesied future king of Israel.

9:21 not to tell anyone. Jesus commanded them be silent about what they know. The problem was that, although they knew He was the Messiah, they did not yet know what *kind* of Messiah He was.

9:22 must suffer. The people did not understand that Messiah was to be a suffering servant. They thought His role meant only glory and victory. They didn't realize salvation would be provided through the suffering and death of the Messiah. **rejected by the elders, the leading priests, and teachers of religious law.** These three groups made up the Sanhedrin, the ruling Jewish body. For the first time, Jesus predicted His rejection by the officials of Israel.

9:23 follow me. This is to take on the role of a disciple, one committed to the teachings of a master. **turn from your selfish ways.** This is to no longer live with self-satisfaction as the primary aim of life. Self must be denied in favor of doing the will of God. **take up your cross.** It is a metaphor emphasizing the call for all Jesus' disciples to put aside one's own desires and interests out of loyalty to Jesus. **daily.** Luke alone included this. Following Jesus is a day-by-day commitment.

9:26 returns in his glory! While His present suffering is real, the future glory of the Son of Man is pictured here (Dan. 7:13-14).

9:28 a mountain. This may be Mt. Hermon, a 9,000-foot mountain located 12 miles from Caesarea Philippi (though early tradition says the transfiguration occurred on Mt. Tabor, located southwest of the Sea of Galilee). In the past, God had revealed Himself on other mountains, such as when He appeared to Moses (Exod. 24) and Elijah (1 Kings 19) on Mt. Sinai (also called Mt. Horeb).

9:30 Moses. It was to Moses God gave the law. **Elijah.** The Jews expected Elijah to return just prior to the coming of the day of the Lord (Mal. 4:5-6).

9:35 a voice. Once again, as He did at the baptism of Jesus (3:22), God proclaimed that Jesus is His Son.

9:41 You faithless and corrupt people! This parallels God's cry when faced with Israel's stubborn refusal to listen to Him in the wilderness (Deut. 32:5,20).

9:42 rebuked . . .healed . . .gave. Jesus displayed the glory, power, and compassion of God by this decisive defeat of the demon.

9:47 brought a little child. Children, like women and slaves, had few rights and little social significance in the eyes of men. By having this child stand beside Him, Jesus placed him in the position of honor that each of the Twelve coveted.

USING THE NAME OF JESUS

49 John said to Jesus, "Master, we saw someone using your name to cast out demons, but we told him to stop because he isn't in our group."

50 But Jesus said, "Don't stop him! Anyone who is not against you is for you."

OPPOSITION FROM SAMARITANS

51 As the time drew near for him to ascend to heaven, Jesus resolutely set out for Jerusalem. 52 He sent messengers ahead to a Samaritan village to prepare for his arrival. 53 But the people of the village did not welcome Jesus because he was on his way to Jerusalem. 54 When James and John saw this, they said to Jesus, "Lord, should we call down fire from heaven to burn them up*?" 55 But Jesus turned and rebuked them.* 56 So they went on to another village.

THE COST OF FOLLOWING JESUS

57 As they were walking along, someone said to Jesus, "I will follow you wherever you go."

58 But Jesus replied, "Foxes have dens to live in, and birds have nests, but the Son of Man has no place even to lay his head."

59 He said to another person, "Come, follow me."

The man agreed, but he said, "Lord, first let me return home and bury my father."

60 But Jesus told him, "Let the spiritually dead bury their own dead!* Your duty is to go and preach about the Kingdom of God."

61 Another said, "Yes, Lord, I will follow you, but first let me say good-bye to my family."

62 But Jesus told him, "Anyone who puts a hand to the plow and then looks back is not fit for the Kingdom of God."

JESUS SENDS OUT HIS DISCIPLES

10 The Lord now chose seventy-two* other disciples and sent them ahead in pairs to all the towns and places he planned to visit. 2 These were his instructions to them: "The harvest is great, but the workers are few. So pray to the Lord who is in charge of the harvest; ask him to send more workers into his fields. 3 Now go, and remember that I am sending you out as lambs among wolves. 4 Don't take any money with you, nor a traveler's bag, nor an extra pair of sandals. And don't stop to greet anyone on the road.

5 "Whenever you enter someone's home, first say, 'May God's peace be on this house.' 6 If those who live there are peaceful, the blessing will stand; if they are not, the blessing will return to you. 7 Don't move around from home to home. Stay in one place, eating and drinking what they provide. Don't hesitate to accept hospitality, because those who work deserve their pay.

8 "If you enter a town and it welcomes you, eat whatever is set before you. 9 Heal the sick, and tell them, 'The Kingdom of God is near you now.' 10 But if a town refuses to welcome you, go out into its streets and say, 11 'We wipe even the dust of your town from our feet to show that we have abandoned you to your fate. And know this—the Kingdom of God is near!' 12 I assure you, even wicked Sodom will be better off than such a town on judgment day.

13 "What sorrow awaits you, Korazin and Bethsaida! For if the miracles I did in you had been done in wicked Tyre and Sidon, their people would have repented of their sins long ago, clothing themselves in burlap and throwing ashes on their heads to show their remorse. 14 Yes, Tyre and Sidon will be better off on judgment day than you. 15 And you people of Capernaum, will you be honored in heaven? No, you will go down to the place of the dead.*"

16 Then he said to the disciples, "Anyone who accepts your message is also accepting me. And anyone who rejects you is rejecting me. And anyone who rejects me is rejecting God, who sent me."

17 When the seventy-two disciples returned, they joyfully reported to him, "Lord, even the demons obey us when we use your name!"

18 "Yes," he told them, "I saw Satan fall from heaven like lightning! 19 Look, I have given you authority over all the power of the enemy, and you can walk among snakes and scorpions and crush them. Nothing will injure you. 20 But don't rejoice because evil spirits obey you; rejoice because your names are registered in heaven."

9:54 Some manuscripts add *as Elijah did.* **9:55** Some manuscripts add an expanded conclusion to verse 55 and an additional sentence in verse 56: *And he said, "You don't realize what your hearts are like. 56For the Son of Man has not come to destroy people's lives, but to save them."* **9:60** Greek *Let the dead bury their own dead.* **10:1** Some manuscripts read *seventy;* also in 10:17. **10:15** Greek *to Hades.*

9:49 someone using your name to cast out demons. The disciples' lack of humility is matched by their lack of acceptance that God is at work outside of their circle. (See Num. 11:24-30 for a similar incident in the life of Moses.) Since a person's name represented his character and power, this exorcist recognized Jesus' authority over demons and called upon that authority in his work.

9:50 Anyone who is not against you is for you. The concern should be whether a person is seeking to glorify Jesus, not whether he or she is part of the "right" organization.

9:52 Samaritans. Samaritans and Jews were bitter enemies. The Samaritans did not want anything to do with someone traveling to Jerusalem, since they believed the true place of worship was on a mountain in *their* province.

9:54 should we call down fire from heaven? Elijah once did this (2 Kings 1:9-12), so the disciples may have thought it was an appropriate fate for those who treated Jesus shabbily.

9:58 no place even to lay his head. Once Jesus began His public ministry He had no settled home but traveled throughout Palestine. To follow Jesus is to be a sojourner in this world (Heb. 11:13).

9:59 let me return home and bury my father. This does not mean that the man's father had just died but that the son was putting off following Jesus until he was free from obligations to his father—the last of which would have been the duty of providing for his burial, a duty that took precedence over all other religious obligations. The kingdom outweighs responsibility even to family.

10:2 harvest. The harvest image was used in the Old Testament as a metaphor for the coming judgment when God would gather together all His people.

10:4 Don't take . . .don't stop to greet. This lack of provisions and the command not to stop to greet anyone highlights the urgency of their task (2 Kings 4:29).

10:8 eat whatever is set before you. The concern here is not for proper etiquette in a host's home. If this trip involved going to the east side of the Jordan River, it would include visiting Gentile towns where the food would not meet Jewish dietary laws. Jesus' point is that the preaching of the kingdom is not to be deterred by religious traditions.

10:12 Sodom. An ancient city whose place in history was preserved because of the severity of God's judgment upon its evil (Gen. 19:1-29).

10:13 What sorrow. In spite of all the evidence concerning Jesus that they had seen and heard, they still had not received Him as Messiah. **Korazin!** Apart from this reference and Matthew 11:21, there is no other mention of Korazin in the Bible. **Bethsaida!** The home of Peter, Andrew, and Philip (John 1:44; 12:21).

10:19 you can walk among snakes. Snakes and scorpions are symbolic of Satan's forces unleashed in nature. These forces, which plague humanity, are rendered powerless at the reign of the Messiah (Ps. 91:13; Isa. 11:8). Nevertheless, the joy of the disciples should not be rooted in acts of supernatural authority but in the assurance that they have a place in heaven (v. 20).

JESUS' PRAYER OF THANKSGIVING

21 At that same time Jesus was filled with the joy of the
Holy Spirit, and he said, "O Father, Lord of heaven and
earth, thank you for hiding these things from those
who think themselves wise and clever, and for reveal-
ing them to the childlike. Yes, Father, it pleased you to
do it this way.
22 "My Father has entrusted everything to me. No
one truly knows the Son except the Father, and no one
truly knows the Father except the Son and those to
whom the Son chooses to reveal him."
23 Then when they were alone, he turned to the dis-
ciples and said, "Blessed are the eyes that see what
you have seen. 24 I tell you, many prophets and kings
longed to see what you see, but they didn't see it. And
they longed to hear what you hear, but they didn't
hear it."

THE MOST IMPORTANT COMMANDMENT

25 One day an expert in religious law stood up to test
Jesus by asking him this question: "Teacher, what
should I do to inherit eternal life?"
26 Jesus replied, "What does the law of Moses say?
How do you read it?"
27 The man answered, "'You must love the LORD
your God with all your heart, all your soul, all your
strength, and all your mind.' And, 'Love your neigh-
bor as yourself.'"*
28 "Right!" Jesus told him. "Do this and you will live!"
29 The man wanted to justify his actions, so he asked
Jesus, "And who is my neighbor?"

THE GOOD SAMARITAN

1. Have you ever helped a stranger or been helped by a stranger? What happened?

LUKE 10:25-37

2. "And who is my neighbor?" What was Jesus' answer to that question according to this passage?
3. How would you answer the question the "expert in religious law" asked in verse 25?
4. Samaritans were like social outcasts in Jesus' day. How did the Samaritan prove to be more like Jesus than the "religious" people in the parable?
5. Who has been a "neighbor" to you? To whom have you been a "neighbor" recently?

ONE NECESSARY THING

1. In your family, who does most of the preparation when company comes? What do you do?

LUKE 10:38-42

2. Why did Mary sit "at the Lord's feet" (v. 39)? Why didn't Martha do that?
3. When is it good to be busy serving others? When is it not the best thing to do?
4. What "details" tend to distract you from spending time with Jesus? How could you balance your schedule to allow more time to listen to Him?
5. In verse 42 Jesus says, "There is only one thing worth being concerned about." What is that thing?

PARABLE OF THE GOOD SAMARITAN

30 Jesus replied with a story: "A Jewish man was trav-
eling from Jerusalem down to Jericho, and he was at-
tacked by bandits. They stripped him of his clothes,
beat him up, and left him half dead beside the road.
31 "By chance a priest came along. But when he saw
the man lying there, he crossed to the other side of
the road and passed him by. 32 A Temple assistant*
walked over and looked at him lying there, but he also
passed by on the other side.
33 "Then a despised Samaritan came along, and
when he saw the man, he felt compassion for him.
34 Going over to him, the Samaritan soothed his
wounds with olive oil and wine and bandaged them.
Then he put the man on his own donkey and took him
to an inn, where he took care of him. 35 The next day
he handed the innkeeper two silver coins,* telling
him, 'Take care of this man. If his bill runs higher than
this, I'll pay you the next time I'm here.'
36 "Now which of these three would you say was a
neighbor to the man who was attacked by bandits?"
Jesus asked.
37 The man replied, "The one who showed him mer-
cy."
Then Jesus said, "Yes, now go and do the same."

JESUS VISITS MARTHA AND MARY

38 As Jesus and the disciples continued on their way
to Jerusalem, they came to a certain village where a
woman named Martha welcomed him into her home.
39 Her sister, Mary, sat at the Lord's feet, listening to

10:27 Deut 6:5; Lev 19:18. **10:32** Greek *A Levite.* **10:35** Greek *two denarii.* A denarius was equivalent to a laborer's full day's wage.

10:25 an expert in religious law. This would have been a scribe, a man charged with the responsibility of interpreting the law and teaching people what was involved in its observance.
10:26-27 What does the law of Moses say? Jesus' question points the lawyer back to the *Shema* (Deut. 6:5), which is recited in verse 27. The scribe also adds Leviticus 19:18 with its stress on the love of neighbor.
10:29 And who is my neighbor? In an attempt to regain the initiative, he asks Jesus another question. Given the understanding of "neighbor" at the time, his follow-up question was perfectly natural. The Jewish religious leaders of the time taught that only other Jews were neighbors.
10:31 A priest. This priest may have been returning home after his period of temple service. He may have passed by to avoid the ritual defilement of touching a dead man.
10:32 a Temple assistant. These were men assigned to aid the priests in various temple duties. Perhaps he was fearful of being attacked himself by the same robbers.
10:33 a Samaritan. These people were despised by most Jews, and hence making him the hero who acted like a neighbor would have caught the Jewish audience off guard.
10:34 soothed his wounds with olive oil and wine. While olive oil and wine were thought to have medicinal benefits, they were also used in acts of worship at the temple.
10:35 two silver coins. Silver coins that would have been enough to care for the man for three weeks.
10:38 village. Bethany, just on the outskirts of Jerusalem, was the home of Martha and Mary and their brother Lazarus. **a woman named Martha.** Martha and Mary also appear in John 11:1-44, where their brother Lazarus dies and is raised from the dead by Jesus.

what he taught. 40 But Martha was distracted by the big dinner she was preparing. She came to Jesus and said, "Lord, doesn't it seem unfair to you that my sister just sits here while I do all the work? Tell her to come and help me."

41 But the Lord said to her, "My dear Martha, you are worried and upset over all these details! 42 There is only one thing worth being concerned about. Mary has discovered it, and it will not be taken away from her."

TEACHING ABOUT PRAYER

11 Once Jesus was in a certain place praying. As he finished, one of his disciples came to him and said, "Lord, teach us to pray, just as John taught his disciples."

2 Jesus said, "This is how you should pray:*

"Father, may your name be kept holy.
May your Kingdom come soon.
3 Give us each day the food we need,*
4 and forgive us our sins,
as we forgive those who sin against us.
And don't let us yield to temptation.*"

5 Then, teaching them more about prayer, he used this story: "Suppose you went to a friend's house at midnight, wanting to borrow three loaves of bread. You say to him, 6 'A friend of mine has just arrived for a visit, and I have nothing for him to eat.' 7 And suppose he calls out from his bedroom, 'Don't bother me. The door is locked for the night, and my family and I are all in bed. I can't help you.' 8 But I tell you this—though he won't do it for friendship's sake, if you keep knocking long enough, he will get up and give you whatever you need because of your shameless persistence.*

9 "And so I tell you, keep on asking, and you will receive what you ask for. Keep on seeking, and you will find. Keep on knocking, and the door will be opened to you. 10 For everyone who asks, receives. Everyone who seeks, finds. And to everyone who knocks, the door will be opened.

11 "You fathers—if your children ask* for a fish, do you give them a snake instead? 12 Or if they ask for an egg, do you give them a scorpion? Of course not! 13 So if you sinful people know how to give good gifts to your children, how much more will your heavenly Father give the Holy Spirit to those who ask him."

JESUS AND THE PRINCE OF DEMONS

14 One day Jesus cast out a demon from a man who couldn't speak, and when the demon was gone, the man began to speak. The crowds were amazed, 15 but some of them said, "No wonder he can cast out demons. He gets his power from Satan,* the prince of demons." 16 Others, trying to test Jesus, demanded that he show them a miraculous sign from heaven to prove his authority.

17 He knew their thoughts, so he said, "Any kingdom divided by civil war is doomed. A family splintered by feuding will fall apart. 18 You say I am empowered by Satan. But if Satan is divided and fighting against himself, how can his kingdom survive? 19 And if I am empowered by Satan, what about your own exorcists? They cast out demons, too, so they will condemn you for what you have said. 20 But if I am casting out demons by the power of God,* then the Kingdom of God has arrived among you. 21 For when a strong man is fully armed and guards his palace, his possessions are safe—22 until someone even stronger attacks and overpowers him, strips him of his weapons, and carries off his belongings.

23 "Anyone who isn't with me opposes me, and anyone who isn't working with me is actually working against me.

24 "When an evil* spirit leaves a person, it goes into the desert, searching for rest. But when it finds none, it says, 'I will return to the person I came from.' 25 So it returns and finds that its former home is all swept and in order. 26 Then the spirit finds seven other spirits more evil than itself, and they all enter the person and live there. And so that person is worse off than before."

27 As he was speaking, a woman in the crowd called out, "God bless your mother—the womb from which you came, and the breasts that nursed you!"

11:2 Some manuscripts add additional phrases from the Lord's Prayer as it reads in Matt 6:9-13. **11:3** Or *Give us each day our food for the day;* or *Give us each day our food for tomorrow.* **11:4** Or *And keep us from being tested.* **11:8** Or *in order to avoid shame,* or *so his reputation won't be damaged.* **11:11** Some manuscripts add *for bread, do you give them a stone? Or [if they ask].* **11:15** Greek *Beelzeboul;* also in 11:18, 19. Other manuscripts read *Beezeboul;* Latin version reads *Beelzebub.* **11:20** Greek *by the finger of God.* **11:24** Greek *unclean.*

10:42 one thing worth being concerned about. Jesus is not saying that a simple meal is all that is needed but that listening and responding to Him is the single most critical thing in life.

11:1 teach us to pray. Various Jewish groups (including John's disciples) had their own distinctive prayers.

11:2 Father. While even the orthodox Jews of the day called God "our Father," this simple, personal form of address was new. Jesus at times used the term "Abba," a term more akin to "Dad" than "Father," which was being much more familiar with God than other rabbis thought appropriate. He taught the disciples to approach God personally. **Your name be kept holy.** The first petition is that the name of God (i.e., His character and nature) be honored by all. **May your kingdom come soon.** The prayer is that God will quickly establish the reign of His kingdom throughout the world. While the kingdom is in some sense already present (10:9), it will only come in its *fullness* when Christ returns.

11:4 as we forgive those who sin against us. This is not an appeal for forgiveness as a reward for our forgiving others but rather a reminder that God's forgiveness produces a willingness to extend that to others. Jesus told the parable of the unmerciful servant (Matt. 18:21-35) to make this point. **don't let us yield to temptation.** The request is that the person will not have to face a trial so difficult that he or she will fall into sin.

11:5-6 I have nothing for him to eat. Hospitality was held in high regard in the ancient Middle East. Hebrews urged Christians to continue to be hospitable to traveling strangers (Heb. 13:2). Since hospitality was such an important duty, it would be imperative that the host in this story provide some food for his surprise visitor.

11:7 The door is locked. A wooden door secured by a wooden or iron bolt thrust through rings. It could not be opened without making a noise. **my family and I are all in bed.** The whole family would sleep together on a mat on the floor of the simple one-room cottage envisioned here. If the man got up, he would disturb the whole household.

11:8 because of your shameless persistence. Literally, "shamelessness."

11:9 keep on asking ... Keep on seeking .... Keep on knocking. Jesus is emphasizing that prayer is a continuous, ongoing process. Prayer is rooted in the assurance that the householder (God) will hear the prayers and meet the needs of his friend.

11:11-13 snake . . . scorpion. These were creatures that Jews were forbidden to eat (Lev. 11:12,42). The snake may be an eel-like fish that likewise was forbidden to the Jews. The scorpion, at least, could be poisonous.

11:13 you sinful people. A strong statement since "evil" is used elsewhere to characterize Satan (Matt. 6:13). Since not even a sinful human father would give such a repulsive, dangerous food to his own son, how much less will the perfect heavenly Father fail to give what His children most need?

11:15 Beelzebul. Probably a slang expression for a demon-prince, meaning something like "The Lord of Dung." It is used here apparently as a synonym for Satan.

28 Jesus replied, "But even more blessed are all who
hear the word of God and put it into practice."

THE SIGN OF JONAH

29 As the crowd pressed in on Jesus, he said, "This evil
generation keeps asking me to show them a miraculous sign. But the only sign I will give them is the sign
of Jonah.
30 What happened to him was a sign to the
people of Nineveh that God had sent him. What happens to the Son of Man* will be a sign to these people
that he was sent by God.
31 "The queen of Sheba* will stand up against this
generation on judgment day and condemn it, for she
came from a distant land to hear the wisdom of Solomon. Now someone greater than Solomon is here—
but you refuse to listen.
32 The people of Nineveh will
also stand up against this generation on judgment
day and condemn it, for they repented of their sins at
the preaching of Jonah. Now someone greater than
Jonah is here—but you refuse to repent.

RECEIVING THE LIGHT

33 "No one lights a lamp and then hides it or puts it
under a basket.* Instead, a lamp is placed on a stand,
where its light can be seen by all who enter the house.
34 "Your eye is like a lamp that provides light for
your body. When your eye is healthy, your whole
body is filled with light. But when it is unhealthy,
your body is filled with darkness.
35 Make sure that
the light you think you have is not actually darkness.
36 If you are filled with light, with no dark corners,
then your whole life will be radiant, as though a
floodlight were filling you with light."

JESUS CRITICIZES THE RELIGIOUS LEADERS

37 As Jesus was speaking, one of the Pharisees invited
him home for a meal. So he went in and took his place
at the table.*
38 His host was amazed to see that he sat
down to eat without first performing the hand-washing ceremony required by Jewish custom.
39 Then
the Lord said to him, "You Pharisees are so careful to
clean the outside of the cup and the dish, but inside
you are filthy—full of greed and wickedness!
40 Fools!
Didn't God make the inside as well as the outside?
41 So
clean the inside by giving gifts to the poor, and you
will be clean all over.
42 "What sorrow awaits you Pharisees! For you are
careful to tithe even the tiniest income from your
herb gardens,* but you ignore justice and the love of
God. You should tithe, yes, but do not neglect the more
important things.
43 "What sorrow awaits you Pharisees! For you love
to sit in the seats of honor in the synagogues and receive respectful greetings as you walk in the marketplaces.
44 Yes, what sorrow awaits you! For you are
like hidden graves in a field. People walk over them
without knowing the corruption they are stepping
on."
45 "Teacher," said an expert in religious law, "you
have insulted us, too, in what you just said."
46 "Yes," said Jesus, "what sorrow also awaits you
experts in religious law! For you crush people with
unbearable religious demands, and you never lift a
finger to ease the burden.
47 What sorrow awaits you!
For you build monuments for the prophets your own
ancestors killed long ago.
48 But in fact, you stand as
witnesses who agree with what your ancestors did.
They killed the prophets, and you join in their crime
by building the monuments!
49 This is what God in his
wisdom said about you:* 'I will send prophets and
apostles to them, but they will kill some and persecute the others.'
50 "As a result, this generation will be held responsible for the murder of all God's prophets from the creation of the world—
51 from the murder of Abel to the
murder of Zechariah, who was killed between the altar and the sanctuary. Yes, it will certainly be charged
against this generation.
52 "What sorrow awaits you experts in religious
law! For you remove the key to knowledge from the
people. You don't enter the Kingdom yourselves, and
you prevent others from entering."
53 As Jesus was leaving, the teachers of religious
law and the Pharisees became hostile and tried to
provoke him with many questions.
54 They wanted
to trap him into saying something they could use
against him.

A WARNING AGAINST HYPOCRISY

12 Meanwhile, the crowds grew until thousands
were milling about and stepping on each other.
Jesus turned first to his disciples and warned them,

11:30 "Son of Man" is a title Jesus used for himself. **11:31** Greek *The queen of the south.* **11:33** Some manuscripts do not include *or puts it under a basket.* **11:37** Or *and reclined.* **11:42** Greek *tithe the mint, the rue, and every herb.* **11:49** Greek *Therefore, the wisdom of God said.*

11:29 the sign of Jonah. This is a reference to Jesus' resurrection. After Jonah spent three days and three nights in the belly of the "great fish," he experienced a miraculous deliverance—which authenticated his call to preach in Nineveh (Jonah 1:17; 2:10).

11:31 The queen of Sheba. She came all the way from Arabia to listen to the wisdom of Solomon (1 Kings 10:1-13). **someone greater.** Jesus claims to be greater than Solomon, under whose reign Israel achieved its apex of power and dominion. He also claims to be greater than Jonah (v. 32), under whose preaching an entire Gentile city was brought to its knees before God.

11:34 Your eye is the lamp that provides light for your body. The comparison is between a lamp that provides light for one's path and a good eye (literally, an eye that is "single") that enables people to find their way toward a purposeful life of obedience to God.

11:38 His host was amazed. Like Simon in 7:39, Jesus' unorthodox actions raised silent questions in the mind of His host. **without first performing the hand-washing ceremony.** This had nothing to do with hygiene but everything to do with religious tradition.

11:41 giving . . .you will be clean all over. They should repent of their greed and give to the poor instead. Such action would reflect a change of heart that would show inner cleanliness.

11:42 to tithe. The Old Testament required a tithe of garden and farm produce (Lev. 27:30-33; Deut. 14:22-29). Jesus attacked the Pharisees for holding fast to this (relatively) insignificant detail while, they had totally neglected concerns like justice and love that dominate the Old Testament Law and prophets.

11:43 the seats of honor. The seats facing the congregation were the most important seats in the synagogue. To be seated there had become a sign of one's status in the congregation.

11:44 hidden graves. Unmarked graves defile those who unknowingly come in contact with them (Num. 19:16).

11:46 crush people with unbearable religious demands. The scribes interpreted the law with a complex system of restrictions. Thus most felt condemned for their continual breaking of God's law. Jesus is incensed that the scribes assumed their duty stopped with interpreting the law. They made no attempt to help the people who struggled under the burden they created.

11:51 Abel. The first person to be murdered. It happened because his brother, like these leaders, refused to listen to God (Gen. 4:3-8). **Zechariah.** The context implies this was Zechariah (son of Jehoiada), who was murdered in the temple by people who refused to hear his word (2 Chron. 24:19-22).

11:52 remove the key of knowledge. Instead of unlocking the Scriptures, the traditions of the scribes have securely locked away such knowledge from the people.

12:1 yeast. Yeast was often used as a metaphor for evil. Here it represents the hypocrisy of the Pharisees.

"Beware of the yeast of the Pharisees—their hypocrisy. [2]The time is coming when everything that is covered up will be revealed, and all that is secret will be made known to all. [3]Whatever you have said in the dark will be heard in the light, and what you have whispered behind closed doors will be shouted from the housetops for all to hear!

[4]"Dear friends, don't be afraid of those who want to kill your body; they cannot do any more to you after that. [5]But I'll tell you whom to fear. Fear God, who has the power to kill you and then throw you into hell.* Yes, he's the one to fear.

[6]"What is the price of five sparrows—two copper coins*? Yet God does not forget a single one of them. [7]And the very hairs on your head are all numbered. So don't be afraid; you are more valuable to God than a whole flock of sparrows.

[8]"I tell you the truth, everyone who acknowledges me publicly here on earth, the Son of Man* will also acknowledge in the presence of God's angels. [9]But anyone who denies me here on earth will be denied before God's angels. [10]Anyone who speaks against the Son of Man can be forgiven, but anyone who blasphemes the Holy Spirit will not be forgiven.

[11]"And when you are brought to trial in the synagogues and before rulers and authorities, don't worry about how to defend yourself or what to say, [12]for the Holy Spirit will teach you at that time what needs to be said."

PARABLE OF THE RICH FOOL

[13]Then someone called from the crowd, "Teacher, please tell my brother to divide our father's estate with me."

[14]Jesus replied, "Friend, who made me a judge over you to decide such things as that?" [15]Then he said, "Beware! Guard against every kind of greed. Life is not measured by how much you own."

[16]Then he told them a story: "A rich man had a fertile farm that produced fine crops. [17]He said to himself, 'What should I do? I don't have room for all my crops.' [18]Then he said, 'I know! I'll tear down my barns and build bigger ones. Then I'll have room enough to store all my wheat and other goods. [19]And I'll sit back and say to myself, "My friend, you have enough stored away for years to come. Now take it easy! Eat, drink, and be merry!"'

BUILDING TRUE WEALTH

1. If you could have fame, fortune, or good looks, which would you choose?

LUKE 12:13-21

2. What was Jesus warning against in verse 15? How does greed lead to spiritual disaster?
3. "Take it easy! Eat, drink, and be merry!" (v. 19). What is your attitude toward this philosophy? The attitude of those in your school?
4. Why did God call the rich man a fool (v. 20): Because he was rich? Because of his attitude? Other?
5. How can you have "a rich relationship with God" (v. 21)? How can you help others whose "life is measured by how much [they] own" (v. 15)?

[20]"But God said to him, 'You fool! You will die this very night. Then who will get everything you worked for?'

[21]"Yes, a person is a fool to store up earthly wealth but not have a rich relationship with God."

TEACHING ABOUT MONEY AND POSSESSIONS

[22]Then, turning to his disciples, Jesus said, "That is why I tell you not to worry about everyday life—whether you have enough food to eat or enough clothes to wear. [23]For life is more than food, and your body more than clothing. [24]Look at the ravens. They don't plant or harvest or store food in barns, for God feeds them. And you are far more valuable to him than any birds! [25]Can all your worries add a single moment to your life? [26]And if worry can't accomplish a little thing like that, what's the use of worrying over bigger things?

[27]"Look at the lilies and how they grow. They don't work or make their clothing, yet Solomon in all his glory was not dressed as beautifully as they are. [28]And if God cares so wonderfully for flowers that are here today and thrown into the fire tomorrow, he will certainly care for you. Why do you have so little faith?

12:5 Greek *Gehenna*. 12:6 Greek *two assaria* [Roman coins equal to 1/16 of a denarius]. 12:8 "Son of Man" is a title Jesus used for himself.

12:2-3 covered up will be revealed . . . secret will be made known to all. In the context of Jesus' warning about the hypocrisy of the Pharisees, He reminds His disciples that everything is open before God's all-seeing gaze. We may pretend to be better than what we are, but God knows. Authentic worship and discipleship live constantly in this realization.

12:4 don't be afraid of those who want to kill your body. Whatever we fear has control of us. Most people's greatest fear is physical death—and by extension—anyone or anything that can bring about our physical death. Jesus says this is a misplaced fear. He died to free us from this slavery (Heb. 2:15). Our only fear should be of Him who has the authority to send those who have died to hell. It was said of the Scottish reformer John Knox that he feared God so much, he feared no man.

12:6 sparrows. These small, common birds were eaten by poor people. **two copper coins.** A penny was worth one sixteenth of a denarius, which was the average day's wage.

12:13 Teacher. Literally, "Rabbi." As men schooled in the law of God, rabbis were often asked to settle legal disputes. **divide our father's estate.** If sons could not peaceably keep the father's estate together, one could sue for the property to be legally divided.

12:14 who made me a judge over you? Jesus refused to be used as a pawn for this man's material gain. Jesus effectively became the judge over both of them, exposing the motivation of their hearts.

12:15 Beware! Guard against every kind of greed. Jesus pinpointed the real motivating factor behind this appeal for justice. **life.** Then, as now, a person's happiness and well-being was often thought to be determined by what he or she owned. Jesus flatly rejected this as a standard for measuring the worth of one's life.

12:18 store all my wheat and other goods. Up to this point in the parable, the listeners would view the man as blessed by God. Even the plan to store the crop for future use could be commended, since the people of the Middle East would periodically suffer from famine. But God redirected the thought. He reminded the rich man that only God directs the future. The man was to live respecting God, not confident in his own resources.

12:19 Eat, drink, and be merry! The man was not following God's ways but living as a pagan, concerned only with his own desires.

12:20 You fool! In the Bible, a fool is someone who lives without regard to God. **You will die this very night.** The word for "demanded" is a word used in banking circles when a loan was being called in for payment.

12:28 you have so little faith? Faith is the opposite of anxiety.

WHERE'S YOUR BEST TREASURE?

1. What "treasure" did you collect as a kid? Do those things still seem valuable to you now?

LUKE 12:22-34

2. Jesus taught this lesson because of the rich man's request for help in verse 13. How might worry have been the motivating factor behind his request?
3. What does it mean to "seek the Kingdom of God" (v. 31)?
4. How do we make "purses of heaven" for [ourselves] that "never get old" (v. 33)?
5. Jesus tells us in verse 34, "Wherever your treasure is, there the desires of your heart will also be." Where is your heart today—with treasures on earth or with Jesus in heaven?

29 "And don't be concerned about what to eat and
what to drink. Don't worry about such things. 30 These
things dominate the thoughts of unbelievers all over
the world, but your Father already knows your needs.
31 Seek the Kingdom of God above all else, and he will
give you everything you need.
32 "So don't be afraid, little flock. For it gives your
Father great happiness to give you the Kingdom.
33 "Sell your possessions and give to those in need.
This will store up treasure for you in heaven! And the
purses of heaven never get old or develop holes. Your
treasure will be safe; no thief can steal it and no moth
can destroy it. 34 Wherever your treasure is, there the
desires of your heart will also be.

BE READY FOR THE LORD'S COMING

35 "Be dressed for service and keep your lamps burn-
ing, 36 as though you were waiting for your master
to return from the wedding feast. Then you will be
ready to open the door and let him in the moment
he arrives and knocks. 37 The servants who are ready
and waiting for his return will be rewarded. I tell you
the truth, he himself will seat them, put on an apron,
and serve them as they sit and eat! 38 He may come
in the middle of the night or just before dawn.* But
whenever he comes, he will reward the servants who
are ready.
39 "Understand this: If a homeowner knew exactly
when a burglar was coming, he would not permit his
house to be broken into. 40 You also must be ready all
the time, for the Son of Man will come when least ex-
pected."
41 Peter asked, "Lord, is that illustration just for us
or for everyone?"
42 And the Lord replied, "A faithful, sensible ser-
vant is one to whom the master can give the respon-
sibility of managing his other household servants
and feeding them. 43 If the master returns and finds
that the servant has done a good job, there will be
a reward. 44 I tell you the truth, the master will put
that servant in charge of all he owns. 45 But what if
the servant thinks, 'My master won't be back for a
while,' and he begins beating the other servants,
partying, and getting drunk? 46 The master will re-
turn unannounced and unexpected, and he will cut
the servant in pieces and banish him with the un-
faithful.
47 "And a servant who knows what the master
wants, but isn't prepared and doesn't carry out those
instructions, will be severely punished. 48 But some-
one who does not know, and then does something
wrong, will be punished only lightly. When some-
one has been given much, much will be required in
return; and when someone has been entrusted with
much, even more will be required.

JESUS CAUSES DIVISION

49 "I have come to set the world on fire, and I wish it
were already burning! 50 I have a terrible baptism of
suffering ahead of me, and I am under a heavy bur-
den until it is accomplished. 51 Do you think I have
come to bring peace to the earth? No, I have come to
divide people against each other! 52 From now on fam-
ilies will be split apart, three in favor of me, and two
against—or two in favor and three against.

53 'Father will be divided against son
and son against father;
mother against daughter
and daughter against mother;
and mother-in-law against daughter-in-law
and daughter-in-law against mother-in-law.'*"

54 Then Jesus turned to the crowd and said, "When
you see clouds beginning to form in the west, you say,
'Here comes a shower.' And you are right. 55 When the
south wind blows, you say, 'Today will be a scorch-
er.' And it is. 56 You fools! You know how to interpret
the weather signs of the earth and sky, but you don't
know how to interpret the present times.
57 "Why can't you decide for yourselves what is
right? 58 When you are on the way to court with
your accuser, try to settle the matter before you get

12:38 Greek *in the second or third watch.* 12:53 Mic 7:6. 12:59 Greek *last lepton* [the smallest Jewish coin].

12:29 Don't be concerned. Literally, "do not seek."

12:31 seek the Kingdom of God. Having warned the disciples not to focus their attention on the material benefits of this life, Jesus encouraged them to seek the spiritual blessings of God's kingdom. **give you everything you need.** The promise is that if the disciples concentrate on doing the will of God, then their basic needs will be met by Him.

12:33 moth. The most expensive clothing is susceptible to insignificant creatures like moths (James 5:1-3; 1 Peter 1:4).

12:35 Be dressed for service. To work or travel a man would gather up the garment with a belt to free his legs for uninhibited movement. This implies the disciples were to be ever ready to serve their Lord.

12:42 sensible servant. When a wealthy homeowner was away, he would appoint one of his servants to be in charge of his affairs during his absence. One of his responsibilities was the management of food rations.

12:46 He will cut the servant in pieces and banish him with the unfaithful. While the method of executing a person by cutting him into pieces is grotesque, the addition of the second phrase may imply that we are to understand it as a metaphor picturing the cutting off of this person from his former household.

12:49 fire. Fire is used both as a symbol of judgment (3:16; Acts 2:19) and of the Holy Spirit (3:16; Acts 2:4).

12:50 baptism. This word was used in a figurative way to describe being overwhelmed by a catastrophe. Before the Spirit's purifying work can begin, the fire of God's judgment must first be experienced by Jesus on the cross. **accomplished.** The death of Jesus was the essential reason for His incarnation, His coming in the flesh (see John 19:30).

there. Otherwise, your accuser may drag you before the judge, who will hand you over to an officer, who will throw you into prison. 59 And if that happens, you won't be free again until you have paid the very last penny.*"

A CALL TO REPENTANCE

13 About this time Jesus was informed that Pilate had murdered some people from Galilee as they were offering sacrifices at the Temple. 2 "Do you think those Galileans were worse sinners than all the other people from Galilee?" Jesus asked. "Is that why they suffered? 3 Not at all! And you will perish, too, unless you repent of your sins and turn to God. 4 And what about the eighteen people who died when the tower in Siloam fell on them? Were they the worst sinners in Jerusalem? 5 No, and I tell you again that unless you repent, you will perish, too."

PARABLE OF THE BARREN FIG TREE

6 Then Jesus told this story: "A man planted a fig tree in his garden and came again and again to see if there was any fruit on it, but he was always disappointed. 7 Finally, he said to his gardener, 'I've waited three years, and there hasn't been a single fig! Cut it down. It's just taking up space in the garden.'

8 "The gardener answered, 'Sir, give it one more chance. Leave it another year, and I'll give it special attention and plenty of fertilizer. 9 If we get figs next year, fine. If not, then you can cut it down.'"

JESUS HEALS ON THE SABBATH

10 One Sabbath day as Jesus was teaching in a synagogue, 11 he saw a woman who had been crippled by an evil spirit. She had been bent double for eighteen years and was unable to stand up straight. 12 When Jesus saw her, he called her over and said, "Dear woman, you are healed of your sickness!" 13 Then he touched her, and instantly she could stand straight. How she praised God!

14 But the leader in charge of the synagogue was indignant that Jesus had healed her on the Sabbath day. "There are six days of the week for working," he said to the crowd. "Come on those days to be healed, not on the Sabbath."

15 But the Lord replied, "You hypocrites! Each of you works on the Sabbath day! Don't you untie your ox or your donkey from its stall on the Sabbath and lead it out for water? 16 This dear woman, a daughter of Abraham, has been held in bondage by Satan for eighteen years. Isn't it right that she be released, even on the Sabbath?"

17 This shamed his enemies, but all the people rejoiced at the wonderful things he did.

PARABLE OF THE MUSTARD SEED

18 Then Jesus said, "What is the Kingdom of God like? How can I illustrate it? 19 It is like a tiny mustard seed that a man planted in a garden; it grows and becomes a tree, and the birds make nests in its branches."

PARABLE OF THE YEAST

20 He also asked, "What else is the Kingdom of God like? 21 It is like the yeast a woman used in making bread. Even though she put only a little yeast in three measures of flour, it permeated every part of the dough."

THE NARROW DOOR

22 Jesus went through the towns and villages, teaching as he went, always pressing on toward Jerusalem. 23 Someone asked him, "Lord, will only a few be saved?"

He replied, 24 "Work hard to enter the narrow door to God's Kingdom, for many will try to enter but will fail. 25 When the master of the house has locked the door, it will be too late. You will stand outside knocking and pleading, 'Lord, open the door for us!' But he will reply, 'I don't know you or where you come from.' 26 Then you will say, 'But we ate and drank with you, and you taught in our streets.' 27 And he will reply, 'I tell you, I don't know you or where you come from. Get away from me, all you who do evil.'

28 "There will be weeping and gnashing of teeth, for you will see Abraham, Isaac, Jacob, and all the prophets in the Kingdom of God, but you will be thrown out. 29 And people will come from all over the world—from east and west, north and south—to take their places in the Kingdom of God. 30 And note this: Some who seem least important now will be the greatest then, and some who are the greatest now will be least important then.*"

13:30 Greek *Some are last who will be first, and some are first who will be last.*

13:1 the people from Galilee as they were offering sacrifices at the Temple. While nothing is known of this specific act, similar acts of violence against worshipping Jews had been done in Jerusalem

13:4 the tower in Siloam. Siloam was a reservoir located near the southeast corner of Jerusalem. The tower Jesus refers to may have been one built for fortification or in conjunction with an aqueduct that was part of the city's water supply. As with the slain Galileans (vv. 2-3), those killed when the tower collapsed were not more sinful than the other residents of the city; indeed, all of them needed to repent.

13:6 fig tree . . .garden. Since vineyards were really more like fruit gardens, the presence of such a tree was not unusual.

13:7-9 If we get figs next year. While the owner wants to cut down the tree, the caretaker of the garden desires to cultivate. Jesus points out God's patience toward His people and the reality that a day of accounting is coming.

13:11 bent double. This woman's disease appears to have been a fusion of the spinal column, causing great pain and making it impossible for her to stand erect.

13:16 a daughter of Abraham. The severity of her infirmity may have led many to assume she was being punished for an especially bad sin and thus was not considered by God as one of His people. Jesus affirms her as a true Israelite (Gal. 3:7). **released, even on the Sabbath?** One of the purposes of the Sabbath was to be a weekly reminder of the freedom for which God had delivered His people from Egypt (Deut. 5:15). By overcoming Satan's grip on this woman on the Sabbath, Jesus, far from defiling the day, demonstrated its true significance.

13:19 mustard seed. The mustard plant is the smallest seed, yet its shrubs grew to about 10 feet high.

13:20-21 yeast. While yeast was generally a symbol of something evil (Mark 8:15), here it is positive, symbolizing growth and transformation.

13:21 three measures of flour. Literally, "three measures"—which would be almost 160 cups of flour! This would make enough bread for over 100 people.

13:23 saved? This word serves as a shorthand way of expressing deliverance from God's judgment and entrance into a relationship of peace with Him (Acts 2:47; 16:29-31; 1 Cor. 1:18; 2 Cor. 2:15). It is synonymous with entering the kingdom of God (12:32) and inheriting eternal life (18:18).

13:25-27 I don't know you. The picture is of people wishing at the last moment to respond to the invitation of a distinguished man holding a dinner party (14:15-24). While they protest that familiarity with the host should be grounds for their admission, the reason for their rejection is found in a paraphrase of Psalm 6:8 ("Depart from me, all evildoers"). They are evildoers shut out from God's presence.

13:30 least important . . .greatest. This saying of Jesus implies that Gentiles, the last to hear of God's grace, may actually respond to His invitation, while many in Israel will find it much more difficult to respond.

JESUS GRIEVES OVER JERUSALEM

31 At that time some Pharisees said to him, "Get away from here if you want to live! Herod Antipas wants to kill you!"

32 Jesus replied, "Go tell that fox that I will keep on casting out demons and healing people today and tomorrow; and the third day I will accomplish my purpose. 33 Yes, today, tomorrow, and the next day I must proceed on my way. For it wouldn't do for a prophet of God to be killed except in Jerusalem!

34 "O Jerusalem, Jerusalem, the city that kills the prophets and stones God's messengers! How often I have wanted to gather your children together as a hen protects her chicks beneath her wings, but you wouldn't let me. 35 And now, look, your house is abandoned. And you will never see me again until you say, 'Blessings on the one who comes in the name of the LORD!'*"

JESUS HEALS ON THE SABBATH

14 One Sabbath day Jesus went to eat dinner in the home of a leader of the Pharisees, and the people were watching him closely. 2 There was a man there whose arms and legs were swollen.* 3 Jesus asked the Pharisees and experts in religious law, "Is it permitted in the law to heal people on the Sabbath day, or not?" 4 When they refused to answer, Jesus touched the sick man and healed him and sent him away. 5 Then he turned to them and said, "Which of you doesn't work on the Sabbath? If your son* or your cow falls into a pit, don't you rush to get him out?" 6 Again they could not answer.

JESUS TEACHES ABOUT HUMILITY

7 When Jesus noticed that all who had come to the dinner were trying to sit in the seats of honor near the head of the table, he gave them this advice: 8 "When you are invited to a wedding feast, don't sit in the seat of honor. What if someone who is more distinguished than you has also been invited? 9 The host will come and say, 'Give this person your seat.' Then you will be embarrassed, and you will have to take whatever seat is left at the foot of the table!

10 "Instead, take the lowest place at the foot of the table. Then when your host sees you, he will come and say, 'Friend, we have a better place for you!' Then you will be honored in front of all the other guests. 11 For those who exalt themselves will be humbled, and those who humble themselves will be exalted."

12 Then he turned to his host. "When you put on a luncheon or a banquet," he said, "don't invite your friends, brothers, relatives, and rich neighbors. For they will invite you back, and that will be your only reward. 13 Instead, invite the poor, the crippled, the lame, and the blind. 14 Then at the resurrection of the righteous, God will reward you for inviting those who could not repay you."

PARABLE OF THE GREAT FEAST

15 Hearing this, a man sitting at the table with Jesus exclaimed, "What a blessing it will be to attend a banquet* in the Kingdom of God!"

16 Jesus replied with this story: "A man prepared a great feast and sent out many invitations. 17 When the banquet was ready, he sent his servant to tell the guests, 'Come, the banquet is ready.' 18 But they all began making excuses. One said, 'I have just bought a field and must inspect it. Please excuse me.' 19 Another said, 'I have just bought five pairs of oxen, and I want to try them out. Please excuse me.' 20 Another said, 'I just got married, so I can't come.'

THE BEST INVITATION EVER

1. What's your favorite excuse to get out of going somewhere you don't want to go?

LUKE 14:15-24

2. Why would people make excuses not to attend a big banquet with free food?
3. What happened to those people who rejected the invitation?
4. What lesson is Jesus teaching in this parable?
5. What excuses do people use to reject Jesus' offer of free salvation?
6. Have you accepted or rejected His invitation? Why or why not?

13:35 Ps 118:26. **14:2** Or *who had dropsy.* **14:5** Some manuscripts read *donkey.* **14:15** Greek *to eat bread.*

13:31 Herod. Herod's dominion included Galilee and Perea, the probable location of Jesus at this point.

13:32 tell that fox. Sometimes the fox was used as a symbol of a cunning person. Note that the image with strength like the lion isn't used here. The reference to the "third day" would bring Jesus' resurrection to mind for Luke's readers.

13:33 killed except in Jerusalem! Prophets, like Jeremiah, did die outside Jerusalem. The force of the saying is that just as the authorities associated with the temple in Jerusalem consistently opposed the prophets and executed some of them, so Jesus will experience the same fate.

13:34-35 O Jerusalem, Jerusalem! . . .look, your house is abandoned. George Santayana observed that those who don't know history are doomed to repeat it. Sometimes even those who know history, repeat it. Nearly 600 years before Jesus spoke these words, the Babylonians leveled Jerusalem and its temple. Now, within forty years Jesus' prophecy will be fulfilled as the Romans utterly destroy the city. "How she sits alone, the city [once] crowded with people" (Lamentations 1:1).

14:2 arms and legs were swollen. This fluid retention was not in actuality a disease but a sign of disease of the heart, kidneys, or liver.

14:5 cow falls into a pit. The first lesson of this dinner party lay in Jesus' exposure of their callous attitude toward people's needs in contrast to their sensitivity to the plight of animals (13:15; Matt. 12:11).

14:8 the seat of honor. The scene envisioned here is that of the embarrassment that would be experienced by someone who assumed he or she should be in a place of honor and took that position apart from the host's invitation. When the guest for whom the host had reserved that spot arrived, the presumptuous guest would be humiliated by having to give up the seat.

14:15 What a blessing. . .! The bliss of life with God was often pictured in terms of a feast (Isa. 25:6; 55:2; 65:13).

14:16-17 sent out invitations . . .sent his servant to tell. In well-to-do circles, invitations to honored guests for a formal dinner were issued well in advance, but the specific time to arrive was communicated on the day of the event when everything was ready (Esther 5:8; 6:14).

14:18-20 excuses. Jesus' listeners would immediately see these excuses as an obvious attempt to insult the host.

14:18 I must inspect it. Then, as now, people would not buy property first and then look at it later!

14:20 now have a wife. Marriage plans were made far in advance; the man certainly would have known of his plans for marriage when he received the original invitation to the banquet. The net effect of all these excuses is that the guests didn't value the relationship enough to come, and so made excuses.

SALT OF THE EARTH

1. Do you like salty food? Bland food?

LUKE 14:25-35

2. What did Jesus mean by teaching that His followers should "hate" their families (v. 26)?
3. Why did Jesus use an illustration of going to war to describe the proper attitude toward possessions (vv. 31-33)?
4. What is so important about salt, especially to Jesus' audience? How are Christians like salt to this world?
5. Are you like good salt in your school, or are you more like salt that has lost its taste? How can you become "saltier" salt?

21"The servant returned and told his master what they had said. His master was furious and said, 'Go quickly into the streets and alleys of the town and invite the poor, the crippled, the blind, and the lame.' 22After the servant had done this, he reported, 'There is still room for more.' 23So his master said, 'Go out into the country lanes and behind the hedges and urge anyone you find to come, so that the house will be full. 24For none of those I first invited will get even the smallest taste of my banquet.'"

THE COST OF BEING A DISCIPLE

25A large crowd was following Jesus. He turned around and said to them, 26"If you want to be my disciple, you must, by comparison, hate everyone else—your father and mother, wife and children, brothers and sisters—yes, even your own life. Otherwise, you cannot be my disciple. 27And if you do not carry your own cross and follow me, you cannot be my disciple.

28"But don't begin until you count the cost. For who would begin construction of a building without first calculating the cost to see if there is enough money to finish it? 29Otherwise, you might complete only the foundation before running out of money, and then everyone would laugh at you. 30They would say, 'There's the person who started that building and couldn't afford to finish it!'

31"Or what king would go to war against another king without first sitting down with his counselors to discuss whether his army of 10,000 could defeat the 20,000 soldiers marching against him? 32And if he can't, he will send a delegation to discuss terms of peace while the enemy is still far away. 33So you cannot become my disciple without giving up everything you own.

34"Salt is good for seasoning. But if it loses its flavor, how do you make it salty again? 35Flavorless salt is good neither for the soil nor for the manure pile. It is thrown away. Anyone with ears to hear should listen and understand!"

PARABLE OF THE LOST SHEEP

15 Tax collectors and other notorious sinners often came to listen to Jesus teach. 2This made the Pharisees and teachers of religious law complain that he was associating with such sinful people—even eating with them!

3So Jesus told them this story: 4"If a man has a hundred sheep and one of them gets lost, what will he do? Won't he leave the ninety-nine others in the wilderness and go to search for the one that is lost until he finds it? 5And when he has found it, he will joyfully carry it home on his shoulders. 6When he arrives, he will call together his friends and neighbors, saying, 'Rejoice with me because I have found my lost sheep.' 7In the same way, there is more joy in heaven over one lost sinner who repents and returns to God than over ninety-nine others who are righteous and haven't strayed away!

PARABLE OF THE LOST COIN

8"Or suppose a woman has ten silver coins* and loses one. Won't she light a lamp and sweep the entire house and search carefully until she finds it? 9And when she finds it, she will call in her friends and neighbors and say, 'Rejoice with me because I have found my lost coin.' 10In the same way, there is joy in the presence of God's angels when even one sinner repents."

PARABLE OF THE LOST SON

11To illustrate the point further, Jesus told them this story: "A man had two sons. 12The younger son told his father, 'I want my share of your estate now before you die.' So his father agreed to divide his wealth between his sons.

15:8 Greek *ten drachmas.* A drachma was the equivalent of a full day's wage.

14:21 streets. These are probably the public squares where beggars gathered, hoping for handouts. **the poor, the crippled, the blind, and the lame!** These people were all social outcasts reduced to begging for survival. Those normally considered unworthy are indeed the ones who are included (1:52-53; 4:18-19; 6:20-22; 7:22).

14:23 urge anyone you find to come. The persuasion in view here is meant to convince these incredulous outcasts that they really are welcomed to the banquet. Middle East etiquette requires people of a low social rank to refuse invitations from those of a higher social status.

14:27 carry your own cross. This does not mean followers of Christ should seek out ways to suffer. It means that a follower of Jesus needs to be willing to go where he is sent and do what God asks of him.

14:28-30 count the cost. This is the first of three parables communicating the need for serious consideration of what it means to be Jesus' disciple. Just as it would be foolish to begin building a tower before contemplating the costs involved, so Jesus is discouraging people from following Him based upon wrong assumptions and ideas of what His kingdom involves.

14:31-32 sitting down with his counselors to discuss. The second parable reinforces the first. Only a foolish king would attempt to wage a war before considering if there is realistic hope for success. A would-be disciple had better consider what is involved in the course he or she is undertaking.

14:33 without giving up everything you own. Just as one should count the costs before beginning, so the disciple must be ready to give up all to follow Jesus.

15:4 the wilderness. This was a desolate area with many cliffs. A lone sheep in such an environment was in great danger from wild animals or from falling over the cliffs.

15:8 ten silver coins. This might represent her dowry. One of these coins was equal to about a day's wage for a laborer and represented a substantial loss for a person who lived a hand-to-mouth existence. **light a lamp.** Peasant homes were poorly illuminated because of a lack of windows. **sweep the entire house.** A coin could easily be obscured since floors were just dirt covered with straw.

15:12 I want my share. Under Jewish law, the younger of two sons would receive one-third of the estate upon his father's death. While a father might divide up his property before he died if he wished, this son's request would be considered unbelievably callous. In essence, he implies that the fact that his father still lives is getting in the way of his plans.

THE WASTEFUL SON

1. Where would you like to be after you graduate?

LUKE 15:11-32

2. Who does the younger son represent in this parable? The father? The older son?
3. Why did the father throw a party for the lost son when he returned? What does that teach us about God?
4. Why was the older son pouting? Why did his father go out to him and plead with him?
5. Who are you most like right now: The younger son living with pigs? The younger son returning home? The older son feeling cheated? How do you need God the Father's love and forgiveness?

13 "A few days later this younger son packed all his
belongings and moved to a distant land, and there
he wasted all his money in wild living. 14 About the
time his money ran out, a great famine swept over
the land, and he began to starve. 15 He persuaded a
local farmer to hire him, and the man sent him into
his fields to feed the pigs. 16 The young man became
so hungry that even the pods he was feeding the pigs
looked good to him. But no one gave him anything.
17 "When he finally came to his senses, he said to
himself, 'At home even the hired servants have food
enough to spare, and here I am dying of hunger! 18 I
will go home to my father and say, "Father, I have
sinned against both heaven and you, 19 and I am no
longer worthy of being called your son. Please take
me on as a hired servant."'
20 "So he returned home to his father. And while he
was still a long way off, his father saw him coming.
Filled with love and compassion, he ran to his son,
embraced him, and kissed him. 21 His son said to him,
'Father, I have sinned against both heaven and you,
and I am no longer worthy of being called your son.*'
22 "But his father said to the servants, 'Quick! Bring
the finest robe in the house and put it on him. Get a
ring for his finger and sandals for his feet. 23 And kill
the calf we have been fattening. We must celebrate
with a feast, 24 for this son of mine was dead and has
now returned to life. He was lost, but now he is found.'
So the party began.
25 "Meanwhile, the older son was in the fields work-
ing. When he returned home, he heard music and
dancing in the house, 26 and he asked one of the ser-
vants what was going on. 27 'Your brother is back,' he
was told, 'and your father has killed the fattened calf.
We are celebrating because of his safe return.'
28 "The older brother was angry and wouldn't go in.
His father came out and begged him, 29 but he replied,
'All these years I've slaved for you and never once re-
fused to do a single thing you told me to. And in all
that time you never gave me even one young goat for
a feast with my friends. 30 Yet when this son of yours
comes back after squandering your money on prosti-
tutes, you celebrate by killing the fattened calf!'
31 "His father said to him, 'Look, dear son, you have
always stayed by me, and everything I have is yours.
32 We had to celebrate this happy day. For your broth-
er was dead and has come back to life! He was lost,
but now he is found!'"

PARABLE OF THE SHREWD MANAGER

16 Jesus told this story to his disciples: "There
was a certain rich man who had a manager
handling his affairs. One day a report came that the
manager was wasting his employer's money. 2 So the
employer called him in and said, 'What's this I hear
about you? Get your report in order, because you are
going to be fired.'
3 "The manager thought to himself, 'Now what?
My boss has fired me. I don't have the strength to dig
ditches, and I'm too proud to beg. 4 Ah, I know how to
ensure that I'll have plenty of friends who will give
me a home when I am fired.'
5 "So he invited each person who owed money to
his employer to come and discuss the situation. He
asked the first one, 'How much do you owe him?' 6 The
man replied, 'I owe him 800 gallons of olive oil.' So the
manager told him, 'Take the bill and quickly change it
to 400 gallons.*'
7 "'And how much do you owe my employer?'
he asked the next man. 'I owe him 1,000 bushels of
wheat,' was the reply. 'Here,' the manager said, 'take
the bill and change it to 800 bushels.*'

15:21 Some manuscripts add *Please take me on as a hired servant.* **16:6** Greek *100 baths . . . 50 [baths].* **16:7** Greek *100 korous . . . 80 [korous].*

15:15 pigs. Ceremonially unclean animals (Lev. 11:7) that Jews would not eat, raise, or touch.

15:16 the pods. While eating the food of pigs sounds terrible even to modern readers, for the Pharisees it would have been utterly horrifying.

15:20 his father saw him. The implication is the father had been waiting and hoping to see his son return one day. **he ran.** It was degrading for an elderly man to run to anyone, especially to someone who had so disgraced him. This presents staggering insight into the response of the Almighty Holy God to a repentant sinner.

15:22 the finest robe. A sign that people should honor him as they honor the father. **a ring.** The signet ring gives the son the authority to represent the father. **sandals. . .** To wear shoes indicated a man was free to go where he pleased.

15:28 wouldn't go in. This son's refusal to enter the house would have been seen as a sign of grave disrespect since the eldest son was expected to play the part of a gracious host at a family feast. As he did with the younger son, the father went out to plead with the older son. This too was an overwhelming display of grace.

15:29 I've slaved for you. Ironically, this son views his ongoing relationship with his father in the way the younger son hoped he might be privileged to have.

15:30 this son of yours. Instead of "my brother."

15:31-32 everything I have is yours. This would assure the older son that he is in no danger of losing his inheritance because of the presence of his younger brother. He, too, should celebrate his brother's homecoming. We are not told what the older son does. Jesus purposely leaves the story open-ended.

16:2. Get your report in order. This is better understood as "turn in your books." Since it would be assumed that a dishonest manager had probably doctored the books, they would not be looked at in order to find evidence to fire him; he is simply to "clean out his desk."

16:5-7 800 gallons . . .change it to 400 gallons. This reduction of debts was done quickly to avoid discovery by the master (v. 6). Since the tenants assumed the manager was still in the employ of the landowner, the renters would be grateful to the manager for his concern for them. The tenants would quickly spread the news throughout the village that the master had been gracious, making it socially impossible for the master to deny that he had authorized such reductions.

16:6-7 The assumption is that the master has let out his land to tenants, who have agreed to pay him a fixed return in grain and oil. The amounts owed indicate that this master was quite wealthy. The reduction of 400 gallons of olive oil and 200 bushels of wheat both amount to the same in cash value, about 500 denarii.

8 "The rich man had to admire the dishonest ras-
cal for being so shrewd. And it is true that the chil-
dren of this world are more shrewd in dealing with
the world around them than are the children of the
light. 9 Here's the lesson: Use your worldly resources
to benefit others and make friends. Then, when your
possessions are gone, they will welcome you to an
eternal home.*

10 "If you are faithful in little things, you will be
faithful in large ones. But if you are dishonest in little
things, you won't be honest with greater responsibil-
ities. 11 And if you are untrustworthy about worldly
wealth, who will trust you with the true riches of
heaven? 12 And if you are not faithful with other peo-
ple's things, why should you be trusted with things of
your own?

13 "No one can serve two masters. For you will hate
one and love the other; you will be devoted to one
and despise the other. You cannot serve God and be
enslaved to money."

14 The Pharisees, who dearly loved their money,
heard all this and scoffed at him. 15 Then he said to
them, "You like to appear righteous in public, but God
knows your hearts. What this world honors is detest-
able in the sight of God.

16 "Until John the Baptist, the law of Moses and the
messages of the prophets were your guides. But now
the Good News of the Kingdom of God is preached,
and everyone is eager to get in.* 17 But that doesn't
mean that the law has lost its force. It is easier for
heaven and earth to disappear than for the smallest
point of God's law to be overturned.

18 "For example, a man who divorces his wife and
marries someone else commits adultery. And anyone
who marries a woman divorced from her husband
commits adultery."

PARABLE OF THE RICH MAN AND LAZARUS

19 Jesus said, "There was a certain rich man who was
splendidly clothed in purple and fine linen and who
lived each day in luxury. 20 At his gate lay a poor man
named Lazarus who was covered with sores. 21 As
Lazarus lay there longing for scraps from the rich
man's table, the dogs would come and lick his open
sores.

22 "Finally, the poor man died and was carried by
the angels to sit beside Abraham at the heavenly ban-
quet.* The rich man also died and was buried, 23 and
he went to the place of the dead.* There, in torment,
he saw Abraham in the far distance with Lazarus at
his side.

24 "The rich man shouted, 'Father Abraham, have
some pity! Send Lazarus over here to dip the tip of his
finger in water and cool my tongue. I am in anguish
in these flames.'

25 "But Abraham said to him, 'Son, remember that
during your lifetime you had everything you wanted,
and Lazarus had nothing. So now he is here being com-
forted, and you are in anguish. 26 And besides, there is a
great chasm separating us. No one can cross over to you
from here, and no one can cross over to us from there.'

27 "Then the rich man said, 'Please, Father Abraham,
at least send him to my father's home. 28 For I have five
brothers, and I want him to warn them so they don't
end up in this place of torment.'

29 "But Abraham said, 'Moses and the prophets
have warned them. Your brothers can read what they
wrote.'

30 "The rich man replied, 'No, Father Abraham! But
if someone is sent to them from the dead, then they
will repent of their sins and turn to God.'

31 "But Abraham said, 'If they won't listen to Moses
and the prophets, they won't be persuaded even if
someone rises from the dead.'"

TEACHINGS ABOUT FORGIVENESS AND FAITH

17 One day Jesus said to his disciples, "There will
always be temptations to sin, but what sorrow
awaits the person who does the tempting! 2 It would
be better to be thrown into the sea with a millstone
hung around your neck than to cause one of these lit-
tle ones to fall into sin. 3 So watch yourselves!

"If another believer* sins, rebuke that person; then
if there is repentance, forgive. 4 Even if that person

HEAVEN AND HELL

1. When can you remember being unbearably thirsty? How did you finally quench it?

LUKE 16:19-31

2. What was Lazarus' life like? What was the rich man's life like?
3. What happened when Lazarus died? What happened when the rich man died? (Note the wording in verse 22.)
4. How are the five brothers going to learn the truth about heaven and hell (v. 28)? How will people today learn that truth?
5. Will you go to heaven when you die? How can you be sure?

16:9 Or *you will be welcomed into eternal homes.* **16:16** Or *everyone is urged to enter in.* **16:22** Greek *to Abraham's bosom.* **16:23** Greek *to Hades.* **17:3** Greek *If your brother.*

16:8 dishonest. The man's moral sense is not being commended; his taking appropriate action to protect himself is. The disciple is likewise called to take action in the face of the coming judgment. **shrewd.** Hebrew and Aramaic translations of this word translate it as "wisdom." If an unjust man shows such wisdom in making provision for his future, how much more ought the children of light show wisdom in preparing for their future in the face of the certain judgment of God?

16:20 Lazarus. His name means "he whom God helps," indicating the poor man's piety before God.

16:26 a great chasm separating us. The impassable gap between them indicated the finality of God's judgment on the matter. It is said earlier that the rich man could see Lazarus and Abraham (v. 23). However, since Lazarus never says anything on his own behalf, it is uncertain how much he is aware of the plight of the rich man.

16:27-28 send him . . . to warn them. This introduces the second lesson of the passage. In light of his fate, the man urges Abraham to send Lazarus as a warning to his brothers who are following in his path. The rich man cared for his family; he just was unable to see poor Lazarus as worthy of the same sort of concern.

16:29 Moses and the prophets. Those who fail to hear Scripture will not be persuaded by resurrection.

17:2 millstone. This would be a large, round grinding stone with a hole in the middle. Such a horrible death is preferable to the judgment that will come upon one who leads another into sin. **cause . . . to fall into sin.** Literally "to scandalize" (v. 1) in the sense of corrupting the life of another by offering an opportunity to sin or making sin appear legitimate.

wrongs you seven times a day and each time turns again and asks forgiveness, you must forgive."

[5] The apostles said to the Lord, "Show us how to increase our faith."

[6] The Lord answered, "If you had faith even as small as a mustard seed, you could say to this mulberry tree, 'May you be uprooted and be planted in the sea,' and it would obey you!

[7] "When a servant comes in from plowing or taking care of sheep, does his master say, 'Come in and eat with me'? [8] No, he says, 'Prepare my meal, put on your apron, and serve me while I eat. Then you can eat later.' [9] And does the master thank the servant for doing what he was told to do? Of course not. [10] In the same way, when you obey me you should say, 'We are unworthy servants who have simply done our duty.'"

TEN HEALED OF LEPROSY

[11] As Jesus continued on toward Jerusalem, he reached the border between Galilee and Samaria. [12] As he entered a village there, ten men with leprosy stood at a distance, [13] crying out, "Jesus, Master, have mercy on us!"

[14] He looked at them and said, "Go show yourselves to the priests."* And as they went, they were cleansed of their leprosy.

[15] One of them, when he saw that he was healed, came back to Jesus, shouting, "Praise God!" [16] He fell to the ground at Jesus' feet, thanking him for what he had done. This man was a Samaritan.

[17] Jesus asked, "Didn't I heal ten men? Where are the other nine? [18] Has no one returned to give glory to God except this foreigner?" [19] And Jesus said to the man, "Stand up and go. Your faith has healed you.*"

THE COMING OF THE KINGDOM

[20] One day the Pharisees asked Jesus, "When will the Kingdom of God come?"

Jesus replied, "The Kingdom of God can't be detected by visible signs.* [21] You won't be able to say, 'Here it is!' or 'It's over there!' For the Kingdom of God is already among you.*"

[22] Then he said to his disciples, "The time is coming when you will long to see the day when the Son of Man returns,* but you won't see it. [23] People will tell you, 'Look, there is the Son of Man,' or 'Here he is,' but don't go out and follow them. [24] For as the lightning flashes and lights up the sky from one end to the other, so it will be on the day* when the Son of Man comes. [25] But first the Son of Man must suffer terribly* and be rejected by this generation.

[26] "When the Son of Man returns, it will be like it was in Noah's day. [27] In those days, the people enjoyed banquets and parties and weddings right up to the time Noah entered his boat and the flood came and destroyed them all.

[28] "And the world will be as it was in the days of Lot. People went about their daily business—eating and drinking, buying and selling, farming and building—[29] until the morning Lot left Sodom. Then fire and burning sulfur rained down from heaven and destroyed them all. [30] Yes, it will be 'business as usual' right up to the day when the Son of Man is revealed. [31] On that day a person out on the deck of a roof must

AN ATTITUDE OF GRATITUDE

1. How are you at writing thank-you notes: Always write them? Sometimes write them? What's a thank-you note?

LUKE 17:11-19

2. How did the faith of the lepers heal them (v. 19)? How did they show faith?
3. The Jewish people considered Samaritans to be outcasts. Why does verse 16 mention that the one leper who was grateful was a Samaritan?
4. Why do you think the other nine healed lepers didn't return to thank Jesus?
5. When it comes to showing gratitude to God, are you more like the one who returned or the nine who didn't?

17:14 See Lev 14:2-32. **17:19** Or *Your faith has saved you.* **17:20** Or *by your speculations.* **17:21** Or *is within you,* or *is in your grasp.* **17:22** Or *long for even one day with the Son of Man.* "Son of Man" is a title Jesus used for himself. **17:24** Some manuscripts do not include *on the day.* **17:25** Or *suffer many things.*

17:6 mustard seed. This was the tiniest of all seeds. **Be uprooted.** This is not an invitation for believers to exercise capricious power in prayer but to illustrate the point that astounding things can result for the person who exercises his or her faith through prayer (Matt. 21:21-22).

17:8-9 The point is not that the master is demanding or ungrateful but simply that the servant's job involves these tasks. The performance of them is a normal, expected part of the role.

17:10 simply done our duty. Obedience to Jesus' commands about purity, radical forgiveness, and faith do not merit special reward from God. They are simply qualities expected of those who follow Him.

17:12 lepers. Most typically, leprosy. Although "leprosy" was used to cover a wide range of skin diseases besides the true leprosy of Hanson's Disease, no diagnosis was dreaded more than leprosy since it brought not only a slow death and physical disfigurement but also social banishment. **stood at a distance.** Lepers were forbidden to approach uninfected people (Lev. 13:45-46).

17:14 show yourselves. Old Testament law required people with skin diseases feared to be leprous to be examined by a priest who would determine if the infection was clearing up or progressing (Lev. 14:1-7). Only upon the priest's declaration of healing could the leper reenter society.

17:15-16 Samaritan. The one man who came back to give thanks to Jesus was the one Jews would least expect to do so—a Samaritan.

17:17-19 Where are the other nine? Only the foreigner caught the significance of his healing and glorified God because of it. The other nine people typify the response of Israel, which saw sign after sign of Jesus' authority but failed to respond to Him with gratitude.

17:21 the kingdom of God is already among you. This phrase has many different translations, all with some relevant meaning here. The Holman Christian Standard translation has "among you," emphasizing that the kingdom of God begins with the community of faith acting in obedience to Christ. The NIV translates the word "within you," which reminds us that it starts with letting God have the throne of our hearts. The ESV translates it "in the midst of you," which emphasizes its present reality. All essentially say that the kingdom of God is not just some future hope. It starts now with our response of obedience.

17:22 the day of when the Son of Man returns. The implication is that before He returns there will be a substantial delay during which his followers will have to wait patiently for Him—even when there is no external evidence of His coming (12:35-48).

17:26-30 enjoyed banquets and parties and weddings. The time of the second coming of Christ is compared to that of Noah (Gen. 6:9-9:17) and Lot (Gen. 18:16-19:29). The activities mentioned here (eating, drinking, marrying, buying, selling, planting) are not evil; instead, the emphasis of the comparison is the unexpected nature of the sudden judgment that came upon the people in the course of their daily lives—as will be the case when Christ returns (1 Thess. 5:1-3).

not go down into the house to pack. A person out in
the field must not return home. [32] Remember what
happened to Lot's wife! [33] If you cling to your life, you
will lose it, and if you let your life go, you will save
it. [34] That night two people will be asleep in one bed;
one will be taken, the other left. [35] Two women will be
grinding flour together at the mill; one will be taken,
the other left.*"

[37] "Where will this happen, Lord?"* the disciples
asked.

Jesus replied, "Just as the gathering of vultures
shows there is a carcass nearby, so these signs indi-
cate that the end is near."*

PARABLE OF THE PERSISTENT WIDOW

18 One day Jesus told his disciples a story to show
that they should always pray and never give up.
[2] "There was a judge in a certain city," he said, "who nei-
ther feared God nor cared about people. [3] A widow of
that city came to him repeatedly, saying, 'Give me justice
in this dispute with my enemy.' [4] The judge ignored her
for a while, but finally he said to himself, 'I don't fear
God or care about people, [5] but this woman is driving
me crazy. I'm going to see that she gets justice, because
she is wearing me out with her constant requests!'"

[6] Then the Lord said, "Learn a lesson from this unjust
judge. [7] Even he rendered a just decision in the end. So
don't you think God will surely give justice to his cho-
sen people who cry out to him day and night? Will he
keep putting them off? [8] I tell you, he will grant justice
to them quickly! But when the Son of Man* returns,
how many will he find on the earth who have faith?"

PARABLE OF THE PHARISEE AND TAX COLLECTOR

[9] Then Jesus told this story to some who had great
confidence in their own righteousness and scorned
everyone else: [10] "Two men went to the Temple to pray.
One was a Pharisee, and the other was a despised tax
collector. [11] The Pharisee stood by himself and prayed
this prayer*: 'I thank you, God, that I am not like other
people—cheaters, sinners, adulterers. I'm certainly
not like that tax collector! [12] I fast twice a week, and I
give you a tenth of my income.'

[13] "But the tax collector stood at a distance and
dared not even lift his eyes to heaven as he prayed.

GOING DOWN TO GO UP

1. How are you at public speaking? At singing a solo? At praying aloud in a group?

LUKE 18:9-14

2. Compare the physical postures of the Pharisee and tax collector as they prayed. What does each man's posture and prayer style show about his true character?
3. Why did the tax collector in this story go home "justified" (v. 14) rather than the Pharisee?
4. What does it mean to exalt yourself? To humble yourself?
5. Is your character more like the tax collector's or the Pharisee's? In what areas of your life do you need to pray for more humility?

Instead, he beat his chest in sorrow, saying, 'O God, be
merciful to me, for I am a sinner.' [14] I tell you, this sin-
ner, not the Pharisee, returned home justified before
God. For those who exalt themselves will be humbled,
and those who humble themselves will be exalted."

JESUS BLESSES THE CHILDREN

[15] One day some parents brought their little children
to Jesus so he could touch and bless them. But when
the disciples saw this, they scolded the parents for
bothering him.

[16] Then Jesus called for the children and said to
the disciples, "Let the children come to me. Don't stop
them! For the Kingdom of God belongs to those who
are like these children. [17] I tell you the truth, anyone
who doesn't receive the Kingdom of God like a child
will never enter it."

THE RICH MAN

[18] Once a religious leader asked Jesus this question:
"Good Teacher, what should I do to inherit eternal
life?"

17:35 Some manuscripts add verse 36, *Two men will be working in the field; one will be taken, the other left.* Compare Matt 24:40.
17:37a Greek *"Where, Lord?"* **17:37b** Greek *"Wherever the carcass is, the vultures gather."* **18:8** "Son of Man" is a title Jesus used for himself.
18:11 Some manuscripts read *stood and prayed this prayer to himself.*

17:37 the gathering of vultures shows there is a carcass nearby. Jesus quotes a common proverb used to illustrate the connection between any two closely related events. Here it means that God's judgment will occur wherever necessary. Such an enigmatic reply forces the disciples to consider their own preparedness for the sudden coming of the Lord in judgment.

18:1-8 The last line of this parable (v. 8) relates what appears to be a general admonition about prayer (11:5–8), specifically to the theme of being prepared for the return of Christ. The disciples are called to pray faithfully and steadfastly for the kingdom of God, never giving up hope for God's justice to be accomplished (v. 1).

18:8 he will grant justice to them quickly! If an unjust judge can be persuaded to act by a persistent widow, how much more will God respond to the prayers of His people.

18:9 great confidence in their own righteousness. This typifies the attitude of a person who assumes that he or she has met God's standards for life. This attitude is marked by a concentration on external performance rather than on humble dependence on God's grace (Gal. 3:10-14; Phil. 3:3-9). **scorned everyone else.** Literally, "to treat with contempt." This was a major flaw of the Pharisees, who would not even associate with those they considered to be "sinners."

18:10 Pharisee . . .tax collector. The Pharisee and tax collector represent opposites in Jewish society. Tax collectors were looked down upon not only because they frequently cheated people but because they raised money for the hated Roman government. Pharisees, on the other hand, were given a place of prestige in Jewish society.

18:12 a tenth of my income. While Jews were only required to fast on the Day of Atonement, Pharisees fasted every Monday and Thursday in an attempt to gain merit with God. Although all Jews were expected to tithe of one's produce, Pharisees carefully tithed even things that were not required (11:42). This man's external performance of religious obligations was exemplary.

18:13 stood at a distance. The tax collector may not even have dared to enter the court of the Jews, remaining in the outermost court of the temple where Gentiles met. **beat his chest in sorrow.** This action, combined with his fear of even following the common custom of looking upwards in prayer, showed his shame and contrition.

18:14 returned home justified before God. The Pharisee left in his self-delusion, while the tax collector was forgiven by God.

18:18 religious leader. Perhaps this person was a leader of a synagogue (like Jairus—8:41), or even a member of the Sanhedrin, the official Jewish ruling council. **what should I do.** The emphasis on gaining the kingdom by virtue of one's religious activities stands in sharp contrast to Jesus' teaching about receiving the kingdom by faith (vv. 16-17).

19 "Why do you call me good?" Jesus asked him.
"Only God is truly good. 20 But to answer your ques-
tion, you know the commandments: 'You must not
commit adultery. You must not murder. You must not
steal. You must not testify falsely. Honor your father
and mother.'*"
21 The man replied, "I've obeyed all these command-
ments since I was young."
22 When Jesus heard his answer, he said, "There is
still one thing you haven't done. Sell all your posses-
sions and give the money to the poor, and you will
have treasure in heaven. Then come, follow me."
23 But when the man heard this he became very
sad, for he was very rich.
24 When Jesus saw this,* he said, "How hard it is for
the rich to enter the Kingdom of God! 25 In fact, it is
easier for a camel to go through the eye of a needle
than for a rich person to enter the Kingdom of God!"
26 Those who heard this said, "Then who in the
world can be saved?"
27 He replied, "What is impossible for people is pos-
sible with God."
28 Peter said, "We've left our homes to follow you."
29 "Yes," Jesus replied, "and I assure you that every-
one who has given up house or wife or brothers or
parents or children, for the sake of the Kingdom of
God, 30 will be repaid many times over in this life, and
will have eternal life in the world to come."

JESUS AGAIN PREDICTS HIS DEATH

31 Taking the twelve disciples aside, Jesus said, "Listen,
we're going up to Jerusalem, where all the predic-
tions of the prophets concerning the Son of Man will
come true. 32 He will be handed over to the Romans,*
and he will be mocked, treated shamefully, and spit
upon. 33 They will flog him with a whip and kill him,
but on the third day he will rise again."
34 But they didn't understand any of this. The signif-
icance of his words was hidden from them, and they
failed to grasp what he was talking about.

JESUS HEALS A BLIND BEGGAR

35 As Jesus approached Jericho, a blind beggar was
sitting beside the road. 36 When he heard the noise of
a crowd going past, he asked what was happening.
37 They told him that Jesus the Nazarene* was going
by. 38 So he began shouting, "Jesus, Son of David, have
mercy on me!"
39 "Be quiet!" the people in front yelled at him.
But he only shouted louder, "Son of David, have
mercy on me!"
40 When Jesus heard him, he stopped and ordered
that the man be brought to him. As the man came
near, Jesus asked him, 41 "What do you want me to do
for you?"
"Lord," he said, "I want to see!"
42 And Jesus said, "All right, receive your sight! Your
faith has healed you." 43 Instantly the man could see,
and he followed Jesus, praising God. And all who saw
it praised God, too.

JESUS AND ZACCHAEUS

19 Jesus entered Jericho and made his way through
the town. 2 There was a man there named Zac-
chaeus. He was the chief tax collector in the region,
and he had become very rich. 3 He tried to get a look at
Jesus, but he was too short to see over the crowd. 4 So
he ran ahead and climbed a sycamore-fig tree beside
the road, for Jesus was going to pass that way.
5 When Jesus came by, he looked up at Zacchaeus
and called him by name. "Zacchaeus!" he said. "Quick,
come down! I must be a guest in your home today."
6 Zacchaeus quickly climbed down and took Jesus
to his house in great excitement and joy. 7 But the peo-
ple were displeased. "He has gone to be the guest of a
notorious sinner," they grumbled.

OUT ON A LIMB

1. Did you like to climb trees when you were little? Do you still like to climb?

LUKE 19:1-10

2. Why were people upset that Jesus was going to stay with Zacchaeus?
3. Tax collectors were notorious for cheating people. Why did Zacchaeus offer to pay back the people he'd cheated?
4. In verse 9 Jesus says, "Salvation has come to this home today." How did salvation come to Zacchaeus?
5. Zacchaeus realized that he needed to make restitution for cheating people. What wrongs do you need to make right?

18:20 Exod 20:12-16; Deut 5:16-20. **18:24** Some manuscripts read *When Jesus saw how sad the man was.* **18:32** Greek *the Gentiles.* **18:37** Or *Jesus of Nazareth.*

18:20 the commandments. Jesus cited five of the Ten Commandments that deal with a person's relationship toward others (Ex. 20:12-16). Significantly, He omits both the first ("You shall have no other gods besides me") and the tenth ("You shall not covet"). Those are the commandments that later prove to be the stumbling blocks for this ruler.

18:22 There is still one thing you haven't done. Jesus did not refute the man's claim to be obedient to the demands of the commandments, but He pointed out that this has not touched his inner attitude of love for God or his neighbor. **sell all your possessions.** Jesus used this command to show the ruler that wealth is his true god and his self-centered use of his money his true love. Jesus was not saying with this teaching that *everyone* who seeks eternal life must sell all their possessions. He was saying to give full allegiance to God. **follow me.** The ultimate demand of the kingdom is for absolute allegiance to Jesus over one's self and possessions (16:13). This the ruler does not accept.

18:24 How hard it is. Jesus contradicted the common assumption that wealth is the verification that one has led a godly life (Job 1:10; Ps. 128:1-2). Instead, wealth is actually a barrier that can prevent people from seeing their need for God.

18:31 up to Jerusalem. Jews used the phrase "going up to Jerusalem" as an idiomatic expression of planning to offer a sacrifice of worship at the temple.

18:35 Jericho. Jericho is 18 miles east of Jerusalem and the place where travelers from Galilee recrossed the Jordan back into Israel.

18:42 Your faith. The blind man demonstrated his faith: (1) by the title he used for Jesus (he grasped who Jesus was); (2) by his persistent pleas for Jesus' help (he would not let this opportunity go by); and (3) by his request for healing (he believed Jesus had the power to heal him).

19:2 rich. The wealth was undoubtedly the result of "legal" but callous exploitation of his own people through inflated tax rates.

19:4 a sycamore fig tree. This tree's short trunk and spreading branches make it easy to climb.

19:5-7 I must be a guest in your home. Jesus invited Himself to Zacchaeus' house, shocking everyone! Not only would the self-righteous Pharisees disapprove, but Zacchaeus' ill-gotten wealth made this association difficult to accept even by the average person.

8 Meanwhile, Zacchaeus stood before the Lord and
said, "I will give half my wealth to the poor, Lord, and
if I have cheated people on their taxes, I will give
them back four times as much!"
9 Jesus responded, "Salvation has come to this home
today, for this man has shown himself to be a true son
of Abraham. 10 For the Son of Man* came to seek and
save those who are lost."

PARABLE OF THE TEN SERVANTS

11 The crowd was listening to everything Jesus said.
And because he was nearing Jerusalem, he told them
a story to correct the impression that the Kingdom of
God would begin right away. 12 He said, "A nobleman
was called away to a distant empire to be crowned
king and then return. 13 Before he left, he called to-
gether ten of his servants and divided among them ten
pounds of silver,* saying, 'Invest this for me while I am
gone.' 14 But his people hated him and sent a delegation
after him to say, 'We do not want him to be our king.'
15 "After he was crowned king, he returned and
called in the servants to whom he had given the mon-
ey. He wanted to find out what their profits were.
16 The first servant reported, 'Master, I invested your
money and made ten times the original amount!'
17 "'Well done!' the king exclaimed. 'You are a good
servant. You have been faithful with the little I en-
trusted to you, so you will be governor of ten cities as
your reward.'
18 "The next servant reported, 'Master, I invested
your money and made five times the original amount.'
19 "'Well done!' the king said. 'You will be governor
over five cities.'
20 "But the third servant brought back only the
original amount of money and said, 'Master, I hid
your money and kept it safe. 21 I was afraid because
you are a hard man to deal with, taking what isn't
yours and harvesting crops you didn't plant.'
22 "'You wicked servant!' the king roared. 'Your own
words condemn you. If you knew that I'm a hard man
who takes what isn't mine and harvests crops I didn't
plant, 23 why didn't you deposit my money in the
bank? At least I could have gotten some interest on it.'
24 "Then, turning to the others standing nearby, the
king ordered, 'Take the money from this servant, and
give it to the one who has ten pounds.'
25 "'But, master,' they said, 'he already has ten
pounds!'
26 "'Yes,' the king replied, 'and to those who use
well what they are given, even more will be given.
But from those who do nothing, even what little they
have will be taken away. 27 And as for these enemies
of mine who didn't want me to be their king—bring
them in and execute them right here in front of me.'"

JESUS' TRIUMPHANT ENTRY

28 After telling this story, Jesus went on toward Jeru-
salem, walking ahead of his disciples. 29 As he came
to the towns of Bethphage and Bethany on the Mount
of Olives, he sent two disciples ahead. 30 "Go into that
village over there," he told them. "As you enter it, you
will see a young donkey tied there that no one has
ever ridden. Untie it and bring it here. 31 If anyone
asks, 'Why are you untying that colt?' just say, 'The
Lord needs it.'"
32 So they went and found the colt, just as Jesus
had said. 33 And sure enough, as they were untying
it, the owners asked them, "Why are you untying
that colt?"
34 And the disciples simply replied, "The Lord needs
it." 35 So they brought the colt to Jesus and threw their
garments over it for him to ride on.
36 As he rode along, the crowds spread out their gar-
ments on the road ahead of him. 37 When he reached
the place where the road started down the Mount of
Olives, all of his followers began to shout and sing as
they walked along, praising God for all the wonderful
miracles they had seen.

38 "Blessings on the King who comes in the name of
the LORD!
Peace in heaven, and glory in highest heaven!"*

39 But some of the Pharisees among the crowd said,
"Teacher, rebuke your followers for saying things like
that!"
40 He replied, "If they kept quiet, the stones along
the road would burst into cheers!"

WEEPING FOR OTHERS

1. Have you ever been in a parade? What was it like? What's the last parade you saw?

LUKE 19:28-44

2. Why did Jesus enter Jerusalem on a donkey? Why not a white horse? Why not walking?
3. What caused Jesus to weep over Jerusalem (v. 41)? How can we show more concern for the souls of those around us?
4. What does Jesus mean that Jerusalem "did not recognize it when God visited you" (v. 44)?
5. Have you recognized Jesus' "visitation" in your own life? Have you brought Him to visit others?

19:10 "Son of Man" is a title Jesus used for himself. **19:13** Greek *ten minas;* one mina was worth about three months' wages. **19:38** Pss 118:26; 148:1.

19:8 half of my wealth to the poor. Zacchaeus immediately did precisely what the ruler refused to do (18:22). **I will give back four times as much!** Giving half of his wealth to the poor did not mean he would keep the other half for himself. Instead, the remaining wealth would be used to recompense those he had defrauded. Zacchaeus was so eager to be restored to God and his community that he pledged to go far beyond what the law required (Lev. 6:1-5).

19:13 servants. Wealthy people who had to travel on business would entrust their resources to servants who would act as managers of the estate. **ten pounds of silver.** This was the equivalent of three months' wages for a laborer.

19:20-21 hid. In contrast to the other two, this servant had simply hidden the money away. In the parable found in Matthew 25, the man buries the money in the ground, an action that would have been considered a safe way to protect what he had been given.

19:21 a hard man. Literally, this is "an exacting man." This is a person who demanded that those who work for him give an unusually good return on investment.

19:29 Bethphage. A village near Jerusalem, probably across a ravine from Bethany. **Bethany.** A small village about two miles east of Jerusalem. **Mount of Olives.** According to Zechariah 14:3-5, it is from the Mt. of Olives that God will commence the final judgment of Israel's enemies. It is not by accident that Jesus chose this place to prepare His entry into Jerusalem.

JESUS WEEPS OVER JERUSALEM

[41] But as he came closer to Jerusalem and saw the city
ahead, he began to weep. [42] "How I wish today that
you of all people would understand the way to peace.
But now it is too late, and peace is hidden from your
eyes. [43] Before long your enemies will build ramparts
against your walls and encircle you and close in on
you from every side. [44] They will crush you into the
ground, and your children with you. Your enemies
will not leave a single stone in place, because you did
not recognize it when God visited you.*"

JESUS CLEARS THE TEMPLE

[45] Then Jesus entered the Temple and began to drive
out the people selling animals for sacrifices. [46] He said
to them, "The Scriptures declare, 'My Temple will be
a house of prayer,' but you have turned it into a den
of thieves."*

[47] After that, he taught daily in the Temple, but the
leading priests, the teachers of religious law, and the
other leaders of the people began planning how to
kill him. [48] But they could think of nothing, because all
the people hung on every word he said.

THE AUTHORITY OF JESUS CHALLENGED

20 One day as Jesus was teaching the people and
preaching the Good News in the Temple, the
leading priests, the teachers of religious law, and the
elders came up to him. [2] They demanded, "By what
authority are you doing all these things? Who gave
you the right?"

[3] "Let me ask you a question first," he replied. [4] "Did
John's authority to baptize come from heaven, or was
it merely human?"

[5] They talked it over among themselves. "If we say
it was from heaven, he will ask why we didn't believe
John. [6] But if we say it was merely human, the people
will stone us because they are convinced John was a
prophet." [7] So they finally replied that they didn't know.

[8] And Jesus responded, "Then I won't tell you by
what authority I do these things."

PARABLE OF THE EVIL FARMERS

[9] Now Jesus turned to the people again and told them
this story: "A man planted a vineyard, leased it to
tenant farmers, and moved to another country to live
for several years. [10] At the time of the grape harvest, he
sent one of his servants to collect his share of the crop.
But the farmers attacked the servant, beat him up, and
sent him back empty-handed. [11] So the owner sent an-
other servant, but they also insulted him, beat him up,
and sent him away empty-handed. [12] A third man was
sent, and they wounded him and chased him away.

[13] "'What will I do?' the owner asked himself. 'I
know! I'll send my cherished son. Surely they will re-
spect him.'

[14] "But when the tenant farmers saw his son, they
said to each other, 'Here comes the heir to this estate.
Let's kill him and get the estate for ourselves!' [15] So they
dragged him out of the vineyard and murdered him.

"What do you suppose the owner of the vineyard
will do to them?" Jesus asked. [16] "I'll tell you—he will
come and kill those farmers and lease the vineyard
to others."

"How terrible that such a thing should ever hap-
pen," his listeners protested.

[17] Jesus looked at them and said, "Then what does
this Scripture mean?

'The stone that the builders rejected
has now become the cornerstone.'*

[18] Everyone who stumbles over that stone will be bro-
ken to pieces, and it will crush anyone it falls on."

[19] The teachers of religious law and the leading
priests wanted to arrest Jesus immediately because
they realized he was telling the story against them—
they were the wicked farmers. But they were afraid
of the people's reaction.

TAXES FOR CAESAR

[20] Watching for their opportunity, the leaders sent
spies pretending to be honest men. They tried to get

19:44 Greek *did not recognize the time of your visitation,* a reference to the Messiah's coming. **19:46** Isa 56:7; Jer 7:11. **20:17** Ps 118:22.

19:43-44 your enemies . . .will not leave a single stone. In A.D. 70 the Romans literally tore Jerusalem apart stone by stone so that absolutely nothing—including the temple—was left standing. The final act of humiliation for the conquered Jews was to watch as the Romans ran a plow through what had been the center of the city as a sign that the Jews were now "plowed under."

19:45 the people selling. Worshippers had to offer an unblemished animal, but inspectors approved only those animals bought from certified vendors who worked for members of the high priest's family. Thus, there was great profiteering as the priests and others took advantage of the religious obligations of the Jews by selling the animals at a huge markup.

19:46 a house of prayer. The outermost area of the temple was intended to be a place where pious Gentiles could pray (Isa. 56:7).

20:1 Luke records several conflicts (vv. 1-47) in which various groups of religious leaders confront Jesus one by one. Thus, the opposition begun in Galilee at the start of Jesus' ministry (5:17-6:11) is continued and completed in Jerusalem. **the leading priests.** These were the key officers of the temple, just below the high priest in rank. **the teachers of religious law.** Originally, it was the scribes' job to make copies of the Old Testament. Because of their familiarity with Scripture, this evolved into their function as teachers of the law. **the elders.** These men served as administrators, judges, military leaders. This group was probably an official committee of the Sanhedrin chosen to confront Jesus for driving the merchants out of the temple (19:45-46).

20:2 They demanded. They asked: Where does He get His authority? While not as subtle as some of their later questions (vv. 20-22,27-33), it is still a trap. If Jesus says He acted on His own authority, they could detain Him as a hopeless megalomaniac. If He said that His authority came from God, they could accuse Him of blasphemy (for which the penalty was death).

20:3-6 Let me ask. Answering a question with a question was a common tactic in rabbinic debate.

20:7-8 they finally replied that they didn't know. To accept that John's authority came from God was to admit that John was a true prophet. They would also have to accept that Jesus came from God, as John said. They would also have to explain why they had not supported John's ministry. On the other hand, to say that John just pretended to be a prophet was to risk an uprising of the crowd.

20:9 moved to another country. Absentee landlords would commonly get tenant-farmers to work their large estates, requiring the tenant farmers to give them a portion of their harvest in payment for use of the land.

20:10 servant. In terms of this parable, the slaves represent the Old Testament prophets.

20:14 estate. The tenants apparently mistook the arrival of the son as a sign that the owner had died. By law, a piece of ownerless property (which it would be if they killed the son) could be kept by those who first seized it.

20:16 Having refused to pay rent three times over, and having killed the owner's son, the farmers suffered severe and immediate action. The owner could muster all the legal power available against these evil tenants. Their judgment would mean their death. The land they had so jealously guarded would be given over to others.

20:17 cornerstone. Stone laid at the corner to bind two walls together and to strengthen them. Used symbolically as a symbol of strength and prominence. The figure is often applied to rulers or leaders (Pss. 118:22; 144:12; Isa. 19:13 NIV, REB, NASB; Zech. 10:4).Here the reference is to Psalm 118 where the Messiah is identified as a cornerstone (Ps. 118:22). Jesus is both the cornerstone and a free-standing stone on which those who reject Him are destroyed.

Jesus to say something that could be reported to the
Roman governor so he would arrest Jesus. 21 "Teach-
er," they said, "we know that you speak and teach
what is right and are not influenced by what others
think. You teach the way of God truthfully. 22 Now tell
us—is it right for us to pay taxes to Caesar or not?"
23 He saw through their trickery and said, 24 "Show
me a Roman coin.* Whose picture and title are
stamped on it?"
"Caesar's," they replied.
25 "Well then," he said, "give to Caesar what belongs
to Caesar, and give to God what belongs to God."
26 So they failed to trap him by what he said in front
of the people. Instead, they were amazed by his an-
swer, and they became silent.

DISCUSSION ABOUT RESURRECTION

27 Then Jesus was approached by some Saddu-
cees—religious leaders who say there is no resur-
rection from the dead. 28 They posed this question:
"Teacher, Moses gave us a law that if a man dies,
leaving a wife but no children, his brother should
marry the widow and have a child who will car-
ry on the brother's name.* 29 Well, suppose there
were seven brothers. The oldest one married and
then died without children. 30 So the second broth-
er married the widow, but he also died. 31 Then the
third brother married her. This continued with all
seven of them, who died without children. 32 Final-
ly, the woman also died. 33 So tell us, whose wife
will she be in the resurrection? For all seven were
married to her!"
34 Jesus replied, "Marriage is for people here on
earth. 35 But in the age to come, those worthy of being
raised from the dead will neither marry nor be given
in marriage. 36 And they will never die again. In this
respect they will be like angels. They are children of
God and children of the resurrection.
37 "But now, as to whether the dead will be raised—
even Moses proved this when he wrote about the
burning bush. Long after Abraham, Isaac, and Jacob
had died, he referred to the Lord* as 'the God of Abra-
ham, the God of Isaac, and the God of Jacob.'* 38 So he
is the God of the living, not the dead, for they are all
alive to him."
39 "Well said, Teacher!" remarked some of the teach-
ers of religious law who were standing there. 40 And
then no one dared to ask him any more questions.

WHOSE SON IS THE MESSIAH?

41 Then Jesus presented them with a question. "Why is
it," he asked, "that the Messiah is said to be the son of
David? 42 For David himself wrote in the book of Psalms:

'The LORD said to my Lord,
Sit in the place of honor at my right hand
43 until I humble your enemies,
making them a footstool under your feet.'*

44 Since David called the Messiah 'Lord,' how can the
Messiah be his son?"
45 Then, with the crowds listening, he turned to his dis-
ciples and said, 46 "Beware of these teachers of religious
law! For they like to parade around in flowing robes and
love to receive respectful greetings as they walk in the
marketplaces. And how they love the seats of honor in
the synagogues and the head table at banquets. 47 Yet
they shamelessly cheat widows out of their property
and then pretend to be pious by making long prayers in
public. Because of this, they will be severely punished."

THE WIDOW'S OFFERING

21 While Jesus was in the Temple, he watched the
rich people dropping their gifts in the collection
box. 2 Then a poor widow came by and dropped in
two small coins.*
3 "I tell you the truth," Jesus said, "this poor widow
has given more than all the rest of them. 4 For they
have given a tiny part of their surplus, but she, poor
as she is, has given everything she has."

JESUS SPEAKS ABOUT THE FUTURE

5 Some of his disciples began talking about the ma-
jestic stonework of the Temple and the memorial
decorations on the walls. But Jesus said, 6 "The time is
coming when all these things will be completely de-
molished. Not one stone will be left on top of another!"
7 "Teacher," they asked, "when will all this happen?
What sign will show us that these things are about to
take place?"

20:24 Greek *a denarius.* 20:28 See Deut 25:5-6. 20:37a Greek *when he wrote about the bush. He referred to the Lord.* 20:37b Exod 3:6. 20:42-43 Ps 110:1. 21:2 Greek *two lepta* [the smallest of Jewish coins].

20:24 Whose picture and title are stamped on it? Jesus did what he did many times—answered a question by asking a question. Those trying to trick Jesus produce a silver denarius minted by the Roman government. On one side was the image of the emperor, Tiberius Caesar. Under Caesar's image was the inscription: "Tiberius, son of the divine Augustus." On the flip side of the coin was an image of Tiberius' mother, Livia.

20:25 give to Caesar what belongs to Caesar. While clearly implying that one's final loyalty must be to God and not the state, Jesus implied that there are things owed to the state and that it was not his mission to detract from the state. In his letter to the Romans Paul clearly articulated God's design for the state: "Everyone must submit to the governing authorities, for there is no authority except from God, and those that exist are instituted by God" (Rom. 13:1).

20:27 Sadducees. There is relatively little information available about this group. However, it seems that they were a small but highly influential party of Jews composed mainly of wealthy, aristocratic priests. The Sadducees accepted only the first five books of the Old Testament as authoritative and denied the resurrection.

20:28-33 in the resurrection? The question they pose has to do with levirate marriage (Deut. 25:5-10), which was designed to ensure the continuation of the family name as well as to keep property within a family. Their case study attempted to show the absurdity of resurrection.

20:34-36 they will be like angels. Jesus affirmed that resurrection life will be more akin to the experience of angels (in which the Sadducees likewise did not believe) than to the social and physical laws that now govern life.

20:39 Well said. The scribes (who were Pharisees) believed in the resurrection and in angels and would be glad to see the cynicism of the Sadducees refuted.

20:46 flowing robes. These were long, white linen garments fringed with tassels touching the ground. In such a stately garment, a person could not run or work and so would be reckoned to be a person of leisure and importance. **greetings.** People considered the teachers of the law to be men of great insight and authority, so they rose when the teachers passed by and called out titles of respect.

20:47 they shamelessly cheat widows out of their property. Since the teachers of the law were forbidden to receive pay for their teaching, they lived off others, including poor widows (21:1-4).

21:1 collection box. This was located in the court of women (which was the first of the inner courts of the temple). It consisted of 13 trumpet-shaped receptacles used to collect donations.

21:2 two small coins. The smallest coins in circulation, worth about 1/8 of a cent. Her donation, while small in amount, represented the depth of her dedication to God (12:22-34).

21:5 Temple. The temple was constructed of huge white stones, some measuring 37 feet long by 12 feet high by 18 feet wide.

8 He replied, "Don't let anyone mislead you, for many
will come in my name, claiming, 'I am the Messiah,'*
and saying, 'The time has come!' But don't believe
them. 9 And when you hear of wars and insurrections,
don't panic. Yes, these things must take place first, but
the end won't follow immediately." 10 Then he added,
"Nation will go to war against nation, and kingdom
against kingdom. 11 There will be great earthquakes,
and there will be famines and plagues in many lands,
and there will be terrifying things and great miraculous signs from heaven.
12 "But before all this occurs, there will be a time
of great persecution. You will be dragged into synagogues and prisons, and you will stand trial before
kings and governors because you are my followers. 13 But this will be your opportunity to tell them
about me.* 14 So don't worry in advance about how
to answer the charges against you, 15 for I will give
you the right words and such wisdom that none of
your opponents will be able to reply or refute you!
16 Even those closest to you—your parents, brothers,
relatives, and friends—will betray you. They will
even kill some of you. 17 And everyone will hate you
because you are my followers.* 18 But not a hair of
your head will perish! 19 By standing firm, you will
win your souls.
20 "And when you see Jerusalem surrounded by
armies, then you will know that the time of its destruction has arrived. 21 Then those in Judea must flee
to the hills. Those in Jerusalem must get out, and those
out in the country should not return to the city. 22 For
those will be days of God's vengeance, and the prophetic words of the Scriptures will be fulfilled. 23 How
terrible it will be for pregnant women and for nursing mothers in those days. For there will be disaster in
the land and great anger against this people. 24 They
will be killed by the sword or sent away as captives
to all the nations of the world. And Jerusalem will be
trampled down by the Gentiles until the period of the
Gentiles comes to an end.
25 "And there will be strange signs in the sun, moon,
and stars. And here on earth the nations will be in
turmoil, perplexed by the roaring seas and strange
tides. 26 People will be terrified at what they see coming upon the earth, for the powers in the heavens will
be shaken. 27 Then everyone will see the Son of Man*
coming on a cloud with power and great glory.* 28 So
when all these things begin to happen, stand and look
up, for your salvation is near!"
29 Then he gave them this illustration: "Notice the
fig tree, or any other tree. 30 When the leaves come
out, you know without being told that summer is
near. 31 In the same way, when you see all these things
taking place, you can know that the Kingdom of God
is near. 32 I tell you the truth, this generation will not
pass from the scene until all these things have taken place. 33 Heaven and earth will disappear, but my
words will never disappear.
34 "Watch out! Don't let your hearts be dulled by
carousing and drunkenness, and by the worries
of this life. Don't let that day catch you unaware,
35 like a trap. For that day will come upon everyone
living on the earth. 36 Keep alert at all times. And
pray that you might be strong enough to escape
these coming horrors and stand before the Son of
Man."
37 Every day Jesus went to the Temple to teach, and
each evening he returned to spend the night on the
Mount of Olives. 38 The crowds gathered at the Temple
early each morning to hear him.

JUDAS AGREES TO BETRAY JESUS

22 The Festival of Unleavened Bread, which is also
called Passover, was approaching. 2 The leading
priests and teachers of religious law were plotting
how to kill Jesus, but they were afraid of the people's
reaction.
3 Then Satan entered into Judas Iscariot, who was
one of the twelve disciples, 4 and he went to the leading priests and captains of the Temple guard to discuss the best way to betray Jesus to them. 5 They were
delighted, and they promised to give him money.
6 So he agreed and began looking for an opportunity to betray Jesus so they could arrest him when the
crowds weren't around.

THE LAST SUPPER

7 Now the Festival of Unleavened Bread arrived, when
the Passover lamb is sacrificed. 8 Jesus sent Peter and
John ahead and said, "Go and prepare the Passover
meal, so we can eat it together."
9 "Where do you want us to prepare it?" they asked
him.
10 He replied, "As soon as you enter Jerusalem, a
man carrying a pitcher of water will meet you. Follow him. At the house he enters, 11 say to the owner,
'The Teacher asks: Where is the guest room where I
can eat the Passover meal with my disciples?' 12 He

21:8 Greek *claiming, 'I am.'* **21:13** Or *This will be your testimony against them.* **21:17** Greek *on account of my name.* **21:27a** "Son of Man" is a title Jesus used for himself. **21:27b** See Dan 7:13.

21:11 terrifying things and great miraculous signs from heaven. This is apocalyptic language—graphic, calamitous, cosmic imagery. Such language was used often in the Old Testament (Isa. 2:6-21; 13:6-22).

21:21 those in Judea must flee. Those who follow Christ are to recognize that this is the sign that God's judgment against Israel is coming to a head. Instead of flocking to the city in anticipation of a messianic appearance, they must run for their lives.

21:24 the period of the Gentiles. Some believe this may refer to the period of the Gentile ingathering to Christ and others to the completion of a time during the tribulation (Rom. 11:25).

22:1 The Festival of Unleavened Bread. This feast was a seven-day period so closely related to Passover (Deut. 16:1-8) that the whole period was often called Passover. Passover, celebrated on the fourteenth day of the Jewish month of Nisan (March–April), was the celebration of God's deliverance of Israel from slavery in Egypt (Ex. 12).

22:2 plotting how to kill Jesus. The religious leadership had long ago decided that Jesus must be silenced (6:11; 20:19). It was only their fear of an uproar by the masses that had prevented them from doing so.

22:4 leading priests and captains of the Temple guard. The management of the temple was under the control of the high priest and those who aligned themselves with him. They controlled the temple guard and held them responsible for maintaining order in the temple area.

22:7–8 the Festival of Unleavened Bread arrived, when the Passover lamb is sacrificed. While the Feast of Unleavened Bread did not officially start until the day after Passover, the day on which the lambs were sacrificed was sometimes referred to as the first day of the Feast of Unleavened Bread. **the Passover meal.** Each pilgrim sacrificed his own lamb in the temple. A priest caught the blood in a bowl and threw it on the altar. The pilgrim then ate the sacrificial lamb for Passover.

22:10 a man carrying a pitcher of water. Such a person would have been easy to spot since it was highly unusual for a man to carry a jar. Women carried jars, while men carried wineskins.

CELEBRATING THE LORD'S SUPPER

1. What special meals does your family celebrate together: Thanksgiving? Sunday dinner? Birthday suppers?

LUKE 22:7-23

2. What is the purpose of the Lord's Supper according to Jesus?
3. What was the disciples' response during this first Lord's Supper (v. 23)? What is your focus at church: Worshiping God? Arguing with others?
4. Why should Christians today celebrate the Lord's Supper?
5. How often do you celebrate the Lord's Supper? What do you do in preparing to receive it?

will take you upstairs to a large room that is already
set up. That is where you should prepare our meal."
13 They went off to the city and found everything just
as Jesus had said, and they prepared the Passover
meal there.
14 When the time came, Jesus and the apostles sat
down together at the table.* 15 Jesus said, "I have been
very eager to eat this Passover meal with you before
my suffering begins. 16 For I tell you now that I won't
eat this meal again until its meaning is fulfilled in the
Kingdom of God."
17 Then he took a cup of wine and gave thanks to
God for it. Then he said, "Take this and share it among
yourselves. 18 For I will not drink wine again until the
Kingdom of God has come."
19 He took some bread and gave thanks to God for it.
Then he broke it in pieces and gave it to the disciples,
saying, "This is my body, which is given for you. Do
this in remembrance of me."
20 After supper he took another cup of wine and
said, "This cup is the new covenant between God and
his people—an agreement confirmed with my blood,
which is poured out as a sacrifice for you.*
21 "But here at this table, sitting among us as a
friend, is the man who will betray me. 22 For it has
been determined that the Son of Man* must die. But
what sorrow awaits the one who betrays him." 23 The
disciples began to ask each other which of them
would ever do such a thing.
24 Then they began to argue among themselves
about who would be the greatest among them. 25 Jesus
told them, "In this world the kings and great men lord
it over their people, yet they are called 'friends of the
people.' 26 But among you it will be different. Those
who are the greatest among you should take the lowest
rank, and the leader should be like a servant. 27 Who is
more important, the one who sits at the table or the one
who serves? The one who sits at the table, of course. But
not here! For I am among you as one who serves.
28 "You have stayed with me in my time of trial.
29 And just as my Father has granted me a Kingdom, I
now grant you the right 30 to eat and drink at my table
in my Kingdom. And you will sit on thrones, judging
the twelve tribes of Israel.

JESUS PREDICTS PETER'S DENIAL

31 "Simon, Simon, Satan has asked to sift each of you
like wheat. 32 But I have pleaded in prayer for you,
Simon, that your faith should not fail. So when you
have repented and turned to me again, strengthen
your brothers."
33 Peter said, "Lord, I am ready to go to prison with
you, and even to die with you."
34 But Jesus said, "Peter, let me tell you something.
Before the rooster crows tomorrow morning, you will
deny three times that you even know me."
35 Then Jesus asked them, "When I sent you out to
preach the Good News and you did not have money,
a traveler's bag, or an extra pair of sandals, did you
need anything?"
"No," they replied.
36 "But now," he said, "take your money and a travel-
er's bag. And if you don't have a sword, sell your cloak
and buy one! 37 For the time has come for this proph-
ecy about me to be fulfilled: 'He was counted among
the rebels.'* Yes, everything written about me by the
prophets will come true."
38 "Look, Lord," they replied, "we have two swords
among us."
"That's enough," he said.

JESUS PRAYS ON THE MOUNT OF OLIVES

39 Then, accompanied by the disciples, Jesus left the
upstairs room and went as usual to the Mount of Ol-
ives. 40 There he told them, "Pray that you will not give
in to temptation."

22:14 Or *reclined together.* **22:19-20** Some manuscripts do not include 22:19b-20, *which is given for you . . . which is poured out as a sacrifice for you.* **22:22** "Son of Man" is a title Jesus used for himself. **22:37** Isa 53:12.

22:14 When the time came. The meal could be eaten only after sunset.

22:16-18 The Passover had a twofold significance: it looked back upon Israel's deliverance from Egypt, and it looked forward to the final redemption that would be ushered in by the Messiah. The comments in verses 16 and 18 refer to that final consummation of the kingdom of God. In a sense, the meal will not be finished until the final messianic banquet. No longer is the Old Testament Passover the supreme act of God's deliverance of His people: From now on spiritual deliverance from the power and penalty of sin is secured by the death and resurrection of Jesus.

22:19 He simply says, "Do this in remembrance of Me." Jesus' use of the bread and the cup in a symbolic way was consistent with the way in which the various elements of the Passover meal were used. The symbols in the Passover meal pointed back to the first covenant God made with Israel, while Jesus' words here at the Last Supper pointed forward to His death and the new covenant.

22:20 covenant. This is a treaty between two parties, often sealed by the sacrifice of an animal. It refers to the agreement that God made with Israel which was dependent on Israel's obedience (Ex. 24:1-8). Now a new covenant (Jer. 31:31-33; Heb. 8:8,13) is established which is dependent on Jesus' obedience and sacrificial death. A covenant of law gives way to a covenant of love.

22:26 the lowest rank. Prestige in this culture went with age and experience. The youngest people had little prestige or honor. Jesus' followers should not think that true greatness requires any more prestige than the youngest person received in that culture.

22:32 I have pleaded in prayer for you. This "you" is singular. While Peter will deny Jesus, he is also the one who will encourage the others to reaffirm their faith in Him. This pictures the conflict between Satan and Jesus in the ongoing life of the church. While Satan has an influence, it is continually checked and countered by the intercession of Jesus as the High Priest of God's people (Heb. 4:14-16). **strengthen your brothers.** In Acts 1:15 and 2:14 Peter was the leading character among the original disciples. His faith and courage exemplified to all the others what it meant to follow Jesus (John 21:15-17).

22:37 counted among the rebels. Jesus will be crucified as a criminal with two criminals (23:32). This is to fulfill the prophecy of Isaiah (Isa. 53:12).

41 He walked away, about a stone's throw, and knelt
down and prayed, 42 **"Father, if you are willing, please
take this cup of suffering away from me. Yet I want
your will to be done, not mine."** 43 Then an angel
from heaven appeared and strengthened him. 44 He
prayed more fervently, and he was in such agony
of spirit that his sweat fell to the ground like great
drops of blood.*

45 At last he stood up again and returned to the disciples, only to find them asleep, exhausted from grief.
46 **"Why are you sleeping?"** he asked them. **"Get up and
pray, so that you will not give in to temptation."**

JESUS IS BETRAYED AND ARRESTED

47 But even as Jesus said this, a crowd approached,
led by Judas, one of the twelve disciples. Judas
walked over to Jesus to greet him with a kiss. 48 But
Jesus said, **"Judas, would you betray the Son of Man
with a kiss?"**

49 When the other disciples saw what was about to
happen, they exclaimed, "Lord, should we fight? We
brought the swords!" 50 And one of them struck at the
high priest's slave, slashing off his right ear.

51 But Jesus said, **"No more of this."** And he touched
the man's ear and healed him.

52 Then Jesus spoke to the leading priests, the captains of the Temple guard, and the elders who had
come for him. **"Am I some dangerous revolutionary,"**
he asked, **"that you come with swords and clubs to arrest me? 53 Why didn't you arrest me in the Temple? I
was there every day. But this is your moment, the time
when the power of darkness reigns."**

PETER DENIES JESUS

54 So they arrested him and led him to the high
priest's home. And Peter followed at a distance.
55 The guards lit a fire in the middle of the courtyard
and sat around it, and Peter joined them there. 56 A
servant girl noticed him in the firelight and began
staring at him. Finally she said, "This man was one of
Jesus' followers!"

57 But Peter denied it. "Woman," he said, "I don't
even know him!"

58 After a while someone else looked at him and
said, "You must be one of them!"

"No, man, I'm not!" Peter retorted.

59 About an hour later someone else insisted, "This
must be one of them, because he is a Galilean, too."

60 But Peter said, "Man, I don't know what you are
talking about." And immediately, while he was still
speaking, the rooster crowed.

61 At that moment the Lord turned and looked at
Peter. Suddenly, the Lord's words flashed through Peter's mind: **"Before the rooster crows tomorrow morning, you will deny three times that you even know
me."** 62 And Peter left the courtyard, weeping bitterly.

63 The guards in charge of Jesus began mocking
and beating him. 64 They blindfolded him and said,
"Prophesy to us! Who hit you that time?" 65 And they
hurled all sorts of terrible insults at him.

JESUS BEFORE THE COUNCIL

66 At daybreak all the elders of the people assembled,
including the leading priests and the teachers of religious law. Jesus was led before this high council,*
67 and they said, "Tell us, are you the Messiah?"

But he replied, **"If I tell you, you won't believe me.
68 And if I ask you a question, you won't answer. 69 But
from now on the Son of Man will be seated in the
place of power at God's right hand.*"**

70 They all shouted, "So, are you claiming to be the
Son of God?"

And he replied, **"You say that I am."**

71 "Why do we need other witnesses?" they said. "We
ourselves heard him say it."

22:43-44 Verses 43 and 44 are not included in the most ancient manuscripts. **22:66** Greek *before their Sanhedrin.* **22:69** See Ps 110:1.

CONFRONTING SIN

1. How do you usually react to failure: Kick yourself for days? Pray about it? Talk to someone about it? Try to learn from it?

LUKE 22:54-62

2. Peter had just told Jesus that he would follow Him to death (v. 33). Why did he suddenly deny Jesus?
3. Have you ever denied Jesus? How? Why?
4. Peter "left the courtyard, weeping bitterly" (v. 62). How do you react when you find that you've somehow failed God?
5. Jesus "turned and looked at Peter" (v. 61). How does God turn and look at you to convict you of sin?

22:42 Father. This distinguishes the nature of the relationship Jesus enjoyed with God. **this cup.** The Old Testament often pictured a person's destiny as related to the nature of the "cup" from which God gave the person to drink. For those who trust Him, it was seen as a cup of blessing (Ps. 16:5; 23:5), but His opponents would be forced to drink a cup full of wrath (Isa. 51:17; Lam. 4:21; Hab. 2:16). **Yet I want your will to be done, not mine.** The wrestling in prayer resolves itself in Jesus' entrustment of Himself to the Father.

22:54 the high priest's home. On the Day of Atonement the high priest alone could enter the most holy place and, with sprinkled blood, make atonement for the sins of the people. Caiaphas was the high priest before whom Jesus came (Matt. 26:57).

22:60 the rooster crowed. Roosters in Palestine might crow anytime between midnight and 3 a.m. (which was the reason that particular watch was called "cock-crow"). Peter's denials therefore occurred in the very early morning hours.

22:61 the Lord turned. The other Gospels make it clear that Jesus was interrogated during the night by the high priest and at least some members of the Sanhedrin (Matt. 26:68). It may be at this point that Jesus was being transferred from the high priest's house to the meeting place of the full Sanhedrin for His early morning trial.

22:66 high council. This was a council consisting of 71 leaders (both priests and laymen) who made up the highest Jewish court. They were given authority by Rome to rule in matters of religious law.

22:67-68 Tell us, are you the Messiah? While the other Gospels record the failure of the Sanhedrin to produce any charges against Jesus (Mark 14:56), Luke zeroes in on the point of contention that most angered the council: They felt Jesus was making false claims to be Messiah.

22:69 the Son of Man. Jesus openly and unequivocally declared His Messiahship. The three titles for Jesus, Christ, Son of Man, Son of God, are combined here for the first time in the Gospel. It becomes clear the Son of Man is the Messiah, who is the Son of God. **seated in the place of power at God's right hand.** This was the place of honor. Jesus, the Son of Man like in Daniel 7:13-14, will be vindicated at the second coming when His accusers see that His claim was true.

22:71 We ourselves heard him say it. The Sanhedrin heard all they needed. The Old Testament penalty for blaspheming God was death by stoning (Lev. 24:10-16), but at this point in history the Sanhedrin did not have the power to carry out a death sentence. They would need to get the Roman procurator to do that for them somehow.

JESUS' TRIAL BEFORE PILATE

23 Then the entire council took Jesus to Pilate, the Roman governor. 2 They began to state their case: "This man has been leading our people astray by telling them not to pay their taxes to the Roman government and by claiming he is the Messiah, a king."

3 So Pilate asked him, "Are you the king of the Jews?"

Jesus replied, "You have said it."

4 Pilate turned to the leading priests and to the crowd and said, "I find nothing wrong with this man!"

5 Then they became insistent. "But he is causing riots by his teaching wherever he goes—all over Judea, from Galilee to Jerusalem!"

6 "Oh, is he a Galilean?" Pilate asked. 7 When they said that he was, Pilate sent him to Herod Antipas, because Galilee was under Herod's jurisdiction, and Herod happened to be in Jerusalem at the time.

8 Herod was delighted at the opportunity to see Jesus, because he had heard about him and had been hoping for a long time to see him perform a miracle. 9 He asked Jesus question after question, but Jesus refused to answer. 10 Meanwhile, the leading priests and the teachers of religious law stood there shouting their accusations. 11 Then Herod and his soldiers began mocking and ridiculing Jesus. Finally, they put a royal robe on him and sent him back to Pilate. 12 (Herod and Pilate, who had been enemies before, became friends that day.)

13 Then Pilate called together the leading priests and other religious leaders, along with the people, 14 and he announced his verdict. "You brought this man to me, accusing him of leading a revolt. I have examined him thoroughly on this point in your presence and find him innocent. 15 Herod came to the same conclusion and sent him back to us. Nothing this man has done calls for the death penalty. 16 So I will have him flogged, and then I will release him."*

18 Then a mighty roar rose from the crowd, and with one voice they shouted, "Kill him, and release Barabbas to us!" 19 (Barabbas was in prison for taking part in an insurrection in Jerusalem against the government, and for murder.) 20 Pilate argued with them, because he wanted to release Jesus. 21 But they kept shouting, "Crucify him! Crucify him!"

22 For the third time he demanded, "Why? What crime has he committed? I have found no reason to sentence him to death. So I will have him flogged, and then I will release him."

23 But the mob shouted louder and louder, demanding that Jesus be crucified, and their voices prevailed. 24 So Pilate sentenced Jesus to die as they demanded. 25 As they had requested, he released Barabbas, the man in prison for insurrection and murder. But he turned Jesus over to them to do as they wished.

THE CRUCIFIXION

26 As they led Jesus away, a man named Simon, who was from Cyrene,* happened to be coming in from the countryside. The soldiers seized him and put the cross on him and made him carry it behind Jesus. 27 A large crowd trailed behind, including many grief-stricken women. 28 But Jesus turned and said to them, "Daughters of Jerusalem, don't weep for me, but weep for yourselves and for your children. 29 For the days are coming when they will say, 'Fortunate indeed are the women who are childless, the wombs that have not borne a child and the breasts that have never nursed.' 30 People will beg the mountains, 'Fall on us,' and plead with the hills, 'Bury us.'* 31 For if these things are done when the tree is green, what will happen when it is dry?*"

32 Two others, both criminals, were led out to be executed with him. 33 When they came to a place called The Skull,* they nailed him to the cross. And the criminals were also crucified—one on his right and one on his left.

ON THE CROSS

1. When have you been punished for something you didn't do? How did it feel? Have you ever taken someone else's punishment? Why?

LUKE 23:26-49

2. Why did Jesus die on the cross? What did His death accomplish?
3. Why did Jesus assure one thief, "today you will be with me in paradise" (v. 43)? Why didn't He promise that to the other thief?
4. When Jesus said, "Father, forgive them" (v. 34), who was he asking God to forgive?
5. When you die, will you be with Jesus in paradise? How do you know?

23:16 Some manuscripts add verse 17, *Now it was necessary for him to release one prisoner to them during the Passover celebration.* Compare Matt 27:15; Mark 15:6; John 18:39. **23:26** *Cyrene* was a city in northern Africa. **23:30** Hos 10:8. **23:31** Or *If these things are done to me, the living tree, what will happen to you, the dry tree?* **23:33** Sometimes rendered *Calvary,* which comes from the Latin word for "skull."

23:1 took Jesus to Pilate. Pilate served as procurator of Judea from A.D. 26 to 36. Historians of the time called him an "inflexible, merciless, and obstinate" man who disliked the Jews and their customs.

23:5-7 sent him to Herod. Pilate decided to pass off the case to Herod who had authority over Galilee. This might have been done since Herod Antipas was Jewish, or simply to get a Jewish opinion of the case or to rid himself of the responsibility.

23:9 Jesus refused to answer. See Isaiah 53:7.

23:18 Barabbas. A genuine resistance leader who was also guilty of murder.

23:20-22 Pilate . . . wanted to release Jesus. Pilate argues again for Jesus' release, but the leaders will hear nothing of this. He then seeks to appease the crowd by punishing Jesus and then releasing Him.

23:25 released Barabbas . . . in prison for . . . murder. The death of the innocent in the place of the guilty is an individual application of the meaning of Jesus' death as a substitutionary atonement for sinners. It explains what Jesus meant in Mark 10:45 when He said that He came to "give His life as a ransom for many."

23:26 Simon. Possibly a Jew, from a Greek city on the north shore of Africa who was in Jerusalem for the Passover feast. **put the cross on him.** The fact that Jesus could not carry His crossbeam reveals the extent to which He had been beaten. Because of Jesus' weakened condition, Simon was grabbed out of the crowds and forced into service by the Roman soldiers.

23:31 For if these things are done when the tree is green, what will happen when it is dry? A proverbial saying that means, "If things are this bad now, what will happen later?"

23:33 The Skull. In Aramaic, this was Golgotha. The name was given because it was a round, bare hillock outside Jerusalem. **they nailed him to the cross.** Crucifixion was the most feared of all punishments in the first-century world.

34 Jesus said, "Father, forgive them, for they don't
know what they are doing."* And the soldiers gam-
bled for his clothes by throwing dice.*
35 The crowd watched and the leaders scoffed. "He
saved others," they said, "let him save himself if he
is really God's Messiah, the Chosen One." 36 The sol-
diers mocked him, too, by offering him a drink of
sour wine. 37 They called out to him, "If you are the
King of the Jews, save yourself!" 38 A sign was fas-
tened above him with these words: "This is the King
of the Jews."
39 One of the criminals hanging beside him scoffed,
"So you're the Messiah, are you? Prove it by saving
yourself—and us, too, while you're at it!"
40 But the other criminal protested, "Don't you fear
God even when you have been sentenced to die? 41 We
deserve to die for our crimes, but this man hasn't done
anything wrong." 42 Then he said, "Jesus, remember
me when you come into your Kingdom."
43 And Jesus replied, "I assure you, today you will be
with me in paradise."

THE DEATH OF JESUS

44 By this time it was about noon, and darkness fell
across the whole land until three o'clock. 45 The light
from the sun was gone. And suddenly, the curtain in
the sanctuary of the Temple was torn down the mid-
dle. 46 Then Jesus shouted, "Father, I entrust my spirit
into your hands!"* And with those words he breathed
his last.
47 When the Roman officer* overseeing the execu-
tion saw what had happened, he worshiped God and
said, "Surely this man was innocent.*" 48 And when
all the crowd that came to see the crucifixion saw
what had happened, they went home in deep sor-
row.* 49 But Jesus' friends, including the women who
had followed him from Galilee, stood at a distance
watching.

THE BURIAL OF JESUS

50 Now there was a good and righteous man named
Joseph. He was a member of the Jewish high council,
51 but he had not agreed with the decision and ac-
tions of the other religious leaders. He was from the
town of Arimathea in Judea, and he was waiting for
the Kingdom of God to come. 52 He went to Pilate and
asked for Jesus' body. 53 Then he took the body down
from the cross and wrapped it in a long sheet of linen
cloth and laid it in a new tomb that had been carved
out of rock. 54 This was done late on Friday afternoon,
the day of preparation,* as the Sabbath was about to
begin.
55 As his body was taken away, the women from
Galilee followed and saw the tomb where his body
was placed. 56 Then they went home and prepared
spices and ointments to anoint his body. But by the
time they were finished the Sabbath had begun, so
they rested as required by the law.

THE RESURRECTION

24 But very early on Sunday morning* the wom-
en went to the tomb, taking the spices they had
prepared. 2 They found that the stone had been rolled
away from the entrance. 3 So they went in, but they
didn't find the body of the Lord Jesus. 4 As they stood
there puzzled, two men suddenly appeared to them,
clothed in dazzling robes.
5 The women were terrified and bowed with their
faces to the ground. Then the men asked, "Why are
you looking among the dead for someone who is
alive? 6 He isn't here! He is risen from the dead! Re-
member what he told you back in Galilee, 7 that the
Son of Man* must be betrayed into the hands of sinful
men and be crucified, and that he would rise again on
the third day."
8 Then they remembered that he had said this. 9 So
they rushed back from the tomb to tell his eleven dis-
ciples—and everyone else—what had happened.
10 It was Mary Magdalene, Joanna, Mary the moth-
er of James, and several other women who told the
apostles what had happened. 11 But the story sound-
ed like nonsense to the men, so they didn't believe it.
12 However, Peter jumped up and ran to the tomb to
look. Stooping, he peered in and saw the empty lin-
en wrappings; then he went home again, wondering
what had happened.

23:34a This sentence is not included in many ancient manuscripts. **23:34b** Greek *by casting lots.* See Ps 22:18. **23:46** Ps 31:5. **23:47a** Greek *the centurion.* **23:47b** Or *righteous.* **23:48** Greek *went home beating their breasts.* **23:54** Greek *It was the day of preparation.* **24:1** Greek *But on the first day of the week, very early in the morning.* **24:7** "Son of Man" is a title Jesus used for himself.

23:34 Father, forgive them. Jesus' call for mercy reflected His radical call to His disciples to forgive their enemies (6:27-28; Acts 7:60). **gambled for his clothes.** The clothes of the condemned person belonged to the four soldiers who carried out the crucifixion (Ps. 22:18; John 19:23-24).

23:35 if he is really God's Messiah. To the leaders, the disgraceful death Jesus was experiencing proved that He could not possibly be the Messiah.

23:44 darkness. This was some sort of supernatural event (Ex. 10:21-23) showing the significance of the crucifixion (22:53; Amos 8:9).

23:45 curtain in the sanctuary. The curtain in the temple was probably the one that separated the holy place (where the priests performed their daily service) and the most holy place. The curtain stood as a visible sign of the barrier between people and God since only the high priest could pass through that curtain once a year on the Day of Atonement. Its rending was another supernatural sign of the significance of Jesus' death: He has opened the way for believers to have immediate and direct access to God (Heb. 10:19-20).

23:50-52 asked for Jesus' body. To ask for the body was to admit allegiance to the now discredited Jesus and was, therefore, potentially dangerous.

23:55 the women from Galilee. See chapter 8:2-3. These women saw where Jesus was laid. Thus, Luke undermines any criticism that the women merely went to the wrong tomb later on.

24:1 on Sunday morning. This was early Sunday morning. **spices.** Aromatic oils to anoint the body, not so much to preserve it as to honor it. Clearly they did not expect Jesus to have risen from the dead.

24:2 The stone was rolled away not so that the resurrected Jesus could leave the tomb but so that His disciples could see that it was empty (John 20:8). **the stone.** It would have been fairly easy to roll the huge, disc-shaped stone down the groove cut for it so that it covered the opening, but once in place it would have been very difficult to push it back up the incline. **tomb.** Typically such tombs had a large antechamber, with a small two-foot-high doorway at the back which led into the six- or seven-foot burial chamber.

24:4 two men. Matthew 28:2-3 says that an angel came down from heaven. The description of their clothing here confirms this is Luke's meaning, too.

24:9 his eleven. Judas had committed suicide for his treachery (Matt. 27:5).

24:10 Mary Magdalene, Joanna. All the Gospel writers include Mary as one of the witnesses of Jesus' empty tomb. Under Jewish law, women were not considered reliable witnesses. **Mary the mother of James.** Literally, "Mary of James." Typically one would understand it to mean James' wife, but Mark 15:40 refers specifically to Mary as the mother of James.

24:12 Peter . . . saw the empty linen wrappings. John reports this curious fact in even greater detail (John 20:1–9). It was the custom to bind a dead body with strips of linen cloth. The head was bound with a separate cloth. Thus, when Jesus rose from the dead He would have passed through the cloth (as He later did through doors) and the whole mass would have collapsed. Had the body been stolen, grave clothes would have been taken or, at least, unwound and tossed aside.

THE WALK TO EMMAUS

13 That same day two of Jesus' followers were walking to the village of Emmaus, seven miles* from Jerusalem. 14 As they walked along they were talking about everything that had happened. 15 As they talked and discussed these things, Jesus himself suddenly came and began walking with them. 16 But God kept them from recognizing him.

17 He asked them, "What are you discussing so intently as you walk along?"

They stopped short, sadness written across their faces. 18 Then one of them, Cleopas, replied, "You must be the only person in Jerusalem who hasn't heard about all the things that have happened there the last few days."

19 "What things?" Jesus asked.

"The things that happened to Jesus, the man from Nazareth," they said. "He was a prophet who did powerful miracles, and he was a mighty teacher in the eyes of God and all the people. 20 But our leading priests and other religious leaders handed him over to be condemned to death, and they crucified him. 21 We had hoped he was the Messiah who had come to rescue Israel. This all happened three days ago.

22 "Then some women from our group of his followers were at his tomb early this morning, and they came back with an amazing report. 23 They said his body was missing, and they had seen angels who told them Jesus is alive! 24 Some of our men ran out to see, and sure enough, his body was gone, just as the women had said."

25 Then Jesus said to them, "You foolish people! You find it so hard to believe all that the prophets wrote in the Scriptures. 26 Wasn't it clearly predicted that the Messiah would have to suffer all these things before entering his glory?" 27 Then Jesus took them through the writings of Moses and all the prophets, explaining from all the Scriptures the things concerning himself.

28 By this time they were nearing Emmaus and the end of their journey. Jesus acted as if he were going on, 29 but they begged him, "Stay the night with us, since it is getting late." So he went home with them. 30 As they sat down to eat,* he took the bread and blessed it. Then he broke it and gave it to them. 31 Suddenly, their eyes were opened, and they recognized him. And at that moment he disappeared!

32 They said to each other, "Didn't our hearts burn within us as he talked with us on the road and explained the Scriptures to us?" 33 And within the hour they were on their way back to Jerusalem. There they found the eleven disciples and the others who had gathered with them, 34 who said, "The Lord has really risen! He appeared to Peter.*"

AN EYE-OPENING EXPERIENCE

1. What's the longest walk you've ever taken?

LUKE 24:13-35

2. Why did Jesus ask the men to tell Him all about His own death and resurrection?
3. Why did the Messiah "have to suffer these things" (v. 26)—that is, dying on the cross and rising again from the dead?
4. Why were the men's eyes "opened" to who Jesus was when "he took the bread and blessed and it. Then he broke it and gave it to them" (vv. 30-31)? What does this teach us about the Lord's Supper?
5. Has Jesus "opened your eyes"? If not, will you ask Him to right now?

JESUS APPEARS TO THE DISCIPLES

35 Then the two from Emmaus told their story of how Jesus had appeared to them as they were walking along the road, and how they had recognized him as he was breaking the bread. 36 And just as they were telling about it, Jesus himself was suddenly standing there among them. "Peace be with you," he said. 37 But the whole group was startled and frightened, thinking they were seeing a ghost!

38 "Why are you frightened?" he asked. "Why are your hearts filled with doubt? 39 Look at my hands. Look at my feet. You can see that it's really me. Touch me and make sure that I am not a ghost, because ghosts don't have bodies, as you see that I do." 40 As he spoke, he showed them his hands and his feet.

41 Still they stood there in disbelief, filled with joy and wonder. Then he asked them, "Do you have anything here to eat?" 42 They gave him a piece of broiled fish, 43 and he ate it as they watched.

24:13 Greek *60 stadia* [11.1 kilometers]. **24:30** Or *As they reclined.* **24:34** Greek *Simon.*

24:13 two of Jesus' followers. These may not have been two of the remaining eleven apostles, but two followers of Jesus who lived in nearby Jerusalem. They were likely returning home after the Passover feast. **Emmaus.** The site of this village is uncertain.

24:14-16 As Jesus came up to the two, they were prevented from recognizing Him. Later on, they recognized Him as He broke bread (vv. 30-31).

24:18 Cleopas. While this man was probably a figure Luke's readers would know, his identity remains uncertain today.

24:21 to rescue Israel. To free the Jewish nation from bondage to Rome and establish the kingdom of God (1:68; 2:38; 21:28,31; Titus 2:14; 1 Peter 1:18). **three days ago.** This could refer to the Jewish belief that after the third day the soul left the body or to Jesus' statement that He would be raised to life on the third day (9:22).

24:25-27 You foolish people! Jesus rebuked them for their lack of understanding about the Old Testament prophecies regarding the Messiah and explained how these Scriptures foretold all that had taken place.

24:26 the Messiah would have to suffer. The need for the Messiah to suffer was proclaimed in Isaiah 53. **before entering his glory?** The messianic glory was a common expectation of the Jews, but His suffering was not.

24:27 Moses and all the Prophets. This was a way of referring to all the Old Testament Scriptures (16:31). Jesus claims that all the Old Testament teachings about the Servant of the Lord, the Son of Man, the Son of David, and the Messiah apply to Him. It is these teachings collectively that explain who He is and what He came to do.

24:30 he took the bread and blessed it. Then he broke it and gave it to them. While this is a simple enough description of how a meal would begin, it is probably meant to carry overtones of the Lord's Supper (22:19).

24:31 he disappeared. The Gospels' accounts of the appearances of the resurrected Jesus indicate that while He was in His earthly form (vv. 39, 42-43; Matt. 28:9), He was not restricted by that body (John 20:19).

24:37-43 ghost. Luke described at some length the way in which Jesus proved to the disciples that He was not a ghost, an angel, nor a product of any hallucinations. The wound marks were still visible even in His resurrected body. When even that evidence seemed insufficient due to the disciples' amazement and shock, He ate before them to again show He was no ghost. Jesus truly, physically, rose from the dead (1 Cor. 15:35-49).

44 Then he said, "When I was with you before, I
told you that everything written about me in the
law of Moses and the prophets and in the Psalms
must be fulfilled." 45 Then he opened their minds to
understand the Scriptures. 46 And he said, "Yes, it
was written long ago that the Messiah would suffer
and die and rise from the dead on the third day. 47 It
was also written that this message would be pro-
claimed in the authority of his name to all the na-
tions,* beginning in Jerusalem: 'There is forgiveness
of sins for all who repent.' 48 You are witnesses of all
these things.

49 "And now I will send the Holy Spirit, just as my
Father promised. But stay here in the city until the
Holy Spirit comes and fills you with power from heav-
en."

THE ASCENSION

50 Then Jesus led them to Bethany, and lifting his hands
to heaven, he blessed them. 51 While he was blessing
them, he left them and was taken up to heaven. 52 So
they worshiped him and then returned to Jerusalem
filled with great joy. 53 And they spent all of their time
in the Temple, praising God.

24:47 Or *all peoples.*

24:49 just as my Father promised. The baptism of the Holy Spirit at Pentecost is what the Father had promised (Joel 2:28; Acts 2:14-18). It is this theme that is picked up and developed throughout the book of Acts in which Luke recorded how the Spirit empowered the early Christians (particularly Peter and Paul) to bear witness for Christ.

24:51 taken up to heaven. This is the first of two descriptions of Jesus' ascension (Acts 1:9-11).

24:53 The book ends with a note of expectancy that provides the setting for the opening of the book of Acts.

INTRODUCTION TO JOHN

PERSONAL READING PLAN

- ☐John 1:1-34
- ☐John 1:35–2:25
- ☐John 3:1-36
- ☐John 4:1-42
- ☐John 4:43–5:47
- ☐John 6:1-59
- ☐John 6:60–7:24
- ☐John 7:25–8:11
- ☐John 8:12-59
- ☐John 9:1-41
- ☐John 10:1-42
- ☐John 11:1-44
- ☐John 11:45–12:19
- ☐John 12:20-50
- ☐John 13:1-38
- ☐John 14:1-31
- ☐John 15:1–16:4
- ☐John 16:5-33
- ☐John 17:1-26
- ☐John 18:1-27
- ☐John 18:28–19:16a
- ☐John 19:16b-42
- ☐John 20:1-31
- ☐John 21:1-25

AUTHOR

Like the other three Gospels, the fourth Gospel is anonymous. The inscription "The Gospel According to John" or "According to John" (as found in some ancient manuscripts) was added to the text by early Christians. Yet the writer identifies himself by calling himself "the disciple who Jesus loved" (21:20-24; see also 13:23-25; 19:26-27; 20:2-8; 21:7). Who was he?

He must have been one of the 12 original disciples because he was present at the Last Supper (13:23-25; 21:20). In fact, the beloved disciple was "reclining close beside" Jesus (13:23). This gives us a valuable clue as to his identity. We know that the person reclining next to Jesus was not Peter because Peter asked this disciple a question (13:24). The person was probably not Andrew since Andrew is explicitly named several times in the text (1:40,44; 6:8; 12:22. Most of the other disciples are also named in this Gospel.

Some have suggested Lazarus as author of the fourth Gospel because in 11:5 Jesus is said to have loved him, but Lazarus is named in chapters 11–12. Of all the possible candidates, James and John are not named in the fourth Gospel. The beloved disciple could not have been James since he died at the hands of Herod Agrippa I (Acts 12:2) early in the development of the church, and the fourth Gospel is written years after his death. Therefore, the author is most likely John. Indeed, early church tradition is unanimous that John the apostle wrote the fourth Gospel.

DATE

Most scholars agree that John was the last of the four Gospels to be written. It was probably composed in A.D. 80 or 90, though estimates range from the A.D. 50s to 90s.

THEME

Jesus is the giver of life.

PURPOSE

Why did John write as he did about Jesus? Two of his own statements provide the answer to this question. First, John claims: "we testify and proclaim to you that he is the one who is eternal life. He was with the Father, and then he was revealed to us. . . . we ourselves have actually seen and heard so that you may have fellowship with us" (1 John 1:1-3). Second, John states at the end of his Gospel: "these are written so that you may continue to believe that Jesus is the Messiah, the Son of God, and that by believing in him you will have life by the power of his name" (John 20:31). John's Gospel also is a witness document. He tells us Jesus' story so that we will understand who Jesus is, put our faith in Him as the unique Son of God, and so experience life in Christ and fellowship with other believers.

HISTORICAL BACKGROUND

What, then, do we know about John the apostle? We know that he and his brother James, along with Peter and his brother Andrew, were the first four disciples called by Jesus (Mark 1:16-20). Furthermore, James and John seem inseparable. On only one occasion is John recorded as acting alone (Luke 9:49-50). Together the two brothers want to call down fire on a village (Luke 9:54). Together they earn the title from Jesus of "Sons of Thunder" (Mark 3:17). The two of them request to be seated on Jesus' right and left in the coming kingdom (Mark 10:35-37). They are both with Jesus on the mountain of Transformation (Mark 9:2), in Gethsemane (Mark 14:33), and when Jairus' daughter is raised from the dead (Mark 5:37). John is right at the heart of Jesus' life and ministry.

CHARACTERISTICS

For those familiar with the Synoptic Gospels (Matthew, Mark, Luke), what strikes one so forcibly about John's Gospel is how different it is. John's account does not contradict the synoptics. Rather, John makes explicit what Matthew, Mark and Luke only hint at. He does not repeat material covered in the Synoptics but adds aspects of Jesus' ministry not included elsewhere. And he records for us some of Jesus' longer discourses (sermons) on great themes such as light, love, life, truth, and abiding. Here in the great I Am sections we listen to Jesus reveal who he is.

THE OMISSIONS

In John's Gospel, we find no information about Jesus' birth or His temptation. In this Gospel, Jesus casts out no demons, cures no lepers, almost never speaks in parables, and does not emphasize the "kingdom of God." John does not mention the institution of the Lord's Supper or Jesus' agony in the Garden of Gethsemane.

THE CONCLUSION

Instead, John tells us about portions of Jesus' ministry not discussed in the synoptics. We hear about Jesus' ministry before John the Baptist's imprisonment and Jesus' visits to Jerusalem. Perhaps most importantly, we read details of Jesus' ministry in Judea (the Synoptic Gospels focus on His Galilean ministry). John's Gospel is particularly rich when it comes to the teachings of Jesus.

John records for us some of the most beloved stories about Jesus: the wedding feast at Cana of Galilee (2:1-11); the night visit of Nicodemus (3:1-15); the conversation with the woman at the well (4:1-42); the raising of Lazarus from the dead (11:1-44); and the washing of the disciples' feet (13:1-17). In John's Gospel, we find the bulk of our Lord's teaching about the Holy Spirit, and here the "I" in the Sermon on the Mount in Matthew 5:21ff ("You have heard it said . . . but I tell you") becomes the majestic "I am" who is God's own Son.

STYLE

John writes in very simple Greek with a relatively small vocabulary. He often repeats words and phrases. Yet the end is a compelling document whose very simplicity makes it impressive. In fact, some scholars suggest that this Greek sounds acquired, not native. Furthermore, the writing has a strong Jewish flavoring. This is exactly what one would expect of John, the son of Zebedee—a Jew who had lived for a long time in Galilee, an area whose population included more Gentiles than Jews.

STRUCTURE

Most scholars agree that John's Gospel begins with a distinct prologue (1:1-18) and then divides into two major parts. The first part of the Gospel concentrates on Jesus' public ministry. It is organized around His miracles, "signs" that reveal who He really is. This part covers most of the three years of Jesus' ministry.

In the second part, the focus shifts from the crowds to the disciples and Jesus' private ministry among them. The theme in this section is the glory that is revealed in Jesus' crucifixion and resurrection. The time period of this segment is short: from the Thursday night of the Last Supper through Jesus' post-resurrection appearances.

Additional themes run through the book. For example, the material is grouped around the major Jewish feasts. Also, the idea of the passion of Jesus is present throughout.

John recounted events from specially selected days in Jesus' life. These events present a Savior who knows "where I came from and where I am going" (8:14). Jesus' repeated references to the One "who sent me" emphasize he is truly God's Son.

John describes Jesus as the "Word" (1:1-14), the sum of all that God wanted to say to us. God communicated in the only way we could truly understand: by becoming one of us.

PASSAGES FOR TOPICAL GROUP STUDY

2:1-11 . . . . . MIRACLES and HELPING OTHERS . . . . . . Wedding Vows
3:1-21 . . . . . . ETERNAL LIFE. . . . . A Spiritual Birth
4:1-26 . . . . . . LIVING WATER and WORSHIP . . . . It's Alive!
5:1-15 . . . . FAITH and HEALING . . . Exercising Faith Muscles
8:1-11 . . . . . . EXAMINE YOURSELF and SIN . . . . Anyone Without Sin?
8:12-20 . . . . LIGHT FOR LIFE . . . . Walking in the Light
9:1-15,24-34. . WEAKNESS and DISABILITIES . . . . Power in Weakness
11:17-44 . . . . . JESUS POWER AND LOVE . . . . . Raising the Dead
13:1-17 . . . . . . LOVE and SERVING OTHERS . . . . Washing Stinking Feet
14:15-27 . . . . . PEACE and THE HOLY SPIRIT . . . . . . Do You Really Love Me?
20:1-18 . . . . . . DEATH AND RESURRECTION . . . . . Tomb Raiders
20:24-31 . . . . . DOUBTS and BELIEVING . . . . . You Gotta Believe
21:1-14 . . . . . . RISKS and FAITH. . . . . Cast Your Nets

PROLOGUE: CHRIST, THE ETERNAL WORD

1 1 In the beginning the Word already existed.
The Word was with God,
and the Word was God.
2 He existed in the beginning with God.
3 God created everything through him,
and nothing was created except through
him.
4 The Word gave life to everything that was
created,*
and his life brought light to everyone.
5 The light shines in the darkness,
and the darkness can never extinguish it.*

6 God sent a man, John the Baptist,* 7 to tell about
the light so that everyone might believe because
of his testimony. 8 John himself was not the light; he
was simply a witness to tell about the light. 9 The one
who is the true light, who gives light to everyone, was
coming into the world.
10 He came into the very world he created, but the
world didn't recognize him. 11 He came to his own
people, and even they rejected him. 12 But to all who
believed him and accepted him, he gave the right to
become children of God. 13 They are reborn—not with
a physical birth resulting from human passion or
plan, but a birth that comes from God.
14 So the Word became human* and made his home
among us. He was full of unfailing love and faithful-
ness.* And we have seen his glory, the glory of the Fa-
ther's one and only Son.
15 John testified about him when he shouted to the
crowds, "This is the one I was talking about when I
said, 'Someone is coming after me who is far greater
than I am, for he existed long before me.'"
16 From his abundance we have all received one
gracious blessing after another.* 17 For the law was
given through Moses, but God's unfailing love and
faithfulness came through Jesus Christ. 18 No one has
ever seen God. But the unique One, who is himself
God,* is near to the Father's heart. He has revealed
God to us.

THE TESTIMONY OF JOHN THE BAPTIST

19 This was John's testimony when the Jewish leaders
sent priests and Temple assistants* from Jerusalem
to ask John, "Who are you?" 20 He came right out and
said, "I am not the Messiah."
21 "Well then, who are you?" they asked. "Are you Eli-
jah?"
"No," he replied.
"Are you the Prophet we are expecting?"*
"No."
22 "Then who are you? We need an answer for those
who sent us. What do you have to say about yourself?"
23 John replied in the words of the prophet Isaiah:

"I am a voice shouting in the wilderness,
'Clear the way for the LORD's coming!'"*

24 Then the Pharisees who had been sent 25 asked
him, "If you aren't the Messiah or Elijah or the Proph-
et, what right do you have to baptize?"
26 John told them, "I baptize with* water, but right
here in the crowd is someone you do not recognize.
27 Though his ministry follows mine, I'm not even wor-
thy to be his slave and untie the straps of his sandal."
28 This encounter took place in Bethany, an area
east of the Jordan River, where John was baptizing.

JESUS, THE LAMB OF GOD

29 The next day John saw Jesus coming toward him and
said, "Look! The Lamb of God who takes away the sin
of the world! 30 He is the one I was talking about when
I said, 'A man is coming after me who is far greater
than I am, for he existed long before me.' 31 I did not
recognize him as the Messiah, but I have been baptiz-
ing with water so that he might be revealed to Israel."
32 Then John testified, "I saw the Holy Spirit descend-
ing like a dove from heaven and resting upon him. 33 I
didn't know he was the one, but when God sent me to
baptize with water, he told me, 'The one on whom you
see the Spirit descend and rest is the one who will bap-
tize with the Holy Spirit.' 34 I saw this happen to Jesus,
so I testify that he is the Chosen One of God.*"

1:3-4 Or *and nothing that was created was created except through him. The Word gave life to everything.* **1:5** Or *and the darkness has not understood it.* **1:6** Greek *a man named John.* **1:14a** Greek *became flesh.* **1:14b** Or *grace and truth;* also in 1:17. **1:16** Or *received the grace of Christ rather than the grace of the law;* Greek reads *received grace upon grace.* **1:18** Some manuscripts read *But the one and only Son.* **1:19** Greek *and Levites.* **1:21** Greek *Are you the Prophet?* See Deut 18:15, 18; Mal 4:5-6. **1:23** Isa 40:3. **1:26** Or *in;* also in 1:31, 33. **1:34** Some manuscripts read *the Son of God.*

1:1 In the beginning. The coming of Jesus inaugurates a new creation (Gen. 1:1). **the Word.** This is the translation of the Greek word *Logos*. The Greeks taught that the *Logos* was a principle that gave order and meaning to the universe. The Old Testament spoke of the *Logos* as the divine wisdom active in creation and human affairs (Prov. 8:12-36).

1:4 life. This has a double meaning, referring to physical life and the supernatural illumination (*"the light"*) that brings spiritual life.

1:5 light . . . darkness. This is another theme borrowed from Greek philosophy that is central to John's portrait of Jesus (8:12; 12:35). The light of God shines in spite of the efforts of the powers of darkness to extinguish it.

1:6 John. John the Baptist's influence was felt from Egypt to Asia Minor (Acts 18:24-26; 19:1-4).

1:10 He came into the very world. This is the radically new dimension the gospel adds to Greek or Jewish ideas about the *Logos*: It is *not* an "it," but a person.

1:11 He came to his own people. Israel, God's own people (Gen. 17:7), especially failed to see who Jesus was (12:37-41).

1:12 children of God. Entrance into God's family does not depend on birthright or race (v. 13) but on following God's will based on belief in Jesus.

1:14 became human. The Greeks believed the flesh was so worthless that the divine would have no relationship with it. They thought of spirituality as a matter of escaping the limits of the body. **made his home among us.** Literally, "set His tent in us." This is an allusion to God's dwelling with Israel in the tabernacle (Ex. 33:7-11). Temporarily, God lived among people in human form. **Only son.** While Israel's kings were sometimes called "Sons of God" (Ps. 2), Jesus is God's Son in a unique sense (v. 18; 3:16,18).

1:17 Moses . . . Jesus. The grace of Jesus brings life, whereas the Law of Moses could only point out the failure of people before God. **Jesus Christ.** "Christ" is the Greek term for the Hebrew title "Messiah," which means "the anointed one."

1:23 Clear the way for the LORD's coming. When a royal figure traveled, a herald was sent ahead announcing the person's arrival so people could be prepared.

1:25 baptize. Prior to John, only Gentiles who converted to Judaism were baptized, as a sign of their cleansing from the pollutions of their Gentile past. **the Messiah.** The popular expectation was that the Messiah would be a military leader who would deliver Israel from the rule of the Romans.

1:29 the Lamb of God. Although Jesus is referred to as a lamb elsewhere in the Bible (1 Pet. 1:19; Rev. 5:6; 13:8), this exact title for Jesus occurs only here and in verse 36.

1:30 he existed long before me. John speaks of the pre-existence of Jesus (vv. 1-3). This is a divine quality that Jesus claimed when He declared that He predates not only John but Abraham (8:58).

1:32 the Holy Spirit . . . and resting upon him. (See Isa. 11:2; 42:1.) God's Spirit would permanently abide with the Messiah unlike the occasional movement of the Spirit on Old Testament kings and prophets.

THE FIRST DISCIPLES

35 The following day John was again standing with two of his disciples. 36 As Jesus walked by, John looked at him and declared, "Look! There is the Lamb of God!" 37 When John's two disciples heard this, they followed Jesus.

38 Jesus looked around and saw them following. "What do you want?" he asked them.

They replied, "Rabbi" (which means "Teacher"), "where are you staying?"

39 "Come and see," he said. It was about four o'clock in the afternoon when they went with him to the place where he was staying, and they remained with him the rest of the day.

40 Andrew, Simon Peter's brother, was one of these men who heard what John said and then followed Jesus. 41 Andrew went to find his brother, Simon, and told him, "We have found the Messiah" (which means "Christ"*).

42 Then Andrew brought Simon to meet Jesus. Looking intently at Simon, Jesus said, "Your name is Simon, son of John—but you will be called Cephas" (which means "Peter"*).

43 The next day Jesus decided to go to Galilee. He found Philip and said to him, "Come, follow me." 44 Philip was from Bethsaida, Andrew and Peter's hometown.

45 Philip went to look for Nathanael and told him, "We have found the very person Moses* and the prophets wrote about! His name is Jesus, the son of Joseph from Nazareth."

46 "Nazareth!" exclaimed Nathanael. "Can anything good come from Nazareth?"

"Come and see for yourself," Philip replied.

47 As they approached, Jesus said, "Now here is a genuine son of Israel—a man of complete integrity."

48 "How do you know about me?" Nathanael asked.

Jesus replied, "I could see you under the fig tree before Philip found you."

49 Then Nathanael exclaimed, "Rabbi, you are the Son of God—the King of Israel!"

50 Jesus asked him, "Do you believe this just because I told you I had seen you under the fig tree? You will see greater things than this." 51 Then he said, "I tell you the truth, you will all see heaven open and the angels of God going up and down on the Son of Man, the one who is the stairway between heaven and earth.*"

THE WEDDING AT CANA

2 The next day* there was a wedding celebration in the village of Cana in Galilee. Jesus' mother was there, 2 and Jesus and his disciples were also invited to the celebration. 3 The wine supply ran out during the festivities, so Jesus' mother told him, "They have no more wine."

4 "Dear woman, that's not our problem," Jesus replied. "My time has not yet come."

5 But his mother told the servants, "Do whatever he tells you."

6 Standing nearby were six stone water jars, used for Jewish ceremonial washing. Each could hold twenty to thirty gallons.* 7 Jesus told the servants, "Fill the jars with water." When the jars had been filled, 8 he said, "Now dip some out, and take it to the master of ceremonies." So the servants followed his instructions.

9 When the master of ceremonies tasted the water that was now wine, not knowing where it had come from (though, of course, the servants knew), he called the bridegroom over. 10 "A host always serves the best wine first," he said. "Then, when everyone has had a lot to drink, he brings out the less expensive wine. But you have kept the best until now!"

WEDDING WOES

1. Have you ever been at a wedding where things didn't go right? What happened?

JOHN 2:1-11

2. Why does Jesus initially tell His mother that her concerns and His are not the same?
3. Why does Jesus, after saying that, turn around and provide more wine?
4. Why would the Son of God concern Himself about whether there's enough wine at a wedding? What does this miracle show about Jesus?
5. How did this miracle display Jesus' glory (v. 11)?
6. How can you help meet a need of someone you know this week?

1:41 *Messiah* (a Hebrew term) and *Christ* (a Greek term) both mean "anointed one." **1:42** The names *Cephas* (from Aramaic) and *Peter* (from Greek) both mean "rock." **1:45** Greek *Moses in the law.* **1:51** Greek *going up and down on the Son of Man;* see Gen 28:10-17. "Son of Man" is a title Jesus used for himself. **2:1** Greek *On the third day;* see 1:35, 43. **2:6** Greek *2 or 3 measures* [75 to 113 liters].

1:38 Rabbi. Rabbis were teachers who gathered disciples around them. **staying.** This word hints that the concern in this question ("Where are you staying?") is on Jesus' true dwelling place. In this Gospel, recognition of Jesus' identity is tied up with recognizing where He is from and where He is going (8:21; 9:30; 14:2-6).

1:39 Come and see. Jesus invites these followers to enter into the journey of discipleship with Him. Only as they commit themselves to follow Him will they learn His true identity.

1:42 Cephas. The Aramaic name Cephas and the Greek name Peter both mean "rock." Although Peter seemed unstable at times (18:15-17,25-27), he eventually became the chief spokesman for the apostles and a leader in the early church (Acts 2:14).

1:43 Galilee. This province where Jesus was raised was 60 miles north of Jerusalem. The Pharisees couldn't believe that the Messiah would come from Galilee (7:41,52).

1:45 the very person Moses and the prophets wrote about! This refers to the Prophet to come (Deut. 18:18), the fulfillment of the Old Testament hope (v. 21).

1:46 Nazareth. This was a small, insignificant village in Galilee. It seemed impossible to Nathanael that the impressive person whom Philip described could come from such a place.

1:47 a genuine son of Israel. Nathanael came to Jesus with sincerity. Israel was supposed to be a people prepared to respond to God, but it failed to reflect that purpose.

1:50 greater things. This is probably an allusion to the miracles Jesus will perform as signs of His divine identity.

1:51 the Son of Man. Of all the titles for Jesus in this chapter, this is the one He uses for Himself. Daniel 7:13 provides its background as the one invested with divine authority to rule the earth.

2:1 a wedding celebration. Jesus' presence at this joyful occasion reminds us that He was not a sour ascetic who avoided the celebrations of life. **Cana.** This village is believed to have been near Nazareth.

2:3 The wine supply ran out. This situation was an embarrassment to the host because it suggested that he was too stingy to provide adequate refreshments for his guests. **Jesus' mother.** Mary appears only here and in 19:25. Her concern for this problem as well as her relationship to the servants (v. 5) indicates she may have been active in the planning of the wedding.

2:8 master of ceremonies. This appears to be an honored guest at the wedding, serving in a role like that of a modern-day toastmaster.

2:10 A host always serves the best wine first. Typically, the best wine was served when the guests were most able to appreciate it.

11 This miraculous sign at Cana in Galilee was the
first time Jesus revealed his glory. And his disciples
believed in him.
12 After the wedding he went to Capernaum for a
few days with his mother, his brothers, and his dis-
ciples.

JESUS CLEARS THE TEMPLE

13 It was nearly time for the Jewish Passover celebra-
tion, so Jesus went to Jerusalem. 14 In the Temple area
he saw merchants selling cattle, sheep, and doves for
sacrifices; he also saw dealers at tables exchanging
foreign money. 15 Jesus made a whip from some ropes
and chased them all out of the Temple. He drove out
the sheep and cattle, scattered the money changers'
coins over the floor, and turned over their tables.
16 Then, going over to the people who sold doves, he
told them, "Get these things out of here. Stop turning
my Father's house into a marketplace!"
17 Then his disciples remembered this prophecy
from the Scriptures: "Passion for God's house will con-
sume me."*
18 But the Jewish leaders demanded, "What are you
doing? If God gave you authority to do this, show us a
miraculous sign to prove it."
19 "All right," Jesus replied. "Destroy this temple, and
in three days I will raise it up."
20 "What!" they exclaimed. "It has taken forty-six
years to build this Temple, and you can rebuild it in
three days?" 21 But when Jesus said "this temple," he
meant his own body. 22 After he was raised from the
dead, his disciples remembered he had said this, and
they believed both the Scriptures and what Jesus had
said.

JESUS AND NICODEMUS

23 Because of the miraculous signs Jesus did in Jerusa-
lem at the Passover celebration, many began to trust
in him. 24 But Jesus didn't trust them, because he knew
all about people. 25 No one needed to tell him about
human nature, for he knew what was in each per-
son's heart.

3 There was a man named Nicodemus, a Jewish
religious leader who was a Pharisee. 2 After dark
one evening, he came to speak with Jesus. "Rabbi," he
said, "we all know that God has sent you to teach us.
Your miraculous signs are evidence that God is with
you."

A SPIRITUAL BIRTH

1. What is the favorite story your parents tell about the day you were born?

JOHN 3:1-21

2. What does it mean to be "born again" (v. 3)?
3. What is the difference between "humans can reproduce only human life" and the "Holy Spirit gives birth to spiritual life" (v. 6)?
4. What does it really mean to believe in Jesus? How would you explain it to Nicodemus?
5. How can a person have eternal life? Is there any other way to eternal life (v. 18)?
6. Are you born again? If so, how do you know? If not, would you like to be?

3 Jesus replied, "I tell you the truth, unless you
are born again,* you cannot see the Kingdom of
God."
4 "What do you mean?" exclaimed Nicodemus. "How
can an old man go back into his mother's womb and
be born again?"
5 Jesus replied, "I assure you, no one can enter the
Kingdom of God without being born of water and the
Spirit.* 6 Humans can reproduce only human life, but
the Holy Spirit gives birth to spiritual life.* 7 So don't
be surprised when I say, 'You* must be born again.'
8 The wind blows wherever it wants. Just as you can
hear the wind but can't tell where it comes from or
where it is going, so you can't explain how people are
born of the Spirit."
9 "How are these things possible?" Nicodemus
asked.
10 Jesus replied, "You are a respected Jewish teach-
er, and yet you don't understand these things? 11 I as-
sure you, we tell you what we know and have seen,
and yet you won't believe our testimony. 12 But if you
don't believe me when I tell you about earthly things,
how can you possibly believe if I tell you about heav-
enly things? 13 No one has ever gone to heaven and
returned. But the Son of Man* has come down from
heaven. 14 And as Moses lifted up the bronze snake on
a pole in the wilderness, so the Son of Man must be

2:17 Or *"Concern for God's house will be my undoing."* Ps 69:9. **3:3** Or *born from above;* also in 3:7. **3:5** Or *and spirit.* The Greek word for *Spirit* can also be translated *wind;* see 3:8. **3:6** Greek *what is born of the Spirit is spirit.* **3:7** The Greek word for *you* is plural; also in 3:12. **3:13** Some manuscripts add *who lives in heaven.* "Son of Man" is a title Jesus used for himself.

2:11 sign. John uses this term frequently to describe Jesus' miracles as more than acts of power. They pointed to God's presence in Jesus.

2:14 merchants selling cattle, sheep, and doves. This commercial activity began as a way to allow travelers to purchase animals for sacrifice at the temple rather than bringing them from long distances. But it had deteriorated into a money making scheme with the sellers charging inflated prices.

2:18 the Jewish leaders. This phrase in the Gospel of John usually refers to the religious leaders in Jerusalem and Judea who were hostile to Jesus. It has more of a political sense (i.e., "the establishment") than an ethnic one.

2:19 Destroy this temple, and in three days I will raise it up. The leaders misunderstood what Jesus means by this statement. After the resurrection, the disciples realized that Jesus was referring to Himself as the true place in which God dwells (1:14,51).

2:25 He knew all about people. The Scriptures (1 Kings 8:39) and the rabbis taught that only God could know this.

3:1 Pharisees. The Pharisees believed that religious and ethical purity was the way to secure God's favor. They were concerned for the fine points of the law, which tended to overshadow its purpose. **Nicodemus.** A respected religious authority (v. 10), Nicodemus also appears in 7:50 and 19:39 but in no other Gospel. **Jewish religious leader.** Nicodemus was a member of the Sanhedrin—the religious and political governing body of Judea.

3:3 born again. This phrase can be translated in two ways—"born again" or "born from above." "Born again" emphasizes the radical reorientation of life that results from trusting Jesus. "Born from above" declares that spiritual life is a gift from God, not something we can earn (1:12-13).

3:13 gone into heaven and returned. This Gospel's witness to Jesus is from the perspective of the whole story already told; hence the author can refer to the ascension of Jesus even at this point.

3:14 snake. Because of the Israelites' rebellion in the wilderness, God sent deadly serpents among them. Then in His mercy He instructed Moses to put a statue of a serpent on a pole. Whoever looked upon that serpent would not die (Num. 21:4-9). In a similar way, when people look with faith upon Jesus who is "lifted up" (on the cross), they are rescued from God's judgment (6:40).

lifted up, 15 so that everyone who believes in him will have eternal life.*

16 "For this is how God loved the world: He gave* his one and only Son, so that everyone who believes in him will not perish but have eternal life. 17 God sent his Son into the world not to judge the world, but to save the world through him.

18 "There is no judgment against anyone who believes in him. But anyone who does not believe in him has already been judged for not believing in God's one and only Son. 19 And the judgment is based on this fact: God's light came into the world, but people loved the darkness more than the light, for their actions were evil. 20 All who do evil hate the light and refuse to go near it for fear their sins will be exposed. 21 But those who do what is right come to the light so others can see that they are doing what God wants.*"

JOHN THE BAPTIST EXALTS JESUS

22 Then Jesus and his disciples left Jerusalem and went into the Judean countryside. Jesus spent some time with them there, baptizing people.

23 At this time John the Baptist was baptizing at Aenon, near Salim, because there was plenty of water there; and people kept coming to him for baptism. 24 (This was before John was thrown into prison.) 25 A debate broke out between John's disciples and a certain Jew* over ceremonial cleansing. 26 So John's disciples came to him and said, "Rabbi, the man you met on the other side of the Jordan River, the one you identified as the Messiah, is also baptizing people. And everybody is going to him instead of coming to us."

27 John replied, "No one can receive anything unless God gives it from heaven. 28 You yourselves know how plainly I told you, 'I am not the Messiah. I am only here to prepare the way for him.' 29 It is the bridegroom who marries the bride, and the bridegroom's friend is simply glad to stand with him and hear his vows. Therefore, I am filled with joy at his success. 30 He must become greater and greater, and I must become less and less.

31 "He has come from above and is greater than anyone else. We are of the earth, and we speak of earthly things, but he has come from heaven and is greater than anyone else.* 32 He testifies about what he has seen and heard, but how few believe what he tells them! 33 Anyone who accepts his testimony can affirm that God is true. 34 For he is sent by God. He speaks God's words, for God gives him the Spirit without limit. 35 The Father loves his Son and has put everything into his hands. 36 And anyone who believes in God's Son has eternal life. Anyone who doesn't obey the Son will never experience eternal life but remains under God's angry judgment."

JESUS AND THE SAMARITAN WOMAN

4 Jesus* knew the Pharisees had heard that he was baptizing and making more disciples than John 2 (though Jesus himself didn't baptize them—his disciples did). 3 So he left Judea and returned to Galilee.

4 He had to go through Samaria on the way. 5 Eventually he came to the Samaritan village of Sychar, near the field that Jacob gave to his son Joseph. 6 Jacob's well was there; and Jesus, tired from the long walk, sat wearily beside the well about noontime. 7 Soon a Samaritan woman came to draw water, and Jesus said to her, "Please give me a drink." 8 He was alone at the time because his disciples had gone into the village to buy some food.

9 The woman was surprised, for Jews refuse to have anything to do with Samaritans.* She said to Jesus,

IT'S ALIVE!

1. When you're really thirsty, what quenches your thirst the best?

JOHN 4:1-26

2. What is the "living water" that Jesus was talking about? What did the woman think He meant?
3. Why did Jesus tell the woman to go get her husband and bring him back? How did that question force the woman to understand what Jesus was saying?
4. What did Jesus mean when He said that "true worshipers will worship the Father in spirit and truth" (v. 23)?
5. What helps you to worship God in spirit and truth?

3:15 Or *everyone who believes will have eternal life in him.* **3:16** Or *For God loved the world so much that he gave.* **3:21** Or *can see God at work in what he is doing.* **3:25** Some manuscripts read *some Jews.* **3:31** Some manuscripts do not include *and is greater than anyone else.* **4:1** Some manuscripts read *The Lord.* **4:9** Some manuscripts do not include this sentence.

3:15 eternal life. This type of life is more than never-ending existence. It also means the quality of fullness, goodness, and perfection of life with God.

3:16 this is how God loved the world. The great motivation behind God's plan of salvation (1 John 4:9-10). **He gave.** This is demonstrated especially in Jesus' incarnation and crucifixion.

3:17 but to save the world through him. The purpose of Jesus' mission was to provide access to God for all who believe.

3:18 already been judged. It is our own behavior that condemns us. Through Jesus, God saves us from the condemnation that results from our own actions. **God's one and only Son.** Jesus is the unique Son of God because He alone fully reflects the Father.

3:19-20 light . . . darkness. Just as 3:16-18 sums up the good news of the gospel, so these verses sum up the human situation that makes the gospel necessary. The problem is not a lack of understanding of the "light" but a preference for the "darkness."

3:21 those who do what is right. This stands in parallel with "everyone who believes in Him" (v. 16) and in contrast with "everyone who practices wicked things" (v. 20). Together these phrases show that belief in Jesus and a lifestyle marked by obedience to God's ways go hand-in-hand (1 John 3:10).

3:22 into the Judean countryside . . . baptizing. The other Gospel writers do not mention this stage of Jesus' ministry. John 4:2 says it was not Jesus who baptized but His disciples.

3:26 everybody is going to him. Some of John's disciples were upset that Jesus was becoming more popular than their master.

3:29 the best man. This refers to John the Baptist, whose purpose was to prepare people for the coming of the Messiah (1:31).

4:1-3 the Pharisees had heard. The Pharisees had already investigated John (1:24-27) because of his challenge to their beliefs and authority (Matt. 3:7-10; Mark 11:27-33). Jesus' popularity fueled their suspicions as well.

4:4 Samaria. This was a territory between the provinces of Judea and Galilee. When the northern kingdom of Israel was conquered in 722 B.C. by the Assyrians, many of its people were deported. Exiles from other areas of the vast Assyrian Empire were brought in (2 Kings 17:22-41). Many of these people intermarried with the remaining Israelites and adopted some of the Jewish religious practices. In Jesus' day, strict Jews avoided Samaria as an unclean area, and the term "Samaritan" was used as an insult (8:48).

4:5 the field that Jacob gave to his son Joseph. Genesis 48:22 tells of Jacob giving some land to Joseph.

4:7 came to draw water. Translations differ in the time of day of this encounter. The Samaritan woman probably came at this time to avoid other women, perhaps because of their criticism of the life she lived.

4:9 Jews do not associate with Samaritans. Since some sects of Judaism regarded Samaritans as unclean from birth, Jesus' request shocks the woman.

"You are a Jew, and I am a Samaritan woman. Why
are you asking me for a drink?"
10 Jesus replied, "If you only knew the gift God has
for you and who you are speaking to, you would ask
me, and I would give you living water."
11 "But sir, you don't have a rope or a bucket," she
said, "and this well is very deep. Where would you get
this living water? 12 And besides, do you think you're
greater than our ancestor Jacob, who gave us this
well? How can you offer better water than he and his
sons and his animals enjoyed?"
13 Jesus replied, "Anyone who drinks this water will
soon become thirsty again. 14 But those who drink the
water I give will never be thirsty again. It becomes
a fresh, bubbling spring within them, giving them
eternal life."
15 "Please, sir," the woman said, "give me this water!
Then I'll never be thirsty again, and I won't have to
come here to get water."
16 "Go and get your husband," Jesus told her.
17 "I don't have a husband," the woman replied.
Jesus said, "You're right! You don't have a hus-
band—18 for you have had five husbands, and you ar-
en't even married to the man you're living with now.
You certainly spoke the truth!"
19 "Sir," the woman said, "you must be a prophet.
20 So tell me, why is it that you Jews insist that Jerusa-
lem is the only place of worship, while we Samaritans
claim it is here at Mount Gerizim,* where our ances-
tors worshiped?"
21 Jesus replied, "Believe me, dear woman, the time
is coming when it will no longer matter whether you
worship the Father on this mountain or in Jerusa-
lem. 22 You Samaritans know very little about the one
you worship, while we Jews know all about him, for
salvation comes through the Jews. 23 But the time is
coming—indeed it's here now—when true worship-
ers will worship the Father in spirit and in truth. The
Father is looking for those who will worship him that
way. 24 For God is Spirit, so those who worship him
must worship in spirit and in truth."
25 The woman said, "I know the Messiah is com-
ing—the one who is called Christ. When he comes, he
will explain everything to us."
26 Then Jesus told her, "I AM the Messiah!"*
27 Just then his disciples came back. They were
shocked to find him talking to a woman, but none of
them had the nerve to ask, "What do you want with
her?" or "Why are you talking to her?" 28 The woman
left her water jar beside the well and ran back to the
village, telling everyone, 29 "Come and see a man who
told me everything I ever did! Could he possibly be
the Messiah?" 30 So the people came streaming from
the village to see him.
31 Meanwhile, the disciples were urging Jesus,
"Rabbi, eat something."
32 But Jesus replied, "I have a kind of food you know
nothing about."
33 "Did someone bring him food while we were
gone?" the disciples asked each other.
34 Then Jesus explained: "My nourishment comes
from doing the will of God, who sent me, and from fin-
ishing his work. 35 You know the saying, 'Four months
between planting and harvest.' But I say, wake up and
look around. The fields are already ripe* for harvest.
36 The harvesters are paid good wages, and the fruit
they harvest is people brought to eternal life. What
joy awaits both the planter and the harvester alike!
37 You know the saying, 'One plants and another har-
vests.' And it's true. 38 I sent you to harvest where you
didn't plant; others had already done the work, and
now you will get to gather the harvest."

MANY SAMARITANS BELIEVE

39 Many Samaritans from the village believed in Jesus
because the woman had said, "He told me everything
I ever did!" 40 When they came out to see him, they
begged him to stay in their village. So he stayed for
two days, 41 long enough for many more to hear his
message and believe. 42 Then they said to the woman,
"Now we believe, not just because of what you told us,
but because we have heard him ourselves. Now we
know that he is indeed the Savior of the world."

JESUS HEALS AN OFFICIAL'S SON

43 At the end of the two days, Jesus went on to Galilee.
44 He himself had said that a prophet is not honored
in his own hometown. 45 Yet the Galileans welcomed
him, for they had been in Jerusalem at the Passover
celebration and had seen everything he did there.

4:20 Greek *on this mountain.* **4:26** Or *"The 'I AM' is here"*; or *"I am the LORD"*; Greek reads *"I am, the one speaking to you."* See Exod 3:14.
4:35 Greek *white.*

4:10 living water. This was a common phrase referring to water that flowed from a brook or spring. Water like this was better than the stagnant water of a well or a pond.

4:17-18 You're right! Women in Bible times could be divorced by their husbands for trivial reasons, but they had no right to divorce their husbands. This Samaritan woman may have been abandoned by one or more of her husbands and was a mistress to the man she was living with at this time.

4:19 prophet. Jesus' knowledge of this woman's life led her to see Him as a prophet who must be taken seriously.

4:21-24 worship the Father in spirit and in truth. In 2:18-22 Jesus had shown that He is the new temple that is superior to the physical building in Jerusalem. Here He shows that He is superior to the religious claims of the Samaritans. The point is not where a person worships but whom.

4:23 the time is coming—indeed it is here now. This captures the tension of the gospel's announcement about the kingdom of God. It is both present and future.

4:29 Come and see. This is the same invitation to discipleship extended to Andrew and Nathanael (1:39-40,46). **Could he possibly be the Messiah?** The phrase in Greek appears to require a negative answer, but it hopes for a positive response.

4:34 God, who sent me. This emphasizes Jesus' awareness of His mission and His sense of operating within His Father's will. This purpose filled Him with satisfaction ("My food").

4:35 four months between planting and harvest. This common saying may have indicated that there was no great rush to finish a task (i.e., no matter what you do, it still takes four months for the harvest to grow). Jesus contradicted that proverb by insisting that, although He has only just "sown the seed" of the gospel with the woman, already a harvest is about to be gathered. The disciples are to see the urgency of the work of the kingdom.

4:37 One plants and another harvests. By talking with this woman, Jesus harvests the work of His Father, the planter. But in verse 38 it will be the disciples who harvest what others (such as Jesus, John the Baptist, and the prophets) have planted.

4:42 Savior. This is the only place in the Gospels where this title is applied to Jesus. In the Old Testament, it refers to God as the one who rescues (Isa. 43:3,11; 49:6; Jer. 14:8). It is another reference to the deity of Christ. **of the world.** The Gospel of John emphasizes that Jesus' mission involves all types of people (3:16; 8:12; 10:16; 17:20). The religious leaders rejected Jesus, but these "unclean Samaritans"—recognizing that God's plan included them—embraced it with joy!

4:44 a prophet is not honored in his own hometown. In the other Gospels this phrase is linked to Jesus' rejection in Nazareth (Matt. 13:57; Mark 6:4; Luke 4:24). Why it is mentioned here is uncertain. It may be in anticipation of the fact that while Jesus' initial reception in Galilee would be positive (v. 45), the people would ultimately reject Him.

46 As he traveled through Galilee, he came to Cana, where he had turned the water into wine. There was a government official in nearby Capernaum whose son was very sick. 47 When he heard that Jesus had come from Judea to Galilee, he went and begged Jesus to come to Capernaum to heal his son, who was about to die.

48 Jesus asked, "Will you never believe in me unless you see miraculous signs and wonders?"

49 The official pleaded, "Lord, please come now before my little boy dies."

50 Then Jesus told him, "Go back home. Your son will live!" And the man believed what Jesus said and started home.

51 While the man was on his way, some of his servants met him with the news that his son was alive and well. 52 He asked them when the boy had begun to get better, and they replied, "Yesterday afternoon at one o'clock his fever suddenly disappeared!" 53 Then the father realized that that was the very time Jesus had told him, "Your son will live." And he and his entire household believed in Jesus. 54 This was the second miraculous sign Jesus did in Galilee after coming from Judea.

JESUS HEALS A LAME MAN

5 Afterward Jesus returned to Jerusalem for one of the Jewish holy days. 2 Inside the city, near the Sheep Gate, was the pool of Bethesda,* with five covered porches. 3 Crowds of sick people—blind, lame, or paralyzed—lay on the porches.* 5 One of the men lying there had been sick for thirty-eight years. 6 When Jesus saw him and knew he had been ill for a long time, he asked him, "Would you like to get well?"

7 "I can't, sir," the sick man said, "for I have no one to put me into the pool when the water bubbles up. Someone else always gets there ahead of me."

8 Jesus told him, "Stand up, pick up your mat, and walk!"

9 Instantly, the man was healed! He rolled up his sleeping mat and began walking! But this miracle happened on the Sabbath, 10 so the Jewish leaders objected. They said to the man who was cured, "You can't work on the Sabbath! The law doesn't allow you to carry that sleeping mat!"

11 But he replied, "The man who healed me told me, 'Pick up your mat and walk.'"

12 "Who said such a thing as that?" they demanded.

13 The man didn't know, for Jesus had disappeared into the crowd. 14 But afterward Jesus found him in the Temple and told him, "Now you are well; so stop sinning, or something even worse may happen to you." 15 Then the man went and told the Jewish leaders that it was Jesus who had healed him.

EXERCISING FAITH MUSCLES

1. How important is it to you to stay physically fit? What are you doing to keep in shape?

JOHN 5:1-15

2. Why did Jesus ask the man if he wanted to get well (vv. 5-6)?
3. Why did Jesus command him to pick up his bedroll and walk? How did that demonstrate the man's faith?
4. In what area of life might Jesus be asking you to exercise some faith?
5. Is there some healing that you need: Physical? Spiritual? Emotional? Other?

JESUS CLAIMS TO BE THE SON OF GOD

16 So the Jewish leaders began harassing* Jesus for breaking the Sabbath rules. 17 But Jesus replied, "My Father is always working, and so am I." 18 So the Jewish leaders tried all the harder to find a way to kill him. For he not only broke the Sabbath, he called God his Father, thereby making himself equal with God.

19 So Jesus explained, "I tell you the truth, the Son can do nothing by himself. He does only what he sees the Father doing. Whatever the Father does, the Son also does. 20 For the Father loves the Son and shows him everything he is doing. In fact, the Father will show him how to do even greater works than healing this man. Then you will truly be astonished. 21 For just as the Father gives life to those he raises from the dead, so the Son gives life to anyone he wants. 22 In addition, the Father judges no one. Instead, he has given the Son absolute authority to judge, 23 so that everyone will honor the Son, just as they honor the Father. Anyone who does not honor the Son is certainly not honoring the Father who sent him.

24 "I tell you the truth, those who listen to my message and believe in God who sent me have eternal life. They will never be condemned for their sins, but they have already passed from death into life.

25 "And I assure you that the time is coming, indeed it's here now, when the dead will hear my voice—the voice of the Son of God. And those who listen will live. 26 The Father has life in himself, and he has granted

5:2 Other manuscripts read *Beth-zatha;* still others read *Bethsaida*. 5:3 Some manuscripts add an expanded conclusion to verse 3 and all of verse 4: *waiting for a certain movement of the water, 4 for an angel of the Lord came from time to time and stirred up the water. And the first person to step in after the water was stirred was healed of whatever disease he had.* 5:16 Or *persecuting.*

4:48 Will you never believe…unless you see miraculous signs and wonders? The reliance on miracles as an evidence to produce faith did not meet with Jesus' approval. Such faith lacked the depth of conviction found in people who believed because of the truth of what He said.

4:50 the man believed. The man stands in contrast to the crowds in verse 48 by becoming an example of what faith in Jesus is all about—to trust His promises upon His authority.

4:54 the second miraculous sign. John's Gospel numbers only the first sign of Jesus at Cana (2:11) and this one—in spite of the fact that many other signs are alluded to and five more are spelled out.

5:2 Bethesda. This pool in Jerusalem has been excavated. Fed by intermittent springs, it was seen as a healing shrine even by second-century Roman cults.

5:7 I have no one to put me in the pool. The man did not expect to be healed by Jesus. He only hoped that Jesus might help him get into the water at the next healing opportunity.

5:10 The law doesn't allow you to carry that sleeping mat! This is one example of the many traditions the rabbis had developed to help people obey the law.

5:13 had disappeared. Apparently Jesus had not identified Himself to this man or others in the crowd. He didn't stay around to make sure He got the credit for this healing.

5:14 stop sinning, or something even worse may happen to you. Jesus did not accept the common idea that all suffering and disease were the result of personal sin (9:1-3), but in some instances sin can have earthly consequences.

5:25 the time is coming, indeed it's here now. Jesus says new life occurs as those who are spiritually dead respond to the Son who will give them true life (1:12).

that same life-giving power to his Son. [27] And he has given him authority to judge everyone because he is the Son of Man.* [28] Don't be so surprised! Indeed, the time is coming when all the dead in their graves will hear the voice of God's Son, [29] and they will rise again. Those who have done good will rise to experience eternal life, and those who have continued in evil will rise to experience judgment. [30] I can do nothing on my own. I judge as God tells me. Therefore, my judgment is just, because I carry out the will of the one who sent me, not my own will.

WITNESSES TO JESUS

[31] "If I were to testify on my own behalf, my testimony would not be valid. [32] But someone else is also testifying about me, and I assure you that everything he says about me is true. [33] In fact, you sent investigators to listen to John the Baptist, and his testimony about me was true. [34] Of course, I have no need of human witnesses, but I say these things so you might be saved. [35] John was like a burning and shining lamp, and you were excited for a while about his message. [36] But I have a greater witness than John—my teachings and my miracles. The Father gave me these works to accomplish, and they prove that he sent me. [37] And the Father who sent me has testified about me himself. You have never heard his voice or seen him face to face, [38] and you do not have his message in your hearts, because you do not believe me—the one he sent to you.

[39] "You search the Scriptures because you think they give you eternal life. But the Scriptures point to me! [40] Yet you refuse to come to me to receive this life.

[41] "Your approval means nothing to me, [42] because I know you don't have God's love within you. [43] For I have come to you in my Father's name, and you have rejected me. Yet if others come in their own name, you gladly welcome them. [44] No wonder you can't believe! For you gladly honor each other, but you don't care about the honor that comes from the one who alone is God.*

[45] "Yet it isn't I who will accuse you before the Father. Moses will accuse you! Yes, Moses, in whom you put your hopes. [46] If you really believed Moses, you would believe me, because he wrote about me. [47] But since you don't believe what he wrote, how will you believe what I say?"

JESUS FEEDS FIVE THOUSAND

6 After this, Jesus crossed over to the far side of the Sea of Galilee, also known as the Sea of Tiberias. [2] A huge crowd kept following him wherever he went, because they saw his miraculous signs as he healed the sick. [3] Then Jesus climbed a hill and sat down with his disciples around him. [4] (It was nearly time for the Jewish Passover celebration.) [5] Jesus soon saw a huge crowd of people coming to look for him. Turning to Philip, he asked, "Where can we buy bread to feed all these people?" [6] He was testing Philip, for he already knew what he was going to do.

[7] Philip replied, "Even if we worked for months, we wouldn't have enough money* to feed them!"

[8] Then Andrew, Simon Peter's brother, spoke up. [9] "There's a young boy here with five barley loaves and two fish. But what good is that with this huge crowd?"

[10] "Tell everyone to sit down," Jesus said. So they all sat down on the grassy slopes. (The men alone numbered about 5,000.) [11] Then Jesus took the loaves, gave thanks to God, and distributed them to the people. Afterward he did the same with the fish. And they all ate as much as they wanted. [12] After everyone was full, Jesus told his disciples, "Now gather the leftovers, so that nothing is wasted." [13] So they picked up the pieces and filled twelve baskets with scraps left by the people who had eaten from the five barley loaves.

[14] When the people saw him* do this miraculous sign, they exclaimed, "Surely, he is the Prophet we have been expecting!"* [15] When Jesus saw that they were ready to force him to be their king, he slipped away into the hills by himself.

JESUS WALKS ON WATER

[16] That evening Jesus' disciples went down to the shore to wait for him. [17] But as darkness fell and Jesus still hadn't come back, they got into the boat and headed across the lake toward Capernaum. [18] Soon a gale swept down upon them, and the sea grew very rough. [19] They had rowed three or four miles* when suddenly they saw Jesus walking on the water toward the boat. They were terrified, [20] but he called out to them, "Don't be afraid. I am here!*" [21] Then they were eager to let him in the boat, and immediately they arrived at their destination!

5:27 "Son of Man" is a title Jesus used for himself. **5:44** Some manuscripts read *from the only One.* **6:7** Greek *Two hundred denarii would not be enough.* A denarius was equivalent to a laborer's full day's wage. **6:14a** Some manuscripts read *Jesus.* **6:14b** See Deut 18:15, 18; Mal 4:5-6. **6:19** Greek *25 or 30 stadia* [4.6 or 5.5 kilometers]. **6:20** Or *The 'I AM' is here;* Greek reads *I am.* See Exod 3:14.

5:32 someone else. This means the Father.

5:35 John was like a burning and shining lamp. A reference to the lamp of Psalm 132:17 which God would set up to light the way for His "Anointed One."

5:45 Moses will accuse you! The Jewish religious leaders believed Jesus had rejected the law, but it was they who had abandoned it. Therefore, it was the law, in which they prided themselves, that would condemn them.

6:1 Sea of Galilee . . . Sea of Tiberias. Tiberias was a city founded on the shore of the Sea of Galilee in A.D. 20 by Herod, Roman ruler of the area. By the time this Gospel was written, this new name for the Sea of Galilee had become well known.

6:4 the Jewish Passover. Passover celebrated Israel's deliverance from Egypt (Ex. 12:1-13). At that time, each family of Israel was to sacrifice a lamb, eat it, and put its blood on the doorframes of their homes so God's avenging angel would "pass over" their houses as Egypt was punished. Hence the lamb's blood was accepted in place of their firstborn, and its flesh nourished them for their escape from Egypt. The Passover theme makes sense of the transition from "bread" to "flesh" later in verse 51 since Jesus is the true Lamb whose blood assures deliverance from God's wrath and whose flesh nurtures believers into life. This assurance is a gift each person must choose on his own.

6:9 five barley loaves and two fish. Barley bread was used by the poor because it was less expensive than wheat. From Luke 11:5 we may assume that three loaves were normally a meal. At most the boy had provisions for two people. **But what good is that with this huge crowd?** The question asked by Andrew and Philip is similar to the response of Moses when the people asked for meat in the wilderness (Num. 11:23).

6:10 numbered about 5,000. According to Matthew 14:21, this number did not include women and children.

6:14-15 surely, he is the Prophet. The people see by this action that Jesus is far more than a healer. He has done far greater things than the prophets of old.

6:16-21 The inadequacy of the crowd's assessment of Jesus as simply a political leader is shown in this scene of Old Testament allusions that reveal Jesus' divine glory to the Twelve.

6:19 three or four miles. This would be about halfway across the lake. The lake, surrounded by high hills, was often buffeted by strong winds and rainstorms.

6:20 I am here. Jesus is calming them by the assurance of His presence. He is the Son of God who controls the wind and sea, so they shouldn't be afraid (Pss. 29:3; 77:19). **Don't be afraid!** The call not to fear echoes God's assurance to Israel of His presence and protection.

JESUS, THE BREAD OF LIFE

22 The next day the crowd that had stayed on the far
shore saw that the disciples had taken the only boat,
and they realized Jesus had not gone with them.
23 Several boats from Tiberias landed near the place
where the Lord had blessed the bread and the peo-
ple had eaten. 24 So when the crowd saw that neither
Jesus nor his disciples were there, they got into the
boats and went across to Capernaum to look for him.
25 They found him on the other side of the lake and
asked, "Rabbi, when did you get here?"
26 Jesus replied, "I tell you the truth, you want to
be with me because I fed you, not because you un-
derstood the miraculous signs. 27 But don't be so con-
cerned about perishable things like food. Spend your
energy seeking the eternal life that the Son of Man*
can give you. For God the Father has given me the seal
of his approval."
28 They replied, "We want to perform God's works,
too. What should we do?"
29 Jesus told them, "This is the only work God wants
from you: Believe in the one he has sent."
30 They answered, "Show us a miraculous sign if
you want us to believe in you. What can you do? 31 Af-
ter all, our ancestors ate manna while they journeyed
through the wilderness! The Scriptures say, 'Moses
gave them bread from heaven to eat.'*"
32 Jesus said, "I tell you the truth, Moses didn't give
you bread from heaven. My Father did. And now he
offers you the true bread from heaven. 33 The true
bread of God is the one who comes down from heaven
and gives life to the world."
34 "Sir," they said, "give us that bread every day."
35 Jesus replied, "I am the bread of life. Whoever
comes to me will never be hungry again. Whoever
believes in me will never be thirsty. 36 But you haven't
believed in me even though you have seen me. 37 How-
ever, those the Father has given me will come to me,
and I will never reject them. 38 For I have come down
from heaven to do the will of God who sent me, not
to do my own will. 39 And this is the will of God, that I
should not lose even one of all those he has given me,
but that I should raise them up at the last day. 40 For it
is my Father's will that all who see his Son and believe
in him should have eternal life. I will raise them up at
the last day."
41 Then the people* began to murmur in disagree-
ment because he had said, "I am the bread that came
down from heaven." 42 They said, "Isn't this Jesus, the
son of Joseph? We know his father and mother. How
can he say, 'I came down from heaven'?"
43 But Jesus replied, "Stop complaining about what
I said. 44 For no one can come to me unless the Father
who sent me draws them to me, and at the last day I
will raise them up. 45 As it is written in the Scriptures,*
'They will all be taught by God.' Everyone who listens
to the Father and learns from him comes to me. 46 (Not
that anyone has ever seen the Father; only I, who was
sent from God, have seen him.)
47 "I tell you the truth, anyone who believes has
eternal life. 48 Yes, I am the bread of life! 49 Your ances-
tors ate manna in the wilderness, but they all died.
50 Anyone who eats the bread from heaven, howev-
er, will never die. 51 I am the living bread that came
down from heaven. Anyone who eats this bread will
live forever; and this bread, which I will offer so the
world may live, is my flesh."
52 Then the people began arguing with each other
about what he meant. "How can this man give us his
flesh to eat?" they asked.
53 So Jesus said again, "I tell you the truth, unless
you eat the flesh of the Son of Man and drink his
blood, you cannot have eternal life within you. 54 But
anyone who eats my flesh and drinks my blood has
eternal life, and I will raise that person at the last day.
55 For my flesh is true food, and my blood is true drink.
56 Anyone who eats my flesh and drinks my blood re-
mains in me, and I in him. 57 I live because of the living

6:27 "Son of Man" is a title Jesus used for himself. **6:31** Exod 16:4; Ps 78:24. **6:41** Greek *Jewish people;* also in 6:52. **6:45** Greek *in the prophets.* Isa 54:13.

6:25 Rabbi, when did you get here? Their real question of course is not "when" but "how"?

6:26 not because you understood the miraculous signs. The crowd saw Jesus only as a way of getting their physical needs met.

6:27 spend your energy seeking . . . eternal life. Jesus challenges the crowd to examine their priorities and to realize that He has come to provide the "food" that will save them from spiritual hunger and death.

6:29 This is the only work God wants from you. The crowd was looking for the laws Jesus wanted them to obey so they might have God's favor (v. 28). Jesus lets them see that only one thing is required (note the singular "work" in contrast to the plural "works"—v. 28)—belief in Him.

6:30 Show us a miraculous sign. Some messianic expectations included the idea that the Messiah would display miracles greater than those that had been performed by Moses in the wilderness. Since Jesus had only fed the people once, they referred to this specific scene in hopes that He might provide for their needs continually as Moses had done. **if you want us to believe in you.** As in 5:44, the problem was not a lack of evidence but a concern for people's praise more than God's. The people were unable to see what was going on because of their preoccupation with the things of this life.

6:34 give us that bread every day. Just as the disciples thought in physical terms when they found Jesus talking with the Samaritan woman, so do these people (4:32-33).

6:37 I will never reject them. Those who come to Jesus are a gift from the Father. As such, they enjoy a sense of ultimate security that no human can offer.

6:39 I should not lose even one of all those. Jesus' purpose was to do the Father's will. God's desire is that none of those who come to His Son would be lost but will be raised from death on the last day.

6:40 My Father's will. Two crucial themes, each emphasizing God's grace, are summed up here: (1) Salvation is open to all who will believe Jesus, and (2) Salvation is a gift to be received. It is God's desire that all people accept His gift (2 Pet. 3:9).

6:42 Isn't this Jesus, the son of Joseph? Jesus' description of Himself as "the bread that came down from heaven" evoked complaints from the religious leaders. A common saying in English is "familiarity breeds contempt." These religious leaders knew the small village Jesus came from and knew his father, Joseph. The very ordinariness of Jesus' background was a stumbling block to their seeing Jesus for Who He was (is). Their expectation was that Messiah would come as a warrior or as a heavenly Son of Man coming on clouds of glory.

6:44 No one can come to me unless. Jesus answers the religious leaders' complaints by reminding them that God draws people to Jesus. Human perception and understanding are insufficient to see what God is doing. The religious leaders and Jesus read the same Scriptures but they weren't seeing or understanding the same thing. Rabbis quoted interpretations of the Scriptures at great length. Jesus' teaching was different. He taught in a direct, authoritative style and not like the religious teachers.

6:45 They will all be taught by God. Jesus alludes to a marvelous promise in Isaiah: "Then all your children will be taught by the LORD, their prosperity will be great" (54:13). **Everyone who listens to the Father and learns from him.** The implication is that those who are listening to God will recognize and receive Jesus. The religious leaders are offended by Jesus because they are out of touch with God. Because Jesus, the Word, is the only one who has seen the Father, those who receive Him will learn much more of God than is possible apart from Jesus.

6:51 so the world may live. Like the Passover lamb, Christ's death means life to those who feed spiritually on Him.

6:54 eternal life. Jesus makes it clear that He is not talking about the Passover. The subject is eternal life.

Father who sent me; in the same way, anyone who feeds on me will live because of me. 58 I am the true bread that came down from heaven. Anyone who eats this bread will not die as your ancestors did (even though they ate the manna) but will live forever."

59 He said these things while he was teaching in the synagogue in Capernaum.

MANY DISCIPLES DESERT JESUS

60 Many of his disciples said, "This is very hard to understand. How can anyone accept it?"

61 Jesus was aware that his disciples were complaining, so he said to them, "Does this offend you? 62 Then what will you think if you see the Son of Man ascend to heaven again? 63 The Spirit alone gives eternal life. Human effort accomplishes nothing. And the very words I have spoken to you are spirit and life. 64 But some of you do not believe me." (For Jesus knew from the beginning which ones didn't believe, and he knew who would betray him.) 65 Then he said, "That is why I said that people can't come to me unless the Father gives them to me."

66 At this point many of his disciples turned away and deserted him. 67 Then Jesus turned to the Twelve and asked, "Are you also going to leave?"

68 Simon Peter replied, "Lord, to whom would we go? You have the words that give eternal life. 69 We believe, and we know you are the Holy One of God.*"

70 Then Jesus said, "I chose the twelve of you, but one is a devil." 71 He was speaking of Judas, son of Simon Iscariot, one of the Twelve, who would later betray him.

JESUS AND HIS BROTHERS

7 After this, Jesus traveled around Galilee. He wanted to stay out of Judea, where the Jewish leaders were plotting his death. 2 But soon it was time for the Jewish Festival of Shelters, 3 and Jesus' brothers said to him, "Leave here and go to Judea, where your followers can see your miracles! 4 You can't become famous if you hide like this! If you can do such wonderful things, show yourself to the world!" 5 For even his brothers didn't believe in him.

6 Jesus replied, "Now is not the right time for me to go, but you can go anytime. 7 The world can't hate you, but it does hate me because I accuse it of doing evil. 8 You go on. I'm not going* to this festival, because my time has not yet come." 9 After saying these things, Jesus remained in Galilee.

JESUS TEACHES OPENLY AT THE TEMPLE

10 But after his brothers left for the festival, Jesus also went, though secretly, staying out of public view. 11 The Jewish leaders tried to find him at the festival and kept asking if anyone had seen him. 12 There was a lot of grumbling about him among the crowds. Some argued, "He's a good man," but others said, "He's nothing but a fraud who deceives the people." 13 But no one had the courage to speak favorably about him in public, for they were afraid of getting in trouble with the Jewish leaders.

14 Then, midway through the festival, Jesus went up to the Temple and began to teach. 15 The people* were surprised when they heard him. "How does he know so much when he hasn't been trained?" they asked.

16 So Jesus told them, "My message is not my own; it comes from God who sent me. 17 Anyone who wants to do the will of God will know whether my teaching is from God or is merely my own. 18 Those who speak for themselves want glory only for themselves, but a person who seeks to honor the one who sent him speaks truth, not lies. 19 Moses gave you the law, but none of you obeys it! In fact, you are trying to kill me."

20 The crowd replied, "You're demon possessed! Who's trying to kill you?"

21 Jesus replied, "I did one miracle on the Sabbath, and you were amazed. 22 But you work on the Sabbath, too, when you obey Moses' law of circumcision. (Actually, this tradition of circumcision began with the patriarchs, long before the law of Moses.) 23 For if the correct time for circumcising your son falls on the Sabbath, you go ahead and do it so as not to break the law of Moses. So why should you be angry with me for healing a man on the Sabbath? 24 Look beneath the surface so you can judge correctly."

IS JESUS THE MESSIAH?

25 Some of the people who lived in Jerusalem started to ask each other, "Isn't this the man they are trying to kill? 26 But here he is, speaking in public, and they say nothing to him. Could our leaders possibly believe that he is the Messiah? 27 But how could he be? For we know where this man comes from. When the Messiah comes, he will simply appear; no one will know where he comes from."

28 While Jesus was teaching in the Temple, he called out, "Yes, you know me, and you know where I come from. But I'm not here on my own. The one who sent me is true, and you don't know him. 29 But I know him because I come from him, and he sent me to you." 30 Then the leaders tried to arrest him; but no one laid a hand on him, because his time* had not yet come.

31 Many among the crowds at the Temple believed in him. "After all," they said, "would you expect the Messiah to do more miraculous signs than this man has done?"

32 When the Pharisees heard that the crowds were whispering such things, they and the leading priests

6:69 Other manuscripts read *you are the Christ, the Holy One of God;* still others read *you are the Christ, the Son of God;* and still others read *you are the Christ, the Son of the living God.* **7:8** Some manuscripts read *not yet going.* **7:15** Greek *Jewish people.* **7:30** Greek *his hour.*

6:67 the Twelve. This is the first mention of the apostolic band in this Gospel (See also Mark 3:13-19). **Are you also going to leave?** In Greek, this question anticipates a negative answer.

6:68 You have the words that give eternal life. When this verse is compared with verse 63, it is clear that Peter has grasped Jesus' meaning.

7:2 Jewish Festival of Shelters. This, along with Passover and Pentecost, was a major feast when Jews from all over the Roman empire gathered in Jerusalem. This feast celebrated God's provision for Israel during their years of wandering in the wilderness (Lev. 23:39). By this time, it had also become a Thanksgiving celebration for the harvest (v. 37).

7:3-5 Jesus' brothers said to him. The urging of Jesus' brothers bears similarities to that of His mother in John 2:3-5. Members of His family members are trying to advise Him about how He should carry out His mission. Verse 5 shows that His brothers, like the crowds in 6:66, misunderstood the nature of Jesus as Messiah and His mission on earth.

7:22-23 circumcision. Circumcision, a sign of God's covenant with His people, was initiated long before Moses by Abraham (Gen. 17). Yet circumcision was reinforced by Moses' Law which required that a male child be circumcised eight days after birth. Pharisaic tradition held that since the law of circumcision was more important than the laws prohibiting work on the Sabbath, it was lawful to circumcise a child on the Sabbath. Jesus uses their logic against them (v. 23). If it is lawful to perform an act that led to a person's ceremonial perfection on the Sabbath, how could it be wrong for Him to restore a person to wholeness on that day?

sent Temple guards to arrest Jesus. 33 But Jesus told them, "I will be with you only a little longer. Then I will return to the one who sent me. 34 You will search for me but not find me. And you cannot go where I am going."

35 The Jewish leaders were puzzled by this statement. "Where is he planning to go?" they asked. "Is he thinking of leaving the country and going to the Jews in other lands?* Maybe he will even teach the Greeks! 36 What does he mean when he says, 'You will search for me but not find me,' and 'You cannot go where I am going'?"

JESUS PROMISES LIVING WATER

37 On the last day, the climax of the festival, Jesus stood and shouted to the crowds, "Anyone who is thirsty may come to me! 38 Anyone who believes in me may come and drink! For the Scriptures declare, 'Rivers of living water will flow from his heart.'"* 39 (When he said "living water," he was speaking of the Spirit, who would be given to everyone believing in him. But the Spirit had not yet been given,* because Jesus had not yet entered into his glory.)

DIVISION AND UNBELIEF

40 When the crowds heard him say this, some of them declared, "Surely this man is the Prophet we've been expecting."* 41 Others said, "He is the Messiah." Still others said, "But he can't be! Will the Messiah come from Galilee? 42 For the Scriptures clearly state that the Messiah will be born of the royal line of David, in Bethlehem, the village where King David was born."* 43 So the crowd was divided about him. 44 Some even wanted him arrested, but no one laid a hand on him.

45 When the Temple guards returned without having arrested Jesus, the leading priests and Pharisees demanded, "Why didn't you bring him in?"

46 "We have never heard anyone speak like this!" the guards responded.

47 "Have you been led astray, too?" the Pharisees mocked. 48 "Is there a single one of us rulers or Pharisees who believes in him? 49 This foolish crowd follows him, but they are ignorant of the law. God's curse is on them!"

50 Then Nicodemus, the leader who had met with Jesus earlier, spoke up. 51 "Is it legal to convict a man before he is given a hearing?" he asked.

52 They replied, "Are you from Galilee, too? Search the Scriptures and see for yourself—no prophet ever comes* from Galilee!"

[The most ancient Greek manuscripts do not include John 7:53–8:11.]

53 Then the meeting broke up, and everybody went home.

A WOMAN CAUGHT IN ADULTERY

8 Jesus returned to the Mount of Olives, 2 but early the next morning he was back again at the Temple. A crowd soon gathered, and he sat down and taught them. 3 As he was speaking, the teachers of religious law and the Pharisees brought a woman who had been caught in the act of adultery. They put her in front of the crowd.

4 "Teacher," they said to Jesus, "this woman was caught in the act of adultery. 5 The law of Moses says to stone her. What do you say?"

6 They were trying to trap him into saying something they could use against him, but Jesus stooped down and wrote in the dust with his finger. 7 They kept demanding an answer, so he stood up again and

ANYONE WITHOUT SIN?

1. Have you ever written with chalk on the sidewalk? What things have you drawn or written?

JOHN 8:1-11

2. How was the Pharisees' question intended to trap Jesus? How did He turn the trap back on them instead?
3. Who in the group had "never sinned" (vv. 7-9)? Who in the group had the right to condemn or forgive sins?
4. What lesson was Jesus teaching here: Adultery is okay? Forgive others? Repent and stop sinning? Examine your own life instead of others?
5. How can you help others who are living in sin?

7:35 Or *the Jews who live among the Greeks?* **7:37-38** Or *"Let anyone who is thirsty come to me and drink. 38 For the Scriptures declare, 'Rivers of living water will flow from the heart of anyone who believes in me.'"* **7:39** Several early manuscripts read *But as yet there was no Spirit.* Still others read *But as yet there was no Holy Spirit.* **7:40** See Deut 18:15, 18; Mal 4:5-6. **7:42** See Mic 5:2. **7:52** Some manuscripts read *the prophet does not come.*

7:37 Anyone who is thirsty may come to me! The vision in Ezekiel 47:1-12 of water flowing from the temple giving life to all the surrounding area is in view as Jesus, the new temple of God (2:19), who provides the water of life to all who believe.

8:3 the teachers of religious law and the Pharisees. The teachers of the law, or scribes, are not mentioned in the Gospel of John, but they play a prominent part in the other Gospels. They were ordained teachers, serving as the representatives of Moses in interpreting the law. They were taught as rabbis and acted as lawyers in legal cases. **a woman . . . caught in the act of adultery.** Since this sin cannot be committed alone, why was only one offender brought before the temple courts? The teachers of the law and the Pharisees likely staged this to trap Jesus (v. 6).

8:5 The law of Moses says to stone her. This was only partially true. Leviticus 20:10 and Deuteronomy 22:22 prescribe that both parties should be put to death. Since it was said that the woman was caught in the act, the man was also there and should have been brought in as well. The Jews, under Roman law, had no authority to carry out such sentences. In Israel's past, this penalty was rarely carried out because capital offenses required two or three witnesses. The normal result of adultery (on the part of a woman) was divorce. Women could not divorce their husbands for any reason.

8:6 They were trying to trap him. See also Matthew 19:3 and 22:15 for other situations where Jesus' enemies attempted to find some reason for making a charge against Him. In this case, if He allowed stoning, He would be in violation of Roman law and would be considered stricter than even the Pharisees in His application of the law. If Jesus tried to release her, He could be faulted for ignoring the Law of Moses. **wrote in the dust with his finger.** It is uncertain what Jesus wrote. But speculation centers on the possibility that He may have been writing the other commandments, which would remind the onlookers of commandments *they* may have broken.

8:7 let the one who has never sinned. Jesus affirms the validity of the law but forces the initiative back on the accusers. Perhaps some of them were reminded of times when they "sowed some wild oats." This statement does not imply that judicial cases can only be tried by sinless people. But it is a rebuke to the motives of these leaders who ignored their own sins while using this woman to implicate Jesus.

said, "All right, but let the one who has never sinned
throw the first stone!" 8 Then he stooped down again
and wrote in the dust.
9 When the accusers heard this, they slipped away one
by one, beginning with the oldest, until only Jesus was
left in the middle of the crowd with the woman. 10 Then
Jesus stood up again and said to the woman, "Where are
your accusers? Didn't even one of them condemn you?"
11 "No, Lord," she said.
And Jesus said, "Neither do I. Go and sin no more."

JESUS, THE LIGHT OF THE WORLD

12 Jesus spoke to the people once more and said, "I am
the light of the world. If you follow me, you won't
have to walk in darkness, because you will have the
light that leads to life."
13 The Pharisees replied, "You are making those
claims about yourself! Such testimony is not valid."
14 Jesus told them, "These claims are valid even
though I make them about myself. For I know where
I came from and where I am going, but you don't
know this about me. 15 You judge me by human stan-
dards, but I do not judge anyone. 16 And if I did, my
judgment would be correct in every respect because
I am not alone. The Father* who sent me is with me.
17 Your own law says that if two people agree about
something, their witness is accepted as fact.* 18 I am
one witness, and my Father who sent me is the other."
19 "Where is your father?" they asked.
Jesus answered, "Since you don't know who I am,
you don't know who my Father is. If you knew me,
you would also know my Father." 20 Jesus made these
statements while he was teaching in the section of the
Temple known as the Treasury. But he was not arrest-
ed, because his time* had not yet come.

THE UNBELIEVING PEOPLE WARNED

21 Later Jesus said to them again, "I am going away.
You will search for me but will die in your sin. You
cannot come where I am going."
22 The people* asked, "Is he planning to commit sui-
cide? What does he mean, 'You cannot come where I
am going'?"
23 Jesus continued, "You are from below; I am from
above. You belong to this world; I do not. 24 That is
why I said that you will die in your sins; for unless
you believe that I AM who I claim to be,* you will die
in your sins."
25 "Who are you?" they demanded.
Jesus replied, "The one I have always claimed to be.*
26 I have much to say about you and much to condemn,
but I won't. For I say only what I have heard from the
one who sent me, and he is completely truthful." 27 But
they still didn't understand that he was talking about
his Father.
28 So Jesus said, "When you have lifted up the Son of
Man on the cross, then you will understand that I AM
he.* I do nothing on my own but say only what the
Father taught me. 29 And the one who sent me is with
me—he has not deserted me. For I always do what
pleases him." 30 Then many who heard him say these
things believed in him.

JESUS AND ABRAHAM

31 Jesus said to the people who believed in him, "You
are truly my disciples if you remain faithful to my

WALKING IN THE LIGHT

1. When have you witnessed an accident or crime? Were you called to testify as a witness?
2. What do you have in common with your dad? What's something important he taught you?

JOHN 8:12-20

3. How is Jesus "the light of the world" (v. 12a)? How does it feel to know that by following Him "you won't have to walk in darkness, because you will have the light that leads to life" (v. 12b)?
4. What did Jesus mean that the Pharisees judge "by human standards" (v. 15)? How can we learn to judge by God's standards?
5. Are you walking in Jesus' light or in darkness?

8:16 Some manuscripts read *The One.* **8:17** See Deut 19:15. **8:20** Greek *his hour.* **8:22** Greek *Jewish people;* also in 8:31, 48, 52, 57. **8:24** Greek *unless you believe that I am.* See Exod 3:14. **8:25** Or *Why do I speak to you at all?* **8:28** Greek *When you have lifted up the Son of Man, then you will know that I am.* "Son of Man" is a title Jesus used for himself.

8:9 beginning with the oldest. The older men may have had the wisdom of experience to recognize their own fallibilities more readily.
8:11 Neither do I. This story illustrates the truth of 3:17. The woman had come face-to-face with condemnation, shame, and death, but she was pardoned by the One to whom all judgment has been given (5:22). **Go and sin no more.** The compassion and mercy of Jesus is related to His call to people to live in obedience to the will of His Father. Paul, likewise, rejects the idea that people can claim God's mercy, while pursuing a lifestyle in opposition to His will (Rom. 6:1-2, 15).
8:12 Jesus spoke to the people once more. The place for this exchange between Jesus and the religious leaders is probably the Feast of Tabernacles (7:2). **I am the light of the world.** Jesus makes another bold assertion coupled with the promise that those who follow Him will not walk in darkness. Because the religious leaders were out of touch with God, they were walking in darkness and leading those who followed them away from the light. There is tragic irony here that the One who had created them and longed to dispel their darkness was viewed as an enemy.
8:13 Such testimony is not valid. The religious leaders viewed Jesus' assertion to be the light of the world as lacking support. They were challenging Him to bring forth evidence to support His claim.
8:14 even though I make them about myself. Jesus answers their challenge by saying that His claim about Himself is based on His knowing where he came from and where he is going.
8:17 Your own law says . . . their witness is accepted as fact. Jesus reminds the religious leaders of the rules of evidence in their law. No one could be put to death on the testimony of just one witness (Num. 35:30). At least two witnesses had to testify to the guilt of the accused. Jesus argues that His claim to be the light of the world has two witnesses: He and the Father, two impeccable witnesses. But from the perspective of the religious leaders, this amounted to no witnesses at all.
8:28 lifted up the Son of Man. This is to say, "crucify" Him.
8:31 if you remain faithful to my teachings. Witnessing Jesus' miracles and hearing His teachings and conversations with the religious leaders, many Jews had come to believe His claims. To these who had come to an intellectual belief, Jesus sets forth the condition of being His followers. The condition is as true today as it was when Jesus first uttered these words: stay in My word. Again, this is more than an intellectual knowledge of His word. The religious leaders of Jesus' time had God's Word. They memorized it and could quote it readily. The problem was that for most of them the Word didn't move from their heads to their hearts. There was nothing wrong with the Word. It had fallen onto hard ground, rocky ground, or among thorns (Mk. 4:1-20). The condition of the hearer will be a limiting or an enriching factor when God's Word is spoken. To stay in Jesus' word is to be transformed.

teachings. 32 And you will know the truth, and the truth will set you free."

33 "But we are descendants of Abraham," they said. "We have never been slaves to anyone. What do you mean, 'You will be set free'?"

34 Jesus replied, "I tell you the truth, everyone who sins is a slave of sin. 35 A slave is not a permanent member of the family, but a son is part of the family forever. 36 So if the Son sets you free, you are truly free. 37 Yes, I realize that you are descendants of Abraham. And yet some of you are trying to kill me because there's no room in your hearts for my message. 38 I am telling you what I saw when I was with my Father. But you are following the advice of your father."

39 "Our father is Abraham!" they declared.

"No," Jesus replied, "for if you were really the children of Abraham, you would follow his example.* 40 Instead, you are trying to kill me because I told you the truth, which I heard from God. Abraham never did such a thing. 41 No, you are imitating your real father."

They replied, "We aren't illegitimate children! God himself is our true Father."

42 Jesus told them, "If God were your Father, you would love me, because I have come to you from God. I am not here on my own, but he sent me. 43 Why can't you understand what I am saying? It's because you can't even hear me! 44 For you are the children of your father the devil, and you love to do the evil things he does. He was a murderer from the beginning. He has always hated the truth, because there is no truth in him. When he lies, it is consistent with his character; for he is a liar and the father of lies. 45 So when I tell the truth, you just naturally don't believe me! 46 Which of you can truthfully accuse me of sin? And since I am telling you the truth, why don't you believe me? 47 Anyone who belongs to God listens gladly to the words of God. But you don't listen because you don't belong to God."

48 The people retorted, "You Samaritan devil! Didn't we say all along that you were possessed by a demon?"

49 "No," Jesus said, "I have no demon in me. For I honor my Father—and you dishonor me. 50 And though I have no wish to glorify myself, God is going to glorify me. He is the true judge. 51 I tell you the truth, anyone who obeys my teaching will never die!"

52 The people said, "Now we know you are possessed by a demon. Even Abraham and the prophets died, but you say, 'Anyone who obeys my teaching will never die!' 53 Are you greater than our father Abraham? He died, and so did the prophets. Who do you think you are?"

54 Jesus answered, "If I want glory for myself, it doesn't count. But it is my Father who will glorify me. You say, 'He is our God,'* 55 but you don't even know him. I know him. If I said otherwise, I would be as great a liar as you! But I do know him and obey him. 56 Your father Abraham rejoiced as he looked forward to my coming. He saw it and was glad."

57 The people said, "You aren't even fifty years old. How can you say you have seen Abraham?*"

58 Jesus answered, "I tell you the truth, before Abraham was even born, I Am!*" 59 At that point they picked up stones to throw at him. But Jesus was hidden from them and left the Temple.

JESUS HEALS A MAN BORN BLIND

9 As Jesus was walking along, he saw a man who had been blind from birth. 2 "Rabbi," his disciples asked him, "why was this man born blind? Was it because of his own sins or his parents' sins?"

3 "It was not because of his sins or his parents' sins," Jesus answered. "This happened so the power of God could be seen in him. 4 We must quickly carry out the tasks assigned us by the one who sent us.* The night is coming, and then no one can work. 5 But while I am here in the world, I am the light of the world."

6 Then he spit on the ground, made mud with the saliva, and spread the mud over the blind man's eyes. 7 He told him, "Go wash yourself in the pool of Siloam" (Siloam means "sent"). So the man went and washed and came back seeing!

8 His neighbors and others who knew him as a blind beggar asked each other, "Isn't this the man who used to sit and beg?" 9 Some said he was, and others said, "No, he just looks like him!"

But the beggar kept saying, "Yes, I am the same one!"

10 They asked, "Who healed you? What happened?"

11 He told them, "The man they call Jesus made mud and spread it over my eyes and told me, 'Go to the pool of Siloam and wash yourself.' So I went and washed, and now I can see!"

8:39 Some manuscripts read *if you are really the children of Abraham, follow his example.* **8:54** Some manuscripts read *You say he is your God.* **8:57** Some manuscripts read *How can you say Abraham has seen you?* **8:58** Or *before Abraham was even born, I have always been alive;* Greek reads *before Abraham was, I am.* See Exod 3:14. **9:4** Other manuscripts read *I must quickly carry out the tasks assigned me by the one who sent me;* still others read *We must quickly carry out the tasks assigned us by the one who sent me.*

8:32 the truth will set you free. Jesus brings together two short but powerful words: *truth and freedom*. This saying is often quoted out of context in academic settings to support the claim that there is a strong link between intellectual pursuits and human freedom. The truth Jesus is talking about is not just intellectual. Being set free is not being able to do as we wish.

8:33 we are descendents of Abraham. The religious leaders responded by saying that they didn't need to be set free. They are children of Abraham.

8:34 everyone who sins is a slave of sin. In this verse, the freedom Jesus spoke of in 8:32 and 8:36 becomes clearer. The freedom that every human being needs is freedom from sin. Sin is a cruel taskmaster. Truth is a gift of God that enables humans to see both the problem and its solution.

8:36 if the Son sets you free. The source of spiritual freedom is found in Jesus. Here He offers the solution to the problem He posed in verse 34.

8:41 your real father. Having denied that they are Abraham's children in verse 40, Jesus' statement here raises the question of whose children they really are. **We aren't illegitimate children!** The crowd was probably referring to the irregular circumstances behind Jesus' birth.

8:59 they picked up stones. Stoning was the punishment for blasphemy against "the name of the Lord" (Lev. 24:16). The incredulity and scorn of verses 52 and 57 turn to fury at Jesus' bold assertion in verse 58.

9:1 As Jesus was walking along. An indefinite time reference. **blind from birth.** The story of the healing of the blind man, which extends through 10:21, illustrates Jesus' ability to give new life to people in hopeless situations and the implications of discipleship in the face of opposition.

9:2 his disciples. These disciples may be the Twelve or a broader group of Judean followers. **his own sins or his parents' sins?** Despite the book of Job's teaching, the rabbis taught that a person's misfortune was the result of his sin or a punishment inherited because of one's parents' sins. Some people taught that such handicaps were a punishment for the sin that the child in the womb had committed (Luke 13:1-5). Ezekiel taught that people would not be punished by God for the sins of their parents, but the belief in such retribution lingered (Ezek. 18). **born blind.** The emphasis is on the fact that this man was born with this disability (vv. 1, 19-20, 32). This not only points out the longevity of his problem but underscores the theological emphasis that people who are not "born again" will not "see the kingdom of God" (3:3). They walk in darkness (8:12).

9:3 not because of his sins or his parents' sins. Jesus is not pronouncing the family sinless but is dismissing the disciples' interest in the *cause* of the man's blindness. He focuses their attention on its *purpose*.

POWER IN WEAKNESS

1. When you were a kid, what was your favorite "mud game?"

JOHN 9:1-15,24-34

2. Why was this man born blind? What does this teach us about one reason for suffering in life?
3. When did the man actually start seeing (v. 11)? What does this teach us about God's healing and our own obedience?
4. How can a weakness in your life turn into an opportunity for God to show His power?
5. The Pharisees asked the blind man who Jesus was. How would you answer that question?

12 "Where is he now?" they asked.
"I don't know," he replied.
13 Then they took the man who had been blind to the Pharisees, 14 because it was on the Sabbath that Jesus had made the mud and healed him. 15 The Pharisees asked the man all about it. So he told them, "He put the mud over my eyes, and when I washed it away, I could see!"
16 Some of the Pharisees said, "This man Jesus is not from God, for he is working on the Sabbath." Others said, "But how could an ordinary sinner do such miraculous signs?" So there was a deep division of opinion among them.
17 Then the Pharisees again questioned the man who had been blind and demanded, "What's your opinion about this man who healed you?"
The man replied, "I think he must be a prophet."
18 The Jewish leaders still refused to believe the man had been blind and could now see, so they called in his parents. 19 They asked them, "Is this your son? Was he born blind? If so, how can he now see?"
20 His parents replied, "We know this is our son and that he was born blind, 21 but we don't know how he can see or who healed him. Ask him. He is old enough to speak for himself." 22 His parents said this because they were afraid of the Jewish leaders, who had announced that anyone saying Jesus was the Messiah would be expelled from the synagogue. 23 That's why they said, "He is old enough. Ask him."
24 So for the second time they called in the man who had been blind and told him, "God should get the glory for this,* because we know this man Jesus is a sinner."
25 "I don't know whether he is a sinner," the man replied. "But I know this: I was blind, and now I can see!"
26 "But what did he do?" they asked. "How did he heal you?"
27 "Look!" the man exclaimed. "I told you once. Didn't you listen? Why do you want to hear it again? Do you want to become his disciples, too?"
28 Then they cursed him and said, "You are his disciple, but we are disciples of Moses! 29 We know God spoke to Moses, but we don't even know where this man comes from."
30 "Why, that's very strange!" the man replied. "He healed my eyes, and yet you don't know where he comes from? 31 We know that God doesn't listen to sinners, but he is ready to hear those who worship him and do his will. 32 Ever since the world began, no one has been able to open the eyes of someone born blind. 33 If this man were not from God, he couldn't have done it."
34 "You were born a total sinner!" they answered. "Are you trying to teach us?" And they threw him out of the synagogue.

SPIRITUAL BLINDNESS

35 When Jesus heard what had happened, he found the man and asked, "Do you believe in the Son of Man?*"
36 The man answered, "Who is he, sir? I want to believe in him."
37 "You have seen him," Jesus said, "and he is speaking to you!"
38 "Yes, Lord, I believe!" the man said. And he worshiped Jesus.
39 Then Jesus told him,* "I entered this world to render judgment—to give sight to the blind and to show those who think they see* that they are blind."
40 Some Pharisees who were standing nearby heard him and asked, "Are you saying we're blind?"
41 "If you were blind, you wouldn't be guilty," Jesus replied. "But you remain guilty because you claim you can see.

THE GOOD SHEPHERD AND HIS SHEEP

10 "I tell you the truth, anyone who sneaks over the wall of a sheepfold, rather than going through the gate, must surely be a thief and a robber! 2 But the one who enters through the gate is the shepherd of the sheep. 3 The gatekeeper opens the gate for him, and the sheep recognize his voice and come to him. He calls his own sheep by name and leads them out. 4 After he has gathered his own flock, he walks ahead of them, and they follow him because they know his

9:24 Or *Give glory to God, not to Jesus;* Greek reads *Give glory to God.* 9:35 Some manuscripts read *the Son of God?* "Son of Man" is a title Jesus used for himself. 9:38-39a Some manuscripts do not include *"Yes, Lord, I believe!" the man said. And he worshiped Jesus. Then Jesus told him.* 9:39b Greek *those who see.*

9:21 He is old enough. The legal age was 13. The parents affirm he is old enough to speak for himself.

9:22 the Jewish leaders. From the account in 12:42, it is clear that the Pharisaic leaders are referred to here. They found Jesus offensive because He broke the traditional interpretations of the Mosaic Law which they attempted to keep in such detail.

9:24 God should get the glory for this. Although this saying is equivalent to the modern-day oath to "tell the truth, the whole truth, and nothing but the truth," the man did indeed give glory to God by affirming his conviction about Jesus, even though this was the exact opposite of what the Pharisees intended.

9:29 we don't even know where this man comes from. This implies that Jesus, unlike Moses, had no connection with God.

9:35 heard what had happened. Jesus said that He would never drive away those who came to Him (6:37). In contrast, the Pharisees reject those who are drawn by the Father.

10:1 sheepfold. At night sheep were herded into enclosures made of stone as a protection against predators and thieves.

10:3 The gatekeeper. Although both the shepherd and the gate clearly represent Jesus (vv. 7, 11), the figure of the watchman is not explained. In a parable, unlike an allegory, not all the details have a meaning. **calls his own sheep by name.** Shepherds had names and distinctive calls for their sheep. These calls helped them separate their flocks from other herds mixed in with their sheep in a sheep pen.

voice. 5 They won't follow a stranger; they will run from him because they don't know his voice."

6 Those who heard Jesus use this illustration didn't understand what he meant, 7 so he explained it to them: "I tell you the truth, I am the gate for the sheep. 8 All who came before me* were thieves and robbers. But the true sheep did not listen to them. 9 Yes, I am the gate. Those who come in through me will be saved.* They will come and go freely and will find good pastures. 10 The thief's purpose is to steal and kill and destroy. My purpose is to give them a rich and satisfying life.

11 "I am the good shepherd. The good shepherd sacrifices his life for the sheep. 12 A hired hand will run when he sees a wolf coming. He will abandon the sheep because they don't belong to him and he isn't their shepherd. And so the wolf attacks them and scatters the flock. 13 The hired hand runs away because he's working only for the money and doesn't really care about the sheep.

14 "I am the good shepherd; I know my own sheep, and they know me, 15 just as my Father knows me and I know the Father. So I sacrifice my life for the sheep. 16 I have other sheep, too, that are not in this sheepfold. I must bring them also. They will listen to my voice, and there will be one flock with one shepherd.

17 "The Father loves me because I sacrifice my life so I may take it back again. 18 No one can take my life from me. I sacrifice it voluntarily. For I have the authority to lay it down when I want to and also to take it up again. For this is what my Father has commanded."

19 When he said these things, the people* were again divided in their opinions about him. 20 Some said, "He's demon possessed and out of his mind. Why listen to a man like that?" 21 Others said, "This doesn't sound like a man possessed by a demon! Can a demon open the eyes of the blind?"

JESUS CLAIMS TO BE THE SON OF GOD

22 It was now winter, and Jesus was in Jerusalem at the time of Hanukkah, the Festival of Dedication. 23 He was in the Temple, walking through the section known as Solomon's Colonnade. 24 The people surrounded him and asked, "How long are you going to keep us in suspense? If you are the Messiah, tell us plainly."

25 Jesus replied, "I have already told you, and you don't believe me. The proof is the work I do in my Father's name. 26 But you don't believe me because you are not my sheep. 27 My sheep listen to my voice; I know them, and they follow me. 28 I give them eternal life, and they will never perish. No one can snatch them away from me, 29 for my Father has given them to me, and he is more powerful than anyone else.* No one can snatch them from the Father's hand. 30 The Father and I are one."

31 Once again the people picked up stones to kill him. 32 Jesus said, "At my Father's direction I have done many good works. For which one are you going to stone me?"

33 They replied, "We're stoning you not for any good work, but for blasphemy! You, a mere man, claim to be God."

34 Jesus replied, "It is written in your own Scriptures* that God said to certain leaders of the people, 'I say, you are gods!'* 35 And you know that the Scriptures cannot be altered. So if those people who received God's message were called 'gods,' 36 why do you call it blasphemy when I say, 'I am the Son of God'? After all, the Father set me apart and sent me into the world. 37 Don't believe me unless I carry out my Father's work. 38 But if I do his work, believe in the evidence of the miraculous works I have done, even if you don't believe me. Then you will know and understand that the Father is in me, and I am in the Father."

39 Once again they tried to arrest him, but he got away and left them. 40 He went beyond the Jordan River near the place where John was first baptizing and stayed there awhile. 41 And many followed him. "John didn't perform miraculous signs," they remarked to one another, "but everything he said about this man has come true." 42 And many who were there believed in Jesus.

THE RAISING OF LAZARUS

11 A man named Lazarus was sick. He lived in Bethany with his sisters, Mary and Martha. 2 This is the Mary who later poured the expensive perfume on the Lord's feet and wiped them with her hair.* Her brother, Lazarus, was sick. 3 So the two sisters sent a message to Jesus telling him, "Lord, your dear friend is very sick."

4 But when Jesus heard about it he said, "Lazarus's sickness will not end in death. No, it happened for the glory of God so that the Son of God will receive glory from this." 5 So although Jesus loved Martha, Mary,

10:8 Some manuscripts do not include *before me.* **10:9** Or *will find safety.* **10:19** Greek *Jewish people;* also in 10:24, 31. **10:29** Other manuscripts read *for what my Father has given me is more powerful than anything;* still others read *for regarding that which my Father has given me, he is greater than all.* **10:34a** Greek *your own law.* **10:34b** Ps 82:6. **11:2** This incident is recorded in chapter 12.

10:7 I am the gate. This symbol is stated forthrightly in 14:6 where Jesus says He is the way to God.

10:8 thieves and robbers. Jesus is referring to the religious leaders who exploit the people for their own advantage (2:14-15; Ezek. 34:1-6)

10:10 rich and satisfying life. The eternal life a person has in Christ means more than length of life. It includes quality of life as well.

10:11 I am the good shepherd. In contrast to the hired hands who run away at danger, the true shepherd cares for the flock at risk of his life (1 Sam. 17:34-35). The image of the ruler as a shepherd was common in Israel (Ps. 23; Ezek. 34).

10:14 I know my own sheep. "To know" means "to love" (v. 17).

10:15 I sacrifice my life. This phrase accents the voluntary nature of Jesus' death (v. 18).

10:16 I have other sheep, too, that are not in this sheepfold. Since the Gospel of John has consistently emphasized that Jesus' mission was not just for Jews but for the entire world, it is likely that this is the meaning here. **one flock with one shepherd.** The Christian community is not to be marred by divisions, but it should model unity across racial and ethnic lines as all people respond to the voice of the Great Shepherd (11:52; Eph. 2:11-22).

10:22 Festival of Dedication. This feast (Hanukkah) commemorated Judas Maccabeus' deliverance of Jerusalem—and the temple—from the tyranny of the Syrian (Selucid) king, Antiochus Epiphanes, who had profaned the temple by placing a statue of the Greek god Zeus in the Most Holy Place. The Pharisees try to get Jesus to proclaim Himself as the Messiah so he will attract the attention and the displeasure of Rome.

10:23 Solomon's Colonnade. This was a large covered porch on the east side of the temple. The porch was constructed on a foundation that was believed to have been part of the original temple built by King Solomon.

11:2 Mary. Apparently the author of the Gospel of John, aware that the story of Jesus' anointing was a familiar one to his readers, used this incident to identify Mary, even though it doesn't occur in this Gospel until chapter 12 (Mark 14:1-11).

11:4 the Son of God will receive glory from this. All the signs in this Gospel were meant as a demonstration of the reality of Jesus' unity with the Father (10:25-30).

and Lazarus, 6 he stayed where he was for the next
two days. 7 Finally, he said to his disciples, "Let's go
back to Judea."
8 But his disciples objected. "Rabbi," they said, "only
a few days ago the people* in Judea were trying to
stone you. Are you going there again?"
9 Jesus replied, "There are twelve hours of daylight
every day. During the day people can walk safe-
ly. They can see because they have the light of this
world. 10 But at night there is danger of stumbling be-
cause they have no light." 11 Then he said, "Our friend
Lazarus has fallen asleep, but now I will go and wake
him up."
12 The disciples said, "Lord, if he is sleeping, he will
soon get better!" 13 They thought Jesus meant Lazarus
was simply sleeping, but Jesus meant Lazarus had
died.
14 So he told them plainly, "Lazarus is dead. 15 And
for your sakes, I'm glad I wasn't there, for now you
will really believe. Come, let's go see him."
16 Thomas, nicknamed the Twin,* said to his fellow
disciples, "Let's go, too—and die with Jesus."
17 When Jesus arrived at Bethany, he was told that
Lazarus had already been in his grave for four days.
18 Bethany was only a few miles* down the road from
Jerusalem, 19 and many of the people had come to con-
sole Martha and Mary in their loss. 20 When Martha
got word that Jesus was coming, she went to meet
him. But Mary stayed in the house. 21 Martha said to
Jesus, "Lord, if only you had been here, my brother
would not have died. 22 But even now I know that God
will give you whatever you ask."
23 Jesus told her, "Your brother will rise again."
24 "Yes," Martha said, "he will rise when everyone
else rises, at the last day."
25 Jesus told her, "I am the resurrection and the
life.* Anyone who believes in me will live, even af-
ter dying. 26 Everyone who lives in me and believes
in me will never ever die. Do you believe this, Mar-
tha?"
27 "Yes, Lord," she told him. "I have always believed
you are the Messiah, the Son of God, the one who has
come into the world from God." 28 Then she returned

RAISING THE DEAD

1. What was the last funeral you attended? What was it like?

JOHN 11:17-44

2. Why had Jesus' "anger welled up within him, and he was deeply troubled" (v. 33) when He saw everyone weeping? What does this teach us about God's view of death? Sin?
3. Why did Jesus Himself weep (v. 35)? What does this show us about God's compassion and love?
4. What does the resurrection of Lazarus prove about Jesus? Why is it important to know that He has power over death?
5. Is there a "resurrection" that you need in your life right now?

to Mary. She called Mary aside from the mourners
and told her, "The Teacher is here and wants to see
you." 29 So Mary immediately went to him.
30 Jesus had stayed outside the village, at the place
where Martha met him. 31 When the people who were
at the house consoling Mary saw her leave so hasti-
ly, they assumed she was going to Lazarus's grave to
weep. So they followed her there. 32 When Mary ar-
rived and saw Jesus, she fell at his feet and said, "Lord,
if only you had been here, my brother would not have
died."
33 When Jesus saw her weeping and saw the oth-
er people wailing with her, a deep anger welled up
within him,* and he was deeply troubled. 34 "Where
have you put him?" he asked them.
They told him, "Lord, come and see." 35 Then Jesus
wept. 36 The people who were standing nearby said,
"See how much he loved him!" 37 But some said, "This
man healed a blind man. Couldn't he have kept Laza-
rus from dying?"

11:8 Greek *Jewish people;* also in 11:19, 31, 33, 36, 45, 54. **11:16** Greek *Thomas, who was called Didymus.* **11:18** Greek *was about 15 stadia* [about 2.8 kilometers]. **11:25** Some manuscripts do not include *and the life.* **11:33** Or *he was angry in his spirit.*

11:6 he stayed . . . for the next two days. At least two views are possible on why Jesus did this: (1) As in 2:3-4, Jesus seemingly ignores an urgent request to act in a needy situation. Jesus' delay communicates that His agenda is set neither by Himself (6:38) nor by the desires of those He loves, but by the Father; (2) He waited in order that through this trial His glory would be revealed in a new and dramatic way.

11:7 Let's go back to Judea. Jesus was in Perea on the other side of the Jordan River (10:40-42).

11:9 There are twelve hours of daylight every day. Jesus responds with a two-sentence parable which indicates there is no need to fear the Jewish leaders since He is living in His Father's will and by His timetable. Until His "hour" comes, He is safe from harm and will do the Father's work. There is the implication, though, that the "night" will soon come when He—the light of the world—is taken away. The parable also calls His disciples to consider whether they will take their cues from the "light of the world" or from those (like the Pharisees) who operate in the darkness.

11:11 fallen asleep. This was a common euphemism for death.

11:13 they thought. Like the Pharisees, the disciples failed to grasp the spiritual implications of Jesus' words (4:33).

11:16 Thomas, nicknamed the "Twin". Although Thomas has become famous for his doubt (20:25), here he demonstrates his deep faith and loyalty.

11:21 if only you had been here, my brother would not have died. This is not a rebuke but an expression of regret. Martha apparently had faith that if Jesus had been there before his death, Lazarus could have survived.

11:23 will rise again. Martha would have understood Jesus' comment as an appropriate expression of comfort at a funeral.

11:25 I am the resurrection and the life. Jesus focuses Martha's attention not on the doctrine of the general resurrection but on Him as the source of resurrection (5:24-29). **will live, even after dying.** In this verse and in verse 26, Jesus is asserting His power over death and His ability to give life "to anyone He wants to" (5:21).

11:26 Do you believe this? Jesus confronts Martha with this claim. Does she see Him only as a healer or as the Lord of life?

11:27 In this verse, Martha declares by using several terms exactly who Jesus is. **the Messiah, the Son of God.** In calling Him the Christ, Martha acknowledges Jesus as the One who delivers and saves His people from sin and death. Her recognition of Him as the Son of God shows her insight into His divine identity. The meaning behind this title is that He is God, sharing the Father's nature just as a child shares the characteristics of his parents.

11:32 Mary. That Mary stayed in the house when Jesus arrived (v. 20) seems to indicate her despair. Mary does not add a statement of faith like Martha expressed—that Jesus could still do something powerful (v. 22). When Mary says, "Lord, if You had been here, my brother would not have died," it may have been an expression of disappointment rather than faith.

11:33 wailing. Funerals were times for loud, public expressions of grief in Bible times.

38 Jesus was still angry as he arrived at the tomb, a cave with a stone rolled across its entrance. 39 "Roll the stone aside," Jesus told them.

But Martha, the dead man's sister, protested, "Lord, he has been dead for four days. The smell will be terrible."

40 Jesus responded, "Didn't I tell you that you would see God's glory if you believe?" 41 So they rolled the stone aside. Then Jesus looked up to heaven and said, "Father, thank you for hearing me. 42 You always hear me, but I said it out loud for the sake of all these people standing here, so that they will believe you sent me." 43 Then Jesus shouted, "Lazarus, come out!" 44 And the dead man came out, his hands and feet bound in graveclothes, his face wrapped in a headcloth. Jesus told them, "Unwrap him and let him go!"

THE PLOT TO KILL JESUS

45 Many of the people who were with Mary believed in Jesus when they saw this happen. 46 But some went to the Pharisees and told them what Jesus had done. 47 Then the leading priests and Pharisees called the high council* together. "What are we going to do?" they asked each other. "This man certainly performs many miraculous signs. 48 If we allow him to go on like this, soon everyone will believe in him. Then the Roman army will come and destroy both our Temple* and our nation."

49 Caiaphas, who was high priest at that time,* said, "You don't know what you're talking about! 50 You don't realize that it's better for you that one man should die for the people than for the whole nation to be destroyed."

51 He did not say this on his own; as high priest at that time he was led to prophesy that Jesus would die for the entire nation. 52 And not only for that nation, but to bring together and unite all the children of God scattered around the world.

53 So from that time on, the Jewish leaders began to plot Jesus' death. 54 As a result, Jesus stopped his public ministry among the people and left Jerusalem. He went to a place near the wilderness, to the village of Ephraim, and stayed there with his disciples.

55 It was now almost time for the Jewish Passover celebration, and many people from all over the country arrived in Jerusalem several days early so they could go through the purification ceremony before Passover began. 56 They kept looking for Jesus, but as they stood around in the Temple, they said to each other, "What do you think? He won't come for Passover, will he?" 57 Meanwhile, the leading priests and Pharisees had publicly ordered that anyone seeing Jesus must report it immediately so they could arrest him.

JESUS ANOINTED AT BETHANY

12 Six days before the Passover celebration began, Jesus arrived in Bethany, the home of Lazarus—the man he had raised from the dead. 2 A dinner was prepared in Jesus' honor. Martha served, and Lazarus was among those who ate* with him. 3 Then Mary took a twelve-ounce jar* of expensive perfume made from essence of nard, and she anointed Jesus' feet with it, wiping his feet with her hair. The house was filled with the fragrance.

4 But Judas Iscariot, the disciple who would soon betray him, said, 5 "That perfume was worth a year's wages.* It should have been sold and the money given to the poor." 6 Not that he cared for the poor—he was a thief, and since he was in charge of the disciples' money, he often stole some for himself.

7 Jesus replied, "Leave her alone. She did this in preparation for my burial. 8 You will always have the poor among you, but you will not always have me."

9 When all the people* heard of Jesus' arrival, they flocked to see him and also to see Lazarus, the man Jesus had raised from the dead. 10 Then the leading priests decided to kill Lazarus, too, 11 for it was because of him that many of the people had deserted them* and believed in Jesus.

JESUS' TRIUMPHANT ENTRY

12 The next day, the news that Jesus was on the way to Jerusalem swept through the city. A large crowd of Passover visitors 13 took palm branches and went down the road to meet him. They shouted,

"Praise God!*
Blessings on the one who comes in the name of the
Lord!
Hail to the King of Israel!"*

11:47 Greek *the Sanhedrin.* **11:48** Or *our position;* Greek reads *our place.* **11:49** Greek *that year;* also in 11:51. **12:2** Or *who reclined.* **12:3** Greek *took 1 litra* [327 grams]. **12:5** Greek *worth 300 denarii.* A denarius was equivalent to a laborer's full day's wage. **12:9** Greek *Jewish people;* also in 12:11. **12:11** Or *had deserted their traditions;* Greek reads *had deserted.* **12:13a** Greek *Hosanna,* an exclamation of praise adapted from a Hebrew expression that means "save now." **12:13b** Ps 118:25-26; Zeph 3:15.

11:38 the tomb. Tombs for people of importance were either vertical shafts covered by a stone or horizontal crevices carved out of a hill. Since this tomb was carved out of a cave, it was the latter type.

11:39 The smell will be terrible. Even if Martha knew of the other people whom Jesus had raised (Matt. 11:5; Mark 5:22-43; Luke 7:11-15), they had been dead for only a short time. By the fourth day the decomposition of the body had begun, so resuscitation was not possible.

11:40 Didn't I tell you? This may be a reference to the message in verse 4 or the implication of what Jesus meant by His declaration to Martha in verse 25. The signs in the Gospel of John have consistently been regarded as demonstrations of Jesus' identity. This final sign will reveal what has been alluded to all along—Jesus is God.

11:44 hands and feet bound in graveclothes. Burial customs included wrapping the body with cloth and spices (19:40). This practice was not intended to preserve the body like the ancient Egyptian process of mummification. It was a sign of honor for the deceased person.

11:48 everyone will believe in him. What bothered these leaders was that people might interpret Jesus' miracles as a sign of His messiahship. Since they have already decided that He could not possibly be the Messiah (7:52), this was something they could not allow to happen.

12:6 he was a thief. This is the only place in the Gospels that we are given any background about Judas. The author's point is not to dismiss legitimate caring for the poor but to point out that in spite of his words Judas' motives were self-serving.

12:7 in preparation for my burial. Jesus uses this incident as a foreshadowing of His death. Bodies were often wrapped with spices for burial (19:39-40). Mary's expression was an act of thanksgiving to Jesus for what He had done for her brother.

12:8 You always have the poor among you. This is not meant to disparage acts of mercy but to shift the focus to the upcoming death of Jesus.

12:10 the leading priests decided to kill Lazarus, too. There is no record that this ironic plot to kill a man who had just been raised from the dead ever got beyond the planning stage.

12:12 a large crowd. This was a large crowd of Jews in town for the Passover celebration.

12:13 Praise God! Originally a one-word prayer for God to save (Ps. 118:25), this had become an expression of praise. **Blessings on the one who comes in the name of the Lord!** Psalm 118:26 was used in the liturgy for Passover and celebrated God's deliverance of Israel from her enemies.

14 Jesus found a young donkey and rode on it, fulfilling the prophecy that said:

15 "Don't be afraid, people of Jerusalem.*
Look, your King is coming,
riding on a donkey's colt."*

16 His disciples didn't understand at the time that this was a fulfillment of prophecy. But after Jesus entered into his glory, they remembered what had happened and realized that these things had been written about him.

17 Many in the crowd had seen Jesus call Lazarus from the tomb, raising him from the dead, and they were telling others* about it. 18 That was the reason so many went out to meet him—because they had heard about this miraculous sign. 19 Then the Pharisees said to each other, "There's nothing we can do. Look, everyone* has gone after him!"

JESUS PREDICTS HIS DEATH

20 Some Greeks who had come to Jerusalem for the Passover celebration 21 paid a visit to Philip, who was from Bethsaida in Galilee. They said, "Sir, we want to meet Jesus." 22 Philip told Andrew about it, and they went together to ask Jesus.

23 Jesus replied, "Now the time has come for the Son of Man* to enter into his glory. 24 I tell you the truth, unless a kernel of wheat is planted in the soil and dies, it remains alone. But its death will produce many new kernels—a plentiful harvest of new lives. 25 Those who love their life in this world will lose it. Those who care nothing for their life in this world will keep it for eternity. 26 Anyone who wants to serve me must follow me, because my servants must be where I am. And the Father will honor anyone who serves me.

27 "Now my soul is deeply troubled. Should I pray, 'Father, save me from this hour'? But this is the very reason I came! 28 Father, bring glory to your name."

Then a voice spoke from heaven, saying, "I have already brought glory to my name, and I will do so again." 29 When the crowd heard the voice, some thought it was thunder, while others declared an angel had spoken to him.

30 Then Jesus told them, "The voice was for your benefit, not mine. 31 The time for judging this world has come, when Satan, the ruler of this world, will be cast out. 32 And when I am lifted up from the earth, I will draw everyone to myself." 33 He said this to indicate how he was going to die.

34 The crowd responded, "We understood from Scripture* that the Messiah would live forever. How can you say the Son of Man will die? Just who is this Son of Man, anyway?"

35 Jesus replied, "My light will shine for you just a little longer. Walk in the light while you can, so the darkness will not overtake you. Those who walk in the darkness cannot see where they are going. 36 Put your trust in the light while there is still time; then you will become children of the light."

After saying these things, Jesus went away and was hidden from them.

THE UNBELIEF OF THE PEOPLE

37 But despite all the miraculous signs Jesus had done, most of the people still did not believe in him. 38 This is exactly what Isaiah the prophet had predicted:

"LORD, who has believed our message?
To whom has the LORD revealed his powerful arm?"*

39 But the people couldn't believe, for as Isaiah also said,

40 "The Lord has blinded their eyes
and hardened their hearts—
so that their eyes cannot see,
and their hearts cannot understand,
and they cannot turn to me
and have me heal them."*

41 Isaiah was referring to Jesus when he said this, because he saw the future and spoke of the Messiah's glory. 42 Many people did believe in him, however, including some of the Jewish leaders. But they wouldn't admit it for fear that the Pharisees would expel them from the synagogue. 43 For they loved human praise more than the praise of God.

44 Jesus shouted to the crowds, "If you trust me, you are trusting not only me, but also God who sent me. 45 For when you see me, you are seeing the one who sent me. 46 I have come as a light to shine in this dark world, so that all who put their trust in me will no longer remain in the dark. 47 I will not judge those who hear me but don't obey me, for I have come to save the world and not to judge it. 48 But all who reject me and my message will be judged on the day of judgment by the truth I have spoken. 49 I don't speak on my own authority. The Father who sent me has commanded me what to say and how to say it. 50 And I know his commands lead to eternal life; so I say whatever the Father tells me to say."

12:15a Greek *daughter of Zion.* 12:15b Zech 9:9. 12:17 Greek *were testifying.* 12:19 Greek *the world.* 12:23 "Son of Man" is a title Jesus used for himself. 12:34 Greek *from the law.* 12:38 Isa 53:1. 12:40 Isa 6:10.

12:20 Some Greeks. These were Gentile converts to Judaism such as the men described in Acts 10:2.

12:23 The time has come. Throughout John's Gospel, the author has anticipated this time (2:4; 7:6; 8:20). From here on, he speaks of how Jesus' "hour had come" (13:1). This is the time of His glorification initiated by His death (v. 28).

12:24 a kernel of wheat. Just as a seed must be buried before it can become fruitful, so Christ's death is necessary so many people may be brought to life.

12:25 love . . . care nothing. The only way to gain life is to be willing to lose it for the sake of Christ (Matt. 10:39; Luke 9:24).

12:27 my soul is deeply troubled. The Gospel of John does not show us Jesus praying in the garden of Gethsemane as the other gospels do, but the same anguish that was expressed at that time is seen here.

12:31 for judging this world. Jesus has said repeatedly that His purpose was not to judge but to save. But His coming *does* bring judgment. His presence brings all people to a crisis point. If they receive Him, they will have life. If they refuse Him, they will experience death. **the ruler of this world.** Satan is often presented as having the world under his domination (Matt. 4:8; Eph. 2:2-3; Heb. 2:14-15).

12:32 when I am lifted up from the earth, I will draw everyone to myself. There is a double meaning here. To be "lifted up" was understood by the crowds to mean crucifixion (v. 34), but it is also reminiscent of the "lifting up" of a military flag or standard as a rallying point for an army (6:40).

12:35-36 the light. Jesus does not answer the question of the crowds, but He describes Himself as "the light of the world" (8:12) to issue them one last call to trust in Him.

12:47 I have come to save the world and not to judge it. Just as to believe in Jesus is to believe in the Father (vv. 44-46), so to refuse Him is to refuse the Father.

JESUS WASHES HIS DISCIPLES' FEET

13 Before the Passover celebration, Jesus knew that his hour had come to leave this world and return to his Father. He had loved his disciples during his ministry on earth, and now he loved them to the very end.* 2 It was time for supper, and the devil had already prompted Judas,* son of Simon Iscariot, to betray Jesus. 3 Jesus knew that the Father had given him authority over everything and that he had come from God and would return to God. 4 So he got up from the table, took off his robe, wrapped a towel around his waist, 5 and poured water into a basin. Then he began to wash the disciples' feet, drying them with the towel he had around him.

6 When Jesus came to Simon Peter, Peter said to him, "Lord, are you going to wash my feet?"

7 Jesus replied, "You don't understand now what I am doing, but someday you will."

8 "No," Peter protested, "you will never ever wash my feet!"

Jesus replied, "Unless I wash you, you won't belong to me."

WASHING STINKING FEET

1. Who cleans the toilet where you live? When it comes to housework, what's the last job you would do?

JOHN 13:1-17

2. Why did Jesus wash the disciples' feet? What does He mean by "wash each other's feet" (v. 14)?
3. How would you have reacted to Jesus washing your feet? Would you have been more like Peter in verse 8 or in verse 9?
4. What does Jesus mean, "Unless I wash you, you won't belong to me" (v. 8)?
5. In practical terms, how can you be "washing someone's feet" this week?

9 Simon Peter exclaimed, "Then wash my hands and head as well, Lord, not just my feet!"

10 Jesus replied, "A person who has bathed all over does not need to wash, except for the feet,* to be entirely clean. And you disciples are clean, but not all of you." 11 For Jesus knew who would betray him. That is what he meant when he said, "Not all of you are clean."

12 After washing their feet, he put on his robe again and sat down and asked, "Do you understand what I was doing? 13 You call me 'Teacher' and 'Lord,' and you are right, because that's what I am. 14 And since I, your Lord and Teacher, have washed your feet, you ought to wash each other's feet. 15 I have given you an example to follow. Do as I have done to you. 16 I tell you the truth, slaves are not greater than their master. Nor is the messenger more important than the one who sends the message. 17 Now that you know these things, God will bless you for doing them.

JESUS PREDICTS HIS BETRAYAL

18 "I am not saying these things to all of you; I know the ones I have chosen. But this fulfills the Scripture that says, 'The one who eats my food has turned against me.'* 19 I tell you this beforehand, so that when it happens you will believe that I AM the Messiah.* 20 I tell you the truth, anyone who welcomes my messenger is welcoming me, and anyone who welcomes me is welcoming the Father who sent me."

21 Now Jesus was deeply troubled,* and he exclaimed, "I tell you the truth, one of you will betray me!"

22 The disciples looked at each other, wondering whom he could mean. 23 The disciple Jesus loved was sitting next to Jesus at the table.* 24 Simon Peter motioned to him to ask, "Who's he talking about?" 25 So that disciple leaned over to Jesus and asked, "Lord, who is it?"

26 Jesus responded, "It is the one to whom I give the bread I dip in the bowl." And when he had dipped it, he gave it to Judas, son of Simon Iscariot. 27 When Judas had eaten the bread, Satan entered into him. Then Jesus told him, "Hurry and do what you're going to do." 28 None of the others at the table knew what

13:1 Or *he showed them the full extent of his love.* **13:2** Or *the devil had already intended for Judas.* **13:10** Some manuscripts do not include *except for the feet.* **13:18** Ps 41:9. **13:19** Or *that the 'I AM' has come;* or *that I am the LORD;* Greek reads *that I am.* See Exod 3:14. **13:21** Greek *was troubled in his spirit.* **13:23** Greek *was reclining on Jesus' bosom.* The "disciple Jesus loved" was probably John.

13:1 Jesus knew. Here and in verses 3 and 11, John points out what Jesus knew. This emphasizes that Jesus was in charge of the events leading to His death (10:18).

13:3 Jesus' self-knowledge was at the heart of His willingness and ability to serve. This verse says that He knew who He was in terms of where He had come from (the Father), where He was going (back to the Father), and what His role was while He was on earth.

13:4-5 to wash the disciples' feet. People's dusty, sandaled feet were usually washed by the lowest-ranking servant of the household before a meal was served. Jesus' action was deliberate. Removing His outer clothing was a sign He was going to do some work, and it identified Him with a lowly servant who was dressed in the same way.

13:6 Lord, are you going to wash my feet? Peter is surprised at this departure from normal procedure.

13:7 don't understand now . . . someday you will. This may refer to verse 17, but more likely it refers to the full understanding of Jesus' servanthood that will be made clear after His resurrection.

13:8 Unless I wash you, you won't belong to me. This lifts the meaning of the footwashing to a higher plane than an object lesson about humility. Jesus' action was a symbol of the spiritual cleansing He would accomplish for His followers through the cross.

13:16 slaves are not greater than their master. If the master serves, how much more should the servants? **the messenger.** This is the same word as "apostle," which occurs only here in the Gospel of John. An apostle was a person sent with authority to represent another. Jesus' followers are to represent His servanthood to others.

13:18 this fulfills the Scripture. Psalm 41:9 is quoted as an example of a person being betrayed by close friends. Like David, Jesus must face being betrayed by His friends. **The one who eats my food has turned against me.** Eating together was a sign of friendship. To lift up one's heel was a gesture of contempt, implying a desire to trample someone underfoot.

13:23 the disciple Jesus loved. This is the first mention of a disciple who will appear several times in these final chapters (19:26-27; 20:2; 21:7,20). This is probably a reference to John, author of this Gospel. This title does not mean that Jesus loved this disciple more than the others but that his identity was defined by Jesus' love for him.

13:26 he gave it to Judas. Although this was a signal that Judas was the person who would betray Jesus, it may also have been His final attempt to call Judas to repentance since the sharing of food was a sign of friendship and peace.

13:27 Satan entered into him. The relationship between Satan's activity and that of Judas is never explained. It is Judas's free choice to betray Jesus no matter his motives, but in so doing he was following the desires of the Devil. **Hurry and do what you're going to do.** Jesus' control of the timing of His death is evident even in Judas's betrayal. His life was not taken from Him by others; He gave it willingly as a sacrifice on our behalf.

Jesus meant. 29 Since Judas was their treasurer, some
thought Jesus was telling him to go and pay for the
food or to give some money to the poor. 30 So Judas left
at once, going out into the night.

JESUS PREDICTS PETER'S DENIAL

31 As soon as Judas left the room, Jesus said, "The time
has come for the Son of Man* to enter into his glory,
and God will be glorified because of him. 32 And since
God receives glory because of the Son,* he will give
his own glory to the Son, and he will do so at once.
33 Dear children, I will be with you only a little longer.
And as I told the Jewish leaders, you will search for
me, but you can't come where I am going. 34 So now I
am giving you a new commandment: Love each other.
Just as I have loved you, you should love each other.
35 Your love for one another will prove to the world
that you are my disciples."

36 Simon Peter asked, "Lord, where are you going?"

And Jesus replied, "You can't go with me now, but
you will follow me later."

37 "But why can't I come now, Lord?" he asked. "I'm
ready to die for you."

38 Jesus answered, "Die for me? I tell you the truth,
Peter—before the rooster crows tomorrow morning,
you will deny three times that you even know me.

JESUS, THE WAY TO THE FATHER

14 "Don't let your hearts be troubled. Trust in God,
and trust also in me. 2 There is more than enough
room in my Father's home.* If this were not so, would
I have told you that I am going to prepare a place for
you?* 3 When everything is ready, I will come and get
you, so that you will always be with me where I am.
4 And you know the way to where I am going."

5 "No, we don't know, Lord," Thomas said. "We have
no idea where you are going, so how can we know
the way?"

6 Jesus told him, "I am the way, the truth, and the
life. No one can come to the Father except through me.
7 If you had really known me, you would know who
my Father is.* From now on, you do know him and
have seen him!"

8 Philip said, "Lord, show us the Father, and we will
be satisfied."

9 Jesus replied, "Have I been with you all this time,
Philip, and yet you still don't know who I am? Anyone
who has seen me has seen the Father! So why are you
asking me to show him to you? 10 Don't you believe that
I am in the Father and the Father is in me? The words I
speak are not my own, but my Father who lives in me
does his work through me. 11 Just believe that I am in
the Father and the Father is in me. Or at least believe
because of the work you have seen me do.

12 "I tell you the truth, anyone who believes in me
will do the same works I have done, and even greater
works, because I am going to be with the Father. 13 You
can ask for anything in my name, and I will do it, so
that the Son can bring glory to the Father. 14 Yes, ask
me for anything in my name, and I will do it!

JESUS PROMISES THE HOLY SPIRIT

15 "If you love me, obey* my commandments. 16 And I
will ask the Father, and he will give you another Ad-
vocate,* who will never leave you. 17 He is the Holy
Spirit, who leads into all truth. The world cannot re-
ceive him, because it isn't looking for him and doesn't
recognize him. But you know him, because he lives
with you now and later will be in you.* 18 No, I will not
abandon you as orphans—I will come to you. 19 Soon
the world will no longer see me, but you will see me.

DO YOU REALLY LOVE ME?

1. What was your most memorable Christmas or birthday gift?

JOHN 14:15-27

2. If we love Jesus, what will we do (vv. 15,21,23)? What does this imply when we deliberately choose to sin?
3. What do you learn about the Holy Spirit in verses 16-17 and 25-27?
4. What sort of "peace" does the world give? What sort does Jesus give?
5. Do you love Jesus? How can you more fully obey Him?
6. Do you know the peace of Jesus, or are you seeking peace with the world?

13:31 "Son of Man" is a title Jesus used for himself. **13:32** Several early manuscripts do not include *And since God receives glory because of the Son.* **14:2a** Or *There are many rooms in my Father's house.* **14:2b** Or *If this were not so, I would have told you that I am going to prepare a place for you.* Some manuscripts read *If this were not so, I would have told you. I am going to prepare a place for you.* **14:7** Some manuscripts read *If you have really known me, you will know who my Father is.* **14:15** Other manuscripts read *you will obey;* still others read *you should obey.* **14:16** Or *Comforter,* or *Encourager,* or *Counselor.* Greek reads *Paraclete;* also in 14:26. **14:17** Some manuscripts read *and is in you.*

13:33 you can't come where I am going. Jesus used this same phrase with the Jewish religious leaders as a warning that they would not see the Father because they were heading in the wrong direction (8:21).

13:34-35 a new commandment. This is the first of several indications that at this meal Jesus is instituting a New Covenant between God and His people.

14:2 more than enough room. The emphasis is on the abundance of room for all who will receive Jesus.

14:3 I will come and get you. This probably refers to the coming of Christ through His Spirit (vv. 15-21) rather than to the second coming, which receives very little attention in this Gospel. Through the Spirit, Jesus returns to the disciples (v. 18), and they are then "in" or "with" Him and the Father (vv. 20, 23). Seen in this way, this promise is not for the distant future, but it will be true for the disciples in a short time (20:22).

14:6 I am the way. The destination to which Jesus is going is not so much a place but a person—the Father (7:33; 8:21). The way for the disciples to come to the Father is through the Son, who opens the way for them through His death (Heb. 10:19-22).

14:12 even greater works. The work Jesus has done is revealing the truth about God. It is this mission that His disciples will inherit after His death. The "greater" things that they will do should be understood in terms of their scope (i.e., they will bring the gospel to the Gentile world) rather than their power.

14:16 another Advocate. The Greek term *paraclete* has no adequate English translation. Words such as "Advocate" or "Helper" or "Comforter" emphasize only one of the many aspects of this term. Since this discourse presents the ministry of the Spirit in the same terms as that of Jesus, the Spirit can be referred to as *another* "Paraclete" like Jesus was (1 John 2:1).

14:17 he lives with you now and later will be in you. This indwelling of the Spirit with God's people ultimately makes the temple and the issue of where to worship irrelevant (4:21).

14:18 I will come to you. The coming of Jesus spoken of here should be understood in terms of the coming of the Spirit. It is in that way that the believers will "see" Him, whereas the world will not (v. 19).

Since I live, you also will live. 20 When I am raised to life again, you will know that I am in my Father, and you are in me, and I am in you. 21 Those who accept my commandments and obey them are the ones who love me. And because they love me, my Father will love them. And I will love them and reveal myself to each of them."

22 Judas (not Judas Iscariot, but the other disciple with that name) said to him, "Lord, why are you going to reveal yourself only to us and not to the world at large?"

23 Jesus replied, "All who love me will do what I say. My Father will love them, and we will come and make our home with each of them. 24 Anyone who doesn't love me will not obey me. And remember, my words are not my own. What I am telling you is from the Father who sent me. 25 I am telling you these things now while I am still with you. 26 But when the Father sends the Advocate as my representative—that is, the Holy Spirit—he will teach you everything and will remind you of everything I have told you.

27 "I am leaving you with a gift—peace of mind and heart. And the peace I give is a gift the world cannot give. So don't be troubled or afraid. 28 Remember what I told you: I am going away, but I will come back to you again. If you really loved me, you would be happy that I am going to the Father, who is greater than I am. 29 I have told you these things before they happen so that when they do happen, you will believe.

30 "I don't have much more time to talk to you, because the ruler of this world approaches. He has no power over me, 31 but I will do what the Father requires of me, so that the world will know that I love the Father. Come, let's be going.

JESUS, THE TRUE VINE

15 "I am the true grapevine, and my Father is the gardener. 2 He cuts off every branch of mine that doesn't produce fruit, and he prunes the branches that do bear fruit so they will produce even more. 3 You have already been pruned and purified by the message I have given you. 4 Remain in me, and I will remain in you. For a branch cannot produce fruit if it is severed from the vine, and you cannot be fruitful unless you remain in me.

5 "Yes, I am the vine; you are the branches. Those who remain in me, and I in them, will produce much fruit. For apart from me you can do nothing. 6 Anyone who does not remain in me is thrown away like a useless branch and withers. Such branches are gathered into a pile to be burned. 7 But if you remain in me and my words remain in you, you may ask for anything you want, and it will be granted! 8 When you produce much fruit, you are my true disciples. This brings great glory to my Father.

9 "I have loved you even as the Father has loved me. Remain in my love. 10 When you obey my commandments, you remain in my love, just as I obey my Father's commandments and remain in his love. 11 I have told you these things so that you will be filled with my joy. Yes, your joy will overflow! 12 This is my commandment: Love each other in the same way I have loved you. 13 There is no greater love than to lay down one's life for one's friends. 14 You are my friends if you do what I command. 15 I no longer call you slaves, because a master doesn't confide in his slaves. Now you are my friends, since I have told you everything the Father told me. 16 You didn't choose me. I chose you. I appointed you to go and produce lasting fruit, so that the Father will give you whatever you ask for, using my name. 17 This is my command: Love each other.

THE WORLD'S HATRED

18 "If the world hates you, remember that it hated me first. 19 The world would love you as one of its own if you belonged to it, but you are no longer part of the world. I chose you to come out of the world, so it hates you. 20 Do you remember what I told you? 'A slave is not greater than the master.' Since they persecuted me, naturally they will persecute you. And if they had listened to me, they would listen to you. 21 They will do all this to you because of me, for they have rejected the one who sent me. 22 They would not be guilty if I had not come and spoken to them. But now they have no excuse for their sin. 23 Anyone who hates me also hates my Father. 24 If I hadn't done such miracu-

---

14:26 the Father sends the Advocate as my representative. Here and in verse 16, it is the Father who sends the Spirit to the believer. In 15:26 and 16:7, Jesus says He will send the Spirit. **will teach you. . . . remind you.** These parallel verbs are two ways of saying the same thing. The purpose of the teaching of the Spirit is not to impart new information but to remind believers of the truth that Jesus taught and to help them apply it to new situations.

15:1 I am the true grapevine. The image of the vine was used to describe Israel in the Old Testament (Ps. 80:14-18; Isa. 5:1-7). But Israel did not produce the fruits God expected (Isa. 5:1-7; Matt. 21:43). Jesus transfers this image to Himself. He is the "true vine" who produces fruit because He always obeys the Father and does what pleases Him (8:29).

15:2 cuts off . . . prunes. A gardener cuts off dead branches that do not contribute to the plant and trims small branches to make them stronger when they grow back.

15:4 produce fruit. Although Paul uses the image of fruit to describe Christian character (Gal. 5:22-23), the fruit here probably relates to 4:35 and 12:24 where a similar agricultural image refers to the many people who would come to Christ. Just as Jesus' fruitfulness was dependent on His doing the Father's will, so the believer's fruitfulness results from following Jesus' teaching.

15:5 For apart from me you can do nothing. The disciples' relationship with Jesus is changing. He will no longer be visibly present to them. But His physical absence makes possible a relationship in which His disciples abide in Him and He in them. This mutual indwelling is not just a nice possibility but a vital necessity. Each of the disciples who heard these words understood clearly the relationship of the grape vine to its branches. They knew what happened when branches are severed from the vine.

15:6 Anyone who does not remain in me. Jesus elaborates on the metaphor of the vine and branches calling to mind a scene that His disciple has probably witnessed numerous times. Severed branches are worthless. Rather than letting them clutter up the vineyard, they are gathered and thrown in the fire.

15:7 ask for anything you want, and it will be granted. Here the promise is in the context of spiritual fruitfulness. In this verse, Jesus gives a further definition to what it means for his disciples to abide in Him and He in them: His words remain in His disciples. Words are the fuel of our lives. Observe yourself and other human beings. The attitudes and actions of every life are fueled by some kind of words. Our destinies are determined by the words that shape us. Jesus cleanses us by His words (15:3). By taking in Jesus' words that we grow into His likeness. Within this context His desires have become our desires, and so whatever we ask, He will do.

15:8 brings great glory to my Father. When God is glorified His weighty importance, divine power, and shining majesty are evident to both believers and nonbelievers. The same concept is seen in Jesus' command to disciples to let their lights shine through their good works. When others see this they recognize that God at work and they praise Him (Matt. 5:16).

15:15 friends. The disciples' relationship with Jesus is modeled upon that of Jesus with His Father. In 5:19-20 Jesus said the Father showed Him all that He does. In the same way, Jesus has now revealed to the disciples all that He has learned from the Father.

15:18 the world. This means that system of thinking and acting that sets humanity against the ways of God. **it hated me first.** The reason for this hatred was "people loved darkness rather than the light because their deeds were evil" (3:19). It hates Jesus because He was from above, while those who opposed Him were of this world and belonged to the Devil (8:23,44).

lous signs among them that no one else could do, they
would not be guilty. But as it is, they have seen every-
thing I did, yet they still hate me and my Father. 25 This
fulfills what is written in their Scriptures*: 'They hat-
ed me without cause.'
26 "But I will send you the Advocate*—the Spirit of
truth. He will come to you from the Father and will
testify all about me. 27 And you must also testify about
me because you have been with me from the begin-
ning of my ministry.

16 "I have told you these things so that you won't
abandon your faith. 2 For you will be expelled
from the synagogues, and the time is coming when
those who kill you will think they are doing a holy
service for God. 3 This is because they have never
known the Father or me. 4 Yes, I'm telling you these
things now, so that when they happen, you will re-
member my warning. I didn't tell you earlier because
I was going to be with you for a while longer.

THE WORK OF THE HOLY SPIRIT

5 "But now I am going away to the one who sent me,
and not one of you is asking where I am going. 6 In-
stead, you grieve because of what I've told you. 7 But
in fact, it is best for you that I go away, because if I
don't, the Advocate* won't come. If I do go away, then
I will send him to you. 8 And when he comes, he will
convict the world of its sin, and of God's righteous-
ness, and of the coming judgment. 9 The world's sin
is that it refuses to believe in me. 10 Righteousness is
available because I go to the Father, and you will see
me no more. 11 Judgment will come because the ruler
of this world has already been judged.
12 "There is so much more I want to tell you, but you
can't bear it now. 13 When the Spirit of truth comes,
he will guide you into all truth. He will not speak on
his own but will tell you what he has heard. He will
tell you about the future. 14 He will bring me glory by
telling you whatever he receives from me. 15 All that
belongs to the Father is mine; this is why I said, 'The
Spirit will tell you whatever he receives from me.'

SADNESS WILL BE TURNED TO JOY

16 "In a little while you won't see me anymore. But a
little while after that, you will see me again."
17 Some of the disciples asked each other, "What does
he mean when he says, 'In a little while you won't see
me, but then you will see me,' and 'I am going to the
Father'? 18 And what does he mean by 'a little while'?
We don't understand."
19 Jesus realized they wanted to ask him about it, so
he said, "Are you asking yourselves what I meant? I
said in a little while you won't see me, but a little while
after that you will see me again. 20 I tell you the truth,
you will weep and mourn over what is going to happen
to me, but the world will rejoice. You will grieve, but
your grief will suddenly turn to wonderful joy. 21 It will
be like a woman suffering the pains of labor. When her
child is born, her anguish gives way to joy because she
has brought a new baby into the world. 22 So you have
sorrow now, but I will see you again; then you will re-
joice, and no one can rob you of that joy. 23 At that time
you won't need to ask me for anything. I tell you the
truth, you will ask the Father directly, and he will grant
your request because you use my name. 24 You haven't
done this before. Ask, using my name, and you will re-
ceive, and you will have abundant joy.
25 "I have spoken of these matters in figures of
speech, but soon I will stop speaking figuratively and
will tell you plainly all about the Father. 26 Then you
will ask in my name. I'm not saying I will ask the Fa-
ther on your behalf, 27 for the Father himself loves you
dearly because you love me and believe that I came
from God.* 28 Yes, I came from the Father into the
world, and now I will leave the world and return to
the Father."
29 Then his disciples said, "At last you are speaking
plainly and not figuratively. 30 Now we understand
that you know everything, and there's no need to
question you. From this we believe that you came
from God."
31 Jesus asked, "Do you finally believe? 32 But the
time is coming—indeed it's here now—when you
will be scattered, each one going his own way, leav-
ing me alone. Yet I am not alone because the Father
is with me. 33 I have told you all this so that you may
have peace in me. Here on earth you will have many
trials and sorrows. But take heart, because I have
overcome the world."

THE PRAYER OF JESUS

17 After saying all these things, Jesus looked up
to heaven and said, "Father, the hour has come.
Glorify your Son so he can give glory back to you. 2 For
you have given him authority over everyone. He gives
eternal life to each one you have given him. 3 And this
is the way to have eternal life—to know you, the only
true God, and Jesus Christ, the one you sent to earth. 4 I
brought glory to you here on earth by completing the
work you gave me to do. 5 Now, Father, bring me into
the glory we shared before the world began.

15:25 Greek *in their law.* Pss 35:19; 69:4. 15:26 Or *Comforter,* or *Encourager,* or *Counselor.* Greek reads *Paraclete.* 16:7 Or *Comforter,* or *Encourager,* or *Counselor.* Greek reads *Paraclete.* 16:27 Some manuscripts read *from the Father.*

15:26 the Advocate . . . will testify all about me. In times of persecution the Spirit will enable the disciples to speak the truth of the Father.

16:1 Throughout this discourse (13:1–17:26) Jesus prepares the disciples for what will be happening when He departs (v. 4; 13:19; 14:29). **abandon your faith.** Literally, "scandalize." The severity of persecution might dissuade the disciples from holding on to Jesus and His teaching. His warning is a corrective to any notions they may have that His kingdom will come about easily.

16:7 it is best for you that I go away. Jesus' departure means the coming of the Counselor (14:16), which really means His return to them in a deep, inner, spiritual way (7:39; 14:15-21).

16:8 he will convict the world of its sin, and of God's righteousness, and of the coming judgment. The "world" held that Jesus was an unrighteous sinner under the judgment of God (9:25). The Spirit will prove that the world is wrong.

16:17-18 We don't understand. The riddle (v. 16) left the disciples confused. Their frustration here sums up the misunderstanding so common in this Gospel (2:21-22; 3:4; 4:15,32; 6:5,41,52; 7:35; 8:22,27,33,43; 10:19; 11:12). His closest followers do not know what He means. It will be resolved as He speaks without using any figurative language (v. 29).

16:20-22 weep and mourn . . . rejoice. This parable explains what the disciples will soon experience. While they are weeping over their loss of Jesus, the world (as personified by the religious authorities) will rejoice that He is gone.

16:22 But I will see you again. Characteristically, this might mean either physically after Jesus' resurrection or spiritually when He comes to them in the Spirit.

16:23 At that time. Again, this might mean the literal day of Jesus' resurrection or the figurative Old Testament "day" of the Lord when salvation and judgment would be fulfilled. In the latter case, the "day" really extends from the first coming of Christ until His return in glory.

16:33 overcome. The powers of evil are overcome by Jesus' death and resurrection (Heb. 2:14; Rev. 5:5; 17:14).

6 “I have revealed you* to the ones you gave me
from this world. They were always yours. You gave
them to me, and they have kept your word. 7 Now they
know that everything I have is a gift from you, 8 for
I have passed on to them the message you gave me.
They accepted it and know that I came from you, and
they believe you sent me.

9 “My prayer is not for the world, but for those you
have given me, because they belong to you. 10 All who
are mine belong to you, and you have given them
to me, so they bring me glory. 11 Now I am depart-
ing from the world; they are staying in this world,
but I am coming to you. Holy Father, you have given
me your name;* now protect them by the power of
your name so that they will be united just as we are.
12 During my time here, I protected them by the power
of the name you gave me.* I guarded them so that not
one was lost, except the one headed for destruction,
as the Scriptures foretold.

13 “Now I am coming to you. I told them many things
while I was with them in this world so they would
be filled with my joy. 14 I have given them your word.
And the world hates them because they do not belong
to the world, just as I do not belong to the world. 15 I’m
not asking you to take them out of the world, but to
keep them safe from the evil one. 16 They do not be-
long to this world any more than I do. 17 Make them
holy by your truth; teach them your word, which is
truth. 18 Just as you sent me into the world, I am send-
ing them into the world. 19 And I give myself as a holy
sacrifice for them so they can be made holy by your
truth.

20 “I am praying not only for these disciples but also
for all who will ever believe in me through their mes-
sage. 21 I pray that they will all be one, just as you and
I are one—as you are in me, Father, and I am in you.
And may they be in us so that the world will believe
you sent me.

22 “I have given them the glory you gave me, so they
may be one as we are one. 23 I am in them and you are
in me. May they experience such perfect unity that
the world will know that you sent me and that you
love them as much as you love me. 24 Father, I want
these whom you have given me to be with me where
I am. Then they can see all the glory you gave me be-
cause you loved me even before the world began!

25 “O righteous Father, the world doesn’t know you,
but I do; and these disciples know you sent me. 26 I
have revealed you to them, and I will continue to do
so. Then your love for me will be in them, and I will
be in them.”

JESUS IS BETRAYED AND ARRESTED

18 After saying these things, Jesus crossed the
Kidron Valley with his disciples and entered a
grove of olive trees. 2 Judas, the betrayer, knew this
place, because Jesus had often gone there with his
disciples. 3 The leading priests and Pharisees had giv-
en Judas a contingent of Roman soldiers and Temple
guards to accompany him. Now with blazing torch-
es, lanterns, and weapons, they arrived at the olive
grove.

4 Jesus fully realized all that was going to happen
to him, so he stepped forward to meet them. “Who are
you looking for?” he asked.

5 “Jesus the Nazarene,”* they replied.

“I Am he,”* Jesus said. (Judas, who betrayed him,
was standing with them.) 6 As Jesus said “I Am he,”
they all drew back and fell to the ground! 7 Once more
he asked them, “Who are you looking for?”

And again they replied, “Jesus the Nazarene.”

8 “I told you that I Am he,” Jesus said. “And since I
am the one you want, let these others go.” 9 He did this
to fulfill his own statement: “I did not lose a single one
of those you have given me.”*

10 Then Simon Peter drew a sword and slashed
off the right ear of Malchus, the high priest’s slave.
11 But Jesus said to Peter, “Put your sword back into its
sheath. Shall I not drink from the cup of suffering the
Father has given me?”

JESUS AT THE HIGH PRIEST’S HOUSE

12 So the soldiers, their commanding officer, and the
Temple guards arrested Jesus and tied him up. 13 First
they took him to Annas, since he was the father-in law
of Caiaphas, the high priest at that time.* 14 Caiaphas
was the one who had told the other Jewish leaders,
“It’s better that one man should die for the people.”

17:6 Greek *have revealed your name;* also in 17:26. **17:11** Some manuscripts read *you have given me these [disciples].* **17:12** Some manuscripts read *I protected those you gave me, by the power of your name.* **18:5a** Or *Jesus of Nazareth;* also in 18:7. **18:5b** Or *“The ‘I Am’ is here”;* or *“I am the Lord”;* Greek reads *I am;* also in 18:6, 8. See Exod 3:14. **18:9** See John 6:39 and 17:12. **18:13** Greek *that year.*

17:6-8 They have accepted it. The disciples’ insight that Jesus had indeed come from God (16:30) was a clue that Jesus’ mission had been successful.

17:9 you have given me. Jesus’ disciples are not His, but the Father’s—since it is because of the Father that they have come to Him (6:65).

17:12 I guarded them. One part of God’s work is protecting us—as He did His disciples—through His great power.

17:17 Make them holy by your truth. Jesus prayed that the Father would keep His disciples from worldly concerns and empower them for service in His kingdom.

17:25 righteous Father! God’s righteousness means that He always does what is right. No matter what happens to us, we can trust Him because He has our best interests at heart.

18:1 Kidron Valley. This valley was one of the borders of Jerusalem. During the rainy season it was a torrent. **a grove.** Luke 22:39 locates this on the Mt. of Olives, while Matthew 26:36 and Mark 14:32 refer to it as Gethsemane. It was a place of refuge that Jesus and the disciples often retreated to during visits to Jerusalem (v. 2; Luke 22:39).

18:2 Judas, the betrayer. The author of the Gospel of John gives no details about Judas’ betrayal (Luke 22:1-6,47-48).

18:3 a contingent of Roman soldiers. The word for “detachment” is a technical term meaning a force of 600 soldiers. Only Pilate would have the authority to dispatch these troops. This strong show of force would make sense if Pilate had been told by the Jewish authorities that Jesus and the disciples were planning an insurrection, which, according to 11:48, is what the authorities feared.

18:9 to fulfill his own statement. This refers to 6:39; 17:12. This phrase is similar to the one used in 13:18; 15:25 when referring to Old Testament passages.

18:10 Simon Peter drew a sword. According to Luke 22:36-38, two of the disciples armed themselves with swords. These were daggers that could have been easy to hide. In John 13:37 Peter had pledged to die for Jesus. In light of the odds here, his attack could easily have caused that to happen. **Malchus.** The name of the servant is mentioned only here in the New Testament. Perhaps he was known to the community to which this Gospel was originally written.

18:11 Put your sword back into its sheath. In verse 36 this refusal to meet force with force is used by Jesus as a sign of the true nature of His kingdom. **the cup.** In the Old Testament, drinking “the cup” is sometimes a symbol of experiencing God’s judgment and wrath against sin (Ezek. 23:32-34; Hab. 2:16). This use of the metaphor reminds us that Jesus Himself will bear God’s judgment against the sins of the people.

18:13 Annas. Annas was the high priest from A.D. 6 until A.D. 15, when he was deposed by the Roman authorities. But he held on to power by controlling the office through the appointment of family members, such as Caiaphas. In Acts 4:6 Annas is called the high priest, even though that was no longer his title.

PETER'S FIRST DENIAL

15 Simon Peter followed Jesus, as did another of the
disciples. That other disciple was acquainted with
the high priest, so he was allowed to enter the high
priest's courtyard with Jesus. 16 Peter had to stay out-
side the gate. Then the disciple who knew the high
priest spoke to the woman watching at the gate, and
she let Peter in. 17 The woman asked Peter, "You're not
one of that man's disciples, are you?"
"No," he said, "I am not."
18 Because it was cold, the household servants and
the guards had made a charcoal fire. They stood
around it, warming themselves, and Peter stood with
them, warming himself.

THE HIGH PRIEST QUESTIONS JESUS

19 Inside, the high priest began asking Jesus about
his followers and what he had been teaching them.
20 Jesus replied, "Everyone knows what I teach. I
have preached regularly in the synagogues and the
Temple, where the people* gather. I have not spo-
ken in secret. 21 Why are you asking me this ques-
tion? Ask those who heard me. They know what I
said."
22 Then one of the Temple guards standing nearby
slapped Jesus across the face. "Is that the way to an-
swer the high priest?" he demanded.
23 Jesus replied, "If I said anything wrong, you must
prove it. But if I'm speaking the truth, why are you
beating me?"
24 Then Annas bound Jesus and sent him to Caia-
phas, the high priest.

PETER'S SECOND AND THIRD DENIALS

25 Meanwhile, as Simon Peter was standing by the fire
warming himself, they asked him again, "You're not
one of his disciples, are you?"
He denied it, saying, "No, I am not."
26 But one of the household slaves of the high priest,
a relative of the man whose ear Peter had cut off,
asked, "Didn't I see you out there in the olive grove
with Jesus?" 27 Again Peter denied it. And immediately
a rooster crowed.

JESUS' TRIAL BEFORE PILATE

28 Jesus' trial before Caiaphas ended in the early
hours of the morning. Then he was taken to the head-
quarters of the Roman governor.* His accusers didn't
go inside because it would defile them, and they
wouldn't be allowed to celebrate the Passover. 29 So Pi-
late, the governor, went out to them and asked, "What
is your charge against this man?"
30 "We wouldn't have handed him over to you if he
weren't a criminal!" they retorted.
31 "Then take him away and judge him by your own
law," Pilate told them.
"Only the Romans are permitted to execute some-
one," the Jewish leaders replied. 32 (This fulfilled Jesus'
prediction about the way he would die.*)
33 Then Pilate went back into his headquarters and
called for Jesus to be brought to him. "Are you the
king of the Jews?" he asked him.
34 Jesus replied, "Is this your own question, or did
others tell you about me?"
35 "Am I a Jew?" Pilate retorted. "Your own people
and their leading priests brought you to me for trial.
Why? What have you done?"
36 Jesus answered, "My Kingdom is not an earthly
kingdom. If it were, my followers would fight to keep
me from being handed over to the Jewish leaders. But
my Kingdom is not of this world."
37 Pilate said, "So you are a king?"
Jesus responded, "You say I am a king. Actually, I was
born and came into the world to testify to the truth. All
who love the truth recognize that what I say is true."
38 "What is truth?" Pilate asked. Then he went out
again to the people and told them, "He is not guilty
of any crime. 39 But you have a custom of asking me
to release one prisoner each year at Passover. Would
you like me to release this 'King of the Jews'?"
40 But they shouted back, "No! Not this man. We
want Barabbas!" (Barabbas was a revolutionary.)

JESUS SENTENCED TO DEATH

19 Then Pilate had Jesus flogged with a lead-tipped
whip. 2 The soldiers wove a crown of thorns and
put it on his head, and they put a purple robe on
him. 3 "Hail! King of the Jews!" they mocked, as they
slapped him across the face.
4 Pilate went outside again and said to the people, "I
am going to bring him out to you now, but understand
clearly that I find him not guilty." 5 Then Jesus came
out wearing the crown of thorns and the purple robe.
And Pilate said, "Look, here is the man!"
6 When they saw him, the leading priests and Tem-
ple guards began shouting, "Crucify him! Crucify him!"
"Take him yourselves and crucify him," Pilate said.
"I find him not guilty."
7 The Jewish leaders replied, "By our law he ought
to die because he called himself the Son of God."

18:20 Greek *Jewish people;* also in 18:38. **18:28** Greek *to the Praetorium;* also in 18:33. **18:32** See John 12:32-33.

18:15 another of the disciples. The identity of this disciple is unknown. Although some interpreters believe this is John, the author of this Gospel, it is unlikely that he is "the beloved disciple" mentioned elsewhere in the Gospel since he is not identified here as such.

18:20 I have not spoken in secret. Jesus' teaching has been public all along. If the religious leaders wanted to know what He taught, they had ample opportunity to find out for themselves (8:43; 10:25). According to Jewish law, people were not required to testify against themselves, but witnesses were required. Jesus' answer and His suggestion that they call on others who had heard what He said (v. 21) may be His way of pointing out that this was an illegal hearing, since no witnesses were present.

18:28 early hours of the morning. Jesus' trial before the high priest was either late at night or very early in the morning. The trial before Pilate probably began around 6:00 to 7:00 a.m., since the Roman courts began early. **headquarters.** The Roman seat of power over Judea was located at Caesarea (Acts 23:33-35). This word refers to Pilate's temporary residence in Jerusalem, a building that Herod the Great had erected as a home for himself years before. **it would defile them.** Rabbinic tradition taught that Gentile homes were unclean, defiling any Jew who entered. **the Passover.** According to the chronology of this Gospel, the Passover would be observed that evening. Any Jew ritually defiled would have to wait a month to observe this feast.

18:31 judge him by your own law. Pilate's contempt for the Jews is seen throughout this account. He knew they had already tried Jesus, or they would not have brought Him before his tribunal.

18:33 Are you the king of the Jews? This was probably asked in sarcasm or surprise. The Jewish religious leaders must have told Pilate that Jesus was claiming to be their king. They tried to portray Him as a threat to Roman rule (vv. 34-35).

19:1 flogged. This Roman punishment involved 39 lashes with a whip imbedded with metal and rock. It sometimes led to death from bleeding and shock.

19:2 a crown of thorns . . . a purple robe. These were mock symbols of royalty.

19:7 he called himself the Son of God. This was the charge that the leaders originally made against Jesus (5:18; 8:53; 10:33).

[8] When Pilate heard this, he was more frightened
than ever. [9] He took Jesus back into the headquarters*
again and asked him, "Where are you from?" But Jesus
gave no answer. [10] "Why don't you talk to me?" Pilate
demanded. "Don't you realize that I have the power to
release you or crucify you?"

[11] Then Jesus said, "You would have no power over
me at all unless it were given to you from above. So
the one who handed me over to you has the greater
sin."

[12] Then Pilate tried to release him, but the Jewish
leaders shouted, "If you release this man, you are no
'friend of Caesar.'* Anyone who declares himself a
king is a rebel against Caesar."

[13] When they said this, Pilate brought Jesus out to
them again. Then Pilate sat down on the judgment
seat on the platform that is called the Stone Pavement
(in Hebrew, *Gabbatha*). [14] It was now about noon on
the day of preparation for the Passover. And Pilate
said to the people,* "Look, here is your king!"

[15] "Away with him," they yelled. "Away with him!
Crucify him!"

"What? Crucify your king?" Pilate asked.

"We have no king but Caesar," the leading priests
shouted back.

[16] Then Pilate turned Jesus over to them to be cru-
cified.

THE CRUCIFIXION

So they took Jesus away. [17] Carrying the cross by him-
self, he went to the place called Place of the Skull (in He-
brew, *Golgotha*). [18] There they nailed him to the cross.
Two others were crucified with him, one on either side,
with Jesus between them. [19] And Pilate posted a sign on
the cross that read, "Jesus of Nazareth,* the King of the
Jews." [20] The place where Jesus was crucified was near
the city, and the sign was written in Hebrew, Latin, and
Greek, so that many people could read it.

[21] Then the leading priests objected and said to Pi-
late, "Change it from 'The King of the Jews' to 'He said,
I am King of the Jews.'"

[22] Pilate replied, "No, what I have written, I have
written."

[23] When the soldiers had crucified Jesus, they divided
his clothes among the four of them. They also took his
robe, but it was seamless, woven in one piece from top
to bottom. [24] So they said, "Rather than tearing it apart,
let's throw dice* for it." This fulfilled the Scripture that
says, "They divided my garments among themselves and
threw dice for my clothing."* So that is what they did.

[25] Standing near the cross were Jesus' mother, and
his mother's sister, Mary (the wife of Clopas), and
Mary Magdalene. [26] When Jesus saw his mother
standing there beside the disciple he loved, he said to
her, "Dear woman, here is your son." [27] And he said to
this disciple, "Here is your mother." And from then on
this disciple took her into his home.

THE DEATH OF JESUS

[28] Jesus knew that his mission was now finished, and
to fulfill Scripture he said, "I am thirsty."* [29] A jar of
sour wine was sitting there, so they soaked a sponge
in it, put it on a hyssop branch, and held it up to his
lips. [30] When Jesus had tasted it, he said, "It is fin-
ished!" Then he bowed his head and gave up his spirit.

[31] It was the day of preparation, and the Jewish
leaders didn't want the bodies hanging there the
next day, which was the Sabbath (and a very spe-
cial Sabbath, because it was the Passover). So they
asked Pilate to hasten their deaths by ordering that
their legs be broken. Then their bodies could be tak-
en down. [32] So the soldiers came and broke the legs of
the two men crucified with Jesus. [33] But when they
came to Jesus, they saw that he was already dead, so
they didn't break his legs. [34] One of the soldiers, how-
ever, pierced his side with a spear, and immediately
blood and water flowed out. [35] (This report is from an
eyewitness giving an accurate account. He speaks
the truth so that you also may continue to believe.*)
[36] These things happened in fulfillment of the Scrip-
tures that say, "Not one of his bones will be broken,"*
[37] and "They will look on the one they pierced."*

THE BURIAL OF JESUS

[38] Afterward Joseph of Arimathea, who had been a
secret disciple of Jesus (because he feared the Jew-

19:9 Greek *the Praetorium.* **19:12** "Friend of Caesar" is a technical term that refers to an ally of the emperor. **19:14** Greek *Jewish people;* also in 19:20. **19:19** Or *Jesus the Nazarene.* **19:24a** Greek *cast lots.* **19:24b** Ps 22:18. **19:28** See Pss 22:15; 69:21. **19:35** Some manuscripts read *that you also may believe.* **19:36** Exod 12:46; Num 9:12; Ps 34:20. **19:37** Zech 12:10.

19:14 the day of preparation. This was Friday. The Sabbath (which was also Passover according to this Gospel) would begin that evening.

19:15 We have no king but Caesar. Even during the period of the Jewish kings, God was considered the only true King of Israel. In 8:33,41 the religious leaders protested against Jesus' implication that they served anyone but God. But they would rather affirm loyalty to a leader they despised than follow Jesus.

19:17 Carrying the cross by himself. Condemned prisoners had to carry at least the crossbar of the cross to the site of their execution, where the vertical posts were probably permanently installed.

19:19 Pilate posted a sign on the cross. Some prisoners were required to wear signs around their necks that declared their crimes. This sign listed the name and origin of Jesus as well as the "crime" for which He was convicted.

19:20 Hebrew, Latin, and Greek. These were the three common languages of the area. Jews from outside of Palestine would not necessarily have been able to read Aramaic (the local language of that area), nor Latin (the official language of the empire), but everyone would have known Greek since that was the common language of commerce.

19:25 Jesus' mother. Particularly touching is the presence of Jesus' mother at the cross. She watches her own son die a horrible death normally reserved for criminals. She had been told that her status as mother of the Son of God would make her blessed (Luke 1:42), but she did not feel "blessed" at this point.

19:26 the disciple he loved. It appears that by this time Joseph, Mary's husband, was dead. As the oldest son, Jesus would have assumed the responsibility of caring for His mother (13:23).

19:29 sour wine. This was cheap wine. It may have been on the scene for the entertainment of the soldiers as they waited for the process of crucifixion to run its course. It would have done little for Jesus' thirst, and its bitterness symbolized the agony of the experience.

19:30 It is finished! Jesus is saying that His work had been accomplished. **released his spirit.** Jesus' death was voluntary. His life was not taken away by others; He sacrificed it freely (10:18).

19:31 the Jewish leaders didn't want the bodies hanging there the next day. Although Roman custom left bodies on crosses as a warning for criminals, Jewish law forbade bodies hung on a tree to remain there overnight (Deut. 21:22-23). **their legs be broken.** By pressing their weight on their legs, victims could ease some of the pressure on their arms and chests, making breathing easier. But once their legs were broken, this relief was no longer possible; death by suffocation and shock would come quickly.

19:36 Not one of his bones will be broken. From the beginning of this Gospel, the ministry of Jesus has been pictured in terms of the Passover lamb (1:29; 6:4). One of the requirements about these lambs was that their bones should not be broken (Ex. 12:46).

19:38 Joseph. Although this Joseph is mentioned in all the Gospels, little is known about him. Luke says he was a member of the Sanhedrin who had opposed the plan of the majority to kill Jesus (Luke 23:50-51). The author's comment here that he was a secret disciple because of his fear of the Jews accords with what he said in 12:42-43.

ish leaders), asked Pilate for permission to take down Jesus' body. When Pilate gave permission, Joseph came and took the body away. 39 With him came Nicodemus, the man who had come to Jesus at night. He brought about seventy-five pounds* of perfumed ointment made from myrrh and aloes. 40 Following Jewish burial custom, they wrapped Jesus' body with the spices in long sheets of linen cloth. 41 The place of crucifixion was near a garden, where there was a new tomb, never used before. 42 And so, because it was the day of preparation for the Jewish Passover* and since the tomb was close at hand, they laid Jesus there.

THE RESURRECTION

20 Early on Sunday morning,* while it was still dark, Mary Magdalene came to the tomb and found that the stone had been rolled away from the entrance. 2 She ran and found Simon Peter and the other disciple, the one whom Jesus loved. She said, "They have taken the Lord's body out of the tomb, and we don't know where they have put him!"

3 Peter and the other disciple started out for the tomb. 4 They were both running, but the other disciple outran Peter and reached the tomb first. 5 He stooped and looked in and saw the linen wrappings lying there, but he didn't go in. 6 Then Simon Peter arrived and went inside. He also noticed the linen wrappings lying there, 7 while the cloth that had covered Jesus' head was folded up and lying apart from the other wrappings. 8 Then the disciple who had reached the tomb first also went in, and he saw and believed—9 for until then they still hadn't understood the Scriptures that said Jesus must rise from the dead. 10 Then they went home.

JESUS APPEARS TO MARY MAGDALENE

11 Mary was standing outside the tomb crying, and as she wept, she stooped and looked in. 12 She saw two white-robed angels, one sitting at the head and the other at the foot of the place where the body of Jesus had been lying. 13 "Dear woman, why are you crying?" the angels asked her.

"Because they have taken away my Lord," she replied, "and I don't know where they have put him."

14 She turned to leave and saw someone standing there. It was Jesus, but she didn't recognize him. 15 "Dear woman, why are you crying?" Jesus asked her. "Who are you looking for?"

She thought he was the gardener. "Sir," she said, "if you have taken him away, tell me where you have put him, and I will go and get him."

16 "Mary!" Jesus said.

She turned to him and cried out, "Rabboni!" (which is Hebrew for "Teacher").

17 "Don't cling to me," Jesus said, "for I haven't yet ascended to the Father. But go find my brothers and tell them, 'I am ascending to my Father and your Father, to my God and your God.'"

18 Mary Magdalene found the disciples and told them, "I have seen the Lord!" Then she gave them his message.

JESUS APPEARS TO HIS DISCIPLES

19 That Sunday evening* the disciples were meeting behind locked doors because they were afraid of the Jewish leaders. Suddenly, Jesus was standing there among them! "Peace be with you," he said. 20 As he spoke, he showed them the wounds in his hands and his side. They were filled with joy when they saw the Lord! 21 Again he said, "Peace be with you. As the Father has sent me, so I am sending you." 22 Then he breathed on them and said, "Receive the Holy Spirit.

TOMB RAIDERS

1. Have you ever seen someone you knew from your past, and you didn't recognize him or her? What happened? How did you feel when you suddenly realized who it was?

JOHN 20:1-18

2. Why did Jesus ask Mary who she was looking for when He undoubtedly knew? Why did she suddenly recognize Him when He said her name?
3. John, "the disciple who had reached the tomb first," "went in, and he saw, and believed" (v. 8). What did he believe? Why did the empty tomb convince him?
4. Do you believe in Jesus' death and resurrection? How does this belief affect your life?

19:39 Greek *100 litras* [32.7 kilograms]. 19:42 Greek *because of the Jewish day of preparation.* 20:1 Greek *On the first day of the week.* 20:19 Greek *In the evening of that day, the first day of the week.*

19:39 about seventy-five pounds of perfumed ointment made from myrrh and aloes. This was a large amount of spices to use in the burial process. Normally, only royal figures were accorded such honor at death.
19:41 A new tomb. Tombs for the wealthy were carved in rock and closed by a stone rolled across the entrance. Matthew 27:59-60 says this was Joseph's own tomb.
20:1 Mary Magdalene. Mary is mentioned in the accounts of the resurrection of Jesus in all four Gospels. Luke 8:2 says that she was one of several women who traveled with the disciples.
20:5-7 linen wrappings. Grave robbers, in search of treasures entombed with the corpse, would either have taken the wrapped body of Jesus or scattered the strips as they tore them off. The fact that the clothes were neatly laid to one side was one of the evidences that led the "other disciple" to faith (v. 8).
20:14 she didn't recognize him. Mary may have been blinded by her grief. Or perhaps there was a difference in Jesus' appearance that caused her not to recognize Him.
20:15 gardener. The tomb was located in a garden owned by Joseph of Arimathea. As an aristocratic member of the Sanhedrin, he probably would have employed a gardener to care for his property.
20:16 Mary. When Jesus speaks Mary's name, she immediately recognizes who is speaking to her, thus proving her discipleship. **Rabbouni.** Literally, "my teacher." This is a title of respect for Jesus as well as one that shows Mary's submission and love for Him.
20:17 Don't cling to me. We need not think that Jesus refused to allow Mary to touch Him. After Mary expressed her joy and relief at seeing Him, He told her that all was not finished yet.
20:19 afraid of the Jewish leaders. The disciples were afraid that the authorities, who had been successful in having Jesus killed, might now turn on them. **Jesus was standing there.** Nothing is said about how Jesus came to be among the disciples, but the implication of the locked doors appears to be that Jesus simply appeared with them (v. 26; Luke 24:31). **Peace be with you.** The promise of peace was given in 14:27 and 16:33. It sums up the blessings and fullness of the New Covenant that Jesus has established between the Father and His people (14:27).
20:22 he breathed on them. As God originally breathed life into Adam at the first creation (Gen. 2:7), so now Jesus breathes spiritual life into His people at the re-creation of the people of God (1:12-13). **Receive the Holy Spirit.** The other Gospels do not mention the coming of the Spirit to the disciples, but Acts 2 indicates that Luke saw this promise being fulfilled on the day of Pentecost, seven weeks after Jesus' resurrection.

23 If you forgive anyone's sins, they are forgiven. If you
do not forgive them, they are not forgiven."

JESUS APPEARS TO THOMAS

24 One of the twelve disciples, Thomas (nicknamed the
Twin),* was not with the others when Jesus came.
25 They told him, "We have seen the Lord!"
But he replied, "I won't believe it unless I see the
nail wounds in his hands, put my fingers into them,
and place my hand into the wound in his side."
26 Eight days later the disciples were together
again, and this time Thomas was with them. The
doors were locked; but suddenly, as before, Jesus
was standing among them. "Peace be with you,"
he said. 27 Then he said to Thomas, "Put your finger
here, and look at my hands. Put your hand into the
wound in my side. Don't be faithless any longer. Be-
lieve!"
28 "My Lord and my God!" Thomas exclaimed.
29 Then Jesus told him, "You believe because you
have seen me. Blessed are those who believe without
seeing me."

PURPOSE OF THE BOOK

30 The disciples saw Jesus do many other miraculous
signs in addition to the ones recorded in this book.
31 But these are written so that you may continue to
believe* that Jesus is the Messiah, the Son of God, and
that by believing in him you will have life by the pow-
er of his name.

EPILOGUE: JESUS APPEARS TO SEVEN DISCIPLES

21 Later, Jesus appeared again to the disciples be-
side the Sea of Galilee.* This is how it happened.
2 Several of the disciples were there—Simon Peter,
Thomas (nicknamed the Twin),* Nathanael from
Cana in Galilee, the sons of Zebedee, and two other
disciples.
3 Simon Peter said, "I'm going fishing."
"We'll come, too," they all said. So they went out in
the boat, but they caught nothing all night.
4 At dawn Jesus was standing on the beach, but the
disciples couldn't see who he was. 5 He called out, "Fel-
lows,* have you caught any fish?"
"No," they replied.
6 Then he said, "Throw out your net on the right-
hand side of the boat, and you'll get some!" So they
did, and they couldn't haul in the net because there
were so many fish in it.
7 Then the disciple Jesus loved said to Peter, "It's the
Lord!" When Simon Peter heard that it was the Lord,
he put on his tunic (for he had stripped for work),
jumped into the water, and headed to shore. 8 The oth-
ers stayed with the boat and pulled the loaded net to
the shore, for they were only about a hundred yards*
from shore. 9 When they got there, they found break-
fast waiting for them—fish cooking over a charcoal
fire, and some bread.
10 "Bring some of the fish you've just caught," Jesus
said. 11 So Simon Peter went aboard and dragged the

YOU GOTTA BELIEVE

1. Are you more likely to believe what someone tells you, or do you have to see to believe?

JOHN 20:24-31

2. Why do you suppose Thomas doubted? If you'd been in his place, what would your response have been?
3. How does Jesus deal with Thomas' doubt (v. 27)?
4. Why does John say that he wrote about Jesus' life, resurrection, and miracles (v. 31)? Why is "believing" such an important thing?
5. Are you an unbeliever or a believer? If you're an unbeliever, what would it take for you to believe?

CAST YOUR NETS

1. What has been your best or worst fishing, camping, or hiking experience?

JOHN 21:1-14

2. Why did Jesus cook breakfast for the disciples? How is this act similar to His washing their feet (13:1-7)?
3. What made John, "the disciple Jesus loved," recognize that it was Jesus on the beach (v. 7)?
4. Why did Peter jump into the lake (v. 7)?
5. Why did Jesus tell the disciples to cast their nets for fish? Why not just miraculously have them swim ashore?
6. Is Jesus calling you to "cast your nets" in faith? How? Where?

20:24 Greek *Thomas, who was called Didymus.* **20:31** Some manuscripts read *that you may believe.* **21:1** Greek *Sea of Tiberias,* another name for the Sea of Galilee. **21:2** Greek *Thomas, who was called Didymus.* **21:5** Greek *Children.* **21:8** Greek *200 cubits* [90 meters].

20:23 If you forgive. . . . If you do not forgive. The disciples are to pronounce forgiveness upon those who receive the gospel. Likewise, to those who refuse the gospel, they are to pronounce the words of warning just as Jesus did (8:24).

20:26 The doors were locked; but suddenly. This indicates that Jesus' resurrected body was not limited in the way a normal physical body is. He was able to enter a locked room and simply appear. Nevertheless His body could be felt (v. 27), and He ate (Luke 24:41-43). **Peace be with you.** The word *peace* reflects the salvation that Christ's redemptive work achieves—total well being and inner rest of spirit, in fellowship with God.

20:28 My Lord and my God! Thomas clearly affirms the deity of Jesus. This is the last of a series of confessions of faith that sum up what the author of John's Gospel wants the reader to recognize about Jesus (11:27).

20:29 Blessed are those who believe without seeing me. The author applies the words of Thomas to the situation of his readers. They are not deprived because of never having seen Jesus. Indeed, He is with them through the Spirit (14:15-20).

21:1 Later. This is actually the same indefinite time reference that John used to begin chapters 5, 6, and 7. When this appearance of Jesus occurred is unclear. Since one of the themes in this section is Jesus' restoration of Peter, and since, like Mary in 20:15, they did not recognize Him at first, it may be that this event actually occurred before Jesus' climactic appearance to the disciples in 20:19.

21:7 the disciple Jesus loved. This is thought to be John, the author of the Gospel of John. **It's the Lord!** Just as Jesus' voice caused Mary to recognize Him (20:16), so here the enormous catch of fish revealed to the beloved disciple that the person with whom they were talking was the Lord.

net to the shore. There were 153 large fish, and yet the net hadn't torn.

12 "Now come and have some breakfast!" Jesus said. None of the disciples dared to ask him, "Who are you?" They knew it was the Lord. 13 Then Jesus served them the bread and the fish. 14 This was the third time Jesus had appeared to his disciples since he had been raised from the dead.

15 After breakfast Jesus asked Simon Peter, "Simon son of John, do you love me more than these?*"

"Yes, Lord," Peter replied, "you know I love you."

"Then feed my lambs," Jesus told him.

16 Jesus repeated the question: "Simon son of John, do you love me?"

"Yes, Lord," Peter said, "you know I love you."

"Then take care of my sheep," Jesus said.

17 A third time he asked him, "Simon son of John, do you love me?"

Peter was hurt that Jesus asked the question a third time. He said, "Lord, you know everything. You know that I love you."

Jesus said, "Then feed my sheep.

18 "I tell you the truth, when you were young, you were able to do as you liked; you dressed yourself and went wherever you wanted to go. But when you are old, you will stretch out your hands, and others* will dress you and take you where you don't want to go." 19 Jesus said this to let him know by what kind of death he would glorify God. Then Jesus told him, "Follow me."

20 Peter turned around and saw behind them the disciple Jesus loved—the one who had leaned over to Jesus during supper and asked, "Lord, who will betray you?" 21 Peter asked Jesus, "What about him, Lord?"

22 Jesus replied, "If I want him to remain alive until I return, what is that to you? As for you, follow me." 23 So the rumor spread among the community of believers* that this disciple wouldn't die. But that isn't what Jesus said at all. He only said, "If I want him to remain alive until I return, what is that to you?"

24 This disciple is the one who testifies to these events and has recorded them here. And we know that his account of these things is accurate.

25 Jesus also did many other things. If they were all written down, I suppose the whole world could not contain the books that would be written.

21:15 Or *more than these others do?* **21:18** Some manuscripts read *and another one.* **21:23** Greek *the brothers.*

21:12 breakfast. The Jesus whom the disciples met was no disembodied spirit. They could see Him, hear Him, and eat with Him. Jesus had been resurrected bodily. He had conquered death.

21:14 the third time. This is the third resurrection account in John's Gospel (20:19-23,24-29). The post-resurrection appearances are part of the proof of Jesus' resurrection. They also show that Jesus had conquered death and describe how the disciples learned of their mission. Their encounter with the living Jesus changed them from frightened men to bold witnesses for their Lord.

21:15 do you love me more than these? Jesus gives Peter three opportunities to pledge his love for Him. **Feed my lambs.** After each query about his love, Jesus calls Peter to demonstrate that love by being a "good shepherd" to Jesus' sheep.

21:18 you will stretch out your hands. The stretching out of a person's hands was an early Christian idiom for crucifixion. This explains the author's comment on this quote in verse 19.

21:19 by what kind of death he would glorify God. Peter would indeed lay down his life for Jesus in the future. Since Peter is believed to have been killed during Nero's persecution of Christians in the early 60s, the manner and reality of his death would have been known by this Gospel's first readers. **Follow me.** The important thing for the disciple, whether Peter or any reader of the Gospel of John, is to keep on following Jesus, no matter where this might lead (12:26).

21:21 what about him, Lord? This question may be a clue about the purpose of this entire chapter. By the time of this writing, the beloved disciple (likely John) was probably old. So something had to be said about a rumor that had begun at the earliest stages of the Christian era which implied that John would live until Jesus' return (v. 23).

21:22 what is that to you? Jesus' response emphasized that Peter should mind his own business. The path of discipleship is different for each follower. We should follow the path He has laid out for us.

21:23 this disciple wouldn't die. . . . But that isn't what Jesus said at all. The narrator thus sets the record straight on Jesus' comment about the beloved disciple. It was not a promise that He would return within this disciple's lifetime.

INTRODUCTION TO

ACTS OF THE APOSTLES

PERSONAL READING PLAN

☐Acts 1:1-26
☐Acts 2:1-47
☐Acts 3:1–4:22
☐Acts 4:23–5:16
☐Acts 5:17–6:15
☐Acts 7:1–8:1a
☐Acts 8:1b-40
☐Acts 9:1-31
☐Acts 9:32–10:23a
☐Acts 10:23b–11:18
☐Acts 11:19–12:25
☐Acts 13:1-52
☐Acts 14:1–15:21
☐Acts 15:22–16:15
☐Acts 16:16–17:15
☐Acts 17:16–18:28
☐Acts 19:1-41
☐Acts 20:1-38
☐Acts 21:1-36
☐Acts 21:37–23:11
☐Acts 23:12–24:27
☐Acts 25:1–26:32
☐Acts 27:1-44
☐Acts 28:1-31

Although unnamed, there is an ancient tradition that Luke wrote Acts as a companion to the third Gospel. Little is known of Luke. He is mentioned only three times in the New Testament (Col. 4:14; Philem. 24; 2 Tim. 4:11). These references tell us that Luke was a physician, a valued companion of Paul, and a Gentile.

Luke's medical background is demonstrated by his use of medical terms, especially in his Gospel, for example, in recounting the story of the camel and the needle's eye in Luke 18:25, Luke's role as Paul's traveling companion is evident in "we" sections, the author suddenly switches from saying, "They did this" to "We did that" (Acts 16:10-17; 20:5–21:18; 27:1–28:16). At these points in Paul's journeys, Luke joined him as a colleague in ministry. And we learn that Luke was a Gentile from the list of greetings with which Paul concludes Colossians (Col. 4:10-11).

DATE

The final events recorded here took place in early A.D. 60, so Acts must have been compiled after that time.

THEME

The spread of the gospel to all the known world (1:8).

HISTORICAL BACKGROUND

Why did Luke write the book of Acts? Possibly he desired to commend Christianity to the Gentile world in general and to the Roman government in particular. We find in Acts not only Jews turning to Jesus (3,000 on the Day of Pentecost, see Acts 2:41) but also Gentiles. We see Peter (the apostle to the Jews) welcoming Cornelius, the Roman centurion, into the church. We see Philip preaching to the Samaritans and Jewish believers and evangelizing Gentiles in Antioch. We find Paul called by Christ to be the apostle to the Gentiles, setting up churches across the Roman Empire. Finally in Acts 15, there is formal affirmation that Gentiles are accepted in the church of Jesus Christ on equal terms with Jews.

Luke's response to the Roman government is fascinating. He seemed to go out of his way to show that Christians were loyal citizens and not lawbreakers and criminals (18:14-16; 19:37; 23:29; 25:25). He also took pains to point out that Roman officials had always treated Christians fairly and courteously (13:12; 18:12-17; 19:31). This was important to state lest Christianity be perceived as a political movement and, therefore, a threat to the Roman Empire.

However, commending Christianity to Gentiles was not Luke's central aim. His main purpose is implied in 1:8, "But you will receive power when the Holy Spirit comes upon you. And you will be my witnesses, telling people about me everywhere—in Jerusalem, throughout Judea, in Samaria, and to the ends of the earth." Luke aims to show how Christianity had spread from Jerusalem to Rome in 30 years.

CHARACTERISTICS

The book of Acts is the bridge between the Gospels and the Epistles. On the one hand, Acts completes the story of Jesus--how his life, death, and resurrection created a whole new community: the church. On the other hand, Acts sets the stage for the correspondence to this church; the letters make up the rest of the New Testament. It would be difficult to fully understand the Epistles without the data found in Acts.

Luke tells the story of the development of the church by opening a series of windows that allows us to glimpse important (and representative) developments in its growth.

1. KEY FIGURE—THE HOLY SPIRIT

One thing that characterizes the entire story is the work of the Holy Spirit. There is little question in Luke's mind how the church spread: the Holy Spirit did it. So we see the church resulting from the baptism of the Holy Spirit (2:38-41). We then see the Holy Spirit gently but directly guide the early church (13:2 and 16:7). In fact, the presence of the Holy Spirit signals that a church is authentic and not false (19:1-6). Some have suggested that this book ought to have been labeled "The Acts of the Holy Spirit" and not "The Acts of the Apostles".

2. LEADING ROLES—PETER AND PAUL

The title "The Acts of the Apostles" is inaccurate for yet another reason. The book of Acts is the story of only two apostles—Peter and Paul. Peter's story is told first. In the initial 12 chapters, he is the central figure. But in chapter 13, the spotlight shifts to Paul, and he holds center stage until Acts concludes.

The stories of these two men are not dissimilar. Both heal cripples (3:1-10; 14:8-12); both have the experience of seeing cures brought about in unusual ways (5:15-16; 19:11-12); both bring people back to life (9:36-42; 20:9-12); both meet a sorcerer (8:9-25; 13:6-12); and both are released from prison as the result of a miracle (12:7; 16:26-28). The author of Acts focuses on Peter and on Paul in their roles as key leaders of the early church. Peter was the chief apostle to the Jews, while Paul was the chief apostle to the Gentiles.

3. KEY SOURCES

Where did Luke get his information about the church's growth? The source of the second half of the book (chapters 13–28) is clear. Luke got this information directly from his friend and companion, Paul. We know Luke was traveling with Paul (the "we" sections), and he may well have kept a journal. We can also guess that during Paul's confinement in prison, the great apostle probably recounted his many adventures to Luke.

But how about the first 12 chapters that center around Peter? Luke tells us in Luke 1:3 that he "carefully investigated everything from the beginning." How? Probably by talking to believers he met through Paul. For example, Luke knew Mark. Both men were with Paul when he wrote Colossians (Col. 4:10, 14). From Mark he would have received valuable information about the growth of the church in Jerusalem and about Peter's role there. And Luke would have heard stories about Peter in the churches he visited. Finally, Luke may have had access to the official records (written and oral) of the key churches mentioned in the first 12 chapters—the churches in Jerusalem, Caesarea, and Antioch.

4. KEEN HISTORIAN

Luke's accuracy as a historian was validated by the archaeological research of Sir William Ramsay. Luke had the mind of a researcher: He was careful and paid attention to details. Thus, when reading his story of the early church, we have confidence that what Luke tells us is just what happened.

PASSAGES FOR TOPICAL GROUP STUDY

1:1-11 ...... HOLY SPIRIT POWER .... Baptism of the Holy Spirit
1:12-26 ..... QUALIFIED SPIRITUAL LEADERS ..... Replacing a Starting Player
2:1-24,36-41 THE HOLY SPIRIT .... Real Fire Power
2:42-47 ..... THE CHURCH .... A Loving Church
3:1-16 ...... COMPASSION and HEALING .... What I Have Is Yours!
5:1-11 ...... HONESTY/INTEGRITY .... Lying to Get in the Spotlight
6:1-7 .... SPIRITUAL GIFTS .... Glamour Ministry
8:26-40 ..... TELLING OTHERS THE GOOD NEWS ...... Sharing Good News
9:1-19 ...... CONVERSION and MENTORING .... Really? That Guy?
9:20-31 ..... DEFENDING YOUR FAITH .... Capable Christianity
10:1-23 ..... CLIQUES and ACCEPTANCE ..... Accepting One Another
12:1-19 ..... PERSECUTION and COURAGE ..... "Get Out of Jail Free" Card
13:1-12 ..... CULTS and DECEIVERS .... False Prophets
15:36-41 .... BROKEN RELATIONSHIPS .... Parting Company
16:6-10 ..... FIGHTING GOD and DECISIONS .... Closed Doors
16:22-40 .... TRUSTING GOD IN TRIALS .... Singing in Prison
19:23-41 .... JESUS ANGERS PEOPLE .... Anger Over the Gospel

THE PROMISE OF THE HOLY SPIRIT

1 In my first book* I told you, Theophilus, about
everything Jesus began to do and teach 2 until the
day he was taken up to heaven after giving his chosen
apostles further instructions through the Holy Spir-
it. 3 During the forty days after he suffered and died,
he appeared to the apostles from time to time, and he
proved to them in many ways that he was actually
alive. And he talked to them about the Kingdom of
God.
4 Once when he was eating with them, he com-
manded them, "Do not leave Jerusalem until the
Father sends you the gift he promised, as I told you
before. 5 John baptized with* water, but in just a few
days you will be baptized with the Holy Spirit."

THE ASCENSION OF JESUS

6 So when the apostles were with Jesus, they kept ask-
ing him, "Lord, has the time come for you to free Israel
and restore our kingdom?"
7 He replied, "The Father alone has the authority to set
those dates and times, and they are not for you to know.
8 But you will receive power when the Holy Spirit comes
upon you. And you will be my witnesses, telling people
about me everywhere—in Jerusalem, throughout Ju-
dea, in Samaria, and to the ends of the earth."
9 After saying this, he was taken up into a cloud
while they were watching, and they could no lon-
ger see him. 10 As they strained to see him rising into
heaven, two white-robed men suddenly stood among
them. 11 "Men of Galilee," they said, "why are you
standing here staring into heaven? Jesus has been
taken from you into heaven, but someday he will re-
turn from heaven in the same way you saw him go!"

MATTHIAS REPLACES JUDAS

12 Then the apostles returned to Jerusalem from the
Mount of Olives, a distance of half a mile.* 13 When
they arrived, they went to the upstairs room of the
house where they were staying.
Here are the names of those who were present:
Peter, John, James, Andrew, Philip, Thomas, Barthol-
omew, Matthew, James (son of Alphaeus), Simon (the
zealot), and Judas (son of James). 14 They all met to-
gether and were constantly united in prayer, along
with Mary the mother of Jesus, several other women,
and the brothers of Jesus.
15 During this time, when about 120 believers* were
together in one place, Peter stood up and addressed
them. 16 "Brothers," he said, "the Scriptures had to be
fulfilled concerning Judas, who guided those who ar-
rested Jesus. This was predicted long ago by the Holy
Spirit, speaking through King David. 17 Judas was one
of us and shared in the ministry with us."
18 (Judas had bought a field with the money he re-
ceived for his treachery. Falling headfirst there, his
body split open, spilling out all his intestines. 19 The
news of his death spread to all the people of Jerusa-
lem, and they gave the place the Aramaic name *Akel-
dama,* which means "Field of Blood.")
20 Peter continued, "This was written in the book of
Psalms, where it says, 'Let his home become desolate,
with no one living in it.' It also says, 'Let someone else
take his position.'*
21 "So now we must choose a replacement for Judas
from among the men who were with us the entire
time we were traveling with the Lord Jesus—22 from
the time he was baptized by John until the day he was

BAPTISM OF THE HOLY SPIRIT

1. What long-awaited prize was worth the wait (concert tickets, driver's license, etc.)?

ACTS 1:1-11

2. What does it mean to be "baptized with the Holy Spirit" (v. 5)? What does that image suggest about the Holy Spirit's work in our lives?
3. Why did Jesus tell the disciples, "The Father alone has the authority to set those dates and times, and they are not for you to know" (v. 7)? What "dates and times" do you sometimes wonder about?
4. What "power" does the Holy Spirit bring to Christians? How do you specifically need the Holy Spirit's help in being a witness to others?

1:1 The reference is to the Gospel of Luke. **1:5** Or *in;* also in 1:5b. **1:12** Greek *a Sabbath day's journey.* **1:15** Greek *brothers.* **1:20** Pss 69:25; 109:8. **2:1** The Festival of Pentecost came 50 days after Passover (when Jesus was crucified). **2:4** Or *in other tongues.* **2:17-21** Joel 2:28-32. **2:22** Or *Jesus of Nazareth.*

1:1 my first book. That is, the Gospel of Luke. Luke authored both works. **everything that Jesus began to do and teach.** Acts is the continuing story of the work of Jesus in the life of the church.

1:2 until the day he was taken up. See Luke 24:50-53. The ascension marks the beginning of a new phase in the work of Jesus. He now exercises His divine reign from heaven. **apostles.** Apostles were ambassadors especially commissioned to represent the one in whose name they were sent. In the Gospels, this term refers only to the Twelve. In Acts, others (like Paul and Barnabas in 14:3–4) are called apostles.

1:4-5 the Father sends you the gift he promised. From the very beginning the expectation was that through Jesus the Spirit of God would be poured out on all His people. **baptized with the Holy Spirit.** Baptism was associated with cleansing. The metaphor would communicate being flooded with God's Spirit. Thus Jesus raised the expectations of the disciples about what the next step in His agenda for them might be.

1:6-8 to free Israel and restore our kingdom? Jesus and the disciples had different ideas about the kingdom of God (Luke 9:46-55; 22:24ff). The question of verse 6 reflects three such misunderstandings: (1) it would not be Jesus who would be doing the work from now on but the disciples empowered by His Spirit; (2) the time of the kingdom's establishment should not concern them; and (3) the kingdom is not a matter of the political destiny of Israel but a spiritual realm involving the whole world.

1:8 the Holy Spirit comes upon you. The mission of Jesus is continued through the work of His Spirit empowering the disciples to bear witness to Him (Luke 12:11-12; Matt. 28:20-21). The result of this empowering will be the spread of the gospel throughout the world.

1:9 he was taken up into a cloud. A declaration of Jesus' deity. The Bible often uses the cloud as a symbol of divine glory (Ex. 16:10; Ps. 104:3).

1:14 Mary . . . and . . . the brothers of Jesus. Before the resurrection, Jesus' brothers had not believed in Him (Mark 3:21; John 7:5). One of His brothers, James, eventually became a leader of the Jerusalem church and the author of the epistle of James.

1:18-19 Falling headfirst there, his body split open. This statement about Judas' death differs considerably from the account in Matthew 27:3-10. It may be that he hanged himself, and then the rope broke, allowing his body to fall to the ground. The field, bought with Judas's betrayal money, may have come to be known as belonging to him.

1:22 from the time he was baptized by John until the day he was taken from us. Since the apostles were to bear witness to all Jesus said and did, it was important that they be eyewitnesses who were involved in His ministry from the very beginning.

taken from us. Whoever is chosen will join us as a wit-
ness of Jesus' resurrection."
23 So they nominated two men: Joseph called Bar-
sabbas (also known as Justus) and Matthias. 24 Then
they all prayed, "O Lord, you know every heart. Show
us which of these men you have chosen 25 as an apos-
tle to replace Judas in this ministry, for he has desert-
ed us and gone where he belongs." 26 Then they cast
lots, and Matthias was selected to become an apostle
with the other eleven.

REPLACING A STARTING PLAYER

1. If you could add any one person to your athletic team now, who would you invite? To your group?

ACTS 1:12-26

2. Why did the disciples decide to find another disciple to replace Judas?
3. Why did Judas commit suicide? Where does going it your own way instead of siding with Jesus lead?
4. Matthias was chosen, but he is never mentioned again; God chose Paul later. What does this suggest about man's views of qualified spiritual leaders?
5. Judas rejected Jesus, while Paul obeyed Him. How can you be a disciple more like Paul?

THE HOLY SPIRIT COMES

2 On the day of Pentecost* all the believers were
meeting together in one place. 2 Suddenly, there
was a sound from heaven like the roaring of a mighty
windstorm, and it filled the house where they were
sitting. 3 Then, what looked like flames or tongues
of fire appeared and settled on each of them. 4 And
everyone present was filled with the Holy Spirit and
began speaking in other languages,* as the Holy Spir-
it gave them this ability.
5 At that time there were devout Jews from every
nation living in Jerusalem. 6 When they heard the
loud noise, everyone came running, and they were
bewildered to hear their own languages being spo-
ken by the believers.
7 They were completely amazed. "How can this be?"
they exclaimed. "These people are all from Galilee,

REAL FIRE POWER

1. What are you usually doing at 9 a.m. on a Sunday? A weekday? A Saturday?

ACTS 2:1-24,36-41

2. What do the images of wind and fire suggest about the Holy Spirit (vv. 2-3)?
3. Why did God "pour out" His Spirit (vv. 17-21)? What is one of the important works of the Holy Spirit (vv. 21,36)?
4. How does a person receive the Holy Spirit (v. 38)? Have you obeyed this step?
5. How have you seen the Holy Spirit at work in your own life? How can you increase His influence in your life?

8 and yet we hear them speaking in our own native
languages! 9 Here we are—Parthians, Medes, Elam-
ites, people from Mesopotamia, Judea, Cappadocia,
Pontus, the province of Asia, 10 Phrygia, Pamphylia,
Egypt, and the areas of Libya around Cyrene, visitors
from Rome 11 (both Jews and converts to Judaism), Cre-
tans, and Arabs. And we all hear these people speak-
ing in our own languages about the wonderful things
God has done!" 12 They stood there amazed and per-
plexed. "What can this mean?" they asked each other.
13 But others in the crowd ridiculed them, saying,
"They're just drunk, that's all!"

PETER PREACHES TO THE CROWD

14 Then Peter stepped forward with the eleven other
apostles and shouted to the crowd, "Listen carefully,
all of you, fellow Jews and residents of Jerusalem!
Make no mistake about this. 15 These people are not
drunk, as some of you are assuming. Nine o'clock in
the morning is much too early for that. 16 No, what you
see was predicted long ago by the prophet Joel:

17 'In the last days,' God says,
'I will pour out my Spirit upon all people.
Your sons and daughters will prophesy.
Your young men will see visions,
and your old men will dream dreams.

1:23 Joseph, called Barsabbas . . .Matthias. Nothing is known of these men. Of all the original 12 apostles, only Peter, James, and John are mentioned outside of the Gospels and Acts 1:13.
1:24 O Lord, you know every heart. Such knowledge is a divine attribute (1 Sam. 16:7; Jer. 17:10) which Jesus shares.
1:26 they cast lots. Making decisions by casting lots was common in biblical times (see Josh. 18:3-8; 1 Chron. 25:6-8; Neh. 10:34.) This was done by shaking stones on which names were written from a container. The person whose name came out of the container first would be selected.
2:1 the day of Pentecost. This was the Feast of Weeks (Ex. 23:16; Lev. 23:15-21; Deut. 16:9-12) held 50 days after Passover. Originally, a kind of Thanksgiving Day for gathered crops, it came to be associated with the commemoration of the giving of the Law at Sinai (Ex. 20:1-17). Pentecost was a celebration attended by thousands of Jews who had settled all over the Roman empire.
2:2-4 the roaring of a mighty windstorm. In both Hebrew (the language in which the Old Testament was originally written) and Greek (the language in which the New Testament was originally written), the word translated as "Spirit" and "wind" and "breath" is all the same word. In Hebrew the word is *rhuah;* in Greek the word is *pneuma.* While this can lead to confusion, it also adds meaning. Is this "wind" from heaven truly a wind, or is it the Spirit of God? Actually, it's both! Note also that it was a violent wind that came at Pentecost. This reminds us that while the Holy Spirit can bring peace to a person's soul, the Spirit is also a powerful force that we cannot control. **like flames or tongues of fire.** Fire is often associated with divine appearances (Ex. 3:2; 19:18). John the Baptist said Jesus would baptize his followers with the Holy Spirit and fire (Luke 3:16), symbolizing the purifying effect of the Spirit. Tongues were a sign to the crowds of a supernatural event, the point of which was Jesus Christ.
2:9-11 Parthians, Medes, Elamites . . . Mesopotamia. Present day Iran and Iraq, to the east of Jerusalem. These Jews traced their roots back to the Assyrian overthrow of Israel and the Babylonian overthrow of Judea several centuries before. **Judea.** Either the immediate environs around Jerusalem are in view, or Luke is referring to the days under David and Solomon when the land of Israel stretched from Egypt on the west to the Euphrates River on the east. **Cappadocia, Pontus, the province of Asia, Phrygia, Pamphylia.** Present day Turkey to the north of Jerusalem. Much of Acts takes place in this region. **Egypt . . . Libya around Cyrene.** To the west of Jerusalem on the northern coast of Africa. **converts to Judaism.** Judaism's high morality and developed spirituality attracted many Gentiles from other religions. **Cretans.** An island south of Greece in the Mediterranean Sea. **Arabs.** The Nabetean kingdom was south of Jerusalem with borders on Egypt and the Euphrates.

18 In those days I will pour out my Spirit
even on my servants—men and women alike—
and they will prophesy.
19 And I will cause wonders in the heavens above
and signs on the earth below—
blood and fire and clouds of smoke.
20 The sun will become dark,
and the moon will turn blood red
before that great and glorious day of the LORD
arrives.
21 But everyone who calls on the name of the LORD
will be saved.'*

22 "People of Israel, listen! God publicly endorsed
Jesus the Nazarene* by doing powerful miracles,
wonders, and signs through him, as you well know.
23 But God knew what would happen, and his pre-
arranged plan was carried out when Jesus was be-
trayed. With the help of lawless Gentiles, you nailed
him to a cross and killed him. 24 But God released him
from the horrors of death and raised him back to life,
for death could not keep him in its grip. 25 King David
said this about him:

'I see that the LORD is always with me.
I will not be shaken, for he is right beside me.
26 No wonder my heart is glad,
and my tongue shouts his praises!
My body rests in hope.
27 For you will not leave my soul among the dead*
or allow your Holy One to rot in the grave.
28 You have shown me the way of life,
and you will fill me with the joy of your
presence.'*

29 "Dear brothers, think about this! You can be sure
that the patriarch David wasn't referring to himself,
for he died and was buried, and his tomb is still here
among us. 30 But he was a prophet, and he knew God
had promised with an oath that one of David's own de-
scendants would sit on his throne. 31 David was looking
into the future and speaking of the Messiah's resur-
rection. He was saying that God would not leave him
among the dead or allow his body to rot in the grave.
32 "God raised Jesus from the dead, and we are all
witnesses of this. 33 Now he is exalted to the place of
highest honor in heaven, at God's right hand. And the
Father, as he had promised, gave him the Holy Spirit to
pour out upon us, just as you see and hear today. 34 For
David himself never ascended into heaven, yet he said,

'The LORD said to my Lord,
"Sit in the place of honor at my right hand
35 until I humble your enemies,
making them a footstool under your feet."'*

36 "So let everyone in Israel know for certain that
God has made this Jesus, whom you crucified, to be
both Lord and Messiah!"
37 Peter's words pierced their hearts, and they said
to him and to the other apostles, "Brothers, what
should we do?"
38 Peter replied, "Each of you must repent of your
sins and turn to God, and be baptized in the name of
Jesus Christ for the forgiveness of your sins. Then you
will receive the gift of the Holy Spirit. 39 This promise
is to you, to your children, and to those far away*—
all who have been called by the Lord our God." 40 Then
Peter continued preaching for a long time, strongly
urging all his listeners, "Save yourselves from this
crooked generation!"
41 Those who believed what Peter said were baptized
and added to the church that day—about 3,000 in all.

THE BELIEVERS FORM A COMMUNITY

42 All the believers devoted themselves to the apostles'
teaching, and to fellowship, and to sharing in meals
(including the Lord's Supper*), and to prayer.

A LOVING CHURCH

1. When have you visited a church that was very different from your own? What was it like? What was so different?

ACTS 2:42-47

2. What does it mean that the church "devoted themselves to the apostles' teaching, and to fellowship, and to sharing in meals (including the Lord's Supper), and to prayer" (v. 42)?
3. How is your church similar to the fellowship described here? How is it different?
4. Why did the early Christians sell "their property and possessions and shared the money with those in need" (v. 45)? How might you help your church to do this today?

2:27 Greek *in Hades;* also in 2:31. **2:25-28** Ps 16:8-11 (Greek version). **2:34-35** Ps 110:1. **2:39** Or *and to people far in the future,* or *and to the Gentiles.* **2:42** Greek *the breaking of bread;* also in 2:46.

2:22 powerful miracles, wonders, and signs through him. The fact of Jesus' miracles is not debated. The stories of His work in Galilee had been widely reported (Mark 3:8; Luke 12:1; Acts 26:26). What was debated was the source of His power: early on some leaders accused Him of being possessed by Satan (Mark 3:22).

2:24-28 Death could not hold Jesus (v. 24) because the Messiah would not be subject to death (v. 27). This is supported by a quote from Psalm 16:8-11 which, in its original setting, was the prayer of a righteous person rejoicing in the fact that because God supported him, he could be assured that he would not be left in Sheol or the Pit but enjoy God's presence forever. Some rabbis viewed this as a Messianic Psalm providing a precedent for Peter to read it as one that foretold the death and resurrection of the Messiah Jesus.

2:36 Lord. The full impact of the deity of Jesus gradually dawned upon the apostles. As the gospel spread beyond Palestine, He is referred to primarily as "the Lord," the title used for God in the Old Testament.

2:38 Repent. Repentance is the act of turning away from all other loyalties to affirm one's allegiance to Jesus (see Mark 1:15). **be baptized.** Baptism is the outward sign of the inward change of heart and mind, which shows the desire to be cleansed from sin. **in the name of Jesus Christ.** The early Christians declared, "Jesus is Lord," as they were baptized (Rom. 10:9; 1 Cor. 12:3), affirming their allegiance and dependence on Him to save them. Recognition of Jesus' Messiahship was critical for a person's inclusion in the church. **receive the gift of the Holy Spirit.** The coming of the Holy Spirit is the distinctive reality that Jesus bestows on those who trust Him.

2:42 teaching. The foundation for the church's life was the instruction of the apostles as the representatives of Jesus. **fellowship.** While this may include the aspect of sharing to meet material needs (v. 45), it most likely refers to their common participation in the Spirit as they worshipped together (1 Cor. 12). **sharing in meals (including the Lord's Supper).** The Lord's Supper in which they remembered Jesus' death (Luke 22:19) and recognized His presence among them (Luke 24:30-31). **prayer.** This may refer to set times and forms of prayer—the typical practice of the Jews.

43 A deep sense of awe came over them all, and the apostles performed many miraculous signs and wonders. 44 And all the believers met together in one place and shared everything they had. 45 They sold their property and possessions and shared the money with those in need. 46 They worshiped together at the Temple each day, met in homes for the Lord's Supper, and shared their meals with great joy and generosity*—47 all the while praising God and enjoying the goodwill of all the people. And each day the Lord added to their fellowship those who were being saved.

PETER HEALS A CRIPPLED BEGGAR

3 Peter and John went to the Temple one afternoon to take part in the three o'clock prayer service. 2 As they approached the Temple, a man lame from birth was being carried in. Each day he was put beside the Temple gate, the one called the Beautiful Gate, so he could beg from the people going into the Temple. 3 When he saw Peter and John about to enter, he asked them for some money.

4 Peter and John looked at him intently, and Peter said, "Look at us!" 5 The lame man looked at them eagerly, expecting some money. 6 But Peter said, "I don't have any silver or gold for you. But I'll give you what I have. In the name of Jesus Christ the Nazarene,* get up and* walk!"

7 Then Peter took the lame man by the right hand and helped him up. And as he did, the man's feet and ankles were instantly healed and strengthened. 8 He jumped up, stood on his feet, and began to walk! Then, walking, leaping, and praising God, he went into the Temple with them.

9 All the people saw him walking and heard him praising God. 10 When they realized he was the lame beggar they had seen so often at the Beautiful Gate, they were absolutely astounded! 11 They all rushed out in amazement to Solomon's Colonnade, where the man was holding tightly to Peter and John.

PETER PREACHES IN THE TEMPLE

12 Peter saw his opportunity and addressed the crowd. "People of Israel," he said, "what is so surprising about this? And why stare at us as though we had made this man walk by our own power or godliness? 13 For it is the God of Abraham, Isaac, and Jacob—the God of all our ancestors—who has brought glory to his servant Jesus by doing this. This is the same Jesus whom you

WHAT I HAVE IS YOURS!

1. What do you do when a beggar asks you for money?

ACTS 3:1-16

2. Why do you think Peter and John "looked at [the lame man] intently" (v. 4)? Why didn't they just drop a coin and keep going?
3. What was the result of their act of faith? How did it affect the lame man (v. 8)? Others (vv. 9-10)?
4. Why did Peter and John heal the man: Out of compassion? They had no money? To glorify God? Other?
5. What was it that healed the man (v. 16)? How can your faith help others in need?

handed over and rejected before Pilate, despite Pilate's decision to release him. 14 You rejected this holy, righteous one and instead demanded the release of a murderer. 15 You killed the author of life, but God raised him from the dead. And we are witnesses of this fact!

16 "Through faith in the name of Jesus, this man was healed—and you know how crippled he was before. Faith in Jesus' name has healed him before your very eyes.

17 "Friends,* I realize that what you and your leaders did to Jesus was done in ignorance. 18 But God was fulfilling what all the prophets had foretold about the Messiah—that he must suffer these things. 19 Now repent of your sins and turn to God, so that your sins may be wiped away. 20 Then times of refreshment will come from the presence of the Lord, and he will again send you Jesus, your appointed Messiah. 21 For he must remain in heaven until the time for the final restoration of all things, as God promised long ago through his holy prophets. 22 Moses said, 'The LORD your God will raise up for you a Prophet like me from among your own people. Listen carefully to everything he tells you.'* 23 Then Moses said, 'Anyone who will not listen to that Prophet will be completely cut off from God's people.'*

2:46 Or *and sincere hearts.* **3:6a** Or *Jesus Christ of Nazareth.* **3:6b** Some manuscripts do not include *get up and.* **3:17** Greek *Brothers.* **3:22** Deut 18:15. **3:23** Deut 18:19; Lev 23:29.

2:43-47 The picture of the church is one of continual growth (v. 47) marked by generous sharing (vv. 44-45) and joyful worship and fellowship (vv. 46-47). The worship at the temple continued as before since the line dividing Christianity from Judaism had not yet been drawn. Christians saw their faith as the natural climax of what the Jewish faith had always declared.

2:44-45 everything they had. The shared life that these early Christians practiced was an outgrowth of the intense love they had for one another through Jesus Christ. They believed that in Christ each person's need should become everyone's need. This attitude is a key component of authentic Christian community.

3:1 the three o'clock prayer service. The two daily times of sacrifice and prayer at the temple were in the early morning and around 3:00 p.m.

3:2 the Temple gate, the one called the Beautiful Gate. This gate was apparently near Solomon's Colonnade (v. 11) on the eastern side of the temple. Beggars would gather about the temple in hopes of receiving alms from passersby.

3:3-5 he asked them for some money. The man probably called out for alms without paying attention to whom he was talking. But Peter and John broke through his routine by insisting that he pay attention to them.

3:6-8 I don't have any silver or gold. To experience life fully is surely more valuable than money, and the healing which Peter was about to do would help this man live more fully. **In the name of Jesus Christ.** This man was healed by the authority of Jesus. Even those who were not Jesus' followers sought to heal by using His name. **jumped up . . .praising God.** This man made no attempt to hide his excitement. That he jumped to his feet is also a sign of how complete the healing was (see Isa. 35:6.)

3:11 Solomon's Colonnade. A long porch extending along the eastern wall of the outer court of the temple. It was the typical gathering place for the early Christians (5:12).

3:17 done in ignorance. The Law of Moses allowed for forgiveness of sins committed unwittingly (Num. 15:27-31). While Peter acknowledges that the people did not really know what they were doing when they had Jesus crucified (see also 13:27, Luke 23:34; 1 Cor. 2:8), he makes the point that if they resist him now, they are guilty of a conscious, willful rejection of the Messiah.

3:22 a Prophet like me. That God would send a new Moses who would restore God's people to Himself was a common expectation among the Jews (John 1:21; 4:25; 6:14).

24 “Starting with Samuel, every prophet spoke
about what is happening today. 25 You are the chil-
dren of those prophets, and you are included in the
covenant God promised to your ancestors. For God
said to Abraham, ‘Through your descendants* all the
families on earth will be blessed.’ 26 When God raised
up his servant, Jesus, he sent him first to you people of
Israel, to bless you by turning each of you back from
your sinful ways.”

PETER AND JOHN BEFORE THE COUNCIL

4 While Peter and John were speaking to the people,
they were confronted by the priests, the captain of
the Temple guard, and some of the Sadducees. 2 These
leaders were very disturbed that Peter and John were
teaching the people that through Jesus there is a res-
urrection of the dead. 3 They arrested them and, since
it was already evening, put them in jail until morning.
4 But many of the people who heard their message be-
lieved it, so the number of believers now totaled 5,000
men, not counting women and children*.
5 The next day the council of all the rulers and el-
ders and teachers of religious law met in Jerusalem.
6 Annas the high priest was there, along with Ca-
iaphas, John, Alexander, and other relatives of the
high priest. 7 They brought in the two disciples and
demanded, “By what power, or in whose name, have
you done this?”
8 Then Peter, filled with the Holy Spirit, said to
them, “Rulers and elders of our people, 9 are we being
questioned today because we’ve done a good deed for
a crippled man? Do you want to know how he was
healed? 10 Let me clearly state to all of you and to all
the people of Israel that he was healed by the power-
ful name of Jesus Christ the Nazarene,* the man you
crucified but whom God raised from the dead. 11 For
Jesus is the one referred to in the Scriptures, where
it says,

‘The stone that you builders rejected
has now become the cornerstone.’*

12 There is salvation in no one else! God has given
no other name under heaven by which we must be
saved.”
13 The members of the council were amazed when
they saw the boldness of Peter and John, for they
could see that they were ordinary men with no spe-
cial training in the Scriptures. They also recognized
them as men who had been with Jesus. 14 But since
they could see the man who had been healed stand-
ing right there among them, there was nothing the
council could say. 15 So they ordered Peter and John
out of the council chamber* and conferred among
themselves.
16 “What should we do with these men?” they asked
each other. “We can’t deny that they have performed a
miraculous sign, and everybody in Jerusalem knows
about it. 17 But to keep them from spreading their pro-
paganda any further, we must warn them not to speak
to anyone in Jesus’ name again.” 18 So they called the
apostles back in and commanded them never again to
speak or teach in the name of Jesus.
19 But Peter and John replied, “Do you think God
wants us to obey you rather than him? 20 We cannot
stop telling about everything we have seen and heard.”
21 The council then threatened them further, but
they finally let them go because they didn’t know how
to punish them without starting a riot. For everyone
was praising God 22 for this miraculous sign—the
healing of a man who had been lame for more than
forty years.

THE BELIEVERS PRAY FOR COURAGE

23 As soon as they were freed, Peter and John returned
to the other believers and told them what the leading
priests and elders had said. 24 When they heard the
report, all the believers lifted their voices together in
prayer to God: “O Sovereign Lord, Creator of heaven
and earth, the sea, and everything in them—25 you
spoke long ago by the Holy Spirit through our ances-
tor David, your servant, saying,

‘Why were the nations so angry?
Why did they waste their time with futile plans?
26 The kings of the earth prepared for battle;
the rulers gathered together
against the LORD
and against his Messiah.’*

27 “In fact, this has happened here in this very city!
For Herod Antipas, Pontius Pilate the governor, the
Gentiles, and the people of Israel were all united
against Jesus, your holy servant, whom you anoint-
ed. 28 But everything they did was determined be-
forehand according to your will. 29 And now, O Lord,
hear their threats, and give us, your servants, great
boldness in preaching your word. 30 Stretch out your
hand with healing power; may miraculous signs and
wonders be done through the name of your holy ser-
vant Jesus.”
31 After this prayer, the meeting place shook, and
they were all filled with the Holy Spirit. Then they
preached the word of God with boldness.

3:25 Greek *your seed;* see Gen 12:3; 22:18. **4:4** Greek *5,000 adult males.* **4:10** Or *Jesus Christ of Nazareth.* **4:11** Ps 118:22. **4:15** Greek *the Sanhedrin.* **4:25-26** Or *his anointed one;* or *his Christ.* Ps 2:1-2.

4:1 the captain of the temple guard. A high-ranking official who had the responsibility of maintaining order in the temple. **the Sadducees.** The Sadducees were a wealthy group who believed only in the first five books of the Old Testament and denied the resurrection (see 23:6-8).

4:2 teaching . . . the resurrection. The Sadducees considered teaching to be a priestly right alone. To further upset things, the disciples were preaching the resurrection, a doctrine that the Sadducees denied.

4:10 Let me clearly state to all of you. The Sanhedrin represented the highest level of authority among the Jews. But Peter is not intimidated by them as he declares that the miracle was not a product of sorcery but of faith in the power of Jesus—the one they had condemned to death a few weeks before.

4:12 salvation. Peter declared that his audience could either repent and believe in order to experience God’s salvation, or they could persist in their rejection of Jesus and forfeit the hope for which Israel had waited so long.

4:13 ordinary men . . . they had been with Jesus. The Sanhedrin identified the boldness with which Peter spoke as reminiscent of the way Jesus had spoken. **no special training in the Scriptures.** As fishermen by trade, Peter and John had not received formal rabbinical training.

4:16-17 we can’t deny. Recognizing the undeniable fact that the man was healed and the widespread popular support for the disciples (v. 21), the Sanhedrin realized there was little they could do but try to intimidate the disciples into silence.

4:19-20 We cannot stop telling everything we have seen and heard. Since the Sanhedrin had set itself against God and His Messiah, the disciples had no choice but to ignore its commands and remain faithful to God.

4:31 the meeting place shook. Earthquakes were a common sign in the Old Testament of God’s presence (Ex. 19:18; Ps. 114:7; Isa. 6:4; Ezek. 38:19). Through this sign, the disciples were assured that their prayer was heard.

THE BELIEVERS SHARE THEIR POSSESSIONS

32 All the believers were united in heart and mind.
And they felt that what they owned was not their
own, so they shared everything they had. 33 The apos-
tles testified powerfully to the resurrection of the
Lord Jesus, and God's great blessing was upon them
all. 34 There were no needy people among them, be-
cause those who owned land or houses would sell
them 35 and bring the money to the apostles to give to
those in need.
36 For instance, there was Joseph, the one the
apostles nicknamed Barnabas (which means "Son
of Encouragement"). He was from the tribe of Levi
and came from the island of Cyprus. 37 He sold a
field he owned and brought the money to the apos-
tles.

ANANIAS AND SAPPHIRA

5 But there was a certain man named Ananias who,
with his wife, Sapphira, sold some property. 2 He
brought part of the money to the apostles, claiming it
was the full amount. With his wife's consent, he kept
the rest.
3 Then Peter said, "Ananias, why have you let Sa-
tan fill your heart? You lied to the Holy Spirit, and you
kept some of the money for yourself. 4 The property
was yours to sell or not sell, as you wished. And after
selling it, the money was also yours to give away. How
could you do a thing like this? You weren't lying to us
but to God!"
5 As soon as Ananias heard these words, he fell to
the floor and died. Everyone who heard about it was
terrified. 6 Then some young men got up, wrapped
him in a sheet, and took him out and buried him.
7 About three hours later his wife came in, not
knowing what had happened. 8 Peter asked her, "Was
this the price you and your husband received for your
land?"
"Yes," she replied, "that was the price."
9 And Peter said, "How could the two of you even
think of conspiring to test the Spirit of the Lord like
this? The young men who buried your husband are
just outside the door, and they will carry you out, too."
10 Instantly, she fell to the floor and died. When the
young men came in and saw that she was dead, they
carried her out and buried her beside her husband.

> ### LYING TO GET IN THE SPOTLIGHT
>
> 1. When has someone caught you in a lie? How did you feel? What did you learn?
>
> **ACTS 5:1-11**
>
> 2. What were Ananias and Sapphira guilty of? Why did God punish them so severely?
> 3. What were they hoping to gain by lying about the price? Were they under some obligation to give any or all of the money to God?
> 4. Why did Peter ask Sapphira what price they had earned? What might she have done differently?
> 5. In your life, where are you most tempted to be dishonest or lack integrity in some way?

11 Great fear gripped the entire church and everyone
else who heard what had happened.

THE APOSTLES HEAL MANY

12 The apostles were performing many miraculous
signs and wonders among the people. And all the be-
lievers were meeting regularly at the Temple in the
area known as Solomon's Colonnade. 13 But no one else
dared to join them, even though all the people had
high regard for them. 14 Yet more and more people be-
lieved and were brought to the Lord—crowds of both
men and women. 15 As a result of the apostles' work,
sick people were brought out into the streets on beds
and mats so that Peter's shadow might fall across some
of them as he went by. 16 Crowds came from the villag-
es around Jerusalem, bringing their sick and those
possessed by evil* spirits, and they were all healed.

THE APOSTLES MEET OPPOSITION

17 The high priest and his officials, who were Saddu-
cees, were filled with jealousy. 18 They arrested the
apostles and put them in the public jail. 19 But an angel
of the Lord came at night, opened the gates of the jail,
and brought them out. Then he told them, 20 "Go to the
Temple and give the people this message of life!"

5:16 Greek *unclean.*

4:32 All the believers were united in heart and mind. Compare with 2:44-45. This sharing was done freely by the early believers as an expression of love for one another; it may be intended as another sign of the Spirit at work (v. 31).
4:34 no needy people among them. While this was the ideal for Old Testament Israel (Deut. 15:4), the generosity of the Christians allowed it to actually be experienced (see Luke 12:32-34; 18:18-30; 19:1-10).
4:35 bring the money to the apostles. The apostles were given the responsibility of distributing the resources so the needs of the people were met.
5:2 he kept the rest. The rare Greek word translated here is used in the Septuagint version of Joshua 7:1 to describe Achan's action of "keeping back" part of the booty from Jericho that was to be devoted to God. Luke may have used this word to make a connection between Achan's sin and that of Ananias.
5:4-10 Many find the death of Ananias and Sapphira disturbing. Capital punishment for an act of deceit seems harsh. But trust was vital to this early Christian community. Those who were not true to their word threatened the community's survival. Whether from heart failure at the exposure of their sin, or from some direct act of God, both Ananias and Sapphira died when their lie was revealed.
5:11 great fear came. The result of this incident was that the entire community recognized the seriousness of the presence of God in their midst (Heb. 10:31; 12:28-29). **church.** This is the first use of the word *ekklesia* in Acts. This word, along with *synagoge,* was commonly used in the Septuagint to translate the Hebrew word *qahal,* referring to the assembly of God's people. Since *synagoge* became tied in with the name for the Jewish places of worship (the synagogue), the Christians used *ekklesia* to refer to themselves. They claimed a common Old Testament term to identify themselves as the true "Israel" of God.
5:12 miraculous signs and wonders. Miracles that point to the reality of God's presence and power.
5:13-14 But no one else dared to join them. The lack of clarity of this passage leads to some questions. There seems to be a contradiction here between verse 13, "None of the rest dared to join them," and verse 14, "Believers were added to the Lord's church in increasing numbers—crowds of both men and women." Verse 13 seems to say that people were still afraid to join with the followers of Christ because of the persecution against them. But it is possible that the word translated here "join them" may be better translated "interfere with them," which makes more sense within the context.
5:15 Peter's shadow. This action reveals the esteem that the common people held for the church (and especially for Peter). The woman in Mark 5:28 had a similar superstitious idea about Jesus' garment which He corrected by telling her it was her faith in Him—not any magical properties about His clothes—that brought her healing (see also 19:11-12 and Mark 6:56).
5:19-20 This is the first of three miraculous escapes from jail reported in Acts (12:6-19 and 16:26.)

21 So at daybreak the apostles entered the Temple, as they were told, and immediately began teaching.

When the high priest and his officials arrived, they convened the high council*—the full assembly of the elders of Israel. Then they sent for the apostles to be brought from the jail for trial. 22 But when the Temple guards went to the jail, the men were gone. So they returned to the council and reported, 23 "The jail was securely locked, with the guards standing outside, but when we opened the gates, no one was there!"

24 When the captain of the Temple guard and the leading priests heard this, they were perplexed, wondering where it would all end. 25 Then someone arrived with startling news: "The men you put in jail are standing in the Temple, teaching the people!"

26 The captain went with his Temple guards and arrested the apostles, but without violence, for they were afraid the people would stone them. 27 Then they brought the apostles before the high council, where the high priest confronted them. 28 "We gave you strict orders never again to teach in this man's name!" he said. "Instead, you have filled all Jerusalem with your teaching about him, and you want to make us responsible for his death!"

29 But Peter and the apostles replied, "We must obey God rather than any human authority. 30 The God of our ancestors raised Jesus from the dead after you killed him by hanging him on a cross.* 31 Then God put him in the place of honor at his right hand as Prince and Savior. He did this so the people of Israel would repent of their sins and be forgiven. 32 We are witnesses of these things and so is the Holy Spirit, who is given by God to those who obey him."

33 When they heard this, the high council was furious and decided to kill them. 34 But one member, a Pharisee named Gamaliel, who was an expert in religious law and respected by all the people, stood up and ordered that the men be sent outside the council chamber for a while. 35 Then he said to his colleagues, "Men of Israel, take care what you are planning to do to these men! 36 Some time ago there was that fellow Theudas, who pretended to be someone great. About 400 others joined him, but he was killed, and all his followers went their various ways. The whole movement came to nothing. 37 After him, at the time of the census, there was Judas of Galilee. He got people to follow him, but he was killed, too, and all his followers were scattered.

38 "So my advice is, leave these men alone. Let them go. If they are planning and doing these things merely on their own, it will soon be overthrown. 39 But if it is from God, you will not be able to overthrow them. You may even find yourselves fighting against God!"

40 The others accepted his advice. They called in the apostles and had them flogged. Then they ordered them never again to speak in the name of Jesus, and they let them go.

41 The apostles left the high council rejoicing that God had counted them worthy to suffer disgrace for the name of Jesus.* 42 And every day, in the Temple and from house to house, they continued to teach and preach this message: "Jesus is the Messiah."

GLAMOUR MINISTRY

1. If you worked in a restaurant, what job would you like to have? What would you not like to do?

ACTS 6:1-7

2. Why should the apostles "spend our time teaching the word of God, not running a food program" (v. 2)?
3. Those who waited on tables needed to be "of good reputation, full of the Spirit and wisdom" (v. 3). What does that suggest about the importance of less glamorous ministries?
4. What ministry do you perform for your church? For your teammates? For your group?

SEVEN MEN CHOSEN TO SERVE

6 But as the believers* rapidly multiplied, there were rumblings of discontent. The Greek-speaking believers complained about the Hebrew-speaking believers, saying that their widows were being discriminated against in the daily distribution of food.

2 So the Twelve called a meeting of all the believers. They said, "We apostles should spend our time teaching the word of God, not running a food program. 3 And so, brothers, select seven men who are well respected and are full of the Spirit and wisdom. We will give them this responsibility. 4 Then we apostles can spend our time in prayer and teaching the word."

5:21 Greek *Sanhedrin;* also in 5:27, 41. 5:30 Greek *on a tree.* 5:41 Greek *for the name.* 6:1 Greek *disciples;* also in 6:2, 7.

5:21–26 The Sanhedrin was bewildered when they discovered the men they had imprisoned were back at the temple preaching!

5:28 you want to make us responsible for his death! The Sanhedrin was concerned that the apostles' teaching would undermine their authority in the public eye. To them, Jesus was a blasphemer who deserved death.

5:29 "We must obey God rather than any human authority." Peter and John had already made this statement in 4:19–20. We are called to be good citizens of the state (Rom. 13:1–7), but we as believers have a higher citizenship. Our loyalty to the kingdom of God extends beyond national borders, and it is not governed by human authority.

5:30 hanging him on a cross. This is a reference to a cross that was sometimes called a "tree." Probably a deliberate reference to Deuteronomy 21:22–23, which taught that a curse rested upon a person whose body was hung on a tree. Peter is highlighting the fact that these leaders are guilty of a serious crime (v. 28) because they condemned the Messiah to a shameful death.

5:34 a Pharisee. In the Gospels the Pharisees are the prime opponents of Jesus because of their conviction that he was a lawbreaker. But in Acts they are more supportive of the church than the Sadducees, who felt that the apostles were encroaching on their power in temple affairs. **Gamaliel.** Other sources confirm Luke's comment that this man was greatly honored and loved by the people.

5:36 Theudas. To prove his point, Gamaliel mentions two former insurrectionists whose crusades fell apart shortly after their leaders died. The Theudas referred to here is unknown.

5:37 Judas of Galilee. This man led a revolt against Roman oppression in A.D. 6 when Judea came under Roman control.

5:40 flogged. "Flogging" referred to being whipped 13 times by a lash with three strands (thus amounting to 39 lashes). Deuteronomy 25:3 allowed a maximum of 40 lashes, but 39 became the norm so the law would not be broken.

6:1 Greek-speaking believers. Jews who came from outside Palestine and for whom Aramaic and Hebrew were relatively unknown languages. Their synagogue worship was also conducted in their native languages. **Hebrew-speaking believers.** Native Palestinians who spoke Aramaic as their daily language. Since all the apostles were Hebraic Jews, it is possible that they were more aware of the needs of those with whom they could easily communicate.

5 Everyone liked this idea, and they chose the fol-
lowing: Stephen (a man full of faith and the Holy
Spirit), Philip, Procorus, Nicanor, Timon, Parmenas,
and Nicolas of Antioch (an earlier convert to the Jew-
ish faith). 6 These seven were presented to the apos-
tles, who prayed for them as they laid their hands on
them.
7 So God's message continued to spread. The num-
ber of believers greatly increased in Jerusalem, and
many of the Jewish priests were converted, too.

STEPHEN IS ARRESTED

8 Stephen, a man full of God's grace and power, per-
formed amazing miracles and signs among the peo-
ple. 9 But one day some men from the Synagogue of
Freed Slaves, as it was called, started to debate with
him. They were Jews from Cyrene, Alexandria, Cili-
cia, and the province of Asia. 10 None of them could
stand against the wisdom and the Spirit with which
Stephen spoke.
11 So they persuaded some men to lie about Stephen,
saying, "We heard him blaspheme Moses, and even
God." 12 This roused the people, the elders, and the
teachers of religious law. So they arrested Stephen
and brought him before the high council.*
13 The lying witnesses said, "This man is always
speaking against the holy Temple and against the law
of Moses. 14 We have heard him say that this Jesus of
Nazareth* will destroy the Temple and change the
customs Moses handed down to us."
15 At this point everyone in the high council stared
at Stephen, because his face became as bright as an
angel's.

STEPHEN ADDRESSES THE COUNCIL

7 Then the high priest asked Stephen, "Are these ac-
cusations true?"
2 This was Stephen's reply: "Brothers and fathers,
listen to me. Our glorious God appeared to our an-
cestor Abraham in Mesopotamia before he settled in
Haran.* 3 God told him, 'Leave your native land and
your relatives, and come into the land that I will show
you.'* 4 So Abraham left the land of the Chaldeans and
lived in Haran until his father died. Then God brought
him here to the land where you now live.
5 "But God gave him no inheritance here, not even
one square foot of land. God did promise, however,
that eventually the whole land would belong to Abra-
ham and his descendants—even though he had no
children yet. 6 God also told him that his descendants
would live in a foreign land, where they would be op-
pressed as slaves for 400 years. 7 'But I will punish the
nation that enslaves them,' God said, 'and in the end
they will come out and worship me here in this place.'*
8 "God also gave Abraham the covenant of circum-
cision at that time. So when Abraham became the fa-
ther of Isaac, he circumcised him on the eighth day.
And the practice was continued when Isaac became
the father of Jacob, and when Jacob became the father
of the twelve patriarchs of the Israelite nation.
9 "These patriarchs were jealous of their brother Jo-
seph, and they sold him to be a slave in Egypt. But God
was with him 10 and rescued him from all his trou-
bles. And God gave him favor before Pharaoh, king of
Egypt. God also gave Joseph unusual wisdom, so that
Pharaoh appointed him governor over all of Egypt
and put him in charge of the palace.
11 "But a famine came upon Egypt and Canaan.
There was great misery, and our ancestors ran out of
food. 12 Jacob heard that there was still grain in Egypt,
so he sent his sons—our ancestors—to buy some.
13 The second time they went, Joseph revealed his
identity to his brothers,* and they were introduced to
Pharaoh. 14 Then Joseph sent for his father, Jacob, and
all his relatives to come to Egypt, seventy-five persons
in all. 15 So Jacob went to Egypt. He died there, as did
our ancestors. 16 Their bodies were taken to Shechem
and buried in the tomb Abraham had bought for a
certain price from Hamor's sons in Shechem.
17 "As the time drew near when God would fulfill
his promise to Abraham, the number of our people in
Egypt greatly increased. 18 But then a new king came
to the throne of Egypt who knew nothing about Jo-
seph. 19 This king exploited our people and oppressed
them, forcing parents to abandon their newborn ba-
bies so they would die.

6:12 Greek *Sanhedrin;* also in 6:15. **6:14** Or *Jesus the Nazarene.* **7:2** *Mesopotamia* was the region now called Iraq. *Haran* was a city in what is now called Syria. **7:3** Gen 12:1. **7:5-7** Gen 12:7; 15:13-14; Exod 3:12. **7:13** Other manuscripts read *Joseph was recognized by his brothers.*

6:5 They chose. The names of the men chosen indicate that all seven were Greek-speaking Jews. They perhaps also served as a bridge between the Palestinian apostles and the Greek-speaking Jews to help avoid further tensions between the two groups. **Stephen.** This man moves to center stage in chapter 7. **Philip.** Like Stephen, Philip demonstrated gifts of evangelism not unlike those of the apostles (see v. 8; 8:4-8; 21:8).

6:9 the Synagogue of Freed Slaves. The Freedmen were former Roman slaves (or their descendants) released by their masters and granted Roman citizenship. The Greek-speaking Jews who left home and family to settle in Jerusalem were especially devoted to the temple and its religious system.

6:14 Jesus . . . will destroy the Temple. The root of the complaint against Stephen was the charge that the followers of Jesus threatened to destroy the temple and replace the laws of Moses with their own ways. Jesus spoke of destroying the temple in a way that was misunderstood (Mark 14:58; John 2:19-22). Jesus spoke of the destruction of the temple that was to come (Luke 21:5-6). Stephen, in repeating this warning of judgment that would result if the Jews rejected Jesus as their Messiah, may have been misunderstood as inferring that the Christians were plotting an attack on the temple.

6:15 face became as bright as an angel's. The only other biblical character who shared this experience was Moses, the man of God whom Stephen was charged with defying (Ex. 34:29-31; 2 Cor. 3:12-13)!

7:6-7 God also told him. This is a combination of quotes issued by God to Abraham and Moses in Genesis 15:13 and Exodus 3:12. God would be with His people in Egypt and, after He delivered them from there, they would worship Him in the desert at Sinai.

7:9-10 These patriarchs were jealous of their brother Joseph. Stephen does not quote directly from Genesis but summarizes the account of Joseph's brothers selling him into slavery. Stephen doesn't refer to them as brothers but as "the patriarchs." His choice of words may be intentional since they weren't acting like brothers. **God was with him.** Joseph suffered greatly in being separated from his father, Jacob, his younger brother, Benjamin. Stephen doesn't go into detail about Joseph's sufferings but chooses to focus on the fact that God was with him. **gave Joseph unusual wisdom.** Joseph's painful losses were offset by great blessings from God. Through Joseph God provided for Egypt and its neighbors, including Joseph's family from Canaan.

7:14 all his relatives . . . seventy-five persons in all. The Hebrew text of Genesis 46:27 says 70, but the Septuagint text reads 75.

7:16 were taken to Shechem. Jacob was buried in Hebron (Gen. 50:13) at the cave that Abraham bought from Ephron. Joseph's bones were eventually laid to rest at Shechem in a field that Jacob bought from the sons of Hamor (Josh. 24:32). The Old Testament does not mention where the bones of the other sons of Jacob were buried, but a Samaritan tradition says it was at Shechem. Stephen appears to have telescoped events in order to get on with his main points.

7:17-34 A major portion of Stephen's sermon is given to what God accomplished through Moses. Stephen divides Moses' life into three segments: (1) his birth and education in Egypt, (2) the years in Midian where he fled as a fugitive after he killed an Egyptian who was dealing harshly with a Hebrew, and (3) the years of the Exodus and journey from Egypt to the Promised Land.

20 "At that time Moses was born—a beautiful child in God's eyes. His parents cared for him at home for three months. 21 When they had to abandon him, Pharaoh's daughter adopted him and raised him as her own son. 22 Moses was taught all the wisdom of the Egyptians, and he was powerful in both speech and action.

23 "One day when Moses was forty years old, he decided to visit his relatives, the people of Israel. 24 He saw an Egyptian mistreating an Israelite. So Moses came to the man's defense and avenged him, killing the Egyptian. 25 Moses assumed his fellow Israelites would realize that God had sent him to rescue them, but they didn't.

26 "The next day he visited them again and saw two men of Israel fighting. He tried to be a peacemaker. 'Men,' he said, 'you are brothers. Why are you fighting each other?'

27 "But the man in the wrong pushed Moses aside. 'Who made you a ruler and judge over us?' he asked. 28 'Are you going to kill me as you killed that Egyptian yesterday?' 29 When Moses heard that, he fled the country and lived as a foreigner in the land of Midian. There his two sons were born.

30 "Forty years later, in the desert near Mount Sinai, an angel appeared to Moses in the flame of a burning bush. 31 When Moses saw it, he was amazed at the sight. As he went to take a closer look, the voice of the LORD called out to him, 32 'I am the God of your ancestors—the God of Abraham, Isaac, and Jacob.' Moses shook with terror and did not dare to look.

33 "Then the LORD said to him, 'Take off your sandals, for you are standing on holy ground. 34 I have certainly seen the oppression of my people in Egypt. I have heard their groans and have come down to rescue them. Now go, for I am sending you back to Egypt.'*

35 "So God sent back the same man his people had previously rejected when they demanded, 'Who made you a ruler and judge over us?' Through the angel who appeared to him in the burning bush, God sent Moses to be their ruler and savior. 36 And by means of many wonders and miraculous signs, he led them out of Egypt, through the Red Sea, and through the wilderness for forty years.

37 "Moses himself told the people of Israel, 'God will raise up for you a Prophet like me from among your own people.'* 38 Moses was with our ancestors, the assembly of God's people in the wilderness, when the angel spoke to him at Mount Sinai. And there Moses received life-giving words to pass on to us.*

39 "But our ancestors refused to listen to Moses. They rejected him and wanted to return to Egypt. 40 They told Aaron, 'Make us some gods who can lead us, for we don't know what has become of this Moses, who brought us out of Egypt.' 41 So they made an idol shaped like a calf, and they sacrificed to it and celebrated over this thing they had made. 42 Then God turned away from them and abandoned them to serve the stars of heaven as their gods! In the book of the prophets it is written,

'Was it to me you were bringing sacrifices and
  offerings
 during those forty years in the wilderness, Israel?
43 No, you carried your pagan gods—
 the shrine of Molech,
 the star of your god Rephan,
 and the images you made to worship them.
So I will send you into exile
 as far away as Babylon.'*

44 "Our ancestors carried the Tabernacle* with them through the wilderness. It was constructed according to the plan God had shown to Moses. 45 Years later, when Joshua led our ancestors in battle against the nations that God drove out of this land, the Tabernacle was taken with them into their new territory. And it stayed there until the time of King David.

46 "David found favor with God and asked for the privilege of building a permanent Temple for the God of Jacob.* 47 But it was Solomon who actually built it. 48 However, the Most High doesn't live in temples made by human hands. As the prophet says,

49 'Heaven is my throne,
 and the earth is my footstool.
Could you build me a temple as good as that?'
 asks the LORD.
'Could you build me such a resting place?
50 Didn't my hands make both heaven and earth?'*

51 "You stubborn people! You are heathen* at heart and deaf to the truth. Must you forever resist the Holy Spirit? That's what your ancestors did, and so do you! 52 Name one prophet your ancestors didn't persecute! They even killed the ones who predicted the coming of the Righteous One—the Messiah whom you betrayed and murdered. 53 You deliberately disobeyed God's law, even though you received it from the hands of angels."

54 The Jewish leaders were infuriated by Stephen's accusation, and they shook their fists at him in rage.* 55 But Stephen, full of the Holy Spirit, gazed steadily into heaven and saw the glory of God, and he saw Jesus standing in the place of honor at God's right hand. 56 And he told them, "Look, I see the heavens opened and the Son of Man standing in the place of honor at God's right hand!"

7:31-34 Exod 3:5-10. **7:37** Deut 18:15. **7:38** Some manuscripts read *to you.* **7:42-43** Amos 5:25-27 (Greek version). **7:44** Greek *the tent of witness.* **7:46** Some manuscripts read *the house of Jacob.* **7:49-50** Isa 66:1-2. **7:51** Greek *uncircumcised.* **7:54** Greek *they were grinding their teeth against him.*

7:22 Moses was taught all the wisdom of the Egyptians. The Old Testament accounts of Moses don't mention his education. The Jewish biblical interpreter, Philo of Alexandria (20 B.C – A.D 50, makes this point in his life of Moses. Philo says that the best teachers of both Egypt and Greece had a part in Moses' education and that Moses excelled them.

7:23 was forty years old. The Exodus account does not mention Moses' age at the time of this event, but rabbinic tradition taught that he was 40.

7:51 stubborn people. The image is that of a people refusing to bow their head before God (Ex. 33:5; Deut. 10:16). **heathen at heart and deaf to the truth.** Physical circumcision was a symbol of a heart set apart for God and ears open to do His will.

7:52 Name one prophet your ancestors didn't persecute? Jewish tradition held that Isaiah was sawn in two by the evil king Manasseh and that Jeremiah was stoned by Jews in Egypt. Jesus also warned the leaders that in rejecting Him they were following in the footsteps of their fathers (Luke 11:47-51).

7:53 disobeyed God's law. The final accusation Stephen makes is that these leaders are the ones who violate Moses' law. **from the hands of angels.** Jewish (and Christian) tradition taught the law was given through the mediation of angels (Gal. 3:19; Heb. 2:2), whereas the gospel is announced directly by the Messiah Himself.

57 Then they put their hands over their ears and began shouting. They rushed at him 58 and dragged him out of the city and began to stone him. His accusers took off their coats and laid them at the feet of a young man named Saul.*

59 As they stoned him, Stephen prayed, "Lord Jesus, receive my spirit." 60 He fell to his knees, shouting, "Lord, don't charge them with this sin!" And with that, he died.

8 Saul was one of the witnesses, and he agreed completely with the killing of Stephen.

PERSECUTION SCATTERS THE BELIEVERS

A great wave of persecution began that day, sweeping over the church in Jerusalem; and all the believers except the apostles were scattered through the regions of Judea and Samaria. 2 (Some devout men came and buried Stephen with great mourning.) 3 But Saul was going everywhere to destroy the church. He went from house to house, dragging out both men and women to throw them into prison.

PHILIP PREACHES IN SAMARIA

4 But the believers who were scattered preached the Good News about Jesus wherever they went. 5 Philip, for example, went to the city of Samaria and told the people there about the Messiah. 6 Crowds listened intently to Philip because they were eager to hear his message and see the miraculous signs he did. 7 Many evil* spirits were cast out, screaming as they left their victims. And many who had been paralyzed or lame were healed. 8 So there was great joy in that city.

9 A man named Simon had been a sorcerer there for many years, amazing the people of Samaria and claiming to be someone great. 10 Everyone, from the least to the greatest, often spoke of him as "the Great One—the Power of God." 11 They listened closely to him because for a long time he had astounded them with his magic.

12 But now the people believed Philip's message of Good News concerning the Kingdom of God and the name of Jesus Christ. As a result, many men and women were baptized. 13 Then Simon himself believed and was baptized. He began following Philip wherever he went, and he was amazed by the signs and great miracles Philip performed.

14 When the apostles in Jerusalem heard that the people of Samaria had accepted God's message, they sent Peter and John there. 15 As soon as they arrived, they prayed for these new believers to receive the Holy Spirit. 16 The Holy Spirit had not yet come upon any of them, for they had only been baptized in the name of the Lord Jesus. 17 Then Peter and John laid their hands upon these believers, and they received the Holy Spirit.

18 When Simon saw that the Spirit was given when the apostles laid their hands on people, he offered them money to buy this power. 19 "Let me have this power, too," he exclaimed, "so that when I lay my hands on people, they will receive the Holy Spirit!"

20 But Peter replied, "May your money be destroyed with you for thinking God's gift can be bought! 21 You can have no part in this, for your heart is not right with God. 22 Repent of your wickedness and pray to the Lord. Perhaps he will forgive your evil thoughts, 23 for I can see that you are full of bitter jealousy and are held captive by sin."

24 "Pray to the Lord for me," Simon exclaimed, "that these terrible things you've said won't happen to me!"

25 After testifying and preaching the word of the Lord in Samaria, Peter and John returned to Jerusalem. And they stopped in many Samaritan villages along the way to preach the Good News.

PHILIP AND THE ETHIOPIAN EUNUCH

26 As for Philip, an angel of the Lord said to him, "Go south* down the desert road that runs from Jerusalem to Gaza." 27 So he started out, and he met the treasurer of Ethiopia, a eunuch of great authority under the Kandake, the queen of Ethiopia. The eunuch had gone to Jerusalem to worship, 28 and he was now returning. Seated in his carriage, he was reading aloud from the book of the prophet Isaiah.

29 The Holy Spirit said to Philip, "Go over and walk along beside the carriage."

30 Philip ran over and heard the man reading from the prophet Isaiah. Philip asked, "Do you understand what you are reading?"

31 The man replied, "How can I, unless someone instructs me?" And he urged Philip to come up into the carriage and sit with him.

7:58 *Saul* is later called Paul; see 13:9. **8:7** Greek *unclean.* **8:26** Or *Go at noon.*

7:58 dragged him out of the city. John 18:31 indicates the Sanhedrin did not have the right to mete out capital punishment, so this may have been an act of mob violence. But Acts 26:10 indicates that perhaps by this time Pilate's ability to control the Sanhedrin had weakened and that it indeed took capital cases into its own hands. **Saul.** This is the person who was to become the great apostle to the Gentiles.

8:1-3 all the believers except the apostles were scattered. That the apostles remained in Jerusalem indicates the persecution was directed mainly against the Greek-speaking converts who shared Stephen's views of the temple. The church's spread to Judea and Samaria shows that God used this persecution to show that He is not limited to Jerusalem (1:8).

8:5 Samaria. When the northern kingdom (Israel) was conquered by the Assyrians in 722 B.C., many of its people were deported while exiles from elsewhere in the vast Assyrian Empire were brought in to settle the land (2 Kings 17:23-41). These people intermarried with the remaining Israelites and adopted some of their religious practices. As a result, the Jews of the southern kingdom (Judah) considered the Samaritans as religious compromisers and racial half-breeds. By Jesus' day, strict Jews avoided Samaria and the word *Samaritan* was an insult (John 8:48). As a Greek-speaking Jew, Philip may have been less prejudiced against the Samaritans than the Palestinian Jews. This allowed him to speak freely with them.

8:9-11 Simon. While biblical information about Simon is limited to this passage, church tradition is rich with stories (vv. 20-24). Superstition and the practice of the occult allow for the demonstration of supernatural powers, which were wrongly assumed to be done by God just because they were powerful.

8:12-13 Simon himself believed. Philip's message and signs even attracted the attention of Simon. His initial interest appears to have been in the miraculous aspect of Philip's ministry more than in the message of the kingdom of God that he preached.

8:14-17 Upon hearing that faith in Jesus had broken out in Samaria, the apostles apparently decided they needed to check out the situation (see also 11:22-23). Thus, Peter and John were sent as representatives to investigate. There are various interpretations for the delay between the Samaritans' response of faith and their reception of the Spirit. But the one that best fits the context of Acts is that it occurred so the apostles would be convinced that the Lord was including the Samaritans as full members of His church (1:8; see also 10:44-45 and 11:15).

8:27 eunuch. Eunuchs (men who were emasculated to protect a king's wives and concubines) were commonly employed as royal officials. Although attracted to Judaism, a eunuch would never be allowed to participate fully in the temple worship (Deut. 23:1). **Kandake.** A title for the queens of Ethiopia.

SHARING GOOD NEWS

1. When did you get your first Bible? Who gave it to you?

ACTS 8:26-40

2. How much time do you spend reading the Bible? How did Bible reading change the Ethiopian's life?
3. What was required for Philip to baptize the Ethiopian (v. 37)?
4. Who, like Philip, helped you understand the Bible? What was the most important thing that person taught you?
5. What is "the good news about Jesus" (v. 35) that Philip described? How would you summarize that good news for someone who asked?

32 The passage of Scripture he had been reading
was this:

"He was led like a sheep to the slaughter.
And as a lamb is silent before the shearers,
he did not open his mouth.
33 He was humiliated and received no justice.
Who can speak of his descendants?
For his life was taken from the earth."*

34 The eunuch asked Philip, "Tell me, was the proph-
et talking about himself or someone else?" 35 So be-
ginning with this same Scripture, Philip told him the
Good News about Jesus.
36 As they rode along, they came to some water, and
the eunuch said, "Look! There's some water! Why can't
I be baptized?"* 38 He ordered the carriage to stop, and
they went down into the water, and Philip baptized him.
39 When they came up out of the water, the Spirit of
the Lord snatched Philip away. The eunuch never saw
him again but went on his way rejoicing. 40 Mean-
while, Philip found himself farther north at the town
of Azotus. He preached the Good News there and in
every town along the way until he came to Caesarea.

SAUL'S CONVERSION

9 Meanwhile, Saul was uttering threats with every
breath and was eager to kill the Lord's followers.*
So he went to the high priest. 2 He requested letters
addressed to the synagogues in Damascus, asking for
their cooperation in the arrest of any followers of the
Way he found there. He wanted to bring them—both
men and women—back to Jerusalem in chains.
3 As he was approaching Damascus on this mission,
a light from heaven suddenly shone down around
him. 4 He fell to the ground and heard a voice saying
to him, "Saul! Saul! Why are you persecuting me?"
5 "Who are you, lord?" Saul asked.
And the voice replied, "I am Jesus, the one you are
persecuting! 6 Now get up and go into the city, and you
will be told what you must do."
7 The men with Saul stood speechless, for they
heard the sound of someone's voice but saw no one!
8 Saul picked himself up off the ground, but when he
opened his eyes he was blind. So his companions led
him by the hand to Damascus. 9 He remained there
blind for three days and did not eat or drink.

REALLY? THAT GUY?

1. What's the most dramatic surprise you've had on a trip? Was it a good or bad surprise?

ACTS 9:1-19

2. How was Saul persecuting Jesus, since Jesus had already ascended to heaven?
3. Saul asked, "Who are You, lord?" (v. 5), while Ananias answered, "Yes, Lord!" (v. 10). What was the difference in these men's lives?
4. Why was Ananias afraid to visit Saul? What does it show of his character that he went?
5. When did Saul become "Brother Saul" (v. 17)? (Consider verses 5-8.)
6. Is there someone God has sent for you to help mentor in the faith?

8:32-33 Isa 53:7-8 (Greek version). **8:36** Some manuscripts add verse 37, *"You can," Philip answered, "if you believe with all your heart." And the eunuch replied, "I believe that Jesus Christ is the Son of God."* **9:1** Greek *disciples.*

8:32-33 He was led like a sheep. The eunuch was reading from Isaiah 53:7-8, a key Old Testament passage that describes Jesus as the "Suffering Servant" or "Servant of the Lord." This passage underlines much of what Luke has already recorded about the apostles' preaching about the identity of Jesus (3:13; 4:27).

8:34 was the prophet talking about himself or someone else? The eunuch's question was a common one in Jewish circles. Some thought the prophet was speaking of his own sufferings as one rejected, while others thought he was speaking figuratively of Israel as a nation that suffered at the hands of its oppressors (Isa. 44:1-2). Still another view of the Servant's identity linked him with Cyrus the King of Persia (see Isa. 44:28-45:1-3). The traditional rabbis had not made any connection between the Suffering Servant of Isaiah 53, the kingly Messiah of Isaiah 11, and the glorified Son of Man in Daniel 13. Only in Jesus' teachings did these concepts finally come together (Luke 24:26).

8:35 the Good News about Jesus. Philip used this passage as a jumping-off point to explain the ministry of Jesus. He undoubtedly referred the eunuch to other verses in Isaiah 53 as well as the other references to the Servant in Isaiah that point out the Servant's suffering for the sake of others and how this Servant would be a light for the Gentiles. All of this would have been related to Jesus' ministry, death, and resurrection.

8:36-38 Why can't I be baptized? The Greek word behind this expression may be part of a baptismal liturgy the early church used with candidates for baptism. Strict Jews would offer at least one reason why this man was ineligible to be considered part of God's people: he was a eunuch. He could never become a Jewish proselyte (v. 27), but he could become a full member of the church through Jesus Christ. This fulfills the prophecy of Isaiah 56:3-8, which anticipated a time when both foreigners and eunuchs would be welcomed into God's household.

9:1 uttering threats . . .to kill the Lord's followers. This reflects Paul's obsessive hatred toward the Christians.

9:2 letters. While the Sanhedrin had no formal authority outside of Judea, its prestige could influence elders in synagogues far from Jerusalem. In this case, the Sanhedrin asked the elders in Damascus to cooperate with Paul by allowing him to arrest as blasphemers those Christians who had fled from Jerusalem to Damascus and bring them for trial in Jerusalem. **Damascus.** A city about 150 miles from Jerusalem. Luke has not told us how the church began among the sizable Jewish community in this important city, but Paul desired to expand his persecution there so it would not spread any further. **the Way.** Unique to Acts as a name for Christianity (19:9,23; 22:4; 24:14,22). It may stem from Jesus' claim in John 14:6.

9:3 a light from heaven suddenly shone down around him. The term is often used of lightning, indicating the brilliance of the light (see also 26:13). Light (glory) is commonly connected with divine appearances (Luke 9:29; Rev. 1:14-16).

10 Now there was a believer* in Damascus named Ananias. The Lord spoke to him in a vision, calling, "Ananias!"

"Yes, Lord!" he replied.

11 The Lord said, "Go over to Straight Street, to the house of Judas. When you get there, ask for a man from Tarsus named Saul. He is praying to me right now. 12 I have shown him a vision of a man named Ananias coming in and laying hands on him so he can see again."

13 "But Lord," exclaimed Ananias, "I've heard many people talk about the terrible things this man has done to the believers* in Jerusalem! 14 And he is authorized by the leading priests to arrest everyone who calls upon your name."

15 But the Lord said, "Go, for Saul is my chosen instrument to take my message to the Gentiles and to kings, as well as to the people of Israel. 16 And I will show him how much he must suffer for my name's sake."

17 So Ananias went and found Saul. He laid his hands on him and said, "Brother Saul, the Lord Jesus, who appeared to you on the road, has sent me so that you might regain your sight and be filled with the Holy Spirit." 18 Instantly something like scales fell from Saul's eyes, and he regained his sight. Then he got up and was baptized. 19 Afterward he ate some food and regained his strength.

SAUL IN DAMASCUS AND JERUSALEM

Saul stayed with the believers* in Damascus for a few days. 20 And immediately he began preaching about Jesus in the synagogues, saying, "He is indeed the Son of God!"

21 All who heard him were amazed. "Isn't this the same man who caused such devastation among Jesus' followers in Jerusalem?" they asked. "And didn't he come here to arrest them and take them in chains to the leading priests?"

22 Saul's preaching became more and more powerful, and the Jews in Damascus couldn't refute his proofs that Jesus was indeed the Messiah. 23 After a while some of the Jews plotted together to kill him. 24 They were watching for him day and night at the city gate so they could murder him, but Saul was told about their plot. 25 So during the night, some of the other believers* lowered him in a large basket through an opening in the city wall.

CAPABLE CHRISTIANITY

1. What skill have you developed the most? What has helped you to improve?

ACTS 9:20-31

2. Why did Saul immediately begin to proclaim, "He [Jesus] is indeed the Son of God!" (v. 20)?
3. Why was Saul's preaching becoming so powerful that the Jews could not refute it (v. 22)?
4. Why did the Jews want to kill him? Since they killed Jesus as well, what does this suggest about being a disciple of Christ?
5. How can you grow "more capable" in defending your faith?

26 When Saul arrived in Jerusalem, he tried to meet with the believers, but they were all afraid of him. They did not believe he had truly become a believer! 27 Then Barnabas brought him to the apostles and told them how Saul had seen the Lord on the way to Damascus and how the Lord had spoken to Saul. He also told them that Saul had preached boldly in the name of Jesus in Damascus.

28 So Saul stayed with the apostles and went all around Jerusalem with them, preaching boldly in the name of the Lord. 29 He debated with some Greek-speaking Jews, but they tried to murder him. 30 When the believers* heard about this, they took him down to Caesarea and sent him away to Tarsus, his hometown.

31 The church then had peace throughout Judea, Galilee, and Samaria, and it became stronger as the believers lived in the fear of the Lord. And with the encouragement of the Holy Spirit, it also grew in numbers.

PETER HEALS AENEAS AND RAISES DORCAS

32 Meanwhile, Peter traveled from place to place, and he came down to visit the believers in the town of Lydda. 33 There he met a man named Aeneas, who had been paralyzed and bedridden for eight years. 34 Peter said to him, "Aeneas, Jesus Christ heals you! Get

9:10 Greek *disciple;* also in 9:26, 36. **9:13** Greek *God's holy people;* also in 9:32, 41. **9:19** Greek *disciples;* also in 9:26, 38. **9:25** Greek *his disciples.* **9:30** Greek *brothers.*

9:10 a believer . . . named Ananias. Apart from Paul's comment in 22:12, nothing is known of this Ananias.
9:11 Straight Street. The "Straight Street" where Saul's host lived is still a main thoroughfare in Damascus, Syria. The house of Judas was traditionally located near the western end of the street. Nothing is known of Judas.
9:15-16 Saul is my chosen instrument to take my message. The Lord overruled Ananias's objections with a final command to "Go!" and a description of what Paul's mission would be. **my chosen instrument.** Literally "a choice vessel." The Servant of Isaiah was God's chosen (Isa. 44:1). Paul would carry on the mission of the Servant by bringing Jesus' light to the Gentiles (Isa. 42:6; 49:6) and by sharing in His suffering.
9:17 Brother Saul. Without further question, Ananias affirms Paul as part of the family through the grace of Jesus. Paul's sight was restored; then he was baptized (presumably by Ananias) and was filled with the Holy Spirit.
9:20 he began preaching about Jesus. That Paul, as a representative from the Sanhedrin, would be invited to speak in the synagogues of Damascus is not unusual. What was unexpected was his message! **He is indeed the Son of God!** This is one of Paul's favorite ways of describing Jesus in his letters.
9:21-22 amazed. The shocked reaction of the Jews in Damascus is understandable, given their previous understanding of why Paul came to the city. **his proofs that Jesus was indeed the Messiah.** This was undoubtedly done by pointing out Old Testament passages about the Messiah that were fulfilled in the life and ministry of Jesus (see also 8:34-35).
9:23-25 After awhile. When Paul returned to Damascus, the leaders of the synagogues were prepared for him. They drew upon the help of the governor of the city in a plot to capture and kill Paul (2 Cor. 11:32-33). The phrase "the Jews" refers to the religious leaders of the Jewish community. **through an opening in the city wall.** Ancient cities were surrounded by walls as a defense against enemies. Although the city gates were being closely observed, Paul escaped from the city by being lowered over the wall in a large basket.
9:27 Barnabas. See 4:36. Barnabas assumes an important role later on as Paul's companion on his missionary trips. Barnabas risked alienating himself from the church by befriending this former persecutor of the early believers.
9:31 grew in numbers. With the persecution over, and the uproar caused by Paul's preaching quieted down, the church throughout Palestine had a period of peace and growth. Perhaps its persecutors thought it would just go away on its own. With this summary, Luke prepares his readers to anticipate the next step of expansion for the church—to the ends of the earth (1:8).
9:32 Meanwhile, Peter traveled. Peter and the other apostles probably made many trips throughout Judea, Samaria, and Galilee to teach and encourage the Christian communities throughout the area (8:25). **Lydda.** A town about 25 miles west of Jerusalem.

up, and roll up your sleeping mat!" And he was healed instantly. 35 Then the whole population of Lydda and Sharon saw Aeneas walking around, and they turned to the Lord.

36 There was a believer in Joppa named Tabitha (which in Greek is Dorcas*). She was always doing kind things for others and helping the poor. 37 About this time she became ill and died. Her body was washed for burial and laid in an upstairs room. 38 But the believers had heard that Peter was nearby at Lydda, so they sent two men to beg him, "Please come as soon as possible!"

39 So Peter returned with them; and as soon as he arrived, they took him to the upstairs room. The room was filled with widows who were weeping and showing him the coats and other clothes Dorcas had made for them. 40 But Peter asked them all to leave the room; then he knelt and prayed. Turning to the body he said, "Get up, Tabitha." And she opened her eyes! When she saw Peter, she sat up! 41 He gave her his hand and helped her up. Then he called in the widows and all the believers, and he presented her to them alive.

42 The news spread through the whole town, and many believed in the Lord. 43 And Peter stayed a long time in Joppa, living with Simon, a tanner of hides.

CORNELIUS CALLS FOR PETER

10 In Caesarea there lived a Roman army officer* named Cornelius, who was a captain of the Italian Regiment. 2 He was a devout, God-fearing man, as was everyone in his household. He gave generously to the poor and prayed regularly to God. 3 One afternoon about three o'clock, he had a vision in which he saw an angel of God coming toward him. "Cornelius!" the angel said.

4 Cornelius stared at him in terror. "What is it, sir?" he asked the angel.

And the angel replied, "Your prayers and gifts to the poor have been received by God as an offering! 5 Now send some men to Joppa, and summon a man named Simon Peter. 6 He is staying with Simon, a tanner who lives near the seashore."

7 As soon as the angel was gone, Cornelius called two of his household servants and a devout soldier, one of his personal attendants. 8 He told them what had happened and sent them off to Joppa.

PETER VISITS CORNELIUS

9 The next day as Cornelius's messengers were nearing the town, Peter went up on the flat roof to pray. It was about noon, 10 and he was hungry. But while a meal was being prepared, he fell into a trance. 11 He saw the sky open, and something like a large sheet was let down by its four corners. 12 In the sheet were all sorts of animals, reptiles, and birds. 13 Then a voice said to him, "Get up, Peter; kill and eat them."

14 "No, Lord," Peter declared. "I have never eaten anything that our Jewish laws have declared impure and unclean.*"

15 But the voice spoke again: "Do not call something unclean if God has made it clean." 16 The same vision was repeated three times. Then the sheet was suddenly pulled up to heaven.

17 Peter was very perplexed. What could the vision mean? Just then the men sent by Cornelius found Simon's house. Standing outside the gate, 18 they asked if a man named Simon Peter was staying there.

19 Meanwhile, as Peter was puzzling over the vision, the Holy Spirit said to him, "Three men have come looking for you. 20 Get up, go downstairs, and go with them without hesitation. Don't worry, for I have sent them."

21 So Peter went down and said, "I'm the man you are looking for. Why have you come?"

22 They said, "We were sent by Cornelius, a Roman officer. He is a devout and God-fearing man, well respected by all the Jews. A holy angel instructed him to summon you to his house so that he can hear your message." 23 So Peter invited the men to stay for the

ACCEPTING ONE ANOTHER

1. Which of these foods would you refuse to eat: Snails? Pickled pigs' feet? Chocolate-covered ants?

ACTS 10:1-23

2. The Old Testament forbids God's people from eating certain types of foods. How was Peter trying to obey God in this passage? What was God trying to teach him?
3. Cornelius was not a Jew. How did Peter treat him when they met (v. 23)? How did Peter's vision help him to behave this way?
4. What does verse 15 mean: "Do not call something unclean if God has made it clean"? How does this principle apply to us today?

9:36 The names *Tabitha* in Aramaic and *Dorcas* in Greek both mean "gazelle." **10:1** Greek *a centurion;* similarly in 10:22. **10:14** Greek *anything common and unclean.*

9:33-35 Aeneas, Jesus Christ heals you! This healing of a paralyzed man is similar to Jesus' healing of a man with the same condition (Luke 5:17-26), affirming Peter as a representative of Jesus.

9:40-43 Get up, Tabitha. Peter followed the pattern of Jesus when he raised Jairus's daughter. This miracle, like the healing of Aeneas, was seen as a sign that pointed to the power of Jesus as Lord. Peter stayed on for some time in Joppa. This sets the stage for his encounter with Cornelius (10:1748).

10:1 Cornelius. This was a popular name taken by the descendants of slaves who were released from slavery by the action of a P. Cornelius Sculla in 82 B.C. **a Roman army officer.** Equivalent to the modern rank of army captain. **the Italian Regiment.** An auxiliary force stationed in the area that was composed of men recruited from Italy.

10:2 God-fearing. The distinction between Gentile God-fearers (who believed in the true God and obeyed His ethical commands) and proselytes (who fully converted to Judaism) lay in the hesitancy of God-fearers to submit to the Jewish ceremonial laws, especially circumcision.

10:4 sir. Cornelius did not yet know about Jesus, so this is an expression of respect for what Cornelius recognized as a divine visitor. **received by God as an offering.** Although as a Gentile Cornelius would not have been allowed to offer animal sacrifices in the temple, the angel lets him know that devotion to God is recognized as a sacrifice that is acceptable to God.

10:13 kill and eat. The voice invites Peter to partake of any of the animals in the sheet, but Peter protests because eating some of these animals would violate the dietary laws of the Jews.

10:15 if God has made it clean. Peter soon understood that if God could pronounce that certain foods which were formerly unclean are now acceptable, He can do the same thing with people.

10:23 So Peter invited the men to stay for the night. While Jews offered Gentiles hospitality, they refused to accept it from Gentiles lest they violate dietary laws. Assuming the messengers from Cornelius arrived in early afternoon (see 10:9), it would have been too late in the day for them to start the 30-mile journey back to Caesarea.

night. The next day he went with them, accompanied
by some of the brothers from Joppa.
24 They arrived in Caesarea the following day. Cor-
nelius was waiting for them and had called together
his relatives and close friends. 25 As Peter entered his
home, Cornelius fell at his feet and worshiped him.
26 But Peter pulled him up and said, "Stand up! I'm a
human being just like you!" 27 So they talked together
and went inside, where many others were assembled.
28 Peter told them, "You know it is against our laws
for a Jewish man to enter a Gentile home like this or
to associate with you. But God has shown me that I
should no longer think of anyone as impure or un-
clean. 29 So I came without objection as soon as I was
sent for. Now tell me why you sent for me."
30 Cornelius replied, "Four days ago I was praying
in my house about this same time, three o'clock in the
afternoon. Suddenly, a man in dazzling clothes was
standing in front of me. 31 He told me, 'Cornelius, your
prayer has been heard, and your gifts to the poor
have been noticed by God! 32 Now send messengers to
Joppa, and summon a man named Simon Peter. He is
staying in the home of Simon, a tanner who lives near
the seashore.' 33 So I sent for you at once, and it was
good of you to come. Now we are all here, waiting be-
fore God to hear the message the Lord has given you."

THE GENTILES HEAR THE GOOD NEWS

34 Then Peter replied, "I see very clearly that God
shows no favoritism. 35 In every nation he accepts
those who fear him and do what is right. 36 This is the
message of Good News for the people of Israel—that
there is peace with God through Jesus Christ, who is
Lord of all. 37 You know what happened throughout
Judea, beginning in Galilee, after John began preach-
ing his message of baptism. 38 And you know that God
anointed Jesus of Nazareth with the Holy Spirit and
with power. Then Jesus went around doing good and
healing all who were oppressed by the devil, for God
was with him.
39 "And we apostles are witnesses of all he did
throughout Judea and in Jerusalem. They put him to
death by hanging him on a cross,* 40 but God raised
him to life on the third day. Then God allowed him to
appear, 41 not to the general public,* but to us whom
God had chosen in advance to be his witnesses. We
were those who ate and drank with him after he rose
from the dead. 42 And he ordered us to preach every-
where and to testify that Jesus is the one appointed
by God to be the judge of all—the living and the dead.
43 He is the one all the prophets testified about, say-
ing that everyone who believes in him will have their
sins forgiven through his name."

THE GENTILES RECEIVE THE HOLY SPIRIT

44 Even as Peter was saying these things, the Holy
Spirit fell upon all who were listening to the mes-
sage. 45 The Jewish believers* who came with Peter
were amazed that the gift of the Holy Spirit had been
poured out on the Gentiles, too. 46 For they heard them
speaking in other tongues* and praising God.
Then Peter asked, 47 "Can anyone object to their be-
ing baptized, now that they have received the Holy
Spirit just as we did?" 48 So he gave orders for them
to be baptized in the name of Jesus Christ. Afterward
Cornelius asked him to stay with them for several
days.

PETER EXPLAINS HIS ACTIONS

11 Soon the news reached the apostles and other
believers* in Judea that the Gentiles had re-
ceived the word of God. 2 But when Peter arrived back
in Jerusalem, the Jewish believers* criticized him.
3 "You entered the home of Gentiles* and even ate
with them!" they said.
4 Then Peter told them exactly what had happened.
5 "I was in the town of Joppa," he said, "and while I
was praying, I went into a trance and saw a vision.
Something like a large sheet was let down by its four
corners from the sky. And it came right down to me.
6 When I looked inside the sheet, I saw all sorts of tame
and wild animals, reptiles, and birds. 7 And I heard a
voice say, 'Get up, Peter; kill and eat them.'
8 "'No, Lord,' I replied. 'I have never eaten anything
that our Jewish laws have declared impure or un-
clean.*'
9 "But the voice from heaven spoke again: 'Do not
call something unclean if God has made it clean.'
10 This happened three times before the sheet and all
it contained was pulled back up to heaven.
11 "Just then three men who had been sent from
Caesarea arrived at the house where we were stay-
ing. 12 The Holy Spirit told me to go with them and not
to worry that they were Gentiles. These six brothers
here accompanied me, and we soon entered the home
of the man who had sent for us. 13 He told us how an

10:39 Greek *on a tree.* **10:41** Greek *the people.* **10:45** Greek *The faithful ones of the circumcision.* **10:46** Or *in other languages.* **11:1** Greek *brothers.* **11:2** Greek *those of the circumcision.* **11:3** Greek *of uncircumcised men.* **11:8** Greek *anything common or unclean.*

10:25-26 fell at his feet and worshiped him. Cornelius was showing great deference to Peter whom he regarded as a special messenger from God. But Peter believed that such respect was to be shown only to God.

10:28 against our laws for a Jewish man. Jews would not associate with Gentiles partly because of the problems associated with their dietary laws. To have such associations rendered the Jew ceremonially unclean. **But God has shown me.** Although the dream Peter had was about food, he realized that it was also about people. He could no longer consider Gentiles unclean.

10:34-35 God shows no favoritism. While this truth is firmly rooted in the Old Testament (Deut. 10:17; Mal. 2:9), the Jews did not apply it to Gentiles. **in every nation he accepts those who fear him and do what is right.** A sense of humility before the Creator and a desire to live in love and justice toward others are the key signs of faith (Mic. 6:8; see also Rom. 2).

10:39 they put him to death. While it was the Jewish leaders who arranged for Jesus' death, the fact that He was crucified implied Roman involvement.

10:45 Jewish believers . . .with Peter. This phenomenon shocked Peter's companions because it violated all they had believed about relations between Jews and Gentiles. It meant that the Gentiles were on equal terms with Jews before God.

10:46 they heard them speaking in other tongues. Luke's mention that these Gentiles spoke in languages or tongues showed the Jewish believers that the Gentiles' experience of the Spirit was no less than that of the apostles. This appears to relate to the outpouring of the Spirit at Pentecost (2:1-8).

10:47 baptized. Baptism with the Spirit usually accompanied (2:38) or followed (8:16-17) baptism with water, but in this groundbreaking situation the Spirit's baptism became the grounds on which water baptism could not be denied. Had the Spirit not come at this point, the Jewish believers may have insisted that before Cornelius and his friends could be baptized as genuine followers of the Messiah, they must observe Jewish traditions about food, the Sabbath, etc.

10:48 ask him to stay with them for several days. Violating custom once again, Peter, a Jew, accepted Gentile hospitality. This was another indication of his acceptance of them as full members of God's family.

11:2 the Jewish believers criticized him. Since at this point all the believers (except Cornelius) were circumcised, Luke may be using a term popular at the time of his writing to describe those Jews who still insisted that Gentiles must first become Jews before they could be Christians.

angel had appeared to him in his home and had told
him, 'Send messengers to Joppa, and summon a man
named Simon Peter. 14 He will tell you how you and
everyone in your household can be saved!'
15 "As I began to speak," Peter continued, "the Holy
Spirit fell on them, just as he fell on us at the begin-
ning. 16 Then I thought of the Lord's words when he
said, 'John baptized with* water, but you will be bap-
tized with the Holy Spirit.' 17 And since God gave these
Gentiles the same gift he gave us when we believed
in the Lord Jesus Christ, who was I to stand in God's
way?"
18 When the others heard this, they stopped object-
ing and began praising God. They said, "We can see
that God has also given the Gentiles the privilege of
repenting of their sins and receiving eternal life."

THE CHURCH IN ANTIOCH OF SYRIA

19 Meanwhile, the believers who had been scattered
during the persecution after Stephen's death trav-
eled as far as Phoenicia, Cyprus, and Antioch of Syr-
ia. They preached the word of God, but only to Jews.
20 However, some of the believers who went to Anti-
och from Cyprus and Cyrene began preaching to the
Gentiles* about the Lord Jesus. 21 The power of the
Lord was with them, and a large number of these
Gentiles believed and turned to the Lord.
22 When the church at Jerusalem heard what had
happened, they sent Barnabas to Antioch. 23 When he
arrived and saw this evidence of God's blessing, he
was filled with joy, and he encouraged the believers
to stay true to the Lord. 24 Barnabas was a good man,
full of the Holy Spirit and strong in faith. And many
people were brought to the Lord.
25 Then Barnabas went on to Tarsus to look for Saul.
26 When he found him, he brought him back to Antioch.
Both of them stayed there with the church for a full
year, teaching large crowds of people. (It was at Anti-
och that the believers* were first called Christians.)
27 During this time some prophets traveled from
Jerusalem to Antioch. 28 One of them named Agabus
stood up in one of the meetings and predicted by the
Spirit that a great famine was coming upon the en-
tire Roman world. (This was fulfilled during the reign
of Claudius.) 29 So the believers in Antioch decided
to send relief to the brothers and sisters* in Judea,
everyone giving as much as they could. 30 This they
did, entrusting their gifts to Barnabas and Saul to
take to the elders of the church in Jerusalem.

JAMES IS KILLED AND PETER IS IMPRISONED

12 About that time King Herod Agrippa* began to
persecute some believers in the church. 2 He had
the apostle James (John's brother) killed with a sword.
3 When Herod saw how much this pleased the Jewish
people, he also arrested Peter. (This took place during
the Passover celebration.*) 4 Then he imprisoned him,
placing him under the guard of four squads of four
soldiers each. Herod intended to bring Peter out for
public trial after the Passover. 5 But while Peter was
in prison, the church prayed very earnestly for him.

PETER'S MIRACULOUS ESCAPE FROM PRISON

6 The night before Peter was to be placed on trial, he
was asleep, fastened with two chains between two
soldiers. Others stood guard at the prison gate. 7 Sud-
denly, there was a bright light in the cell, and an an-

"GET OUT OF JAIL FREE" CARD

1. What's your closest encounter with the police or other law-enforcement authority?

ACTS 12:1-19

2. Why was Herod persecuting Christians? What were his motives?
3. The church was praying for Peter (vv. 5,12). Why didn't they believe Peter was at the door? When have you been surprised by an answer to prayer?
4. Herod and his guards expected to execute Peter. What happened instead? What does this show about God's control when His people are persecuted?
5. Have you ever faced persecution for your belief in Jesus? How did you respond? How can this passage give you courage?

11:16 Or *in;* also in 11:16b. 11:20 Greek *the Hellenists* (i.e., those who speak Greek); other manuscripts read *the Greeks.* 11:26 Greek *disciples;* also in 11:29. 11:29 Greek *the brothers.* 12:1 Greek *Herod the king.* He was the nephew of Herod Antipas and a grandson of Herod the Great. 12:3 Greek *the days of unleavened bread.*

11:17 gift. The gift of the Holy Spirit taking up residence in a person's heart is the indisputable mark of the Christian. Peter highlights that the Spirit is given to all (Jew or Gentile) who believe in the Lord Jesus (see also Gal. 3:2).

11:18 God has also given the Gentiles the privilege of repenting. While the Jerusalem church realized that Gentiles were to be included in the church, tradition and prejudice prevented it from acting on that truth to any great extent (see Acts 15). Instead, it was the church at Antioch, to which Luke now turns his attention, that spearheaded the missionary movement among Gentiles.

11:19 had been scattered. Since there were Jewish communities through the Roman Empire, it is not unusual that the Jewish believers would have spread throughout such a large area.

11:20-21 went to Antioch . . . and began preaching. The synagogues in Antioch were probably attended by Gentile God-fearers (like Cornelius). They were attracted to the ethics and values of Judaism but did not accept its customs about food, circumcision, and Sabbath regulations. It is probably with these Gentiles that the believers shared the gospel.

11:23 he arrived and saw the evidence of God's blessing. Barnabas did not require the Gentile converts to submit to Jewish traditions, but he encouraged them to maintain loyalty to Jesus as Lord.

11:24 Barnabas was a good man. Barnabas is first mentioned in Acts 4:36 as one who sold a field and brought the money to the apostles. He is there said to have been a Levite, and it is noted that his name meant "Son of Encouragement." He encouraged the disciples to take a chance on Saul after Saul's conversion (9:26-27), and he encouraged Paul to take a chance on John Mark after John Mark's desertion on a missionary journey (15:36-41). The manner in which he is eulogized here ("he was a good man") may indicate that he had died by the time of this writing.

11:26 the believers were first called Christians. By the time of Luke's writing, this Latin term was a widespread name for the believers. The only other places in the New Testament where this term is used are situations of ridicule and persecution (Acts 26:28; 1 Pet. 4:16). It may have originally been used to mock the believers.

11:28 great famine. There were at least five localized famines during this period, including one that struck Judea around A.D. 46.

12:1 King Herod. This is Herod Agrippa I, the grandson of Herod the Great, who ruled when Jesus was born, and the nephew of Herod Antipas who governed Galilee during Jesus' ministry. Herod Agippa I was popular with the Jews. To further cultivate this popularity, he resumed the persecution of the church that had come to a stop upon Paul's conversion (9:31).

12:7 was a bright light. Peter was guarded by four soldiers on six-hour shifts (vv. 4,6). Such intense security measures may have been implemented to prevent any further "unexplainable" release such as that which happened when the Sanhedrin imprisoned him earlier (5:19ff). The description of the light underscores that this was a miraculous intervention of God.

gel of the Lord stood before Peter. The angel struck
him on the side to awaken him and said, "Quick! Get
up!" And the chains fell off his wrists. 8 Then the angel
told him, "Get dressed and put on your sandals." And
he did. "Now put on your coat and follow me," the an-
gel ordered.
9 So Peter left the cell, following the angel. But all
the time he thought it was a vision. He didn't realize
it was actually happening. 10 They passed the first
and second guard posts and came to the iron gate
leading to the city, and this opened for them all by
itself. So they passed through and started walking
down the street, and then the angel suddenly left
him.
11 Peter finally came to his senses. "It's really true!"
he said. "The Lord has sent his angel and saved me
from Herod and from what the Jewish leaders* had
planned to do to me!"
12 When he realized this, he went to the home of
Mary, the mother of John Mark, where many were
gathered for prayer. 13 He knocked at the door in the
gate, and a servant girl named Rhoda came to open
it. 14 When she recognized Peter's voice, she was so
overjoyed that, instead of opening the door, she ran
back inside and told everyone, "Peter is standing at
the door!"
15 "You're out of your mind!" they said. When she in-
sisted, they decided, "It must be his angel."
16 Meanwhile, Peter continued knocking. When
they finally opened the door and saw him, they
were amazed. 17 He motioned for them to quiet
down and told them how the Lord had led him out
of prison. "Tell James and the other brothers what
happened," he said. And then he went to another
place.
18 At dawn there was a great commotion among the
soldiers about what had happened to Peter. 19 Herod
Agrippa ordered a thorough search for him. When he
couldn't be found, Herod interrogated the guards and
sentenced them to death. Afterward Herod left Judea
to stay in Caesarea for a while.

THE DEATH OF HEROD AGRIPPA

20 Now Herod was very angry with the people of Tyre
and Sidon. So they sent a delegation to make peace
with him because their cities were dependent upon
Herod's country for food. The delegates won the sup-
port of Blastus, Herod's personal assistant, 21 and an
appointment with Herod was granted. When the
day arrived, Herod put on his royal robes, sat on his
throne, and made a speech to them. 22 The people gave
him a great ovation, shouting, "It's the voice of a god,
not of a man!"
23 Instantly, an angel of the Lord struck Herod with
a sickness, because he accepted the people's worship
instead of giving the glory to God. So he was con-
sumed with worms and died.
24 Meanwhile, the word of God continued to spread,
and there were many new believers.
25 When Barnabas and Saul had finished their mis-
sion to Jerusalem, they returned,* taking John Mark
with them.

BARNABAS AND SAUL ARE COMMISSIONED

13 Among the prophets and teachers of the church
at Antioch of Syria were Barnabas, Simeon
(called "the black man"*), Lucius (from Cyrene), Mana-
en (the childhood companion of King Herod Antipas*),
and Saul. 2 One day as these men were worshiping the
Lord and fasting, the Holy Spirit said, "Appoint Bar-
nabas and Saul for the special work to which I have
called them." 3 So after more fasting and prayer, the
men laid their hands on them and sent them on their
way.

FALSE PROPHETS

1. Have you ever taken a sailing cruise? Where did you go? What was it like?

ACTS 13:1-12

2. The name Bar-Jesus (v. 6) means "son of Jesus." What kind of false doctrine might this sorcerer have been preaching? What modern "prophets" do the same thing?
3. How did Paul react when he met the sorcerer (vv. 10-11)?
4. Who are the "false prophets" today who are trying to turn people "from the faith" (v. 8)?
5. How should a Christian respond to false teachers? When have you encountered a false teacher?

12:11 Or *the Jewish people.* **12:25** Or *mission, they returned to Jerusalem.* Other manuscripts read *mission, they returned from Jerusalem;* still others read *mission, they returned from Jerusalem to Antioch.* **13:1a** Greek *who was called Niger.* **13:1b** Greek *Herod the tetrarch.*

12:11 the Lord . . .saved me from Herod. In Acts, there is no predictable pattern of how God might work. While Peter was released from prison, James, for whom the church undoubtedly prayed just as earnestly, was killed. The call to the church is to be faithful and take responsible action whether or not God chooses to act in a miraculous way.

12:12 Mary, the mother of John Mark. This is the Mark who later wrote the Gospel that bears his name (see v. 25; 13:5).

12:13–17 Luke recounts humorously how Peter was left standing at the gate of the courtyard while the disciples who were praying for just such a release could not believe he was there!

12:15 It must be his angel. Assuming that Peter had been killed, the disciples could come up with only one solution—that Peter's angel had taken on the form of Peter.

12:17 James. This is a half brother of Jesus (Mark 6:3). James did not believe in Jesus as the Messiah during Jesus' ministry (John 7:5), but after the resurrection, Jesus appeared to James in a special way (1 Cor. 15:7), qualifying him to be an apostle. James became a leader in the Jerusalem church (15:13; 21:18; Gal. 2:9); his piety and devotion to God gained the respect of the Jewish community. When executed by the Sadducean high priest in A.D. 61, his death was mourned by many Pharisaic Jews as well as Christians.

12:18-19 Herod interrogated the guards. The release of Peter threw the officials into confusion. Unable to explain how Peter could possibly escape without the cooperation of the guards, Herod ordered them to be executed. Under Roman law, a guard who allowed his prisoner to escape suffered the fate intended for the prisoner.

12:22 the voice of a god. The Gentiles listening to Herod probably intended this chant as nothing more than royal flattery. But Herod should have repudiated such a blasphemous gesture.

12:23 consumed with worms and died. While this may refer to tapeworms or roundworms as the cause of death, this phrase also appears to be a stock way for ancient writers to describe the death of disreputable leaders.

13:1 prophets and teachers. Teachers were church leaders who interpreted and applied the Old Testament Scriptures and the words of Jesus to the life of the church.

13:3 laid their hands on them. The laying on of hands was a sign of solidarity between the church and the missionaries, as well as a sign that the church was committing them to God's grace.

PAUL'S FIRST MISSIONARY JOURNEY

4 So Barnabas and Saul were sent out by the Holy
Spirit. They went down to the seaport of Seleucia and
then sailed for the island of Cyprus. 5 There, in the
town of Salamis, they went to the Jewish synagogues
and preached the word of God. John Mark went with
them as their assistant.

6 Afterward they traveled from town to town
across the entire island until finally they reached Pa-
phos, where they met a Jewish sorcerer, a false proph-
et named Bar-Jesus. 7 He had attached himself to the
governor, Sergius Paulus, who was an intelligent
man. The governor invited Barnabas and Saul to visit
him, for he wanted to hear the word of God. 8 But Ely-
mas, the sorcerer (as his name means in Greek), inter-
fered and urged the governor to pay no attention to
what Barnabas and Saul said. He was trying to keep
the governor from believing.

9 Saul, also known as Paul, was filled with the Holy
Spirit, and he looked the sorcerer in the eye. 10 Then
he said, "You son of the devil, full of every sort of
deceit and fraud, and enemy of all that is good! Will
you never stop perverting the true ways of the Lord?
11 Watch now, for the Lord has laid his hand of pun-
ishment upon you, and you will be struck blind. You
will not see the sunlight for some time." Instantly mist
and darkness came over the man's eyes, and he began
groping around begging for someone to take his hand
and lead him.

12 When the governor saw what had happened, he
became a believer, for he was astonished at the teach-
ing about the Lord.

PAUL PREACHES IN ANTIOCH OF PISIDIA

13 Paul and his companions then left Paphos by ship
for Pamphylia, landing at the port town of Perga.
There John Mark left them and returned to Jerusa-
lem. 14 But Paul and Barnabas traveled inland to An-
tioch of Pisidia.*

On the Sabbath they went to the synagogue for the
services. 15 After the usual readings from the books of
Moses* and the prophets, those in charge of the ser-
vice sent them this message: "Brothers, if you have
any word of encouragement for the people, come and
give it."

16 So Paul stood, lifted his hand to quiet them, and
started speaking. "Men of Israel," he said, "and you
God-fearing Gentiles, listen to me.

17 "The God of this nation of Israel chose our ances-
tors and made them multiply and grow strong during
their stay in Egypt. Then with a powerful arm he
led them out of their slavery. 18 He put up with them*
through forty years of wandering in the wilderness.
19 Then he destroyed seven nations in Canaan and
gave their land to Israel as an inheritance. 20 All this
took about 450 years.

"After that, God gave them judges to rule until the
time of Samuel the prophet. 21 Then the people begged
for a king, and God gave them Saul son of Kish, a man
of the tribe of Benjamin, who reigned for forty years.
22 But God removed Saul and replaced him with Da-
vid, a man about whom God said, 'I have found Da-
vid son of Jesse, a man after my own heart. He will do
everything I want him to do.'*

23 "And it is one of King David's descendants, Jesus,
who is God's promised Savior of Israel! 24 Before he
came, John the Baptist preached that all the people
of Israel needed to repent of their sins and turn to
God and be baptized. 25 As John was finishing his
ministry he asked, 'Do you think I am the Messiah?
No, I am not! But he is coming soon—and I'm not
even worthy to be his slave and untie the sandals on
his feet.'

26 "Brothers—you sons of Abraham, and also you
God-fearing Gentiles—this message of salvation has
been sent to us! 27 The people in Jerusalem and their
leaders did not recognize Jesus as the one the proph-
ets had spoken about. Instead, they condemned him,
and in doing this they fulfilled the prophets' words
that are read every Sabbath. 28 They found no legal
reason to execute him, but they asked Pilate to have
him killed anyway.

29 "When they had done all that the prophecies said
about him, they took him down from the cross* and
placed him in a tomb. 30 But God raised him from the
dead! 31 And over a period of many days he appeared
to those who had gone with him from Galilee to Je-
rusalem. They are now his witnesses to the people of
Israel.

32 "And now we are here to bring you this Good
News. The promise was made to our ancestors, 33 and
God has now fulfilled it for us, their descendants,
by raising Jesus. This is what the second psalm says
about Jesus:

'You are my Son.
  Today I have become your Father.*'

34 For God had promised to raise him from the dead,
not leaving him to rot in the grave. He said, 'I will
give you the sacred blessings I promised to David.'*
35 Another psalm explains it more fully: 'You will not

13:13-14 *Pamphylia* and *Pisidia* were districts in what is now Turkey. **13:15** Greek *from the law.* **13:18** Some manuscripts read *He cared for them;* compare Deut 1:31. **13:22** 1 Sam 13:14. **13:29** Greek *from the tree.* **13:33** Or *Today I reveal you as my Son.* Ps 2:7. **13:34** Isa 55:3.

13:5 Salamis. A Greek city with a substantial Jewish population on the island of Cyprus.
13:6 Paphos. The Roman seat of power on the Island of Cyprus, about 90 miles from the port of Salamis.
13:10 son of the devil. Although Elymas was also called Bar-Jesus (meaning "son of a savior"), Paul does not hesitate to clarify the reality of the situation. Elymas' opposition to the gospel meant he reflected the characteristics of Satan.
13:11-12 you will be struck blind. This was a temporary blindness meant as a warning for Elymas to repent.
13:13 Paul and his companions. Up to verse 7, Barnabas was regarded as the leader of this team; from here on Paul is given the leadership position. **by ship.** A 160-mile boat trip followed by a difficult journey of over 100 miles across the Tarsus Mountains brought the missionaries to Antioch. **John Mark left them.** No reason is given, but Paul's reaction in 15:38 indicates that he at least viewed this as some sort of failure on John (Mark's) part.
13:20 450 years. This was approximately the period of time when the Israelites lived in Egypt, traveled in the desert, and conquered the land of Canaan.
13:24-25 John. Acts 18:24-25 and 19:3 hint that the influence of John the Baptist had spread among Jews throughout the Roman Empire, from North Africa through Asia Minor. It may be that at Pisidian Antioch there were those who acknowledged that John was a prophet sent by God.
13:26 sons of Abraham. The wall between Jew and Gentile was broken down as Paul proclaimed that the message of God's salvation was sent to the "the sons of Abraham's race, and those among you who fear God." These God-fearing Gentiles (10:2) would form a natural bridge from the synagogue to pagan Gentile society.

allow your Holy One to rot in the grave.'* 36 This is not
a reference to David, for after David had done the will
of God in his own generation, he died and was buried
with his ancestors, and his body decayed. 37 No, it was
a reference to someone else—someone whom God
raised and whose body did not decay.
38*"Brothers, listen! We are here to proclaim that
through this man Jesus there is forgiveness for your
sins. 39 Everyone who believes in him is made right in
God's sight—something the law of Moses could never
do. 40 Be careful! Don't let the prophets' words apply to
you. For they said,

41 'Look, you mockers,
be amazed and die!
For I am doing something in your own day,
something you wouldn't believe
even if someone told you about it.'*"

42 As Paul and Barnabas left the synagogue that
day, the people begged them to speak about these
things again the next week. 43 Many Jews and devout
converts to Judaism followed Paul and Barnabas, and
the two men urged them to continue to rely on the
grace of God.

PAUL TURNS TO THE GENTILES

44 The following week almost the entire city turned
out to hear them preach the word of the Lord. 45 But
when some of the Jews saw the crowds, they were
jealous; so they slandered Paul and argued against
whatever he said.
46 Then Paul and Barnabas spoke out boldly and
declared, "It was necessary that we first preach the
word of God to you Jews. But since you have rejected
it and judged yourselves unworthy of eternal life, we
will offer it to the Gentiles. 47 For the Lord gave us this
command when he said,

'I have made you a light to the Gentiles,
to bring salvation to the farthest corners of the
earth.'*"

48 When the Gentiles heard this, they were very
glad and thanked the Lord for his message; and all
who were chosen for eternal life became believers.
49 So the Lord's message spread throughout that re-
gion.
50 Then the Jews stirred up the influential religious
women and the leaders of the city, and they incited a
mob against Paul and Barnabas and ran them out of
town. 51 So they shook the dust from their feet as a sign
of rejection and went to the town of Iconium. 52 And
the believers* were filled with joy and with the Holy
Spirit.

PAUL AND BARNABAS IN ICONIUM

14 The same thing happened in Iconium.* Paul and
Barnabas went to the Jewish synagogue and
preached with such power that a great number of
both Jews and Greeks became believers. 2 Some of the
Jews, however, spurned God's message and poisoned
the minds of the Gentiles against Paul and Barnabas.
3 But the apostles stayed there a long time, preach-
ing boldly about the grace of the Lord. And the Lord
proved their message was true by giving them power
to do miraculous signs and wonders. 4 But the people
of the town were divided in their opinion about them.
Some sided with the Jews, and some with the apostles.
5 Then a mob of Gentiles and Jews, along with their
leaders, decided to attack and stone them. 6 When the
apostles learned of it, they fled to the region of Lyca-
onia—to the towns of Lystra and Derbe and the sur-
rounding area. 7 And there they preached the Good
News.

PAUL AND BARNABAS IN LYSTRA AND DERBE

8 While they were at Lystra, Paul and Barnabas came
upon a man with crippled feet. He had been that way
from birth, so he had never walked. He was sitting
9 and listening as Paul preached. Looking straight at
him, Paul realized he had faith to be healed. 10 So Paul
called to him in a loud voice, "Stand up!" And the man
jumped to his feet and started walking.
11 When the crowd saw what Paul had done, they
shouted in their local dialect, "These men are gods
in human form!" 12 They decided that Barnabas was
the Greek god Zeus and that Paul was Hermes, since
he was the chief speaker. 13 Now the temple of Zeus
was located just outside the town. So the priest of the

13:35 Ps 16:10. **13:38** English translations divide verses 38 and 39 in various ways. **13:41** Hab 1:5 (Greek version). **13:47** Isa 49:6. **13:52** Greek *the disciples.* **14:1** *Iconium,* as well as *Lystra* and *Derbe* (14:6), were towns in what is now Turkey.

13:36-37 David. Paul reminds his listeners that David's death and subsequent decay proves that the passages refer to one who would not be left to "rot in the grave" (GNB).

13:38 forgiveness for your sins. This phrase sums up all that salvation involves. It means the believer's guilt is atoned for so that he enjoys a restored relationship with God, free from shame or anxiety over the past. It also means the believer is being freed from the power of sin as his desires conform more and more to God's will. Finally, it means the believer can experience a relationship of peace with God.

13:39 declared right. This term brings to mind a courtroom scene in which a judge, after hearing the accusations against a defendant, declares that he is not guilty. Because Jesus' death was a sacrifice for sin, the believer is set right before God and pronounced not guilty of sin.

13:43 devout converts to Judaism. These were Gentiles who had submitted to the Jewish traditions on circumcision, dietary laws, and Sabbath observance.

13:48 all who were chosen for eternal life became believers. The fact that these Gentiles responded to the gospel with faith is evidence that their names had also been written in God's figurative book of life (Ex. 32:32; Rev. 13:8; 21:27).

13:50 influential religious women. Palestinian women were allowed little social mobility, but women in Gentile regions could hold official offices and run businesses.

13:51 shook the dust from their feet. Jews entering Palestine from a Gentile area wiped off their feet as a symbol that they were getting rid of Gentile contamination. Paul and Barnabas used this custom to indicate that they were exempt from the judgment to come upon the Jews at Antioch who had rejected the gospel.

14:5 decided to attack and stone them. Opposition to Paul and Barnabas in Antioch proceeded through official channels. But the fact that a stoning was planned here indicates that Jewish leaders were responsible for this plot. They intended to bypass the Roman court system to get rid of Paul and Barnabas.

14:6 the region of Lycaonia—to the towns of Lystra and Derbe. Iconium had originally been a Phrygian settlement and was in the province of Lycaonia. Lystra was about 20 miles southwest of Iconium, and Derbe lay 60 miles further southeast.

14:8 Lystra. The small Jewish community in Lystra (16:1–3) apparently did not have a synagogue. Adopting a new strategy that brought the gospel directly to the Gentiles, Paul probably preached in the Greek forum, the site of the local marketplace and gathering place for public discussion.

14:12 Hermes . . . the chief speaker. Zeus was the chief god among the Greek deities, while Hermes was the herald of the gods. The fact that Paul was identified with Hermes shows that he was the leading figure in this missionary enterprise. Paul was also of much smaller stature than Barnabas, who would have appeared more like the regal Zeus.

temple and the crowd brought bulls and wreaths of flowers to the town gates, and they prepared to offer sacrifices to the apostles.

[14] But when the apostles Barnabas and Paul heard what was happening, they tore their clothing in dismay and ran out among the people, shouting, [15] "Friends,* why are you doing this? We are merely human beings—just like you! We have come to bring you the Good News that you should turn from these worthless things and turn to the living God, who made heaven and earth, the sea, and everything in them. [16] In the past he permitted all the nations to go their own ways, [17] but he never left them without evidence of himself and his goodness. For instance, he sends you rain and good crops and gives you food and joyful hearts." [18] But even with these words, Paul and Barnabas could scarcely restrain the people from sacrificing to them.

[19] Then some Jews arrived from Antioch and Iconium and won the crowds to their side. They stoned Paul and dragged him out of town, thinking he was dead. [20] But as the believers* gathered around him, he got up and went back into the town. The next day he left with Barnabas for Derbe.

PAUL AND BARNABAS RETURN TO ANTIOCH OF SYRIA

[21] After preaching the Good News in Derbe and making many disciples, Paul and Barnabas returned to Lystra, Iconium, and Antioch of Pisidia, [22] where they strengthened the believers. They encouraged them to continue in the faith, reminding them that we must suffer many hardships to enter the Kingdom of God. [23] Paul and Barnabas also appointed elders in every church. With prayer and fasting, they turned the elders over to the care of the Lord, in whom they had put their trust. [24] Then they traveled back through Pisidia to Pamphylia. [25] They preached the word in Perga, then went down to Attalia.

[26] Finally, they returned by ship to Antioch of Syria, where their journey had begun. The believers there had entrusted them to the grace of God to do the work they had now completed. [27] Upon arriving in Antioch, they called the church together and reported everything God had done through them and how he had opened the door of faith to the Gentiles, too. [28] And they stayed there with the believers for a long time.

THE COUNCIL AT JERUSALEM

15 While Paul and Barnabas were at Antioch of Syria, some men from Judea arrived and began to teach the believers*: "Unless you are circumcised as required by the law of Moses, you cannot be saved." [2] Paul and Barnabas disagreed with them, arguing vehemently. Finally, the church decided to send Paul and Barnabas to Jerusalem, accompanied by some local believers, to talk to the apostles and elders about this question. [3] The church sent the delegates to Jerusalem, and they stopped along the way in Phoenicia and Samaria to visit the believers. They told them—much to everyone's joy—that the Gentiles, too, were being converted.

[4] When they arrived in Jerusalem, Barnabas and Paul were welcomed by the whole church, including the apostles and elders. They reported everything God had done through them. [5] But then some of the believers who belonged to the sect of the Pharisees stood up and insisted, "The Gentile converts must be circumcised and required to follow the law of Moses."

[6] So the apostles and elders met together to resolve this issue. [7] At the meeting, after a long discussion, Peter stood and addressed them as follows: "Brothers, you all know that God chose me from among you some time ago to preach to the Gentiles so that they could hear the Good News and believe. [8] God knows people's hearts, and he confirmed that he accepts Gentiles by giving them the Holy Spirit, just as he did to us. [9] He made no distinction between us and them, for he cleansed their hearts through faith. [10] So why are you now challenging God by burdening the Gentile believers* with a yoke that neither we nor our ancestors were able to bear? [11] We believe that we are all saved the same way, by the undeserved grace of the Lord Jesus."

[12] Everyone listened quietly as Barnabas and Paul told about the miraculous signs and wonders God had done through them among the Gentiles.

[13] When they had finished, James stood and said, "Brothers, listen to me. [14] Peter* has told you about the time God first visited the Gentiles to take from them a people for himself. [15] And this conversion of Gentiles is exactly what the prophets predicted. As it is written:

14:15 Greek *Men.* **14:20** Greek *disciples;* also in 14:22, 28. **15:1** Greek *brothers;* also in 15:3, 23, 32, 33, 36, 40. **15:10** Greek *disciples.* **15:14** Greek *Simeon.*

14:23 elders. This is the first mention of elders outside of Palestine. The early churches adopted the synagogue form of leadership in selecting leaders who were responsible for the spiritual oversight of the members. How Paul and Barnabas selected these leaders, or whether the entire church was involved in the process, is not clear.

14:27 reported. The tense of the Greek word implies they "kept on reporting" what had happened. This was probably because the church was actually a combination of small house groups that met throughout the city; at this point Christians had no common meeting places. **opened the door of faith to the Gentiles.** It is precisely the nature of this report that led to the conflict in chapter 15 and the important meeting of the church that resulted from it.

15:1-4 The controversy surrounding circumcision stirred up such a debate that the church felt it necessary to call together the church leaders from Jerusalem and Antioch to settle the issue.

15:5 the believers who belonged to the sect of the Pharisees. The resistance to allowing Gentiles into the church originated with Jewish Christians who had formerly been Pharisees. This small but influential sect was widely respected for its adherence to the law and traditions. Their concern arose from a genuine desire to ensure that God's honor was not violated through disregard of His law. To them, the offer of the gospel apart from the law was inconceivable since for centuries their people had been taught to discern God's will by examining the law. Paul's ministry seemed like a slap in Israel's face—an unthinkable rejection of all the covenant responsibilities of God's chosen people throughout their history.

15:7-8 Peter stood and addressed them. As part of the discussion, Peter recounted his experience with Cornelius (10:1–11:18). The fact that Cornelius experienced the presence of the Spirit in the same way the disciples did was proof that God accepted the Gentiles apart from the practice of Jewish law.

15:10 yoke. A reference to the Law of Moses. Peter declared that requiring Gentile converts to be circumcised would be like putting a yoke around the necks of these believers.

15:13-21 James was the leader of the Jerusalem church (see 12:17). The ultimate decision as to the position of the Jerusalem church was his to make. Since in Galatians 2:11-13, James appears to have represented those who believed that Gentiles could not be considered equal members of the church with Jews, it may be that this council was the turning point when he realized the scope of Jesus' mission. James's affirmation of God's plan to save all types of people through faith in Jesus is his last statement in the book of Acts.

15:16-18 rebuild its ruins. The original context of the prophecy was the anticipation of the destruction of Israel (722 B.C.) after which God, at a future time, would return the nation to its former glory that it had enjoyed in David's time.

PARTING COMPANY

1. Who was your closest friend when you were 7 years old? Are you still friends?

ACTS 15:36-41

2. Why did Paul and Barnabas part company? What were the strengths and weaknesses of each person's reasons?
3. John Mark may have written the Gospel of Mark, and Paul later reunited with him. What does this suggest about Barnabas? About Paul's willingness to admit an error?
4. What good can you see coming out of Paul and Barnabas parting ways in this story?
5. How should you deal with a broken relationship with someone in the Christian community?

16 'Afterward I will return
and restore the fallen house* of David.
I will rebuild its ruins
and restore it,
17 so that the rest of humanity might seek the LORD,
including the Gentiles—
all those I have called to be mine.
The LORD has spoken—
18 he who made these things known so long ago.'*

19 "And so my judgment is that we should not
make it difficult for the Gentiles who are turning
to God. 20 Instead, we should write and tell them to
abstain from eating food offered to idols, from sex-
ual immorality, from eating the meat of strangled
animals, and from consuming blood. 21 For these
laws of Moses have been preached in Jewish syn-
agogues in every city on every Sabbath for many
generations."

THE LETTER FOR GENTILE BELIEVERS

22 Then the apostles and elders together with the
whole church in Jerusalem chose delegates, and
they sent them to Antioch of Syria with Paul and
Barnabas to report on this decision. The men chosen
were two of the church leaders*—Judas (also called
Barsabbas) and Silas. 23 This is the letter they took
with them:

"This letter is from the apostles and elders, your
brothers in Jerusalem. It is written to the Gentile
believers in Antioch, Syria, and Cilicia. Greetings!
24 "We understand that some men from here
have troubled you and upset you with their teach-
ing, but we did not send them! 25 So we decided,
having come to complete agreement, to send you
official representatives, along with our beloved
Barnabas and Paul, 26 who have risked their lives
for the name of our Lord Jesus Christ. 27 We are
sending Judas and Silas to confirm what we have
decided concerning your question.
28 "For it seemed good to the Holy Spirit and to
us to lay no greater burden on you than these few
requirements: 29 You must abstain from eating food
offered to idols, from consuming blood or the meat
of strangled animals, and from sexual immorality.
If you do this, you will do well. Farewell."

30 The messengers went at once to Antioch, where
they called a general meeting of the believers and de-
livered the letter. 31 And there was great joy through-
out the church that day as they read this encouraging
message.
32 Then Judas and Silas, both being prophets, spoke
at length to the believers, encouraging and strength-
ening their faith. 33 They stayed for a while, and then
the believers sent them back to the church in Jerusa-
lem with a blessing of peace.* 35 Paul and Barnabas
stayed in Antioch. They and many others taught and
preached the word of the Lord there.

PAUL AND BARNABAS SEPARATE

36 After some time Paul said to Barnabas, "Let's
go back and visit each city where we previously
preached the word of the Lord, to see how the new be-
lievers are doing." 37 Barnabas agreed and wanted to
take along John Mark. 38 But Paul disagreed strongly,
since John Mark had deserted them in Pamphylia and
had not continued with them in their work. 39 Their
disagreement was so sharp that they separated. Bar-
nabas took John Mark with him and sailed for Cy-
prus. 40 Paul chose Silas, and as he left, the believers
entrusted him to the Lord's gracious care. 41 Then he
traveled throughout Syria and Cilicia, strengthening
the churches there.

15:16 Or *kingdom;* Greek reads *tent.* **15:16-18** Amos 9:11-12 (Greek version); Isa 45:21. **15:22** Greek *were leaders among the brothers.* **15:33** Some manuscripts add verse 34, *But Silas decided to stay there.*

15:20 eating food offered to idols. In Gentile areas meat was sold only after the animal had been sacrificed as part of a worship service to an idol. The eating of such food later became a source of controversy between Jewish and Gentile believers in Rome (Rom. 14:1-8) and Corinth (1 Cor. 8). **sexual immorality.** This may be related to "the pollution of idols" since idolatry sometimes involved ritual prostitution (1 Cor. 6:12-20). **eating the meat of strangled animals, and from consuming blood.** Jews were forbidden to eat meat that contained blood (Lev. 17:10,13). Gentiles would make the sharing of meals with Jewish believers easier if they would respect this tradition.

15:27 Judas. Probably a leader in the Jerusalem church, but nothing more is known about him. **Silas.** Probably also a leader, but one who played a prominent role in the rest of Acts (see also 1 Thess. 1:1; 2 Cor. 1:19; 1 Pet. 5:12).

15:28 lay no greater burden on you. The council of church leaders meeting in Jerusalem recognized that these regulations were over and above what was needed for salvation. It was not necessary that the Gentiles submit to these standards to be right with God, but it was important that they do so to avoid alienating Jews from the gospel.

15:29 If you do this, you will do well. The implication is that no other requirement—especially circumcision (v. 5)—is to be imposed on Gentile believers.

15:32 encouraging and strengthening. The ministry involved in the prophetic gift of Silas and Judas is captured by the word *encouraged*.

15:38 John Mark had deserted them. Luke does not tell us why Mark left Paul and Barnabas during the first missionary journey, but Paul viewed it as a serious problem and was unwilling to let Mark go with them again.

15:39-40 Their disagreement was so sharp. Paul and Barnabas disagreed on whether Mark should be allowed to accompany them on this journey. Barnabas wanted him to join them, while Paul did not. Mark's earlier departure had placed increased demands on Paul and Barnabas, and Paul was unwilling to risk that again. This disagreement caused the missionaries to go their separate ways.

15:41–16:5 The limits of Paul's first journey were reached by an overland trek westward to the border of Cilicia. But this time he went east, going overland through the provinces until he came to Derbe.

PAUL'S SECOND MISSIONARY JOURNEY

16 Paul went first to Derbe and then to Lystra,
where there was a young disciple named Tim-
othy. His mother was a Jewish believer, but his father
was a Greek. 2 Timothy was well thought of by the
believers* in Lystra and Iconium, 3 so Paul wanted
him to join them on their journey. In deference to
the Jews of the area, he arranged for Timothy to be
circumcised before they left, for everyone knew that
his father was a Greek. 4 Then they went from town to
town, instructing the believers to follow the decisions
made by the apostles and elders in Jerusalem. 5 So the
churches were strengthened in their faith and grew
larger every day.

A CALL FROM MACEDONIA

6 Next Paul and Silas traveled through the area of
Phrygia and Galatia, because the Holy Spirit had pre-
vented them from preaching the word in the province
of Asia at that time. 7 Then coming to the borders of
Mysia, they headed north for the province of Bithyn-
ia,* but again the Spirit of Jesus did not allow them to
go there. 8 So instead, they went on through Mysia to
the seaport of Troas.
9 That night Paul had a vision: A man from Macedo-
nia in northern Greece was standing there, pleading
with him, "Come over to Macedonia and help us!" 10 So
we* decided to leave for Macedonia at once, having
concluded that God was calling us to preach the Good
News there.

LYDIA OF PHILIPPI BELIEVES IN JESUS

11 We boarded a boat at Troas and sailed straight
across to the island of Samothrace, and the next day
we landed at Neapolis. 12 From there we reached
Philippi, a major city of that district of Macedonia
and a Roman colony. And we stayed there several
days.
13 On the Sabbath we went a little way outside the
city to a riverbank, where we thought people would
be meeting for prayer, and we sat down to speak with
some women who had gathered there. 14 One of them
was Lydia from Thyatira, a merchant of expensive
purple cloth, who worshiped God. As she listened to
us, the Lord opened her heart, and she accepted what
Paul was saying. 15 She and her household were bap-
tized, and she asked us to be her guests. "If you agree
that I am a true believer in the Lord," she said, "come
and stay at my home." And she urged us until we
agreed.

PAUL AND SILAS IN PRISON

16 One day as we were going down to the place of
prayer, we met a slave girl who had a spirit that en-
abled her to tell the future. She earned a lot of mon-
ey for her masters by telling fortunes. 17 She followed
Paul and the rest of us, shouting, "These men are ser-
vants of the Most High God, and they have come to tell
you how to be saved."
18 This went on day after day until Paul got so exas-
perated that he turned and said to the demon within
her, "I command you in the name of Jesus Christ to
come out of her." And instantly it left her.
19 Her masters' hopes of wealth were now shat-
tered, so they grabbed Paul and Silas and dragged
them before the authorities at the marketplace. 20 "The
whole city is in an uproar because of these Jews!" they
shouted to the city officials. 21 "They are teaching cus-
toms that are illegal for us Romans to practice."
22 A mob quickly formed against Paul and Silas, and
the city officials ordered them stripped and beaten
with wooden rods. 23 They were severely beaten, and
then they were thrown into prison. The jailer was or-
dered to make sure they didn't escape. 24 So the jailer

CLOSED DOORS

1. If you could visit any country in the world, where would you visit?

ACTS 16:6-10

2. Why did Paul not preach in Asia and Bithynia? What does it mean that the Holy Spirit prevented him from speaking (v. 6)?
3. How did this setback turn out to be a good thing?
4. When has God prevented you from pursuing a course of action, even when it seemed like a good choice? What was the result?
5. Do you struggle to pry open a door that God has closed? What closed doors are you struggling with right now?

16:2 Greek *brothers;* also in 16:40. **16:6-7** *Phrygia, Galatia, Asia, Mysia,* and *Bithynia* were all districts in what is now Turkey. **16:10** Luke, the writer of this book, here joined Paul and accompanied him on his journey.

16:1–3 Timothy to be circumcised. For Paul to allow Timothy, a Jew, to accompany him without first following the Jewish custom of circumcision would communicate to other Jews that Paul had no regard for their traditions. This shows Paul's willingness to accommodate himself to cultural sensitivities.

16:6–7 had prevented them. Why Jesus would not allow Paul and Silas to preach in Asia and Bithyna is not known.

16:8 Troas. An important seaport city on the Aegean Sea. While it appears that Paul did not conduct any evangelistic work here at this time, he did so later on (2 Cor. 2:12).

16:9–10 we. Verses 10-17 comprise the first of four passages written in the first person (20:1-15; 21:1-18; 27:1–28:16), indicating that Luke himself, the author of Acts, was accompanying Paul at these points.

16:13 meeting for prayer. Ten men were required to form a synagogue. The fact that there was no synagogue in Philippi indicates the Jewish population in this city was small. **outside the city to a riverbank.** The Jews may have been forbidden to meet inside the city limits, or they may have wanted to be near a river to perform their ceremonial washings.

16:14–15 Lydia. Lydia was a businesswoman who sold purple cloth, a luxury item indicating that she was a woman of wealth. **Thyatira.** A city in the province of Asia noted for its cloth-dyeing industry.

16:16 a spirit that enabled her to tell the future. Literally "a spirit, a python." A snake was supposed to guard the oracle of Delphi, and thus the snake was a symbol of a fortuneteller.

16:18 come out of her. While the girl, who was a fortuneteller, uttered the truth, the spirit that motivated her was not what Paul desired as a collaborator in his mission. Proclamations from this girl attracted attention, but it made Paul and Silas appear more as magicians than as representatives of God. Therefore, Paul commanded the spirit to leave her.

16:19 Her masters' hopes of wealth were now shattered. The girl's worth to her masters was only in her gift of fortunetelling. To them, Paul had not delivered a girl from the power of evil but had violated their property rights.

16:22 stripped and beaten. The authorities should have put Paul and Silas in custody to be formally tried, but they beat them publicly without a trial.

16:24 clamped their feet in the stocks. The stocks were locked wooden boards that clamped about the ankles, making movement impossible.

SINGING IN PRISON

1. When you're down, what song or type of music lifts your spirits?

ACTS 16:22-40

2. Why were Paul and Silas "praying and singing hymns to God" (v. 25) when they were in prison? What does this suggest about their attitude toward God?
3. Why did Paul and Silas stay when they could have left? What was the result?
4. If someone asked you, "What must I do to be saved?" (v. 30), what would you say?
5. How can this passage encourage you to trust more in God during times of trial?

put them into the inner dungeon and clamped their feet in the stocks.

25 Around midnight Paul and Silas were praying and singing hymns to God, and the other prisoners were listening. 26 Suddenly, there was a massive earthquake, and the prison was shaken to its foundations. All the doors immediately flew open, and the chains of every prisoner fell off! 27 The jailer woke up to see the prison doors wide open. He assumed the prisoners had escaped, so he drew his sword to kill himself. 28 But Paul shouted to him, "Stop! Don't kill yourself! We are all here!"

29 The jailer called for lights and ran to the dungeon and fell down trembling before Paul and Silas. 30 Then he brought them out and asked, "Sirs, what must I do to be saved?"

31 They replied, "Believe in the Lord Jesus and you will be saved, along with everyone in your household." 32 And they shared the word of the Lord with him and with all who lived in his household. 33 Even at that hour of the night, the jailer cared for them and washed their wounds. Then he and everyone in his household were immediately baptized. 34 He brought them into his house and set a meal before them, and he and his entire household rejoiced because they all believed in God.

35 The next morning the city officials sent the police to tell the jailer, "Let those men go!" 36 So the jailer told Paul, "The city officials have said you and Silas are free to leave. Go in peace."

37 But Paul replied, "They have publicly beaten us without a trial and put us in prison—and we are Roman citizens. So now they want us to leave secretly? Certainly not! Let them come themselves to release us!"

38 When the police reported this, the city officials were alarmed to learn that Paul and Silas were Roman citizens. 39 So they came to the jail and apologized to them. Then they brought them out and begged them to leave the city. 40 When Paul and Silas left the prison, they returned to the home of Lydia. There they met with the believers and encouraged them once more. Then they left town.

PAUL PREACHES IN THESSALONICA

17 Paul and Silas then traveled through the towns of Amphipolis and Apollonia and came to Thessalonica, where there was a Jewish synagogue. 2 As was Paul's custom, he went to the synagogue service, and for three Sabbaths in a row he used the Scriptures to reason with the people. 3 He explained the prophecies and proved that the Messiah must suffer and rise from the dead. He said, "This Jesus I'm telling you about is the Messiah." 4 Some of the Jews who listened were persuaded and joined Paul and Silas, along with many God-fearing Greek men and quite a few prominent women.*

5 But some of the Jews were jealous, so they gathered some troublemakers from the marketplace to form a mob and start a riot. They attacked the home of Jason, searching for Paul and Silas so they could drag them out to the crowd.* 6 Not finding them there, they dragged out Jason and some of the other believers* instead and took them before the city council. "Paul and Silas have caused trouble all over the world," they shouted, "and now they are here disturbing our city, too. 7 And Jason has welcomed them into his home. They are all guilty of treason against Caesar, for they profess allegiance to another king, named Jesus."

8 The people of the city, as well as the city council, were thrown into turmoil by these reports. 9 So the officials forced Jason and the other believers to post bond, and then they released them.

PAUL AND SILAS IN BEREA

10 That very night the believers sent Paul and Silas to Berea. When they arrived there, they went to the Jewish synagogue. 11 And the people of Berea were more open-minded than those in Thessalonica, and they listened eagerly to Paul's message. They searched the Scriptures day after day to see if Paul and Silas were teaching the truth. 12 As a result, many Jews believed, as did many of the prominent Greek women and men.

13 But when some Jews in Thessalonica learned that Paul was preaching the word of God in Berea, they went there and stirred up trouble. 14 The believers

17:4 Some manuscripts read *quite a few of the wives of the leading men.* **17:5** Or *the city council.* **17:6** Greek *brothers;* also in 17:10, 14.

16:27-28 he drew his sword to kill himself. The penalty for a guard who allowed his prisoners to escape was the punishment the prisoner was to receive. The jailer preferred sudden death by his own hand rather than going through the humiliation of a trial and execution by the authorities.

16:31-32 Believe in the Lord Jesus and you will be saved. Paul's statement to the jailer promised deliverance from divine judgment.

16:35-40 The magistrates wanted to expel Paul and Silas from Philippi to avoid any further trouble. But they refused to leave without a personal apology from the magistrates for their breach of justice. This was important for the protection of the young church in Philippi. By being escorted out of the prison by the magistrates, a signal would be communicated to the community that the charges against Paul and Silas had been false. Then the community would be more likely to leave the young church alone.

16:37 without a trial. While local magistrates could execute punishment upon troublemakers without a trial, this practice was never permitted in the case of a Roman citizen. The magistrates had overlooked the possibility that these two Jews might be Roman citizens.

17:5 the Jews were jealous. In Philippi economic interest had motivated the opposition against Paul and Silas. Here it was the jealousy of the Jews.

17:7 guilty of treason against Caesar. In Philippi, the anger of the owner of the slave girl over his economic loss was masked by a charge of public disturbance. Here, the Jews' jealousy is masked by a charge of sedition against Rome.

17:9 post bond. Since Paul could not be brought before the local officials, they insisted that Jason post a bond. This assured them that Jason would no longer be a host to Paul so he would have to leave the city.

acted at once, sending Paul on to the coast, while Si-
las and Timothy remained behind. 15 Those escorting
Paul went with him all the way to Athens; then they
returned to Berea with instructions for Silas and Tim-
othy to hurry and join him.

PAUL PREACHES IN ATHENS

16 While Paul was waiting for them in Athens, he was
deeply troubled by all the idols he saw everywhere
in the city. 17 He went to the synagogue to reason with
the Jews and the God-fearing Gentiles, and he spoke
daily in the public square to all who happened to be
there.

18 He also had a debate with some of the Epicure-
an and Stoic philosophers. When he told them about
Jesus and his resurrection, they said, "What's this
babbler trying to say with these strange ideas he's
picked up?" Others said, "He seems to be preaching
about some foreign gods."

19 Then they took him to the high council of the city.*
"Come and tell us about this new teaching," they said.
20 "You are saying some rather strange things, and we
want to know what it's all about." 21 (It should be ex-
plained that all the Athenians as well as the foreign-
ers in Athens seemed to spend all their time discuss-
ing the latest ideas.)

22 So Paul, standing before the council,* addressed
them as follows: "Men of Athens, I notice that you are
very religious in every way, 23 for as I was walking
along I saw your many shrines. And one of your al-
tars had this inscription on it: 'To an Unknown God.'
This God, whom you worship without knowing, is the
one I'm telling you about.

24 "He is the God who made the world and every-
thing in it. Since he is Lord of heaven and earth, he
doesn't live in man-made temples, 25 and human
hands can't serve his needs—for he has no needs. He
himself gives life and breath to everything, and he
satisfies every need. 26 From one man* he created all
the nations throughout the whole earth. He decided
beforehand when they should rise and fall, and he
determined their boundaries.

27 "His purpose was for the nations to seek after
God and perhaps feel their way toward him and
find him—though he is not far from any one of us.
28 For in him we live and move and exist. As some of
your* own poets have said, 'We are his offspring.'
29 And since this is true, we shouldn't think of God
as an idol designed by craftsmen from gold or silver
or stone.

30 "God overlooked people's ignorance about these
things in earlier times, but now he commands every-
one everywhere to repent of their sins and turn to
him. 31 For he has set a day for judging the world
with justice by the man he has appointed, and he
proved to everyone who this is by raising him from
the dead."

32 When they heard Paul speak about the resur-
rection of the dead, some laughed in contempt, but
others said, "We want to hear more about this later."
33 That ended Paul's discussion with them, 34 but some
joined him and became believers. Among them were
Dionysius, a member of the council,* a woman named
Damaris, and others with them.

PAUL MEETS PRISCILLA AND AQUILA IN CORINTH

18 Then Paul left Athens and went to Corinth.*
2 There he became acquainted with a Jew
named Aquila, born in Pontus, who had recently ar-
rived from Italy with his wife, Priscilla. They had left
Italy when Claudius Caesar deported all Jews from
Rome. 3 Paul lived and worked with them, for they
were tentmakers* just as he was.

4 Each Sabbath found Paul at the synagogue, trying
to convince the Jews and Greeks alike. 5 And after Si-
las and Timothy came down from Macedonia, Paul
spent all his time preaching the word. He testified to
the Jews that Jesus was the Messiah. 6 But when they
opposed and insulted him, Paul shook the dust from
his clothes and said, "Your blood is upon your own
heads—I am innocent. From now on I will go preach
to the Gentiles."

7 Then he left and went to the home of Titius Justus,
a Gentile who worshiped God and lived next door to
the synagogue. 8 Crispus, the leader of the synagogue,
and everyone in his household believed in the Lord.
Many others in Corinth also heard Paul, became be-
lievers, and were baptized.

9 One night the Lord spoke to Paul in a vision and
told him, "Don't be afraid! Speak out! Don't be silent!
10 For I am with you, and no one will attack and harm
you, for many people in this city belong to me." 11 So
Paul stayed there for the next year and a half, teach-
ing the word of God.

17:19 Or *the most learned society of philosophers in the city.* Greek reads *the Areopagus.* **17:22** Traditionally rendered *standing in the middle of Mars Hill;* Greek reads *standing in the middle of the Areopagus.* **17:26** Greek *From one;* other manuscripts read *From one blood.* **17:28** Some manuscripts read *our.* **17:34** Greek *an Areopagite.* **18:1** *Athens* and *Corinth* were major cities in Achaia, the region in the southern portion of the Greek peninsula. **18:3** Or *leatherworkers.*

17:17 to reason . . .in the public square. Paul preached not only in the synagogue at Athens but also in their marketplace where, three centuries before, Socrates had debated with anyone who would listen.

17:18 Epicurean and Stoic philosophers. Epicurus maintained that a tranquil life free from pain, passions, and fears was the highest good. This could be achieved only by detaching oneself from the world. The Epicureans were practical atheists since they believed the gods had no interest in everyday affairs. **this babbler.** A derisive term stemming from the actions of a bird that picks up seeds wherever it can find them. To the philosophers, Paul seemed like someone who picked up scraps of ideas here and there and then had the audacity to teach them to others.

17:19 high council of the city. Athens was a free city within the Roman Empire, so the council (the Areopagus) had legal and judicial authority over what went on in the city. It does not appear that Paul was on trial as much as his message was being evaluated on its credibility and worth.

17:21 latest ideas. Luke's sarcastic observation about the nature of the Athenians in general is an echo of what the Greek orator Demosthenes had said 400 years earlier: "You are the best people at being deceived by something new that is said."

17:24 he doesn't live in man-made temples. Euripides, a Greek philosopher, recognized this when he wrote, "What house built by craftsman could enclose the . . . divine within enfolding walls?"

17:25 and human hands cannot serve his needs. With this observation of Paul, the philosophers would also agree. Plato had written, "What advantage accrues to the gods from what they get from us?"

17:27 he is not far from any one of us. Challenging the Epicurean assumption that God was unknowable, Paul says that God is knowable by those who seek Him.

17:28 your own poets. Paul supports his points by quoting two Greek authors, Epimenides and Aratus, indicating he recognized that God revealed truth about Himself even through other religions and philosophies.

17:32–34 some joined him and became believers. The converts in Athens included Dionysius, a member of the Athenian council. Nothing more is said in the New Testament about Athens, so it is unlikely that these believers established a church in this city.

18:2 Aquila . . . Priscilla. This couple, apparently converted to Christianity in Rome prior to meeting Paul, became important coworkers with him (Rom. 16:3; 1 Cor. 16:19; 2 Tim. 4:19).

12 But when Gallio became governor of Achaia,
some Jews rose up together against Paul and brought
him before the governor for judgment. 13 They ac-
cused Paul of "persuading people to worship God in
ways that are contrary to our law."
14 But just as Paul started to make his defense, Gallio
turned to Paul's accusers and said, "Listen, you Jews,
if this were a case involving some wrongdoing or a
serious crime, I would have a reason to accept your
case. 15 But since it is merely a question of words and
names and your Jewish law, take care of it yourselves.
I refuse to judge such matters." 16 And he threw them
out of the courtroom.
17 The crowd* then grabbed Sosthenes, the leader of
the synagogue, and beat him right there in the court-
room. But Gallio paid no attention.

PAUL RETURNS TO ANTIOCH OF SYRIA

18 Paul stayed in Corinth for some time after that, then
said good-bye to the brothers and sisters* and went to
nearby Cenchrea. There he shaved his head accord-
ing to Jewish custom, marking the end of a vow. Then
he set sail for Syria, taking Priscilla and Aquila with
him.
19 They stopped first at the port of Ephesus, where
Paul left the others behind. While he was there,
he went to the synagogue to reason with the Jews.
20 They asked him to stay longer, but he declined. 21 As
he left, however, he said, "I will come back later,* God
willing." Then he set sail from Ephesus. 22 The next
stop was at the port of Caesarea. From there he went
up and visited the church at Jerusalem* and then
went back to Antioch.
23 After spending some time in Antioch, Paul went
back through Galatia and Phrygia, visiting and
strengthening all the believers.*

APOLLOS INSTRUCTED AT EPHESUS

24 Meanwhile, a Jew named Apollos, an eloquent
speaker who knew the Scriptures well, had arrived
in Ephesus from Alexandria in Egypt. 25 He had been
taught the way of the Lord, and he taught others
about Jesus with an enthusiastic spirit* and with ac-
curacy. However, he knew only about John's baptism.
26 When Priscilla and Aquila heard him preaching
boldly in the synagogue, they took him aside and ex-
plained the way of God even more accurately.
27 Apollos had been thinking about going to Acha-
ia, and the brothers and sisters in Ephesus encour-
aged him to go. They wrote to the believers in Acha-
ia, asking them to welcome him. When he arrived
there, he proved to be of great benefit to those who,
by God's grace, had believed. 28 He refuted the Jews
with powerful arguments in public debate. Using the
Scriptures, he explained to them that Jesus was the
Messiah.

PAUL'S THIRD MISSIONARY JOURNEY

19 While Apollos was in Corinth, Paul traveled
through the interior regions until he reached
Ephesus, on the coast, where he found several be-
lievers.* 2 "Did you receive the Holy Spirit when you
believed?" he asked them.
"No," they replied, "we haven't even heard that
there is a Holy Spirit."
3 "Then what baptism did you experience?" he
asked.
And they replied, "The baptism of John."
4 Paul said, "John's baptism called for repentance
from sin. But John himself told the people to believe
in the one who would come later, meaning Jesus."
5 As soon as they heard this, they were baptized
in the name of the Lord Jesus. 6 Then when Paul laid
his hands on them, the Holy Spirit came on them, and
they spoke in other tongues* and prophesied. 7 There
were about twelve men in all.

PAUL MINISTERS IN EPHESUS

8 Then Paul went to the synagogue and preached
boldly for the next three months, arguing persuasive-
ly about the Kingdom of God. 9 But some became stub-
born, rejecting his message and publicly speaking

18:17 Greek *Everyone;* other manuscripts read *All the Greeks.* **18:18** Greek *brothers;* also in 18:27. **18:21** Some manuscripts read *"I must by all means be at Jerusalem for the upcoming festival, but I will come back later."* **18:22** Greek *the church.* **18:23** Greek *disciples;* also in 18:27. **18:25** Or *with enthusiasm in the Spirit.* **19:1** Greek *disciples;* also in 19:9, 30. **19:6** Or *in other languages.*

18:12 Gallio. A highly respected Roman official who served as proconsul in Archia for one year—from A.D. July 51 to A.D. June 52.

18:13 our law. The Jews probably did not expect that the proconsul could distinguish between Jews and Christians any better than the Emperor Claudius (v. 2). So it is probable that they accused Paul of violating the Roman laws against advocating religions that threatened the state.

18:18 he shaved his head . . . marking the end of a vow. Pious Jews would take vows, based on the pattern of the Nazarites (Num. 6:1–21), as an indication of their devotion to God. Since the cutting of one's hair indicated the termination of the vow, Paul may have made a vow of dedication to God for as long as he was in Corinth to express his thanks for God's promise of protection (v. 10). Vows normally were terminated by shaving one's head and offering a sacrifice in the temple at Jerusalem. People far from Jerusalem could shave their heads where they were and carry the trimmings to the temple to be presented along with a sacrifice. Luke may have included this incident as evidence that Paul did not abandon the traditions of his people. **taking Priscilla and Aquila with him.** It is significant that Priscilla's name is listed ahead of her husband's. This probably indicates that Priscilla was the more influential and outspoken of the two.

18:25 he knew only about John's baptism. While Apollos was an articulate believer in Jesus, he had not received the full story of the gospel. Just what he was lacking is unclear, but, as the story in 19:1–7 indicates, he may not have heard of the coming of the Holy Spirit promised to those who are baptized in the name of Jesus.

19:2 Did you receive the Holy Spirit when you believed? As Paul talked with these men, something must have seemed out of place that led him to ask this question. Since John spoke of the coming of the Holy Spirit (Luke 3:16), it is likely that the intent of their response is more that they were not aware that the Holy Spirit had been given. Or perhaps they had responded to some other teaching of John's and his words about the Spirit had not registered with them.

19:3 the baptism of John. John baptized people upon their repentance, symbolizing their cleansing from sin in anticipation of the coming of the Messiah. Jesus' baptism is a symbol of the pouring out of the Spirit in fulfillment of the Old Testament promises about the Messiah.

19:4 baptism called for repentance. John's baptism symbolized cleansing from sin. It may have been based on the baptism of the Essene sect at Qumran, a desert community where the Dead Sea Scrolls were found. Or it may have been a refinement of Jewish baptism of Gentile converts. Such were baptized to symbolize their turning away from their sinful Gentile ways. John taught that Jews also needed repentance and cleansing from sin. The baptism that Jesus practiced also involved repentance. But by itself a baptism of repentance focuses only on the past and finding forgiveness for one's sins. Christian baptism also includes the gift of the Spirit, which empowers believers for the future.

19:6 laid his hands on them. The last time this action was mentioned was when the gospel broke through into Samaria (see 8:17). The laying on of hands and the manifestation of tongues was reminiscent of Pentecost in Acts 2. The laying on of hands here may indicate an assurance that these people were now fully included in the church and that Ephesus was to be a major new site for the proclamation of the gospel.

19:8–20 Ephesus became the hub of Paul's ministry for two years. During this time churches were founded in Colossae, Laodecia, and the cities mentioned in Revelation 1:11. It was also at Ephesus that Paul wrote 1 Corinthians.

against the Way. So Paul left the synagogue and took
the believers with him. Then he held daily discus-
sions at the lecture hall of Tyrannus. 10 This went on
for the next two years, so that people throughout the
province of Asia—both Jews and Greeks—heard the
word of the Lord.
11 God gave Paul the power to perform unusual
miracles. 12 When handkerchiefs or aprons that had
merely touched his skin were placed on sick people,
they were healed of their diseases, and evil spirits
were expelled.
13 A group of Jews was traveling from town to town
casting out evil spirits. They tried to use the name of
the Lord Jesus in their incantation, saying, "I com-
mand you in the name of Jesus, whom Paul preaches,
to come out!" 14 Seven sons of Sceva, a leading priest,
were doing this. 15 But one time when they tried it,
the evil spirit replied, "I know Jesus, and I know Paul,
but who are you?" 16 Then the man with the evil spir-
it leaped on them, overpowered them, and attacked
them with such violence that they fled from the
house, naked and battered.
17 The story of what happened spread quickly all
through Ephesus, to Jews and Greeks alike. A solemn
fear descended on the city, and the name of the Lord
Jesus was greatly honored. 18 Many who became be-
lievers confessed their sinful practices. 19 A number of
them who had been practicing sorcery brought their
incantation books and burned them at a public bon-
fire. The value of the books was several million dol-
lars.* 20 So the message about the Lord spread widely
and had a powerful effect.
21 Afterward Paul felt compelled by the Spirit* to
go over to Macedonia and Achaia before going to
Jerusalem. "And after that," he said, "I must go on
to Rome!" 22 He sent his two assistants, Timothy and
Erastus, ahead to Macedonia while he stayed awhile
longer in the province of Asia.

THE RIOT IN EPHESUS

23 About that time, serious trouble developed in Eph-
esus concerning the Way. 24 It began with Demetrius,
a silversmith who had a large business manufactur-
ing silver shrines of the Greek goddess Artemis.* He
kept many craftsmen busy. 25 He called them together,
along with others employed in similar trades, and ad-
dressed them as follows:
"Gentlemen, you know that our wealth comes from
this business. 26 But as you have seen and heard, this
man Paul has persuaded many people that hand-
made gods aren't really gods at all. And he's done this
not only here in Ephesus but throughout the entire
province! 27 Of course, I'm not just talking about the
loss of public respect for our business. I'm also con-
cerned that the temple of the great goddess Artemis
will lose its influence and that Artemis—this magnif-
icent goddess worshiped throughout the province of
Asia and all around the world—will be robbed of her
great prestige!"
28 At this their anger boiled, and they began shout-
ing, "Great is Artemis of the Ephesians!" 29 Soon the
whole city was filled with confusion. Everyone
rushed to the amphitheater, dragging along Gaius
and Aristarchus, who were Paul's traveling compan-
ions from Macedonia. 30 Paul wanted to go in, too, but
the believers wouldn't let him. 31 Some of the officials
of the province, friends of Paul, also sent a message to
him, begging him not to risk his life by entering the
amphitheater.
32 Inside, the people were all shouting, some one thing
and some another. Everything was in confusion. In fact,
most of them didn't even know why they were there.
33 The Jews in the crowd pushed Alexander forward
and told him to explain the situation. He motioned for
silence and tried to speak. 34 But when the crowd real-
ized he was a Jew, they started shouting again and kept
it up for about two hours: "Great is Artemis of the Ephe-
sians! Great is Artemis of the Ephesians!"
35 At last the mayor was able to quiet them down
enough to speak. "Citizens of Ephesus," he said.

ANGER OVER THE GOSPEL

1. Who is the best craftsman that you know? What does that person make? How did he or she become so skillful?

ACTS 19:23-41

2. How did Demetrius and the other artisans make their living? Why were they upset about Paul?
3. What does verse 26 show about Demetrius' beliefs and priorities?
4. He described Artemis as "this magnificent goddess worshiped throughout the province of Asia and all around the world" (v. 27). What does this suggest about how the gospel or "good news" of Jesus affects the world?
5. How does the world today get angry over the gospel of Jesus Christ?

19:19 Greek *50,000 pieces of silver,* each of which was the equivalent of a day's wage. **19:21** Or *decided in his spirit.* **19:24** *Artemis* is otherwise known as Diana.

19:11 unusual miracles. See the similar miracles wrought by Peter in 5:15. Ephesus was known for its magic arts. Some scrolls of magic spells from this ancient city can be seen today in museum collections. Perhaps for that reason, this type of evidence was necessary to convince people that the gospel was more powerful than magic.

19:14 Sceva, a leading priest. Other historical records never identify a high priest in Jerusalem by this name, although he may have been a member of the high priest's family. He was probably a successful exorcist who assumed the title to command respect (and business) from people in the area.

19:18 became believers. The tense of the word implies that these were Christians who secretly practiced magic arts. The incident with Sceva's sons showed them that they needed to give up these practices.

19:19 the value of the books was several million dollars. A piece of silver was called a drachma. This would have been an incredible amount of money, since a drachma was equal to a day's wages.

19:21 I must go on to Rome! Paul intended to visit Rome and then go on to Spain after delivering an offering from the Gentile churches he had founded to Jerusalem (Rom. 1:11; 15:23-25). The letter to the Romans was written from Corinth after Paul left Ephesus and just before his trip to Jerusalem (20:1-6).

19:24 a silversmith. Silversmiths in Ephesus made a great deal of money through the manufacture and sale of models of the goddess Artemis. This goddess combined belief in the Roman virgin goddess Diana with an Asian fertility goddess. The center for her worship was in Ephesus.

19:35 the mayor. This was the highest-ranking official in the city. He was accountable to the Roman provincial government for keeping the peace in Ephesus.

"Everyone knows that Ephesus is the official guard-
ian of the temple of the great Artemis, whose image
fell down to us from heaven. 36 Since this is an unde-
niable fact, you should stay calm and not do anything
rash. 37 You have brought these men here, but they
have stolen nothing from the temple and have not
spoken against our goddess.
38 "If Demetrius and the craftsmen have a case
against them, the courts are in session and the offi-
cials can hear the case at once. Let them make formal
charges. 39 And if there are complaints about other
matters, they can be settled in a legal assembly. 40 I
am afraid we are in danger of being charged with
rioting by the Roman government, since there is no
cause for all this commotion. And if Rome demands
an explanation, we won't know what to say." 41*Then
he dismissed them, and they dispersed.

PAUL GOES TO MACEDONIA AND GREECE

20 When the uproar was over, Paul sent for the
believers* and encouraged them. Then he said
good-bye and left for Macedonia. 2 While there, he
encouraged the believers in all the towns he passed
through. Then he traveled down to Greece, 3 where
he stayed for three months. He was preparing to sail
back to Syria when he discovered a plot by some Jews
against his life, so he decided to return through Mac-
edonia.
4 Several men were traveling with him. They were
Sopater son of Pyrrhus from Berea; Aristarchus and
Secundus from Thessalonica; Gaius from Derbe; Tim-
othy; and Tychicus and Trophimus from the province
of Asia. 5 They went on ahead and waited for us at
Troas. 6 After the Passover* ended, we boarded a ship
at Philippi in Macedonia and five days later joined
them in Troas, where we stayed a week.

PAUL'S FINAL VISIT TO TROAS

7 On the first day of the week, we gathered with the
local believers to share in the Lord's Supper.* Paul
was preaching to them, and since he was leaving the
next day, he kept talking until midnight. 8 The upstairs
room where we met was lighted with many flicker-
ing lamps. 9 As Paul spoke on and on, a young man
named Eutychus, sitting on the windowsill, became
very drowsy. Finally, he fell sound asleep and dropped
three stories to his death below. 10 Paul went down,
bent over him, and took him into his arms. "Don't wor-
ry," he said, "he's alive!" 11 Then they all went back up-
stairs, shared in the Lord's Supper,* and ate together.
Paul continued talking to them until dawn, and then
he left. 12 Meanwhile, the young man was taken home
alive and well, and everyone was greatly relieved.

PAUL MEETS THE EPHESIAN ELDERS

13 Paul went by land to Assos, where he had arranged
for us to join him, while we traveled by ship. 14 He
joined us there, and we sailed together to Mitylene.
15 The next day we sailed past the island of Kios. The
following day we crossed to the island of Samos, and*
a day later we arrived at Miletus.
16 Paul had decided to sail on past Ephesus, for he
didn't want to spend any more time in the province of
Asia. He was hurrying to get to Jerusalem, if possible,
in time for the Festival of Pentecost. 17 But when we
landed at Miletus, he sent a message to the elders of
the church at Ephesus, asking them to come and meet
him.
18 When they arrived he declared, "You know that
from the day I set foot in the province of Asia until
now 19 I have done the Lord's work humbly and with
many tears. I have endured the trials that came to me
from the plots of the Jews. 20 I never shrank back from
telling you what you needed to hear, either publicly
or in your homes. 21 I have had one message for Jews
and Greeks alike—the necessity of repenting from
sin and turning to God, and of having faith in our
Lord Jesus.
22 "And now I am bound by the Spirit* to go to Jeru-
salem. I don't know what awaits me, 23 except that the
Holy Spirit tells me in city after city that jail and suf-
fering lie ahead. 24 But my life is worth nothing to me
unless I use it for finishing the work assigned me by
the Lord Jesus—the work of telling others the Good
News about the wonderful grace of God.
25 "And now I know that none of you to whom I
have preached the Kingdom will ever see me again.
26 I declare today that I have been faithful. If anyone
suffers eternal death, it's not my fault,* 27 for I didn't
shrink from declaring all that God wants you to know.
28 "So guard yourselves and God's people. Feed and
shepherd God's flock—his church, purchased with his

19:41 Some translations include verse 41 as part of verse 40. 20:1 Greek *disciples.* 20:6 Greek *the days of unleavened bread.* 20:7 Greek *to break bread.* 20:11 Greek *broke the bread.* 20:15 Some manuscripts read *and having stayed at Trogyllium.* 20:22 Or *by my spirit,* or *by an inner compulsion;* Greek reads *by the spirit.* 20:26 Greek *I am innocent of the blood of all.*

19:39 legal assembly. The people could gather for meetings to discuss issues that concerned them, but these were to be held at scheduled times and with specific procedures. Such an irregular, chaotic meeting as this one could have led to Roman suppression of their right to assemble.

20:4 Several men were traveling with him. Although Luke does not say why Paul was accompanied by so many men from such different areas, it must be remembered that he was carrying the collection he had gathered for the church in Jerusalem from the churches in Macedonia, Achaia, and Asia (see 19:21-22). First Corinthians 16:3 indicates that some men from Corinth accompanied him as well. These men served as protection for Paul against robbers and as a means of accountability to their home churches for Paul's deliverance of the offering as promised (2 Cor. 8:19-21).

20:7 the first day of the week. This meeting probably occurred on a Sunday evening. Meetings were held in the evenings because Sunday, like every day, was a work day for slaves, who made up a large percentage of the believers (Eph. 6:5). This also may have contributed to the weariness of Eutychus.

20:8 many flickering lamps. These would have been oil lamps giving off fumes that would add to a sense of drowsiness.

20:19 humbly. In the Greek world, humility was a weakness, a sign of a slave. For Paul, who saw himself as a slave for God (Rom. 1:1; Col. 3:24), humility was essential for being a disciple or follower of Jesus Christ (Phil. 2:3; Col. 3:12).

20:23 the Holy Spirit tells me in city after city that jail and suffering lie ahead. Paul was undertaking this journey in the conviction that God wanted him to go but also with an awareness that it would lead to difficulty. All along the way, the Spirit was preparing him for the hardships he would face in Jerusalem. This sense of foreboding led him to ask the Roman church to pray for him as he went (Rom. 15:30-32).

20:24 finishing the work. Just before his death, Paul wrote to Timothy at Ephesus using this same metaphor to describe his ministry (2 Tim. 4:7). **the wonderful grace of God.** Just as repentance and faith sum up what it means to respond to God, so grace sums up the news of what God has done for us (Rom. 5:1-11; Eph. 2:8-9).

20:25 none of you . . .will ever see me again. A few weeks earlier, Paul wrote to the Romans that after he went to Jerusalem he hoped to visit them and proceed to Spain, since his work in Macedonia and Achaia (and presumably Asia) was finished (Rom. 15:23). Whether this is why he declared he would not see these people again or whether he felt that the warnings of the Spirit (v. 23) were to prepare him for death is uncertain.

own blood*—over which the Holy Spirit has appoint-
ed you as leaders.* 29 I know that false teachers, like
vicious wolves, will come in among you after I leave,
not sparing the flock. 30 Even some men from your
own group will rise up and distort the truth in order
to draw a following. 31 Watch out! Remember the three
years I was with you—my constant watch and care
over you night and day, and my many tears for you.
32 "And now I entrust you to God and the message of
his grace that is able to build you up and give you an
inheritance with all those he has set apart for himself.
33 "I have never coveted anyone's silver or gold or
fine clothes. 34 You know that these hands of mine have
worked to supply my own needs and even the needs of
those who were with me. 35 And I have been a constant
example of how you can help those in need by work-
ing hard. You should remember the words of the Lord
Jesus: 'It is more blessed to give than to receive.'"
36 When he had finished speaking, he knelt and
prayed with them. 37 They all cried as they embraced
and kissed him good-bye. 38 They were sad most of all
because he had said that they would never see him
again. Then they escorted him down to the ship.

PAUL'S JOURNEY TO JERUSALEM

21 After saying farewell to the Ephesian elders, we
sailed straight to the island of Cos. The next day
we reached Rhodes and then went to Patara. 2 There
we boarded a ship sailing for Phoenicia. 3 We sighted
the island of Cyprus, passed it on our left, and landed
at the harbor of Tyre, in Syria, where the ship was to
unload its cargo.
4 We went ashore, found the local believers,* and
stayed with them a week. These believers prophesied
through the Holy Spirit that Paul should not go on to
Jerusalem. 5 When we returned to the ship at the end of
the week, the entire congregation, including women*
and children, left the city and came down to the shore
with us. There we knelt, prayed, 6 and said our fare-
wells. Then we went aboard, and they returned home.
7 The next stop after leaving Tyre was Ptolema-
is, where we greeted the brothers and sisters* and
stayed for one day. 8 The next day we went on to Caes-
area and stayed at the home of Philip the Evangelist,
one of the seven men who had been chosen to distrib-
ute food. 9 He had four unmarried daughters who had
the gift of prophecy.
10 Several days later a man named Agabus, who
also had the gift of prophecy, arrived from Judea.
11 He came over, took Paul's belt, and bound his own
feet and hands with it. Then he said, "The Holy Spirit
declares, 'So shall the owner of this belt be bound by
the Jewish leaders in Jerusalem and turned over to
the Gentiles.'" 12 When we heard this, we and the local
believers all begged Paul not to go on to Jerusalem.
13 But he said, "Why all this weeping? You are
breaking my heart! I am ready not only to be jailed
at Jerusalem but even to die for the sake of the Lord
Jesus." 14 When it was clear that we couldn't persuade
him, we gave up and said, "The Lord's will be done."

PAUL ARRIVES AT JERUSALEM

15 After this we packed our things and left for Jerusa-
lem. 16 Some believers from Caesarea accompanied
us, and they took us to the home of Mnason, a man
originally from Cyprus and one of the early believers.
17 When we arrived, the brothers and sisters in Jerusa-
lem welcomed us warmly.
18 The next day Paul went with us to meet with
James, and all the elders of the Jerusalem church
were present. 19 After greeting them, Paul gave a de-
tailed account of the things God had accomplished
among the Gentiles through his ministry.
20 After hearing this, they praised God. And then
they said, "You know, dear brother, how many thou-
sands of Jews have also believed, and they all follow
the law of Moses very seriously. 21 But the Jewish be-
lievers here in Jerusalem have been told that you are
teaching all the Jews who live among the Gentiles to
turn their backs on the laws of Moses. They've heard
that you teach them not to circumcise their children
or follow other Jewish customs. 22 What should we do?
They will certainly hear that you have come.
23 "Here's what we want you to do. We have four
men here who have completed their vow. 24 Go with
them to the Temple and join them in the purification
ceremony, paying for them to have their heads ritually
shaved. Then everyone will know that the rumors are
all false and that you yourself observe the Jewish laws.
25 "As for the Gentile believers, they should do what
we already told them in a letter: They should abstain
from eating food offered to idols, from consuming
blood or the meat of strangled animals, and from sex-
ual immorality."

PAUL IS ARRESTED

26 So Paul went to the Temple the next day with the other
men. They had already started the purification ritual, so
he publicly announced the date when their vows would
end and sacrifices would be offered for each of them.
27 The seven days were almost ended when some
Jews from the province of Asia saw Paul in the Temple

20:28a Or *with the blood of his own [Son].* **20:28b** Or *overseers,* or *bishops.* **21:4** Greek *disciples;* also in 21:16. **21:5** Or *wives.* **21:7** Greek *brothers;* also in 21:17.

20:35 remember the words of the Lord Jesus. This beatitude is not found in the Gospels. Paul quotes Jesus only two other times in his letters (1 Cor. 7:10; 1 Tim. 5:18).

21:2-3 boarded a ship for Phoenicia. Paul and his companions found a ship that was sailing directly to Phoenicia, an area in Syria of which Tyre was the chief city. Tyre was only about 100 miles from Jerusalem.

21:10-11 Agabus. Many years earlier, Paul had met Agabus in Antioch where he had prophesied about a coming famine that would affect Judea (11:28). Agabus acted out his prophecy to accent its impact. The form of this prophecy brings out the similarity between what happened to Jesus and what would happen to Paul.

21:16 Mnason. Nothing more is known of this man who may have been one of the original converts at Pentecost. His home became the residence of Paul and his companions during their stay in Jerusalem.

21:17-19 the brothers. It was undoubtedly at this meeting with James (Jesus' half brother and the spokesperson for the church in Jerusalem) that Paul and his companions presented the offering from the Gentile churches. This meeting also allowed Paul an opportunity to update James and other church leaders on everything that had happened since his last visit to Jerusalem.

21:20-21 turn their backs on the laws of Moses. If Jewish believers in Rome could still be rigid about the Jewish dietary and Sabbath laws (Rom. 14:2,4), how much more would these Judean believers since they had lived all their lives in a strictly Jewish environment? Paul's letters reveal that even after the council's decision in Acts 15, he was consistently troubled by Palestinian believers who insisted that his gospel was deficient because he did not require Christian converts to observe Jewish laws (Col. 2:16; Phil. 3:2-3; Rom. 14:5).

21:22-24 vow. To prove that Paul still honored Jewish customs, it was suggested that he participate in a vow that four of the local Jewish elders had made.

21:27-29 Jews from the province of Asia. These Jews assumed that Paul had brought Trophimus, a Gentile, into the temple. While Gentiles could enter the outermost court of the temple, they were banned from the inner courts.

and roused a mob against him. They grabbed him, 28 yelling, "Men of Israel, help us! This is the man who preaches against our people everywhere and tells everybody to disobey the Jewish laws. He speaks against the Temple—and even defiles this holy place by bringing in Gentiles.*" 29 (For earlier that day they had seen him in the city with Trophimus, a Gentile from Ephesus,* and they assumed Paul had taken him into the Temple.)

30 The whole city was rocked by these accusations, and a great riot followed. Paul was grabbed and dragged out of the Temple, and immediately the gates were closed behind him. 31 As they were trying to kill him, word reached the commander of the Roman regiment that all Jerusalem was in an uproar. 32 He immediately called out his soldiers and officers* and ran down among the crowd. When the mob saw the commander and the troops coming, they stopped beating Paul.

33 Then the commander arrested him and ordered him bound with two chains. He asked the crowd who he was and what he had done. 34 Some shouted one thing and some another. Since he couldn't find out the truth in all the uproar and confusion, he ordered that Paul be taken to the fortress. 35 As Paul reached the stairs, the mob grew so violent the soldiers had to lift him to their shoulders to protect him. 36 And the crowd followed behind, shouting, "Kill him, kill him!"

PAUL SPEAKS TO THE CROWD

37 As Paul was about to be taken inside, he said to the commander, "May I have a word with you?"

"Do you know Greek?" the commander asked, surprised. 38 "Aren't you the Egyptian who led a rebellion some time ago and took 4,000 members of the Assassins out into the desert?"

39 "No," Paul replied, "I am a Jew and a citizen of Tarsus in Cilicia, which is an important city. Please, let me talk to these people." 40 The commander agreed, so Paul stood on the stairs and motioned to the people to be quiet. Soon a deep silence enveloped the crowd, and he addressed them in their own language, Aramaic.*

22 "Brothers and esteemed fathers," Paul said, "listen to me as I offer my defense." 2 When they heard him speaking in their own language,* the silence was even greater.

3 Then Paul said, "I am a Jew, born in Tarsus, a city in Cilicia, and I was brought up and educated here in Jerusalem under Gamaliel. As his student, I was carefully trained in our Jewish laws and customs. I became very zealous to honor God in everything I did, just like all of you today. 4 And I persecuted the followers of the Way, hounding some to death, arresting both men and women and throwing them in prison. 5 The high priest and the whole council of elders can testify that this is so. For I received letters from them to our Jewish brothers in Damascus, authorizing me to bring the followers of the Way from there to Jerusalem, in chains, to be punished.

6 "As I was on the road, approaching Damascus about noon, a very bright light from heaven suddenly shone down around me. 7 I fell to the ground and heard a voice saying to me, 'Saul, Saul, why are you persecuting me?'

8 "'Who are you, lord?' I asked.

"And the voice replied, 'I am Jesus the Nazarene,* the one you are persecuting.' 9 The people with me saw the light but didn't understand the voice speaking to me.

10 "I asked, 'What should I do, Lord?'

"And the Lord told me, 'Get up and go into Damascus, and there you will be told everything you are to do.'

11 "I was blinded by the intense light and had to be led by the hand to Damascus by my companions. 12 A man named Ananias lived there. He was a godly man, deeply devoted to the law, and well regarded by all the Jews of Damascus. 13 He came and stood beside me and said, 'Brother Saul, regain your sight.' And that very moment I could see him!

14 "Then he told me, 'The God of our ancestors has chosen you to know his will and to see the Righteous One and hear him speak. 15 For you are to be his witness, telling everyone what you have seen and heard. 16 What are you waiting for? Get up and be baptized. Have your sins washed away by calling on the name of the Lord.'

17 "After I returned to Jerusalem, I was praying in the Temple and fell into a trance. 18 I saw a vision of Jesus* saying to me, 'Hurry! Leave Jerusalem, for the people here won't accept your testimony about me.'

19 "'But Lord,' I argued, 'they certainly know that in every synagogue I imprisoned and beat those who believed in you. 20 And I was in complete agreement when your witness Stephen was killed. I stood by and kept the coats they took off when they stoned him.'

21 "But the Lord said to me, 'Go, for I will send you far away to the Gentiles!'"

21:28 Greek *Greeks.* **21:29** Greek *Trophimus, the Ephesian.* **21:32** Greek *centurions.* **21:40** Or *Hebrew.* **22:2** Greek *in Aramaic,* or *in Hebrew.* **22:8** Or *Jesus of Nazareth.* **22:18** Greek *him.*

21:31-32 all Jerusalem was in an uproar. Paul was probably dragged outside the temple and beaten. A group of Roman soldiers was quartered on the northwest side of the temple. The commander of this squad and some of his soldiers raced through the crowd to the center of the action.

21:38 Aren't you the Egyptian? A notorious Egyptian had led a revolt against Rome a couple of years earlier. Josephus gives an account of a messianic Egyptian terrorist, who, in A.D. 54, led a movement against Rome to take the city of Jerusalem. **Assassins.** In Latin, the *sicarri*—so called because they carried the short dagger known as the *sica* under their robes. The sicarri were an anti-Roman guerilla group.

21:39-40 let me talk to these people. Paul spoke to the people who had assembled in Aramaic, the common language of Jews in Palestine, but a language not widely spoken outside that area. This got the crowd's attention.

22:3 brought up and educated here. Although a citizen of Tarsus, Paul spent most of his life in Jerusalem. Acts 23:16 implies that Paul's sister and her family lived in the city. **Gamaliel.** See 5:34. Gamaliel was a highly respected Pharisee. To study under him was to receive the best possible Jewish education.

22:4-5 the Way. This word is unique to Acts as a name for Christianity (19:9,23; 22:4; 24:14,22). It may stem from Jesus' claim in John 14:6. **to death.** Although Stephen's death is the only one recorded in Acts, there may well have been other believers who suffered death as a result of the persecution instigated by Paul (see also 26:10).

22:17-18 fell into a trance. This account of why Paul left Jerusalem differs from that in 9:19-30. Chapter 9 tells of the external opposition Paul faced; here Paul recounts the inner direction he received from the Lord. **praying in the temple.** The situation in chapter 9 leads us to assume Paul was praying for direction from God in light of the opposition he was facing. The mention of the temple would be a reminder to his audience that, far from defiling the temple, he considered it a refuge for prayer.

22 The crowd listened until Paul said that word.
Then they all began to shout, "Away with such a fel-
low! He isn't fit to live!" 23 They yelled, threw off their
coats, and tossed handfuls of dust into the air.

PAUL REVEALS HIS ROMAN CITIZENSHIP

24 The commander brought Paul inside and ordered
him lashed with whips to make him confess his
crime. He wanted to find out why the crowd had be-
come so furious. 25 When they tied Paul down to lash
him, Paul said to the officer* standing there, "Is it le-
gal for you to whip a Roman citizen who hasn't even
been tried?"
26 When the officer heard this, he went to the com-
mander and asked, "What are you doing? This man is
a Roman citizen!"
27 So the commander went over and asked Paul,
"Tell me, are you a Roman citizen?"
"Yes, I certainly am," Paul replied.
28 "I am, too," the commander muttered, "and it cost
me plenty!"
Paul answered, "But I am a citizen by birth!"
29 The soldiers who were about to interrogate Paul
quickly withdrew when they heard he was a Roman
citizen, and the commander was frightened because
he had ordered him bound and whipped.

PAUL BEFORE THE HIGH COUNCIL

30 The next day the commander ordered the leading
priests into session with the Jewish high council.* He
wanted to find out what the trouble was all about, so
he released Paul to have him stand before them.

23 Gazing intently at the high council,* Paul be-
gan: "Brothers, I have always lived before God
with a clear conscience!"
2 Instantly Ananias the high priest commanded
those close to Paul to slap him on the mouth. 3 But
Paul said to him, "God will slap you, you corrupt hyp-
ocrite!* What kind of judge are you to break the law
yourself by ordering me struck like that?"
4 Those standing near Paul said to him, "Do you
dare to insult God's high priest?"
5 "I'm sorry, brothers. I didn't realize he was the
high priest," Paul replied, "for the Scriptures say, 'You
must not speak evil of any of your rulers.'*"
6 Paul realized that some members of the high
council were Sadducees and some were Pharisees,
so he shouted, "Brothers, I am a Pharisee, as were my
ancestors! And I am on trial because my hope is in the
resurrection of the dead!"
7 This divided the council—the Pharisees against
the Sadducees—8 for the Sadducees say there is no
resurrection or angels or spirits, but the Pharisees
believe in all of these. 9 So there was a great uproar.
Some of the teachers of religious law who were Phari-
sees jumped up and began to argue forcefully. "We see
nothing wrong with him," they shouted. "Perhaps a
spirit or an angel spoke to him." 10 As the conflict grew
more violent, the commander was afraid they would
tear Paul apart. So he ordered his soldiers to go and
rescue him by force and take him back to the fortress.
11 That night the Lord appeared to Paul and said,
"Be encouraged, Paul. Just as you have been a witness
to me here in Jerusalem, you must preach the Good
News in Rome as well."

THE PLAN TO KILL PAUL

12 The next morning a group of Jews* got together and
bound themselves with an oath not to eat or drink
until they had killed Paul. 13 There were more than
forty of them in the conspiracy. 14 They went to the
leading priests and elders and told them, "We have
bound ourselves with an oath to eat nothing until we
have killed Paul. 15 So you and the high council should
ask the commander to bring Paul back to the council
again. Pretend you want to examine his case more
fully. We will kill him on the way."
16 But Paul's nephew—his sister's son—heard
of their plan and went to the fortress and told Paul.
17 Paul called for one of the Roman officers* and said,
"Take this young man to the commander. He has
something important to tell him."
18 So the officer did, explaining, "Paul, the prisoner,
called me over and asked me to bring this young man
to you because he has something to tell you."

22:25 Greek *the centurion;* also in 22:26. 22:30 Greek *Sanhedrin.* 23:1 Greek *Sanhedrin;* also in 23:6, 15, 20, 28. 23:3 Greek *you whitewashed wall.* 23:5 Exod 22:28. 23:12 Greek *the Jews.* 23:17 Greek *centurions;* also in 23:23.

22:22 He isn't fit to live! For Paul to claim that he was divinely inspired to minister among the Gentiles appeared as rank heresy—a slap in the face to God and the Jews. This was justification for their charges that he was anti-Jewish, lacked respect for the law, and would defile the temple.

22:25 a Roman citizen. Flogging was a severe punishment since leather thongs weighted with pieces of bone, metal, or rocks were used to administer a beating. Because Roman citizens were protected from punishment without trial and were sheltered from this form of punishment, Paul once again brought up his Roman citizenship (see also 16:37).

22:28 I am too . . .and it cost me plenty! Citizenship was not supposedly a matter of money but of birthright or notable service. But bribes and other means of influence were used to gain the privilege. **I am a citizen by birth.** Paul's response turns the table on the commander. His citizenship was not a matter of bribery but of natural right. How Paul's family earned their Roman citizenship is unknown.

22:29-30 the commander was frightened. The fact that Paul, a Roman citizen, had been imprisoned without charge and had been almost flogged was a dangerous breach of policy that could have cost the commander his rank (and perhaps his life).

23:2 Ananias the high priest. Ananias was appointed to this office by Herod Agrippa II (25:13) in A.D. 47, and he held the position until A.D. 58 or 59. He had a reputation as a violent, greedy, and unscrupulous man. **commanded those close to Paul to slap him on the mouth.** It was against Jewish law for a defendant to be treated like this.

23:3 God will slap you. Paul's word came true. In A.D. 66 Jews who were leading a revolt against Rome captured Ananias and murdered him for his pro-Roman policies. **you corrupt hypocrite!** The picture is of a person trying to fix up a wall about to collapse just by covering it with a thin coat of paint.

23:8 resurrection. The resurrection was rejected by the Sadducees.

23:11 the Lord appeared to Paul. For the fourth and final time in Acts (see also 18:9), the Lord addresses Paul personally to encourage him in a time of crisis (an angel comforts him in the midst of a storm in 27:23). **witness to me.** The issue at stake for Paul was speaking about Jesus, not defending himself against false charges.

23:12-13 until they had killed Paul. A group of radical Jewish nationalists decided Paul must die for his alleged anti-Jewish sentiments. **bound themselves with an oath.** If they failed to kill Paul, they acknowledged by this curse that they ought to be struck down by God.

23:14-15 leading priests and elders. The would-be assassins drew at least some members of the Sanhedrin into the plot. Under pretense of wanting another hearing with Paul, they were to ask the Roman commander to bring Paul to them, at which time he would be ambushed. Since Paul was escorted by Roman soldiers, these men were willing to risk death to kill Paul.

23:16 Paul's nephew—his sister's son. This is the only glimpse the New Testament gives us about Paul's family. Perhaps his sister and her family lived in Jerusalem, or perhaps his nephew was sent there to receive his education as Paul had been (22:3). How his nephew got wind of the plot is not revealed. **went to the fortress and told Paul.** Paul was held in custody pending charges on the near-riot, but as a Roman citizen he was permitted visitors.

19 The commander took his hand, led him aside, and asked, "What is it you want to tell me?"

20 Paul's nephew told him, "Some Jews are going to ask you to bring Paul before the high council tomorrow, pretending they want to get some more information. 21 But don't do it! There are more than forty men hiding along the way ready to ambush him. They have vowed not to eat or drink anything until they have killed him. They are ready now, just waiting for your consent."

22 "Don't let anyone know you told me this," the commander warned the young man.

PAUL IS SENT TO CAESAREA

23 Then the commander called two of his officers and ordered, "Get 200 soldiers ready to leave for Caesarea at nine o'clock tonight. Also take 200 spearmen and 70 mounted troops. 24 Provide horses for Paul to ride, and get him safely to Governor Felix." 25 Then he wrote this letter to the governor:

26 "From Claudius Lysias, to his Excellency, Governor Felix: Greetings!

27 "This man was seized by some Jews, and they were about to kill him when I arrived with the troops. When I learned that he was a Roman citizen, I removed him to safety. 28 Then I took him to their high council to try to learn the basis of the accusations against him. 29 I soon discovered the charge was something regarding their religious law—certainly nothing worthy of imprisonment or death. 30 But when I was informed of a plot to kill him, I immediately sent him on to you. I have told his accusers to bring their charges before you."

31 So that night, as ordered, the soldiers took Paul as far as Antipatris. 32 They returned to the fortress the next morning, while the mounted troops took him on to Caesarea. 33 When they arrived in Caesarea, they presented Paul and the letter to Governor Felix. 34 He read it and then asked Paul what province he was from. "Cilicia," Paul answered.

35 "I will hear your case myself when your accusers arrive," the governor told him. Then the governor ordered him kept in the prison at Herod's headquarters.*

PAUL APPEARS BEFORE FELIX

24 Five days later Ananias, the high priest, arrived with some of the Jewish elders and the lawyer* Tertullus, to present their case against Paul to the governor. 2 When Paul was called in, Tertullus presented the charges against Paul in the following address to the governor:

"You have provided a long period of peace for us Jews and with foresight have enacted reforms for us. 3 For all of this, Your Excellency, we are very grateful to you. 4 But I don't want to bore you, so please give me your attention for only a moment. 5 We have found this man to be a troublemaker who is constantly stirring up riots among the Jews all over the world. He is a ringleader of the cult known as the Nazarenes. 6 Furthermore, he was trying to desecrate the Temple when we arrested him.* 8 You can find out the truth of our accusations by examining him yourself." 9 Then the other Jews chimed in, declaring that everything Tertullus said was true.

10 The governor then motioned for Paul to speak. Paul said, "I know, sir, that you have been a judge of Jewish affairs for many years, so I gladly present my defense before you. 11 You can quickly discover that I arrived in Jerusalem no more than twelve days ago to worship at the Temple. 12 My accusers never found me arguing with anyone in the Temple, nor stirring up a riot in any synagogue or on the streets of the city. 13 These men cannot prove the things they accuse me of doing.

14 "But I admit that I follow the Way, which they call a cult. I worship the God of our ancestors, and I firmly believe the Jewish law and everything written in the prophets. 15 I have the same hope in God that these men have, that he will raise both the righteous and the unrighteous. 16 Because of this, I always try to maintain a clear conscience before God and all people.

17 "After several years away, I returned to Jerusalem with money to aid my people and to offer sacrifices to God. 18 My accusers saw me in the Temple as I was completing a purification ceremony. There was no crowd around me and no rioting. 19 But some Jews from the province of Asia were there—and they ought to be here to bring charges if they have anything against me! 20 Ask these men here what crime the Jewish high council* found me guilty of, 21 except for the one time I shouted out, 'I am on trial before you today because I believe in the resurrection of the dead!'"

22 At that point Felix, who was quite familiar with the Way, adjourned the hearing and said, "Wait until Lysias, the garrison commander, arrives. Then I will

23:35 Greek *Herod's Praetorium.* 24:1 Greek *some elders and an orator.* 24:6 Some manuscripts add an expanded conclusion to verse 6, all of verse 7, and an additional phrase in verse 8: *We would have judged him by our law, [7]but Lysias, the commander of the garrison, came and violently took him away from us, [8]commanding his accusers to come before you.* 24:20 Greek *Sanhedrin.*

23:23 Get 200 soldiers ready . . . 200 spearmen and 70 mounted troops. Having witnessed the severity of the reaction against Paul, the Roman commander was taking no chances with this radical group. He placed Paul under the protection of almost half his soldiers and sent him off under cover of darkness.

23:24 Governor Felix. The Roman historian Tacitus described Felix as a self-indulgent ruler who used forceful measures to put down Jewish uprisings and who was cruel toward the people he was supposed to govern. Once in Caesarea, Paul would be under the custody of Felix.

23:27 I arrived . . .removed him to safety. The Roman commander Lysias may have inverted a couple of facts in order to save face. He did not find out about Paul's Roman citizenship until he was about to have him beaten (22:25), but here he says he rescued Paul from the mob because he learned that Paul was a Roman citizen.

23:34 asked what province he was from. By the second century A.D. prisoners were normally tried in the province they were from, regardless of where the crime was committed.

24:1 the lawyer. Literally, "an orator." Tertullus, who bears a Roman name, may have been a Greek-speaking Jew with more knowledge and experience in Roman law and customs than the Palestinian Jews had.

24:5 a troublemaker . . .all over the world. Since Felix was known for his impatience with Jewish uprisings, Tertullus tried to present Paul as an instigator of such movements. **the cult known as the Nazarenes.** Just as the name "Christian" appears to have been a derogatory term for early believers (see note on 11:26), so "the Nazarenes" was also used as an insult (see John 1:46; 7:41).

24:6 trying to desecrate the Temple. The charge has been changed from the accusation in 21:28 that Paul had defiled the temple by bringing a Gentile into the inner court.

24:14-15 follow the Way . . . I worship the God of our ancestors. While Paul denied the charges of insurrection and temple defilement, he agreed he was a follower of "the Way," but he did so as a Jew who was loyal to the God of his ancestors. There was nothing heretical about his views.

decide the case." 23 He ordered an officer* to keep Paul in custody but to give him some freedom and allow his friends to visit him and take care of his needs.

24 A few days later Felix came back with his wife, Drusilla, who was Jewish. Sending for Paul, they listened as he told them about faith in Christ Jesus. 25 As he reasoned with them about righteousness and self-control and the coming day of judgment, Felix became frightened. "Go away for now," he replied. "When it is more convenient, I'll call for you again." 26 He also hoped that Paul would bribe him, so he sent for him quite often and talked with him.

27 After two years went by in this way, Felix was succeeded by Porcius Festus. And because Felix wanted to gain favor with the Jewish people, he left Paul in prison.

PAUL APPEARS BEFORE FESTUS

25 Three days after Festus arrived in Caesarea to take over his new responsibilities, he left for Jerusalem, 2 where the leading priests and other Jewish leaders met with him and made their accusations against Paul. 3 They asked Festus as a favor to transfer Paul to Jerusalem (planning to ambush and kill him on the way). 4 But Festus replied that Paul was at Caesarea and he himself would be returning there soon. 5 So he said, "Those of you in authority can return with me. If Paul has done anything wrong, you can make your accusations."

6 About eight or ten days later Festus returned to Caesarea, and on the following day he took his seat in court and ordered that Paul be brought in. 7 When Paul arrived, the Jewish leaders from Jerusalem gathered around and made many serious accusations they couldn't prove.

8 Paul denied the charges. "I am not guilty of any crime against the Jewish laws or the Temple or the Roman government," he said.

9 Then Festus, wanting to please the Jews, asked him, "Are you willing to go to Jerusalem and stand trial before me there?"

10 But Paul replied, "No! This is the official Roman court, so I ought to be tried right here. You know very well I am not guilty of harming the Jews. 11 If I have done something worthy of death, I don't refuse to die. But if I am innocent, no one has a right to turn me over to these men to kill me. I appeal to Caesar!"

12 Festus conferred with his advisers and then replied, "Very well! You have appealed to Caesar, and to Caesar you will go!"

13 A few days later King Agrippa arrived with his sister, Bernice,* to pay their respects to Festus. 14 During their stay of several days, Festus discussed Paul's case with the king. "There is a prisoner here," he told him, "whose case was left for me by Felix. 15 When I was in Jerusalem, the leading priests and Jewish elders pressed charges against him and asked me to condemn him. 16 I pointed out to them that Roman law does not convict people without a trial. They must be given an opportunity to confront their accusers and defend themselves.

17 "When his accusers came here for the trial, I didn't delay. I called the case the very next day and ordered Paul brought in. 18 But the accusations made against him weren't any of the crimes I expected. 19 Instead, it was something about their religion and a dead man named Jesus, who Paul insists is alive. 20 I was at a loss to know how to investigate these things, so I asked him whether he would be willing to stand trial on these charges in Jerusalem. 21 But Paul appealed to have his case decided by the emperor. So I ordered that he be held in custody until I could arrange to send him to Caesar."

22 "I'd like to hear the man myself," Agrippa said.

And Festus replied, "You will—tomorrow!"

PAUL SPEAKS TO AGRIPPA

23 So the next day Agrippa and Bernice arrived at the auditorium with great pomp, accompanied by military officers and prominent men of the city. Festus ordered that Paul be brought in. 24 Then Festus said, "King Agrippa and all who are here, this is the man whose death is demanded by all the Jews, both here and in Jerusalem. 25 But in my opinion he has done nothing deserving death. However, since he appealed his case to the emperor, I have decided to send him to Rome.

26 "But what shall I write the emperor? For there is no clear charge against him. So I have brought him before all of you, and especially you, King Agrippa, so that after we examine him, I might have something to write. 27 For it makes no sense to send a prisoner to the emperor without specifying the charges against him!"

24:23 Greek *a centurion.* **25:13** Greek *Agrippa the king and Bernice arrived.*

24:24 Drusilla. A daughter of Herod Agrippa, Drusilla was barely 20 years old at this time. She had divorced another man to become Felix's third wife. Since she was Jewish and in a position to hear a lot about the Christians, she may have been the source of Felix's information about their beliefs.

24:26 hoped that Paul would bribe him. The offering and acceptance of a bribe in such cases was illegal.

24:27 Porcius Festus. Felix's administration ended when he was found guilty of using excessive violence in crushing a civil strife between Jews and Greeks in Caesarea. Even when forced to leave office (probably about A.D. 58), he refused to dispense with Paul's case but left him imprisoned as a favor to the Jews. Festus replaced him and was governor of the area until his death two or three years later in A.D. 61.

25:5 if Paul had done anything wrong. Festus reopened Paul's case in an attempt to win the favor of the Jewish leaders.

25:8 the Roman government. (i.e. Caesar) The first five emperors of Rome (from Octavian to Nero) were descendants of Julius Caesar and thus kept his name, although it was commonly used as a title. At the time of this trial, Nero was the emperor. The cruelties for which he is remembered would not occur until several years later.

25:9 wanting to please the Jews. If Paul was sent to Jerusalem for trial, the Sanhedrin would be responsible for charging him on matters of Jewish law. Festus would have only to ratify a decision for capital punishment if that is what the Sanhedrin decided upon. This action was a tacit admission that Paul was innocent of having violated Roman law. Since that was the only reason Paul could be held in a Roman prison, this suggestion showed that Festus was willing to sacrifice Paul for the sake of some political advantage with the Sanhedrin.

25:10-11 this is the official Roman court. Paul knew there was no chance of a fair hearing in Jerusalem, even if he could make it there alive. Recognizing that his only hope for justice lay in getting out of an area where the Sanhedrin exercised great influence, he exercised his right as a Roman citizen to appeal his case to the emperor in Rome.

25:13 King Agrippa. The son of Herod Agrippa I. Agrippa II had been appointed as a puppet king (under Roman authority) over some provinces northeast of Palestine. When Judea was returned to the control of Roman governors after the death of his father, Herod Agrippa was given the right to appoint the Jewish high priest. **Bernice.** Agrippa's sister. After her first husband died, she lived with her brother, prompting rumors of incest. She also maintained loyalty to Rome and later was the mistress of Titus, who became the emperor.

25:26-27 no clear charge against him. It would have been unreasonable for Festus to send on to Rome a prisoner with no statement of the charges against. It also would have made a travesty of Roman justice. He hoped that Agrippa might provide some insight that would allow him to better explain the nature of Paul's case to the Roman authorities.

26 Then Agrippa said to Paul, "You may speak in your defense."

So Paul, gesturing with his hand, started his defense: 2 "I am fortunate, King Agrippa, that you are the one hearing my defense today against all these accusations made by the Jewish leaders, 3 for I know you are an expert on all Jewish customs and controversies. Now please listen to me patiently!

4 "As the Jewish leaders are well aware, I was given a thorough Jewish training from my earliest childhood among my own people and in Jerusalem. 5 If they would admit it, they know that I have been a member of the Pharisees, the strictest sect of our religion. 6 Now I am on trial because of my hope in the fulfillment of God's promise made to our ancestors. 7 In fact, that is why the twelve tribes of Israel zealously worship God night and day, and they share the same hope I have. Yet, Your Majesty, they accuse me for having this hope! 8 Why does it seem incredible to any of you that God can raise the dead?

9 "I used to believe that I ought to do everything I could to oppose the very name of Jesus the Nazarene.* 10 Indeed, I did just that in Jerusalem. Authorized by the leading priests, I caused many believers* there to be sent to prison. And I cast my vote against them when they were condemned to death. 11 Many times I had them punished in the synagogues to get them to curse Jesus.* I was so violently opposed to them that I even chased them down in foreign cities.

12 "One day I was on such a mission to Damascus, armed with the authority and commission of the leading priests. 13 About noon, Your Majesty, as I was on the road, a light from heaven brighter than the sun shone down on me and my companions. 14 We all fell down, and I heard a voice saying to me in Aramaic,* 'Saul, Saul, why are you persecuting me? It is useless for you to fight against my will.*'

15 "'Who are you, lord?' I asked.

"And the Lord replied, 'I am Jesus, the one you are persecuting. 16 Now get to your feet! For I have appeared to you to appoint you as my servant and witness. Tell people that you have seen me, and tell them what I will show you in the future. 17 And I will rescue you from both your own people and the Gentiles. Yes, I am sending you to the Gentiles 18 to open their eyes, so they may turn from darkness to light and from the power of Satan to God. Then they will receive forgiveness for their sins and be given a place among God's people, who are set apart by faith in me.'

19 "And so, King Agrippa, I obeyed that vision from heaven. 20 I preached first to those in Damascus, then in Jerusalem and throughout all Judea, and also to the Gentiles, that all must repent of their sins and turn to God—and prove they have changed by the good things they do. 21 Some Jews arrested me in the Temple for preaching this, and they tried to kill me. 22 But God has protected me right up to this present time so I can testify to everyone, from the least to the greatest. I teach nothing except what the prophets and Moses said would happen— 23 that the Messiah would suffer and be the first to rise from the dead, and in this way announce God's light to Jews and Gentiles alike."

24 Suddenly, Festus shouted, "Paul, you are insane. Too much study has made you crazy!"

25 But Paul replied, "I am not insane, Most Excellent Festus. What I am saying is the sober truth. 26 And King Agrippa knows about these things. I speak boldly, for I am sure these events are all familiar to him, for they were not done in a corner! 27 King Agrippa, do you believe the prophets? I know you do—"

28 Agrippa interrupted him. "Do you think you can persuade me to become a Christian so quickly?"*

29 Paul replied, "Whether quickly or not, I pray to God that both you and everyone here in this audience might become the same as I am, except for these chains."

30 Then the king, the governor, Bernice, and all the others stood and left. 31 As they went out, they talked it over and agreed, "This man hasn't done anything to deserve death or imprisonment."

32 And Agrippa said to Festus, "He could have been set free if he hadn't appealed to Caesar."

PAUL SAILS FOR ROME

27 When the time came, we set sail for Italy. Paul and several other prisoners were placed in the custody of a Roman officer* named Julius, a captain of the Imperial Regiment. 2 Aristarchus, a Macedonian from Thessalonica, was also with us. We left on a ship whose home port was Adramyttium on the northwest coast of the province of Asia;* it was scheduled to make several stops at ports along the coast of the province. 3 The next day when we docked at Sidon, Julius was very kind to Paul and let him go ashore to visit with

26:9 Or *Jesus of Nazareth.* **26:10** Greek *many of God's holy people.* **26:11** Greek *to blaspheme.* **26:14a** Or *Hebrew.* **26:14b** Greek *It is hard for you to kick against the oxgoads.* **26:28** Or *"A little more, and your arguments would make me a Christian."* **27:1** Greek *centurion;* similarly in 27:6, 11, 31, 43. **27:2** *Asia* was a Roman province in what is now western Turkey.

26:4 among my own people. This may refer to Paul's early childhood among the Jewish community in Tarsus or to a family home somewhere in Judea. **in Jerusalem.** The fact that Paul was sent to Jerusalem as a boy to be educated by Gamaliel showed the commitment of his parents to his Jewish heritage (see 22:3).

26:6 God's promise made to our ancestors. Paul identified with his own Jewish heritage. He believed in the promise of the Messiah that God had made to Israel.

26:7 twelve tribes of Israel. While 10 of the original 12 tribes that formed the nation of Israel (northern kingdom) had been dispersed by the Assyrians seven centuries before, there were still traceable links to these tribes among the Jews in Paul's day (see also Luke 2:36; Jas. 1:1). **they accuse me for having this hope.** The only point where Paul differed from his Jewish brothers was in the conviction that the hope of the Messiah had already been fulfilled in the coming of Jesus.

26:10 I cast my vote against them. Taken literally, this may imply that Paul had been a member of the Sanhedrin. But the fact that he does not mention this affiliation in his writings makes that doubtful. It is more probable that he meant he approved of such actions (8:1).

26:14 It is useless for you to fight against my will. There are several examples of this proverb in classical Greek literature. It expresses the difficulty involved in resisting one's destiny—the probable meaning here as well.

26:21-23 Jews. Of course, Paul, Jesus, and many other believers were also Jews. But by this phrase Luke probably means the Jewish religious leaders.

26:24 has made you crazy! Festus, probably bewildered by Paul's conviction that "a dead man named Jesus" (25:19) was alive, and by his talk of a vision that so radically changed his life, broke in with the exasperated cry that Paul must be out of his mind. This reaction was not very different than that of many Jews (John 10:20) and even Jesus' own family when He was beginning His ministry (see Mark 3:20-21). Jesus had come with such a radically different message than they were expecting—and such a radically different approach to life—that they saw it as madness.

26:32 He could have been set free if he hadn't appealed to Caesar. Once an appeal to the Roman emperor had been made, it was considered an insult against Roman law to short-circuit the process.

27:2 We. Luke is again in the picture. Some believe that he and Aristarchus may have come along on this journey to Rome as Paul's servants.

27:3 Sidon. A day's sail of about 70 nautical miles from Caesarea. Paul was allowed (probably under the supervision of a soldier) to visit the Christian community there.

friends so they could provide for his needs. 4 Putting out to sea from there, we encountered strong headwinds that made it difficult to keep the ship on course, so we sailed north of Cyprus between the island and the mainland. 5 Keeping to the open sea, we passed along the coast of Cilicia and Pamphylia, landing at Myra, in the province of Lycia. 6 There the commanding officer found an Egyptian ship from Alexandria that was bound for Italy, and he put us on board.

7 We had several days of slow sailing, and after great difficulty we finally neared Cnidus. But the wind was against us, so we sailed across to Crete and along the sheltered coast of the island, past the cape of Salmone. 8 We struggled along the coast with great difficulty and finally arrived at Fair Havens, near the town of Lasea. 9 We had lost a lot of time. The weather was becoming dangerous for sea travel because it was so late in the fall,* and Paul spoke to the ship's officers about it.

10 "Men," he said, "I believe there is trouble ahead if we go on—shipwreck, loss of cargo, and danger to our lives as well." 11 But the officer in charge of the prisoners listened more to the ship's captain and the owner than to Paul. 12 And since Fair Havens was an exposed harbor—a poor place to spend the winter—most of the crew wanted to go on to Phoenix, farther up the coast of Crete, and spend the winter there. Phoenix was a good harbor with only a southwest and northwest exposure.

THE STORM AT SEA

13 When a light wind began blowing from the south, the sailors thought they could make it. So they pulled up anchor and sailed close to the shore of Crete. 14 But the weather changed abruptly, and a wind of typhoon strength (called a "northeaster") burst across the island and blew us out to sea. 15 The sailors couldn't turn the ship into the wind, so they gave up and let it run before the gale.

16 We sailed along the sheltered side of a small island named Cauda,* where with great difficulty we hoisted aboard the lifeboat being towed behind us. 17 Then the sailors bound ropes around the hull of the ship to strengthen it. They were afraid of being driven across to the sandbars of Syrtis off the African coast, so they lowered the sea anchor to slow the ship and were driven before the wind.

18 The next day, as gale-force winds continued to batter the ship, the crew began throwing the cargo overboard. 19 The following day they even took some of the ship's gear and threw it overboard. 20 The terrible storm raged for many days, blotting out the sun and the stars, until at last all hope was gone.

21 No one had eaten for a long time. Finally, Paul called the crew together and said, "Men, you should have listened to me in the first place and not left Crete. You would have avoided all this damage and loss. 22 But take courage! None of you will lose your lives, even though the ship will go down. 23 For last night an angel of the God to whom I belong and whom I serve stood beside me, 24 and he said, 'Don't be afraid, Paul, for you will surely stand trial before Caesar! What's more, God in his goodness has granted safety to everyone sailing with you.' 25 So take courage! For I believe God. It will be just as he said. 26 But we will be shipwrecked on an island."

THE SHIPWRECK

27 About midnight on the fourteenth night of the storm, as we were being driven across the Sea of Adria,* the sailors sensed land was near. 28 They dropped a weighted line and found that the water was 120 feet deep. But a little later they measured again and found it was only 90 feet deep.* 29 At this rate they were afraid we would soon be driven against the rocks along the shore, so they threw out four anchors from the back of the ship and prayed for daylight.

30 Then the sailors tried to abandon the ship; they lowered the lifeboat as though they were going to put out anchors from the front of the ship. 31 But Paul said to the commanding officer and the soldiers, "You will all die unless the sailors stay aboard." 32 So the soldiers cut the ropes to the lifeboat and let it drift away.

33 Just as day was dawning, Paul urged everyone to eat. "You have been so worried that you haven't touched food for two weeks," he said. 34 "Please eat something now for your own good. For not a hair of your heads will perish." 35 Then he took some bread, gave thanks to God before them all, and broke off a piece and ate it. 36 Then everyone was encouraged and began to eat—37 all 276 of us who were on board. 38 After eating, the crew lightened the ship further by throwing the cargo of wheat overboard.

39 When morning dawned, they didn't recognize the coastline, but they saw a bay with a beach and wondered if they could get to shore by running the ship aground. 40 So they cut off the anchors and left them in the sea. Then they lowered the rudders, raised the fore-

27:9 Greek *because the fast was now already gone by.* This fast was associated with the Day of Atonement (*Yom Kippur*), which occurred in late September or early October. 27:16 Some manuscripts read *Clauda.* 27:27 The *Sea of Adria* includes the central portion of the Mediterranean. 27:28 Greek *20 fathoms . . . 15 fathoms* [37 meters . . . 27 meters].

27:5-6 landing at Myra. At Myra, Paul and the other prisoners were transferred to another ship heading to Italy because their original ship was continuing north to Adramyttium.

27:9 the weather was becoming dangerous for sea travel. According to one Roman military writer, sailing on the Mediterranean Sea was dangerous after September 15, and it usually was halted from mid-November until at least early February.

27:10-11 trouble ahead if we go on. It is unclear whether Paul's comment was in response to a prophetic word he had received or a foreboding based on the difficulties they had already experienced.

27:14 (called a "northeaster"). The Greek word behind this expression is the source of the English word *typhoon*.

27:16 Cauda. A small island, known today as Gavaho or Gozzo, about 20 miles south of Crete. **the lifeboat.** This small boat was normally towed, but in a storm it was brought on board.

27:17 around the hull of the ship to strengthen it. Literally "they used helps to undergird the ship." The "helps" were block and tackle used to pull ropes or cables tightly around the ship to keep it from breaking apart. **Syrtis.** A dangerous shoal off the coast of Africa. **lowered the sea anchor.** Literally, "the tackle." This phrase may refer to taking down the mainsail or to dragging an anchor to slow the ship's speed.

27:21 No one had eaten for a long time. Much of the food on board was probably spoiled by seawater, and conditions were such that eating must have been impossible.

27:29 the back of the ship. If anchors had been dropped from the bow (which was the usual practice), the ship would have swung around and been facing the wrong way for the crew to attempt a beaching on shore in the morning.

27:30–32 tried to abandon. At least some of the sailors planned to make a run for shore that night under pretense of securing the ship. Paul was concerned that the safety of the other passengers depended on the experience of the sailors.

27:38 throwing the cargo of wheat overboard. All portable cargo had already been thrown overboard (v. 18), but now the main load was removed to lighten the ship for its approach to land.

sail, and headed toward shore. 41 But they hit a shoal
and ran the ship aground too soon. The bow of the ship
stuck fast, while the stern was repeatedly smashed by
the force of the waves and began to break apart.
42 The soldiers wanted to kill the prisoners to make
sure they didn't swim ashore and escape. 43 But the
commanding officer wanted to spare Paul, so he
didn't let them carry out their plan. Then he ordered
all who could swim to jump overboard first and make
for land. 44 The others held on to planks or debris from
the broken ship.* So everyone escaped safely to shore.

PAUL ON THE ISLAND OF MALTA

28 Once we were safe on shore, we learned that
we were on the island of Malta. 2 The people of
the island were very kind to us. It was cold and rainy,
so they built a fire on the shore to welcome us.
3 As Paul gathered an armful of sticks and was laying
them on the fire, a poisonous snake, driven out by the
heat, bit him on the hand. 4 The people of the island saw
it hanging from his hand and said to each other, "A mur-
derer, no doubt! Though he escaped the sea, justice will
not permit him to live." 5 But Paul shook off the snake
into the fire and was unharmed. 6 The people waited for
him to swell up or suddenly drop dead. But when they
had waited a long time and saw that he wasn't harmed,
they changed their minds and decided he was a god.
7 Near the shore where we landed was an estate
belonging to Publius, the chief official of the island.
He welcomed us and treated us kindly for three days.
8 As it happened, Publius's father was ill with fever
and dysentery. Paul went in and prayed for him, and
laying his hands on him, he healed him. 9 Then all the
other sick people on the island came and were healed.
10 As a result we were showered with honors, and
when the time came to sail, people supplied us with
everything we would need for the trip.

PAUL ARRIVES AT ROME

11 It was three months after the shipwreck that we
set sail on another ship that had wintered at the is-
land—an Alexandrian ship with the twin gods* as
its figurehead. 12 Our first stop was Syracuse,* where
we stayed three days. 13 From there we sailed across to
Rhegium.* A day later a south wind began blowing,
so the following day we sailed up the coast to Puteoli.
14 There we found some believers,* who invited us to
spend a week with them. And so we came to Rome.
15 The brothers and sisters* in Rome had heard we
were coming, and they came to meet us at the Forum*
on the Appian Way. Others joined us at The Three Tav-
erns.* When Paul saw them, he was encouraged and
thanked God.
16 When we arrived in Rome, Paul was permitted to
have his own private lodging, though he was guarded
by a soldier.

PAUL PREACHES AT ROME UNDER GUARD

17 Three days after Paul's arrival, he called together
the local Jewish leaders. He said to them, "Brothers,
I was arrested in Jerusalem and handed over to the
Roman government, even though I had done nothing
against our people or the customs of our ancestors.
18 The Romans tried me and wanted to release me,
because they found no cause for the death sentence.
19 But when the Jewish leaders protested the decision,
I felt it necessary to appeal to Caesar, even though I
had no desire to press charges against my own peo-
ple. 20 I asked you to come here today so we could get
acquainted and so I could explain to you that I am
bound with this chain because I believe that the hope
of Israel—the Messiah—has already come."
21 They replied, "We have had no letters from Judea
or reports against you from anyone who has come
here. 22 But we want to hear what you believe, for the
only thing we know about this movement is that it is
denounced everywhere."
23 So a time was set, and on that day a large number
of people came to Paul's lodging. He explained and
testified about the Kingdom of God and tried to per-
suade them about Jesus from the Scriptures. Using the
law of Moses and the books of the prophets, he spoke
to them from morning until evening. 24 Some were
persuaded by the things he said, but others did not
believe. 25 And after they had argued back and forth
among themselves, they left with this final word from
Paul: "The Holy Spirit was right when he said to your
ancestors through Isaiah the prophet,

26 'Go and say to this people:
When you hear what I say,
you will not understand.

27:44 Or *or were helped by members of the ship's crew.* **28:11** The *twin gods* were the Roman gods Castor and Pollux. **28:12** *Syracuse* was on the island of Sicily. **28:13** *Rhegium* was on the southern tip of Italy. **28:14** Greek *brothers.* **28:15a** Greek *brothers.* **28:15b** *The Forum* was about 43 miles (70 kilometers) from Rome. **28:15c** *The Three Taverns* was about 35 miles (57 kilometers) from Rome. **28:26-27** Isa 6:9-10 (Greek version).

27:41 bow of the ship stuck fast. The traditional site of St. Paul's Bay on the island of Malta is composed of mud and clay that would trap a stuck ship. The pounding of the waves soon began to break the ship apart.

27:42-43 kill the prisoners. Since the soldiers were responsible for making sure prisoners did not escape in transit, some of the soldiers planned to kill the prisoners on the spot rather than face the possibility that some might escape. Because of the centurion's respect for Paul, he prevented that from happening.

28:1-10 The ship's crew and passengers landed at Malta, a small island 60 miles south of Sicily.

28:4 justice will not permit him to live! The natives of the island thought that Paul, who had been spared by such a disaster as a shipwreck only to be bitten by a viper, must have committed a serious crime for which he was being punished by the gods.

28:11 three months after. The ship sailed again in February.

28:14 we found some believers. At Puteoli, Paul and the others were able to spend a week with some Christians. **And so we came to Rome.** Rome was still about 140 miles away, but Paul's safe arrival in Italy marked the fulfillment of God's promise that Paul would preach the gospel in the imperial city.

28:15 came to meet us. News of Paul's arrival reached the church at Rome. Some of the believers traveled to the Forum of Appius (about 43 miles from Rome) and others to the Three Taverns (33 miles from Rome) to accompany him into the city.

28:16 Paul was permitted to have his own private lodging. Paul was kept under guard in a type of house arrest while he awaited trial. He may have been able to work as a leather worker during this time, or gifts from the churches may have provided for his needs (Phil. 4:14-18).

28:19 my own people. Notice also "brothers" and "our people" (v. 17). Once again, Luke presents Paul as a faithful Jew. His commitment to Jesus as the Messiah was to be seen as a natural outgrowth of his trust in the Old Testament Scriptures and his loyalty to God (v. 20; 23:6; 24:15; 26:22-23). His appeal to Caesar was not an attempt to cause problems for the Jews in Rome or Jerusalem.

28:23 tried to persuade them about Jesus. Examples of how Paul argued for the gospel from the Old Testament Scriptures are given in 13:16-41; 22:3-21; 26:4-27. **the Kingdom of God** (see also v. 31). This phrase serves as summary of all that the gospel is about. It announces the present and coming reign of God in human affairs and calls people to affirm their loyalty to Jesus as God's appointed King.

When you see what I do,
you will not comprehend.
27 For the hearts of these people are hardened,
and their ears cannot hear,
and they have closed their eyes—
so their eyes cannot see,
and their ears cannot hear,
and their hearts cannot understand,
and they cannot turn to me
and let me heal them.'"

28 So I want you to know that this salvation from God
has also been offered to the Gentiles, and they will
accept it."*
30 For the next two years, Paul lived in Rome at his
own expense.* He welcomed all who visited him,
31 boldly proclaiming the Kingdom of God and teach-
ing about the Lord Jesus Christ. And no one tried to
stop him.

28:28 Some manuscripts add verse 29, *And when he had said these words, the Jews departed, greatly disagreeing with each other.* 28:30 Or *in his own rented quarters.*

28:30 welcomed all who visited him. Luke concludes Acts with the picture of Paul continuing his missionary activities with everyone who would listen.

28:31 boldly proclaiming. . . . And no one tried to stop him. In this last statement in Acts, the emphasis in the Greek sentence falls on the boldness and freedom with which Paul preached the gospel. During this period of house arrest, Paul wrote the letter of Philippians and probably the letters of Ephesians, Colossians, and Philemon. Philippians 1:12-13 gives insight into his situation during this time as he carried on an extensive ministry to the soldiers assigned to guard him, undoubtedly resulting in the conversion of many. While some believe that Paul was executed at the end of these two years, other scholars contend that at the end of these two years Paul was released and enjoyed freedom for another two years. During this time he traveled once again to Crete, Asia, and Macedonia. It was probably during this time that he wrote the letters of 1 Timothy and Titus. According to this second perspective, at some point after this, Paul was again arrested and imprisoned at Rome. The Roman emperor, Nero, widely suspected of starting the great fire of Rome in A.D. 64, needed to shift the blame from himself to others, and Christians were chosen as the scapegoats. This brought an outburst of cruel persecution against the church, resulting in the execution of both Paul and Peter by Roman authorities.

INTRODUCTION TO

ROMANS

PERSONAL READING PLAN

☐Romans 1:1-32
☐Romans 2:1-29
☐Romans 3:1-31
☐Romans 4:1–5:11
☐Romans 5:12–6:23
☐Romans 7:1–8:17
☐Romans 8:18–9:29
☐Romans 9:30–10:21
☐Romans 11:1-36
☐Romans 12:1–13:14
☐Romans 14:1–15:13
☐Romans 15:14–16:27

AUTHOR

The writer is the Apostle Paul.

DATE

Paul wrote his letter during a three-month period during the winter spent in Corinth at the home of his friend and convert Gaius (16:23). The time was probably A.D. 56–57 (though it was certainly sometime between A.D. 54–59).

THEME

Being right with God through faith in Christ.

HISTORICAL BACKGROUND

For nearly 10 years Paul evangelized the Gentile territories ringing the Aegean Sea. Now that there were established churches throughout the region, he turns his eyes to fresh fields. He plans a trip to Spain, the oldest Roman colony in the West. But first there was unfinished business: he had taken up a collection to aid the poor in Jerusalem—a fine gesture on the part of the newer churches—and now he would deliver it to Jerusalem, though he did so with some misgiving (15:31).

After Jerusalem, he planned to travel to Spain, stopping en route to fulfill a long-held dream to visit Rome—the capital of the world. He wrote the letter to the Romans by way of introduction (the Roman Christians did not know him, though—as chapter 16 reveals—he had friends there). He was eager to assure the Roman Christians, contrary to false rumors they might have heard, that the gospel he was preaching was, indeed, the gospel of Jesus Christ.

Paul's plan did not work as he intended. He did visit Rome but not for three more years, and then he went not as a tourist but as a prisoner. His misgivings about his Jerusalem trip proved accurate. Once there, he was quickly arrested and eventually sent to Rome for trial. Paul remained in Rome under house arrest for at least two years. Ultimately, according to reliable tradition, he was executed at a place just outside Rome. He never made it to Spain.

It is not known how the Roman church began. It is not unlikely that some Roman Jews, converted on the Day of Pentecost (Acts 2:10), began the church. The Roman historian, Suetonius, writes that Jews were expelled from Rome about A.D. 50 for rioting, probably as a result of preaching Jesus in synagogues. As for the Gentile Christians in Rome, it is known that other Christian missionaries besides Paul were active in founding churches.

CHARACTERISTICS

Romans is Paul's most complete theological statement—precise and painstakingly logical. This is not to say that Romans is boring and burdensome; it is vibrant, colorful, and sweeping in scope. The magnitude of its themes makes Romans heavy going at times. Even the Apostle Peter sometimes found Paul's writing hard to understand (2 Peter 3:16)!

Paul's main focus is the question of how God will judge each of us on the final day. Will it be on the basis of how "good" we were and how well we kept the law? Acutely aware of repeated failure, we would never have any assurance of salvation, but this is not God's intention. Thus, the great theme of Romans emerges that we can have assurance of right standing before God and a positive verdict on Judgment Day. Such confidence does not come because of what we have done; it comes because of what God does. Thanks to Christ's death in our place, He freely offers us grace.

Paul sets this theme against the teaching of certain Jewish Christians, legalists who would add circumcision to grace (thus nullifying grace). Salvation cannot be both the result of our works and a gracious gift, freely given by God. In the course of his argument, Paul sets up a series of opposites: faith versus works, Spirit versus flesh, and liberty versus bondage.

As to how we gain right standing before God, Paul argues first that both pagans and religious people stand condemned before God (1:18–3:20). Right standing comes only by God's grace shown in Christ's sacrificial death and accepted by faith (3:21–5:21). This righteousness leads to a whole new lifestyle (6:1–8:39). He then deals with the question of why Israel rejected Christ (9:1–11:36), ending with practical exhortations for a life of faith (12:1–15:13). The impact of Romans on the history of the church can hardly be overstated. From Augustine to Luther to Wesley, many lives were changed as the result of reflecting on this book.

PASSAGES FOR TOPICAL GROUP STUDY

1:1-7 .... SLAVES OF JESUS .... Serving Jesus
1:8-17 ... STANDING WITH JESUS............. Not Ashamed
1:18-32 .. SEXUAL IMPURITY................ Homosexuality
2:1-16 ... JUDGING OTHERS .... Playing Judge
2:17-29 .. BOASTING OR GLOATING ....Bragging Rights
3:9-24 ... GETTING RIGHT WITH GOD ...... We've All Blown It
5:1-11 ... STRESSES AND TRIALS ..... Finding Joy in Troubles
5:12-21 .. THE ONLY WAY TO GOD..........Justified by Jesus
6:1-14 ... TEMPTATION and SIN .... A New Way of Life
6:15-23 .. GIVING OURSEVES TO GOD .... The Perfect Offering
7:7-25 ... SIN OR GRACE? ..... I Do What I Don't Want to Do
8:1-17 ... NEW WAY OF THINKING ..... Walking by the Spirit
8:18-27 .. SHATTERED DREAMS and HOPE.......... Suffering and Hoping
8:28-39 .. PAIN AND GOD'S LOVE .... The Point of Pain
9:1-29 ... SHOWING MERCY .... Rage or Mercy?
11:1-36 .. RELYING ON GOD, NOT SELF .... Works vs. Faith
12:1-8 ... DON'T CONFORM TO THE WORLD ....You Will Be Assimilated

12:9-21 . . . . . SHOWING HONOR and HUMILITY . . . . . . Honoring Others
13:1-7 . . . . . . RELATING TO AUTHORITY . . . . God-given Authority
13:8-14 . . . . . . HOW TO LOVE OTHERS . . . . The Power of Love
14:1–15:13 . . ARGUING and EXCUSES . . . . Doubtful Issues
15:14-33 . . . . PLANS FOR THE FUTURE . . . . Future Plans
16:1-27 . . . . . GUARD AGAINST DECIEVERS . . . . . Smooth Talkers

PASSAGES FOR GENERAL GROUP STUDY

4:1-25 . . . . . . Getting on God's Good side . . . . . (Finding His Favor)
7:1-6 . . . . "It's Like Being Married" . . . . . (The New Way of the Spirit)
9:30–10:21 . . Calling Heaven's Number . . . . . (Calling on and Sharing Jesus)

GREETINGS FROM PAUL

1 This letter is from Paul, a slave of Christ Jesus, cho-
sen by God to be an apostle and sent out to preach
his Good News. 2 God promised this Good News long
ago through his prophets in the holy Scriptures. 3 The
Good News is about his Son. In his earthly life he
was born into King David's family line, 4 and he was
shown to be* the Son of God when he was raised from
the dead by the power of the Holy Spirit.* He is Jesus
Christ our Lord. 5 Through Christ, God has given us
the privilege* and authority as apostles to tell Gen-
tiles everywhere what God has done for them, so that
they will believe and obey him, bringing glory to his
name.
6 And you are included among those Gentiles who
have been called to belong to Jesus Christ. 7 I am writ-
ing to all of you in Rome who are loved by God and
are called to be his own holy people.

May God our Father and the Lord Jesus Christ give you grace and peace.

SERVING JESUS

1. From whom do you look forward to getting texts or e-mails? What makes them worth waiting for?

ROMANS 1:1-7

2. Why does Paul refer to himself as "a slave of Christ Jesus" (v. 1)? What rights does a slave have? What role?
3. What is the calling of all Christians, according to this passage?
4. What facts do you learn about Jesus Christ in this passage?
5. Do you consider yourself a "slave" of Jesus Christ? How obedient are you to the faith (v. 5)?

GOD'S GOOD NEWS

8 Let me say first that I thank my God through Jesus
Christ for all of you, because your faith in him is be-
ing talked about all over the world. 9 God knows how
often I pray for you. Day and night I bring you and
your needs in prayer to God, whom I serve with all
my heart* by spreading the Good News about his
Son.
10 One of the things I always pray for is the oppor-
tunity, God willing, to come at last to see you. 11 For
I long to visit you so I can bring you some spiritu-
al gift that will help you grow strong in the Lord.
12 When we get together, I want to encourage you
in your faith, but I also want to be encouraged by
yours.
13 I want you to know, dear brothers and sisters,*
that I planned many times to visit you, but I was
prevented until now. I want to work among you and
see spiritual fruit, just as I have seen among other
Gentiles. 14 For I have a great sense of obligation to
people in both the civilized world and the rest of the
world,* to the educated and uneducated alike. 15 So I
am eager to come to you in Rome, too, to preach the
Good News.
16 For I am not ashamed of this Good News about
Christ. It is the power of God at work, saving every-
one who believes—the Jew first and also the Gentile.*

NOT ASHAMED

1. What was the best piece of good news you heard this past week? The worst bad news?

ROMANS 1:8-17

2. Nero ruled the Christians in Rome, and he soon became famous for persecuting them. Why might the news of the Christians' faith be "talked about all over the world" (v. 8)? Why might Paul want to travel there?
3. Why does Paul say, "I am not ashamed of this Good News" (v. 16)? How might the Christians in Rome have been "ashamed of the gospel"? How about you?
4. How can you learn to live more "by faith" (v. 17)?

1:4a Or *and was designated.* **1:4b** Or *by the Spirit of holiness;* or *in the new realm of the Spirit.* **1:5** Or *the grace.* **1:9** Or *in my spirit.* **1:13** Greek *brothers.* **1:14** Greek *to Greeks and barbarians.* **1:16** Greek *also the Greek.*

1:1 Paul. In introducing himself, Paul uses his Roman name and not his Jewish name (Saul). **slave.** Or bond servant. Paul states that he is choosing to be a servant of Jesus whom he identifies as "Lord" (v. 4), a Master in authority over all believers. **chosen.** Paul did not just decide to be an apostle and declare himself one. He is an apostle because God appointed him to this task. **apostle.** In the broad sense, an apostle is anyone sent on a mission with a message. **sent out.** In Galatians 1:15 Paul is set apart by God from birth for a special task, and in Acts 13:2 the church at Antioch appoints him, along with Barnabas, for a special mission of evangelization in the Gentile world.

1:2 promised . . . long ago. Having defined the gospel (good news of salvation through Christ) as being from God in verse 1, Paul further specifies that the gospel was a fulfillment of prophecy. It was not a new thought with God or an invention of man. God had always sought to bring man into fellowship with Him.

1:3-4 about his Son. A short, creedal statement of faith probably familiar to the Roman Christians (4:24-25; 10:8-10; 16:25-26). **born into King David's family line . . . Son of God.** Jesus belongs to two spheres of existence: the human, in which He is the descendant of King David (from whose line the Messiah was to come); and the divine, in which He is God's Son (this having been verified through His resurrection).

1:5 privilege. Grace is God's love reaching out to people who do not deserve it but are loved by God anyway. The gospel is the full expression of God's grace. Paul refers to God's grace throughout Romans as well as his other epistles. **authority as apostles.** Paul did not earn his apostleship or deserve to be an apostle. Unlike other apostles, he had never seen Jesus in the flesh. He was one because of God's "undeserved favor" ("grace"). He considered the churches he founded a mark of his apostleship (1 Cor. 9:2). He also stated that he bore in his body the marks of Jesus that come through his apostolic suffering (1 Cor. 15:10). **Gentiles everywhere.** Paul's apostolic commission is to evangelize the non-Jewish world. **obey him.** This is active response to God—faith that shows itself in obedience (Gal. 5:6-8).

1:14 great sense of obligation. Paul was obligated to God for the price Christ paid for his salvation. Second, because he had been given this incalculable gift, he felt a strong obligation to tell this good news to all mankind.

1:16 saving. This word carries the Hebrew idea of salvation as wholeness and healing (in the here and now), as well as the idea of spiritual rescue (which will be realized in the future). **everyone who believes.** For those seeking a relationship with God, the required response to the good news of salvation is faith.

[17] This Good News tells us how God makes us right in his sight. This is accomplished from start to finish by faith. As the Scriptures say, "It is through faith that a righteous person has life."*

GOD'S ANGER AT SIN

[18] But God shows his anger from heaven against all sinful, wicked people who suppress the truth by their wickedness.* [19] They know the truth about God because he has made it obvious to them. [20] For ever since the world was created, people have seen the earth and sky. Through everything God made, they can clearly see his invisible qualities—his eternal power and divine nature. So they have no excuse for not knowing God.

[21] Yes, they knew God, but they wouldn't worship him as God or even give him thanks. And they began to think up foolish ideas of what God was like. As a result, their minds became dark and confused. [22] Claiming to be wise, they instead became utter fools. [23] And instead of worshiping the glorious, ever-living God, they worshiped idols made to look like mere people and birds and animals and reptiles.

[24] So God abandoned them to do whatever shameful things their hearts desired. As a result, they did vile and degrading things with each other's bodies. [25] They traded the truth about God for a lie. So they worshiped and served the things God created instead of the Creator himself, who is worthy of eternal praise! Amen. [26] That is why God abandoned them to their shameful desires. Even the women turned against the natural way to have sex and instead indulged in sex with each other. [27] And the men, instead of having normal sexual relations with women, burned with lust for each other. Men did shameful things with other men, and as a result of this sin, they suffered within themselves the penalty they deserved.

[28] Since they thought it foolish to acknowledge God, he abandoned them to their foolish thinking and let them do things that should never be done. [29] Their lives became full of every kind of wickedness, sin, greed, hate, envy, murder, quarreling, deception, malicious behavior, and gossip. [30] They are backstabbers, haters of God, insolent, proud, and boastful. They invent new ways of sinning, and they disobey their parents. [31] They refuse to understand, break their promises, are heartless, and have no mercy. [32] They know God's justice requires that those who do these things deserve to die, yet they do them anyway. Worse yet, they encourage others to do them, too.

HOMOSEXUALITY

1. What are some things you have observed in nature that confirm to you "there is a God"?

ROMANS 1:18-32

2. How does God reveal His wrath against unrighteousness (v. 18)?
3. Who suppresses the truth in today's culture?
4. Homosexuality is now known as an "alternative lifestyle." What does Paul say about that?
5. According to this passage, why does God permit homosexuality? Where does it come from? To what does it lead?
6. How do people today "not think it worthwhile to have God in their knowledge" (v. 28)?

GOD'S JUDGMENT OF SIN

2 You may think you can condemn such people, but you are just as bad, and you have no excuse! When you say they are wicked and should be punished, you are condemning yourself, for you who judge others do these very same things. [2] And we know that God, in his justice, will punish anyone who does such things. [3] Since you judge others for doing these things, why do you think you can avoid God's judgment when you do the same things? [4] Don't you see how wonderfully kind, tolerant, and patient God is with you? Does this mean nothing to you? Can't you see that his kindness is intended to turn you from your sin?

1:17 Or *"The righteous will live by faith."* Hab 2:4. **1:18** Or *who, by their wickedness, prevent the truth from being known.*

1:17 God makes us right in his sight. In Hebrew thought, righteousness is not so much a moral quality as a legal judgment. The idea is not that a person is made righteous (in the ethical sense) or proved righteous (virtuous) by such a pronouncement. Rather, a person is counted, or reckoned, as righteous or pardoned, even though he is actually guilty. Then he has the right to stand before God and enter into a relationship with Him. **God.** This declaration of righteousness comes from God to us—it is a reflection of His character. He is righteous, and this is proved by His saving activity. **from start to finish by faith.** What faith is becomes clear as the epistle unfolds, though in verse 5 its primary meaning has already been made clear—it is believing obedience. The person who has faith trusts in the life, death, and resurrection of Jesus Christ. In these actions He sees the power of God at work. He then responds to God by submitting to Christ and trusting solely in God's saving work. **It is through faith that a righteous person has life.** This citation from Habakkuk 2:4 is the first of many quotes that Paul uses from the Old Testament to demonstrate and prove his point.

1:18 God shows his anger. God's anger is toward evil, including human sin and rebellion.

1:24 God abandoned them. This phrase is used three times (see also vv. 26,28) to indicate that God allowed people to carry out their rebellion and experience the fruit of their choices.

1:24-27 shameful things their hearts desired. Refusing to embrace and reverence the revealed nature of their Creator, those who rebel against God are not protected from evil assault. This lack of protection is expressed in a distorted sexuality. Greek and Roman writers agree with Paul's description; it was an age of unparalleled immorality.

1:29 wickedness. The opposite of justice: robbing God and others of their due. **sin.** The deliberate attempt to harm or to corrupt; such a person is not only intentionally bad, but he seeks to make others evil. **greed.** Taking whatever one wants without regard for the rights of others. **hate.** The most general term for badness; a vicious person devoid of any good quality. **envy.** Grudging resentment of (and desire for) another's accomplishments or possessions. **murder.** Jesus teaches that people must avoid the spirit of hatred, which causes such a deed (Matt. 5:21-26). **quarreling.** Contention or disagreement born of envy. **deception.** Underhanded, devious actions designed to get one's own way. **malicious behavior.** Literally "evil-nature"; always thinking the worst of another.

1:29-30 gossip . . .backstabbers. The gossiper spreads ill news about others secretly, while the slanderer openly accuses other people.

1:30 haters of God. These are people who hate God because they believe He suppresses pleasure. **insolent.** A type of pride that defies God and hurts others just for the delight in doing so. **inventing new ways of sinning.** People who create new ways of sinning.

1:31 refused to understand. One who does not learn from experience. **break their promises.** One who breaks agreements. **are heartless.** One without love for others, even members of his own family. **have no mercy.** One without pity who harms or even kills without thought.

2:4 wonderfully kind. Jews are presuming upon the mercy of God, taking His kindness as a sign of their immunity from judgment (when, in fact, such kindness was meant to lead them to change their lives, not to serve as an excuse for continued sinning).

PLAYING JUDGE

1. If you were a judge, what famous trial would you like to re-try? What would your verdict be, and why?

ROMANS 2:1-16

2. What is the difference between "judging" and identifying sin when it is present?
3. What does Paul mean in verse 11? What does this have to do with judging others?
4. In the last chapter, Paul discussed homosexuality. How can we stand up for what is true without judging others?
5. When have you assumed that God would "play favorites," giving you special grace? How can you guard against this?

5 But because you are stubborn and refuse to turn from your sin, you are storing up terrible punishment for yourself. For a day of anger is coming, when God's righteous judgment will be revealed. 6 He will judge everyone according to what they have done. 7 He will give eternal life to those who keep on doing good, seeking after the glory and honor and immortality that God offers. 8 But he will pour out his anger and wrath on those who live for themselves, who refuse to obey the truth and instead live lives of wickedness. 9 There will be trouble and calamity for everyone who keeps on doing what is evil—for the Jew first and also for the Gentile.* 10 But there will be glory and honor and peace from God for all who do good—for the Jew first and also for the Gentile. 11 For God does not show favoritism.

12 When the Gentiles sin, they will be destroyed, even though they never had God's written law. And the Jews, who do have God's law, will be judged by that law when they fail to obey it. 13 For merely listening to the law doesn't make us right with God. It is obeying the law that makes us right in his sight. 14 Even Gentiles, who do not have God's written law, show that they know his law when they instinctively obey it, even without having heard it. 15 They demonstrate that God's law is written in their hearts, for their own conscience and thoughts either accuse them or tell them they are doing right. 16 And this is the message I proclaim—that the day is coming when God, through Christ Jesus, will judge everyone's secret life.

THE JEWS AND THE LAW

17 You who call yourselves Jews are relying on God's law, and you boast about your special relationship with him. 18 You know what he wants; you know what is right because you have been taught his law. 19 You are convinced that you are a guide for the blind and a light for people who are lost in darkness. 20 You think you can instruct the ignorant and teach children the ways of God. For you are certain that God's law gives you complete knowledge and truth.

21 Well then, if you teach others, why don't you teach yourself? You tell others not to steal, but do you steal? 22 You say it is wrong to commit adultery, but do you commit adultery? You condemn idolatry, but do you use items stolen from pagan temples?* 23 You are so proud of knowing the law, but you dishonor God by breaking it. 24 No wonder the Scriptures say, "The Gentiles blaspheme the name of God because of you."*

25 The Jewish ceremony of circumcision has value only if you obey God's law. But if you don't obey God's law, you are no better off than an uncircumcised Gentile. 26 And if the Gentiles obey God's law, won't God declare them to be his own people? 27 In fact, uncircumcised Gentiles who keep God's law will condemn you Jews who are circumcised and possess God's law but don't obey it.

28 For you are not a true Jew just because you were born of Jewish parents or because you have gone through the ceremony of circumcision. 29 No, a true Jew is one whose heart is right with God. And true circumcision is not merely obeying the letter of the law; rather, it is a change of heart produced by the Spirit. And a person with a changed heart seeks praise* from God, not from people.

BRAGGING RIGHTS

1. What accomplishment in your life are you most proud of? What are you most tempted to boast about?

ROMANS 2:17-29

2. What principle is Paul stating in verses 17-24?
3. What does it mean to be "proud of knowing the law" (v. 23)? What is the risk of doing so?
4. What does it mean in verse 29 that "a true Jew is one whose heart is right with God"? That "circumcision is a change of heart"?
5. How often do you boast or gloat when you "win" or accomplish something? How can you have a "purified heart"?

2:9 Greek *also for the Greek;* also in 2:10. **2:22** Greek *do you steal from temples?* **2:24** Isa 52:5 (Greek version). **2:29** Or *receives praise.*

2:11 favoritism. This is the point of Paul's argument. The means by which a person gains "wrath and indignation" (v. 8) or "eternal life" (v. 7) has nothing to do with national or racial heritage.

2:12 the Gentiles . . . the Jews . . . will be judged. Everyone will be held accountable according to his or her particular awareness of God. The Jews had the written law; the Gentiles had their conscience (v. 15) and the revelation of nature (1:20).

2:14-15 God's law is written in their hearts. Gentiles not only know about God from His creation, but their conscience tells them that He is the judge of the difference between right and wrong.

2:17 Jews. To be a Jew was to be special—to be a child of God. Paul attacked this intense nationalistic pride, stating that it is not enough for salvation. **relying on God's law.** Literally to "rest upon the law"; to believe that one is right with God because of his heritage and culture as a Jew.

2:25 circumcision. This was the sign of the covenant between the Jewish people and God (Gen. 17:1-14).

2:28-29 true circumcision. The Old Testament teaches in Deuteronomy 30:6 that true circumcision is not an outward, physical mark, but an inward spiritual work by God. Paul teaches that it is possible to neglect circumcision and still be counted as obedient to God's law. This would be interpreted by Paul's Jewish readers as a radical new teaching.

GOD REMAINS FAITHFUL

3 Then what's the advantage of being a Jew? Is
there any value in the ceremony of circumcision?
2 Yes, there are great benefits! First of all, the Jews
were entrusted with the whole revelation of God.*
3 True, some of them were unfaithful; but just be-
cause they were unfaithful, does that mean God will
be unfaithful? 4 Of course not! Even if everyone else is
a liar, God is true. As the Scriptures say about him,

"You will be proved right in what you say,
and you will win your case in court."*

5 "But," some might say, "our sinfulness serves a
good purpose, for it helps people see how righteous
God is. Isn't it unfair, then, for him to punish us?"
(This is merely a human point of view.) 6 Of course
not! If God were not entirely fair, how would he be
qualified to judge the world? 7 "But," someone might
still argue, "how can God condemn me as a sinner
if my dishonesty highlights his truthfulness and
brings him more glory?" 8 And some people even
slander us by claiming that we say, "The more we
sin, the better it is!" Those who say such things de-
serve to be condemned.

ALL PEOPLE ARE SINNERS

9 Well then, should we conclude that we Jews are bet-
ter than others? No, not at all, for we have already
shown that all people, whether Jews or Gentiles,* are
under the power of sin. 10 As the Scriptures say,

"No one is righteous—
not even one.
11 No one is truly wise;
no one is seeking God.
12 All have turned away;
all have become useless.
No one does good,
not a single one."*
13 "Their talk is foul, like the stench from an open
grave.
Their tongues are filled with lies."
"Snake venom drips from their lips."*
14 "Their mouths are full of cursing and
bitterness."*

WE'VE ALL BLOWN IT

1. What laws do you frequently ignore: Speed limits? School rules? Coach's demands? Other?

ROMANS 3:9-24

2. Who does Paul consider a sinner? Who has never sinned?
3. Who has been saved from sin? How?
4. In verse 20 Paul says, "For no one can ever be made right with God by doing what the law commands." How is a person justified (made right)?
5. Have you gotten right with God? Are you trying to earn your way into His favor through good works?
6. How does disregard for rules show the attitude of your heart?

15 "They rush to commit murder.
16 Destruction and misery always follow them.
17 They don't know where to find peace."*
18 "They have no fear of God at all."*

19 Obviously, the law applies to those to whom it
was given, for its purpose is to keep people from
having excuses, and to show that the entire world is
guilty before God. 20 For no one can ever be made right
with God by doing what the law commands. The law
simply shows us how sinful we are.

CHRIST TOOK OUR PUNISHMENT

21 But now God has shown us a way to be made right
with him without keeping the requirements of the
law, as was promised in the writings of Moses* and
the prophets long ago. 22 We are made right with
God by placing our faith in Jesus Christ. And this is
true for everyone who believes, no matter who we
are.
23 For everyone has sinned; we all fall short of
God's glorious standard. 24 Yet God, in his grace, freely
makes us right in his sight. He did this through Christ
Jesus when he freed us from the penalty for our sins.

3:2 Greek *the oracles of God.* **3:4** Ps 51:4 (Greek version). **3:9** Greek *or Greeks.* **3:10-12** Pss 14:1-3; 53:1-3 (Greek version). **3:13** Pss 5:9 (Greek version); 140:3. **3:14** Ps 10:7 (Greek version). **3:15-17** Isa 59:7-8. **3:18** Ps 36:1. **3:21** Greek *in the law.*

3:1 what's the advantage. Paul raises a question he has heard or that he knows is on the minds of some readers: "Do you really mean that there is no significant difference between a Jew and a Gentile?" Questions like this arise out of an accurate understanding that God had set Israel apart from all other nations.

3:2 there are great benefits! We might assume that Paul would reply: "Jews have no advantage." But this would not be accurate. They had an important place in God's plan. It was through the Jewish people that God worked out the redemption of the world through His Son Jesus, who was a Jew. **revelation of God.** It is a great advantage to have known the mind and will of God.

3:20 be made right by God. God's perspective is the only one that matters.

3:21 But now. Paul moves from the revelation of God's wrath (1:18) to the revelation of God's righteousness. **without keeping the requirements of the law.** God's righteousness as revealed in the law leads only to wrath (4:15), but God's righteousness as revealed in Jesus Christ leads to right standing before Him. **promised in the writings of Moses and the prophets.** The Old Testament, if rightly understood, does contain such a message. Paul has already used Habakkuk 2:4 when describing the gospel (1:17).

3:22 faith. Individuals are not counted as righteous because of faith, as if it were an attitude on their part that forces God to accept them. Rather, they are counted as righteous (justified) because of grace through faith (or on the basis of faith). Faith, then, is a profound trust and hope in God's work in Christ. It is the opposite of works. Works give people a sense of self-confidence. They assume that their religious and moral activities will cause God to pronounce them justified. **in Jesus Christ.** Paul writes not about faith in general but about faith in a specific person—Jesus Christ. **for everyone.** The gospel is for Jew and Gentile alike.

3:23 fall short. The picture is of arrows that have failed to reach their target. **God's glory.** This is God's divine splendor, which is reflected in the law.

3:24 freely and graciously declares. This is a phrase drawn from the law courts. The image is of humanity on trial before God. To be justified is to be granted acquittal on the day of judgment. That a guilty person would be reckoned as not guilty was shocking to the Jew (Ex. 23:7; Prov. 17:15). Such assurance of acquittal, coming as it does at the beginning of the Christian life (the Jew hoped for acquittal at the end of life), brings a sense of personal freedom since a person is released from the nagging questions: Am I good enough? Will I merit heaven? Now, by grace, people are pronounced "righteous" and are freed to do good works out of love for God, not out of fear of His wrath. **freed us from the penalty.** This refers to the act of buying the freedom of a slave—in this case, a slave in bondage to sin (Mark 10:45; 1 Pet. 1:18-19).

[25] For God presented Jesus as the sacrifice for sin. People are made right with God when they believe that Jesus sacrificed his life, shedding his blood. This sacrifice shows that God was being fair when he held back and did not punish those who sinned in times past,
[26] for he was looking ahead and including them in what he would do in this present time. God did this to demonstrate his righteousness, for he himself is fair and just, and he makes sinners right in his sight when they believe in Jesus.
[27] Can we boast, then, that we have done anything to be accepted by God? No, because our acquittal is not based on obeying the law. It is based on faith. [28] So we are made right with God through faith and not by obeying the law.
[29] After all, is God the God of the Jews only? Isn't he also the God of the Gentiles? Of course he is. [30] There is only one God, and he makes people right with himself only by faith, whether they are Jews or Gentiles.*
[31] Well then, if we emphasize faith, does this mean that we can forget about the law? Of course not! In fact, only when we have faith do we truly fulfill the law.

THE FAITH OF ABRAHAM

4 Abraham was, humanly speaking, the founder of our Jewish nation. What did he discover about being made right with God? [2] If his good deeds had made him acceptable to God, he would have had something to boast about. But that was not God's way. [3] For the Scriptures tell us, "Abraham believed God, and God counted him as righteous because of his faith."*
[4] When people work, their wages are not a gift, but something they have earned. [5] But people are counted as righteous, not because of their work, but because of their faith in God who forgives sinners. [6] David also spoke of this when he described the happiness of those who are declared righteous without working for it:

[7] "Oh, what joy for those
whose disobedience is forgiven,
whose sins are put out of sight.
[8] Yes, what joy for those
whose record the LORD has cleared of sin."*

[9] Now, is this blessing only for the Jews, or is it also for uncircumcised Gentiles?* Well, we have been saying that Abraham was counted as righteous by God because of his faith. [10] But how did this happen? Was he counted as righteous only after he was circumcised, or was it before he was circumcised? Clearly,

GETTING ON GOD'S GOOD SIDE

1. What was your first paying job outside of the house? How much did you make?

ROMANS 4:1-25

2. What is the distinction that Paul makes between something earned and something given as a gift? Which applies to salvation and forgiveness of sins?
3. Circumcision here refers to earning God's favor by works or outward obedience. How do we receive God's favor? What does God actually owe us?
4. Why do we need faith to receive God's forgiveness (v. 16)?
5. How did Abraham find favor with God? How can you?

God accepted Abraham before he was circumcised!
[11] Circumcision was a sign that Abraham already had faith and that God had already accepted him and declared him to be righteous—even before he was circumcised. So Abraham is the spiritual father of those who have faith but have not been circumcised. They are counted as righteous because of their faith.
[12] And Abraham is also the spiritual father of those who have been circumcised, but only if they have the same kind of faith Abraham had before he was circumcised.
[13] Clearly, God's promise to give the whole earth to Abraham and his descendants was based not on his obedience to God's law, but on a right relationship with God that comes by faith. [14] If God's promise is only for those who obey the law, then faith is not necessary and the promise is pointless. [15] For the law always brings punishment on those who try to obey it. (The only way to avoid breaking the law is to have no law to break!)
[16] So the promise is received by faith. It is given as a free gift. And we are all certain to receive it, whether or not we live according to the law of Moses, if we have faith like Abraham's. For Abraham is the father of all who believe. [17] That is what the Scriptures mean when God told him, "I have made you the father of many nations."* This happened because Abraham believed in the God who brings the dead back to life and who creates new things out of nothing.

3:30 Greek *whether they are circumcised or uncircumcised.* **4:3** Gen 15:6. **4:7-8** Ps 32:1-2 (Greek version). **4:9** Greek *is this blessing only for the circumcised, or is it also for the uncircumcised?* **4:17** Gen 17:5.

3:25 sacrifice for sin. The removal of divine wrath. Christ's death is the ultimate, final, and complete sacrifice for sin. Christ is the victim who takes upon Himself the wrath intended for sinful humanity. **his blood.** In terms of atonement, the importance of Jesus' death is that His blood was offered to God as a sacrifice on our behalf.

3:26 demonstrate his righteousness. The sacrificial death of Christ exhibits God's justice in two ways: First, by vindicating Jesus—He has taken sin so seriously that He sent His own Son to die. Second, by showing a whole new way of living that Christ's sacrifice has opened up for humanity.

4:1 Abraham. As the first patriarch and thus the founder of the Jewish nation, Abraham was revered by all Jews.

4:3 Abraham believed God. It was the condition of Abraham's heart demonstrated through obedience that caught the favorable attention of God.

4:5 faith. The Jews saw faith as a definite activity, as faithful action in accordance with God's will. Thus, they understood that God responded to Abraham's faith by declaring him "righteous." In contrast, Paul understood faith as a person's response to God's action (1:17; 3:21-26). **people are counted as righteous.** That God would do this contradicts Jewish expectations. God was supposed to condemn the guilty (Ex. 23:7). Paul makes this point because everyone would agree that acquitting the guilty could only be seen as an act of grace, not as a response by God to good works. God was able to justify the wicked because of the future sacrifice of the Messiah (Isa. 53:4-12).

4:9 Abraham was counted as righteous by God because of his faith. This is a financial reference communicating the idea that Abraham, in a sense, borrowed against the future atonement achieved through the death, burial, and resurrection of Jesus.

4:16 promise. The word Paul uses in this verse describes an unconditional promise made out of the generosity of a person's heart. God's promise is a gift of grace, not a contract with certain obligations. **by faith.** By the very nature of a promise, a person must wait for the fulfillment of a promised inheritance.

18 Even when there was no reason for hope, Abra-
ham kept hoping—believing that he would become
the father of many nations. For God had said to him,
"That's how many descendants you will have!"* 19 And
Abraham's faith did not weaken, even though, at
about 100 years of age, he figured his body was as
good as dead—and so was Sarah's womb.
20 Abraham never wavered in believing God's
promise. In fact, his faith grew stronger, and in this
he brought glory to God. 21 He was fully convinced
that God is able to do whatever he promises. 22 And
because of Abraham's faith, God counted him as righ-
teous. 23 And when God counted him as righteous, it
wasn't just for Abraham's benefit. It was recorded
24 for our benefit, too, assuring us that God will also
count us as righteous if we believe in him, the one
who raised Jesus our Lord from the dead. 25 He was
handed over to die because of our sins, and he was
raised to life to make us right with God.

FAITH BRINGS JOY

5 Therefore, since we have been made right in God's
sight by faith, we have peace* with God because of
what Jesus Christ our Lord has done for us. 2 Because
of our faith, Christ has brought us into this place of
undeserved privilege where we now stand, and we
confidently and joyfully look forward to sharing
God's glory.
3 We can rejoice, too, when we run into problems
and trials, for we know that they help us develop
endurance. 4 And endurance develops strength of
character, and character strengthens our confident
hope of salvation. 5 And this hope will not lead to
disappointment. For we know how dearly God loves
us, because he has given us the Holy Spirit to fill our
hearts with his love.
6 When we were utterly helpless, Christ came at
just the right time and died for us sinners. 7 Now, most
people would not be willing to die for an upright
person, though someone might perhaps be willing
to die for a person who is especially good. 8 But God
showed his great love for us by sending Christ to die
for us while we were still sinners. 9 And since we have
been made right in God's sight by the blood of Christ,
he will certainly save us from God's condemnation.

FINDING JOY IN TROUBLES

1. When has someone sacrificed something costly for your benefit? When have you done that for someone else?

ROMANS 5:1-11

2. How does Paul describe humanity in verses 6, 8, and 10?
3. What does "reconciled" mean? How does it change things in our relationship with God?
4. What does it mean to "rejoice when we run into problems" (v. 3)? How does one do this?
5. How does this change the way a Christian is to look upon suffering and stress?
6. How do you view your present stresses and trials?

10 For since our friendship with God was restored by
the death of his Son while we were still his enemies,
we will certainly be saved through the life of his Son.
11 So now we can rejoice in our wonderful new rela-
tionship with God because our Lord Jesus Christ has
made us friends of God.

ADAM AND CHRIST CONTRASTED

12 When Adam sinned, sin entered the world. Adam's
sin brought death, so death spread to everyone, for
everyone sinned. 13 Yes, people sinned even before
the law was given. But it was not counted as sin
because there was not yet any law to break. 14 Still,
everyone died—from the time of Adam to the time of
Moses—even those who did not disobey an explicit
commandment of God, as Adam did. Now Adam is
a symbol, a representation of Christ, who was yet to
come. 15 But there is a great difference between Ad-
am's sin and God's gracious gift. For the sin of this one
man, Adam, brought death to many. But even greater
is God's wonderful grace and his gift of forgiveness
to many through this other man, Jesus Christ. 16 And
the result of God's gracious gift is very different from

4:18 Gen 15:5. **5:1** Some manuscripts read *let us have peace.*

5:1-4 We have been made right in God's sight by faith. Paul points out the fourfold fruit of justification: the past blessing of peace with God (v. 1), the present blessing of grace (v. 2), the future hope of glory (v. 2), and the redeeming value of affliction (v. 3).
5:1 peace. This is not some sort of inner experience of harmony but the objective fact of a new relationship with God. The root image is of war. Those who were in rebellion against God, their rightful King, are now reconciled to Him through Christ. This is the basis for the Christian's access to God's grace and hope for the future. In the Bible the term *peace* often describes the total blessing of salvation.
5:2 brought us in. This word is used to describe ushering someone into the presence of royalty. **undeserved privilege** . To be at peace with God is to come into the sphere of His grace and thus experience the new kind of life described in 5:12–8:39. **confidently.** This is a sense of confidence based on the fact of justification. **God's glory.** That for which people were created and from which they have fallen, but which they will experience again someday.
5:3 problems and trials. Literally, "pressure" or "tribulation." This is not sorrow or pain, but the negative reaction of an unbelieving world. In New Testament times, suffering was the normal and expected lot of Christians (Acts 14:22). Thus, suffering was seen as a sign of true Christianity (2 Thess. 1:4-5). **endurance.** This word describes positive action taken against misfortune rather than passive acceptance.
5:4 character. A word used of metal that has been so heated by fire that all the impurities are removed. **hope.** The confidence born out of suffering that God is transforming a person's character and that He will keep on doing so until he is glorified.
5:12 Adam sinned, sin entered the world. Jews thought of themselves not as isolated individuals, but as part of a family, a tribe, and a nation. The actions and consequences of one person were the actions and consequences of all. So when Adam sinned by doubting God and eating the forbidden fruit (Gen. 2–3), all humanity sinned. **Adam's sin brought death.** Death is the consequence of sin (Gen. 2:17), and so all people die because Adam sinned.
5:14 died. More than the physical end of life is meant here, since the contrast is always with eternal life (v. 21). Death brings a person to judgment and to condemnation (v. 18)—since all have sinned—and thus to punishment. It is spiritual death as well as physical death that concerns Paul. **as Adam did.** Adam disobeyed God's clear instructions (Gen. 2:17). **symbol.** Literally, a mark or impression that has been left by something. Adam and his impact on humanity was a representation of Christ, who would also impact all people.
5:15 gift. This could refer to Christ and His work on behalf of humanity. But in light of verses 18, 20, and 21, it probably indicates the status conferred on people who are made righteous before God.
5:16 led to condemnation . . . being made right with God. One act of disobedience by Adam brought judgment and condemnation to all people. But Christ's gift brings justification and forgiveness not only for that sin, but for all sins across the centuries.

JUSTIFIED BY JESUS

1. Whom do you take after in your temperament, your mother or your father? How about in your body build? Your talents and abilities?

ROMANS 5:12-21

2. What does Paul mean when he says "When Adam sinned, sin entered the world" (v. 12)? Why did sin enter through one man? Why not through Eve's sin?
3. What does "justification" mean? How does a person become "justified"?
4. Who is the "one man" who brought justification, or gift of forgiveness (v. 15)? What does this say about the worldview that there are many ways to God?
5. Have you been justified, "resulting in eternal life through Jesus Christ our Lord" (v. 21)?

the result of that one man's sin. For Adam's sin led to
condemnation, but God's free gift leads to our being
made right with God, even though we are guilty of
many sins. 17 For the sin of this one man, Adam, caused
death to rule over many. But even greater is God's
wonderful grace and his gift of righteousness, for all
who receive it will live in triumph over sin and death
through this one man, Jesus Christ.
18 Yes, Adam's one sin brings condemnation for
everyone, but Christ's one act of righteousness brings
a right relationship with God and new life for every-
one. 19 Because one person disobeyed God, many be-
came sinners. But because one other person obeyed
God, many will be made righteous.
20 God's law was given so that all people could see
how sinful they were. But as people sinned more and
more, God's wonderful grace became more abundant.
21 So just as sin ruled over all people and brought them
to death, now God's wonderful grace rules instead,
giving us right standing with God and resulting in
eternal life through Jesus Christ our Lord.

SIN'S POWER IS BROKEN

6 Well then, should we keep on sinning so that
God can show us more and more of his wonder-
ful grace? 2 Of course not! Since we have died to sin,
how can we continue to live in it? 3 Or have you for-
gotten that when we were joined with Christ Jesus
in baptism, we joined him in his death? 4 For we died
and were buried with Christ by baptism. And just as
Christ was raised from the dead by the glorious pow-
er of the Father, now we also may live new lives.
5 Since we have been united with him in his death,
we will also be raised to life as he was. 6 We know
that our old sinful selves were crucified with Christ
so that sin might lose its power in our lives. We are no
longer slaves to sin. 7 For when we died with Christ
we were set free from the power of sin. 8 And since
we died with Christ, we know we will also live with
him. 9 We are sure of this because Christ was raised
from the dead, and he will never die again. Death no
longer has any power over him. 10 When he died, he
died once to break the power of sin. But now that he
lives, he lives for the glory of God. 11 So you also should
consider yourselves to be dead to the power of sin and
alive to God through Christ Jesus.
12 Do not let sin control the way you live;* do not give
in to sinful desires. 13 Do not let any part of your body
become an instrument of evil to serve sin. Instead,
give yourselves completely to God, for you were dead,
but now you have new life. So use your whole body as
an instrument to do what is right for the glory of God.
14 Sin is no longer your master, for you no longer live
under the requirements of the law. Instead, you live
under the freedom of God's grace.

A NEW WAY OF LIFE

1. What is the closest you have come to losing your life? What happened? What did you learn from the experience?

ROMANS 6:1-14

2. What does Paul mean that "when we were joined with Christ Jesus in baptism, we joined him in his death" (v. 3)? How does this concept relate to sin and temptation?
3. What does it mean to "live new lives" (v. 4)? How does this relate to sin and temptation?
4. How are we "dead to the power of sin" (v. 11)?
5. In practical terms, how can you "not let sin control" (v. 12) in your life?

6:12 Or *Do not let sin reign in your body, which is subject to death.*

5:18-19 one person disobeyed . . . one other person obeyed. With the lack of similarity between Adam and Christ established, Paul can return to the formal comparison he began in verse 12: One man's disobedience brought condemnation and death to all people, just as one man's obedience now brings justification to all who choose it. The only similarity between Christ and Adam is that by one deed, each had a great impact on humanity.
5:18 one act of righteousness. The obedience of Christ's entire life, which led to His sacrificial death on our behalf.
5:20 law. When the law came, it defined what was "sinful." It brought sin into clear view by functioning as a mirror.
6:1-2 Should we keep on sinning. Paul poses a rhetorical question, stating the typical cynical attitude of the day: "If grace is the most wonderful thing there is and if grace abounds in the presence of sin (5:20), then shouldn't we sin all the more in order to produce more grace?"
6:2 died to sin. Paul's point is that the question is absurd. To be a Christian is to have died to sin; therefore it is impossible to live in a state to which one has died!
6:3 in baptism. Baptism was mostly an adult rite in the early church, occurring generally at the moment when a person confessed faith in Christ. It served as a public declaration that a person was no longer an unbeliever but was now identified with Christ.
6:4 buried with Christ. When family and friends bury a loved one, they acknowledge publicly the reality of that death. To be baptized provides an experience in a direct (though symbolic) way to the reality of Christ's death. The experience of baptism marks the end of the old way of life and acknowledges that a person has committed himself to follow the new way of life in Christ.
6:6 old sinful selves. This refers to the unregenerate life before salvation—what a person was before turning his life over to Christ. **lose its power.** The Greek word means "to be defeated," not "to become extinct." The sinful part of a person's nature is not destroyed, but it is deprived of power; its domination is broken. **in our lives.** This reference is to a person's lower self—the sinful nature that belongs to his body (v. 12
6:7 free from the power of sin. The only way to be freed from sin (literally, "justified from sin") is by paying its penalty. But for the Christian, resurrection follows death, and a believer is freed to rise to new life in which sin cannot overpower and dominate.

15 Well then, since God's grace has set us free from
the law, does that mean we can go on sinning? Of
course not! 16 Don't you realize that you become the
slave of whatever you choose to obey? You can be a
slave to sin, which leads to death, or you can choose
to obey God, which leads to righteous living. 17 Thank
God! Once you were slaves of sin, but now you whole-
heartedly obey this teaching we have given you.
18 Now you are free from your slavery to sin, and you
have become slaves to righteous living.
19 Because of the weakness of your human nature, I
am using the illustration of slavery to help you under-
stand all this. Previously, you let yourselves be slaves
to impurity and lawlessness, which led ever deeper
into sin. Now you must give yourselves to be slaves to
righteous living so that you will become holy.
20 When you were slaves to sin, you were free from
the obligation to do right. 21 And what was the result?
You are now ashamed of the things you used to do,
things that end in eternal doom. 22 But now you are
free from the power of sin and have become slaves
of God. Now you do those things that lead to holiness
and result in eternal life. 23 For the wages of sin is
death, but the free gift of God is eternal life through
Christ Jesus our Lord.

THE PERFECT OFFERING

1. Who was your first "boss"? Was this person easy or hard to work for?

ROMANS 6:15-23

2. What does it mean to be a slave to sin? To righteousness?
3. What are the results of being a slave to sin? To righteousness?
4. Why does Paul say that sin pays wages, while Christ gives a gift (v. 23)? What does this suggest about working for one's salvation?
5. Slaves have no choice but to obey, but Paul speaks of "offering" ourselves (v. 19). To what things do you frequently offer yourself? How can you offer yourself more to God?

NO LONGER BOUND TO THE LAW

7 Now, dear brothers and sisters*—you who are fa-
miliar with the law—don't you know that the law
applies only while a person is living? 2 For example,
when a woman marries, the law binds her to her hus-
band as long as he is alive. But if he dies, the laws of
marriage no longer apply to her. 3 So while her hus-
band is alive, she would be committing adultery if she
married another man. But if her husband dies, she
is free from that law and does not commit adultery
when she remarries.
4 So, my dear brothers and sisters, this is the point:
You died to the power of the law when you died with
Christ. And now you are united with the one who was
raised from the dead. As a result, we can produce a
harvest of good deeds for God. 5 When we were con-
trolled by our old nature,* sinful desires were at work
within us, and the law aroused these evil desires that
produced a harvest of sinful deeds, resulting in death.
6 But now we have been released from the law, for we
died to it and are no longer captive to its power. Now
we can serve God, not in the old way of obeying the
letter of the law, but in the new way of living in the
Spirit.

"IT'S LIKE BEING MARRIED"

1. Describe your ideal mate. What things are most important to you? What things are "negotiable"?

ROMANS 7:1-6

2. Put Paul's "marriage" analogy into your own words. What point is he making?
3. What does "the law" mean to us today: Working for God's favor? Earning our salvation? Following rules? Other?
4. What does it mean that we have been "released from the law" (v. 6)?
5. When do you get caught up "in the old way of obeying the letter of the law"? In practical terms, how can you "serve . . . in the new way of the Spirit" (v. 6)?

GOD'S LAW REVEALS OUR SIN

7 Well then, am I suggesting that the law of God is sin-
ful? Of course not! In fact, it was the law that showed
me my sin. I would never have known that coveting
is wrong if the law had not said, "You must not cov-
et."* 8 But sin used this command to arouse all kinds
of covetous desires within me! If there were no law,

7:1 Greek *brothers;* also in 7:4. **7:5** Greek *When we were in the flesh.* **7:7** Exod 20:17; Deut 5:21.

6:18 free from your slavery to sin. Freed in the sense of having a new master—God—in place of the old master—sin. Paul is not teaching that Christians do not sin but that they have a greater capacity to commit themselves to following Christ.
6:19 slaves. In contrast to a servant, a slave was the absolute possession of his master. A slave's time was not his own. It was literally impossible for a slave to serve two masters. **become holy.** The process by which a person is conformed to God's ways is the theme of chapters 5–8.
6:23 wages of sin. Literally, "wages with which to buy food"—a phrase used to describe the rations eaten by soldiers. **gift of God.** In contrast to the wage of death that sin pays, God does not pay wages. He is under obligation to no one. He gives eternal life freely.
7:2-3 a woman marries. A wife is bound to her husband for the duration of his life. If she goes off ("consorts," NEB) with another man while her husband is living, she "incurs the stigma of adultery" (J. B. Phillips). But if he dies, she is free to remarry without any fault or stigma.
7:5-6 But now we have been released from the law. Paul now contrasts life without Christ (v. 5) with the new life in Christ (v. 6) experienced by a believer.
7:5 old nature. That is, when a person's direction in life was determined by his fallen or sinful nature. **sinful desires were at work.** Our sinful nature, inherited from Adam when he fell into sin, affects every area of our lives.
7:6 released from the law. The death of Christ has delivered us from the tyranny of the law. **serve.** A Christian is freed from the law to serve and not to sin—free for obedience, but not license. **not in the old way . . . but in the new way.** The Christian does not serve the law in its crippling and binding details, but he follows the liberating way of the Spirit.
7:8 used. This word describes a military base or the bridgehead from which an assault is launched. **sin.** Paul personifies sin as a great power with an evil intention.

I DO WHAT I DON'T WANT TO DO

1. When have you been pressured into doing something that you didn't really want to do? Who or what pressured you? Why did you do it?

ROMANS 7:7-25

2. Explain in your own words what Paul is saying about how the law actually produces sin. How have you seen this happen in your own life?
3. What does Paul mean in verse 15, "I want to do what is right, but I don't do it. Instead, I do what I hate"? How have you experienced this?
4. What is reigning in your life right now—sin or grace? How can you get on the right track?

sin would not have that power. [9] At one time I lived without understanding the law. But when I learned the command not to covet, for instance, the power of sin came to life, [10] and I died. So I discovered that the law's commands, which were supposed to bring life, brought spiritual death instead. [11] Sin took advantage of those commands and deceived me; it used the commands to kill me. [12] But still, the law itself is holy, and its commands are holy and right and good.

[13] But how can that be? Did the law, which is good, cause my death? Of course not! Sin used what was good to bring about my condemnation to death. So we can see how terrible sin really is. It uses God's good commands for its own evil purposes.

STRUGGLING WITH SIN

[14] So the trouble is not with the law, for it is spiritual and good. The trouble is with me, for I am all too human, a slave to sin. [15] I don't really understand myself, for I want to do what is right, but I don't do it. Instead, I do what I hate. [16] But if I know that what I am doing is wrong, this shows that I agree that the law is good. [17] So I am not the one doing wrong; it is sin living in me that does it.

[18] And I know that nothing good lives in me, that is, in my sinful nature.* I want to do what is right, but I can't. [19] I want to do what is good, but I don't. I don't want to do what is wrong, but I do it anyway. [20] But if I do what I don't want to do, I am not really the one doing wrong; it is sin living in me that does it.

[21] I have discovered this principle of life—that when I want to do what is right, I inevitably do what is wrong. [22] I love God's law with all my heart. [23] But there is another power* within me that is at war with my mind. This power makes me a slave to the sin that is still within me. [24] Oh, what a miserable person I am! Who will free me from this life that is dominated by sin and death? [25] Thank God! The answer is in Jesus Christ our Lord. So you see how it is: In my mind I really want to obey God's law, but because of my sinful nature I am a slave to sin.

LIFE IN THE SPIRIT

8 So now there is no condemnation for those who belong to Christ Jesus. [2] And because you belong to him, the power* of the life-giving Spirit has freed you* from the power of sin that leads to death. [3] The law of Moses was unable to save us because of the weakness of our sinful nature.* So God did what the law could not do. He sent his own Son in a body like the bodies we sinners have. And in that body God declared an end to sin's control over us by giving his Son as a sacrifice for our sins. [4] He did this so that the just requirement of the law would be fully satisfied for us, who no longer follow our sinful nature but instead follow the Spirit.

[5] Those who are dominated by the sinful nature think about sinful things, but those who are controlled by the Holy Spirit think about things that please the Spirit. [6] So letting your sinful nature control your mind leads to death. But letting the Spirit control your mind leads to life and peace. [7] For the sinful nature is always hostile to God. It never did obey God's laws, and it never will. [8] That's why those who are still under the control of their sinful nature can never please God.

[9] But you are not controlled by your sinful nature. You are controlled by the Spirit if you have the Spirit of God living in you. (And remember that those who do not have the Spirit of Christ living in them do not belong to him at all.) [10] And Christ lives within you, so even though your body will die because of sin, the Spirit gives you life* because you have been made right with God. [11] The Spirit of God, who raised Jesus from the dead, lives in you. And just as God raised Christ Jesus from the dead, he will give life to your mortal bodies by this same Spirit living within you.

[12] Therefore, dear brothers and sisters,* you have no obligation to do what your sinful nature urges you to do. [13] For if you live by its dictates, you will die. But if through the power of the Spirit you put

7:18 Greek *my flesh;* also in 7:25. 7:23 Greek *law;* also in 7:23b. 8:2a Greek *the law;* also in 8:2b. 8:2b Some manuscripts read *me.* 8:3 Greek *our flesh;* similarly in 8:4, 5, 6, 7, 8, 9, 12. 8:10 Or *your spirit is alive.* 8:12 Greek *brothers;* also in 8:29. 8:13 Greek *deeds of the body.*

7:9 I died. Though living physically after the law came, Paul fell under its judgment—the sentence of death.

7:13 sin . . . my condemnation to death. Sin reveals its true colors by bringing death through what is good. The law offered life if it was obeyed, but it lacked the power to enable people to overcome sin.

7:24 Oh, what a miserable person I am! The nearer people get to God, the more aware they are of how far short they fall. **Who will free me . . . ?** People are helpless to deliver themselves from sin. They need someone else to rescue them. This is precisely what God has done through Christ (v. 25).

8:1 no condemnation. Christians are free from the guilt that sin produces (and therefore have no anxiety about being condemned on the future day of judgment) as well as the enslaving power of sin (so they can live in God's way in the here and now).

8:2 life-giving Spirit. The Holy Spirit is the third person of the Trinity who indwells believers in power. In chapter 8, Paul will refer to the Spirit over 20 times—more references to the Spirit than in any other chapter of the New Testament. **has freed you.** There is at work in believers a power greater than sin—a power that enables them to resist sin. They are no longer slaves of sin.

8:3 sinful nature. Human nature was unable to keep God's law. Therefore, the law could not save anyone. In response to this plight, Christ, as God's representative, bore the punishment of sin in place of those who deserved it. **in a body like the bodies we sinners have.** Jesus took on weak human nature, but this did not take away His divine nature. He was fully God *and* fully man.

8:6 death ... life. The two outlooks lead to two patterns of conduct, which result in two spiritual states—death to God (because sin separates us from Him), or life in the Spirit.

8:13 put to death. In 7:4 Paul says that Christians are dead to the law through Christ's act of dying on the cross in their place. Believers are to "put to death" the sinful practices they know to be wrong.

to death the deeds of your sinful nature,* you will live. 14 For all who are led by the Spirit of God are children* of God.

15 So you have not received a spirit that makes you fearful slaves. Instead, you received God's Spirit when he adopted you as his own children.* Now we call him, "Abba, Father."* 16 For his Spirit joins with our spirit to affirm that we are God's children. 17 And since we are his children, we are his heirs. In fact, together with Christ we are heirs of God's glory. But if we are to share his glory, we must also share his suffering.

WALKING BY THE SPIRIT

1. When have you been set free from some rule that applied to others? How did you use your freedom?

ROMANS 8:1-17

2. What does it mean to "follow our sinful nature" (v. 4)? The Spirit?
3. What does it mean to "put to death the deeds of your sinful nature" (v. 13)? How does a person do this? What is the result?
4. Does the flesh or the Spirit govern your responses when you are facing stress? How can you more fully develop the mind-set of the Spirit?

THE FUTURE GLORY

18 Yet what we suffer now is nothing compared to the glory he will reveal to us later. 19 For all creation is waiting eagerly for that future day when God will reveal who his children really are. 20 Against its will, all creation was subjected to God's curse. But with eager hope, 21 the creation looks forward to the day when it will join God's children in glorious freedom from death and decay. 22 For we know that all creation has been groaning as in the pains of childbirth right up to the present time. 23 And we believers also groan, even though we have the Holy Spirit within us as a foretaste of future glory, for we long for our bodies to be released from sin and suffering. We, too, wait with eager hope for the day when God will give us our full rights as his adopted children,* including the new bodies he has promised us. 24 We were given this hope when we were saved. (If we already have something, we don't need to hope* for it. 25 But if we look forward to something we don't yet have, we must wait patiently and confidently.)

26 And the Holy Spirit helps us in our weakness. For example, we don't know what God wants us to pray for. But the Holy Spirit prays for us with groanings that cannot be expressed in words. 27 And the Father who knows all hearts knows what the Spirit is saying, for the Spirit pleads for us believers* in harmony with God's own will. 28 And we know that God causes everything to work together* for the good of those who love God and are called according

SUFFERING AND HOPING

1. When have you endured suffering in order to gain something you wanted? What was the suffering? Did you get what you wanted?

ROMANS 8:18-27

2. What are sufferings we experience now (v. 18)? What is "the glory he will reveal to us later"?
3. What is it that Christians "look forward to" (v. 25)? Why must we wait with patience?
4. How does the Holy Spirit help us in waiting and hoping (v. 26)?
5. In what ways have you been "suffering" lately? How might these sufferings be leading to God's blessings?

8:14 Greek *sons;* also in 8:19. **8:15a** Greek *you received a spirit of sonship.* **8:15b** *Abba* is an Aramaic term for "father." **8:23** Greek *wait anxiously for sonship.* **8:24** Some manuscripts read *wait.* **8:27** Greek *for God's holy people.* **8:28** Some manuscripts read *And we know that everything works together.*

8:15 a spirit that makes you fearful of slaves. The Holy Spirit unites us with Christ, enabling us to share in His sonship. **you received.** The verb tense indicates that this is a one-time, past action—something that happened at conversion. **God's Spirit when he adopted you.** For a child to be adopted into a new family, he was first symbolically "sold" by his father to the adopting father. Then the legal case for adoption was taken to the magistrate.

8:16 his Spirit . . . to affirm. In the Roman adoptive proceedings, there were several witnesses to the ceremony who could verify that the child had actually been adopted. The Holy Spirit verifies a person's adoption into the family of God.

8:17 heirs. If a person is a child of God, he is an heir, and he will share in God's riches. In fact, Jesus is God's true heir (v. 3). But since believers are "in Christ," they become sons and daughters of God by adoption and thus are joint-heirs with Christ.

8:18 what we suffer now. This refers to the persecutions (5:3) that Christians face in the time between Jesus' first coming and His return. These sufferings are minor in comparison with the glory we will experience.

8:19 waiting eagerly. The image is of a person scanning the horizon for the first sign of the coming dawn of glory. The only other occurrence of this word in the New Testament is in Philippians 1:20. **when God will reveal who his children really are.** Christians are sons and daughters of God in this life. What Paul refers to here is that believers are incognito. At the second coming of Jesus, those who are the children of God will be revealed for everyone to see.

8:20 God's curse. The inability of creation to achieve the goal for which it was created—glorifying God—because the key actor in this drama of praise (mankind) has fallen. **with eager hope.** There was divine judgment at the original fall of mankind in Eden, but this was not without hope. One day the woman's offspring would strike the serpent (Gen. 3:15).

8:21 glorious freedom. Creation will be freed from its bondage at the second coming of Christ when the children of God are freed from the last vestiges of sin.

8:22 pains of childbirth. Such pain is intense, but it is only temporary. The image is not of the annihilation of the present universe but of the emergence of a transformed order (Rev. 21:1). Childbirth was a Jewish metaphor for the suffering that would precede the coming of the new age (Isa. 26:17).

8:23 foretaste. The experience by the believer of the work of the Holy Spirit is a pledge that God will one day grant all He has promised. **we long for our bodies to be released.** Believers' bodies are still subject to weakness, pain, and death. We long for the suffering to end and for the redemption of the body to be complete.

8:28 everything to work together. God takes that which is painful (the groans, the persecution, and even death—vv. 35-36) and brings profit out of it. **for the good of those who love God.** This does not mean things work out so believers preserve their comfort and convenience. Rather, such action on God's part enables these difficult experiences to assist in the process of salvation and growth. **those who love God and are called according to his purpose.** The love that people have for God is a reflection of the reality of God's love for them as expressed in His call to follow Christ.

THE POINT OF PAIN

1. When did you experience a painful separation from family or friends? How long did it take to get over it?

ROMANS 8:28-39

2. What does it mean to be "called according to his purpose" (v. 28)? What people are "called"?
3. According to verse 29, how does "everything to work together for the good" (v. 28)? What is the purpose of suffering?
4. If God "did not spare even his own Son" (v. 32), what does that mean about His willingness to bring good into your life?
5. Read verses 38-39. What can separate you from God's love? Is anything left out of that list?

to his purpose for them. 29 For God knew his people in
advance, and he chose them to become like his Son,
so that his Son would be the firstborn* among many
brothers and sisters. 30 And having chosen them, he
called them to come to him. And having called them,
he gave them right standing with himself. And hav-
ing given them right standing, he gave them his glo-
ry.

NOTHING CAN SEPARATE US FROM GOD'S LOVE

31 What shall we say about such wonderful things as
these? If God is for us, who can ever be against us?
32 Since he did not spare even his own Son but gave
him up for us all, won't he also give us everything
else? 33 Who dares accuse us whom God has chosen for
his own? No one—for God himself has given us right
standing with himself. 34 Who then will condemn us?
No one—for Christ Jesus died for us and was raised
to life for us, and he is sitting in the place of honor at
God's right hand, pleading for us.
35 Can anything ever separate us from Christ's love?
Does it mean he no longer loves us if we have trou-
ble or calamity, or are persecuted, or hungry, or des-
titute, or in danger, or threatened with death? 36 (As
the Scriptures say, "For your sake we are killed every
day; we are being slaughtered like sheep."*) 37 No, de-
spite all these things, overwhelming victory is ours
through Christ, who loved us.
38 And I am convinced that nothing can ever sepa-
rate us from God's love. Neither death nor life, neither
angels nor demons,* neither our fears for today nor
our worries about tomorrow—not even the powers
of hell can separate us from God's love. 39 No power in
the sky above or in the earth below—indeed, nothing
in all creation will ever be able to separate us from
the love of God that is revealed in Christ Jesus our
Lord.

GOD'S SELECTION OF ISRAEL

9 With Christ as my witness, I speak with utter
truthfulness. My conscience and the Holy Spirit
confirm it. 2 My heart is filled with bitter sorrow and
unending grief 3 for my people, my Jewish brothers
and sisters.* I would be willing to be forever cursed—
cut off from Christ!—if that would save them. 4 They
are the people of Israel, chosen to be God's adopted
children.* God revealed his glory to them. He made
covenants with them and gave them his law. He gave
them the privilege of worshiping him and receiving
his wonderful promises. 5 Abraham, Isaac, and Jacob
are their ancestors, and Christ himself was an Isra-
elite as far as his human nature is concerned. And he

RAGE OR MERCY?

1. When have you unexpectedly received mercy instead of punishment? What did you learn from that experience?

ROMANS 9:1-29

2. Paul says that not all Jews are children of God (vv. 6-7). Why? Who are the true children of God?
3. What does God mean when He says, "I will show mercy to anyone I choose" (v. 15)?
4. What does it mean that we cannot choose or work for God's mercy (v. 16)? What does it depend on?
5. Are you a child of God? How can you show mercy to others as God has shown it to you?

8:29 Or *would be supreme.* **8:36** Ps 44:22. **8:38** Greek *nor rulers.* **9:3** Greek *my brothers.* **9:4** Greek *chosen for sonship.*

8:29 knew . . . in advance. God knew even before the world was created who would have faith (Eph. 1:4; 2 Tim. 1:9). For God to know someone is for Him to love and have a purpose for that person. **chose.** God puts into effect what He foreknew. **to become like his Son.** While Paul has in mind that time of glorification (when believers will be brought into full conformity to the image of Christ), he is also thinking of sanctification. This is the process by which believers grow closer and closer to the image of Christ.

8:30 called. Foreknowledge and predestination are God's prerogatives. They enter the realm of history at the point of His calling or initiative with each person, bringing that person to hear the gospel and responds in faith. The end result is justification.

8:31 If God . . . against us? Paul does not ask, "Who is against us?" In response, many enemies could be named: hostile society, Satan, sin, suffering, and death. Rather, he prefaces the question with an assertion that "God is for us" and then asks, "Who is against us?" All potential enemies fade into insignificance.

8:32 not spare even his own Son. Again Paul does not ask, "Will not God give us all things?" He indicates that God has already given the supreme gift—His Son who died on our behalf.

8:33-34 Who dares. Paul's next two questions are set in the context of a law court. The point of these questions is that there is no charge that can be leveled against Christians to cause their condemnation since God is the Judge who has already justified them.

8:35 Can anything separate us. In response to this question, Paul names those enemies that might appear powerful enough to separate believers from God's love.

8:37 overwhelming victory. Literally, super-conquerors.

8:38 death . . . life. For Paul, to die was not a threat—it was to "be with Christ" (Phil. 1:21-23). Life is used here in the sense of trials, distractions, and enticements that could lead a person away from God. **angels . . . demons.** Continuing his pairing of opposites, Paul says that neither benevolent nor evil spiritual powers need be feared. **today . . . tomorrow.** Neither this age nor the events in the future age (after the end time) are to be feared.

8:39 sky above . . . earth below. The reference could also be to the influence of a star at the height or depth of its zenith. It may simply mean that neither heaven nor hell can separate Christians from God's love.

9:4 adopted. Israel has a special relationship with God. The word *adoption* emphasizes that this relationship is by grace—a product of God's action and not the result of natural succession. **worshipping him.** Through the sacrificial system, Israel had special access to God. **promises.** Old Testament prophecies, which emphasized that God had a great and noble task for Israel.

is God, the one who rules over everything and is wor-
thy of eternal praise! Amen.*
6 Well then, has God failed to fulfill his promise to
Israel? No, for not all who are born into the nation
of Israel are truly members of God's people! 7 Being
descendants of Abraham doesn't make them truly
Abraham's children. For the Scriptures say, "Isaac
is the son through whom your descendants will be
counted,"* though Abraham had other children, too.
8 This means that Abraham's physical descendants
are not necessarily children of God. Only the children
of the promise are considered to be Abraham's chil-
dren. 9 For God had promised, "I will return about this
time next year, and Sarah will have a son."*
10 This son was our ancestor Isaac. When he mar-
ried Rebekah, she gave birth to twins.* 11 But before
they were born, before they had done anything good
or bad, she received a message from God. (This mes-
sage shows that God chooses people according to his
own purposes; 12 he calls people, but not according to
their good or bad works.) She was told, "Your older
son will serve your younger son."* 13 In the words of
the Scriptures, "I loved Jacob, but I rejected Esau."*
14 Are we saying, then, that God was unfair? Of
course not! 15 For God said to Moses,

"I will show mercy to anyone I choose,
and I will show compassion to anyone I
choose."*

16 So it is God who decides to show mercy. We can nei-
ther choose it nor work for it.
17 For the Scriptures say that God told Pharaoh, "I
have appointed you for the very purpose of display-
ing my power in you and to spread my fame through-
out the earth."* 18 So you see, God chooses to show
mercy to some, and he chooses to harden the hearts of
others so they refuse to listen.
19 Well then, you might say, "Why does God blame
people for not responding? Haven't they simply done
what he makes them do?"
20 No, don't say that. Who are you, a mere human
being, to argue with God? Should the thing that was
created say to the one who created it, "Why have you
made me like this?" 21 When a potter makes jars out
of clay, doesn't he have a right to use the same lump
of clay to make one jar for decoration and another to
throw garbage into? 22 In the same way, even though
God has the right to show his anger and his power,
he is very patient with those on whom his anger falls,
who are destined for destruction. 23 He does this to
make the riches of his glory shine even brighter on
those to whom he shows mercy, who were prepared
in advance for glory. 24 And we are among those
whom he selected, both from the Jews and from the
Gentiles.
25 Concerning the Gentiles, God says in the proph-
ecy of Hosea,

"Those who were not my people,
I will now call my people.
And I will love those
whom I did not love before."*

26 And,

"Then, at the place where they were told,
'You are not my people,'
there they will be called
'children of the living God.'"*

27 And concerning Israel, Isaiah the prophet cried out,

"Though the people of Israel are as numerous as
the sand of the seashore,
only a remnant will be saved.
28 For the LORD will carry out his sentence upon the
earth
quickly and with finality."*

29 And Isaiah said the same thing in another place:

"If the LORD of Heaven's Armies
had not spared a few of our children,
we would have been wiped out like Sodom,
destroyed like Gomorrah."*

9:5 Or *May God, the one who rules over everything, be praised forever. Amen.* **9:7** Gen 21:12. **9:9** Gen 18:10, 14. **9:10** Greek *she conceived children through this one man.* **9:12** Gen 25:23. **9:13** Mal 1:2-3. **9:15** Exod 33:19. **9:17** Exod 9:16 (Greek version). **9:25** Hos 2:23. **9:26** Greek *sons of the living God.* Hos 1:10. **9:27-28** Isa 10:22-23 (Greek version). **9:29** Isa 1:9 (Greek version).

9:8 children of the promise. To be a physical descendant of Abraham is not necessarily to be a part of the true Israel. Paul will soon point out that there has always been a remnant of Jews within the larger nation of Israel who were true to God (11:1-15).

9:15-16 God who decides to show mercy. Paul used Exodus 33:19 to show the freedom of God's mercy. God is free to offer His mercy to whomever He chooses.

9:21 a potter . . . have right to use . . .? Paul draws on an image that both Isaiah and Jeremiah used in picturing the relationship of God to human beings. The clay is what it is. It doesn't argue with the potter about how it is shaped. One of the illusions that sin creates is that we can show that God is unjust. Even Job, whom God characterized as a man of perfect integrity (Job 1:1), thought he could bring God to court and demonstrate that God had treated him unfairly. Through an agonizing process Job learned what it means that God is God and we are not. As people whose minds and hearts have been corrupted by sin, we have difficulty grasping the infinite distance between God and ourselves. Only by God's mercy do we begin to recognize how totally dependent we are on Him for everything.

9:22 destined for destruction. The Greek verb translated "destined" carries the sense that destruction is the natural outcome for objects of wrath.

9:23 on those to whom he shows mercy, who were prepared in advance. The Greek verb translated "prepared in advance" is a different Greek work than is translated "destined" in v. 22. While v. 22 has the connotation that destruction is the natural course of objects of wrath, v. 23 gives the sense that for objects of mercy there has been an interruption to change the outcome from destruction to glory. In their commentary on Romans, Ken Boa and William Kruidenier ask us to "picture the flow of God's action, before any mercy is exercised, as a river. His justice sees that all people are flowing in the direction of judgment. That is his will because it is consistent with his justice. None in the flow of that river are resisting his will because there are none who seek God. It is the flow (the purpose) of his will that is carrying them along, and all are acting in concert with his will, not resisting his will. God is not standing on the banks crying out for them to turn to him and be saved, only to discover that they are resisting his will. When his purpose for some changes, and his hand of mercy is extended to them, they are given a new heart, a clean heart, and are saved willingly. The not-chosen do not remain where they are against either their own will or God's will. Therefore, none resist his will."

9:27 only a remnant will be saved. Remnant is a key Bible concept. A remnant is something left over, especially the righteous people of God after divine judgment. Several activities of everyday life are associated with these words. Objects or people may be separated from a larger group by selection, assignment, consumption (eating food), or by destruction. What is left over is the residue, or, in the case of people, those who remain after an epidemic, famine, drought, or war. One of the first cases of this in the Bible is God's saving Noah and his family from the flood. In this verse, Paul makes a distinction between Israel and the remnant who will be saved out of Israel.

CALLING HEAVEN'S NUMBER

1. When have you called on someone in authority for help? Did you get the help you needed? Why did you need it in the first place?

ROMANS 9:30–10:21

2. What is the only way to be saved, according to Paul in 10:9-10? How does this compare with other religious teachings? With the teachings of the world around you?
3. What does it mean to "call on the name of the LORD" (10:13)?
4. What does verse 14 suggest about the importance of sharing Jesus with others? How often do you tell others about Jesus? How can you do this more often?

ISRAEL'S UNBELIEF

30 What does all this mean? Even though the Gentiles
were not trying to follow God's standards, they were
made right with God. And it was by faith that this
took place. 31 But the people of Israel, who tried so
hard to get right with God by keeping the law, nev-
er succeeded. 32 Why not? Because they were trying
to get right with God by keeping the law* instead of
by trusting in him. They stumbled over the great rock
in their path. 33 God warned them of this in the Scrip-
tures when he said,

"I am placing a stone in Jerusalem* that makes
people stumble,
a rock that makes them fall.
But anyone who trusts in him
will never be disgraced."*

10 Dear brothers and sisters,* the longing of my
heart and my prayer to God is for the people
of Israel to be saved. 2 I know what enthusiasm they
have for God, but it is misdirected zeal. 3 For they don't
understand God's way of making people right with
himself. Refusing to accept God's way, they cling to
their own way of getting right with God by trying to
keep the law. 4 For Christ has already accomplished
the purpose for which the law was given.* As a result,
all who believe in him are made right with God.

SALVATION IS FOR EVERYONE

5 For Moses writes that the law's way of making a
person right with God requires obedience to all of
its commands.* 6 But faith's way of getting right with
God says, "Don't say in your heart, 'Who will go up to
heaven?' (to bring Christ down to earth). 7 And don't
say, 'Who will go down to the place of the dead?' (to
bring Christ back to life again)." 8 In fact, it says,

"The message is very close at hand;
it is on your lips and in your heart."*

And that message is the very message about faith that
we preach: 9 If you openly declare that Jesus is Lord
and believe in your heart that God raised him from
the dead, you will be saved. 10 For it is by believing in
your heart that you are made right with God, and it
is by openly declaring your faith that you are saved.
11 As the Scriptures tell us, "Anyone who trusts in him
will never be disgraced."* 12 Jew and Gentile* are the
same in this respect. They have the same Lord, who
gives generously to all who call on him. 13 For "Every-
one who calls on the name of the LORD will be saved."*
14 But how can they call on him to save them un-
less they believe in him? And how can they believe
in him if they have never heard about him? And how
can they hear about him unless someone tells them?
15 And how will anyone go and tell them without be-
ing sent? That is why the Scriptures say, "How beauti-
ful are the feet of messengers who bring good news!"*
16 But not everyone welcomes the Good News, for
Isaiah the prophet said, "LORD, who has believed our
message?"* 17 So faith comes from hearing, that is,
hearing the Good News about Christ. 18 But I ask, have
the people of Israel actually heard the message? Yes,
they have:

"The message has gone throughout the earth,
and the words to all the world."*

19 But I ask, did the people of Israel really understand?
Yes, they did, for even in the time of Moses, God said,

"I will rouse your jealousy through people who
are not even a nation.
I will provoke your anger through the foolish
Gentiles."*

20 And later Isaiah spoke boldly for God, saying,

"I was found by people who were not looking for
me.
I showed myself to those who were not asking
for me."*

21 But regarding Israel, God said,

"All day long I opened my arms to them,
but they were disobedient and rebellious."*

9:32 Greek *by works.* **9:33a** Greek *in Zion.* **9:33b** Isa 8:14; 28:16 (Greek version). **10:1** Greek *Brothers.* **10:4** Or *For Christ is the end of the law.* **10:5** See Lev 18:5. **10:6-8** Deut 30:12-14. **10:11** Isa 28:16 (Greek version). **10:12** Greek *and Greek.* **10:13** Joel 2:32. **10:15** Isa 52:7. **10:16** Isa 53:1. **10:18** Ps 19:4. **10:19** Deut 32:21. **10:20** Isa 65:1 (Greek version). **10:21** Isa 65:2 (Greek version).

9:32 great rock. Jesus identifies himself as "the stone that the builders rejected" (Ps. 118:22-23; Matt. 21:42). In not recognizing Jesus as the inner meaning of the law, Israel can do little else than stumble over Him.
10:6 Who will go up to heaven? This phrase means that Israel does not have to go all the way up to heaven to find God's law (Deut. 30:12). The righteousness of the law is found in Christ—Christ had come to them. Now, righteousness is obtained only through our faith.
10:7 bring Christ back to life again. There is no need to bring Christ up from the dead, since He has already been inside the abyss after His death on the cross. He conquered sin and death, and then was raised from the dead.
10:12 are the same. In 3:23, when Jews and non-Jews are discussed, the emphasis is negative—all are sinners. Here, the positive comparison is given: The Lord is available to all people who call on Him.
10:15 go and tell. This means to proclaim like a herald. Proclamation or preaching came to refer to declaring the gospel message of Jesus' salvation to all who believe (16:28-26).

GOD'S MERCY ON ISRAEL

11 I ask, then, has God rejected his own people, the nation of Israel? Of course not! I myself am an Israelite, a descendant of Abraham and a member of the tribe of Benjamin.

[2] No, God has not rejected his own people, whom he chose from the very beginning. Do you realize what the Scriptures say about this? Elijah the prophet complained to God about the people of Israel and said, [3] "LORD, they have killed your prophets and torn down your altars. I am the only one left, and now they are trying to kill me, too."*

[4] And do you remember God's reply? He said, "No, I have 7,000 others who have never bowed down to Baal!"*

[5] It is the same today, for a few of the people of Israel* have remained faithful because of God's grace—his undeserved kindness in choosing them. [6] And since it is through God's kindness, then it is not by their good works. For in that case, God's grace would not be what it really is—free and undeserved.

[7] So this is the situation: Most of the people of Israel have not found the favor of God they are looking for so earnestly. A few have—the ones God has chosen—but the hearts of the rest were hardened. [8] As the Scriptures say,

"God has put them into a deep sleep.
To this day he has shut their eyes so they do not see,
and closed their ears so they do not hear."*

[9] Likewise, David said,

"Let their bountiful table become a snare,
a trap that makes them think all is well.
Let their blessings cause them to stumble,
and let them get what they deserve.
10 Let their eyes go blind so they cannot see,
and let their backs be bent forever."*

[11] Did God's people stumble and fall beyond recovery? Of course not! They were disobedient, so God made salvation available to the Gentiles. But he wanted his own people to become jealous and claim it for themselves. [12] Now if the Gentiles were enriched because the people of Israel turned down God's offer of salvation, think how much greater a blessing the world will share when they finally accept it.

[13] I am saying all this especially for you Gentiles. God has appointed me as the apostle to the Gentiles. I stress this, [14] for I want somehow to make the people of Israel jealous of what you Gentiles have, so I might save some of them. [15] For since their rejection meant that God offered salvation to the rest of the world, their acceptance will be even more wonderful. It will be life for those who were dead! [16] And since Abraham and the other patriarchs were holy, their descendants will also be holy—just as the entire batch of dough is holy because the portion given as an offering is holy. For if the roots of the tree are holy, the branches will be, too.

[17] But some of these branches from Abraham's tree—some of the people of Israel—have been broken off. And you Gentiles, who were branches from a wild olive tree, have been grafted in. So now you also receive the blessing God has promised Abraham and his children, sharing in the rich nourishment from the root of God's special olive tree. [18] But you must not brag about being grafted in to replace the branches that were broken off. You are just a branch, not the root.

[19] "Well," you may say, "those branches were broken off to make room for me." [20] Yes, but remember—those branches were broken off because they didn't believe in Christ, and you are there because you do believe. So don't think highly of yourself, but fear what could happen. [21] For if God did not spare the original branches, he won't* spare you either.

[22] Notice how God is both kind and severe. He is severe toward those who disobeyed, but kind to you if you continue to trust in his kindness. But if you stop trusting, you also will be cut off. [23] And if the people of Israel turn from their unbelief, they will be grafted in again, for God has the power to graft them back into the tree. [24] You, by nature, were a branch cut from a wild olive tree. So if God was willing to do something contrary to nature by grafting you into his cultivated tree, he will be far more eager to graft the original branches back into the tree where they belong.

WORKS VS. FAITH

1. When have you fallen for a trap: In sports? From a friend or enemy? What did you learn?

ROMANS 11:1-36

2. How can good works "become a snare and a trap" (v. 9)?
3. How do you balance works and grace? What can good works never accomplish? In what ways are works still important?
4. Are you relying more on performance of rituals than on God's grace? Are you taking God's grace for granted?
5. What are you depending on for your own salvation? Are you obedient even though you've been saved by faith?

11:3 1 Kgs 19:10, 14. **11:4** 1 Kgs 19:18. **11:5** Greek *for a remnant.* **11:8** Isa 29:10; Deut 29:4. **11:9-10** Ps 69:22-23 (Greek version). **11:21** Some manuscripts read *perhaps he won't.*

11:1 I myself am a Israelite. Paul, who remains a zealous Jew who happens to be a believing Christian, is proof that God has not cast off Israel. He is still using Israel, through Paul and others, to fulfill its God-given task of bearing God's redemptive message to the world.

11:5 few. There was always at least a small number of people who were true to God. Through history, God has preserved a faithful remnant of His people, even in wicked times. They were like a nation within a nation.

11:7 have not found the favor of God they are looking for. The nation of Israel was looking for righteousness, but they thought they earned righteous by keeping the law. The blood of Jesus is now the channel through which righteousness is obtained.

11:14 jealous. Jealousy or envy is usually something that is negative. In this case it brings about good. **save.** God's goal was to convert people to the Christian faith and redeem them.

11:17 branches ... broken off. Paul is referring here to unbelieving Israel. **a wild olive tree.** The Gentile (non-Jewish) Christians.

GOD'S MERCY IS FOR EVERYONE

25 I want you to understand this mystery, dear broth-
ers and sisters,* so that you will not feel proud about
yourselves. Some of the people of Israel have hard
hearts, but this will last only until the full number of
Gentiles comes to Christ. 26 And so all Israel will be
saved. As the Scriptures say,

"The one who rescues will come from Jerusalem,*
  and he will turn Israel* away from ungodliness.
27 And this is my covenant with them,
  that I will take away their sins."*

28 Many of the people of Israel are now enemies
of the Good News, and this benefits you Gentiles. Yet
they are still the people he loves because he chose
their ancestors Abraham, Isaac, and Jacob. 29 For God's
gifts and his call can never be withdrawn. 30 Once, you
Gentiles were rebels against God, but when the peo-
ple of Israel rebelled against him, God was merciful
to you instead. 31 Now they are the rebels, and God's
mercy has come to you so that they, too, will share*
in God's mercy. 32 For God has imprisoned everyone in
disobedience so he could have mercy on everyone.
33 Oh, how great are God's riches and wisdom and
knowledge! How impossible it is for us to understand
his decisions and his ways!

34 For who can know the LORD's thoughts?
  Who knows enough to give him advice?*
35 And who has given him so much
  that he needs to pay it back?*

36 For everything comes from him and exists by his
power and is intended for his glory. All glory to him
forever! Amen.

A LIVING SACRIFICE TO GOD

12 And so, dear brothers and sisters,* I plead with
you to give your bodies to God because of all he
has done for you. Let them be a living and holy sac-
rifice—the kind he will find acceptable. This is truly
the way to worship him.* 2 Don't copy the behavior
and customs of this world, but let God transform you
into a new person by changing the way you think.
Then you will learn to know God's will for you, which
is good and pleasing and perfect.
3 Because of the privilege and authority* God has
given me, I give each of you this warning: Don't think
you are better than you really are. Be honest in your
evaluation of yourselves, measuring yourselves by
the faith God has given us.* 4 Just as our bodies have
many parts and each part has a special function, 5 so it
is with Christ's body. We are many parts of one body,
and we all belong to each other.
6 In his grace, God has given us different gifts for
doing certain things well. So if God has given you the
ability to prophesy, speak out with as much faith as
God has given you. 7 If your gift is serving others, serve
them well. If you are a teacher, teach well. 8 If your gift
is to encourage others, be encouraging. If it is giving,
give generously. If God has given you leadership abil-
ity, take the responsibility seriously. And if you have a
gift for showing kindness to others, do it gladly.

YOU WILL BE ASSIMILATED!

1. When have you thought of yourself more highly than you should have? How did you discover your error?

ROMANS 12:1-8

2. What does Paul mean in verse 2 when he says, "Don't copy the behavior and customs of this world, but let God transform you into a new person by changing the way you think"?
3. How can you offer your body as "a living and holy sacrifice" (v. 1)?
4. According to this passage, what is required of you to discover God's will for your life?
5. How much are you conforming to the world's standards? Are you working to transform your mind to God's way of thinking?

11:25 Greek *brothers.* **11:26a** Greek *from Zion.* **11:26b** Greek *Jacob.* **11:26-27** Isa 59:20-21; 27:9 (Greek version). **11:31** Other manuscripts read *will now share;* still others read *will someday share.* **11:34** Isa 40:13 (Greek version). **11:35** See Job 41:11. **12:1a** Greek *brothers.* **12:1b** Or *This is your spiritual worship;* or *This is your reasonable service.* **12:3a** Or *Because of the grace;* compare 1:5. **12:3b** Or *by the faith God has given you;* or *by the standard of our God-given faith.*

11:25 mystery. This is something that is hidden in the mind of God, but which He is now pleased to reveal to all who are willing to seek Him.

12:1 all he has done for you. Paul has just declared God's amazing mercy (11:30-32). A Christian's motivation to obedience is gratitude for God's mercy. **bodies.** The Christian lifestyle is not a matter of mystical spirituality that transcends one's bodily nature but an everyday, practical exercise of love (6:13). The idea of "bodies" also emphasizes the metaphor of sacrifice since animal bodies were put on the altar. **living . . . holy . . . the kind he would find acceptable.** In Greek, these three phrases are attached with equal weight as requirements for "sacrifices."

12:2 Don't copy. Literally, "stop allowing yourself to be conformed." Believers are no longer helpless victims of natural and supernatural forces that shape them into a distorted pattern; they now have the ability and help to resist such powers. **transform.** The force of the verb is "continue to let yourself be transformed"—a continuous action by the Holy Spirit that goes on for a lifetime. A Christian's responsibility is to stay open to this sanctification process as the Spirit works to teach him or her to look at life from God's view of reality. **changing the way you think.** Developing a spiritual sensitivity and perception—learning to look at life on the basis of God's view of reality. Paul emphasizes the need to develop understanding of God's ways. **you will learn to know God's will for you.** Christians are called to a responsible freedom of choice and action based on the inner renewing work of the Holy Spirit.

12:3 each of you. The truth about spiritual gifts applies to every believer. **be honest in your evaluation.** The command is to know oneself accurately rather than to have too high an opinion of oneself in comparison to others.

12:5 We are many parts of one body. Paul is speaking here of believers in the church, the body of Christ. The church is like a family. Although individual members of the family are distinct and different, they belong to one another because of the common Lord whom they serve.

12:6 gifts. Those endowments given by God to every believer by grace (the words *grace* and *gifts* come from the same root word) to be used in God's service. The gifts listed here (or elsewhere in the New Testament) are not meant to be exhaustive or absolute since no gift list overlaps completely. **to prophesy.** Inspired utterances, distinguished from teaching by their immediacy and spontaneous nature, the source of which is direct revelation by God.

12:7 serving others. The special capacity for rendering practical service to the needy. **a teacher.** In contrast to the prophet (with direct revelation from God), the teacher relied on the Old Testament Scriptures and the teachings of Jesus to instruct others.

12:8 encourage. This is supporting and assisting others to live a life of obedience to God. **giving.** A person with this gift takes delight in giving away his or her possessions. **leadership ability.** Those with special ability to guide a congregation are called upon to do so with zeal. **showing kindness.** Serving those who need care with cheerfulness.

9 Don't just pretend to love others. Really love them.
Hate what is wrong. Hold tightly to what is good.
10 Love each other with genuine affection,* and take
delight in honoring each other. 11 Never be lazy, but
work hard and serve the Lord enthusiastically.* 12 Re-
joice in our confident hope. Be patient in trouble, and
keep on praying. 13 When God's people are in need, be
ready to help them. Always be eager to practice hos-
pitality.
14 Bless those who persecute you. Don't curse them;
pray that God will bless them. 15 Be happy with those
who are happy, and weep with those who weep.
16 Live in harmony with each other. Don't be too proud
to enjoy the company of ordinary people. And don't
think you know it all!
17 Never pay back evil with more evil. Do things in
such a way that everyone can see you are honorable.
18 Do all that you can to live in peace with everyone.
19 Dear friends, never take revenge. Leave that to
the righteous anger of God. For the Scriptures say,

"I will take revenge;
I will pay them back,"*
says the LORD.

20 Instead,

"If your enemies are hungry, feed them.
If they are thirsty, give them something to drink.
In doing this, you will heap
burning coals of shame on their heads."*

21 Don't let evil conquer you, but conquer evil by doing
good.

RESPECT FOR AUTHORITY

13 Everyone must submit to governing authorities.
For all authority comes from God, and those
in positions of authority have been placed there by
God. 2 So anyone who rebels against authority is re-
belling against what God has instituted, and they will
be punished. 3 For the authorities do not strike fear
in people who are doing right, but in those who are
doing wrong. Would you like to live without fear of
the authorities? Do what is right, and they will hon-
or you. 4 The authorities are God's servants, sent for
your good. But if you are doing wrong, of course you
should be afraid, for they have the power to punish
you. They are God's servants, sent for the very pur-
pose of punishing those who do what is wrong. 5 So
you must submit to them, not only to avoid punish-
ment, but also to keep a clear conscience.
6 Pay your taxes, too, for these same reasons. For
government workers need to be paid. They are serv-
ing God in what they do. 7 Give to everyone what you

HONORING OTHERS

1. To whom do you find yourself showing real honor? Why do you honor that person? How do you express it?

ROMANS 12:9-21

2. How do we sometimes show love with hypocrisy (v. 9)? What does love without hypocrisy look like?
3. What does it mean to "take delight in honoring each other" (v. 10)? How can we honor others in this way?
4. What can you do this week, in a practical way, to "live at peace" with someone who irritates you?
5. How have you sometimes thought you know it all (v. 16)? How can you avoid this?

GOD-GIVEN AUTHORITY

1. What is the closest you have come to having a "run-in" with the police?

ROMANS 13:1-7

2. What does it mean that "all authority comes from God" (v. 1)? What about people who abuse their authority? Those who are incompetent?
3. According to this passage, what should our response be to all people in authority over us?
4. If a law passed by Congress was contrary to God's law, what would you do?
5. Do you ever try to cheat on taxes, tolls, and school or team rules? What does Paul say about this?

12:10 Greek *with brotherly love.* **12:11** Or *but serve the Lord with a zealous spirit;* or *but let the Spirit excite you as you serve the Lord.* **12:19** Deut 32:35. **12:20** Prov 25:21-22.

12:9 Love. The Greek word *agape*—self-giving love in action on behalf of others—which is made possible by God's Spirit. **pretend.** Genuine, not counterfeit or showy.

12:10 genuine affection. The word for love used here, *philadelphia*, denotes the tender affection expressed in families, now said to be appropriate to those in the church—which is the believer's new family. **honoring.** Since other Christians are in union with Christ, they are to be honored.

12:11 enthusiastically. This Greek word is also used of water when it has been brought to a boil (or of metal, like copper, which glows red-hot in the refining or shaping process).

13:1 Everyone. That is, every Christian in Rome; no one is exempt. **submit.** Submission must be understood in light of 12:10 (honoring others above oneself) and Philippians 2:3-4 (considering others as more important). Christians must recognize the God-given claim that the authorities have upon them.

13:3-4 authorities are God's servants. Paul, both a Roman citizen and a Jew, was not being naive when he wrote this. Although he grew up in Tarsus of Cilicia, he lived in Jerusalem as a student of Gamaliel. From his wide reading and first hand experience, he knew the character of the Roman emperors, and he was aware of the suffering of occupied peoples at the hands of Roman authorities. Christians had lived under Caligula (A.D. 37-41) and Claudius (A.D 41-54). As Paul wrote this letter (A.D. 57), Nero was 18 and had been Emperor for three years. How can these pagans be God's servant and why should Christians submit to them? The answer lies in the sovereignty of God. God brought the Roman emperors to power, and he deposed of them. **punishing those who do what is wrong.** Governments can't make bad people good, but they can use force to restrain evil. That's what God has charged them to do whether they know it or not.

13:5 submit . . .to avoid punishment. Paul gives two motivations for submitting to the government. The first is to avoid punishment. **to keep a clear conscience.** A higher motive for submission is to maintain a clear conscience. Although a clear conscience is not infallible, a bad conscience will adversely affect one's relationship with God, with fellow believers and with those outside the family of faith.

13:7 taxes. Local taxes such as duty, import and export taxes, taxes for the use of roads or for the right to drive a cart, etc.

owe them: Pay your taxes and government fees to those who collect them, and give respect and honor to those who are in authority.

LOVE FULFILLS GOD'S REQUIREMENTS

[8]Owe nothing to anyone—except for your obligation to love one another. If you love your neighbor, you will fulfill the requirements of God's law. [9]For the commandments say, "You must not commit adultery. You must not murder. You must not steal. You must not covet."* These—and other such commandments—are summed up in this one commandment: "Love your neighbor as yourself."* [10]Love does no wrong to others, so love fulfills the requirements of God's law.

[11]This is all the more urgent, for you know how late it is; time is running out. Wake up, for our salvation is nearer now than when we first believed. [12]The night is almost gone; the day of salvation will soon be here. So remove your dark deeds like dirty clothes, and put on the shining armor of right living. [13]Because we belong to the day, we must live decent lives for all to see. Don't participate in the darkness of wild parties and drunkenness, or in sexual promiscuity and immoral living, or in quarreling and jealousy. [14]Instead, clothe yourself with the presence of the Lord Jesus Christ. And don't let yourself think about ways to indulge your evil desires.

THE POWER OF LOVE

1. Who supports you with their love?

ROMANS 13:8-14

2. How does love fulfill all of the other commandments (v. 9)?
3. The Bible teaches us to love others as we love ourselves. How does this compare with the world's teaching that we must love ourselves?
4. Paul says, "Love does no wrong to others" (v. 10). How does this compare with the world's teaching that we should look after our own interests?
5. What does it mean to "live decent lives" (v. 13)?
6. How can you work harder at loving others more than yourself?

THE DANGER OF CRITICISM

14 Accept other believers who are weak in faith, and don't argue with them about what they think is right or wrong. [2]For instance, one person believes it's all right to eat anything. But another believer with a sensitive conscience will eat only vegetables. [3]Those who feel free to eat anything must not look down on those who don't. And those who don't eat certain foods must not condemn those who do, for God has accepted them. [4]Who are you to condemn someone else's servants? Their own master will judge whether they stand or fall. And with the Lord's help, they will stand and receive his approval.

[5]In the same way, some think one day is more holy than another day, while others think every day is alike. You should each be fully convinced that whichever day you choose is acceptable. [6]Those who worship the Lord on a special day do it to honor him. Those who eat any kind of food do so to honor the Lord, since they give thanks to God before eating. And those who refuse to eat certain foods also want to please the Lord and give thanks to God. [7]For we don't live for ourselves or die for ourselves. [8]If we live, it's to honor the Lord. And if we die, it's to honor the Lord. So whether we live or die, we belong to the Lord. [9]Christ died and rose again for this very purpose—to be Lord both of the living and of the dead.

[10]So why do you condemn another believer*? Why do you look down on another believer? Remember, we will all stand before the judgment seat of God. [11]For the Scriptures say,

"'As surely as I live,' says the LORD,
'every knee will bend to me,
and every tongue will declare allegiance to God.*'"

[12]Yes, each of us will give a personal account to God. [13]So let's stop condemning each other. Decide instead

13:9a Exod 20:13-15, 17. **13:9b** Lev 19:18. **14:10** Greek *your brother;* also in 14:10b, 13, 15, 21. **14:11** Or *declare praise for God.* Isa 49:18; 45:23 (Greek version).

13:10 love fulfills the requirements of God's law. Jesus summarized the law with two love-commands (Matt 22:37,39).

13:11 time. Although the distinction is not absolute, there are two words in the NT that emphasize these two dimensions of time. *Chronos* is the Greek term usually referring simply to the chronological measurement of time, while *kairos* usually refers to the spiritual significance of an era (Rom. 5:6, 13:11; Titus 1:3; Rev. 1:3). Christians should be careful to discern the meaning and significance of their time, comprehending both the reality of evil and the movement of God in history. **salvation.** Here understood as a divine event that will take place at a particular time in the future. Although a person enters into salvation upon conversion, this is a state to be realized fully only when Christ returns at the second coming.

13:12 night. The present age. **daylight.** The coming age inaugurated by Christ's second coming, in which God's new order will appear. **the day of salvation will soon be here.** The early church understood that the life, death, and resurrection of Jesus had ushered in the last days—the end time. But because of His patience, God had provided an interval before the culmination of the "night," in order to allow other people to come to faith. During this interval Christians are to remain alert and expectant, knowing that the second coming may occur at any time. **shining armor of right living.** Character and behavior that a person obtains from God and which will also be appropriate to wear when the new age dawns (Eph. 6:11-12).

13:13 sexual promiscuity. In the first century, prior to Christianity, chastity or sexual purity was almost unknown and was not considered a virtue by most people. **immoral living.** Public display, without shame, of immoral acts. **quarreling.** The desire for power and prestige demonstrated by a willingness to stir up trouble if one is not in charge. **jealousy.** Envy that begrudges another's place or gifts.

14:1 Accept other believers. This is the basic imperative addressed to the "strong" majority in the church: receive the "weak" into fellowship. **who are weak in faith.** Those who are not sure their faith is adequate to do certain things. The issue is not a lack of faith in Christ. Both the "weak" and the "strong" are authentically Christian. **what they think is right or wrong.** Do not judge the principles of others that are not essential to following Christ.

14:3 look down . . . condemn. Two forms of judgment: the tendency of the "strong" not to take seriously the moral convictions of the weak (to laugh at them or even to despise them); and the tendency of the "weak" to act superior and become hypercritical (because they felt that not doing certain things made them better Christians). Both attitudes are wrong. **God has accepted them.** The person who abstains cannot condemn those who indulge since no one should judge a person whom God has accepted.

14:13 stumble and fall. A new theme is introduced into the discussion: the liberty of the strong can be detrimental to others. What appears to the strong as an innocent action may cause the more scrupulous or morally rigid people to suffer pain, shock, outrage, or even hurt.

DOUBTFUL ISSUES

1. What foods do you avoid eating? Why? What foods do you eat freely?

ROMANS 14:1–15:13

2. Why does Paul say, "don't argue . . . about what they think is right or wrong" (v. 1)? How do you know the difference between minor issues and important ones?
3. What are some issues that Christians have argued about in your church? Are any of those minor issues?
4. If someone disagrees with you about a minor issues what is the correct response: To argue back? To give up your rights for his or her benefit? Other?
5. Do you use Christian liberty as an excuse to do what you want? Why or why not?

to live in such a way that you will not cause another
believer to stumble and fall.
14 I know and am convinced on the authority of the
Lord Jesus that no food, in and of itself, is wrong to eat.
But if someone believes it is wrong, then for that per-
son it is wrong. 15 And if another believer is distressed
by what you eat, you are not acting in love if you eat
it. Don't let your eating ruin someone for whom Christ
died. 16 Then you will not be criticized for doing some-
thing you believe is good. 17 For the Kingdom of God is
not a matter of what we eat or drink, but of living a
life of goodness and peace and joy in the Holy Spirit.
18 If you serve Christ with this attitude, you will please
God, and others will approve of you, too. 19 So then,
let us aim for harmony in the church and try to build
each other up.
20 Don't tear apart the work of God over what you
eat. Remember, all foods are acceptable, but it is
wrong to eat something if it makes another person
stumble. 21 It is better not to eat meat or drink wine or
do anything else if it might cause another believer to
stumble.* 22 You may believe there's nothing wrong
with what you are doing, but keep it between your-
self and God. Blessed are those who don't feel guilty
for doing something they have decided is right. 23 But
if you have doubts about whether or not you should
eat something, you are sinning if you go ahead and
do it. For you are not following your convictions. If
you do anything you believe is not right, you are sin-
ning.*

LIVING TO PLEASE OTHERS

15 We who are strong must be considerate of those
who are sensitive about things like this. We
must not just please ourselves. 2 We should help others
do what is right and build them up in the Lord. 3 For
even Christ didn't live to please himself. As the Scrip-
tures say, "The insults of those who insult you, O God,
have fallen on me."* 4 Such things were written in the
Scriptures long ago to teach us. And the Scriptures
give us hope and encouragement as we wait patiently
for God's promises to be fulfilled.
5 May God, who gives this patience and encourage-
ment, help you live in complete harmony with each
other, as is fitting for followers of Christ Jesus. 6 Then
all of you can join together with one voice, giving
praise and glory to God, the Father of our Lord Jesus
Christ.
7 Therefore, accept each other just as Christ has ac-
cepted you so that God will be given glory. 8 Remem-
ber that Christ came as a servant to the Jews* to show
that God is true to the promises he made to their an-
cestors. 9 He also came so that the Gentiles might give
glory to God for his mercies to them. That is what the
psalmist meant when he wrote:

"For this, I will praise you among the Gentiles;
I will sing praises to your name."*

10 And in another place it is written,

"Rejoice with his people,
you Gentiles."*

11 And yet again,

"Praise the LORD, all you Gentiles.
Praise him, all you people of the earth."*

14:21 Some manuscripts read *to stumble or be offended or be weakened.* **14:23** Some manuscripts place the text of 16:25-27 here. **15:3** Greek *who insult you have fallen on me.* Ps 69:9. **15:8** Greek *servant of circumcision.* **15:9** Ps 18:49. **15:10** Deut 32:43. **15:11** Ps 117:1.

14:14 I know and am convinced. Paul comes down clearly on the side of the "strong" (see Mark 7:15). **wrong to eat.** That is, in the ritual sense. There is no food that has power to harm a person's relationship with God. **someone believes it is wrong.** For those believers who have not been convinced that Christ abolished the ceremonial law of the Old Testament (even though the food is not objectively unclean), it is subjectively unclean for that person.

14:15 not acting in love. If the "strong" exercise their liberty even when they know such actions are considered sinful by the "weak," they are failing to act lovingly toward them. To do so jeopardizes the faith of the weak and disturbs the delicate harmony of the body of Christian believers. To act lovingly is more vital than exercising one's freedom. **ruin.** By exercising this liberty, it is possible that the weaker Christian could be caused great harm in his faith.

14:17-18 the Kingdom of God is not a matter of what we eat and drink. Such matters as eating or drinking are trivial in kingdom terms; to cause spiritual ruin over such minor issues is scandalous.

14:19 build each other up. Our pursuits must be focused on helping individual Christians and the church body to grow in faith and practice.

14:21 It is better not. The "strong" are called on not to eat or drink when doing so would cause harm. **drink wine.** The Bible does not specifically forbid the drinking of wine except for priests on duty (Lev. 10:9) or for Nazirites (Num. 6:2-3), but drunkenness is clearly condemned. Wisdom suggests abstinence from strong drink as a logical precaution against falling into sin.

14:22 believe. Here faith signifies a sort of inner freedom or liberty that comes from knowing that what one is doing is in accord with Christian faith in general.

14:23 sinning. When a Christian acts without a sense of inner liberty, such an act, even though in itself morally neutral (neither inherently bad or good), is sin to that believer.

15:1 We who are strong. Paul is not talking about physical strength but about conscience. Some believers' consciences allow them options on nonessential issues. Paul was such a believer. He was able to eat meat that had been offered to idols and then sold in the marketplace at Corinth (1 Cor. 8). Some believers, who were new to the faith or had worshipped idols, would feel guilty if they ate meat that had been offered to idols. The principle Paul articulates is that the strong need to be mindful of the weak and not flaunt their strong conscience before them.

15:3 Christ didn't live to please himself. Jesus is our model in these matters. He did not come to be served but to be a servant. Paul quotes Psalm 69 that foreshadows the Messiah. This is the second most frequently quoted psalm in the New Testament.

12 And in another place Isaiah said,

"The heir to David's throne* will come,
and he will rule over the Gentiles.
They will place their hope on him."*

13 I pray that God, the source of hope, will fill you completely with joy and peace because you trust in him. Then you will overflow with confident hope through the power of the Holy Spirit.

PAUL'S REASON FOR WRITING

14 I am fully convinced, my dear brothers and sisters,* that you are full of goodness. You know these things so well you can teach each other all about them. 15 Even so, I have been bold enough to write about some of these points, knowing that all you need is this reminder. For by God's grace, 16 I am a special messenger from Christ Jesus to you Gentiles. I bring you the Good News so that I might present you as an acceptable offering to God, made holy by the Holy Spirit. 17 So I have reason to be enthusiastic about all Christ Jesus has done through me in my service to God. 18 Yet I dare not boast about anything except what Christ has done through me, bringing the Gentiles to God by my message and by the way I worked among them. 19 They were convinced by the power of miraculous signs and wonders and by the power of God's Spirit.* In this way, I have fully presented the Good News of Christ from Jerusalem all the way to Illyricum.*

20 My ambition has always been to preach the Good News where the name of Christ has never been heard, rather than where a church has already been started by someone else. 21 I have been following the plan spoken of in the Scriptures, where it says,

"Those who have never been told about him will see,
and those who have never heard of him will understand."*

22 In fact, my visit to you has been delayed so long because I have been preaching in these places.

PAUL'S TRAVEL PLANS

23 But now I have finished my work in these regions, and after all these long years of waiting, I am eager to visit you. 24 I am planning to go to Spain, and when I do, I will stop off in Rome. And after I have enjoyed your fellowship for a little while, you can provide for my journey.

25 But before I come, I must go to Jerusalem to take a gift to the believers* there. 26 For you see, the believers in Macedonia and Achaia* have eagerly taken up an offering for the poor among the believers in Jerusalem. 27 They were glad to do this because they feel they owe a real debt to them. Since the Gentiles received the spiritual blessings of the Good News from the believers in Jerusalem, they feel the least they can do in return is to help them financially. 28 As soon as I have delivered this money and completed this good deed of theirs, I will come to see you on my way to Spain. 29 And I am sure that when I come, Christ will richly bless our time together.

30 Dear brothers and sisters, I urge you in the name of our Lord Jesus Christ to join in my struggle by praying to God for me. Do this because of your love for me, given to you by the Holy Spirit. 31 Pray that I will be rescued from those in Judea who refuse to obey God. Pray also that the believers there will be willing to accept the donation* I am taking to Jerusalem. 32 Then, by the will of God, I will be able to come to you with a joyful heart, and we will be an encouragement to each other.

33 And now may God, who gives us his peace, be with you all. Amen.*

PAUL GREETS HIS FRIENDS

16 I commend to you our sister Phoebe, who is a deacon in the church in Cenchrea. 2 Welcome her in the Lord as one who is worthy of honor among God's people. Help her in whatever she needs, for she has been helpful to many, and especially to me.

FUTURE PLANS

1. What things are you most tempted to boast about? What are you most likely not to boast about?

ROMANS 15:14-33

2. What motivates and inspires Paul (vv. 16-22)? What motivates and inspires you?
3. What is Paul's "ambition" in life (v. 20)? What is your aim in life? How concerned are you about the needs of others?
4. How fully are you presently fulfilling God's will for your life? What can you do to be more fully obedient?
5. In your plans for the future, how much does God's will fit in? How much do your own desires fit in?

15:12a Greek *The root of Jesse.* David was the son of Jesse. **15:12b** Isa 11:10 (Greek version). **15:14** Greek *brothers;* also in 15:30. **15:19a** Other manuscripts read *the Spirit;* still others read *the Holy Spirit.* **15:19b** *Illyricum* was a region northeast of Italy. **15:21** Isa 52:15 (Greek version). **15:25** Greek *God's holy people;* also in 15:26, 31. **15:26** *Macedonia* and *Achaia* were the northern and southern regions of Greece. **15:31** Greek *the ministry;* other manuscripts read *the gift.* **15:33** Some manuscripts do not include *Amen.* One very early manuscript places 16:25-27 here.

15:14 you are full. These are not words of flattery designed to win over a hostile audience. One sentence would hardly suffice in light of the preceding chapters. Paul seems to feel that writing such specific instructions for behavior (as he has done in 12:1–15:13) to a church he has never visited might seem overly bold (v. 15), even presumptuous. So he hastens to assure the Roman Christians that he does consider them to be mature Christians.

15:24 Spain. The Roman colony of Spain was situated at the edge of the civilized world—no doubt the reason why Paul's pioneering spirit was drawn there.

15:25-27 the poor among the believers. The collection for the poor in Jerusalem is like a debt in Paul's thinking. When he was commissioned by the church to serve as the apostle to the Gentiles, they requested that he remember the poor (Gal. 2:10).

15:26 Macedonia and Achaia. Two Roman provinces located south of Illyricum, on a peninsula bordering the Adriatic and Aegean Seas (in the region of modern Greece).

16:1-2 I commend . . .Phoebe. Phoebe probably carried Paul's letter from Corinth to the church at Rome. Typical in letters of his day, Paul includes a note of commendation in which he makes two requests: that they receive Phoebe as a sister in the Lord and that they assist her because she has helped many others. Phoebe was probably a woman of wealth and influence who had committed herself to God's kingdom.

[3]Give my greetings to Priscilla and Aquila, my
co-workers in the ministry of Christ Jesus. [4]In fact,
they once risked their lives for me. I am thankful to
them, and so are all the Gentile churches. [5]Also give
my greetings to the church that meets in their home.
Greet my dear friend Epenetus. He was the first
person from the province of Asia to become a fol-
lower of Christ. [6]Give my greetings to Mary, who
has worked so hard for your benefit. [7]Greet Andro-
nicus and Junia,* my fellow Jews,* who were in pris-
on with me. They are highly respected among the
apostles and became followers of Christ before I did.
[8]Greet Ampliatus, my dear friend in the Lord. [9]Greet
Urbanus, our co-worker in Christ, and my dear friend
Stachys.
[10]Greet Apelles, a good man whom Christ approves.
And give my greetings to the believers from the
household of Aristobulus. [11]Greet Herodion, my fellow
Jew.* Greet the Lord's people from the household of
Narcissus. [12]Give my greetings to Tryphena and Try-
phosa, the Lord's workers, and to dear Persis, who has
worked so hard for the Lord. [13]Greet Rufus, whom the
Lord picked out to be his very own; and also his dear
mother, who has been a mother to me.
[14]Give my greetings to Asyncritus, Phlegon, Her-
mes, Patrobas, Hermas, and the brothers and sisters*
who meet with them. [15]Give my greetings to Philolo-
gus, Julia, Nereus and his sister, and to Olympas and
all the believers* who meet with them. [16]Greet each
other with a sacred kiss. All the churches of Christ
send you their greetings.

PAUL'S FINAL INSTRUCTIONS

[17]And now I make one more appeal, my dear brothers
and sisters. Watch out for people who cause divisions
and upset people's faith by teaching things contrary
to what you have been taught. Stay away from them.
[18]Such people are not serving Christ our Lord; they
are serving their own personal interests. By smooth
talk and glowing words they deceive innocent peo-
ple. [19]But everyone knows that you are obedient to
the Lord. This makes me very happy. I want you to be
wise in doing right and to stay innocent of any wrong.
[20]The God of peace will soon crush Satan under your
feet. May the grace of our Lord Jesus* be with you.
[21]Timothy, my fellow worker, sends you his greet-
ings, as do Lucius, Jason, and Sosipater, my fellow
Jews.
[22]I, Tertius, the one writing this letter for Paul, send
my greetings, too, as one of the Lord's followers.
[23]Gaius says hello to you. He is my host and also
serves as host to the whole church. Erastus, the city
treasurer, sends you his greetings, and so does our
brother Quartus.*
[25]Now all glory to God, who is able to make you
strong, just as my Good News says. This message
about Jesus Christ has revealed his plan for you Gen-
tiles, a plan kept secret from the beginning of time.
[26]But now as the prophets* foretold and as the eter-
nal God has commanded, this message is made known
to all Gentiles everywhere, so that they too might be-
lieve and obey him. [27]All glory to the only wise God,
through Jesus Christ, forever. Amen.*

SMOOTH TALKERS

1. When have you seen someone causing problems with "bad mouthing" and negative talk: On your team? In your school? In your own life?

ROMANS 16:1-27

2. What does it mean to "cause divisions" (v. 17)? How can a person cause such things just by talking?
3. What does it mean to serve "their own personal interests" (v. 18)? Do you sometimes do this?
4. How can "smooth talk and glowing words" (v. 18) actually deceive people? When have you seen this happen? How can you guard against being deceived?

16:7a *Junia* is a feminine name. Some late manuscripts accent the word so it reads *Junias,* a masculine name; still others read *Julia* (feminine). **16:7b** Or *compatriots;* also in 16:21. **16:11** Or *compatriot.* **16:14** Greek *brothers;* also in 16:17. **16:15** Greek *all of God's holy people.* **16:20** Some manuscripts read *Lord Jesus Christ.* **16:23** Some manuscripts add verse 24, *May the grace of our Lord Jesus Christ be with you all. Amen.* Still others add this sentence after verse 27. **16:26** Greek *the prophetic writings.* **16:25-27** Various manuscripts place the doxology (shown here as 16:25-27) after 14:23 or after 15:33 or after 16:23.

16:3-16 Of the 26 people named in these verses, at least four are women. Thirteen of these names occur in manuscripts or inscriptions related to the imperial household, giving rise to speculation that the gospel of Christ had penetrated even into the royal palace (Phil. 4:22).

16:3-5 Prisca and Aquila. Aquila, a Jew born in Pontus in Asia Minor, and his wife Priscilla appear regularly in the New Testament. They are often involved in Paul's work of sharing Christ, planting new churches, and training new converts.

16:5 the church . . .in their home. During the first two centuries, there were no special church buildings, so Christians met in the homes of their members (1 Cor. 16:19; Col. 4:15; Philem. 2). The growth of these churches was overwhelming.

16:13 Rufus. Quite possibly the son of Simon of Cyrene, who carried Jesus' cross. Simon is identified (Mark 15:21) as the father of Alexander and Rufus.

16:17 Watch out for people who cause divisions. Paul must have heard that some troublemakers were causing a problem in the church at Rome. The nature of this problem is a mystery. Even at this early point in Christian history, the church was not perfect. Believers must act decisively to protect the harmony and fellowship of the church.

16:22 Tertius. The only time the name of one of Paul's secretaries is revealed.

16:23 Gaius. This name is mentioned several times in the New Testament. It probably refers to the Gaius mentioned in 1 Corinthians 1:14, with whom Paul was staying in Corinth while he wrote this letter to the Romans.

16:25-27 able to make you strong. This closing doxology is a single, complex sentence in which God is praised for the salvation that He freely offers in Christ Jesus.

16:25 a plan kept secret. In the New Testament, this refers to truths about God's plan that were unknown until God disclosed them. They are insights about God that could not be achieved through reasoning or deduction (1 Cor. 1:18-20) but are known solely because God has revealed them.

16:26 all Gentiles everywhere, so they . . . might believe. This is the goal of the gospel message: it is for all nations, not just for the Jews. Since Jesus' death and resurrection, people of all backgrounds and nationalities are invited to become the people of God.

INTRODUCTION TO

1 CORINTHIANS

PERSONAL READING PLAN

- ☐ 1 Corinthians 1:1–2:5
- ☐ 1 Corinthians 2:6–3:23
- ☐ 1 Corinthians 4:1–5:13
- ☐ 1 Corinthians 6:1-20
- ☐ 1 Corinthians 7:1-40
- ☐ 1 Corinthians 8:1–9:27
- ☐ 1 Corinthians 10:1–11:1
- ☐ 1 Corinthians 11:2-34
- ☐ 1 Corinthians 12:1–13:13
- ☐ 1 Corinthians 14:1-40
- ☐ 1 Corinthians 15:1-58
- ☐ 1 Corinthians 16:1-24

AUTHOR

The writer is the Apostle Paul.

DATE

Paul wrote 1 Corinthians sometime between A.D. 53–55.

THEME

Christian lifestyle in a pagan society.

PURPOSE

First Corinthians is a practical, issue-oriented letter in which Paul tells his readers what they ought or ought not to do. Paul's typical pattern in other letters is to begin with a strong theological statement and then to follow up by applying this insight to daily life. But that is not the case in the letter, which has come to be known as 1 Corinthians. Here we find little direct theological teaching. Rather Paul discusses, in turn, a number of practical life issues.

The problem was that these proud, materialistic, independent ex-pagans were having a most difficult time learning how to live as Christians. It was at this level of lifestyle that paganism directed its attack on the newly emerging Christian faith. Christian behavior was the underlying issue. Where were the lines to be drawn? How much of one's culture had to be abandoned to become a Christian? Residual paganism was mounting a frontal attack on Christianity. If Christianity lost in Corinth, its existence would be threatened throughout the Roman Empire. So just as he did in Galatians, when residual Judaism attacked Christianity over the issue of whether or not one must keep the law, Paul struck back decisively and directly with this letter to the Corinthians.

HISTORICAL BACKGROUND

Paul visited Corinth during his second missionary journey, probably in A.D. 50. Having been in some peril in Macedonia, he fled by ship to Athens (Acts 17:1-15). Not meeting with great success there (Acts 17:16-34), he then journeyed the short distance to Corinth where he met Priscilla and Aquila (Acts 18:1-3). At first he preached in the synagogue with some success (even the ruler of the synagogue was won to Christ). But then the Jews forced him to leave, so he moved next door into the home of a Gentile. Hoping to silence him, the Jews eventually hauled Paul before the governor Gallio, but Gallio threw the case out of court as having no merit. After some 18 months (his longest stay anywhere except Ephesus), Paul left and continued his missionary work in Syria.

Two events sparked the writing of 1 Corinthians some three or four years later. First, Paul heard that a divisive spirit was loose in the church (1 Cor. 1:11). Second, he received a letter in which the Corinthians asked him questions about marriage and other matters (1 Cor. 7:1). In addition, a delegation from Corinth completed his knowledge of the problems there (1 Cor. 16:15-17). Being unable to visit Corinth personally, Paul sought to deal with the issues by letter. Thus the Corinthian correspondence was begun.

THE CITY OF CORINTH

Corinth was an unusual city. After its capture by the Roman legions in 146 B.C., the city was leveled. It lay in ruins for nearly 100 years until Julius Caesar rebuilt it in 44 B.C. Then it grew rapidly, thanks largely to its unique geographical location. Because it lay at the neck of a narrow isthmus connecting the Peloponnesus with central Greece, it controlled all north-south land traffic. To the east and the west of the city were two fine harbors. Both goods and ships were hauled across the four-mile-wide isthmus of Corinth. Thus Corinth also controlled most east-west sea routes. This strategic location commanded wealth and influence. By the time of Paul's visit some 100 years after its rebuilding, Corinth had become the capital of the province of Achaia and the third most important city in the Roman Empire, after Rome and Alexandria.

In this wealthy young city, excess seemed to be the norm. The city was stocked with art purchased from around the Roman Empire. It became a center of philosophy, though apparently few citizens were seriously interested in studying philosophy, preferring rather to listen to stirring orations on faddish topics delivered by the city's numerous itinerant philosophers. Even in religion, this excess was obvious. The Greek author Pausanias describes 26 pagan shrines and temples, including the great temples of Apollo and Aphrodite. In Old Corinth, 1,000 temple prostitutes had served Aphrodite, the goddess of love, and New Corinth continued this tradition of sexual worship practices. The city developed a worldwide reputation for vice and debauchery.

Luxury was the hallmark of Corinth. Because storms in the Aegean Sea were frequent and treacherous, sailors preferred to put into one of the harbors and transport their ship overland to the other harbor, despite the exorbitant tolls charged by the Corinthians. Consequently, goods from around the world passed through Corinthian ports, and some 400,000 slaves were kept in the city to provide the labor for this arduous job.

Into Corinth flowed people from around the Roman Empire. There were "Greek adventurers and Roman bourgeois, with a tainting infusion of Phoenicians, a mass of Jews, ex-soldiers, philosophers, merchants, sailors, freed men, slaves, tradespeople, hucksters and agents of every form of vice" (Farrar, quoted by William Barclay, The Letters to the Corinthians, p. 4). Not surprisingly, it was in Corinth that Paul had to fight this battle to prevent Christianity from giving in to debilitating enticements offered by paganism.

PASSAGES FOR TOPICAL GROUP STUDY

1:10-17 . . . CLIQUES and DIVISIONS . . . . Divided We Fall
1:18–2:5 . . STANDING FOR YOUR FAITH . . . . . . Looking Foolish
2:6-16 . . . . THE MIND OF CHRIST . . . . Conflicting Spirits
4:1-21 . . . . TREATED BADLY . . . . The World's Garbage
5:1-13 . . . . SEXUALITY . . . . Sex and the Christian
6:1-11 . . . . HEAVEN OR HELL . . . . Judging Others
6:12-20 . . . SEXUAL TEMPTATION . . . . Run From Sex
7:1-40 . . . . MARRIAGE and DIVORCE . . . . The Question of Marriage
8:1-13 . . . . CHOICES and CHRISTIAN LIBERTY . . . Careful Choices
9:24-27 . . . DISCIPLINE AND TRAINING . . . . The Ultimate Qualification
10:1-13 . . . SEXSUAL PURITY . . . . Standing and Falling
11:2-16 . . . GENDER ROLES . . . . Roles of Men and Women
11:17-34 . . THE LORD'S SUPPER . . . . Evaluate Yourself
12:12-31 . . . UNIQUENESS and TEAMWORK . . . . All for One
13:1-13 . . . LOVING OTHERS . . . . True Love
14:26-40 . . ORDERLY WORSHIP . . . . Order vs. Chaos
15:1-11 . . . . PEER PRESSURE and STAYING TRUE . . . Holding Firm
15:12-34 . . RESURRECTION . . . . The Vital Statistic
15:35-58 . . VICTORY OVER SIN AND DEATH . . . . Victory Over Death
16:1-24 . . . BRAVERY and PRESSURE . . . . . . Bravery Under Fire

PASSAGES FOR GENERAL GROUP STUDY

3:1-23 . . . . Building with Gold (God's Co-workers in Building Eternity)
10:14–11:1 . . . . Handling Our Freedom as Christians
14:1-25 . . . . Gifted and Talented (Spiritual Gifts)

GREETINGS FROM PAUL

1 This letter is from Paul, chosen by the will of God to
be an apostle of Christ Jesus, and from our brother
Sosthenes.
2 I am writing to God's church in Corinth,* to you
who have been called by God to be his own holy peo-
ple. He made you holy by means of Christ Jesus,* just
as he did for all people everywhere who call on the
name of our Lord Jesus Christ, their Lord and ours.
3 May God our Father and the Lord Jesus Christ give
you grace and peace.

PAUL GIVES THANKS TO GOD

4 I always thank my God for you and for the gracious
gifts he has given you, now that you belong to Christ
Jesus. 5 Through him, God has enriched your church
in every way—with all of your eloquent words and
all of your knowledge. 6 This confirms that what I told
you about Christ is true. 7 Now you have every spiri-
tual gift you need as you eagerly wait for the return
of our Lord Jesus Christ. 8 He will keep you strong to
the end so that you will be free from all blame on the
day when our Lord Jesus Christ returns. 9 God will do
this, for he is faithful to do what he says, and he has
invited you into partnership with his Son, Jesus Christ
our Lord.

DIVISIONS IN THE CHURCH

10 I appeal to you, dear brothers and sisters,* by the
authority of our Lord Jesus Christ, to live in harmo-
ny with each other. Let there be no divisions in the
church. Rather, be of one mind, united in thought
and purpose. 11 For some members of Chloe's house-
hold have told me about your quarrels, my dear
brothers and sisters. 12 Some of you are saying, "I
am a follower of Paul." Others are saying, "I fol-
low Apollos," or "I follow Peter,*" or "I follow only
Christ."
13 Has Christ been divided into factions? Was I,
Paul, crucified for you? Were any of you baptized
in the name of Paul? Of course not! 14 I thank God
that I did not baptize any of you except Crispus and
Gaius, 15 for now no one can say they were baptized
in my name. 16 (Oh yes, I also baptized the house-
hold of Stephanas, but I don't remember baptizing
anyone else.) 17 For Christ didn't send me to baptize,
but to preach the Good News—and not with clever
speech, for fear that the cross of Christ would lose
its power.

DIVIDED WE FALL

1. When there is an argument, do you quickly take sides or do you try to stay out of it? How do you decide?

1 CORINTHIANS 1:10-17

2. Reading between the lines, what would seem to be causing the arguments and division in the Corinthian church?
3. Why does Paul suggest (v. 12) that it's wrong to say, "I'm with so and so" even "I'm with Christ"?
4. Why are cliques and divisions, especially within the church, so damaging to the Christian community (vv. 10,13,17)?
5. What issues cause the biggest division between people in your school? Your church? Your group or team?

THE WISDOM OF GOD

18 The message of the cross is foolish to those who are
headed for destruction! But we who are being saved
know it is the very power of God. 19 As the Scriptures
say,

"I will destroy the wisdom of the wise
and discard the intelligence of the intelligent."*

20 So where does this leave the philosophers, the
scholars, and the world's brilliant debaters? God has
made the wisdom of this world look foolish. 21 Since
God in his wisdom saw to it that the world would
never know him through human wisdom, he has used
our foolish preaching to save those who believe. 22 It
is foolish to the Jews, who ask for signs from heaven.

1:2a *Corinth* was the capital city of Achaia, the southern region of the Greek peninsula. **1:2b** Or *because you belong to Christ Jesus.* **1:10** Greek *brothers;* also in 1:11, 26. **1:12** Greek *Cephas.* **1:19** Isa 29:14.

1:1 an apostle. Paul does not always identify himself an apostle: "one who is sent," an office held by those who witnessed the resurrected Christ (1 Thess. 1:1). He may have done so here because his authority as an apostle was an issue with the Corinthians. **Sosthenes.** Possibly mentioned in Acts 18:17.

1:2 made holy. Dedicated to God's service. **holy people.** Set apart to serve God's purposes. All believers are saints, holy persons.

1:3 grace. Grace is the unmerited gift of God by which a person receives salvation.

1:7 spiritual gift. *Charismata,* special gifts given by God to build up the church. **revelation.** Literally, the unveiling of Jesus Christ as He comes in glory.

1:10 divisions. *Schismata* ("schism"); a word often used to describe an incision in a piece of clothing. **united.** Their disunity is rooted in differing ideas (doctrines).

1:11 Chloe's household. Paul is writing from Ephesus. The slaves (or freedmen) of an Ephesian woman named Chloe had visited Corinth and brought back the story of disunity there.

1:12 I am a follower of Paul. Paul does not commend those "on his side." No better than any other faction, these people had probably exaggerated and falsified his actual viewpoints. (This was probably the Gentile party.) **I follow Apollos.** After he had been instructed in the gospel by Priscilla and Aquila, Apollos, a bright, articulate Jew from Alexandria with great skill in debate (Acts 18:24-28), went to Corinth to assist the church there. A natural leader for those who attempted to intellectualize Christianity. **I follow Peter.** Peter probably visited Corinth. This faction would have been oriented toward a more Jewish Christianity. **I follow only Christ.** Possibly those who look with disdain on the others who profess allegiance to the Christ preached by Paul, Apollos, or Cephas. In other words, "holier-than-thou." This may even be a mystical or Gnostic-like party, given to inner visions and revelations.

1:17 clever speech. *Sophia,* the Greek word for "wisdom," is a key word in 1 Corinthians, which Paul uses in both positive and negative ways. Here the idea is the negative use of human reason with a view to convincing the hearer of a position. **the cross of Christ would lose its power.** Paul is eager that people be persuaded by the actual truth and not mere eloquence.

1:18 foolish. It is absurd to many that God's redemptive activity involves death by crucifixion. **perishing.** Unless they repent (turn around and go the other way), they will not be acquitted on the Day of Judgment. **being saved.** Salvation is a process, begun at conversion, consummated at the second coming of Jesus, and fulfilled in heaven .

1:22 Jews . . . ask for signs. The Jews expected a divine-warrior Messiah of mega-miracles, not a Jesus executed by His enemies. **Greeks . . . seek human wisdom.** Their delight was in clever, cunning logic delivered with compelling persuasiveness.

LOOKING FOOLISH

1. When have you felt or looked foolish for believing something that others didn't believe? What was your belief? Was it true or false?

1 CORINTHIANS 1:18–2:5

2. Who are those "who are being saved" (v. 18)? Why "being saved" rather than "saved"?
3. How has God "made the wisdom of the world look foolish" (v. 20)? What is the "world's wisdom"? What is God's wisdom?
4. How is "Christ crucified . . . nonsense" to the Gentiles" (v. 23)?
5. On what issue do you need to take a stand for your faith, even though you might look foolish?

And it is foolish to the Greeks, who seek human wisdom. 23 So when we preach that Christ was crucified, the Jews are offended and the Gentiles say it's all nonsense.

24 But to those called by God to salvation, both Jews and Gentiles,* Christ is the power of God and the wisdom of God. 25 This foolish plan of God is wiser than the wisest of human plans, and God's weakness is stronger than the greatest of human strength.

26 Remember, dear brothers and sisters, that few of you were wise in the world's eyes or powerful or wealthy* when God called you. 27 Instead, God chose things the world considers foolish in order to shame those who think they are wise. And he chose things that are powerless to shame those who are powerful. 28 God chose things despised by the world,* things counted as nothing at all, and used them to bring to nothing what the world considers important. 29 As a result, no one can ever boast in the presence of God.

30 God has united you with Christ Jesus. For our benefit God made him to be wisdom itself. Christ made us right with God; he made us pure and holy, and he freed us from sin. 31 Therefore, as the Scriptures say, "If you want to boast, boast only about the LORD."*

PAUL'S MESSAGE OF WISDOM

2 When I first came to you, dear brothers and sisters,* I didn't use lofty words and impressive wisdom to tell you God's secret plan.* 2 For I decided that while I was with you I would forget everything except Jesus Christ, the one who was crucified. 3 I came to you in weakness—timid and trembling. 4 And my message and my preaching were very plain. Rather than using clever and persuasive speeches, I relied only on the power of the Holy Spirit. 5 I did this so you would trust not in human wisdom but in the power of God.

6 Yet when I am among mature believers, I do speak with words of wisdom, but not the kind of wisdom that belongs to this world or to the rulers of this world, who are soon forgotten. 7 No, the wisdom we speak of is the mystery of God*—his plan that was previously hidden, even though he made it for our ultimate glory before the world began. 8 But the rulers of this world have not understood it; if they had, they would not have crucified our glorious Lord. 9 That is what the Scriptures mean when they say,

"No eye has seen, no ear has heard,
  and no mind has imagined
what God has prepared
  for those who love him."*

10 But* it was to us that God revealed these things by his Spirit. For his Spirit searches out everything and shows us God's deep secrets. 11 No one can know a person's thoughts except that person's own spirit, and no one can know God's thoughts except God's own Spirit. 12 And we have received God's Spirit (not the world's spirit), so we can know the wonderful things God has freely given us.

13 When we tell you these things, we do not use words that come from human wisdom. Instead, we speak words given to us by the Spirit, using the Spirit's words to explain spiritual truths.* 14 But people who aren't spiritual* can't receive these truths from

1:24 Greek *and Greeks.* **1:26** Or *high born.* **1:28** Or *God chose those who are low born.* **1:31** Jer 9:24. **2:1a** Greek *brothers.* **2:1b** Greek *God's mystery;* other manuscripts read *God's testimony.* **2:7** Greek *But we speak God's wisdom in a mystery.* **2:9** Isa 64:4. **2:10** Some manuscripts read *For.* **2:13** Or *explaining spiritual truths in spiritual language,* or *explaining spiritual truths to spiritual people.* **2:14** Or *who don't have the Spirit;* or *who have only physical life.*

1:23 Jews are offended. Literally, a scandal. Jesus' crucifixion "proved" to the Jews that He could not be of God (Deut. 21:23 says those hanging from a tree are cursed of God). A suffering, dying Messiah was totally outside first-century Jewish expectations. **nonsense.** Both Jesus' incarnation (human birth) and His crucifixion were actions that Greeks felt were unworthy of their gods.

1:26 Remember . . . when God called you. In their own calling they see the paradox of the all-powerful God using the "weak things of the world." **few.** The early church had special appeal to the poor and to those with little social standing. This was part of its offensiveness—the "wrong" people were attracted to it. **wise.** This refers to people with education or philosophical training. **powerful.** This means people in high positions politically or socially. **wealthy.** These were people of distinguished families who may have held Roman citizenship.

1:28 the things despised. . . bring to nothing what the world considers important. God chooses "nobodies" and thus exposes the foolishness of the way the world defines "somebodies."

1:30 For our benefit. They owe the fact that they are related to God solely to Jesus Christ. **him to be wisdom.** God's plan of salvation through Christ. **right with God.** Christ is their righteousness in that He took upon Himself the guilt of human sin. On the Last Day when Christians stand before the Judge, they are viewed not in terms of their own failure and inadequacy but as being "in Christ." **pure and holy.** Christ provides the holiness people lack enabling them to appear before God. **freed us from sin.** It is by Christ's redeeming work on the cross that wisdom, righteousness, and holiness are mediated to humankind.

2:4 power of the Holy Spirit. People were moved by the convicting power of the Holy Spirit.

2:6 I do speak with words of wisdom. Not the false wisdom in 1:17. **mature.** A potential that all Christians have (Col. 1:28), though not all experience (3:1). **wisdom that belongs to this world.** "This age" is person-centered and corrupted by rebellion against God, while "the age to come" is when God's kingdom will be present and visible.

2:7 wisdom . . . mystery of God. In contrast to the "wisdom of the world" no one could have guessed God's plan. Even when it was revealed, many shunned it as "foolish" and/or scandalous (1:23).

2:10 by his Spirit. Insight not by reasoning but as a result of revelation. **his Spirit searches out everything.** In Corinth, people believed one could discover the nature of God through philosophy. Paul indicates that only the Spirit communicates accurate knowledge about God.

2:12 world's spirit. An equivalent phrase to "the wisdom of this age" (v. 6). **has freely given us.** These gifts of God (v. 9) are not merely for the future, but are the present experience of Christians.

CONFLICTING SPIRITS

1. What is your favorite mystery movie or book? Who is your favorite fictional detective?

1 CORINTHIANS 2:6-16

2. What does it mean that "the wisdom we speak of is the mystery of God" (v. 7)? What is the "mystery" to which Paul is referring?
3. What is the "the world's spirit" (v. 12)? How does it compare with "God's Spirit"?
4. What is "the mind of Christ" (v. 16)? What do you need to do to have Christ's wisdom more fully in your life?
5. Whose spirit governs your decisions: the spirit of the world or of God? Why?

God's Spirit. It all sounds foolish to them and they
can't understand it, for only those who are spiritual
can understand what the Spirit means. 15 Those who
are spiritual can evaluate all things, but they them-
selves cannot be evaluated by others. 16 For,

"Who can know the LORD's thoughts?
Who knows enough to teach him?"*

But we understand these things, for we have the mind of Christ.

PAUL AND APOLLOS, SERVANTS OF CHRIST

3 Dear brothers and sisters,* when I was with you I
couldn't talk to you as I would to spiritual people.*
I had to talk as though you belonged to this world
or as though you were infants in Christ. 2 I had to
feed you with milk, not with solid food, because you
weren't ready for anything stronger. And you still ar-
en't ready, 3 for you are still controlled by your sinful
nature. You are jealous of one another and quarrel
with each other. Doesn't that prove you are controlled
by your sinful nature? Aren't you living like people of
the world? 4 When one of you says, "I am a follower of
Paul," and another says, "I follow Apollos," aren't you
acting just like people of the world?

5 After all, who is Apollos? Who is Paul? We are
only God's servants through whom you believed the
Good News. Each of us did the work the Lord gave us.
6 I planted the seed in your hearts, and Apollos wa-
tered it, but it was God who made it grow. 7 It's not im-
portant who does the planting, or who does the wa-
tering. What's important is that God makes the seed
grow. 8 The one who plants and the one who waters
work together with the same purpose. And both will
be rewarded for their own hard work. 9 For we are
both God's workers. And you are God's field. You are
God's building.

10 Because of God's grace to me, I have laid the foun-
dation like an expert builder. Now others are building
on it. But whoever is building on this foundation must
be very careful. 11 For no one can lay any foundation
other than the one we already have—Jesus Christ.

12 Anyone who builds on that foundation may use a
variety of materials—gold, silver, jewels, wood, hay,
or straw. 13 But on the judgment day, fire will reveal
what kind of work each builder has done. The fire
will show if a person's work has any value. 14 If the
work survives, that builder will receive a reward.
15 But if the work is burned up, the builder will suffer
great loss. The builder will be saved, but like someone
barely escaping through a wall of flames.

16 Don't you realize that all of you together are the
temple of God and that the Spirit of God lives in* you?
17 God will destroy anyone who destroys this temple.
For God's temple is holy, and you are that temple.

18 Stop deceiving yourselves. If you think you are
wise by this world's standards, you need to become a
fool to be truly wise. 19 For the wisdom of this world is
foolishness to God. As the Scriptures say,

"He traps the wise
in the snare of their own cleverness."*

BUILDING WITH GOLD

1. Did you ever plant a garden? What did you grow? Who did most of the weeding? Watering? Harvesting?

1 CORINTHIANS 3:1-23

2. What is Paul saying about Christian workers in verses 5-8? How does this apply to different "jobs" and ministries in the church?
3. What does it mean that "we are both God's workers" (v. 9)?
4. What kinds of work are like "gold, silver, jewels" (v. 12)? What are like "wood, hay, or straw"?
5. Name one thing you can do this week to build "the temple of God" (you) with the gems of holiness (vv. 16-17).

2:16 Isa 40:13 (Greek version). **3:1a** Greek *Brothers.* **3:1b** Or *to people who have the Spirit.* **3:16** Or *among.* **3:19** Job 5:13.

3:1 you belonged to this world. Immature Christians who are molded more by the spirit of the age than by the Spirit of God.
3:3 people of the world? By exalting certain teachers, they betray their lack of understanding of the gospel. Paul's point is that although they have the Spirit, they are acting precisely like people without the Spirit.
3:6 Apollos watered. Paul preached salvation. Apollos gave instruction on holy living.
3:10 expert builder. (In Greek, *architekton.*) The one who plans and supervises the construction of a building, not a laborer. **I have laid the foundation.** By preaching Christ the foundation (vv. 6, 11).
3:12 gold, silver, jewels. These works or materials will survive the test of fire. **wood, hay, or straw.** These are inferior or inadequate materials: works that will burn up.
3:13 the judgment day. On the Day of Judgment the quality of labor will be revealed. **fire will reveal.** The idea is not of fire as punishment but as a means of testing the "quality of each one's work."
3:16 temple of God. This reference is not to individual believers' bodies as the temple of the Spirit; that comes in 6:19. The sanctuary is the community they are becoming—wherever it gathered— a particularly vivid and exciting image for the Corinthians, surrounded as they were by pagan temples, because Paul shows them that God's Spirit is creating a new people.
3:17 destroys. The idea has shifted from losing one's pay for having used inferior building materials (vv. 12-15) to being punished for destroying the church.

[20] And again,

"The LORD knows the thoughts of the wise;
he knows they are worthless."*

[21] So don't boast about following a particular hu-
man leader. For everything belongs to you—[22] wheth-
er Paul or Apollos or Peter,* or the world, or life and
death, or the present and the future. Everything be-
longs to you, [23] and you belong to Christ, and Christ
belongs to God.

PAUL'S RELATIONSHIP WITH THE CORINTHIANS

4 So look at Apollos and me as mere servants of
Christ who have been put in charge of explaining
God's mysteries. [2] Now, a person who is put in charge
as a manager must be faithful. [3] As for me, it matters
very little how I might be evaluated by you or by any
human authority. I don't even trust my own judgment
on this point. [4] My conscience is clear, but that doesn't
prove I'm right. It is the Lord himself who will exam-
ine me and decide.

THE WORLD'S GARBAGE

1. Are you a pack rat, or do you easily get rid of things? What item do you still have from your childhood?

1 CORINTHIANS 4:1-21

2. What does Paul mean in verse 3? When are the opinions of other people unimportant? When are they important?
3. Why does Paul emphasize humility so often? How does the realization in verse 7 bring true humility?
4. In what way was Jesus treated "like the world's garbage, like everybody's trash" (v. 13)?
5. When have others treated you like "garbage" due to your faith? How did you react? How can Paul's counsel help you deal with this?

[5] So don't make judgments about anyone ahead of
time—before the Lord returns. For he will bring our
darkest secrets to light and will reveal our private
motives. Then God will give to each one whatever
praise is due.
[6] Dear brothers and sisters,* I have used Apollos
and myself to illustrate what I've been saying. If you
pay attention to what I have quoted from the Scrip-
tures,* you won't be proud of one of your leaders at
the expense of another. [7] For what gives you the right
to make such a judgment? What do you have that God
hasn't given you? And if everything you have is from
God, why boast as though it were not a gift?
[8] You think you already have everything you need.
You think you are already rich. You have begun to reign
in God's kingdom without us! I wish you really were
reigning already, for then we would be reigning with
you. [9] Instead, I sometimes think God has put us apostles
on display, like prisoners of war at the end of a victor's
parade, condemned to die. We have become a spectacle
to the entire world—to people and angels alike.
[10] Our dedication to Christ makes us look like fools,
but you claim to be so wise in Christ! We are weak, but
you are so powerful! You are honored, but we are rid-
iculed. [11] Even now we go hungry and thirsty, and we
don't have enough clothes to keep warm. We are often
beaten and have no home. [12] We work wearily with
our own hands to earn our living. We bless those who
curse us. We are patient with those who abuse us.
[13] We appeal gently when evil things are said about
us. Yet we are treated like the world's garbage, like
everybody's trash—right up to the present moment.
[14] I am not writing these things to shame you, but
to warn you as my beloved children. [15] For even if you
had ten thousand others to teach you about Christ,
you have only one spiritual father. For I became your
father in Christ Jesus when I preached the Good News
to you. [16] So I urge you to imitate me.
[17] That's why I have sent Timothy, my beloved and
faithful child in the Lord. He will remind you of how I
follow Christ Jesus, just as I teach in all the churches
wherever I go.
[18] Some of you have become arrogant, thinking
I will not visit you again. [19] But I will come—and
soon—if the Lord lets me, and then I'll find out

3:20 Ps 94:11. **3:22** Greek *Cephas.* **4:6a** Greek *Brothers.* **4:6b** Or *If you learn not to go beyond "what is written."*

4:1 So look at Apollos and me as mere servants. How Christians should relate to their ministers or church leaders. **servants of Christ.** First and foremost, a minister who does the work given him or her under Christ's authority. **put in charge.** Literally, stewards. In a Greek household this was the slave who directed the staff, saw to securing supplies, and, in effect, ran the entire household for his master. **God's mysteries.** As in 2:7, these are the plans of God once known only by Him, but now revealed to all. It is the minister's task to share and coordinate work in accord with these mysteries.

4:3-4 evaluated. Neither the Corinthians nor Paul himself is fit to judge Paul's faithfulness as God's steward. Only God can, and Paul is content to rest in that knowledge and not let criticism bother him.

4:5 before the Lord returns. At the second coming of Christ, the Day of Judgment will occur. Paul cautions about making premature judgments. Let the Lord judge. He is the only one able to do it properly. **private motives.** Not just actions but also one's personal intentions will be made plain when Christ returns.

4:8 already. The Corinthians are acting as if the kingdom of God itself had already arrived. **we would be reigning with you.** Paul wishes they were right because, in fact, his present experience was quite grim (vv. 11-12; 2 Cor. 6:4-10).

4:9 condemned to die. The image is of the triumphal return of a Roman general who parades before the people his trophies who will be taken into the arena to fight and die.

4:10 Christ makes us look like fools. By the standards of the world's wisdom, Paul is indeed foolish. This is the pathway to God's wisdom (3:18). **you claim to be so wise in Christ!** In ironic contrast Paul points out that the worldly Corinthians are acting as if they are wise and superior. **We are weak.** In fact, in God's economy, weakness is strength. Christ came not as a conquering hero, but to be crucified as a common criminal. In the suffering Savior one finds the model for the Christian life.

4:12 we work. Covering all of his expenses by making tents, sometimes with the tent-making missionary couple Aquila and Priscilla (Acts 18:3; 20:34).

4:14-21 Paul ends the section begun in 1:10. The Corinthians preference for worldly wisdom has resulted in patronizing their missionaries and ministers and in attempting to play them off against one another. In this context, Paul uses the metaphor of a father correcting his children.

4:14 to shame you. Indeed, though Corinthians ought to be blushing in acute distress over their ungodliness, it is not shame Paul intends. **warn.** The word means "to admonish," as a father might do, in hope that his children will see their error.

4:16 imitate me. They can look to Paul: a servant eager to do Christ's bidding and a man who walks in the footsteps of a despised, crucified Savior (vv. 11-12).

4:17 That's why. Since Paul himself cannot come yet (though he is planning a trip), he will send his convert and disciple Timothy who will model the Christian life for them.

whether these arrogant people just give pretentious
speeches or whether they really have God's power.
20 For the Kingdom of God is not just a lot of talk; it is
living by God's power. 21 Which do you choose? Should
I come with a rod to punish you, or should I come with
love and a gentle spirit?

PAUL CONDEMNS SPIRITUAL PRIDE

5 I can hardly believe the report about the sexual
immorality going on among you—something that
even pagans don't do. I am told that a man in your
church is living in sin with his stepmother.* 2 You are
so proud of yourselves, but you should be mourning
in sorrow and shame. And you should remove this
man from your fellowship.
3 Even though I am not with you in person, I am
with you in the Spirit.* And as though I were there,
I have already passed judgment on this man 4 in the
name of the Lord Jesus. You must call a meeting of
the church.* I will be present with you in spirit, and
so will the power of our Lord Jesus. 5 Then you must
throw this man out and hand him over to Satan so
that his sinful nature will be destroyed* and he him-
self* will be saved on the day the Lord* returns.
6 Your boasting about this is terrible. Don't you real-
ize that this sin is like a little yeast that spreads through
the whole batch of dough? 7 Get rid of the old "yeast" by
removing this wicked person from among you. Then
you will be like a fresh batch of dough made without
yeast, which is what you really are. Christ, our Passover
Lamb, has been sacrificed for us.* 8 So let us celebrate
the festival, not with the old bread* of wickedness and
evil, but with the new bread* of sincerity and truth.
9 When I wrote to you before, I told you not to as-
sociate with people who indulge in sexual sin. 10 But I
wasn't talking about unbelievers who indulge in sexual
sin, or are greedy, or cheat people, or worship idols. You
would have to leave this world to avoid people like that.
11 I meant that you are not to associate with anyone who
claims to be a believer* yet indulges in sexual sin, or is
greedy, or worships idols, or is abusive, or is a drunkard,
or cheats people. Don't even eat with such people.
12 It isn't my responsibility to judge outsiders, but it
certainly is your responsibility to judge those inside
the church who are sinning. 13 God will judge those
on the outside; but as the Scriptures say, "You must
remove the evil person from among you."*

SEX AND THE CHRISTIAN

1. What do you think of the dress code at your school? What would you change?

1 CORINTHIANS 5:1-13

2. How can handing someone over to Satan result in that person's salvation on the Day of the Lord (v. 5)?
3. What happens when Christians are more concerned with judging those around them than with evaluating their own behavior and motives?
4. What distinction does Paul draw between sexually immoral Christians and non-Christians? Why is the Christian treated more severely?
5. Are you examining your own life or comparing yourself with others, especially in the area of sexual morality?

AVOIDING LAWSUITS WITH CHRISTIANS

6 When one of you has a dispute with another be-
liever, how dare you file a lawsuit and ask a sec-
ular court to decide the matter instead of taking it to
other believers*! 2 Don't you realize that someday we
believers will judge the world? And since you are go-
ing to judge the world, can't you decide even these little
things among yourselves? 3 Don't you realize that we
will judge angels? So you should surely be able to re-
solve ordinary disputes in this life. 4 If you have legal
disputes about such matters, why go to outside judges
who are not respected by the church? 5 I am saying this
to shame you. Isn't there anyone in all the church who
is wise enough to decide these issues? 6 But instead, one
believer* sues another—right in front of unbelievers!
7 Even to have such lawsuits with one another is a
defeat for you. Why not just accept the injustice and
leave it at that? Why not let yourselves be cheated?
8 Instead, you yourselves are the ones who do wrong
and cheat even your fellow believers.*
9 Don't you realize that those who do wrong will
not inherit the Kingdom of God? Don't fool yourselves.
Those who indulge in sexual sin, or who worship

5:1 Greek *his father's wife.* **5:3** Or *in spirit.* **5:4** Or *In the name of the Lord Jesus, you must call a meeting of the church.* **5:5a** Or *so that his body will be destroyed;* Greek reads *for the destruction of the flesh.* **5:5b** Greek *and the spirit.* **5:5c** Other manuscripts read *the Lord Jesus;* still others read *our Lord Jesus Christ.* **5:7** Greek *has been sacrificed.* **5:8a** Greek *not with old leaven.* **5:8b** Greek *but with unleavened [bread].* **5:11** Greek *a brother.* **5:13** Deut 17:7. **6:1** Greek *God's holy people;* also in 6:2. **6:6** Greek *one brother.* **6:8** Greek *even the brothers.*

5:1 sexual immorality. Literally, "fornication." Since Paul does not label this "adultery," the man's father was probably either dead or divorced from his wife. The Corinthians had been newly converted from a pagan environment that was notoriously lax regarding sexual standards. **even pagans don't do.** Incest was also condemned by pagans (as well as by Jews: Lev. 18:8; 20:11), who were shocked at the idea of a father and a son having sexual relations with the same woman. **his stepmother.** Probably not the man's actual mother but rather his stepmother.

5:3-6 Clearly intending discipline, not destruction, Paul orders the church to cut off the man from fellowship.

5:4 call a meeting of the church. Such excommunication (removal from the church) should not be done by Paul or the leaders but by the whole church gathered together under the guidance of Jesus (Matt. 18:17-18).

5:5 his sinful nature will be destroyed. He hopes that by exclusion from the church, the man may see clearly the enormity of his loss and then repent (1 Tim. 1:20).

5:11 Don't even eat. Dining together was an important practice among early Christians (10:14-22; 11:17-34). In excommunication all contact is severed.

6:1 dare. The implication is that such action is an affront to God and to the church. **file a lawsuit.** The bench from which justice was dispensed was located in the marketplace at Corinth. In hauling a brother or sister into court, a Christian was not simply settling a dispute, but holding the church itself up to public scrutiny and ridicule. **secular.** Here this term simply means "non-Christian."

6:7 a defeat. A lawsuit is a clear sign that love in the church has been replaced by selfishness. **Why not just accept the injustice?** Paul counsels non-retaliation as Jesus had taught (Matt. 5:38-42; Rom. 12:17-21; 1 Thess. 5:15) because the Christian knows that his or her true life is to be found in the coming age. **Why not let yourselves be cheated?** An indication that Paul is writing about financial and property cases.

6:9 do wrong. Paul illustrates typical destructive lifestyles in Corinth and elsewhere in the Greco-Roman world by the list that follows. **Kingdom of God.** Paul continues with this idea of living out the ethic of the age to come when all evil is undone and God reigns visibly. **male prostitutes . . . practice homosexuality.** The passive and active partners in male homosexual activity (Lev 18:22; 20:13; Rom 1:27; 1 Tim 1:10). Homosexuality was widespread in the Greco-Roman world; 14 of the first 15 Roman emperors practiced it.

idols, or commit adultery, or are male prostitutes, or
practice homosexuality, 10 or are thieves, or greedy
people, or drunkards, or are abusive, or cheat peo-
ple—none of these will inherit the Kingdom of God.
11 Some of you were once like that. But you were
cleansed; you were made holy; you were made right
with God by calling on the name of the Lord Jesus
Christ and by the Spirit of our God.

JUDGING OTHERS

1. If you could judge the whole world for one day, what crimes would you address?

1 CORINTHIANS 6:1-11

2. Why should Christians "accept the injustice" and "be cheated" (v. 7) than take another Christian to court? Why is it so damaging for Christians to sue one another?
3. Look at the list of people in verses 9-10 who will not inherit God's kingdom. Why are "greedy people" listed with "thieves"? What does this suggest?
4. Why will homosexuals not inherit God's kingdom? How does this differ from the world's teachings? How do you deal with this issue?

AVOIDING SEXUAL SIN

12 You say, "I am allowed to do anything"—but not
everything is good for you. And even though "I am
allowed to do anything," I must not become a slave
to anything. 13 You say, "Food was made for the stom-
ach, and the stomach for food." (This is true, though
someday God will do away with both of them.) But
you can't say that our bodies were made for sexual
immorality. They were made for the Lord, and the
Lord cares about our bodies. 14 And God will raise us
from the dead by his power, just as he raised our Lord
from the dead.
15 Don't you realize that your bodies are actually
parts of Christ? Should a man take his body, which is
part of Christ, and join it to a prostitute? Never! 16 And
don't you realize that if a man joins himself to a pros-
titute, he becomes one body with her? For the Scrip-
tures say, "The two are united into one."* 17 But the per-
son who is joined to the Lord is one spirit with him.
18 Run from sexual sin! No other sin so clearly af-
fects the body as this one does. For sexual immorality
is a sin against your own body. 19 Don't you realize that
your body is the temple of the Holy Spirit, who lives in
you and was given to you by God? You do not belong
to yourself, 20 for God bought you with a high price. So
you must honor God with your body.

RUN FROM SEX

1. What food would be the hardest for you to give up eating?

1 CORINTHIANS 6:12-20

2. Explain in your own words what Paul means in verse 12. How does this apply to behaviors such as drinking or smoking?
3. How does a person "Run from sexual sin" (v. 18)? Why are we to do this according to this passage?
4. In what way is "sexual immorality a sin against your own body" (v. 18)?
5. How does this passage compare with the world's view of sex? With your view of sex?

INSTRUCTION ON MARRIAGE

7 Now regarding the questions you asked in your
letter. Yes, it is good to abstain from sexual rela-
tions.* 2 But because there is so much sexual immo-
rality, each man should have his own wife, and each
woman should have her own husband.
3 The husband should fulfill his wife's sexual needs,
and the wife should fulfill her husband's needs. 4 The
wife gives authority over her body to her husband,
and the husband gives authority over his body to his
wife.
5 Do not deprive each other of sexual relations, un-
less you both agree to refrain from sexual intimacy
for a limited time so you can give yourselves more
completely to prayer. Afterward, you should come
together again so that Satan won't be able to tempt
you because of your lack of self-control. 6 I say this as
a concession, not as a command. 7 But I wish everyone
were single, just as I am. Yet each person has a special
gift from God, of one kind or another.
8 So I say to those who aren't married and to wid-
ows—it's better to stay unmarried, just as I am.
9 But if they can't control themselves, they should go
ahead and marry. It's better to marry than to burn
with lust.

6:16 Gen 2:24. **7:1** Or *to live a celibate life;* Greek reads *It is good for a man not to touch a woman.*

6:12 I'm allowed to do anything. This was probably the slogan of a libertarian party at Corinth, which felt that since the body was insignificant (in comparison with the "spirit"), it did not really matter what one did. **not everything is good . . . I must not become a slave to anything.** Paul argues that while everything may be permissible, not everything is good. The principle of freedom must be guided by the principle of love. We should ask: (1) Is what I am doing beneficial for myself or others; and (2) What does my activity show about whom or what I honor as Lord? Without guiding principles, Christian freedom becomes a cover for self-indulgence. **a slave.** To indulge one's appetites in unsuitable ways opens the possibility of slavery to a harmful habit.
6:13 Food was made for the stomach. Diet is a matter of indifference—especially in that it has no impact on one's salvation. **bodies.** The Corinthians fail to see that the body is the means by which one serves and honors the Lord.
6:18 Run. Paul's counsel regarding sexual temptation is simple and direct.
7:5 Abstinence is allowed under two conditions: both partners agree, and it is for a limited time. **deprive.** Literally, "rob." For one partner to opt out of sexual relations under the guise of spirituality is a form of robbery. **prayer.** The purpose of such abstinence is prayer. **lack of self-control.** Paul assumes that a couple would not have married if they did not feel any legitimate sexual desire, which they ought to fulfill lest they be tempted to commit adultery.
7:7 just as I am. That is, celibate. Paul is not advocating celibacy as much as resistance against inappropriate sexual expression. **gift.** Celibacy is a spiritual gift that not everyone has.
7:8 stay unmarried, just as I am. Paul was more likely a widower than a bachelor, since it was quite rare for a rabbi to be unmarried. In fact, marriage was virtually obligatory for a Jew. His point applies to unmarried and widowed people.
7:9 can't control. Abstinence would be problematical for those who had once experienced an active married life. **to burn.** It is difficult to lead a devoted Christian life when one is consumed with desire.

THE QUESTION OF MARRIAGE

1. Who do you know that has remained single? What do you admire about that person?

1 CORINTHIANS 7:1-40

2. What does Paul mean that "The wife gives authority over her body to her husband" and vice versa (v. 4)? What does this say about marriage?
3. Why is it better for some people to remain unmarried? For others to marry?
4. What do verses 10-11 and 39 teach about divorce and remarriage? How does this compare with the world's beliefs?
5. How can you be sure to follow God's plan for your life regarding marriage?

10 But for those who are married, I have a command that comes not from me, but from the Lord.* A wife must not leave her husband. 11 But if she does leave him, let her remain single or else be reconciled to him. And the husband must not leave his wife.

12 Now, I will speak to the rest of you, though I do not have a direct command from the Lord. If a fellow believer* has a wife who is not a believer and she is willing to continue living with him, he must not leave her. 13 And if a believing woman has a husband who is not a believer and he is willing to continue living with her, she must not leave him. 14 For the believing wife brings holiness to her marriage, and the believing husband* brings holiness to his marriage. Otherwise, your children would not be holy, but now they are holy. 15 (But if the husband or wife who isn't a believer insists on leaving, let them go. In such cases the believing husband or wife* is no longer bound to the other, for God has called you* to live in peace.) 16 Don't you wives realize that your husbands might be saved because of you? And don't you husbands realize that your wives might be saved because of you?

17 Each of you should continue to live in whatever situation the Lord has placed you, and remain as you were when God first called you. This is my rule for all the churches. 18 For instance, a man who was circumcised before he became a believer should not try to reverse it. And the man who was uncircumcised when he became a believer should not be circumcised now. 19 For it makes no difference whether or not a man has been circumcised. The important thing is to keep God's commandments.

20 Yes, each of you should remain as you were when God called you. 21 Are you a slave? Don't let that worry you—but if you get a chance to be free, take it. 22 And remember, if you were a slave when the Lord called you, you are now free in the Lord. And if you were free when the Lord called you, you are now a slave of Christ. 23 God paid a high price for you, so don't be enslaved by the world.* 24 Each of you, dear brothers and sisters,* should remain as you were when God first called you.

25 Now regarding your question about the young women who are not yet married. I do not have a command from the Lord for them. But the Lord in his mercy has given me wisdom that can be trusted, and I will share it with you. 26 Because of the present crisis,* I think it is best to remain as you are. 27 If you have a wife, do not seek to end the marriage. If you do not have a wife, do not seek to get married. 28 But if you do get married, it is not a sin. And if a young woman gets married, it is not a sin. However, those who get married at this time will have troubles, and I am trying to spare you those problems.

29 But let me say this, dear brothers and sisters: The time that remains is very short. So from now on, those with wives should not focus only on their marriage. 30 Those who weep or who rejoice or who buy things should not be absorbed by their weeping or their joy or their possessions. 31 Those who use the things of the world should not become attached to them. For this world as we know it will soon pass away.

32 I want you to be free from the concerns of this life. An unmarried man can spend his time doing the Lord's work and thinking how to please him. 33 But a married man has to think about his earthly responsibilities and how to please his wife. 34 His interests are divided. In the same way, a woman who is no longer married or has never been married can be devoted to the Lord and holy in body and in spirit. But a married woman has to think about her earthly responsibilities and how to please her husband. 35 I am saying this for your benefit, not to place restrictions on you. I want you to do whatever will help you serve the Lord best, with as few distractions as possible.

36 But if a man thinks that he's treating his fiancée improperly and will inevitably give in to his passion, let him marry her as he wishes. It is not a sin. 37 But

7:10 See Matt 5:32; 19:9; Mark 10:11-12; Luke 16:18. **7:12** Greek *a brother.* **7:14** Greek *the brother.* **7:15a** Greek *the brother or sister.* **7:15b** Some manuscripts read *us.* **7:23** Greek *don't become slaves of people.* **7:24** Greek *brothers;* also in 7:29. **7:26** Or *the pressures of life.*

7:10 not from me, but from the Lord. Paul is probably referring to statements by Jesus, as in Mark 10:2-12. **A wife.** Paul writes (vv. 10-11) primarily to women because they were probably advocating sexual abstinence in order to remain "spiritually pure." **must not leave her husband.** Despite preferring the single life, Paul does not encourage those who are already married to be divorced (see Mal. 2:16).

7:12-14 he must not leave . . . she must not leave. A Christian must not take the initiative to divorce his or her non-believing spouse.

7:15 let them leave. But should the non-Christian partner leave, the prohibition against divorce does not apply.

7:16 saved because of you. Christians who remain in a mixed marriage may have the joy of seeing their spouses converted to Christ (see also 1 Pet. 3:1-2).

7:17-24 Paul now gives the general principle (stay as one was when called into service by God), repeated three times (vv. 17, 20, 24), upon which he based his arguments in verses 1-16 and then verses 25-40. He illustrates this principle by references to circumcision and slavery.

7:25 young women. Those persons without sexual experience. **wisdom that can be trusted.** Paul does not have a clear word from the Lord about whether single people ought to marry, but he does offer his Spirit-directed advice (v. 40).

7:26 the present crisis. Written when the gospel was spreading rapidly, Christians were being persecuted for their faith, and they expected Christ's return would come very soon. In light of these circumstances, it was felt that it would be proper to put aside the responsibilities of marriage to devote oneself to furthering God's kingdom. **it is best to remain as you are.** Again Paul appears to be quoting a truism or maxim from Corinth.

7:28 it is not a sin. The Corinthians have probably been insisting that unmarried men remain single. While Paul sees the wisdom of this, it is not a command but good advice that the Christian is free to accept or reject.

7:34 divided. The married man is rightly concerned about how to please the Lord and please his wife. This is the problem: how to be fully faithful to both legitimate commitments. **a married woman.** The same is true of a married woman: her attention is divided in a way that is not true of a single woman.

if he has decided firmly not to marry and there is no urgency and he can control his passion, he does well not to marry. 38 So the person who marries his fiancée does well, and the person who doesn't marry does even better.

39 A wife is bound to her husband as long as he lives. If her husband dies, she is free to marry anyone she wishes, but only if he loves the Lord.* 40 But in my opinion it would be better for her to stay single, and I think I am giving you counsel from God's Spirit when I say this.

FOOD SACRIFICED TO IDOLS

8 Now regarding your question about food that has been offered to idols. Yes, we know that "we all have knowledge" about this issue. But while knowledge makes us feel important, it is love that strengthens the church. 2 Anyone who claims to know all the answers doesn't really know very much. 3 But the person who loves God is the one whom God recognizes.*

4 So, what about eating meat that has been offered to idols? Well, we all know that an idol is not really a god and that there is only one God. 5 There may be so-called gods both in heaven and on earth, and some people actually worship many gods and many lords. 6 But for us,

There is one God, the Father,
by whom all things were created,
and for whom we live.
And there is one Lord, Jesus Christ,
through whom all things were created,
and through whom we live.

7 However, not all believers know this. Some are accustomed to thinking of idols as being real, so when they eat food that has been offered to idols, they think of it as the worship of real gods, and their weak consciences are violated. 8 It's true that we can't win God's approval by what we eat. We don't lose anything if we don't eat it, and we don't gain anything if we do.

9 But you must be careful so that your freedom does not cause others with a weaker conscience to stumble. 10 For if others see you—with your "superior knowledge"—eating in the temple of an idol, won't they be encouraged to violate their conscience by eating food that has been offered to an idol? 11 So because of your superior knowledge, a weak believer* for whom Christ died will be destroyed. 12 And when you sin against other believers* by encouraging them to do something they believe is wrong, you are sinning against Christ. 13 So if what I eat causes another believer to sin, I will never eat meat again as long as I live—for I don't want to cause another believer to stumble.

CAREFUL CHOICES

1. Do you think a Christian should ever drink alcohol? Why or why not?

1 CORINTHIANS 8:1-13

2. Why might Christians in Paul's day have refrained from eating food offered to idols? Why might others have felt free to do so?
3. What sorts of choices today are like the choice to eat "food offered to idols"?
4. Put into your own words the principle of "Christian liberty" that Paul addresses here and the principle of "dying to self."
5. Have you done anything lately to wound the conscience of a fellow Christian (v. 12)? How will you choose differently next time?

PAUL GIVES UP HIS RIGHTS

9 Am I not as free as anyone else? Am I not an apostle? Haven't I seen Jesus our Lord with my own eyes? Isn't it because of my work that you belong to the Lord? 2 Even if others think I am not an apostle, I certainly am to you. You yourselves are proof that I am the Lord's apostle.

3 This is my answer to those who question my authority.* 4 Don't we have the right to live in your homes and share your meals? 5 Don't we have the right to bring a believing wife* with us as the oth-

7:39 Greek *but only in the Lord.* **8:3** Some manuscripts read *the person who loves has full knowledge.* **8:11** Greek *brother;* also in 8:13. **8:12** Greek *brothers.* **9:3** Greek *those who examine me.* **9:5a** Greek *a sister a wife.* **9:5b** Greek *Cephas.*

7:39 only if he loves the Lord. It is also possible to translate this phrase, "remembering that she is a Christian." In any case, Christian widows (or widowers) may remarry other Christians.

8:1 food . . . offered to idols. In ancient cities, most of the meat for sale came from the temples where it had first been offered to an idol, since only priests were allowed by the Romans to function as butchers. Jews were absolutely forbidden to eat such idol-food, and the question is whether the same prohibition applied to Christians. **we all have knowledge.** Once again, Paul appears to be quoting from their letter which argued that eating such food should be all right in view of their new position in Christ. Paul agrees with the assertion but then goes on to qualify it sharply. **knowledge makes us feel important, it is love that strengthens the church.** While knowledge is useful, the basic aim of the Christian must be love. When people feel "superior" because they have special insights, this attitude may make it hard to reach out in love to others.

8:9 be careful. Love for others is the limitation placed upon one's freedom in Christ. **stumble.** If "strong" Christians exercise their right to eat idol-meat at a temple, this may induce "weak" Christians to violate their consciences to their detriment. **weaker.** These are people whose faith is still relatively immature or ill-informed.

8:10 eating in the temple of an idol. Temples were the "restaurants" of the time. Social life involved invitations to join friends at a temple for a meal held in honor of the god of that temple. Therefore, to eat at such a temple implied involvement with that god. If a Christian with "knowledge" that "an idol is nothing" (v. 4) exercised his or her knowledge by eating at such an occasion, this could induce weaker Christians who are not so informed to compromise or abandon their faith by again falling into idolatry and immorality.

8:12 sinning against Christ. Instead of proving oneself to be "strong" and "spiritual," a Christian who ignores the concerns of the "weak" has offended the more important law of love.

9:1 Am I not as free? He is certainly as free as any Christian, but because of his commitment to the way of love, he restricts his lifestyle (as he showed in ch. 8). **Haven't I seen Jesus our Lord?** A person could not become an apostle unless he had witnessed firsthand the resurrected Christ (15:7-8; Acts 1:22). This was the primary evidence that he was a legitimate apostle (15:3-11; Gal. 1:11-24).

9:4 the right . . . to share your meals. Paul is certainly free to eat idol-food, but he refuses to exercise this right because it would harm the "weaker" Christians in the community.

9:5 bring a believing wife. All Christians have the right to a wife (ch. 7). Apparently the Christian community they were serving would support both an apostle and his wife. **Peter.** Peter is singled out because he had probably visited Corinth along with his wife.

er apostles and the Lord's brothers do, and as Peter*
does? 6 Or is it only Barnabas and I who have to work
to support ourselves?
7 What soldier has to pay his own expenses? What
farmer plants a vineyard and doesn't have the right to
eat some of its fruit? What shepherd cares for a flock
of sheep and isn't allowed to drink some of the milk?
8 Am I expressing merely a human opinion, or does
the law say the same thing? 9 For the law of Moses
says, "You must not muzzle an ox to keep it from eat-
ing as it treads out the grain."* Was God thinking only
about oxen when he said this? 10 Wasn't he actually
speaking to us? Yes, it was written for us, so that the
one who plows and the one who threshes the grain
might both expect a share of the harvest.
11 Since we have planted spiritual seed among you,
aren't we entitled to a harvest of physical food and
drink? 12 If you support others who preach to you,
shouldn't we have an even greater right to be sup-
ported? But we have never used this right. We would
rather put up with anything than be an obstacle to
the Good News about Christ.
13 Don't you realize that those who work in the temple
get their meals from the offerings brought to the temple?
And those who serve at the altar get a share of the sacri-
ficial offerings. 14 In the same way, the Lord ordered that
those who preach the Good News should be supported
by those who benefit from it. 15 Yet I have never used any
of these rights. And I am not writing this to suggest that
I want to start now. In fact, I would rather die than lose
my right to boast about preaching without charge. 16 Yet
preaching the Good News is not something I can boast
about. I am compelled by God to do it. How terrible for
me if I didn't preach the Good News!
17 If I were doing this on my own initiative, I would
deserve payment. But I have no choice, for God has
given me this sacred trust. 18 What then is my pay?
It is the opportunity to preach the Good News with-
out charging anyone. That's why I never demand my
rights when I preach the Good News.
19 Even though I am a free man with no master, I have
become a slave to all people to bring many to Christ.
20 When I was with the Jews, I lived like a Jew to bring
the Jews to Christ. When I was with those who follow
the Jewish law, I too lived under that law. Even though
I am not subject to the law, I did this so I could bring to
Christ those who are under the law. 21 When I am with
the Gentiles who do not follow the Jewish law,* I too live
apart from that law so I can bring them to Christ. But I
do not ignore the law of God; I obey the law of Christ.
22 When I am with those who are weak, I share
their weakness, for I want to bring the weak to Christ.
Yes, I try to find common ground with everyone, do-
ing everything I can to save some. 23 I do everything
to spread the Good News and share in its blessings.
24 Don't you realize that in a race everyone runs, but
only one person gets the prize? So run to win! 25 All
athletes are disciplined in their training. They do it to
win a prize that will fade away, but we do it for an
eternal prize. 26 So I run with purpose in every step. I
am not just shadowboxing. 27 I discipline my body like
an athlete, training it to do what it should. Otherwise,
I fear that after preaching to others I myself might be
disqualified.

THE ULTIMATE QUALIFICATION

1. Who is your favorite Olympic athlete, and why?

1 CORINTHIANS 9:24-27

2. What does it mean that athletes compete for "a prize that will fade away" (v. 25)? What is an "eternal prize"?
3. What does Paul do to assure "that after preaching to others, I myself will not be disqualified" (v. 27)? How can we avoid being disqualified?
4. What kinds of discipline are required in your own sport? How costly is it for you to follow those disciplines?
5. What kinds of discipline are required in serving Christ? Do you follow those disciplines as faithfully as your sport's disciplines?

LESSONS FROM ISRAEL'S IDOLATRY

10 I don't want you to forget, dear brothers and
sisters,* about our ancestors in the wilderness
long ago. All of them were guided by a cloud that
moved ahead of them, and all of them walked through
the sea on dry ground. 2 In the cloud and in the sea,
all of them were baptized as followers of Moses. 3 All
of them ate the same spiritual food, 4 and all of them
drank the same spiritual water. For they drank from
the spiritual rock that traveled with them, and that
rock was Christ. 5 Yet God was not pleased with most
of them, and their bodies were scattered in the wil-
derness.

9:9 Deut 25:4. **9:21** Greek *those without the law.* **10:1** Greek *brothers.*

9:12 we have never used this right. This is the point Paul wants to get across to the Corinthians so that they might follow his example. While he has the right to financial support (vv. 7-12), he has chosen not to exercise this right. **obstacle to the Good News.** If Paul had accepted financial reward, potential converts might have misunderstood this as the major motive for his ministry. Paul had the right to support; instead he supported himself making tents.

9:15 these rights. Though Paul had the right to be supported just as priests were supported in temple service, he forwent these privileges so that it would not be perceived that he was rendering services for its material benefits or was under obligation to anyone. Thus, receiving no reward was his reward!

9:19 Even though I am a free man. In verse 1, this appears to have referred to Paul's freedom from dietary concerns based on religious principles. While it carries the same meaning here, it also includes the fact that since he refuses financial support from those he teaches, he is "owned" by no one (6:20). He is obligated to no system or group.

9:22 weak. Those with weak consciences (8:7-13) who are not yet free from legalism or from the power of paganism.

9:26 run with purpose. *Unlike* such a runner who has no fixed goal. Paul's activities are not without a point. Everything he does is for the sake of the gospel. **shadowboxing.** In the same way that he pictured pointless running, now he switches to the image of futile boxing.

10:1 I don't want you to forget. They claimed to have "knowledge" (8:1-2), but the Corinthians had really misunderstood the meaning of baptism and Communion (the Eucharist). **our ancestors.** Though his readers are largely Gentiles, Paul considers them to be the spiritual heirs of Israel. **cloud . . . sea.** Paul reminds them of the Exodus (Ex. 13:21; 14:19-31), using the engulfing presence of the cloud of God and their passing through the sea as analogies to baptism.

10:3-4 spiritual food . . . water. Not only did these gifts from God nourish their physical bodies, they had an additional spiritual function (in that they were symbols that prefigured Christian Communion, and therefore, the benefits of Christ's death).

10:5 not pleased. Paul gives an example of those who were direct benefactors of God's grace but who ultimately proved themselves to be imposters. A stern warning to be sure of one's salvation.

STANDING AND FALLING

1. Have you ever been winning a competition only to lose at the very end? Did overconfidence play a part in that loss?

1 CORINTHIANS 10:1-13

2. What is "sexual immorality" (v. 8)? How far is too far? What physical actions are appropriate?
3. Why would complaining (v. 10) bring the same punishment as sexual immorality?
4. What does Paul mean by "If you think you are standing strong, be careful not to fall" (v. 12)?
5. Are you being sexually pure? Uncomplaining? How can you avoid becoming overconfident in your own abilities and strength?

6 These things happened as a warning to us, so that we would not crave evil things as they did, 7 or worship idols as some of them did. As the Scriptures say, "The people celebrated with feasting and drinking, and they indulged in pagan revelry."* 8 And we must not engage in sexual immorality as some of them did, causing 23,000 of them to die in one day.

9 Nor should we put Christ* to the test, as some of them did and then died from snakebites. 10 And don't grumble as some of them did, and then were destroyed by the angel of death. 11 These things happened to them as examples for us. They were written down to warn us who live at the end of the age.

12 If you think you are standing strong, be careful not to fall. 13 The temptations in your life are no different from what others experience. And God is faithful. He will not allow the temptation to be more than you can stand. When you are tempted, he will show you a way out so that you can endure.

14 So, my dear friends, flee from the worship of idols. 15 You are reasonable people. Decide for yourselves if what I am saying is true. 16 When we bless the cup at the Lord's Table, aren't we sharing in the blood of Christ? And when we break the bread, aren't we sharing in the body of Christ? 17 And though we are many, we all eat from one loaf of bread, showing that we are one body. 18 Think about the people of Israel. Weren't they united by eating the sacrifices at the altar?

19 What am I trying to say? Am I saying that food offered to idols has some significance, or that idols are real gods? 20 No, not at all. I am saying that these sacrifices are offered to demons, not to God. And I don't want you to participate with demons. 21 You cannot drink from the cup of the Lord and from the cup of demons, too. You cannot eat at the Lord's Table and at the table of demons, too. 22 What? Do we dare to rouse the Lord's jealousy? Do you think we are stronger than he is?

23 You say, "I am allowed to do anything"*—but not everything is good for you. You say, "I am allowed to do anything"—but not everything is beneficial. 24 Don't be concerned for your own good but for the good of others.

HANDLING OUR FREEDOM

1. What freedom would you like to have that your parents now deny you? From what are they protecting you?

1 CORINTHIANS 10:14–11:1

2. What things has the world today "offered to demons" (v. 20)? Consider popular music, entertainment, video games, and so forth.
3. What does Paul mean, "You cannot drink from the cup of the Lord and from the cup of demons" (v. 21)? How might we sometimes fall into that in the world today?
4. In what ways is a Christian free (vv. 23-24)? How can you exercise that freedom properly? What is the highest priority?

10:7 Exod 32:6. **10:9** Some manuscripts read *the Lord.* **10:23** Greek *All things are lawful;* also in 10:23b.

10:8 sexual immorality. Paul now explicitly condemns the sexual vice associated with pagan religion (6:12-20). **23,000.** Paul is referring to the story of the Israelites' fornication with the Moabite women as recorded in Numbers 25:1-9 (the figure there is 24,000).

10:9 put Christ to the test. The Corinthians (as had the Israelites before them) were testing God by these actions.

10:10 grumble. They were also grumbling against Paul for telling them not to engage in temple feasts and ritual prostitution.

10:11 written down to warn us. One of the great values of Scripture is to keep before us the danger and consequences of sin. One habit of the human heart is to keep hidden from itself the certain consequences of sin. God's Word is designed to remind us constantly of the danger that accompanies sinful attitudes and actions.

10:12 think you are standing strong. The person at greatest risk is the person who believes he is immune from danger.

10:13 Paul encourages the Corinthians to stand firm by reminding them that when Christians resist sin, they do so in the knowledge that they will be able to endure. **temptation.** Paul has identified various temptations that Israel faced: idolatry, sexual immorality, the temptation to test God, and the temptation to grumble about where God led them. To be tempted is to be tested. Facing the choice of deserting God's will or doing God's will, the person must either resist or yield. Temptation is not sin. Yielding is. **a way out.** Temptation is not unusual or unexpected. Resisting temptation is not pleasant, but the Christian can do it with God's help.

10:14 So. Paul will now draw the logical conclusions from his survey of Israel's past. **flee from the worship of idols.** In the same way that he unequivocally forbids fornication (6:18), he forbids Christians to participate in idol worship. While Paul urges Christians to "stand fast" in the face of evil (Eph. 6:10-18), he counsels flight (not a fight) when it comes to "sins of the flesh." Constant temptations are too strong to resist.

10:16 bless the cup at the Lord's Table. This refers to the cup of wine drunk at the conclusion of the meal in a Jewish home, over which a blessing was spoken. During the Last Supper, Jesus made this cup a symbol of His soon-to-be-shed blood, to be drunk regularly in remembrance of Him.

10:18 eating the sacrifices. The priests were allowed to eat parts of the sacrificial offerings (Lev. 10:12-15), as were others in certain instances (1 Sam. 9:10-24).

10:20 participate with demons. Just as Paul and Scripture (Exod. 22:20; 32:8; Deut. 28:64; 32:17; Ps. 106:36-37) are explicitly clear that the worship of pagan gods and the offering of sacrifices to them is condemned, so too must the Christian be extremely conscientious in avoiding divided loyalties.

10:23 allowed. In 6:12, Paul addresses the correct attitude towards what is permissible to each individual "body of Christ," that is, each individual member. Here, Paul explains what is permissible in view of the body of Christ as a whole, represented by the Corinthian church. First, Christians are not to defile themselves or the church in what they participate in publicly.

25 So you may eat any meat that is sold in the mar-
ketplace without raising questions of conscience.
26 For "the earth is the LORD's, and everything in it."*
27 If someone who isn't a believer asks you home
for dinner, accept the invitation if you want to. Eat
whatever is offered to you without raising questions
of conscience. 28 (But suppose someone tells you, "This
meat was offered to an idol." Don't eat it, out of consid-
eration for the conscience of the one who told you. 29 It
might not be a matter of conscience for you, but it is
for the other person.) For why should my freedom be
limited by what someone else thinks? 30 If I can thank
God for the food and enjoy it, why should I be con-
demned for eating it?
31 So whether you eat or drink, or whatever you
do, do it all for the glory of God. 32 Don't give offense
to Jews or Gentiles* or the church of God. 33 I, too, try
to please everyone in everything I do. I don't just do
what is best for me; I do what is best for others so that
many may be saved. 11:1 And you should imitate me,
just as I imitate Christ.

INSTRUCTIONS FOR PUBLIC WORSHIP

11 2 I am so glad that you always keep me in your
thoughts, and that you are following the teach-
ings I passed on to you. 3 But there is one thing I want
you to know: The head of every man is Christ, the
head of woman is man, and the head of Christ is God.*
4 A man dishonors his head* if he covers his head
while praying or prophesying. 5 But a woman dis-
honors her head* if she prays or prophesies without
a covering on her head, for this is the same as shaving
her head. 6 Yes, if she refuses to wear a head covering,
she should cut off all her hair! But since it is shameful
for a woman to have her hair cut or her head shaved,
she should wear a covering.*
7 A man should not wear anything on his head
when worshiping, for man is made in God's image
and reflects God's glory. And woman reflects man's
glory. 8 For the first man didn't come from woman,
but the first woman came from man. 9 And man was
not made for woman, but woman was made for man.
10 For this reason, and because the angels are watch-
ing, a woman should wear a covering on her head to
show she is under authority.*
11 But among the Lord's people, women are not in-
dependent of men, and men are not independent of
women. 12 For although the first woman came from
man, every other man was born from a woman, and
everything comes from God.
13 Judge for yourselves. Is it right for a woman to
pray to God in public without covering her head?
14 Isn't it obvious that it's disgraceful for a man to have
long hair? 15 And isn't long hair a woman's pride and
joy? For it has been given to her as a covering. 16 But
if anyone wants to argue about this, I simply say that
we have no other custom than this, and neither do
God's other churches.

ORDER AT THE LORD'S SUPPER

17 But in the following instructions, I cannot praise
you. For it sounds as if more harm than good is done
when you meet together. 18 First, I hear that there are
divisions among you when you meet as a church, and
to some extent I believe it. 19 But, of course, there must
be divisions among you so that you who have God's
approval will be recognized!
20 When you meet together, you are not really in-
terested in the Lord's Supper. 21 For some of you hurry
to eat your own meal without sharing with others.
As a result, some go hungry while others get drunk.
22 What? Don't you have your own homes for eating
and drinking? Or do you really want to disgrace God's

EVALUATE YOURSELF

1. How do you evaluate how well you are progressing in your sport, artistic pursuits, or job?

1 CORINTHIANS 11:17-34

2. What is the purpose of the Lord's Supper? How is it "announcing the Lord's death" (v. 26)?
3. What does it mean that someone "drinks this cup of the Lord unworthily" (v. 27)? What is the result of that? How does one guard against this?
4. In verses 31 and 32, Paul discusses the inescapable aspect of judgment from either God or ourselves. What area of your life do you need to "properly evaluate" so that God doesn't have to discipline you?

10:26 Ps 24:1. **10:32** Greek *or Greeks.* **11:3** Or *to know: The source of every man is Christ, the source of woman is man, and the source of Christ is God.* Or *to know: Every man is responsible to Christ, a woman is responsible to her husband, and Christ is responsible to God.* **11:4** Or *dishonors Christ.* **11:5** Or *dishonors her husband.* **11:6** Or *should have long hair.* **11:10** Greek *should have an authority on her head.*

10:27 Eat whatever is offered to you. Paul shifts his focus to the related question of what one might eat or not eat at the home of a non-Christian friend. Christians can eat whatever is placed before them in such a setting, although the conscience of one's dinner companions must also be considered. It could be a greater evil to reject a host's food.

10:28 someone. It is probably a pagan who points out that what is being offered is idol-food. Pagans viewed Christianity as a Jewish sect and so assumed Christians followed the same dietary laws.

11:3 head of. Paul uses this metaphor and cites three examples: Christ as head of man, man as head of woman, and God as head of Christ. "Head of" has two different connotations. One is "source of." The other is "authority." There are times when "source" needs to be emphasized. At other times, "authority" should be emphasized. Paul's point in using this metaphor with these three examples is to point to a divine order—even between God the Father and God the Son. Father and Son are equal but they are distinct persons and have different roles. Husband and wife have equal worth before God. They both bear the image of God. The husband is charged with being head of that relationship as Christ is head of the church. A wife is to be submissive to the servant leadership of her husband in the same way that the church submits to Christ, her head.

11:11 not independent. While verses 2-16 do not directly mention the context of marriage, the relationship between husband and wife is clearly in view here. Paul points out the mutual interdependence that exists between men and women and their equal dependence on God.

11:18 I hear. Paul had heard what was going on from other sources (1:11; 16:17). He's shocked that it is as bad as reported ("in part I believe it").

11:20 not really interested in the Lord's Supper. The Corinthians have so badly abused the Lord's Supper that it was more like a pagan temple celebration than a meal held in honor of the Lord.

11:21 some of you hurry to eat . . . without sharing with others. The purpose of the meal was for the body of believers to remember the Lord and His victory over sin and death on the cross. **hungry . . . drunk.** The contrast could not be more stark. The poor in the church went hungry during this meal, while others indulged themselves to the point of drunkenness.

11:22 Don't you have your own homes. If the rich can't wait to indulge in their food and drink, at least they should do this at home and not demean the common meal at church.

ROLES OF HUSBANDS AND WIVES

1. What is your ideal for how you'd like to relate with your future spouse?

1 CORINTHIANS 11:22-16

2. A husband can't properly love and lead his wife until Christ is his "head" (v.3). What can you do to make Christ your head?
3. As a wife follows the lead of her husband, is she any less valuable to God because she takes the role of a supportive and helping partner? (See Gal. 3:27-28.)
4. Is the husband of any more value to God because it is his role to lead in marriage?
5. Should a wife follow her husband's lead if he is disobeying God?

church and shame the poor? What am I supposed to
say? Do you want me to praise you? Well, I certainly
will not praise you for this!
23 For I pass on to you what I received from the Lord
himself. On the night when he was betrayed, the Lord
Jesus took some bread 24 and gave thanks to God for it.
Then he broke it in pieces and said, "This is my body,
which is given for you.* Do this in remembrance of
me." 25 In the same way, he took the cup of wine af-
ter supper, saying, "This cup is the new covenant be-
tween God and his people—an agreement confirmed
with my blood. Do this in remembrance of me as often
as you drink it." 26 For every time you eat this bread
and drink this cup, you are announcing the Lord's
death until he comes again.
27 So anyone who eats this bread or drinks this cup
of the Lord unworthily is guilty of sinning against*
the body and blood of the Lord. 28 That is why you
should examine yourself before eating the bread and
drinking the cup. 29 For if you eat the bread or drink
the cup without honoring the body of Christ,* you are
eating and drinking God's judgment upon yourself.
30 That is why many of you are weak and sick and
some have even died.
31 But if we would examine ourselves, we would
not be judged by God in this way. 32 Yet when we are
judged by the Lord, we are being disciplined so that
we will not be condemned along with the world.
33 So, my dear brothers and sisters,* when you gath-
er for the Lord's Supper, wait for each other. 34 If you
are really hungry, eat at home so you won't bring
judgment upon yourselves when you meet together.
I'll give you instructions about the other matters after
I arrive.

SPIRITUAL GIFTS

12 Now, dear brothers and sisters,* regarding your
question about the special abilities the Spirit
gives us. I don't want you to misunderstand this. 2 You
know that when you were still pagans, you were led
astray and swept along in worshiping speechless
idols. 3 So I want you to know that no one speaking by
the Spirit of God will curse Jesus, and no one can say
Jesus is Lord, except by the Holy Spirit.
4 There are different kinds of spiritual gifts, but the
same Spirit is the source of them all. 5 There are differ-
ent kinds of service, but we serve the same Lord. 6 God
works in different ways, but it is the same God who
does the work in all of us.
7 A spiritual gift is given to each of us so we can
help each other. 8 To one person the Spirit gives the
ability to give wise advice*; to another the same Spir-
it gives a message of special knowledge.* 9 The same
Spirit gives great faith to another, and to someone else
the one Spirit gives the gift of healing. 10 He gives one
person the power to perform miracles, and another
the ability to prophesy. He gives someone else the
ability to discern whether a message is from the Spir-
it of God or from another spirit. Still another person
is given the ability to speak in unknown languages,*
while another is given the ability to interpret what is
being said. 11 It is the one and only Spirit who distrib-
utes all these gifts. He alone decides which gift each
person should have.

ONE BODY WITH MANY PARTS

12 The human body has many parts, but the many
parts make up one whole body. So it is with the body
of Christ. 13 Some of us are Jews, some are Gentiles,*
some are slaves, and some are free. But we have all
been baptized into one body by one Spirit, and we all
share the same Spirit.*
14 Yes, the body has many different parts, not just
one part. 15 If the foot says, "I am not a part of the body

11:24 Greek *which is for you;* other manuscripts read *which is broken for you.* 11:27 Or *is responsible for.* 11:29 Greek *the body;* other manuscripts read *the Lord's body.* 11:33 Greek *brothers.* 12:1 Greek *brothers.* 12:8a Or *gives a word of wisdom.* 12:8b Or *gives a word of knowledge.* 12:10 Or *in various tongues;* also in 12:28, 30. 12:13a Greek *some are Greeks.* 12:13b Greek *we were all given one Spirit to drink.*

11:24 "This is my body." Jesus interprets for the disciples the new meaning He is giving to these ordinary acts. He himself will become the Passover lamb for them, to be slain for their sins. **remember.** Paul repeats this phrase twice, to stress that the Lord's Supper is a memorial feast (Luke 22:19).

11:25 This cup is the new covenant. This statement is not found in the four Gospels. It is Paul's summary of the meaning of the Lord's Supper.

11:26 announcing the Lord's death. The Lord's Supper proclaims the fact and meaning of Jesus' death in several ways: the broken bread and outpoured wine symbolically proclaim His death; the words spoken at such a meal (formally and informally) recall the Jesus' crucifixion; and the whole event "proclaims" His atoning death.

11:29 without honoring. When the meal turned into a time of drunkenness, division, and gluttony, people lost sight of the meaning of the event. **the body.** Here, "the body" in view is the body of the Lord remembered in the supper and, secondarily, the church (12:12), both of which the Corinthians were abusing.

12:8 wise advice . . . special knowledge. Exposition of biblical truth with practical, ethical application.

12:9 faith. To believe God for extraordinary results. Saving faith, which all Christians share, is not in view here. **healing.** The special ability to effect miraculous cures. Paul apparently had this gift (Acts 14:8-10).

12:10 to perform miracles. This could refer to miraculous powers of kind witnessed in Acts (5:1-10; 9:40-41; 13:10 11; 16:0; 20:9-10). **to prophesy.** Inspired utterances given in ordinary (not ecstatic) speech, distinguished from teaching and wisdom by its unprepared nature. **discern whether a message is from the Spirit of God or . . . another spirit.** Just because a person claimed to be inspired by the Holy Spirit did not make it true. Those who possessed this gift of discernment were able to identify the source of an utterance—the Holy Spirit or another spirit. **to speak in unknown languages.** Some interpret this to be ecstatic speech, unintelligible except by those with the gift of interpretation of tongues. Others believe it refers to the supernatural ability to speak in real, known languages (as at Pentecost in Acts 2). **interpret what is being said.** This gift allowed a person to understand and explain to others what was being said by someone else in a different tongue or language.

ALL FOR ONE

1. Have you ever broken a bone? How did it affect the rest of your body?

1 CORINTHIANS 12:12-31

2. Put into your own words what Paul is saying in this passage. Why does he use the analogy of a body?
3. What body part is the most "glamorous"? Which is most important to survival? Which is "weaker"?
4. Describe yourself as a "part" of the body of Christ (an eye, hand, etc.). Why did you select that part?
5. How do you treat some of your "weaker" or less desirable brothers and sisters in Christ? How can you make them feel more loved?

because I am not a hand," that does not make it any less a part of the body. 16 And if the ear says, "I am not part of the body because I am not an eye," would that make it any less a part of the body? 17 If the whole body were an eye, how would you hear? Or if your whole body were an ear, how would you smell anything?

18 But our bodies have many parts, and God has put each part just where he wants it. 19 How strange a body would be if it had only one part! 20 Yes, there are many parts, but only one body. 21 The eye can never say to the hand, "I don't need you." The head can't say to the feet, "I don't need you."

22 In fact, some parts of the body that seem weakest and least important are actually the most necessary. 23 And the parts we regard as less honorable are those we clothe with the greatest care. So we carefully protect those parts that should not be seen, 24 while the more honorable parts do not require this special care. So God has put the body together such that extra honor and care are given to those parts that have less dignity. 25 This makes for harmony among the members, so that all the members care for each other. 26 If one part suffers, all the parts suffer with it, and if one part is honored, all the parts are glad.

27 All of you together are Christ's body, and each of you is a part of it. 28 Here are some of the parts God has appointed for the church:

first are apostles,
second are prophets,
third are teachers,
then those who do miracles,
those who have the gift of healing,
those who can help others,
those who have the gift of leadership,
those who speak in unknown languages.

29 Are we all apostles? Are we all prophets? Are we all teachers? Do we all have the power to do miracles? 30 Do we all have the gift of healing? Do we all have the ability to speak in unknown languages? Do we all have the ability to interpret unknown languages? Of course not! 31 So you should earnestly desire the most helpful gifts.

But now let me show you a way of life that is best of all.

LOVE IS THE GREATEST

13 If I could speak all the languages of earth and of angels, but didn't love others, I would only be a noisy gong or a clanging cymbal. 2 If I had the gift of prophecy, and if I understood all of God's secret plans and possessed all knowledge, and if I had such faith that I could move mountains, but didn't love others, I would be nothing. 3 If I gave everything I have to the poor and even sacrificed my body, I could boast about it;* but if I didn't love others, I would have gained nothing.

4 Love is patient and kind. Love is not jealous or boastful or proud 5 or rude. It does not demand its own way. It is not irritable, and it keeps no record of being wronged. 6 It does not rejoice about injustice but rejoices whenever the truth wins out. 7 Love never gives up, never loses faith, is always hopeful, and endures through every circumstance.

8 Prophecy and speaking in unknown languages* and special knowledge will become useless. But love will last forever! 9 Now our knowledge is partial and incomplete, and even the gift of prophecy reveals only part of the whole picture! 10 But when the time of perfection comes, these partial things will become useless.

11 When I was a child, I spoke and thought and reasoned as a child. But when I grew up, I put away childish things. 12 Now we see things imperfectly, like puzzling reflections in a mirror, but then we will see everything with perfect clarity.* All that I know now is partial and incomplete, but then I will know

13:3 Some manuscripts read *sacrificed my body to be burned.* **13:8** Or *in tongues.* **13:12** Greek *see face to face.*

12:28 Paul offers a second list of the types of gifts given by the Holy Spirit (see the parallel list in Eph. 4:11)—mixing together ministries (apostles) with spiritual gifts (the gift of healing). **apostles.** These individuals were responsible for founding new churches. **prophets.** Those who were inspired to speak God's Word to the church, in plain language. **teachers.** Those gifted to instruct others in the meaning of the Christian faith. Having first focused on those gifts whereby the church is established and nurtured, Paul then shifts to other gifts. **help others.** The gift of support; those with this gift often function to aid the needy (e.g., the poor, the widow, the orphan). **leadership.** This is gift of direction, literally, the process of steering a ship through the rocks and safely to shore.

13:1 languages of earth and of angels. This seems to refer again to the gift of tongues (ecstatic speech or speaking in other languages)—highly prized in Corinth and an authentic gift of the Holy Spirit (see also note for 12:10).

13:2 prophecy. Such activity is highly commended by Paul (14:1), yet without love a prophet is really nothing. **understood all of God's secret plans.** In Corinth, special and mysterious knowledge was highly valued (1:18–2:16). **faith that I could move mountains.** Paul refers to Jesus' words in Mark 11:23—even such massive faith is not enough to make a person significant without love.

13:8 love will last forever. It functions both now and in the age to come without ceasing or being held back. By contrast, spiritual gifts are relevant only to this age. **will become useless.** One day, when Christ comes again in fullness, the prophecy will be fulfilled (and so the gift of prophecy will come to an end), indirect communication with God through languages or tongues will no longer be needed (so they cease), and since all will be revealed and be evident, the gift of knowledge will be unnecessary (and so will come to an end).

13:12 Now . . . then. Paul is thinking of the second coming of Christ. The here-and-now experience is contrasted to the complete reality when Christ's kingdom is revealed in its fullness. **imperfectly.** Corinth was famous for the mirrors it made out of highly polished metal. Still, no mirror manufactured in the first century was without imperfections. All of them distorted the image somewhat, and so this is an apt metaphor for the present knowledge of God—it lacks clarity (until the day we see the Lord clearly in heaven).

everything completely, just as God now knows me completely.

[13] Three things will last forever—faith, hope, and love—and the greatest of these is love.

TRUE LOVE

1. What is your favorite love story from a movie, book, TV show, or fairy tale? Why is it a favorite?

1 CORINTHIANS 13:1-13

2. Why does Paul use the analogy of "a noisy gong or a clanging cymbal" (v. 1) to describe someone who is gifted but unloving?
3. How does verse 5 compare with our modern idea of "loving yourself"? What would Paul say about that concept in light of this passage?
4. Why is love greater than the virtues of faith and hope?
5. Name one specific thing you can do in the coming week to be more loving toward others.

TONGUES AND PROPHECY

14 Let love be your highest goal! But you should also desire the special abilities the Spirit gives—especially the ability to prophesy. [2] For if you have the ability to speak in tongues,* you will be talking only to God, since people won't be able to understand you. You will be speaking by the power of the Spirit,* but it will all be mysterious. [3] But one who prophesies strengthens others, encourages them, and comforts them. [4] A person who speaks in tongues is strengthened personally, but one who speaks a word of prophecy strengthens the entire church.

[5] I wish you could all speak in tongues, but even more I wish you could all prophesy. For prophecy is greater than speaking in tongues, unless someone interprets what you are saying so that the whole church will be strengthened.

[6] Dear brothers and sisters,* if I should come to you speaking in an unknown language,* how would that help you? But if I bring you a revelation or some special knowledge or prophecy or teaching, that will be helpful. [7] Even lifeless instruments like the flute or the harp must play the notes clearly, or no one will recognize the melody. [8] And if the bugler doesn't sound a clear call, how will the soldiers know they are being called to battle?

GIFTED AND TALENTED

1. Do you speak any foreign languages? Which ones do you wish you could speak fluently?

1 CORINTHIANS 14:1-25

2. What is the difference between speaking in tongues and prophesying (vv. 2-4)? What is the most important thing about such gifts?
3. What does it mean to "be childish in your understanding" (v. 20)? To "be innocent as babies when it comes to evil, but be mature in understanding matters of this kind"?
4. What is the purpose of spiritual gifts according to this passage? What is their most important function?
5. What do you think your main spiritual gift is? How can you develop it more?

[9] It's the same for you. If you speak to people in words they don't understand, how will they know what you are saying? You might as well be talking into empty space.

[10] There are many different languages in the world, and every language has meaning. [11] But if I don't understand a language, I will be a foreigner to someone who speaks it, and the one who speaks it will be a foreigner to me. [12] And the same is true for you. Since you are so eager to have the special abilities the Spirit gives, seek those that will strengthen the whole church.

[13] So anyone who speaks in tongues should pray also for the ability to interpret what has been said. [14] For if I pray in tongues, my spirit is praying, but I don't understand what I am saying.

[15] Well then, what shall I do? I will pray in the spirit,* and I will also pray in words I understand. I will sing in the spirit, and I will also sing in words I understand. [16] For if you praise God only in the spirit, how can those who don't understand you praise God along with you? How can they join you in giving thanks when they don't understand what you are saying? [17] You will be giving thanks very well, but it won't strengthen the people who hear you.

14:2a Or *in unknown languages;* also in 14:4, 5, 13, 14, 18, 22, 26, 27, 28, 39. **14:2b** Or *speaking in your spirit.* **14:6a** Greek *brothers;* also in 14:20, 26, 39. **14:6b** Or *in tongues;* also in 14:19, 23. **14:15** Or *in the Spirit;* also in 14:15b, 16.

13:13 last forever. Many spiritual gifts will cease because they bring only partial knowledge of God; but three things will carry over into the new age: faith, hope, and love. **the greatest of these is love.** Love is the greatest because God is love (1 John 4:8). After everything else is no longer necessary, love will still be the governing principle.

14:5 but even more. While affirming the value of both tongues and prophecy, Paul stresses prophecy because of its value when the church is gathered. **tongues.** In verses 2-5, Paul gives insight into just what tongues are. They seem to be a gift from the Holy Spirit whereby an individual "utters mysteries" to God by (or in) the Spirit, from which great personal benefit is gained. Uninterpreted tongues, however, are meant to be part of private devotions, not public worship. **greater.** "Greater" in the sense that prophecy edifies, and is, therefore, an act of love. Interpreted tongues have the same use and value as prophecy.

14:6-12 Now the real issue comes out: intelligibility (v. 9). It appears that it is not just prophecy that Paul is commending (v. 6). Prophecy is just the example he has chosen of an intelligible gift. Paul examines the value of various gifts from the point of view of what will build the body.

14:13 So. Connects the previous sentence with what follows.

14:14-17 In the same way that Paul has described that spiritual gifts without love are useless, he goes on to explain that the exercise of the gift of tongues must always keep in mind the ultimate benefit for believers and non-believers alike. The amount of time Paul spends on this subject speaks to its potential abuse for the purpose of self-glory.

14:15 pray in the spirit. Paul adds another insight into tongues: this is prayer that bypasses the mind. It is, according to verse 15, one quite legitimate (and edifying—v. 4) means of prayer, but it is meant to be complemented with prayer that engages the mind.

18 I thank God that I speak in tongues more than any of you. 19 But in a church meeting I would rather speak five understandable words to help others than ten thousand words in an unknown language.

20 Dear brothers and sisters, don't be childish in your understanding of these things. Be innocent as babies when it comes to evil, but be mature in understanding matters of this kind. 21 It is written in the Scriptures*:

"I will speak to my own people
  through strange languages
  and through the lips of foreigners.
But even then, they will not listen to me,"*
  says the LORD.

22 So you see that speaking in tongues is a sign, not for believers, but for unbelievers. Prophecy, however, is for the benefit of believers, not unbelievers. 23 Even so, if unbelievers or people who don't understand these things come into your church meeting and hear everyone speaking in an unknown language, they will think you are crazy. 24 But if all of you are prophesying, and unbelievers or people who don't understand these things come into your meeting, they will be convicted of sin and judged by what you say. 25 As they listen, their secret thoughts will be exposed, and they will fall to their knees and worship God, declaring, "God is truly here among you."

A CALL TO ORDERLY WORSHIP

26 Well, my brothers and sisters, let's summarize. When you meet together, one will sing, another will teach, another will tell some special revelation God has given, one will speak in tongues, and another will interpret what is said. But everything that is done must strengthen all of you.

27 No more than two or three should speak in tongues. They must speak one at a time, and someone must interpret what they say. 28 But if no one is present who can interpret, they must be silent in your church meeting and speak in tongues to God privately.

29 Let two or three people prophesy, and let the others evaluate what is said. 30 But if someone is prophesying and another person receives a revelation from the Lord, the one who is speaking must stop. 31 In this way, all who prophesy will have a turn to speak, one after the other, so that everyone will learn and be encouraged. 32 Remember that people who prophesy are in control of their spirit and can take turns. 33 For God is not a God of disorder but of peace, as in all the meetings of God's holy people.*

34 Women should be silent during the church meetings. It is not proper for them to speak. They should be submissive, just as the law says. 35 If they have any questions, they should ask their husbands at home, for it is improper for women to speak in church meetings.*

36 Or do you think God's word originated with you Corinthians? Are you the only ones to whom it was given? 37 If you claim to be a prophet or think you are spiritual, you should recognize that what I am saying is a command from the Lord himself. 38 But if you do not recognize this, you yourself will not be recognized.*

39 So, my dear brothers and sisters, be eager to prophesy, and don't forbid speaking in tongues. 40 But be sure that everything is done properly and in order.

ORDER VS. CHAOS

1. What was the most disciplined and organized team you've ever been on? The most disorderly and chaotic? Which team played better?

1 CORINTHIANS 14:26-40

2. According to this passage, how should Christians properly use the gift of tongues? What are improper uses of that gift?
3. Why does Paul insist that worship times together be done in an orderly way (vv. 26, 31-33)?
4. When you gather as a group, how can you use your God-given gifts to build up one another?

THE RESURRECTION OF CHRIST

15 Let me now remind you, dear brothers and sisters,* of the Good News I preached to you before. You welcomed it then, and you still stand firm in it. 2 It is this Good News that saves you if you continue to believe the message I told you—unless, of course, you believed something that was never true in the first place.*

3 I passed on to you what was most important and what had also been passed on to me. Christ died for our sins, just as the Scriptures said. 4 He was buried, and he was raised from the dead on the third day, just

14:21a Greek *in the law.* **14:21b** Isa 28:11-12. **14:33** The phrase *as in all the meetings of God's holy people* could instead be joined to the beginning of 14:34. **14:35** Some manuscripts place verses 34-35 after 14:40. **14:38** Some manuscripts read *If you are ignorant of this, stay in your ignorance.* **15:1** Greek *brothers;* also in 15:31, 50, 58. **15:2** Or *unless you never believed it in the first place.*

14:19 rather speak five understandable words. Simply put, don't major on the minors. In line with the other imbalances manifested in the church at Corinth, far too much emphasis was being placed on the demonstration of languages. It may be that the Corinthians' familiarity with "mystery" religions and the ecstatic languages expressed in such meetings caused them to believe that the same should be the hallmark of Christianity as well. Paul is careful here to refocus their concentration on the message of the gospel. In 12:28-29 apostles, prophets, and teachers head the list of spiritual gifts and are indispensable to the establishment and continuance of the church. Many would say that, beyond these primary gifts, the other gifts are simply evidences of the words of the apostles, prophets, and teachers having been spoken and received. And that word directly revolved around the Word Himself, Jesus Christ (John 1:1-5). Therefore, it is understandable why Paul would declare that five intelligible words such as these outweigh the 10,000 words of ecstatic speech. As Paul says, ultimately all spiritual gifts will pass away (13:10), but the Word is eternal.

14:26 one will. Paul reiterates that each believer has a gift to offer during times when the church gathers, that there are a variety of gifts, and that gifts are to be used to build up other people in the body of believers. **sing.** Like church services today, worship begins with songs followed by teaching. Paul makes a point by placing these in such order.

14:29-33 Here Paul gives guidelines for prophecy: two or three speak, followed by discerning interpretation.

14:37-38 As to those who are teaching this, if they are really inspired by the Holy Spirit, they cannot help but agree. God is the author of peace, not confusion.

15:1-3 passed on to me. Paul uses the same word to describe what he received from the Lord when he gave the Corinthians the instruction on the Lord's Supper (11:23) as he does here to describe the instruction he is again reminding them of in regards to the Lord's resurrection. What he received, they in turn have received.

as the Scriptures said. [5]He was seen by Peter* and
then by the Twelve. [6]After that, he was seen by more
than 500 of his followers* at one time, most of whom
are still alive, though some have died. [7]Then he was
seen by James and later by all the apostles. [8]Last of
all, as though I had been born at the wrong time, I
also saw him. [9]For I am the least of all the apostles. In
fact, I'm not even worthy to be called an apostle after
the way I persecuted God's church.
[10]But whatever I am now, it is all because God
poured out his special favor on me—and not with-
out results. For I have worked harder than any of
the other apostles; yet it was not I but God who was
working through me by his grace. [11]So it makes no
difference whether I preach or they preach, for we
all preach the same message you have already be-
lieved.

HOLDING FIRM

1. Who has best helped you to understand God's Word? How did that person effectively pass on God's message to you?

1 CORINTHIANS 15:1-11

2. What does Paul list as the most important aspects of the gospel?
3. In previous passages, Paul has warned against divisions and disagreements. Why might the list in verses 3-8 be the things on which all Christians need to agree?
4. How are you holding firmly to the important things of God's Word when friends or teammates pressure you?

THE RESURRECTION OF THE DEAD

[12]But tell me this—since we preach that Christ rose
from the dead, why are some of you saying there
will be no resurrection of the dead? [13]For if there
is no resurrection of the dead, then Christ has not
been raised either. [14]And if Christ has not been
raised, then all our preaching is useless, and your
faith is useless. [15]And we apostles would all be ly-

THE VITAL STATISTIC

1. What would your coach say is the single most important rule in your sport? What would happen if you broke that rule?

1 CORINTHIANS 15:12-34

2. Why is Christ's resurrection so vitally important to the Christian faith? What would be the implications if He had not really risen again?
3. According to 15:1-8, how can we be assured that Jesus really did rise again?
4. Why would Paul suggest that "Let's feast and drink, for tomorrow we die" (v. 32) would be an appropriate attitude if there were no resurrection?
5. How should your own eternal life affect your behavior today in sports and in life?

ing about God—for we have said that God raised
Christ from the grave. But that can't be true if there
is no resurrection of the dead. [16]And if there is no
resurrection of the dead, then Christ has not been
raised. [17]And if Christ has not been raised, then
your faith is useless and you are still guilty of your
sins. [18]In that case, all who have died believing in
Christ are lost! [19]And if our hope in Christ is only
for this life, we are more to be pitied than anyone
in the world.
[20]But in fact, Christ has been raised from the dead.
He is the first of a great harvest of all who have died.
[21]So you see, just as death came into the world
through a man, now the resurrection from the dead
has begun through another man. [22]Just as everyone
dies because we all belong to Adam, everyone who
belongs to Christ will be given new life. [23]But there is
an order to this resurrection: Christ was raised as the
first of the harvest; then all who belong to Christ will
be raised when he comes back.
[24]After that the end will come, when he will turn
the Kingdom over to God the Father, having destroyed
every ruler and authority and power. [25]For Christ
must reign until he humbles all his enemies beneath
his feet. [26]And the last enemy to be destroyed is death.

15:5 Greek *Cephas*. 15:6 Greek *the brothers*.

15:4 He was buried. Jesus was really dead, and so He really rose from the dead. It was a real resurrection, not just resuscitation. **he was raised.** Paul shifts the tense of the verb in Greek (completed past action—"died/buried") to the perfect tense in order to convey the idea that what once happened is even now still in force.

15:6 more than 500 of his followers . . . most of whom are still alive. Paul is inviting people to check out for themselves the reality of Christ's resurrection. What he is saying is: "There are more than 500 people who some 20 years ago saw Jesus after His resurrection. Ask one of them."

15:8 Last of all . . . I also saw him. This appearance came several years after the resurrection of Christ (Acts 9:1-8). **born at the wrong time.** This probably refers to the fact that, unlike Peter and James, circumstances were such that Paul never knew Jesus during His earthly ministry.

15:9 I persecuted. As the book of Acts records, Paul, a devout Pharisee, persecuted the Christians (Acts 8:1-3) immediately following the stoning of Stephen for preaching the gospel (Acts 7:54-60). Through God's gracious sovereignty, Paul now finds himself preaching the very same gospel. For, on the Damascus Road, Lord Jesus Christ appeared to him and said, "Saul, Saul, Why are you persecuting Me?" Perhaps Paul says he is unworthy to be called an apostle because, by that time, other apostles were being put to death. Eventually, Paul too would seal his love of Christ with his life on the banks of the Tiber.

15:16 if there is no resurrection of the dead. This is the first of three times in this section (vv. 12-34) that Paul uses this phrase that summarizes the implications of their errant view about the resurrection of the body. If the dead are not raised, then: (a) Christ could not have been resurrected (and they believe He was); (b) there would be no point in baptizing people for the dead (as they were apparently doing—v. 29); and (c) believers might as well "live it up," since they had no future (v. 32).

15:17-19 if Christ has not been raised. Relentlessly, Paul points out to his readers the implications of no resurrection: (a) they are still lost and dead in sin; (b) those who have died are lost; (c) their "hope" is groundless; and (d) they are pitiable people. Without the resurrection, Christianity crumbles.

15:20-28 The future resurrection of believers is the logical outcome of Christ's past resurrection. First Thessalonians 4:13-18 refers also to this future resurrection of believers. Paul returns to the metaphor of the "firstfruits," showing how it relates to the second coming. In order for the Corinthians to understand the future resurrection, Paul must place it in the context of the time when Christ returns.

27 For the Scriptures say, "God has put all things under
his authority."* (Of course, when it says "all things are
under his authority," that does not include God him-
self, who gave Christ his authority.) 28 Then, when all
things are under his authority, the Son will put him-
self under God's authority, so that God, who gave his
Son authority over all things, will be utterly supreme
over everything everywhere.
29 If the dead will not be raised, what point is there
in people being baptized for those who are dead?
Why do it unless the dead will someday rise again?
30 And why should we ourselves risk our lives hour
by hour? 31 For I swear, dear brothers and sisters, that
I face death daily. This is as certain as my pride in
what Christ Jesus our Lord has done in you. 32 And
what value was there in fighting wild beasts—those
people of Ephesus*—if there will be no resurrection
from the dead? And if there is no resurrection, "Let's
feast and drink, for tomorrow we die!"* 33 Don't be
fooled by those who say such things, for "bad compa-
ny corrupts good character." 34 Think carefully about
what is right, and stop sinning. For to your shame I
say that some of you don't know God at all.

THE RESURRECTION BODY

35 But someone may ask, "How will the dead be
raised? What kind of bodies will they have?" 36 What
a foolish question! When you put a seed into the
ground, it doesn't grow into a plant unless it dies
first. 37 And what you put in the ground is not the
plant that will grow, but only a bare seed of wheat
or whatever you are planting. 38 Then God gives it
the new body he wants it to have. A different plant
grows from each kind of seed. 39 Similarly there are
different kinds of flesh—one kind for humans, an-
other for animals, another for birds, and another for
fish.
40 There are also bodies in the heavens and bodies
on the earth. The glory of the heavenly bodies is dif-
ferent from the glory of the earthly bodies. 41 The sun
has one kind of glory, while the moon and stars each
have another kind. And even the stars differ from
each other in their glory.
42 It is the same way with the resurrection of the
dead. Our earthly bodies are planted in the ground
when we die, but they will be raised to live forever.
43 Our bodies are buried in brokenness, but they will
be raised in glory. They are buried in weakness, but
they will be raised in strength. 44 They are buried as
natural human bodies, but they will be raised as spir-
itual bodies. For just as there are natural bodies, there
are also spiritual bodies.
45 The Scriptures tell us, "The first man, Adam, be-
came a living person."* But the last Adam—that is,
Christ—is a life-giving Spirit. 46 What comes first is
the natural body, then the spiritual body comes later.
47 Adam, the first man, was made from the dust of the
earth, while Christ, the second man, came from heav-
en. 48 Earthly people are like the earthly man, and
heavenly people are like the heavenly man. 49 Just as
we are now like the earthly man, we will someday be
like* the heavenly man.
50 What I am saying, dear brothers and sisters, is
that our physical bodies cannot inherit the Kingdom
of God. These dying bodies cannot inherit what will
last forever.
51 But let me reveal to you a wonderful secret. We
will not all die, but we will all be transformed! 52 It
will happen in a moment, in the blink of an eye, when

VICTORY OVER DEATH

1. What is the sweetest victory you have experienced? How did you celebrate?

1 CORINTHIANS 15:35-58

2. What does it mean that our bodies are "planted in the ground" and "raised to live forever" (v. 42)?
3. Who is "the last Adam" (v. 45)? How did He become "a life-giving Spirit"?
4. Why can't "dying bodies . . . inherit what will last forever" (v. 50)? How should this affect the way we live?
5. How did Jesus win victory over death? How can you share in this victory (see John 5:24)?

15:27 Ps 8:6. 15:32a Greek *fighting wild beasts in Ephesus.* 15:32b Isa 22:13. 15:45 Gen 2:7. 15:49 Some manuscripts read *let us be like.*

15:27 put all things under his authority. Psalm 8:6, quoted here, continues the allusion to Psalm 110:1 in verse 25. That the final obstacle, death (v. 26), is already considered a done deal still to be realized gives reason for the Corinthians to hope in resurrection.

15:29-34 Thus far, Paul has shown that there is a resurrection for believers in the future. Here he points out that both his actions and theirs demonstrate a belief in the resurrection of the dead.

15:29 baptized for those who are dead. It seems that among the strange things that happened at Corinth was the practice (by some) of vicarious baptism. A living person was immersed in water on behalf of a dead person to secure, as if by magic, the benefits of baptism for the departed friend. This practice may also have been for believers who died without first being baptized. In this case, it would have been merely a symbolic act.

15:36-38 put a seed. Death brings transformation, not extinction. Here, Paul probes the nature of the transformation; his point being that what one plants is not what one gets in the end. A small grain of wheat grows mysteriously into a tall, grain-bearing stalk (John 12:24). So, too, with the bodies of believers.

15:39-41 heavenly bodies. A second analogy is used to show that there are a host of different kinds of bodies, and it is not unreasonable to expect the resurrection body to be quite different from the natural body.

15:42-44 resurrection of the dead. Paul reinforces the idea of verse 36: what is sown in one way is raised in another. He makes this point by means of a series of antithetical comparisons: corruption/incorruption; dishonor/glory; weakness/power; natural/spiritual.

15:43 glory. Paul now describes the nature of the changed body. The resurrection body is characterized by glory (brightness, radiance, splendor). This is a quality ascribed to God, in which believers will somehow share (Phil. 3:21).

15:44 natural . . . spiritual. The natural body is that which is animated by the soul of the person, while the spiritual body has as its animating source the Holy Spirit.

15:49 the heavenly man. This is Jesus, whose image Christians will reflect both in terms of character and glory.

15:50 physical bodies. That is, living people cannot inherit the kingdom. **dying bodies.** Nor can the unchanged dead inherit the kingdom. What Paul is saying is that at the second coming neither the living nor the dead can take part in the kingdom without being changed.

15:51 secret. A truth about the end times, once hidden but now revealed. **We.** Paul expected to be alive at the Second Coming. **not all die.** Some Christians will be alive at the Second Coming. **all be transformed.** Both the living and the dead will be changed.

15:52 in a moment. This change will occur instantaneously. **the last trumpet is blown.** The sounding of the trumpet was used to rally an army for action. This image is used to describe God's calling of His people together (1 Thess. 4:16). **who have died will be raised.** Those who are in the grave at the second coming will be transformed as will the living.

the last trumpet is blown. For when the trumpet
sounds, those who have died will be raised to live for-
ever. And we who are living will also be transformed.
53 For our dying bodies must be transformed into
bodies that will never die; our mortal bodies must be
transformed into immortal bodies.
54 Then, when our dying bodies have been trans-
formed into bodies that will never die,* this Scripture
will be fulfilled:

"Death is swallowed up in victory.*
55 O death, where is your victory?
O death, where is your sting?*"

56 For sin is the sting that results in death, and the
law gives sin its power. 57 But thank God! He gives us
victory over sin and death through our Lord Jesus
Christ.
58 So, my dear brothers and sisters, be strong and
immovable. Always work enthusiastically for the
Lord, for you know that nothing you do for the Lord
is ever useless.

THE COLLECTION FOR JERUSALEM

16 Now regarding your question about the money
being collected for God's people in Jerusalem.
You should follow the same procedure I gave to the
churches in Galatia. 2 On the first day of each week,
you should each put aside a portion of the money
you have earned. Don't wait until I get there and
then try to collect it all at once. 3 When I come, I will
write letters of recommendation for the messengers
you choose to deliver your gift to Jerusalem. 4 And if it
seems appropriate for me to go along, they can travel
with me.

PAUL'S FINAL INSTRUCTIONS

5 I am coming to visit you after I have been to Mace-
donia,* for I am planning to travel through Macedo-
nia. 6 Perhaps I will stay awhile with you, possibly
all winter, and then you can send me on my way
to my next destination. 7 This time I don't want to
make just a short visit and then go right on. I want
to come and stay awhile, if the Lord will let me. 8 In
the meantime, I will be staying here at Ephesus un-
til the Festival of Pentecost. 9 There is a wide-open
door for a great work here, although many oppose
me.
10 When Timothy comes, don't intimidate him. He is
doing the Lord's work, just as I am. 11 Don't let anyone
treat him with contempt. Send him on his way with
your blessing when he returns to me. I expect him to
come with the other believers.*
12 Now about our brother Apollos—I urged him to
visit you with the other believers, but he was not will-
ing to go right now. He will see you later when he has
the opportunity.
13 Be on guard. Stand firm in the faith. Be coura-
geous.* Be strong. 14 And do everything with love.
15 You know that Stephanas and his household
were the first of the harvest of believers in Greece,*
and they are spending their lives in service to God's
people. I urge you, dear brothers and sisters,* 16 to sub-
mit to them and others like them who serve with such
devotion. 17 I am very glad that Stephanas, Fortunatus,
and Achaicus have come here. They have been pro-
viding the help you weren't here to give me. 18 They
have been a wonderful encouragement to me, as they
have been to you. You must show your appreciation to
all who serve so well.

PAUL'S FINAL GREETINGS

19 The churches here in the province of Asia* send
greetings in the Lord, as do Aquila and Priscilla*
and all the others who gather in their home for
church meetings. 20 All the brothers and sisters here
send greetings to you. Greet each other with a sa-
cred kiss.
21 HERE IS MY GREETING IN MY OWN HANDWRITING—
PAUL.

BRAVERY UNDER FIRE

1. Who is the bravest person you know? What has that person done to show real courage?

1 CORINTHIANS 16:1-24

2. What does it mean to "Be on guard" (v. 13)? To "stand firm in the faith"?
3. Why do Christians need to "Be Courageous. Be Strong" (v. 13)? When has obedience required that you be brave?
4. Are you spiritually alert? Brave? Strong? How can you improve in these areas?
5. When you get under fire—and pressure or competition heats up—how does your bravery stand up?

15:54a Some manuscripts add *and our mortal bodies have been transformed into immortal bodies.* **15:54b** Isa 25:8. **15:55** Hos 13:14 (Greek version). **16:5** *Macedonia* was in the northern region of Greece. **16:11** Greek *with the brothers;* also in 16:12. **16:13** Greek *Be men.* **16:15a** Greek *in Achaia,* the southern region of the Greek peninsula. **16:15b** Greek *brothers;* also in 16:20. **16:19a** *Asia* was a Roman province in what is now western Turkey. **16:19b** Greek *Prisca.*

15:56 the law gives sin its power. By this Paul meant that the law of God has the unfortunate result of arousing sin within people. As he shows from his own example in Romans 7, the law's command not to covet did not put an end to his wanting what others had. The command, holy in itself, actually stirred him up to covet all the more.

15:57 victory. In great joy, Paul exults in the fact that sin and the law (that by which sin is made known) do not have the last word. Christ's death was a victory over sin and death.

15:58 be strong. His letter is at an end; his chastening is finished, and so it is appropriate that he challenge his readers to allow this same Christ who has won victories for them to win victories through them. **nothing you do for the Lord is ever useless.** Because the resurrection is real, the future is secure and magnificent.

16:1 the money. When in Jerusalem, Paul had agreed to help support the poor there (Gal. 2:10). In this way, the Gentile and the Jewish wings of the church would be bound together in a new fashion.

16:2 On the first day. Sunday, when Christians typically met for worship (Jewish Christians often went to the worship with Jews in a Synagogue on Saturdays). **put aside a portion.** Paul is not calling for a collection to be taken each Sunday for his purpose. Rather, he asks individual Christians to set aside funds on their own. **Don't wait until I get there.** Paul hoped that each person would have a sum of money set aside, ready to hand over when he came, so that he would not have to bother with the time-consuming process of taking a collection.

16:20 a sacred kiss. This was a custom used in the early church as part of the worship service. Kisses were a common form of greeting in biblical times, especially in the Middle Eastern culture.

[22] If anyone does not love the Lord, that person is cursed. Our Lord, come!*

[23] May the grace of the Lord Jesus be with you.
[24] My love to all of you in Christ Jesus.*

16:22 From Aramaic, *Marana tha.* Some manuscripts read *Maran atha,* "Our Lord has come." **16:24** Some manuscripts add *Amen.*

16:22 that person is cursed. Paul calls for God's judgment upon those who fail to love Jesus and, by implication, follow Him. The Lord is then invoked as a witness to the judgment. **come!** *Maranatha!* This is an Aramaic expression, translated *"Come, O Lord!"* transliterated by Paul into Greek (see also Rev. 22:20). This was an expression used by the early Christians referring to the fact that Christ would soon return. The Lord's return would mark the moment when the curse on those who had refused to love Him would be put into effect.

INTRODUCTION TO

2 CORINTHIANS

PERSONAL READING PLAN

☐2 Corinthians 1:1–2:4
☐2 Corinthians 2:5–3:18
☐2 Corinthians 4:1-18
☐2 Corinthians 5:1–6:2
☐2 Corinthians 6:3–7:1
☐2 Corinthians 7:2-16
☐2 Corinthians 8:1–9:5
☐2 Corinthians 9:6-15
☐2 Corinthians 10:1-18
☐2 Corinthians 11:1-15
☐2 Corinthians 11:16–12:10
☐2 Corinthians 12:11–13:14

AUTHOR

The Apostle Paul was the writer of 2 Corinthians.

DATE

Paul wrote this letter around A.D. 55–56.

THEME

The strength of weakness.

HISTORICAL BACKGROUND

Paul founded a church on his first visit to Corinth during his second missionary journey. In 2 Corinthians 13:1, Paul proposes a third visit to the city. It seems that his second visit was the cause of much trouble and the reason he wrote 2 Corinthians.

This second visit had been promised in 1 Corinthians 16:1-9. Paul wrote that he would leave Ephesus, journey to Macedonia, and then come down to Corinth on his way to Jerusalem with the collection. But Paul traveled straight to Corinth, intending to go from there up to Macedonia and then back to Corinth once again. He anticipated visiting Corinth as mutual pleasure (1:15-16). But his unexpected visit proved so painful (due to conflict with false apostles) that he canceled his return trip from Macedonia. Instead he went back to Ephesus, then north again to Troas, and finally back once more to Macedonia. At Macedonia, he wrote 2 Corinthians to prepare them for a third visit.

Reconstructing the events surrounding the writing of 2 Corinthians is further complicated because it seems Paul wrote two other letters to the Corinthians that have not been preserved (see 1 Cor. 5:9; 2 Cor. 2:3-4,9; 7:8-13). Paul wrote one of these letters prior to 1 Corinthians and another (the "sorrowful" letter) in between 1 and 2 Corinthians, probably to explain why he was not returning to Corinth from Macedonia (1:23; 2:4).

Some believe that 2 Corinthians may be two letters. The fierce tone of chapters 10–13 stands in sharp contrast to the gentle, reconciling tone of chapters 1–9. According to this theory, the first nine chapters (Paul's fourth letter) seem to be based on the report of Titus (7:6-16) that the situation in Corinth had been rectified. But when Titus returned to Corinth with chapters 1–9, he found to his horror that the "super-apostles" were back in charge, so he quickly returned to Macedonia. Reacting to the new situation, Paul penned chapters 10–13 (his fifth letter). The fourth and fifth letters were later copied together, since they were so closely related in subject matter, and they became what we know as 2 Corinthians.

PAUL'S NEW OPPONENTS

Who then opposed Paul with such vigor during his second "painful" visit? The best guess is that the troublemakers were not from the Corinthian church itself. Rather, they were a band of outside "apostles" (called cynically by Paul "super apostles" in 11:5 and 12:11) probably Jewish Christians from Palestine, who sought to conform the Corinthian church to Jewish Law. They attacked Paul vigorously, calling him two-faced (10:1-11); they questioned his credentials as an apostle, and they criticized him for drawing no financial support from the Corinthians (the way a real apostle would). Apparently Paul's real pain came because the Corinthians did not rally to his support in this conflict.

PAUL'S PAIN

In many ways, 2 Corinthians is Paul's most personal letter. He reveals his pain and his joy, his outrage and his suffering, and his love and his convictions. Second Corinthians is filled with profound feeling. As C. K. Barrett said: "Writing 2 Corinthians must have come near to breaking Paul, and . . . a church that is prepared to read it with him and understand it, may find itself broken too" (The Second Epistle to the Corinthians: Harper New Testament Commentaries).

Not only is Paul's pain evident in this letter but also his toughness. He was willing to fight to wrest the Corinthians from the corrupting influence of the false apostles. "It would have been natural for Paul simply to give up the ungrateful, unruly, unloving, unintelligent Corinthians and leave them to their destiny. There is no indication that this thought ever crossed his mind" (Barrett, The Second Epistle to the Corinthians, pp. 32-33). The reason for his tenacity is found in the strength of his calling. He was an apostle—called by God to bring men and women into the kingdom. No band of petty pretenders was going to defeat him in that God-given purpose.

PASSAGES FOR TOPICAL GROUP STUDY

1:3-11	HURTING and COMFORT	God's Comfort
1:12–2:11	GOD'S PROMISE and SIN	Yes, No, Maybe
3:7-18	THE LAW VS. GRACE	The Old and New Covenants
4:1-18	CHRIST-CONFIDENCE	Unwavering Confidence
5:1-10	TAKING CARE OF OURSELVES	Camping Out on Earth
5:11–6:2	DRAWING PEOPLE TO GOD	A Ministry of Reconciliation
6:3-13	ENDURING IN TRIALS	The Test of Faith
6:14–7:1	FRIENDSHIPS WITH UNBELIVERS	An Uneven Match
7:2-16	TURNING BACK TO GOD	Godly Grief
8:1-15	USING YOUR BLESSINGS	Using What You Have
8:16–9:5	MONEY and GIVING	Generous Giving

9:6-15 .... GIVING .... Cheerful Giving
10:1-18 ... SPIRITUAL WAR .... Weapons of War
11:1-15 ... SATAN'S SCHEMES .... Evil in Disguise
12:1-10 ... WEAKNESS AND PROBLEMS.... Thorn in the Flesh
12:11-21 .. PERSISTING IN LOVE .... Unselfish Sacrifice
13:1-14 ... TESTING YOURSELF............ Passing the Test

PASSAGES FOR GENERAL GROUP STUDY

2:12–3:6..... Fragrant Letters (Scent of "Life" or of "Death")
11:16-33..... Tolerating Fools (Handling Foolish Teaching)

GOD'S COMFORT

1. What was your favorite "comforter" as a child: Teddy bear? Blanket? Thumb? Other?

2 CORINTHIANS 1:3-11

2. From what "mortal danger" (v. 10) has Jesus delivered us? How does that lead to the comfort and hope that Paul speaks of here?
3. How does our "comfort overflow through Christ" (v. 5)?
4. Are you in need of God's comfort? Do you know someone else to whom you can show God's comfort?

GREETINGS FROM PAUL

1 This letter is from Paul, chosen by the will of God to
be an apostle of Christ Jesus, and from our brother
Timothy.
I am writing to God's church in Corinth and to all of
his holy people throughout Greece.*
2 May God our Father and the Lord Jesus Christ give
you grace and peace.

GOD OFFERS COMFORT TO ALL

3 All praise to God, the Father of our Lord Jesus Christ.
God is our merciful Father and the source of all comfort.
4 He comforts us in all our troubles so that we can
comfort others. When they are troubled, we will be
able to give them the same comfort God has given us.
5 For the more we suffer for Christ, the more God will
shower us with his comfort through Christ. 6 Even
when we are weighed down with troubles, it is for
your comfort and salvation! For when we ourselves
are comforted, we will certainly comfort you. Then
you can patiently endure the same things we suffer.
7 We are confident that as you share in our sufferings,
you will also share in the comfort God gives us.
8 We think you ought to know, dear brothers and
sisters,* about the trouble we went through in the
province of Asia. We were crushed and overwhelmed
beyond our ability to endure, and we thought we
would never live through it. 9 In fact, we expected to
die. But as a result, we stopped relying on ourselves

YES, NO, MAYBE

1. From which parent can you rely on a "no" reply? A "yes" reply? Which one waffles? Why is that?

2 CORINTHIANS 1:12–2:11

2. In what does Paul boast (1:12)? What is the basis for his integrity?
3. What does it mean that Jesus is the "Yes" of God's promise to us (1:20)?
4. Paraphrase the "business deal" of 1:22 in modern terms. How have you experienced this spiritual "new deal"?
5. What can we learn from 2:5-11 about dealing with fellow Christians in sin? How should they be corrected? What completes the restoration?

and learned to rely only on God, who raises the dead.
10 And he did rescue us from mortal danger, and he
will rescue us again. We have placed our confidence
in him, and he will continue to rescue us. 11 And you
are helping us by praying for us. Then many people
will give thanks because God has graciously answered
so many prayers for our safety.

PAUL'S CHANGE OF PLANS

12 We can say with confidence and a clear conscience
that we have lived with a God-given holiness* and
sincerity in all our dealings. We have depended on
God's grace, not on our own human wisdom. That is
how we have conducted ourselves before the world,
and especially toward you. 13 Our letters have been
straightforward, and there is nothing written between
the lines and nothing you can't understand. I
hope someday you will fully understand us, 14 even if
you don't understand us now. Then on the day when
the Lord Jesus* returns, you will be proud of us in the
same way we are proud of you.
15 Since I was so sure of your understanding and
trust, I wanted to give you a double blessing by visiting
you twice—16 first on my way to Macedonia and

1:1 Greek *Achaia,* the southern region of the Greek peninsula. 1:8 Greek *brothers.* 1:12 Some manuscripts read *honesty.* 1:14 Some manuscripts read *our Lord Jesus.*

1:1 by the will of God . . . an apostle of Christ Jesus. While this is a stock phrase Paul often used to identify himself (1 Cor. 1:1; Eph. 1:1; Col. 1:1; 2 Tim. 1:1), in this letter the title takes on special force since it is precisely Paul's apostleship that is being called into question. **Timothy.** Timothy was Paul's coworker and colleague who had also been involved with the Corinthian church (Acts 18:5; 1 Cor. 4:17; 16:10). **Greece.** Roughly equivalent to what today is southern Greece, Achaia was the Roman province of which Corinth was the capital city.

1:4 our troubles. Literally, "our trials." This includes both the internal anguish and the physical hardships that Christians experience because of following Jesus. **we will be able to give them the same comfort.** The purpose of God's aid is to enable those so helped to aid others who are afflicted.

1:5 suffer for Christ. Those who follow Christ share in His sufferings. Rejection, injustice, and bearing the affliction of others are all common experiences for the Christian.

1:6 patiently endure. Not a grim, bleak acceptance of difficulties but a hopeful steadfastness in the midst of trial.

1:8 trouble. The Book of Acts has no record of what was obviously an extremely difficult experience for Paul in Asia. Some commentators think it may refer to the imprisonment mentioned in Philippians 1:12-20 where Paul was not certain whether he would live or die. **Asia.** This was the Roman province located in the western part of modern Turkey. Ephesus was its leading city. **overwhelmed beyond of our ability.** This is to be weighed down like an overloaded ship.

1:12 confidence. Paul begins the defense of his integrity by pointing out that he has nothing to be ashamed of—despite this criticism of him. "Boast" literally means, "confidence." Paul uses this word (or a derivative of it) 29 times in this letter. This may be in response to the "boasting" done by the itinerant teachers who were promoting themselves over him. **especially toward you.** Paul had taken great pains to act with integrity toward the Corinthians: he took no payment from them (11:7-9); he also worked to ensure that the collection for the needy in Jerusalem was not misappropriated (1 Cor. 16:1-4). **sincerity.** The Corinthians have charged him with deception. On the contrary, he says, his actions were characterized throughout by sincerity. **human wisdom.** Such "wisdom" guides one's actions in the ways of self-interest or self-promotion. In contrast, Paul focused on God and the needs of others.

1:15-16 I was so sure. Paul addresses the charge that he was unreliable. He had written that he intended to go to Macedonia and then to Corinth (1 Cor. 16:5-9). However, perhaps in response to a report from Timothy (1 Cor. 16:10-11), he changed his plans and visited Corinth first, sooner than expected. His intention at the time was to go from there to Macedonia and then return to Corinth again. However, since this unexpected visit was so difficult (2:1), it is thought that he returned to Ephesus and wrote another letter (now lost) to Corinth (2:1-4). Then he went to Macedonia and chose not to return to Corinth at all (v. 23). The changes in Paul's plans opened the way for him to be charged as being untrustworthy.

again when I returned from Macedonia.* Then you could send me on my way to Judea.

[17]You may be asking why I changed my plan. Do you think I make my plans carelessly? Do you think I am like people of the world who say "Yes" when they really mean "No"? [18]As surely as God is faithful, our word to you does not waver between "Yes" and "No." [19]For Jesus Christ, the Son of God, does not waver between "Yes" and "No." He is the one whom Silas,* Timothy, and I preached to you, and as God's ultimate "Yes," he always does what he says. [20]For all of God's promises have been fulfilled in Christ with a resounding "Yes!" And through Christ, our "Amen" (which means "Yes") ascends to God for his glory.

[21]It is God who enables us, along with you, to stand firm for Christ. He has commissioned us, [22]and he has identified us as his own by placing the Holy Spirit in our hearts as the first installment that guarantees everything he has promised us.

[23]Now I call upon God as my witness that I am telling the truth. The reason I didn't return to Corinth was to spare you from a severe rebuke. [24]But that does not mean we want to dominate you by telling you how to put your faith into practice. We want to work together with you so you will be full of joy, for it is by your own faith that you stand firm.

2 So I decided that I would not bring you grief with another painful visit. [2]For if I cause you grief, who will make me glad? Certainly not someone I have grieved. [3]That is why I wrote to you as I did, so that when I do come, I won't be grieved by the very ones who ought to give me the greatest joy. Surely you all know that my joy comes from your being joyful. [4]I wrote that letter in great anguish, with a troubled heart and many tears. I didn't want to grieve you, but I wanted to let you know how much love I have for you.

FORGIVENESS FOR THE SINNER

[5]I am not overstating it when I say that the man who caused all the trouble hurt all of you more than he hurt me. [6]Most of you opposed him, and that was punishment enough. [7]Now, however, it is time to forgive and comfort him. Otherwise he may be overcome by discouragement. [8]So I urge you now to reaffirm your love for him.

[9]I wrote to you as I did to test you and see if you would fully comply with my instructions. [10]When you forgive this man, I forgive him, too. And when I forgive whatever needs to be forgiven, I do so with Christ's authority for your benefit, [11]so that Satan will not outsmart us. For we are familiar with his evil schemes.

[12]When I came to the city of Troas to preach the Good News of Christ, the Lord opened a door of opportunity for me. [13]But I had no peace of mind because my dear brother Titus hadn't yet arrived with a report from you. So I said good-bye and went on to Macedonia to find him.

MINISTERS OF THE NEW COVENANT

[14]But thank God! He has made us his captives and continues to lead us along in Christ's triumphal procession. Now he uses us to spread the knowledge of Christ everywhere, like a sweet perfume. [15]Our lives are a Christ-like fragrance rising up to God. But this fragrance is perceived differently by those who are being saved and by those who are perishing. [16]To those who are perishing, we are a dreadful smell of death and doom. But to those who are being saved, we are a life-giving perfume. And who is adequate for such a task as this?

[17]You see, we are not like the many hucksters* who preach for personal profit. We preach the word of God with sincerity and with Christ's authority, knowing that God is watching us.

3 Are we beginning to praise ourselves again? Are we like others, who need to bring you letters of recommendation, or who ask you to write such letters on their behalf? Surely not! [2]The only letter of recommendation we need is you yourselves. Your lives are a letter written in our* hearts; everyone can read it and recognize our good work among you. [3]Clearly, you are a letter from Christ showing the result of our ministry among you. This "letter" is written not with pen and ink, but with the Spirit of the living God. It is carved not on tablets of stone, but on human hearts.

FRAGRANT LETTERS

1. What is your favorite fragrance? Favorite perfume or cologne? What smells always make you gag?

2 CORINTHIANS 2:12–3:6

2. How can the same gospel be either the "dreadful smell" or the "life-giving perfume" (2:16)?
3. Until Titus returns with "a report" (see 7:6-13), Paul has no peace of mind (2:13). What does that say about Paul's concern for this church?
4. What does Paul mean by "Your lives are a letter" (3:2)? What sort of a "letter" are you?
5. How can you spread the aroma of Christ in the environment of your home? In your school?

1:16 *Macedonia* was in the northern region of Greece. **1:19** Greek *Silvanus.* **2:17** Some manuscripts read *the rest of the hucksters.* **3:2** Some manuscripts read *your.*

1:19 Silas and Timothy. Paul's coworkers in Corinth during his original trip (Acts 18:5). **Yes.** The sending of Jesus, God's Son, is God's guarantee to humanity that He is for us; that He will fulfill all His promises; that He can be trusted absolutely.

2:3 I wrote. Paul was in a bind. If he came again as proposed, he would cause pain. If he didn't come, he would be charged with fickleness. **I won't be grieved.** Paul was concerned both that they would be grieved by another visit (vv. 1-2) and that he too would find it painful. His fear, perhaps, was that indeed they had been subverted by the false teachers and had embraced a false gospel.

2:12-13 When I came. Leaving Corinth as a result of the painful incident, Paul went to Macedonia, then to Ephesus, and then to Troas (a city 150 miles north of Ephesus). Finally, he returned to Macedonia.

2:13 Titus. Although not mentioned in Acts, Titus traveled with Paul and was entrusted with several important missions.

2:14 triumphal procession. This phrase may simply mean "displays us," or it may refer to the Roman practice of a military general leading a victory march with those he had conquered following behind.

3:1 letters of recommendation. It was common for itinerant teachers to get such letters as a means of introducing and validating their work in a new area.

[4]We are confident of all this because of our great trust in God through Christ. [5]It is not that we think we are qualified to do anything on our own. Our qualification comes from God. [6]He has enabled us to be ministers of his new covenant. This is a covenant not of written laws, but of the Spirit. The old written covenant ends in death; but under the new covenant, the Spirit gives life.

THE GLORY OF THE NEW COVENANT

[7]The old way,* with laws etched in stone, led to death, though it began with such glory that the people of Israel could not bear to look at Moses' face. For his face shone with the glory of God, even though the brightness was already fading away. [8]Shouldn't we expect far greater glory under the new way, now that the Holy Spirit is giving life? [9]If the old way, which brings condemnation, was glorious, how much more glorious is the new way, which makes us right with God! [10]In fact, that first glory was not glorious at all compared with the overwhelming glory of the new way. [11]So if the old way, which has been replaced, was glorious, how much more glorious is the new, which remains forever!

THE OLD AND NEW COVENANTS

1. Who is the boldest person you know? What has that person done that is so bold? Was it a good boldness or just arrogance?

2 CORINTHIANS 3:7-18

2. How does Paul contrast the old and new covenants (see also 3:3,6)?
3. Why did the everlasting covenant of Christ have to replace the once-glorious covenant of Moses?
4. What are the practical results of this new covenant (vv. 16-18)?
5. In what sense is the law (such as the Ten Commandments referred to in verse 7) "replaced" (v. 11)? In what sense does that law still apply today?

[12]Since this new way gives us such confidence, we can be very bold. [13]We are not like Moses, who put a veil over his face so the people of Israel would not see the glory, even though it was destined to fade away. [14]But the people's minds were hardened, and to this day whenever the old covenant is being read, the same veil covers their minds so they cannot understand the truth. And this veil can be removed only by believing in Christ. [15]Yes, even today when they read Moses' writings, their hearts are covered with that veil, and they do not understand.

[16]But whenever someone turns to the Lord, the veil is taken away. [17]For the Lord is the Spirit, and wherever the Spirit of the Lord is, there is freedom. [18]So all of us who have had that veil removed can see and reflect the glory of the Lord. And the Lord—who is the Spirit—makes us more and more like him as we are changed into his glorious image.

TREASURE IN FRAGILE CLAY JARS

4 Therefore, since God in his mercy has given us this new way,* we never give up. [2]We reject all shameful deeds and underhanded methods. We don't try to trick anyone or distort the word of God. We tell the truth before God, and all who are honest know this.

[3]If the Good News we preach is hidden behind a veil, it is hidden only from people who are perishing. [4]Satan, who is the god of this world, has blinded the minds of those who don't believe. They are unable to see the glorious light of the Good News. They don't understand this message about the glory of Christ, who is the exact likeness of God.

[5]You see, we don't go around preaching about ourselves. We preach that Jesus Christ is Lord, and we ourselves are your servants for Jesus' sake. [6]For God, who said, "Let there be light in the darkness," has made this light shine in our hearts so we could know the glory of God that is seen in the face of Jesus Christ.

[7]We now have this light shining in our hearts, but we ourselves are like fragile clay jars containing this great treasure.* This makes it clear that our great power is from God, not from ourselves.

[8]We are pressed on every side by troubles, but we are not crushed. We are perplexed, but not driven to

3:7 Or *ministry;* also in 3:8, 9, 10, 11, 12. **4:1** Or *ministry.* **4:7** Greek *We now have this treasure in clay jars.*

3:6 new covenant. A covenant is an agreement initiated and defined by God between Himself and His people. This covenant is quite different from the old one. Jeremiah clearly prophesied about this new covenant (Jer. 31:31-34). **written laws . . . Spirit.** "Letter" refers to the words of the Old Covenant law; "Spirit" is the Holy Spirit. The Old Covenant law kills because we are sinful. The law is good and spiritual, but in itself it only shows that people don't measure up. The Old Covenant condemns. The New Covenant forgives and empowers.

3:7-11 Paul uses what we might call a "how much more" argument here. If there was great glory when the Law—an instrument of condemnation—was given, how much more or how much greater glory attends the ministry of the Spirit through which we are made righteous.

3:7 glory. This refers to the radiance in Moses' face that reflected God's presence when he came down from Mount Sinai.

3:12-13 confidence. Paul's point is not that he is superior to Moses. Rather, he simply uses the thought of Moses' veiling himself as a contrast with his open approach to ministry. While Moses hid the diminishing glory of the Old Covenant behind the veil, Paul hides nothing of the permanent glory of the New Covenant of the Spirit. This imagery serves to highlight the superiority and permanence of the New Covenant

3:13 a veil. To cover one's face or head was to hide something, or a sign of shame; to unveil the head and face was to be completely open and bold.

3:14-16 the people's minds were hardened. Paul now uses the veil of Moses as an illustration to describe why those who hold to the Old Covenant are unable to see the glory of the new. Their minds and hearts are only unveiled (and thus able to see) when they turn to the Lord.

3:17 the Lord is the Spirit. The Holy Spirit is Jesus' Agent within us bringing to completion in us all that Jesus did for us in His death and resurrection. **wherever the Spirit of the Lord . . . freedom.** We were slaves to sin. The law only made us acutely aware of that. Because of Jesus death, we are free from both the condemnation of the law and the power of sin. We are freed from our past and freed for our future, freed to be what God always intended us to be.

3:18 reflect. As believers see the glory of God in Jesus (who is the image of God—4:4,6), they are themselves continually being transformed by that encounter so that they will ultimately reflect the character and glory of Jesus (Rom. 8:29; Phil. 3:21).

4:8-10 We are pressed. God's power is seen, not in that Paul rides above suffering, but that in the midst of suffering he is continually sustained by God. The hardships experienced by the apostles reflect the opposition and, ultimately, the death (v. 10) experienced by Jesus (Rom. 8:17; Phil. 3:10). The ministry of the glory of the gospel requires all of its messengers—all of Christ's followers—to share in the suffering of Christ. These verses should bring us all hope in the midst of suffering.

4:8 pressed. The affliction (the idea behind this word) was real but not fatal (he was not "crushed").

UNWAVERING CONFIDENCE

1. When have you accidentally broken something very valuable? How did it happen?

2 CORINTHIANS 4:1-18

2. Why is it important to "reject all shameful deeds" (v. 2)?
3. Who is "the god of this world" (v. 4)? How has he "blinded the minds of those who don't believe. They are unable to see the glorious light of the Good News"?
4. In verse 7, what are the "clay jars"? What is the "treasure"?
5. Paul had unwavering confidence in the Lord and his work for the Lord (vv. 13-14). Where do you draw confidence in your life?

despair. 9 We are hunted down, but never abandoned
by God. We get knocked down, but we are not de-
stroyed. 10 Through suffering, our bodies continue to
share in the death of Jesus so that the life of Jesus may
also be seen in our bodies.
11 Yes, we live under constant danger of death be-
cause we serve Jesus, so that the life of Jesus will be
evident in our dying bodies. 12 So we live in the face
of death, but this has resulted in eternal life for you.
13 But we continue to preach because we have the
same kind of faith the psalmist had when he said, "I
believed in God, so I spoke."* 14 We know that God, who
raised the Lord Jesus,* will also raise us with Jesus
and present us to himself together with you. 15 All of
this is for your benefit. And as God's grace reaches
more and more people, there will be great thanks-
giving, and God will receive more and more glory.
16 That is why we never give up. Though our bodies
are dying, our spirits are* being renewed every day. 17 For
our present troubles are small and won't last very long.
Yet they produce for us a glory that vastly outweighs
them and will last forever! 18 So we don't look at the trou-
bles we can see now; rather, we fix our gaze on things
that cannot be seen. For the things we see now will soon
be gone, but the things we cannot see will last forever.

NEW BODIES

5 For we know that when this earthly tent we live
in is taken down (that is, when we die and leave
this earthly body), we will have a house in heaven, an
eternal body made for us by God himself and not by
human hands. 2 We grow weary in our present bodies,
and we long to put on our heavenly bodies like new
clothing. 3 For we will put on heavenly bodies; we will
not be spirits without bodies.* 4 While we live in these
earthly bodies, we groan and sigh, but it's not that
we want to die and get rid of these bodies that clothe
us. Rather, we want to put on our new bodies so that
these dying bodies will be swallowed up by life. 5 God
himself has prepared us for this, and as a guarantee
he has given us his Holy Spirit.
6 So we are always confident, even though we know
that as long as we live in these bodies we are not at
home with the Lord. 7 For we live by believing and not
by seeing. 8 Yes, we are fully confident, and we would
rather be away from these earthly bodies, for then we
will be at home with the Lord. 9 So whether we are
here in this body or away from this body, our goal is
to please him. 10 For we must all stand before Christ to
be judged. We will each receive whatever we deserve
for the good or evil we have done in this earthly body.

WE ARE GOD'S AMBASSADORS

11 Because we understand our fearful responsibility
to the Lord, we work hard to persuade others. God
knows we are sincere, and I hope you know this, too.
12 Are we commending ourselves to you again? No, we
are giving you a reason to be proud of us,* so you can
answer those who brag about having a spectacular
ministry rather than having a sincere heart. 13 If it
seems we are crazy, it is to bring glory to God. And if

CAMPING OUT ON EARTH

1. Have you ever lived in a tent? For how long? Why? What was it like?

2 CORINTHIANS 5:1-10

2. What is Paul referring to as "this earthly tent" (v. 1)? Why does he call it a tent? What does this suggest about our earthly life?
3. What does it mean that we "long to put on our heavenly bodies" (v. 2)?
4. Why must we "all stand before Christ to be judged" (v. 10)? How should this knowledge affect your daily life?
5. Are you disciplined in taking care of your earthly "tent"? How about your eternal "house"?

4:13 Ps 116:10. **4:14** Some manuscripts read *who raised Jesus.* **4:16** Greek *our inner being is.* **5:3** Greek *we will not be naked.* **5:12** Some manuscripts read *proud of yourselves.*

4:9 hunted down. The opposition Paul faced—both from Jewish and Gentile sources—was very real and very intense, yet in it all, God enabled him to prevail. **knocked down.** Even when the blow was overwhelming, Paul was preserved by God.

4:12 we live in. Paul absorbs the brunt of the persecution (as a key leader in the Christian movement) so that the church might be able to thrive (Col. 1:24).

4:16 we never give up. Paul again states his confidence in his ministry (v. 1).

4:18 fix. This is a dedicated striving, like a runner pursuing the goal (Heb. 12:1-2). The prize for a race, in ancient times, was placed at the end of the race so the runners could focus upon it, motivating them to win. Paul is calling on Christians to focus on the unseen rewards of God's Kingdom. **seen . . . cannot see.** Christians are not to shape their lives on the basis of visible standards of success (5:12) but in light of Christ's Kingdom.

5:1 this earthly tent. The tent, as a temporary home, is a metaphor for the mortal body which is destroyed by suffering, weakness, and, finally, death. **house in heaven.** A heavenly building was a common end of the time image representing all the fullness of God's Kingdom (Rev. 21:2). In this case Paul refers to our resurrected, transformed bodies.

5:10 stand before Christ. This is the specific evaluation of believers in the end times during which rewards are given or withheld. The judgment of unbelievers is at the "great white throne" (Rev. 20:11-15).

5:11 fearful responsibility to the Lord. The word translated *fearful* can also be translated *terror.* Even when we come to know God's grace and love, God's awesomeness stirs a reverential awe within it. Contemplating judgment before a Holy God, **we persuade men.**

A MINISTRY OF RECONCILIATION

1. Who is the most persuasive person you know? What does that person persuade people to do?

2 CORINTHIANS 5:11–6:2

2. According to 5:15, what is the purpose of Christ's death? What does it mean, in practical terms, to live for ourselves? To live for Christ?
3. What does it mean to be reconciled (v. 18)? How does God reconcile us to Himself?
4. Why did God give us "the task of reconciling" (v. 18)? How can you carry out this ministry in practical terms?

THE TEST OF FAITH

1. What is the greatest physical hardship you've been through? What did it accomplish?

2 CORINTHIANS 6:3-13

2. How does Paul defend the authenticity of his ministry?
3. By appealing to these things instead of his supernatural conversion or miracles (Acts 9:3-5; 19:11-12), what is he saying the real test of faith is?
4. What is Paul asking the Corinthians (and us) to do in verses 11-13 (see 3:2-3)?
5. What does it mean to "own nothing, and yet . . . have everything." (v. 10)? How did this attitude help Paul to endure all that is listed in verses 4-10? How could it help you?

we are in our right minds, it is for your benefit. [14] Ei-
ther way, Christ's love controls us.* Since we believe
that Christ died for all, we also believe that we have
all died to our old life.* [15] He died for everyone so that
those who receive his new life will no longer live for
themselves. Instead, they will live for Christ, who
died and was raised for them.
[16] So we have stopped evaluating others from a hu-
man point of view. At one time we thought of Christ
merely from a human point of view. How differently
we know him now! [17] This means that anyone who be-
longs to Christ has become a new person. The old life
is gone; a new life has begun!
[18] And all of this is a gift from God, who brought us
back to himself through Christ. And God has given us
this task of reconciling people to him. [19] For God was
in Christ, reconciling the world to himself, no longer
counting people's sins against them. And he gave us
this wonderful message of reconciliation. [20] So we
are Christ's ambassadors; God is making his appeal
through us. We speak for Christ when we plead,
"Come back to God!" [21] For God made Christ, who nev-
er sinned, to be the offering for our sin,* so that we
could be made right with God through Christ.

6 As God's partners,* we beg you not to accept this
marvelous gift of God's kindness and then ignore
it. [2] For God says,

"At just the right time, I heard you.
On the day of salvation, I helped you."*

Indeed, the "right time" is now. Today is the day of
salvation.

PAUL'S HARDSHIPS

[3] We live in such a way that no one will stumble
because of us, and no one will find fault with our
ministry. [4] In everything we do, we show that we
are true ministers of God. We patiently endure trou-
bles and hardships and calamities of every kind.
[5] We have been beaten, been put in prison, faced an-
gry mobs, worked to exhaustion, endured sleepless
nights, and gone without food. [6] We prove ourselves
by our purity, our understanding, our patience, our
kindness, by the Holy Spirit within us,* and by our
sincere love. [7] We faithfully preach the truth. God's
power is working in us. We use the weapons of
righteousness in the right hand for attack and the
left hand for defense. [8] We serve God whether peo-
ple honor us or despise us, whether they slander
us or praise us. We are honest, but they call us im-

5:14a Or *urges us on.* **5:14b** Greek *Since one died for all, then all died.* **5:21** Or *to become sin itself.* **6:1** Or *As we work together.* **6:2** Isa 49:8 (Greek version). **6:6** Or *by our holiness of spirit.*

5:14 Christ died for all. This (v. 15) is an adaptation of a creedal statement of belief (Rom. 5:8; 1 Cor. 15:3; 1 Thess. 5:10). They can no longer be evaluated on the basis of an old, worldly standard (1:12,17; 5:12,16). **all died.** In the sense that when Christ died, He opened up a new way of life to everyone. They could be free from the law of sin and death—and instead live for Christ. They could die to the old life of futility and self-centeredness.
5:17 to (or "in") **Christ.** A favorite phrase of Paul's, signifying the union of the believer with Jesus Christ and hence with Jesus' death and resurrection; it is by this union that the believer enters into new life. **a new person.** To be in Christ is to be new. A believer has died to the old life and is raised to a whole new sphere of existence by this act of recreation.
5:19 this wonderful message of reconciliation. All the work of reconciliation—bringing us back into relationship with God—has been done. Now it is simply a matter of people accepting the finished work of Christ.
5:20 ambassadors. In Roman territories considered dangerous and not fully loyal, the key administrator was the ambassador. He was a direct representative of the emperor. Ambassadors were also those individuals who arranged the terms of peace between a hostile country and Rome. Paul, therefore, understands his role to be that of one acting on behalf of God to offer reconciliation and peace to a hostile, alienated people. **we plead.** Reconciliation will not take place until God's offer is accepted; thus the urgency of Paul's appeal.
5:21 Christ, who never sinned. A key to Christ's power to reconcile is His own lack of sin (John 8:46; Rom. 8:3; Heb. 4:15). **to be the offering for our sin.** Because He had no sin of His own, He could therefore bear the sins of others. He exchanged His righteousness for our sin. As He became the sins of humanity, He stood in relationship to God as we should have: cut off and the object of wrath. As He became sin for us, He cried out, "My God, My God, why have You forsaken Me?"
6:5 worked to exhaustion. Paul generally earned his own living, toiling to the point of exhaustion. **endured sleepless nights . . . gone without food.** His hardships led to physical deprivation.
6:6 by the Holy Spirit. Paul demonstrated the presence of the Spirit in his life through the qualities of love, kindness, etc. (refer to Gal. 5:22-23). **sincere love.** This is an active goodwill toward others.
6:7 the truth. A shorthand way of referring to the gospel. **weapons.** A Roman soldier carried a spear or sword in his right hand and a shield in his left. Likewise, Paul was fully equipped with God's righteousness to each out and minister to others.
6:8 honor . . . despise . . . slander . . . praise. Neither rejection nor praise distracted him from his ministry (1 Cor. 4:12-13; 1 Thess. 2:2). **imposters.** This begins a series of contrasts in which Paul renounces the charges that have been made against him.

AN UNEVEN MATCH

1. What's the dirtiest you've ever been? How did you get that way?

2 CORINTHIANS 6:14–7:1

2. What does it mean to not "team up with those who are unbelievers" (v. 14)? What relationships does this include?
3. What does it mean to "come out from among unbelievers" (v. 17)? How does a Christian "come out from among" non-Christians?
4. How can you be a friend to an unbeliever and still be "separate"?
5. What are things that "defile our body or spirit" (7:1)? How can you wash yourself from them?

postors. 9 We are ignored, even though we are well
known. We live close to death, but we are still alive.
We have been beaten, but we have not been killed.
10 Our hearts ache, but we always have joy. We are
poor, but we give spiritual riches to others. We own
nothing, and yet we have everything.
11 Oh, dear Corinthian friends! We have spoken hon-
estly with you, and our hearts are open to you. 12 There
is no lack of love on our part, but you have withheld
your love from us. 13 I am asking you to respond as if
you were my own children. Open your hearts to us!

THE TEMPLE OF THE LIVING GOD

14 Don't team up with those who are unbelievers. How
can righteousness be a partner with wickedness?
How can light live with darkness? 15 What harmony
can there be between Christ and the devil*? How can
a believer be a partner with an unbeliever? 16 And
what union can there be between God's temple and
idols? For we are the temple of the living God. As God
said:

"I will live in them
and walk among them.
I will be their God,
and they will be my people.*
17 Therefore, come out from among unbelievers,
and separate yourselves from them, says the
LORD.
Don't touch their filthy things,
and I will welcome you.*
18 And I will be your Father,
and you will be my sons and daughters,
says the LORD Almighty.*"

7 Because we have these promises, dear friends, let
us cleanse ourselves from everything that can de-
file our body or spirit. And let us work toward com-
plete holiness because we fear God.
2 Please open your hearts to us. We have not done
wrong to anyone, nor led anyone astray, nor taken
advantage of anyone. 3 I'm not saying this to condemn
you. I said before that you are in our hearts, and we
live or die together with you. 4 I have the highest con-
fidence in you, and I take great pride in you. You have
greatly encouraged me and made me happy despite
all our troubles.

PAUL'S JOY AT THE CHURCH'S REPENTANCE

5 When we arrived in Macedonia, there was no rest
for us. We faced conflict from every direction, with
battles on the outside and fear on the inside. 6 But
God, who encourages those who are discouraged,

GODLY GRIEF

1. What finally gets your attention: Tough talk? Slammed door? Tears? Letter? Walkout? Give a recent example.

2 CORINTHIANS 7:2-16

2. Why does Paul want this church to open up to him (vv. 2-4; see 6:11-13)?
3. What was the result of Paul's previous letter to them (vv. 8-13; see 2:3-4)?
4. In light of his previous hurtful letter, why would he underscore his present joy and confidence (v. 16)?
5. What is "sorry God wants us to experience" (v. 10)? What produces such grief? To what does it lead?
6. What grief in your life could be resolved with repentance (turning back to God)?

6:15 Greek *Beliar;* various other manuscripts render this proper name of the devil as *Belian, Beliab,* or *Belial.* 6:16 Lev 26:12; Ezek 37:27. 6:17 Isa 52:11; Ezek 20:34 (Greek version). 6:18 2 Sam 7:14.

6:9 ignored . . . well-known. While some did not recognize Paul as a legitimate apostle, God and the Corinthian church knew his genuineness (5:11).
6:10 poor, but we give spiritual riches to others. While financially poor, Paul gave others the gift of life in Christ. This too reflects the ministry of Jesus (8:9). **have everything.** Though in this life he may have nothing, the fullness of God's Kingdom is given to him (Luke 6:20; 1 Cor. 3:21-23).
6:14 team up. Or "yoked together." The idea of the double yoke has Old Testament roots, as in Deuteronomy 22:10 where it is forbidden to put an ox and a donkey in the same harness. The point is that the fundamental incompatibility of an ox and a donkey would make it very difficult to plow in a straight line, besides causing strain to both animals and their driver. This is also true for believers and unbelievers.
6:15 devil. (Belial)This name for Satan, not used elsewhere in the New Testament, is common in the writings from the ancient community of Qumran.
7:2 led . . . astray. Literally, "ruined." This may refer either to financial or moral ruin. **taken advantage.** This implies taking advantage of someone.
7:3 I'm not saying this to condemn you. Paul is not interested in striking back at the church by accusing them of being in the wrong. He simply wants to clear himself of the suspicions that have been raised by his opponents.
7:5 conflict in every direction. Paul had already mentioned how he came near to death in the province of Asia (1:8-10). His troubles evidently followed him into Macedonia. **battles on the outside and fear on the inside.** He faced external pressures from his enemies as well as inner anxiety such as his concern over Titus and the situation in Corinth.
7:6 God, who encourages. Paul returns to the description of God with which he began this letter (1:3-5; Isa. 49:13). To "encourage" does not mean simply to console but to actively help, encourage, and strengthen someone undergoing trial. **encouraged us by the arrival of Titus.** Paul had a lot of confidence in Titus, who had the ability to deal with tough situations. He was entrusted with the delicate task of delivering Paul's severe letter (2:1-4) to Corinth and correcting problems within the church there (7:13-15). Titus' genuine concern for and evenhanded dealing with the Corinthians (8:16-17; 12:18) no doubt contributed to his success, which he reported in person to Paul, anxiously awaiting word in Macedonia.

encouraged us by the arrival of Titus. 7 His presence
was a joy, but so was the news he brought of the en-
couragement he received from you. When he told us
how much you long to see me, and how sorry you are
for what happened, and how loyal you are to me, I
was filled with joy!
8 I am not sorry that I sent that severe letter to you,
though I was sorry at first, for I know it was painful
to you for a little while. 9 Now I am glad I sent it, not
because it hurt you, but because the pain caused you
to repent and change your ways. It was the kind of
sorrow God wants his people to have, so you were
not harmed by us in any way. 10 For the kind of sor-
row God wants us to experience leads us away from
sin and results in salvation. There's no regret for that
kind of sorrow. But worldly sorrow, which lacks re-
pentance, results in spiritual death.
11 Just see what this godly sorrow produced in you!
Such earnestness, such concern to clear yourselves,
such indignation, such alarm, such longing to see me,
such zeal, and such a readiness to punish wrong. You
showed that you have done everything necessary to
make things right. 12 My purpose, then, was not to
write about who did the wrong or who was wronged.
I wrote to you so that in the sight of God you could
see for yourselves how loyal you are to us. 13 We have
been greatly encouraged by this.

In addition to our own encouragement, we were es-
pecially delighted to see how happy Titus was about
the way all of you welcomed him and set his mind* at
ease. 14 I had told him how proud I was of you—and you
didn't disappoint me. I have always told you the truth,
and now my boasting to Titus has also proved true!
15 Now he cares for you more than ever when he re-
members the way all of you obeyed him and welcomed
him with such fear and deep respect. 16 I am very happy
now because I have complete confidence in you.

A CALL TO GENEROUS GIVING

8 Now I want you to know, dear brothers and sis-
ters,* what God in his kindness has done through
the churches in Macedonia. 2 They are being tested by
many troubles, and they are very poor. But they are
also filled with abundant joy, which has overflowed
in rich generosity.
3 For I can testify that they gave not only what they
could afford, but far more. And they did it of their

USING WHAT YOU HAVE

1. With what are you generous: Your money? Time? Talents? Toys? With what are you stingy?

2 CORINTHIANS 8:1-15

2. What do we learn about the Macedonians from their giving?
3. How can the equality principle (vv. 13-15) help us decide what cause needs our immediate attention?
4. What does this principle say about getting our own needs met?
5. Verse 15 is a quotation from Exodus 16:18, where God provided manna in the desert. What does this principle show you about the blessings you enjoy? How should you use those blessings?

own free will. 4 They begged us again and again for
the privilege of sharing in the gift for the believers in
Jerusalem.* 5 They even did more than we had hoped,
for their first action was to give themselves to the
Lord and to us, just as God wanted them to do.
6 So we have urged Titus, who encouraged your giv-
ing in the first place, to return to you and encourage you
to finish this ministry of giving. 7 Since you excel in so
many ways—in your faith, your gifted speakers, your
knowledge, your enthusiasm, and your love from us*—I
want you to excel also in this gracious act of giving.
8 I am not commanding you to do this. But I am test-
ing how genuine your love is by comparing it with
the eagerness of the other churches.
9 You know the generous grace of our Lord Jesus
Christ. Though he was rich, yet for your sakes he be-
came poor, so that by his poverty he could make you
rich.
10 Here is my advice: It would be good for you to fin-
ish what you started a year ago. Last year you were
the first who wanted to give, and you were the first to
begin doing it. 11 Now you should finish what you start-
ed. Let the eagerness you showed in the beginning be
matched now by your giving. Give in proportion to
what you have. 12 Whatever you give is acceptable if

7:13 Greek *his spirit.* 8:1 Greek *brothers.* 8:4 Greek *for God's holy people.* 8:7 Some manuscripts read *your love for us.*

7:10 kind of sorrow God wants . . . leads us away from sin. Two different Greek words are translated *repentance*. Judas' repentance for betraying Jesus was more regret. The repentance produced by godly grief stems from a person's awareness of sin in their lives and an intention to change—to be in conformity with God's ways. The Corinthians became aware of how out of line their actions were, and this insight brought sorrow, which in turn led to a change of attitude and behavior. **worldly sorrow.** Worldly grief does not lead to the positive change of heart and life that repentance implies but brings only bitterness and resentment.

7:11 earnestness. Having realized their sin, the Corinthians went to extreme lengths to clear themselves. **zeal.** They now took the problem seriously and passionately wanted to correct it.

8:1 the churches in Macedonia. Macedonia was the Roman province just north of the province of Achaia where Corinth was located. The churches in mind were probably those located at Philippi, Thessalonica, and Berea (Acts 16:6–17:15). These churches were planted by Paul, Silvanus, and Timothy on Paul's second missionary journey. At least two of the three churches began with severe persecution that didn't let up but intensified. The impact of the gospel in the Macedonia is seen in the fact that though they were experiencing persecution and poverty, they responded with great generosity. Difficult circumstances have the potential for bringing out the best in those in whom the Spirit of Christ dwells.

8:4 They begged us. This verse contains three words that show how the motivation for this offering sprang not only from humanitarian concerns but from distinctly Christian convictions as well. **privilege.** Literally, "grace." **sharing.** The Greek word is *koinonia*, often translated as "fellowship." Giving is an expression of partnership in other believers in Christ. **ministry.** Giving is a way of serving and ministering to the needs of others, a Christian responsibility (5:15).

8:5 to give themselves to the Lord. Here is the source of generosity. Seeing what God has done for us, we give ourselves to Him and consequently give to support His work here on earth. A person's priorities can be seen in his checkbook and his calendar.

8:7 excel. Paul exhorts the Corinthians to participate in giving as wholeheartedly as they participate in the exercise of other spiritual gifts (1 Cor. 12:7-11; 14:1) and as a reflection of their desire to affirm his apostleship (7:11).

8:11 Now you should finish what you started. This is reminiscent of Christ's parable of the two sons, one of whom said he was going to do something (work in the vineyard) but didn't, and the other of whom said he would not but did (Matt. 21:28-32). Following through on good intentions is vital. **to what you have.** One reason the Corinthians may have stalled is that they felt they could not make a significant contribution. The issue is not how much one gives but simply that one gives out of love for God and people.

you give it eagerly. And give according to what you
have, not what you don't have. 13 Of course, I don't
mean your giving should make life easy for others and
hard for yourselves. I only mean that there should be
some equality. 14 Right now you have plenty and can
help those who are in need. Later, they will have plen-
ty and can share with you when you need it. In this
way, things will be equal. 15 As the Scriptures say,

"Those who gathered a lot had nothing left over,
and those who gathered only a little had
enough."*

TITUS AND HIS COMPANIONS

16 But thank God! He has given Titus the same enthusi-
asm for you that I have. 17 Titus welcomed our request
that he visit you again. In fact, he himself was very
eager to go and see you. 18 We are also sending anoth-
er brother with Titus. All the churches praise him as
a preacher of the Good News. 19 He was appointed by
the churches to accompany us as we take the offering
to Jerusalem*—a service that glorifies the Lord and
shows our eagerness to help.
20 We are traveling together to guard against any
criticism for the way we are handling this generous
gift. 21 We are careful to be honorable before the Lord,
but we also want everyone else to see that we are
honorable.
22 We are also sending with them another of our
brothers who has proven himself many times and
has shown on many occasions how eager he is. He
is now even more enthusiastic because of his great
confidence in you. 23 If anyone asks about Titus, say
that he is my partner who works with me to help
you. And the brothers with him have been sent by the
churches,* and they bring honor to Christ. 24 So show
them your love, and prove to all the churches that our
boasting about you is justified.

THE COLLECTION FOR CHRISTIANS IN JERUSALEM

9 I really don't need to write to you about this min-
istry of giving for the believers in Jerusalem.* 2 For
I know how eager you are to help, and I have been
boasting to the churches in Macedonia that you in
Greece* were ready to send an offering a year ago. In
fact, it was your enthusiasm that stirred up many of
the Macedonian believers to begin giving.
3 But I am sending these brothers to be sure you
really are ready, as I have been telling them, and that
your money is all collected. I don't want to be wrong
in my boasting about you. 4 We would be embar-
rassed—not to mention your own embarrassment—
if some Macedonian believers came with me and
found that you weren't ready after all I had told them!
5 So I thought I should send these brothers ahead of
me to make sure the gift you promised is ready. But I
want it to be a willing gift, not one given grudgingly.
6 Remember this—a farmer who plants only a few
seeds will get a small crop. But the one who plants
generously will get a generous crop. 7 You must each
decide in your heart how much to give. And don't give
reluctantly or in response to pressure. "For God loves

GENEROUS GIVING

1. Do you like to save your money or spend it? Why?

2 CORINTHIANS 8:16–9:5

2. Why did the churches choose Titus to deliver this offering to Jerusalem and ensure its use for mission-relief work?
3. Why does Paul expect the Corinthians to be generous (9:1-5)? In what ways?
4. If the Macedonians came to visit you, would they find your generosity lacking or overflowing? With what else besides money are you generous?
5. What is the difference between a "a willing gift" and an "one give grudgingly" (9:5)? Which is more typical of your own generosity to others?

CHEERFUL GIVING

1. How much money do you have on you right now? Under what conditions would you give it all away?

2 CORINTHIANS 9:6-15

2. What does Paul mean in verse 6? If you give $100, you will get $1,000 back? Why or why not?
3. Why do you think God cares about our attitudes when we give?
4. In what ways, other than money, can you give to your church?
5. What is something you are cheerfully willing to give to God?

8:15 Exod 16:18. 8:19 See 1 Cor 16:3-4. 8:23 Greek *are apostles of the churches.* 9:1 Greek *about the offering for God's holy people.*
9:2 Greek *in Achaia,* the southern region of the Greek peninsula. *Macedonia* was in the northern region of Greece. 9:7 See footnote on Prov 22:8.

8:13 equality. In their abundance the Corinthians share what they have with those who are in need. Likewise, in the future, it could be the other way around, and the Corinthians could expect aid if they needed it from Christians in Jerusalem and elsewhere.
8:18 brother. An unnamed fellow worker known for acts of Christian service.
8:19 He was appointed. This brother comes not merely on his own initiative, but as a representative of the churches (probably in Macedonia).
8:22 We are also sending. There will also be a third traveling companion. Paul is going to great lengths to ensure his enemies and critics cannot charge him with profiting personally from this collection. Titus is his friend and fellow worker, so it is vital to have two other respected traveling companions appointed by the churches to accompany Titus.
9:2 boasting. Apparently in the same way that Paul used the Macedonians as examples to the Corinthians (8:1-5), so too he has used the readiness of the Corinthians to give as an example to the Macedonians. **Greece.** (Achaia) Corinth was the largest city in the province of Achaia and probably the site of the largest church.
9:6 the one who plants generously will get a generous crop. Paul may be quoting a proverb (similar sayings were known in both Jewish and Greek literature) as support for his encouragement for generous giving. It is not that a person can be assured of financial security by giving (and thus obligating God in some way) but rather that the exercise of giving leads to the growth in grace in the life of the giver.
9:7 don't give reluctantly or in response to pressure. Unlike the temple tax, this voluntary offering required people to consider for themselves what they would contribute. **God loves a person who gives cheerfully.** It is not that giving earns God's love but that God "approves of" the character of a person who is generous.

a person who gives cheerfully."* [8] And God will generously provide all you need. Then you will always have everything you need and plenty left over to share with others. [9] As the Scriptures say,

"They share freely and give generously to the poor.
Their good deeds will be remembered forever."*

[10] For God is the one who provides seed for the farmer and then bread to eat. In the same way, he will provide and increase your resources and then produce a great harvest of generosity* in you.

[11] Yes, you will be enriched in every way so that you can always be generous. And when we take your gifts to those who need them, they will thank God. [12] So two good things will result from this ministry of giving—the needs of the believers in Jerusalem* will be met, and they will joyfully express their thanks to God.

[13] As a result of your ministry, they will give glory to God. For your generosity to them and to all believers will prove that you are obedient to the Good News of Christ. [14] And they will pray for you with deep affection because of the overflowing grace God has given to you. [15] Thank God for this gift* too wonderful for words!

PAUL DEFENDS HIS AUTHORITY

10 Now I, Paul, appeal to you with the gentleness and kindness of Christ—though I realize you think I am timid in person and bold only when I write from far away. [2] Well, I am begging you now so that when I come I won't have to be bold with those who think we act from human motives.

[3] We are human, but we don't wage war as humans do. [4]*We use God's mighty weapons, not worldly weapons, to knock down the strongholds of human reasoning and to destroy false arguments. [5] We destroy every proud obstacle that keeps people from knowing God. We capture their rebellious thoughts and teach them to obey Christ. [6] And after you have become fully obedient, we will punish everyone who remains disobedient.

WEAPONS OF WAR

1. If you were to fight in a war, what weapons would you want to have? Why?

2 CORINTHIANS 10:1-18

2. What does Paul mean when he says, "we are human" (v. 3)? What, in practical terms, does it mean to wage a spiritual war "as humans do"?
3. What are the weapons of our warfare (v. 4)?
4. What "strongholds" does the Word of God demolish? What arguments? Give examples of modern "strongholds" and "arguments" that are contrary to the Word of God.
5. What would you say if you were to "boast only about the Lord" (v. 17)?

[7] Look at the obvious facts.* Those who say they belong to Christ must recognize that we belong to Christ as much as they do. [8] I may seem to be boasting too much about the authority given to us by the Lord. But our authority builds you up; it doesn't tear you down. So I will not be ashamed of using my authority.

[9] I'm not trying to frighten you by my letters. [10] For some say, "Paul's letters are demanding and forceful, but in person he is weak, and his speeches are worthless!" [11] Those people should realize that our actions when we arrive in person will be as forceful as what we say in our letters from far away.

[12] Oh, don't worry; we wouldn't dare say that we are as wonderful as these other men who tell you how important they are! But they are only comparing themselves with each other, using themselves as the standard of measurement. How ignorant!

[13] We will not boast about things done outside our area of authority. We will boast only about what has happened within the boundaries of the work God has

9:9 Ps 112:9. **9:10** Greek *righteousness.* **9:12** Greek *of God's holy people.* **9:15** Greek *his gift.* **10:4** English translations divide verses 4 and 5 in various ways. **10:7** Or *You look at things only on the basis of appearance.*

9:8 everything. The stress on "every" in this verse emphasizes God's lavish generosity.

9:11 you will be enriched. The purpose of such riches is not to pamper personal indulgences but to facilitate generosity. **in every way.** God might not reward faithfulness with material wealth but with a wealth of spiritual and emotional resources. James 2:5 reminds us, "Hasn't God chosen the poor in this world to be rich in faith? Aren't they the ones who will inherit the Kingdom he has promised to those who love him?"

9:12 ministry. Giving is a way of ministering to the needs of others, a Christian responsibility (5:15). **needs of the believers.** The poor are actually helped. This is one fruit of generosity.

10:1 I, Paul appeal to you. This verse begins the final section of the letter. From his extravagant hope of what might be in the future as expressed in 9:12-15 (based probably on Titus' report mentioned in 7:6-16), Paul moves to what is happening in Corinth. Paul begins his case by defending himself against the charge that he has a weak character. Paul was charged with being unimpressive (v. 10) and thus not an authoritative apostle of Christ. The fact that Paul begins the final section of this letter by invoking the meekness and gentleness of Jesus (Matt. 11:29) immediately shows that he rejects authoritarianism and aggressive behavior as a sign of apostleship. His opponents saw this as weakness, not Christlikeness.

10:3 We are human. Paul acknowledges his humanity. **don't wage war as humans do.** God's work can't be done just any way. We err if we think we can bring about God's kingdom using fleshly methods.

10:4 not worldly weapons. Sheer intellect, cleverness, marketing savvy, organizational genius, and persuasive rhetoric in themselves can never accomplish God's purposes. He does not accept the self-oriented lifestyle of the world. He refuses to live life relying solely on his own resources and with an eye only to increasing his own power and prestige. **God's mighty weapons . . . to knock down the strongholds of human reasoning.** In contrast to the weapons of the world, Paul relies on Christ's extremely powerful spiritual weapons to bring about change. The picture is of a situation where a city attempts to protect itself from invasion by constructing various defensive barriers. The spiritual walls can only be breeched by divine weapons that seem weak to those have a fleshly outlook. Spiritual warfare is real. Those who fully give themselves to Christ will experience opposition that is not merely human.

10:7 Look at the obvious facts. Since they view what is happening on the basis of human wisdom, they misinterpret the situation. **belong to Christ.** Quite possibly Paul's opponents in Corinth are claiming to be Christ's true apostles which, by inference or direct accusation, would make Paul a false apostle—a claim he rejects.

10:8 builds you up. Paul's commission as an apostle was to preach the gospel and so to build churches. His commission is not to destroy churches (as his opponents were doing; 1 Cor. 3:17).

10:10 his speeches are worthless! Paul was probably in ill health, and he had long ago rejected the art of rhetoric (1 Cor. 2:1-5). But in Corinth, which had many educated citizens, both powerful speech and a persuasive personality were highly valued, which may account for why the church started to listen to these new teachers.

given us, which includes our working with you. [14] We
are not reaching beyond these boundaries when we
claim authority over you, as if we had never visited
you. For we were the first to travel all the way to Co-
rinth with the Good News of Christ.
[15] Nor do we boast and claim credit for the work
someone else has done. Instead, we hope that your
faith will grow so that the boundaries of our work
among you will be extended. [16] Then we will be able
to go and preach the Good News in other places far
beyond you, where no one else is working. Then there
will be no question of our boasting about work done
in someone else's territory. [17] As the Scriptures say, "If
you want to boast, boast only about the LORD."*
[18] When people commend themselves, it doesn't
count for much. The important thing is for the Lord
to commend them.

PAUL AND THE FALSE APOSTLES

11 I hope you will put up with a little more of my
foolishness. Please bear with me. [2] For I am jeal-
ous for you with the jealousy of God himself. I prom-
ised you as a pure bride* to one husband—Christ.
[3] But I fear that somehow your pure and undivided
devotion to Christ will be corrupted, just as Eve was
deceived by the cunning ways of the serpent. [4] You
happily put up with whatever anyone tells you,
even if they preach a different Jesus than the one we
preach, or a different kind of Spirit than the one you
received, or a different kind of gospel than the one
you believed.

EVIL IN DISGUISE

1. What's the most memorable encounter you ever had with a snake?

2 CORINTHIANS 11:1-15

2. Read Genesis 3. How did Satan (the serpent) deceive Eve? How does he use those same arguments to deceive people today?
3. What "different kind of gospel" has pulled you away from Jesus in the past? How did you become aware of its deceitfulness?
4. How does Satan disguise himself as an "angel of light" today (v. 14)?
5. Sin rarely approaches us as evil but as "virtue in disguise." From verses 2-4, how can you guard yourself against this satanic strategy?

[5] But I don't consider myself inferior in any way
to these "super apostles" who teach such things. [6] I
may be unskilled as a speaker, but I'm not lacking in
knowledge. We have made this clear to you in every
possible way.
[7] Was I wrong when I humbled myself and honored
you by preaching God's Good News to you without ex-
pecting anything in return? [8] I "robbed" other church-
es by accepting their contributions so I could serve
you at no cost. [9] And when I was with you and didn't
have enough to live on, I did not become a financial
burden to anyone. For the brothers who came from
Macedonia brought me all that I needed. I have never
been a burden to you, and I never will be. [10] As surely
as the truth of Christ is in me, no one in all of Greece*
will ever stop me from boasting about this. [11] Why?
Because I don't love you? God knows that I do.
[12] But I will continue doing what I have always
done. This will undercut those who are looking for an
opportunity to boast that their work is just like ours.
[13] These people are false apostles. They are deceit-
ful workers who disguise themselves as apostles of
Christ. [14] But I am not surprised! Even Satan disguises
himself as an angel of light. [15] So it is no wonder that
his servants also disguise themselves as servants of
righteousness. In the end they will get the punish-
ment their wicked deeds deserve.

PAUL'S MANY TRIALS

[16] Again I say, don't think that I am a fool to talk like
this. But even if you do, listen to me, as you would to a
foolish person, while I also boast a little. [17] Such boast-
ing is not from the Lord, but I am acting like a fool.

TOLERATING FOOLS

1. When have you put up with someone's bullying or abuse? Why did you tolerate it? What would you do now if you had it to do over?

2 CORINTHIANS 11:16-33

2. What does Paul mean in verse 19, "After all, you think you are so wise, but you enjoy putting up with fools"? How do Christians do this today?
3. Why does Paul say this is a weakness (v. 21)? What should Christians do when confronted with foolish teaching?
4. How can you discern foolish teaching from sound, wise teaching?

10:17 Jer 9:24. **11:2** Greek *a virgin.* **11:10** Greek *Achaia,* the southern region of the Greek peninsula.

10:16 in other places far beyond you. Paul had no desire to hang onto any power or position in Corinth. He wanted to resolve the difficulties in Corinth so he could get on with the business of preaching the gospel in the parts of the empire that had not yet heard the good news of Jesus Christ. In fact, his plans were to leave the region around the Aegean Sea, to push on to Rome, and then head into Spain (Rom. 15:23-29).

11:5 "super apostles." This is a sarcastic label for the false apostles.

11:6 unskilled as a speaker. A popular style of rhetoric had developed among the Greeks that utilized rhetorical form as a means of manipulating people rather than communicating truth. It was this abuse of rhetoric that Paul rejected. **knowledge.** This was more than understanding information; Paul brought revelation from God with spiritual insight.

11:7 without expecting anything. In 1 Corinthians 9, Paul makes it clear that he believed it was appropriate for apostles to be supported by the churches they served. He refused the support of the Corinthians so that he would not be a burden to them (v. 9).

11:14 angel of light. Paul has already referred to Satan as the arch-deceiver (v. 3), masquerading as something he is not.

11:16 a foolish person . . . while I also boast a little. By comparison to the super apostles, the false teachers, Paul seemed incredibly weak and ineffective. The Corinthians came to this conclusion about Paul because they were judging by worldly standards. So Paul with ironic sarcasm says in the following section (11:22-33), if you want to play the game on this field, I can do that. Paul takes this tact not to show how great he is but to show that worldly standards of measuring God's representatives collapse.

[18] And since others boast about their human achieve-
ments, I will, too. [19] After all, you think you are so wise,
but you enjoy putting up with fools! [20] You put up with
it when someone enslaves you, takes everything you
have, takes advantage of you, takes control of every-
thing, and slaps you in the face. [21] I'm ashamed to say
that we've been too "weak" to do that!
But whatever they dare to boast about—I'm
talking like a fool again—I dare to boast about it,
too. [22] Are they Hebrews? So am I. Are they Israelites?
So am I. Are they descendants of Abraham? So am
I. [23] Are they servants of Christ? I know I sound like
a madman, but I have served him far more! I have
worked harder, been put in prison more often, been
whipped times without number, and faced death
again and again. [24] Five different times the Jewish
leaders gave me thirty-nine lashes. [25] Three times I
was beaten with rods. Once I was stoned. Three times
I was shipwrecked. Once I spent a whole night and
a day adrift at sea. [26] I have traveled on many long
journeys. I have faced danger from rivers and from
robbers. I have faced danger from my own people,
the Jews, as well as from the Gentiles. I have faced
danger in the cities, in the deserts, and on the seas.
And I have faced danger from men who claim to be
believers but are not.* [27] I have worked hard and long,
enduring many sleepless nights. I have been hungry
and thirsty and have often gone without food. I have
shivered in the cold, without enough clothing to keep
me warm.
[28] Then, besides all this, I have the daily burden of
my concern for all the churches. [29] Who is weak with-
out my feeling that weakness? Who is led astray, and I
do not burn with anger?
[30] If I must boast, I would rather boast about the
things that show how weak I am. [31] God, the Father of
our Lord Jesus, who is worthy of eternal praise, knows
I am not lying. [32] When I was in Damascus, the gover-
nor under King Aretas kept guards at the city gates to
catch me. [33] I had to be lowered in a basket through a
window in the city wall to escape from him.

PAUL'S VISION AND HIS THORN IN THE FLESH

12 This boasting will do no good, but I must go on.
I will reluctantly tell about visions and reve-
lations from the Lord. [2] I* was caught up to the third
heaven fourteen years ago. Whether I was in my body
or out of my body, I don't know—only God knows.
[3] Yes, only God knows whether I was in my body or
outside my body. But I do know [4] that I was caught
up* to paradise and heard things so astounding that
they cannot be expressed in words, things no human
is allowed to tell.
[5] That experience is worth boasting about, but I'm
not going to do it. I will boast only about my weak-
nesses. [6] If I wanted to boast, I would be no fool in
doing so, because I would be telling the truth. But I
won't do it, because I don't want anyone to give me
credit beyond what they can see in my life or hear
in my message, [7] even though I have received such
wonderful revelations from God. So to keep me from
becoming proud, I was given a thorn in my flesh, a
messenger from Satan to torment me and keep me
from becoming proud.

THORN IN THE FLESH

1. What is the greatest weakness that you face in your sport? How do you compensate for it?

2 CORINTHIANS 12:1-10

2. What does Paul mean by "a thorn in my flesh" (v. 7)? Why does he refer to it as "a messenger from Satan"?
3. How has Paul's "thorn" affected his life?
4. How do you react when God appears to be silent in answering your urgent requests? How do you feel about God's promise in verse 9? Why doesn't God simply take your problem away?

11:26 Greek *from false brothers.* **12:2** Greek *I know a man in Christ who.* **12:3-4** Greek *But I know such a man, [4] that he was caught up.*

11:22 descendants of Abraham. Often a synonym for "Israelites." Paul points out that he shares all the ethnic, social, and religious claims of the false teachers regarding their background. **Israelites.** This emphasizes the religious and cultural dimension of their backgrounds. This was the nation God had chosen to be his representatives to the nations. Through Abraham's seed, the Messiah would come, and the Scriptures were given. Paul was born into all the privileges of God's people and prior to his conversion had distinguished himself as a zealous Israelite of the tribe of Benjamin.

11:23-27 Paul reveals his weaknesses rather than his strengths.

11:25 beaten with rods. This was a common Roman punishment (Acts 16:22-23). **shipwrecked.** One shipwreck is described in Acts 27:14-44, but that had not yet occurred when Paul wrote this letter. Since Paul traveled frequently by ship and since shipwrecks were by no means uncommon in those days, it appears that Paul endured several shipwrecks.

11:26 dangers from rivers. Not all rivers had bridges or safe ferries. **and robbers.** This could have been a special problem when Paul was transporting collections taken in aid of poorer churches. **danger from my own people.** Such danger came from mobs, from the courts, and from personal attacks (Acts 9:23,29; 13:6-8,45; 14:2,19; 17:5; 18:6,12; 20:3,19; 21:11,27). **danger from men who claim to be believers .** Not only did he face the possibility of harm (bodily and otherwise) from Jews and Gentiles but also from those claiming to be Christ-followers.

11:29 weak. In his "boasting" he now boasts of being weakest of all. **burn.** In his concern for the churches, Paul has a constant source of anguish over those who have been led astray from the faith.

11:30-33 Because it seems absurd that one could be both weak and be an apostle, Paul asserts that he has indeed been telling the truth (v. 31). To wrap up the accounts of his weakness, he recounts a final incident that was especially humiliating (Acts 9:23-25). The mighty apostle, far from being heralded with glory, was reduced to hiding in a basket. **King Aretas.** This Arab king ruled from 9 B.C to A.D 39.

12:1 visions and revelations. It is difficult to distinguish between these two. Perhaps "vision" refers to what was seen in the experience, while "revelation" refers to what was heard (the content). These are ecstatic experiences of some sort, whereby for a brief time the limitations of space, time, and sense perception are removed so that one experiences firsthand immediate, direct access to the supernatural.

12:2 fourteen years ago. This was probably around A.D 42, well before he planted the Corinthian church. This is the only time in any letter that Paul mentions such an experience. While Paul doesn't indicate that this was his vision (so as not to draw the attention to himself), it seems clear that he is referring to himself. **caught up.** Visions were often spoken of in terms of a journey to another place. Whether Paul was literally transported to a new place or simply found himself in a new reality is impossible to know. **third heaven.** Jewish literature spoke of heaven having various levels, although the number of levels differs. **in my body or out of my body.** Paul refuses to speculate on how this experience occurred.

12:6 telling the truth. This may infer that his opponents had fabricated tales of their visions.

12:7 a thorn in my flesh. It is unknown what Paul means here, but the reference may be unclear so that we can all apply these truths to our won struggles. **messenger of Satan.** Sickness was thought to be caused by Satan, but the false apostles in Corinth are also referred to as servants of Satan (11:13-15). **torment me.** Literally, "to continually torment me." Whatever the problem was, it was chronic, though not debilitating.

UNSELFISH SACRIFICE

1. What is one way your parents have sacrificed for you? How do you feel about that unselfish sacrifice?

2 CORINTHIANS 12:11-21

2. What led Paul to write this letter (vv. 11-13)? How have the false "super apostles" distorted his ministry (see 2:17; 11:7)?
3. How would you respond if fellow Christians you love were behaving like the Corinthians in verses 20-21? How persistent would you be in loving them?
4. To whom is God leading you to reach out and help? How can you show the spirit of verses 14-15 to this person?

8 Three different times I begged the Lord to take it
away. 9 Each time he said, "My grace is all you need.
My power works best in weakness." So now I am glad
to boast about my weaknesses, so that the power of
Christ can work through me. 10 That's why I take pleasure in my weaknesses, and in the insults, hardships,
persecutions, and troubles that I suffer for Christ. For
when I am weak, then I am strong.

PAUL'S CONCERN FOR THE CORINTHIANS

11 You have made me act like a fool. You ought to be
writing commendations for me, for I am not at all
inferior to these "super apostles," even though I am
nothing at all. 12 When I was with you, I certainly
gave you proof that I am an apostle. For I patiently
did many signs and wonders and miracles among
you. 13 The only thing I failed to do, which I do in the
other churches, was to become a financial burden to
you. Please forgive me for this wrong!
14 Now I am coming to you for the third time, and
I will not be a burden to you. I don't want what you
have—I want you. After all, children don't provide
for their parents. Rather, parents provide for their
children. 15 I will gladly spend myself and all I have
for you, even though it seems that the more I love you,
the less you love me.
16 Some of you admit I was not a burden to you. But
others still think I was sneaky and took advantage of
you by trickery. 17 But how? Did any of the men I sent
to you take advantage of you? 18 When I urged Titus to
visit you and sent our other brother with him, did Titus take advantage of you? No! For we have the same
spirit and walk in each other's steps, doing things the
same way.
19 Perhaps you think we're saying these things
just to defend ourselves. No, we tell you this as
Christ's servants, and with God as our witness.
Everything we do, dear friends, is to strengthen
you. 20 For I am afraid that when I come I won't like
what I find, and you won't like my response. I am
afraid that I will find quarreling, jealousy, anger,
selfishness, slander, gossip, arrogance, and disorderly behavior. 21 Yes, I am afraid that when I come
again, God will humble me in your presence. And I
will be grieved because many of you have not given up your old sins. You have not repented of your
impurity, sexual immorality, and eagerness for
lustful pleasure.

PAUL'S FINAL ADVICE

13 This is the third time I am coming to visit you
(and as the Scriptures say, "The facts of every
case must be established by the testimony of two or
three witnesses"*). 2 I have already warned those
who had been sinning when I was there on my second visit. Now I again warn them and all others,
just as I did before, that next time I will not spare
them.
3 I will give you all the proof you want that Christ
speaks through me. Christ is not weak when he deals
with you; he is powerful among you. 4 Although he
was crucified in weakness, he now lives by the power
of God. We, too, are weak, just as Christ was, but when
we deal with you we will be alive with him and will
have God's power.
5 Examine yourselves to see if your faith is genuine.
Test yourselves. Surely you know that Jesus Christ is

13:1 Deut 19:15. 13:5 Or *in you.*

12:8 three different times. There are parallels between Paul's experience and that of Jesus in the Garden of Gethsemane. Like Jesus, Paul was not delivered of the hardship that faced him but received strength to remain faithful in the midst of the suffering.

12:9 My grace is all you need. This sentence is the lens through which 2 Corinthians must be understood. It reflects the fundamental misunderstanding that the false teachers and the Corinthians had about the gospel. They thought the power of God meant that Christians should escape or avoid the experiences of weakness, vulnerability, suffering, and hardship that are common to life. Paul's emphasis has been that the power of God does not mean such trials are avoided but that God empowers believers to love, bring healing, serve others, and remain faithful in the midst of such times (1:3-11).

12:11 act like a fool. Paul is forced to boast because the Corinthians refused to speak up on his behalf and stand with him.

12:12 signs and wonders and miracles. While there is no record of Paul performing any miracles in Corinth, he did do so elsewhere (Acts 14:8-10; 20:9-12).

12:13-16 Since Paul's desire to minister without thought of profiteering was seen as a lack of love (11:9-11), he offers a mock apology. Yet he asserts that when he visits again, he still will refuse their financial support because his intent is to serve them as a parent does a child.

12:13 become a financial burden. Once again, it seems that what most rankled the Corinthians was Paul's refusal to allow them to support him.

12:21 God will humble me. Paul is aware that this could be another very painful visit because he will see that the people will not have repented and his work has not been as effective as he would like. **impurity, sexual immorality and eagerness for lustful pleasure.** These three terms describe sexual sin of all types. Sexual sins were an especially prevalent problem in Corinth (1 Cor. 5:1; 6:12-20).

13:1-4 The Old Testament Law required that there be at least two witnesses before anyone could be accused of a crime (Deut. 19:15). Paul adapts this principle to justify the rightness of his coming with judgment on his next visit, since he has already warned the people twice (through his second visit and his sorrowful letter—2:3-4) of their need to correct their ways.

13:2 warn them and all others. Paul intends to deal both with the long-standing problems in the Corinthian church (detailed in 1 Corinthians), and with the newer problems arising as a result of their seduction by false apostles (12:20-21).

13:3 powerful. Paul may have not been all they expected, but the resurrected Christ is. The power of Christ has been readily visible to the Corinthians in miracles (12:12; Rom. 15:19; Gal. 3:5), in Paul's preaching (1 Cor. 2:4), and in the conversion of sinners to the faith in Christ (1 Cor. 6:11).

13:4 in weakness. It is not that Christ was killed because He was powerless to prevent His crucifixion. Rather, He was killed because He allowed Himself to be weak for our sakes. He renounced the power that could have saved Him and so died to save us. **alive with him and will have God's power.** God's power was displayed in Christ's resurrection from the dead.

PASSING THE TEST

1. What do you do to prepare yourself for big exams?

2 CORINTHIANS 13:1-14

2. Paul prefers to come to the Corinthians in "the gentleness and kindness of Christ" (10:1), and as a loving parent (12:14-15). How will he come, instead, if repentance has not occurred? How does this relate to the ministry of Jesus?
3. What does Paul hope for as he considers his upcoming visit (vv. 10-11)?
4. In which area of your spiritual life will you be "strong" (13:9) this week? In which area will you be content with being "weak" (12:9-10)?

among you*; if not, you have failed the test of genuine
faith. 6 As you test yourselves, I hope you will recog-
nize that we have not failed the test of apostolic au-
thority.
7 We pray to God that you will not do what is wrong
by refusing our correction. I hope we won't need to
demonstrate our authority when we arrive. Do the
right thing before we come—even if that makes it
look like we have failed to demonstrate our authori-
ty. 8 For we cannot oppose the truth, but must always
stand for the truth. 9 We are glad to seem weak if it
helps show that you are actually strong. We pray that
you will become mature.
10 I am writing this to you before I come, hoping
that I won't need to deal severely with you when I
do come. For I want to use the authority the Lord
has given me to strengthen you, not to tear you
down.

PAUL'S FINAL GREETINGS

11 Dear brothers and sisters,* I close my letter with
these last words: Be joyful. Grow to maturity. Encour-
age each other. Live in harmony and peace. Then the
God of love and peace will be with you.
12 Greet each other with a sacred kiss. 13 All of God's
people here send you their greetings.
14*May the grace of the Lord Jesus Christ, the love
of God, and the fellowship of the Holy Spirit be with
you all.

13:11 Greek *Brothers.* **13:14** Some English translations include verse 13 as part of verse 12, and then verse 14 becomes verse 13.

INTRODUCTION TO

GALATIANS

PERSONAL READING PLAN

☐Galatians 1:1-24
☐Galatians 2:1-21
☐Galatians 3:1-25
☐Galatians 3:26–4:20
☐Galatians 4:21–5:15
☐Galatians 5:16–6:18

AUTHOR

The Apostle Paul was the author of Galatians.

DATE

The date of Paul's epistle depends on whether he was writing to churches in North or South Galatia. If Paul had been writing to congregations in North Galatia, the letter could not have been written before his third missionary expedition after the journey mentioned in Acts 16:6 and 18:23, around A.D. 55. On the other hand, if Paul were writing to the churches in the southern region, the epistle to the Galatians is his earliest letter—written in A.D. 48 or 49, possibly while he was in Syrian Antioch just prior to the Council in Jerusalem (Acts 15:6-21).

THEME

Justification by faith alone.

HISTORICAL BACKGROUND

Paul tells us he is writing "to the churches of Galatia" (1:2). But where are these churches located? This is unclear because in 25 B.C. the Romans created a new imperial province that they named Galatia. This new province was made up of the original kingdom of Galatia plus a new region to the south forged out of territory originally belonging to six other regions. So when a first-century writer speaks of Galatia, it is not always clear whether he is referring to the original territory in the north or the new province extending southward—which included the cities of Pisidian, Antioch, Iconium, Lystra, and Derbe that Paul visited during his first missionary journey described in Acts 13–14.

CHARACTERISTICS

Paul writes in anger: "Oh, foolish Galatians! Who has cast an evil spell on you?" (3:1). He felt it strongly because the issue he was addressing in this letter was not a minor matter of church policy; it struck right to the heart of the gospel. Apparently some legalistic Jewish Christians (Judaizers) had been stirring up trouble. They had twisted the gospel into something Jesus never intended, and then they had made false charges against Paul. "Who is that fellow, anyway. He wasn't one of the Twelve. He is a self-appointed apostle. No wonder he left out some crucial parts of the message. Let us set you straight . . ." And the Galatians seemingly believed their words against Paul. Paul wrote, "I am shocked that you are turning away so soon from God, who called you to himself through the loving mercy of Christ. You are following a different way that pretends to be the Good News . . ." (1:6).

What were the Judaizers saying? At first glance, they seemed to be adding only a little to the message. "Believe in Christ," they were saying (they were Christians), "but also be circumcised" (6:12). Paul saw the implications: if the Galatians let themselves be circumcised, it would be but the first step back to keeping the whole law (5:3), which Paul called slavery (4:9). This is not the gospel. The gospel asserts that salvation is a free gift by grace. If you add anything else to grace, salvation is no longer free. It then becomes a matter of doing the "other thing."

The core issue in Galatians is justification. How does a person gain right standing before God? The Judaizers said that Christ (grace) plus circumcision (law-keeping) equals right standing. Paul's equation was different; Christ (grace) plus nothing else equals right standing. Works are excluded from Paul's equation. "Yet we know that a person is made right with God by faith in Jesus Christ, not by obeying the law. And we have believed in Christ Jesus, so that we might be made right with God because of our faith in Christ, not because we have obeyed the law. For no one will ever be made right with God by obeying the law" (2:16). This key verse sums up Paul's argument.

THE IMPLICATIONS

To the modern reader, it may sound as if Paul is getting worked up over a small issue. The important thing is to believe in Jesus, and all the parties agreed to that. But history demonstrated that Paul's concerns were valid. Was Christianity for all people in all cultures (as Paul was arguing), or was it only a Jewish sect? To be a Christian, did you have to accept Jewish customs and submit to Jewish laws? If the Judaizers had won, Christianity would probably have died out in the first century.

Instead, the church was able to expand into the Graeco-Roman world because the gospel was truly universal. It was not tied to temple sacrifice and the Law of Moses, about which most pagans neither knew nor cared. The Judaizers wanted a Christianity circumcised by Jewish exclusiveness, taboos, and customs—in which Gentile believers would always be second-class citizens. Paul fought this with vehemence and passion, as had other believers from Stephen onward; so Christianity became the transcultural world religion Christ intended (Matt. 28:19-20).

THE RELATIONSHIP BETWEEN GALATIANS AND ROMANS

It is obvious that there is a close thematic connection between Galatians and Romans. Galatians appears to be Paul's first attempt at wrestling with the issue of justification by faith alone. Paul does so in the context of having to deal with a local problem. Romans, on the other hand, is a more studied consideration of the same issue. It is an eloquent, carefully stated, logical argument, which stands as one of the finest pieces of theological writing ever penned.

STRUCTURE

After a terse greeting (1:1-5) and pronouncement of condemnation against the troublemakers (1:6-10), Paul launches into his first major theme: his personal defense, in which he deals with the charge that he is not a real apostle (1:11–2:21). This is followed by a doctrinal defense, in which he shows that Christianity lived under the law is inferior to Christianity lived by faith (3:1–4:31). On the basis of these two arguments, he then shows what true Christian freedom is (5:1–6:10), ending with an unusual conclusion written in his own hand (6:11-18).

PASSAGES FOR TOPICAL GROUP STUDY

1:1-10 . . . . CULTS and DECEIVERS . . . . A Different Gospel
1:11-24 . . . GOD'S AUTHORITY . . . . The Final Authority
2:1-10 . . . . CARING FOR THE POOR . . . . Caring for All
2:11-21 . . . WHO CONTROLS YOUR LIFE? . . . . . The Big "I" or JC?
3:1-14 . . . . GOD'S GRACE FOR SALVATION . . . . . . Grasping Grace
3:15-25 . . . CHRIST VS. OTHER RELIGIONS . . . . The Only Seed
3:26–4:7 . . CHILD OF GOD and PUT ON CHRIST . . . . . Leveling the Field
4:8-20 . . . . BAD HABITS and ADDICTIONS . . . . Enslaved
4:21-31 . . . TEMPTATION and OBEDIENCE . . . . Freedom vs. Obedience
5:1-15 . . . . LOVING AND SERVING . . . . Love, Not Slavery
5:16-26 . . . FRUIT OF THE SPIRIT . . . . Fruit Inspection
6:1-10 . . . . ACCOUNTABILITY and HELP . . . . Carrying Your Load

GREETINGS FROM PAUL

1 This letter is from Paul, an apostle. I was not ap-
pointed by any group of people or any human
authority, but by Jesus Christ himself and by God the
Father, who raised Jesus from the dead.
2 All the brothers and sisters* here join me in send-
ing this letter to the churches of Galatia.
3 May God the Father and our Lord Jesus Christ*
give you grace and peace. 4 Jesus gave his life for our
sins, just as God our Father planned, in order to rescue
us from this evil world in which we live. 5 All glory to
God forever and ever! Amen.

THERE IS ONLY ONE GOOD NEWS

6 I am shocked that you are turning away so soon from
God, who called you to himself through the loving
mercy of Christ.* You are following a different way
that pretends to be the Good News 7 but is not the
Good News at all. You are being fooled by those who
deliberately twist the truth concerning Christ.
8 Let God's curse fall on anyone, including us or even
an angel from heaven, who preaches a different kind
of Good News than the one we preached to you. 9 I say
again what we have said before: If anyone preaches
any other Good News than the one you welcomed, let
that person be cursed.
10 Obviously, I'm not trying to win the approval of
people, but of God. If pleasing people were my goal, I
would not be Christ's servant.

PAUL'S MESSAGE COMES FROM CHRIST

11 Dear brothers and sisters, I want you to understand
that the gospel message I preach is not based on mere
human reasoning. 12 I received my message from no
human source, and no one taught me. Instead, I re-
ceived it by direct revelation from Jesus Christ.*
13 You know what I was like when I followed the Jew-
ish religion—how I violently persecuted God's church.
I did my best to destroy it. 14 I was far ahead of my fel-
low Jews in my zeal for the traditions of my ancestors.
15 But even before I was born, God chose me and
called me by his marvelous grace. Then it pleased him
16 to reveal his Son to me* so that I would proclaim the
Good News about Jesus to the Gentiles.
When this happened, I did not rush out to consult
with any human being.* 17 Nor did I go up to Jerusa-
lem to consult with those who were apostles before
I was. Instead, I went away into Arabia, and later I
returned to the city of Damascus.
18 Then three years later I went to Jerusalem to get
to know Peter,* and I stayed with him for fifteen days.

A DIFFERENT GOSPEL

1. What subject do you have the most trouble learning? What lessons do you find yourself forgetting soon after you leave class?

GALATIANS 1:1-10

2. What did Jesus voluntarily do for Paul, the Galatians, and us (v. 4)?
3. What does Paul say will happen to anyone who promotes a "gospel" other than that which Paul preached—the good news of grace (vv. 8-9)?
4. What are some modern teachings that promote a different "gospel"? How do some teachings claim to have special "authority" from enlightened teachers?

THE FINAL AUTHORITY

1. Who is the "final authority" on your sport or hobby? Whose opinions carry the most weight? Why?

GALATIANS 1:11-24

2. What does Paul mean in verse 11, "the gospel message I preach is not based on mere human reasoning"? On what is the gospel based?
3. How does the gospel run counter to human logic and opinion? Why does the world react in anger to the gospel?
4. By whom (and what) was Paul called (v. 15)? What was he specifically called to do (v. 16)?
5. For what has God called you? Are you fulfilling His calling?

1:2 Greek *brothers;* also in 1:11. **1:3** Some manuscripts read *God our Father and the Lord Jesus Christ.* **1:6** Some manuscripts read *through loving mercy.* **1:12** Or *by the revelation of Jesus Christ.* **1:16a** Or *in me.* **1:16b** Greek *with flesh and blood.* **1:18** Greek *Cephas.*

1:1 Paul. Virtually everyone accepts that he was the author of Galatians. **apostle.** This New Testament word means "a special messenger." **not appointed by any group of people . . . but by Jesus Christ.** Paul emphasizes that his apostleship derives not from any human intermediary. Rather, his commission and authority were received directly from the resurrected Christ on the Damascus road.

1:2 Galatia. The Roman province of Galatia was located in what is now the central part of Turkey (see a Bible map).

1:4 gave his life. The idea is one of voluntary sacrifice for a specific purpose. **rescue.** To be rescued from bondage is a key idea in the letter.

1:6 shocked. Typically at this place in a letter, Paul would commend the church (e.g. Rom. 1:8; Phil. 1:3). But here he launches straight into his remonstration, expressing indignation at the news that they have been persuaded by the teaching of people referred to as Judaizers. **turning away.** The word means, literally, a removal from one place to another. The word can also be used for those who "change sides"—for example, army deserters. **loving mercy.** This pinpoints the nature of their turning—from a gospel of unmerited favor to a gospel of works. **Good News.** The proclamation of the good news that in the life, death, and resurrection of Jesus, the kingdom of God has been made clearly evident and is open to all who by faith trust in His atoning work on the cross.

1:8 God's curse fall on anyone. This stands as the direct opposite of God's grace and is used by Paul as a solemn calling down of judgment on the Judaizers, who insisted that to become a good Christian, one had to accept the demands of Jewish law.

1:12 revelation. It was only after Jesus Christ revealed the truth and meaning of these facts to him following the Damascus road experience that Paul accepted the gospel.

1:15 God chose me. Paul's experience is similar to that of Old Testament prophets (Isa. 49:1-6; Jer. 1:5). He could see the special calling and hand of God throughout his life.

1:16 to the Gentiles. With Paul's conversion came his commission to preach to the Gentiles (Acts 9:15). In encountering Christ, he came to the realization that the Law was bankrupt insofar as its ability to save anyone. There was no barrier to prevent Gentiles from coming to the all-sufficient Christ for eternal salvation.

1:18 three years later. A significant interval of time elapsed between his conversion and his first visit to Jerusalem. **Jerusalem.** It was a courageous act by Paul to return here—to his former friends who might well try to harm him (because of his conversion to Christianity) and to new friends who might not even receive him (because of their suspicions about him). **fifteen days.** This was a short visit, and Paul spent much of his time preaching (Acts 9:28-29).

19 The only other apostle I met at that time was James,
the Lord's brother. 20 I declare before God that what I
am writing to you is not a lie.
21 After that visit I went north into the provinces
of Syria and Cilicia. 22 And still the churches in Christ
that are in Judea didn't know me personally. 23 All
they knew was that people were saying, "The one
who used to persecute us is now preaching the very
faith he tried to destroy!" 24 And they praised God be-
cause of me.

THE APOSTLES ACCEPT PAUL

2 Then fourteen years later I went back to Jerusalem
again, this time with Barnabas; and Titus came
along, too. 2 I went there because God revealed to me
that I should go. While I was there I met privately
with those considered to be leaders of the church and
shared with them the message I had been preaching
to the Gentiles. I wanted to make sure that we were in
agreement, for fear that all my efforts had been wast-
ed and I was running the race for nothing. 3 And they
supported me and did not even demand that my com-
panion Titus be circumcised, though he was a Gentile.*
4 Even that question came up only because of some
so-called believers there—false ones, really*—who
were secretly brought in. They sneaked in to spy on
us and take away the freedom we have in Christ Jesus.
They wanted to enslave us and force us to follow their
Jewish regulations. 5 But we refused to give in to them
for a single moment. We wanted to preserve the truth
of the gospel message for you.
6 And the leaders of the church had nothing to add
to what I was preaching. (By the way, their reputa-
tion as great leaders made no difference to me, for
God has no favorites.) 7 Instead, they saw that God
had given me the responsibility of preaching the gos-
pel to the Gentiles, just as he had given Peter the re-
sponsibility of preaching to the Jews. 8 For the same
God who worked through Peter as the apostle to the
Jews also worked through me as the apostle to the
Gentiles.
9 In fact, James, Peter,* and John, who were known
as pillars of the church, recognized the gift God had
given me, and they accepted Barnabas and me as
their co-workers. They encouraged us to keep preach-
ing to the Gentiles, while they continued their work
with the Jews. 10 Their only suggestion was that we
keep on helping the poor, which I have always been
eager to do.

PAUL CONFRONTS PETER

11 But when Peter came to Antioch, I had to oppose
him to his face, for what he did was very wrong.
12 When he first arrived, he ate with the Gentile be-
lievers, who were not circumcised. But afterward,
when some friends of James came, Peter wouldn't eat
with the Gentiles anymore. He was afraid of criticism
from these people who insisted on the necessity of
circumcision. 13 As a result, other Jewish believers fol-
lowed Peter's hypocrisy, and even Barnabas was led
astray by their hypocrisy.
14 When I saw that they were not following the
truth of the gospel message, I said to Peter in front of
all the others, "Since you, a Jew by birth, have discard-
ed the Jewish laws and are living like a Gentile, why
are you now trying to make these Gentiles follow the
Jewish traditions?
15 "You and I are Jews by birth, not 'sinners' like the
Gentiles. 16 Yet we know that a person is made right
with God by faith in Jesus Christ, not by obeying the
law. And we have believed in Christ Jesus, so that we
might be made right with God because of our faith in

CARING FOR ALL

1. Are you the type of person who usually "goes with the crowd" or "does your own thing"?

GALATIANS 2:1-10

2. If Paul's converts had to become Jews to be Christians, what would have happened to Paul's ministry to the Gentiles (v. 2)? What would be different about the church today?
3. What did the spiritual "pillars" of the Jerusalem church recognize about Paul (v. 9)?
4. How does caring for the poor (v. 10) relate to proclaiming the gospel of grace?
5. What can you do this week to help care for the poor?

2:3 Greek *a Greek.* 2:4 Greek *some false brothers.* 2:9 Greek *Cephas;* also in 2:11, 14. 2:16 Some translators hold that the quotation extends through verse 14; others through verse 16; and still others through verse 21.

1:19 James. James, the brother of Jesus, eventually became the leader of the Jerusalem church (Mark 6:3; Acts 1:14; 15:13; 21:18).
1:21 Syria and Cilicia. After leaving Jerusalem, Paul went north into Syria and then into the adjacent area of Cilicia to the city of Tarsus, his birthplace.
2:1 fourteen years later. It is not clear whether Paul means 14 years after his conversion or after his first visit to Jerusalem. In any case, the significant factor is that Paul had little contact with the leaders in Jerusalem. He was not their missionary. He did not take orders from them. **I went back.** In 14 years Paul made only two visits to Jerusalem. The first was for the purpose of meeting Peter. The second was necessary in order to deliver to the mother church a famine collection donated by Christians at Antioch. **Barnabas.** A Levite from Cyprus, whose name was actually Joseph but who had been nicknamed Barnabas (Son of Encouragement) by the apostles (Acts 4:36). When the church in Jerusalem heard that a great number of people in Antioch had turned to Jesus, they sent Barnabas to verify what was happening. Barnabas in turn, having seen this to be an authentic work of God, sought out Paul in Tarsus and brought him back to Antioch, where the two of them labored together to establish the church (Acts 11:19-30). **Titus.** A Gentile Christian from Antioch. Titus became an important coworker with Paul and later was the recipient of a pastoral letter.
2:2 wasted. Paul preached that Gentiles could become Christians without first becoming Jews, i.e., that there was one church made up of both Jews and Gentiles. If the leaders in Jerusalem disputed this, his 14 years of work would have been wasted.
2:11-14 oppose him. Paul concludes his autobiographical sketch by recounting an incident in which he had to rebuke the Apostle Peter for his inconsistency. This incident probably occurred after Paul's return to Antioch following his second visit to Jerusalem (vv. 1-10) but prior to his first missionary journey (Acts 13-14) during which he founded the Galatian churches.
2:15 'sinners' like the Gentiles. Jews did look down rather arrogantly on all Gentiles. But Paul's point is that both Jew and Gentile come to God by faith, not by works. Being "better" morally has nothing to do with justification before God.
2:16 made right. Behind this word stands the image of the Judgment Day. The Jew was preoccupied with how one obtained a positive verdict (justification) from God the Judge. The opposite of justification is condemnation—to be declared guilty—on Judgment Day. This is the language of the courtroom where people are either found guilty or innocent. If you ask most people why God will let them into heaven, they will say He will do so because their good deeds outweighed the bad. This common understanding is dangerously wrong. Only God can justify people based on the work of Christ on the cross.

THE BIG "I" OR JC?

1. Have you ever "told off" your parents, teacher, coach, or some other adult? Why? What was the outcome?

GALATIANS 2:11-21

2. Why did Paul confront Cephas? How was Cephas being a hypocrite?
3. What is the difference between "obeying the law" and "faith in Jesus Christ" (v. 16)?
4. In the Christian life, what dies and what gets resurrected (vv. 19-20)? How is that made possible?
5. Applying the spiritual concept of verse 20, who is "alive" in your life right now—the big "I" or "Christ in me"?

GRASPING GRACE

1. Have you ever seen someone hypnotized? What was it like? Was it real or fake?

GALATIANS 3:1-14

2. What is the answer to Paul's question in verse 2? Give some Scripture verses to support your answer.
3. According to verse 5, what is required of us to have God's Spirit doing miraculous things in our lives?
4. Did God consider Abraham righteous through his faith or through his works (vv. 5-9)?
5. Who are those "those who depend on the law" (v. 10)?
6. Do you rely on your own good works or on God's grace for your salvation?

Christ, not because we have obeyed the law. For no one will ever be made right with God by obeying the law."*

17 But suppose we seek to be made right with God through faith in Christ and then we are found guilty because we have abandoned the law. Would that mean Christ has led us into sin? Absolutely not! 18 Rather, I am a sinner if I rebuild the old system of law I already tore down. 19 For when I tried to keep the law, it condemned me. So I died to the law—I stopped trying to meet all its requirements—so that I might live for God. 20 My old self has been crucified with Christ.* It is no longer I who live, but Christ lives in me. So I live in this earthly body by trusting in the Son of God, who loved me and gave himself for me. 21 I do not treat the grace of God as meaningless. For if keeping the law could make us right with God, then there was no need for Christ to die.

THE LAW AND FAITH IN CHRIST

3 Oh, foolish Galatians! Who has cast an evil spell on you? For the meaning of Jesus Christ's death was made as clear to you as if you had seen a picture of his death on the cross. 2 Let me ask you this one question: Did you receive the Holy Spirit by obeying the law of Moses? Of course not! You received the Spirit because you believed the message you heard about Christ. 3 How foolish can you be? After starting your new lives in the Spirit, why are you now trying to become perfect by your own human effort? 4 Have you experienced* so much for nothing? Surely it was not in vain, was it?

5 I ask you again, does God give you the Holy Spirit and work miracles among you because you obey the law? Of course not! It is because you believe the message you heard about Christ.

6 In the same way, "Abraham believed God, and God counted him as righteous because of his faith."* 7 The real children of Abraham, then, are those who put their faith in God.

8 What's more, the Scriptures looked forward to this time when God would make the Gentiles right in his sight because of their faith. God proclaimed this good news to Abraham long ago when he said, "All nations will be blessed through you."* 9 So all who put their faith in Christ share the same blessing Abraham received because of his faith.

10 But those who depend on the law to make them right with God are under his curse, for the Scriptures say, "Cursed is everyone who does not observe and obey all the commands that are written in God's Book of the Law."* 11 So it is clear that no one can be made right with God by trying to keep the law. For the Scriptures say, "It is through faith that a righteous person has life."* 12 This way of faith is very different from the way of law, which says, "It is through obeying the law that a person has life."*

13 But Christ has rescued us from the curse pronounced by the law. When he was hung on the cross, he took upon himself the curse for our wrongdoing. For it is written in the Scriptures, "Cursed is everyone who is hung on a tree."* 14 Through Christ Jesus, God has blessed the Gentiles with the same blessing he promised to Abraham, so that we who are believers might receive the promised* Holy Spirit through faith.

2:20 Some English translations put this sentence in verse 19. **3:4** Or *Have you suffered.* **3:6** Gen 15:6. **3:8** Gen 12:3; 18:18; 22:18. **3:10** Deut 27:26. **3:11** Hab 2:4. **3:12** Lev 18:5. **3:13** Deut 21:23 (Greek version). **3:14** Some manuscripts read *the blessing of the.*

2:20 no longer I who live. Paul died in relationship to the Law. **Christ lives in me.** That which now activates the believer is the resurrection life and power of Jesus. **trusting.** Faith is that which bonds together the believer and the risen Christ. Paul will also refer to this as living by the Spirit (5:25).

3:1 foolish. Paul's feelings of exasperation and indignation flare up. How could they have been so stupid (as the NEB translates the word)? It is not that they were unable to understand what was happening. They simply failed to use their minds. **cast an evil spell.** Their actions were so bizarre it seemed that their minds were altered.

3:6-9 the Scriptures. Paul turns from his argument based on their experience to an argument based on Scripture. Here he shows that it has always been by faith that men and women became God's children.

3:6 believed God. God promised Abraham that he would have descendants as numerous as the stars, even though his wife Sarah was barren. Despite the improbability of this ever happening, Abraham still trusted God that it would be so. **counted him as righteous.** For Abraham, right standing before God came by faith, not by law-keeping.

3:10-14 under his curse. Paul's next point is that law-keeping is ultimately futile because no one is able to fulfill the whole Law—therefore no one is justified by the Law. Rather a curse hangs heavy upon them. Blessing comes by faith.

THE LAW AND GOD'S PROMISE

[15] Dear brothers and sisters,* here's an example from
everyday life. Just as no one can set aside or amend
an irrevocable agreement, so it is in this case. [16] God
gave the promises to Abraham and his child.* And
notice that the Scripture doesn't say "to his children,*"
as if it meant many descendants. Rather, it says "to
his child"—and that, of course, means Christ. [17] This
is what I am trying to say: The agreement God made
with Abraham could not be canceled 430 years lat-
er when God gave the law to Moses. God would be
breaking his promise. [18] For if the inheritance could be
received by keeping the law, then it would not be the
result of accepting God's promise. But God graciously
gave it to Abraham as a promise.
[19] Why, then, was the law given? It was given along-
side the promise to show people their sins. But the law
was designed to last only until the coming of the child
who was promised. God gave his law through angels
to Moses, who was the mediator between God and the
people. [20] Now a mediator is helpful if more than one
party must reach an agreement. But God, who is one,
did not use a mediator when he gave his promise to
Abraham.
[21] Is there a conflict, then, between God's law and
God's promises?* Absolutely not! If the law could give
us new life, we could be made right with God by obey-
ing it. [22] But the Scriptures declare that we are all pris-
oners of sin, so we receive God's promise of freedom
only by believing in Jesus Christ.

GOD'S CHILDREN THROUGH FAITH

[23] Before the way of faith in Christ was available to
us, we were placed under guard by the law. We were
kept in protective custody, so to speak, until the way of
faith was revealed.
[24] Let me put it another way. The law was our
guardian until Christ came; it protected us until we
could be made right with God through faith. [25] And
now that the way of faith has come, we no longer
need the law as our guardian.
[26] For you are all children* of God through faith in
Christ Jesus. [27] And all who have been united with
Christ in baptism have put on Christ, like putting on
new clothes.* [28] There is no longer Jew or Gentile,*
slave or free, male and female. For you are all one
in Christ Jesus. [29] And now that you belong to Christ,
you are the true children* of Abraham. You are his
heirs, and God's promise to Abraham belongs to
you.

THE ONLY SEED

1. Have you ever been inside a jail? What was it like? How did you feel there?

GALATIANS 3:15-26

2. Can the Old Testament Law give "new life" (v. 21)? Who can? How (v. 22)?
3. Why does Paul make a distinction in verse 16 between one seed and many "seeds"?
4. If Christ is the only "seed" of God's salvation, what does that say about other world religions? How does this compare with what the world teaches us about religion?
5. How do you share your faith with someone from another religion?

LEVELING THE FIELD

1. In what ways does your sport make equals of all players? How does it bring out inequalities?

GALATIANS 3:27–4:7

2. What does it take to become a child of God?
3. What does it mean to "put on Christ" (3:27)? How does that happen on the field and off?
4. What does Paul mean that all are one in Christ Jesus (3:28)? What effect does being "in Christ" have on relationships among believers?
5. What is the difference between being a slave and an heir? Which have you felt more like lately?

3:15 Greek *Brothers.* **3:16a** Greek *seed;* also in 3:16c, 19. See notes on Gen 12:7 and 13:15. **3:16b** Greek *seeds.* **3:21** Some manuscripts read *and the promises?* **3:26** Greek *sons.* **3:27** Greek *have put on Christ.* **3:28** Greek *Jew or Greek.* **3:29** Greek *seed.*

3:15-18 example from everyday life. Having argued from experience and from Scripture, Paul now argues the same point from human reason. He asks the Galatians to think about how wills are made. His point is that once established, no one can alter a will. Likewise, the covenant given by God to Abraham cannot be altered. The promised blessings came to Abraham's true children, not because they earned them through law-keeping but because they came by grace without conditions.
3:16 his child. God's promises to Abraham were not for all his many descendants, but more specifically, for his one crucial descendant: the Messiah. The blessings are then channeled outward to all who believe—Jew or Gentile—through Jesus the Messiah.
3:17 The prior Abrahamic covenant is unaffected by the later Law. **430 years later.** The Law was given much later during the time of Moses.
3:18 inheritance. Promises, along with material possessions, given to a person's descendants. **promise.** God's promise to Abraham had nothing to do with law or obligations. It was a pure gift without conditions.
3:19 Why . . . was the law given? If the promises came by faith, what about the Law? What purpose did it have? This was a burning question to the Judaizers, because they felt that it perfectly reflected God's will. **to last . . . until.** Paul answers that the Law was temporary. Its purpose was to make people aware of their sin, but when the Messiah came, its function would cease. **a mediator.** On the basis of Deuteronomy 33:2, it was concluded that the Law was given to Moses at Mount Sinai by the angels who accompanied God. Paul's point is that a word that came indirectly from God is of less significance than one that came directly as did God's promise to Abraham.
3:24 our guardian. The Law is now pictured as a tutor. The same word is used for household slaves whose responsibility it was to look after the young men in the family until they reached the age of accountability.
3:27 baptism. A common water rite in Judaism. One of three acts by which a person became a Jew, it was picked up and given new meaning (repentance and remission of sins) by John the Baptist, and later used by the Christian church as the visible, outward sign of admission into the Christian community. **put on.** This image may spring from the practice by the early church of removing old garments prior to baptism and then donning a new white robe after baptism.
3:28 no longer Jew or Gentile. The Jewish contempt for the non-Jew was immense. **slave or free.** Although some 60 million slaves virtually ran the Roman Empire, they were generally regarded as mere things, without rights. This was another barrier broken down by Christ. **male and female.** A woman had few, if any, rights in either first-century Judaism or Greco-Roman culture. She belonged to her husband, and he could treat her as he chose, including divorcing her with ease. **one in Christ Jesus.** In morning prayer, a Jewish man thanked God that he had not been made a Gentile, a slave, or a woman. The traditional distinctions are finished. In Christ all are one.

ENSLAVED

1. What is one of your most compulsive habits? How are you trying to break it?

GALATIANS 4:8-20

2. Overall, was Paul more concerned for himself or the Galatians? Why?
3. Do you show deep concern for the welfare of others as Paul did for the Galatians?
4. In what ways does sin "enslave" us? How can a Christian break out of such slavery?
5. Like the Galatians, have you slipped back into any bad habits or old ways from which Christ once delivered you? Which ones? What can you do about it?

4 Think of it this way. If a father dies and leaves an inheritance for his young children, those children are not much better off than slaves until they grow up, even though they actually own everything their father had. 2 They have to obey their guardians until they reach whatever age their father set. 3 And that's the way it was with us before Christ came. We were like children; we were slaves to the basic spiritual principles* of this world.

4 But when the right time came, God sent his Son, born of a woman, subject to the law. 5 God sent him to buy freedom for us who were slaves to the law, so that he could adopt us as his very own children.* 6 And because we* are his children, God has sent the Spirit of his Son into our hearts, prompting us to call out, "Abba, Father."* 7 Now you are no longer a slave but God's own child.* And since you are his child, God has made you his heir.

PAUL'S CONCERN FOR THE GALATIANS

8 Before you Gentiles knew God, you were slaves to so-called gods that do not even exist. 9 So now that you know God (or should I say, now that God knows you), why do you want to go back again and become slaves once more to the weak and useless spiritual principles of this world? 10 You are trying to earn favor with God by observing certain days or months or seasons or years. 11 I fear for you. Perhaps all my hard work with you was for nothing. 12 Dear brothers and sisters,* I plead with you to live as I do in freedom from these things, for I have become like you Gentiles—free from those laws.

You did not mistreat me when I first preached to you. 13 Surely you remember that I was sick when I first brought you the Good News. 14 But even though my condition tempted you to reject me, you did not despise me or turn me away. No, you took me in and cared for me as though I were an angel from God or even Christ Jesus himself. 15 Where is that joyful and grateful spirit you felt then? I am sure you would have taken out your own eyes and given them to me if it had been possible. 16 Have I now become your enemy because I am telling you the truth?

17 Those false teachers are so eager to win your favor, but their intentions are not good. They are trying to shut you off from me so that you will pay attention only to them. 18 If someone is eager to do good things for you, that's all right; but let them do it all the time, not just when I'm with you.

19 Oh, my dear children! I feel as if I'm going through labor pains for you again, and they will continue until Christ is fully developed in your lives. 20 I wish I were with you right now so I could change my tone. But at this distance I don't know how else to help you.

ABRAHAM'S TWO CHILDREN

21 Tell me, you who want to live under the law, do you know what the law actually says? 22 The Scriptures say that Abraham had two sons, one from his slave wife and one from his freeborn wife.* 23 The son of the slave wife was born in a human attempt to bring about the fulfillment of God's promise. But the son of the freeborn wife was born as God's own fulfillment of his promise.

24 These two women serve as an illustration of God's two covenants. The first woman, Hagar, represents Mount Sinai where people received the law that enslaved them. 25 And now Jerusalem is just like Mount Sinai in Arabia,* because she and her children

4:3 Or *powers;* also in 4:9. 4:5 Greek *sons;* also in 4:6. 4:6a Greek *you.* 4:6b *Abba* is an Aramaic term for "father." 4:7 Greek *son;* also in 4:7b. 4:12 Greek *brothers;* also in 4:28, 31. 4:22 See Gen 16:15; 21:2-3. 4:25 Greek *And Hagar, which is Mount Sinai in Arabia, is now like Jerusalem;* other manuscripts read *And Mount Sinai in Arabia is now like Jerusalem.*

4:2 guardians. In his will, a Roman father appointed a guardian who looked after the child until he came of age at 14. Then a curator looked after the child's affairs until age 25. **until they grow up.** The father had some discretion as to when the child received the inheritance.

4:3 spiritual principles. This concept has been interpreted in two ways. (1) It could be basic religious and moral principles or (2) it may be spirits, spiritual powers that were thought to move the heavenly bodies. No matter which interpretation one favors, Paul was speaking of people who were enslaved by some force other than the Holy Spirit of God, the Spirit of Christ.

4:4 when the right time came. Finally, the long history of God's revelation reached the culminating point: Jesus was sent. From a human point of view, Jesus was born at a favorable time. Roman law, the wonderful system of Roman highways, the political stability maintained throughout the Mediterranean world by Rome, the widespread use of the Greek language by people of diverse cultures, and the growing interest in Jewish religious teaching all combined to create a situation in which the gospel could spread.

4:10 observing. Paul observed certain sacred events (Acts 20:16; 1 Cor. 16:8). It is one thing for a Jew to continue in his ethnic tradition in a nonbinding way, and another for a group of Gentiles to be forced to adopt the Jewish calendar.

4:14 my condition. While there has been speculation about malaria, epilepsy, and other ailments, there is no way to be certain about the exact nature of Paul's illness. **an angel.** Perhaps there is an allusion to the time when Paul and Barnabas went to Lystra and were mistaken for gods (Acts 14:11-13). In any case, the contrast is between the greeting given an angel or Christ Jesus and their present attitude toward Paul.

4:15 taken out your own eyes. At that time there was nothing the Galatians would not have done for Paul.

4:19 labor pains. Paul often refers to himself as the father of spiritual children (1 Cor. 4:15). Here he plays the mother role and expresses his deep love and concern. **My dear children.** Paul cannot mask his deep affection for them despite his distress over their actions. **again.** For the second time he must endure the pangs of childbirth—first, when he sought to bring them out of paganism and into new birth in Christ, and now as he seeks to bring them out of legalism. **Christ is fully developed.** The metaphor is mixed but the point is clear. Paul's desire is that they come to possess Christ-like characteristics.

4:25 now Jerusalem. For Paul, this represents contemporary Judaism with all its legalism. **in slavery.** Just as Jerusalem was in slavery to Rome, the Jews were enslaved to the Law.

FREEDOM VS. OBEDIENCE

1. Were you an obedient child? How did your parents discipline you?

GALATIANS 4:21-31

2. What was extraordinary about Isaac's birth (Gen. 21:1-7)?
3. Why does Paul turn the tables on this story and indicate that the Jews are actually the ones in slavery with Hagar—their slave mother (vv. 25-26)?
4. Read verse 29, and explain how it applies to the struggle between flesh (temptation) and spirit (obedience).
5. How can you live out your "freedom" in Christ and still please Him with your sacrificial obedience?

LOVE, NOT SLAVERY

1. How do you feel when others cut in front of you in line? What do you do?

GALATIANS 5:1-15

2. What does Paul mean by a "slavery to the law" (v. 1)?
3. Since our own efforts and achievements aren't the way to God, what is (vv. 5-6)?
4. What does it mean to "love your neighbor as yourself" (v. 14)? Does "loving yourself" look more like verse 15 or 1 Corinthians 13?
5. How do we "serve one another in love" (v. 13)? What fellow Christian can you serve through love in the coming week?

live in slavery to the law. 26 But the other woman, Sarah, represents the heavenly Jerusalem. She is the free woman, and she is our mother. 27 As Isaiah said,

"Rejoice, O childless woman,
 you who have never given birth!
Break into a joyful shout,
 you who have never been in labor!
For the desolate woman now has more children
 than the woman who lives with her husband!"*

28 And you, dear brothers and sisters, are children of the promise, just like Isaac. 29 But you are now being persecuted by those who want you to keep the law, just as Ishmael, the child born by human effort, persecuted Isaac, the child born by the power of the Spirit. 30 But what do the Scriptures say about that? "Get rid of the slave and her son, for the son of the slave woman will not share the inheritance with the free woman's son."* 31 So, dear brothers and sisters, we are not children of the slave woman; we are children of the free woman.

FREEDOM IN CHRIST

5 So Christ has truly set us free. Now make sure that you stay free, and don't get tied up again in slavery to the law.

2 Listen! I, Paul, tell you this: If you are counting on circumcision to make you right with God, then Christ will be of no benefit to you. 3 I'll say it again. If you are trying to find favor with God by being circumcised, you must obey every regulation in the whole law of Moses. 4 For if you are trying to make yourselves right with God by keeping the law, you have been cut off from Christ! You have fallen away from God's grace.

5 But we who live by the Spirit eagerly wait to receive by faith the righteousness God has promised to us. 6 For when we place our faith in Christ Jesus, there is no benefit in being circumcised or being uncircumcised. What is important is faith expressing itself in love.

7 You were running the race so well. Who has held you back from following the truth? 8 It certainly isn't God, for he is the one who called you to freedom. 9 This false teaching is like a little yeast that spreads through the whole batch of dough! 10 I am trusting the Lord to keep you from believing false teachings. God will judge that person, whoever he is, who has been confusing you.

11 Dear brothers and sisters,* if I were still preaching that you must be circumcised—as some say I do—why am I still being persecuted? If I were no longer preaching salvation through the cross of Christ, no one would be offended. 12 I just wish that those troublemakers who want to mutilate you by circumcision would mutilate themselves.*

13 For you have been called to live in freedom, my brothers and sisters. But don't use your freedom to satisfy your sinful nature. Instead, use your freedom to serve one another in love. 14 For the whole law can be summed up in this one command: "Love your neighbor as yourself."* 15 But if you are always biting and devouring one another, watch out! Beware of destroying one another.

4:27 Isa 54:1. **4:30** Gen 21:10. **5:11** Greek *Brothers;* similarly in 5:13. **5:14** Lev 19:18. **5:12** Or *castrate themselves,* or *cut themselves off from you;* Greek reads *cut themselves off.*

4:26 heavenly Jerusalem. The heavenly city that was thought to provide the pattern for the physical city. The heavenly Jerusalem is the real thing—uncorrupted, perfect (Heb. 12:22; Rev. 3:12; 21:2,9-27).

5:2 I, Paul. Paul speaks with the full weight of his apostolic authority.

5:4 grace. Grace is not grace (a freely given gift) if there is any requirement at all for receiving it. **trying to make yourselves right.** Paul has said repeatedly that it is impossible to gain right standing through the Law (Rom. 11:5-7). The only thing the Law brings (in this context) is a curse (3:10-14).

5:5 Spirit. It is the Holy Spirit who fosters such assurances of acquittal. **righteousness.** The Christian can confidently expect a positive verdict on the Judgment Day. To have such a hope in advance of the event brings great liberty and rejoicing. This stands in contrast to the anxiety of one who is never sure if he or she has done quite enough "good works" or has been faithful to all points of the Law.

5:7 running the race so well. Paul uses an athletic metaphor to describe what happened to the Galatians. **held you back.** A word originally referring to the breaking up of roads by armies so as to hinder the progress of the enemy; it came to carry the idea of cutting in front of a runner to trip him up. **the truth.** The gospel (2:5, 14-16).

5:13 freedom . . . But. What Paul has written about freedom from the Law could be misunderstood to be a license to indulge in one's appetites, and certainly he does not mean that. He begins this new section on Christian living by examining the use of freedom.

FRUIT INSPECTION

1. What is your favorite fruit? What is your least favorite?

GALATIANS 5:16-26

2. How are the Spirit and the sinful nature in conflict (vv. 16-18)?
3. How does society today encourage the behaviors listed in verses 19-21?
4. Consider each item in the fruit of the Spirit list (vv. 22-23), and explain how they are opposite to those in 19-21. (For example, patience is opposite to anger; love is opposite to selfish ambition, etc.)
5. Are you allowing any of the behaviors from verses 19-21 in your own life? Does all the fruit of the Spirit show in your life? How about in the heat of competition?

CARRYING YOUR LOAD

1. What's the heaviest thing you've ever tried to lift? Did you need help to carry it? Did you succeed?

GALATIANS 6:1-10

2. How are we to help "restore" a brother or sister who is caught up in sin? Why must we take care about this?
3. What does it mean to "satisfy their own sinful nature" (v. 8)?
4. As outlined in this passage, what responsibilities do we have for our brothers and sisters in Christ?
5. Why does God also call us to be accountable for ourselves? How are you doing at carrying your "own conduct" (v. 5)?

LIVING BY THE SPIRIT'S POWER

16 So I say, let the Holy Spirit guide your lives. Then you
won't be doing what your sinful nature craves. 17 The
sinful nature wants to do evil, which is just the oppo-
site of what the Spirit wants. And the Spirit gives us
desires that are the opposite of what the sinful nature
desires. These two forces are constantly fighting each
other, so you are not free to carry out your good inten-
tions. 18 But when you are directed by the Spirit, you
are not under obligation to the law of Moses.
19 When you follow the desires of your sinful nature,
the results are very clear: sexual immorality, impuri-
ty, lustful pleasures, 20 idolatry, sorcery, hostility, quar-
reling, jealousy, outbursts of anger, selfish ambition,
dissension, division, 21 envy, drunkenness, wild par-
ties, and other sins like these. Let me tell you again, as
I have before, that anyone living that sort of life will
not inherit the Kingdom of God.
22 But the Holy Spirit produces this kind of fruit in
our lives: love, joy, peace, patience, kindness, goodness,
faithfulness, 23 gentleness, and self-control. There is
no law against these things!
24 Those who belong to Christ Jesus have nailed the
passions and desires of their sinful nature to his cross
and crucified them there. 25 Since we are living by the
Spirit, let us follow the Spirit's leading in every part
of our lives. 26 Let us not become conceited, or provoke
one another, or be jealous of one another.

WE HARVEST WHAT WE PLANT

6 Dear brothers and sisters, if another believer* is
overcome by some sin, you who are godly* should
gently and humbly help that person back onto the
right path. And be careful not to fall into the same
temptation yourself. 2 Share each other's burdens,
and in this way obey the law of Christ. 3 If you think
you are too important to help someone, you are only
fooling yourself. You are not that important.
4 Pay careful attention to your own work, for then
you will get the satisfaction of a job well done, and
you won't need to compare yourself to anyone else.
5 For we are each responsible for our own conduct.

6:1a Greek *Brothers, if a man.* **6:1b** Greek *spiritual.*

5:20 idolatry. The worship of any idol, be it a carved image of God (a statue) or an abstract substitute for God (a status symbol). An idol can be defined as anything that takes a person's time, attention, and devotion away from God and influences a person to follow its leading first when faced with a choice. Money, for instance, becomes an idol when a person will do anything to gain it. **hostility.** This is the underlying political, social, and religious hostility which drives individuals and communities apart. **strife.** This is the type of contention which leads to factions. **selfish ambition.** This word has come to refer to anyone who works only for his or her own good and not for the benefit of others. **division.** This refers to the partisan spirit that leads people to regard those with whom they disagree as enemies.

5:21 drunkenness. In the first century, diluted wine was drunk, but drunkenness was condemned. **sins like these.** The list is representative, not exhaustive—touching, in order, upon the sins of sensuality, idolatry, social dissension, and intemperance. **not inherit.** The issue here is not sins into which one falls, but sin as a lifestyle. These are evidence of a life not controlled by the Spirit.

5:22 fruit in our lives. These are the traits which characterize the child of God. The list is representative and not exhaustive. **love.** The Greek *agape* (self-giving, active benevolence); in contrast, there is *eros* (sexual love), *philos* (warm feelings to friends and family), and *storge* (family affection). **joy.** The Greek word is *chara* and comes from the same root as "grace" (*charis*). It is not based on earthly things or human achievement; it is a gift from God based on a right relationship with Him. **peace.** The prime meaning of this word is not negative ("an absence of conflict") but positive ("the presence of that which brings wholeness and well-being"). **patience.** This is the ability to be steadfast with people, refusing to give up on them. **kindness.** This is the compassionate use of strength for the good of another. **goodness.** This implies moral purity which reflects the character of God. **faithfulness.** This refers to firm conviction, which leads to being reliable and trustworthy.

5:23 gentleness. According to Aristotle, this is the virtue that lies between excessive proneness to anger and the inability to be angry; it implies control of oneself. **self-control.** This is control of one's sensual passions, emotions, and physical desires.

6:1 overcome by sin. A temporary lapse (as compared to an active lifestyle). **you who are godly.** Those whose lives bear the mark of the Spirit. This is not a clique of "special" Christians but is a call to all Christians (followers of Christ; 5:24-25). **help.** A medical term, used to describe the resetting of a fractured bone. The verb tense (in Greek) implies that this is not a single act but a continuous action. **gently and humbly.** This is an evidence of control by the Spirit (5:23).

6:2 Share each other's burdens. Mutual burden-bearing lies at the heart of Christian fellowship. **burdens.** A heavy, crushing weight, which a single individual cannot carry. **law of Christ.** The law of love (5:14), which stands in sharp contrast to the Jewish Law.

6:5 our own conduct. This is not the same as the crushing burden in verse 2. Rather, the word is used to describe the small individual pack a hiker or soldier carries. This is the same word used by Jesus in Matthew 11:30 to describe the burden (load) of His yoke, signifying that each of us has a burden (load) to carry.

6 Those who are taught the word of God should pro-
vide for their teachers, sharing all good things with
them.
7 Don't be misled—you cannot mock the justice of
God. You will always harvest what you plant. 8 Those
who live only to satisfy their own sinful nature will
harvest decay and death from that sinful nature. But
those who live to please the Spirit will harvest ever-
lasting life from the Spirit. 9 So let's not get tired of do-
ing what is good. At just the right time we will reap
a harvest of blessing if we don't give up. 10 Therefore,
whenever we have the opportunity, we should do
good to everyone—especially to those in the family
of faith.

PAUL'S FINAL ADVICE

11 Notice what large letters I use as I write these
closing words in my own handwriting.
12 Those who are trying to force you to be cir-
cumcised want to look good to others. They don't
want to be persecuted for teaching that the cross
of Christ alone can save. 13 And even those who
advocate circumcision don't keep the whole law
themselves. They only want you to be circumcised
so they can boast about it and claim you as their
disciples.
14 As for me, may I never boast about anything
except the cross of our Lord Jesus Christ. Because of
that cross,* my interest in this world has been cruci-
fied, and the world's interest in me has also died. 15 It
doesn't matter whether we have been circumcised
or not. What counts is whether we have been trans-
formed into a new creation. 16 May God's peace and
mercy be upon all who live by this principle; they are
the new people of God.*
17 From now on, don't let anyone trouble me with
these things. For I bear on my body the scars that
show I belong to Jesus.
18 Dear brothers and sisters,* may the grace of our
Lord Jesus Christ be with your spirit. Amen.

6:14 Or *Because of him.* **6:16** Greek *this principle, and upon the Israel of God.* **6:18** Greek *Brothers.*

INTRODUCTION TO
EPHESIANS

PERSONAL READING PLAN

☐Ephesians 1:1-23 ☐Ephesians 3:1-21 ☐Ephesians 4:17–5:21
☐Ephesians 2:1-22 ☐Ephesians 4:1-16 ☐Ephesians 5:22–6:24

AUTHOR

The Apostle Paul was the writer of Ephesians.

DATE

Paul probably wrote this letter in the early A.D. 60s, some 30 years after Jesus' crucifixion and only a few years before Paul's death.

THEME

God's new society.

HISTORICAL BACKGROUND

Paul is in prison once again, and Epaphras has come to visit him bearing news about the church at Colosse that was disturbing. Paul sends a letter in which he addresses the Colossian heresy. Onesimus, (now converted), carries the letter and returns to his owner Philemon, in the Colossian Church, Paul also writes two more letters: one to Philemon and one to a neighboring area, the letter to the Ephesians. These three epistles form the core of what we now know as the Prison Epistles or the Captivity Letters. It is unclear which imprisonment produced these letters (see 2 Cor. 11:23), but most likely Paul was at Rome (Acts 28).

Ephesians and Colossians are more similar in language and content than any other two letters in the New Testament. Seventy-five of the 155 verses in Ephesians are found in parallel form in Colossians. It seems that Paul first developed those themes in Colossians while dealing with a local problem, and then expanded them, explained them and cast them into a universal setting in Ephesians.

CHARACTERISTICS

In Ephesians, Paul focuses on Jesus Christ who breaks down the wall between God and humanity. We see Jesus creating the church, a new social order of love and unity that transcends the racial, ethnic, and social distinctions between people. In conveying this vision, Paul reaches into eternity past and eternity future to demonstrate how God, out of his love and glory, calls people to be reconciled to himself and to one another through the cross of Christ. The cross provides forgiveness of sins, a new life, and a new people. Between Paul's greeting (1:1-2) and salutation (6:21-24), the letter divides easily into two parts. Part one (chaps. 1–3) focuses on doctrine, specifically, the new life and new society God has created through Jesus. Part two (chaps. 4–6) focuses on ethics--specifically, the new standards and new relationships expected of believers.

THE CITY OF EPHESUS

The city of Ephesus was the capital of the Roman province of Asia. It was a large, bustling, secular city situated on the west coast of Asia Minor (modern Turkey) on the Aegean Sea. Originally a Greek colony, by Roman times it had become a center for international trade, largely as a result of its fine, natural harbor. Its key architectural feature was the Temple of Artemis (of Diana), considered to be one of the seven wonders of the ancient world. The image of Artemis was thought to have descended from heaven (Acts 19:35). There was also a huge, outdoor Greek theatre, capable of holding 50,000 people as well as a stadium where fights, races, and other athletic contests were held.

Paul's first visit to Ephesus was brief—little more than a reconnaissance trip (Acts 18:18-22). He later returned during his third missionary journey and spent over two years there. His ministry was both effective and controversial. After three months in the synagogue, he was forced out and took up residence in the lecture hall of Tyrannus (Acts 19:8-9). Paul probably worked as a tentmaker in the mornings and lecturer in the afternoons. News of his message spread throughout Asia Minor (Acts 19:10) and extraordinary things happened. Handkerchiefs touched by him were used to cure the sick (Acts 19:11-12). Demons were cast out in the name of Jesus, even by Jewish exorcists (Acts 19:13-17). Pagan converts burned their books of magic (Acts 19:18-20). Eventually, a riot broke out in Ephesus because of Paul. Demetrius, a silversmith, organized a citywide protest. He charged that Paul's success posed a threat to the economic well-being of craftsmen who made their living from the worshipers of Artemis (Acts 19:23-41). As a result, Paul moved on to Macedonia. But by this time the church was firmly established.

Paul never visited Ephesus again. He did, however, stop at the nearby port of Miletus on his return to Jerusalem. He called the Ephesian elders to him there and gave a moving farewell address (Acts 20:13-38). Later on, Paul would write 1 and 2 Timothy in an attempt to deal with false teaching that had arisen in Ephesus—as he had warned in his farewell address might happen (Acts 20:28-31). His words and Timothy's ministry were apparently successful. The apostle John's book of Revelation records that the Ephesians resisted false teaching—though they had lost their first love (Rev. 2:1-7). Tradition says that John spent the final years of his life in Ephesus—as the beloved bishop and last surviving apostle.

PASSAGES FOR TOPICAL GROUP STUDY

1:3-14 . . . ADOPTED BY GOD . . . . Picked for the Team
1:15-23 . . SEEING WITH OUR HEARTS . . . . Open Your Eyes!
2:1-10 . . . FREE GIFT OF SALVATION . . . . The Greatest Gift
2:11-22 . . PEACEMAKERS . . . . Making Peace
3:1-21 . . . GOD'S LOVE . . . . The Power of Love
4:1-16 . . . UNITY and THE CHURCH . . . . Building Up and Hanging Out
4:17-32 . . ANGER and BAD ATTITUDES . . . . . . A New Uniform
5:1-21 . . . FRIENDSHIPS and TIME . . . . Follow the Light
5:22-33 . . MARRIAGE and DATING . . . . Marriage Matters
6:1-4 . . . . RELATING TO PARENTS . . . . Parental Expectations
6:10-20 . . SPIRITUAL BATTLE and SATAN . . . . Life on the Front Line

GREETINGS FROM PAUL

1 This letter is from Paul, chosen by the will of God to be an apostle of Christ Jesus.

I am writing to God's holy people in Ephesus,* who are faithful followers of Christ Jesus.

[2] May God our Father and the Lord Jesus Christ give you grace and peace.

SPIRITUAL BLESSINGS

[3] All praise to God, the Father of our Lord Jesus Christ, who has blessed us with every spiritual blessing in the heavenly realms because we are united with Christ. [4] Even before he made the world, God loved us and chose us in Christ to be holy and without fault in his eyes. [5] God decided in advance to adopt us into his own family by bringing us to himself through Jesus Christ. This is what he wanted to do, and it gave him great pleasure. [6] So we praise God for the glorious grace he has poured out on us who belong to his dear Son.* [7] He is so rich in kindness and grace that he purchased our freedom with the blood of his Son and forgave our sins. [8] He has showered his kindness on us, along with all wisdom and understanding.

[9] God has now revealed to us his mysterious will regarding Christ—which is to fulfill his own good plan. [10] And this is the plan: At the right time he will bring everything together under the authority of Christ—everything in heaven and on earth. [11] Furthermore, because we are united with Christ, we have received an inheritance from God,* for he chose us in advance, and he makes everything work out according to his plan.

[12] God's purpose was that we Jews who were the first to trust in Christ would bring praise and glory to God. [13] And now you Gentiles have also heard the truth, the Good News that God saves you. And when you believed in Christ, he identified you as his own* by giving you the Holy Spirit, whom he promised long ago. [14] The Spirit is God's guarantee that he will give us the inheritance he promised and that he has purchased us to be his own people. He did this so we would praise and glorify him.

PAUL'S PRAYER FOR SPIRITUAL WISDOM

[15] Ever since I first heard of your strong faith in the Lord Jesus and your love for God's people everywhere,* [16] I have not stopped thanking God for you. I pray for you constantly, [17] asking God, the glorious Father of our Lord Jesus Christ, to give you spiritual wisdom* and insight so that you might grow in your knowledge of God. [18] I pray that your hearts will be flooded with light so that you can understand the confident hope he has given to those he called—his holy people who are his rich and glorious inheritance.*

PICKED FOR THE TEAM

1. Under what circumstances would you be willing to adopt a child, and what qualities would you look for in that child?

EPHESIANS 1:3-14

2. What is the significance of God choosing us before "he made the world" (v. 4)? How are we "holy and without fault in his eyes"?
3. Who is the "agent" through which God adopts us (v. 5)? How did this "agent" accomplish our adoption (v. 7)?
4. With all that God has done for you, what do you think He expects in return?

OPEN YOUR EYES!

1. What magic trick have you seen that left you speechless?

EPHESIANS 1:15-23

2. What major change does Paul include in his prayer for the Ephesians, and how would it benefit them?
3. What is the benefit of seeing more with our hearts (v. 18), and how can that happen for us?
4. If everything is "under the authority of Christ" and we are part of His body, the church, how should that affect our struggles (vv. 22-23)?
5. If God answered Paul's prayer completely in you, how would it change the way you live?

1:1 The most ancient manuscripts do not include *in Ephesus.* **1:6** Greek *to us in the beloved.* **1:11** Or *we have become God's inheritance.* **1:13** Or *he put his seal on you.* **1:15** Some manuscripts read *your faithfulness to the Lord Jesus and to God's people everywhere.* **1:17** Or *to give you the Spirit of wisdom.* **1:18** Or *called, and the rich and glorious inheritance he has given to his holy people.*

1:1 apostle. Apostles are much like ambassadors. This was the title that was given to the original Twelve (Luke 6:13) and then later to Paul (Gal. 1:11-24). By using this title, Paul indicates that he is writing with the authority of the Lord Jesus Christ.
1:2 give you grace and peace. Grace refers to the undeserved favor of God freely given as a gift. Peace refers to the reconciliation of sinners to God and others.
1:3 praise. The verb translated "bless" or "praise" can also be translated "to speak well of" and carries the idea of thanking, glorifying, and singing the praises of the one who is the object of this gratitude. **God.** God is the subject of virtually every main verb in this passage. **Jesus Christ.** It is in and through Jesus that God's work of love, grace, and redemption is performed. **has blessed us.** The tense of the Greek verb indicates that what is in view here is a single, past action on God's part. **in the heavenly realms.** The unseen world of spiritual reality.
1:5 decided in advance. Literally, "marked out beforehand." **to adopt.** This was a common Roman custom, in which a child was given all the rights of the adoptive family by grace, not by birth. **what he wanted to do.** This phrase is also translated "pleasure and will," and carries with it the sense that God goes about such choosing with great joy.
1:7 purchased our freedom. The setting free (originally of prisoners or slaves) by payment of a ransom (in this case, Jesus' death in place of the sinner).
1:9 mysterious plan. Contrary to the normal use of the word (with its emphasis on a secret being kept), here the word focuses on the disclosure of what was once hidden but is now revealed by God.
1:13 identified. A mark placed by an owner on a package, a cow, or even a slave. The cults in the first century sometimes tattooed a mark on their devotees. For the Jews, circumcision was such a seal (Rom. 4:11); the Holy Spirit is the Christian's seal.
1:14 guarantee. A deposit, or "earnest money," that guarantees ultimate ownership by God.
1:17 wisdom and insight. God must do a work within individuals to enable them to "see" and understand what is going on.
1:18 your hearts. Paul wants this illumination to strike right to the core of a person's being.

19 I also pray that you will understand the incredible greatness of God's power for us who believe him. This is the same mighty power 20 that raised Christ from the dead and seated him in the place of honor at God's right hand in the heavenly realms. 21 Now he is far above any ruler or authority or power or leader or anything else—not only in this world but also in the world to come. 22 God has put all things under the authority of Christ and has made him head over all things for the benefit of the church. 23 And the church is his body; it is made full and complete by Christ, who fills all things everywhere with himself.

MADE ALIVE WITH CHRIST

2 Once you were dead because of your disobedience and your many sins. 2 You used to live in sin, just like the rest of the world, obeying the devil—the commander of the powers in the unseen world.* He is the spirit at work in the hearts of those who refuse to obey God. 3 All of us used to live that way, following the passionate desires and inclinations of our sinful nature. By our very nature we were subject to God's anger, just like everyone else.

4 But God is so rich in mercy, and he loved us so much, 5 that even though we were dead because of our sins, he gave us life when he raised Christ from the dead. (It is only by God's grace that you have been saved!) 6 For he raised us from the dead along with Christ and seated us with him in the heavenly realms because we are united with Christ Jesus. 7 So God can point to us in all future ages as examples of the incredible wealth of his grace and kindness toward us, as shown in all he has done for us who are united with Christ Jesus.

8 God saved you by his grace when you believed. And you can't take credit for this; it is a gift from God. 9 Salvation is not a reward for the good things we have done, so none of us can boast about it. 10 For we are God's masterpiece. He has created us anew in Christ Jesus, so we can do the good things he planned for us long ago.

ONENESS AND PEACE IN CHRIST

11 Don't forget that you Gentiles used to be outsiders. You were called "uncircumcised heathens" by the Jews, who were proud of their circumcision, even though it affected only their bodies and not their hearts. 12 In those days you were living apart from Christ. You were excluded from citizenship among the people of Israel, and you did not know the covenant promises God had made to them. You lived in this world without God and without hope. 13 But now you have been united with Christ Jesus. Once you were far away from God, but now you have been brought near to him through the blood of Christ.

14 For Christ himself has brought peace to us. He united Jews and Gentiles into one people when, in his own body on the cross, he broke down the wall of hostility that separated us. 15 He did this by ending the system of law with its commandments and regulations. He made peace between Jews and Gentiles by creating in himself one new people from the two groups. 16 Together as one body, Christ reconciled both groups to God by means of his death on the cross, and our hostility toward each other was put to death.

17 He brought this Good News of peace to you Gentiles who were far away from him, and peace to the Jews who were near. 18 Now all of us can come to the Father through the same Holy Spirit because of what Christ has done for us.

THE GREATEST GIFT

1. What is a really great gift you've received? What did you do to deserve it? How did you express thanks to the giver?
2. What is the unpardonable sin in your family? At your school?

EPHESIANS 2:1-10

3. How does Paul describe the person who is "dead" in his or her trespasses (vv. 1-3)?
4. What does Paul want to make sure people understand about salvation (v. 9), and why is it so important to understand?
5. How is your life different now than it was before you became a Christian? What do you still need to change?

2:2 Greek *obeying the commander of the power of the air.*

1:19 incredible greatness of God's power. Seeing this makes a world of difference in one's life as a Christian.
1:20 raised Christ from the dead. Jesus was really dead and buried in a tomb. But so mighty is God's power that it burst the bonds of death. **seated him . . . at God's right hand.** Jesus is now the King who reigns in absolute power. One day that reign will result in the bringing together of all things under him (1:10; Heb. 2:5-9).
1:21 ruler or authority or power or leader or anything else. Paul wants to be quite clear that there is no power by any name—be it angelic or demonic, natural or supernatural, from the past or in the future—that stands outside the scope of Christ's powerful reign.
2:1 dead. They were spiritually dead. **disobedience and . . . sins.** These two words refer, respectively, to active wrongdoing (sins of commission) and passive failure (sins of omission).
2:2 commander of the powers in the unseen world. This is the first of several references in Ephesians to Satan, the Devil. **at work.** Satan's activity is not only past, nor only in the future. It is here and now in this present evil age. **those who refuse to obey.** They are, in fact, in active rebellion against God.
2:3 passionate desires. The word here is literally "the flesh," and it refers to self-centered human nature that expresses itself in destructive activities of both body and mind.
2:5 gave us life. Paul coins this phrase to describe exactly what happens to us when we are "in Christ"; namely, we share in Christ's resurrection, ascension, and enthronement
2:8 God saved you by grace. This is the second time Paul acclaims this amazing fact (v. 5). **when you believed.** Salvation does not come about because of faith in and of itself. Salvation comes by grace (from God) through faith (from us).
2:8-9 can't take credit for this . . . not a reward for good things. Salvation is not a reward for being good or keeping the Law.
2:10 good things. Although good works do not save a person, they are a result of salvation.
2:11 Don't forget. In verses 1-3, Paul reminded his Gentile readers that once they were trapped in their transgressions and sins and so were spiritually dead and alienated from God.
2:14 peace to us. Jesus brings peace between human beings and God. He also creates harmony in human relationships, bringing people into peace with one another. **wall of hostility.** Paul might have in mind an actual wall that existed in the temple in Jerusalem beyond which Gentiles could not go. They were cut off by a stonewall ("the dividing wall")—a wall bearing signs that warned in Greek and Latin that trespassing foreigners would be killed.
2:17 He brought this Good News of peace. Christ's first words to the stunned apostles after His resurrection were, in fact, "Peace be with you!" (John 20:19).

A TEMPLE FOR THE LORD

[19] So now you Gentiles are no longer strangers and
foreigners. You are citizens along with all of God's
holy people. You are members of God's family. [20] To-
gether, we are his house, built on the foundation of
the apostles and the prophets. And the cornerstone
is Christ Jesus himself. [21] We are carefully joined to-
gether in him, becoming a holy temple for the Lord.
[22] Through him you Gentiles are also being made part
of this dwelling where God lives by his Spirit.

MAKING PEACE

1. What was your favorite wall, fence, or playground equipment to climb over when you were little?
2. Who is the peacemaker among your family or group, and how does this person do it?

EPHESIANS 2:11-22

3. Who do you think the two groups are in verse 14, and what barriers did they have to overcome?
4. How does Christ put "hostility . . . to death" (v. 16)?
5. What role does the Holy Spirit play in helping us to be peacemakers (vv. 18-22)?
6. What relationship in your life still has walls that need knocking down? How can the Holy Spirit help?

GOD'S MYSTERIOUS PLAN REVEALED

3 When I think of all this, I, Paul, a prisoner of Christ
Jesus for the benefit of you Gentiles* . . . [2] assuming,
by the way, that you know God gave me the special
responsibility of extending his grace to you Gentiles.
[3] As I briefly wrote earlier, God himself revealed his
mysterious plan to me. [4] As you read what I have writ-
ten, you will understand my insight into this plan re-
garding Christ. [5] God did not reveal it to previous gen-
erations, but now by his Spirit he has revealed it to his
holy apostles and prophets.

[6] And this is God's plan: Both Gentiles and Jews
who believe the Good News share equally in the rich-
es inherited by God's children. Both are part of the
same body, and both enjoy the promise of blessings
because they belong to Christ Jesus.* [7] By God's grace
and mighty power, I have been given the privilege of
serving him by spreading this Good News.

[8] Though I am the least deserving of all God's
people, he graciously gave me the privilege of
telling the Gentiles about the endless treasures
available to them in Christ. [9] I was chosen to ex-
plain to everyone* this mysterious plan that God,
the Creator of all things, had kept secret from the
beginning.

[10] God's purpose in all this was to use the church to
display his wisdom in its rich variety to all the unseen
rulers and authorities in the heavenly places. [11] This
was his eternal plan, which he carried out through
Christ Jesus our Lord.

[12] Because of Christ and our faith in him,* we can
now come boldly and confidently into God's presence.
[13] So please don't lose heart because of my trials here. I
am suffering for you, so you should feel honored.

PAUL'S PRAYER FOR SPIRITUAL GROWTH

[14] When I think of all this, I fall to my knees and pray
to the Father,* [15] the Creator of everything in heaven
and on earth.* [16] I pray that from his glorious, un-
limited resources he will empower you with inner
strength through his Spirit. [17] Then Christ will make
his home in your hearts as you trust in him. Your roots
will grow down into God's love and keep you strong.
[18] And may you have the power to understand, as all
God's people should, how wide, how long, how high,

THE POWER OF LOVE

1. What is the hardest thing you have tried to teach another person?
2. What is the last thing you remember praying very hard about?

EPHESIANS 3:14-21

3. What does it look like when God gives us "inner strength" (v. 16)?
4. What does Paul mean by a "love . . . too great to understand fully," and what is the point of experiencing this love (v. 19)?
5. When have you felt overwhelmed by the love of God?
6. What needs to change in you to fully comprehend and experience God's love?

3:1 Paul resumes this thought in verse 14: "When I think of all this, I fall to my knees and pray to the Father." **3:6** Or *because they are united with Christ Jesus.* **3:9** Some manuscripts do not include *to everyone.* **3:12** Or *Because of Christ's faithfulness.* **3:14** Some manuscripts read *the Father of our Lord Jesus Christ.* **3:15** Or *from whom every family in heaven and on earth takes its name.*

2:19 foreigners. Nonresident aliens were disliked by the native population and often held in suspicion. **strangers.** These are residents in a foreign land. They pay taxes, but have no legal standing and few rights. **citizens.** Whereas once the Gentiles were "excluded from citizenship in Israel" (v. 12), now they are members of God's kingdom. **members of God's family.** In fact, their relationship is far more intimate.

2:20 cornerstone. The stone that rested firmly on the foundation and anchored two walls together, giving each its correct alignment.

2:21 joined together. A term used by a mason to describe how two stones were prepared so that they would bond tightly together. **holy temple.** The new temple is not like the old one, carved out of dead stone—beautiful, but forbidding and exclusive. Rather, it is alive all over the world, inclusive of all, and made up of the individuals in whom God dwells.

3:3 mysterious plan. In Greek, a mystery is something that is beyond human reason to figure out, but once revealed by God, it is open and plain to all. **revealed.** This new reality was given by God.

3:9 to explain. Paul's original commission, given by Jesus on the Damascus Road, carried this idea: "I am sending you to open their eyes and turn them from darkness to light . . ." (see also Acts 26:17-18)

3:10 unseen rulers and authorities in the heavenly places. The supernatural powers see what God is doing in His church.

3:16 empower . . . with inner strength. Paul asks that Christians be fortified or invigorated within by the Holy Spirit. He asks that they experience this awesome power of God about which he has written so eloquently. **inner.** By this term, Paul may be referring to the deepest part of the human personality, where a person's true essence lies.

3:17 make his home. This means "to settle down," and it implies a permanent residency (in a house) versus a temporary stopover (in a tent or hotel). In other words, Christ has come to stay. **love.** *Agape* love is selfless giving to others, regardless of how one feels. Such love is the foundation upon which the church will grow.

and how deep his love is. [19] May you experience the
love of Christ, though it is too great to understand ful-
ly. Then you will be made complete with all the full-
ness of life and power that comes from God.
[20] Now all glory to God, who is able, through his
mighty power at work within us, to accomplish in-
finitely more than we might ask or think. [21] Glory to
him in the church and in Christ Jesus through all gen-
erations forever and ever! Amen.

UNITY IN THE BODY

4 Therefore I, a prisoner for serving the Lord, beg
you to lead a life worthy of your calling, for you
have been called by God. [2] Always be humble and
gentle. Be patient with each other, making allowance
for each other's faults because of your love. [3] Make
every effort to keep yourselves united in the Spirit,
binding yourselves together with peace. [4] For there is
one body and one Spirit, just as you have been called
to one glorious hope for the future.

[5] There is one Lord, one faith, one baptism,
[6] one God and Father of all,
who is over all, in all, and living through all.

[7] However, he has given each one of us a special
gift* through the generosity of Christ. [8] That is why
the Scriptures say,

"When he ascended to the heights,
he led a crowd of captives
and gave gifts to his people."*

[9] Notice that it says "he ascended." This clearly means
that Christ also descended to our lowly world.* [10] And
the same one who descended is the one who ascended
higher than all the heavens, so that he might fill the
entire universe with himself.
[11] Now these are the gifts Christ gave to the church:
the apostles, the prophets, the evangelists, and the
pastors and teachers. [12] Their responsibility is to
equip God's people to do his work and build up the
church, the body of Christ. [13] This will continue until
we all come to such unity in our faith and knowledge
of God's Son that we will be mature in the Lord, mea-
suring up to the full and complete standard of Christ.
[14] Then we will no longer be immature like chil-
dren. We won't be tossed and blown about by every
wind of new teaching. We will not be influenced
when people try to trick us with lies so clever they

BUILDING UP AND HANGING OUT

1. What activities can draw together a large crowd of your friends?
2. What problems can pull your friends apart?

EPHESIANS 4:1-16

3. What are the things that bind us together (vv. 4-6), and which one is most underutilized?
4. What is the ultimate purpose of having people in specific positions (v. 11), and how can that be abused?
5. What is keeping your church or team from modeling the church as it was meant to be? What can you do to help bring unity?

sound like the truth. [15] Instead, we will speak the truth
in love, growing in every way more and more like
Christ, who is the head of his body, the church. [16] He
makes the whole body fit together perfectly. As each
part does its own special work, it helps the other parts
grow, so that the whole body is healthy and growing
and full of love.

LIVING AS CHILDREN OF LIGHT

[17] With the Lord's authority I say this: Live no longer
as the Gentiles do, for they are hopelessly confused.
[18] Their minds are full of darkness; they wander far
from the life God gives because they have closed their
minds and hardened their hearts against him. [19] They
have no sense of shame. They live for lustful pleasure
and eagerly practice every kind of impurity.
[20] But that isn't what you learned about Christ.
[21] Since you have heard about Jesus and have learned
the truth that comes from him, [22] throw off your old
sinful nature and your former way of life, which is
corrupted by lust and deception. [23] Instead, let the
Spirit renew your thoughts and attitudes. [24] Put on
your new nature, created to be like God—truly righ-
teous and holy.
[25] So stop telling lies. Let us tell our neighbors the
truth, for we are all parts of the same body. [26] And
"don't sin by letting anger control you."* Don't let the
sun go down while you are still angry, [27] for anger
gives a foothold to the devil.

4:7 Greek *a grace.* **4:8** Ps 68:18. **4:9** Some manuscripts read *to the lower parts of the earth.* **4:26** Ps 4:4.

4:2 humble. Humility is an absence of pride and self-assertion based upon accurate self-knowledge and on an understanding of the God-given worth of others. Humility is the key to the growth of healthy relationships between people. **gentle.** Paul is not urging people to be timid and without convictions. Gentleness is the quality of strength under control, like a thoroughbred horse. **patient.** Patience with others is also called long-suffering. **making allowance for . . . faults.** This is tolerance of the faults of others that springs from humility, gentleness, and patience.

4:8 When he ascended. Paul quotes Psalm 68:18, which describes the triumphal procession of a conquering Jewish king up Mt. Zion and into Jerusalem. The king is followed by a procession of prisoners in chains. As he marches up the hill, he is given gifts of tribute and in turn disperses spoils of victory. Paul uses this verse to describe Christ's ascension into heaven.

4:9 descended. Paul is referring to Christ's incarnation, whereby He came down from heaven and into our space and time (Phil. 2:5-11).

4:11 Christ gave. This is one of several lists of gifts in the New Testament. The emphasis in this list is on teaching gifts. **apostles.** Paul probably had in mind the small group of individuals who had seen the resurrected Christ and had been commissioned by Him to launch His church (Acts 1:21-22; 1 Cor. 9:1), but some take this to be a more general gift of "missions". **prophets.** In contrast to teachers who relied upon the Old Testament Scripture and the teaching of Jesus to instruct others, prophets offered words of instruction, exhortation, and admonition, which were immediate and unpremeditated. Their source was direct revelation from God. **evangelists.** Those with the special gift of making the gospel clear and convincing to people. **pastors and teachers.** The way in which this is expressed in Greek indicates that these two functions reside in one person.

4:15 we will speak the truth in love. Truth without love becomes harsh. Love without truth becomes weak.

4:18 hardened their hearts. The center of their being (the heart) has become "stone-like."

4:26 by letting anger. Literally "be angry and do not sin." Paul recognizes that there is such a thing as legitimate anger. But once admitted, anger is to be dealt with, and so Paul identifies ways to deal with anger. Do not let anger develop into resentment.

A NEW UNIFORM

1. When it comes to getting angry, do you tend to have a short or long fuse?
2. How can someone tell when you are angry? When you are lying?

EPHESIANS 4:17-32

3. What do verses 22 and 24 mean by taking off "the old sinful nature" and putting on "your new nature"?
4. What are some of the reasons we do not speak the truth?
5. How do you usually deal with anger? What do you learn about anger from verses 26-27?
6. Which attitude or behavior that grieves God (vv. 31-32) do you struggle with most? How can you take off this old, smelly uniform?

---

28 If you are a thief, quit stealing. Instead, use your
hands for good hard work, and then give generous-
ly to others in need. 29 Don't use foul or abusive lan-
guage. Let everything you say be good and helpful, so
that your words will be an encouragement to those
who hear them.
30 And do not bring sorrow to God's Holy Spirit by
the way you live. Remember, he has identified you as
his own,* guaranteeing that you will be saved on the
day of redemption.
31 Get rid of all bitterness, rage, anger, harsh words,
and slander, as well as all types of evil behavior. 32 In-
stead, be kind to each other, tenderhearted, forgiving
one another, just as God through Christ has forgiven
you.

LIVING IN THE LIGHT

5 Imitate God, therefore, in everything you do, be-
cause you are his dear children. 2 Live a life filled
with love, following the example of Christ. He loved
us* and offered himself as a sacrifice for us, a pleasing
aroma to God.
3 Let there be no sexual immorality, impurity, or
greed among you. Such sins have no place among
God's people. 4 Obscene stories, foolish talk, and coarse
jokes—these are not for you. Instead, let there be
thankfulness to God. 5 You can be sure that no immor-
al, impure, or greedy person will inherit the Kingdom
of Christ and of God. For a greedy person is an idola-
ter, worshiping the things of this world.
6 Don't be fooled by those who try to excuse these
sins, for the anger of God will fall on all who disobey
him. 7 Don't participate in the things these people do.
8 For once you were full of darkness, but now you have
light from the Lord. So live as people of light! 9 For this
light within you produces only what is good and right
and true.
10 Carefully determine what pleases the Lord.
11 Take no part in the worthless deeds of evil and dark-
ness; instead, expose them. 12 It is shameful even to
talk about the things that ungodly people do in secret.
13 But their evil intentions will be exposed when the
light shines on them, 14 for the light makes everything
visible. This is why it is said,

"Awake, O sleeper,
rise up from the dead,
and Christ will give you light."

LIVING BY THE SPIRIT'S POWER

15 So be careful how you live. Don't live like fools,
but like those who are wise. 16 Make the most of
every opportunity in these evil days. 17 Don't act
thoughtlessly, but understand what the Lord
wants you to do. 18 Don't be drunk with wine, be-
cause that will ruin your life. Instead, be filled
with the Holy Spirit, 19 singing psalms and hymns
and spiritual songs among yourselves, and making
music to the Lord in your hearts. 20 And give thanks
for everything to God the Father in the name of our
Lord Jesus Christ.

FOLLOW THE LIGHT

1. Who is your best friend right now? What makes this person such a good friend?
2. Who has had the biggest influence on your life? What good advice did this person give you?

EPHESIANS 5:1-21

3. What kind of people and what kind of advice should we avoid, and how do we stay friends while avoiding the "partner" trap (vv. 5-7)?
4. When Paul says, "Make the most of every opportunity" (v. 16), what do you think he is talking about?
5. What have you found helpful in resisting pressure to do something you shouldn't?

4:30 Or *has put his seal on you.* 5:2 Some manuscripts read *loved you.*

4:29-30 foul or abusive language. Paul turns to the use of one's mouth. The word "rotten" is elsewhere used to describe spoiled fruit (Matt. 12:33). Instead of rancid words that wound others, the words of Christians ought to edify ("building up"), be appropriate ("of someone in need"), bring grace (in other words, be of benefit to those who hear), and not cause distress for the Holy Spirit (by unholy words).

4:31 Get rid of. Paul identifies six negative attitudes that must be erased from the Christian life. **bitterness.** Spiteful, long-standing, resentment. **rage, anger.** These two attitudes are related. Anger may be a quick flare up, or a longer term, sullen hostility. Wrath often carries the connotation of violence and punishment. **harsh words, and slander.** Saying hurtful and untrue things about another person.

5:4 coarse jokes. Vulgar talk is out of place because it demeans God's good gift of sex (which is a subject for thanksgiving, not joking).

5:5 greedy person. The reference is to the sexually greedy person. **idolater.** When vice has become an obsession, it functions in a person's life as a "god" (or idol), drawing forth passionate commitment of time and energy.

5:8-14 live as people of light. A second reason why Christians should not get involved in immoral practices (v. 11) is that they have become "children of light" (v. 8). In fact, it is not just that they walk in the light; they "are light in the Lord" (v. 8). To be such a child of light implies a lifestyle of "goodness, righteousness, and truth" (v. 9).

5:18 be filled. This is a command, not an option. It means, "let the Spirit fill you."

SPIRIT-GUIDED RELATIONSHIPS: WIVES AND HUSBANDS

21 And further, submit to one another out of reverence
for Christ.
22 For wives, this means submit to your husbands as
to the Lord. 23 For a husband is the head of his wife as
Christ is the head of the church. He is the Savior of his
body, the church. 24 As the church submits to Christ, so
you wives should submit to your husbands in every-
thing.
25 For husbands, this means love your wives, just as
Christ loved the church. He gave up his life for her 26 to
make her holy and clean, washed by the cleansing of
God's word.* 27 He did this to present her to himself as a
glorious church without a spot or wrinkle or any oth-
er blemish. Instead, she will be holy and without fault.
28 In the same way, husbands ought to love their wives
as they love their own bodies. For a man who loves his
wife actually shows love for himself. 29 No one hates his
own body but feeds and cares for it, just as Christ cares
for the church. 30 And we are members of his body.
31 As the Scriptures say, "A man leaves his father
and mother and is joined to his wife, and the two are
united into one."* 32 This is a great mystery, but it is an
illustration of the way Christ and the church are one.
33 So again I say, each man must love his wife as he
loves himself, and the wife must respect her husband.

MARRIAGE MATTERS

1. Who was your first "true love"?
2. Who has a marriage that you admire? What makes it work?

EPHESIANS 5:22-33

3. Guys: How do you feel about the standard for husbands in verses 25 and 28? Ladies: How do you feel about the standard for wives in verses 22 and 33?
4. As you look at the phrase "the two are united into one" (v. 31), what do you think it means and doesn't mean?
5. What is the best way to know if someone is right for you?
6. What is God saying to you about dating and marriage?

CHILDREN AND PARENTS

6 Children, obey your parents because you belong
to the Lord,* for this is the right thing to do. 2 "Hon-
or your father and mother." This is the first command-
ment with a promise: 3 If you honor your father and
mother, "things will go well for you, and you will have
a long life on the earth."*
4 Fathers,* do not provoke your children to anger by
the way you treat them. Rather, bring them up with
the discipline and instruction that comes from the
Lord.

PARENTAL EXPECTATIONS

1. Which TV family best reflects your family?
2. When you are away from home, how often do your parents expect you to check in? Do you feel this is a reasonable expectation?

EPHESIANS 6:1-4

3. What does God ask of children? What does the phrase "belong to the Lord" mean (v. 1)?
4. Do you look at verse 3 as a promise or a threat? Why?
5. If you have kids, how will you apply the lesson in verse 4?
6. In what way can you honor your parents this week?

5:26 Greek *washed by water with the word.* **5:31** Gen 2:24. **6:1** Or *Children, obey your parents who belong to the Lord;* some manuscripts read simply *Children, obey your parents.* **6:2-3** Exod 20:12; Deut 5:16. **6:4** Or *Parents.*

5:21 submit to one another. Another aspect of being filled with the Spirit involves mutual submission within the Christian community.

5:22 submit to your husbands. The verb in 5:21 ("submit") is linked grammatically both backward to 5:18 and forward to this verse. Looking backward, "submit" describes what is involved in being filled with the Spirit (speaking, singing, giving thanks, submitting). Looking forward, "submit" provides the verb for this verse, which has no verb of its own. Submitting goes against our sinful natures but is specifically commanded by God, in this case of a wife to her husband and to the Lord.

5:23 Christ is the head of the church. Paul has already described in 4:15-16 the way in which Christ is the head of the church. He is head in that the rest of the body derives from Him the health and strength that allows each part to play its own distinctive role. It is a headship of love, not of control; of nurture, not of suppression. The word "head" when used today has the sense of "ruler" or "authority." However, in Greek when "head" is used in a metaphorical sense as it is here, it also means "origin" as in the "source (head) of a river." Woman has her origins in man (Gen. 2:18-23) just as the church has its origins in Christ. **the Savior.** The emphasis in this analogy is not on Christ as Lord but on Christ as Savior. Paul is not saying that husbands are to express "headship" through the exertion of authority (as befits a "lord"), but through the expression of sacrificial love (as characterized by the Savior).

5:25 love your wives. This is the main thing Paul says to husbands. It is so important that he repeats this injunction three times (vv. 25,28,33). In Greek culture, although certain philosophers such as Aristotle taught that men ought to love their wives, they used a mild word for love (*phileo*), signifying the sort of affection a person has for family and friends. Here, however, Paul urges a far stronger type of love: agape, which is characterized by sacrificial, self-giving action. **just as Christ loved the church. He gave up his life for her.** Two actions characterize Christ's role for the church: love and sacrifice. The husband is called upon to act toward his wife in the same way. A husband is never instructed to force submission to his leadership of tyrannical authority, but to lead as Jesus did through sacrificial love. In the case of domestic abuse, it is role of the church and civil authorities to step with discipline.

5:28 their own bodies. The deep-rooted instinct to care for and protect oneself is to be carried over to the wife who has become one flesh with her husband.

5:31 united into one. Paul does not view marriage as some sort of spiritual covenant devoid of sexuality. His illustration of how a husband is to love his wife (vv. 28-31) revolves around their sexual union as is made explicit here by his quotation of Genesis 2:24.

6:1 Children. That he addresses children in this public letter means that children were in attendance with their families at worship when such a letter would have been read. **obey.** Paul tells the children to "obey" ("follow," "be subject to," literally, "listen to").

6:4 Just as children have a duty to obey, parents have the duty to instruct children with gentleness and restraint. **Fathers.** The ultimate model for a father is God, the "Father of all" (4:6). This view of fatherhood stands in sharp contrast to the harsh Roman father, who had the power of life and death over his children. **provoke . . . to anger.** Parents are to be responsible for not provoking hostility on the part of their children, or exasperating them. By humiliating children, being cruel to them, over-indulging them, or being unreasonable, parents squash children rather than encouraging them. **bring them up.** This verb is literally "nourish" or "feed" them. **discipline.** This word can be translated "discipline." **instruction.** The emphasis here is on what is said verbally to children.

SLAVES AND MASTERS

5 Slaves, obey your earthly masters with deep respect
and fear. Serve them sincerely as you would serve
Christ. 6 Try to please them all the time, not just when
they are watching you. As slaves of Christ, do the will
of God with all your heart. 7 Work with enthusiasm, as
though you were working for the Lord rather than for
people. 8 Remember that the Lord will reward each
one of us for the good we do, whether we are slaves
or free.
9 Masters, treat your slaves in the same way. Don't
threaten them; remember, you both have the same
Master in heaven, and he has no favorites.

THE WHOLE ARMOR OF GOD

10 A final word: Be strong in the Lord and in his mighty
power. 11 Put on all of God's armor so that you will be
able to stand firm against all strategies of the devil.
12 For we* are not fighting against flesh-and-blood
enemies, but against evil rulers and authorities of
the unseen world, against mighty powers in this dark
world, and against evil spirits in the heavenly places.
13 Therefore, put on every piece of God's armor so
you will be able to resist the enemy in the time of evil.
Then after the battle you will still be standing firm.
14 Stand your ground, putting on the belt of truth and
the body armor of God's righteousness. 15 For shoes,
put on the peace that comes from the Good News so
that you will be fully prepared.* 16 In addition to all of
these, hold up the shield of faith to stop the fiery ar-
rows of the devil.* 17 Put on salvation as your helmet,
and take the sword of the Spirit, which is the word
of God.
18 Pray in the Spirit at all times and on every occa-
sion. Stay alert and be persistent in your prayers for
all believers everywhere.*
19 And pray for me, too. Ask God to give me the right
words so I can boldly explain God's mysterious plan
that the Good News is for Jews and Gentiles alike.*

LIFE ON THE FRONT LINE

1. What is the scariest situation you have ever experienced?
2. What do you think the Devil's most successful strategy is right now in your team, your school, or the world in general?

EPHESIANS 6:10-20

3. What makes up "Gods armor" (vv. 14-17)? Which piece of armor are you most likely to forget to put on?
4. How important is prayer to the battle strategy (v. 18), and what makes this kind of prayer so effective?
5. What would you say to a friend who is losing the unseen battle? How would you explain this teaching in your own words?

20 I am in chains now, still preaching this message as
God's ambassador. So pray that I will keep on speak-
ing boldly for him, as I should.

FINAL GREETINGS

21 To bring you up to date, Tychicus will give you a full
report about what I am doing and how I am getting
along. He is a beloved brother and faithful helper in
the Lord's work. 22 I have sent him to you for this very
purpose—to let you know how we are doing and to
encourage you.
23 Peace be with you, dear brothers and sisters,* and
may God the Father and the Lord Jesus Christ give you
love with faithfulness. 24 May God's grace be eternally
upon all who love our Lord Jesus Christ.

6:12 Some manuscripts read *you*. **6:15** Or *For shoes, put on the readiness to preach the Good News of peace with God.* **6:16** Greek *the evil one.* **6:18** Greek *all of God's holy people.* **6:19** Greek *explain the mystery of the Good News*; some manuscripts read simply *explain the mystery.* **6:23** Greek *brothers.*

6:10 Be strong . . . in his mighty power. In order to wage successful warfare against Satan, the Christian must draw upon God's own power.
6:11 Put on. It is not enough to rely passively on God's power. The Christian must do something. He or she must "put on" God's armor. **all strategies of the devil.** Evil does not operate in the light. It lurks in shadows and strikes unexpectedly with cleverness and subtlety.
6:12 evil rulers and authorities . . . mighty powers . . . evil spirits. By these various titles, Paul names the diverse spiritual forces which rage against believers and which can't be fought by solely human means. **mighty powers in this dark world.** It was no empty boast on Satan's part when during Jesus' temptations he claimed to be able to give Him "all the kingdoms of the world." These world rulers have real power, and even though Christ has defeated them, they refuse to concede their defeat.
6:13 time of evil. The immediate reference is to those special times of pressure and testing that come to all Christians. **standing firm.** Fully-equipped soldiers were virtually invulnerable to enemy onslaught—unless they panicked and broke ranks. As long as they "stood firm" when the enemy attacked, they would prevail in the long run.
6:14 belt of truth. The leather belt on which the Roman soldier hung his sword, and by which he secured his tunic and armor (so he would be unimpeded in battle). The "truth" referred to is the inner integrity and sincerity by which the Christian fights evil. Lying and deceit are tactics of the enemy. **body armor of God's righteousness.** The breastplate (or "mail") was the major piece of armor for the Roman soldier. Made of metal and leather, it protected his vital organs. "Righteousness" refers to the right standing before God that is the status of the Christian, out of which moral conduct and character emerges.
6:15 For shoes. These are the leather half-boots worn by the Roman legionnaire, with heavy studded soles that enabled him to dig in and resist being pushed out of place. **fully prepared.** This term can be translated as "firmness" or "steadfastness," in which case the "gospel of peace" is understood to provide the solid foundation on which the Christian stands in the fight against evil.
6:16 the shield of faith. A large, oblong shield constructed of layers of wood on an iron frame, which was then covered with linen and hide. When wet, such a shield could absorb "flaming arrows." **fiery arrows.** These were pitch-soaked arrows. Their aim was not so much to kill a soldier as to set him aflame and cause him to break rank and create panic.
6:17 salvation as your helmet. A heavy, metal head covering lined with felt or sponge, which gave substantial protection to the soldier's head. **sword.** A short, stabbing sword used for personal combat. The sword is the only piece of offensive equipment in the armor.
6:18 Pray. Paul does not consider prayer a seventh weapon. Rather, it underlies the whole process of spiritual warfare. **in the Spirit.** Prayer is guided by the Spirit. This is, after all, spiritual warfare.

INTRODUCTION TO
PHILIPPIANS

PERSONAL READING PLAN

☐Philippians 1:1-30 ☐Philippians 3:1–4:1
☐Philippians 2:1-30 ☐Philippians 4:2-23

AUTHOR

The Apostle Paul was the writer of Philippians.

DATE

Philippians was probably written around A.D. 61–63, a dozen or so years after Paul had founded the church in Philippi (the first church in Europe; see Acts 16).

THEME

The joy of knowing Jesus.

HISTORICAL BACKGROUND

Paul founded the church at Philippi around A.D. 50 as the result of a vision during the night in which a "man from Macedonia" pleaded with him to "Cross over to Macedonia and help us!" (Acts 16:9). He sailed immediately from Asia, thus launching Christianity in Europe. Paul's stay at Philippi was marked by joy and trial. Positive results were the conversion of Lydia, the dealer in purple cloth, as well as the conversion of the jailer and his family after an earthquake unexpectedly released Paul from prison. Unfortunately it was in Philippi that the first recorded conflict between Christians and Gentiles occurred, and Paul was thrown in jail for casting out a demon from a fortuneteller's slave girl.

Paul is in prison (probably in Rome) when Epaphroditus, an old friend from Philippi, arrives bearing yet another gift from the church. Unfortunately, Epaphroditus falls gravely ill. His home church hears about it and is grieved. Eventually he recovers, and Paul is anxious for him to return home and relieve their fears. This affords Paul an opportunity to send along a letter.

So he writes these old friends in the warmest and most personal of his epistles. There is no need for him to assert his authority as an apostle like he usually does when beginning a letter. There is no formality in his outline either. Paul puts down ideas as they occur to him, interspersed with strong declarations of emotion.

Basically, Philippians is a letter of thanksgiving (1:3-11 and 4:14-20) and a report on his imprisonment (1:12-26; 2:19-30; 4:10-13). Philippians reads like a thank you for all that this, perhaps his favorite church, has done for him (particularly their gift, as seen in 4:10-19). Still, Paul has two concerns: a tendency in the church toward disunity (1:27–2:18 and 4:2-3) and potential dangers from Judaizers (3:2-16) and false teachers (3:17-21).

THE CITY OF PHILIPPI

Located in the Roman province of Macedonia (a territory corresponding to northern Greece and parts of several other Balkan countries), Philippi was a historic city founded by Alexander the Great's father in 360 B.C. so he could mine its gold to pay for his army. Philippi eventually came to prominence as the result of two battles. In 42 B.C. on the plains of Philippi, the Caesarean forces of Anthony and Octavian defeated the Republican forces led by the assassins of Julius Caesar— Brutus and Cassius. Then in 31 B.C., Octavian (who later became the Emperor Caesar Augustus) became sole ruler by defeating his former colleague, Anthony, who was in alliance with the Egyptian Queen Cleopatra. Veterans from these conflicts were given land in Philippi, and Octavian declared it to be a Roman colony with all the accompanying rights, tax breaks, and privileges. To be in Philippi was to be in a miniature Rome.

CHARACTERISTICS

Joy permeates Philippians from start to finish. And yet this is not joy forged out of privilege and abundance. It is not the joy of people who have no problems. This is joy in the midst of hard situations. Paul is writing from prison where he faces the very real possibility of execution. The Philippian church is confronted with internal dissension and with false teachers who would seduce it away from the gospel. Furthermore, both Paul and the Philippians live with the sense that the world might end any day. The second coming of Jesus was a living reality for them.

How can you be joyful in that kind of world? How can you urge joy when you are in prison? How can you be joyful when the world is about to end? Since most of us are puzzled by the emphasis in this epistle, it is therefore important to listen carefully to Paul's words. The hardship would not go away for either Paul or the Philippians. Yet they could write Philippians, brimming with joy.

STRUCTURE

There is a question about whether the epistle to the Philippians is one letter or two. It opens in a traditional way: Paul talks about his imprisonment and about how the gospel is advancing. He makes an appeal for harmony among the members of the Philippian church. He tells them that he will be sending both Epaphroditus and Timothy to see them. And in 3:1 he says, "Whatever happens, my dear brothers and sisters . . ." as if he is about to close the letter. But then he abruptly launches into a warning about dangerous men who will harm the church (3:2-21). This is followed by more exhortations (4:1-9) and by thanks for their gifts (4:10-20), after which he actually concludes his letter.

Most commentators regard Philippians as a single letter, but it is instructive to note the two sections that could be separate letters. First, there is the warning about troublemakers that begins in 3:2 and goes to at least 4:1 (and possibly to 4:9). Then, second, there is Paul's note of thanks in 4:10-20.

PASSAGES FOR TOPICAL GROUP STUDY

1:1-11 . . . GOD'S WORK IN YOUR LIFE . . . . A Work in Progress
1:12-30 . . THE BIGGER PICTURE . . . . A Reason to Live

GREETINGS FROM PAUL

1 This letter is from Paul and Timothy, slaves of
Christ Jesus.
I am writing to all of God's holy people in Phil-
ippi who belong to Christ Jesus, including the church
leaders* and deacons.
2 May God our Father and the Lord Jesus Christ give
you grace and peace.

PAUL'S THANKSGIVING AND PRAYER

3 Every time I think of you, I give thanks to my God.
4 Whenever I pray, I make my requests for all of you
with joy, 5 for you have been my partners in spread-
ing the Good News about Christ from the time you
first heard it until now. 6 And I am certain that God,
who began the good work within you, will continue
his work until it is finally finished on the day when
Christ Jesus returns.
7 So it is right that I should feel as I do about all of
you, for you have a special place in my heart. You
share with me the special favor of God, both in my
imprisonment and in defending and confirming the
truth of the Good News. 8 God knows how much I love
you and long for you with the tender compassion of
Christ Jesus.
9 I pray that your love will overflow more and more,
and that you will keep on growing in knowledge and
understanding. 10 For I want you to understand what
really matters, so that you may live pure and blame-
less lives until the day of Christ's return. 11 May you
always be filled with the fruit of your salvation—the
righteous character produced in your life by Jesus
Christ*—for this will bring much glory and praise to
God.

PAUL'S JOY THAT CHRIST IS PREACHED

12 And I want you to know, my dear brothers and sis-
ters,* that everything that has happened to me here
has helped to spread the Good News. 13 For everyone
here, including the whole palace guard,* knows that
I am in chains because of Christ. 14 And because of
my imprisonment, most of the believers* here have
gained confidence and boldly speak God's message*
without fear.
15 It's true that some are preaching out of jealou-
sy and rivalry. But others preach about Christ with
pure motives. 16 They preach because they love me,
for they know I have been appointed to defend the
Good News. 17 Those others do not have pure motives
as they preach about Christ. They preach with selfish
ambition, not sincerely, intending to make my chains
more painful to me. 18 But that doesn't matter. Wheth-
er their motives are false or genuine, the message
about Christ is being preached either way, so I rejoice.

A WORK IN PROGRESS

1. When you care for someone, are you more likely to send a funny card or a touching one?

PHILIPPIANS 1:1-11

2. What are Paul's feelings for this church? What does that show about his leadership style?
3. How is God at work in a Christian's life, according to verses 6 and 9-11?
   How does this make you feel about uncertainties in your life?
4. Who was the "Apostle Paul" in your spiritual life that introduced you to Jesus Christ and cared about your spiritual growth?
5. What is God saying to you about your identity in this passage?

A REASON TO LIVE

1. When you were little, what helped you get through the night: A flashlight? Teddy bear? Special blanket? Other?
2. Paul was in prison but joyful. What trying circumstances are you dealing with? What is your attitude toward them?

PHILIPPIANS 1:12-30

3. What was Paul's reason for wanting to "live" (v. 22)? What does today's culture teach about the reason for living?
4. What do you think Paul would consider a life "worthy of the Good News" (v. 27)?
5. What is something that opposes you and your progress with Jesus right now?

1:1 Or *overseers*, or *bishops*. **1:11** Greek *with the fruit of righteousness through Jesus Christ*. **1:12** Greek *brothers*. **1:13** Greek *including all the Praetorium*. **1:14a** Greek *brothers in the Lord*. **1:14b** Some manuscripts read *speak the message*.

1:1 Timothy. Timothy had long been a companion of Paul. Timothy was with Paul when he visited Philippi for the first time and was well known there. Paul may have dictated this letter to Timothy.
1:3 Every time I think of you. During times of prayer, Paul was compelled by love to mention his Philippian friends.
1:4 with joy. "Joy" is a theme that pervades Philippians. This is the first of 14 times that Paul will refer to "joy" or "rejoice" in this letter.
1:5 you have been my partners. The Greek word rendered here as "partners" is the familiar word *koinonia*, translated elsewhere as "fellowship." It means, literally, "having something in common."
1:6 I am certain that. This is confidence that springs out of faith in who God is and what He is doing. **the day when Christ Jesus.** This is the moment when Christ will return in glory and triumph to establish His kingdom on earth.
1:7 defending and confirming. This references Paul's defense before the Roman court. In court, he hopes not only to vindicate himself and the gospel from false charges but also to proclaim the gospel and its life-changing power to those in the courtroom.
1:9 I pray that. He prays that this love will increase (i.e., that it will go on developing) and that it will be regulated by knowledge and discernment. **knowledge and understanding.** This growing love is to be focused by intellectual, practical, and moral insight.
1:10 to understand what really matters. Literally "to determine." The word translated "determine" is used to describe the process of testing coins in order to distinguish between those that are real and those that are counterfeit.
1:13 palace guard. The elite soldiers in the Roman army; the bodyguards of the emperor.
1:18 motives are false. The three words by which Paul characterizes the motivation of his rivals—envy, strife, and rivalry—are all words he has used in other contexts to describe those actions and attitudes that are to be shunned by Christians. They are "vices that always adversely affect, even endanger, the life of the church" (Hawthorne).

And I will continue to rejoice. 19 For I know that as you
pray for me and the Spirit of Jesus Christ helps me,
this will lead to my deliverance.

PAUL'S LIFE FOR CHRIST

20 For I fully expect and hope that I will never be
ashamed, but that I will continue to be bold for Christ,
as I have been in the past. And I trust that my life will
bring honor to Christ, whether I live or die. 21 For to
me, living means living for Christ, and dying is even
better. 22 But if I live, I can do more fruitful work for
Christ. So I really don't know which is better. 23 I'm
torn between two desires: I long to go and be with
Christ, which would be far better for me. 24 But for
your sakes, it is better that I continue to live.
25 Knowing this, I am convinced that I will remain
alive so I can continue to help all of you grow and expe-
rience the joy of your faith. 26 And when I come to you
again, you will have even more reason to take pride in
Christ Jesus because of what he is doing through me.

LIVE AS CITIZENS OF HEAVEN

27 Above all, you must live as citizens of heaven, con-
ducting yourselves in a manner worthy of the Good
News about Christ. Then, whether I come and see you
again or only hear about you, I will know that you
are standing together with one spirit and one pur-
pose, fighting together for the faith, which is the Good
News. 28 Don't be intimidated in any way by your ene-
mies. This will be a sign to them that they are going to
be destroyed, but that you are going to be saved, even
by God himself. 29 For you have been given not only
the privilege of trusting in Christ but also the privi-
lege of suffering for him. 30 We are in this struggle to-
gether. You have seen my struggle in the past, and you
know that I am still in the midst of it.

HAVE THE ATTITUDE OF CHRIST

2 Is there any encouragement from belonging to
Christ? Any comfort from his love? Any fellowship
together in the Spirit? Are your hearts tender and com-
passionate? 2 Then make me truly happy by agreeing
wholeheartedly with each other, loving one another,
and working together with one mind and purpose.
3 Don't be selfish; don't try to impress others. Be
humble, thinking of others as better than yourselves.
4 Don't look out only for your own interests, but take
an interest in others, too.
5 You must have the same attitude that Christ Jesus
had.

6 Though he was God,*
he did not think of equality with God
as something to cling to.
7 Instead, he gave up his divine privileges*;
he took the humble position of a slave*
and was born as a human being.
When he appeared in human form,*
8 he humbled himself in obedience to God
and died a criminal's death on a cross.

9 Therefore, God elevated him to the place of highest
honor
and gave him the name above all other names,
10 that at the name of Jesus every knee should bow,
in heaven and on earth and under the earth,
11 and every tongue declare that Jesus Christ is Lord,
to the glory of God the Father.

WHO'S NUMBER ONE?

1. Growing up, who was your role model—someone you respected and wanted to be like?
2. When has another person put your needs before his or her own? How did you feel?

PHILIPPIANS 2:1-11

3. What does verse 3 mean? Can that attitude go too far, resulting in others taking advantage of us?
4. What is Christ's attitude (vv. 6-11)? How does your attitude compare?
5. How would the relationships with your friends or teammates be different if you practiced the humility demonstrated by Jesus?

SHINE BRIGHTLY FOR CHRIST

12 Dear friends, you always followed my instruc-
tions when I was with you. And now that I am
away, it is even more important. Work hard to
show the results of your salvation, obeying God
with deep reverence and fear. 13 For God is working

2:6 Or *Being in the form of God.* **2:7a** Greek *he emptied himself.* **2:7b** Or *the form of a slave.* **2:7c** Some English translations put this phrase in verse 8.

1:20 continue to be bold. Paul's desire is the courage to speak boldly during his trial. **will bring honor.** This word means literally "to make something or someone large." **whether I live or die.** By this phrase, Paul simply means that his single goal is to bring praise to Christ . . . no matter what happens.

1:21 living means living for Christ. For Paul, his entire existence revolves around Christ. He is inspired by Christ; he works for Christ; his sole focus in life is Christ. He is a man with a single, all-consuming passion. **dying is even better.** Death is the door into the presence of Christ. Death is not so much escape from hardship as it is entrance into joy.

1:23 to go and be with Christ. Death would be a gain for Paul since being with, in, and for Christ meant everything to him.

1:27 standing together. This is a military term used for Roman soldiers standing back-to-back, protecting each other while resisting the enemy. **for the faith, which is the Good News.** The goal is not victory on the battlefield but the preservation of the Christian faith.

1:28 Don't be intimidated. The Greek word used here is rare, appearing only once in the Bible. Its original reference was to horses that were timid and shied easily. The Philippians must not let their opponents spook them into an uncontrolled stampede.

2:1 Is there. In Greek, this construction assumes a positive response, e.g., "Is there any encouragement from belonging to Christ? And of course, there is . . ."

2:3 selfish. This is the second time in this letter that Paul has used this word (1:17). It means working to advance oneself without thought for others. **impress others.** This is the only occurrence of this word in the New Testament. Translated literally, it means "vain glory" (*kendoxia*), which is asserting oneself over God who alone is worthy of true glory (*doxa*). **humble.** This was not a virtue that was valued by the Greeks in the first century. They considered this to be the attitude of a slave (i.e., servility).

2:7 as a human being. The point is not that Jesus just seemed to be human. He assumed the identity of a person and was in actuality a human being.

2:8 he humbled himself. Jesus is the ultimate model of One who lived a life of self-sacrifice, self-renunciation, and self-surrender. **died . . . on a cross.** Crucifixion was a harsh, demeaning, and utterly painful way to die. According to the Old Testament, those who died by hanging on a tree were considered to have been cursed by God.

2:11 Jesus Christ is Lord. This is the earliest and most basic confession of faith on the part of the church (Acts 2:36; Rom. 10:9; 1 Cor. 12:3). **Lord.** This is the name that was given to Jesus—the name that reflects who He really is (v. 9). This is the name of God. Jesus is the supreme Sovereign of the universe.

WORKING OUT

1. Who demands the most from you: Your dad? Your mom? Your coach? A teacher?
2. What training do you find most difficult, and why: Physical? Spiritual? Academic? Other?

PHILIPPIANS 2:12-18

3. Verse 12 says, "Work hard to show the results of your salvation," and verse 13 says, "God is working in you." How does this apparent contradiction work?
4. Why do you think it is important that God works on the "desire" and the "power" (v. 13)? Which one is harder for you?
5. What is God saying to you about your spiritual training in this passage?

TEAMING UP

1. Are you more like your mother or father? In what way?
2. What is the most important message you have ever delivered?

PHILIPPIANS 2:19-30

3. Consider verses 20-22 and 30. Give some examples of how verse 21 is true today.
4. Epaphroditus has five roles listed in verse 25. Which one do you think is best to have, and why?
5. Is it easy or hard for you to give praise? Where do you need to improve?
6. What does this passage teach about the importance of teamwork?

in you, giving you the desire and the power to do
what pleases him.
14 Do everything without complaining and arguing,
15 so that no one can criticize you. Live clean, innocent
lives as children of God, shining like bright lights in
a world full of crooked and perverse people. 16 Hold
firmly to the word of life; then, on the day of Christ's
return, I will be proud that I did not run the race in
vain and that my work was not useless. 17 But I will
rejoice even if I lose my life, pouring it out like a liquid
offering to God,* just like your faithful service is an
offering to God. And I want all of you to share that
joy. 18 Yes, you should rejoice, and I will share your joy.

PAUL COMMENDS TIMOTHY

19 If the Lord Jesus is willing, I hope to send Timothy to
you soon for a visit. Then he can cheer me up by tell-
ing me how you are getting along. 20 I have no one else
like Timothy, who genuinely cares about your welfare.
21 All the others care only for themselves and not for
what matters to Jesus Christ. 22 But you know how
Timothy has proved himself. Like a son with his father,
he has served with me in preaching the Good News. 23 I
hope to send him to you just as soon as I find out what
is going to happen to me here. 24 And I have confidence
from the Lord that I myself will come to see you soon.

PAUL COMMENDS EPAPHRODITUS

25 Meanwhile, I thought I should send Epaphroditus
back to you. He is a true brother, co-worker, and fellow
soldier. And he was your messenger to help me in my
need. 26 I am sending him because he has been longing
to see you, and he was very distressed that you heard
he was ill. 27 And he certainly was ill; in fact, he almost
died. But God had mercy on him—and also on me, so
that I would not have one sorrow after another.
28 So I am all the more anxious to send him back to
you, for I know you will be glad to see him, and then
I will not be so worried about you. 29 Welcome him in
the Lord's love* and with great joy, and give him the
honor that people like him deserve. 30 For he risked his
life for the work of Christ, and he was at the point of
death while doing for me what you couldn't do from
far away.

THE PRICELESS VALUE OF KNOWING CHRIST

3 Whatever happens, my dear brothers and sisters,*
rejoice in the Lord. I never get tired of telling you
these things, and I do it to safeguard your faith.
2 Watch out for those dogs, those people who do
evil, those mutilators who say you must be circum-
cised to be saved. 3 For we who worship by the Spirit
of God* are the ones who are truly circumcised. We
rely on what Christ Jesus has done for us. We put no
confidence in human effort, 4 though I could have
confidence in my own effort if anyone could. Indeed,
if others have reason for confidence in their own ef-
forts, I have even more!
5 I was circumcised when I was eight days old. I am
a pure-blooded citizen of Israel and a member of the
tribe of Benjamin—a real Hebrew if there ever was
one! I was a member of the Pharisees, who demand
the strictest obedience to the Jewish law. 6 I was so
zealous that I harshly persecuted the church. And as
for righteousness, I obeyed the law without fault.

2:17 Greek *I will rejoice even if I am to be poured out as a liquid offering.* **2:29** Greek *in the Lord.* **3:1** Greek *brothers;* also in 3:13, 17.
3:3 Some manuscripts read *worship God in spirit;* one early manuscript reads *worship in spirit.*

2:25 Epaphroditus. Epaphroditus had been sent by the Philippian church to convey a gift to Paul and then to stay on as a member of Paul's apostolic group. However, he fell ill. The church heard about this and became quite anxious about him. In addition, Epaphroditus was homesick. For both reasons, Paul sensed that it was time for Epaphroditus to return to Philippi.

2:30 risked his life. A gambling term, it denotes one who risked everything on the roll of the dice.

3:2 those mutilators. Paul is saying that their circumcision is really mutilation.

3:4 confidence in my own effort. This is what these Jews are promoting: a righteousness based on their heritage and many accomplishments.

3:5 eight days old. It was on the eighth day after birth that a Jewish child (as opposed to a proselyte) was circumcised. Paul was a true Jew right from the time of his birth. **the tribe of Benjamin.** The members of the tribe of Benjamin constituted an elite group within Israel. **a member of the Pharisees.** He was one of the spiritual elite in Israel.

3:6 I was so zealous . . . persecuted the church. Zeal was a highly prized virtue among the Jews. Paul had demonstrated his zeal for the Law by ferreting out Christians and bringing them to trial (Acts 22:4-5; 26:9-11). **without fault.** To the best of his ability, Paul tried to observe the whole Law. Taken together, all these attributes mean that Paul was in every way the match to his opponents in Philippi. He had lived at the very pinnacle of Judaism.

THE SECRET TO SUCCESS

1. What person in your school would you vote "most likely to succeed"? Why?
2. What is it going to take for you to be a success in the eyes of your parents? Your friends? God?

PHILIPPIANS 3:1-11

3. According to Paul, what is the secret to success (v. 8)?
4. Paul desires to know Christ better by experiencing things He experienced (vv. 10-11). How does that change the way we look at suffering?
5. What "garbage" (v. 8) do you need to give up to know Christ better?
6. How would you compare your life goals to the Apostle Paul's goals in this passage?

7 I once thought these things were valuable, but
now I consider them worthless because of what
Christ has done. 8 Yes, everything else is worthless
when compared with the infinite value of knowing
Christ Jesus my Lord. For his sake I have discarded
everything else, counting it all as garbage, so that I
could gain Christ 9 and become one with him. I no lon-
ger count on my own righteousness through obeying
the law; rather, I become righteous through faith in
Christ.* For God's way of making us right with him-
self depends on faith. 10 I want to know Christ and ex-
perience the mighty power that raised him from the
dead. I want to suffer with him, sharing in his death,
11 so that one way or another I will experience the res-
urrection from the dead!

PRESSING TOWARD THE GOAL

12 I don't mean to say that I have already achieved
these things or that I have already reached perfec-
tion. But I press on to possess that perfection for
which Christ Jesus first possessed me. 13 No, dear
brothers and sisters, I have not achieved it,* but
I focus on this one thing: Forgetting the past and
looking forward to what lies ahead, 14 I press on to
reach the end of the race and receive the heavenly
prize for which God, through Christ Jesus, is calling
us.
15 Let all who are spiritually mature agree on these
things. If you disagree on some point, I believe God
will make it plain to you. 16 But we must hold on to the
progress we have already made.
17 Dear brothers and sisters, pattern your lives
after mine, and learn from those who follow our
example. 18 For I have told you often before, and I
say it again with tears in my eyes, that there are
many whose conduct shows they are really ene-
mies of the cross of Christ. 19 They are headed for
destruction. Their god is their appetite, they brag
about shameful things, and they think only about
this life here on earth. 20 But we are citizens of
heaven, where the Lord Jesus Christ lives. And we
are eagerly waiting for him to return as our Savior.
21 He will take our weak mortal bodies and change
them into glorious bodies like his own, using the
same power with which he will bring everything
under his control.

REACH FOR THE PRIZE

1. If you could compete in the Olympics, what sport would you choose?
2. When have you had a hard time moving on and letting go of the past?

PHILIPPIANS 3:12-21

3. What "prize" is Paul trying to win (v. 14)? How did this goal guide his life?
4. Why is it so hard to maintain the balance between earthly things and spiritual things (vv. 19-20)?
5. What might God be calling you to do for Him in your athletics or other interests? How about with your life?

3:9 Or *through the faithfulness of Christ.* **3:13** Some manuscripts read *not yet achieved it.*

3:7 valuable . . . worthless. Paul describes his change in outlook in terms of a balance sheet. What was once on the "profit" side of the ledger (when he was a Pharisee) has been shifted over to the "loss" side (now that he is a Christian).
3:8 compared with the infinite value. Paul discovered only one thing had any ultimate value—knowing Christ Jesus. Knowing Christ did not come as a result of any personal accomplishment.
3:10 know. The knowledge about which Paul speaks is personal knowledge and not just intellectual knowledge (i.e., not just knowing "about" someone). **the mighty power that raised him.** Paul wants to personally experience the resurrected Christ in all His power (Eph. 1:18-21). **sharing in his death.** Paul coins a new phrase by which he expresses that he wants to be obedient to God just as Christ was . . . even to the point of death.
3:11 one way or another I will experience. In humility, he expresses his sense that it is solely by God's grace that he would gain such a gift.
3:12 don't mean to say . . . already achieved. He has not gained full possession of what Christ has for him. **perfection.** This is the only time in his letters that Paul uses this word. Paul indicates he has not yet fully understood Jesus Christ. There is simply too much to know of Christ ever to grasp it all this side of heaven. **press on.** In contrast to those groups that claim it is possible to attain spiritual perfection here and now, the Christian life is one of relentless striving to know Christ in His fullness. **to possess.** Winning a prize, as for example, in a race, or also to understand or comprehend something. **that perfection for which Christ first possessed me.** Paul refers here to his conversion experience on the Damascus Road.
3:13 Forgetting the past. In order to press on to a successful conclusion of his spiritual pilgrimage, Paul must first cease looking at what he has accomplished in the past. **what lies ahead.** If the first movement in the spiritual pilgrimage is to forget the past, the second is to concentrate totally on what lies ahead—full comprehension of Jesus Christ.
3:14 end of the race. The mark on the track that signifies the end of the race. Paul had apparently experienced the Greek games first hand. He draws a number of parallels between the Christian life and athletic contests. Both require training, discipline, courage, endurance, concentration, and strong commitment. **prize.** What Paul seems to have in mind is the moment at the end of the race, when the winner is called forward by the games master to receive the victory palm or wreath.
3:20 we are citizens of heaven. This metaphor was especially meaningful to the Christians in Philippi. In 42 B.C. Philippi became a Roman colony, and the Philippians could truly say and took pride in saying "our citizenship is in Rome," even though they were far removed from it geographically. In the same way as Christians their citizenship was not just on earth. Their true and lasting citizenship was in heaven. **eagerly waiting.** Paul captures the keen anticipation and happy expectation of the Christians who long for Christ's return.
3:21 weak mortal bodies. In contrast to those who taught that perfection was possible here and now, Christians knew that it was only at the second coming, by the work of Christ, that their frail, weak, and corrupt bodies would be transformed into a spiritual body akin to Christ's body.

DON'T WORRY—BE HAPPY!

1. What makes you anxious: A trip to the dentist? A big test? A date? Other?

PHILIPPIANS 4:2-9

2. What makes Paul's challenge to rejoice so difficult (v. 4)?
3. What are some things people do to relieve stress from worry in their lives? What does Paul say to do (vv. 6,8)?
4. How does what you think about affect how you feel? How does it affect your relationship with God?
5. What is something you are anxious about right now? Present these worries to God in prayer.

4 Therefore, my dear brothers and sisters,* stay true
to the Lord. I love you and long to see you, dear
friends, for you are my joy and the crown I receive for
my work.

WORDS OF ENCOURAGEMENT

2 Now I appeal to Euodia and Syntyche. Please, be-
cause you belong to the Lord, settle your disagree-
ment. 3 And I ask you, my true partner,* to help these
two women, for they worked hard with me in telling
others the Good News. They worked along with Clem-
ent and the rest of my co-workers, whose names are
written in the Book of Life.
4 Always be full of joy in the Lord. I say it again—
rejoice! 5 Let everyone see that you are considerate in
all you do. Remember, the Lord is coming soon.*
6 Don't worry about anything; instead, pray about
everything. Tell God what you need, and thank him
for all he has done. 7 Then you will experience God's
peace, which exceeds anything we can understand.
His peace will guard your hearts and minds as you
live in Christ Jesus.
8 And now, dear brothers and sisters, one final
thing. Fix your thoughts on what is true, and honor-
able, and right, and pure, and lovely, and admirable.
Think about things that are excellent and worthy of
praise. 9 Keep putting into practice all you learned
and received from me—everything you heard from
me and saw me doing. Then the God of peace will be
with you.

PAUL'S THANKS FOR THEIR GIFTS

10 How I praise the Lord that you are concerned
about me again. I know you have always been con-
cerned for me, but you didn't have the chance to
help me. 11 Not that I was ever in need, for I have
learned how to be content with whatever I have. 12 I
know how to live on almost nothing or with every-
thing. I have learned the secret of living in every
situation, whether it is with a full stomach or emp-
ty, with plenty or little. 13 For I can do everything
through Christ,* who gives me strength. 14 Even so,
you have done well to share with me in my present
difficulty.

CAREFREE CONTENTMENT

1. What would you say causes the most stress among students at your school?

PHILIPPIANS 4:10-20

2. What is the great value of Paul's complete contentment (vv. 11-13)?
3. What "reward" do you think Paul is referring to in verse 17, and what is he really saying?
4. In what ways are you feeling insecure with your life? How do verses 13 and 19 help you?
5. What is Paul's secret to contentment? What needs to change in your life for you to find true contentment in all circumstances?

4:1 Greek *brothers;* also in 4:8. **4:3** Or *loyal Syzygus.* **4:5** Greek *the Lord is near.* **4:13** Greek *through the one.*

4:2 appeal. This is a strong verb, meaning "to exhort, to implore, to beg." **Euodia . . . Syntyche.** Apparently these two women had carried their quarrel into the body, and it was threatening to split the church. Peace between them was crucial to the unity of the whole body. **to the Lord.** The only hope for this kind of unity to develop between these two women is found in the fact and power of their common commitment to Jesus.

4:3 true partner. Can be descriptive or it may be a proper name, *Syzgus* or *Suzuge*. Some commentators have speculated that it might be Lydia, the first convert in the church at Philippi (Acts 16:14,15,40). In any case, Paul had great confidence in this person and saw them as a peacemaker.

4:4 Always be full of joy in the Lord. Paul emphasizes this command by repeating it. The object of their rejoicing is the Lord who is constant in an ever-changing world, a God faithful to his people.

4:5 considerate. This word can also be translated *gentleness*. A person with this quality isn't a doormat but neither does he go around asserting his rights. He's able to see and care for not only his own interests but that of others.

4:6 Don't worry. They are to stop being anxious. To worry is to display a lack of confidence in God's care and in God's control over a situation (Matt. 6:25-34). **pray . . . Tell God what you need.** In the Greek, Paul uses three synonyms in a row for prayer to describe the alternative to anxiety. Instead of worrying, a person ought to converse directly with God and lay out before Him all that is on his or her mind, confident that God will hear and respond.

4:7 God's peace. This is supernatural peace that comes from God and is focused on Him. **exceeds anything we can understand.** Such peace can never fully be understood by human beings. **guard.** This is a military term. It describes a garrison of soldiers, such as those stationed at Philippi, whose job it is to stand watch over the city and protect it.

4:8 true. Sincerity and accuracy, not only in thought and word, but also in deed and attitude. **honorable.** Those majestic things that command respect and lift up one's mind from the mundane. **right.** Giving to God and others that which is their due. **pure.** In all spheres of life—ideas, actions, motives, etc. **lovely.** A warmth that calls forth love from others. **admirable.** What people admire and think well of. **excellent.** The best; without fault. **worthy of praise.** Behavior that is universally praised.

4:12 almost nothing. This word refers to the lowering of water in a river. As such, it is a reference to fundamental needs which are basic to life (such as food and water). Paul has learned to live even in the midst of abject poverty. **with everything.** This is the opposite state of "a little." It means literally, "to overflow," that is, to have enough for one's own daily needs plus something left over. **with a full stomach.** This describes force-fed animals that are stuffed to capacity in order to fatten them for slaughter. It is used by Paul to define one of the extremes: having more than enough to eat. **with plenty or little.** Another set of contrasting words. It is by the experience of these extremes that Paul has come to know the secret of coping with all circumstances.

4:13 everything. Paul is referring to what he has just described: his ability to live in all types of material circumstances—wealth or poverty, abundant food or no food, etc. **through Christ who gives me strength.** The source of Paul's ability to live successfully in all circumstances is his union with Christ. This is his secret.

[15] As you know, you Philippians were the only
ones who gave me financial help when I first
brought you the Good News and then traveled on
from Macedonia. No other church did this. [16] Even
when I was in Thessalonica you sent help more
than once. [17] I don't say this because I want a gift
from you. Rather, I want you to receive a reward for
your kindness.
[18] At the moment I have all I need—and more! I am
generously supplied with the gifts you sent me with
Epaphroditus. They are a sweet-smelling sacrifice
that is acceptable and pleasing to God. [19] And this
same God who takes care of me will supply all your
needs from his glorious riches, which have been giv-
en to us in Christ Jesus.
[20] Now all glory to God our Father forever and ever!
Amen.

PAUL'S FINAL GREETINGS

[21] Give my greetings to each of God's holy people—all
who belong to Christ Jesus. The brothers who are
with me send you their greetings. [22] And all the rest of
God's people send you greetings, too, especially those
in Caesar's household.
[23] May the grace of the Lord Jesus Christ be with
your spirit.*

4:23 Some manuscripts add *Amen.*

4:22 the rest of God's people. The Christians in Rome are the third group that sends greetings.

INTRODUCTION TO

COLOSSIANS

PERSONAL READING PLAN

- ☐Colossians 1:1-23
- ☐Colossians 1:24–2:23
- ☐Colossians 3:1–4:1
- ☐Colossians 4:2-18

AUTHOR

The Apostle Paul was the writer of Colossians.

DATE

Tradition has it that Paul wrote Colossians, Ephesians, and Philemon during his imprisonment in Rome. This would mean these letters were written in the early A.D. 60s. However, other sites, including Caesarea and Ephesus, have been proposed as the place of Paul's confinement, so that neither date nor place is certain.

THEME

Fullness and freedom in Christ.

HISTORICAL BACKGROUND

Paul did not found this church, at least not directly. It was probably established as a result of his ministry in Ephesus, since during Paul's two or three years in Ephesus the whole province of Asia was evangelized (Acts 19:10). Paul evidently never visited the churches at Colosse or Laodicea (2:1). Epaphras probably founded the Colossian church. A native of Colosse (4:12), he worked hard on behalf of the church there (4:13). In fact, in 1:6-7 Paul says, "This same Good News that came to you is going out all over the world. It is bearing fruit everywhere by changing lives, . . . You learned about the Good News from Epaphras . . ."Paul then commends Epaphras as his dear friend and a faithful minister of Christ. In fact, because of their friendship, Epaphras stayed with Paul during his imprisonment (Philem. 23) and so was unable to deliver the letter to the Colossians personally. We also meet the church at Colosse in Paul's letter to Philemon, where he requests that the runaway slave Onesimus (converted through Paul's ministry) be accepted back.

The church at Colosse was probably Gentile in composition. In 1:21 Paul speaks of the Colossian Christians as having once been "enemies" from God and having "evil thoughts"—phrases he uses elsewhere to describe those who are not part of God's covenant with Israel. Then in 1:27, he talks about making the mystery of God clear to the Gentiles; the reference is obviously to the Colossians. Finally in 3:5-7, Paul lists their past sins, which are characteristic of Gentiles rather than Jews.

RELIGION IN COLOSSE

A large number of Jews had lived in the region of Colosse, ever since the second century B.C. when Antiochus III brought 2,000 Jews from Mesopotamia and Babylon to settle there. By Paul's time there may have been as many as 50,000 Jews living in the region and practicing their religion. However, their synagogue had a "reputation for laxity and openness to speculation drifting in from the hellenistic world" (Ralph P. Martin, Colossians and Philemon: New Century Bible Commentary, p. 18).

But freethinking Judaism was not the major religious force in the Lycus Valley. The Greek religions also flourished there. The fertility cult of Cybele was highly popular; it was characterized by ecstasy and excessive enthusiasm Throughout the Roman Empire, the worship of Isis, Apollo, Dionysus, Asclepius, and other gods was widespread. The cult of Mithras, a mystery religion based on astrology and sacrifice, abounded in Colosse. The church at Colosse, therefore, grew up in an atmosphere that blended a variety of religious traditions that may have been sources of heresy within the church.

CHARACTERISTICS

As Paul does so often, he begins his letter with a strong doctrinal statement and concludes with behavioral implications. Here his doctrinal emphasis is on the cosmic nature of Jesus Christ. Jesus is the divine Lord of the universe who reconciles all things to Himself through his death, not by rules and regulations. Paul sets this strong statement of Christ's deity (1:15-23) over against the mystical, ritualistic religion of the false teachers (2:8-23). (Apparently, these teachings had something to do with astrology. The "star-deities" could only be pleased by a life of abstinence and self-denial.) Once the truth about Christ is stated, Paul turns to the implications of Christ's lordship over all and describes how Christ's followers ought to live (3:1–4:6).

The epistle to the Colossians begins, like most of Paul's letters, with a lengthy introduction (1:1-14). In the first major division on doctrine, Paul establishes the preeminence of Christ (1:15–2:23). He follows this with an exhortation to the Colossians to live in union with Christ (3:1–4:6). He concludes with personal greetings (4:7-18).

THE CITY OF COLOSSE

About 100 miles west of Ephesus in the Lycus River Valley lay the city of Colosse. In Paul's time, it was located in the Roman province of Asia (in what today is Turkey). It was one of three major population centers that flourished in the region. Hierapolis and Laodicea (4:13) stood on opposite sides of the Lycus River, about six miles apart, while Colosse straddled the river 12 miles upstream.

Since it was located on a major trade route from Ephesus, Colosse was considered a great city in the days of Xerxes, the Persian king (fifth century B.C.). One hundred years later, it had developed into a prosperous commercial center on account of its weaving industry. In fact, "Colossian" came to mean a specific color of dyed wool.

By the time of Paul, however, Colosse's prominence had diminished; though its sister cities, Laodicea and Hierapolis, were still prospering. Laodicea had become the seat of Roman government in the region, and Hierapolis was famous for its healing waters. But Colosse, when Paul wrote, was no longer even a city. In fact, Colosse was the least important town to which Paul ever wrote.

PASSAGES FOR TOPICAL GROUP STUDY

1:15-23 . . . JESUS CHRIST. . . . . Supernatural Hero
1:24–2:5 . . SPIRITUAL DISCIPLINE AND TRAINING . . . . No Pain... No Gain
3:1-25 . . . . FORGIVENESS. . . . . Take Out the Trash
4:1-18 . . . . THANKFULNESS and PRAYER . . . . Open Doors

PASSAGES FOR GENERAL GROUP STUDY

1:1-14 . . . . The Lasting Hope (from Jesus)
2:6-23 . . . . Victory over the Enemy (by Walking with Christ)

GREETINGS FROM PAUL

1 This letter is from Paul, chosen by the will of God to
be an apostle of Christ Jesus, and from our brother
Timothy.
2 We are writing to God's holy people in the city
of Colosse, who are faithful brothers and sisters* in
Christ.
May God our Father give you grace and peace.

PAUL'S THANKSGIVING AND PRAYER

3 We always pray for you, and we give thanks to God,
the Father of our Lord Jesus Christ. 4 For we have
heard of your faith in Christ Jesus and your love for
all of God's people, 5 which come from your confident
hope of what God has reserved for you in heaven. You
have had this expectation ever since you first heard
the truth of the Good News.
6 This same Good News that came to you is going
out all over the world. It is bearing fruit everywhere
by changing lives, just as it changed your lives from
the day you first heard and understood the truth
about God's wonderful grace.
7 You learned about the Good News from Epaphras,
our beloved co-worker. He is Christ's faithful servant,
and he is helping us on your behalf.* 8 He has told us
about the love for others that the Holy Spirit has giv-
en you.
9 So we have not stopped praying for you since we
first heard about you. We ask God to give you complete
knowledge of his will and to give you spiritual wis-
dom and understanding. 10 Then the way you live will
always honor and please the Lord, and your lives will
produce every kind of good fruit. All the while, you
will grow as you learn to know God better and better.
11 We also pray that you will be strengthened with
all his glorious power so you will have all the endur-
ance and patience you need. May you be filled with
joy,* 12 always thanking the Father. He has enabled
you to share in the inheritance that belongs to his
people, who live in the light. 13 For he has rescued us
from the kingdom of darkness and transferred us into
the Kingdom of his dear Son, 14 who purchased our
freedom* and forgave our sins.

CHRIST IS SUPREME

15 Christ is the visible image of the invisible God.
He existed before anything was created and is
supreme over all creation,*
16 for through him God created everything
in the heavenly realms and on earth.
He made the things we can see
and the things we can't see—
such as thrones, kingdoms, rulers, and authorities
in the unseen world.

THE LASTING HOPE

1. What were you the most thankful for when you got up this morning?

COLOSSIANS 1:1-14

2. Why are faith and love the result of hope (vv. 4-5)? Why must hope exist first?
3. How does what Paul prays for (vv. 9-11) compare with what he thanks God for (vv. 12-14)?
4. Where is Paul saying real spiritual growth comes from (vv. 9-14)?
5. When did you first come to know the hope offered through Christ in the gospel (when He rescued you from darkness)? What life situation caused you to need hope?

SUPERNATURAL HERO

1. As a kid, who was your favorite superhero? What special power did he or she have?
2. Do you tend to think of Jesus as a superhero? Why or why not?

COLOSSIANS 1:15-23

3. How does Jesus hold all things together (vv. 16-17)? What does that mean for our lives, both now and in eternity?
4. How did Jesus reconcile us to God (v. 20)? Why was this necessary (v. 21)?
5. Considering who Jesus is (vv. 15-20) and what He did for you (vv. 21-23), how will you live your life? How can you give Him "first place in everything"?

1:2 Greek *faithful brothers.* **1:7** Or *he is ministering on your behalf;* some manuscripts read *he is ministering on our behalf.* **1:11** Or *all the patience and endurance you need with joy.* **1:14** Some manuscripts add *with his blood.* **1:15** Or *He is the firstborn of all creation.*

1:2 give you grace and peace. Right from the beginning, this letter highlights the reality of God's grace through Christ and the reconciliation (peace) that results.

1:4-5 faith . . . love . . . hope. This triad of Christian graces is arranged and expanded upon in various ways throughout the New Testament. The center of the Christian faith is Jesus Christ; the essence of its lifestyle is love; and the sure hope of a future with Christ is its motivation.

1:6 all over the world. Within 30 years after Jesus' resurrection, the gospel had spread from Palestine throughout the Roman Empire.

1:9 knowledge . . . spiritual wisdom and understanding. The false teachers (combining elements of Christianity, Greek mystery religions, and Judaism) defined salvation in terms of secret, divine knowledge, and ecstatic experiences which could only be gained by following their regimen of ascetic disciplines and ceremonies.

1:10 the way you live. Rather than esoteric knowledge and experiences, true spirituality is seen in a lifestyle that reflects the love and holiness of Jesus. **grow as you learn to know God.** Knowing and obeying God is the key to ongoing spiritual growth.

1:11 strengthened with all his glorious power. The false teachers taught that spiritual power was a matter of gaining control over the celestial forces that dominated human life (Eph. 2:2; 6:12). Paul teaches instead that true spiritual power is shown by patiently enduring life's hardships with a spirit of thankfulness to God (v. 12).

1:13 the kingdom of darkness. Darkness is an appropriate image for the influence of the hostile spiritual forces (v. 16) since their domination only leads to spiritual and moral blindness (Luke 22:53; John 1:5; Eph. 5:8-14). Paul reminds the Colossians that these astral powers are not a threat to the Christian because He has rescued us from their kingdom and transferred us into Jesus' eternal kingdom.

1:15 image of the invisible God. "Image" does not mean a second-hand representation (as a photograph is an image of a person) but rather a complete representation. All that God is, Jesus is (John 1:18; 14:9; 2 Cor. 4:4-6; Heb. 1:3). One need not look anywhere else but to Christ in order to fully know God.

1:16 thrones, kingdoms, rulers, and authorities. Christ is Lord over all authorities, physical or spiritual.

Everything was created through him and for
him.
17 He existed before anything else,
and he holds all creation together.
18 Christ is also the head of the church,
which is his body.
He is the beginning,
supreme over all who rise from the dead.*
So he is first in everything.
19 For God in all his fullness
was pleased to live in Christ,
20 and through him God reconciled
everything to himself.
He made peace with everything in heaven and on
earth
by means of Christ's blood on the cross.

21 This includes you who were once far away
from God. You were his enemies, separated from
him by your evil thoughts and actions. 22 Yet now
he has reconciled you to himself through the death
of Christ in his physical body. As a result, he has
brought you into his own presence, and you are
holy and blameless as you stand before him with-
out a single fault.
23 But you must continue to believe this truth and
stand firmly in it. Don't drift away from the assur-
ance you received when you heard the Good News.
The Good News has been preached all over the world,
and I, Paul, have been appointed as God's servant to
proclaim it.

PAUL'S WORK FOR THE CHURCH

24 I am glad when I suffer for you in my body, for I am
participating in the sufferings of Christ that contin-
ue for his body, the church. 25 God has given me the
responsibility of serving his church by proclaiming
his entire message to you. 26 This message was kept
secret for centuries and generations past, but now it
has been revealed to God's people. 27 For God want-
ed them to know that the riches and glory of Christ
are for you Gentiles, too. And this is the secret: Christ
lives in you. This gives you assurance of sharing his
glory.
28 So we tell others about Christ, warning everyone
and teaching everyone with all the wisdom God has
given us. We want to present them to God, perfect* in
their relationship to Christ. 29 That's why I work and
struggle so hard, depending on Christ's mighty power
that works within me.

NO PAIN, NO GAIN

1. When have you worked very hard in sports or in school to achieve a goal? How did you feel when you were done?

COLOSSIANS 1:24–2:5

2. In what sense are Paul's sufferings a continuation of Jesus' sufferings? Why would this lead him to rejoice (see 2 Cor. 12:9-10)?
3. How can we make Paul's stated purpose (1:28; 2:2) a reality in our lives?
4. What "well-crafted arguments" (2:4) from others or the world's system hinder you in following Jesus? How does Paul speak to your concerns?
5. What is God saying to you in this passage about the training necessary to achieve your spiritual goals?

2 I want you to know how much I have agonized for
you and for the church at Laodicea, and for many
other believers who have never met me personally.
2 I want them to be encouraged and knit together by
strong ties of love. I want them to have complete con-
fidence that they understand God's mysterious plan,
which is Christ himself. 3 In him lie hidden all the
treasures of wisdom and knowledge.
4 I am telling you this so no one will deceive you
with well-crafted arguments. 5 For though I am far
away from you, my heart is with you. And I rejoice
that you are living as you should and that your faith
in Christ is strong.

FREEDOM FROM RULES AND NEW LIFE IN CHRIST

6 And now, just as you accepted Christ Jesus as your
Lord, you must continue to follow him. 7 Let your roots
grow down into him, and let your lives be built on him.
Then your faith will grow strong in the truth you were
taught, and you will overflow with thankfulness.
8 Don't let anyone capture you with empty philos-
ophies and high-sounding nonsense that come from
human thinking and from the spiritual powers* of
this world, rather than from Christ. 9 For in Christ
lives all the fullness of God in a human body.* 10 So you
also are complete through your union with Christ,
who is the head over every ruler and authority.

1:18 Or *the firstborn from the dead.* **1:28** Or *mature.* **2:8** Or *the spiritual principles;* also in 2:20. **2:9** Or *in him dwells all the completeness of the Godhead bodily.*

1:17 He existed before anything else. Christ's preexistence and preeminence means He is Lord over everything.
1:18 the head of the church. This emphasizes the organic, living relationship between Christ and His people. **beginning.** As Jesus is Lord over the original creation, so also He is Lord over the new creation (v. 15).
1:19 fullness. Paul declares that Christ is fully God and that there is nothing else other than Christ needed in our lives to have right standing before God.
1:20 reconcile everything to himself. Jesus seeks the eventual goal of not only reconciling humanity to Himself but to creation, which has been thrown out of kilter by sin (Rom. 8:19-25). **Christ's blood on the cross.** The irony of the gospel is that this work of redemption was completed through the gory, earthly act of crucifixion.
1:21 separated. Jews viewed Gentile idolatry and immorality as the chief evidence that humanity was in revolt against God. Paul utilizes that idea to contrast the Colossians' "before" and "after" status in Christ.
1:22 his physical body. The stress here is on Jesus' actual body, which died, rather than the church as the expression of Christ's body (v. 18). **holy and blameless . . . without a single fault.** While the false teachers taught that the Colossians needed something more in order to be truly spiritual, Paul uses the language both of sacrifice and the law court to emphasize that believers are completely acceptable to God through Christ (Rom. 8:1ff).
1:24 sufferings of Christ. Given Paul's stress on the once-for-all sufficiency of Christ's death as a sacrifice for sin (v. 22), he cannot mean that his sufferings add to the value of Christ's death. Rather, believers will continue to suffer as Christ would if He were still here. Paul's suffering results in the spread of the good news of redemption.
1:26 kept secret . . . has been revealed. The "mystery" of the gospel is revealed by God to all—including Gentiles—who believe. It is not a secret form of spiritual power as the false teachers claimed but the hope for eternity guaranteed by the presence of Christ within the believer.
1:28 perfect . . . Christ. Each Christian is perfect in Christ. Jesus stands wholly righteous on our behalf before God. We mature in our relationship with Him through obedience as we continue moving toward the goal of the completed work of Christ in us.

VICTORY OVER THE ENEMY

1. Do you consider your parents "permissive" or "strict"?

COLOSSIANS 2:6-23

2. What does "following him" (v. 6) involve (see 1:10-12)?
3. What are "the spiritual powers of this world" (vv. 8,20) and the "rulers and authorities" (vv. 10,15)? How did Christ give the Colossians victory over these?
4. What is the result of trying to base one's relationship with God on rule-keeping or private visions, as the false teachers were doing?
5. What is God saying to you in this passage about the key to a victorious and growing faith?

11 When you came to Christ, you were "circumcised," but not by a physical procedure. Christ performed a spiritual circumcision—the cutting away of your sinful nature.* 12 For you were buried with Christ when you were baptized. And with him you were raised to new life because you trusted the mighty power of God, who raised Christ from the dead.

13 You were dead because of your sins and because your sinful nature was not yet cut away. Then God made you alive with Christ, for he forgave all our sins. 14 He canceled the record of the charges against us and took it away by nailing it to the cross. 15 In this way, he disarmed* the spiritual rulers and authorities. He shamed them publicly by his victory over them on the cross.

16 So don't let anyone condemn you for what you eat or drink, or for not celebrating certain holy days or new moon ceremonies or Sabbaths. 17 For these rules are only shadows of the reality yet to come. And Christ himself is that reality. 18 Don't let anyone condemn you by insisting on pious self-denial or the worship of angels,* saying they have had visions about these things. Their sinful minds have made them proud, 19 and they are not connected to Christ, the head of the body. For he holds the whole body together with its joints and ligaments, and it grows as God nourishes it.

20 You have died with Christ, and he has set you free from the spiritual powers of this world. So why do you keep on following the rules of the world, such as, 21 "Don't handle! Don't taste! Don't touch!"? 22 Such rules are mere human teachings about things that deteriorate as we use them. 23 These rules may seem wise because they require strong devotion, pious self-denial, and severe bodily discipline. But they provide no help in conquering a person's evil desires.

LIVING THE NEW LIFE

3 Since you have been raised to new life with Christ, set your sights on the realities of heaven, where Christ sits in the place of honor at God's right hand. 2 Think about the things of heaven, not the things of earth. 3 For you died to this life, and your real life is hidden with Christ in God. 4 And when Christ, who is your* life, is revealed to the whole world, you will share in all his glory.

5 So put to death the sinful, earthly things lurking within you. Have nothing to do with sexual immorality, impurity, lust, and evil desires. Don't be greedy, for a greedy person is an idolater, worshiping the things of this world. 6 Because of these sins, the anger of God is coming.* 7 You used to do these things when your life was still part of this world. 8 But now is the time to get rid of anger, rage, malicious behavior, slander, and dirty language. 9 Don't lie to each other, for you have stripped off your old sinful nature and all its wicked deeds. 10 Put on your new nature, and be renewed as you learn to know your Creator and become like him. 11 In this new life, it doesn't matter if you are a Jew or a Gentile,* circumcised or uncircumcised, barbaric, uncivilized,* slave, or free. Christ is all that matters, and he lives in all of us.

12 Since God chose you to be the holy people he loves, you must clothe yourselves with tenderhearted

2:11 Greek *the cutting away of the body of the flesh.* **2:15** Or *he stripped off.* **2:18** Or *or worshiping with angels.* **3:4** Some manuscripts read *our.* **3:6** Some manuscripts read *is coming on all who disobey him.* **3:11a** Greek *a Greek.* **3:11b** Greek *Barbarian, Scythian.*

2:8 from human thinking. The false teachings were not based on the teachings of Christ but upon faulty ideas influenced by the "elemental forces" of the world, angelic beings that manipulated human affairs in opposition to God (1:16; 1 Cor. 2:6,8; Gal. 3:19; 4:3,9; Eph. 6:12).
2:10 complete . . . with Christ. Christ is fully God. **the head.** This stresses Christ's lordship over all creation (1:15-17). To go "beyond" Christ is to go backwards spiritually.
2:11 circumcised. True circumcision is through Christ spiritually, and not the removal of flesh.
2:14 the record of charges. This refers to a written agreement to pay back a debt or to obey a law. When fulfilled, the document was blotted out and canceled.
2:16 holy days or new moon ceremonies or Sabbaths. While this serves as a summary of the annual, monthly, and weekly Jewish holy days (1 Chron. 23:31), pagans also observed cycles of worship determined by astrological practices. The false teachers probably used the Jewish traditions to support their astrological calendar.
2:17 shadows . . . that reality. Hebrews 8:3-13 and 10:1-18 compared the work of Christ to the Old Testament sacrificial system (1 Cor. 5:7). While the false teachers claimed their ascetic practices were the pathway that led to the reality of spiritual experience, Paul asserts they only lead to the shadow-lands and not to a true spiritual life found in Christ.
2:23 evil desires. Paul plays with the false teacher's fondness for spiritual fulfillment by pointing out that their ascetic rules about the body ironically only fill up the "body" or the "flesh" (v. 18)."
3:1 raised . . . with the Messiah. As the Christian's *death* with Christ cut the bonds to the old authorities (2:20), so one's *life* with Christ creates new bonds with God and others. **set your sights on.** This is not encouraging escapism from earthly affairs. The point is that Christians are to shape their lives by the values of the heavenly world in which Christ sits enthroned as King rather than heeding rules based on the elemental spirits.
3:3 hidden with Christ. What God did in the past is now a present reality in Christ.
3:5 put to death. Believers are to daily turn away from attitudes and actions that reflect the old way of life. **sexual immorality . . . greedy.** This list of sins begins with external actions and proceeds to internal motives and attitudes (see also v. 8).
3:8 get rid of. Anger, slander, abusive talk, and the like have no place in the life of a Christian.
3:9 stripped off your old sinful nature. Literally, "to strip off." This phrase is also used to describe the putting off of the sinful nature through Christ's death (2:11), and Christ's victory over spiritual powers (2:15).
3:10 Put on your new nature. The lifestyle of Christians is patterned after the attitudes and actions of Christ who is at work within them (1 Cor. 15:45; Gal. 3:27). It's not enough to put off the old; the "new man" must be put on to replace the old.
3:11 uncivilized. Literally Scythian. The Greeks considered Scythians to be especially uncouth barbarians. Allegiance to Christ eradicates prideful divisions based on race, religion, culture, or social class (and gender—Gal. 3:28).
3:12-17 clothe yourselves. Paul uses the image of putting on new clothes to show how true spirituality involves "wearing" the Christ-like qualities of love, peace, and thankfulness (Rom. 13:14).

TAKE OUT THE TRASH

1. What did you really want as a child that you never got?

COLOSSIANS 3:1-25

2. How does God's forgiveness affect our willingness to forgive others (vv. 12-13)?
3. How does the message and truth from God help us to get along with others (vv.16-17)?
4. What do you need to "get rid of" (v. 8)? What should you "clothe yourself with" instead (v. 12)?
5. Verse 13 says, "Remember, the Lord forgave you." Whom do you need to forgive? How can you reach out to this person in the coming week?

mercy, kindness, humility, gentleness, and patience.
13 Make allowance for each other's faults, and forgive
anyone who offends you. Remember, the Lord forgave
you, so you must forgive others. 14 Above all, clothe
yourselves with love, which binds us all together in
perfect harmony. 15 And let the peace that comes from
Christ rule in your hearts. For as members of one
body you are called to live in peace. And always be
thankful.
16 Let the message about Christ, in all its richness,
fill your lives. Teach and counsel each other with all
the wisdom he gives. Sing psalms and hymns and
spiritual songs to God with thankful hearts. 17 And
whatever you do or say, do it as a representative of
the Lord Jesus, giving thanks through him to God the
Father.

INSTRUCTIONS FOR CHRISTIAN HOUSEHOLDS

18 Wives, submit to your husbands, as is fitting for
those who belong to the Lord.
19 Husbands, love your wives and never treat them
harshly.
20 Children, always obey your parents, for this
pleases the Lord. 21 Fathers, do not aggravate your
children, or they will become discouraged.
22 Slaves, obey your earthly masters in everything
you do. Try to please them all the time, not just when
they are watching you. Serve them sincerely because
of your reverent fear of the Lord. 23 Work willingly at
whatever you do, as though you were working for
the Lord rather than for people. 24 Remember that the
Lord will give you an inheritance as your reward,
and that the Master you are serving is Christ.* 25 But
if you do what is wrong, you will be paid back for the
wrong you have done. For God has no favorites.

4 Masters, be just and fair to your slaves. Remember
that you also have a Master—in heaven.

AN ENCOURAGEMENT FOR PRAYER

2 Devote yourselves to prayer with an alert mind
and a thankful heart. 3 Pray for us, too, that God will
give us many opportunities to speak about his mys-
terious plan concerning Christ. That is why I am here
in chains. 4 Pray that I will proclaim this message as
clearly as I should.
5 Live wisely among those who are not believers,
and make the most of every opportunity. 6 Let your
conversation be gracious and attractive* so that you
will have the right response for everyone.

PAUL'S FINAL INSTRUCTIONS AND GREETINGS

7 Tychicus will give you a full report about how I am
getting along. He is a beloved brother and faithful
helper who serves with me in the Lord's work. 8 I
have sent him to you for this very purpose—to let
you know how we are doing and to encourage you.
9 I am also sending Onesimus, a faithful and beloved
brother, one of your own people. He and Tychicus will
tell you everything that's happening here.

OPEN DOORS

1. In elementary school, who were two of your best friends? What was one quality about each one that stands out to you?

COLOSSIANS 4:1-18

2. In "speaking about his mysterious plan" of Jesus with others (vv. 2-6), what is the role of prayer?
3. Why is thankfulness such a key ingredient in a Christian's life (see 2:7; 3:15,17)?
4. What has helped you to grow the most in your prayer life?
5. What would happen at school if you and some of your friends followed Paul's model in verses 2-6?

3:24 Or *and serve Christ as your Master.* **4:6** Greek *and seasoned with salt.*

3:16 the message about Christ. While the false teachers don't "hold on to the head" (2:19), the message that the Colossians teach must be centered on Jesus. **in all its richness, fill your lives.** Spiritual fullness is rooted in a commitment to Christ. **Teach . . . each other.** The Christian faith is lived in community, not held in as a solely personal faith. All the aspects of worship listed here are to be carried out to build one another up as well as directing our hearts toward God.

3:18-22 submit. In Christ, this is transformed from a passive obedience to an authority to a specific, active application of Christ's call to put the needs and interest of others before one's own (Eph. 5:21-24; Phil. 2:4).

3:21 Fathers. This applies to both parents (Heb. 11:23).

4:2 Devote yourselves to prayer. See the example of the church in Acts 1:14; 2:42; and 6:4. **with an alert mind.** An allusion to Matthew 26:41 and Luke 18:1. This call to vigilance and spiritual alertness became part of the Apostles' teaching to Christians in general (Acts 20:31; 1 Cor. 16:13; 1 Thess. 5:6; 1 Peter 5:8).

4:3 in chains. Paul, imprisoned several times because Jewish opponents considered his missionary activity as subversive to their interests, probably wrote this letter while under the house arrest described in Acts 28.

4:5 make the most of every opportunity. An emphasis on being alert to God-given opportunities to bear witness to Christ in the course of daily life is in view.

4:7 Tychicus. Personal name meaning "fortunate." One of Paul's fellow workers in the ministry. A native of Asia Minor (Acts 20:4), he traveled with the apostle on the third missionary journey. Tychicus and Onesimus carried the Colossian letter from Paul (Col. 4:7-9) and were to relate to the church Paul's condition. Paul also sent Tychicus to Ephesus on one occasion (2 Tim. 4:12) and possibly to Crete on another (Titus 3:12). Tradition holds that he died a martyr.

4:9 Onesimus. The slave for whom Paul wrote his letter to Philemon. In his letter Paul pled with Philemon to free the servant because Onesimus had been so helpful to the apostle. Onesimus accompanied Tychicus in bearing Paul's letter to the church at Colossae .

10 Aristarchus, who is in prison with me, sends you his
greetings, and so does Mark, Barnabas's cousin. As you
were instructed before, make Mark welcome if he comes
your way. 11 Jesus (the one we call Justus) also sends his
greetings. These are the only Jewish believers among
my co-workers; they are working with me here for the
Kingdom of God. And what a comfort they have been!
12 Epaphras, a member of your own fellowship and
a servant of Christ Jesus, sends you his greetings. He
always prays earnestly for you, asking God to make
you strong and perfect, fully confident that you are
following the whole will of God. 13 I can assure you
that he prays hard for you and also for the believers
in Laodicea and Hierapolis.
14 Luke, the beloved doctor, sends his greetings,
and so does Demas. 15 Please give my greetings to our
brothers and sisters* at Laodicea, and to Nympha and
the church that meets in her house.
16 After you have read this letter, pass it on to the
church at Laodicea so they can read it, too. And you
should read the letter I wrote to them.
17 And say to Archippus, "Be sure to carry out the
ministry the Lord gave you."
18 HERE IS MY GREETING IN MY OWN HANDWRITING—
PAUL.

Remember my chains.
May God's grace be with you.

4:15 Greek *brothers*.

4:12 Epaphras. Personal name meaning "lovely." A native Colossian who established the church there and throughout the Lycus valley (1:7; Philem. 23). Paul's commendation here and in Colossians 1:7 substantiates his claim that the church had already heard the gospel. His ministry also included the churches at Laodicea and Hierapolis.

4:13 Laodicea. A city near Colosse. **Hierapolis.** A city about 12 miles northwest of Colosse and six miles north of Laodicea.

4:14 Luke, the beloved doctor. It is from this reference that we learn of Luke's profession. The various "we" passages in the book of Acts (16:10-17; 20:5–21:18; 27:1–28:16) indicate that Luke accompanied Paul at several points during his missionary work.

4:15 Nympha and the church that meets in her house. The Laodicean church, or at least part of it, followed the custom of other early churches in meeting in the homes of members who could accommodate them. Philemon's home was one of the sites of the congregation in Colosse (Philem. 1-2).

4:17 Archippus. In Philemon 2 he is called a "fellow soldier."

4:18 HERE IS MY GREETING IN MY OWN HANDWRITING—PAUL. Typically, others actually wrote Paul's letters at his dictation (Rom. 16:22), while he penned the final greeting as a mark of the letter's genuineness (1 Cor. 16:21; Gal. 6:11; 2 Thess. 3:17; Philem. 19). 2 Thessalonians 2:2 hints at the possibility that forged letters had been circulated in Paul's name.

INTRODUCTION TO

1 THESSALONIANS

PERSONAL READING PLAN

☐ 1 Thessalonians 1:1–2:16
☐ 1 Thessalonians 2:17–3:13
☐ 1 Thessalonians 4:1-12
☐ 1 Thessalonians 4:13–5:28

AUTHOR

The Apostle Paul wrote 1 Thessalonians.

DATE

First Thessalonians may well be the first document written in the New Testament. Many scholars believe that it is Paul's earliest letter, although a few say that Galatians has that honor. It is generally agreed that 1 Thessalonians was written about A.D. 50, during Paul's second missionary journey, not long after the founding of the church in Thessalonica. Paul probably wrote from Corinth, where he went after he left Athens. Timothy had returned with news from Thessalonica, and this letter was Paul's response to his report.

THEME

Living in the light of the coming of Christ.

HISTORICAL BACKGROUND

When Paul crossed over into Macedonia in A.D. 50, a new era began for Christianity. Now the gospel had spread to Europe and from there it flowed west through Greece into Italy, on to Spain and the limits of the Roman Empire. After the vision that sent Paul across the Aegean Sea to Philippi, he came to Thessalonica, which turned out to be a key stop in his pioneering work in Europe.

His stay in Thessalonica was brief and stormy. After he preached in the synagogue three Sabbaths, the Jews were so jealous of his success that they organized a mob by rounding up "some troublemakers from the marketplace" (Acts 17:5). The mob then rushed around looking for Paul and Silas. Failing to find them, they dragged Jason (at whose home Paul was staying) and a few other Christians before the city officials. They claimed that these men were associates of Paul who was preaching that Jesus, not Caesar, was king. That night after Jason and the others were released on bail, Paul and Silas slipped away to Berea.

PAUL'S CONCERNS ABOUT THE CHURCH AT THESSALONICA

Could three weeks of ministry produce a viable church at Thessalonica? Apparently this question troubled Paul. After ministering in Berea, Paul went on to Athens. He attempted to return to Thessalonica, but his efforts were frustrated (2:17-18). In his place he sent Timothy to see how they were doing and to give them what help he could (3:1-5).

What Timothy found was twofold. Generally the news was good. The converts were standing fast in their faith despite persecution and Paul's hasty departure from the city. In fact, they were even doing evangelistic work on their own. On the other hand, some of the converts had not fully understood the ethical implications of the gospel. In particular, there was laxity in sexual matters (4:3-8). Some felt it unnecessary to work and had become a burden to the others (4:11-12; 5:14). There was also misunderstanding about the second coming. They knew Christ would return again and rescue them from the "coming judgment" (1:9-10; 5:9-10). But some worried about those Christians who died prior to the Lord's return (4:13-14). Quite possibly Paul and the others had departed from Thessalonica before their teaching on this subject was complete. So Paul assures them that the dead in Christ were at no disadvantage. In fact, the first event of the second coming would be the resurrection of the dead (4:16).

In his letter to them, Paul expresses his relief and joy at their good progress in the gospel. He calls them "an example to all the believers in Greece" (1:7). Paul explains why he never returned to them and ends his letter with further instruction about the life of holiness and about the second coming.

THE CONVERTS

Who were these believers? Luke says (in Acts 17:1-4) that the church had its roots in the Jewish community. Some members of the synagogue where Paul preached, along with a large number of God-fearing Greeks—Gentiles who worshiped at the synagogue—and several prominent women had become convinced that Jesus was the Messiah and so became Christians. These included Jason, who opened his home to Paul and his companions, and Aristarchus, who was later Paul's traveling companion and prison mate (Acts 19:29; 20:4; 27:2; Col. 4:10; Philem. 24).

In fact, throughout Paul's ministry in Macedonia many prominent women were converted. Lydia, the businesswoman, was his first convert in Philippi (Acts 16:14). Many "prominent Greek women" were converted in Berea (Acts 17:12). Unlike most other women in the first century, the women in Macedonia were noted for their competence and the active role they played in society. As it turns out, they were crucial to the growth of the church in Europe.

The greater part of the church, however, consisted of converted pagans, as Paul's comment in 1:9 indicates: "... you turned away from idols to serve the living and true God."

THE CITY OF THESSALONICA

Thessalonica was a great city. Originally named Therme, its famous harbor became the base for the Persian fleet during Xerxes' invasion of Europe. In 315 B.C., Cassander, the Macedonian king, renamed the city Thessalonica after his wife, the half-sister of Alexander the Great. In 146 B.C. after Rome had taken over Greece, Thessalonica was made the capital of the Roman province of Macedonia. In 42 B.C., Rome granted it the status of a free city, which gave Thessalonica a high degree of autonomy.

The key to its importance was Thessalonica's location astride the famous Via Egnatia—the great Roman military road across northern Greece, which stretched from the Adriatic Sea on the west to Constantinople in the east. Hence trade between Rome and Asia Minor and points farther east flowed through Thessalonica, making it very wealthy. This was a crucial site for a church if Christianity were to spread throughout the world.

CHARACTERISTICS

First Thessalonians stands out from the four books that precede it because, unlike them, this letter does not emphasize theology and doctrine as much as some of the others. Rather, it reflects the concern, gratitude, disappointment, and joy of a beloved missionary who can't stop thinking about the church he left behind.

PASSAGES FOR TOPICAL GROUP STUDY

1:1-10 . . . . . HOLY SPIRIT and MODEL OF FAITH . Real-Life Power
2:1-16 . . . . . OPPOSITION and PERSECUTION . . . Misunderstood
2:17–3:13 . . ENCOURAGEMENT . . . . Encouragement to Press On
4:1-12 . . . . . DESIRES and SEXUAL PURITY . . . . Choosing the Best Way
4:13–5:11 . . JESUS' RETURN . . . . . . Heaven's Gonna Be a Blast

PASSAGES FOR GENERAL GROUP STUDY

5:12-28 . . . . God's Incredible Gifts to Us

GREETINGS FROM PAUL

1 This letter is from Paul, Silas,* and Timothy.
We are writing to the church in Thessalonica, to
you who belong to God the Father and the Lord Jesus
Christ.
May God give you grace and peace.

THE FAITH OF THE THESSALONIAN BELIEVERS

2 We always thank God for all of you and pray for you
constantly. 3 As we pray to our God and Father about
you, we think of your faithful work, your loving deeds,
and the enduring hope you have because of our Lord
Jesus Christ.
4 We know, dear brothers and sisters,* that God
loves you and has chosen you to be his own people.
5 For when we brought you the Good News, it was not
only with words but also with power, for the Holy
Spirit gave you full assurance* that what we said
was true. And you know of our concern for you from
the way we lived when we were with you. 6 So you
received the message with joy from the Holy Spirit
in spite of the severe suffering it brought you. In this
way, you imitated both us and the Lord. 7 As a result,
you have become an example to all the believers in
Greece—throughout both Macedonia and Achaia.*
8 And now the word of the Lord is ringing out from
you to people everywhere, even beyond Macedo-
nia and Achaia, for wherever we go we find people
telling us about your faith in God. We don't need to
tell them about it, 9 for they keep talking about the
wonderful welcome you gave us and how you turned
away from idols to serve the living and true God.
10 And they speak of how you are looking forward to
the coming of God's Son from heaven—Jesus, whom
God raised from the dead. He is the one who has res-
cued us from the terrors of the coming judgment.

PAUL REMEMBERS HIS VISIT

2 You yourselves know, dear brothers and sisters,*
that our visit to you was not a failure. 2 You know
how badly we had been treated at Philippi just before
we came to you and how much we suffered there. Yet
our God gave us the courage to declare his Good News
to you boldly, in spite of great opposition. 3 So you can
see we were not preaching with any deceit or impure
motives or trickery.
4 For we speak as messengers approved by God to
be entrusted with the Good News. Our purpose is to
please God, not people. He alone examines the mo-
tives of our hearts. 5 Never once did we try to win you
with flattery, as you well know. And God is our wit-
ness that we were not pretending to be your friends
just to get your money! 6 As for human praise, we have
never sought it from you or anyone else.
7 As apostles of Christ we certainly had a right to
make some demands of you, but instead we were like
children* among you. Or we were like a mother feed-
ing and caring for her own children. 8 We loved you
so much that we shared with you not only God's Good
News but our own lives, too.
9 Don't you remember, dear brothers and sisters,
how hard we worked among you? Night and day we
toiled to earn a living so that we would not be a bur-
den to any of you as we preached God's Good News
to you. 10 You yourselves are our witnesses—and so is
God—that we were devout and honest and faultless
toward all of you believers. 11 And you know that we
treated each of you as a father treats his own chil-
dren. 12 We pleaded with you, encouraged you, and
urged you to live your lives in a way that God would
consider worthy. For he called you to share in his
Kingdom and glory.

REAL-LIFE POWER

1. How do you stay motivated to improve in your chosen sport or field of study?

1 THESSALONIANS 1:1-10

2. What do you think Paul was referring to in verse 5 when he said, "The Good News it was not only with words, but also with power"?
3. How did the Thessalonians first become imitators of, and then models for, the faith (vv. 6-10)? What does this demonstrate about their growth in Christ?
4. In a time without any mass media, how do you suppose their faith became so legendary?
5. How can you tap into and experience the power of the Holy Spirit in your life?

1:1 Greek *Silvanus,* the Greek form of the name. 1:4 Greek *brothers.* 1:5 Or *with the power of the Holy Spirit, so you can have full assurance.* 1:7 *Macedonia* and *Achaia* were the northern and southern regions of Greece. 2:1 Greek *brothers;* also in 2:9, 14, 17. 2:7 Some manuscripts read *we were gentle.*

1:1 Silas. Silas was a representative of the Jerusalem church to the Christians at Antioch (Acts 15:22). He accompanied Paul on his second missionary journey during which they met Timothy, a young man highly spoken of by the Christians in his area (Acts 16:1-5). **Thessalonica.** Thessalonica was an important city in northern Greece, the capital of the province of Macedonia. Paul, Silvanus, and Timothy came to Thessalonica from Philippi where they planted the first church in Europe. As was Paul's custom, he went first to the Jewish synagogue where he reasoned with the Jews. He showed them from the Hebrew Scriptures that Messiah had to die and be raised from death. He further argued that this prophecy had been fulfilled in Jesus of Nazareth.

1:2 We always thank God for all of you. Paul most often began his letters with an affirmation of the recipients (Rom. 1:8; 1 Cor. 1:4; Eph. 1:15-16; Phil. 1:3; Col. 1:3; 2 Thess. 1:3).

1:3 faithful work . . . loving deeds . . . enduring hope. Paul and other New Testament writers use these words (or a combination of them) as a way of summing up the essentials of the Christian life (5:8; Rom. 5:1-5; 1 Cor. 13:13; Gal. 5:5-6; Eph. 4:2-5; Col. 1:4-5; Heb. 6:10-12; 10:22-24; 1 Peter 1:21-22). Faith in Christ, rooted in the promise (hope) of eternal life, is expressed by love to others. These are active concepts, the presence of which is evidenced by the tangible activities of sacrifice and service.

1:4 We know . . . God . . . has chosen you. Paul's purpose in reminding them of God's initiative in their salvation is to strengthen their hope in light of the pressures of external persecution (2:14) and internal uncertainty (4:13). **to be his own people.** This is a reminder of the intimacy with which "God the Father" relates to His people.

1:5 not only with words. Sometimes Paul's and the other apostles' preaching was accompanied by signs and miracles. That wasn't so in Thessalonica. But God's Spirit was strongly present with Paul and his listeners as he opened their Scriptures and showed them their Messiah had come.

2:2 God gave us the courage to declare his Good News to you boldly. Paul was as susceptible to fear in difficult situations as anyone (Acts 18:9-10; Phil. 1:20). His strength, as he continually declares, is found in God.

2:7 like children . . . like a mother. Paul eloquently described his love for his spiritual children.

2:11 as a father treats his own children. In some respects Paul was what a single parent must be—both mother (v. 7) and father. In the ancient world, the father's role was to see that his children learned how to live as responsible citizens.

MISUNDERSTOOD

1. When have you felt completely misunderstood or falsely accused?

1 THESSALONIANS 2:1-16

2. Judging from the way Paul was defending himself from the "opposition" (vv. 1-6), what was he most likely being accused of?
3. Why do you think it was so important for Paul to clear his name of these false accusations?
4. What difficulties were the Thessalonians facing (vv. 14-15)? How would Paul's example of "hanging in there" through persecution encourage them?
5. In what situation do you need to persevere—to press on? What person can be an example or help to get you through?

ENCOURAGEMENT TO PRESS ON

1. What struggle, competitive situation, or worry has hit you recently? How did you deal with it?

1 THESSALONIANS 2:17–3:13

2. What do you think Paul meant when he called the Thessalonian church his "hope," "joy," and "crown" (2:19)?
3. What in Timothy's report particularly encouraged Paul?
4. In what specific ways have you been encouraged by someone else's faith? Have you told that person about it?
5. Where do you need some encouragement in your life right now? (Be sure to talk to God about it too.) How can you encourage someone in your group, team, or circle of friends?

13 Therefore, we never stop thanking God that when
you received his message from us, you didn't think of
our words as mere human ideas. You accepted what
we said as the very word of God—which, of course,
it is. And this word continues to work in you who be-
lieve.
14 And then, dear brothers and sisters, you suffered
persecution from your own countrymen. In this way,
you imitated the believers in God's churches in Judea
who, because of their belief in Christ Jesus, suffered
from their own people, the Jews. 15 For some of the
Jews killed the prophets, and some even killed the
Lord Jesus. Now they have persecuted us, too. They
fail to please God and work against all humanity 16 as
they try to keep us from preaching the Good News of
salvation to the Gentiles. By doing this, they continue
to pile up their sins. But the anger of God has caught
up with them at last.

TIMOTHY'S GOOD REPORT ABOUT THE CHURCH

17 Dear brothers and sisters, after we were separated
from you for a little while (though our hearts never
left you), we tried very hard to come back because of
our intense longing to see you again. 18 We wanted
very much to come to you, and I, Paul, tried again
and again, but Satan prevented us. 19 After all, what
gives us hope and joy, and what will be our proud
reward and crown as we stand before our Lord Jesus
when he returns? It is you! 20 Yes, you are our pride
and joy.

3 Finally, when we could stand it no longer, we de-
cided to stay alone in Athens, 2 and we sent Timo-
thy to visit you. He is our brother and God's co-work-
er* in proclaiming the Good News of Christ. We sent
him to strengthen you, to encourage you in your faith,
3 and to keep you from being shaken by the troubles
you were going through. But you know that we are
destined for such troubles. 4 Even while we were
with you, we warned you that troubles would soon
come—and they did, as you well know. 5 That is why,
when I could bear it no longer, I sent Timothy to find
out whether your faith was still strong. I was afraid
that the tempter had gotten the best of you and that
our work had been useless.
6 But now Timothy has just returned, bringing us
good news about your faith and love. He reports that
you always remember our visit with joy and that
you want to see us as much as we want to see you.
7 So we have been greatly encouraged in the midst of
our troubles and suffering, dear brothers and sisters,*
because you have remained strong in your faith. 8 It
gives us new life to know that you are standing firm
in the Lord.
9 How we thank God for you! Because of you we
have great joy as we enter God's presence. 10 Night
and day we pray earnestly for you, asking God to let
us see you again to fill the gaps in your faith.
11 May God our Father and our Lord Jesus bring us
to you very soon. 12 And may the Lord make your love

3:2 Other manuscripts read *and God's servant;* still others read *and a co-worker,* or *and a servant and co-worker for God,* or *and God's servant and our co-worker.* 3:7 Greek *brothers.*

2:14 suffered from their own people, the Jews. As in John's Gospel, Paul often uses the term "Jews" when referring to the entrenched opposition of the Jewish religious leaders to Christianity. While the prime opposition to Jesus and the early church came from these leaders, it must be remembered that the first church was almost entirely Jewish in its makeup.

2:15-16 against all humanity . . . try to keep us from preaching . . . to the Gentiles. Prior to his visit to Thessalonica, Paul had encountered Jewish opposition in Antioch of Pisidia (Acts 13:50), Iconium (Acts 14:2), and Lystra, where he was stoned (Acts 14:19). The Thessalonian Jews forced Paul not only to leave that city, but also chased him out of Beroea (Acts 17:5,13). In Corinth, where he was probably living when he wrote this letter, he likewise suffered at the hands of Jewish opposition (Acts 18:12).

2:17 separated from you. Literally, this is "to be bereaved." It describes the anguish of a parent being forcibly separated from his or her children.

2:18 Satan prevented us. Whether Paul's forced change of plans was due to sickness, inability to make travel arrangements, or some other factor is unknown, but ultimately he attributes this frustration to Satan, God's adversary. At other times, Paul sees roadblocks to his plans as the leading of the Holy Spirit or the Spirit of Jesus (Acts 16:7). The difference may be that whereas one set of difficulties ends up in the spread of the gospel, at another time those difficulties would hinder that process and delay the mission that Paul was trying to accomplish.

3:10 to fill the gaps in your faith. The prayer that follows (vv. 11-13) and the final two chapters, which are full of both ethical and doctrinal instructions, give us hints about what Paul felt was lacking.

for one another and for all people grow and overflow,
just as our love for you overflows. 13 May he, as a re-
sult, make your hearts strong, blameless, and holy as
you stand before God our Father when our Lord Jesus
comes again with all his holy people. Amen.

LIVE TO PLEASE GOD

4 Finally, dear brothers and sisters,* we urge you in
the name of the Lord Jesus to live in a way that
pleases God, as we have taught you. You live this way
already, and we encourage you to do so even more.
2 For you remember what we taught you by the au-
thority of the Lord Jesus.
3 God's will is for you to be holy, so stay away from
all sexual sin. 4 Then each of you will control his
own body* and live in holiness and honor—5 not
in lustful passion like the pagans who do not know
God and his ways. 6 Never harm or cheat a fellow
believer in this matter by violating his wife,* for
the Lord avenges all such sins, as we have solemnly
warned you before. 7 God has called us to live holy
lives, not impure lives. 8 Therefore, anyone who re-
fuses to live by these rules is not disobeying human
teaching but is rejecting God, who gives his Holy
Spirit to you.
9 But we don't need to write to you about the im-
portance of loving each other,* for God himself has
taught you to love one another. 10 Indeed, you already
show your love for all the believers* throughout Mac-
edonia. Even so, dear brothers and sisters, we urge
you to love them even more.
11 Make it your goal to live a quiet life, minding your
own business and working with your hands, just as
we instructed you before. 12 Then people who are not
believers will respect the way you live, and you will
not need to depend on others.

THE HOPE OF THE RESURRECTION

13 And now, dear brothers and sisters, we want you
to know what will happen to the believers who have
died* so you will not grieve like people who have no
hope. 14 For since we believe that Jesus died and was
raised to life again, we also believe that when Jesus
returns, God will bring back with him the believers
who have died.
15 We tell you this directly from the Lord: We
who are still living when the Lord returns will not
meet him ahead of those who have died.* 16 For the
Lord himself will come down from heaven with a

CHOOSING THE BEST WAY

1. What teacher, coach, or other person has really challenged you to live up to your best?

1 THESSALONIANS 4:1-12

2. What is "God's will" regarding sexual conduct (v. 3)?
3. How can we control our bodies in "holiness and honor—not in lustful desires" (vv. 4-5)? What pressures at school and with your friends make it hard to maintain self-control?
4. What would you say to a Christian who tries to push physical intimacy, or take advantage of you on a date? How about a non-Christian?
5. What lines have you drawn and what decisions have you made for yourself about sexual purity?

HEAVEN'S GONNA BE A BLAST!

1. Who do you look forward to seeing in heaven someday?
2. What question would you like to ask God when you get to heaven?

1 THESSALONIANS 4:13—5:11

3. How can we have hope when it comes to death (4:13-14)? What's the importance of Jesus' resurrection?
4. On a scale of 1 ("This can't be happening now!") to 10 ("Let's do it!"), how prepared are you if Christ returned right now?
5. What can you do to better prepare yourself for His return (5:6-10)? How can you help to prepare others?

4:1 Greek *brothers;* also in 4:10, 13. 4:4 Or *will know how to take a wife for himself;* or *will learn to live with his own wife;* Greek reads *will know how to possess his own vessel.* 4:6 Greek *Never harm or cheat a brother in this matter.* 4:9 Greek *about brotherly love.* 4:10 Greek *the brothers.* 4:13 Greek *those who have fallen asleep;* also in 4:14. 4:15 Greek *those who have fallen asleep.* 4:16 Greek *the dead in Christ.*

3:12 may the Lord make your love for one another . . . grow and overflow. This petition highlights love as the defining element in a Christian's relationships with others.

4:1 live in a way that pleases God. Just as a spouse desires to please his or her mate, so the Christian's concern is how to please God.

4:3 be holy. This is an act and a process of being set apart for God's use. The emphasis here is that Christians are not to passively wait for God to make them holy but to pursue holiness in dependence upon the Spirit (Rom. 6:13; 8:13). **sexual sin.** This term is an inclusive one for sexual sin—including fornication, adultery, prostitution, and homosexuality, all of which were routine realities in pagan life. New Christians from this environment did not automatically give up the sexual sins that were part of their previous life but had to be instructed on the new way to live in Christ (1 Cor. 5:1-2; 6:9-18).

4:4 control his own body. Paul insists on sexual self-control in contrast to being controlled by lustful sexual impulses. He is saying that sexual activity must be only within marriage and is to be carried out in a way that respects the dignity and worth of the woman and the man.

4:10 all the believers throughout Macedonia. At this time, churches had been established at least in Philippi and Beorea. **even more.** A Christian lifestyle grows out of a desire to please God and love others. Paul encourages these new believers to press on in that direction, unfolding the limitless possibilities within each directive.

4:13 who have no hope. While Greek philosophy and some pagan cults speculated about the immortality of the soul and the afterlife, the rank and file among the people saw death as the end of everything

4:14 we believe that Jesus died and was raised to life again. This was probably a creedal statement Paul had passed on to this church earlier. He now draws out its implications for those who have died. **God will bring back with him the believers who have died.** Rather than being "left out" of the return of the Lord, those who have died in Christ will be the first to join the Lord in the air.

4:16 with a commanding shout . . . the voice of the archangel . . . the trumpet call of God. These elements of a military advance are used throughout Scripture as a picture of the manifestation of God's presence and glory when He comes to deliver His people and bring judgment upon their enemies (Ex. 19:13, 16, 19; Isa. 27:13; Zeph. 1:14-16; Matt. 24:31; 1 Cor. 15:52; Rev. 19:17).

commanding shout, with the voice of the archangel,
and with the trumpet call of God. First, the believers
who have died* will rise from their graves. 17 Then,
together with them, we who are still alive and re-
main on the earth will be caught up in the clouds
to meet the Lord in the air. Then we will be with the
Lord forever. 18 So encourage each other with these
words.

5 Now concerning how and when all this will
happen, dear brothers and sisters,* we don't
really need to write you. 2 For you know quite well
that the day of the Lord's return will come unex-
pectedly, like a thief in the night. 3 When people are
saying, "Everything is peaceful and secure," then
disaster will fall on them as suddenly as a pregnant
woman's labor pains begin. And there will be no
escape.
4 But you aren't in the dark about these things,
dear brothers and sisters, and you won't be surprised
when the day of the Lord comes like a thief.* 5 For
you are all children of the light and of the day; we
don't belong to darkness and night. 6 So be on your
guard, not asleep like the others. Stay alert and be
clearheaded. 7 Night is the time when people sleep
and drinkers get drunk. 8 But let us who live in the
light be clearheaded, protected by the armor of faith
and love, and wearing as our helmet the confidence
of our salvation.
9 For God chose to save us through our Lord Jesus
Christ, not to pour out his anger on us. 10 Christ died
for us so that, whether we are dead or alive when he
returns, we can live with him forever. 11 So encourage
each other and build each other up, just as you are
already doing.

PAUL'S FINAL ADVICE

12 Dear brothers and sisters, honor those who are your
leaders in the Lord's work. They work hard among
you and give you spiritual guidance. 13 Show them
great respect and wholehearted love because of their
work. And live peacefully with each other.
14 Brothers and sisters, we urge you to warn those
who are lazy. Encourage those who are timid. Take
tender care of those who are weak. Be patient with
everyone.
15 See that no one pays back evil for evil, but always
try to do good to each other and to all people.
16 Always be joyful. 17 Never stop praying. 18 Be
thankful in all circumstances, for this is God's will for
you who belong to Christ Jesus.
19 Do not stifle the Holy Spirit. 20 Do not scoff at
prophecies, 21 but test everything that is said. Hold on
to what is good. 22 Stay away from every kind of evil.

GOD'S INCREDIBLE GIFTS

1. What people, things, and circumstances are you particularly thankful for now, and why?

1 THESSALONIANS 5:12-28

2. From this passage, what are the ways we should help one another, especially other Christians (vv. 14-15)?
3. What is the goal and hope of the Christian life (vv. 23-24)? What assurance do we have that we will receive these incredible gifts?
4. Which command from verses 16-22 will you work on this week? Give a specific example of what you will do.
5. God's gifts are so much better and lasting than the stuff of this life. Thank Him now for His incredible gifts!

5:1 Greek *brothers;* also in 5:4, 12, 14, 25, 26, 27. 5:4 Some manuscripts read *comes upon you as if you were thieves.*

4:17 together with them . . . we . . . will be caught up in the clouds. When a royal figure came to a city, its inhabitants (or a delegation of them) went out of the city to greet this person and escort the royal procession into their town.
5:4 you aren't in the dark. The Apostle John as well as Paul often referred to people who lived with disregard to God as living in "darkness" (John 8:12; 2 Cor. 6:14; Eph. 6:12).
5:5 children of the light and of the day. In the Hebrew idiom, to be a "son of" someone or something meant to share in the characteristics of that person or thing. Christians who believe in the One who is the "light of the world" share the characteristics of that light.
5:6 not asleep. Continuing on with the metaphor of day and night, Christians, since they operate in "the day," must not "sleep" as are those who live in "the night." Whereas in 4:14, the metaphor of sleep meant death, here it refers to spiritual indifference and unawareness (Eph. 5:14).
5:7 drinkers get drunk. Paul is not talking about literal sobriety and drunkenness but uses it as a metaphor of how the Christian life of purpose, awareness, and direction contrasts with the "worldly" life of excess, spiritual insensitivity, and folly.
5:8 protected by the armor of faith and love, and wearing as our helmet the confidence of our salvation. Elsewhere Paul uses other virtues to describe the various parts of the Christian's armor (Rom. 13:12; 2 Cor. 6:7; 10:4; Eph. 6:13-17). Here faith, love, and confidence are the primary pieces of the spiritual armor that Christians need in order to stand at watch for the Day of the Lord. The "confidence of our salvation" is not a wish, but a firm confidence and expectation that give courage in the face of struggle.
5:9 save us through. Salvation includes both the present experience of God's grace and the confident fulfillment of that grace in the future.
5:10 Christ died for us. The Christian's hope for life is rooted in Jesus' death on their behalf (Rom. 5:6-8; 2 Cor. 5:15; 1 Peter 2:21-24). **whether we are dead or alive.** This most likely refers to the issue of whether we are alive or dead at the time of Christ's coming.
5:14 lazy. Second Thessalonians 3:6-15 is a strong admonition against idleness that stemmed from a "watching" for the Lord's return and which precluded doing anything else. Such people not only failed to pull their own weight but became a nuisance and weight upon others.
5:15 See that no one pays back evil for evil. The temptation to retaliate against persecution would have been strong but is admonished in Scripture (Prov. 25:21; Matt. 5:43-44; Rom. 12:17-20; 1 Peter 3:9).
5:16 Always be joyful. Joy springs not from circumstances but from the Holy Spirit giving believers a confidence of God's presence no matter what happens (Rom. 5:3-5; 2 Cor. 6:10; Gal. 5:22-23; Phil. 4:4; Col. 1:24).
5:17 Never stop praying. This does not mean one is literally to pray all the time in exclusion of other activities but that one continually approaches life with the spirit of prayer; that is, with a sense of dependency upon God and thankfulness to Him.
5:18 Be thankful in all circumstances. One has the confidence that all things are under the sovereign hand of God. **this is God's will.** God's will is not simply to get believers to do what is right but to produce a spirit of joy, dependence, and thankfulness within them.
5:19 Do not stifle the Holy Spirit. Fire is often used as an image of the Holy Spirit (Matt. 3:11; Acts 2:3). This "fire" can be dampened by disobedience (Eph. 4:30).
5:20 Do not scoff at prophecies. Whereas in Corinth the problem was an undiscerning obsession with spiritual gifts, perhaps here the problem was an undiscerning repression of them. Paul advocates a discerning acceptance instead (v. 21). It may be that "prophecies" about the Lord's return caused some of the anxiety in this church about this topic.

PAUL'S FINAL GREETINGS

[23] Now may the God of peace make you holy in every
way, and may your whole spirit and soul and body
be kept blameless until our Lord Jesus Christ comes
again. [24] God will make this happen, for he who calls
you is faithful.
[25] Dear brothers and sisters, pray for us.
[26] Greet all the brothers and sisters with a sacred
kiss.
[27] I command you in the name of the Lord to read
this letter to all the brothers and sisters.
[28] May the grace of our Lord Jesus Christ be with you.

5:26 a sacred kiss. Kissing on the cheek was a common greeting in this culture and still is in many Mediterranean and Middle Eastern countries. This kiss is similar to a handshake in Western cultures.

INTRODUCTION TO

2 THESSALONIANS

PERSONAL READING PLAN

☐2 Thessalonians 1:1-12 ☐2 Thessalonians 2:1-17 ☐2 Thessalonians 3:1-18

AUTHOR

The Apostle Paul wrote 2 Thessalonians.

DATE

Paul probably wrote 2 Thessalonians around A.D. 51; 1 and 2 Thessalonians or Galatians are the earliest letters of Paul.

THEME

Living in the light of the coming of Christ.

HISTORICAL BACKGROUND

See the Introduction to 1 Thessalonians.

CHARACTERISTICS

First and Second Thessalonians are very much alike. In fact, 2 Thessalonians covers almost the same content as 1 Thessalonians. There is thanksgiving for the faith and love of the Thessalonians, encouragement to them in the midst of their persecution, teaching about the second coming, and a warning against idleness. Second Thessalonians was probably written within months, if not weeks, of 1 Thessalonians. Why was it necessary?

Perhaps Paul's first letter to these young, untaught Christians produced a serious misunderstanding that necessitated a second, clarifying letter. Specifically, his teaching that "the day of the Lord's return will come unexpectedly, like a thief in the night" (1 Thess. 5:2) may have encouraged people to abandon normal pursuits to prepare for the second coming. Thus, he wrote 2 Thessalonians 2:1-12, outlining the events that must take place prior to the return of Christ. "The second coming is imminent," he seems to be saying, "but not so imminent that you have to stop everything else." Then he goes on to reiterate what he said in his earlier letter: Stand firm and do not be idle.

In fact, 1 and 2 Thessalonians complement one another concerning the second coming. Paul's teaching in 1 Thessalonians is mainly on a personal level, and it is given in response to questions about the lot of believers who have died before the second coming. In 2 Thessalonians believers are given further instructions on how they may be prepared for the great day. The ungodly will be taken by surprise, but believers will be awake and prepared for Christ's return.

PASSAGES FOR TOPICAL GROUP STUDY

3:6-15 ... MANAGING OUR TIME .... Who's Responsible

PASSAGES FOR GENERAL GROUP STUDY

1:1-12 .... Worthy of God's Kingdom
2:1-17 .... The Man of Lawlessness

GREETINGS FROM PAUL

1 This letter is from Paul, Silas,* and Timothy.
We are writing to the church in Thessalonica, to
you who belong to God our Father and the Lord Jesus
Christ.
2 May God our Father* and the Lord Jesus Christ
give you grace and peace.

ENCOURAGEMENT DURING PERSECUTION

3 Dear brothers and sisters,* we can't help but thank
God for you, because your faith is flourishing and
your love for one another is growing. 4 We proudly
tell God's other churches about your endurance and
faithfulness in all the persecutions and hardships you
are suffering. 5 And God will use this persecution to
show his justice and to make you worthy of his King-
dom, for which you are suffering. 6 In his justice he
will pay back those who persecute you.
7 And God will provide rest for you who are be-
ing persecuted and also for us when the Lord Jesus
appears from heaven. He will come with his mighty
angels, 8 in flaming fire, bringing judgment on those
who don't know God and on those who refuse to obey
the Good News of our Lord Jesus. 9 They will be pun-
ished with eternal destruction, forever separated
from the Lord and from his glorious power. 10 When
he comes on that day, he will receive glory from his
holy people—praise from all who believe. And this
includes you, for you believed what we told you about
him.
11 So we keep on praying for you, asking our God to
enable you to live a life worthy of his call. May he give
you the power to accomplish all the good things your
faith prompts you to do. 12 Then the name of our Lord
Jesus will be honored because of the way you live, and
you will be honored along with him. This is all made
possible because of the grace of our God and Lord,
Jesus Christ.*

EVENTS PRIOR TO THE LORD'S SECOND COMING

2 Now, dear brothers and sisters,* let us clarify
some things about the coming of our Lord Jesus
Christ and how we will be gathered to meet him.
2 Don't be so easily shaken or alarmed by those who
say that the day of the Lord has already begun. Don't
believe them, even if they claim to have had a spiri-
tual vision, a revelation, or a letter supposedly from

WORTHY OF GOD'S KINGDOM

1. What have your parents done right in raising you? What rewards and punishments worked best?

2 THESSALONIANS 1:1-12

2. What has happened to this church since Paul wrote 1 Thessalonians (v. 4)? How has persecution affected them?
3. Why is God waiting until the second coming to punish these persecutors? Who benefits from this delayed justice? How?
4. What quality do you think Paul admires most in these Christians?
5. Are your faith and endurance "worthy of God's Kingdom" right now? Why or why not?

THE MAN OF LAWLESSNESS

1. Who is the worst bad guy or nasty woman that you've seen on TV or in the movies?

2 THESSALONIANS 2:1-17

2. What must have been happening in Thessalonica to lead Paul to write this passage?
3. What is God's ultimate purpose in allowing the "man of lawlessness" to deceive people? What signs will mark his appearing?
4. How and why will God save His people (vv. 13-14)? In response to God's initiative and Paul's ministry, what are the people to do?
5. When is it difficult for you to "stand firm" (v. 15)? How does knowing the end of the story encourage you?

1:1 Greek *Silvanus,* the Greek form of the name. 1:2 Some manuscripts read *God the Father.* 1:3 Greek *Brothers.* 1:12 Or *of our God and our Lord Jesus Christ.* 2:1 Greek *brothers;* also in 2:13, 15.

1:1 Silas. Silas was a representative of the Jerusalem church to the Christians at Antioch (Acts 15:22). He accompanied Paul on his second missionary journey. Silas is mentioned again in 1 Peter 5:12 as the one who penned that letter under the authority of the Apostle Peter. **church.** In the New Testament, "church" can refer either to the whole, worldwide Christian community (1 Cor. 10:32; Col. 1:18), a gathering of believers that met in a house (Rom. 16:5), or all such gatherings within a given locality (Rom. 16:1; 1 Cor. 1:2). It is unlikely that this community had the time to develop a formal organizational structure. **Thessalonica.** Thessalonica was an important city in northern Greece, the capital of the province of Macedonia. Wealth, trade, and news flowed freely through this city between Rome on the west and Asia Minor on the east. **belong to God our Father and the Lord Jesus Christ.** The terms "Father" and "Lord" highlight the relationship of God and Jesus to the believer.

1:3-10 persecutions and hardships. This church is facing persecution and is unsure how to interpret its meaning: Is it a sign of God's disfavor? Or is it a sign of the nearness of the return of the Lord? Paul reassures them that their response to the suffering is notable and comforts them with the thought that the Lord will one day make right all the wrongs and provide the strength to endure.

1:5 will use this persecution. Their faithfulness in suffering for Christ and Paul's sharing of it with others is an evidence of their new life in Christ.

1:7-8 the Lord Jesus. Paul uses this term more in the Thessalonian letters than he does elsewhere. It stresses the royal authority of Jesus as the true King. It was this teaching that caused the original trouble in Thessalonica (Paul's opponents claimed he was proclaiming a rival king to Caesar—Acts 17:7) and may still have been the source of tension. **with his mighty angels, in flaming fire.** Fire and angels are commonly associated with God's presence with His people in the Old Testament.

1:9 will be punished with eternal destruction. *Paying the penalty* carries the sense of justice being done rather than that of vengeance. *Everlasting destruction* doesn't mean annihilation but rather eternal separation from God.

2:1-12 This passage, the heart of the letter, is meant to correct some erroneous ideas that had developed about the return of the Lord.

2:2 a spiritual vision, a revelation, or a letter supposedly from us. The false teaching was being supported by either a mistaken view of what Paul had written or preached, or by a forged letter that distorted his views. **the day of the Lord has already begun.** The nature of the false teaching here is not clear, but it apparently led some people to think the presence (*parousia*) of the Lord had already come in all its fullness. This led them to overlook the mundane issues of being a disciple, things such as work (3:6-15).

us. 3 Don't be fooled by what they say. For that day
will not come until there is a great rebellion against
God and the man of lawlessness* is revealed—the
one who brings destruction.* 4 He will exalt himself
and defy everything that people call god and every
object of worship. He will even sit in the temple of
God, claiming that he himself is God.
5 Don't you remember that I told you about all this
when I was with you? 6 And you know what is hold-
ing him back, for he can be revealed only when his
time comes. 7 For this lawlessness is already at work
secretly, and it will remain secret until the one who is
holding it back steps out of the way. 8 Then the man of
lawlessness will be revealed, but the Lord Jesus will
slay him with the breath of his mouth and destroy
him by the splendor of his coming.
9 This man will come to do the work of Satan with
counterfeit power and signs and miracles. 10 He will
use every kind of evil deception to fool those on their
way to destruction, because they refuse to love and
accept the truth that would save them. 11 So God will
cause them to be greatly deceived, and they will be-
lieve these lies. 12 Then they will be condemned for
enjoying evil rather than believing the truth.

BELIEVERS SHOULD STAND FIRM

13 As for us, we can't help but thank God for you, dear
brothers and sisters loved by the Lord. We are al-
ways thankful that God chose you to be among the
first* to experience salvation—a salvation that came
through the Spirit who makes you holy and through
your belief in the truth. 14 He called you to salvation
when we told you the Good News; now you can share
in the glory of our Lord Jesus Christ.
15 With all these things in mind, dear brothers and
sisters, stand firm and keep a strong grip on the teach-
ing we passed on to you both in person and by letter.
16 Now may our Lord Jesus Christ himself and God
our Father, who loved us and by his grace gave us
eternal comfort and a wonderful hope, 17 comfort you
and strengthen you in every good thing you do and
say.

PAUL'S REQUEST FOR PRAYER

3 Finally, dear brothers and sisters,* we ask you
to pray for us. Pray that the Lord's message will
spread rapidly and be honored wherever it goes, just

WHO'S RESPONSIBLE?

1. What was your first paying job?
2. How do you typically spend your free time?

2 THESSALONIANS 3:6-15

3. How does the "command" in verse 10 apply to Christians today?
4. Why is the way we manage our time and energies important to God according to this passage?
5. In light of the command in verse 6, what changes, if any, do you need to make regarding the people you hang out with?
6. What's one thing you would like to change this week in how you spend your time?

as when it came to you. 2 Pray, too, that we will be res-
cued from wicked and evil people, for not everyone is
a believer. 3 But the Lord is faithful; he will strengthen
you and guard you from the evil one.* 4 And we are
confident in the Lord that you are doing and will con-
tinue to do the things we commanded you. 5 May the
Lord lead your hearts into a full understanding and
expression of the love of God and the patient endur-
ance that comes from Christ.

AN EXHORTATION TO PROPER LIVING

6 And now, dear brothers and sisters, we give you this
command in the name of our Lord Jesus Christ: Stay
away from all believers* who live idle lives and don't
follow the tradition they received* from us. 7 For you
know that you ought to imitate us. We were not idle
when we were with you. 8 We never accepted food
from anyone without paying for it. We worked hard
day and night so we would not be a burden to any
of you. 9 We certainly had the right to ask you to feed
us, but we wanted to give you an example to follow.
10 Even while we were with you, we gave you this
command: "Those unwilling to work will not get to
eat."
11 Yet we hear that some of you are living idle lives,
refusing to work and meddling in other people's

2:3a Some manuscripts read *the man of sin.* **2:3b** Greek *the son of destruction.* **2:13** Some manuscripts read *chose you from the very beginning.* **3:1** Greek *brothers;* also in 3:6, 13. **3:3** Or *from evil.* **3:6a** Greek *from every brother.* **3:6b** Some manuscripts read *you received.*

2:3 great rebellion against God . . . man of lawlessness. Other passages foresee a time when the powers of evil will rise up (Matt. 24; 1 Tim. 4:1-3), and this will be centered on the rise of an antichrist (1 John 4:3), or false prophets (Matt. 24:5; Rev. 16:13).

2:4 He will even sit in the temple of God. Paul's description of this figure here is steeped in Old Testament apocalyptic imagery (Ezek. 28:2; Dan. 7:25; 8:9-12; 11:36-37; Zech. 3:1). The "man of lawlessness" sets himself in total opposition to God by claiming the prerogatives of God (Mark 13:14).

2:6-7 you know what is holding him back . . . steps out of the way. God restrains sin and the man of lawlessness through the work of the Holy Spirit.

2:11 God will cause them to be greatly deceived. Because people refuse to embrace the gospel, God acts in such a way as to confirm their disbelief. First Kings 22:23 and Ezekiel 14:9 tell of God sending a "lying spirit" into so-called prophets who only served to confirm the rebellion that was in the hearts of their listeners.

2:13 God chose you to be among the first. Paul often refers to God's initiative in bringing people to salvation as a way of reassuring Christians in times of suffering.

3:2 wicked and evil people. The Thessalonians would be well aware of the opposition that Paul encountered time and time again, since he met with such resistance in their own city (Acts 17:1-9; 1 Thess. 2:1-2). In Corinth, where Paul was living when he wrote this letter, he faced such strong resistance that he needed a special word from the Lord to keep on (Acts 18:9). The news of their faithfulness was an encouragement (1 Thess. 3:7).

3:5 patient endurance that comes from Christ. The prayer is that the Thessalonians realize the fullness of God's love for them so that they draw courage from Christ's perseverance as a model for their own.

3:6 Stay away from all believers who live idle lives. While these people are not to be considered as enemies of the gospel (v. 15), they need to be disciplined so they will give up their mistaken practice. The purpose of such discipline is a "tough love" approach to correcting a potentially serious problem, yet it is to be carried out in a way that communicates that the "family ties" are still strong.

3:11 refusing to work and meddling in other people's business. These people are bothering others with their false notions, probably trying to convince them to wait for the Day of the Lord with them. Such action would also give a negative impression of the Christian community to outsiders as it would appear that they are lazy and content to live off the income of others.

business. 12 We command such people and urge them in the name of the Lord Jesus Christ to settle down and work to earn their own living. 13 As for the rest of you, dear brothers and sisters, never get tired of doing good.

14 Take note of those who refuse to obey what we say in this letter. Stay away from them so they will be ashamed. 15 Don't think of them as enemies, but warn them as you would a brother or sister.*

PAUL'S FINAL GREETINGS

16 Now may the Lord of peace himself give you his peace at all times and in every situation. The Lord be with you all.

17 HERE IS MY GREETING IN MY OWN HANDWRITING—PAUL. I DO THIS IN ALL MY LETTERS TO PROVE THEY ARE FROM ME.

18 May the grace of our Lord Jesus Christ be with you all.

3:15 Greek *as a brother.*

3:12 settle down and work. Throughout church history there have been groups that have set the date for the return of the Lord, and responded by abandoning the normal pursuits of life in a feverish state of religious excitement. The end result is disenchantment and a discrediting of the gospel. In contrast, Paul wants them to live in peace, providing for their own needs (1 Thess. 4:11-12).

3:16 may the Lord of peace himself give you his peace at all times. At times, "peace" is used as a summary of all the benefits that Christ gives to His people (John 20:21,26; Rom. 15:33; Phil. 4:9). Paul prays that peace would mark their lives both personally and as a church.

3:17 Here is my greeting is my own handwriting—Paul. Paul typically used a secretary to write his letters. Tertius wrote Romans (Rom. 16:22). Tychicus, who delivered the letters of Ephesians and Colossians, may have penned those as well, and Silas (1 Peter 5:12) may have written the Thessalonian letters. Sometimes Paul calls attention to the fact that he has actually penned the final greeting (1 Cor. 16:21; Gal. 6:11), which may be to assure the recipients of the authenticity of the letter that he is sending them.

INTRODUCTION TO

1 TIMOTHY

PERSONAL READING PLAN

☐ 1 Timothy 1:1–2:15
☐ 1 Timothy 3:1–4:16
☐ 1 Timothy 5:1–6:2
☐ 1 Timothy 6:3-21

AUTHOR

The Apostle Paul was most likely the author of 1 Timothy. However, based on considerations of vocabulary and style, the Pauline authorship of the Pastoral Epistles (1 and 2 Timothy, and Titus) has been questioned by some scholars.

DATE

First Timothy was written about A.D. 63–65.

THEME

A faithful ministry.

HISTORICAL BACKGROUND

When Paul first met Timothy, he was living at Lystra in the Roman province of Galatia (modern Turkey). Timothy was the child of a mixed marriage. His father was a Gentile, and his mother was Jewish (Acts 16:1). Timothy, along with his mother Eunice and his grandmother Lois, was probably converted during Paul's first missionary journey (Acts 14:8-25; compare 2 Tim. 3:10-11). By the time of Paul's second visit to the area a year or two later, Timothy had matured so quickly that the local church recommended Timothy to Paul as a helpful traveling companion (Acts 16:2). However, Paul decided that Timothy must be circumcised first to legitimize him in the eyes of Paul's Jewish critics. Without circumcision, they would have considered him a Gentile.

From this point on, Timothy works alongside Paul (Rom. 16:21; 1 Cor. 16:10; Phil. 2:22; 1 Thess. 3:2). He collaborated in the writing of six of Paul's letters (1 and 2 Thess., 2 Cor., Phil., Col. and Philem.). He was Paul's trusted representative on three missions before this one in Ephesus (to Thessalonica around A.D. 50; to Corinth between A.D. 53 and 54; and to Philippi around A.D. 60–62).

Timothy was more than a colleague of Paul's. Paul called him "my beloved and faithful child in the Lord" (1 Cor. 4:17). In Philippians 2:20-22, the aging apostle says: "I have no one else like Timonty . . . But you know how Timothy has proved himself. Like a son with his father, he has served with me in preaching the Good News."

AUDIENCE

The three so-called Pastoral Epistles (plus Philemon) are set apart from the other letters written by Paul; they are addressed to persons, not churches. In 1 Timothy, Paul wrote his instructions to the church via Timothy, since the local church leadership was itself the problem. There are few personal remarks in 1 Timothy, and all of these are directed toward Timothy's commission to restore proper order in the church (see 1:18-19; 4:6-16; 6:11-21).

PURPOSE

Paul tells us why he wrote 1 Timothy: "When I left for Macedonia, I urged you to stay there in Ephesus and stop those whose teaching is contrary to the truth" (1:3).

"I am writing these things to you now, even though I hope to be with you soon, so that if I am delayed, you will know how people must conduct themselves in the household of God. This is the church of the living God, which is the pillar and foundation of the truth" (3:14-15).

Timothy had been left in Ephesus to prevent those whose faith was "shipwrecked" (1:19) from corrupting the rest of the church (see 2 Tim. 2:17-18). He was Paul's apostolic delegate, taking temporary charge of the Ephesian church during the crises it was facing.

THE FALSE TEACHERS

Who were these false teachers who had so upset the Ephesian church? The best guess is that they were elders of that church! It is clear that the teaching in Ephesians was done by the elders (3:2; 5:17). Furthermore, Paul devotes considerable space to outlining qualifications for leaders in the church. These qualifications contrast sharply with what he says about the false teachers. For example, the false teachers said it was "wrong to be married" (4:3). Paul says that an overseer (elder), in contrast, "must be . . . faithful to his wife" and he "must manage his own family well" (3:2,4-5; see also 3:12). The false teachers believed "a show of godliness is just a way to become wealthy" (6:5), whereas an elder must "not love money" (3:3). In other words, Paul is saying: "Here is what true elders should be like, in contrast to your erring elders." Finally in 5:17-25, he outlines the process of selection and discipline of elders "who sin" (5:20).

Paul had a sense that this might happen in Ephesus. In his farewell address he said, "Even some men from your own group will rise up and distort the truth in order to draw a following" (Acts 20:30).

From various references (2:9-15; 5:11-15; 2 Tim. 3:6-7), it appears that these false teachers were listened to, supported, and encouraged by some of the women in the church, especially younger widows. Also, it is likely that the church in Ephesus was not a single large body that met together on Sunday. Rather, it consisted of a number of house churches, some of which had been taken over by the false teachers.

THE NATURE OF THE FALSE TEACHING

Since we have only Paul's response to the problem, we are forced to figure out the nature of the false teaching. From the text, it appears that the false teachers were involved in questionable speculation rather than the teaching of accepted Christian doctrine. Furthermore, the teachers were proud, arrogant, argumentative, and greedy. They used religion to make money and gain power. Their false teaching was connected with the Old Testament, but it also had an aspect of self-denial and a strong Greek element. It sounds much like the false teaching in the Lycus Valley churches (see the Introduction to Colossians).

PASSAGES FOR TOPICAL GROUP STUDY

1:1-11 . . . FALSE TEACHERS . . . . Watch Out for False Teachers
1:12-20 . . FAILURE EVER . . . . Beyond God's Love
3:1-16 . . . STRONG LEADERS . . . . Stepping Up to Lead
4:1-16 . . . YOUNG and GIFTS TO SERVE . . . . . No Guts, No Glory
5:1–6:2 . . HELPING OTHERS and AUTHORITY . . . . Lending a Helping Hand
6:3-21 . . . MONEY and WEALTH . . . . Money Issues

PASSAGES FOR GENERAL GROUP STUDY

2:1-15 . . . . Finding Worth in Christ

GREETINGS FROM PAUL

1 This letter is from Paul, an apostle of Christ Jesus, appointed by the command of God our Savior and Christ Jesus, who gives us hope.

2 I am writing to Timothy, my true son in the faith.

May God the Father and Christ Jesus our Lord give you grace, mercy, and peace.

WARNINGS AGAINST FALSE TEACHINGS

3 When I left for Macedonia, I urged you to stay there in Ephesus and stop those whose teaching is contrary to the truth. 4 Don't let them waste their time in endless discussion of myths and spiritual pedigrees. These things only lead to meaningless speculations,* which don't help people live a life of faith in God.*

5 The purpose of my instruction is that all believers would be filled with love that comes from a pure heart, a clear conscience, and genuine faith. 6 But some people have missed this whole point. They have turned away from these things and spend their time in meaningless discussions. 7 They want to be known as teachers of the law of Moses, but they don't know what they are talking about, even though they speak so confidently.

8 We know that the law is good when used correctly. 9 For the law was not intended for people who do what is right. It is for people who are lawless and rebellious, who are ungodly and sinful, who consider nothing sacred and defile what is holy, who kill their father or mother or commit other murders. 10 The law is for people who are sexually immoral, or who practice homosexuality, or are slave traders,* liars, promise breakers, or who do anything else that contradicts the wholesome teaching 11 that comes from the glorious Good News entrusted to me by our blessed God.

PAUL'S GRATITUDE FOR GOD'S MERCY

12 I thank Christ Jesus our Lord, who has given me strength to do his work. He considered me trustworthy and appointed me to serve him, 13 even though I used to blaspheme the name of Christ. In my insolence, I persecuted his people. But God had mercy on me because I did it in ignorance and unbelief. 14 Oh, how generous and gracious our Lord was! He filled me with the faith and love that come from Christ Jesus.

15 This is a trustworthy saying, and everyone should accept it: "Christ Jesus came into the world to save sinners"—and I am the worst of them all. 16 But God had mercy on me so that Christ Jesus could use me as a prime example of his great patience with even the worst sinners. Then others will realize that they, too, can believe in him and receive eternal life. 17 All honor and glory to God forever and ever! He is the eternal King, the unseen one who never dies; he alone is God. Amen.

TIMOTHY'S RESPONSIBILITY

18 Timothy, my son, here are my instructions for you, based on the prophetic words spoken about you earlier. May they help you fight well in the Lord's battles. 19 Cling to your faith in Christ, and keep your conscience clear. For some people have deliberately violated their consciences; as a result, their faith has

WATCH OUT FOR FALSE TEACHERS!

1. What is your favorite topic to debate? How often do you win?

1 TIMOTHY 1:1-11

2. Why does Paul consider Timothy to be his "true son in the faith" (v. 2)?
3. What kind of problem is Timothy facing? What do you think is motivating the people causing the problem (vv. 4,7)?
4. What is the major contrast in motive between Paul and Timothy and these false teachers (v. 5)?
5. What does this passage teach you regarding the proper response to false teachers? How should your response be different in different situations, i.e., school vs. church?

NEVER BEYOND GOD'S LOVE

1. What is the worst thing you've gotten busted for by your parents or a teacher? What did you learn from it?
2. Who has shown you the most patience when you've failed?

1 TIMOTHY 1:12-20

3. Why did Jesus come to this world (v. 15)? Why was Paul reminding Timothy about this belief?
4. What was causing Paul to talk about himself as he does in verses 13 and 15? Do you think it hurt the way the church thought about him as their leader, and why?
5. How can you let God use your failures the way He used Paul's (v. 16)?

1:4a Greek *in myths and endless genealogies, which cause speculation.* **1:4b** Greek *a stewardship of God in faith.* **1:10** Or *kidnappers.*

1:1 Paul, an apostle. When Paul uses the designation "an apostle" in his salutation, it is because his authority is in question or because he has an "official" word for the recipients of the letter

1:3 stay there in Ephesus. Paul had to go on to Macedonia, leaving Timothy behind in Ephesus. As he indicates in 3:15, the purpose of this letter is to instruct Timothy in his role while there in case Paul is delayed in returning to Ephesus (which according to 2 Timothy is exactly what happened). **Ephesus.** The capital of the Roman Province of Asia. Ephesus was one of the largest and most impressive cities in the ancient world. The church in Ephesus apparently flourished. It was not a single congregation but rather a collection of house churches (1 Cor. 16:19). Paul's ministry in Ephesus was strategic in the spread of Christianity to the entire province of Asia (Acts 19:10).

1:10 sexually immoral, or who practice homosexuality. The seventh commandment was interpreted by the Jewish teachers (as well as Christian orthodoxy) to refer to all types of sexual sin.

1:13 used to. Paul is utterly amazed that he of all people was chosen for this high calling, given his past record. **blaspheme.** Paul had denied Christ and tried to force others to do the same (Acts 26:11). **in ignorance and in unbelief.** Paul is clearly not saying that he had received mercy because he was without guilt. All he is saying is that he acted "unintentionally" instead of "defiantly," using a common Old Testament distinction (Num. 15:22-31; Luke 23:34).

been shipwrecked. 20 Hymenaeus and Alexander are two examples. I threw them out and handed them over to Satan so they might learn not to blaspheme God.

INSTRUCTIONS ABOUT WORSHIP

2 I urge you, first of all, to pray for all people. Ask God to help them; intercede on their behalf, and give thanks for them. 2 Pray this way for kings and all who are in authority so that we can live peaceful and quiet lives marked by godliness and dignity. 3 This is good and pleases God our Savior, 4 who wants everyone to be saved and to understand the truth. 5 For,

> There is one God and one Mediator who can reconcile God and humanity—the man Christ Jesus. 6 He gave his life to purchase freedom for everyone.

FINDING WORTH

1. How did you feel about church or Sunday School as a little kid?

1 TIMOTHY 2:1-15

2. Who are the people Paul is asking us to pray for—that they would "be saved and to understand the truth" (vv. 1,4,6,7)?
3. In this letter, Paul was dealing with a special cultural problem involving women in ministry at Ephesus (see 1:3-4; 2 Tim. 3:6-7). How should we then apply verses 9-15 to worship in the 21st century?
4. How do verses 12-15 compare with what Paul said in Galatians 3:28? Why the difference?
5. What have you found in Christ that affirms your worth, even when others put you down?

This is the message God gave to the world at just the right time. 7 And I have been chosen as a preacher and apostle to teach the Gentiles this message about faith and truth. I'm not exaggerating—just telling the truth.

8 In every place of worship, I want men to pray with holy hands lifted up to God, free from anger and controversy.

9 And I want women to be modest in their appearance.* They should wear decent and appropriate clothing and not draw attention to themselves by the way they fix their hair or by wearing gold or pearls or expensive clothes. 10 For women who claim to be devoted to God should make themselves attractive by the good things they do.

11 Women should learn quietly and submissively. 12 I do not let women teach men or have authority over them.* Let them listen quietly. 13 For God made Adam first, and afterward he made Eve. 14 And it was not Adam who was deceived by Satan. The woman was deceived, and sin was the result. 15 But women will be saved through childbearing,* assuming they continue to live in faith, love, holiness, and modesty.

LEADERS IN THE CHURCH

3 This is a trustworthy saying: "If someone aspires to be a church leader,* he desires an honorable position." 2 So a church leader must be a man whose life is above reproach. He must be faithful to his wife.* He must exercise self-control, live wisely, and have a good reputation. He must enjoy having guests in his home, and he must be able to teach. 3 He must not be a heavy drinker* or be violent. He must be gentle, not quarrelsome, and not love money. 4 He must manage his own family well, having children who respect and obey him. 5 For if a man cannot manage his own household, how can he take care of God's church?

6 A church leader must not be a new believer, because he might become proud, and the devil would cause him to fall.* 7 Also, people outside the church

2:9 Or *to pray in modest apparel.* **2:12** Or *teach men or usurp their authority.* **2:15** Or *will be saved by accepting their role as mothers,* or *will be saved by the birth of the Child.* **3:1** Or *an overseer,* or *a bishop;* also in 3:2, 6. **3:2** Or *must have only one wife,* or *must be married only once;* Greek reads *must be the husband of one wife;* also in 3:12. **3:3** Greek *must not drink too much wine;* similarly in 3:8. **3:6** Or *he might fall into the same judgment as the devil.*

1:20 Hymenaeus and Alexander. Hymenaeus is mentioned again in 2 Timothy 2:17 (along with Philetus) as one who taught that the resurrection was already past. An Alexander (a coppersmith) is also mentioned in 2 Timothy 4:14-15 as having done great harm to Paul. **handed them over to Satan.** Paul excommunicated them from the church; i.e., they were expelled from the fellowship of other followers of Christ and sent back into the world, which is Satan's realm (1 Cor. 5:5).

2:9 appropriate. Also translated "propriety." This is the central issue for Paul in this area (vv. 10, 15). He is concerned that the women in the church live in a way that is considered decent and modest by the culture.

2:12 I do not let. The issue of the role of women in the church is complex, and often causes disagreements among believers. Scripture affirms that women functioned in the early church with service, influence, leadership, and teaching. Mark's mother, Mary, and Lydia of Thyatira opened their homes for meetings of believers and practiced hospitality (Acts 12:12; 16:14-15). Pricilla, with here husband Aquila, instructed Apollos in individual ministry (Acts 18:26). Women offered themselves in special ministries to Jesus (John 12:1-11). Paul obviously did not feel that women could not engage in ministry, as evidenced by his statements in Romans 16:1-3 and Philippians 4:2-3. He encouraged women to work within the divinely given framework based on the natural order of creation and appropriateness of function. He commended women for learning (2:11) but didn't allow women to teach men or rule over men—and that within two spheres, the home and church.

3:1 elder. Sometimes translated "bishop." The words "overseer" and "elder" were used interchangeably.

3:2 above reproach. Paul begins with an all-encompassing category: there should be no obvious defect in the character of the overseer that would cause people to question the appointment. **faithful to his wife.** Literally, "a one-woman man." Paul could mean four things by this phrase. First, that church leaders must be married, in contrast to the false teachers who forbade marriage. Second, that polygamy was forbidden. Third, that second marriages were forbidden whether due to divorce or death of one's spouse. (Yet, he gives in 5:14 what amounts almost to a "command" to young widows to remarry.) Fourth, the most likely meaning, that sexual faithfulness to one's spouse was demanded; that is, the married life of the overseer must be exemplary—in contrast to the widespread infidelity of that day. **self-control.** This was considered in Greek literature to be a great virtue. If people are self-controlled in their outer conduct, it is because they are respectable in their inner lives. **enjoy having guests.** Overseers must be willing to open up their homes to guests. It was a common practice in the first century to offer hospitality to travelers since the inns were notorious for dirtiness and immorality, not to mention expense (5:10; Rom. 12:13; 1 Pet. 4:9). **be able to teach.** This is the one quality that implies a function. Paul says more about this in 5:17.

3:3 not be a heavy drinker. Paul is not forbidding all drinking of wine (which was widely used in his time due to poor water supplies), but he is forbidding over-indulgence. **must be gentle, not quarrelsome.** "Gentle" refers to those who do not seek to apply the letter of the law in cases where to do so would bring injustice.

3:6 new believer. It is a temptation for a church to unwisely put into office people of worldly standing and influence who have been recently converted.

STEPPING UP TO LEAD

1. When have you served as a leader (in school, athletics, a club, a job)? What did you enjoy about it?

1 TIMOTHY 3:1-16

2. Why is this list of qualifications for leadership focused on the outward as well as on inward character traits? How does this list line up with your idea of a good leader?
3. Verse 8 says leaders in the church must be "well respected," and verse 10 says they must be "closely examined" before they can lead. In what areas do you need to step up so you can become a strong leader?
4. What can you do to prepare yourself to be a leader in God's work—both for the future and right now?

must speak well of him so that he will not be dis-
graced and fall into the devil's trap.
8 In the same way, deacons must be well respected
and have integrity. They must not be heavy drinkers
or dishonest with money. 9 They must be committed to
the mystery of the faith now revealed and must live
with a clear conscience. 10 Before they are appointed
as deacons, let them be closely examined. If they pass
the test, then let them serve as deacons.
11 In the same way, their wives* must be respect-
ed and must not slander others. They must exercise
self-control and be faithful in everything they do.
12 A deacon must be faithful to his wife, and he must
manage his children and household well. 13 Those
who do well as deacons will be rewarded with re-
spect from others and will have increased confidence
in their faith in Christ Jesus.

THE TRUTHS OF OUR FAITH

14 I am writing these things to you now, even though I
hope to be with you soon, 15 so that if I am delayed, you
will know how people must conduct themselves in
the household of God. This is the church of the living
God, which is the pillar and foundation of the truth.
16 Without question, this is the great mystery of our
faith*:

Christ* was revealed in a human body
and vindicated by the Spirit.*
He was seen by angels
and announced to the nations.
He was believed in throughout the world
and taken to heaven in glory.

WARNINGS AGAINST FALSE TEACHERS

4 Now the Holy Spirit tells us clearly that in the last
times some will turn away from the true faith;
they will follow deceptive spirits and teachings that
come from demons. 2 These people are hypocrites and
liars, and their consciences are dead.*
3 They will say it is wrong to be married and wrong
to eat certain foods. But God created those foods to
be eaten with thanks by faithful people who know
the truth. 4 Since everything God created is good, we
should not reject any of it but receive it with thanks.
5 For we know it is made acceptable* by the word of
God and prayer.

A GOOD SERVANT OF CHRIST JESUS

6 If you explain these things to the brothers and sis-
ters,* Timothy, you will be a worthy servant of Christ
Jesus, one who is nourished by the message of faith
and the good teaching you have followed. 7 Do not
waste time arguing over godless ideas and old wives'
tales. Instead, train yourself to be godly. 8 "Physical
training is good, but training for godliness is much
better, promising benefits in this life and in the life
to come." 9 This is a trustworthy saying, and every-
one should accept it. 10 This is why we work hard and

NO GUTS, NO GLORY

1. How often do you exercise? Are you in better physical or spiritual shape?
2. What is one bad habit you would like to break? What healthy habit would you like to start?

1 TIMOTHY 4:1-16

3. What are some parallels between physical training and spiritual training (v. 8)? Why is training in godliness even more important than physical training alone?
4. When have you felt ignored or looked down on because you are young? How can you still influence others for Christ (v.12)?
5. What gifts (capacity for serving in His work) do you feel God has given you? How can you more fully use these gifts to please God?

3:11 Or *the women deacons.* The Greek word can be translated *women* or *wives.* 3:16a Or *of godliness.* 3:16b Greek *He who;* other manuscripts read *God.* 3:16c Or *in his spirit.* 4:2 Greek *are seared.* 4:5 Or *made holy.* 4:6 Greek *brothers.* 4:10 Some manuscripts read *continue to suffer.*

3:8 deacons. Paul often describes himself and others as a *diakonos* ("deacon"), a word also translated as "servant" or "minister."

4:1 the Holy Spirit tells us clearly. Paul does not identify the specific prophecy he has in mind. However, the idea that there will be apostasy in the last days is found at other places in Scripture (Mark 13:22; 2 Tim. 3:1-5). **deceptive spirits . . . come from demons.** This is the real source of the false doctrine. Satan (with his minions) is behind the chaos in the Ephesian church as he has been in other churches (2 Cor. 2:11).

4:2 consciences are dead. Their moral judgment has been cauterized so that they are no longer able to distinguish between truth and falsehood.

4:3 wrong to be married. Paul identifies two specific errors in their teaching. They were saying that people ought not to get married and that they should not eat certain foods.

4:4 everything God created is good. This is the theological basis on which Paul says what he does about food (v. 3).

4:6 explain these things. Paul's gentle tone is evident right from the beginning. He does not instruct Timothy to "order" or "command" the brothers and sisters in the church. What he is to do is more akin to "suggesting" and "persuading" than it is to "instructing."

4:7 train yourself to be godly. In contrast to the unchristian asceticism (v. 3), Paul now proposes a genuinely Christian form of self-discipline.

4:8 Physical training. While affirming the value of physical exercise, Paul's real interest is in spiritual exercise ("godliness"). **promising benefits in this life and in the life to come.** The "life" Paul refers to is the "eternal life" one receives through belief in Jesus (1:16).

continue to struggle,* for our hope is in the living God, who is the Savior of all people and particularly of all believers.

11 Teach these things and insist that everyone learn them. 12 Don't let anyone think less of you because you are young. Be an example to all believers in what you say, in the way you live, in your love, your faith, and your purity. 13 Until I get there, focus on reading the Scriptures to the church, encouraging the believers, and teaching them.

14 Do not neglect the spiritual gift you received through the prophecy spoken over you when the elders of the church laid their hands on you. 15 Give your complete attention to these matters. Throw yourself into your tasks so that everyone will see your progress. 16 Keep a close watch on how you live and on your teaching. Stay true to what is right for the sake of your own salvation and the salvation of those who hear you.

ADVICE ABOUT WIDOWS, ELDERS, AND SLAVES

5 Never speak harshly to an older man,* but appeal to him respectfully as you would to your own father. Talk to younger men as you would to your own brothers. 2 Treat older women as you would your mother, and treat younger women with all purity as you would your own sisters.

3 Take care of* any widow who has no one else to care for her. 4 But if she has children or grandchildren, their first responsibility is to show godliness at home and repay their parents by taking care of them. This is something that pleases God.

5 Now a true widow, a woman who is truly alone in this world, has placed her hope in God. She prays night and day, asking God for his help. 6 But the widow who lives only for pleasure is spiritually dead even while she lives. 7 Give these instructions to the church so that no one will be open to criticism.

8 But those who won't care for their relatives, especially those in their own household, have denied the true faith. Such people are worse than unbelievers.

9 A widow who is put on the list for support must be a woman who is at least sixty years old and was faithful to her husband.* 10 She must be well respected by everyone because of the good she has done. Has she brought up her children well? Has she been kind to strangers and served other believers humbly?* Has she helped those who are in trouble? Has she always been ready to do good?

11 The younger widows should not be on the list, because their physical desires will overpower their devotion to Christ and they will want to remarry. 12 Then they would be guilty of breaking their previous pledge. 13 And if they are on the list, they will learn to be lazy and will spend their time gossiping from house to house, meddling in other people's business and talking about things they shouldn't. 14 So I advise these younger widows to marry again, have children, and take care of their own homes. Then the enemy will not be able to say anything against them. 15 For I am afraid that some of them have already gone astray and now follow Satan.

16 If a woman who is a believer has relatives who are widows, she must take care of them and not put the responsibility on the church. Then the church can care for the widows who are truly alone.

LENDING A HELPING HAND

1. What kind of human suffering is hardest for you to look at? When have you been extremely moved to want to help?

1 TIMOTHY 5:1–6:2

2. What possible abuses of care for the needy does Paul imply in verses 3-15? Is a different response to each person in need appropriate in today's world as well?
3. What should be the Christian's/church's response to the welfare issue?
4. According to Paul, how are we to treat our bosses or authorities ("masters" in 6:1-2)? Why is this important?
5. Who in your church needs some help that you or your group can provide?

5:1 Or *an elder.* 5:3 Or *Honor.* 5:9 Greek *was the wife of one husband.* 5:10 Greek *and washed the feet of God's holy people?*

4:11 Teach. Paul instructs that Timothy must speak with authority. The impression given here in verses 11-12 and elsewhere (1 Cor. 16:10-11; 2 Tim. 1:6-9) is that Timothy was a somewhat diffident, even timid, person.
4:12 young. The problem may have to do with Timothy's age. He is probably only in his early 30s. Yet, he is living in a culture that respects age. **Be an example.** There is little he can do about his age, but Timothy can lead by example. Paul identifies five areas in which he is to model Christian conduct. "Speech" and "conduct" refer to day-by-day conversation and behavior. "Love" (*agape*), "faith" (faithfulness), and "purity" (not only chastity but general integrity) refer to inner qualities that show themselves by an outer lifestyle.
4:13 reading the Scriptures. This is the first reference to the use of Scripture in Christian worship, although this was common in Jewish worship. **teaching.** This is instruction in Christian doctrine.
4:14 laid their hands on. Appointment to office (ordination) was accompanied by the laying on of hands (literally, the "pressing of hands") by the commissioning body (here, the elders).
5:1 speak harshly . . . appeal. Timothy will have to confront older men over the issue of false teaching. Paul tells him how to do it. It is not by means of harsh "rebuke"; instead, he is to appeal to them.
5:3 widow. The early church—following the pattern of the Jewish nation before them—was committed to caring for those women who had lost their husbands (Deut. 24:17,19-21; Ps. 68:5; Isa. 1:17; Acts 6:1-6; 9:36-41; Jas. 1:27).
5:4 has children or grandchildren. The first group of widows who do not qualify for help are those who have family and friends that can care for them (vv. 8, 16).
5:5-6 truly alone . . . lives only for pleasure. Paul next contrasts two types of widows: those who put their hope in God (v. 5) and those who by their sensual living give no evidence of trusting God to meet their needs (v. 6). The first group is really "all alone" and so must trust God. The second group is "self-indulgent." It may be that Paul is contrasting those women who refuse to be compromised (and so put their trust in God) with those women who live by sensual means (whether in actual prostitution or by being involved with individual men).
5:9 sixty years old. In the first century, 60 was considered the age of retirement and the point at which "old age" began. It was also considered to be the age beyond which remarriage was not a real possibility.
5:11-15 younger widows. Paul now comes to the real issue—the problematic younger widows. He gives two reasons for not putting them on the list for support. First, because their sexual desires are such that they do not want to remain widows (vv. 11-12) and second, because they are not really living according to the model of the godly widow that he has just sketched (v. 13). His advice is that they remarry (v. 14) lest they fall away from the faith (v. 15).
5:14 not be able to say anything against. The younger widows' behavior had become the grounds on which others were speaking evil of the church. Paul continues with his concern that the church not be judged negatively by the surrounding culture.

17 Elders who do their work well should be respect-
ed and paid well,* especially those who work hard at
both preaching and teaching. 18 For the Scripture says,
"You must not muzzle an ox to keep it from eating as
it treads out the grain." And in another place, "Those
who work deserve their pay!"*
19 Do not listen to an accusation against an elder un-
less it is confirmed by two or three witnesses. 20 Those
who sin should be reprimanded in front of the whole
church; this will serve as a strong warning to others.
21 I solemnly command you in the presence of God
and Christ Jesus and the highest angels to obey these
instructions without taking sides or showing favorit-
ism to anyone.
22 Never be in a hurry about appointing a church
leader.* Do not share in the sins of others. Keep your-
self pure.
23 Don't drink only water. You ought to drink a little
wine for the sake of your stomach because you are
sick so often.
24 Remember, the sins of some people are obvious,
leading them to certain judgment. But there are oth-
ers whose sins will not be revealed until later. 25 In the
same way, the good deeds of some people are obvious.
And the good deeds done in secret will someday come
to light.

6 All slaves should show full respect for their mas-
ters so they will not bring shame on the name of
God and his teaching. 2 If the masters are believers,
that is no excuse for being disrespectful. Those slaves
should work all the harder because their efforts are
helping other believers* who are well loved.

FALSE TEACHING AND TRUE RICHES

Teach these things, Timothy, and encourage every-
one to obey them. 3 Some people may contradict our
teaching, but these are the wholesome teachings
of the Lord Jesus Christ. These teachings promote a
godly life. 4 Anyone who teaches something different
is arrogant and lacks understanding. Such a person
has an unhealthy desire to quibble over the meaning
of words. This stirs up arguments ending in jealousy,
division, slander, and evil suspicions. 5 These people
always cause trouble. Their minds are corrupt, and
they have turned their backs on the truth. To them,
a show of godliness is just a way to become wealthy.

MONEY ISSUES

1. What was your first job where you made real money? Why were you working?
2. If you suddenly had lots of money, what is the first thing you would buy?

1 TIMOTHY 6:3-21

3. Why does "true godliness with contentment" lead to "great wealth" (v. 6)?
4. What is dangerous about wanting to be rich (v. 9)? Why is it dangerous?
5. What should we focus on in life instead of the pursuit of wealth (vv. 11-12)?
6. What is your biggest concern about money right now? How can you use your money for the good even now (vv. 17-19)?

6 Yet true godliness with contentment is itself great
wealth. 7 After all, we brought nothing with us when
we came into the world, and we can't take anything
with us when we leave it. 8 So if we have enough food
and clothing, let us be content.
9 But people who long to be rich fall into temptation
and are trapped by many foolish and harmful desires
that plunge them into ruin and destruction. 10 For the
love of money is the root of all kinds of evil. And some
people, craving money, have wandered from the true
faith and pierced themselves with many sorrows.

PAUL'S FINAL INSTRUCTIONS

11 But you, Timothy, are a man of God; so run from all
these evil things. Pursue righteousness and a godly life,
along with faith, love, perseverance, and gentleness.
12 Fight the good fight for the true faith. Hold tightly to
the eternal life to which God has called you, which you
have declared so well before many witnesses. 13 And I
charge you before God, who gives life to all, and before
Christ Jesus, who gave a good testimony before Pontius
Pilate, 14 that you obey this command without waver-
ing. Then no one can find fault with you from now until
our Lord Jesus Christ comes again. 15 For,

5:17 Greek *should be worthy of double honor.* **5:18** Deut 25:4; Luke 10:7. **5:22** Greek *about the laying on of hands.* **6:2** Greek *brothers.*

5:18 the Scripture says. Paul justifies his assertion that elders deserve remuneration from the community by means of two citations, one from the Old Testament (Deut. 25:4) and the other from Jesus (Luke 10:7).
5:19-20 Do not listen to an accusation. Paul next addresses the matter of discipline with two points. First, no unsubstantiated charge is to be made about an elder. Second, if valid charges are made, those found guilty are to be rebuked publicly, serving as a warning to other elders who are in error, as well as the whole church.
5:23 a little wine. Having told him to remain "pure," Paul quickly adds that what he has in mind is not the sort of abstinence from food and drink taught by the false teachers (4:3). He recommends that Timothy follow the common medical practice of using wine as a treatment for his stomach problems.
6:4 arrogant and lacks understanding. These teachers are swollen with pride despite the fact that they are really quite ignorant. **quibble.** This refers to a sort of idle speculation. **arguments.** This is literally a "battle of words," which Paul sharply criticizes. **stirs up.** Paul identifies two negative results of this sick preoccupation with word battles. First, it produces strife within the church, and second, it brings about a kind of corruption or decay to the minds of the teachers themselves. **jealousy.** Controversy produces jealousy as people take up sides (see Romans 1:29, and Galatians 5:21, where envy is said to be one of the evidences of the sinful nature). **slander, and evil suspicions.** This quarreling drives people to tell lies about one another and question one another's motives.
6:5 minds are corrupt. "Mind" refers to one's whole way of thinking.
6:6 contentment. This word refers to a person who is not impacted by circumstances. Such a person is self-contained and thus able to rise above all conditions. For Paul, however, this sort of contentment is derived from the Lord (Phil. 4:11).
6:7-8 brought nothing . . . have enough food. There are two reasons why "godliness with contentment" is a great gain. First, at death people can take nothing with them (so why worry about material gain that has to be given up in the end anyway?). Second, if people have the essentials in life, this should be enough.
6:9 temptation. Greed causes people to notice and desire what they might not otherwise have paid attention to.
6:10 For the love of money is the root of all kinds of evil. This verse is often misquoted as "money is the root of all evil." While Paul clearly sees the danger of money, he is not contending that all evil can be traced to greed.
6:12 Fight the good fight. Paul again uses an athletic metaphor to encourage Timothy to persevere in the faith. The verb tense emphasizes the ongoing nature of the struggle. **Hold tightly to the eternal life.** The focus shifts from the contest to the prize. A person can grasp eternal life in a single act.

At just the right time Christ will be revealed from
heaven by the blessed and only almighty God, the
King of all kings and Lord of all lords. 16 He alone
can never die, and he lives in light so brilliant that
no human can approach him. No human eye has
ever seen him, nor ever will. All honor and power
to him forever! Amen.

17 Teach those who are rich in this world not to be
proud and not to trust in their money, which is so
unreliable. Their trust should be in God, who richly
gives us all we need for our enjoyment. 18 Tell them
to use their money to do good. They should be rich
in good works and generous to those in need, al-
ways being ready to share with others. 19 By doing
this they will be storing up their treasure as a good
foundation for the future so that they may experi-
ence true life.

20 Timothy, guard what God has entrusted to you.
Avoid godless, foolish discussions with those who op-
pose you with their so-called knowledge. 21 Some peo-
ple have wandered from the faith by following such
foolishness.

May God's grace be with you all.

6:17 those who are rich. This is the only place in his letters that Paul addresses the wealthy directly. His consistent "command" is that the rich share their wealth with the poor (Rom. 12:8, 13; 2 Cor. 9:6-15). **not to be arrogant or to set their hope on . . . wealth.** These are the twin dangers of wealth—that it will cause people to think of themselves as better than others and that they might put their trust in their riches (and not in God). **to enjoy.** But Paul is no ascetic. That the wealthy should not place confidence in their wealth does not carry with it an attitude of total rejection of wealth.

INTRODUCTION TO

2 TIMOTHY

PERSONAL READING PLAN

2 Timothy 1:1–2:13
2 Timothy 2:14–3:9
2 Timothy 3:10–4:8
2 Timothy 4:9-22

AUTHOR

The Apostle Paul was most likely the author of 2 Timothy. However, based on considerations of vocabulary and style, the Pauline authorship of the Pastoral Epistles (1 and 2 Timothy, and Titus) has been questioned by some scholars.

DATE

Second Timothy is probably the last epistle Paul ever wrote. The date is thought to be around A.D. 67–68. He is an old man now, in prison once again, deserted by most all of his friends, and facing the likely prospect of death. "As for me, my life has already been poured out as an offering to God. The time of my death is near. I have fought the good fight, I have finished the race, and I have remained faithful. And now the prize awaits me—the crown of righteousness, which the Lord, the righteous Judge, will give me on the day of his return. And the prize is not just for me but for all who eagerly look forward to his appearing" (4:6-8).

THEME

Guard the gospel.

PURPOSE

Second Timothy is deeply moving as Paul writes Timothy, imploring him to come and be with him in the last days of his life. In 2 Timothy, the urgency of the problem in Ephesus is in the background. Paul's more pressing need is to have Timothy at his side once again. Even more than personal comfort, Paul wants to pass on the torch of his ministry to Timothy.

Timothy was the logical choice for this new responsibility. He had been Paul's trusted colleague for over 15 years, and he really cared for the welfare of the churches (Phil. 2:20-22). This was a crucial time for the churches in Europe and Asia. They seemed fragile in the face of their opposition. For one thing, Nero seemed bent on destroying the church. Furthermore, in the Roman province of Asia there had been widespread desertion (1:15). Only a generation after Christ's resurrection, Christianity appeared to be on the verge of annihilation. But Paul's ministry was over. No longer could he travel through the Roman Empire, troubleshooting, correcting, or, establishing order. Now it was up to Timothy and the new leaders.

In many ways Timothy was an unlikely leader. He was relatively young by Roman standards, in his mid-thirties (1 Tim. 4:12; 2 Tim. 2:22). He was prone to illness (1 Tim. 5:23). And he was, apparently, somewhat shy and in need of encouragement (1 Cor. 16:10; 2 Tim. 1:7-8; 2:1,3; 3:12-14). To his credit, Timothy overcame his natural inclination and tackled risky assignments for Paul (for example, in Corinth).

If Timothy did not make it to Rome in time, these instructions in 2 Timothy would have to suffice. Paul's last letter was a crucial one.

HISTORICAL BACKGROUND

It is difficult to trace Paul's movements during the period when he wrote the Pastoral Epistles. The best guess is that after being released from the house arrest in Rome (described at the end of Acts), Paul went on another preaching tour, taking with him Timothy and Titus. In the course of their travels, they came to Crete. When it came time to move on, Paul left Titus behind to appoint leaders for the new church there. Paul and Timothy went to Macedonia via Ephesus. At Ephesus, Paul discovered that heresy was rotting away the church. So he excommunicated Hymenaeus and Alexander, two of the erring leaders (1 Tim. 1:19-20), and he left Timothy behind to help the church through its difficulties (1 Tim. 1:3-4). Paul himself went on to Macedonia. Once there he wrote 1 Timothy and Titus (hence the similarity between the two letters).

Paul wintered in the Adriatic seacoast town of Nicopolis where he was (presumably) joined by Titus. In the spring, Paul started back to Ephesus, only to be arrested along the way—probably at Troas—at the instigation of Alexander the metalworker (2 Tim. 4:14-15).

Paul was eventually taken back to Rome and thrown into prison. This time he was not allowed the relative comfort of a rented house with twenty-four-hour-a-day guards as was the case during his first imprisonment. Instead he was chained and thrown into a dark, damp dungeon (1:16), "like a criminal" (2:9). Onesiphorus was able to find Paul only after a long search (1:17). Paul was cold ("bring the coat," 4:13), bored ("bring my books, and especially my papers," 4:13), and lonely ("Only Luke is with me," 4:11). He had already had a preliminary hearing (4:16-17). His full trial was yet to come, and he did not expect to be acquitted. Nero's insane persecution of the Christians was at its height.

So Paul wrote Timothy to come to him in Rome. He sent this important letter (2 Timothy) via Tychicus, who was to replace Timothy in Ephesus.

CHARACTERISTICS

Although 2 Timothy is similar in content and focus to both 1 Timothy and Titus, there are some marked differences. Second Timothy is far more personal than 1 Timothy. First Timothy has the feel of a business letter containing important instructions to be heeded by the local congregation. But in 2 Timothy, Paul is writing to Timothy and not to the church, and he reminisces about the work he and Timothy did together. His primary purpose is not combating heresy (although that is a background concern) but to call Timothy to join him in Rome.

In fact, it is Paul's altered situation that gives 2 Timothy its distinct flavor. There is an urgency to his writing. His ministry is over. He tells Timothy to "fan into flames the spiritual gift God gave you" (1:6). Timothy must never "be ashamed to tell others about our Lord" (1:8). He must "guard the previous truth" given to him (1:14). "Preach the word" (4:2), Paul says, "whether the time is favorable or not."

Second Timothy is also characterized, somewhat surprisingly, by a note of triumph. Paul knows that despite all the difficulties he is facing, despite the pressure on the church, the gospel will prevail. It cannot be chained, even if he is chained (2:9). Nor will the church ultimately be hampered. It, too, will prevail (2:11-13; 4:8). Therefore, Paul writes to Timothy to carry on the work of the gospel despite persecution, despite Paul's death, because God's kingdom will prevail (3:10–4:8).

PASSAGES FOR TOPICAL GROUP STUDY

1:1-12 . . . POWER, LOVE, SOUND MIND. . . . . Fired Up
2:14-26 . . REPENTANCE and RIGHT LIVING . . . Positive Pursuits
4:9-18 . . . LONELINESS and LOSING FRIENDS . . . . . Never Alone

PASSAGES FOR GENERAL GROUP STUDY

3:1-9 . . . . The Dark Side (False Teachers)
3:10–4:8. . . . . The Living Word (the Bible)

GREETINGS FROM PAUL

1 This letter is from Paul, chosen by the will of God to be an apostle of Christ Jesus. I have been sent out to tell others about the life he has promised through faith in Christ Jesus.

2 I am writing to Timothy, my dear son.

May God the Father and Christ Jesus our Lord give you grace, mercy, and peace.

ENCOURAGEMENT TO BE FAITHFUL

3 Timothy, I thank God for you—the God I serve with a clear conscience, just as my ancestors did. Night and day I constantly remember you in my prayers. 4 I long to see you again, for I remember your tears as we parted. And I will be filled with joy when we are together again.

5 I remember your genuine faith, for you share the faith that first filled your grandmother Lois and your mother, Eunice. And I know that same faith continues strong in you. 6 This is why I remind you to fan into flames the spiritual gift God gave you when I laid my hands on you. 7 For God has not given us a spirit of fear and timidity, but of power, love, and self-discipline.

8 So never be ashamed to tell others about our Lord. And don't be ashamed of me, either, even though I'm in prison for him. With the strength God gives you, be ready to suffer with me for the sake of the Good News. 9 For God saved us and called us to live a holy life. He did this, not because we deserved it, but because that was his plan from before the beginning of time—to show us his grace through Christ Jesus. 10 And now he has made all of this plain to us by the appearing of Christ Jesus, our Savior. He broke the power of death and illuminated the way to life and immortality through the Good News. 11 And God chose me to be a preacher, an apostle, and a teacher of this Good News.

12 That is why I am suffering here in prison. But I am not ashamed of it, for I know the one in whom I trust, and I am sure that he is able to guard what I have entrusted to him* until the day of his return.

13 Hold on to the pattern of wholesome teaching you learned from me—a pattern shaped by the faith and love that you have in Christ Jesus. 14 Through the power of the Holy Spirit who lives within us, carefully guard the precious truth that has been entrusted to you.

15 As you know, everyone from the province of Asia has deserted me—even Phygelus and Hermogenes.

16 May the Lord show special kindness to Onesiphorus and all his family because he often visited and encouraged me. He was never ashamed of me because I was in chains. 17 When he came to Rome, he searched everywhere until he found me. 18 May the Lord show him special kindness on the day of Christ's return. And you know very well how helpful he was in Ephesus.

A GOOD SOLDIER OF CHRIST JESUS

2 Timothy, my dear son, be strong through the grace that God gives you in Christ Jesus. 2 You have heard me teach things that have been confirmed by many reliable witnesses. Now teach these truths to other trustworthy people who will be able to pass them on to others.

3 Endure suffering along with me, as a good soldier of Christ Jesus. 4 Soldiers don't get tied up in the affairs of civilian life, for then they cannot please the officer who enlisted them. 5 And athletes cannot win the prize unless they follow the rules. 6 And hardworking farmers should be the first to enjoy the fruit of their labor. 7 Think about what I am saying. The Lord will help you understand all these things.

8 Always remember that Jesus Christ, a descendant of King David, was raised from the dead. This is the Good News I preach. 9 And because I preach this Good News, I am suffering and have been chained like a criminal. But the word of God cannot be chained. 10 So

FIRED UP

1. How does your team get ready for an important game or event?

2 TIMOTHY 1:1-12

2. Judging by what Paul exhorts Timothy to keep doing in verse 6, what kinds of examples do you suppose Timothy's mother and grandmother demonstrated (v. 5)?
3. Verse 7 says that God gives us a spirit of power, not fearfulness. How do you think your life would be different if you really grabbed hold of that promise in your life?
4. What are you doing to "fan into flames" the gift that God has given you?
5. In what area do you need to get "fired up"? Where do you most need God to give you power, love, and a sound mind?

1:12 Or *what has been entrusted to me.*

1:4 remember your tears. Paul is probably recalling that when they parted the last time, he was to go on to Macedonia, while Timothy stayed in Ephesus (see Acts 20:37 for a similar situation). **I long to see you.** This is the main reason he writes this letter: to urge Timothy to join him (4:9). **joy.** Once again, as he did in the Philippian letter, Paul sounds a note of joy, even though he is in prison.

1:5 Eunice. Timothy's mother was a Jewish Christian (Acts 16:1). His father was a Gentile, probably not a believer.

1:6 fan into flames. "Rekindle." Paul uses the image of a fire, not to suggest that his spiritual gift has "gone out," but that it needs constant stirring up so that it always burns brightly. **the spiritual gift of God.** Paul reminds Timothy not only of his spiritual roots (the faith of his mother and grandmother) but also of the gift he has been given for ministry.

1:7 spirit of fear. Paul makes this sort of appeal because Timothy is not a forceful person (1 Tim. 4:12).

1:8 ashamed to tell others about our Lord. The gospel message about a dying Savior was not immediately popular in the first-century world. The Greeks laughed at the idea that the Messiah could be a convicted criminal and that God was so weak He would allow His own Son to die. The Jews could not conceive of a Messiah (whom they knew to be all-powerful) dying on a cross (which they felt disqualified Him from acceptance by God). It was not easy to preach the gospel in the face of such scorn.

2:2 You have heard me teaching. Just as the gospel has been committed to Timothy (1:14; 1 Tim. 6:20), so he is to commit it to others who, in turn, teach it to still more people. This whole process of "committing" is made doubly important by the fact that Paul will soon call Timothy to join him in Rome (which means that others will have to take over his teaching ministry in Ephesus).

2:3-6 soldier . . . athletes . . . farmers. Paul uses three metaphors (drawn from the military, athletics, and agriculture) to encourage Timothy to work hard and endure suffering with the knowledge that he will be rewarded.

2:9 criminal. This is the term used for those who committed serious crimes (such as murder and theft).

POSITIVE PURSUITS

1. What happened the last time your coach changed game plans due to the opposing team's strategies?

2 TIMOTHY 2:14-26

2. Looking over this passage, especially verses 15-16 and 22-24, what should we pursue? What should we run from?
3. Since repentance means "changing directions," how does repentance (v. 25) relate to fleeing and pursuing (v. 22)?
4. What seems to be the main goal of all of this righteous living (v. 26)?
5. How do you need to change your strategies for pursuing "faithfulness, love, and peace" (v. 22) and "escape from the devil's trap" (v. 26) in the coming week?

I am willing to endure anything if it will bring sal-
vation and eternal glory in Christ Jesus to those God
has chosen.
11 This is a trustworthy saying:

If we die with him,
    we will also live with him.
12 If we endure hardship,
    we will reign with him.
If we deny him,
    he will deny us.
13 If we are unfaithful,
    he remains faithful,
    for he cannot deny who he is.

14 Remind everyone about these things, and com-
mand them in God's presence to stop fighting over
words. Such arguments are useless, and they can ruin
those who hear them.

AN APPROVED WORKER

15 Work hard so you can present yourself to God and
receive his approval. Be a good worker, one who does
not need to be ashamed and who correctly explains
the word of truth. 16 Avoid worthless, foolish talk that
only leads to more godless behavior. 17 This kind of talk
spreads like cancer,* as in the case of Hymenaeus and
Philetus. 18 They have left the path of truth, claiming that
the resurrection of the dead has already occurred; in this
way, they have turned some people away from the faith.
19 But God's truth stands firm like a foundation
stone with this inscription: "The LORD knows those
who are his,"* and "All who belong to the LORD must
turn away from evil."*
20 In a wealthy home some utensils are made of
gold and silver, and some are made of wood and clay.
The expensive utensils are used for special occasions,
and the cheap ones are for everyday use. 21 If you keep
yourself pure, you will be a special utensil for honor-
able use. Your life will be clean, and you will be ready
for the Master to use you for every good work.
22 Run from anything that stimulates youthful lusts.
Instead, pursue righteous living, faithfulness, love,
and peace. Enjoy the companionship of those who call
on the Lord with pure hearts.
23 Again I say, don't get involved in foolish, ignorant
arguments that only start fights. 24 A servant of the
Lord must not quarrel but must be kind to everyone,
be able to teach, and be patient with difficult people.
25 Gently instruct those who oppose the truth. Perhaps
God will change those people's hearts, and they will
learn the truth. 26 Then they will come to their senses
and escape from the devil's trap. For they have been
held captive by him to do whatever he wants.

THE DANGERS OF THE LAST DAYS

3 You should know this, Timothy, that in the last
days there will be very difficult times. 2 For people
will love only themselves and their money. They will
be boastful and proud, scoffing at God, disobedient
to their parents, and ungrateful. They will consider
nothing sacred. 3 They will be unloving and unforgiv-
ing; they will slander others and have no self-control.
They will be cruel and hate what is good. 4 They will

2:17 Greek *gangrene*. 2:19a Num 16:5. 2:19b See Isa 52:11.

2:10 those God has chosen. God's chosen people; Christ-followers.
2:14 Remind everyone about these things. Timothy's first task is to keep people in touch with the truth of the gospel. The verb tense indicates that this is something he will have to do over and over again. **fighting over words.** Literally, "word battle." This lies at the heart of the false teaching.
2:15 receive his approval. Literally, "one who has stood the test." A word used to describe gold or silver that had been purified in fire, or a stone that has been cut without a flaw (examined and then pronounced fit to be used in a building). **a good worker.** The picture is of a farm laborer who has done a good job and is therefore not afraid to show his boss what he has accomplished. **who correctly explains the word of truth.** In contrast to the false teachers and their "word battles," Timothy is called upon to teach and preach the gospel correctly. The phrase "word of truth" refers not to Scripture specifically but to the gospel message as a whole.
2:17 cancer. Literally gangrene, which is disease that "gnaws away" at healthy tissue, causing its decay. Likewise, false teaching eats away at the healthy life in a church. **Hymenaeus and Philetus.** False teachers who have been a real problem. Paul had mentioned Hymenaeus in 1 Timothy 1:20 as one he had "delivered over to Satan." It appears he is still at work "overturning the faith of some" (v. 18).
2:18 the resurrection of the dead has already occurred. They were probably teaching that the resurrection of believers was a spiritual or mystical event that had already taken place (1 Cor. 15:20-23; 2 Thess. 2:2).
2:19 foundation stone. Paul is probably referring to God's truth (Isa. 40:8). **with this inscription.** Paul has in mind the practice of placing an inscription on the foundation stone of a building to indicate the purpose of the building or the name of the owner.
2:22 Run from . . . pursue. Simply trying to avoid evil desires isn't enough to keep us pure: we have to replace the evil desires and strive for positive virtues. **youthful lusts.** Part of what Paul has in mind is the impatience and arrogance of self-assertive youth, who love novelty and indulge in argument for argument's own sake.
3:2 people. Although he casts this list into general terms ("people"), Paul implies that these vices characterize (at least in part) the false teachers. **love . . . their money.** The path is short from love of self to love of money. Self-interest leads to self-indulgence. **boastful and proud.** These two terms are connected. The first refers to outward expressions of unrealistic pride, while the second to an inner attitude of superiority. These words can also be translated as "braggart" and "conceited." This second term has already been applied to the false teachers (1 Tim. 6:4). **disobedient to their parents.** Duty to parents was considered obligatory by both Greeks and Jews. **ungrateful.** To be "ungrateful" is to refuse to honor the debt one owes to others. **nothing sacred.** Such a person violates the unwritten laws that stand at the core of life.
3:3 unloving. The lack of natural, human affection. **unforgiving.** Such a person finds it impossible to forgive or to be reconciled to others. This sort of person is harsh and often bitter. **no self-control.** This is the person who is a slave to a habit or desire.
3:4 reckless. To be swept along by impulse or passion into bad decisions. **puffed up with pride.** Such people are swollen with pride at the sense of their own importance.

THE DARK SIDE

1. What crimes have you seen reported in the news that really made you angry?

2 TIMOTHY 3:1-9

2. How are the sins listed in this passage a failure of the true love Jesus described in Matthew 22:37-39?
3. What does it mean to "act religious, but they will reject the power that could make them godly" (v. 5)? Why should we avoid people who do this?
4. According to verses 6-9, what is the character, danger, and fate of false teachers?
5. What do you think is the right thing to do with people like the ones described in this passage? Is there someone you need to avoid?

betray their friends, be reckless, be puffed up with
pride, and love pleasure rather than God. 5 They will
act religious, but they will reject the power that could
make them godly. Stay away from people like that!
6 They are the kind who work their way into peo-
ple's homes and win the confidence of* vulnerable
women who are burdened with the guilt of sin and
controlled by various desires. 7 (Such women are
forever following new teachings, but they are never
able to understand the truth.) 8 These teachers oppose
the truth just as Jannes and Jambres opposed Moses.
They have depraved minds and a counterfeit faith.
9 But they won't get away with this for long. Someday
everyone will recognize what fools they are, just as
with Jannes and Jambres.

PAUL'S CHARGE TO TIMOTHY

10 But you, Timothy, certainly know what I teach, and
how I live, and what my purpose in life is. You know
my faith, my patience, my love, and my endurance.
11 You know how much persecution and suffering I
have endured. You know all about how I was per-
secuted in Antioch, Iconium, and Lystra—but the
Lord rescued me from all of it. 12 Yes, and everyone
who wants to live a godly life in Christ Jesus will suf-
fer persecution. 13 But evil people and impostors will
flourish. They will deceive others and will themselves
be deceived.
14 But you must remain faithful to the things you
have been taught. You know they are true, for you
know you can trust those who taught you. 15 You
have been taught the holy Scriptures from child-
hood, and they have given you the wisdom to re-
ceive the salvation that comes by trusting in Christ
Jesus. 16 All Scripture is inspired by God and is use-
ful to teach us what is true and to make us realize
what is wrong in our lives. It corrects us when we
are wrong and teaches us to do what is right. 17 God
uses it to prepare and equip his people to do every
good work.

4 I solemnly urge you in the presence of God and
Christ Jesus, who will someday judge the living
and the dead when he comes to set up his Kingdom:
2 Preach the word of God. Be prepared, whether the
time is favorable or not. Patiently correct, rebuke, and
encourage your people with good teaching.
3 For a time is coming when people will no longer
listen to sound and wholesome teaching. They will
follow their own desires and will look for teachers
who will tell them whatever their itching ears want
to hear. 4 They will reject the truth and chase after
myths.
5 But you should keep a clear mind in every situa-
tion. Don't be afraid of suffering for the Lord. Work at
telling others the Good News, and fully carry out the
ministry God has given you.
6 As for me, my life has already been poured
out as an offering to God. The time of my death is

THE LIVING WORD

1. What is your all-time favorite book?
2. How old were you when you first started learning about the Bible? Who taught you?

2 TIMOTHY 3:10–4:8

3. What type of literature would the average student in your school call the Bible: Fiction? History? Mystery? Nonfiction?
4. In what ways has the Bible taught, rebuked, corrected, or encouraged you?
5. Comparing your spiritual life to a race, are you: Just getting out of the blocks? Really hitting your stride? Ready to drop?
6. What would you like to accomplish for God in the future? How can the Word of God help?

3:6 Greek *and take captive.*

3:5 act religious. These teachers missed out on the real power of God by substituting an outward religiosity for the inner reality of a relationship with God.
3:6 controlled by various desires. There may have been some sort of sexual involvement between the false teachers and the women they influenced.
3:8 Jannes and Jambres. These were Pharaoh's magicians, who by means of their secret arts duplicated the miracles of Moses and Aaron.
3:10 what I teach. This is the first of nine characteristics of Paul's life and ministry that Timothy is asked to note and reproduce. These nine make up a sort of "virtue list" that stands in sharp contrast to the "vice list" in verses 2-5 (2 Cor. 6:4-10).
3:15 wisdom to receive the salvation . . . in Christ Jesus. The Old Testament Scriptures lead one to salvation; i.e., to an understanding of God's saving purpose.
3:16 All Scripture is inspired by God. Scripture has a divine origin. It comes from God (2 Peter 1:21). **is useful to.** By means of two contrasting pairs of phrases, Paul names four ministry tasks in which Scripture plays a vital part. **to teach.** Scripture is the source of what Timothy teaches in contrast to the speculative nature of the erring elders' doctrine. **to make . . . realize.** Not only does Scripture teach that which is true, it also reveals that which is in error. **corrects.** Scripture also defines how to live. It is thus a measuring stick against which to assess behavior and change what is found wanting. **teaches.** This is the positive side of "correcting."
4:2 Preach the word of God. Above all else, Timothy is to proclaim the message of the gospel. This is the main command and controls the next four. **Be prepared, whether the time is favorable or not.** Probably Paul is encouraging Timothy to keep on preaching whether his hearers find it convenient or not, though he may be urging Timothy to continue with this task whether or not it is convenient to him. **correct, rebuke, and encourage.** In preaching the gospel he is to "correct" those who are in error, "rebuke" them if they fail to heed his correction, and "encourage" or "urge" them all to respond to what the gospel says.

near. 7 I have fought the good fight, I have finished
the race, and I have remained faithful. 8 And now
the prize awaits me—the crown of righteousness,
which the Lord, the righteous Judge, will give me
on the day of his return. And the prize is not just
for me but for all who eagerly look forward to his
appearing.

PAUL'S FINAL WORDS

9 Timothy, please come as soon as you can. 10 Demas
has deserted me because he loves the things of this
life and has gone to Thessalonica. Crescens has gone
to Galatia, and Titus has gone to Dalmatia. 11 Only Luke
is with me. Bring Mark with you when you come, for
he will be helpful to me in my ministry. 12 I sent Tychi-
cus to Ephesus. 13 When you come, be sure to bring the
coat I left with Carpus at Troas. Also bring my books,
and especially my papers.*
14 Alexander the coppersmith did me much harm,
but the Lord will judge him for what he has done. 15 Be
careful of him, for he fought against everything we
said.
16 The first time I was brought before the judge,
no one came with me. Everyone abandoned me.
May it not be counted against them. 17 But the Lord
stood with me and gave me strength so that I might
preach the Good News in its entirety for all the
Gentiles to hear. And he rescued me from certain
death.* 18 Yes, and the Lord will deliver me from
every evil attack and will bring me safely into his
heavenly Kingdom. All glory to God forever and
ever! Amen.

NEVER ALONE

1. If you were in prison, who would come to visit you?
2. When have you been stranded somewhere? Who finally came to your rescue?

2 TIMOTHY 4:9-18

3. What can we learn from Paul's attitude toward the coppersmith (v. 14)?
4. When everyone deserted Paul, to whom did he turn (vv. 17-18)?
5. In what ways are you feeling deserted? How can Paul's words in verses 17-18 help you the next time you feel all alone?
6. How can you help someone who is lonely and in need of a friend in the coming week?

PAUL'S FINAL GREETINGS

19 Give my greetings to Priscilla and Aquila and those
living in the household of Onesiphorus. 20 Erastus
stayed at Corinth, and I left Trophimus sick at Miletus.
21 Do your best to get here before winter. Eubulus
sends you greetings, and so do Pudens, Linus, Claudia,
and all the brothers and sisters.*
22 May the Lord be with your spirit. And may his
grace be with all of you.

4:13 Greek *especially the parchments.* **4:17** Greek *from the mouth of a lion.* **4:21** Greek *brothers.*

4:9 come as soon as you can. Paul highlights his main request. He wants Timothy to leave his post at Ephesus and join him in Rome, a journey of over 1,000 miles.

4:10-11 deserted . . . gone. All his colleagues have left him (with the exception of Luke), either by reason of defection (Demas) or because of ministry needs (Crescens and Titus).

4:11 Bring Mark with you. It is a remarkable testimony to the power of the Holy Spirit that after the argument over Mark, which had resulted in the split between Paul and Barnabas (because Mark had deserted them in Perga—Acts 13:13; 15:36-41), reconciliation has taken place. Mark is now once again a valued coworker with Paul (Col. 4:10; Philem. 24).

4:13 coat. A heavy wool cape that was worn in the cold and rain, consisting of a single piece of material with a hole in the middle for the head. Winter was coming and Paul needed his cloak to stay warm while in jail. **books . . . papers.** Various suggestions have been made about what these were: portions of the Old Testament, blank writing materials, early copies of the Gospels, official documents (such as Paul's birth certificate).

INTRODUCTION TO

TITUS

PERSONAL READING PLAN

☐Titus 1:1-16 ☐Titus 2:1-15 ☐Titus 3:1-15

AUTHOR

The Apostle Paul was most likely the writer of Titus. However, based on considerations of vocabulary and style, the Pauline authorship of the Pastoral Epistles (1 and 2 Timothy, and Titus) has been questioned by some scholars.

DATE

Titus was written about A.D. 63–65 (at the same time 1 Timothy was written).

THEME

Be devoted to what is good.

HISTORICAL BACKGROUND

Paul and Titus, along with Timothy, went to Crete as part of a preaching tour following Paul's release from his first imprisonment in Rome. When Paul and Timothy left for Macedonia, Titus stayed behind to establish firmly the new church on Crete. When Paul reached Macedonia he wrote two letters—one to Timothy who had remained in Ephesus and the other to Titus.

In his letter to Titus, Paul reminds the younger man of his role: to appoint good leaders who will guide the church wisely. He also urges Titus to combat the false teachers found on the island. Finally, he tells him that either Artemas or Tychicus will come to relieve him (3:12), after which he is to join Paul for the winter. (See details of Paul's itinerary during this period in the Introduction to 2 Timothy.)

Titus was a Greek (Gal. 2:3) who was probably converted through Paul's ministry. He was a trusted colleague of Paul's and was often sent on difficult assignments. For example, when the conflict between Paul and the Corinthian church had reached a breaking point, it was Titus who delivered Paul's "harsh" letter and restored order in that community (2 Cor. 7:5-7). At some point, Titus was sent to Dalmatia (modern Yugoslavia) for yet another mission.

Titus is strikingly similar to 1 Timothy. Apart from the greeting and two pieces of theological writing in 2:11-14 and 3:3-7 (which appear to be creeds), all the material is parallel to 1 Timothy. The main difference is found in the contrasting situation of Titus and Timothy. Timothy had been left to straighten out a mess in an already established church. Titus, on the other hand, had the job of appointing elders in a new church. As a result, there is less intensity in Titus. There are few imperatives ("Do this"); there is no mention of endurance (as one finds in 1 Timothy); and there are no appeals to "keep the faith." Establishing order in a new church was quite different from restoring order to an established church.

PASSAGES FOR TOPICAL GROUP STUDY

1:5-16 ... LIVING YOUR FAITH .... Walking the Talk
2:1-15 ... GODLY LIVING and MENTORS .... Just Say No
3:1-15 ... GOOD WORKS REQUIRED .... Doing Good

PASSAGES FOR GENERAL GROUP STUDY

1:1-4 .... Powerful Knowledge of the Truth of Christ

GREETINGS FROM PAUL

1 This letter is from Paul, a slave of God and an apostle of Jesus Christ. I have been sent to proclaim faith to* those God has chosen and to teach them to know the truth that shows them how to live godly lives. [2] This truth gives them confidence that they have eternal life, which God—who does not lie—promised them before the world began. [3] And now at just the right time he has revealed this message, which we announce to everyone. It is by the command of God our Savior that I have been entrusted with this work for him.

[4] I am writing to Titus, my true son in the faith that we share.

May God the Father and Christ Jesus our Savior give you grace and peace.

POWERFUL KNOWLEDGE

1. What subject or hobby would you like to learn more about?

TITUS 1:1-4

2. In verse 1, Paul explains that God called him as an apostle to help people come "to know the truth that shows them how to live godly lives." When did you come to the knowledge of the truth of Christ? What happened?
3. After coming to faith in Christ, did your new knowledge lead to godliness? In what ways?
4. When have you questioned your own "eternal life"? How does verse 2 speak to someone questioning his or her position with God?

TITUS'S WORK IN CRETE

[5] I left you on the island of Crete so you could complete our work there and appoint elders in each town as I instructed you. [6] An elder must live a blameless life. He must be faithful to his wife,* and his children must be believers who don't have a reputation for being wild or rebellious. [7] A church leader* is a manager of God's household, so he must live a blameless life. He must not be arrogant or quick-tempered; he must not be a heavy drinker,* violent, or dishonest with money. [8] Rather, he must enjoy having guests in his home, and he must love what is good. He must live wisely and be just. He must live a devout and disciplined life. [9] He must have a strong belief in the trustworthy message he was taught; then he will be able to encourage others with wholesome teaching and show those who oppose it where they are wrong.

[10] For there are many rebellious people who engage in useless talk and deceive others. This is especially true of those who insist on circumcision for salvation. [11] They must be silenced, because they are turning whole families away from the truth by their false teaching. And they do it only for money. [12] Even one of their own men, a prophet from Crete, has said about them, "The people of Crete are all liars, cruel animals, and lazy gluttons."* [13] This is true. So reprimand them sternly to make them strong in the faith. [14] They must stop listening to Jewish myths and the commands of people who have turned away from the truth.

[15] Everything is pure to those whose hearts are pure. But nothing is pure to those who are corrupt and unbelieving, because their minds and consciences are corrupted. [16] Such people claim they know God,

WALKING THE TALK

1. Who in your family, group of friends, or team is the most disciplined?

TITUS 1:5-16

2. Why is Paul's list of leadership qualifications focused mostly on "being" and not on "doing" (vv. 6-9)?
3. Which of the qualities in verses 7-9 do you feel you need to develop in your own life?
4. How, in the past or present, have your actions not fit with your profession to "know God" (v. 16)?
5. Are there some areas where you aren't truly living out your beliefs? How can you become more disciplined?

1:1 Or *to strengthen the faith of.* **1:6** Or *must have only one wife,* or *must be married only once;* Greek reads *must be the husband of one wife.* **1:7a** Or *An overseer,* or *A bishop.* **1:7b** Greek *must not drink too much wine.* **1:12** This quotation is from Epimenides of Knossos.

1:1-4 an apostle. The salutation that begins the letter to Titus is different from those that open 1 and 2 Timothy. The most notable difference is the way in which Paul defines the purpose of his apostleship.

1:5-16 Crete. The problem in Crete has to do with the erroneous teaching of the circumcision party (see note for 1:10), which Paul strenuously opposed in the book of Galatians as well. Paul urges Titus to deal with this problem by appointing elders who will resist the false teachers.

1:5 complete . . . appoint. The reason he left Titus behind was to complete the task of organizing the churches, specifically, to appoint and train up elders.

1:6 Paul begins this list of characteristics by focusing on the home life of the potential elder. **blameless.** This is a general term covering a variety of behaviors, some of which Paul will identify. **faithful to his wife.** The most likely meaning is that sexual faithfulness to one's spouse was demanded.

1:7 elder. Sometimes translated "bishop" (*episkopoi*), this title probably did not mean in the first century what "bishop" has come to mean today. It seems likely that in Paul's day the terms "overseers" and "elders" were interchangeable. **dishonest with money.** The Cretans had a reputation for making money in shady ways.

1:8 Paul follows the list of five vices (v. 7) with a list of six virtues. **enjoy having guests in his home.** Overseers must be willing to open up their homes to guests. It was a common practice in the first century to offer hospitality to travelers (Rom. 12:13; 1 Tim. 5:10; 1 Pet. 4:9). **live wisely.** The Greek word, *sophron*, is hard to translate into English and has been variously rendered as "prudent," "of sound mind," and "chaste." **just.** Such a person acts justly toward others. **self-controlled.** Overseers must have worked to master their desires and behaviors.

1:10 For. Paul connects the character required of elders to the problem facing the church. **those who insist on circumcision.** Literally, "of the circumcision." This group of Christian Jews was insisting that before Gentiles could become Christians, they must first become Jews by undergoing the rite of circumcision.

1:13 reprimand them sternly. This is the only time in this letter that Paul calls upon Titus to directly confront the false teachers (v. 9 indicates the elders confronting them).

1:15-16 pure . . . corrupt. Food prohibitions, important to Jewish tradition, are probably in view here (1 Tim. 4:3).

1:15 Everything is pure. This is a common New Testament theme. What people eat does not defile them (Mark 7:1-23; Rom. 14:20; 1 Tim. 4:4).

but they deny him by the way they live. They are detestable and disobedient, worthless for doing anything good.

PROMOTE RIGHT TEACHING

2 As for you, Titus, promote the kind of living that reflects wholesome teaching. 2 Teach the older men to exercise self-control, to be worthy of respect, and to live wisely. They must have sound faith and be filled with love and patience.

3 Similarly, teach the older women to live in a way that honors God. They must not slander others or be heavy drinkers.* Instead, they should teach others what is good. 4 These older women must train the younger women to love their husbands and their children, 5 to live wisely and be pure, to work in their homes,* to do good, and to be submissive to their husbands. Then they will not bring shame on the word of God.

6 In the same way, encourage the young men to live wisely. 7 And you yourself must be an example to them by doing good works of every kind. Let everything you do reflect the integrity and seriousness of your teaching. 8 Teach the truth so that your teaching can't be criticized. Then those who oppose us will be ashamed and have nothing bad to say about us.

9 Slaves must always obey their masters and do their best to please them. They must not talk back 10 or steal, but must show themselves to be entirely trustworthy and good. Then they will make the teaching about God our Savior attractive in every way.

11 For the grace of God has been revealed, bringing salvation to all people. 12 And we are instructed to turn from godless living and sinful pleasures. We should live in this evil world with wisdom, righteousness, and devotion to God, 13 while we look forward with hope to that wonderful day when the glory of our great God and Savior, Jesus Christ, will be revealed. 14 He gave his life to free us from every kind of sin, to cleanse us, and to make us his very own people, totally committed to doing good deeds.

15 You must teach these things and encourage the believers to do them. You have the authority to correct them when necessary, so don't let anyone disregard what you say.

DO WHAT IS GOOD

3 Remind the believers to submit to the government and its officers. They should be obedient, always ready to do what is good. 2 They must not slander anyone and must avoid quarreling. Instead, they should be gentle and show true humility to everyone.

JUST SAY NO

1. In what area do you need to learn more self-control?

TITUS 2:1-15

2. What one quality in each of the groups mentioned is most important for Christians in our society (see vv. 2-7)?
3. What is Paul implying about the importance of mentors (trusted guides or models)? How important have mentors been in your life?
4. What difference does our salvation make in our behavior in this "evil world" (vv. 11-12)? What is it hardest for you to say "No" to?
5. How can you live with "wisdom, righteousness, and devotion to God" (v. 12) in the coming week?

DOING GOOD

1. What memory comes to mind when you think of being disobedient as a child?

TITUS 3:1-15

2. Why do you think Paul again stresses devotion to "doing good" (vv. 1,8,14)? What is there about human nature that makes such reminders necessary (v. 3)?
3. When can "doing good" become a problem?
4. What do verses 4-7 say about God's character? About His work in us?
5. Over the past year, where do you sense growth in "doing good" for God in the key areas you give you life to (relationships, school, sports, activities, etc.)?

2:3 Greek *be enslaved to much wine.* 2:5 Some manuscripts read *to care for their homes.*

2:2 older men. These would be men over 50. Paul's words to them parallel what he said to the potential elders (1:6-9) since most church leaders would be elders in age as well.

2:3 teach . . . what is good. Formal instruction is probably not intended. Rather, the idea is that the older women would mentor, modeling "what is good" for younger women in terms of a woman's character and in her role as a wife and mother.

2:5 submissive to their husbands. Paul is not placing women under the authority of all men. Instead he has in mind submission to the woman's own husband.

2:7 integrity. This means "without corruption," "sincere." In contrast to the false teachers, Titus' motivation must not be mercenary. **of your teaching.** The focus is on the activity of teaching. The three words that Paul uses to describe how Titus should teach relate to the motive, demeanor, and content of his teaching.

2:8 truth . . . can't be criticized. Literally, "healthy" or "wholesome" speech—a medical metaphor that Paul probably borrowed from the itinerant philosophers of the day. By this, he refers to teaching that is in accord with the gospel proclaimed by the apostles (v. 2; 1:9,13; 1 Tim. 1:10; 6:3; 2 Tim. 1:13; 4:3).

2:9 Slaves must always obey their masters. Slavery was widespread in the first century. To be a slave was to be at the bottom of the social system.

2:10 they will make the teaching about God our Savior attractive. What Paul urges for slaves is, in fact, what he wants from all Christians in Crete, namely, the kind of behavior that honors the Lord and that society in general will count as respectable. This will make the Christian message attractive to those outside the church (v. 5).

2:13 that wonderful hope. This refers to the second coming of Jesus. **our great God and Savior, Jesus Christ.** This is a clear statement of the deity of Christ.

2:14 to free us . . . and to cleanse us. Paul identifies the connection between the salvation Jesus brought and their lifestyle. Jesus died in order to: (1) rescue them from wickedness (therefore they ought not to live that way any longer); (2) make them a pure people (which defines how they are now to live). A godly lifestyle is, therefore, a response to the saving work of Jesus and a testimony to the power He has to change lives.

3:1-11 Remind the believers. Paul now returns to his main concern in the letter: the behavior of Christians. Previously, his focus was on the relationships between Christians and how this was viewed by the world (2:5,10). Now he turns to the question of how Christians are to behave to outsiders.

[3] Once we, too, were foolish and disobedient. We
were misled and became slaves to many lusts and
pleasures. Our lives were full of evil and envy, and we
hated each other. [4] But—

When God our Savior revealed his kindness and
love, [5] he saved us, not because of the righteous
things we had done, but because of his mercy. He
washed away our sins, giving us a new birth and
new life through the Holy Spirit.* [6] He generously
poured out the Spirit upon us through Jesus Christ
our Savior. [7] Because of his grace he made us right
in his sight and gave us confidence that we will
inherit eternal life.

[8] This is a trustworthy saying, and I want you to insist
on these teachings so that all who trust in God will
devote themselves to doing good. These teachings are
good and beneficial for everyone.

[9] Do not get involved in foolish discussions about
spiritual pedigrees* or in quarrels and fights about
obedience to Jewish laws. These things are useless
and a waste of time. [10] If people are causing divisions
among you, give a first and second warning. After
that, have nothing more to do with them. [11] For people
like that have turned away from the truth, and their
own sins condemn them.

PAUL'S FINAL REMARKS AND GREETINGS

[12] I am planning to send either Artemas or Tychi-
cus to you. As soon as one of them arrives, do your
best to meet me at Nicopolis, for I have decided to
stay there for the winter. [13] Do everything you can
to help Zenas the lawyer and Apollos with their
trip. See that they are given everything they need.
[14] Our people must learn to do good by meeting the
urgent needs of others; then they will not be un-
productive.

[15] Everybody here sends greetings. Please give my
greetings to the believers—all who love us.

May God's grace be with you all.

3:5 Greek *He saved us through the washing of regeneration and renewing of the Holy Spirit.* 3:9 Or *spiritual genealogies.*

3:5 he saved us. This is the main focus of verses 4-7. The tense of the verb indicates that this is a once-for-all act. **because of his mercy.** The mercy of God, not their character or works, is the basis for salvation. **new birth.** This is the first of three metaphors that describe salvation. Believers become new persons; they are reborn. **new life.** The second metaphor is similar to the first. It expresses the fact that they have been transformed into newness of life (2 Cor. 5:14-17).

3:7 declared us righteous. The third salvation metaphor emphasizes that believers are made right with God.

3:9 Do not get involved. Paul contrasts the good deeds, to which they are to devote themselves, with the evil deeds, which they are to flee. **spiritual pedigrees.** Some Jewish scholars took the family trees in the Old Testament and devoted great energy to constructing "biographies" for each character. **quarrels.** Literally, "word-battles," probably between those who disagree about genealogies and other such matters.

3:12 to meet me. Titus is to be replaced as soon as Paul can send someone to take over his work. **Artemas.** Nothing is known about this individual. **Tychicus.** Tychicus was a trusted fellow worker, who often traveled with or for Paul (Acts 20:4; Eph. 6:21; Col. 4:7). **Nicopolis.** This city was located several hundred miles northwest of Athens near the Adriatic Sea.

3:13 Zenas the lawyer and Apollos. These men probably carried this letter to Titus. Zenas was an expert in Roman law. Apollos is probably the well-known orator from Alexandria (Acts 18:24–19:1; 1 Cor. 1:12; 3:4,22; 16:12).

3:14 Our people. These are the believers on Crete as opposed to the false teachers.

INTRODUCTION TO

PHILEMON

PERSONAL READING PLAN

☐Philemon 1-25

AUTHOR

The Apostle Paul wrote Philemon.

DATE

Paul probably wrote Philemon in the early A.D. 60s.

THEME

Radical forgiveness.

HISTORICAL BACKGROUND

At this point in history, the 60 million slaves in the Roman Empire made up a critical component of Rome's social and economic structure. Runaways were considered criminals who were punishable by severe measures, including death. Philemon, a member of the church at Colosse, was the owner of a slave (Onesimus) who had run away. Somehow Onesimus got to Rome, met Paul, and became a Christian. We may wonder why Paul did not take this opportunity simply to condemn slavery. The reason is partially clear; conditions were not yet right for such a massive social upheaval. The Romans would never have voluntarily freed their slaves. Any revolt would have been savagely crushed. Also, Roman slavery was not a permanent condition based on race. This meant that slaves could purchase their freedom and enter the mainstream of society. Still, Paul did strike the first note for emancipation by his teaching on how Christians, regardless of race or economic condition, are one "family" in Christ (v. 16; Col. 3:11). This letter is Paul's attempt to persuade Philemon to forgive the crime and receive Onesimus as he would receive Paul himself. Onesimus carried this letter (and possibly Colossians and Ephesians) back to his home (Col. 4:9). The outcome of this story is not recorded in Scripture, but about A.D. 110 Bishop Ignatius of Antioch wrote a letter to the bishop of Ephesus, who was a man named Onesimus. In it, he used the same wordplay on his name as Paul does here in verses 10-11. Since many scholars think that Paul's letters were first collected at Ephesus, Bishop Ignatius may have included this personal note as a vivid demonstration of how Christ can transform and use even a runaway slave.

CHARACTERISTICS

Philemon is the shortest of Paul's New Testament letters, and it is his only private letter preserved in Scripture. All his other letters, whether to churches or to coworkers, relate to Paul's ministry. But Philemon is a personal plea written to a friend about a private matter—the fate of Onesimus, a runaway slave. As such, it gives us a valuable glimpse into Paul's personality. He is deeply sympathetic to the plight of Onesimus, so much so that he is willing to deprive himself of Onesimus' help and to pay Philemon for any loss Onesimus has caused him (vv. 18-19). This is certainly Christian compassion in action.

PASSAGES FOR TOPICAL GROUP STUDY

1-25 . . . . . STANDING WITH A FRIEND . . . . . Faithful Friendships

GREETINGS FROM PAUL

This letter is from Paul, a prisoner for preaching the
Good News about Christ Jesus, and from our brother
Timothy.
I am writing to Philemon, our beloved co-worker,
[2]and to our sister Apphia, and to our fellow soldier
Archippus, and to the church that meets in your*
house.
[3]May God our Father and the Lord Jesus Christ give
you grace and peace.

PAUL'S THANKSGIVING AND PRAYER

[4]I always thank my God when I pray for you, Phile-
mon, [5]because I keep hearing about your faith in the
Lord Jesus and your love for all of God's people. [6]And
I am praying that you will put into action the gener-
osity that comes from your faith as you understand
and experience all the good things we have in Christ.
[7]Your love has given me much joy and comfort, my
brother, for your kindness has often refreshed the
hearts of God's people.

PAUL'S APPEAL FOR ONESIMUS

[8]That is why I am boldly asking a favor of you. I could
demand it in the name of Christ because it is the right
thing for you to do. [9]But because of our love, I prefer
simply to ask you. Consider this as a request from
me—Paul, an old man and now also a prisoner for
the sake of Christ Jesus.*
[10]I appeal to you to show kindness to my child, Ones-
imus. I became his father in the faith while here in pris-
on. [11]Onesimus* hasn't been of much use to you in the
past, but now he is very useful to both of us. [12]I am send-
ing him back to you, and with him comes my own heart.
[13]I wanted to keep him here with me while I am
in these chains for preaching the Good News, and he
would have helped me on your behalf. [14]But I didn't
want to do anything without your consent. I wanted
you to help because you were willing, not because
you were forced. [15]It seems you lost Onesimus for a
little while so that you could have him back forever.
[16]He is no longer like a slave to you. He is more than
a slave, for he is a beloved brother, especially to me.
Now he will mean much more to you, both as a man
and as a brother in the Lord.
[17]So if you consider me your partner, welcome him
as you would welcome me. [18]If he has wronged you
in any way or owes you anything, charge it to me. [19]I,
PAUL, WRITE THIS WITH MY OWN HAND: I WILL REPAY IT.
AND I WON'T MENTION THAT YOU OWE ME YOUR VERY
SOUL!
[20]Yes, my brother, please do me this favor* for the
Lord's sake. Give me this encouragement in Christ.
[21]I am confident as I write this letter that you will
do what I ask and even more! [22]One more thing—
please prepare a guest room for me, for I am hoping
that God will answer your prayers and let me return
to you soon.

PAUL'S FINAL GREETINGS

[23]Epaphras, my fellow prisoner in Christ Jesus, sends
you his greetings. [24]So do Mark, Aristarchus, Demas,
and Luke, my co-workers.
[25]May the grace of the Lord Jesus Christ be with
your spirit.

FAITHFUL FRIENDSHIPS

1. Who was your best friend in grade school? What made this person such a good friend?

PHILEMON 1-25

2. What qualities in Philemon does Paul commend (vv. 4-7)?
3. Does the fact that Onesimus has become a Christian lessen the seriousness of his crime? Why or why not?
4. Why does Paul take such a strong stand with Philemon about forgiving and accepting Onesimus (vv. 9-12)?
5. Have you had an opportunity to "stand" for someone with a troubled background, but who has been changed by Christ? Would you stand up for somebody like this?

2 Throughout this letter, *you* and *your* are singular except in verses 3, 22, and 25. 9 Or *a prisoner of Christ Jesus.* 11 *Onesimus* means "useful." 20 Greek *onaimen,* a play on the name Onesimus.

1 prisoner. Paul may have written this letter during his imprisonment in Rome (Acts 28) or from an unrecorded imprisonment somewhere closer to Colosse, perhaps in Ephesus. **Philemon.** This man, not mentioned anywhere else in the New Testament, was obviously someone close to Paul.
2 Apphia. It is assumed she was Philemon's wife. **the church that meets in your house.** How Philemon responded to Onesimus was a matter that would affect the life of the church to which both of them now belonged.
8-9 because of our love. Christian love, not a grudging obedience to Paul's command, was the only basis on which a true brotherly relationship could be built between Philemon and Onesimus. **old man . . . prisoner.** While not appealing to his apostolic authority, Paul certainly appeals to the respect Philemon has for him.
11 hasn't been of much use . . . very useful. There is a play on words here. These two words, which sound very similar in Greek, share a root word that sounds like the word for "Christ" (*christos* means Christ; *euchrestos* means useful). Through Christ, Onesimus (whose name means useful), formerly a useless, disobedient slave, has now become truly useful as a brother in the Lord.
12 sending him back to you. In spite of his love, Paul had to send Onesimus back since harboring a runaway slave was a serious crime. The reality of his conversion would be seen in his willingness to return to Philemon and face up to the consequences of what he had done. Christian slaves were expected to view their work for their master as work done as unto the Lord (Col. 3:22-25).
16 both as a man and as a brother in the Lord. "In the flesh" Onesimus is just a slave, but "in the Lord" he is now Philemon's spiritual brother.
18 wronged you . . . owes you. Onesimus may have stolen some money before running away. Besides that, his escape caused economic loss through lost services.
19 I will repay it. This first part of this verse is a promissory note whereby Paul obligates himself to carry out the pledge he made in verse 18. The latter half of the verse reminds Philemon of the spiritual debt that he owes to Paul for the treasure of the gospel to which Paul introduced him.

INTRODUCTION TO

HEBREWS

PERSONAL READING PLAN

☐Hebrews 1:1–2:18
☐Hebrews 3:1-19
☐Hebrews 4:1-13
☐Hebrews 4:14–6:12
☐Hebrews 6:13–7:10
☐Hebrews 7:11-28
☐Hebrews 8:1–9:10
☐Hebrews 9:11-28
☐Hebrews 10:1-39
☐Hebrews 11:1-40
☐Hebrews 12:1-29
☐Hebrews 13:1-25

AUTHOR

No one knows who wrote the epistle to the Hebrews. The author is nowhere named within it, nor is there any strong external evidence pointing to a particular person. At least eight good candidates have been proposed.

Paul is listed as the author in the King James Version, even though no evidence is found in any of the ancient manuscripts. It is unlikely that Paul wrote Hebrews since the style and language is quite unlike Paul's. Hebrews is a polished piece of writing. Its transitions are neatly in place and its argument carefully spelled out. This sharply contrasts Paul's more expansive style.

Other suggested authors include Barnabas (Acts 4:36), Luke, Priscilla, Silas (1 Peter 5:12), Apollos (Acts 18:24), and Clement of Rome. Origen, a third-century Christian scholar, had the last word on this issue: saying that "only God knows certainly" (recorded in Eusebius, Historia Ecclesiastica).

DATE

It is difficult to be certain about its date as well. If the persecution referred to is that of Nero, then Hebrews was written after A.D. 64. Some believe it had to be written prior to the fall of Jerusalem and the destruction of the temple in A.D. 70, for such a dramatic event would have been mentioned as the end of the sacrificial system. Others argue for a later date nearer to the persecution by Emperor Domitian in A.D. 85, probably somewhere around A.D. 80.

THEME

The superiority of Jesus.

HISTORICAL BACKGROUND

This letter was probably written to a particular assembly of Jewish-Christian believers (perhaps a house church) that was part of a larger community, quite possibly in Rome. Whoever they were, it is clear that they had suffered great persecution (10:32-34) and that they were being tempted to abandon Christianity. What was weighing on them? Perhaps the constant injustices they suffered as Christians were beginning to take their toll. Or perhaps they were facing the prospect of severe persecution in the near future. Maybe they were being enticed away from Christ by false teaching that seemed to offer relief from their struggles. Whatever the temptation, Hebrews was written to encourage these beleaguered Christians to "keep . . . courage" (3:6), to have "endurance" (10:36), and to "hold tightly without wavering to the hope we affirm" (10:23) lest they compromise Christ and lose all the enormous blessings of the new covenant.

CHARACTERISTICS

To modern readers, Hebrews is a strange book filled with references to ancient traditions of a foreign culture. It is true that to understand Hebrews, the reader must understand the Old Testament. Yet for all its strangeness, Hebrews contains compelling themes and images, stirring remembrances of the heroes of the faith, and a breathtaking portrait of Jesus—the ultimate priest.

Hebrews has been called an epistle but in fact, it lacks several key features of a true letter: no introductory greeting, nor names of a sender or recipients. Its ending is typical of a letter, however, with personal greetings and a standard conclusion.

PURPOSE

How does one write to suffering Christians and tell them to stay faithful despite the price they are paying? The writer points them to Jesus, the only one who is worth such costly allegiance. As a result, in the book of Hebrews, we get a marvelous portrait of Christ—the prophet, priest and king whose new covenant is so superior to the old covenant that to fall away from Him would be unthinkable. The central theme of Hebrews, therefore, is the superiority of Christ. He is superior to the great religious leaders of the past such as Moses, Joshua, and Aaron. He is superior to the great supernatural powers like angels. The new covenant he established and the new order he inaugurated are superior to the old beliefs and practices of the Jewish religion.

PASSAGES FOR TOPICAL GROUP STUDY

3:1-19 . . . . HARDENED HEARTS and COMMUNITY . . . . Help for the Heart
4:1-13 . . . . OBEDIENCE AND REWARD . . . . The Ultimate Reward
4:14–5:10 . . JESUS' PERFECTION . . . . Bold Confessions
5:11–6:12 . . MATURITY . . . . Keep Moving Forward
8:1-13 . . . . . NEW COVENANT . . . . The Best Game Plan
10:19-39 . . . HOLDING ONTO FAITH . . . Draw Near and Hold On
11:1-16 . . . . FUTURE DREAMS and FAITH . . . Faith Hall of Fame
12:1-13 . . . . PERSEVERANCE and DISCIPLINE . . . Running Wide Open
12:14-29 . . . REJECTING GOD or ACCEPTING GRACE . . . . Pursuing Peace

PASSAGES FOR GENERAL GROUP STUDY

1:1-14 . . . . The Role of Angels
2:1-18 . . . . . Power of Shared Experiences (Jesus one of us)
6:13-20 . . . . The Promise (Trusting God)
7:1-28 . . . . Jesus is #1 (Superior Qualifications)
9:1-10 . . . . A Guilty Pleas (and Restoration)
9:11-28 . . . . Passionate Sacrifice (Once-For-All)
10:1-18 . . . . The Perfect Sacrifice
13:1-25 . . . . Lifestyle of the Rich in Faith

JESUS CHRIST IS GOD'S SON

1 Long ago God spoke many times and in many ways
to our ancestors through the prophets. [2] And now in
these final days, he has spoken to us through his Son.
God promised everything to the Son as an inheritance,
and through the Son he created the universe. [3] The Son
radiates God's own glory and expresses the very char-
acter of God, and he sustains everything by the mighty
power of his command. When he had cleansed us from
our sins, he sat down in the place of honor at the right
hand of the majestic God in heaven. [4] This shows that
the Son is far greater than the angels, just as the name
God gave him is greater than their names.

THE SON IS GREATER THAN THE ANGELS

[5] For God never said to any angel what he said to Jesus:

"You are my Son.
Today I have become your Father.*"

God also said,

"I will be his Father,
and he will be my Son."*

[6] And when he brought his supreme* Son into the
world, God said,*

"Let all of God's angels worship him."*

[7] Regarding the angels, he says,

"He sends his angels like the winds,
his servants like flames of fire."*

[8] But to the Son he says,

"Your throne, O God, endures forever and
ever.
You rule with a scepter of justice.
[9] You love justice and hate evil.
Therefore, O God, your God has anointed
you,
pouring out the oil of joy on you more than on
anyone else."*

[10] He also says to the Son,

"In the beginning, Lord, you laid the foundation of
the earth
and made the heavens with your hands.
[11] They will perish, but you remain forever.
They will wear out like old clothing.
[12] You will fold them up like a cloak
and discard them like old clothing.
But you are always the same;
you will live forever."*

[13] And God never said to any of the angels,

"Sit in the place of honor at my right hand
until I humble your enemies,
making them a footstool under your feet."*

[14] Therefore, angels are only servants—spirits sent to
care for people who will inherit salvation.

A WARNING AGAINST DRIFTING AWAY

2 So we must listen very carefully to the truth we
have heard, or we may drift away from it. [2] For
the message God delivered through angels has al-
ways stood firm, and every violation of the law
and every act of disobedience was punished. [3] So
what makes us think we can escape if we ignore
this great salvation that was first announced by
the Lord Jesus himself and then delivered to us by
those who heard him speak? [4] And God confirmed
the message by giving signs and wonders and var-
ious miracles and gifts of the Holy Spirit whenever
he chose.

THE ROLE OF ANGELS

1. What is your favorite movie, TV show, or story about an angel or angels?

HEBREWS 1:1-14

2. What is this writer's main reason for bringing up angels (vv. 5-8)?
3. Why might someone be tempted to worship angels instead of Jesus?
4. What is the difference between the biblical view of angels and some modern ideas about angels?
5. What does verse 14 say about the purpose of angels? How does that make you feel?
6. How do you need one of God's angels to minister to you right now?

1:5a Or *Today I reveal you as my Son.* Ps 2:7. **1:5b** 2 Sam 7:14. **1:6a** Or *firstborn.* **1:6b** Or *when he again brings his supreme Son* [or *firstborn Son*] *into the world, God will say.* **1:6c** Deut 32:43. **1:7** Ps 104:4 (Greek version). **1:8-9** Ps 45:6-7. **1:10-12** Ps 102:25-27. **1:13** Ps 110:1.

1:1 through the prophets. God spoke to His people through his representatives at different times and in various ways.
1:2 he has spoken . . . through his Son. In contrast to the partial, limited revelation of the prophets, the Son fully reveals God to the world. The author intends to show that Jesus is superior to all the forms of communication used in the past. **final days.** This term signifies the time after Jesus' resurrection.
1:3 radiates God's own glory. God's glory is like light that radiates from its source. Jesus' miracles revealed God's glory (John 2:11) and thus made God known to people (John 1:18). **expresses . . . character of God.** The Greek word *charakter* was used to refer to an impression made by a stamping die (such as the inscription on the face of a coin). The image on a coin exactly matches the image engraved on the die. **sustains everything.** The Son's role in creation was not limited to creation's origin or its future. It is His powerful word that keeps order and stability in creation (Col. 1:17).
1:14 servants. In contrast to the ruling authority of the Son, the function of the angels is to serve God's people at the Son's command. **sent to care.** This describes the priestly service at the tabernacle (8:4-6). In the New Testament, angels perform tasks such as interceding for children (Matt. 18:10), protecting the apostles (Acts 12:7-10), revealing God's will (Luke 1:11-38; Acts 8:26), and carrying out God's judgment (Rev. 7:1). **salvation.** Later passages indicate salvation as a deliverance (from the devil's power — 2:14; the fear of death — 2:15; and the power of sin — 9:26). Salvation also leads to holiness (10:10), forgiveness (10:18), free access to God (10:22), and the eternal inheritance that God provides for those who have faith (9:15).
2:2-4 The author appeals to four things that show the divine origin of the message of the gospel: (1) it was the Lord, the Son, who first announced this message; (2) this message was supported by that of the apostles, men commissioned by the Son; (3) the signs, wonders, and various miracles that have come through the apostles (v. 4) show the divine authorization of the message; and (4) the gifts of the Holy Spirit, personally experienced by these people and given for their mutual encouragement (1 Cor. 12; Eph. 4), give God's confirmation to this message.

POWER OF SHARED EXPERIENCES

1. What is some good news you've recently had that you couldn't wait to share with someone else?

HEBREWS 2:1-18

2. In what respects was Jesus "a little lower than the angels" (v. 9)? What elevated Him above them?
3. Why did we need someone with flesh and blood like us—not an angel—to die in our place (vv. 14-18)? What is the goal of our salvation (vv. 10-11)?
4. What do you think Jesus gained from His earth-bound experience that He didn't already have?
5. How can you use your own experiences to share Christ with others?

JESUS, THE MAN

5 And furthermore, it is not angels who will control
the future world we are talking about. 6 For in one
place the Scriptures say,

"What are mere mortals that you should think
about them,
or a son of man* that you should care for him?
7 Yet for a little while you made them a little lower
than the angels
and crowned them with glory and honor.*
8 You gave them authority over all things."*

Now when it says "all things," it means nothing is left
out. But we have not yet seen all things put under their
authority. 9 What we do see is Jesus, who for a little
while was given a position "a little lower than the an-
gels"; and because he suffered death for us, he is now
"crowned with glory and honor." Yes, by God's grace,
Jesus tasted death for everyone. 10 God, for whom and
through whom everything was made, chose to bring
many children into glory. And it was only right that
he should make Jesus, through his suffering, a perfect
leader, fit to bring them into their salvation.
11 So now Jesus and the ones he makes holy have the
same Father. That is why Jesus is not ashamed to call
them his brothers and sisters.* 12 For he said to God,

"I will proclaim your name to my brothers and
sisters.
I will praise you among your assembled people."*
13 He also said,

"I will put my trust in him,"
that is, "I and the children God has given me."*

14 Because God's children are human beings—
made of flesh and blood—the Son also became flesh
and blood. For only as a human being could he die,
and only by dying could he break the power of the
devil, who had* the power of death. 15 Only in this
way could he set free all who have lived their lives as
slaves to the fear of dying.
16 We also know that the Son did not come to help
angels; he came to help the descendants of Abraham.
17 Therefore, it was necessary for him to be made in
every respect like us, his brothers and sisters,* so that
he could be our merciful and faithful High Priest be-
fore God. Then he could offer a sacrifice that would
take away the sins of the people. 18 Since he himself
has gone through suffering and testing, he is able to
help us when we are being tested.

JESUS IS GREATER THAN MOSES

3 And so, dear brothers and sisters who belong to
God and* are partners with those called to heav-
en, think carefully about this Jesus whom we declare

HELP FOR THE HEART

1. What or who can cheer you up when you are down or disappointed?

HEBREWS 3:1-19

2. In what ways are Jesus and Moses similar (vv. 1-6)? In what ways is Jesus greater? Why is that important?
3. What does it mean to "enter [God's] rest" (vv. 11,18-19; 4:1-11; Matt. 11:28-30)?
4. What is the ultimate danger of allowing our hearts to be hardened?
5. What role does the Christian community play in keeping its fellow members true to God (v. 13)?
6. Are there any areas of your life where you are in danger of being "hardened by sin's deception"?

2:6 Or *the Son of Man.* **2:7** Some manuscripts add *You gave them charge of everything you made.* **2:6-8** Ps 8:4-6 (Greek version). **2:11** Greek *brothers;* also in 2:12. **2:12** Ps 22:22. **2:13** Isa 8:17-18. **2:14** Or *has.* **2:17** Greek *like the brothers.* **3:1a** Greek *And so, holy brothers who.*

2:9 crowned with glory . . . Jesus tasted death. Jesus' death was not a denial of His glory but the means through which this glory was revealed.
2:10 it was only right. While the idea of a suffering Messiah was unacceptable to the Jews, the author maintains that the idea is appropriate. **leader.** Literally, "pioneer" (12:2). The image is of one who blazes the way, making it possible for others to follow. **perfect.** This does not imply that Jesus had faults that needed to be purged.
2:16 descendants of Abraham. Since Jewish converts were the primary audience, the author points out that it is only through Jesus that the ancient promise to Abraham is fulfilled (Gen. 12:3; Rom. 2:28-29; 4:9, 13-23; Gal. 3:6-14).
2:17 like us. Because of God's choice of Israel to be His people, the Son became a flesh and blood Jew. Only in this way could He truly serve as a representative of the people before God. **our merciful and faithful High Priest.** The idea of the Messiah as a high priest is this author's unique way of communicating the identity of Jesus. This picture is found only in this New Testament book. **offer a sacrifice.** A priest's main function was to offer the blood of a sacrifice in place of the blood of the sinner. Chapters 9–10 interpret Jesus' death in this framework.
2:18 he himself has gone through . . . testing. Jesus is more, not less, able to help those who are currently tempted. Jesus' humanity, rather than detracting from His elevated status, fully qualifies Him to enter into the struggles of His people. He can help them in a way angels never could (4:15).
3:1 think carefully about this Jesus. Two phrases are used to remind the readers of who they are in Christ. **dear brothers and sisters.** Not morally perfect but "set apart" by God as His people (2:11-13). **partners.** Since the readers share together in God's call, they have special responsibilities toward God and one another. **think carefully.** This implies concentrated attention and reflection. While Jesus helps believers deal with temptations, they are to focus their attention on Him so they will not be distracted by temptations to follow another course (12:2).

to be God's messenger* and High Priest. 2 For he was
faithful to God, who appointed him, just as Moses
served faithfully when he was entrusted with God's
entire* house.
3 But Jesus deserves far more glory than Moses, just
as a person who builds a house deserves more praise
than the house itself. 4 For every house has a builder,
but the one who built everything is God.
5 Moses was certainly faithful in God's house as a
servant. His work was an illustration of the truths
God would reveal later. 6 But Christ, as the Son, is in
charge of God's entire house. And we are God's house,
if we keep our courage and remain confident in our
hope in Christ.*
7 That is why the Holy Spirit says,

"Today when you hear his voice,
8 don't harden your hearts
as Israel did when they rebelled,
when they tested me in the wilderness.
9 There your ancestors tested and tried my patience,
even though they saw my miracles for forty
years.
10 So I was angry with them, and I said,
'Their hearts always turn away from me.
They refuse to do what I tell them.'
11 So in my anger I took an oath:
'They will never enter my place of rest.'"*

12 Be careful then, dear brothers and sisters.* Make
sure that your own hearts are not evil and unbeliev-
ing, turning you away from the living God. 13 You must
warn each other every day, while it is still "today," so
that none of you will be deceived by sin and hardened
against God. 14 For if we are faithful to the end, trust-
ing God just as firmly as when we first believed, we
will share in all that belongs to Christ. 15 Remember
what it says:

"Today when you hear his voice,
don't harden your hearts
as Israel did when they rebelled."*

16 And who was it who rebelled against God,
even though they heard his voice? Wasn't it the
people Moses led out of Egypt? 17 And who made
God angry for forty years? Wasn't it the people who
sinned, whose corpses lay in the wilderness? 18 And
to whom was God speaking when he took an oath
that they would never enter his rest? Wasn't it the
people who disobeyed him? 19 So we see that be-
cause of their unbelief they were not able to enter
his rest.

THE ULTIMATE REWARD

1. What is your favorite way to spend a Sunday afternoon?

HEBREWS 4:1-13

2. What efforts (v. 11) can help us enter into God's rest (John 6:27-29)?
3. How would you explain the "promised rest" to someone who is not a Christian?
4. What does it mean that, "the word of God is alive" (v. 12)? "Powerful"? That it penetrates?
5. Is there anything in your life that you are trying to hide from God (v. 13)? If so, how do you think you can you break this disobedience like that of the people of Israel (v. 11)?

PROMISED REST FOR GOD'S PEOPLE

4 God's promise of entering his rest still stands, so
we ought to tremble with fear that some of you
might fail to experience it. 2 For this good news—that
God has prepared this rest—has been announced to
us just as it was to them. But it did them no good be-
cause they didn't share the faith of those who listened
to God.* 3 For only we who believe can enter his rest.
As for the others, God said,

"In my anger I took an oath:
'They will never enter my place of rest,'"*

even though this rest has been ready since he made
the world. 4 We know it is ready because of the place
in the Scriptures where it mentions the seventh day:
"On the seventh day God rested from all his work."*
5 But in the other passage God said, "They will never
enter my place of rest."*
6 So God's rest is there for people to enter, but those
who first heard this good news failed to enter be-
cause they disobeyed God. 7 So God set another time
for entering his rest, and that time is today. God an-
nounced this through David much later in the words
already quoted:

"Today when you hear his voice,
don't harden your hearts."*

8 Now if Joshua had succeeded in giving them this
rest, God would not have spoken about another day of

3:1b Greek *God's apostle.* **3:2** Some manuscripts do not include *entire.* **3:6** Some manuscripts add *faithful to the end.* **3:7-11** Ps 95:7-11. **3:12** Greek *brothers.* **3:15** Ps 95:7-8. **4:2** Some manuscripts read *they didn't combine what they heard with faith.* **4:3** Ps 95:11. **4:4** Gen 2:2. **4:5** Ps 95:11. **4:7** Ps 95:7-8.

3:3-6 Two analogies substantiate the claim that Jesus is worthy of far more honor than even Moses: (1) In terms of a house (or dynasty), Jesus is the builder (God made the universe through Jesus as indicated in 1:2), whereas Moses is part of the house itself; and (2) Moses was faithful as a servant, but Jesus is the Son who owns the estate.
3:6 our hope. Not a wish, but an expectation that is guaranteed to come about.
3:11 my place of rest. In the context of the Israelites, this meant the promised land of Canaan where they would have prosperity and peace (4:1).
3:12 turning you away. Literally, "abandons" or "defects." Whereas the warning in 2:1 was against drifting from the Lord, this is a deliberate turning from God's way.
3:16-19 Through the five questions based on events in Numbers 14:26-35, the author hammers home the importance of maintaining faith.
4:1 promise. God's promise was to bring Israel into a "good and spacious land" where they would have peace (Ex. 3:8). However, the generation who originally received this promise never experienced its fulfillment. **his rest.** Not a state of idleness but a condition in which one is free to live in peace, joy, security, and freedom. Israel thought of rest in terms of dwelling securely in their own land in freedom and prosperity (Deut. 5:33; 8:6-9). Later on, this developed into the hope of an eternal kingdom under the wise, compassionate leadership of a Davidic king (Ezek. 34:24-31; Dan. 7:13-14). It is likely some of the original readers thought of this rest in such national, physical terms (Acts 1:6). **tremble with fear.** This is reverence that produces careful behavior.

BOLD CONFESSIONS

1. When you "blow it," how do you feel about the mistake? About yourself? About others involved?

HEBREWS 4:14–5:10

2. What characteristic about Jesus' priesthood is most encouraging (4:14-15; see 2:17; 3:1)?
3. What are two qualities of Jesus that allow Him to be compared to Melchizedek (5:6,10; see chap. 7)?
4. What is the significance for our eternal salvation, as well as our current situations, that Jesus was fully human? That Jesus was without sin?
5. How does this passage affect your feelings about your relationship with Jesus? What sins do you need to confess to your "High Priest"?

---

rest still to come. 9 So there is a special rest* still wait-
ing for the people of God. 10 For all who have entered
into God's rest have rested from their labors, just as
God did after creating the world. 11 So let us do our
best to enter that rest. But if we disobey God, as the
people of Israel did, we will fall.
12 For the word of God is alive and powerful. It is
sharper than the sharpest two-edged sword, cutting
between soul and spirit, between joint and marrow. It
exposes our innermost thoughts and desires. 13 Noth-
ing in all creation is hidden from God. Everything is
naked and exposed before his eyes, and he is the one
to whom we are accountable.

CHRIST IS OUR HIGH PRIEST

14 So then, since we have a great High Priest who
has entered heaven, Jesus the Son of God, let us hold
firmly to what we believe. 15 This High Priest of ours
understands our weaknesses, for he faced all of the
same testings we do, yet he did not sin. 16 So let us
come boldly to the throne of our gracious God. There
we will receive his mercy, and we will find grace to
help us when we need it most.

5 Every high priest is a man chosen to represent
other people in their dealings with God. He pre-
sents their gifts to God and offers sacrifices for their
sins. 2 And he is able to deal gently with ignorant and
wayward people because he himself is subject to the
same weaknesses. 3 That is why he must offer sacrific-
es for his own sins as well as theirs.
4 And no one can become a high priest simply be-
cause he wants such an honor. He must be called by
God for this work, just as Aaron was. 5 That is why
Christ did not honor himself by assuming he could
become High Priest. No, he was chosen by God, who
said to him,

"You are my Son.
Today I have become your Father.*"

6 And in another passage God said to him,

"You are a priest forever in the order of
Melchizedek."*

7 While Jesus was here on earth, he offered prayers
and pleadings, with a loud cry and tears, to the one
who could rescue him from death. And God heard
his prayers because of his deep reverence for God.
8 Even though Jesus was God's Son, he learned obe-
dience from the things he suffered. 9 In this way, God
qualified him as a perfect High Priest, and he became
the source of eternal salvation for all those who obey
him. 10 And God designated him to be a High Priest in
the order of Melchizedek.

4:9 Or *a Sabbath rest.* 5:5 Or *Today I reveal you as my Son.* Ps 2:7. 5:6 Ps 110:4.

4:9 special rest. This term, found only here in the New Testament, is a play on words—the Greek words for "sabbath" and "rest" sound alike. The term identifies this rest with the traditional Jewish Sabbath rest yet emphasizes that this rest fulfills the reality that the Jewish Sabbath only symbolized. Once again Jesus' superiority over all elements of traditional Jewish faith is evidenced. **people of God.** This includes all people, Jew or Gentile, who entrust themselves to Jesus.

4:11 do our best. Literally, "strive." The life of faith is not a passive waiting for God but an urgent, determined resolve to push on in the pursuit of God.

4:12 word of God is alive and powerful. The comparison of God's Word to a sword was first made by Isaiah (Isa. 49:2). It shows the piercing, discerning power of God's Word to cut through people's thoughts, intentions, and motivations (Eph. 6:17; Rev. 1:16). **cutting between soul and spirit, between joint and marrow. . . . innermost thoughts and desires.** The whole person is spoken to by God's Word—spirit, body, and mind.

4:13 naked and exposed. Three possibilities exist as to the meaning of this graphic image. It may refer to: (1) a wrestler whose head has been thrust back rendering him vulnerable to being pinned; (2) a soldier without armor to cover his throat; (3) a sacrificial animal whose neck is bared so that a knife can be drawn across its throat. All three images portray a frightening picture of being defenseless before an opponent.

4:14 a great High Priest. The high priest served as the spiritual leader (and often as the civil leader) of the Jews. His most unique function was to bring a sacrifice to God in the Most Holy Place on the Day of Atonement (9:3,8; Lev. 16:17). **entered heaven.** As the high priest would pass through a curtain into the Most Holy Place in the tabernacle, so Jesus entered into the presence of God as the representative of those who trust in Him.

4:15 same testings we do. Jesus was tempted in the desert by Satan (Luke 4:1-13). Here we find that He experienced every kind of temptation that we face. **he did not sin.** Technically, every high priest was without sin before offering atonement for the people. This was achieved by offering a sacrifice for himself prior to offering those for the people (5:3). Jesus was superior to the Old Testament priesthood because He had no sin for which to offer sacrifice.

4:16 come boldly to the throne. Jesus sits at the right hand of God, interceding for us. The readers are urged to approach God, knowing they have a compassionate, perfect high priest who is gracious and merciful to the needy (6:20).

5:5-6 High Priest. Jesus, the God-appointed priestly-king. Psalms 2:7 and 110:4 are linked to show that Jesus' priesthood can be traced to the mysterious Old Testament figure of Melchizedek, a king-priest who lived long before Aaron was born (Gen. 14:18-19). This connection between Jesus and Melchizedek (first identified in Psalm 110) was unique to the author of Hebrews.

5:5 Christ did not honor himself. For the second time (1:5) in Hebrews the author quotes Psalm 2 to show that Jesus did not place on Himself the honor of being high priest but responded to God's call to that appointment.

5:6 a priest forever in the order of Melchizedek. The high priesthood in Israel was a hereditary office based on descent from Aaron who was of the tribe of Levi. The priesthood of Christ was of a different order—the order of Melchizedek who was both king and priest. Jesus, too, is both king and priest. Unlike the Aaronic priesthood, Jesus was of the tribe of Judah. His priesthood is both perfect and will last always.

5:7 prayers and pleadings. The two words overlap, but the latter most often indicates an intense pleading. **loud cry and tears.** Western culture does not typically associate such emotion with prayer, but this would be a normal part of sincere intercession by the faithful Jew. Jesus' prayer in Gethsemane may be in view (Matt. 26:36-42). **rescue him from death.** In one sense Jesus was not "saved from death." He had to pass through it to experience resurrection and victory over death. **reverence.** Literally, "godly fear."

A CALL TO SPIRITUAL GROWTH

11 There is much more we would like to say about this,
but it is difficult to explain, especially since you are
spiritually dull and don't seem to listen. 12 You have
been believers so long now that you ought to be
teaching others. Instead, you need someone to teach
you again the basic things about God's word.* You are
like babies who need milk and cannot eat solid food.
13 For someone who lives on milk is still an infant and
doesn't know how to do what is right. 14 Solid food is
for those who are mature, who through training have
the skill to recognize the difference between right
and wrong.

KEEP MOVING FORWARD

1. What do you like hot out of the oven with a glass of cold milk: Chocolate chip cookies? Pound cake? Homemade bread? Apple pie?
2. What skill did you learn when you were younger that caused you to realize you were growing up?

HEBREWS 5:11–6:12

3. What effect does "solid food" have on the believer (5:14)?
4. What is wrong with this prolonged immaturity (6:4-6)?
5. How and why does the author encourage his readers to do "better things" to increase in maturity (6:9-12)?
6. What is the overarching warning you see here? How does it apply to your life?

6 So let us stop going over the basic teachings about
Christ again and again. Let us go on instead and
become mature in our understanding. Surely we don't
need to start again with the fundamental importance
of repenting from evil deeds* and placing our faith in
God. 2 You don't need further instruction about bap-
tisms, the laying on of hands, the resurrection of the
dead, and eternal judgment. 3 And so, God willing, we
will move forward to further understanding.
4 For it is impossible to bring back to repentance
those who were once enlightened—those who have
experienced the good things of heaven and shared in
the Holy Spirit, 5 who have tasted the goodness of the
word of God and the power of the age to come—6 and
who then turn away from God. It is impossible to
bring such people back to repentance; by rejecting
the Son of God, they themselves are nailing him to the
cross once again and holding him up to public shame.
7 When the ground soaks up the falling rain and
bears a good crop for the farmer, it has God's blessing.
8 But if a field bears thorns and thistles, it is useless.
The farmer will soon condemn that field and burn it.
9 Dear friends, even though we are talking this way,
we really don't believe it applies to you. We are confi-
dent that you are meant for better things, things that
come with salvation. 10 For God is not unjust. He will
not forget how hard you have worked for him and
how you have shown your love to him by caring for
other believers,* as you still do. 11 Our great desire is
that you will keep on loving others as long as life lasts,
in order to make certain that what you hope for will
come true. 12 Then you will not become spiritually dull
and indifferent. Instead, you will follow the example
of those who are going to inherit God's promises be-
cause of their faith and endurance.

GOD'S PROMISES BRING HOPE

13 For example, there was God's promise to Abraham.
Since there was no one greater to swear by, God took
an oath in his own name, saying:

14 "I will certainly bless you,
and I will multiply your descendants beyond
number."*

15 Then Abraham waited patiently, and he received
what God had promised.
16 Now when people take an oath, they call on
someone greater than themselves to hold them to it.
And without any question that oath is binding. 17 God
also bound himself with an oath, so that those who
received the promise could be perfectly sure that he
would never change his mind. 18 So God has given
both his promise and his oath. These two things are
unchangeable because it is impossible for God to lie.
Therefore, we who have fled to him for refuge can
have great confidence as we hold to the hope that
lies before us. 19 This hope is a strong and trustworthy
anchor for our souls. It leads us through the curtain
into God's inner sanctuary. 20 Jesus has already gone
in there for us. He has become our eternal High Priest
in the order of Melchizedek.

5:12 Or *about the oracles of God.* **6:1** Greek *from dead works.* **6:10** Greek *for God's holy people.* **6:14** Gen 22:17.

5:12 milk . . . solid food. While these readers have been believers long enough to have become "teachers," their uncertain faithfulness is more akin to that of "babies" just beginning to walk with Christ.

5:13-14 infant . . . doesn't know how to do what is right. Spiritual maturity, like emotional maturity, is developed through practicing that which leads to responsible development.

6:1-2 become mature. The only way to become trained (5:14) is to start exercising. The author wants to move on to weightier matters. **repenting . . . faith, baptisms . . . laying on of hands, the resurrection of the dead . . . eternal judgment.** These three couplets focus on basic elements of the Christian life, church practices, and doctrine. All could be found in Judaism and the readers may have lost sight of how Jesus had changed their meaning. The themes that dominate the rest of the book, Jesus' role as high priest and sacrifice, will remind them. **basic teachings.** Acts that stem from sin and lead to death. Repentance from sin was the first note of the gospel message (Mark 1:14-15). **baptisms.** Some Jewish sects practiced ceremonies for cleansing far beyond what the Law required.

6:4-6 back to repentance. Western Christians often think of the terms in this warning in a subjective, individual sense and wonder how someone who has been touched by God like this could give up faith. The author was likely not referring to subjective experiences at all but to "tasted the heavenly gift" as the Lord's Supper; "became companions with the Holy Spirit" as the laying on of hands (a sign that the person was included in the community of the Spirit); "tasted God's good word " as hearing gospel preaching; and "tasted the powers of the coming age" as observing the use of spiritual gifts within the church. Jewish Christians viewed these rituals as vital expressions of faith. To partake in them and then deliberately choose not to live up to the obligations they represented was unthinkable. **impossible . . . back to repentance.** Since to leave required a deliberate, conscious act, there could be no reasonable expectation that such people would ever return.

6:9-12 He will not forget . . . you have worked. The warning gives way to encouragement. Their works of love indicate that they have not fallen away (v. 10). They are urged to stay on that course, following the example of others in the past who held on to God's promises (v. 12)

THE PROMISE

1. What tries your patience more: Slow elevators? Slow food service? Traffic jams? How do you react?
2. What is one goal you would like to accomplish this year?

HEBREWS 6:13-20

3. How does Abraham's example help these people understand God's promise (3:12; 6:6)?
4. What effect did God's promise and oath have on Abraham's descendants? How does this affect Christians now?
5. What is the source of our hope (vv. 17-19)?
6. Where in your life does trusting in God come hardest? Easiest? Why?

JESUS IS #1

1. If you could live to be 100 but could retain either the body or the mind of a 30-year-old, which would you choose? Why?

HEBREWS 7:1-28

2. From verses 1-10, what do we know about Melchizedek? How did Abraham regard him?
3. In what ways is Jesus like the Melchizedek portrayed here (vv. 12-17)?
4. In what ways is Jesus a better priest than those under the Old Testament system (vv. 20-28)?
5. Why is the writer emphasizing Jesus' superior qualifications as a priest?
6. How do you need Jesus to intercede for you (v. 25) this week?

MELCHIZEDEK IS GREATER THAN ABRAHAM

7 This Melchizedek was king of the city of Salem
and also a priest of God Most High. When Abra-
ham was returning home after winning a great battle
against the kings, Melchizedek met him and blessed
him. 2 Then Abraham took a tenth of all he had cap-
tured in battle and gave it to Melchizedek. The name
Melchizedek means "king of justice," and king of Sa-
lem means "king of peace." 3 There is no record of his
father or mother or any of his ancestors—no begin-
ning or end to his life. He remains a priest forever,
resembling the Son of God.

4 Consider then how great this Melchizedek was.
Even Abraham, the great patriarch of Israel, recog-
nized this by giving him a tenth of what he had taken
in battle. 5 Now the law of Moses required that the
priests, who are descendants of Levi, must collect a
tithe from the rest of the people of Israel,* who are
also descendants of Abraham. 6 But Melchizedek,
who was not a descendant of Levi, collected a tenth
from Abraham. And Melchizedek placed a blessing
upon Abraham, the one who had already received
the promises of God. 7 And without question, the per-
son who has the power to give a blessing is greater
than the one who is blessed.

8 The priests who collect tithes are men who die,
so Melchizedek is greater than they are, because
we are told that he lives on. 9 In addition, we might
even say that these Levites—the ones who collect the
tithe—paid a tithe to Melchizedek when their ances-
tor Abraham paid a tithe to him. 10 For although Levi
wasn't born yet, the seed from which he came was
in Abraham's body when Melchizedek collected the
tithe from him.

11 So if the priesthood of Levi, on which the law
was based, could have achieved the perfection God
intended, why did God need to establish a different
priesthood, with a priest in the order of Melchizedek
instead of the order of Levi and Aaron?*

12 And if the priesthood is changed, the law must
also be changed to permit it. 13 For the priest we are
talking about belongs to a different tribe, whose
members have never served at the altar as priests.
14 What I mean is, our Lord came from the tribe of Ju-
dah, and Moses never mentioned priests coming from
that tribe.

JESUS IS LIKE MELCHIZEDEK

15 This change has been made very clear since a dif-
ferent priest, who is like Melchizedek, has appeared.
16 Jesus became a priest, not by meeting the physical
requirement of belonging to the tribe of Levi, but by
the power of a life that cannot be destroyed. 17 And the
psalmist pointed this out when he prophesied,

> "You are a priest forever in the order of
> Melchizedek."*

18 Yes, the old requirement about the priesthood was
set aside because it was weak and useless. 19 For the
law never made anything perfect. But now we have
confidence in a better hope, through which we draw
near to God.

7:5 Greek *from their brothers.* **7:11** Greek *the order of Aaron?* **7:17** Ps 110:4.

7:1 Melchizedek. Probably not as obscure a figure to the original readers as he is to readers today. **king . . . of Salem.** This city was associated with the site of Jerusalem. **winning a great battle.** Abraham had fought against a coalition of tribal rulers.

7:2 took a tenth. The tribute may have been given as an acknowledgment of Melchizedek's relationship with Abraham's God. In any case Abraham recognized Melchizedek as a superior, worthy of a tithe (tenth) of all he owned. **king of Salem . . . king of peace.** Since vowels were never written in Hebrew, both "Salem" and "peace [*shalom*]" were spelled *slm*— allowing for an easy identification of the two words.

7:4-10 Melchizedek's priesthood is compared to that of Levi (Num. 8). In the mindset of an Israelite, what my ancestor did was what I did—for I was part of him or her; what I do reflects what my ancestor did since he or she lives on in me. Since Abraham paid tribute to Melchizedek, the Levitical priests as Abraham's descendants also paid tribute to him. Since tribute is paid from the lesser to the greater Melchizedek's priesthood is superior to that of the Levites.

7:11-19 The need for a new High Priest is the theme of this section.

7:16-17 physical requirement. The Levitical priesthood was based solely on ancestry. The new priesthood is based on one's eternal nature. Jesus' resurrection thus qualified Him to be the better High Priest foretold in Psalm 110.

7:18-19 never made . . . perfect. While the endless repetition of sacrifices served to remind people of their sin, it was powerless to change their condition (10:3-4; Rom. 3:20).

[20]This new system was established with a solemn
oath. Aaron's descendants became priests without
such an oath, [21]but there was an oath regarding Jesus.
For God said to him,

"The LORD has taken an oath and will not break
his vow:
'You are a priest forever.'"*

[22]Because of this oath, Jesus is the one who guaran-
tees this better covenant with God.
[23]There were many priests under the old system,
for death prevented them from remaining in office.
[24]But because Jesus lives forever, his priesthood lasts
forever. [25]Therefore he is able, once and forever, to
save* those who come to God through him. He lives
forever to intercede with God on their behalf.
[26]He is the kind of high priest we need because he
is holy and blameless, unstained by sin. He has been
set apart from sinners and has been given the highest
place of honor in heaven.* [27]Unlike those other high
priests, he does not need to offer sacrifices every day.
They did this for their own sins first and then for the
sins of the people. But Jesus did this once for all when
he offered himself as the sacrifice for the people's sins.
[28]The law appointed high priests who were limited
by human weakness. But after the law was given, God
appointed his Son with an oath, and his Son has been
made the perfect High Priest forever.

CHRIST IS OUR HIGH PRIEST

8 Here is the main point: We have a High Priest who
sat down in the place of honor beside the throne
of the majestic God in heaven. [2]There he ministers in
the heavenly Tabernacle,* the true place of worship
that was built by the Lord and not by human hands.
[3]And since every high priest is required to offer
gifts and sacrifices, our High Priest must make an
offering, too. [4]If he were here on earth, he would
not even be a priest, since there already are priests
who offer the gifts required by the law. [5]They serve
in a system of worship that is only a copy, a shad-
ow of the real one in heaven. For when Moses was
getting ready to build the Tabernacle, God gave him
this warning: "Be sure that you make everything ac-
cording to the pattern I have shown you here on the
mountain."*
[6]But now Jesus, our High Priest, has been given
a ministry that is far superior to the old priesthood,
for he is the one who mediates for us a far better cov-
enant with God, based on better promises.
[7]If the first covenant had been faultless, there would
have been no need for a second covenant to replace it.
[8]But when God found fault with the people, he said:

"The day is coming, says the LORD,
when I will make a new covenant
with the people of Israel and Judah.
[9] This covenant will not be like the one
I made with their ancestors
when I took them by the hand
and led them out of the land of Egypt.
They did not remain faithful to my covenant,
so I turned my back on them, says the LORD.
[10] But this is the new covenant I will make
with the people of Israel on that day,* says the
LORD:
I will put my laws in their minds,

THE BEST GAME PLAN

1. What game plan has best helped your team to win? What game plan would you like your coach to try?
2. What are you best at forgetting: Names? Chores? Birthdays? Scripture references?

HEBREWS 8:1-13

3. What is a covenant? What is the significance of the fact that God initiates and guarantees it?
4. What is the main difference between the old and new covenants (vv. 5-6)?
5. What four promises does this new covenant involve (vv. 10-12)?
6. Which aspect of the new covenant do you wish to experience more? Why?

7:21 Ps 110:4. **7:25** Or *is able to save completely.* **7:26** Or *has been exalted higher than the heavens.* **8:2** Or *tent;* also in 8:5. **8:5** Exod 25:40; 26:30. **8:10** Greek *after those days.* **8:11** Greek *their brother.* **8:8-12** Jer 31:31-34.

7:20-21 oath. The Levitical priests were appointed by divine command (Num. 8), but there was no oath involved. In contrast, as the full quote from Psalm 110:4 reveals, God's promise of a new High Priest is sealed with an oath.

7:22 guarantees. This literally means "surety." Covenants were sealed with a pledge as a token that their terms would be carried out. Jesus' sacrifice is God's pledge of the new covenant. **better covenant.** A covenant was a binding commitment of mutual obligations between two parties. In the case of ancient kings, covenants were unilateral in that the king determined what both he and his subjects would do for one another.

7:23-24 priesthood lasts forever. Naturally, priests died, and so their service was only temporary; they had to be replaced. Jesus' superior priesthood is evidenced by the fact that His is permanent.

7:25 able, once and forever, to save. One of this letter's main themes is that Jesus has the power to truly cleanse believers from sin and thus enable them to draw near to God.

8:1-6 This passage begins to consider the value of Jesus' priestly offering, a theme taken up in detail in chapters 9–10.

8:2 heavenly Tabernacle. This refers to the Most Holy Place (9:3). God gave Moses a pattern for how to build a copy of the true heavenly tabernacle (Ex. 26). Jesus' greatness is seen in that He serves in this true tabernacle, not in an earthly copy. The tabernacle, an elaborate movable tent, gave way to Solomon's Temple and, later still, to the Herodian Temple destroyed by the Romans in A.D. 70. The fact that the author does not refer to its destruction as proof that the old order had passed away (v. 13) is a strong clue that the letter was written prior to that date. The focus on the tabernacle may have been because some Jewish sects considered the current administration of the temple services to be corrupted and invalid.

8:3 gifts and sacrifices. A primary function of the Old Testament high priests was to offer sacrifice on the Day of Atonement (Lev. 16). Jesus, as a priest, must likewise have a sacrifice to offer—namely, Himself (7:27).

8:5 copy, a shadow. These words communicate the difference between the physical, visible nature of the old covenant and the spiritual, heavenly nature of the new. The quote, "Be sure . . ." is from Exodus 25:40.

8:6 a ministry . . . far superior. Jesus' ministry supersedes that of the old priests because the new covenant accomplishes that which the old never could (vv. 7-13). **one who mediates.** Since a covenant involved two parties, the mediator served as a go-between to work out the various terms of the covenant between the two parties. **better promises.** The new covenant promises are "better" in that they promise far more than was ever promised in the old.

8:8-12 Jeremiah prophesied just prior to Babylon's conquest of Judah in 586 B.C. When the Jews were free to return to Jerusalem about 70 years later, expectations ran high that his prophecy quoted here was being fulfilled. Christians by contrast saw it fulfilled in the covenant established by Christ.

and I will write them on their hearts.
I will be their God,
and they will be my people.
11 And they will not need to teach their neighbors,
nor will they need to teach their relatives,*
saying, 'You should know the LORD.'
For everyone, from the least to the greatest,
will know me already.
12 And I will forgive their wickedness,
and I will never again remember their sins."*

13 When God speaks of a "new" covenant, it means he has made the first one obsolete. It is now out of date and will soon disappear.

OLD RULES ABOUT WORSHIP

9 That first covenant between God and Israel had regulations for worship and a place of worship here on earth.
2 There were two rooms in that Tabernacle.* In the first room were a lampstand, a table, and sacred loaves of bread on the table. This room was called the Holy Place.
3 Then there was a curtain, and behind the curtain was the second room* called the Most Holy Place.
4 In that room were a gold incense altar and a wooden chest called the Ark of the Covenant, which was covered with gold on all sides. Inside the Ark were a gold jar containing manna, Aaron's staff that sprouted leaves, and the stone tablets of the covenant.
5 Above the Ark were the cherubim of divine glory, whose wings stretched out over the Ark's cover, the place of atonement. But we cannot explain these things in detail now.
6 When these things were all in place, the priests regularly entered the first room* as they performed their religious duties.
7 But only the high priest ever entered the Most Holy Place, and only once a year. And he always offered blood for his own sins and for the sins the people had committed in ignorance.
8 By these regulations the Holy Spirit revealed that the entrance to the Most Holy Place was not freely open as long as the Tabernacle* and the system it represented were still in use.

A GUILTY PLEA

1. How often were you told, "Don't touch!" when you were a little kid? What were you trying to touch?

HEBREWS 9:1-10

2. How do you picture the earthly sanctuary described in verses 1-5?
3. Why were the gifts and sacrifices of the Old Testament worshipers not sufficient to clear their consciences (vv. 9-10)?
4. What is the "better system" (v. 10)? Why do we have "physical regulations" prior to that time?
5. When you feel guilty, how do you try to clear your conscience and restore your peace of mind?

9 This is an illustration pointing to the present time. For the gifts and sacrifices that the priests offer are not able to cleanse the consciences of the people who bring them.
10 For that old system deals only with food and drink and various cleansing ceremonies—physical regulations that were in effect only until a better system could be established.

CHRIST IS THE PERFECT SACRIFICE

11 So Christ has now become the High Priest over all the good things that have come.* He has entered that greater, more perfect Tabernacle in heaven, which was not made by human hands and is not part of this created world.
12 With his own blood—not the blood of goats and calves—he entered the Most Holy Place once for all time and secured our redemption forever.
13 Under the old system, the blood of goats and bulls and the ashes of a heifer could cleanse people's bodies from ceremonial impurity.
14 Just think how much more the blood of Christ will purify our consciences from sinful deeds* so that we can worship the living

9:2 Or *tent;* also in 9:11, 21. 9:3 Greek *second tent.* 9:6 Greek *first tent.* 9:8 Or *the first room;* Greek reads *the first tent.* 9:11 Some manuscripts read *that are about to come.* 9:14 Greek *from dead works.*

9:2 the Holy Place. The tabernacle, a flat-roofed tent about 15 by 45 feet, had two curtains forming separate rooms (Ex. 26). Priests entering the tabernacle through the first curtain came into the "Holy Place" where they carried out their daily functions. **a lampstand.** A seven-branched lampstand (Ex. 25:31-40) provided the only light in the otherwise dark tent. **a table, and sacred loaves of bread.** Twelve loaves of fresh bread were placed daily upon this table (Ex. 25:30; Lev. 24:5-9).
9:3 the Most Holy Place. Behind the second curtain was a small (about 9 by 15 feet), dark, mysterious place reserved for God, and at special times, the high priest. Here God said He would meet Moses (Ex. 25:22).
9:4 Ark of the Covenant. A box in which was placed: (1) the jar of manna—a reminder of God's care for the people during their time in the wilderness; (2) Aaron's staff—a reminder of God's election of his sons as priests; and (3) the stone tablets (the Ten Commandments)—a reminder of Israel's covenant responsibilities.
9:5 the cherubim. Two winged statues, representative of the angelic protection of God's honor, stood over the ark (Ex. 25:18). **divine glory.** A reverent way of referring to God (1:3). **the place of atonement.** Located on top of the ark (Ex. 25:17-22) and upon which the high priest sprinkled blood on the Day of Atonement.
9:7-8 revealed that the entrance . . . was not freely open. The entire setup of the tabernacle reinforced this point. The altar for sacrifice, where the people brought their sacrifices, was outside the tabernacle. Directly in line with that, but inside the first curtain of the tabernacle, was the altar where only priests could go. Behind that was the Most Holy Place into which only the high priest could enter, only on the Day of Atonement, and only if he first offered a sacrifice for himself (Lev. 16).
9:11 greater, more perfect Tabernacle. In contrast to the temple worship, Jesus entered a "tabernacle" that is not a part of the sin-infected creation.
9:12 once for all time. The finality of Christ's ministry stands in marked contrast with the ongoing cycle of sacrifices represented in the old covenant: Christ was sacrificed one time only (v. 26); He as the ultimate and eternal High Priest brought the blood of this sacrifice into God's presence (v. 21); His sacrifice secures the forgiveness of the sins of His people once and for all (10:10). **redemption forever.** The liberation from sin that Christ has secured, by contrast, is spiritual and permanent.
9:13 the blood of goats and bulls. A reference to the sacrifices on the Day of Atonement (Lev. 16). **ashes of a heifer.** Israelites who were ceremonially defiled through contact with a dead body were cleansed by being sprinkled with water mixed with the ashes of a burned heifer. Without this cleansing, they could not worship at the tabernacle (Num. 19). **cleanse people's bodies.** This is outward or bodily cleanness set in opposition to the cleanness of the spirit (v. 14).
9:14 how much more. If the sacrifice of an animal could effect some change in a person's standing with God, obviously the sacrifice of the royal Son of God would be far more effective. **the blood of Christ.** Blood represents sacrifice and death. **the eternal Spirit.** Literally, "an eternal spirit." This does not refer to the Holy Spirit but to Christ's eternal nature. Because Christ Himself is eternal in nature, the redemption He secured is likewise everlasting (v. 12). The phrase also contrasts the spiritual nature of Christ's sacrifice to the fleshly nature of the old (v. 13). While they only ceremonially cleansed the body, the new sacrifice actually cleanses the conscience. **perfect sacrifice.** Sacrificial animals had to be of the best quality. What was true of them physically was true of Jesus morally.

PASSIONATE SACRIFICE

1. Have you ever seen a movie with lots of blood and gore? Which one? How did you feel about watching it?

HEBREWS 9:11-28

2. What distinguishes the priesthood of Christ from the old system (vv. 12-14)?
3. Why the emphasis on shed blood (vv. 19-22)? Whose blood? What for?
4. In verses 27-28, how is the once-and-for-all sacrifice of Christ's death illustrated?
5. How should this new covenant affect the way we relate to Jesus on a daily basis?
6. What sacrifice is Jesus calling you to make to help others come to know Him?

God. For by the power of the eternal Spirit, Christ of-
fered himself to God as a perfect sacrifice for our sins.
15 That is why he is the one who mediates a new cov-
enant between God and people, so that all who are
called can receive the eternal inheritance God has
promised them. For Christ died to set them free from
the penalty of the sins they had committed under that
first covenant.
16 Now when someone leaves a will,* it is necessary
to prove that the person who made it is dead.* 17 The
will goes into effect only after the person's death.
While the person who made it is still alive, the will
cannot be put into effect.
18 That is why even the first covenant was put into
effect with the blood of an animal. 19 For after Moses
had read each of God's commandments to all the
people, he took the blood of calves and goats,* along
with water, and sprinkled both the book of God's
law and all the people, using hyssop branches and
scarlet wool. 20 Then he said, "This blood confirms
the covenant God has made with you."* 21 And in the
same way, he sprinkled blood on the Tabernacle and
on everything used for worship. 22 In fact, according
to the law of Moses, nearly everything was purified
with blood. For without the shedding of blood, there
is no forgiveness.
23 That is why the Tabernacle and everything in it,
which were copies of things in heaven, had to be pu-
rified by the blood of animals. But the real things in
heaven had to be purified with far better sacrifices
than the blood of animals.
24 For Christ did not enter into a holy place made
with human hands, which was only a copy of the true
one in heaven. He entered into heaven itself to appear
now before God on our behalf. 25 And he did not en-
ter heaven to offer himself again and again, like the
high priest here on earth who enters the Most Holy
Place year after year with the blood of an animal. 26 If
that had been necessary, Christ would have had to die
again and again, ever since the world began. But now,
once for all time, he has appeared at the end of the
age* to remove sin by his own death as a sacrifice.
27 And just as each person is destined to die once
and after that comes judgment, 28 so also Christ was
offered once for all time as a sacrifice to take away the
sins of many people. He will come again, not to deal
with our sins, but to bring salvation to all who are ea-
gerly waiting for him.

CHRIST'S SACRIFICE ONCE FOR ALL

10 The old system under the law of Moses was only
a shadow, a dim preview of the good things to
come, not the good things themselves. The sacrifices
under that system were repeated again and again,
year after year, but they were never able to provide
perfect cleansing for those who came to worship. 2 If
they could have provided perfect cleansing, the sacri-
fices would have stopped, for the worshipers would
have been purified once for all time, and their feelings
of guilt would have disappeared.
3 But instead, those sacrifices actually reminded
them of their sins year after year. 4 For it is not possi-
ble for the blood of bulls and goats to take away sins.
5 That is why, when Christ* came into the world, he
said to God,

"You did not want animal sacrifices or sin
offerings.
But you have given me a body to offer.
6 You were not pleased with burnt offerings
or other offerings for sin.
7 Then I said, 'Look, I have come to do your will,
O God—
as is written about me in the Scriptures.'"*

8 First, Christ said, "You did not want animal sacrifices
or sin offerings or burnt offerings or other offerings
for sin, nor were you pleased with them" (though
they are required by the law of Moses). 9 Then he said,
"Look, I have come to do your will." He cancels the
first covenant in order to put the second into effect.
10 For God's will was for us to be made holy by the sac-
rifice of the body of Jesus Christ, once for all time.
11 Under the old covenant, the priest stands and
ministers before the altar day after day, offering the

9:16a Or *covenant;* also in 9:17. **9:16b** Or *Now when someone makes a covenant, it is necessary to ratify it with the death of a sacrifice.* **9:19** Some manuscripts do not include *and goats.* **9:20** Exod 24:8. **9:26** Greek *the ages.* **10:5** Greek *he;* also in 10:8. **10:5-7** Ps 40:6-8 (Greek version).

9:20 This blood confirms. This paraphrase of Exodus 24:8 would remind the readers of Jesus' words as He instituted the new covenant (Matt. 26:28).
9:22 without the shedding of blood. This is the main point of the argument. Just as there is no inheritance from a will without a death, so the covenant promises cannot be fulfilled without a sacrifice. God accepts the death of the sacrifice in place of the deserved death of the sinner (Lev. 17:11).
9:26 to remove sin. Literally, "to effect an annulment." Christ not only brings forgiveness of sin but also breaks its power.
9:28 He will come again. Unlike the old high priests, Christ will not have to come again to bear sin. Instead, He will come to usher in the fullness of salvation.
10:2 purified once. The continuous repetition of the sacrifices indicated that the root problem of sin was never addressed until Christ.
10:4 it is not possible. No amount of animal sacrifices could change the moral imperfection within people. The main purpose of the old covenant was to point out the need for One who is finally able to "take away sins" of believers forever.
10:9 cancels the first. Literally, "to abolish." The old sacrificial system, which could not accomplish God's will of making people holy (v. 10), was superseded by the Messiah who was devoted to doing God's will.
10:10 That is, God's will (v. 9). **sacrifice of the body of Jesus Christ.** Cleansing from sin is a matter of complete identification with Jesus, whose once-for-all sacrifice merits full redemption.

GIVING IT UP

1. What part of your daily routine do you enjoy the most? The least?
2. During your teen or young adult years, who has inspired you to strive for holiness?

HEBREWS 10:1-18

3. In what ways does Christ replace the inadequate sacrifices of the Law?
4. How does Jesus' obedience relate to our ability to be holy and "to made holy" (vv. 9-10)?
5. How would you define holiness to a person who doesn't know God but is interested?
6. Do you live your life as if you "are being made holy" (v. 14)? In what way is God calling you to practice greater holiness?

same sacrifices again and again, which can never take away sins. 12 But our High Priest offered himself to God as a single sacrifice for sins, good for all time. Then he sat down in the place of honor at God's right hand. 13 There he waits until his enemies are humbled and made a footstool under his feet. 14 For by that one offering he forever made perfect those who are being made holy.

15 And the Holy Spirit also testifies that this is so. For he says,

16 "This is the new covenant I will make
with my people on that day,* says the LORD:
I will put my laws in their hearts,
and I will write them on their minds."*

17 Then he says,

"I will never again remember
their sins and lawless deeds."*

18 And when sins have been forgiven, there is no need to offer any more sacrifices.

A CALL TO PERSEVERE

19 And so, dear brothers and sisters,* we can boldly enter heaven's Most Holy Place because of the blood of Jesus. 20 By his death,* Jesus opened a new and life-giving way through the curtain into the Most Holy Place. 21 And since we have a great High Priest who rules over God's house, 22 let us go right into the presence of God with sincere hearts fully trusting him. For our guilty consciences have been sprinkled with Christ's blood to make us clean, and our bodies have been washed with pure water.

23 Let us hold tightly without wavering to the hope we affirm, for God can be trusted to keep his promise. 24 Let us think of ways to motivate one another to acts of love and good works. 25 And let us not neglect our meeting together, as some people do, but encourage one another, especially now that the day of his return is drawing near.

26 Dear friends, if we deliberately continue sinning after we have received knowledge of the truth, there is no longer any sacrifice that will cover these sins. 27 There is only the terrible expectation of God's judgment and the raging fire that will consume his enemies. 28 For anyone who refused to obey the law of Moses was put to death without mercy on the testimony of two or three witnesses. 29 Just think how much worse the punishment will be for those who have trampled on the Son of God, and have treated the blood of the covenant, which made us holy, as if it were common and unholy, and have insulted and disdained the Holy Spirit who brings God's mercy to us. 30 For we know the one who said,

"I will take revenge.
I will pay them back."*

DRAW NEAR AND HOLD ON

1. Which of your possessions would be the hardest for you to give away? Why?

HEBREWS 10:19-39

2. Note the three "let us" statements in verses 22-25. What does each one mean? What incentives are given?
3. In rejecting Christ, what are the three big mistakes a person would be guilty of (v. 29)? What would the consequence be for these mistakes (v. 31)?
4. After such a dire warning, how does the author encourage the people to whom he is writing (vv. 32-39)? Which appeal do you find persuasive?
5. What encouragement do you need in order to hold on to your faith?

10:16a Greek *after those days.* 10:16b Jer 31:33a. 10:17 Jer 31:34b. 10:19 Greek *brothers.* 10:20 Greek *Through his flesh.* 10:30a Deut 32:35. 10:30b Deut 32:36.

10:15-18 As the final proof that Jesus' sacrifice brings about the true cleansing God requires, Jeremiah's promise of the new covenant is again considered (8:8-12). Since under this covenant the peoples' sins are forgiven (v. 18) and they now live according to the law embedded in their hearts, there is no longer any need for sacrifices (v. 18).

10:19 enter heaven's Most Holy Place. In the old covenant only the high priest could draw near to God. In contrast, all Christians can do so with assurance.

10:20 life-giving way. Not "new" as opposed to "old," but rather something fresh and alive.

10:22 guilty consciences . . . sprinkled. Priestly garments were consecrated for use by being sprinkled with the blood of a sacrifice (Ex. 29:19-21).

10:26 no longer any sacrifice. The Levitical sacrifices covered ceremonial uncleanness, moral lapses for which one repented (Lev. 6:1-7), and sins of ignorance and passion (Lev. 5:17-19; 19:20-22). Sins that were a defiant rejection of the Law were not covered by the sacrifices (Num. 15:30). The author transfers this principle to the new covenant as well. The God-appointed sacrifice must be met with an attitude of repentance and dedication. To reject Christ's sacrifice is to reject the only sacrifice for sins.

10:29 trampled on the Son of God, and have treated the blood of the covenant . . . insulted and disdained the Holy Spirit. These three phrases amplify the nature of the sin warned against. It is a deliberate rejection of Jesus as the Messiah, a decision to abandon the covenant that comes through His sacrifice, and a resistance to the Spirit who applies God's grace to those who trust.

He also said,

"The LORD will judge his own people."*

[31] It is a terrible thing to fall into the hands of the liv-
ing God.
[32] Think back on those early days when you first
learned about Christ.* Remember how you remained
faithful even though it meant terrible suffering.
[33] Sometimes you were exposed to public ridicule and
were beaten, and sometimes you helped others who
were suffering the same things. [34] You suffered along
with those who were thrown into jail, and when all
you owned was taken from you, you accepted it with
joy. You knew there were better things waiting for
you that will last forever.
[35] So do not throw away this confident trust in the
Lord. Remember the great reward it brings you! [36] Pa-
tient endurance is what you need now, so that you
will continue to do God's will. Then you will receive
all that he has promised.

[37] "For in just a little while,
the Coming One will come and not delay.
[38] And my righteous ones will live by faith.*
But I will take no pleasure in anyone who turns
away."*

[39] But we are not like those who turn away from God
to their own destruction. We are the faithful ones,
whose souls will be saved.

GREAT EXAMPLES OF FAITH

11 Faith shows the reality of what we hope for; it is
the evidence of things we cannot see. [2] Through
their faith, the people in days of old earned a good
reputation.
[3] By faith we understand that the entire universe
was formed at God's command, that what we now see
did not come from anything that can be seen.
[4] It was by faith that Abel brought a more accept-
able offering to God than Cain did. Abel's offering
gave evidence that he was a righteous man, and
God showed his approval of his gifts. Although Abel
is long dead, he still speaks to us by his example of
faith.
[5] It was by faith that Enoch was taken up to heaven
without dying—"he disappeared, because God took
him."* For before he was taken up, he was known
as a person who pleased God. [6] And it is impossible
to please God without faith. Anyone who wants to
come to him must believe that God exists and that he
rewards those who sincerely seek him.
[7] It was by faith that Noah built a large boat to save
his family from the flood. He obeyed God, who warned
him about things that had never happened before. By
his faith Noah condemned the rest of the world, and
he received the righteousness that comes by faith.
[8] It was by faith that Abraham obeyed when God
called him to leave home and go to another land that
God would give him as his inheritance. He went with-
out knowing where he was going. [9] And even when
he reached the land God promised him, he lived
there by faith—for he was like a foreigner, living in
tents. And so did Isaac and Jacob, who inherited the
same promise. [10] Abraham was confidently looking
forward to a city with eternal foundations, a city de-
signed and built by God.
[11] It was by faith that even Sarah was able to have
a child, though she was barren and was too old. She
believed* that God would keep his promise. [12] And so
a whole nation came from this one man who was as
good as dead—a nation with so many people that,
like the stars in the sky and the sand on the seashore,
there is no way to count them.
[13] All these people died still believing what God had
promised them. They did not receive what was prom-
ised, but they saw it all from a distance and welcomed
it. They agreed that they were foreigners and nomads

FAITH HALL OF FAME

1. What is the riskiest thing you have done recently?
2. Who has inspired you the most by his or her example of faith?

HEBREWS 11:1-16

3. How do you define faith? How does your answer compare with verse 1?
4. What is the essential ingredient in a life that is pleasing to God (v. 6)? Does this seem unreasonable to you?
5. What are some of the risks the heroes of faith took in order to follow God's will?
6. If you knew you could not fail, what big dream would you pursue? What is keeping you from going for this?

10:32 Greek *when you were first enlightened.* **10:38** Or *my righteous ones will live by their faithfulness;* Greek reads *my righteous one will live by faith.* **10:37-38** Hab 2:3-4. **11:5** Gen 5:24. **11:11** Or *It was by faith that he [Abraham] was able to have a child, even though Sarah was barren and he was too old. He believed.*

10:32 terrible suffering. Jewish Christians (the most likely recipients of this letter) had suffered persecution from their fellow Jews. This ranged from harassment (Acts 18:17) to murder (Acts 7:59). Some experienced family rejection, economic boycotts, and physical abuse, which lead to forced relocation and the resultant loss of property.

11:3 the entire universe was formed at God's command. The stories of faith begin with creation, which in itself dramatically exemplifies how God brought into being things that were unseen.

11:4 Abel. Abel's faith is not mentioned in Genesis, but it is clear that the reason God accepted his sacrifice and not Cain's had to do with a matter of attitude (Gen. 4:4-7).

11:5 Enoch. The main facts about Enoch were his mysterious disappearance and that "he pleased God" (Gen. 5:21-24). Enoch was a popular figure in Jewish legends, which taught that his purity was such that God "took him" because he had no sin.

11:7 Noah. Noah's faith is not mentioned in the Old Testament but is seen in his obedience to God (Gen. 6:9–9:17). **had never happened.** Acting upon that which God promises (or warns), even when unseen, is the essence of faith (v. 1). **righteousness.** Faith lives in recognition of the awesome power of God. **condemned.** In that he acted in obedience to God, while others did not.

11:8-10 Abraham . . . was like a foreigner. In contrast to his settled life in Ur, Abraham's nomadic life in Canaan showed that his eyes were fixed upon a vision of something greater than could be found in this world.

11:13 All these. Abraham, Sarah, Isaac, Jacob. **died still believing.** None of the patriarchs saw the fulfillment of God's promise regarding the land or the vast nation Abraham would father. **foreigners and nomads.** Both terms describe how believers are to view their lives in the world (John 17:14)

here on earth. 14 Obviously people who say such
things are looking forward to a country they can call
their own. 15 If they had longed for the country they
came from, they could have gone back. 16 But they
were looking for a better place, a heavenly homeland.
That is why God is not ashamed to be called their God,
for he has prepared a city for them.
17 It was by faith that Abraham offered Isaac as a
sacrifice when God was testing him. Abraham, who
had received God's promises, was ready to sacrifice his
only son, Isaac, 18 even though God had told him, "Isaac
is the son through whom your descendants will be
counted."* 19 Abraham reasoned that if Isaac died, God
was able to bring him back to life again. And in a sense,
Abraham did receive his son back from the dead.
20 It was by faith that Isaac promised blessings for
the future to his sons, Jacob and Esau.
21 It was by faith that Jacob, when he was old and
dying, blessed each of Joseph's sons and bowed in
worship as he leaned on his staff.
22 It was by faith that Joseph, when he was about to
die, said confidently that the people of Israel would
leave Egypt. He even commanded them to take his
bones with them when they left.
23 It was by faith that Moses' parents hid him for
three months when he was born. They saw that God
had given them an unusual child, and they were not
afraid to disobey the king's command.
24 It was by faith that Moses, when he grew up, re-
fused to be called the son of Pharaoh's daughter. 25 He
chose to share the oppression of God's people instead
of enjoying the fleeting pleasures of sin. 26 He thought
it was better to suffer for the sake of Christ than to
own the treasures of Egypt, for he was looking ahead
to his great reward. 27 It was by faith that Moses left
the land of Egypt, not fearing the king's anger. He
kept right on going because he kept his eyes on the
one who is invisible. 28 It was by faith that Moses com-
manded the people of Israel to keep the Passover and
to sprinkle blood on the doorposts so that the angel of
death would not kill their firstborn sons.
29 It was by faith that the people of Israel went
right through the Red Sea as though they were on dry
ground. But when the Egyptians tried to follow, they
were all drowned.
30 It was by faith that the people of Israel marched
around Jericho for seven days, and the walls came
crashing down.
31 It was by faith that Rahab the prostitute was not de-
stroyed with the people in her city who refused to obey
God. For she had given a friendly welcome to the spies.
32 How much more do I need to say? It would take
too long to recount the stories of the faith of Gide-
on, Barak, Samson, Jephthah, David, Samuel, and
all the prophets. 33 By faith these people overthrew
kingdoms, ruled with justice, and received what God
had promised them. They shut the mouths of lions,
34 quenched the flames of fire, and escaped death by
the edge of the sword. Their weakness was turned to
strength. They became strong in battle and put whole
armies to flight. 35 Women received their loved ones
back again from death.

But others were tortured, refusing to turn from
God in order to be set free. They placed their hope in a
better life after the resurrection. 36 Some were jeered
at, and their backs were cut open with whips. Others
were chained in prisons. 37 Some died by stoning, some
were sawed in half,* and others were killed with the
sword. Some went about wearing skins of sheep and
goats, destitute and oppressed and mistreated. 38 They
were too good for this world, wandering over des-
erts and mountains, hiding in caves and holes in the
ground.
39 All these people earned a good reputation be-
cause of their faith, yet none of them received all that
God had promised. 40 For God had something better in
mind for us, so that they would not reach perfection
without us.

GOD'S DISCIPLINE PROVES HIS LOVE

12 Therefore, since we are surrounded by such a
huge crowd of witnesses to the life of faith, let us
strip off every weight that slows us down, especially
the sin that so easily trips us up. And let us run with
endurance the race God has set before us. 2 We do
this by keeping our eyes on Jesus, the champion who

11:18 Gen 21:12. **11:37** Some manuscripts add *some were tested.* **12:2a** Or *Jesus, the originator and perfecter of our faith.* **12:2b** Or *Instead of the joy.*

11:16 a heavenly homeland. In the new covenant a superior territory to the land of Canaan is to be achieved (8:5). **called their God.** God openly identifies with these people, pledging Himself to them (Ex. 3:6,15).

11:17 offered Isaac. Since child sacrifice was part of the worship life of the surrounding cultures, this may not have seemed as outrageous to Abraham as it does to modern readers. That does not minimize his anxiety regarding the death of his son, however. It also would generate tension in Abraham in that it was through Isaac that God had said the promise would come true (v. 18; Gen. 21:12).

11:19 bring him back to life. Abraham believed God would keep His promise, even if it meant resurrecting Isaac from the dead.

11:21 Jacob. Looking two generations ahead, the elderly Jacob passed on the blessing and promise to Ephraim and Manasseh (Gen. 48:20). **leaned on his staff.** A reference back to Joseph's oath to Jacob in Genesis 47:31.

11:22 Joseph. His faith was evidenced by his belief in God's promise to one day deliver Israel from Egypt (Gen. 15:13-16).

11:24 refused to be called the son of Pharaoh's daughter. Moses was raised by the Pharaoh's daughter (Ex. 2:5-10), but he chose not to identify with the oppressor of his people, even though that would have been an easier, more comfortable option.

11:26 the sake of the Christ. Literally, "the anointed." In the Old Testament, Israel as a nation was sometimes called "the anointed one" (Ps. 89:51). The author uses Moses' loyalty to "God's anointed" nation as a model for how the individual believer ought to be loyal to God's anointed Messiah, Jesus Christ.

11:28 Passover. This action demonstrated faith that God would keep the promise to "pass over" the homes of the Israelites as the destroying angel came through the land (Ex. 12). **sprinkle blood.** Blood from the Passover lamb was sprinkled on the doorframe of each Jewish home.

11:31 Rahab. All the previous examples of faith were men held in high esteem by the Jews. Rahab was a Gentile prostitute who had faith to see that the God of Israel was the God of the whole earth (Josh. 2:11).

11:39 none of them received all that God had promised. All that was included in the coming of the Messiah and His sacrifice occurred after their deaths.

12:1 witnesses. This is the same word used for "martyrs." It is probably a deliberate play on words in which both meanings are intended. The heroes of faith are pictured as a cheering section of former runners in a race urging the contemporary readers to persevere as they did. **strip off every weight.** In Greek games at the time, runners ran with no clothes so that they could move freely without hindrance. **the sin that so easily trips us up.** Just as a flowing robe makes it impossible to run well, so sin makes the Christian life difficult.

12:2 keeping our eyes on Jesus. In races of the time, the prize for the race was placed at the end to motivate the runners. Jesus is here described as the focus of the Christian life. **joy awaiting him.** Jesus knew the joy His mission of reconciliation would bring and so pursued it whatever the cost. **disregarding its shame.** Crucifixion was considered so degrading that no Roman citizen could be crucified, regardless of the crime committed.

RUNNING WIDE OPEN

1. What discipline did you sometimes resent as a child that you appreciate now: Practicing? Turning in homework on time? Not overspending your allowance? Other?

HEBREWS 12:1-13

2. How should Christians run the "race" (v. 1) in sports, in school, and in life?
3. What does it mean to keep "our eyes on Jesus" (v. 2)? Why is this often difficult?
4. How does Christ's discipline differ from human discipline? What benefits does discipline bring?
5. What is the hardest thing you're going through right now? How is God using this in your life?

initiates and perfects our faith.* Because of the joy*
awaiting him, he endured the cross, disregarding its
shame. Now he is seated in the place of honor beside
God's throne. 3 Think of all the hostility he endured
from sinful people;* then you won't become weary
and give up. 4 After all, you have not yet given your
lives in your struggle against sin.
5 And have you forgotten the encouraging words
God spoke to you as his children?* He said,

"My child,* don't make light of the LORD's discipline,
and don't give up when he corrects you.
6 For the LORD disciplines those he loves,
and he punishes each one he accepts as his child."*

7 As you endure this divine discipline, remember that
God is treating you as his own children. Who ever
heard of a child who is never disciplined by its fa-
ther? 8 If God doesn't discipline you as he does all of
his children, it means that you are illegitimate and
are not really his children at all. 9 Since we respected
our earthly fathers who disciplined us, shouldn't we
submit even more to the discipline of the Father of our
spirits, and live forever?*
10 For our earthly fathers disciplined us for a few years,
doing the best they knew how. But God's discipline is al-
ways good for us, so that we might share in his holiness.
11 No discipline is enjoyable while it is happening—it's
painful! But afterward there will be a peaceful harvest
of right living for those who are trained in this way.
12 So take a new grip with your tired hands and
strengthen your weak knees. 13 Mark out a straight
path for your feet so that those who are weak and
lame will not fall but become strong.

A CALL TO LISTEN TO GOD

14 Work at living in peace with everyone, and work at
living a holy life, for those who are not holy will not
see the Lord. 15 Look after each other so that none of
you fails to receive the grace of God. Watch out that no
poisonous root of bitterness grows up to trouble you,
corrupting many. 16 Make sure that no one is immoral
or godless like Esau, who traded his birthright as the
firstborn son for a single meal. 17 You know that after-
ward, when he wanted his father's blessing, he was
rejected. It was too late for repentance, even though
he begged with bitter tears.
18 You have not come to a physical mountain,* to a
place of flaming fire, darkness, gloom, and whirlwind,
as the Israelites did at Mount Sinai. 19 For they heard
an awesome trumpet blast and a voice so terrible that
they begged God to stop speaking. 20 They staggered
back under God's command: "If even an animal touch-
es the mountain, it must be stoned to death."* 21 Moses
himself was so frightened at the sight that he said, "I
am terrified and trembling."*
22 No, you have come to Mount Zion, to the city
of the living God, the heavenly Jerusalem, and to
countless thousands of angels in a joyful gathering.

PURSUING PEACE

1. If you could move to any city with the right job, what criteria would you use to choose: Friends or family? Climate? Housing? Cultural or athletic pursuits? Other?

HEBREWS 12:14-29

2. What is the point of the comparison between Mount Sinai (vv. 18-21) and Mount Zion (vv. 22-24)?
3. What happens to any who refuse to hear God's voice (vv. 18-21,25-29)? To those who heed His call?
4. What efforts have you made to "[w]ork at living in peace with everyone" (v. 14)? Does the world's view of competition help or hinder?
5. How can you live a life of grace in the same way that God has extended grace to you (vv.14-15,28)?

12:3 Some manuscripts read *Think of how people hurt themselves by opposing him.* 12:5a Greek *sons;* also in 12:7, 8. 12:5b Greek *son;* also in 12:6, 7. 12:5-6 Prov 3:11-12 (Greek version). 12:9 Or *and really live?* 12:18 Greek *to something that can be touched.* 12:20 Exod 19:13. 12:21 Deut 9:19.

12:14 holy life. To be holy is to be dedicated to God. The word does not have the connotation many associate with it today of being self righteous or having a "better than thou" attitude. **those . . . not holy will not see the Lord.** Faith and holiness are essential for life with God. Faith without the pursuit of holiness is only intellectual assent; holiness without faith is self-righteousness (11:6).

12:16 immoral or godless. Jewish tradition viewed Esau both as sexually immoral and ungodly. The latter was especially seen in his trading his right as the firstborn son for the immediate pleasure of a single meal (Gen. 25:27-34). Sexual sin and choosing the short-term benefits of turning from Christ over the long-term benefits of faithfulness are two types of defiling activity in this community (13:4).

12:17 too late for repentance. This phrase is better understood as "he had no opportunity to bring about a change of mind." The blessing had already been given to Esau's brother Jacob and could not be revoked (Gen. 27:34-40).

12:18-21 This retelling of the Israelites' experience at Mount Sinai is based on Exodus 19. Even the old covenant, limited as it has been shown to be, was accompanied by overwhelming signs of God's authority that emphasized how seriously it must be taken.

12:21 I am terrified and trembling. This is actually from the time when Moses sought God's forgiveness over Israel's idolatry with the golden calf (Ex. 32:7-14).

12:22 Mount Zion. This was the site of a fortress King David conquered and made his home (2 Sam. 5:6-9). Later it referred to Jerusalem as the site of God's temple. Symbolically, it stood for the place of God's residence.

23 You have come to the assembly of God's firstborn
children, whose names are written in heaven. You
have come to God himself, who is the judge over all
things. You have come to the spirits of the righteous
ones in heaven who have now been made perfect.
24 You have come to Jesus, the one who mediates the
new covenant between God and people, and to the
sprinkled blood, which speaks of forgiveness instead
of crying out for vengeance like the blood of Abel.
25 Be careful that you do not refuse to listen to the
One who is speaking. For if the people of Israel did
not escape when they refused to listen to Moses, the
earthly messenger, we will certainly not escape if we
reject the One who speaks to us from heaven! 26 When
God spoke from Mount Sinai his voice shook the earth,
but now he makes another promise: "Once again I
will shake not only the earth but the heavens also."*
27 This means that all of creation will be shaken and
removed, so that only unshakable things will remain.
28 Since we are receiving a Kingdom that is unshak-
able, let us be thankful and please God by worshiping
him with holy fear and awe. 29 For our God is a de-
vouring fire.

CONCLUDING WORDS

13 Keep on loving each other as brothers and sis-
ters.* 2 Don't forget to show hospitality to strang-
ers, for some who have done this have entertained an-
gels without realizing it! 3 Remember those in prison, as
if you were there yourself. Remember also those being
mistreated, as if you felt their pain in your own bodies.
4 Give honor to marriage, and remain faithful to
one another in marriage. God will surely judge peo-
ple who are immoral and those who commit adultery.
5 Don't love money; be satisfied with what you
have. For God has said,

"I will never fail you.
I will never abandon you."*

6 So we can say with confidence,

"The LORD is my helper,
so I will have no fear.
What can mere people do to me?"*

7 Remember your leaders who taught you the word
of God. Think of all the good that has come from their
lives, and follow the example of their faith.
8 Jesus Christ is the same yesterday, today, and for-
ever. 9 So do not be attracted by strange, new ideas.

LIFESTYLE OF THE RICH IN FAITH

1. In a word, how would you describe the relationship you have with your siblings?
2. If you were to write a good-bye letter to your high school, what top three points would you include?

HEBREWS 13:1-25

3. In what areas should "loving each other as brothers and sisters" define Christians (vv. 1-7)?
4. What "strange, new ideas" was a particular temptation to the Hebrew Christians (vv. 9-10)? What rituals, traditions, and other forms of legalism tempt believers of any age?
5. From verses 1-19, how would you sum up the Christian lifestyle? Which command do you most need to work on?

Your strength comes from God's grace, not from rules
about food, which don't help those who follow them.
10 We have an altar from which the priests in the
Tabernacle* have no right to eat. 11 Under the old sys-
tem, the high priest brought the blood of animals into
the Holy Place as a sacrifice for sin, and the bodies of
the animals were burned outside the camp. 12 So also
Jesus suffered and died outside the city gates to make
his people holy by means of his own blood. 13 So let us
go out to him, outside the camp, and bear the disgrace
he bore. 14 For this world is not our permanent home;
we are looking forward to a home yet to come.
15 Therefore, let us offer through Jesus a continual
sacrifice of praise to God, proclaiming our allegiance
to his name. 16 And don't forget to do good and to
share with those in need. These are the sacrifices that
please God.
17 Obey your spiritual leaders, and do what they say.
Their work is to watch over your souls, and they are
accountable to God. Give them reason to do this with
joy and not with sorrow. That would certainly not be
for your benefit.
18 Pray for us, for our conscience is clear and we want
to live honorably in everything we do. 19 And especially
pray that I will be able to come back to you soon.

20 Now may the God of peace—
who brought up from the dead our Lord Jesus,

12:26 Hag 2:6. 13:1 Greek *Continue in brotherly love.* 13:5 Deut 31:6, 8. 13:6 Ps 118:6. 13:10 Or *tent.*

12:23 spirits of righteous ones . . . made perfect. These are the "cloud of witnesses" (v. 1), who, while still awaiting their final completion (11:40), have already reached their destination with God.
12:26-27 I will shake not only the earth but the heavens. Haggai 2:6 is a reminder that God will one day shake not only the earth (as at Mount Sinai) but also the heavens. Thus the old order, which is earthly, partial, and temporary, will fully give way to the new, which is heavenly, complete, and eternal.
12:28 a Kingdom. The kingdom of God inaugurated by Jesus and consummated in the new heavens and new earth (Mark 1:15; Isa. 65:17-19).
13:2 entertained angels. The concept that a stranger might be an angelic visitor can be traced back to the story of the angels who were sent to rescue Lot from the doomed cities of Sodom and Gomorrah (Gen. 18–19).
13:4 marriage. The denial of legitimate sexual desire led to incidents of sexual immorality (1 Cor. 6:15-20). Here, marriage is validated, and people are warned not to be involved in any form of immorality (12:16).
13:8 the same yesterday, today, and forever. The same trustworthy Jesus preached by the original leaders is the one the readers should continue to pursue "today and forever." Since Jesus and the gospel are stable and eternal, the readers should not be distracted by any new teachings that differ from what they originally received (v. 9).
13:9-14 Just what "strange teaching" is involved is unclear. Various food regulations created different types of problems in many early churches, so something of that nature may be in view (Acts 11:1-18; Rom. 14; 1 Cor. 8; Col. 2:21; 1 Tim. 4:3).
13:17 watch over. The leaders' responsibility was to teach true doctrine and guard against error infiltrating the church (Acts 20:28-31). **they are accountable.** As a shepherd is responsible to the owner of the flock, so the church leader is responsible to Jesus, the head of the church.
13:20 an eternal covenant with his blood. This phrase is rich in Old Testament allusions; Ezekiel 37:26 (everlasting covenant); Zechariah 9:11 (blood of the covenant). **Shepherd.** This title for Jesus highlights His high-priestly ministry of comfort and guidance (4:15-16).

the great Shepherd of the sheep,
and ratified an eternal covenant with his blood—
21 may he equip you with all you need
for doing his will.
May he produce in you,*
through the power of Jesus Christ,
every good thing that is pleasing to him.
All glory to him forever and ever! Amen.

22 I urge you, dear brothers and sisters,* to pay attention to what I have written in this brief exhortation.
23 I want you to know that our brother Timothy has been released from jail. If he comes here soon, I will bring him with me to see you.
24 Greet all your leaders and all the believers there.*
The believers from Italy send you their greetings.
25 May God's grace be with you all.

13:21 Some manuscripts read *in us.* **13:22** Greek *brothers.* **13:24** Greek *all of God's holy people.*

13:21 may he equip you . . . doing his will. Another translation is: "May He make you complete in all goodness to do the will of Him who does in us those things pleasing before Him . . ." **All glory to him.** Typically, this would refer to God, the main subject of the whole clause, but the Greek word order and the author's theology certainly allow this to refer to Jesus (1:3,8). **forever and ever.** This covenant will never be replaced.

13:23 Timothy. Timothy was Paul's trusted companion. There is no other reference to his imprisonment in the New Testament.

13:25 grace be with you all. This was a typical way to end a letter, although for Christians grace had a specific reference point in Christ.

INTRODUCTION TO

JAMES

PERSONAL READING PLAN

☐James 1:1-27
☐James 2:1-26
☐James 3:1–4:12
☐James 4:13–5:20

AUTHOR

In the New Testament there are apparently two men by the name of James, who might have written this epistle—either James the apostle, or James the brother of Jesus. Since it is almost certain that the Apostle James (the son of Zebedee) was killed by Herod in A.D. 44 (before the epistle could have been written), traditionally the author has been assigned to James, the leader of the church in Jerusalem and the brother of Jesus (Mark 6:3).

The pilgrimage of James to faith is fascinating. At first Jesus' family was hostile to his ministry (John 7:5) and, in fact, tried to stop it at one point (Mark 3:21). Yet after Jesus' ascension, Jesus' mother and brothers are listed among the early believers (Acts 1:14). For James, this coming to faith may have resulted from Jesus' post-resurrection appearance to him (1 Cor. 15:7).

James emerged as a leader of the church in Jerusalem, presiding over the first Jerusalem Council, which decided whether to admit Gentiles to the church (Acts 15, especially vv. 13-21). And it is to James that Paul later brought the collection for the poor in Jerusalem (Acts 21:17-25).

DATE

Some place it very early, around A.D. 45, making it the first New Testament book. Others date it quite late.

THEME

Christianity in action.

AUDIENCE

James is one of the General Epistles (along with 1 and 2 Peter, John's epistles and Jude), so called because it has no single destination. It appears that he is writing to Jewish Christians dispersed around the Greek world: "to the 'twelve tribes'—Jewish believers scattered abroad" (1:1). But since Peter uses the same sort of inscription (1 Peter 1:1-2), James' destination remains unclear.

PURPOSE

While James clearly stands in the tradition of other Christian writers, he has some special concerns. The relationship between rich and poor crops up at various points (1:9-11; 5:1-6)—an issue of special significance to the modern affluent West. He is concerned about the use and abuse of speech (1:19,26; 2:12; 3:3-12; 5:12). He gives instruction on prayer (1:5-8; 4:2-3; 5:13-18). Above all, he is concerned with ethical behavior. How believers act, he says, has significance for the Day of Judgment; future reward or punishment depends on it. In this regard, James bemoans the inconsistency of human behavior (1:6-8,22-24; 2:14-17; 4:1,3). Human beings are "unstable" or "divided" (1:8; 4:8) in sharp contrast to God who is one (2:19) and does not change (1:17).

James has been incorrectly understood by some to be contradicting Paul's doctrine of justification of faith (2:14-26). In fact if James had Paul in mind at all, he was addressing himself to those who had perverted Paul's message—insisting that it doesn't matter what you do as long as you have faith. James responded by asserting that works are the outward evidence of inner faith. Works make faith visible to others. In contrast, Paul was concerned with our standing before God. As is evident from Romans 12–15, Paul certainly agreed with James that faith in Christ has direct implications for how believers live.

ITS OMISSIONS

James contains no mention of the Holy Spirit and no reference to the redemptive work or resurrection of Christ. In fact, it contains only two references to the name Jesus Christ (1:1 and 2:1). Furthermore, examples are drawn from the lives of Old Testament prophets, not from the experiences of Jesus. Although the title Lord appears 11 times, it generally refers to the name of God (in Old Testament fashion) and not to the kingly authority of Jesus. Indeed, it is God the Father who is the focus of the book of James.

HISTORICAL BACKGROUND

James draws his language, images, and ideas from three worlds: Judaism, Greek culture, and early Christianity. From Christianity, he uses language referring to the second coming (5:7-9); common patterns of Christian ethical instruction, which parallel those in 1 Peter (1:2-4,21; 4:7-10); and especially the teachings of Jesus (1:5,17; 2:5,8,19; 4:3; 5:12). From Judaism, he draws his insistence on the unity of God, concern for keeping the Law, and quotations from Jewish Scriptures (2:8,11,21-25; 4:6; 5:11,17-18) along with his use of Jewish terms (e.g., the word translated "hell" in 3:6 is the Hebrew word gehenna). Christianity and Judaism shared his concern for the poor and oppressed

STRUCTURE

Written in epistle (letter) form, James is loosely structured and rambling in style. James shares many characteristics of the sermonic style of both Greek philosophers and Jewish rabbis. James carries on a conversation with a hypothetical opponent (2:18-26; 5:13-16), switches subjects by means of a question (2:14; 4:1), uses many commands (60 of the 108 verses in James are imperatives), relies on vivid images from everyday life (3:3-6; 5:7), illustrates points by reference to famous people (2:21-23,25; 5:11,17), uses vivid opposites in which the right way is set alongside the wrong way (2:13,26). (James Hardy Ropes, The International Critical Commentary; William Barclay, The Letters of James and Peter). Jewish sermons had many of the same characteristics. But rabbis also had the habit, as did James, of constructing sermons that were deliberately disconnected—a series of moral truths and commands strung together like beads.

PASSAGES FOR TOPICAL GROUP STUDY

1:2-18 ... TEMPTATIONS and TRIALS .... Passing the Test
1:19-27 .. DOER OF THE TRUTH .... Just Do It
2:1-13 ... FAVORITISM and ACCEPTANCE .... Been Misjudged Lately?
2:14-26 .. PERFECTING YOUR FAITH .... Talk is Cheap
3:1-18 ... HARSH WORDS and GOSSIP .... Tongue Trouble
4:1-12 ... FRIENDSHIPS and CHOICES .... Favorable Friendship
4:13-17 .. FUTURE PLANS .... One Day at a Time
5:7-20 ... PATIENCE AND WAITING .... It's Tough to Wait

PASSAGES FOR GENERAL GROUP STUDY

5:1-6 .... Money Concerns (and Management)

GREETINGS FROM JAMES

1 This letter is from James, a slave of God and of the
Lord Jesus Christ.
I am writing to the "twelve tribes"—Jewish believ-
ers scattered abroad.
Greetings!

FAITH AND ENDURANCE

2 Dear brothers and sisters,* when troubles of any
kind come your way, consider it an opportunity for
great joy. 3 For you know that when your faith is
tested, your endurance has a chance to grow. 4 So
let it grow, for when your endurance is fully de-
veloped, you will be perfect and complete, needing
nothing.
5 If you need wisdom, ask our generous God, and he
will give it to you. He will not rebuke you for asking.
6 But when you ask him, be sure that your faith is in
God alone. Do not waver, for a person with divided
loyalty is as unsettled as a wave of the sea that is
blown and tossed by the wind. 7 Such people should
not expect to receive anything from the Lord. 8 Their
loyalty is divided between God and the world, and
they are unstable in everything they do.
9 Believers who are* poor have something to boast
about, for God has honored them. 10 And those who are
rich should boast that God has humbled them. They
will fade away like a little flower in the field. 11 The hot
sun rises and the grass withers; the little flower droops
and falls, and its beauty fades away. In the same way,
the rich will fade away with all of their achievements.
12 God blesses those who patiently endure testing
and temptation. Afterward they will receive the
crown of life that God has promised to those who love
him. 13 And remember, when you are being tempted,
do not say, "God is tempting me." God is never tempt-
ed to do wrong,* and he never tempts anyone else.
14 Temptation comes from our own desires, which en-
tice us and drag us away. 15 These desires give birth
to sinful actions. And when sin is allowed to grow, it
gives birth to death.
16 So don't be misled, my dear brothers and sisters.
17 Whatever is good and perfect is a gift coming down
to us from God our Father, who created all the lights
in the heavens.* He never changes or casts a shifting
shadow.* 18 He chose to give birth to us by giving us
his true word. And we, out of all creation, became his
prized possession.*

LISTENING AND DOING

19 Understand this, my dear brothers and sisters: You
must all be quick to listen, slow to speak, and slow to
get angry. 20 Human anger* does not produce the righ-
teousness* God desires. 21 So get rid of all the filth and
evil in your lives, and humbly accept the word God
has planted in your hearts, for it has the power to save
your souls.
22 But don't just listen to God's word. You must do
what it says. Otherwise, you are only fooling your-
selves. 23 For if you listen to the word and don't obey, it
is like glancing at your face in a mirror. 24 You see your-
self, walk away, and forget what you look like. 25 But
if you look carefully into the perfect law that sets you
free, and if you do what it says and don't forget what
you heard, then God will bless you for doing it.
26 If you claim to be religious but don't control your
tongue, you are fooling yourself, and your religion is

PASSING THE TEST

1. What is your usual approach to a test: Fear? Joy? Prayer? Study all night?

JAMES 1:2-18

2. How is it that we can "consider it an opportunity for great joy" when we are going through difficult times (v. 2)?
3. What reward comes with persevering in the faith (v. 12)?
4. What does James say is the origin of temptation, and why is it so important to understand this (vv. 13-15)?
5. How are you dealing with the trials and temptations in your life? Who or what can help you to persevere?

1:2 Greek *brothers;* also in 1:16, 19. **1:9** Greek *The brother who is.* **1:13** Or *God should not be put to a test by evil people.* **1:17a** Greek *from above, from the Father of lights.* **1:17b** Some manuscripts read *He never changes, as a shifting shadow does.* **1:18** Greek *we became a kind of firstfruit of his creatures.* **1:20a** Greek *A man's anger.* **1:20b** Or *the justice.*

1:3 endurance. This could also be translated as "perseverance." It is used in the sense of active overcoming, rather than passive acceptance.
1:4 fully developed. Perfection is not automatic—it takes time and effort. **perfect and complete.** What James has in mind here is wholeness of character. **needing nothing.** The opposite of mature and complete. This word is used of an army that has been defeated or a person who has failed to reach a standard.
1:5 wisdom. This is not just abstract knowledge but God-given insight that leads to right living.
1:6 But. Both here and in 4:3, unanswered prayer is connected to the quality of our asking, not the unwillingness of God to give. **be sure your faith is in God alone.** To be *single-minded* about God's ability to answer prayer.
1:8 divided. To doubt is to be double-minded—to both believe and disbelieve.
1:12 blesses. Happy is the person who has withstood all the trials to the end. **endure.** Such a person is like metal that has been purged by fire and is purified of all foreign substances. **crown of life.** Crowns were worn at weddings and feasts (signifying joy); were given to winners of athletic competitions (signifying victory); and worn by royalty (as befits children of God the King).
1:13 tempted. The focus shifts from enduring outward trials (v. 12) to resisting inner temptations. **"God is tempting me."** The natural tendency is to blame others for our failure. In this case, God is blamed for sending a test that is too hard to bear. **he never tempts anyone else.** God does not lure anyone into a tempting situation just to see whether that person will stand or fall.
1:14 our own desires. The true source of evil is a person's own inner inclinations (Mark 7:21-23).
1:19 slow to speak. One needs to consider carefully what is to be said rather than impulsively and carelessly launching into unwise words. **slow to get anger.** James does not forbid anger. He does caution against responding in anger at every opportunity.
1:21 get rid of. This verb means literally, "to lay aside" or "to strip off," as one would do with filthy clothing. **the word . . . planted in your hearts.** They are Christians already. They have the life of God in them. It is now up to them to act upon what is already theirs.
1:26 If you claim. The focus is on a person's own self-assessment of his or her religious commitment. By contrast, in verse 27, James states what God considers as truly religious. **religious.** The emphasis here is probably on the overt acts of religion, such as scrupulous observance of the details of worship and personal piety. **don't control your tongue.** The inability to control one's speech (as in gossip and criticism) is the mark of the person who thinks he or she is religious but really is not.

JUST DO IT

1. When have you forgotten to do something important your parents, teacher, or coach asked you to do? What happened?

JAMES 1:19-27

2. What would James recommend as a solution to conflicts in relationships (v. 19)?
3. How do we prepare ourselves to receive God's word fully in our lives (v. 21)? What do you need to "get rid of"?
4. What does the mirror illustration say about the importance of doing and not just hearing (vv. 22-25)?
5. What is one way this week that you can practice being a "doer" this week—a person who lives the way God says?

worthless. 27 Pure and genuine religion in the sight of
God the Father means caring for orphans and widows
in their distress and refusing to let the world corrupt
you.

A WARNING AGAINST PREJUDICE

2 My dear brothers and sisters,* how can you claim
to have faith in our glorious Lord Jesus Christ if
you favor some people over others?
2 For example, suppose someone comes into your
meeting* dressed in fancy clothes and expensive jew-
elry, and another comes in who is poor and dressed in
dirty clothes. 3 If you give special attention and a good
seat to the rich person, but you say to the poor one,
"You can stand over there, or else sit on the floor"—
well, 4 doesn't this discrimination show that your
judgments are guided by evil motives?
5 Listen to me, dear brothers and sisters. Hasn't God
chosen the poor in this world to be rich in faith? Ar-
en't they the ones who will inherit the Kingdom he
promised to those who love him? 6 But you dishonor
the poor! Isn't it the rich who oppress you and drag
you into court? 7 Aren't they the ones who slander
Jesus Christ, whose noble name* you bear?
8 Yes indeed, it is good when you obey the royal law
as found in the Scriptures: "Love your neighbor as
yourself."* 9 But if you favor some people over others,
you are committing a sin. You are guilty of breaking
the law.
10 For the person who keeps all of the laws except
one is as guilty as a person who has broken all of
God's laws. 11 For the same God who said, "You must
not commit adultery," also said, "You must not mur-
der."* So if you murder someone but do not commit
adultery, you have still broken the law.
12 So whatever you say or whatever you do, remem-
ber that you will be judged by the law that sets you
free. 13 There will be no mercy for those who have not
shown mercy to others. But if you have been merciful,
God will be merciful when he judges you.

BEEN MISJUDGED LATELY?

1. Who are the kids at your school or on your team you have the hardest time accepting?
2. When have you either misjudged someone or been misjudged yourself based on appearance?

JAMES 2:1-13

3. What is the connection between being poor and being rich in verse 5?
4. How does God look upon favoritism (v. 9)?
5. What is the significance of James' statement, "... if you have been merciful, God will be merciful ..." (v. 13) in the context of verses 8-11?
6. What can you do to be more accepting of others in the coming week?

FAITH WITHOUT GOOD DEEDS IS DEAD

14 What good is it, dear brothers and sisters, if you say
you have faith but don't show it by your actions? Can
that kind of faith save anyone? 15 Suppose you see a
brother or sister who has no food or clothing, 16 and
you say, "Good-bye and have a good day; stay warm
and eat well"—but then you don't give that person
any food or clothing. What good does that do?

2:1 Greek *brothers;* also in 2:5, 14. **2:2** Greek *your synagogue.* **2:7** Greek *slander the noble name.* **2:8** Lev 19:18. **2:11** Exod 20:13-14; Deut 5:17-18.

1:27 religion. True religion has more to do with acts of charity than acts of piety. It involves caring for others and avoiding the corrupting influence of one's culture. **orphans and widows.** In the Old Testament, orphans and widows were the poor and oppressed, whom God's people were to care for because God cared for them (Deut. 10:17-18; 24:17-22). **corrupt.** Unpolluted; pure; undefiled. **world.** This refers to the world system that is in opposition to God.

2:1 favor. The practice James addresses in these verses keeps one's religion from being pure and undefiled. The motive for this partiality to the rich is likely self-serving.

2:2 expensive jewelry. This is the mark of those who belonged to the equestrian order—the second level of Roman aristocracy. These noblemen were typically wealthy. Rings, in general, were signs of wealth. Early Christians were urged to wear only one ring on the little finger, bearing the image of a dove, fish, or anchor. **fancy clothes.** These are literally "bright and shining" garments like those worn by the angels in Acts 10:30. **poor.** The word used here denotes a beggar, a person from the lowest level of society. **dirty clothes.** In contrast to the spotless garments of the rich man, the beggar wears filthy rags, probably because this is all he owns. Our treatment of others should not be based on outward appearances.

2:6 oppress you. In a day of abject poverty the poor were often forced to borrow money at exorbitant rates of interest just to survive. The rich profited from their need. **drag you into court.** This was probably over the issue of a debt.

2:7 noble name. The early followers of Jesus were dubbed with the name "Christians" (Acts 11:26). At baptism they formally took upon themselves the name of Christ, knowing that they might well be vilified simply for bearing that name.

2:12 the law that sets you free. Judaism had become encrusted with countless rules that bound people. Christians had only one key principle to follow: to love others freely as Christ freely loved them (v. 8; 1:25).

2:14 faith. James uses this word in a special way. The faith he speaks of here is mere intellectual affirmation. Such a mind-oriented profession stands in sharp contrast to the comprehensive, whole-life commitment that characterizes true New Testament faith. New Testament faith involves believing with one's full being: mind, emotions, body (behavior), and spirit. The people James has in mind differ from their pagan and Jewish neighbors only in what they *profess* to believe. **don't show . . . by your actions.** Just as James uses the word "faith" in his own way, so too he uses "works" in a unique way. For James, works have to do with proper ethical behavior. **Can that kind of faith save anyone?** The implied answer is "No," based on what James just said in verses 12-13. Intellectual faith cannot save one from judgment when one has not been merciful.

TALK IS CHEAP

1. Are you a doer or a thinker? Are you more likely to act without thinking or think without acting?

JAMES 2:14-26

2. Is James saying that faith or belief doesn't really matter? If not, why does it matter?
3. What is the significance of verse 22? In what way does faith need to be "perfected"?
4. What is God really saying with the Rahab example in verse 25? How would you apply this to your thoughts and actions in everyday life?
5. Give some examples of works you can do to help perfect your faith.

17 So you see, faith by itself isn't enough. Unless it
produces good deeds, it is dead and useless.
18 Now someone may argue, "Some people have
faith; others have good deeds." But I say, "How can
you show me your faith if you don't have good deeds?
I will show you my faith by my good deeds."
19 You say you have faith, for you believe that there
is one God.* Good for you! Even the demons believe
this, and they tremble in terror. 20 How foolish! Can't
you see that faith without good deeds is useless?
21 Don't you remember that our ancestor Abraham
was shown to be right with God by his actions when
he offered his son Isaac on the altar? 22 You see, his faith
and his actions worked together. His actions made his
faith complete. 23 And so it happened just as the Scrip-
tures say: "Abraham believed God, and God counted
him as righteous because of his faith."* He was even
called the friend of God.* 24 So you see, we are shown
to be right with God by what we do, not by faith alone.
25 Rahab the prostitute is another example. She was
shown to be right with God by her actions when she
hid those messengers and sent them safely away by
a different road. 26 Just as the body is dead without
breath,* so also faith is dead without good works.

CONTROLLING THE TONGUE

3 Dear brothers and sisters,* not many of you should
become teachers in the church, for we who teach
will be judged more strictly. 2 Indeed, we all make
many mistakes. For if we could control our tongues,
we would be perfect and could also control ourselves
in every other way.

TONGUE TROUBLE

1. In your family or group, are you more likely to tease or be teased? Whom do you tease or who teases you?

JAMES 3:1-18

2. How does James illustrate the power of the tongue (vv. 3-6)? When have you been hurt by harsh words or gossip?
3. What is the ultimate solution for controlling our speech (vv. 10-12)? How does our heart need to change?
4. How does "the wisdom from above" (v. 17) guide us in how we talk to others?
5. When has your mouth gotten you into trouble lately? Competition or stress has a way of bringing that out. How can you correct this?

3 We can make a large horse go wherever we want
by means of a small bit in its mouth. 4 And a small
rudder makes a huge ship turn wherever the pilot
chooses to go, even though the winds are strong. 5 In
the same way, the tongue is a small thing that makes
grand speeches.
But a tiny spark can set a great forest on fire. 6 And
among all the parts of the body, the tongue is a flame
of fire. It is a whole world of wickedness, corrupting
your entire body. It can set your whole life on fire, for
it is set on fire by hell itself.*
7 People can tame all kinds of animals, birds, rep-
tiles, and fish, 8 but no one can tame the tongue. It is
restless and evil, full of deadly poison. 9 Sometimes it
praises our Lord and Father, and sometimes it curses
those who have been made in the image of God. 10 And
so blessing and cursing come pouring out of the same
mouth. Surely, my brothers and sisters, this is not
right! 11 Does a spring of water bubble out with both
fresh water and bitter water? 12 Does a fig tree pro-
duce olives, or a grapevine produce figs? No, and you
can't draw fresh water from a salty spring.*

TRUE WISDOM COMES FROM GOD

13 If you are wise and understand God's ways, prove
it by living an honorable life, doing good works with
the humility that comes from wisdom. 14 But if you
are bitterly jealous and there is selfish ambition in

2:19 Some manuscripts read *that God is one;* see Deut 6:4. **2:23a** Gen 15:6. **2:23b** See Isa 41:8. **2:26** Or *without spirit.* **3:1** Greek *brothers;* also in 3:10. **3:6** Or *for it will burn in hell* (Greek *Gehenna*). **3:12** Greek *from salt.*

2:17 faith . . . Unless it produces good deeds . . . is dead. An inevitable result of faith is good works. Jesus said you can recognize a person by the fruit he's bearing. Grapes don't come from thornbushes nor do figs come from thistles. Good fruit comes from a good tree and bad fruit from a bad tree (Mt 7:15-20).

2:19 the demons believe this. James clinches his argument against faith as just intellectual assent by pointing out that even the demons believe in God. They shudder, but they don't repent and have authentic faith from which good works flow.

2:21-25 Abraham . . . Rahab. James concludes with two illustrations from the Old Testament, which contain the evidence demanded by the fool in verse 20. In both cases, faith is demonstrated by means of concrete action. Abraham actually had the knife raised over his beloved son Isaac, and Rahab actually hid the spies. Without faith, Abraham would never have even considered sacrificing his only son, nor would Rahab have defied her king at great personal risk.

2:24 not by faith alone. James declares that saying you have faith isn't the same as sharing your faith. Real faith produces a changed life, which in turn, does good works.

3:14 bitterly jealous. The word "bitterly" is the same word that was used in verse 12 to describe brackish water unfit for human consumption. It is now applied to zeal (the word translated "envy" is literally *zelos*). Zeal that has gone astray becomes jealousy. **in your heart.** This is the issue: What lies at the core of the person's being? **don't cover up the truth with boasting and lying.** Those whose hearts are filled with this sense of rivalry and party-spirit ought not to pretend they are speaking God's wisdom. This merely compounds the wrong that is taking place.

FAVORABLE FRIENDSHIP

1. When has a "friend" gotten you in trouble? What did you learn from that experience?

JAMES 4:1-12

2. What are two reasons we don't get what we want (vv. 2-3)? What does this reveal about God's heart toward answered prayer?
3. How does the statement, "friendship with the world makes you an enemy of God" (v. 4), balance with, "For God loved the world" (John 3:16)? What is James trying to communicate?
4. Where do you need to submit yourself to God and resist the Devil this week (v. 7)? Are there any friends that are making it harder for you to resist temptation?

ONE DAY AT A TIME

1. What is your favorite way to spend a weekend?
2. How far into the future have you planned your life?

JAMES 4:13-17

3. What attitude should you have toward planning (v. 15)? How do you balance having faith about the future and being presumptuous?
4. Whom do you admire for the way he or she lives one day at a time—making every day count for God?
5. Where do you need God's guidance in your plans for the future? How will you get this guidance?

your heart, don't cover up the truth with boasting
and lying. [15] For jealousy and selfishness are not God's
kind of wisdom. Such things are earthly, unspiritual,
and demonic. [16] For wherever there is jealousy and
selfish ambition, there you will find disorder and evil
of every kind.
[17] But the wisdom from above is first of all pure.
It is also peace loving, gentle at all times, and willing to yield to others. It is full of mercy and the
fruit of good deeds. It shows no favoritism and is
always sincere. [18] And those who are peacemakers
will plant seeds of peace and reap a harvest of righteousness.*

DRAWING CLOSE TO GOD

4 What is causing the quarrels and fights among
you? Don't they come from the evil desires at war
within you? [2] You want what you don't have, so you
scheme and kill to get it. You are jealous of what others have, but you can't get it, so you fight and wage
war to take it away from them. Yet you don't have
what you want because you don't ask God for it. [3] And
even when you ask, you don't get it because your motives are all wrong—you want only what will give
you pleasure.
[4] You adulterers!* Don't you realize that friendship with the world makes you an enemy of God? I
say it again: If you want to be a friend of the world,
you make yourself an enemy of God. [5] Do you think
the Scriptures have no meaning? They say that God
is passionate that the spirit he has placed within us
should be faithful to him.* [6] And he gives grace generously. As the Scriptures say,

"God opposes the proud
but gives grace to the humble."*

[7] So humble yourselves before God. Resist the devil,
and he will flee from you. [8] Come close to God, and God
will come close to you. Wash your hands, you sinners;
purify your hearts, for your loyalty is divided between God and the world. [9] Let there be tears for what
you have done. Let there be sorrow and deep grief. Let
there be sadness instead of laughter, and gloom instead of joy. [10] Humble yourselves before the Lord, and
he will lift you up in honor.

WARNING AGAINST JUDGING OTHERS

[11] Don't speak evil against each other, dear brothers and sisters.* If you criticize and judge each other, then you are criticizing and judging God's law.
But your job is to obey the law, not to judge whether it applies to you. [12] God alone, who gave the law,
is the Judge. He alone has the power to save or to
destroy. So what right do you have to judge your
neighbor?

3:18 Or *of good things*, or *of justice*. **4:4** Greek *You adulteresses!* **4:5** Or *They say that the spirit God has placed within us is filled with envy;* or *They say that the Holy Spirit, whom God has placed within us, opposes our envy.* **4:6** Prov 3:34 (Greek version). **4:11** Greek *brothers.*

3:15 earthly, unspiritual, demonic. Wisdom that springs from envy is not of God but ultimately has its source in Satan.
3:16 disorder and evil of every kind. It was out of envy that Cain murdered his brother Abel. Many of the evils of this world can be traced to this spirit of envy that produces disorder.
3:17 peace loving. This is the opposite of envy and ambition. True wisdom produces right relationships between people, and this is the root idea behind the word "peace" in the New Testament. **willing to yield.** True wisdom is willing to listen, learn, and then yield when persuaded. **full of mercy and fruit of good deeds.** True wisdom reaches out to the unfortunate in practical ways, a point James never tires of making. **no favoritism.** Literally, "undivided." True wisdom does not vacillate back and forth. It is the opposite of the wavering in 1:6-8. **always sincere.** True wisdom does not act or pretend. It is honest and genuine.
4:1 quarrels and fights. Literally, "wars and battles." These are long-term conflicts, not sudden explosions. **among you.** The struggle is within a believer—between the part of him or her that is controlled by the Holy Spirit and that which is controlled by the flesh.
4:2 You desire. This is desire at work (1:14). **and do not have.** This is desire frustrated. **murder and covet.** This is how frustrated desire responds. It lashes out at others in anger and abuse. (This is "killing" in the sense of heart attitude—Matt. 5:21-22.) It responds in jealousy to those who have what it wants. **fight and war.** This mad desire-driven quest causes a person to disregard other people, trampling over them to get what they want. **you don't ask.** One reason for this frustrated desire is a lack of prayer.
4:3 your motives are all wrong. Jesus teaches us to ask for our daily bread, for our earthly needs. But he doesn't stop there. We may ask wrongly, failing to pray the other petitions in the Model Prayer (Mt 6:9-13).
4:7 humble yourselves before God. His first and primary command is that they must submit to God. **Resist the Devil.** Submission to God begins with resistance to Satan. Thus far they have been giving in to the Devil's enticements. **he will flee from you.** Since the Devil has no ultimate power over a Christian, when resisted, he can do little but withdraw.

MONEY CONCERNS

1. If you won the lottery, how would you spend your first $100,000?

JAMES 5:1-6

2. How do you think the rich people reacted to this warning from James?
3. What are the abuses the rich committed (vv. 4-6)? How do these injustices happen in the world today? How should Christians respond and be involved?
4. What do you think James would say about the concerns most people have for saving money, preparing for retirement, estate planning, etc.?
5. How does this passage challenge you in the way you manage your money?

IT'S TOUGH TO WAIT

1. For what do you hate waiting?
2. Rate yourself on the patience meter from 1 (none) to 10 (plenty).

JAMES 5:7-20

3. As Christians, for what are we waiting (vv. 7-8)? How easy is it to wait?
4. What do you think verse 12 is really saying about making promises? Why is swearing by heaven or earth a bad thing to do?
5. What is something in your life for which you've been waiting a long time? How do verses 13-18 encourage you?

WARNING ABOUT SELF-CONFIDENCE

13 Look here, you who say, "Today or tomorrow we are
going to a certain town and will stay there a year. We
will do business there and make a profit." 14 How do
you know what your life will be like tomorrow? Your
life is like the morning fog—it's here a little while,
then it's gone. 15 What you ought to say is, "If the Lord
wants us to, we will live and do this or that." 16 Oth-
erwise you are boasting about your own pretentious
plans, and all such boasting is evil.
17 Remember, it is sin to know what you ought to do
and then not do it.

WARNING TO THE RICH

5 Look here, you rich people: Weep and groan with
anguish because of all the terrible troubles ahead
of you. 2 Your wealth is rotting away, and your fine
clothes are moth-eaten rags. 3 Your gold and silver
are corroded. The very wealth you were counting on
will eat away your flesh like fire. This corroded trea-
sure you have hoarded will testify against you on the
day of judgment. 4 For listen! Hear the cries of the field
workers whom you have cheated of their pay. The
cries of those who harvest your fields have reached
the ears of the LORD of Heaven's Armies.
5 You have spent your years on earth in luxu-
ry, satisfying your every desire. You have fattened
yourselves for the day of slaughter. 6 You have con-
demned and killed innocent people,* who do not re-
sist you.*

PATIENCE AND ENDURANCE

7 Dear brothers and sisters,* be patient as you wait for
the Lord's return. Consider the farmers who patiently
wait for the rains in the fall and in the spring. They
eagerly look for the valuable harvest to ripen. 8 You,
too, must be patient. Take courage, for the coming of
the Lord is near.
9 Don't grumble about each other, brothers and
sisters, or you will be judged. For look—the Judge is
standing at the door!
10 For examples of patience in suffering, dear broth-
ers and sisters, look at the prophets who spoke in the
name of the Lord. 11 We give great honor to those who
endure under suffering. For instance, you know about
Job, a man of great endurance. You can see how the
Lord was kind to him at the end, for the Lord is full of
tenderness and mercy.
12 But most of all, my brothers and sisters, never
take an oath, by heaven or earth or anything else. Just
say a simple yes or no, so that you will not sin and be
condemned.

THE POWER OF PRAYER

13 Are any of you suffering hardships? You should
pray. Are any of you happy? You should sing praises.

5:6a Or *killed the Righteous One.* **5:6b** Or *Don't they resist you?* or *Doesn't God oppose you?* or *Aren't they now accusing you before God?*
5:7 Greek *brothers;* also in 5:9, 10, 12, 19.

4:13 Boasting about the future is arrogant because God is the only One who knows what will happen in the future.
4:14 tomorrow. All such planning presupposes that tomorrow will unfold like any other day, when in fact, the future is anything but secure (Prov. 27:1). **what your life will be.** Hosea 13:3 says, "Therefore, they will be like the morning mist, like the early dew that vanishes."
4:15 If the Lord wants us to. The uncertainty of the future ought not to be a terror to the Christian. Instead, it ought to force on him or her an awareness of how vital dependence upon God is. **we will live and do this or that.** James is not ruling out planning. He says, "Go ahead and plan, but involve God in your plans and be flexible."
4:16 boasting. The problem with this boasting is that they are claiming to have the future under control when, in fact, only God holds time in His hands. These are empty claims.
5:1 rich people. In the first century there was a great gulf between rich and poor. **Weep.** This is a strong word meaning, "to shriek" or "howl," and is used to describe the terror that will be felt by the damned.
5:4 have cheated their pay. The Old Testament insisted that it was wrong to withhold wages. A worker was to be paid immediately. **the field workers.** In Palestine, day laborers were used to plant and harvest crops. They were cheaper than slaves. **fields.** The Greek word means "estates." These were large tracts of land owned by the very wealthy. **cries of those.** This is a word used to describe the wild, incoherent cry of an animal.
5:5 in luxury. In contrast to the hunger of the laborers is the soft and easy living of the landowners (Amos 6:1-7). **satisfying.** Not just luxury but also vice is in view here. **day of slaughter.** Cattle were pampered and fattened for one purpose only: to be slaughtered. On the day when this took place a great feast was held.
5:12 never take an oath. The issue is not that of using foul language but of taking an oath to guarantee a promise. **Just say a simple yes or no.** Christians have no need for oaths. They are expected to speak only truth.

14 Are any of you sick? You should call for the elders
of the church to come and pray over you, anointing
you with oil in the name of the Lord. 15 Such a prayer
offered in faith will heal the sick, and the Lord will
make you well. And if you have committed any sins,
you will be forgiven.
16 Confess your sins to each other and pray for each
other so that you may be healed. The earnest prayer
of a righteous person has great power and produces
wonderful results. 17 Elijah was as human as we are,
and yet when he prayed earnestly that no rain would
fall, none fell for three and a half years! 18 Then, when
he prayed again, the sky sent down rain and the earth
began to yield its crops.

RESTORE WANDERING BELIEVERS

19 My dear brothers and sisters, if someone among
you wanders away from the truth and is brought
back, 20 you can be sure that whoever brings the
sinner back from wandering will save that person from death and bring about the forgiveness of
many sins.

5:14 sick. Illness is not something anybody else does to you. Especially in the first century, when only a minimum of medical help was available, illness made one feel vulnerable. What could be done? Where could a believer go for help? **call for the elders.** Illness was to be dealt with in the context of the Christian community. The elders were to be called to minister to the ill person. They had two things to do: pray over the person and anoint him or her with oil. **anointing him with oil.** When a Jew was ill, he or she first went to a rabbi to be anointed with oil. Oil was used not only for ritual purposes but also for cleaning wounds, for paralysis, and for toothaches. In this case, the olive oil is not being used as a medicine but as a part of the healing prayer (Mark 6:13; Luke 10:34).

5:15 the Lord will make you well. James is quite clear about the source of the healing. It is not the oil, it is not the laying on of hands by the elders, nor is it even prayer in some sort of magical sense. It is God who heals!

5:16 Confess your sins. Confessing your sins to one another removes barriers between people and promotes honesty in the Christian community. Prayer is directed to *God*, who is all-powerful and who works in this world.

5:17 as human as we are. Elijah knew depression, despair, and doubt, just as did the Christians (1 Kings 19). And yet, God answered his prayer in a mighty way. All Christians can pray like this, not just prophets.

INTRODUCTION TO
1 PETER

PERSONAL READING PLAN

☐ 1 Peter 1:1–2:3
☐ 1 Peter 2:4–3:7
☐ 1 Peter 3:8–4:11
☐ 1 Peter 4:12–5:14

AUTHOR

Traditionally, the Apostle Peter is credited with writing this letter. Peter was one of the first disciples called by Jesus. From Galilee, he was by trade a fisherman. His father was Jonah. His brother was Andrew the apostle. He was married, and his wife accompanied him on some of his preaching tours. Peter quickly became one of the leaders among the 12 apostles; later, he was a leader of the church in Jerusalem. He was the apostle to the Jews, yet because of his response to a vision, the first Gentile convert, Cornelius, was admitted to the church (Acts 10). Tradition says that Peter was martyred in Rome around A.D. 68 by crucifixion upside down.

DATE

First Peter was written sometime between the fire in Rome (A.D. 64) and Peter's death (A.D. 68).

THEME

Hope in the midst of suffering.

AUDIENCE

First Peter is a circular letter to Christians living in the northwest section of Asia Minor (in what is now modern Turkey). Pontus, Galatia, Cappadocia, Asia, and Bithynia (1:1) are all Roman provinces. This area had a large population, and the fact that Christians were living throughout the region testifies to the success of early Christian missionaries.

That these Christians were mainly Gentiles is clear from the way Peter describes their pre-conversion life; he uses categories and phrases typically applied to pagans but not to Jews (1:14; 2:9-10; 4:3-4). Peter also uses the Greek form of his name, Cephas, in this letter, and not Simon, his Jewish name.

HISTORICAL BACKGROUND

One hot July night in A.D. 64, Rome caught fire. For three days and nights the fire blazed out of control. Ancient temples and landmarks were swept away; homes were destroyed. Ten of the 14 city sections suffered damage; three sections were reduced to rubble. The people of Rome were distraught and angry, especially because some of Nero's officers were caught with firebrands trying to rekindle the waning fire. Many felt that Nero's passion for building caused him to want the city destroyed so he might rebuild it. No matter what Nero did to refute this rumor—and he aided the homeless extensively—nothing reduced the suspicion that the fire was his doing. Clearly he needed a scapegoat on which to blame the fire.

The Christians were accused of setting fire to Rome. Up to this time, they were thought to be simply a Jewish sect and were hardly noticed by Roman authorities. In fact, the Roman courts protected Christians against the wrath of the synagogue and others. But now all this changed. Nero introduced the church to martyrdom. What began in Rome would soon burn across the Roman Empire.

Under Roman law there were two types of religious systems: those that were legal, such as Judaism, and those that were forbidden. Anyone who practiced a forbidden religion was considered a criminal and was subject to harsh penalties. After the great fire, Christianity was judged to be distinct from Judaism, and it was quickly prohibited. This meant that throughout the Roman Empire, Christians were now technically outlaws and thus subject to persecution. Just such persecution was taking place in Asia Minor among the Christians to whom Peter writes (4:12).

PURPOSE

In the midst of the "fiery trials" (4:12) Peter writes to comfort and encourage. He says, "be very glad—for these trials make you partners with Christ in his suffering." How can they rejoice at such a difficult time? Because of the great hope they have as Christians. Hope is the theme of Peter's letter to these suffering believers.

CHARACTERISTICS

When reading 1 Peter, one hears echoes from the Old Testament, particularly from Isaiah. For example in 1:24-25, he quotes Isaiah 40:6-8; in 2:6, Isaiah 28:16; in 2:8, Isaiah 8:14; and in 2:22, Isaiah 53:9. He also alludes to Old Testament ideas and stories.

Peter is also familiar with Paul's writings. This letter contains parallels to Romans and, in particular, Ephesians. For example, compare 1:3 with Ephesians 1:3 and 1:20 with Ephesians 1:4. Note also the similarity between Peter and Paul in their instructions to family members and slaves (2:18–3:7; Eph. 5:21–6:9; Col. 3:18-25). In addition, there are parallels to Hebrews, James, and to Peter's own sermons in Acts.

First Peter is written in excellent Greek, which has caused scholars to question whether a Galilean fisherman like Peter could have had such a sophisticated command of the language. First Peter contains some of the best Greek in the New Testament. Its style is smoother even than Paul's with his years of training; its rhythmic structure is not unlike that of the Greek masters.

The answer to this question is found in 5:12: "I have written . . . with the help of Silas, . . ." Silas could well be the source of the excellent style as he helped Peter draft the letter and polish up the language.

PASSAGES FOR TOPICAL GROUP STUDY

1:3-12 . . . SPIRITUAL STRUGGLES and TRIALS . Hanging Tough
1:13–2:3 . PURE HEART and HOLY LIVING. . . . . Choosing to Do It Right
2:4-12 . . . LIVING TO GLORIFYING GOD . . . . Made for God
2:13-25 . . SUFFERING AND HARDSHIPS . . . . . .Facing Hardship
3:1-7 . . . . MARRIAGE and DATING. . . . . Marriage that Works
3:8-22 . . . SET APART and HOPE . . . . .Changing Behavior
4:1-11 . . . PRIORITIES . . . . .Changing Priorities
4:12-19 . . SUFFERING and PERSECUTION. . . . . No Big Surprise
5:1-11 . . . STRESS and LIFE'S STORMS . . . . .Stressed Out

GREETINGS FROM PETER

1 This letter is from Peter, an apostle of Jesus Christ.
I am writing to God's chosen people who are
living as foreigners in the provinces of Pontus, Gala-
tia, Cappadocia, Asia, and Bithynia.* 2 God the Father
knew you and chose you long ago, and his Spirit has
made you holy. As a result, you have obeyed him and
have been cleansed by the blood of Jesus Christ.

May God give you more and more grace and peace.

THE HOPE OF ETERNAL LIFE

3 All praise to God, the Father of our Lord Jesus Christ.
It is by his great mercy that we have been born again,
because God raised Jesus Christ from the dead. Now we
live with great expectation, 4 and we have a priceless
inheritance—an inheritance that is kept in heaven for
you, pure and undefiled, beyond the reach of change
and decay. 5 And through your faith, God is protecting
you by his power until you receive this salvation, which
is ready to be revealed on the last day for all to see.

6 So be truly glad.* There is wonderful joy ahead,
even though you must endure many trials for a little
while. 7 These trials will show that your faith is genu-
ine. It is being tested as fire tests and purifies gold—
though your faith is far more precious than mere
gold. So when your faith remains strong through
many trials, it will bring you much praise and glory
and honor on the day when Jesus Christ is revealed to
the whole world.

8 You love him even though you have never seen
him. Though you do not see him now, you trust him;
and you rejoice with a glorious, inexpressible joy.
9 The reward for trusting him will be the salvation of
your souls.

10 This salvation was something even the prophets
wanted to know more about when they prophesied
about this gracious salvation prepared for you. 11 They
wondered what time or situation the Spirit of Christ
within them was talking about when he told them in
advance about Christ's suffering and his great glory
afterward.

12 They were told that their messages were not for
themselves, but for you. And now this Good News has
been announced to you by those who preached in the
power of the Holy Spirit sent from heaven. It is all so
wonderful that even the angels are eagerly watching
these things happen.

A CALL TO HOLY LIVING

13 So prepare your minds for action and exercise
self-control. Put all your hope in the gracious salva-
tion that will come to you when Jesus Christ is re-
vealed to the world. 14 So you must live as God's obe-
dient children. Don't slip back into your old ways of
living to satisfy your own desires. You didn't know
any better then. 15 But now you must be holy in every-
thing you do, just as God who chose you is holy. 16 For
the Scriptures say, "You must be holy because I am
holy."*

HANGING TOUGH

1. What is the worst sport's injury you've had? How did you recover?
2. When have you felt like quitting the team or sport in which you participate? What kept you going?

1 PETER 1:3-12

3. What purpose do life's trials serve (v. 7)?
4. In what can we rejoice, despite the trials we face (vv. 3-5)?
5. What does verse 12 tell us about the place of humanity in God's grand design?
6. What have you found helpful when you are dealing with struggles?
7. What spiritual struggles are you going through right now?

CHOOSING TO DO IT RIGHT

1. What do you do to keep in shape physically? Mentally? Emotionally?

1 PETER 1:13–2:3

2. According to Peter, what does it mean to be holy (vv. 13-16)?
3. Why does Peter talk about the mind first (vv. 13-16) and then about conduct (v. 17)?
4. What is a good test to see if a Christian really has "sincere love" (v. 22)?
5. What makes loving others deeply and actively possible (vv. 22-23)?
6. Which of the characteristics of holy living listed in verses 13-16 is the greatest challenge for you?

1:1 *Pontus, Galatia, Cappadocia, Asia,* and *Bithynia* were Roman provinces in what is now Turkey. **1:6** Or *So you are truly glad.* **1:16** Lev 11:44-45; 19:2; 20:7.

1:1 Peter. Peter was the leader of the 12 apostles. Before joining Jesus' band of disciples he, along with his brother Andrew, was a fisherman on the Sea of Galilee. **an apostle.** This means, literally, "one who is sent." It is the term used in the New Testament to identify those who were selected for the special task of founding and guiding the new church. **living . . . in the provinces of.** This word originally referred to the Jews who were scattered in exile throughout the world. **Pontus, Galatia, Cappadocia, Asia, and Bithynia.** These are Roman provinces located in Asia Minor (now modern Turkey). The order in which they are named is the order in which a traveler would visit each.

1:2 God the Father knew . . . and chose. Israel knew itself to be chosen by God to be His people (Ezek. 20:5; Hos. 11:1). They were to be the people through whom He would reveal Himself to the rest of the world. The first Christians knew that they too had been chosen by God.

1:4 pure and undefiled . . . beyond the reach of change or decay. The first phrase, "pure and undefiled," refers to a land that has not been polluted or defiled by a conquering army. The second phrase, "beyond the reach of change or decay," paints a picture of a land without change or decay. It refers especially to flowers that do not fade.

1:14 Don't slip back . . . living to satisfy your own desires. They are not to allow themselves to be shaped by the sensuality of their pre-Christian existence. **You didn't know any better.** Not only was their pre-Christian life dominated by physical desires of all sorts, they also lived in ignorance of God. Pagans believed there was a god but thought him to be unknowable and disinterested in human beings.

1:18 ransom. To ransom, or redeem, someone is to rescue that person from bondage. This is a technical term for the money paid to buy freedom for a slave.

17 And remember that the heavenly Father to whom
you pray has no favorites. He will judge or reward
you according to what you do. So you must live in
reverent fear of him during your time here as "tem-
porary residents." 18 For you know that God paid a
ransom to save you from the empty life you inherited
from your ancestors. And it was not paid with mere
gold or silver, which lose their value. 19 It was the
precious blood of Christ, the sinless, spotless Lamb of
God. 20 God chose him as your ransom long before the
world began, but now in these last days he has been
revealed for your sake.

21 Through Christ you have come to trust in God.
And you have placed your faith and hope in God be-
cause he raised Christ from the dead and gave him
great glory.

22 You were cleansed from your sins when you
obeyed the truth, so now you must show sincere love
to each other as brothers and sisters.* Love each other
deeply with all your heart.*

23 For you have been born again, but not to a life
that will quickly end. Your new life will last forever
because it comes from the eternal, living word of God.
24 As the Scriptures say,

"People are like grass;
their beauty is like a flower in the field.
The grass withers and the flower fades.
25 But the word of the Lord remains forever."*

And that word is the Good News that was preached
to you.

2 So get rid of all evil behavior. Be done with all
deceit, hypocrisy, jealousy, and all unkind speech.
2 Like newborn babies, you must crave pure spiritual
milk so that you will grow into a full experience of
salvation. Cry out for this nourishment, 3 now that you
have had a taste of the Lord's kindness.

LIVING STONES FOR GOD'S HOUSE

4 You are coming to Christ, who is the living corner-
stone of God's temple. He was rejected by people, but
he was chosen by God for great honor.

MADE FOR GOD

1. What is something you've made or built recently?
2. How does it make you feel to know you are chosen by God—that you belong to Him?

1 PETER 2:4-12

3. What kind of process is necessary for God to use you as His blocks that he is "building into his spiritual temple" (v. 5)? What is the wisdom of this strategy by God?
4. Peter talks about things "that wage war against your souls" (v. 11). What are you fighting against right now?
5. How can you "give honor to God" (v. 12) and show others that you belong to Him?

5 And you are living stones that God is building
into his spiritual temple. What's more, you are his
holy priests.* Through the mediation of Jesus Christ,
you offer spiritual sacrifices that please God. 6 As the
Scriptures say,

"I am placing a cornerstone in Jerusalem,*
chosen for great honor,
and anyone who trusts in him
will never be disgraced."*

7 Yes, you who trust him recognize the honor God has
given him.* But for those who reject him,

"The stone that the builders rejected
has now become the cornerstone."*

8 And,

"He is the stone that makes people stumble,
the rock that makes them fall."*

1:22a Greek *must have brotherly love.* **1:22b** Some manuscripts read *with a pure heart.* **1:24-25** Isa 40:6-8. **2:5** Greek *holy priesthood.* **2:6a** Greek *in Zion.* **2:6b** Isa 28:16 (Greek version). **2:7a** Or *Yes, for you who believe, there is honor.* **2:7b** Ps 118:22. **2:8** Isa 8:14.

1:19 blood. In the Old Testament, the blood of the sacrificial animal was offered to God in place of the life of the sinner. In the New Testament, it is not the sacrifice of animals that secures forgiveness; it is the death of Jesus who gave Himself once for all. **sinless, spotless.** Jesus was able to be such a sacrifice because He was without sin.

1:22 obeyed the truth. In the context of Peter's writings this is a reference to one's conversion which involves repentance and faith in Christ. **love each other deeply.** This command for love that is both earnest, sincere, and from a pure heart is possible because of the cleansing that comes through conversion. The word translated *deeply* is used to describe the intense prayer of the church in Jerusalem when Peter was imprisoned (Acts 12:5). It is also used to describe Jesus' agonizing prayer in Gethsemane (Lk. 22:44).

1:23 not to a life that will quickly end. Literally, *not of perishable seed*. The seed of a human father is "perishable and earthly, and even if it produces children, they too will die eventually. The seed God uses to beget his people is invincible and incorruptible" (Schreiner). **the eternal, living word of God.** God's Word is the agent that gives us new birth. The result of our being born again is life that doesn't perish but continues forever.

2:1 get rid of. This verb was used to describe taking off one's clothes. Christians must strip off, like spoiled and dirty clothes, their old lifestyle. An essential practice in maintaining one's house is to regularly take out the trash. This is also true in our lives as Christians. This is the daily maintenance required to keep the command of loving one another earnestly and with a pure heart. **evil behaviour . . . all deceit, hypocrisy.** Evil behaviour is an attitude of ill will toward others. Deceit and hypocrisy undermine trust between people and so disrupt community. **jealousy, and all unkind speech.** Jealousy is divisive and robs love of the earnestness and purity of heart that come from a right relationship with Christ. It takes a dim view of someone having something that it lacks and is pleased with others fail. Unkind speech may mean to lie about people, but it may also mean to tell the truth in such a way that other people are placed in a bad light.

2:2 crave . . . spiritual milk. The word translated *crave* conveys the sense of craving nourishment. Milk has all the components infants need to help them grow and mature.

2:4 the living cornerstone. He gets this metaphor from two Old Testament texts: Isaiah 28:16 (quoted in verse 6) speaks of "a firm and tested stone" and Psalm 118:22 (quoted in verse 7) speaks of the rejection of that stone. Both verses point out the supreme value of the cornerstone. Peter's point is that, despite His rejection, Christ is the chosen One of God, and in the end He prevails.

2:5 is building into. Stones by themselves serve no function. But shaped together into a structure by a master builder, they become something of use and importance. **a spiritual temple.** The church is the temple of God, made up of a close-knit community of men and women. **his holy priests.** Not only are they a "spiritual temple," they **are the priests or ministers set apart to serve in it.**

They stumble because they do not obey God's word,
and so they meet the fate that was planned for them.
9 But you are not like that, for you are a chosen peo-
ple. You are royal priests,* a holy nation, God's very
own possession. As a result, you can show others the
goodness of God, for he called you out of the darkness
into his wonderful light.

10 "Once you had no identity as a people;
now you are God's people.
Once you received no mercy;
now you have received God's mercy."*

11 Dear friends, I warn you as "temporary residents
and foreigners" to keep away from worldly desires
that wage war against your very souls. 12 Be careful
to live properly among your unbelieving neighbors.
Then even if they accuse you of doing wrong, they
will see your honorable behavior, and they will give
honor to God when he judges the world.*

RESPECTING PEOPLE IN AUTHORITY

13 For the Lord's sake, submit to all human authority—
whether the king as head of state, 14 or the officials he
has appointed. For the king has sent them to punish
those who do wrong and to honor those who do right.
15 It is God's will that your honorable lives should
silence those ignorant people who make foolish ac-
cusations against you. 16 For you are free, yet you are
God's slaves, so don't use your freedom as an excuse
to do evil. 17 Respect everyone, and love the family of
believers.* Fear God, and respect the king.

SLAVES

18 You who are slaves must submit to your masters
with all respect.* Do what they tell you—not only
if they are kind and reasonable, but even if they are
cruel. 19 For God is pleased when, conscious of his will,
you patiently endure unjust treatment. 20 Of course,
you get no credit for being patient if you are beaten
for doing wrong. But if you suffer for doing good and
endure it patiently, God is pleased with you.
21 For God called you to do good, even if it means
suffering, just as Christ suffered* for you. He is your
example, and you must follow in his steps.

22 He never sinned,
nor ever deceived anyone.*
23 He did not retaliate when he was insulted,
nor threaten revenge when he suffered.
He left his case in the hands of God,
who always judges fairly.
24 He personally carried our sins
in his body on the cross
so that we can be dead to sin
and live for what is right.
By his wounds
you are healed.
25 Once you were like sheep
who wandered away.
But now you have turned to your Shepherd,
the Guardian of your souls.

WIVES

3 In the same way, you wives must accept the au-
thority of your husbands. Then, even if some
refuse to obey the Good News, your godly lives will
speak to them without any words. They will be won
over 2 by observing your pure and reverent lives.
3 Don't be concerned about the outward beauty
of fancy hairstyles, expensive jewelry, or beautiful
clothes. 4 You should clothe yourselves instead with
the beauty that comes from within, the unfading
beauty of a gentle and quiet spirit, which is so pre-
cious to God. 5 This is how the holy women of old made
themselves beautiful. They put their trust in God and
accepted the authority of their husbands. 6 For in-

FACING HARDSHIP

1. In what job or task have you felt like a slave?

1 PETER 2:13-25

2. How are Christians to act toward governmental authority, and why?
3. What kind of suffering is pleasing to God (v. 20)?
4. How does Christ's death have both an ending and a beginning effect on our lives (v. 24)?
5. What example did Jesus give us to follow when we have to endure suffering (vv. 21-25)?
6. How can Jesus' example help you when you face hardships you cannot change?

2:9 Greek *a royal priesthood.* **2:10** Hos 1:6, 9; 2:23. **2:12** Or *on the day of visitation.* **2:17** Greek *love the brotherhood.* **2:18** Or *because you fear God;* Greek reads *in all fear.* **2:21** Some manuscripts read *died.* **2:22** Isa 53:9.

2:9 God's very own possession. The church is a community chosen by God. **you can show others the goodness of God.** This is what our "spiritual sacrifices" are all about: making God known in the world.
2:11 temporary residents and foreigners. They may be a chosen nation and a royal priesthood, but they are also outsiders in terms of the world and culture in which they live. **keep away from worldly desires.** "worldly desires" are literally "fleshly lusts." In the New Testament, "sins of the flesh" encompass a far wider sphere than just sexual sin, including pride, envy, hatred, greed, gluttony, etc. (see Gal. 5:19-21).
2:13 Submit. This is the key concept in the next two passages. What Peter urges is voluntary subordination in all spheres of human life.
2:13-14 king . . . officials. The first situation in which Peter applies this general principle is with civil authorities.
2:16 God's slaves. The paradox is that Christians are both free and bound. They are to "live as free people," while simultaneously they are "slaves of God."
2:18 You who are slaves must submit. Slaves were the legal property of their masters. This fact, though inherently wrong, defined the reality within which they had to live. Peter does not counsel rebellion or even "passive resistance." What gave slaves the freedom to submit in this way was the sense that they as Christians were, in fact, members of a heavenly family and of a kingdom far more significant than the earthly reality within which they lived.
2:21 For God called you to do good . . . just as Christ suffered for you. The example of Jesus, who gave His life for us, is the basis on which Peter says what he does about accepting unjust treatment. Christian slaves are to imitate Christ.
2:24 carried our sins. In a key passage about Christ's saving work, Peter points out that Jesus was their substitute. He bore their sins. He took upon Himself the penalty, which they deserved because of their sin. **so that.** Peter points to two results of Jesus' death on the cross: (1) because of it they are able to be free of sin and (2) they can now live for righteousness. It is the moral impact of the cross which Peter chooses to highlight here. **healed.** Christ's wounds bring restoration to our sin-scarred lives.
3:1 In the same way, wives. By this phrase Peter makes a transition from slaves to wives. Just as the behavior of Christ was the model for slaves, so too is it for women. **must accept the authority of.** Again, as he did for slaves, Peter counsels submission to husbands, not rebellion. **won over.** Peter (like Paul) does not counsel Christian women to leave unbelieving husbands. His desire is that the husbands be converted, perhaps by the example of their wives.

MARRIAGE THAT WORKS

1. How would you rate your parents' marriage?

1 PETER 3:1-7

2. How does Peter define beauty? When appreciating or striving for beauty, which kind do you tend to focus on—that in verses 3 or 4?
3. What a wife is as an "equal partner in God's gift of new life" with her husband (v. 7), what does this say about their equality in the eyes of God?
4. How should men and women today follow the spirit of Peter's teaching on submission in this passage and in 2:13-15?
5. What does this passage tell you about the type of person you should look for in a spouse?

stance, Sarah obeyed her husband, Abraham, and
called him her master. You are her daughters when
you do what is right without fear of what your hus-
bands might do.

HUSBANDS

7 In the same way, you husbands must give honor to
your wives. Treat your wife with understanding as
you live together. She may be weaker than you are,
but she is your equal partner in God's gift of new life.
Treat her as you should so your prayers will not be
hindered.

ALL CHRISTIANS

8 Finally, all of you should be of one mind. Sympathize
with each other. Love each other as brothers and sis-
ters.* Be tenderhearted, and keep a humble attitude.
9 Don't repay evil for evil. Don't retaliate with insults
when people insult you. Instead, pay them back with
a blessing. That is what God has called you to do, and
he will grant you his blessing. 10 For the Scriptures say,

"If you want to enjoy life
and see many happy days,
keep your tongue from speaking evil
and your lips from telling lies.
11 Turn away from evil and do good.
Search for peace, and work to maintain it.
12 The eyes of the LORD watch over those who do right,
and his ears are open to their prayers.
But the LORD turns his face
against those who do evil."*

SUFFERING FOR DOING GOOD

13 Now, who will want to harm you if you are eager
to do good? 14 But even if you suffer for doing what is
right, God will reward you for it. So don't worry or
be afraid of their threats. 15 Instead, you must worship
Christ as Lord of your life. And if someone asks about
your hope as a believer, always be ready to explain
it. 16 But do this in a gentle and respectful way.* Keep
your conscience clear. Then if people speak against
you, they will be ashamed when they see what a good
life you live because you belong to Christ. 17 Remem-
ber, it is better to suffer for doing good, if that is what
God wants, than to suffer for doing wrong!
18 Christ suffered* for our sins once for all time. He
never sinned, but he died for sinners to bring you

CHANGING BEHAVIOR

1. Was there ever a time you unfairly got "caught holding the bag"? What happened? Did justice prevail in the end?

1 PETER 3:8-22

2. How is it possible to live like verses 8-12: Prayer? Effort? Obedience no matter what? A deepening relationship with Christ? Other?
3. How can suffering for what is right be a means of blessing (v. 14)?
4. How does hope change your everyday behavior (v. 15)? What situation seemed hopeless to you until God brought hope?

3:8 Greek *Show brotherly love.* **3:10-12** Ps 34:12-16. **3:16** Some English translations put this sentence in verse 15. **3:18a** Some manuscripts read *died.*

3:7 Husbands. In contrast to verses 1-2, where the focus is on Christian wives and unbelieving husbands, here Peter discusses how Christian husbands should relate to Christian wives. Peter reminds husbands that the respect they are to show to all people (2:17) is also due to their own wives. **in the same way.** As he did when he addressed wives (v. 1), Peter points back to the example of Christ who voluntarily gave Himself for the sake of others (2:21). **with understanding.** This phrase is literally "according to knowledge;" it is also translated "treat them with respect." In other words, the husband is not supposed to ride rough shod over his wife's needs and desires, but rather he is supposed to know her, to understand her, and to treat her with respect. The culture of the time, both pagan and Jewish, considered women to be inferior to men. The idea that the "superior" should show honor to the "inferior" by seeking to understand her was a strange teaching. **their weaker nature.** Literally, the "weaker vessel." There has been much debate as to what this means. It might refer to anatomical differences between men and women (this phrase was used in Greek to refer to the woman's body), to the inferior position of women in that society, or to the comparative lack of physical strength on the part of the woman. **equal partner in God's gift of new life.** Literally, "joint heirs." Both husband and wife are equal participants in the grace of God, again reinforcing the idea that men and women have equal value in God's eyes (Gal. 3:26-29).

3:8 be of one mind. The phrase is literally "all of one mind." By it Peter encourages the kind of unity that is vital in a hostile environment. There must be no divisions within the church. **love each other as brothers and sisters.** Peter uses the verb related to *philadelphia* (love amongst family) instead of the verb related to *agape* (self-giving love).

3:15 you must worship. Literally, "sanctify" Christ. Christ is to be acknowledged as holy and worshiped as Lord. They are to open themselves to His inner presence. **of your life.** At the core of their being, Christ must reign. **be ready to explain.** Although this may refer to an official inquiry in which they are called upon to defend the fact they are Christians, it probably is more general in reference. When anybody asks about the hope they have, they are to explain why they are followers of Jesus. **to explain.** Greeks valued a logical, intelligent statement as to why one held certain beliefs.

3:16 in a gentle and respectful way. This reply should not be given in a contentious or defensive way.

3:18 suffered for our sins. Christ died—as have men and women down through the ages. But His death was different in that it was a full, sufficient, and adequate sacrifice that atones for the sins of all people. **once for all time.** The sacrifices in the temple had to be repeated over and over again; Christ's sacrifice was the final and perfect sacrifice through which all people in all ages may obtain salvation (Heb. 10:14). **He never sinned, but he died for sinners.** His death was vicarious; He died in the place of others.

safely home to God. He suffered physical death, but he
was raised to life in the Spirit.*
19 So he went and preached to the spirits in pris-
on—20 those who disobeyed God long ago when God
waited patiently while Noah was building his boat.
Only eight people were saved from drowning in that
terrible flood.* 21 And that water is a picture of bap-
tism, which now saves you, not by removing dirt from
your body, but as a response to God from* a clean con-
science. It is effective because of the resurrection of
Jesus Christ.
22 Now Christ has gone to heaven. He is seated in
the place of honor next to God, and all the angels and
authorities and powers accept his authority.

LIVING FOR GOD

4 So then, since Christ suffered physical pain, you
must arm yourselves with the same attitude he
had, and be ready to suffer, too. For if you have suf-
fered physically for Christ, you have finished with
sin.* 2 You won't spend the rest of your lives chasing
your own desires, but you will be anxious to do the
will of God. 3 You have had enough in the past of the
evil things that godless people enjoy—their immoral-
ity and lust, their feasting and drunkenness and wild
parties, and their terrible worship of idols.
4 Of course, your former friends are surprised when
you no longer plunge into the flood of wild and de-
structive things they do. So they slander you. 5 But re-
member that they will have to face God, who stands
ready to judge everyone, both the living and the dead.
6 That is why the Good News was preached to those
who are now dead*—so although they were destined
to die like all people,* they now live forever with God
in the Spirit.*
7 The end of the world is coming soon. Therefore, be
earnest and disciplined in your prayers. 8 Most import-
ant of all, continue to show deep love for each other, for
love covers a multitude of sins. 9 Cheerfully share your
home with those who need a meal or a place to stay.
10 God has given each of you a gift from his great
variety of spiritual gifts. Use them well to serve one
another. 11 Do you have the gift of speaking? Then
speak as though God himself were speaking through
you. Do you have the gift of helping others? Do it with
all the strength and energy that God supplies. Then
everything you do will bring glory to God through
Jesus Christ. All glory and power to him forever and
ever! Amen.

SUFFERING FOR BEING A CHRISTIAN

12 Dear friends, don't be surprised at the fiery trials
you are going through, as if something strange were
happening to you. 13 Instead, be very glad—for these
trials make you partners with Christ in his suffering,
so that you will have the wonderful joy of seeing his
glory when it is revealed to all the world.

CHANGING PRIORITIES

1. Where do the party kids in your school go after a ball game, and what do they do? Have they ever gotten in trouble?

1 PETER 4:1-11

2. When has someone slandered you (v. 4) because you didn't join them in something you considered wrong?
3. What are some priorities that a Christian should have in his or her life (vv. 7-10)?
4. How have your priorities changed since becoming a Christian or since you got serious about your faith?
5. Right now, are you living more for yourself or for God? In what ways?

NO BIG SURPRISE

1. What kind of pain affects you the most: physical or emotional?
2. How do you feel when you hear that your country is sending military troops into conflict around the world?

1 PETER 4:12-19

3. What false assumption does Peter set straight in verse 12? How often are you surprised at the trials of life?
4. What is the first and most important course of action amidst suffering (v. 19)? How will this lift some of the burden of suffering?
5. Our society does not physically persecute Christians. What form, then, does your suffering for Christ take?

3:18b Or *in spirit.* **3:20** Greek *saved through water.* **3:21** Or *as an appeal to God for.* **4:1** Or *For the one* [or *One*] *who has suffered physically has finished with sin.* **4:6a** Greek *preached even to the dead.* **4:6b** Or *so although people had judged them worthy of death.* **4:6c** Or *in spirit.*

3:19 preached. The nature of Jesus' proclamation has been interpreted as: (1) The gospel which was proclaimed to those who lived before Christ came, or as (2) The announcement to the rebellious spirits that their power had been broken. **the spirits.** Who these spirits were is not clear. They have been variously identified as: (1) sinners who lived before the incarnation of Christ, or (2) the rebellious angels of Genesis 6:1-4.

4:3 evil things. The list of vices here parallels the lists in Romans 13:13 and Galatians 5:19-21. The picture it paints is of an out of control lifestyle characterized by sexual and alcoholic addictions and cultic practices. **had enough in the past.** Christians have two views of time: (1) time past, in which they gave themselves over to a destructive lifestyle, and (2) "the remaining time" (v. 2)—that time following conversion in which they live in accord with God's will. **immorality and lust.** "Excesses;" "debauchery," "outrages against decency;" "living in sensualities." **drunkenness.** Literally, "overflowings of wine." **wild parties.** Literally, "drinking bouts;" "drunken parties."

4:6 the Good News was preached to those who are now dead. The meaning of this phrase is quite difficult and has been much debated. It probably refers to those members of the church who have heard and accepted the gospel but who have since died. Some scholars, however, connect this verse to 3:19-20 and conclude that this is a reference to Christ's descent into hell, during which He proclaimed the gospel to those who were there.

4:10 gift. This word is *charisma* and refers to the different gifts which the Holy Spirit gives to individual Christians for the sake of the whole body. **to serve one another.** The point of these gifts is to use them for the sake of others. **his great variety of spiritual gifts.** Each one has a gift, but not all have the same gift (see also Rom. 12:6-8; 1 Cor. 12:7-10; and Eph. 4:11-12 for lists of various gifts).

14 If you are insulted because you bear the name of
Christ, you will be blessed, for the glorious Spirit of
God* rests upon you.* 15 If you suffer, however, it must
not be for murder, stealing, making trouble, or prying
into other people's affairs. 16 But it is no shame to suf-
fer for being a Christian. Praise God for the privilege
of being called by his name! 17 For the time has come
for judgment, and it must begin with God's house-
hold. And if judgment begins with us, what terrible
fate awaits those who have never obeyed God's Good
News? 18 And also,

"If the righteous are barely saved,
  what will happen to godless sinners?"*

19 So if you are suffering in a manner that pleases God,
keep on doing what is right, and trust your lives to the
God who created you, for he will never fail you.

ADVICE FOR ELDERS AND YOUNG MEN

5 And now, a word to you who are elders in the
churches. I, too, am an elder and a witness to the
sufferings of Christ. And I, too, will share in his glory
when he is revealed to the whole world. As a fellow
elder, I appeal to you: 2 Care for the flock that God has
entrusted to you. Watch over it willingly, not grudg-
ingly—not for what you will get out of it, but because
you are eager to serve God. 3 Don't lord it over the
people assigned to your care, but lead them by your
own good example. 4 And when the Great Shepherd
appears, you will receive a crown of never-ending
glory and honor.
5 In the same way, you who are younger must ac-
cept the authority of the elders. And all of you, dress
yourselves in humility as you relate to one another,
for

"God opposes the proud
  but gives grace to the humble."*

6 So humble yourselves under the mighty power of
God, and at the right time he will lift you up in honor.
7 Give all your worries and cares to God, for he cares
about you.

STRESSED OUT

1. What do you do when you are anxious or stressed out: Bite your nails? Eat? Stop eating? Withdraw?
2. Where do you turn for help in times of stress: Friends? Teammates? Parents? Coach?

1 PETER 5:1-11

3. During storms in your life, what are some good things to do (vv. 6-9)?
4. What would the opposite teaching of verse 6 be?
5. Among your Christian friends, what is the greatest cause for spiritual collapse?
6. What anxiety in your life do you need to turn over to God?

8 Stay alert! Watch out for your great enemy, the
devil. He prowls around like a roaring lion, looking
for someone to devour. 9 Stand firm against him, and
be strong in your faith. Remember that your family
of believers* all over the world is going through the
same kind of suffering you are.
10 In his kindness God called you to share in his
eternal glory by means of Christ Jesus. So after you
have suffered a little while, he will restore, support,
and strengthen you, and he will place you on a firm
foundation. 11 All power to him forever! Amen.

PETER'S FINAL GREETINGS

12 I have written and sent this short letter to you with
the help of Silas,* whom I commend to you as a faith-
ful brother. My purpose in writing is to encourage
you and assure you that what you are experiencing
is truly part of God's grace for you. Stand firm in this
grace.
13 Your sister church here in Babylon* sends you
greetings, and so does my son Mark. 14 Greet each oth-
er with a kiss of love.
Peace be with all of you who are in Christ.

4:14a Or *for the glory of God, which is his Spirit.* **4:14b** Some manuscripts add *On their part he is blasphemed, but on your part he is glorified.* **4:18** Prov 11:31 (Greek version). **5:5** Prov 3:34 (Greek version). **5:9** Greek *your brotherhood.* **5:12** Greek *Silvanus.* **5:13** Greek *The elect one in Babylon.* Babylon was probably symbolic for Rome.

4:16 Christian. Apart from two references in Acts (11:26; 26:28), this is the only other use of "Christian" in the New Testament.
4:19 trust your lives. This is a technical term which refers to the act of depositing money with a trusted friend. This is the same word Jesus used in Luke 23:46: "Father, I entrust my spirit into your hands!"
5:3 Don't lord it over . . . but lead them by . . . example. Mutual respect, submission, humility, and love are attitudes that should characterize the Christian community. The elders would be expected to set an example in displaying these attitudes.
5:5 you who are younger. The Greek social order was such that young men were considered subordinate to older men. **must accept the authority of.** Submission and respect are called for once again. **dress yourselves in humility.** This is a rare verb, meaning "wrap yourselves" or "gird yourselves." It is derived from the name for the apron which was worn by slaves when working.
5:6 humble yourselves. The same humility that is owed to one another is owed to God as well. **at the right time he will lift you up in honor.** This will happen when Christ returns and they experience His glory.
5:7 Give all your worries and cares to God. This is connected to the imperative "humble yourself." It is not a separate commandment.
5:8 Stay alert! Watch out. That they are not to be passive in the face of trouble is seen in this command. Coupled with conscious reliance on God, there must also be diligent effort on their part. **the devil.** Behind all their trials stands the Devil (*diabolos*). In the Old Testament he is known by the Hebrew name Satan. In the New Testament he is seen as the one who tempts (as he did with Jesus), as the prince of evil who rebels against God, and as the one who seeks to undo God's purposes.
5:9 Stand firm against him. Peter's advice is plain: do not run away, but stand your ground and face him, refusing to give in to his purposes, and trusting in God (Eph. 6:10-13; James 4:7; Rev. 12:9-11). **your family of believers . . . is going through the same kind of suffering.** Solidarity with Christian brothers and sisters around the world is a strong motivation for standing firm.
5:12 Silas. Like Paul (and others), Peter used an amanuensis (secretary/scribe) to write this letter. In this case, Silas (also known as Silvanus) seems to have had an active part in shaping the final form of the letter with its rather polished Greek. The Silas referred to here was probably Paul's companion on his second missionary trip (Acts 15:40–18:5), a minister of the gospel (2 Cor. 1:19), and the co-author with Paul of 1 and 2 Thessalonians.
5:13 Your sister church here in Babylon. Peter is probably referring to the church (2 John 1,13) in Rome, where he was when he wrote this letter. **my son Mark.** Tradition has it that Mark was another of Peter's secretaries, and, in writing the Gospel that bears his name, Mark was expressing Peter's experience of Jesus. Certainly this phrase reflects a warm relationship between the two.

INTRODUCTION TO

2 PETER

PERSONAL READING PLAN

☐2 Peter 1:1-21 ☐2 Peter 2:1-22 ☐2 Peter 3:1-18

AUTHOR

Traditionally, the Apostle Peter is thought to have authored this letter. However, questions about his authorship have existed since the earliest times. It was not uncommon in the first century to attribute pieces of writing to famous people. In fact, Peter's name is attached to several other books that clearly were not written by him (e.g., the Gospel of Peter, the Preaching of Peter, and the Apocalypse of Peter).

So questions arise when the language and thought of 1 and 2 Peter are compared. In their original Greek form, these two books are strikingly different. Could the same man have written both? This difference in style, of course, may simply be the result of Peter's use of several different secretaries. Peter indicates in his first letter that Silas helped him write it (1 Peter 5:12), and it is known that Peter had other secretaries (e.g., Mark and Glaucias.)

DATE

Second Peter was probably written near the time of Peter's death in A.D. 68 (see 1:12-15).

THEME

Be eager and on your guard.

AUDIENCE

On the basis of 1:1, it appears that there were no specific recipients of the letter. It seems intended for all Christians everywhere (hence its description as a General Epistle). However, in the body of the letter it becomes clear that 2 Peter was sent to a church or group of churches that had previously received 1 Peter (3:1). This would make the recipients Gentile Christians in Asia Minor. Furthermore, the tone of the letter makes it clear that a specific problem and specific false teachers are in view—which implies that 2 Peter is written for a specific people living in a particular area.

PURPOSE

Second Peter is a very important book for today because it deals with similar issues confronting the modern church, such as a lax lifestyle based on weak theology. Some church members in Peter's time argued that the doctrine of the second coming needed to be reconsidered. "The plain fact is that Christ has not returned yet," they said, "and he probably won't" (see 3:4,9). In fact, they suggested that this doctrine may have been invented by the apostles rather than revealed by God (1:16). It was suggested that the doctrine of the second doming was a moral restriction used to inhibit one's lifestyle. In contrast, the false teachers were saying that behavior does not matter. "Freedom" was their catchword, and evidently they felt free to indulge in sexual immorality and drunkenness.

"Not so!" exclaims Peter in this letter. We, too, need to remain firmly established within the truth we received from the prophets and from our Lord (chap. 1). We, too, need to be warned against those who would lead people away from that truth (chap. 2).

CHARACTERISTICS

Chapter 1 is an exhortation to grow in the Christian virtues. Chapter 2 is very similar to the epistle of Jude (see the Introduction to Jude). A marked contrast is drawn there between the character and teaching of true apostles (like Peter and Paul) and that of false teachers whose lives are marked by their denial of Jesus, immorality, rejection of authority, enslavement to sin, and misuse of Scripture. Chapter 3 addresses the second coming of Jesus Christ.

STRUCTURE

Second Peter begins like a typical first-century letter (1:1-2) by identifying sender and recipients and offering a Christian greeting. And then, in typical fashion, it announces its theme (1:3-11) and tells the occasion of writing (1:12-15). The only thing 2 Peter lacks is personal greetings at the end, but these were not characteristic of all first-century letters.

Second Peter is also a farewell speech. It sounds like the last words of a great leader. In the New Testament Paul's farewell speech to the Ephesian elders had this character (Acts 20:17-35) as does the book of 2 Timothy.

In 1:12-15, Peter says that his death is soon to take place, and the way he writes his letter is typical of testament literature in general. The letter contains ethical instructions in which the author summarizes his view, and then he makes predictions about the future.

THE EARLY CHURCH

Controversies abounded in the early church. One group denied Jesus was God, and another theory declared him God but not fully man. The apostles denounced obtaining salvation by works, only to encounter those who took it to the extreme and assumed "anything goes." Members of one church quit working and gathered together to await Jesus' return, while others gave up on His coming again at all.

Second Peter was written in response to a young church's questioning and doubting tendencies. Where 1 Peter centered on dangers from outside the church, this letter speaks to dangers from within. False teachers were stirring up problems, casting doubt on doctrine, and leading Christians into immoral behavior.

PASSAGES FOR TOPICAL GROUP STUDY

1:1-11 . . . . MUSIC and ENTERTAINMENT. . . Maturing in the Faith

PASSAGES FOR GENERAL GROUP STUDY

1:12-21 . . . . Pay Attention to God and His Word
2:1-22 . . . . Dangerous Lies
3:1-18 . . . . Anticipation (of Jesus' Return)

MATURING IN THE FAITH

1. How does music influence the lifestyle of kids in your school?

2 PETER 1:1-11

2. How much of today's music, movies, and entertainment emphasizes the qualities listed in verses 5-7?
3. Do you think there is any purpose to the progressive order in verses 5-7? Which one of these qualities are you adding to your faith currently? How? On which quality do you need to work?
4. How does your commitment to Christ affect your choice of movies and music? How difficult is it to avoid listening to or watching things that undermine your faith, and why?

GREETINGS FROM PETER

1 This letter is from Simon* Peter, a slave and apostle of Jesus Christ.

I am writing to you who share the same precious faith we have. This faith was given to you because of the justice and fairness* of Jesus Christ, our God and Savior.

2 May God give you more and more grace and peace as you grow in your knowledge of God and Jesus our Lord.

GROWING IN FAITH

3 By his divine power, God has given us everything we need for living a godly life. We have received all of this by coming to know him, the one who called us to himself by means of his marvelous glory and excellence. 4 And because of his glory and excellence, he has given us great and precious promises. These are the promises that enable you to share his divine nature and escape the world's corruption caused by human desires.

5 In view of all this, make every effort to respond to God's promises. Supplement your faith with a generous provision of moral excellence, and moral excellence with knowledge, 6 and knowledge with self-control, and self-control with patient endurance, and patient endurance with godliness, 7 and godliness with brotherly affection, and brotherly affection with love for everyone.

8 The more you grow like this, the more productive and useful you will be in your knowledge of our Lord Jesus Christ. 9 But those who fail to develop in this way are shortsighted or blind, forgetting that they have been cleansed from their old sins.

10 So, dear brothers and sisters,* work hard to prove that you really are among those God has called and chosen. Do these things, and you will never fall away. 11 Then God will give you a grand entrance into the eternal Kingdom of our Lord and Savior Jesus Christ.

PAYING ATTENTION TO SCRIPTURE

12 Therefore, I will always remind you about these things—even though you already know them and are standing firm in the truth you have been taught. 13 And it is only right that I should keep on reminding you as long as I live.* 14 For our Lord Jesus Christ has shown me that I must soon leave this earthly life,* 15 so I will work hard to make sure you always remember these things after I am gone.

16 For we were not making up clever stories when we told you about the powerful coming of our Lord Jesus Christ. We saw his majestic splendor with our own eyes 17 when he received honor and glory from

PAY ATTENTION

1. What event in your life this past year was the most memorable?

2 PETER 1:12-21

2. What event of Jesus' life does Peter recall (vv. 16-18)?
3. Why do you think it was so important for Peter to emphasize the divine inspiration of God's Word in verses 20-21? How can this teaching be misused?
4. If you could have been with Jesus at one event in His life, which would you choose? Why?
5. What is God saying to you about His Word (the Bible) in this passage?

1:1a Greek *Simeon.* **1:1b** Or *to you in the righteousness.* **1:10** Greek *brothers.* **1:13** Greek *as long as I am in this tent* [or *tabernacle*]. **1:14** Greek *I must soon put off my tent* [or *tabernacle*].

1:1 Simon Peter. Probably Peter wrote the letter shortly before his death in the mid 60s. The letter was most likely written to the same readers who received 1 Peter (cp. 3:2). In this letter, Peter alludes to his being an eye witness of Jesus' transfiguration (1:16-18). **justice and fairness.** This means that this second-generation audience of Christians had a faith that was in no way inferior ("of equal privilege") to that of the apostles.

1:3 everything we need. Nothing is more frustrating than setting to work on a project or an assignment and realizing that you don't have what you need to complete the task. Likewise, nothing is as encouraging as realizing that you have all that's needed to complete the project. For Christians, God's power has provided everything needed for living a godly life. **coming to know him.** God's power is imparted to us through our knowledge of Christ. This knowledge refers to our initial encounter with Christ at conversion, but it doesn't stop their. Knowledge increases, and Peter will soon describe this process of growth (1:5).

1:4 great and precious promises. This refers to the many promises found in Scripture based on having Christ making His home within us (John 14:23). **share his divine nature.** We are now new creations in Christ. We are being transformed into His image (2 Cor. 3:18).

1:5 make every effort. Peter's command is built on God's provision. This is no self help approach to the Christian life. God has provided all that is needed, therefore "make every effort." What follows is a chain of eight virtues that begins with faith, the root of these virtues, and ends with love, the goal of the Christian life. It's doubtful that Peter is calling on believers to work on these virtues one at a time. **supplement your faith.** Faith in Christ, the starting point for the Christian life, must produce a new quality of life. **moral excellence.** Literally, "virtue," an ethical term meaning moral excellence. **knowledge.** This is the wisdom and discernment gained from life experiences.

1:6 self-control. This is the self-discipline that leads to the pursuit of a virtuous life. It was often used in regard to sexual behavior. **endurance.** This is steadiness and faithfulness in the face of suffering and trials.

1:7 brotherly affection. The Greek word here (*philadelphia*) refers to family affection. It was commonly used to describe how Christians should relate to other members of the church, their spiritual family. **love.** *Agape*, which is the quality of showing loving actions toward even those who are one's enemies. This type of love is the chief aim of the Christian faith.

DANGEROUS LIES

1. If people have pets that are like them in some way, what does your choice of pet say about you?

2 PETER 2:1-22

2. If it is so plain that judgment awaits these false teachers, why does anyone follow them (vv. 2-3,14,18-19)?
3. Who are the gross sinners in verses 13-16? What are they like? On what basis is Peter assured they will be paid back for what they've done?
4. How can you help a "brother" or "sister" in Christ who is "tangled up" (v. 20) in the ways of the world?

God the Father. The voice from the majestic glory of God said to him, "This is my dearly loved Son, who brings me great joy."* 18 We ourselves heard that voice from heaven when we were with him on the holy mountain.

19 Because of that experience, we have even greater confidence in the message proclaimed by the prophets. You must pay close attention to what they wrote, for their words are like a lamp shining in a dark place—until the Day dawns, and Christ the Morning Star shines* in your hearts. 20 Above all, you must realize that no prophecy in Scripture ever came from the prophet's own understanding,* 21 or from human initiative. No, those prophets were moved by the Holy Spirit, and they spoke from God.

THE DANGER OF FALSE TEACHERS

2 But there were also false prophets in Israel, just as there will be false teachers among you. They will cleverly teach destructive heresies and even deny the Master who bought them. In this way, they will bring sudden destruction on themselves. 2 Many will follow their evil teaching and shameful immorality. And because of these teachers, the way of truth will be slandered. 3 In their greed they will make up clever lies to get hold of your money. But God condemned them long ago, and their destruction will not be delayed.

4 For God did not spare even the angels who sinned. He threw them into hell,* in gloomy pits of darkness,* where they are being held until the day of judgment. 5 And God did not spare the ancient world—except for Noah and the seven others in his family. Noah warned the world of God's righteous judgment. So God protected Noah when he destroyed the world of ungodly people with a vast flood. 6 Later, God condemned the cities of Sodom and Gomorrah and turned them into heaps of ashes. He made them an example of what will happen to ungodly people. 7 But God also rescued Lot out of Sodom because he was a righteous man who was sick of the shameful immorality of the wicked people around him. 8 Yes, Lot was a righteous man who was tormented in his soul by the wickedness he saw and heard day after day. 9 So you see, the Lord knows how to rescue godly people from their trials, even while keeping the wicked under punishment until the day of final judgment. 10 He is especially hard on those who follow their own twisted sexual desire, and who despise authority.

These people are proud and arrogant, daring even to scoff at supernatural beings* without so much as trembling. 11 But the angels, who are far greater in power and strength, do not dare to bring from the Lord* a charge of blasphemy against those supernatural beings.

12 These false teachers are like unthinking animals, creatures of instinct, born to be caught and destroyed. They scoff at things they do not understand, and like animals, they will be destroyed. 13 Their destruction is their reward for the harm they have done. They love to indulge in evil pleasures in broad daylight. They are a disgrace and a stain among you. They delight in deception* even as they eat with you in your fellowship meals. 14 They commit adultery with their eyes, and their desire for sin is never satisfied. They lure unstable people into sin, and they are well trained in greed. They live under God's curse. 15 They have wandered off the right road and followed the footsteps of Balaam son of Beor,* who loved to earn money by doing wrong. 16 But Balaam was stopped from his mad course when his donkey rebuked him with a human voice.

17 These people are as useless as dried-up springs or as mist blown away by the wind. They are doomed to blackest darkness. 18 They brag about themselves with empty, foolish boasting. With an appeal to twisted sexual desires, they lure back into sin those who have

1:17 Matt 17:5; Mark 9:7; Luke 9:35. **1:19** Or *rises.* **1:20** Or *is a matter of one's own interpretation.* **2:4a** Greek *Tartarus.* **2:4b** Some manuscripts read *in chains of gloom.* **2:10** Greek *at glorious ones,* which are probably evil angels. **2:11** Other manuscripts read *to the Lord;* still others do not include this phrase at all. **2:13** Some manuscripts read *in fellowship meals.* **2:15** Some manuscripts read *Bosor.*

1:19 message proclaimed by the prophets. The whole Old Testament was seen as a prophetic anticipation of the Messiah. **greater confidence.** Rather than dismiss the prophecies as the false teachers did, the readers ought to consider them very seriously. **lamp shining in a dark place.** God's Word was often compared to a light (Ps. 119:105). **the Morning Star shines.** This refers to Numbers 24:17 and is considered a prophecy of the Messiah. When the morning star (Venus) arises, daybreak is soon to come.

1:20-21 they spoke from God. While the false teachers claimed prophetic words of a future judgment were made up, the Peter asserts that the prophets were empowered by the Holy Spirit (Jer. 20:9).

1:21 moved by the Holy Spirit. The same verb describes how God's voice came to the apostles at the transfiguration (v. 17). What they heard and what the Old Testament authors wrote came from God.

2:1 false prophets. The presence of Israel's lying prophets (Deut. 18:20; Jer. 14:13-16) is used to expose the presence of false teachers within the Christian community. The major problem of these teachers was their rejection of the Lord (1:16-21; 2:18-21; 3:3-11). **destructive heresies.** Literally, "teachings of destruction."

2:2 shameful immorality. Since these false teachers denied accountability, they assumed they had freedom (v. 19) to indulge in immorality.

2:3 greed. The motivation for these false teachers is to teach what people will pay to hear.

2:5 Noah warned the world. Noah's righteous living set against the backdrop of the sinful world was a strong statement about God's ways. Those around him were indifferent.

2:7 a righteous man. Lot was not willing to participate in the sin of Sodom and Gomorrah. Peter describes him three times here as righteous. Righteousness is not based on works.

2:10-12 proud and arrogant. Like those mentioned in verses 4-9, the false teachers follow the corrupt desire of the sinful nature and despise authority. This involves blatant sexual immorality (v. 14) and a wholesale rejection of Christ's lordship.

2:13 a disgrace and a stain. These people are like animals unfit to be offered in sacrifice to God. **deception.** Literally, "deceits" or perversions of pleasure.

barely escaped from a lifestyle of deception. 19 They promise freedom, but they themselves are slaves of sin and corruption. For you are a slave to whatever controls you. 20 And when people escape from the wickedness of the world by knowing our Lord and Savior Jesus Christ and then get tangled up and enslaved by sin again, they are worse off than before. 21 It would be better if they had never known the way to righteousness than to know it and then reject the command they were given to live a holy life. 22 They prove the truth of this proverb: "A dog returns to its vomit."* And another says, "A washed pig returns to the mud."

THE DAY OF THE LORD IS COMING

3 This is my second letter to you, dear friends, and in both of them I have tried to stimulate your wholesome thinking and refresh your memory. 2 I want you to remember what the holy prophets said long ago and what our Lord and Savior commanded through your apostles.

3 Most importantly, I want to remind you that in the last days scoffers will come, mocking the truth and following their own desires. 4 They will say, "What happened to the promise that Jesus is coming again? From before the times of our ancestors, everything has remained the same since the world was first created."

5 They deliberately forget that God made the heavens long ago by the word of his command, and he brought the earth out from the water and surrounded it with water. 6 Then he used the water to destroy the ancient world with a mighty flood. 7 And by the same word, the present heavens and earth have been stored up for fire. They are being kept for the day of judgment, when ungodly people will be destroyed.

8 But you must not forget this one thing, dear friends: A day is like a thousand years to the Lord, and a thousand years is like a day. 9 The Lord isn't really being slow about his promise, as some people think. No, he is being patient for your sake. He does not want anyone to be destroyed, but wants everyone to repent. 10 But the day of the Lord will come as unexpectedly as a thief. Then the heavens will pass away with a terrible noise, and the very elements themselves will disappear in fire, and the earth and everything on it will be found to deserve judgment.*

11 Since everything around us is going to be destroyed like this, what holy and godly lives you should live, 12 looking forward to the day of God and hurrying it along. On that day, he will set the heavens on fire, and the elements will melt away in the flames. 13 But we are looking forward to the new heavens and new earth he has promised, a world filled with God's righteousness.

14 And so, dear friends, while you are waiting for these things to happen, make every effort to be found living peaceful lives that are pure and blameless in his sight.

15 And remember, our Lord's patience gives people time to be saved. This is what our beloved brother Paul also wrote to you with the wisdom God gave him—16 speaking of these things in all of his letters. Some of his comments are hard to understand, and those who are ignorant and unstable have twisted his letters to mean something quite different, just as they do with other parts of Scripture. And this will result in their destruction.

PETER'S FINAL WORDS

17 You already know these things, dear friends. So be on guard; then you will not be carried away by the errors of these wicked people and lose your own secure footing. 18 Rather, you must grow in the grace and knowledge of our Lord and Savior Jesus Christ.

All glory to him, both now and forever! Amen.

ANTICIPATION

1. When did an important person in your life promise a fishing trip, a ball game, or a graduation present and then fail to deliver? How did that make you feel?

2 PETER 3:1-18

2. What frustrations are produced by God's patience in coming again? How is God's patience beneficial (vv. 9,15)?
3. In verses 10-16, is Peter addressing the certainty, the timing, or the manner of Christ's coming?
4. How can you best occupy your time while you await Jesus' coming (v. 14)?

2:22 Prov 26:11. 3:10 Other manuscripts read *will be burned up;* one early manuscript reads *will be found destroyed.*

2:19 freedom. In light of the false teachers' denial of the second coming (3:4), this probably refers to the "freedom" from the moral implications of preparing for His imminent return. They may have used Paul's teaching on freedom in Christ (Rom. 6:1-18) to justify their position (3:15-16). **you are a slave to whatever controls you.** This was a common saying based on what actually happened to people conquered in war (John 8:34; Rom. 6:16). Their supposed "freedom" is simply slavery to sin.

3:3 scoffers. In the book of 2 Peter, these are the teachers who mock the idea of the Lord's return (v. 4).

3:4 What happened to the promise that Jesus is coming again? Since Jesus stressed the imminence of His return (Matt. 24:34), the death of those followers of Jesus raised the critical problem of whether His promise could be trusted. **since the world was first created.** The scoffers argued that the world has always just gone on and on with no divine intervention or judgment, a belief shared by much of Greek philosophy as well.

3:6 water to destroy. In the flood, it was God who released the waters to deluge the earth.

3:10 as a thief. Like a thief, the Lord will come without warning (Matt. 24:43-44; 1 Thess. 5:4). **heavens will pass away with a terrible noise.** The coming of God in judgment is always described in graphic images. The roar here may be the sound of the heavens being rolled up (Heb. 1:12) or the shout of God pronouncing judgment upon the cosmos. **elements . . . disappear . . . earth . . . will be found.** There will be nothing to hide the wickedness of the earth from the eyes of the heavenly Judge (Isa. 2:19).

3:16 comments are hard to understand. In the context of the problems at this church, this might refer either to Paul's teaching about Christian freedom (Gal. 5:1), or to passages in his letters that indicated the imminent return of Christ (Rom. 13:11-12; Phil. 4:5; 1 Thess. 4:15). Both may have been distorted to provide the false teachers with justification for their acceptance of immorality.

3:17 secure footing. A secure position, in contrast to the instability of the false teachers (v. 16).

3:18 Lord and Savior. In the New Testament, these two names are found together as titles for Jesus only in 2 Peter; 2 Peter refers to Jesus as Savior more than any other New Testament book. **to him.** Typically doxologies were ascribed to God, but this one is clearly ascribed to the Son. Second Peter stands out in the New Testament as a letter that clearly affirms the divine nature of Jesus.

INTRODUCTION TO

1 JOHN

PERSONAL READING PLAN

- ☐ 1 John 1:1–2:17
- ☐ 1 John 2:18–3:24
- ☐ 1 John 4:1-21
- ☐ 1 John 5:1-21

AUTHOR

Although the author is nowhere named in the epistle, it is likely the beloved Apostle John, now an old man living in Asia Minor and pastoring the churches in and around Ephesus. There are a number of reasons for attributing this anonymous epistle to John:

1. A strong tradition dating back to the early days of the church holds that John is the author.

2. There are many similarities in style and content between the Gospel of John and this epistle. The same sharp contrasts appear in light and darkness, truth and falsehood, love and hate. The differences between them can be traced to differences in purpose and to the length of time that elapsed between the composition of each.

3. The internal information in the epistle points to John. For example, the author tells us that he was one of the original eyewitnesses of Jesus (1:1-2). Also, the author writes with the air of authority that would be expected of an apostle (4:6).

DATE

There is little clear evidence by which to date this letter accurately. Although it can be dated as early as A.D. 60, it was probably written toward the end of the New Testament era (A.D. 90–95), by which time many false teachings had flourished.

THEME

Walking in the light.

THE PROBLEM OF FALSE TEACHERS

Apparently a group of Christians got involved in false teaching, split off from the church (2:19), and were hassling their former friends, trying to convince them to accept their new views (2:26). This deeply troubled the church, and thus John, as pastor, wrote to assure the Christians in and around Ephesus that they were, indeed, true Christians with the assurance of eternal life.

The nature of the false teaching is not completely clear. John does not describe it. The recipients of his letter knew well enough what was being taught. As John defends orthodox Christianity, certain features of the incorrect doctrine emerge.

In particular, the false teachers had a low view of Jesus. They did not believe he was the Messiah (2:22; 5:1). They did not believe he was the Son of God (5:5). They denied that Jesus had come in the flesh (4:2). They apparently claimed they did not need Jesus because they already knew God (2:4) and had fellowship with him (1:6). They did not believe that sin separated a person from God (1:6,8,10), and thus they had no need of Jesus' atoning death (5:6) to provide forgiveness and a way back to God. It is not by accident that John calls such a person an "antichrist" (2:22).

SPIRITUAL "SUPERIORITY"

This group had come to think of themselves as some sort of spiritual elite, claiming that they had a "deeper" understanding of Christianity (4:1-6). As an antidote to such spiritual pride, John reminded his readers over and over that Christians are called to love one another, not to look down on their brothers and sisters.

It is not clear what to call this group of false teachers. They were probably related to what later became Gnosticism—a philosophy in which matter (including the body) was impure and spirit was all that counted. Therefore, these false teachers denied that Christ was fully human. They kept his deity but at the expense of his humanity. To them, salvation came by illumination. Thus, secret "knowledge" was eagerly sought, often at the expense of apostolic doctrine.

PURPOSE

John's central concerns are quite clear. He wants to define the marks of a true Christian against the claims of the false teachers. He wants his congregation to have assurance that they have eternal life (5:13). He wants them to know the characteristics of a true Christian: right belief (the doctrinal test), righteousness (the moral test), and love (the social test).

CHARACTERISTICS

First John is written in the simplest Greek of all the New Testament. Although 5,437 different Greek words appear in the New Testament, only 303 are used in the three letters of John—less than six percent. This is not to say, however, that 1 John is a superficial book. On the contrary, the apostle John, now an old man, is writing a summary of all he has learned. "This is what Christianity is all about," he is saying. "This is what it all boils down to: God is light (1:5); God is love (4:16); Jesus is the Messiah (2:22), the Son of God (4:15), who has come in the flesh (4:2). We are to be God's children (3:1); as such we have eternal life (2:25). We do not continue in sin (2:1), but we love one another (3:11). I repeat, we are to love one another (4:7-12)."

STRUCTURE

First John is not a letter like 2 and 3 John or most of Paul's writings. It lacks identification of writer and recipients, a salutation and a final greeting. Still, it is not a generalized document written to all Christians. John has a specific audience in mind, probably the churches in his charge in Asia Minor. Despite the lack of usual greetings, he writes in personal terms. Many see 1 John as a tract, perhaps intended to be read as a sermon, in which John deals with a specific problem.

PASSAGES FOR TOPICAL GROUP STUDY

1:1-4 . . . . . . KNOWING AND SHARING JESUS . . On Jesus' Team
1:5–2:6 . . . . FAILURE and SIN . . . . Living in the Light
2:7-14 . . . . . LOVING AND OBEYING GOD . . . . . The Test of Faith
2:15-27 . . . . LOVE FOR THE WORLD . . . . Love is the Key
2:28–3:10 . CHILDREN OF GOD . . . . God is My Dad
3:11-24 . . . . ASSURANCE and COMPASSION . . . . True Love
4:1-6 . . . . . . CULTS . . . . Seeking Truth
4:7-21 . . . . . GOD'S LOVE and FEAR . . . . Fear vs. Love
5:1-15 . . . . . DOUBTS . . . . Confidence in Eternity

INTRODUCTION

1 We proclaim to you the one who existed from the
beginning,* whom we have heard and seen. We
saw him with our own eyes and touched him with
our own hands. He is the Word of life. 2 This one who
is life itself was revealed to us, and we have seen him.
And now we testify and proclaim to you that he is the
one who is eternal life. He was with the Father, and
then he was revealed to us. 3 We proclaim to you what
we ourselves have actually seen and heard so that
you may have fellowship with us. And our fellowship
is with the Father and with his Son, Jesus Christ. 4 We
are writing these things so that you may fully share
our joy.*

ON JESUS' TEAM

1. What is the most unbelievable thing you have personally witnessed?

1 JOHN 1:1-4

2. John makes a point of saying that he has heard, seen, and touched Jesus. What were your "beginnings" with Jesus like? In what ways have you "seen," "heard," and "touched" Him?
3. Who has been like the Apostle John in your life—a person who has convinced you of Jesus' love and cared about your spiritual growth and maturity?
4. A key part of being on Jesus' team is revealing the truth about Him to others. How could you help someone else "see" Jesus?

LIVING IN THE LIGHT

5 This is the message we heard from Jesus* and now
declare to you: God is light, and there is no darkness in
him at all. 6 So we are lying if we say we have fellow-

LIVING IN THE LIGHT

1. When was the last time the lights went out in your house and you were plunged into darkness?

1 JOHN 1:5–2:6

2. When you've blown it, what should you do to "clean up" (1:9)? Does that work for every sin?
3. How does it make you feel to know Jesus speaks to God "in our defense" (2:1)?
4. What are two ways you can tell if you are walking in the light (1:7; 2:3)?
5. Where have you been walking lately—in the light or in the darkness? How can you live more in the "light"?

ship with God but go on living in spiritual darkness;
we are not practicing the truth. 7 But if we are living
in the light, as God is in the light, then we have fellow-
ship with each other, and the blood of Jesus, his Son,
cleanses us from all sin.
8 If we claim we have no sin, we are only fooling
ourselves and not living in the truth. 9 But if we con-
fess our sins to him, he is faithful and just to forgive us
our sins and to cleanse us from all wickedness. 10 If we
claim we have not sinned, we are calling God a liar
and showing that his word has no place in our hearts.

2 My dear children, I am writing this to you so that
you will not sin. But if anyone does sin, we have
an advocate who pleads our case before the Father.
He is Jesus Christ, the one who is truly righteous. 2 He
himself is the sacrifice that atones for our sins—and
not only our sins but the sins of all the world.
3 And we can be sure that we know him if we obey
his commandments. 4 If someone claims, "I know God,"
but doesn't obey God's commandments, that person is

1:1 Greek *What was from the beginning.* 1:4 Or *so that our joy may be complete;* some manuscripts read *your joy.* 1:5 Greek *from him.*

1:1 from the beginning. The initial clause makes the assertion that this "Word of life" was pre-existent (John 1:1). Since only divine beings pre-existed, John affirms Jesus' deity.
1:2 testify. This is a legal term describing what an eyewitness does while in court. Such a person makes a public declaration of what he or she has experienced firsthand.
1:3 fellowship. This word has the dual sense of participation together in shared activity or outlook and union together because of this shared experience.
1:5 God is light. Within the context of the Bible, "light" was connected to two basic ideas. First, on the intellectual level, it was a symbol of truth. John is saying that God is truth. Second, on the moral level, light is a symbol of purity.
1:6 If we say. Here is the first of three false claims that John will refute. He will measure the validity of each claim against the apostolic proclamation that God is light and in Him is no darkness whatsoever. **have fellowship with God . . . living in spiritual darkness.** It is claimed by the false teachers that it is possible to be in union with God and yet habitually sin.
1:7 are living in the light. The image here is of a person confidently striding forth, illuminated by the light of God's truth, in contrast to the person who stumbles around in darkness. **cleanses.** If the first result of "walking in the light" is fellowship with one another. The second result is cleansing from sin.
1:8 If we claim we have no sin. The second false claim is that they are sinless. It is one thing to deny that sin breaks fellowship with God (vv. 6-7). At least the existence of sin is admitted (even if its impact is denied); but it is another thing to deny the fact of sin altogether. **we are only fooling ourselves.** This assertion goes beyond a mere lie (v. 6). This is self-deception. **not living in the truth.** Not only do they not live by the truth (v. 6), but they demonstrate that they do not even know the truth.
1:9 If we confess our sins. Rather than denying their sinful natures, they need to admit their sin to God and so gain forgiveness. **faithful.** God will keep His promise to forgive (Mic. 7:18-20). **just.** The granting of forgiveness is not merely an act of unanticipated mercy but a response of justice, since the conditions for forgiveness have been fulfilled as a result of the death of Christ. **cleanse.** Sin makes a person unclean; Christ cleanses us of our sin (v. 7).
1:10 If we claim we have not sinned. The third false claim: not only do they say that at the present moment they are without sin (v. 8), they actually claim never to have sinned! **we are calling God a liar.** By claiming sinlessness they are, in essence, saying that God is lying about human nature and about His claim to forgive people. **his word has no place in our hearts.** Contrary to what they might claim, they are, in fact, alienated from God (Col. 1:21).
2:1 so that you will not sin. John quickly points out that sin is not compatible with Christian commitment. **if anyone does sin.** The provision for sin is found in Jesus, who is the Advocate, "the righteous One," and the atoning sacrifice for believers.
2:2 the sacrifice. Jesus, the Advocate, bases His plea (that their sins should be forgiven) on the fact that His death legally and fully paid for their sin. Propitiation is one of the key concepts in the New Testament. Propitiation is not just the removal of our sins and their effects. Propitiation is required because of God's wrath toward sin. God's wrath is not a whimsical, out-of control outburst. Wrath is God's eternal opposition to sin and evil. We are strongly offended when someone in authority overlooks wrong. We say they are unjust. In order for God to be just and to offer mercy to those who had sinned, someone must take the punishment due. That someone is Jesus Christ.
2:3 if we obey his commandments. The first test to determine whether a person knows God is moral in nature: Does that person keep God's commands?

a liar and is not living in the truth. [5]But those who
obey God's word truly show how completely they
love him. That is how we know we are living in him.
[6]Those who say they live in God should live their lives
as Jesus did.

A NEW COMMANDMENT

[7]Dear friends, I am not writing a new commandment
for you; rather it is an old one you have had from the
very beginning. This old commandment—to love one
another—is the same message you heard before. [8]Yet
it is also new. Jesus lived the truth of this command-
ment, and you also are living it. For the darkness is
disappearing, and the true light is already shining.
[9]If anyone claims, "I am living in the light," but
hates a fellow believer,* that person is still living in
darkness. [10]Anyone who loves a fellow believer* is
living in the light and does not cause others to stum-
ble. [11]But anyone who hates a fellow believer is still
living and walking in darkness. Such a person does
not know the way to go, having been blinded by the
darkness.

[12] I am writing to you who are God's children
because your sins have been forgiven through
Jesus.*
[13] I am writing to you who are mature in the faith*
because you know Christ, who existed from the
beginning.
I am writing to you who are young in the faith
because you have won your battle with the evil
one.
[14] I have written to you who are God's children
because you know the Father.
I have written to you who are mature in the faith
because you know Christ, who existed from the
beginning.
I have written to you who are young in the faith
because you are strong.
God's word lives in your hearts,
and you have won your battle with the evil one.

DO NOT LOVE THIS WORLD

[15]Do not love this world nor the things it offers you,
for when you love the world, you do not have the
love of the Father in you. [16]For the world offers only
a craving for physical pleasure, a craving for every-
thing we see, and pride in our achievements and pos-
sessions. These are not from the Father, but are from
this world. [17]And this world is fading away, along
with everything that people crave. But anyone who
does what pleases God will live forever.

WARNING ABOUT ANTICHRISTS

[18]Dear children, the last hour is here. You have heard
that the Antichrist is coming, and already many
such antichrists have appeared. From this we know
that the last hour has come. [19]These people left our
churches, but they never really belonged with us; oth-
erwise they would have stayed with us. When they
left, it proved that they did not belong with us.
[20]But you are not like that, for the Holy One has giv-
en you his Spirit,* and all of you know the truth. [21]So
I am writing to you not because you don't know the

THE TEST OF FAITH

1. What game did you play as a child where you were blindfolded? What was the experience like?

1 JOHN 2:7-14

2. How can the command to love God and others be both old and new at the same time (vv. 7-8)?
3. John makes a very bold claim (vv. 9-11) about who really loves God. What is it about loving others that becomes such solid evidence? Does that seem like a fair test? Why or why not?
4. What three things does John stress again in verses 12-13? Which one of these do you most need to hear this week, and why?

LOVE IS THE KEY

1. What do you love to do most with your free time?

1 JOHN 2:15-27

2. What does John mean by "the world" (vv. 15-16)? Is it wrong to love the outdoors or our pets? Are all human desires contrary to God's will? Why?
3. Why can't love for the world and love for God coexist in our lives (v. 17)?
4. How can we be sure that we "remain" in the truth (vv. 24-27)?
5. In what areas of your life does love for the world compete with love for God: In your use of money? Time? Priorities? Relationships? Ambitions?

2:9 Greek *hates his brother;* also in 2:11. **2:10** Greek *loves his brother.* **2:20** Greek *But you have an anointing from the Holy One.* **2:12** Greek *through his name.* **2:13** Or *to you fathers;* also in 2:14.

2:12 children . . . have been forgiven. The verb tense indicates John is thinking of the forgiveness that comes at the time of conversion. In 1:9, his concern was with ongoing forgiveness for subsequent sins based on the confession of sins.
2:15 world. The word John uses here is *kosmos,* and in this context it means that which is alienated from God and is contrary to who God is. It refers to pagan culture which is alien to God.
2:16 craving for physical pleasure. That part of human nature which demands gratification—be it for sexual pleasure, for luxury, for possessions, for expensive food, or for whatever. **Craving for everything we see.** Greed, which is aroused by sight. A person sees something and wants it. (Gen. 3:6; Josh. 7:21; 2 Sam. 11:2-4.) **pride.** Pride in one's possessions; an attitude of arrogance because one has acquired so much.
2:18 the last hour. They knew that His second coming (the *parousia*) would bring to a close the "last days" and usher in a new age in which God's rule would be visible and universal. **Antichrist.** In the last days an evil opponent will arise under the control of Satan. **antichrists.** John points out that the coming of the Antichrist was not just some future threat. Even at that moment the "spirit of the antichrist" (4:3) was loose in the world and active in those who denied Christ and His teachings (v. 22).
2:19 These people left our churches. John now identifies those who are imbued with the spirit of the antichrist. They are none other than the secessionists who left the church and even now seek to win over their former friends and colleagues to their point of view (v. 26).

truth but because you know the difference between
truth and lies. 22 And who is a liar? Anyone who says
that Jesus is not the Christ.* Anyone who denies the
Father and the Son is an antichrist.* 23 Anyone who
denies the Son doesn't have the Father, either. But
anyone who acknowledges the Son has the Father
also.
24 So you must remain faithful to what you have
been taught from the beginning. If you do, you will
remain in fellowship with the Son and with the Fa-
ther. 25 And in this fellowship we enjoy the eternal life
he promised us.
26 I am writing these things to warn you about
those who want to lead you astray. 27 But you have
received the Holy Spirit,* and he lives within you, so
you don't need anyone to teach you what is true. For
the Spirit* teaches you everything you need to know,
and what he teaches is true—it is not a lie. So just as
he has taught you, remain in fellowship with Christ.

LIVING AS CHILDREN OF GOD

28 And now, dear children, remain in fellowship with
Christ so that when he returns, you will be full of
courage and not shrink back from him in shame.
29 Since we know that Christ is righteous, we also
know that all who do what is right are God's children.

3 See how very much our Father loves us, for he
calls us his children, and that is what we are! But
the people who belong to this world don't recognize
that we are God's children because they don't know
him. 2 Dear friends, we are already God's children, but

GOD IS MY DAD

1. How would you feel if Jesus returned right now: Excited? Relieved? Ashamed?

1 JOHN 2:28–3:10

2. How easy is it for you to see God as your loving Father (3:1-2)? God is the perfect Father—far beyond any earthly father—and He loves you. How does that make you feel?
3. When John says, "Anyone who continues to live in him will not sin" (3:6), do you think he's referring to occasional sins or a lifestyle of continuous sin?
4. How can you know you are a child of God (3:10)? When has it recently been difficult for you to love?

he has not yet shown us what we will be like when
Christ appears. But we do know that we will be like
him, for we will see him as he really is. 3 And all who
have this eager expectation will keep themselves
pure, just as he is pure.
4 Everyone who sins is breaking God's law, for all
sin is contrary to the law of God. 5 And you know that
Jesus came to take away our sins, and there is no sin
in him. 6 Anyone who continues to live in him will not
sin. But anyone who keeps on sinning does not know
him or understand who he is.
7 Dear children, don't let anyone deceive you
about this: When people do what is right, it shows
that they are righteous, even as Christ is righteous.
8 But when people keep on sinning, it shows that
they belong to the devil, who has been sinning since
the beginning. But the Son of God came to destroy
the works of the devil. 9 Those who have been born
into God's family do not make a practice of sinning,
because God's life* is in them. So they can't keep on
sinning, because they are children of God. 10 So now
we can tell who are children of God and who are
children of the devil. Anyone who does not live righ-
teously and does not love other believers* does not
belong to God.

LOVE ONE ANOTHER

11 This is the message you have heard from the be-
ginning: We should love one another. 12 We must not
be like Cain, who belonged to the evil one and killed
his brother. And why did he kill him? Because Cain
had been doing what was evil, and his brother had
been doing what was righteous. 13 So don't be sur-
prised, dear brothers and sisters,* if the world hates
you.
14 If we love our brothers and sisters who are be-
lievers,* it proves that we have passed from death to
life. But a person who has no love is still dead. 15 Any-
one who hates another brother or sister* is really a
murderer at heart. And you know that murderers
don't have eternal life within them.
16 We know what real love is because Jesus gave up
his life for us. So we also ought to give up our lives
for our brothers and sisters. 17 If someone has enough
money to live well and sees a brother or sister* in
need but shows no compassion—how can God's love
be in that person?
18 Dear children, let's not merely say that we love
each other; let us show the truth by our actions. 19 Our
actions will show that we belong to the truth, so we
will be confident when we stand before God. 20 Even
if we feel guilty, God is greater than our feelings, and
he knows everything.

2:22a Or *not the Messiah.* **2:22b** Or *the antichrist.* **2:27a** Greek *the anointing from him.* **2:27b** Greek *the anointing.* **3:9** Greek *because his seed.* **3:10** Greek *does not love his brother.* **3:13** Greek *brothers.* **3:14** Greek *the brothers;* similarly in 3:16. **3:15** Greek *hates his brother.* **3:17** Greek *sees his brother.*

2:22 denies. John now reveals the master lie in the secessionists' false teaching: they deny that Jesus is the Messiah and the Son of God.

3:2 no yet shown us what we will be like. The precise nature of what Christians will become when they meet Christ is not fully clear yet. However, they can get an idea of what they will be like by looking at Jesus ("we will be like Him"). In some way, Christians will become like Jesus when the process of glorification—which began at rebirth—is completed at Jesus' second coming.

3:6 will not sin. John appears to be saying here (and in vv. 8-10) that a Christian cannot sin. Yet in other passages, he points out that Christians can and do sin (1:8,10; 2:1; 5:16). Some scholars feel that what John has in mind here is willful and deliberate sin (as opposed to involuntary error). Other scholars stress the tense of the verb that John uses: a Christian does not keep on sinning. In other words, Christians do not habitually sin.

3:9 God's life. John probably is referring to the Word of God (Luke 8:11; Jas. 1:18; 1 Pet. 1:23), to the Holy Spirit (John 3:6), or to both, by which the Christian is kept from sin.

3:19-20 God is greater than our feelings. John seems to be saying that Christians can be at peace with themselves, even when troubled by their consciences. But, as John points out, the basis of their confidence is the fact that it is God who will judge them and not their own hearts. They can trust themselves to His all-knowing justice because they have sought and found His forgiveness (1 Cor. 4:3-5).

TRUE LOVE

1. How do you know when someone really loves you?

1 JOHN 3:11-24

2. What is the definition of love in this passage (vv. 16-18)? How does this compare with the definition of love at your school or among your friends?
3. What kind of comfort should we receive from verses 21 and 22?
4. How does the Spirit help us to have assurance that God remains in us and loves us (v. 27)?
5. What can you do to share God's love with someone this week: Visit someone who is lonely? Help your brother or sister with homework? Other?

SEEKING TRUTH

1. What is the strangest story you have heard about a religious cult?
2. When you are unsure, how do you determine if someone is telling you the truth?

1 JOHN 4:1-6

3. How are we to determine if a spirit is the "Spirit of God" or the "spirit of the Antichrist" (vv. 2-3)?
4. What power equips us to overcome false teachings and prophets (v. 4)?
5. Why do you think some students are attracted to strange groups?
6. What have you found is the best strategy in resisting cults?

21 Dear friends, if we don't feel guilty, we can come
to God with bold confidence. 22 And we will receive
from him whatever we ask because we obey him and
do the things that please him.
23 And this is his commandment: We must believe in
the name of his Son, Jesus Christ, and love one anoth-
er, just as he commanded us. 24 Those who obey God's
commandments remain in fellowship with him, and
he with them. And we know he lives in us because the
Spirit he gave us lives in us.

DISCERNING FALSE PROPHETS

4 Dear friends, do not believe everyone who claims
to speak by the Spirit. You must test them to see
if the spirit they have comes from God. For there are
many false prophets in the world. 2 This is how we
know if they have the Spirit of God: If a person claim-
ing to be a prophet* acknowledges that Jesus Christ
came in a real body, that person has the Spirit of God.
3 But if someone claims to be a prophet and does not
acknowledge the truth about Jesus, that person is not
from God. Such a person has the spirit of the Anti-
christ, which you heard is coming into the world and
indeed is already here.
4 But you belong to God, my dear children. You have
already won a victory over those people, because
the Spirit who lives in you is greater than the spirit
who lives in the world. 5 Those people belong to this
world, so they speak from the world's viewpoint, and
the world listens to them. 6 But we belong to God, and
those who know God listen to us. If they do not be-
long to God, they do not listen to us. That is how we
know if someone has the Spirit of truth or the spirit
of deception.

LOVING ONE ANOTHER

7 Dear friends, let us continue to love one another, for
love comes from God. Anyone who loves is a child of
God and knows God. 8 But anyone who does not love
does not know God, for God is love.
9 God showed how much he loved us by sending
his one and only Son into the world so that we might
have eternal life through him. 10 This is real love—not
that we loved God, but that he loved us and sent his
Son as a sacrifice to take away our sins.
11 Dear friends, since God loved us that much, we
surely ought to love each other. 12 No one has ever
seen God. But if we love each other, God lives in us,
and his love is brought to full expression in us.
13 And God has given us his Spirit as proof that
we live in him and he in us. 14 Furthermore, we have
seen with our own eyes and now testify that the Fa-
ther sent his Son to be the Savior of the world. 15 All
who declare that Jesus is the Son of God have God
living in them, and they live in God. 16 We know how
much God loves us, and we have put our trust in his
love.
God is love, and all who live in love live in God, and
God lives in them. 17 And as we live in God, our love

4:2 Greek *If a spirit;* similarly in 4:3.

3:21 confidence. Confidence is necessary in order to come before God. Without confidence a person does not feel free to enter into prayer.

3:22 receive . . . whatever we ask. Once again, John states a truth in a stark, unqualified way: if we ask, we will receive. **we obey him.** Obedience does not cause prayer to be answered; it is a condition that motivates Christians to pray.

3:23-24 believe . . . love . . . obey God's commandments. In these verses, John brings together the three issues underlying the three tests by which believers can know they are truly children of God. He shows the connection between obedience (the moral test), love (the social test), and belief (the doctrinal test) and how these relate to the question of union with God.

4:1 do not believe everyone who claims. It is dangerous to accept uncritically everything that is said "in the name of God." Not everyone claiming inner revelation is hearing God's voice. **test.** The test that John suggests by which to distinguish between spirits is doctrinal in nature. It has to do with who Jesus is. False spirits will not acknowledge that Jesus of Nazareth (a fully human man) is the incarnate Messiah (the divine Son of God).

4:2 This is how we know. By the strong claims Jesus made, He will not be one option among many. His assertion that "no one comes to the Father except through me (John 14:6) is clear and calls for a decision from each person who hears the claim. Knowing if a prophet has the Spirit of God can be tested by the content of what he confesses publicly.

4:3 Antichrist. In this context, *Antichrist* doesn't refer to a political ruler but to the spirit of evil that leads men to promote a religion contrary to God's revelation. In 2:18-27 John's concern was that believers not be led astray by those who are filled with the spirit of the Antichrist.

4:10 as a sacrifice to take away our sins. By this phrase, John describes the saving work of Jesus. The idea of atonement is tied up with the Old Testament concept of substitution and sacrifice. In the Old Testament, sin was dealt with when a person symbolically placed his sins on an animal that he had brought to the temple. This animal had to be perfect—without spot or blemish. It was then sacrificed in place of the sinful (imperfect) person. Such substitutionary sacrifices were a picture of the final sacrifice Jesus would one day make.

FEAR VS. LOVE

1. When was the last time you were truly afraid? What happened?
2. How do you show your friends and family that you love them?

1 JOHN 4:7-21

3. How has God demonstrated that He is love (vv. 9-10)? How can we know God and experience His love (vv. 15-17)?
4. In what way does God's love motivate us to love others (v. 11)? How big of a challenge is that?
5. What is some fear you need to trade in for love (v. 18)?

CONFIDENCE IN ETERNITY

1. What is one thing that you take for granted?
2. Which part of your church worship service helps to strengthen your faith the most?

1 JOHN 5:1-15

3. Judging by the standard in verse 2, how loved would you say God feels by you?
4. What would you say to a friend who has doubts that he or she is really a Christian (vv. 11-12)?
5. With how much confidence can you say you "know you have eternal life" (v. 13)? What would help you to increase your confidence level?

grows more perfect. So we will not be afraid on the
day of judgment, but we can face him with confidence
because we live like Jesus here in this world.
[18]Such love has no fear, because perfect love expels
all fear. If we are afraid, it is for fear of punishment, and
this shows that we have not fully experienced his per-
fect love. [19]We love each other* because he loved us first.
[20]If someone says, "I love God," but hates a fellow
believer,* that person is a liar; for if we don't love
people we can see, how can we love God, whom we
cannot see? [21]And he has given us this command:
Those who love God must also love their fellow be-
lievers.*

FAITH IN THE SON OF GOD

5 Everyone who believes that Jesus is the Christ*
has become a child of God. And everyone who
loves the Father loves his children, too. [2]We know we
love God's children if we love God and obey his com-
mandments. [3]Loving God means keeping his com-
mandments, and his commandments are not burden-
some. [4]For every child of God defeats this evil world,
and we achieve this victory through our faith. [5]And
who can win this battle against the world? Only those
who believe that Jesus is the Son of God.
[6]And Jesus Christ was revealed as God's Son by his
baptism in water and by shedding his blood on the
cross*—not by water only, but by water and blood. And
the Spirit, who is truth, confirms it with his testimony.
[7]So we have these three witnesses*—[8]the Spirit, the
water, and the blood—and all three agree. [9]Since we be-
lieve human testimony, surely we can believe the great-
er testimony that comes from God. And God has testified
about his Son. [10]All who believe in the Son of God know
in their hearts that this testimony is true. Those who
don't believe this are actually calling God a liar because
they don't believe what God has testified about his Son.
[11]And this is what God has testified: He has given
us eternal life, and this life is in his Son. [12]Whoever
has the Son has life; whoever does not have God's Son
does not have life.

CONCLUSION

[13]I have written this to you who believe in the name
of the Son of God, so that you may know you have
eternal life. [14]And we are confident that he hears

4:19 Greek *We love.* Other manuscripts read *We love God;* still others read *We love him.* **4:20** Greek *hates his brother.* **4:21** Greek *The one who loves God must also love his brother.* **5:1** Or *the Messiah.* **5:6** Greek *This is he who came by water and blood.* **5:7** A few very late manuscripts add *in heaven—the Father, the Word, and the Holy Spirit, and these three are one. And we have three witnesses on earth.*

4:18 Such love has no fear. People cannot love and fear at the same moment. The love casts out the fear. **fear of punishment.** This is the root of the fear: they think God is going to punish them. They forget that they are His forgiven children.

5:1 believes. Belief on the part of Christians is clear proof that they have been born of God.

5:3 burdensome. Obedience to the thousands of often picayune rules and regulations promulgated by the scribes and Pharisees was indeed a heavy burden. But obedience to God does not exasperate the Christian, since God enables the believer through the Holy Spirit to respond in obedience.

5:4 our faith. This is the source of the overcoming power of the Christian—confidence and trust that Jesus is the Son of God (v. 5).

5:6 his baptism ... shedding his blood. By these two phrases, John is probably referring to Jesus' baptism and His death. These two events are crucial in understanding who Jesus really is. The secessionists felt that Jesus, the man, became the Christ at His baptism and that the Christ then departed prior to the death of Jesus. In contrast, the apostolic witness (as recorded in the New Testament) asserts that at His baptism, Jesus publicly identified Himself with the sins of the people (even though He Himself was without sin). By His death, Jesus took away those sins. **not by water only.** The secessionists agreed that the baptism of Jesus was important. They felt it was then that the heavenly Christ infused the man Jesus. (In fact, it was the Holy Spirit who descended on Jesus at His baptism.) John is insistent that both the Jesus' baptism and crucifixion are crucial in understanding Him. **the Spirit, who is truth.** The Holy Spirit is the third witness and is qualified to be such because the Spirit is, in His essence, truth Himself.

5:7 three witnesses. There are two kinds of testimony: the objective historical witnesses of the water and the blood and the subjective, experiential witness of the Spirit (Christians experience within themselves the reality of these events). These two types of witness complement one another. Believers know in their hearts the truthfulness and power of the historical facts of Jesus' life and death.

5:10 believe in. It is one thing to believe Jesus. It is another to believe in Jesus. To believe Jesus is to accept what He says as true. To believe in Jesus is to accept who He is. It involves trusting him completely and committing one's life to Him.

5:11 eternal life. The Greek word that is here translated "eternal" means "that which belongs to the coming age." But since that age has already broken into the present age, eternal life can be enjoyed even now (John 17:3)

5:13 so that you may know. This verse parallels John 20:31 which is the concluding verse of that Gospel. John wrote his Gospel in order to witness about Jesus and so inspire faith in those who did not yet know Christ. By believing in Jesus, they would discover "life." His purpose in the letter is similar, except that now his words are directed to those who have, in fact, come to believe in Jesus. His purpose is no longer to tell them how to find "life" but, instead, to assure them that they do have eternal life.

5:14 confident. Originally this word meant "freedom of speech." It was used to describe the right of all those in a democracy to speak their mind. By this word John refers to the bold confidence Christians have—that they can approach God in prayer and freely speak their minds. **that pleases him.** In 3:22, John says that a condition for answered prayer is obedient behavior. Here John adds another condition: what we ask must be in accord with God's purposes (Matt. 26:39,42).

us whenever we ask for anything that pleases him.
[15] And since we know he hears us when we make our
requests, we also know that he will give us what we
ask for.
[16] If you see a fellow believer* sinning in a way that
does not lead to death, you should pray, and God will
give that person life. But there is a sin that leads to
death, and I am not saying you should pray for those
who commit it. [17] All wicked actions are sin, but not
every sin leads to death.
[18] We know that God's children do not make a
practice of sinning, for God's Son holds them se-
curely, and the evil one cannot touch them. [19] We
know that we are children of God and that the
world around us is under the control of the evil
one.
[20] And we know that the Son of God has come, and
he has given us understanding so that we can know
the true God.* And now we live in fellowship with the
true God because we live in fellowship with his Son,
Jesus Christ. He is the only true God, and he is eternal
life.
[21] Dear children, keep away from anything that
might take God's place in your hearts.*

5:16 Greek *a brother.* **5:20** Greek *the one who is true.* **5:21** Greek *keep yourselves from idols.*

5:15 he hears. By this phrase John means, "He hears us favorably." To know that God hears us is to know that "we have what we have asked for."
5:16 sin that leads to death. Although John's readers probably understood what he was referring to, it is not at all clear to the modern reader just what this phrase means. A specific kind of sin is probably not in view here but rather a lifestyle of habitual, willing, and persistent sinning.
5:18 We know. John concludes with a final list of assurances. The first affirmation relates to Christian behavior. The new birth results in new behavior. Sin and the child of God are incompatible.
5:19 children of God. The second affirmation that John makes is that they are, indeed, "children of God." They are part of the family of God and in relationship with the other children of God.
5:20 that we can know the true God. The third affirmation is that they really do know what is true. **understanding.** This is the power or ability to know what is actually so. Specifically, Jesus gave Christians the power to perceive the one and only true God over and against false idols (v. 21).

INTRODUCTION TO

2 JOHN / 3 JOHN

PERSONAL READING PLAN

☐ 2 John 1-13 ☐ 3 John 1-14

AUTHOR

There is much similarity of style and content between 2 and 3 John. For example, compare 2 John 1 with 3 John 1, 2 John 4 with 3 John 4; 2 John 12 with 3 John 13-14. Undoubtedly, both were written by the same person. There is also a close connection between 1 John and these two shorter letters (compare, for example, 1 John 4:3 with 2 John 7). All three epistles seem to deal with the same situation. Therefore, it seems very likely that the "elder" who wrote 2 and 3 John is, indeed, the Apostle John.

DATE

The dates are uncertain, but both letters were probably written in the late A.D. 80s or early 90s when the false doctrine that they rebuke began to flourish.

THEME

Hospitality for traveling missionaries.

PURPOSE

The issue addressed by 2 and 3 John is that of wandering missionaries. In a time when Roman inns were notorious for being dirty and flea-infested, visiting Christian teachers would turn to the local church for hospitality. The problem was that some of the people seeking room and board were false teachers, expounding erroneous doctrines; others were phony, pretending to be true prophets to get free hospitality. Even a pagan Greek author like Lucian noticed this sort of abuse. In his satirical work, *Peregrinus*, he wrote about a religious charlatan who lived off the generosity of the church simply as a way to avoid working. In an attempt to cope with this problem, the Didache, an early church manual, laid down a series of regulations, guiding the reception of itinerant ministers. It said, for example, that true prophets were indeed to be entertained—for a day or two. But if a prophet stayed three days, this was a sign that he was false. Likewise, if a prophet under the inspiration of the Spirit asked for money, he was a false prophet.

These concerns are found in 2 and 3 John. In 2 John, the author worries about false prophets who are teaching erroneous doctrine, such as Gnosticism (salvation is a product of special knowledge). "Don't invite that person into your home," he says (2 John 10). But in 3 John, he addresses the opposite problem: Christians who failed to provide hospitality for genuine teachers.

PASSAGES FOR TOPICAL GROUP STUDY

2 John 1-13. . . . . CULTS. . . . . . . Truth or Consequences
3 John 1-14. . . . . FRIENDS . . . . Picking Your Friends

GREETINGS

This letter is from John, the elder.*

I am writing to the chosen lady and to her children,* whom I love in the truth—as does everyone else who knows the truth—2 because the truth lives in us and will be with us forever.

3 Grace, mercy, and peace, which come from God the Father and from Jesus Christ—the Son of the Father—will continue to be with us who live in truth and love.

LIVE IN THE TRUTH

4 How happy I was to meet some of your children and find them living according to the truth, just as the Father commanded.

5 I am writing to remind you, dear friends,* that we should love one another. This is not a new commandment, but one we have had from the beginning. 6 Love means doing what God has commanded us, and he has commanded us to love one another, just as you heard from the beginning.

7 I say this because many deceivers have gone out into the world. They deny that Jesus Christ came* in a real body. Such a person is a deceiver and an antichrist. 8 Watch out that you do not lose what we* have worked so hard to achieve. Be diligent so that you receive your full reward. 9 Anyone who wanders away from this teaching has no relationship with God. But anyone who remains in the teaching of Christ has a relationship with both the Father and the Son.

10 If anyone comes to your meeting and does not teach the truth about Christ, don't invite that person into your home or give any kind of encouragement. 11 Anyone who encourages such people becomes a partner in their evil work.

CONCLUSION

12 I have much more to say to you, but I don't want to do it with paper and ink. For I hope to visit you soon and talk with you face to face. Then our joy will be complete.

13 Greetings from the children of your sister,* chosen by God.

TRUTH OR CONSEQUENCES

1. Whose home could you drop in on unexpectedly and know that you would be welcome?

2 JOHN 1-13

2. How do John's exhortations to true Christ-followers (vv. 4-6) help them resist the deception and wickedness of the religious frauds (vv. 7-11)?
3. Have you ever been involved in a deep relationship that had to end because of an overriding issue involving your faith? What happened?
4. When was the last time you spent time with someone who was hurting, lonely, or needing help (no names)? What is stopping you from doing this more often?

1a Greek *From the elder.* **1b** Or *the church God has chosen and its members.* **5** Greek *I urge you, lady.* **7** Or *will come.* **8** Some manuscripts read *you.* **13** Or *from the members of your sister church.*

1-3 the elder. As was the custom in first-century letters, the writer of this letter first identifies himself, then names the recipients of the letter, and finally concludes his salutation by pronouncing a blessing.

4-11 your children. This is the heart of John's message. In verses 4-6 he focuses on the internal life of the local church. He points out its need to walk in truth, obedience, and love. In verses 7-11 he focuses on the external life of the local church, specifically the threat posed by false teachers who espouse erroneous doctrine. John makes a sharp distinction between what is true (vv. 4-6) and what is false (vv. 7-11).

7-11 deceivers. John now turns from true believers to false deceivers. He warns Christians not to be deceived (vv. 7-8). He tells them not to encourage false teachers by giving them hospitality (vv. 10-11). If his exhortations in verses 4-6 to walk in truth, obedience, and love are followed, the believers will be able to resist the heresy being taught by these false teachers.

7 Many. In contrast to "some" children who walk in truth, there are the "many" who deceive. **have gone out.** John may be saying that these false teachers were once in the church but have now left (1 John 2:19). Or he may be saying that in the same way that the emissaries of God are sent out into the world (John 17:18; 20:21), Satan sends out his own emissaries. **deny that Jesus Christ came in a real body.** John defines the deceivers' error. They deny His incarnation.

8 receive a full reward. The Greek word translated "reward" refers to "the wages of a workman." John's concern is not with the loss of salvation which one does not earn in any case (it is a free gift) but with the loss of reward due for faithful service.

10 don't invite ... into your home. John now issues his second warning: do not receive or welcome false teachers into your home. This injunction sounds harsh in the light of the New Testament's insistence upon hospitality—including John's own words on the subject (Rom. 12:13; 1 Tim. 3:2; Titus 1:8; Heb. 13:2; 1 Pet. 4:8-10; 3 John 5-8). However, it is important to notice that John refers to teachers and not believers who might hold errant views.

3 JOHN

GREETINGS

This letter is from John, the elder.*
I am writing to Gaius, my dear friend, whom I love
in the truth.
2 Dear friend, I hope all is well with you and that
you are as healthy in body as you are strong in spirit.
3 Some of the traveling teachers* recently returned
and made me very happy by telling me about your
faithfulness and that you are living according to the
truth. 4 I could have no greater joy than to hear that
my children are following the truth.

CARING FOR THE LORD'S WORKERS

5 Dear friend, you are being faithful to God when you
care for the traveling teachers who pass through,
even though they are strangers to you. 6 They have
told the church here of your loving friendship. Please
continue providing for such teachers in a manner
that pleases God. 7 For they are traveling for the Lord,*
and they accept nothing from people who are not
believers.* 8 So we ourselves should support them so
that we can be their partners as they teach the truth.
9 I wrote to the church about this, but Diotrephes,
who loves to be the leader, refuses to have anything
to do with us. 10 When I come, I will report some of the
things he is doing and the evil accusations he is mak-
ing against us. Not only does he refuse to welcome the
traveling teachers, he also tells others not to help them.
And when they do help, he puts them out of the church.
11 Dear friend, don't let this bad example influence
you. Follow only what is good. Remember that those
who do good prove that they are God's children, and
those who do evil prove that they do not know God.*

PICKING YOUR FRIENDS

1. Did you ever run out of money when you were away from home? What happened?

3 JOHN 1-14

2. Why is John urging that these teachers be cared for in their travels?
3. What is John's big problem with Diotrephes, and why does he take it so seriously?
4. How would you explain what John is saying in verse 11? Does this seem too black and white?
5. When picking close friends (as Gaius was to John), what do you look for? How can you be that kind of friend to others?

12 Everyone speaks highly of Demetrius, as does the
truth itself. We ourselves can say the same for him,
and you know we speak the truth.

CONCLUSION

13 I have much more to say to you, but I don't want to
write it with pen and ink. 14 For I hope to see you soon,
and then we will talk face to face.
15* Peace be with you.
Your friends here send you their greetings. Please
give my personal greetings to each of our friends
there.

1 Greek *From the elder.* 3 Greek *the brothers;* also in verses 5 and 10. 7a Greek *They went out on behalf of the Name.* 7b Greek *from Gentiles.* 11 Greek *they have not seen God.* 15 Some English translations combine verses 14 and 15 into verse 14.

1 the elder. Both 2 and 3 John were written by the same person, identified only as "the Elder"—the Apostle John. **my dear friend.** This is one of only two personal letters in the New Testament (the other is Philemon). While other letters do bear the name of an individual recipient—Timothy and Titus, for example—they are, in fact, letters meant to be read publicly. **Gaius.** There are several men by this name mentioned in the New Testament (Acts 19:29; 20:4; Rom. 16:23; 1 Cor. 1:14). "Gaius" was one of the most common names in the Roman Empire. As a result, it is not possible to identify with certainty the Gaius to whom John writes with any other Gaius in the New Testament.
3 your faithfulness. This was one of several characteristics of Gaius that John singled out for commendation.
4 my children. Paul used this phrase to describe those he assisted in converting to Christ. Perhaps, therefore, Gaius was John's spiritual son. **following the truth.** Gaius did not just know the truth; he lived what he believed. He let his theological convictions guide his moral behavior.
5-8 being faithful to God. Here John commends Gaius for showing hospitality to the visiting teachers. John's words in verses 5-8 stand in sharp contrast to what he wrote in 2 John 10-11, where he warned against offering hospitality to certain teachers. The difference is that in 2 John he was concerned about false teachers, and here he discusses "brothers" who went out "for the sake of the name" and who are "co-workers with the truth." Second and Third John must be read together to get a balanced picture of the situation in the early church related to itinerant teachers.
9 Diotrephes. He and Gaius may have been members of the same congregation or, more likely, of neighboring congregations. In any case, they act in opposite ways when it comes to hospitality. Gaius welcomes visiting teachers. Diotrephes refuses to receive them. This may have to do with his desire "to be first."
12 Demetrius. Demetrius probably delivered this letter to Gaius. Since he was unknown to Gaius, John wrote this threefold recommendation. Demetrius may himself have been a wandering missionary whom John wished the house-church to receive.

INTRODUCTION TO

JUDE

PERSONAL READING PLAN

☐Jude 1-25

AUTHOR

Traditionally Jude, the brother of Jesus, is considered the author of Jude (see Matt. 13:55, Jude is a form of the name "Judas"). In the New Testament there are five people by the name of Jude or Judas (Mark 6:3; Luke 6:16; John 14:22; Acts 9:11; 15:22,27,32), but only the brother of Jesus is a serious candidate as author. Little is known about Jude other than that he was one of four brothers (Mark 6:3). He was probably not a follower of Jesus during the years of his brother's ministry (Mark 3:21,31-35; John 7:5). It was only after the Resurrection that Jude became a believer (Acts 1:14). The brothers of Jesus eventually became itinerant missionaries (1 Cor. 9:5). Tradition says they spread the gospel throughout Palestine. Jude's brother, James the Just, was leader of the church in Jerusalem. Jude gives us a view of the early church under Jesus' own brothers' leadership.

DATE

The date of Jude is hard to determine. If the author of 2 Peter made use of it, then it would be dated around A.D. 65; otherwise it could be dated as late as A.D. 80.

THEME

Contend for the faith.

PURPOSE

Jude gives an overview of his book in verses 3-4. He makes two points: Christians are "to defend the faith"; and secondly, they are to contend with false Christians who "have wormed their way into your churches." The rest of the book develops these two points. In verses 5-19, the nature of the false teachers is explained. Jude makes it clear that false teachers are not a new problem. In verses 20-23, Jude's main point is an appeal to the Christians to hold on to the Christian faith despite false teachers.

THE FALSE TEACHERS

Jude's opponents are a band of smooth-talking teachers who go from church to church, receiving hospitality in return for their instruction. Such itinerant teachers were often a source of trouble in the early church (Matt. 7:15; 2 Cor. 10–11; 1 John 4:1; 2 John 10). These teachers were antinomians, those who rejected all moral standards (since they misunderstood grace) and indulged in all manner of immoral behavior, particularly sexual. Their teaching was derived largely from individual subjective experiences.

CHARACTERISTICS

Most people know Jude only because of its benediction (vv. 24-25):

Now all glory to God, who is able to keep you from falling away and will bring you with great joy into his glorious presence without a single fault. All glory to him who alone is God, our Savior through Jesus Christ our Lord. All glory, majesty, power, and authority are his before all time, and in the present, and beyond all time! Amen.

Today, Jude is less frequently read than the other New Testament letters. To its first readers, however, Jude was anything but obscure. It was heard as a fiery call to defend the faith against the heretics who had wormed their way into the church (v. 4).

In true sermonic fashion, Jude quotes (or alludes to) various texts and then explains them. What sets Jude's sermon apart from contemporary Christian sermons is his choice of texts. His first references are to Old Testament stories (vv. 5-7,11), and his concluding reference is to "what the apostles of our Lord Jesus Christ predicted" (v. 17). This is familiar material. But in between, Jude quotes 1 Enoch (vv. 14-15), a Jewish apocryphal book, and alludes to the Assumption of Moses (v. 9), probably to the Testament of Naphtali (v. 7), and to the Testament of Asher (v. 8).

The Apocryphal books Jude quotes were written during the time between the Old and New Testament. They were not accepted as orthodox and so never became part of the Bible itself.

Some of the church fathers concluded (wrongly) that any book that used apocryphal literature could not be genuine. But this view says more about the presuppositions of those theologians than it does about what can and cannot be included within Scripture.

Certainly, other New Testament authors used nonbiblical Jewish writing (such as 2 Tim. 3:8). Paul quotes the heathen poets in Acts 17:28; 1 Corinthians 15:32-33; and Titus 1:12. The author of Hebrews echoes the works of Philo; James makes reference to nonbiblical sources. The issue is not where the specific words came from but how the New Testament writer used these words to reveal God's truth.

RELATIONSHIP TO 2 PETER

It is clear that Jude and 2 Peter are somehow related. Of the 25 verses in Jude, 15 of them appear in whole or in part in 2 Peter. The question is: What is the nature of the relationship between Jude and 2 Peter? Did Jude quote from 2 Peter? Or was the reverse true? Or did they both quote from the same outside source?

OLD TESTAMENT LINK IN JUDE

1. The way of Cain (v. 11)—Adam and Eve's first son, Cain, consumed with jealousy and anger, murdered his brother, Abel (Gen. 4:3-8).

2. Balaam's error (v. 11)—Balaam was an ancient pagan sorcerer hired to curse God's people. Though God compelled him to bless Israel instead, his greed apparently motivated him to give advice that proved destructive to the Israelites (Num. 22–24; 31:16).

3. Korah's rebellion (v. 11)—Korah was a Levite who led a rebellion against the authority God had given to Moses and Aaron (Num. 16:1-3,11).

STRUCTURE

Jude is a genuine letter with a standard opening (vv. 1-2). Verses 3-4 develop the theme and occasion of the epistle. But Jude is also a short sermon. The bulk of the book (vv. 5-25) consists of an exposition of certain texts as related to a particular problem facing the church. Thus, Jude is a sermon sent by mail to be read before the congregation(s).

The book of Jude is a painstakingly crafted document. Jude packs a lot of content into a few words by carefully choosing his words and images. Verses 11-13 are particularly vivid in imagery, evoking a wide range of thought in remarkably few words.

PASSAGES FOR TOPICAL GROUP STUDY

1-25 . . . . . TROUBLE and PROTECTION . . . . Bad News, Good News

GREETINGS FROM JUDE

This letter is from Jude, a slave of Jesus Christ and a
brother of James.
I am writing to all who have been called by God the
Father, who loves you and keeps you safe in the care
of Jesus Christ.*
2 May God give you more and more mercy, peace,
and love.

THE DANGER OF FALSE TEACHERS

3 Dear friends, I had been eagerly planning to write to
you about the salvation we all share. But now I find
that I must write about something else, urging you
to defend the faith that God has entrusted once for
all time to his holy people. 4 I say this because some
ungodly people have wormed their way into your
churches, saying that God's marvelous grace allows
us to live immoral lives. The condemnation of such
people was recorded long ago, for they have denied
our only Master and Lord, Jesus Christ.
5 So I want to remind you, though you already know
these things, that Jesus* first rescued the nation of Israel
from Egypt, but later he destroyed those who did not re-
main faithful. 6 And I remind you of the angels who did
not stay within the limits of authority God gave them
but left the place where they belonged. God has kept
them securely chained in prisons of darkness, waiting
for the great day of judgment. 7 And don't forget Sod-
om and Gomorrah and their neighboring towns, which
were filled with immorality and every kind of sexual
perversion. Those cities were destroyed by fire and
serve as a warning of the eternal fire of God's judgment.
8 In the same way, these people—who claim au-
thority from their dreams—live immoral lives, defy
authority, and scoff at supernatural beings.* 9 But
even Michael, one of the mightiest of the angels,* did
not dare accuse the devil of blasphemy, but simply
said, "The Lord rebuke you!" (This took place when
Michael was arguing with the devil about Moses'
body.) 10 But these people scoff at things they do not
understand. Like unthinking animals, they do what-
ever their instincts tell them, and so they bring about
their own destruction. 11 What sorrow awaits them!
For they follow in the footsteps of Cain, who killed his
brother. Like Balaam, they deceive people for money.
And like Korah, they perish in their rebellion.
12 When these people eat with you in your fellow-
ship meals commemorating the Lord's love, they are
like dangerous reefs that can shipwreck you.* They
are like shameless shepherds who care only for
themselves. They are like clouds blowing over the
land without giving any rain. They are like trees in
autumn that are doubly dead, for they bear no fruit
and have been pulled up by the roots. 13 They are
like wild waves of the sea, churning up the foam of
their shameful deeds. They are like wandering stars,
doomed forever to blackest darkness.
14 Enoch, who lived in the seventh generation after
Adam, prophesied about these people. He said, "Lis-
ten! The Lord is coming with countless thousands of
his holy ones 15 to execute judgment on the people
of the world. He will convict every person of all the
ungodly things they have done and for all the insults
that ungodly sinners have spoken against him."*
16 These people are grumblers and complainers,
living only to satisfy their desires. They brag loudly
about themselves, and they flatter others to get what
they want.

A CALL TO REMAIN FAITHFUL

17 But you, my dear friends, must remember what the
apostles of our Lord Jesus Christ predicted. 18 They
told you that in the last times there would be scoff-
ers whose purpose in life is to satisfy their ungodly
desires. 19 These people are the ones who are creating
divisions among you. They follow their natural in-
stincts because they do not have God's Spirit in them.

BAD NEWS, GOOD NEWS

1. Share a time when you really fell for a lie or got "taken for a ride."

JUDE 1-25

2. How does Jude describe himself and his fellow Christians (vv. 3-5)? From this description, what does it mean to be a Christian?
3. What is the challenge that these young Christians face (vv. 17-21)?
4. Which part of Jude's speech do people in your school, team, or community most need to hear?
5. In light of the warnings in Jude, what hope do you find in verses 24-25? How does that help as you struggle with sin in groups or teams, at home, or even when you're alone?

1 Or *keeps you for Jesus Christ.* **5** Other manuscripts read *[the] Lord,* or *God,* or *God Christ.* **8** Greek *at glorious ones,* which are probably evil angels. **9** Greek *Michael, the archangel.* **12** Or *they are contaminants among you;* or *they are stains.* **14-15** The quotation comes from intertestamental literature: Enoch 1:9.

1 **brother of James.** James was the leader of the Jerusalem church (Acts 12:17; Gal. 2:9). **called, who loves . . . keeps.** These terms, drawn from Isaiah 40–45, are a marked contrast to the description of the false teachers later on.

4 **grace allows us to live immoral lives.** The critical problem with the false teachers is their manipulation of the gospel's emphasis on God's grace into an excuse for living an immoral lifestyle (Rom. 6:1,15; Gal. 5:13; Phil. 3:2; 2 Tim. 3:1-9; 1 Pet. 2:16; 1 John 1:6; Rev. 2:4).

7 **Sodom and Gomorrah.** These were two Old Testament towns whose wickedness was legendary (Gen. 18–19).

8 **people . . . claim authority from their dreams.** This mocks the false teachers' claim to special revelations that justify their actions (v. 19; Col. 2:18). **live immoral lives.** Like the fallen angels, they indulge in illicit sexual activities. **despise authority.** Literally, "lordship." As in all the examples above, they defy Jesus' lordship over their lives (v. 4). **scoff at supernatural beings.** Jewish tradition taught that the Law was mediated through and guarded by angels (Gal. 3:19; Heb. 2:2). To justify their rejection of the Law, these people may have taught that the Law originated with the angels as well and could be discarded by people like them who had special revelations from God.

11 **Cain . . . Balaam . . . Korah.** Their lifestyle reflects that of Cain (Gen. 4—the first murderer, viewed as a man full of lust, violence and greed); their motivations those of Balaam (Num. 31:16—he led Israel into idolatry and immorality by allowing his gift of prophecy to be bought by the highest bidder); and their future that of Korah (Num. 16—his rebellion against Moses was ended by God's judgment).

12 **dangerous reefs.** Just as a submerged reef endangers a ship, so these teachers threaten the church. **fellowship meals.** These were communal meals eaten by the church as a celebration of their unity and love in Christ. Six images from nature are used to accent how the immorality of the false teachers threatened the very meaning of that common meal.

[20] But you, dear friends, must build each other up
in your most holy faith, pray in the power of the Holy
Spirit,* [21] and await the mercy of our Lord Jesus Christ,
who will bring you eternal life. In this way, you will
keep yourselves safe in God's love.
[22] And you must show mercy to* those whose faith
is wavering. [23] Rescue others by snatching them from
the flames of judgment. Show mercy to still others,*
but do so with great caution, hating the sins that contaminate their lives.*

A PRAYER OF PRAISE

[24] Now all glory to God, who is able to keep you from
falling away and will bring you with great joy into
his glorious presence without a single fault. [25] All glory to him who alone is God, our Savior through Jesus
Christ our Lord. All glory, majesty, power, and authority are his before all time, and in the present, and beyond all time! Amen.

20 Greek *pray in the Holy Spirit.* 22 Some manuscripts read *must reprove.* 22-23a Some manuscripts have only two categories of people: (1) those whose faith is wavering and therefore need to be snatched from the flames of judgment, and (2) those who need to be shown mercy. 23b Greek *with fear, hating even the clothing stained by the flesh.*

INTRODUCTION TO

REVELATION

PERSONAL READING PLAN

☐Revelation 1:1-20
☐Revelation 2:1-29
☐Revelation 3:1-22
☐Revelation 4:1–5:14
☐Revelation 6:1-17
☐Revelation 7:1-17
☐Revelation 8:1–9:21
☐Revelation 10:1–11:19
☐Revelation 12:1–13:1a
☐Revelation 13:1b-18
☐Revelation 14:1-20
☐Revelation 15:1–16:21
☐Revelation 17:1-18
☐Revelation 18:1-24
☐Revelation 19:1-21
☐Revelation 20:1-15
☐Revelation 21:1-27
☐Revelation 22:1-21

AUTHOR

The "John" of 1:4 has traditionally been interpreted as John the apostle. John writes in his own name, and only an apostle could expect to hold authority. Furthermore, the Gospel of John and the three letters of John contain striking similarities in ideas, theology, and language.

John wrote from the island of Patmos, a barren island in the Aegean Sea where he had been exiled because of his Christian witness. Tradition says that he was eventually released from Patmos and spent the remaining years of his long life in Ephesus.

DATE

Most scholars believe the book of Revelation was written near the end of the reign of Domitian around A.D. 90–95. Evidence also exists for a date during the last years of Nero's reign (between A.D. 65 and 68) or possibly when Vespasian was emperor (A.D. 69–79).

THEME

Christ shall overcome!

HISTORICAL BACKGROUND

Rome is a central, negative image in the Book of Revelation. This view of the Roman government stands in sharp contrast to most of the rest of the New Testament, where Rome is seen as the protector of Christianity. In the early days of missionary activity, Roman judges protected Christians from Jewish mobs (Acts 18:1-17; 19:13-41). Roman justice aided Paul on several occasions (Acts 23:12-35; 25:10-11). As a result, the apostles urged submission to Rome (Rom. 13:1-7; 1 Peter 2:13-17). But in Revelation, the attitude is quite different. Rome is seen as a whore, drunk with the blood of Christians (17:5-6), deserving nothing but destruction.

This shift in attitude was due to Caesar worship. Although Roman rulers were long considered divine, their centrality in Roman civil religion was not enforced until the end of the first century. Then Roman citizens were required to appear annually to burn a pinch of incense and declare, "Caesar is Lord." To Romans a mere formality, but Christians could not declare loyalty to anyone except Jesus. Thus, civil authorities hounded them mercilessly. Revelation reminds Christians they may suffer now, but ahead lies unimaginable glory when Jesus, the true Lord, comes in power.

APOCALYPTIC LITERATURE

The book of Revelation is unique as the only apocalyptic book in the New Testament despite the fact that during the period between the Old and New Testaments, apocalyptic literature was the most common type of Jewish religious writing.

At the heart of apocalyptic literature was hope—hope that God would right wrongs and rescue the righteous. The Jews, God's chosen people, had been subject to ungodly rulers for so long that they longed for God to intervene in history. Their hopes are clear in the apocalyptic writings (apocalypse is a Greek word meaning an "unveiling" or "uncovering" of future events or hidden realms, like heaven).

Apocalyptic literature dealt with God's return: how He would burst into history, who He would destroy, and how He would set up His kingdom. These books were, of necessity, the products of dreams and visions. They were filled with swirling images and vivid pictures of death, supernatural creatures, destruction, and redemption. Since the events described were unlike anything ever seen, they could only be alluded to, often in cryptic language—thus our difficulty in interpreting the author's original meanings.

THE APOCALYPTIC WORLDVIEW

Underlying both Jewish and Christian apocalyptic literature was the view that history is divided into two ages: the present age of evil, which will be destroyed, and the future that is characterized by God's presence and power. The turning point comes on the Day of the Lord, when the present age will give way to the new age.

Christian writers understood the Day of the Lord as Christ's second coming. When he came again, it would not be as an infant but as a king before whom the whole creation would bow. Christians must live in the in-between time.

The similarities in Christian and Jewish apocalyptic literature are striking. Beyond the obvious difference over the role of Christ, the same outline is found in Jewish literature as in Revelation. Specifically:

1. The Messiah will be the central figure in the Day of the Lord.

2. The coming of the new age will be preceded by a terrible time in history filled with war, famine, and calamity of all sorts.

3. The Day of the Lord will be the time when judgment is rendered.

4. After judgment will come a time of great peace and joy. The New Jerusalem will descend. The dead will rise, and the Messiah will reign.

INTERPRETATON

There are widely varying interpretations for Revelation. Some limit its meaning to the first-century struggle between the church and Rome. Others see Revelation as a collection of symbols that predict future events (e.g., the locusts from the bottomless pit represents the invasion of Europe by Islam). Most likely Revelation speaks both to first-century struggle of Christians and also to the future when the Lord will return.

PASSAGES FOR TOPICAL GROUP STUDY

2:1–3:22 ...... LUKEWARM FAITH .... Letters of Warning
4:1–5:14 ...... ONLY JESUS IS WORTHY ...... Lion and Lamb
6:1–7:17 ...... PROTECTION AT THE END ..... Sealed by Jesus from Wrath
12:1–13:18 ... DEVIL CONQUERED .... Dragon Slayer
14:1–15:8..... JOYS OF FOLLOWING GOD .... Wrath and Rejoicing
18:1–19:1..... THE END OF EVIL ... Heaven's Marriage Feast
19:11–20:10 .. FINAL SPIRITUAL BATTLE ....The Last Battle
20:11–21:8 ... HEAVEN AND HELL .... Lake of Fire or Eternal Life
22:7-21....... PREPARE FOR CHRIST'S RETURN ....Come!

PASSAGES FOR GENERAL GROUP STUDY

1:1-20 .... A Strange Vision (of the Risen Lord)
8:1–9:21............Incense and Death (Final Judgments)
10:1–11:19 .... Two Witnesses Persecuted
16:1–17:18 .... Plagues and Prostitutes (The Seven Bowl Judgments)
21:9–22:6...........................Heavenly Citizenship

PROLOGUE

1 This is a revelation from* Jesus Christ, which God
gave him to show his servants the events that must
soon* take place. He sent an angel to present this rev-
elation to his servant John, 2 who faithfully reported
everything he saw. This is his report of the word of
God and the testimony of Jesus Christ.
3 God blesses the one who reads the words of this
prophecy to the church, and he blesses all who listen
to its message and obey what it says, for the time is
near.

JOHN'S GREETING TO THE SEVEN CHURCHES

4 This letter is from John to the seven churches in the
province of Asia.*
Grace and peace to you from the one who is, who
always was, and who is still to come; from the seven-
fold Spirit* before his throne; 5 and from Jesus Christ.
He is the faithful witness to these things, the first to
rise from the dead, and the ruler of all the kings of
the world.
All glory to him who loves us and has freed us from
our sins by shedding his blood for us. 6 He has made us
a Kingdom of priests for God his Father. All glory and
power to him forever and ever! Amen.

7 Look! He comes with the clouds of heaven.
    And everyone will see him—
    even those who pierced him.
And all the nations of the world
    will mourn for him.
Yes! Amen!

8 "I am the Alpha and the Omega—the beginning
and the end,"* says the Lord God. "I am the one who
is, who always was, and who is still to come—the Al-
mighty One."

VISION OF THE SON OF MAN

9 I, John, am your brother and your partner in suf-
fering and in God's Kingdom and in the patient en-
durance to which Jesus calls us. I was exiled to the
island of Patmos for preaching the word of God and
for my testimony about Jesus. 10 It was the Lord's Day,
and I was worshiping in the Spirit.* Suddenly, I heard
behind me a loud voice like a trumpet blast. 11 It said,
"Write in a book* everything you see, and send it to
the seven churches in the cities of Ephesus, Smyrna,
Pergamum, Thyatira, Sardis, Philadelphia, and Laod-
icea."
12 When I turned to see who was speaking to me,
I saw seven gold lampstands. 13 And standing in the
middle of the lampstands was someone like the Son of
Man.* He was wearing a long robe with a gold sash
across his chest. 14 His head and his hair were white
like wool, as white as snow. And his eyes were like
flames of fire. 15 His feet were like polished bronze
refined in a furnace, and his voice thundered like
mighty ocean waves. 16 He held seven stars in his
right hand, and a sharp two-edged sword came from
his mouth. And his face was like the sun in all its bril-
liance.
17 When I saw him, I fell at his feet as if I were dead.
But he laid his right hand on me and said, "Don't be
afraid! I am the First and the Last. 18 I am the living
one. I died, but look—I am alive forever and ever!
And I hold the keys of death and the grave.*
19 "Write down what you have seen—both the
things that are now happening and the things that
will happen.* 20 This is the meaning of the mystery of
the seven stars you saw in my right hand and the sev-
en gold lampstands: The seven stars are the angels*

A STRANGE VISION

1. How often do you remember your dreams? What dream is most vivid in your memory right now?

REVELATION 1:1-20

2. Alpha and Omega (v. 8) are the first and last letters of the Greek alphabet. Why does God describe Himself that way? What does this suggest about His character?
3. Look at the description of Jesus in verses 13-16, and consider each part individually. Why does He have "eyes were like flames of fire" (v. 14)? Feet like fine bronze? What does each thing tell us about Jesus?
4. How does this view of Jesus make you feel about Him?

1:1a Or *of.* **1:1b** Or *suddenly,* or *quickly.* **1:4a** *Asia* was a Roman province in what is now western Turkey. **1:4b** Greek *the seven spirits.* **1:8** Greek *I am the Alpha and the Omega,* referring to the first and last letters of the Greek alphabet. **1:10** Or *in spirit.* **1:11** Or *on a scroll.* **1:13** Or *like a son of man.* See Dan 7:13. "Son of Man" is a title Jesus used for himself. **1:18** Greek *and Hades.* **1:19** Or *what you have seen and what they mean—the things that have already begun to happen.* **1:20** Or *the messengers.*

1:1 The revelation. Literally, *apokalupsis*—an unveiling or uncovering of something that was hidden; supernatural truths that could not be known had God not spoken them.
1:4 seven churches. Those named in verse 11. There were other churches in this region, and (Acts 20:5-6; Col. 1:2; 4:13) why only these seven are addressed is not clear. They may have been the key churches in seven regions in Asia. Number seven is important (it represented perfection) and used often in Revelation. The seven churches were located 30 to 50 miles from each other on a circular road that connected them. **province of Asia.** Western half of Asia Minor (western part of modern Turkey). **the one who is, who always was, and who is to come.** An elaboration of the name of God in Exodus 3:14-15. **the sevenfold Spirits.** This may be an unusual way of speaking about the Holy Spirit (number seven referring to a complete manifestation of the Holy Spirit). Or it could refer to seven angels who minister to the Lamb (4:5; 5:6).
1:8 the Alpha and the Omega. The first and last letters in the Greek alphabet. **says the Lord God.** One of the two places where God speaks directly (21:5-8)
1:9 Patmos. A small island in the Aegean Sea off the coast of modern Turkey; probably a Roman penal colony.
1:10 in the Spirit. A trance, an ecstatic experience; a type of mystical experience (Acts 10:10; 11:5; 22:17; 2 Cor. 12:2-4). **the Lord's day.** The first day of the week (Sunday) when Christians met to worship together.
1:12 seven gold lampstands. These stand for the seven churches (v. 20), a fitting symbol for the church, which is meant to be a light to the world (Matt. 5:14-16).
1:13 someone like the Son of Man. See Daniel 7:13. **wearing in a long robe.** Jesus wore the full-length robe of a high priest. In verses 1-20, Jesus is presented in the threefold office of Prophet (v. 1), Priest (v. 13), and King (v. 5).
1:16 sword. The sword that came from the mouth of Jesus represents the fact of divine judgment.
1:20 angels. This word means "messengers." It is possible that this word refers to leaders of the seven congregations. However, because of the use of the word throughout the book, it probably refers to heavenly beings that are associated with the churches (compare Dan. 10:13,20-21; Matt. 18:10; Acts 12:15).

LETTERS OF WARNING

1. Do you write many letters or e-mails? To whom do you write, and about what?

REVELATION 2:1–3:22

2. To whom is God talking in 2:7? What does He want us to learn from these letters to the churches?
3. What strengths did each church have? What weaknesses?
4. What does it mean that Laodicea was "neither cold nor hot" (3:15)? Why did this make God vomit them out of His mouth (3:16)?
5. Are you lukewarm about Jesus? What will you do to heat up your walk with the Lord?

of the seven churches, and the seven lampstands are the seven churches.

THE MESSAGE TO THE CHURCH IN EPHESUS

2 "Write this letter to the angel* of the church in
Ephesus. This is the message from the one who
holds the seven stars in his right hand, the one who
walks among the seven gold lampstands:

2"I know all the things you do. I have seen
your hard work and your patient endurance. I
know you don't tolerate evil people. You have
examined the claims of those who say they are
apostles but are not. You have discovered they
are liars. 3 You have patiently suffered for me
without quitting.
4"But I have this complaint against you. You
don't love me or each other as you did at first!*
5 Look how far you have fallen! Turn back to me
and do the works you did at first. If you don't
repent, I will come and remove your lampstand
from its place among the churches. 6 But this is in
your favor: You hate the evil deeds of the Nicolai-
tans, just as I do.
7"Anyone with ears to hear must listen to the
Spirit and understand what he is saying to the
churches. To everyone who is victorious I will
give fruit from the tree of life in the paradise of
God.

THE MESSAGE TO THE CHURCH IN SMYRNA

8"Write this letter to the angel of the church in
Smyrna. This is the message from the one who is
the First and the Last, who was dead but is now
alive:

9"I know about your suffering and your poverty—
but you are rich! I know the blasphemy of those
opposing you. They say they are Jews, but they
are not, because their synagogue belongs to Satan.
10 Don't be afraid of what you are about to suffer.
The devil will throw some of you into prison to test
you. You will suffer for ten days. But if you remain
faithful even when facing death, I will give you
the crown of life.
11"Anyone with ears to hear must listen to
the Spirit and understand what he is saying to
the churches. Whoever is victorious will not be
harmed by the second death.

THE MESSAGE TO THE CHURCH IN PERGAMUM

12"Write this letter to the angel of the church in Per-
gamum. This is the message from the one with the
sharp two-edged sword:

13"I know that you live in the city where Satan
has his throne, yet you have remained loyal to me.
You refused to deny me even when Antipas, my
faithful witness, was martyred among you there
in Satan's city.
14"But I have a few complaints against you. You
tolerate some among you whose teaching is like
that of Balaam, who showed Balak how to trip
up the people of Israel. He taught them to sin by
eating food offered to idols and by committing
sexual sin. 15 In a similar way, you have some
Nicolaitans among you who follow the same
teaching. 16 Repent of your sin, or I will come to
you suddenly and fight against them with the
sword of my mouth.
17"Anyone with ears to hear must listen to the
Spirit and understand what he is saying to the
churches. To everyone who is victorious I will give
some of the manna that has been hidden away
in heaven. And I will give to each one a white
stone, and on the stone will be engraved a new
name that no one understands except the one who
receives it.

2:1 Or *the messenger;* also in 2:8, 12, 18. 2:4 Greek *You have lost your first love.*

2:1 the seven stars . . . the seven gold lampstands. Here Jesus is the One who holds control over the seven angels, and He walks among the seven churches. He has come to inspect His church.

2:6 Nicolaitans. It is hard to say for certain who these individuals are. They are some sort of heretical sect who mixed Christianity with pagan practices such as idolatry and immorality.

2:7 churches. The plural is significant. These words are not intended only for the church at Ephesus but as a challenge to all churches. **tree of life in the paradise of God.** This anticipates the New Jerusalem (21:10-11; 22:1-5).

2:8 Smyrna. A beautiful city approximately 35 miles north of Ephesus on the eastern shore of the Aegean Sea. **the First and the Last.** Smyrna had strong ties to Rome. The imperial cult, with its emperor worship, was strong there. **was dead but is now alive.** His second title assures them that they too can overcome death, an important promise given the persecution they faced.

2:9 suffering. This is a church under siege. **rich.** Though they were experiencing material poverty, they were rich spiritually (Matt. 5:11-12). **say they are Jews.** These may be Jewish proselytes. But also, the New Testament sense is that being Jewish (a descendant of Abraham) has far more to do with sharing Abraham's faithfulness than it does with simply sharing his lineage (Rom. 2:28-29).

2:11 second death. The promised reward is that the victors will be unhurt by the second death, eternal death in the "lake of fire" (20:14-15).

2:12 Pergamum. Located approximately 40 miles north of Smyrna and 10 miles inland from the Aegean Sea, the city sat atop a thousand-foot high cone-shaped hill. It was the site of a famous library.

2:13 where Satan has his throne. Pagan religion flourished in Pergamum. Four gods were worshiped there—including Zeus, for whom a spectacular altar had been built jutting out from the top of the mountain (some identify this as Satan's throne).

2:14 Balaam. Reference to the Old Testament story where Balaam advised the Moabite women to seduce the Israelites into leaving their God (v. 20; Num. 25:1-3; 31:16).

2:17 manna that has been hidden away. Supernatural food given to the Israelites during their wanderings in the wilderness.

THE MESSAGE TO THE CHURCH IN THYATIRA

18 "Write this letter to the angel of the church in Thyatira. This is the message from the Son of God, whose eyes are like flames of fire, whose feet are like polished bronze:

19 "I know all the things you do. I have seen your
love, your faith, your service, and your patient
endurance. And I can see your constant improvement in all these things.
20 "But I have this complaint against you. You are
permitting that woman—that Jezebel who calls
herself a prophet—to lead my servants astray. She
teaches them to commit sexual sin and to eat food
offered to idols. 21 I gave her time to repent, but she
does not want to turn away from her immorality.
22 "Therefore, I will throw her on a bed of
suffering,* and those who commit adultery with
her will suffer greatly unless they repent and
turn away from her evil deeds. 23 I will strike her
children dead. Then all the churches will know
that I am the one who searches out the thoughts
and intentions of every person. And I will give to
each of you whatever you deserve.
24 "But I also have a message for the rest of you
in Thyatira who have not followed this false teaching ('deeper truths,' as they call them—depths of
Satan, actually). I will ask nothing more of you
25 except that you hold tightly to what you have
until I come. 26 To all who are victorious, who obey
me to the very end,

To them I will give authority over all the nations.
27 They will rule the nations with an iron rod
and smash them like clay pots.*

28 They will have the same authority I received
from my Father, and I will also give them the
morning star!
29 "Anyone with ears to hear must listen to the
Spirit and understand what he is saying to the
churches.

THE MESSAGE TO THE CHURCH IN SARDIS

3 "Write this letter to the angel* of the church in
Sardis. This is the message from the one who has
the sevenfold Spirit* of God and the seven stars:

"I know all the things you do, and that you have a
reputation for being alive—but you are dead. 2 Wake
up! Strengthen what little remains, for even what
is left is almost dead. I find that your actions do not
meet the requirements of my God. 3 Go back to what
you heard and believed at first; hold to it firmly.
Repent and turn to me again. If you don't wake up, I
will come to you suddenly, as unexpected as a thief.
4 "Yet there are some in the church in Sardis
who have not soiled their clothes with evil. They
will walk with me in white, for they are worthy.
5 All who are victorious will be clothed in white.
I will never erase their names from the Book of
Life, but I will announce before my Father and his
angels that they are mine.
6 "Anyone with ears to hear must listen to the
Spirit and understand what he is saying to the
churches.

THE MESSAGE TO THE CHURCH IN PHILADELPHIA

7 "Write this letter to the angel of the church in Philadelphia.

This is the message from the one who is holy and
true,
the one who has the key of David.
What he opens, no one can close;
and what he closes, no one can open:*

8 "I know all the things you do, and I have opened
a door for you that no one can close. You have little
strength, yet you obeyed my word and did not
deny me. 9 Look, I will force those who belong to
Satan's synagogue—those liars who say they are
Jews but are not—to come and bow down at your
feet. They will acknowledge that you are the ones
I love.
10 "Because you have obeyed my command to
persevere, I will protect you from the great time
of testing that will come upon the whole world
to test those who belong to this world. 11 I am
coming soon.* Hold on to what you have, so that
no one will take away your crown. 12 All who are
victorious will become pillars in the Temple of my
God, and they will never have to leave it. And I
will write on them the name of my God, and they
will be citizens in the city of my God—the new
Jerusalem that comes down from heaven from my
God. And I will also write on them my new name.
13 "Anyone with ears to hear must listen to the
Spirit and understand what he is saying to the
churches.

2:22 Greek *a bed.* **2:26-27** Ps 2:8-9 (Greek version). **3:1a** Or *the messenger;* also in 3:7, 14. **3:1b** Greek *the seven spirits.* **3:7** Isa 22:22. **3:11** Or *suddenly,* or *quickly.*

2:18 Thyatira. City southeast of Pergamum; a manufacturing and marketing center with numerous trade guilds. Lydia, a dealer of purple cloth, was from Thyatira (Acts 16:14).

2:20 permitting . . . Jezebel. The original Jezebel was the wicked wife of Israel's King Ahab who promoted the detestable worship of Baal (1 Kings 16:29-33; 2 Kings 9:30-37). Her first-century counterpart played the same role in the church, promoting false practices. **food offered to idols.** Trade guilds were pagan in orientation, requiring participation in meals involving meat dedicated to idols. To refuse to participate would have great economic consequences since it would have been difficult to work without being a member of one of the guilds.

2:28 the morning star. No clear understanding about what this refers to.

3:1 Sardis. Sardis, located 50 miles east of Ephesus atop a 1,500-foot citadel, had once been a powerful city but by the first century had lost much of its influence. The temple in Sardis was dedicated to the goddess Cybele who was thought to have the power to bring dead people back to life—possibly the reason Jesus spoke to them about being dead and the need to be made alive again.

3:4 not soiled their clothes. In a place like Sardis, where making and dyeing wool cloth was a central occupation, the reference to clothing is appropriate. The image of defiled garments hints that sin of some sort had been allowed to stain the church.

3:5 Book of Life. Some sort of divine ledger where the names of the people who have eternal life are written. This picture was first found in the Old Testament (Ex. 32:32-33; Ps. 69:28; Dan. 12:1). In the first century, the names of citizens were recorded in a register. To have your name removed was to lose your citizenship.

3:7 Philadelphia. This was the newest of the seven cities. It was located 28 miles southeast of Sardis in a region of severe earthquakes.

3:12 pillars. This metaphor speaks of stability and permanence (Gal. 2:9; 1 Tim. 3:15).

THE MESSAGE TO THE CHURCH IN LAODICEA

14 "Write this letter to the angel of the church in La-
odicea. This is the message from the one who is the
Amen—the faithful and true witness, the beginning*
of God's new creation:

15 "I know all the things you do, that you are
neither hot nor cold. I wish that you were one
or the other! 16 But since you are like lukewarm
water, neither hot nor cold, I will spit you out of
my mouth! 17 You say, 'I am rich. I have everything
I want. I don't need a thing!' And you don't realize
that you are wretched and miserable and poor
and blind and naked. 18 So I advise you to buy gold
from me—gold that has been purified by fire.
Then you will be rich. Also buy white garments
from me so you will not be shamed by your
nakedness, and ointment for your eyes so you will
be able to see. 19 I correct and discipline everyone
I love. So be diligent and turn from your indiffer-
ence.
20 "Look! I stand at the door and knock. If you
hear my voice and open the door, I will come in,
and we will share a meal together as friends.
21 Those who are victorious will sit with me on my
throne, just as I was victorious and sat with my
Father on his throne.
22 "Anyone with ears to hear must listen to the
Spirit and understand what he is saying to the
churches."

WORSHIP IN HEAVEN

4 Then as I looked, I saw a door standing open in
heaven, and the same voice I had heard before
spoke to me like a trumpet blast. The voice said, "Come
up here, and I will show you what must happen after
this." 2 And instantly I was in the Spirit,* and I saw a
throne in heaven and someone sitting on it. 3 The one
sitting on the throne was as brilliant as gemstones—
like jasper and carnelian. And the glow of an emer-
ald circled his throne like a rainbow. 4 Twenty-four
thrones surrounded him, and twenty-four elders sat
on them. They were all clothed in white and had gold
crowns on their heads. 5 From the throne came flash-
es of lightning and the rumble of thunder. And in
front of the throne were seven torches with burning
flames. This is the sevenfold Spirit* of God. 6 In front
of the throne was a shiny sea of glass, sparkling like
crystal.

LION AND LAMB

1. What wild animals have you seen up close: Lion? Bear? Eagle? Other?

REVELATION 4:1—5:14

2. Jesus is pictured here as a victorious Lion (5:5). What does that suggest about His character?
3. Jesus is also pictured as a slaughtered Lamb (5:6). What does that suggest about His character? How can He be both a powerful Lion and a meek Lamb?
4. Why is Christ the only one worthy to open the scroll (5:4-9; see John 1:29)? What does this suggest about other religions in the world?
5. How can this passage help you to worship Jesus in a new way?

In the center and around the throne were four
living beings, each covered with eyes, front and
back. 7 The first of these living beings was like a
lion; the second was like an ox; the third had a hu-
man face; and the fourth was like an eagle in flight.
8 Each of these living beings had six wings, and
their wings were covered all over with eyes, inside
and out. Day after day and night after night they
keep on saying,

"Holy, holy, holy is the Lord God, the Almighty—
the one who always was, who is, and who is still
to come."

9 Whenever the living beings give glory and honor
and thanks to the one sitting on the throne (the one
who lives forever and ever), 10 the twenty-four elders
fall down and worship the one sitting on the throne
(the one who lives forever and ever). And they lay
their crowns before the throne and say,

11 "You are worthy, O Lord our God,
to receive glory and honor and power.
For you created all things,
and they exist because you created what you
pleased."

3:14 Or *the ruler,* or *the source.* **4:2** Or *in spirit.* **4:5** Greek *They are the seven spirits.*

3:14 Laodicea. A wealthy city, situated at the intersection of three major roads, known for its banking and industry. Paul wrote a letter to this church, which unfortunately has been lost (Col. 4:16). Like the church at Sardis, this church seems to be prosperous and without persecution or heresy. **Amen.** The word "amen" was used in the Old Testament as an acknowledgment that something was true.

3:18 gold. Thinking themselves "rich" (v. 17), they will become truly rich only with the spiritual gold they can get from Christ. **nakedness.** A startling image for a people who lived in a city famous for its textile industry. At Laodicea, they raised sheep with a glossy black wool that they made into a popular black fabric. What the church has need of, however, are the white garments of heaven. **ointment.** Laodicea was the site of a famous medical school. One of its well-known products was an eye ointment.

3:19 discipline. Rebuke and discipline are expressions not of hatred but of love (Prov. 3:11-12; Heb. 12:5-6). **love.** The Greek word used here is *phileō* warm and tender affection, rather than *agapaō*, that means to value unconditionally.

3:20 I stand at the door and knock. The call here is to those within the church to return to the Lord. **share a meal together.** Sharing a meal was a sign that an intimate bond existed between people.

4:2 I was in the Spirit. John is caught up in an ecstatic vision. Such visions are not uncommon in Scripture (1 Kings 22:19). **in heaven . . . one sitting on the throne.** John is granted a vision of God on His throne. The image of the throne pervades Revelation, occurring more than 40 times.

4:3 jasper. As it is known today, jasper is opaque, while this heavenly gem is described in 21:11 as a transparent crystal. **carnelian.** A fiery red mineral found in Sardis.

4:4 Twenty-four elders. There are various interpretations of these figures. Some say they represent the 24 orders of God's people of the Old and New Testament (the 12 patriarchs of Israel and the 12 apostles). Others hold that they are angels who assist in the ruling of the universe. In any case, they function to worship and serve God.

4:6 four living beings. These are similar to the creatures ("seraphim," "cherubim") seen in the vision of Isaiah (Isa. 6:1-3) and Ezekiel (Ezek. 10:9-14). They are some sort of angelic order that serve God.

THE LAMB OPENS THE SCROLL

5 Then I saw a scroll* in the right hand of the one
who was sitting on the throne. There was writing
on the inside and the outside of the scroll, and it was
sealed with seven seals. 2 And I saw a strong angel,
who shouted with a loud voice: "Who is worthy to
break the seals on this scroll and open it?" 3 But no one
in heaven or on earth or under the earth was able to
open the scroll and read it.
4 Then I began to weep bitterly because no one was
found worthy to open the scroll and read it. 5 But one
of the twenty-four elders said to me, "Stop weeping!
Look, the Lion of the tribe of Judah, the heir to David's
throne,* has won the victory. He is worthy to open the
scroll and its seven seals."
6 Then I saw a Lamb that looked as if it had been
slaughtered, but it was now standing between the
throne and the four living beings and among the
twenty-four elders. He had seven horns and sev-
en eyes, which represent the sevenfold Spirit* of
God that is sent out into every part of the earth.
7 He stepped forward and took the scroll from the
right hand of the one sitting on the throne. 8 And
when he took the scroll, the four living beings
and the twenty-four elders fell down before the
Lamb. Each one had a harp, and they held gold
bowls filled with incense, which are the prayers
of God's people. 9 And they sang a new song with
these words:

"You are worthy to take the scroll
and break its seals and open it.
For you were slaughtered, and your blood has
ransomed people for God
from every tribe and language and people and
nation.
10 And you have caused them to become
a Kingdom of priests for our God.
And they will reign* on the earth."

11 Then I looked again, and I heard the voices of
thousands and millions of angels around the throne
and of the living beings and the elders. 12 And they
sang in a mighty chorus:

"Worthy is the Lamb who was slaughtered—
to receive power and riches
and wisdom and strength
and honor and glory and blessing."

13 And then I heard every creature in heaven and
on earth and under the earth and in the sea. They
sang:

"Blessing and honor and glory and power
belong to the one sitting on the throne
and to the Lamb forever and ever."

14 And the four living beings said, "Amen!" And
the twenty-four elders fell down and worshiped the
Lamb.

THE LAMB BREAKS THE FIRST SIX SEALS

6 As I watched, the Lamb broke the first of the seven
seals on the scroll.* Then I heard one of the four
living beings say with a voice like thunder, "Come!"
2 I looked up and saw a white horse standing there.
Its rider carried a bow, and a crown was placed on
his head. He rode out to win many battles and gain
the victory.
3 When the Lamb broke the second seal, I heard the
second living being say, "Come!" 4 Then another horse
appeared, a red one. Its rider was given a mighty
sword and the authority to take peace from the earth.
And there was war and slaughter everywhere.
5 When the Lamb broke the third seal, I heard the
third living being say, "Come!" I looked up and saw

SEALED BY JESUS FROM WRATH

1. Have you ever been in an earthquake? What was it like? Where were you?

REVELATION 6:1–7:17

2. Authority and instructions were given to each of the four horsemen (6:1-8). Who gave them their power and instructions? What does this suggest about suffering and death—who has control?
3. Who are "[God's] servants" (7:3)? What does the seal on their foreheads mean?
4. Jesus was the only one who could open the seals on the scroll. What does this suggest about the seals on the slaves' foreheads? How does this bring comfort to you?

5:1 Or *book;* also in 5:2, 3, 4, 5, 7, 8, 9. **5:5** Greek *the root of David.* See Isa 11:10. **5:6** Greek *which are the seven spirits.* **5:10** Some manuscripts read *they are reigning.* **6:1** Or *book.*

5:1 seals. The scroll is rolled up and sealed along its edge with seven wax seals (that ensure the secrecy of its contents), which must be broken in order for the contents to be read. As each seal is broken, a momentous event takes place.
5:5 the Lion of the tribe of Judah. An ancient title for the Messiah (Gen. 49:9-10) that was in use in the first century. The image is of a conquering King. **the heir of David's throne.** Another messianic title, referring this time to the fact that the Messiah will come from the royal family of David (Isa. 11:1).
5:6 seven horns. A horn is a symbol of power in the Old Testament (Deut. 33:17; Ps. 18:2). **seven eyes.** He has fullness of vision, omniscience (Zech. 4:10). **the sevenfold Spirit of God.** The work of Christ on earth is done by the Holy Spirit Who is pictured by means of this symbol (4:5).
5:8 harp. The instrument of praise in the Psalms (Ps. 33:2). **incense.** Incense was used in Old Testament worship (Deut. 33:10). Here it stands for the prayers of God's people.
5:9 a new song. A special song praises the Lamb for His worthiness and His redemptive work. **has ransomed.** Redeemed—a word used to describe the freeing of a slave from bondage by the payment of a price. The purchase price, in this case, was the blood of Christ. What it bought was the freedom of men and women from the bondage of sin. **from every tribe and language and people and nation.** Christ redeems believers from the whole of humankind—past, present, and future—by this great and terrible payment.
6:2 a white horse. There has been much debate about the identity of the rider on the white horse. One suggestion is that he symbolizes military conquest, an image in line with the identity of the other three riders. Another suggestion is that the rider on a white horse symbolizes the preaching of the gospel throughout the world prior to the end. The bow is used in the Old Testament as a symbol of divine victories (Hab. 3:9). In Revelation, white is generally a symbol of Christ (1:14; 14:14; 19:11, 14). Furthermore, unlike the coming of the other three horsemen, no calamities follow after this rider.
6:3-4 second seal. The second seal is broken and a red horse and rider appear, a symbol of bloodshed and war.
6:5 third seal. The third seal is broken and a black horse and rider are called forth, symbolizing a time of great scarcity, verging on famine. **pair of scales.** A device used for measuring out grain.

a black horse, and its rider was holding a pair of
scales in his hand. 6 And I heard a voice from among
the four living beings say, "A loaf of wheat bread or
three loaves of barley will cost a day's pay.* And don't
waste* the olive oil and wine."
7 When the Lamb broke the fourth seal, I heard the
fourth living being say, "Come!" 8 I looked up and saw
a horse whose color was pale green. Its rider was
named Death, and his companion was the Grave.*
These two were given authority over one-fourth of
the earth, to kill with the sword and famine and dis-
ease* and wild animals.
9 When the Lamb broke the fifth seal, I saw under
the altar the souls of all who had been martyred
for the word of God and for being faithful in their
testimony. 10 They shouted to the Lord and said,
"O Sovereign Lord, holy and true, how long before
you judge the people who belong to this world and
avenge our blood for what they have done to us?"
11 Then a white robe was given to each of them. And
they were told to rest a little longer until the full
number of their brothers and sisters*—their fellow
servants of Jesus who were to be martyred—had
joined them.
12 I watched as the Lamb broke the sixth seal, and
there was a great earthquake. The sun became as
dark as black cloth, and the moon became as red
as blood. 13 Then the stars of the sky fell to the earth
like green figs falling from a tree shaken by a strong
wind. 14 The sky was rolled up like a scroll, and all of
the mountains and islands were moved from their
places.
15 Then everyone—the kings of the earth, the rul-
ers, the generals, the wealthy, the powerful, and ev-
ery slave and free person—all hid themselves in the
caves and among the rocks of the mountains. 16 And
they cried to the mountains and the rocks, "Fall on
us and hide us from the face of the one who sits on
the throne and from the wrath of the Lamb. 17 For the
great day of their wrath has come, and who is able to
survive?"

GOD'S PEOPLE WILL BE PRESERVED

7 Then I saw four angels standing at the four cor-
ners of the earth, holding back the four winds so
they did not blow on the earth or the sea, or even on
any tree. 2 And I saw another angel coming up from
the east, carrying the seal of the living God. And he
shouted to those four angels, who had been given
power to harm land and sea, 3 "Wait! Don't harm the
land or the sea or the trees until we have placed the
seal of God on the foreheads of his servants."
4 And I heard how many were marked with the seal
of God—144,000 were sealed from all the tribes of Is-
rael:

5 from Judah 12,000
from Reuben 12,000
from Gad 12,000
6 from Asher 12,000
from Naphtali 12,000
from Manasseh 12,000
7 from Simeon 12,000
from Levi 12,000
from Issachar 12,000
8 from Zebulun 12,000
from Joseph 12,000
from Benjamin 12,000

PRAISE FROM THE GREAT CROWD

9 After this I saw a vast crowd, too great to count, from
every nation and tribe and people and language,
standing in front of the throne and before the Lamb.
They were clothed in white robes and held palm
branches in their hands. 10 And they were shouting
with a great roar,

"Salvation comes from our God who sits on the throne
and from the Lamb!"

11 And all the angels were standing around the
throne and around the elders and the four living be-
ings. And they fell before the throne with their faces
to the ground and worshiped God. 12 They sang,

"Amen! Blessing and glory and wisdom
and thanksgiving and honor
and power and strength belong to our God
forever and ever! Amen."

13 Then one of the twenty-four elders asked me,
"Who are these who are clothed in white? Where did
they come from?"

6:6a Greek *A choinix* [1 quart or 1 liter] *of wheat for a denarius, and 3 choinix of barley for a denarius.* A denarius was equivalent to a laborer's full day's wage. **6:6b** Or *harm.* **6:8a** Greek *was Hades.* **6:8b** Greek *death.* **6:11** Greek *their brothers.*

6:6 A loaf of wheat bread . . . will cost a day's pay. Food is sold at inflated prices—over 10 times what it should cost. **don't waste the olive oil and the wine.** A limitation is placed upon the rider of the black horse. Grain is easily destroyed by drought, but the drought is not to be so severe as to damage the deeper roots of the olive trees or grapevines.

6:7-8 fourth seal. The fourth horse and rider represent death from various causes. These are the "four devastating judgments" in Ezekiel 14:21.

6:8 a horse whose color was pale green. Pale greenish gray, the color of a corpse. **Grave.** It is not clear whether Hades is following behind Death on foot, on another horse, or on the same horse. Still, the image is clear. After Death comes the grave or the underworld. Hades was understood to be the place where the dead resided as they awaited the final judgment. **one-fourth of the earth.** There is a limitation placed upon Death. It threatens all of life but is not permitted to totally do away with all of it. **kill with the sword.** This is death by murder, war, or violence. **famine.** The issue is no longer scarcity (as with the black horse) but a severe lack of food that leads to death.

6:9 fifth seal. A new scene unfolds with the breaking of the fifth seal. Those who have been martyred in the name of God are pictured under the altar.

6:12-14 sixth seal. The sixth seal is broken, and John sees cosmic disturbances, which herald the coming of the last days.

6:12-13 earthquake. The very trembling of the earth is often associated with the presence of God (Ex. 19:18; Hag. 2:6). **sun . . . moon . . . stars.** Even the predictable, well-ordered movement of the heavenly bodies goes awry (Isa. 34:4; Acts 2:20).

7:1-4 The earth is pictured as a great square with an angel at each corner holding back a lethal wind until the 144,000 can be sealed.

7:3 seal . . . on the foreheads. Probably similar to the signet ring that kings used to authenticate documents by its imprint. The purpose of this seal is to mark God's people so that they will be spared from the plagues that are to come (9:4).

7:5 12,000. This number is symbolic, as is the total number of 144,000 (12 squared times a thousand), and conveys the idea of completeness: 12,000 are sealed from each of the 12 tribes.

7:12 glory. A reference to the brightness of God, His divine luminous presence.

7:13-14 Who are these. The question of the identity of the great multitude is raised and then answered, a process often used in prophetic literature when a vision is to be explained (Jer. 1:11,13; 24:3; Amos 7:8; 8:2; Zech. 4:4-14).

14 And I said to him, "Sir, you are the one who knows."

Then he said to me, "These are the ones who died in* the great tribulation.* They have washed their robes in the blood of the Lamb and made them white.

15 "That is why they stand in front of God's throne
and serve him day and night in his Temple.
And he who sits on the throne
will give them shelter.
16 They will never again be hungry or thirsty;
they will never be scorched by the heat of the sun.
17 For the Lamb on the throne*
will be their Shepherd.
He will lead them to springs of life-giving water.
And God will wipe every tear from their eyes."

THE LAMB BREAKS THE SEVENTH SEAL

8 When the Lamb broke the seventh seal on the scroll,* there was silence throughout heaven for about half an hour. 2 I saw the seven angels who stand before God, and they were given seven trumpets.

3 Then another angel with a gold incense burner came and stood at the altar. And a great amount of incense was given to him to mix with the prayers of God's people as an offering on the gold altar before the throne. 4 The smoke of the incense, mixed with the prayers of God's holy people, ascended up to God from the altar where the angel had poured them out. 5 Then the angel filled the incense burner with fire from the altar and threw it down upon the earth; and thunder crashed, lightning flashed, and there was a terrible earthquake.

THE FIRST FOUR TRUMPETS

6 Then the seven angels with the seven trumpets prepared to blow their mighty blasts.

7 The first angel blew his trumpet, and hail and fire mixed with blood were thrown down on the earth. One-third of the earth was set on fire, one-third of the trees were burned, and all the green grass was burned.

8 Then the second angel blew his trumpet, and a great mountain of fire was thrown into the sea. One-third of the water in the sea became blood, 9 one-third

INCENSE AND DEATH

1. When have you experienced excruciating pain? What happened?

REVELATION 8:1–9:21

2. What do we learn about prayer from the use of altars and incense (8:3-5)? When was the last time you cried for justice or mercy?
3. What events does the sixth trumpet begin? Why did this woe fail to bring the majority to repentance as originally intended?
4. What do you see in our society that fits with the actions listed in 9:20-21? Which of these actions do you see in your own life? In what way? What can you do about this in the coming week?

of all things living in the sea died, and one-third of all the ships on the sea were destroyed.

10 Then the third angel blew his trumpet, and a great star fell from the sky, burning like a torch. It fell on one-third of the rivers and on the springs of water. 11 The name of the star was Bitterness.* It made one-third of the water bitter, and many people died from drinking the bitter water.

12 Then the fourth angel blew his trumpet, and one-third of the sun was struck, and one-third of the moon, and one-third of the stars, and they became dark. And one-third of the day was dark, and also one-third of the night.

13 Then I looked, and I heard a single eagle crying loudly as it flew through the air, "Terror, terror, terror to all who belong to this world because of what will happen when the last three angels blow their trumpets."

THE FIFTH TRUMPET BRINGS THE FIRST TERROR

9 Then the fifth angel blew his trumpet, and I saw a star that had fallen to earth from the sky, and he was given the key to the shaft of the bottomless pit.* 2 When he opened it, smoke poured out as though

7:14a Greek *who came out of.* 7:14b Or *the great suffering.* 7:17 Greek *on the center of the throne.* 8:1 Or *book.* 8:11 Greek *Wormwood.* 9:1 Or *the abyss,* or *the underworld;* also in 9:11.

7:14 the ones who died. These are the martyrs from the great tribulation: those who maintained their faith to the point of death. **the great tribulation.** This event is mentioned in both the Old and New Testaments. Daniel 12:1 refers to the "time of distress" (literally, "tribulation" in Hebrew) that will come. See Matthew 24:21-22.

7:17 the Lamb . . . will be their Shepherd. The Lamb becomes the shepherd (who tends the flock of lambs); Jesus is pictured as the Good Shepherd (John 10:1-30; 21:15-17).

8:1 seventh seal. The breaking of the seventh seal opens the scroll so that the events of the end times can be revealed. Unlike the other seals (with the possible exception of the first seal), the breaking of this seal brings no judgment, simply silence.

8:2 trumpets. In the Old Testament, trumpets are used for various purposes: to signal various activities (Num. 10:1-10); as part of worship and celebration (Num. 10:10; 29:1); in war (Josh. 6); and at coronations (1 Kings 1:34). Here in Revelation, however, they have the more ominous purpose of announcing and loosing the plagues of the end times.

8:7 One-third of the earth was set on fire. The first plague destroys a third of the earth's vegetation. The fact that only a third of the earth is pictured as being afflicted represents a severe, but limited, act of judgment. This is similar to the seventh Egyptian plague (Ex. 9:13-35).

8:8-9 second . . . trumpet. The second plague is unique; it is impossible to parallel it with any known natural event, such as a volcano. It destroys a third of the sea along with a third of the fish in the sea and a third of the boats on the sea. This plague is similar to what happened to the Nile in Exodus 7:20-21.

8:10-11 third . . . trumpet. During the third plague, a great meteor falls from the sky and poisons a third of the fresh water.

8:12 fourth . . . trumpet. The fourth plague strikes the heavenly bodies. A third of the sun, moon, and stars go dark. This is similar to the ninth plague in Egypt (Ex. 10:21-23).

8:13 Terror. The triple "Woe" corresponds to the final three trumpets (9:12). **all who belong to this world.** These plagues will come upon those who are hostile to God.

9:1 a star. An angel, a demon, or Satan himself with the power to unlock the underworld. **the bottomless pit.** In the way the Bible speaks of the cosmos, there are said to be three levels: the heavens, the earth, and the underworld (which is a huge, bottomless pit). It is the realm of the dead (Rom. 10:7); it is where the beast abides (11:7); it is the place of demons (Luke 8:31); it will be used as the prison of Satan during the millennium (20:3); and in this case, it is the home of the demon locusts.

from a huge furnace, and the sunlight and air turned dark from the smoke.

3 Then locusts came from the smoke and descended on the earth, and they were given power to sting like scorpions. 4 They were told not to harm the grass or plants or trees, but only the people who did not have the seal of God on their foreheads. 5 They were told not to kill them but to torture them for five months with pain like the pain of a scorpion sting. 6 In those days people will seek death but will not find it. They will long to die, but death will flee from them!

7 The locusts looked like horses prepared for battle. They had what looked like gold crowns on their heads, and their faces looked like human faces. 8 They had hair like women's hair and teeth like the teeth of a lion. 9 They wore armor made of iron, and their wings roared like an army of chariots rushing into battle. 10 They had tails that stung like scorpions, and for five months they had the power to torment people. 11 Their king is the angel from the bottomless pit; his name in Hebrew is *Abaddon,* and in Greek, *Apollyon*—the Destroyer.

12 The first terror is past, but look, two more terrors are coming!

THE SIXTH TRUMPET BRINGS THE SECOND TERROR

13 Then the sixth angel blew his trumpet, and I heard a voice speaking from the four horns of the gold altar that stands in the presence of God. 14 And the voice said to the sixth angel who held the trumpet, "Release the four angels who are bound at the great Euphrates River." 15 Then the four angels who had been prepared for this hour and day and month and year were turned loose to kill one-third of all the people on earth. 16 I heard the size of their army, which was 200 million mounted troops.

17 And in my vision, I saw the horses and the riders sitting on them. The riders wore armor that was fiery red and dark blue and yellow. The horses had heads like lions, and fire and smoke and burning sulfur billowed from their mouths. 18 One-third of all the people on earth were killed by these three plagues—by the fire and smoke and burning sulfur that came from the mouths of the horses. 19 Their power was in their mouths and in their tails. For their tails had heads like snakes, with the power to injure people.

20 But the people who did not die in these plagues still refused to repent of their evil deeds and turn to God. They continued to worship demons and idols made of gold, silver, bronze, stone, and wood—idols that can neither see nor hear nor walk! 21 And they did not repent of their murders or their witchcraft or their sexual immorality or their thefts.

THE ANGEL AND THE SMALL SCROLL

10 Then I saw another mighty angel coming down from heaven, surrounded by a cloud, with a rainbow over his head. His face shone like the sun, and his feet were like pillars of fire. 2 And in his hand was a small scroll* that had been opened. He stood with his right foot on the sea and his left foot on the land. 3 And he gave a great shout like the roar of a lion. And when he shouted, the seven thunders answered.

4 When the seven thunders spoke, I was about to write. But I heard a voice from heaven saying, "Keep secret* what the seven thunders said, and do not write it down."

5 Then the angel I saw standing on the sea and on the land raised his right hand toward heaven. 6 He swore an oath in the name of the one who lives forever and ever, who created the heavens and everything in them, the earth and everything in it, and the sea and everything in it. He said, "There will be no more delay. 7 When the seventh angel blows his trumpet, God's mysterious plan will be fulfilled. It will happen just as he announced it to his servants the prophets."

8 Then the voice from heaven spoke to me again: "Go and take the open scroll from the hand of the angel who is standing on the sea and on the land."

9 So I went to the angel and told him to give me the small scroll. "Yes, take it and eat it," he said. "It will be sweet as honey in your mouth, but it will turn sour in your stomach!" 10 So I took the small scroll from the hand of the angel, and I ate it! It was sweet in my mouth, but when I swallowed it, it turned sour in my stomach.

11 Then I was told, "You must prophesy again about many peoples, nations, languages, and kings."

10:2 Or *book;* also in 10:8, 9, 10. **10:4** Greek *Seal up.*

9:3 locusts. These are not actual locusts but some sort of demonic entity. Their coming is similar to the plague of (real) locusts in Exodus 10:1-20.

9:4 harm . . . only the people. Real locusts consume plants, trees, and grass. These locusts lack that ability, attacking only humans.

9:8 hair like women's hair. Perhaps a reference to the antennae of locusts, or to the hair on their legs or bodies.

9:9 armor made of iron. The scales on the body of locusts are shaped like this. **their wings roared.** When locusts swarm into an area, they make a loud noise by beating their wings.

9:11 *Abaddon*. A Hebrew word meaning "destruction." In the Old Testament, this word is used along with "Sheol" for the place of destruction and death (Job 26:6; 28:22; Prov. 15:11; 27:20).

9:12 first terror is past. This refers back to 8:13. The first woe is passed. The second will be described in verses 13-21 when the sixth trumpet is sounded. The third woe will come when the seventh trumpet is sounded in 11:14-19.

9:13-21 The plague of the fifth trumpet brought pain and suffering; plague six brings death. The Old Testament parallel for such an invasion of horses is found in Ezekiel 38:14-16 (Isa. 5:26-30; Jer. 6:22-26).

9:17 horses. The demon locusts in the previous plague are followed by demon horses in this plague. There is a difference. While the locusts had the power to torture, the horses have the power to kill. **fire and smoke and burning sulfur.** Fire, smoke, and sulfur (brimstone) of this sort are straight out of hell (14:10-11; 19:20; 21:8).

9:20-21 refused to repent. The intent of the plagues is not vengeance—it is to lead humankind to repentance. Despite the horror of the plagues, people still refuse to turn from their worship of demons and the lifestyle that such a commitment brings.

10:1 another mighty angel. The description of this angel is so similar to that of Christ in chapter 1 that some commentators have identified him as such. However, in verse 6 he shows himself to be a genuine angel by swearing by "the One who lives forever and ever." **surrounded by a cloud.** Celestial beings are often described as ascending and descending with clouds (Ps. 104:3; Dan. 7:13; Acts 1:9). **rainbow.** This can be understood as a kind of crown or as the reflection of His brilliance ("His face was like the sun") through the clouds.

10:2 a small scroll. This is an unusual word, used nowhere else in Greek literature prior to this time. John probably coined it himself. Unlike the scroll of 5:1 that was a book, this scroll was more akin to a booklet.

10:4 seven thunders. John understood what the seven thunders communicated, but he was told not to record them. What these thunders convey is unknown, but in the three other instances where there is thunder, it is the precursor to judgment (8:5; 11:19; 16:18).

10:7 when. The sounding of the seventh trumpet is not a single act but a period of time. As will emerge, it includes the events of the seven bowls (16:1-21). **God's mysterious plan.** "Mysterious plan" in the New Testament does not refer to something that is secret but to the purpose of God that has been revealed.

10:8 the angel who is standing on the sea and on the land. For the third time the tremendous size of this angel is emphasized. His coming has something to do with all of the earth (vv. 2,5).

TWO WITNESSES PERSECUTED

1. Where would you least like to live: An area prone to earthquakes? Hurricanes? Floods?

REVELATION 10:1–11:19

2. Why is God's Word "sweet as honey" in John's mouth but bitter in his stomach (10:9)?
3. Why was this scroll lying open (10:2) instead of closed and sealed like other scrolls? What does this suggest about God's Word?
4. Why were the two witnesses dressed in "burlap" (11:3)? What does this suggest about those who preach God's Word?
5. Why did the world rejoice when the two witnesses had died? Have you seen this happen in the world today?

THE TWO WITNESSES

11 Then I was given a measuring stick, and I was
told, "Go and measure the Temple of God and
the altar, and count the number of worshipers. 2 But
do not measure the outer courtyard, for it has been
turned over to the nations. They will trample the holy
city for 42 months. 3 And I will give power to my two
witnesses, and they will be clothed in burlap and will
prophesy during those 1,260 days."
4 These two prophets are the two olive trees and the
two lampstands that stand before the Lord of all the
earth. 5 If anyone tries to harm them, fire flashes from
their mouths and consumes their enemies. This is
how anyone who tries to harm them must die. 6 They
have power to shut the sky so that no rain will fall for
as long as they prophesy. And they have the power to
turn the rivers and oceans into blood, and to strike the
earth with every kind of plague as often as they wish.
7 When they complete their testimony, the beast
that comes up out of the bottomless pit* will declare
war against them, and he will conquer them and kill
them. 8 And their bodies will lie in the main street of
Jerusalem,* the city that is figuratively called "Sod-
om" and "Egypt," the city where their Lord was cruci-
fied. 9 And for three and a half days, all peoples, tribes,
languages, and nations will stare at their bodies. No
one will be allowed to bury them. 10 All the people
who belong to this world will gloat over them and
give presents to each other to celebrate the death of
the two prophets who had tormented them.
11 But after three and a half days, God breathed life
into them, and they stood up! Terror struck all who
were staring at them. 12 Then a loud voice from heaven
called to the two prophets, "Come up here!" And they
rose to heaven in a cloud as their enemies watched.
13 At the same time there was a terrible earthquake
that destroyed a tenth of the city. Seven thousand peo-
ple died in that earthquake, and everyone else was
terrified and gave glory to the God of heaven.
14 The second terror is past, but look, the third terror
is coming quickly.

THE SEVENTH TRUMPET BRINGS THE THIRD TERROR

15 Then the seventh angel blew his trumpet, and there
were loud voices shouting in heaven:

"The world has now become the Kingdom of our
Lord and of his Christ,*
and he will reign forever and ever."

16 The twenty-four elders sitting on their thrones be-
fore God fell with their faces to the ground and wor-
shiped him. 17 And they said,

"We give thanks to you, Lord God, the Almighty,
the one who is and who always was,
for now you have assumed your great power
and have begun to reign.
18 The nations were filled with wrath,
but now the time of your wrath has come.
It is time to judge the dead
and reward your servants the prophets,
as well as your holy people,
and all who fear your name,
from the least to the greatest.
It is time to destroy
all who have caused destruction on the earth."

19 Then, in heaven, the Temple of God was opened and
the Ark of his covenant could be seen inside the Tem-
ple. Lightning flashed, thunder crashed and roared,
and there was an earthquake and a terrible hailstorm.

THE WOMAN AND THE DRAGON

12 Then I witnessed in heaven an event of great sig-
nificance. I saw a woman clothed with the sun,
with the moon beneath her feet, and a crown of twelve

11:7 Or *the abyss*, or *the underworld*. 11:8 Greek *the great city*. 11:15 Or *his Messiah*.

11:1 Temple of God. The Greek word refers to the temple building itself and not the outer courtyard. The temple itself consisted of a building at the center containing the Holy Place and the Holy of Holies, bordered by the court of the priests, the court of Israel, and the court of the women where the people of Israel assembled. This temple complex was surrounded by a huge outer court where Gentiles were allowed to come.

11:2 42 months. Three and a half years, the length of time evil is allowed to dominate (Dan. 7:25; 12:6-7, 11-12; Rev. 12:6, 14; 13:5).

11:3 two witnesses. What is clear is that these two men are similar to Moses and Elijah (Ex. 7:14-18; 1 Kings 17:1; 2 Kings 1:10-12; Mal. 4:5; Mark 9:4). In this context, they may represent those who preach repentance during the tribulation. **1,260 days.** Three and a half years = 42 months = 1,260 days (a solar month had 30 days).

11:4 the two olive trees and the two lampstands. John's imagery comes from Zechariah 4:1-14, "two anointed ones" produced a united witness represented by one lampstand. John's witnesses have separate lampstands. The olive oil alludes to the power of the Holy Spirit (Zech. 4:6).

11:7 the beast. This is the first time that this figure appears. He will become the major threat in the last days. His origins are clear: he is a demon out of the abyss.

11:13 terrible earthquake. This devastating earthquake that levels a tenth of the city can be linked to the prophecy in Ezekiel 38:19-20.

11:18 destroy all who have caused destruction on the earth. People were created to be the stewards of the earth (Gen. 1:26), but the results of human sin have led creation to groan (Rom. 8:19-22). God's final judgment will be a time when judgment is directed against those who have worked against Him.

11:19 the Ark of his covenant. In the Old Testament the ark of the covenant was a wooden chest that stood in the Holy of Holies and symbolized the presence of God.

12:1 a woman. The first participant in this heavenly drama is introduced: the radiant woman who represents the church, Israel, or believing Jews (Isa. 54:1; 66:7-8; Gal. 4:26). The details of her dress indicate her magnificence. Psalm 104:2 describes God in such terms.

DRAGON SLAYER

1. What is your favorite book about dragons? Movie about monsters?

REVELATION 12:1–13:18

2. Who or what does the dragon represent? The woman's Son (12:5)?
3. Why is the Devil in a "great anger" (12:12)? How is this bad news for humanity?
4. How was the Devil conquered (12:11)? How is this good news for humanity?
5. What does the description of the second beast refer to in 13:11? What real people or forces in history have appeared like a lamb but spoken like a dragon?
6. Is your name written in the Book of Life (13:8)? How do you know?

---

stars on her head. 2 She was pregnant, and she cried out because of her labor pains and the agony of giving birth.

3 Then I witnessed in heaven another significant event. I saw a large red dragon with seven heads and ten horns, with seven crowns on his heads. 4 His tail swept away one-third of the stars in the sky, and he threw them to the earth. He stood in front of the woman as she was about to give birth, ready to devour her baby as soon as it was born.

5 She gave birth to a son who was to rule all nations with an iron rod. And her child was snatched away from the dragon and was caught up to God and to his throne. 6 And the woman fled into the wilderness, where God had prepared a place to care for her for 1,260 days.

7 Then there was war in heaven. Michael and his angels fought against the dragon and his angels. 8 And the dragon lost the battle, and he and his angels were forced out of heaven. 9 This great dragon—the ancient serpent called the devil, or Satan, the one deceiving the whole world—was thrown down to the earth with all his angels.

10 Then I heard a loud voice shouting across the heavens,

"It has come at last—
salvation and power
and the Kingdom of our God,
and the authority of his Christ.*
For the accuser of our brothers and sisters*
has been thrown down to earth—
the one who accuses them
before our God day and night.
11 And they have defeated him by the blood of the Lamb
and by their testimony.
And they did not love their lives so much
that they were afraid to die.
12 Therefore, rejoice, O heavens!
And you who live in the heavens, rejoice!
But terror will come on the earth and the sea,
for the devil has come down to you in great anger,
knowing that he has little time."

13 When the dragon realized that he had been thrown down to the earth, he pursued the woman who had given birth to the male child. 14 But she was given two wings like those of a great eagle so she could fly to the place prepared for her in the wilderness. There she would be cared for and protected from the dragon* for a time, times, and half a time.

15 Then the dragon tried to drown the woman with a flood of water that flowed from his mouth. 16 But the earth helped her by opening its mouth and swallowing the river that gushed out from the mouth of the dragon. 17 And the dragon was angry at the woman and declared war against the rest of her children—all who keep God's commandments and maintain their testimony for Jesus.

18 Then the dragon took his stand* on the shore beside the sea.

THE BEAST OUT OF THE SEA

13 Then I saw a beast rising up out of the sea. It had seven heads and ten horns, with ten crowns on its horns. And written on each head were names that blasphemed God. 2 This beast looked like a leopard, but it had the feet of a bear and the mouth of a lion! And the dragon gave the beast his own power and throne and great authority.

3 I saw that one of the heads of the beast seemed wounded beyond recovery—but the fatal wound was healed! The whole world marveled at this miracle and gave allegiance to the beast. 4 They worshiped the dragon for giving the beast such power, and they also worshiped the beast. "Who is as great as the beast?" they exclaimed. "Who is able to fight against him?"

5 Then the beast was allowed to speak great blasphemies against God. And he was given authority to

12:10a Or *his Messiah.* **12:10b** Greek *brothers.* **12:14** Greek *the serpent;* also in 12:15. See 12:9. **12:18** Greek *Then he took his stand;* some manuscripts read *Then I took my stand.* Some translations put this entire sentence into 13:1.

12:3 large red dragon. The second participant comes on stage: the great dragon, Satan (v. 9). **seven heads.** Indicating great intelligence. **seven crowns.** Seven is the number of completeness; a crown is the sign of power.

12:4 devour her baby. The purpose of Satan is revealed: he wants to destroy the Messiah.

12:5 a son. The third participant is the Messiah (Ps. 2:9; Rev. 2:27; 19:15).

12:6 wilderness. Not a wasteland but a place of refuge (as it often was for the children of Israel). **1,260 days.** This is the period when evil is allowed to do its work upon earth.

12:9 the ancient serpent. An allusion to Genesis 3:1-5. **the devil.** Literally, *diabolos*, a Greek term for Satan meaning "accuser," "adversary," or "slanderer" (Zech. 3:1-2; 1 Pet. 5:8). **Satan.** A Hebrew term meaning "accuser."

12:12 terror . . . on the earth. Some say this is the third woe announced in 8:13.

12:14 a time, times, and half a time. One year plus two years plus a half year. This phrase is taken from Daniel 7:25, the same time period as three and a half years = 42 months = 1,260 days.

13:1 seven heads . . . with ten crowns on its horns. Like the dragon, the beast has multiple heads and horns. There is a difference; the dragon has seven diadems on his heads, while the beast has 10 diadems on his horns. These 10 diadems represent 10 kings (17:12). **on each head were names that blasphemed God.** The beast has taken to himself divine names. In verse 4 he is worshiped. This accords with Paul's description of "the man of lawlessness" (2 Thess. 2:3-4).

13:2 This beast. This beast has all the attributes of the four beasts in Daniel 7. He is the complete embodiment of evil, his power derived from Satan. In Daniel, these beasts represent four dominant kingdoms of the world that were hostile to God.

13:5 speak great blasphemies. Thus the beast speaks as if he were God, in accord with Daniel 7:8,20,25.

do whatever he wanted for forty-two months. [6] And
he spoke terrible words of blasphemy against God,
slandering his name and his dwelling—that is, those
who dwell in heaven.* [7] And the beast was allowed to
wage war against God's holy people and to conquer
them. And he was given authority to rule over every
tribe and people and language and nation. [8] And all
the people who belong to this world worshiped the
beast. They are the ones whose names were not writ-
ten in the Book of Life that belongs to the Lamb who
was slaughtered before the world was made.*

9 Anyone with ears to hear
should listen and understand.
10 Anyone who is destined for prison
will be taken to prison.
Anyone destined to die by the sword
will die by the sword.

This means that God's holy people must endure perse-
cution patiently and remain faithful.

THE BEAST OUT OF THE EARTH

[11] Then I saw another beast come up out of the earth. He
had two horns like those of a lamb, but he spoke with
the voice of a dragon. [12] He exercised all the authority
of the first beast. And he required all the earth and its
people to worship the first beast, whose fatal wound
had been healed. [13] He did astounding miracles, even
making fire flash down to earth from the sky while
everyone was watching. [14] And with all the miracles he
was allowed to perform on behalf of the first beast, he
deceived all the people who belong to this world. He
ordered the people to make a great statue of the first
beast, who was fatally wounded and then came back
to life. [15] He was then permitted to give life to this statue
so that it could speak. Then the statue of the beast com-
manded that anyone refusing to worship it must die.
[16] He required everyone—small and great, rich and
poor, free and slave—to be given a mark on the right
hand or on the forehead. [17] And no one could buy or
sell anything without that mark, which was either
the name of the beast or the number representing his
name. [18] Wisdom is needed here. Let the one with un-
derstanding solve the meaning of the number of the
beast, for it is the number of a man.* His number is
666.*

WRATH AND REJOICING

1. What is one of your favorite pop tunes? One of your favorite worship songs or hymns?

REVELATION 14:1–15:8

2. Who is the Lamb? What has He done? Why are the people following Him?
3. What determines who will "drink the wine of God's anger" (14:10) and who will "rest from their hard work" (14:13)?
4. Look at the pictures used for God's wrath (strong wine, fire, sickles, etc.). What does each suggest about His anger? Why is He so angry about humanity's wickedness?
5. Are you following God with your whole heart? What can you praise God for today?

THE LAMB AND THE 144,000

14 Then I saw the Lamb standing on Mount Zion,
and with him were 144,000 who had his name
and his Father's name written on their foreheads.
[2] And I heard a sound from heaven like the roar of
mighty ocean waves or the rolling of loud thunder.
It was like the sound of many harpists playing to-
gether.
[3] This great choir sang a wonderful new song in
front of the throne of God and before the four living
beings and the twenty-four elders. No one could learn
this song except the 144,000 who had been redeemed
from the earth. [4] They have kept themselves as pure as
virgins,* following the Lamb wherever he goes. They
have been purchased from among the people on the
earth as a special offering* to God and to the Lamb.
[5] They have told no lies; they are without blame.

THE THREE ANGELS

[6] And I saw another angel flying through the sky, car-
rying the eternal Good News to proclaim to the peo-
ple who belong to this world—to every nation, tribe,
language, and people. [7] "Fear God," he shouted. "Give
glory to him. For the time has come when he will sit

13:6 Some manuscripts read *and his dwelling and all who dwell in heaven.* **13:8** Or *not written in the Book of Life before the world was made—the Book that belongs to the Lamb who was slaughtered.* **13:18a** Or *of humanity.* **13:18b** Some manuscripts read *616.* **14:4a** Greek *They are virgins who have not defiled themselves with women.* **14:4b** Greek *as firstfruits.*

13:8 All . . . worshiped the beast. All are required to worship the beast. Those who belong to the Lamb will die as martyrs because of their refusal to worship.

13:11-18 A second beast arises who is a servant to the first beast. His purpose is to cause people to worship the first beast. He is probably meant to represent organized religion. He is later called "the false prophet" (16:13; 19:20; 20:10). With the coming of this beast, the evil trinity is complete. Satan, the antichrist, and the false prophet oppose God the Father, Son, and the Holy Spirit.

13:14 allowed to perform. In verses 5-7 (when speaking about the first beast) the passive "was given" is used four times (in the Greek text) to show that the first beast was a front for Satan. Here too the point is made that this second beast has no independent power. It also is controlled by Satan.

13:15 commanded . . . must die. It is the statue that commands the death of those who will not worship it in this battle between God and Satan.

13:16 mark. Satan causes people to be sealed with the name of the beast, just as God's people were sealed with God's mark in 7:3. Now there are people sealed for God and those sealed for Satan.

13:17 no one could buy or sell. There are severe economic consequences for failing to have the mark of the beast. Such people cannot purchase anything or engage in trade.

13:18 666. Many attempts have been made to translate this number into a name. None really succeed, since all such translation is, in the end, guesswork. Some suggest that this is a symbol, not a cryptogram; since 7 is the perfect number, each number in the mark falls short of such perfection.

14:1 Mount Zion. In the vision of Joel, this is the place of deliverance for those who call upon the name of the Lord (Joel 2:32). This is either the temple site in Jerusalem or the heavenly Zion, the Jerusalem that is above (Gal. 4:26; Heb. 12:22) since this whole scene takes place in a heavenly context.

14:4 following the Lamb. Many take this verse to mean that the 144,000 are a special class of people who enjoy a special relationship with God and who are characterized by three things: abstinence from marriage (celibacy); following of the Lamb; and special consecration to God. **kept . . . as pure as virgins.** It is true that both Jesus and Paul spoke approvingly of those who abstained from marriage (Matt. 19:12; 1 Cor. 7:1, 32), but they also spoke approvingly of marriage (Matt. 19:4-6; Eph. 5:31-32). Furthermore, Israel was spoken of as a virgin in the Old Testament (Jer. 18:13; Lam. 2:13; Amos 5:2) as was the church in the New Testament (2 Cor. 11:2). **special offering.** Originally this was an offering to God of some of the fruit from the beginning of the harvest (Lev. 23:9-14).

as judge. Worship him who made the heavens, the
earth, the sea, and all the springs of water."
8 Then another angel followed him through the sky,
shouting, "Babylon is fallen—that great city is fall-
en—because she made all the nations of the world
drink the wine of her passionate immorality."
9 Then a third angel followed them, shouting, "Any-
one who worships the beast and his statue or who ac-
cepts his mark on the forehead or on the hand 10 must
drink the wine of God's anger. It has been poured full
strength into God's cup of wrath. And they will be tor-
mented with fire and burning sulfur in the presence of
the holy angels and the Lamb. 11 The smoke of their tor-
ment will rise forever and ever, and they will have no
relief day or night, for they have worshiped the beast
and his statue and have accepted the mark of his name."
12 This means that God's holy people must endure
persecution patiently, obeying his commands and
maintaining their faith in Jesus.
13 And I heard a voice from heaven saying, "Write
this down: Blessed are those who die in the Lord from
now on. Yes, says the Spirit, they are blessed indeed,
for they will rest from their hard work; for their good
deeds follow them!"

THE HARVEST OF THE EARTH

14 Then I saw a white cloud, and seated on the cloud
was someone like the Son of Man.* He had a gold
crown on his head and a sharp sickle in his hand.
15 Then another angel came from the Temple and
shouted to the one sitting on the cloud, "Swing the
sickle, for the time of harvest has come; the crop on
earth is ripe." 16 So the one sitting on the cloud swung
his sickle over the earth, and the whole earth was
harvested.
17 After that, another angel came from the Temple
in heaven, and he also had a sharp sickle. 18 Then an-
other angel, who had power to destroy with fire, came
from the altar. He shouted to the angel with the sharp
sickle, "Swing your sickle now to gather the clusters
of grapes from the vines of the earth, for they are ripe
for judgment." 19 So the angel swung his sickle over
the earth and loaded the grapes into the great wine-
press of God's wrath. 20 The grapes were trampled in
the winepress outside the city, and blood flowed from
the winepress in a stream about 180 miles* long and
as high as a horse's bridle.

THE SONG OF MOSES AND OF THE LAMB

15 Then I saw in heaven another marvelous
event of great significance. Seven angels
were holding the seven last plagues, which would
bring God's wrath to completion. 2 I saw before me
what seemed to be a glass sea mixed with fire. And
on it stood all the people who had been victorious
over the beast and his statue and the number rep-
resenting his name. They were all holding harps
that God had given them. 3 And they were singing
the song of Moses, the servant of God, and the song
of the Lamb:

"Great and marvelous are your works,
O Lord God, the Almighty.
Just and true are your ways,
O King of the nations.*
4 Who will not fear you, Lord,
and glorify your name?
For you alone are holy.
All nations will come and worship before you,
for your righteous deeds have been revealed."

THE SEVEN BOWLS OF THE SEVEN PLAGUES

5 Then I looked and saw that the Temple in heaven,
God's Tabernacle, was thrown wide open. 6 The sev-
en angels who were holding the seven plagues came
out of the Temple. They were clothed in spotless white
linen* with gold sashes across their chests. 7 Then one
of the four living beings handed each of the seven
angels a gold bowl filled with the wrath of God, who
lives forever and ever. 8 The Temple was filled with
smoke from God's glory and power. No one could en-
ter the Temple until the seven angels had completed
pouring out the seven plagues.

16 Then I heard a mighty voice from the Temple
say to the seven angels, "Go your ways and pour
out on the earth the seven bowls containing God's
wrath."
2 So the first angel left the Temple and poured out
his bowl on the earth, and horrible, malignant sores
broke out on everyone who had the mark of the beast
and who worshiped his statue.
3 Then the second angel poured out his bowl on
the sea, and it became like the blood of a corpse. And
everything in the sea died.

14:14 Or *like a son of man.* See Dan 7:13. "Son of Man" is a title Jesus used for himself. **14:20** Greek *1,600 stadia* [300 kilometers]. **15:3** Some manuscripts read *King of the ages.* **15:6** Other manuscripts read *white stone;* still others read *white [garments] made of linen.*

14:8 another angel. This is another announcement of what is yet to come (11:15; 12:10) as if it had just happened (17:1–18:24). **Babylon.** The original Babylon was a great city in Mesopotamia, renowned for its luxury and its corruption. It was also the traditional enemy of Israel.

14:9-11 third angel. The third angel discloses the fate of those who do not leave the beast and worship God. In contrast to 13:15-17, here those who worship the beast and bear his mark will be the objects of God's wrath.

14:10 fire and burning sulfur. The lake of fire and sulfur is the description used in Revelation for the final resting place of Satan, his cohorts, and followers (20:10, 14-15).

14:14 someone like the Son of Man. This title was also used in Daniel 7:13-14; it was used extensively by Jesus as a title for Himself (Mark 2:10).

14:15 the time of harvest. Harvest in the New Testament carries the idea both of gathering people into God's kingdom (Matt. 9:37-38) and gathering the wicked for divine judgment (Matt. 13:30,40-42).

14:18 gather the clusters of grapes. Harvesting grapes is used elsewhere in the Bible as an image for judgment (Isa. 63:2-6; Joel 3:13).

14:19 great winepress of God's wrath. Clearly judgment, not salvation, since the grapes are tossed into a huge winepress to be trampled on.

14:20 blood flowed from the winepress. The image shifts from wine to blood. The amount of blood is enormous. **as high as a horse's bridles.** About four feet deep. **about 180 miles.** The approximate length of Palestine.

15:1 another marvelous event. This is the third such sign. The first was of the radiant woman (12:1); the second was of the fiery red dragon (12:3). **the seven last plagues.** This is the third and final set of calamities.

15:2 all the people who had been victorious. They won over the demands of the beast (13:15-17) by refusing to disown the name of Christ, by remaining steadfast in their faith, and by refusing to worship the beast or receive his mark (14:12). They died instead, frustrating the purposes of the beast. What seemed like defeat became victory.

15:3 Lord God, the Almighty. God is called Almighty nine times in Revelation and only once in the rest of the New Testament (2 Cor. 6:18). This is appropriate since His overwhelming power is a central feature in this book.

15:8 filled with smoke. When God appeared in the Old Testament, there was often smoke (Ex. 19:18; Isa. 6:4). It signified God's power and His judgment.

16:2 first . . . bowl. The first plague falls upon those who bear the mark of the beast, marking them with painful sores.

16:3 second . . . bowl. The second plague turns the oceans and seas into blood, killing all the sea life.

PLAGUES AND PROSTITUTES

1. If you could rule the world for just one hour, what would you do?

REVELATION 16:1–17:18

2. What might these plagues represent? If they turn out to be literal, how might they come about?
3. Who is in control of the plagues? Why is He pouring them out?
4. How did the world respond to the plagues? How might things have been different if the world's response had been different?
5. Who or what is like the "great prostitute" (17:1) in today's world? In your own life?

4 Then the third angel poured out his bowl on the
rivers and springs, and they became blood. 5 And I
heard the angel who had authority over all water
saying,

"You are just, O Holy One, who is and who always was,
because you have sent these judgments.
6 Since they shed the blood
of your holy people and your prophets,
you have given them blood to drink.
It is their just reward."

7 And I heard a voice from the altar,* saying,

"Yes, O Lord God, the Almighty,
your judgments are true and just."

8 Then the fourth angel poured out his bowl on
the sun, causing it to scorch everyone with its fire.
9 Everyone was burned by this blast of heat, and they
cursed the name of God, who had control over all
these plagues. They did not repent of their sins and
turn to God and give him glory.
10 Then the fifth angel poured out his bowl on the
throne of the beast, and his kingdom was plunged
into darkness. His subjects ground their teeth* in an-
guish, 11 and they cursed the God of heaven for their
pains and sores. But they did not repent of their evil
deeds and turn to God.
12 Then the sixth angel poured out his bowl on the
great Euphrates River, and it dried up so that the kings
from the east could march their armies toward the
west without hindrance. 13 And I saw three evil* spirits
that looked like frogs leap from the mouths of the drag-
on, the beast, and the false prophet. 14 They are demon-
ic spirits who work miracles and go out to all the rulers
of the world to gather them for battle against the Lord
on that great judgment day of God the Almighty.

15 "Look, I will come as unexpectedly as a thief! Blessed are all who are watching for me, who keep their clothing ready so they will not have to walk around naked and ashamed."

16 And the demonic spirits gathered all the rulers
and their armies to a place with the Hebrew name
Armageddon.*
17 Then the seventh angel poured out his bowl into
the air. And a mighty shout came from the throne in
the Temple, saying, "It is finished!" 18 Then the thun-
der crashed and rolled, and lightning flashed. And
a great earthquake struck—the worst since people
were placed on the earth. 19 The great city of Babylon
split into three sections, and the cities of many na-
tions fell into heaps of rubble. So God remembered all
of Babylon's sins, and he made her drink the cup that
was filled with the wine of his fierce wrath. 20 And ev-
ery island disappeared, and all the mountains were
leveled. 21 There was a terrible hailstorm, and hail-
stones weighing as much as seventy-five pounds* fell
from the sky onto the people below. They cursed God
because of the terrible plague of the hailstorm.

THE GREAT PROSTITUTE

17 One of the seven angels who had poured out the
seven bowls came over and spoke to me. "Come
with me," he said, "and I will show you the judgment
that is going to come on the great prostitute, who
rules over many waters. 2 The kings of the world have

16:7 Greek *I heard the altar.* **16:10** Greek *gnawed their tongues.* **16:13** Greek *unclean.* **16:16** Or *Harmagedon.* **16:21** Greek *1 talent* [34 kilograms]. **17:3** Or *in spirit.*

16:4 third . . . bowl. The third plague does the same to all the fresh water, thus no water to drink in the land.

16:8-9 fourth . . . bowl. The fourth plague strikes the sun so that it flares up, scorching and searing people. The impact of the fourth trumpet (8:12) also fell on the sun, moon, and stars, but it brought the opposite effect (darkness, not intense light).

16:9 they cursed the name of God. They know full well who is behind these calamities. **They did not repent.** Even at this point, it seems, repentance is possible. Still, they will not turn to God. Like Pharaoh, who saw the plagues and yet would not change, their hearts are hard.

16:10-11 fifth . . . bowl. The fifth plague directly attacks the heart of the problem. It assaults the throne of the beast and plunges his kingdom into darkness. This darkness parallels the ninth Egyptian plague (Ex. 10:21-29).

16:12-16 The sixth plague dries up the great river Euphrates. Since it is no longer a barrier, an invasion is planned (Ex. 14:21-22; Josh. 3:14-17 for other examples of God drying up water). The sixth trumpet plague (9:13-14) was also centered on the Euphrates. This plague is different from the others in that it does not directly bring suffering to people. It does, however, pave the way for war.

16:14 sixth . . . bowl. The frogs are identified as the "spirits of demons." In the sixth trumpet plague (9:16-19), demon locusts were loosed on the world. In this case, the demons cause people to follow the beast. These deceiving spirits go over to the kings of the world in anticipation of the final great battle.

16:16 Armageddon. In Hebrew, this word means "the mountain of Megiddo." However, in Palestine, Megiddo is a plain that stretches from the Sea of Galilee to the Mediterranean, so it is not clear where, precisely, this is. The region of Megiddo was the site of many battles in the history of Israel (Judg. 5:19; 2 Kings 9:27; 23:29; 2 Chron. 35:22).

16:17-21 seventh . . . bowl. The seventh and final plague brings about the overthrow of Babylon. This was announced in 14:8 and will be described in detail in chapters 17 and 18.

16:19 The great city. The city of the beast is undone as are the cities of those who aligned themselves with the beast. **the cup that was filled with the wine of his fierce wrath.** Babylon caused the nations to drink from the cup of her sexual immorality, and they grew rich from this adultery (18:3). Now Babylon is forced to drink from another cup—the cup of God's wrath (14:8, 10).

17:1 who rules over many waters. The Babylon of history was built on a network of canals (Jer. 51:13). John interprets the meaning of these "many waters" in verse 15 as "peoples, multitudes, nations, and languages."

17:2 immorality. In this context, this term describes the corrupting influence of Babylon, which enticed the nations to prostitute everything for the sake of riches, luxury, and pleasure (Isa. 23:16-17; Jer. 51:7; Nah. 3:4).

committed adultery with her, and the people who belong to this world have been made drunk by the wine of her immorality."

3 So the angel took me in the Spirit* into the wilderness. There I saw a woman sitting on a scarlet beast that had seven heads and ten horns, and blasphemies against God were written all over it. 4 The woman wore purple and scarlet clothing and beautiful jewelry made of gold and precious gems and pearls. In her hand she held a gold goblet full of obscenities and the impurities of her immorality. 5 A mysterious name was written on her forehead: "Babylon the Great, Mother of All Prostitutes and Obscenities in the World." 6 I could see that she was drunk—drunk with the blood of God's holy people who were witnesses for Jesus. I stared at her in complete amazement.

7 "Why are you so amazed?" the angel asked. "I will tell you the mystery of this woman and of the beast with seven heads and ten horns on which she sits. 8 The beast you saw was once alive but isn't now. And yet he will soon come up out of the bottomless pit* and go to eternal destruction. And the people who belong to this world, whose names were not written in the Book of Life before the world was made, will be amazed at the reappearance of this beast who had died.

9 "This calls for a mind with understanding: The seven heads of the beast represent the seven hills where the woman rules. They also represent seven kings. 10 Five kings have already fallen, the sixth now reigns, and the seventh is yet to come, but his reign will be brief.

11 "The scarlet beast that was, but is no longer, is the eighth king. He is like the other seven, and he, too, is headed for destruction. 12 The ten horns of the beast are ten kings who have not yet risen to power. They will be appointed to their kingdoms for one brief moment to reign with the beast. 13 They will all agree to give him their power and authority. 14 Together they will go to war against the Lamb, but the Lamb will defeat them because he is Lord of all lords and King of all kings. And his called and chosen and faithful ones will be with him."

15 Then the angel said to me, "The waters where the prostitute is ruling represent masses of people of every nation and language. 16 The scarlet beast and his ten horns all hate the prostitute. They will strip her naked, eat her flesh, and burn her remains with fire. 17 For God has put a plan into their minds, a plan that will carry out his purposes. They will agree to give their authority to the scarlet beast, and so the words of God will be fulfilled. 18 And this woman you saw in your vision represents the great city that rules over the kings of the world."

THE FALL OF BABYLON

18 After all this I saw another angel come down from heaven with great authority, and the earth grew bright with his splendor. 2 He gave a mighty shout:

"Babylon is fallen—that great city is fallen!
She has become a home for demons.
She is a hideout for every foul* spirit,
a hideout for every foul vulture
and every foul and dreadful animal.*
3 For all the nations have fallen*
because of the wine of her passionate
immorality.
The kings of the world
have committed adultery with her.
Because of her desires for extravagant luxury,
the merchants of the world have grown rich."

HEAVEN'S MARRIAGE FEAST

1. What is the most romantic or unusual wedding proposal you've ever heard of? What was the most interesting wedding you've attended?

REVELATION 18:1–19:10

2. Are there any cities or societies today that remind you of Babylon? How are they similar? How are they different?
3. Read the list of things bought and sold in Babylon (18:11-13). What sort of city is this? How might a city buy and sell "bodies—that is, human slaves"?
4. Who are the blessed people invited to the marriage feast of the Lamb? Are you one of the blessed?

17:8 Or *the abyss,* or *the underworld.* 18:2a Greek *unclean;* also in each of the two following phrases. 18:2b Some manuscripts condense the last two lines to read *a hideout for every foul [unclean] and dreadful vulture.* 18:3 Some manuscripts read *have drunk.*

17:3 took me. The angel then takes John to a desert. **in the Spirit.** John is in the midst of a vision (1:10; 4:2). **a scarlet beast.** The same beast as in 13:1—the antichrist. His scarlet color identifies him with his master, Satan, the fiery red dragon (12:3). It is the beast that has made the city (the prostitute) great.

17:4 purple and scarlet. The high cost of these dyes made clothing of this color expensive, so that it could only be worn by the wealthy.

17:5 on her forehead. Prostitutes in Rome wore headbands bearing the name of their owners. **Mother of All Prostitutes.** Not content simply to pursue her own adulteries, she made her daughters into prostitutes.

17:8 was once alive but isn't now . . . will soon come up. A description that mimics that of the Lamb (1:18; 2:8).

17:9 seven hills. Rome was famed as a city built on seven hills along the east bank of the Tiber River.

17:10 seven kings. The identity of these kings has been hotly debated. Some scholars take the number seven to represent (as it often does in Revelation) the fullness of imperial power so that the seven kings stand for a succession of kingdoms.

17:11 the beast that was, but is no longer. The eighth king is the Antichrist (Dan. 7:24). This is a difficult verse with complex symbolism. A best guess is that the seventh king with the short reign will reappear a second time as the eighth king (who is therefore one of the seven) and will be a particularly virulent manifestation of the beast.

17:14 go to war against the Lamb. They are even willing to fight against the Lamb. This final conflict at Armageddon is discussed in 19:11-21. **because he is Lord of lords and King of kings.** Given the nature of the Messiah's sovereign power as captured in this title, the outcome of the battle is certain (19:16; Deut. 10:17; Ps. 136:2-3; Dan. 2:47). His victory will be shared by those who have remained faithful to Him even to the point of death.

18:2 Babylon is fallen. The language used to describe the fall of this Babylon is similar to the language used to describe the fall of Babylon in the Old Testament as well as the fall of Edom and Nineveh (Isa. 34:11-15; Zeph. 2:15). This phrase (also in 14:8) echoes the words of Isaiah 21:9.

18:3 committed adultery with her. Sexual promiscuity is used in the Old Testament as a metaphor for spiritual unfaithfulness on the part of the people of Israel (Isa. 1:21; Jer. 2:20-30; 3:1; Ezek. 16:15; Hos. 2:5; 4:15). She has seduced the nations to follow the beast. What she used was the lure of riches and luxury.

4 Then I heard another voice calling from heaven,

"Come away from her, my people.
Do not take part in her sins,
or you will be punished with her.
5 For her sins are piled as high as heaven,
and God remembers her evil deeds.
6 Do to her as she has done to others.
Double her penalty* for all her evil deeds.
She brewed a cup of terror for others,
so brew twice as much* for her.
7 She glorified herself and lived in luxury,
so match it now with torment and sorrow.
She boasted in her heart,
'I am queen on my throne.
I am no helpless widow,
and I have no reason to mourn.'
8 Therefore, these plagues will overtake her in a single day—
death and mourning and famine.
She will be completely consumed by fire,
for the Lord God who judges her is mighty."

9 And the kings of the world who committed adul-
tery with her and enjoyed her great luxury will
mourn for her as they see the smoke rising from her
charred remains. 10 They will stand at a distance, ter-
rified by her great torment. They will cry out,

"How terrible, how terrible for you,
O Babylon, you great city!
In a single moment
God's judgment came on you."

11 The merchants of the world will weep and mourn
for her, for there is no one left to buy their goods. 12 She
bought great quantities of gold, silver, jewels, and pearls;
fine linen, purple, silk, and scarlet cloth; things made of
fragrant thyine wood, ivory goods, and objects made of
expensive wood; and bronze, iron, and marble. 13 She
also bought cinnamon, spice, incense, myrrh, frank-
incense, wine, olive oil, fine flour, wheat, cattle, sheep,
horses, wagons, and bodies—that is, human slaves.

14 "The fancy things you loved so much
are gone," they cry.
"All your luxuries and splendor
are gone forever,
never to be yours again."

15 The merchants who became wealthy by selling
her these things will stand at a distance, terrified by
her great torment. They will weep and cry out,

16 "How terrible, how terrible for that great city!
She was clothed in finest purple and scarlet linens,
decked out with gold and precious stones and pearls!
17 In a single moment
all the wealth of the city is gone!"

And all the captains of the merchant ships and
their passengers and sailors and crews will stand at a
distance. 18 They will cry out as they watch the smoke
ascend, and they will say, "Where is there another
city as great as this?" 19 And they will weep and throw
dust on their heads to show their grief. And they will
cry out,

"How terrible, how terrible for that great city!
The shipowners became wealthy
by transporting her great wealth on the seas.
In a single moment it is all gone."
20 Rejoice over her fate, O heaven
and people of God and apostles and prophets!
For at last God has judged her
for your sakes.

21 Then a mighty angel picked up a boulder the size
of a huge millstone. He threw it into the ocean and
shouted,

"Just like this, the great city Babylon
will be thrown down with violence
and will never be found again.
22 The sound of harps, singers, flutes,
and trumpets
will never be heard in you again.
No craftsmen and no trades
will ever be found in you again.
The sound of the mill
will never be heard in you again.
23 The light of a lamp
will never shine in you again.
The happy voices of brides and grooms
will never be heard in you again.
For your merchants were the greatest in the world,
and you deceived the nations with your sorceries.
24 In your* streets flowed the blood of the prophets
and of God's holy people
and the blood of people slaughtered all over the world."

18:6a Or *Give her an equal penalty.* **18:6b** Or *brew just as much.* **18:24** Greek *her.*

18:7 I am no helpless widow, and I have no reason to mourn. Babylon is so secure in her power and invincibility that she boasts. She denies that her armies will die on the battlefield. Others may experience loss, but she will not (Isa. 47:7-9). Her self-deception will end with her fall.

18:9-10 kings of the world. Not the 10 kings of 17:12-14, who are utterly loyal to the beast and join with him in his war against the Lamb. These represent the nations who have allowed themselves to be seduced by the prostitute of Babylon into a life of excess.

18:12-13 goods. The 29 items are divided into seven types of merchandise: precious minerals, fabrics used for expensive clothing, ornamental decorations, aromatic substances, food, animals, and slaves. Fifteen of the items in this catalog of imports are mentioned in the lament over the destruction of Tyre, another great trading nation (Ezek. 27).

18:15-17 the merchants. It is now the turn of the merchants to lament the loss of the great city in the same way as did the kings. This is the second dirge.

18:20 Rejoice over her fate. This song of praise from heaven stands in contrast to the lament that has just ended. The reason for such praise is that the judgment of God has come upon the city that persecuted His people.

18:21 mighty angel picked up a boulder. It all happens so suddenly. Babylon was there in her arrogance and power, and then she is gone like a stone dropped into the sea. This is a large stone used for grinding wheat and weighing thousands of pounds.

18:22 The sound of harps, singers, flutes, and trumpets. Babylon was known as a great patron of the arts. Flutes were used for festivals and funerals (Isa. 30:29; Matt. 9:23). Trumpets were sounded at the games and in the theater. **mill.** A small millstone used in the home to grind wheat into flour for bread in contrast to the massive commercial millstone in verse 21.

SONGS OF VICTORY IN HEAVEN

19 After this, I heard what sounded like a vast crowd in heaven shouting,

"Praise the LORD!*
Salvation and glory and power belong to our God.
2 His judgments are true and just.
He has punished the great prostitute
who corrupted the earth with her immorality.
He has avenged the murder of his servants."

3 And again their voices rang out:

"Praise the LORD!
The smoke from that city ascends forever and ever!"

4 Then the twenty-four elders and the four living
beings fell down and worshiped God, who was sitting
on the throne. They cried out, "Amen! Praise the LORD!"
5 And from the throne came a voice that said,

"Praise our God,
all his servants,
all who fear him,
from the least to the greatest."

6 Then I heard again what sounded like the shout of
a vast crowd or the roar of mighty ocean waves or the
crash of loud thunder:

"Praise the LORD!
For the Lord our God,* the Almighty, reigns.
7 Let us be glad and rejoice,
and let us give honor to him.
For the time has come for the wedding feast of the Lamb,
and his bride has prepared herself.
8 She has been given the finest of pure white linen to wear."
For the fine linen represents the good deeds of God's holy people.

9 And the angel said to me, "Write this: Blessed are
those who are invited to the wedding feast of the
Lamb." And he added, "These are true words that
come from God."
10 Then I fell down at his feet to worship him, but
he said, "No, don't worship me. I am a servant of God,
just like you and your brothers and sisters* who tes-
tify about their faith in Jesus. Worship only God. For
the essence of prophecy is to give a clear witness for
Jesus.*"

THE LAST BATTLE

1. If you could travel back in time 1,000 years, what would you do?

REVELATION 19:11–20:10

2. Who is the rider who is called "Faithful and True" (19:11)?
3. Why is the rider's robe stained with blood? Why are His followers wearing "pure white linen" (19:14)? What does this suggest about salvation and redemption?
4. There was no struggle when the angel "seized the dragon" (20:2). What does this suggest about Satan's power in heaven? What about his power on earth?
5. Which side of this final battle will you be on when the crisis comes? Choose sides now while you can.

THE RIDER ON THE WHITE HORSE

11 Then I saw heaven opened, and a white horse was
standing there. Its rider was named Faithful and
True, for he judges fairly and wages a righteous war.
12 His eyes were like flames of fire, and on his head
were many crowns. A name was written on him that
no one understood except himself. 13 He wore a robe
dipped in blood, and his title was the Word of God.
14 The armies of heaven, dressed in the finest of pure
white linen, followed him on white horses. 15 From
his mouth came a sharp sword to strike down the
nations. He will rule them with an iron rod. He will

19:1 Greek *Hallelujah;* also in 19:3, 4, 6. *Hallelujah* is the transliteration of a Hebrew term that means "Praise the LORD." **19:6** Some manuscripts read *the Lord God.* **19:10a** Greek *brothers.* **19:10b** Or *is the message confirmed by Jesus.*

19:1-5 The story of the destruction of Babylon is concluded by a shout of thanksgiving on the part of the heavenly company. The fall of Babylon and the removal of her corrupting influence is celebrated. This contrasts sharply with the preceding dirges of the kings, merchants, and seafarers who mourn their loss of income.

19:1 Praise the LORD! An exclamation of praise derived from two Hebrew words meaning, "Praise the Lord." It is used frequently in the Psalms (Ps. 106; 111–113), though never in the New Testament apart from the four occurrences in this passage (vv. 1,3-4,6).

19:6-10 John announces the marriage of the Lamb, though he does not describe it. It is announced here and assumed in later chapters (21:2-3,9-10). The metaphor used here is based on Jewish wedding customs of the first century.

19:7 his bride. Israel was regularly spoken of as the wife of Yahweh (Isa. 54:5; 62:5; Jer. 31:32; Ezek. 16:8-14; Hos. 2:19-20). Jesus spoke of Himself as the bridegroom (Mark 2:19-20), and John the Baptist used this same language to describe Jesus (John 3:29). Jesus also used the idea of the wedding feast in His parables (Matt. 22:1-14; 25:1-13). Paul picks up the idea of Israel as the bride of God and applies it to the church as the bride of Christ (Rom. 7:1-4; 1 Cor. 6:17; 2 Cor. 11:2; Eph. 5:25-27).

19:8 finest of pure white linen. This contrasts sharply to the gaudy robes of the prostitute (17:4). The wedding clothes of the bride are similar to the white robes of the martyrs washed in the blood of the Lamb (7:14).

19:9 The focus shifts to the wedding guests. In the fluid language of metaphor, the church is both bride and guests. This same fluidity is seen elsewhere in the New Testament. In Mark 2:19-20, the disciples are pictured as guests at the wedding. Likewise in the parable of the wedding banquet, the bride is not mentioned. The issue there has to do with who the guests will be. However, in Ephesians 5:25-27 the church is spoken of as the bride who is made ready for her Husband, Christ. **the wedding feast.** This is the great messianic banquet about which Jesus spoke (Matt. 8:11; 26:29).

19:13 a robe dipped in blood. Not His own blood. Here Jesus comes not as the Redeemer who dies for sins but as the Warrior who conquers evil. This parallels Isaiah 63:1-6 where the Messiah has the blood of His enemies on His garments.

19:14 The armies of heaven. May be an army of angels or an army of the redeemed as 17:14 suggests (Zech. 14:5; Mark 8:38; 1 Thess. 3:13; 2 Thess. 1:7). The army does not engage in battle. That is left to Christ (v. 21).

19:15 sword . . . iron rod . . . winepress. Three symbols in this verse, all taken from the Old Testament, describe the actions of the Warrior. First, the weapon that He uses in this battle issues from His mouth, an image that is drawn from Isaiah 11:4 (1:16; 2:12,16). His sword is His Word; the same Word that was the source of all creation (John 1:1-3; Heb. 1:2). Second, He rules with a rod of iron, an image taken from Psalm 2:9, a rod not of governing but of destruction. Third, He treads the winepress, a familiar image in Revelation (14:19), drawn originally from Isaiah 63:3.

release the fierce wrath of God, the Almighty, like juice flowing from a winepress. 16 On his robe at his thigh* was written this title: King of all kings and Lord of all lords.

17 Then I saw an angel standing in the sun, shouting to the vultures flying high in the sky: "Come! Gather together for the great banquet God has prepared. 18 Come and eat the flesh of kings, generals, and strong warriors; of horses and their riders; and of all humanity, both free and slave, small and great."

19 Then I saw the beast and the kings of the world and their armies gathered together to fight against the one sitting on the horse and his army. 20 And the beast was captured, and with him the false prophet who did mighty miracles on behalf of the beast—miracles that deceived all who had accepted the mark of the beast and who worshiped his statue. Both the beast and his false prophet were thrown alive into the fiery lake of burning sulfur. 21 Their entire army was killed by the sharp sword that came from the mouth of the one riding the white horse. And the vultures all gorged themselves on the dead bodies.

THE THOUSAND YEARS

20 Then I saw an angel coming down from heaven with the key to the bottomless pit* and a heavy chain in his hand. 2 He seized the dragon—that old serpent, who is the devil, Satan—and bound him in chains for a thousand years. 3 The angel threw him into the bottomless pit, which he then shut and locked so Satan could not deceive the nations anymore until the thousand years were finished. Afterward he must be released for a little while.

4 Then I saw thrones, and the people sitting on them had been given the authority to judge. And I saw the souls of those who had been beheaded for their testimony about Jesus and for proclaiming the word of God. They had not worshiped the beast or his statue, nor accepted his mark on their foreheads or their hands. They all came to life again, and they reigned with Christ for a thousand years.

5 This is the first resurrection. (The rest of the dead did not come back to life until the thousand years had ended.) 6 Blessed and holy are those who share in the first resurrection. For them the second death holds no power, but they will be priests of God and of Christ and will reign with him a thousand years.

LAKE OF FIRE OR ETERNAL LIFE?

1. Have you ever been scuba diving? How deep did you go? What did you see?

REVELATION 20:11–21:8

2. What is the "lake of fire" (20:14)? Who will be thrown into it? What will that be like?
3. What will life be like when "there will be no more death" (21:4)?
4. Who is heaven reserved for (21:7)? Who is hell reserved for (21:8)?
5. How can the person described in 21:8 still find eternal life?
6. What must you do to overcome and share in God's eternal inheritance (see 1 John 5:5,11-12)?

THE DEFEAT OF SATAN

7 When the thousand years come to an end, Satan will be let out of his prison. 8 He will go out to deceive the nations—called Gog and Magog—in every corner of the earth. He will gather them together for battle—a mighty army, as numberless as sand along the seashore. 9 And I saw them as they went up on the broad plain of the earth and surrounded God's people and the beloved city. But fire from heaven came down on the attacking armies and consumed them.

10 Then the devil, who had deceived them, was thrown into the fiery lake of burning sulfur, joining the beast and the false prophet. There they will be tormented day and night forever and ever.

THE FINAL JUDGMENT

11 And I saw a great white throne and the one sitting on it. The earth and sky fled from his presence, but they found no place to hide. 12 I saw the dead, both great and small, standing before God's throne. And the books were opened, including the Book of Life. And the dead were judged according to what they had done, as recorded in the books. 13 The sea gave up its dead, and death and the grave* gave up their dead. And all were judged according to their deeds. 14 Then death and the grave were thrown into the lake of fire. This lake of fire is the second death. 15 And anyone

19:16 Or *On his robe and thigh.* 20:1 Or *the abyss,* or *the underworld;* also in 20:3. 20:13 Greek *and Hades;* also in 20:14.

19:18 humanity. All who bear the mark of the beast, a number that includes all kinds of people who have not stood as a witness for God.

20:1-3 The meaning of this passage has been the subject of great debate in the church. There are three main schools of thought when it comes to the Millennium (the thousand-year reign of Christ). Postmillennialists feel that the return of Christ will not occur until the kingdom of God has been established here on earth, in history as we know it. This will be the "golden age" of the church, a long reign of peace and prosperity. It will be followed by the second coming, the resurrection of the dead, the final judgment, and the eternal kingdom. Amillennialists do not believe there will be a literal thousand-year reign of Christ. They see it as a metaphor for the history of the church between the resurrection of Christ and His second coming during which those believers who have died will reign with Christ in heaven. When Christ returns there will be a general resurrection, the final judgment, and the start of Christ's reign over the new heaven and earth. They consider the binding of Satan to be what Christ did when He died on the cross (Matt. 12:29). Premillennialists believe that the events described in verses 1-6 will literally take place. Christ will remove believers from the earth before He returns. Christ will return, the first resurrection will occur, and there will be a thousand years of peace in which Christ reigns here on earth. Then will come the final resurrection, the last judgment, and the new heaven and earth. The millennial reign is seen (by some premillennialists) as a special reward to the martyrs of chapter 6 (6:9-11).

20:6 the second death. The first death is the death of the body; the second death involves being cast into the lake of fire (v. 14; 21:8).

20:8 Gog and Magog. In Ezekiel 38–39, there is an extended prophecy about "Gog, of the land of Magog" (38:2). As in Ezekiel, the final battle follows the establishment of the messianic kingdom that Israel has looked forward to for centuries (Ezek. 36–37).

20:10 the fiery lake of burning sulfur. In the rest of the New Testament this is called Gehenna in Greek—translated "hell" in English (Matt. 5:22; Mark 9:43). The Valley of Hinnom, from which Gehenna is drawn, was a place where human sacrifice took place (2 Kings 16:3; 23:10; Jer. 7:31-32). It eventually became a kind of town dump where a fire perpetually smoldered, and thus it became a metaphor for hell.

20:13 the grave. This is not the same as Gehenna (v. 10). It is the place where departed souls go. It was thought of as an intermediate state (Luke 16:23; Acts 2:27).

whose name was not found recorded in the Book of Life was thrown into the lake of fire.

THE NEW JERUSALEM

21 Then I saw a new heaven and a new earth, for the old heaven and the old earth had disappeared. And the sea was also gone. 2 And I saw the holy city, the new Jerusalem, coming down from God out of heaven like a bride beautifully dressed for her husband.

3 I heard a loud shout from the throne, saying, "Look, God's home is now among his people! He will live with them, and they will be his people. God himself will be with them.* 4 He will wipe every tear from their eyes, and there will be no more death or sorrow or crying or pain. All these things are gone forever."

5 And the one sitting on the throne said, "Look, I am making everything new!" And then he said to me, "Write this down, for what I tell you is trustworthy and true." 6 And he also said, "It is finished! I am the Alpha and the Omega—the Beginning and the End. To all who are thirsty I will give freely from the springs of the water of life. 7 All who are victorious will inherit all these blessings, and I will be their God, and they will be my children.

8 "But cowards, unbelievers, the corrupt, murderers, the immoral, those who practice witchcraft, idol worshipers, and all liars—their fate is in the fiery lake of burning sulfur. This is the second death."

9 Then one of the seven angels who held the seven bowls containing the seven last plagues came and said to me, "Come with me! I will show you the bride, the wife of the Lamb."

10 So he took me in the Spirit* to a great, high mountain, and he showed me the holy city, Jerusalem, descending out of heaven from God. 11 It shone with the glory of God and sparkled like a precious stone—like jasper as clear as crystal. 12 The city wall was broad and high, with twelve gates guarded by twelve angels. And the names of the twelve tribes of Israel were written on the gates. 13 There were three gates on each side—east, north, south, and west. 14 The wall of the city had twelve foundation stones, and on them were written the names of the twelve apostles of the Lamb.

15 The angel who talked to me held in his hand a gold measuring stick to measure the city, its gates, and its wall. 16 When he measured it, he found it was a square, as wide as it was long. In fact, its length and width and height were each 1,400 miles.* 17 Then he measured the walls and found them to be 216 feet thick* (according to the human standard used by the angel).

18 The wall was made of jasper, and the city was pure gold, as clear as glass. 19 The wall of the city was built on foundation stones inlaid with twelve precious stones:* the first was jasper, the second sapphire, the third agate, the fourth emerald, 20 the fifth onyx, the sixth carnelian, the seventh chrysolite, the eighth beryl, the ninth topaz, the tenth chrysoprase, the eleventh jacinth, the twelfth amethyst.

21 The twelve gates were made of pearls—each gate from a single pearl! And the main street was pure gold, as clear as glass.

22 I saw no temple in the city, for the Lord God Almighty and the Lamb are its temple. 23 And the city has no need of sun or moon, for the glory of God illuminates the city, and the Lamb is its light. 24 The nations will walk in its light, and the kings of the world will enter the city in all their glory. 25 Its gates will never be closed at the end of day because there is no night there. 26 And all the nations will bring their glory and honor into the city. 27 Nothing evil* will be

HEAVENLY CITIZENSHIP

1. What is the biggest city you've been in? Would you like to live there?

REVELATION 21:9–22:6

2. What does the wealth and beauty of the city suggest?
3. What did John mean in 21:22 that he "saw no temple in the city, for the Lord God Almighty and the Lamb are its temple"? Why would there be no "temple"? How is the Lamb our temple?
4. What does it mean that in heaven "no longer will there be a curse upon anything" (22:3)?
5. What will you like most about being a citizen in the New Jerusalem?

21:3 Some manuscripts read *God himself will be with them, their God.* **21:10** Or *in spirit.* **21:16** Greek *12,000 stadia* [2,220 kilometers]. **21:17** Greek *144 cubits* [65 meters]. **21:19** The identification of some of these gemstones is uncertain. **21:27** Or *ceremonially unclean.*

21:1 the old earth had disappeared. This event occurred in 20:11, described by means of a few terse words. **the sea was also gone.** In ancient times the sea was often pictured as dark and mysterious; it was an enemy, not a friend. The lack of any seas in the new earth indicates how radically different the new will be.

21:6 the Alpha and the Omega. The first and last letters in the Greek alphabet. **the Beginning and the End.** God encompasses the whole of time. **To all who are thirsty I will give.** He satisfies the deepest needs—physical and spiritual—of humanity.

21:16 1,400 miles. It is an enormous city, beyond what any earthly city will be or could be. Each of its four sides was approximately 1,400 miles long. John struggles to convey the vastness of the city. **its length and width and height were each.** The new Jerusalem is a cube, as high as it is wide. The inner sanctuary of the temple was a perfect cube (1 Kings 6:20), a symbol of perfection.

21:17 216 feet. The walls will be over 200 feet thick. Of course, such a city will not need walls which, in ancient days, were a defense against enemies. This is God's city, and all His enemies will have been destroyed.

21:18 was made of. This city is built of materials unlike those used in any human city. **jasper.** A green, translucent crystal. This is the third time this mineral has been mentioned (vv. 11, 19; 4:3). In verse 11, jasper was said to glow with the radiance of God. The whole city would be aglow with God. The word jasper was used for various gemstones. **pure gold, as clear as glass.** Gold has long been considered very precious, and here is a city of gold! This is unlike ordinary gold, however, since it is transparent.

21:19 sapphire. A deep blue, transparent gem. **agate.** Green silicate of copper found near Chalcedon in Asia Minor. **emerald.** A green gemstone.

21:20 onyx. An agate made up of layers of a red mineral by the name of sard, and white onyx. **carnelian.** Blood red. **chrysolite.** Yellow topaz or golden jasper. **beryl.** A sea-green mineral. **topaz.** A greenish-gold or yellow mineral. **chrysoprase.** A type of quartz that was apple-green. **jacinth.** A bluish-purple mineral. **amethyst.** Another variety of quartz; it was purple and transparent.

21:21 twelve gates. The gates of ancient cities were an important part of their defense. They were built into the wall, often with a tower as part of their construction. **made of pearls.** Pearls were of great value in the ancient world (Matt. 13:45-46; 1 Tim. 2:9). The pearls from which these gates will be built will have to be enormous; again, quite beyond anything on this earth.

allowed to enter, nor anyone who practices shame-
ful idolatry and dishonesty—but only those whose
names are written in the Lamb's Book of Life.

22 Then the angel showed me a river with the
water of life, clear as crystal, flowing from the
throne of God and of the Lamb. 2 It flowed down the
center of the main street. On each side of the river
grew a tree of life, bearing twelve crops of fruit,* with
a fresh crop each month. The leaves were used for
medicine to heal the nations.
3 No longer will there be a curse upon anything. For
the throne of God and of the Lamb will be there, and
his servants will worship him. 4 And they will see his
face, and his name will be written on their foreheads.
5 And there will be no night there—no need for lamps
or sun—for the Lord God will shine on them. And
they will reign forever and ever.
6 Then the angel said to me, "Everything you have
heard and seen is trustworthy and true. The Lord God,
who inspires his prophets,* has sent his angel to tell
his servants what will happen soon.*"

JESUS IS COMING

7 "Look, I am coming soon! Blessed are those who
obey the words of prophecy written in this book.*"

8 I, John, am the one who heard and saw all these
things. And when I heard and saw them, I fell down
to worship at the feet of the angel who showed them
to me. 9 But he said, "No, don't worship me. I am a
servant of God, just like you and your brothers the
prophets, as well as all who obey what is written in
this book. Worship only God!"
10 Then he instructed me, "Do not seal up the pro-
phetic words in this book, for the time is near. 11 Let the
one who is doing harm continue to do harm; let the
one who is vile continue to be vile; let the one who is
righteous continue to live righteously; let the one who
is holy continue to be holy."

12 "Look, I am coming soon, bringing my reward
with me to repay all people according to their
deeds. 13 I am the Alpha and the Omega, the First
and the Last, the Beginning and the End."

14 Blessed are those who wash their robes. They
will be permitted to enter through the gates of the
city and eat the fruit from the tree of life. 15 Outside the

COME!

1. When you see Jesus face-to-face, what is the one question you'd most like to ask Him?

REVELATION 22:7-21

2. Regarding Jesus' claims in verses 12-17, how is the final state of humanity determined: By some arbitrary reward system fixed from eternity? By what we have done in this present life? By our response to his universal and undeserved invitation to simply "come"?
3. Is it ever too late for people to change their ways and come to Christ? Why?
4. How have you prepared yourself for Christ's second coming? In what way has this study of Revelation helped to prepare you?

city are the dogs—the sorcerers, the sexually immor-
al, the murderers, the idol worshipers, and all who
love to live a lie.

16 "I, Jesus, have sent my angel to give you this
message for the churches. I am both the source of
David and the heir to his throne.* I am the bright
morning star."

17 The Spirit and the bride say, "Come." Let any-
one who hears this say, "Come." Let anyone who is
thirsty come. Let anyone who desires drink freely
from the water of life. 18 And I solemnly declare to
everyone who hears the words of prophecy writ-
ten in this book: If anyone adds anything to what
is written here, God will add to that person the
plagues described in this book. 19 And if anyone re-
moves any of the words from this book of prophecy,
God will remove that person's share in the tree of
life and in the holy city that are described in this
book.
20 He who is the faithful witness to all these things
says, "Yes, I am coming soon!"
Amen! Come, Lord Jesus!
21 May the grace of the Lord Jesus be with God's
holy people.*

22:2 Or *twelve kinds of fruit.* 22:6a Or *The Lord, the God of the spirits of the prophets.* 22:6b Or *suddenly*, or *quickly;* also in 22:7, 12, 20. 22:7 Or *scroll*; also in 22:9, 10, 18, 19. 22:16 Greek *I am the root and offspring of David.* 22:21 Other manuscripts read *be with all;* still others read *be with all of God's holy people.* Some manuscripts add *Amen.*

22:2 a tree of life. The great story ends where it began, with the tree of life. In Genesis the tree of life in the garden of Eden was lost to humanity by reason of sin (Gen. 2:9; 3:22). In Revelation it is restored.

22:7 Look! I am coming soon! Jesus affirms what He said at the beginning of the book (2:16; 3:11). In light of this fact, His people must always be alert, always prepared for His return. **Blessed.** This is the sixth of seven beatitudes. **obey the words of prophecy.** The important thing for believers is to realize that the aim of the book is not so much to inform the church about the details of the last days as it is to call the church to faithful living in the midst of the struggle it faces with evil in whatever historical context it finds itself.

22:14 wash their robes. An allusion to 3:4 and 7:14. Those who are blessed are those who, by faith, have benefited from the redeeming death of Jesus. **eat the fruit from the tree of life.** Those who are thus clad in the righteousness of Jesus have access to the very life of God (vv. 1-5). **enter through the gates of the city.** Furthermore, they have access to the city of God, the new Jerusalem where they will live eternally.

22:16 the source of David and the heir to his throne. He is the messianic King from the line of David (5:5; Matt. 1:1; 9:27; 15:22; 21:9; Rom. 1:3). The image of a shoot that grows out of the stump of David is taken from Isaiah 11:1. **the bright morning star.** See Numbers 24:17, which is understood to be a prophecy about the Messiah.

22:18-19 plagues . . . will remove that person's share. A warning is affixed to the book. No one is to tamper with its contents, either to add to or take away from it (Deut. 4:2). This would be a real temptation with a book like this, whose message is mysterious, harsh at times, and often hard to understand. The temptation would be to leave out or explain away the parts that do not conform to one's views.

22:20 Yes, I am coming soon! For the third time in this epilogue, the reader is reminded that Jesus is coming soon. **Amen! Come, Lord Jesus!** John's response to this declaration is enthusiastic: "So be it; let it happen; please come Lord Jesus."

SUBJECT INDEX

SUBJECT INDEX

Page numbers in **bold** are Old Testament, in ***bold italics*** are New Testament. For example: **12** Gen. 16:7-11; **18** Gen. 22:11,16; ***243*** 1 Cor. 16:24; ***269*** Gal. 6:18

A

B

T

PEOPLE AND PLACES

A

AARON—Levite, brother of Moses (Exod. 4:14; 6:16-20). Spokesman for Moses (4:14-16; 7:1-2). Consecrated (Exod. 29) and ordained (Lev. 8) as priest (Exod. 28:1; 1 Chron. 6:49; Heb. 5:1-4; 7). Made golden calf (Exod. 32). Died outside the promised land (Num. 20:1-12,22-29; 33:38-39).

ABADDON—The Hb name of the angel of the bottomless pit whose Gk name was Apollyon.

Your faithfulness in **A**? . Ps. 88:11
Sheol and **A** lie open . . Prov. 15:11
his name in Hebrew is **A**, Rev. 9:11

ABEL—Shepherd, second son of Adam; brought acceptable sacrifice; was murdered (Gen. 4:2-8; Matt. 23:35; Heb. 11:4).

ABRAHAM—Born Abram son of Terah in Ur, Mesopotamia, then lived in Haran (Gen. 11:31; Acts 7:2-4). Called to Canaan and given a promise of progeny and prosperity (Gen. 12:1-3). God declared him righteous because of his faith (15:6; Rom. 4:3,20-22; Gal. 3:6; Jas. 2:23). Fathered Ishmael by Hagar (Gen. 16). Promised a son with Sarah (18:9-14; cp. 17:15-19; 21:1-7). Tested by God concerning Isaac (Gen. 22; Heb. 11:17-19; Jas. 2:21-24). John and Paul showed that salvation does not come from descent from Abraham, but from emulating his faith (Matt. 3:9; Rom. 4; 9; Gal. 3). Also see Subject Index.

ADAM AND EVE—First man and woman; created by God (Gen. 1:26-2:25). Their failure in the Garden of Eden resulted in the fall (Gen. 3). The corruption that permeates our world and our lives is the direct result of Adam's decision to disobey God (Rom. 5:14; 1 Cor. 15:22).

AHAB—The seventh king of Israel, he married a foreigner, Jezebel, and incited God's anger more than any of Israel's previous kings by serving other gods (1 Kings 20:13-14, 22, 28; 22:8, 16; Mic. 6:16).

AMOS—Prophet from Judah who ministered in Israel about 750 B.C. (Amos 7:14-15). He opposed the moral and religious evils of his day (5:24).

ANANIAS—**1**. Husband of Sapphira (Acts 5:1-6). They sold property, lied to the Holy Spirit about the amount they were contributing, and were both struck dead (5:5, 10). **2**. Disciple who lived in Damascus (9:10-19; 22:12). He laid his hands on Paul, and he received the Holy Spirit. **3**. Jewish high priest and president of the Sanhedrin that tried Paul in Jerusalem (Acts 23).

ANDREW—A fisherman and one of Jesus' first apostles, he led his brother Simon to Jesus (John 1:40-41; 6:8-9; 12:12; Acts 1:13).

APOLLOS—Jewish Christian who used the Scriptures to demonstrate that Jesus was the Christ (Acts 18:28; cp. 1 Cor. 1:12; 3:4-6, 22; 4:6; 16:12; Titus 3:13).

AQUILA AND PRISCILLA—Married couple of Corinth who assisted Paul in his ministry (Acts 18; Rom. 16:3; 1 Cor. 16:19; 2 Tim. 4:19).

ARABAH—Desert region with a hot climate and sparse rainfall.

ARMAGEDON—Site of future final battle between forces of good and evil (Rev. 16:16).

ASHERAH—Phoenician and Canaanite fertility goddess represented by a wooden pole.

ASHTAROTH, ASHTORETHS—A Canaanite goddess of fertility, love, and war (1 Sam. 31:10).

ASSYRIA—Nation in northern Mesopotamia north of Babylonia along the banks of the upper Tigris River (Gen. 10:11; Isa. 10:5; Jer. 50:18). Nineveh became its capital. The Assyrians conquered Samaria in 721 B.C. (2 Kings 18:11).

B

BAAL—Canaanite false god of thunderstorms and fertility (Num. 25:3; 1 Kings 18:19; 19:18; Jer. 2:8).

BABEL—A tower and city intended to be a monument of human pride, where people sought to "make a name" for themselves (Gen. 11:4-9); it is also the Hb word for Babylon.

BABYLON—City-state in southern Mesopotamia on the Euphrates River. One of the largest and most magnificent cities that ever existed. Babylon became symbolic of man's decadence and God's judgment. "Babylon" in Rev. 14:8; 16:19; 17:5; 18:2 and probably in 1 Pet. 5:13 refers to Rome, the city which personified this idea for early Christians. Also see Subject Index.

from a distant country,
from **B**. . . . . .2 Kings 20:14
serve the king of **B** for
70 years. . . . . .Jer. 25:11
It has fallen, **B** the Great Rev. 14:8

BALAAM—Non-Israelite prophet whom Balak, king of Moab, hired to curse the invading Israelites (Num. 22:1-21; 2 Pet. 2:16). God made him bless Israel instead (Num. 23–24; Neh. 13:2). He was condemned for promoting Baal worship (2 Pet. 2:15-16; Jude 11; Rev. 2:14).

BARABBAS—A murderer and insurrectionist. When Pilate offered to release Jesus or Barabbas, the crowd demanded Barabbas (Mark 15:6-15).

BARNABAS—Co-worker with Paul on his first missionary journey (Acts 13–15; see also 4:36; 9:26-27; 11:19-30; 1 Cor. 9:6; Gal. 2:1,9,13; Col. 4:10).

BARTHOLOMEW—One of the 12 apostles (Mark 3:18).

BATHSHEBA—Wife of Uriah the Hittite (2 Sam. 11). David had an adulterous relationship with her then arranged for the death of Uriah so he could take her as his wife. She was the mother of Solomon (1 Kings 1:11–2:19).

BEELZEBUL—Name for Satan based on Hb Baal-zebub, "lord of the flies."

if I drive out demons by
B, ... Matt. 12:27

BENJAMIN—The last son of Jacob, second by Rachel (Gen. 35:17-18,24). The tribe occupied the smallest territory (Josh. 18:11-20; 1 Sam. 9:21; see also Josh. 20–21; 1 Sam. 9:1; Rom. 11:1; Phil. 3:5).

BETHANY— Home of Jesus' friends Mary, Martha, and Lazarus (Matt. 21:17; Mark 11:11-12).

BETHEL—City in Ephraim where Abraham built an altar (Gen. 12:8; 13:3), Jacob spent the night (28:10-22; 35:1-16; Hos. 12:4-5), and Jeroboam I erected a golden calf (1 Kings 12:29-33).

BETHLEHEM—Hometown of David (1 Sam. 16:1-13; 17:12, 15) and birthplace of Jesus the Messiah (Mic. 5:2; Matt. 2:1; Luke 2:4; John 7:42; see also Gen. 35:19; Ruth 1:22).

C

CAESAR—Family name of Julius Caesar assumed as a title by the emperors who followed him.

CAIAPHAS—High Priest at the time of the trial and crucifixion of Jesus (Matt. 26:3, 57; Luke 3:2; John 11:49-52; Acts 4:6).

CAIN— Firstborn son of Adam and Eve. He murdered Abel (Gen. 4; Heb. 11:4; 1 John 3:12; Jude 11).

CALEB—The spy representing Judah sent by Moses to scout out the territory of Canaan (Num. 13:6). He brought back a positive report (13:30; Deut. 1:36; Josh. 14:13).

CANAAN—The promised land, from the Mediterranean Sea to the Jordan River and from the Brook of Egypt to Syria or to the Euphrates. Named for a son of Ham (Gen. 9:18-27; 10:15-19).

CAPERNAUM—City on the northwest shore of the Sea of Galilee where Jesus began His ministry.

CHALDEANS—People who lived on the lower Tigris and Euphrates Rivers, central and southeastern Mesopotamia (Gen. 11:31; 2 Kings 25:10; Ezra 5:12).

CHRIST—The "anointed one," the Messiah, who is Jesus of Nazareth, the Son of God.

The birth of Jesus **C** came about..................Matt. 1:18
I know that Messiah is coming (who is called **C**) ..... John 4:25
God and Savior, Jesus **C**. Titus 2:13

CORINTH—A city in Greece (Acts 18:1; 19:1; 1 Cor. 1:2; 2 Cor. 1:1, 23; 2 Tim. 4:20).

CORNELIUS—Centurion in the Roman army who lived at Caesarea (Acts 10).

CYRUS—King of the Persians and Medes who permitted the Jews to return and rebuild the temple and city of Jerusalem (2 Chron. 36:22-23; Ezra 1:1-4; cp. Isa. 44:28-45:6; Dan. 6:28).

D

DANIEL—A young man of nobility taken captive by the king of Babylon and elevated to high rank (Dan. 1). In addition to wisdom, he was gifted in dream interpretation (2:25-45; 4:19; cp. 5:25). Throughout his entire life he demonstrated an unshakable faith in his God (1:8; 6). Also see Subject Index.

DAVID—Shepherd, musician, poet, warrior, and loyal subject of King Saul, David became Israel's second king. He received the promise of a royal Messiah in his line (2 Sam. 7:11-16). Though he was not perfect (2 Sam. 11), he was a man who pursued God's heart (1 Sam. 13:14; Acts 13:22). Also see Subject Index.

DEAD SEA—Inland lake at the end of the Jordan Valley with no outlet. The surface is 1,292 feet below sea level.

DEBORAH—A prophetess and judge who delivered Israel (Judg. 4–5).

DEVIL—A personal being in direct opposition to God, His purposes, and His people. Also see Subject Index.

don't give the **D** an opportunity ....Eph. 4:27
against the tactics of the **D**....................Eph. 6:11
But resist the **D**, and he will.......................Jas. 4:7
adversary the **D** is prowling ....1 Pet. 5:8

E

EARTH—The planet created by God for mankind.

In the beginning God created the heavens and the **E**. .... Gen. 1:1
may know the **E** is the Lord's................Exod. 9:29
The **E** and everything in it, ... Ps. 24:1
they will inherit the **E**... Matt. 5:5
new heavens and a new **E**,................2 Pet. 3:13

EDEN—Garden of God, the idyllic place of creation (Gen. 2:8-15; 3:22-24; Isa. 51:3; Ezek. 28:13). Located somewhere near the source of the Tigris and Euphrates rivers.

EDOM—Another name for Esau, his descendants, and the land they lived in south of the Dead Sea (Gen. 25:30; 32:3).

EGYPT—Land in northeastern Africa, an important cultural and political influence on ancient Israel (Gen. 12:10; 37:36; 46:6).

Israelites lived in **E** ... 430 years. ....Exod. 12:40
and out of **E** I called My son. .Hos. 11:1;Matt. 2:15

ELIJAH—A prophet of Israel who condemned baalism (1 Kings 18), confronted kings prophetically, and passed his mantle to Elisha (19:19) before he ascended to heaven in a whirlwind (2 Kings 2:11). He was a forerunner to the Messiah, embodied in John the Baptist (Mal. 4:5; Matt. 11:14; 17:10-13; Luke 1:17). He appeared with Jesus (Matt. 17:3-4).

ELISHA—An Israelite prophet, he completed the assignment God had given Elijah (1 Kings 19:11-16; 2 Kings 8:7-15; 9:1-13). Elisha performed many miracles during his life (2:14, 19-24; 3:13-22; 4–7) and one even after his death (13:21).

ELIZABETH—Descendant of Aaron and wife of Zacharias the priest (Luke 1:5) and mother of John the Baptist.

EMMAUS—A village about seven miles from Jerusalem (Luke 24:13).

ENOCH—Methuselah's father, taken up to God without dying (Gen. 5:24; Heb. 11:5; Jude 14).

EPHESUS—One of the largest and most impressive cities in the ancient world, a political, religious, and commercial center in Asia Minor. Associated with the ministries of Paul, Timothy, and the Apostle John, the city played a significant role in the spread of early Christianity (Acts 18:19; 19:1; 1 Cor. 16:8; Eph. 1:1). One of the seven churches in Revelation (Rev. 1:11; 2:1).

EPHRAIM—A son of Joseph (Gen. 41:52) and the tribe and territory named for him (Gen. 48; Josh. 14:4; 16:4-5). Used as another name for the northern kingdom of Israel (Isa. 11:13; Jer. 7:15; Ezek. 37:16; Hos. 5:13).

ESAU—Son of Isaac and Rebekah; elder twin brother of Jacob; father of the Edomites. Sold his birthright (Gen. 25:30-34; Heb. 12:16) and was tricked out of his blessing (Gen. 27; Heb. 11:20).

ESTHER—Mordecai's niece who became queen of Persia and was used by God to protect His people from genocide.

EUPHRATES AND TIGRIS RIVERS—Two great rivers of Western Asia (Gen. 2:14; 15:18; Exod. 23:31; Mic. 7:12; Zech. 9:10; Rev. 9:14; 16:12). They originate in the mountains of Armenia and unite about 90 miles from the Persian Gulf.

EVE—See Adam and Eve.

EZEKIEL—Prophet who ministered to Judean exiles in Babylon. He related striking visions (Ezek. 1; 8–11; 37:1-14; 40–48), crafted powerful word pictures (17:1-24; 19:1-14; 27:1-9), and performed symbolic acts (4–5; 12:1-20; 37:15-28).

EZRA—Priest and scribe who was sent with a large company of Israelites to Jerusalem by King Artaxerxes of Persia in 458 B.C. (Ezra 7:1; Neh. 8:1; 12:1). His mission was "to study the law of the Lord, obey it, and teach its statutes and ordinances in Israel" (Ezra 7:10).

G

GABRIEL—Angel sent to Daniel (Dan. 8:15-27; 9:20-27), Zechariah (Luke 1:8-20), and Mary (1:26-38).

GALILEE—1. Northern part of Palestine. Jesus devoted most of His earthly ministry to Galilee, being known as the Galilean (Matt. 26:69). 2. A freshwater sea along the Jordan River area (Matt. 4:18; 15:29).

GENTILES—People who are not part of God's chosen family by birth.
a light for revelation to the **G** .... Luke 2:32
full number of the **G**. Rom. 11:25

GIDEON—After God gave him a sign, he delivered the Israelites from the Midianites and Amalekites and judged for 40 years (Judg. 6:11–8:35; Heb. 11:32).

GOD—Personal Creator and Lord of the universe. When not capitalized or when plural, it refers to other so-called gods. Also see Subject Index.
In the beginning **G** Ωcreated the .... Gen. 1:1
Do not have other **G-S** . Exod. 20:3
G is not a man who lies, or a .... Num. 23:19
G is a consuming fire, ... Deut. 4:24
they had worshiped other **G-S**.......... 2 Kings 17:7
I will be their **G**, and they will .... Jer. 31:33
was with **G**, and the Word was **G**. .... John 1:1
For **G** loved the world in this way:.......... John 3:16
G is spirit, and those who worship .... John 4:24
I said, you are **G-S**?.... John 10:34
We must obey **G** rather than men .... Acts 5:29
If **G** is for us, who is against............... Rom. 8:31
not know **G**, because **G** is love............. 1 John 4:8

GOLIATH—The huge Philistine champion who baited the Israelite army and was slain by David (1 Sam. 17).

H

HABAKKUK—Preexilic prophet who asked God for justice and praised His sovereignty.

HADES—A place of torment for wicked souls.
forces of **H** will not overpower it....... Matt. 16:18
I hold the keys of death and **H**.................. Rev. 1:18

HAGAR—Sarah's personal servant, given as a concubine to Abraham and became the mother of Ishmael (Gen. 16:1-16; 25:12; Gal. 4:24-25).

HAGGAI—Postexilic prophet who roused the people of Judah to finish rebuilding the Temple (Ezra 5:1; 6:14; Hag. 1–2).

HAM—Youngest of Noah's three sons (Gen. 5:32). He discovered his father naked and reported it to Shem and Japheth, so Noah cursed Ham's son Canaan (9:20-29).

HEAVEN—See Subject Index.

HEBREW—A designation for Israelites (Gen. 14:13; Jonah 1:9; Phil. 3:5) and the language they spoke and wrote (2 Kings 18:26; John 19:20).

HELL—See Subject Index.

HEROD—Name given to the family ruling Palestine around the time of Christ: Herod the Great (Matt. 2:1-19), Archelaus (2:22), Antipas (14:1-12), Philip (14:3), Agrippa I (Acts 12:20-23) and II (25:13).

HERODIAS—Wife of Herod Antipas; called for the head of John the Baptist (Matt. 14:3-11).

HEZEKIAH—King of Judah who promoted religious reforms, reopened the temple, and removed the idols from it. He fortified the city of Jerusalem and constructed a tunnel from the spring of Gihon to the Siloam pool (2 Kings 18–20; Matt. 1:9-10).

HOLY SPIRIT—Third person of the Trinity through whom God acts, reveals His will, empowers individuals, and discloses His personal presence in the OT and NT. Also see Subject Index.
or take Your **H** from me. .... Ps. 51:11
they were all filled with the **H** .... Acts 2:4
your body is a sanctuary of the **H** .... 1 Cor. 6:19
were sealed with the promised **H**. ....Eph. 1:13
don't grieve God's **H**, ...Eph. 4:30
moved by the **H**, men spoke 2 Pet. 1:21

HOSEA—Prophet who illustrated God's unfailing love for unfaithful Israel and called for repentance.

I

ISAAC—Only son of Abraham by Sarah, he was the child of a promise from God, born when Abraham and Sarah were very old (Gen. 17:17; 21:5). God tested Abraham's faith by commanding him to sacrifice Isaac (22:1-19). Isaac married Rebekah (Gen. 24), who bore him twin sons, Esau and Jacob (25:21-28).

ISAIAH—Prophet who predicted the exile of Judah because of their rebellion against God. He also predicted the Messiah as a branch (Isa. 11:1), a kingly figure (9:6-7), and a suffering servant (50:6; 53:3-6). Jesus fulfilled all of these.

ISHMAEL—Son of Abraham by the Egyptian concubine Hagar (Gen. 16:11).

ISRAEL—Name that God gave Jacob after he wrestled with the divine messenger (Gen. 32:28). It was also the name of the nation made up of his descendants—chosen by God and delivered from slavery in Egypt—as well as the land they occupied. Later it was the name of the northern kingdom when they separated from Judah (1 Kings 12). Also see Subject Index.

Lord saved I from the power of the Egyptians ..... Exod. 14:30
go to the lost sheep of the house of I.................... Matt. 10:6
not all who are descended from I are I. .... Rom. 9:6

J

JABEZ—Israelite who asked God for a blessing and received it (4:9-10).

JACOB—The son of Isaac and Rebekah, he cheated his older twin Esau out of the rights of the first-born. At Peniel he wrestled with a stranger who gave him the name Israel, "he struggles with God." As father of the 12 ancestors of the 12 tribes of Israel, he was the progenitor of the nation (Gen. 25:26–Exod. 1:5).

JAMES—**1.** An apostle, the son of Zebedee and brother of John the apostle (Matt. 4:21; 10:2). **2.** An apostle, Alphaeus's son (Matt. 10:3; Acts 1:13). **3.** The half brother of Jesus. He assumed the leadership of the Jerusalem church (15:13) and is probably the author of the book of James.

JAPHETH—One of Noah's three sons(Gen. 5:32).

JEREMIAH—Hilkiah's son, called to be a prophet in Judah (Jer. 1:2). He constantly proclaimed God's judgment upon Judah and Jerusalem, recommended surrender to Babylon, and called Nebuchadnezzar the "servant of the Lord" (25:9; 27:6). Yet he wrote aggressive oracles against Babylon (50–51).

JERICHO The first city Israel conquered in Canaan west of the Jordan (Josh. 6).

JEROBOAM—First king of the northern kingdom Israel. Jeroboam previously had managed the laborers for Solomon (1 Kings 11:28). He became the example of evil kings in Israel because he set up idols in Dan and Bethel (12:25-33).

JERUSALEM—A city set high on a plateau in the hills of Judah, Yahweh's chosen center of His divine kingship and of the human kingship of David and his sons. It was originally named Jebus and was also called "the City of David" and "Zion." Also see Subject Index.

J, the city I chose for Myself ....1 Kings 11:36
Pray for the peace of J:.. Ps. 122:6
you will be My witnesses in J, in all .... Acts 1:8
the Holy City, new J, coming down .... Rev. 21:2

JESSE—Father of David (Ruth 4:17-22; 1 Sam. 16:1; Acts 13:22).

JESUS—The Son of God, the Messiah, the Savior; the only way to God (John 14:6; Acts 4:12). Also see Subject Index.

you are to name Him J, because .... Matt. 1:21
confess with your mouth, "J is Lord," .... Rom. 10:9
name of J every knee should bow .... Phil. 2:10

JEW—Judahite, a person from the southern kingdom; Judean.

has been born King of the J-S? .... Matt. 2:2
salvation is from the J-S. .... John 4:22
There is no J or Greek, slave or .... Gal. 3:28

JEZEBEL—Wife of King Ahab of Israel, she brought the worship of Baal from Sidon (1 Kings 16:31) and tried to destroy all God's prophets in Israel (18:4).

JOB—A wealthy nomad (Job 1:3; 42:12) who was an example of patient and persistent faith in the face of hardships (Jas. 5:11). God allowed him to lose his possessions, his children, and his health, yet he did not turn away from God.

JOHN—**1.** John the Baptist was a prophet who preached a message of repentance, announced the coming of the Messiah, baptized Jesus, and was beheaded by Herod Antipas (Matt. 3; 14). **2.** The apostle, brother of James, and leader in the early church (Gal. 2:9). He wrote a Gospel, three letters, and Revelation. Also see Subject Index.

JOHN MARK—See Mark, John.

JONAH—A prophet, a reluctant messenger of God to Nineveh. Jesus said Jonah's three days in the belly of the fish was a sign concerning Jesus' death and resurrection (Matt. 12:39-41; 16:4; Luke 11:29-30, 32).

JONATHAN—Eldest son of King Saul, friend of David (1 Sam. 18–20). When he was killed by the Philistines, David mourned (2 Sam. 1:17-27).

JOPPA—City on the coast northwest of Jerusalem.

JORDAN—The longest and most important river of Palestine, it flows south through the Sea of Galilee to the Dead Sea.

dry ground in the middle of the J .... Josh. 3:17
Jesus came ... to John at the J .... Matt. 3:13

JOSEPH—**1.** Son of Jacob by his favorite wife, Rachel, he became Jacob's favorite son. This and the dreams that showed his rule over his family inspired the envy of his brothers, who sold him into slavery (Gen. 37). In Egypt he eventually became second in command to the pharaoh (41:39-45). Later, Jacob moved the rest of his family to Egypt (46:1–47:12). **2.** Husband of Mary, mother of Jesus (Luke 2:8-33). **3.** Joseph of Arimathea, a rich member of the Sanhedrin and a disciple of Jesus, he requested Jesus' body from Pilate and laid it in his own unused tomb (Matt. 27:57-60; John 19:38-42).

JOSHUA—Moses' successor. He was on Matt.. Sinai when Moses received the Law (Exod. 32:17). He was the spy representing Ephraim sent to investigate Canaan (Num. 13:8, 16). He and Caleb returned with a positive, minority report; of all the adults alive at that time, only the two of them were allowed to enter Canaan (14:28-30, 38). He led the Israelites to conquer the promised land (Josh. 1–12) and to divide it among the tribes (Josh. 13–22).

JOSIAH—Judah's king who led the people to renew their loyalty to the Lord (2 Kings 21:19–23:30).

JUDAH—**1.** Fourth son of Jacob (Gen. 29:35) and ancestor of David and Jesus (49:10; 1 Sam. 17:12; Matt. 1:3,6,16; Rev. 5:5). **2.** A tribe of Israel.

3. When the kingdom was divided, the southern kingdom, including Judah and Benjamin, was called Judah.

JUDAS—**1.** Half brother of Jesus (Matt. 13:55; Mark 6:3), also called Jude (Jude 1). **2.** An apostle, also called Lebbaeus or Thaddaeus (Matt. 10:3; Mark 3:18; John 14:22). **3.** Judas Iscariot, who betrayed Jesus (Matt. 26:21-25, 44-50; Luke 22:3-6; John 13:21-30). He acted as treasurer for the disciples but was known as a miser and a thief (12:4-6). Also see Subject Index.

JUDEA—Judah, from the area around Jerusalem and south to the Negev, was called Judea after the exile (Ezra 5:8).

Jesus was born in Bethlehem of **J** .... Matt. 2:1
in Jerusalem, in all **J** and Samaria, ... Acts 1:8

L

LAZARUS—**1.** One of the principal characters in a parable Jesus told to warn the selfish rich that justice will eventually prevail (Luke 16:19-31). **2.** A personal friend of Jesus and the brother of Mary and Martha (John 11:1-3). Jesus raised him from the dead (11:38-44).

LEAH—Older daughter of Laban (Gen. 29:16); Jacob's first wife. She bore six sons (Reuben, Simeon, Levi, Judah, Issachar, Zebulun) (29:31-35; 35:23) and a daughter (Dinah).

LEVI—**1.** Son of Jacob and Leah (Gen. 29:34), ancestor of priestly tribe (Exod. 32:25-29; Num. 3:11-13; Deut. 10:6-9). **2.** Apostle, called Matthew (Mark 2:14; Luke 5:27-29; cp. Matt. 9:9).

LEVITES—Descendants of Levi, and assistants to the priests in Israel's sacrificial system (Num. 3:11-13; 2 Chron. 17:7-9; 29:12-21; Neh. 8:9-12). They did not receive a land allotment; God was their inheritance (Num. 18:20).

LOT—Nephew of Abraham (Gen. 11:27) who accompanied him to Canaan (12:5). Lot chose to live in the Jordan Valley in the city of Sodom (13:8-12).

LUKE—Author of the Third Gospel and the Acts of the Apostles in the NT; Paul's traveling companion (Col. 4:14; 2 Tim. 4:11; Philem. 24).

M

MACEDONIA—A mountainous country north of Greece to which Paul was beckoned in a vision (Acts 16:9-10) and where he founded the first Christian community in Europe (19:21-22; 20:1,3; Rom. 15:26; 2 Cor. 1:16; 8:1; 11:9; Phil. 4:15; 1 Thess. 1:7-8; 4:10).

MALACHI—Author of the last book of the OT, he calls the people to turn from their spiritual apathy, honor the Lord with tithes and offerings, and be faithful to covenants, especially marriage.

MANASSEH—**1.** A son of Joseph (Gen. 41:50-51). Along with his brother Ephraim, he became one of the 12 tribes of Israel. **2.** King of Judah who led the people to worship false gods (2 Kings 21; 24:3).

MARK, JOHN—Author of the Second Gospel. He was a cousin of Barnabas (Col. 4:10) and a companion of Barnabas and Paul on their first missionary journey (Acts 12:12,25). On the second journey, Paul refused to take Mark since he had left them on the first (15:37, 39). Later, however, Mark was with Paul (Col. 4:10; Philem. 24).

MARTHA—Sister of Mary and Lazarus, she was concerned with being a hostess (Luke 10:38-42; John 11).

MARY—**1.** Mother of Jesus (Matt. 2; Luke 1–2; Acts 1:14). **2.** Magdalene, from whom seven demons were driven (Luke 8:2). She was a key witness to Jesus' death (Matt. 27:56), burial (Mark 15:47), the empty tomb (Luke 24:1-10), and was the first to encounter the risen Christ (John 20:1-18). **3.** Sister of Martha and Lazarus, she anointed the feet of Jesus with perfume (John 12:1-8). **4.** Mother of James the Younger and Joses (Mark 15:40–16:1). **5.** Wife of Clopas (John 19:25). **6.** Mother of Mark (Acts 12). **7.** A believer greeted by Paul (Rom. 16:6). Also see Subject Index.

MATTHEW—A tax collector who became an apostle of Jesus (Matt. 9:9; 10:3). Also called Levi (Luke 5:27).

MELCHIZEDEK—Priest and king of Salem who blessed Abraham in the name of "God Most High" (Gen. 14:18-20), he symbolized the undying priesthood fulfilled by Jesus (Ps. 110:4; Heb. 5–7).

MESOPOTAMIA—The area between the Tigris and Euphrates rivers (Acts 2:9; 7:2).

MESSIAH—The anointed one, Christ. This title carried overtones of political power. Only after the resurrection did the disciples see how Jesus was truly a royal Messiah (Luke 24:45-46).

until **M** the Prince will be seven .... Dan. 9:25
You are the **M**, the Son of the................. Matt. 16:16
proving that this One is the **M**.................. Acts 9:22
who denies that Jesus is the **M**?............... 1 John 2:22

METHUSELAH—Noah's grandfather who died at the age of 969 (Gen. 5:25-29).

MICHAEL—Archangel who served as the guardian of the nation of Israel (Dan. 12:1; Jude 9; Rev. 12:7).

MIRIAM—Sister of Moses and Aaron (Num. 20:1; 26:59). After crossing the Red Sea, she led the women in singing a song of victory (Exod. 15:20-21). When she rebelled against Moses, God struck her with leprosy but healed her after Moses' intercession (Num. 12:1, 4-5, 10, 15; Deut. 24:8-9).

MOSES—Son of Amram and Jochabed, and brother of Miriam and Aaron; leader of the Israelites in their exodus from Egyptian slavery and in their journey toward the promised land. He was the author of the Pentateuch and Ps. 90. Also see Subject Index.

N

NAAMAN—Syrian general cured of leprosy under the direction of the prophet Elisha (2 Kings 5).

NAOMI—Mother-in-law to Orpah and Ruth (Ruth 1–4). Her matchmaking between Ruth and Boaz was successful, and she became a forebear of David (4:21-22).

NAPHTALI—Sixth son of Jacob and second son by Rachel's slave Bilhah (Gen. 30:7-8).

NATHAN—Prophet in David's court, he confronted David about Uriah and Bathsheba (2 Sam. 12).

NATHANAEL—Possibly another name for the apostle Bartholomew, he was an Israelite whom Jesus complimented as being guileless and who, in turn, confessed Jesus as the Son of God and King of Israel (John 1:45-49).

NAZARENE—A person from Nazareth, the hometown of Jesus. It is in lower Galilee about halfway between the Sea of Galilee and the Mediterranean.

that He will be called a **N**... Matt. 2:23
of the sect of the **N-S**!.... Acts 24:5

NAZIRITE—An individual especially devoted to God by taking a vow. Lifelong Nazirites included Samson (Judg. 13:5, 7; 16:17), Samuel (1 Sam. 1), and John the Baptist (Luke 1:15-17). The essential elements of the Nazirite vow were abstention from wine or any other product of grapes, not touching a dead body, and not cutting one's hair (Num. 6). Also see Subject Index.

NEBUCHADNEZZAR—King of Babylon who conquered Jerusalem and exiled its inhabitants (1 Chron. 6:15; 2 Chron. 36; Neh. 7:6; Esth. 2:6).

NEGEV—An arid region in southern Palestine.

NEHEMIAH—Cupbearer to Artaxerxes, king of Persia (Neh. 1:11). He repaired the walls of Jerusalem then led a revival.

NICODEMUS—A "ruler of the Jews" who came to Jesus at night and was told he must be born again (John 3:1-20; 7:50-51; 19:39).

NILE—The major river considered the "life" of ancient Egypt. Also see Subject Index.

NINEVEH—The capital of the ancient Assyrian Empire, it was the enemy city to which God called the reluctant Prophet Jonah (Gen. 10:11-12; 2 Kings 19:36; Isa. 37:37; Jonah 3:2-7; Nah. 1:1; Zeph. 2:13; Matt. 12:41; Luke 11:30-32).

NOAH—A righteous man, God gave him specific instructions for building the ark by which he and his family survived the flood (Gen. 5:28–10:1; Ezek. 14:14; Matt. 24:37-38; Heb. 11:7; 1 Pet. 3:20; 2 Pet. 2:5). His sons were Shem, Ham, and Japheth.

P

PALESTINE—The land west of Jordan River that God allotted to Israel for an inheritance (Josh. 13–19).

PAUL—His Jewish name was Saul. He was educated in the Jewish religion and became a Pharisee (23:6; 26:5). Initially he rejected Jesus and persecuted Christians, but he was converted when the resurrected Christ appeared to him. He became an outstanding missionary, theologian, and writer of the early church; he wrote 13 letters that comprise the most important theological interpretation of the teachings of Christ and of the significance of His life, death, and resurrection. Also see Subject Index.

PERSIA—In ancient times, a vast collection of states and kingdoms reaching from Asia Minor to India and from Russia to Egypt and the Persian Gulf.

PETER—Simon was his given name; he was called Peter, Gk for "rock," by Jesus (Matt. 16:18); also called Simeon and Cephas (Aramaic for "rock"). He was a leader among the 12 disciples. He contessed "You are the Messiah" (Matt. 16:16) but later said "I don't know this man" (Mark 14:71). After Pentecost (Acts 2:1) he was a bold evangelist even when persecuted. Also see Subject Index.

PHARAOH—1. Of Abraham (Gen. 12:10-20). 2. Of Joseph (Gen. 39–50). 3. Of the oppression (Exod. 1). 4. Of the exodus (2:23–15:19). 5. Of Solomon (1 Kings 3–11). 6. Of Rehoboam, called Shishak (14:25). 7. Of Hezekiah and Isaiah (2 Kings 18:21; Isa. 36). 8. Of Josiah (2 Kings 23:29). 9. Other (1 Chron. 4:18; Jer. 44:30; Ezek. 29:1-16).

PHARISEES—Religious group that insisted on obedience to the law and numerous strict rules. Also see Subject Index.

unless your righteousness surpasses that of the scribes and **P-S**................ Matt. 5:20
I am a **P**, a son of **P-S**!.... Acts 23:6

PHILIP—1. One of 12 apostles (Matt. 10:3). 2. One of first seven deacons (Acts 6:5), and an evangelist (8:5-13, 26-39). 3. Philip Herod, a tetrarch.

PHILISTINES—Enemies of Israel from Joshua's conquest to the time of David and beyond. Also see Subject Index.

PILATE, PONTIUS—Roman governor of Judea under whom Christ "suffered" (Mark 15:1-15; 1 Tim. 6:13).

R

RACHEL—Laban's younger daughter, second wife and cousin of Jacob, and mother of Joseph and Benjamin (Gen. 29–31; 33:1-2, 7; 35:16-25).

RAHAB—Prostitute in Jericho who hid the Israelite spies (Josh. 2; 6:17,22-25; Heb. 11:31); mother of Boaz (Matt. 1:5).

REBEKAH—Isaac's wife and mother of Jacob and Esau (Gen. 24; 25:25-26).

RED SEA—Body of water God divided in the exodus (Exod. 13:18; 14:15-31; Deut. 11:4; Josh. 2:10; 4:23; 24:6; Neh. 9:9; Ps. 106:9-11; Acts 7:36; Heb. 11:29). The Hb yam suph means "sea of reeds."

REUBEN—Eldest son of Jacob and the tribe descended from him.

ROME—The name of the empire in control of Europe and the Near East at the time of Christ, and the name of its capital city in Italy.

RUTH—Moabite widow who pledged loyalty to her mother-in-law, Naomi, and her people (Ruth 1:16-17). There she "happened to" end up in the field of Boaz (2:3). Boaz married Ruth and provided Naomi with a family heir, and an ancestor of David and Jesus.

S

SADDUCEES—A Jewish group that took the Pentateuch as their authority. They did not believe in the afterlife (Matt. 22:23), so were focused on temporal rewards.

SAMARITANS—The few Israelites that remained after the fall of Samaria intermarried with the Assyrian captives from distant places who were settled there (2 Kings 17:23-24) becoming hated half-breeds who did not worship in the same manner as the Jews. In the days of Christ, the animosity was so great that the Jews bypassed Samaria as they traveled between Galilee and Judea. Also see Subject Index.

But a **S** on his journey came up..............Luke 10:33
Jews do not associate with **S-S**..................John 4:9

SAMSON—Last of the major judges; a lifelong Nazirite (Judg. 13:3-7). Samson's legendary strength came from the Spirit of the Lord (14:6, 19; 15:14; Heb. 11:32, 34). Delilah betrayed him (Judg. 16).

SAMUEL—Priest and prophet who linked the period of the judges with the monarchy. He was raised by the priest Eli (1 Sam. 2:11). Israel appealed to Samuel to appoint a king (8:3, 5, 20). He warned Israel of the dangers of a monarchy before anointing Saul (10:1). After God rejected Saul, Samuel anointed David (16:13).

SARAH—Abraham's wife (1 Pet. 3:6). Originally named Sarai, when she was almost 90 years old God changed her name to Sarah and promised her a son (Gen. 17:15-16; cp. 18:10; Rom. 9:9). A year later, she bore Isaac (Gen. 21:1-7; Heb. 11:11).

SATAN—Adversary or accuser; the Devil.

told Peter, "Get behind Me, **S**! ....Matt. 16:23
For **S** himself is disguised...........2 Cor. 11:14
messenger of **S** to torment me.....................2 Cor. 12:7
I watched **S** fall from heaven..............Luke 10:18

SAUL—1. First king of Israel. His presumptuous offering (1 Sam. 13:8-14) and violation of a holy war ban led to his rejection by God (15:7-23). 2. Paul's Hebrew name.

SHEM—Noah's oldest son and ancestor of the Semitic peoples, including the Israelites.

SHEOL—Abode of the unrighteous dead.

You will not abandon me to **S** Ps. 16:10
make my bed in **S**, You are there.......... Ps. 139:8

SILAS—A leader in the Jerusalem church, he traveled with Paul and also served as Peter's scribe (Acts 15:22, 32, 40-41; 16:19-40; 17:10-15; 18:5; 2 Cor. 1:19; 1 Thess. 1:1; 2 Thess. 1:1; 1 Pet. 5:12).

SIMON—1. The father of Judas Iscariot. 2. See Peter. 3. Pharisee who hosted Jesus. 4. Native of Cyrene forced to carry Jesus' cross (Mark 15:21). 5. Tanner who lived in Joppa. 6. One of Jesus' twelve apostles, also called "the Canaanite" (Matt. 10:4) or the Zealot (Luke 6:15). 7. Half brother of Jesus (Matt. 13:55). 8. Leper who hosted Jesus. 9. Sorcerer from Samaria who believed Philip's preaching, was baptized, and then tried to buy the power of the gospel (Acts 8:9-24).

SINAI, MOUNT—Mountain on the Sinai Peninsula where God gave the Ten Commandments to Moses (Exod. 19:1-3,20; 31:18; Lev. 25:1; Acts 7:38; Gal. 4:25).

SODOM AND GOMORRAH—Two cities destroyed by God because of their wickedness (Gen. 19).

SOLOMON—David's son and successor as king of Israel (1 Kings 1–2). He was granted wisdom and wealth from God (3:12-13), and he built the temple (1 Kings 5–8). But his "700 wives who were princesses and 300 concubines ... turned his heart away from the Lord" (11:3).

STEPHEN—One of seven men chosen to serve in the Jerusalem church (Acts 6:5), and the first Christian martyr (7:54-60).

T

THADDAEUS—Another name for the Apostle Judas, not Iscariot (Matt. 10:3; Mark 3:18).

THOMAS—One of the apostles (Mark 3:18). He sought evidence of Jesus' resurrection, and when shown, expressed faith (John 20:25-28).

TIGRIS—See Euphrates and Tigris Rivers.

TIMOTHY—Paul's friend and trusted coworker. He may have been converted on Paul's first missionary journey (Acts 14:6-23). When Paul came to Lystra on his second journey, Timothy was a disciple who was well respected by the believers (Acts 16:1-2). Timothy not only accompanied Paul but also was sent on many crucial missions (17:14-15; 18:5; 19:22; 20:4; Rom. 16:21; 1 Cor. 16:10; 2 Cor. 1:19; 1 Thess. 3:2, 6).

TITUS—Gentile companion of Paul (Gal. 2:3). Paul spoke highly of Titus and entrusted him with ministry (2 Cor. 2:13; 7:6, 13-14; 8:6, 16, 23; 12:18; cp. Gal. 2:1; 2 Tim. 4:10).

Y

YAHWEH—God's name that He revealed to Moses. In most English translations it is represented by Lord in small caps.

Y, the God of your fathers .. Exod. 3:15
I am **Y**, that is My name . Isa. 42:8

Z

ZACCHAEUS—Corrupt tax collector whom Jesus visited in Jericho (Luke 19:2-9).

ZEALOT—Member of the Jewish group that wanted to liberate Judea from Rome by force.

ZECHARIAH—1. Prophet who urged the people of Judah to rebuild the temple. 2. Father of John the Baptist (Luke 1:5-64).

ZION—Originally, the fortified hill of Jebus, also called the City of David; Jerusalem (2 Sam. 5:7; Ps. 48:2; Ps. 137:3; Joel 2:1; Zech. 9:9; Matt. 21:5; Rom. 9:33).

I have consecrated My King on **Z** .... Ps. 2:6
laid a stone in **Z**, a tested stone .... Isa. 28:16
The Liberator will come from **Z**........ Rom. 11:26

DICTIONARY
CONCORDANCE

A

ABBA—Aramaic word for "father" used by Jesus and Paul to speak an intimate relationship with God.
He said, "**A**, Father!" .. Mark 14:36
we cry out, "**A**, Father!". Rom. 8:15
crying, "**A**, Father!" .... Gal. 4:6

ABOMINATION—That which is detestable to God.
Milcom, the **A** of the Ammonites. ...... 2 Kings 23:13
and set up the **A** of desolation. .... Dan. 11:31
see the **A** that causes desolation, ... Matt. 24:15

ABORTION—Induced miscarriage. Prohibited by implication from God's dealings with the unborn (Judg. 13:7; Isa.. 49:1; Jer. 1:5; Luke 1:15,41).

ABSTINENCE—Voluntarily refraining from some action, such as sexual relations, eating certain foods, or drinking alcoholic beverages.

ABYSS—The dark abode of the dead (Ps. 140:10; Luke 8:31; Rom. 10:7).

ACROSTIC—Literary device by which each section of a literary work begins with the succeeding letter of a certain word or of the alphabet. Pss. 9–10; 25; 34; 37; 111–112; 119; 145; Prov. 31:10-31; Lam. 1–4 are alphabetic acrostics.

ADOPTION—Legal process whereby one person receives another into his family and confers upon that person familial privileges and advantages (Rom. 8:15,23; 9:4).

ADULTERY—Act of unfaithfulness in marriage. The Bible addresses literal adultery—both actual (Exod. 20:14; Deut. 5:18) and in the thought life of a person (Matt. 5:28)—and also uses adultery figuratively for unfaithfulness to God (Ezek. 16:32; Matt. 12:39; 16:4; Jas. 4:4).

ADVERSARY—Enemy; one who is against another. The devil is the greatest adversary (1 Pet. 5:8-9).

ADVOCATE—One who intercedes in behalf of another. Abraham (Gen. 18:23-33), Moses (Exod. 32:11-14), and Samuel interceded with God on behalf of Israel (1 Sam. 7:8-9), and Christ intercedes with the Father on behalf of sinners (1 John 2:1).

AFFLICTION—Condition of physical or mental distress. It ultimately shows the power of God (Rom. 5:3; 2 Cor. 4:17).

ALIEN—Person living in a society other than his own. The patriarchs (Abraham, Isaac, Jacob) were aliens in Canaan but owned large material resources (20:1; 26:3; 32:5). God loves aliens (Deut. 10:19). They could observe Passover (Num. 9:14) and offer sacrifices (Lev. 17:8) just as any Israelite.
the land where you l ive as an **A**, ... Gen. 28:4
if you no longer oppress the **A**, ... Jer. 7:6
I urge you as **A-S** .... 1 Pet. 2:11

ALLOTMENT—Land allocation either by God directly or by casting lots. Num. 32; Josh. 13–19; Ezek. 48.

ALMIGHTY—Title of God expressing His power.
I am God **A**. .... Gen. 17:1
Can ... discover the limits of the **A**? .... Job 11:7

ALPHA AND OMEGA—First and last letters of the Greek alphabet, used in Revelation to describe God or Christ (Rev. 1:8; 21:6; 22:13).

ALTAR—Structure used in worship as the place for presenting sacrifices to God or gods (Exod. 20:25; 27:1-4; 30:1-6; 1 Kings 7:48-50;2 Chron. 4:1).

AMBASSADOR—Representative of one government to another.
we are **A-S** for Christ; . 2 Cor. 5:20
For this I am an **A** in chains. .... Eph. 6:20

AMEN—Transliteration of Hb word signifying something as certain, truthful, or faithful.
The **A**, the faithful and true .... Rev. 3:14

ANCIENT OF DAYS—Phrase used to describe the everlasting God, implying age, dignity, endurance, and wisdom (Dan. 7:9,13,22).

ANGEL—Created being whose primary function is to serve and worship God.
He will send His **A** before you, ... Gen. 24:7
the **A** Gabriel was sent. Luke 1:26
we will judge **A-S**. .... 1 Cor. 6:3
disguised as an **A** of light. .... 2 Cor. 11:14

ANOINT, ANOINTED—Procedure of rubbing or smearing a person or thing, usually with olive oil, for the purpose of grooming, healing, setting apart, or embalming (Exod. 30:30; 1 Sam. 15:1; Matt. 6:17; Mark 16:1; Luke 10:34).

ANTICHRIST—One who opposes God and His purpose (1 John 2:18,22; 4:3; 2 John 7).

ANXIETY—State of mind ranging from genuine, legitimate concern (Phil. 2:28) to obsessions that originate from a distorted perspective of life (Prov. 12:25; Luke 12:22-31).

APOSTLE—**1.** One of the Twelve whom Jesus chose. Paul was also an apostle because he had seen the risen Christ. **2.** A person sent to perform a task.
12—He also named them **A-S** .... Mark 3:14
received grace and **A-SHIP** .... Rom. 1:5
I am an **A** to the Gentiles, ... Rom. 11:13
unworthy to be called an **A**, ... 1 Cor. 15:9

ARAMAIC—North Semitic language similar to Phoenician and Hebrew; the language of the Arameans of northwestern Mesopotamia, used widely in commerce and diplomacy (2 Kings 18:26). Jesus and the Apostles probably spoke in Aramaic.

ARCHANGEL—Chief angel; functions as a messenger on God's spiritual business (1 Thess. 4:16; Jude 9).

ARK—Water vessel (Gen. 6–9; Matt. 24:38; Luke 17:27; Heb. 11:7; 1 Pet. 3:20).

ARK OF THE COVENANT—Also called ark of the LORD and ark of the testimony. Original container for the Ten Commandments (Deut. 10:1-5; Exod. 25:10-22; Jer. 3:16-17; Ps. 132:7-8; Heb. 9:1-10).

ARMOR—Defensive tools of warfare (Eph. 6:10-17; cp. Isa. 59:16-17).

ASCENTS—Word used in the titles of 15 psalms (Pss. 120–134); probably a reference to pilgrims going up to Jerusalem for the festivals.

ASCRIBE—To consider something as coming from or belonging to somebody (Ps. 96:7-8).

ASSAY—To test ore for its silver and gold content (Jer. 6:27).

ASSEMBLY—Official gathering of the people of Israel or of the church; congregation.

ATONEMENT—God's reconciling of sinners to Himself through the sacrificial work of Jesus Christ (Ps. 79:9; Prov. 16:6; 2 Cor. 5:20).
priest will make **A** on their behalf,.................. Lev. 4:20
is the Day of **A**.......... Lev. 23:27

AUTHORITY—The rightful and legitimate exercise of power by virtue of position. Delegated authority is given from one who has intrinsic authority to one serving in an office or carrying out a function.
Son of Man has **A** on earth................... Matt. 9:6
gave them **A** over unclean spirits.................. Matt. 10:1
All **A** has been given to Me.................. Matt. 28:18
submit to the governing **A-IES**,................ Rom. 13:1
teach or to have **A** over a man;................ 1 Tim. 2:12
be submissive to rulers and **A-IES**,............. Titus 3:1

AVENGER—Person with the legal responsibility to punish a wrongdoer (Num. 35:12,19; Rom. 12:19; 13:4).

AWE—Honor, fear, and respect for a superior.
the great, mighty, and **A-SOME** God,.................. Deut. 10:17
stand in **A** of the God of Israel,.................. Isa. 29:23

AZAZEL—A "scapegoat" or a desert demon (Lev. 16:8,10,26).

B

BALANCE—A type of scale for weighing.
You are to have honest **B-S**,..................... Lev. 19:36
B-S and scales are the Lord's;................ Prov. 16:11
weighed the mountains in a **B**................. Isa. 40:12

BALM—Aromatic resin or gum used for cosmetic and medical purposes.
Is there no **B** in Gilead? .. Jer. 8:22

BANNER—Sign carried to identify a group, to give it a rallying point, and to make signals.

BAPTISM—Immersion in water as a symbol of cleansing from sin and as a public confession of faith in Jesus the Savior.
preaching a **B** of repentance.............Mark 1:4
we were buried with Him by **B**.................. Rom. 6:4

BARREN—Unable to bear children (Gen. 11:30; 25:21; 29:31; Judg. 13:2; 1 Sam. 1:5; Luke 1:7,36).

BEASTS—Symbolic enemies of God's people in Daniel and Revelation.
Four huge **B-S** came up .. Dan. 7:3
B that comes up out of the abyss.................... Rev. 11:7
a **B** coming up out of the sea...................... Rev. 13:1

BEER—Intoxicating drink made from grain, traditionally called "strong drink."
he is to abstain from wine and **B**.................... Num. 6:3
Wine is a mocker, **B** is a brawler,.............. Prov. 20:1

BESIEGE—To apply a military siege.

BIRTHRIGHT—Special privileges that belonged to the firstborn male child in a family, including a double portion of the inheritance and the father's major blessing (Gen. 27:36; Deut. 21:17; cp. 2 Kings 2:9).
First sell me your **B**... Gen. 25:31
B in exchange for one meal..................... Heb. 12:16

BLASPHEMY—Speech or actions that show disrespect for God (Lev. 24:11-16). Jesus was regarded by the Jewish leaders as a blasphemer (Matt. 9:3; 26:65; Mark 2:7; 14:64; Luke 5:21; John 10:33).
B against the Spirit will not................... Matt. 12:31

BLEMISH—Deformity or defect that disqualifies an animal as a sacrifice (Lev. 22:17-25) or a man from priestly service (21:17-24).
Messiah who ... offered Himself without **B** to God,..... Heb. 9:14

BLESS—To fill with benefits; or to "praise," as if filling something with honor and good words.
I will **B** you,............... Gen. 12:2
has **B-ED** us with every spiritual.................. Eph. 1:3

BLIND—Unable to see. The Bible addresses spiritual blindness as the great human problem.
the eyes of the **B** will be opened,.................. Isa. 35:5
Woe to you, **B** guides,. Matt. 23:16
are wretched, pitiful, poor, **B**,................... Rev. 3:17

BLOOD—In OT it was intimately associated with physical life (Lev. 17:11,14; Deut. 12:23; Acts 15:20). The blood of Christ represents atonement in His death (Heb. 9:12-14, 22; 13:20; 1 Pet. 1:1-2, 19).
this is My **B** ... the covenant;.............. Matt. 26:28
through faith in His **B**, . Rom. 3:25
redemption through His **B**,..................... Eph. 1:7
by making peace through the **B**.................... Col. 1:20
B of Jesus His Son cleanses us.......... 1 John 1:7

BOOK OF LIFE—Heavenly record (Luke 10:20; Phil. 4:3; Heb. 12:23; Rev. 3:5) written by God before the foundation of the world (13:8; 17:8) containing names of those who are destined because of God's grace and their faithfulness to participate in God's heavenly kingdom (cp. Exod. 32:32; Ps. 69:28; Isa. 4:3; Dan. 12:1; Mal. 3:16).

BOOTH—Temporary shelter constructed for cattle (Gen. 33:17) and people (Lev. 23:40-43; 2 Sam. 11:11; 1 Kings 20:12,16; Neh. 8:15; Isa. 1:8; Jonah 4:5).

BOUNDARY MARKER—Pillar or heap of stones indicating the edge of a field (Deut. 19:14; 27:17; Job 24:2; Hos. 5:10).

BREAD—A cake or loaf made from wheat or barley flour, the basic food of most people in Bible times.
man does not live on **B** alone................ Deut. 8:3
Give us today our daily **B**.................. Matt. 6:11
I am the **B** of life,........ John 6:35

BREASTPIECE—Piece of elaborate embroidery about nine inches square worn by the high priest upon his breast (Exod. 28; Lev. 8:8).

BREATH—Source and evidence of life.
breathed the **B** of life into Gen. 2:7
gives everyone life and **B** .... Acts 17:25

BRIDE—A woman getting married; an image of the church and its relationship to Christ (John 3:29).

BROTHER—This usually refers to siblings (Exod. 4:14; Judg. 9:5) but is also used to signify kinsmen, allies, and members of the same country or community.
Am I my **B-'S** guardian? . Gen. 4:9
a **B** is born for a difficult time.................. Prov. 17:17
Whoever does the will of God is My **B** and sister and mother................ Mark 3:35

BUCKLER—Small, round shield.

BURDEN—A heavy weight to carry.
My yoke is easy and My **B** is light. .... Matt. 11:30

C

CAMEL—Large hump-backed mammal of Asia and Africa used for desert travel to bear burdens or passengers.
it is easier for a **C** to go through the eye of a needle Matt. 19:24
gulp down a **C**!........ Matt. 23:24

CENSER—Vessel used for offering incense before the Lord (Lev. 10:1).

CENSUS—A count of population for the purpose of taxation or for the determination of manpower for war (Num. 1:2; 2 Sam. 24:10).

CENTURION—Officer in the Roman army, nominally in command of 100 soldiers.

CHAFF—Husks and other materials separated from the kernel of grain during the threshing and winnowing process.
But the **C** He will burn up with fire...................... Matt. 3:12

CHARIOT—Two-wheeled, horse-drawn vehicle.
even though they have iron **C-S** .... Josh. 17:18
Some take pride in a **C**, ... Ps. 20:7

CHERUB, plural **CHERUBIM**—A class of winged angels who functioned primarily as guards (Gen. 3:24) or attendants (Ezek. 10:1-22).

CHOSEN PEOPLE—The group God has selected in order to bless them (Deut. 7:6; 1 Pet. 2:9).

CHRISTIAN—Slave or follower of Christ(Acts 11:26).

CHRONICLE—A written report of events in chronological order, such as that written by the court historian (1 Kings 14:19).

CHURCH—A local group of people who believe in Christ (Matt. 18:17; Rom. 16:5; Rev. 2:1) or the universal body of all believers (Matt. 16:18; 1 Cor. 15:9). The description of the church as the body of Christ (Eph. 5:23; Col. 1:18,24) designates Jesus' rule over the community.

CIRCUMCISION—Removal of the foreskin of the penis as a sign of the covenant between God and mankind (Gen. 17:11). The Jerusalem Council determined that circumcision was not essential to Christian faith (Acts 15:1-12; cp. Gal. 5:2).
and **C** is of the heart.... Rom. 2:29

CISTERN—A well or a reservoir into which water could drain from a roof, tunnel, or courtyard.

CITY OF REFUGE—Safe place to flee for a person who had accidentally killed another (Num. 35:11; Josh. 20). The city provided asylum until a trial could be held to determine his guilt or innocence.

CITIZEN—Officially recognized status in political state bringing certain rights and responsibilities (Acts 16:37; 22:26-28).

CITY OF DAVID—In the OT the phrase refers to Jerusalem; its original reference may have been only to the southeastern hill and the Jebusites' military fortress there (2 Sam. 5:6-10). In Luke 2:4,11 the reference is to Bethlehem, the birthplace of David (John 7:42).

CLAN—A kinship group more extensive than "household" or "family" but smaller than "tribe."

CLEAN—Ceremonially acceptable to God. People must be clean to participate in worship(Lev. 22:2-9; Num. 8:15; Ps. 24:3-4). Certain animals were considered clean and therefore suitable for food or for sacrifice (Lev. 11; Deut. 14:3-21). Jesus cleansed His people by His blood (1 John 1:7,9; cp. John 15:3; Titus 2:14).

COMMON—In the context of the law, it means profane, the opposite of holy (Lev. 10:10; Acts 10:14-15).

COMPASSION—Deep sympathy for one who is in sorrow and pain. Jesus had compassion for people (Matt. 9:36; 14:14; 15:32; 20:34). Compassion is evidence that one is a child of God (1 John 3:17).
the LORD your God is a **C-ATE** God. ....Deut. 4:31

CONCUBINE—A wife of lower status than a primary wife.
He had 700 wives ... and 300 **C-S**, ... 1 Kings 11:3

CONDEMN—To pronounce someone guilty after weighing the evidence.
He c-s a man who schemes.............. Prov. 12:2
who believes in Him is not **C-ED**, ... John 3:18

CONFESS—1. To admit sin (Lev. 16:21; 1 Sam. 7:6; Neh. 1:6; 9:2-3; Ps. 32:5; Dan. 9:4-5; Matt. 3:6). 2. To acknowledge faith and commitment to God (Rom. 10:9-10; 1 Tim. 6:12-13; Heb. 13:15; 1 John 4:15; 2 John 7). One's public acknowledgment of Jesus is the basis for Jesus' own acknowledgment of that believer to God (Matt. 10:32-33; cp. 1 John 4:2-3; Rev. 3:5).
C that Jesus Christ is Lord,.................... Phil. 2:11
C your sins to one another .... Jas. 5:16
If we **C** our sins, He is faithful.................. 1 John 1:9
he who **C-ES** the Son has the Father as well. .... 1 John 2:23

CONSCIENCE—The capacity to know whether one's behavior is good or bad, right or wrong.
at night my **C** instructs me......................... Ps. 16:7
a clear **C** toward God and men...................... Acts 24:16
of liars whose **C-S** are seared. .... 1 Tim. 4:2

CONSECRATE—Give to God or set apart for the service of God.
C every firstborn male to Me, ... Exod. 13:2
C yourselves and be holy, for I.................... Lev. 20:7

CONVERT—Turn or return to God.
C-ED and become like..Matt. 18:3
be **C-ED** ... John 12:40; Acts 28:27

CONVICT—Cause a sense of guilt and shame leading to repentance.
He will **C** the world about sin,............ John 16:8

CORBAN—Gift particularly designated for the Lord, and so forbidden for any other use.

might have received from
me is **C** .... Mark 7:11

CORNERSTONE—Stone laid at the corner to bind two walls together, symbolic of strength and prominence. Christ is the only sure foundation of faith.
rejected has become
the **C**.................. Ps. 118:22
a precious **C**, a sure
foundation;.......... Isa. 28:16
This Jesus ... has become
the **C**..................Acts 4:11
Christ Jesus Himself as
the **C**...................Eph. 2:20

COUNSELOR—John used this word to describe the Holy Spirit as one who teaches (John 14:16), reminds the disciples of what Jesus taught (14:26), testifies (15:26), and convicts of sin (16:7-8). Jesus was the first Counselor (14:16) and is for the Christian an Advocate in heaven (1 John 2:1).

COURT HISTORIAN—Person in the palace who wrote down the king's daily business.

COVENANT—Oath-bound promise whereby one party solemnly pledges to bless or serve another party in some specified way.
the Lord made a **C** with
Abram,............... Gen. 15:18
will never break My **C**
with you. .... Judg. 2:1
I will make a new **C**
with .... Jer. 31:31
This cup is the new **C** . Luke 22:20
He is the mediator of a
new **C**,................ Heb. 9:15

COVET—To inordinately desire to possess what belongs to another.
Do not **C** your
neighbor's......... Exod. 20:17

CREATION—The act of God in bringing the world and everything in it into existence (Gen. 1–2; John 1:1-3; Heb. 11:3) and the result of that act (Col. 1:15, 23), which proclaims the glory of God (Ps. 8; 19:1-4).
From the **C** of the world
His.................. Rom. 1:20
For the **C** eagerly waits
with .... Rom. 8:19
For we are His **C**—created
in .... Eph. 2:10

CROSS—Method the Romans used to execute Jesus Christ. It was seen by the Jews as a curse (Deut. 21:23; Gal. 3:13). For Paul the message of the cross is the heart of the gospel (1 Cor. 1:17-18, 23; 2:2). Jesus Himself established the primary figurative interpretation of the cross as a call to complete surrender to God (Matt. 10:38; 16:24; cp. Rom. 12:1; Gal. 6:14).

CROWN—Special headdress worn by royalty and other persons of high merit and honor.
A capable wife is her
husband's **C**,......... Prov. 12:4
twisted together a **C** of
thorns, ... Matt. 27:29
do it to receive a
perishable **C**, ... 1 Cor. 9:25
for me the **C** of
righteousness, ... 2 Tim. 4:8
will receive the
unfading **C** of glory... 1 Pet. 5:4
cast their **C-S** before the
throne,................. Rev. 4:10

CRUCIBLE—Melting pot used in the refining of silver, a figure for testing of people (Prov. 17:3; 27:21).

CUBIT—The distance from a person's elbow to the tip of the middle finger, approximately 18 inches.

CUPBEARER—An officer of the royal court who had charge of wines and other beverages and who helped prevent the poisoning of the king.
king of Egypt's **C** and his
baker.................. Gen. 40:1
I was the king's **C**....... Neh. 1:11

CURSE—To predict, pray for, or cause misfortune on someone. Since belonging to God and His people meant blessing, being cursed often meant separation from God and the community of faith.
come and put a **C** on
these people........... Num. 22:6
an undeserved **C** goes
nowhere. .... Prov. 26:2

D

DAY—**1.** The time of daylight from sunrise to sunset. **2.** The 24-hour period, usually defined as one sunset to the next, but also as starting at sunrise. **3.** An undetermined time period or era associated with a particular person, event, or characteristic.
God called the light "**D**," Gen. 1:5
can endure the **D** of His
coming?................. Mal. 3:2
Give us each **D** our
daily bread. .... Luke 11:3
now is the **D** of salvation. 2 Cor. 6:2
one **D** is like 1,000 years, 2 Pet. 3:8

DAY OF THE Lord—Time when God reveals His sovereignty; day of divine judgment (Joel 2:31; Amos 5:18; 1 Thess. 5:2).

DEACON—Title for an office in the local church (Phil. 1:1; 1 Tim. 3:8-13). The events of Acts 6:1-6 may be the origin of the office.

DEATH—The cessation of life. The Bible talks about physical, spiritual, and eternal death.
He will destroy **D**
forever.................. Isa. 25:8
he will never see
D—ever!............. John 8:51
For the wages of sin is **D**,
............................Rom. 6:23
that neither **D** nor life, . Rom. 8:38
O **D**, where is your
victory?............ 1 Cor. 15:55
D will exist no longer; .. Rev. 21:4

DECREE—Command or decision made by someone of authority.

DEDICATE—To set apart for special purposes.

DEFILE—To make something unclean or impure.
things that **D** a man, . Matt. 15:20

DELIVER—To rescue from danger.

DELUGE—A great flood (Gen. 6–9).

DEMONS—Fallen angels who joined Satan in his rebellion.
drive out **D** in Your
name .... Matt. 7:22
D also believe—and they
shudder................ Jas. 2:19

DENARIUS—Coin representing a day's wage for a soldier or an ordinary laborer (Matt. 20:2).

DESECRATE—To take away sacredness, or to treat something as if it were not sacred (Dan. 11:31; Acts 24:6).

DEVOTED—Set apart for something, such as God's use.

DEVOUT—Careful in fulfilling religious duties.
This man was righteous
and **D**,................ Luke 2:25

DIE—To become lifeless. To die to something is to give up any association to it.

you eat from it, you will certainly **D**.............Gen. 2:17
eat and drink, for tomorrow we **D**!....................Isa. 22:13
will never **D**—ever.....John 11:26
moment, Christ **D-D** for the ungodly..................Rom. 5:6
How can we who **D-D** to sin still..................Rom. 6:2
living is Christ and **DYING** is gain..........Phil. 1:21
appointed for people to **D** once....................Heb. 9:27

DISCERN—The ability to see differences and make choices (Rom. 12:2; Eph. 5:10; Phil. 1:9). One of the spiritual gifts (1 Cor. 12:10).
and to **D** between good and evil...............1 Kings 3:9

DISCIPLE—An adherent of a particular teacher or school. The primary reference is to followers of Jesus Christ (Matt. 10:1; 27:57; 28:19; Acts 6:7).
and make **D-S** of all nations,............Matt. 28:19
He summoned His **D-S**, and He chose 12 of them..... Luke 6:13

DISCIPLINE—Moral training, and the punishment inflicted to effect it. God disciplines His children for their own good in love (Deut. 8:5).
happy is the man You **D** and teach.....................Ps. 94:12
for the LORD **D-S** the one He loves..............Prov. 3:12
What son is there whom a father does not **D**?...........Heb. 12:7

DISPOSSESS—To drive residents out.

DISSIPATION—Recklessness; lack of discipline (1 Pet. 4:4).

DISSENSION—Contention; quarreling; discord (Rom. 16:17; Gal. 5:20).

DISTAFF—Either part of the spindle or a stick used to hold the unspun fibers, used in spinning thread (Prov. 31:19).

DIVINATION—The practice of making decisions or telling the future by means of reading signs and omens (Lev. 19:26; Ezek. 21:21).

DIVINE—Having to do with God.
His eternal power and **D** nature,.....................Rom. 1:20
For His **D** power has given us...............2 Pet. 1:3
you may share in the **D** nature,.....................2 Pet. 1:4

DIVORCE—Breaking of the marriage covenant.
may write her a **D** certificate,..............Deut. 24:1
If he hates and **D-S** {his wife},..............Mal. 2:16
Permitted you to **D** your wives...................Matt. 19:8

DOCTRINE—Christian truth and teaching passed on from generation to generation.
teaching as **D-S** the commands............Matt. 15:9
they will not tolerate sound **D**,..............2 Tim. 4:3

DOMINION—Political authority.
His **D** is an everlasting **D**,..............Dan. 4:34; 7:14
power and **D**, and every title.....................Eph. 1:21

DOOR—Opening into a house or room.
and the **D** will be opened to you..............Matt. 7:7
to enter through the narrow **D**,..........Luke 13:24
a **D** was opened to me 2 Cor. 2:12
I stand at the **D** and knock. Rev. 3:20

DOUBLE-MINDED—Lacking purity of heart or failing to trust only God (Ps. 119:1-13; Jas. 4:8).

DOUBT—Uncertainty; failure to believe.
of little faith, why did you **D**?..............Matt. 14:31
whoever **D-S** stands condemned......... Rom. 14:23
let him ask in faith without **D-ING**......................Jas. 1:6

DREAMS—One of the ways people sought to know God's will, see the future, and make decisions. Interpretation was often necessary (Gen. 40:8; 41:8; Dan. 2:3), and dreams could be false (Deut. 13:1-3).
your old men will have **D-S**, and.................Joel 2:28
appeared to Joseph in a **D**, ...Matt. 2:13

DROSS—Waste products that float to the top of molten metal in the refining process.
Israel has become **D** into Me...........................Ezek. 22:18

DUST—Fine, loose earth.
man out of the **D** from the ground...................Gen. 2:7
remembering that we are **D**.....................Ps. 103:14
and all return to **D**........Eccl. 3:20

E

EDIFICATION—Encouragement and consolation with the goal of establishment in the faith.
speaks to people for **E**, 1 Cor. 14:3

ELDER—Title for a leader in both Jewish and early Christian communities.
to appoint **E-S** in every town:.........................Titus 1:5
thrones sat 24 **E-S** dressed in ....Rev. 4:4

ELECTION—The plan of God whereby He chooses certain individuals and groups through whom He fulfills His purpose of salvation.
God's purpose according to **E**.........................Rom. 9:11
knowing your **E**, brothers loved 1 Thess. 1:4
to confirm your calling and **E**, ...2 Pet. 1:10

ELEMENTS, ELEMENTAL FORCES—1. The primary or elementary points of learning, especially for a religion or philosophy (Heb. 6:1). 2. The four basic elements: fire, air, water, and earth (2 Pet. 3:10, 12). 3. Spirits who were thought by some to exercise a certain amount of control over the heavenly bodies (Gal. 4:3, 9; Col. 2:8, 20).

ENDURE—To bear something difficult and keep on going.
the one who **E-S** to the end will............Matt. 10:22
hopes all things, **E-S** all things...................1 Cor. 13:7
if we **E**, we will also reign ....2 Tim. 2:12
joy that lay before Him **E-D** a cross.......Heb. 12:2
testing of your faith produces **E-ANCE**.......Jas. 1:3

ENEMY—An opponent.
me in the presence of my **E-IES**;......................Ps. 23:5
love your **E-IES** and pray for those ....Matt. 5:44
The last **E** He abolishes is death ....1 Cor. 15:26

ENGAGEMENT—Solemn promise to marry; in Bible times, engagement was as binding as marriage.

ENVOY—Representative; ambassador.

ENVY—To resent another's perceived advantage.
Don't **E** evil men ....Prov. 24:1

Love does not **E**; is not boastful............1 Cor. 13:4

EPHOD—Priestly garment, possibly a short apron or loincloth (Exod. 28; 1 Sam. 2:18; 2 Sam. 6:14).

ETERNAL LIFE—Life at its best, having infinite duration, characterized by abiding fellowship with God.
will awake, some to **E**.. Dan. 12:2
what good must I do to have **E**?..............Matt. 19:16
will not perish but have **E**..................John 3:16
the gift of God is **E** in Christ Jesus..........Rom. 6:23

EUNUCH—A castrated male; the term came to be used of officials without regard to emasculation.
The **E** replied to Philip, "I ask...................Acts 8:34

EVERLASTING—Unending; eternal.
Yahweh is the **E** God, the Creator.................Isa. 40:28
the penalty of **E** destruction,........2 Thess. 1:9

EVIL—Wicked, immoral; malevolent, malicious, harmful; contrary to the goodness of God.
tree of the knowledge of good and **E**..................Gen. 2:9
To fear the LORD is to hate **E**....................Prov. 8:13
but deliver us from the **E** one......................Matt. 6:13
Do not repay anyone **E** for **E**...............Rom. 12:17
from every form of **E**..................1 Thess. 5:22
root of all kinds of **E**, ..1 Tim. 6:10
For God is not tempted by **E**,.......................Jas. 1:13

EXALT—To elevate in rank, honor, or power; to praise.
let us **E** His name together.....................Ps. 34:3
Righteousness **E-S** a nation, but..........Prov. 14:34
humbles himself will be **E-ED**.................Matt. 23:12

EXECRATION—Cursing (Jer. 42:18; 44:12).

EXHORTATION—Argument or advice intended to incite hearers to action (1 Tim. 5:1).
with many other **E-S**, he proclaimed the good news Luke 3:18

EXILE—Forced deportation from one's homeland (2 Kings 17; 24–25).

EXODUS—The departure or emigration of a large number of people. The book of Exodus tells about Israel's escape from slavery in Egypt.

EXORCISM—Expelling demons by means of some ritual act (Acts 19:13).

EXPANSE—A way the ancients described the sky or atmosphere (Gen. 1; Ps. 19:1; 150:1; Ezek. 1:22-26; 10:1; Dan. 12:3).

EXPLOIT—To take unfair advantage of (Exod. 22:21).

EXTORTION—Obtaining something by force, threat, or abuse of authority.

F

FABLE—Short, fictitious story that uses animals or inanimate objects as characters to teach ethical or practical lessons. There are only two fables in the Bible (Judg. 9:8-15; 2 Kings 14:8-10; 2 Chron. 25:17-19).

FAIRNESS—Justice with integrity and without bias (Ps. 96:10; Ezek. 18:25; 33:17; Col. 4:1).

FAITH—Trust or dependence on a person or thing.
righteous one will live by his **F**.................Hab. 2:4
F the size of a mustard seed,................Matt. 17:20
is justified by **F** apart from works..........Rom. 3:28
So **F** comes from what is heard,..........Rom. 10:17
is not from **F** is sin.... Rom. 14:23
if I have all **F**, so that I can move...........1 Cor. 13:2
for we walk by **F**, not by sight...................2 Cor. 5:7
by grace you are saved through **F**,............Eph. 2:8
one Lord, one **F**, one baptism,...............Eph. 4:5
finished the race, I have kept the **F**.............2 Tim. 4:7
Now **F** is the reality of what is.................Heb. 11:1
Now without **F** it is impossible............Heb. 11:6
source and perfecter of our **F**,...................Heb. 12:2
F, if it doesn't have works, is dead ....Jas. 2:17

FAITHFUL—Constant; true to one's word.
great is Your **F-NESS**! .. Lam. 3:23
Well done, good and **F** slave!.............Matt. 25:21
God is **F** and He will not allow...............1 Cor. 10:13
He who calls you is **F**, who also...........1 Thess. 5:24
commit to **F** men who will be able..........2 Tim. 2:2
for He who promised is **F**......................Heb. 10:23
He is **F** and righteous to forgive ....1 John 1:9
Its rider is called **F** and True, ...Rev. 19:11

FAITHLESS—Having distrusted or stopped trusting; without faith.
if we are **F**, He remains faithful,...............2 Tim. 2:13

FALSE—Deceptive, misleading; phony, fake.
Do not give **F** testimony against............Exod. 20:16
F messiahs and **F** prophets will..................Matt. 24:24
there will be **F** teachers .2 Pet. 2:1

FAMINE—Extreme shortage of food (Amos 4:6).
There was a **F** in the land,..................Gen. 12:10
not a **F** of bread or a thirst for ....Amos 8:11
or persecution or **F** or nakedness ....Rom. 8:35

FAST—To refrain from eating food (Ezra 8:23; Isa. 58; Joel 2:12; Zech. 7:5; Acts 13:2-3).
Whenever you **F**, don't be sad-faced like the hypocrites.............Matt. 6:16

FATE—That which must necessarily happen.

FATHER—Male parent; progenitor, provider, and person of responsibility and authority. Sometimes it means "ancestor" (Deut. 26:5). One of the titles of God, the first person in the Trinity, expressing kinship, compassion, and loving discipline.
Honor your **F** and your mother ....Exod. 20:12
You are my **F**, my God, the rock..........Ps. 89:26
Our **F** in heaven, Your name be ....Matt. 6:9
What **F** among you, if his son ....Luke 11:11
The **F** and I are one....John 10:30
F-S, do not exasperate your ....Col. 3:21
son is there whom a **F** does not...............Heb. 12:7

FEAR—1. Natural emotional response of terror when facing a perceived threat. 2. Respect, honor; awe, reverence.
- **F** the LORD your God, worship Him....................Deut. 6:13
- The **F** of the LORD is the beginning....................Prov. 1:7
- Do not **F**, for I am with you;............Isa. 41:10
- **F** Him who is able to destroy both...............Matt. 10:28
- salvation with **F** and trembling.............Phil. 2:12
- There is no **F** in love; instead, perfect love drives out **F**,. 1 John 4:18

FEAST—A meal given to celebrate a joyous event, either a singular event such as a wedding (Judg. 14:10) or periodic events such as harvest or sheep-shearing (1 Sam. 25:7-8) or the Jewish festivals.
- to the marriage **F** of the Lamb!.................Rev. 19:9

FELLOWSHIP—A bond of common purpose and devotion, a close association, a good relationship.
- teaching, to **F**, to the breaking...............Acts 2:42
- Or what **F** does light have with.................2 Cor. 6:14
- we say, "We have **F** with Him,"..................1 John 1:6

FERTILE—Able to produce fruit.

FESTIVAL—Regular religious celebration remembering God's great acts of salvation.
- a **F** in My honor three times a year.........Exod. 23:14

FETTER—A constraint, especially a foot shackle (Jer. 2:20; 5:5; 27:2; 30:8).

FIG—Important fruit and tree of the Holy Land. Fruits could be eaten fresh (Isa. 28:4; Jer. 24:2) or dried and stored as cakes (1 Sam. 25:18; 30:12).
- At once the **F** tree withered...........Matt. 21:19

FIRSTBORN—The first son born to a newly married couple. In memory of the death of Egypt's firstborn, all the firstborn of Israel belonged to the LORD (Exod. 13:2). The birthright of a firstborn included a double portion of the estate and leadership of the family.
- she gave birth to her **F** Son,....................Luke 2:7
- the **F** from the dead and the ruler.................Rev. 1:5

FIRSTFRUITS—Choice portions of a crop harvested first and dedicated to God (Exod. 23:19). Used figuratively of the Spirit as the beginning of our salvation (Rom. 8:23), of Christ as the first man to rise from the dead (1 Cor. 15:20, 23), and of certain Christians as the first of humanity to enter the kingdom (16:15; Jas. 1:18; Rev. 14:4).

FLESH—The skin, meat, or the body as a whole of humans or animals. It can also mean all mankind, or one's relatives. In the NT, especially in Paul's writings, it stands for the fallen human nature, which is incapable of conforming to God's holy expectations.
- spirit is willing, but the **F** is weak...........Matt. 26:41
- The Word became **F**.... John 1:14
- are not in the **F**, but in the Spirit,............Rom. 8:9
- the works of the **F** are obvious:................Gal. 5:19

FLOCK—A group of sheep, goats, or both. Figuratively, people in need of care and guidance.
- sheep of the **F** will be scattered...........Matt. 26:31
- watch at night over their **F**...................Luke 2:8

FLOG—Punish by repeated blows of a whip or rod.
- after having Jesus **F-GED**,.............Matt. 27:26

FODDER—Feed for domestic animals (Job 6:5; 24:6; Isa. 30:24).

FOLLY, FOOLISHNESS—Lack of wisdom.
- answer a fool according to his **F**,..............Prov. 26:4,5
- the message of the cross is **F**,..................1 Cor. 1:18
- wisdom of this world is **F**,..................1 Cor. 3:19

FOOL—Unwise and ungodly person.
- The **F** says in his heart, "God...............Ps. 14:1; 53:1
- whoever says to his brother, '**F**!'............Matt. 5:22
- Claiming to be wise, they became **F-S**.....Rom. 1:22

FOREKNOWLEDGE—God's omniscience with regard to the future (Isa. 42:9; 46:10; Rom. 8:29; 11:2; 1 Pet. 1:2).

FORGIVE—Pardon a fault or offense; excuse payment for a debt owed.
- **F** their sin, and heal their land.................2 Chron. 7:14
- And **F** us our debts, as we alsohave **F-N** our debtors....................Matt. 6:12
- **F-ING** one another, just as Godalso **F-GAVE** you in Christ..................Eph. 4:32
- the **F-NESS** of sins.........Col. 1:14

FORSAKE—Abandon.
- I will not leave you or **F** you.....................Josh. 1:5
- My God, why have You **F-N** Me?............ Matt. 27:46

FORTIFIED CITIES—Strategically located walled cities guarding travel routes or borders (Josh. 19:35-38; 2 Chron. 11:5-12).

FOWLER—One who traps birds (Prov. 6:5; Jer. 5:26; Hos. 9:8).

FRANKINCENSE—A resinous substance derived from certain trees in the balsam family (Matt. 2:11).

FREE—Not captive or enslaved.
- and the truth will set you **F**....................John 8:32
- Jesus has set you **F** from the law .... Rom. 8:2
- slave or **F**, male or female;................Gal. 3:28
- Christ has liberated us into **F-DOM**...................Gal. 5:1

FREEDMEN—Former slaves (Acts 6:9; 1 Cor. 7:22).

FREEWILL OFFERING—Gift given at the impulse of the giver.

FRIEND—Person with a close, trusting relationship with another. The "king's friend" was his adviser (1 Kings 4:5 KJV).
- Now when Job's three **F-S**—Eliphaz ....Job 2:11
- A **F** loves at all times,..Prov. 17:17
- a **F** of tax collectors and.................Matt. 11:19
- I have called you **F-S**, John 15:15
- the world's **F** becomes God's enemy. .... Jas. 4:4

FRUIT—Literally, the useful product of a plant; figuratively, the product of anything.
- recognize them by their **F**. ....Matt. 7:16
- But the **F** of the Spirit is love, joy,...................Gal. 5:22

FULFILL—To bring about what was promised, predicted, or foreshadowed.
F what you vow.......... Eccl. 5:4
not come to destroy but to **F**.................Matt. 5:17
this Scripture has been **F-ED**.................. Luke 4:21
entire law is **F-ED** in one statement........ Gal. 5:14

FULLNESS—Completeness; the entire essence.
filled with all the **F** of God.....................Eph. 3:19

G

GALL—Bitter, poisonous herb (Ps. 69:21; Matt. 27:34).

GARRISON—Body of troops stationed for defense, often in the sense of occupying forces.

GATE—Point of access to a walled town. The space near the gate was used for public proceedings.

GENEALOGY—A family tree, sometimes selective.
to myths and endless **G-IES**.................. 1 Tim. 1:4

GIFT—Favor, item, or ability bestowed on someone.
but the **G** of God is eternal life....................Rom. 6:23
Now there are different **G-S**,................ 1 Cor. 12:4
every perfect **G** is from above,....................Jas. 1:17

GLEAN—Gather remnants of grain or fruit.
you must not **G** what is left................... Deut. 24:21
saw what she had **G-ED**.................... Ruth 2:18

GLORIFY—Praise, recognize the honor or importance of another.
the Son of Man is **G-IED**, andGod is **G-IED** in Him................John 13:31
those He justified, He also **G-IED**...................Rom. 8:30

GLORY—Weighty importance and shining majesty that accompany God's presence.
Declare His **G** among ...nations........ 1 Chron. 16:24
ascribe to the LORD **G** and strength.................Ps. 96:7
observed His **G**, the **G** as the One.............. John 1:14
and fall short of the **G** of God.................Rom. 3:23
do everything for God's **G**............1 Cor. 10:31
Christ in you, the hope of **G**.................Col. 1:27

GNASH—Grate (one's teeth) together as an expression of anger or despair.
they **G-ED** their teeth at me...................Ps. 35:16
weeping and **G-ING** of teeth...................Matt. 8:12

GOAD—Rod with a pointed end used to control oxen (Eccl. 12:11; Acts 26:14).

GOAT—Hollow-horned, cud-chewing mammal with long, floppy ears. Milk, meat, skin, and hair were utilized, and it was used as a sacrifice.

GOD-FEARERS—Gentiles who were drawn to the Jewish religion and practices.

GODLESS—Excluding God from thought and ignoring or deliberately violating God's laws.

GODLY—Respecting God, resulting in obedience and piety.
But **G-INESS** with contentment is a..... 1 Tim. 6:6

GOSPEL—The good news about salvation provided for all through the life, death, and resurrection of Jesus the Messiah.
and preach the **G** to the whole ....Mark 16:15
For I am not ashamed of the **G**,..............Rom. 1:16

GOSPELS—The first four books of the NT.

GRACE—Undeserved acceptance and love, usually from a superior to an inferior. In the Bible, the favor of God in providing salvation in Christ for those who deserve condemnation.
G and truth came through Jesus..................John 1:17
For by **G** you are saved through................Eph. 2:8
having been justified by His **G**,...................Titus 3:7

GRIEVE—To express or to cause sorrow.
And don't **G** God's Holy Spirit,...........Eph. 4:30
you will not **G** like the rest,................1 Thess. 4:13

GUARDIAN—Adult responsible for the person and property of a minor.
law, then, was our **G** until Christ,................ Gal. 3:24

GUILT—Responsibility for an offense or wrongdoing; guilt requires either punishment or expiation.
You took away the **G** of my sin....................Ps. 32:5

H

HALF TRIBE—Part of Manasseh, usually the part dwelling east of the Jordan (Num. 32:33; Deut. 3:13; Josh. 1:12; 4:12; 22:1).

HALLELUJAH—Exclamation meaning "Praise Yahweh!"
H! My soul, praise the LORD.................... Ps. 146:1
multitude in heaven, saying: **H**!............. Rev. 19:1

HARDNESS OF HEART—Resistance to and rejection of the Word and will of God.
He rebuked their unbelief and **H**,..............Mark 16:14

HARP—Musical instrument with strings.
who knows how to play the **H**............1 Sam. 16:16
praise Him with **H** and lyre............... Ps. 150:3

HATE—Strong negative reaction implying volatile hostility. Sometimes hate means to love less than something better (Matt. 10:37; Luke 14:26; John 12:26).
To fear the LORD is to **H** evil........................Prov. 8:13
I loved Jacob, but I **H-D** Esau.................... Mal. 1:3
does not **H** his own .... Luke 14:26
want to do, but I do what I **H**.............Rom. 7:15

HAUGHTY—Proud.
You humble those with **H** eyes............ Ps. 18:27

HEAD—The uppermost part of the body; the first, top, or chief.
Christ is the **H** of every man, theman is the **H** of the woman, ... 1 Cor. 11:3
He is also **H** of the body,.....................Col. 1:18

HEAL—Bring health to persons who are sick physically, emotionally, and spiritually.
For I am the LORD who

H-S you. . . . . Exod. 15:26
gifts of H-ING by the one Spirit,. . . . . 1 Cor. 12:9
by His wounding you have been H-ED . . . . . . 1 Pet. 2:24

HEART—Center of intellectual, moral, emotional, and spiritual life.
LORD your God with all your H, ... Deut. 6:5
but the LORD sees the H. . . . . 1 Sam. 16:7
create a clean H for me and. . . . . Ps. 51:10
Your word in my H so that I may . . . . Ps. 119:11
Search me, God, and know my H; . . . . Ps. 139:23
them and write it on their H-S. . . . . Jer. 31:33
I will give you a new H . . . . Ezek. 36:26
there your H will be also. . . . . Matt. 6:21

HEAVEN—The part of God's creation above the earth, including air and space, serving as the home of God and the final abode of the righteous.
God created the H-S and the earth. . . . . Gen. 1:1
The H-S declare the glory of God,. . . . . Ps. 19:1
for yourselves treasures in H, ... Matt. 6:20
but our citizenship is in H, ... Phil. 3:20
I saw a new H and a new earth . . . . Rev. 21:1

HEIFER—Young cow, especially one that has not yet calved (Heb. 9:13).

HEIR—One who inherits the property, blessing, or position of a predecessor.
if children, also H-S—H-S of God . . . . Rom. 8:17
H-S according to the promise. . . . . Gal. 3:29
the Gentiles are co-H-S, members . . . . Eph. 3:6

HELL—The final abode of the unrighteous dead wherein they suffer eternal punishment.
to have two hands and go to H. . . . . Mark 9:43
authority to throw {people} into H . . . . . . Luke 12:5

HIGH PLACE—Elevated site, usually on the top of a mountain or hill. Most high places were places of pagan worship and idolatry, and God commanded that they be destroyed.

HIGH PRIEST—One in charge of the temple (or tabernacle) worship, a hereditary office based on descent from Aaron.
led Him away to Caiaphas the H, ... Matt. 26:57
become a merciful and faithful H . . . . Heb. 2:17
this is the kind of H we need: . . . . Heb. 7:26

HILL COUNTRY—High ground west of the Jordan Valley, differentiated from the Shephelah (foothills) and coastal plain on the west and the Negev on the south.

HOLY—Separated from the world and dedicated to God; separated from worldliness.
you are standing is H ground. . . . . Exod. 3:5
and be H because I am H. . . . . Lev. 11:44
H, H, H is the Lord of Hosts;Isa. 6:3
and called us with a H calling, ... 2 Tim. 1:9

HOLY OF HOLIES—Innermost sanctuary of the temple (Heb. 9:3), also called the most holy place.

HOLY PLACE—Courts, inner room, and outer room of the tabernacle (Exod. 26:33).

HONOR—Respect, recognition.
H your father and your mother . . . . Exod. 20:12
Your name be H-ED as holy. . . . . Matt. 6:9
is not without H except in his . . . . Matt. 13:57

HOPE—Trustful expectation, particularly with reference to the fulfillment of God's promises.
Put your H in God, for I will . . . . Ps. 42:5
This H does not disappoint, ... Rom. 5:5
Christ in you, the H of glory. . . . . Col. 1:27
the rest, who have no H. . . . . 1 Thess. 4:13
the reality of what is H-D for, ... Heb. 11:1
reason for the H that is in you . . . . 1 Pet. 3:15

HORN—Metaphorically, strength and honor.
My shield, the H of my salvation2 Sam. 22:3

HOSANNA—A Hb or Aramaic word originally meaning "Save now," or "Save, we plead of You," used as an exclamation of praise.
H in the highest heaven! . . . . Matt. 21:9

HOSTILE—Opposed, antagonistic, against.
I will put H-ITY between you and the . . . . Gen. 3:15
mind-set of the flesh is H to God. . . . . Rom. 8:7
tore down the dividing wall of H-ITY. . . . . Eph. 2:14

HUMANITY—Humankind, male and female, created in the image of God (Gen. 1:27), having a body and soul (2:7).

HUMBLE—Free from arrogance and pride.
Moses was a very H man, ... Num. 12:3
and to walk H-Y with your God. Mic. 6:8
whoever H-S himself like this child. . . . . Matt. 18:4
He H-D Himself by becoming . . . . Phil. 2:8
but gives grace to the H. . . . . . Jas. 4:6

HUMILITY—Absence of pride.
and H comes before honor. . . . . Prov. 15:33
but in H consider others as more . . . . Phil. 2:3

HUNGER—Literally, a desire for food (Gen. 41:55). Figuratively, any strong desire (Mic. 6:14; Matt. 5:6).

HYMNS—Songs of praise.
singing psalms, H, and . . . Col. 3:16

HYPOCRITE—One who pretends to be better than he really is.
you must not be like the H-S, ... Matt. 6:5
H! First take the log out of .Matt. 7:5

HYSSOP—Small bushy plant used to apply ritually cleansing blood.
Purify me with H, and I will be clean; . . . . Ps. 51:7

I

I AM—The way God identified or described Himself to Moses (Exod. 3:13-14). Jesus spoke the same phrase, claiming equality with God (John 8:58).

IDOL—Image or form representing a divine being and thus an object of worship in place of God.
Do not make an I for yourself, ... Exod. 20:4

we know that "an I is nothing ....1 Cor. 8:4
and greed, which is I-ATRY......................Col. 3:5

IMAGE—Likeness.
Let Us make man in Our I,......................Gen. 1:26
He is the I of the invisible God ....Col. 1:15

IMMANUEL—"God with us"; name of a son to be born in Isaiah's prophecy to King Ahaz (Isa. 7:14; cp. 8:8), fulfilled in the birth of Jesus (Matt. 1:23).

IMMORALITY—Wickedness; what is not right.
Flee from sexual I!..... 1 Cor. 6:18

IMMORTAL—Exempt from death: the gift of God to mankind.
mortal must be clothed with I-ITY......................1 Cor. 15:53
the King eternal, I, invisible ....1 Tim. 1:17

IMPERISHABLE—Not subject to decay.
into an inheritance that is I, ...1 Pet. 1:4

IMPURITY—Uncleanness; imperfection.
I will remove all your I-IES......................Isa. 1:25
God has not called us to I, ... 1 Thess. 4:7

INCENSE—Mixture of aromatic spices burned during sacrificial worship (Exod. 30:1-10, 34-38).
prayer be set before You as I,................ Ps. 141:2

INDIGNATION—Displeasure at something offensive; righteous, justified anger.

INHERIT—Receive assets from someone who died.
they will I the earth..... Matt. 5:5
must I do to I eternal life?.......... Luke 10:25; 18:18

INHERITANCE—Assets received from someone who died.
to be a people for His I,.Deut. 4:20
Levi has no I among his brothers,the LORD is his I,..Deut. 18:2
In Him we were also made His I,..............Eph. 1:11

INIQUITY—Sin.
crushed because of our I-IES;......................Isa. 53:5

INQUIRE OF GOD—Seek God's guidance and will regarding such things as battles (1 Sam. 23:2), illness (2 Kings 1:2-3, 16), and other decisions (2 Sam. 2:1).

INSCRIPTION—Words or letters carved, engraved, or printed on a surface (Exod. 31:18; Dan. 5:8; Mark 15:26).

INSTRUCT—Teach or exhort; disciple.
Your good Spirit to I them......................Neh. 9:20
are able to I you for salvation..............2 Tim. 3:15

INSTRUCTION—The act or content of teaching or exhortation; discipleship.
This book of I must not depart......................Josh. 1:8
Listen to I and be wise; Prov. 8:33

INTEGRITY—Unwavering support of a standard of values; singleness of heart or mind.
if you walk before Me ... with I......................1 Kings 9:4
You desire I in the inner self......................Ps. 51:6

INTERCEDE—Intervene or mediate between differing parties, particularly to pray to God on behalf of another person.
But Moses I-D with the LORD his......................Exod. 32:11
the Spirit Himself I-S for us with......................Rom. 8:26
He always lives to I for them......................Heb. 7:25

INTERCESSION—Act of interceding.
perseverance and I for all the ....Eph. 6:18
prayers, I-S, and thanksgivings........ 1 Tim. 2:1

INTERMARRY—Marry someone from another culture or religion.
Do not I with them.........Deut. 7:3

INTERPRET—Explain the meaning of something.
and the ability to I dreams,......................Dan. 5:12
Do all speak in languages? Do all I?..............1 Cor. 12:30

INVOKE—To call on by name for help.
must not I the names of other gods;.........Exod. 23:13

J

JEALOUSY—1. Intolerance of rivalry or unfaithfulness. God is jealous for His people Israel in this first sense: He is intolerant of rival gods (Deut. 4:24; 5:9; Ezek. 8:3). 2. A disposition suspicious of rivalry or unfaithfulness (Num. 5:11-31). 3. Hostility toward a rival or one believed to enjoy an advantage; envy (Acts 5:17; 13:45).
provoked His J with foreign gods........ Deut. 32:16

JUDAISM—Religion and way of life of the Jews.

JUDGE—1. An official with authority to administer justice by trying cases (Exod. 2:14) and condemning the guilty (Ps. 1:5). 2. A military deliverer in the period between Joshua and David (Judg. 2:16).
He J-S the world with righteousness; ....Ps. 9:8
Do not J, so that you won't be J-D. ....Matt. 7:1
I did not come to J the world but..........John 12:47
before the J-MENT seat of Christ,..........2 Cor. 5:10
who is going to J the living and .. 2 Tim. 4:1
die once—and after this, J-MENT—..........Heb. 9:27

JUST—Fair, impartial, legally correct.
Won't the Judge of all the earth do what is J?..............Gen. 18:25
Only to act J-LY, to love .. Mic. 6:8
whatever is J, whatever is pure ....Phil. 4:8

JUSTICE—Fair and impartial treatment.
He will bring J to the nations.................Isa. 42:1
But let J flow like water,..............Amos 5:24
will proclaim J to the nations..............Matt. 12:18

JUSTIFICATION—Divine, forensic act of God whereby a sinner is pronounced righteous by the imputation of the righteousness of Christ.
and raised for our J..... Rom. 4:25

JUSTIFIED—Pronounced righteous.
who believes in Him is J..............Acts 13:39
They are J freely by His grace ....Rom. 3:24
no one is J by the works of the law ....Gal. 2:16

K

KEY—Instrument for gaining access.
give you the **K-S** of the kingdom .... Matt. 16:19
and I hold the **K-S** of death and .... Rev. 1:18
the One who has the **K** of David, ... Rev. 3:7

KIND—Compassionate, gentle, gracious.
with ropes of **K-NESS**.... Hos. 11:4
God's **K-NESS** is intended to lead .... Rom. 2:4
Love is patient; love is **K**......... 1 Cor. 13:4
And be **K** and compassionate .... Eph. 4:32

KING—Male monarch of a country.
said, "Give us a **K** to judge us .... 1 Sam. 8:6
who has been born **K** of the Jews? .... Matt. 2:2
K OF **K-S** AND LORD OF .... Rev. 19:16

KINGDOM—The realm over which rule is exerted and the exercise of authority to reign. Jesus preached that God's kingdom was at hand (Matt. 11:12). Jesus' miracles, preaching, forgiving sins, and resurrection were an inbreaking of God's sovereign rule in this dark, evil age.
you will be My **K** of priests and .... Exod. 19:6
But seek first the **K** of God .... Matt. 6:33
I will give you the keys of the **K**............. Matt. 16:19
the **K** of God is among you.......... Luke 17:21
My **K** is not of this world, ... John 18:36
transferred us into the **K** of the Son .... Col. 1:13

KISS—The touching of the lips to another person's lips, cheeks, shoulders, hands, or feet as a gesture of friendship, acceptance, respect, and reverence.
betraying the Son of Man with a **K**? .... Luke 22:48
Greet one another with a holy **K**....... Rom. 16:16

KNOWLEDGE—Awareness of facts, truths, and principles. Right knowledge gives direction, conviction, and assurance to faith (2 Cor. 4:14).
fear of the LORD is the beginning of **K**; .... Prov. 1:7
K inflates with pride, but love .... 1 Cor. 8:1

L

LAMB—Young sheep, used for sacrifice during Passover (Exod. 12:1-36) as well as in the daily sacrifices of Israel (Lev. 14:12-21). Christ was the Lamb of God who provided salvation for the world.
God Himself will provide the **L** .... Gen. 22:8
Like a **L** led to the slaughter .... Isa. 53:7
L of God, who takes away the sin.......... John 1:29
L who was slaughtered is worthy .... Rev. 5:12

LAMENT, LAMENTATION—Expression of grief and mourning.

LAMP—An open bowl for oil with a pinched spout to support a wick.
Your word is a **L** for my feet and .... Ps. 119:105
No one lights a **L** and puts it .... Matt. 5:15
like 10 virgins who took their **L-S**......... Matt. 25:1

LANGUAGE—System of communication.
the whole earth had the same **L** .... Gen. 11:1
began to speak in different **L-S**, ... Acts 2:4
different kinds of **L-S**, to another, interpretation of **L-S**................ 1 Cor. 12:10
do not forbid speaking in {other} **L-S**. .... 1 Cor. 14:39
every tribe and **L** and people .... Rev. 5:9

LATTICE—Structure of crisscrossed strips used as window covering to allow some light to penetrate while keeping heat and rain to a minimum.

LAW—Term used for commandments, customs, legal judgments, collections of regulations and ordinances, the book of Deuteronomy (which means "second law"), the entire complex of regulations revealed at Sinai, the first five books of the OT, and the OT as a whole as opposed to the NT.
Moses wrote down this **L** .... Deut. 31:9
I will place My **L** within them .... Jer. 31:33
All the **L** and the Prophets depend on these ... Matt. 22:40
are not under **L** but under grace .... Rom. 6:14
The **L**, then, was our guardian until .... Gal. 3:24
sin is the breaking of **L**. 1 John 3:4

LEAVEN—Natural yeast used to make dough rise.

LEWDNESS—Lust; sexual unchastity (Mark 7:22).

LIFE—The animating force in both animals and humans (Gen. 1:20). Just as physical life is the gift of God, so is eternal life (Rom. 6:23).
breathed the breath of **L** into his .... Gen. 2:7
the **L** of a creature is in the blood, ... Lev. 17:11
gains the whole world yetloses his **L**? ...... Matt. 16:26
I am the resurrection and the **L**. .... John 11:25
I am the way, the truth, and the **L**. .... John 14:6

LIGHT—Radiant energy, illumination. Symbolic of instruction (Ps. 119:105,130), truth (43:3), good (Isa. 5:20), salvation (49:6), life (Job 33:28,30), peace (Isa. 45:7), rejoicing (Ps. 97:11), covenant (Isa. 42:6), justice and righteousness (59:9), God's presence and favor (Ps. 89:15; 1 John 1:5), and the glory of the LORD (Isa. 60:1-3; Rev. 21:23).
"Let there be **L**," and there was **L**. .... Gen. 1:3
in darkness have seen a great **L**; .... Isa. 9:2
You are the **L** of the world. .... Matt. 5:14
I am the **L** of the world. John 8:12

LINEN—Common fabric spun from the flax plant.

LION—Large meat-eating cat.
and the **L** will eat straw like an ox. .... Isa. 11:7
prowling around like a roaring **L**, ... 1 Pet. 5:8
The **L** from the tribe of Judah, ... Rev. 5:5

LIVE—Be physically or spiritually alive.
for no one can see Me and **L**. .... Exod. 33:20
man does not **L** on bread alone .... Deut. 8:3
The one who believes in Me, even if he dies, will **L**....... John 11:25
The righteous will **L** by faith. .... Rom. 1:17
I no longer **L**, but Christ **L-S** in me. The life I now **L** in the flesh, I **L** by faith ...... Gal. 2:20

LOCUST—An insect, similar to the grasshopper, that periodically multiplies to astronomical numbers devouring vegetation.

What the devouring **L** has left, the .... Joel 1:4
his food was **L-S** and wild honey.................. Matt. 3:4

LORD—A title of God. Yahweh is the name of God (Exod. 3:15), commonly represented by Lord (in small caps; "Ld" below). *'Adonai* is another important Hb designation for God as Lord and master in the OT. In the NT, the Gk word *kurios* is used of God as well as Jesus. *'Adonai* and *kurios* are also used of humans (Gen. 18:12; 39:2; Num. 21:28; Isa. 26:13; Matt. 13:27; 21:30; 27:63; Luke 14:22).
The **LD** is my shepherd; ... Ps. 23:1
The **LD** declared to my **L**: Ps. 110:1
who says to Me, '**L**, **L**!' will enter .... Matt. 7:21
to Him, "My **L** and my God!" .... John 20:28
crucified, both **L** and Messiah! .... Acts 2:36
with your mouth, "Jesus is **L**," .... Rom. 10:9
one can say, "Jesus is **L**," except .... 1 Cor. 12:3
confess that Jesus Christ is **L**, ... Phil. 2:11
King of kings, and the **L** of **L-S**, ... 1 Tim. 6:15
obeyed Abraham, calling him **L**.......... 1 Pet. 3:6
but set apart the Messiah as **L**.......... 1 Pet. 3:15

LOT—Object used to discover God's will. Person casting lots would first pray to God asking for a correct answer (1 Sam. 14:41; Acts 1:26).
The land must be divided by **L**; .... Num. 26:55
The **L** is cast into the lap, ... Prov. 16:33
His clothes by casting **L-S**.......... Matt. 27:35

LOVE—Unselfish, loyal, and benevolent intention and commitment toward another person. Gk word agape was used in the NT to denote the unconditional love of God (John 3:16; Rom. 5:8).
showing faithful **L** to a thousand .... Exod. 20:6
but **L** your neighbor as yourself; .... Lev. 19:18
L the LORD your God with all your .... Deut. 6:5
A friend **L-S** at all times, ... Prov. 17:17
L your enemies and pray for .... Matt. 5:44
For God **L-D** the world in this way.................... John 3:16
give you a new commandment: **L** one another.......... John 13:34
No one has greater **L** than this, ... John 15:13
God proves His own **L** for us in that .... Rom. 5:8
L is patient; **L** is kind. **L** does not........... 1 Cor. 13:4
Husbands, **L** your wives, just as .... Eph. 5:25
For the **L** of money is a root of .... 1 Tim. 6:10
Do not **L** the world or the things .... 1 John 2:15
L one another, because **L** is from God.................. 1 John 4:7
God is **L**, ... 1 John 4:16

LUST—Strong craving or desire for something wrong, especially illicit sexual desire.
looks at a woman to **L** for her has.......... Matt. 5:28
the **L** of the flesh, the **L** of the eyes .... 1 John 2:16

LYRE—A stringed instrument similar to a harp.

M

MAGIC—The manipulation of natural or supernatural events through incantation or other means (Exod. 7:22; Prov. 17:8; Acts 19:19).

MAJESTY—Imposing, regal dignity.
Splendor and **M** are before Him; .... 1 Chron. 16:27
He is robed in **M**; .... Ps. 93:1
right hand of the **M** on high. .... Heb. 1:3
we were eyewitnesses of His **M**. .... 2 Pet. 1:16

MALICE—Hatred; harmful intentions.
put away ... wrath, **M**, slander, ... Col. 3:8

MANNA—Food from heaven that sustained the Israelites in the wilderness.
Israel named the substance **M**........ Exod. 16:31
fathers ate the **M** in the desert, ... John 6:31,49

MANTLE—Robe worn as an outer garment (1 Kings 19:19; 2 Kings 2:13-14).

MARRIAGE—The covenantal union of one man and one woman enacted with an oath before God of lifelong loyalty and love for each other.
nor are given in **M** but are like .... Matt. 22:30
M must be respected by all, ... Heb. 13:4
the **M** of the Lamb has come, ... Rev. 19:7

MARRY—Form a marriage.
it is better to **M** than to burn .... 1 Cor. 7:9

MASTER—One in authority over others (Mark 13:35; Luke 13:25; 14:21; 16:13; Eph. 6:9).
if I am a **M**, where is {your} fear .... Mal. 1:6
No one can be a slave of two **M-S**........... Matt. 6:24
slave is not greater than his **M**, ... John 13:16

MATTOCK—Tool used for digging (1 Sam. 13:20-21).

MEDIATOR—One who stands between two or more parties to negotiate and reconcile. Jesus was the perfect mediator between God and man.
one God and one **M** between God......... 1 Tim. 2:5

MEDITATE—Think deeply or reflect upon some truth or supposition.
he **M-S** on it day and night. Ps. 1:2
mouth and the **M-ION** of my heart .... Ps. 19:14

MEDIUM—A person possessed by (Lev. 20:6) or consulting (Deut. 18:11) a ghost or spirit of the dead.
Do not turn to **M-S** or consult .... Lev. 19:31
a woman at Endor who is a **M**......... 1 Sam. 28:7

MERCY—Compassionate action towards someone over whom one has the advantage.
for His **M-IES** never end..................... Lam. 3:22
I desire **M** and not sacrifice.............. Matt. 9:13
I will show **M** to whom I show **M**, ... Rom. 9:15
M triumphs over judgment.............. Jas. 2:13

MERCY SEAT—Slab of pure gold that sat atop the ark of the covenant, it symbolized the throne from which God ruled Israel (Lev. 16:2; Num. 7:89; Heb. 9:5).

MIDWIFE—Woman who assisted in the delivery of a baby (Gen. 35:17; 38:28; Exod. 1:15-21).

MILLSTONE—Either of a pair of circular stones used to grind grain.
or an upper **M** as security for a ....Deut. 24:6
better for him if a heavy **M** were................Matt. 18:6

MIRACLE—Event which involves an immediate and powerful action of God designed to reveal His character or purposes.
and do many **M-S** in Your name? ....Matt. 7:22
testified by signs ... various **M-S**,..........Heb. 2:4

MONEY—Medium of exchange.
loves **M** is never satisfied with **M** ....Eccl. 5:10
without **M**, come, buy, and eat! ....Isa. 55:1
cannot be slaves of God and of **M**..............Matt. 6:24
For the love of **M** is a root of ....1 Tim. 6:10

MORTAL—Human; susceptible to death.
this **M** must be clothed with immortality.........1 Cor. 15:53

MOURN—Express sorrow and grief.
a time to **M** and a time to dance;..................Eccl. 3:4
Blessed are those who **M**, because.................Matt. 5:4

MURDER—Intentional, illegal taking of human life.
Do not **M**..............Exod. 20:13
who hates his brother is a **M-ER** ....1 John 3:15

MUTE—Unable to speak.
Who makes him **M** or deaf, seeing...................Exod. 4:11

MYRRH—Aromatic resin used as an ingredient in anointing oil (Exod. 30:23), applied as perfume (Esth. 2:12; Prov. 7:17; Songs 1:13; 3–5), given as a gift (Matt. 2:11; cp. Rev. 18:13), and used in embalming (John 19:39; cp. Mark 15:23).

MYSTERY—A revealed secret that could not have been understood apart from divine revelation.
The **M** was then revealed to Daniel.................Dan. 2:19
the **M** hidden for ages....Col. 1:26
the **M** of godliness is great:......1 Tim. 3:16

MYTH—An unproven but popular belief; a contrived tale that does not adhere to facts.
not ... to pay attention to **M-S**....................1 Tim. 1:4

N

NARD—Expensive fragrance (Songs 4:13-14; Mark 14:3; John 12:3).

NEIGHBOR—A nearby person. Jesus expanded the definition to any person in need(Luke 10:29-37).
but love your **N** as yourself;..................Lev. 19:18

O

OATH—Invoking of God's name or something else of value to promise that a vow will be kept or that a statement is true.

OFFENSE—That which causes indignation or disgust (Gen. 31:36; Matt. 18:7; Gal. 5:11).

OFFERING—A gift to God as an act of worship.
Lord had regard for Abel and his **O**,...............Gen. 4:4
and fragrant **O** to God.... Eph. 5:2
You did not want sacrifice and **O**,..................Heb. 10:5

OIL—A product of olives, it had many uses including the treatment of wounds (Isa. 1:6;Luke 10:34) and anointing (Exod. 29:7; 30:25; cp. Matt. 26:7, 12).
You anoint my head with **O**;Ps. 23:5
sensible ones took **O** in their flasks.....................Matt. 25:4
anointing him with olive **O** in the name of the Lord.............Jas. 5:14

OPPRESS—Burden with unjust restraints.
raises up those who are **O-ED**.....................Ps. 146:8
He was **O-ED** and afflicted,.................Isa. 53:7

ORACLE—A communication from God.

ORDAIN—1. Determine ahead of time what will happen. 2. Commission a person for special service to the Lord and His people.

ORDINANCE—A law, especially one from God.

OVERSEER—1. Secular superintendent or supervisor (Exod. 5:10). 2. A church office (Acts 20:28; Phil. 1:1; 1 Tim. 3:1-2; Titus 1:7; 1 Pet. 5:2).

OX—Large bovine used as a work animal, as food, and as a sacrifice.
Do not muzzle an **O** while it.... Deut. 25:4; 1 Cor. 9:9

P

PAGAN—One who worships a god or gods other than the LORD.

PARABLE—A story that puts one thing alongside another for purposes of comparison and new insight (cp. John 10:6).
He told them many things in **P-S**.........Matt. 13:3

PARADISE—Literally a garden (Songs 4:13); another word for heaven (Rev. 2:7).
you will be with Me in **P**....................Luke 23:43
was caught up into **P**.. 2 Cor. 12:4

PARALYTIC—One who has lost use of a body part.
brought to Him a **P** lying on a..............Matt. 9:2

PARENTS—Fathers and mothers.
who sinned, this man or his **P**, ...John 9:2
Children, obey your **P** in the Lord,.....................Eph. 6:1

PASSOVER—Israelite festival commemorating deliverance from Egyptian bondage (Exod. 12:11).
Christ our **P** has been sacrificed. ....1 Cor. 5:7

PATIENCE—Endurance of opposition; perseverance, steadfastness, forbearance.
endured with much **P** objects of ....Rom. 9:22
love, joy, peace, **P**, kindness,...............Gal. 5:22

PATIENT—Displaying patience.
Love is **P**; love is kind.. 1 Cor. 13:4

PATRIARCH—An ancestor, the founding father of a family, clan, or nation.

PEACE—A condition or sense of security, harmony, well-being, and prosperity.
who proclaims **P**, who brings news ....Isa. 52:7
P, **P**, when there is no **P**. Jer. 6:14; 8:11
P I leave with you.
My **P** I give ....John 14:27
And the **P** of God, which surpasses.......................Phil. 4:7

by making **P** through the blood..................Col. 1:20

PENTECOST—A Jewish festival fifty days after Passover. The Holy Spirit came to dwell with the disciples on this day (Acts 2:1-4).

PEOPLE—**1.** Human beings. **2.** Persons in a particular ethnic, cultural, or geographical group.
your **P** will be my **P**,.... Ruth 1:16
My **P** who are called by My name.............2 Chron. 7:14
a holy nation, a **P** for His possession,...................1 Pet. 2:9
and language and **P** and nation...............Rev. 5:9

PERFECT—Whole or complete, without defect and lacking nothing; also mature.
Be **P**, therefore, as your heavenly..............Matt. 5:48

PERISH—Die, disappear, cease to exist, be destroyed.
and they will never **P**—ever!.............John 10:28
not wanting any to **P**, but all to ....2 Pet. 3:9

PERSECUTE—Harass and cause suffering for being different in faith, culture, or race.
Princes have **P-D** me without............ Ps. 119:1-61
and pray for those who **P** you,..........Matt. 5:44
they **P-D** Me, they will also **P** you............John 15:20
in Christ Jesus will be **P-D**....................2 Tim. 3:12

PERSEVERE—Maintain Christian faith through the trying times of life.
P in these things, for by doing.................1 Tim. 4:16

PERVERTED—Bent, crooked, twisted; inverted.
P men of the city surrounded......... Judg. 19:22
in a crooked and **P** generation,............Phil. 2:15

PESTILENCE—Devastating epidemic sent by God.
or the **P** that ravages at noon.........................Ps. 91:6

PETITION—Formal request.

PHARAOH—Title for the ancient kings of Egypt. See *People and Places*.

PLAGUE—Widespread disease or calamity implying divine judgment.
to send all My **P-S** against you,.................. Exod. 9:14
angels with the seven last **P-S**......................Rev. 15:1

PLEDGE—Something given as a deposit or guarantee of a debt. The Holy Spirit is a down payment or pledge on our souls guaranteeing Jesus' "purchase" of our souls (2 Cor. 1:22; 5:5; Eph. 1:14).

PLOWSHARE—A metal tip for a wooden plow (1 Sam. 13:20-21; Isa. 2:4; Joel 4:10; Mic. 4:3).

PLUMB LINE—Weighted cord that assures vertical accuracy (Amos 7:8).

PLUNDER—Loot after victory in battle.
So you will **P** the Egyptians........... Exod. 3:22

POMEGRANATE—A fruit with many seeds and juicy, red pulp.

POOR—People with little or no money.
there will never cease to be **P**.............. Deut. 15:11
Me to bring good news to the **P**. ....Isa. 61:1
Blessed are the **P** in spirit,.................. Matt. 5:3
if I donate all my goods to feed the **P**................ 1 Cor. 13:3

PORTICO—Covered entrance; porch or vestibule.
P in front of the temple sanctuary....................1 Kings 6:3

PRAISE—Proclaim the merit or worth of someone or something in worship and thanksgiving.
This is my God, and I will **P** Him,............... Exod. 15:2
and His courts with **P**... Ps. 100:4
have prepared **P** from the mouths............... Matt. 21:16
up to God a sacrifice of **P**,........... Heb. 13:15

PRAY—Engage in dialogue with God.
I will not sin against the LORD by ceasing to **P** for you.......... 1 Sam. 12:23
humble themselves, **P** andseek My.................2 Chron. 7:14
P for those who persecute you,..................Matt. 5:44
you should **P** like this:... Matt. 6:9
know what to **P** for as we should................Rom. 8:26
P constantly..........1 Thess. 5:17

PREACH—Tell about God's acts of salvation through Jesus Christ.
Go into all the world and **P** the gospel ....Mark 16:15
but we **P** Christ crucified, ... 1 Cor. 1:23

PRECEPT—Command, decree.
How I long for Your **P-S**! .... Ps. 119:40

PRECIOUS—Valuable, costly; dear.
their lives are **P** in his sight......................Ps. 72:14
but with the **P** blood of Christ,.................1 Pet. 1:19

PREDESTINE—Determine or decree ahead of time.
Your plan had **P-D** to take place...............Acts 4:28
He also **P-D** to be conformed to............Rom. 8:29
He **P-D** us to be adopted through....................Eph. 1:5

PREPARATION DAY—Sixth day of the week, in which Jews prepared life's necessities in order to avoid work on the Sabbath (John 19:31).

PREVAIL—Succeed; conquer.

PRIDE—Undue confidence in and attention to one's own skills, accomplishments, possessions, or position.
P comes before destruction, ...Prov. 16:18
Knowledge inflates with **P**,......................1 Cor. 8:1

PRIEST—Person who represented God to human beings and human beings to God (1 Tim. 2:5).
you will be My kingdom of **P-S**................. Exod. 19:6
you are a chosen race, a royal **P-HOOD**, ... 1 Pet. 2:9

PROCLAIM—Declare, announce.
P His salvation fromday to day........... 1 Chron. 16:23
and the sky **P-S** the work of His.............................Ps. 19:1
to **P** the year of the LORD's favor,............Isa. 61:2
you **P** the Lord's death until He..............1 Cor. 11:26

PROFANE—Treat what is holy as if it were common.

they **P-D** My holy name............ Ezek. 36:20

PROMISE—A declaration of the gifts and deeds that God will bestow. All the promises of God were fulfilled in Jesus Christ.
of God's **P-S** is "Yes" in Him................ 2 Cor. 1:20

PROPHECY—A message from the Lord through the Holy Spirit.
P-IES, they will come to an end;................ 1 Cor. 13:8
no **P** of Scripture comes from................ 2 Pet. 1:20

PROPHESY—Deliver a prophecy.
your sons and your daughters will **P**,................ Joel 2:28
and above all that you may **P**... 1 Cor. 14:1

PROPHET, PROPHETESS—A person who receives a prophecy.
God will raise up for you a **P** like .... Deut. 18:15
A **P** is not without honor except....... Matt. 13:57
some to be apostles, some **P-S**, ... Eph. 4:11

PROPITIATION—The satisfaction of an offended party—in this case, God (Rom. 3:25; Heb. 2:17; 1 John 2:2; 4:10).

PROSELYTE—Convert to a religion, especially a non-Jew who accepted the Jewish faith.
over land and sea to make one **P**,........ Matt. 23:15

PROSTITUTE—One who trades sexual services for pay.
who consorts with **P-S** destroys his .... Prov. 29:3

PROUD—Having pride.
God resists the **P**, but gives grace to .... Jas. 4:6

PROVERB—A wise observation.
Solomon composed 3,000 **P-S**, ... 1 Kings 4:32

PROVOKE—Arouse anger or exasperation.
tested God and **P-D** the Holy One............ Ps. 78:41

PRUDENT—Wise and practical.

PRUNE—To remove branches from a plant in order to improve its health or productivity.

PSALM—A hymn or poem of praise.
speaking to one another in **P-S**,................Eph. 5:19

PUNISHMENT—Penalty for wrongdoing.
P for our peace was on Him,................Isa. 53:5
they will go away into eternal **P**, ... Matt. 25:46

PURE—Clean; without fault or contamination.
eyes are too **P** to look on evil,................Hab. 1:13
whatever is just, whatever is **P**,......... Phil. 4:8

PURGE—To cleanse from impurity.

PURIFY—Make pure.
P me with hyssop, and I will be clean;................Ps. 51:7

PURIM—A Jewish holiday celebrating Esther's rescue of Israel from destruction (Esth. 9:26).

PURPLE—Color often designating luxury or royalty.

PURSUE—Follow in order to capture or obtain.
seek peace and **P** it. ..... Ps. 34:14
who did not **P** righteousness, have................Rom. 9:30

R

RABBI—One learned in the law of Moses.

RAM—Male sheep.

RANSOM—The price paid to gain the freedom of a captive or slave.
to give His life—a **R** for many.......... Matt. 20:28
gave Himself—a **R** for all,............... 1 Tim. 2:6

REAP—To harvest grain; figuratively, to receive the product of one's actions.
who sows injustice will **R** disaster,................Prov. 22:8
whatever a man sows he will also **R**,................Gal. 6:7

REBUKE—Reprimand, admonish.
profitable for teaching, for **R-ING**,..............2 Tim. 3:16
many as I love, I **R** and discipline.............. Rev. 3:19

RECONCILE—Bring together two parties that are estranged or in dispute. Jesus Christ brings together God and man.
First go and be **R-D** with your brother,............Matt. 5:24
on Christ's behalf, "Be **R-D** to God."............ 2 Cor. 5:20

REDEEM—Pay a price in order to secure the release of something or someone.
He **R-S** your life from the Pit;................Ps. 103:4
Christ has **R-ED** us from the curse .... Gal. 3:13

REDEMPTION—The act or result of redeeming.
In Him we have **R** through His .... Eph. 1:7

REFUGE—Place of safety.
God is our **R** and strength,Ps. 46:1

REGARD—Notice, consider, pay attention.

REGENERATION—Rebirth, renewal (Titus 3:5).

REGULATION—Rule dictating procedure.
Why do you submit to **R-S**:...............Col. 2:20

REIGN—Rule, exercise sovereign authority.
do not let sin **R** in your mortal body,................Rom. 6:12
and He will **R** forever and ever!..............Rev. 11:15

REJOICE—Express joy.
let us **R** and be glad in it. ....Ps. 118:24
but **R** that your names are written................Luke 10:20
I will say it again: **R**!...... Phil. 4:4

REMNANT—Something left over, especially the people who remain after divine judgment.
only the **R** will be saved; ....Rom. 9:27

REPENT—Change one's mind; turn to God and away from sin.
R, because the kingdom of heaven................Matt. 3:2
R ... and be baptized,.....Acts 2:38

REPENTANCE—Turning from sin to God.
fruit consistent with **R**. . Matt. 3:8
godly grief produces a **R** 2 Cor. 7:10

REPROACH—Disgrace, dishonor, discredit.

REQUIRE—Demand, deem as necessary.
what it is the LORD
R-S of you: .... Mic. 6:8
given us everything
R-D for life .... 2 Pet. 1:3

RESCUE—Save, free, liberate.
He has **R-D** us from the domain
of .... Col. 1:13

RESTORE—Reinstate, rectify; return something to its former state.
R the joy of Your salvation
to me, ... Ps. 51:12

RESURRECTION—Bodily rising and returning to life after being dead.
the **R** of life ... the **R** of
judgment .... John 5:29
I am the **R** and the life. John 11:25
if there is no **R** of the
dead, ... 1 Cor. 15:13

RETRIBUTION—Punishment for evil.

REVELATION—Act of disclosing, making known.
light for **R** to the Gentiles
.... Luke 2:32
was made known to me
by **R**, ... Eph. 3:3

REVERE—Show respect and awe.

REVILE—Speak abusively.
When we are **R-D**, we
bless; .... 1 Cor. 4:12
when **R-D**, He did not
R in return; .... 1 Pet. 2:23

REWARD—Compensation for goodness.
your **R** is great in
heaven. .... Matt. 5:12

RIGHTEOUSNESS—Justice and rightness; conformity to divine law and morality.
He credited it to him
as **R**. .... Gen. 15:6
R exalts a nation,
but sin is .... Prov. 14:34
apart from the law,
God's **R** has .... Rom. 3:21
reserved for me the
crown of **R**, ... 2 Tim. 4:8

ROD—A short stick used for walking or defense.

S

SABBATH—Day of rest, a time for sacred assembly and worship (Lev. 23:1-3), and a symbol of Israel's covenant with God (Exod. 31:12-17).
Remember to dedicate
the **S** day: .... Exod. 20:8
The **S** was made for man
and not .... Mark 2:27

SACKCLOTH—Garment of coarse material made from goat or camel hair and worn as a sign of mourning (Isa. 15:3) or repentance (58:5; Jonah 3:5-8).

SACRED—Holy; set apart for God.

SACRIFICE—A slaughtered animal given to God during worship to express devotion, thanksgiving, or the need for forgiveness (Lev. 1–7). Christ fulfilled the law as the sinless high priest who offered Himself up as a sacrifice for sinners (Heb. 7:27).
to obey is better
than **S**, ... 1 Sam. 15:22
present your bodies as a
living **S**, ... Rom. 12:1
removal of sin by the **S** of Himself. .... Heb. 9:26
offer up to God a **S** of
praise, ... Heb. 13:15

SAINTS—Holy people; a title for all believers in Christ. In the Book of Revelation, saints are faithful and true witnesses for Jesus.
He intercedes for
the **S-S** .... Rom. 8:27
Greet every **S** in Christ
Jesus. .... Phil. 4:21

SALVATION—Rescue from danger or death. Biblical salvation is a free gift from God through Jesus Christ that rescues the believer from sin and its consequences.
He has become my **S**.... Ps. 118:14
For my eyes have seen
Your **S**. .... Luke 2:30
There is **S** in no one else, Acts 4:12
work out your own **S** with fear
and .... Phil. 2:12
escape if we neglect
such a great **S**? .... Heb. 2:3

SANCTIFICATION—Process of being made holy and growing into the likeness of Jesus Christ through the work of the Holy Spirit.
For this is God's will,
your **S**: .... 1 Thess. 4:3

SANCTUARY—Place set aside as sacred and holy, especially a place of worship (Exod. 25:8).
your body is a **S** of the Holy
Spirit .... 1 Cor. 6:19

SANHEDRIN—Highest Jewish council in NT times. The Great Sanhedrin at the Jerusalem temple had 71 members and was presided over by the high priest. They did not have the authority to condemn people to death (John 18:31).

SATRAP—Political official who governed a province of the Persian Empire.

SAVE—Rescue from danger.
come to seek and to **S**
the lost. .... Luke 19:10
everyone who calls on the name
of the Lord will be
S-D. .... Rom. 10:13
by grace you are **S-D** through
faith, ... Eph. 2:8

SAVIOR—God is the only true Savior (Ps. 106:21; Isa. 45:15, 21-22). Jesus is also the Savior because He is God incarnate.
a **S**, who is Messiah the
Lord. .... Luke 2:11
our great God and **S**,
Jesus Christ. .... Titus 2:13

SCEPTER—Official staff or baton of a king that symbolized his authority (Isa. 14:5).
The **S** will not depart from
Judah, ... Gen. 49:10

SCOFF—Show contempt or disrespect for others.

SCORN—Consider something to be of low value.
S-ED by men and despised by
people. .... Ps. 22:6

SCOURGE—An affliction (Isa. 28:15, 18), or a severe form of corporal punishment involving whipping and beating (Josh. 23:13; Acts 22:24-25; Heb. 11:36).

SCRIBE—Person trained in writing skills (Jer. 36:32). During the exile in Babylon, scribes apparently copied, preserved, and taught the law.

SCRIPTURE—Sacred writings that reveal God's redemption. For the NT authors, "Scripture" was the OT. Now the NT is also Scripture (2 Pet. 3:15-16).
concerning Himself in all
the **S-S**. .... Luke 24:27
All **S** is inspired by God
and is. .... 2 Tim. 3:16
no prophecy of **S** comes from
one's own
interpretation. .... 2 Pet. 1:20

SEAL—Ring, stamp, or small cylinder containing a distinctive engraving. An object marked with a seal implied ownership. A letter marked with a seal was considered an official dispatch.
S-ED with the promised Holy Spirit....................Eph. 1:13
to open the scroll and break its **S-S**?".......................Rev. 5:2

SEER—Prophet; one whom God has enabled to see the future.

SELAH—Term of unknown meaning appearing in Psalms and Hab. 3:3,9,13. The word probably called for a pause or an intensification of instruments or voices in worship.

SELF-CONTROL—Mastery of personal desires and passions.
gentleness, **S.** Against such....................Gal. 5:23
knowledge with **S**, **S** with endurance,...........2 Pet. 1:6

SELFISH—Concerned with one's own needs rather than the needs of others and the purpose of God.
is not **S**; is not provoked; .1 Cor. 13:5

SEXUAL IMMORALITY—Sexual activity outside the context of the marital covenant, including premarital sex (fornication) and adultery(Exod. 20:14, 1 Cor. 6:9-10).
Flee from **S**!............1 Cor. 6:18
works of the flesh are obvious: s,.............Gal. 5:19

SHAME—Painful emotion arising from the consciousness of improper conduct.
on Him will not be put to **S**...............Rom. 9:33
a cross and despised the **S**,..................Heb. 12:2

SHEEP—A prominent animal in the sacrificial system of Israel, also a source for food and clothing.
His people, the **S** of His pasture.................Ps. 100:3
separates the **S** from the goats................Matt. 25:32
I lay down My life for the **S**.................John 10:15

SHEKEL—A weight of about four-tenths of an ounce; a coin of that weight.

SHEPHERD—Keeper of sheep. Used figuratively for kings (2 Sam. 5:2), other political and religious leaders (Ezek. 34), and God Himself (Ps. 23:1).
like sheep without a **S**.... 1 Kings 22:17; Matt. 9:36
The LORD is my **S**; there is Ps. 23:1
I am the good **S**. The good **S** lays..............John 10:11

SHIELD—Protective devise used in battle.
LORD is my strength and my **S**; ....Ps. 28:7
In every situation take the **S** of faith,.........Eph. 6:16

SHRINE—Small building or part of a building devoted to the worship of a god.

SICKLE—Curved blade of flint or metal used to cut down stalks of grain (Joel 3:13; Rev. 14:14).

SIEGE—Battle tactic in which an army surrounds an objective and cuts off all supplies.

SIGNET—A ring used as a seal.

SIN—Rebellion against God; a violation of the righteous nature of God; unbelief.
forgive their **S**, and heal their land...............2 Chron. 7:14
so that I may not **S** against You.......................Ps. 119:11
yet He bore the **S** of many.................Isa. 53:12
authority on earth to forgive **S-S**...............Matt. 9:6
takes away the **S** of the world!..............John 1:29
For all have **S-NED** and fall short...........Rom. 3:23
For the wages of **S** is death,..................Rom. 6:23
Christ died for our **S-S** 1 Cor. 15:3
as we are, yet without **S**.................Heb. 4:15
If we confess our **S-S**, ... forgive us.......................1 John 1:9
If we say, "We have not **S-NED**," we make Him a liar, ...1 John 1:10

SINNER—Person who sins.
or take the path of **S-S**,..... Ps. 1:1
Don't be jealous of **S-S**;..................Prov. 23:17
joy in heaven over one **S** who repents...............Luke 15:7
while we were still **S-S** Christ died.....................Rom. 5:8
came into the world to save **S-S**..............1 Tim. 1:15

SLACKER—Lazy person.
Go to the ant, you **S**!......Prov. 6:6

SLANDER—To speak critically and maliciously of another person (Lev. 19:16). In a court of law, it means to accuse another person falsely (Deut. 5:20).
Don't **S** a servant to his master,.............Prov. 30:10
to **S** no one, to avoid fighting,...............Titus 3:2

SLAVE—A person bonded to work for another and dependent on that other for daily needs.
No one can be a **S** of two masters..............Matt. 6:24
be first among you must be your **S**;...........Matt. 20:27
Well done, good and faithful **S**!..........Matt. 25:21
who commits sin is a **S** of sin..............John 8:34
you used to be **S-S** of sin,.......................Rom. 6:17
no Jew or Greek, **S** or free, male.....................Gal. 3:28
by assuming the form of a **S**,......................Phil. 2:7

SLAY, SLAIN—Kill violently.

SLING—Weapon consisting of two long straps with a pouch at the end to hold a stone.
defeated the Philistine with a **S**............1 Sam. 17:50

SLUMBER—Sleep, doze, nod off.
your Protector will not **S**.....................Ps. 121:3
A little sleep, a little **S**,........Prov. 6:10; 24:33

SNARE—Trap that lures birds and animals.

SON—Male descendant.
This man really was God's **S**!.............Matt. 27:54
will be called **S-S** of the living God.....................Rom. 9:26
slave, but a **S**; and if a **S**, then an heir.........................Gal. 4:7
The one who has the **S** has life.............. 1 John 5:12

SON OF MAN—1. A poetic synonym for "human." Jesus sometimes used the title in the context of His humanity. 2. In Dan. 7:13 it was a reference to the Messiah (Matt. 24:27; 25:31).
S did not come to be served, but..........................Mark 10:45
the **S** seated at the right hand of.............Mark 14:62

SONS OF THE PROPHETS—Members of a band or guild of prophets (2 Kings 2:3, 5, 7, 15; Amos 7:14).

SORCERY—Magic by appeal to evil spirits.
interpret omens, practice S, ... Deut. 18:10

SOUL—The inner part of the person; the non-physical aspect of being that does not die.
all your S, and with all your strength................ Deut. 6:5
Him who is able to destroy both S and body in hell.. Matt. 10:28
as far as to divide S, spirit, joints,..................Heb. 4:12
the salvation of your S-S................1 Pet. 1:9

SOVEREIGN—Possessing all power and authority.
{He is} the blessed and only S,................1 Tim. 6:15

SOW—To scatter seeds on the ground.
As he was S-ING, some seeds fell..............Matt. 13:4
One S-S and another reaps...................John 4:37
whatever a man S-S he will also..................Gal. 6:7

SPIRIT—1. The animating force from God in a living being. 2. The part of a human being associated with thinking and understanding, emotions; a compelling notion or tendency in a person. 3. The Spirit of God. 4. An evil spirit or demon.
renew a steadfast S within me.............. Ps. 51:10
pour out My S on all humanity................Joel 2:28
The S is willing, but the flesh.................Matt. 26:41
God is S, and those who worship Him must worship in S and truth...................John 4:24
distinguishing between S-S,......................1 Cor. 12:10
Don't stifle the S......1 Thess. 5:19

SPLENDOR—Brilliant or magnificent appearance.

SPOILS—Items taken by a victorious army.

STAFF—A long stick used for walking, defense, or herding sheep, or as a symbol of office.
rod and Your S—they comfort me...........................Ps. 23:4

STAG—Adult male deer.

STATUTE—Law or commandment.

STEADFAST—Immovable and patient.
me and renew a S spirit within....................Ps. 51:10
grounded and S in the faith,................Col. 1:23

STEAL—Take someone's property without permission. Seize illegally.
Do not S................Exod. 20:15
The thief must no longer S................Eph. 4:28

STEWARDSHIP—Management of resources on behalf of someone else (1 Cor. 9:17).

STIFF-NECKED—Stubborn, obstinate.

STONING—Capital punishment carried out by throwing stones at a person.

STRENGTH—Power, potency.
The Lord is my S and my song; ....Exod. 15:2
with all your soul, and with all your S. .... Deut. 6:5
in the Lord will renew their S; ....Isa. 40:31
Not by S or by might, but by My .... Zech. 4:6

STRIFE—Conflict, lack of harmony.
than a house full of feasting with S. .... Prov. 17:1

STRONGHOLD—Secure place.
the God of Jacob is our S.................. Ps. 46:7,11

SUBMISSION—Voluntary placement of oneself under the authority and leadership of another.
learn in silence with full S....................1 Tim. 2:11

SUBMIT—Voluntarily yield to another.
S to the governing authorities,...........Rom. 13:1
Wives, S to your own husbands.............Eph. 5:22
Therefore, S to God. But resist .... Jas. 4:7
S to every human institution ....1 Pet. 2:13

SUFFER—Go through something difficult or painful.
He was . . . a man of S-ING....................Isa. 53:3
Son of Man must S many things,............... Mark 8:31
we S with Him so that we also may........Rom. 8:17
one member S-S, all ... S with it;...........1 Cor. 12:26
it is better to S for doing good,...............1 Pet. 3:17

SUSTAIN—Provide what is needed to carry on.
wake again because the LORD S-S me ....Ps. 3:5
and He S-S all things by His Heb. 1:3

SWEAR—Take an oath.
Neither should you S by your head,...........Matt. 5:36

SYMBOL—Token or sign; a thing that represents something else.
a S on your forehead Exod. 13:16; Deut. 6:8

SYNAGOGUE—Local meeting place and assembly of the Jewish people.
He entered the S on the Sabbath............... Luke 4:16
reasoned in the S every Sabbath...............Acts 18:4

T

TABERNACLE—Sacred tent, portable and provisional sanctuary, where the God of Israel revealed Himself to and dwelled among His people. It was built in accordance with directions given to Moses by God on Sinai (Exod. 25–40).
glory of the LORD filled the T. ....Exod. 40:34

TALENT—In the OT, a weight of about 75 pounds; in the NT, a coin worth that much in gold.
one who owed 10,000 T-S ....Matt. 18:24
To one he gave five T-S;.................. Matt. 25:15

TAXES—Regular payments to a government.
lawful to pay T to Caesar or not?.............. Matt. 22:17
T to those you owe T, ... Rom. 13:7

TEACH—Instruct, pass on knowledge or skill.
T them to your children Deut. 4:9; 11:19
T us to pray.................. Luke 11:1
Holy Spirit ... will T you all things ....John 14:26
who will be able to T others also.............. 2 Tim. 2:2

TEMPEST—Violent storm.

TEMPLE—Place of worship, especially the temple Solomon built in Jerusalem.

But the LORD is in His holy T; ....Hab. 2:20
something greater than the T is here! ....Matt. 12:6

TEMPTATION—The enticement to do evil.
And do not bring us into T, ...Matt. 6:13
No T has overtaken you except..........1 Cor. 10:13

TENANT—Person who rents land or other property.

TESTIMONY—Solemn affirmation of fact; statement of a witness.
Do not give false T against your ....Exod. 20:16

TETRARCH—Roman political office, originally over the "fourth part" of a territory.

THANKS—Expression of gratitude.
Give T to the LORD, for He is good. ....Ps. 136:1
and after giving T, He gave it ....Matt. 26:27
But T be to God, who gives us ....1 Cor. 15:57
Give T in everything, for this ....1 Thess. 5:18

THANKSGIVING—Acknowledgement of a benefactor.
Enter His gates with T and ....Ps. 100:4
through prayer and petition with T, ...Phil. 4:6

THRESH—Separate seeds from plants by beating or dragging something across the stalks.

THUMMIM—See Urim and Thummim.

TITHE—Tenth part.

TOMB—Natural or man-made cave, with a stone door, used for burial.
You are like whitewashed T-S, ...Matt. 23:27
stone rolled away from the T. ....Luke 24:2

TONGUE—1. Organ of speech. 2. See language.
and a gentle T can break a bone. ....Prov. 25:15
and every T should confess that ....Phil. 2:11
but no man can tame the T. ....Jas. 3:8

TORMENT—Persecute with injurious intent.
come here to T us before the time? ....Matt. 8:29

TRADITION—Doctrine or ritual which is handed down from generation to generation.
You revoke God's word by your T .... Mark 7:13

TRANSFORM—Change in appearance or nature.
He was T-ED in front of them, ...Matt. 17:2
be T-ED by the renewing of your ....Rom. 12:2

TRANSGRESSION—Sin; overstepping the limits of God's law.
How happy is the one whose T is forgiven, ...Ps. 32:1
was pierced because of our T-S, ...Isa. 53:5

TREACHEROUS—Faithless, untrustworthy; unreliable with the result that harm may result.

TREASURE—Something highly esteemed or valued.
I have T-D Your word in my heart ....Ps. 119:11
For where your T is, there your ....Matt. 6:21

TREATY—Agreement between two nations.
Make no T with them ... Deut. 7:2

TRESPASS—Sin.
He was delivered up for our T-ES. ....Rom. 4:25
when you were dead in T-ES ....Col. 2:13

TRIBE—Group of people of common ancestry.
These are the T-S of Israel, 12 ....Gen. 49:28

TRIBULATION—1. Suffering; affliction; distress. 2. The eschatological time of trouble that will usher in the second coming of Christ (Matt. 24:15-22; Rev. 2:22; 7:14; cp. Dan. 12:1).

TRIBUTE—Any payment exacted by a superior power, usually a country, from an inferior one.

TRIUMPH—Decisive and exultant victory.
He T-ED over them by Him. ....Col. 2:15
Mercy T-S over judgment. ....Jas. 2:13

TRUE—Conforming to fact, standard, or reality.
He is righteous and T... Deut. 32:4
God must be T, but everyone is a liar, ...Rom. 3:4
whatever is T, whatever is. ....Phil. 4:8
these words are faithful and T ...Rev. 21:5; 22:6

TRUST—Have faith in, rely on, believe.
in God I T; ... What can man do ....Ps. 56:4,11
T in the LORD with all your ....Prov. 3:5
those who T in the LORD will renew their strength; .. Isa. 40:31

TRUTH—That which accurately reflects facts or reality.
The entirety of Your word is T, ...Ps. 119:160
worship the Father in spirit and T. ....John 4:23
the T, and the T will set you free. ....John 8:32
am the way, the T, and the life. ....John 14:6
exchanged the T of God for a lie.................Rom. 1:25
But speaking the T in love, ...Eph. 4:15
teaching the word of T. ....2 Tim. 2:15
and the T is not in us. .. 1 John 1:8

TUNIC—Loose-fitting, knee-length garment worn next to the skin (John 19:23).

TURBAN—Headdress formed by wrapping long strips of cloth around the head.

U

UNBELIEF—Skepticism or doubt.
I do believe! Help my U... Mark 9:24

UNBELIEVER—Skeptic; one who does not believe the gospel of Jesus.
he has denied the faith and is worse than an U. .... 1 Tim. 5:8

UNCIRCUMCISED—Not Jewish.
called "the U" by those called. ....Eph. 2:11

UNCLEAN—Not ceremonially clean; food not acceptable to eat, or a person not admissible for worship.
I have never eaten anything ... U! .... Acts 10:14
nothing is U in itself.. Rom. 14:14

UNITY—Full and perfect agreement.
until we all reach **U** in the faith ....Eph. 4:13
love—the perfect bond of **U**. ....Col. 3:14

UNLEAVENED BREAD—Bread prepared without a substance such as yeast that produces fermentation and rising in dough.
observe the {Festival of} **U** Bread ....Exod. 12:17

UPRIGHT—Doing what is morally right.
The **U** will see His face. ... Ps. 11:7

URIM AND THUMMIM—Objects Israel, and especially the high priest, used to determine God's will (Num. 27:21; Deut. 33:8; 1 Sam. 28:6; Ezra 2:63; Neh. 7:65). They were kept by the high priest in a "breastplate of judgment" (Exod. 28:15-30; Lev. 8:8).

V

VAIN—Without value or significance; "in vain" means without a worthwhile result.
and the peoples plot in **V**? . Ps. 2:1
its builders labor over it in **V**; .... Ps. 127:1
They worship Me in **V**,.Matt. 15:9
labor in the Lord is not in **V**. ....1 Cor. 15:58
be running, or have run, in **V**. ....Gal. 2:2
I didn't run in **V** or labor for ....Phil. 2:16

VALIANT—Fearless, courageous.

VENGEANCE—Retaliation or punishment of crime for the sake of justice and deliverance.
V belongs to Me; I will repay..............Deut. 32:35

VIGOR—Strength, as in one's prime.

VINDICATE—Justify, clear; defend.
wisdom is **V-ED** by all her children............... Luke 7:35

VIPER—Poisonous snake.
he said to them, "Brood of **V-S**! .... Matt. 3:7

VIRGIN—Person who has not had sexual intercourse.
The **V** will conceive, have a son,.............Isa. 7:14
The **V-'S** name was Mary.................. Luke 1:27

VISION—One method that God used to communicate with mankind, either literally through one's eyes, in a dream, or by prophetic inspiration.
your young men will see **V-S**. Joel 2:28; Acts 2:17

VOW—Voluntary promise, as an expression of devotion, usually fulfilled after some condition had been met.
I will fulfill my **V-S** before those ....Ps. 22:25
Fulfill what you **V**. ......Eccl. 5:4

W

WADI—A rocky watercourse that is dry except during rainy seasons.

WAGES—Terms of employment or compensation for services rendered.
For the **W** of sin is death, ...Rom. 6:23

WALK—To travel at a normal pace on foot. Used figuratively for a person's conduct or way of life (Gen. 5:24; Rom. 8:4; Eph. 5:15; 1 John 1:6-7).
and to **W** humbly with your God. .... Mic. 6:8
we too may **W** in a new way of life............. Rom. 6:4
we **W** by faith, not by sight ....2 Cor. 5:7
But if we **W** in the light as He ....1 John 1:7

WANDER—Travel aimlessly and without a plan.
will be a restless **W-ER** on the earth..................Gen. 4:12
have **W-ED** away from the faith ....1 Tim. 6:10

WASH—Cleanse.
but you were **W-ED**, you were .. 1 Cor. 6:11
the **W-ING** of water by the word....................Eph. 5:26

WATCH—1. Division of time during which soldiers or others were on duty (1 Chron. 26:16; Ps. 63:6; 119:1-48; Jer. 51:12; Luke 2:8). 2. Be vigilant, alert.
unless the LORD **W-ES** over a city, ... Ps. 127:1
W! Be alert! For you don't know ....Mark 13:33

WATCHMAN—One who stands guard to sound a warning if trouble approaches (Ezek. 3; 33).

WAY—Path, route; manner of conduct.
See if there is any offensive **W** in me;lead me in the everlasting **W**. ....Ps. 139:24
There is a **W** that seems right..................Prov. 14:12
we all have turned to our own **W**;.............Isa. 53:6
I am the **W**, the truth, and the life. ....John 14:6
will show you an even better **W**............1 Cor. 12:31

WEAPON—Device used in battle.
No **W** formed against you will .... Isa. 54:17
the **W-S** of our warfare are not ....2 Cor. 10:4

WEARY—Being drained of strength or of patience.
they will run and not grow **W**;................ Isa. 40:31
Come to Me, all of you who are **W**......... Matt. 11:28

WELCOME—Greet; invite in, accept.
whoever **W-S** one child like this ....Matt. 18:5

WHOLEHEARTED—Genuine and without reservation or hesitation.

WICKED—Immoral, sinful.
does not follow the advice of the **W**, ... Ps. 1:1
no pleasure in the death of the **W**, ...Ezek. 33:11

WIDOW—Woman whose husband has died.

WILDERNESS—Area with little rainfall and sparse population.

WILL—Desire.
I delight to do Your **W**, my God; ....Ps. 40:8
Your **W** be done on earth as it is ....Matt. 6:10
My food is to do the **W** of Him.................... John 4:34
and He hardens whom He **W-S**...............Rom. 9:18
say, "If the Lord **W-S**, we will ....Jas. 4:15
ask anything according to His **W**, ... 1 John 5:14

WINEPRESS—Place for squeezing or treading grapes, usually a pit or vat.

WINESKIN—Animal skin formed into a bag by sewing, made to contain wine.

WISDOM—Insight, discernment, understanding.
The fear of the LORD is the beginning of **W**, ... Prov. 9:10
depth of the riches both of the **W** ... Rom. 11:33

WISE MEN—Astrologers from Arabia, Persia, or Babylon whose interpretation of the stars led them to visit the baby Jesus (Matt. 2:1-12).

WITHER—Dry up and wilt, as from a lack of moisture.

WITNESS—One that bears testimony to things seen, heard, transacted, or experienced.
the testimony of two or three **W-ES**. ... Deut. 19:15
will be My **W-ES** in Jerusalem, ... Acts 1:8

WOE—Anguish, misery, wretchedness.
W is me, for I am ruined, .. Isa. 6:5
W to you, scribes and Pharisees, ... Matt. 23:13

WOMB—Uterus, where a baby develops before birth.
You knit me together in my mother's **W**. ... Ps. 139:13
before I formed you in the **W**; ... Jer. 1:5

WORD—1. A single term. 2. A short statement. 3. A message or prophecy or command. 4. A speech or story. 5. The entire law. 6. The gospel message. 7. Scripture. 8. Christ.
My **W** ... will not return to Me empty ... Isa. 55:11
In the beginning was the **W**, and the **W** was with God, and the **W** was God. ... John 1:1
the **W** of God is living and effective ... Heb. 4:12

WORK—Act, deed, accomplishment, effort.
six days and do all your **W**, ... Exod. 20:9
do even greater **W-S** than these, ... John 14:12
by faith apart from **W-S** of law. ... Rom. 3:28
test the quality of each one's **W**. ... 1 Cor. 3:13
W out your own salvation with ... Phil. 2:12
isn't willing to **W**, he should not eat. ... 2 Thess. 3:10
has faith, but does not have **W-S**? ... Jas. 2:14
judged according to their **W-S**. ... Rev. 20:13

WORLD—1. The planet earth. 2. All mankind. 3. The environment or spirit of evil and enmity toward God.
the **W** and everything in it is Mine. ... Ps. 50:12
For God loved the **W** in this way: ... John 3:16
Do not love the **W** or the things ... 1 John 2:15

WORMWOOD—Nonpoisonous but bitter plant.

WORRY—Be anxious or burdened.
Don't **W** about anything, but ... Phil. 4:6

WORSHIP—Attribute honor or value to someone or something.
W the LORD in the splendor of ... 1 Chron. 16:29
who **W** Him must **W** in spirit and truth ... John 4:24

WORTHY—Deserving; having sufficient merit.
the LORD, who is **W** of praise, ... 2 Sam. 22:4
urge you to walk **W** of the calling ... Eph. 4:1
Lamb who was slaughtered is **W** ... Rev. 5:12

WRATH—Anger, indignation, and fury. The punitive righteousness of God by which He maintains His moral order.
but a harsh word stirs up **W**. ... Prov. 15:1
God's **W** is revealed from heaven ... Rom. 1:18
by nature we were children under **W** ... Eph. 2:3

Y

YEARN—Want very much, desire earnestly.

YEAST—A fungus that permeates dough and makes it rise.
beware of the **Y** of the Pharisees ... Matt. 16:6
know that a little **Y** permeates ... 1 Cor. 5:6

YOKE—Wooden frame placed on the backs of draft animals to make them pull in tandem.
take up My **Y** and learn from Me, ... Matt. 11:29
don't submit again to a **Y** of slavery. ... Gal. 5:1

YOUTH—Period between childhood and maturity, characterized by freshness and vigor.
Y is renewed like the eagle. ... Ps. 103:5
Teach a **Y** about the way he should go ... Prov. 22:6

Z

ZEAL—Intense eagerness that compels action.
Z for Your house will consume Me. ... John 2:17
that they have **Z** for God, but not ... Rom. 10:2

ONE

PHILIPPIANS 1:27

INDEX

FCA ANNUAL THEME/ONE

"I will know that you are standing together with one spirit and one purpose, fighting together for the faith, which is the Good News." —Philippians 1:27

The Power of One. One passion, one purpose and one goal can drive an athlete, coach, or team to be their very best. The Impact of One. One player, one play, and one game-changing moment can transform the course of competition and bring victory. Everything comes down to One. There is power in One Gospel. There is power in One Truth. And there is power in our One Great God who transforms hearts and brings victory in our lives. As Christian athletes, when we stand together with one passion, one power, and one purpose, there is great impact! Let's stand together as One!

FOUR STUDIES TO HELP YOU BE ONE

SESSION 1: One Passion

"And I am convinced that nothing can ever separate us from God's love. Neither death nor life, neither angels nor demons, neither our fears for today nor our worries about tomorrow—not even the powers of hell can separate us from God's love."—Romans 8:38

SESSION 2: One Pain

"For everyone has sinned; we all fall short of God's glorious standard."—Romans 3:23

SESSION 3: One Power

"I also pray that you will understand the incredible greatness of God's power for us who believe him. This is the same mighty power that raised Christ from the dead and seated him in the place of honor at God's right hand in the heavenly realms."—Ephesians 1:19-20

SESSION 4: One Purpose

"'I pray that they will all be one, just as you and I are one—as you are in me, Father, and I am in you. And may they be in us so that the world will believe you sent me.'"—John 17:21

IF YOU HAVE FEWER THAN FOUR MEETINGS

These four topics were designed to fit together for a complete message. It's not recommended to completely skip any of the topics. If you need to cover the contents in fewer than four meeting times, consider these options:

- Depending on your emphasis and group makeup, you may decide to focus a bit more on one or two topics while hitting the highlights in the others.
- If you cover two topics in a meeting, choose only one "Warm-Up" section for the time.

WELCOME

"And I am convinced that nothing can ever separate us from God's love. Neither death nor life, neither angels nor demons, neither our fears for today nor our worries about tomorrow—not even the powers of hell can separate us from God's love."
—Romans 8:38

Passion.

It drives us. It moves us forward. It pushes us toward our goals. It keeps us from giving up. It fuels our fire.

Passion is often used with the word *love*, but it's not the same thing. Love is certainly a key component, but more specifically, passion is a very strong feeling or a compelling enthusiasm about a person or thing. That feeling usually leads to action.

Stephen Curry
© Noah Salzman | Wikimedia Commons

NBA champion Stephen Curry has been passionate about basketball ever since he was a child. That passion led to a lot of hard work throughout grade school, high school, college, and into the professional ranks where he has become known as one of the greatest three-point shooters in the history of the game.

But initially, not many saw value in Curry. He was an undersized prep athlete playing at a small Christian school in Charlotte. Davidson College, however, pursued Curry relentlessly and helped launch a future All-Star's career. During his 2015 NBA MVP acceptance speech, Curry explained the importance of his number one passion—God—and how that powers everything he does:

"ALL YOU NEED TO HAVE IS FAITH IN GOD, AND UNDYING PASSION FOR WHAT YOU DO, WHAT YOU CHOOSE TO DO IN THIS LIFE, AND A RELENTLESS DRIVE AND THE WILL TO DO WHATEVER IT TAKES TO BE SUCCESSFUL AT WHATEVER YOU PUT YOUR MIND TO."

ONE PASSION

WARM-UP

What's Your Passion?

We are all made uniquely with different passions that drive us to get out of bed every morning and chase our dreams. Listed below are 10 common passions that people have. From 1 to 10, rank the list from the things you are most passionate about (1) to the least passionate about (10):

	Competitive success (winning)		Friends
	Academic success (making good grades)		Material success (making money, possessions)
	Higher education (getting a college scholarship)		God
	Serving others		Personal happiness
	Family		Activism (social causes, community)

Q: Which things ranked highest on your list? Which things ranked lowest?

Q: What does the order of your list say about who you are as a person? As an athlete?

Q: Are there any things you wish were ranked higher or lower on your list? Explain.

WORKOUT

An Unlikely Hero

In biblical Hebrew culture, women were not highly valued. So it must have seemed strange to a young girl named Mary when an angel visited her and revealed that she would play a pivotal role in God's plan to restore His relationship with mankind.

It was a plan that had been set into motion thousands of years earlier after Earth's first people (Adam and Eve) sinned against God and turned a place of peace into a place of chaos. God needed to send a Savior (His Son Jesus) to serve as the perfect sacrifice for that sin, and He was going to send Him in the most unexpected way—as a human baby born to a virgin.

You would think God would use someone more obvious to play the hero in this story—perhaps a dynamic leader or maybe a great warrior. But instead, He chose Mary. He saw value in her when no one else did. Because of that, she bravely put her reputation (and her relationship with her fiancé Joseph) on the line to accept the call.

Mary is just one example of an unlikely hero in the Bible. God continues to look for people just like her who may not be perfect in the world's eyes but have a willing heart and a desire to use their passions for a higher purpose.

Q: Have you ever felt undervalued or looked over? Explain.

Q: How does Mary's story give you hope that God can use you no matter what circumstances you might currently be facing?

Purpose in the Passion

God is never random. He always has a specific purpose in mind. The purpose behind His passion is evident in three specific ways:

1. God sent His Son for you: This radical plan was born out of His passion for mankind. That passion sent God into action and drove Him to send His only Son to earth to die for the sins of the world. That's how much He loves you.

"For this is how God loved the world: He gave his one and only Son, so that everyone who believes in him will not perish but have eternal life."—John 3:16

2. God never gives up on you: In Matthew 18:12-14, Jesus shares a story about a shepherd who leaves behind 99 sheep so he can go find his one lost sheep. Jesus wasn't just telling a story. He was illustrating how His passionate love for every lost soul moves Him to action. God pursues you. He desperately wants you to be saved, and His love will follow you everywhere you go.

"And I am convinced that nothing can ever separate us from God's love. Neither death nor life, neither angels nor demons, neither our fears for today nor our worries about tomorrow—not even the powers of hell can separate us from God's love."
—Romans 8:38

3. God has a plan for you: Mary is proof that you don't have to be deemed special in the world's eyes to become a part of God's big plan. He has a plan for you too, and it's a special plan with a significant purpose.

"For I know the plans I have for you, says the Lord. They are plans for good and not for disaster, to give you a future and a hope."—Jeremiah 29:11

Q: What is one thing you have passionately chased after in your sport? What drove you to engage in that pursuit?

Q: How does it make you feel to know that God is actively pursuing you? How do you think you should respond to God's active pursuit?

Earlier in the Warm-Up section, we had you personally rank some common passions. Using the space below, write out your three biggest passions. Then, in the adjacent columns, briefly describe your plan for pursuing that passion (under "My Plan") and your thoughts on how God might be able to use that passion (under "God's Plan"):

MY PASSIONS

1.

2.

3.

MY PLAN:

GOD'S PLAN:

Q: Do you believe that God has a plan for you as an athlete? How does that truth change the way you view God and yourself?

KEY TRAINING POINTS

- **We Are God's Passion**: We are the center of His universe. We are the most important thing to God.
- **Our Passion Starts With God**: Everything we do in life (including sports) should be a reflection of His love for us and our love for Him.
- **God Has a Plan For Our Passion**: God has given you your passions for a purpose. He has given you all the talents and abilities you need to walk out that plan.

WRAP-UP

One Passion

So often, we look to sports as an outlet for our passion and fail to realize that the Source of that passion desires a relationship with us and desires to use our passions for something so much greater.

Perhaps you have yet to enter into a relationship with God through His Son Jesus. If you want to make Him the Lord of your life, turn to page 1369 and review "More Than Winning."

If you have already made that commitment, ask God to give you a greater passion to pursue Him and His purposes. As He fills you up with His love, you will then be better equipped to live out our theme verse on a daily basis:

"I will know that you are standing together with one spirit and one purpose, fighting together for the faith, which is the Good News."—Philippians 1:27

Before the Next Meeting:

Go back and look at that list of passions and how you ranked each item. Ask God to reveal which of those passions are out of order. And if you aren't sure what your true passion is, ask God to reveal that to you as well. Then, stay alert for open doors and nudges from the Holy Spirit that will help you better understand how God wants His passion and your passion to intersect.

If you gave your heart to Christ for the first time or if you have recommitted your life to Him, make sure to talk to your group leader or another staff member and tell them about your exciting decision.

WELCOME

"For everyone has sinned; we all fall short of God's glorious standard."—Romans 3:23

Our world is full of pain. That pain affects us in every way imaginable—physically, emotionally, and mentally. While there are many causes, there is really just one true source of that pain—sin.

Sin is anything that separates us from God. It's based in mankind's disobedience and willful turning away from God's plan for our lives. No matter how big or how small, sin always results in actions that hurt us or hurt others.

When Dave Bliss was an NCAA Division I basketball coach, he admittedly allowed the sin of pride to slowly creep into his life. Although he got into coaching as a way to help young people grow, he eventually developed a thirst for winning and wealth.

Dave Bliss
© Elsa | Getty Images Sport

It all came to a head in 2003 when he was forced to resign as Baylor's head coach amid an ugly scandal that involved illegal payments for players and an attempted cover-up. While suffering through the scandal, Bliss came to an awful realization about the man he had become.

Bliss is now the head coach at Southwestern Christian University where he uses his story as a warning to others about the pitfalls of the sin of pride. He is also thankful for the opportunity to share the hope and restoration that he has found in his renewed relationship with Jesus Christ.

// I HAD COMPROMISED MY INTEGRITY AND MY CHARACTER AND MADE CHOICES THAT NOT ONLY HURT MY FAMILY, IT HURT THE SCHOOL THAT I CARED A GREAT DEAL ABOUT. I HAD A BAD METAPHOR FOR WHO GOD WAS IN MY LIFE. AND SO MY DAILY WALK WAS PRONE TO FAIL AT A CERTAIN TIME. AND OF COURSE, IT HURT A LOT OF PEOPLE.

WARM-UP

The Injury Report

In every sport, there's always the chance that an athlete might get hurt. Go around the group and have each person tell about the worst injury they have ever experienced during training, practice, or competition.

INJURY REPORT

Date	Location	Injury

Q: Do you think most injuries are the fault of the individual, the fault of someone else, or accidents that happen for no apparent reason?

Q: What are some difficult aspects of getting injured (e.g., physical pain, loss of playing time, disappointment, etc.)?

WORKOUT

An Ultimate Sacrifice

In the previous meeting, we learned that God wanted to restore His relationship with mankind. His radical plan was set into motion as He sent His Son Jesus to earth. For 33 years, Jesus lived a perfect life as an example to the world. He healed the sick, taught truth to the masses, and set people free from sin. But His work wasn't complete until He gave the ultimate sacrifice—His very life.

The crucifixion of Christ is the Bible's most heart-wrenching story. Even though He was sinless and an innocent of any crime, Jesus was sentenced to death in the middle of political and cultural unrest in Jerusalem. He was whipped, beaten, mocked, cursed, and spit on. The Son of God was completely humiliated and then mercilessly nailed to a cross and hung high for everyone to see.

Before He died, however, Jesus had a profound conversation with two criminals who were hanging alongside Him (Luke 23:39-43). The first man lashed out in anger. But the other man recognized that Jesus was the Messiah and repented of his sin.

Those two men represent the two ways we can respond to sin and pain in our lives. We can either turn further away from God and fall deeper into sin, or we can recognize our brokenness and surrender our hurts to the Savior.

Q: What emotions do you feel as you imagine the events that took place on the day Jesus was crucified?

Q: Can you relate to one or both of the criminals in this story? Explain.

Purpose in the Pain

We were born into this world with sin and Jesus paid the ultimate price so that we could be forgiven and restored back to a relationship with the Father. Because of our sin, pain has been a running thread throughout the course of humanity.

But thankfully, God has provided three incredible responses to the hopelessness and despair that sin and pain bring into our lives:

1. Jesus suffered pain and even death for your sins: This is the greatest miracle in the history of the world. Jesus willingly chose to step out of His perfect home in heaven and come to earth as a man so He could take on the sins of the world and give us the chance to be with Him in eternity someday.

"But God showed his great love for us by sending Christ to die for us while we were still sinners."—Romans 5:8

2. Jesus can take away your pain: Suffering is inevitable, but it isn't permanent. Jesus can heal our physical, emotional, and mental hurts. And in heaven, the pain we so often experience in this world will be gone forever.

"He heals the brokenhearted and bandages their wounds."—Psalm 147:3

ONE PAIN

3. Your pain has a purpose: It doesn't always make sense why we have to go through so much heartache in our lives, but God brings purpose to our pain and gives us a testimony that we can share with others as a result.

"And we know that God causes everything to work together for the good of those who love God and are called according to his purpose for them."—Romans 8:28

Using the journal page below, identify the three most painful things (physical, emotional, or mental) that you have experienced so far in your life. Find someone you trust with whom you can share your pains.

Q: Which of these pains do you need to turn over to God by repenting and asking forgiveness?

Q: Which of the pains do you need to give to God by forgiving someone else?

Q: Do you believe that God can use painful situations in your life to help others and glorify Him? Explain.

KEY TRAINING POINTS

- **Jesus Bore Your Pain**: His great love for you led Him all the way to the cross.
- **Jesus Is the Painkiller**: He doesn't want you to be bound by sin or by the consequences of sin. Jesus wants to heal you and set you free.
- **Jesus Can Use Your Pain**: He can take those things that have hurt you temporarily and change someone else's life for eternity.

WRAP-UP

One Pain

There's no escaping pain. Because sin is the one source of all pain and because we were all born with sin, pain and suffering will always be an unfortunate and uncomfortable aspect of our lives. But as we also learned, there is some great news thanks to the sacrifice Jesus made on the cross. He has overcome our sin and offers forgiveness, restoration, and healing.

In yesterday's meeting, you were given the chance to ask Jesus into your heart and to make him the Lord of your life. If you didn't make that commitment and are ready to do so today, turn to page 1369 and review "More Than Winning." Go through the steps provided and enter into a life-changing relationship with God.

If you have already made that commitment, meditate on the fact that you can bring God all the pain and all the hurts you are carrying around. As He heals you with His perfect love, you will be better equipped to walk in the truth of this week's theme verse:

"I will know that you are standing together with one spirit and one purpose, fighting together for the faith, which is the Good News."—Philippians 1:27

Before the Next Meeting:

Go back over your list of pains. Ask God if you need to ask forgiveness from Him and from someone else for a sin that may have caused them pain, or if you need to forgive someone else of a sin that has caused you pain. If you are going through something deeply hurtful, take time to talk to one of the leaders about it so they can agree with you in prayer and believe for complete healing and restoration in your life.

WELCOME

"I also pray that you will understand the incredible greatness of God's power for us who believe him. This is the same mighty power that raised Christ from the dead and seated him in the place of honor at God's right hand in the heavenly realms."
—Ephesians 1:19-20

Allyson Felix
© Grosremy | Dreamstime.com

When it comes to physical training, all sports are different. Some require a focus on speed, and others require a focus on agility, while other sports require a focus on endurance. But one common characteristic that all athletes need to be successful is power.

For elite sprinter Allyson Felix, that explosive power needed to compete at a high level is achieved through countless hours on the track and an equal amount of time in the weight room. Through the 2015 season, her methods had yielded four Olympic gold medals, two Olympic silver medals, and 13 World Championships medals, including nine gold.

But more importantly, she is committed to staying connected to the one power Source that gives her spiritual fortitude.

// MY GOAL IS TO BE MORE CHRISTLIKE EACH AND EVERY DAY AND THAT IS NOT AN EASY TASK. I TRY TO STAY IN THE WORD OF GOD AND I PRAY A LOT, JUST TALKING TO GOD. HE PROVIDES MY STRENGTH AND WISDOM.

WARM-UP

Power Up

Choose a partner and sit on the ground back-to-back. Try and stand straight up without using your hands. Add one person to the game every time you stand up successfully.

Q: Why is power needed to stand up successfully?

Q: Did you need to rely on others' power to stand up? Why or why not?

Q: Why do you think athletic power is so difficult to achieve?

WORKOUT

An Ultimate Victory

After Jesus died on the cross, He was buried in a tomb as His followers mourned the loss of their spiritual leader and friend. Even though Jesus had told them what was going to happen, they were still shocked and amazed when He rose from the grave three days later. Jesus is alive!

This was a significant event not just because of the miraculous power that God displayed in that moment, but also because of what it represented for mankind. Jesus had defeated death with His resurrection power and had fulfilled the very purpose for which He had come to earth in the first place.

"I tell you the truth, those who listen to my message and believe in God who sent me have eternal life. They will never be condemned for their sins, but they have already passed from death into life."—John 5:24

And we don't just have the promise of eternal life in heaven, but we also have the promise of fulfillment here on earth as Jesus also promised.

"The thief's purpose is to steal and kill and destroy. My purpose is to give them a rich and satisfying life."—John 10:10

That means we have victory over sin and the opportunity to be everything that God called us to be if we walk in fellowship with Him through the redemption that Jesus paid for on the cross and the power He proclaimed through His resurrection. That's great news! Jesus overcame the world so that now we can do the same.

"I have told you all this so that you may have peace in me. Here on earth you will have many trials and sorrows. But take heart, because I have overcome the world."
—John 16:33

ONE POWER

Using the journal page below, identify three things that you need victory over in your life (e.g. pride, past hurts, unforgiveness, distrust, etc.).

Q: If you feel comfortable doing so, share something from your list and explain why that thing has kept you from claiming complete victory in Christ.

Q: How does the revelation that Jesus overcame the world through His resurrection empower you to live victoriously over those things that have been holding you back?

Purpose in the Power

Hearing the story of Jesus' resurrection is inspiring. But sometimes, we struggle to apply the victory He achieved that day to our personal lives. Thankfully, God has given us clear instruction and some powerful tools to help us stay on course.

1. There is power in prayer: This is an amazing gift—the ability to have a two-way conversation with the Creator. God is always faithful to listen *and* respond.

"The earnest prayer of a righteous person has great power and produces wonderful results."—James 5:16b

2. There is power in the Bible: Every piece of advice and every piece of instruction can be found in God's inerrant Word. It may have been written thousands of years ago, but it still applies to all of us in today's times.

"All Scripture is inspired by God and is useful to teach us what is true and to make us realize what is wrong in our lives. It corrects us when we are wrong and teaches us to do what is right. God uses it to prepare and equip his people to do every good work."—2 Timothy 3:16-17

3. There is power in fellowship: Christians weren't meant to walk alone. Jesus came to establish the church so that we might learn from each other, encourage each other, and serve the needs of each other and the needs of those around us.

"Let us think of ways to motivate one another to acts of love and good works. And let us not neglect our meeting together, as some people do, but encourage one another, especially now that the day of his return is drawing near."—Hebrews 10:24-25

4. There is power in the Holy Spirit: Not long after Jesus left the earth, He fulfilled another promise by sending the Holy Spirit to the disciples. Today, we still have access to the Holy Spirit as a source of guidance, courage, boldness, and comfort.

"And I will ask the Father, and he will give you another Advocate, who will never leave you. He is the Holy Spirit, who leads into all truth."—John 14:16-17a

Q: Which of those three spiritual tools listed above do you struggle to engage in on a regular basis? How have you seen them work in your life when consistently applied?

Q: What do you think a life led by the Holy Spirit should look like?

Q: What is keeping you from experiencing the power of the Holy Spirit in your life?

KEY TRAINING POINTS

- **Jesus overcame the world**: Death is the ultimate consequence of sin, but when Jesus was raised from the dead, He not only overcame death, but also overcame anything that the world might throw our way.
- **We can overcome the world**: Because Jesus conquered death, we now have the power to be victorious through the Holy Spirit. That power is strengthened through the spiritual disciplines of prayer, Bible study, and fellowship with other believers.

WRAP-UP

One Power

Just like in sports, victory over our spiritual Enemy and the things of this world is never instantaneous. It requires a long-term commitment. But God has given us an amazing gift. He has given us the power over death and the promise of abundant life on earth and eternal life in heaven.

Once we understand just how much power we can access through the Holy Spirit and through the spiritual disciplines, we will be better equipped to live out our theme verse:

"I will know that you are standing together with one spirit and one purpose, fighting together for the faith, which is the Good News."—Philippians 1:27

Before the Next Meeting:

Go back and look at the list of things that you need to overcome. Ask the Holy Spirit for guidance on steps you need to take to win the victory over those things. Then, put together a plan for daily prayer and Bible study that will strengthen your faith and increase your power over the world. Make sure to talk to one of your leaders about this commitment so they can agree with you in prayer and help keep you accountable.

ONE PURPOSE

WELCOME

" I pray that they will all be one, just as you and I are one—as you are in me, Father, and I am in you. And may they be in us so that the world will believe you sent me."
—John 17:21

Turner Gill
© Grant Halverson | Getty Images Sport

Every athlete has a mission. For some athletes, that mission might be to show improvement from the previous season or win more games. For other athletes, it might be about developing chemistry and better team cohesion. And of course, there are always those big-picture goals like winning a tournament or a conference championship.

But for athletes that are led by the Spirit, there should always be a much greater mission.

Such is the case for Liberty University head football coach Turner Gill who certainly wants to win championships, but more importantly wants people to see what it looks like when a group of athletes and coaches come together for a higher cause.

// "I BELIEVE THAT EVERYTHING THAT HAPPENS IS FOR GOD TO GET THE GLORY. I KNOW THAT THE FOOTBALL TEAM WILL PROCEED WHERE GOD GETS THE GLORY, NOT TURNER GILL. WE'RE HERE TO BE SERVANTS AND TO OBEY. I WANT TO HONOR JESUS CHRIST AS MY LORD AND SAVIOR."

ONE PURPOSE

WARM-UP

Tight-Knit Team

Gather the huddle into a tight circle of five to ten people. While in the circle, everyone must look down at the ground and may not raise their head to make eye contact with others in their group. The goal of this game is to count the numbers 1 to 15 in order, with each person in the group saying at least one number. The students are not allowed to count around the circle consecutively. If two people say the same number at the same time, they must start over again at one.

Q: Is it easy or hard to count to 15 without looking at anyone? Why or why not?

Q: How does knowing your purpose or role on the team make a difference in achieving the goal?

WORKOUT

An Ultimate Mission

During Jesus' ministry on earth, He put together His own dream team, which ironically wasn't really much of a dream team in the world's eyes. This rag-tag group of 12 disciples was made up of a tax collector, a physician, several fishermen, and even a traitor.

But just as He was about to go back to the heavens, Jesus sent them on the most important mission in the history of mankind. In what is now commonly known as "the Great Commission," they were given the incredible task of spreading the good news of Jesus' life, death, and resurrection throughout the world

"Jesus came and told his disciples, 'I have been given all authority in heaven and on earth. Therefore, go and make disciples of all the nations, baptizing them in the name of the Father and the Son and the Holy Spirit. Teach these new disciples to obey all the commands I have given you. And be sure of this: I am with you always, even to the end of the age.'"—Matthew 28:18-20

Shortly thereafter, the Holy Spirit came and gave the disciples that power we discussed in the last meeting. Suddenly, this team of Christ-followers began preaching the gospel to thousands of people and performing many miracles. There was no denying that this team was special—and everyone who crossed their path was compelled to believe in Jesus.

"They worshiped together at the Temple each day, met in homes for the Lord's Supper, and shared their meals with great joy and generosity—all the while praising God and enjoying the goodwill of all the people. And each day the Lord added to their fellowship those who were being saved."—Acts 2:46-47

Q: Imagine for a moment what it might have been like to be one of the pioneers of the early church. What are some key elements of a great team that helped them be so effective in walking out their mission?

Q: Do you think your team has these same key elements? Why or why not?

God's Team

When you accept Jesus as your Lord and Savior, you instantly become a member of God's team. It doesn't matter if you feel qualified or not, being a part of this team means you are now part of a higher purpose and expected to work together with other believers to fulfill that purpose. Here are three key aspects to being a part of God's team:

1. God's team has one mission: Our entire purpose as the church is to show the world God's love and to draw people to Christ.

"So we are Christ's ambassadors; God is making his appeal through us. We speak for Christ when we plead, 'Come back to God!'"—2 Corinthians 5:20

2. God's team has one heart: To be effective as a team, we must share the same passion for Jesus and demonstrate that love within the church.

"Then make me truly happy by agreeing wholeheartedly with each other, loving one another, and working together with one mind and purpose."—Philippians 2:2

3. God's team stands out: Our love should be so radiant and bold that people should take notice and be drawn to us.

"Your love for one another will prove to the world that you are my disciples."
—John 13:35

ONE PURPOSE

Q: What are some reasons teams don't get along? What about Christians?

Q: In what ways do you think the world is discouraged or disappointed when they see disunity within the church?

Using the journal page below, give five ways that your sports team might impact the world for Christ if it were truly unified for one purpose. Create a similar list that pertains to the church.

UNIFIED TEAM

1.

2.

3.

4.

5.

UNIFIED CHURCH

1.

2.

3.

4.

5.

Q: How do you think your community would change if those things took place within your sports teams and within your local churches?

KEY TRAINING POINTS

- **God wants us to be unified**: It pleases Him when His children love each other and work together as a team.
- **Our unity draws others to God**: That is our ultimate mission—to draw people to Christ through our love for God, through our love for each other, and through our love for the lost.

WRAP-UP

One Purpose

All week long, we've talked about the passion that God showed in saving us, the pain that caused the need for that salvation, the power God has given us to live victoriously, and finally, the ultimate purpose behind it all.

As individuals, we were made to worship God. As a body of believers, we were made to tell the world about Jesus. The only way that can effectively happen is if we are willing to sacrifice our personal desires and sell out to God's passion for the people who don't know Jesus personally and work together as a powerful, unstoppable force that was created to change the world.

Winning games is amazing. Having athletic success is fulfilling. Impacting the community in a positive way is a noble goal. But none of those things matter if we miss out on fulfilling the command found in our theme verse:

"I will know that you are standing together with one spirit and one purpose, fighting together for the faith, which is the Good News."—Philippians 1:27

ONE PURPOSE

Before You Go Home:

Think of the most important things in your life—your team, your family, your church, your community, etc.

Create separate mission statements that indicate how you use your renewed passion and your empowered faith in order to make a significant impact on each of those areas of your life. Share those mission statements with a fellowship leader and ask them to pray with you so that you will stay the course and live out the one purpose to which you were called.

ONE

PHILIPPIANS 1:27

Every [redacted] aside a special time called “Quiet Time” or spiritual “Training [redacted] this time, you can talk to God and let Him talk to you [redacted] nd His Spirit. There are many effective [redacted] for your daily time with [redacted] hod is one way we [redacted] ed. Examine, [redacted] nd Share.

TRAINING TIME: P.R.E.S.S. METHOD

PRAY . . .

Begin by thanking God for the new day, and then asking Him to help you learn from what you read. Prepare yourself by:

- **CLEARING** your mind and being quiet before the Lord
- **ASKING** God to settle your heart
- **LISTENING** to worship music to prepare your spirit
- **ASKING** God for a teachable heart

READ . . .

A great way to start is to read a Proverb each day (there are 31 chapters in Proverbs, so you have one per day), a Psalm, and a chapter out of the New Testament or Old Testament. Another way is to begin with one of the Gospels such as John or one of the shorter letters such as Ephesians or James. You might also start with the first four devotions in this section: "ONE Passion" (p. 1372), "ONE Pain" (p. 1373), "ONE Power" (p. 1374), "ONE Purpose" (p. 1375).

Journaling can help your spiritual development and is an effective way of building your faith, reminding you of how God is working in your life.

EXAMINE . . .

Ask yourself the following questions in regard to the Bible passage you read:

- **TEACHING:** What do I need to KNOW about God, myself, and others?
- **REBUKING:** What do I need to STOP doing—sins, habits, or selfish patterns?
- **CORRECTING:** What do I need to CHANGE in my thoughts, attitudes, or actions?
- **TRAINING:** What do I need to DO in obedience to God's leading?

SUMMARIZE . . .

Do one of the following to solidify the key insights in your mind and heart:

- Discover what the passage reveals about God and His character, what it says or promises about you, and what it says or promises about others—your parents, friends, teammates, strangers, and enemies. Write this in a personal journal.
- Rewrite one or two key verses in your own words.
- Outline what each verse is saying.
- Give each verse a one-word title that summarizes what it's saying.

SHARE . . .

Talk with God about what you've learned. Also, take time each day to share with someone from your group what you gained from your "Training Time."

A daily "Training Time" is extremely important. It is one of the keys to developing spiritually.

This is why we've prepared 31 devotions for you. If you commit to doing these over the next month, you will establish a powerful habit for your spiritual growth.

FCA is excited to present devotions that will keep you "ONE" in your life. Each is written from the athletic perspective to encourage you to be like Christ in your life on and off the field or court. In life and sports, there is always the need to take a TIME-OUT to think about your purpose in living and playing for God.

I will commit to establishing this daily habit.

Signed

____

Today's date

____

WRITERS

There are many writers and editors who have contributed their time, talents, and experience to writing these devotions. Writers include representatives from the world of sports. Our writing team consists of coaches, athletes, team chaplains, and FCA staff—all from very diverse backgrounds.

TOPICS

Topics covered in the "Training Time" devotions were created to support this year's theme, "ONE."

FORMAT

- **READY:** The Focus—a verse, passage, or thought to direct your heart and mind. (It will help to turn to the Scripture reference in your Bible so you can read it within the overall context of the passage.)
- **SET:** Teaching—a story, training point, or thought taken from a sports perspective.
- **GO:** Application—a prayer, question, thought, or action to direct you to be like Christ.
- **OVERTIME:** Additional Bible reading to help you dig deeper and a prayer to help you connect with God.

To receive a daily e-mail sports devotion, go to *www.FCAImpactPlay.org*.

One Passion By Sarah Roberts

READY:

"We love each other because he loved us first." —1 John 4:19

SET:

Eric Liddell was and Olympic athlete and extremely passionate about his sport. He was quoted as saying "God made me fast, and when I run I feel His pleasure." Although he loved running, his passion for God was greater. In the 1924 Paris Summer Olympics, Liddell refused to run in the 100 meters in which he was favored because the event was on a Sunday. His personal obedience to God was greater than his need of acceptance by the world. He ran the 400 meters and won. He ran for One . . . the ONE TRUE GOD.

The passion he had for God was because of the love he knew his God had for him. Passion and love go hand in hand. Liddell showed his passion for God when he ran. God showed his love for us when He lived . . . and died. God is passionate about us because of the love He has for us!

GO:

1. When you play the game you love, do you feel God is pleased?
2. As an athlete, it can be so easy to play for the acceptance of others. How freeing would it be if you had nothing to prove and only One to please?
3. How do you show love and passion for the game you play?
4. How does the passion for the game you play compare to the love you have for God?

WORKOUT:

Zephaniah 3:17; John 3:16; 1 John 4:9

OVERTIME:

Dear Lord, thank You for loving me. I know it because of the love and passion You have for me that You died for my sins. Help me to love the way You love in all that I do. May I live full of passion for You, my Lord and Savior. Amen.

One Pain By Julie Martin

READY:

"For everyone has sinned; we all fall short of God's glorious standard. Yet God, in his grace, freely makes us right in his sight. He did this through Christ Jesus when he freed us from the penalty for our sins."—Romans 3:23-24

SET:

Every athlete at one time or another has suffered pain while competing. I was notorious for turning my right ankle. Even now as an adult I have to be careful of it!

When in physical pain, what do most people do? They find something that will take away the pain, right? It might be ice, heat, pain medicine or the best pain reliever of all: Mom.

Sadly, there is no pain medicine that can take away that of our sin. The ultimate outcome of that pain is death. But there is good news! Jesus Christ became the "Painkiller" to our sin when He was crucified on the cross, thereby relieving us of our punishment.

All of us sin. There is no denying that. Because of the work Jesus did on the cross, we can now spend our eternity with God in heaven. Our own personal sin is still painful, and the consequences of our actions can cause a lot of pain. But God freely gives us His grace, not due to anything we have done, but because He loves us. Therefore, just by believing that Jesus Christ died on the cross for our sin and that God raised Him from the grave, we will be saved! And on that day, all our pain will be relieved.

GO:

1. Until now, who or what has been your "painkiller"? Has it been a relationship, a person, alcohol, drugs, etc.?
2. Why are those poor sources of pain relief?
3. Can you trust Jesus Christ to become your "Painkiller"? If so, what will you do to let Him?

WORKOUT:

Romans 10:9; Ephesians 2:8-9

OVERTIME:

Dear Jesus, I know that I am a sinner and need Your forgiveness. Please come into my heart and be my Lord and Savior. In Your name, amen.

One Power By Julie Martin

READY:

"I also pray that you will understand the incredible greatness of God's power for us who believe him. This is the same mighty power that raised Christ from the dead and seated him in the place of honor at God's right hand in the heavenly realms."
—Ephesians 1:19-20

SET:

There's a sense of power and passion when it comes to defending your home court or field. This is your house, and no one comes in and steals a victory on your turf!

The same kind of power (only a degree more intense) is displayed in a mother grizzly bear when protecting her cubs. Standing 12 feet tall when on her hind legs, she can decapitate lions, wolves and, yes, humans, with a swipe of her paw. This makes her one of the fiercest animals in North America. The only competition she faces is a male grizzly bear, which is normally 30 percent larger in size. Even a male grizzly will relent, though, when faced with the ferociousness of a momma grizzly bear protecting her young. What the momma grizzly lacks in size, she makes up for in power.

Did you know that God has the same power and passion for us? Unlike the grizzly bear or an athletic team, though, God has no competition. God is the competition!

In the book of Ephesians, Paul prays that we'll understand the greatness of God's power. This same power that raised Jesus Christ from the dead is alive and active inside of us! We are protected by faith in the salvation that comes from Jesus Christ, and our faith in Him gives us direct access to God's power—the power that raised Christ from the dead! And that same power protects us as we carry out His perfect plan for our lives.

GO:

1. How does knowing God's power is at work in your life affect the way you face obstacles in sports? In life?
2. What does it mean for you to know God has you protected?

WORKOUT:

Romans 8:38; 1 Peter 1:5, 9, 13

OVERTIME:

God, help me to live my life with power and to face obstacles with courage and strength knowing I am protected by Your power through Christ. Amen

One Purpose By Dan Britton

READY:

"I pray that they will all be one, just as you and I are one—as you are in me, Father, and I am in you. And may they be in us so that the world will believe you sent me."
—John 17:21

SET:

Just give up. It should become a daily practice for all of us. If more athletes and coaches would give up, the sports world would be better off.

I'm not talking about giving up as in quitting. I'm talking about giving up our rights and surrendering them to the Lord. God hates the "quitting-giving-up," but He loves the "surrendering-giving-up." What does God truly want most from us? For us to give up our lives for the sake of His kingdom and be unified. Our whole life we are taught to hold on tight to what we have earned, to defend what is ours, and not let people take advantage of us.

Giving up should become a part of who we are when it comes to our sports teams, families, churches, ministries, organizations, and businesses. True teamwork is when God's kingdom comes together to transform vision into reality. When you give up your rights and join together, the reward is great. When the body of Christ joins together and operates with one purpose, it fires up the Lord Jesus Christ. The nature of Christ is demonstrated in a real, tangible way to a lost world when we give up, unite together, and do the work of the kingdom.

It's time to give up. Surrender, team up with others today, and see what God will do with your life. You will become the channel for God's greatest work.

GO:

1. What does it look like to give up on your team the way God desires? What would happen to your team?
2. Why is God pleased when we unite with others?

WORKOUT:

John 15:12-13; 2 Corinthians 6:14; Galatians 1:10

OVERTIME:

Father, I ask for the power to give up. I don't want to be a quitter but someone who surrenders to do Your will. In Jesus' name I pray, amen.

Daily Surrender By Sarah Rennicke

READY:

"For I swear, dear brothers and sisters, that I face death daily. This is as certain as my pride in what Christ Jesus our Lord has done in you."—1 Corinthians 15:31

SET:

"Why can't I get it right?"

We've all asked ourselves this when wanting to do well in sports and daily life. But we're human, and we so easily entangle ourselves in slip-ups without even trying.

As followers of Christ, we long to live in obedience to our Lord, but we often find ourselves living out of the flesh rather than the Spirit. There's always that inner tugging to go our own way—whether that's thinking we should get more playing time, or that we really know what's best for the team instead of our coach. And going a level deeper, we face the same struggle with our stubborn sin habits. We know we are a new creation in Christ, but try as we might, we feel bound to mess up.

Thankfully, God has a short memory when it comes to our mistakes, and today is a great day to wipe the slate clean—to go about practice, life, and relationships with renewed vigor. And we do that by turning our hearts over to Him, asking for forgiveness, and entrusting ourselves to His will.

It's all about daily surrender to God's plan and a continuous sacrifice of our self for the sake of His Spirit. We're quick to hold tight to the sin of our flesh, but when we lose control of our carnal nature and embrace His grace, God will set us free.

GO:

1. How do you fight the battle of self vs. spirit?
2. In what ways can you keep surrendering yourself to God?
3. Ask God to show you the areas of your heart you need to turn over to Him.

WORKOUT:

2 Corinthians 5:17; Galatians 5:25

OVERTIME:

Lord, help me to dig into those private places I hide and hand them over to Your care. Let me die daily to myself for the sake of Your Spirit. Amen.

Is Your "But" Holding You Back?

By Kerry O'Neill

READY:

"Now Jephthah of Gilead was a great warrior. He was the son of Gilead, but his mother was a prostitute."—Judges 11:1

SET:

It seems like any scouting report contains a "but." He's a good shooter, *but* he is too slow to guard anyone. She is fast, *but* she is skinny and not very strong. He's a good coach with the X's and O's, *but* he does not relate well to his players. The girls like her as a coach, *but* they really don't learn a lot about soccer from her.

Imagine the huge "but" that Jephthah had to face from birth. He "was a great warrior . . . but his mother was a prostitute." It's likely he was teased, called horrible names, and judged by others. Perhaps being picked on and learning to defend himself is what helped him become a mighty warrior.

Here are some of the "but" labels that were placed on me by others: broken home, divorce, single mom, poor, alcoholism, ADD, skinny, weak, can't jump—just to name a few. But those labels, even though part of my background, didn't need to define me. And none of them are my identity.

You too are a great warrior, but you have weaknesses and labels like every other person on earth. In which truth will you walk? Let your identity in Christ and the strengths He gave you be your identity, not your weaknesses. Ultimately, let the Lord's opinion of you outweigh the opinion of man.

GO:

1. What are the "but's" in your life?
2. Which ones have you allowed to negatively define you?
3. How can you walk in the truth of God's opinion of you and overcome any negative labels?

WORKOUT:

Isaiah 41:13; Colossians 3:1-3; 1 John 3:1-2

OVERTIME:

Lord, help me to walk in the truth of Your opinion of me. In Jesus' name, amen.

Bold Belief Moments By Clay Elliott

READY:

"One day Jonathan said to his armor bearer, 'Come on; let's go over to where the Philistines have their outpost.'"—1 Samuel 14:1a

SET:

The Israelite warrior Jonathan made this suggestion to his armor bearer almost on a whim. We really have no idea how the thought came to him, but when you look at the context you realize that he'd decided to go to battle and that the odds were against him. The enemy had 20 warriors in a well-protected garrison, and Jonathan was going in to fight them with one measly teammate.

I would call this a "bold belief moment." This situation oozes with courage (or craziness)! Jonathan just decided to get after it with no guarantees and almost certain death. The two were not only outmanned, they were out weaponed and out positioned, and every move they made could be seen by the enemy. How could they win?

Have you ever made a bold belief move as a Christian athlete? Maybe not as crazy as Jonathan's, but maybe something like going out to the middle of the field before a game and kneeling in prayer? Or inviting your entire team to FCA or church? Or writing a note to your coach saying how your faith makes you the player you are?

A few verses later, the Bible tells us that this one bold belief moment by Jonathan resulted in other crazy happenings:

- The enemy ran away in fear.
- The Israelite traitors rejoined the team.
- Israelite cowards that had been hiding in the trees entered the battle.

Sometimes one bold belief moment by one person can wreck the world! Why not be that one?

GO:

1. Can you think of other bold belief moments that inspired many?
2. Can you think of bold belief moments that you could go and do?
3. Would you choose one today and implement it?

WORKOUT:

2 Samuel 14:15-23; Luke 19:45

OVERTIME:

Father, compel me to make a bold belief moment for You! In Jesus' name I pray, amen.

Work Hard By Rebekah Trittipoe

READY:

"Work brings profit, but mere talk leads to poverty!"—Proverbs 14:23

SET:

A multi-sport athlete in high school and college, I was accustomed to working hard and striving for excellence. I was a leader. I was that kid who went to extremes not to disappoint a coach. A true competitor, I led the charge and never looked back.

What caught me off guard was this. It was the fall of 1977, and I was playing college field hockey. My position was out on the right wing, placed there because of my speed. Few players on any team could outrun me, but on this particular day, the ball was stolen from me. Of course, my job was to pursue with fury. But to this very day, I distinctly remember just jogging to catch up. That had NEVER happened before. It was like I was in a trance; perhaps a slow-motion dream. And then . . .

"TRITTIPOE! WHAT ARE YOU DOING?!?!?!?" My coach was screaming from the sidelines! In all my athletic years, I had never failed so miserably in effort. I was mortified! And that's all it took. The afterburners lit, and I caught my opponent, tackled back and played feverishly the rest of the game—and season.

Reading through Romans 16, I'm amazed to see the value of hard work so highly commended. Paul asked that Mary be greeted as a woman *"who has worked so hard for your benefit."* A few verses later, he scribes, *"Give my greetings to Tryphena and Tryphosa, the Lord's workers, and to dear Persis, who has worked so hard for the Lord"* (Romans 16:6, 12).

There are many other character traits that can be lauded, but the fact remains, hard work is admirable. Be intentional. Be an example.

GO:

1. Why is hard work important for Christ-followers?
2. Can hard work become sin if taken to extremes?

WORKOUT:

1 Corinthians 4:12; 2 Corinthians 11:23; 1 Thessalonians 2:9; 5:12

OVERTIME:

God, Help me work hard so that all glory reflects back to You. Amen.

Run the Play! By Rex Stump

READY:

"As evening came, Jesus said to his disciples, 'Let's cross to the other side of the lake.'"—Mark 4:35

SET:

"Run the play!" These simple yet piercing words encourage athletes to obey and trust the instructions of the coach. In the moments that follow, coaches watch and hope that the athletes trust their words and execute the play.

Jesus and His disciples had finished teaching the masses and were retreating across the Sea of Galilee. Without warning, a terrible storm rocked their boat—and their world! Where was Jesus? He was resting like a baby in the midst of a mini hurricane! Where were the disciples? They were scrambling, panicking and wondering if Jesus cared whether or not they sank!

Read Mark 4:35 again, which is just before the storm. Jesus didn't say, "Let's cross the lake and sink," or, "Let's cross halfway." He said, "Let's cross to the other side of the lake." He called the play in the huddle, and it was up to the disciples to run it. Get in the boat, sail across the lake, exit the boat. But when the storm appeared, the sound of the wind and waves deafened the words of Jesus.

That happens in life. God tells us one thing, but when life gets hard, we hear the storm, the doubters, and the evil one before we hear God's words.

When you read the Word of God, realize He's calling the play. I encourage you to hear God, trust Him, and act on those words of truth!

GO:

1. Which do you tend to hear more: crisis words or Christ's words?
2. Do you trust the Words of God and act on them daily?
3. Recall a time when Jesus sailed with you through a storm, and share it with a friend.

WORKOUT:

Isaiah 50:9-10; Proverbs 3:5-6; 2 Timothy 3:14-17

OVERTIME:

Father, thank You for being with me in all the storms of life. Forgive me for not trusting You fully. Help me trust You and execute the plays You give me! Amen

Keep Moving Forward By Mark Jones

READY:

"No, dear brothers and sisters, I have not achieved it, but I focus on this one thing: Forgetting the past and looking forward to what lies ahead . . ."—Philippians 3:13

SET:

Have you ever made a big mistake on the field of play that you couldn't get out of your mind? In the regional track meet during my senior year, I faulted on my first throw. While the others all did their throws, I kept thinking about what I did to disqualify my first attempt. By the time it was my turn again, I did not have a good mind-set. I was too focused on not faulting again instead of on the next throw. I ended up faulting twice in three throws, and my season ended.

In Philippians chapter 3, Paul recounts the days before he turned his life to Jesus. One of the things he remembers is being a persecutor of the church. The very people he used to hunt and arrest were now his co-missionaries and partners. Then in verse 13, he says he focuses on *"forgetting the past and looking forward."* Paul didn't stay focused on his past. His focus was on what God was laying in front of him.

We all make mistakes, in athletics and in our spiritual lives. But Jesus died to take away the punishment of our mistakes! Through His death and resurrection, we can stop regretting and worrying about yesterday, seek forgiveness, and follow Jesus as we move ahead.

GO:

1. Think of a big mistake that you made during competition.
2. Were you able to move past it? Why or why not?
3. What can help you keep your spiritual walk moving forward when you make mistakes?

WORKOUT:

2 Corinthians 5:17; Hebrews 12:1

OVERTIME:

Father, thank You for forgiving me for the mistakes of my past. Please help me keep following You in obedience. In Jesus' name, amen.

Strength Built in Secret By Chanda Rigby

READY:

"But when you pray, go away by yourself, shut the door behind you, and pray to your Father in private. Then your Father, who sees everything, will reward you."
—Matthew 6:6

SET:

As athletes, we all know that long before our shining moments in front of cheering crowds, there are hours and hours of preparation performed in much less public and glamorous environments. How many hours of practicing in silence does the gymnast invest, and how many practice shots are taken in an empty gym before the shooter is able to hit the shots that make the crowd go wild? Public moments of glory make up a very small amount of the time we spend in our athletic endeavors. Countless more, however, are spent alone and in secret, grinding out the work that greatness requires.

How we build athletic strength can be compared to how we build spiritual strength. Though public acts of spiritual obedience such as attending church and donating our resources to good causes can be positive steps toward spiritual growth, it is our time spent alone in prayer with God that builds the bulk of our spiritual muscle. Matthew 6:6 teaches us that we need to spend time with God in private. Scripture gives us many examples of Jesus modeling this important behavior by stepping away from others to spend alone time with His Father.

Just as the athlete must be disciplined to strengthen his or her body, so must a believer make time to spend alone with God, building spiritual strength.

GO:

1. Try to estimate how many hours you've invested in spending time alone working to get better at your sport.
2. How much time you are spending alone with God to strengthen your spiritual life?
3. How will you respond today?

WORKOUT:

Matthew 26:36; Mark 1:35; Luke 6:12

OVERTIME:

Lord, please help me be diligent in meeting with You alone so I can build the strength to be a conqueror when I am in the presence of others. Amen.

Complainer or Contributor? By Rex Stump

READY:

"Do everything without complaining and arguing, so that no one can criticize you. Live clean, innocent lives as children of God, shining like bright lights in a world full of crooked and perverse people."—Philippians 2:14-15

SET:

In Mark chapter 2, Jesus heals a paralytic on a mat who has been dropped through the roof of a house. When reading this story, it's easy to skip over some important verses because, like the crowd in the house, we're totally amazed with the whole scene. But verses 6-7 say, *"But some of the teachers of religious law who were sitting there thought to themselves, 'What is he saying? This is blasphemy! Only God can forgive sins!'"*

These religious men were not amazed, nor were they excited. They were just sitting there complaining! Instead of finding joy in new life, healing, and exuberant teaching, they just sat there and whined to themselves. Instead, as representatives of God, they should have been contributing to His kingdom by . . .

- contributing not complaining.
- praising not protesting.
- commending not criticizing.
- giving not grumbling.

Do we sit in the stands and complain about the coaches or the referees? Do we sit around the dinner table and complain about our teachers? Do we complain about our classes, our church, or the government? Do we really find joy in a complaining lifestyle? I don't think so. So, let's encourage one another to stand, contribute, commend, and give God praise!

GO:

1. Would you identify more with the religious leaders, or the one being healed?
2. Are you a complainer or a contributor?
3. How can you make a habit of contributing with positive words?

WORKOUT:

Philippians 2:14; 1 Thessalonians 5:11; 2 Timothy 4:2

OVERTIME:

Heavenly Father, forgive me for being a complainer. Give me the power to speak powerful and encouraging words. In Jesus' name I pray, amen.

Reaching Higher By Charles Gee

READY:

"And you must Love the Lord your God with all your heart, all your soul, all your mind, and all your strength."—Mark 12:30

SET:

Being fit is one thing; being an athlete is another. Experts say 30 minutes of exercise at a comfortable pace four times a week will make us fit. That means two hours a week of running, walking, biking, or swimming will allow an individual to meet the requirements of maintaining basic fitness.

Being an athlete requires taking training to another level. We must push our abilities to the limit, giving the maximum our bodies can give. Being an athlete is not something we do for two hours a week; it's part of our lifestyle, requiring a greater commitment. What we eat, how much rest we get, and the intensity of our training all have a direct impact on our success. Fitness is good, but for an athlete, it won't cut it. We have to be all in.

Calling ourselves Christians is one thing, but giving God everything is another. Going to church each Sunday and being active in youth group allows us to maintain a comfortable level of spiritual "fitness." And while those things are good, they alone won't yield the abundant life God has for us. God doesn't want us to settle for being spiritually fit; He wants us to be spiritual athletes. That requires 24-hour-a-day commitment. We must daily give Him all our heart, soul, mind, and strength.

Being spiritually fit helps us see the life we should lead. Being a spiritual athlete means we have found it.

GO:

1. Do you consider yourself an athlete? Does your level of training verify your answer?
2. Are you spiritually "fit" or a spiritual "athlete"?
3. What does it mean to love God with all your heart, soul, mind, and strength?

WORKOUT:

Deuteronomy 10:12; Joshua 22:5

OVERTIME:

God, take me to a new level of spiritual fitness today. Teach me to give You all my heart, soul, mind, and strength daily. In Jesus' name I pray, amen.

Befriend Your Limitations By Amanda Tewksbury

READY:

"There's a young boy here with five barley loaves and two fish. But what good is that with this huge crowd?"—John 6:9

SET:

Is it easy for you to see your weaknesses in sport and in life solely as problems to be avoided? I've found this to be very true in the sports world. As a lefty basketball player, I avoided dribbling with my right hand at all costs because I felt weak as a player when I used it. I saw my limitation as something to be eluded. And don't get me started on how many times I see players I coach avoiding their weaknesses!

Jesus' disciples during His ministry seemed to be no different. A large crowd of 5,000 men (not including women and children) followed the disciples and Jesus after a long day of ministry and arrived at their destination hungry. The disciples told Jesus, "There's a young boy here with five barley loaves and two fish. But what good is that with this huge crowd?" They saw their limitations not as an opportunity to see God at work, but as a limitation that was a nuisance for them. Thankfully, Jesus didn't agree. Luke 9:14-17 tells us that Jesus had them divide up the people and that everyone was fed with the fish and loaves. There were even leftovers!

If we see our limitations as an opportunity to improve and see more of God's kingdom of love and abundance at work, then there will be a shift to befriending our limitations instead of condemning them. We'll know they aren't our enemies; they're opportunities!

GO:

1. Identify one limitation in your life as an athlete and one limitation in your walk with Jesus can motivate you to grow and see God at work.
2. What are the gifts you've already been given that you can thank God for today?

WORKOUT:

Luke 9:10-17; 2 Corinthians 12:5-10

OVERTIME:

Lord Jesus, help me see my limitations as chances to see more of You at work. In Your name, amen.

Attitude in Difficulty By Kristy Makris

READY:

"The angel of the Lord said to her, 'Return to your mistress, and submit to her authority.'"—Genesis 16:9

SET:

Pause for a moment and read Genesis 16. Here we find the story of Hagar—a woman, a foreigner, a slave. How could a woman like her have any dignity?

Did you know that dignity is not dependent on a person, position, culture, gender, or appearance? It's given to us by God. He created us in His image, He sent His Son to die so we could be reconciled to Him, and He displays His love toward us even though we don't deserve it. To Sarai, Hagar was property with no rights and no dignity. But to the angel who appeared to her in the wilderness, she was God's image-bearer with great value and purpose.

Hagar returned to her difficult circumstances with promises from God regarding her yet-to-be-born son and an accurate view of herself in God's sight. When she returned to Sarai, she understood that she was not just serving her, but serving God.

It's very likely that God also was sending her back to Abram and Sarai because there were things He wanted to teach her that she could only learn through difficulty—which is something He still does in our lives today. Often we are tempted to pray and ask for a life of ease, but what if we learn things about God in our sufferings that we otherwise would not have known? God uses suffering redemptively and purposefully in the lives of those who trust Him.

GO:

1. Have you ever felt "used" by maybe a coach or teammate to accomplish what they wanted (e.g. a statistic, championship, popularity, etc.)?
2. How did that affect you and the way you played?
3. How can you, like Hagar, change your attitude in difficulties even if you can't change your circumstances?

WORKOUT:

Proverbs 31:25; James 1:2-3

OVERTIME:

Lord, help me believe that what You withhold is for my good and what You give is for my blessing. Amen.

What Is Your Name? By Kerry O'Neill

READY:

"Then Jesus demanded, 'What is your name?' And he replied, 'My name is Legion, because there are many of us inside this man.'"—Mark 5:9

SET:

There are distinct differences in cultures of teams who practice put-downs and teams that practice put-ups. Sadly, however, the biggest put-downs tend to come from ourselves.

Imagine a coach asking an athlete her name, and she replies, "Slow." Another player answers, "Fat," and another answers "Average." Or you introduce yourself to a coach and ask him his name, and he says, "Loser."

The truth is, Jesus likely asked this man his name not because He didn't know, but because He wanted to see what name the man gave himself. Legion is a term for a Roman army unit consisting of 6,000 soldiers. This man had obvious, serious problems he was battling. And to me, it appears that he allowed his problem to become a label with which he self-identified.

Jesus ends up healing this man, setting him free from the demons inside him, restoring him to his family and giving him back his self-worth. And Jesus wants to do the same with you. You are not who the crowd, your opponent, or anyone else says you are. You are His child—the one He created with His own hands for a good purpose!

GO:

1. What labels have others given you?
2. In what ways does the Lord desire to restore you and raise your self-worth?
3. How can you grow to accept the compliments and praise of others without putting yourself down?

WORKOUT:

Judges 6:12; Isaiah 43:1; John 10:3

OVERTIME:

Jesus, may "Child of God" be the identity in which I compete and live. In Your name I pray,. amen.

It's No Big Thing By Rex Stump

READY:

"But if you refuse to do what is right, then watch out! Sin is crouching at the door, eager to control you. But you must subdue it and be its master."—Genesis 4:7

SET:

"It's no big thing." Have you heard that phrase from a friend, a teammate, or even yourself? Maybe it was a false start on the track, your first foul in a basketball game, or a flag in a football game. Maybe it was an angry word spoken to your opponent or your disrespectful actions toward an official. "It's no big thing." Right?

It could be one incomplete homework assignment. Maybe it was simply skipping church. Maybe it was a small drink, a quick glance at a website, a few choice words placed on social media, or an R-rated movie with 20-plus F-bombs. "It's no big thing." Right?

What if I told you that little things can quickly escalate into big things? Would you then be so nonchalant about those little things?

Adam and Eve's disobedience brought sin into the human race (Genesis 3). Just eating the wrong piece of fruit seemed like "no big thing," but their sinful nature quickly developed in their children. God warned Cain before his murderous act, but jealousy led to anger, anger led to action, and his action lead to murder.

Our "little" sins can become something big if we aren't careful. Watch out! Sin is crouching at the door, eager to control us. And it will lead you places you never thought you wanted to go or dreamed you would.

GO:

1. What was something little that became something big in your life?
2. What little thing do you need to confess and quit?
3. What plan of discipline do you have to combat the little things?

WORKOUT:

Matthew 26:69-75; Galatians 5:9-10; Hebrews 12:14-16

OVERTIME:

Father, I don't always realize that sin is at my door. Please give me strength to overcome sin by the power and strength of Your Spirit. Guard me from all my sinful actions—big and little. Amen.

Trials By Donna Noonan

READY:

"Dear friends, don't be surprised at the fiery trials you are going through, as if something strange were happening to you."—1 Peter 4:12

SET:

We often hear that God has a wonderful plan for our lives, and He does; but we often think it will result in a successful life on earth. Unfortunately, that's not always the case. Players get injured, top recruits go elsewhere, we lose ballgames. Things that are out of our control happen all the time, and responding to those trials tests our faith.

Answering the "why" questions during trials is hard. The most honest answer often is, "I don't know," but that doesn't usually help the questioner. The best thing we can do is to remind ourselves and others what we do know about God.

Here's what I know:

- **Compared to God's, our view is very small and shortsighted.** He sees the big picture. We may not know why something is happening, but we can trust that He does and believe that He will work all things for our good (Romans 8:28).
- **It's OK to cry out to God and tell Him what we're feeling.** Sometimes we fear doing that, but it helps to get it out. The key is not to stay there.
- **Get into His Word to recall the promises and character of God.** Psalms are a great place to go. Remember, He wastes nothing and is always at work to take ashes and turn them to glory (Romans 5:3-5).
- **Seek community.** We may try to isolate from others and God, but it's important to let others in so that God can work through them.
- **Make a choice to trust God's power and plan more than your own.** This can truly set us free.

GO:

1. What promises has God shown you?
2. He might fix it for you to see or He may not. What's your response?
3. Do you trust Him enough to live not knowing the "why"?

WORKOUT:

Habakkuk 3:17-19 (Amplified); Romans 5:3-5; Philippians 3:8-10; 1 Peter 4:12-19

OVERTIME:

Father, help me choose joy, trusting You in trials. In Jesus' name I pray, amen.

At First Look By Chanda Rigby

READY:

"Then Pilate had Jesus flogged with a lead-tipped whip. The soldiers wove a crown of thorns and put it on his head, and they put a purple robe on him. 'Hail! King of the Jews!' they mocked, as they slapped him across the face."—John 19:1-3

SET:

In championship training, one of the most important lessons for an athlete to learn is that winners don't always appear to be winning. Though applause and trophies are common images of championships, it's important to remember that for every glamorous championship moment, there have been countless unglamorous moments.

The reality is that sacrificing and stumbling are necessary when building strength for victory. Often, when we're going through seasons of failure and defeat, we forget that they could be part of our future championship.

John 19:1-3 is taken from the account of Jesus' crucifixion. I'm quite certain that Christ didn't *look* like a champion when He was being mocked, slapped, and scourged. But though He appeared to be at His very weakest, He was actually on the verge of becoming the world's most accomplished champion by defeating death itself.

Stay encouraged when you appear to be losing. Though at first look you may appear to be defeated, you may be on the verge of your biggest championship yet! Keep in mind that the Lord has promised to work all things for your good (Romans 8:28)—even those that could be considered defeat.

GO:

1. Think of some times when you felt like a failure.
2. Consider how these times could be a part of your future success.
3. Visualize how Jesus must have appeared to be losing at His crucifixion and then what He conquered three days later.

WORKOUT:

Ecclesiastes 3:1; Romans 8:28

OVERTIME:

Jesus, help me remember that even You did not always appear to be winning, but that, like You, I can push through temporary pain and the appearance of failure to be a champion if I focus on doing the will of my Father. Amen.

Knuckleballs and Knuckleheads

By Charles Gee

READY:

"I know, Lord, that our lives are not our own. We are not able to plan our own course."—Jeremiah 10:23

SET:

In baseball, the knuckleball is probably the hardest pitch to throw, hit, and catch. The pitcher doesn't know where it's going when he throws it, the hitter has difficulty adjusting to the ball's random movement, and the poor catcher can only try his best to knock it down as it crosses the plate. The knuckleball is slow by Major League standards, only traveling between 60 and 75 miles per hour. It seems to have a mind of its own as it moves, dips, and drops in every direction. That's one reason knuckleball pitchers give up a high number of walks and throw a lot of wild pitches.

Jeremiah 10:23 reminds us that we can be a great deal like the knuckleball. How often do we find ourselves in trouble as a result of trying to direct our own lives? Like the knuckleball, we move this way, dip that way and flutter in every possible direction. Have you ever been called or acted like a "knucklehead"?

Jeremiah tells us we don't have to be that way. When we surrender our lives to Jesus, they are no longer our own. We no longer determine our own path; we give Him that right.

Trying to direct our own lives is as hopeless as trying to direct a knuckleball, anyway. If we want any sort of direction, we need to surrender our will to God. He will show us the way, directing us to His best plan and His best purpose.

GO:

1. Are you making all the plans in your life and leaving God out of the process? How's that working?
2. Are you ready to surrender your life to God? Who can you talk to about this decision?

WORKOUT:

1 Corinthians 1:25; 2 Corinthians 1:12

OVERTIME:

Lord, thank You for loving me even when I act like a knucklehead. Help me today to surrender to Your will and not my own. Amen.

The Little Things

By Sarah Rennicke

READY:

"The master was full of praise. 'Well done, my good and faithful servant. You have been faithful in handling this small amount, so now I will give you many more responsibilities. Let's celebrate together!'"—Matthew 25:21

SET:

Another missed free throw. Another slip of the tongue that falls on a teammate. Friction with that coach who can't see your value beyond your ability. Sometimes we're just one explosion away from ruining our refinement.

Often when we are in tough spots as athletes, we take a quick breath, readjust our sights, and focus on what's before us. It's almost like tunnel-vision concentration—follow-through, check our tongue, focus on getting the next play right. While it may seem menial, over time it makes a big difference.

How we react to the little things of life shapes our hearts. God has great plans for us, yet we must first take responsibility for what we do now. He's training our hearts to serve Him with gladness no matter what. While we may not think much of the mundane, in God's eyes, nothing is too small. When we shift our heart posture to love in the little things, we change as He brings us greater responsibility.

First we master the basics. We must be found faithful with the small before He entrusts us with much, even when little is the last thing we want to work on. But because our eyes are on the cross and what Jesus did for us, we can give our all in everything.

GO:

1. What are "small things" you can do today for God?
2. What role does pride play in keeping you from serving in small ways?
3. How has God promised to be with you in this season of life?

WORKOUT:

Proverbs 22:4; Luke 16:10-12

OVERTIME:

Lord, I get frustrated when I can't master a play or get along with my teammate, and it's hard for me to submit to the small tasks that will make me better. Please help me do the little things for Your glory today. Amen.

Wise Words By Roger Lipe

READY:

"A word spoken at the right time is like gold apples on a silver tray."
—Proverbs 25:11 (HCSB)

SET:

We all know the value of gold and silver, even if we can't afford to own any. We also know how sweet to the taste apples are. How valuable and how sweet to our souls would apples be that were made of gold and served on plates made of pure silver?

The point of this proverb is that our words, spoken at just the right time, are of immeasurable value. You probably have teammates who have followed you all season, and you have followed others, possibly for your whole career. Tell them what you want for them, challenge them to excellence, call them to be athletes of great character. Build a tradition through speaking carefully chosen words to your leaders and to those who follow you.

GO:

1. Have you ever wanted to say something to a friend or teammate, but chickened out at the last minute because you thought it might seem silly or embarrassing? Did you later regret not saying it? Tell the story.
2. What have you heard God nudging you to say to a teammate, coach, or friend this week? How valuable would your words be to that person?
3. How will you go about serving these golden apple words on a silver tray of proper timing to this person? When seems to be the right time for this conversation?

WORKOUT:

Proverbs 16:21; Proverbs 18:21; 1 Thessalonians 5:11

OVERTIME:

Wise and loving Father, thank You for the teammates, coaches, friends, and family you have graciously given me. May I be given opportunities to serve them wise words like apples made of gold on the finest silver platters. I commit my heart's intentions and the purpose of my will to deliver them with grace, love, and joy. I pray with expectation in Jesus' strong name, amen.

Content By Rebekah Trittipoe

READY:

"I have learned the secret of being content in any and every situation."
—Philippians 4:12b (NIV)

SET:

It was a perfect evening for a laid-back training run. A light breeze, low humidity, and the sweet smell of freshly cut hay provided an optimal venue. My pace was casual, somewhere between a Ninja Turtle and Speed Racer. While I was meandering down the country road, a little girl and her daddy emerged from a farmhouse. "Hello! How ya doing tonight?" the half-pint child's honeyed voice wafted across the yard.

With a smile and wave, I replied, "Very fine, thank you." Within a few minutes, a car slowed and pulled alongside. It was the same father and daughter. "Wow. You sure run fast. How old are you, anyway?" he asked. I hardly felt fast, but suppressing a giggle I answered, "59." Startled, he shook his head, mumbled something and drove off. He seemed to appreciate my ability to run, regardless of the pace. Me? I was just content to be running at all!

The incident reminded me of a time when I finished a competitive 50-mile race in third place. To most, that was an admirable position. However, I was disappointed and sourly communicated as much when congratulated by those who finished behind me. I suppose I wanted people to know I hadn't performed up to expectations. I was better than that. My "Thanks, but . . ." was hardly gracious and likely insulting.

As athletes, we're driven to excellence and are responsible to optimize our talents for God's glory. But we also need to be content and gracious no matter the circumstance. We should be thankful that He gifted us to run, to throw things far or to kick a ball with precision. Let's be grateful that even a sub-par performance is better than no performance at all.

GO:

1. How can being content and striving to be better coexist?
2. Why should/can we thank God even in disappointment?

WORKOUT:

Proverbs 19:23; Philippians 4:11-13; 1 Timothy 6:6

OVERTIME:

Father, thank You for the privilege of being Your ambassador through sport regardless of my performance. Amen.

Your Gift, His Ministry By Rex Stump

READY:

"God has given each of you a gift from his great variety of spiritual gifts. Use them well to serve one another."—1 Peter 4:10

SET:

It's no secret that I'm not fast, nor do I have the ability to jump high. To top it off, I'm average height. So when I played collegiate volleyball, I obviously was not a strong front-row player. I also hated receiving serves, because passing was one of my weaknesses. So what were my strengths? Setting and serving. I was confident when finding my hitters and when serving the ball at my opponent. On the court, I believed God gave me the tools to compete. At the time I didn't realize that through volleyball, God also was giving me tools to glorify Him as a coach.

In Judges 6, we read that God chose a man named Gideon to free the Israelites from their opponents, the Amalekites. One day while Gideon was threshing wheat, the angel of the Lord approached him and told him of this choosing. Not convinced of his ability, Gideon debated the angel. Could God really use *him*? Seeking proof that it was really God recruiting him, Gideon made an offering. In response, the angel took Gideon's staff, touched his offering, and immediately fire rose out from the rock it was sitting on and consumed everything! Using Gideon's staff, God demonstrated His power!

Could it be that God wants to demonstrate His power through the tools He gives us? Yield yourself and your talents to God and allow Him to work through you for His glory!

GO:

1. Do you doubt God's ability to use you?
2. Have you ever considered your talent as a tool to glorify God?
3. How can you use your talent to give God glory?

WORKOUT:

Judges 6; Romans 12:1-9; Ephesians 4:7

OVERTIME:

Father, thank You for giving me specific skills. Help me use them for Your glory. I take no credit, and I pray that others will turn to You by watching me use these talents for Your glory. Amen.

When the Crowd Isn't Cheering Your Name

By Adrienne Sherwood

READY:

"Never let loyalty and kindness leave you! Tie them around your neck as a reminder. Write them deep within your heart."—Proverbs 3:3

SET:

After college I began working for FCA. The leadership there was very encouraging and supported me in following God's call to start an inner-city soccer league. It has been one of the most rewarding and challenging things God has ever asked me to do! It felt like there was great interest among others to see if God could really use me to start something great. After three years, we had a real soccer league. We were in four different neighborhoods, and youth were coming to Christ through the ministry.

Soon thereafter the excitement had worn. I had a hard time continuing to be disciplined in the work because I wanted to start the ministry and then let someone else maintain it. Author Lysa Terkeurst says, "Feelings are indicators, not dictators. They can indicate where your heart is in the moment, but that doesn't mean they have the right to dictate your behavior and boss you around."

When emotions are high and everyone's watching, it's easy to work hard. But what happens when you win the championship or earn the MVP and yet it's still time to work hard? Or maybe the time has passed for you to win that championship, but it's still your responsibility to be faithful. We should work faithfully to please the Father, not those around us. That's a calling that will never stop.

GO:

1. How does your athletic performance change depending on your emotions?
2. Do you find yourself seeking the approval of others more than God's?
3. Share a time when you really wanted to quit but stayed faithful.

WORKOUT:

Galatians 1:10; 6:9; Colossians 3:17

OVERTIME:

Lord, help me not let my emotions control my work ethic. Help me want Your approval more than the praise of others. Amen.

Anxiety By Roger Lipe

READY:

"Worry weighs a person down; an encouraging word cheers a person up."
—Proverbs 12:25

SET:

Anxiety seems to coat our hearts with lead and turn our legs to limp spaghetti when we compete. Suddenly doubt, confusion, and frustration weigh us down. All these lead to a performance on the court, field, mat, track, or in the pool that's far less than our best.

But there is a great promise in Proverbs 12:25; it says that a good word cheers one up. And this can be so key in the field of competition.

Encouragement is a powerful tool for an athlete. A simple word, a kind expression, or a well-timed compliment can put a charge into a teammate or a coach, thus lifting the weight he or she had been carrying. And it can make all the difference both in the game and in their heart.

GO:

1. In the hours prior to a competition, what are the things that bring anxiety to your mind and heart?
2. What is the usual effect of such anxiety? How do you deal with it?
3. How does a good word from a coach or teammate affect your feelings of anxiety?
4. How and when do you deliver similar powerful and good words?

WORKOUT:

Philippians 4:6-7; 1 Thessalonians 5:11

OVERTIME:

Merciful Father of Peace, I confess my heart is bent toward anxiety and worry. Those thieves rob my body of its strength, my heart of its faith, and my soul of its resolve. Thank You for my teammates, coaches, family, and friends who speak good and kind words to me. Their words of counsel and cheer encourage my heart, they embolden my spirit, and they renew my mind. With renewed strength and emboldened spirit I will compete to honor and to worship You. I pray In Jesus' strong name. Amen.

Little Bump. Big Change. By Rebekah Trittipoe

READY:

"Let all that I am wait quietly before God, for my hope is in him."—Psalm 62:5

SET:

I'm not used to sitting around. I am a woman of action—working, meeting people, planning, being a wife, gardener, pool attendant, coach, and running (literally) a lot of miles around town and in the mountains. I enjoy being productive and often pride myself on the volume of work I can do in a short amount of time. But the emergency brake was pulled for me this week. Everything came to an abrupt halt.

I ran a 35-mile mountain trail race five days ago. Now I sit on my bed contemplating how a little bump discovered along my jawline several months ago could reset my normal.

Two days ago I had a tumor removed, leaving six inches of incisions that need to heal. I'm told to do nothing active for a week or two. Now I'm trying to figure out how to do nothing. That's harder than running 35 mountain miles.

As athletes, we can get so wrapped up in our training and goal-achieving that we miss out on something both beautiful and restorative: quietness and rest. In reality, if we fail to have these periods, we will eventually blow up, and our effectiveness will lessen.

You don't need a major surgical intervention to take some down time. But we all should be intentional to take well-planned rest from the fray so that we come back better equipped to use our talents for God's glory.

GO:

1. How is resting different than being lazy?
2. Is it possible to optimize physical training without effective rest?
3. What are some benefits of rest?

WORKOUT:

Genesis 2:2-3; Psalm 23; Matthew 11:28, 29; Hebrews 4:9-11

OVERTIME:

Father, resting is hard. Help me see resting in You as a necessary component of my training. Please restore me, Lord. In Jesus' name I pray, amen.

Relation Migration By Clay Elliott

READY:

"But those who wish to boast should boast in this alone: that they truly know me and understand that I am the Lord."—Jeremiah 9:24a

SET:

How would you describe God? Maybe as Creator? Warrior? Father? Of course we know all of these to be true, but limiting Him to just one or two of these really shortchanges Him. The truth is, the more we know Him the more we realize His depth and breadth. The more we discover about Him the more we understand Him. I call this a "relation migration" in which we study and abide with God, getting to know Him intimately.

As athletes we place ourselves—willingly or unwillingly—under the headship of our coaches. We hope they know what they're talking about. We hope they know how to lead us. We hope they understand the game and how to train us in its nuances. And sometimes, when we get connected to a really good coach, we might brag, "This coach knows what's what!"

Jeremiah gives us a challenge here: If you brag at all, you should brag about knowing and understanding God. This knowing and understanding means traveling from the simple to the complex—journeying from the basic to the intricate. And this relation migration can be a sweet lifetime pursuit of God.

Boasting is a selfish proposition. It's about telling others that *we're* what's what. But wouldn't it be exciting to be able to brag about God? I challenge you to go on a relation migration with Him so you can brag to others about the amazingness of God . . . and that He truly knows what's what!

GO:

1. How would you describe your coach?
2. How would you describe God?
3. How would you begin a relation migration with God if you were to start one?

WORKOUT:

Genesis 1–3; Psalm 23; John 1

OVERTIME:

Father, I have a lifetime to go on this relation migration with You. Journey with me. Let me experience You more so I can know and understand You better. In Jesus' name I pray, amen.

I Can't By Amanda Tewksbury

READY:

"He is the one all the prophets testified about, saying that everyone who believes in him will have their sins forgiven through his name."—Acts 10:43

SET:

I've noticed that for athletes there is a very common belief known as **"I can't."** Even little things like trying a new ball-handling drill. If the athlete has experienced failure with a similar drill or with that hand, he or she often responds with the classic, "I can't," and stops pushing toward improvement.

The irony of this negative phrase is that God embraces our brokenness in failures because of our resulting humility. Read the Bible long enough and you'll see there are many examples of tremendous leaders who followed God and brought others to Him who also failed often.

Take Peter, for example, who was one of Jesus' disciples. Peter told Jesus that he would never deny Him, yet he did so in Jesus' darkest hour (three times, just as Jesus predicted). There's also the time he fell asleep the night of Jesus' arrest when Jesus asked him to pray. **But Peter didn't wallow in the "I can't" for long after that. He ended up becoming one of the forerunners of the early church and did incredible things for God and people.** The humility he had from his failures allowed him to yearn for and receive Christ's love and forgiveness and to say, "I can."

As athletes and coaches both in and out of competition, a wonderful motivation, then, for us to lead and love comes from the love and forgiveness we continually receive from God. Our failures can actually become the motivation for our success in sports and as followers of Christ!

GO:

1. What "I can't" is hindering you from improvement in sports?
2. What "I can't" from your past failures do you need to receive forgiveness for to allow you to move forward in following Christ?

WORKOUT:

Acts 10:34-43; Matthew 26:31-74

OVERTIME:

God, please give me the faith to receive Your love and forgiveness and to keep pressing on. In Jesus' name, amen.

Walking in the Valley

By Adrienne Sherwood

READY:

"When you go through deep waters, I will be with you. When you go through rivers of difficulty, you will not drown."—Isaiah 43:2a

SET:

I was a second-year collegiate basketball player when I found out that our women's soccer team was heading to the playoffs with a freshmen backup goalkeeper. Upon discovering this, I approached the soccer coach to let him know that I'd played keeper in high school and could be a great alternative to his backup.

After a conversation with the athletic director and basketball coach, I went on to start in the first round of the playoffs! As a result of this crazy experience, I felt like God was leading me to switch to soccer for the remainder of my college years. I left friendships and traditions from basketball behind to pursue this new path. So when I didn't make the varsity team I was absolutely devastated! I felt like God had abandoned me, and I was very resentful.

Are you in a season in your sport or in life where you feel like God has abandoned you? Are you questioning His goodness, care, concern, and best interest for your life? I have found that these are the seasons in life when we learn the most about God because He has our attention. It certainly worked that way with me!

Although suffering is not always a result of God trying to get our attention, I believe He does use it to teach us more about His character. He is a loving Father who disciplines His children and a jealous God who is with us always.

GO:

1. Do you struggle to worship God in the valley of suffering?
2. Share what God has taught/is teaching you in the valley.
3. What are some of God's characteristics that you can focus on when going through a trial?

WORKOUT:

Joshua 1:9; Hebrews 12:6

OVERTIME:

God, help me praise You in the best and worst of times and believe that You are with me. In Jesus' name I pray, amen.

Finish By Sarah Roberts

READY:

"I have fought the good fight, I have finished the race, and I have remained faithful."
—2 Timothy 4:7

SET:

In 1968, a marathon runner from Tanzania named John Stephen Akwari entered the Olympic Games in Mexico. As Tanzania's only athlete in the Games, he was their hero. Unfortunately, about halfway through his race, Akwari took a horrible fall and messed up his knee. Still, he pulled himself together, got up and started hobbling.

During the marathon in the Olympics, the runners always finish the race in track and field arena. That day, Akwari made his way into the arena in last place. The story had gotten around about his fall and that he was still determined to finish. So once he was done, the news reporters surrounded him. One reporter asked him why he wanted to finish the race, and Akwari replied, "My country did not send me here to start a race. My country sent me here to finish one."

Finish. It's a word used a lot as athletes, but it also signifies the greatest moment in the history of the world. Jesus showed us not only how to live for God but to finish well because of God. In the midst of His greatest pain as He hung on the cross, He managed to utter the words, "It is finished."

What was finished? The job He was sent to this earth to do. The role He was sent to fulfill. If Jesus didn't finish what He started during His life, none of us would have the love, hope, strength or ability to finish in ours. God did not send us here to start a practice, a game, or a season in life but to finish it.

GO:

1. Describe a time you had a hard time finishing a practice, game, or season.
2. How does Jesus and the way He finished inspire you as a Christian athlete?

WORKOUT:-

Ecclesiastes 7:8; 2 Corinthians 8:10-11

OVERTIME:

Lord, thank You for setting the example regarding how to finish strong. Teach me to finish with passion, energy, and integrity. Amen.

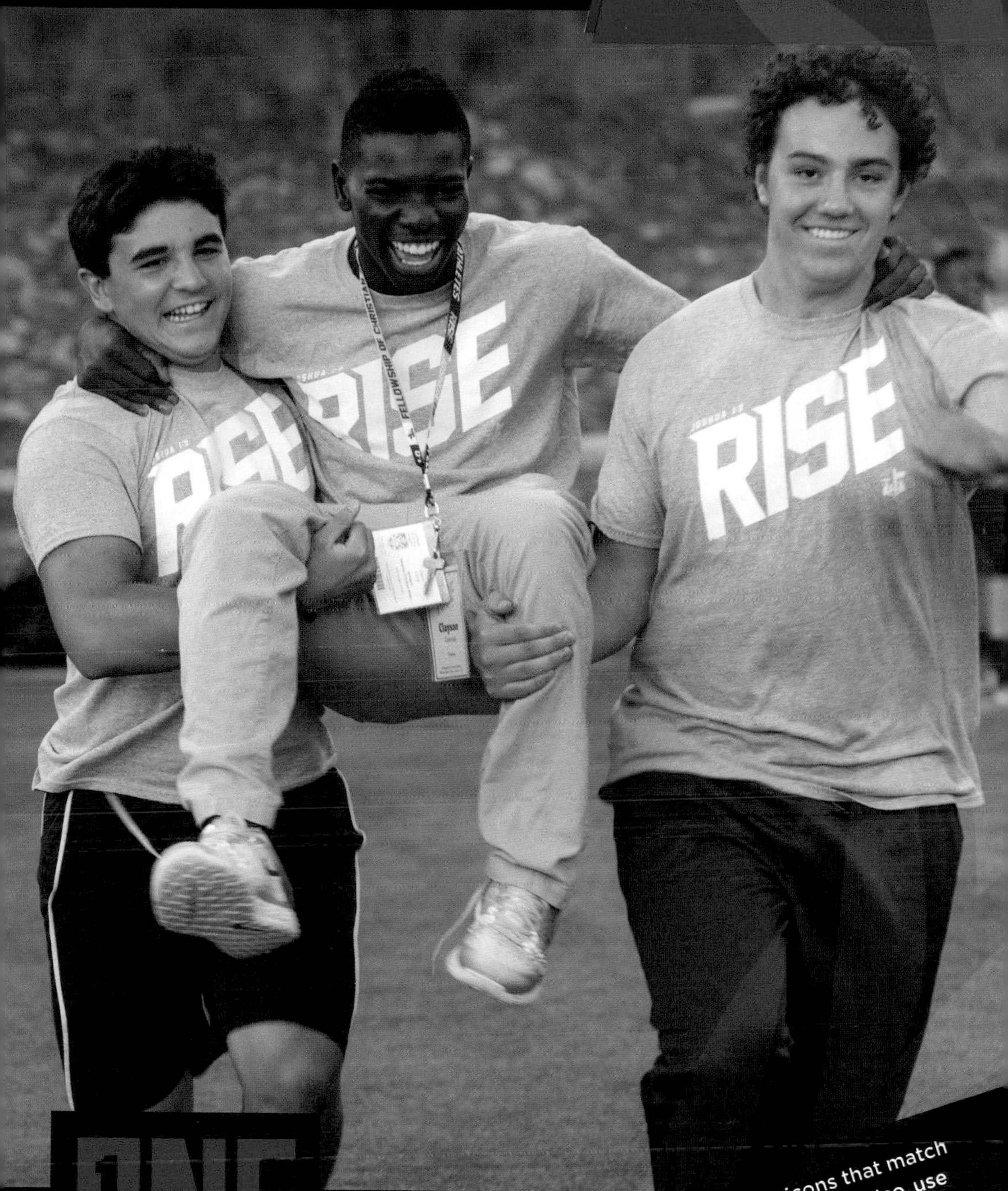

ONE

PHILIPPIANS 1:27

The team-building "Warm-ups" on the following pages have icons that match the icons for the "Life Topics" in the front of the Bible. You can also use these "Warm-ups" with any of the "Athlete Topics" to kick off or enhance your group discussions.

PAIRS:

GROUPS OF AROUND FOUR:

TABLE OF CONTENTS

CIRCLES OF EIGHT:

WHOLE GROUP:

MOST LIKELY

GROUP BELIEFS DISCIPLESHIP

Get in groups of about eight. You may be staring your final year of high school in the face or it may seem like-light years away. Regardless of how long it will be before you accept that diploma, it's likely that the days ahead will be filled with some great (as well as some not-so-great) experiences.

Thinking about the persons in your group, what are they most likely to accomplish in the future? Some things may seem obvious. Many will surprise you. Read each of the following statements then call out the names of persons in your group who would be most likely to accomplish these deeds.

Walk across the country for charity

Become a millionaire

Make their living as a stand-up comedian

Go to Mars

Live in a jungle

Have a decorated military career

Write a best-selling novel

Make a movie

Star in a movie

Become a professional athlete

Have a big family

Serve as a missionary

Be awarded top salesman of their company

Invent something that will change the world

Become a school counselor

Discover a new planet

Find a cure for cancer

Set a world record

Become a nationally known media personality

Sell out every one of their concerts

FAMILY MATTERS

Ask, "What was the funniest thing you ever did that got you in trouble at home?" After sharing responses, place everyone in four or more groups of approximately equal size. Consider grouping students according to birth order, size of immediate family, or some other family-themed grouping. In these groups, reflect on the following questions from your childhood then discuss responses.

What have you learned from having conflicts with your parents and siblings?

- ⬡ Listening to each other clears up many conflicts.
- ⬡ Always apologize (even if you're right).
- ⬡ It's best to talk it out.
- ⬡ Even parents can be wrong sometimes.
- ⬡ What your parents don't know won't hurt them (or you).
- ⬡ It's better to face a conflict and get it over with than to try to hide or ignore it.

In your normal style of handling family conflict, which are you most like?

- ⬡ A hawk—I fly above it all and pick my targets.
- ⬡ An ostrich—I hide my head in the sand until it goes away.
- ⬡ A cat—I timidly slip away then scratch up the couch when no one's looking.
- ⬡ A dolphin—I can fight if necessary, but would rather swim away.
- ⬡ A fox—I use my brains to win.

ROOTED

The Bible declares: "the love of money is a root of all kinds of evil" (1 Timothy 6:10). Money can play a powerful role in your life — both positive and negative. The same is true for success. What keeps you rooted? In your group, answer and discuss the following questions.

My attitude toward money is best expressed by the following motto:

- ⬡ Save, save, save.
- ⬡ Spend, spend, spend!
- ⬡ There's never enough.
- ⬡ It's a necessary evil.
- ⬡ It's a source of arguments.
- ⬡ It's a source of fun.

My feelings about getting ahead can be summed by the following statement:

- ⬡ Look out for number one.
- ⬡ What else is there in life?
- ⬡ It's a high priority.
- ⬡ Keep a balanced life instead.
- ⬡ Don't neglect your family.
- ⬡ It's not worth it.

My idea of a successful person is represented by the following type of person:

- ⬡ Healthcare professional
- ⬡ Scholar
- ⬡ Technological genius
- ⬡ Spiritual guide
- ⬡ Politician
- ⬡ Professional athlete

WARM-UPS

WIN. LOSE. TIE.

Few things in life seem to be neutral. Most of the time people either like or dislike things. And (it seems) most people prefer winning to losing.

Find a partner. Read through the following list of situations. As you read each situation, decide if it represents a win, lose, or tie for you. Indicate your choice by circling the corresponding letter: "W" for win, "L" for lose, or "T" for tie. After you've marked a choice for each situation, share your responses. Note similarities and differences. Do you and your partner define winning and losing the same way?

W L T I've got plans with friends for this weekend.
W L T I barely passed a test that I didn't study for.
W L T It looks like I have multiple chances to take the SAT and ACT.
W L T My parent travels a lot on business.
W L T I scored highest in my class on a test.
W L T According to the results of my physical, I'm perfectly healthy.
W L T Our family may adopt.
W L T There's going to be a substitute in class all week.
W L T It looks like I'm on track to get into the college of my choice.
W L T I had to sit out a game.

FLAVOR OF THE MONTH

Get in groups of around four and share your favorite ice cream flavors and combinations. Whether it's a single, double, or triple scoop, places like Baskets of Robins and Bob and Terry's can make your wildest frozen fantasy a reality. If you've got the funds, they've got the flavors.

Choose up to three of your favorite flavors — from plain vanilla to banana-rama-extravaganza. You can write them on each scoop, if you like.

Compare your favorites with other members of your group.

Now think of three words that distinctively describe you. Whether you write them down or not, share and compare your responses.

MAPPING ME

On the map below, indicate some of the significant events that have happened in your life as well as those you anticipate happening in your future. A few of those events have been provided for you. After using the letters provided to indicate those life occurrences, add other events that you consider to be an important part of your past, present, and future experiences. If any of those events occurred outside of the United States, estimate their location to the US.

Then gather in groups of four and discuss your maps and significant events.

B WHERE I WAS BORN

C WHERE I SPENT MOST OF MY CHILDHOOD

V MY FAVORITE VACATION

G WHERE GOD BECAME REAL TO ME

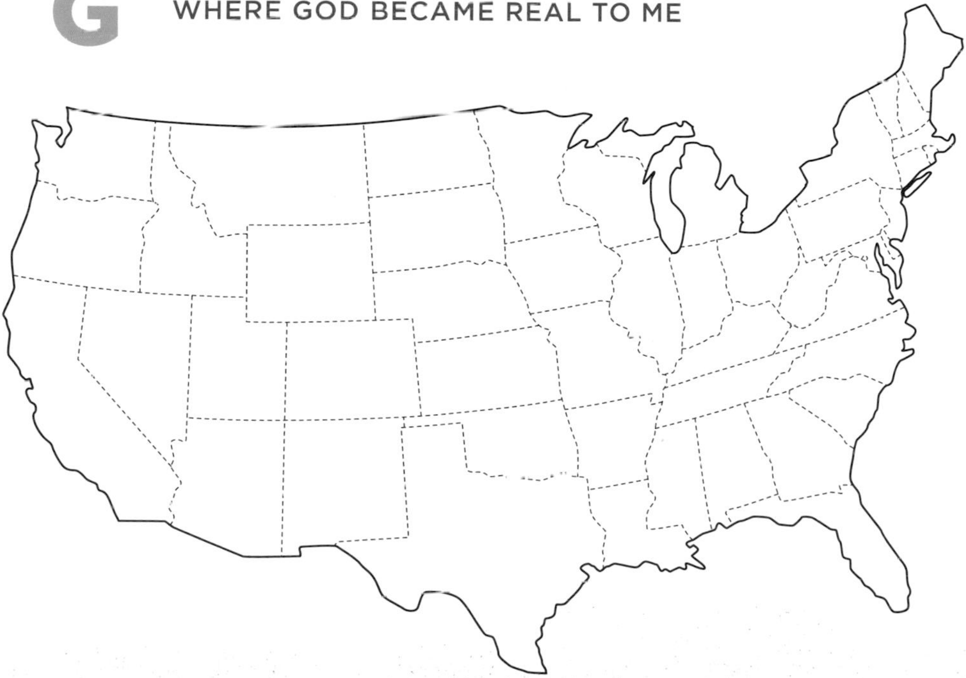

WARM-UPS

ON MY LAST NERVE

OMLN. On my last nerve.

When something is on your last nerve you are close to being completely fed up. You risk losing your temper. When someone is on your last nerve he or she is trying your patience to its limit and better back off before feeling the wrath of your anger.

What annoys you to the point of “losing it”? Consider the following list. Get together in groups of up to eight. Begin by having one group member read the first line. Before giving an answer let others group members guess what the response will be. Take turns reading each line, having others guess the response, and then sharing answers.

On My Nerves

	Always	Never	Depends
Drivers who tailgate			
Someone who chews with his or her mouth open			
An annoying song that gets stuck in your head			
Obnoxious fans			
Students who want to know your grades			
People who change plans at the last minute			
A phone that rings in a movie theater			
Having one sock on and not being able to locate the other one			
Running out of toilet paper when you really need it			
Someone who is always late			
Riding in the back seat			
A monotone teacher			
A person who talks and talks ad talks			
When your favorite show is canceled for a special announcement			
Liars			
Coughers who never cover their mouths			
Cracking knuckles			
Standing in line			
Siblings who borrow your clothes without asking			

YOU DECIDE

In groups of around four, discuss who most influences the decisions you make. Some decisions you may make on your own. But don't be fooled. Even if you aren't aware of the influences on your life, someone is always speaking into your life. Think long and hard below your answer. Think about the people in the different areas of your life. Think about the media in your life.

Your decisions	My parents	My brother/sister	My friends	My teachers/coaches	My church group/ FCA group	Music/movies/ social media
How I spend my time						
How I spend my money						
What I watch and listen to. . .						
What I wear						
Where I draw the line						
What I believe						
What I want out of life						
How I see myself						
How I handle fear, failure, and guilt						

FACTS AND FICTION

Get together in a group of four. Here's a chance to share some interesting facts about yourself — and a piece of fiction. One at a time, complete the four sentences below. Read through the four phrases first, before quietly choosing the one to be a work of fiction. Then share the four statements, keeping a straight face throughout. Let others in the group try to guess which is the fictitious statement. When everyone has guessed, reveal the fictitious response then complete phrase with a true piece of information. Take enough time so that everyone has a chance to share.

When I was five years old, I wanted to grow up to be a ____________________.

When I was ten, my hero was ____________________.

My favorite thing to do when I am not in school (or studying) is ____________________.

One day, I hope to change the world by ____________________.

FOR YOU

Get in groups of about eight. Think about what you value about each person in your small group. You may not know some as well as others, but you can always find a word of appreciation or affirmation to offer. As you consider each person, think about something you could give them that symbolizes what you most value about them.

For example, you might symbolically give them your driver's license because you trust their leadership and feel safe when you are with them. Or; you could symbolically give them a bandage to represent how they have helped you when you were hurting or in need. Or a photo of a fun time you shared could symbolically represent the fun times you've shared.

Begin by asking yourself, "If I could give something to each person in this group to express my feelings for them, what would I give?"

Listen as each person "gives" his or her symbolic gifts to members of the group. Enjoy sharing your gifts too. Although none of them cost anything, their value is likely to last a long time. After each person "receives" the gifts, he or she can simply say, "Thanks."

LIVE IT UP

Though life can sometimes be difficult, it is a gift from God. Each day provides challenges and opportunities to make the most of each day. How would you complete the following three statements? Share your responses in your group of four.

For me, a great day includes:

- curling up with a good book
- going to a party
- attending a concert
- curling up with technology
- watching a movie
- eating my favorite food
- competing in my favorite sport
- hanging out at the mall
- pulling for my favorite team
- going on a date

I would have a lousy day because:

- it's Monday
- the weather is crummy
- my team lost
- it's a bad hair day
- I have to work
- of dating problems
- of hassles with my parents
- things are bad with a friend
- I have no money
- school is wearing me out

If I only had three months on earth, I would:

- ⬭ give everything away
- ⬭ empty my bank account
- ⬭ be angry
- ⬭ spend more time with family
- ⬭ travel the world
- ⬭ do exactly what I'm doing now
- ⬭ do all I can for God
- ⬭ party
- ⬭ disappear
- ⬭ spend more time with friends

EMERGENCY CONTACTS

Discuss recent national or community crises that are on students' minds. Acknowledge the pain and suffering, but try to focus on hope and the way the nation or community has made or can make a positive difference in the situation. Remember that God is present in the worst of circumstances and can bring good out of the worst of situations.

Read the following five situations aloud. Discuss how a personal crisis can seem as monumental as a national disaster when it's happening to you. Take time to discuss the best person or group of people to seek help from in each circumstance. Discuss why certain assistance would be sought. What makes these emergency contacts so sought after in crisis situations? Write helpful names and contact information in the spaces provided.

Emergency: You have a life-changing decision to make. You need good counsel.

Name/Contact: ______________________________

Emergency: You had a huge fight with your parents. You need to talk to someone who understands.

Name/Contact: ______________________________

Emergency: You just received a break-up text. You need someone to talk to.

Name/Contact: ______________________________

Emergency: You just found out that you have a serious disease. You need someone to pray for you.

Name/Contact: ______________________________

Emergency: Someone you thought was a friend has been spreading rumors about you. You need advice.

Name/Contact: ______________________________

WARM-UPS

ADVANCED PLACEMENT

GROUP AWARENESS CHOICES

You have an opportunity to check out some college classes at no cost. You have to take all eight classes and you'll get full credit for each course, regardless of your final grade. However, you have to enroll by listing your class preferences from first choice to last. Get in groups of four and take turns reading each course.

Rank classes by placing a number in the box to the left of each course title.

⬭ **Sociology 101: AMERICAN TV VIEWING.**
A fascinating study of viewing habits focusing on becoming an expert couch potato, snacking, and channel surfing.

⬭ **Calculus 401: THE MATHEMATICS OF CHAOS.**
Classes meet in several different locations, at several different times, and are taught by several different professors.

⬭ **Archeology 200: BONES DOWN UNDER.**
The study of aboriginal fossils. Class spends summer in the outback of Australia.

⬭ **Bird Watching 100: OUR FEATHERED FRIENDS.**
In this introductory class, you'll learn how to spot a bird, how many wings it has, and how to identify a feather.

⬭ **Political Science 300: THE MANAGEMENT OF BUREAUCRACY.**
An introduction to bureaucratic language, form making, and standing in line. Special segment on how to obtain a driver's license.

⬭ **Creative Writing 222: THE LIMERICK.**
Learn to rhyme in the Irish tradition. In lieu of a trip to the Emerald Isle, study will focus on reading limericks and composing original rhymes.

⬭ **Automotive Repair 420: ADVANCED AUTO ELECTRONICS.**
The first part of the semester will be devoted to setting the buttons on your sound system. Second semester will address the proper use of intermittent wipers.

⬭ **Cultural Studies 301: STUDY ABROAD.**
A study of the music and culture of Great Britain, including concerts and personal audiences with Britain's music royalty.

CAR CHASE

The next best thing to getting your license to drive is having a car to drive. You may be sharing a car with a parent or sibling, enjoying a brand-new vehicle, getting around in a not-so-new-but-you-paid-for-it-yourself automobile, or watching your license discolor as you wait to put it to the test.

What vehicle would you drive if you were going:

interstate driving? ____________________

on a date? ____________________

to school? ____________________

on a mandatory family vacation? ____________________

to the beach? ____________________

off-roading? ____________________

camping? ____________________

MAJOR IMPACT

Every person makes an impact. You influence others and others influence you. Even though you may not be aware of it, what you do and say makes an impact. Look at the following "impact list." Beside each description, write the names or initials of at least five people in your life who make an impact on your life as described. Then get together in groups of four and discuss your responses.

- **Believer:** Listens to and appreciates my dreams.
- **Confronter:** Loves me enough to say what I might not want to hear.
- **Consoler:** Calms me down when life gets out of control.
- **Crazy Friend:** Does something wild to bring out my fun side.
- **Encourager:** Helps me look on the bright side of things.
- **Inspirer:** Reminds me that God has everything under control
- **Listener:** Hears what I have to say without trying to change me.
- **Mentor:** Sticks with me and guides me on life's journey.
- **Prayer Partner:** Joins me when I seek God in prayer.
- **Role Model:** Sets a good example for me in actions, character, and reputation.

CASE CLOSED

Get together in groups of up to eight. Discuss cases, issues, and participants found in a trial or court of law. Share examples from history and current events. What were the verdicts and sentences?

1. If you had an attorney to argue your right to enter heaven before God, what would you most want him or her to say on your behalf?

2. Which of your weaknesses do you have the hardest time believing Jesus could empathize with or understand?

3. If you fully grasped Jesus' willingness and ability to empathize with you, how might it impact the way you prejudge yourself?

4. How confident do you feel accepting God's free gift of forgiveness?

HEALTH FAN OR HEALTH FOE?

Get in groups of four or more. Consider one area at a time then mark an X where you would rate yourself for each of area. Share the results of your checkup with members of your group.

HEALTH FOOD	**NUTRITION**	JUNK FOOD
MARATHON RUNNER	**EXERCISE**	COUCH POTATO
"GOOD MORNING, LORD!"	**SLEEP**	"OH LORD , IT'S MORNING!"
ABOVE THE INFLUENCE	**DRUG USE**	UNDER THE INFLUENCE
CHILLED	**STRESS**	FREAKED OUT
SHARP	**MENTAL ALERTNESS**	CLUELESS
SUPER CHARGED	**OVERALL FITNESS**	DEAD BATTERY

TELL-IT-LIKE-IT-IS TRIAGE

A triage unit, in an emergency room or other medical facility, prioritizes the injured or ailing for treatment according to the seriousness of their condition. None of the following conditions are life-threatening but they may have some lifelong effects. As one person reads each "ailment," share with group members if you "suffer" from it.

Shop-itis:

A strong compulsion to spend hours and dollars at a store or boutique.

Choco-holism:

Giving bad looks when someone asks for some of your chocolate dessert or candy.

Socialmedia-itis:

Staring at a screen for hours every day typing messages to both people you know and those you've never met.

Channelsurf-itis:

Cramping feeling in your index finger from pushing the remote control buttons so much.

Involuntaryleadfoot Reflex:

Always finding yourself in a rush in the vehicle and usually traveling at a faster speed than most drivers.

Which of these "ailments" do you believe to be at a point of crisis in your life? Is there anything you can do to alleviate the situation?

WARM-UPS

BESTIES

GROUP | RELATIONSHIPS | AWARENESS

Get together in groups of about eight. Reflect on the best experiences you have had. Think of the "bests" in your life using the following list.

1. The best movie I ever saw was

______________________________.

2. The best teacher I ever had was

______________________________.

3. The best concert I ever went to was

______________________________.

4. The best game I ever played in was

______________________________.

5. The best babysitter I ever had was

______________________________.

6. The best class in school I ever had was

______________________________.

7. The best pet I ever had was

______________________________.

8. The best birthday I ever had was

______________________________.

9. The best vacation I ever went on was

______________________________.

10. The best book I ever read was

______________________________.

11. The best summer of my life was

______________________________.

12. The best friend I ever had was

______________________________.

Choose two or three items from the list and talk about the highlights with members of your group. Discuss why some experiences were better than others.

What role did relationships play in making these the best experiences of your life?

I'M NOT COMPETIVE . . . AM I?

GROUP AWARENESS RELATIONSHIPS CHOICES

Get with one other person. Does your partner know how competitive and cooperative you are? How would the people who know you most classify you?

Look at the following list of activities. In which are you more likely to compete? In which are you more likely to cooperate? Take turns with your partner going through the list and selecting *Competes* or *Cooperates* for each situation.

Competes		Cooperates
⬡	playing a board game	⬡
⬡	playing a game of pick-up ball with friends	⬡
⬡	playing on a school sports team	⬡
⬡	working with a group on a school project	⬡
⬡	discussing an issue in class	⬡
⬡	driving	⬡
⬡	using social media	⬡
⬡	making a family decision	⬡

SHIELDED

GROUP CHOICES

Throughout history, families have used symbols, usually in the shape of a shield, to represented their family heritage. Though a family may not post a coat of arms in their home or property, there has always been an interest in genealogy: the study of family history. Get in groups of around four. Using the coat of arms here, list five strengths about your parents and yourself on the shield.

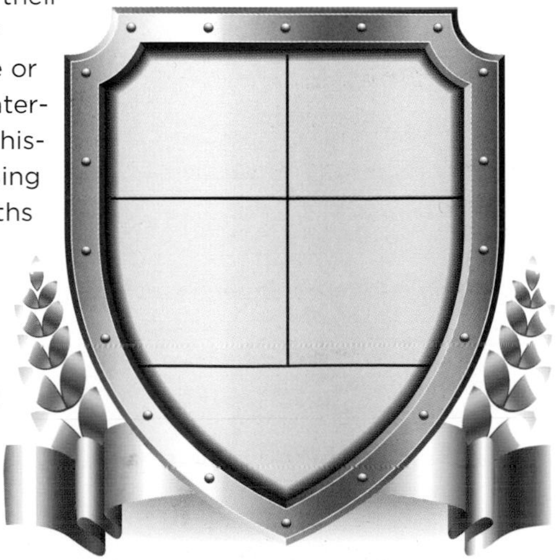

After you share the strengths that make up your family coat of arms with your group, share what you liked about what you heard and then complete the following statement:

If I could add another strength that I have seen in you, it would be:

LIKES AND LOVES

Make one sign that reads **"LIKE"** and another that reads **"LOVE."** Post these signs on opposite sides of your meeting space, or have two students hold the signs in different areas. Read the following words and have students move to the sign that best represents their feelings.

Eating Sleeping Staying busy Weekends Sports Social media Music

Then share that you are now going to discuss likable and lovable relationships. Ask for volunteers to come forward who are willing to answer some personal questions in front of the group. Ask the following questions:

1. Who was your first love?

2. What TV show, movie, or book do you like because it shows a relationship you admire?

3. What TV show, movie, or book do you not like because it celebrates a negative relationship?

4. What three words describe your relationship with God?

5. What does it mean to you to "follow Jesus"?

POTATO HEAD GONE WILD

Get together in groups of up to four. If possible, use a Mr. Potato Head to illustrate the following discussion.
Pass Mr. Potato Head around and let each group member design a better body.

1. If you could change anything about your appearance what would it be?

2. Is the human body an imperfect creation? Why?

3. What makes sense about the way God designed you? What doesn't make sense?

4. Wouldn't it be better to have eyes in the back of your head or an extra hand every now and then?

DIFFICULT PEOPLE

GROUP STRESS RELATIONSHIPS

Some people just seem to be more difficult than other people. Whether it's true or not, you can almost guarantee that at some point in your day-to-day activities you are bound to encounter someone in a less-than-perfect situation.

Ask a member of the group to read the first "If I were to encounter" statement and briefly describe how he or she would likely respond. Invite others to respond. Read each statement, allowing several responses for each. After allowing time for group members to respond to all the statements, ask, "How are our responses a result of the things that cause us stress? What if we imagined ourselves—or someone we care deeply about—in the other person's place? Would we respond differently? If so, how?

If I were to encounter someone who chews with his or her mouth open, I would likely . . .

If I were to encounter someone who is boring me with endless conversation, I would likely . . .

If I were to encounter a server who gets my order wrong, I would likely . . .

If I were to encounter a driver who cuts me off, I would likely . . .

If I were to encounter a telemarketer who won't take no for an answer, I would likely . . .

If I were to encounter a person who flirts with me, I would likely . . .

If I were to encounter a cashier who talks on the phone while waiting on me, I would likely . . .

If I were to encounter a homeless person begging for money, I would likely . . .

If I were to encounter a person who cuts ahead in a long line, I would likely . . .

If I were to encounter someone who is being rude to an elderly person, I would likely . . .

If I were to encounter someone whose political views are the opposite of mine, I would likely . . .

If I were to encounter a person who seems very shallow, I would likely . . .

ALMOST OVERWHELMED

It you ever wanted to have the lowest score on a test this would be the one. Get in groups of about eight. Read each stressor listed. If, in the last year, you have experienced any of the things listed, circle the corresponding number to the right. After everyone in your group has gone through the list and circled responses, share scores and compare answers. If your score is more than 150, you have likely been living with a lot of stress. You may need to talk to someone who can help you. This test is not a professional or reliable test. But it may help you recognize that you can't handle everything in life by yourself.

Stressor	**Stress Points**
Death of a parent	100
Death of a family member	75
Death of a friend	65
Divorce of parents	60
Breakup with girlfriend/boyfriend	55
Major personal injury or illness	53
Failed a class	50
Got in trouble at school	45
Lost your driver's license	40
Moved to a new community	37
Failed a big test	35
Conflict with parents	33
Changed schools	30
Got in an argument with a friend	27
Experienced a family health or financial problem	23
Had a bad hair day	10
Discovered a blemish on your face	5

TOTAL

WHEN I WAS TEN

Get in groups of around four. Use the following questions to talk about the person you were when you were ten years old. As you complete each statement, remember do so as a ten-year-old you. Make sure everyone has a chance to respond before moving to the next statement.

- My first pet: ______________________________
- My favorite subject in elementary school: ______________________________
- The person I went to when I got hurt: ______________________________
- The chore I dreaded doing most: ______________________________
- My first big trip: ______________________________
- My favorite room in the house: ______________________________
- The fun thing we often did as a family: ______________________________
- My favorite thing to do on a summer day: ______________________________
- The friend who got in trouble with me: ______________________________
- My favorite uncle or aunt: ______________________________
- The best Christmas present I received: ______________________________
- My favorite thing to eat: ______________________________

WILDERNESS ADVENTURE

Play wilderness adventure charades. Rather than allowing students to call out answers, invite those who think they know the answer to join you in the charade. Even if they are wrong allow them to continue acting alongside you. After several students have joined in the charade reveal the answer. Allow several students to pantomime a bear, deer, owl, hawk, whitewater rapids, campfire, backpacker, sunset, tent, mountain, blizzard, sleeping bag, forest fire, and so on. Some charades may require more than one person.

Point out that the great outdoors can be awesome, but also unpredictable and risky—like sharing Christ. Ask students to share how they would share the gospel with the following people: close friends, people in crisis, teammates, people who seem to have it all together, strangers who ask, family members, people you try to avoid.

YOUR LIFE'S WORK

What do you think you will do with the rest of your life? It's not too early to be making preparations for your life's work.

From the list below choose your first and second career choices. If your life's passion is not listed below, add it. Get in groups of around four and share your top choices.

______ Social Worker	______ Novelist	______ Veterinarian
______ Professional Athlete	______ I T Specialist	______ Pilot
______ Actor	______ Engineer	______ Police Officer
______ Physician	______ Missionary	______ Fashion Designer
______ Politician	______ Astronaut	______ Teacher
______ Psychologist	______ Banker	______ Minister
______ Attorney		

LIFETIME GUARANTEE

If you could guarantee three things in your life, which three would you choose from the list below? Get together with one other person and share your choices with each other.

- ⬡ Financially independent so you never have to work a day in your life
- ⬡ Secure and rewarding job guaranteed for life with benefits
- ⬡ An attractive appearance that always gets you noticed in a crowd
- ⬡ Stress-free life without pain, struggles, or tension
- ⬡ Deep, satisfying relationship with God
- ⬡ So popular that everybody wants to spend time with you
- ⬡ Romantic relationship with the person of your dreams
- ⬡ Close family with no hassles, unconditional love, and lots of support
- ⬡ Good health and a long life
- ⬡ One deep friendship with someone who will always be there
- ⬡ Success, fame, and recognition in your chosen field

LIKE CHRIST

GROUP DISCIPLESHIP

LIKE CHRIST

Every Christian reflects the character of Christ in some way. As your group has gotten to know each other, you begin to see how others demonstrate Christ in their personality and actions. Take time to affirm each other in the way they are letting Jesus live His life through your friends. This might feel odd at first, but God is sure to honor your time of sincere affirmation.

If your group is too large to affirm each other, divide the large group into smaller ones. Then use the descriptions of Jesus listed below to share how you see Christ at work in the lives of others.

Servant:
There's nothing you wouldn't do for someone.

Healer:
You're able to touch lives with your compassion, then all is well.

Preacher:
You share your faith in a way that challenges and inspires people.

Leader:
Just like Jesus had a plan for the disciples, you're able to lead others well.

Reconciler:
Like Jesus, you are a peacemaker.

Teacher:
You have a gift of bringing understanding to God's Word.

DECISION TIME

You make decisions every day. You are aware of many of them, but some are so much a part of your daily routine that you don't give them much thought. Get together in groups of about eight. Read through each of the following questions, one at a time, and share your answers with the members in your group.

WHEN IT COMES TO MAKING TOUGH DECISIONS, I USUALLY:

- ask for advice
- decide quickly
- go for a walk
- struggle for days
- wait to see what someone else will do
- never ask for advice
- hope it will go away

THE MOST DIFFICULT DECISIONS FOR ME ARE USUALLY INVOLVE MY:

- reputation
- popularity
- money
- friendships
- morals

MY BIGGEST FEAR WHEN IT COMES TO STANDING UP FOR WHAT I BELIEVE IS:

- being wrong
- losing my friends
- getting someone in trouble
- being laughed at
- standing alone

IN MY FAMILY, WHEN WE TALK ABOUT MORALITY, IT IS DESCRIBED AS:

- a matter of black and white
- the mark of a gentleman or lady
- dependent on the circumstances
- the results of being a Christian
- an individual thing

YOUR FRIEND DOESN'T STUDY. EVER. HE PREFERS TO CHEAT OFF YOUR PAPER. WHAT WILL YOU DO?

- let him copy
- tell the teacher
- let your friend know that it's not cool
- cover your paper

WHEN I DON'T AGREE WITH WHAT ONE OF MY FRIENDS IS DOING, I:

- ignore it
- confront him or her about it
- take a break from hanging out with him or her
- talk to someone else about it
- permanently end the friendship

YOUR FRIEND DOESN'T MAKE THE INVITE LIST TO A PARTY, BUT YOU DO. WHAT WILL YOU DO?

- go to the party
- do something with your friend
- ask why your friend wasn't invited

ALCOHOL AND DRUGS ARE AT A PARTY. IF YOU'RE REALLY BEING HONEST, YOU'LL PROBABLY:

- enjoy the party but not drink or do drugs
- tell their parents
- make an excuse not to go
- enjoy the party, the alcohol, and the drugs
- tell your parents

MAYBE, MAYBE NOT.

GROUP AWARENESS CRISIS

Get together with one other person. Take turns sharing answers to each of the following statements. Discuss your responses to each statement before moving on to the next one. (Or, if you think you know your partner pretty well, respond privately then try to guess how your partner responded.)

I would probably	Yes	No	Maybe
Sneak into a movie or concert	⬡	⬡	⬡
Go on a blind date	⬡	⬡	⬡
Forget my gym clothes on purpose	⬡	⬡	⬡
Pig out on chocolate	⬡	⬡	⬡
Save money now for later	⬡	⬡	⬡
Come home after curfew	⬡	⬡	⬡
Be embarrassed by an inappropriate image	⬡	⬡	⬡
Cry at a sad movie	⬡	⬡	⬡
Stalk someone on social media	⬡	⬡	⬡
Skydive	⬡	⬡	⬡
T.P. (or roll) a friend's house with toilet paper	⬡	⬡	⬡
Forge my parent's signature	⬡	⬡	⬡
Post multiple selfies each day	⬡	⬡	⬡

WALK IT OFF

GROUP CHOICES RELATIONSHIPS

Do you like to walk? For each pair, choose the type of walking you prefer. Think about what your choices say about you.

- Walk in fresh snow / Walk on the beach
- Hike a mountain trail / Walk in a shopping mall
- Walk in a political rally / Walk in a charity walkathon
- Tour the Smithsonian / Cover Disney World
- Tour a BMW plant / Walk through the Hershey chocolate factory
- Walk to an ice cream shop / Walk to Starbucks
- Walk across the Golden Gate Bridge / Climb to the top of the Statue of Liberty
- Hike to the base of the Grand Canyon / Traverse a rope across the Colorado River

The way you live your life can be called your "walk."
Which of the following statements is most true about you right now?

⬡ I walk in front.
⬡ I walk alone.
⬡ I walk in a crowd.
⬡ I am picky about who I walk with.

IN A DILEMMA

Imagine you find yourself facing one of the following decisions. Have one group member take the first situation and explain what he or she would do and why.

Then have the next person take the second situation, and so on, until each person has shared.

What would you do if you:

- Read an incriminating letter or e-mail?
- Saw a house on fire?
- Hit a dog while driving on a dark and deserted street?
- Were given too much change from a cashier?
- Found someone else's purse or wallet?
- Heard someone calling for help in a sketchy area of town?
- Lost your purse or wallet?

WITH GRATITUDE

Giving thanks is a great thing to do—even if you're not staring face-to-face with a turkey on your dinner table. Take a few minutes to say thanks to God. Look at the list below and choose the things for which you are thankful. There is no limit on your choices or your gratitude.

Share with the group some of the things for which you are thankful.

- ⬡ accomplishments
- ⬡ appearance
- ⬡ calling
- ⬡ car
- ⬡ character
- ⬡ church
- ⬡ courage
- ⬡ creativity
- ⬡ education
- ⬡ emotions
- ⬡ faith
- ⬡ family
- ⬡ friends
- ⬡ future
- ⬡ health
- ⬡ heritage
- ⬡ hobby
- ⬡ home
- ⬡ job
- ⬡ memories
- ⬡ mind
- ⬡ nationality
- ⬡ neighborhood
- ⬡ pets
- ⬡ reputation
- ⬡ school
- ⬡ sense of purpose
- ⬡ spiritual gifts
- ⬡ talents
- ⬡ wisdom

Now that you've expressed your gratitude, choose from the verses listed below the one that best expresses your gratefulness to God. Say it out loud and then share why you made your choice. Listen as others read their verses and share.

Give thanks to the LORD, for He is good; His faithful love endures forever. — 1 Chronicles 16:34

I will thank the Lord because he is just; I will sing praise to the name of the Lord Most High. — Psalm 7:17

Enter his gates with thanksgiving; go into his courts with praise. Give thanks to him and praise his name. — Psalm 100:4

Let them praise the Lord for his great love and for the wonderful things he has done for them. Let them offer sacrifices of thanksgiving and sing joyfully about his glorious acts.. — Psalm 107:21-22

Don't worry about anything; instead, pray about everything. Tell God what you need, and thank him for all he has done. — Philippians 4:6

After group members have shared verses, close with a prayer of thanksgiving.

WHO'S YOUR BUDDY?

GROUP RELATIONSHIPS

Assume one of the following identities. You don't have to keep it a secret, and it's likely others in your group will choose the same identity you choose.

Now that you've chosen who you will be for this activity, meet as many people as you can. Pretend that you are meeting them for the first time as the new person they have chosen to be. Introduce yourself according to the identity you have chosen.

- ⬡ Scientist
- ⬡ Seamstress
- ⬡ Quadriplegic
- ⬡ Minister, pastor, or priest
- ⬡ Doctor or nurse
- ⬡ Soldier
- ⬡ Musician
- ⬡ Exchange student
- ⬡ History teacher
- ⬡ Millionaire
- ⬡ Girl scout
- ⬡ Chef
- ⬡ Boy scout
- ⬡ Model
- ⬡ Hearing impaired
- ⬡ Environmental engineer
- ⬡ Police officer
- ⬡ Mechanic
- ⬡ Professional athlete
- ⬡ Sailor

Now here's where all of these new identities come into play. You've been selected to participate in an experiment in which you and three others will live in tents for three months in a remote area. You will be provided with a bed and enough clothes to get you through the adventure. Food, water, and personal hygiene will be available, complements of the great outdoors, but you'll have to hunt and gather them. What three people do you choose for your camp?

When you have formed your group, discuss what each person brings to the group.

HOLD ON

GROUP RELATIONSHIPS DISCIPLESHIP

Get in groups of about eight and complete this simple ten-question inventory. All you have to do is circle numbers. But before you start, have someone in your group read Romans 12:9-21 aloud. Then take turns reading each statement and description. After each is read, circle the number that is most true for you, 1 being very low and 10 being very high.

Love must be without hypocrisy.

I'm learning to sincerely care for others in meaningful ways without personal prejudice or putting my needs first. **1 2 3 4 5 6 7 8 9 10**

Detest evil; cling to what is good.

I'm learning to stand up for my convictions, to say no to something I know is wrong and say yes to God. **1 2 3 4 5 6 7 8 9 10**

Show family affection to one another with brotherly love.

I'm learning to reach out and hug my Christian brothers and sisters warmly—in a way that pleases God. **1 2 3 4 5 6 7 8 9 10**

Be fervent in spirit; serve the Lord.

I'm eager to do anything I can do for Christ because I'm grateful for what He has done for me. **1 2 3 4 5 6 7 8 9 10**

Rejoice in hope.

I'm experiencing new freedom, overflowing with praise because God is in control. **1 2 3 4 5 6 7 8 9 10**

Be patient in affliction.

Problems don't often get me down. Under pressure, I'm usually able to stay cool. **1 2 3 4 5 6 7 8 9 10**

Be persistent in prayer.

I'm learning to give every need to Christ and to share every decision I have to make with Him. I'm learning to wait on God and let Him work everything out in His time. **1 2 3 4 5 6 7 8 9 10**

Share with the saints (fellow Christians) in their needs; pursue hospitality.

I'm learning that my possessions, my time, and my abilities belong to God to be shared with those in need. **1 2 3 4 5 6 7 8 9 10**

Bless those who persecute you.

I'm learning to respond with kindness to those who put me down and to pray for them. I'm becoming less defensive. **1 2 3 4 5 6 7 8 9 10**

Rejoice with those who rejoice; weep with those who weep.

I celebrate when others are celebrating and grieve when others are hurting. I'm not afraid to show my feelings. **1 2 3 4 5 6 7 8 9 10**

THINK ABOUT IT

Your thoughts are important because they influence what you say and do. Words and actions impact others. Take turns reading the verses from Proverbs 15 then rate yourself in each category. Discuss responses with group members.

	VERY LOW 1	2	3	4	VERY HIGH 5
I talk about things that help others know God better. (v. 2)					
I try to bring healing instead of harm. (v. 4)					
I can teach others the truths of Scripture. (v. 7)					
I always want to know more about God's Word. (v. 14)					
I control my temper. (v. 18)					
I try to encourage others. (v. 23)					
I try to consider how my words might affect others. (v. 28)					
I try to change my thinking when impure thoughts enter my mind. (v. 26)					
I try to learn from criticism and improve my character. (v. 31)					

ALARMING

Security is big business. Whether in the form of electronic systems or personal guards, everyone sleeps a little better knowing they and their possessions are safe—and they'll pay for peace of mind. The amount of time and attention given to someone or something indicates value.

If you could invest in only one security system what would you choose?

- ⬭ Car alarm system
- ⬭ Bodyguard
- ⬭ Home alarm
- ⬭ Electric fence

How does your alarm system reflect your priorities? What concerns you most? Do you feel that you can take on anything that life throws at you? If not, to whom will you turn for help?

RIGHT & WRONG

GROUP CHOICES STRESS

Get in groups of about eight and stand in a circle. Then give the following commands. If anyone acts on a "wrong" command, ask him or her to sit down. (Students may choose to act on commands marked "wrong" to get a laugh.)

Compliment the person on your right. (RIGHT)

Compliment the person on your left. (RIGHT)

Smile at the person directly across from you. (RIGHT)

Wave at someone you haven't interacted with yet. (RIGHT)

Politely cover your mouth then cough. (RIGHT)

Tell the person across from you that his or her real name is "Stinky." (WRONG)

Gently tug the hair of the person to your right. (WRONG)

Quickly blink three times at anyone in the group. (RIGHT)

Cover your mouth and belch loudly. (WRONG)

Slowly turn in a circle while humming "The Star Spangled Banner." (RIGHT)

Shout, "You are a warthog!" to the person on your left. (WRONG)

After the activity, discuss the following questions.

1. For some reason, it can be tempting to follow the "wrong" instructions just to get a laugh or liven things up. In the real world, we are often tempted to do the wrong thing for the sake of covering up mistakes or making ourselves look better. What are some examples?

2. Even if you managed to do all the "right" things and none of the "wrong" things in our game, you will sometimes mess up in life. Think about how you felt when a group member had to sit down for having done a "wrong" thing. How did you feel toward that person? How do you feel when a friend makes a poor moral choice?

3. How do you think God feels when we give in to the temptation to rebel against Him? Why do you think He gave us the free will to make mistakes and poor choices?

TREE OF MY LIFE

Some trees populate forests and produce oxygen. Some are used for lumber. Others are harvested and decorated for Christmas, Valentines Day, and even Easter.

How would you decorate a tree of your life?

What ornaments, decorations, and colors would you use? How would you top it?

What would the tree of your life say about your interests and relationships?

What would the colors represent? What would top your tree?

LIVING WILL

A living will is a written document that lets people know the type of care you want, in the event that your health at the time prevents you from deciding for yourself.

Get in groups of four and discuss your personal preferences and why. Use the following questions to get the discussion going.

1. Would you like to be made well, regardless of the cost?

2. How would you want your pain to be managed? Would you want to be "out of it" or aware of your environment and those around you?

3. Would you be willing to try an experimental treatment?

4. In poor health, would you rather be in a care facility or at home surrounded by family and friends?

5. How would you expect to grow in your Christian walk through these tough times? In what way would you hope to follow Jesus' example

AMITY ASSESSMENT

Amity is a synonym for friendship. Get together in groups of up to four. Discuss personal preferences in friends. For each of the following qualities place an X on the line somewhere between the two extremes and be prepared to explain your responses. Then allow group members time to explain the importance of each of the ten qualities.

PERSONALITY

SIMILAR TO MINE ← → *DIFFERENT FROM MINE*

COMMUNICATION

MOTOR MOUTH ← → *QUIET AS A MOUSE*

TEMPERMENT

LAID BACK ← → *INTENSE*

COMPATIBILITY

LIKE DOING THE SAME THINGS ← → *NOT AFRAID TO DISAGREE AND GO OWN WAY*

LOYALTY

ALWAYS GOES ALONG WITH ME ← → *CHALLENGES ME WHEN I NEED IT*

SELF-ESTEEM

PUTS SELF DOWN ALL THE TIME ← → *BRAGS ABOUT SELF ALL THE TIME*

FAMILY RELATIONSHIPS

SPEAKS HIGHLY OF PARENTS AND SIBLINGS ← → *ALWAYS COMPLAINING ABOUT FAMILY*

MORAL STANDARDS

WILD AND FREE ← → *STICKS TO THE RULES*

CHURCH

COULDN'T CARE LESS ← → *VERY COMMITTED*

LIFE ATTITUDE

OPTIMISTIC ← → *PESSIMISTIC*

LOCATION, LOCATION, LOCATION

Get in groups of four and share about your childhood neighborhood. Though you may still live in the same neighborhood, it has probably changed since you were a child.

1. The neighborhood where I lived as a child was like:

- ⬭ The Great Plains: spread out but close-knit
- ⬭ New Delhi: distinctively ethnic
- ⬭ Manhattan: urban and multicultural
- ⬭ Rome: a great place to explore

2. Where did the kids gather in your neighborhood?

3. What were your favorite things to do together?

4. Who was the one-of-a-kind kid who stood out from the rest of the crowd?

5. Who was the kid who always got into trouble (or got you in trouble)?

6. Where were the special places—the places to climb, skateboard, or hide?

7. Where were the dangerous places—mean dogs, grumpy neighbors, and "haunted houses"?

CAR TALK

As one person in the group reads each of the following automotive parts or accessories, listen carefully to each description. Think of the person (or persons) in the group best represented by each description. Call out the names of people who fit. As time allows, affirm each person who is recognized, but make sure you have time to read the entire list. Be careful that everyone in the group is recognized at least once.

Windshield. Keeps the vision clear.
Gasoline. Consumed for the benefit of others and keeping things moving.
Airbag. Protects others from being hurt worse than they already are.
Seatbelt. Helps keep others in line for their best.
Cup holder. A servant who is always meeting a need.
Muffler. Reduces unnecessary noise.
Sound system. Makes everything more enjoyable.
Shock. Smoothes out the bumps and makes things easier.
Spark plug. Provides the initial start to get things moving.
Battery. Dependable source of energy.

DO I HEAR FIFTY?

GROUP CHOICES BELIEFS

Appoint one student to be the auctioneer. Tell the rest of the group to bid on the following list of items. Conduct the auction as follows: Everybody starts with $1,000. Start each item at $50. The auctioneer not only calls and announces the bids, but may also get in on the bidding. Write winning bids in the left column and the winners' names in the right column. Remind everyone that they only have $1,000 to spend for the entire auction.

WINNING BID	ITEMS	WINNER'S NAME
______	Two Super Bowl tickets on the 50-yard line	______
______	All-expense-paid vacation for four to Disney World	______
______	Huge flat screen TV with surround sound	______
______	Date with your favorite celebrity	______
______	Freedom from household chores for one year	______
______	Complete wardrobe of latest fashions	______
______	Guaranteed college degree	______
______	Backstage passes with your favorite band	______
______	Season pass to the ski resort of your choice	______
______	Lead role in a major motion picture	______
______	Unlimited use of your car of choice	______
______	Ten-minute shopping spree in an electronics store	______
______	One year to do anything you want	______

FRIENDLY CHOICE

GROUP CHOICES RELATIONSHIPS

Find a partner. Read through the list of qualities that you look for in a friend. Note the qualities both of you agree on.

Discuss the descriptions that only one of you has marked.

- ◯ fun to be with
- ◯ same musical taste
- ◯ personally shares about himself/herself
- ◯ intellectual
- ◯ laid-back
- ◯ comes from a solid family
- ◯ has a nice smile
- ◯ common interests
- ◯ good personality
- ◯ attractive
- ◯ good sense of fashion
- ◯ athletic
- ◯ sense of humor
- ◯ plenty of money
- ◯ honest
- ◯ strong morals
- ◯ drives a cool vehicle
- ◯ spiritual depth
- ◯ similar background to me
- ◯ popular
- ◯ plenty of time for me
- ◯ generous

WINNING CATEGORIES

Get together in groups of up to four. Imagine you're one of four contestants on a TV game show and it's down to the final round. The following categories are the topics from which you may choose. You need to get more right answers than your three opponents in order to win. Which categories will be "winners" for you? Which categories will you most likely lose?

In your group share your best and worst category.

See who can come up with the most answers in each category.

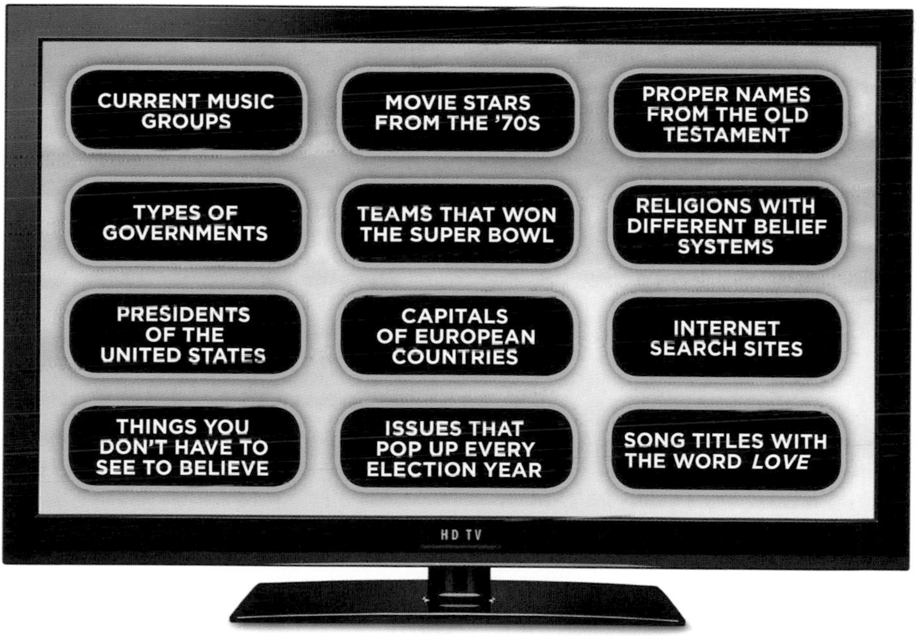

BLESSED

GROUP ISSUES

Get into groups of up to eight and read the Beatitudes as recorded in Matthew 5:3-10. Discuss each type of "blessed" person and the positive results of being that kind of person. Talk about what each beatitude means in real, day-to-day life. For example, "What does it mean to be 'poor in spirit' when I'm trying to get along with my family?" or "What does it mean to me to be given 'the kingdom of heaven'?" After everyone has time to discuss, have each group member rate how he or she is doing with living out that beatitude. Use a scoring system of 1 ("I'm having a hard time") to 5 ("I think I've got this one down"). Then share examples of people who live out each.

1. "Poor in spirit" means

____

____

A great example is

____

How I rate myself:

1 2 3 4 5

2. "Those who mourn" means

____

____

A great example is

____

How I rate myself:

1 2 3 4 5

3. "The gentle" means

____

____

A great example is

____

How I rate myself:

1 2 3 4 5

4. "Those who hunger and thirst for righteousness" means

____

____

A great example is

____

How I rate myself:

1 2 3 4 5

5. "The merciful" means

____

____

A great example is

____

How I rate myself:

1 2 3 4 5

6. "The pure in heart" means

____

____

A great example is

____

How I rate myself:

1 2 3 4 5

7. "The peacemakers" means

____

____

A great example is

____

How I rate myself:

1 2 3 4 5

8. "Those who are persecuted for righteousness" means

____

____

A great example is

____

How I rate myself:

1 2 3 4 5

C.O.D.

Get together in groups of about eight. Read the first situation then share what your initial C.O.D. response would be and why. "Cash on Delivery" responses are "me first" responses. "Call of Duty" responses are "others first" responses. Allow each group member to share, then respond to the second situation, and so on.

CASH ON DELIVERY		CALL OF DUTY
⬡	**The Titanic has hit an iceberg and is going down.**	⬡
⬡	**Your parents accuse you and a sibling of having a party while they were out of town.**	⬡
⬡	**A child wanders into oncoming traffic. If you attempt a rescue you could be hit.**	⬡
⬡	**A rough group of opposing fans accosts you and a friend. You can run faster.**	⬡
⬡	**You are at a party with a friend and are offered a beer. Your friend does not drink.**	⬡
⬡	**You help a friend cheat on an exam.**	⬡

Are you a taker or a giver? How do you react in a crisis? Is your initial thought to take care of number one, or to first do what you can to help others?

WARM-UPS

MY LIFE IN A SONG

Get together in groups of around four. Read the statements. Mark an X somewhere between the two extremes to indicate how you feel. Think of a song that best describes how you feel about each area of your life. For each, briefly explain why you marked each statement as you did and why you selected that song.

In my EMOTIONAL LIFE, I'm feeling . . . TERRIBLE — GREAT
This area of my life would best be summed up by the song: ______________________

In my FAMILY LIFE, I'm feeling . . . TERRIBLE — GREAT
This area of my life would best be summed up by the song: ______________________

In my ATTITUTE TOWARD SCHOOL OR WORK, I'm feeling . . . TERRIBLE — GREAT
This area of my life would best be summed up by the song: ______________________

In my SPIRITUAL LIFE, I'm feeling . . . TERRIBLE — GREAT
This area of my life would best be summed up by the song: ______________________

In my CLOSE RELATIONSHIPS, I'm feeling . . . TERRIBLE — GREAT
This area of my life would best be summed up by the song: ______________________

As I look toward THE FUTURE, I'm feeling . . . TERRIBLE — GREAT
This area of my life would best be summed up by the song: ______________________

BEST IN SHOW

Gather in a group of four. In God's eyes everyone is extraordinary and the world has no way, right, or wisdom to place one individual in a place of ultimate importance over anyone else. How you see yourself is not necessarily the way others see you. And you can be sure that your Father in heaven values you over the most magnificent riches the world can provide or the greatest artisan can design. Rank yourself on each category by marking an X on the line nearest the appropriate description.

POPULARITY
HOMECOMING COURT MATERIAL ←——→ INVISIBLE

NEATNESS
CARL/CARLA CLEAN ←——→ MESSY MARVIN/MARY

FASHION
WELL-DRESSED ←——→ WELL-WORN

SENSITIVITY
GOOD LISTENER ←——→ DON'T CARE AT ALL

FITNESS
FRANK/FRAN FITNESS ←——→ SAMMY/SARAH SLOTH

MANNERS
MIKE/MOLLY MANNERS ←——→ RUDE RUDY/RUBY

ATHLETICISM
MVP ←——→ BEST BENCH WARMER EVER

STRESS POINT

Get together with one other person and go through the following list. Share what stresses you out in each situation. Suggestions are provided to help you get started, but they may not be right for you. Be honest about your own experiences. After you share what causes you stress in each area, share what you do to relieve that stress.

Major tests and exams	The feeling of doom that hangs over me Drawing a blank on an answer that I should know Other:
Important athletic competitions	Sitting on the sidelines waiting to get in the game Seeing a teammate make a really bad play Other:
Friendships	Fear of rejection Being used or manipulated Other:
Family interactions	Getting along with my siblings Having very strict rules and restrictions Other:

Daily frustrations	Having unreliable or nonexistent transportation Feeling that I don't have enough time to do everything Other:
Athletic training	Having a coach who is way too demanding Being disciplined to stay in training Other:

REASSURANCE

GROUP AWARENESS BELIEFS

Have you ever wanted to ask God a question? If so, what would it be?

What helps you to deal with the bad stuff that life throws your way?

What is something you know for certain that reassures you God cares deeply about you and is actively involved in the world?

NEW GAME

GROUP BELIEFS

Look at the partial list of team sports below and rank them in order from 1 (most favorite) to 8 (least favorite).

____ Football ____ Softball ____ Basketball ____ Baseball

____ Soccer ____ Hockey ____ Lacrosse ____ Volleyball

In a group of eight, discuss what you like most about each of the sports listed. Combine the best elements of each sport to make a new sport.

What would you call your new sport?

What equipment and uniforms would be required to play it?

How would you play and win?

What kind of penalties would be assessed?

Would it be easier to create a new sport from existing ones or to start from scratch?

Read Genesis 1:1–2:3. God created something out of nothing. What did God create in those first six days?

First Day: ____________________	Fourth Day: ____________________
Second Day: ____________________	Fifth Day: ____________________
Third Day: ____________________	Sixth Day: ____________________

On the seventh day God had completed His work of creation. God rested. He blessed the seventh day and declared it holy.

Read Genesis 1:2 and 2:1 again. What changed?

First there was nothing; then there was everything.

At first the earth was formless; then things were completed.

God can do anything. And everything He does is good and perfect.

Read 2 Corinthians 5:17 and discuss how belief in the mighty creative power of God makes all things new.

BAD THINGS HAPPEN

Gather in a group of four. Use your computers or phones to search for articles or headlines that show the prevalence of evil and injustice in society. Be careful not to dwell on the bad and use godly discernment when searching and discussing your results. You may not even need to search online if you stay current with local and world news. Discuss the stories you found or of which you are already aware.

- ⬡ Jump in the middle and try to help.
- ⬡ Get mad.
- ⬡ Hope someone else decides to do something.
- ⬡ Try to ignore it.
- ⬡ Pray for God to intervene.
- ⬡ Feel helpless.
- ⬡ I want to do something to stop it.
- ⬡ Other:

How do you typically respond when you see evil or injustice? Check all that apply.

What is an example of an injustice you've seen recently?

When someone wrongs you, how do you typically respond?

JESUS AND ME

Get together in groups of around eight. Before sharing your answers, silently read over the following list and check the box next to the three most important things in your life right now. Then write the appropriate letter (D, I, or N) to indicate how much influence Jesus has on each area of your life.

D—My relationship with Jesus **DIRECTLY** influences this area of my life.

I—My relationship with Jesus **INDIRECTLY** influences this area of my life.

N—My relationship with Jesus has **NO** influence in this area of my life.

You only have to check three from the list below.

- ⬡ Getting good grades
- ⬡ Going to heaven
- ⬡ Having a job
- ⬡ Having a car
- ⬡ Dating
- ⬡ Doing what is right
- ⬡ Being accepted by my peers and friends
- ⬡ Getting along with my family at home
- ⬡ Feeling good about myself
- ⬡ Knowing who I am and what I want to do in my life

STRANDED

Get together in a group of four. Imagine that you are on a tropical island. Sounds great, until you look around and realize that you are the only one on the island. Yes, you are stranded on a deserted island. Besides adequate food and clothing—and, of course, the shade of your trusty palm tree—choose three of the following items that you would consider necessary for your survival. Be careful to choose only three. It's a really small island. After you make your choices, compare your list with the lists of other group members.

- ⬡ bait
- ⬡ bed
- ⬡ Bible
- ⬡ books
- ⬡ deck of card
- ⬡ exercise equipment
- ⬡ first-aid kit
- ⬡ fishing pole
- ⬡ four wheeler
- ⬡ harpoon
- ⬡ pet
- ⬡ really, really smart phone
- ⬡ satellite television
- ⬡ solar-powered computer
- ⬡ surfboard

GAUGING HOW YOU FEEL

How do you feel? How do you really feel? Do you feel the same way you felt last week at this time? Do you think you know how you'll feel tomorrow? Do you feel differently at the beginning of a practice or athletic event than you do when it's over? What makes you feel the way you do and change the way you feel? Indicate on the image below where you are right now emotionally.

How high are your stress, frustration, and relationship levels? Is your love tank full or empty?

	LOW	AVERAGE	HIGH
Love Tank			
Stress Indicator			
Frustration Level			
Enthusiasm			
Relationships			

WOULD YOU RATHER

GROUP AWARENESS CHOICES

Get together in groups of around eight. This is a simple game of choice. All you have to do is decide between the two options given.

Pause after each pair is read so everyone can respond. After everyone in the group has responded, move to the next pair, then the next, and so on.

FIRST OPTION	SECOND OPTION
Spend my inheritance	Put the money in the bank
Take a lap around the track with a professional racecar driver	Sit in the stands
Go scuba diving	Go bowling
Lead a group	Blend in with the crowd
Study hard for a test	Wing it
Say what I think	Keep my opinions to myself
Explore the city	Stay close to home
Watch a scary movie	Watch an animated feature
Live in confidence because I know God has control of my future	Live in uncertainty because I can't control or know what the future holds for me

ALONG THE WAY

Get in groups of about eight and prepare to respond to seven statements. Before you begin, have someone in your group read Ephesians 6:10-18 aloud. God doesn't promise us an easy life. Paul calls the Christian life a struggle and compares the spiritual equipment needed for the struggle to that of a soldier. Take turns reading each statement and description. After each is read, circle the number that is most true for you, 1 being very low and 10 being very high.

TRUTH LIKE A BELT

I'm prepared to stake my life on the fact that Jesus Christ is the Son of God. I've thought through what I believe, and I am willing to take a stand.

1 2 3 4 5 6 7 8 9 10

RIGHTEOUSNESS LIKE ARMOR

I'm prepared to put my life where my mouth is—in clean and right living with genuine integrity as Christ did. I'm serious about being God's child.

1 2 3 4 5 6 7 8 9 10

FEET SANDALED WITH READINESS FOR THE GOSPEL OF PEACE

I'm willing to publically affirm my faith in Christ at school, work, on the field, or wherever. I find it easy to talk about my personal faith.

1 2 3 4 5 6 7 8 9 10

SHIELD OF FAITH

I'm willing to publically affirm my faith in Christ, to risk my life and my future for Him, whatever the cost or consequences. Through faith, I am taking a stand against the Evil One.

1 2 3 4 5 6 7 8 9 10

HELMET OF SALVATION

I know I'm part of the family of God because of Jesus Christ. I have a strong inner peace because I am at peace with God.

1 2 3 4 5 6 7 8 9 10

SWORD OF THE SPIRIT (GOD'S WORD)

I actively seek to know more about God and His will for my life through an ongoing study of His guidebook, the Bible. I am disciplined to reflect on it daily.

1 2 3 4 5 6 7 8 9 10

PRAYER

I set aside time regularly to talk with God and to listen to Him speak to me. I consciously try to submit every decision in my life to God.

1 2 3 4 5 6 7 8 9 10

CHECK IN

Get together in groups of eight. Read each statement and then respond by circling the number that best describes the way you feel.

1. **never** 2. **rarely** 3. **sometimes** 4. **most of the time** 5. **always**

Discuss responses as a group. Remember that no group is perfect, and all groups need time to grow together.

I feel that this group:	**1**	**2**	**3**	**4**	**5**
understands what I am trying to say					
can tell when something is bothering me					
accepts me for who I am					
feels free to let me know when I'm bothering them					
encourages my comments and opinions					
is fulfilling its potential					
helps me understand God better					
includes me in what's going on					
encourages me to grow in my Christian faith					
succeeds with problem solving					

WARM-UPS

GOD'S WORD ON LOVE

One of the most familiar Bible passages about love is found in 1 Corinthians 13:4–7. Ask group members to locate it in their Bibles and read aloud as they follow along.

Read the first statement from the list that follows. Then ask everyone to choose a number between 1 (does not describe me at all) and 5 (describes me exactly) to rate the way they love. Take turns reading each statement and then rating it.

1 2 3 4 5 Love is patient. I don't take out my frustrations on those I love. I'm calm under pressure and careful with my tongue.

1 2 3 4 5 Love is kind. I go out of my way to say nice words and do thoughtful things for others.

1 2 3 4 5 Love is not jealous. I'm not envious of others' abilities or possessions. Neither am I jealous with my time for those in need.

1 2 3 4 5 Love is not boastful. I don't consider myself more important than those I love. I don't brag.

1 2 3 4 5 Love is not proud. I don't think of myself as better than those I love.

1 2 3 4 5 Love is not rude. I don't make cutting or crude remarks when I don't get my way—or become silent and withdrawn.

1 2 3 4 5 Love does not demand its own way. I don't put myself first. I give those I love spiritual and emotional support.

1 2 3 4 5 Love is not irritable. I don't let little things bother me. I work to control my mouth.

1 2 3 4 5 Love keeps no record of being wronged. I don't keep score of unkind things said or done to me.

1 2 3 4 5 Love does not rejoice about injustice. I accept others but don't have to approve of all they do.

1 2 3 4 5 Love rejoices whenever the truth wins out. With compassion, I say what needs to be said, even if it's difficult.

1 2 3 4 5 Love never gives up. I'm always there for those I love—even when they upset me.

1 2 3 4 5 Love never loses faith. I believe in those I love. I'm willing to let God shape and mold them.

1 2 3 4 5 Love is always hopeful. I'm good at expecting and thinking the best about those I love.

1 2 3 4 5 Love endures through every circumstance. I'm committed to those I love and prepared to see things through.

WHAT'S IN A NAME?

GROUP AWARENESS RELATIONSHIPS

Names have meaning. Some parents spend hours thinking about the name they will give their newborn, sometimes far in advance of the child's birth. Many times children are named after relatives. Some names are passed down for generations. *Sophia* means "wisdom." *Angel* means "messenger." *Jack* is a form of John and means "God is gracious."

What do you think of when you see the following names?

Virginia	Georgia	Stormie	Noel	Wilma	Wendy
Beau	Oscar	Leonardo	Jude	Dash	Dallas

A child's name might be changed when he enters adulthood—not unlike little Bobby wanting to be called Bob or Robert. Sit in a circle. Beginning with one student, provide a new name that reflects his or her character, lifestyle, or relationships. For example, if he is not a big talker but is aggressive in competition you might call him Silent Warrior. Use consensus in creating each new name. Continue until all students have been renamed.

Discuss that *Christian* means "follower of Christ." Though their new name might not have been a popular name to the pagan world it did identify them with their Lord and His call on their lives. How does the name Christian fit you?

I GOT IT!

GROUP AWARENESS

Get in groups of eight. If you have a backpack, wallet, or purse use the first set of questions below. If you don't have a backpack, wallet, or purse with you use the second set of questions. You have two minutes in silence to go through your possessions or think about your answers. After two minutes, you break the silence and share what you have. But first, you have to work silently by yourself. It's likely you won't have all (or any) of the items listed.

If you have items from your backpack, wallet, or purse:

1. The thing that reminds me of a fun time is . . .
2. The thing I have had for the longest time is . . .
3. The most revealing thing about me is . . .
4. The thing that is most sentimental to me is . . .

If you don't have your backpack, wallet, or purse:

1. The cheapest thing I'm wearing is . . .
2. The most expensive thing I'm wearing is . . .
3. The thing I carry with me all the time is . . .
4. The thing I wear that has sentimental value is . . .

UNDER THE LIGHTS

GROUP AWARENESS ISSUES

Find a partner. Think about your answers to the following questions. Don't share your answers yet.

How would you judge your confidence level? Are you overconfident? Or do you lack confidence?

What makes you feel confident about you? List two or three causes here. Share with your partner how you think others would answer the following questions.

How do others judge your confidence level? Do people consider you to be over-confident? Or would they say that you lack confidence?

Look at the causes you listed above and share them with your partner. Do you share similar causes? Are you different as different as night and day?

We tend to want to be in the light when we feel good about who we are and how we're doing—or performing. Jesus reminds us, "***'In the same way, let your light shine before men, so that they may see your good works and give glory to your Father in heaven'"*** —Matthew 5:16 (HCSB).

Maybe you should be less worried about your own confidence level and more aware of how God wants to use you and what He wants to do through you.

DIVINE DIFFUSION

GROUP CHOICES DISCIPLESHIP

Fill a clear glass mug with hot water and hold a tea bag above it. Quickly dip the tea bag into the water then remove it immediately. Explain that the mug of water represents us and the tea bag represents the Word of God. Share that every time you hear God's Word it is like dipping the tea bag into the water. Show the contents of the mug to the group and ask, "Does this look like tea to you?" (It shouldn't.) Point out that tea takes time. The tea bag has to steep in the water. Likewise, it takes time to be transformed by God's Word.

Drop the tea bag in the water and leave it. Share that meditating on the Word of God is like leaving the bag in the water until the tea permeates the water. Dip the tea bag in and out of the water three or four times, leaving the tea bag in the water.

1. What happens to the water as the tea bag is left for a longer period of time?
2. What did you learn about Christian mediation from the tea bag example?
3. How much of your life is currently absorbed by the Word of God?

⬡ Some ⬡ Most ⬡ All ⬡ None

2050

GROUP BELIEFS CHOICES

Get together in groups of up to four. Reflect on the following questions about the future and then discuss responses.

1. Which phrase best describes your philosophy about the future?

"One day at a time."

"Sometimes you're the bug; sometimes you're the windshield."

"Only the good die young."

"Back to the future."

"The future is so bright you need sunglasses."

"I don't want to grow up."

"He who isn't busy being born is busy dying."

"The future belongs to those who plan for it."

"I don't know what the future holds, but I know who holds the future."

"You can't ever go home again."

2. What would you like to be doing in 2050?
3. What is one thing you expect to have in the future that you do not have now?

UNBROKEN

GROUP STRESS

A broken promise could result in a broken relationship. At the very least, it might create unnecessary stress. But there is One who keeps every promise He makes. Scripture is full of God's promises for you. Read the 12 promises listed below. Choose one—only one—of the promises and share why you chose it. Then restate the promise in first-person language. For example, if you chose the first promise you would say aloud, "This means that *I* who belong to Chris have become a new person. *My* old life is gone; a new life has begun *for me*."

- This means that anyone who belongs to Christ has become a new person. The old life is gone; a new life has begun!—2 Corinthians 5:17
- And I am certain that God, who began the good work within you, will continue his work until it is finally finished on the day when Christ Jesus returns. —Philippians 1:6
- Ask me and I will tell you remarkable secrets you do not know about things to come. —Jeremiah 33:3
- And God will generously provide all you need. Then you will always have everything you need and plenty left over to share with others.—2 Corinthians 9:8
- For I can do everything through Christ, who gives me strength.—Philippians 4:13
- And we know that God causes everything to work together for the good of those who love God and are called according to his purpose for them. —Romans 8:28
- "Keep on asking, and you will receive what you ask for. Keep on seeking, and you will find. Keep on knocking, and the door will be opened to you. For everyone who asks, receives. Everyone who seeks, finds. And to everyone who knocks, the door will be opened."—Matthew 7:7-8
- The temptations in your life are no different from what others experience. And God is faithful. He will not allow the temptation to be more than you can stand. When you are tempted, he will show you a way out so that you can endure.—1 Corinthians 10:13
- "Look! I stand at the door and knock. If you hear my voice and open the door, I will come in, and we will share a meal together as friends."—Revelation 3:20
- "I am leaving you with a gift—peace of mind and heart. And the peace I give is a gift the world cannot give. So don't be troubled or afraid."—John 14:27
- Trust in the LORD with all your heart; do not depend on your own understanding. Seek his will in all you do, and he will show you which path to take. —Proverbs 3:5-6
- The LORD keeps you from all harm and watches over your life. The LORD keeps watch over you as you come and go, both now and forever. —Psalm 121:7-8

CRISIS AVERTED

Gather in a group of four. Look at the list below. It's a list of personal qualities based on positive values. Think about each member of your small group and write his or her name next to the quality that best describes them. You can use each person's name only once, and you must use everyone's name once. (So, most of the spaces beside the listed qualities will remain unfilled.) Allow one person to share the qualities they assigned to each group member. Repeat until everyone has shared.

__________ **Community Builder:** God uses you to bring people together in unity.

__________ **Compassionate:** You have the ability to feel what others feel.

__________ **Contented:** You know that your worth is based on who you are rather than on what you have.

__________ **Faithful:** You are faithful to uphold godly morality even under pressure.

__________ **Generous:** You give freely, not for attention or praise—but for the joy of giving.

__________ **Gentle:** You can be outwardly tender because you are inwardly strong.

__________ **Humble:** You demonstrate what humility is all about.

__________ **Joyful:** Regardless of the circumstances, you have a smile on your face and a positive outlook about life.

__________ **Loving:** You have a Christ-like capacity to love others unconditionally.

__________ **Patient:** You never seem to be in a hurry or to get irritated by others.

__________ **Peacemaker:** You have a gift from God to help people overcome.

__________ **Pure in Heart:** Your life is marked by integrity before God and others.

__________ **Spiritually Hungry:** You have a longing in your heart to grow in a relationship with God.

__________ **Transparent:** You can be yourself without any pretense and let the light of Christ shine through.

Now that you have recognized group members by the values they possess, think about how each of these people could use these personal qualities to address a crisis that might come up. Begin by thinking about realistic crises that your group could actually face. Then match the crises you have identified to the persons who are most likely to help deal with each situation.

Thinking about other members and yourself, what is a good name to call your group that would communicate what you are best equipped to do? Salvation Army? Fellowship of Christian Athletes? Those names are already taken.

WARM-UPS

WHAT'S YOUR P.R.Q.?

Get in groups of about eight and consider the idea of a Personal Risk Quotient (P.R.Q.). The six questions below are a fun way to get you thinking about how much of a risk-taker you may be. After you answer all six, figure out your score. There's nothing scientific about this. It's just for fun!

1. When playing a board game, I usually
   - **a.** play it safe
   - **b.** stay cool and hold back a little
   - **c.** go for broke—risking everything
2. With my parents, I usually
   - **a.** do exactly as I'm asked
   - **b.** test the boundaries
   - **c.** do my own thing despite the cost
3. On a menu, I usually pick
   - **a.** an item I know I like
   - **b.** an item that's a little different
   - **c.** an item I've never tried
4. In most social settings, I usually
   - **a.** stick with my friends
   - **b.** mix with strangers
   - **c.** see how many new people I can meet
5. In meeting someone for the first time, I usually
   - **a.** let them do the talking
   - **b.** share the conversation
   - **c.** take the initiative
6. I would prefer my life to include
   - **a.** no risks and lots of safety
   - **b.** some risks and some safety
   - **c.** lots of risks and little safety

Now, give yourself one point for every "a" response, two points for every "b" response, and three points for every "c" response. Then circle the total on the line below to get your P.R.Q.

MAY LIKE TO PLAY IT SAFE ← → **I THINK I LIKE TO TAKE CHANCES**

6 7 8 9 10 11 12 13 14 15 16 17 18

TEN GRAND

Lucky you. A wealthy relative has given you $10,000. How will you spend it? Just in case you have trouble coming up with a spending plan, that same relative has provided the following categories to help you decide.

Get together in groups of four and compare the ways you would spend ten grand. See if others can guess which category you would spend the most in before you share answers.

$ Amount	Response	$ Amount	Response
________	Clothes	________	Technology
________	Athletic equipment	________	My family
________	Going out with friends	________	Sporting event tickets
________	Savings	________	Music
________	Concert tickets	________	Church

WARM-UPS

HANG TIME

GROUP ISSUES

Invite volunteers to give examples of hang time in sports. What was the outcome? Hang time can be good; hang time can be not so good. At kickoff it's great to have extra time to run down the field and make it to the receiver before he heads down the field toward you. Alternatively, as a receiver, you have the option to signal a fair catch, but as you stare at that spiraling ball as it drops from the sky in slow motion you might be thinking, "If I could just get my hands on that ball before anyone gets close I can shorten the distance between my team and the goal line." Hang time goes both ways. Hang time also goes both ways in social circles.

Obtain a tennis ball. Share that you are going to toss the ball into the air. While it is in the air students are to think about the following questions.

The person who catches the ball may answer the question or toss it to someone else who must answer. To move to the next question the ball must be held, the next question asked, then tossed high into the air.

What is a current issue that personally impacts you? What issue do you stand alone on in contrast to the majority of your friends? What is an issue you will personally defend even if it costs you your reputation? What makes it difficult to choose one particular side of an issue over another? At what point does a social issue become a personal conviction?

RULES: KEEP, BEND, OR BREAK?

GROUP DISCIPLESHIP CHOICES

Get together in groups of up to four. Share that games are a great way to have fun and pass the time. Provide as many board games (checkers, chess, and other table games) as you can and distribute one to each group. Tell students to set up the games in preparation to play, but to wait until your signal to begin. When all games are set, tell students to play with only one rule in mind: There are no rules.

After a few minutes of playing call groups together and discuss the following questions about their favorite games: **What specifically did you like about your favorite game? What were some of the rules of your favorite game? What are some of the rules of the game your group was given? Which rules really got on your nerves?** After students share answers to these questions discuss why creators of games include rules. Ask students if they have ever thought about the fact that it's the rules of play that really give games their entertainment value. **How you do you feel about following rules, both in games and in life? Do you stay within the boundaries, or do you push to the limits?**

ONE

PHILIPPIANS 1:27

Use these [redacted]te-focused studies for your personal Bible reading, team Bible stud[redacted]up meetings, or chapels. Read the Scripture passages carefully, an[redacted]ke[redacted]ditate on the study questions. This will help you [redacted]d the [redacted]ible's message and learn to apply [redacted]our everyday life.

THIS SECTION OF ATHLETE STUDIES FOCUSES ON COMPETITION. IF CHRISTIANS ARE SUPPOSED TO BE SERVANTS OF OTHERS, WHERE DOES THE CONCEPT OF COMPETING FIT? CAN A CHRISTIAN ATHLETE REALLY BE FULLY COMPETITIVE? WHERE'S THE BALANCE? GOD DESIGNED US FOR ADVENTURE AND FOR COMPETITION, BUT HE'S VERY CONCERNED ABOUT OUR ATTITUDES AND ABOUT HOW WE COMPETE.

AVOID THE KILLJOY

WARM-UP

1. Do your friends consider you more of an optimist or a pessimist? With what kind of people do you surround yourself?
2. When have you surprised others with your optimism? When have you dragged others down with a can't-win-never-gonna-make-it attitude?

WORKOUT

John 10:10

3. Jesus reminds us that Satan is in direct opposition to Himself. When have you witnessed the battle between Christ and Satan in the world?
4. How might the reality that evil kills and steals impact your love of life and playing your favorite sport?
5. Knowing that Jesus has conquered evil and has come to give you abundant life, how will you approach victories and challenges on and off the field?

SETTING THE STANDARD

WARM-UP

1. What do your fellow teammates expect from you? What does your coach expect of you?
2. Describe a time when you or someone else surprised fans in a game by doing something unexpected. How did others respond?

WORKOUT

Romans 12:9-21

3. How are love and life described in verses 9-16?
4. According to verses 17-21, how are we to deal with life's injustices?
5. Which description in these verses seems most difficult for you to imitate? Why?

READY. SET.

WARM-UP

1. How do you mentally prepare yourself for competition?
2. Have you ever been so nervous before a competition that fear made you freeze up? How did this impact your performance?

WORKOUT

Joshua 2:1-24

3. How does Joshua prepare for battle? How does Rahab prepare?
4. What is Rahab's motivation? Fear? Desire for safety? Respect for God's power?
5. How can God help you prepare for your next battle?

REALIZE YOUR POTENTIAL

WARM-UP

1. When did you first realize you had the potential to excel in athletics? Was it something you saw in yourself or did someone else point it out to you?
2. What gave you the confidence to work hard and turn potential into something tangible?

WORKOUT

Ephesians 1:3-14

3. What do God's promises (vv. 3-5) say to you about the potential with which you were born?
4. How might being adopted by God change the way you view your talents and abilities?
5. How does it make you feel to realize that God has big plans for you and knows you're more than you've become?

LESSONS FROM DEFEAT

WARM-UP

1. Describe a humiliating defeat that you or your team suffered. What was the worst part?
2. What lessons did you learn from that defeat? How did those lessons help in future competitions?

WORKOUT

Psalm 51:1-19

3. According to Psalm 51, what lessons did David learn from his humiliating defeat?
4. What character qualities does God desire in His people (vv. 5-12)? What steps can you take to gain those character qualities in your own life?

CUT IT OUT

WARM-UP

1. How do you know when you've really done your best in your sport? How often does that happen?
2. Have you ever felt ashamed after competing because you hadn't given your best effort?

WORKOUT

2 Timothy 2:15-16, 22-26

3. What is required of God for you to do your best?
4. What does "correctly explains the word of truth" mean?
5. What choices will you make this week to "run from anything that stimulates youthful lusts" and, instead, "pursue righteous living, faithfulness, love and peace"?

SELF DISCIPLINE

WARM-UP

1. How is self-discipline important in your sport? Is there a particular mind-set or routine that you use to develop self-discipline?
2. What things most frequently tempt you to be undisciplined?

WORKOUT

Judges 16:1-22

3. In what ways did Samson lack discipline? How might more self-discipline have changed his life?
4. What areas of your own spiritual life need greater passion or discipline? What benefits could result from increased passion and discipline?

FANS IN THE STANDS

WARM-UP

1. What disciplines associated with your favorite sport do you find most difficult to maintain? Which ones seem easy?
2. How does the crowd impact your performance? Do you perform better or worse in front of fans?
3. What are your tactics for tuning out the crowd so you can focus on your performance?

WORKOUT

Hebrews 12:1-2

4. How does knowing you have a "huge crowd of witnesses" watching you live your life on and off the field enhance your performance?
5. What hinders you in your race for Christ? What do you need to do to rid yourself of those things that weigh you down and keep you from living the life Christ wants for you?

GOT HEART?

WARM-UP

1. How often do you check your pulse? Do you know what your resting heart rate is?
2. When has your heart felt like it was going to come out of your chest because it was beating so hard?

WORKOUT

Colossians 3:23-24

3. The Bible instructs you to work at whatever you do with all your heart. When you give something your best effort do you do so to impress others or to honor the Lord?
4. Christ promises you an eternal inheritance. With His promise in mind, how are you investing today?
5. Are you giving your heart to the right things? If not, what adjustments do you need to make in order to do so?

THE PEOPLE I TRUST

WARM-UP

1. Who are three people you trust with your life? Why do you trust them?
2. How can lack of trust in coaches or leadership affect a team's confidence? How can it affect individual performance?

WORKOUT

Jeremiah 17:5-8

3. According to these verses, what are your two options for determining whom you can trust?
4. What are the results for a person who places his or her trust in people? What are the results for a person who places his or her trust in God?
5. How can trusting God give you confidence in other areas of your life?

RESPECTING THE REF

WARM-UP

1. Would you ever consider being a professional referee? Why or why not?
2. What is your usual reaction to rules, regulations, and official decisions?

WORKOUT

Hebrews 12:11-13

3. How do these verses define the old adage "no pain, no gain"?
4. What are the results of God's discipline? What do these benefits look like in your life?
5. Discipline is a necessary part of life. How can you benefit most from God's training? Drop to your "weakened knees" and confess any resistance to God's loving discipline.

END IN SIGHT

WARM-UP

1. How important is to have a game plan before going into competition? What might be the result if no plan is in place?
2. How does having a clearly defined role motivate you to do your best?

WORKOUT

Jeremiah 29:4-12

3. What were some of the instructions God gave the Israelites who were exiled in Babylon?
4. How might God's "game plan" have helped them through this difficult time?
5. How might God's promises affect the way you look at life?

DO IT FOR HIM

WARM-UP

1. Who has not ever seen you compete but if they could it would mean the world to you?
2. If that person were to be present the next time you compete, how do you think you would feel? Would you be excited? Nervous?

WORKOUT

Psalm 105:4

3. The psalmist knew what it was like to walk with the Lord. He leaned on God time and time again. Where does your strength and encouragement come from? If not from God, why?
4. In what practical ways can you "continually seek him"—as you make preparations to be the best athlete that you can be for the Lord?

I WANT IT

WARM-UP

1. What keeps you motivated to work hard when practicing your sport?
2. How important is winning to you? How important is it to you to do your best?

WORKOUT

Matthew 6:25-33

3. According to verse 31, what are some of the motivating factors in many peoples' lives?
4. In what ways has worry ever motivated you? What was the end result of your worrying?
5. How can following the priorities Jesus laid out in verse 33 impact your motivation? In what ways would changing your focus like this benefit both your sport and your life?

THEY NEVER WIN

WARM-UP

1. When have you been tempted to cheat at school or on the field?
2. Have you ever suspected or known that a competitor had cheated? How did it make you feel?
3. What are some of the reasons people cheat?

WORKOUT

Acts 5:1-11

4. What do you think motivated Ananias and Sapphira to cheat the church? What impact did their deaths have on other people in the church?
5. What are some ways you can resist the temptation to cheat in order to get ahead?

THIS SECTION OF ATHLETE STUDIES FOCUSES ON COMPETITION. IF CHRISTIANS ARE SUPPOSED TO BE SERVANTS OF OTHERS, WHERE DOES THE CONCEPT OF COMPETING FIT? CAN A CHRISTIAN ATHLETE REALLY BE FULLY COMPETITIVE? WHERE'S THE BALANCE? GOD DESIGNED US FOR ADVENTURE AND FOR COMPETITION, BUT HE'S VERY CONCERNED ABOUT OUR ATTITUDES AND ABOUT HOW WE COMPETE.

FAULT

WARM-UP

1. Do those you compete against respect you or dislike you? Why?
2. How do you respond when a competitor tries to cheat against you?

WORKOUT

Daniel 6:1-24

3. Why do the people set a trap for Daniel, hoping to kill him? Why do they insist the king make a decree?
4. How do you measure up to Daniel's record? Are you faultless? Blameless? Or somewhere in between?

IT'S HOW YOU PLAY

WARM-UP

1. How do you feel about the phrase, "It's not whether you win or lose, it's how you play the game"? Do you think most athletes believe this phrase is true?
2. How important is it for you to win? How bad does it feel to lose?

WORKOUT

Colossians 3:23-24

3. What do these two verses say about the value of hard work? How might knowing you are doing everything for God change the way you approach competition?
4. How do Paul's words to the Colossians radically differ from the world's view of winning?
5. What effect might this perspective on winning and losing have on the way you deal with the unpredictable results of competition?

CELEBRATE

WARM-UP

1. Have you ever experienced an accomplishment or victory that made you, teammates, coaches, fans, or parents jump up and down for joy? What were the circumstances?

WORKOUT

2 Samuel 6:1-5, 12-15

2. What happened in 2 Samuel 6:1-5? Verse 12 reports that God blessed a family because of the ark. In your own words, describe the celebration recorded in verses 14-15.
3. Into what area of your team's life could God bring His presence and blessing? Do you think God really wants to do this?
4. Into what area of your personal life could God bring His presence and blessing that would cause you to leap for joy?

KNOW YOUR COMPETITION

WARM-UP

1. How does it help to know your opponent before going into a game? Can you think of a recent example when having that information helped you gain an advantage?
2. What are some of the ways you can learn more about your competition?

WORKOUT

John 8:42-44; 1 Peter 5:8

3. What are some characteristics of Satan described in Scripture?
4. In what ways can you gain an advantage over Satan, your mortal enemy?
5. How might knowing your enemy's strengths and weaknesses—as well as your own—help you stand up to his attacks?

STRENGTH FROM FAILURE

WARM-UP

1. When was the last time you failed while attempting something in practice or competition? How did it make you feel?
2. How did that failure influence the way you approached future practices and competitions?

WORKOUT

Judges 16:21-30

3. What conditions did Samson face in his defeat? How did his enemies respond to his situation?
4. What did Samson request of God? What final act established his legacy?
5. How does Samson's story reflect God's faithfulness? How might past mistakes and failures make you stronger?

THE HUMBLE ATHLETE

WARM-UP

1. What is the first thought that goes through your mind when you excel in competition or outdo everyone else in practice?

WORKOUT

Philippians 2:3-8

2. What advice does Paul give when it comes to humility?
3. How can keeping others in mind help you remain humble in any situation?
4. How might your attitude about competition and personal achievement change if you were to follow Jesus' example?

HOW ARE YOU HOLDING UP?

WARM-UP

1. Are you ever afraid when you think about your future in athletics?
2. What scares you more: next week's game or the possibility of a career in athletics? If you do not have your sights set on being a professional athlete, what makes you fear the future?

WORKOUT

Isaiah 41:10

3. God tells Isaiah, "Don't be afraid, for I am with you. Don't be discouraged, for I am your God." How can these words give you hope for the future?
4. The verse continues with the promise: "I will strengthen you and help you. I will hold you up with my victorious right hand." How can these words calm your fears about your present position?

MORE THAN A FEELING

WARM-UP

1. What are some of the emotions you feel heading into competition? How can your emotions help your performance? How can they hurt?
2. How do you control your emotions so that you can keep your focus when you are competing?

WORKOUT

Matthew 15:18-19; Proverbs 28:26; Jeremiah 17:9

3. What are some of the characteristics of the heart Jesus describes in Matthew? How might those characteristics slow you down when relying solely on your emotions?
4. What kind of trouble might you face if you trust in your emotions rather than in God's truth? Give specific examples.
5. How can understanding the nature of your heart help you make better life decisions?

KEEP IT CLEAN

WARM-UP

1. Have you ever allowed a referee or line judge to make a bad call in your favor?
2. Have you cheated in competition? Did winning justify your actions? Did losing make your efforts seem even worse?

WORKOUT

Proverbs 12:13, 17

3. According to these verses what you say can trap you if your words are contrary to God's purpose for your life. How might you be trapped by your words or actions?
4. Right words and actions will help you avoid trouble. Do you need to come clean before God and others? If not, what actions will you take to avoid falling into the trap of dishonesty?

LOUDER THAN WORDS

WARM-UP

1. Has your name ever been dragged through the mud? Did you deserve it? Does anyone actually deserve that kind of treatment?
2. How difficult it is to clean a tarnished reputation? How might lashing out in the process hinder your efforts at rebuilding your character?

WORKOUT

Psalm 119:69-70

3. What do you think the writer of this psalm was feeling when he wrote these words?
4. The "precepts" mentioned are God's absolute truths recorded in Scripture. What do you know to be absolutely true about God?
5. How does knowing the truth help you when you are up against a powerful—and possibly arrogant and uncaring—competitor?

UNDERDOG

WARM-UP

1. Have you ever beaten a competitor despite overwhelming odds against you? Describe the victory or one like this you can recall?
2. When you're a spectator do you usually support a favored team or the underdog?

WORKOUT

Judges 7:1-25

3. Why do you think God told Gideon to reduce his forces so that he was terribly outnumbered?
4. How did God accomplish this victory recorded in Judges?
5. How has God demonstrated His miraculous power in your life? Where might He be asking you now to rely on His strength instead of your own?

AGAIN AND AGAIN

WARM-UP

1. How do you feel when an opponent mocks you or ridicules your team?
2. When others have ridiculed you and threatened to humiliate you in competition, how have you or your teammates responded? Did you respond with similar taunts, or did you ignore them?

WORKOUT

Nehemiah 4:1-23

3. What types of opposition does Nehemiah face?
4. How does Nehemiah respond to the verbal taunts? How does he respond to threats of physical harm?
5. How can you adapt Nehemiah's attitude toward verbal abuse? How can a prayerful attitude transform your personal response to legitimate threats of defeat?

SHOW-OFF!

WARM-UP

1. Think of an example when an athlete—known to you or not—showed off during competition. How did it make you feel?
2. How do you feel about showing off? Could it have any impact on the outcome of a game or match?

WORKOUT

Luke 18:10-14

3. What two approaches to prayer are described in these verses? What does the Pharisee's prayer reveal about his character? What does the tax collector's reveal about his character?
4. What did Jesus say was God's response to the two prayers?
5. How might this parable impact the way you view others? After reading these verses, will you approach your conversation with God any differently?

NY GIANTS (NOT YOUR GIANTS)

WARM-UP

1. When have you exhibited courage?
2. In what ways have you witnessed players demonstrating courage through sports?

WORKOUT

1 Samuel 17:20-24, 31-51

3. What are the most striking features of David's courage?
4. To what extent can you relate to David's courage? In what ways is your experience with courage different from his?
5. What action do you need to take to turn the giants in your life over to God so they're not your giants?

WIN OVER WILL

WARM-UP

1. How does it make you feel when you compete against someone who is an equal match? Do you go for a quick victory or even match?
2. Does taking on someone equally matched push you to improve or frustrate you?

WORKOUT

Genesis 32:24-32

3. Why does God wrestle Jacob? God is almighty and omnipotent so why doesn't He just pin Jacob?
4. Why does Jacob want to know God's name? Why does God change Jacob's name to Israel?
5. In what area of your life are you wrestling with God? Are you willing to allow God to win over your will?

BEING A GOOD TEAM PLAYER IS CRITICAL TO MOST ATHLETES' PERFORMANCE. EACH OF US MUST LEARN HOW TO COOPERATE WITH OTHERS, WORK TOGETHER, AND SHARE TOGETHER ALL OUR WINS AND LOSSES. THIS IS VITALLY TRUE OF THE CHRISTIAN LIFE AS WELL. NOBODY IS A SUPERSTAR; WE EACH PLAY A UNIQUE AND SIGNIFICANT ROLE ON GOD'S TEAM. SPEND SOME TIME REFLECTING ON TEAMWORK AND YOUR PART IN THE TEAM AS YOU EXAMINE THE FOLLOWING ATHLETE STUDIES.

TEAM EFFORT

WARM-UP

1. Who do you consider to be your greatest teammates?
2. What are the most important factors in working together as a team?

WORKOUT

Luke 9:10-17

3. Where is teamwork demonstrated in this passage?
4. What is Jesus' role in the team effort?
5. What can you learn from Jesus' promotion of teamwork that you can apply to your team?

CARE ENOUGH TO CONFRONT

WARM-UP

1. Are you a confronter, or do you avoid confrontation like the plague?
2. Which is better: to let something hurtful go on without being addressed, or to bring it out into the open? What might be the benefit of confronting it? What is the risk?

WORKOUT

Ephesians 4:11-16

3. It takes all types to make up the family of God. Do you have the making of an apostle, prophet, evangelist, pastor, or teacher? If not, do you appreciate those who do?
4. Whether you know it or not, as a Christian you have been gifted by God to help other Christians. As you mature spiritually you will learn more about your unique giftedness. In what ways has God used you to impact your teammates in a way that points them to Christ?
5. One of the measures of a maturing believer in Christ is the ability to speak the truth in love. Who do you need to talk to in order to mend a relationship? Are you willing to trust God to bring healing instead of division?

FOR REAL?

WARM-UP

1. What is the most unbelievable thing your coach has ever told you? Was it directed at you or another teammate? Was it about an opponent? How did you react?
2. When has a coach or teacher "opened your mind" to some idea or technique that you had struggled to understand? What did he or she do that helped you?

WORKOUT

Luke 24:36-45

3. What are the circumstances around Jesus' appearance? Why are His words significant?
4. To what area of your life would you like your mind opened so you can truly see things as they really are? How might seeing things for what they are impact your relationships with teammates?

TEAM OF TEAMS

WARM-UP

1. If you could choose anyone, whom would you choose to make up your team of teams?
2. What goals would you want to accomplish with this team?

WORKOUT

Matthew 10:1-10

3. What was key to the disciples' ability to work together to accomplish miraculous things?
4. What might you be able to accomplish for God by teaming up with other Christians?

WORTH THE RISK

WARM-UP

1. Have you ever been on a team with someone, or had a friend, who you were so close to that he or she felt like a member of your family? What made the relationship so special?
2. What kind of sacrifices did you and your friend make for one another?

WORKOUT

1 Samuel 20:1-17

3. How did Jonathan and David's friendship affect them? What did Jonathan risk for David?
4. How has Jesus been this kind of friend to you? What risks or sacrifices are you willing to make for Him?

DRAGGING THE TEAM DOWN

WARM-UP

1. What are some ways in which a teammate's mistake can affect the outcome of a game?
2. Have you ever made a mistake that had a negative impact on someone else? Can you remember a time when someone else's mistake had a negative impact on you?

WORKOUT

Jonah 1:1-15

3. What was Jonah's sin? How did his sin affect the lives of innocent people?
4. What is a recent example of how an individual's sin resulted in serious consequences for others?
5. How might Jonah's story provide the strength you need to resist giving into temptation?

THE GREATEST

WARM-UP

1. Every coach looks for that player whose value exceeds all others. What qualities make a player so valuable?
2. What is the greatest team you have ever been a part of? What made it that way?

WORKOUT

Acts 15:22-41

3. Why did Paul and Barnabas disagree?
4. How did Paul and Barnabas's conflict have a positive impact on the early church?
5. Do you value yourself as God values you? How can your friends help you be more like the person God wants you to be?

GET IT AND GO

WARM-UP

1. Are you better at listening or talking? Are you better at doing or observing?
2. What is your definition of a hypocrite? Do you know anyone who fits the bill?

WORKOUT

James 1:22

3. The theme of James can be summed up in two letters: D and O. The message of James is that faith without works is dead. How do you live out your faith?
4. Teammates and friends are always watching you. What will help you to match your actions to what you know to be true?
5. What will it take for you to become a more authentic person?

FORGIVE AND FORGET

WARM-UP

1. Have you ever been betrayed or hurt by a teammate or a coach? How difficult was it to forgive that person? How did his or her action affect your ability to trust again?

WORKOUT

Luke 15:11-32

2. How did the younger son in the parable hurt his family? (vv. 12-13).
3. What was his father's response when he finally came home? (vv. 22-24). How did the older brother react to the way his father handled the situation? (vv. 28-30).
4. Which of those responses reflects God's heart of forgiveness? How could embracing the father's attitude affect the way you deal with your own betrayal or hurt?

KISS WHOM?

WARM-UP

1. What do teammates consider appropriate expressions of appreciation on and off the field?
2. Your gender and personality play a large part in how you show friendship and affection to others. How comfortable are you openly sharing victories and disappointments with members of your team?

WORKOUT

1 Thessalonians 5:23-28

3. When Paul wrote to the home team in Thessalonica he instructed them to be set apart for God's work. What role might you play in helping your team to be all God wants them to be?
4. A team that is whole is made up of whole people. Paul addressed the spirit, soul, and body of the Thessalonians. If one part of a person is unhealthy, how might it affect the other parts?
5. It is not necessary that you meet and greet teammates with the biblical practice of a holy kiss. But how can you demonstrate your love and support for each other, especially as children of God?

SHARE THE LOAD

WARM-UP

1. When have you had to stand in for a teammate who was injured or not playing well? Have you ever had to rely on a teammate to pick up your slack?
2. How valuable are good friends and teammates during bad times?

WORKOUT

Ecclesiastes 4:9-12; Galatians 6:2

3. What does Ecclesiastes tell us about the value of friends?
4. What are some situations in which you could be a good friend to someone else?
5. How does Galatians 6:2 impact your view of the responsibility you have to help others?

RUMORS

WARM-UP

1. Have you ever been part of a team where rumors were consistently spread? Have you ever been the subject of gossip or been tempted to start or pass along a rumor?
2. How can rumors and gossip affect a team's chemistry? How about an individual's confidence and performance?

WORKOUT

Proverbs 11:12-13; 16:28; 19:5; 21:23

3. According to Proverbs 16:28, what are some of the long-term dangers of getting involved with rumors?
4. According to Proverbs 19:5, what kinds of punishment might a gossiper face? How can guarding your words (see Proverbs 21:23) keep you from facing certain troubles?
5. What character qualities can help a person resist the temptation to spread rumors?

NO ONE LEFT BEHIND

WARM-UP

1. What would happen to your team if you lost just one member? Is there anyone on your team who is expendable? It there anyone who is completely irreplaceable?
2. What happens to a team's performance if one player feels he or she is of no value?
3. How do you and your teammates maintain team spirit and loyalty? How do you encourage all members of the team to feel valuable?

WORKOUT

Ephesians 4:1-6

4. According to these verses how can you maintain unity in Christ? Why is Jesus' type of unity so important?
5. How well are you doing at demonstrating humility, gentleness, patience, and acceptance?

PULLING TOGETHER

WARM-UP

1. When have you been part of a team where the players didn't get along? What effect did that have on your performance as a team? How did it impact your personal performance?
2. What do you do to try to resolve conflicts on your team?

WORKOUT

James 4:1-12

3. What causes Christians to fight other Christians? What does James say are the results of such conflicts?
4. What attitudes should Christians have toward one another?
5. Who are people in your life whom you need to treat differently? Are you willing to take the first step toward reconciliation?

WHAT AM I DOING?

WARM-UP

1. Why do you participate in certain sports instead of others?
2. Rank the following in order of importance from one to three in deciding which specific sports to participate in:
   - ⬡ What I am doing
   - ⬡ Who I am doing it with
   - ⬡ What kind of recognition I might get

WORKOUT

Genesis 4:1-16

3. Why did Cain murder Abel?
4. What were the consequences of Cain's action?
5. Is there anything you need to do to make things right with one of your teammates or another person?

ANY SPORT REQUIRES TIME IN TRAINING. AN ATHLETE NEEDS TRAINING TO LEARN THE BASIC RULES AND SKILLS OF A SPORT AND TO TEACH THE BODY TO ADAPT TO NEW MOVES AND SKILLS. IT'S THE SAME IN THE CHRISTIAN LIFE. WE NEED TO MASTER THE BASICS AND ALSO TEACH OUR BODIES, MINDS, AND SPIRITS TO THINK AND ACT IN NEW WAYS SO WE CAN LIVE AND COMPETE AS JESUS WOULD DESIRE FROM HIS TEAM.

JUST LET GO

WARM-UP

1. What is something you have had to let go of before you could get serious about your commitment to your sport? How was holding onto it keeping you from reaching your full potential?
2. Was it difficult to let go of? What were the benefits that came with letting go of it? What helped you keep your commitment to move forward without it?

WORKOUT

Mark 10:17-30

3. What spiritual reward is the man seeking? What acts has he been faithful to keep?
4. What motivated Jesus' response? Why do you think the man was disappointed?
5. How does the promise in verses 29-30 help you to handle the challenges that make it difficult to commit your whole life to God?

PAIN THRESHOLD

WARM-UP

1. What is the worst pain you have experienced from your training or competition? What was your initial reaction? Did you learn anything from your experience?
2. Are there any benefits you might gain as an athlete from an injury or physical suffering? If so, what?

WORKOUT

Romans 5:1-5; James 1:2-4

3. How do Paul and James, the writers of these passages, contradict human nature with regard to human suffering? (See Romans 5:3 and James 1:2.)
4. According to the two writers, what are some of the benefits of suffering for the cause of Christ?
5. How might understanding the biblical view of pain and suffering change your perspective on your past, present, and future trials?

CONFIDENT APPROACH

WARM-UP

1. Describe a time when you wanted to change your role within a team. How did you approach the coach with your request? Were you anxious?
2. How did your coach respond? How has your experience impacted the way you might approach future wants or concerns?

WORKOUT

Luke 11:1-13

3. What are some key components of the prayer Jesus taught His disciples? (vv. 2-4)
4. In the story Jesus shares in verses 5-8, what principle of prayer does He reveal?
5. How does the promise in verses 9-10 change the way you view your communication with God? How does it affect the way you view your physical and spiritual needs?

WATCH AND LEARN

WARM-UP

1. Have you watched a video of yourself in competition or worked out in front of a mirror? How did these images help you improve your technique?
2. After seeing your own technique, how long does it take for you to slip back into poor form? How many times do you need to see yourself—your weaknesses and areas that need growth—before you begin to experience real change?

WORKOUT

James 1:19-27

3. How is the Word of God like a mirror or a training video?
4. What steps are necessary if you are to improve your spiritual "technique"? What are some practical helps James provides to help improve one's spiritual technique?

GET FIRED UP

WARM-UP

1. When was the last time you and your teammates were totally pumped up for a game? What did you do, or what happened, to get you fired up as a team?
2. How did being fired up make you ready for the competition? In the end how did things turn out?

WORKOUT

Ephesians 6:10-18

3. According to these verses, what is the actual battle in which we are engaged?
4. Why is truth described like a belt? Why is righteousness positioned over our chests?
5. How can faith be used effectively as a defensive shield?
6. Why is the Word of God the only offensive weapon? How can God's Word be used offensively?

BOLD ASSURANCE

WARM-UP

1. When have you experienced defeat due to lack of confidence?
2. Prior to competing, what do you do to increase your confidence?

WORKOUT

Numbers 13:26-33

3. Joshua sends 12 spies into the land to scout it before engaging in battle to take it. Why does he do this? Why do 10 spies lack confidence but two are filled with it?
4. What's the relationship between lack of confidence and good preparation?
5. Where does your confidence come from? Is it true confidence?

ETHICS IN ATHLETICS

WARM-UP

1. What part does your work ethic play in your performance? How about when you are competing?
2. Who do you know who exhibits a strong work ethic? How does it show up in his or her approach to athletics?

WORKOUT

Proverbs 10:4; 12:2; 14:2; 22:29

3. Which proverb best illustrates your personal conviction about hard work?
4. In a practical sense, how can this be an important factor for success in competition?
5. How can you encourage others to build a stronger work ethic for their sport?

INSIDE YOUR HEAD

WARM-UP

1. Name three athletes whose heads you'd like to get inside and find out their thought process. Why do you want to know these three so well?
2. What would you hope to learn from seeing inside the heads of these athletes?
3. How would thinking like one of these athletes help you achieve your goals?

WORKOUT

1 Corinthians 2:11-16

4. What is one thing that can give you insight into the thoughts of God? What are some benefits of understanding the blessings available to us through a relationship with God?
5. How can thinking like Jesus change the way you look at your circumstances? What are some of the ways it can change the way you view the world?

CHAMPIONSHIP BOUND

WARM-UP

1. Have you ever been part of a dramatic and decisive win? How did it feel?
2. What factors contributed to the win? What was your part in the victory?

WORKOUT

Romans 8:31-39

3. What brings victory in the Christian life? How can a person attain it?
4. In what areas of your life can you attain complete victory? How can you be confident of obtaining real spiritual victory in Christ?

PUSH TO THE LIMIT

WARM-UP

1. When have you pushed your body to do something related to your sport that it just couldn't do? What was the result?
2. What is the greatest weakness you most struggle with in your sport?
3. What do you do to train your body to push beyond your limitation?

WORKOUT

Romans 7:7-28

4. What weaknesses does Paul address in his letter to the Romans? Can you relate?
5. What does Paul present as the answer to these limitations? What do you need to do in order to push yourself past your spiritual weakness?

GIVE IT A REST

WARM-UP

1. How can you tell when you've been training too hard? What physical, mental, and emotional benefits can come from taking time off from practice and training?

WORKOUT

Exodus 18:13-23

2. What does Moses' father-in-law, Jethro, observe (vv. 15, 17-18)? What advice does he give Moses about how to alleviate some of his stress (vv. 19-23)?
3. Describe a time when—like Moses—you felt burned out because you were working too hard or trying to do too much. How did this impact your effectiveness?
4. How can Jethro's advice help you avoid burnout in your walk and work with
5. God? What other things could you do to keep from wearing down spiritually and emotionally?

DON'T BE LATE

WARM-UP

1. We all have times when we don't feel like working hard. Describe a time when you procrastinated in your training. What impact did your choice have on your performance?
2. What are some of the physical benefits of maintaining a routine training schedule? How can it help you keep your competitive edge and winning attitude?

WORKOUT

Matthew 25:1-13

3. What are some of the characteristics that describe the wise virgins in the parable? How about the foolish ones?
4. What did the procrastination of the foolish virgins cost them (v. 10)? What spiritual truth is Jesus teaching through this parable?
5. How does Jesus' warning in verse 13 challenge you to avoid procrastinating in spiritual things? How can taking Jesus' advice change the way you approach all areas of your life?

TROUBLE-FREE TRAINING

WARM-UP

1. Do you ever worry about pulling a muscle while you are training? How do you prevent harming your body?
2. Do you train with the same intensity you use when you perform?

WORKOUT

John 14:1-3

3. This passage is commonly used at funerals and memorial services. What comfort does it provide you as you think about day-to-day living?
4. How do your belief in God and the saving power of Jesus help you focus on what is most important?
5. God is preparing you right now for a great service until you arrive at that place in heaven He has prepared for you. How will you invest your life?

SOBER LIVING

WARM-UP

1. What parts of your athletic ability do you consider superb? What parts do you consider awful?
2. When was a time you felt like a superstar? When have you felt like a benchwarmer?

WORKOUT

Romans 12:3

3. What does it mean to view yourself soberly? Do you know someone who sincerely does this? How do you measure up to the sobriety test?
4. How can the words of this one verse affect the way you practice, play, and compete? If you try to live by these words, how would you interact with teammates and opponents?

SELLING OUT

WARM-UP

1. Describe a time when you've been required to put some of your personal desires aside to obtain a bigger reward. What did you do to stay focused on that longer-term goal?

WORKOUT

Matthew 16:24-27

2. Why do you think it's so difficult for us to follow the advice Jesus gives in verse 24? What spiritual truth do you think He's revealing in verse 25?
3. In what ways does verse 26 remind you of how many successful people—including professional athletes—approach their lives? What are some examples of this principle?
4. How can grasping the truth of verse 27 motivate you to deny your self-centered or distorted desires, take up your cross, and follow Jesus?

ANY ATHLETE KNOWS THAT ALL THE TRAINING AND PRACTICE IN THE WORLD IS ONLY AS GOOD AS HIS OR HER PERFORMANCE IN COMPETITION. PUTTING TRAINING INTO ACTUAL PRACTICE IS THE ATHLETE'S ULTIMATE GOAL. IT'S THE SAME IN OUR WALK WITH JESUS. ALL THE BOOK LEARNING AND PREACHING IN THE WORLD IS OF NO VALUE UNLESS WE TAKE THOSE TRUTHS AND PUT THEM INTO PRACTICE IN DAILY LIFE. FOCUS IN THESE STUDIES TO PERFORM ON AND OFF THE FIELD FOR THE GLORY OF GOD.

COOLING THE HOT HEAD

WARM-UP

1. When have you lost your cool in the heat of competition? Have you ever gotten angry during a practice or competition but managed to keep your cool?
2. What were the different outcomes of these two situations? In the instance when you kept your cool, what helped you do so?

WORKOUT

Ephesians 4:26-32

3. Is it possible to be angry and not sin? Why does Jesus warn against remaining angry?
4. What are some of the behaviors that anger prompts? What are the consequences that result for the one who is angry and those on the receiving end?
5. What makes it difficult to live according to Jesus' command in verse 32? How can you follow Jesus' example on and off the field?

YOU CAN DO IT

WARM-UP

1. Who is the most encouraging member of your team? Who is the most discouraging?
2. Have you ever felt the impact of negative words on your own performance? What noticeable results did you experience?

WORKOUT

James 3:1-12

3. Why does James use the analogies of a ship and a horse? What is the lesson to take away from these two examples?
4. Do you usually tend to encourage or discourage others with your words? What will you say this week that will bring glory to God?

FOR GOD'S GLORY

WARM-UP

1. When you or your team wins a competition, who gets the glory and recognition?
2. What are some things that are permissible on your team and yet are not really helpful to all teammates?

WORKOUT

1 Corinthians 10:23–11:1

3. What kinds of things might Paul be calling "permissible" but not "helpful"? What "permissible" things do you do that might cause someone else to struggle with his or her conscience?
4. What would our lives look like if we committed to give our all for God's glory in every area of our lives?

GOAL ORIENTED

WARM-UP

1. What athletic goal has been the most difficult for you to reach?
2. What has it cost you in striving to achieve the goal? What rewards have you (or will you) receive upon reaching it?

WORKOUT

Philippians 3:12-21

3. What goal did Paul strive toward? What did it cost him? What did he receive?
4. What is the most important goal in your life right now? How you will go about achieving it?

PERSONAL RESPONSIBILITY

WARM-UP

1. What aspect of your athletic participation requires the greatest amount of physical control?
2. Have you been able to teach yourself this area of control? How?

WORKOUT

1 Thessalonians 4:1-8

3. In what specific ways does Paul call us to control our own bodies? What reasons does Paul give for self-control?
4. Sexual immorality is not only physical. It is mental and spiritual as well. What decisions will you make to control your thoughts, attitudes, and actions this week?

OFF THE BENCH

WARM-UP

1. Have you ever spent an entire game sitting on the bench? What did it feel like the first time you were called into the game?
2. When you're waiting to be called into competition, what do you think about? What do you do to be ready at a moment's notice?

WORKOUT

1 Samuel 3:1-21

3. Samuel may have been only 12 years old when the Lord called him. How did he demonstrate a readiness to answer God's call? How did Samuel continue—as he grew up—to be always ready for God's call?
4. How can you make yourself ready for whatever God calls you to be or do this week?

TAKE A TIME OUT

WARM-UP

1. Give a recent example of a game when your team needed to take a time-out. How did taking a time-out help the team's performance?

WORKOUT

Proverbs 18:13; Ephesians 5:17

2. What are some everyday life situations that might require taking a time-out? Describe a time when you had to think twice before taking action or speaking.
3. What kind of "disgrace" awaits someone who falls into the trap of speaking before thinking (see Proverbs 18:13 HCSB)? How did Paul instruct the Ephesians to avoid such dangers?
4. How can taking Paul's advice in Ephesians 5:17 help you make better decisions?

OUT IN THE OPEN

WARM-UP

1. How have you seen athletes publicly display their faith during a game? Have you ever displayed your faith on the playing field?
2. What are your thoughts about displaying one's faith during competition? Can you think of a situation when it would be inappropriate to do so?

WORKOUT

Matthew 5:13-16

3. How can a Christian athlete be "salt of the earth" or a "light of the world"?
4. How does what Jesus says in verse 16 influence your thoughts about publicly displaying Christian faith during an athletic contest?

YOU KNOW ME

WARM-UP

1. Everyone goes through a slump—even the most famous of athletes. It's a time when you're not performing at your highest potential. When have you experienced a slump?
2. What steps did you take to get out of your slump? How did taking those steps help you perform at a more competitive level?

WORKOUT

Psalm 139

3. What does David, the writer of this psalm, say about how God understands you? How do these truths affect your confidence in God's ability to understand your challenges and struggles?
4. When you aren't on top of your game, what can you learn from these verses about the best way to tackle the problem?
5. How can following the example in these verses help you discover both your problems and their solutions?

GIVE IT TO 'EM

WARM-UP

1. Have you played alongside a selfish teammate, someone who always wanted to be the star? If so, how did it affect the way other members viewed their roles on the team?
2. Have you ever turned the spotlight from yourself to a fellow teammate? What did it feel like to give someone else the chance to shine?

WORKOUT

Proverbs 11:24-25; Luke 6:30

3. Toward whom does Jesus say we should have a giving attitude? How is His command different than what the world promotes?
4. Scripture points out that there are benefits from giving. What role should these promised benefits play in your actions to be a giver?
5. What are specific actions you will take to become more of a giver?

NO SHORTCUTS

WARM-UP

1. What is the greatest sacrifice you've made to play your sport or serve your team?
2. Is it more important to sacrifice everything for your team or to do what your coach tells you to do?

WORKOUT

1 Samuel 15:1-23

3. What was Saul commanded to do? What did he actually do?
4. What was Saul's logic for not obeying God exactly?
5. What motivates you to take a shortcut in what you've been coached to do? How should you respond to God's instructions?

PRIORITY PLAYER

WARM-UP

1. Are you secure in your position? On what do you base your personal value?
2. What would it take for you to become number one? Are you willing to do it regardless of the cost to you or others?

WORKOUT

1 Corinthians 6:19-20

3. These verses are commonly used to remind us not to abuse our bodies but to keep them pure as God has commanded. We should live this way. How does this verse relate to priorities?
4. How does the treatment of your body relate to your personal importance to God?
5. God bought you at the price of His Son. How will you honor God with your body and be His star player in living the Christian life?

GOLD STANDARD

WARM-UP

1. Eric Liddell, a devout Christian who lived during the first half of the last century, gave up a chance for Olympic gold because he refused to race on the Sabbath. Have you ever been confronted with a choice between honoring God and honoring your sport?
2. What would you have done if you had been Eric Liddell? Would the glimmer of Olympic gold blind you to your convictions?

WORKOUT

Daniel 3:1-10

3. Shadrach and his friends were successful government officials. What do their positions suggest about their characters and work ethics?
4. Why do the young men refuse to obey the king in this one matter of the law? Would you feel different about their decision if they had died in the furnace?
5. In what area of your life might God be calling you to obey Him above all else?

THIS ONE DESIRE

WARM-UP

1. What do you want right now more than anything in the world? If you were to get what you most want, how would your life be different?
2. If you never received what you most want, would you be able to survive? Is your life and future truly dependent on this one desire being fulfilled?

WORKOUT

Psalm 37:4

3. God will give you the desires of your heart—if you take delight in Him. What does it look like to delight in the Lord?
4. The more you enjoy God the closer you come to seeing your desires fulfilled. You begin to desire the same things God desire for you. How is God transforming what you want into what He wants for you?
5. Even when things aren't going your way you can be thankful for and enjoy what God has provided for you. Are you willing to trust God for His best for you? How can you honor Him while you wait?

FLEX

WARM-UP

1. When has someone's stubbornness caused problems for your team? When has your stubbornness been a problem?
2. What causes a person to be stubborn? What motivates you to be obstinate?

WORKOUT

Exodus 7:14-24; 12:28-30

3. What motivated Pharaoh to be so immovable?
4. What effect did his stubborn heart have on Egypt? How would things have been different for the entire nation if Pharaoh had not been so stubborn?
5. How is the attitude of the Israelites different from Pharaoh's attitude? In what one specific way do you need to be more like the Israelites and less like Pharaoh this week?

NO ATHLETIC ENDEAVOR IS COMPLETE WITHOUT A DETAILED GAME PLAN MADE WELL IN ADVANCE OF THE GAME! SAME WITH THE WALK OF FAITH: IT'S IMPORTANT FOR EACH OF US TO KNOW IN ADVANCE WHAT WE WILL DO WHEN FACED WITH TEMPTATIONS AND TRIALS. THIS SECTION ADDRESSES THAT TOPIC, HELPING YOU KNOW WHAT TO DO WHETHER YOU'RE IN THE MIDDLE OF A BIG MATCH OR ON A NIGHT OUT WITH FRIENDS.

WAKE-UP CALL

WARM-UP

1. As an athlete, what might warn you about possible dangers ahead? What can happen if you choose to ignore warnings? What are the benefits of the "wake-up calls" in your life?
2. We all have times when we're going down the wrong path in life. Describe a time when a negative situation helped you realize that you were heading the wrong way.

WORKOUT

Acts 9:1-18; Proverbs 29:1

1. In Acts 9, what was Saul doing that was displeasing to God? What extraordinary "wake-up call" did Saul receive? What miraculous effect did it have on him?
2. According to Proverbs 29:1, what will happen to the person who fails to heed God's warnings? How does this principle encourage you to stay on the right path?
3. What are some things you can do to avoid the need for a spiritual "wake-up call"?

RISK IT

WARM-UP

1. What's the greatest risk you've ever taken for your sport?
2. Who is an athlete who sacrificed greatly for his or her team?

WORKOUT

Esther 4:1-17

1. What danger did Esther face? What danger did the Jews face?
2. How might Esther have avoided danger if she'd chosen the safe route? What would have happened if she'd chosen safety?
3. Would you be willing to risk your life for Christ and the people He loves? Is He calling you to take some risks for His kingdom this week?

WISE GUY

WARM-UP

1. What do you consider to be more important: good players or a good game plan? Why?
2. If God were to fulfill one request, what would it be?

WORKOUT

1 Kings 3:4-14

3. Why did Solomon ask God for wisdom?
4. Why do you think God not only gave Solomon wisdom but also bestowed on him wealth and honor?
5. In what area do you most need wisdom right now? Ask God for wisdom and He will give it to you.

DRAWS AND DRAWBACKS

WARM-UP

1. What has been the greatest achievement in your athletic career to date? How did you feel immediately after accomplishing it?
2. What motivates you to excel in your sport? What are some of the benefits that come from winning? What are some of the drawbacks that can accompany athletic success?

WORKOUT

Luke 16:19-24

3. What might have motivated the rich man to achieve his wealth? How is his motivation most likely different than Lazarus's?
4. At his death, what hard lesson did the rich man learn? How does this reality help put worldly success into perspective?
5. What does the Bible say about misplaced value? How can you balance your physical and spiritual needs

GAME FORECAST

WARM-UP

1. What game have you watched or participated in that was won or lost because of severe weather conditions?
2. What game have you participated in that took an unusually long time to end or involved the most overtime?

WORKOUT

Joshua 10:6-14

3. What great miracle does God perform for the Israelites? Why does God do this?
4. The God who makes the sun stand still knows you personally, hears your voice, and answers your prayers. What great miracle do you need in your life?

NOTHING LASTS FOREVER

WARM-UP

1. Can you name any athletes who died before they fulfilled their potential? If so, how did you feel when you learned that their lives had been cut short?
2. Has this had an impact on the way you think about your own life?

WORKOUT

James 4:13-17

3. Why is it a bad idea to trust in yourself? Where should you place your trust?
4. How does living by the principle stated in verse 14 change the way you approach each day?
5. In what ways can you live to the fullest while first glorifying God?

POWER PLAY

WARM-UP

1. When have you seen great power demonstrated by a team or athlete? How did you react to what you saw?
2. Have you ever watched a game with players or spectators from all over the world? If so, what was most memorable about the experience?

WORKOUT

Acts 2:1-13

3. If you had been present at Pentecost, how would you have reacted?
4. What role does the Holy Spirit play in your life? Ask God to show you His power and help this week.

WHO POWERS YOU?

WARM-UP

1. Who is the most powerful athlete you know? What has he or she accomplished?
2. When have you seen a team or athlete greatly affected by something seemingly insignificant?

WORKOUT

Zechariah 4:6-10

3. What does the Lord mean when He asks, "Do not despise these small beginnings?" (v. 10).
4. What does "Not by strength or by might, but by my Spirit" mean (v. 6 HCSB)?
5. In what ways have you tried to live by your own power rather than by the Spirit's power? What do you need to do to change this?

MY BLIND SPOT

WARM-UP

1. Have you ever gotten upset with a coach or teammate who was trying to help you? How did you feel afterward?
2. Who are the people who have helped you most to discover and fix your "blind spots" in your game? What are those blind spots?

WORKOUT

Numbers 22:21-34

3. What is suggested by the fact that Balaam couldn't see the angel but his donkey could?
4. Why was the Lord angry with Balaam?
5. What is the Lord trying to make you see in your own life? What "donkey" is he using to open your eyes?

SATISFACTION GUARANTEED

WARM-UP

1. What are the three main reasons you are presently involved in athletics?
2. What would you do if you were offered an athletic scholarship? What if you became a sports celebrity? What if all of this came crashing down due to an injury?

WORKOUT

Hebrews 13:5

3. The Bible doesn't say money is the root of evil; it says that the love of money is the root of evil. What do you love so much that it has the potential of (or already is) coming between you and God?
4. Jesus promises He will always be there for you. How are your earthly relationships—as good as they may be—limited? How does having Jesus as your forever Friend help you approach the uncertainties ahead?
5. Ask God to free you from the love of material things and to help you to be satisfied with what you have. Pray that He will help you live in the present and have hope for the future.

GOD'S LOVE LETTER

WARM-UP

1. Have you ever received a love letter? Have you ever written one? Did you save the letter you received? Did you deliver the one you wrote?
2. Have you received a love letter from a parent, grandparent, or other special relative?

WORKOUT

Song of Solomon 7:10

3. The Bible is God's love letter to you. The entire Bible speaks of His plan to recapture your heart and take you as His very own forever. Believing that God is love, how would you restate this verse in your own words? What do you belong to now that is keeping you from being with God?
4. Who besides God has your best interests at heart? What can God do for you that no one else can?

SOLDIER ON THE FIELD

WARM-UP

1. When have you had to make a choice to stand up for what was right or do nothing at all? Was the decision difficult to make?
2. Why can it be so difficult sometimes to do the right thing? What are some other situations that might require you to defend what's true and just?

WORKOUT

2 Timothy 2:1-13

3. What is the first piece of advice Paul gives his young friend Timothy? What would taking this same advice look like in your life?
4. What does Paul say defenders of Christ will likely face? What are some ways that this reality can affect the way you live your life for Christ?
5. How do these verses help you face the challenges of standing up for the gospel, no matter the cost?

TRUST TIME

WARM-UP

1. How do you usually react when your coach designs a play or strategy that seems strange?
2. When has your team won, not because of you, but in spite of you?

WORKOUT

Exodus 13:23-31

3. Imagine you are walking with the Israelites when you see Pharaoh's army racing toward you. How will you react?
4. What did the Israelites learn from the experience?
5. In what way is God asking you to trust Him? How will you respond?

HERE'S THE PLAN

WARM-UP

1. When was the last time your coach or trainer made a game plan that seemed doomed to fail?
2. Did you follow the plan? What was the result?

WORKOUT

Genesis 6:13-22

3. What is God's plan? Why has He come to this decision?
4. With the possibility that it had never rained prior to the flood, what sort of mockery and abuse might Noah have endured while obeying God?
5. Are you willing to follow God's plan, even if it doesn't make sense to you?

HOMECOMING

WARM-UP

1. Describe a time when you had to leave a familiar and comfortable situation because of your commitment to a sport. Was it difficult to separate yourself from your former surroundings? Explain.

WORKOUT

Hebrews 11:8-16; 13:14; John 14:2-3

2. According to Hebrews 11, what did Abraham and Sarah have to do to gain the blessings God promised them? What kind of homeland were they ultimately seeking? (vv. 10, 16)
3. How does Hebrews 13:14 alter the level of importance you place on personal achievements? What are some of the benefits of understanding the promise given in John 14?
4. Identify ways you can maintain an eternal perspective as you live in the present.

MORE THAN WINNING

YOUR GAME PLAN FOR LIFE

ONE

PHILIPPIANS 1:27

GOD'S PLAN

IN MOST ATHLETIC CONTESTS A COACH PREPARES A GAME PLAN AHEAD OF TIME. GOD DESIGNED A PLAN FOR OUR LIVES BEFORE THE WORLD BEGAN. GOD IS HOLY AND PERFECT. HE CREATED US TO LOVE HIM, GLORIFY HIM, AND ENJOY HIM FOREVER.

WHAT IS GOD'S STANDARD?

The Bible, God's playbook, states that the standard for being on His team is to:

BE HOLY

"You must be holy because I am holy."

—1 Peter 1:16b

BE PERFECT

"But you are to be perfect, even as your Father in heaven is perfect."

—Matthew 5:48

WHAT IS GOD'S PLAN?

God created us to:

LOVE HIM

Jesus replied, "You must love the Lord your God with all your heart, all your soul, and all your mind."

—Matthew 22:37

GLORIFY (HONOR) HIM

You are worthy, O Lord our God, to receive glory and honor and power. For you created all things, and they exist because you created what you pleased.

—Revelation 4:11

ENJOY HIM FOREVER

My purpose is to give them a rich and satisfying life —John 10:10b

Why is it that we cannot live up to God's standard of holiness and perfection and fulfill God's plan for our lives?

BECAUSE OF . . .

WHAT IS SIN?

Sin means missing the mark, falling short of God's standard. It is not only doing wrong and failing to do what God wants (lying, gossip, losing our temper, lustful thoughts, and so forth), but it is also an attitude of ignoring or rejecting God, which is a result of our sinful nature.

For I was born a sinner.
—Psalm 51:5a

WHO HAS SINNED?

For everyone has sinned; we all fall short of God's glorious standard.
—Romans 3:23

WHAT'S THE RESULT OF SIN?

SEPARATION FROM GOD

It's your sins that have cut you off from God.—Isaiah 59:2a

DEATH

For the wages of sin is death.
—Romans 6:23a

JUDGMENT

Each person is destined to die once and after that comes judgment.
—Hebrews 9:27

This illustration shows that God is holy and we are sinful and separated from Him. Man continually tries to reach God through his own efforts (being good, religious activities, philosophy, and so forth) but, while these can be good things, they all fall short of God's standard.

We are all infected and impure with sin. When we display our righteous deeds, they are nothing but filthy rags.
—Isaiah 64:6

THERE IS ONLY ONE WAY TO BRIDGE THIS GAP BETWEEN GOD AND MAN . . .

GOD'S SUBSTITUTE

God provided the only way to be on His team by sending His Son, Jesus Christ, as the holy and perfect substitute to die in our place.

WHO IS JESUS CHRIST?

HE IS GOD

[Jesus said,] "The Father and I are one."—John 10:30

HE IS MAN

The Word [Jesus] was God . . . The Word became human and made his home among us.—John 1:1c, 14

WHAT HAS JESUS DONE?

HE DIED AS OUR SUBSTITUTE

But God showed his great love for us by sending Christ to die for us while we were still sinners.—Romans 5:8

HE ROSE FROM THE DEAD

Christ died for our sins, just as the Scriptures said. He was buried, and he was raised from the dead on the third day, just as the Scriptures said. He was seen by Peter and then by the Twelve. After that, he was seen by more than 500 of his followers at one time.
—1 Corinthians 15:3b-6a

HE IS THE ONLY WAY TO GOD

Jesus told him, "I am the way, the truth, and the life. No one can come to the Father except through me."—John 14:6

This diagram shows that God has bridged the gap between Himself and man by sending Jesus Christ to die in our place as our substitute. Jesus defeated sin and death and rose from the grave. Yet, it isn't enough just to know these facts. The following page tells how to become part of God's team and experience His plan.

MAN'S RESPONSE

Knowing a lot about a sport and "talking the game" doesn't make you a member of a team. The same is true in becoming a Christian. It takes more than just knowing about Jesus Christ; it requires a total commitment by faith in Him.

FAITH IS NOT

JUST KNOWING THE FACTS

You say you have faith, for you believe that there is one God. Good for you! Even the demons believe this, and they tremble in terror.—James 2:19

JUST AN EMOTIONAL EXPERIENCE

Raising your hand or repeating a prayer is not enough.

FAITH IS

REPENTING

Turning to God from sin.

For the kind of sorrow God wants us to experience leads us away from sin and results in salvation.—2 Corinthians 7:10a

RECEIVING JESUS CHRIST

Trusting in Christ alone for salvation.

But to all who believed him and accepted him, he gave the right to become children of God.—John 1:12

LOOK AT THE DIAGRAM

On which side do you see yourself? Where would you like to be?

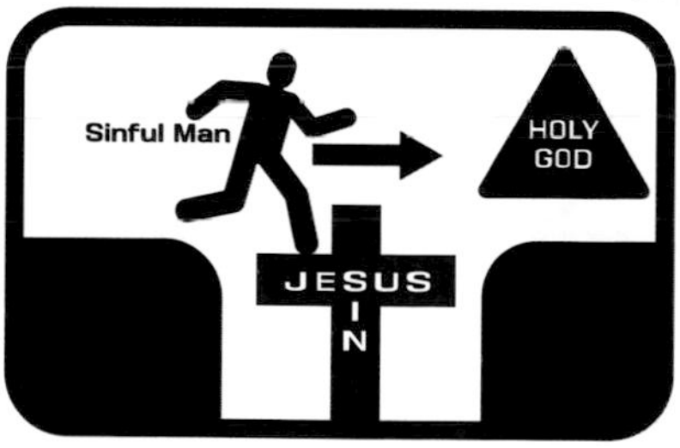

"I tell you the truth, those who listen to my message and believe in God who sent me have eternal life. They will never be condemned for their sins, but they have already passed from death into life."—John 5:24

REPLAY OF GOD'S PLAN

REalize God is holy and perfect; we are sinners and cannot save ourselves.

REcognize who Jesus is and what He's done as our substitute.

REceive Jesus Christ by faith as Savior and Lord.

But to all who believed him and accepted him, he gave the right to become children of God.—John 1:12

REspond to Jesus Christ in a life of obedience.

"If any of you wants to be my follower, you must turn from your selfish ways, take up your cross daily, and follow me."—Luke 9:23

Does God's plan make sense to you? Are you willing to repent and receive Jesus Christ? If so, express to God your need for Him. Consider the "Suggested Prayer of Surrender" below. Remember that God is more concerned with your attitude than with the words you say.

SUGGESTED PRAYER OF SURRENDER

Lord Jesus, I need You. I realize I'm a sinner and I can't save myself.

I need Your forgiveness. I believe that You loved me so much that You died on the cross for my sins and rose from the dead. I repent of my sins and put my faith in You as Savior and Lord. Today, I surrender my life. I am all in, Jesus. Take control of my life and help me to follow You in obedience. I love you Jesus. In Jesus' name, Amen.

If you openly declare that Jesus is Lord and believe in your heart that God raised him from the dead, you will be saved. . . . For "Everyone who calls on the name of the Lord will be saved."—Romans 10:9, 13

ONCE YOU HAVE COMMITTED YOUR LIFE TO JESUS CHRIST, IT IS IMPORTANT TO UNDERSTAND WHAT YOUR POSITION IS ON THIS TEAM . . .

KNOW YOUR POSITION

Too many people make the mistake of measuring the certainty of their salvation by their feelings instead of the facts of God's Word. In Jesus Christ you have a new life. See what God's Word says about your new position on His team.

I am a **new creation** in Christ. (2 Corinthians 5:17; Galatians 2:20)

I have **everything** I need for life and godliness. (2 Peter 1:3; Ephesians 1:3)

I am a **witness** for Christ and am His **workmanship**, created for good works. (Acts 1:8; Ephesians 2:10)

I am **loved** and accepted completely in Christ. (Ephesians 1:4-6; Romans 8:39)

I am **indwelt** by the Holy Spirit. (1 Corinthians 6:19-20; 1 John 4:4)

I am **forgiven** and **free** from condemnation. (1 John 1:9; Romans 8:1-2)

I have **eternal life** in Christ. (John 5:24; 1 John 5:11-13)

Trust God! Put your faith in His Word, not in your feelings:

I have written this to you who believe in the name of the Son of God, so that you may know you have eternal life.
—1 John 5:13

FOUR DAILY EXERCIES

JUST AS PHYSICAL GROWTH DEMANDS PHYSICAL EXERCISE, SPIRITUAL GROWTH AS A CHRISTIAN DEMANDS SPIRITUAL EXERCISE. TO BUILD SPIRITUAL MUSCLE, HERE ARE FOUR DAILY EXERCISES.

1. SEEK CHRIST

Spend time every day reading God's Word and devoting time in prayer.

They searched the Scriptures day after day to see if Paul and Silas were teaching the truth.—Acts 17:11b

I praise you seven times a day.
—Psalm 119:164a

2. SHARE CHRIST

Share Jesus every day through your words and actions.

Every day, in the Temple and from house to house, they continued to teach and preach this message: "Jesus is the Messiah."—Acts 5:42

We are Christ's ambassadors; God is making his appeal through us.
—2 Corinthians 5:20

3. LEAD OTHERS

Lead others by serving as Christ did. Every day die to self and yield complete control of your life to Jesus Christ.

The greatest among you must be a servant.—Matthew 23:11

If any of you wants to be my follower, you must turn from your selfish ways, take up your cross daily, and follow me.—Luke 9:23

4. LOVE OTHERS

Take every opportunity to show others around you that you love them.

. . . and to love my neighbor as myself.—
Mark 12:33b

You must warn each other every day, while it is still "today."—Hebrews 3:13a

Do these exercises and you will grow strong in your Christian life and be an effective member of God's team.

If you made a commitment to Christ, or rededicated your life to Christ, FCA wants to know. Please do one of the following so we can help you:

1. Log onto www.morethanwinning.org and record your decision.
2. Contact us at 1-800-289-0909 or fca@fca.org.
3. Contact your local FCA office.

ONE
PHILIPPIANS 1:27

INDEX

TAKE THE CHALLENGE TO START FAST AND FINISH STRONG!

The Starting Line may be the most life-changing study you'll ever complete. It will set the foundation for your relationship with Jesus. Whether you're a new Christian or in need of a spiritual "jump start," the Starting Line will bring focus and direction as you come out of the blocks in your "run" with Christ—both on and off the field of competition. Going through this study is just the starting point of a lifelong race of adventure, sacrifice, and commitment in your life with Jesus.

WHAT IS THIS?

It's a comprehensive eight-week discipleship study for athletes who are new or experienced Christ-followers and want to understand the vital basics of the Christian faith. Many people accept Christ and decide to follow Him, but they don't fully understand what comes next. This study is designed to ground you in what it means to be a disciple and live your life for Jesus.

This resource is designed to help athletes, coaches, parents, youth leaders, and volunteers to experience dramatic growth in their new faith in Christ. As you engage each session, you will be equipped, encouraged, and motivated to run with Jesus the race—the adventure—that God has already marked out for your life.

HOW CAN I USE IT?

The Starting Line can be utilized in three different ways:

1. **One-on-One:** Two people can commit to walk through this study together. In order to get the most from the one-on-one approach, it's best for a more mature Christ-follower to mentor a newer believer throughout the eight sessions. The benefit of this approach is that it allows more discussion and personal connection.
2. **Small Group:** This study is also designed to work well for a small group that wants to interact with this material together. You can use this resource in an existing group or begin a new one. It's best to keep your group size no larger than six people to enable everyone to be fully involved. If necessary, divide the group into two smaller groups with separate discussion leaders to create a better environment for interaction.
3. **Individually:** This study can also be used personally to help you grow in your faith and walk with Christ. If you study these eight sessions on your own, be sure you share with someone what God is showing you during your time of study.

Training for your sport requires self-discipline, enthusiasm, and energy. Investing quality time into this study will yield huge results for you personally.

WHAT IS SALVATION ALL ABOUT?

READY

Athletes have a strong desire to compete—whether we're trying to make the team, set a personal best, win a championship, or simply outplay our buddies in a friendly game.

1. What are some things that motivate you to compete? What does it mean to you when you're successful in winning a competition?

2. How do you feel when you lose or fail to reach your competitive goals?

For the serious athlete, the competitive spirit seems wired into our DNA—and that's because it is. God uses that very fact to draw us closer to Him. As we work for excellence in sports and other areas of life, we eventually realize that true satisfaction doesn't come from winning trophies, medals, applause, or high-dollar contracts. No achievement or award can equal the rush or deep satisfaction of discovering new life—real life in Jesus.

SET

The Bible often refers to our new life as Christ-followers in athletic and military terms.

Read Colossians 1:12-14.

3. According to Colossians 1:12-14, what incredible things are part of the big win God has provided for us?

Read Ephesians 2:1-9.

Ephesians 2:1-9 highlights three major differences between prizes earned on earth and the ultimate prize our salvation gives us: a personal relationship with our God and Creator.

Difference 1:

This ultimate prize of salvation is based solely on GOD'S EXTREME LOVE for us (vv. 1-4).

4. After reading verses 1-3, how do you think people can be "dead" while they're still alive? What defined your dead life before you turned to Jesus?

Unlike our athletic accomplishments—which we achieve thanks to God-given talent—we have not earned the privilege of salvation. God knows that no matter how much we push, we'll always fall short of His standard: perfection. But God made a way to rescue us from the dominion of darkness because He longs for us to be with Him forever.

Difference 2:

We are saved by GRACE (vv. 5-7).

5. God's grace is His favor toward us who don't deserve it. How has choosing to accept God's incredible free gift of salvation in Jesus changed your life? How do you feel about your life now and looking to the future?

Even though we don't deserve God's grace because of our failures, He still offers it to anyone willing to accept Jesus as Rescuer and Redeemer.

Difference 3:

We are saved through FAITH (vv. 8-9).

6. How does someone receive God's free gift of salvation (v. 8)? According to verse 9, what has no bearing at all on your salvation?

God doesn't stop with saving us from judgment. He also elevates us to a level of greatness on His team, lavishing us with "immeasurable riches" in His kingdom.

Read John 3:16 and Romans 8:14-17.

7. According to John 3:16 and Romans 8:14-17, what privileges do you gain from your relationship with God? How do these gifts make you feel?

The word *suffering* seems out of place in the Romans 8:17 discussion about being glorified as God's heirs. While our salvation is assured when we accept Jesus by faith, the game is not over. We're still in the race and our enemy is hot on our heels.

Read 1 Corinthians 9:24-27.

8. What life lessons from athletics are highlighted in 1 Corinthians 9:24-27?

9. How might understanding the ultimate prize God offers you and grasping the unique role He designed you to fill affect the way you live at home?

at practice or during competition?

while hanging out with friends or teammates?

in your school and community?

10. God has marked out a unique race and unique role for each of us. How ready are you to give everything you've got to the race He's laid out before you?

Ask God to give you a vision of the big win—the "imperishable crown" He has for you—so you'll stay motivated to discipline yourself and run your race well.

HOW CAN I EXPERIENCE ETERNAL LIFE?

1 READY

Time is always a major factor. We live in a world of 60-minute games, 30-second time-outs, 3-second lane violations, 2-minute warnings, and other time crunchers like having 2 outs and 2 strikes in the bottom of the 9th inning.

1. Describe a situation when time played a role in the outcome of a competition. What adjustments were you or your team forced to make as the clock ran down?

2. List three emotions that you've felt when under pressure. What impact did those emotions have on your ability to perform?

No one likes to think about it, but our time on earth is temporary. Thanks to the big win Jesus achieved on the cross, however, we don't have to feel the kind of pressure that comes during the crucial last moments of competition. Instead, we can focus on the quality of our relationship with Him now and on the awesome rewards that await us in heaven.

1 SET LINE

WHAT WE DESERVE

When you break a law, the seriousness of the offense increases with the level of damage. The penalty is more severe if you steal a car than a candy bar. The seriousness also increases depending on the importance of the person you offend. Hit your sister and she'll hit you back; try hitting a police officer and you'll get more than a slap.

Read Romans 3:23 and Romans 6:23.

3. According to Romans 3:23, what is true about all people? What would you say is a just punishment for offending and deeply hurting a perfect God?

4. What does Romans 6:23 say we deserve for sinning against God? God cares so deeply about us and doesn't give us what we deserve. What does God offer us instead?

WHAT WE GET

When it comes to serving Christ, there's way more to look forward to than trophies, medals, and record-breaking performances. In fact, at the end of our lives here on earth, those of us who've accepted God's ultimate gift will hear the final buzzer. In that instant, all the pressures, disappointments, and pains of this life will be gone forever.

Read John 3:16-17 and 1 John 5:11-12.

5. According to John, why was Jesus sent into our world? What's the one thing we need in order to receive the unbelievable gift of eternal life?

Read Revelation 21:1-4, 18-21.

6. What will the quality of life be like in heaven as described in Revelation 21? List at least five cool things about the life God has planned for His people—His team.

As awesome as heaven will be, it's even more exciting to realize that our eternity will allow us to actually see and touch Jesus, our Rescuer and Redeemer. We'll have forever to be treasured by Him and to explore the infinite depths and beauty of God Himself.

As athletes, we go to great lengths to achieve great things in the field of competition. We do it for the love of the game and for the love of the sport. Our Creator gave us those desires because He created us in His image. He has also gone to great lengths to chase His dream and fulfill His desire—to have a close, personal relationship with each of us.

Read John 17:2-3.

7. What does Jesus say is the true meaning of eternal life (v. 3)? How soon can it begin?

8. How does it feel to realize God wants to connect with you so badly that He gave the ultimate gift, sending His only Son to give His life for our sins and to rescue us from sin?

Scripture tells us that nobody knows when we will hear that final buzzer and go to heaven, but when we do, we'll finally see God in all His glory (1 Corinthians 13:12). Meanwhile, ask God to draw you closer into a more personal connection with Him.

HOW DOES GOD FORGIVE ME? HOW CAN I FORGIVE?

Imagine that the game or match is on the line and your number is called. You make the free throw or you don't. You make the penalty kick or you don't. You make the hole big enough so the four yards can be gained or you don't. You make a birdie or you don't. If you succeed, you win; if you miss, you lose. You either become the hero or the "goat."

1. Describe a time when you dropped the ball, fell short, or really messed up when everybody was counting on you. What did it feel like to be the "goat"? What broke down?

2. Why do you think we feel so bad when we fail or miss the mark?

God never intended for us to be the "goats." God created us to live as heroes and champions. But in our messed-up world we all fail and fall short of the glory God desires. Sooner or later, everyone blows it. The amazing thing is that we don't have to live in failure and sin!

MESSED UP

In living for God, it seems we drop the ball a lot. In times when we need to love, we treat someone badly. When our thoughts need to be pure, we lust. When we should tell the truth, we lie. When we should honor our parents and listen to their advice, we do our own thing. When we should give our all in practice, we give in to comfort and slack off. When we should love God and our neighbors, we ignore them.

Read Isaiah 64:5-6.

3. According to verse 5, how do our failures and sins affect God's feelings? What does verse 6 state about our best efforts to hit the mark?

MISSING THE MARK

The Hebrew word for *sin* is an athletic term that means missing the mark. God has a bull's-eye that we miss regularly. Missing God's mark could leave us discouraged and feeling like God should kick us off His team. Thankfully, God doesn't work that way! God knows what we're made of and recognizes that we're not capable of saving ourselves. Because of His deep desire to be in relationship with His children, however, God made a way.

GOD LONGS TO FORGIVE AND RESTORE US

Read Ephesians 1:7 and Colossians 1:13-14.

4. According to Ephesians 1:7 and Colossians 1:13-14, only God has the power to rescue, redeem, and forgive us. From what things does He rescue us? What is the attitude of His heart toward each of His people?

Once we invite Jesus into our lives, He releases us from the guilt of our failures. He redeems—buys or wins back—our freedom, totally canceling any debt we owe.

STAYING ON TARGET

Our heart's desire not to be the "goat" helps us realize how our relationship with God works. If you blow a big play, you're not off the team, but your relationships with your teammates and coach can be affected. Likewise, if you blow it in life with God, your wrong choices will affect your relationship with Him and your effectiveness in life.

Read 1 John 1:6-9.

5. How does 1 John 1:6-7 describe the impact of our sins? When we blow it, what do we have to do to receive God's forgiveness and gain a fresh start?

To keep open our relationship with God and to maintain our freedom from the sinful garbage that would ruin our lives, all we're asked to do is confess our sins. Confession means to agree with. God simply wants you to agree that you fell back into an old rut—a wrong, hurtful attitude or behavior pattern. Each time you do that, God promises to forgive you, to wash out the junk, and to help you start clean. Believe it!

THE TRAPS OF UNFORGIVENESS

Just as God's enemy and ours—the Great Deceiver, Satan—wants to mess up our relationship with God, so too he hopes to ruin our other relationships and keep us from experiencing the freedom that Jesus won for us on the cross.

Read Matthew 6:14-15; 2 Corinthians 2:5-11; and Hebrews 12:15.

6. Look carefully at each of these three passages. What traps are set for us when we don't take the path toward forgiving those who have offended us?

Matthew 6:14-15 ______________________________

2 Corinthians 2:5-11 ______________________________

Hebrews 12:15 ______________________________

FREEDOM FROM THE TRAPS

God doesn't minimize our offenses or sins, and we shouldn't minimize the offenses or hurts that others inflict on us. Authentic forgiveness does not deny hurt or ignore anger. It doesn't excuse a person's wrong or hurtful actions. Forgiveness does not forget, but it does make room for another's humanness.

Read Colossians 3:12-15.

7. Verses 14-15 highlight three godly traits that we need to put on like clothing if we're going to be able to forgive. What are the traits and from where do they come? How strong are these traits in your life right now?

8. Verse 13 states, "Just as the Lord forgave you." Why do you think this phrase is included? Consider the implications on the way you respond to people who've hurt you.

Read Romans 12:16-19.

9. A destructive cycle begins when we hurt people and they in turn hurt us. How do we break out of this destructive cycle (vv. 16-18)?

10. What does it mean to "leave room for [God's] wrath"? Why do you think God is so possessive and assertive about vengeance belonging to Him (v. 19 HCSB)?

We can only forgive because God first forgave us. Forgiveness doesn't come naturally. It's a process that can take some time, but once we've allowed ourselves to truly feel anger, sadness, and hurt, we can move toward forgiveness. As we forgive, we take our offender off our hook and put him or her on God's. God is far more protective of us than we are, and He's far more qualified to avenge our hurts. As we release the desire for revenge, we can live in freedom, love, and hope. In forgiveness, we prevent a root of bitterness from destroying our hearts, joy, relationships, and effectiveness.

WHAT ARE THE BASIC SKILLS FOR GROWTH?

Every sport requires players to learn fundamental skills that lay the foundation for excellence. At times, the basics can be unexciting and unglamorous. They can even be difficult to learn. But in any sport, mastering these basics is always the key to success.

1. What three basics have you mastered in your sport or your position?

2. What has motivated you to work on the basics? How has this helped your performance?

Much like fundamental skills in sports, a core set of basics will guide you in living a life focused on Christ. There are three areas of basic training essential to a successful endurance run with God.

BASICS 1

STUDY GOD'S TRAINING MANUAL—THE BIBLE

Each sport has its training manual or training program to develop excellence. For the Christ-follower, the Bible is like a rule book, playbook, and training manual rolled into one. Its inspired words come from the heart and mind of God.

Read 2 Timothy 3:16-17 and Hebrews 4:12.

1. From 2 Timothy 3:16-17, list four benefits of reading and studying the Bible. What are some specific ways these benefits might equip you and impact your life?

2. Why do you think Hebrews 4 describes the words of God as "alive" and actively "powerful"? How does the Bible differ from other books?

The Bible has power because it's God's words. It contains piercing truth about God, life, who we really are, our mission and destiny, and the condition of our individual hearts. Its message is basically simple and yet deeply powerful. Studying the Bible may feel like studying a complicated playbook. At times, it might seem confusing and overwhelming, but it's living and active so God can reveal new insights each time you open it.

BASICS 2

STAY IN CONSTANT COMMUNICATION WITH YOUR LIFE COACH—PRAY

Whether we play a team sport or compete individually, success on the field becomes increasingly difficult without a mentor, coach, or trainer to guide us. The same is true in our lives. We need to meet personally with God through direct communication—prayer.

Read Matthew 6:5-15.

3. In Matthew 6, Jesus gives us a model for communicating with God. What attitude should we have when we pray (vv. 5-6)? What should we avoid doing (vv. 7-8)?

4. Rephrase Jesus' prayer (vv. 9-13) in your own words, noting specific things for which Jesus prayed. How might sincerely praying those things impact your life and your relationships with others?

Prayer is a powerful tool that can change your life and the lives of those around you. Prayer is about sharing your heart with God and allowing Him to speak into your life. Learn to relax and be totally open with God. Learn to slow down long enough to listen for His voice.

BASICS 3

LOCK ARMS WITH A WINNING TEAM—FIND A CHURCH

As athletes, we must depend on the support of others to reach our competitive goals. A church is a supportive team focused on serving God. From the beginning, God has always put people together with different talents, abilities, life experiences, and strengths.

Read 1 Corinthians 12:12-31.

5. What does Paul tell us about the importance of teamwork in the church (vv. 12-20)?

6. What attitudes should we exhibit to others in the church (vv. 21-26)? How can this build up unity and make the church more effective in impacting the world for Christ?

Keep a daily routine of prayer and Bible reading just like you follow a basic training schedule in your athletic life. Start by following the PRESS method described in the first "Training Time" devotional. Learn more about your new identity under "Your Identity in Christ."

7. How will taking time to talk with God and read the Bible each day make you a better athlete? teammate? student? friend? son or daughter? brother or sister?

HOW DO I WALK IN THE POWER OF THE SPIRIT?

READY

As athletes, many factors play into our success on the court or field of competition. Fitness, nutrition, rest, proper attitude, and mental focus are just some of the less visible factors that determine how we'll perform. Even though these things are not as visible as skills training or weight training, they play a vital role in being game ready.

1. What does your daily fitness and nutrition routine look like? In what ways do those things empower you to perform at the highest level?

2. There's so much we don't understand about how to fully prepare ourselves for success on and off the field. Name a person who has been instrumental in helping you to improve in your sport. What advice or counsel did he or she give you?

SET

Just as coaches teach us the finer points of our sports, when Jesus walked on earth, He taught His disciples how to follow His lead and grow into maturity. But as Jesus prepared to leave earth and return to heaven, He knew that His followers couldn't thrive or carry on the mission He called them to without someone else to guide them. We still need that source of power to help give us the inner strength, courage, and wisdom to keep moving forward even when no one else seems to be on our side.

Read John 14:16-18, 26.

3. Who did Jesus say was coming to take His place in the lives of His followers? What are some of the words Jesus used to describe this representative of heaven?

Read John 16:7-14.

4. Just as our heavenly Father is fully God and Jesus is fully God, the Holy Spirit is fully God. Also, just as Jesus takes a unique role in our lives, so does the Holy Spirit. According to John 16, what's the Spirit's role and why is the Spirit so important?

5. Describe a time when you were with friends, teammates, or family and you could have benefited from the Holy Spirit in His role as:

Counselor—
Comforter—
Guide—

Read Romans 8:12-15.

When the Bible talks about the flesh, it's not referring to our bodies. Think about cleaning up after a practice and putting on clean clothes, but carrying around your smelly sweat socks inside your fresh, clean clothes. Your flesh is like those smelly socks that still stay with you after you become totally new. Jesus made you a new creation when you accepted Him as your Savior, but you still carry around the flesh—those old habit patterns and well-worn ruts of thinking and behavior you keep falling back into when you become weak or tired.

6. According to Romans 8:12-13, what will happen to those who live "according to the flesh"? How about those who live "by the Spirit"? What do you think it means to live "by the Spirit"?

7. Romans 8:14-15 states those led by God's Spirit are God's children, with the rights and privileges of a firstborn son. How does it feel to be "adopted" by God? How does being His son or daughter empower you to keep going even in the face of difficult times?

POWER UP

We all have times when we feel like we can't live a Christian life in a world so full of temptations and distractions. But thanks to the work of the Holy Spirit, we have the power to say no to our wrong desires. The Spirit also empowers us to say yes to our deepest desires for connection to God and the great adventure He has for us.

Read Galatians 5:16-23.

8. What are some ways we can give in to our flesh and fail in our walk with God (vv. 19-21)? What will the consequence be for those who refuse to stop doing these things (v. 21)?

9. What are some characteristics that show up in our lives as we follow the Holy Spirit (vv. 22-23)? Which of these do you most need the Spirit to develop in your life?

Allow the Spirit to be your constant Guide. Tap into real power as you listen for and accept His direction, encouragement, and power. Take a moment now to ask the Holy Spirit to do the following things in your life:

- Lead me in the right direction.
- Teach me how to be more like Jesus.
- Give me the courage and boldness to share my faith with others.
- Empower me to resist the urge to give in to temptations.

WHAT'S THE SECRET TO A LIFE OF VICTORY?

It seems most of us are born competitors, with the quest for challenge, adventure, and victory arising from deep inside us. As athletes, we're willing to give our blood, sweat, and tears to defeat an opponent.

1. How do you prepare for a game or competition against a ruthless rival who wants to take you down? What motivates you to push yourself to gain the victory?

Competition gives a clear picture of the two opposing sides in the spiritual realm that are battling fiercely to win the prize. Good and evil—God's army and Satan's forces—are battling for your allegiance and your heart. Because of your value to God, you are the prize.

OUR RUTHLESS OPPONENT

Read Ephesians 6:10-12 and 1 Peter 5:8.

2. Who is our unseen adversary and what does he intend for our lives and relationships? Do you think we'll ever be free from temptation and the need to fight to retain the freedom we've been given?

Although God has already sealed Satan's fate through Jesus' death and resurrection, Satan is still "prowling around" (1 Peter 5:8), using his primary tactic of deception to take us out! He tries to get us to believe that God is not good, he puts a twisted perspective on every event, he wreaks pain and havoc in our lives, and he ultimately works to destroy us. The Bible makes it clear that the devil and his demons are ruthless and purposeful.

STRONG OFFENSE AND DEFENSE

To protect against enemy attacks, we need disciplined preparation, a strong defense, and a strong offense. Seven strategies built around the word *PREVENT** will be our allies as we resist the enemy and the temptations from our own distorted desires (the "flesh").

P PREVENT STRATEGY 1: PREPARE

Read Ephesians 5:15-17 and 1 Peter 1:3.

3. What are some ways highlighted in Ephesians 5:15-17 and 1 Peter 1:3 that will help us prepare before we face the temptations that will come?

R PREVENT STRATEGY 2: REEVALUATE AND REPENT

We must continue to evaluate ourselves. When we're wrong, we promptly admit it and turn back to truth and light. Turning away from sin and to God is called repenting. The word *repent* comes from the Greek word *metanoia*, which means to change (*meta*) our mind-set or understanding (*noia*).

Read 2 Corinthians 4:1-2, 6 and Romans 12:1-2.

4. According to 2 Corinthians 4, what is God's part in radically changing us from the inside out? What's our part? What two decisions do we need to make in order to allow God to renew our minds and transform us (Romans 12:1-2)?

E PREVENT STRATEGY 3: ENVISION YOUR FUTURE GLORY

It's easy to get bogged down in routines and struggles. We must continually shift our focus back to the larger story in life and long for all that awaits us.

Read Romans 8:16-19.

*Adapted from *Stop the Madness* by Serendipity.

V PREVENT STRATEGY 4: VALUE YOUR HEART

If we value and guard our hearts, we set protective boundaries, and we connect our hearts to God.

Read Proverbs 4:23 and Psalm 119:9-11,15-16.

5. Why is it so important to guard our hearts (Proverbs 4:23)? What are some ways that we stay connected with our hearts and with God (Psalm 119)?

E PREVENT STRATEGY 5: ESCAPE TEMPTATION

Read 1 Corinthians 10:12-13.
Sometimes temptation jumps into your lap, and there's no avoiding it. When you find yourself in a tempting situation, take off in the opposite direction as fast as you can!

N PREVENT STRATEGY 6: NO PROVISION FOR THE FLESH

Spit into the wind, and you'll regret it. Eat contaminated food, and you'll pay dearly. Live in a way that leads to trouble, and you'll find it. Beware of falling back into your old ways.

Read Romans 13:12-14 and Ephesians 5:6-8, 10-11.

6. The "flesh" is old baggage we still carry—distorted desires and old habit patterns. How can we "make no plans to satisfy the fleshly desires" and "live as children of light"?

T PREVENT STRATEGY 7: TEAMWORK & ACCOUNTABILITY

There's great power in a team of people who can lift up one another. Christianity is a team sport. The enemy would like nothing more than to isolate us and take us out!

1 GO ONE

Read Hebrews 10:24-25 and James 5:19-20.
We're engaged in a brutal competition for our hearts and our legacies. However, as children of God, we have access to divinely powerful weapons. Stay in tune with the Holy Spirit at all times, and execute the plays as He directs the action.

Read 2 Corinthians 10:3-5.

7. How can we "capture rebellious thoughts" and make them obedient to Christ?

Taking one day at a time, dumping the garbage, and maintaining accountability will be the core of your program for the rest of your life. God never intended us to push through hardships on our own. He designed us to lock arms and take the journey together.

HOW CAN I DISCOVER THE DEEPER THINGS OF GOD?

What is it that allows some athletes to soar to the top of their sport? Many athletes have strong skills, are disciplined, and strive with determination, but a few rise above the crowds into glory and greatness.

1. Describe a time when you found your authentic swing, when you were "in the zone," or when you rose into a level of play beyond your normal experience. During that time, what was the focus of your heart, soul, mind, and strength?

2. Which outside factors or internal beliefs tend to distract you from playing "in the zone" or playing out of your own glory?

In the same way that passion and single-minded focus on the goal help us find our authentic swing or get into "the zone" in sports, passion and single-mindedness will take us into God's "zone" in a way that discipline and techniques never will.

As competitors, it's easy for us to focus on performance, but the key to rising into the glory of our lives is not about performance. It's about heart and soul. It's about realizing who we really are, about connecting deeply and personally with God, and about living out of the individual glory God created within each of us.

GOD'S HEART TOWARD YOU

If you're going to trust God to direct your life, then you need to understand His heart toward you. We all, at times, have doubts about whether God really cares.

Read Isaiah 49:15-16 and Zephaniah 3:17.

3. Sure, God loves everybody because He's God. But how personal is His love for each of His children—for you—according to Isaiah 49:15-16 and Zephaniah 3:17?

4. How does it make you feel that God has "written your name on the palms" of His hands where you're always before His eyes?

YOUR FAVORED POSITION ON GOD'S TEAM

God lavishes His love on His children who place their faith in Jesus. Because of nothing except God's extreme love, we've been given an incredible position that few of us understand, and even fewer live in. The enemy clearly wants to keep this hidden.

Read Romans 8:14-17 and Colossians 3:1-4.

5. What amazing privileges do each of us receive when we become children of God, with the full status of a firstborn son (Romans 8:14-17 and Colossians 3:1-4)?

GOD PURSUES US

We now know how much God really enjoys each one of us. He also longs for deep relationships and has deep feelings for us. That's a new revelation to many of us.

Read Song of Songs 2:8-10.

6. The "love" or "lover" in Song of Songs 2:8-10 refers to God, and the object of His affection is you. Which words in this poem illustrate God's love toward you? How does this compare with your current views of God?

Read Ezekiel 34:12, 15-16.

7. According to Ezekiel 34, how does God deal with us when we get lost in the fog or confused by the darkness in life? How does God's personal promise apply to our own life issues, hurts, and spiritual struggles?

God is thrilled about you and longs to see you excited about life with Him. He also wants you to rest in His arms, comforted in those times when you're unable to pursue God because you're tired, trapped, or struggling. In those times, He's still pursuing!

PURSUING GOD

We also need to be pursuing God to deepen our relationship with Him.

Read Psalm 42:1-2; Matthew 7:7-8, 13-14; and 2 Corinthians 4:16-18.

8. Each of these passages has emotion and passion; that's what God wants from us. What key passion do you see in each of the following verses? How is it demonstrated?

- Psalm 42:1-12 ____________________
- Matthew 7:7-8 ____________________
- Matthew 7:13-14 ____________________
- 2 Corinthians 4:16-18 ____________________

9. What's our motivation to press on through the hard things of life (2 Corinthians 4:16-18)? How do the struggles we experience now compare to the unseen reality that awaits?

God created you so that your deepest desires would be satisfied only through a close personal relationship with Him. There's no doubt that we can get very excited and passionate about our favorite teams or winning a competition. Discovering the deeper things of God is a lifelong journey powered by passion. Spend an extended time with God this week, and ask Him how He feels about you and what He enjoys about you.

WHAT'S MY ROLE IN THE GREAT COMMISSION?

With pride, we look back on past accomplishments. It will be even more fulfilling to look back at the end of the journey and know for sure that our lives counted for something big.

1. How do you think it would feel to be accepted into the Hall of Fame for your sport?

Read Hebrews 11:30-39 for God's Faith Hall of Fame.

If we allow fear—fear of change, the unknown, failure, ridicule, not following the crowd, our own inadequacies, or dozens of other things—to set the course for our lives, we'll miss many rich, fulfilling opportunities. God has a spot in His Faith Hall of Fame waiting for you.

YOU WERE CREATED WITH A PURPOSE

Read Romans 8:28-30 and 2 Timothy 1:9.

2. When did God set your purpose and destiny? Each person saved by faith in Jesus has an eternal purpose. What do you think God's "holy calling" for you might be now?

TAKE THE CHALLENGE

THE GREAT MISSION

We're drawn to stories of heroic deeds and great sacrifice because Ecclesiastes 3:11 states that God "planted eternity in the human heart." We were created for a great eternal purpose and destiny, but our purpose now is to join Jesus in His mission.

Read Isaiah 61:1-3 to see Jesus' mission statement.

3. What are the key elements of Jesus' mission outlined in this passage? Reread Isaiah 61:1-3 aloud and replace the word *me* with your name.

YOUR GREAT COMMISSION

Jesus has invited each of us to play a heroic role in His Great Mission. In the early church, people called Jesus' followers Christians (little Christs).

Read Matthew 28:18-20.

4. Matthew 28:18-20 records Jesus' final words, often called "the Great Commission." With what great task did He charge us? What needs to be our focus as His disciples?

Read Hebrews 12:1-3 and 1 Peter 3:13-15.

5. People don't end up in the Hall of Fame by sitting on the sidelines. They go for it! What characteristics of a winner do you see in Hebrews 12:1-3 and 1 Peter 3:13-15?

Every athlete who follows Jesus has a unique story; no two are the same. Your story will impact people whom nobody else could reach.

IF YOU'RE READY FOR AN EXTREME ADVENTURE AND THE CHANCE OF A LIFETIME, ACCEPT JESUS' INVITATION TO JOIN HIM IN HIS MISSION!

WILL YOU TAKE THE CHALLENGE?

YOUR IDENTITY IN CHRIST

This means that anyone who belongs to Christ has become a new person. The old life is gone; a new life has begun!
—2 Corinthians 5:17

What good news! If you're a believer, you've become "new," and the following is already true of you:

YOU ARE A NEW CREATION

- You were crucified with Christ. You no longer live, spiritually, but Christ lives in you. The life you are now living is Christ's life (Galatians 2:20).
- You died with Christ, spiritually, and died to the power of sin's rule over your life (Romans 6:1-7).
- You've been given the mind of Christ (1 Corinthians 2:16).
- Christ Himself is in you (Colossians 1:27).
- You've been forgiven of all your sins. The debt of sin against you has been canceled (Colossians 1:13 14).
- You've already been made complete in Christ (Colossians 2:10).
- You've been given a spirit of power, love, and self-discipline (2 Timothy 1:7).

YOU ARE ACCEPTED

- You are God's child (John 1:12).
- You are Christ's friend (John 15:15).
- You are united with Christ and one with Him in spirit (1 Corinthians 6:17).
- You've been bought with a price. You belong to God (1 Corinthians 6:19-20).
- You are a member of Christ's body (1 Corinthians 12:27).
- You are holy and blameless (Ephesians 1:4).
- You are adopted as God's child (Ephesians 1:5).
- You have direct access to God through the Holy Spirit (Ephesians 2:18).
- You may approach God with freedom and confidence (Ephesians 3:12).

YOU ARE SECURE

- You are free forever from condemnation (Romans 8:1).
- You can be assured that all things in your life will work together for good (Romans 8:28).
- You can never be separated from the love of God (Romans 8:35-39).
- You are hidden with Christ in God (Colossians 3:3).
- The good work that God has begun in you will be completed (Philippians 1:6).
- You are a citizen of heaven (Philippians 3:20).
- You will find grace and mercy in time of need (Hebrews 4:16).
- You are born of God, and the evil one cannot touch you (1 John 5:18).

YOU ARE SIGNIFICANT

- You are the salt and light of the earth (Matthew 5:13-16).
- You are a branch of the true vine, a channel of His life (John 15:5).
- You have been chosen and appointed to bear fruit (John 15:16).
- You are a personal witness of Christ's (Acts 1:8).
- You are God's temple (1 Corinthians 3:16).
- You are seated with Christ in the heavenly realm (Ephesians 2:6).
- You are God's "work of art," created to do good works (Ephesians 2:10).
- You can do all things through Christ who will give you strength (Philippians 4:13).

Adapted from *Living Free in Christ and Victory Over the Darkness* by Dr. Neil Anderson

GETTING INVOLVED WITH FCA

FCA CAMPS

FCA.org

fcacamps.org

FIELDS OF FAITH

fieldsoffaith.com

FCAResources.com

fb

facebook.com/FCAfans

twitter.com/fcanews

FCA MAGAZINE

www.fca.org/fca-magazine

3DIMENSIONAL COACHING

fcacoachesacademy.com

COACHES MINISTRY:

FCA Coaches Ministry is the ministry method for coaches through Huddles, events, training, and resources. FCA Coaches Ministry focuses on ministering to the heart of the coach first, and then supporting the coach as they engage with the Four C's of Ministry.

CAMPUS MINISTRY:

The school campus is one of the most strategic mission fields with more than 98 percent of all youth passing through this portal. FCA focuses on equipping, enabling, empowering, and encouraging student athletes, coaches, and adult leaders to impact and influence their campus for Christ.

CAMPS MINISTRY:

Camp is a time of "inspiration and perspiration" for coaches and athletes to reach their potential. Camps offer comprehensive athletic, spiritual, and leadership training. In FCA we offer seven types of camps: Sports Camps, Leadership Camps, Coaches Camps, Power Camps, Partnership Camps, Team Camps, and International Camps.

COMMUNITY MINISTRY:

FCA Community Ministry is the off- campus opportunities to reach coaches and athletes for Christ through the club and recreation sport environment.

FCA VISION: TO SEE THE WORLD IMPACTED FOR JESUS CHRIST THROUGH THE INFLUENCE OF COACHES AND ATHLETES.

For general questions on FCA and how to find local FCA staff, visit www.FCA.org or call 1-800-289-0909.

One Way 2 Play
DRUG FREE

I'VE MADE THE COMMITMENT!

I've accepted the challenge to strive for excellence as a student athlete by choosing the lifestyle of One Way 2 Play—Drug Free!

FAITH IN JESUS CHRIST.

We believe Christ forgives us, gives us the wisdom to make good decisions, and gives us the strength to carry them out.

COMMITMENT TO SAY NO! TO ALCOHOL AND DRUGS.

We pledge to be strong in our commitment and to help others be strong too.

ACCOUNTABILITY TO ONE ANOTHER.

We will regularly ask each other the five hard questions.

THE FIVE HARD QUESTIONS:

1. Are you living and playing alcohol and drug free?
2. Are you encouraging others to live and play that way?
3. Are you being honest with at least one mature person about your feelings and temptations?
4. Are you trusting Christ to meet your needs?
5. Are you honoring Him in your thoughts, words, and actions?

I, ____
(name)

made my

ONE WAY 2 PLAY—DRUG FREE!

commitment on ______________________________ (date)